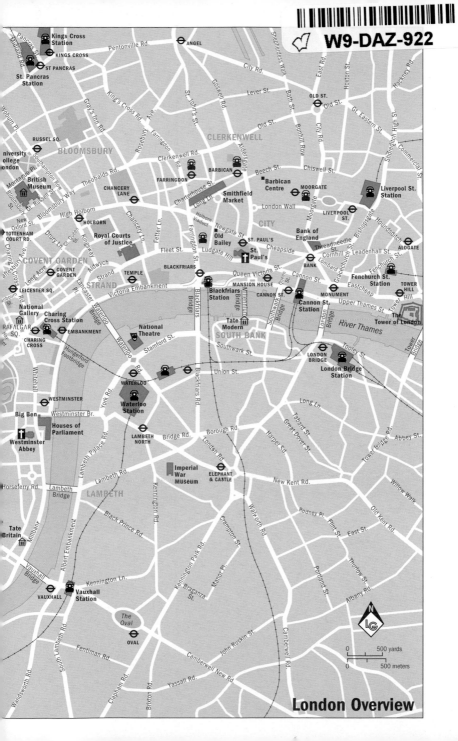

W9-DAZ-922

London Overview

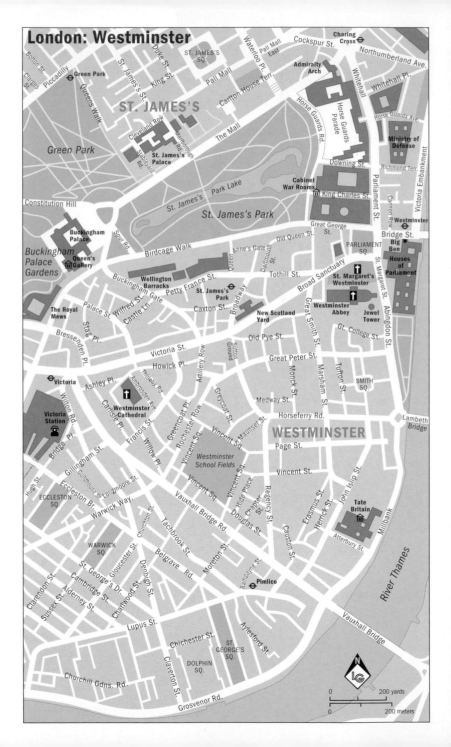

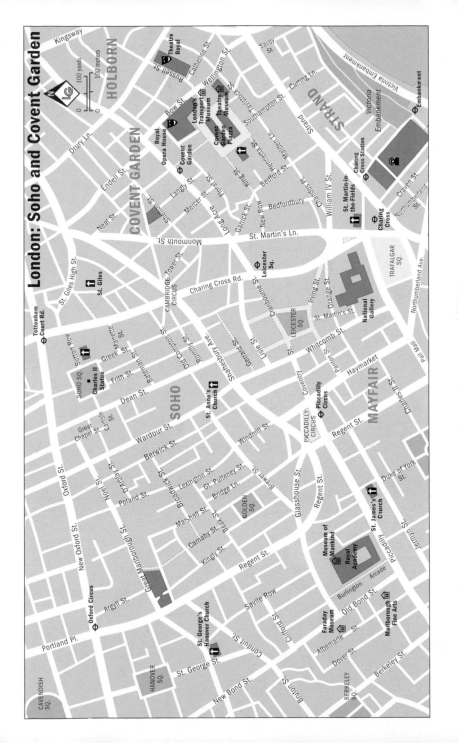

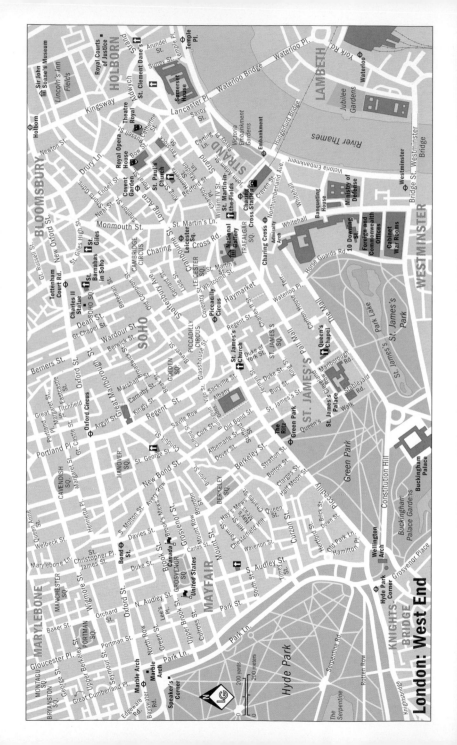

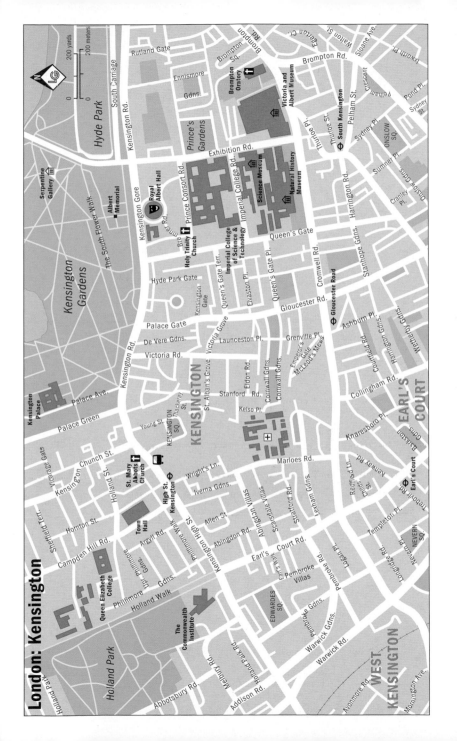

London: Kensington

Hyde Park

Rutland Gate

South Carriage

South Carriage

Kensington Rd.

Ennismore Gdns.

Brompton Rd.

Brompton Rd.

Brompton Oratory

Victoria and Albert Museum

South Kensington

Pelham St.

Thurloe Pl.

Thurloe St.

Sumner Pl.

ONSLOW SQ.

Sydney Pl.

Sydney St.

Pond Pl.

Pelham Crescent

Onslow Gdns.

Cranley Pl.

Prince's Gardens

Exhibition Rd.

Imperial College Rd.

Science Museum

Natural History Museum

Queen's Gate

Serpentine Gallery

Albert Memorial

The South Flower Walk

Kensington Gore

Royal Albert Hall

Prince Consort Rd.

Holy Trinity Church

Imperial College of Science & Technology

Harrington Rd.

Stanhope Gdns.

Cromwell Rd.

Gloucester Rd.

Gloucester Road

Ashburn Pl.

Kensington Gardens

Hyde Park Gate

Kensington Gate

Queen's Gate Terr.

Queen's Gate

Elvaston Pl.

Queen's Gate Pl.

Palace Gate

De Vere Gdns.

Victoria Rd.

Victoria Grove

Launceston Pl.

Grenville Pl.

Emperor's Gate

McLeod's Mews

Collingham Rd.

Courtfield Rd.

Harrington Gdns.

Wetherby Gdns.

EARL'S COURT

Kensington Rd.

Kensington Palace

Palace Ave.

Palace Green

Young St.

KENSINGTON SQ.

Thackeray St.

KENSINGTON

St. Alban's Grove

Stanford Rd.

Eldon Rd.

Cornwall Gdns.

Cornwall Gdns.

Kelso Pl.

Marloes Rd.

Lexham Gdns.

Knaresboro Pl.

Earl's Court

Airway Rd.

Redfield Ln.

Child's St.

Trebovir Rd.

Templeton Pl.

NEVERN SQ.

Nevern Pl.

Longridge Rd.

Barkston Gdns.

Vicarage Gate

Kensington Church St.

Holland St.

St. Mary Abbots Church

High St. Kensington

Wright's Ln.

Iverna Gdns.

Allen St.

Stratford Rd.

Lexham Gdns.

Sheffield Terr.

Hornton St.

Campden Hill Rd.

Queen Elizabeth College

Phillimore Gdns.

Un. Gdns.

Town Hall

Argyll Rd.

Phillimore Walk

Phillimore Pl.

Kensington High St.

Abingdon Rd.

Abingdon Villas

Scarsdale Villas

Earl's Walk

Earl's Court Rd.

Pembroke Rd.

Logan Pl.

Holland Park

Holland Walk

Melbury Rd.

The Commonwealth Institute

Holland Park Rd.

Abbotsbury Rd.

Addison Rd.

EDWARDES SQ.

Pembroke Gdns.

Pembroke Villas

Warwick Gdns.

Warwick Rd.

WEST KENSINGTON

Avonmore Rd.

Mornington Ave.

0   200 yards
0   200 meters

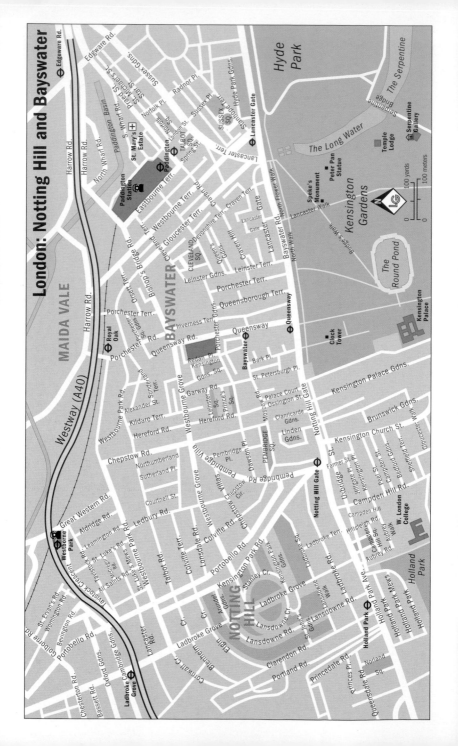

London: Notting Hill and Bayswater

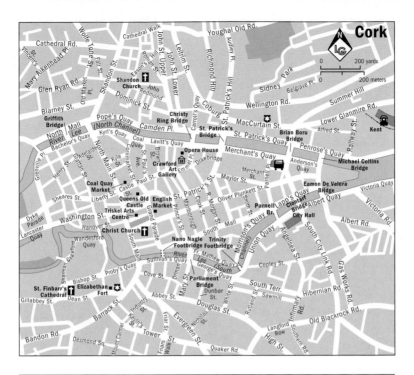

Cork

N
LG

0   200 yards
0   200 meters

Cathedral Rd.
Cathedral Walk
Youghal Old Rd.
Wolfe Tone St.
St. Vincent's Bridge
Mary Aikenhead Pl.
John St. Upper
John St. Lower
Leitrim St.
Richmond Hill
Audley Pl.
Glen Ryan Rd.
Fair Hill
Shandon St.
Roman St.
St. Patrick's Hill
Sidney Park
Belgrave Pl.
Blarney St.
Old Market Place
Shandon Church
John Redmond
Coburg St.
Wellington Rd.
Summer Hill
Dominick St.
Griffith Bridge
Pope's Quay (North Channel)
Christy Ring Bridge
Camden Pl.
St. Patrick's Bridge
MacCurtain St.
Lower Glanmire Rd.
Alfred St.
Railway St.
Kent
North Mall
North River Lee
Kyrl's Quay
Lavitt's Quay
St. Patrick's Bridge
St. Patrick's Quay
Brian Boru Bridge
Penrose's Quay
Bachelor's Quay
Greenville Pl.
Adelaide St.
Henry St.
Grattan St.
North Main St.
Cornmarket St.
Kyle St.
Paul's Ave.
St. Paul's
Browny Quay
Opera House
Merchant's Quay
Anderson's Quay
Michael Collins Bridge
Victoria Quay
Crawford Art Gallery
Emmet Pl.
Drawbridge
Merchant St.
Maylor St.
Coal Quay Market
Castle St.
Castle Paul St.
Liberty
Maylor St.
Eamon De Valera Bridge
Sheares St.
Queens Old Castle
English Market
St. Patrick's St.
Prince's St.
Oliver Plunkett St.
R. Morgan St.
Smith St.
Parnell Br.
Lapp's Quay
Clontarf Bridge
Albert Quay
Albert Rd.
Dyke Parade
Triskel Arts Centre
Hanover St.
Grand Parade
Marlborough St.
South Mall
Morrison's Quay
Union Quay
Angelesa St.
South City Link Rd.
Lancaster Quay
Christ Church
Washington St.
Nano Nagle Footbridge
Trinity Footbridge
Fr. Mathew Quay
George's Quay
Copley St.
Gas Works Rd.
Wandesford Quay
South Main
Sharman Crawford St.
Sullivan's Quay
River Lee (South Channel)
South Terr.
Bishop St.
Proby's Quay
Cove St.
Parliament Bridge
Dunbar St.
St. Finbarr's Cathedral
Elizabethan Fort
Gillabbey St.
Dean St.
Abbey St.
White St.
Sawmill
Rutland St.
Hibernian Rd.
Old Blackrock Rd.
Barrack St.
Industry St.
Helen's Tower
Friar St.
Nicholas St.
Douglas St.
Langford Row
Southern Rd.
Infirmary Rd.
Bandon Rd.
Desmond Sq.
Mount Carmel
Friars Walk
Evergreen St.
Quaker Rd.
High St.

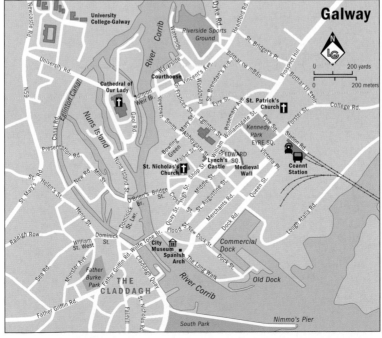

Galway

N
LG

0   200 yards
0   200 meters

Newcastle Rd.
University College-Galway
Dyke Rd.
Headford Rd.
River Corrib
Riverside Sports Ground
St. Bridget's Pl.
Prospect Hill
Bóthar Uí mBán
Bóthar Uí Eithir
University Rd.
N59
Eglinton Canal
Cathedral of Our Lady
Courthouse
Salmon Weir Br.
Waterside
St. Vincent's Ave.
St. Frances's Ave.
St. Brendan's Ave.
St. Patrick's Church
College Rd.
Canal Rd.
Nuns Island
Gaol Rd.
Newtown Smith
Eyre St.
Forster St.
Station Rd.
Presentation Rd.
Nuns Island St.
Bowling Green
Mary St.
Abbeygate St.
Eglinton St.
Rosemary Ave.
Williamsgate St.
William St.
Kennedy Park
EYRE SQ.
Victoria Pl.
Ceannt Station
St. Mary's Rd.
St. Helen's St.
New Rd. Mill St.
St. Nicholas's Church
Market St.
Shop St.
EDWARD SQ.
Lynch's Castle
Medieval Wall
Raleigh Row
Henry St.
O'Brien's Bridge
Dominick St. Lwr.
Cross St.
Middle St.
St. Augustine St.
Queen St.
Merchants Rd.
Dock Rd.
Lough Atalia Rd.
William St. West
Dominick St.
Quay St.
Flood St.
New Dock St.
Commercial Dock
Sea Rd.
Munster Ave.
Wolfe Tone Br.
City Museum
Spanish Arch
The Long Walk
Dock St.
Old Dock
Father Burke Park
Griffith Rd.
Claddagh Quay
THE CLADDAGH
River Corrib
St. Nicholas Rd.
Father Griffin Rd.
Fairhill
South Park
Nimmo's Pier

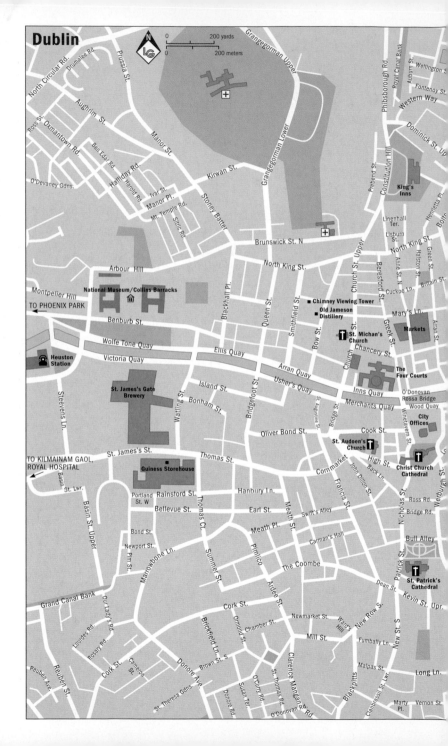

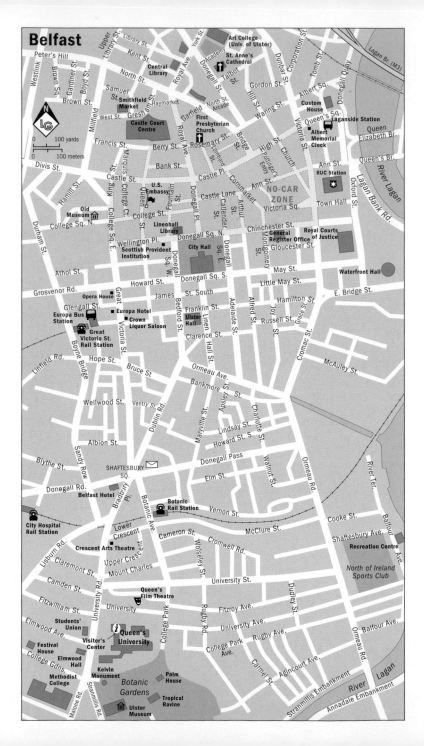

Paris Metro

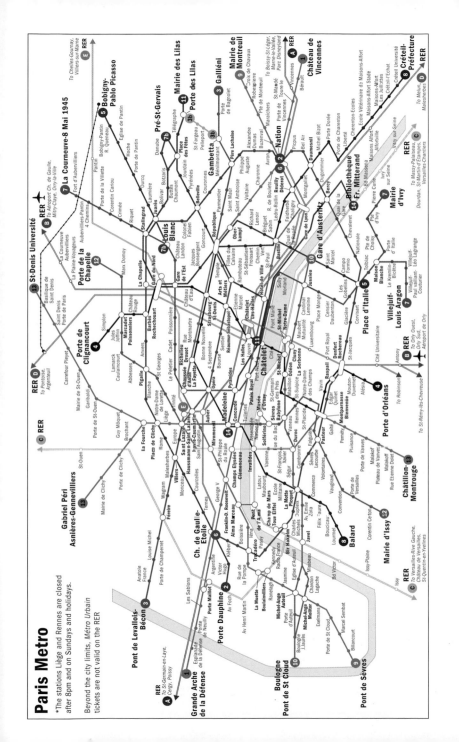

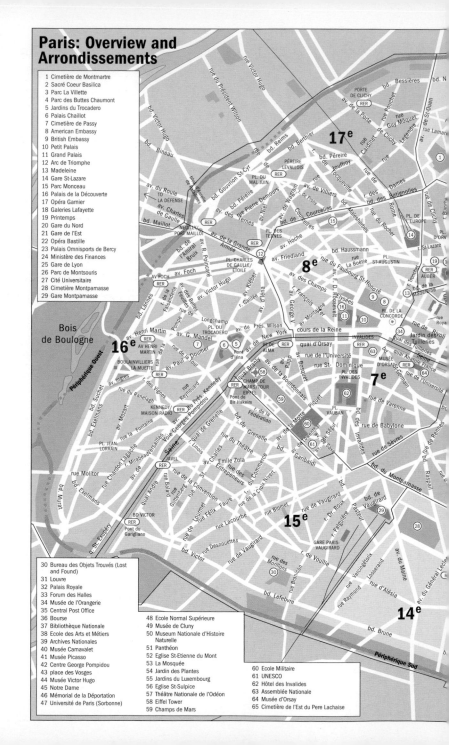

Paris: Overview and Arrondissements

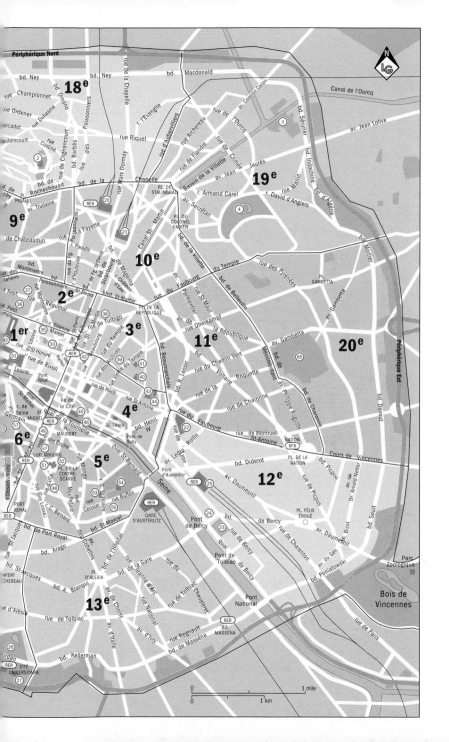

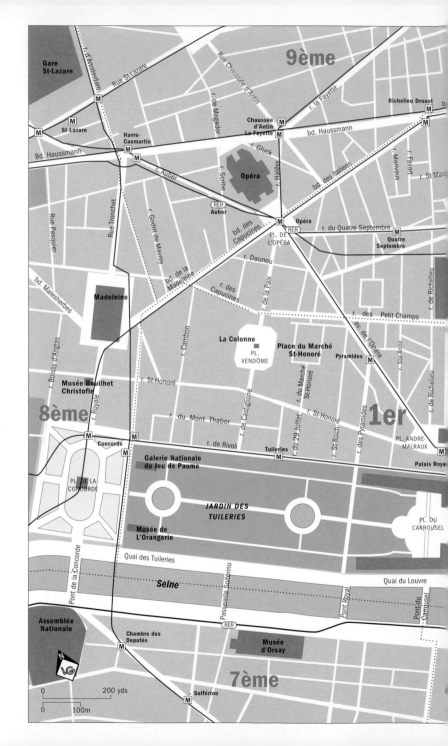

Paris: 1er & 2ème

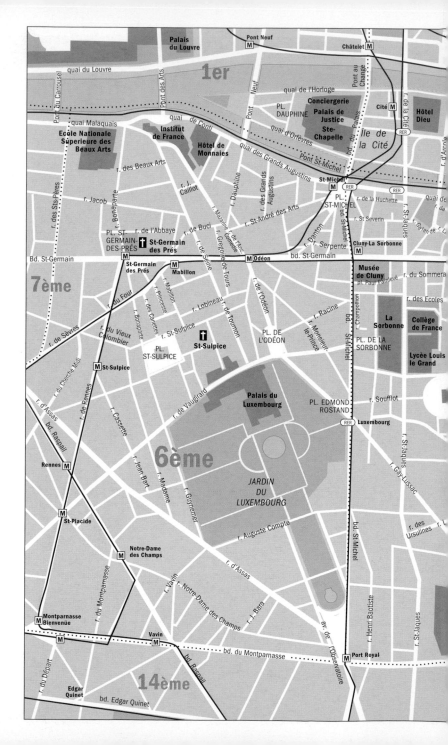

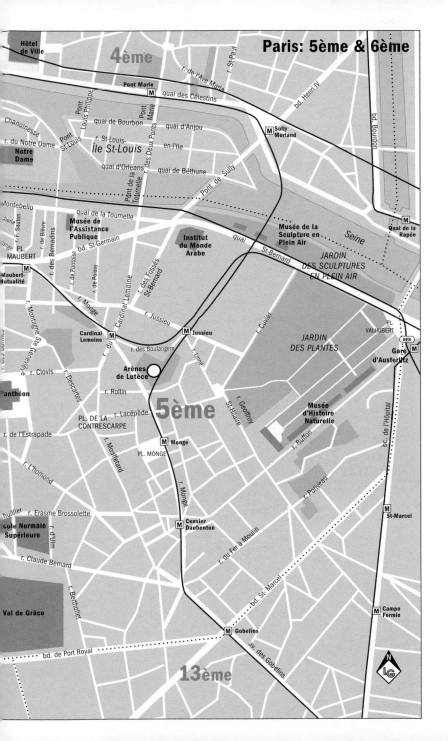

Paris: 5ème & 6ème

4ème

5ème

13ème

Hôtel de Ville

Pont Marie

quai des Célestins

r. de l'Ave Maria

r. St-Paul

bd. Henri IV

bd. Bourdon

Pont Louis Philippe

Pont Marie

quai de Bourbon

quai d'Anjou

Sully Morland

Chanoinesse

r. du Notre Dame

Notre Dame

Pont St-Louis

r. St-Louis-

Île St-Louis

en-l'Île

Pont des Deux Ponts

quai d'Orléans

quai de Béthune

Pont de la Tournelle

Pont. de Sully

Seine

Quai de la Rapée

Montebello

quai de la Tournelle

Musée de l'Assistance Publique

Musée de la Sculpture en Plein Air

cherie

r. F. Sauton

r. de Bièvre

bd. St-Germain

Institut du Monde Arabe

quai

St-Bernard

JARDIN DES SCULPTURES EN PLEIN AIR

ange

PL. MAUBERT

r. des Bernadins

r. de Pontoise

r. de Poissy

r. des Fossés St-Bernard

Cardinal Lemoine

Maubert-Mutualité

r. Monge

r. Jussieu

Jussieu

r. Cuvier

PL. VALHUBERT

Gare d'Austerlitz

RER

Cardinal Lemoine

r. du

r. des Boulangers

r. Linné

JARDIN DES PLANTES

r. Montagne Ste Geneviève

Arènes de Lutèce

r. Clovis

r. Descartes

r. Rollin

5ème

r. Geoffroy St-Hilaire

Musée d'Histoire Naturelle

bd. de l'Hôpital

'anthéon

r. Lacépède

PL. DE LA CONTRESCARPE

r. Buffon

r. de l'Estrapade

r. Mosftard

Monge

PL. MONGE

r. L'homond

r. Monge

r. Poliveau

St-Marcel

huillier

r. Erasme Brossolette

cole Normale Supérieure

r. d'Ulm

Censier Daubenton

r. Claude Bernard

r. du Fer à Moulin

r. Berthollet

Val de Grâce

bd. St-Marcel

Campo Formio

Gobelins

bd. de Port Royal

av. des Gobelins

13ème

N

LG

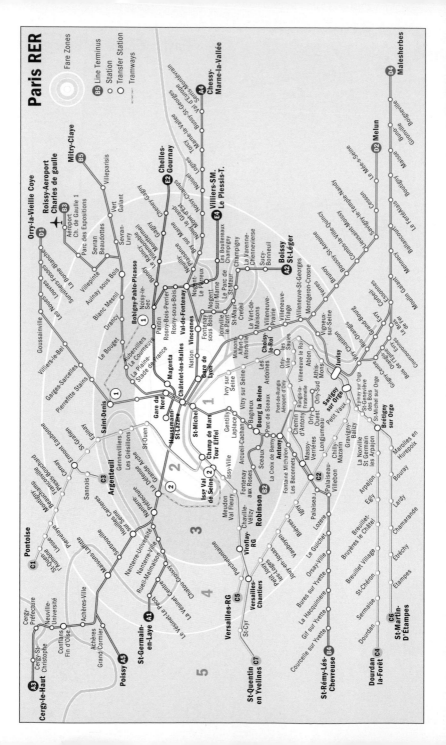

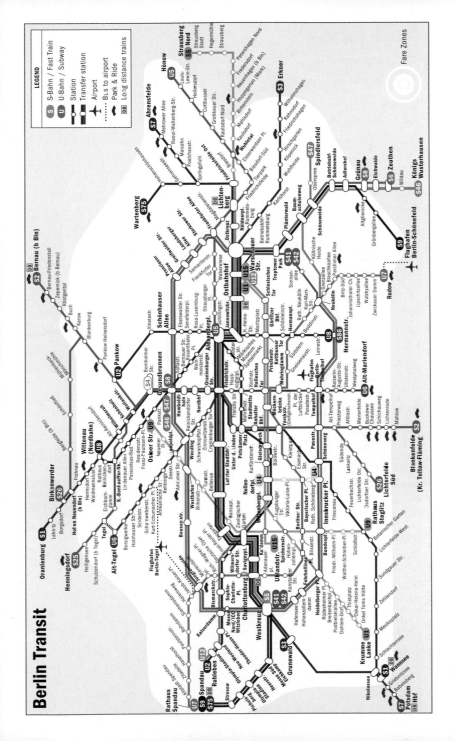

Berlin Transit

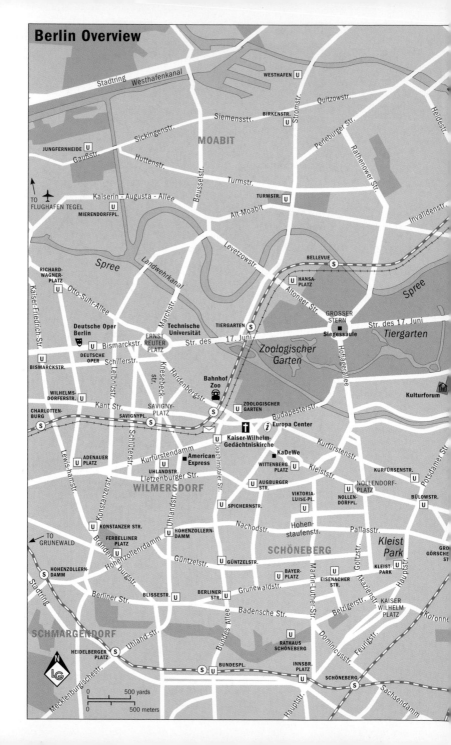

Berlin Overview

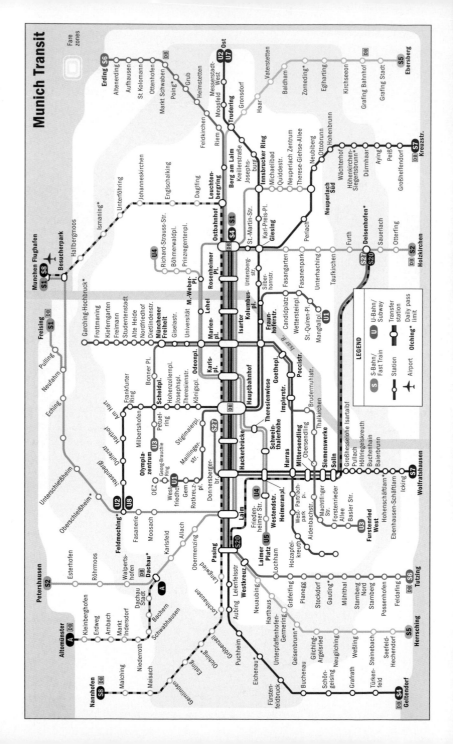

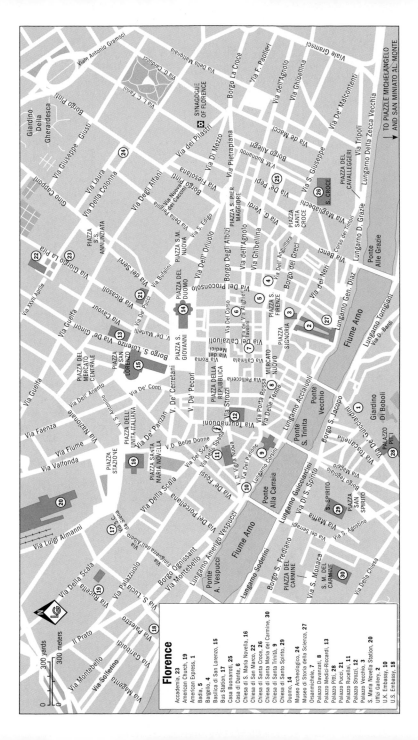

Florence

Accademia, **23**
American Church, **19**
American Express, **1**
Badia, **5**
Bargello, **4**
Basilica di San Lorenzo, **15**
Bus Station, **17**
Casa Buonarroti, **25**
Casa di Dante, **1**
Chiesa di S. Maria Novella, **16**
Chiesa di San Marco, **22**
Chiesa di Santa Croce, **26**
Chiesa di Santa Maria del Carmine, **30**
Chiesa di Santa Trinita, **9**
Chiesa di Santo Spirito, **29**
Duomo, **14**
Museo Archeologico, **24**
Museo di Storia della Scienza, **27**
Orsanmichele, **7**
Palazzo Davanzati, **8**
Palazzo Medici-Riccardi, **13**
Palazzo Pitti, **28**
Palazzo Pucci, **21**
Palazzo Rucellai, **11**
Palazzo Strozzi, **12**
Palazzo Vecchio, **3**
S. Maria Novella Station, **20**
Uffizi Gallery, **2**
U.K. Embassy, **10**
U.S. Embassy, **18**

TO PIAZZE MICHELANGELO
AND SAN MINIATO AL MONTE

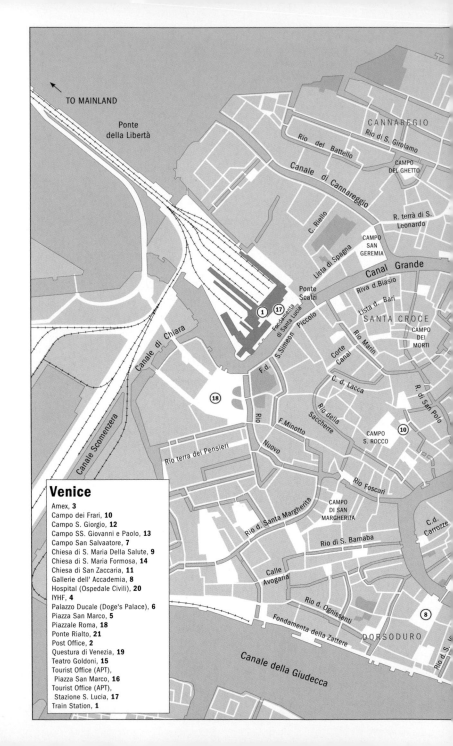

Venice

Amex, **3**
Campo dei Frari, **10**
Campo S. Giorgio, **12**
Campo SS. Giovanni e Paolo, **13**
Campo San Salvaatore, **7**
Chiesa di S. Maria Della Salute, **9**
Chiesa di S. Maria Formosa, **14**
Chiesa di San Zaccaria, **11**
Gallerie dell' Accademia, **8**
Hospital (Ospedale Civili), **20**
IYHF, **4**
Palazzo Ducale (Doge's Palace), **6**
Piazza San Marco, **5**
Piazzale Roma, **18**
Ponte Rialto, **21**
Post Office, **2**
Questura di Venezia, **19**
Teatro Goldoni, **15**
Tourist Office (APT),
  Piazza San Marco, **16**
Tourist Office (APT),
  Stazione S. Lucia, **17**
Train Station, **1**

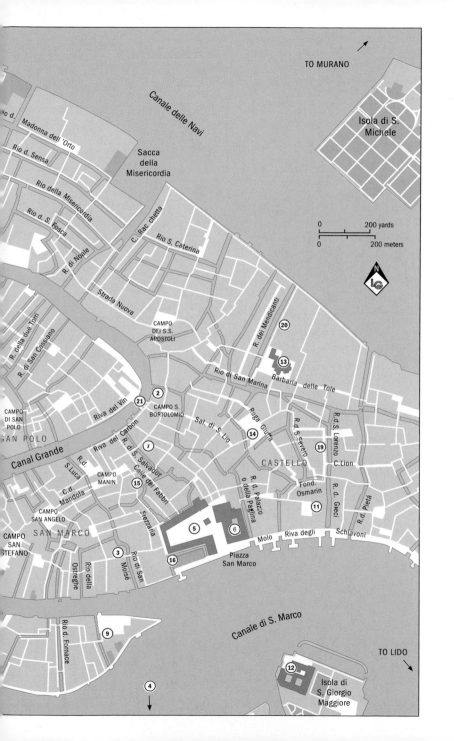

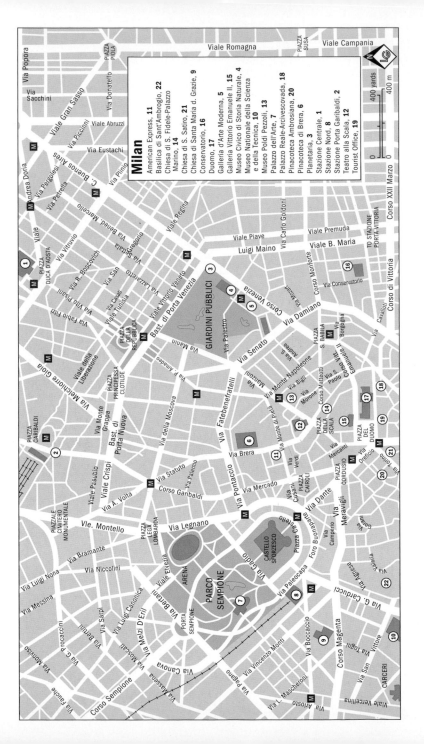

Milan

American Express, **11**
Basilica di Sant'Ambrogio, **22**
Chiesa di S. Fidele-Palazzo
Marino, **14**
Chiesa di S. Satiro, **21**
Chiesa di Santa Maria d. Grazie, **9**
Conservatorio, **16**
Duomo, **17**
Galleria d'Arte Moderna, **5**
Galleria Vittorio Emanuele II, **15**
Museo Civico di Storia Naturale, **4**
Museo Nazionale della Scienza
e della Tecnica, **10**
Museo Poldi Pezzoli, **13**
Palazzo dell'Arte, **7**
Palazzo Reale-Arcivescovada, **18**
Pinacoteca Ambrosiana, **20**
Pinacoteca di Brera, **6**
Planetaria, **3**
Stazione Centrale, **1**
Stazione Nord, **8**
Stazione Porta Garibaldi, **2**
Teatro alla Scala, **12**
Tourist Office, **19**

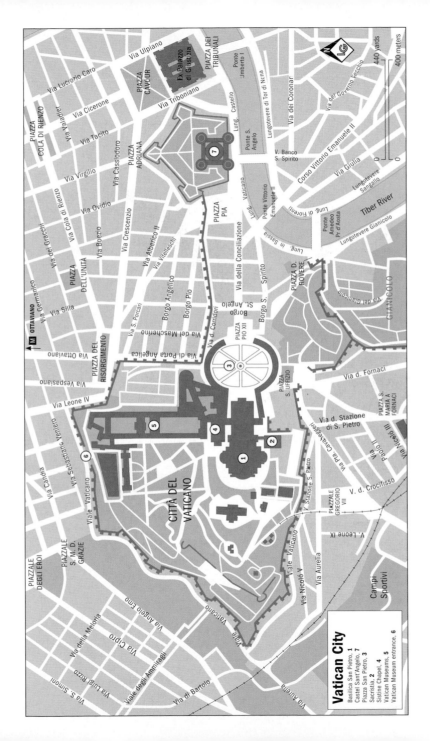

Vatican City

Basilica San Pietro, 1
Castel Sant'Angelo, 7
Piazza San Pietro, 3
Sacristia, 2
Sistine Chapel, 4
Vatican Museums, 5
Vatican Museum entrance, 6

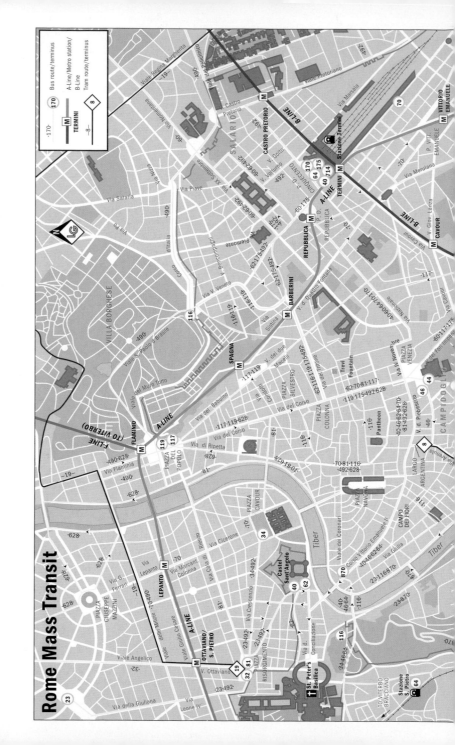

Rome Mass Transit

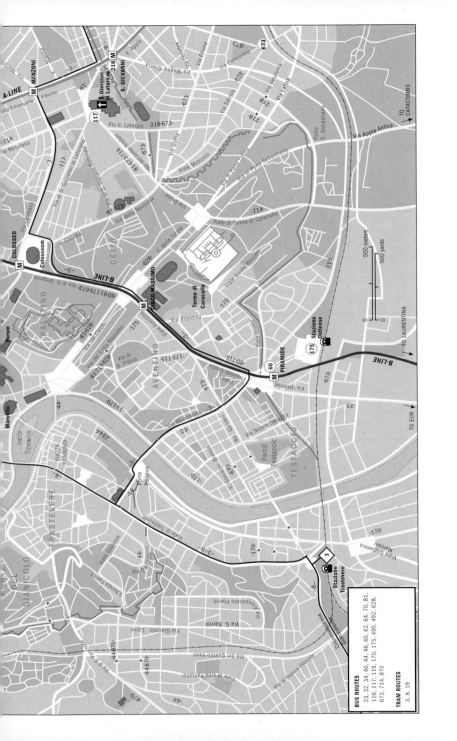

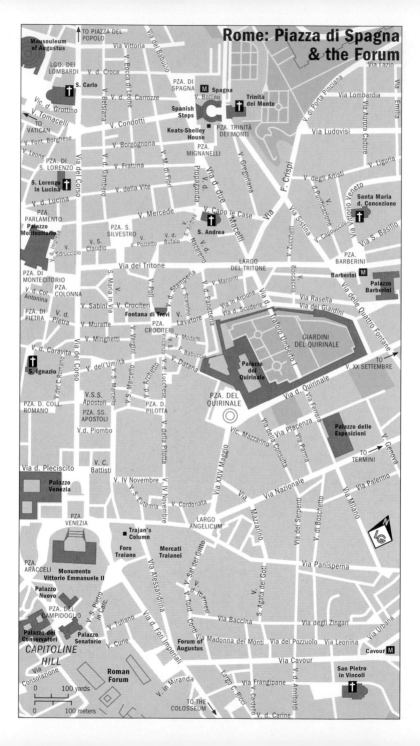

Rome: Piazza di Spagna & the Forum

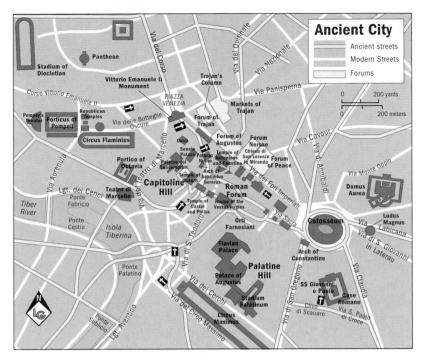

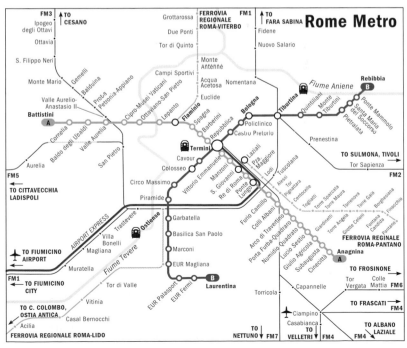

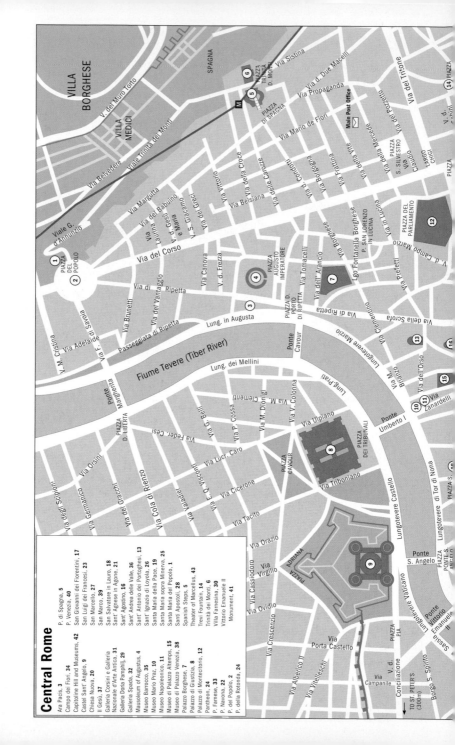

Central Rome

Ara Pacis, 3
Campo dei Fiori, 34
Capitoline Hill and Museums, 42
Castel Sant' Angelo, 9
Chiesa Nuova, 20
Il Gesù, 37
Galleria Corsini e Galleria
 Nazionale d'Arte Antica, 31
Galleria Doria Pamphilj, 29
Galleria Spada, 32
Mausoleum of Augustus, 4
Museo Barrocco, 35
Museo Mario Praz, 10
Museo Napoleonico, 11
Museo di Palazzo Altemps, 15
Museo di Palazzo Venezia, 38
Palazzo Borghese, 7
Palazzo di Giustizia, 8
Palazzo di Montecitorio, 12
Pantheon, 24
P. Farnese, 33
P. Navona, 22
P. del Popolo, 24
P. della Rotonda, 24

P. di Spagna, 5
P. Venezia, 40
San Giovanni dei Fiorentini, 17
San Luigi dei Francesi, 23
San Marcello, 27
San Marco, 39
San Salvatore in Lauro, 18
Sant' Agnese in Agone, 21
Sant' Agostino, 16
Sant' Andrea delle Valle, 36
Sant' Antonio dei Portoghesi, 13
Sant' Ignazio di Loyola, 26
Santa Maria della Pace, 19
Santa Maria sopra Minerva, 25
Santa Maria del Popolo, 1
Santi Apostoli, 28
Spanish Steps, 5
Theater of Marcellus, 43
Trevi Fountain, 14
Trinità dei Monti, 6
Villa Farnesina, 30
Vittorio Emanuele II
 Monument, 41

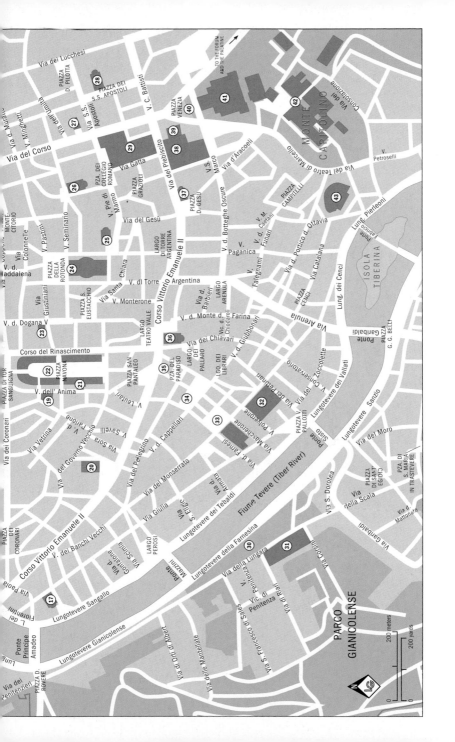

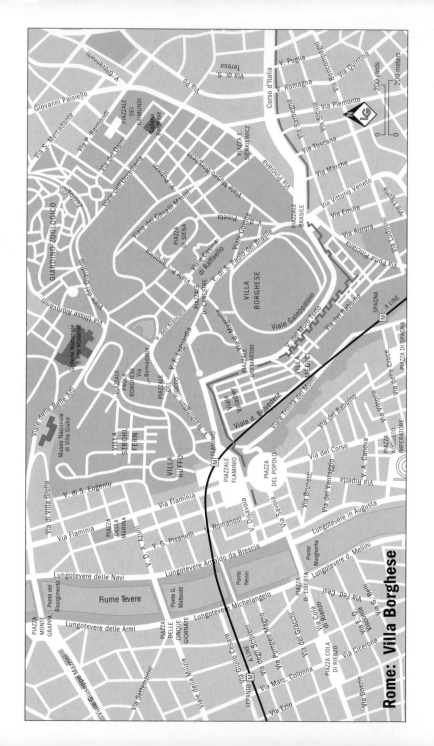

Rome: Villa Borghese

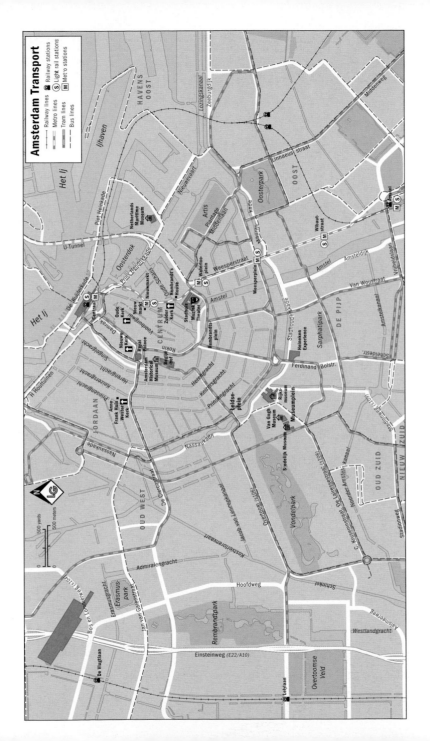

Amsterdam Transport

Railway lines
Ⓡ Railway stations
Metro lines
Ⓢ Light rail stations
Ⓢ Light rail stations
Tram lines
Ⓜ Metro stations
Bus lines

Het Ij

Havens Oost

Ijhaven

Het Ij

Loingskanaal

Zeeburgdijk

Linnaeust straat

Oosterpark

Oost

Piet Heinkade

Netherlands Maritime Museum

Artis

Plantage Middenlaan

U-Tunnel

Oosterdok

Prins Hendrikkade

De Ruijterkade

Nieuwevaart

kade

Centraal Ⓢ Ⓜ

Oude Kerk

Nieuwmarkt Ⓜ

Nieuw kade

Rembrandt's House

Waterlooplein Ⓜ Ⓢ

Weesperstraat

Weesperplein Ⓜ Ⓢ

Wibaut-straat Ⓢ Ⓜ

Amsteldijk

Amstel Ⓜ Ⓢ

Amstel

Het Ij

Damrak

Singelgracht

Nieuw Kerk

Royal Palace

Zuider Kerk

Stadhuis Muziek Theater

Amstel

Van Woustraat

H Houtuinen

Keizersgracht

Herengracht

Amsterdam Historical Museum

Begijnhof

Rokin

Rembrandts plein

De Pijp

Heineken Experience

Stadhouderskade

Sarphatipark

Jordan

Prinsengracht

Anne Frank Huis

Westerkerk

Herengracht

Keizersgracht

Prinsengracht

Leidse plein

Ferdinand Bolstr.

Sobelastr.

Amstelkanaal

Nassaukade

Van Gogh Museum

Stedelijk Museum

Rijks-museum

Museumplein

Nieuw Zuid

Oud Zuid

Nassaukade

De Clercqstraat

Leidse van Leeuwenhoekstraat (510)

Overtoom (510)

Vondelpark

C. Krusemanstraat

De Lairessestraat

Noorder Amstel kanaal

Stadionweg

Oud West

Admiralengracht

Kostverlorenvaart

Hoofdweg

Schinkel

Aalsmeerweg

Erasmusgracht

Erasmus park

Jan van Galenstraat

Bos en Lommerplantsoen & (510)

Rembrandtpark

Westlandgracht

Overtoomse Veld

Einsteinweg (E22/A10)

De Vlugtlaan Ⓡ

Lelylaan Ⓡ

0   500 meters
0   500 yards

Amsterdam Overview

0 200 yards
0 200 meters

Het Ij

Ij Tunnel

e Ruijterkade

Sumatrakade

Javakade

Piet Heinkade

Dijksgracht

TIONS IN t

Oosterdokskade

Oosterdok

Oosterdokskade

Geldersekade

Gelderse
Waalsstr
Binnen
Bantammerstr

Nieuwe
Jonkerstr

Binnenkant
Eilandsgracht

Rapenburgstr.

Scheep-
vaart-
museum 🏛

Kattenburgstr.

Kattenburgerkade

Wittenburgervaart

JWE
RKT

Keizerstr.
Konfigsstr
Korte Koni
Koni

Prins Hendrikkade

Kattenburger
vaart

Oostenburgervaart

Oude Schans

Zuider-
kerk

Nieuwe Uilenburgerstr.

Foeliestr.

Kattenburgergracht

Kattenburger

Uilenburgerstr.

Anne Frankstr.

Hoogte Kadijk

Wittenburgergracht

Oostenburgergracht

Museum
Rembrandt

Jodenbreestr.

Valkenburgerstr.

Rapenburgerstr.

Laagte Kadijk

Czaar Peterstr.

dhuis

MR VISSER-
PLEIN

Muiderstr.

Herengracht

Plantage
Pakhlaan

Entrepotdok

Nieuwevaart

Zeeburgstr.

uziek-
eater

Waterlooplein

Nieuwe
Amstelstr.

Wertheim
Park

Henri
Polaklaan

Plantage Doklaan

Entrepotdok

Jewish Historical
Museum 🏛

Hortus
Botanicus

Artis Zoo

Nieuwe

Hortus Plantsoen

Plantage Middenlaan

Nieuwe Kerkstr.

Keizersgracht

Nieuwe
Keizersgracht

Dapperstr.

Nieuwe Prinsengracht

Roetersstr.

Plantage Muidergracht

Plantage Muidergracht

ALEXANDER-
PLEIN

Von Zesenstr.

Commelinstr.

Nieuwe Achtergracht

Wagenaarstr.

1e van Swindenstr.

Binnen Amstel

Nieuwe

Marnixstr

Tappelstr

WEESPER-
PLEIN

Sarphatistr.

Tropenmuseum 🏛

Achtergracht

Mauritskade

Linnaeusstr.

Spinozastr.

Andrea Bonnstr.

's Gravesandestr.

Oosterpark

Wijttenbachstr.

Domselaerstr.

Rhijnspoorplein

Boer Campenstr.

tadhouderskade

monylaan

Amsteldijk

Swammerdamstr.

Weesperzijde

Wibautstr.

Ruyschstr.

Oosterparkstr.

2e Oosterparkstr.

Hemonystr.

Amstel

1e Oosterparkstr.

3e Oosterparkstr.

Vrolikstr.

Populierenweg

Ceintuurbaan

Tugelaweg

Retiefstr.

STEVE
BIKO-
PLEIN

Woust.

Pretoriusstr.

Transvaalstr.

Ringvaart

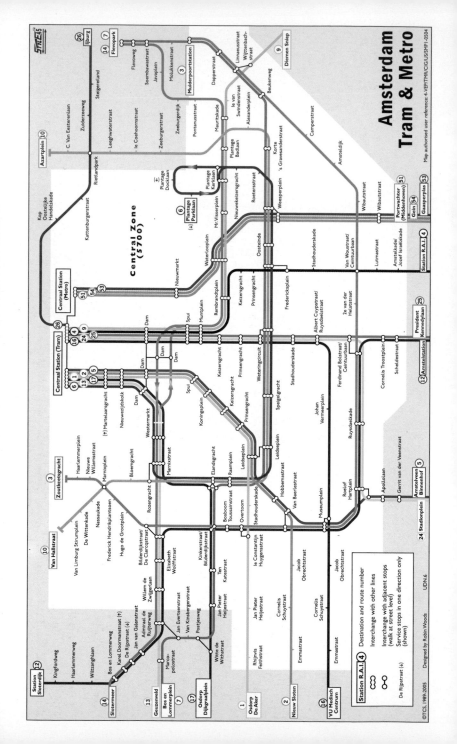

Amsterdam Tram & Metro

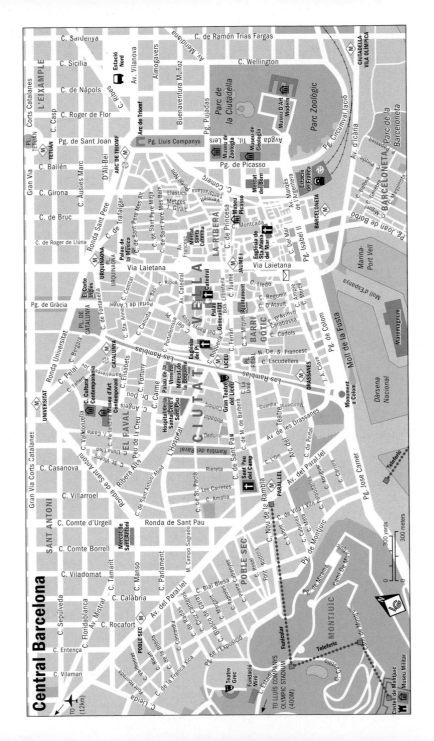

Central Barcelona

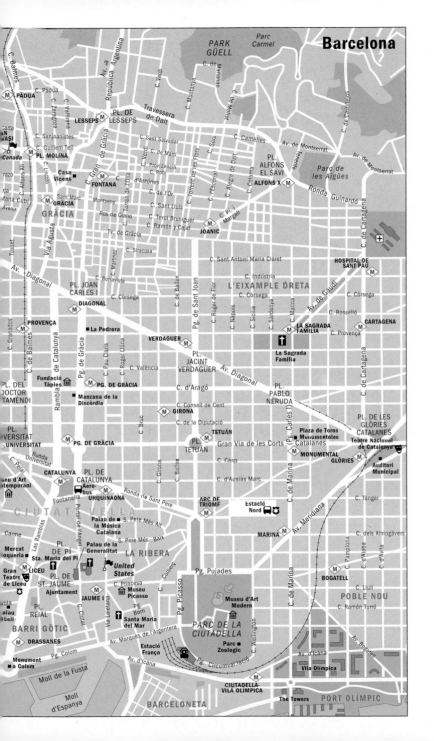

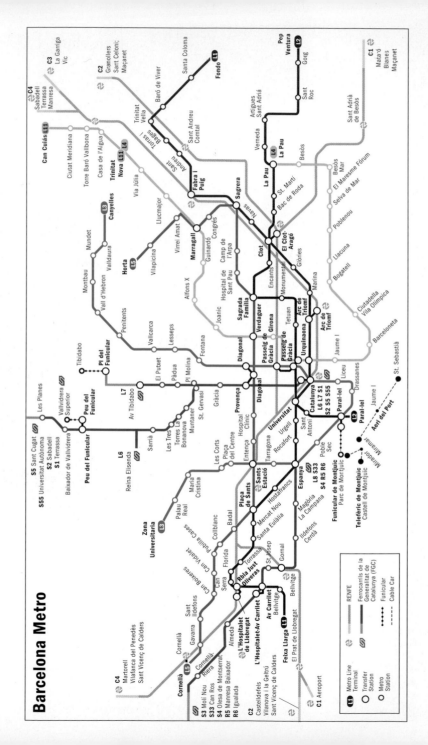

Barcelona Metro

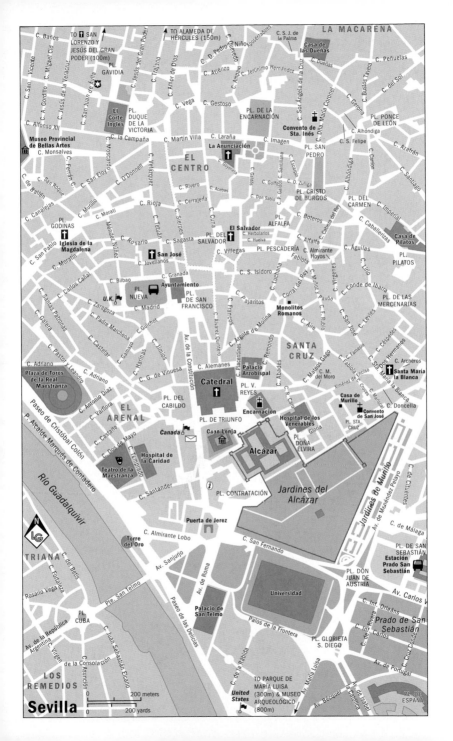

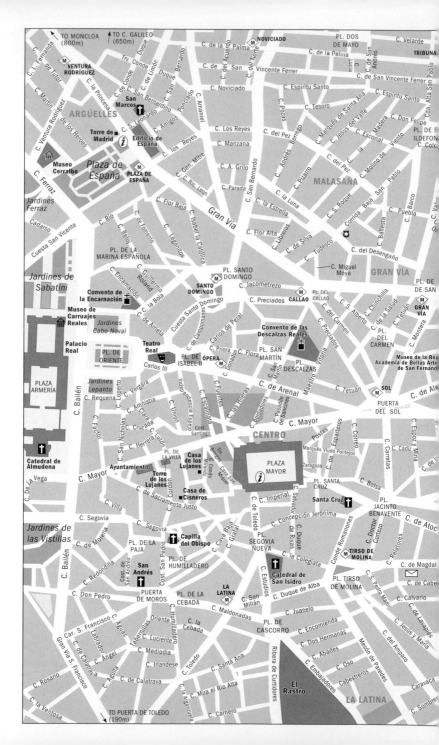

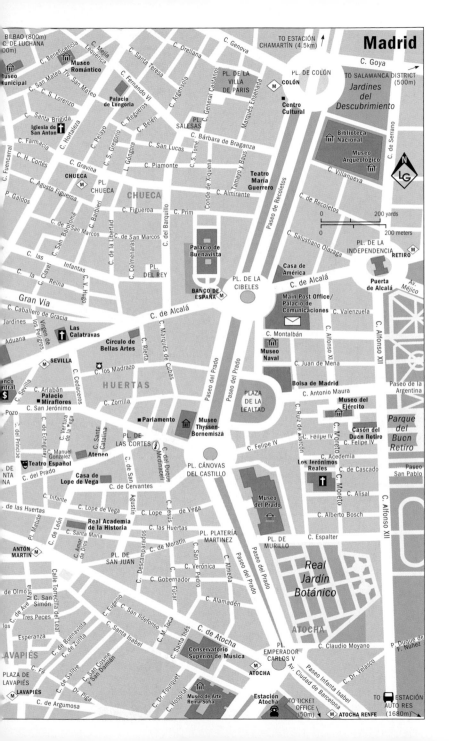

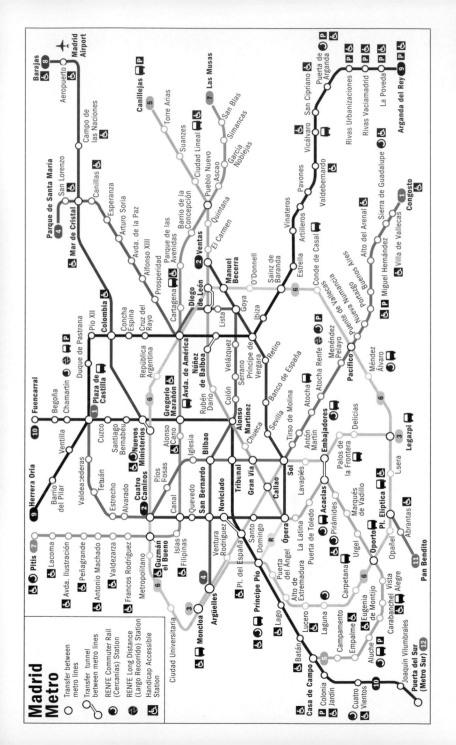

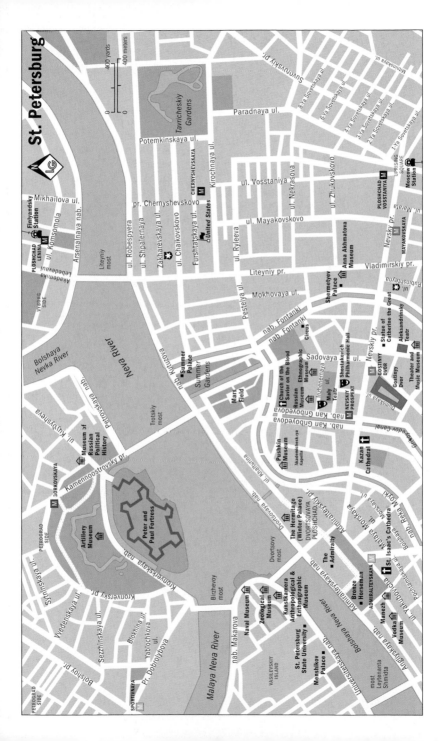

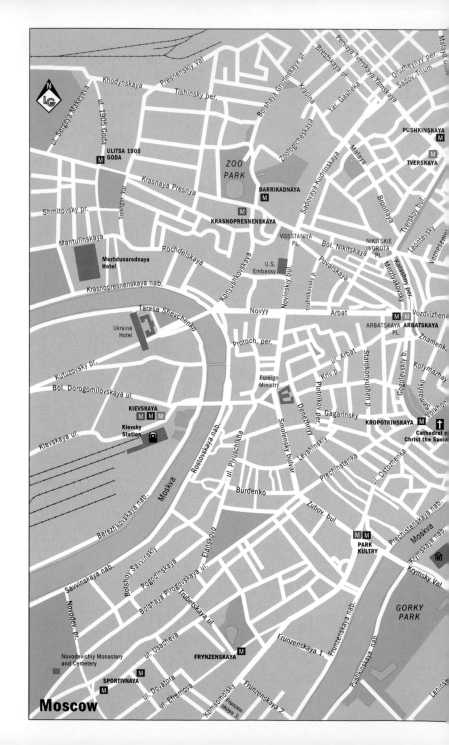

Moscow

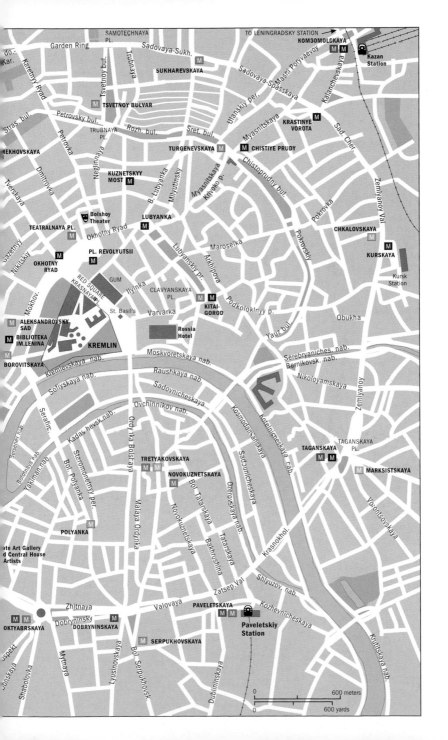

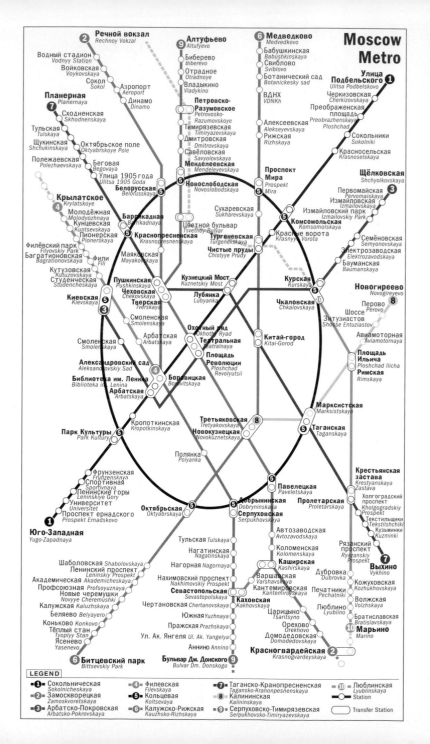

Moscow Metro

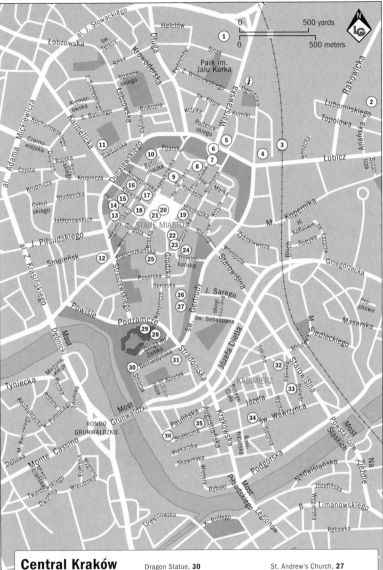

Central Kraków

Akademia Ekonomiczna, **2**
Almatur Office, **22**
Barbican, **6**
Bernardine Church, **31**
Bus Station, **4**
Carmelite Church, **11**
Cartoon Gallery, **9**
Collegium Maius, **14**
Corpus Christi Church, **34**
Czartoryski Art Museum, **8**
Dominican Church, **24**

Dragon Statue, **30**
Filharmonia, **12**
Franciscan Church, **25**
Grunwald Memorial, **5**
History Museum of Kraków, **17**
Jewish Cemetery, **32**
Jewish Museum, **33**
Kraków Glowny Station, **3**
Monastery of the
   Reformed Franciscans, **10**
Pauline Church, **36**
Police Station, **18**
Politechnika Krakowska, **1**

St. Andrew's Church, **27**
St. Anne's Church, **15**
St. Catherine's Church, **35**
St. Florian's Gate, **7**
St. Mary's Church, **19**
St. Peter and Paul Church, **26**
Stary Teatr (Old Theater), **16**
Sukiennice (Cloth Hall), **20**
Town Hall, **21**
United States Embassy, **23**
University Museum, **13**
Wawel Castle, **28**
Wawel Cathedral, **29**

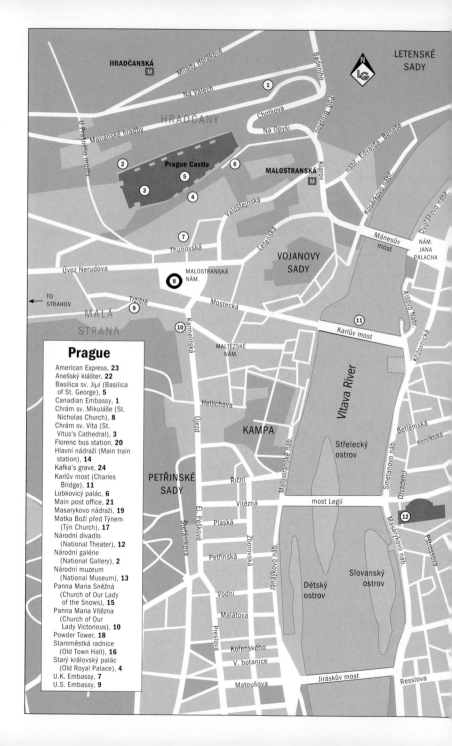

Prague

American Express, **23**
Anešský klášter, **22**
Basilica sv. Jiųí (Basilica of St. George), **5**
Canadian Embassy, **1**
Chrám sv. Mikuláše (St. Nicholas Church), **8**
Chrám sv. Víta (St. Vitus's Cathedral), **3**
Florenc bus station, **20**
Hlavní nádraží (Main train station), **14**
Kafka's grave, **24**
Karlův most (Charles Bridge), **11**
Lobkovicý palác, **6**
Main post office, **21**
Masarykovo nádraží, **19**
Matka Boží před Týnem (Týn Church), **17**
Národní divadlo (National Theater), **12**
Národní galérie (National Gallery), **2**
Národní muzeum (National Museum), **13**
Panna Maria Sněžná (Church of Our Lady of the Snows), **15**
Panna Maria Vítězna (Church of Our Lady Victorious), **10**
Powder Tower, **18**
Staroměstská radnice (Old Town Hall), **16**
Starý královský palác (Old Royal Palace), **4**
U.K. Embassy, **7**
U.S. Embassy, **9**

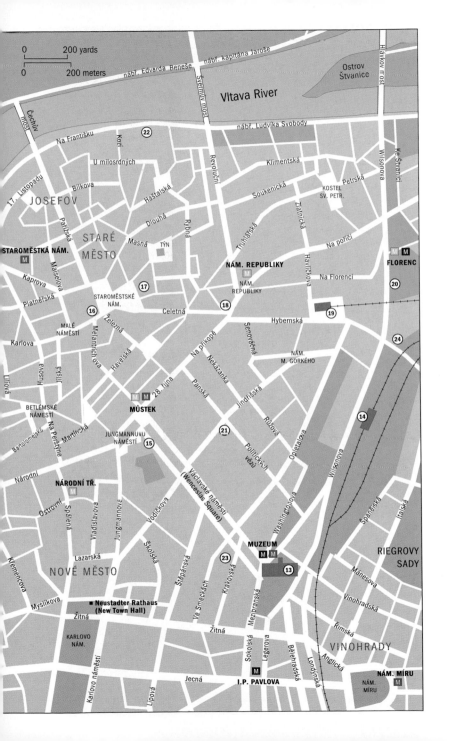

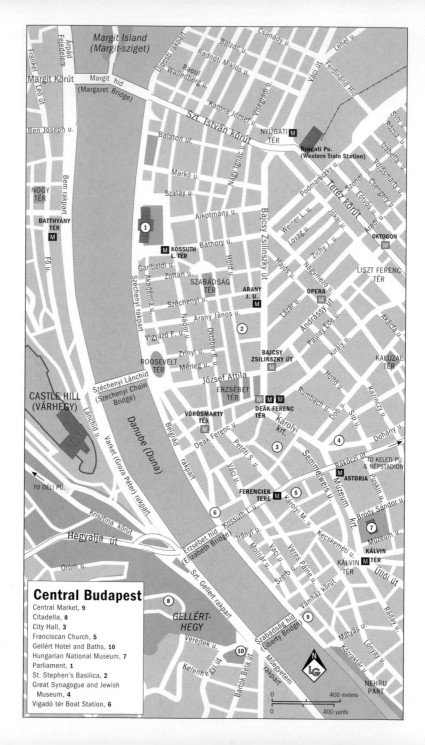

Central Budapest

Central Market, 9
Citadella, 8
City Hall, 3
Franciscan Church, 5
Gellért Hotel and Baths, 10
Hungarian National Museum, 7
Parliament, 1
St. Stephen's Basilica, 2
Great Synagogue and Jewish
  Museum, 4
Vigadó tér Boat Station, 6

LET'S GO

■ THE RESOURCE FOR THE INDEPENDENT TRAVELER

"The guides are aimed not only at young budget travelers but at the indepedent traveler; a sort of streetwise cookbook for traveling alone."
—*The New York Times*

"Unbeatable; good sight-seeing advice; up-to-date info on restaurants, hotels, and inns; a commitment to money-saving travel; and a wry style that brightens nearly every page."
—*The Washington Post*

"Lighthearted and sophisticated, informative and fun to read. [Let's Go] helps the novice traveler navigate like a knowledgeable old hand."
—*Atlanta Journal-Constitution*

"A world-wise traveling companion—always ready with friendly advice and helpful hints, all sprinkled with a bit of wit."
—*The Philadelphia Inquirer*

■ THE BEST TRAVEL BARGAINS IN YOUR PRICE RANGE

"All the dirt, dirt cheap."
—*People*

"Anything you need to know about budget traveling is detailed in this book."
—*The Chicago Sun-Times*

"Let's Go follows the creed that you don't have to toss your life's savings to the wind to travel—unless you want to."
—*The Salt Lake Tribune*

■ REAL ADVICE FOR REAL EXPERIENCES

"The writers seem to have experienced every rooster-packed bus and lunar-surfaced mattress about which they write."
—*The New York Times*

"Value-packed, unbeatable, accurate, and comprehensive."
—*The Los Angeles Times*

"[Let's Go's] devoted updaters really walk the walk (and thumb the ride, and trek the trail). Learn how to fish, haggle, find work—anywhere."
—*Food & Wine*

LET'S GO PUBLICATIONS

TRAVEL GUIDES

Australia 8th edition
Austria & Switzerland 12th edition
Brazil 1st edition
Britain & Ireland 2005
California 10th edition
Central America 9th edition
Chile 2nd edition
China 5th edition
Costa Rica 2nd edition
Eastern Europe 2005
Ecuador 1st edition **NEW TITLE**
Egypt 2nd edition
Europe 2005
France 2005
Germany 12th edition
Greece 2005
Hawaii 3rd edition
India & Nepal 8th edition
Ireland 2005
Israel 4th edition
Italy 2005
Japan 1st edition
Mexico 20th edition
Middle East 4th edition
Peru 1st edition **NEW TITLE**
Puerto Rico 1st edition
South Africa 5th edition
Southeast Asia 9th edition
Spain & Portugal 2005
Thailand 2nd edition
Turkey 5th edition
USA 2005
Vietnam 1st edition **NEW TITLE**
Western Europe 2005

ROADTRIP GUIDE

Roadtripping USA **NEW TITLE**

ADVENTURE GUIDES

Alaska 1st edition
New Zealand **NEW TITLE**
Pacific Northwest **NEW TITLE**
Southwest USA 3rd edition

CITY GUIDES

Amsterdam 3rd edition
Barcelona 3rd edition
Boston 4th edition
London 2005
New York City 15th edition
Paris 13th edition
Rome 12th edition
San Francisco 4th edition
Washington, D.C. 13th edition

POCKET CITY GUIDES

Amsterdam
Berlin
Boston
Chicago
London
New York City
Paris
San Francisco
Venice
Washington, D.C.

EUROPE

2005

STUART J. ROBINSON EDITOR

RACHEL M. BURKE ASSOCIATE EDITOR
JOSIAH CHILD ASSOCIATE EDITOR
MARCEL A.Q. LaFLAMME ASSOCIATE EDITOR
KATHERINE PLOTNICK ASSOCIATE EDITOR
EMILY C. ZAZULIA ASSOCIATE EDITOR

WILL GARRIGUES MAP EDITOR
JOEL AUGUST STEINHAUS MANAGING EDITOR

ST. MARTIN'S PRESS ❤ NEW YORK

HELPING LET'S GO. If you want to share your discoveries, suggestions, or corrections, please drop us a line. We read every piece of correspondence, whether a postcard, a 10-page email, or a coconut. **Address mail to:**

> Let's Go: Europe
> 67 Mount Auburn Street
> Cambridge, MA 02138
> USA

Visit Let's Go at **http://www.letsgo.com**, or send email to:

> **feedback@letsgo.com**
> **Subject: "Let's Go: Europe"**

In addition to the invaluable travel advice our readers share with us, many are kind enough to offer their services as researchers or editors. Unfortunately, our charter enables us to employ only currently enrolled Harvard students.

HOW TO USE THIS BOOK

If you're reading this, you're probably about to embark on a grand tour of Europe—maybe your first, maybe your 17th. For the 45th year in a row, *Let's Go: Europe* is here to guide you to the most magnificent cathedrals, the cleanest hostels, and the finest €1.20 wines. Things are changing in Europe: You can now travel between half the countries on the continent without so much as pulling out your passport, and you're more likely to come across an Internet terminal than a coin-operated pay phone. It's a pretty different place than you may remember—but don't worry, we've been keeping up. Whether you're a long-time expat or an international newbie, the freshly reformatted and always updated *Let's Go: Europe 2005* will tell you everything you need to know.

ORGANIZATION. *Let's Go: Europe 2005* is arranged to make the information you need easy to find. The **Discover** chapter offers highlights of the region, tips on when to travel (including a calendar of festivals), and suggested itineraries. The **Essentials** chapter details the nitty-gritty of passports, money, communications, and more—everything you'll need to plan your trip and stay safe on the road. The **Transportation** section will get you to and around Europe, while the ensuing **Alternatives to Tourism** chapter gives advice on how to work or volunteer your way across the continent. Next come 36 jam-packed **country chapters**, from Andorra to Ukraine; each begins with essential information on traveling in that specific country. Don't overlook the **language phrasebook** (p. 1057), offering a crash course in the local tongues you're sure to encounter. The black tabs on the side of the book separate the chapters and should help you navigate your way through.

PRICE RANGES AND RANKINGS. Our 65 indefatigable researchers list establishments in order of value from best to worst; absolute favorites are denoted by the *Let's Go* thumbs-up (🖐). Since the best value does not always mean the cheapest price, we have incorporated a system of **price ranges (❶❷❸❹❺)** into our coverage of accommodations and restaurants. At a glance, you can compare the cost of a night's stay in towns a mile apart or halfway across the country. The price ranges for each country can be found in the introductory sections of each chapter, and for more information on what to expect from each ranking, see p. xix.

NEW FEATURES. Long-time readers will notice a number of other changes in our series, most notably the sidebars that accompany much of our coverage. At the end of the Discover chapter, you'll also find a series of longer **Scholarly Articles** focused on issues affecting Europe as a whole. Whether read on a long train ride or in a quiet hostel, we hope these articles will entertain as well as inform.

ENJOY YOUR TRIP. Need we say more?

A NOTE TO OUR READERS. The information for this book was gathered by *Let's Go* researchers from May through August of 2004. Each listing is based on one researcher's opinion, formed during his or her visit at a particular time. Those traveling at other times may have different experiences since prices, dates, hours, and conditions are always subject to change. You are urged to check the facts presented in this book beforehand to avoid inconvenience and surprises.

Europe: Chapters

CONTENTS

FINLAND (SUOMI) 318

FRANCE 337

REGIONAL EDITORS AND RESEARCHER-WRITERS

CONTRIBUTING WRITERS

Patrice M. Dabrowski — *Celebrating the New Europe (p. 13)*

Dr. Patrice M. Dabrowski is a postdoctoral fellow at Brown University's Watson Institute for International Studies.

Derek Glanz — *Maintaining Borders in an Expanding EU (p. 14)*

Derek Glanz is a doctoral candidate in political science at the University of North Carolina at Chapel Hill. He was the Editor of *Let's Go: Spain & Portugal 1998.*

Brian Palmer and Kathleen Holbrook — *The Continent in Black and White (p. 15)*

Dr. Brian Palmer lectures on ethnography and ethics, and Kathleen Holbrook researches globalization and human values.

Marcel A. Q. LaFlamme — *Learning from the City of Lights (p. 81)*

Marcel LaFlamme was an Associate Editor for *Let's Go: Europe* and *Let's Go: Western Europe.*

Barbara Richter — *Test Tubes and Teutons (p. 82)*

Barbara Richter was a Researcher-Writer for *Let's Go: Austria & Switzerland.*

ACKNOWLEDGEMENTS

TEAM EUROPE THANKS: ⬛Joel, for being all that an ME should be and more. Vicki, for fulfilling the role of personal proddess. Will, for map-making magic. Regional editors and researchers, whose hard work made it all possible. Emma and Teresa, for foodstuffs and fishnets. Jesse, for superfluous coffee breaks. Nalgenes, headphones, and SEAS, all of which somehow made our lives more livable.

STUART THANKS: The indefatigable Europe AEs: Rachel, for poise in the face of chocolate-eating monsters; Josiah, for lunches and patiently taming the Cyrillic beast; Marcel, for incredible prose and much-needed optimism; Kat, for java jaunts and a wonderful sense of humor; and Emily, for musical insights and eagle-eye edits. To Joel, for being true. Emma and Teresa, for being an impossible act to follow. Seth, Chris, Kiernan, Aaron, and Alex for reasonableness. Anne, for making time. To my family, Nana, and Papa, for unwavering support in all my endeavors.

RACHEL THANKS: Stuart, for knowing glances, witty remarks, and constant support; Josiah, Kat, Emily, and Marcel, for putting up with the nonsensical remarks I make when over-caffeinated and under-rested; Will, for handsome maps; Joel, for Advil and radish-edits; Anne, for the ergonomic equipment; EEUR, for providing distraction; all of my lovely roommates—N42 and Dewolfe 62—for jumping, dance parties, and biscuit-cookies; and always, Mom, Dad, Daniel, and Emma—all my love.

JOSIAH THANKS: Stuart, for my introduction to dim sum and the iced Vietnamese; Emily Z., Kat, Marcel, and Rachel, for their work ethic; Seth, Alexandra, Emily G., and Molly, my fellow-travelers in font issues; Katherine and Will, for the moments spent reminiscing about places we never visited together; Matt and Zach and Steve, for putting me up at various points; and Malia and DL for keeping it real.

MARCEL THANKS: Stuart, the brains behind the operation; Rachel, Josiah, Kat, and Emily for bolding every comma; Will for making the compass point north; Gina, Laura, and Patrick for their unfaltering dedication; Team SEAS, without whom 4:30pm was never the same; and Ryan, for whom cable, hot water, and Vietnamese food were really no substitute.

KATHERINE THANKS: Stuart, for vision, moral support, and a constant sense of humor; Rachel, Josiah, Marcel, and Emily, for hard work and late-night laughs; Vicki, for pillow fights and "frame" advice; Teams France and B&I, for their help along the way; Meghan and Leanne, for keeping me sane this summer; Leena and Adam, for wide-eyed Euro-enthusiasm; and especially Mom, Dad, and Ben.

EMILY THANKS: Stuart, ever-thorough, for keeping this whole operation together; Marcel, Kat, Rachel, and Josiah, for redefining the phrase "Type A," (no hyphen); Will, for untangling our streets; team Italy, for amusing marginalia; team SEAS, for putting everything in perspective; Dan, for sunshine and plans of future travel; and, of course, Mom, Nicholas, and the Zeiders for everything along the way.

WILL THANKS: The Europe team, especially Stu and Marcel—for running this thing so smoothly; my parents who put up with me for 18 years and without me for four more; Jim and his adopted accent; Joe and his travels; Grant who is the greatest.

PRICE RANGES >> EUROPE

Our researchers list establishments in order of value from best to worst; our favorites are denoted by the Let's Go thumbs-up (🖐). Since the best value is not always the cheapest price, however, we have also incorporated a system of price ranges, based on a rough expectation of what you will spend. For **accommodations,** we base our range on the cheapest price for which a single traveler can stay for one night. For **restaurants** and other dining establishments, we estimate the average amount a traveler will spend. The table below tells you what you will *typically* find in Europe at the corresponding price range; keep in mind that no system can allow for every individual establishment's quirks.

ACCOMMODATIONS	WHAT YOU'RE *LIKELY* TO FIND
❶	Camping; most dorm rooms, such as HI or other hostels or university dorm rooms. Expect bunk beds and a communal bath; you may have to provide or rent towels and sheets.
❷	Upper-end hostels or small hotels. You may have a private bathroom, or there may be a sink in your room and communal shower in the hall.
❸	A small room with a private bath. Should have decent amenities, such as phone and TV. Breakfast may be included in the price of the room.
❹	Similar to 3, but may have more amenities or be in a more touristed area.
❺	Large hotels or upscale chains. If it's a 5 and it doesn't have the perks you want, you've paid too much.

FOOD	WHAT YOU'RE *LIKELY* TO FIND
❶	Mostly street-corner stands, falafel and shwarma huts, or fast-food joints. Most of the Dutch snack food, including *tostis* and *broodjes*. Desserts like *stropwafels* and *pannekoeken*. Soups and simple noodle dishes in minimalist surroundings. You may have the option of sitting down or getting take-out.
❷	Sandwiches, appetizers at a bar, or low-priced entrees and *tapas*. Ethnic eateries and pan-Asian noodle houses. Take-out is less frequent; generally a sit-down meal, sometimes with servers, but only slightly more upscale decor.
❸	Mid-priced entrees, seafood and exotic pasta dishes. More upscale ethnic eateries. Tip'll bump you up a couple dollars, since you will have a waiter.
❹	A somewhat fancy restaurant or a steakhouse. Either way, you'll have a special knife. Few restaurants in this range have a dress code, but some may look down on t-shirt and jeans.
❺	Food with foreign names and a decent wine list. Slacks and dress shirts may be expected. Don't order PB&J.

ABOUT LET'S GO

GUIDES FOR THE INDEPENDENT TRAVELER

At Let's Go, we see every trip as the chance of a lifetime. If your dream is to grab a machete and forge through the jungles of Brazil, we can take you there. If you'd rather bask in the Riviera sun at a beachside cafe, we'll set you a table. We write for readers who know that there's more to travel than sharing double deckers with tourists and who believe that travel can change both themselves and the world—whether they plan to spend six days in London or six months in Latin America. We'll show you just how far your money can go, and prove that the greatest limitation on your adventures is not your wallet, but your imagination. After all, traveling close to the ground lets you interact more directly with the places and people you've gone to see, making for the most authentic experience.

BEYOND THE TOURIST EXPERIENCE

To help you gain a deeper connection with the places you travel, our researchers give you the heads-up on both world-renowned and off-the-beaten-track attractions, sights, and destinations. They engage with the local culture, writing features on regional cuisine, local festivals, and hot political issues. We've also opened our pages to respected writers and scholars to hear their takes on the countries and regions we cover, and asked travelers who have worked, studied, or volunteered abroad to contribute first-person accounts of their experiences. We've also increased our coverage of responsible travel and expanded each guide's Alternatives to Tourism chapter to share more ideas about how to give back to local communities and learn about the places you travel.

FORTY-FIVE YEARS OF WISDOM

Let's Go got its start in 1960, when a group of creative and well-traveled students compiled their experience and advice into a 20-page mimeographed pamphlet, which they gave to travelers on charter flights to Europe. Four and a half decades later, we've expanded to cover six continents and all kinds of travel—while retaining our founders' adventurous attitude toward the world. Our guides are still researched and written entirely by students on shoestring budgets, experienced travelers who know that train strikes, stolen luggage, food poisoning, and marriage proposals are all part of a day's work. This year, we're expanding our coverage of South America and Southeast Asia, with brand-new *Let's Go: Ecuador*, *Let's Go: Peru*, and *Let's Go: Vietnam*. Our adventure guide series is growing, too, with the addition of *Let's Go: Pacific Northwest Adventure* and *Let's Go: New Zealand Adventure*. And we're immensely excited about our new *Let's Go: Roadtripping USA*—two years, eight routes, and sixteen researchers and editors have put together a travel guide like none other.

THE LET'S GO COMMUNITY

More than just a travel guide company, Let's Go is a community. Our small staff comes together because of our shared passion for travel and our desire to help other travelers see the world. We love it when our readers become part of the Let's Go community as well—when you travel, drop us a postcard (67 Mt. Auburn St., Cambridge, MA 02138, USA) or send us an e-mail (feedback@letsgo.com) to tell us about your adventures and discoveries.

For more information, visit us online: www.letsgo.com.

DISCOVER EUROPE

DISCOVER

The most popular tourist destination in the world, Europe offers as many unique journeys as it has travelers to take them. The continent's fame is age-old, and some things never change. Aspiring writers still spin impassioned romances in Parisian alleyways; a glass of sangria at twilight on the Plaza Mayor tastes as sweet as ever; and iconic treasures, from the onion domes of St. Basil's cathedral to the behemoth slabs of Stonehenge, inspire wonder in another generation of wayfarers. Yet against this ancient backdrop, a freshly costumed continent takes the stage at the beginning of a new act. As the European Union has expanded from a small clique of nations trading coal and steel to a 25-member commonwealth with a parliament and a central bank, Eastern and Western Europe find themselves more intimately connected than ever before.

The results are impressive: While Prague and Budapest may have been the hot spots of the 90s, emerging cities like Kraków and Stockholm are poised to lure travelers off the beaten path in the early years of the new millennium. Just-minted cultural meccas like Bilbao's Guggenheim and London's Tate Modern have breezily joined the ranks of timeless galleries like the Louvre and the Hermitage, while a constant influx of students and DJs who verge on pop icons keep the nightlife dependably hot. Whether it's the pubs of Dublin, the upscale bistros of Lyon, the frozen north country of Sweden, or the dazzling beaches of Croatia's Dalmation Coast that call to you, *Let's Go: Europe 2005* has the answer.

WHEN TO GO

To the delight of skiing and ice-climbing enthusiasts, traveling during the low season (mid-Sept. to June) brings cheaper airfares and accommodations, in addition to freeing you from the hordes of fanny-pack-toting tourists. On the flip side, many attractions, hostels, and tourist offices close in the winter, and in some rural areas local transportation dwindles or shuts down altogether. Most of Europe's best **festivals** (see below) also take place during the summer months. For more info on the best time to make your excursion, see the **Weather Chart** on p. 1067.

WHAT TO DO

We've compiled a few launching pads from which you can start drawing up a custom itinerary: **Themed categories** let you know where to find your museums, your mountains, and your madhouses; **Let's Go Picks** point you toward some of the quirkiest gems you could uncover; **suggested itineraries** outline the common paths across Europe. After getting a general impression of the continent, make sure to turn to the country-specific **Discover** section at the beginning of each chapter for more detailed info.

🏛 MUSEUMS

It is a truism to say that Europe has bred all the masterworks of Western art from ancient Greece through the Renaissance to Impressionism and beyond, but what a breathtaking truism it is. Not only did it breed them, it has also kept most of them close to home in cultural strongholds like the Louvre, the Prado, and the Vatican Museums. Imperial conquest certainly helped Britain to compile the marvels that outfit the British Museum and Russia to amass the wealth so picturesquely on display in the galleries of the Hermitage. European museums do not merely house art, however. They also shelter torture instruments, marijuana, puppets, erotica, marzipan, leprosy, secret police, and spirits both literal and figurative—in short, whatever can be classified and captioned. A trip across Europe qualifies as little more than a stopover without an afternoon spent among some of the paintings and artifacts below—whether they include the pinnacles of Western culture, or its morbid or risqué dregs.

THE PICTURESQUE	AND THE OFTEN GROTESQUE
🖼 **FRANCE: THE LOUVRE** (p. 361). Along with troves of work by nearly every other master, Da Vinci's *Mona Lisa* smiles out from behind her glass case and her crowds of beady-eyed tourists.	🖼 **SWITZERLAND: COLLECTION DE L'ART BRUT** (p. 1042). Inspiration and madness have never been harder to separate than in these artworks by institutionalized schizophrenics and criminals.
🖼 **RUSSIA: THE HERMITAGE** (p. 891). In the palatial St. Petersburg home of the Tsars resides the world's largest art collection. Only 5% of its 3 million pieces is on display at any one time.	🖼 **CZECH REPUBLIC: MUSEUM OF MEDIEVAL TORTURE INSTRUMENTS** (p. 271). Save lunch for after visiting these exhibits and the accompanying explanations, all in meticulous detail.
🖼 **SPAIN: MUSEO DEL PRADO** (p. 930). It's an art-lover's heaven to harrow the hell painted by Hieronymus Bosch. Also here are works by El Greco, Goya, Rubens, Titian, and Velázquez.	🖼 **GERMANY: MUSEUM FÜR PUPPENTHEATER** (p. 471). Thousands of hand, string, shadow, and stick puppets from around the globe make up the largest private puppet collection in the world.
🖼 **BRITAIN: THE BRITISH MUSEUM** (p. 176). Gathering world artifacts like Egypt's Rosetta Stone or Iran's Oxus Treasure, the British Museum ironically has almost nothing British in it at all.	🖼 **THE NETHERLANDS: CANNABIS COLLEGE** (p. 757). Cannabis College is just like college, except there are no libraries, no lectures, no studying, no liquor, no dorms, and no full-time students.
🖼 **ITALY: VATICAN MUSEUMS** (p. 642). Look for the *School of Athens* here, in Rome; the painting crowns a wealth of Renaissance and other art, including the incredible Raphael Rooms.	🖼 **FRANCE: MUSÉE DU VIN** (p. 420). See the vats and winepresses housed in the 15th-century Hôtel des Ducs de Bourgogne for free before splurging on the age-ripened vintages themselves.
🖼 **AUSTRIA: KUNSTHISTORISCHES MUSEUM** (p. 101). Venetian paintings are the highlights of the world's 4th-largest art collection, while the Hof-jagd- und Rustkammer gathers medieval arms.	🖼 **LITHUANIA: DEVIL MUSEUM** (p. 725). Devil-worshippers can practice idolatry in 2000 different ways in this museum, which has amassed that many depictions of devils in various media.
🖼 **GREECE: NATIONAL ARCHAEOLOGICAL MUSEUM** (p. 517). Athens itself may be museum enough for some, but this building collects what's too small to be seen with a placard on the street.	🖼 **GERMANY: EROTIC ART MUSEUM** (p. 471). Picasso's visual imagination seems tame next to *Kama Sutra* poses and Victorian pornography, not to mention—but hush, this is a family publication.
🖼 **BRITAIN: TATE GALLERIES** (p. 177). While the Tate Modern collects Picassos, Duchamps, and others, the Tate Britain assembles the works of Blake, Hockney, Rosetti, and Turner.	🖼 **RUSSIA: KGB MUSEUM** (p. 884). Quiz a current FSB agent and learn everything about Russia's secret police from Ivan the Terrible to the present. Everything, that is, except for its secrets.
🖼 **ITALY: GALLERIA BORGHESE** (p. 642). Sculpture and paintings by Bernini, Caravaggio, Rubens, and Titian are a sight for sore eyes after staring at the paltry canvases of the Vatican Museums.	🖼 **NORWAY: LEPROSY MUSEUM** (p. 791). Ancient treatments of this fabled disease are exhibited here in cells that housed as many as three patients at once into the 1950s.
🖼 **THE NETHERLANDS: RIJKSMUSEUM** (p. 759). Renovations should not deter anyone from seeing the pinnacles of the Dutch Golden Age, like Rembrandt and Vermeer, line up along the walls.	🖼 **HUNGARY: SZABÓ MARZIPAN MUSEUM** (p. 559). Only one statuette on display at this museum is not composed of marzipan: an 80kg white chocolate effigy of Michael Jackson.

👁 ARCHITECTURE

European history is legible not only in textbooks, but also in the architecture bequeathed by millennia of secular and religious tradition. Royal lines from the early Welsh dynasties and Polish kings to the Bourbons, Hapsburgs, and Romanovs have all been outlasted by the emblems of their magnificence—castles, palaces, and chateaux. Monarchs were careless of expense, and jealous of each other: Louis XIV's palace at Versailles, which has become a byword for opulence, whet the ambition of rival monarchs and spurred the construction of rival domiciles, among them Peter the Great's Peterhof, Charles III's Reggia, and Ludwig II's Herreninsel. No expense was spared for God, either, as attest the many splendid cathedrals, monasteries, synagogues, temples, and mosques that rise skyward from their low cityscapes. Córdoba's Mezquita mosque and Budapest's Great Synagogue are among the finest of their kind, while Chartres's Cathédrale de Notre Dame and Cologne's Dom are pinnacles—no pun intended—of the Gothic style.

HUMBLE ABODES	THE HOLIEST OF HOLIES
GERMANY: NEUSCHWANSTEIN (p. 504). A waterfall, an artificial grotto, a byzantine throne room, and a Wagnerian opera hall deck out the inspiration for Disney's Cinderella Castle.	**ITALY: SISTINE CHAPEL** (p. 640). Since the 16th century, white smoke has risen from the chapel after the election of a new pope. Michelangelo's ceiling frescoes are also worth a glance.
FRANCE: VERSAILLES PALACE (p. 370). Little can compare to Versailles, testimony to the extravagance of pre-Revolutionary France and the prototype for regal self-indulgence down the ages.	**SPAIN: MEZQUITA** (p. 944). Córdoba's Mezquita, one of the most important Islamic monuments in the West, is supported by 850 pink-and-blue marble and alabaster columns.
BRITAIN: BUCKINGHAM PALACE (p. 165). Queen Elizabeth still resides here, among the Throne Room, the Music Room, the opulent White Room, the gardens, and the galleries.	**FRANCE: CHARTRES CATHEDRAL** (p. 370). Arguably the world's finest example of early Gothic architecture has intact stained-glass windows from the 12th century, and a crypt from the 9th.
RUSSIA: PETERHOF (p. 894). Nothing was too good for the tsars, or too holy to have been built by more than serf labor. Peter the Great's project stretches magnificently along the Gulf of Finland.	**HUNGARY: THE GREAT SYNAGOGUE** (p. 556). Europe's largest synagogue can hold 3000 faithful. Inscribed leaves of a metal tree in the courtyard commemorate the victims of the Holocaust.
ITALY: THE REGGIA (p. 702). Decorating Charles III's Reggia are a man-made waterfall and, in the English Gardens, man-made ruins modeled on those in Pompeii and Paestum.	**BRITAIN: WESTMINSTER ABBEY** (p. 166). Royal weddings and coronations take place in the sanctuary; nearby poets and politicians from the earliest kings to Winston Churchill rest in peace.
SPAIN: THE ALHAMBRA (p. 956). At an impressionistic distance, the Alhambra looks like a worn-out toy; zoom in, and its wood, stucco, and ceramics reveal exquisite beauty.	**ITALY: THE DUOMO** (p. 687). It is hard to know which to be more impressed by, the massive nave built by Arnolfo di Cambrio, or the dome built by Filippo Brunelleschi that crowns it.
POLAND: WAWEL CASTLE (p. 820). Kraków's hillside masterpiece includes a castle begun in the 900s, as well as a cathedral that was once the seat of the archbishopric of Pope John Paul II.	**GERMANY: KÖLNER DOM** (p. 477). With a ceiling 44m high and 1350 sq. m of stained glass illuminating the interior with particolored sunlight, Cologne's cathedral is Germany's greatest.
AUSTRIA: SCHLOß SCHÖNBRUNN (p. 100). It's hard to tell which is more impressive, the palace or the classical gardens that extend behind it and stretch a full four times the length of the structure.	**RUSSIA: SERGIEV POSAD** (p. 885). Under the trademark Orthodox onion domes, Russia's most celebrated pilgrimage site now thrives again after seven decades of state-propagated atheism.
BRITAIN: CAERNARFON CASTLE (p. 214). Edward I began this architectural feat in 1283 in order to maintain control over northern Wales, but left it unfinished when he ran out of money.	**GREECE: THE PARTHENON** (p. 515). Keeping vigil over Athens from the Acropolis, the Parthenon is a needful pilgrimage for any culture-worshiper; the Greek mythology has become common to all.
FRANCE: CHENONCEAU (p. 379). A series of noblewomen crafted one of the most graceful chateaux in France, which arches elegantly over the Cher river.	**AUSTRIA: STEPHANSDOM** (p. 99). Work on the north tower of Vienna's cathedral stopped, according to legend, after a pact with the devil went awry and the builder plunged to his death.

DISCOVER

⚠ OUTDOORS

Granted, it may not be what you came for. Europe, as the seat of modern civilization, tends to draw people to its museums and ruins more than its mountains and rivers. But for any traveler, budget or prodigal, solo or companioned, expert or neophyte, an excursion to the courtly outdoors can round-off (or salvage, as the case may be) any journey. Fjords, volcanoes, vales, gorges, plateaus, and upthrusts pock the spots where the Earth's plates wreck and unwreck at their edges. Waters of innumerable shades of blue wash up on uninhabited shores of black-, white-, and red-sand beaches. Mountains, sprawling with trees or culminating in icy apexes, continue to challenge mankind and dwarf the man-made, just as they, and the rest of the European landscape, did when civilization began.

LANDSCAPES	SEAVIEWS
▨ **GERMANY: THE SCHWARZWALD** (p. 489). The eerie darkness pervading this tangled expanse of evergreen, once the inspiration of the Brothers Grimm, continues to lure hikers and skiers alike.	▨ **ITALY: THE AMALFI COAST** (p. 703). The azure waters that make up the coastline south of Naples are second only to the gravity-defying, jagged rocks which overlook them.
▨ **SWITZERLAND: INTERLAKEN** (p. 1026). Thanks to its mild climate and pristine landscape, Interlaken quenches the thirst for anything outdoors, whether it be hiking, bungee jumping, or skydiving.	▨ **NORWAY: SOGNEFJORD** (p. 794). Thundering waterfalls give way to halcyon lakes, sweeping green meadows, and regal glaciers at the longest fjord in the world.
▨ **GREECE: MOUNT OLYMPUS** (p. 527). Erupting out of the Thermaic Gulf, the 3000m height and formidable slopes of Olympus so awed the ancients that they believed it to be the divine dwelling of their immortal pantheon.	▨ **FRANCE: D-DAY BEACHES** (p. 372). The heroism of the Allied forces is tastefully preserved on the beaches near Bayeux, where thousands of soldiers were killed or wounded in battle over 60 years ago.
▨ **PORTUGAL: PARQUE NATURAL DE DOURO** (p. 855). Flowering almond trees soften the rough terrain of Portugal's most esteemed park, offering insights into the country's wildlife, flora, and fauna.	▨ **DENMARK: ÆRØSKØBING** (p. 303). Economic stagnation and recent conservation efforts have successfully fossilized the 19th-century lifestyle and charm of this tiny island.
▨ **THE NETHERLANDS: HOGE VELUWE NATIONAL PARK** (p. 769). Wild boars and red deer inhabit the 13,500 acres of forestry, while the park's museum houses works by Van Gogh and Picasso.	▨ **BRITAIN: LAKE DISTRICT NATIONAL PARK** (p. 207). Four million sheep have cast their votes for the loveliest park in England—an equal number of summertime tourists seem to agree.
▨ **ICELAND: ÞINGVELLIR NATIONAL PARK** (p. 576). Few sights in the world allow visitors to straddle separating tectonic plates amidst lava fields.	▨ **FRANCE: CANNES** (p. 399). Never mind the annual film festival; the essence of Cannes is found on its stunning beaches and palm-lined boardwalks.
▨ **SLOVAKIA: SLOVENSKÝ RAJ NATIONAL PARK** (p. 905). Hikers who tire of the views overlooking the Tatras can rest in the frozen columns, gigantic walls, and hardened waterfalls of the Dobšinská Ice Caves, which date back to the last Ice Age.	▨ **SWEDEN: SKÄRGÅRD ARCHIPELAGO** (p. 1004). A popular daytrip from the capital city, this archipelago has become a favorite of sailing enthusiasts and less-than-overzealous hikers and picnickers.
▨ **ITALY: MT. VESUVIUS** (p. 702). The only active volcano on the continent is overdue for another eruption. Scientists claim that the next tantrum the ancient mountain throws will be more violent than the one which buried Pompeii in AD 79.	▨ **SPAIN: SITGES** (p. 975). One of the many destinations vying for the title of "Jewel of the Mediterranean," Sitges's maintains its credibility as a must-see beach town with prime tanning grounds baked by over 300 sunny days a year.
▨ **AUSTRIA: THE HOHE TAUERN NATIONAL PARK** (p. 110). Saturated with glaciers, mountains, lakes, and endangered species, the largest park in Europe offers ice-free mountain paths once trod by Celts and Romans.	▨ **BRITAIN: LOCH LOMOND** (p. 226). While tales of monsters are generally reserved for another Loch, Lomond still manages to attract travelers with the largest lake in Britain, along with the 38 islands which dot it.
▨ **POLAND: WIELICZKA SALT MINES** (p. 822). Discovered by monks digging a well, miners and artists transformed the salt deposits into a maze of chambers full of sculptures and carvings.	▨ **CROATIA: HVAR ISLAND** (p. 253). Hordes of sun-soaked and salt-licked revelers descend upon Hvar, internationally regarded as one of the 10 most beautiful beaches in the world.

✤FÊTES! FIESTAS! FESTIVALS!

COUNTRIES	APR. – JUNE	JULY – AUG.	SEPT. – MAR.
AUSTRIA AND SWITZERLAND	Vienna Festival (mid-May to mid-June) Open-Air St. Gallen (late June)	Salzburger Festspiele (July 24-Aug. 31)	Escalade (Geneva; early Dec.) Fasnacht (Basel; Feb. 14-16)
BELGIUM	Festival of Fairground Arts (Wallonie; late May)	Gentse Feesten (Ghent; July 16-25)	International French Language Film Festival (Namur; late Sept.)
BRITAIN AND IRELAND	Bloomsday (Dublin; June 16) Wimbledon (London; June 20-July 3)	Fringe Festival (Aug. 7-29) Edinburgh Int'l Festival (Aug.14-Sept. 4)	Matchmaking Festival (Lisdoonvarna; Sept.) St. Patrick's Day (Mar. 17)
CROATIA	World Festival of Animated Film (Zagreb; May)	Int'l Folklore Festival (July) Dubrovnik Summer Fest. (July and Aug.)	Int'l Puppet Festival (Sept.) Zagreb Fest (Nov.)
CZECH REPUBLIC	Prague Spring Festival (May)	Český Krumlov Int'l Music Fest (Aug.)	Int'l Organ Fest (Olomouc; Sept.)
FRANCE	Cannes Film Festival (May)	Tour de France (July) Festival d'Avignon (July-Aug.) Bastille Day (July 14)	Carnevale (Nice, Nantes; Feb.)
GERMANY	May Day (Berlin; May 1) Christopher St. Day (late June)	Love Parade (Berlin; mid-July) Rhine in Flames Festival (Rhine Valley; Aug. 9)	Oktoberfest (Munich; Sept. 17-Oct. 2) Fasching (Munich; Jan. 7-Feb. 4)
HUNGARY	Golden Shell Folklore (Siófok; June)	Sziget Rock Fest (Budapest; July) Baroque Festival (Eger; July)	Eger Vintage Days (Sept.) Festival of Wine Songs (Pécs; Sept.)
ITALY	Maggio Musicale (Florence; Apr. 30-June 28) Festa di San Gennaro (Naples; May 7, Dec. 16, Sept. 19)	Il Palio (Siena; July 2 and Aug. 16) Umbria Jazz Festival (July)	Dante Festival (Ravenna; mid-Sept.) Carnevale (late Feb.) Scoppio del Carro (Florence; Easter Su)
THE NETHERLANDS	Queen's Day (Apr. 30) Holland Festival (June)	Gay Pride Parade (Aug.)	Flower Parade (Aalsmeer; Sept. 3) Cannabis Cup (Nov.)
POLAND	Int'l Short Film (Kraków; May) Festival of Jewish Culture (Kraków; June)	Street Theater (Kraków; July) Highlander Folklore (Zakopane; Aug.)	Kraków Jazz Fest (Oct.) Nat'l Blues Music (Torún; Nov.)
PORTUGAL	Burning of the Ribbons (Coimbra; early May)	Feira Popular (mid-July)	Carnival (Mar. 4) Semana Santa (Mar. 20-27)
SCANDINAVIA	Midsummer (June 21-23) Bergen Festival (May 21-June 1)	Savonlinna Opera Festival (July 2-29) Quart Music Festival (Kristiansand; early July)	Helsinki Festival (Aug. 22-Sept. 7)
SPAIN	Feria de Abril (Seville; late Apr.)	San Fermines (Pamplona; July 6-14)	Las Fallas (Valencia; Mar.) Carnaval (Mar.)

DISCOVER

DISCOVER

SUGGESTED ITINERARIES

There is no formula for the perfect itinerary in Europe. Here we humbly suggest a few routes to give you an idea of what is possible. The **Basics** below outlines our skeletal suggestions for the best of Europe. We've also included some regional itineraries to help you plan a few extra forays. These other itineraries can be thought of as **Building Blocks** to tack onto a basic route. For more in-depth suggestions, see the **Suggested Itineraries** in the individual country chapters, as well as **Themed** and **Featured Itineraries** scattered throughout the book.

THE BASICS

THE BEST OF EUROPE IN 2 MONTHS
From **London** (4 days; p. 155), catch a cheap flight to energetic **Dublin** (2 days; p. 584). Get studious in **Oxford** (1 day; p. 192), then take in the natural beauty of the **Cotswolds** (1 day; p. 197) en route to elegant **Bath** (2 days; p. 189). Meet the continent in the museums and cafes of **Paris** (4 days; p. 342) and the gorgeous chateaux of the **Loire Valley** (1 day; p. 376). Venture south to worldly **Madrid** (2 days; p. 921) and then hook around to otherworldly **Barcelona** (3 days; p. 960). After a night in

Marseille (1 day; p. 391), soak up the Riviera's rays in **Nice** (1 day; p. 400). Embrace the Tuscan sun in **Florence** (2 days; p. 681) and pause at stunning **Siena** (1 day; p. 692) en route to **Rome** (3 days; p. 620). Wind through **Venice** (2 days; p. 665) and continue on to posh **Milan** (1 day; p. 646). Stop in **Lyon** (1 day; p. 414) for your trip's best meal before heading to international **Geneva** (1 day; p. 1038). Scale the Swiss Alps around **Zermatt** (1 day; p. 1037) and **Interlaken** (1 day; p. 1026). Move on to cultured **Zurich** (1 day;

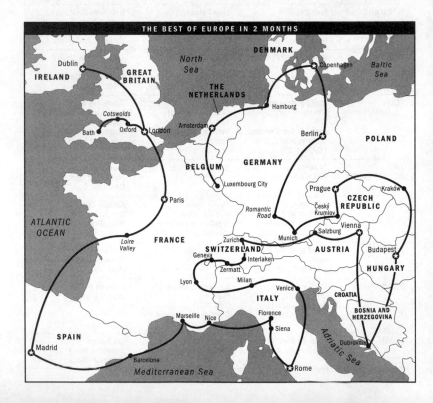

p. 1028) and classical **Salzburg** (1 day; p. 104) before taking in an opera in **Vienna** (2 days; p. 90). Go south toward Croatia's beautiful **Dalmatian Coast** and up-and-coming **Dubrovnik** (2 days; p. 254). Soak in the baths of **Budapest** (2 days; p. 548) and then turn to historical **Kraków** (2 days; p. 816). **Prague** (3 days; p. 260) and gorgeous **Český Krumlov** (1 day; p. 278) may convince you never to leave Central Europe, but it's onward for a beer in **Munich** (3 days; p. 490). The **Romantic Road** (2 days; p. 503) will steer you to **Berlin** (3 days; p. 433). Head north to cosmopolitan **Copenhagen** (2 days; p. 288) before dropping down to restless **Hamburg** (2 days; p. 466). Succumb to hedonism in **Amsterdam** (3 days; p. 746), then earn your virtue back in unjustly neglected **Luxembourg City** (1 day; p. 731).

THE BEST OF EUROPE IN 1 MONTH

THE BEST OF EUROPE IN 1 MONTH

Start in **London** (3 days; p. 155), spinning from theaters to museums to pubs, then chunnel to rejuvenating **Paris** (3 days; p. 342). Sample the cuisine of **Lyon** (1 day; p. 414) en route to animated **Barcelona** (2 days; p. 960). Graze the Mediterranean shoreline, hitting the French Riviera in **Nice** (1 day; p. 400) and taking in the Renaissance art of **Florence** (2 days; p. 681). Discover the one and only **Rome** (3 days; p. 620) before gliding through **Venice** (2 days; p. 665). Pick up fashion pointers in **Milan** (1 day; p. 646), then don your banker's suit in **Geneva** (1 day; p. 1038). Continue north for a frothy pint in **Munich** (2 days; p. 490) and a cup of coffee in **Vienna** (2 days; p. 90) before following the crowds to enrapturing **Prague** (2 days; p.

260) and hip **Kraków** (2 days; p. 816). Overwhelm yourself in sprawling **Berlin** (2 days; p. 433), continue the revelry in libertine **Amsterdam** (2 days; p. 746), and then settle down to a soft landing in demure **Brussels** (1 day; p. 127).

THE BEST OF THE MEDITERRANEAN IN 6 WEEKS

Begin in the flower-filled *terrazas* of **Seville** (2 days; p. 945) before basking on the soft-sand beaches of **Cádiz** (2 days; p. 951). Stand on the imposing Rock of **Gibraltar** (1 day; p. 952) en route to the Costa del Sol town of **Málaga** (1 day; p. 953). Skip inland to **Granada** (2 days; p. 954) and wind your way through Moorish fortresses. From **Valencia** (2 days; p. 958), hop around the **Balearic Islands** between **Ibiza's** foam parties and **Menorca's** raw beaches (3 days; p. 984). Ferry to vibrant **Barcelona** (3 days; p. 960) before hitting the **Costa Brava** and the Dalí museum in

THE BEST OF THE MEDITERRANEAN IN 6 WEEKS

Figueres (2 days; p. 974). Head to France's Provençal **Nîmes** (1 day; p. 388) and then to Roman **Arles** (1 day; p. 389). Great theater awaits in **Avignon** (1 day; p. 388), before you revel in **Aix-en-Provence** (1 day; p. 390). Taste the *bouillabaisse* in **Marseille** (1 day; p. 391) and move on to the glitter of the Côte d'Azur: Movie stars await you in **Cannes** (2 days; p. 399) and nonstop parties in **Nice** (2 days; p. 400). Explore the gorgeous cliff-top villages of the **Corniches** (1 day; p. 406) before hitting the world-famous casinos of **Monte-Carlo** (1 day; p. 407). Take a breather by relaxing in the placid waters of **Finale Ligure** (1 day; p. 656) and hiking through the colorful villages of Italy's **Cinque Terre** (1 day; p. 658). Admire the architecture of **Genoa** (1 day; p. 655) before ooh-ing and aah-ing over **Florence's** magnificent art collections (3 days; p. 681). Check out the two-toned duomo of **Siena** (2 days; p. 692) before indulging your gladiatorial fantasies in capital city **Rome** (4 days; p. 620). From **Naples** (2 days; p. 697), home of pizza and pickpockets, finish off your trip in sun-drenched **Capri** (2 days; p. 704).

SCANDINAVIA IN 3 WEEKS From modern **Copenhagen** (4 days; p. 288), daytrip to the castle of Frederiksborg Slot in **Hillerød** (1 day; p. 297). Head into Sweden through **Malmö** (1 day; p. 1007) to reach elegant **Gothenburg** (2 days; p. 1010). Zip to Norway's lively capital, **Oslo** (2 days; p. 778), and take the haunting train ride west to laid-back **Bergen** (2 days; p. 787) before dipping your toes in icy, dramatic **Sognefjord** (1 day; p. 794) and **Geirangerfjord** (1 day; p. 797). Head back to Oslo to

catch the night train to Sweden's **Stockholm** (3 days; p. 993), the jewel of Scandinavia's cities. Take a daytrip to brainy **Uppsala** (1 day; p. 1004), home of Sweden's oldest university. Hop the ferry to Finland's **Helsinki** (2 days; p. 322), where east meets west, and end your travels among the seaside villas of unassuming **Hanko** (1 day; p. 329). Take the ferry to Estonia's **Tallinn** (p. 312) to link with the Baltic Sea itinerary.

THE ENGLISH CHANNEL (31 DAYS)
After visiting **London** (4 days; p. 155), punt on the Isis in **Oxford** (1 day; p. 192). From there, explore elegant **Bath** (1 day; p. 189) before strolling in the quaint **Cotswolds** (1 day; p. 197). Check out Shakespeare's hometown, **Stratford-upon-Avon** (1 day; p. 196). Breeze through **Manchester** (1 day; p. 201) on your way to Beatles worship in **Liverpool** (1 day; p. 202). Cross the Irish Sea to **Dublin** (2 days; p. 584), home to James Joyce and Guinness, and then discover the charming villages of rural Ireland in the **Ring of Kerry** (2 days; p. 601). From **Galway** (1 day; p. 605), a center of Irish culture, forge on to neighborly **Belfast** (2 days; p. 609). From there, it's back across the Irish Sea to Stranraer, trainbound for historic

SCANDINAVIA IN 3 WEEKS

NORWAY · Geirangerfjord · Sognefjord · Bergen · Oslo · SWEDEN · FINLAND · Uppsala · Helsinki · Hanko · Stockholm · Gothenburg · DENMARK · Hillerød · Malmö · Copenhagen

THE ENGLISH CHANNEL

NORTHERN IRELAND · SCOTLAND · North Sea · Edinburgh · Belfast · Lake District · GREAT BRITAIN · Galway · IRELAND · Dublin · Liverpool · Manchester · Ring of Kerry · ENGLAND · WALES · Stratford-upon-Avon · Cotswolds · Oxford · Bath · London · St-Malo · Mont-St-Michel · Rennes · Paris · Tours · Loire Valley · ATLANTIC OCEAN · FRANCE

Edinburgh (2 days; p. 216) and the sublime **Lake District** (2 days; p. 207). Head back to London and hop a train for carefree **Paris** (4 days; p. 342). Use **Tours** (2 days; p. 378) as a hub for exploring the fertile **Loire Valley** before pressing on to **Rennes** (1 day; p. 373). The fortified island of **Mont-St-Michel** (1 day; p. 373) gives you a chance to stretch your legs and imagination before you settle into the seaside paradise of **St-Malo** (2 days; p. 374). A train will whisk you back to Paris and your homebound airline of choice. But should your travel bug persist, a train to **Marseille** (p. 391) leaves you at the heart of the Mediterranean itinerary.

CENTRAL EUROPE (31 DAYS) Begin in glamorous, Bohemian **Prague** (3 days; p. 260), then stop in stately **Wrocław** (1 day; p. 824) on the way to the seaport of **Gdańsk** (1 day; p. 828). Continue to nononsense **Warsaw** (2 days; p. 808), then to trendy **Kraków** (2 days; p. 816). Hike in the Tatras surrounding **Zakopane** (2 days; p. 823) and **Starý Smokovec** (1 day; p. 904). Next, visit vibrant **Budapest** (3 days; p. 548), followed by the warm, shallow waters of **Lake Balaton** (2 days; p. 564). Wander the streets of **Zagreb** (2 days; p. 246), then stop over in **Sarajevo** (2 days; p. 147) before returning to Croatia to explore the heavenly islands of the **Dalmatian Coast** (3 days; p. 251), between Dubrovnik and Split. Continue on to lovely **Ljubljana** (2 days; p. 910), then experience the grandeur of **Vienna** (3 days; p. 90), ending up in blossoming **Bratislava** (2 days; p. 899).

THE BALTIC SEA (22 DAYS) Begin in the bustling, medieval streets of **Tallinn** (2 days; p. 312), then relax on the tranquil and secluded **Estonian Islands** (4 days; p. 316). Move on to the lively university town of **Tartu** (2 days; p. 316), before immersing yourself in glitzy **Rīga** (2 days; p. 711). Head down the coast of Lithuania to **Palanga, Klaipėda,** and dreamy **Nida** (3 days; p. 727). Continue to up-and-coming **Vilnius** (2 days; p. 721), one of the many "New Pragues," then wake up from the night train in **Moscow's** historic Red Square (4 days; p. 874). Cap it off spending some time in **St. Petersburg,** home of the ornate delights of the Hermitage (3 days; p. 886). Connect to the Scandinavian route via **Helsinki** (p. 322).

THE BEST OF SOUTHERN ITALY AND GREECE IN 4 WEEKS

THE BEST OF SOUTHERN ITALY AND GREECE IN 4 WEEKS

View the rubble of the Roman Empire, the cathedrals of high Christianity, and the art of the Renaissance in **Rome** (5 days; p. 620). From **Naples** (2 days; p. 697), daytrip to **Pompeii** (1 day; p. 702) and check out Roman remains buried in AD 79. Then escape to the sensuous paradise of **Capri** (2 days; p. 704). Hop off the boot at Brindisi or Bari, from which overnight ferries (1 day) go to Greece. Get off at **Corfu** (1 day; p. 530), beloved by literary luminary Oscar Wilde and partiers alike, and continue on to **Patras** (1 day; p. 519). Wrestle in **Olympia** (1 day; p. 520) before beginning your Peloponnesian adventure with a survey of the ancient ruins in **Naf-**plion, **Mycenae,** and **Epidavros** (3 days; p. 523). Get initiated in the "mysteries of love" in equally ruinous **Corinth** (1 day; p. 523). On to chaotic **Athens,** a jumble of things ancient and modern (2 days; p. 509). Succumb to your longing in the Cyclades: Party all night long on **Mykonos** (1 day; p. 532), repent the morning after at the Temple of Apollo in **Delos** (1 day; p. 533), and continue on to the earthly paradise of **Santorini** (2 days; p. 535). Catch the ferry to **Crete,** where chic **Iraklion** and the home of the Minotaur await (2 days; p. 536). Base yourself in **Hania** and hike the **Samaria Gorge** (2 days; p. 538).

THEMED ITINERARIES

THE ULTIMATE PUB CRAWL (25 DAYS) A beery romp through Europe should begin in Dublin. Let the bartender at **The Stag's Head** (p. 593) pour you a slow, dark pint of Guinness beneath the pub's stained-glass windows, and then it's on to Oxford via London. Swap yarns with the young scholars at **Turf's Tavern** (p. 195), and then hop the ferry in Hull for Zeebrugge. It's hard to choose among the 300 brews at Bruges's **'t Brugs Beertje** (p. 138), but Cologne's **Brauhaus Früh am Dom** (p. 477) beckons and so does **Café 't Smalle** (p. 763), one of Amsterdam's venerable *bruin cafés*. The Thalys will whisk you down to Paris, where you can nurse a mojito in the dim, second-story salon of **Les Etages** (p. 366). Angle your way south and west to Salamanca, where the tall *chupito* shots at **Bar La Chupiteria** (p. 940) will set you back just €1. Savor the acrid bite of *agave* at Lisbon's **A Tasca Tequila Bar** (p. 845), and

then sip your way through a snifter of absinthe at Barcelona's **Casa Almirall** (p. 973). **Dan Racing** (p. 397), in Marseille, dares you to take the stage for a jangly, communal jam session, but you can recover your dignity under the high ceilings of **Enoteca Alessi** (p. 687), a classy Florentine wine bar. The leafy **Augustinerkeller** beer garden (p. 497) in Munich is dwarfed by Salzburg's enormous **Augustiner Bräustübl-Mülln** (p. 108), which has been irrigating western Austria since 1621. Pay a visit to the labyrinthine **wine cellars** (p. 563) of Eger, and then make your pilgrimage to the **Pilsner Urquell brewery** (p. 277) in Plzen. Duck into the cellar at Prague's **Kozička** (p. 272), and then stop by the incongruously authentic Irish pub **Morgan's** (p. 815) in downtown Warsaw. From here, it's a straight shot to **Trys Mylimos** (p. 726) in Klaipeda, for a round of Lithuanian porter and a vow to stay on the wagon this time.

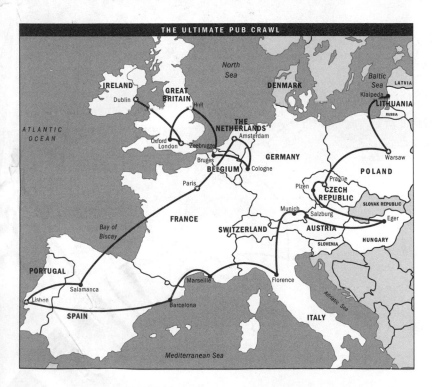

THE ULTIMATE PUB CRAWL

MUSIC FESTIVALS TOUR 2005

Europe comes alive every summer with seemingly endless festivals representing every musical genre. Kick off your summer tour on July 1 at Birmingham's **International Jazz Festival** (July 1-3; p. 198), where admission to many of the concerts is free. Make your way to **Echternach** (July 4-7; p. 730) to soak up classical strains in a town who's history and music have been intertwined for centuries. Catch a train to Beaune for the **Beaune Festival** (July 8-10; p. 420) which specializes in baroque opera. Fast forward 300 years at Bern's **Gurten Festival** (July14-17; p. 1023), where previous headliners including Oasis, Erykah Badu, and Ani DiFranco are evidence of their eclectic programs. Lucerne's **Blue Balls Festival** (July 22-25; p. 1034) offers eager crowds a mix of jazz, blues, and pop. Head south to Verona's ancient Roman amphitheater, which hosts a summer-long **opera festival** (July 28-Aug. 3; p. 678). The 2005 season will feature *Nabucco, Aida, and La Boheme.* In addition to opera and concerts, **Salzburg's** annual festival regularly offers first-class drama (Aug. 5-9; p. 104). Isaac was so distraught at leaving Innsbruck that he composed his enduring "Innsbruck, Ich muss dich lassen" (Innsbruck, I must leave you). Today, Isaac and his contemporaries are celebrated at the annual **Early Music Festival** (Aug. 12-17; p. 104). The **European Music Festival** (Aug. 18-22; p. 488) in Stuttgart usually focuses on large-scale orchestral and choral works. Round out your tour in Cologne for the **Musikfest am Ring,** one of the world's largest pop music festivals featuring up to 1000 bands in a single weekend (Aug. 26-28; p. 475). Be sure to confirm festival dates in early spring, as dates are subject to change.

MUSIC FESTIVALS TOUR 2005

Manufacturing Continental Unity

As midnight approached on April 30th, 2004, corks could be heard popping across much of what used to be known as Eastern Europe. May 1st marked the beginning of a new era: Ten new countries— Cyprus, the Czech Republic, Estonia, Hungary, Latvia, Lithuania, Malta, Poland, the Slovak Republic, and Slovenia—were admitted into the European Union. The union, now 25 strong, set about commemorating its expansion across what had long been a divided continent. Concerts were held in Berlin and Warsaw, and all of Europe was able to watch televised broadcasts of the fireworks in Malta. All of this testified to the transformation of a Europe no longer divided into East and West.

Celebrations such as these can be quite enlightening. What and how we commemorate often tells more about who we are and what we claim to value than about the event or person being commemorated. May 1 had traditionally been a day to celebrate the working class (in the East) or labor more generally (in the West). This time, these themes were overshadowed by a different kind of internationalism: a sense on the part of the 10 inductees that they had finally become full-fledged members of "Europe." Examining this new Europe's celebrations tells us a good deal about just what the reinvented continent aspires to be.

What Europeans choose to remember or forget, how they recast their past and imagine the future can all be gleaned from commemorations choreographed and spontaneous, solemn and joyous, permanent and ephemeral. Take, for example, the 60th anniversary of D-Day, celebrated in 2004. Those festivities brought not only aging war veterans and their families, but numerous international dignitaries to the coasts of Normandy for a week's worth of events. American president George W. Bush underscored the contributions the United States had made to the security of Europe and the world as a whole, doubtless hoping that the luster of Normandy would rub off on his country's latest attempts at ridding the world of tyranny. Indeed, the American invasion of Normandy has long been a symbol of the larger Pax Americana that followed World War II, and although this vision has come under siege in recent years, it continues to be trumpeted in the public realm.

The festivities of 2004 brought changes to the D-Day anniversary, which had been celebrated regularly in previous decades. For the first time, the heads of Germany and Russia were present. The participation of both tells us much more about current alliances than about those that prevailed during the war. Recall that 20 years earlier, Ronald Reagan had been criticized for his visit to the Bitburg cemetery, where slain Nazi fighters lay buried. This time, the presence of Chancellor Gerhard Schroeder at the joint festivities reflected the fact that a united Germany lies at the center of the new Europe. Russian participation in the D-Day festivities is even more interesting, since it amounted to recognition of one of the Allied Powers not often given its due. In the Cold War decades, after the Axis Powers were vanquished, Soviet efforts in World War II were conveniently "forgotten" in the West. Given the improved relations between post-Communist Russia and the West, it had become acceptable to recall the Soviet Union's wartime sacrifices as well as those of Britain, France, and America.

Of course, Not only battles are commemorated. A newly-minted tradition, initiated by the European Union, is the designation of European Capitals of Culture. Each year, the designated city organizes festivities, exhibits, and events to showcase its artistic and cultural heritage. Genoa, Italy and Lille, France split the honor in 2004, while Cork, Ireland enjoys top billing in 2005. Such commemorations say much about the identity of these particular urban centers, and to some extent about how they situate themselves within European culture as a whole. The same is true of the European Heritage Days set aside each autumn, again celebrated in diverse ways in cities and towns across the continent. That the European Union promotes such local expressions of cultural inheritance suggests that it values the rich cultural mosaic that comprises Europe.

Thus, the second half of the European Union's slogan "unity in diversity" continues to receive attention. However, the first half of the slogan— unity—still lacks its own celebration. Is not European Unity Day—"E-Day"—equally worth celebrating in the aftermath of May 1, 2004? Perhaps Europeans will take it upon themselves to transform May Day into E-Day on a permanent basis. This might make up for the fact that the revolutions of 1989, which helped to initiate the reunification of Europe's two halves, received so little notice on their 15th anniversary. With the tearing down of the Berlin Wall, Europe lost one site for spontaneous celebrations such as those that took place on November 9, 1989. One fitting tribute to both 1989 and to the European reunification of 2004 might be fireworks over Budapest's Statue Park, with its collection of monuments to Karl Marx and V.I. Lenin. Here, perhaps, one could best appreciate the irony of Europe's slogan for the 21st century: "Europeans of the world, unite!"

Patrice M. Dabrowski is a postdoctoral fellow at Brown University's Watson Institute for International Studies. She is the author of Commemorations and the Shaping of Modern Poland, *published by Indiana University Press in 2004 and hailed by fellow scholars for its "tremendous erudition."*

The Struggle for a European Immigration Policy

In June of 2003, 200 would-be European immigrants believed to have embarked from Libya drowned in the rough waters south of Sicily; that same month, 2666 migrants from Africa survived the journey, landing on the isolated Italian island Lampedusa and creating a study in contrasts in the ongoing EU immigration debate. In the annals of European immigration, tragedies of this caliber are far from rare: The Sicily drowning occurred four years to the month after 58 Chinese refugees were asphyxiated in a container lorry at the English port of Dover. Even the illegal immigrants who beat the odds and the border control do not always escape tragic circumstances. Many are forced into black-market labor, such as prostitution, to pay back smugglers for their passage. While it is fairly clear that current EU immigration policies are harmful to refugees, opening the floodgates on legal immigration is not only in the best interests of those seeking entrance—it now appears that the EU needs immigrants as desperately as immigrants need the EU.

Western European birth-rates have crashed to an all-time low, averaging only 1.5 children per woman, and dipping as low as Spain's scant 1.1. At the other end of things, Europe's aging population has become a major strain on its pension systems. French Parliamentarian Elisabeth Guigou reports that, if present demographic trends continue, without relaxing immigration constraints, the mighty new 25-nation European Union will experience a net decline in population of 50 million people by 2050. Even now Europe is facing shortages in both its skilled and unskilled labor pools, making even more apparent its need for immigrants for economic prosperity to continue.

With so much at stake, it may seem confusing to witness the recent immigration policy swing to the political right experienced by much of Europe. Some of the most developed, prosperous nations, such as Germany and France, worry that an influx of immigrants will destabilize their economies and jeopardize publicly-funded medical and social programs. Tensions have been primarily focused on African and Arab ghettos, commonly seen as drags on the welfare state and

feared to be security threats in the wake of September 11. This explosive combination of fear and uncertainty has fueled the popularity of far-right populist political candidates running on anti-immigration platforms, spawning legislation severely restricting legal immigration.

During June-July 2003 at the Thessaloniki Summit, Germany, Britain, and Italy were the most vocal and influential players in the debate over how to manage illegal immigration while integrating legal immigrants. Some leaders, such as German Interior Minister Otto Schily, think agreements with countires of origin are the best way to curbing illegal immigration. Supporters of such efforts point to Italy's bilateral agreements with Lybia, a hub for human trafficking from Africa to Europe, and Albania as models. In the former scenario, Italy will provide technical assistance to Libya, and the two countries will cooperate on offshore patrols. The 1997 Italian-Albanian cooperation deal contains a simplified repatriation scheme, quotas for seasonal workers, and joint patrols in Albanian waters of the Adriatic Sea that separate Italy and the former Stalinist state.

The stage is set for what promises to be an ongoing debate, as Germany leads the fight to retain autonomous control of its border policies while nations like Britain and Italy attempt to institute centralized, EU-wide control of immigration policy and enforcement. For the moment, a stopgap EU program intended to "promote a tolerant and inclusive society by raising awareness of fundamental European values" and to project accurate information about immigrants' culture, traditions, and religion underscores the two-sided complexity of the situation. By educating immigrants in the cultural, social, and political characteristics of their adoptive state—and providing EU citizens with accurate information about immigrants' cultures—there is hope that some of the elements of mistrust and misunderstanding that have plagued the discussion thus far can be mitigated, and that the frustrated desperation that costs the lives of so many refugees will give way to a peaceful, legal, and mutually beneficial solution.

Derek Glanz is a doctoral candidate in political science at the University of North Carolina at Chapel Hill. He was the Editor of Let's Go: Spain & Portugal *1998.*

The Prevalence of Xenophobia in Modern Europe

In Europe as in America, cultural racism has long been a tale of bodies told as a story about minds—an evaluation of hair and skin behind claims about culture and language. This is evident to every child who, though born and raised in Europe, is perceived as an immigrant because she "looks Middle Eastern" or "looks African."

Anti-immigrant agitators have caused several recent electoral earthquakes. In 1999, the ultra-nationalist party of Jörg Haider shocked the European Union by attracting more than one-fourth of Austria's voters and becoming part of the country's governing coalition. Regimes in Italy, Portugal, and Denmark also depend on the extreme right to maintain parliamentary majorities. Osama bin Laden's September 11th gift to reactionary forces worldwide aided the Dutch Muslim-baiting party of the late Pim Fortuyn as well as France's Jean-Marie Le Pen, who was supported by 17% of the electorate in the first round of the 2002 presidential election.

Political entrepreneurs of the far right fan xenophobic fires by framing immigrants and native workers as rival claimants to material resources and social respect. In a western Europe of advanced general-welfare policies, resources for health-care, education, and housing, as well as unemployment benefits, have been squeezed during recent decades of retrenchment. Some politicians portray immigrants as getting something for nothing, receiving social support without having contributed to society. The immigrants themselves are in a catch-22: they are resented if they are unemployed (and thus seen as living off other people's taxes), but also if they find jobs (seen as taking them from natives).

Support for anti-immigrant parties comes largely from the working classes; bourgeois racism also exists, but wealthy citizens often value the inexpensive labor provided by immigrants even while looking down on them. Working-class opposition to immigration arises above all from the humiliations that workers have suffered. A man who welds fenders eight hours a day at a Renault factory, barely supporting his family in a dreary suburban flat—then finds himself unemployed when production is shifted abroad—is unlikely to welcome a Rwandan refugee, much less to empathize with her own biography of humiliations.

Immigration is also debated as part of Europe's ongoing cultural globalization. Multinational products perceived as American—from food to news to movies—have saturated the continent. Citizens of many countries (not least France) see this development as jeopardizing national integrity. Non-European immigrants may be framed as further eroding an imagined cultural homogeneity due to their different diets, clothing, religion, and language.

The more extreme right-wing politicians supplement economic and cultural discourses with imagery of bodily and sexual danger. As in racisms the world over, men of the disfavored groups are presented as violent, criminal, and predatory toward women—invaders, Le Pen once said, "who want to sleep in my bed, with my wife." In fact, it is the immigrants who are often the victims of crimes, committed largely by the underemployed sons of marginalized workers. Here racism is at its most obvious: those targeted may not be "foreign" at all, but native citizens who happen not to be white.

A politician who opposes anti-immigrant parties and the violence they sometimes condone faces a political obstacle course. How to protect asylum seekers arriving from a war-torn world while at the same time reassuring the public that the nation is strictly guarding its borders? How to reduce unemployment while also encouraging immigration of needed workers in such sectors as high technology and care of the expanding elderly population? How to balance respect for cultural and religious differences with the need to socialize new arrivals in the values and habits of the host society? In the hard-won answers to these questions lies the fate of the European Dream, a vision of an inclusive and egalitarian society extending across a continent.

Dr. Brian Palmer lectures on ethics in an era of globalization, and Kathleen Holbrook researched religious diversity in Utah as a graduate student at Harvard Divinity School. They were voted Harvard's best young faculty member and best teaching fellow for a course which the New York Times nicknamed "Idealism 101."

ESSENTIALS

PLANNING YOUR TRIP

ENTRANCE REQUIREMENTS

Passport (below). Required for almost all non-EU citizens traveling in Europe.

Visa (p. 18). Not required for citizens of Australia, Canada, Ireland, New Zealand, the UK, and the US for stays shorter than 90 days in most European countries.

Inoculations (p. 26). Visitors to Europe should be up to date on vaccines for diptheria, haemophilus influenza B, hepatitis A, hepatitis B, measles, mumps, pertussis, polio, rabies, rubella, tetanus, and typhoid.

Work Permit (p. 18). Required for all foreigners planning to work in any European country.

EMBASSIES AND CONSULATES

CONSULAR SERVICES

Information about European consular services at home and foreign consular services in Europe is located in individual country chapters; it can also be found at www.embassyworld.com and www.tyzo.com/planning/embassies.html.

TOURIST OFFICES

Information about national tourist boards in Europe is located in individual country chapters; it can also be found at www.towd.com.

DOCUMENTS AND FORMALITIES

PASSPORTS

REQUIREMENTS

Citizens of Australia, Canada, Ireland, New Zealand, the UK, and the US need valid passports to enter European countries and to re-enter their home countries. Most countries do not allow entrance if the holder's passport expires within six months; returning home with an expired passport is illegal, and may result in a fine.

NEW PASSPORTS

Citizens of Australia, Canada, Ireland, New Zealand, the UK, and the US can apply for a passport at any passport office and most post offices and courts of law. Any new passport or renewal applications must be filed well in advance of the departure date, though most passport offices offer rush services for a very steep fee. Citizens living abroad who need a passport or renewal should contact the nearest passport office of their home country.

ONE EUROPE. European unity has come a long way since 1958, when the European Economic Community (EEC) was created to promote European solidarity and cooperation. Since then, the EEC has become the European Union (EU), a mighty political, legal, and economic institution. On May 1, 2004, ten Southern, Central, and Eastern European countries—Cyprus, the Czech Republic, Estonia, Hungary, Latvia, Lithuania, Malta, Poland, the Slovak Republic, and Slovenia—were admitted to the EU, joining 15 other member states: Austria, Belgium, Denmark, Finland, France, Germany, Greece, Ireland, Italy, Luxembourg, the Netherlands, Portugal, Spain, Sweden, and the UK.

What does this have to do with the average non-EU tourist? The EU's policy of **freedom of movement** means that border controls between the first 15 member states (minus Ireland and the UK, but plus Norway and Iceland) have been abolished, and visa policies harmonized. While you're still required to carry a passport (or government-issued ID card for EU citizens) when crossing an internal border, once you've been admitted into one country, you're free to travel to other participating states. Britain and Ireland have also formed a **common travel area,** abolishing passport controls between the UK and the Republic of Ireland.

For more important consequences of the EU for travelers, see **The Euro** (p. 20) and **Customs in the EU** (p. 19).

PASSPORT MAINTENANCE

Photocopy the page of your passport with your photo, as well as your visas, traveler's checks' serial numbers, and any other important documents. Carry one set of copies in a safe place, apart from the originals, and leave another set at home. Consulates also recommend that you carry an expired passport or an official copy of your birth certificate in a part of your baggage separate from other documents.

If you lose your passport, immediately notify the local police and the nearest embassy or consulate of your home government. To expedite its replacement, you will need to know all information previously recorded, and show ID and proof of citizenship. In some cases, a replacement may take weeks to process, and it may be valid only for a limited time. Any visas stamped in your old passport will be irretrievably lost. In an emergency, ask for immediate temporary traveling papers that will permit you to re-enter your home country.

VISAS, INVITATIONS, AND WORK PERMITS

VISAS

As of June 2004, citizens of Australia, Canada, Ireland, New Zealand, the UK, or the US do not need a visa to visit the following countries for less than 90 days: Andorra, Austria, Belgium, Denmark, Finland, Germany, Greece, Iceland, Italy, Liechtenstein, Luxembourg, Morocco, the Netherlands, Norway, Portugal, Slovenia, Spain, Switzerland, and Sweden. Furthermore, citizens of Australia, Canada, New Zealand, and the US do not need visas to enter Ireland or the UK for less than 90 days. Visitors to Andorra should contact the French embassy with any inquiries, while those headed for Liechtenstein should contact a Swiss embassy. Please refer to the chart below for information regarding visas to Eastern European countries.

For travelers planning to spend more than three months in any European country, visas cost US$35-200 and typically allow you to spend six months in that country. Visas can usually be purchased at a consulate or at www.itseasypassport.com/services/visas/visas.htm.

Double-check entrance requirements at the nearest embassy or consulate of your destination for up-to-date info before departure. US citizens can also consult http://travel.state.gov/foreignentryreqs.html.

VISA REQUIREMENTS						
	AUS	**CAN**	**IRE**	**NZ**	**UK**	**US**
BELARUS	Y^3	Y^3	Y^3	Y^3	Y^3	Y^3
BOSNIA	Y	N	N	Y	N	N
BULGARIA	N^1	N^1	N^1	N^1	N^1	N
CZECH REPUBLIC	Y	N	N	N	N	N^1
ESTONIA	N	Y	N	N	N	N
HUNGARY	Y	N	N	Y	N	N
LATVIA	Y^2	Y	N	Y^2	N	N
LITHUANIA	N	N	N	Y	N	N
POLAND	N	N	N	N	N	N
ROMANIA	Y	Y	Y	Y	Y	N^1
RUSSIA	Y^3	Y^3	Y^3	Y^3	Y^3	Y^3
SLOVAKIA	Y	N	N	Y	N	N^1
TURKEY	N	N	Y	N	Y	Y
UKRAINE	Y^3	Y^3	Y^3	Y^3	Y^3	Y^3

KEY: 1 tourists can stay up to 30 days without visa; **2** tourists can stay up to 10 days without visa; **3** invitation required

INVITATIONS
In addition to a visa, Belarus, Russia, and Ukraine currently require that visitors from Australia, Canada, Ireland, New Zealand, the UK, and the US obtain an invitation from a sponsoring individual or organization. You can obtain one by writing to each country's consulate or embassy in America.

WORK PERMITS
Admission as a visitor does not include the right to work, which is authorized only by a work permit. Entering a country in Europe to study typically requires a special study visa, though many study-abroad programs are able to subsidize it. For more information, see **Alternatives to Tourism** (p. 73).

IDENTIFICATION
When you travel, always carry at least two forms of identification on your person, including a photo ID; a passport and a driver's license or birth certificate is usually adequate. Never carry all of your IDs together; split them up in case of theft or loss, and keep photocopies of all of them in your luggage and at home.

STUDENT, TEACHER, AND YOUTH IDENTIFICATION
The **International Student Identity Card (ISIC),** the most widely accepted form of student ID, provides discounts on some sights, accommodations, food, and transport; access to a 24hr. emergency helpline; and insurance benefits for US cardholders (see **Insurance,** p. 27). Applicants must be full-time secondary or post-secondary school students at least 12 years of age. Because of the proliferation of fake ISICs, some services (particularly airlines) require additional proof of student identity.

The **International Teacher Identity Card (ITIC)** offers teachers the same insurance coverage as the ISIC and similar but limited discounts. For travelers who are 25 years old or under but are not students, the **International Youth Travel Card (IYTC)** also offers many of the same benefits as the ISIC.

Each of these identity cards costs US$22 or equivalent. ISICs and ITICs are valid until the new year, or if you get them in Sept.-Dec., they become valid for the rest of that year plus the next calendar year; IYTC cards are valid for one year from the date of issue. Many student travel agencies issue the cards; for a list of issuing agencies or more information, see the **International Student Travel Confederation (ISTC)** website (www.istc.org).

The **International Student Exchange Card (ISE)** is a similar identification card available to students, faculty, and youth aged 12 to 26. The card provides discounts, medical benefits, access to a 24hr. emergency helpline, and the ability to purchase student airfares. The card costs US$25; call US ☎ 800-255-8000 for more info, or visit www.isecard.com.

CUSTOMS

Upon entering a European country, you must declare certain items from abroad and pay a duty on the value of those articles if they exceed the allowance established by that country's customs service. Goods and gifts purchased at **duty-free** shops abroad are not exempt from duty or sales tax; "duty-free" merely means that you need not pay a tax in the country of purchase. Upon returning home, you must likewise declare all articles acquired abroad and pay a duty on the value of articles in excess of your home country's allowance. In order to expedite your return, make a list of any valuables brought from home and register them with customs before traveling abroad, and be sure to keep receipts for all goods acquired abroad.

Every country covered by *Let's Go: Europe* has a **Value Added Tax (VAT)** which can be claimed upon departure. Policies granting such refunds to travelers are set by individual countries (see **Taxes**, p. 22).

 CUSTOMS IN THE EU. As well as freedom of movement of people within the EU (p. 17), travelers in the 15 original EU member countries (Austria, Belgium, Denmark, Finland, France, Germany, Greece, Ireland, Italy, Luxembourg, the Netherlands, Portugal, Spain, Sweden, and the UK) can also take advantage of the freedom of movement of goods. This means that there are no customs controls at internal EU borders (i.e., you can take the blue customs channel at the airport), and travelers can transport whatever legal substances they like as long as it is for their own personal (non-commercial) use—up to 800 cigarettes, 10L of spirits, 90L of wine (60L of sparkling wine), and 110L of beer. You should also be aware that duty-free allowances were abolished on July 1, 1999 for travel between EU member states; however, travelers between the EU and the rest of the world still get a duty-free allowance when passing through customs.

MONEY

CURRENCY AND EXCHANGE

As a general rule, it's cheaper to convert money in Europe than at home. However, you should bring enough foreign currency for the first few days of a trip to avoid being cashless if you arrive after bank hours or on a holiday.

When changing money abroad, try to go only to banks or change bureaus that have at most a 5% margin between their buy and sell prices. Since you lose money with every transaction, convert large sums (unless the currency is depreciating rapidly), but no more than you'll need. Use **ATM, debit,** or **credit cards** for the lowest exchange rates.

ESSENTIALS

ESSENTIALS

If you use traveler's checks or bills, carry some in small denominations (the equivalent of US$50 or less) for times when you are forced to exchange money at disadvantageous rates, but bring a range of denominations since charges may be levied per check cashed. Store your money in a variety of forms; ideally, at any given time you will be carrying some cash, some traveler's checks, and an ATM and/or credit card. All travelers should also consider carrying some US dollars (about US$50 worth), which are often preferred by local tellers.

For more info on currency and exchange rates, see individual country chapters.

THE EURO. The official currency of 12 members of the European Union—Austria, Belgium, Finland, France, Germany, Greece, Ireland, Italy, Luxembourg, the Netherlands, Portugal, and Spain—is now the euro.

The currency has some important—and positive—consequences for travelers hitting more than one euro-zone country. For one thing, money-changers across the euro-zone are obliged to exchange money at the official, fixed rate (see below), and at no commission (though they may still charge a small service fee). Second, euro-denominated travelers cheques allow you to pay for goods and services across the euro-zone, again at the official rate and commission-free.

At the time of printing, €1=US$1.23=CDN$1.60=NZ$1.83 For more info, check a currency converter (such as www.xe.com/ucc) or www.europa.eu.int.

TRAVELER'S CHECKS

Traveler's checks are one of the safest and least troublesome means of carrying funds. American Express and Visa are the most recognized brands. If you are traveling to remote areas, lesser known brands may not be accepted. Many banks and agencies sell traveler's checks for a small commission. Check issuers provide refunds if the checks are lost or stolen, and many provide additional services, such as toll-free refund hotlines abroad, emergency message services, and stolen credit card assistance. They are readily accepted throughout Europe. Ask about toll-free refund hotlines and the location of refund centers when purchasing checks, and always carry emergency cash. Note that if you pay for traveler's checks with a credit card, it may count as a cash advance, carrying hefty fees and interest.

American Express: Checks available with commission at select banks, at all AmEx offices, and online (www.americanexpress.com; US residents only). American Express cardholders can also purchase checks by phone (☎800-721-9768). Checks available in Australian, Canadian, Euro, Japanese, British, and US currencies. For purchase locations or more information contact AmEx's service centers: in Australia ☎800 68 80 22; in New Zealand 0508 555 358; in the UK 0800 587 6023; in the US and Canada 800-221-7282; elsewhere, call the US collect at 1 801-964-6665.

Visa: Checks available (generally with commission) at banks worldwide. AAA offers commission-free checks to its members. For the location of the nearest office, call Visa's service centers: in the US ☎800-227-6811; in the UK 0800 89 5078; elsewhere call the UK collect 44 020 7937 8091.

Travelex/Thomas Cook: Issues Visa traveler's checks. Members of AAA and affiliated automobile associations receive a 25% commission discount on check purchases. In the US and Canada call ☎800-287-7362; in the UK call 0800 62 21 01; elsewhere call the UK collect at 44 1733 31 89 50.

CREDIT, ATM, AND DEBIT CARDS

Where they are accepted, credit cards often offer superior exchange rates—up to 5% better than the retail rate used by banks and other currency exchange establishments. Credit cards may also offer services such as insurance or emergency help, and are sometimes required to reserve hotel rooms or rental cars. **Mastercard** (a.k.a. EuroCard or Access in Europe) and **Visa** (a.k.a. Carte Bleue or Barclaycard) are the most welcomed; **American Express** cards work at AmEx offices, most major airports, and some ATMs.

ATM cards are commonplace in Europe. Depending on the system that your home bank uses, you can most likely access your personal bank account from abroad. ATMs get the same wholesale exchange rate as credit cards, but there is often a limit on the amount of money you can withdraw per day (usually around US$500). Also, there is typically a surcharge of US$1-5 per withdrawal.

Debit cards are as convenient as credit cards but have a more immediate impact on your funds. A debit card can be used wherever its associated credit card company (usually Mastercard or Visa) is accepted, yet the money is withdrawn directly from the holder's checking account. Debit cards also often function as ATM cards and can be used to withdraw cash from associated banks and ATMs throughout Europe. Ask your local bank about obtaining one.

One drawback of using plastic is that some banks have begun adding extra conversion fees (1-4%) on international purchases. Read your card agreement carefully to avoid such hidden fines. Also, be sure to have backup finances if you will be traveling extensively in Eastern Europe or rural areas of Western Europe, as many places do not accept credit cards, and functional ATMs may be hard to find.

The two major international money networks are **Cirrus** (to locate ATMs US ☎ 800-424-7787 or www.mastercard.com) and **Visa/PLUS** (to locate ATMs US ☎ 800-843-7587 or www.visa.com). Most ATMs charge a transaction fee that is paid to the bank that owns the ATM.

ATMS AND PINS. To use a cash or credit card to withdraw money from an ATM in Europe, you must have a four-digit **Personal Identification Number (PIN).** If your PIN is longer than four digits, ask your bank whether you can just use the first four, or whether you'll need a new one. **Credit cards** don't usually come with PINs, so if you intend to hit up ATMs in Europe with a credit card to get cash advances, call your credit card company before leaving to request one.

Travelers with alphabetic, rather than numerical, PINs may also be thrown off by the lack of letters on European cash machines. The following are the corresponding numbers to use: 1=QZ; 2=ABC; 3=DEF; 4=GHI; 5=JKL; 6=MNO; 7=PRS; 8=TUV; and 9=WXY. Note that if you mistakenly punch the wrong code into the machine three times, it will swallow your card for good.

GETTING MONEY FROM HOME

If you run out of money while traveling, the easiest and cheapest solution is to have someone back home make a deposit to the bank account linked to your credit card or ATM card. Failing that, consider one of the options below. The online **International Money Transfer Consumer Guide** (http://international-money-transfer-consumer-guide.info) may also be of help.

WIRING MONEY

It is possible to arrange a **bank money transfer,** which means asking a bank back home to wire money to a bank in Europe. This is the cheapest way to transfer cash, but it's also the slowest, usually taking several days or more. Note that some banks may only release your funds in local currency, potentially sticking you with a poor exchange rate; inquire about this in advance. Money transfer services like **Western Union** are faster and more convenient than bank transfers—but also much pricier. Western Union has many locations worldwide. To find one, visit www.westernunion.com, or call in Australia ☎800 501 500, in Canada 800-235-0000, in the UK 0800 83 38 33, and in the US 800-325-6000. Money transfer services are also available at **American Express** and **Thomas Cook** offices.

US STATE DEPARTMENT (US CITIZENS ONLY)

In serious emergencies only, the US State Department will forward money within hours to the nearest consular office, which will then disburse it according to instructions for a US$30 fee. If you wish to use this service, you must contact the Overseas Citizens Service division of the US State Department (☎317-472-2328; nights, Sundays, and holidays 202-647-4000).

COSTS

The cost of your trip will vary considerably, depending on where you go, how you travel, and where you stay. The most significant expenses will probably be your round-trip (return) **airfare** to Europe (see **Getting to Europe: By Plane**, p. 51) and a **railpass** or **bus pass** (see **Getting around Europe**, p. 56). Before you go, spend some time calculating a reasonable **daily budget.**

STAYING ON A BUDGET

Your daily budget will vary greatly from country to country. A bare-bones day in Europe would include camping or sleeping in hostels/guesthouses and buying food at supermarkets. A slightly more comfortable day would include sleeping in hostels or guesthouses and the occasional budget hotel, eating one meal per day at a restaurant, and going out at night. For a luxurious day, the sky's the limit. In any case, don't forget to factor in emergency reserve funds (at least US$200) when planning how much money you'll need.

TIPS FOR SAVING MONEY

Some simple ways to save include searching out opportunities for free entertainment, splitting accommodation and food costs with trustworthy fellow travelers, and buying food in supermarkets rather than eating out. Bring a **sleepsack** (p. 23) to save on sheet charges in European hostels, and do your **laundry** in the sink (unless you're explicitly prohibited from doing so). That said, don't go overboard. Though staying within your budget is important, don't do so at the expense of your health or a great travel experience.

TIPPING AND BARGAINING

In most European countries, the 5-10% gratuity is already included in the food service bill, but an additional 5-10% tip for very good service is often also polite. Note that in some countries (e.g., Germany), the tip is handed directly to the server instead of being left on the table. For other services such as taxis or hairdressers, a 10-15% tip is recommended. Watch other customers to gauge what is appropriate. Bargaining is especially useful in Greece and outdoor markets in Italy, Britain, and Ireland. See individual country chapters for specific info.

TAXES

The EU imposes a Value Added Tax (VAT) on goods and services, usually included in the sticker price. Non-EU citizens visiting Europe may obtain a refund for taxes paid on unused retail goods, but not for taxes paid on services. As the VAT is 15-

25%, it might be worthwhile to file for a refund. To do so, you must obtain Tax-Free Shopping Cheques, available from shops sporting the Europe Tax-Free Shopping logo, and save your receipts. Upon leaving the EU, present your goods, invoices, and passport to customs and have your checks stamped. Then go to an ETS cash refund office or file for a refund once back home. Keep in mind that goods must be taken out of the country within three months of the end of the month of purchase, and that some stores require minimum purchase amounts to become eligible for a refund.

PACKING

Pack lightly. Lay out only what you absolutely need, then take half the clothes and twice the money. The Travelite FAQ (www.travelite.org) is a good resource for tips on traveling light. The online **Universal Packing List** (http://upl.codeq.info) will generate a customized list of suggested items based on your trip length, the expected climate, your planned activities, and other factors. If you plan to do a lot of hiking, also consult **Camping and the Outdoors,** p. 41.

Luggage: If you plan to cover most of your itinerary by foot, a sturdy **frame backpack** is unbeatable. (For the basics on buying a pack, see p. 43.) Toting a **suitcase** or **trunk** is fine if you plan to live in one or two cities and explore from there, but not a great idea if you plan to move around frequently. In addition to your main piece of luggage, a **daypack** (a small backpack or courier bag) is useful.

Clothing: No matter when you're traveling, it's a good idea to bring a warm jacket or wool sweater, a rain jacket (Gore-Tex® is both waterproof and breathable), sturdy shoes or hiking boots, and thick socks. Flip-flops or waterproof sandals are must-haves for grubby hostel showers. You may also want one outfit for going out, and maybe a nicer pair of shoes. If you plan to visit religious or cultural sites, remember that you will need modest and respectful dress.

Sleepsack: Some hostels require that you either provide your own linens or rent sheets from them. Save cash by making your own sleepsack: fold a full-size sheet in half the long way, then sew it closed along the long side and one of the short sides.

Converters and Adapters: In Europe, electricity is 230 volts AC, enough to fry any 120V North American appliance. 220/240V electrical appliances won't work with a 120V current, either. Americans and Canadians should buy an adapter (which changes the shape of the plug; US$20) and a converter (which changes the voltage; US$20). Don't make the mistake of using only an adapter (unless appliance instructions explicitly state otherwise). Australians and New Zealanders (who use 230V at home) won't need a converter, but will need a set of adapters to use anything electrical. For more on all things adaptable, check out http://kropla.com/electric.htm.

Toiletries: Toothbrushes, towels, cold-water soap, talcum powder (to keep feet dry), deodorant, razors, tampons, and condoms are often available, but may be difficult to find; bring extras. **Contact lenses** are likely to be expensive and difficult to find, so bring enough extra pairs and solution for your entire trip. Also bring your glasses and a copy of your prescription in case you need emergency replacements. If you use heat-disinfection, either switch temporarily to a chemical disinfection system (check first to make sure it's safe with your brand of lenses), or buy a converter to 220/240V.

First-Aid Kit: For a basic first-aid kit, pack bandages, a pain reliever, antibiotic cream, a thermometer, a Swiss Army knife, tweezers, moleskin, decongestant, motion-sickness remedy, diarrhea or upset-stomach medication (e.g., Pepto Bismol or Imodium), an antihistamine, sunscreen, insect repellent, burn ointment, and a syringe for emergencies (get an explanatory letter from your doctor).

Film: Film and developing in Europe can be expensive, so consider bringing along enough film for your entire trip and developing it at home. Less serious photographers may want to bring a disposable camera or two. Despite disclaimers, airport security X-rays can fog film, so buy a lead-lined pouch at a camera store or ask security to hand-inspect it. Always pack film in your carry-on luggage, since higher-intensity X-rays are used on checked luggage.

Other Useful Items: For safety purposes, you should bring a **money belt** and **small padlock.** Basic **outdoors equipment** (i.e., plastic water bottle, compass, waterproof matches, pocketknife, sunglasses, sunscreen, and hat) may also prove useful. Quick repairs of torn garments can be done on the road with a needle and thread; also consider bringing electrical tape for patching tears. If you want to do laundry by hand, bring detergent, a small rubber ball to stop up the sink, and string for a makeshift clothes line. **Other things** you're liable to forget are an umbrella; sealable plastic bags (for damp clothes, soap, food, shampoo, and other spillables); an alarm clock; safety pins; rubber bands; a flashlight; earplugs; garbage bags; and a small calculator. A **cell phone** can be a lifesaver (literally) on the road; see p. 35 for information on acquiring one that will work at your destination.

Important Documents: Don't forget your passport, traveler's checks, ATM and/or credit cards, adequate ID, and photocopies of all of the aforementioned in case these documents are lost or stolen (p. 18). Also check that you have any of the following that might apply to you: a hostelling membership card (p. 37); driver's license (p. 18); travel insurance forms (p. 27); ISIC (p. 18), and/or rail or bus pass (p. 56).

SAFETY AND HEALTH

GENERAL ADVICE

In any type of crisis situation, the most important thing to do is **stay calm.** Your country's embassy abroad is usually your best resource when things go wrong; registering with that embassy upon arrival in the country is often a good idea. The government offices listed in the **Travel Advisories** box below can provide information on the services they offer their citizens in case of emergencies abroad.

DRUGS AND ALCOHOL

Drug and alcohol laws vary widely throughout Europe. In the Netherlands you can buy "soft" drugs on the open market; in much of Eastern Europe drug possession may lead to a heavy prison sentence. If you carry **prescription drugs,** you must carry both a copy of the prescriptions themselves and a note from a doctor, especially at border crossings. **Public drunkenness** is culturally unacceptable and against the law in many countries; it can also jeopardize your safety.

TERRORISM AND CIVIL UNREST

In the wake of 9/11 and the war in Iraq, exercise increased vigilance near embassies and be wary of big crowds and demonstrations. Keep an eye on the news, heed travel warnings, and comply with security measures.

Overall, risks of civil unrest tend to be localized and rarely directed toward tourists. Though the peace process in Northern Ireland is progressing, tension tends to surround the July "marching season." Notoriously violent separatist movements include ETA, a Basque group that operates in France and Spain, and FLNC, a Corsican separatist group in France. The November 17 group in Greece is known for anti-Western acts, though they do not target tourists. For now, it is safest to avoid conflict-ridden Macedonia, Serbia, Montenegro, and Bosnia-Herzegovina.

The **travel advisories** box lists offices to contact and webpages to visit to get the most updated list of your home country's government's advisories about travel.

TRAVEL ADVISORIES. The following government offices provide travel information and advisories by telephone, by fax, or via the web:

Australian Department of Foreign Affairs and Trade: ☎13 00 555135; faxback service 02 6261 1299; www.dfat.gov.au.

Canadian Department of Foreign Affairs and International Trade (DFAIT): In Canada and the US call ☎800-267-8376, elsewhere call 1 613-944-4000; www.dfait-maeci.gc.ca. Call for their free booklet, *Bon Voyage...But.*

New Zealand Ministry of Foreign Affairs: ☎04 439 8000; fax 494 8506; www.mft.govt.nz/travel/index.html.

United Kingdom Foreign and Commonwealth Office: ☎020 7008 0232; fax 7008 0155; www.fco.gov.uk.

US Department of State: ☎202-647-5225, faxback service 202-647-3000; http://travel.state.gov. For *A Safe Trip Abroad,* call ☎202-512-1800.

PERSONAL SAFETY

EXPLORING AND TRAVELING

To avoid unwanted attention, try to blend in as much as possible. Respecting local customs (in many cases, dressing more conservatively than you would at home) may placate would-be hecklers. Familiarize yourself with your surroundings before setting out, and carry yourself with confidence. Check maps in shops and restaurants rather than on the street. If you are traveling alone, be sure someone at home knows your itinerary, and never admit that you're by yourself. When walking at night, stick to busy, well-lit streets and avoid dark alleyways. If you ever feel uncomfortable, leave the area as quickly and directly as you can.

There is no sure fire way to avoid all the threatening situations you might encounter while traveling, but a good **self-defense course** will give you concrete ways to react to unwanted advances. **Impact, Prepare, and Model Mugging** can refer you to local self-defense courses in the US (☎800-345-5425). Visit the website at www.impactsafety.org for a list of nearby chapters. Workshops (1½-3hr.) start at US$75; full courses (20-25hr.) run US$350-400.

If you are using a **car,** learn local driving signals and wear a seatbelt. Children under 40 lbs. should ride only in specially-designed carseats, available for a small fee from most car rental agencies. Study route maps before you hit the road, and if you plan on spending a lot of time driving, consider bringing spare parts. If your car breaks down, wait for the police to assist you. For long drives in desolate areas, invest in a cellular phone and a roadside assistance program. Park your vehicle in a garage or well traveled area, and use a steering wheel locking device in larger cities. **Sleeping in your car** is one of the most dangerous (and often illegal) ways to get your rest. For info on the perils of **hitchhiking,** see p. 72.

POSSESSIONS AND VALUABLES

Never leave your belongings unattended; crime occurs in even the most demure-looking hostel or hotel. Bring your own **padlock** for hostel lockers, and don't ever store valuables in a locker. Be particularly careful on **buses** and **trains** (especially in Eastern Europe); horror stories abound about determined thieves who wait for travelers to fall asleep. Carry your backpack in front of you where you can see it.

When traveling with others, sleep in alternate shifts. When alone, use good judgment in selecting a train compartment: never stay in an empty one, and use a lock to secure your pack to the luggage rack. Try to sleep on top bunks with your luggage stored above you (if not in bed with you), and keep important documents and other valuables on your person.

There are a few steps you can take to minimize the financial risk associated with traveling. First, **bring as little with you as possible.** Second, buy a few **combination padlocks** to secure your belongings in either your pack or a hostel or train station locker. Third, **carry as little cash as possible.** Keep your traveler's checks and ATM/credit cards in a **money belt**—not a "fanny pack"—along with your passport and ID cards. Fourth, **keep a small cash reserve separate from your primary stash.** This should be about US$50 (US$ or euros are best) sewn into or stored in the depths of your pack, along with your traveler's check numbers and important photocopies. Photocopies of all important documents (i.e., passport, credit cards, plane tickets, identification, and any other crucial information) will prove an invaluable resource if any of these is lost or stolen.

In large cities **con artists** often work in groups and may involve children. Beware of certain classics: sob stories that require money, rolls of bills "found" on the street, mustard spilled (or saliva spit) onto your shoulder to distract you while they snatch your bag. **Never let your passport and your bags out of your sight.** Beware of **pickpockets** in city crowds, especially on public transportation. Also, be alert in public telephone booths: If you must say your calling card number, do so very quietly; if you punch it in, make sure no one can look over your shoulder.

If you will be traveling with electronic devices, such as a laptop computer or a PDA, check whether your homeowner's insurance covers loss, theft, or damage when you travel. If not, you might consider purchasing a low-cost separate insurance policy. **Safeware** (☎ US 800-800-1492; www.safeware.com) specializes in covering computers and charges US$90 for 90-day comprehensive international travel coverage up to $4000.

PRE-DEPARTURE HEALTH

In your **passport,** write the names of any people you wish to be contacted in case of a medical emergency, and list any allergies or medical conditions you have. Matching a prescription to a foreign equivalent is not always easy, safe, or possible, so if you take prescription drugs, consider carrying up-to-date, legible prescriptions or a doctor's statement listing the medication's trade name, manufacturer, chemical name, and dosage. See www.rxlist.com for what to ask for at the pharmacy counter. While traveling, keep all medication with you in your carry-on luggage. For tips on packing a basic **first-aid kit** and other health essentials, see p. 23.

IMMUNIZATIONS AND PRECAUTIONS

Travelers over two years old should make sure that they are up to date on the following vaccines: MMR (for measles, mumps, and rubella); DTaP or Td (for diphtheria, tetanus, and pertussis); IPV (for polio); Hib (for *haemophilus* influenza B); and HepB (for Hepatitis B). For travelers going to Eastern Europe or Morocco, a Hepatitis A and/or immune globulin (IG) vaccine is also recommended, as well as typhoid and rabies vaccines. Some countries may deny access to travelers arriving from parts of South America and sub-Saharan Africa without a certificate of vaccination for yellow fever. For recommendations on immunizations and prophylaxis, consult the CDC (see below) in the US or the equivalent in your home country, and check with a doctor for guidance.

INSURANCE

Travel insurance covers four basic areas: medical/health problems, property loss, trip cancellation/interruption, and emergency evacuation. Though regular insurance policies may well extend to travel-related accidents, you may consider purchasing separate travel insurance if the potential cost of trip cancellation, or emergency medical evacuation is greater than you can absorb. Prices for travel insurance purchased separately generally run about US$50 per week for full coverage, while trip cancellation/interruption may be purchased separately at a rate of US$3-5 per day depending on length of stay.

Medical insurance (especially university policies) often covers costs incurred abroad; check with your provider. **Australians** traveling in Finland, Ireland, Italy, the Netherlands, the UK, or Sweden are entitled to many of the services that they would receive at home as part of the Reciprocal Health Care Agreement. **Canadian** provincial health insurance plans increasingly do not cover foreign travel; check with the provincial Ministry of Health or Health Plan Headquarters for details. **US Medicare** does not cover foreign travel. **Homeowners' insurance** (or your family's coverage) often covers theft during travel and loss of travel documents (passport, plane ticket, railpass, etc.) up to US$500.

ISIC and **ITIC** (p. 18) provide basic insurance benefits to US cardholders, including US$100 per day of in-hospital sickness for up to 60 days and US$5000 of accident-related medical reimbursement (see www.isicus.com for details). Cardholders have access to a toll-free 24hr. helpline for medical, legal, and financial emergencies overseas. **American Express** (US ☎ 800-528-4800) grants most cardholders automatic collision and theft car rental insurance and ground travel accident coverage of US$100,000 on flight purchases made with the card.

INSURANCE PROVIDERS

STA (p. 51) offers a range of plans that can supplement your basic coverage. Other private insurance providers in the US and Canada include: Access America (☎ 800-284-8300; www.accessamerica.com); Berkely Group (☎ 800-797-4514; www.berkely.com); Globalcare Travel Insurance (☎ 800-821-2488; www.globalcare-cocco.com), Travel Assistance International (☎ 800-821-2828; www.travelassistance.com); and Travel Guard (☎ 800-826-4919; www.travelguard.com). AFTA (☎ 02 9264 3299; www.afta.com.au) operates in Australia and Columbus Direct (☎ 020 7375 0011; www.columbusdirect.co.uk) in the UK.

USEFUL ORGANIZATIONS AND PUBLICATIONS

The US **Centers for Disease Control and Prevention;** ☎ 877-FYI-TRIP; www.cdc.gov/travel) maintains an international travelers' hotline and an informative website. The CDC's comprehensive booklet *Health Information for International Travel* (The Yellow Book), an annual rundown of disease, immunization, and general health advice, is free online or US$29-40 via the Public Health Foundation (☎ 877-252-1200; http://bookstore.phf.org). Consult the appropriate government agency of your home country for consular info sheets on health, entry requirements, and other issues for various countries (see the listings in the box on **Travel Advisories,** p. 25). For quick info on health and other travel warnings, call the **Overseas Citizens Services** (☎ 888-407-4747 M-F 8am-8pm; 202-647-4000; after-hours 317-472-2328 from overseas), or contact a passport agency, embassy, or consulate abroad. For information on medical evacuation services and travel insurance firms, see the US government's website at http://travel.state.gov/medical.html or the **British Foreign and Commonwealth Office** (www.fco.gov.uk). For general health info, contact the **American Red Cross** (☎ 800-564-1234; www.redcross.org).

STAYING HEALTHY

Common sense is the simplest prescription for good health while you travel. Drink lots of fluids to prevent dehydration and constipation, and wear sturdy, broken-in shoes and clean socks. Travelers face very different health risks in different regions of Europe, and the quality of health care available also varies widely. Many of the country chapters in this book contain more specific information and advice to help you stay healthy on the road.

ONCE IN EUROPE

ENVIRONMENTAL HAZARDS

Heat exhaustion and dehydration: Heat exhaustion leads to nausea, excessive thirst, headaches, and dizziness. Avoid it by drinking plenty of fluids, eating salty foods (e.g. crackers), abstaining from dehydrating beverages (e.g., alcohol and caffeinated beverages), and always wearing sunscreen. Continuous heat stress can eventually lead to heatstroke, characterized by a rising temperature, severe headache, delirium and cessation of sweating. Victims should be cooled off with wet towels and taken to a doctor.

Sunburn: Always wear sunscreen (SPF 30) when spending excessive amounts of time outdoors. If you are planning on spending time at altitude, near water, in the desert, or in the snow, you are at a higher risk of getting burned, even through clouds. If you get sunburned, drink more fluids than usual and apply an aloe-based lotion. Severe sunburns can lead to sun poisoning, a condition that affects the entire body, causing fever, chills, nausea, and vomiting. Sun poisoning should always be treated by a doctor.

Hypothermia and frostbite: A rapid drop in body temperature is the clearest sign of overexposure to cold. Victims may also shiver, feel exhausted, have poor coordination or slurred speech, hallucinate, or suffer amnesia. *Do not let hypothermia victims fall asleep.* To avoid hypothermia, keep dry, wear layers, and stay out of the wind. When the temperature is below freezing, watch out for frostbite. If skin turns white or blue, waxy, and cold, do not rub the area. Drink warm beverages, stay dry, and slowly warm the area with dry fabric or steady body contact until a doctor can be found.

High Altitude: Allow your body a couple of days to adjust to less oxygen before exerting yourself. Note that alcohol is more potent and UV rays are stronger at high elevations.

INSECT-BORNE DISEASES

Many diseases are transmitted by insects—mainly mosquitoes, fleas, ticks, and lice. Be aware of insects in wet or forested areas, especially while hiking and camping; wear long pants and long sleeves, tuck your pants into your socks, and use a mosquito net. Use insect repellents such as DEET and soak or spray your gear with permethrin (licensed in the US only for use on clothing). **Mosquitos** are most concerning in wet, swampy, or wooded areas. **Ticks**—responsible many diseases including Lyme—can be especially dangerous in rural and forested regions.

Tick-borne encephalitis: A viral infection of the central nervous system transmitted during the summer by tick bites (primarily in wooded areas) or by consumption of unpasteurized dairy products. The risk of contracting the disease is relatively low, especially if precautions are taken against tick bites.

Leishmaniasis: a parasite transmitted by sand flies; can occasionally occur in Southern Europe and the eastern Mediterranean, usually in rural rather than urban areas. Common symptoms are fever, weakness, and swelling of the spleen, as well as skin sores weeks to months after the bite. There is a treatment but no vaccine.

Lyme disease: A bacterial infection carried by ticks and marked by a circular bull's-eye rash of 2 in. or more. Later symptoms include fever, headache, fatigue, and aches and pains. Antibiotics are effective if administered early. Left untreated, Lyme can cause problems in joints, the heart, and the nervous system. If you find a tick attached to your skin, grasp the head with tweezers as close to your skin as possible and apply slow, steady traction. Removing a tick within 24 hours greatly reduces the risk of infection. Do not try to remove ticks with petroleum jelly, nail polish remover, or a hot match. Tick bites usually occur in moist, shaded environments and heavily wooded areas. If you are going to be hiking in these areas, wear long clothes and DEET.

FOOD- AND WATER-BORNE DISEASES

Prevention is the best cure: be sure that your food is properly cooked and the water you drink is clean. Unpeeled fruit and vegetables and tap water should be safe throughout most of Europe, particularly Western Europe. In some parts of Southern and Eastern Europe, and especially in Morocco, you'll need to peel fruits and vegetables and avoid tap water (including ice cubes and anything washed in tap water, like salad). Watch out for food from markets or street vendors that may have been cooked in unhygienic conditions. Other culprits are raw shellfish, unpasteurized milk, and sauces containing raw eggs. Buy bottled water, or purify your own water by bringing it to a rolling boil or treating it with **iodine tablets;** note, however, that some parasites such as *giardia* have exteriors that resist iodine treatment, so boiling is more reliable. Always wash your hands before eating or bring a quick-drying purifying liquid hand cleaner.

Cholera: An intestinal disease caused by a bacteria found in contaminated food. There is no risk for travelers in Western Europe, and the risk in Eastern Europe is normally very low. Symptoms include severe diarrhea, dehydration, vomiting, and muscle cramps. See a doctor immediately; if left untreated, it may be deadly, even within a few hours. Antibiotics are available, but the most important treatment is rehydration. There is no vaccine available in the US.

Giardiasis: Transmitted through parasites (microbes, tapeworms, etc., in contaminated water and food) and acquired by drinking untreated water from streams or lakes. Symptoms include diarrhea, abdominal cramps, bloating, fatigue, weight loss, and nausea. If untreated it can lead to severe dehydration. Giardiasis occurs worldwide.

Hepatitis A: A viral infection of the liver acquired primarily through contaminated water, including shellfish from contaminated water. Symptoms include fatigue, fever, loss of appetite, nausea, dark urine, jaundice, vomiting, aches and pains, and light stools. There is a moderate risk in Eastern Europe, mainly in rural areas and the countryside, but also present in urban areas. Ask your doctor about the Hepatitis A vaccine (Havrix or Vaqta) or an injection of immune globulin (IG; formerly called gamma globulin).

Traveler's diarrhea: Results from drinking fecally contaminated water or eating uncooked and contaminated foods. Symptoms include nausea, bloating, and urgency. Try quick-energy, non-sugary foods with protein and carbohydrates to keep your strength up. Over-the-counter anti-diarrheals (e.g., Imodium) may counteract the problems. The most dangerous side effect is dehydration; drink 8 oz. of water with ½ tsp. of sugar or honey and a pinch of salt, try uncaffeinated soft drinks, or eat salted crackers. If you develop a fever or your symptoms don't go away after 4-5 days, consult a doctor. Consult a doctor immediately for treatment of diarrhea in children.

Typhoid fever: Caused by the salmonella bacteria. Travelers to villages and rural areas in Eastern Europe may be at risk. While mostly transmitted through contaminated food and water, typhoid may also be acquired by direct contact with another person. Early symptoms include a persistent, high fever, headaches, fatigue, loss of appetite, constipation, and sometimes a rash on the abdomen or chest. Antibiotics can treat typhoid, but a vaccination (70-90% effective) is recommended.

OTHER INFECTIOUS DISEASES

AIDS and HIV: For detailed information on Acquired Immune Deficiency Syndrome (AIDS) in the regions you will be visiting, call the US Centers for Disease Control's 24hr. hotline at ☎800-342-2437, or contact the Joint United Nations Programme on HIV/AIDS (UNAIDS), 20, ave. Appia, CH-1211 Geneva 27, Switzerland (☎41 22 791 3666; fax 22 791 4187). Note that Belarus, Bulgaria, Hungary, Latvia, Lithuania, Russia, Slovak Republic, and Ukraine screen incoming travelers for AIDS, primarily those planning extended visits for work or study, and deny entrance to those who test HIV-positive. Contact the country's consulate for information.

Hepatitis B: A viral infection of the liver transmitted via blood or other bodily fluids. Symptoms, which may not surface until years after infection, include jaundice, loss of appetite, fever, and joint pain. It is transmitted through activities like unprotected sex, injections of illegal drugs, and unprotected health work. A 3-shot vaccination sequence is recommended for health-care workers, sexually-active travelers, and anyone planning to seek medical treatment abroad; it must begin 6 months before traveling.

Hepatitis C: Like Hepatitis B, but the mode of transmission differs. IV drug users, those with occupational exposure to blood, hemodialysis patients, and recipients of blood transfusions are at the highest risk, but the disease can also be spread through sexual contact or sharing items like razors and toothbrushes that may have traces of blood on them. No symptoms are usually exhibited, but if there are any, they can include loss of appetite, abdominal pain, fatigue, nausea, and jaundice. If untreated, Hepatitis C can lead to liver failure.

Rabies: Transmitted through the saliva of infected animals; fatal if untreated. By the time symptoms (thirst and muscle spasms) appear, the disease is in its terminal stage. If you are bitten, wash the wound thoroughly, seek immediate medical care, and try to have the animal located. A rabies vaccine, which consists of 3 shots given over a 21-day period, is available and recommended for developing world travel, but is only semi-effective. Rabies is found all over the world, and is often transmitted through dogs.

Sexually transmitted diseases (STDs): Chlamydia, genital warts, gonorrhea, herpes, syphilis, and other STDs are more common than HIV and can cause serious complications. Hepatitis B and C can also be transmitted sexually. Though condoms may protect you from some STDs, oral or even tactile contact can lead to transmission. If you think you may have contracted an STD, see a doctor immediately.

OTHER HEALTH CONCERNS

MEDICAL CARE ON THE ROAD

While health care systems in Western Europe tend to be quite accessible and of high quality, medical care varies greatly across Eastern and Southern Europe. Major cities such as Prague and Budapest will have English-speaking medical centers or hospitals for foreigners, whereas English-speaking facilities are nearly nonexistent in relatively untouristed countries like Belarus or Latvia. In general, medical service in these regions is not up to Western standards; though basic supplies are always there, specialized treatment is not. Private hospitals tend to have better facilities than state-operated ones. Tourist offices may have names of local doctors who speak English. In the event of a medical emergency, you should also contact your embassy for aid and recommendations. All EU citizens can receive free first-aid and emergency services by presenting a **European Health Insurance Card**, which will be available in all Member States of the EU by the end of 2005. Travelers from EU countries that haven't yet introduced this card should fill out an **E111 form** (available at most post offices).

If you are concerned about obtaining medical assistance while traveling, you may wish to employ special support services. The *MedPass* from **GlobalCare, Inc.,** 6875 Shiloh Rd. East, Alpharetta, GA 30005, USA (☎800-860-1111; fax 678-341-1800; www.globalcare.net), provides 24hr. international medical assistance, support, and medical evacuation resources. The **International Association for Medical Assistance to Travelers** (US ☎716-754-4883, Canada 519-836-0102; www.cybermall.co.nz/NZ/IAMAT) has free membership, lists English-speaking doctors worldwide, and offers detailed info on immunization requirements and sanitation. If your regular **insurance** policy does not cover travel abroad, you may wish to purchase additional coverage (p. 27).

Those with medical conditions (e.g., diabetes, allergies to antibiotics, epilepsy, heart conditions) may want to obtain a **Medic Alert** membership (first year US$35, annually thereafter US$20), which includes a stainless steel ID tag among other benefits, like a 24hr. collect-call number. Contact the Medic Alert Foundation, 2323 Colorado Ave, Turlock, CA 95382, USA (☎888-633-4298; outside US 209-668-3333; www.medicalert.org).

WOMEN'S HEALTH

Women traveling in unsanitary conditions are vulnerable to **urinary tract (including bladder and kidney) infections.** Over-the-counter medicines can sometimes alleviate symptoms, but see a doctor if they persist. **Vaginal yeast infections** may flare up in hot and humid climates. Wearing loosely fitting trousers or a skirt and cotton underwear will help, as will over-the-counter remedies like Monostat or Gynelotrimin. Bring supplies from home if you are prone to infection, as they may be difficult to find on the road. **Tampons, pads,** and reliable **contraceptive devices** are widely available in most of Western Europe, but they can be hard to find in areas of Eastern Europe—bring supplies with you. **Abortion** laws vary from country to country. In most of Europe, abortion is legal up to the first 10-12 weeks of pregnancy, but it remains illegal in Andorra, Ireland, Liechtenstein, Monaco, Morocco, Poland, and Portugal, except in extreme circumstances.

KEEPING IN TOUCH

BY MAIL

SENDING MAIL

Airmail is the best way to send mail home from Europe. From Western Europe to North America, airmail averages seven days; from Central or Eastern Europe, allow anywhere from seven days to three weeks. **Aerogrammes,** printed sheets that fold into envelopes and travel via airmail, are available at post offices. Write "par avion" (or *por avion, mit Luftpost, via aerea,* etc.) on the front. Most post offices will charge exorbitant fees or simply refuse to send aerogrammes with enclosures. **Surface mail** is the cheapest and slowest way to send mail. It takes one to two months to cross the Atlantic and one to three to cross the Pacific—good for heavy items you won't need for a while, such as souvenirs or other articles you've acquired along the way that are weighing down your pack. See the beginning of each chapter for country-specific info on local postal services.

ESSENTIALS

To send mail abroad from home, mark envelopes "airmail" in your country's language; otherwise, your letter may never arrive. In addition to the postage systems whose rates are listed below, **Federal Express** (Australia ☎ 13 26 10; Canada and US 800-463-3339; Ireland 1800 535 800; New Zealand 0800 733 339; UK 0800 123 800; www.fedex.com) handles express mail services from most countries to Europe.

Australia: Allow 5-7 days for regular airmail to Europe. Postcards and letters up to 20g cost AUS$1 and letters up to 50g cost AUS$1.65; packages up to 0.5kg AUS$14.50, up to 2kg AUS$50.50. EMS can get a letter to Western Europe in 2-3 days for AUS$35. www.auspost.com.au/pac.

Canada: Allow 4-7 days for regular airmail to Europe. Postcards and letters up to 30g cost CDN$1.40; packages up to 0.5kg CDN$12.20, up to 2kg CDN$37.35. Purolator International can get a letter to Western Europe in 2 days for CDN$43.90. www.canada-post.ca/personal/rates/default-e.asp.

Ireland: Allow 2-6 days for regular airmail to the UK and Western Europe. Postcards and letters up to 50g cost €0.65 to the UK, €0.60 to the continent; packages up to 0.5kg €4, up to 2kg €13. Swiftpost International can get a letter to some major European countries in 2-6 days for €7. www.letterpost.ie.

New Zealand: Allow 4-10 days for regular airmail to Europe. Postcards cost NZ$1.50; letters up to 200g NZ$2-5; packages up to 0.5kg NZ$17.23, up to 2kg NZ$55.25. International Express can get a letter to Europe in 2-4 days for NZ$2. www.nzpost.co.nz/nzpost/inrates.

UK: Allow 2-3 days for regular airmail to Europe. Letters up to 20g cost UK£0.40; packages up to 0.5kg UK£2.98, up to 2kg UK£10.48. Airsure or International Signed For will get letters to most major European countries at least a day faster for UK£4 and UK£3.30, respectively, more. www.royalmail.co.uk/calculator.

US: Allow 4-10 days for regular airmail to Europe. Postcards/aerogrammes cost US$0.70; letters up to 1 oz. cost US$0.80; packages up to 1 lb. US$14, up to 5 lb. US$22.75. Global Express Mail takes 3-5 days and costs US$17 for a letter. http://ircalc.usps.gov.

RECEIVING MAIL

There are several ways to arrange pick-up of letters sent to you by friends and relatives while you are abroad. Mail can be sent via **Poste Restante** (General Delivery; *Lista de Correos, Fermo Posta, Postlagernde Briefe*, etc.) to almost any city or town in Europe with a post office. See individual country chapters to find out how to address *Poste Restante* letters. The mail will go to a special desk in the central post office, unless you specify a post office by street address or postal code. It's best to use the largest post office, since mail may be sent there regardless. It is usually safer and quicker, though more expensive, to send mail express or registered. Bring your passport (or other photo ID) for pick-up; there may be a small fee. If the clerks insist that there is nothing for you, have them check under your first name as well. *Let's Go* lists post offices in the **Practical Information** section for each city and most towns.

BY TELEPHONE

CALLING HOME

A **calling card** is probably your cheapest bet. Calls are billed collect or to your account. You can frequently call collect without even possessing a company's calling card just by calling their access number and following the instructions. You

can also purchase cards from your national telecommunications companies. Keep in mind that phone cards can be problematic in Russia, Ukraine, Belarus, and Slovenia—double-check with your provider before setting out.

You can usually also make direct international calls from pay phones, but if you aren't using a calling card, you may need to drop your coins as quickly as your words. Where available, prepaid phone cards and occasionally major credit cards can be used for direct international calls, but they are generally less cost-efficient. Placing a collect call through an international operator is even more expensive, but may be necessary in case of emergency.

CALLING WITHIN EUROPE

Many travelers are opting to buy mobile phones for placing calls within Europe. (For more info, see **Cellular Phones** below.) Beyond that, perhaps the simplest way to call within a country is to use a coin-operated phone. However, much of Europe has switched to a **prepaid phone card** system, and in some countries you may have a hard time finding any coin-operated phones at all. Prepaid phone cards (available at newspaper kiosks and tobacco stores), which carry a certain amount of phone time depending on the card's denomination, usually save time and money in the long run. The computerized phone will tell you how much time, in units, you have left on your card. Another kind of prepaid telephone card comes with a Personal Identification Number (PIN) and a toll-free access number. Instead of inserting the card into the phone, you call the access number and follow the directions on the card. These cards can be used to make international as well as domestic calls. Phone rates tend to be highest in the morning, lower in the evening, and lowest on Sunday and late at night. Before settling on a calling card plan, be sure to research your options in order to pick the one that best fits both your needs and your destination.

CELLULAR PHONES

Cell phones are an increasingly popular option for travelers calling within Europe. In addition to greater convenience and safety, mobile phones often provide an economical alternative to expensive landline calls. Unlike North America, virtually all areas of Europe receive excellent coverage, and the widespread use of the **Global System for Mobiles (GSM)** allows one phone to function in multiple countries. To make and receive calls in Europe, you will need a GSM-compatible phone and a **SIM (subscriber identity module) card,** a country-specific, thumbnail-sized chip that gives you a local phone number and plugs you into the local network. SIM cards can be purchased from carriers in any European country to provide a local number for any GSM phone. However, some companies lock their phones to prevent switches to competitor carriers, so inquire about using the phone in other countries before buying. Phones in Europe cost around US$100, and instead of requiring a service contract, they often run on prepaid minutes that are easily purchased in many locations. Incoming calls are frequently free. When you use up the prepaid time, you can buy additional cards or vouchers (usually available at convenience stores) to get more. For more information on GSM phones, check out www.telestial.com, www.vodafone.com, www.orange.co.uk, www.roadpost.com, www.t-mobile.com, or www.planetomni.com. Companies like **Cellular Abroad** (www.cellularabroad.com) and **Telestial** (www.telestial.com) rent cell phones that work in a variety of destinations around the world, providing a simpler option than picking up a phone in-country.

ESSENTIALS

 GSM PHONES. Just having a GSM phone doesn't mean you're necessarily good to go when you travel abroad. The majority of GSM phones sold in the United States operate on a different **frequency** (1900) than international phones (900/1800) and will not work abroad. Tri-band phones work on all three frequencies (900/1800/1900) and will operate through most of the world. As well, some GSM phones are **SIM-locked** and will only accept SIM cards from a single carrier. You'll need a **SIM-unlocked** phone to use a SIM card from a local carrier when you travel.

TIME DIFFERENCES

All of Europe falls within three hours of **Greenwich Mean Time (GMT)**. For more info, consult the **time zone chart** on the inside back cover. GMT is five hours ahead of New York time, eight hours ahead of Vancouver and San Francisco time, 10 hours behind Sydney time, and 12 hours behind Auckland time. Some countries ignore **Daylight Saving Time;** fall and spring switchover times vary.

BY EMAIL AND INTERNET

Email is popular and easily accessible in most of Europe. Though in some places it's possible to forge a remote link with your home server, in most cases this is a much slower (and thus more expensive) option than taking advantage of free **web-based email accounts** (e.g., www.hotmail.com and www.yahoo.com). **Internet cafes** and the occasional free Internet terminal at a public library or university are listed in the **Practical Information** sections of major cities. For lists of additional cybercafes in Europe, check www.cypercaptive.com or www.world66.com/netcafeguide.

Increasingly, travelers find that taking their **laptop computers** on the road with them can be a convenient option for staying connected. Laptop users can call an Internet service provider via a modem using long-distance phone cards specifically intended for such calls. They may also find Internet cafes that allow them to connect their laptops to the Internet. And most excitingly, travelers with wireless-enabled computers may be able to take advantage of an increasing number of Internet "hotspots," where they can get online for free or for a small fee. Newer computers can detect these hotspots automatically; otherwise, websites like www.wi-fihotspotlist.com and www.locfinder.net can help you find them. For information on insuring your laptop while traveling, see p. 26.

ACCOMMODATIONS

HOSTELS

In the summer Europe is overrun by young budget travelers drawn to hostels' low prices and communal meeting spaces. Many hostels are laid out dorm-style, often with large single-sex rooms and bunk beds, although private rooms that sleep two to four are becoming more common. They sometimes have kitchens and utensils for your use, bike or moped rentals, storage areas, transportation to airports, breakfast and other meals, laundry facilities, and Internet access. However, there can be drawbacks: some hostels close during certain daytime "lockout" hours, have a curfew, don't accept reservations, impose a maximum stay, or, less frequently, require that you do chores. In Western and Eastern Europe a hostel bed will average around US$10-25 and US$5-25, respectively, and a private room around US$30 and US$20, respectively.

 A HOSTELER'S BILL OF RIGHTS. There are certain standard features that we do not include in our hostel listings. Unless we state otherwise, you can expect that every hostel has no lockout, no curfew, a kitchen, free hot showers, some system of secure luggage storage, and no key deposit.

HOSTELLING INTERNATIONAL

Joining the youth hostel association in your own country (listed below) automatically grants you membership privileges in **Hostelling International (HI),** a federation of national hostelling associations. Non-HI members may be allowed to stay in some hostels, but will have to pay extra to do so. HI hostels are scattered throughout Europe, and are typically less expensive than private hostels. HI's umbrella organization's web page (www.hihostels.com), which lists the web addresses and phone numbers of all national associations, can be a great place to begin researching hostelling in a specific region. Other comprehensive hostelling websites include www.hostels.com, www.hostelplanet.com, www.youth-hostels-in.com, and www.hostelseurope.com.

Most HI hostels also honor **guest memberships**—you'll get a blank card with space for six validation stamps. Each night you'll pay a nonmember supplement (one-sixth the membership fee) and earn one guest stamp; get six stamps, and you're a member. This system works well in most of Western Europe, but in some countries you may need to remind the hostel reception. A new membership benefit is the FreeNites program, which allows hostelers to gain points toward free rooms. Most student travel agencies sell HI cards, as do all of the national hostelling organizations listed below. All prices listed below are valid for individual **one-year memberships** unless otherwise noted.

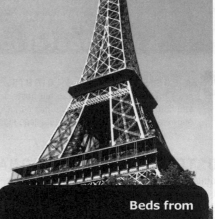

Australian Youth Hostels Association (AYHA), 422 Kent St., Sydney, NSW 200 (☎02 9261 1111; www.yha.com.au). AUS$52, under 18 AUS$19.

Hostelling International-Canada (HI-C), 205 Catherine St. #400, Ottawa, ON K2P 1C3 (☎613-237-7884; www.hihostels.ca). CDN$35, under 18 free.

An Óige (Irish Youth Hostel Association), 61 Mountjoy St., Dublin 7 (☎830 4555; www.irelandyha.org). €20, under 18 €10.

Hostelling International Northern Ireland (HINI), 22 Donegal Rd., Belfast BT12 5JN (☎02890 31 54 35; www.hini.org.uk). UK£13, under 18 UK£6.

Youth Hostels Association of New Zealand (YHANZ), Level 1, Moorhouse City, 166 Moorhouse Ave., P.O. Box 436, Christchurch (☎0800 278 299 (NZ only) or 03 379 9970; www.yha.org.nz). NZ$40, under 18 free.

Scottish Youth Hostels Association (SYHA), 7 Glebe Cres., Stirling FK8 2JA (☎01786 89 14 00; www.syha.org.uk). UK£6, under 17 £2.50.

Youth Hostels Association (England and Wales), Trevelyan House, Dimple Rd., Matlock, Derbyshire DE4 3YH, UK (☎0870 770 8868; www.yha.org.uk). UK£14, under 18 UK£6.

Hostelling International-USA, 8401 Colesville Rd., Ste. 600, Silver Spring, MD 20910 (☎301-495-1240; fax 495-6697; www.hiayh.org). US$28, under 18 free.

ESSENTIALS

BOOKING HOSTELS ONLINE. One of the easiest ways to ensure you've got a bed for the night is by reserving online. Click to the **Hostelworld** booking engine through **www.letsgo.com,** and you'll have access to bargain accommodations from Argentina to Zimbabwe with no added commission.

OTHER TYPES OF ACCOMMODATIONS

YMCAS AND YWCAS

Young Men's Christian Association (YMCA) lodgings are usually cheaper than a hotel but more expensive than a hostel. Not all YMCA locations offer lodging. Many YMCAs accept women and families; some will not lodge those under 18 without parental permission. **World Alliance of YMCAs,** 12 Clos Belmont, 1208 Geneva, Switzerland (☎41 22 849 5100; www.ymca.int) has more info and a register of European YMCAs with housing options.

HOTELS, GUESTHOUSES, AND PENSIONS

In Western Europe, **hotels** generally start at a hefty US$35 per person. Elsewhere or for couples and larger groups, however, hotels can be a more reasonable option. You'll typically share a hall bathroom; a private bathroom will cost extra, as may hot showers. Some hotels offer "full pension" (all meals) and "half pension" (no lunch). Smaller **guesthouses** and **pensions** are often cheaper than hotels. If you make **reservations** in writing, indicate your night of arrival and the number of nights you plan to stay. The hotel will send you a confirmation and may request payment for the first night. Often it is easiest to make reservations over the phone with a credit card. For letters, enclosing two **International Reply Coupons** will encourage a prompt reply (each US$1.75; available at any post office).

BED & BREAKFASTS (B&BS)

For a cozy alternative to impersonal hotel rooms, B&Bs (private homes with rooms available to travelers) range from the acceptable to the sublime. B&Bs are particularly popular in Britain and Ireland, where rooms average UK£20/€30 per person. For more information, check out **InnFinder** (www.inncrawler.com), **InnSite** (www.innsite.com), or **BedandBreakfast.com** (www.bedandbreakfast.com).

UNIVERSITY DORMS

Many **colleges** and **universities** open their residence halls to travelers when school is not in session; some do so even during term-time. Getting a room may take a couple of phone calls and require advanced planning, but rates tend to be low, and many offer free local calls and Internet access.

HOME EXCHANGES AND HOSPITALITY CLUBS

Home exchange offers the traveler various types of homes (houses, apartments, condominiums, villas, and even castles), plus the opportunity to live like a native and to reduce housing fees. For more information, contact Intervac International Home Exchange (www.intervac.com; see site for phone listings by country).

Hospitality clubs link their members with individuals or families abroad who are willing to host travelers for free or for a small fee to promote cultural exchange and general good karma. In exchange, members usually must be willing to host travelers in their own homes; a small membership fee may also be required. **The Hospitality Club** (www.hospitalityclub.org) and **GlobalFreeloaders.com** (www.global-freeloaders.com) are good places to start. **Servas** (www.servas.org) is an established, more formal, peace-based organization, and requires a fee and an interview to join. An Internet search will find many similar organizations, some of which cater to special interests (e.g., women, gay and lesbian travelers, or members of certain professions). As always, use common sense when planning to stay with or host someone you do not know.

LONG-TERM ACCOMMODATIONS

Travelers planning to stay in Europe for extended periods of time may find it most cost-effective to rent an **apartment.** Rents vary widely by region, season, and quality. Beyond the rent itself, prospective tenants are often required to front a security deposit (frequently one month's rent) and the last month's rent. Typically, it is most efficient to find an apartment through regional contacts or agencies. Out of session, it may be possible to arrange to sublet rooms from departed students; university listings are a good place to begin.

CAMPING AND THE OUTDOORS

Camping can be a thrilling if rugged way to see Europe on the cheap. **Organized campgrounds** exist just outside most European cities. Showers, bathrooms, and a small restaurant or store are common; some have more elaborate facilities. Prices are low, usually running US$5-15 per person plus additional charges for tents and/or cars. While camping is cheaper than hostelling, the cost of transportation to and from campsites can add up. Certain parks and public grounds allow **free camping,** but check local regulations before you pitch your tent. Many areas have additional park-specific rules. The **Great Outdoor Recreation Pages** (www.gorp.com) provides general information for travelers planning on camping or spending time outdoors.

LEAVE NO TRACE. *Let's Go* encourages travelers to embrace the "Leave No Trace" ethic, minimizing their impact on natural environments and protecting them for future generations. Trekkers and wilderness enthusiasts should set up camp on durable surfaces, use cookstoves instead of campfires, bury human waste away from water supplies, bag trash and carry it out with them, and respect wildlife and natural objects. For more detailed information, contact the **Leave No Trace Center for Outdoor Ethics,** PO Box 997, Boulder, CO 80306, USA (☎800-332-4100 or 303-442-8222; www.lnt.org).

USEFUL PUBLICATIONS AND RESOURCES

A variety of publishing companies offer hiking guidebooks to meet the educational needs of novice or expert. For information about camping, hiking, and biking, write or call the publishers listed below to receive a free catalog. Campers heading to Europe should consider buying an **International Camping Carnet**. Similar to a hostel membership card, it's required at a few campgrounds and provides discounts at others. It is available in North America from the **Family Campers and RVers Association** and in the UK from **The Caravan Club** (see below). **Auto Camper Service International** lists campsites throughout Europe at www.eurocampings.net.

Automobile Association, Contact Centre, Carr Ellison House, William Armstrong Dr., Newcastle-upon-Tyne NE4 7YA, UK. (☎0870 600 0371; www.theAA.com). Publishes *Caravan and Camping Europe* and *Britain* (both UK£8) as well as Big Road Atlases for certain European countries.

The Caravan Club, East Grinstead House, East Grinstead, West Sussex, RH19 1UA, UK (☎44 01342 326 944; www.caravanclub.co.uk). For UK£30, members receive travel equipment discounts, maps, and a monthly magazine.

The European Federation of Campingsite Organizations, EFCO Secretariat, 6 Pullman Court, Great Western Rd., Gloucester GL1 3ND (UK ☎014 5252 6911; www.campingeurope.com). The website has links to campsites in most European countries, though not all links are in English.

The Mountaineers Books, 1001 SW Klickitat Way, Ste. 201, Seattle, WA 98134, USA (☎206-223-6303; www.mountaineersbooks.org). Boasts over 600 titles on hiking, biking, mountaineering, natural history, and conservation.

Sierra Club Books, 85 Second St., 2nd fl., San Francisco, CA 94105, USA (☎415-977-5500; www.sierraclub.org). Publishes general resource books on hiking and camping.

WILDERNESS SAFETY

Staying **warm, dry, and well-hydrated** is key to a happy and safe wilderness experience. For any hike, prepare yourself for an emergency by packing a first-aid kit, a reflector, a whistle, high energy food, extra water, raingear, a hat, and mittens. For warmth, wear wool or insulating synthetic materials designed for the outdoors. Cotton is a bad choice since it dries painfully slowly. Check **weather forecasts** often and pay attention to the skies when hiking, as weather patterns can change suddenly. Always let someone, either a friend, your hostel, a park ranger, or a local hiking organization, know when and where you are going hiking. Know your physical limits and don't attempt hikes beyond your ability. There is a risk of landmines still buried in parks and the wilderness in parts of Eastern Europe; to minimize the risk, stay on the beaten path and consider buying a local landmine map. See **Safety and Health,** p. 24, for information on outdoor ailments and medical concerns.

CAMPING AND HIKING EQUIPMENT

WHAT TO BUY

Good camping equipment is both sturdy and light. North American suppliers tend to offer the most competitive prices.

Sleeping Bags: Most sleeping bags are rated by season; "summer" means 30-40°F (around 0°C) at night; "four-season" or "winter" often means below 0°F (-17°C). Bags are made of **down** (warm and light, but expensive, and miserable when wet) or of **synthetic** material (heavy, durable, and warm when wet). Prices range US$50-250 for a summer synthetic to US$200-300 for a good down winter bag. **Sleeping bag pads** include foam pads (US$10-30), air mattresses (US$15-50), and self-inflating mats (US$30-120). Bring a **stuff sack** to store your bag and keep it dry.

Tents: The best tents are free-standing (with their own frames and suspension systems), set up quickly, and only require staking in high winds. Low-profile dome tents are the best all-around. Worthy 2-person tents start at US$100, 4-person at US$160. Make sure your tent has a rain fly and seal its seams with waterproofer. Other useful accessories include a **battery-operated lantern,** a plastic **groundcloth,** and a nylon **tarp.**

Backpacks: Internal-frame packs mold well to your back, keep a lower center of gravity, and flex adequately to allow you to hike difficult trails, while **external-frame packs** are more comfortable for long hikes over even terrain, as they carry weight higher and distribute it more evenly. Make sure your pack has a strong, padded hip-belt to transfer weight to your legs. There are models designed specifically for women. Any serious backpacking requires a pack of at least 4000 in^3 (16,000cc), plus 500 in^3 for sleeping bags in internal-frame packs. Sturdy backpacks cost anywhere from US$125 to 420—your pack is an area where it doesn't pay to economize. On your hunt for the perfect pack, fill up prospective models with something heavy, strap it on correctly, and walk around the store to get a sense of how the model distributes weight. Either buy a **rain cover** (US$10-20) or store all of your belongings in plastic bags inside your pack.

Boots: Be sure to wear hiking boots with good **ankle support.** They should fit snugly and comfortably over 1-2 pairs of **wool socks** and a pair of thin **liner socks.** Break in boots over several weeks before you go to spare yourself blisters.

Other Necessities: Synthetic layers, like those made of polypropylene or polyester, and a pile jacket will keep you warm even when wet. A **space blanket** (US$5-15) will help you to retain body heat and doubles as a groundcloth. Plastic **water bottles** are vital; look for shatter- and leak-resistant models. Carry **water-purification tablets** for when you can't boil water. Although most campgrounds provide campfire sites, you may want to bring a small **metal grate** or **grill.** For those places (including virtually every organized campground in Europe) that forbid fires or the gathering of firewood, you'll need a **camp stove** (the classic Coleman starts at US$50) and a propane-filled **fuel bottle** to operate it. Also bring a **first-aid kit, insect repellent, pocketknife,** and **waterproof matches** or a **lighter.**

WHERE TO BUY IT

The mail-order/online companies listed below offer lower prices than many retail stores. A visit to a local camping or outdoors store will give you a good sense of the look and weight of certain items.

Campmor, 28 Parkway, P.O. Box 700, Upper Saddle River, NJ 07458, USA (US ☎888-226-7667; www.campmor.com).

Discount Camping, 880 Main North Rd., Pooraka, South Australia 5095, Australia (☎08 8262 3399; www.discountcamping.com.au).

Eastern Mountain Sports (EMS), 1 Vose Farm Rd., Peterborough, NH 03458, USA (☎888-463-6367; www.ems.com).

L.L. Bean, Freeport, ME 04033 (US and Canada ☎800-441-5713; UK ☎0800 891 297; www.llbean.com).

Mountain Designs, 51 Bishop St., Kelvin Grove, Queensland 4059, Australia (☎07 3856 2344; www.mountaindesigns.com).

Recreational Equipment, Inc. (REI), Sumner, WA 98352, USA (US and Canada ☎800-426-4840, elsewhere 253-891-2500; www.rei.com).

YHA Adventure Shop, 19 High St., Staines, Middlesex, TW18 4QY, UK (☎1784 458 625; www.yhaadventure.com).

CAMPERS AND RVS

Renting an RV costs more than tenting or hostelling but less than staying in hotels while renting a car (see **Renting**, p. 67). The convenience of bringing along your own bedroom, bathroom, and kitchen makes RVing an attractive option, especially for older travelers and families with children. Rates vary widely by region, season (July and August are the most expensive months), and type of RV. Rentals can cost as little as US$800 per week for a standard RV, and may require a security deposit. **Motorhome.com** (www.motorhome.com/rentals.html) lists rental companies for 13 European countries. **Auto Europe** (UK ☎0800 169 6414, US 888-223-5555; www.autoeurope.com) rents RVs in France, Germany, Italy, Spain and the UK.

ORGANIZED ADVENTURE TRIPS

Organized adventure tours offer another way of exploring the wild. Activities include hiking, biking, skiing, canoeing, kayaking, rafting, climbing, photo safaris, and archaeological digs. Tourism bureaus often can suggest parks, trails, and outfitters. Organizations that specialize in camping and outdoor equipment like REI and EMS (see above) are also good sources for info. The **Specialty Travel Index**, 305 San Anselmo Ave., Ste. 309, San Anselmo, CA 94960 (US ☎888-624-4030, elsewhere 415-455-1643; www.specialtytravel.com) compiles tours worldwide.

SPECIFIC CONCERNS

SUSTAINABLE TRAVEL

As the number of travelers on the road continues to rise, the detrimental effect they can have on natural environments becomes an increasing concern. With this in mind, *Let's Go* promotes a philosophy of **sustainable travel.** Through a sensitivity to issues of ecology and sustainability, today's travelers can be a powerful force in preserving and restoring the places they visit.

Ecotourism, a growing trend in sustainable travel, focuses on the conservation of natural habitats and using them to build up the economy without exploitation or overdevelopment. Travelers can make a difference by doing advance research and by supporting organizations and establishments that pay attention to their impact on their natural surroundings and strive to be environmentally-friendly. Coastal and marine areas, riverbanks, islands, mountain ranges and watersheds receive the most attention from conservationists, and travelers should approach these areas with particular care. **International Friends of Nature** (www.nfi.at) has info about sustainable travel in Europe and offers a directory of links to member nations' sites, though not all of these are in English. (For more information, see **Alternatives to Tourism,** p. 73.)

ECOTOURISM RESOURCES. For more information on environmentally responsible tourism, contact one of the organizations below:

The Centre for Environmentally Responsible Tourism (www.c-e-r-t.org).

Earthwatch, 3 Clock Tower Place, Ste. 100, Box 75, Maynard, MA 01754, USA (☎800-776-0188 or 978-461-0081; www.earthwatch.org).

International Ecotourism Society, 733 15th St. NW, Washington, D.C. 20005, USA (☎202-347-9203; www.ecotourism.org).

TRAVELING ALONE

There are many benefits to traveling alone, including independence and greater interaction with locals. On the other hand, any solo traveler is a more vulnerable target for harassment and street theft. As a lone traveler, try not to stand out as a tourist, look confident, and be especially careful in empty or very crowded areas. If questioned, never admit that you are traveling alone. Maintain regular contact with someone at home who knows your itinerary. For more tips, visit www.travelalone-andloveit.com, pick up *Traveling Solo* by Eleanor Berman (Globe Pequot Press, US$18), or subscribe to **Connecting: Solo Travel Network,** 689 Park Rd., Unit 6, Gibsons, BC V0N 1V7, Canada (☎604-886-9099; www.cstn.org; membership US$28-45).

WOMEN TRAVELERS

Women exploring on their own inevitably face some additional safety concerns, but it's easy to be adventurous without taking undue risks. If you are concerned, consider staying in hostels which offer single rooms that lock from the inside or in religious organizations with rooms for women only. Stick to centrally located accommodations and avoid solitary late-night treks or metro rides.

Always carry extra money for a phone call, bus, or taxi. **Hitchhiking** is never safe for lone women, or even for two women traveling together. Look as if you know where you're going and approach older women or couples for directions if you're lost or uncomfortable. Generally, the less you look like a tourist, the better off you'll be. Dress conservatively, especially in rural areas. Wearing a conspicuous **wedding band** sometimes helps to prevent unwanted overtures.

Your best answer to verbal harassment is no answer at all; pretending not to hear the speaker, sitting motionless, and staring straight ahead at nothing in particular will often defuse situations that more pointed reactions may only exacerbate. The extremely persistent can sometimes be dissuaded by a firm, loud, and very public "Go away!" in the appropriate language. Don't hesitate to seek out a police officer or a passerby if you are being harassed. Memorize the emergency numbers in places you visit, and consider carrying a whistle on your keychain. A self-defense course will both prepare you for a potential attack and raise your level of awareness of your surroundings (p. 26). Also be sure you are aware of the health concerns that women face when traveling (p. 31). For more information, consult *Safety and Security for Women Who Travel*, by Sheila Swan and Peter Laufer (Travelers' Tales, US $13).

GLBT TRAVELERS

Attitudes toward gay, lesbian, bisexual, and transgendered (GLBT) travelers are particular to each region in Europe. On the whole, Northern and Western Europe (especially the Netherlands) tends to be queer-friendly, while Central and Eastern Europe consists of enclaves of tolerance in major cities amid stretches of cultural conservatism. Still, countries like Romania and Armenia that outlawed homosexuality as recently as 2002 are becoming more liberal today, and can be considered viable destinations for the GLBT traveler. **Out and About** (www.planetout.com) offers a bi-weekly newsletter addressing travel concerns and a comprehensive site addressing gay travel concerns. The online newspaper **365gay.com** (www.365gay.com/travel/travelchannel.htm) has a solid travel section, while the sleek French-language site **netgai.com** (netgai.com/international/Europe) includes links to a host of country-specific resources, including many in English.

To avoid hassles at airports and border crossings, transgendered travelers should make sure that all of their travel documents consistently report the same gender. Many countries (including Australia, Canada, Ireland, New Zealand, the UK, and the US) will amend the passports of post-operative transsexuals to reflect their true gender, although governments are generally less willing to amend documents for pre-operative transsexuals and other transgendered individuals.

Listed below are contact organizations, mail-order bookstores, and publishers that offer materials addressing some specific concerns.

Gay's the Word, 66 Marchmont St., London WC1N 1AB, UK (☎44 20 7278 7654; www.gaystheword.co.uk). The largest gay and lesbian bookshop in the UK, with both fiction and non-fiction titles. Mail-order service available.

Giovanni's Room, 1145 Pine St., Philadelphia, PA 19107, USA (☎215-923-2960; www.queerbooks.com). An international lesbian/feminist and gay bookstore with mail-order service (carries many of the publications listed below).

International Lesbian and Gay Association (ILGA), 81 rue Marché-au-Charbon, B-1000 Brussels, Belgium (☎32 2 502 2471; www.ilga.org). Provides political information, such as homosexuality laws of individual countries.

FURTHER READING: GLBT TRAVEL.
Damron Men's Travel Guide, Damron Accommodations Guide, Damron City Guide, and *Damron Women's Traveller.* Damron Travel Guides (US$11-19). For info, call ☎800-462-6654 or visit www.damron.com.
Ferrari Guides' Gay Travel A to Z, Ferrari Guides' Men's Travel in Your Pocket, Ferrari Guides' Women's Travel in Your Pocket, and *Ferrari Guides' Inn Places.* Ferrari Publications (US$16-20).
Spartacus 2004-2005: International Gay Guide. Bruno Gmünder Verlag (US$33).

TRAVELERS WITH DISABILITIES

European countries vary in accessibility to travelers with disabilities. Some national and regional tourist boards, particularly in Western and Northern Europe, provide directories on the accessibility of various accommodations and transportation services. If these services are not available, contact institutions of interest directly. Travelers should inform airlines and hotels of their disabilities when making reservations; some time may be needed to prepare special accommodations. Call ahead to restaurants, museums, and other facilities to find out if they are handicapped-accessible. **Guide dog owners** should inquire as to the quarantine policies of each destination country. At the very least, you will need to provide a certificate of immunization against rabies.

Rail is probably the most convenient form of travel for disabled travelers in Europe: many stations have ramps, and some trains have wheelchair lifts, special seating areas, and specially equipped toilets. Large stations in Britain are equipped with wheelchair facilities, and the French national railroad offers wheelchair compartments on all TGV (high speed) and Conrail trains. (All Eurostar, some InterCity (IC), and some EuroCity (EC) trains are wheelchair-accessible; CityNightLine trains, French TGV (high speed), and Conrail trains feature special compartments.) In general, the countries with the most **wheelchair-accessible rail networks** are Denmark (IC and Lyn trains), France (TGVs and other long-distance trains), Germany (ICE, EC, IC, and IR trains), Italy (all Pendolino and many EC and IC trains), the Netherlands (most trains), the

Republic of Ireland (most major trains), Sweden (X2000s, most IC and IR trains), and Switzerland (all IC, most EC, and some regional trains). Austria, Poland, and Great Britain offer accessibility on selected routes. Bulgaria, the Czech Republic, Greece, Hungary, the Slovak Republic, Spain, and Turkey's rail systems have limited resources for wheelchair accessibility. For those who wish to rent cars, many major **car rental** agencies (including Hertz, Avis, and National) offer hand-controlled vehicles.

USEFUL ORGANIZATIONS

Access Abroad, www.umabroad.umn.edu/access. A website devoted to making study abroad available to students with disabilities. The site is maintained by Disability Services Research and Training, University of Minnesota, University Gateway, Ste. 180, 200 Oak St. SE, Minneapolis, MN 55455, USA (☎612-626-1333).

Accessible Journeys, 35 West Sellers Ave., Ridley Park, PA 19078, USA (☎800-846-4537; www.disabilitytravel.com). Designs tours for wheelchair users and slow walkers. The site has tips and forums for all travelers.

Flying Wheels, 143 W. Bridge St., P.O. Box 382, Owatonna, MN 55060, USA (☎507-451-5005; www.flyingheelstravel.com). Specializes in escorted trips to Europe for people with physical disabilities; plans custom accessible trips worldwide.

The Guided Tour Inc., 7900 Old York Rd., #114B, Elkins Park, PA 19027, USA (☎800-783-5841; www.guidedtour.com). Organizes travel programs for persons with developmental and physical challenges in Iceland, Ireland, Spain, London, Paris, and Rome.

Mobility International USA (MIUSA), P.O. Box 10767, Eugene, OR 97440, USA (☎541-343-1284; www.miusa.org). Provides a variety of books and other publications containing information for travelers with disabilities.

Society for Accessible Travel & Hospitality (SATH), 347 Fifth Ave., #610, New York, NY 10016, USA (☎212-447-7284; www.sath.org). An advocacy group that publishes free online travel information and the travel magazine *OPEN WORLD* (annual subscription US$13, free for members). Annual membership US$45, students and seniors US$30.

MINORITY TRAVELERS

In general, minority travelers will find a high level of tolerance in large cities; small towns and the countryside are more unpredictable. The increasingly mainstream reality of anti-immigrant sentiments means that travelers of African or Arab descent (regardless of their citizenship) may be the object of unwarranted assumptions and even hostility. The September 11 terrorist attacks on the United States corresponded to an upsurge in anti-Muslim sentiments in Europe, while anti-Semitism also remains a very real problem in many countries, most visibly in France and Germany. Jews, Muslims, and other minority travelers should keep an eye out for skinheads, who have been linked to racist violence in Central Europe, Eastern Europe, and elsewhere. **The European Monitoring Centre on Racism and Xenophobia,** Rahlgasse 3, A-1060 Vienna, Austria (☎43 15 80 30; eumc.eu.int) publishes a wealth of country-specific statistics and reports. Travelers can also consult **United for Intercultural Action,** Postbus 413, NL-1000 AK, Amsterdam, Netherlands (☎31 20 6834778; www.unitedagainstracism.org) for a list of 500+ country-specific organizations that work against racism and discrimination, or **Youth United Against Racism in Europe,** P.O. Box 858, London E11 1YG, England (☎020 8558 7947) for educational resources. Minority travelers should also consult **Personal Safety** (p. 25) for tips on how to avoid unwanted attention.

DIETARY CONCERNS

Vegetarians will find no shortage of meat-free dining options throughout most of Northern and Western Europe, although **vegans** may have a trickier time away from urban centers, where eggs and dairy can dominate traditional cuisine. The cuisine of Eastern Europe still tends to be heavy on meat and gravy, although major cities are often enclaves of surprisingly inventive vegetarian and ethnic fare.

The travel section of The Vegetarian Resource Group's website, at www.vrg.org/travel, has a comprehensive list of organizations and websites that are geared toward helping vegetarians and vegans traveling abroad. The website for the **European Vegetarian Union (EVU)**, at www.europeanvegetarian.org, includes links to organizations in 26 European countries, and gives free access to archived issues of the now-defunct *European Vegetarian* quarterly. A 20-euro yearly membership to the EVU includes regular email updates on vegetarian news and events. For more information, visit your local bookstore or health food store, and consult *The Vegetarian Traveler: Where to Stay if You're Vegetarian, Vegan, Environmentally Sensitive*, by Jed and Susan Civic (Larson Publications; US$16). Other promising resources include *Vegetarian Europe*, by Alex Bourke (Vegetarian Guides; US$17) and the indispensably multilingual *Vegan Passport* (The Vegan Society; US$5), along with websites www.vegdining.com, www.happycow.net, and www.vegetariansabroad.com.

Travelers who keep **kosher** should find abundant dining options across Europe, and they should contact synagogues in larger cities for information, or else consult www.kashrut.com/travel/Europe for country-specific resources. Hebrew College Online also offers a searchable database of kosher restaurants at www.shamash.org/kosher. Another good resource is the *Jewish Travel Guide*, edited by Michael Zaidner (Vallentine Mitchell; US$18). Travelers looking for **halal** groceries and restaurants will have the most success in France and Eastern European nations with substantial Muslim populations. These travelers should consult www.zabihah.com for establishment reviews. Keep in mind that if you are strict in your observance, you may have to prepare your own food on the road.

OTHER RESOURCES

Let's Go tries to cover all aspects of budget travel, but we can't put *everything* in our guides. Listed below are books and websites that can serve as jumping-off points for your own research.

TRAVEL PUBLISHERS AND BOOKSTORES

Globe Corner Bookstore, 28 Church St., Cambridge, MA 02138 (☎617-492-6277; www.globecorner.com), sponsors an Adventure Travel Lecture Series and carries a vast selection of guidebooks and maps. Online catalog also includes atlases and monthly staff picks for outstanding travel writing.

Hippocrene Books, 171 Madison Ave., New York NY 10016 (☎212-454-2366; www.hippocrenebooks.com), publishes foreign language dictionaries and learning guides, along with ethnic cookbooks and a smattering of guidebooks.

Rand McNally, 8255 N. Central Park, Skokie, IL 60076 (☎800-275-7263; outside of the US, call 847-329-6656; www.randmcnally.com), sells its own International Series of country maps (US$10), along with maps from well-respected European companies including Michelin, Hallwag, and Freytag & Berndt.

WORLD WIDE WEB

Almost every aspect of budget travel is accessible via the web. In 10min. at the keyboard, you can make a hostel reservation, get advice on travel hotspots from other travelers, or find out how much a train from Geneva to Nice costs.

Listed here are some regional and travel-related sites to start off your surfing; other relevant web sites are listed throughout the book. Because website turnover is high, use search engines (such as www.google.com) to strike out on your own.

WWW.LETSGO.COM Our freshly redesigned website features extensive content from our guides; community forums where travelers can connect with each other and ask questions or advice—as well as share stories and tips; and expanded resources to help you plan your trip. Visit us soon to browse by destination, find information about ordering our titles, and sign up for our e-newsletter!

THE ART OF TRAVEL

Backpacker's Ultimate Guide: www.bugeurope.com. Tips on packing, employment opportunities, and lots of country-specific travel information. Affiliate site europe.bugride.com facilitates ride-sharing, as a safer alternative to hitchhiking.

BootsnAll.com: www.bootsnall.com. A wide array of resources for independent travelers, from travelogues and discussion boards to tips on booking hostels. Free membership includes a bimonthly newsletter, and an open invitation to crash for a night with the founders outside of Portland, OR.

How to See the World: www.artoftravel.com. Free online version of independent traveler John Gregory's terse, copiously researched book on world travel. Recommendations on everything from binoculars to instructions on finding safe drinking water.

World Hum: www.worldhum.com. The site cribs its name from a Don Delillo novel, and features thoughtful travel essays, along with a daily weblog highlighting recent news and commentary in other publications.

INFORMATION ON EUROPE

BBC News: news.bbc.co.uk/europe. The latest coverage, free, from one of Europe's most reputable sources for English-language news.

CIA World Factbook: www.odci.gov/cia/publications/factbook. An indispensable source of hard info on countries' geography, government, economy, and people.

European Visits: www.eurodata.com. An online magazine of European travel, including feature articles, an advice column, and the odd book review.

EUROPA: europa.eu.int/index_en.htm. English-language gateway to the European Union, featuring recent news articles and a citizen's guide to EU institutions.

TRANSPORTATION

GETTING TO EUROPE

BY PLANE

When it comes to airfare, a little effort can save you a bundle. If your plans are flexible enough to deal with the restrictions, courier fares are the cheapest. Tickets bought from consolidators and standby seating are also good deals, but last-minute specials, airfare wars, and charter flights often beat these fares. The key is to hunt around, be flexible, and ask persistently about discounts. Students, seniors, and those under 26 should never pay full price for a ticket.

AIRFARES

Airfares to Europe peak between mid-June and early September; holidays are also expensive. The cheapest times to travel are November to mid-December and early January to March. Midweek (M-Th morning) round-trip flights run US$40-50 cheaper than weekend flights, but they are generally more crowded and less likely to permit frequent-flier upgrades. Not fixing a return date ("open return") or arriving in and departing from different cities ("open-jaw") can be pricier than round-trip flights. Patching one-way flights together is the most expensive way to travel. Flights between Europe's capitals or regional hubs—Amsterdam, Frankfurt, London, and Paris—will tend to be cheaper.

If your European destinations are part of a more extensive globe-hop, consider a round-the-world (RTW) ticket. Tickets usually include at least five stops and are valid for about a year; prices range US$1200-5000. Try **Northwest Airlines/KLM** (US ☎800-447-4747; www.nwa.com) or **Star Alliance,** a consortium of 15 airlines including United Airlines (US ☎ 800-864-8331; www.staralliance.com).

Fares for round-trip flights to major European hubs from the US or Canadian East Coast cost US$600-900, US$250-400 in the low season; from the US or Canadian West Coast US$800-1000/US$400-500; from the UK to the continent, UK£50-100; from Australia AUS$1700-2300/AUS$2100-2400; from New Zealand NZ$1800-2200/NZ$1500-1800.

BUDGET AND STUDENT TRAVEL AGENCIES

While knowledgeable agents specializing in flights to Europe can make your life easy and help you save, they may not spend the time to find you the lowest possible fare—they get paid on commission. Travelers holding **ISICs** and **IYTCs** (p. 18) qualify for big discounts from student travel agencies. Most flights from budget agencies are on major airlines, but in peak season some may sell seats on less reliable chartered aircrafts.

CTS Travel, 30 Rathbone Pl., London W1T 1GQ, UK (☎0207 209 0630; www.ctstravel.co.uk). A British student travel agent with offices in 39 countries including the US, Empire State Building, 350 Fifth Ave., Suite 7813, New York, NY 10118 (☎877-287-6665; www.ctstravelusa.com).

STA Travel, 5900 Wilshire Blvd., Ste. 900, Los Angeles, CA 90036, USA (24hr. reservations and info ☎800-781-4040; www.sta-travel.com). A student and youth travel organization with over 150 offices worldwide (check their website for a listing of all their offices), including US offices in Boston, Chicago, L.A., New York, San Francisco, Seattle, and Washington, D.C. Ticket booking, travel insurance, railpasses, and more. Walk-in offices are located throughout Australia (☎03 9349 4344), New Zealand (☎09 309 9723), and the UK (☎0870 1 600 599).

Travel CUTS (Canadian Universities Travel Services Limited), 187 College St., Toronto, ON M5T 1P7 (☎416-979-2406; www.travelcuts.com). Offices across Canada and the US including L.A., New York, San Francisco, and Seattle.

USIT, 19-21 Aston Quay, Dublin 2 (☎01 602 1777; www.usitworld.com), Ireland's leading student/budget travel agency has 22 offices throughout Northern Ireland and the Republic of Ireland. Offers programs to work in North America.

Wasteels, Skoubogade 6, 1158 Copenhagen K. (☎3314 4633; www.wasteels.com). A huge chain with 180 locations across Europe. Sells Wasteels BIJ tickets discounted 30-45% off regular fare, 2nd-class international point-to-point train tickets with unlimited stopovers for those under 26 (sold only in Europe).

 FLIGHT PLANNING ON THE INTERNET. The Internet may be the budget traveler's dream when it comes to finding and booking bargain fares, but the array of options can be overwhelming. Many airline sites offer special last-minute deals on the web, although some may require membership logins or email subscriptions. Try www.icelandair.com, www.airfrance.com, www.lufthansa.de, and www.britishairways.com. (For a great set of links to practically every airline in every country, see www.travelpage.com.) **STA** (www.statravel.com) and **StudentUniverse** (www.studentuniverse.com) provide quotes on student tickets, while **Expedia** (www.expedia.com), **Orbitz** (www.orbitz.com), **Opodo** (www.opodo.com), and **Travelocity** (www.travelocity.com) offer full travel services. **Priceline** (www.priceline.com) lets you specify a price, and obligates you to buy any ticket that meets or beats it; **Hotwire** (www.hotwire.com) offers bargain fares but won't reveal the airline or flight times until you buy. Other sites that compile deals for you include www.bestfares.com, www.flights.com, www.lowestfare.com, www.onetravel.com, and www.travelzoo.com. Increasingly, there are online tools available to help sift through multiple offers; **Booking Buddy** (www.bookingbuddy.com) and **SideStep** (www.sidestep.com; download required) let you enter your trip information once and search multiple sites. An indispensable resource on the Internet is the **Air Traveler's Handbook** (www.faqs.org/faqs/travel/air/handbook), a comprehensive listing of links to everything you need to know before you board a plane.

COMMERCIAL AIRLINES

The commercial airlines' lowest regular offer is the **APEX** (Advance Purchase Excursion) fare, which provides confirmed reservations and allows "open-jaw" tickets. Generally, reservations must be made seven to 21 days ahead of departure, with seven- to 14-day minimum-stay and up to 90-day maximum-stay restrictions. These fares carry hefty cancellation and change penalties. Book peak-season APEX fares early. Use **Microsoft Expedia** (http://msn.expedia.com) or **Travelocity** (www.travelocity.com) to get an idea of the lowest published fares, then use the resources outlined here to try and beat those fares. Low-season fares should be appreciably cheaper than the high-season (mid-June to Aug.) ones listed here.

TRAVELING FROM NORTH AMERICA

Basic round-trip fares to Europe range from roughly US$200-750: to Frankfurt, US$350-750; London, US$200-600; Paris, US$250-750. Standard commercial carriers like American (☎800-433-7300; www.aa.com), Northwest (☎800-447-4747;

www.nwa.com), and United (☎800-538-2929; www.ual.com) will probably offer convenient flights, but they may not be the cheapest. Check Air France (☎800-237-2747; www.airfrance.us), Alitalia (☎800-223-5730; www.alitaliausa.com), British Airways (☎800-247-9297; www.britishairways.com), and Lufthansa (☎800-399-5838; http://cms.lufthansa.com) for cheap tickets from locations throughout the US to all over Europe. You might find an even better deal on one of the following airlines, if any of their limited departure points is convenient for you.

Finnair: ☎800-950-5000; www.us.finnair.com. Cheap round-trips from New York, San Francisco, and Toronto to Helsinki; connections throughout Europe.

Icelandair: ☎800-223-5500; www.icelandair.com. Stopovers in Iceland for no extra cost on most transatlantic flights. New York to Frankfurt May-Sept. US$500-800; Oct.-May US$390-$500. For last-minute offers, subscribe to their email Lucky Fares.

Martinair: ☎800-627-8462; www.martinair.com. Fly from Florida to Amsterdam mid-June to mid-Aug. US$880; mid-Aug. to mid-June US$730.

TRAVELING FROM THE UK AND IRELAND
Because of the many carriers flying from the British Isles to the continent, we only include discount airlines or those with cheap specials here. The **Air Travel Advisory Bureau** in London (☎020 7306 3000; www.atab.co.uk) provides referrals to travel agencies and consolidators that offer discounted airfares out of the UK. **Cheapflights** (www.cheapflights.co.uk) publishes airfare bargains.

Aer Lingus: Ireland ☎0818 365 000; www.aerlingus.ie. Return tickets from Dublin, Cork, and Shannon to Amsterdam, Brussels, Düsseldorf, Frankfurt, Helsinki, Madrid, Munich, Paris, Rome, and Zurich (€44-135). Also serving smaller European cities.

bmibaby: UK ☎0870 264 22 29; www.bmibaby.com. Departures throughout the UK. London to Cork (UK£60) and Prague (UK£70).

easyJet: UK ☎0871 750 01 00; www.easyjet.com. London to Athens, Barcelona, Madrid, Nice, Palma, and Zurich (UK£72-141). Online tickets.

KLM: UK ☎0870 507 40 74; www.klmuk.com. Cheap tickets from the UK to Amsterdam, Brussels, Frankfurt, Düsseldorf, Milan, Paris, Rome, and other destinations.

Ryanair: Ireland ☎0818 303 030, UK 0871 246 00 00; www.ryanair.com. From Dublin, London, and Glasgow to destinations in Austria, Belgium, France, Germany, Italy, the Netherlands, Portugal, Scandinavia, and elsewhere.

TRAVELING FROM AUSTRALIA AND NEW ZEALAND
Air New Zealand: New Zealand ☎0800 737 000; www.airnz.co.nz. Auckland to London.

Qantas Air: Australia ☎13 11 31, New Zealand 0800 101 500; www.qantas.com.au. Flights from Australia and New Zealand to London for around AUS$2400.

Singapore Air: Australia ☎13 10 11, New Zealand 0800 808 909; www.singaporeair.com. Flies from Auckland, Sydney, Melbourne, and Perth to European cities.

Thai Airways: Australia ☎1300 65 19 60, New Zealand 09 377 38 86; www.thaiair.com. Auckland, Melbourne, and Sydney to Amsterdam, London, and elsewhere.

AIR COURIER FLIGHTS
Those who travel light should consider courier flights. Couriers help transport cargo on international flights by using their checked luggage space for freight. Generally, couriers must travel with carry-ons only and deal with complex flight restrictions. Most flights are round-trip only, with short fixed-length stays (usually 1 week) and a limit of one ticket per issue. Most of these flights also operate only out of major gateway cities, mostly in North America. Generally, you must be over

21 (in some cases 18). In summer, the most popular destinations usually require an advance reservation of two weeks (you can usually book up to 2 months ahead). Super-discounted fares are common for "last-minute" flights (3-14 days ahead).

FROM NORTH AMERICA

Round-trip courier fares from the US to Europe run about US$200-500. Most flights leave from Miami, New York, Los Angeles, or San Francisco in the US; and from Montreal, Toronto, or Vancouver in Canada. The organizations below provide members with lists of opportunities and courier brokers for an annual fee. Prices quoted below are round-trip.

> **Air Courier Association,** 1767 A Denver West Blvd., Golden, CO 80401 (☎800-280-5973; www.aircourier.org). 10 departure cities throughout the US and Canada to London, Madrid, Paris, Rome, and throughout Europe (high-season US$130-640). One-year membership US$20.

> **International Association of Air Travel Couriers (IAATC),** P.O. Box 847, Scottsbluff, NE 69363 (☎308-632-3273; www.courier.org). From 9 North American cities to European cities, including London, Madrid, Paris, and Rome. One-year membership US$45.

FROM THE UK AND IRELAND

The minimum age for couriers from the **UK** is usually 18. **Brave New World Enterprises,** P.O. Box 22212, London SE5 8WB (www.courierflights.com), publishes a directory of all the companies offering courier flights in the UK (UK£10, in electronic form UK£8). The **International Association of Air Travel Couriers** (see listing above) often offers courier flights from London to Budapest.

STANDBY FLIGHTS

Traveling standby requires considerable flexibility in arrival and departure dates and cities. Companies dealing in standby flights sell vouchers rather than tickets, with the promise to get you to your destination (or near your destination) within a certain window of time (typically 1-5 days). You call in before your specific window of time to hear flight options and the probability that you will be able to board each flight. You can then decide which flights you want to try to make, show up at the appropriate airport at the appropriate time, present your voucher, and board if space is available. Vouchers can usually be bought for both one-way and round-trip travel. You may receive a monetary refund only if every available flight within your date range is full; if you opt not to take an available (but perhaps less convenient) flight, you can only get credit toward future travel. Carefully read agreements with any company offering standby flights as tricky fine print can leave you in the lurch. To check on a company's service record in the US, call the Better Business Bureau (☎703-276-0100). It is difficult to receive refunds, and clients' vouchers will not be honored when an airline fails to receive payment in time.

TICKET CONSOLIDATORS

Ticket consolidators, or **"bucket shops,"** buy unsold tickets in bulk from commercial airlines and sell them at discounted rates. The best place to look is in the Sunday travel section of any major newspaper (e.g., *The New York Times*), where many bucket shops place tiny ads. Call quickly, as availability is typically extremely limited. Not all bucket shops are reliable, so insist on a receipt that gives full details of restrictions, refunds, and tickets, and pay by credit card (in spite of the 2-5% fee) so you can stop payment if you never receive your tickets. For more info, see www.travel-library.com/air-travel/consolidators.html.

Travel Avenue (☎ 800-333-3335; www.travelavenue.com) searches for best available published fares and then uses several consolidators to attempt to beat that fare. Other consolidators worth trying are **Rebel** (☎ 800-732-3588; www.rebeltours.com) and **Cheap Tickets** (☎ 800-652-4327; www.cheaptickets.com). Yet more consolidators on the web include **Flights.com** (www.flights.com) and **TravelHUB** (www.travelhub.com). Keep in mind that these are just suggestions to jump-start to your research; *Let's Go* does not endorse any of these agencies. As always, be cautious, and research companies before you hand over your credit card number.

CHARTER FLIGHTS

Charters are flights a tour operator contracts with an airline to fly extra loads of passengers during peak season. Charter flights fly less frequently than major airlines, make refunds particularly difficult, and are almost always fully booked. Schedules and itineraries may also change or be cancelled at the last moment (as late as 48 hours before the trip and without a full refund), and check-in, boarding, and baggage claim are often much slower. However, they can also be cheaper.

Discount clubs and fare brokers offer members savings on last-minute charters and tours. Study contracts closely; don't end up with an unwanted overnight layover. Travelers Advantage, 7 Cambridge Dr., Trumbull, CT 06611, USA (☎ 877-259-2691; www.travelersadvantage.com; US$90 annual fee includes discounts and cheap flight directories), specializes in European travel and tour packages.

BY CHUNNEL FROM THE UK

Traversing 43km under the sea, the Chunnel is undoubtedly the fastest, most convenient, and least scenic route from England to France.

BY TRAIN

Eurostar, Eurostar House, Waterloo Station, London SE1 8SE (UK ☎ 08705 186 186, Belgium 02 528 28 28, France 08 92 35 35 39; www.eurostar.com) runs frequent trains between London and the continent. Ten to 28 trains per day run to 100 destinations including Paris (4hr., US$75-300, 2nd class), Disneyland Paris, Brussels, Lille, and Calais. Book at major rail stations in the UK or at the office above.

BY BUS

Both **Eurolines** and **Eurobus** provide bus-ferry combinations (p. 66).

BY CAR

Eurotunnel (UK ☎ 08705 353 535; Customer relations, P.O. Box 2000, Folkestone, Kent CT18 8XY; www.eurotunnel.co.uk) shuttles cars and passengers between Kent and Nord-Pas de Calais. Return fares for vehicle and all passengers range from UK£283-317 with car. Same-day return costs UK£19-34, five-day return for either a car or a campervan UK£163-197. Book online or via phone. Travelers with cars can also look into sea crossings by ferry (see below).

BY BOAT FROM THE UK AND IRELAND

The fares below are **one-way** for **adult foot passengers** unless otherwise noted. Though standard return fares are usually just twice the one-way fare, **fixed-period returns** (usually within five days) are almost invariably cheaper. Ferries run **year-round** unless otherwise noted. **Bikes** are usually free, although you may have to pay up to UK£10 in high season. For a **camper/trailer** supplement, you will have to add

UK£20-140 to the "with car" fare. If more than one price is quoted, the quote in UK£ is valid for departures from the UK, etc. A directory of ferries in this region can be found at www.seaview.co.uk/ferries.html.

Brittany Ferries: UK ☎08703 665 333, France 08 25 82 88 28; www.brittany-ferries.com. **Plymouth** to **Roscoff, France** (6hr.; in summer 1-3 per day, off-season 1 per week; UK£20-58 or €21-46) and **Santander, Spain** (24hr., 1-2 per week, return UK£80-145). **Portsmouth** to **St-Malo** (8¾hr., 1-2 per day, €23-49) and **Caen, France** (6hr, 1-3 per day, €21-44). **Poole** to **Cherbourg, France** (4¼hr., 1-2 per day, EUR€21-44). **Cork** to **Roscoff, France** (14hr., Apr.-Sept. 1 per week, €52-99).

DFDS Seaways: UK ☎08705 33 30 00; www.dfdsseaways.co.uk. **Harwich** to **Hamburg** (19½hr.) and **Esbjerg, Denmark** (18hr.). **Newcastle** to **Amsterdam** (16hr.); **Kristiansand, Norway** (18¼hr.); and **Gothenburg, Sweden** (26hr.).

Fjord Line: UK ☎0191 296 1313; www.fjordline.no. **Newcastle, England** to **Stavanger** (19½hr.) and **Bergen, Norway** (26hr.) for UK£60-120, students £30-120.

Hoverspeed: UK ☎0870 240 8070, France 008 00 1211 1211; www.hoverspeed.co.uk. Dover to Calais (1 hr., every 1-2hr., UK£15). Newhaven to Dieppe, France (2¼-4¼hr., 1-3 per day, UK£25).

Irish Ferries: France ☎01 44 88 54 50, Ireland 1890 31 31 31, UK 08705 17 17 17; www.irishferries.ie. **Rosslare** to **Cherbourg** and **Roscoff** (18hr.; €50-120, students €40-96); and **Pembroke, UK** (3¾hr.; UK£20-24, students £15-18). **Holyhead, UK** to **Dublin** (2-3hr.; UK£26-30, students £20-23).

P&O North Sea Ferries: UK ☎0870 520 2020; www.ponsf.com. Daily ferries from **Hull** to **Rotterdam, Netherlands** (11hr.) and **Zeebrugge, Belgium** (13hr.). Both UK£38-48, cars UK£63-78. Online bookings.

P&O Stena Line: UK ☎087 0600 0611; from Europe 44 13 04 86 40 03; www.posl.com. **Dover** to **Calais** (1¼hr., every 30min.-1hr. 30 per day, UK£17).

SeaFrance: UK ☎08705 711 711, France 08 03 04 40 45; www.seafrance.com. **Dover** to **Calais** (1½hr., 15 per day, UK£18).

Stena Line: UK ☎ 08704 00 67 98; www.stenaline.co.uk. **Harwich** to **Hook of Holland** (3½-6hr., UK£26). **Fishguard** to **Rosslare** (1½-3½hr., UK£20-24). **Holyhead** to **Dublin** or **Dún Laoghaire** (1½-3hr., UK£26-30). **Stranraer** to **Belfast** (1¾-3¼hr.; UK£16-24, students £11-19).

GETTING AROUND EUROPE

Fares are either **single** (one-way) or **return** (round-trip). "Period returns" require you to return within a specific number of days; "day return" means you must return on the same day. Unless stated otherwise, *Let's Go* always lists single fares. Round-trip fares on trains and buses in Europe are simply twice the one-way fare.

BY PLANE

The recent emergence of no-frills airlines has made traveling Europe by air increasingly affordable and convenient. Though these flights often feature inconvenient hours or serve less-popular regional airports, with one-way flights averaging about US$50, it's never been faster or easier to traverse the Continent. For info on cheap flights from Britain to the continent, see **Traveling from the UK and Ireland**, p. 53. For links to regional budget airlines, check out www.lowcostairlines.org.

easyJet: UK ☎0871 750 01 00; www.easyjet.com. Serves 44 destinations in the Czech Republic, Denmark, France, Germany, Greece, Hungary, Italy, the Netherlands, Portugal, the UK, Slovenia, Spain, Switzerland.

Ryanair: Ireland ☎0818 303 030, UK 0871 246 00 00; www.ryanair.com. Serves 86 destinations in Austria, Belgium, France, Germany, Ireland, Italy, the Netherlands, Portugal, Scandinavia, Spain, and the UK.

The **Star Alliance European Airpass** offers economy-class fares as low as US$65 for travel within Europe to more than 200 destinations in 43 countries. The pass is available to transatlantic passengers on Star Alliance carriers, including Air Canada, Austrian Airlines, BMI British Midland, Lufthansa, Mexicana, Scandinavian Airlines System, THAI, United Airlines, US Airways, and Varig, as well as on certain partner airlines. See www.staralliance.com for more information. In addition, a number of European airlines offer discount coupon packets. Most are only available as tack-ons for transatlantic passengers, but some are stand-alone offers. Most must be purchased before departure, so research in advance.

Europe by Air: ☎888-387-2479; www.europebyair.com. *FlightPass* allows you to country-hop to over 150 European cities. US$99 per flight.

Iberia: ☎800-772-4642; www.iberia.com. *Europass* allows Iberia passengers flying from the US to Spain to add a minimum of 2 more destinations in Europe. US$139 each.

BY TRAIN

Trains in Europe are generally comfortable, convenient, and reasonably swift. Second-class compartments, which seat two to six, are great places to meet fellow travelers. Trains, however, are not always safe; for safety tips, see p. 25. For long trips, make sure you are on the correct car, as trains sometimes split at crossroads. Towns listed in parentheses on European train schedules require a train switch at the town listed immediately before the parentheses.

You can either buy a **railpass**, which allows you unlimited travel within a particular region for a given period of time, or rely on buying individual **point-to-point** tickets as you go. Almost all countries give students or youths (usually defined as anyone under 26) direct discounts on regular domestic rail tickets, and many also sell a student or youth card that provides 20-50% off all fares for up to a year.

RESERVATIONS

While seat reservations are required only for selected trains (usually on major lines), you are not guaranteed a seat without one (usually US$4-11). You should strongly consider reserving in advance during peak holiday and tourist seasons (at the very latest, a few hours ahead). You will have to purchase a **supplement** (US$10-50) or special fare for high-speed or high-quality trains such as Spain's AVE, Cisalpino, Finland's Pendolino S220, Italy's ETR500 and Pendolino, Germany's ICE, and certain French TGVs. InterRail holders must also purchase supplements (US$10-25) for trains like EuroCity, InterCity, Sweden's X2000, and many French TGVs; supplements are unnecessary for Eurailpass holders.

OVERNIGHT TRAINS

On night trains, you won't waste valuable daylight hours traveling and you can avoid the hassle and expense of staying at a hotel. However, the main drawbacks include discomfort, sleepless nights, and lack of scenery. **Sleeping accommodations** on trains differ from country to country, but typically you can either sleep upright in your seat (for free) or pay for a separate space. **Couchettes** (berths) typically

Rail prices and times are subject to wide variation, and student or other discounts may be available. This map gives only a general picture of train travel in Europe. Consult *Thomas Cook's European Timetable* for accurate schedule info.

Rail Planner

FINLAND

ORWAY

SWEDEN

Oslo

Helsinki | $50 5½hr. | St. Petersburg

| $136-165 5-6hr.
| $58-85 4½hr.

Stockholm | $16-30 10hr. | Tallinn | $22 14hr. | $23 8hr.

Göteborg

ESTONIA

Rīga | Moscow

| $85-103 2¾-3½hr.
| $118-144 4½-6¾hr.

LATVIA | $20 8hr.

Baltic Sea

LITHUANIA | $66 16hr. | RUSSIA

| $80 4½hr. Malmö Copenhagen

Vilnius | $25 10hr.

RUSSIA

| $133 7½hr.
| $60 2¼hr.

Gdańsk | $20 5½hr. | $51 10-10½hr. | Minsk | $32 14hr.

BELARUS

Berlin | $40 3hr. | POLAND | $52 8½hr. | $30 4hr. | $41 8hr.

| $102 4½hr. | $61 6¾hr. Poznań | $25 3¼hr. Warsaw | $57 17hr. | Kyiv | Kharkiv

Wrocław | $31 4¾hr. | $29 2½-5hr.

Prague | $43 6hr. | $28 4½hr. | $9 10hr.

| $199-128 6½-7hr. | $55 9hr. Kraków | $41 12hr. | Lviv | UKRAINE

CZECH REPUBLIC

Dnieper River

| $97 7hr. | $50 5-5½hr. | $62 4¼hr. SLOVAK REPUBLIC | $8 11hr.

Munich | $71 4¾hr. | $20 1¼hr. Bratislava | MOLDOVA

| $08 5½hr. AUSTRIA | $82 6½hr. | $42 3hr. | $76 13½hr. | Chişinău

Vienna | Sea of Azov

| $70 6½hr. Budapest

| $22 1½hr. Ljubljana | $44 7hr. HUNGARY | $120 13hr. | Odessa

| $44 5½hr. SLOVENIA | $48 7½hr. | ROMANIA | Yalta

Venice | $25 2½hr. Zagreb

| $35 2½hr. CROATIA | Bucharest | Black Sea

SAN MARINO BOSNIA AND HERZEGOVINA | Belgrade

| Sarajevo | $48 6hr. | $52 10hr.

ITALY Dubrovnik SERBIA AND MONTENEGRO | Sofia | BULGARIA

Rome | Skopje | $22 8hr.

| $31 1¾hr. | $16 4hr. F.Y.R. MACEDONIA

Adriatic Sea Tiranë | Thessaloniki

Naples | $48 7hr. ALBANIA

Brindisi | $45 7¾hr.

Tyrrhenian Sea | Aegean Sea

| $52 6hr. GREECE

Palermo | Ionian Sea | Athens

| $33 3½hr. Messina

Sicily

MALTA Sea of Crete

TRANSPORTATION

have four to six seats per compartment (about US$20 per person); **sleepers** (beds) in private sleeping cars offer more privacy and comfort, but are considerably more expensive (US$40-150). If you're using a railpass valid only for a restricted number of days, inspect train schedules to maximize the use of your pass: An overnight train or boat journey uses up only one of your travel days if it departs after 7pm.

SHOULD YOU BUY A RAILPASS?

Railpasses were conceived to allow you to jump on any train in Europe, go wherever you want whenever you want, and change your plans at will. In practice, however, it's not so simple. You still must stand in line to validate your pass and pay for supplements and seat and couchette reservations. More importantly, railpasses don't always pay off. Consult our railplanner (p. 58) to estimate the point-to-point cost of each leg of your journey; add them up and compare the total with the cost of a railpass. If you're planning to spend extensive time on trains, hopping between big cities, a railpass will probably be worth it. But in many cases, especially if you are under 26, point-to-point tickets may prove a cheaper option.

You may find it tough to make your railpass pay for itself in Belgium, Greece, Ireland, Italy, Luxembourg, the Netherlands, Portugal, Spain, Eastern Europe, or the Balkans, where train fares are reasonable, distances short, or buses preferable. If, however, the total cost of your trips nears the price of the pass, the convenience of avoiding ticket lines may be worth the difference.

MULTINATIONAL RAILPASSES

EURAILPASS. Eurail is valid in most of Western Europe: Austria, Belgium, Denmark, Finland, France, Germany, Greece, Hungary, Italy, Luxembourg, the Netherlands, Norway, Portugal, the Republic of Ireland, Spain, Sweden, and Switzerland. It is not valid in the UK. Standard **Eurailpasses,** valid for a consecutive given number of days, are best for those planning on spending extensive time on trains every few days. **Flexipasses,** valid for any 10 or 15 (not necessarily consecutive) days within a two-month period, are more cost-effective for those traveling longer distances less frequently. **Saverpacooo** provide first-class travel for travelers in groups of two to five (prices are per person). **Youthpasses** and **Youth Flexipasses** provide parallel second-class perks for those under 26.

EURAILPASSES	15 DAYS	21 DAYS	1 MONTH	2 MONTHS	3 MONTHS
1st class Eurailpass	US$588	US$762	US$946	US$1338	US$1654
Eurail Saverpass	US$498	US$648	US$804	US$1138	US$1408
Eurail Youthpass	US$414	US$534	US$664	US$938	US$1160

EURAIL FLEXIPASSES	10 DAYS IN 2 MONTHS	15 DAYS IN 2 MONTHS
1st class Eurail Flexipass	US$694	US$914
Eurail Saver Flexipass	US$592	US$778
Eurail Youth Flexipass	US$488	US$642

Passholders receive a timetable for major routes and a map with details on possible ferry, steamer, bus, car rental, hotel, and Eurostar discounts (p. 55). Passholders often also receive reduced fares or free passage on many bus and boat lines.

EURAIL SELECT PASS. The Eurail Select Pass is a slimmed-down version of the Eurailpass: it allows five to 15 days of unlimited travel in any two-month period within three, four, or five bordering countries of the 17 Eurail network countries plus Romania. (For the purposes of the Select Pass, Belgium, the Netherlands, and Luxembourg are considered one country, called "Benelux".) **First-Class passes** (for individuals) and **Saverpasses** (for people traveling in groups of 2-5) range from

US$356/US$304 per person (5 days) to US$794/US$674 (15 days). **Second-Class Youthpasses** for those aged 12-25 cost US$249-556. For a fee, you can add additional zones (Austria/Hungary; Belgium/Luxembourg/Netherlands; Greece Plus, including the ADN/HML ferry between Italy and Greece; and/or Portugal). You are entitled to the same freebies afforded by the Eurailpass, but only when they are within or between countries that you have purchased.

SHOPPING AROUND FOR A EURAIL. Eurailpasses are designed by the EU itself, and can be bought only by non-Europeans almost exclusively from non-European distributors. These passes must be sold at uniform prices determined by the EU. However, some travel agents tack on a US$10 handling fee, and others offer certain bonuses with purchase, so shop around. Also, keep in mind that pass prices usually go up each year, so if you're planning to travel early in the year, you can save cash by purchasing before January 1 (you have three months from the purchase date to validate your pass in Europe).

It is best to buy your Eurail before leaving; only a few places in major European cities sell them, and at a marked-up price. You can get a replacement for a lost pass only if you have purchased insurance on it under the Pass Protection Plan (US$14-17). Eurailpasses can now be ordered online directly from the **Eurail Group** (www.eurail.com). They are also available through travel agents, student travel agencies like STA, and **Rail Europe** (Canada ☎ 800-361-7245, UK 08 705 848 848, US 877-257-2887; www.raileurope.com) or **DER Travel Services,** whose services are available at several outfits across the US (☎ 800-782-2424; www.der.com).

OTHER MULTINATIONAL PASSES. If your travels will be limited to one area, regional passes are often good values. They include the **France 'n' Italy Pass** (standard/under 26 passes for 4-10 days in 2 months of 2nd-class travel US$259-421/US$199-325); the **France 'n' Spain Pass** (standard/under 26 passes for 4-10 days in 2 months 2nd-class US$259-433/US$199-331); the **ScanRail Pass** for Denmark, Finland, Norway, and Sweden (standard/under 26 passes for 5 days in 2 months 2nd-class US$291/US$203; 10 days in 2 months US$390/ US$273; 21 consecutive days US$453/US$316; 1st class passes $100 extra); the **Benelux Tourrail Pass** for Belgium, the Netherlands, and Luxembourg (5 days in 1 month 2nd-class US$163, under 26 US$109; 50% discount for companion traveler); the **Balkan Flexipass,** which is valid for travel in Bulgaria, Greece, the Former Yugoslav Republic of Macedonia, Montenegro, Romania, Serbia, and Turkey (5 days in 1 month 1st-class only US$189, under 26 US$112); and the **European East Pass** that covers Austria, the Czech Republic, Hungary, Poland, and Slovakia (5 days in 1 month 2nd-class US$158).

If you have lived for at least six months in one of the European countries where **InterRail Passes** are valid, or in Algeria, Belarus, Estonia, Latvia, Lithuania, Moldova, Russia, Tunisia, or Ukraine, they prove an economical option. There are eight InterRail **zones.** The **Under 26 InterRail Card** allows 16 consecutive days, 22 consecutive days, or one month of unlimited travel within one, two, three or all of the eight zones; the cost is determined by the number of zones the pass covers (UK£159-295). The **Over 26 InterRail Card** provides the same services as the Under 26 InterRail Card, but at higher prices: UK£223-415. The new **Child Pass** (ages 4-11) offers the same services for 50% off the adult fare. Passholders receive **discounts** on rail travel, Eurostar journeys, and most ferries to Ireland, Scandinavia, and the rest of Europe. Most exclude **supplements** for high-speed trains. For info and ticket sales in Europe contact **Student Travel Centre,** 24 Rupert St., 1st fl., London W1D 6DQ (☎ 020 74 37 81 01; www.student-travel-centre.com). Tickets are also available from travel agents, at major train stations throughout Europe, or through online vendors (www.railpassdirect.co.uk).

DOMESTIC RAILPASSES

If you are planning to spend a significant amount of time within one country or region, a national pass—valid on all rail lines of a country's rail company—may be more cost-effective than a multinational pass. But many national passes are limited and don't provide the free or discounted travel on private railways and ferries that Eurail does. Some of these passes can be bought only in Europe, some only outside of Europe; check with a railpass agent or with national tourist offices.

NATIONAL RAILPASSES. The domestic analogs of the Eurailpass, national rail-passes (called "flexipasses" in some countries) are valid either for a given number of consecutive days or for a specific number of days within a given time period. Usually, they must be purchased before you leave. Though they will usually save travelers some money, in some cases (particularly in Eastern Europe) you may find that they are actually a more expensive alternative to point-to-point tickets. For more information on national railpasses, check out www.raileurope.com/us/rail/passes/single_country_index.htm.

EURO DOMINO. Like the Interrail Pass, the Euro Domino pass is available to anyone who has lived in Europe for at least six months; however, it is only valid in one country (which you designate when buying the pass). It is available for 28 European countries plus Morocco. Reservations must still be paid for separately. **Supplements** are required for some high-speed trains (e.g., German ICE). The pass must be bought within your country of residence; each destination country has its own price for the pass. Ask your national rail company for more info.

REGIONAL PASSES. This type of pass covers a specific area within a country or a round-trip from any border to a particular destination and back; these are useful as supplements when your main pass isn't valid. The Prague Excursion Pass is a common purchase for Eurailers, whose passes are not valid in the Czech Republic; it covers travel from any Czech border to Prague and back out of the country (round trip must be completed within 7 days; 2nd-class US$40, under 26 US$35).

RAIL-AND-DRIVE PASSES. In addition to simple railpasses, many countries (as well as Eurail) offer rail-and-drive passes, which combine car rental with rail travel—a good option for travelers who wish both to visit cities accessible by rail and to make side trips into the surrounding areas. Prices range per person from $295-539, depending on the type of pass, type of car, and number of people included. Children under the age of 11 cost $123, and adding more days costs $49-95 per day (see **By Car,** p. 66).

DISCOUNTED TICKETS

For travelers under 26, **BIJ** tickets (Billets Internationales de Jeunesse; operated by **Wasteels**) are a great alternative to railpasses. Available for international trips within Europe and most ferry services, they knock 20-40% off 1st- and 2nd-class fares. Tickets are good for two months after purchase allow stopovers along the normal direct route of the train journey. Issued for a specific international route between two points, they must be used in the direction and order of the designated route and must be bought in Europe. The equivalent for those over 26, **BIGT** tickets provide a 20-30% discount on 1st- and 2nd-class international tickets. Both types of tickets are available from European travel agents, at Wasteels offices (usually in or near train stations), or directly at the ticket counter in some nations. For more info and to locate offices in different European countries, see www.wasteels.com.

> **FURTHER READING AND RESOURCES ON TRAIN TRAVEL.**
> **Info on rail travel and railpasses:** www.raileurope.com.
> **Point-to-point fares and schedules:** www.raileurope.com/us/rail/
> fares_schedules/index.htm. Calculate whether buying a railpass would save
> you money. For a more portable resource, see our railplanner on p. 58.
> **European Railway Server:** mercurio.iet.unipi.it/home.html. Links to rail servers
> throughout Europe.
> *Thomas Cook European Timetable,* updated monthly, covers all major and most
> minor train routes in Europe. Buy it online directly from Thomas Cook
> (www.thomascooktimetables.com) or find it at any Thomas Cook Money
> Exchange Center in Europe.
> *On the Rails Around Europe: A Comprehensive Guide to Travel by Train,* Melissa
> Shales. Thomas Cook Ltd. (US$19).

BY BUS

Though European trains and railpasses are extremely popular, buses may prove a better option. In Spain, buses are on par with trains; in Britain, Greece, Ireland, and Portugal, bus networks are more extensive, more efficient, and often more comfortable than train routes; and in Iceland and parts of Scandinavia, bus service is the only ground transportation available. In the rest of Europe, scattered offerings from private companies can be inexpensive but sometimes unreliable. Often cheaper than railpasses, **international bus passes** typically allow unlimited travel on a hop-on, hop-off basis between major European cities. In general, these services tend to be more popular among non-American backpackers.

Eurolines, 52 Grosvenor Gardens, London, WSWIW OAU (UK ☎015 8240 4511; www.eurolines.com). The largest operator of Europe-wide coach services, Eurolines offers unlimited peak-season 15-day (€285, under 26 €240), 30-day (€425/€345), and 60-day (€490/€380) travel between 35 European cities in 25 countries; low-season prices are lower.

Busabout, 258 Vauxhall Bridge Rd., London SW1V 1BS (UK ☎020 7950 1661; www.busabout.com) covers 41 European cities in 11 countries. Sells consecutive-day passes for 2 weeks (€359, under 26 €329), 4 weeks (€589/€519), 6 weeks (€729/€649), 8 weeks (€859/€759), 12 weeks (€1059/€939), and 6-month seasons (€1239/€1109). Flexipasses, valid for the entire operating season, are also available for 8 days (€419/€379), 12 days (€589/€579), 16 days (€729/€649), and 20 days (€879/€789).

BY CAR

Cars offer speed, freedom, access to the countryside, and an escape from the town-to-town monotony of trains. Before setting out, familiarize yourself with the laws of the countries in which you'll be driving (e.g., both seat belts and headlights must be on at all times in Scandinavia, and cars must keep left in Ireland and the UK). For an informal primer on European road signs and conventions, check out http://travlang.com/signs. A good resource for information on road conditions and general safety is the **Association for Safe International Road Travel** (www.asirt.org).

RENTING

Although a single traveler won't save money by renting a car, a group of four usually will. If you can't decide between train and car travel, you may benefit from a combination of the two; RailEurope and other railpass vendors offer rail-and-drive packages (p. 65). Fly-and-drive packages are also often available from travel agents or airline/rental agency partnerships. When comparing prices, consider that cheaper cars tend to be less reliable and harder to handle on difficult terrain. Less expensive four-wheel-drive (4WD) vehicles in particular tend to be more top-heavy and are more dangerous when navigating particularly bumpy roads.

RENTAL AGENCIES

You can rent a car from a US-based firm (e.g., Alamo, Avis, Budget, or Hertz) with European offices, from a European-based company with local representatives (e.g., Europcar), or from a tour operator (e.g., Auto Europe, Europe By Car, and Kemwel Holiday Autos) that will arrange a rental for you from a European company at its own rates. Multinationals offer greater flexibility, but tour operators often strike better deals. Some chains allow you to choose a drop-off location different from your pick-up city, but there is often a minimum rental period and an extra charge. Expect to pay more for larger cars and for four-wheel-drive.

You can generally make reservations before you leave by calling major international offices in your home country. However, occasionally the price and availability information they give doesn't jive with what the local offices in your country will tell you. Try checking with both phone numbers to make sure you get the best price and accurate information. Local desk numbers are included in town listings; for home-country numbers, call your toll-free directory.

Minimum age requirements vary but tend to fall in the range of 21-25, with some as low as 18; there may be an additional insurance fee for drivers under 25. Policies and prices vary from agency to agency; often all you need to rent a car is a license from home and proof that you've had it for a year. Small local operations occasionally rent to people under 21, but be sure to ask about the insurance coverage and deductible (see below), and always check the fine print. Rental agencies operating in Europe include:

Auto Europe: US and Canada ☎ 888-223-5555; www.autoeurope.com.

Avis: Australia ☎ 136 333, Canada 00-272-5871, New Zealand 0800 655 111, UK 087 0606 0100, US 800-230-4898; www.avis.com.

Budget: UK ☎ 013 4448 4100, US and Canada 800-527-0700; www.budgetrentacar.com.

Europe by Car: US ☎ 800-223-1516; www.europebycar.com.

Europcar International: UK ☎ 087 0607 5000, US and Canada 877-940-6900; www.europcar.com.

Hertz: Australia ☎ 9698 2555, Canada 800-263-0600, UK 020 7026 0077, US 800-654-3131; www.hertz.com.

COSTS AND INSURANCE

Rental rates vary widely by region and agency; expect to pay around US$80-400 per week, plus tax (5-25%), for a tiny car. Larger vehicles and 4WD will raise prices. Reserve ahead and pay in advance if possible. It is less expensive to reserve a car from the US than from Europe. During the summer, rental in parts of Eastern Europe and Scandinavia, as well as in Ireland and Italy, can be comparatively expensive. Pickup location matters; for instance, it is usually cheaper to rent a car in Germany, or the Netherlands than in Paris. Some companies charge extra fees for traveling into Eastern Europe. National chains often allow one-way rentals, picking up in one city and dropping off in another. There is usually a minimum hire period and sometimes an extra drop-off charge of several hundred dollars.

Cars with **automatic transmission** are more expensive than manuals (stick shift), and are more difficult to find in most of Europe. It is virtually impossible to obtain an automatic 4WD. Many rental packages offer unlimited kilometers, while others offer a fixed distance per day with a per-kilometer surcharge after that. Be sure to ask whether the price includes **insurance** against theft and collision. Remember that if you are driving a conventional vehicle on an **unpaved road** in a rental car, you are almost never covered by insurance; ask about this before leaving the rental agency. Beware that cars rented on an **American Express** or **Visa/ Mastercard Gold or Platinum** credit cards in Europe might *not* carry the automatic insurance that they would in some other countries; check with your credit card company. Insurance plans almost always come with an **excess** (or deductible) for conventional vehicles; excess is usually higher for younger drivers and for 4WD. This provision means you pay for all damages up to the specified sum, unless they are the fault of another vehicle. The excess you will be quoted applies to collisions with other vehicles; collisions with non-vehicles like trees ("single-vehicle collisions") will cost you even more. The excess can often be reduced or waived for an additional charge. Remember to return the car with a full tank of **gasoline** to avoid high fuel charges in the end. Gas prices vary by country and are generally highest in Scandinavia. Throughout Europe fuel tends to be cheaper in cities than in outlying areas. Western Europeans and Scandinavians use unleaded gas almost exclusively, but it's not available in many gas stations in Eastern Europe.

LEASING A CAR

For trip durations longer than three weeks, leasing can be cheaper than the daily cost of renting; it is often the only option for those ages 18-21. The cheapest leases are agreements to buy the car and then sell it back to the manufacturer at a prearranged price. As far as you're concerned, though, it's a lease and doesn't entail enormous financial transactions. Leases generally include insurance coverage and are not taxed. The most affordable ones tend to originate in Belgium, France, and Germany. Expect to pay upward of US$1400, depending on the model of vehicle, for 60 days. Many rental agencies have leasing plans, in particular **Auto Europe, Europe by Car,** and **Kemwel** (see above).

BUYING A CAR

If you're brave and know what you're doing, **buying** a used car or van in Europe and selling it just before you leave can provide the cheapest wheels for longer trips. Check with consulates for import-export laws concerning used vehicles, registration, and safety and emission standards.

ON THE ROAD

Road conditions and **regional hazards** are variable throughout Europe. They tend to fluctuate with seasons; winter weather will make driving difficult in some countries, while in others, spring thaws cause flooding due to melted ice. Roads in mountainous areas are often steep and curvy and may be closed in the winter. Owing to maintenance issues and inadequately enforced traffic laws, road conditions in Eastern Europe are often poor, and many travelers prefer public transportation. Western European roads are generally excellent, but keep in mind that each area has its own dangers. In Scandinavia, for example, drivers should be on the lookout for moose and elk, while on the Autobahn the threat will come from cars speeding at 150kph. In this book, region-specific hazards are listed in country introductions. The Association for Safe International Road Travel (see above) can provide more extended info on road safety. Carry emergency equipment with you (see **Driving Precautions,** below) and know what to do in case of a breakdown. Car rental companies will often have phone numbers for emergency service.

DRIVING PRECAUTIONS. When traveling in the summer or in the desert, bring substantial amounts of water (a suggested 5L of **water** per person per day) for drinking and for the radiator. For long drives to unpopulated areas, register with police before beginning the trek, and again upon arrival at the destination. Check with the local automobile club for details. When traveling for long distances, make sure tires are in good repair and have enough air, and get good maps. A **compass** and a **car manual** can also be very useful. Always carry a **spare tire** and **jack, jumper cables, extra oil, flares, a flashlight (torch),** and **heavy blankets** (in case your car breaks down at night or in the winter). If you don't know how to **change a tire,** learn before heading out, especially if you are planning on traveling in deserted areas. Blowouts on dirt roads are exceedingly common. If you do have a breakdown, **stay with your car;** if you wander off, there's less likelihood trackers will find you.

DRIVING PERMITS AND CAR INSURANCE

INTERNATIONAL DRIVING PERMIT (IDP)

If you plan to drive a car while in Europe, you must be over 18 and have an International Driving Permit (IDP), though certain countries (such as the UK) allow travelers to drive with a valid American or Canadian license for a limited number of months. It may be a good idea to get one anyway, in case you're in a situation (e.g., an accident or stranded in a small town) where the police do not know English; information on the IDP is printed in ten languages, including French, German, Italian, Portuguese, Russian, Spanish, and Swedish.

Your IDP, valid for one year, must be issued in your own country before you depart. An application for an IDP usually requires one or two photos, a current local license, an additional form of identification, and a fee. To apply, contact the national or local branch of your home country's automobile association. Be careful when purchasing an IDP online or anywhere other than your home automobile association. Many vendors sell permits of dubious legitimacy for higher prices.

CAR INSURANCE

Most credit cards cover standard insurance. If you rent, lease, or borrow a car, you will need a **green card,** or **International Insurance Certificate,** to certify that you have liability insurance and that it applies abroad. Green cards can be obtained at car rental agencies, car dealers (for those leasing cars), some travel agents, and some border crossings. Rental agencies may require you to purchase theft insurance in countries that they consider to have a high risk of auto theft.

BY BOAT

Most European ferries are quite comfortable; the cheapest ticket typically still includes a reclining chair or couchette. Fares jump in July and August. Ask for discounts; ISIC holders often can get student fares, and Eurailpass holders get many reductions and free trips. You may have to pay a port tax (usually under US$10).

ENGLISH CHANNEL AND IRISH SEA FERRIES

Ferries are frequent and dependable. The main route across the **English Channel,** from England to France, is Dover-Calais. The main ferry port on the southern coast of England is Portsmouth, with connections to France and Spain. Ferries also cross the **Irish Sea,** connecting Northern Ireland with Scotland and England, and the Republic of Ireland with Wales. For more info on sailing (or "hovering") in this region, see **By Boat from the UK and Ireland,** p. 55.

NORTH AND BALTIC SEA FERRIES

Ferries in the **North Sea** are reliable and go everywhere. Those content with deck passage rarely need to book ahead. For ferries heading to and from the UK, see p. 55. **Baltic Sea** ferries service routes between Poland and Scandinavia.

Polferries: Poland ☎48 94 35 52 102; www.polferries.se. Ferries run between Poland and Denmark or Sweden.

Color Line: Norway ☎47 22 94 44 00; www.colorline.com. Offers ferries between Norway and Denmark, Sweden, and Germany.

Silja Line: US sales ☎800-533-3755, Finland 358 09 18041; www.silja.com. Helsinki to Stockholm; St. Petersburg; Tallinn, Estonia; and Visby, Sweden. Also St. Petersburg to Rostock, Germany; and Turku to Stockholm.

DFDS Seaways: US ☎800-533-3755; www.seaeurope.com. Offers routes within Scandinavia and from Scandinavia to England or Germany.

MEDITERRANEAN AND AEGEAN FERRIES

Mediterranean ferries may be the most glamorous, but they can also be the most rocky; bring toilet paper. Ferries run from Spain to Morocco, from Italy to Tunisia, and from France to Morocco and Tunisia. Reservations are recommended, especially in July and August. Schedules are erratic, with similar routes and varying prices. Shop around, and beware of dinky, unreliable companies that don't take reservations. Ferries float across the **Adriatic** from Ancona and Bari, Italy to Split and Dubrovnik, respectively, in Croatia.

Ferries also run across the **Aegean,** from Ancona, Italy to Patras, Greece (19hr.), and from Bari, Italy to Igoumenitsa (9hr.) and Patras (15hr.), Greece. **Eurail** is valid on certain ferries between Brindisi, Italy and Corfu (8hr.), Igoumenitsa (11½hr.), and Patras (14½hr.), Greece. Countless ferry companies operate these routes simultaneously; websites such as www.ferries.gr list various schedules. See specific country chapters for more information.

BY BICYCLE

With a mountain bike, you can do some serious natural sightseeing. Many airlines will count your bike as your second free piece of luggage; a few charge extra (US$60-110 one-way). Bikes must be packed in a cardboard box with the pedals and front wheel detached; many airlines sell bike boxes at the airport (US$10). Most ferries let you take your bike for free or for a nominal fee, and you can always ship your bike on trains. Renting a bike beats bringing your own if you plan to stay in one or two regions. Some youth hostels rent bicycles for low prices, and in Switzerland, train stations rent bikes and often allow you to drop them off elsewhere; check train stations throughout Europe for similar details. In addition to **panniers** to hold your luggage, you'll need a good **helmet** (US$25-50) and a **sturdy lock** (from US$30). For more country-specific books on biking through France, Germany, Ireland, or the UK, try **Mountaineers Books,** 1001 S.W. Klickitat Way, Suite 201, Seattle, WA 98134 (☎800-553-4453; www.mountaineersbooks.org).

If you are nervous about striking out on your own, **Blue Marble Travel** (Canada ☎519-624-2494, France 42 36 02 34, US 215-923-3788; www.bluemarble.org) offers bike tours for small groups of ages 20 to 49 throughout Europe. **CBT Tours,** 2506 N. Clark St. #150, Chicago, IL 60614 (☎800-736-2453; www.cbttours.com), offers full-package biking, mountain biking, hiking, and multi-sport tours (US$1500-2500) to Belgium, the Czech Republic, England, France, Germany, Italy, Ireland, the Netherlands, Scotland, and Switzerland. **Cycle Rides** (☎800-389-3384; www.cyclerides.co.uk) offers various one- to two-week tours throughout Europe. **EURO Bike and Walking Tours** (☎800-321-6060; www.eurobike.com) gives many six-day to two-week biking, walking, and multi-sport tours across Central and Western Europe.

BY MOPED AND MOTORCYCLE

Motorized bikes and **mopeds** don't use much gas, can be put on trains and ferries, and are a good compromise between costly car travel and the limited range of bicycles. However, they're uncomfortable for long distances, dangerous in the rain, and unpredictable on rough roads. Always wear a helmet, and never ride with a backpack. If you've never ridden a moped before, a twisting Alpine road is not the place to start. Expect to pay about US$20-35 per day; try auto repair shops, and remember to bargain. **Motorcycles** are more expensive and normally require a license, but are better for long distances. Before renting, ask if the price includes tax and insurance, or you may be hit with an unexpected fee. Avoid handing your passport over as a deposit; if you have an accident or mechanical failure you may not get it back until you cover all repairs, so pay ahead of time instead. For more info, try: *Motorcycle Journeys through the Alps and Corsica*, by John Hermann (US$24.95); *Motorcycle Touring and Travel*, by Bill Stermer (US$19.95); or *Europe by Motorcycle*, by Gregory W. Frazier (US$19.95).

BY FOOT

Some of Europe's best scenery can be seen only by foot. *Let's Go* features many daytrips, but native inhabitants, hostel owners, and fellow travelers are the best source for tips. Many countries have hiking and mountaineering organizations; alpine clubs in Austria, Germany, Italy, and Switzerland, as well as tourist organizations in Scandinavia, provide simple accommodations in splendid settings.

BY THUMB

> *Let's Go* never recommends hitchhiking as a safe means of transportation, and none of the information presented here is intended to do so.

No one should hitch without considering the risks involved. Hitching means entrusting your life to a stranger who happens to stop beside you on the road; you risk theft, assault, sexual harassment, and unsafe driving. Some travelers report that hitchhiking allows them to meet local people and travel in areas where public transportation is sketchy. The choice is yours.

Britain and **Ireland** are probably the easiest places in Western Europe to get a lift. Hitching in **Scandinavia** is slow but steady. Long-distance hitching in the developed countries of **northwestern Europe** demands close attention to expressway junctions, rest stop locations, and often a destination sign. Hitching in **Southern Europe** is generally mediocre; **France** is the worst. In some **Central** and **Eastern European** countries, the line between hitching and taking a taxi is quite thin.

Hitchhiking at night can be particularly dangerous; experienced hitchers stand in well-lit places. For women traveling alone, hitching is just too dangerous. A man and a woman are a safer combination, two men will have a harder time, and three will go nowhere. Experienced hitchers pick a spot outside of built-up areas, where drivers can stop, return to the road without causing an accident, and have time to look over potential passengers as they approach. Hitching (or even standing) on super-highways is usually illegal: one may only thumb at rest stops or at the entrance ramps to highways. Most Europeans signal with an open hand, not a thumb; many write their destination on a sign. Finally, success will depend on appearance. Drivers prefer hitchers who are neat and wholesome-looking.

Most Western European countries offer a ride service, which pairs drivers with riders; the fee varies according to destination. **Eurostop International** (**Verband der Deutschen Mitfahrzentralen** in Germany and **Allostop** in France) is one of the largest in Europe. Not all organizations screen drivers and riders; ask in advance.

ALTERNATIVES TO TOURISM

A PHILOSOPHY FOR TRAVELERS

Let's Go believes that the connection between travelers and their destinations is an important one. We've watched the growth of the 'ignorant tourist' stereotype with dismay, knowing that many travelers care passionately about the communities and environments they explore—but also knowing that even conscientious tourists can inadvertently damage natural wonders and harm cultural environments. With this "Alternatives to Tourism" chapter, *Let's Go* hopes to promote a better understanding of Europe and enhance your experience there.

There are several different options for those who seek to participate in Alternatives to Tourism. Opportunities for **volunteering** abound, both with local and international organizations. **Studying** can also be instructive, either in the form of direct enrollment in a local university or in an independent research project. **Working** is a way to both immerse yourself in the local culture and finance your travels.

As a **volunteer** in Europe, you can participate in projects from castle-cleaning in France to protecting the endangered Loggerhead turtles in Greece, either on a short-term basis or as the main component of your trip. Later in this section, we recommend organizations that can help you find the opportunities that best suit your interests, whether you're looking to pitch in for a day or a year.

Studying at a college or language program is another option. Those who choose to study abroad in Europe often find the immersion in the region's educational environment to be much more rewarding and genuine than the typical camera-toting tourist's experience. With hundreds of programs to choose from, students are can select from a full spectrum of fields that cater to their individual interests.

Many travelers also structure their trips by the **work** that they can do along the way—either odd jobs as they go, or full-time stints in cities where they plan to stay for longer periods of time. Many big cities are eager to employ foreigners, especially for work which requires interaction with tourists. For information on the legality of short-term work, see p. 80.

 Start your search at ■ **www.beyondtourism.com,** Let's Go's brand-new searchable database of Alternatives to Tourism, where you can find exciting feature articles and helpful program listings divided by country, continent, and program type.

VOLUNTEERING

Volunteering can be one of the most fulfilling experiences you have in life, especially if it is combined with the thrill of traveling in a new place. Whether your passion is for ecological, political, or social work, opportunities to volunteer abound.

Most people who volunteer in Europe do so on a short-term basis, at organizations that make use of drop-in or once-a-week volunteers. The best way to find opportunities that match up with your interests and schedule may be to check with local or national volunteer centers.

More intensive volunteer services may charge you a fee to participate. These costs can be surprisingly hefty, although they frequently cover airfare and most living expenses. Most people choose to go through a parent organization that takes care of logistical details and often provides a group environment and support system. There are two main types of organizations—religious and non-sectarian—although there are rarely restrictions on participation for either.

Opportunities for volunteer work are more abundant in Eastern Europe than in other areas of the continent. Habitat for Humanity and Peace Corps placements, for example, are not usually available in Western Europe.

ONLINE DIRECTORIES

www.alliance-network.org. Umbrella website bringing together various international service organizations from around the world.

www.idealist.org. Provides extensive listings of service opportunities.

www.volunteerabroad.com. Searchable database of opportunities around the world.

www.worldvolunteerweb.org. Lists organizations and events around the world.

PROGRAMS

COMMUNITY DEVELOPMENT

Cross-Cultural Solutions, 2 Clinton Pl., New Rochelle, NY 10801 (☎800-380-4777; http://crossculturalsolutions.org). 2- to 12-week education and social service placements in Russia and many other countries. 17+. From US$2175.

Global Volunteers, 375 E. Little Canada Rd., St. Paul, MN 55117 (☎800-487-1074; www.globalvolunteers.org). A variety of 1- to 3-week volunteer programs throughout Europe. Fees range from US$1995-2395 including room and board but not airfare.

Service Civil International Voluntary Service (SCI-IVS), SCI USA Main Office, 5474 Walnut Level Rd., Crozet, VA 22932 (☎206-350-6585; www.sci-ivs.org). Arranges placement in outdoor work camps throughout Europe. 18+. Registration fee US$175.

CONSERVATION

Archaeological Institute of America, 656 Beacon St., Boston, MA 02215 (☎617-353-9361; www.archaeological.org). The *Archaeological Fieldwork Opportunities Bulletin,* available on the organization's website, lists field sites throughout Europe.

Business Enterprises for Sustainable Travel (www.sustainabletravel.org). Supports travel to help communities preserve natural and cultural resources and create sustainable livelihoods. Listings of local programs, innovative opportunities, and internships.

Club du Vieux Manoir, Abbaye Royale du Moncel, 60700 Pontpoint, France (☎03 44 72 33 98; http://cvmclubduvieuxmanoir.free.fr). Offers year-long and summer programs restoring castles and churches throughout France. €14 membership/insurance fee; €16 per day, including food and tent.

Earthwatch Institute, 3 Clocktower Pl., Ste. 100, Box 75, Maynard, MA 01754 (☎800-776-0188; www.earthwatch.org). Arranges 1- to 3-week programs to promote conservation of natural resources. Fees vary based on program location and duration. Costs range from US$700-4000 plus airfare.

The National Trust, Volunteering and Community Involvement Office, Rowan, Kembrey Park, Swindon, Wiltshire, SN2 8YL, UK (☎08706 095 383; www.nationaltrust.org.uk/volunteers). Arranges numerous volunteer opportunities, including Working Holidays.

World Wide Opportunities on Organic Farms (WWOOF), Main Office, P.O. Box 2675, Lewes BN7 1RB, England, UK (www.wwoof.org). Arranges volunteer work with organic and eco-conscious farms around the world.

MEDICAL OUTREACH

AIDS Take Care, Schlossstr. 15, D-82269 Geltendorf, Germany (☎8193 93000; www.aidstakecare.com). Supports AIDS education and patient treatment throughout the world.

Doctors Without Borders, 333 7th Ave., 2nd fl., New York, NY 10001 (☎212-679-6800; www.doctorswithoutborders.org/volunteer). Medical and non-medical volunteer assignments wherever there is need.

HUMANITARIAN AND SOCIAL SERVICES

Coalition for Work with Psychotrauma and Peace, Gunduliceva 18, 32000 Vukovar, Croatia (☎32 444 662; www.cwwpp.org). Work in a group for 1½-2 years in education and health care related to long-term conflict stress in Bosnia, Croatia, and Serbia.

Simon Wiesenthal Center, 1399 South Roxbury Dr., Los Angeles, CA 90035 (☎800-900-9036; www.wiesenthal.org). Fights anti-Semitism and Holocaust denial throughout Europe. Small, variable donation required for membership.

United Nations High Commission for Refugees (UNHCR), Case Postale 2500, CH-1211 Genève 2 Dépôt, Switzerland (☎22 739 8111; www.unhcr.org). Gladly provides advice on how and where to help.

Volunteers for Peace, 1034 Tiffany Rd., Belmont, VT 05730 (☎802-259-2759; www.vfp.org). Arranges placement in work camps throughout Europe. Membership (US$20) required for registration. Programs average US$200-400 for 2-3 weeks.

STUDYING

VISA INFORMATION. Different countries have different requirements for students wishing to study abroad. Ask the local consulate for specific information about acquiring the proper visa. Generally speaking, applicants must be able to provide a passport and give proof of enrollment, medical insurance, and financial support before their visa can be issued. Since the process may take months to complete, it is advisable to apply for a visa well in advance of your departure date.

Study abroad programs range from basic language and culture courses to college-level classes, often for credit. In order to choose a program that best fits your needs, research as much as you can before making your decision—determine costs and duration, as well as what kind of students participate in the program and what sort of accommodations are provided.

In programs that have large groups of students who speak the same language, there is a trade-off. You may feel more comfortable in the community, but you will not have the same opportunity to practice a foreign language or to befriend other international students. For accommodations, dorm life provides a better opportunity to mingle with fellow students, but there is less of a chance to experience the local scene. If you live with a family, there is a potential to build lifelong friendships with natives and to experience day-to-day life in more depth, but conditions can vary greatly from family to family.

UNIVERSITIES

Most university-level study-abroad programs are meant as language and culture enrichment opportunities, and therefore are conducted in the local language. Still, many programs offer classes in English and beginner- and lower-level language courses. Those relatively fluent in a foreign language may find it cheaper to enroll directly in a university abroad, although getting college credit may be more difficult. You can search www.studyabroad.com for various semester-abroad programs that meet your criteria, including your desired location and focus of study. The following is a list of organizations that can help place students in university programs abroad, or have their own branch in Europe.

ONLINE DIRECTORIES

The following websites are good resources for finding programs that cater to your particular interests. Each has links to various study-abroad programs broken down by a variety of criteria, including desired location and focus of study.

> **www.studyabroad.com.** A great starting point for finding college- or high school-level programs in foreign languages or specific academic subjects. Also maintains a page of links to several other useful websites.
>
> **www.petersons.com/stdyabrd/sasector.html.** Lists summer and term-time study-abroad programs at accredited institutions that usually offer cross-credit.
>
> **www.westudyabroad.com/europe.htm.** Lists language courses and college-level programs in a number of European countries.

AMERICAN PROGRAMS

American Institute for Foreign Study, College Division, River Plaza, 9 West Broad St., Stamford, CT 06902 (☎800-727-2437; www.aifsabroad.com). Organizes programs for high school and college study at universities in Austria, Britain, the Czech Republic, France, Ireland, Italy, Russia, and Spain.

American Field Service (AFS), 71 W. 23rd St., 17th fl., New York, NY 10010 (☎212-807-8686; www.afs.org), has branches in over 50 countries. Summer-, semester-, and year-long homestay exchange programs for high school students and graduating seniors in locations including the Czech Republic, Hungary, Latvia, Russia, and the Slovak Republic. Community service programs also offered for young adults, 18+. Teaching programs available for current and retired teachers. Financial aid available.

American School of Classical Studies (ASCSA), Souidias 54, 10676 Athens, Greece (☎210 72 36 313; www.ascsa.edu.gr). Offers a variety of archaeological and classical studies programs to undergraduates, graduate students, and doctoral candidates. Visit the website to find a list of publications and links to other archaeological programs.

Arcadia University for Education Abroad, 450 S. Easton Rd., Glenside, PA 19038 (☎866-927-2234; www.arcadia.edu/cea). Operates programs in Britain, Greece, Ireland, Italy, and Spain. Costs range from US$2750 (summer) to US$36,000 (full-year).

Central College Abroad, Box 0140, 812 University, Pella, IA 50219 (☎800-831-3629 or 641-628-5375; www.central.edu/abroad). Offers internships, as well as summer-, semester-, and year-long programs in Austria, Britain, France, the Netherlands, and Spain. US$30 application fee.

Council on International Educational Exchange (CIEE), 7 Custom House St., 3rd fl., Portland, ME 04101 (☎800-407-8839; www.ciee.org). Sponsors academic, internship, volunteer, and work programs in Belgium, Britain, the Czech Republic, France, Hungary, Ireland, Italy, the Netherlands, Poland, Romania, Russia, Spain, and Turkey.

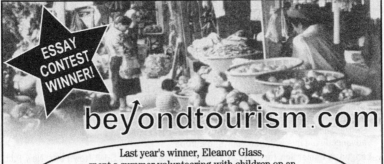

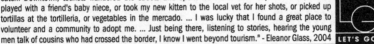

Last year's winner, Eleanor Glass, spent a summer volunteering with children on an island off the Yucatan Peninsula. Read the rest of her story and find your own once-in-a-lifetime experience at www.beyondtourism.com!

"... I was discovering elements of life in Mexico that I had never even dreamt of. I regularly had meals at my students' houses, as their fisherman fathers would instruct them to invite the nice gringa to lunch after a lucky day's catch. Downtown, tourists wandered the streets and spent too much on cheap necklaces, while I played with a friend's baby niece, or took my new kitten to the local vet for her shots, or picked up tortillas at the tortilleria, or vegetables in the mercado. ... I was lucky that I found a great place to volunteer and a community to adopt me. ... Just being there, listening to stories, hearing the young men talk of cousins who had crossed the border, I know I went beyond tourism." - Eleanor Glass, 2004

Institute for the International Education of Students (IES), 33 N. LaSalle St., 15th fl., Chicago, IL 60602 (☎800-995-2300; www.IESabroad.org). Offers year-long, semester, and summer programs in Austria, England, France, Germany, Ireland, Italy, the Netherlands, and Spain for college students. Internship opportunities. US$50 application fee. Scholarships available.

International Association for the Exchange of Students for Technical Experience (IAESTE), 10400 Little Patuxent Pkwy. Suite 250, Columbia, MD 21044 (☎410-997-2200; www.iaste.org). Offers 8- to 12-week programs in Europe for college students who have completed 2 years of technical study. US$50 application fee.

The International Kitchen, 1 IBM Plaza, 330 N. Wabash #3005, Chicago, IL 60611 (☎800-945-8606 or 312-726-4525; www.theinternationalkitchen.com). Leading provider of cooking school vacations to Italy and France. Traditional cooking instruction in beautiful settings. Program locations include the Amalfi Coast, Liguria, and Tuscany. Courses run 2-7 nights. Prices vary.

School for International Training, College Semester Abroad, Admissions, Kipling Rd., P.O. Box 676, Brattleboro, VT 05302, (☎800-257-7751 or 802-257-7751; www.sit.edu). Semester- and year-long programs in Europe run US$12,775-15,725. Also runs the **Experiment in International Living** (☎800-345-2929; www.usexperiment.org), 3- to 5-week summer programs that offer high-school students cross-cultural homestays, community service, ecological adventure, and language training in Europe and cost US$4100-5200.

Youth for Understanding International Exchange (YFU), 6400 Goldsboro Rd., Ste. 100, Bethesda, MD 20817 (☎800-833-6243 or 866-493-8872; www.yfu.org). Places US high school students with host families throughout Europe for a year, semester, or summer. US$75 application fee plus $500 enrollment deposit.

ALTERNATIVES TO TOURISM

LANGUAGE SCHOOLS

Language schools can be divisions of foreign universities or independently run international or local organizations. Though they rarely offer college credit, they are a good alternative to university study if you desire a deeper focus on the language or a slightly less rigorous courseload. These programs are also good for younger high school students who might not feel comfortable with older students in a university program. Some good programs include:

Eurocentres, 101 N. Union St. Suite 300, Alexandria, VA 22314, USA (☎703-684-1494; www.eurocentres.com) or in Europe, Head Office, Seestr. 247, CH-8038 Zurich, Switzerland (☎41 1 485 50 40; fax 481 61 24). Language programs for beginning to advanced students with homestays in Europe.

Language Immersion Institute, 75 South Manheim Blvd., SUNY-New Paltz, New Paltz, NY 12561 (☎845-257-3500; www.newpaltz.edu/lii). 2- to 8-week summer language courses and some overseas courses in foreign languages. Program fees are around US$600 for a 2-week course.

LanguagesPLUS, 413 Ontario St., Toronto, Ontario M5A 2V9, Canada (US ☎888-526-4758; outside US 416-925-7117; www.languagesplus.com), runs 2- to 12-week programs in Britain, France, Germany, Ireland, Italy, and Spain. 18+. US$350-3000; includes tuition and accommodations with host families or in apartments.

WORKING

VISA INFORMATION. Generally speaking, **EU citizens** have the right to work anywhere in the EU for up to three months without a visa; longer-term employment usually requires some sort of **residency** or **work permit.** By law, all EU citizens must be given equality of opportunity when applying to jobs not directly related to national security. Different countries have different laws for non-EU foreigners wishing to work abroad; inquire at the local embassy or consulate for specific information. Non-EU foreigners will usually have more difficulty finding work opportunities than EU citizens.

As with volunteering, work opportunities tend to fall into two categories: long-term and short-term. Some travelers want long-term jobs that allow them to get to know another part of the world as a member of the community, while other travelers seek out short-term jobs to finance the next leg of their travels. In Europe, people who want to work long-term might find success where their language skills are in demand, such as in teaching or working with tourists. Employment opportunities for those who want to work short-term may be more limited and are generally contingent upon the economic needs of the city or region.

In additional to local papers, international English-language newspapers, such as the *International Herald Tribune* (www.int.com), often list job opportunities in their classified sections. If applicable, travelers should also consult federally run employment offices and be aware of possible visa restrictions (see above).

Generally speaking, acquiring the appropriate work permits is easier for EU citizens than for others. Non-EU citizens planning to work in Europe must carefully research country-specific requirements and limitations before their departure.

LONG-TERM WORK

If you're planning on spending a substantial amount of time (more than three months) working in Europe, search for a job well in advance. International placement agencies are often the easiest way to find employment abroad, especially for teaching English. **Internships,** usually for college students, are a good way to segue into working abroad, although they often offer no or low wages (many say the experience, however, is well worth it). Be wary of companies that claim the ability to get you a job abroad for a fee—often the same listings are available online or in newspapers, or are even out-of-date. Some reputable organizations include:

Council Exchanges, 7 Custom House St., Portland, ME 03101 (☎800-407-8839; www.councilexchanges.org). Charges a US$300-475 fee for arranging 3- to 6-month work authorizations in France, Germany, and Ireland.

Escapeartist.com (http://jobs.escapeartist.com). International employers post directly to this website; various European jobs advertised.

Fruitful Ltd., Unit 3 Ind. Est., Honeybourne, Evesham, Worcester, WR117QF, UK (☎01386 83255; www.fruitfuljobs.com). Sets up farm work in the UK for backpackers and students; online application available.

International Cooperative Education, 15 Spiros Way, Menlo Park, CA 94025 (☎650-323-4944; www.icemenlo.com). Finds summer jobs for students in Belgium, Britain, Germany, and Switzerland. Participants must be between the ages of 18 and 30. Costs include a US$250 application fee and a US$700 placement fee.

International Employment Gazette, 423 Townes St., Greenville, SC 29601 (☎800-882-9188; www.intemployment.com). An online subscription service that publishes available overseas jobs every 2 weeks. US$20 per month.

ResortJobs.com (www.resortjobs.com). Searchable database of service and entertainment jobs at resorts around the world.

StepStone, StepStone ASA, 2 Bell Court, Leapale Lane, Guildford, Surrey GU1 4LY (☎44 14 83 73 94 50; www.stepstone.com). An online database covering international employment openings for most of Europe. Several search options and a constantly changing list of openings.

TEACHING ENGLISH

Teaching jobs abroad are rarely well-paid, although some elite private American schools can pay more competitive salaries. Volunteering as a teacher in lieu of getting paid is also a popular option; even in those cases, teachers often get some sort of a daily stipend to help with living expenses. In almost all cases, you must have at least a bachelor's degree to be a full-fledged teacher, although college undergraduates can often get summer positions teaching or tutoring.

Many schools require teachers to have a **Teaching English as a Foreign Language (TEFL)** certificate. Not having this certification does not necessarily exclude you from finding a teaching job, but certified teachers often find higher-paying positions. Native English speakers working in private schools are most often hired for English-immersion classrooms where not of word of the local language is spoken. Those volunteering or teaching in poorer, public schools are more likely to be working in both English and the native tongue. Placement agencies and university fellowship programs are the best resources for finding teaching jobs. The alternative is to make contact directly with schools or just to try your luck once you get there. If you are going to try the latter, the best time to look is several weeks before the start of the school year. The following organizations are extremely helpful in placing teachers in Europe.

Central European Teaching Program (CETP), 3800 NE 72nd Ave., Portland, OR 97213 (www.ticon.net/~cetp). College graduates only. Half- and full-year periods in Hungary and Romania. $2000 (academic year) or $1250 (semester), placement fee.

International Schools Services (ISS), 15 Roszel Rd., Box 5910, Princeton, NJ 08543-5910 (☎609-452-0990; www.iss.edu). Hires teachers for more than 200 overseas schools; candidates should have experience teaching or with international affairs, 2-year commitment expected.

Teaching English as a Foreign Language (TEFL), TEFL Professional Network Ltd., 72 Pentyla Baglan Rd., Port Talbot SA12 8AD, UK (www.tefl.com). Maintains the most extensive database of openings throughout Europe. Offers job training and certification.

AU PAIR WORK

Au pairs are typically women (although sometimes men), aged 18-27, who work as live-in nannies, caring for children and doing light housework in foreign countries in exchange for room, board, and a small spending allowance or stipend. Most former au pairs speak favorably of their experience. One perk of the job is that it allows you to get to know the country without the high expenses of traveling. Drawbacks, however, often include long hours of constantly being on duty and mediocre pay. Au pairs in Europe typically work 25-35 hours per week and receive US$200-350 per month. Much of the au pair experience really does depend on the family with whom you're placed. The agencies below are a good starting point for looking for employment as an au pair.

Au Pair Homestay, World Learning, Inc., 1015 15th St. NW, Suite 750, Washington, DC 20005, (☎800-287-2477; fax 202-408-5397).

Au Pair in Europe, P.O. Box 68056, Blakely Postal Outlet, Hamilton, Ontario, Canada L8M 3M7 (☎905-545-6305; www.princeent.com/aupair).

Childcare International, Ltd., Trafalgar House, Grenville Pl., London NW7 3SA (☎ 020 8906-3116; www.childint.co.uk).

InterExchange, 161 Sixth Ave., New York, NY 10013 (☎212-924-0446; www.interexchange.org).

SHORT-TERM WORK

Traveling for long periods of time can get expensive; therefore, many travelers try their hand at odd jobs for a few weeks at a time to help finance another month or two abroad. Another popular option is to work several hours a day at a hostel in exchange for free or discounted room and/or board. Most often, these short-term jobs are found by word of mouth or simply by talking to the owner of a hostel or restaurant. Due to the high turnover in the tourism industry, many places are eager for help, even if it is only temporary.

The availability and legality of temporary work vary widely across Europe. If you are interested in working your way through the continent, we recommend picking up *Let's Go* city and country guides. These books contain thorough information on local work opportunities at specific hostels and restaurants.

FOR FURTHER READING ON ALTERNATIVES TO TOURISM

Alternatives to the Peace Corps: A Directory of Third World and U.S. Volunteer Opportunities, by Joan Powell. Food First Books, 2000 (US$10).

How to Get a Job in Europe, by Matherly and Sanborn. Surrey Books, 1999 (US$22).

How to Live Your Dream of Volunteering Overseas, by Collins, DeZerega, and Heckscher. Penguin Books, 2002 (US$17).

International Directory of Voluntary Work, by Pybus. Peterson's Guides and Vacation Work, 2000 (US$19).

International Jobs, by Kocher and Segal. Perseus Books, 1999 (US$18).

Overseas Summer Jobs 2002, by Collier and Woodworth. Peterson's Guides and Vacation Work, 2002 (US$18).

Work Abroad: The Complete Guide to Finding a Job Overseas, by Hubbs, Griffith, and Nolting. Transitions Abroad Publishing, 2000 ($16).

Work Your Way Around the World, by Susan Griffith. US Worldview Publishing Services, 2001 (US$18).

LEARNING FROM THE CITY OF LIGHTS
On Belonging and Not Belonging in Paris

The first time Paris felt like home to me was a blustery week in November when I barely left my apartment. Sure, there were other indications along the way, like the first expensive sneakers I bought in a city that stacks shoes in windows like towers of candied fruit. But I think of that week in November because so much of what we call tourism involves speed—a frantic dash through a dozen museums, a precise ratio of *arrondissements* per hour. We want to see all that we can in the short time we have. Yet in Paris or anywhere else, alternatives to tourism mean surrendering to a sense of daily life, the mundane and the quietly memorable and even the stationary. My third month in Paris was the first time I let go in this way: yes, there were still corners of the city to explore, but the afternoons were chilly and the light was leaking out of the sky earlier and earlier. So for four days, I stayed in my pajamas and padded downstairs for little quiches to heat up in the oven. The baker made fun of my flip-flops, and told me that I would catch pneumonia.

I spent 13 weeks in Paris during what would have been the fall semester of my senior year in college. I took a leave of absence from school rather than studying abroad for credit, and while I can't make a case for one over the other, students should know that there's more than one way to spend time overseas. Study-abroad programs that strand you in special English-language classes hinder you from becoming proficient in a second language and insulate you from meeting locals. The programs that let you enroll directly are at least innocent of those two charges, although they still involve a fixed schedule that makes it hard for you to pick up and spend a random week in Budapest. The research stipend that my university gave me meant that I could set my own timeline for completing my project. And while not all schools earmark funds for student research, it's a possibility that's worth checking into—especially if you can get a tenured faculty member to sponsor you.

My stipend didn't pay for everything, but I made ends meet by working for an online tutoring company. Helping business-school hopefuls gussy up their application essays wasn't too fulfilling, but freelance work done online for a company based in your home country is a great way to finance a short-term stay overseas. It dodges the question of applying for a work visa. And in a country like France where unemployment hovers around 10%, it frees up one more entry-level job for a local who may need it more than you do. When you visit Paris as a tourist, you do your part to buoy the local economy just by spending money at cafes and bookstores. But when you come for a longer period of time, it's worth thinking about ways to support yourself that also have a positive impact on a community into which you have essentially invited yourself.

The EU tends to think that Europe would be a better place if people didn't think of nations as places that are or aren't their own. And between the right-wing political parties popping up across Europe and America's brief flirtation with "freedom fries," I tend to agree. But 13 weeks in Paris also gave me perspective on just how thoroughly American I am. I remember going out for drinks with two graduate students, bright young women with witty things to say about film and politics. Then someone brought up the issue of Muslim headscarves, which French schools have prevented students from wearing in the classroom since early in 2004. I believe in the separation of church and state, but I'm also a fan of freedom of expression, so I brashly denounced the policy, sure that my new friends would agree. Their blank stares assured me that they did not. "Your president," one of them explained almost apologetically, "swears an oath of office with his right hand on the Bible. *That would never happen here.*"

I have thought about this exchange for a long time, because it showed me that no matter how glib we become about the blurring of national borders, there are still very real, fascinating differences between people across an ocean that go beyond who drinks beer with dinner and who drinks wine. It's exchanges like these that lead us to pursue alternatives to tourism, to plunk ourselves down in a city we can't know no matter how many times we read through a travel guide like this one. So yes, take a stroll through the Tuileries and go make eyes at the Mona Lisa. (She's too pretty to write off as kitsch.) Then if there are still unanswered questions lingering in your mind, rent an apartment and stay a while. These things take time.

Marcel LaFlamme was an Associate Editor of Let's Go: Europe and Let's Go: Western Europe. He spent a semester researching boulevard life in Paris and is currently writing a senior thesis on gender politics at all-male boarding schools.

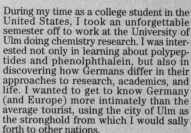

TEST TUBES AND TEUTONS
Research in Germany

During my time as a college student in the United States, I took an unforgettable semester off to work at the University of Ulm doing chemistry research. I was interested not only in learning about polypeptides and phenolphthalein, but also in discovering how Germans differ in their approaches to research, academics, and life. I wanted to get to know Germany (and Europe) more intimately than the average tourist, using the city of Ulm as the stronghold from which I would sally forth to other nations.

For centuries, Germany has been known for its rigorous intellectual tradition, especially in the physical sciences. After sitting in on a mind-blowing statistical mechanics lecture in Ulm, I learned that the professor was also deeply interested in history. In particular, he emphasized Einstein's variegate contributions to the field and the fact that Ulm was his birthplace. Germany may have lost some of its academic luster since the times of Boltzmann, Leibniz, and Hegel, but its academic research is still as vital as the flow of the mighty Rhine.

I began my search for a position in a German lab by talking to my academic advisor in the States about potential contacts in Germany. Finding professors who wanted an American protégé ended up being much easier than finding a reliable, sufficient, and legal method of financing my trip. I eventually was lucky enough to come upon a professor whose university could fund my studies, which meant I could stop trying to arrange my own funding through the **German Academic Exchange Program** (www.daad.de).

Undertaking academic research in Germany had several advantages over participating in a mere study abroad program, the biggest being the financial backing. I also appreciated the interaction afforded by eating with students in their dining hall. During my time in Germany, I lived in university housing with visiting scholars from many different countries, all of whom had very different academic and personal backgrounds, and fascinating stories. The true highlight of my research experience, however, was the opportunity to get involved in intense, focused scholarship, which can be far more intellectually rewarding than the academic dabbling of broad overview classes.

To pursue academic research in Germany, you usually have to be a university student or graduate with a strong interest in pursuing a narrow research topic in a rigorous academic setting. In most fields, especially scientific ones, you do not need to speak any German at all, let alone know how to decline an unpreceded adjective in front of a feminine noun in the dative case. Everyone in my lab spoke some heartfelt variant of English, and I was actually required to give my presentations in English.

My six-month stay in Germany was one of the most rewarding experiences I've had abroad. Academically, my project succeeded beyond our wildest dreams. I worked hard, but received unending support from my labmates. I survived the student dining hall, sat in on sundry classes, and went to a few raging university parties. But even as we climbed scientific mountains together, I saw firsthand the ways in which German students differed from Americans. One day I arrived at work to find that the students had gone on strike (by refusing to attend classes, a tough move for the industrious Germans) to protest an administrative fee that the university was planning to establish.

While based in Ulm, I also had the opportunities to explore Munich and Stuttgart and spend a strenuous but rewarding weekend biking at the glorious Chiemsee in Bavaria. Since I was a wage-earning chemist instead of a starving backpacker, my quick trips to Austria, France, and England had a more generous budget than they otherwise would have, and the superb European train system and new discount airlines helped make them relatively hassle-free. Academic research was a phenomenal way for me to get to know Germany, change the shape of my life for a while, see much of Europe, and even learn a little bit of science.

Barbara Richter was a Researcher-Writer for Let's Go: Austria & Switzerland. A native Austrian, then New Jersian, she'll be continuing her studies in chemistry and physics as a graduate student.

ANDORRA

Andorra, the tiny country sandwiched between France and Spain, did not have its own democratic constitution until 1993; it spent its first 12 centuries caught in a tug-of-war between the Spanish Counts of Urgell, the Church of Urgell, and the French King. Catalan is the official language, but French and Spanish are widely spoken. Because Andorra is so petite, one day can include sniffing aisles of duty-free perfume, hiking through a pine-scented valley, and relaxing in a luxury spa.

ESSENTIALS

WHEN TO GO

Andorra possesses a temperate climate and offers a variety of outdoor and indoor activities, making visits enjoyable during any season. Accommodations will be at their fullest during ski season (Dec.-Mar.) and summer (July-Aug.).

DOCUMENTS AND FORMALITIES

VISAS. There are no specific visa requirements for Andorra, but visitors must follow the regulations of France or Spain, depending on where they enter Andorra.

EMBASSIES. The few foreign embassies in Andorra are in Andorra la Vella. For Andorran embassies at home, contact: **Canada** and **US,** 2 United Nations Plaza, 25th fl., New York, NY, 10017 (☎212-750-8064); **UK,** 63 Westover Rd., London SW, 18 2RF (☎208 874 48 06).

TRANSPORTATION

The only way to get to Andorra is by **car** or **bus.** All traffic from Spain enters through the town of La Seu d'Urgell; the gateway from France is Pas de la Casa. Samar buses (Andorra ☎82 62 89, Madrid 914 68 41 90, Toulouse 561 16 49 00)

run from Andorra la Vella to **Madrid** (9hr.; Tu-Th and Su 11:30am, F and Su 10pm; €40) and to **Toulouse**. Nadal (Andorra ☎80 51 51) also has buses between Andorra la Vella and Toulouse (2½hr.; W, F, Su 6 per day). Alsina Graells (Andorra ☎826 567) runs from Barcelona to Andorra la Vella (3½-4hr., 5 per day, €19.50). Eurolines (Andorra ☎80 51 51, Barcelona 934 90 40 00) also runs between Barcelona and Andorra la Vella (4hr., 4-7 per day, €20). To go anywhere else in Spain, first go to the town of La Seu d'Urgell on a La Hispano-Andorra bus (☎82 13 72). From La Seu, Alsina Graells buses continue into Spain via Puigcerdà (1hr., 4 per day, €5). **Driving** in Andorra la Vella is an adventure for some, but navigating the streets, which often lack signs, can be maddening; it's best to ditch the car in a parking lot as soon as possible. Intercity buses connect the villages along the three major highways that converge in Andorra la Vella; the country's cities can be seen in a single day. The tourist office offers a schedule of the **bus** routes throughout the valley, and will tell you where to wait for specific destinations. Rides cost €0.70-1.70.

TOURIST SERVICES AND MONEY

EMERGENCY	Police: ☎110. Ambulance: ☎118. Fire: ☎118.

TOURIST OFFICES. Andorra operates an official tourism website at www.andorra.ad. **Tourist offices** in Andorra stock maps and brochures.

MONEY. On January 1, 2002, the **euro (€)** replaced the **peseta** and the **franc** as the unit of currency used in Andorra. For more information, see p. 20. As a general rule it's cheaper to exchange money in Andorra than at home. Prices in restaurants usually include a 10-15% service charge; customers should tip an additional 10%. Andorra has no duties or VAT, making it a favorite destination of shoppers. *Let's Go* uses the same **price diversity** range in Andorra as in Spain (p. 916).

COMMUNICATION

PHONE CODES	Country code: 376. International dialing prefix: 00. From outside Andorra, dial int'l dialing prefix (see inside back cover) + 376 + local number. Within Andorra, simply dial the local number.

Andorra's telephone company is **Servei de Telecomunicacions d'Andorra (STA)**. It sells phone cards in denominations of €3 and €6. For information on using a **cell phone** in Andorra, see p. 35. Mail from Andorra is sent via either the French or the Spanish mail system. Postage within Andorra is free. Address mail to be held as you would in France or Spain. For more information, refer to the **Essentials** sections of the France (p. 337) or Spain (p. 916) chapters. Internet access in Andorra la Vella is listed under **Practical Information.**

Although the official language of Andorra is Catalan, most inhabitants are bi- or even trilingual. Castilian Spanish is widely spoken and is often the language of business. French is the predominant language in Pas de la Casa; elsewhere it is less common. Portuguese is also spoken, but much less frequently.

HOLIDAYS AND FESTIVALS

Holidays: New Year's Day (Jan. 1); Epiphany (Jan. 6); Constitution Day (Mar. 6); Holy Thursday through Easter Monday (Mar. 24-28); Labor Day (May 1); Ascension (May 5); Pentecost (May 15); Whit Monday (May 16); St. John's Day (June 24); Assumption Day

(Aug. 15); National Day (Sept. 8); All Saints' Day (Nov. 1); St. Charles's Day (Nov. 4); Feast of the Immaculate Conception (Dec. 8); Christmas Eve through 2nd day of Christmas (Dec. 24-26); New Year's Eve (Dec. 31).

Festivals: Andorrans celebrate St. George's Day by giving gifts of books and flowers on April 23. The *Festa del Poble* is celebrated on St. John's Day (June 24) and marks the summer solstice. Escaldes-Engordany hosts an International Jazz Festival every July.

FACTS AND FIGURES: ANDORRA	
Official Name: Principality of Andorra.	**Land Area:** 470 sq. km.
Capital: Andorra la Vella.	**Time Zone:** GMT + 1.
Major Cities: Escaldes.	**Language:** Catalan (official), Spanish (Castilian), French, Portuguese.
Population: 70,000 (39% Spanish, 38% Andorran, 10% Portuguese, 6.4% French, 6.6% other).	**Religions:** Roman Catholic.

ANDORRA LA VELLA

Andorra la Vella (pop. 20,760), the country's capital, is effectively a single road flanked by shop after duty-free shop. This city is anything but *vella* (old); shiny new stores have upstaged the more aged buildings. After shopping, you're best off escaping to the mountainous countryside, where you can find excellent hiking.

🖪🚹 ORIENTATION AND PRACTICAL INFORMATION. Several blocks into the city, the main thoroughfare **Avinguda Santa Coloma** becomes **Avinguda Príncep Benlloch,** which in turn becomes **Avinguda Meritxell** at Pl. Príncep Benlloch. There are several **tourist offices** scattered throughout Andorra la Vella; the largest is in Pl. de la Rotonda. Its multilingual staff offers free *Sports Activities* and *Hotels i Restaurants* guides. (☎82 71 17. Open July-Aug. M-Sa 9am-9pm, Su 9am-7pm; Sept.-June daily 9:30am-1:30pm and 3:30-7:30pm.) For **weather** and **ski conditions,** call Ski Andorra (☎86 43 89). The Spanish **post office** is at C. Joan Maragall 10. (☎82 02 57. *Lista de Correos.* Open M-F 8:30am-2:30pm, Sa 9:30am-1pm.) **Internet** access is available at **Future@Point,** C. de la Sardana 6. (☎82 82 02. €1 per 15min., €3 per hr. Open M-Sa 10am-11pm, Su 10am-10pm. MC/V.) **Postal Code:** AD500.

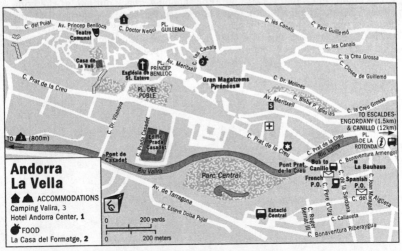

Andorra La Vella

🏠🏠 ACCOMMODATIONS
Camping Valira, 3
Hotel Andorra Center, 1

🍴 FOOD
La Casa del Formatge, 2

⌐⌐ ACCOMMODATIONS AND FOOD. There is no middle ground when it comes to accommodations in Andorra la Vella. Places are either run-down and overpriced, or extravagant and luxurious. At the high end, check out **Hotel Andorra Center ❸**, C. Doctor Nequi 12, which offers beautiful, fully furnished rooms as well as in-house restaurants and a fitness center with pool and sauna. (☎82 48 00. Breakfast included. Prices change frequently; expect to pay €25-35 per person. AmEx/MC/V.) You don't exactly rough it at **Camping Valira ❶**, Av. Salou, which has TV, hot showers, a restaurant, and a pool. (☎72 23 84; www.campvalira.com. Call ahead. €4.20 per person, per tent, and per car.) ▨**La Casa del Formatge ❷**, C. les Canals 4, is entirely dedicated to cheese. (☎80 75 75. Entrees €5-10. Open M-F 10am-8pm, Sa 9:30am-9pm, Su 9:30am-7pm.) A supermarket is located on the second floor of the **Grans Magatzems Pyrénées** (see below).

▨▨ HIKING AND SKIING. The tourist office brochure *Mountain Activities* has 41 suggested hiking itineraries, nine mountain biking itineraries, and several rock-climbing routes, as well as bike rental services and cabin and *refugio* (refuge; a cabin with bunks) listings. For organized hiking trips, try the **La Rabassa Sports and Nature Center** (☎32 38 68; www.campdeneudelarabassa.ad) in southwestern Andorra. In addition to *refugio*-style accommodations, the center has mountain biking, guided hikes, horseback riding, archery, and other field sports.

Andorra offers skiing opportunities galore. (Nov.-Apr. Lift tickets €25-40.) **Pal** (☎73 70 00), 10km from La Massana, is accessible by **bus** from La Massana (5 per day, €1). Nearby **Arinsal** (☎73 70 00) can be reached by bus from Andorra la Vella (1 per hr., €1). On the French border, **Pas de la Casa Grau Roig** (☎80 10 60), boasts 53 slopes. Buses run from Andorra la Vella (4 per day, €5). **La Rabassa** (☎84 38 98) is Andorra's only cross-country ski resort. Call **SKI Andorra** (☎86 43 89; www.skiandorra.ad) or the tourist office for more information.

▨ DAYTRIPS. The best thing to do in Andorra la Vella is drop your bags in a hostel and get out. **Caldea-Spa**, in **Escaldes-Engordany,** is the largest in Europe, with luxurious treatments and prices to match. (☎80 09 99. €25 for 3hr., plus fees. Open daily 9am-11pm.) Have some fun in **Canillo's** colossal **Palau de Gel D'Andorra,** a recreational complex with a swimming pool and an ice-skating rink. (☎80 08 40. Open daily 10am-11:30pm; each facility has its own hours. €5.50-8 each. €12.50 for all in 1 day. Equipment rental €2.30-4.50.) For shopping, check out one of the complexes in Santa Coloma, or the **Grans Magatzems Pyrénées,** Av. Meritxell 11, the country's biggest department store, where an entire aisle is dedicated to chocolate bars. (Open Sept.-July M-F 9:30am-8pm, Sa 9:30am-9pm, Su 9:30am-7pm; Aug. and holidays M-Sa 9:30am-9pm, Su 9:30am-7pm.)

AUSTRIA (ÖSTERREICH)

At the peak of Habsburg megalomania, the Austrian Empire was one of the largest in history. Though the empire crumbled during World War II, Austria remains a complex, multiethnic country. Drawing on centuries of Habsburg political maneuvering, Austria has become a skillful mediator between Eastern and Western Europe. Today, Austria owes much of its allure to the overpowering Alps, which dominate two-thirds of its surface. The mention of Austria evokes images of onion-domed churches set against snow-capped Alpine peaks, castles rising from meadows of golden flowers, and monasteries towering over the majestic Danube.

 DISCOVER AUSTRIA: SUGGESTED ITINERARIES

THREE DAYS Spend all three days in **Vienna,** the Imperial headquarters of romance. From the stately **Staatsoper** to the majestic **Hofburg,** Vienna's attractions will leave you with enough sensory stimulation to last until your next trip.

ONE WEEK Begin in **Kitzbühel** (1 day; p. 115) to take advantage of its hiking and skiing. Stop in **Salzburg** (2 days; p. 104) and see the home of Mozart and the Festung Hohensalzburg (p. 107). Move on to the **Salzkammergut** region for the Dachstein Ice Caves (1 day; p. 110). End by basking in the glory of **Vienna** (3 days).

TWO WEEKS Start in **Innsbruck,** where museums and mountains meet (2 days; p. 111), then swing by **Kitzbühel** (2 days). Spend another two days wandering **Hohe Tauern National Park** (p. 110), visiting the Krimml Waterfalls and the Großglockner Hochalpenstraße. Next, tour **Hallstatt** and its nearby ice caves (2 days; p. 109). Follow your ears to **Salzburg** (3 days) before heading to the throbbing nightlife of **Graz** (2 days; p. 115). Finally, make your way to **Vienna** for a grand finale of romance, waltzes, and high coffeehouse culture (4 days).

Austria

ESSENTIALS

WHEN TO GO

November to March is peak ski season; prices in western Austria double and travelers need reservations months in advance. The situation reverses in the summer, when the eastern half fills with vacationers. Accommodations are cheaper and less crowded in the shoulder season (May-June and Sept.-Oct.). However, some Alpine resorts close in May and June—call ahead. The Vienna State Opera, the Vienna Boys' Choir, and many major theaters don't perform during the summer.

DOCUMENTS AND FORMALITIES

VISAS. EU Citizens do not need a visa. Citizens of Australia, Canada, New Zealand, the UK, and the US do not need a visa for stays of up to 90 days.

EMBASSIES. All foreign embassies in Austria are in Vienna (p. 94). Austrian embassies at home include: **Australia,** 12 Talbot St., Forrest, Canberra ACT 2603 (☎00 6295 1533; www.austriaemb.org.au); **Canada,** 445 Wilbrod St., Ottawa, ON K1N 6M7 (☎613-789-1444; www.austro.org); **Ireland,** 15 Ailesbury Court, 93 Ailesbury Rd., Dublin 4 (☎01 269 45 77); **New Zealand,** Level 2, Willbank House, 57 Willis St., Wellington (☎04 499 63 93); **UK,** 18 Belgrave Mews West, London SW1X 8HU (☎020 7235 3731; www.austria.org.uk); **US,** 3524 International Ct. NW, Washington, D.C. 20008 (☎202-895-6700; austrianembassy@washington.nu).

TRANSPORTATION

BY PLANE. The only major international airport is Vienna's Schwechat Flughafen (VIE). Others are in Graz, Innsbruck, Klagenfurt, Linz, and Salzburg. From London-Stansted, **Ryanair** (☎3531 303 030; www.ryanair.com) flies to the latter three.

BY TRAIN. The **Österreichische Bundesbahn (ÖBB),** Austria's state railroad, operates an efficient system with fast and comfortable trains. **Eurail, InterRail,** and **Europe East** are valid in Austria; however, they do not guarantee a seat without a reservation (US$3-10). The **Austrian Railpass** allows three days of travel within any 15-day period on all rail lines; it also entitles holders to 40% off on bike rentals at train stations (2nd-class US$107, each additional day US$15).

BY BUS. The Austrian bus system consists mainly of orange **BundesBuses,** which cover areas inaccessible by train (but cost about as much as trains). Buy tickets at the station or from the driver. For info, call ☎0222 711 01 between 7am-8pm.

BY CAR. Driving is a convenient way to see more isolated parts of Austria, but gas is costly, an international license is required, and some small towns prohibit cars. The roads are well-maintained and well-marked, and Austrian drivers are quite careful. **Mitfahrzentrale** (ride-sharing services) in larger cities pair drivers with riders for a small fee. Riders then negotiate fares with the drivers. Be aware that not all organizations screen their drivers or riders; ask in advance.

BY BIKE. Bikes are a great way to get around Austria; roads are generally smooth and safe. Many train stations rent bikes and allow you to return them to any participating station. Consult local tourist offices for bike routes and maps.

TOURIST SERVICES AND MONEY

EMERGENCY	Police: ☎133. Ambulance: ☎144. Fire: ☎122.

TOURIST OFFICES. Tourist offices are marked by signs with a green "i;" most brochures are available in English. Visit www.austria-tourism.at for more info.

MONEY. In 2002, the **euro (€)** replaced the **Schilling (ATS)** as the unit of currency in Austria. As a general rule, it's cheaper to exchange money in Austria than at home. Railroad stations, airports, hotels, and most travel agencies offer exchange services, as do banks. If you stay in hostels and prepare most of your own food, expect to spend anywhere from €30-60 per person per day. Accommodations start at about €12, while a basic sit-down meal usually costs around €10. Menus will say whether service is included (*Preise inclusive* or *Bedienung inclusiv*); if it is, you don't have to **tip**. If it's not, 10% will do. Austrian restaurants expect you to seat yourself, and servers will not bring the bill until you ask them to do so. Say "*Zahlen bitte*" (TSAHL-en BIT-uh) to settle your accounts, and don't leave tips on the table. Don't expect to bargain except at flea markets and the Naschmarkt in Vienna. Austria has a 10-20% **Value Added Tax (VAT)**, which is applied to purchased goods. You can get refunds for purchases of over €75 at one store.

COMMUNICATION

TELEPHONES. Wherever possible, use a calling card for international phone calls, as the long-distance rates for national phone services are often exorbitant. Prepaid phone cards and major credit cards can be used for direct international calls, but they are still less cost-efficient. For info on cell phones, see p. 35. Direct dial access numbers include **AT&T** (☎0800 20 02 88), **British Telecom** (☎0800 20 02 09), **Canada Direct** (☎0800 20 02 17), **Ireland Direct** (☎0800 40 00 00), **MCI** (☎0800 20 02 35), **Sprint** (☎0800 20 02 36), and **Telecom New Zealand** (☎0800 20 02 22).

PHONE CODES	**Country code: 43. International dialing prefix: 00** (from Vienna, 900). From outside Austria, dial int'l dialing prefix (see inside back cover) + 43 + city code + local number.

MAIL. Letters take one or two days within Austria. Airmail to North America takes four to seven days, up to nine days to Australia and New Zealand. Mark all letters and packages "*mit Flugpost.*" Aerogrammes are the cheapest option.

LANGUAGE. German is the official language. English is the most common second language; outside of cities and among older residents, English is less common. For basic German words and phrases, see p. 1061.

ACCOMMODATIONS AND CAMPING

AUSTRIA	❶	❷	❸	❹	❺
ACCOMMODATIONS	under €15	€15-25	€25-34	€34-55	over €55

Always ask if your lodging provides a **guest card** (*Gästekarte*), which grants discounts on activities, museums, and public transportation. The **Österreiches Jugendherbergsverband-Hauptverband (ÖJH)** runs the over 80 HI **hostels** in Austria. Due to the rigorous standards of the national organizations, these are usually very clean and orderly. Most charge €12-22 per night for dorms; nonmembers usually pay a surcharge. **Independent hostels** vary in quality, but often have more personality and a more lively backpacking culture. **Hotels** are expensive (singles €40-100; doubles €80-150). The cheapest have "*Gasthof,*" "*Gästehaus,*" or "*Pension-Garni*" in the name. Renting a **Privatzimmer** (room in a family home) is a cheaper option. Rooms range from €25-60 per person; contact the local tourist office for a list. Slightly more expensive, **Pensionen** are similar to British B&Bs. Most camping sites in Austria are large plots glutted with RVs and are open in summer only. Prices run €4-6 per person and €4-8 per tent. In the high Alps, hikers and mountaineers can retire to the well-maintained system of **mountain huts** (*Hütten*).

FOOD AND DRINK

AUSTRIA	❶	❷	❸	❹	❺
FOOD	under €5	€5-10	€10-16	€16-25	over €25

Loaded with fat, salt, and cholesterol, traditional Austrian cuisine is a cardiologist's nightmare but a delight to the palate. Austria's best known dish, *Wiener-Schnitzel*, is a breaded meat cutlet (usually veal or pork) fried in butter. Vegetarians should look for *Spätzle* (noodles), *Eierschwammerl* (yellow mushrooms), or anything with the word "*Vegi*" in it. Natives nurse their sweet tooth with *Kaffee und Kuchen* (coffee and cake), *Sacher Torte* (a rich chocolate cake layered with marmalade), and *Linzer Torte* (a light yellow cake with currant jam). Austrian beers are outstanding—try *Stiegl Bier*, a Salzburg brew; *Zipfer Bier*, from Upper Austria; and Styrian *Gösser Bier*.

OUTDOOR ACTIVITIES. Nearly every town has **hiking** trails in its vicinity; consult the local tourist office. Trails are usually marked with either a red-white-red marker (only sturdy boots and hiking poles necessary) or a blue-white-blue marker (mountaineering equipment needed). Due to snow in the higher passes, most mountain hiking trails and mountain huts are open only from late June to early September. Western Austria is one of the world's best **skiing** regions. High season runs from mid-December to mid-January and from February to March. Tourist offices have info and can suggest agencies that offer ski packages.

HOLIDAYS AND FESTIVALS

Holidays: Just about everything closes on public holidays, so plan accordingly. New Year's Day (Jan. 1); Epiphany (Jan. 6); Good Friday (Mar. 25); Easter Monday (Mar. 28); Labor Day (May 1); Ascension (May 5); Corpus Christi (June 10); Assumption Day (Aug. 15); Austrian National Day (Oct. 26); All Saints' Day (Nov. 1); Immaculate Conception (Dec. 8); Christmas (Dec. 25); Boxing Day (Dec. 26).

Festivals: Vienna celebrates Fasching (Carnival) during the first 2 weeks of Feb. Austria's most famous summer music festivals are the Wiener Festwochen (mid-May to mid-June) and the Salzburger Festspiele (late July-late Aug.).

FACTS AND FIGURES: AUSTRIA

Official Name: Republic of Austria.
Capital: Vienna.
Major Cities: Graz, Innsbruck, Salzburg.
Population: 8,030,000.
Land Area: 83,858 sq. km.

Time Zone: GMT +1.
Language: German.
Religions: Roman Catholic (74%), Protestant (5%), Muslim (4%), other (17%).

VIENNA (WIEN)   ☎ 01

From its origins as a Roman camp along the Danube, Vienna (pop. 1,500,000) was catapulted by war, marriage, and Habsburg maneuvering into the political linchpin of the continent. The melodies of Beethoven, Mahler, Mozart, and Schönberg have made Vienna an everlasting arbiter of high culture. So high, at times, that it seemed inflated: During its *fin-de-siècle* coffeehouse era, bohemian Viennese self-mockingly referred to their city as the "merry apocalypse." Although the city has a reputation and a grand past, the recently opened Museumsquartier, an ultramodern theater venue, proves that Vienna is still writing its own dynamic history.

⚑ INTERCITY TRANSPORTATION

Flights: The **Wien-Schwechat Flughafen** (VIE; ☎ 7007 0) is home to **Austrian Airlines** (☎ 051 17 89; www.aua.com). The airport is 18km from the city center; the cheapest way to reach the city is S7 Flughafen/Wolfsthal, which stops at **Wien Mitte** (30min., every 30min. 5am-11pm, €3). The heart of the city, **Stephansplatz**, is a short metro ride from Wien Mitte on the U3 line. The **Vienna Airport Lines Shuttle Bus** (http://english.viennaairport.com/bus.html), which runs between the airport and the City Air Terminal, at the Hilton opposite Wien Mitte, is convenient but expensive (every 30min. 6:30am-6am, €6). The **City Airport Train** (CAT; ☎ 25 250; www.cityairporttrain.com) takes only 16min. to reach **Wien Mitte** (every 30min. 6:06am-11:36pm; €9, round-trip €16, children under 15 free when traveling with an adult; Eurail not valid).

Trains: Vienna has 2 main train stations with international connections. For general train info, dial ☎ 05 17 17 (24hr.) or check www.oebb.at.

Westbahnhof, XV, Mariahilferstr. 132. To: **Amsterdam** (14hr., 1 per day, €152.30); **Berlin** (11hr., 1 per day, €108); **Budapest** (3-4hr., 6 per day, €38); **Hamburg** (9hr., 2 per day, €125); **Innsbruck** (5-6hr., every 2hr., €49); **Munich** (4hr., 5 per day, €63); **Paris** (14hr., 2 per day, €156); **Salzburg** (3hr., 1 per hr., €37); **Zurich** (9hr., 3 per day, €78). Info counter open M-F 7:30am-9:20pm, Sa 7:30am-8:50pm, Su and holidays 8am-9pm.

Südbahnhof, X, Wiener Gürtel 1a. Trains generally go south and east. To: **Graz** (2½hr., 1 per hr., €27); **Kraków** (7-8hr., 4 per day, €46); **Prague** (4hr., 5 per day, €41); **Rome** (14hr., 1 per day, €111); **Venice** (9-10hr., 2 per day, €72). Info counter open daily 7am-8pm.

Buses: Buses in Austria are seldom cheaper than trains; compare prices before buying a ticket. **City bus terminals** at Wien Mitte/Landstr., Hütteldorf, Heiligenstadt, Floridsdorf, Kagran, Erdberg, and Reumannpl. **BundesBuses** run from these stations. Ticket counters open M-F 6am-5:50pm, Sa-Su 6am-3:50pm. Many international bus lines also have agencies in the stations. For info, call BundesBus (☎ 711 01; 7am-10pm).

Hitchhiking: Those headed for Salzburg, take U4 to Hütteldorf; the highway is 10km farther. Though *Let's Go* does not recommend hitchhiking, some travelers report riding tram #67 to the last stop and waiting at the rotary near Laaerberg.

⚑ ORIENTATION

Vienna is divided into 23 **districts** (*Bezirke*). The first is Innenstadt (city center), defined by the **Ringstraße** on three sides and the Danube Canal on the fourth. The Ringstraße (or "Ring") consists of many different segments, each with its own name, such as Opernring or Kärntner Ring. Many of Vienna's major attractions are in District I and immediately around the Ringstraße. Districts II-IX spread out from the city center following the clockwise traffic of the Ring. The remaining districts expand from yet another ring, the **Gürtel** ("Belt"). Like the Ring, this major thoroughfare has numerous segments, including Margaretengürtel, Währinger Gürtel, and Neubaugürtel. Street signs indicate the district number in Roman or Arabic numerals *before* the street and number. *Let's Go* includes district numbers for establishments in Roman numerals before the street address.

⚑ LOCAL TRANSPORTATION

Public transportation: call ☎ 790 91 00 (general info). The **subway** (U-Bahn), **tram** (Straßenbahn), **elevated train** (S-Bahn), and **bus** lines operate under a 1-ticket system. A **single fare** (€2 on board; €1.50 in advance from a ticket machine, ticket office, or tobacco shop) lets you travel to any destination in the city and switch from bus to U-Bahn to tram to S-Bahn, as long as your travel is uninterrupted. To **validate a ticket,** punch it in the machine upon entering the 1st vehicle, but don't stamp it

OTTO-WAGNERPL.

Ostarichi-Park

Alser Str.

Wickenburgg.

Garellig. Gamisong. Frankg.

Wähinger Str.

Votivkirche

ROOSEVELT-PL.

Sigmund Freud Park

Universitätsstr.

Rathaustr.

Liebigg.

Universität Wien

VIII

Floriang.

Tulpeng.

Felderstr.

Ebendorferstr.

Rathausplatz

Grillparzerstr.

RATHAUS

Schmidg.

Lenaug.

Landesgerichtstr.

Auersperggg.

Rathaust.

Bartensteing.

Stadlong.

Doblhoffg.

Trautsong.

Lerchenfelderstr.

Reichsratstr.

Parlament

SCHMERLINGPL.

Justizpalast

Museumstr.

WEGHUBERPARK

Neustiftg.

Zitterh.-g.

Gardeg.

Burgg.

Volkstheater

VOLKSTHEATER

Kirchbergg.

Breite-G.

Museum Moderner Kunst

Kunsthalle Wien

MUSEMS-QUARTIER

Spittelbergg.

Stift

Siebensterng.

VII

Stifts-kaserne

Schweighoferg.

Gurtengg.

Messe Palast

Leopold Museum

Jugend-Info Wien

Lindeng.

Stiftg.

Mariahilfer Str.

Theobaldg.

Königskosterg.

Gumpendorferstr.

Comic-Treff Steiner

Windmühlg.

VI

Lehärg.

Fillgraderg.

Girardig.

Laimgrubeng.

Kösterg.

Steigentg.

Joaneumg.

Alfred Grünwald Park

Linke Wienzeile

Majolikahaus

IX

Koling.

Wasag.

Maria Theresien Str.

Schottenring

Neutorg. Zelinkag. Gonzaga.

Börse (Stock Exchange)

BÖRSEPL.

Eßlingg.

Wippingerstr.

CONCORDIAP

Schottentor

Schottengg.

Schottenbastei

Schottenderferstr.

Helfersterferstr.

Hohenstaufeng.

Schottenstift

Freyung

Renng.

Wächterg.

Wippingerstr.

Färberg.

Graben

Judisches Museum

JUDENPL.

Palais Ferstel

AM HOF

Kirche am Hof

Tiefer

Strauchg.

Kung.

Minoriten Kirche

Landhausg.

MINORITENPL.

Bundes-kanzleramt

Landes-museum

HERRENG.

Löwelstr.

Schenkenstr.

Bankg.

Schauflerg.

MICHAELERPL.

Looshaus

Peterskirche

PETERSPL.

Graben

Bräunerstr.

Dorotheerg.

Michaelerkirche

Spanische Reitschule

Alte Burg

In der Burg

Hofburg

Jüdisches Museum

Lipizzaner Museum

JOSEFSPL.

Salvador Dali Museum

National-bibliothek

NEUERMARKT

Kapuziner-Kirche

HELDENPL.

Neue Burg

Augustiner-kirche

Monument gegen Hitler

Albertina Museum

ALBERTINAPL.

Burggarten

Führiche

Maysederg.

Hotel Sacher

Philharmonikerstr.

Opernring

ROBERT STOLZ PL.

Staatsoper

Kärntner Str.

Elizabethstr.

SCHILLERPL.

Nibelungeng.

Makartg.

Gauermanng.

AVIS

Opern-Passage

Bösendorferstr.

Akademie der Bildenden Künste

Secession Building

KARLSPLATZ

KARLSPL.

Otto-Wagner-Pavilion

Resselpark

IV

Technische Universität

Pagáßg.

Rechte Wienzeile

Theater an der Wien

Naschmarkt

Treitlstr.

Resselg.

Wiedner Hauptstr.

Paniglg.

Margaretenstr.

Frankenberg.

RATHAUS

Burg-theater

RATHAUSPL.

Dr. Karl-Lueger-Ring

Rathauspark

Volksgarten

Dr. Karl-Renner-Ring

BALLHAUSPL.

Theseus Tempel

Natur-historisches Museum

Burgring

MARIA THERESIENPL.

Kunsthistorisches Museum

Babenbergstr.

MUSEUMS-QUARTIER

Getreidemarkt

Burggasse

AUSTRIA

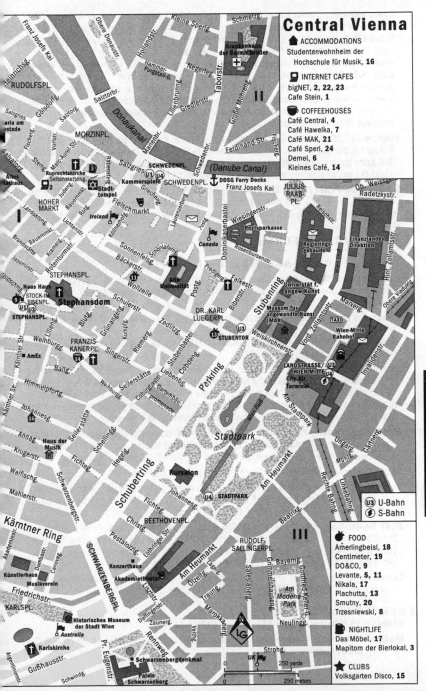

Central Vienna

🏠 ACCOMMODATIONS
Studentenwohnheim der
Hochschule für Musik, **16**

💻 INTERNET CAFES
bigNET, **2, 22, 23**
Cafe Stein, **1**

☕ COFFEEHOUSES
Café Central, **4**
Café Hawelka, **7**
Café MAK, **21**
Café Sperl, **24**
Demel, **6**
Kleines Café, **14**

Ⓤ U-Bahn
Ⓢ S-Bahn

🍴 FOOD
Amerlingbeisl, **18**
Centimeter, **19**
DO&CO, **9**
Levante, **5, 11**
Nikala, **17**
Plachutta, **13**
Smutny, **20**
Trzesniewski, **8**

🍺 NIGHTLIFE
Das Möbel, **17**
Mapitom der Bierlokal, **3**

⭐ CLUBS
Volksgarten Disco, **15**

AUSTRIA

again when you switch trains. Otherwise, plainclothes inspectors may fine you €60. Other ticket options (available at the same places as pre-purchased single tickets) include a **1-day pass** (€5), a **3-day rover ticket** (€12), and a **7-day pass** (€12.50; valid M 9am to the next M 9am), and an **8-day pass** (€24; valid any 8 days, not necessarily consecutive; valid also for several people traveling together). The **Vienna Card** (€16.90) offers free travel for 72hr. as well as discounts at sights and events. Regular trams and subway cars stop running midnight-5am. **Nightbuses** run every 30min. along most routes; "N" signs designate night bus stops. Single-fare €1.50; day transport passes not valid. A complete night bus schedule is available at bus counters in U-Bahn stations.

Taxis: ☎313 00, 401 00, 601 60, or 814 00. Stands are at Westbahnhof, Südbahnhof, Karlspl. in the city center, and by the Bermuda Dreieck for late-night revelers. Accredited taxis have yellow-and-black signs on the roof. Base rate €2.50, €0.20 per additional 0.2km; slightly more expensive holidays and 11pm-6am.

Bike Rental: Pedal Power, II, Ausstellungsstr. 3 (☎729 72 34). Rents bikes (€17 per 4hr., €32 for 24hr.) and offers bike tours (€19-23). Student and Vienna Card discounts. Open daily May-Oct. 8am-7pm. Pick up *Vienna By Bike* at the tourist office.

🛈 PRACTICAL INFORMATION

TOURIST, LOCAL, AND FINANCIAL SERVICES

Main Tourist Office: I, Albertinapl. (☎211 14 0). Follow Operng. up 1 block from the Opera House. The staff gives a free map of the city and the pamphlet *Youth Scene,* and books rooms for a €3 fee plus a 1-night deposit. Open daily 9am-7pm.

Embassies and Consulates: Australia, IV, Mattiellistr. 2 (☎506 74). **Canada,** I, Laurenzerberg 2 (☎531 38 30 00). **Ireland,** I, Rotenturmstr. 16 (☎71 54 24 6). **New Zealand,** XIX, Karl-Tomay-g. 34 (☎318 85 05). **UK,** III, Jauresg. 10 (☎716 13 51 51). **US,** IX, Boltzmanng. 16 (☎313 39 0).

Currency Exchange: ATMs are your best bet. Nearly all accept Cirrus, MC, and V. **Banks** and **airport exchanges** use the same official rates. Most open M-W and F 8am-12:30pm and 1:30-3pm, Th 8am-12:30pm and 1:30-5:30pm. **Train station** exchanges (daily 7am-10pm at the Westbahnhof) offer a min. fee of €6 for the 1st 3 checks (€300 max.). Stay away from the 24hr. bill-exchange machines in Innenstadt.

American Express: I, Kärntnerstr. 21-23 (☎515 40), down the street from Stephanspl. Cashes AmEx and Thomas Cook (min. €7 commission) checks, sells event tickets, and holds mail for 4 weeks (members only). Open M-F 9am-5:30pm, Sa 9am-noon.

Luggage Storage: Lockers are €2 per 24hr. at all train stations.

Bookstores: Shakespeare & Company, I, Bezriksterng. 2. International magazine selection. Open M-Sa 9am-7pm. **British Bookshop,** I, Weihburgg. 24, has an extensive travel section. Open M-F 9:30am-6:30pm, Sa 9:30am-5pm.

GLBT Resources: Pick up the *Vienna Gay Guide* (www.gayguide.at), *Extra Connect,* or *Bussi* from any tourist office or gay bar, cafe, or club. **Rosa Lila Tip,** VI, Linke Wienzeile 102 (☎585 4343), is a resource and social center for homosexual Viennese and visitors alike. Friendly staff speaks English. Open M-W 5-8pm.

Laundromat: Most hostels offer laundry service for €4. **Schnell und Sauber,** VII, Westbahnhofstr. 60. Wash €4.50, dry €1 per 20min. Soap included. Open 24hr.

EMERGENCY AND COMMUNICATION

Police: ☎133. **Ambulance:** ☎144. **Fire:** ☎122.

Medical Assistance: Allgemeines Krankenhaus, IX, Währinger Gürtel 18-20 (☎404 00 19 64). **Emergency care:** ☎141.

Crisis Hotlines: All have English speakers. **Rape Crisis Hotline:** ☎523 22 22. Staffed M and Th 1-6pm, Tu and F 10am-3pm. **24hr. immediate help for women:** ☎ 717 19.

24hr. Pharmacy: ☎ 15 50. Consulates have lists of English-speaking doctors, or call Wolfgang Molnar ☎330 34 68.

Internet Access: bigNET.internet.cafe, I, Kärntnerstr. 61 or I, Hoher Markt 8-9. €3.70 per 30min. Cafe Stein, IX, Wahringerstr. 6-8. €4 per 30min.

Post Office: Hauptpostamt, I, Fleischmarkt 19. Open 24hr. **Branches** throughout the city and at the train stations; look for the yellow signs with the trumpet logo. Address Poste Restante as in the following example: SURNAME, Firstname, Postlagernde Briefe; Hauptpostamt; Fleischmarkt 19, A-1010 Wien AUSTRIA. **Postal Codes:** 1st district A-1010, 2nd A-1020, 3rd A-1030, etc., to the 23rd A-1230.

▛ ACCOMMODATIONS AND CAMPING

Hunting for cheap rooms in Vienna during high season can be unpleasant; call for reservations at least five days in advance. Otherwise, plan on calling between 6 and 9am to put your name down for a reservation. The summer crunch for budget rooms is slightly alleviated in July, when dorms convert into makeshift hostels.

HOSTELS

▨ **Hostel Ruthensteiner (HI)**, XV, Robert-Hamerlingg. 24 (☎893 42 02). Exit Westbahnhof, turn right onto Mariahilferstr., and continue until Haidmannsg. Turn left, then right on Robert-Hamerlingg. Knowledgeable staff, spotless rooms, a rose-filled courtyard, and a kitchenette. Breakfast €2.50. Internet €2 per 25min. Sheets included (except for 10-bed dorms). 4-night max. stay. Reception 24hr. 32-bed "Outback" summer dorm €11; 4- to 10-bed dorms €11.50-13; singles, doubles, and triples €14-25. AmEx/MC/V. ❷

Wombats City Hostel, XIV, Grang. 6 (☎897 23 36). Exit Westbahnhof, turn right on Mariahilferstr., right on Rosinag., and left on Grang. While near train tracks, Wombats compensates with an in-house pub and other perks. Internet €1 per 12min. In-line skate rental €8 per day, bike rental €13. 3- to 6-bed dorms €16; doubles €42. ❷

Westend City Hostel, VI, Fügerg. 3, near Westbahnhof. Exit on Aussere Mariahilferstr., cross the large intersection, go right on Mullerg. and left on Fügerg. Very plain, but its location is ideal. Breakfast included. Internet €2.60 per 30min. Reception 24hr. Check-out 10:30am. Curfew 11:30pm. 12-bed dorms €17; 8- to 10-bed dorms €17.80; 4-bed dorms €19; singles €41; doubles €49. ❷

Myrthengasse (HI), VII, Myrtheng. 7, and **Neustiftgasse (HI)**, VII, Neustiftg. 85 (☎523 63 16). These simple, modern hostels, are a 20min. walk from Innenstadt. Same-sex rooms. Breakfast included. Locks €4. Reception 24hr. at Myrtheng. Curfew 1am. 2- to 6-bed dorms €15-18. Nonmembers add €3.50. AmEx/MC/V. ❷

Believe It Or Not, VII, Myrtheng. 10, Apt. #14 (☎526 46 58). Take U6 to Burgg./ Stadthalle, then bus #48A (dir.: Ring) to Neubaug. Backtrack on Burgg. 1 block and take the 1st right on Myrtheng. A converted apartment with kitchen and 2 bunkrooms. Ages 18-30. 2-night min. stay. Reception 8am-1pm. Dorms €13; smaller dorms €15. ❶

HOTELS AND PENSIONS

Pension Kraml, VI, Brauerg. 5 (☎587 85 88). U3: Zierierg. Exit on Otto-Bauerg., take 1st left, then 1st right. Near the Naschmarkt. Large rooms, a lounge, and cable TV. Breakfast included. Singles €28; doubles €48, with shower €58; triples €68/€75. Apartment with bath €90-120 for 3-5 people. ❸

Pension Hargita, VII, Andreasg. (☎526 19 28). U3: Zieglerg. and exit on Andreasg. Hardwood floors, sea-foam walls, cozy beds, and quiet. Breakfast €3. Reception 8am-10pm. Singles €35, with shower €40; doubles €48/€55; triples €70/€76. MC/V. ❹

Lauria Apartments, VII, Kaiserstr. 77, Apt. #8 (☎522 25 55). From Westbahnhof, take tram #5 to Burgg. 2-night min. stay. Reception 8am-2pm. Lockout 10am-2pm. Doubles €46; triples €63; quads €80. MC over €100. ❷

UNIVERSITY DORMITORIES

From July through September, many university dorms become hotels. Their cleanliness and low cost make them particularly suited to longer stays.

Porzellaneum der Wiener Universität, IX, Porzellang. 30 (☎317 728 20). From Südbahnhof, take tram D (dir.: Nußdorf) to Fürsteng. Clean dorms with desks. Reception 24hr. Reserve 1 week in advance. Singles €18-20; doubles €34-38; quads €64-72. ❸

Katholisches Studentenhaus, XIX, Peter-Jordanstr. 29 (☎369 55 85). U6: Nußdorferstr., then bus #35A or tram #38 to Hardtg. In a calm, quiet district. Free Internet. Reception daily until 10pm. Dorms €20, 1-month stay €250; doubles €34/€420. ❸

Studentenwohnheim der Hochschule für Musik, I, Johannesg. 8 (☎514 84). Walk 3 blocks down Kärntnerstr. from Stephansdom and turn left on Johannesg. Breakfast included. Reception 24hr. Reserve in advance. Singles €33-39; doubles €58-70; triples €66; quads €80; quints €100. Apartment for 4 €28.50 per person. ❹

CAMPING

Wien-West, Hüttelbergstr. 80 (☎914 23 14; www.wiencamping.at). Take U4 to Hütteldorf, then bus #14B or 152 (dir.: Campingpl.) to Wien West. 8km from the city center. Hikes through the Vienna Woods. Crowded but clean. Laundry, groceries, and cooking facilities. Reception daily 7:30am-9:30pm. Open Mar.-Jan. July-Aug. and New Year's €6.50 per person, €5 per tent; Sept.-June €5.50/€4; €3.50-4 per child ages 4-15. 2-person bungalows €23-27; 4-person €33-37. Electricity €3. ❶

Wien Süd, Breitenfurterstr. 269 (☎867 36 49). U6: Philadelphiabrücke, then bus #62A to Wien Süd. This former imperial park encompasses 25 sq. km of woods and meadows. Laundry, cafe, playground, supermarket, and kitchen. Open May-Sept. €5.50-6.50 per person, €4-5 per tent, €7-8 per car. Electricity €3.50-4. ❶

🄵 FOOD

For the Viennese, food is not mere fuel for the body: It is a multi-faceted traditional experience that begins when you wish someone *"Mahlzeit"* and ends with one of the city's renowned pastries. The eateries near Kärntnerstr. are expensive—a cheaper area is the neighborhood north of the university, near the Votivkirche (U2: Schottentor), where Universitätsstr. and Währingerstr. meet. Cafes also line **Burggasse** in District VI. The area radiating from the Rechte and Linke Wienzeile near Naschmarkt (U4: Kettenbrückeg.) has affordable restaurants. The **Naschmarkt** has the city's biggest market. Supermarkets include **Zielpunkt, Hofer,** and **Spar.** Kosher groceries are available at the **Kosher** supermarket, II, Hollandstr. 10 (☎216 96 75).

INSIDE THE RING

🄼 **Nikala,** I, Grünangerg. 10, off Singerstr. near Stephanspl. The sensual decor of this restaurant, a former burlesque theater, complements the scrumptious crepes, both sweet and savory (€4-15). Open M-F 4pm-midnight, Sa-Su 11am-midnight. AmEx/MC/V. ❸

🄼 **Trzesniewski,** I, Dorotheerg. 1, 3 blocks down the Graben from Stephansdom. This famous stand-up establishment has been serving open-faced mini-sandwiches (€0.80) for over 100 years. Toppings include salmon, onion, paprika, and egg. This was Kafka's favorite place to eat. Open M-F 8:30am-7:30pm, Sa 9am-5pm. ❷

Smutny, I, Elisabethstr. 8, off Karlspl. A delicious traditional Austrian restaurant offering schnitzel and goulash (around €10). *Menü* €6. Open 10am-midnight. AmEx/MC/V. ❷

Plachutta, I, Wollzeile 38 (☎512 15 77; www.plachutta.at). Take the U3 to Stubentor and walk down Wollzeile. This restaurant serves Vienna's best *Tafelspitz* (€20). Other entrees €12-24. Open daily 11:30am-11:15pm. ❺

DO&CO, I, Stephanspl. 12, 7th fl. (☎535 39 69). Set above the Stephanspl. cathedral in the *Haas Haus*, this gourmet eatery has both local and international dishes (€18-24). Reservations recommended. Open daily noon-3pm and 6pm-1am. V. ❷

Levante, I, Wallnerstr. 2. Walk down Graben away from Stephansdom, turn left on Kohlmarkt and right onto Wallnerstr. Greek-Turkish franchise featuring street-side dining and some vegetarian dishes. Entrees €7-12. Open daily 11am-11:30pm. MC/V. ❷

Zimolo, I, Ballg. 5, near Stephanspl. off Weihburgg. Italian food served in a sexy ambience. Entrees €7-19. Open M-Sa noon-3pm and 6pm-midnight. AmEx/MC/V. ❸

OUTSIDE THE RING

▨ **Centimeter,** IX, Liechtensteinstr. 42. Tram D to Bauernfeldpl. This chain offers huge portions of greasy Austrian fare and an unbelievable selection of beers. Cold (€0.10 per cm) and warm sandwiches (€0.15 per cm) by the centimeter. Open M-Th 10am-1am, F 10am-2am, Sa 11am-2am, Su 11am-midnight. AmEx/MC/V. ❷

▨ **OH Pot, OH Pot,** IX, Währingerstr. 22. U2: Schottentor. This adorable eatery serves filling "pots," stew-like veggie or meat concoctions (€8.20). Fusion fare ranging from Chilean to Ethiopian. Open M-F 11am-midnight, Sa-Su 6pm-midnight. AmEx/MC/V. ❷

Sato Café-Restaurant, XV, Mariahilferstr. 151 (☎897 54 97). Take U3 (orange) or U6 (brown) to Westbahnhof. Conveniently near the Ruthensteiner and Wombats hostels, this family-run restaurant offers excellent Turkish fare, including vegetarian dishes. Entrees (€5-9). Delicious breakfast omelettes €3-4. Open daily 8am-midnight. ❶

Amerlingbeisl, VII, Stiftg. 8. U3: Neubaug. The grapevine-covered courtyard resembles a *Heuriger*. Entrees €6-8. Open daily 9am-2am. Kitchen open until 1am. ❷

Fischerbräu, XIX, Billrothstr. 17. U6 to Nußdorfer Str., exit on Wahringer Gurtel, continue until Döblinger Hauptpl., take a left, and left again onto Billrothstr. Try the home-brewed beer (0.3L €2.30) and various breads (€4-5). Open July-Aug. daily 4pm-1am; Sept.-June M-Sa 4pm-1am, Su 11am-1am. ❷

Vegetasla, III, Ungarg. 57. Take the O tram to Neulingg. A vegetarian nirvana, this Taiwanese restaurant offers seitan and many forms of soy. Lunch buffet M-Sa €6.80.

Servieten Stüberl, IX. Servieteng. 7 (☎317 53 36; www.servietenstueberl.at). Take U4 to Rossauer Lände, walk down Grünentorg. and make a right onto Servieteng. With a courtyard overlooking the Servientenkirche, this family-run restaurant serves its own wine and Austrian entrees (€7-14). Open M-F 10am-midnight. MC/V. ❸

COFFEEHOUSES

In Vienna, the coffeehouse is not simply the place to resolve your midday caffeine deficit. For years these establishments have been havens for artists, writers, and thinkers: Peter "the cafe writer" Altenberg scribbled, exiles Lenin and Trotsky played chess, Theodor Herzl made plans for a Zionist Israel, and Kafka came to visit the Herrenhof. The most serious dictate of coffeehouse etiquette is that you linger; the waiter (*Herr Ober*) will serve you when you sit down, then leave you to sip and cogitate. When you're ready to leave, just ask to pay ("*Zahlen bitte*").

▨ **Kleines Café,** I, Franziskanerpl. 3. Turn off Kärtnerstr. onto Weihburg. and follow it to the Franziskanerkirche. The cafe is situated in the courtyard of the Franziskanerkirche, with low ceilings and colorful posters. Sandwiches €2.80-4. Open daily 10am-2am.

▨ **Café Central,** I, at the corner of Herreng. and Strauchg. inside Palais Fers. Arched ceilings and wall frescoes: every bit the mecca of the cafe world. Open M-Sa 8am-10pm, Su 10am-6pm. AmEx/MC/V.

■ **Café Sperl,** VI, Gumpendorferstr. 11. U2: Museumsquartier. Walk 1 block on Getreide-markt and turn right on Gumpendorferstr. One of Vienna's oldest and most elegant cafes. Open July-Aug. M-Sa 7am-11pm; Sept.-June M-Sa 7am-11pm, Su 11am-8pm.

Café Hawelka, I, Dorotheerg. 6, off Graben. Josephine and Leopold Hawelka put this legendary cafe on the map in 1939. Today, at 90 and 92 years, respectively, they still make a mean *Buchteln* (bohemian doughnut with plum marmalade; fresh at 10pm; €3). Open M and W-Sa 8am-2am, Su 4pm-2am.

Demel, I, Kohlmarkt 14. 5min. from the Stephansdom down Graben. The most lavish *Konditorei,* Demel was confectioner to the imperial court. The chocolate is made fresh every morning, and the desserts are legendary. Open daily 10am-7pm. AmEx/MC/V.

Café MAK, I, Stubenring 3-5 (☎714 01 21), inside the Museum für Angewandte Kunst. Take tram #1 or 2 to Stubenring. Fitted with funky Bauhaus furniture. Students crowd in after 10pm. Open Tu-Su 10am-midnight.

Café Griensteidl, I, Michaelerpl. 2 (☎535 26 92), down the street from Café Central toward the Hofburg. Vienna's 1st literary cafe. Open daily 8am-11:30pm. AmEx/MC/V.

🗷 HEURIGEN (WINE TAVERNS)

Heurigen, marked by a hanging branch of evergreen, sell wine and savory Austrian buffet-style delicacies in a unique ambience. The wine, also called *Heuriger,* is from the most recent harvest and is typically grown and pressed by the owner himself. Good *Heuriger* wine is white, fruity, and full of body. The most famous region, **Grinzing,** in District XIX, is where the tour buses go; you'll find better atmosphere in the hills of **Sievering, Neustift am Walde** (both in District XIX), and **Neuwaldegg** (in XVII). Authentic *Heurigen* abound on Hochstr. in **Perchtoldsdorf,** southwest of the city. Take U4 to Hietzing and tram #6 to Rodaun. Walk down Ketzerg. until Hochstr. and continue for a few minutes. True *Heuriger* devotees make the trip to **Gumpoldskirchen.** Take the S-Bahn from the Südbahnhof.

■ **Buschenschank Heinrich Niersche,** XIX, Strehlg. 21. Take U6 to Währingerstr., and tram #41 to Pötzleing. Walk up Pötzleing. which becomes Khevenhuller Str.; go right on Strehlg. *Weiße G'spritzter* (white wine spritzer) €1.60. Open M and Th-Su 3pm-midnight.

■ **Zum Krottenbach'l,** XIX, Krottenbachstr. 148. U6 to Nußdorferstr., then bus #35A (dir.: Salmannsdorf) to Kleingartenverein. Larger but more touristy than Buschenschank. 0.25L of wine about €2. Open daily in winter 3pm-midnight; summer 4:30pm-midnight.

🗷 SIGHTS

Vienna's streets are by turns stately, residential, and decaying. Don't miss the **Hofburg, Schloß Schönbrunn, Schloß Belvedere,** or any of the buildings along the **Ringstraße.** To wander on your own, grab the brochure *Vienna from A to Z* (€4 with Vienna Card) from the tourist office. The range of available **tours** is overwhelming—there are 50 themed walking tours alone in the brochure *Walks in Vienna.* Contact **Pedal Power,** II, Ausstellungsstr. 3 (☎729 72 34; www.pedalpower.at.), for **bike rental** (€5) or **cycling tours** (€20). **Bus tours** (€30) are given by **Vienna Sightseeing Tours,** IV, Graf Starhemberg (☎712 46 83), and **Cityrama,** I, Börgeg. 1 (☎534 13).

INSIDE THE RING
District I is Vienna's social and geographical epicenter; with its Romanesque arches, Gothic portals, *Jugendstil* apartments, and modern *Haas Haus,* it's also a gallery of the history of aesthetics.

STEPHANSPLATZ, GRABEN, AND PETERSPLATZ. Right in the heart of Vienna, this square is home to the massive **Stephansdom** (St. Stephen's Cathedral), Vienna's most treasured symbol. For a view of Vienna, take the elevator up the North Tower or climb the 343 steps of the South Tower. *(North Tower open daily July-Aug. 9am-6:30pm; Apr.-June and Sept.-Oct. 9am-6pm; Nov.-Mar. 8:30am-5pm. €4. South Tower open daily 9am-5:30pm. €3.)* Downstairs, skeletons of plague victims fill the **catacombs**. The **Gruft** (vault) stores all of the Habsburg innards. *(Tours M-Sa every 30min. 10-11:30am and 1:30-4:30pm, Su and holidays 1:30-4:30pm. €4.)* From Stephanspl., follow Graben for *Jugendstil* architecture, including the **Ankerhaus** (#10), Otto Wagner's red-marble **Grabenhof,** and the underground public toilet complex designed by Adolf Loos. Graben leads to Petersplatz and the 1663 **Pestsaüle** (Plague Column), built to celebrate the passing of the Black Death. *(U1 or 3 to Stephanspl.)*

HOHER MARKT AND STADTTEMPEL. Once both a market and an execution site, Hoher Markt was the heart of the Roman encampment, Vindobona. Roman ruins lie beneath the shopping arcade across from the fountain. *(From Stephanspl., walk down Rotenturmstr. and turn left on Lictenstr. Open Tu-Su 9am-12:15pm and 1:30-4:30pm. €2, students €1.)* The biggest draw is the 1914 *Jugendstil* **Ankeruhr** (clock), whose 3m figures—from Marcus Aurelius to Maria Theresia—rotate past the Viennese coat of arms accompanied by the tunes of their times. *(1 figure per hr. At noon all figures appear. Follow Judeng. from Hoher Markt to Ruprechtspl.)* Hidden on Ruprechtspl. at Seitenstetteng. 2, the Stadttempel is the only synagogue in Vienna to escape Nazi destruction during *Kristallnacht*. *(Bring passport. Open M-Th 10am-4pm. Free.)*

AM HOF AND FREYUNG. Once a medieval jousting square, Am Hof now houses the **Kirche am Hof** (Church of the Nine Choirs of Angels) and **Collalto Palace,** where Mozart gave his first public performance. *(From Stephanspl., walk down Graben until it ends, go right and continue on Bognerg.; Am Hof is on the right.)* Just west of Am Hof is Freyung, the "square" with the **Austriabrunnen** (Austria Fountain) in the center. Freyung (sanctuary) took its name from the **Schottenstift** (Monastery of the Scots), where fugitives could claim asylum in medieval times. The annual **Christkindl market** held here blots out unpleasant memories of this former execution site.

HOFBURG. The sprawling Hofburg was the winter residence of the Habsburgs. Construction began in 1275, and additions continued until the end of the family's reign in 1918. Coming through the Michaelertor, you'll first enter the courtyard called **"In der Burg"** (within the fortress). On your left is the red-and-black-striped **Schweizertor** (Swiss Gate), erected in 1552. The **Silberkammer,** on the ground floor, displays the gold, silver, goblets, and 100 ft. gilded candelabra that once adorned the imperial table. *(Open daily 9am-5pm. €7.50, students €6.)*

Behind the Schweizertor lies the **Schweizerhof,** the inner courtyard of the **Alte Burg** (Old Fortress), which stands on the same site as the original 13th-century palace. Take a right at the top of the stairs for the Gothic **Burgkapelle** (chapel), where the members of the **Wiener Sängerknaben** (Vienna Boys' Choir) raise their heavenly voices every Sunday. Beneath the stairs is the entrance to the **Weltliche und Geistliche Schatzkammer,** containing the Habsburg jewels, crowns, and Napoleon's cradle. *(Open M and W-Su 10am-6pm. €8, students and seniors €6. Free audioguide available in English.)* Northeast of the Alte Burg, the **Stallburg** is home to the Lipizzaner stallions and the **Spanische Reitschule** (Spanish Riding School). The cheapest way to see the steeds is to watch them train. *(Mid-Feb. to June and late Aug.-early Nov. Tu-F. Check ahead for exact dates and times. Tickets sold at the door at Josefspl., Gate 2. About €20.)*

Built between 1881 and 1913, the **Neue Burg** is the youngest wing of the palace. The double-headed golden eagle crowning the roof symbolizes the double empire of Austria-Hungary. Today, the Neue Burg houses Austria's largest library, the **Österreichische Nationalbibliothek.** *(Open July-Sept. M-F 9am-4pm, Sa 9am-12:45pm; Oct.-June M-F 9am-9pm, Sa 9am-12:45pm; closed Sept. 1-7.)*

High Mass is still held in 14th-century **Augustinerkirche** (St. Augustine's Church) on Josefspl. The hearts of the Habsburgs are stored in the **Herzgrüftel.** *(Head through the Michaelertor in Michaelerpl. Mass 11am. Open M-Sa 8am-5pm, Su 11am-6pm. Free.)*

OUTSIDE THE RING

Some of Vienna's most famous modern architecture is outside the Ring, where 20th-century designers found more space to build. This area is also home to a number of Baroque palaces and parks that were once beyond the city limits.

KARLSPLATZ AND NASCHMARKT. Karlspl. is home to Vienna's most beautiful Baroque church, the **Karlskirche,** an eclectic masterpiece combining a Neoclassical portico with a Baroque dome and towers on either side. *(U1, 2, or 4 to Karlspl. Open M-Sa 9am-12:30pm and 1-6pm, Su 1-6pm. €4, students €2.)* West of Karlspl., along Linke Wienzeile, is the colorful **Naschmarkt** food bazaar. On Saturdays, the Naschmarkt becomes a massive flea market. *(Open M-F 6am-6:30pm, Sa 6am-2pm.)*

SCHLOß BELVEDERE. The Schloß Belvedere was originally the summer residence of Prince Eugène of Savoy, one of Austria's greatest military heroes. The grounds, stretching from Schwarzenberg Palace to the Südbahnhof, contain three excellent museums (p. 102) and an equal number of spectacular sphinx-filled gardens. *(Take tram D or #71 one stop past Schwarzenbergpl.)*

SCHLOß SCHÖNBRUNN. From its humble beginnings as a hunting lodge, Schönbrunn was Maria Theresia's favorite residence. The **Grand Tour** passes through the **Great Gallery,** where the Congress of Vienna met, and the **Hall of Mirrors,** where six-year-old Mozart played. *(U4: Schönbrunn. Apartments open daily July-Aug. 8:30am-6pm; Apr.-June and Sept.-Oct. 8:30am-5pm; Nov.-Mar. 8:30am-4:30pm. Imperial Tour €8, students €7.40. Grand Tour €10.50/€8.60. Audioguides in English included.)* As impressive as the palace itself are the classical **gardens** behind it, which contain the **Schmetterlinghaus** (Butterfly House), among other attractions. *(Park open 6am-dusk. Free.)*

ZENTRALFRIEDHOF. The Viennese like to describe the Central Cemetery as half the size of Geneva but twice as lively. **Tor I** (Gate 1) leads to the old **Jewish Cemetery.** Many of the headstones are cracked and neglected because the families of most of the dead have left Austria. Behind **Tor II** (Gate 2) are Beethoven and Strauss, and an honorary monument to Mozart, whose true resting place is an unmarked pauper's grave in the **Cemetery of St. Mark,** III, Leberstr. 6-8. **Tor III** (Gate 3) leads to the Protestant section and the new Jewish cemetery. *(XI, Simmeringer Hauptstr. 234. Take tram #71 from Schwarzenbergpl or tram #72 from Schlachthausg. Open daily May-Aug. 7am-7pm; Mar.-Apr. and Sept.-Oct. 7am-6pm; Nov.-Feb. 8am-5pm. Free.)*

▥ MUSEUMS

Vienna owes its vast selection of masterpieces to the acquisitive Habsburgs and to the city's own crop of art schools and world-class artists. An exhaustive list is impossible to include here, but the tourist office's free *Museums* brochure lists all opening hours and admission prices. All museums run by the city are free Friday before noon (except on public holidays). If you're going to be in town for a while, invest in the **Museum Card** (ask at any museum ticket window).

INSIDE THE RING

KUNSTHISTORISCHES MUSEUM (MUSEUM OF FINE ARTS). One of the world's largest art collections features Venetian and Flemish paintings, Classical art, and an Egyptian burial chamber. The **Ephesos Museum** exhibits findings of excavations in Turkey, the **Hofjagd- und Rustkammer** is the second-largest collection of arms in the world, and the **Sammlung alter Musikinstrumente** includes Beethoven's harpsichord and Mozart's piano. *(U2: Museumsquartier. Across from the Burgring and Heldenpl. on Maria Theresia's right. Open M and W-Su 10am-6pm. €8, students €6. Audioguide included.)*

HAUS DER MUSIK. Science meets music in this über-interactive museum. Experience the physics of sound, learn about famous Viennese composers, and entertain yourself with a fascinating invention called the Brain Opera. *(I, Seilerstatte 30, near the opera house. Open daily 10am-10pm. €10, students €8.50.)*

KUNST HAUS WIEN. Artist-environmentalist Friedenreich Hundertwasser built this museum without straight lines—even the floor bends. It also hosts contemporary art from around the world. *(III, Untere Weißgerberstr. 13. U1 or 4 to Schwedenpl., then tram N to Hetzg. Open daily 10am-7pm. €9, students €7; M half-price, except holidays.)*

AKADEMIE DER BILDENDEN KUNST (ACADEMY OF FINE ARTS). This building houses the art academy famous for having rejected Hitler's application. Offers an excellent collection, including several works by Peter Paul Rubens and Hieronymus Bosch's *The Last Judgment. (I, Schillerpl. 3. From Karlspl. turn left onto Friedrichstr., right onto Operng., and left on Nibelungeng. Open Tu-Su and holidays 10am-6pm. €5, students €3. Call ahead for guided tours in English. Audioguides €2.)*

ÖSTERREICHISCHES MUSEUM FÜR ANGEWANDTE KUNST (MAK). Dedicated to beautiful design, from the smooth curves of Thonet bentwood chairs to the intricacies of Venetian glass. Klimt-lovers will warm to *The Embrace. (I, Stubenring 5. U3: Stubentor. Open Tu 10am-midnight, W-Su 10am-6pm. €7.90, students €4, Sa free.)*

ALBERTINA. First an Augustinian monastery and then the largest of the Habsburg residences, the Albertina now houses the **Collection of Graphic Arts.** Past exhibits have included Rembrandt and various Pop artists. *(Open M-Tu and Th-Su 10am-6pm, W 10am-9pm. €9, students €6.50.)*

A PRINCELY GIFT

After a 66-year hiatus, what may be the world's most significant private art collection has reopened to the public; on March 29, 2004, Liechtenstein's Prince Hans-Adam II opened the Liechtenstein Museum in Vienna's 9th district.

Hans-Adam II and his predecessors have acquired a collection of some 1600 works. The history of the collection can be traced back to Prince Karl I of Liechtenstein (1569-1627), whose heirs continued what quickly became a Liechtenstein tradition of art collecting. From 1807-1938 Liechtenstein's private collection was displayed in the Garden Palace in the Rossau.

However, World War II brought financial troubles for the royal family. In 1938 the museum in Vienna was closed and some of its artwork sold. When Hans-Adam II restructured the family's finances, the art collection once again became a priority. In 1985, the Liechtenstein collection was temporarily exhibited at the New York Metropolitan Museum of Art, but only returned to its former and permanent home in the Garden Palace in Vienna in 2004.

A particularly impressive part of the palace is the Hercules Hall, which is Vienna's largest secular Baroque room and contains an extraordinary ceiling fresco by Andrea Pozzo. The museum also contains works by Franz Xaver Messerschmidt, Raphael, Rembrandt, and Peter Paul Rubens.

JÜDISCHES MUSEUM (JEWISH MUSEUM). Jewish culture and history told through holograms and more traditional displays. Temporary exhibits focus on prominent Jewish figures and contemporary Jewish art. *(I, Dorotheerg. 11, near Stephanspl. Open M-W, F, and Su 10am-6pm; Th and Sa 10am-8pm. €5, students €2.90.)*

OUTSIDE THE RING

■ **ÖSTERREICHISCHE GALERIE (AUSTRIAN GALLERY).** The Schloß Belvedere houses 19th- and 20th-century European art, including Klimt's *The Kiss*. The Unteres Belvedere contains the **Austrian Museum of Baroque Art** and the **Austrian Museum of Medieval Art,** which showcase an extensive collection of sculptures and altarpieces. *(III, Prinz-Eugen-Str. 27, in the Belvedere Palace behind Schwarzenbergpl. Walk up from the Südbahnhof, then take tram D to Schloß Belvedere or tram #71 to Unteres Belvedere. Both Belvederes open Tu-Su 10am-6pm. €7.50, students €5.)*

MUSEUMSQUARTIER. At 60 sq. km, it's one of the 10 biggest art districts in the world. Central Europe's largest collection of modern art, the **Museum Moderner Kunst,** highlights Classical Modernism, Pop Art, Photo Realism, Fluxus, and Viennese Actionism in a building made from basalt lava. 20th-century masters include Kandinsky, Klee, Magritte, Miró, Motherwell, Picasso, Pollock, and Warhol. *(Open Tu-Su 10am-7pm, Th 10am-9pm. €8, students €6.50.)* The **Leopold Museum** has the world's largest Schiele collection, plus works by Egger-Lienz, Gerstl, Klimt, and Kokoschka. *(Open M, W, and F-Su 10am-7pm; Th 10am-9pm. €9, students €5.50.)* Themed exhibits of contemporary artists fill **Kunsthalle Wien.** *(Take U2 to Museumsquartier. Open M-Tu and F-Su 10am-7pm, Th 10am-10pm. Exhibition Hall 1 €7.50, students €6; Exhibition Hall 2 €6/€4.50; both €10.50/€8.50; students €2 on M.)*

HISTORISCHES MUSEUM DER STADT WIEN. In the Historical Museum of Vienna, artifacts and paintings document Vienna's evolution from a Roman encampment to the center of 640 years of Habsburg rule. *(IV, Karlspl., to the left of the Karlskirche. Open Tu-Su 9am-6pm. €4, students €2. Permanent exhibit on Su free.)*

FREUD MUSEUM. Freud's former home has lots of bric-a-brac, including his report cards and circumcision certificate. *(IX, Bergg. 19. U2: Schottentor; walk up Währingerstr. to Bergg. Open daily July-Sept. 9am-6pm; Oct.-June 9am-4pm. €5, students €3.)*

◪◪ ♫ FESTIVALS AND ENTERTAINMENT

Vienna hosts an array of important annual **festivals,** mostly musical. The **Vienna Festwochen** (mid-May to mid-June) has a diverse program of exhibitions, plays, and concerts. (☎58 92 20; www.festwochen.or.at.) The Staatsoper and Volkstheater host the annual **Jazzfest Wien** (☎503 5647; www.viennajazz.org) during the first weeks of July. The Social Democrats host the late-June **Danube Island Festival,** which draws millions of revelers for fireworks and concerts. From mid-July to mid-August, the **Im-Puls Dance Festival** (☎523 55 58; www.impulstanz.com) attracts some of the world's greatest dance troupes and offers seminars to enthusiasts. In mid-October, the annual city-wide film festival, the **Viennale,** kicks off.

While Vienna offers all the standard entertainment in the way of festivals, film, and theater, the heart of the city beats to music. All but a few of classical music's marquee names lived, composed, and performed in Vienna. Beethoven, Haydn, and Mozart wrote their greatest masterpieces in Vienna, creating the First Viennese School; a century later, Berg, Schönberg, and Webern formed the Second Viennese School. Every Austrian child must learn to play an instrument during school, and the Vienna Konservatorium and Hochschule are world-renowned conservatories. All year, Vienna hosts many performances accessible to the budget traveler. None of the venues listed below have performances in July or August.

Staatsoper, I, Opernring 2 (www.wiener-staatsoper.at). Vienna's premiere opera performs nearly every night Sept.-June. No shorts. The box office (Bundestheaterkasse; ☎ 514 44 78 80), I, Hanuschg. 3, is around the corner. Open M-F 8am-6pm, Sa-Su 9am-noon; 1st Sa of each month 9am-5pm. Seats €5-254. 500 standing-room tickets available for every show (1 per person; €2-3.50); arrive 2hr. before curtain.

Wiener Philharmoniker (Vienna Philharmonic Orchestra) plays in the **Musikverein**, Austria's premiere concert hall. Even if you only want standing-room tickets, visit the box office (Bösendorferstr. 12; www.wienerphilharmoniker.at) well in advance.

Wiener Sängerknaben (Vienna Boys' Choir) sings during mass every Su at 9:15am (mid-Sept. to late June) in the Hofburgkapelle (U3: Herreng.). Despite rumors to the contrary, standing-room is free; arrive before 8am.

◨ NIGHTLIFE

With one of the highest bar-to-cobblestone ratios in the world, Vienna is the place to party, whether you're looking for a quiet evening with a glass of wine or a wild night in a disco. Take U1 or 4 to Schwedenpl., which will drop you within blocks of the **Bermuda Dreieck** (Bermuda Triangle), an area packed with crowded clubs. If you make it out, head down **Rotenturmstraße** toward Stephansdom or walk around the areas bounded by the synagogue and Ruprechtskirche. Slightly outside the Ring, the streets off **Burggasse** and **Stiftgasse** in District VII and the **university quarter** in Districts XIII and IX have outdoor courtyards and hip bars. Viennese nightlife starts late, often after 11pm. For listings, pick up the indispensable *Falter* (€2).

▨ Das Möbel, VII, Burgg. 10. U2 or 3 to Volkstheater. Metal couches, car-seat chairs, and Swiss-army tables are filled by an artsy crowd. Open M-F noon-1am, Sa-Su 10am-1am.

Volksgarten Disco, I, Volksgarten. U2: Volkstheater. Hip-hop and a teenage crowd F; house and a somewhat older crowd Sa. Cover €6-13. Open Su Th-Su 10pm-5am.

Mapitom der Bierlokal, I, Seitenstetteng. 1. This bar has large tables in a warehouse-style interior. Beer and mixed drinks from €3. Open Su-Th 5pm-3am, F-Sa 5pm-4am.

Flex, I, Donaulände, near the Schottenring II-Bahn station. Danoc, grab a beer (€4), or bring your own and sit by the river like everyone else. DJs start spinning at 10pm. Cover starts at €4, free after 3:30am. Open daily 8pm-4am.

Chelsea, VIII, Lerchenfeldergürtel U-Bahnbögen 29-30 (☎ 407 93 09; www.chelsea.co.at), under the U-Bahn, between Thaliastr. and Josefstädterstr. Bands from all over Austria rock this underground club 3-4 times per week (fewer July-Aug.). When live acts are not scheduled, expect a techno-pop atmosphere. Cover €7-11 if a band is playing. Beer (0.5L) €3.10. Wine (0.13L) €1.50. Open daily 6pm-4am.

Kaktus, I, Seitenstetteng. 5, in the heart of the Bermuda Triangle. Packed with 20-somethings dripping with alcohol and dancing to mainstream music. Dress to impress. Beer (0.5L) €3.40. Happy Hour (all drinks half-price) M-Th 7-10pm. Topless bartenders F-Sa. Open Su-Th 7pm-3am, F-Sa 7pm-4am.

Porgy & Bess, I, Riemerg. 11. U1: Stubentor. The best jazz club in Vienna. Prices vary—shows generally €15-20. Open M-Th and Su 8pm-2am, F-Sa 8pm-4am. MC/V.

SALZBURGER LAND AND UPPER AUSTRIA

Salzburger Land derives its name from the German *Salz* (salt), and it was this white gold that first drew visitors to the region. Combined with Upper Austria, this region encompasses the shining lakes and rolling hills of the Salzkammergut, where Salzburg and Hallstatt are among the more enticing destinations.

SALZBURG ☎ 0662

Graced with Baroque wonders, Salzburg is overflowing with fascinating stories waiting to be heard. In the 17th and 18th centuries it was the ecclesiastical center of Austria. Governed by Prince-Archbishops, this Golden Age produced architectural masterpieces and fostered a rich musical culture. The city's love for native genius Mozart reaches a climax in summer during the Salzburger Festspiele.

▐ TRANSPORTATION

Trains: Hauptbahnhof, in Südtirolerpl. (24hr. reservations ☎05 17 17). To: **Graz** (4hr., 8 per day, €37); **Innsbruck** (2hr., 11 per day, €30); **Munich** (2hr., 30 per day, €26); **Vienna** (3½hr., 26 per day, €37); **Zurich** (6hr., 7 per day, €65.20).

Public Transportation: Get bus info. at the **Lokalbahnhof** (☎44 80 61 66), next to the train station. Single tickets (€1.70) available at automatic machines or from the drivers. Books of **5 tickets** (€7), **day passes** (€3.20), and **week passes** (€9) are available at machines, the ticket office, or *Tabak* (newsstand/tobacco) shops. Punch your ticket when you board or risk a €36 fine. Buses usually make their last run 10:30-11:30pm, but **BusTaxi** fills in when the public buses stop. Get on at Hanuschpl. or Theaterg. and tell the driver where you need to go (every 30min. Su-Th 11:30pm-1:30am, F-Sa 11:30pm-3am; €3 for anywhere within the city limits).

✚ ▐ ORIENTATION AND PRACTICAL INFORMATION

Just a few kilometers from the German border, Salzburg covers both banks of the **Salzach River.** Two hills abut the river: the **Mönchsberg** over the **Altstadt** (old city) on the southern side and the **Kapuzinerberg** by the **Neustadt** (new city) on the northern side. The Hauptbahnhof is on the northern side of town beyond the Neustadt; buses #1, 5, 6, 51, and 55 connect it to downtown. On foot, turn left out of the station onto Rainerstr. and follow it straight under the tunnel and on to Mirabellpl.

Tourist Office, Mozartpl. 5 (☎88 98 73 30), in the Altstadt. From the station, take bus #3, 5, 6, or 55 to Mozartsteg, head away from the river, and curve right around the building into Mozartpl. The office gives free hotel maps, guided tours of the city (daily 12:15pm, €8), and sells the **Salzburg Card,** which grants admission to all museums and sights as well as unlimited public transportation (1-day card €19, 2-day €27, 3-day €32). Room reservation service €2.20. Open daily 9am-8pm.

Currency Exchange: Banks offer good rates but higher commissions. Banking hours M-F 8am-12:30pm and 2-4:30pm. Train station's exchange open 7am-9pm.

American Express: Mozartpl. 5 (☎80 80). Provides all banking services; no commission on AmEx cheques. Holds mail and books tours. Open M-F 9am-5:30pm, Sa 9am-noon.

Luggage Storage: At the train station. 24hr. lockers €2-3.50.

Emergency: Police: ☎133. **Ambulance:** ☎144. **Fire:** ☎122.

Pharmacies: Elisabeth-Apotheke, Elisabethstr. 1a (☎87 14 84). Pharmacies in the city center open M-F 8am-6pm, Sa 8am-noon. There are always 3 pharmacies open; check the list on the door of any closed pharmacy.

Internet Access: Internet Café, Mozartpl. 5 (☎84 48 22), near the tourist office. €0.15 per min. Open daily Sept.-June 10am-11pm; July-Aug. 9am-midnight.

Post Office: ☎88 30 30. At the train station. Address *Poste Restante* mail with the specific Postal Code 5021 and it will be held at the post office for 3 weeks. Open M-F 7am-8:30pm (counter closes 6pm), Sa 8am-2pm, Su 1-6pm. **Postal Code:** A-5021.

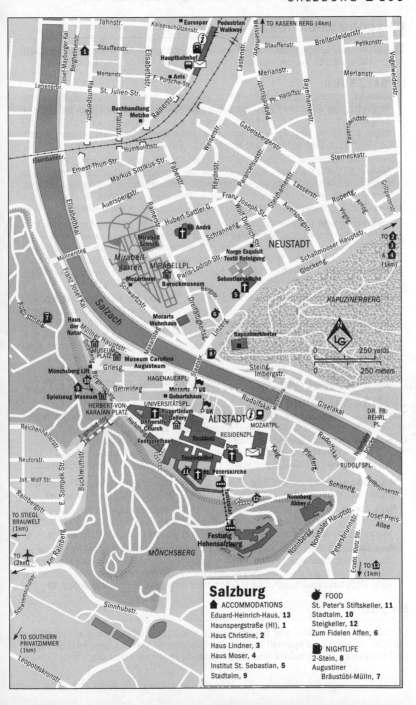

Salzburg

ACCOMMODATIONS
Eduard-Heinrich-Haus, **13**
Haunspergstraße (HI) **1**
Haus Christine, **2**
Haus Lindner, **3**
Haus Moser, **4**
Institut St. Sebastian, **5**
Stadtalm **9**

FOOD
St. Peter's Stiftskeller, **11**
Stadtalm, **10**
Steigkeller, **12**
Zum Fidelen Affen, **6**

NIGHTLIFE
2-Stein, **8**
Augustiner
Bräustübl-Mülln, **7**

AUSTRIA

ACCOMMODATIONS

Though hostels are plentiful, other housing in the city center is expensive; affordable options also lie on the outskirts of town or just outside it on **Kasern Berg.**

IN SALZBURG

Stadtalm, Mönchsberg 19c (☎/fax 84 17 29). Take bus #1 (dir.: Maxglan) to Mönchsbergaufzug, go down the street and through the stone arch on the left to the Mönchsberg lift, and ride up (daily 9am-9pm, round-trip €2.40). At the top, turn right, climb the steps, and follow signs for Stadtalm. Communal showers. Breakfast included. Reception 9am-9pm. Curfew 1am. Open Apr.-Sept. Dorms €13. AmEx/MC/V. ❷

Institut St. Sebastian, Linzerg. 41 (☎87 13 86). From the station, bus #1, 3, 5, or 6 to Mirabellpl. Cross the street, continue in the same direction as the bus, turn left onto Bergstr., and left again onto Linzerg.; the hostel is through the arch. Breakfast included. Sheets €2 for dorms. Laundry €3. Reception 8am-noon and 4-9pm. Dorms €15; singles €21, with shower €33; doubles €40/€54; triples €60/€69; quads €72/€84. ❷

Haunspergstraße (HI), Haunspergstr. 27 (☎87 96 49; fax 88 34 77), near the train station. Take bus #1 (dir.: Messezentrum) or 2 (dir.: Walserfeld) to Jahnstr. Walk in the same direction as the bus to the corner; the hostel is directly across the street. Spacious 2- to 4-bed rooms. Breakfast and sheets included. All rooms either have a private shower or share with 1 other room. Reception 7am-2pm and 5pm-midnight. Open early July to early Aug. 4-person dorms €18; 2-person dorms €21. MC/V. ❷

Eduard-Heinrich-Haus (HI), Eduard-Heinrich-Str. 2 (☎62 59 76; hostel.eduard-heinrich@salzburg.co.at). Take bus #3 (dir.: Salzburg-Süd) or 8 (dir.: Alpensiedlung) to Polizeidirektion. Cross over Alpenstr., continue down Billrothstr., turn left on Robert-Stolz-Promenade footpath, walk 200m, and take the 1st right; the hostel is the big pink building on the left. Big rooms and lobbies with leather couches on each floor. Private bathrooms. Breakfast and lockers included. Internet €2.60 per 20min. Reception M-F 7am-midnight, Sa-Su 7-10am and 5pm-midnight. Rooms of 1-2 people €21.42 per person; 3-4 people €18.42 per person; 5-6 people €15.42 per person. MC/V. ❸

OUTSIDE SALZBURG

The rooms on **Kasern Berg** are officially outside Salzburg, which means the tourist office can't recommend them, but the personable hosts and bargain prices make these *Privatzimmer* (rooms in a family home) a terrific housing option. All northbound trains run to Kasern Berg (4min., every 30min. 6:15am-11:15pm, €1.60; Eurail valid). Get off at Salzburg-Maria Plain and take the road that leads uphill.

Haus Lindner, Panoramaweg 5 (☎45 66 81). Offers homey rooms, some with mountain views. Breakfast included. Call for pickup from the station. €15-17 per person. ❷

Haus Moser, Turnerbühel (☎45 66 76). Climb the hidden stairs on the right side of Kasern Berg road across from Germana Kapeller. Charming couple offers comfortable rooms in their dark-timbered home. Breakfast and laundry included. €15 per person. ❷

Haus Christine, Panoramaweg 3 (☎/fax 45 67 73; haus.christine@gmx.at), just before Haus Lindner. Spacious, clean triples and quads with a country motif. Breakfast served on a glass-enclosed patio overlooking the countryside—the best view on the block. 1st night €15, subsequent nights €14. Credit cards accepted, but cash preferred. ❷

FOOD

Countless beer gardens and pastry-shop patios make Salzburg a great place for outdoor dining. Local specialties include *Salzburger Nockerl* (egg whites, sugar, and raspberry filling baked into three mounds that represent the three hills of

Salzburg) and the world-famous *Mozartkugeln* (hazelnuts coated in marzipan, nougat, and chocolate). **Supermarkets** cluster on the Mirabellpl. side of the river, and **open-air markets** are held on Universitätpl. (Open M-F 6am-7pm, Sa 6am-1pm.)

Zum Fidelen Affen, Priesterhausg. 8, off Linzerg. Hearty, honest Austrian food keeps everyone coming back "To the Faithful Ape." Try the toasted black bread with various toppings, the farmer's salad (€10), or the "Monkey Steak," (a roasted pork dish). Vegetarian options like spinach dumplings (€10). Open M-Sa 5pm-midnight. MC/V. ❸

Stadtalm, Mönchsberg 19c. Even if you aren't staying in the Stadtalm youth hostel, consider making a trip to the Mönchsberg lift to eat at the delightful cafe of the same name. Enjoy chicken cordon bleu (€10), Greek salad (€6), or a glass of Stiegl (€3) while soaking up a view of the Altstadt. Open daily Mar.-Oct. 10am-10pm. ❸

St. Peter's Stiftskeller, St.-Peter-Bezirk 1/4. Tucked away behind the fortress at the foot of the cliffs is the oldest restaurant in Central Europe, established in 803. Most entrees €18-20. Open M-F 11am-midnight, during the Festspiele until 1am. MC/V. ❹

Stiegkeller, Festungsg. 10. A short walk up the Festungsg. from the bottom of the Festungsbahn. A Salzburg favorite since 1492. Seating for 1600 both outside under shady trees and inside under imposing antlers. Open daily May-Sept. 11am-11pm. MC/V. ❸

SIGHTS

THE ALTSTADT

FESTUNG HOHENSALZBURG. Built between 1077 and 1681 by the ruling archbishops, Hohensalzburg Fortress, which looms over Salzburg from atop Mönchsberg, is the largest completely preserved castle in Europe—partly because it was never successfully attacked. The castle contains formidable Gothic state rooms, an organ (nicknamed the "Bull of Salzburg" for its off-key snorting), and a watchtower that affords an unmatched view of the city. The **Burgmuseum** inside the fortress displays medieval instruments of torture and has side-by-side histories of Salzburg, the fortress, and the world. *(Take the trail or the Festungsbahn funicular up to the fortress from Festungsg. Funicular every 10min. 9am-9pm. Ascent €5.60, round-trip €8.50; includes fortress admission. Grounds open daily mid-June to mid-Sept. 9am-7pm; mid-Sept. to mid-Mar. 9am-5pm; mid-Mar. to mid-June 9:30am-6pm. Interior open daily mid-June to mid-Sept. 9am-5:30pm; mid-Sept. to mid-Mar. 9am-4:30pm; mid-Mar. to mid-June 9:30am-5pm. If you walk, fortress €3.60. Combo ticket including fortress, interiors, and museums €7.20.)*

MOZARTS GEBURTSHAUS. Mozart's birthplace holds an impressive collection of the child genius's belongings, including his first viola and violin and a pair of keyboard instruments. Several rooms recreate his young years as a traveling virtuoso. Come before 11am to avoid the crowd. *(Getreideg. 9. Open daily July-Aug. 9am-7pm; Sept.-June 9am-5:30pm. €5.50, students and seniors €4.50.)*

UNIVERSITY CHURCH. In Mozart's backyard stands the **Universitätskirche,** one of the largest Baroque chapels on the continent and designer Fischer von Erlach's masterpiece. Sculpted clouds coat the nave, while pudgy cherubim frolic all over the church's immense apse. *(Hours vary, although generally open daily 9am-5pm. Free.)*

TOSCANINIHOF, CATACOMBS, AND THE DOM. Steps lead from Toscaninihof, the courtyard of **St. Peter's Monastery,** up the Mönchsberg cliffs. **Stiftskirche St. Peter,** a church within the monastery, features a marble portal from 1244. In the 18th century, the building was remodeled in Rococo style. *(Open daily 9am-12:15pm and 2:30-6:30pm.)* Near the far end of the cemetery, against the Mönchsberg, is the entrance to the Catacombs. In the lower room (St. Gertrude's Chapel), a fresco commemorates the martyrdom of Thomas à Becket. *(Open May-Sept. Tu-Su 10:30am-5pm; Oct.-Apr. W-Th 10:30am-3:30pm. €1, students €0.60.)* The exit at the other end of the cemetery leads to the immense baroque *Dom* (cathedral), where Mozart was christened in 1756 and later worked as concert master and court organist. The square leading out of the cathedral, **Domplatz,** features a statue of the Virgin Mary and figures representing Wisdom, Faith, the Church, and the Devil. *(Free.)*

RESIDENZ. The archbishops of Salzburg have resided in the magnificent Residenz since 1595. Stunning baroque **Prunkräume** (state rooms) have huge ceiling frescoes, gilded furniture, and ornate stucco work. A **gallery** exhibits 16th- to 19th-century art. *(Open daily 10am-5pm, closed some M. €5, students €4. Audioguide included.)*

THE NEUSTADT

MIRABELL PALACE AND GARDENS. Mirabellpl. holds the marvelous **Mirabell Schloß,** which the supposedly celibate Archbishop Wolf Dietrich built for his mistress and their 10 children in 1606. Behind the palace, the **Mirabellgarten** is a maze of seasonal flower beds. The garden contains the moss-covered **Zauberflötenhäuschen,** where Mozart purportedly composed *The Magic Flute* in just five months.

MOZARTS WOHNHAUS. Mozart moved here at age 17 with his family, staying from 1773-1780. Hear excerpts from his music. *(Makartpl. 8. Open daily July-Aug. 9am-6:30pm; Sept.-June 9am-5:30pm. €5.50, students €4.50. Audioguide included.)*

🎵 ENTERTAINMENT

Max Reinhardt, Richard Strauss, and Hugo von Hofmannsthal founded the renowned **Salzburger Festspiele** in 1920. Ever since, Salzburg has become a musical mecca from late July to the end of August. On the eve of the festival's opening, over 100 dancers don regional costumes and perform a *Fackeltanz* (torch dance) on Residenzpl. Operas, plays, films, concerts, and tourists overrun every available public space. Info and tickets for Festspiele events are available through the *Festspiele Kartenbüro* (ticket office) and *Tageskasse* (daily box office) in Karajanpl., against the mountain and next to the tunnel. (Open late July-late Aug. M-F 9:30am-6:30pm; early to mid-July M-Sa 9:30-5pm; Sept.-June 9:30am-3pm.)

Even when the Festspiele is not on, many concerts and events occur around the city. The **Salzburg Academy of Music and Performing Arts** performs in the **Mozarteum** (next to the Mirabell gardens), and the **Dom** has a concert program in July and August. (€8.80, students €7.37.) From May to August there are **outdoor performances,** including concerts, folk-singing, and dancing, around the Mirabellgarten. The tourist office has leaflets on scheduled events, but an evening stroll through the park might answer your questions just as well. **Mozartplatz** and **Kapitelplatz** are also popular stops for street musicians and touring school bands.

🍺 PUBS AND BEER GARDENS

Munich may be known as the world's beer capital, but much of that liquid gold flows south to Austria's pubs and *Biergärten* (beer gardens). These lager oases cluster in the city center by the Salzach River. The more boisterous stick to Rudolfskai, between the Staatsbrücke and Mozartsteg. Elsewhere, especially along Chiemseeg. and around Anton-Neumayr-Pl., you can throw back a few drinks in a more reserved *Beisl* (pub). Refined bars with older patrons can be found along Steing. and Giselakai on the other side of the river. 🍺**Augustiner Bräustübl-Mülln,** Augustinerg. 4, has been serving home-brewed beer in the halls of a former monastery since 1621. (Beer €2.40-2.70. Open M-F 3-11pm, Sa-Su 2:30-11pm.) **2-Stein,** Giselakai 9, is the place to come for Salzburg's gay and lesbian scene. (☎87 71 79. Mixed drinks from €5. Open M-W 6pm-4am, Th-Su 6pm-5am.)

ⓩ DAYTRIP FROM SALZBURG: LUSTSCHLOß HELLBRUNN

South of Salzburg lies **Lustschloß Hellbrunn,** a sprawling estate with a large palace, fish ponds, flower gardens, and the **Wasserspiele,** which consist of water-powered figurines and a booby-trapped table that spouts water on surprised guests. (Open May-June and Sept. daily 9am-6pm; July-Aug. 9am-6pm; Apr. and Oct. 9am-4:30pm. Castle tour, gardens, and Wasserspiele €7.50; students €5.50.) Take bus #25 (dir.: Hellbrunn; 30min.) to Hellbrun from the train station, Mirabellpl., or Mozartsteg.

HALLSTATT   ☎06134

Teetering on the banks of the Hallstättersee, tiny Hallstatt (pop. 960) is easily the most striking lakeside village in the Salzkammergut. Hallstatt's salt-rich earth has helped preserve its archaeological treasures, which are so extensive that one era in Celtic studies (800-400 BC) is dubbed "the Hallstatt era."

ⓕⓩ TRANSPORTATION AND PRACTICAL INFORMATION. Buses are the cheapest way (€15) to get to Hallstatt from Salzburg but require layovers in both Bad Ischl and Gosaumühle. The **train station,** across the lake, is not staffed. All trains come from Attnang-Puchheim in the north or Stainach-Irdning in the south. **Trains** run hourly to Bad Ischl (30min., €3) and Salzburg via Attnang-Puchheim (2½hr., €17). The **tourist office,** Seestr. 169, finds the confusing system of street numbers. (☎82 08. Open July-Aug. M-F 9am-5pm, Sa 10am-5pm; Nov.-May M-F 9am-noon and 2-5pm.) There is an **ATM** by the post office. The **post office,** Seestr. 160, is below the tourist office. (Open M-Tu and Th-F 8am-noon and 1:30-5:30pm, W 8am-noon.) **Postal Code:** A-4830.

ⓕⓒ ACCOMMODATIONS AND FOOD. To reach **Gästehaus Zur Mühle ❷,** Kirchenweg 36, from the tourist office, walk uphill and head for a short tunnel at the upper right corner of the square; it's at the end of the tunnel by the waterfall. (☎83 18. Breakfast €2.50. Reception 10am-2pm and 4-10pm. Closed Nov. Dorms €10.) **Frühstückspension Sarstein ❸,** Gosamühlstr. 83, offers glorious views and a beachside lawn. From the ferry, turn right on Seestr. and walk 10min. (☎82 17. Breakfast included. Showers €1 per 10min. Singles €18; doubles €36.) To get to **Camping Klausner-Höll ❶,** Lahnstr. 201, turn right out of the tourist office and follow Seestr. for 10min. (☎832 24. Showers available. Laundry €8. Gate closed daily noon-3pm and 10pm-7:30am. Open mid-Apr. to mid-Oct. €5.80 per person, €3.70 per tent, €2.90 per car.) The cheapest eats are at **Konsum** supermarket, across from the bus stop; the butcher prepares sandwiches on request. (Open M-Tu and Th-F 7:30am-noon and 3-6pm, W 7:30am-12:30pm, Sa 7:30am-noon.)

ⓖⓝ SIGHTS AND HIKING. Back when Rome was still a village, the "white gold" from the salt mines made Hallstatt a world-famous settlement; the 2500-year-old **Salzbergwerk** is the oldest salt mine in the world. Take the 1hr. guided tour (in English and German), and zip down a wooden mining slide on a burlap sack to an eerie lake deep inside the mountain. (☎200 2400. Open daily May-Sept. 9:30am-4:30pm; Oct. 9:30am-3pm. €14.50, students €8.70.)

In the 19th century, Hallstatt was also the site of an immense and well-preserved Iron Age archaeological find. The **Charnel House** next to St. Michael's Chapel is a bizarre repository filled with the remains of over 610 villagers dating back as early

AUSTRIA

as the 16th century; the latest were added in 1995. From the ferry dock, follow the signs marked *"Katholische Kirche."* (Open daily June-Sept. 10am-6pm; May and Oct. 10am-4pm; Nov.-Apr. call ☎82 79 for an appointment. €1.)

Hallstatt offers some of the most spectacular day hikes in the Salzkammergut. The tourist office has an excellent Dachstein hiking guide in English (€6), which details 38 hikes in the area, as well as bike trail maps (€7). The **Salzbergwerk hike** is a simple 1hr. gravel hike leading to the salt-mine tour; walk to the Salzbergbahn and take the road to the right upward, turning at the black and yellow Salzwelten sign. The **Waldbachstrub Waterfall hike** is a light 1¾hr. walk along a tumbling stream and up to a spellbinding waterfall. From the bus station, follow the brown Malerweg signs near the supermarket until you reach the Waldbachstrub sign (about 40min.). The waterfall is in the **Echental**, a valley carved out by glaciers and now blazed with trails leading deep into the valley. The **Gangsteig**, a slippery stairway carved into the side of a cliff, requires sturdy shoes and a strong will to climb.

⊠ DAYTRIP FROM HALLSTATT: DACHSTEIN ICE CAVES. Above **Obertraun**, opposite the lake from Hallstatt, the famed **Riesenhöhle** (Giant Ice Cave) is part of the largest system of ice caves in the world. Slide by its frozen waterfalls and palaces on a sheet of green ice. The Riesenhöhle and the **Mammuthöhle** (Mammoth Cave) are up on the mountain, while the **Koppenbrüllerhöhle**, a giant spring, is in the valley. Mandatory tours are offered in English and German; you'll be assigned to a group at the Schönbergalm station. The cave temperatures are near freezing, so wear good footwear and warm clothes. *(From Hallstatt, walk to the Lahn station by heading down Seestr. with the lake to your left. Catch the bus to Obertraun (10min., 1 per hr. 9am-5pm, €1.90). Stop at Dachstein, then ride the cable car (every 15min. 8:40am-5:30pm; round-trip €13.40, children €8) up to Schönbergalm to reach the ice caves. The Koppenbrüller cave is a 15min. walk from the Dachstein bus stop in Obertraun. ☎06131 84 00. Open daily May to mid-Oct. 9am-5pm. Admission to each cave €8.20, children €4.80.)*

HOHE TAUERN NATIONAL PARK

The enormous Hohe Tauern range, the largest national park in Europe, boasts 246 glaciers and 304 mountains over 3km. The best way to explore the rare preserve is to take one of the many hikes, which range from pleasant ambles to difficult ascents. *An Experience in Nature*, available at park centers and most area tourist offices, describes 84 different hikes. The center of the park is Franz-Josefs-Höhe and the Pasterze glacier, which hovers above the town of Heiligenblut.

◨ TRANSPORTATION. Trains arrive in Zell am See from: Innsbruck (1½-2hr., 3:45am-9:27pm, €20); Kitzbühel (45min., 7:17am-9:27pm, €8.70); and Salzburg (1½hr., 1-2 per hr., €11.30). From Zell am See, a rail line runs west along the northern border of the park, terminating in Krimml (1¾hr., 6am-8:55pm, €7.60). A bus also runs directly to the Höhe (2hr., 2 per day, €10). The park itself is criss-crossed by **bus** lines that operate on a complicated timetable.

◪ FRANZ-JOSEFS-HÖHE. This tourist center, stationed above the Pasterze glacier, has a great view of the Großglockner (3797m). The Höhe has its own **park office** in the parking area. (☎04824 27 27. Open daily mid-May to mid-Oct. 10am-4pm.) The elevator next to the info center leads to the **Swarovski Observation Center**, with binoculars for viewing the surrounding terrain. (Open daily 10am-4pm. Free.)

◪ HEILIGENBLUT. The closest town to the highest mountain in Austria is a great starting point for hikes. Reach Heiligenblut by **bus** from Franz-Josefs-Höhe (30min., €3.60) and Lienz (1hr., 2-6 per day, €6). The **tourist office**, Hof 4, up the street from the bus stop, dispenses info on rooms, hikes, and transport. (☎20 01 21. Open July-Aug. M-F 9am-6pm, Sa 9am-noon and 4-6pm; Sept.-June M-F 9am-noon and 2-6pm, Sa 9am-noon and 4-6pm.) To reach the **Jugendgäste- haus (HI) ❸**, Hof 36, take the path down from the wall behind the bus stop parking lot. (☎22 59. Breakfast included. Reception daily July-Aug. 7-11am and 5-10 pm; Sept.-June 7-10am and 5-9pm. Lockout 10am-4pm. Curfew 10pm. €16.50. HI members only.)

◪ KRIMML. Over 400,000 visitors per year arrive here to see the extraordinary Krimml Waterfalls, a set of three 380m-high cascades. (8am-6pm €1.50; free after 6pm.) These waterfalls are usually enjoyed as a daytrip from Zell am See; **buses** run from Zell am See to Maustelle Ort (1½ hr., 5:45am-8:55pm, €7.60), the start of the path to the falls. To reach the **tourist office,** Oberkrimml 37, follow the road from the Krimml Ort bus stop and turn right down the hill in front of the church. (☎723 90. Open M-F 8am-noon and 2:30-5:30pm, Sa 8:30-10:30am.)

TYROL (TIROL)

Tyrol's mountains overwhelm the average mortal with their celestial scale. In the east, the mighty Hohe Tauern range is protected as a national park. In the center of it all, stylish Innsbruck flaunts Baroque facades and bronze statues, showcasing why Tyrol has become one of the world's most celebrated mountain playgrounds.

INNSBRUCK   ☎0512

The 1964 and 1976 winter Olympics were held in Innsbruck (pop. 128,000), bring- ing international recognition to this beautiful mountain city. The nearby Tyrolean Alps await skiers and hikers, and the tiny cobblestone streets of the Altstadt are peppered with fancy facades and relics of the Habsburg Empire.

▬ ▰ TRANSPORTATION AND PRACTICAL INFORMATION

Trains: Hauptbahnhof, Südtirolerpl. (☎05 17 17). To: **Munich** (2hr., 20 per day, €32); **Salzburg** (2½hr., 21 per day, €30); **Vienna Westbahnhof** (5½-7hr., 23 per day, €49); **Zurich** (4hr., 15 per day, €44).

Public Transportation: The **IVB** Office, Stainerstr. 2 (☎530 17 99), near Maria-There- sien-Str., has bus schedules. Open M-F 7:30am-6pm. The main bus station is in front of the entrance to the train station. Most buses stop running around 11:30pm, but 2 *Nachtbus* lines continue through the night.

Bike Rental: Sport Neuner, Maximillianstr. 23 (☎56 15 01). Mountain bikes and hel- mets €20 per day, €16 per half-day. Open M-F 9am-6pm, Sa 9am-noon.

Tourist Office: Innsbruck Tourist Office, Burggraben 3, 3rd fl. (☎53 56), off Museum- str. Sells the **Innsbruck Card,** which grants unlimited access to public transportation and most museums. 1-day card €21, 2-day €26, 3-day €31. Open daily 9am-6pm.

Emergency: Police: ☎133. **Ambulance:** ☎144 or 142. **Fire:** ☎122. **Mountain Res- cue:** ☎140.

Internet Access: International Telephone Discount, Bruneckstr. 12 (☎59 42 72 61). Turn right from the Hauptbahnhof; it's on the left, just past the end of Südtirolerpl. €0.90 per min. Open daily 9am-11pm.

Post Office: Maximilianstr. 2 (☎500 79 00). Open M-F 7am-9pm, Sa 7am-3pm, Su 10am-8pm. **Postal Code:** A-6010.

Innsbruck

🏠 **ACCOMMODATIONS**
Camping Innsbruck
Kranebitten, **8**
Gasthof Innbrücke, **5**
Hotel Fritz Prior-
Schwedenhaus (HI), **2**
Jugendherberge
Innsbruck (HI), **3**

🍎 **FOOD**
Dom, **1**
Noi Original Thaiküche, **4**
Salute Pizzeria, **6**
Theresianbräu, **7**

Alpenzoo

Waltherpark

Herreng.

Dom St. Jakob

Herzog-Otto-Str.

Inn

Rennweg

Badg.

Pfarrg.

Helblinghaus

Hofburg

Goldenes
Dachl

Maximaleneum

Hofg.

Hotel
Goldener
Adler

Stadtturm

Rieseng.

Hofkirche

Tiroler
Volkskunst-
museum

Herzog-
Friedrich-Str.

Kiebachg.

Schlosserg.

Seilerg.

Markgraben

Burggraben

Stiftg.

Weiherburgg.

Hoher Weg

Inn

Rennweg

✝ St. Nikolas

Innstr.

Inngstg.

Walterpark

St.-Nikolaus-G.

Karl-Kapferer-Str.

Elisabethstr.

Kaiserjägerstr.

Falkstr.

Claudiastr.

Schillerstr.

TO ❸
(1.5km)

Bienerstr.

Siebererstr.

Kochstr.

Herzog-Otto-Str.

HÖTTING

Höttingerg.

Congress

Landestheater

UK

Hofgarten

Kapuziner-
kirche

Etzel Str.

Jahnstr.

Kärntnerstr.

**BRÜCKEN-
PLATZ**

Dreiheiligenstr.

Universitätsstr.

Mariahilfstr.

Inn
Brücke

Hofburg

Angerzellg.

Meinhardstr.

Sillg.

Ingenieur

Weinhartstr.

König Laurin Str.

Sill

PRADL

Pradlerstr.

Höttinger Au

Inn

Herzog-Siegmund Ufer

Volksgarten

See
Inset

ℹ

Burggraben

M-Preis

Museumstr.

Stadt
Park

Komstr.

Universitäts-
brücke

Innrain

Burgerstr.

❻

Bubblepoint
Waschsalon

Hertz

Bruneckerstr.

Amraserstr.

Brixner-Hueber-Str.

Meraner Str.

Erlerstr.

BOZNERPL

Brixnerstr.

Hunoldstr.

Silluler

Sill

Anton Eder-Str.

**University
Library**

Anichstr.

Kaiser Josef Str.

Stainerstr.

Landhaus

ÖAV

W.-Greil-Str.

Adamg.

**SÜDTI-
ROLERPL**

Haupt-
bahnhof

Anzengruberstr.

TO HOMOSEXUELLE
INITIATIVE TIROL (2km)

Maximilianstr.

M-Preis

❼

Salurnerstr.

Denzel Cars

Sport Neuner

Triumphpforte

Heiliggeiststr.

Müllerstr.

Templstr.

Andreas-Hofer-Str.

Speckbacherstr.

Schöpfstr.

Peter-Mayr-Str.

Fritz-Pregl-Str.

Michael-Gaismayr-Str.

Frauenzentrum
Innsbruck

Liebenggstr.

Leopoldstr.

Südbahnstr.

Olympiastr.

Olympic Ice
Stadium

WILTEN

Neuhauserstr.

Franz-Fischer-Str.

Westfriedhof

Stafflerstr.

Olympiabrücke

Egger-Lienz-Str.

Tschamlerstr.

Anton Melzer Str.

Fritz Konzert-Str.

Grassmayr
Bell-Foundry

Karwendel Str.

Feldstr.

0   200 yards

0   200 meters

Westbahnhof

Pastorstr.

Basilika
Wilten ✝

Stiftskirche
Wilten ✝

TO ❽ (5km)

TO SCHLOß AMBRAS (2km)

Autobahn A12

A12

AUSTRIA

ACCOMMODATIONS

Budget accommodations are scarce in June, when some hostels close. The opening of student dorms to backpackers in July and August somewhat alleviates the crunch. Visitors can join the free **Club Innsbruck** at any Innsbruck accommodation; membership gives discounts on skiing, tours, and the club's hiking program.

Hostel Fritz Prior-Schwedenhaus (HI), Rennweg 17b (☎58 58 14; www.tirol.com/youth-hostel). From the station, take bus #4 to Handelsakademie, continue to the end and across Rennweg to the river. Spacious rooms with private bath. Sheets €2.10. Reception daily 7-9:30am and 5-10:30pm. Check-in before 6pm. Curfew 10:30pm, but with a key guests can stay out later. Open July-Aug. and late Dec.-early Jan. Dorms €10; doubles €28; triples €41.25. ❷

Jugendherberge Innsbruck (HI), Reichenauer Str. 147 (☎34 61 79). Take tram #3 to Sillpark and bus O to Jugendherberge. Bare-bones rooms with locking closets. Bikes €11 per day. Breakfast included. Reception daily 5-10pm. 6-bed dorms €15; 4-bed dorms €17; singles with shower €28; doubles with shower €41. Nonmembers add €3. ❷

Gasthof Innbrücke, Innstr. 1 (☎28 19 34). From the Altstadt, cross the Innbrücke. The 575-year-old inn has a riverside and mountain view. Breakfast included. Singles €28, with shower €36; doubles €47/€62; quads €110. MC/V. ❸

Camping Innsbruck Kranebitten, Kranebitter Allee 214 (☎28 41 80). Take bus O to Technik and then bus LK to Klammstr. Walk downhill to the right. Pleasant grounds in the shadow of a snow-capped mountain. Restaurant open 8-11am and 4pm-midnight. Showers included. If reception is closed, find a site and check in the next morning. €5.50 per adult, €3.50 per child; €3 per tent; €3 per car. Bike rental €5 per day. ❶

FOOD

The delis on Maria-Theresien-Str. are good but overpriced. Cross the Inn River to Innstr., in the university district, for ethnic restaurants and cheap pizzerias. There are **M-Preis** supermarkets at Museumstr. 34 and across from the train station. (Open M-F 7:30am-6:30pm, Sa 7:30am-5pm.)

Theresianbräu, Maria-Theresien-Str. 51, is built around giant copper brewing kettles. Try the dark house lager (0.5L stein €3.30) alongside traditional Austrian meals. Open M-W 10:30am-1am, Th-Sa 10:30am-2am, Su 10:30am-midnight. MC/V. ❷

Noi Original Thaiküche, Kaiserjägerstr. 1. Cooks up Thai soups (€4.20-9) and spicy dishes from the wok (€8-11). Open M-F 11:30am-3pm and 6-11pm, Sa 5-11pm. ❷

Salute Pizzeria, Innrain 35, on the side of the street farthest from the river. A popular student hangout. Some of the best and least expensive pizza in town (€3-8). Salads €3-4.50. Pasta €4.50-6.50. Open 11am-midnight. ❷

Dom, Pfarrg. 3. Located in the heart of the Altstadt and diagonally across from the cathedral, this restaurant-cafe offers light fare. Soups €3.10. Salads €4-8. Sandwiches €2.40-5. Wide selection of ice cream desserts €2-4.30. The arched ceilings and red interior give this place the feel of a wine cellar. Open daily 11am-2am. AmEx/MC/V. ❶

SIGHTS

THE OLD TOWN. The Altstadt is a cobbled mix of old buildings, churches, and museums on the river. Its centerpiece is the **Goldenes Dachl** (Golden Roof) on Herzog Friedrichstr., a gold-shingled balcony honoring Maximilian. The nearby *Helbinghaus* is graced with pale-green floral detail and intricate stucco work. Its contemporary, Hotel Goldener Adler (Golden Eagle Inn), has hosted Camus, Goethe, Mozart, Sartre, and Wagner. Innsbruck's most distinctive street is **Maria-Theresien-Straße,** which begins at the edge of the Altstadt and runs south. At its far end stands the Triumphpforte (Triumphal Arch), built in 1765 after the betrothal of Emperor Leopold II. Up the street, the Annasäule (Anna Column) commemorates the Tyroleans' victory against the Bavarians on St. Anne's Day, 1703.

DOM ST. JAKOB. The *Dom's* unassuming gray facade conceals a riot of pink-and-white High Baroque ornamentation within. *Trompe-l'oeil* ceiling murals depict the life of St. James. The cathedral's prized possession is the small altar painting of *Our Lady of Succor* by Lukas Cranach the Elder. *(1 block behind the Goldenes Dachl. Open daily Apr.-Sept. 7:30am-7:30pm; Oct.-Mar. 8am-6:30pm. Free.)*

HOFBURG. The imperial palace was built in 1460 but completely remodeled under Maria Theresia. Imposing furniture, large portraits, and elaborate chandeliers fill the rooms. Don't miss the gilded Augusta Family tableau in the Audience Room, depicting the whole Habsburg gang in gold medallions. *(Behind the Dom St. Jakob. Open daily 9am-5pm. €5.45, students €3.63. English guidebook €1.82.)*

HOFKIRCHE. Twenty-eight statues of saints and emperors line the nave, and the elegant Silver Chapel holds the tomb of Archduke Ferdinand II. *(In the Volkskunstmuseum building. Open July-Aug. daily 9am-5:30pm; Sept.-June M-Sa 9am-5pm, Su noon-5pm.)*

HOFGARTEN. The imperial garden is complete with ponds, a concert pavilion, and an oversize chess set with 1m-tall pieces. *(Walk down Museumstr. toward the river, turning right onto Burggraben and continuing as it becomes Rennweg. Open daily 6am-10:30pm. Free.)*

■ ◢ HIKING AND SKIING

A ◧**Club Innsbruck** membership lets you in on one of the best deals in Austria. The club's excellent and popular **hiking** program provides free guides, transportation, and equipment (including boots). To hike on your own, take the J bus to Patscherkofel Seilbahnen (20min.). The lift provides access to moderate 1½-5hr. hikes near the summit of the Patscherkofel. (Open in winter 9am-4pm; summer 9am-5pm. Round-trip €15.) For more challenging hikes, head to the lifts ferrying passengers to the **Nordkette** mountains. Those interested in flying should check out Innsbruck-Information, which has a €95 **paragliding** package, including transport and equipment. For Club-led **ski excursions,** take the free ski shuttle (schedules at the tourist office) to any cable car. The **Innsbruck Gletscher Ski Pass** (available at all cable cars) is valid for all 60 lifts in the region (with Club Innsbruck membership: 3-day €87, 6-day €150). The tourist office also rents **ski equipment** (€9-18 per day). One day of winter glacier skiing costs €32. Both branches of **Innsbruck-Information,** Burggraben 3, offer summer ski packages (bus, lift, and rental €49).

◪ DAYTRIP FROM INNSBRUCK:SCHLOß AMBRAS

In the late 16th century, Ferdinand II transformed a hunting lodge into one of Austria's most beautiful castles, **Schloß Ambras.** Don't miss the famous **Spanischer Saal** (Spanish Room) and the **Habsburg Portrait Gallery** (summer only). The **gardens** outside vary from manicured shrubs to forested hillsides. (From Innsbruck, take the Sightseer bus from the Arch on Maria-Theresien-Str. (20min., €1. 60), or take tram #3 or 6 (dir.: Igls) to Schloß Ambras (20min., €1.60). Schloßstr. 20. Open Apr.-Oct. daily 10am-5pm; Nov.-Mar. closed Tu. €8; students and seniors €6. Tours €2; reservations required for tours in English.)

KITZBÜHEL   ☎ 05356

Kitzbühel's **Ski Circus** is one of the best ski areas in the world. A one-day **ski pass** (€33) or a three- or six-day summer **vacation pass** (€35/€48) include all 64 lifts and the shuttles that connect them; purchase either at any lift. In the summer, 77 **hiking trails** snake up the mountains; trail maps are free at the tourist office. **Trains** leave from the Hauptbahnhof for Innsbruck (1hr., 1 per 2hr., €12); Salzburg (2½hr., 9 per day, €21) and Vienna (6hr., 3 per day, €42). To reach the *Fußgängerzone* (pedestrian zone) from the Hauptbahnhof, head straight down Bahnhofstr.; turn left at the main road, go right at the traffic light, and follow the road uphill. The **tourist office,** Hinterstadt 18, is by the Rathaus in the *Fußgängerzone*. (☎ 62 15 50. Open July-Aug. and Christmas to mid-Mar. M-F 8:30am-6:30pm, Sa 9am-6pm, Su 10am-6pm; Nov.-Christmas and mid-Mar. to June M-F 8:30am-12:30pm and 2:30-6pm, Sa 8:30am-noon.) Snag a free **guest card,** which provides guided hikes (June-Oct. M-F 8:45am) and tours (M 10am) in English. Consider staying at **Pension Hörl ❷,** Joseph-Schmidlstr. 60. From Hotel Kaiser, turn left onto Joseph-Schmidlstr. (☎ 631 44. Breakfast included. Singles €20-25.) **Postal Code:** A-6370.

STYRIA (STEIERMARK)

Many of southern Austria's folk traditions live on in this, "The Green Heart of Austria." Even its largest city, Graz, remains relatively untouristed. The crumbling medieval strongholds and Lipizzaner stallions are among the region's notable attractions. The Styrian vineyards are also essential to any wine tour of Europe.

GRAZ   ☎ 0316

The second largest of Austria's cities, Graz (pop. 226,000) also offers an under-touristed Altstadt and an energetic nightlife thanks to 45,000 university students.

▣ ▨ TRANSPORTATION AND PRACTICAL INFORMATION. From the Hauptbahnhof, **trains** run to: Innsbruck (5-6hr., 7 per day, €44); Munich (6¼hr., 4 per day, €63); Salzburg (4¼hr., €37); Vienna Südbahnhof (2½hr., 19 per day, €27); and Zurich (10hr., 2 per day, €74). From the train station, go down Annenstr. and cross the main bridge to reach **Hauptplatz,** the city center. Five minutes away is **Jakominiplatz,** the hub of the public transportation system. **Herren-**

PAYING HOMAGE TO HANGOVERS

There is more than enough homebrew in Zell am Ziller to keep every resident feeling tipsy for months. The town is home to the Zillertal Bier factory, and every May its inhabitants pay homage to their local brewery with a weekend of drunken festivities. The Braumeister's vats, Tyrol's oldest, concoct the beloved and potent *Gauderbock* especially for the occasion. The celebration even has its own jingle: *Gauderwurst und G'selchts mit Kraut / hai, wia taut dosmunden / und 10 Halbe Bockbier dauf / mehr braucht's nit zum G'sundsein!* (Gauder sausage and smoked pork with sauerkraut / hey, how good it tastes / and 10 pints of beer to go with it / what more could you need for your health!)

One of the highlights of the festival is the Ranggein, a type of traditional wrestling cheered on by an exctited, and more-than-somewhat sloshed, group of revelers. Though wrestlers used to challenge animals like pigs, sheep, and goats, today they only pick on animals of their own species.

On Sunday, the entire town dons their best *lederhosen* and most colorful dresses—called "*trachten*"—for the concluding parade, the *Trachtenumzug.* Everyone marches behind "Gaudl," the spirit of the Gauderfest clad in the traditional (electric pink and blue) duds while riding in style high atop a giant vat of Zillertal Beer.

gasse, a pedestrian street lined with cafes and boutiques, connects the two squares. The **university** is tucked away past the Stadtpark, in the northeastern part of Graz. The **tourist office**, Herreng. 16, has free maps and a walking tour. The staff offers English-language **tours** of the Altstadt (2hr.; Apr.-Oct. Tu-W and F-Su 2:30pm; €7.50) and books rooms for free. (☎807 50. Open June-Sept. M-F 9am-7pm, Sa 9am-6pm, Su 10am-6pm; Oct.-May M-Sa 9am-6pm, Su 10am-6pm.) **Postal Code:** A-8010.

▐▐ ▐ ACCOMMODATIONS AND FOOD. In Graz, most accommodations are pricey and far from the city center. Luckily, local transportation provides an easy commute to the outlying neighborhoods. To reach **░Jugendgästehaus Graz (HI) ❸**, Idlhofg. 74, from the station, cross the street, head right on Eggenberger Gürtel, turn left on Josef-Huber-G., then take the first right; the hostel is through the parking lot on your right. Buses #31 and 32 run from Jakominipl. (☎71 48 76. All rooms with bath. Breakfast included. Laundry €2. Internet €1.50 per 20min. Reception daily 7am-11pm. 4-bed dorms €17; singles €24; doubles €40. MC/V.) **Hotel Strasser ❸**, Eggenberger Gürtel 11, is 5min. from the train station. Exit, cross the street, and head right on Eggenberger Gürtel. (☎71 39 77. Breakfast included. Singles €29, with shower €36; doubles €45/€54; triples with shower €65. AmEx/MC/V.) Find an inexpensive meal on **Hauptplatz**, where concession stands sell sandwiches, *Wurst* (€2-3), and other fast food. Cheap student hangouts line **Zinzendorfgasse** near the university. **Braun de Praun ❹**, Morellenfeldg. 32, is unafraid of a little culinary experimentation. (☎32 20 03. Open M-Sa 8am-2am. AmEx/MC/V.)

▣ ▐ SIGHTS AND NIGHTLIFE. The tourist office, in the **Landhaus**, is a sight in itself; the building was remodeled in the Lombard style by architect Domenico dell'Allio in 1557. The **Landeszeughaus** (Provincial Arsenal), Herreng. 16, details the history of Ottoman attacks on the arsenal and has enough spears, muskets, and armor to outfit 28,000 mercenaries. (Open Apr.-Oct. Tu-Su 10am-6pm, Th 10am-8pm; Nov.-Mar. Tu-Su 10am-3pm. €1.40.) North of Hauptpl., the wooded **Schloßberg** (Castle Mountain) rises 123m above Graz. Climb the zig-zagging stone steps of the **Schloßbergstiege**, built by WWI prisoners, for views of the Styrian plain. The newest addition to the Graz riverscape is the **Murinsel**, shaped like a mussel shell; it houses a cafe, open-air theater, and playground. The magnificent **Opernhaus** was built in less than two years by Viennese architects Fellner and Helmer. *(At Opernring and Burgg., down the street from the mausoleum.* ☎80 08.*)* The hub of after-hours activity is the so-called **Bermuda Triangle**, an area of the old city behind Hauptpl. and bordered by Mehlpl., Färberg., and Prokopig. Check out **Kulturhauskeller**, Elisabethstr. 30, where dance music throbs all night. (19+. Cover €2. Open Tu-Sa 9pm-late.)

▐ DAYTRIP FROM GRAZ: LIPIZZANER STUD FARM. One kilometer outside the town of Köflach is the **Gestüt Piber** (Piber Stud Farm), home to the world-famous **Lipizzaner** horses, whose snow-white coats are the pride of the Spanish Riding School in Vienna. (☎03144 33 23. Open daily Apr.-Oct. 9am-5:30pm. €11, students €6.) Take the **train** from Graz (50min., 8 per day 5:26am-1:40pm, €5.40), then the **bus** (€1.60) to Piber. Sign up at the tourist office in Graz for a ride and English-language tour. (Sa 2pm. €24, children €9.)

BELARUS (БЕЛАРУСЬ)

Flattened by the Germans during WWII, then exploited by the Soviets until 1990, Belarus has become the unwanted stepchild of Mother Russia. While the concrete high-rises of the capital, Minsk, still evoke the glory days of the USSR, the untouched villages of the countryside harken back to an earlier era of agricultural beauty. For those willing to endure the difficulties of travel in Belarus, the country presents a unique look at a people in transition.

ESSENTIALS

DOCUMENTS AND FORMALITIES

VISAS. Visitors to Belarus need a visa, an invitation, and medical insurance. With an **official invitation** from an acquaintance, from an embassy or consulate you can obtain a single-entry (US$100), double-entry (US$200), triple-entry (US$300), or multiple-entry (US$350) visa. Rush service adds to costs. **SMOK Travel** (www.smoktravel.com) and **Alatan Tour** (www.alatantour.com) offer invitations and visa services. **Transit**

visas (US$20), valid for 48 hours, are issued at consulates and at the border. Belarus requires travelers to purchase **medical insurance** at the port of entry, whatever their separate policies. Costs vary with the length of the stay. Be sure to register your passport within three business days at the nearest **Passport and Visa Office** of the Ministry of the Interior; hotel receptions can take care of this.

EMBASSIES. Foreign embassies are in Minsk (p. 119). Embassies at home include: **Canada,** 130 Albert St., Ste. 600, Ottawa, ON K1P 5G4 (☎613-233-9994; belamb@iqs.net); **Ireland** and the **UK,** 6 Kensington Ct., London, W8 5DL (☎0171 938 3677; www.belemb.freeserve.co.uk); **US,** 1619 New Hampshire Ave. NW, Washington, D.C. 20009 (☎202-986-1606; www.belarusembassy.org).

TRANSPORTATION

The national airline, **Belavia** (www.belavia.by), flies into Minsk from many European capitals; Lufthansa also offers daily flights from Frankfurt. Minsk's airport, **Minsk-II,** now meets international safety standards. Some international train tickets must be paid partly in Belarussian rubles (see below); **Eurail** is not valid. All immigration and customs formalities are performed on the trains. **Trains** and **buses** transit between Minsk and most European capitals, the Baltic states, and CIS countries. **Taxis** can be run-down and often overcharge. The E30 highway runs from Paris through Berlin, Warsaw, and Brest to Minsk, and then on to Moscow.

TOURIST SERVICES AND MONEY

EMERGENCY	**Police:** ☎02. **Ambulance:** ☎03. **Fire:** ☎01.

Belintourist (p. 121) is a helpful resource. **Hotel Belarus** in Minsk has a private travel agency. **Traveler's checks** are rarely accepted, and outside Minsk there are few **ATMs.** Belarus's national currency is the **Belarussian ruble (BR),** but Russian rubles, euros, and US dollars may be preferred. Other currencies are difficult to exchange. Posted prices often omit the final three zeros; *Let's Go* prices follow that convention, and because **inflation** is rampant, many prices are listed in US dollars.

BEL. RUBLES (BR)		
AUS$1 = 1546.58BR		1000BR = AUS$0.65
CDN$1 = 1642.06BR		1000BR = CDN$0.61
EUR€1 = 2654.80BR		1000BR = EUR€0.38
NZ$1 = 1411.12BR		1000BR = NZ$0.71
UK£1 = 3983.27BR		1000BR = UK£0.25
US$1 = 2164.16BR		1000BR = US$0.46

COMMUNICATION

PHONE CODES	**Country code: 375. International dialing prefix: 810.** From outside Belarus, dial int'l dialing prefix (see inside back cover) + 375 + city code + local number.

Avoid the **postal system**—almost everything is opened by the authorities and mail is often discarded. Local calls require **tokens** sold at kiosks or **magnetic cards,** available at the post office and some hotels (from 1500BR). International calls must be placed at the telephone office and paid for in advance in cash. Calls to the US and Western Europe tend to cost from US$1-3 per minute. International access numbers include **AT&T Direct** (☎8800 101), **Canada Direct** (☎8800 111), **MCI WorldPhone** (☎8800 103), **NZ Direct** (☎8800 641), and **Sprint** (☎8800 102). After entering the first 8, wait for a second dial tone. Post offices may offer **Internet** access; email is usually the best way to communicate across the border. **Belarussian** is the official language; it helps to have some familiarity with the **Cyrillic alphabet** (p. 1057).

ACCOMMODATIONS AND FOOD

BELARUS	❶	❷	❸	❹	❺
ACCOMMODATIONS	under US$12	US$12-20	US$20-28	US$28-55	over US$55
FOOD	under US$2	US$2-5	US$5-10	US$10-20	over US$20

Keep all receipts from **hotels;** when exiting the country, you may have to produce them to avoid fines. For foreigners, hotel prices are outrageous. To find a **private room,** look for postings at stations, or ask taxi drivers. Older women at train stations will usually feed and house you for US$10 or less. Belarus has limited facilities for **camping** but permits it anywhere in the countryside. **Cuisine** consists of whatever farmers can grow or fatten: potatoes, bread, chicken, and pork.

SAFETY AND SECURITY

Medical care is inadequate at best. Due to a shortage of basic health supplies—antibiotics, vaccines, and anesthetics—travelers with **existing health problems** are at high risk. In a **medical emergency,** try to make it to the nearest major city in Western Europe. A medical evacuation to the United States may cost up to US$50,000. Nearly two decades after the 1986 **Chernobyl** accident, it is often possible to travel through formerly contaminated areas; nonetheless, avoid cheap Belarussian dairy products, mushrooms, berries, and **tap water.**

HOLIDAYS

New Year's Day (Jan. 1); Orthodox Christmas (Jan. 7); International Women's Day (Mar. 8); Constitution Day (Mar. 15); Easter (Mar. 27); Good Friday (Apr. 9); Orthodox Easter/Labor Day (May 1); Victory Day (May 9); Independence Day (July 3); Remembrance Day (Nov. 2); October Revolution Day (Nov. 7); Christmas (Dec. 25).

FACTS AND FIGURES: BELARUS

Official Name: Republic of Belarus.
Capital: Minsk.
Major Cities: Brest, Gomel, Hrodna.
Population: 10,311,000.

Land Area: 207,600 sq. km.
Time Zone: GMT +2.
Language: Belarussian, Russian.
Religion: Orthodox (80%).

BELARUS

MINSK (MИHCK)　　　　　☎8017

Moscow is less a true Soviet city than Minsk (pop. 1,800,000), which was rebuilt after WWII in the "grand" Stalinist style: surreal cityscapes of gray concrete highrises towering over flat expanses. Superficially, little may have changed since the dissolution of the USSR, but in his decade of leadership President Lukashenka has improved transportation and cleaned up the streets. Now, at night, lights cast a soft glow over the monuments of the city center in a display of Belarussian pride.

Svislach

Peramohi Park

Varvaseni

Varvaseni

Very Kharuzay

Maksima Bagdanovica

Krapotkina

Kvrtubysheva

vul. Kulman

Laundromat

TO CENTRAL STORE (50m)

■ Hero-City Monument

2

Kahatny

Kamunistychnaya

Starazhenskaya

Starazhenskaya

Cyceryna

Varvaseni

PL. YAKUBA KOLASA M

Belinturist

i

Pr. Masherava

3

Zaslaŭskaya
Jewish
Memorial ■

Carlson Wagonlit

i

Island
of Tears

OLD
TOWN

Opera and
Ballet

Maksima Bogdanovica

Kisialeva

Franciska Skaryny

St. Rokha
Cathedral

OVIR

M

PL.
PERAMOHI
(VICTORY SQ.)

i

vul. Zolotaja Gorke

M

Palace of
Sports

Paddle Boat
Rental

Kamunistychnaya

M

PL. PERAMOHI

Carlson
Wagonlit

i

Maksima Tanka

Melnikate

Spalernaya

Cathedral of
St. Peter and Paul

NYAMIHA

M

M FRUNZENSKAYA

M

Romanovskaya Sloboda

Rakovskaya

Rakovskaya

Nyamiha

Maryinsky
Cathedral

Cathedral of
the Holy Spirit

PL.
SVABODY

Janki Kupaly

Janki-
Kupaly Park

Paddle Boat
Rental

Circus

Gorky
Park

Karava

Kalektarnaya

Miasnikova

Haradski Val

Town
Hall

Revalucijnaya

Internacianalnaya

Kamsamolskaya

4

PL.
KASTRYCHNITSKAYA

Museum of the
Great Patriotic War

PL.

KUPALAVSKAYA/
KASTRYTCHINSKAYA
(JUNCTION)

M

Kirava

Persamayskaya

Azgura

Siesamaya

Pulihava

Chyrvonaarmeyskaya

Nyamiha

Barsa na B.

Central Ticket Office ■

Frantsishka Skaryny

Church of
St. Simon

R

Sudzdaskaya

Karla Marksa

S

5

UK

National Arts
Museum

Kirava

Pr. Lenina

Enhersa

Svislach

PL. NEZALEZHNASTSI
(INDEPENDENCE
SQUARE)

Savetskaya

Leningradskaya

Kirava

Stad.
Dynamo

PERSHAMAYSKAYA

M

PL.
NEZALEZHNASTSI

M

PRIVAKZALNAYA
PL.

Uljanaskaya

M USKHOD

Kastrysniskaya

PRALETARSKAYA

M

Maskavskaya

Talstoho

Druznaya

Rabkorauskaya

Vakzalnaya

Belarussian
Polytechnical
University

Babrujskaya

Sverdlova

Belaruskaya

INSTITUT
KULTURY

Mahileuskaya

Oranskaha

Partizansky

TO 🏛 (3km)

TO MIR CASTLE (90km),
STATE MUSEUM OF FOLK
ARCHITECTURE AND PEASANT LIFE (15km)

TO
MINSK II AIRPORT (50km)
& MINSK I AIRPORT (3km)

Mahileuskaya

Minsk

🏠 ACCOMMODATIONS
Gastsinitsa Tourist, 6
Gastsinitsa Yubileny, 3
Hotel Belarus, 2

🍎 FOOD
Grill-Bar Pechki-Lavochki, 5
Krinitsa, 4

📻 NIGHTLIFE
Reactor Disco, 1

BELARUS

▮▮ TRANSPORTATION AND PRACTICAL INFORMATION. Trains run from Chigunachny Vokzal (Чыгуначны Вокзал; info ☎ 005), on pl. Privakzalnaya, to: Brest (3-5hr., 8 per day, 15,000BR); Hrodna (6-9hr., 2-3 per day, 19,000BR); Kyiv (12hr., 9:07pm, 42,000BR); Moscow (10-11hr., 15 per day, 38,000BR); St. Petersburg (12hr., 2 per day, 41,350BR); and Vilnius (4hr., 3 per day, 25,000BR). Tickets are sold on the first floor of the station and at Belinturist (see below). **Buses** run from Avtovakzal Tsentralny (Автовакзал Центральны; info ☎ 004), vul. Babruyskaya 6 (Бабруйская), by the train station, to Hrodna (4-5 hr., 2-3 per hr., 22,000BR) and Vilnius (4hr., 4 per day, 12,000BR). To reach the city center, walk up vul. Leningradskaya from the square, turn left on Sverdlova (Свердлова) to pl. Nezalezhnastsi, and continue down pr. F. Skaryny. **Belinturist** (Белінтурíст), pr. Masherava 19, next to Gastsinitsa Yubileny, has general info in English. (☎ 226 90 56; www.belintourist.by. M-red: Nyamiha. Ticket office open M-Sa 8am-1pm.) **Embassies: UK,** vul. Karla Marksa 37 (Карла Маркса; ☎ 210 59 20; fax 229 23 11; open M-F 9am-1pm and 2-5:30pm); **US,** vul. Staravilenskaya 46 (☎ 210 12 83; fax 234 78 53; open M-F 8:30am-5:30pm). Apteka 13, a **pharmacy,** is at pr. F. Skaryny 16. (Open 24hr.; ring bell for late-night service.) **Ekomedservis** (Эломедсервис), at vul. Talstoho 4 (Толстого), is a hospital. (☎ 207 74 74; **ambulance** toll-free 003.) Add an initial "2" to numbers listed in six digits. Check email and make phone calls at **Beltelekom** (Белтелеком), vul. Engelsa 14. (☎ 219 06 79; www.beltelecom.by. Internet 1200BR per 30min. Open 24hr.)

▮▮ ACCOMMODATIONS AND FOOD. Gastsinitsa Yubileny ❹, pr. Masherava 19, next to Belinturist, is clean and centrally located. (☎ 226 90 56; www.belintourist.by. Breakfast included. ATM outside. Currency exchange in the lobby. Singles with bath US$50; doubles US$65.) **Hotel Belarus ❹,** vul. Storozhevskaya 15, is a 22-story hotel with over 500 rooms, located along the Svislach riverside near the Nyamiha metro station. (☎ 209 76 93; www.hotel-belarus.com. Rooms in two classes: singles US$46/$86; doubles US$60/$90.) Somewhat distant from the center but conveniently located near M: Partizanskaya is **Gastsinitsa Tourist ❹,** pr. Partizansky 81, a typical Soviet-style cement block hotel. (☎ 295 40 31. Breakfast included. Singles 70,000BR; doubles 120,000BR. First night costs an additional 10,000BR for visa registration.) Serving outstanding Belarussian specialties, ▰**Krinitsa ❷** (Криница), vul. Lenina 2, is between M-red/blue: Kupalavskaya and Nyamiha. (Entrees 5000-8000BR. Cheaper lunch menus M-F noon-4pm for 5600-6660BR. Open daily noon-midnight.) Watch chefs prepare your food on a flaming grill at **Grill-Bar Pechki-Lavochki ❸** (Печки-Лавочки), F. Skaryny 22, near M-red/blue: Pl. Kastrylchitskaya. (☎ 227 78 79. Entrees 8000-25,000BR. Open daily 8am-midnight.) At night, check out **Reactor Disco,** vul. Very Kharuzay 29, up the street from M: Pl. Yakuba Kolasa. (Open daily noon-6am.)

▮▮ SIGHTS AND ENTERTAINMENT. After the obliteration of most of Minsk in WWII, the city was rebuilt under the influence of Stalin. The crimson **Church of St. Simon,** Savetskaya 15, stands behind a statue of the saint slaying a dragon. The **Jewish Memorial,** vul. Melnikaite (Мельникайте), commemorates 5000 Jews who were shot and buried there by the Nazis in 1942. (M-blue: Frunzenskaya; фрунзенская.) The **State Museum of Folk Architecture and Peasant Life** (Белоруский Государственный Музей Народной Архитектуры и Быта; Belorusskiy Gosudarstvennyy Muzey Narodnoy Arkhitektury i Byta) features a collection of nailless 17th-century houses and churches near the site of 9th-century Minsk. (M-blue: Institut Kultury. The museum is near the village Azyatso (Азяцо); take minibus #81 to Gorodishe and indicate "Muzey" to the driver. Open Tu-Sa 10am-4:30pm. 10,000BR.) The grim **Museum of the Great Patriotic War** (Музей Велíкой

Отечественной Войны; Muzey Velikoy Otechestvennoy Voyny), at pr. Skaryny 25a, M-red/blue: Kastrychnitskaya, has photographs from WWII and celebrates the heroism of the Soviet army. (Open Tu-Su 10am-5pm. 3000BR.) The **National Arts Museum** (Нацыянальны Мастацкі Музей Распублікі Беларусь; Natsyanalny Mastatski Muzey Raspubliki Belarus), pr. Lenina 20, exhibits Belarussian and Russian art and furniture. (M-red/blue: Kastrytchnitskaya. Open M and W-Su 11am-7pm. 5000BR.) Walk down vul. F. Skarny past the 40m obelisk in **Victory Square** to reach the **National Opera and Ballet Theater,** vul. Paryzhskai Kamuny 1 (Парыжскай Камуны), one of the best ballets in the former USSR. The season runs from late September to May. (M-blue: Nyamiha; Няміга. ☎234 06 66. 1000-10,000BR. Theater box office open Tu-Su 11:30am-7:30pm. Advance tickets available from the Central Ticket Office, pr. Skaryny 13. Open M-F 9:30am-8pm, Sa 10am-7pm, Su noon-5pm.)

🔁 DAYTRIP FROM MINSK: MIR CASTLE. Take a bus from Minsk to Mir (Мир; 2hr., 5500BR) and get off at Mirski Zamak (Мирски Замак; Mir Castle). Deep in the Belarussian countryside, the 16th-century **Mir Castle** is the only well-preserved castle in the country. It was begun on Gothic models by Duke Ilich in the early 16th century, but finished in the Renaissance style after the Radzivil family took control in 1568. Despite thick earthen ramparts and a moat, the castle was severely damaged by warfare several times; Napoleon's army savaged it in 1812. Luckily no one has yet removed the stone ram's head in the wall, which (as legend has it) keeps the castle from falling. Tall, tortuous stairs provide a glimpse into the castle's past: a small museum, located in one of the five towers, displays relics, including weapons, clay pots, coins, and traditionally embroidered garments. A panorama of the countryside—as seen through arrow-slits—greets those who ascend the tower. Guided tours are recommended, as much of the castle's beauty lies in its rich history. (Open W-Su. Guided tours 10,000BR. Museum 5000BR.)

BELGIUM
(BELGIQUE, BELGIË)

Tucked in between the two superpowers of Western Europe, Belgium can come off as little more than a pretty land bridge connecting France and Germany. And while Brussels does play an important role in connecting other nations as the seat of NATO and the European Union, neither Belgium nor its capital city wants for an identity of its own. Gothic towers crane their necks above the cobblestone squares of Flanders, while visitors below souse themselves on the canvases of Old Masters by day and the perfumed ales of hop-slinging monks by night. French-speaking Wallonie may not have a polished tourist shtick down pat yet, but the caves of the Lesse Valley and the forested trails of the Ardennes can speak for themselves.

 DISCOVER BELGIUM: SUGGESTED ITINERARIES

Plan for at least two days in **Brussels** (p. 127), the capital whose **Grand-Place** Victor Hugo called "the most beautiful square in the world." Head north to the elegant boulevards of **Antwerp** (p. 139) and the historic districts of **Ghent** (p. 140), then angle west to the winding streets and canals of romantic **Bruges** (p. 134). Connect to eastbound trains in the gritty university town of **Liège** (p. 142), or else take your time exploring the leafy Ardennes, using **Namur** (p. 143) as a base for hikes or bike rides into Belgium's rural south country.

ESSENTIALS

WHEN TO GO

May, June, and September may be the most appealing months to visit Belgium, since July and August tend to be humid and rainy, with temperatures hovering around 18-22°C (64-72°F). Winters are cloudy and cool, with temperatures aver-

Belgium

YOU SAY TOMATO...

As long as Belgium has called itself an independent nation, it has been governed by a French-speaking minority. By the mid-19th century, members of the urban literati had formed a "Flemish Movement" that agitated for the rights of Dutch speakers. One early victory was the passage of an 1873 law that guaranteed defendants who could not understand French the right to a Dutch-language trial. Early 20th-century activists became more interested in consolidating regional unity than in swaying all of Belgium, laying the groundwork for the 1963 "linguistic frontier" that froze the boundaries between Dutch-speaking Flanders and French-speaking Wallonie. Almost immediately, both sides accused each other of gerrymandering the borders to gain political clout, and a French-language university was even evicted from the city of Leuven for its "Frenchifying" influence on the Flemish community.

It was out of this historical and cultural context that the Flemish nationalist party Vlaams Blok emerged in 1978. Party leaders tapped into Walloon resentment over their region's flagging post-industrial economy, even as Flanders fine-tuned the tourist and high-tech industries that would catapult it to prosperity. In April 2004 a court in Ghent charged Vlaams Blok with sustained "incitement to segregation and racism," but less than two

aging 2-7°C (36-45°F), and somewhat colder in the eastern Ardennes. Bring a sweater and umbrella whenever you go.

DOCUMENTS AND FORMALITIES

VISAS. EU citizens do not need a visa. Citizens of Australia, Canada, New Zealand, and the US do not need a visa for stays of up to 90 days, although this three-month period begins upon entry into any of the countries that belong to the EU's freedom of movement zone. For more information, see p. 17.

EMBASSIES AND CONSULATES. All foreign embassies are in Brussels. For Belgian embassies at home: **Australia,** 19 Arkana St., Yarralumla, ACT 2600 (☎62 73 25 02; www.diplomatie.be/canberra); **Canada,** 360 Albert St., Ste. 820, Ottawa, ON K1R 7X7 (☎613-236-7267; www.diplobel.org/canada); **Ireland,** 2 Shrewsbury Rd., Ballsbridge, Dublin 4 (☎269 20 82; www.diplomatie.be/dublin); **UK,** 103-105 Eaton Sq., London SW1W 9AB (☎7470 3700; www.diplobel.org/uk/uk.htm); **US,** 3330 Garfield St. NW, Washington, D.C. 20008 (☎202-333-6900; www.diplobel.us). **New Zealanders** should contact the Belgian Honorary Consul for Auckland (☎915 91 50; imackenzie@farrow-jamieson.co.nz), or the Australian embassy.

TRANSPORTATION

BY PLANE. Several major airlines fly into **Brussels** from Europe, North America, and Australia. The recently reconstituted **SN Brussels Airlines** (Belgium ☎070 35 11 11, UK 0870 735 2345; www.flysn.com) flies into Brussels from most major European cities, while budget airline **RyanAir** (☎353 1249 7851; www.ryanair.com) flies into Brussels South Charleroi Airport from across Europe.

BY TRAIN AND BUS. The extensive and reliable **Belgian Rail** (www.b-rail.be) network traverses the country. **Eurail** is valid in Belgium. A **Benelux Tourrail Pass** allows five days of unlimited train travel in a one-month period in Belgium, the Netherlands, and Luxembourg, and is discounted 33% for travelers under 26. Travelers who have time to explore the nooks and crannies of Belgium might consider the **Rail Pass** (€60), which allows 10 single trips within the country over a six-month period, though it is invalid in July, August, and on weekends. The similar **Go Pass** (€40) for travelers under 26 carries the same restrictions, and both passes may be used by more than one person. Because trains are so widely available, **buses** are used primarily for municipal transport (€1-2).

BY FERRY. P&O Ferries (UK ☎087 05 20 20 20, Belgium 027 10 64 44; www.poferries.com) cross the Channel from **Hull, England** to **Zeebrugge,** north of Bruges (11hr., departure at 7pm, from €140).

BY CAR, BIKE, AND THUMB. Belgium honors most foreign driver's licenses, including those from Australia, Canada, the EU, and the US. **New Zealanders** must contact the New Zealand Automobile Association (☎0800 822 422; www.aa.co.nz) for an International Driving Permit. **Speed limits** are 120kph on motorways, 90kph on main roads, and 50kph elsewhere. **Biking** is popular, and many roads in Flanders have dedicated bike lanes, while Wallonie has started to convert old railroad beds into paths for pedestrians and cyclists. **Hitchhiking** is both illegal and uncommon, and *Let's Go* does not recommend it as a safe means of transport.

EMERGENCY	Ambulance: ☎100. Fire: ☎100. Police: ☎101.

TOURIST SERVICES AND MONEY

TOURIST OFFICES. **Bureaux de Tourisme,** marked by green-and-white or blue signs labeled "i," are supplemented by **Infor-Jeunes/Info-Jeugd,** networks of youth information centers that help young people find work and secure accommodations in Wallonie and Flanders respectively.

MONEY. On January 1, 2002, the **euro (€)** replaced the **Belgian Franc** as the unit of currency in Belgium. For exchange rates and more info on the euro, see p. 20. A bare-bones day in Belgium might cost €25-35; a more comfortable day might cost €45-50. All countries who are members of the European Union impose a **Value Added Tax (VAT)** on goods and services purchased within the EU. Prices in Belgium already include the country's stiff 21% VAT rate, although partial refunds are available for visitors who are not EU citizens (p. 22). Restaurant bills usually include a service charge, although an extra 5-10% tip can be a classy gesture.

BUSINESS HOURS. **Banks** are generally open Monday through Friday 9am-4pm, but some break for lunch noon-2pm. **Stores** are open Monday to Saturday 10am to 6pm; in larger towns and cities, stores stay open Friday nights until 9pm. Most **sights** are closed Mondays except in Tournai, where museums close on Tuesday.

months later the party registered its strongest showing ever in regional elections. A net gain of 10 seats meant that Vlaams Blok would send 32 representatives to the 124-seat Flemish Parliament. While none of the more moderate parties have been willing to bring them into a coalition government, the Vlaams Blok delegation is still in a position to use their seats as a bully pulpit for expressing anti-French sentiments.

All of this means that 2005 is shaping up to be a tense year for Belgium. Level-headed scholars have long concluded that a deep-seated "conflict culture" around language is part and parcel of what it means to be Belgian. The real challenge, they maintain, is to find respectful, pluralistic ways to account for cultural differences without exploiting them for political gain. So when in the city of Brussels or the region of Flanders, English-speaking travelers should make a point of hailing locals in English, whether or not they also speak French. French will tend to get better results in Wallonie, although English and German are also worth a try. Just remember that if you are breakfasting at a cafe in Antwerp, the home base of Vlaams Blok, don't go trying to impress your waiter by ordering a *chocolat chaud;* you'll find yourself on the receiving end of a steely stare, and your *chocolat* may be decidedly *froid* by the time it finally arrives.

COMMUNICATION

TELEPHONES. Most public phones require a phone card (starting at €5), available at post offices, supermarkets, and magazine stands. Coin-operated phones are rare. Calls are cheapest from 6:30pm-8am and on weekends. Mobile phones are an increasingly popular and economical alternative (p. 35). For operator assistance within Belgium, dial ☎ 12 07; for international assistance, ☎ 12 04 (€0.25). International direct dial numbers include: **AT&T** (☎ 0800 100 10); **British Telecom** (☎ 0800 89 0032); **Canada Direct** (☎ 0800 100 19); **MCI** (☎ 0800 100 12); **Sprint** (☎ 0800 100 14); **Telecom New Zealand** (☎ 0800 100 64); **Telstra Australia** (☎ 0800 100 61).

MAIL. Most post offices open Monday to Friday 9am to 5pm (sometimes with a midday break), and some also open Saturdays from 9am to noon. A postcard or letter (up to 50g) sent to a destination within Belgium costs €0.44-0.50, within the EU €0.55-0.60, and to the rest of the world €0.65-0.80.

INTERNET ACCESS. There are cybercafes in the larger towns and cities in Belgium. For access to the Web, expect to pay €2-3 per 30min. Many hostels have Internet access for €0.08-0.10 per min.

LANGUAGES. Belgium is a nation of three official languages, each one clearly associated with a particular area and often with fierce regionalist sentiments as well. Flemish, a variant of Dutch, is spoken in Flanders, the northern half of the country; French is spoken in Wallonie, the southern region; German is spoken in a few districts east of Liège. Both Flemish and French are spoken in Brussels, and most people (especially in Flanders) speak English. For basic French words and phrases, see p. 1060; for German, see p. 1061.

PHONE CODES	**Country code: 32. International dialing prefix:** 00. From outside Belgium, dial int'l dialing prefix (see inside back cover) + city code + local number.

ACCOMMODATIONS AND CAMPING

BELGIUM	❶	❷	❸	❹	❺
ACCOMMODATIONS	under €10	€10-18	€18-25	€25-33	over €33

Hotels in Belgium are fairly expensive, with rock-bottom singles from €25 and doubles from €35-40. The country's 31 **HI youth hostels**, which charge about €15 per night, are generally modern and many boast cheap bars. **Private hostels,** however, often cost about the same but are much nicer. Most receptionists speak some English, and reservations are a good idea, particularly in the summer and on weekends. **Campgrounds** charge about €4 per night.

FOOD AND DRINK

BELGIUM	❶	❷	❸	❹	❺
FOOD	under €5	€5-8	€8-10	€10-15	over €15

Belgian cuisine, influenced by both France and Germany, is praised throughout Western Europe, although an authentic evening meal may cost as much as the night's accommodations. Moules or mosselen (steamed mussels), regarded as the national dish, are usually tasty and reasonably affordable (€14 is the cheapest, usually €17-20). Frites (french fries), get dipped into mayonnaise and consumed alongside plates of mussels. Belgian beer is both a source of national pride and a national pastime; the country produces over 300 varieties, ranging from ordinary pilsners (€1) to religiously brewed Trappist ales (€3). Sample chocolate pralines from Leonidas, and leave room for Belgian waffles (*gaufres*)—soft, warm, glazed ones on the street (€1.50) and thin, crispier ones piled high with toppings at cafes (€2-5). See p. 131 for a guide to the best waffle destinations in Brussels.

HOLIDAYS AND FESTIVALS

Holidays: New Year's Day (Jan. 1); Easter (Mar. 27); Easter Monday (Mar. 28); Labor Day (May 1); Feast of the Ascension (May 5); Whit Sunday and Monday (May 15-16); Flemish Community Holiday (July 11); National Holiday (July 21); Feast of the Assumption (Aug. 15); French Community Holiday (Sept. 27); All Saints Day (Nov. 1); Armistice Day (Nov. 11); Christmas (Dec. 25).

Festivals: Ghent hosts the Gentse Feesten cultural festival, which includes live music, street theater, and the dance party 10 Days Off (July 16-25). Antwerp runs open-air films throughout Aug. as part of its summer-long Zomer van Antwerpen festival. Music events include Bruges's up-and-coming Cactusfestival (mid-July) as well as eastern Belgium's Pukkelpop (late Aug.) for the alternative set. Dinant draws in visitors with the delightfully ramshackle International Bathtub Regatta (mid-Aug.).

FACTS AND FIGURES: BELGIUM

Official Name: Kingdom of Belgium.

Capital: Brussels.

Major Cities: Antwerp, Ghent, Liège.

Population: 10,350,000.

Land Area: 30,000 sq. km.

Time Zone: GMT +1.

Language: Flemish and French; pockets of German in the east.

Religions: Roman Catholic (75%).

BRUSSELS (BRUXELLES, BRUSSEL) ☎02

As the city that headquarters both NATO and the EU, Brussels (pop. 1,200,000) has become known for its white-collar population of earnest, terminally bland functionaries. Yet these civil servants aren't the only ones who speak for Belgium's capital, and beneath the drone of parliamentary procedure you'll hear the witty clamor of local life if you listen closely. These voices echo throughout the city's architecture, alternately Gothic and Art Nouveau, and they jabber in both French and Flemish into the waning, red-eyed hours of Brussels nightlife.

▟ TRANSPORTATION

Flights: Brussels International Airport (BRU; ☎ 753 42 21 or 723 31 11; www.brusselsairport.be) is 14km from the city. See www.flysn.be for info on **SN Brussels Airline,** the Belgian national carrier. Trains run to the airport from Gare du Midi (25min., every 20min., €2.60) stopping at Gare Centrale and Gare du Nord. Bus #12 traces the same route (every 30min.; 5am-11pm, Sept.-June until midnight; €3). **Brussels South Charleroi** (CRL; ☎71 25 12 11; www.charleroi-airport.com) is 46km outside the city, between Brussels and Charleroi, and services a number of European airlines. Buses run to the airport from r. de France just outside the Gare du Midi in Brussels (2½hr. before each RyanAir flight, €10).

BELGIUM

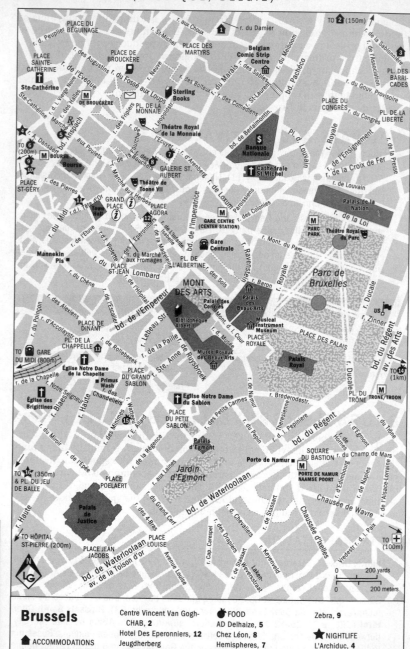

Brussels

BELGIUM

Trains: Info ☎555 25 55. All international trains stop at the **Gare du Midi;** most also stop at the **Gare Centrale** (near Grand Place) or the **Gare du Nord** (near the Botanical Gardens). To: **Amsterdam** (3hr.; €32, under 26 €21); **Antwerp** (45min., €6); **Bruges** (45min., €11); **Cologne** (2¾hr.; €37, under 26 €19); **Luxembourg City** (1¾hr., €26); **Paris** (1½hr.; €69, under 26 €34). **Eurostar** goes to **London** (2¾hr.; from €79, under-26 from €60, with Eurail or Benelux pass from €75).

Public Transportation: The **Metro (M), buses,** and **trams** run daily 6am-midnight. 1hr. ticket €1.40, day pass €3.80, 5 trips €6.50, 10 trips €9.80. All three are run by the **Société des Transports Intercommunaux Bruxellois (STIB),** Gare du Midi (☎515 20 00; www.stib.irisnet.be). Open M-F 7:30am-5:30pm. STIB also offers the **Carte 3/5** (€9), providing three 24hr. periods of unlimited intracity transport within 5 days' time.

✈🛈 ORIENTATION AND PRACTICAL INFORMATION

Most major attractions are clustered around **Grand Place,** between the **Bourse** (Stock Market) to the west and the **Parc de Bruxelles** to the east. Two **Metro** lines circle the city, while efficient trams run north-south. Signs list both street names in both French and Flemish, but *Let's Go* gives the French name for all addresses.

Tourist Offices: The **Belgian Tourist Office,** Grasmarkt 63 (☎504 30 90; www.visitbelgium.com), one block from Grand Place, books rooms all over Belgium and offers free copies of the indispensable *What's On.* Open July-Aug. M-F 9am-7pm, Sa-Su 9am-1pm and 2-7pm; Sept.-June M-F 9am-6pm, Sa-Su 9am-1pm and 2-6pm; Nov.-Apr. closed Su afternoon. The **Brussels International Tourism and Congress** (BITC; ☎513 89 40; www.brusselsinternational.be), on Grand Place in the Town Hall, is the official tourist office of the city of Brussels. The BITC books rooms within the city for no extra charge, and sells the Brussels card, which provides free public transportation and access to 30 museums for 3 days (€30). Open daily 9am-6pm; Jan.-Easter closed Su.

Budget Travel: Infor-Jeunes Bruxelles, 155 r. Van Arteveld (☎514 41 11; bruxelles@inforjeunes.be). M: Bourse. Offers budget travel info for students and helps to find jobs and apartments. Free **Internet** for students. Open M-F noon-5:30pm.

Embassies and Consulates: Australia, 6-8 r. Guimard (☎286 05 00). **Canada,** 2 av. Tervuren (☎741 06 11). **Ireland,** 50 r. Wiertz (☎235 66 76). **New Zealand,** 1 sq. de Meeus (☎512 10 40). **UK,** 85 r. d'Arlon (☎287 62 11). **US,** 27 bd. du Régent (☎508 21 11; www.usembassy.be).

Currency Exchange: Many exchange booths near Grand Place stay open until 11pm. Most banks and booths charge a commission (€2.50-3.75) to cash checks. **CBC-Automatic Change,** 7 Grand Place (☎547 12 11), exchanges cash and checks and is open 24hr. Exchange booths are also available in the train stations.

GLBT Services: Call ☎736 26 81 for info on local events. Staffed Tu 8-10pm, W and F 8-11pm. The tourist office offers the *Safer Guide* to gay nightlife.

English-Language Bookstore: Sterling Books, Wolvengracht 38, r. du Fossé aux Loups. M: De Brouckère. Open M-Sa 10am-7pm, Su noon-6:30pm.

Laundromat: Primus Wash, 50 r. Haute, around the corner from the hostel on r. de St-Esprit. M: Gare Centrale. Wash €3.50, dry €0.50 per 10min. Open daily 7am-11pm.

Emergency: Ambulance: ☎112. **Fire:** ☎112. **Police:** ☎101.

Pharmacy: Neos-Bourse Pharmacie (☎218 06 40), bd. Anspach at r. du Marché aux Polets. M: Bourse. Open M-Sa 8:30am-6:30pm.

BELGIUM

Medical Assistance: Free Clinic, 154a Chaussée de Wavre (☎512 13 14). M: Porte de Namur. Ignore the name—you'll have to pay. Open M-F 9am-6pm, Sa 10am-noon. **Centre Hospitalier Universitaire St. Pierre,** 322 r. Haute (☎535 31 11). M: Porte de Namur. You can also call ☎479 18 18 to reach an on-call doctor 24hr. a day.

Internet Access: A bevy of Internet cafes can be found on Chaussée de Wavre (M: Porte de Namur), generally charging €1-1.50 per hr. **Call Center,** in the De Brouckère Metro station, is €1.50 per hr. Open M-F 8am-11pm, Sa-Su 10am-10pm.

Post Office: pl. de la Monnaie, Centre Monnaie, 2nd fl. (☎226 21 11). M: de Brouckère. Open M-F 8am-6pm, Sa 9:30am-3pm. Address mail to be held in the following format: First name SURNAME, *Poste Restante,* pl. de la Monnaie, 1000 Bruxelles, BELGIUM.

Women navigating Brussels on their own are often the target of unwanted advances from male admirers, ranging from playful requests for a kiss to cruder overtures. While sexual harassment is illegal in Belgium, isolated incidents are rarely prosecuted. Consider venturing out with a companion, and see p. 46 for further tips specific to women travelers.

ACCOMMODATIONS

Accommodations can be difficult to find in Brussels, especially on weekends in June and July. In general, however, accommodations are well-kept and centrally located. A good bet for finding low rates is to contact the BITC; they book rooms for free, sometimes at a discount approaching 50%. If a hotel or hostel is booked, the staff will sometimes call other establishments on behalf of prospective guests.

Centre Vincent Van Gogh-CHAB, 8 r. Traversière (☎217 01 58). M: Botanique. Exit on r. Royale, head right and turn right onto Chaussée d'Haecht, which becomes r. Traversière. Simple rooms are gussied up by a candlelit bar and sunroom lounge where guests congregate around the clock to play cards. Breakfast included. Sheets €3.60. Laundry €4.50. Internet €1 per 20min. Lockers €5 deposit. Reception daily 7:30am-2am. Under 35 only. Dorms €12-16; singles €27; doubles €40. AmEx/MC/V. ●

Sleep Well, 23 r. du Damier (☎218 50 50), near Gare du Nord. M: Rogier. Exit on r. Neuve, take the first left onto r. de la Blanchisserie and the next right onto r. du Damier. Sponge-painted walls add some spice to the basic, pleasant rooms. Breakfast and sheets included. Internet €0.50 per 5min. Lockout 11am-3pm. Dorms €16-20; singles €27; doubles €48; triples €64. Prices reduced by €2.75 after 1st night. MC/V. ●

Auberge de Jeunesse "Jacques Brel" (HI), 30 r. de la Sablonnière (☎218 01 87), on pl. des Barricades. M: Botanique. Follow r. Royale, with the botanical gardens to your right, and take the 1st left onto r. de la Sablonnière. Clean, spacious rooms. Breakfast and sheets included. Reception daily 8am-1am. Lockout noon-3pm. Laundry €7. HI members only. Dorms €15.50-17.30; singles €26; doubles €41; triples €50. MC/V. ●

Hotel Des Eperonniers, 1 r. des Eperonniers (☎513 53 66). M: Gare Centre. Choose between basic singles and spacious studios just around the corner from Grand Place. Reception daily 7am-midnight. Singles €25-55; doubles €42-70. AmEx/MC/V. ●

Jeugdherberg Bruegel (HI), 2 r. de St-Esprit (☎511 04 36). M: Gare Centre. From the station, walk down bd. de l'Empereur until you reach pl. de la Chapelle. Clean and close to the city's museums, if lacking in atmosphere. Breakfast and sheets included. Internet €1 per 30min. Reception daily 7am-1am. Lockout 10am-2pm. Curfew 1am. Dorms €17; singles €26; doubles €41; quads €64. Nonmembers add €3. MC/V. ●

⬛ FOOD

Brussels has earned its reputation as one of the culinary capitals in Europe, although the city's gastronomy caters more to the five-star port-wine-reduction set than to the budget traveler. Inexpensive restaurants cluster around **Grand Place,** while to the south **Rue du Marché aux Fromages** offers cheap Middle Eastern food. Shellfish, paella, and other seafood are served along the narrow, luminous **Rue des Bouchers,** where the *maîtres d'* of adjoining restaurants will literally quarrel with each other for your business. Seafood can also be found at the small restaurants on **Quai aux Briques,** in the Ste-Catherine area behind pl. St-Géry. An **AD Delhaize** supermarket is on the corner of bd. Anspach and r. du Marché aux Polets. (M: Bourse. Open M-Th and Sa 9am-9pm, F 9am-4pm, Su 9am-6pm.)

⬛ **'t Spinnekopke,** 1 pl. du Jardin aux Fleurs (☎511 86 95). M: Bourse. Few tourists venture "in the spider's head" (an English translation of the restaurant's name), but locals savor an authentically Belgian, game-heavy menu in a woodsy, candlelit decor. Entrees €13-24. Open M-F noon-3pm and 6-11pm, Sa noon-3pm. AmEx/MC/V. ❹

Hemispheres, 65 r. de l'Ecuyer (☎513 93 70). Middle Eastern and Asian cuisine amid cozy furnishings and a peacenik vibe. Entrees €9-13; plenty of vegetarian fare. Open M-F noon-3pm and 6:30-10:30pm, Sa 6:30pm-midnight. MC/V. ❸

Zebra, 33-35 pl. St-Géry. M: Bourse. Although known for its cocktails, this chic, centrally located cafe also serves light, tasty sandwiches and generous portions of pasta (€2-6). Kitchen closes at 11pm. Open M-Th and Su 11am-2am, F-Sa 11am-3am. MC/V. ❶

Maison Antoine, 1 pl. Jourdan. M: Schuman. From the rotary, walk down r. Froissart; it's the brown kiosk in the middle of pl. Jourdan. The best *frites* (€1.60-1.80) in town, and they only improve with a side of tartar sauce (€0.50). Also offers sandwiches and fried kebabs (€1-3). Open M-Th and Su 11:30am-1am, F-Sa 11:30am-2am. Cash only. ❶

Chez Léon, 18 r. des Bouchers (☎511 14 15). Though it's surrounded by competitors, locals swear allegiance to Chez Léon's generous plate of *moules frites* (mussels; €13-22). Open daily noon-11pm. AmEx/MC/V. ❹

Le Perroquet, 31 r. Watteau (☎512 99 22). A convenient stop for anyone exploring the southern half of the city, Le Perroquet does the trick for lunch, an afternoon beer, or a late-night pastry. Salads and pitas €5-10. Open daily 10:30am-1am. MC/V. ❷

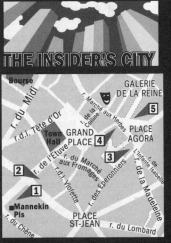

THE INSIDER'S CITY

WAFFLE WALK

Instead of breakfasting on their waffles, Belgians nab the golden-brown confections from street carts as an afternoon snack. The vendors around Grand-Place pour sweet batter into crackling hot irons day and night.

1 Start off with a *gaufre natur* sprinkled with sugar at **Funambule,** 42 r. de l'Etuve.

2 Head down the street to **The Waffle Factory,** 21b r. de l'Etuve, for dense, unleavened Liège waffles served with stracciatella ice cream

3 **Australian Homemade Ice Cream,** 2 r. de la Colline, is always generous with pecans and warm chocolate sauce.

4 Yes, they're corporate. And yes, they're expensive. But **Häagen-Dazs,** 1 Galerie de la Reine, tops waffles with their irresistibly rich ice cream.

5 Finish with a fluffy Brussels waffle at **Gaufre de Bruxelles,** 113 r. du Marché aux Herbes. A dollop of freshly whipped *crème de Chantilly* is a must.

👁 SIGHTS

GRAND-PLACE AND ENVIRONS. Victor Hugo once called the gold-trimmed **Grand-Place** "the most beautiful square in the world." By night, the densely statued **town hall** takes center stage in a swirling lights show, illuminated by 800 colored floodlights set to classical music. By day, the **Carpet of Flowers** festival (even-numbered years, around Aug. 15) fills the square with blossoms. *(Lights show daily Apr.-Aug. and Dec. around 10:30pm. Town hall tours €3, students €2.50.)* Three blocks behind the town hall, on the corner of r. de l'Etuve and r. du Chêne, is Brussels's most giggled-at sight, the **Mannekin Pis,** a statue of an impudent boy (with an apparently gargantuan bladder) continuously peeing. Legend has it that the statue commemorates a boy who ingeniously defused a bomb destined for the Grand-Place. In reality, the fountain was installed to supply the neighborhood with drinking water during the reign of Archduke Albert and Archduchess Isabelle. Locals have created hundreds of outfits for him, vying to dress him in the ritual coats of different organizations and regions, each with a strategically placed hole for his you-know-what. His wardrobe is on display on the third floor of the **Museum of the City of Brussels (Maison de Roi).** *(Open Tu-Su 10am-5pm. €3, students €2.50.)* In the glorious **Galerie Saint-Hubert** arcade, one block behind Grand-Place, you can window-shop for everything from square umbrellas to marzipan frogs. Just north of Gare Centrale, the Gothic and Romanesque architecture of the **Cathédrale Saint-Michel et Sainte-Gudule** was the backdrop for the 1999 wedding of Crown Prince Philippe to his bride Mathilde d'Udekem d'Acoz. *(Pl. St-Gudule. Open daily 7am-6pm. Free.)*

MONT DES ARTS. The ▓**Musées Royaux des Beaux-Arts** encompass the **Musée d'Art Ancien,** the **Musée d'Art Moderne,** a **sculpture gallery,** and temporary exhibitions. Together, the museums steward a huge collection of Belgian art from across the centuries, including Bruegel the Elder's *Landscape with the Fall of Icarus* and pieces by Rubens and Brussels native René Magritte. Just the view of Brussels's cityscape from the fourth floor of the 19th-century wing would make the admission fee a worthwhile investment. *(3 r. de la Régence. M: Parc. ☎ 508 32 11; www.fine-arts-museum.be. Open Tu-Su 10am-5pm. Some wings close noon-2pm. €5, students €3.50; 1st W of each month 1-5pm free.)* The **Musical Instrument Museum (MIM),** located in a six-story Art Nouveau building, houses over 1500 instruments. Stand in front of any instrument and your headphones automatically play a sample of its music. There is a fabulous panoramic view of the city from a corner turret on the third floor, and in the overpriced restaurant upstairs. *(2 r. Montagne de la Cour. One block from the Musées des Beaux-Arts. ☎ 545 01 30; www.mim.fgov.be. Open Tu-F 9:30am-5pm, Sa-Su 10am-5pm. €5, students €3.50. 1st W of each month 1-5pm free.)*

BELGIAN CENTER FOR COMIC STRIP ART. Comic strips (*"les BD"*) are serious business in Belgium, and today a restored Art Nouveau warehouse in the center of the capital pays tribute to what Belgians call the Ninth Art. The **museum library** makes thousands of books available to scholarly researchers, while the museum store hawks enchantingly kitschy merchandise festooned with Tintin and a whole cast of lesser characters. *(20 r. des Sables. M: Gare Centre. From the station, take bd. de l'Impératrice until it becomes bd. de Berlaimont, and turn left onto r. des Sables. ☎ 219 19 80. Open Tu-Su 10am-6pm. €6.20, students €5.)*

OTHER SIGHTS. The enormous **Musées Royaux d'Art et d'Histoire** dredges up artifacts from the catacombs of history—Roman torsos without heads, Syrian heads without torsos, and Egyptian caskets with feet. The eerily illuminated *Salle au Tresor* (Treasure Room) and the Greco-Roman collection are the museum's main attractions. *(10 Parc du Cinquantenaire. M: Mérode. From the station, it's next to the big arch.*

☎ 741 72 11. Open Tu-F 9:30am-5pm, Sa-Su 10am-5pm. €4, students €3.) Master architect Victor Horta's home, today the **Musée Horta**, is a graceful application of his Art Nouveau style to a domestic setting. (25 r. Américaine. M: Horta. Take a right out of the stop, walk 7min. uphill on ch. de Waterloo, then turn left onto ch. de Charleroi and right onto r. Américaine. ☎ 543 04 90; www.hortamuseum.be. Open Tu-Su 2-5:30pm. €5, students €3.70.)

🎵 🎭 ENTERTAINMENT AND NIGHTLIFE

For information on events, check the weekly *What's On*, available at the tourist office. The flagship of Brussels's theater network is the beautiful **Théâtre Royal de la Monnaie**, on pl. de la Monnaie, renowned throughout the world for its opera and ballet. Its performance of the opera *Muette de Portici* in August of 1830 sparked the revolt that led to Belgium's independence from the Dutch. (M: de Brouckère. ☎ 229 12 00; www.lamonnaie.be. Tickets from €8.) The **Théâtre Royal de Toone VII**, 21 Petite r. des Bouchers, is a 7th-generation puppet theater that stages marionette performances, a distinctly Belgian art form. The theater also houses a unique bar with marionettes hanging from the ceiling. (☎ 513 54 86. French-language shows F-Sa 8:30pm, occasionally T-Th as well. €10, students €7.) The resolutely out-there **Nova**, 3 r. d'Arenberg, is a vibrant one-screen cinema that shows foreign, indie, and experimental films. B-grade movies are shown every Friday at midnight, and Nova holds free summertime film screenings at construction sites around the city. (☎ 503 57 57; www.nova-cinema.com. €5, students €3.50. Showtimes vary.)

On summer nights, **Grand Place** and the **Bourse** come to life with street performers and **live concerts** in every imaginable genre. For outdoor patios jammed with a laid-back crowd of students and backpackers, the **Place Saint Géry** is the place to be. **Zebra** and a host of other bars are located within a few steps of one another, and are lively until late. **L'Archiduc**, 6 r. Antoine Dansaert, unites live jazz, swanky cocktails (€7-8), and a horseshoe-shaped Art Deco balcony for a sophisticated vibe that somehow avoids descending into snobbery. (☎ 512 06 52. Open daily 4pm-late.) For dancing, try **La Salsa**, 9 r. Borgval, which offers daily salsa lessons, free on Fridays. (Lessons 8-10pm, prices vary. Open daily 8pm-late.) For throbbing techno amid a sea of pretty young things, all roads lead to **Le Fuse**, 208 r. Blaes. (☎ 511 97 89; www.fuse.be. Open daily 10pm-late. €3 before midnight, €8 after.) Gay nightlife centers around r. des Pierres and r. du Marché-au-Charbon, next to Grand Place. **L'Homo Erectus**, 57 r. des Pierres, is extremely popular, especially on Sunday nights, when you can win prizes playing Love Trivial Pursuit. (☎ 514 74 93; www.lhomoerectus.com. Open M-F noon-5am, Sa-Su 4pm-late.) Another hot spot is **Tel Quels**, 81 r. du Marché-au-Charbon, which hosts a ladies' night on Monday and draws a younger crowd Wednesday and Saturday. (☎ 512 32 34; www.telsquels.be. M-Tu, Th, and Su 5pm-2am, W 2pm-2am, F-Sa 5pm-4am.)

🔲 DAYTRIP FROM BRUSSELS: MECHELEN (MALINES)

Just north of Brussels, Mechelen (pop. 78,000), once the ecclesiastical capital of Belgium, is best known today for its treasure-filled churches and its grim role in the Holocaust. The stately **St. Rombouts Cathedral,** down Consciencestr. from Centraal Station, features gorgeous stained-glass windows and **St. Rombouts Tower,** which rises 97m over the **Grote Markt** and houses two 49-bell carillons. (Cathedral open daily 9:30am-5pm. Climb the tower July-Aug. M 2:15 and 7pm, Tu-Su 2:15pm; June and Sept. M 7pm, Sa-Su 2:15pm. €5. ◼Carillon recitals June-Sept. M 11:30am and 8:30pm, Sa 11:30am, Su 3pm.) The 15th-century **Church of St. John** boasts Rubens's magnificent triptych *The Adoration of the Magi*. From the Grote Markt, walk down Fr. de Merodestr. and turn left onto St-Janstr. (Open Tu-Su 1:30-5pm.) To reach the **Jewish Museum of Deportation and Resistance**, 153 Goswin de Stassart-str., follow Wollemarkt from behind St. Rumbouts; it becomes Goswin de Stassart-str. The museum is housed in 18th-century barracks that were used as a holding pen for Jews en route to Auschwitz-Birkenau. (Open M-Th and Su 10am-5pm, F 10am-1pm. Free.) **Trains** arrive from Antwerp (20min., every 5-15min., €2.90) and Brussels (20min., every 5-10min., €3.30). The **tourist office,** on the Grote Markt, calls hotels to check for vacancies. Walk 10min. down Consciencestr. to the Grote Markt. (☎015 29 76 55; www.mechelen.be. Open Easter-Oct. M-F 8am-6pm, Sa 9:30am-12:30pm and 1:30-5pm, Su 1:30-5pm; Nov.-Easter reduced hours.) Restaurants cluster around the Grote Markt. Try *mechelse koekoek,* spiced chicken that's been braised in beer, or mild white asparagus during the springtime.

FLANDERS (VLAANDEREN)

Flanders, the moneyed, Flemish-speaking half of Belgium, spans fussy, quaint cities and a short coastline firmly in the grip of the leisure industry. Historically, the mouth of the Schelde River at Antwerp provided the region with a major port, and trade in linen, wool, and diamonds created great prosperity. Today, tourism buoys the region's economy, although its highly-skilled workforce also continues to innovate in fields from biotechnology to video game graphic design.

BRUGES (BRUGGE)   ☎50

Famed for its lace and its relationship with noted Flemish painter Jan van Eyck, Bruges (pop. 116,000) is also the most touristed city in Belgium and one of the most romantic cities in Europe. Canals carve their way through rows of stone houses and cobblestone streets en route to the breathtaking Gothic Markt. The city remains one of the best-preserved examples of Northern Renaissance architecture, although the violence of World War I did not quite leave Bruges untouched; eight decades after the war, farmers on the outskirts of the city still uncover 200 tons of artillery shells every year as they plow their fields.

■ ? TRANSPORTATION AND PRACTICAL INFORMATION

Bruges is enclosed by a circular canal, with its main train station, **Stationsplein,** just beyond its southern extreme. The compact historic district is entirely accessible on foot. The dizzying **Belfort** (belfry) towers high over the center of town, presiding over the handsome **Markt.** The windmill-lined **Kruisvestraat** and serene **Minnewater Park** are great for a walk or picnic.

Trains: Leave from **Stationsplein** (☎38 23 82), a 15min. walk south of the city. Trains head to: **Antwerp** (1¼hr., 1 per hr., €12); **Brussels** (50min., 1-3 per hr., €11); **Ghent** (40min., 1-2 per hr., €4.80); **Ostend** (13min., 3-6 per hr., €3).

Bike Rental: At the train station (☎30 23 29). €6.50 per half-day, €9 per day. **Koffieboontje,** Hallestr. 4, off the Markt by the belfry. €6 for 4hr.; €9 per day, students €6 per day. Open daily 9am-11pm. Some hostels and hotels also rent bikes for €5-9 per day.

Tourist Office: Burg 11 (☎44 86 86; www.brugge.be). From the train station, head left to 't Zand, turn right on Zuidzandstr., and walk through the Markt to Breidelstr. (20min.). Books rooms (€2.50 service fee, €20 deposit) and sells maps and ▨ **info guides** (€1). Open Apr.-Sept. M-F 9:30am-6:30pm, Sa-Su 10am-12:30pm and 2-6:30pm; Oct.-Mar. M-F 9:30am-5pm, Sa-Su 9:30am-1pm and 2-5:30pm.

Tours: The tourist office leads **walking tours** (June and Sept. Sa-Su 2:30pm; July-Aug. daily 2:30pm; €5). Five companies offer **boat tours** that traverse Bruges's canals and glide by corners of the city that would otherwise be inaccessible (Mar.-Nov. 10am-6pm,

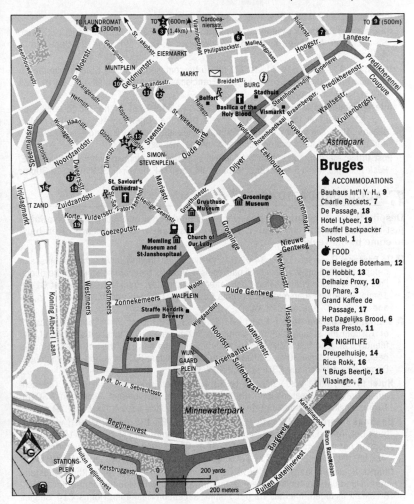

Bruges

🏠 ACCOMMODATIONS
Bauhaus Int'l Y. H., **9**
Charlie Rockets, **7**
De Passage, **18**
Hotel Lybeer, **19**
Snuffel Backpacker
  Hostel, **1**

🍴 FOOD
De Belegde Boterham, **12**
De Hobbit, **13**
Delhaize Proxy, **10**
Du Phare, **3**
Grand Kaffee de
  Passage, **17**
Het Dagelijks Brood, **6**
Pasta Presto, **11**

⭐ NIGHTLIFE
Dreupelhuisje, **14**
Rica Rokk, **16**
't Brugs Beertje, **15**
Vlissinghe, **2**

every 30min., €5.20); pick up tickets at any of the boat symbols on the maps from the tourist office. **QuasiMundo Tours** offers 4 different **bike tours**, including one through the countryside and another at dusk; all include a drink in a local pub. Bike tours depart daily from the Burg. (☎ 33 07 75; www.quasimundo.com. Tours Mar.-Oct. €18, under 26 €16.) **Pink Bear Bicycle Company** also leads 2 fun, informative tours, one to the neighboring town of Damme and another through the countryside; both leave daily from the Markt. (☎ 61 66 86; www.pinkbear.freeservers.com. €16, under 26 €14.)

ATMs: One located at Simon Stevenplein, another outside of the post office in the Markt, and one in the KBC Bank, Steenstr. 38.

Luggage Storage: At the train station, €1.50-3.30. **Lockers** at the tourist office, €1. Only accessible during regular hours.

Laundromat: Belfort, Ezelstr. 51. Wash €2.50-3.50. Dry €1. Open daily 7am-10pm.

BELGIUM

Emergency: ☎100. **Police:** ☎101. Station at Hauwerstr. 7.

Pharmacies: Apotheek Dryepondt, Wollestr. 7. Open M-F 9am-12:30pm and 2-6:30pm, Sa until 6pm. **Apotheek K. Dewolf,** Zuidzandstr. 1. Open M-F 9am-12:30pm and 2-6:30pm, Sa until 6pm.

Hospitals: A. Z. St.-Jan (☎41 21 11; not to be confused with Oud St-Janshospitaal, a museum), St.-Lucas (☎36 91 11), St.-Franciscus Xaverivskliniek (☎47 04 70). Call tourist office for doctors on call.

Internet Access: The Coffee Link, Mariastr. 38 (☎34 99 73), in the Oud St-Janshospitaal. €1.25 for first 15min., €0.07 per min. thereafter. Open July-Aug. 10am-9pm; low season 10am-7pm. Many hostels also offer Internet access for around €1 per 30min., and a number of them extend access to anyone, not just guests.

Post Office: Markt 5. Address mail to be held in the following format: First name SURNAME, *Poste Restante,* Markt 5, 8000 Brugge, BELGIUM. Open M-F 9am-6pm, Sa 9:30am-12:30pm.

▟ ACCOMMODATIONS

Despite Bruges's popularity, reasonably-priced accommodations are available just blocks from the city center. Reserve in advance, as rooms are often hard to come by on weekends.

▨ **De Passage,** Dweersstr. 26 (☎34 02 32). Ideal location, friendly service, great rooms, and a popular cafe. Trust in fellow backpackers is a must, as there are no locks on the doors. Free beer with dinner and a free T-shirt after a 3-night stay. Breakfast €3. Internet €1 per 15min. Reception 9am-midnight. Dorms €12; singles €25-40; doubles €40-60; triples and quads €60. AmEx/MC/V. ❷

▨ **Snuffel Backpacker Hostel,** Ezelstr. 47-49 (☎33 31 33; www.snuffel.be). Take bus #3 or 13 from the station. Colorful rooms, each decorated by a local artist. Helpful and friendly staff lead free walking tours twice a week, and serve up their own tasty Snuffel beer. Internet €1 per 30min. Bikes €5 per day. Breakfast €2. Reception 8am-midnight. Dorms €11-13; doubles €30. AmEx/MC/V. ❷

Hotel Lybeer, Korte Vuldersstr. 31 (☎33 43 55; hotellybeer@hotmail.com). Old-fashioned charm in a great location. Breakfast included. Free Internet. Reception 7:30am-11pm. Singles €25; doubles €44-54; triples €73; quads €89. AmEx/MC/V. ❸

Bauhaus International Youth Hotel, Langestr. 133-137 (☎34 10 93; www.bauhaus.be). Take bus #6 or 16 from the station. Internet cafe (€1.30 per 15min.) and popular bar. Lockers €1. Breakfast €2. Bikes €7 per day. Reception 8am-midnight, or until the bar closes. Dorms €11-14; singles €24; doubles €30-36. AmEx/MC/V. ❷

Charlie Rockets, Hoogstr. 19 (☎33 06 60; www.charlierockets.com). Rooms upstairs from a popular, centrally-located restaurant and bar with wooden barrels for tables. Breakfast included. Internet €2 per 20min. Reception 8am-4am. Dorms €14; singles €32; doubles €42. AmEx/MC/V. ❷

Camping St-Michiel, Tillegemstr. 55 (☎38 08 19). From the station, take bus #7 to Jagerstr. Facing the road, head left and then turn left on Jagerstr. Bear left at the first intersection, staying on Jagerstr. and going around the rotary to Tillegemstr. €3 per person, €3.50 per tent. Showers €2. ❶

◖ FOOD

Inexpensive food can be hard to find in Bruges, but seafood lovers should splurge at least once on Belgium's famous *mosselen* (mussels; usually €15-22) or buy fresh raw seafood at the **Vismarkt.** From the Burg, cross the river and turn left. (Open Tu-Sa 8am-1pm.) Those spooked by the maritime world can get groceries at **Delhaize Proxy,** Noordzandstr. 4, near the Markt. (Open M-Sa 9am-7pm.)

Grand Kaffee de Passage, Dweerstr. 26-28 (☎34 02 32). Attached to the De Passage hotel. Traditional Belgian cuisine in a romantic, candlelit setting, including the highly recommended Flemish stew (€9.50). Open daily 6am-11:30pm. AmEx/MC/V. ❸

Du Phare, Sasplein 2 (☎34 35 90). From the Burg, walk down Hoogstr. and turn left at the canal onto Verversdijk. Follow the canal for 15min. to reach Sasplein. A jazz and blues bistro serving plentiful international fare (€10-17) between pink and purple walls. Open M and W-Th 11:30am-2:30pm and 7pm-midnight, F-Sa 11:30am-2:30pm and 6:30pm-midnight, Su 11:30am-3pm and 6pm-midnight. MC/V. ❹

Het Dagelijks Brood, Philipstockstr. 21 (☎33 60 60). Quiches and soups (€4.50-9) are the house specialties, although sandwiches, salads, pastries, and organic yogurt also grace the long, family-style wooden table at this gourmet chain. Great for breakfast and lunch. Open M and W-Su 8am-6pm. Cash only. ❷

De Hobbit, Kemelstr. 8 (☎33 55 20). Big portions of hearty food, from pasta (€7.50-10) to meat (€15) and salads (€9-14), ordered from clever newsprint menus. Open daily 6pm-1am. AmEx/MC/V. ❸

Pasta Presto, St. Amandsstr. 17 (☎34 55 36). Nicely priced Italian fare, just off the Markt. Takeout available. Opt for the pasta with choice of 9 sauces (€5-7), or choose from soups, sandwiches, salads, and meat dishes. Open M, W-Th, and Su 11:30am-8:30pm, F and Sa 11:30am-9:30pm. Cash only. ❷

De Belegde Boterham, Kleine St-Amandstr. 5. Health-conscious spot serves up sandwiches (€6) and innovative salads (€10) on a series of small, lovingly mismatched tables. Open M-Sa noon-5pm. Cash only. ❸

◉ SIGHTS

Lined with gorgeous canals, and small enough to be explored on a short walk, Bruges is best seen on foot. Avoid visiting Bruges on Mondays, when all of the museums are closed. If you plan to visit many museums, consider a cost-saving **combination ticket** (€15, includes admission to five museums).

MARKT AND BURG. Over the **Markt** looms the **Belfort,** an 88m medieval bell tower. During the day, climb its dizzying 366 steps for a great view, or stroll by after twilight to bask in its yellowy glow. *(Belfort open Tu-Su 9:30am-5pm. Tickets sold until 4:15pm. €5, students €3. Bell concerts Oct. to mid-June W and Sa-Su 2:15pm; mid-June to -Sept. Su only.)* Behind the Markt, the **Burg** is dominated by the massive, yet finely detailed Gothic facade of the **Stadhuis.** Inside, wander through two rooms of paintings and wood carvings, as well as the gilded hall where many residents of Bruges still get married. *(Open Tu-Su 9:30am-4:30pm. €2.50, students €1.50.)*

MUSEUMS. From the Burg, follow Wollestr. left and then head right on Dijver to reach the **Groeninge Museum,** which has a comprehensive collection of Belgian and Dutch paintings from the last six centuries. Highlights include Hieronymous Bosch's fantastically lurid *Last Judgment,* and works by both Jan Van Eyck and Bruges-born Hans Memling. *(Dijver 12. Open Tu-Su 9:30am-5pm. €8, students €5.)* Once a palace, the nearby **Gruuthuse Museum** houses a collection of intricate 16th- and 17th-century tapestries. The museum's small chapel, which protrudes into the Church of Our Lady (see below), was built so that the palace residents could attend church services in the comfort of their home. *(Dijver 17. Open Tu-Su 9:30am-5pm. €6, students €4.)* Continue on Dijver as it becomes Gruuthusestr. and walk under the stone archway to reach **St-Janshospitaal,** one of the oldest surviving medieval hospitals in Europe. Inside, the **Memling Museum** reconstructs everyday life in the hospital and has several paintings by its namesake, Hans Memling. *(Mariastr. 38. Open Tu-Su 9:30am-5pm. €8, students €5.)* To get to the **Lace Center,** Peperstr.

3A, walk down Hoogstr. from the Burg, which turns into Langestr. Turn left onto Peperstr.; the center is beside the 15th-century **Jerusalem Chapel.** The spidery lace on display isn't terribly impressive inside a frame, but a brood of wrinkled octogenarians gives lace demonstrations every afternoon. *(www.kantcentrum.com. Open M-F 10am-noon and 2-6pm, Sa-Su 10am-noon and 2-5pm. €2.50, students €1.50.)*

OTHER SIGHTS. The 14th-century **Church of Our Lady,** at Mariastr. and Gruuthusestr., contains Michelangelo's *Madonna and Child* as well as fresco fragments from the 16th-century tombs of Mary of Burgundy and Charles the Bold. *(Open M-F 9am-12:20pm and 1:30-4:50pm, Sa 9am-12:20pm and 1:30-3:50pm, Su 1:30-4:50pm. Church free. Tomb viewing €2.50, students €1.50.)* Beer aficionados will enjoy the informative tour and free samples at the **Straffe Hendrik Brewery,** a beer museum and brewery built in 1856. *(From the Church of Our Lady, turn left, follow Mariastr., turn right onto Wijngaardstr., and turn right onto Welplein. Tours 45min. Apr.-Sept. every hr. 11am-4pm; Oct.-Mar. 11am and 3pm. €4.)* Inside the **Beguinage,** a grassy cove encircled by medieval cloisters, you can saunter through the gardens or stop to ponder the small pigeon tower. The Beguine's House displays furnishings typical of ancient Flemish households, although it's free (and just as enjoyable) to simply wander about the grounds. *(From Simon Stevenplein, follow Mariastr., turn right onto Wijngaardstr.; at the canal, turn right and cross the footbridge. Open daily Mar.-Nov. 10am-noon and 1:45-5:30pm; gate closes at sunset. Admission to house €2, students €1.)* On the southern edge of the city, the **Minnewater** (Lake of Love) is cradled by a beautiful park perfect for an afternoon picnic; you'd never know it was once used as an ammunition dump.

ENTERTAINMENT AND NIGHTLIFE

For three days during July, Bruges hosts the **Cactusfestival,** a series of concerts with musicians from all over the world; 2004's lineup included soul chanteuse Macy Gray and everyone's favorite Angry Young Man, Elvis Costello. For information on 2005 dates, tickets, and performers, visit www.cactusfestival.be. The city also sponsors **Klinkers,** an open-air music and film series that's free to the public throughout July and August. Otherwise, the best nighttime activity in Bruges may be a walk through the city's picturesque streets and over its cobblestoned bridges. There are some lively late-night options, however, including the popular **bar** at the Bauhaus Hostel (see above) or the 300 varieties of beer at **'t Brugs Beertje,** Kemelstr. 5, off Steenstr. (Open M-Tu, Th, and Su 4pm-1am, F-Sa 4pm-2am.) Next door, the candlelit **Dreupelhuisje** dishes out fruity *jenever,* a flavored Dutch gin (€2). Be careful though—it packs a wallop at upwards of 70 proof. (Open M and Th-Su 6pm-1am.) For a quieter atmosphere, check out the oldest of Bruges's 420-odd pubs, **Vlissinghe,** Blekersstr. 2, established in 1515. From the Burg, take Hoogstr. and turn left onto Verversdijk. Cross the second bridge, onto Blekerstr. (Open W-Th 11am-midnight, F-Sa 11am-late, Su 11am-7pm.) Or head down to the area of Eiermarkt and Kuipersstr., behind the Markt, where many tourist bars pump loud, commercial music that can be heard halfway across the city. Belgian students tend to prefer the dance floor of **Rica Rokk,** 't Zand 6, where shots are €3 and a meter of beer starts at €20. (Open M-Th and Su 10am-4am, F-Sa 10am-5am.)

 THE LONG ARM OF THE LAW. If you're wobbling back to your hostel with a bellyful of beer, think twice before yielding to nature's call en route. Bruges has started cracking down on public urination inside the city limits, and police will fine you €152 if they catch you in the act. Make it a point to relieve yourself before you head home, or keep a €0.50 coin handy for the public toilets.

▶ DAYTRIP FROM BRUGES: OSTEND (OOSTENDE)

On the coast of the North Sea, Ostend (pop. 68,000) is a slightly tawdry, heavily touristed beach town, centered around a promenade lined with restaurants and bars. **Viserkaai** (Fisherman's Quay) marks the entrance to the harbor that brings in most of Belgium's fresh fish. Near the bustling **Vitrap** (fish market), vendors set up stands selling steaming bowls of *caricoles* (sea snails). To get to the main **beach,** cross the bridge directly in front of the station, turn right on Visserkaai and follow the promenade for 20min. The sand isn't especially soft, and the vistas are cluttered with high-rises, but the beaches of Ostend still offer a welcome breath of fresh air when summer in Bruges gets torrid. **Trains** run to Ostend from Bruges (15min., 3 per hr., €3). To get to the **tourist office,** Monacoplein 2, follow the directions to the beach, but walk on the promenade for 10min. and turn left onto Langestr.; follow it to the end. (☎70 11 99. Open June-Aug. M-Sa 9am-7pm, Su 10am-7pm; Sept.-May M-Sa 10am-6pm, Su 10am-5pm.) Don't even bother asking for a menu at **Taverne Koekoek ❶,** Langestr. 38-40, because they do just one thing: tender, perfectly spiced rotisserie chicken. (Half-chicken €4.90. Open 24hr. AmEx/MC/V.)

ANTWERP (ANTWERPEN, ANVERS)   ☎03

Home of the Golden Age master painter Peter Paul Rubens, Antwerp (pop. 455,000) remains distinctly cosmopolitan. The city's nightlife has calmed down considerably in the last three years, and Benelux hipsters are less likely to dip into town for the weekend than they once were, but an afternoon window-shopping in the city's gritty diamond quarter reveals that Antwerp still has a sparkle all its own. The city's main promenades, **De Keyserlei** and the **Meir,** run east-west through the downtown area, and are lined by elegant department stores. On the western edge of the buying spree, the **Cathedral of Our Lady,** Groenpl. 21, boasts a magnificent Gothic tower and Rubens's *Descent from the Cross.* (Open M-F 10am-5pm, Sa 10am-3pm, Su 1-4pm. Guided tours each day, usually at 11am and 2:15pm, are included with entrance fee. €2.) Take in the exterior of the dignified **Stadhuis,** just to the west, and then hop tram #11 to see the wildly opulent mansions lining the **Cogels Osylei.** A stroll by the Schelde River leads to the 13th-century **Steen Castle,** which houses the extensive collections of the **National Maritime Museum.** (Open Tu-Su 10am-4:30pm. €4, students €2.) The **Royal Museum of Fine Arts,** Leopold De Waelpl. 1-9, has one of the world's finest collections of Old Flemish Master paintings. (☎238 78 09. Open Tu-Sa 10am-5pm, Su 10am-6pm. €5, under 25 €4. Audioguides €1.50.) The **Mayer van den Bergh Museum,** Lange Gasthuisstr. 19, showcases Bruegel's apocalyptic *Mad Meg,* along with other works from the 14th to 16th centuries. (Open Tu-Su 10am-5pm. €4, students €2.) The **Rubens Huis,** Wapper 9, off Meir, was built by Antwerp's favorite son and is filled with his works. (Open Tu-Su 10am-5pm. €5, students €2.50.) While scenesters once spoke about Antwerp's nightclubs in the same breathless tone they reserved for London and Barcelona, the lone vestige of this era is **Café d'Anvers,** Verversrui 15, in the middle of Antwerp's red light district, north of the Grote Markt. (☎226 38 70. Open F-Sa 11pm-late.) Otherwise, **bars** are the place to be, either behind the cathedral, or in the trendy southern neighborhood around the Museum of Fine Arts. For live jazz and a chill atmosphere, hole up in the loft of **De Muze,** Melkmarkt 15, or else sip your glass of abbey beer at one of the tables outside. (Open daily 11am-3am.)

Antwerp has two train stations: **Berchem,** which handles international traffic, and **Centraal,** the domestic station. **Trains** go from Berchem to: Amsterdam (2hr., 1 per hr., €27); Brussels (1hr., 5 per hr., €6); and Rotterdam (1hr., 1 per hr., €16). To get from Berchem to the **tourist office,** Grote Markt 15, take tram #8 (€1) to Groenplaats. The **tourist office,** Grote Markt 13, books rooms for a small deposit. (☎232

01 03; www.visitantwerpen.be. Open M-Sa 9am-6pm, Su 9am-5pm). The **New International Youth Hotel and Hostel ❷**, Provinciestr. 256, is a 15min. walk from Centraal Station. Turn left out of the station onto Pelikaanstr., which becomes Simonsstr.; turn left on Plantin en Moretus, walk under the bridge, and then turn right onto Provinciestr. Rooms are clean and carpeted, if a bit worn in places. (☎230 05 22; www.youthhotel.be. Breakfast included. Sheets €4. Dorms €14.50; singles €31; doubles €46-58; quads €78-90. MC/V.) To get to the conveniently located **Scoutel ❹**, Stoomstr. 3, from Centraal Station, turn left on Pelikaanstr. and take your first left under the bridge; once through, the entrance is on the right. (☎226 46 06; www.scoutel.be. Breakfast and sheets included. Reception 8am-11pm. Singles €28, under 26 €25; doubles €45/€40; triples €56/€50; quads €75/€65. MC/V.) Both **Grote Markt** and **Groenplaats** are surrounded by restaurants, while **Suikerrui**, off Grote Markt, is the street for those seeking seafood. Hearty pizza (€4.50-10) and multilingual service await at **Pizzeria Ristorante Da Giovanni ❷**, Jan Blomstr. 8. (Open daily 11am-1am. 20% student discount. AmEx/MC/V.) The **GB** supermarket is in the Grand Shopping Bazar; enter on the corner of Beddenstr. and Schoenmarkt. (Open M-Th and Sa 8:30am-8pm, F 8:30am-9pm.) **Postal Code:** 2000.

GHENT (GENT) ☎09

Once the heart of the Flemish textile industry, modern Ghent (pop. 228,000) celebrates the memory of its industrial past. Awe-inspiring buildings in the city's main square stand in proud testament to its former grandeur, while the summertime Gentse Feesten commemorates the first vacation granted to laborers in 1860. The streets fill with performers, carnival rides, and rivers of beer, while international DJs drop eleven nights of rambunctious beats. (July 16-25, 2005. ☎269 46 00; www.gentsefeesten.be.) Steer clear of Ghent on Mondays, when museums close and nightlife is slow, as well as during the last two weeks of August, when most of the city's sights shut down. The **Leie canal** runs through the center of the city and wraps around the **Gravensteen**, St-Veerlepl. 11, a medieval fortress whose shadowy halls and spiral staircases will give you chills before you even reach the weapons room and torture museum. (Open daily Apr.-Sept. 9am-5:15pm; Oct.-Mar. 9am-4:15pm. €6, students €1.20.) The castle is near the historic **Partershol** quarter and **Vrijmarkt,** a bank of well-preserved 16th- to 18th-century houses. One block away on Limburgstr., **▧Saint Bavo's Cathedral** boasts van Eyck's many-paneled *Adoration of the Mystic Lamb* and Rubens's *St. Bavo's Entrance into the Monastery of Ghent.* (Cathedral and crypt open daily Apr.-Oct. 8:30am-6pm; Nov.-Mar. 8:30am-5pm. Free. *Mystic Lamb* exhibition open Apr.-Oct. M-Sa 9:30am-4:45pm, Su 1-4:30pm; Nov.-Mar. M-Sa 10:30am-3:45pm, Su 1-3:30pm. €3.) Walk across **Saint Michael's Bridge** for the best view of the steeples and belfry that make up Ghent's skyline, and then along the **Graslei**, a medieval port street lined by handsome guild houses and frequented during the summer by raffish young locals. The **Church of St. Nicholas,** the church of the rich merchants in days gone by, was built with blue-gray limestone drawn from quarries along the nearby Schelde River. (Open M 2-5pm, Tu-Su 10am-5pm. Free.) Sadly, the **Museum voor Schone Kunsten** (Museum of Fine Arts), in Citadel Park, is closed for renovations until fall 2006, although many of its paintings are on display elsewhere in the city. **Korenmarkt** and **Vrijdagmarkt** are filled with restaurants and pubs, and the staff at Use-It (see below) can direct you to live music just about every night. One popular haunt is the murky **Charlatan,** Vlasmarkt 6, which features live bands and DJs. (Open Tu-Su 4pm-late.)

Trains run from St-Pietersstation (accessible by tram #1, 10, or 11) to: Antwerp (50min., 2 per hr., €7); Brussels (35min., 4-5 per hr., €6.60); and Bruges (25min., 5-6 per hr., €4.80). The **tourist office,** Botermarkt 17A, in the crypt of the belfry, books rooms for free. (☎266 52 32; www.visitgent.be. Open daily Apr.-Oct. 9:30am-

6:30pm; Nov.-Mar. 9:30am-4:30pm.) **Use-It,** 43 Bagattenstr., is also a great service for young, budget-conscious backpackers, shelling out quirky maps and offering free **Internet** access. Check their website for a searchable database of available rooms, including university dorms (€25) in summer. (☎324 39 06; www.use-it.be. Open M-F 1-6pm.) To reach **De Draeke (HI) ❷,** St-Widostr. 11, from the station, take tram #1, 10, 11, 12, or 13 to Gravensteen. Facing the castle, head left over the canal, then go right on Gewad and turn right on St-Widostr. Double-check that you are getting the correct door code to avoid getting stranded outside after hours. (☎233 70 50. Breakfast and sheets included. Internet access €0.08 per min. Reception 7am-11pm. Dorms €16.30; singles €26; doubles €41. Nonmembers add €3. AmEx/MC/V.) **Oudburg,** near Patershol, and **St-Pietersnieuwstraat,** by the university, have inexpensive kebab and pita restaurants that stay open until late. **Magazijn ❷,** Penitentenstr. 24, has cheap and hearty fare with abundant vegetarian options. (☎234 07 08. Open M-Th noon-2pm and 6-11pm, Sa-Su 6-11pm.)

YPRES (IEPER)   ☎57

"In Flanders fields the poppies grow
Between the crosses, row on row
That mark our place; and in the sky
The larks, still bravely singing, fly
Scarce heard amid the guns below."
—John McCrae

Canadian soldier John McCrae wrote these famous lines during WWI at the Second Battle of Ypres. What the Germans believed would be a quick victory soon became a bitter stalemate punctuated by the first use of chemical warfare in Western history. Once a medieval textile center, Ypres (pop. 35,000) was completely destroyed by four years of combat, but was soon rebuilt as a near-perfect replica of its former self. Today, the town is surrounded by over 150 **British cemeteries** and filled with memorial sites, drawing soldiers' families as well as many British tourists and school groups. In the **Cloth Hall,** one of the grand guild halls that preside over **Grote Markt,** the ◪**In Flanders Field Museum,** Grote Markt 34, documents the gruesome history and bloody battles of the Great War. (☎23 92 20; www.inflandersfields.be. Open Apr.-Sept. daily 10am-6pm; Oct.-Mar. Tu-Su 10am-5pm. €7.50.) Next door stands splendid **St. Martin's Cathedral.** Cross the street in front of St. Martin's and head right to reach the Anglican **St. George's Memorial Church,** Elverdingsestr. 1. Each brass plaque and kneeling pillow in the church commemorates a specific individual or unit. (Open daily 9:30am-dusk. Free.) Across the Markt, the names of 54,896 British soldiers who were lost in the trenches are inscribed on the somber **Menin Gate.** At 8pm each evening, the **Last Post** bugle ceremony honors those who defended Ypres. You can easily walk the circumference of Ypres along the old ramparts. From Menin Gate, take the **Rose Coombs Walk** to visit the nearby **Ramparts Cemetery,** where white crosses stare blankly at the river.

Trains run to: Bruges (2hr., 1 per hr., €9); Brussels (1½hr., 1 per hr., €14); and Ghent (1¼hr., 1 per hr., €8.50). To get to the **Visitors Center,** inside the Cloth Hall, head straight from the station all the way down Stationsstr.; turn left onto Tempelstr., then right onto Boterstr. (☎23 92 20; www.ieper.be. Open Apr.-Sept. M-Sa 9am-6pm, Su 10am-6pm; Oct.-Mar. M-Sa 9am-5pm, Su 10am-5pm.) **Zonneweelde ❸,** Masscheleinlaan 18, has just four guest rooms, but they are spacious and the cheapest in town. From the Grote Markt, walk 5min. down Diksmuidestr., and turn left onto Masscheleinlaan. (☎20 27 23. Singles €24; doubles €45. Cash only.) Spend a more rustic night in the huts at canalside **Camping Jeugdstadion ❶,** 16

Leopold III laan. (☎21 72 82. Huts with 4 beds and kitchenette €32. Camping €3 per person, €1.50 per tent. Open Mar.-Oct.) Restaurants line the **Grote Markt,** and dessert comes in the form of free samples at **Vandaele,** Grote Markt 9, a family-run chocolatier well into its second century of operation. You can also stock up on groceries at **Super GB,** Vandepeereboompl. 15. (Open M-Sa 9am-7pm.)

WALLONIE

Wallonie, the French-speaking region of Belgium, enjoys less wealth than its Flemish counterpart; nonetheless, its bigger towns can claim a muscular, forthright charm all their own. The wooded hamlets of the Ardennes are gateways to a network of hiking trails, while visitors to the region's southeastern corner will find little-known breweries and acres of peaceful farmland clustered around minor river valleys. Nature-lovers will want to spend at least a night in this part of the Wallonie wilderness, although those pressed for time can enjoy the scenery from a train on the way to Brussels, Luxembourg City, or Paris.

LIEGE (LUIK)   ☎04

The largest city in Wallonie, Liège (pop. 200,000) is often dismissed as a mere transportation hub for travelers heading east into Germany—or as a sprawling industrial armpit. It takes time to penetrate the surface of this underappreciated city, but Liège's student haunts and vibrant art scene have a gritty integrity all their own. The city spans a large land area, but most of the main sights are accessible on foot. The **Coeur Historique** is a knot of cobblestone lanes and medieval architecture, and it contains the **Musée de L'Art Wallon,** 86 Féronstrée, with eastern Belgian paintings and sculptures dating back to the Renaissance. (Open Tu-Sa 1-6pm, Su 11am-4:30pm. €3.80, students €2.50.) Walk down r. Hors-Chateau and turn right onto the Impasse des Ursulines to reach the **Montagne de Bueren.** Scale the 367 steps for a spectacular view of the city. Across the Meuse River, the **Musée d'Art Moderne et d'Art Contemporain (MAMAC),** 3 Parc de la Boverie, shows minor works by Picasso and Chagall, and will host a major engraving exhibition during the spring of 2005. From the Pont des Arches in the working-class district of Outremeuse, follow the river toward quai Sur-Meuse until you reach the Parc de la Boverie. (☎343 04 03; www.mamac.org. Open Tu-Sa 1-6pm, Su 11am-4:30pm. €3.80, students €2.50.) **Flea markets** are big business on the weekends in Liège; **La Batte** is the oldest and largest in Belgium, with stalls stretching 4km between and around the Quai Roosevelt and Quai de Maastricht. (Open Su 8am-2pm.) Students at the University of Liège literally pack the streets at night, particularly in the area known as **Le Carré**—a pedestrian-only quadrant bisected by r. du Pot-d'Or, with narrow, bar-lined streets extending out to the northwest and southeast.

Trains go to: Aachen, Germany (45min., 1-2 per hr., €11); Brussels (1½hr., 2-5 per hr., €11); Luxembourg City (2½hr.; every 2hr.; €28, under 26 €21); and Maastricht (30min.; 1 per hr.; €7, under 26 €5). To get to the **tourist office,** 92 Féronstrée, take bus #1 or 4. (☎221 92 21; www.liege.be. Open M-F 9am-5pm.) On weekends, the **Maison du Tourisme** on Place St. Lambert picks up the slack. (☎237 92 92. Open daily June-Sept. 9:30am-5:30pm.) The **Auberge de Jeunesse de Liège (HI) ❷,** 2 r. Georges Simenon, is conveniently located in the Outremeuse, just across the Pont des Arches from the Coeur Historique. Take bus #4 from the station and ask to get off at Auberge de Jeunesse. (☎344 56 89. Breakfast and sheets included. Internet €0.08 per min. Laundry €6. Reception 7:30am-1am. Dorms €15.75; singles €24; doubles €38. Nonmembers add €3. MC/V.) Outremeuse teems with inexpensive kebab stands, and **Newave à la Passerelle ❷,** 13 bvd. Saucy, serves up vegetarian couscous (€8) in bright, cheery surroundings. (Open M-F noon-10pm, Su noon-5pm. Cash only.) Pick up groceries at **Contact GB**, 4 r. Pont St. Nicholas, down the street from the Auberge de Jeunesse. (Open M-Sa 8:30am-7pm.)

TOURNAI (DOORNIK)   ☎069

The first city liberated from the Nazis by Allied forces, Tournai (pop. 68,000) has a history of being bounced between various empires; it was once a Roman trading post and later served as the capital of Gaul. The city's most spectacular sight is the 800-year-old **Cathédrale Notre-Dame,** the only cathedral in the world to have five steeples. A 1999 tornado left the landmark in need of emergency repairs, but visitors are still welcome as renovations continue. Climb the 257 steps of the **belfry** for a stunning view of the city. (Open Mar.-Oct. Tu-Sa 10am-1pm and 2-5:30pm, Su 11am-1pm and 2-6:30pm; Nov.-Feb. Tu-Sa 10am-noon and 2-5pm, Su 2-5pm. €2, students €1.) Two blocks away, Victor Horta's sunlit **Musée des Beaux-Arts,** enclos St-Martin, houses a small collection of Belgian and Dutch paintings. (Open Apr.-Sept. Tu-Su 9:30am-12:30pm and 2-5:30pm; Oct.-Mar. Tu-Sa 10am-noon and 2-5pm, Su 2-5pm. €3, students €1.) At night, check out medieval-chic **▩Hangar,** 6 r. de l'Arbalète, located just off of r. de l'Hôpital de Notre Dame. (Open Tu-Su 9pm-late.) **Trains** arrive at pl. Crombez from Brussels' Gare du Midi (1hr., 1 per hr., €9.60). To get to the **tourist office,** 14 Vieux Marché aux Poteries, exit the station, walk 10min. to the city center, and go around the left side of the cathedral. (☎22 20 45; www.tournai.be. Open Apr.-Sept. M-F 8:30am-6pm, Sa 9:30am-noon and 2-5pm, Su 10am-noon and 2:30-6pm; Oct.-Mar. M-F 8:30am-5:30pm, Sa 10am-noon and 2-5pm, Su 2:30-6pm.) To get to the **Auberge de Jeunesse (HI) ❷,** 64 r. St-Martin, continue straight up the hill from the tourist office or take bus #7 or 88 (€1.10) from the station. (☎21 61 36. Breakfast and sheets included. Reception 8am-noon and 5-10pm. Closed Jan. Dorms €14; singles €24; doubles €38. Nonmembers add €2.50.) The area around **Grand Place** has plenty of options for cheap food, but to avoid getting mauled by tourists, head down to the riverside **Quai du Marché Poisson.**

NAMUR   ☎081

The quiet and friendly city of Namur (pop. 110,000), in the heart of Wallonie, is the last sizable outpost before the wilderness of the Ardennes. Given the proximity of opportunities for **hiking, biking, caving,** and **kayaking,** it is the most convenient base for exploration. The foreboding **citadel,** on top of a cliff to the south, was built by the Spanish in the Middle Ages, expanded by the Dutch in the 19th century, and besieged by an invading German army during WWI; it remained an active Belgian military base until 1978. Footpaths and bike paths thread their way through the surrounding **Parc de Champeau,** and are open to the public year-round. **Trains** link Namur to: Brussels (1hr., 1 per hr., €7), Dinant (30min., 1 per hr., €5); and Luxembourg City (2 hr., 1 per hr., €15). The **tourist office** is on the Square Léopold. (☎24 64 49. Open daily 9:30am-6pm.) Turn left out of the train station, and walk 100m down r. de la Gare. (☎24 64 48. Open Apr.-Nov. 9:30am-6pm.) The cheapest place to rent **bikes** is at **Maison des Cyclistes,** 16 r. Muzet. (☎81 38 48. €2 per hr., €8 per day, €14 for 2 days.) Flocks of geese dally on the banks of the Meuse not ten paces away from the **Auberge Félicien Rops (HI) ❷,** 8 av. Félicien Rops, accessible by bus #3 from the train station. (☎22 36 88. Breakfast and sheets included. Laundry €6.50. Free Internet. Reception 7:30am-11:30pm. Lockout 11am-4pm. Dorms €14-16. Nonmembers add €3.) To **camp** at **Les Trieux ❶,** 99 r. des Tris, 6km away, take bus #6. (☎44 55 83. Open Apr.-Oct. €4 per person, €4.50 per tent.) Restaurants cluster in the lanternlight of the **Place Marché-aux-Legumes** on r. St-Jean.

DINANT
☎ **082**

Razed by the German army in 1914 and reeling from mill closings through the 60s and 70s, the scrappy town of Dinant (pop. 13,000) has managed to reinvent itself as a tourist destination. Its imposing **citadel** towers over the Meuse River. (☎ 22 36 70. Citadel open daily Mar.-Sept. 10am-6pm. Required tour in French and Dutch, 45min., every 35min., €5.50.) Pick your way through stalactites and stalagmites at the caves of the **Grotte Merveilleuse,** 142 rte. de Phillippeville. Bring a jacket. (Open daily July-Aug. 10am-6pm; Sept.-Apr. 11am-5pm. Tours every hr. €5.50, students €4.50.) Smoky, aromatic Leffe ale is no longer brewed at the 13th-century **Leffe Abbey,** 1 pl. de l'Abbaye, but the **Musée Histoire de la Leffe** has information on the abbey's history as well as beer tastings. (☎ 64 75 83. Open July-Aug. Tu-Su 1-6pm; Apr.-June and Sept.-Oct. Sa-Su 1-6pm. €3.50.) A number of companies offer kayaking on the Meuse, while **Dakota Raid Adventure,** 6 r. Cousot, bends over backwards to sponsor rappelling, mountain biking, and moonlit hikes into the Ardennes. (☎ 22 32 43. €14 per half-day, €20 per full day. Reserve in advance.) The **tourist office,** 8 Quai Cadoux, charges a €2 fee to book rooms, which tend to be pricey. (☎ 22 28 70; www.dinant-tourisme.be. Open M-Sa 9:30am-7pm, Su 10am-6pm; low season reduced hours.) From the station, turn right, take the first left, and another immediate left. Dinant is accessible by **train** from Brussels (1hr., 1 per hr., €9.60) and Namur (30min., 1 per hr., €3.60) or by **bike** from Namur (approx. 3hr.); on summer weekends, take a one-way river cruise from Namur (3hr.; €14).

ROCHEFORT
☎ **084**

A charming town with hospitable residents, Rochefort (pop. 12,000) is hidden within the rolling hills and woods of the Lesse Valley. The main attraction is the **Grotte de Lorette,** a fairly deep cave that descends 65m into the earth. (☎ 21 25 37. Tours July-Aug. daily 11am-5:30pm, every 45min; low season reduced hours. €7, students €3.45.) No less touristed but a good deal more spectacular are the famous caves at **Han-sur-Lesse,** 6km from Rochefort on bus #29, which leaves every hour from the Square Crépin. (☎ 37 72 13. Open July-Aug. 10am-noon and 1:30-5:30pm; low season reduced hours. €11.50, students 10% off.) Back in Rochefort, walk up r. Jacquet to the crumbled **Château Comtal** for a breathtaking view of the Northern Ardennes. (☎ 21 44 09. Site open daily Apr.-Oct. 10am-6pm. €1.80.) To reach Rochefort, take the **train** from Namur to Jemelle (40min., every 40min., €6.60) and **bus** #29 from Jemelle (1 per hr., usually 34min. after the hr., €1.10). The **tourist office,** 5 r. de Behogne, sells hiking maps. To get there from the bus drop-off point, turn left down r. de France, and then left on r. de Behogne. (☎ 21 25 37. Open M-F 8am-5pm, Sa-Su 9:30am-5pm; low season reduced hours.)

BOSNIA AND HERZEGOVINA
(BOSNA I HERCEGOVINA)

In June 2004, the US State Department reiterated its **Travel Warning** against visits to certain regions in Bosnia. Before departure, consult the Embassy in Sarajevo and see http://travel.state.gov/travel/bosnia_warning.html.

The mountainous centerpiece of former Yugoslavia, Bosnia and Herzegovina today stands as an independent nation but remains a contentious mixing ground for Muslim Bosniaks, Catholic Croats, and Orthodox Serbs. Sarajevo, the capital, maintains a verbal ideal of tolerance, but ethnic tensions continue in the country-side. Although recent years have been unkind to the country, leaving its lush valleys punctuated by abandoned houses and gaping rooftops, Bosnia's resilient people are optimistic and reconstruction has begun.

ESSENTIALS

DOCUMENTS AND FORMALITIES

VISAS. Citizens of Australia, Canada, Ireland, New Zealand, the UK, and the US do not need visas for stays of up to 90 days. A valid passport is required to enter and leave the country. Occasionally, travelers will encounter police checkpoints within the country. All must **register** with the police within 24hr. of arrival; hotels will often take care of this automatically. It is also wise to register with your embassy, and to keep your papers with you at all times.

EMBASSIES. Foreign embassies in Bosnia are in Sarajevo (p. 147). Bosnian embassies at home include: **Australia,** 5 Beale Crescent, Deakin, ACT 2600 (☎02 6232 4646; www.bosnia.webone.com.au); **Canada,** 130 Albert St. Ste. 805, Ottawa, ON K1P 5G4 (☎613-236-0028; fax 613-236-1139); **UK,** 4th Floor, Morley House, 320 Regent St., London W1R 5AB (☎020 7255 3758; fax 020 7255 3760); **US,** 2109 E St. NW, Washington, D.C. 20037 (☎202-337-6473; www.bhembassy.org).

Bosnia and Herzegovina

TRANSPORTATION

Commercial **plane** service into Sarajevo is limited and expensive; **Croatia Airlines** (www.croatiaairlines.hr) has regular service to Sarajevo from Zagreb. **Buses** are reliable, uncrowded, and clean, but road travel in the Balkans can be nerve-wracking. **Railways** suffered in wartime and should not be considered an option. **Driving, biking,** and **hitch-hiking** should be avoided if possible.

TOURIST SERVICES AND MONEY

EMERGENCY	Police: ☎92. Ambulance: ☎94. Fire: ☎93.

Introduced in 1998, the **convertible mark (KM)** is fixed to the euro at a rate of 1KM to €0.51. Bosnia also named the Croatian **kuna** an official currency in 1997; while not legal tender in Sarajevo, it is accepted in the western (Croatian) area of divided Mostar. The old Bosnian *dinar* is no longer valid. Change your money to euros before leaving, as the convertible mark is not so convertible outside Bosnia. Banks are the best places to exchange money; a few in Sarajevo cash traveler's checks. **Western Union** in Sarajevo has very helpful English-speaking staff. **ATMs** are also available in the capital. Bring euros along if you venture outside Sarajevo. **Tip** restaurant waitstaff only for outstanding service.

CONV. MARKS (KM)		
AUS$1 = 1.14KM		1KM = AUS$0.87
CDN$1 = 1.22KM		1KM = CDN$0.82
EUR€1 = 1.96KM		1KM = EUR€0.51
NZ$1 = 1.06KM		1KM = NZ$0.94
UK£1 = 2.90KM		1KM = UK£0.35
US$1 = 1.58KM		1KM = US$0.63

COMMUNICATION

PHONE CODES	**Country code: 387. International dialing prefix:** 00. From outside Bosnia-Herzegovina, dial int'l dialing prefix (see inside back cover) + 387 + city code + local number.

TELEPHONES AND INTERNET ACCESS. Phones are troublesome and expensive; the best option is to call collect from the Sarajevo post office. An international access number is available for **AT&T** (☎00 800 0010). **Internet** access is becoming widely available in larger cities.

MAIL. Yellow-and-white "PTT" signs indicate post offices. Mail service is improving in efficiency. Mail to Europe takes three to five days, to North America seven to ten days. Address mail to be held as follows: First name SURNAME, *Post Restante*, Zmaja od Bosne 88, Sarajevo 71000 BOSNIA AND HERZEGOVINA.

ACCOMMODATIONS AND FOOD

BOSNIA	❶	❷	❸	❹	❺
ACCOMMODATIONS	under 35KM	35-40KM	40-50KM	50-60KM	over 60KM
FOOD	under 4KM	4-7KM	7-10KM	10-14KM	over 14KM

Accommodations options are limited in Bosnia. **Hotels** are most common, going for around 30-80KM per night. **Private rooms** usually cost as much as cheaper hotels and exist only in Sarajevo (30-50KM). **Camping** should be avoided for safety reasons, except as arranged through special organizations. Cheap **meals** average 4KM.

SAFETY AND SECURITY

Likely over half a million **land mines** and **unexploded ordnance (UXO)** still litter the country, many on road shoulders and in abandoned houses. Outside Sarajevo, *always* stay on hard-covered surfaces and never pick up any objects off the ground. More info is available from the **Mine Action Center (MAC)**, Zmaja od Bosne 8 KMT, Sarajevo (☎033 253 3800; www.bhmac.org). It is not difficult to find **medical help** and supplies in Sarajevo; national embassies are the best resource. Peacekeeping has brought English-speaking doctors but not insurance, so be prepared to pay in cash. Always check the latest security warnings before departure.

HOLIDAYS

Holidays: New Year's (Jan. 1); Orthodox Christmas (Jan. 7); Orthodox New Year (Jan. 14); Independence Day (Mar. 1); Labor Day (May 1); Orthodox Easter (May 1-2); St. George's Day (May 6); Vidovdan (Jun. 28); Petrovdan (Jul. 12); Ilindan (Aug. 2); Orthodox Assumption (Aug. 28); Orthodox Nativity (Sept. 21); All Saints' Day (Nov. 1); All Souls' Day (Nov. 2); Mitrovdan (Nov. 8); National Day (Nov. 25); Christmas (Dec. 25).

FACTS AND FIGURES: BOSNIA AND HERZEGOVINA

Official Name: Bosnia and Herzegovina.

Capital: Sarajevo.

Major City: Mostar.

Population: 4,000,000 (40% Bosniak, 31% Serb, 15% Croat, 14% other).

Land Area: 51,129 sq. km.

Languages: Bosnian, Serbian, Croatian.

Time Zone: GMT +1.

Religions: Muslim (43%), Orthodox (30%), Catholic (18%), other (9%).

SARAJEVO   ☎033

Sarajevo lives again. Although it takes work not to see the suffering the city faced during the brutal siege of 1992-1995, the enchantments of this "big village" (pop. 450,000) make it easy to forget the massive destruction it faced then, and reconstruction is methodically healing the physical scars. A burgeoning arts scene, the old Turkish Quarter's lively marketplace, and revived nightlife all promise a return to Sarajevo's prewar glory. Today, the city's residents are not aloof—pension owners, shopkeepers, and even taxi drivers welcome visitors like old friends.

The following outlying areas of Sarajevo were battlegrounds during the war and still contain land mines: Dobrinja, Grbavica, Illidža, and Lukavica.

▐▓ TRANSPORTATION AND PRACTICAL INFORMATION. Buses (☎21 31 00) run from Put Života 2, at the corner with Halida Kajtaza, to: Dubrovnik (7hr., 1 per day, 44KM); Frankfurt (23hr., 1 per day, 198KM); Ljubljana (10hr., 3 per week, 74KM); Split (7hr., 5 per day, 34KM); and Zagreb (7hr., 3 per day, 54KM). To reach the main street, **Maršala Tita,** turn left from the station and follow Kranjčevića for 20min., or take a cab (7-8KM). To reach the tourist bureau, **Turistička Zajednica,** Zelenih Beretki 22a, bear right at the Eternal Flame on Maršala Tita. At the church on the left, turn right on Štrosmajerova, then left onto Zelenih Beretki. (☎22 07 24. Open in summer M-Sa 9am-8pm, Su 10am-2pm; in winter M-Sa 9am-6pm, Su 10am-2pm.) **Embassies** include: **Canada,** Grbavička 4 (☎22 20 33; open M-F 8:30am-5pm); **UK,** Petrakijina 11 (☎20 82 29; open M-F 8:30am-5pm); and **US,** Alipašina 43 (☎44 57 00; www.usembassy.ba;

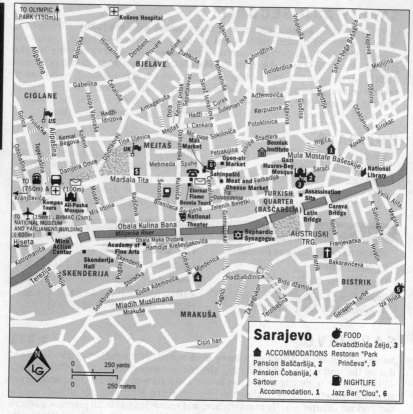

Sarajevo

🍎 FOOD
Čevabdžinića Željo, 3
Restoran "Park
Prinčeva", 5

🔺 ACCOMMODATIONS
Pansion Baščaršija, 2
Pansion Čobanija, 4
Sartour
Accommodation, 1

🍸 NIGHTLIFE
Jazz Bar "Clou", 6

open M-F 2-3:30pm, Tu and Th 8am-noon). Citizens of **Australia** should contact their embassy in Vienna (p. 94), citizens of **New Zealand** their embassy in Rome (p. 625). **Central Profit Banka**, Zelenih Beretki 24, cashes **traveler's checks** and changes money. (Open M-F 8am-7pm, Sa 8am-noon.) **ATMs** are everywhere. **Internet** cafes lie along Ferhadija (2-3KM per hr.). **Postal Code:** 71000.

🚪🛏 **ACCOMMODATIONS AND FOOD.** **Private rooms** (30-50KM) are available all over town; taxi drivers can help find these. To reach ▓**Pansion Baščaršija** ❺, Veliki Čurčiluk 41, walk down Ferhadija away from the Eternal Flame, go right onto Gazi Huzrev-Begova, and take the third left. (☎23 21 85. Singles 60KM; doubles 100KM; triples 120KM.) **Sartour Accommodation** ❶, Mula Mustafe Baseskije 63, just before the intersection with Kovaći, runs two excellent guesthouses. (☎23 86 80. Singles 30KM; doubles 60KM.) To get to modern **Pansion Čobanija** ❺, Čobanija 29, from the Eternal Flame, take the first left onto Kulovića, which crosses the river to become Čobanija. (☎44 17 49. Reserve ahead. Singles 80KM; doubles 120KM.) Take a taxi (5KM) up to ▓**Restoran "Park Prinčeva"** ❹, Iza Hrida 7, for an unmatchable view of Sarajevo. (☎061 22 27 08. Entrees 10-20KM. Open daily 9am-11pm.) **Čevabdžinića Željo** ❷, Kundurdžiluk 19, is the most popular *čevabdžinića* (kebab; 4KM) shop in the Turkish Quarter. (Open daily 8am-10pm.) Don't miss the Bosnian coffee at cafes in the Turkish Quarter's central square.

◙ SIGHTS. The **Eternal Flame,** where Maršala Tita splits into Ferhadija and Mula Mustafe Bašeskije, was lit in 1945 as a memorial to all Sarajevans who died in WWII; its homage to South Slav unity now seems painfully ironic. Reconstruction has obscured most signs of the recent siege in the center, but the **treeline** in the hills still marks the war's front lines; trapped Sarajevans cut down all the safely available wood for winter heat. From Maršala Tita, walk riverward to Obala Kulina Bana and turn left to find the **National Library,** at the tip of the Turkish Quarter. Once Sarajevo's most beautiful building, the library was firebombed on August 25, 1992, the centennial of its construction. As it burned, citizens risked their lives to salvage its treasures, but most of the collection was destroyed. Walk toward the center to the third bridge on Obala Kulina Bana, where Serbian terrorist Gavrilo Princip shot Austrian Archduke Franz Ferdinand on June 28, 1914, triggering WWI.

Several religions have places of worship in the city center. Walk right at the Eternal Flame on Ferhadija, which becomes Sarači, to find the 16th-century **Gazi Husrev-Bey mosque,** Sarači 12, one of Sarajevo's most famous buildings. Inside, brightly-colored Bosnian carpets complement intricate designs on the walls and dome. (Women must cover heads and shoulders. Open daily 9am-noon, 2:30-4pm, and 5:30-7pm. 1KM.) Low, red-roofed buildings surrounding the mosque make up **Baščaršija,** the Turkish Quarter, at the center of which is a traditional bazaar. The **National Museum** and the **History Museum** are at Zmaja od Bosne 3 and 5, respectively. The former houses impressive ethnographic and natural history exhibitions, the latter an exhibit on the recent siege. (National Museum open Tu-F, Su 10am-2pm. 5KM. History Museum open M-F 9am-2pm and 4-8pm, Sa-Su 9am-1pm. 1KM.) Next to the National Museum, the shattered tower of the **Parliament Building** is a shocking reminder of how most of Sarajevo looked after the war. War ignited in 1992 when a peace rally began from Parliament and marched on ul. Vrbanja across the bridge; Serb snipers opened fire, causing the first casualties. A small monument to the rally's victims can now be found beside the bridge.

▣▣ ENTERTAINMENT AND NIGHTLIFE. Sarajevo has begun a steady ascent toward its former position as the cultural capital of the Balkans. For a monthly schedule of theater, opera, ballet, and concert events, stop by Turistička Zajednica (see above) and pick up a *Program of Cultural Events* (Program Kulturnih Događaja). Sarajevo's revived **National Theater** (Narodno Pozorište Sarajevo), Obala Kulina Bana 9, hosts theater, opera, ballet, and concerts. From the Eternal Flame, walk down Maršala Tita to Kulovića and turn left; one block down on the left is Pozorišni Trg (Theater Square). Enter on Branilaca Sarajeva. (☎22 16 82; www.npsa.org. Box office open daily 9am-noon and 4-7:30pm.) Every July, the Turkish Quarter hosts the **Turkish Nights** (Baščaršija Noci), featuring open-air music, theater, and film. In late August, the **Sarajevo Film Festival** rolls into theaters city-wide. (☎22 15 16; www.sff.ba. 5KM per film.) A celebration of culture that continued even during the siege, the **Sarajevan Winter** (Sarajevska Zima; ☎20 79 48) takes place from February 7 to March 21. Underground events are always happening; find out about them by word of mouth. The best nightlife is found in clubs along **Štrosmajerova** and in basement bars on **Baščaršija.** At Mula Mustafe Bašeskije 5, through an unmarked door near the Eternal Flame, **◙Jazz Bar "Clou"** hosts local bands on Friday and Saturday nights. (Beer 3-4KM. Open daily 8:30pm-5am.)

BRITAIN

Having spearheaded the Industrial Revolution, colonized two-fifths of the globe, and won every foreign war in its history but two, Britain seems intent on making the world forget its tiny size. It's hard to believe that the rolling farms of the south and the rugged cliffs of the north are only a day's train ride apart, or that people as diverse as London clubbers, Cornish miners, Welsh students, and Gaelic monks all occupy a land area half the size of Spain. Beyond the stereotypical fairy-tale cottages and quaint sheep farms of "Merry Olde England," today's Britain is a cosmopolitan destination driven by international energy. Though the sun may have set on the British Empire, a colonial legacy survives in multicultural urban centers and a dynamic arts and theater scene. Brits now eat kebab and curry as often as they do scones, and five-story dance clubs in post-industrial settings draw as much attention as picturesque views of country inns.

Travelers should be aware that names hold political force. The term "Great Britain" refers to England, Scotland, and Wales; "United Kingdom" encompasses Northern Ireland as well. *Let's Go* uses "Britain" to refer to England, Scotland, and Wales because of legal and monetary distinctions.

 DISCOVER BRITAIN: SUGGESTED ITINERARIES

THREE DAYS: Spend it all in **London** (p. 155), the city of tea, royalty, and James Bond. After a stroll through **Hyde Park,** head to **Buckingham Palace** for the changing of the guard. Check out the renowned collections of the **British Museum** and the **Tate Modern.** Stop at storied **Westminster Abbey** and catch a play at **Shakespeare's Globe Theatre** before sipping a drink in the **East End.**

ONE WEEK: Begin in **London** (3 days), then immerse yourself in academia at the colleges in **Oxford** (1 day; p. 192). Travel north to Scotland for a day in the museums and galleries of **Glasgow** (p. 223) and finish off with pubs and parties in lively **Edinburgh** (2 days; p. 216).

THREE WEEKS: Start in **London** (4 days), where you'll explore the museums, theaters, and clubs. Tour the college greens in **Cambridge** (2 days; p. 198) and **Oxford** (2 days), then amble through the rolling hills of the **Cotswolds** (1 day; p. 197). Don't miss Shakespeare's hometown, **Stratford-upon-Avon** (1 day; p. 196), or that of the Beatles, **Liverpool** (1 day; p. 202). Head to **Manchester** for its nightlife (1 day; p. 201) before moving on to **Glasgow** (1 day) and nearby **Loch Lomond** (1 day; p. 226). Exuberant **Edinburgh** (4 days) will keep you busy, especially during festival season. Finally, enjoy the beautiful **Lake District** (2 days; p. 207) and historic **York** (1 day; p. 204).

ESSENTIALS

WHEN TO GO

It may be wise to plan around the high season (June-Aug.). Spring or autumn (Apr.-May and Sept.-Oct.) are more appealing times to visit; the weather is still reasonable and flights are cheaper, though there may be fewer services in rural areas. If you intend to visit the large cities and linger indoors at museums and theaters, the off season (Nov.-Mar.) is most economical. Keep in mind, however, that sights and accommodations often close or run reduced hours, especially in rural regions.

Another factor to consider is hours of daylight. In Scotland, summer light lasts almost to midnight, but in winter the sun may set as early as 3:45pm. Regardless of when you go, it will rain—have warm, waterproof clothing on hand.

DOCUMENTS AND FORMALITIES

VISAS. EU citizens do not need a visa. Citizens of Australia, Canada, New Zealand, and the US do not need a visa for stays up to six months.

EMBASSIES. Foreign embassies in Britain are in London (see p. 159.) British embassies at home include: **Australia,** British High Commission, Commonwealth Ave., Yarralumla, ACT 2600 (☎02 6270 6666; www.britaus.net); **Canada,** British High Commission, 80 Elgin St., Ottawa, ON K1P 5K7 (613-237-1530; www.britain-in-canada.org); **Ireland,** British Embassy, 29 Merrion Rd., Ballsbridge, Dublin 4 (01 205 3700; www.britishembassy.ie); **New Zealand,** British High Commission, 44 Hill St., Thorndon, Wellington 1 (04 924 2888; www.britain.org.nz); **US,** British Embassy, 3100 Massachusetts Ave. NW, Washington, D.C. 20008 (202-588-6500; www.britainusa.com).

TRANSPORTATION

BY PLANE. For info on flying to Britain from the Continent, see p. 51. Most flights into Britain that originate outside Europe land at London's Heathrow (☎0870 000 0123) and Gatwick (0870 000 2468) airports, but some fly directly to regional airports such as Manchester (0161 489 3000) and Edinburgh (0870 040 0007).

BY TRAIN. Trains run to Britain from the Continent through the **Chunnel** (see p. 55). Britain's train network is extensive. Prices and schedules often change; find up-to-date information from **National Rail Enquiries** (☎08457 484 950; www.nationalrail.co.uk/planmyjourney) or **Network Rail** (www.networkrail.co.uk; schedules only). The **BritRail Pass,** only sold outside Britain, allows unlimited travel in England, Wales, and Scotland (8-day US$270, under 26 US$202; 22-day US$510/US$382); in Canada and the US, contact **Rail Europe** (Canada ☎800-361-7245; US 800-257-2887; www.raileurope.com). Rail discount cards (£20) grant 33% off most point-to-point fares and are available at stations and travel agencies to those ages 16-25, full-time students, seniors over 60, and families. **Eurail** is not valid in Britain.

BY BUS. The British distinguish between **buses,** which cover short local routes, and **coaches,** which cover long distances; *Let's Go* uses the term "buses" to refer to both. **National Express** (☎08705 808 080; www.nationalexpress.com) is the principal long-distance coach service operator in Britain, although **Scottish Citylink** (☎08705 505 050; www.citylink.co.uk) has coverage in Scotland. **Discount Coachcards** (£10) are available online for those ages 16-25, students, and seniors over 50; they reduce fares by up to 30%. The **Brit Xplorer Pass** offers unlimited travel on National Express buses. (4-day £70, 14-day £120; 28-day £190.)

BY FERRY. Several ferry lines provide service between Britain and the Continent. Ask for discounts; ISIC holders can sometimes get student fares, and Eurail passholders are eligible for reductions and free trips. In the summer, book ahead. For information on boats from Wales to Dublin, Dún Laoghaire, and Rosslare, Ireland; from Scotland to Belfast; or from England to the Continent, see p. 55.

BY CAR. To drive, you must be 17 and have a valid license from your home country; to rent, you must be over 21. Britain is covered by a high-speed system of **motorways** ("M-roads") that connect London with other major cities. Visitors may not be accustomed to **driving on the left,** and automatic transmission is rare in rental cars. In London, traffic is slow and parking is impossible. Roads are generally well-maintained, but petrol (gasoline) prices are high.

BY BIKE AND BY THUMB. Much of Britain's countryside is well suited for **biking.** Many cities and villages have bike rental shops and maps of local cycle routes. Large-scale Ordnance Survey maps, often available at tourist offices, detail the extensive system of long-distance **hiking** paths. Tourist offices and National Park Information Centres can provide extra information about routes. Hitchhiking is illegal on M-roads; *Let's Go* does not recommend hitchhiking.

TOURIST SERVICES AND MONEY

EMERGENCY   Police: ☎ 999. Ambulance: ☎ 999. Fire: ☎ 999.

TOURIST OFFICES. Formerly known as the British Tourist Authority, **Visit Britain** (☎ 020 8563 3000; www.visitbritain.com) is an umbrella organization for the separate UK tourist boards. **Tourist offices** within Britain usually stock maps and information on sights and accommodations.

MONEY. The **pound sterling** is the main unit of currency in the United Kingdom. It is divided into 100 pence, issued in standard denominations of 1p, 2p, 5p, 10p, 20p, 50p, £1, and £2 in coins, and £5, £10, £20, and £50 in notes. Scotland has its own bank notes, which can be used interchangeably with English currency, though you may have difficulty using Scottish £1 notes outside Scotland. As a general rule, it's cheaper to exchange money in Britain than at home. Expect to spend anywhere from £22-50 per day. London in particular is a budget-buster, with the bare minimum for accommodations, food, and transport costing £30-40. **Tips** in restaurants are often included in the bill, sometimes as a "service charge." If gratuity is not included, you should tip about 15%. Taxi drivers should receive a 10-15% tip, and bellhops and chambermaids usually expect somewhere between £1 and £3. There is a **Value Added Tax (VAT)** of 17.5% on goods and services purchased within Britain, which is included in the price (see p. 22).

BRITISH POUNDS (£)		
AUS$1 = UK£0.39		UK£1 = AUS$2.55
CDN$1 = UK£0.42		UK£1 = CDN$2.38
EUR€1 = UK£0.68		UK£1 = EUR€1.48
NZ$1 = UK£0.36		UK£1 = NZ$2.74
US$1 = UK£0.55		UK£1 = US$1.82

COMMUNICATION

TELEPHONES. For information on buying a cell phone, see p. 35. Most public pay phones in Britain are run by British Telecom (BT). Public phones charge a minimum of 30p and don't accept 1p, 2p, or 5p coins. A BT Chargecard will bill phone calls to your credit card, but most pay phones now have readers where you can swipe credit cards directly, including AmEx/MC/Visa. For directory inquiries, which are free from pay phones, call ☎ 192. International direct dial numbers include: AT&T ☎ 0800 013 0011; British Telecom 0800 14 41 44; Canada Direct 0800 096 0634 or 0800 559 3141; MCI 0800 279 5088; and Sprint 0800 890 877.

MAIL. To send a postcard or letter within Europe costs £0.40; a postcard to any other international destination costs £0.43, while a letter costs £0.68. Address mail to be held according to the following example: First name SURNAME, *Poste Restante*, New Bond St. Post Office, Bath BA1 1AJ, UK.

INTERNET ACCESS. Britain is one of the world's most wired countries. **Cybercafes** or public terminals can be found almost everywhere; they usually cost £4-6 per hour, but you often pay only for the time used. Public **libraries** usually have free or inexpensive Internet access, but you might have to wait or call ahead. Online guides to cybercafes in Britain, updated daily, include the **Cybercafe Search Engine** (http://cybercaptive.com) and **Cybercafes.com** (www.cybercafes.com).

ACCOMMODATIONS AND CAMPING

BRITAIN	❶	❷	❸	❹	❺
ACCOMMODATIONS	under £11	£11-20	£20-30	£30-60	over £60

Hostels are run by the **Youth Hostels Association (YHA) of England and Wales** (☎0870 770 8868; www.yha.org.uk) and the **Scottish Youth Hostels Association (SYHA;** ☎01786 89 14 00; www.syha.org.uk). Hostel dorms will cost around £10 in rural areas, £14 in larger cities, and £15-25 in London. You can book **B&Bs** by calling directly, or by asking the local tourist office to help you find accommodations. Tourist offices usually charge a 10% deposit on the first night's or the entire stay's price, deductible from the amount you pay the B&B proprietor; often a flat fee of £1-3 is added on. **Campsites** tend to be privately owned and cost £3-10 per person per night. It is illegal to camp in national parks.

FOOD AND DRINK

BRITAIN	❶	❷	❸	❹	❺
FOOD	under £5	£5-10	£10-15	£15-20	over £20

A pillar of traditional British fare, the famous, cholesterol-filled, meat-anchored English breakfast is still served in most B&Bs across the country. The best native dishes for lunch or dinner are roasts—beef, lamb, and Wiltshire hams—and puddings, including the standard Yorkshire. Pubs often serve meat pies or a "ploughman's lunch" consisting of cheese, bread, and pickles. Fish and chips (french fries) are traditionally drowned in malt vinegar and salt. To escape English food, try Chinese, Greek, or Indian cuisine. British "tea" refers to both a drink, served strong and milky, and a social ritual. An afternoon tea might include cooked meats, salad, sandwiches, and pastries. Cream tea, a specialty of Cornwall and Devon, includes toast, shortbread, crumpets, scones, jam, and clotted cream.

HOLIDAYS AND FESTIVALS

Holidays: New Year's Day (Jan. 1); Good Friday (Mar. 25); Easter Sunday and Monday (Apr. 27and 28); May Day (May 2); Bank Holidays (May 30 and Aug. 29); Christmas (Dec. 25); and Boxing Day (Dec. 26).

Festivals: Scotland's New Year's Eve celebration, Hogmanay, takes over the streets in Edinburgh and Glasgow. Muddy fun abounds at the Glastonbury Festival, Britain's biggest homage to rock (June 24-26). The National Eisteddfod of Wales (July 6-Aug. 5) has brought Welsh writers, musicians, and artists together since 1176. One of the largest music and theater festivals in the world is the Edinburgh International Festival (Aug. 14-Sept. 5); also highly recommended is the Fringe Festival (Aug. 3-25). Manchester's Gay Village hosts Manchester Pride (Aug. 19-29), and London talks back with the Notting Hill Carnival (Aug. 27-29).

FACTS AND FIGURES: BRITAIN

Official Name: United Kingdom of Great Britain and Northern Ireland.
Capital: London.
Major Cities: Cardiff, Glasgow, Edinburgh, Liverpool, Manchester.
Population: 60,000,000.

Land Area: 241,590 sq. km
Time Zone: GMT.
Language: English; also Welsh, Scottish, and Gaelic.
Religions: Anglican and Roman Catholic (72%), Muslim (3%), other (25%).

ENGLAND

In a land where the stately once prevailed, conservatism has been booted in two successive elections and a wild profusion of the avant-garde has emerged from hallowed academic halls. At the cutting edge of art, music, film, and eclecticism, England is a youthful, hip, and forward-looking nation. But traditionalists can rest easy; for all the moving and shaking in large cities, around the corner there are still scores of ancient towns, opulent castles, and comforting cups of tea.

LONDON ☎020

London offers the visitor a bewildering array of choices: Leonardo at the National or Hirst at the Tate Modern; Rossini at the Royal Opera or Les Mis at the Queen's; Bond Street couture or Camden cutting-edge—you could spend your entire stay just deciding what to do and what to leave out. London is often described as a conglomeration of villages, whose traditions are still alive and evolving. Thanks to the independence and diversity of each, the London "buzz" is continually on the move.

◼ INTERCITY TRANSPORTATION

Flights: Heathrow (LON; ☎0870 000 0123) is London's main airport. The **Piccadilly Line** heads from the airport to central London (50min.-1hr.; every 4-5min.; £3.80, under 16 £1.50). The expensive **Heathrow Express** train speeds to Paddington (15min.; every 15min.; £13, round-trip £25). From **Gatwick Airport** (LGW; ☎0870 000 2468), the **Gatwick Express** heads to Victoria (30min., every 15min., £12), as do cheaper **Connex** commuter trains (40min., £9.80).

Trains: London has 8 major stations: **Charing Cross** (serves south England); **Euston** (the northwest); **King's Cross** (the northeast); **Liverpool Street** (East Anglia); **Paddington** (the west and south Wales); **St. Pancras** (the Midlands and the northwest); **Victoria** (the south); and **Waterloo** (the south, the southwest, and the Continent). All stations are linked by the Underground (Tube; ⊖). Itineraries involving a change of stations in London usually include a cross-town transfer by Tube. Get info at the station ticket office or from the **National Rail Enquiries Line** (☎08457 484 950; www.britrail.com).

Buses: Long-distance buses (a.k.a **coaches**) arrive in London at **Victoria Coach Station,** 164 Buckingham Palace Rd. ⊖Victoria. National Express (☎0870 580 8080; www.nationalexpress.com) is the largest operator of intercity services.

◢ ORIENTATION

The **West End** is the heart of London. It stretches east from Park Lane to Kingsway and south from Oxford St. to the River Thames; within this area you'll find aristocratic **Mayfair,** the shopping streets near **Oxford Circus,** the clubs of **Soho,** and the boutiques of **Covent Garden.** Heading east of the West End, you'll pass legalistic **Holborn** before hitting the ancient **City of London** ("the City"), the site of the original Roman settlement and home to St. Paul's Cathedral and the Tower of London. The City's eastern border jostles the ethnically diverse, working-class **East End.**

Westminster encompasses the grandeur of **Trafalgar Square** and extends south along the Thames; this is the heart of royal and political London, with the Houses of Parliament, Buckingham Palace, and Westminster Abbey. Farther west lies rich, snooty **Chelsea.** Across the river from Westminster and the West End, the **South Bank** has an incredible variety of entertainment and museums. The huge expanse

Central London

● SIGHTS

Albert Memorial, **1**	B4
Apsley House, **2**	C4
The Barbican, **3**	E3
British Library, **4**	D2
British Museum, **5**	D3
Buckingham Palace, **6**	C4
Cabinet War Rooms, **7**	D4
Chelsea Physic Garden, **8**	C5
Chinatown, **9**	D4

Courtauld Institute, **10**	D4
Design Museum, **11**	F4
The Gilbert Collection, **12**	D4
Guildhall, **13**	E3
Hayward Gallery, **14**	D4
The Houses of Parliament, **15**	D4
ICA, **16**	D4
Imperial War Museum, **17**	E5
Kensington Palace, **18**	B4
London Eye, **19**	D4
London Planetarium, **20**	C3
London Transport Museum, **21**	D3

Madame Tussaud's, **22**	C3
Marble Arch, **23**	C3
Millennium Bridge, **24**	E4
Monument, **25**	F4
Museum of London, **26**	E3
National Gallery, **27**	D4
Natural History Museum, **28**	B5
National Portrait Gallery, **29**	D4
Royal Academy, **30**	D4
Royal Albert Hall, **31**	B4
Royal Courts of Justice, **32**	E3
The Royal Hospital, **33**	C5

BRITAIN

The Royal Mews, **34**   C4
Royal Opera House, **35**   D3
St. Bartholomew the Great, **36**   E3
St. Bride's, **37**   E3
St. Etheldreda's, **38**   E3
St. James's Palace, **39**   D4
St. John's Square, **40**   E3
St. Margaret's Westminster, **41**   D4
St. Martin-in-the-Fields, **42**   D4
St. Mary-le-Bow, **43**   E3
St. Pancras Station, **44**   D2
St. Paul's Cathedral, **45**   E3

St. Paul's Church, **46**   D3
Savile Row, **47**   D3
Science Museum, **48**   B5
Shakespeare's Globe
  Theatre, **49**   E4
Sir John Soane's Museum, **50**   E3
Smithfield Market, **51**   E3
South Bank Centre, **52**   D4
Southwark Cathedral, **53**   E4
Tate Britain, **54**   D5
Tate Modern, **55**   E4
The Temple, **56**   E3

Theatre Royal Dury Lane, **57**   D3
Tower Bridge, **58**   F4
The Tower of London, **59**   F4
Trafalgar Square, **60**   D4
University College London, **61**   D3
Victoria and Albert Museum, **62**   B5
The Wallace Collection, **63**   C3
The Wellington Arch, **64**   C4
Westminster Abbey, **65**   D4
Westminster Cathedral, **66**   D5
Whitehall, **67**   D4

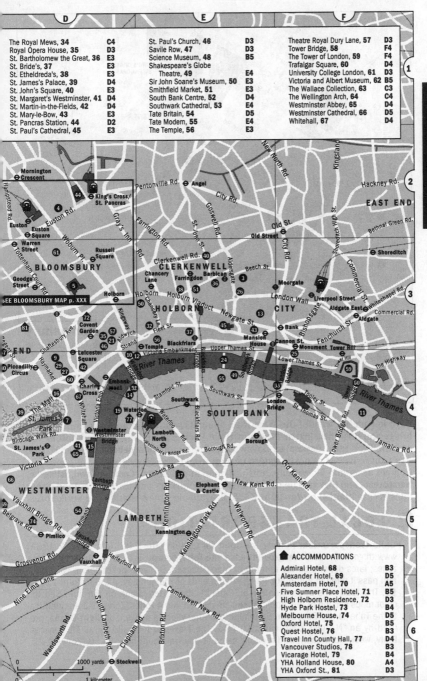

ACCOMMODATIONS

Admiral Hotel, **68**	B3
Alexander Hotel, **69**	D5
Amsterdam Hotel, **70**	A5
Five Sumner Place Hotel, **71**	B5
High Holborn Residence, **72**	D3
Hyde Park Hostel, **73**	B4
Melbourne House, **74**	D5
Oxford Hotel, **75**	B5
Quest Hostel, **76**	B3
Travel Inn County Hall, **77**	D4
Vancouver Studios, **78**	B3
Vicarage Hotel, **79**	B4
YHA Holland House, **80**	A4
YHA Oxford St., **81**	D3

SEE BLOOMSBURY MAP p. XXX

0   1000 yards   ⊖ Stockwell
0   1 kilometre

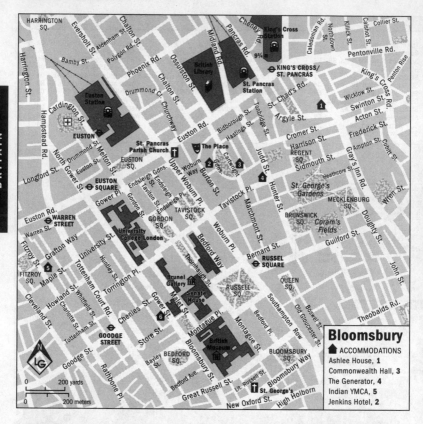

Bloomsbury

🏠 ACCOMMODATIONS
Ashlee House, 1
Commonwealth Hall, 3
The Generator, 4
Indian YMCA, 5
Jenkins Hotel, 2

of **Hyde Park** lies west of the West End; along its southern border are chic **Knightsbridge** and posh **Kensington.** North of Hyde Park is the media-infested **Notting Hill** and the B&B-filled **Bayswater.** Bayswater, Mayfair, and **Marylebone** meet at Marble Arch, on Hyde Park's northeastern corner; from there, Marylebone stretches west to meet academic **Bloomsbury,** north of Soho and Holborn. **Camden Town, Islington, Hampstead,** and **Highgate** lie to the north of Bloomsbury and the City. A good street atlas is essential; ▧*London A to Z* (£5) is available at newsstands and bookstores.

☰ LOCAL TRANSPORTATION

Public Transportation: Run by Transport for London (TfL; 24hr. info ☎7222 1234; www.tfl.gov.uk). The **Underground** (a.k.a. the **Tube**) network is divided into 6 concentric zones; fares depend on the number of zones crossed. Buy your ticket before you board and pass it through automatic gates at both ends of your journey. A trip in Zone 1 costs £2. The Tube runs approximately 5:30am-12:30am, depending on the line. See the color maps section of this book. **Buses** are divided into 4 zones. Zones 1-3 are identical to the Tube zones. Buses run 6am-midnight, after which a network of **Night Buses**, prefixed by an "N," take over. Fares £0.70-1. The **Travelcard** is valid for all TfL services. Daily, weekend, weekly, and monthly cards. 1-day Travelcard from £5.30 (Zones 1-2).

Licensed Taxicabs: An illuminated "taxi" sign on the roof of a black cab signals availability. Very expensive, but drivers know their stuff. Tip 10%. For pick-up (min. £2 extra charge), call **Computer Cabs** (☎ 7286 0286), **Dial-a-Cab** (☎ 7253 5000), or **Radio Taxis** (☎ 7272 0272).

Minicabs: Private cars. Cheaper than black cabs, but less reliable—stick to a reputable company. **London Radio Cars** (☎ 8905 0000) offers 24hr. pick-up.

⑦ PRACTICAL INFORMATION

TOURIST, FINANCIAL, AND LOCAL SERVICES

Tourist Offices: Britain Visitor Centre, 1 Regent St. (www.visitbritain.com). ⊖Oxford Circus. Open M 9:30am-6:30pm, Tu-F 9am-6:30pm, Sa-Su 10am-4pm. **London Information Centre**, 1 Leicester Pl. (☎ 7930 6769; www.londoninformation.org). ⊖Leicester Sq. Open M 9:30am-6:30pm, Tu-F 9am-6:30pm, Sa-Su 10am-4pm.

Embassies: Australia, Australia House, Strand (☎ 7379 4334). ⊖Temple. Open M-F 9:30am-3:30pm. **Canada**, MacDonald House, 1 Grosvenor Sq. (☎ 7258 6600). ⊖Bond St. Open M-F 8:30am-5pm. **Ireland**, 17 Grosvenor Pl. (☎ 7235 2171). ⊖Hyde Park Corner. Open M-F 9:30am-4:30pm. **New Zealand**, New Zealand House, 80 Haymarket (☎ 7930 8422). ⊖Piccadilly Circus. Open M-F 9am-5pm. **US**, 24 Grosvenor Sq. (☎ 7499 9000). ⊖Bond St. Open M-F 8:30am-5:30pm, phones answered till 10pm.

Financial Services: The best rates for **currency exchange** are found at banks, such as **Barclays, HSBC, Lloyd's,** and **National Westminster** (NatWest). **Branches** open M-F 9:30am-4:30pm. Call ☎ 0800 52 13 13 for the nearest **American Express** location.

Bi-Gay-Lesbian Resources: London Lesbian & Gay Switchboard (☎ 7837 7324; www.queery.org.uk). 24hr. helpline and information service.

EMERGENCY AND COMMUNICATIONS

Emergency: ☎ 999, free from any payphone.

Hospitals: Charing Cross, Fulham Palace Rd. (☎ 8846 1234), entrance on St. Dunstan's Rd. ⊖Hammersmith. **Royal Free**, Pond St. (☎ 7794 0500). ⊖Belsize Park. **St. Thomas's**, Lambeth Palace Rd. (☎ 7188 7982). ⊖Waterloo. **University College Hospital**, Grafton Way (☎ 7387 9300). ⊖Warren St.

Pharmacies: Usually M-Sa 9:30am-5:30pm; a "duty" chemist in each neighborhood opens Su, though hours may be limited. Late-night and 24hr. chemists are rare; one 24hr. option is **Zafash Pharmacy**, 233 Old Brompton Rd. (☎ 7373 2798). ⊖Earl's Ct.

Police: London is covered by 2 police forces: the **City of London Police** (☎ 7601 2222) for the City and the **Metropolitan Police** (☎ 7230 1212) for the rest. At least 1 station in each of the 32 boroughs is open 24hr. Call ☎ 7230 1212 to find the nearest station.

Internet Access: Some B&Bs and hostels now offer Internet access, but rates are lower at cybercafes. If you're paying more than £2 per hour, you're paying too much. Try the ubiquitous **easyEverything** (☎ 7241 9000; www.easyeverything.com). Locations include 9-16 Tottenham Court Rd. (⊖Tottenham Court Rd.); 456/459 The Strand (⊖Charing Cross); 358 Oxford St. (⊖Bond St.); 9-13 Wilson Rd. (⊖Victoria); 160-166 Kensington High St. (⊖High St. Kensington). All open 24hr.

Post Office: Post offices are on almost every major road. When sending mail to London, be sure to include the full Postal Code. The largest office is the **Trafalgar Square Post Office**, 24-28 William IV St. (☎ 7484 9304). ⊖Charing Cross. All mail sent Poste Restante or general delivery to unspecified post offices ends up here. Open M-Th and Sa 8am-8pm, F 8:30am-8pm. **Postal Code:** WC2N 4DL.

ACCOMMODATIONS

No matter where you stay, it's essential to plan ahead, especially in summer. Hostels frequently hold a few beds—it's always worth checking. Sheets are included at all YHAs, but towels are not; buy one from reception ($3.50). YHAs also sell discount tickets to theaters and major attractions. The best deals in town are student residence halls, which rent out rooms over the summer and sometimes Easter vacations. In London, "B&B" encompasses accommodations of wildly varying quality, personality, and price. Be aware that in-room showers are often prefabricated units jammed into a corner.

BAYSWATER

The streets between Queensway and Paddington station house London's highest concentration of cheap accommodations.

Vancouver Studios, 30 Prince's Sq. (☎7243 1270; www.vancouverstudios.co.uk). ⊖Bayswater. "Convenience of a hotel, with the privacy of an apartment." Rooms come with kitchenette, TV, phone, private bath, laundry facilities, and daily maid service. Single studios £65; doubles £85-95; triples £120. AmEx/MC/V. ❺

Quest Hostel, 45 Queensborough Terr. (☎7229 7782; www.astorhostels.com). ⊖Bayswater. Dorms are mostly coed (2 female-only rooms available), and nearly all are ensuite. Laundry, luggage storage, and kitchen available. Continental breakfast, lockers, and sheets included. Internet £0.50 for 15min. 4- to 8-bed dorms £14-17; doubles £42. MC/V. ❷

Admiral Hotel, 143 Sussex Gdns. (☎7723 7309; www.admiral-hotel.com). ⊖Paddington. Beautifully kept family-run B&B; all rooms with bath and TV. English breakfast included. Call 10-14 days ahead in summer. Singles £40-50; doubles £58-75; triples £75-90; quads £88-110; quints £100-130. Winter and long-stay discounts. MC/V. ❹

Hyde Park Hostel, 2-6 Inverness Terr. (☎7229 5101; www.astorhostels.com). ⊖Queensway or Bayswater. The basement bar and dance space hosts DJs and parties (W-Sa 8pm-3am). Kitchen, laundry, TV lounge, secure luggage room. Continental breakfast and sheets included. Internet access. Reception 24hr. Reserve 2 weeks ahead. Dorms £11-18; doubles £43-50. Ages 16-35 only. 10% ISIC discount. MC/V. ❷

BLOOMSBURY AND MARYLEBONE

Bloomsbury's proximity to Soho makes it well suited to those who want to stay near nightlife. The neighborhood is also close to the British Museum and plenty of cheap restaurants. Many B&Bs are on busy roads, so be wary of noise levels. The area becomes seedier closer to King's Cross.

The Generator, Compton Pl. (☎7388 7655; www.generatorhostels.com), off 37 Tavistock Pl. ⊖Russell Sq. or King's Cross. The ultimate party hostel. Luggage storage, lockers, and laundry. Internet access. Continental breakfast included. Reserve 1 week ahead. Mar.-Oct. 4- to 8-bed dorms £13-17; singles £42; doubles £53; triples £68; quads £90; quints £113. 18+ unless part of a family group. MC/V. ❷

Ashlee House, 261-265 Gray's Inn Rd. (☎7833 9400; www.ashleehouse.co.uk). ⊖King's Cross St. Pancras. Quiet, mellow, and laid-back. Coed and female-only dorms are airy and bright. Private rooms include sink, luggage room, safe, laundry, and kitchen. Continental breakfast included. Internet access. Reception 24hr. May-Sept. dorms £15-19; singles £36; doubles £48. Oct.-Apr. £2 less. MC/V. ❷

Jenkins Hotel, 45 Cartwright Gdns. (☎7387 2067; www.jenkinshotel.demon.co.uk), entry on Barton Pl. ⊖Euston or King's Cross St. Pancras. Rooms are airy and pleasant, with TV, phone, fridge, and safe. English breakfast included. Non-smoking. Reserve 1-2 months ahead for summer. Singles £52, with bath £72; doubles with bath £85; triples with bath £105. MC/V. ❺

Indian YMCA, 41 Fitzroy Sq. (☎ 7387 0411; www.indianymca.org). ⊖Warren St. or Great Portland St. Standard student-dorm affair with an institutional feel. Laundry and games room. Deluxe rooms have TV, fridge, and desk. Continental breakfast and dinner included. Reserve ahead in summer; 1-night deposit required with reservations. Dorms £20; singles £34, with bath £52; doubles £49/£55-72. AmEx/MC/V. ❸

Commonwealth Hall, 1-11 Cartwright Gdns. (☎ 7685 3500; www.lon.ac.uk/services/students/halls1/halls2/vacrates.asp). ⊖Russeil Sq. Bar, cafeteria, tennis and squash courts. English breakfast included. Open mid-Mar. to late Apr. and mid-June to mid-Sept. No walk-ins. Singles £24, half-board £28, UK students half-board £20. MC/V. ❸

KENSINGTON AND EARL'S COURT

▨ **Oxford Hotel,** 24 Penywern Rd. (☎ 7370 1161; www.the-oxford-hotel.com). Mid-sized, bright rooms, all with shower. Continental breakfast included. Reception 24hr. Reserve 2-3 weeks ahead for June. Singles £38, with bath £53; doubles £59/£69; triples £72/£81; quads £90/£96; quints £110/£120. AmEx/MC/V. ❹

▨ **Vicarage Hotel,** 10 Vicarage Gate (☎ 7229 4030; www.londonvicaragehotel.com). ⊖High St. Kensington. Beautifully kept Victorian house with charming rooms. English breakfast included. Reserve several months ahead with 1 night's deposit. Singles £46, with bath £75; doubles £78/£102; triples £95/£130; quads £102/£140. ❹

YHA Holland House, Holland Walk (☎ 7937 0748; hollandhouse@yha.org.uk). ⊖High St. Kensington or Holland Park. Ultra-clean, standard 12- to 20-bed single-sex dorms in the middle of Holland Park. TV room, luggage storage, lockers, laundry, and kitchen. Internet access. Breakfast included. Reception 24hr. Dorms £22, under 18 £20; singles £30; doubles £50; triples £70; quads £90; 6-beds £135. Book private rooms 14 days in advance. £3 student discount. MC/V. ❸

Amsterdam Hotel, 7 Trebovir Rd. (☎ 7370 5084; www.amsterdam-hotel.com). Suites have a kitchenette and sitting area. Rooms have bath, TV, kettle, and phone. Continental breakfast included. Singles standard £62, executive £84; doubles £87/£97; triples £114/£124. Suites: studios standard £102, executive £108; doubles £108/£120; triples £146/£156; 2-bedroom £173/£180. AmEx/MC/V. ❺

Five Sumner Place Hotel, 5 Sumner Pl. (☎ 7584 7586; www.sumnerplace.com). ⊖South Kensington. The amenities of a luxury hotel with a fantastic location. Spacious rooms have elegant ceilings, large windows, private bath, fridge, and phone. Book 1 month ahead. Singles £85; doubles £130. Extra bed £22. AmEx/MC/V. ❺

WESTMINSTER

Quiet **Pimlico,** south of Victoria station, is full of budget hotels; **Belgrave Road** has the highest number. Quality tends to improve farther from the station. Though the area is fairly close to major sights such as Parliament and Buckingham Palace, there's little in the way of restaurants or nightlife.

▨ **Melbourne House,** 79 Belgrave Rd. (☎ 7828 3516; www.melbournehousehotel.co.uk). ⊖Pimlico. All rooms with TV, phone, coffee-maker, and kettle. Luxurious basement double has a triangular bathtub. No smoking. Continental breakfast included. Reserve 2 weeks ahead. Singles £38, with bath £60; doubles with bath £85; triples with bath £95; quad with bath £100. MC/V. ❹

Alexander Hotel, 13 Belgrave Rd. (☎ 7834 9738; www.alexanderhotel.co.uk). ⊖Victoria. Eclectically furnished rooms with quality fittings and satellite TV. Breakfast included. Singles £45; doubles £65; triples from £75; quads and quints £110. MC/V. ❹

OTHER NEIGHBORHOODS

▨ **YHA Oxford Street,** 14 Noel St. (☎0870 770 5984; oxfordst@yha.org.uk). ⊖Oxford Circus. An unbeatable location for Soho nightlife. The double rooms have bunk beds, sink, mirror, and wardrobe. Continental breakfast £3.60. Internet access. Reserve 1 month ahead. Dorms £23-25, under 18 £19. ❸

▨ **Travel Inn County Hall,** Belvedere Rd. (☎0870 238 3300; www.travelinn.co.uk). ⊖Westminster or Waterloo. Seconds from the South Bank and Westminster. Rooms with full bath. Facilities include restaurant and bar. English breakfast £7. Reserve 1 month ahead. Singles, doubles, and family rooms M-Th £85, F-Su £80. AmEx/MC/V. ❺

High Holborn Residence, 178 High Holborn (☎7379 5589; www.lse.ac.uk/collections/vacations). ⊖Holborn or Tottenham Court Rd. Perfect location for West End exploits. Rooms are organized into clusters of 4-5 singles (some doubles) with shared kitchen and bath. Rooms with private bath are much larger. Bar, laundry, TV room, and game room. Continental breakfast included. Open Aug.-Sept. 2005. Singles £30; doubles £48, with bath £58; triples with bath £68. MC/V. ❸

◻ FOOD

Forget stale stereotypes about British food: London's restaurants offer a gastronomic experience as diverse, stylish, and satisfying as you'll find anywhere on the planet. Any restaurant charging under £10 for a main course is relatively cheap; add drinks and service and you're nudging £15. That said, it *is* possible to eat cheaply—and well—in London. Lunchtime and early-evening **special offers** save cash. For the best and cheapest **ethnic restaurants,** head to the source: **Whitechapel** for Bengali *baltis,* **Islington** for Turkish *meze,* **Marylebone** for Lebanese *shwarma.* Often the cheapest places to get your own ingredients in London are local **street markets.** For all your food under one roof, London's largest supermarket chains are **Tesco, Safeway,** and **Sainsbury's. Asda, Kwik-Save,** and **Somerfield** are "budget" supermarkets, while **Waitrose** and **Marks & Spencer** are more upscale.

Afternoon tea is a ritual as much as a meal. It involves a long afternoon of sandwiches, scones, pastries, and restrained conversation. The main attraction of afternoon tea is the chance to lounge in sumptuous surroundings and mingle with the upper crust for a few hours. Most major hotels and hoity-toity department stores serve tea, but for the ultimate in old-fashioned luxury, take tea at the **Ritz,** Piccadilly. (⊖Green Park. ☎7493 5181. Dress smart. Tea served M-F noon, 1:30, 3:30, and 5pm. £32. Reservations are highly recommended.)

BAYSWATER

▨ **Mr. Jerk,** 19 Westbourne Grove (☎7221 4678). ⊖Bayswater or Royal Oak. **Branch** at 189 Wardour St. in the West End (☎7287 2878). No snickering, children: the name refers to their house specialty "jerk chicken" (£6.50). Guinness Punch or Soursap £2.50. Open M-Sa 10am-11pm, Su noon-8pm. AmEx/MC/V. ❷

Levantine, 26 London St. (☎7262 1111). ⊖Paddington. A beautiful, elegant Lebanese restaurant, with loads of vegetarian options, featured nights of belly-dancing and *shisha* (hookah); this is a splurge well worth making. Set-menu lunch £8.50-15, dinner £20-28. *A la carte* dishes from £3.25. Cover £1. Open daily noon-1am. Kitchen open until midnight. MC/V. ❺

BLOOMSBURY AND MARYLEBONE

▨ **ICCo (Italiano Coffee Company),** 46 Goodge St. (☎7580 9688). ⊖Goodge St. Buy any hot drink before noon and get a free fresh-baked croissant. 11" pizza £3. Pre-packaged sandwiches and baguettes from £1.50; sandwiches half-off after 4pm. Pasta £2. Open M-F 7am-11pm, Sa-Su 9am-11pm. MC/V. ❶

North Sea Fish Restaurant, 7-8 Leigh St. (☎7387 5892). ⊖Russell Sq. or King's Cross St. Pancras. Fish 'n' chips done right. The takeout shop sells heaping portions of the same for unbeatable prices (£3.50-5). Entrees £8-17. Open M-Sa noon-2:30pm and 5:30-10:30pm. Takeout M-Sa noon-2:30pm and 5-11pm. AmEx/MC/V. ❸

Vats, 51 Lambs Conduit St. (☎7242 8963). ⊖Russell Square. Vats has too many wines to fit them all on the list; its friendly staff is happy to let you taste before you commit. Entrees £10-16. "Good ordinary claret" £3.50 per glass, £14.50 per bottle. Open M-F noon-11pm. Kitchen open noon-2:30pm and 6-9:30pm. AmEx/MC/V. ❸

CHELSEA

■ **Chelsea Bun,** 9a Limerston St. (☎7352 3635). Extensive vegetarian and vegan options include a full English breakfast with faux sausages. Early-bird specials available 7am-noon (£2-3). Breakfast from £4. Sandwiches £1.80-4. Pasta, salads, burgers, and omelettes £6-8. Open M-Sa 7am-11:30pm, Su 9am-7pm. MC/V. ❶

Chelsea Kitchen, 98 King's Rd. (☎7589 1330). One of the cheapest sit-down meals in London. Entrees £3.30-5. Soup, salads, and sandwiches £2-4. Wine £1.40 per glass, £6.80 per bottle. Open daily 7am-midnight. MC/V (£10 min.). ❶

Gordon Ramsay, 68 Royal Hospital Rd. (☎7352 4441). Gordon Ramsay—eccentric artist, former footballer, and celebrity chef. The purple and glass-trimmed interior manages to avoid pretension. Lunch menu £35. Multi-course dinners £65-80. Don't show up in anything but a jacket and tie. Reserve 1 month ahead. Open M-F noon-2:50pm and 6:30-11pm. AmEx/MC/V. ❺

THE CITY OF LONDON

■ **Futures,** 8 Botolph Alley (☎7623 4529), between Botolph Ln. and Lovat Ln. ⊖Monument. Weekly-changing vegetarian soups (£2-3), salads (£1.50-£3), pre-packaged smoothies (£1.40), and hot dishes (£4). For breakfast you'll find pastries (£0.80), or porridges and cereals (£1). Open M-F 7:30-10am and 11:30am-3pm. Cash only. ❶

Cafe Spice Namaste, 16 Prescot St. (☎7488 9242). ⊖Tower Hill or DLR: Tower Gateway. Hard to find, but worth the trek. Entrees £11-13. Vegetarian entrees £7-9. Open M-F noon-3pm and 6:15-10:30pm, Sa 6:30-10:30pm. AmEx/MC/V. ❸

HOLBORN AND CLERKENWELL

■ **Anexo,** 61 Turnmill St. (☎7250 3401). ⊖Farringdon. This Spanish-flavored restaurant and bar serves up tasty Iberian concoctions all day long. Lunch £7.50-9.50. "Tapas Menu" £15. Happy Hour M-Sa 5-7pm. Kitchen open M-F 10am-10pm, Sa 6-11pm, Su 4:30-10pm. Bar open until 2am most nights. AmEx/MC/V. ❸

Bleeding Heart Tavern (☎7404 0333) at the corner of Greville St. and Bleeding Heart Yard. ⊖Farringdon. This "tavern" is in fact a restaurant, and a good one. Highlights include the roast pig with apple (£11). Entrees £8-12. Open M-F 7-10:30am, noon-2:30pm, and 6-10:30pm. Upstairs pub open M-F 11:30am-11pm. AmEx/MC/V. ❸

KENSINGTON AND EARL'S COURT

■ **Zaika,** 1 Kensington High St. (☎7795 6533). ⊖High St. Kensington. One of London's best Indian restaurants. Excellent wine list. Entrees £12-20. Desserts £4-5. Lunch menu £15-18. 5-course dinner menu £38, with wine £57. Dress smart. Reservations recommended. Open M-F noon-2:45pm and 6:30-10:45pm, Sa 6:30-10:45pm, Su noon-2:45pm and 6:30-9:45pm. AmEx/MC/V. ❹

Raison d'Être, 18 Bute St. (☎7584 5008). ⊖South Kensington. Catering to the local French community, this comfortable, quiet eatery offers a bewildering range of filled *baguettes* and *foccacia* (£2.50-5). Salads made to order £3.20-5.20. Open M-F 8am-6pm, Sa 9:30am-4pm. Cash only. ❷

KNIGHTSBRIDGE AND BELGRAVIA

■ **Jenny Lo's Teahouse,** 14 Eccleston St. (☎7259 0399). ⊖Victoria. The small, modern interior bustles on weekdays, but the delicious pork noodle soup (£5.75) and the broad selection of Asian noodles (£5.75-7.50) make it well worth the wait. Vegetarian options abound. Open M-F 11:30am-3pm and 6-10pm. Cash only. ❷

MARYLEBONE AND REGENT'S PARK

■ **Mandalay,** 444 Edgware Rd. (☎7258 3696). ⊖Edgware Rd. Walk 5min. north from the Tube. Lunch specials £4-6. Entrees £3-7.50. No smoking. Reservations recommended at peak hours. Open M-Sa noon-2:30pm and 6-10:30pm. AmEx/MC/V. ❶

Giraffe, 6-8 Blandford St. (☎7935 2333; www.giraffe.net). ⊖Bond St. or Baker St. Food from noodle dishes to Mexican burgers (£7-9) at cheerful communal tables. Open M-F 8am-4pm and 5-10:45pm, Sa-Su 9am-4pm and 5-10:45pm. AmEx/MC/V. ❷

NOTTING HILL

■ **George's Portobello Fish Bar,** 329 Portobello Rd. (☎8969 7895). ⊖Ladbroke Grove. George opened in 1961. It's now a 50s-style diner, and the fish 'n' chips (£4-5) are still delicious. Open M-F 11am-midnight, Sa 11am-9pm, Su noon-9:30pm. Cash only. ❶

Books for Cooks, 4 Blenheim Crescent (☎7221 1992). ⊖Ladbroke Grove. At lunchtime, owner Eric and his crew of culinary pros "test" recipes from new titles. There's no telling what will be on offer. Daily cookery workshops £25; reservations essential. Bookstore open Tu-Sa 10am-6pm. Kitchen open Tu-Sa 10 am-2:30pm. Cash only. ❷

THE SOUTH BANK

■ **Cantina del Ponte,** 36c Shad Thames, Butler's Wharf (☎7403 5403). ⊖Tower Hill or London Bridge. Given the quality of the Italian food, the set menu is a bargain at £11 for 2 courses, £14 for 3 (M-F noon-3pm and 6-7:30pm). Pizza £6-8. Entrees £10-15. Open M-Sa noon-3pm and 6-10:45pm, Su noon-3pm and 6-9:45pm. AmEx/MC/V. ❸

Tas, 33 The Cut (☎7928 2111). ⊖Southwark. Also at 72 Borough High St. (☎7928 3300). **Tas Cafe,** 76 Borough High (☎7403 8559). **Tas Pide,** 20-22 New Globe Walk (☎7928 3300). ⊖London Bridge. A group of stylish, affordable Turkish restaurants. Entrees £6-9. Menus £7-10. Live music daily from 7:30pm. Evening reservations recommended. Open M-Sa noon-11:30pm, Su noon-10:30pm. AmEx/MC/V. ❷

THE WEST END

■ **Mô,** 23 Heddon St. (☎7434 3999). ⊖Piccadilly Circus or Oxford Circus. A restaurant, tea room, and bazaar all in one, Mô is an aesthetic slice of Marrakesh. Mix and match from their tapas-style dishes (£6-£7.50). *Shisha* (hookah) is also available (£9-20). Lunch is cheaper. Open M-W 11am-11pm, Th-Sa noon-midnight. AmEx/MC/V. ❸

Masala Zone, 9 Marshall St. (☎7287 9966). ⊖Oxford Circus. South-Indian fare is cooked in a kitchen visible from anywhere in the restaurant. The menu has typical favorites (£5-6) as well as "street food," which comes in small bowls (£3-5) and large platters that allow you to try a variety of dishes (£8-11). Open M-F noon-2:45pm and 5:30-11pm, Sa 12:30-3pm and 5-11pm, Su 12:30-3:30pm and 6-10:30pm. MC/V. ❷

busaba eathai, 106-110 Wardour St. (☎7255 8686). Locals and students queue up for marvelous Thai cuisine (£5-8) served at communal tables in a sea of polished wood. Open M-Th noon-11pm, F-Sa noon-11:30pm, Su noon-10pm. AmEx/MC/V. ❷

Golden Dragon, 28-29 Gerrard St. (☎7734 2763). It's the ritziest and best-known dim sum joint in Chinatown. Dishes range from veggie staples to minced prawn and sugarcane treats (£2-3). Regular dinner items £5.50-9. Set dim sum meal £12.50-22.50. Open M-Th noon-11:30pm, F-Sa noon-midnight, Su 11am-11pm. AmEx/MC/V. ❷

WESTMINSTER

■ **Goya,** 34 Lupus St. (☎7976 5309). ⊖Pimlico. 1of 2 corner Goya tapas bars. Plentiful vegetarian options. Generous, diverse tapas £3-5. Sangria £3. Open daily noon-11:30pm. AmEx/MC/V. ❶

NORTH LONDON

▨ **Gallipoli,** 102 Upper St. (☎ 7359 0630). **Gallipoli Again,** 120 Upper St. (☎ 7359 1578) **Gallipoli Bazaar,** 107 Upper St. (☎ 7226 5333). Deep-hued walls, patterned tiles and hanging lamps provide the backdrop for Turkish delights like *Iskender Kebap* (grilled lamb with yogurt and marinated pita bread; £6). Reservations recommended F-Sa. Open M-Th 10:30am-11pm, F-Sa 10:30am-midnight, Su 10:30am-11pm. MC/V. ❷

Mango Room, 10-12 Kentish Town Rd. (☎ 7482 5065). The Caribbean menu favors fish with mango, avocado, and coconut sauces. Potent tropical drinks are served from the tiny bar at night. Entrees £9-12. Reservations recommended for weekends. Open M 6pm-midnight, Tu-Sa noon-3pm and 6pm-midnight, Su noon-11pm. MC/V. ❸

Le Crêperie de Hampstead, 77 Hampstead High St. Metal stand on the side of the King William IV. Don't let the line deter you; these phenomenal crepes (from £2.60) are worth any wait. Open M-Th 11:45am-11pm, F-Su 11:45am-11:30pm. Cash only. ❶

OTHER NEIGHBORHOODS

▨ **Bug** (☎ 7738 3366), in the crypt of St. Matthew's Church, Brixton Hill, South London. ❷Brixton. Eerie lighting gives this small dining room a gothic atmosphere. North African lamb and Cajun chicken £7.50-13. Su "Bug Roast" gets you 2 courses for £12. Evening reservations essential. Open Tu-Th 5-11pm, F-Sa 5-11:30pm, Su 1-9pm. MC/V. ❸

Aladin, 132 Brick Ln. (☎ 7247 8210), in East London. Food that's a cut above the rest makes Aladin one of Brick Ln.'s more popular *balti* joints. Even the Prince of Wales has been here; a large commemorative photo rests in the window. 3-course lunch £6. Entrees £3-8.50. Open M-Th and Su noon-11:30pm, F-Sa noon-midnight. Cash only. ❷

◳ SIGHTS

ORGANIZED TOURS

The classic London **bus tour** is on an open-top double-decker; in good weather, it's undoubtedly the best way to get a good overview of the city. Tickets for the **Big Bus Company,** 48 Buckingham Palace Rd., are valid for 24hr. on three hop-on, hop-off routes, with 1hr. walking tours and a short Thames cruise included. (❷Victoria. ☎ 7233 9533; www.bigbus.co.uk. £18, children £12.) For a more in-depth account, you can't beat a **walking tour** led by a knowledgeable guide. **Original London Walks** runs 12-16 walks (most 2hr.) per day, from the "Beatles Magical Mystery Tour" to the nighttime "Jack the Ripper's Haunts" and guided visits to larger museums. (☎ 7624 3978; www.walks.com. £6, students £4, children free.)

WESTMINSTER

The City of Westminster, now a borough of London, has been the seat of British power for over a thousand years. William the Conqueror was crowned in Westminster Abbey on Christmas Day, 1066, and his successors built the Palace of Westminster that would one day house Parliament.

BUCKINGHAM PALACE

Originally built for the Dukes of Buckingham, Buckingham House was acquired by George III in 1762 and converted into a full-scale palace by George IV. During the summer opening of the **State Rooms,** visitors have access to the **Throne Room,** the **Galleries** (with works by Rubens and Rembrandt), and the **Music Room,** where Mendelssohn played for Queen Victoria, among others. In the opulent **White Room,** the large mirrored fireplace hides a door used by the Royal Family at formal dinners. Since 2001, Queen Elizabeth has also allowed visitors into the **gardens.** *(At the end of the Mall, between Westminster, Belgravia, and Mayfair.* ❷*St. James's Park, Victoria, Green Park, or Hyde Park Corner. State room tickets available at* ☎ *7766 7300. Book ahead. Open daily Aug.-late Sept. 9:30am-4:15pm. £13, students £11, under 17 £6.50.)*

CHANGING OF THE GUARD. The Palace is protected by **Foot Guards** in full uniform. Accompanied by a band, the "New Guard" starts marching down Birdcage Walk from Wellington Barracks around 10:30am, while the "Old Guard" leaves St. James's Palace around 11:10am. When they meet at the central gates of the palace, the officers of the regiments touch hands, symbolically exchanging keys, and *voilà!* The guard is officially changed. Show up well before 11:30am and stand directly in front of the palace, or watch from the steps of the Victoria Memorial. *(Apr.-Oct. daily; Nov.-Mar. every other day, provided the Queen is in residence, it's not raining, and there are no pressing state functions. Call ☎ 7766 7300 to hear about any interruptions. Free.)*

OTHER PALACE SIGHTS. The **Royal Mews'** main attraction is the collection of coaches, from the "glass coach" used to carry Diana to her wedding to the four-ton Gold State Coach and the carriage horses. *(Open daily Apr.-July and Sept. 11am-4pm; Aug.-Sept. 10am-5pm. Last admission 45min. before close. £5.50, under 17 £3.)*

WESTMINSTER ABBEY

On December 28, 1065, Edward the Confessor was buried in the church of the West Monastery; a year later, the Abbey saw the coronation of William the Conqueror, thus establishing its twin traditions as the figurative birthplace and literal resting place of royalty. It was this connection that allowed Westminster, uniquely among England's great monasteries, to escape destruction by Henry VIII. Early English kings are buried around the Confessor's tomb in the **Shrine of St. Edward,** behind which the **Coronation Chair** stands at the entry to the Tudor **Lady Chapel. Poet's Corner** begins with Geoffrey Chaucer, buried in 1400; plaques at his feet commemorate both poets and prose writers, as does the stained-glass window above. The simple memorial to **Winston Churchill** is just beyond the **Tomb of the Unknown Warrior.** The **Old Monastery** houses the **Great Cloister,** festooned with monuments and plaques, from which passages lead to the **Chapter House,** the original meeting place of Parliament, the **Pyx Chamber,** and the **Abbey Museum,** which features an array of royal funeral effigies. The pleasant **gardens** are reached from the Cloisters. *(Parliament Sq., in Westminster. Access Old Monastery, Cloister, and Gardens from Dean's Yard, behind the Abbey. ⊖Westminster. ☎ 7654 4900. Open M-Tu and Th-F 9:30am-3:45pm, W 9:30am-3:45pm and 6-7pm, Sa 9:30am-1:45pm, Su for services only. Museum open daily 10am-4pm. Chapter House open daily 10am-4pm. Cloister open daily 8am-6pm. Gardens open Apr.-Sept. Tu-Th 10am-6pm; Oct.-Mar. daily 10am-4pm. Old Monastery £3. Abbey and Museum £6, students £4. Services, Cloister, and Gardens free.)*

THE HOUSES OF PARLIAMENT

The Palace of Westminster, as the Parliament building is officially known, has been at the heart of English governance since the 11th century, when Edward the Confessor established his court here. William the Conqueror liked the site, and under the Normans the palace was greatly extended. Westminster Hall aside, little of the Norman palace remained after the massive fire of October 16, 1834; rebuilding began in 1835 under the joint command of Charles Barry and Augustus Pugin.

The ostentatious **House of Lords** is dominated by the **Throne of State.** The Lord Chancellor presides from the giant red **Woolsack.** In contrast is the restrained **House of Commons,** with simple green-backed benches under a plain wooden roof. The **Speaker** sits at the rear of the chamber, with government MPs to his right and the opposition to his left. With seating for only 437 out of 635 MPs, things get hectic when all are present. *(Parliament Sq. ⊖Westminster. ☎ 7219 3107. Debates open to the public while Parliament is in session (Oct.-July). Advance tickets required for Prime Minister's Question Time (W 3-3:30pm). Lords usually sits M-W from 2:30pm, Th 3pm, occasionally F 11:30am; closing times vary. Commons sits M-W 2:30-9:30pm, Th 11:30am-7:30pm, F 9:30am-3pm. Free. Tours Aug.-Sept. M-Sa 9:15am-4:30pm; call ☎ 0870 906 3773. £7, students £5.)*

OUTSIDE THE HOUSES. A statue of Oliver Cromwell stands in front of the mid-point of the complex, **Westminster Hall,** the only statue to survive the 1834 fire. During its centuries as a court of law, famous defendants included Saint Thomas More and Charles I. The **Clock Tower** is universally miscalled **Big Ben,** which actually refers only to the bell within. It's named after the robustly proportioned Sir Benjamin Hall, who served as Commissioner of Works when the bell was cast in 1858.

OTHER WESTMINSTER SIGHTS

WHITEHALL. A long stretch of imposing facades housing government ministries, Whitehall is synonymous with the British civil service. From 1532 until a fire in 1698, Whitehall was the main royal palace. All that remains is Inigo Jones's **Banqueting House,** which features magnificent ceiling paintings by Rubens. Charles I was executed on a scaffold outside the house in 1649. *(Between Trafalgar Sq. and Parliament Sq. ⊖Westminster, Embankment, or Charing Cross.)* Opposite Banqueting House, tourists line up to be photographed with the Household Cavalry at **Horseguards;** the guard is changed Monday to Friday at 11am and Saturday at 10am. Just off Whitehall, King James St. leads to the **Cabinet War Rooms** (p. 179). Current Prime Minister Tony Blair lives on **Downing Street,** separated from Whitehall by steel gates. The Prime Minister traditionally lives at #10, but Blair's family is so big that he's had to swap with the Chancellor, Gordon Brown, at #11.

WESTMINSTER CATHEDRAL. Westminster, London's first Catholic cathedral after Henry VIII espoused Protestantism, was started in 1887. In 1903, money ran out, leaving the interior only partially completed. The blackened brick domes contrast dramatically with the swirling marble of the lower walls and the magnificence of the side chapels. An elevator carries visitors up the striped 90m **bell tower.** *(Cathedral Piazza, off Victoria St. ⊖Victoria. Cathedral open daily 7am-7pm. Suggested donation £2. Bell Tower open Mar.-Nov. daily 9am-12:30pm and 1-5pm; Dec.-Feb. Tu-Sa 9am-12:30pm. £3, students £1.50.)*

TRAFALGAR SQUARE AND THE STRAND

John Nash suggested the design of Trafalgar Square in 1820 to commemorate Nelson's 1805 victory over Napoleon's navy at the Battle of Trafalgar. But it took years to get its current appearance: Nelson only arrived in 1843, the bronze lions in 1867. The reliefs at the column's base are cast from captured French and Spanish cannons. Every December, the square hosts a giant **Christmas Tree,** donated by Norway to thank the British for assistance against the Nazis. *(⊖Charing Cross.)*

ST. MARTIN-IN-THE-FIELDS. James Gibbs's 1720s creation was the model for Georgian churches in Britain and America. It's still the Queen's parish church; the royal box is to the left of the altar. The **crypt** downstairs houses a cafe, a bookshop, an art gallery, and the **London Brass Rubbing Centre.** *(St. Martin's Ln., at the northeastern corner of Trafalgar Sq.; crypt entrance on Duncannon St. ⊖Charing Cross. ☎7766 1100.)*

THE CITY OF LONDON

The City of London **("the City")** is the oldest part of the capital—for most of its 2000 years, this *was* London, the rest merely outlying villages. Following the Great Fire of 1666 and the Blitz of 1940-43, the area underwent a cosmetic rearrangement that left little of its medieval history behind.

ST. PAUL'S CATHEDRAL

Christopher Wren's masterpiece is the fifth cathedral to occupy the site; the original was built in AD 604. Wren's succeeded "Old St. Paul's," begun in 1087, whose steeple was just one-third higher than the current 111m dome. After three designs were rejected by the bishops, Wren, with Charles II's support, just started building—sneakily, he had persuaded the king to let him make "necessary alterations" as work progressed, and the building that emerged from the scaffolding in 1708 bore little resemblance to the model Charles II had approved. With space to seat 2500 worshippers, the **nave** is festooned with monuments to great Britons. The tombs are downstairs, in the **crypt**. Christopher Wren lies beneath the epitaph *Lector, si monumentum requiris circumspice:* "Reader, if you seek his monument, look around." To see the inside of the second-tallest freestanding **dome** in Europe (after St. Peter's in the Vatican), climb the 259 steps to the **Whispering Gallery**. From here, 119 more steps lead to **Stone Gallery**, on the outer base of the dome, and it's another 152 to the summit's **Golden Gallery**. Back inside, the mosaic of *Christ Seated in Majesty* overlooks the **High Altar**. *(St. Paul's Churchyard. ❷St. Paul's or Mansion House. Open M-Sa 8:30am-4:30pm. Open for worship daily 7:15am-6pm. Dome and galleries open M-Sa 9:30am-4pm. Cathedral £7, students £6, worshippers free. 1½hr. tours M-F 11, 11:30am, 1:30, and 2pm. £2.50, students £2.)*

THE TOWER OF LONDON

The Tower of London, palace and prison of English monarchs for over 900 years, is steeped in blood and history. Conceived by William the Conqueror in 1067 to provide protection *from* rather than *for* his new subjects, the original wooden palisade was replaced by a stone structure in 1078 that over the next 20 years would grow into the **White Tower**. From the western entrance near the **Middle Tower**, you pass over the old moat, now a garden, entering the **Outer Ward** through **Byward Tower**. Just beyond Byward Tower is a massive **Bell Tower;** the curfew bell has been rung nightly for over 500 years. The stretch of the Outer Ward along the Thames is **Water Lane,** which was adjacent to the river until the 16th century. **Traitor's Gate** was built by Edward I for his personal use, but is now associated with the prisoners who passed through it on their way to execution at **Tower Green**. Some victims are buried in the **Chapel Royal of St. Peter and Vincula,** including Catholic martyr St. Thomas More and Henry VIII's wives Catherine Howard and Anne Boleyn. **White Tower** houses a huge display of arms and armor from the Royal Armory. Across the green is the **Bloody Tower,** so named because Richard III allegedly imprisoned and murdered his nephews here before usurping the throne in 1483.

The most famous sights in the Tower are the **Crown Jewels;** moving walkways ensure that no awestruck gazers hold up the queue. While eyes are naturally drawn to the **Imperial State Crown,** featuring the Stuart Sapphire along with 16 others, 2876 diamonds, 273 pearls, 11 emeralds, and a mere five rubies, don't miss the **Sceptre with the Cross,** topped with the First Star of Africa, the largest quality-cut diamond in the world. This was hewn from an even larger monster, the 3106-carat Cullinan diamond. Other famous gems include the **Koh-i-Noor,** set into the **Queen Mother's Crown;** legend claims the stone will bring luck only to women. Numerous retired crowns and other treasures are displayed in the **Martin Tower,** at the end of **Wall Walk.** *(❷Tower Hill. ☎0870 756 6060. Open Mar.-Oct. M 10am-6pm, Tu-Sa 9am-6pm, Su 10am-6pm; Nov.-Feb. closes 1hr. earlier. Tickets also sold at Tube stations; buy ahead to avoid queues. £14, students £11. Audio tours £3.)*

OTHER CITY OF LONDON SIGHTS

■ **MONUMENT.** Raised in 1677, Christopher Wren's 61m column stands exactly that distance from the bakery on Pudding Lane where the Great Fire started in 1666. The view of the surrounding city from the top is astounding. *(Monument St. ❷Monument. Open 9:30am-5pm; last admission 4:40pm. £2, children £1.)*

■ ALL HALLOWS-BY-THE-TOWER. All Hallows bears its longevity proudly, incorporating a Saxon arch from AD 675. The undercroft is home to an array of archaeological finds, including Roman pavement and some stunning Celtic carvings. *(Byward St. ⊖ Tower Hill. ☎ 7481 2928. Church open daily 9am-6pm. Crypt and museum open M-Sa 11am-4pm, Su 1-4pm. Free.)*

TOWER BRIDGE. This iconic symbol of London is often mistaken for its plain upriver sibling, London Bridge—the story goes that when an Arizona millionaire bought the previous London Bridge and shifted it stone-by-stone to the US, he thought he was getting Tower Bridge. The **Tower Bridge Experience** offers a cutesy introduction to the history and technology of the unique lifting mechanism, though the view isn't all it's cracked up to be. *(Enter Tower Bridge Experience through the western side (upriver) of the North Tower. ⊖ Tower Hill or London Bridge. ☎ 7940 3985, lifting schedule 7940 3984. Open daily 10am-6pm. Last admission 5:30pm. £5, students £4.25.)*

THE SOUTH BANK

From the Middle Ages until Cromwell's arrival, the South Bank was London's center of amusement. Banished from the strictly regulated City, all manner of illicit attractions sprouted in "the Borough" at the southern end of London Bridge. Today, the South Bank is once again at the heart of London entertainment, with some of the city's top concert halls, theaters, cinemas, and galleries.

■ LONDON EYE. At 135m, the London Eye is the world's biggest observational wheel. The ellipsoid glass "pods" give uninterrupted views at the top of each 30min. revolution; on clear days, Windsor is visible to the west. *(Jubilee Gardens. ⊖ Waterloo. ☎ 0870 444 5544. Open daily late May-early Sept. 9:30am-10pm; Apr.-late May and late Sept. 10:30am-8pm; Jan.-Mar. and Oct.-Dec. 10:30am-7pm. Ticket office open daily 8:30am-6:30pm. £12, students £9, under 16 £5.75.)*

TATE MODERN AND THE MILLENNIUM BRIDGE. Squarely opposite each other on Bankside are the most glorious success and most abject failure of London's millennial celebrations. **Tate Modern** (p. 177), created from the shell of the Bankside power station, is as visually arresting as its contents are thought-provoking. The **Millennium Bridge,** built to link the Tate to the City, was completed six months too late for the Y2K festivities and, following a literally shaky debut, has only recently been stabilized. *(Queen's Walk, Bankside. ⊖ Southwark.)*

SHAKESPEARE'S GLOBE THEATRE. In the shadow of Tate Modern, the half-timbered Globe, opened in 1997, sits just 640m from where the original burned down in 1613. Try to arrive in time for a tour of the theater, given on mornings during the performance season and 10am-5pm otherwise. Tours include the **Rose Theatre,** where both Shakespeare and Marlowe performed; not much of it is left. *(Bankside. ⊖ Southwark or London Bridge. ☎ 7902 1500. Open daily May-Sept. 9am-noon and 1-4pm; Oct.-Apr. 10am-5pm. £8, students £6.50. For performances, see p. 180.)*

OTHER SIGHTS. ■ Vinopolis is a Dionysian Disneyland offering patrons an interactive (yes, that means samples) tour of the world's wine regions. *(1 Bank End. ⊖ London Bridge. ☎ 7940 8301. Open M noon-9pm, Tu-Su noon-6pm. Last admission 2hr. before close. £13, seniors £12.)* The **Old Operating Theatre and Herb Garret** is located in the loft of an 18th-century church. The oldest operating theater in the world is accompanied by a fearsome array of saws, knives, and primitive surgical instruments. *(9a St. Thomas's St. ⊖ London Bridge. ☎ 7955 4791. Open daily 10:30am-4:45pm. Closed Dec. 12-Jan. 5. £4.25, students £3.25.)* A less authentic horror is the **London Dungeon,** whose most effective instrument of torture is the interminable queue. The interior offers weak imitations of some London atrocities. *(28-34 Tooley St. ⊖ London Bridge. ☎ 7403 7224. Open daily in summer 9:30am-7:30pm; in winter 10am-5:30pm. £14, students £12.)*

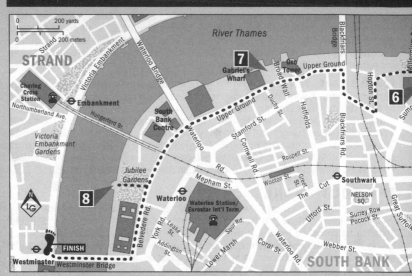

Once a somewhat seedy neighborhood, the South Bank is now home to London's densest concentration of cultural centers. The Tate Modern's cutting-edge design showcases the best of British contemporary art. Shakespeare's Globe Theatre had its first season in 1997, and each subsequent season brings bolder interpretations of the Bard's works.

DISTANCE: 4km

WHEN TO GO: Start early morning

START: ⊖Tower Hill

FINISH: ⊖Westminster

Concert halls host every genre of music and theaters present an unparalleled range of new works. Commercial Gabriel's Wharf adds to the vibrant atmosphere. Fantastic city views from Tate Modern, OXO Wharf and, of course, the London Eye, are constant draws, but so is the understated grace of the Thames itself. Meanwhile, the Jubilee Line Extension—including a revamped interior at London Bridge—has greatly facilitated transportation to the South Bank and helped to ensure the area's role as a cultural haven.

1 TOWER OF LONDON. Begin your trek to the Tower (p. 168) early to avoid the crowds. Tours given by the Yeomen Warders meet every 1½hr. near the entrance. Listen as they expertly recount tales of royal conspiracy, treason, and murder. See the **White Tower,** once both the fortress and residence of kings. Shiver at the executioner's stone on the tower green and pay your respects at the Chapel of St. Peter ad Vinculum, which holds the remains of three queens. Get the dirt on the gemstones at **Martin Tower,** then wait in line to see the **Crown Jewels,** which include such glittering lovelies as the First Star of Africa, the largest cut diamond in the world.

2 TOWER BRIDGE. Tower Bridge (p. 169) is an engineering wonder that puts its plainer sibling, the London Bridge, to shame. Marvel at its beauty, but skip the Tower Bridge Experience. Or better yet, call ahead to find out what times the Tower drawbridge is lifted.

3 DESIGN MUSEUM. On Butler's Wharf, let the Design Museum (p. 179) introduce you to the latest innovations in contemporary design, from marketing to movements in *haute couture*. See what's to come in the forward-looking Review Gallery or hone in on individual designers and products in the Temporary Gallery. From the DM, move on to the **Queen's Walk.** To your left, you'll find the **HMS Belfast,** which was launched upon Normandy, France, on D-Day, 1938.

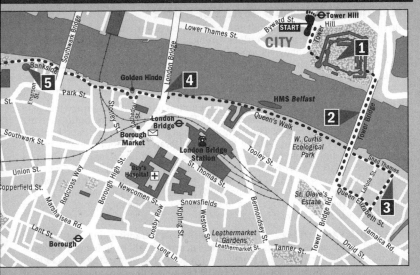

🄳 LONDON BRIDGE. This is the fifth incarnation of a London classic, hopefully more sturdy than its predecessors. The 1832 Old London Bridge is now relocated in Lake Havasu City, Arizona. The **Golden Hinde** is docked on the other side of London Bridge, a full-size and functional replica of Sir Francis Drake's 16th-century war ship. Stop by **Borough Market** for fresh fruit.

🄵 SHAKESPEARE'S GLOBE THEATRE. "I hope to see London once ere I die," says Shakespeare's Davy in *Henry IV, Part II*. In time, he may see it from the beautiful recreation of Will's most famous theater (p. 169). Excellent exhibits describe how Shakespearean actors dressed, the secrets of their stage effects, and the painstaking process of rebuilding the theater almost 400 years after the original burned down. You might be able to catch a matinee performance if you time your visit right. Call ahead for tour and show times.

🄶 TATE MODERN. It's hard to imagine anything casting a shadow over the Globe Theatre, but the former Bankside Power Station, now the massive Tate Modern (p. 169), does just that. One of the world's premier modern art museums, the Tate's arrangements promise a new conceptual spin on well-known favorites and works by emerging artists. Be sure to catch one of the informative docent tours and don't miss the rotating installation in the Turbine Room.

🄷 GABRIEL'S WHARF. Check out the cafes, bars, and boutiques of colorful **Gabriel's Wharf.** If you missed the top floor of the Tate Modern, go to the public viewing gallery on the 8th floor of the **OXO Tower Wharf.** On your way to the London Eye stop by the **South Bank Centre.** Established as a primary cultural center in 1951, it now features music ranging from Philharmonic extravaganzas to low-key jazz. Call ahead to find out the dates and times of free lunchtime and afternoon events.

🄸 LONDON EYE. Once known as the Millennium Wheel, the London Eye (p. 169) has firmly established itself as one of London's top attractions, popular with locals and tourists alike. The Eye offers amazing 360° views from its glass pods. With the right timing, you can see all of London illuminated by the sunset. Book in advance to avoid the long queues, but be sure to check the weather forecast.

BLOOMSBURY AND MARYLEBONE

Marylebone's most famous resident (and address) never existed. 221b Baker St. was the fictional lodging of Sherlock Holmes, but 221 Baker St. is actually the headquarters of the Abbey National Bank. Bloomsbury's intellectual reputation was bolstered in the early 20th century with the philosophizing and womanizing of the **Bloomsbury Group**, an early 20th-century coterie of intellectuals that included John Maynard Keynes, Bertrand Russell, Lytton Strachey, and Virginia Woolf.

■ **BRITISH LIBRARY.** Since its 1998 opening, the new British Library has won acclamation from visitors and users alike. The 320km of underground shelving hold up to 12 million books. The library also has a dramatic glass cube containing the 65,000 volumes of George III's **King's Library,** and books, manuscripts, and artifacts that range from the 2nd-century *Unknown Gospel* to Joyce's handwritten draft of *Finnegan's Wake*. For more info, see p. 178. *(96 Euston Rd. ⊖King's Cross. ☎ 7412 7332. Open M and W-F 9:30am-6pm, Tu 9:30am-8pm, Sa 9:30am-5pm, Su 11am-5pm. Free. Tours M, W, F 3pm; Sa 10:30am and 3pm. £6, students £4.50. Tours with reading rooms Tu 6:30pm, Su 11:30am and 3pm. £7, students £5.50. Reservations recommended.)*

■ **REGENT'S PARK.** This is perhaps London's most attractive and most popular park, with landscapes ranging from football-scarred fields to Italian-style formal plantings. It's all very different from John Nash's vision of wealthy villas hidden among exclusive gardens; fortunately for us common folk, Parliament intervened in 1811 and guaranteed the space would remain open to all. *(⊖Baker St., Regent's Park, Great Portland St., or Camden Town. ☎ 7486 7905. Open daily 6am-dusk. Free.)*

ACADEMIA. The strip of land along **Gower Street** and immediately to its west is London's academic heartland. Established in 1828, **University College London** was the first in Britain to admit Catholics, Jews, and women. The embalmed body of founder **Jeremy Bentham** has been on display in the South Cloister since 1850. *(Main entrance on Gower St. South Cloister entrance through the courtyard. ⊖Warren St.)* Now the administrative headquarters of the University of London, **Senate House** was the model for the Ministry of Truth in *1984;* George Orwell worked there as part of the BBC propaganda unit in WWII. *(At the southern end of Malet St. ⊖Goodge St.)*

HOLBORN AND CLERKENWELL

Squeezed between the capitalism of the City and the commercialism of the West End, Holborn is the historical home of two of the world's least-loved professions—journalists and lawyers.

■ **THE TEMPLE.** South of Fleet St., this labyrinthine compound encompasses the inns of the **Middle Temple** to the west and the neighboring **Inner Temple** to the east—there was once an Outer Temple, but it's long gone. The Inner Temple was leveled during the Blitz; with the exception of the Tudor **Inner Temple Gateway,** 16-17 Fleet St., all is reconstruction. **Middle Temple Hall,** closed to the public, still has its 1574 hammerbeam ceiling as well as a dining table made from the hatch of Sir Francis Drake's *Golden Hinde. (Between Fleet St., Essex St., Victoria Embankment, and Temple Ave./Bouvier St. ⊖Temple or Blackfriars.)* From 1185 until the order was dissolved in 1312, this land belonged to the crusading Knights Templar; the sole remnant of this time is the **Temple Church.** Adjoining the round church is a Gothic nave, built in 1240, with an altar screen by Wren. *(☎ 7353 3470. Hours vary depending on services and are posted outside the door of the church for the coming week. No services Aug.-Sept. Organ recitals W 1:15-1:45pm. Free.)*

According to Shakespeare's *Henry VI*, the red and white flowers that served as emblems in the Wars of the Roses were plucked in **Middle Temple Garden,** south of the hall. *(Open May-Sept. M-F noon-3pm. Free.)*

ST. ETHELDREDA'S. The only pre-Reformation Catholic church in the city, bought back from the Church of England in 1870 after centuries of captivity, is also one of London's most beautiful. Inside, the surprisingly high ceiling swallows up the bustle of the streets, creating an island of calm in the midst of Holborn Circus. *(☎ 7405 1061. Open daily 7:30am-7pm. Free.)*

■ **SOMERSET HOUSE.** A magnificent Palladian structure completed in 1790, Somerset House was London's first intended office block. Originally home to the Royal Academy and the Royal Society, the building now harbors the magnificent **Courtauld Institute** (p. 178). From mid-December to mid-January, the central **Fountain Courtyard** is iced over to make an open-air rink. *(On the Strand. ⊖ Charing Cross. Courtyard open daily 7:30am-11pm. Free. Tours Sa 1:30 and 3:45pm. £2.80.)*

KENSINGTON

Nobody took much notice of Kensington before 1689, when the newly crowned William III and Mary II moved into Kensington Palace. In 1851, the Great Exhibition brought in enough money to finance museums and colleges. Now the neighborhood is home to expensive stores like Harrods and Harvey Nichols—it's hard to imagine the days when the area was known for taverns and highwaymen.

KENSINGTON PALACE. Remodeled by Christopher Wren for William III and Mary II, parts of the palace are still in use today as a royal residence. Princess Diana lived here until her death. The **Royal Ceremonial Dress Collection** features 19th-century court costumes along with the Queen's demure evening gowns and some of Diana's sexier numbers. Hanoverian economy is evident in the *trompe l'oeil* decoration in the **State Apartment,** carried out by William Kent for George I. *(On the western edge of Kensington Gardens; enter through the park. ⊖ High St. Kensington. Open daily Mar.-Oct. 10am-6pm; Nov.-Feb. 10am-5pm. £11, students £8.20.)*

HYDE PARK AND KENSINGTON GARDENS. Surrounded by London's wealthiest neighborhoods, giant **Hyde Park** has served as the model for city parks around the world, including Central Park in New York and Bois de Boulogne in Paris. **Kensington Gardens,** to the west, is contiguous with Hyde Park. The 41-acre **Serpentine** was created in 1730; innumerable people pay to row and swim here. At the northeastern corner of the park, near Marble Arch, proselytizers, politicos, and flat-out crazies dispense their knowledge to bemused tourists at **Speaker's Corner** on Sundays. *(Framed by Kensington Rd., Knightsbridge, Park Ln., and Bayswater Rd. ⊖ Queensway, or High St. Kensington. Park open daily 5am-midnight. Gardens open daily dawn-dusk. Both free.)*

KNIGHTSBRIDGE

APSLEY HOUSE AND WELLINGTON ARCH. Apsley House, with the convenient address of "No. 1, London," was bought in 1817 by the Duke of Wellington. On display is Wellington's outstanding collection of art, much of it given by grateful European royalty following the battle of Waterloo. The majority of the paintings hang in the **Waterloo Gallery.** *(Hyde Park Corner. ⊖ Hyde Park Corner. Open Apr.-Oct. Tu-Su 10am-5pm; Nov.-Mar. 10am-4pm. £4.50, students £3, children £2.30)* Across from Apsley House, the Wellington Arch was built in 1825. In 1838 it was dedicated to the Duke of Wellington; later, to the horror of its architect, Decimus Burton, an enormous statue of the Duke was placed on top. *(Hyde Park Corner. ⊖ Hyde Park Corner. Open Apr.-Oct. W-Su 10am-5pm; Nov.-Mar. 10am-4pm. £3, students £2.30)*

BRITAIN

THE WEST END

MAYFAIR AND ST. JAMES'S

OXFORD AND REGENT STREETS. Oscar Wilde famously quipped that London's famous shopping strip, **Oxford Street** (p. 181), is "all street and no Oxford." **Regent Street** is more imposing, though none of John Nash's original Regency arcades remain. To the north, near Oxford Circus, **Carnaby Street** was the heart of Swinging London in the 60s. After that psychedelic high followed 30 years as a tourist trap; now Carnaby swings again with an influx of trendy boutiques. *(⊖Oxford Circus.)*

PICCADILLY, BOND STREET, AND SAVILE ROW. Frilly ruffs were big business in the 16th century—one local tailor named his house after these "piccadills," and the name stuck. Clogged with traffic, **Piccadilly** is no longer the preferred address of gentlemen as it was in the late 18th century, but it's still posh with a capital P. *(⊖Piccadilly Circus or Green Park.)* Running into Piccadilly is **Old Bond Street,** London's swankiest shopping street; this end is dominated by art and jewelry dealers, while most of the designer boutiques are on **New Bond Street.** *(⊖Bond St. or Green Park.)* **Savile Row,** running parallel to Bond St., is synonymous with elegant and expensive tailoring; less well-known is that the **Beatles** performed their last ever live gig on the roof of No. 3 while filming *Let It Be. (⊖Piccadilly Circus.)*

ST. JAMES'S PALACE. St. James's, constructed in 1536, is London's only remaining purpose-built palace. The massive gateway is one of the few original parts of the palace remaining. Unless your name starts with HRH, the only part you're likely to get into is the **Chapel Royal.** *(Services Oct.-Easter Su 8:30 and 11:30am.)* From Easter to September, services are held in the Inigo Jones-designed **Queen's Chapel,** across Marlborough Rd. *(Between the Mall and Pall Mall. ⊖Green Park.)*

SOHO

Soho's first settlers were French Huguenots fleeing religious persecution in the 17th century. These days, a concentration of gay-owned restaurants and bars has turned **Old Compton Street** into the heart of gay London.

PICCADILLY CIRCUS. In the glow of lurid neon signs, five of the West End's major arteries merge and swirl round the **Statue of Eros,** dedicated to the Victorian philanthropist, Lord Shaftesbury. Eros originally pointed down Shaftesbury Ave., but recent restoration work has put his aim significantly off. *(⊖Piccadilly Circus.)*

LEICESTER SQUARE. Amusements at this entertainment nexus range from London's largest cinema to the **Swiss Centre** glockenspiel, whose atonal renditions of Beethoven's *Moonlight Sonata* are enough to make even the tone-deaf weep. *(Rings M-F noon, 6, 7, and 8pm; Sa-Su noon, 2, 4, 5, 6, 7, and 8pm.)* Indulge your inner tourist by having your name engraved on a grain of rice and sitting for a caricature. *(⊖Leicester Sq. or Piccadilly Circus.)*

CHINATOWN. The pedestrian, tourist-ridden **Gerrard Street,** with dragon gates and pagoda-capped phone booths, is the heart of London's tiny slice of Canton, but gritty **Lisle Street,** one block to the south, has a more authentic feel. Chinatown is most exciting during the raucous Chinese New Year in February. *(Between Leicester Sq., Shaftesbury Ave., and Charing Cross Rd.)*

COVENT GARDEN

The Covent Garden piazza, designed by Inigo Jones in the 17th century, is one of the few parts of London popular with locals and tourists alike. On the very spot where England's first Punch and Judy show was performed, street entertainers delight the thousands who flock here year-round. *(⊖Covent Garden.)*

NORTH LONDON

CAMDEN TOWN

An island of honest tawdriness in an increasingly affluent sea, Camden Town has thrown off attempts at gentrification thanks to the ever-growing **Camden Market** (p. 181), London's fourth most popular attraction, centered in **Camden Lock Market.**

HAMPSTEAD

Hampstead caught the attention of well-heeled Londoners in the 17th century, when it became fashionable to take the waters at Hampstead Wells on the site of today's **Well Walk.** In the 1930s, Hampstead saw many European avant-garde luminaries in flight from fascism: residents Sigmund Freud, Aldous Huxley, and Piet Mondrian have lent the area an enduring cachet.

HAMPSTEAD HEATH. Hampstead Heath is one of the last remaining traditional commons in England, open to all since at least 1312. **Parliament Hill** is the highest open space in London, with excellent views across the city. (⊖*Hampstead. Open 24hr.; be careful after dark.)* Farther north, ◪**Kenwood House** is a picture-perfect 18th-century country estate, designed by Robert Adams and home to the impressive **Iveagh Bequest** (p. 179) of Old Masters. (⊖*Hampstead. Open daily Apr.-Oct. 8am-8:30pm; Oct.-Mar. 8am-4:45pm.)*

KEATS HOUSE. While living here (1818-20), John Keats produced some of his finest work, including *Ode to a Nightingale.* Inside, poems lie scattered about reconstructed rooms. *(Keats Grove.* ⊖*Hampstead.* ☎*7435 2062. Open Apr.-Nov. Tu-Su noon-5pm; Nov.-Mar. noon-4pm. £3, students £1.50, under 16 free.)*

EAST LONDON

THE EAST END AND DOCKLANDS

The boundary between the East End and the City of London is as sharp today as it was when Aldgate and Bishopsgate were literal gateways in the wall separating the rich and powerful City from the poorer quarters to the east. **Whitechapel** is the oldest part of the East End. In the 19th century, it was thronged with Jewish refugees from Eastern Europe; today it's the heart of London's Bangladeshi community, which centers around **Brick Lane. Christ Church,** on Commercial St., opposite Spitalfields market, is Nicholas Hawksmoor's largest, and is considered by many to be his masterpiece; it is slowly being restored to its former glory. *(⊖Liverpool St. Open M-F 12:30-2:30pm.)* The area of the East End along the river is known as the **Docklands.** This man-made archipelago of docks was the commercial heart of the British Empire for centuries. In 1981, the government decided to redevelop the area; the showpiece of the regeneration is **Canary Wharf,** with Britain's highest skyscraper, the 243m pyramid-topped **One Canada Square.** Under the tower, the **Canada Place** and **Cabot Square** malls draw shoppers from all over London. *(⊖Canary Wharf.)*

GREENWICH

Seat of the Royal Navy until 1998, Greenwich's position as the "home of time" is intimately connected to its maritime heritage—the Royal Observatory was originally founded to produce the accurate star-charts essential to navigation. Charles II founded the **Royal Observatory Greenwich** in 1675 to find a way of calculating longitude at sea. Though the problem was eventually solved without reference to the sky, the connection lives on—the **Prime Meridian** (marking 0° longitude) started out as the axis along which astronomers' telescopes swung. Next to the meridian, is Wren's **Flamstead House,** whose **Octagon Room** has long windows designed to accommodate telescopes. Climb the Observatory Dome to see the 28" scope, constructed in 1893. It hasn't been used since 1954, but you can see the stars at the **Planetarium** in the South Building. *(At the top of Greenwich Park. DLR: Cutty Sark. A tram leaves from the back of the museum every 30min. Open daily 10am-5pm. Free.)*

CUTTY SARK. Even landlubbers will appreciate the **Cutty Sark,** the last of the great tea clippers. Launched in 1869, she was the fastest ship of her time, making the trip to and from China in only 120 days. *(King William Walk, by Greenwich Pier. Open daily 10am-5pm. £4.25, students and under 16 £3.25.)*

WEST LONDON

■ **HAMPTON COURT PALACE.** Although a monarch hasn't lived here for 250 years, Hampton Court still exudes regal charm. Cardinal Wolsey built the first palace here in 1514, showing the young Henry VIII how to act the part of a ruler. In 1689, William III and Mary II employed Christopher Wren to bring Hampton Court up to date. In addition to touring the sumptuous rooms of the palace, including Henry's **State Apartments** and William's **King's Apartments,** be sure to leave time for the vast gardens, including the devilishly difficult **maze.** Take the train from Waterloo (35min., every 30min., round-trip £4) or a boat from Westminster Pier (4hr.; 4 per day; £10, round-trip £14); to leave time to see the palace, take the boat one way and return by train. *(Open late Mar.-late Oct. M 10:15am-6pm, Tu-Su 9:30am-6pm; late Oct.-late Mar. closes 4:30pm. Last admission 45min. before close. Gardens open until 9pm or dusk. £12, students £9. Maze only £3.50. Gardens only free.)*

KEW GARDENS. The Kew Gardens (a.k.a. the Royal Botanic Gardens) feature thousands of flowers, fruits, trees, and vegetables from around the globe. The three **conservatories,** housing a staggering variety of plants ill-suited to the English climate, are the highlight. Most famous is the steamy **Palm House,** home to "The Oldest Pot Plant In The World," which is not at all what it sounds like but interesting nonetheless. The **Temperate House** is the largest ornamental glasshouse in the world. The interior of the **Princess of Wales Conservatory** is divided into 10 different climate zones, including one entirely devoted to orchids. *(Main entrance at Victoria Gate. ♦Kew Gardens. Open Apr.-Aug. M-F 9:30am-6:30pm, Sa-Su 9:30am-7:30pm; Sept.-Oct. daily 9:30am-6pm; Nov.-Jan. daily 9:30am-4:15pm; Feb.-Mar. daily 9:30am-5:30pm. Last admission 30min. before close. £7.50, students £5.50.)*

🏛 MUSEUMS

Centuries spent as the capital of an empire, together with a decidedly English penchant for collecting, have given London a spectacular set of museums. Art lovers, history buffs, and amateur ethnologists won't know which way to turn when they arrive. And there's even better news for museum lovers: In celebration of the Queen's Golden Jubilee, all major museums are free indefinitely.

■ BRITISH MUSEUM

The funny thing about the British Museum is that there's almost nothing British in it. The **Western Galleries** house the most famous items in the collection. Room 4 harbors Egyptian sculpture, including the **Rosetta Stone,** and Room 18 is entirely devoted to the Athenian **Elgin Marbles.** Other highlights include giant Assyrian and Babylonian **reliefs,** the Roman **Portland Vase,** and bits and bobs from two Wonders of the Ancient World, the **Temple of Artemis** at Ephesus and the **Mausoleum of Halikarnassos.** The **Northern Galleries** feature eight rooms of mummies and sarcophagi and nine of artifacts from the ancient Near East, including the **Oxus Treasure** from Iran. The northern wing also houses the excellent African and

Islamic galleries, the giant Asian collections, and the Americas collection. The upper level of the **South** and **East Galleries** is dedicated to ancient and medieval Europe. Famous remains include the preserved body of **Lindow Man,** an Iron Age Celt (Room 50), along with treasures excavated from the **Sutton Hoo Burial Ship** (Room 41). Room 42 is home to the enigmatic **Lewis Chessmen,** an 800-year-old chess set mysteriously abandoned in Scotland. *(Great Russell St. ⊖Tottenham Court Rd. ☎ 7323 8000. Great Court open M-W and Su 9am-6pm, Th-Sa 9am-11pm. Galleries open daily 10am-5:30pm. Free tours at the Enlightenment Desk daily 12:30pm. 1½hr. Highlights Tour daily 10:30am, 1, 3pm. £8, students £5. Audio tours £3.50. Temporary exhibitions £5, students £3.50.)*

■ NATIONAL GALLERY

The National Gallery was founded by an Act of Parliament in 1824, with 38 pictures displayed in a townhouse; it grew so rapidly in size and popularity that a new gallery was constructed in 1838. If you're pressed for time, head to the **Micro Gallery** in the **Sainsbury Wing,** where you can design and print out a personalized tour of the paintings you want to see. Climate-controlled rooms house the oldest, most fragile paintings, including the 14th-century English *Wilton Diptych,* Botticelli's *Venus and Mars,* and the *Leonardo Cartoon,* a detailed preparatory drawing by da Vinci for a never-executed painting. With paintings that date from 1510 to 1600, the **West Wing** is dominated by the Italian High Renaissance, both Roman and Venetian, and the first flowering of German and Flemish art. The **North Wing** spans the 17th century, with an exceptional display of Flemish and Spanish Renaissance works spread over 17 rooms. The **East Wing,** home to paintings from 1700 to 1900, is the most crowded, housing the most famous works and the Impressionist galleries. The focus is primarily on room 45, which features one of van Gogh's *Sunflowers*. *(Main entrance on north side of Trafalgar Sq., Westminster. ⊖Charing Cross or Leicester Sq. ☎ 7747 2885. Open M-Tu and Th-Su 10am-6pm, W 10am-9pm. Special exhibitions occasionally open until 10pm. Free 1hr. gallery tours daily 11:30am and 2:30pm, W also 6:30pm. Audio tours free. Temporary exhibitions £5-7, students and ages 12-18 £2-3.)*

■ TATE MODERN

Since opening in May 2000, Tate Modern has been credited with single-handedly reversing the long-term decline in museum attendance in Britain. One of the largest modern art museums in the world, its most striking aspect is the building itself, formerly Bankside Power Station. The conversion to a gallery added a seventh floor, with wraparound views of north and south London, and turned the old **Turbine Hall** into an immense atrium that often overpowers the installations commissioned for it. The Tate groups works according to theme rather than period or artist—the four overarching divisions are **Still Life/Object/Real Life** and **Landscape/ Matter/Environment** on Level 3, and **Nude/Action/Body** and **History/Memory/Society** on Level 5— even skeptics admit that this arrangement throws up some interesting contrasts and forces visitors into contact with an exceptionally wide range of art. It's now impossible to see the Tate's more famous pieces, which include Picasso's *Nude Woman with Necklace,* without also confronting challenging and invigorating works by less well-known contemporary artists. *(Bankside, on the South Bank. ⊖Southwark or Blackfriars. ☎ 7887 8000. From Southwark Tube, turn left up Union then left on Great Suffolk, then left on Holland. Open M-Th and Su 10am-6pm, F-Sa 10am-10pm. Free tours meet on the gallery concourses. Audio tours £2.)*

TATE BRITAIN

The original Tate opened in 1897 as a showcase for modern British art. Before long, it had expanded to include contemporary art from all over the world, as well as British art from the Middle Ages on. Despite many expansions, it was clear that the dual role was too much for one building; the problem was resolved with the relocation of almost all the contemporary art to the new Tate Modern at Bankside (see above). At the same time, the original Tate was rechristened and rededicated to British art. The **Clore Gallery** continues to display the Turner Bequest of 282 oils and 19,000 watercolors; other painters featured heavily are William Blake, John Constable, Lucien Freud, David Hockney, and Dante Gabriel Rossetti. Despite the Tate Modern's popular explosion, the annual **Turner Prize** for contemporary art is still held here. *(Millbank, in Westminster. ⊖Pimlico. Open daily 10am-5:50pm. Last admission 5pm. Free tours M-F 11am, noon, 2, and 3pm; Sa-Su noon and 3pm. Audio tours £3, students £2.50. Special exhibitions £3-10.)*

VICTORIA & ALBERT MUSEUM

The V&A is dedicated to displaying "the fine and applied arts of all countries, all styles, and all periods." The subject of a £31 million refit, the vast **British Galleries** hold a series of recreated rooms from every period between 1500 and 1900, mirrored by the vast **Dress Collection,** a dazzling array of the finest *haute couture* through the ages. The ground-floor **European** collections range from 4th-century Byzantine tapestries to Alfonse Mucha posters; if you only see one thing, make it the **Raphael Gallery,** hung with six massive paintings commissioned by Pope Leo X in 1515. The **Sculpture Gallery,** home to Canova's *Three Graces* (1814-17) and voluptuous *Sleeping Nymph* (1820-24), is not to be confused with the **Cast Courts,** a plaster-replica collection of the world's greatest sculptural hits, from Trajan's Column to Michelangelo's *David*. The V&A's **Asian** collections are particularly formidable. The number one to see here is **Tippoo's Tiger,** the graphically fascinating 1799 model of a tiger eating a man—complete with organ sounds and crunching noises.

In contrast to the geographically laid-out ground floor, the **upper levels** are mostly arranged by material; here you'll find specialist galleries devoted to everything from jewelry to musical instruments to stained glass. Two exceptions to the material-y themed galleries are the **Leighton gallery,** with a fresco by the eponymous Victorian painter, and the sprawling **20th-century** collections, a trippy highlight. The six-level **Henry Cole wing** is home to British paintings, including some 350 works by Constable and numerous Turners. Also here is a display of Rodin bronzes, donated by the artist in 1914, and the "world's greatest collection" of miniature portraits. *(Main entrance on Cromwell Rd. ⊖South Kensington. ☎7942 2000. Open daily 10am-5:45pm, W and last F of month until 10pm. Free tours meet at rear of main entrance. Last F of month features live performances, guest DJs, bar, and food.)*

OTHER MUSEUMS AND GALLERIES

British Library Galleries, 96 Euston Rd. (☎7412 7332). ⊖King's Cross. A stunning display of texts, from the 2nd-century *Unknown Gospel* to the Beatles' hand-scrawled lyrics. Other highlights include a Gutenberg Bible and pages from da Vinci's notebooks. Open M and W-F 9:30am-6pm, Tu 9:30am-8pm, Sa 9:30am-5pm, Su 11am-5pm. Free.

Museum of London, London Wall, The City of London (☎7600 3699). ⊖Barbican. Enter through the Barbican. The engrossing collection traces the history of London from its foundations to the present day, with a particular focus on Roman objects. Open M-Sa 10am-6pm, Su noon-6pm. Last admission 5:30pm. Free.

Courtauld Institute, Somerset House, The Strand, Westminster (☎7420 9400). ⊖Charing Cross. Small, outstanding collection. 14th- to 20th-century abstractions, focusing on Impressionism. Cézanne's *The Card Players,* Manet's *A Bar at the Follies Bergères,* and van Gogh's *Self Portrait with Bandaged Ear*. Open daily 10am-6pm. £6.50, students £4; M 10am-2pm free.

Natural History Museum, on Cromwell Rd., Kensington (☎ 7942 5000). ⊖South Kensington. Cathedral-like building home to an array of minerals and stuffed animals. Highlights include a frighteningly realistic T-Rex and the engrossing, interactive Human Biology gallery. Open M-Sa 10am-5:50pm, Su 11am-5:50pm. Free.

Royal Academy of Art, Burlington House, Piccadilly, The West End (☎ 7300 8000). ⊖Piccadilly Circus. Founded in 1768 as both an art school and a meeting place for Britain's foremost artists. Outstanding exhibitions on all manner of art. Open daily 10am-6pm, F until 10pm. Around £7; students £6.

Dulwich Picture Gallery, Gallery Rd., Dulwich (☎ 8299 8700). 10min. from North or West Dulwich rail station, or bus P4 from ⊖Brixton. Designed by Sir John Soane, this marvelous array of Old Masters was England's 1st public art gallery. Rubens and van Dyck feature prominently, as does Rembrandt's *A Girl at a Window.* Open Tu-F 10am-5pm, Sa-Su 11am-5pm. £4, seniors £3, students and under 16 free.

Cabinet War Rooms, Clive Steps, Westminster (☎ 7766 0130). ⊖Westminster. The rooms where Churchill and his ministers, generals, and support staff lived and worked underground from 1939 to 1945. Highlights include the small room containing the top-secret trans-Atlantic hotline—the official story was that it was Churchill's personal toilet. Open daily Apr.-Sept. 9:30am-6pm; Oct.-Mar. 10am-6pm. £7.50, students £5.50.

The Gilbert Collection, Somerset House, The Strand (☎ 7420 9400). ⊖Charing Cross or Temple. Pick up a free audio tour and magnifying glass as you enter—the latter is invaluable for studying the displays of micro-mosaics and ornate snuffboxes. Open daily 10am-6pm. £6.50, students £6.

The Iveagh Bequest, Kenwood House (☎ 8348 1286). ⊖Hampstead. A large collection bequeathed by Edward Guinness, Earl of Iveagh. The Kenwood setting and the magnificent pictures make it one of London's finest small galleries. Highlights include works by Botticelli, Rembrandt, Turner, and Vermeer. Open Apr.-Sept. M-Tu, Th, Sa-Su 10am-6pm; W and F 10:30am-6pm. Oct. until 5pm. Nov.-Mar. until 4pm. Free.

Design Museum, 28 Shad Thames, Butler's Wharf (☎ 7403 6933). ⊖Tower Hill or London Bridge. This contemporary museum explores the development of mass-market design with a constantly changing selection of objects; most fun are the funky chairs that you can try out. Open daily 10am-5:45pm. Last admission 5:15pm. £6, students £4.

🔲 ENTERTAINMENT

The West End is the world's theater capital, supplemented by an adventurous "Fringe" and a justly famous National Theatre. New bands spring eternal from the fountain of London's many music venues. Whatever you're planning to do, the listings in *Time Out* (£2.35; every W) are indispensable.

THEATER

The stage for a dramatic tradition over 800 years old, London theaters maintain unrivaled breadth of choice. At a **West End theater** (a term referring to all the major stages, even outside the West End), you can expect a professional production and top-quality performers. **Off-West End** theaters tend to present more challenging works, while remaining as professional as their West End brethren. The **Fringe** refers to scores of smaller, less commercial theaters, often just rooms in pub basements with a few benches and a team of dedicated amateurs. **tkts,** on the southern side of Leicester Sq., is run jointly by London theaters and is the only place where you can be sure your discount tickets are genuine. Buy on the day of the performance, in person, on a first-come, first-served basis. Notice boards display which shows have tickets available. (Open M-Sa 10am-7pm, Su noon-3pm. Most tickets £15-25. Booking fee £2.50 per ticket.)

BRITAIN

■ **Shakespeare's Globe Theatre,** 21 New Globe Walk (☎ 7401 9919). ⊖Southwark or London Bridge. Opt for backless wooden benches or stand as a "groundling." For tours, see p. 169. Performances mid-May to late Sept. Tu-Sa 7:30pm, Su 6:30pm; from June also Tu-Sa 2pm, Su 1pm. Box office open M-Sa 10am-6pm, 8pm on performance day. Seats £12-27, students £10-24; standing tickets £5.

Barbican Theatre (☎ 7382 7000), main entrance on Silk St. A huge, futuristic auditorium with steeply raked, forward-leaning balconies. Hosts touring companies and short-run shows, as well as frequent contemporary dance performances. The Pit is largely experimental, while Barbican Hall houses the London Symphony Orchestra (p. 181). Tickets £7-30. Same-day student and senior standbys available from 9am.

The Almeida, Almeida St. (☎ 7359 4404; www.almeida.co.uk). ⊖Angel or Highbury & Islington. Top fringe in London, if not the world. Stars Nicole Kidman and Kevin Spacey have established acting credentials here. Tickets £6-28; concessions standbys £10.

Donmar Warehouse, 41 Earlham St. (☎ 7369 1732; www.donmarwarehouse.com). ⊖Covent Garden. Serious contemporary theater. Tickets £14-29; concessions standbys available 30min. before curtain £12.

COMEDY

Capital of a nation famed for its sense of humor, London takes comedy seriously. On any given night, you'll find at least 10 comedy clubs in operation. However, the city empties of comedians in August, when most head to Edinburgh's annual festival. Check listings in *Time Out* or a newspaper to get up to speed. ■**Comedy Store,** 1a Oxendon St., the UK's top comedy club, sowed the seeds that gave rise to *Ab Fab*, *Whose Line is it Anyway?*, and *Blackadder*. (⊖Piccadilly Circus. ☎0870 060 2340. 18+. Shows Tu-Su 8pm, F-Sa also midnight. Book ahead. Tickets £12-15, students £8.) East London's ■**Comedy Cafe,** 66 Rivington St., merits a health warning: prolonged exposure may lead to uncontrollable laughter. (☎ 7739 5706. Shows from 9pm, dancing until 1am. Cover W free, Th £5, F £10, Sa £14. Reserve F-Sa.)

MUSIC

ROCK AND POP

Birthplace of the Stones, the Sex Pistols, Madness, and the Chemical Brothers, home to Madonna (sort of) and McCartney, London is a town steeped in rock.

■ **The Water Rats,** 328 Grays Inn Rd. (☎ 7837 7269). ⊖King's Cross St. Pancras. Pub-cafe by day, stomping ground for top new talent after 8pm. Oasis was signed here after their 1st London gig. Cover £5-6, with band flyer £4-5.

Brixton Academy, 211 Stockwell Rd. (Ticketweb ☎ 7771 3000). ⊖Brixton. 1929 ex-theater; sloping floor ensures everyone can see the band. Covers all the bases, from the Pogues to Senegalese stars. 4300 seat capacity. Box office open only on performance evenings. Tickets £15-33.

Dublin Castle, 94 Parkway (☎ 7485 1773). ⊖Camden Town. There's music in the back of this pub every night 8:45-11pm. Doors open 8:30pm. Cover M-Th and Su £5, students £4.50, F-Sa £6/£4.50.

CLASSICAL

Home to four world-class orchestras, three major concert halls, two opera houses, two ballet companies, and more chamber ensembles than you could Simon Rattle your baton at, London is ground zero for serious music—and there's no need to break the bank. To hear some of the world's top choirs for free, head to Westminster Abbey (p. 166) or St. Paul's Cathedral (p. 167) for **Evensong.**

Barbican Hall (see **Barbican Theatre**, p. 180). ⊖Barbican or Moorgate. One of Europe's leading concert halls. The resident London Symphony Orchestra (www.lso.co.uk) plays over 80 concerts a year. Tickets £5-35.

English National Opera, the Coliseum, St. Martin's Ln. (☎7632 8300; www.eno.org). ⊖Charing Cross or Leicester Sq. Known for both innovative productions of the classics and contemporary, avant-garde work. All performances in English. Box office open M-Sa 10am-8pm. Tickets £5-15, students £13, under 18 half-price with adult. Cheap standbys bookable by phone from 12:30pm or in person at 10am on performance days.

The Proms (☎7589 8212), at the Royal Albert Hall. This summer season of classical music has been held since 1895, with concerts every night from mid-July to mid-Sept. "Promenade" refers to the tradition of selling dirt-cheap standing tickets, but it's the presence of up to 1000 dedicated prommers that gives the concerts their unique atmosphere. Lines for standing places often start mid-afternoon. Tickets (£5-75) go on sale in mid-May; standing room from 1½hr. before the concert £4.

JAZZ, FOLK, AND WORLD

This isn't Chicago, but top **jazz** clubs still pull in big-name performers. **Folk** (which in London usually means Irish) and **world** music keep an even lower profile, mostly restricted to pubs and community centers. International performers occasionally perform at major concert halls like the **Barbican** and the **Wigmore Hall** (above).

■ **Jazz Café**, 5 Parkway (☎7344 0044; www.jazzcafe.co.uk). ⊖Camden Town. Shows can be pricey at this night spot but the top roster of jazz, hip-hop, funk, and Latin performers (£10-30) explains it. Jazzy DJs spin on club nights following the show F-Sa (cover £8-9, £5 with flyer). Awesome jam session open to all young musicians Su noon-4pm (cover £3 or £1 with musical instrument). Open M-Th 7pm-1am, F-Sa 7pm-2am, Su 7pm-midnight.

606 Club, 90 Lots Rd. (☎7352 5953; www.606club.co.uk). Hard to find; look for the brick arch labeled 606 opposite the "Fire Access" garage across the street; ring the doorbell to be let in. Entrance F-Su with meal only. Music M-Th £7, F £9, Sa-Su £8. M-W doors open 7:30pm, music 8pm-1am; Th-Sa doors open 8pm, music 9:30pm-1:30am; Su doors open 8pm, music 9pm-midnight. Closing times are for the kitchen—the music continues until the musicians don't want to play anymore. Reservations recommended.

⬛ SHOPPING

London shopping centers around the department stores and mainstream chains of **Oxford** and **Regent Streets**. ■**Selfridges**, 400 Oxford St., is the total department store. It also features 14 eateries, a hair salon, a bureau de change, and a hotel. (⊖Bond St. ☎0870 837 7377. Open M-W 10am-7pm, Th-F 10am-8pm, Sa 9:30am-7pm, Su noon-6pm.) **Hamley's**, 188-189 Regent St., fills seven floors with every conceivable toy and game. (⊖Bond St. ☎7734 3161. Open M-F 10am-8pm, Sa 9:30am-8pm, Su noon-6pm.) Fashionable boutiques line pedestrian **South Molton Street**, stretching south into Mayfair from Bond St. Tube, and **Foubert's Place**, near youth-oriented Carnaby St. The area also has a number of excellent sale shops.

In aristocratic **Mayfair**, many high-priced shops bear Royal Warrants to indicate their status as official palace suppliers. **Bond Street** is the location of choice for the biggest names. **Paul Smith Sale Shop**, 23 Avery Row (⊖Bond St.); has a smallish range of last-season and clearance items from the acknowledged master of modern British menswear. The ■**Waterstone's** at 203-206 Piccadilly (⊖Piccadilly Circus; ☎7851 2400) is Europe's largest bookshop. **Covent Garden** is increasingly mainstream, but there are enough quirky shops left to make it worth a look, especially north of the piazza on **Floral Street**. A best bet for women's clothing is ■**Apple Tree**, 51 and 62 Neal St. (☎7836 6088), which offers colorful clothing that verges on punk. Treat your feet at **Office**, 57 Neal St. (☎7379 1896), the largest outlet of London's foremost fashion footwear retailer. No serious shopper can ignore **Chelsea**, where the **King's Road** is all things to all shoppers. The main shopping arteries of **Knightsbridge** are the **Old Brompton Road**, with upscale chains, and **Sloane Street**, full of exclusive boutiques. **World's End**, 430 King's Rd. (☎ 7352 6551) gave birth to the Sex Pistols, but has since gone mainstream. The best reason to visit **Notting Hill** is **Portobello Market** (◉Notting Hill Gate, Westbourne Park, or Ladbroke Grove), actually several distinct markets occupying different parts of the street and operating on different days; Saturday, when all come together in a 1½km-long row, is the best day to visit. Nearby is ◙**The Travel Bookshop**, 13-15 Blenheim Cres. (☎ 7229 5260), the specialty bookshop featured in *Notting Hill*, today besieged by Grantophiles. North London's **Camden markets** are located off Camden High St. and Chalk Farm Rd. (◉Camden Town). The **Stables Market** (most shops open daily) is the best of the bunch, offering good clothes and some of the most outrageous club- and fetish-wear ever made.

◙ NIGHTLIFE

The **West End**—especially **Soho**—is the scene of much of Central London's after-dark action, from glitzy Leicester Sq. tourist traps to semi-secret underground clubs. The other major axes of London nightlife are East London's **Shoreditch** and **Hoxton** (known as Shoo) and South London's **Brixton**, which is quickly becoming London's top neighborhood for nightlife.

PUBS

Pubs might close at 11pm, but they're still an essential part of the London social scene. There are hundreds of pubs in London; these are some of our favorites.

◙ **Ye Olde Mitre Tavern,** 1 Ely Ct. (☎ 7405 4751), off #8 Hatton Garden. ◉Chancery Ln. To find the alley where this pub hides, look for the street lamp on Hatton Garden bearing a sign of a mitre. This classic pub fully merits its "ye olde"—it was built in 1546 by the Bishop of Ely. With dark oak beams and spun glass, the 2 rooms are perfect for nestling up to a bitter. Open M-F 11am-11pm. AmEx/MC/V (£10 min.).

◙ **Ye Olde Cheshire Cheese,** Wine Office Ct. (☎ 7353 6170), by 145 Fleet St. ◉Blackfriars or St. Paul's. Once a haunt of Charles Dickens, Theodore Roosevelt, and Mark Twain. Open M-F 11am-11pm, Sa 11am-3pm and 5:30-11pm, Su noon-3:30pm. AmEx/MC/V. 1.5% credit card surcharge.

The Troubadour, 265 Old Brompton Rd. (☎ 7370 1434). ◉Earl's Court. A combination pub/cafe/deli; each wing is uniquely fantastic. Breakfast all day £3-5. Pub grub £5.50-10. Open daily 9am-midnight. MC/V.

The Jerusalem Tavern, 55 Britton St. (☎ 7490 4281). ◉Farringdon. Tiny and ancient, this Dickensian pub offers many niches in which to get your drink on, including a bizarre 1-table balcony right across from the bar. Specialty ales £2.40. Pub grub £5-8. Open M-F 11am-11pm, Sa 5-11pm, Su 11am-5pm. MC/V.

BARS

An explosion of **club-bars** has bridged the gap between pubs and clubs, offering seriously stylish surroundings and top-flight DJs together with plentiful lounging space. Club-bars are usually open from either noon or early evening, allowing you to skip the cover charge by arriving early and staying put. They tend to close earlier than clubs, usually between midnight and 2am.

◙ **Na Zdrowie,** 11 Little Turnstile (☎ 7831 9679). ◉Holborn. Hidden in the pub-filled alleyways behind the Holborn Tube station—when you see Pu's Brasserie, look to the left. The name (pronounced nah-ZDROVE-yeh) is a Polish toast. Over 65 types of vodka £2.10. Open M-F 12:30-11pm, Sa 6-11pm.

The Market, 240A Portobello Rd. (☎ 7229 6472). ⊖Ladbroke Grove. Look for the strange sculpture above the door. It's consistently the loudest spot on Portobello, and that's saying a lot. Thai food served weekdays noon-3pm. Cuban punch £3. Open M-Sa 11am-11pm, Su noon-12:30am.

Filthy MacNasty's Whiskey Café, 68 Amwell St. (☎ 7837 6067). ⊖Angel or King's Cross. Shane MacGowan, U2, and the Libertines have all played here. The last 2 still drop by periodically; Shane just lives here. Live music and occasional literary readings add to the bad-boy-*cum*-intellectual atmosphere. 14 varieties of whisky £2. Food £5-6. Open M-Sa noon-11pm, Su noon-10:30pm.

NIGHTCLUBS

Every major DJ in the world either lives in London or makes frequent visits. The UK has taken the lead in developing and experimenting with new types of dance music. Even weekly publications have trouble keeping up with the club scene—*Time Out* (£2.35; every W), the Londoner's clubbing bible, only lists about half the happenings any given night. The scene revolves around promoters and the nights they organize rather than the clubs themselves; top nights come, go, and move around unpredictably. To stay on top of things, comb through *Time Out*, which also prints the "TOP" pass, giving you discounts on the week's shenanigans.

Working out how to get home afterwards is crucial; remember that the Tube and regular buses stop shortly after **midnight,** and after **1am** black cabs are rare. If there's no **Night Bus** home, ask the club in advance if they can order a **minicab** for you; otherwise, order your own before you leave. Although it's technically illegal for minicabs to ply for hire, whispered calls of "taxi" or honking horns signal their presence—but there's no guarantee that the driver is reputable or even insured. Agree on a price before you get in, and never ride alone.

▨ **Fabric,** 77a Charterhouse St. ⊖Farringdon. One of London's premier clubbing venues; expect lines. Fabric is large, loud, and boasts a vibrating "bodysonic" dance floor that is actually one giant speaker. Cover £12-15.

▨ **Strawberry Moons,** 15 Heddon St. ⊖Piccadilly Circus or Oxford Circus. Loud, eccentric, hip bar/club with theatrical lighting effects. Cover £5-9. Open M and W 5pm-11pm, Tu and Th-Sa 5pm-3am.

▨ **Trap,** 201 Wardour St. ⊖Oxford Circus or Tottenham Court Rd. The coolest new club-bar in town, Trap took the place of the now-defunct Propaganda. Tu-W bar and food available. Cover Th-F £10, Sa £15.

Notting Hill Arts Club, 21 Notting Hill Gate. ⊖Notting Hill Gate. Excellent place for relaxed grooving: turntables on folding tables, a dance floor, and minimal decoration, this no-frills basement still manages to rock. Not at all touristy, and very chill. Cover M £4, before 9pm free; Tu-Th £5, before 8pm free; F £6, before 8pm free; Sa-Su £5, before 6pm free. Open M-W 6pm-1am, Th-F 6pm-2am, Sa 4pm-2am, Su 4pm-12:30am.

Tongue&Groove, 50 Atlantic Rd. ⊖Brixton. Unself-consciously trendy club-bar so popular and narrow that people dance on the speakers. Don't underestimate the cocktails (£5 doubles). Cover Th £2, F-Sa £3. Open M-W and Su 7pm-3am, Th-Sa 7pm-5am.

Ministry of Sound, 103 Gaunt St. ⊖Elephant and Castle. Take the exit for South Bank University. Mecca for serious clubbers worldwide—arrive before it opens or queue all night. Cover £13-17. No jeans or sneakers. Open F 10:30pm-5am, Sa 11pm-8am.

Bar Rumba, 36 Shaftesbury Ave. ⊖Piccadilly Circus. Rumba has weathered 11 years of London existence, impressive for any club. Tu salsa and merengue dance class 6:30-8:30; £7. Cover £3-8. Open Tu and Th 8:30pm-3am, W 10pm-3am, F 10pm-4am, Sa 10pm-6am £12, Su 8pm-1am.

GAY AND LESBIAN NIGHTLIFE

London has a very visible gay scene, ranging from flamboyant to mainstream. *Time Out* devotes a section to gay listings, and gay newspapers include the *Pink Paper*. *Boyz* magazine, free from gay bars, and the *Ginger Beer* website (www.gingerbeer.co.uk) track gay and lesbian nightlife respectively. Soho—especially **Old Compton Street**—is the heart of gay London, with much smaller scenes in Islington, Earl's Court, and Brixton.

Ku Bar, 75 Charing Cross Rd. ⊖Leicester Sq. Don't be fooled by the naked-lady mosaic; this stylish hangout is definitely gay. Happy Hour noon-9pm offers discounted cocktail jugs (£7) and beer refills (£1). Beer from £2.90. Open M-Sa 1-11pm, Su 1-10:30pm.

Vespa Lounge, 15 St. Giles Ct. ⊖Tottenham Court Rd. Above the Conservatory, a gay bar/restaurant, at the foot of Centrepoint tower. Small, relaxed lesbian lounge bar with blue walls, comfy seats, and big-screen TV. Gay men welcome. Spirits and mixers from £2.40. Th live music, F-Sa DJ from 8pm. Open Su-Th noon-midnight, F-Sa noon-1am.

G-A-Y, 157 Charing Cross Rd. ⊖Tottenham Court Rd. London's biggest gay/lesbian night, 4 nights a week. G-A-Y (you spell it out when you say it) is a bouncing bit of fluff that enjoys mainstream popularity. Sa G-A-Y Big Night Out rocks the capacity crowd with commercial-dance DJs and live performances. Cover £3-10. Discounts with flyer or ad. Open M 10:30pm-4am, Th-F 11pm-4am, Sa 10:30pm-5am.

⚡ DAYTRIP FROM LONDON

WINDSOR AND ETON

Windsor has two train stations, both within walking distance of the castle. Trains (☎084 5748 4950) to Windsor and Eton Central arrive from both Victoria and Paddington stations (40min., 2 per hr., round-trip £7.30) via Slough, while those to Windsor and Eton Riverside come from Waterloo (50min., 2 per hr., round-trip £6.90).

Built by William the Conqueror in the 1070 and 80s as a fortress rather than a residence, Windsor is the largest inhabited castle in the world. The castle's main attractions are found in the **Upper Ward.** The **state apartments** are filled with works by Holbein, Rembrandt, Rubens, Van Dyck, and Queen Victoria herself. A stroll to the **Lower Ward** brings you to the 15th-century **St. George's Chapel,** with delicate vaulting and exquisite stained glass. The site of Edward and Sophie's wedding, 10 sovereigns lie here, including George V, Edward IV, Charles I, and Henrys VI and VIII. (24hr. info ☎017 5383 1118. As a "working castle," large areas may be closed on short notice. Open daily Mar.-Oct. 9:45am-5:30pm; Nov.-Feb. 9:45am-4pm. Last admission 1¾hr. before close. £12.) **Eton College** was founded by Henry VI in 1440 as a school for paupers, and is now England's preeminent "public" (i.e. private) school. Pupils still wear tailcoats to every class and raise one finger in greeting to any teacher they pass. For all its air of privilege, Eton has shaped some notable dissidents, including Aldous Huxley and George Orwell. (Across Windsor Bridge, and along Eton High St. ☎017 05367 1177. Open daily late Mar. to mid-Apr. and July-Aug. 10:30am-4:30pm; mid-Apr. to June and Sept. to late Mar. 2-4:30pm. Schedule varies due to academic calendar. £3. Daily tours 2:15 and 3:15pm; £4.)

SOUTHERN ENGLAND

History and myth cloak Southern England as densely as the Atlantic fog. Cornwall, the alleged birthplace of King Arthur, was the last stronghold of the Celts in England, but traces of even older Neolithic communities linger in the massive stone circles they left behind. During WWII, German bombings uncovered long-

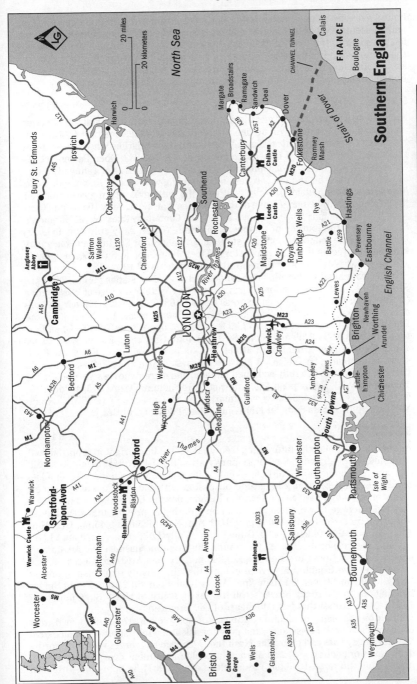

Southern England

buried evidence of an invasion by Caesar, whose Romans dotted the countryside with settlements that include the elaborate spas at Bath. William the Conqueror left his mark in the form of awe-inspiring castles and cathedrals. Apart from all this pomp and circumstance is another, less palpable, presence: The voices of such British literati as Jane Austen, Geoffrey Chaucer, Charles Dickens, and E. M. Forster still seem to echo above the sprawling pastures and seaside cliffs.

CANTERBURY   ☎ 01227

Archbishop Thomas Becket met his demise at ⬛**Canterbury Cathedral** in 1170 after an irate Henry II asked, "Will no one rid me of this troublesome priest?" Later, in his famed *Canterbury Tales*, Chaucer caricatured the pilgrims who traveled from London to England's most famous execution site. (☎ 762 862. Open Easter-Oct. M-Sa 9am-6:30pm, Su 12:30-2:30pm and 4:30-5:30pm; Oct.-Easter reduced hours. £4.50, students £3.50.) Soaring arches and crumbling walls are all that remain of **St. Augustine's Abbey**, outside the city wall near the cathedral. St. Augustine himself lies in a humble tomb under a pile of rocks. (Open Apr.-Sept. daily 10am-6pm; Oct.-Mar. W-Su 10am-4pm. £3.50, students £2.60.) **The Canterbury Tales**, on St. Margaret's St., simulates the journey of Chaucer's pilgrims. (Open daily July-Aug. 9:30am-5pm; Sept.-June reduced hours. £7, students £6.) On Stour St., the **Canterbury Heritage Museum** recounts the town's history. (Open June-Sept. M-Sa 10:30am-5pm, Su 1:30-5pm; Nov.-May M-Sa 10:30am-5pm. £3.10, students £2.10.)

Trains from London Victoria arrive at Canterbury's **East Station** (1¾hr., 2 per hr., £18), while trains from London Charing Cross and Waterloo arrive at **West Station** (1½hr., 1 per hr., £18). National Express **buses** (☎ 08705 808 080) arrive from London at St. George's Ln. (2hr., 2 per hr., £11). The **tourist office**, 12-13 Sun St., in the Buttermarket, books rooms for a £2.50 fee and 10% deposit. (☎ 378 100. Open Easter-Christmas M-Sa 9:30am-5:30pm, Su 10am-4pm; Christmas-Easter M-Sa 10am-4pm.) **B&Bs** cluster around **High Street,** and on **New Dover Road.** For a laid-back social atmosphere, try ⬛**Kipps, A Place to Sleep ❷**, 40 Nunnery Fields, home to a friendly management, a fully-equipped kitchen, and a great movie selection. (☎ 786 121. Laundry £3. Key deposit £10. Internet £1 for 30min. Dorms £13; singles £19; doubles £32.) There's a **Safeway** supermarket on St. George's Pl. (☎ 769 335. Open M-F 8am-9pm, Sa 8am-8pm, Su 11am-5pm.) **Postal Code:** CT1 2BA.

BRIGHTON   ☎ 01273

According to legend, the future King George IV sidled into Brighton (pop.180,000) for some decidedly common hanky-panky around 1784. Today, Brighton is still the unrivaled home of the "dirty weekend"—it sparkles with a tawdry luster all its own. Check out England's long-time obsession with the Far East at the excessively ornate **Royal Pavilion**, on Pavilion Parade, next to Old Steine. Rumor has it that King George IV wept tears of joy upon entering it, proving that wealth does not give you taste. (☎ 292 880. Open daily Apr.-Sept. 9:30am-5:45pm; Oct.-Mar. 10am-5:15pm. £6, students £4.20. Guided tours daily 11:30am and 2:30pm. £1.50.) Around the corner on Church St. stands the **Brighton Museum and Art Gallery,** showcasing Art Nouveau paintings, English pottery, and Art Deco pieces, as well as an extensive Brighton historical exhibit that thoroughly explains the phrase "dirty weekend." (Open Tu 10am-7pm, W-Sa 10am-5pm, Su 2-5pm. Free.) Before heading out to the rocky **beach,** stroll the **Lanes,** south of North St., a jumble of 17th-century streets that form the heart of Old Brighton.

Brighton has plenty of nightlife options. For tips, pick up *The Punter* or *What's On* at music stores, newsstands, and pubs; or ask at the tourist office for an extensive list of gay bars and clubs. **The Mash Tun,** 1 Church St., serves up a noteworthy dark rum concoction (£3) and attracts an eclectic student crowd. (Open M-Sa noon-11pm, Su noon-10:30pm.) Most **clubs** are open M-Sa 9pm-2am. Brighton native Fatboy Slim still mixes occasionally at **The Beach,** 171-181 King's Rd., a hopping shore-side club. (Cover £4-10.) **Casablanca,** on Middle St., plays live jazz, funk and Latin tunes. (Th-Sa cover £7.) The lesbian venue **Candy Bar,** 129 St. James's St., draws an all-female crowd for nightly entertainment. (Cover £3-5.)

Trains (☎ 08457 484 950) leave from the northern end of Queen's Rd. for London Victoria (1hr., 2 per hr., £14.40) and Portsmouth (1½hr., 2 per hr., £13). National Express **buses** (☎ 08705 808 080) arrive at Pool Valley from London Victoria (2¼hr., 1 per hr., £9). The **tourist office** is at 10 Bartholomew Sq. (☎ 0906 711 2255; www.visitbrighton.com. Open June-Sept. M-F 9am-5:30pm, Sa 10am-5pm, Su 10am-4pm; Oct.-May reduced hours.) West of West Pier along King's Rd., ■**Baggies Backpackers ❷,** 33 Oriental Pl., offers exquisite murals, frequent live music, and many spontaneous parties. (☎ 733 740. Dorms £12; doubles £30. Cash only.) A cultish following praises ■**Bombay Aloo ❶,** 39 Ship St., for flawless Indian vegetarian cuisine and an unbeatable £5 all-you-can-eat special. (Entrees from £3.50. Open daily noon-midnight.) Get groceries at **Safeway,** 6 St. James's St. (☎ 570 363. Open M-Sa 8am-9pm, Su 11am-5pm.) **Postal Code:** BN1 1BA.

PORTSMOUTH
☎023

Though its reputation has been tainted by a 900-year history of prostitutes, drunkards, and foul-mouthed sailors, Portsmouth (pop. 190,500) has recently come into its own as a respectable vacationing destination. War buffs and historians will want to plunge head-first into the **Portsmouth Historic Dockyard,** in the Naval Base, which houses a trio of Britain's most storied ships: Henry VIII's *Mary Rose,* the HMS *Victory,* and the HMS *Warrior.* The entrance is next to the TIC on The Hard. (Ships open daily Mar.-Oct. 10am-5:30pm; Nov.-Feb. 10am-4:45pm. Individual site tickets £9.70, seniors and children £8. Combination ticket £15.50/£12.50.) The **D-Day Museum,** on Clarence Esplanade, leads visitors through life-size dioramas of the 1944 invasion. (☎ 9282 7261. Open daily Apr.-Sept. 10am-5:30pm; Oct.-Mar. 10am-5pm. Last admission 30min. before closing. £5, children and students £3, seniors £3.75, families £13. Admission and special events during the D-Day anniversary week £2.50.)

Trains (☎ 08457 484 950) run to Southsea Station, on Commercial Rd., from London Waterloo (1¾hr., 4 per hr., £21). National Express **buses** (☎ 08705 808 080) arrive from London Victoria (2½hr., 1 per hr., £18.50). The **tourist office,** which books accommodations for a £2 fee, is on The Hard, by the historic ships. (☎ 9282 6722; www.visitportsmouth.co.uk. Open daily Apr.-Sept. 9:30am-5:45pm; Oct.-Mar. 9:30am-5:15pm.) Moderately priced **B&Bs** (around £20) clutter **Southsea,** 2km southeast of The Hard along the coast. Take any Southsea bus and get off at the Strand to reach the **Portsmouth and Southsea Backpackers Lodge ❷,** 4 Florence Rd., which offers immaculate rooms, energetic owners, and a pan-European crowd. (☎/fax 9283 2495. Internet £1 for 30min. Dorms £12; doubles £26, with bath £29.) **Country Kitchen ❶,** 59a Marmion Rd., has vegetarian and vegan entrees. (£2.40-3.95. Open daily 9:30am-5pm.) **Pubs** near The Hard provide galley fare and grog, while those on Albert Rd. cater to students. **Postal Code:** PO1 1AA.

WINCHESTER
☎01962

Once the center of William the Conqueror's kingdom, Winchester (pop. 32,000) revels in its storied past. **Winchester Cathedral,** 5 The Close, is the longest medieval building in Europe at 169m The interior holds a shrine to St. Swithun that made it a spiritual capital of medieval England, as well as the tomb of Winchester resident Jane Austen. The 12th-century Winchester Bible resides in the library. (☎ 857 200. Open M-Sa 8:30am-6pm, Su 8:30am-5:30pm; east end closes 5pm. Suggested donation £3.50, students £2.50. Free tours 10am-3pm.) About 25km north of Winchester is the meek village of **Chawton,** where Jane Austen lived. In her cottage, she penned *Pride and Prejudice, Emma, Mansfield Park,* and *Persuasion,* among others.

Many of her manuscripts are on display. Take Hampshire **bus** #X64 (M-Sa 11 per day, round-trip £5.30), or the London and Country bus #65 from the bus station (Su); ask to be let off at the Chawton roundabout, and follow the signs. (☎0142 083 262. Open Mar.-Nov. daily 11am-4pm; Dec.-Feb. Sa-Su only. £4, students £3.)

Trains (☎08547 484 950) arrive at Winchester's Station Hill from London Waterloo (1hr., 3-4 per hr., £20) and Portsmouth (1hr., 1 per hr., £7.50). National Express **buses** (☎08705 808 080) run from London via Heathrow (1½hr., 7 per day, £12) and Oxford (2½hr., 2 per day, £7). The **tourist office,** the Guildhall, Broadway, is across from the bus station. (☎840 500; www.winchester.gov.uk. Open May-Sept. M-Sa 9:30am-5:30pm, Su 11am-4pm; Oct.-Apr. M-Sa 10am-5pm.) **YHA Winchester ❷,** 1 Water Ln., is located in an 18th-century water mill and offers creative bed arrangements between the mill's roof beams. (☎08707 706 092. Continental breakfast £2.40. Lockout 10am-5pm. Curfew 11pm. Open Mar.-June and Oct. M-Sa; July-Sept. daily; Nov.-Dec. on request. Dorms £11, students £8, under 18 £7.20.) **Royal Oak ❶,** on Royal Oak Passage, next to the Godbegot House off High St., is yet another pub touting itself as the UK's oldest. The locally brewed hogshead cask ale (£1.75) is delicious. (Pub food £4-6. Open daily 11am-11pm; kitchen open M-Th and Su noon-9pm, F-Sa noon-7pm.) A **Sainsbury's** supermarket is on Middle Brook St., off High St. (Open M-Sa 7am-8pm, Su 11am-5pm.) **Postal Code:** SO23 8WA.

SALISBURY

☎01722

Salisbury (pop. 37,000) centers around the mammoth structure of ⬛**Salisbury Cathedral,** built between 1220 and 1258. Its astounding 123m spire was the tallest of medieval England, and the bases of its pillars actually bend inward under 6400 tons of limestone. The cathedral also houses the oldest functioning mechanical clock. (☎555 120. Open June-Aug. M-Sa 7:15am-8:15pm, Su 7:15am-6:15pm; Sept.-May daily 7:15am-6:15pm. Tours of cathedral free; roof and tower £3, students £2. Call ahead. Suggested donation £3.80, students and seniors £3.30.) Nearby, the best surviving copy of the **Magna Carta** rests in the **Chapter House.** (Open June-Aug. M-Sa 9:30am-5:30pm, Su noon-5:30pm; Sept.-May daily 9:30am-5:30pm. Free.)

Trains go from South Western Rd. to London Waterloo (1½hr., 2 per hr., £22-30) and Winchester (1 hr., 2 per hr., £11). National Express **buses** (☎08705 808 080) leave 8 Endless St. for London (3hr., 3per day, £13); Wilts & Dorset buses (☎336 855) go to Bath (#X4; 1 per hr. M-Sa 8am-4pm, £3). The **Tourist office** is on Fish Row, in the Guildhall in Market Sq. (☎334 956; www.visitsalisbury.com. Open June-Sept. M-Sa 9:30am-6pm, Su 10:30am-4:30pm; Oct.-May M-Sa 9:30am-5pm.) From the TIC, head left on Fish Row, right on Queen St., left on Milford St., and under the overpass for **YHA Salisbury ❷,** in Milford Hill House, on Milford Hill, which offers 4 kitchenettes and a cafeteria. (☎327 572. Breakfast included. Internet access £2.50 for 30min. Lockout 10am-1pm. Dorms £15, under 18 £12.) At ⬛**Harper's "Upstairs Restaurant" ❷,** 6-7 Ox Rd., the "Early Bird" (2 courses for £8.50 before 8pm) buys a heap of food. (Open M-F noon-2pm and 6-9:30pm, Sa noon-2pm and 6-10pm, Su 6-9pm; Oct.-May closed Su.) **Postal Code:** SP1 1AB.

STONEHENGE AND AVEBURY

A sunken colossus amid swaying grass and indifferent sheep, **Stonehenge** has been battered for millennia by winds whipping at 80 kilometers per hour and visited by legions of people for over 5000 years. The monument, which has retained its present shape since about 1500 BC, was at one point a complete circle of 6½m tall stones weighing up to 45 tons. Though the construction of Stonehenge has been attributed to builders as diverse as Merlin and extraterrestrials, and an attractive mythology surrounds the site, the more plausible explanation—Neolithic builders using still unknown methods—is perhaps the most astonishing of all. You may admire Stonehenge for free from nearby Amesbury Hill, 2½km up A303, or pay admission at the site. (☎01980 624 715. Open daily June-Aug. 9am-7pm; mid-Mar. to May and Sept. to mid-Oct. 9:30am-6pm; mid-Oct. to mid-Mar. 9:30am-4pm. £5.20, students £4.) For those looking for less touristy stone circles, the neighboring megaliths at **Avebury** are a good alternative. With stones that date from 2500 BC, Avebury's titans are older and larger than their favored cousins at Stonehenge. Wilts & Dorset **buses** (☎336 855) connect from Salisbury's center and train station, and run to both sites (#3, 5, and 6; round-trip £4-6). An **Explorer** ticket (£6) allows travel all day on any bus. The closest accommodations are in **Salisbury** (see above).

BATH   ☎01225

A place of pilgrimage and an architectural masterwork, Bath (pop. 83,000) has been a must-see for travelers ever since AD 43, when the Romans built an elaborate complex to house the town's curative waters. The **■Roman Baths Museum,** Stall St., showcases the complexity of Roman architecture and engineering, which included central heating and internal plumbing. (☎447 785; www.romanbaths.co.uk. Open daily July-Aug. 9am-10pm; Sept.-Oct. and Mar.-June 9am-6pm; Jan.-Feb. and Nov.-Dec. 9:30am-5:30pm. Last admission 1hr. before closing. Hourly guided tours included. £9, seniors £8, children £5, families £29.) Next to the baths, the towering 16th-century **Bath Abbey** fulfills masons George and William Vertue's promise to build "the goodliest vault in all England and France." (Open Apr.-Oct. M-Sa 9am-6pm, Su 1-2:30pm and 4:30-5:30pm; Nov.-Mar. M-Sa 9am-4pm, Su between services. Requested donation £2.50.) Head north up Stall St., turn left on Westgate St., and turn right on Saw Close to reach Queen Sq.; the **Jane Austen Centre,** 40 Gay St., describes the city as it was when Austen lived there, and explains the references she made to Bath in works like *Persuasion* and *Northanger Abbey*. (Open M-Sa 10am-5:30pm, Su 10:30am-5:30pm. £5, students and seniors £4.20, ages 6-16 £2.50, under 6 free.) The dazzling **Museum of Costume,** on Bennet St. to the left of the Circus, parades 400 years of catwalk fashions. (Open daily Mar.-Oct. 10am-5pm; Nov.-Feb. 11am-4pm. Last admission 30min. before closing. £6, joint ticket with Roman Baths £12.)

Trains leave from Dorchester St. for: Birmingham (2hr., 1 per hr., £27); Bristol (15min., 3 per hr., £5); and London Paddington (1½hr., 2 per hr., £45). National Express **buses** (☎08705 808 080) run to London (3½hr., every 1½hr., £14.50) and Oxford (2¼hr., 1 per day, £11). Walk toward the town center and turn left on York St. to reach the **tourist office,** in Abbey Chambers. (☎0870 444 6442; www.visitbath.co.uk. Open May-Sept. M-Sa 9:30am-6pm, Su 10am-4pm; Oct.-Apr. M-Sa 9:30am-5pm, Su 10am-4pm.) Many **B&Bs** cluster on Pulteney Rd. and Pulteney Gardens. At **■Prior House ❹,** 3 Marlborough Ln., warm owners conjure up a homey feel. (☎313 587; www.greatplaces.co.uk/priorhouse. Continental breakfast included. Doubles £50-55. AmEx/MC/V.) Take bus #18 or 418 from the bus station to reach **YHA Bath ❷,** Bathwick Hill, housed in a beautiful Italianate mansion. (☎465 674. Internet access. Dorms £14, HI members £12.) **Demuths Restaurant ❸,** 2 North Parade Passage, serves exotic vegetarian and vegan creations, including delicious chocolate fudge cake (£4.80) and Andalusian tapas. (☎446 059. Entrees £8-12. Open M-F and Su 10am-5pm and 6-9pm, Sa 9:30am-5:30pm and 6-9pm.) **Guildhall Market,** between High St. and Grand Parade, has fresh fruit and vegetables. (☎447 945. Open M-Sa 9am-5:30pm.) **Postal Code:** BA1 1AJ.

GLASTONBURY   ☎01458

The seat of Arthurian legend and the reputed cradle of Christianity in England, Glastonbury (pop. 6900) is an amalgam of myth and religion. Legend has it that Joseph of Arimathea founded present-day **Glastonbury Abbey,** on Magdalene St., in

AD 63. For Arthurians, **Glastonbury Tor** is a must-see. The 160m Tor is reputedly the site of the Isle of Avalon, where King Arthur sleeps until his country needs him. To reach the Tor, take the bus in summer from St. Dunstan's Car Park (£1), or turn right at the top of High St. onto Lambrook, which becomes Chilkwell St.; turn left onto Wellhouse Ln. and follow the path up the hill. On your way, visit the **Chalice Well,** on Chilkwell St., where it is said that Joseph of Arimathea washed the Holy Grail; legend holds that the well once ran red with Christ's blood. Pilgrims of a different sort flock to the annual **Glastonbury Festival.** Britain's largest music event takes place at the end of June and has featured some of the world's biggest bands. (Tickets ☎ 834 596; www.glastonburyfestivals.co.uk.)

First **buses** (☎ 08706 082 608) run from Bath via Wells (1¼hr.; M-Sa 1 per hr., Su 7 per day; £4). From the bus stop, turn right on High St. to reach the **tourist office,** the Tribunal, 9 High St., which books rooms for a £3 fee plus a 10% deposit. (☎ 832 954; www.glastonburytic.co.uk. Open Apr.-Sept. M-Th and Su 10am-5pm, F-Sa 10am-5:30pm; Oct.-Mar. reduced hours.) Buses stop near 🖻**Glastonbury Backpackers ❷,** 4 Market Pl., at the corner of Magdalene St. and High St. Friendly staff and a lively cafe-bar complement a great location. (☎ 833 353; www.glastonburybackpackers.com. Internet £2.50 for 30min. Reception 9am-11pm. Dorms £12; doubles £30, with bath £35.) **Heritage Fine Foods,** 34 High St., has groceries. (Open M-W 7am-9pm, Th-Sa 9am-10pm, Su 8am-9pm.) **Postal Code:** BA6 9HG.

CHANNEL ISLANDS

Situated in the waters between England and France, Jersey and Guernsey (along with Guernsey's seven smaller islands) comprise the 190 sq. km known as the Channel Islands. Borrowing from the cultures of England and France, they offer visitors an unrivaled combination of history and elegance. Museums and once-formidable fortresses rest amidst the striking landscape, constantly reminding sunsoaked travelers of the islands' intriguing role in their neighbors' affairs.

🄲 **FERRIES TO THE CHANNEL ISLANDS. Condor Ferries** (☎ 01202 207 216) runs various options from Poole, Portsmouth, and Weymouth, docking at St. Peter Port, Guernsey and the Elizabeth Harbor at St. Helier, Jersey. Times, frequencies, and ticket prices are affected by the season and the tides. Call ☎ 0845 124 2003 or check www.condorferries.co.uk for up-to-date scheduling. ISIC holders are eligible for a 20% discount; ask before purchasing your ticket.

🄹 **JERSEY.** The largest of the Channel Islands, Jersey offers an array of options: a bustling city center (St. Helier), rocky coastlines, sandy beaches, and gorgeous countryside. Across from Liberation Sq. by St. Helier Marina, the 🖻**Maritime Museum** provides information about the seas surrounding the island. For a daunting view, climb to the top of Mont Orgueil castle, Gorey Pier, initially built in the 13th century to protect the island from the French. (☎ 01534 853 292. £5.10. Open daily in summer 10am-6pm; in winter 10am-dusk.) The **Opera House,** Gloucester St., presents the latest in theater. (Box office ☎ 01534 511 115. Open M-Sa 10am-6pm, 8pm on show nights, 1 hr. before a show on Su.) In autumn, Jersey plays host to **Tennerfest,** challenging local restaurants to come up with the best menu for around £10. Check out www.jersey.com for more on festivals throughout the year.

An elaborate system of **buses** makes travel around the island painless. **Connex** buses are based at the station on Weighbridge, St. Helier, and travel all over the island. (☎ 01534 877 772. £0.85-1.60.) **Easylink** offers a hop on/hop off tour service. (☎ 01534 721 201. M-F and Su.) Exit the harbor, follow signs to the Esplanade, and turn right for the **tourist office,** Liberation Sq., St. Helier. (☎ 01534 500 700; www.jersey.com. Open daily 8:30am-7pm.) Handsome B&Bs line the Havre des Pas, stretching to the beach. **Camping** is also an option. **Rozel Camping Park ❶**, St. Martin, has a view of the French coast. (☎ 01534 856 797; www.jerseyhols.com/rozel. £5.60-8 per person per night, pitch only.) Jersey boasts everything from seafood to ethnic restaurants. **City Bar and Brasserie ❷**, 75-77 Halkett Pl., offers sizable portions and free Internet access during meals. (☎ 01534 510 096. Entrees £7-14.50. Sandwiches £4.50-6.25. Open M-Sa 11:30am-10pm.)

◪ **GUERNSEY.** Smaller in stature but not in charm, Guernsey flaunts its French roots more than neighboring Jersey—cultural fusion is evident in the architecture, cuisine, and speech of the locals. ◪**Hauteville House,** 38 Hauteville, Victor Hugo's home during his exile from France, is as nuanced as his writing. Paid for by his successful poetry compilation *Contemplations*, the house is full of secret passages, inverted decorations (e.g., doors for tables, and table legs for pillars), and hidden inscriptions. Preserved in their original state, the grounds on which *Les Misérables* was born should not be missed. (☎ 01481 721 911. £4. Open July-Aug. daily 10am-5pm; Apr.-June and Sept. M-Sa 10am-noon and 2-5pm.)

Island Coachways (☎ 01481 720 210; www.buses.gg.) operates **buses** throughout the island and offers tours from May-Sept.; call the office for fares and information. Routes 7 and 7a circle the coast for £0.50. A **Tourist office** awaits you as you exit the ferry; its larger office is located across the harbor on North Esplanade. The TIC books rooms for a £2 fee and 10% deposit, and distributes maps. *Naturally Guernsey* is a helpful guide to the island. (☎ 01481 723 552; www.guernseytouristboard.com. Open M-F 9am-5pm, Sa 9am-6pm, Su 9:30am-12:30pm.) For an option near town with views of nearby Sark and Herm, try **St. George's Hotel ❸**, St. George's Esplanade, St. Peter Port. (☎ 01481 721 027. Breakfast included. Apr.-Oct. £29-34 per person; Nov.-Mar. £27.) **La Cucina ❶**, North Plantation, above Yugo's Take-Out, cooks up delicious sandwiches (£4.50-5) with a Mediterranean influence. (☎ 01481 715 166. Open Tu-Sa 11:30am-2:30pm and 7pm-late.)

THE CORNISH COAST

With lush cliffsides stretching out into the Atlantic, Cornwall's terrain doesn't feel quite like England. Years ago, the Celts fled westward in the face of Saxon conquest; today, the movement to Cornwall continues in the form of artists, vacationers, and surfers. Though the Cornish language is no longer spoken, the area remains as protective of its distinctive past as of its ubiquitous pasties.

NEWQUAY. Known to the locals as "the new California," Newquay (NEW-key; pop. 20,000) is an incongruous slice of surfer culture in the middle of Cornwall. Winds descend with a vengeance on **Fistral Beach,** creating what some consider the best surfing conditions in Europe. Tamer waters beckon from the bay side at **Lusty Glaze Beach.** Drink up at **Central Inn,** 11 Central Sq., where outdoor seating is packed with partygoers. (Open M-Sa 11am-11pm, Su noon-10:30pm.) **Trains** (☎ 08457 484 950) to Newquay go through Par (50min., summer 5-8 per day, £4.50) before connecting to Plymouth (50min., 15 per day, £8.40) and Penzance (1½hr., 12 per day, £9.50). **Buses** leave from Manor Rd. for St. Ives (#301; 2¼hr., 4 per day, return £5.30); National Express (☎ 08705 808 080) runs to London (7hr., 2-4 per day, £33). The **tourist office** is on Marcus Hill, a few blocks toward the city center from the train station. (☎ 01637 854 020; www.newquay.co.uk. Open June-Sept. M-Sa 9:30am-5:30pm, Su 9:30am-12:30pm; Oct.-May reduced hours.) An international crowd parties late into the night at **Newquay Backpackers ❷**, 16 Beachfield Ave. (☎ 01637 874 668. Kitchen and laundry £2.50. July-Aug. 7 night min. stay. Dorms £9-15; twins £10-16; doubles with bath £13-19. MC/V.)

PENZANCE. Penzance is the very model of an ancient English pirate town. A Benedictine monastery, **St. Michael's Mount,** marks the spot where the archangel St. Michael is said to have appeared in AD 495. The interior is modest, but the grounds are lovely and the 30-story views are worth the climb. (Open Apr.-Oct. M-F, most Sa, and Su 10:30am-5:30pm; Nov.-Mar. M, W, F by appointment only. £5.20, families £13.) During low tide, visitors can walk to the Mount; during high tide, take the ferry (£1). Penzance boasts many **art galleries;** pick up the *Cornwall Gallery Guide* (£1) at the tourist office. **Trains** (☎ 08457 484 950) go to London (5½hr., 7 per day, £59) and Plymouth (2hr., every hr., £11). National Express (☎ 08705 808 080) **buses** also run to London (8½hr., 7 per day, £33) and Plymouth (3hr., 5 per day, £6). The **tourist office** is between the train and bus stations on Station Rd. (☎ 01736 362 207. Open May-Sept. M-Sa 9am-5:30pm, Su 9am-1pm; Oct.-Apr. M-F 9am-5pm, Sa 10am-1pm.) **Blue Dolphin Penzance Backpackers ❷,** on Alexandra Rd., is relaxed and well-kept. (☎ 01736 363 836; www.pzbackpack.com. Dorms £11-13; doubles £26-28. MC/V.) ■**Admiral Benbow,** 46 Chapel St., is a pub decorated with paraphernalia from local shipwrecks. (Open M-Sa 11am-11pm, Su noon-10:30pm.)

ST. IVES. Medieval St. Ives (pop. 11,400) is on a spit of land edged by pastel beaches and azure waters. The town was colonized by painters and sculptors in the 1920s; Virginia Woolf's *To the Lighthouse* is thought to refer to the Godrevy Lighthouse, visible in the distance. The *Cornwall Gallery Guide* (£1) will help you navigate the dozens of galleries here, but St. Ives's real attractions are its beaches. ■**Porthminster Beach,** downhill from the train station, is a magnificent stretch of golden sand and tame waves. **Trains** (☎ 08457 484 950) to St. Ives usually pass through St. Erth (15min., every hr., £1.70). First (☎ 0870 608 2608) **buses** run to Penzance (#16, 16B, 17B; 40min.; 2 per hr.; round-trip £3) and Newquay (#301; 2¾hr., 4 per day, £4.70). From the stations, walk down to the foot of Tregenna Hill and turn right to reach the **tourist office,** in the Guildhall on Street-an-Pol. (☎ 01736 796 297. Open Easter-Sept. M-Sa 9am-5:30pm, Su 10am-4pm; Oct.-Easter M-F 9am-5pm, Sa 10am-4pm.) **St. Ives International Backpackers ❷,** The Stennack, is covered with bright murals. (☎ 01736 799 444; www.backpackers.co.uk/st-ives. Internet £1 for 15min. July-Aug. 7 night min. stay. Dorms £11-16; twins £28-36. AmEx/MC/V.)

EAST ANGLIA AND THE MIDLANDS

The rich farmland and watery flats of East Anglia stretch northeast from London. Literally England's newest landscape, the vast plains of the fens were drained as late as the 1820s. Mention of "The Midlands" inevitably evokes grim urban images, but there is a unique heritage and quiet grandeur to this smoke-stacked pocket. Even Birmingham, the region's much-maligned center, has its saving graces, among them lively nightlife and the Cadbury chocolate empire.

OXFORD   ☎ 01865

A near-millennium of scholarship at Oxford (pop. 120,000) has seen the education of 25 British Prime Ministers and numerous other world leaders. A scholarly community founded in 1167 by Henry II, Oxford is not only Britain's first university, but the world's as well. Despite the crowds of tourists, Oxford has an irrepressible grandeur and pockets of tranquility that lift the spirits: the basement room of Blackwell's Bookshop, the impeccable galleries of the Ashmolean, and the perfectly maintained quadrangles of the university's 39 colleges.

BRITAIN

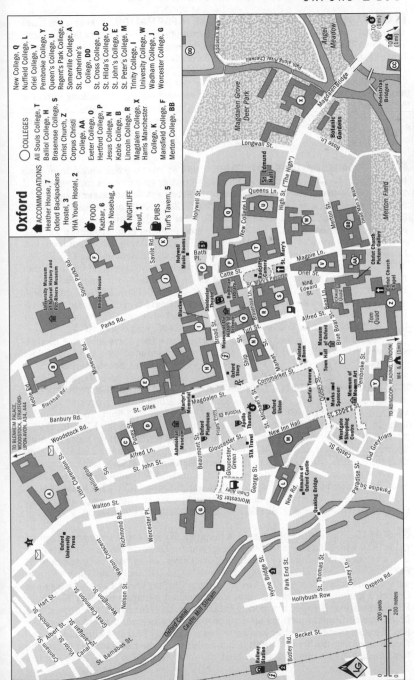

Oxford

▲ ACCOMMODATIONS
Heather House, 7
Oxford Backpackers Hostel, 3
YHA Youth Hostel, 2

🍴 FOOD
Kazbar, 6
The Nosebag, 4

★ NIGHTLIFE
Freud, 1

🍺 PUBS
Turf's Tavern, 5

◯ COLLEGES
All Souls College, T
Balliol College, H
Brasenose College, S
Christ Church, Z
Corpus Christi College, AA
Exeter College, O
Hertford College, P
Jesus College, N
Keble College, B
Lincoln College, R
Magdalen College, X
Harris Manchester College, K
Mansfield College, F
Merton College, BB

New College, Q
Nuffield College, L
Oriel College, V
Pembroke College, Y
Queen's College, U
Regent's Park College, C
Somerville College, A
St. Catherine's College, DD
St. Cross College, D
St. Hilda's College, CC
St. John's College, E
St. Peter's College, M
Trinity College, I
University College, J
Wadham College, W
Worcester College, G

BRITAIN

█▐ TRANSPORTATION AND PRACTICAL INFORMATION. Trains run from Botley Rd., which is down Park End St., to: Birmingham (1¼hr., every 30min., £18); Glasgow (7hr., every hr., £70); London Paddington (1hr., 2-4 per hr., £15); and Manchester (3¼hr., 1-2 per hr., £39). Oxford CityLink **buses** (☎785 400) depart from Gloucester Green for: London Gatwick (2hr., every hr., £21); Heathrow (1½hr., 2 per hr., £14); and Victoria (1¾hr.; 3 per hr.; £9, students £7). The **tourist office**, 15-16 Broad St., books rooms for a £4 fee and offers 2hr. walking tours for £6.50. (☎726 871. Open Easter-Oct. M-Sa 9:30am-5:30pm, Su 10am-3:30pm; low season closed Su.) You can access the **Internet** for free at the **Oxford Central Library**, on Queen St. near Westgate Shopping Center. (☎815 549. Open M-Th 9:15am-7pm, F-Sa 9:15am-5pm.) **Postal Code:** OX1 1ZZ.

▐ █ ACCOMMODATIONS AND FOOD. Book at least a week ahead from June to September and be prepared to mail in a deposit or give a credit card number. If you're homeless, call the **Oxford Association of Hotels and Guest Houses** at one of the following numbers: ☎721 561 (East Oxford), 862 138 (West Oxford), 244 691 (North Oxford), or 244 268 (South Oxford). Make a right from the train station to reach the █**YHA Oxford ❷**, 2a Botley Rd., which features bright rooms, a kitchen, and lockable wardrobes. (☎727 275. Internet £0.50 for 10min. Breakfast included. Laundry £3. Dorms £19.50, under 18 £14.40; twins £46. Student discount £3. MC/V.) The **Oxford Backpackers Hostel ❷**, 9a Hythe Bridge St., between the bus and train stations, has an inexpensive bar, a pool table, and constant music. (☎721 761. Passport required. Internet £1 for 30min. Laundry £2.50. Dorms £13-14; quads £64. MC/V.) Sparkling, modern rooms await at **Heather House ❹**, 192 Iffley Rd. Walk 10-15min. from Magdalen Bridge, or take the bus marked "Rose Hill" from the bus or train stations or Carfax Tower. (☎/fax 249 757. £33-35 per person. MC/V.)

The proprietors of Oxford's bulging eateries know they have a captive market; students fed up with fetid college food are easily seduced by a bevy of budget options. If you're cooking for yourself, try █**Gloucester Green Market,** which abounds with tasty treats, well-priced wares, and fabulous finds. (Open W 8am-3:30pm.) The **Covered Market** between Market St. and Carfax has fresh produce, deli goods, and breads. (Open M-Sa 8am-5pm.) Stock up on groceries at **Sainsbury's**, in the Westgate Shopping Center. (Open M-Sa 7am-8pm, Su 11am-5pm.) Keep an eye out for after-hours **kebab vans,** usually at Broad St., High St., Queen St., and St. Aldates. **Kazbar ❶**, 25-27 Cowley Rd., is a Mediterranean tapas bar with Spanish-style decor and a posh atmosphere. (☎202 920. Tapas £2.20-4.50. Open daily noon-11pm. MC/V.) Head to cozy **Pierre Victoire Bistrot ❸**, 9 Little Clarendon St., for delicious French cuisine. (☎316 616. Lunch £5-7. Dinner £9-14. Open M-Sa noon-2:30pm and 6-11pm, Su noon-3:30pm and 6-10pm. MC/V.) **The Nosebag ❷**, 6-8 St. Michael's St., offers vegan and vegetarian options and tasty soups. (☎721 033. Open M-Th 9:30am-10pm, F-Sa 9:30am-10:30pm, Su 9:30am-9pm. MC/V.)

◘ SIGHTS. The tourist office sells a map (£1.25) and the *Welcome to Oxford* guide (£1), which lists the variable visiting hours of Oxford's **colleges.** Don't bother trying to sneak in outside opening hours; even after hiding your pack and copy of *Let's Go*—bouncers, affectionately known as "bulldogs," will squint their eyes and kick you out. Just down St. Aldate's St. from Carfax, **Christ Church College** has Oxford's grandest quad and its most distinguished alumni, including 13 former Prime Ministers. It's also a shooting location for the *Harry Potter* movies. The **Christ Church Chapel** functions as the university's cathedral. It was here that the Rev. Charles Dodgson (better known as Lewis Carroll) first met Alice Liddell, the dean's daughter; the White Rabbit is immortalized in the hall's stained glass. The **Tom Quad** takes its name from Great Tom, the seven-ton bell in Tom Tower that has faithfully rung 101 strokes at 9:05pm, the original undergraduate curfew, every evening since 1682. (Open M-Sa 9am-12:45pm and 2-5pm, Su noon-5:30pm. £4, students £3.) Tolkien lectured at **Merton College**, Merton St., whose library houses the first printed Welsh Bible. Nearby **St. Alban's Quad** has some of the university's best gargoyles. (Open M-F 2-4pm, Sa-Su 10am-4pm.) Soot-blackened **University College**, High St., was built in 1249 and vies with Merton for the title of oldest, claiming Alfred the Great as its founder. Percy Bysshe Shelley was expelled, then immortalized in a prominent monument, to the right as you enter. (Open to tours only.) **Oriel College**, wedged between High St. and Merton St., was once the turf of Sir Walter Raleigh. (Open to tours only.) South of Oriel, **Corpus Christi College**, the smallest of Oxford's colleges, surrounds a sundialed quad where a garden gate was built for visits between Charles I and his queen, residents at adjacent Christ Church and Merton colleges during the Civil Wars. (Open daily 1:30-4:30pm.) The prestigious **All Souls College**, at the corner of High St. and Cattle St., admits only the best—and stores only the best in its wine cellar. (Open Apr.-Oct. daily 2-4:30pm; Oct.-Apr. M-F 2-4pm.) At **The Queen's College**, High St., a boar's head graces the table at Christmas to commemorate an early student who, attacked by a boar on the outskirts of Oxford, choked the animal to death with a volume of Aristotle. Alumni include Edmund Halley, Jeremy Bentham, and the celebrated Mr. Bean. (Open to tours only.) With extensive grounds, flower-edged quads, and a deer park, **Magdalen College** (MAUD-lin), on High St. near the Cherwell, is considered Oxford's handsomest. The college's decadent spiritual patron is alumnus Oscar Wilde. (Open daily July-Sept. noon-6pm; Oct.-Mar. 1pm-dusk; Apr.-June 1-6pm. £3, students £2.) The imposing **▓Ashmolean Museum**, on Beaumont St., houses works by van Gogh, Matisse, Monet, Michelangelo, Rodin, and da Vinci. Opened in 1683, the Ashmolean was Britain's first public museum and still possesses one of its finest collections. (Open Tu-Sa 10am-5pm, Su noon-5pm; in summer Th until 7:30pm. Free.) **Bodleian Library**, on Catte St. off High St., is Oxford's principal reading and research library with over five million books and 50,000 manuscripts; no one has ever been permitted to check one out. (Open fall-spring M-F 9am-10pm, Sa 9am-1pm; summer M-F 9am-7pm, Sa 9am-1pm. Tours £4.) Next door is the **Sheldonian Theatre**, a Romanesque auditorium designed by a teenaged Christopher Wren. The Sheldonian conducts graduation ceremonies in Latin and hosts world-class opera performances. The cupola affords a picturesque view of Oxford's scattered quads. (Open in summer M-Sa 10am-12:30pm and 2-4:30pm; in winter until 3:30pm. £1.50.) According to the *Guinness Book of Records*, **Blackwell's Bookstore**, 53 Broad St., is the world's largest room devoted to bookselling, with nine kilometers of bookshelves. (☎792 792. Open M and W-Sa 9am-6pm, Tu 9:30am-6pm, Su 11am-5pm.)

▓▓ ENTERTAINMENT AND NIGHTLIFE. Punting on the River Thames, known in Oxford as the "Isis," or on the River Cherwell (CHAR-wul) is a traditional Oxford pastime. **Magdalen Bridge Boat Company**, just under Magdalen Bridge, rents boats. (☎202 643. £10-12 per hr.; deposit £30 plus ID. Open daily Mar.-Oct. 7:30am-9pm. Cash and checks only.) Music and drama at Oxford are cherished arts. *This Month in Oxford* and *Daily Information* (www.dailyinfo.co.uk), both available at the tourist office, list upcoming events. **Pubs** far outnumber colleges in Oxford. Many are so small that a single band of students will squeeze out other patrons—luckily, there's usually another place around the corner, so be ready to crawl. Known as "the Turf," **▓Turf's Tavern**, 4 Bath Pl., off Holywell St., is a wildly popular 13th-century pub tucked in the alley of an alley, against the ruins of the city wall. (☎243 235. Open M-Sa 11am-11pm, Su noon-10:30pm. Kitchen open daily noon-7:30pm. AmEx/MC/V.) **The Eagle and Child**, 49 St. Giles, moistened the tongues of C. S. Lewis and J. R. R. Tolkien for 25 years; *The Chronicles of Narnia* and *The Hobbit* were first read aloud here. (☎302 925. Open M-Sa noon-11pm, Su noon-10:30pm. Kitchen open M-F noon-3:30pm and 5-

8pm, Sa-Su noon-4pm. AmEx/MC/V.) In a former church, ▓**Freud,** 119 Walton St., is a cafe by day and a cocktail bar by night. (☎311 171. Open M and Su 11am-midnight, Tu 11am-1am, W 11am-1:30am, Th-Sa 11am-2am. MC/V.) **Jongleurs,** on Hythe Park St., is a comedy club with an attached bar. (☎722 437. Cover £5-15. Open Th-Sa 7pm-2am, shows 8:30-10:30pm. Bar open M-Th noon-11pm, F-Sa noon-2am, Su noon-10:30pm.)

STRATFORD-UPON-AVON ☎01789

Former native William Shakespeare is the area's industry, and even his most tenuous connections are fully exploited. Fortunately, beyond the tour buses and "Will Power" t-shirts is such stuff as dreams are made of: the enduring grace of the Avon and the pin-drop silence before a soliloquy in the Royal Shakespeare Theatre.

▐**7** **TRANSPORTATION AND PRACTICAL INFORMATION. Trains** (☎08457 484 950) arrive at Station Rd., off Alcester Rd., from Birmingham (50min., every hr., £5) and London Paddington (2¼hr., 5 per day, £34). National Express (☎08705 808 080) runs **buses** to London Victoria (3hr., 3 per day, £13.50). Local Stratford Blue bus #X20 stops at Wood St. and Bridge St., and serves Birmingham (1¼hr., every hr., £3.50). The **tourist office,** Bridgefoot, across Warwick Rd., books rooms for a £3 charge and a 10% deposit. (☎0870 160 7930. Open Apr.-Sept. M-Sa 9am-5:30pm, Su 10:30am-4:30pm; Oct.-Mar. M-Sa 9am-5pm.) Surf the **Internet** at **Cyber Junction,** 28 Greenhill St. (Open M-F 10am-6pm, Sa 10:30am-5:30pm, Su 11am-5pm. £2.50 for 30min., £4 per hr.; students £2/£3.50.) **Postal Code:** CV37 6PU.

▐▐ **ACCOMMODATIONS AND FOOD.** B&Bs line **Evesham Place, Evesham Road, Grove Road,** and **Shipston Road.** ▓**Carlton Guest House ❸,** 22 Evesham Pl., has spacious rooms and spectacular service. (☎293 548. £20-26 per person. Cash only.) Follow B4086 from the town center (35min.), or take bus #X18, X77, or 618 from Bridge St. (10min., every 30min., £1.60) to reach **YHA Stratford ❷,** Wellsbourne Rd., 3km from Clopton Bridge in a gorgeous 200-year-old house. (☎297 093. Breakfast included. Dorms £17, under 18 £13. MC/V.) **Riverside Caravan Park ❶,** Tiddington Rd., 30min. east of Stratford on B4086, offers **camping** with beautiful but crowded views of the Avon. (☎292 312. Open Easter-Oct. Free electricity and showers. Tent and up to 4 people £11. AmEx/MC/V.) Classy yet cozy, **The Oppo ❸,** 13 Sheep St., receives rave reviews from locals for its varied cuisine. (Open M-Sa noon-2pm and 5-10pm, Su noon-2pm and 6-9pm. MC/V.) **Hussain's Indian Cuisine ❷,** 6a Chapel St., has fantastic chicken tikka masala. (Entrees from £6.50. Open M-W 5pm-midnight, Th-Su 12:30-2:30pm and 5pm-midnight. AmEx/MC/V.) A **Somerfield** supermarket is in Town Sq. (Open M-W 8am-7pm, Th-Sa 8am-8pm, Su 10am-4pm.)

◖**♫** **SIGHTS AND ENTERTAINMENT.** Summer traffic at the Shakespeare sights peaks around 2pm, so try to hit them before 11am or after 4pm. Die-hard fans can buy a ticket for admission to all five official Shakespeare properties: Anne Hathaway's cottage, Mary Arden's House and Countryside Museum, Hall's Croft, New Place and Nash's House, and Shakespeare's Birthplace. (£13, students £12.) The Three In-Town Houses Pass covers only the latter three sights. (£10, students £8.) **Shakespeare's Birthplace,** on Henley St., is part period re-creation and part exhibition of Shakespeare's life and works. (Open June-Aug. M-Sa 9am-5pm, Su 9:30am-5pm; Apr.-May and Sept.-Oct. M-Sa 10am-5pm, Su 10:30am-5pm; Nov.-Mar. M-Sa 10am-4pm, Su 10:30am-4pm.) **New Place,** on High St., was Stratford's finest home when Shakespeare bought it in 1597—now only the foundations remain. They can be viewed from **Nash's House,** on Chapel St., which belonged to the first husband of Shakespeare's granddaughter. **Hall's Croft** and **Mary Arden's House** also capitalize on connections to Shakespeare's extended family and provide exhibits on Elizabethan daily life. Pay homage to the Bard's tiny **grave** in the **Holy Trinity Church,** on Trinity St. (Open Apr.-Sept. M-Sa 8:30am-6pm, Su noon-5pm; low season reduced hours. Requested donation £1.) The world-famous **⊠Royal Shakespeare Company** sells over a million tickets each year; recent sons include Kenneth Branagh and Ralph Fiennes. Tickets are sold through the box office in the foyer of the Royal Shakespeare Theatre, on the Waterside. (☎01789 403 444, ticket hotline 0870 609 1110; www.rsc.org.uk. Open M-Sa 9:30am-8pm. Tickets £5-40. Students and under 30 eligible for half-price tickets available in advance for M-W performances, same day for Th-Su. Standbys £12-15. Tours ☎403 405. £5, students £4.)

THE COTSWOLDS

The Cotswolds have deviated little from their etymological roots—"Cotswolds" means "sheep enclosure in rolling hillsides." Grazing sheep and cattle roam 500sq. km of verdant hills, which hide tiny towns barely touched by modern times. These Roman settlements and Saxon villages, hewn from the famed Cotswold stone, demand a place on any itinerary, although their relative inaccessibility via public transportation will necessitate extra effort to get there.

📠🎫 TRANSPORTATION AND PRACTICAL INFORMATION. Useful gateway cities are Cheltenham, Oxford, and Bath. **Moreton-in-Marsh,** one of the bigger villages, has **trains** to London (1½hr., every 1-2hr., £22) via Oxford (30min., £8.20). The Cotswolds are much easier to reach by **bus.** The Cheltenham tourist office's free *Getting There* pamphlet has detailed bus information. *Explore the Cotswolds by Public Transport,* available at most tourist offices in the area, lists timetables. Pulham's Coaches (☎01451 820 369) run from Cheltenham to Moreton-in-Marsh (1hr., M-Sa 7 per day, £1.75) via Stow-on-the-Wold (50min., £1.70).

Local roads are perfect for **biking. The Toy Shop,** on High St. in Moreton-in-Marsh, rents bikes. (☎01608 650 756. Open M and W-Sa 9am-1pm and 2-5pm. £14 per day.) Visitors can also experience the Cotswolds as the English have for centuries, by treading the well-worn footpaths from village to village. The **Cotswold Way,** spanning over 160 km. from Bath to Chipping Camden, gives **hikers** glorious vistas of hills and dales. Contact the **National Trails Office** (☎01865 810 224) for details on this and other trails. The *Cotswold Events* booklet lists anything from music festivals and antique markets to cheese-rolling and woolsack races. A newer way of seeing the region, the **Cotswold Discovery Tour** is a full-day bus tour that starts in Bath and visits five of the most scenic villages. (☎01225 477 101. £25.)

WINCHCOMBE, MORETON-IN-MARSH, AND STOW-ON-THE-WOLD. Six miles north of Cheltenham on A46, **Sudeley Castle,** once the manor of King Ethelred the Unready, crowns the town of **Winchcombe.** (Open daily Mar.-Oct. 11am-5pm. £7, students £6.) The Winchcombe **tourist office** is on High St., next to Town Hall. (☎01242 602 925. Open Apr.-Oct. M-Sa 10am-1pm and 2-5pm, Su 10am-1pm and 2-4pm; Nov.-Mar. Sa-Su 10am-1pm and 2-4pm.) With a train station, relatively frequent bus service, and bike shop, **Moreton-in-Marsh** is a convenient base for exploring the Cotswolds. Its **tourist office** is in the District Council Building. (☎01608 650 881. Open M 8:45am-4pm, Tu-Th 8:45am-5:15pm, F 8:45am-4:45pm, Sa 10am-1pm.) **Warwick House B&B ❸,** on London Rd., offers many luxuries, including a pleasant garden and access to a nearby leisure center. (☎01608 650 733; www.snoozeand-sizzle.com. Book 2 weeks in advance. £21-25 per person. Cash only.) **Stow-on-the-Wold,** the self-proclaimed "Heart of the Cotswolds," sits atop a hill, offering visitors fine views and a sense of the Cotswold pace of life. The **tourist office** is in Hollis House on The Square. (☎01451 831 082. Open Easter-Oct. M-Sa 9:30am-5:30pm; Nov.-Easter M-Sa 9:30am-4:30pm.) The **YHA ❷** is beside the tourist office on The

Square. (☎01451 830 497. Open mid-Feb. to Oct. daily; Nov.-Dec. F-Sa. Dorms £14, under 18 £10. AmEx/MC/V.) A **Tesco** supermarket is on Fosse Way. (Open M-F 6am-midnight, Sa 6am-10pm, Su 10am-4pm.)

BIRMINGHAM   ☎0121

As the industrial heart of the Midlands, Birmingham (pop. 1,000,000) is steadily overcoming its reputation for lack of urban charm. At night, the city truly comes alive, fueled by world-class entertainers and a young university crowd. The most popular attractions may be its extensive **shopping** districts. The sprawling **Bullring** is Europe's largest retail project. (☎632 1500. Open M-F 9:30am-8pm, Sa 9am-8pm, Su 11am-5pm.) Twelve minutes south of town by rail lies **█Cadbury World,** an unabashed, cavity-inducing celebration of the famed chocolate company. Take a train from New St. to Bournville, or bus #11A, 11C, 27, or 84 from the city center. (☎451 4159. Open Mar.-Oct. daily 10am-3pm; Nov.-Feb. Tu-Th and Sa-Su. £9, students £7.20, children £7.) The **Birmingham Jazz Festival** brings over 200 performers to town during the first two weeks of July. (☎454 7020. Most events free.) **Broad Street** is lined with trendy cafe-bars and clubs. Pick up the bimonthly *What's On* to discover the hot spots. **9 Bar,** 192 Broad St., has dark decor and a futuristic warehouse motif. (Cover F £1, Sa £3-5. Open F-Sa 9pm-2am.) A thriving gay-friendly scene has arisen around **Essex Street.**

Birmingham is at the center of a web of train and bus lines between London, central Wales, southwest England, and all destinations north. **Trains** arrive in New St. Station (☎08457 484 950) from: Liverpool Lime St. (1½hr., every hr., £19); London Euston (2hr., 2 per hr., £36); Manchester Piccadilly (2hr., every hr., £20); and Oxford (1¼hr., 2 per hr., £18). National Express **buses** (☎08705 808 080) arrive in Digbeth Station from: Cardiff (2½hr., 3 per day, £19); Liverpool (3hr., 4 per day, £13); London (3hr., every hr., £13); and Manchester (2½hr., 2 per hr., £11). The **tourist office,** in The Rotunda, 150 New St., books rooms. (☎202 5099; www.bein-birmingham.com. Open M-Sa 9:30am-5:30pm, Su 10:30am-4:30pm.) Birmingham has no hostels, and inexpensive B&Bs are rare. **Hagley Road** is your best bet. **Wentworth Hotel ❹,** 103 Wentworth Rd., has spacious rooms and a warm atmosphere. (☎427 2839. Singles £38; doubles £58. MC/V.) Get groceries at **Sainsbury's,** Martineau Pl., 17 Union St. (Open M-Sa 7am-8pm, Su 11am-5pm.) **Postal Code:** B2 4TU.

CAMBRIDGE   ☎01223

In contrast to metropolitan Oxford, Cambridge is determined to retain its pastoral academic robes—the city manages, rather than encourages, visitors. No longer the exclusive preserve of sons of privilege, the university now welcomes women and state-school pupils. During May Week, which marks term's end, Cambridge shakes off its reserve with gin-soaked glee.

█▐ TRANSPORTATION AND PRACTICAL INFORMATION. Trains (☎08457 484 950) run from Station Rd. to London King's Cross (45min., 3 per hr., £17) and London Liverpool St. (1¼hr., 5 per hr., £17). From Drummer St., National Express (☎08705 808 080) **buses** go to London Victoria (2hr., 2 per hr., from £9), and Stagecoach Express (☎01604 676 060) buses go to Oxford (3hr., every hr., from £6). The **tourist office,** on Wheeler St., is south of Market Sq. (☎09065 862 526; www.visit-cambridge.org. Open M-Sa 10am-5pm, Su 11am-4pm.) **Postal Code:** CB2 3AA.

▐▐ ACCOMMODATIONS AND FOOD. Rooms are scarce in Cambridge, which makes prices high and quality low. Most **B&Bs** aren't in the town center. Those around **Portugal Street** and **Tenison Road** are often open only in July and August, since they house students during the academic terms. Check the list at the tourist

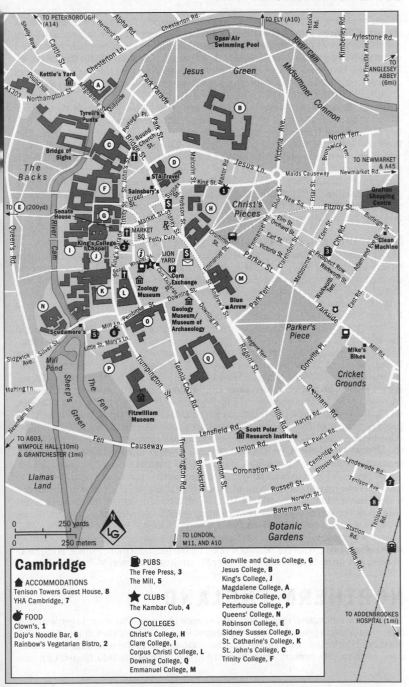

Cambridge

ACCOMMODATIONS
Tenison Towers Guest House, **8**
YHA Cambridge, **7**

FOOD
Clown's, **1**
Dojo's Noodle Bar, **6**
Rainbow's Vegetarian Bistro, **2**

PUBS
The Free Press, **3**
The Mill, **5**

CLUBS
The Kambar Club, **4**

COLLEGES
Christ's College, **H**
Clare College, **I**
Corpus Christi College, **L**
Downing College, **Q**
Emmanuel College, **M**
Gonville and Caius College, **G**
Jesus College, **B**
King's College, **J**
Magdalene College, **A**
Pembroke College, **O**
Peterhouse College, **P**
Queens' College, **N**
Robinson College, **E**
Sidney Sussex College, **D**
St. Catharine's College, **K**
St. John's College, **C**
Trinity College, **F**

office, or pick up its guide to accommodations (£0.50). Two blocks from the train station, ◪**Tenison Towers Guest House ❸**, 148 Tenison Rd., has impeccable, airy rooms with fresh flowers. (☎566 511. Breakfast includes homemade bread and marmalade. Singles and doubles £25-28 per person. Cash only.) **YHA Cambridge ❷**, 97 Tenison Rd., has a welcoming atmosphere, well-equipped kitchen, and laundry facilities. (☎354 601; cambridge@yha.org.uk. Breakfast included. Internet £0.50 for 7min. Call ahead. Dorms £18, under 18 £14.)

Market Square has pyramids of fruit and vegetables. (Open M-Sa 9:30am-4:30pm.) Students buy their gin and cornflakes at **Sainsbury's** supermarket, 44 Sidney St. (Open M-F 8am-9pm, Sa 7:30am-9pm, Su 11am-5pm.) South of town, **Hills Road** and **Mill Road** have good budget options. ◪**Dojo's Noodle Bar ❶**, 1-2 Mill Ln., whips up enormous plates of noodles for less than £6. (☎363 471. Open M-Th noon-2:30pm and 5:30-11pm, F-Su noon-4pm and 5:30-11pm.) Childrens' drawings plaster the walls at **Clown's ❶**, 54 King St., which has a variety of pasta and European cuisine. (☎355 711. Entrees £3-7. Open daily 7:30am-midnight.) **Rainbow's Vegetarian Bistro ❷**, 9a King's Parade, is a tiny, creative spot featuring delicious vegan and vegetarian fare. (☎321 551. Entrees £7.25. Open Tu-Sa 10am-10pm.)

🎦 🎭 **SIGHTS AND ENTERTAINMENT.** Cambridge is an architect's dream—it packs some of England's most breathtaking monuments into less than three square kilometers. Many colleges at the **University of Cambridge** close to sightseers during Easter term (Apr.-June), and virtually all are closed during exams (mid-May to mid-June); your best bet is to call ahead (☎331 100) for hours. Sir Isaac Newton originally measured the speed of sound by stamping his foot in the cloister along the north side of the Great Court at **Trinity College.** Trinity houses the **Wren Library,** on Trinity St., with A.A. Milne's handwritten manuscript of *Winnie the Pooh* and the original copy of Newton's *Principia.* (Chapel and courtyard open daily 10am-5pm. Free. Wren Library open M-F noon-2pm. Easter-Oct. £2, students £1.) **King's College,** south of Trinity on King's Parade, is E. M. Forster's alma mater. Rubens's *Adoration of the Magi* hangs behind the altar of its spectacular Gothic chapel. (Open M-Sa 9:30am-4:30pm, Su 10am-5pm. Book tours through the tourist office. £4, students £3.) Established in 1511 by the mother of Henry VIII, **St. John's College,** on St. John's St., is one of seven colleges founded by women. It boasts the 12th-century School of Pythagoras, thought to be the oldest building in Cambridge. (Open daily 10am-5:30pm. £2, students £1.20.) A welcome break from academia, the ◪**Fitzwilliam Museum,** on Trumpington St., displays Egyptian, Greek, and Asian treasures. (Open Tu-Sa 10am-5pm, Su noon-5pm. Suggested donation £3.)

The best source of info on student activities is the student newspaper *Varsity* (£0.20). **Pubs** constitute the core of Cambridge nightlife, but clubs and bars are also on the curriculum. **The Mill,** 14 Mill Ln., off Silver St. Bridge, takes over a riverside park for punt- and people-watching. (Open M-Sa 11am-11pm, Su noon-10:30pm.) Locals haunt **The Free Press,** Prospect Row. (No smoking. Open M-F noon-2:30pm and 6-11pm, Sa noon-3pm and 6-11pm, Su noon-3pm and 7-10:30pm.) **The Kambar Club,** 1 Wheeler St., has weekly nights for indie rock, garage, goth, electronica, and drum 'n' bass music. (Cover £5, students £3. Open M-Sa 10pm-2am.)

NORTHERN ENGLAND

The north's innovative music and arts scenes are world-famous: Liverpool and Manchester alone produced four of *Q Magazine's* 10 biggest rock stars of the 20th century. Its principal urban areas may have grown out of the wool and coal industries, bearing 19th-century scars to prove it, but their newly refurbished city centers have redirected energy toward accommodating visitors. When the urban pace becomes overwhelming, poets can find respite in the Peak District's green hills or the Lake District's crags and waters.

MANCHESTER
☎ 0161

Teeming with electronic beats and post-industrial glitz, Manchester (pop. 430,000) has risen from factory soot to savor a reputation as one of the hippest spots in England. "Madchester" is also a cradle for pop music—bands like New Order, Joy Division, and Oasis got their start here during the New Wave of the 80s. Though still dodgy in parts, the city is increasingly accessible to the street smart, who revel in its vibrant arts scene and notorious nightclubs.

BRITAIN

▐▌ TRANSPORTATION AND PRACTICAL INFORMATION. Flights arrive at **Manchester International Airport** (MAN; ☎ 489 3000). **Trains** leave **Piccadilly Station,** on London Rd., and **Victoria Station,** on Victoria St., for: Birmingham (1¾hr., every hr., ₤20); Edinburgh (4hr., 5 per day, ₤49); Liverpool (50min., 2 per hr., ₤8); London Euston (2½-3hr., every hr., ₤51); and York (40min., 2 per hr., ₤16.10). National Express **buses** (☎ 0870 580 8080) go from Chorlton St. to Liverpool (55min., every hr., ₤5.25) and London (4-5hr., 7-12 per day, ₤19). **Piccadilly Gardens** is home to about 50 stops for local bus routes; pick up a route map at the tourist office. (All-day bus ticket ₤3.30.) **Manchester Visitor Centre,** in the Town Hall Extension on Lloyd St., books accommodations for ₤2.50 plus a 10% deposit. (☎ 234 3157. Open M-Sa 10am-5:30pm, Su 10:30am-4:30pm.) **Postal Code:** M2 1BB.

▐▌ ACCOMMODATIONS AND FOOD. Most budget lodgings are concentrated 1-2km south in the suburbs of **Didsbury, Fallowfield,** and **Withington;** take bus #40, 42, or 157. Check out the TIC's *Where to Stay* (free) Take the metro to G-Mex Station or bus #33 (dir.: Wigan) from Piccadilly Gardens to Deansgate to reach the clean, spacious **YHA Manchester ❷,** Potato Wharf, Castlefield. (☎ 0870 770 5950; www.yhamanchester.org.uk. Breakfast included. Laundry ₤1.50. Internet ₤0.50 for 6min. Reception 24hr. Dorms ₤20. MC/V.) In the dorm-style accommodations at **Student Village ❷,** Lower Chatham St., groups of 3-7 single rooms share a common space, kitchen, and bathrooms. (☎ 236 1776. Open mid-June to Sept. Singles ₤15, students ₤10. MC/V.) Restaurants in **Chinatown** can be pricey, but most offer a reasonable "Businessman's Lunch" (M-F noon-2pm, ₤4-8). Better yet, visit **Curry Mile,** a stretch of Asian restaurants on Wilmslow Rd. A **Tesco** supermarket is at 58-66 Market St. (Open M-F 6am-midnight, Sa 7am-10pm, Su 11am-5pm.) ▐**Tampopo Noodle House ❷,** 16 Albert Sq., is one of Manchester's favorites, serving up noodles from Indonesia, Japan, Malaysia, Thailand, and Vietnam. (☎ 819 1966. Noodles ₤4-8. Open daily noon-11pm. AmEx/MC/V.) **Dimitri's ❸,** Campfield Arcade, Tonman St., offers Greek delicacies in a bright atmosphere. (☎ 839 3319. Entrees ₤8-13. 20% off drinks during 5-7pm Happy Hour. Open daily 11am-11:30pm. AmEx/MC/V.)

▐▌ SIGHTS AND ENTERTAINMENT. Few of Manchester's buildings are notable—postcards mostly portray the fronts of trams—but an exception is the neo-Gothic **Manchester Town Hall,** at Albert St. Behind the Town Hall Extension, the **Central Library** is the city's jewel. One of the largest municipal libraries in Europe, the domed building has a music and theater library, a language and literature library, and the UK's second-largest Judaica collection. Reopened in 2002 after a three-year, ₤35-million renovation, the **Manchester Art Gallery,** Nicholas St., holds Rossetti's stunning *Astarte Syriaca* in its huge collection. (☎ 235 8888. Open Tu-Su and bank holidays 10am-5pm. Free.) In the **Museum of Science and Industry,** Liverpool Rd., in Castlefield, steam engines and looms illustrate Britain's industrialization. (☎832 2244. Open daily 10am-5pm. Museum free. Special exhibits ₤3-5.) Loved and reviled, Manchester United is England's reigning football team. From the Old Trafford metro stop, follow signs up Warwick Rd. to reach the **Manchester United Museum and Tour Centre,** Sir Matt Busby Way, at the Old Trafford football stadium. (☎0870 442 1994. Open daily 9:30am-5pm. Tours every 10min. ₤9.)

The **Manchester Festival** (☎234 3157) runs all summer with dramatic, musical, and multimedia events. The Gay Village hosts a number of festivals, most notably **Manchester Pride** (☎238 4548; Aug. 19-29 2005), which raises money for GLBT organizations and AIDS relief. At **The Temple,** on Bridgewater St., an entrance in the middle of the street leads downstairs to a small, smoky bar, once a toilet. (Open M-Sa noon-11pm, Su 5-10:30pm.) Centered around **Oldham Street,** the **Northern Quarter** is the city's outlet for live music. Partiers flock to **Oxford Street** for late-night clubbing. Don't forget to collect flyers—they'll often score you a discount. Be cautious after dark. There's no shame in short taxi trips at night in this town. **⬛Music Box,** 65 Oxford St. is a small, underground venue that hosts live bands and enormously popular parties. (Cover ₤5-8. Open Th-Sa from 10pm, closes between 3am and 6am.) Gay and lesbian clubbers will want to check out the **Gay Village,** northeast of Princess St., which centers around the bars on **Canal Street.**

LIVERPOOL ☎0151

Many Brits still scoff at once-industrial Liverpool, but Scousers—as Liverpudlians are colloquially known—hardly seem to mind. In recent years, their metropolis has undergone a face-lift, trading in working-class grit for offbeat vitality. With free museums, two near-deified football squads, countless reminders of the Beatles, and top-notch nightlife, the city was named European Capital of Culture 2008.

🖪🎵 TRANSPORTATION AND PRACTICAL INFORMATION. Trains (☎08457 484 950) leave Lime Street Station for: Birmingham (1¾hr., every hr., ₤20); London Euston (3hr., every hr., ₤85); and Manchester Piccadilly (1hr., 2-4 per hr., ₤8). National Express **buses** (☎08705 808 080) run from Norton Street Coach Station to: Birmingham (3hr., 5 per day, ₤9.30); London (4½-5½hr., 5-6 per day, ₤20); and Manchester (1hr., 1-3 per hr., ₤5.25). The Isle of Man Steam Packet Company (☎08705 523 523; www.steam-packet.com) runs **ferries** from Princess Dock to Dublin, Ireland. The **tourist office,** in Queen Square Centre, gives away the handy *Visitor Guide to Liverpool and Merseyside,* and books rooms for a 10% deposit. (☎0906 680 6886; www.visitliverpool.com. Open M and W-Sa 9am-5:30pm, Tu 10am-5:30pm, Su 10:30am-4:30pm.) Expert guide Phil Hughes runs personalized 3-4hr. **Beatles tours** (☎228 4565; ₤12) for the lucky eight that fit in his van. Surf the **Internet** for free at the **Central Library** on William Brown St. (Open M-Th 9am-8pm, F 9am-7pm, Sa 9am-5pm, Su noon-4pm.) **Postal Code:** L1 1AA.

🖍🍽 ACCOMMODATIONS AND FOOD. Most budget hotels are located around **Lord Nelson Street,** next to the train station, and **Mount Pleasant,** one block from Brownlow Hill. At **⬛Embassie Backpackers ❷,** 1 Falkner Sq., relax by using some of the numerous amenities (including a pool table, three lounges, and a kitchen), or carouse with a young crowd over free toast and coffee. (☎707 1089; www.embassie.com. Laundry facilities. Dorms ₤13.50, ₤12.50 each additional night. Cash only.) Clean rooms and a relaxing bar await at **Aachen Hotel ❹,** 89-91 Mt. Pleasant. (☎709 3477. Breakfast included. Singles ₤32-40; doubles ₤46-54. AmEx/MC/V.) Trendy cafes and well-priced Indian restaurants line **Bold Street** and **Hardman Street.** Many of the fast-food joints on **Berry Street** stay open until 3am. A **Tesco Metro** supermarket is in Clayton Sq., across from St. John's Shopping Centre. (Open M-F 6am-midnight, Sa 6am-10pm, Su 11am-5pm.) At ▨**Country Kitchen ❶**, Drury Ln., delicious toasties, salads, and pasta cost a mere £1. (☎236 0509. Open daily 7:30am-3:30pm.)

◪▧ **SIGHTS AND NIGHTLIFE.** The tourist office's **Beatles Map** (£3) leads visitors through Beatles-themed sights that include **Strawberry Fields** and **Penny Lane.** At Albert Dock, **The Beatles Story** traces the rise and fall of the band through Hamburg, the Cavern Club, and a pseudo-shrine to John's legacy of love. (Open daily 10am-6pm. £8, students £5.50.) Completed in 1978, the **Liverpool Cathedral,** on Upper Duke St., boasts the heaviest bells in the world. Climb the tower for a view that extends to Wales. (Cathedral open daily 8am-6pm. Suggested donation £2.50. Tower open daily Mar.-Sept. 11am-5pm; Oct.-Feb. 11am-4pm. Suggested donation £3.) The Liverpool branch of the **Tate Gallery,** also on Albert Dock, contains a select collection of 20th-century artwork. (Open Tu-Su 10am-6pm. Free. Special exhibits £4.) Neon-blue stained glass casts a glow over the controversial, modern interior of the **Metropolitan Cathedral of Christ the King,** on Mt. Pleasant. (Open in summer M-F 7:30am-6pm, Sa-Su 8:30am-6pm; low season M-F 8am-6pm, Sa 8:30am-6pm, Su 8:30am-5pm. Free.) The **Liverpool** and **Everton football clubs**—intense rivals—offer tours of their grounds. Bus #26 runs from the city center to both stadiums. (Book in advance. Everton ☎330 2277; tour £9. Liverpool ☎260 6677; tour £8.50.)

Consult the *Liverpool Echo* (£0.35), an evening paper sold by street vendors, for up-to-date information on nightlife. **Slater Street** in particular brims with £1 pints. **Matthew Street, Church Street,** and **Bold Street** overflows with clubbers. John Lennon once said that the worst thing about fame was "not being able to get a quiet pint at the Phil." Fortunately, the rest of us can sip with an old-boy crowd at **The Philharmonic,** 36 Hope St. (Open M-Sa noon-11pm, Su noon-10:30pm.) The outdoor beer garden at **Modo,** 23-25 Fleet St., comes alive around 10pm on Saturdays. (Open M-Sa 11:30am-2am, Su noon-12:30am.) **The Jacaranda,** 21-23 Slater St., the site of the Beatles' first paid gig, has live bands and a dance floor. (Open M-Th noon-11pm, F-Sa noon-2am, Su noon-10:30pm.) Fabulous **Society,** 47 Fleet St., draws decadent crowds and posh VIPs to its steamy dance floor. (Cover F £7, Sa £10, Su £5. Open F 10:30pm-2am, Sa 10:30pm-4am, Su 10:30pm-1am.)

PEAK DISTRICT NATIONAL PARK

A green cushion trapped between the industrial giants of Manchester, Sheffield, and Nottingham, Britain's first national park is one of the most visited in the world—over 20 million frustrated urbanites come each year. Though the region can't lay claim to any true mountains, its 555 square miles offer a bit of almost everything else: deep gullies, green pastures, rocky hillsides, and soft peat moorland. Transportation is easiest in the south and near outlying cities, but hikers should head north for a more isolated escape.

▣▨ **TRANSPORTATION AND PRACTICAL INFORMATION.** The invaluable *Peak District Timetable* (£0.60), available at tourist offices, has transport routes and a map. Two **train** lines originate in Manchester and enter the park from the west. One stops at Buxton, near the park's edge (1hr., every hr., £5.70), but planned construction will force travelers to connect by bus (free with rail ticket) to Hazel Grove. The other crosses the park (11-16 per day) via Edale (55min., £7), Hope (1hr., £7.20), and Hathersage (1hr., £7.20), terminating in Sheffield (1½hr., £11.20). Trent (☎01773 712 265) **bus** TP, the "Transpeak," runs from Manchester to Derby (3hr., 5-6 per day), stopping at Bakewell, Buxton, Matlock, and other towns in between. First North Staffordshire (☎01782 207 999) #X18 leaves from Sheffield for Bakewell (45min., 5 per day). First South Yorkshire (☎01709 515 151) #272 and

BRITAIN

Stagecoach East Midland (☎01246 211 007) #273 and 274 depart from Sheffield to Castleton (40-55min., 12-15 per day). The **Derbyshire Wayfarer** ticket (£7.50; available at tourist offices) allows one day of train and bus travel through the Peak District as far north as Sheffield and as far south as Derby.

The **National Park Information Centres (NPICs)** at Bakewell, Castleton, and Edale offer walking guides. Info is also available at the **tourist offices** in Buxton (☎01298 25 106) and Matlock Bath (☎01629 55 082). **YHA** operates 19 **hostels ❷** in the park. (Dorms £9-15.) For Bakewell, Castleton, and Edale, see below; the Matlock YHA, 40 Bank Rd., can be contacted at ☎01629 582 983. For the 11 **YHA Camping Barns ❶** in the park (£4 per person), book at the **Camping Barns Reservation Office**, 6 King St., Clitheroe, Lancashire BB7 2EP (☎0870 770 8868). The park has 10 **Cycle Hire Centres** (£13 per day); a free brochure, *Cycle Derbyshire*, available at NPICs, includes phone numbers, hours, locations, and a map with on- and off-road tracks.

CASTLETON. Lying 3.2km west of Hope, Castleton (pop. 705) lays claim to an unnatural amount of natural beauty. Its main attraction is the █**Treak Cliff Cavern**, which hides purple seams of Blue John, a semi-precious mineral found only in these hills. (Open daily Easter-Oct. 10am-4:20pm; Nov.-Feb. 10am-3:20pm; Mar.-Easter 10am-4:20pm. 40min. tours every 15-30min. £6, students and YHA members £5.) The Castleton **NPIC** is on Buxton Rd. (☎01433 620 679. Open daily Apr.-Oct. 9:30am-5:30pm; Nov.-Mar. 10am-5pm.) **YHA Castleton ❷** is in Castleton Hall, in the heart of town. (☎01433 620 235. Internet access. Book 2-3 weeks in advance. Open Feb.-late Dec. Dorms £12, under 18 £8.50. Members only. Cash only.)

BAKEWELL AND EDALE. The town of **Bakewell,** 50km southeast of Manchester, is the best base from which to explore the region. Several scenic walks through the **White Peaks** begin nearby. Bakewell's **NPIC** is in Old Market Hall, on Bridge St. (☎01629 813 227. Open daily Mar.-Oct. 9:30am-5:30pm; Nov.-Feb. 10am-5pm.) The cozy **YHA Bakewell ❷,** on Fly Hill, is 5min. from the town center. (☎01629 812 313. Dorms £11, under 18 £7.20. Cash only.) An **Extra Foodstore** peddles groceries at the corner of Granby Rd. and Market St. (Open M-Sa 8am-10pm, Su 10am-4pm.)

The northern Dark Peak area contains some of the wildest and most rugged hill country in England, including spectacular peat marshes around **Edale.** For details on **trails** nearby, check out the National Park Authority's *8 Walks Around Edale* (£1.20). The town itself offers little more than a church, pub, school, and the nearby **YHA ❷,** Rowland Cote. (☎01433 670 302. Dorms £12, under 18 £8.50. Cash only.)

YORK   ☎01904

Although its well-preserved city walls have foiled many, York (pop. 105,000) is defenseless against present-day hordes of tourists. Now marauders brandish cameras instead of swords, and the plunder is York's compact collection of rich historical sights, including Britain's largest Gothic cathedral.

🖂🗗 **TRANSPORTATION AND PRACTICAL INFORMATION. Trains** leave Station Rd. for: Edinburgh (2½hr., 2 per hr., £56); London King's Cross (2hr., 2 per hr., £66); Manchester Piccadilly (1½hr., 3 per hr., £17); and Newcastle (1hr., 4 per hr., £17). National Express **buses** (☎08705 808 080) go from Rougier St. to: Edinburgh (5½hr., 1 per day, £29); London (5hr., 4 per day, £22); and Manchester (2¾hr., 3 per day, £8). Follow Station Rd. as it becomes Museum St., cross the bridge, and go left on St. Leonard's Pl. for the **tourist office,** Exhibition Sq. (Open June-Oct. M-Sa 9am-8pm, Su 9am-5pm; Nov.-May daily 9am-5pm.) **Cafe of the Evil Eye,** 42 Stonegate, has **Internet.** (☎640 002. £2 per hr.) **Postal Code:** YO1 8DA.

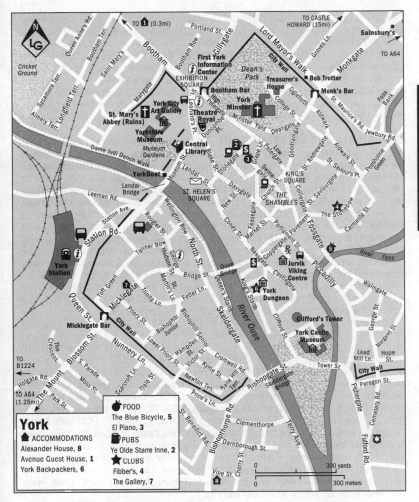

York

🏠 **ACCOMMODATIONS**
Alexander House, **8**
Avenue Guest House, **1**
York Backpackers, **6**

🍴 **FOOD**
The Blue Bicycle, **5**
El Piano, **3**

🍺 **PUBS**
Ye Olde Starre Inne, **2**

⭐ **CLUBS**
Fibber's, **4**
The Gallery, **7**

🏠🍴 **ACCOMMODATIONS AND FOOD.** B&Bs are concentrated on the side streets along **Bootham** and **Clifton,** in the Mount area down **Blossom Street,** and on **Bishopthorpe Road,** south of town. In summer, competition for all types of accommodations is fierce. Try to book rooms weeks in advance. 📱**York Backpackers ❷,** 88-90 Micklegate, is an 18th-century mansion with a kitchen, laundry, and a social atmosphere. Its "Dungeon Bar" stays open long after the pubs have closed for the night. (☎627 720; www.yorkbackpackers.co.uk. Internet £1 for 20min. Dorms £13-14; doubles £34. MC/V.) **Avenue Guest House ❸,** 6 The Avenue, off Clifton, is immaculate and comfortable. (☎620 575; www.avenuegh.fsnet.co.uk. Singles £22; doubles £42, with bath £50. MC/V.) Five minutes from the train station, **Alexander House ❺,** 94 Bishopthorpe Rd., has luxurious ensuite rooms. (☎625 016. Singles £63; doubles £73.) **Newgate Market** is between Parliament St. and the Shambles. (Open Apr.-

Dec. M-Sa 9am-5pm, Su 9am-4:30pm; Jan.-Mar. closed Su.) Buy groceries at **Sainsbury's,** at the intersection of Foss Bank and Heworth Green. (Open M-Sa 8am-8pm, Su 11am-5pm.) Smooth-talking waiters, French bread, and carefully prepared entrees (£16-20) await at **The Blue Bicycle ❹,** 34 Fossgate. (☎673 990. Open daily noon-2:30pm and 6-10pm. AmEx/MC/V.) The city's oldest pub, **Ye Olde Starre Inne ❶,** 40 Stonegate, serves sausages and bursting pies. (☎623 063. Meals £5-7. Open M-Sa 11am-11pm, Su noon-10:30pm. AmEx/MC/V.) **El Piano ❷,** 15 Grape Ln., has Latin-inspired veggie dishes in a corner of the medieval city. (☎610 676. Entrees £6. Open M-Sa 10am-midnight, Su noon-midnight. Cash only.)

◙ �🔎 SIGHTS AND ENTERTAINMENT. The best introduction to York is the 4km walk along its medieval **walls.** Beware of the tourist stampede, which slows only in the early morning and just before the walls and gates close at dusk. The **Association of Voluntary Guides** (☎630 284) offers free 2hr. **walking tours,** which leave at 10:15am, 2:15, and 6:45pm in summer from the York City Art Gallery, across from the tourist office. Everything in York converges at the ◙**York Minster,** the largest Gothic cathedral in Britain. An estimated half of all the medieval stained glass in England lines the walls; the Great East Window depicts the beginning and end of the world in over 100 scenes. (☎639 347. Open daily 9am-6pm. £4.50, combined ticket with Undercroft £6.50; students £3/£4.50.) The **Chapter House** has grotesque medieval carvings of everything from demons to a three-faced woman. (Open daily 9am-6pm. Free.) Climb the 275 steps of **Central Tower** for a view of York's rooftops. (Open daily 9:30am-6:30pm. £2.50.) The **Undercroft, Treasury,** and **Crypt** are filled with interesting sights, including the 12th-century **Doomstone** upon which the cathedral was built. (Open daily 9:30am-6:30pm. £3, students £2.)

The ◙**York Castle Museum,** at the Eye of York, between Tower St. and Picadilly St., is arguably Britain's premier museum dedicated to daily life. It contains Kirkgate, a reconstructed Victorian shopping street, and Half Moon Court, its Edwardian counterpart. (Open daily 9:30am-5pm. £6, students £4.50.) The **Jorvik Viking Centre,** on Coppergate, is one of the busiest places in York; arrive early or late to avoid lines, or call at least 24hr. in advance. Visitors float in "time cars" through the York of AD 948, past authentic artifacts, life-like mannequins, and painfully accurate smells. (☎643 211, advance booking 543 403. Open daily Apr.-Oct. 9am-6pm; Nov.-Mar. 10am-5pm. £7.20, students £6.10, families £22-27.) **Clifford's Tower,** Tower St., is one of the last remaining pieces of **York Castle** and a chilling reminder of the worst outbreak of anti-Jewish violence in English history. In 1190, Christian merchants tried to erase their debts by destroying York's Jewish community. Faced with the prospect of starvation or butchery, 150 Jews took refuge in the tower, where they committed mass suicide. (Open daily Apr.-Sept. 10am-6pm; Oct.-Mar. reduced hours. £2.50, students £2.)

The monthly *What's On* and *Artscene* guides, available at the tourist office, publish info on live music, theater, cinema, and exhibitions. In the evenings, barbershop quartets share the pavement of **King's Square** and **Stonegate** with jugglers, magicians, and soapboxers. York's dressy new club **The Gallery,** 12 Clifford St., has two dance floors and six bars. (No sneakers. Cover £3.50-8. Open M-Th and Su 10pm-2am, F-Sa 10pm-3am.) **Fibber's,** Stonebow House, the Stonebow, hosts high-quality live music nightly at 8pm. (☎466 148. Check *What's On* for events.)

NEWCASTLE-UPON-TYNE   ☎0191

The largest city in the northeast, Newcastle (pop. 278,000) has emerged into the 21st century determined to forge itself a new identity. Ambitious building efforts have lent the city genuine daytime energy, and its nightlife is hotter than ever as locals, students, and tourists swarm to its pubs and clubs. The largely intact **Castle**

Garth Keep, at the foot of St. Nicholas St., is all that remains of the 12th-century New Castle complex. Oddly enough, the city derives its name from a castle that existed over 100 years earlier. (☎232 7938. Open daily Apr.-Sept. 9:30am-5:30pm; Oct.-Mar. 9:30am-4:30pm. £1.50, students £0.50.) The ▨BALTIC Centre for Contemporary Art, housed in a renovated grain warehouse, is the largest center for contemporary art outside of London; it showcases current artists at the cutting edge of their fields. (☎478 1810; www.balticmill.com. Open M-W and F-Sa 10am-7pm, Th 10am-10pm, Su 10am-5pm. Free.) Rowdy **Bigg Market** features the highest concentration of pubs in England, while **Quayside** attracts students to its packed clubs. *The Crack* (free at record stores) is the best source for nightlife listings. **Chase,** 10-15 Sandhill, is a flashy pub with neon lights and a fluorescent bar. (Open M-Sa 11am-11pm, Su noon-10:30pm.) The **Head of Steam,** 2 Neville St., near the train station, has live soul, funk, and jazz reggae. (Open M-Su noon-1:30am.) Students dance the night away at **Ikon,** 49 New Bridge St. (Cover £3-7. Open M and W-Sa 10pm-2am.) For a happening gay and lesbian scene, head to Waterloo St. for a night of drinking and dancing at **The Powerhouse.** (Cover £5-8. Open M-F 10:30pm-3am, Sa 10am-4am, Su 10:30am-1am.) No matter what your plans, be sure to finish the night Newcastle-style with a kebab and extra chili sauce.

Trains leave from Central Station, Neville St., for Edinburgh (1½hr., approx. every hr., £36) and London King's Cross (3½hr., 1 per hr., £83). National Express **buses** (☎08705 808 080) leave Percy St. for Edinburgh (3hr., 4 per day, £14) and London (6½hr., 5 per day, £25). The **tourist office** is at 132 Grainger St., facing Grey's Monument. (☎277 8000. Open June-Sept. M-F 9:30am-5:30pm, Sa 9am-5:30pm, Su 10am-4pm; Oct.-May closed Su.) To get to the friendly **YHA Newcastle ❷,** 107 Jesmond Rd., take the metro to Jesmond, turn left onto Jesmond Rd., and walk past the traffic lights. Call well in advance. (☎0870 770 5972. Internet access. Curfew 11pm. Open mid-Jan. to mid-Dec. Dorms £12, under 18 £8.50. MC/V.) Located in an underground grotto, **Gershwins ❷,** 54 Dean St., serves continental cuisine at a great price. (Full meals £7-11. Open M-F noon-2:30pm and 5:30-11pm, Sa noon-11pm. MC/V.) **Safeway** is on Clayton St., in the city center. (Open M-Sa 8am-7pm, Su 11am-5pm.) **Postal Code:** NE1 7AB.

LAKE DISTRICT NATIONAL PARK

Quite possibly the loveliest place in England, the Lake District owes its jagged peaks, windswept fells, and serene mountain lakes to a thorough glacier-gouging during the last Ice Age. Use Windermere, Ambleside, Grasmere, and Keswick as bases from which to ascend into the hills—the farther west you go from the A591, which connects these towns, the more countryside you'll have to yourself.

▐▼ TRANSPORTATION AND PRACTICAL INFORMATION. Trains (☎08457 484 950) run to Oxenholme, the primary gateway to the lakes, from: Birmingham (2hr., every 2hr., £40); Edinburgh (2hr., 6 per day, £29); London Euston (3½hr., 11-16 per day, £62); and Manchester Piccadilly (1½hr., 9-10 per day, £13). Trains also run from Oxenholme to Windermere (20min., 1 per hr., £3.25), and from Manchester Piccadilly to Windermere (1¾hr., 1 per hr., £13). National Express **buses** (☎08705 808 080) arrive in Windermere from Birmingham (4½hr., 1 per day, £29) and London (7½hr., 1 per day, £27), then continue north through Ambleside and Grasmere to Keswick. **Stagecoach in Cumbria** (☎0870 608 2608) is the primary bus service in the region; a complete timetable, *The Lakeland Explorer*, is available at tourist offices. An **Explorer ticket** offers unlimited travel on all area Stagecoach buses (1-day £8; 4-day £18). YHA Ambleside offers a convenient **minibus** service (☎01539 432 304) between hostels (2 per day, £2.50) as well as free service from the Windermere train station to the hostels in Windermere and Ambleside. The

National Park Visitor Centre is in **Brockhole,** halfway between Windermere and Ambleside. (☎01539 446 601. Open daily Apr.-Oct. 10am-5pm.) **National Park Information Centres (NPICs)** book accommodations and dispense free information and maps. Although B&Bs line every street in every town and there's a hostel around every bend, lodgings fill up in summer; book ahead.

WINDERMERE AND BOWNESS. Windermere and its sidekick **Bowness-on-Windermere** fill with vacationers in summer, when sailboats and waterskiers swarm the lake. **Windermere Lake Cruises** (☎01539 443 360), at the northern end of Bowness Pier, sends boats north to Waterhead Pier in Ambleside (30min., round-trip £6.65) and south to Lakeside (40min., round-trip £6.85). The short, steep climb to **Orrest Head** (2km round-trip) is moderately difficult, but affords one of the best views in the Lake District. It begins opposite the TIC on A591. Lakeland Experience **bus** #599 (3 per hr., £1) leaves for Bowness from the train station in Windermere. The **tourist office** is next door. (☎01539 446 499. Open daily July-Aug. 9am-6:30pm; Easter-June and Sept.-Oct. 9am-6pm; Nov.-Easter 9am-5pm.) The local **NPIC,** on Glebe Rd., is beside Bowness Pier. (☎01539 442 895. Open daily mid-July to Aug. 9:30am-6pm; low season reduced hours.) **Brendan Chase ❸**, 1-3 College Rd., is a family- and biker-friendly B&B with large, attractive rooms. (☎01539 445 638. Singles £25; doubles from £40. Cash only.) To **camp** at **Park Cliffe ❷**, Birks Rd., 7km south of Bowness, take bus #618 from Windermere. (☎01539 531 344. £11-12 per tent.)

AMBLESIDE. About 1½km north of Lake Windermere, Ambleside is an attractive village with convenient access to the southern lakes. **Hiking** trails extend in all directions. Splendid views of high fells can be had from the top of **Loughrigg,** a moderately difficult climb (11km round-trip). An easy trek from town is the lovely waterfall **Stockghyll Force.** The tourist office has guides to these and other walks. Lakeslink **bus** #555 (☎01539 432 231) leaves from Kelsick Rd. for Grasmere, Keswick, and Windermere (1 per hr., £2-6.50). The **tourist office** is in the Central Building on Market Cross. (☎01539 432 582. Open daily 9am-5pm.) To reach the **NPIC,** on Waterhead, walk south on Lake Rd. or Borrans Rd. to the pier. (☎01539 432 729. Open daily Easter-Oct. 9:30am-5:30pm.) Bus #555 stops in front of ▨YHA **Ambleside ❷**, 1½km south of Ambleside and 5km north of Windermere, a very social spot with refurbished rooms, great food, and swimming off the pier. (☎01539 432 304. Bike rentals. Internet £2.50 for 30min. Dorms £15, under 18 £11.)

GRASMERE. The peace that William Wordsworth enjoyed in the village of Grasmere is still tangible on quiet mornings. The 17th-century **Dove Cottage,** 10min. from the center of town, was the poet's home from 1799 to 1808 and remains almost exactly as he left it; next door is the outstanding **Wordsworth Museum.** (Both open daily mid-Feb. to mid-Jan. 9:30am-5pm. £6, students and YHA members £4.60.) The **Wordsworth Walk** (9½km) circumnavigates the two lakes of the Rothay River, passing the cottage, the poet's grave in St. Oswald's churchyard, and **Rydal Mount,** where he lived until his death in 1850. (Rydal open Mar.-Oct. daily 9:30am-5pm; Nov.-Feb. M and W-Su 10am-4pm. £4, students £3.25.) A steep, strenuous scramble leads to the top of **Helm Cragg** (6½km round-trip). **Bus** #555 stops in Grasmere every hour on its way south to Ambleside or north to Keswick. The combined **tourist office** and **NPIC** is on Redbank Rd. (☎01539 435 245. Open Easter-Oct. daily 9:30am-5:30pm; Nov.-Easter F-Su 10am-4pm.) **YHA Butharlyp Howe ❷**, on Easedale Rd., is a large Victorian house with Internet access. (☎01539 435 316. Open Mar.-Oct. Tu-Su; call for availability. Dorms £13, under 18 £9. Cash only.)

KESWICK. Between towering Skiddaw peak and the northern edge of Lake Derwentwater, Keswick (KEZ-ick) rivals Windermere as the Lake District's tourist capital. A great 6½km day-hike from Keswick culminates with the eerily striking

Castlerigg Stone Circle, a 5000-year-old neolithic henge. Another short walk hits the beautiful Friar's Crag, on the shore of Derwentwater, and Castlehead, a viewpoint encompassing the town, the lakes, and the peaks beyond. Both of these walks are fairly easy, with only a few strenuous moments. Maps and information on these and other walks are available at the NPIC, in Moot Hall, Market Sq. (☎01768 772 645. Open daily Apr.-Oct. 9:30am-5:30pm; Nov.-Mar. 9:30am-4:30pm.) YHA Derwentwater ❷, in Barrow House, Borrowdale, is in a 200-year-old house with a waterfall. Take bus #79 (1 per hr.) 3km south out of Keswick. (☎01768 777 246. Open Feb. to early Oct. daily; Dec.-Jan. F-Sa only. Dorms £11.50, under 18 £8. Cash only.)

WALES (CYMRU)

Wales may border England, but many of the 2.9 million Welsh people would rather it were oceans away. Ever since England solidified its control over Wales with the murder of Prince Llywelyn ap Gruffydd in 1282, relations between the two countries have been marked by a powerful unease. Wales clings steadfastly to its Celtic heritage, and the Welsh language endures in conversation, commerce, and literature. As coal, steel, and slate mines fell victim to Britain's faltering economy in the mid-20th century, Wales turned its economic eye from heavy industry to tourism. Travelers today come for the sandy beaches, grassy cliffs, dramatic mountains, and brooding castles that typify this corner of Britain.

CARDIFF (CAERDYDD)   ☎029

The "Come on, Cardiff!" signs that flutter all around the city speak to the vigor with which Cardiff (pop. 306,000) is reinventing itself. Formerly the main port of call for Welsh coal, Cardiff is now the port of arrival for a colorful international population. "Europe's Youngest Capital" stakes its reputation on its progressive attitudes, yet tradition—apparent in the Welsh language or the red dragons emblazoned on every flag and store window—remains as strong as ever.

▐▐ TRANSPORTATION AND PRACTICAL INFORMATION. Trains (☎08457 484 950; ticket office open M-Sa 5:45am-9:30pm, Su 6:45am-9:30pm) leave Central Station, Central Sq., for: Bath (1-1½hr., 1-3 per hr., £12); Birmingham (2¼hr., 2 per hr., £22); Edinburgh (7-7½hr., 3 per hr., £7.20); and London Paddington (2hr., 1 per hr., £54). National Express buses (☎08705 808 080) leave Wood St. for: Birmingham (2¼hr., 8 per day, £19); London (3½hr., 9 per day, £17); and Manchester (6hr., 8 per day, £26). Pick up a free Wales Bus, Rail, and Tourist Map and Guide at the TIC. Cardiff Bus (Bws Caerdydd), St. David's House, Wood St. (☎2066 6444), runs city buses in Cardiff and surrounding areas. (Service ends M-Sa 11:20pm, Su 11pm. £0.65-£1.55, week-long pass £16.) The tourist office, The Old Library, The Hayes, books rooms for a £2 fee and a 10% deposit. (☎2022 7281; www.visitcardiff.info. Open M-Sa 10am-6pm, Su 10am-4pm.) The public county library, at Frederick St. and Bridge St. offers free Internet access in 30min. slots. (☎2038 2116. Open M-W and F 9am-6pm, Th 9am-7pm, Sa 9am-5:30pm. Sign up in advance.) Postal Code: CF10 2SJ.

▐▐ ACCOMMODATIONS AND FOOD. Budget accommodations are hard to come by in Cardiff; the cheapest B&Bs (£18-20) are on the outskirts of the city. The picturesque Victorian B&Bs on Cathedral Rd. are pricier (from £25), but the location is much more convenient, with easy access by buses #60 and 62. ◪Cardiff International Backpacker ❷, 98 Neville St., is a backpacker's dream, with a Happy

BRITAIN

ON THE MENU

WELSH RABBIT

Switzerland has gooey fondue, Italy hot pizza, and Mexico tangy *quesadillas*, but none of these are quite as delicious as Wales's contribution to the world of cheese. Take a piece of wheat bread, smear it ▮th a thick concoction of cheese▮ beer, mustard, and spices, ▮elt it all under high heat until brown and bubbly, and there you have it—a traditional Welsh rabbit.

Sometimes erroneously called "rarebit," the dish's name has a contested etymology. Some claim it was coined by patronizing Englishmen who considered the Welsh so hopeless that they couldn't even catch a hare for supper, and instead were forced to eat bread and cheese. Another story contends that St. Peter lured the Welsh people out of heaven using a "rabbit" of sorts—a bait of roasted cheese (*caws pobi*)—to get them outside the pearly gates.

But the Welsh can't exclusively take credit for this dish: Old cookbooks also contain Scottish and even English rabbit recipes. The instructions for these rabbits of yore o▮ ▮ll for a "salamander▮ ▮e iron slab on a stick, si▮▮▮ ▮o a pizza peel. The heated salamander rested just inches above the bread and acted as a rudimentary broiler. Now, toaster ovens do the trick, and rabbit is still common throughout Wales in cafes and vegetarian hangouts.

Hour (Su-Th 7-9pm) and a rooftop patio complete with hammocks. (☎2034 5577. Only international students in summer. Dorms ₤16; doubles ₤38; triples ₤48; quads ₤60.) **Acorn Camping and Caravaning ❶**, near Rosedew Farm, Ham Ln. South, Llantwit Major, is one hour by bus #X91 from Central Station or a 15min. walk from the Ham Ln. stop. (☎01446 794 024. ₤6 per adult, reduced rates for groups. Electricity ₤2.75.) Cardiff's downtown is full of coffee shops and pubs. ▨**Europa Cafe ❶**, 25 Castle St., across from Cardiff Castle, combines live music performances with red plush couches and an eclectic bookshelf. (☎2066 7776. Drinks ₤1-3. Open M-W 8am-8pm, Th-Sa 8am-11pm, Su 12pm-6pm.) ▨**Celtic Cauldron Wholefoods ❶**, 47-49 Castle Arcade, is the place to gorge on traditional Glamorganshire sausage, seaweed-based laverbread, and Welsh rabbit. (☎2238 7185. Open in summer M-Sa 8:30am-9pm; in winter M-Sa 8:30am-6pm, Su 11am-4pm. MC/V.) Stock up at **Central Market,** between St. Mary St. and Trinity St. (Open M-Sa 8am-5:30pm.)

◧ ♫ **SIGHTS AND ENTERTAINMENT.** Over the past 2000 years, ▨**Cardiff Castle,** Castle St., has changed drastically from pre-Roman to Victorian. However, its buildings, including an impressive keep, are still as flamboyant as the peacocks that strut on the green. Watch out for owls Billy and Floyd during falconry shows. (☎2087 8100. Open daily Mar.-Oct. 9:30am-6pm; Nov.-Feb. 9:30am-5pm. ₤6, children and seniors ₤3.70, students ₤4.85, families ₤17.60.) The **Civic Centre,** in Cathays Park, includes Alexandra Gardens, the City Hall, and the **National Museum and Gallery.** Exhibits range from carved Celtic crosses to a walkthrough of Wales's flora and fauna. (☎2039 7951. Open Tu-Su 10am-5pm. Free.) After 11pm, the action migrates from downtown pubs to an array of nearby clubs, most located on or around **St. Mary Street.** The **Itchy Cardiff Guide** (₤3.50), available at the TIC, has up-to-date, accurate nightlife info. Locals love ▨**The Toucan,** 95-97 St. Mary St. for its receptiveness to both hard-core veterans and clubbing newbies. (☎2037 2212; www.toucanclub.co.uk. Open Tu 6pm-12:30am, W 6pm-1am, Th and Sa 6pm-2am, F 5pm-2am, Su 8pm-12:30am.)

↗ **DAYTRIP FROM CARDIFF: CAERPHILLY CASTLE.** Visitors to ▨**Caerphilly Castle,** eight miles north of Cardiff, may find the 30-acre castle easy to navigate. However, 13th-century warriors had to contend with pivoting drawbridges, trebuchets, crossbows, and catapults when attacking this menacing stronghold, the most technologically advanced fortification of its time. Take the train (20min., M-Sa 2 per hr., £3) or bus #26 from Central Station. (Open daily June-Sept. 9:30am-6pm; low season reduced hours. £3, students £2.50.)

WYE VALLEY   ☎01291

It's no wonder that Wordsworth mused on the tranquility and pastoral majesty that suffuse this once-troubled Welsh-English border territory. As the Wye River (Afon Gwy) meanders through a tranquil valley riddled with sheep farms, trails, abbeys, and castles, much of the landscape still seems utterly untouched by human encroachment and the passage of time.

▐ **TRANSPORTATION.** The valley is best entered from the south at Chepstow. **Trains** run to Chepstow from Cardiff (45min., 1-2 per hr., £5.50) and Newport (20min., 1 per hr., £4.20). National Express **buses** (☎08705 808 080) arrive from Cardiff (50min., 13 per day, £4.25) and London (2½hr., 7 per day, £17). For schedules, pick up *Discover the Wye Valley on Foot and by Bus* in tourist offices. Over 330 sq. km of the valley have been named an Area of Outstanding Natural Beauty; **hiking** is a great way to explore. The 350km **Wye Valley Walk** treks north from Chepstow, through Hay-on-Wye, and on to Prestatyn along wooded cliffs and farmland. **Offa's Dyke Path** consists of 285km of hiking and biking paths along the Welsh-English border. For info, consult the **Offa's Dyke Association** (☎01547 528 753).

CHEPSTOW AND TINTERN. Chepstow's strategic position at the mouth of the river and the base of the English border made it an important fortification in Norman times. Flowers spring from the cliffside ruins of **Castell Casgwent,** Britain's oldest datable stone castle (c. 1070), which offers stunning views of the Wye from its tower walls. (☎624 065. Open daily 9:30am-6pm. £3, students £2.50, families £8.50.) **Trains** arrive on Station Rd.; **buses** stop in front of Somerfield supermarket. Buy tickets at **The Travel House,** 9 Moor St. (☎623 031. Open M-Sa 9am-5:30pm.) The **tourist office** is on Bridge St. (☎623 772; www.chepstow.co.uk. Open daily Apr.-Oct. 10am-5:30pm; Nov.-Mar. 10am-3:30pm.) Visit **Mrs. Presley ❸,** 30 Kingsmark Ave., a 10min. walk from the town center, for beautiful rooms. (☎624 466. Breakfast included. Singles £20; doubles £40.) The **Tesco** on Station Rd. is open 24hr. but closes Sa 10pm-Su 10am and Su 4pm-M 8am. **Postal Code:** NP16 5DA.

Five miles north of Chepstow on A466, the haunting Gothic arches of ▧**Tintern Abbey** "connect the landscape with the quiet of the sky"—as described in Wordsworth's famous poem, written just a few miles away. (☎689 251. Open June-Sept. daily 9:30am-6pm; Apr.-May and Oct. daily 9:30am-5pm; Nov.-Mar. M-Sa 9:30am-4pm, Su 11am-4pm. £3.) A 5km hike along **Monk's Trail** will get you to **Devil's Pulpit,** from which Satan is said to have tempted the monks as they worked in the fields. One kilometer to the north on A466, the **tourist office** is in a train carriage at the Old Station. (☎689 566. Open daily Apr.-Oct. 10:30am-5:30pm.) **YHA St. Briavel's Castle ❷,** 6½km northeast of Tintern across the English border, occupies a 13th-century fortress. While a unique experience, St. Briavel's is somewhat remote, and should only be booked by those prepared for a nearly 5km uphill hike. From A466 (bus #69 from Chepstow) or Offa's Dyke, follow signs from the edge of the bridge. (☎01594 530 272. Dorms £12, under 18 £8.50.) The cozy **Holmleigh B&B ❷** is near the edge of Tintern Village on A466. (☎689 521. £18.) Try **The Moon and Sixpence ❷,** next to Holmleigh B&B, for rich country food in a pub atmosphere. (☎689 284.)

BRECON BEACONS NATIONAL PARK

The *Parc Cenedlaethol Bannau Brycheiniog* encompasses 520 dramatic square miles of red sandstone crags, shaded forests, and breathtaking waterfalls. The park is divided into four regions: **Brecon Beacons,** where King Arthur's fortress is thought to have stood; **Fforest Fawr,** with the spectacular waterfalls of Ystradfellte; the eastern, Tolkien-esque **Black Mountains;** and the remote, western **Black Mountain** (singular). Brecon, on the fringe of the park, makes the best touring base.

⌐ TRANSPORTATION. Trains (☎ 08457 484 950) run from London Paddington via Cardiff to Abergavenny, at the park's southeastern corner, and to Merthyr Tydfil, on the southern edge. National Express (☎ 08705 808 080) **bus** #509 runs to Brecon from London (5hr., 1 per day, £21) via Cardiff (1¼hr., £3.25). Stagecoach Red and White (☎ 01633 838 856) bus #21 arrives in Brecon from Abergavenny (50min., 6 per day, £4.50). The free *Brecon Beacons: A Visitor's Guide*, available at TICs, details bus coverage and lists walks accessible by public transportation.

BRECON (ABERHONDDU). Most hikers start from Brecon, at the northern edge of the mountains. **Buses** arrive at the **Bulwark** in the central square from Cardiff (1¼hr., 1 per day, £3.25). The **tourist office** is in the Cattle Market parking lot with the **National Park Information Centre (NPIC);** walk through Bethel Square off Lion St. (☎ 01874 622 485. Open daily 9:30am-5pm.) Accommodations fill up far in advance during the mid-August Jazz Festival—remember to book ahead. Delightful **Mrs. J. Thomas ❷,** 13 Alexandra Rd., behind the TIC, has traveled to 27 countries and displays exotic memorabilia in her well-kept rooms. (☎ 01874 624 551. Breakfast included. £20-22 per person. Cash and checks only.) Camp at **Brynich Caravan Park ❶,** one and a half miles east on the A40. (☎ 01874 623 325; www.brynich.co.uk. Open Easter-Oct. £5 per person, £11 for 2 people with car.)

FFOREST FAWR. Forests abound with moss and ferns and funnel water over spectacular falls near **Ystradfellte** (uh-strahd-FELTH-tuh), about seven miles southwest of the Beacons. The **YHA Ystradfellte ❶** is a perfect launching pad for those willing to make the hike. (☎ 01639 720 301. Open Easter-late Sept. Call 48hr. in advance. Dorms £9.50, under 18 £7.) From the hostel, 16km of trails pass **Fforest Fawr,** the headlands of the Waterfall District, on their way to the somewhat touristy **Dan-yr-Ogof Showcaves.** (☎ 01639 730 284. Open daily Apr.-Oct. 10am-5pm. £8.50, children £6.) Stagecoach Red and White **bus** #63 (1½hr., 2-3 per day, £4-5) stops at the hostel and caves en route to Brecon.

THE BLACK MOUNTAINS. Located in the easternmost section of the park, the Black Mountains are a group of long, lofty ridges offering 207 sq. km of solitude and unsurpassed ridge-walks. Begin forays from **Crickhowell,** on the A40, or travel the eastern boundary along **Offa's Dyke Path,** which is dotted with impressive ruins. The **YHA Capel-y-ffin ❶** (kap-EL-uh-fin), along Offa's Dyke Path, is eight miles from Hay-on-Wye. Take Stagecoach Red and White **bus** #39 from Hereford to Brecon, stop before Hay, and walk uphill. (☎ 01873 890 650. Lockout 10am-5pm. Open July-Sept. daily; Oct.-Dec. and Mar.-June M-Tu and F-Sa. Dorms £9.30, under 18 £6.70.)

THE BRECON BEACONS. These peaks at the center of the park lure hikers with idyllic farmland and pastoral slopes. The most convenient route to the top begins at **Storey Arms** (a carpark on the A470) and offers views of **Llyn Cwm Llwch** (HLIN koom hlooch), a 600-meter-deep glacial pool. Because this route is the most convenient, however, it is also the most overcrowded. Consult guides at the NPICs in Brecon or Abergavenny for recommendations on alternate trails.

ST. DAVID'S (TYDDEWI)   ☎01437

The quaintness of St. David's tiny city center is strangely in sync with the austere immensity of ■St. David's Cathedral, a major medieval pilgrimage site, built in the 6th century to offer protection from marauding Vikings. The bones of St. David are still kept in the cathedral's reliquary. (Open M-Sa 8:30am-6pm, Su 12:45-5:45pm.) The Bishop's Palace, across the stream from the cathedral, with lavish carvings and arches, evokes a past when the bishopric was the military and religious community center. (Open daily June-Sept. 9:30am-6pm; Sept.-May reduced hours. £2.50.)

To reach St. David's from Cardiff, take the train to Haverfordwest (3hr., up to 10 per day, £14.50), and then take Richards Bros. bus #411 (50min., M-Sa 12 per day, £2.15). The tourist office is on the Grove. (☎720 392; www.stdavids.co.uk. Open Easter-Oct. daily 9:30am-5:30pm; Nov.-Easter M-Sa 10am-4pm.) Beautiful Alandale ❸, 43 Nun St., has cathedral views, warm hosts, and filling breakfasts. (☎720 404. £30 per person.) For excellent Welsh food, head to Cartref ❸, in Cross Sq. Try the Celtic pie (£7), a Welsh dish that combines cheese, oats, flan, spinach, and bread. (Dinner from £10. Open daily June-Aug. 11am-3pm and 6-8:30pm; Mar.-May 11am-2:30pm and 6:30-8:30pm.) Postal Code: SA62 6SW.

SNOWDONIA NATIONAL PARK

Amid Edward I's impressive man-made battlements in Northern Wales lies the 2175 sq. km natural fortress of Snowdonia National Park. Snowdonia's craggy peaks, the highest in England and Wales, yield surprisingly diverse terrain—pristine lakes etch glittering outlines onto green fields and desolate slate cliffs slope into thickly wooded hills. Although these lands have largely fallen into private hands, endless public footpaths accommodate droves of visitors.

▐▀❷ TRANSPORTATION AND PRACTICAL INFORMATION. Trains (☎08457 484 950) stop on the park's outskirts at towns like Conwy (p. 215). The Conwy Valley Line runs from Llandudno through Betws-y-Coed to Blaenau Ffestiniog (1hr., 2-7 per day). At Blaenau Ffestiniog the Conwy Valley Line connects with the narrow-gauge Ffestiniog Railway (p. 214), which runs through the mountains to Porthmadog, meeting the Cambrian Coaster to Llanberis and Aberystwyth. Buses run to the interior of the park from Conwy and Caernarfon; consult the *Gwynedd Public Transport Maps and Timetables* and *Conwy Public Transport Information*, available in all regional tourist offices. The Snowdonia National Park Information Headquarters, Penrhyndeudraeth, Gwynedd (☎01766 770 274; www.gwynedd.gov.uk), provides hiking info and can direct you to the seven quality YHAs in the park, as well as the region's other tourist offices and National Park Information Centres (NPICs).

▐ HIKING. The highest peak in England and Wales at 1085m, Mount Snowdon is the park's most popular destination. Its Welsh name is *Yr Wyddfa* ("the burial place")—local lore holds that Rhita Gawr, a giant cloaked with the beards of kings he slaughtered, is buried here. Six paths of varying difficulties wind their way up Snowdon; tourist offices and NPICs can provide guides on these ascents. Pick up Ordnance Survey Landranger Map #115 (£6) and Outdoor Leisure Map #17 (£7), as well as individual path guides, at tourist offices and park centers. It will always be cold and wet, with unpredictable shifts, in the high mountains—dress accordingly. Contact Mountaincall Snowdonia (☎09068 500 449) or check at NPICs for local forecasts and ground conditions.

BRITAIN

LLANBERIS   ☎ 01286

Llanberis owes its outdoorsy bustle to the appeal of Mt. Snowdon, whose ridges and peaks unfurl just south of town. The immensely popular **Snowdon Mountain Railway** has been helping visitors "climb" to Snowdon's summit since 1896. (☎ 0870 458 0033. Open mid-Mar. to Oct. Round-trip £20.) KMP (☎ 870 880) **bus** #88 runs from Caernarfon (25min.; 1-2 per hr.; £1.50, round-trip £2). The **tourist office** is at 41b High St. (☎ 870 765. Open Easter-Oct. daily 9:30am-5:30pm; Nov.-Easter W and F-Su 11am-4pm.) Plenty of sheep keep hostelers company at the **YHA Llanberis ❷**, 2¼km up Capel Goch Rd. Follow the signs from Main St. (☎ 0870 770 5928. Curfew 11pm. Open Apr.-Oct. daily; Nov.-Dec. F-Sa. Dorms £12, under 18 £8.50. Membership fee £14.)

HARLECH   ☎ 01766

This tiny hillside town just south of the Llyn Peninsula commands panoramic views of sea, sand, and Snowdonian summits. ▓**Harlech Castle** was built by Edward I to keep an eye on troublemakers, but later served as the insurrection headquarters of Welsh rebel Owain Glyndŵr. (Open June-Sept. daily 9:30am-6pm; low season reduced hours. £3, students £2.50.) Harlech lies midway on the Cambrian Coaster line; **trains** arrive from Machynlleth (1¼-1½hr., 3-7 per day, £6.20) and connect to Pwllheli and other spots on the Llyn Peninsula. The **tourist office**, on Stryd Fawr, doubles as a **NPIC**. (☎ 780 658. Open daily Apr.-Oct. 9:30am-5:30pm.) Enjoy spacious rooms and breakfast served in a glassed-in patio overlooking the ocean and castle at ▓**Arundel ❷**, Stryd Fawr. Call ahead for pick-up. (☎ 780 637. £16 per person. Cash only.) At the **Plâs Cafe ❷**, Stryd Fawr, guests linger over cream tea (£3.50) and sunset dinners (from £7) on a grassy patio. (☎ 780 204. Open daily Mar.-Oct. 10am-8:30pm; Nov.-Feb. 10am-5:30pm. AmEx/MC/V.) **Postal Code:** LL46 2YA.

LLYN PENINSULA   ☎ 01766

The seclusion and sublime tranquility of the Llyn have always brought visitors to reverence. **Porthmadog,** on the southeastern part of the peninsula, is the main gateway. This travel hub's attraction is the **Ffestiniog Railway** (☎ 516 000; call for hours), which runs from Harbour Station, High St., into the hills of Snowdonia (round-trip 2½hr., 2-10 per day, £14). **Trains** run from Aberystwyth (2hr., 3-7 per day) via Machynlleth. Express Motors **bus** #1 stops in Porthmadog on its way from Blaenau Ffestiniog to Caernarfon (1hr., M-Sa 1 per hr. 7:05am-11:05pm, £2.60). The **tourist office** is on High St. by the harbor. (☎ 512 981. Open daily Easter-Oct. 10am-6pm; Nov.-Easter 10am-5pm.) The birthplace of Lawrence of Arabia is now the huge, comfortable ▓**Snowdon Backpackers Hostel ❷**, with a cafe, a kitchen, and a bar. (☎ 515 354. Dorms £12-13; doubles £29-33. MC/V.) **Postal Code:** LL49 9AD.

CAERNARFON   ☎ 01286

Majestic and fervently Welsh, the walled city of Caernarfon (car-NAR-von) has a world-famous castle at its prow and mountains in its wake. Begun by Edward I in 1283, ▓**Caernarfon Castle** was left unfinished when Eddie ran out of money, but is still an architectural feat; its walls withstood a 1404 siege with only 28 defenders. (☎ 677 617. Open daily June-Sept. 9:30am-6pm; low season reduced hours. £4.50, students £3.50.) Arriva Cymru **buses** #5 and 5x arrive from Conwy. (☎ 08706 082 608; 1¼hr., 1-3 per hr.) National Express (☎ 08705 808 080) runs to London (9hr., 1 per day, £26). The **tourist office** is on Castle St. (☎ 672 232. Open Apr.-Oct. daily 9:30am-5:30pm, Nov.-Mar. M-Sa 10am-4:30pm.) ▓**Totter's Hostel ❷**, 2 High St., has huge rooms, a full kitchen, and awesome owners. (☎ 672 963. Dorms £12. Cash only.) **Hole-in-the-Wall Street** offers a tremendous collection of bistros, cafes, and restaurants. **Postal Code:** LL55 2ND.

CONWY

☎ 01492

The central attraction of this tourist mecca is the imposing, 13th-century ▓Conwy Castle, another link in Edward I's chain of Welsh fortresses. (Open June-Sept. daily 9:30am-6pm; Apr.-May and Oct. daily 9:30am-5pm; Nov.-Mar. M-Sa 9:30am-4pm, Su 11am-4pm. £3.75, students £3.25. Tours £1.) Arriva Cymru buses (☎ 08706 082 608) stop in Conwy on their way to Caernarfon from Llandudno (#5 and 5X; 2-3 per hr.). National Express buses (☎ 08705 808 080) arrive from: Liverpool (2¾hr., 1 per day, £8.25); Manchester (4½hr., 1 per day, £13); and Newcastle (10hr., 1 per day, £44). The tourist office is at the castle entrance. (☎ 592 248. Open daily June-Sept. 9:30am-6pm; Oct.-Nov. and May 9:30am-5pm; Dec.-Apr. 9:30am-4pm.) Cozy rooms and timber ceilings await at Swan Cottage ❷, 18 Berry St. (☎ 596 840.Singles £19; doubles £38. Cash only.) Bistro Conwy ❸ serves inspired Welsh fare on wooden plates. (☎ 596 326. Dinner £13. Open Tu-Su 6:30-9pm.) Postal Code: LL32 8H7.

SCOTLAND

A little over half the size of England but with only one-tenth of its population, Scotland possesses open spaces and natural splendor its southern neighbor cannot hope to rival. The craggy, heathered Highlands and the luminescent mists of the Hebrides elicit any traveler's awe, while farmlands and fishing villages harbor a gentler beauty. Scotland at its best is a world apart from the rest of the UK, whose people revel in a culture all their own. The Scots doggedly defended their independence for hundreds of years before reluctantly joining with England in 1707. In 1999, they regained a separate parliament, which gave them more power over domestic tax laws and strengthened their national identity. While the kilts, bagpipes, and souvenir clan paraphernalia of the big cities may grow tiresome, a visit to the less touristed regions of Scotland will allow you to rub elbows with the inheritors of ancient traditions: a B&B owner speaking Gaelic to her grandchildren, a crofter cutting peat, or a fisherman setting out in his skiff at dawn.

✈ ☐ GETTING THERE AND AROUND

Bus travel from London is cheaper than train fares. British Airways (☎ 0845 773 3377; www.ba.com) sells a limited number of round-trip tickets starting at £70. British Midland (☎ 0870 607 0555; www.flybmi.com) offers Saver fares from London to Glasgow (from £70 round-trip). Cheap fares are available through easyJet (☎ 0870 600 0000; www.easyjet.com), which flies to Edinburgh and to Glasgow from London (prices vary). For info on ferries from Stranraer to Belfast, see p. 55.

In the Lowlands (south of Stirling and north of the Borders), train and bus connections are frequent. In the Highlands, trains routes are restricted and bypass the northwest almost entirely. Many stations are unstaffed or nonexistent—buy tickets onboard. The Freedom of Scotland Travelpass allows unlimited train travel, transportation on most Caledonian MacBrayne ferries, and discounts on some other ferry lines. Purchase the pass *before* traveling to Britain from any BritRail distributor (p. 152). Buses tend to be the best way to travel; Scottish Citylink (☎ 08705 505 050) provides most intercity service. HAGGiS (☎ 0131 557 9393; www.haggisadventures.com) and MacBackpackers (☎ 0131 558 9900; www.macbackpackers.com) cater to the young and adventurous with witty and informative pre-packaged or hop-on/hop-off tours that reach spots no public transportation can.

EDINBURGH   ☎ 0131

A city of elegant stone amid rolling hills and ancient volcanoes, Edinburgh (ED-in-bur-ra; pop. 500,000) is the jewel of Scotland. The Stuarts made it into a center for poetry and music. That tradition lives on during the festivals in August, which draw global performers and crowds. Meanwhile, the city endures as a cultural beacon, its medieval spires calling travelers to the cosmopolitan mecca beneath.

▐ TRANSPORTATION

BRITAIN

Flights: Edinburgh International Airport (EDI; ☎ 333 1000), 11km west of the city. Lothian's Airlink (☎ 555 6363) shuttles between the airport and Waverley Bridge (25min.; every 10-15min. all day, 1 per hr. after midnight; £3). An **Airsaver** ticket (£4.20) scores a trip on Airlink plus 1 day unlimited travel on Lothian buses.

Trains: Waverley Station (☎ 08457 484 950), between Princes St., Market St., and Waverley Bridge. Trains to: **Aberdeen** (2½hr.; M-Sa 1 per hr., Su 8 per day; £32); **Glasgow** (1hr., 4 per hr., £8-9); **Inverness** (3½hr., every 2hr., £32); **London King's Cross** (4¾hr., 1 per hr., £83-89); **Stirling** (50min., 2 per hr., £5.30).

Buses: Edinburgh Bus Station, on the eastern side of St. Andrew Sq. Open daily 6am-midnight. National Express (☎ 08705 808 080) to **London** (10hr., 4 per day, £29). Scottish Citylink (☎ 08705 505 050) to: **Aberdeen** (4hr., 1 per hr., £15); **Glasgow** (1hr., 2-3 per hr., £3.80); **Inverness** (4½hr., 8-10 per day, £15). A combination bus-ferry route via Stranraer goes to **Belfast** (2 per day, £20) and **Dublin** (1 per day, £28).

Public Transportation: Lothian (☎ 555 6363; www.lothianbuses.co.uk) buses provide most services. Exact change required (£0.50-£1). Buy a 1-day **Daysaver** ticket (M-F £2.70, Sa-Su £1.80) from any driver. **Night buses** cover selected routes after midnight (£2). **First Edinburgh** (☎ 0870 872 7271) also operates locally. **Traveline** (☎ 0800 232 323) has information on all area public transport.

✳ ▞ ORIENTATION AND PRACTICAL INFORMATION

Edinburgh is a glorious city for walking. **Princes Street** is the main thoroughfare in **New Town,** the northern section of the city. From there you can view the impressive stone facade of the towering **Old Town** to the south. The **Royal Mile** (Castle Hill, Lawnmarket, High St., and Canongate) is the major road in the Old Town and connects Edinburgh Castle in the west to the Palace of Holyroodhouse in the east. **North Bridge, Waverley Bridge,** and **The Mound** connect Old and New Town. Two miles northeast, **Leith** is the city's seaport on the Firth of Forth.

Tourist Office: Waverley Market, 3 Princes St. (☎ 473 3800; www.edinburgh.org), on the northern side of the Waverley Station complex. Books rooms for a £3 charge plus a 10% deposit; sells bus, museum, tour, and theater tickets. Open July-Aug. M-Sa 9am-8pm, Su 10am-8pm; May-June and Sept. until 7pm; Oct.-Apr. M-W 9am-5pm, Th-Sa 9am-6pm, Su 10am-5pm. In summer, look for blue-jacketed **Guiding Stars** who wander through the city center and answer questions in several languages.

Emergency: ☎ 999 or 112; free from any payphone.

Police: 14 St. Leonard's St. (☎ 662 5000).

Hospital: Royal Infirmary of Edinburgh, 41 Lauriston Pl. (☎ 536 1000).

Internet Access: Free at the **Central Library** (☎ 242 8000) on George IV Bridge. Open M-Th 10am-8pm, F 10am-5pm, Sa 9am-1pm. **easyInternet Cafe,** 58 Rose St. (☎ 220 3577), inside Caffe Nero. (£1 for 30min. Open M-Sa 7am-10pm, Su 9am-10pm.)

Post Office: (☎ 556 9546), in the St. James Centre beside the Bus Station. Open M-Sa 9am-5:30pm. **Postal Code:** EH1 3SR.

BRITAIN

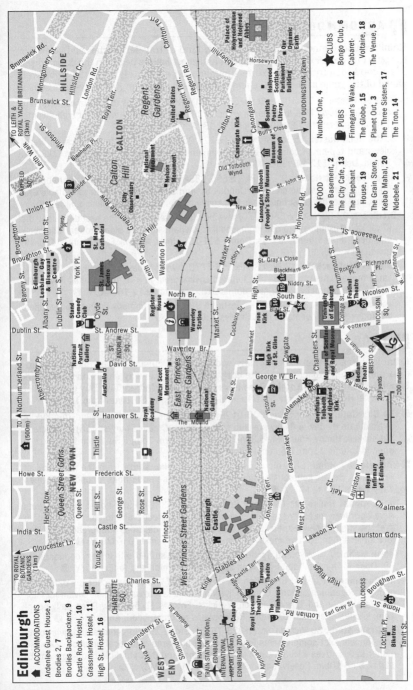

Edinburgh

▲ ACCOMMODATIONS
Ardenlee Guest House, **1**
Brodies 2, **7**
Brodies Backpackers, **9**
Castle Rock Hostel, **10**
Grassmarket Hostel, **11**
High St. Hostel, **16**

★ CLUBS
Bongo Club, **6**
Cabaret-Voltaire, **18**
The Venue, **5**

Number One, **4**

🍴 FOOD
The Basement, **2**
The City Cafe, **13**
The Elephant House, **19**
The Grain Store, **8**
Kebab Mahal, **20**
Ndebele, **21**

🍺 PUBS
Finnegan's Wake, **12**
The Globe, **15**
Planet Out, **3**
The Three Sisters, **17**
The Tron, **14**

ACCOMMODATIONS

Edinburgh accommodations cater to every kind of traveler. **Hostels** and **hotels** are the only city-center options, while **B&Bs** and **guest houses** begin on the outer edges. It's a good idea to book ahead in summer, and absolutely essential to be well ahead of the game at New Year's and during festival season (late July-early Sept.).

■ **High St. Hostel,** 8 Blackfriars St. (☎557 3984). Good facilities, party atmosphere, and convenient Royal Mile location have made this hostel a long-time Edinburgh favorite. Continental breakfast £1.90. Dorms £11-13. AmEx/MC/V. ❷

■ **Castle Rock Hostel,** 15 Johnston Terr. (☎225 9666), just steps from the castle. Regal views and top-notch common areas. Continental breakfast £1.90. Internet £0.80 for 30min. Dorms £12-14. AmEx/MC/V. ❷

Ardenlee Guest House, 9 Eyre Pl. (☎556 2838). Take bus #23 or 27 (northbound) from Hanover St. to the corner of Dundas St. and Eyre Pl. Near the Royal Botanic Gardens, this friendly guest house has big, comfy rooms. £30-40 per person. MC/V. ❹

Brodies 2, 93 High St. (☎556 6770; www.brodieshostels.co.uk). The best deal along the Royal Mile. Luxurious common room, spotless kitchen, stainless steel showers, and heavenly beds. Free Internet access. Dorms £11-16, during festival £18; doubles £34-45; quads from £55. MC/V. ❷

Brodies Backpackers, 12 High St. (☎556 6770; www.brodieshostels.co.uk). Under the same management as Brodies 2. Relaxed environment at a relatively small Royal Mile hostel. Free Internet access. Aug. dorms £18; Sept.-July £11-16. MC/V. ❷

Grassmarket Hotel, 94 Grassmarket (☎0870 990 6400), formerly Premier Lodge, offers tiny rooms at an unbeatable rate. Singles £30. MC/V. ❸

FOOD

Edinburgh features an exceptionally wide range of cuisines. Many **pubs** offer student and hosteler discounts in the early evening. Takeaway shops on **South Clerk Street, Leith Street,** and **Lothian Road** have Chinese and Indian fare. Buy groceries at **Sainsbury's,** 9-10 St. Andrew Sq. (Open M-Sa 7am-10pm, Su 10am-8pm.)

■ **The City Cafe,** 19 Blair St. (☎220 0125), right off the Royal Mile behind Tron Kirk. A relaxed cafe by day, a flashy pre-club spot by night. Creative burgers (£6) and incredible shakes. Happy Hour daily 5-8pm. Open M-Th 11am-1am, F-Su 11am-1am; kitchen open M-Th until 11pm, F-Su until 10pm. MC/V. ❷

■ **Ndebele,** 57 Home St., Tolcross (☎221 1141), 1km south from the west end of Princes St. Serves generous portions of African cuisine and drinks for under £5. Open daily 10am-10pm. MC/V. ❶

The Elephant House, 21 George IV Bridge (☎220 5355). Harry Potter and Hogwarts were born here as hasty scribblings on napkins. A perfect place to chill, chat, or pore over the stack of newspapers. Exotic teas and coffees, delicious shortbread, and filling fare for less than £5. Live music Th 7pm. Open daily 8am-11pm. MC/V. ❶

Kebab Mahal, 7 Nicolson Sq. (☎667 5214). You'll be stuffed with Indian food for under £5. Open M-Th noon-1am, F-Sa noon-2am, Su noon-midnight. AmEx/MC/V. ❶

The Basement, 10a-12a Broughton St. (☎557 0097). The menu changes daily, with plenty of vegetarian options. Draws a lively mix of locals to its candlelit cavern for Mexican fare Sa-Su and Thai cuisine on W nights. Entrees £5.50-7.50. Open daily noon-1am; kitchen open until 10:30pm. Reservations recommended. AmEx/MC/V. ❷

The Grain Store, 30 Victoria St. (☎225 7635). Stone-vaulted ceilings and quiet comfort. The wine list complements French cuisine prepared with local produce. 2-course dinner £20. Entrees £18-30. Open M-Th noon-2pm and 6-10pm, F-Sa noon-3pm and 6-11pm, Su 6-10pm. Reservations recommended. AmEx/MC/V. ❹

Number One, 1 Princes St. (☎557 6727), underneath the Balmoral Hotel. One of Edinburgh's most exclusive restaurants. Modern Scottish cuisine, local seafood, and seasonal game. 6-course dinner £41. Open M-Th noon-2pm and 7-10pm, F noon-2pm and 7-10:30pm, Sa 7-10:30pm, Su 7-10pm. Reserve 1 week in advance. AmEx/MC/V. ❺

🄶 SIGHTS

A boggling array of Edinburgh tour companies tout themselves as "the original" or "the scariest," but the most worthwhile is the ▧**Edinburgh Literary Pub Tour.** Led by professional actors, this alcohol-sodden 2hr. crash course in Scottish literature meets outside the Beehive Inn in the Grassmarket. (☎226 6665; www.edinburghliterarypubtour.co.uk. June-Sept. daily 7:30pm; Apr.-May and Oct. Th-Su 7:30pm; Nov.-Mar. F 7:30pm. £8, students £6. £1 discount for online booking.)

THE OLD TOWN AND THE ROYAL MILE

Edinburgh's medieval center, the fascinating **Royal Mile** defines **Old Town** and passes many worthwhile sights. Once lined with narrow shopfronts and slums towering to a dozen stories, this famous strip is now a playground for hostelers and locals alike, buzzing with bars, attractions, and the inevitable souvenir shops.

▧ **EDINBURGH CASTLE.** Perched atop an extinct volcano and dominating the city center, Edinburgh castle is a testament to the city's past strategic importance. The castle is the result of centuries of renovation and rebuilding; the most recent additions date to the 1920s. The **One O'Clock Gun** fires M-Sa at 1pm. (☎225 9846. Open daily Apr.-Oct. 9:30am-6pm; Nov.-Mar. 9:30am-5pm. Last admission 45min. before close. Guided tour included. £9.50. Audio tours £3.)

CASTLE HILL AND LAWNMARKET AREA. Staffed with knowledgeable guides, the oldest surviving house on the Royal Mile (c. 1617) has been carefully preserved and holds a collection of 17th-century Dutch art. (477b Lawnmarket. ☎226 5856. Open Apr.-Oct. M-Sa 10am-5pm, Su 2-5pm. £5, students £3.75.) Nearby, the 17th-century **Lady Stair's House** contains the **Writer's Museum,** with memorabilia belonging to three of Scotland's greatest literary figures: Robert Burns, Sir Walter Scott, and Robert Louis Stevenson. (Lawnmarket. ☎529 4901. Open M-Sa 10am-5pm; during Festival also Su 2-5pm. Free.) The **Outlook Tower** on Castle Hill has a 150-year-old **camera obscura** that captures a moving image of the streets below. (Open daily Apr.-June and Sept.-Oct. 9:30am-6pm; July-Aug. 9:30am-7:30pm; Nov.-Mar. 10am-5pm. £6, students £4.70.)

HIGH STREET AND CANONGATE AREA. At the beautiful ▧**High Kirk of St. Giles** (St. Giles Cathedral), Scotland's principal church, John Knox delivered the fiery Presbyterian sermons that drove Mary, Queen of Scots, into exile. Most of the present structure was built in the 15th century, but parts date as far back as 1126. The kirk hosts free concerts throughout the year. (Where Lawnmarket becomes High St. ☎225 4363. Open Easter to mid-Sept. M-F 9am-7pm, Sa 9am-5pm, Su 1-5pm; mid-Sept. to Easter M-Sa 9am-5pm, Su 1-5pm. Suggested donation £1.) The 17th-century **Canongate Kirk,** on the hill at the end of the Mile, is the resting place of economist Adam Smith; royals used to worship here when in residence. (Same hours as High Kirk. Free.)

THE PALACE OF HOLYROODHOUSE. This Stuart palace, at the base of the Royal Mile beside Holyrood Park, remains Queen Elizabeth II's official Scottish residence; as a result, only parts of the ornate interior are open to the public. On the palace grounds lie the 12th-century ruins of **Holyrood Abbey,** built by David I in 1128 and ransacked during the Reformation. Only a single doorway remains from the original construction; most of the ruins date from the 13th century. Located in a recently renovated 17th-century schoolhouse near the palace entrance, the **Queen's Gallery** displays rotating exhibits from the royal art collection. (☎556 5100.

Open Apr.-Oct. daily 9:30am-6pm; Nov.-Mar. M-Sa 9:30am-4:30pm. Last admission 45min. before close. Closed to visitors while royals are in residence (often late May-early July). £8, students £6.50. Queen's Gallery £5/£4. Joint ticket £11/£9. Audio tours free.)

HOLYROOD SCOTTISH PARLIAMENT BUILDING. The new Scottish Parliament Building, designed by the late Catalan architect Enric Miralles, was scheduled to open—after years of controversy and massive budget overruns—in October 2004. *(☎ 348 5000; www.scottish.parliament.uk. Open M and F-Su 10am-4pm, Tu-Th 9am-7pm. Guided tours will be available; check website for information.)*

OTHER SIGHTS IN THE OLD TOWN. The ▓**Museum of Scotland** and the connected **Royal Museum,** on Chambers St., just south of the George IV Bridge, are not to be missed. The former houses a definitive collection of Scottish artifacts in a stunning contemporary building; highlights include the working Corliss Steam Engine and the **Maiden,** Edinburgh's pre-French Revolution guillotine. The Royal Museum has a varied mix of European art and ancient Roman and Egyptian artifacts. *(Both open M and W-Sa 10am-5pm, Tu 10am-8pm, Su noon-5pm. Free.)* Across the street, a statue of Greyfriar's loyal pooch, Bobby, marks the entrance to 17th-century **Greyfriar's Kirk,** surrounded by a beautiful, supposedly haunted churchyard. *(Off Candlemaker Row. Open Apr.-Oct. M-F 10:30am-4:30pm, Sa until 2:30pm; Nov.-Mar. Th 1:30-3:30pm. Free.)*

THE NEW TOWN

Edinburgh's New Town is a masterpiece of Georgian design. James Craig, a 23-year-old architect, won the city-planning contest in 1767; his rectangular grid of three parallel streets (**Queen, George,** and **Princes**) linking two large squares (**Charlotte** and **St. Andrew**) reflects the Scottish Enlightenment's belief in order.

THE GEORGIAN HOUSE AND THE WALTER SCOTT MONUMENT. The elegantly restored Georgian House gives a fair picture of how Edinburgh's elite lived 200 years ago. *(7 Charlotte Sq. ☎ 226 3318. Open daily Apr.-Oct. 10am-5pm; Mar. and Nov.-Dec. 11am-3pm. Last admission 30min. before close. £5, students £3.75.)* The ▓**Walter Scott Monument** is a Gothic "steeple without a church"; climb the 287-step staircase for views stretching out to Princes St., the castle, and the surrounding city. *(Princes St. between The Mound and Waverley Bridge. ☎ 529 4068. Open Mar.-Oct. M-Sa 9am-6pm, Su 10am-6pm; Nov.-Feb. until 3pm. £2.50.)*

▓**ROYAL YACHT BRITANNIA.** Northeast of the city center floats one of Edinburgh's top tourist attractions, the Royal Yacht *Britannia.* Used by the Queen and her family from 1953 to 1997, *Britannia* sailed around the world on state visits and royal holidays before going into permanent retirement here. Visitors can follow an audio tour of the entire flagship, which remains exactly as it was when decommissioned. *(Entrance on the Ocean Terminal's 3rd fl. Take bus #22 from Princes St. or #35 from the Royal Mile to Ocean Terminal; £1. ☎ 555 5566. Open daily Apr.-Sept. 9:30am-4:30pm; Oct.-Mar. 10am-3:30pm. £8.50, students £4.50.)*

THE NATIONAL GALLERIES

Edinburgh's National Galleries of Scotland form an elite group, with excellent collections housed in stately buildings and connected by a free shuttle every hour. The flagship is the ▓**National Gallery of Scotland,** on The Mound, which houses a superb collection of works by Renaissance, Romantic, and Impressionist masters, including Degas, Gauguin, Monet, Raphael, and Titian. Be sure not to miss the octagonal room which displays Poussin's entire *Seven Sacraments.* The basement houses a fine spread of Scottish art. The **Scottish National Portrait Gallery,** 1 Queen St., north of St. Andrew Sq., features the faces of famous Scots. Among its notable members are wordsmith Robert Louis Stevenson, renegade Bonny Prince Charlie, and royal troublemaker Mary, Queen of Scots. The gallery also hosts excellent visiting exhibits of contemporary artists. Take the free bus #13 from George St., or walk to the **Scottish National Gallery of Modern Art,** 75 Belford Rd., west of town, to see works by Braque, Matisse, and Picasso. The new **Dean Gallery,** 73 Belford Rd., specializes in Dadaist and Surrealist art. *(All open M-W and F-Su 10am-5pm, Th 10am-7pm; extended hours during festival season. Free.)*

GARDENS AND PARKS

Just off the eastern end of the Royal Mile, the oasis of **Holyrood Park** is a natural wilderness replete with hills, moorland, and lochs. **Arthur's Seat,** once a holy place for Picts, is the park's highest point; the walk to the summit takes about 45min. Traces of forts and Bronze-Age terraces dot the surrounding hillside. Located directly in the city center and affording fantastic views of the Old Town and the castle, the **Princes Street Gardens** are on the site of now-drained Nor'Loch, where Edinburghers used to drown their accused witches. The loch has been replaced with impeccably manicured lawns and stone fountains. On fine summer days all of Edinburgh eats lunch here. The lovely **Royal Botanic Gardens** are north of the city center. Guided tours wander across the lush grounds and greenhouses. *(Take bus #23 or 27 from Hanover St. ☎552 7171. Open daily Apr.-Sept. 10am-7pm; Mar. and Oct. 10am-6pm; Nov.-Feb. 10am-4pm. Free.)*

🎵 🎭 ENTERTAINMENT AND NIGHTLIFE

The summer sees an especially joyful string of events—music in the gardens, plays and films, and *ceilidhs* (traditional Scottish dances) even before the Festival. In winter, shorter days and the crush of students promote a flourishing nightlife. For the most up-to-date info on what's going on, check out *The List* (£2.20), a comprehensive bi-weekly guide to events, available from any local newsstand.

THEATER, FILM, AND MUSIC

The **Festival Theatre,** 13-29 Nicholson St., stages ballet and opera, while the affiliated **King's Theatre,** 2 Leven St., hosts comedy, drama, musicals, and opera. (☎529 6000. Box office open M-Sa 10am-6pm. Tickets £8-52.) **The Stand Comedy Club,** 5 York Pl., has nightly acts. (☎558 7272. Tickets £1-8.) The **Filmhouse,** 88 Lothian Rd., offers quality European, arthouse, and Hollywood cinema. (☎228 2688. Tickets £3.50-5.50.) For a run-down of live music, look to *The List.* Free live jazz can be found at **Henry's Jazz Bar,** 8 Morrison St. (Open W-Su 8pm-3am. £5.) **Whistle Binkie's,** 4-6 South Bridge, off High St., is a subterranean pub with two live music shows every night. (Open daily until 3am.)

PUBS

Students and backpackers gather in force each night in the **Old Town.** Pubs on the **Royal Mile** attract a mixed crowd of old and young, tourist and local. Casual pubgoers groove to live music on **Grassmarket, Candlemaker Row,** and **Victoria Street.** Historical pubs in the New Town cluster on **Rose Street,** parallel to Princes St.

🍺 **The Tron,** 9 Hunter Sq., behind the Tron Kirk. Wildly popular for its incredible deals. Frequent live music on 3 hopping floors. Students and hostelers get £1 drinks on W nights. A mix of alcoves and pool tables can be found downstairs. Open daily 11:30am-1am.

The Globe, 13 Niddry St. This backpacker's abode is recommended up and down the Royal Mile. Airs international sports, hosts DJs, and holds quiz nights and karaoke. Open M-F 4pm-1am, Sa noon-1am, Su 12:30pm-1am; during festivals until 3am.

The Three Sisters, 139 Cowgate. Loads of space for dancing, drinking, and chilling. Attracts a young crowd to its 3 bars (Irish, Gothic, and Style). Beer garden and barbecue sees close to 1000 pass through on Sa nights. Open daily 9am-1am.

FRINGE FUN

Once confined to the margins while more traditional festivities took center stage, the **Edinburgh Fringe Festival** has become an international magnet in its own right. Impatient visitors can whet their artistic appetites before the International Festival begins: The Fringe starts roughly two weeks earlier and encompasses everything from Shakespeare to coconut-juggling dwarves to symphony-trained violinists. Theaters spring up everywhere as churches, stores, bars, and community centers convert their floors to stages. Even the Royal Mile turns into an action-packed artistic platform where actors and exhibitionists recite monologues, bang cymbals, and thrust fliers in pedestrians' faces to promote their shows.

Since any performer who can afford the small registration fee can participate, the number of events at the Fringe is dizzying. It can be a challenge to navigate your way through the good, the bad, and the ugly; many newspapers (especially *The Scotsman*) publish brutally honest daily reviews that provide rapid, critical guidance.

Aug. 3-25 in 2005. Book tickets online, by phone, or in person at the Fringe Festival Office, 180 High St., Edinburgh EH1 1QS. (☎ 226 0000; www.edfringe.com. Open daily June-Aug. Tickets £20 and under.)

Finnegan's Wake, 9b Victoria St. Drink Ireland-style with several stouts on tap, road signs from Cork, and live Irish music every weekend. Open daily 1pm-1am.

CLUBS

Club venues are constantly closing down and reopening under new management; consult *The List* for updated info. Clubs cluster around the historically disreputable **Cowgate,** just downhill from and parallel to the Royal Mile. Most close at 3am. The Broughton St. area of the New Town (better known as the **Broughton Triangle**) is the center of Edinburgh's gay community.

■ **Cabaret-Voltaire,** 36-38 Blair St. Hosting a wide range of live music, dance, and art, this innovative club throws a great party. Cover free-£15, depending on event.

Bongo Club, 14 New St. A fun and very safe club. Noted for its hip-hop, including the long-running and immensely popular Messenger and Headspin nights, which run on alternate Saturdays from each other. Cover free-£10.

The Venue, 17-23 Calton Rd. 3 dance floors run the musical gamut throughout the month. The Venue also hosts top live gigs. Cover £2-8.

Planet Out, 6 Baxter's Pl. Prepare for wildness at this gay-friendly club, especially on M when all drinks are £1.

❄ FESTIVALS

In August, Edinburgh is *the* place to be in Europe. What's commonly referred to as "the Festival" actually encompasses a number of independently organized events. For more info, check out www.edinburghfestivals.co.uk. The **Edinburgh International Festival** (Aug. 14-Sept. 3 in 2005), the largest of them all, features a kaleidoscopic program of music, drama, dance, and art. Tickets (£7-57, 50% discount for students) are sold beginning in April, but you can usually get them at the door. Look for half-price tickets from 9am on performance days at **The HUB** (☎ 473 2000), Edinburgh's Festival Centre, Castlehill. Around the established festival has grown a less formal ■**Fringe Festival** (Aug. 7-29 in 2005; see **Fringe Fun,** p. 222.) The **Edinburgh Jazz and Blues Festival** is in late July (☎ 467 5200; tickets on sale in June). The **Military Tattoo** (Aug. 5-27 in 2005) is a spectacle of military bands, bagpipes, and drums. For tickets (£9-31), contact the Tattoo Ticket Sale Office, 33-34 Market St. (☎ 225 1188; www.edintattoo.co.uk). The excellent **Edinburgh International Film Festival** is also in August at The Filmhouse (☎ 229 2550; tickets on sale starting late July). ■**Hogmanay,** the traditional New Year's Eve festival, is a serious street party with a week of associated events. (www.edinburghshogmanay.org.)

🧭 DAYTRIP FROM EDINBURGH: ST. ANDREWS

Golf overruns the small city of St. Andrews, where the rules of the sport were formally established. Today, a mix of golfers, college students, beach bums, castlehunters, ruin-seekers, and royalty-spotters all converge on its three medieval streets. The **Old Course** frequently hosts the British Open. (☎01334 466 666 for reservations or enter a same-day lottery for starting times. Apr.-Oct. £90 per round; Nov.-Mar. £56.) The budget option, still lovely, is the nine-hole **Balgove Course** (£7-10). **St. Andrews Cathedral** was once the greatest in Scotland; its stones are now mostly in the houses along South St. The nearby **St. Andrews Castle** hides medieval siege tunnels and bottle-shaped dungeons. (Cathedral and castle open daily Apr.-Sept. 9:30am-6:30pm; Oct.-Mar. 9:30am-4:30pm. Joint ticket £4, students £3.)

 Trains (☎08457 484 590) stop 8km away in Leuchars (1hr., 1 per hr., £8.10), where buses #94 and 96 depart for St. Andrews (£1.60). **Buses** (☎01383 621 249) also pull in from Edinburgh (#X59 or X60; 2hr., 1-2 per hr., £5.70) and Glasgow (#X24; 2½hr., M-Sa 1 per hr., £5.50). From the bus station, turn right on City Rd. and take the first left for the **tourist office**, 70 Market St. (☎01334 472 021. Open July-Aug. M-Sa 9:30am-5pm, Su 10:30am-5pm; low season reduced hours.)

GLASGOW ☎0141

Glasgow (pop. 700,000), Scotland's largest urban center, has reinvented itself many times and retains the mark of each transformation. Stately architecture recalls Queen Victoria's reign, while cranes littering the river Clyde bear witness to a sooty past as a major industrial hub. Today, world-class art museums and collections, give Glasgow a thriving creative pulse. The city comes alive at night, fueled by football-happy locals and the largest student population in Scotland.

📳 **TRANSPORTATION AND PRACTICAL INFORMATION. Flights** land at **Glasgow Airport** (GLA; ☎887 1111), 16km west in Abbotsinch. Citylink buses connect to Buchanan Station (25min., 6 per hr., £3.40). **Glasgow Prestwick International Airport** (☎02192 511 000), 51½km away, has its own train station, which offers half-price fares to Glasgow with plane ticket (45min., 2-3 per hr., £5.20). **Trains** pull into Central Station, on Gordon St. (U: St. Enoch), from London King's Cross (5-6hr., 1 per hr., £100). From Queen St. Station, on George Sq. (U: Buchanan St.), trains go to: Aberdeen (2½hr., 11 per day, £33); Edinburgh (50min., 2 per hr., £9); and Inverness (3¼hr., 5 per day, £33). Scottish Citylink (☎08705 505 050) **buses** leave Buchanan Station, on Hanover St., for: Aberdeen (4hr., 1 per hr., £17); Edinburgh (1hr., 2 per hr., £9); Inverness (3½hr., 1 per hr., £33). National Express (☎08705 808 080) goes to London (8hr.; 1 per hr.; £29). Local transportation includes the circular **Underground (U)** subway line (M-Sa 6:30am-11pm, Su 11am-5:30pm; £1). A **Discovery Ticket** (£1.70) allows one day of unlimited travel. The **tourist office,** 11 George Sq., south of Queen St. Station and northeast of Central Station, books rooms for a £2 fee plus 10% deposit. (U: Buchanan St. ☎204 4400; www. seeglasgow.com. Open July-Aug. M-Sa 9am-8pm, Su 10am-6pm; Sept.-June M-Sa 9am-7pm, Su 10am-6pm.) Access the **Internet** at **easyInternet Cafe**, 57-61 St. Vincent St. (☎222 2365. £1 for 40min.-3hr. Open daily 7am-10:45pm.) **Postal Code:** G2 5QX.

📳 **ACCOMMODATIONS AND FOOD.** Reserve B&Bs and hostels in advance, especially in August. B&Bs cluster on **Argyle Street,** near the university, or on **Westercraigs Road,** east of the Necropolis. The newly renovated ensuite rooms of the ▨SYHA Glasgow ❷, 7-8 Park Terr., are the best in town. (U: St. George's Cross. ☎332 3004. Laundry, Internet access, and kitchen. June-Sept. dorms £14, under 18

BRITAIN

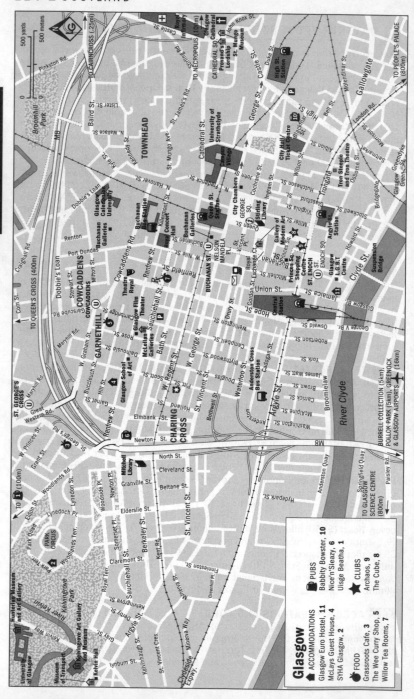

Glasgow

▲ ACCOMMODATIONS
Glasgow Euro Hostel, **11**
McLays Guest House, **4**
SYHA Glasgow, **2**

🍴 FOOD
Grassroots Cafe, **3**
The Wee Curry Shop, **5**
Willow Tea Rooms, **7**

🍺 PUBS
Babbity Bowster, **10**
Nice'n'Sleazy, **6**
Uisge Beatha, **1**

★ CLUBS
Archaos, **9**
The Cube, **8**

£12; Oct.-May £13/£11. MC/V.) The **Glasgow Euro Hostel ❶**, on the corner of Clyde St. and Jamaica St., is near the city center, and includes a bar. (☎222 2828; www.euro-hostels.com. Breakfast included. Internet access. Dorms from £10. MC/V.) **McLays Guest House ❸**, 268 Renfrew St., has a TV and phone in each room. (☎332 4796. Singles from £24, with bath £32; doubles £40/£48. MC/V.)

The area bordered by Otago St. in the west, St. George's Rd. in the east, and along Great Western Rd., Woodlands Rd., and Eldon St. brims with cheap kebab-and-curry joints. **Byres Road** and **Ashton Lane** (a tiny cobblestoned alley parallel to Byres Rd.) thrive with cheap, trendy cafes. The 🖼**Willow Tea Rooms ❷**, 217 Sauchie-hall St., upstairs from Henderson the Jewellers, are a Glasgow landmark. (U: Buchanan St. ☎332 0521. Tea £1.70 per pot. 3-course high tea £9.50. Open M-Sa 9am-4:30pm, Su noon-4:15pm. MC/V.) Glasgow's best vegetarian food is at the 🖼**Grassroots Cafe ❷**, 97 St. George's Rd. (U: St. George's Cross. ☎333 0534. Open daily 10am-10pm. AmEx/MC/V.) **The Wee Curry Shop ❶**, 7 Buccleuch St., off Sauchiehall St., is a good deal in this town full of *pakora* and *poori*. (☎353 0777. U: Cowcaddens. Lunch £4.80. Open M-Sa noon-2:30pm and 5:30-10:30pm. Cash only.)

🖼 **SIGHTS.** Glasgow is a budget sightseer's paradise, with splendid period architecture, grand museums, and chic galleries, many of which are free. Your first stop should be the Gothic 🖼**Glasgow Cathedral**, the only full-scale cathedral spared by the fury of the 16th-century Scottish Reformation. (Open Apr.-Sept. M-Sa 9:30am-6pm, Su 1-5pm; Oct.-Mar. until 4pm. Ask for free personal tours.) On the same street is the **St. Mungo Museum of Religious Life and Art**, 2 Castle St., which surveys every religion from Islam to Yoruba, and displays Dali's *Christ of St. John's Cross*. (Open M-Sa 10am-5pm, Su 11am-5pm. Free.) Built in 1471, **Provand's Lord-ship**, 3-7 Castle St., is the oldest house in Glasgow and has the creaky floors to prove it. (Open M-Th and Sa 10am-5pm, F and Su 11am-5pm. Free.) Behind the cathedral is the **necropolis**, a terrifying hilltop cemetery. (Open 24hr. Free.)

In the West End, **Kelvingrove Park** lies on the banks of the River Kelvin. In the south-western corner of the park, at Argyle and Sauchiehall St., the magnificent **Kelvingrove Art Gallery and Museum** shelters works by Monet, Rembrandt, and van Gogh. Due to renovation, the museum's collection will be on display until 2006 at the **McLellan Galleries**, 270 Sauchiehall St. (Open M-Th and Sa 10am-5pm, F and Su 11am-5pm. Free.) Farther west rise the Gothic edifices of the **University of Glasgow**. The main building is on University Ave., which runs into Byres Rd. While walking through campus, stop by the **Hunterian Museum**, home to the death mask of Bonnie Prince Charlie, or see 19th-century Scottish art at the **Hunterian Art Gallery**, across the street. (U: Hillhead. Both open M-Sa 9:30am-5pm. Free.) The **Glasgow School of Art**, 167 Renfrew St., reflects a uniquely Glaswegian Modernist style. (Tours July-Aug. M-F 11am and 2pm; Sa-Su 10:30, 11:30am, and 1pm. Sept.-June M-F 11am and 2pm, Sa 10:30am. £5, students £3.)

Take bus #45, 47, 48, or 57 from Jamaica St. (15min., £1.20) to reach the famous 🖼**Burrell Collection**, 5km south of the city in the Pollok Country park. Once the private stash of ship magnate William Burrell, the collection includes paintings by Cezánne and Degas, needlework from European tapestries and Persian textiles, and fine china. (☎287 2550. Open M-Th and Sa 10am-5pm, F and Su 11am-5pm. Tours daily 11am and 2pm. Free.) Also in the park is the less spectacular **Pollok House**, a Victorian mansion with a small collection of paintings, some by El Greco and Goya. (Open daily 10am-5pm. Apr.-Oct. £5, students £3.75; Nov.-Mar. free.)

🎶🖼 **ENTERTAINMENT AND NIGHTLIFE.** Glaswegians have a reputation for partying hard. *The List* (£2.20 at newsstands) has detailed nightlife and entertainment listings. The infamous **Byres Road** pub crawl slithers past the University area, starting at Tennant's Bar and proceeding toward the River Clyde. With its 100 varieties, 🖼**Uisge Beatha**, 232 Woodlands Rd., reminds you that in Scotland, it's spelled "whisky." (Whisky £1.30-1.60. Open M-Sa noon-midnight, Su 12:30pm-midnight.)

Go to ■**Babbity Bowster,** 16-18 Blackfriar St., for the authentic Glasgow experience. (Open M-Sa 10am-midnight, Su 11am-midnight.) **Nice'n'Sleazy,** 421 Sauchiehall St., features local bands in its underground lair. (Open daily 11:30am-midnight.) At **Archaos,** 25 Queen St., students get 2-for-1 whiskies. (Cover £3-7. Open Tu and Th-Su 11pm-3am.) **The Cube,** 34 Queen St., has Glasgow's longest lines; arrive early or know someone important. (Cover £8, Th students £6. Open daily 10:30pm-3am.)

STIRLING ☎01786

The third point of a strategic triangle completed by Glasgow and Edinburgh, Stirling has historically presided over north-south travel in the region; it was once said that "he who controlled Stirling controlled Scotland." At the 1297 Battle of Stirling Bridge, William Wallace (of Braveheart fame) overpowered the English army, enabling Robert the Bruce to finally overthrow the English at **Bannockburn,** 3¼km south of town. Take bus #51 or 52 from Murray Pl. in Stirling. (Visitor center open daily Apr.-Oct. 10am-5:30pm; low season reduced hours. £3.50. Battlefield open year-round.) ■**Stirling Castle,** situated on a defunct volcano, recalls a history of royal residence and military might. (Open daily Apr.-Oct. 9:30am-6pm; Nov.-Mar. 9:30am-5pm. £8, concessions £6.) **Argyll's Lodging,** a 17th-century mansion below the castle, has been impressively restored. (Open daily Apr.-Sept. 9:30am-6pm; Oct.-Mar. 9:30am-5pm. £3.30, with castle admission free.)

Trains (☎08457 484 950) run from Goosecroft Rd. to: Aberdeen (2hr.; M-Sa 1 per hr., Su 6 per day; £31); Edinburgh (50min., 2 per hr., £5.30); Glasgow (40min., 2-3 per hr., £5.40); Inverness (3hr., 3-4 per day, £31); and London King's Cross (5½hr., 1 per hr., £44-84). **Buses** also run from Goosecroft Rd. to: Edinburgh (1¼hr., 1 per hr., £4); Fort William (2¾hr., 1 per day, £15); Glasgow (40min., 2-3 per hr., £4); and Inverness (3¾hr., 1 per hr., £13). The **tourist office** is at 41 Dumbarton Rd. (☎475 019. Open July-Aug. M-Sa 9am-7pm, Su 9:30am-6pm; Apr.-May and Sept.-Oct. daily 9am-5pm; Oct.-Mar. M-F 10am-5pm, Sa 10am-4pm.) The excellent **SYHA Stirling ❷,** St. John St., is halfway up the hill to the castle and occupies the shell of the first Separatist Church in Stirling. (☎473 442. Laundry, kitchen, and Internet access available. Curfew 2am. Dorms £12-14, under 18 £9-12. MC/V.) Buy groceries at **Iceland,** 5 Pitt Terr. (Open M-F 8:30am-8pm, Sa 8:30am-6pm, Su 10am-5pm.) Hearty, homemade fare awaits at **The Cottage Cafe ❶,** 52 Spittal St. (☎446 124. Open M-Tu and Th-Su 11am-3pm, Th-Sa also 5:30-9pm. Cash only.) **Postal Code:** FK8 2BP.

THE TROSSACHS ☎01877

The most accessible tract of Scotland's wilderness, the mountains and misty lochs of the Trossachs (from the Gaelic for "bristly country") are as popular now as they were under the reign of Queen Victoria. The Trossachs and Loch Lomond form Scotland's first national park, justifiably billed as the "Highlands in miniature." You'll find long cycle routes winding through dense forest, peaceful loch-side walks, and some of Scotland's more manageable peaks.

▐ **TRANSPORTATION.** Access to the Trossachs is easiest from Stirling. First (☎01324 613 777) **buses** connect to the region's two main towns, running from Stirling to Aberfoyle (#11; 45min., 4 per day, £2.50) and Callander (#59; 45min., 12 per day, £3). Scottish Citylink also runs a bus from Edinburgh to Callander (1¾hr., 1 per day, £8) via Stirling. In summer, the useful Trossachs Trundler (☎01786 442 707) travels between Callander, Aberfoyle, and the Trossachs Pier at Loch Katrine; one daily trip begins and ends in Stirling (June-Sept. M-Tu and Th-Su 4 per day; Day Rover £5, students £4; including travel from Stirling £7.50/£6).

CALLANDER. Beside the quiet River Teith, the town of Callander makes a good base for exploring the Trossachs. Dominating the horizon, **Ben Ledi** (878m) provides a strenuous but not overly challenging trek. A trail up the mountain (9½km) begins just north of town along A84. A number of walks depart from Callander itself. **The Crags** (10½km) heads up to the ridge above town, while the walk to **Bracklinn Falls** (8km) crosses a picturesque glen. In Callander, **cyclists** can join a lovely stretch of **The Lowland Highland Trail**, which runs north to Strathyre along an old railway line. Callander's **Rob Roy and Trossachs Visitor Centre**, Main St., is a combined **tourist office** and exhibit on the 17th-century hero. (☎330 342. Open daily June-Aug. 9am-6pm; low season reduced hours. Exhibit £3.25, students £2.50.) Rent bikes at **Cycle Hire Callander**, beside the tourist office. (☎331 052. £10 per day. Open daily 9am-6pm. MC/V.) The hidden gem of the region's lodgings is ▓**Trossachs Backpackers ❷**, Invertrossachs Rd., 1km south of Callander. This hostel's forest-clearing location makes it an ideal base. The owners will pick you up from Callander. (☎331 100. Breakfast included. Bikes £13 per day. Dorms £14. MC/V.)

ABERFOYLE. Aberfoyle, another springboard into the wilderness, is at the heart of the **Queen Elizabeth Forest Park**. The park covers territory from the shore of Loch Lomond to the slopes of the Strathyre Mountains. For more information on **trails,** visit the **Trossachs Discovery Centre**, right in town. (☎382 352. Open July-Aug. daily 9:30am-6pm; Apr.-June and Sept.-Oct. daily 10am-5pm; Nov.-Mar. Sa-Su 10am-5pm.) Ann and John Epps welcome visitors to **Crannaig House ❹**, Trossachs Rd., which boasts spacious rooms. (☎382 276. Singles from £30; doubles £50-60. MC/V.)

LOCH KATRINE. The A821 winds through the heart of the Trossachs between Aberfoyle and Callander. Named the **Trossachs Trail**, this scenic drive passes near majestic Loch Katrine, the Trossachs' original lure and the setting of Sir Walter Scott's "The Lady of the Lake." The popular **Steamship Sir Walter Scott** cruises from Trossachs Pier and tours the loch, stopping at Stronachlachar, on the northwestern bank. (☎376 316. Apr.-Oct. daily 11am, 1:45, and 3:15pm; W no 11am tour. £6-7.) At the pier, rent bikes from **Katrinewheelz**. (☎376 284. £12 per day.) For a good daytrip, take the ferry to Stronachlachar and then walk or ride back along the 22½km wooded shore road to the pier. Above the loch hulks **Ben A'an** (460m), a reasonable 3¼km ascent that begins from a carpark 1½km along A821.

LOCH LOMOND   ☎01389

Immortalized by the famous ballad, the pristine wilderness surrounding Loch Lomond continues to awe visitors. Britain's largest lake is dotted by some 38 islands. Given their proximity to Glasgow, parts of these bonnie, bonnie banks can get crowded, especially during summer when daytrippers pour into **Balloch,** the area's largest town. Hikers adore the **West Highland Way,** which snakes along the entire eastern side of the Loch and stretches north 150km from Milngavie to Fort William. At the southern tip of the lake is Balloch, the most important tourist center. Attractions and services at the new **Loch Lomond Shores** in Balloch include a giant-screen film about the loch, a **National Park Gateway Centre,** a tourist office, and bike and canoe rentals. (☎722 406. Shores open daily June-Sept. 10am-6pm; Oct.-May 10am-5pm. £5.) Departing from Loch Lomond Shores and the Balloch tourist office on the River Leven, hour-long **Sweeney's Cruises** provide excellent introductions to the area. (☎752 376. 1 per hr. 10:30am-5:30pm. £9.)

   Trains leave Balloch Rd. for Glasgow's Queen St. (45min., 2 per hr., £3.50). Scottish Citylink (☎08705 505 050) **buses** serve Glasgow (45min., 3-5 per day, £3.60). First (☎0141 423 6600) buses go to Stirling (1½hr., 4 per day, £3.80). **Tourist offices** are at Loch Lomond Shores (above) and in the Old Station building. (☎753 533. Open daily Apr.-Sept. 9:30am-6pm.) The ▓**SYHA Loch Lomond ❷**, 3¼km north of town, is in a stunning 19th-century mansion. From the train station, follow the main road for 1km, turn right at the roundabout, continue 2½km, and follow signs to the hostel. (☎850 226. Internet access. Completely self-catering; bring food with you. Open Mar.-Oct. Dorms £12-14, under 18 £10-12. MC/V.)

BRITAIN

INVERNESS AND LOCH NESS   ☎ 01463

Inverness is rightfully termed the "hub of the Highlands." The city is both the main gateway to the area from the rest of the UK and the easiest link between most points within the region. ◪**Loch Ness,** 8km south of Inverness, guards its secrets well. In 565, St. Columba repelled a savage sea beast as it attacked a monk; the monster has captivated the world's imagination ever since. The easiest way to see the loch is with a tour group, departing from the Inverness tourist office. **Jacobite Cruises,** Tomnahurich Bridge, Glenurquhart Rd., whisks you around on coach or boat trips. (☎ 233 999. £8-20. Student discounts available.) **Kenny's Tours** circles the loch on a minibus. (☎ 252 411. Tours 10:30am-2:20pm and 2:30-5pm. £13, students £10.) Three miles south on A82 sits ◪**Urquhart Castle** (URK-hart), one of the largest in Scotland before it was blown up in 1692 to prevent Jacobite occupation. A number of Nessie photos have been fabricated there. (☎ 01456 450 551. Open June-Aug. daily 9:30am-6:30pm; Apr.-May and Sept. daily 9:30am-5:45pm; Oct.-Mar. M-Sa 9:30am-3:45pm. £5.) The Jacobite cause died in 1746 on **Culloden Battlefield,** east of Inverness, when Bonnie Prince Charlie lost 1200 men in 40min. To get there, take Highland County bus #12 from the post office at Queensgate (round-trip £2). Just 2½km south of Culloden, the stone circles and chambered cairns (mounds of rough stones) of the **Cairns of Clava** recall the Bronze Age. Bus #12 will also take you to **Cawdor Castle,** home of the Cawdors since the 15th century. Don't miss the family maze. (Open daily May-Sept. 10am-5pm. £6.50, students £5.30.)

    Trains (☎ 08457 484 950) run from Academy St. in Inverness's Station Sq., to: Aberdeen (2¼hr., 10 per day, £20); Edinburgh (3½hr., 11 per day, £33); Glasgow (3½hr., 8 per day, £33); and London (8hr., 3 per day, £84-110). Scottish Citylink (☎ 08705 505 050) **buses** run from Farraline Park, off Academy St., to Edinburgh and Glasgow (both 4½hr., 5-6 per day, £16). To reach the **tourist office,** Castle Wynd, from the stations, turn left on Academy St. and then right onto Union St. (☎ 234 353. Internet £1 for 20min. Open mid-June to Aug. M-Sa 9am-7pm, Su 9:30am-5pm; Sept. to mid-June M-Sa 9am-5pm, Su 10am-4pm.) The ideally located **Inverness Tourist Hostel ❷,** 34 Rose St., is brand-spanking-new with kitchen, couches, and flat-screen TV. (☎ 241 962. May-Aug. dorms £11-14; Oct.-Apr. £10. MC/V.) Try the **Lemon Tree ❶,** 18 Inglis St., for fabulously cheap and tasty soups (£1.80) and baked goods. (Open M-Sa 8:30am-5:45pm.)

FORT WILLIAM AND BEN NEVIS   ☎ 01397

In 1654, General Monck founded the town of Fort William on the banks of Loch Linnhe, among Britain's highest peaks, to keep out "savage clans and roving barbarians." His scheme backfired: Today thousands of Highlands-bound hikers regularly invade Fort William, which makes an excellent base for exploring some of Scotland's most impressive wilderness. Just outside of town, beautiful **Glen Nevis** runs southeast into Britain's tallest mountain. The breathtaking **Ben Nevis** (1343m), by far the biggest draw to the region, offers a challenging but manageable hike. One trail originates from the **Glen Nevis Visitor Centre,** where hikers stock up on maps and useful advice. (☎ 705 922. Open daily Apr.-Sept. 9am-5pm.) The ascent (13km; 5-7hr. round-trip) is difficult for its length rather than its terrain, but harsh conditions near the summit can prove deadly to the unprepared. Bring water and warm, waterproof clothes, and be sure to inform someone of your route.

    Trains (☎ 08457 484 950) come from Glasgow Queen St. (3¾hr., 2-3 per day, £19) on the magnificent ◪**West Highland Railway.** Built at the turn of the last century and traversing some of Scotland's finest scenery, you might recognize stretches of it from the recent *Harry Potter* films. The overnight sleeper train runs to London Euston (12hr., 1 per day, £70-110). **Buses** arrive next to the **Safeway** supermarket by the train station. Scottish Citylink (☎ 08705 505 050) travels to: Edinburgh (4hr., 3 per day, £16.20); Glasgow (3hr., 4 per day, £12.30); Inverness (2hr., 7-8 per day, £8.40); and Kyle of Lochalsh (2hr., 3 per day, £11.20). The **tourist office,** Cameron Sq., off of High St., books accommodations for a £3 charge plus a 10% deposit. (☎703 781. Open July-Aug. M-Sa 9am-7pm, Su 10am-6pm; low season reduced hours.) Fort William's accommodations fill up quickly in the summer. From the train station, turn left onto Belford Rd. and right onto Alma Rd., then bear left at the split to reach **Fort William Backpackers ❷**, 6 Alma Rd., a welcoming hostel removed from the hustle below. (☎700 711. Breakfast £1.90. Laundry £2.50. Internet and kitchen available. Curfew 2am. Dorms £11-14. AmEx/MC/V.) Before heading for the hills, pick up a packed lunch (£3) at the **Nevis Bakery ❶**, 49 High St. (☎704 101), across from the TIC, or groceries at **Tesco,** at the north end of High St. (Open M-Sa 8am-9pm, Su 9am-6pm.) **Postal Code:** PH33 6AR.

ISLE OF SKYE

Often called the shining jewel in the Hebridean crown, the misty Isle of Skye possesses unparalleled natural beauty, from the serrated peaks of the Cuillin Hills to the rugged Trotternish Peninsula. Although the island's charms are no secret, Skye won't give up all of its character to tourism. A strong Scottish Gaelic influence is still present in bilingual signs and genealogy centers.

◨ TRANSPORTATION. The **Skye Bridge** links the island to the mainland's Kyle of Lochalsh (toll £5.70 each way). **Trains** (☎08457 484 950) run to Kyle from Inverness (2½hr.; M-Sa 3 per day, Su 2 per day; £14.60). Scottish Citylink **buses** arrive from: Fort William (2hr., 3 per day, £12); Glasgow (6hr., 3 per day, £20); and Inverness (2hr., 2 per day, £12). **Pedestrians** can take either the bridge's 2½km footpath or the **shuttle bus** (2 per hr., £1.70). Buses on Skye are infrequent and expensive; grab the handy *Public Transport Guide to Skye* (£1) at any tourist office.

KYLE OF LOCHALSH AND KYLEAKIN. Kyle of Lochalsh ("Kyle" for short) and Kyleakin (Ky-LOCK-in) bookend the Skye Bridge. Kyle, on the mainland, wishes travelers would dally, but is best used *en route* to Skye. Though Kyleakin is short on conveniences, it operates three hostels and countless tours, making it a boisterous backpacker's hub. ▧**MacBackpackers Skye Trekker Tour,** departing from the hostel in Kyleakin, offers a 1-day tour emphasizing the history and legends of the island and a 2-day eco-conscious hike into the Cuillin Hills, with all necessary gear provided. (☎01599 534 510. 1-day £15, 2-day £45. Call ahead.) Located between Kyle of Lochalsh and Inverness, **Eilean Donan Castle** is the restored 13th-century seat of the MacKenzie family and the most photographed monument in Scotland. (☎01599 555 202. Open daily Apr.-Oct. 10am-5:30pm; Nov. and Mar. 10am-3pm. £4.50, students £3.60.) The Kyle of Lochalsh **tourist office** is on the hill above the train station. (☎01599 534 276. Open May-Oct. M-Sa 9am-5:30pm.) The friendly owners of ▧**Dun Caan Hostel ❷** in Kyleakin, have masterfully renovated a 200-year-old cottage. (☎01599 534 087. Bikes £10 per day. Dorms £10. Book ahead.) The **Pier Coffee Shop ❶,** also in Kyleakin, serves toasties (£2) and breakfast (£4.50) all day long. (☎01599 534 641. Open M-F 9am-8pm, Su 10:30am-8pm. Cash only.)

SLIGACHAN. Renowned for their hiking and their cloud and mist formations, the **Cuillin Hills** (COO-leen), the highest peaks in the Hebrides, are visible from nearly every part of Skye. Legend says the warrior Cúchulainn was the lover of the Amazon ruler of Skye, who named the hills for him after he returned to Ireland to die. *Walks from Sligachan and Glen Brittle* (£1), available at tourist offices, suggests routes. West of Kyleakin, the smooth, conical Red Cuillin and the rough, craggy Black Cuillin Hills meet in Sligachan, a hiker's hub in a jaw-dropping setting. The Cuillins are great for experienced hikers, but can be risky for beginners. For a room, try the **Sligachan Hotel ❹,** a classic hill-walker and -climber's haunt. (☎01478 650 204. Breakfast included. Singles £30-40; doubles £60-80. MC/V.) To camp at **Glenbrittle Campsite ❶,** in Glenbrittle at the foot of the Black Cuillins, take bus #53 (M-Sa 2 per day) from Portree or Sligachan to Glenbrittle. (☎01478 640 404. Open Apr.-Sept. £4.50 per person. Cash only.)

PORTREE. The island's capital has busy shops and an attractive harbor. **Dunvegan Castle,** the seat of the clan MacLeod, holds the record for the longest-inhabited Scottish castle, with continual residence since the 13th century. The castle holds the **Fairy Flag,** a 1500-year-old silk, and **Rory Mor's Horn,** capable of holding two liters of claret. Take Highland Country **bus** #56 (1-3 per day) from Portree. (☎01478 521 206. Open daily Apr.-Oct. 10am-5:30pm; Nov.-Mar. 11am-4pm. £6.) Buses to Portree from Kyle of Lochalsh (5 per day, £8) stop at Somerled Sq. The **tourist office** is on Bayfield Rd. (☎01478 612 137. Open July-Aug. M-Sa 9am-7pm, Su 10am-4pm; low season reduced hours.) The **Portree Independent Hostel ❶,** The Green, has a prime location. (☎01478 613 737. Dorms £11; doubles £23. MC/V.)

■**TROTTERNISH PENINSULA.** The rugged peaks and valleys of Trotternish are usually empty, often foggy, and always stunning. The eastern side is a geological masterpiece punctuated by thundering waterfalls, while the western side has a softer landscape of endless hills. Northeast of Portree, the A855 snakes along the east coast past the **Old Man of Storr** and the **Quirang** rock pinnacles, one of Mother Nature's most spectacular playing fields. The Old Man of Storr is accessible by a steep **hike** (1hr. round-trip). Take Highland Country bus #57 on the Portree-Staffin route (M-Sa 4-6 per day, June-Sept. also Su 3 per day; Day Rover £5) and ask the driver to let you off at the carpark.

ISLE OF LEWIS (LEODHAS)   ☎01851

Long-gone inhabitants have left a collection of tombs, standing stones, and other relics in the far-flung Outer Hebrides. Lewis is the most populous of these islands; more than 8000 people live in **Stornoway,** a splash of urban life in the untouched miles of moorland and half-cut fields of peat. The ■**Callanish Stones,** 22½km west of Stornoway on the A858, are second only to Stonehenge in grandeur and considerably less overrun. (Always open. Free.) Most of Lewis's biggest attractions, including the Callanish Stones and other archaeological sites, line the west coast and can be reached via the #W2 **bus,** which operates on a circuit beginning at the Stornoway bus station (M-Sa 4-12 per day in either direction). Maclennan Coaches offers a Day Rover pass on this route (£5), or a round-trip ticket to see one, two, or three of the sights (May-Oct.; £3.50-4.50). Alternatively, travel with **Out and About Tours** (☎612 288; individually designed day tours from £20) or **Albannach Guided Tours** (☎830 433; from £10), both departing from the tourist office. Lewis is also home to "the most consistent surf in Europe." Warm currents and long daylight hours further conspire to draw **surfers** to spots like the popular **Dalmor Beach,** near the village of Dalbeg, which has hosted several competitions.

CalMac **ferries** sail to Stornoway from Ullapool (2¾hr., 2-3 per day; £14, 5-day round-trip £24; with car £69/£117). Western Isles **buses** depart from Stornoway's Beach St. station; pick up a *Lewis and Harris Bus Timetable* (£0.50). The **tourist office** is at 26 Cromwell St. From the ferry terminal, turn left, then right onto Cromwell St. (☎703 088. Open Apr.-Oct. M, Tu, Th 9am-6pm and 8-9pm; W and F 9am-8pm; Sa 9am-6pm. Nov.-Mar. M-F 9am-5pm.) Rent bikes at **Alex Dan's Cycle Centre,** 67 Kenneth St. (☎704 025. £10 per day, £30 per week. Open M-Sa 9am-6pm.) **Internet** access is free at the **Stornoway Library.** (Open M-Sa 10am-5pm.) The best place to rest your head is ■**Fairhaven Hostel ❶,** at the intersection of Francis St. and Keith St., which also rents surf equipment. From the pier, turn left on Shell St., which becomes South Beach, then right onto Kenneth St. and right again onto Francis St. (☎705 862. Breakfast £2.50. Dorms £10, full board £20. Wetsuits £10 per day, surfboards £10-20. Cash only.) Buy groceries at the **Co-op** on Cromwell St. (☎702 703. Open M-Sa 8am-8pm.) **Postal Code:** HS1 2AA.

BULGARIA (БЪЛГАРИЯ)

Bulgaria's history is not as serene as its landscape. Once the most powerful state in the Balkans, Bulgaria fell to the Turks in the late-14th century. In their 500 years of rule, the Ottomans obliterated Bulgaria's nobility and enserfed its peasants. Underground monasteries, however, preserved the former culture, enabling the construction during the 1870s' National Revival of much of the majestic architecture that now graces Bulgarian cities. Today, in the wake of the recent Balkan wars, the country struggles to increase its economic output and accede to the EU. During this time of transition, many travelers will be rewarded by journeys to cosmopolitan Sofia, the lush countryside, or the beautiful Black Sea Coast.

DISCOVER BULGARIA

Trips to Bulgaria are convenient from Greece. In the capital city of **Sofia** (p. 235), admire Orthodox Churches and wander cobblestone alleyways. Just to the south, **Rila Monastery** (p. 239), in the highest mountains of the Balkan Peninsula, is the masterpiece of Bulgarian religious art. Move east to the art museums and Roman ruins of **Plovdiv** (p. 240); from there, the splendid **Bachkovo Monastery** (p. 240) is only 30min. away. Before traveling coastward, head north to beautiful, hillside **Veliko Tŭrnovo** (p. 240). End your trip with the raucous discos and beaches of **Varna** (p. 241) or the fortified old town of **Nesebŭr** (p. 242), both on the Black Sea.

ESSENTIALS

WHEN TO GO

Year-round, Bulgaria is milder than other Balkan countries due to the proximity of the Mediterranean and Black Seas. Temperatures average −2°C (28°F) in mid-winter, 25°C (77°F) in mid-summer. Spring and fall weather is generally ideal, as winter can be quite cold. For the Black Sea Coast, summer is the best time to visit.

DOCUMENTS AND FORMALITIES

VISAS. Citizens of Australia, Canada, New Zealand, and the US do not need visas for stays of up to 30 days, citizens of the EU for stays of up to 90 days. All non-EU residents staying longer than 30 days must obtain a 90-day visa from their local embassy or consulate. US citizens may obtain a visa for free, though a US$20 processing fee still applies. Without rush service, single-entry visas for non-US citizens cost around US$50; multiple-entry visas US$120. Transit visas are US$40 and are valid for 24hr.; double transit (valid 24hr.) US$60. Prices include a **border tax** of around US$20; those not needing visas must pay the tax upon entering the country.

EMBASSIES. Foreign embassies in Bulgaria are in Sofia (p. 235). Bulgarian embassies at home include: **Australia** (consulate), 4 Carlotta Rd., Double Bay, Sydney, NSW 2028 (☎02 9327 7581; www.users.bigpond.com/bulcgsyd); **Canada,** 325 Stewart St., Ottawa, ON K1N 6K5 (☎613-789-3215; mailmn@storm.ca); **Ireland,** 22 Bulington Rd., Dublin 4 (☎01 660 3293; fax 01 660 3915); **UK,** 186-188 Queensgate, London SW7 5HL (☎020 7584 9433; www.bulgarianembassy.org.uk); **US,** 1621 22nd St. NW, Washington, D.C. 20008 (☎202-387-0174; www.bulgaria-embassy.org).

TRANSPORTATION

BY PLANE. All flights to Sofia connect through England or Western Europe. Tickets to the capital can run over US$3000 during the summer months. Budget travelers might want to fly into a nearby capital—Athens or Bucharest—and take a bus.

BY TRAIN. Bulgarian trains run to Hungary, Romania, and Turkey and are most useful for travel in the north; **Rila** is the main international train company. The train system is comprehensive but slow, crowded, and smoke-filled. There are three types of trains: express (експрес; ekspres), fast (бърз; burz), and slow (пътнически; putnicheski). Avoid *putnicheski* like the plague—they stop at anything that looks inhabited. *Purva klasa* (първа класа; first-class seating) is very similar to *vtora klasa* (втора класа; second-class) and not worth the extra money. Arrive well in advance if you want a seat. Stations are often marked only in Cyrillic, so it's best to know beforehand when to disembark.

BY BUS. Buses are better for travel in eastern and western Bulgaria and are often faster than trains, but are also less frequent and less comfortable. Buses head north from Ruse, to Istanbul from anywhere on the Black Sea Coast, and to Greece from Blagoevgrad. For long distances, **Group Travel** and **Etap** offer modern buses with A/C, bathrooms, and VCRs at prices 50% higher than trains. Some buses have set departure times; others leave when full. Grueling local buses stop everywhere and make for a bumpy, sweaty ride.

BY TAXI AND BY CAR. Yellow taxis are everywhere in cities. Refuse to pay in dollars and insist that the trip be metered (*sus apparata*) or fix a lump sum beforehand. Ask the distance and price per kilometer and pay attention to the sums. Some taxi drivers accrue extra mileage by fixing the meters; bargaining is not done. Tipping taxi drivers usually means rounding up to the nearest lev or half-lev. Some Black Sea towns can only be reached by taxi or by car. Rural roads tend to be in need of repair, and rocks and landslides can pose a threat in mountainous areas. Seat belts are mandatory in Bulgaria.

BY BIKE, BY FOOT, AND BY THUMB. Motoroads (www.motoroads.com) and travel agencies offer bike tours; when biking in urban areas, stay alert as drivers disregard traffic signals. Cars, not pedestrians, have the right of way; faithfully obey crosswalk signs, and cross roads quickly. Hitchhiking is rare because drivers hardly ever stop, but many who do hitchhike say it is generally safe. *Let's Go* does not recommend hitchhiking.

TOURIST SERVICES AND MONEY

EMERGENCY	Police: ☎166. Ambulance: ☎150. Fire: ☎160.

TOURIST OFFICES. Tourist offices are fairly common, as are local travel agencies. Staffs are helpful and usually speak English; often they reserve rooms, but some only plan itineraries. In larger hotels you can often find an English-speaking receptionist and maps.

MONEY. The **lev** (lv; plural *leva*) is the standard monetary unit; it subdivides into 100 stotinki. Given high inflation, prices may be volatile. Some places may accept US dollars or euros. It is illegal to exchange money on the street. **Banks** are the most reliable way to exchange money. They cash traveler's checks and often give Visa cash advances. Use exchange bureaus only when banks are closed. Credit cards are rarely accepted except at larger hotels and expensive resorts. **ATMs** offer the best exchange rates and are common throughout Bulgaria; they usually accept Cirrus, MasterCard, Plus, and Visa. Restaurant meals cost 6lv on average. **Tipping** is not obligatory, as most people just round up to the nearest lev, but 10% doesn't hurt. Occasionally a 10% service charge will be added; check the bill or the menu.

BUSINESS HOURS. Businesses open at 8 or 9am and there is a one-hour lunch break between 11am and 2pm. Banks are usually open 8:30am to 4pm, but some close at 2pm. Tourist offices, post offices, and shops stay open until 6 or 8pm; in tourist areas and big cities, shops may close as late as 10pm. *Vseki den* (всеки ден; every day) usually means Monday through Friday, and "non-stop" doesn't always mean open 24hr.

LEVA (LV) AS OF AUGUST 2004		
AUS$1 = 1.14LV		1LV = AUS$0.88
CDN$1 = 1.20LV		1LV = CDN$0.83
EUR€1 = 1.96LV		1LV = EUR€0.51
NZ$1 = 1.05LV		1LV = NZ$0.95
UK£1 = 2.91LV		1LV = UK£0.34
US$1 = 1.60LV		1LV = US$0.63

COMMUNICATION

PHONE CODES	Country code: 359. International dialing prefix: 00. From outside Bulgaria, dial int'l dialing prefix (see inside back cover) + 359+ city code + local number.

TELEPHONES AND INTERNET ACCESS. Opt first for phone offices; **pay phones** are ludicrously expensive. If using them for either local or international calls, it is best to purchase a 400 unit **phone card.** One brand of telephone services two brands of cards: BulFon (orange) and Mobika (blue). BulFon is better and more prevalent. To call collect (*za tyahna smetka;* за тяхна сметка), dial ☎01 23 for the international operator. Post offices also may have telephones; a clerk assigns you a booth, a meter records your bill, and you pay when finished. International access codes include **AT&T Direct** (☎00 800 0010), **British Telecom** (☎00 800 9727), and **MCI** (☎00 800 0001). Internet cafes can be found throughout urban centers, cost around 1lv per hr., and are often open 24hr.

MAIL. Overseas mail requires a Bulgarian return address, and costs: 0.60lv to any European destination; 0.90lv to the US; 0.80-1lv to Australia and New Zealand. Write "С въздушна поща" for airmail. Packages must be unwrapped for inspection; register important ones and allow for a two-week transit period. *Poste Restante* is unreliable. Address mail to be held according to the following example: First name SURNAME, *Poste Restante*, Gen. Gurko 6, Sofia 1000, BULGARIA.

LANGUAGES. Bulgarian is a South Slavic language similar to Russian; it is helpful to learn the Cyrillic alphabet (p. 1057). English is spoken mostly by young people and in tourist areas. German is also understood in many places.

 YES AND NO. To indicate "yes" and "no," Bulgarians shake their heads in the opposite directions from Brits and Yankees. If you are uncoordinated, it's easier just to hold your head still and say *dah* or *neh*.

ACCOMMODATIONS AND CAMPING

BULGARIA	❶	❷	❸	❹	❺
ACCOMMODATIONS	under 20lv	20-35lv	35-50lv	50-70lv	over 70lv

Foreigner registration is required as of March 2002 in response to 9/11. If you are staying in Bulgaria for more than 48 hours, you must register with the police. Hotels and hostels will do this for you, and may ask for your passport, but should return it immediately. Keep the registration with your passport, and be sure to re-register when changing accommodations. If staying with friends, register with the **Bulgarian Registration Office;** see the consular section of your embassy for details.

Private rooms are indicated by signs marked "частни квартири" (*tschastnee kvartiri*). Rooms can be arranged through **Balkantourist** (www.balkantourist.bg) or other tourist offices for US$6-12 per night (be sure to ask for a central location), or from individuals in train and bus stations. Be careful if alone, and don't hand over any money until you've checked out the place. *Babushki* (older women) are your best bet, but try to bargain them down. Bulgarian **hotels** are classed on a star system; one-star hotels differ from two- and three-star hotels mainly by lacking private bathrooms. Hotels fall in the range of US$9-50 per night, although foreigners are often charged more. The majority of Bulgarian **youth hostels** are in the countryside. Almost all include free breakfast and many offer amenities like Internet access and laundry facilities. Outside major towns, most **campgrounds** provide tent space or spartan bungalows (call ahead to reserve these in summer). It is advisable to check out the site before it is too late to stay elsewhere.

FOOD AND DRINK

BULGARIA	❶	❷	❸	❹	❺
FOOD	under 4lv	4-8lv	9-14lv	15-18lv	over 18lv

Tap water is generally safe for drinking. Bulgaria is known for cheese and yogurt; try *shopska salata* (шопска салата), a mix of tomatoes, peppers, and cucumbers with feta cheese, or *tarator* (таратор), a cold soup made with yogurt, cucumber, garlic, and sometimes walnuts. Baklava and *sladoled* (сладолед; ice cream) are sold in *sladkarnitsy* (сладкарници). Fruit and vegetables are sold in a *plod-zelenchuk* (плод-зеленчук; fruit store), *pazar* (пазар; market), and on the street. Kiosks sell *kebabcheta* (кебабчета; sausage burgers), sandwiches, pizzas, and *banitsa sus sirene* (баница със сирене; cheese-filled pastries). *Skara* (скара; grill restaurants) serve *kavarma* (каварма), meat dishes with onions, spices, and egg. In restaurants, seat yourself and ask for the bill when you are finished.

SAFETY AND SECURITY

Emergency care is far better in Sofia than in the rest of the country. Services at the Pirogov State Hospital are free, some doctors speak English, and the tourist office will send someone to translate. Travelers must carry proof of health insurance; most doctors expect cash payment. In the case of extreme emergency, air evacuation runs about US$50,000. UK nationals receive free medical care with a valid passport and NHS medical card. **Pharmacies** are labeled "Аптека" (*apteka*). A late-night pharmacy always stays open in larger towns; its address is posted on the doors of the others. Prescription drugs can be difficult to obtain. **Public bathrooms** ("Ж" for women, "М" for men) are often holes in the ground; pack a small bar of soap and toilet paper and expect to pay 0.05-0.20lv. Fiber tablets help against constipation, very much a possibility on the Bulgarian diet. Don't buy **alcohol** from street vendors, and beware homemade liquor. Only young girls wear sneakers, tank tops, or shorts outside big cities; **women** who wish to avoid unwanted attention should wear skirts and blouses. While hate crimes are rare and **discrimination** focuses on Roma (Gypsies), persons of a non-European ethnicity might receive stares. Although the government has recognized **homosexuality,** acceptance is slow in coming.

HOLIDAYS

New Year's Day (Jan. 1); Baba Marta (Mar. 1); Liberation Day (Mar. 3); Good Friday (Mar. 25); Labor Day (May 1); Orthodox Easter (May 1-2); St. George's Day (May 6); Day of Slavic Heritage (May 24); Day of Union (Sept. 6); Independence Day (Sept. 22); Day of the Leaders (Nov. 1); Christmas (Dec. 24-26).

FACTS AND FIGURES: BULGARIA

Official Name: Republic of Bulgaria.

Capital: Sofia.

Major Cities: Varna, Burgas, Ruse.

Population: 7,518,000.

Land Area: 110,910 sq. km.

Time Zone: GMT +2.

Language: Bulgarian.

Religion: Orthodox (83%).

SOFIA (СОФИЯ) ☎02

A history of assimilation has left Bulgaria unsure of its identity. In Sofia (pop. 1,100,000), spray-painted skateboarding ramps front the Soviet Army monument, while older women tote home their bread in *Harry Potter* shopping bags. Though McDonald's arches keep surfacing, the dome of St. Alexander Nevsky Cathedral remains Sofia's most visible golden landmark, and opportunities still abound to indulge in traditional cuisine, listen to folk music, and buy handmade crafts.

⌷ TRANSPORTATION

Flights: Airport Sofia (☎ 79 80 35). Bus #84 (tickets 0.50lv) runs to Eagle Bridge (Орлов Мост), a 10min. walk from the city center. Cab rides (see below) to destinations downtown should cost no more than 5lv.

Trains: Tsentralna Gara (Централна Гара; Central Train Station; www.razpisanie.bdz.bg), Knyaginya Mariya Luiza St. (Мария Луиза). **Ticket office** (☎931 11 11). Open M-F 7am-7pm. To **Burgas** (5 per day, 9.60-17.90lv) and **Plovdiv** (14 per day, 4.20-8.30lv). Left of the main entrance, **Rila Travel Bureau** (Рила; ☎932 33 46) sells tickets to **Athens** via **Thessaloniki** (1 per day, 65-90lv) and to **Budapest** via **Bucharest** (1 per day, 110-135lv). Open daily 6am-11pm.

BULGARIA

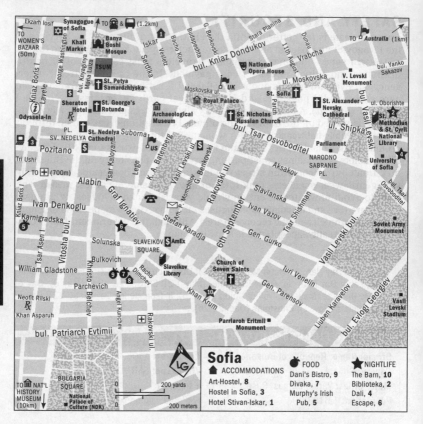

Sofia

▲ ACCOMMODATIONS
Art-Hostel, **8**
Hostel in Sofia, **3**
Hotel Stivan-Iskar, **1**

♦ FOOD
Dani's Bistro, **9**
Divaka, **7**
Murphy's Irish
Pub, **5**

★ NIGHTLIFE
The Barn, **10**
Biblioteka, **2**
Dali, **4**
Escape, **6**

Buses: Private buses, which leave from the parking lot directly across from the train station, are reasonably priced and usually fast. **Group Travel** (☎931 81 23) sends buses to: **Burgas** (2 per day, 17lv); **Varna** (3 per day, 21lv); **Veliko Tŭrnovo** (4 per day, 11lv). Arrive 30-45min. before departure to get a seat. Open daily 6am-11pm.

Local Transportation: Trams, trolleybuses, and buses cost 0.50lv per ride, 2.00 lv for 5 rides, 1-day pass 2.20lv, 5-day pass 10lv. Buy tickets at kiosks with Билети (*bileti;* tickets) signs or from the driver. Punch them on board to avoid a 5lv fine. If you put your backpack on a seat, you may be fined 5lv. Trams #1 and 7 run from the train station through pl. Sveta Nedelya (Света Неделя) to bul. Vitosha (Витоша). Officially, public transportation runs 5:30am-11:00pm, but rides are scarce after 9pm.

Taxis: Taxi S-Express (☎912 80), **OK Taxi** (☎973 21 21), and **INEX** (☎919 19) are reliable. Calling a taxi is always cheaper than hailing one from the street. At night, prefer cabs. Fares are 0.40-0.45lv per km, slightly more 10pm-6am. Make sure the ride is metered or fix a lump sum beforehand. Drivers almost never speak English.

✦❓ ORIENTATION AND PRACTICAL INFORMATION

The city center, **pl. Sveta Nedelya** (Света Неделя), is a triangle formed by the Tsurkva (church) Sv. Nedelya, the wide Sheraton Hotel, and the department store Tsentralen Universalen Magazin. **Bul. Knyaginya Mariya Luiza** (Княгиня Мария

Луиза) connects pl. Sveta Nedelya to the train station. Bul. Vitosha, one of the main shopping and nightlife thoroughfares, links pl. Sveta Nedelya to **pl. Bŭlgaria** and the huge, concrete **Natsionalen Dvorets na Kulturata** (Национален Дворец Култура; NDK, National Palace of Culture). On your right as you go down bul. Mariya Luiza, historic **bul. Tsar Osvoboditel** (Цар Освободител; Tsar the Liberator) leads to **Sofia University.** The *Inside & Out Guide* (free at the Sheraton Hotel and at tourist centers) has tourist info in English. **Maps** are also available in the Sheraton Hotel lobby (open 24hr.) and the open-air book market at Slaveikov Sq. (Славейков) on Graf Ignatiev (Граф Игнатиев).

Tourist Office: Odysseia-In/Zig Zag Holidays, bul. Stamboliiski 20-B (Стамболийски; ☎980 51 02; http://zigzag.dir.bg). From pl. Sv. Nedelya, head down Stamboliskii and take the 2nd right on Lavele; Odysseia is halfway down on the left. Consultation 5lv per session. Open M-Sa 9am-6:30pm, Su also in summer.

Embassies: Australia (consulate), ul. Trakiya 37 (☎946 13 34). **Canada,** ul. Assen Zlatarov 11 (☎943 37 04). **Ireland, New Zealand** and the **UK,** ul. Moskovska 9 (Московска; ☎933 92 22). Register either by phone or in person upon arrival in Bulgaria. Open M-Th 8am-12:30pm and 2-5pm, F 9am-noon. **US,** ul. Suborna 1a (Сиборна; ☎937 51 004), 3 blocks from pl. Sv. Nedelya behind the Sheraton. Open M-Th 8:30am-5pm, F 8:30am-1pm. Consular section at Kapitan Andreev 1 (Капитан Андреев; ☎963 20 22), behind the NDK. Open M-F 9am-5pm.

Currency Exchange: Bulbank (Булбанк), pl. Sv. Nedelya 7 (☎923 21 11), cashes **traveler's checks** with a minimum US$3 fee and gives Visa cash advances for a 4% commission. Open M-F 8am-6pm.

American Express: D. Ignatiy 21, 2nd fl. (☎988 49 53), on the left past the post office heading toward Slaveikov Sq. Issues (1% commission) and cashes (3.5% commission) **American Express Traveler's Cheques.** Open daily M-F 9am-6pm, Sa 9am-noon.

Luggage Storage: Downstairs at the central train station. 0.80lv per piece. Claim bags 30min. before departure. Open daily 6am-midnight.

Emergency: Police: ☎166. **Ambulance:** ☎150. **Fire:** ☎160.

24hr. Pharmacies: Apteka Sv. Nedelya, pl. Sv. Nedelya 5 (☎950 50 26). **Apteka Vassil Levski,** bul. Vassil Levski 70, around the corner from Popa (☎986 17 55).

Medical Assistance: State-owned hospitals offer foreigners free 24hr. emergency aid; staff might not speak English. **Pirogov Emergency Hospital,** bul. Gen. Totleben 21 (Ген. Тотлебен; ☎915 44 11), opposite Hotel Rodina. Take trolley #5 or 19 from the city center. Open 24hr.

Telephones: Telephone Center, ul. General Gurko 4. From the post office, turn right onto Vasil Levski then left onto Gurko; it's a white building 1 block down. Phone, fax, photocopy, email, Internet access.

Internet Access: Stargate, Pozitano 20 (Позитано), 30m on the left if facing Hostel Sofia. 1lv per hr. Open 24hr.

Post Office: Ul. General Gurko 6 (Гурко). Send international mail at windows #6-8; *Poste Restante* at window #12. Open M-Sa 7am-8:30pm, Su 8am-1pm.

ACCOMMODATIONS AND FOOD

Big hotels are rarely worth the exorbitant price; hostels or private rooms are the best option. **Hostel in Sofia ❶,** Pozitano 16 (Позитано), has a great location and a friendly staff. From pl. Sv. Nedelya, walk down Vitosha, and turn right on Pozitano. (☎/fax 989 85 82. Reception 24hr. €9 per person.) The spacious **Art-Hostel ❶,** ul. Angel Kunchev 21A (Ангел Кънчев), is part hostel, part art gallery. From pl. Sv. Nedelya, take Vitosha to William Gladstone (Уилям Гладстон), turn left, and after two blocks turn right onto Angel Kunchev. (☎987 05 45. Free Internet. Reception

24hr. €10 per person.) To reach **Hotel Stivan-Iskar ❸**, ul. Iskar 11B, walk up bul. Mariya Luiza and turn right on ul. Ekzah Iosif (Екзарх Йосиф), then walk two blocks and turn right on Bacho Kiro, then left on Iskar. (☎986 67 50; www.hoteliskar.com. Check-out noon. Doubles €25-37; apartment €50-55.)

Cheap meals are easy to find. Across bul. Mariya Luiza from TSUM are two large **markets,** the **Women's Bazaar** (Жени Пазар) and **Khali** (Хали). **❿Dani's Bistro ❸**, Angel Kunchev 18A, is a streetside cafe with friendly staff and simple, savory fare. (☎987 45 48. Open daily 10am-10pm.) Facing McDonald's in pl. Slaveikov, take the left side street and continue right at the fork to **Divaka ❷**, ul. William Gladstone 54, for huge salads (1.50-3.50lv) and sizzling veggie and meat *sacheta* (6.50lv) on iron plates. (☎989 95 43. Open 24hr.) **Murphy's Irish Pub ❷**, Karnigradska 6 (Кърниградска), is a haven for homesick English-speakers. (☎980 28 70. Entrees from 6.50lv. Live music F. Open M-Th and Su noon-12:30am, F-Sa noon-1:30am.)

👁 SIGHTS

PLOSHAD ALEXANDER NEVSKY. With the tsar-liberator for its patron saint, the golden-domed **St. Alexander Nevsky Cathedral** (Св. Александр Невски; Sv. Aleksandr Nevsky) was erected as a memorial to the 200,000 Russians who died in the 1877-78 Russo-Turkish War. Through a separate entrance left of the main church, the **crypt** contains an array of painted icons and religious artifacts from the past 1500 years. *(Cathedral open daily 7am-7pm. Free. Crypt open M and W-Su 10:30am-6:30pm. 4lv, students 2lv. Guided tours of the crypt 25lv for 5 or more persons, 20lv for fewer than 5.)*

AROUND PLOSHAD SVETA NEDELYA. The focal point of pl. Sveta Nedelya, the **Cathedral of St. Nedelya** (Катедрален Храм Св. Неделя; Katedralen Hram Sv. Nedelya), is filled with frescoes blackened by soot from visitors' candles (0.10-2lv). The church is a reconstruction of a 14th-century original destroyed by a bomb detonated in an attempt on Tsar Boris III's life in 1925. Sunday liturgy shows off the church's great acoustics. *(Open daily 7am-6pm.)* In the courtyard behind the Sheraton Hotel stands the 4th-century **St. George's Rotunda** (Св. Георги; Sv. Georgi), adorned with beautiful 11th- to 14th-century murals. *(Open daily in summer 8am-6pm, in winter 8am-5pm. Services daily 9am.)* Walk up bul. Mariya Luiza and take a left on Ekzarh Iosif to reach the recently-renovated **Synagogue of Sofia** (Софийски Синагога; Sofiiska Sinagoga), Sofia's only synagogue, where a museum upstairs outlines the history of Jews in Bulgaria. *(Open M-F 9am-5pm. Services F 7pm, Sa 10am. Synagogue 2lv. Museum free.)*

ALONG BULEVARD TSAR OSVOBODITEL. Sofia's first paved street, bul. Tsar Osvoboditel stretches between the **House of Parliament** and the **Royal Palace.** Midway sits the **St. Nicholas Russian Church** (Св. Николай; Sv. Nikolai), built in 1913. Icons from the Novgorod school ornament the interior, Russian Orthodox onion domes the exterior. *(Open daily 9am-10:30pm. Services W and Sa 5-7pm.)*

MUSEUMS. The Royal Palace houses the **National Museum of Ethnography** (Национален Етнографски Музей; Natsionalen Etnografski Muzey), devoted to four centuries of Bulgarian folk history. *(Open Tu-Su 10am-6pm. 4lv, students 2lv. Guided tours 10lv.)* The **National Art Gallery** (Национална Художествена Галериа; Natsionalna Hudozhestvena Galeriya) gathers artwork in the same building. *(Open Tu-Su 10:30am-6:30pm. 4lv, students 2lv. English tours 20lv.)* To reach the **National History Museum,** Residence Boyana, Palace 1 (Национален Исторически Музей; Natsionalen Istoricheski Muzey), take minibus #21, trolley #2, or bus #63 or 111 to Boyana. The museum showcases archaeological finds and cultural artifacts from prehistory to the present. *(☎955 42 80. Open daily 9:30am-5:30pm. 10lv, students 5lv, guided tour 10lv.)*

♫ 🎭 ENTERTAINMENT AND NIGHTLIFE

Half a dozen theaters lie on **Rakovski** (Раковски), Bulgaria's theater hub. A left on Rakovski leads to the columns of the National Opera House, Rakovski 59. (☎987 13 66. Performances Tu-Sa 6pm. Box office open M-Tu 9:30am-2pm and 2:30-6:30pm, W-F 8:30am-7:30pm, Sa 10:30am-6:30pm, Su 10am-6pm. Tickets 5-20lv.)

At night, smartly dressed Sofians roam the main streets, filling the outdoor bars along **bulevard Vitosha** and the cafes around the **National Palace of Culture**. For the younger set, nightlife centers around Sofia University at the intersection of Vasil Levski and Tsar Osvoboditel. **█Biblioteka** (Библиотека), in St. Cyril and Methodius Library, has live bands and karaoke. (Cover M-F and Su 3lv, Sa 4lv. Open daily 8:30pm-6am.) Dance with Sofia's hotties at **Escape,** Angel Kunchev 1. (Cover 3lv. Open W-Sa 10:30pm-4am.) **Dali,** behind the University on Khristo Georgiev, is the best Latin club in town. (☎946 51 29. Call ahead to reserve a table. Cover 3lv. Open daily 8pm-5am.) Hidden away at 22 Sixth September, **█The Barn** (Хамбара; Khambara) is a former communist newspaper turned tavern. (Open 8pm-late.)

🔲 DAYTRIPS FROM SOFIA

RILA MONASTERY. Holy Ivan of Rila built the 10th-century Rila Monastery (Рилски Манастир; Rilski Manastir), the largest and most famous in Bulgaria, as a refuge from worldly temptation. The monastery sheltered the arts of icon painting and manuscript copying during the Byzantine and Ottoman occupations, and remained a bastion of Bulgarian culture during five centuries of foreign rule. Today's monastery, decorated with 1200 brilliantly colored **frescoes,** was built between 1834 and 1837, after raids and the destruction of the earlier structure, little of which now remains. Signs outside the monastery display maps and suggested hiking routes through nearby **Rila National Park.**

To get to the monastery, take **tram** #5 from Hostel Sofia to Ovcha Kŭpel Station (Овча КЪпел) and take the **bus** to Rila Town (2hr., 1 per day 10:20am, 5lv). From Rila Town, catch the bus to the monastery (30min., 3 per day, 1.50lv). Inquire at room #170 in the monastery about staying in a spartan but heated **monastic cell ❷.** (☎07054 22 08. Curfew midnight. US$15 per person.) Behind the monastery is a cluster of restaurants, cafes, and a mini-market.

KOPRIVSHTITSA. Todor Kableshkov's 1876 "letter of blood," urging rebellion against Ottoman rule, incited the War of Liberation in this little village in the Sredna Gora mountains. Today, Koprivshtitsa (Копривщица; pop. 2600) is a historical center and home to Bulgaria's popular **folk festival,** which attracts international crowds in mid-August. The well-preserved **National Revival houses** were built by the town's first settlers. Many homes have enclosed verandas and delicate woodwork, and six have been turned into **museums** of history and ethnography; buy tickets and maps at the tourist office. (Each 3lv, students 1.50lv. Combination ticket 5lv, students 3lv. Open daily 10am-6pm.)

Trains run to Plovdiv (3½hr., 5 per day, 2.60-3.20lv) via Sofia (2hr., 3 per day, 5lv). **Private buses** also run to Plovdiv (2½hr., daily, 5lv) and Sofia (2hr., 2 per day, 5.50lv). Backtrack along the river bisecting town to the main square, where the **tourist office** sells maps (2lv), rents mountain bikes (3lv per hr.), and finds **private rooms** (€10-12) in the center of town. (☎07184 21 91. Open daily 10am-6pm.) Small **hotels,** often with "Kushta" (КЪща) in the name, are also easy to find (15-30lv).

PLOVDIV (ПЛОВДИВ)　　　　　　　　　　☎032

Although smaller than Sofia, Plovdiv (pop. 376,000) is widely hailed as the cultural capital of Bulgaria. Plovdiv's historical and cultural treasures are concentrated among the **Trimondium** (three hills) of **Stariya Grad** (Стария Град; old town). Stariya Grad itself is filled with churches and National Revival houses. To reach the 2nd-century ◼**Roman amphitheater** (Античен Театър; Antichen Teatŭr) from pl. Tsentralen (Централен), take a right off Knyaz Aleksandr (Княз Александр) onto Suborna (Съборна), then go right up the steps along Mitropolit Paisii to the steps next to the music academy. Dating from the early Roman occupation of the Balkans, this marble masterpiece now hosts concerts and shows, such as the **Opera Festival** in June and the **Festival of the Arts** in summer and early fall. (Amphitheater open daily 9am-7pm. 3lv.) Return to Knyaz Aleksandr and follow it to the end to pl. Dzhumaya (Джумая), home to the **Dzhumaya Mosque** and the ancient **Philipopolis Stadium,** which has an intact gladiator's entrance. (Both free.) At the end of Suborna, the **Museum of Ethnography** (Етнографски Музей; Etnografski Muzey) exhibits artifacts such as *kukerski maski,* masks used to scare away evil spirits. (Open Tu-Th and Sa-Su 9am-noon and 2-5pm, F 9am-noon. 3lv, students 2lv.)

Trains run to: Burgas (5hr., 6 per day, 4.70-6.70lv); Sofia (2½hr., 14 per day, 2.90-4.20lv); and Varna (5½hr., 3 per day, 5.90-8.40lv). Buy international tickets at **Rila,** bul. Khristo Botev 31a. (Open M-F 8am-7:30pm, Sa 8am-2pm.) **Buses** from Sofia (2hr., every 30min., 8lv) arrive at Yug (Юг) station, bul. Khristo Botev 47 (☎62 69 37), opposite the train station. An up-to-date map is absolutely essential; street vendors sell good ones in Cyrillic for 3lv. Check email at **Speed,** Kryaz Aleksandr 12, on the left before the mosque. (1lv per hr. Open 24hr.) ◼**Bed and Breakfast Queen Mary Elizabeth ❶,** Gustav Vaigand Str. 7, is clean, backpacker-friendly, and cheap. From Ruski, turn left onto Gustav Vaigand; it's on the right, 100m down. (☎62 93 06. Free laundry. Reception 24hr. A/C. 15lv per person. Cash only.) **Hotel Bulgaria ❹,** Patriarch Evtimii 13, has rooms with private bath, TV, and A/C. (☎63 35 99. Reception 24hr. Singles €35. Cash only.) **Postal Code:** 4000.

◪ DAYTRIP FROM PLOVDIV: BACHKOVO MONASTERY.

In the Rodopi mountains 28km south of Plovdiv is Bulgaria's second-largest monastery, **Bachkovo Monastery** (Бачковски Манастир; Bachkovski Manastir), built in 1083. The main church holds the **Icon of the Virgin Mary and Child** (Икона Света Богородица; Ikona Sveta Bogoroditsa), which is said to have miraculous healing power. (Open daily 7am-8pm. Free.) Well-maintained hiking paths lie uphill from the monastery. **Buses** run from Yug station in Plovdiv to Asenovgrad (25min., every 30min., 0.80lv). **Trains** also run there from Plovdiv (25min., 17 per day, 0.80lv). From Asenovgrad, take a bus headed to Lŭki (Лъки) for the monastery (20min., 4 per day, 0.60lv).

VELIKO TŬRNOVO (ВЕЛИКО ТЪРНОВО)　　　　☎062

Veliko Tŭrnovo (pop. 75,000), on the steep hills above the Yantra River, has watched over Bulgaria for over 5000 years. The city's residents led the national uprising against Byzantine rule in 1185; its revolutionaries wrote the country's first constitution here in 1879. The remains of the ◼**Tsarevets** (Царевец), a fortress that once housed the royal palace and a cathedral, span a hillside outside the city. (Open daily 8am-7pm. 4lv.) Climb uphill to the beautiful **Church of the Ascension** (Църква Възнесениегосподне; Tsŭrkva Vŭzneseniegospodne), which was restored for Bulgaria's 1300th anniversary in 1981. (Open daily 7am-6:30pm. Free.) From the center, go down Nezavisimost, which becomes Nikola Pikolo, and turn right at ul. Ivan Vazov (Иван Вазов) to reach the **National Revival Museum** (Музей на Възраждането; Muzey na Vŭzrazhdaneto), which documents Bulgaria's 19th-century National Revival and has a copy of the first constitution. (Open M and W-Su 8am-6pm. 4lv.) On summer evenings, there is often a ■**sound-and-light show** above Tsarevets Hill. (Begins between 9:45 and 10pm and lasts 20min.)

All **trains** stop at nearby Gorna Oryakhovitsa (Горна Оряховица; 20min., 10 per day, 0.60lv), where connecting trains leave for: Burgas (6hr., 5 per day, 6.40lv); Sofia (5hr., 9 per day, 8.30lv); and Varna (4hr., 4 per day, 7.30lv). Minibuses and city bus #10 go from the station to **ploshad Maika Bŭlgaria** (Майка Българиа), the town center. Just off the square is the **tourist office,** Khristo Botev 5. (Maps 2.50lv. Open M-Sa 9am-6pm.) Check email at nearby **Bezdnata** (Бездната), Khristo Botev 3. (Noon-10pm 0.80lv per hr., 10pm-noon 0.50lv per hr. Open 24hr.) ■**Hostel Trapezitsa (HI)** ❶, Stefan Stambolov 79, has rooms with private bath; from the town center, walk down Nezavisimost toward the post office and follow the street to the right. (☎ 220 61. Singles 17lv; doubles 20lv.) **Hotel Comfort** ❸, Panayot Tipografov 5 (Панайот Типографов), has an amazing view of Tsarevets. From Stambolov, turn left on Rakovski (Раковски), left again into the small square, and look for the signs. (☎ 287 28. Singles €25; doubles €30.) **Postal Code:** 5000.

BLACK SEA COAST (ЧЕРНО МОРЕ)

Bulgaria's most popular vacation spot, the Black Sea Coast is covered with secluded bays, seaside towns, and pricey resorts. Sometimes the bronzed tourists and modern luxury seem to contrast too starkly with folk tradition, but tiny, centuries-old fishing villages are always just a step off the beaten path.

VARNA (ВАРНА) ☎052

Visitors are drawn to Varna (pop. 290,000) by its expansive beaches, Mediterranean-like climate, and frequent summer festivals. Go right on bul. Primorski (Приморски) from the train station to reach the **beaches** and **seaside gardens.** Despite Varna's sprawl, most sights are within a 30min. walk of one another. In the city's old quarter, **Grutska Makhala** (Гръцка Махала), the well-preserved ruins of the ■**Roman Thermal Baths** (Римски Терми; Rimski Termi) sit on San Stefano. (Open Tu-Su 10am-5pm. 3lv, students 2lv.) The **Archaeological Museum** (Археологически Музей, Arkheologicheski Muzey), in the park on Mariya Luiza, has the world's oldest gold artifacts. (Open in summer Tu-Su 10am-5pm; low season Tu-Sa 10am-5pm. 4lv.) Varna's cultural events include the **International Jazz Festival** in late August as part of **Varna Summer,** a chamber music, theater, and folk festival from early June to mid-August. For schedules and tickets, check the **Festival and Congress Center,** on bul. Primorski, which also has a cinema where the international film festival **"Love is Folly"** takes place from August to September.

Trains depart from near the commercial harbor for Plovdiv (7hr., 3 per day, 8-11lv) and Sofia (8hr., 6 per day, 12-15lv). **Buses,** at ul. Vladislav Varenchik (Владислав Варенчик), go to Burgas (2½hr., 4 per day, 7lv) and Sofia (6hr., 16 per day, 19lv). **Megatours,** in the Hotel Cherno More, Slivnitsa 33, has tourist info. (Open M-F 8:45am-6:30pm, Sa 8:45am-2pm.) **Astra Tour,** near track #6 at the train station, finds private rooms that run for about 22lv. (☎ 60 58 61; astratur@yahoo.com. Open daily in summer 6am-10pm.) **Hotel Trite Delfina** ❹ (Трите Делфина; Three Dolphins), ul. Gabrovo 27, is convenient. Go up Simeon from the station and turn right on Gabrovo. (☎ 60 09 11. Call ahead. Singles 50lv; doubles 60lv.) **Postal Code:** 9000.

BALCHIK (БАЛЧИК) ☎0579

Balchik (Балчик), a fishing village with houses carved into its chalky cliffs, makes a good daytrip from Varna. From pl. Ribarski (Рибарски), turn right and walk 20min. along the boardwalk or Primorska (Приморска) to reach Romanian Queen

Maria's ▓**Summer Palace,** where visitors can sit on a marble throne or explore the botanical garden. (Open daily 8am-8pm. 5lv, children 1lv.) Take a taxi (4lv) from pl. Ribarski to the mud baths of **Tuzlata,** 6km north, for a grand bath (грязни баня; grazni banya). Bask in the sun while covered in drying mud. (Open daily in summer 8:30am-7pm. Costs vary by procedure.) **Tourist Agency Chaika** (Чайка), pl. Ribarski 2, arranges **private rooms.** (☎7 20 53; www.chaikabg.com. Rooms 10-15lv. Open daily in summer 8am-8pm.) **Minibuses** run from Mladost station in Varna (40min., 1 per hr. 6:30am-7:30pm, 2.50lv). **Postal Code:** 9600.

BURGAS (БУРГАС) ☎056

Though mostly used as a transport hub for the southern Black Sea Coast, Burgas (pop. 230,000) also has its own pleasant **beaches** and **seaside gardens.** The bus and train stations are near the port at pl. Garov (Гаров). **Trains** go to Sofia (6-8hr., 5 per day, 9lv) and Varna (5hr., 4 per day, 5-10lv). From a stop to the left as you face the train station, **minibuses** run to coastal resorts; note that many smaller resorts don't have places to change money. **Bulbank,** across the street from Hotel Bulgaria on Aleksandrovska, cashes traveler's checks and has an **ATM.** (Open M-F 8:30am-4pm.) If you stay overnight, **Primoretz Tourist Bourgas,** across from the train station, can secure a private room. (☎84 27 27. Open daily 7am-7pm. Rooms from 11lv.) Or, go up Aleksandrovska from the station, take a right on Bogoridi (Богориди), and take the second left onto Lermontov to the affordable **Hotel Mirage ❷** (Мираж), Lermontov 48. (☎84 56 47. Doubles €20.) **Postal Code:** 8000.

NESEBŬR (НЕСЕБЪР) ☎0554

A popular resort town, Nesebŭr (Несебър; pop. 10,000) tops the peninsula at the southern end of Sunny Beach. A walk through the ancient **Stariya Grad** (old town) begins along the 3rd-century stone **fortress walls.** The Byzantine gate and port date from the 5th century. The **Archaeological Museum** (Археологически Музей; Arkheologicheski Muzey), to the right of the town gate, displays ancient ceramics and relics, such as a 13th-century stone anchor. (☎460 18. Open M-F 9am-1pm and 1:30-7pm, Sa-Su 9am-1pm and 2-6pm. 2.50lv, students 1.20lv. English tours 5lv per group.) From the center, take Mitropolitska to reach the 10th-century **Temple of John the Baptist** (Йоан Кръстител; Yoan Krŭstitel), a UNESCO-protected site that is now an art gallery. (Open daily 10am-10pm. Free.) In the main square, the 13th-century **Church of Christ the Almighty** (Христос Пантократор; Khristos Pantokrator) also doubles as an art gallery. (☎450 00. Open daily 9am-9pm. Free.) **Buses** run to Burgas (40min., every 40min. 6am-9pm, 2.40lv). **Postal Code:** 8230.

SOZOPOL (СОЗОПОЛ) ☎05514

Sozopol (Созопол), settled in 610 BC, was once the resort of choice for Bulgaria's artistic community, and is still a haven for the creative set. Take a **boat cruise** (7 and 8:15pm, 6lv) from the seaport behind the bus station to get a closer look at the two nearby islands, **St. Peter** and **St. Ivan.** To explore some less-crowded beaches, rent a motorbike near the new town beach and cruise along the shoreline (10lv per hr.). **Minibuses** arrive from Burgas (45min., every 30min. 6am-9:30pm, 2.40lv). Turn left on Apoloniya (Аполония) to reach the **old town.** To get to the **new town,** go right from the station and bear left at the fork onto Republikanska (Републиканска). Walk until Republikanska runs into a pedestrian street and then go down the blocked street to reach **Imperial Tour,** Ropotamo St. 5, which arranges **private rooms.** (☎/fax 224 63. Open daily 9am-10pm. Singles 10-12lv per person; doubles 20-24lv.) After walking into the old town, take the right-most fork along the seacoast to reach **Orfei ❸** (Орфеи), which offers a panoramic view and a long list of seafood specialties. (☎224 41. Open daily 10am-midnight.) **Postal Code:** 8130.

CROATIA (HRVATSKA)

Croatia is a land of preternatural beauty, endowed with dense forests, barren mountains, and crystal-clear waters. At the convergence of the Mediterranean, the Alps, and the Pannonian Plain, the country has also been situated along dangerous political boundaries—those between the Frankish and Byzantine empires in the 9th century, the Catholic and Orthodox churches since the 11th century, and Christian Europe and Islamic Turkey from the 15th to the 19th centuries. In the past decade, the list has extended to its own fractious ethnic groups. After the devastating 1991-1995 war, however, the country achieved full independence for the first time in 800 years, leaving natives and visitors alike to enjoy Croatia in peace.

DISCOVER CROATIA

In **Zagreb** (p. 246), Croatia's lively capital, sip a latte at a hip cafe amid the city's Habsburg splendor. Catch a concert in the world's second-largest Roman amphitheater in **Pula** (p. 250), the 2000-year-old heart of the Istrian Peninsula, before proceeding to

Croatia

Croatia's true highlight, the **Dalmatian Coast** (p. 251), where pristine beaches meet the clearest waters of the Mediterranean. Bask on the sands of **Split** (p. 252), then head offshore to breathtaking **Hvar Island** (p. 253). Return to land to conclude with the white limestone buildings and city walls of **Dubrovnik** (p. 254).

ESSENTIALS

WHEN TO GO

The mildness of the Dalmatian Coast means that there is no wrong time to visit. Warm, sunny July and August bring crowds to the coast; travelers will find more breathing room, and lower prices, from June to September. Areas further inland see higher rainfall year-round, comparable to the Eastern European norm.

DOCUMENTS AND FORMALITIES

VISAS. Citizens of Australia, Canada, Ireland, New Zealand, the UK, and the US do not need visas for stays of up to 90 days. On pain of expulsion or fines, all visitors must **register** with the police within 48 hours of arrival; hotels, campsites, and accommodations agencies will usually do this for you. Police may check passports anywhere. There is no entry fee at the border.

EMBASSIES. Foreign embassies in Croatia are all in Zagreb (p. 246). Croatian embassies at home include: **Australia,** 14 Jindalee Crescent, O'Malley ACT 2606 (☎ 02 6286 6988; croemb@dynamite.com.au); **Canada,** 229 Chapel St., Ottawa, ON K1N 7Y6 (☎ 613-562-7820; www.croatiaemb.net); **New Zealand** (consulate), 291 Lincoln Rd., Henderson; mail to: P.O. Box 83-200, Edmonton, Auckland (☎ 09 836 5581; cro-consulate@xtra.co.nz); **UK,** 21 Conway St., London W1P 5HL (☎ 020 7387 2022; amboffice@croatianembassy.co.uk; consular dept. 020 7387 1144; consulardept@croatianembassy.co.uk); **US,** 2343 Massachusetts Ave. NW, Washington, D.C. 20008 (☎ 202-588-5899; www.croatiaemb.org).

TRANSPORTATION

BY PLANE. Zračna Luka Zagreb (www.zagreb-airport.hr) receives most incoming flights. **Croatia Airlines** (www.croatiaairlines.hr) flies from many cities, including Frankfurt, London, and Paris, to Dubrovnik, Split, and Zagreb. Rijeka, Zadar, and Pula also have tiny international airports.

BY TRAIN AND BY BUS. Trains (www.hznet.hr) travel to Zagreb from Budapest, Ljubljana, Venice, and Vienna. Train connections are *very* slow and nonexistent south of Split. *"Odlazak"* means departures, *"dolazak"* arrivals. **Buses** (www.akz.hr) are best domestically; buy tickets onboard for the lowest rates.

BY BOAT. If on the coast, take one of the ferries run by **Jadrolinija** (www.jadrolinija.hr), which traverse the Rijeka-Split-Dubrovnik route with island stops. Ferries also run from Split to Ancona, Italy, and from Dubrovnik to Bari, Italy (4½hr. by train from Naples). Cheap beds sell out fast, so buy in advance. A basic ticket provides only a place on the deck. If you have one, run—literally—to get a bed.

BY CAR, BY BIKE, AND BY THUMB. Anyone over 18 can rent a **car** (350-400kn per day) in larger cities, but parking and gas can be expensive. Rural roads are in poor condition; in the Krajina region and other conflict areas, drivers should be wary of off-road land mines. **Moped** and **bicycle** rentals (50-80kn per day) are a cheap option in resort or urban areas. *Let's Go* does not recommend hitchhiking.

TOURIST SERVICES AND MONEY

EMERGENCY	Police: ☎092. Ambulance: ☎094. Fire: ☎093.

TOURIST OFFICES AND MONEY. Even small towns have a branch of the excellent, English-speaking tourist board **turistička zajednica** (www.htz.hr). Accommodations are handled by private agencies (*turistička/putnička agencija*), the largest of which is **Atlas.** Croatia's monetary unit is the **kuna (kn),** which is divided into 100 *lipa;* the *kuna* is virtually impossible to exchange abroad except in Bosnia, Hungary, and Slovenia. Banks usually have the best rates, and most give MasterCard or Visa cash advances. Credit cards are widely accepted and **ATMs** are common. **Tipping** is rare, but many round up to the nearest whole *kuna;* certain places do this for you. **Bargaining** is acceptable only for informal transactions.

KUNA (KN)
–AS OF AUGUST 2004

AUS$1 = 4.29KN	1KN = AUS$0.23
CDN$1 = 4.51KN	1KN = CDN$0.22
EUR€1 = 7.35KN	1KN = EUR€0.14
NZ$1 = 3.95KN	1KN = NZ$0.25
UK£1 = 10.94KN	1KN = UK£0.09
US$1 = 6.00KN	1KN = US$0.17

COMMUNICATION

PHONE CODES	**Country code: 385. International dialing prefix: 00.** From outside Croatia, dial int'l dialing prefix (see inside back cover) + 385 + city code + local number.

TELEPHONES. Post offices usually have public phones; pay after you talk. All payphones require phone cards (*telekarta*), sold at newsstands and post offices. 50 "impulses" cost 23kn (1 impulse equals 3min. domestic, 36sec. international; 50% discount 10pm-7am and Sundays). Calls to the US and Europe are expensive (20kn per min.). International access numbers include **AT&T** (☎0800 22 01 11), **BT Direct** (☎0800 22 10 44), **Canada Direct** (☎0800 22 01 01), **MCI Worldphone** (☎0800 22 01 12), and **Sprint** (☎0800 22 01 13). Dialing ☎901 reaches an international **operator.**

MAIL. "*Avionski*" and "*zrakoplovom*" indicate airmail. *Poste Restante* is held for 30 days at a city's main post office. Address mail to be held as follows: First name SURNAME, *Poste Restante*, Pt. Republike 28, 2000, Dubrovnik, CROATIA.

LANGUAGE. Croatian is now distinct from Serbo-Croatian. Younger generations typically have some English, but commoner second languages are German and Italian. Noun inflections mean that street designations on maps may differ from those on signs by "-va" or "-a." Croatian basics are listed on p. 1058.

ACCOMMODATIONS AND FOOD

CROATIA	❶	❷	❸	❹	❺
ACCOMMODATIONS	under 100kn	100-150kn	150-210kn	210-360kn	over 360kn
FOOD	under 40kn	40-70kn	70-110kn	110-190kn	over 190kn

Croatia only has a handful of youth hostels (in Dubrovnik, Pula, Punat, Šibenik, Zadar, and Zagreb); for info, contact the **Croatian Youth Hostel Association,** Savska 5, 10000 Zagreb (☎01 482 92 94; www.hfhs.hr). **Private rooms** are also affordable; look

CROATIA

for *sobe* signs, especially near stations. Agencies generally charge 30-50% more if you stay fewer than three nights. If you opt for a **hotel**, call in advance, above all in summer. **Camping** is usually a good, cheap option; for info, contact the **Croatian Camping Union**, HR-52440 Poreč, Pionirska 1 (☎52 451 324; www.camping.hr). All accommodations are subject to a **tourist tax** of 5-10kn.

Croatian **cuisine** varies with the country's geography. In continental Croatia east of Zagreb, heavy meals featuring meat and creamy sauces predominate. *Purica s mlincima* (turkey with pasta) is the regional dish near Zagreb. Also popular is the spicy Slavonian *kulen*, which is considered one of the world's best sausages by the panel of German men who decide such things. On the coast, textures and flavors change with the presence of seafood and Italian influence. *Lignje* (squid) or *Dalmatinski pršut* (Dalmatian smoked ham) are not to be missed. If your budget is tight, *slane sardele* (salted sardines) are a tasty substitute. Croatia has excellent wines; price is the best indicator of quality. *Šlivovica* is a hard-hitting plum brandy found in many small towns. *Karlovačko* and *Ožujsko* are popular beers.

SAFETY AND SECURITY

Unexploded landmines means that travel to the Slavonia and Krajina regions remains dangerous, even though Croatia is no longer at war. **Pharmacies** are generally well stocked with Western products. Croatians are friendly to foreigners and sometimes a little too friendly to **women** travelers; companions can help ward off unwanted advances. Discretion remains wise for **GLBT** travelers, as Croatians are just beginning to accept homosexuality.

HOLIDAYS AND FESTIVALS

Holidays: New Year's Day (Jan. 1); Epiphany (Jan. 6); Easter (Mar. 27-28); May Day (May 1); Corpus Christi (May 26); Independence Day (May 30); Anti-Fascist Struggle Day (June 22); Statehood Day (June 25); National Thanksgiving Day (Aug. 5); Assumption (Aug. 15); All Saints' Day (Nov. 1); Christmas (Dec. 25-26).

Festivals: Zagreb hosts many festivals: street performers swarm in for Cest is D'best in June; the International Children's Festival in late June and early July features a children's derby and puppet performances; the International Folklore Festival in July is the premier gathering of European folk dancers and singing groups. On Korčula Island, the Festival of Sword Dances (Festival Viteških Igara) takes place from July-Aug. Dubrovnik Summer Festivals in July and Aug. feature theater, ballet, opera, classical music, and jazz.

FACTS AND FIGURES: CROATIA

Official Name: Republic of Croatia.

Capital: Zagreb.

Major Cities: Split, Dubrovnik.

Population: 4,497,000 (88% Croat, 4% Serb, 1% Bosniak, 6% other).

Land Area: 56,414 sq. km.

Time Zone: GMT +1.

Language: Croatian.

Religions: Catholic (77%), Orthodox (11%), Muslim (1%), other (11%).

ZAGREB ☎01

In Zagreb (pop. 750,000), Mediterranean breezes blow past churches and lively outdoor cafes and the external scars of civil war have all but vanished. Despite its wide boulevards, sprawling parks, and Habsburg architecture, the seemingly untouristed Croatian capital retains a small-town charm. Yet, as the city's many international festivals attest, Zagreb is more cosmopolitan than it appears.

CROATIA

Zagreb

ACCOMMODATIONS
Evistas, **5**
Omladinski Turistički
Centar (HI), **4**
Ravnice Youth Hostel, **1**

FOOD
Baltazar, **2**
Restaurant Boban, **3**

NIGHTLIFE
Aquarius, **6**
Pivnica Medvedgrad, **7**

300 yards
300 meters

TO MAKSIMIR PARK,
ZAGREB ZOO,
& (2km)

TO MIROGOJ CEMETERY (3km)

TO BUS (0.6km)

TO SAVA RIVER (1.6km)
& NOVI ZAGREB (3km)

TO 6 7 &
JARUN LAKE

Domjaničeva
Guljufova
Gotočeva
Petrova
Kamaufova
TRG PETRETIČEV
Petrićev
Derenčinova
Pavla Šubića
Crvenog Križa
Ljudevita
Kršimirov TRG
KVATERNIKOV TRG
Držićeva
Autobusni Kolodvor ■ Tram

Vončinina
Voćarska
Jurkovićeva
Antuna
Bauera
Laginjina
Vojnovićeva
Stančičeva
Zvonimirova
Višeslavova
Hvrojeva
Kraljice Jelene
TRG ŽRTAVA FAŠIZMA

Salata
Novakova
Ribnjak
Šalata
Srce Šalata
Rubetićeva UK
Schlosserove Stube
Vlaška
Smičiklasova
Martićeva
Račioga
Janka
Jurišićeva
HRVATSKIH VELIKANA
TRG
Palmotićeva
Amruševa
Đorđićeva
Draškovićeva
Dráslavova
Predom Laundromat
Bornina
Trpimirova
Mišlovska
Domagojeva
Branimirova
Trpimirova
Cinestar Cinema
Boškovićeva
Hatzova
Senoina
5

KAPTOL
Nova Ves
Australia
Tkalčićeva
Vinoteka Bornstein
Milkovićeva
Priest's Tower
Observatory
Broadway Cinema
Opatovina
Kaptol
Radićeva
Opatička
Stone Gate
Dvori Gallery
Klovićevi
Dolac
Marketplaca
Bakačeva
Cesarčeva
Cathedral of the Assumption
Ribnjak Park
Pod Zidom
Skalinska
TRG BANA Tram
JOSIPA
Bogovi
PETRICA PETRETIĆA
Berislavićeva ZRINJEVAC
Teslina
TIC
Croatia Airlines
AmEX
Strossmayer Gallery
STROSSMAYEROV TRG
Petrinjska
Exhibition Pavilion
TRG KRALJA TOMISLAVA
Trenkova
Glavni Kolodvor ■ Tram
Vatroslav Lisinski Concert Hall

GORNJI GRAD
Ban's Palace
St. Mart's
Parliament
Kata Mama
Rasch Palace
Lotrščak Towers
Strossmayerov
St. Catherine's
Ilica
Funicular
Mesnička
Tkalčićeva
JELAČIĆA
RG PETRA PETRETIĆA
Masarykova
Jadranská Ferrieta
Gundulićeva
Preradovićeva
DONJI GRAD
Hebrangova
TRG KRALJA PETRA SVAČIĆA
Gajeva
Haulikova
Kumičićeva ulica
Gallery of Modern Art
Puppet Theater
Miramarska ulica
Mihanovićeva

Demetrova
Kerempuh Satirical Theater
Dezmanova
Frankopanska
Daimatinska
Canada
Medulićeva
Valšavská
TRG MARŠALA TITA
Croatian National Theater
Museum of Arts and Crafts
Mimara Museum
ROOSEVELTOV TRG
Ethnographic Museum
TRG BRAĆE MAŽURANIĆA
Žerjavićeva
MARULIĆEV TRG
BOTANIČKI VRT
Vodnikova
Savska
Mihanovićeva
Kumičićeva

BRITANSKI TRG
Kačićeva
Klaićeva
Kršnjavoga
Brozova

Radnički dol
Pantovčak ul.
Primorska
Kordunska
Prilaz Gjure Deželiča
Krajiška
Republike Austrije
Kranjčevićeva
Jagićeva
Crpatkova
Zapadni Kolodvor
Rudolfova Vojarna

EUROPEAN DREAMS

After a year-long application process, Croatia was given the go-ahead in June 2004 to begin negotiations for entering the European Union. Admission to the EU is seen as crucial to Croation economic development—acceptance is predicted to contribute several hundred million euros to the national economy. Just as significantly, it is also expected to help stabilize the riven Balkan region. Incorporation would also be seen as a cultural triumph for Croatia. Having undergone centuries of Roman, Italian, and Austrian rule, most Croatians already think of themselves as more European than their fellow Slavs. Many consider admission a long-overdue affirmation of their Western cultural heritage.

Croatia still has a long road to travel before it is accepted, however. A major barrier is its treatment of Serbian refugees. During the recent conflict with Serbia, about 300,000 ethnic Serbs fled Croatia. Many have since returned, but they continue to face discrimination and everyday hostility. Now, the EU is calling for the country to facilitate the repatriation of these refugees. It remains to be seen whether Croatia can surmount this and other challenges by its 2007 deadline, but in light of its tremendous economic and political growth, it is likely to be included in the next round of EU expansion.

TRANSPORTATION AND PRACTICAL INFORMATION. Trains leave the Glavni Kolodvor (main station), Trg Kralja Tomislava 12 (☎060 333 444, international info 378 25 32; www.hznet.hr), for: Budapest (7hr., 4 per day, 224kn); Ljubljana (2½hr., 4 per day, 106kn); Split (9hr., 2 per day, 149kn); Venice (7hr., 2 per day, 320kn); Vienna (6½hr., 2 per day, 355kn); and Zurich (8hr., 1 per day, 647kn). From the station, to reach the main square, Trg bana Josipa Jelačića, cross the street, walk along the left side of the park to the end, then follow Praška. **Buses** (☎060 313 333) leave Autobusni Kolodvor (bus station), Držićeva bb, to: Dubrovnik (11hr., 17 per day, 185kn); Ljubljana (2½hr., 2 per day, 115kn); Sarajevo (9hr., 3 per day, 220kn); Split (6½-8½hr., 29 per day, 120kn); and Vienna (8hr., 2 per day, 250kn). To reach Trg b. Jelačića, exit on Držićeva, turn left, continue past Trg Žrtava Fašizma, and turn left onto Jurišićeva. The **tourist office** is at Trg b. Jelačića 11. (☎481 40 51; www.zagreb-touristinfo.hr. Open M-F 9am-9pm, Sa 9am-5pm, Su 9am-2pm.) In Zagreb, **register** at the Department for Foreign Visitors in the central police station, Petrinjska 30, 2nd fl., room 103. Bring your passport and use form #14. (☎456 36 23, after hours 456 31 11. Open M-F 8am-4pm.) Hotels and hostels will register guests automatically. **Internet** access is most convenient at **Charlie Net,** Gajeva 4. (☎488 02 33. Open M-Sa 8am-10pm. 16kn per hr.) **Postal Code:** 10000.

ACCOMMODATIONS AND FOOD. It can be hard to find a cheap room in Zagreb. Impeccably clean ▓**Ravnice Youth Hostel ❶,** 1 Ravnice 38d, is a 20min. ride from the city center. Take tram #11 or 12 from Trg bana Jelačica, tram #4 from the train station, or tram #7 from the bus station (dir.: Dubrava or Dubec). Get off at the unmarked Ravnice stop, one block past football stadium Dinamo. (☎233 23 25; fax 234 56 07. Kitchen available. Laundry 15kn. Internet 16kn per hr. Dorms 99kn.) Although noisy and run-down, the **Omladinski Turistički Centar (HI) ❶,** Petrinjska 77, is cheap and convenient from the train station; turn right onto Branimirova, and Petrinjska is on the left. (☎484 12 61; www.hfhs.hr. Reception 24hr. Dorms 80kn; singles 158kn, with bath 218kn; doubles 211kn/286kn. Cash only.) **Evistas ❸,** Šenoina 28, books private rooms in the center. From the station, turn right on Branimirova, left on Petrinjska, and then right onto Augusta Šenoe. (☎483 95 46; evistas@zg.hinet.hr. Open M-F 9am-1:45pm and 3-8pm, Sa 9:30am-5pm. Singles 185kn; doubles 264kn; apartments (2-day min.) 390-750kn. Prices rise 20% for 1-night stays. Under 26 10% off. Tax 7kn.) **▓Baltazar ❷,** Nova Ves 4, serves traditional Croatian meat dishes for 35-80kn. (Open daily noon-midnight.). Vegetarians will prefer **Restaurant Boban ❷,** Gajeva 9, which serves pastas and fresh salads. (Entrees 28-70kn. Open daily 10am-11pm.) **Konzum,** on the corner of Preradovićeva and Hebrangova, has groceries. (Open M-F 7am-8pm, Sa 7am-3pm.)

◙ 🏛 SIGHTS AND MUSEUMS. Zagreb is best seen on foot. From Trg b. Jelačića, take Ilica, then turn right on Tomiceva to the funicular (3kn), which gives access to many sights on the hills of Gornji Grad (upper town). **Lotrščak Tower** has a spectacular view of the city. (Open May-Sept. Tu-Su 11am-8pm. 10kn, students 5kn.) The 17th-century **St. Catherine's Church** is to the right of the tower. (Open M-F and Su 7am-11pm, Sa 7am-6:30pm.) Follow ul. Cirilometodska to Markov Trg; the colorful roof tiles of Gothic **St. Mark's Church** (Crkva Sv. Marka) depict the coats of arms of Croatia, Dalmatia, and Slavonia on the left and of Zagreb on the right. (Open daily 7am-1:30pm and 5:30-7pm. Free.) Visible from anywhere in Zagreb, the neo-Gothic bell towers of the 11th-century **▓Cathedral of the Assumption** loom over Kaptol Hill. (Open daily 10am-5pm. Free.) Take a short bus ride (8min., every 15min.) from Kaptol to **Mirogoj,** the country's largest and most beautiful cemetery; Croatia's first President, Franjo Tudjman, is buried beyond the grand mausoleum at the entrance. (Open M-F 6am-8pm, Su 7:30am-6pm. Free.)

Zagreb's museums focus on Croatian artwork. The **▓Museum of Arts and Crafts,** Trg Maršala Tita 10, has timepieces, antique furniture, and more from the 15th century onward. (Open Tu-F 10am-6pm, Sa-Su 10am-1pm. 20kn, students 10kn.) The **Gallery of Modern Art,** Herbrangova 1, features rotating exhibitions of Croatia's best artists in a small, attractive gallery. (Open Tu-Sa 10am-6pm, Su 10am-1pm. Prices vary by exhibition.) The **Mimara Museum,** Rooseveltov Trg 5, contains a vast collection ranging from prehistoric Egyptian art to European masters. (Open Tu-W and F-Sa 10am-5pm, Th 10am-7pm, Su 10am-2pm. 20kn, students 15kn.)

▐ 🌸 NIGHTLIFE AND FESTIVALS. Zagreb has a lively night scene. Dance and swim at the lakeside club **▓Aquarius,** on Lake Jarun. Take tram #17 to Srednjaci, the third unmarked stop after Studenski dom "S. Radić" (15min.). Cross the street, follow any dirt path to the lake, and walk left along the boardwalk; Aquarius is the last building. (☎364 02 31. Cover 30kn. Club open Tu-Su 10pm-4am. Cafe open daily 9am-9pm.) **Indy's,** Vranicanijeva 4, is closer to the center and has an extensive cocktail menu. (Mixed drinks 18-55kn. Open daily 9am-11pm). Locals chug cheap but good-quality homemade beer at **▓Pivnica Medvedgrad,** Savska 56. Take tram #13, 14, or 17 from Trg b. Jelačića to the corner of Avenija Vukovar and Savska. (Beer 18kn per L. Open M-Sa 10am-midnight, Su noon-midnight.)

January kicks off each year with a **blues festival.** In late June, the city bursts with performances for the street festival **Cest is d'Best** (The Streets are the Best), and the **Eurokaz Avant-Garde Theaters Festival.** June also sees the **Satire Days,** hosted by the Kerempuh Satirical Theater, Ilica 31, which performs satirical plays almost daily. Folk-culture mavens will flock to Zagreb in mid-July for the 39th **International Folklore Festival,** the premier gathering of European folk dancers and singing groups. A huge **International Puppet Festival** begins September, and Zagreb's **International Jazz Days** end October. Zagreb's **Christmas Fair** sets mid-December awash in twinkling colored light. Check www.zagreb-touristinfo.hr for updated schedules.

▶ DAYTRIP FROM ZAGREB: TRAKOŠĆAN CASTLE. Built in the 13th century as a defense tower, Trakošćan was acquired by the Drašković nobility, who enlarged and refurbished it, retaining ownership of the castle until WWII. Today, it exhibits family portraits, tapestries, a collection of firearms, and

CROATIA

THE BRIJUNI ARCHIPELAGO

Although expensive to reach, the Brijuni Archipelago, a short bus and ferry ride from Pula, is one of Croatia's most beautiful regions. It also has something for everyone: politics for the history buff, animals for the kids, and ruins for the romantics. Accessible only by a guided tour, **Veli Brijun**, the archipelago's largest island, was once a Roman resort and later a Venetian colony. More recently, it hosted the opulent residence of former Yugoslav president Josip Brož Tito.

Tours begin with a mini-trolley ride through a safari park of curiosities, including a pair of elephants given to Tito by Indira Gandhi, and then continue on foot though a gallery of adoring publicity photos of Tito. For those interested, it's worth the steep 25kn per hour (100kn per day) to explore the island's deserted beaches by bike. Look for the rental agency on the far side of Hotel Neptune.

Veli Brijun can only be seen on a guided tour run by the Brijuni Agency, Brijunska 10 (☎52 58 83; www.np-brijuni.hr), in Fazana. To get to the agency, take a local bus (20min.; M-Sa 1 per hr., Su 1 per 2-3hr.; 12kn) from Ulica 43 Istarske Divizije in Pula, and get off in at the supermarket. Cross the street and walk to the water; it's 1 block to the right. English tours leave daily at 11:30am; call 1 day ahead. Round-trip ferry and 4hr. tour 180kn. Open daily 8am-7pm.

suits of armor from the 15th through 19th centuries. Leave time to wander around the quiet lake and to hike through the hills surrounding the castle. Bring a sandwich; the restaurant at the bottom of the hill is expensive. (☎042 79 62 81. Castle open daily Apr.-Oct. 9am-6pm; Nov.-Mar. 9am-3pm. 20kn, students 10kn. Free guided tours in English; call ahead. English booklet 20kn.) **Buses** run from the Zagreb bus station to Varaždin (1¾hr., 20 per day, 50kn), where a local bus (1½hr., 7-11 per day, 26kn) continues to Trakošćan. Leave early in order to make the connection and still have plenty of time at the castle before the last bus back to Varaždin (M-F 9pm, Sa-Su 5pm).

NORTHERN COAST

As you approach the coast from Zagreb, you'll encounter the islands of the **Gulf of Kvarner,** blessed by long summers and gentle breezes; Rab in particular is graced with rare sand beaches. Roman ruins at Pula, on the **Istrian Peninsula,** lie farther north along the coast where the Mediterranean laps at the foot of the Alps.

PULA ☎052

If you visit only one city in Istria, it should be Pula—not only for its cool, clear water, but also for its winding medieval corridors, outdoor cafes, and breathtaking Roman ▓amphitheater. The second largest in the world, it is now often used as a concert venue. (Open daily 8am-9pm. 16kn, students 8kn.) To get there from the bus station, take a left on Istarska. Following Istarska in the opposite direction will bring you to the **Arch of the Sergians** (Slavoluk obitelji Sergii), a stone arch that dates from 29 BC. Go through the gates and down bustling ulica Sergijevaca to the **Forum,** which holds the remarkably well-preserved **Temple of Augustus** (Augustov hram.), finished in AD 14. To reach the private coves of Pula's **beaches,** buy a bus ticket from any newsstand (8kn) and take bus #1 to the Stója campground.

Trains (☎54 19 82) run from Kolodvorska 5 to Ljubljana (7½hr., 3 per day, 127kn) and Zagreb (7hr., 4 per day, 112-125kn). **Buses** (☎50 29 97) run from Trg Istarske Brigade to: Dubrovnik (15hr., 1 per day, 408kn); Trieste (3hr., 4 per day, 85-103kn); and Zagreb (5-6hr., 15 per day, 136kn). The **tourist office,** Forum 3, can help find private rooms. (☎21 29 87; www.pulainfo.hr. Open M-Sa 9 8am-midnight, Su 10am-6pm.) To reach beachside **Omladinski Hostel (HI) ❶,** Zaljev Valsaline 4, take bus #2 (dir.: Veruda) from the bus station. Get off at the first stop on

Veruda and follow the signs. (☎39 11 33; www.hfhs.hr. Call ahead. Dorms 89-110kn; 10kn registration.) Close to the hostel, ☒Biska ❶, Sisplac 15 (☎38 73 33), has superb seafood and pasta for a third of Stari Grad prices. **Postal Code:** 52100.

RAB ISLAND: RAB TOWN   ☎051

After centuries of Byzantine, Venetian, and Hungarian rule, Rab still has ruins dating from the time of its construction in Augustan Age Rome. Stroll along **Gornja Ulica** from the remains of **St. John's Church** (Crkva sv. Jvana), a Roman basilica, to **St. Justine's Church** (Crkva sv. Justine), which houses a museum of Christian art. (Open daily 10am-12:30pm and 7:30-10pm. 5kn.) Atop the bell tower of the 13th-century **St. Mary's Church** (Crkva sv. Marije), behold the sunset on the horizon or the nuns' lush garden below. (Open daily 10am-1pm and 7:30-10pm. 5kn.) **Beaches** dot the perimeter of Rab Island; the tourist office has transportation info. Most sand beaches, among the few in Croatia, are on the northern end of the island, while rocky beaches lie on the western edge and pebble beaches on the eastern.

  Buses arrive from Zagreb (5½hr., M-Sa 4 per day, 157kn). On the other side of the bus station can be found the friendly **tourist office.** (☎77 11 11; www.tzg-rab.hr. Open daily 8am-10pm.) **Katurbo ❶**, M. de Dominisa, on the waterfront between the bus station and town center, arranges private rooms. (☎72 44 95; www.katurbo.hr. Open daily July-Aug. 8am-9pm; Sept.-June 8am-1pm and 4-9pm. Singles 80-120kn. 30% discount on stays longer than 3 nights.) **Hotel Istria ❷** has clean, modern rooms. (☎72 41 34. 90-160kn per person.) Walk 2km east along the bay from the bus station to reach **Camping Padova ❶**, which has lovely beaches. (☎72 43 55. 23-37kn per person, 18-26kn per tent. Tax 4.50-7.50kn. Registration 4.50kn.) ☒**St. Maria ❷**, Dinka Dokule 6, serves Hungarian specialties in a medieval courtyard. (Entrees 50-90kn. Open daily 10am-2pm and 5pm-midnight.) A **supermarket** neighbors the post office at Dalit 88. (Open daily 6am-10pm). **Postal Code:** 51280.

DALMATIAN COAST

After his last visit to Dalmatia, George Bernard Shaw wrote: "The gods wanted to crown their creation and on the last day they turned tears, stars and the sea breeze into the isles of Kornati." Shaw's words speak to the entire Dalmatian Coast—a stunning seascape of unfathomable beauty set against a backdrop of dramatic mountains. With more than 1100 islands, Dalmatia is not only Croatia's largest archipelago, but also has the cleanest and clearest waters in the Mediterranean.

TROGIR   ☎021

In Trogir (pop. 1500), made up of Trogir and Čiovo Islands, medieval buildings crowd into winding streets and palmed promenades open onto lush parks. The Renaissance **North Gate** on Trogir Island frames the entrance to the **Stari Grad** (old town). **Trg Ivana Pavla,** the central square, contains most sights, including the **Cathedral of St. Lawrence** (Crkva sv. Lovre). Trogir's stone-carving tradition is chronicled in two buildings of the **City Museum of Trogir:** in the **lapidary**, through the arch in front of the North Gate, and in the **convent of St. Nicholas,** off Kohl-Genscher past Trg Ivana Pavla. (Lapidary open M-Sa 9am-1pm and 5-9pm. Convent open M-Sa 8am-12:30pm and 3-7:30pm. Each 10kn, students 5kn.) At the tip of the island lie the remains of the **Fortress of Kamerlengo,** now an open-air cinema. (Open M-Sa 9am-11pm. 10kn, students free. Movies 20kn.) Trogir's best beaches lie on **Čiovo Island,** accessible from Trogir Island by the Čiovski bridge, past Trg Ivana Pavla.

Buses from Zagreb stop in front of the station on the mainland on their way south to Split (30min., 22kn). Local bus #37 also runs to Split (45min., 2-3 per hr., 18kn). Across Čiovski bridge, **Atlas**, Obala kralja Zvonimira 10, has bus schedules and ferry info. (☎88 42 79. Open in summer M-Sa 8am-9pm, Su 8am-noon.) The **tourist office**, Trg Ivana Pavla 2, gives out free maps of the city. (☎88 14 12. Open M-Sa 8am-9pm, Su 8am-noon and 5-7pm.) **Čipko ❸**, Gradska 41, across from the cathedral, arranges private rooms in town. (☎88 15 54. Open daily 8am-8pm. July-Aug. singles 200kn; doubles 330kn; tax 7.50kn. May-June and Sept. singles 150kn; doubles 250kn; tax 5.50kn.) To get to the beach-side hotel **Prenočište Saldun ❶**, Sv. Andrije 1, cross Čiovski bridge and take Put Balana up the hill, keeping right; Saldun is at the top. (☎80 60 53. Call ahead. Singles 76kn; tax 6kn.) **Čiovka** supermarket is next to Atlas. (Open M-Sa 5:30am-9pm, Su 6:30am-8pm.) Lively waterfront cafes line Obala b. Berislavića. **Postal Code:** 21220.

SPLIT   ☎021

With a welter of activities and nightlife, this palatial city by the sea is more a cultural center than a beach resort. The **Stari Grad** (old town), wedged between a high mountain range and palm-lined waterfront, sprawls around a luxurious **palace** where the Roman emperor Diocletian summered when not persecuting Christians. City **cellars** are near the entrance to the palace, across from the taxis on thoroughfare **Obala hrvatskog narodnog preporoda;** turn either way to wander around this haunting labyrinth. (Open M-F 9am-9pm, Sa-Su 10am-6pm. 8kn.) Through the cellars and up the stairs is the open-air **peristyle.** The Catholic **cathedral** to its right is the world's oldest; ironically, it was once Diocletian's mausoleum. The view from atop the adjoining **Bell Tower of St. Dominus** (Zvonik sv. Duje) is incredible. (Cathedral and tower open daily 8:30am-9:30pm. Tower 5kn.) A 25min. walk away along the waterfront, the **⧉Meštrović Gallery** (Galerija Ivana Meštrovića), Šetaliste Ivana Meštrovića 46, gathers works by Croatia's most famous modern sculptor. (Open June-Aug. Tu-Sa 9am-1pm and 5-8pm, Su 9am-2pm; Sept.-May Tu-Sa 10am-4pm, Su 10am-2pm. 15kn, students 10kn.) At night, locals skinny-dip at **Bačvice beach,** the starting point for a strip of waterfront bars.

Buses (☎33 84 83; schedule info 060 32 73 27) run to: Dubrovnik (4½hr., 17 per day, 125kn); Ljubljana (11hr., 1 per day, 260kn); Sarajevo (7½hr., 6 per day, 142kn); and Zagreb (8hr., 2 per hr., 140kn). **Ferries** (☎33 83 33) head from the terminal across from the train and bus stations to Dubrovnik (8hr., 5 per week, 97kn) and Ancona, Italy (10hr., 4 per week, 274kn). From the bus station, follow Obala kneza Domagoja (also called Riva) until it meets Obala hrvatskog narodnog preporoda, which runs roughly east-west. The **tourist office** is at Obala hrv. 12. (☎34 71 00. Open M-F 8am-9pm, Sa 8am-10pm.) Near the train station, the **Daluma Travel Agency,** Obala kneza domagoja 1, helps find private rooms. (☎33 84 84; www.daluma-travel.htnet.hr. May-Oct. singles 150-200kn; doubles 240-300kn; Nov.-Apr. singles 100-120kn/200kn. Open M-F 7am-9pm, Sa 8am-2pm.) To get from the station to the newly renovated **Prenočište Slavija ❹**, Buvinova 2, follow Obala hrv., turn right on Trg Braće Radića, then go right on Mihovilova širina; signs lead up the stairs. (☎34 70 53. Breakfast included. Singles 320-400kn; doubles 460-500kn.) There is a **supermarket** at Svačićeva 4. (Open daily 7am-10pm.) To see one of the best views in Split, at **⧉Jugo Restoran ❷**, Uvala Baluni bb, face the water on Obala hrv. and walk right along the waterfront for 10min., following the curves onto Branimirova Obala; pass the marina, ascend the hill, and follow the signs. (Entrees 30-200kn. Open daily 9am-midnight.) **Postal Code:** 21000.

HVAR ISLAND ☎021

One of the most glorious isles in Europe, the thin, 88km Hvar Island gifts its visitors with breathtaking views of mainland mountains from its own high, rugged hills; below these lies beach enough for all the tourists that swarm here in July and August. From mid-June to early October, the **Hvar Summer Festival** includes outdoor drama performances (30-50kn) in the island's Franciscan monastery and elsewhere. Virtually the only place with a name is the main square, **Trg Sv. Stjepana,** directly below the bus station by the waterfront. From here, facing the sea, take a left along the waterfront to reach the tourist office, ferry terminal, and, after 20min., the less-crowded beaches; a right leads to gravel beaches and the major hotels. Also to the right, stairs lead to a 13th-century **Venetian fortress** with marine archaeological relics. (Open daily 8am-midnight. 10kn.) At the end of Riva past the Jadrolinija office, waterfront ▣**Carpe Diem** has a hip crowd and loud, live DJs. (Open daily 9am-2am.) Nearby, the **Hellish Islands** (Pakleni Otoci) include Palmižana beach, which has sparse sand and a nudist area at the far tip of the cove. (Taxi boats every 30min. 10am-6:30pm, round-trip 20-40kn.)

Ferries run from Split to Hvar's old town (2hr.; June 21-Sept. 9 M-Th 3 per day, F-Su 5 per day; 32kn); from there, **buses** go to Hvar Town (15min., 7 per day, 15kn). Also, directly from Split run a catamaran (1hr., 1 per day, 32kn) and a ferry (2hr., 2 per day, 32kn). To reach the bus station from the marina, walk through Trg Sv. Stjepana, keeping left of the church. **Jadrolinija,** Riva bb, on the left tip of the waterfront, sells ferry tickets. (☎ 74 11 32. Open M-Sa 5:30am-1pm and 3-8pm; Su 8-9am, noon-1pm, and 3-4pm.) The **tourist office,** Trg Sv. Stjepana 16, has island maps (20kn) and bus schedules. (☎ 74 10 59; www.tzhvar.hr. Open M-F 8am-8pm, Sa-Su 8am-1pm and 4-8pm; low season daily 8:30am-noon.) **Pelegrini Tours,** Riva bb, books rooms. (☎ 74 27 43; pelegrini@inet.hr. Open M, W, and F-Sa 7:15am-1pm and 5pm-8pm, Tu and Th 8:30am-1pm and 5-8pm. High season singles and doubles 200-350kn.) "*Sobe*" (private room) signs litter the area down the waterfront from the main square. ▣**Luna ❷,** up the steps from the square to the fortress, has a gorgeous rooftop terrace. (☎ 74 86 95. Open daily noon-3pm and 6pm-midnight). **Postal Code:** 21450.

BRAČ ISLAND: BOL ☎021

Central Dalmatia's largest island, Brač is an ocean-lover's paradise. Most visitors come here for **Zlatni rat,** a peninsula of white pebble beach and emerald waters, just a short walk from the town center of Bol. The 1475 **Dominican Monastery,** on the eastern tip of Bol, displays Tintoretto's altar painting of the Madonna with Child. (Open daily 10am-noon and 5-7pm. 10kn.) The **ferry** from Split docks at Supetar (1hr., 7-13 per day, 23kn). From there, take a **bus** to Bol (1hr., 7-13 per day, 15kn). The last bus back to the ferry leaves at 5:50pm. From the bus station, walk left for 5min. to reach the **tourist office,** Porad bolskich pomorca bb, on the far side of the small marina. (☎ 63 56 38; www.bol.hr.) **Adria Tours,** Obala Vladimira Nazora 28, to the right facing the sea from the bus station, books rooms and rents vehicles. (☎ 63 59 66; www.adria-bol.hr. Rooms July-Aug. 60-170kn. Tax 10kn. 20% surcharge for stays under 4 nights. Cars 400-500kn per day. Small motorcycles 200kn per day. Open daily 8am-9pm.) There are five **campsites** around Bol; the largest is **Kito ❶,** Bračka cesta bb, on the road into town. (☎ 63 55 51. Open May-Sept. 44kn per person, tent included.) **Postal Code:** 21420.

KORČULA ☎020

Within sight of the mainland are the macchia thickets and slender cypresses of Korčula, the birthplace of Marco Polo. Sacred monuments and churches here date from the time of the Apostles. The **Festival of Sword Dances** enlivens the entire island in July-Aug. (www.moreska.hr. 60kn; tickets available from tourist agencies.) **Buses** board ferries to the mainland and head to: Dubrovnik (3½hr., 1 per day, 77kn); Sarajevo (6½hr., 4 per week, 145kn); and Zagreb (11-13hr., 1 per day, 209kn). **Ferries** run to Dubrovnik (3½hr., 5 per week, 67kn) and Split (4½hr., 1 per day, 82kn). To reach the **tourist office,** face the water and walk left along the main street as it curves from the marina; look for the glass building just before the hotel. (Open M-Sa 8am-3pm and 4-8pm, Su 9am-1pm.) Private rooms are the only budget lodgings; it's good to shop around. **Marko Polo,** Biline 5, can arrange rooms. (☎71 54 00; www.korcula.com. Singles 150-188kn; doubles 210-263kn. Open daily 8am-9pm.) ▓**Adio Mare ❷,** Marka Pola bb, serves authentic local specialties. (Entrees 40-80kn. Open M-Sa 5:30pm-midnight, Su 6pm-midnight.) **Postal Code:** 20260.

DUBROVNIK ☎020

George Bernard Shaw once wrote: "Those who seek Paradise on earth should come to Dubrovnik." Nearly scarless despite recent wars, the city continues to draw visitors with azure waters and sunsets just beyond its 14th-century Italian limestone walls. If you make it as far south as Dubrovnik, you might never leave.

▐▞ TRANSPORTATION AND PRACTICAL INFORMATION. Jadrolinija **ferries** (☎41 80 00; www.jadrolinija.hr) depart from opposite Obala S. Radica 40 for Bari, Italy (9hr., 5 per week, 315kn) and Split (8hr., 1 per day, 97kn). **Buses** (☎35 70 88) run from Pt. Republike 19 to: Ljubljana (14hr., 1 per day, 380kn); Sarajevo (6hr., 1 per day, 157kn); Split (4½hr., 16 per day, 125kn); Trieste (15hr., 1 per day, 340kn); and Zagreb (11hr., 8 per day, 180kn). To reach Stari Grad, face away from the station and turn left onto Ante Starčevića; follow it uphill to the Pile Gate (25min.). To reach the ferries from the station, head left and then bear right at the fork (5min.). All local buses *except* #5, 7, and 8 go to the Pile Gate (8kn at kiosks, 10kn from the driver). From there, walk away from Stari Grad to reach the **Tourist Board,** Ante Starčevića 7, for free maps and cheap Internet access. (☎42 75 91; ured.pile@tzdubrovnik.hr. Open June-Sept. M-Sa 8am-8pm; Oct.-May 8am-3pm.) **Turistička Zajednica Grada Dubrovnika,** Cvijete Zuzorić 1/2, 2nd floor, distributes the free but invaluable *City Guide*. (☎32 38 87; www.tzdubrovnik.hr. Open June-Aug. M-F 8am-4pm, Sa 9am-3pm, Su 9am-noon; Sept.-May M-F 8am-4pm.) **Postal Code:** 20108.

▐▌ ACCOMMODATIONS AND FOOD. For two people, a private room tends to be the cheapest and most comfortable option; arrange one through **Atlas ❷,** Lučarica 1, next to St. Blasius's Church. (☎44 25 28; www.atlas-croatia.com. Open June-Aug. M-Sa 8am-9pm, Su 8am-1pm; Sept.-May M-Sa 8am-7pm. Singles 100-150kn; doubles 120-375kn.) For cheaper rooms, try haggling with the locals holding "*sobe*" signs around the ferry and bus terminals. To get to cozy ▓**Begović Boarding House ❷,** Primorska 17, from the bus station, take bus #6 toward Dubrava and tell the driver you want to get off at post office Lapad. Facing the pedestrian walkway, turn right at the intersection. Bear left at the fork and take the first right onto Primorska. (☎43 51 91. Doubles 100-120kn per person.) Call ahead and Sado, the hospitable owner, will pick you up from the bus or ferry terminal. The **HI Youth Hostel ❶,** b. Josipa Jelačića 15/17, is one of the best in Croatia. With your back to the bus station, turn left onto Ante Starčevića, turn right at ul. Pera Rudenjaka, and left at the end of the street onto b. Josipa Jelačića. Look for the hidden HI sign on your left immediately after #17. (☎42 32 41. Dorms 75-100kn, 10kn extra without HI membership.) ▓**Lokarda Peskarija ❶,** on Na Ponti bb, has the freshest and cheapest seafood in Stari Grad. From the bell tower, turn right out on Pred Dvorum and take the first left out of the city

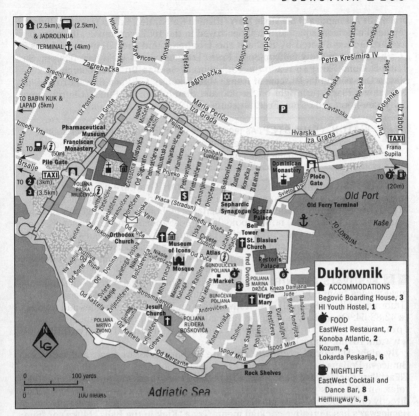

Dubrovnik

▲ ACCOMMODATIONS
Begović Boarding House, **3**
HI Youth Hostel, **1**

🍴 FOOD
EastWest Restaurant, **7**
Konoba Atlantic, **2**
Kozum, **4**
Lokarda Peskarija, **6**

🍸 NIGHTLIFE
EastWest Cocktail and
Dance Bar, **8**
Hemingway's, **5**

CROATIA

walls. (☎32 47 50. Open daily 8am-midnight. Seafood 30-35kn.) ▨**Konoba Atlantic ❷**, Kardinala Stopinga 42, dishes up some of the best pasta in Croatia (49-160kn). Take bus #6 to post office Labad, walk straight on the walkway, and then turn right on the staircase just before the Hotel Kompas, which will take you up to the restaurant. (☎098 185 96 25. Open daily noon-11pm.) See the sun set over the Adriatic from the sprawling outdoor terrace of **EastWest Restaurant ❸**, on Frana Supila bb. From the bell tower, turn left onto Svetog Dominika, bear right after the footbridge and continue along Frana Supila, descending the stairs next to the post office. (☎41 22 20. Open daily 11am-midnight.) Small supermarket **Kozum** faces the open-air market on Gundulićeva Poljana. (Open M-Sa 7am-10pm, Su 8am-9pm.) **Kerum**, Kralja Tomislava 7, has a more extensive selection. (Open M-Sa 7am-10pm, Su 8am-9pm.)

🔳 **SIGHTS. Stari Grad** (old town) packs in the churches, museums, monasteries, palaces, and fortresses; the most popular sights are along **Placa**. The entrance to the staggering 2km-long city walls (*gradske zidine*) lies just inside the **Pile Gate**, on the left. Go at dusk to be dazzled by the sunset. (Open daily May-Oct. 9am-7pm; Nov.-Apr. 10am-3pm. 30kn.) The 14th-century **Franciscan Monastery** (Franjevački samostan), next to the city wall entrance on Placa, houses the oldest pharmacy in Europe (est. 1317) and a related museum. (Open daily 9am-6pm. 10kn.) The **Cathe-**

dral of the Assumption of the Virgin Mary (Riznica Katedrale), Kneza Damjana Jude 1, replaced a Romanesque cathedral destroyed in the 1667 earthquake. Its reliquary has artifacts collected by Richard the Lionheart and the "Diapers of Jesus." (Cathedral open daily 6:30am-8pm. Free. Treasury open M-Sa 8am-5:30pm, Su 11am-5:30pm. 7kn.) To reach the 19th-century **Serbian Orthodox Church** (Pravoslavna Crkva) and its **Museum of Icons** (Muzej Ikona), Od Puča 8, walk from Pile Gate down Placa, turn right on Široka, and then left on Od Puča. (Church open daily 8am-noon and 5-7pm. Free. Museum open M-Sa 9am-1pm. 10kn.)

WATCH YOUR STEP. As tempting as it may be to stroll in the hills above Dubrovnik or wander the unpaved paths on Lopud, both may still be laced with **landmines.** Stick to the paved paths and beach.

BEACHES. Outside the fortifications of Stari Grad are a number of **rock shelves** for sunning and swimming. For a surreal seaside experience, take a swim in the cove at the foot of the old **Hotel Libertas.** The hotel was damaged during the war and then abandoned; now it looks like a post-apocalyptic movie set. Ferries shuttle daily from the Old Port (20min.; 9am and every 30min. 10am-6pm; round-trip 35kn) to the nearby island of **Lokrum,** which has a nude beach; once there, look for the FKK signs. More modest travelers can stroll through the **nature preserve.**

FESTIVALS AND NIGHTLIFE. Dubrovnik becomes a party scene and cultural mecca from mid-July to mid-August during the **Dubrovnik Summer Festival** (Dubrovački Ijetni Festival). The **festival office** on Placa has schedules and tickets. (☎42 88 64. Open daily during the festival 8:30am-9pm, tickets 9am-2pm and 3-7pm. 50-300kn.) In low season, contact the head office. (☎32 34 00; www.dubrovnik-festival.hr.)

By night Dubrovnik's crowds gravitate to bars in Stari Grad and cafes on Buničeva Poljana, where live bands and street performers turn up in summer. At **EastWest Cocktail and Dance Bar,** Frana Supila bb, dressed-to-impress clientele relax on the bar's plush white divans, while hipsters recline on leather sofas directly on the beach. (Beer 12-30kn. Mixed drinks 33-78kn. Open daily 8am-3am.) **Hemingway's** has a creative cocktail menu. Try a "Kick in the Balls" (40kn) or "She is Paying" (48kn) on the patio, with a view of Dubrovnik. (Open daily 10am-1am.)

DAYTRIP FROM DUBROVNIK: LOPUD ISLAND. Less than an hour from Dubrovnik is Lopud, an enchanting island of the Elafiti Archipelago. The tiny village is dotted with white buildings, chapels, and parks stretching along the island's waterfront (*obala*). A short walk along the shore leads to an abandoned **monastery,** which can be explored—just be careful of crumbling floors. The island's highlight is its **beach,** Plaža Šunj. Arguably the best beach in Croatia, this cove has one thing that most of the Dalmatian Coast lacks: sand.

Ferries run from Dubrovnik to the Elafiti islands (50min.; in summer M-Sa 4 per day, Su 1 per day; round-trip 22kn). The beach is on the opposite side of the island from the village. Facing the water, walk left for 5min. and turn left onto the road between the high wall and the palm park; look for the Konoba Barbara sign and continue over the hill for 15min., keeping right when the path forks.

CZECH REPUBLIC
(ČESKÁ REPUBLIKA)

From the Holy Roman Empire through the USSR, the Czechs have long stood at a crossroads of international affairs. Unlike many of their neighbors, the citizens of this small, landlocked country have rarely resisted as armies marched across their borders, often choosing to fight with words instead of weapons. As a result, Czech towns and cities are among the best-preserved and most beautiful in Europe. Today, the Czechs face a different kind of invasion, as enamored tourists sweep in to savor the magnificent capital, the welcoming locals, and the world's best beers.

DISCOVER CZECH REPUBLIC: SUGGESTED ITINERARIES

THREE DAYS If you have three days, spend the bulk of your time in **Prague** (p. 260) exploring the Baroque and Art Nouveau architecture of the Staré Město. Take a daytrip out to see the bone church in **Kutná Hora** (p. 274), where human femurs and crania hang from chandeliers.

TEN DAYS Spend the first three days in

Prague before heading south to **ČeskýKrumlov** (1 day; p. 278). Stop in to see the Pilsner-Urquell brewery in **Plzeň** (1 day; p. 277) en route to **Karlovy Vary** (2 days; p. 275), known for its summer film festival and for its *Becherovka*, an herb liqueur with "curative powers" rivaled only by those of the local hot springs. Spend your last day back in **Prague**.

ESSENTIALS

WHEN TO GO

Since summer tourists mob the country, spring and fall are the best times to visit, although spring can be rainy. Winters are cold, damp, and snowy.

258 ■ CZECH REPUBLIC (ČESKÁ REPUBLIKA)

DOCUMENTS AND FORMALITIES

VISAS. Citizens of Australia, Canada, Ireland, New Zealand, and the US may visit the Czech Republic without a visa for up to 90 days, UK citizens for up to 180 days. To check a specific country's policy, consult the regional Czech Embassy. Travelers on a visa must **register** with the Czech Immigration Police within three days of arrival; hotels register their guests automatically.

EMBASSIES. All foreign embassies are in Prague (p. 260). Czech embassies at home include: **Australia,** 8 Culgoa Circuit, O'Malley, Canberra, ACT 2606 (☎ 02 6290 1386; www.mfa.cz/canberra); **Canada,** 251 Cooper St., Ottawa, ON K2P OG2 (613-562-3875; www.mfa.cz/ottawa); **Ireland,** 57 Northumberland Rd., Ballsbridge, Dublin 4 (01 668 1135; www.mfa.cz/dublin); **UK,** 26 Kensington Palace Gardens, London W8 4QY (020 7243 1115; www.mfa.cz/london); **US,** 3900 Spring of Freedom St. NW, Washington, D.C. 20008 (202-274-9100; www.mzv.cz/washington).

TRANSPORTATION

BY PLANE AND BY TRAIN. Many major carriers fly into Prague's Ruzyně Airport, but the best way to enter and travel through the Czech Republic is by train. **Eastrail** is accepted, but **Eurail** is only valid up to the Czech border. The fastest international trains are EuroCity and InterCity (*expresní,* marked in blue on schedules). Rychlík, or *zrychlený vlak,* are fast domestic trains (marked in red). Avoid slow *osobní* trains (marked in white). Seat reservations (*místenka;* 10Kč) are recommended on express and international trains and for all first-class seating.

BY BUS. Buses are efficient and convenient for domestic travel, but schedules are often confusing. **ČSAD** runs national and international bus lines. Consult the timetables posted at stations or buy your own schedule (25Kč) from kiosks.

BY CAR AND BY TAXI. Roads in the Czech Republic are well-maintained and **roadside assistance** is usually available. In addition to an International Driving Permit, US citizens must have a US driver's license. **Taxis** are a safe means of travel, though many tourists complain of exorbitant rates, especially in Prague. Phoning a taxi company is generally more affordable than flagging a cab on the street.

BY THUMB. Although it is a common way for young people to travel in the Czech Republic, *Let's Go* does not recommend hitchhiking.

TOURIST SERVICES AND MONEY

EMERGENCY	Police: ☎ 158. Ambulance: ☎ 155. Fire: ☎ 150.

TOURIST OFFICES. CKM (☎ 222 721 595; www.ckm-praha.cz), a national student tourist agency, books hostel beds and issues ISIC and HI cards. **Municipal tourist offices** provide info on sights and events, maintain lists of accommodations, and often book rooms.

MONEY. The Czech unit of currency is the **koruna** (crown; Kč), plural *koruny.* Banks offer good exchange rates; **Komerční banka** and **Česká spořitelna** are common chains. **ATMs,** which have the best rates, are everywhere; look for the red-and-black *Bankomat* signs. Traveler's checks can be exchanged almost everywhere, though rarely without commission. MasterCard and Visa are accepted at most high-priced establishments, but rarely at hostels. To **tip,** add 10-20% to the cost of your meal and tell the waiter the new amount; simply leaving *koruny* on the table is considered rude.

BUSINESS HOURS. Banks are usually open Monday to Friday 8am to 4pm, shops Monday to Friday 9am to 5pm and Saturday 9am to noon. Almost all museums and galleries close on Mondays.

CZECH KORUNY (Kč) AS OF AUGUST 2004		
AUS$1 = 18.53Kč	10Kč = AUS$0.54
CDN$1 = 19.74Kč	10Kč = CDN$0.51
EUR€1 = 31.68Kč	10Kč = EUR€0.32
NZ$1 = 17.20Kč	10Kč = NZ$0.58
UK£1 = 46.94Kč	10Kč = UK£0.21
US$1 = 25.60Kč	10Kč = US$0.39

COMMUNICATION

PHONE CODES	**Country code: 420. International dialing prefix: 00.** From outside the Czech Republic, dial int'l dialing prefix (see inside back cover) + 420 + city code + local number.

TELEPHONES AND INTERNET ACCESS. Card-operated phones (175Kč per 50 units; 320Kč per 100 units) are simpler to use than coin phones. **Phone cards** are sold at most *Tábaks* and *Trafika* (convenience stores). Calls run 8Kč per minute to Australia, Canada, the UK, and the US; and 12Kč per minute to New Zealand. Dial ☎1181 for English info or dial 0800 12 34 56 for the international operator. International access codes include: **AT&T** (☎00 420 00 101); **British Telecom** (00 420 04 412); **Canada Direct** (00 420 00 151); **MCI** (☎00 420 00 112); **Sprint** (00 420 87 187); **Telkom Telstra Australia** (00 420 06 101). **Internet** access is readily available throughout the Czech Republic, with rates around 2Kč per minute.

MAIL. The Czech Republic has an efficient postal system. A postcard to the US costs 12Kč, to Europe 9Kč. When sending by airmail, stress that you want it to go on a *letecky* (plane). Go to the customs office to send international packages heavier than 2kg. Address mail to be held as in the following example: First name SURNAME, *Poste Restante*, Jindřišská 14, 1 110 00 Praha, CZECH REPUBLIC.

LANGUAGES. Czech is a Western Slavic language, most closely related to Slovak and Polish. English is widely understood, and German phrases may be useful, especially in the western spas. Russian is also commonly understood but is not always welcome. For Czech words and phrases, see p. 1058.

ACCOMMODATIONS AND CAMPING

CZECH REPUBLIC	❶	❷	❸	❹	❺
ACCOMMODATIONS	under 320Kč	320-500Kč	501-800Kč	801-1200Kč	over 1200Kč

Hostels are consistently clean and safe; **university dorms** are the cheapest lodgings in July and August, with two- to four-bed rooms running 250-400Kč per person. **Pensions** are the next most affordable option; expect to pay 600Kč, including breakfast. **Hotels** start at around 1000Kč. From June to September reserve rooms at least one week ahead in Prague, Český Krumlov, and Brno. If you can't keep a reservation, always call to cancel. **Private homes,** indicated by *Zimmer frei* signs at train stations, are not nearly as popular (or as cheap) as in the rest of Eastern Europe. **Campgrounds** are strewn throughout the countryside, though most are open only mid-May to September.

FOOD AND DRINK

CZECH REPUBLIC	❶	❷	❸	❹	❺
FOOD	under 80Kč	80-110Kč	111-150Kč	151-200Kč	over 200Kč

Thick, pasty *knedlíky* dough is a staple of Czech meals. The national meal, known as *vepřo-knedlo-zelo*, consists of *vepřové* (roast pork), *knedlíky*, and *zelí* (sauerkraut). If you're in a hurry, try *párky* (frankfurters) or *sýr* (cheese) from food stands. Vegetarian restaurants serving *bez masa* (meatless) dishes are uncommon; at most restaurants, vegetarian options will be limited to *smažený sýr* (fried cheese) or *saláty* (salad). Ask for *káva espresso* rather than *káva* to avoid the mud that Czechs call coffee. The most beloved dessert is *koláč*—a tart with poppy-seed jam or sweet cheese. *Plzeňský Prazdroj* (Pilsner Urquell) is the most prominent beer, though many Czechs are loyal to *Budvar* or *Krušovice*.

HOLIDAYS AND FESTIVALS

Holidays: New Year's Day (Jan. 1); Easter (Mar. 25-27); May Day (May 1); Liberation Day (May 8); Cyril and Methodius Day (July 5); Jan Hus Day (July 6); St. Wenceslas Day (Sept. 28); Independence Day (Oct. 28); Day of Student Struggle for Freedom and Democracy (Nov. 17); Christmas (Dec. 24-25).

Festivals: The Spring Festival (mid-May to early June) attracts international classical music lovers to Prague. In June, Český Krumlov hosts the boisterous Five-Petaled Rose Festival, which features music, dancing, and a jousting tournament. Masopust is a version of Mardi Gras celebrated across the country from Epiphany to Ash Wednesday.

FACTS AND FIGURES: CZECH REPUBLIC

Official Name: Czech Republic.

Capital: Prague.

Major Cities: Brno, Ostrava.

Population: 10,250,000.

Land Area: 80,000 sq. km.

Time Zone: GMT +1.

Language: Czech.

Religion: Roman Catholic (40%), Atheist (40%), Protestant (5%), other (15%).

PRAGUE (PRAHA)

According to legend, Countess Libuše stood above the Vltava and declared, "I see a grand city whose glory will touch the stars." Medieval kings, benefactors, and architects fulfilled that prophecy, building soaring cathedrals and lavish palaces that reflected the status of Prague (pop. 1,200,000) as capital of the Holy Roman Empire. Prague's maze of alleys spawned legends of demons and occult forces, giving this "city of dreams" the dark mystique that inspired Franz Kafka's tales of paranoia. Yet since the fall of the Iron Curtain, hordes of foreigners have flooded the city; in summer, tourists pack streets so tightly that crowd-surfing seems a viable method of transportation. Walk a few blocks away from the major sights, and you'll be a lone backpacker among cobblestone alleys and looming churches.

▣ INTERCITY TRANSPORTATION

Flights: Ruzyně Airport (☎220 111 111), 20km northwest of the city. Take bus #119 to Metro A: Dejvická (daily 5am-midnight; 12Kč, luggage 6Kč per bag); buy tickets from kiosks or machines. **Airport buses** run by **Cedaz** (☎220 114 296) collect travelers from metro stops (5:30am-9:30pm every 30min.; Nám. Republiky 90Kč, Dejvická 60Kč). **Taxis** to the airport are expensive (400-600Kč); try to settle on a price before departing.

Central Prague

♠ ACCOMMODATIONS
Apple Hostel, **9**
Dlouhá 33, **3**
Dům U Krále Jiřího, **19**
Hostel Týn, **8**
Husova 3, **20**
U Lilie, **16**

● FOOD
Cafe Bambus, **5**
Jáchymka, **7**
Klub architektů, **22**
Roma Due, **17**
U Špirků, **14**

☕ NIGHTLIFE AND CAFES
Bakeshop Praha, **2**
Bugsy's Bar, **6**
Cafe Ebel, **11, 18**
Cafe Marquis de Sade, **13**
Karlovy Lázně, **15**
Kavárna Imperial, **10**
Kozička, **4**
Roxy, **1**
U staré paní, **21**
Ungelt, **12**

Trains: Domestic ☎221 111 122, international 224 615 249; www.vlak.cz. Prague has 4 main terminals. **Hlavní nádraží** (☎224 615 786; Metro C: Hlavní nádraží) and **Nádraží Holešovice** (☎224 624 632; Metro C: Nádraží Holešovice) are the largest and cover most international service. Domestic trains leave from **Masarykovo nádraží** (☎840 112 113; Metro B: Nám. Republiky), on the corner of Hybernská and Havlíčkova, and from **Smíchovské nádraží** (☎972 226 150; Metro B: Smíchovské nádraží). International trains run to: **Berlin** (5hr., 5 per day, 1400Kč); **Budapest** (7-9hr., 4 per day, 1400Kč); **Kraków** (7hr., 4 per day, 874Kč); **Moscow** (31hr., 1 per day, 3000Kč); **Munich** (7hr., 5 per day, 1650Kč); **Vienna** (4½hr., 6 per day, 925Kč); **Warsaw** (9½hr., 3 per day, 1290Kč). **BIJ Wasteels** (☎224 641 954; www.wasteels.cz), on the 2nd fl. of Hlavní nádraží, to the right of the stairs, sells discounted international tickets to those under 26; they also book couchettes and bus tickets. Open M-F 9am-7pm, Sa 9am-4pm. Wasteels tickets are also available from the **Czech Railways Travel Agency** (☎224 239 464) at Nádraží Holešovice. Open M-F 9am-5pm, Sa-Su 8am-4pm.

Buses: Schedule info ☎900 149 044; www.vlak-bus.cz. Open daily 6am-9pm. The state-run **ČSAD** (Česká státní automobilová doprava; Czech National Bus Transport; ☎257 319 016) has several bus terminals. The biggest is **Florenc**, Křižíkova 4 (☎900 149 044). Metro B or C: Florenc. Info office open daily 6am-9pm. Buy tickets in advance. To: **Berlin** (7hr., 1 per day, 850Kč); **Budapest** (8hr., 1 per day, 1550Kč); **Paris** (14hr., 3 per day, 2200Kč); **Vienna** (5hr., 1 per day, 600Kč). 10% ISIC discount. The **Tourbus** office (☎224 218 680; www.eurolines.cz), at the terminal, sells tickets for **Eurolines** and airport buses. Open M-F 7am-7pm, Sa 8am-7pm, Su 9am-7pm.

✦ ORIENTATION

Shouldering the river **Vltava,** greater Prague is a mess of suburbs and maze-like streets. Fortunately, nearly everything of interest to the traveler lies within the compact downtown. The Vltava runs south-northeast through central Prague, separating **Staré Město** (old town) and **Nové Město** (new town) from **Malá Strana** (lesser side). On the right bank of the river, **Staroměstské Náměstí** (Old Town Square) is the heart of Prague. From the square, the elegant **Pařížská ulice** (Paris Street) leads north into **Josefov,** the old Jewish ghetto in which only six synagogues and the Old Jewish Cemetery remain. South of Staré Město, the more modern Nové Město houses **Václavské Náměstí** (Wenceslas Square), the commercial core of the city. West of Staroměstské nám., the picturesque **Karlův most** (Charles Bridge) spans the Vltava, connecting Staré Město with **Malostranské náměstí** (Lesser Town Square). **Pražský Hrad** (Prague Castle) looks over Malostranské nám. from **Hradčany** hill.

Prague's **train station,** Hlavní nádraží, and Florenc **bus station** lie northeast of Václavské nám. All train and bus terminals are on or near the excellent metro system. To get to Staroměstské nám., take the Metro A line to Staroměstská and head down Kaprova away from the river. Kiosks and bookstores sell an indexed *plán města* (map), which is essential for newcomers to the city.

▐ LOCAL TRANSPORTATION

Public Transportation: Buy **metro, tram,** or **bus** tickets from newsstands, *tabák* kiosks, machines in stations, or **DP** (*Dopravní Podnik;* transport authority) kiosks. The basic 8Kč ticket is good for 15min. on a tram or 4 stops on the metro; the 12Kč ticket is valid for 1hr. during the day, with unlimited connections between buses, trams, and metro in any single direction. Large bags require an extra 6Kč ticket. Validate tickets in machines above the escalators or face a 400Kč fine. The 3 metro lines run daily 5am-midnight: A is green on maps, B is yellow, and C is red. **Night trams** #51-58 and **buses** #502-514 and 601 run all night after the last metro and cover the same areas as day trams and buses (every 30min.; look for dark blue signs with white lettering at bus stops). The 24hr. tourist office in the Old Town Hall sells **multi-day passes** valid for the entire network. (1-day 70Kč, 3-day 200Kč, 7-day 250Kč.)

Taxis: Radiotaxi (☎272 731 848) or **AAA** (☎140 14). 30Kč flat rate plus 22Kč per km and 4Kč per min. waiting. Hail a cab anywhere on the street, but call one of the above numbers to avoid getting ripped off.

 To avoid the taxi scams that run rampant through the city, always ask for a receipt *("Prosím, dejte mi paragon")* with distance traveled and price paid.

◪ PRACTICAL INFORMATION

TOURIST AND FINANCIAL SERVICES

Tourist Offices: Green "i"s mark tourist agencies, which book rooms and sell maps. **Pražská Informační Služba** (PIS; Prague Info Service; ☎12 444; www.pis.cz) is in the Old Town Hall. Branches at Na příkopě 20 and Hlavní nádraží (summer M-F 9am-7pm, Sa-Su 9am-5pm; low season M-F 9am-6pm, Sa 9am-3pm), as well as in the tower by the Charles Bridge. (Open daily Apr.-Oct. 10am-6pm, closed Nov.-Mar.)

Budget Travel: CKM, Manesova 77 (☎222 721 595; www.ckm-praha.cz). Metro A: Jiřího z Poděbrad. Budget air tickets for those under 26. Also books accommodations (dorms from 250Kč). Open M-Th 10am-6pm, F 10am-4pm.

Passport Office: Foreigner Police Headquarters, Olšanská 2 (☎974 811 111). Metro A: Flora. From the metro, turn right on Jičínská with the cemetery on your right and turn right again on Olšanská. Or take tram #9 from Václavské nám. toward Spojovací and get off at Olšanská. For a **visa extension,** get a 90Kč stamp inside. Line up at doors #2-12, and prepare to wait up to 2hr. Little English spoken. Open M-Tu and Th 7:30-11:30am and 12:15-3pm, W 8am-12:15pm and 1-5pm, F 7.30-11:30am.

Embassies: Canada, Mickiewiczova 6 (☎272 101 800; www.canada.cz). Metro A: Hradčanská. Open M-F 8:30am-12:30pm and 1:30-4:30pm. **Ireland,** Tržiště 13 (☎257 530 061). Metro A: Malostranská. Open M-F 9:30am-12:30pm and 2:30-4:30pm. **UK,** Thunovská 14 (☎257 402 111; www.britain.cz). Metro A: Malostranská. Open M-F 9am-noon. **US,** Tržiště 15 (☎257 530 663; after-hours emergency ☎253 12 00; www.usembassy.cz). Metro A: Malostranská. Open M-F 8am-4:30pm. **Australia,** Klimentskà 10 (☎296 578 350) and **New Zealand,** Dykova 19 (☎222 514 672) have consuls, but citizens should contact the UK embassy in an emergency.

Currency Exchange: Exchange counters are everywhere but their rates vary wildly. Never change money on the street. **Chequepoints** are convenient and open late, but usually charge a large commission or fee. **Komerční banka,** Na příkopě 33 (☎222 432 111), buys notes and checks for a 2% commission. Open M-W 9am-6pm, Th-F 9am-5pm. **ATMs** *(Bankomats)* abound and can offer the best rates, but often charge large fees.

American Express: Václavské nám. 56 (☎222 800 224). Metro A or C: Muzeum. AmEx **ATM** outside. Grants MC/V cash advances for a 3% commission. Western Union services available. Open daily 9am-7pm. **Branches** on Mostecká 12 (☎257 313 638; open daily 9:30am-7:30pm), Celetná 17 (☎/fax 222 481 205; open daily 8:30am-7:15pm), and Staroměstské nám. 5 (☎224 818 388; open daily 9am-7:30pm).

LOCAL SERVICES

Luggage Storage: Lockers in all train and bus stations take two 5Kč coins. If these are full or if you need to store your cargo longer than 24hr., use the luggage offices to the left in the basement of **Hlavní nádraží** (15-30Kč per day; open 24hr.) or halfway up the stairs at **Florenc** (30Kč per day; open daily 5am-11pm).

Laundromat: Laundry Kings, Dejvická 16 (☎233 343 743), Metro A: Hradčanská. Exit metro to Dejvická, cross the street, and turn left. Internet access 55Kč per 30min. Wash 70Kč per 6kg, dry 15Kč per 8min. Open M-F 6am-10pm, Sa-Su 8am-10pm.

EMERGENCY AND COMMUNICATION

Medical Assistance: Na Homolce (Hospital for Foreigners), Roentgenova 2 (☎257 272 146, after hours 257 211 111; www.homolka.cz). Bus #168 and 184. Open M-F 8am-4pm. 24hr. emergency service. **American Medical Center,** Janovského 48 (☎220 807 756). Major foreign insurance accepted. On call 24hr. Appointments M-F 9am-4pm. Average consultation 50-200Kč.

24hr. pharmacy: U. Lékárna Andwla, Štefánikova 6 (☎257 320 918, after hours ☎257 320 194). Metro B: Anděl. For after-hours service, press the button marked *"Pohotovost"* to the left of the main door.

Telephones: Phone cards sell for 175Kč per 50 units and 350Kč per 100 units at kiosks, post offices, and some exchange places. Don't let kiosks rip you off.

Internet Access: Prague is an Internet nirvana. ■ **Bohemia Bagel,** Masna 2 (www.bohemiabagel.cz). Metro A: Staroměstská. 1.80Kč per min. Open M-F 7am-midnight, Sa-Su 8am-midnight. **Branch** at Újezd 16. Open daily 9am-midnight. **Cafe Net,** Havelská 27. Metro A: Staroměstská. Full bar. Internet 20Kč per 15min. Open daily 10am-10pm.

Post Office: Jindřišská 14 (☎221 131 445). Metro A: Můstek. Airmail to the US takes 7-10 days. Open daily 2am-midnight. For *Poste Restante,* address mail to be held as in the following example: First name SURNAME, Poste Restante, Jindřišská 14, Praha 1 110 00, CZECH REPUBLIC.

⌐ ACCOMMODATIONS AND CAMPING

Although hotel prices are through the roof, rates in the glutted hostel market have stabilized at around 300-600Kč per night. Reservations are a must at hotels, which can be booked solid months in advance; they are also a good idea at the few hostels that accept them. Most accommodations have 24hr. reception and require check-out by 10am. A growing number of Prague residents rent affordable rooms.

ACCOMMODATIONS AGENCIES

Apartments go for 600-1200Kč per day, depending on proximity to the city center. If you don't want to bargain on the street, try a **private agency.** Ask where the nearest bus or metro stop is, and don't pay until you know what you're getting; ask for details in writing. Some travel agencies also book lodgings (p. 263).

HOSTELS

If you tote a backpack in Hlavní nádraží or Holešovice, you will most likely be approached by hostel runners offering cheap beds. Many of these hostels are university dorms that students vacate from June to August, and often you'll be offered free transportation. These rooms are convenient options for those arriving in the middle of the night without reservations. If you prefer more than just a place to sleep, smaller establishments are a safer bet. It's a good idea to call as soon as you know your plans, even if only the night before or the morning of your arrival when hostel owners know who's checking out that day. In Prague, the staff typically speaks English, and hostels rarely have curfews.

STARÉ MĚSTO

Dlouhá 33, Dlouhá 33 (☎224 826 662). Metro B: Nám. Republiky. Follow Revoluční toward the river, turn left on Dlouhá. Unbeatable location in the same building as the Roxy (p. 273). Book 2-3 weeks in advance in summer. Dorms 370-430Kč; doubles 1240Kč; triples 1440Kč. ISIC discount 40Kč. MC/V. ❷

Apple Hostel, Krádlodvorská 16 (☎224 231 050; www.applehostel.cz). Metro B: Nám. Republiky. At the corner of Revoluční and Nám. Republiky. Social hostel with a helpful staff and prime location. Breakfast included. Internet available. Mar.-Oct. dorms 360-450Kč, Nov.-Feb. 300-350Kč; Singles 1950Kč/1150Kč; doubles 1240Kč/1040Kč. ❷

Husova 3, (☎222 220 078), in Staré Město. Metro B: Národní třída. Turn right on Spálená (which becomes Na Perštýně after Národní), and again on Husova. Quiet location in the middle of Staré Město. Open July-Aug. Dorms 450Kč; doubles 620Kč. ❷

Hostel Týn, Týnská 19 (☎/fax 224 828 519), in Staré Město. Metro A: Staroměstská. From Old Town Sq., head down Dlouhá, bear right at Masná, then right onto Týnská. A quiet getaway with immaculate facilities. Dorms 400Kč; doubles 1100Kč. ❷

NOVÉ MĚSTO AND VINOHRADY

Hostel U Melounu, Ke Karlovu 7 (☎224 918 322). Metro C: I. P. Pavlova. Follow Sokolská and go right on Na Bojišt then left onto Ke Karlovu. A historic building with great facilities. Breakfast included. Dorms 380Kč; singles 540Kč; doubles 900Kč. ❷

Hostel Advantage, Sokolská 11-13 (☎224 914 062; www.advantagehostel.cz). Metro C: IP Pavlova. From the metro, take the stairs on the left leading to Ječná, take a left onto Sokolská; the hostel will be 100m down on your right. This beautifully cared for hostel has simple rooms in a homey atmosphere. Bathrooms sparkle. Breakfast included. Dorms 400Kč; doubles 500Kč. 10% ISIC discount. MC/V. ❷

Hostel Elf, Husitská 11 (☎222 540 963). From Metro C: Hlavní nadrazi, turn left through the park, then cross the tram tracks, and turn right, then immediately left. Cross the street and turn left onto Husitska. The hostel is on the left, near the station. Spacious rooms and a fully equipped kitchen. Bring a lock for cabinets. Breakfast included. 9-bed dorms 290Kč; singles 700Kč, with private bath 1000Kč; doubles 840Kč/1200Kč. ❷

OUTSIDE THE CENTER

Hostel Boathouse, Lodnická 1 (☎241 770 051), south of the city center. Take tram #21 from Nářodni south toward Sídliště. Get off at Černý Kůň (20min.), go down the ramp to the left, and follow the yellow signs. Social atmosphere and caring staff generate a carefree atmosphere. Breakfast included. Dorms 300-340Kč. ❶

Penzion v podzámčí, V podzámčí 27 (☎241 444 609; www.sleepinprague.com), south of the city center. From Metro C: Budějovická, take bus #192 to the 3rd stop (Nad Rybníky), by request only. Kitchen and laundry facilities. Dorms Sept.-June 310Kč, July-Aug. 330Kč; doubles 690Kč/790Kč; triples 960Kč/1080Kč. 30Kč student discount. ❶

Welcome Hostel, Zíkova 13 (☎224 320 202; www.bed.cz). Metro A: Dejvická. Cheap, tidy, and convenient university dorm. Near airport shuttle stop. Singles 400Kč; doubles 540Kč. 10% ISIC discount. DC/MC/V. ❷

Welcome Hostel at Strahov Complex, Vaníčkova 7 (☎224 320 202), outside the center. Take bus #217 or 149 from Metro A: Dejvická to Koleje Strahov. Reception in Block 3. Basic rooms in high-rise dorms near Prague Castle. Not convenient, but there's always space. Open July-Sept. Singles 300Kč; doubles 440Kč. 10% ISIC discount. ❶

CZECH REPUBLIC

HOTELS AND PENSIONS

As tourists colonize Prague, hotels are upgrading their services and their prices; budget hotels are now quite scarce. Call several months ahead to book a room in summer and confirm by fax with a credit card.

▓ **Dům U krále Jiřího,** Liliová 10 (☎222 220 925). Metro A: Staroměstská. Exit onto Nám. Jana Palacha, walk down Křížovnická toward the water, and turn left onto Karlova; Liliová is on the right. All rooms with private bath. Breakfast included. Apr.-Oct. singles 1800Kč; doubles 3100Kč. Nov.-Mar. singles 1500Kč; doubles 2700Kč. AmEx/MC/V. ❺

U Lilie, Liliová 15 (☎222 220 432; www.pensionulilie.cz), in Staré Město. Metro A: Staroměstská. See directions for Dům U krále Jiřího (above). Lovely courtyard. Breakfast included. Singles with showers 1850Kč; doubles 2150-2800Kč. ❺

Pension Museum, Mezibranská 15 (☎296 325 186). Metro C: Muzeum. From the metro, turn right on Mezibranská and walk up the hill. This luxurious B&B near Wenceslas Sq. has elegant rooms with TV and bath. Breakfast included. Apr.-Dec. singles 2240Kč; doubles 2650Kč. Jan.-Mar. 1450Kč; doubles 1800Kč. AmEx/DC/MC/V. ❺

Pension Unitas/Cloister Inn, Bartolomějská 9 (☎224 221 802; www.unitas.cz), in Nové Město. Metro B: Národní třída. Cross Národní, head up Na Perštýně away from Tesco, and turn left on Bartolomějská. Renovated rooms in the cells of the former Communist prison where Václav Havel was incarcerated. Breakfast included. Dorms 400Kč; singles 1200Kč; doubles 1500Kč; triples 1950Kč. ❹

CAMPING

Campsites can be found on the Vltava islands as well as on the outskirts of Prague. Bungalows must be reserved in advance, but tent space is generally available without prior notice. Tourist offices sell a guide to sites near the city (15Kč).

Sokol Troja, Trojská 171 (☎/fax 233 542 908), north of the center in the Troja district. Metro C: Nádraží Holešovice. Take bus #112 to Kazanka. Similar places line the road. July-Aug. 130Kč per person, 90-180Kč per tent; Oct.-June 70-150Kč per tent. Private rooms available. July-Aug. singles 320Kč; doubles 640Kč. Oct.-June 290Kč/580Kč. ❶

Caravan Park, Císařská louka 599 (☎257 318 681), on the Císařská louka peninsula. Metro B: Smíchovské nádraží, then take any of the buses numbered in the 300sto Lihovar. Alternatively, a ferry service leaves every hr. on the hour from the small landing 1 block from Smíchovské nádraží (10Kč). Small, tranquil campground on the banks of the Vltava. 95Kč per person, 90-140Kč per tent. ❶

◘ FOOD

The nearer you are to the center, the more you'll pay. Away from the center, a meal of pork, cabbage, dumplings, and a half-liter of beer costs about 50Kč. You will be charged for everything the waiter brings to the table; check your bill carefully. Most restaurants accept only cash. **Tesco,** Národní třída 26, right next to Metro B: Národní třída, has groceries. (Open M-F 8am-9pm, Sa 9am-8pm, Su 10am-8pm.) Look for the **daily market** in Staré Město where Havelská and Melantrichova intersect. After a night out, grab a *párek v rohlíku* (hot dog) or a *smažený sýr* (fried cheese sandwich) from a Václavské nám. vendor.

RESTAURANTS

STARÉ MĚSTO

▓ **Jáchymka,** Jáchymova 4 (☎224 819 621). From Old Town Sq., walk up Pařížská and take a right on Jáchymova. A local favorite, Jáchymka serves heaping portions of traditional Czech cuisine in a lively, informal atmosphere. Try the goulash with dumplings (95Kč) or one of their massive meat *escalopes* (95-150Kč). Open daily 11am-11pm. ❸

Klub architektů, Betlémské nám. 52A (☎224 401 214). Metro B: Národní třída. A 12th-century cellar with 20th-century ambience. Veggie options 120-150Kč. Meat dishes 160-190Kč. Open daily 11:30am-midnight. AmEx/MC/V. ❸

Cafe Bambus, Benediktska 12 (☎224 828 110). Metro B: Nám. Republiky. An African oasis with an international menu. Entrees 55-228Kč. Czech pancakes 55-75Kč. Open M-Th 10am-1am, F 10am-2am, Sa 11am-2am, Su 11am-11pm. ❷

U Špirků, ul. Kožná 12 (☎224 238 420). Metro A: Staroměstská. Authentic Czech decor and great food at very low prices. Entrees about 100Kč. Open daily 11am-midnight. ❶

Roma Due, Liliová 18 (☎777 268 145). Metro A: Staroměstská. Perfect to cap off a night out. Pasta 89-155Kč until 10pm. Pizza 89-175Kč until 5am. Open 24hr. ❸

NOVÉ MĚSTO

▨ **Radost FX,** Bělehradská 120. Metro C: I. P. Pavlova. Both a dance club and a late-night cafe with an imaginative menu and great vegetarian food. Entrees 105-195Kč. Brunch Sa-Su 95-140Kč. Open daily 11am-late. See also **Clubs and Discos.** ❸

U Sádlů, Klimentskà 2 (☎224 813 874). Metro B: Nám. Republiky. From the square, walk down Revoluční toward the river, then go right on Klimentskà. Medieval-themed restaurant with bountiful portions; call ahead. Czech-only menu lists traditional meals (105-235Kč). Open M-Sa 11am-1am, Su noon-midnight. AmEx/MC/V. ❸

Velryba (The Whale), Opatovická 24. Metro B: Národní třída. Cross the tram tracks and follow Ostrovní, then go left onto Opatovická. Relaxed restaurant with art gallery downstairs. Entrees 62-145Kč. Open daily 11am-midnight. Gallery open daily 11am-9pm. ❷

MALÁ STRANA

U Švejků, Újezd 22. Metro A: Malostranská. Head down Klárov and turn right onto Letenská. Bear left through Malostranské nám. and follow Karmelitská until it becomes Újezd. Named after the lovable Czech cartoon hero from Hasek's novel The Good Soldier Svejk. Entrees 118-148Kč. Open daily 11am-midnight. AmEx/MC/V. ❸

Kajetanka, Hradčanskó nám. Metro A: Malostranská. Walk down Letenská through Malostranské nám., climb Nerudova until it curves to Ke Hradu, and continue up the hill. Terrace cafe with a spectacular view. Meat dishes 129-369Kč. Salads 49-09Kč. Open daily Apr.-Sept. 10am-8pm; Oct.-Mar. 10am-6pm. ❹

CAFES AND TEAHOUSES

▨ **Cafe Ebel,** Týn 2 (☎603 441 434). Metro A or B: Staroměstská. Under the Ungelt Arches. The best coffee in town and an affordable continental breakfast. Additional location at Retezova 9. Both open daily 9am-10pm. AmEx/MC/V.

▨ **Bakeshop Praha,** Kozí 1. From Old Town Sq., follow Dlouhá to the intersection with Kozí. Mouthwatering breads, pastries, salads, sandwiches, quiche, and a multitude of coffee and tea drinks. Branch at Lázenska 19 in Malá Strana. Both open daily 7am-7pm.

▨ **The Globe Coffeehouse,** Pštrossova 6. Metro B: Národní třída. At the Globe Bookstore. Exit metro left on Spálená, turn right on Ostrovní, then left on Pštrossova. Smoothies (55-70Kč), coffee (25Kč), and salads (70-120Kč). Open daily 10am-midnight.

Kavárna Medúza, Belgická 17. Metro A: Nám. Míru. Walk down Rumunská and turn left at Belgická. Cafe masquerading as an antique shop. Fluffed-up Victorian seats and lots of coffee (19-30Kč). Open M-F 11am-1am, Sa-Su noon-1am.

Kavarná Imperial, Na Poříčí 15. Metro B: Nám. Republiky. Pillared cafe with a courtly air. Live jazz F-Sa 9pm. Open M-Sa 9am-midnight, Su 9am-11pm.

U Malého Glena, Karmelitská 23. Metro A: Malostranská. Take tram #12 to Malostranské nám. Their motto is: "Eat, Drink, Drink Some More." Killer margaritas 90Kč. Jazz or blues daily 9pm. Cover 100-150Kč. Open daily 10am-2am. AmEx/MC/V.

🖸 SIGHTS

One of the only major Central European cities unscathed by WWII, Prague is a well-preserved blend of labyrinthine alleys and Baroque architecture. You can easily escape the crowds by venturing away from **Staroměstské náměstí, Karlův Most** (Charles Bridge), and **Václavské náměstí.** Compact central Prague is best explored on foot. There are plenty of opportunities for exploration in the back alleys of **Josefov,** the hills of **Vyšehrad,** and the maze of streets in **Malá Strana.**

NOVÉ MĚSTO (NEW TOWN)

Established in 1348 by Charles IV, Nové Město has become the commercial center of Prague, complete with American chain stores, but a stroll through the Franciscan Gardens will remind you of the natural beauty that Prague has to offer.

WENCESLAS SQUARE. More a boulevard than a square, Wenceslas Square (Václavské nám ̂stí) owes its name to the equestrian statue of Czech ruler and patron St. Wenceslas (Václav) that stands in front of the National Museum. Wenceslas has presided over a century of turmoil and triumph, witnessing no fewer than five revolutions in his pedestal: the declaration of the new Czechoslovak state in 1918, the invasion by Hitler's troops in 1939, the arrival of Soviet tanks in 1968, the self-immolation of Jan Palach in protest of the Soviet invasion, and the 1989 Velvet Revolution. The square stretches from the statue past department stores, thumping discos, posh hotels, and glitzy casinos. **Radio Free Europe,** which gives global news updates and advocates peace, has been broadcasting from its glass building behind the National Museum since WWII. *(Metro A or C: Muzeum.)*

FRANCISCAN GARDEN AND VELVET REVOLUTION MEMORIAL. Monks somehow manage to preserve the immaculate and serene **rose garden** (františkánská zahrada) in the heart of Prague's bustling commercial district. A plaque under the arcades halfway down Národní, across from the Black Theatre, memorializes the hundreds of citizens beaten by police on November 17, 1989. A subsequent wave of mass protests led to the total collapse of Communism in Czechoslovakia during the Velvet Revolution. *(Metro A or B: Můstek. Enter through the arch to the left of Jungmannova and Národní, behind the statue. Open daily mid-Apr. to mid-Sept. 7am-10pm; mid-Sept.to mid-Oct. 7am-8pm, mid-Oct. to mid-Apr. 8am-7pm. Free.)*

THE DANCING HOUSE. American architect Frank Gehry (of Guggenheim-Bilbao fame; p. 983) built the undulating "Dancing House" (Tančící dům) at the corner of Resslova and Rašínovo nábřeží. Since its 1996 unveiling, it has been called an eyesore by some and a shining example of postmodern design by others. *(Metro B: Karlovo nám. As you walk down Resslova toward the river, the building is on the left.)*

STARÉ MĚSTO (OLD TOWN)

Getting lost among the narrow roads and old-world alleys of Staré Město is probably the best way to appreciate the 1000-year-old neighborhood's charm.

CHARLES BRIDGE. Thronged with tourists and the hawkers who feed on them, the Charles Bridge (Karlův Most) is Prague's most recognizable landmark. On each side of the bridge, defense towers offer splendid views of the city and the river. Five stars and a cross mark the spot where St. Jan Nepomucký was tossed over the side of the bridge for guarding the queen's extramarital secrets from a suspicious King Wenceslas IV. *(Metro A: Malostranská on the Malá Strana side and Metro A: Staroměstská on the Staré Město side. Open daily 10am-10pm. 40Kč, students 30Kč.)*

OLD TOWN SQUARE. The heart of Staré Město is Staroměstské náměstí (Old Town Square), surrounded by eight magnificent towers. Next to the grassy knoll stands the **Old Town Hall** (Staroměstské Radnice). The multi-facaded building is missing a piece of the front facade where the Nazis partially demolished it in the final days of WWII. Crowds gather on the hour to watch the **astronomical clock** chime as the skeletal Death empties his hourglass and a procession of apostles marches by. *(Metro A: Staroměstská or Metro A or B: Můstek. Town Hall open in summer M 10am-7pm, Tu-F 9am-7pm, Sa-Su 9am-6pm. Clock tower open daily 10am-6pm. 50Kč, students 40Kč.)* Opposite the Old Town Hall, the spires of **Týn Church** (Chrám Matka Boží před Týnem) rise above a mass of medieval homes. Buried inside is famous astronomer Tycho Brahe, whose overindulgence at one of Emperor Rudolf's lavish dinner parties cost him his life. Since it was deemed improper to leave the table unless the emperor himself did so, poor Tycho had to remain in his chair while his bladder filled until it finally burst. The bronze statue of theologian **Jan Hus**, the country's most famous martyr, stands in the middle of the square. In front of the Jan Hus statue sits the flowery **Goltz-Kinský Palace,** the finest of Prague's Rococo buildings. *(Open Tu-F 10am-6pm; closes early in summer for daily concerts.)*

POWDER TOWER AND MUNICIPAL HOUSE. One of the original eight city gates, the Gothic **Powder Tower** (Prašná Brána) looms at the edge of Nám. Republiky as the entrance to Staré Město. A steep climb to the top rewards you with expansive views. Next door, on the former site of a royal court, is the **Municipal House** (Obecnídům), where the Czechoslovak state declared independence on October 28, 1918. *(Nám. Republiky 5. Metro B: Nám. Republiky. Tower open daily July-Aug. 10am-10pm; Apr.-June and Sept.-Oct. 10am-6pm. Top of tower 40Kč, students 30Kč. House open daily 10am-6pm. Guided tours Sa noon and 2pm. 150Kč.)*

CATHEDRAL OF ST. NICHOLAS. While smaller and less impressive than its brother cathedral across the Vltava, this church is still worth a visit, if only for the stunning crystal chandelier in the center, complete with a giant iron cross. The ceiling frescoes are also noteworthy. *(Metro A: Staroměstská. Next to the Kafka Museum. Open M noon-4pm, Tu-Sa 10am-4pm, Su noon-3pm. Mass Su 10:30am. Free.)*

JOSEFOV

Josefov, the oldest Jewish settlement in Central Europe, lies north of Staroměstské nám., along Maiselova. In 1180, Prague's citizens built a 12 ft. wall around the area. The closed neighborhood bred exotic tales, many of which centered around Rabbi Loew ben Bezalel (1512-1609) and his legendary *golem*—a mud creature that supposedly came to life to protect Prague's Jews. The city's Jews remained clustered in Josefov until WWII when the ghetto was vacated as residents were sent to death camps. Ironically, Hitler's wish to create a "museum of an extinct race" sparked the preservation of Josefov's cemetery and synagogues. Though it's only a fraction of its former size, there is still an active Jewish community. *(Metro A: Staroměstská. Synagogues and cemetery open Apr.-Oct. M-F and Su 9am-6pm; Nov.-Mar. 9am-4:30pm. Closed Jewish holidays. Admission to all 6 synagogues except Starnová charge 300Kč, students 200Kč. Starnová Synagogue 200Kč/140Kč.)*

THE SYNAGOGUES. The **Maisel Synagogue** (Maiselova synagoga) displays artifacts from the Jewish Museum's collections, which were only returned to the city's Jewish community in 1994. *(On Maiselova, between Široká and Jáchymova.)* Some 80,000 names line the walls of the **Pinkas Synagogue** (Pinkasova), a requiem for Czech Jews persecuted during the Holocaust. Turn left down Široká to reach this sobering memorial. Upstairs, drawings by children interred at the Terezín camp further memorialize the inhumanity of the Holocaust. Backtrack up Široká and go left on Maiselova to visit the oldest operating synagogue in Europe, the 700-year-old **Old-New Synagogue** (Staronová), which remains the religious center of Prague's Jewish community. Farther up Široká on Dušní is the **Spanish Synagogue** (Španělská), which has an ornate Moorish interior modeled after Granada's Alhambra.

OLD JEWISH CEMETERY. The Old Jewish Cemetery (Starý židovský hřbitov) remains Josefov's most-visited site. Between the 14th and 18th centuries, 20,000 graves were laid in 12 layers. The striking clusters of tombstones visible today were formed as older stones rose from underneath. Rabbi Loew is buried by the wall opposite the entrance. *(At the corner of Široká and Žatecká.)*

MALÁ STRANA

A seedy hangout for criminals and counter-revolutionaries for nearly a century, the cobblestone streets of Malá Strana have become prized real estate. Malá Strana is centered around **Malostranské Náměstí** and its centerpiece, the Baroque **St. Nicholas's Cathedral** (Chrám sv. Mikuláše), whose towering dome is one of Prague's most prominent landmarks. The cathedral hosts nightly concerts of classical music. *(Metro A: Malostranská; follow Letenská to Malostranské nám. Open daily 9am-4:45pm. 50Kč, students 25Kč.)* Along Letenská, a wooden gate opens into the beautiful **Wallenstein Garden** (Valdštejnská zahrada), one of Prague's best-kept secrets. *(Letenská 10. Metro A: Malostranská. Open daily Apr.-Oct. 10am-6pm. Free.)* **Church of Our Lady Victorious** (Kostel Panna Marie Vítězné) is known for its famous wax statue of the **Infant Jesus of Prague,** said to bestow miracles on the faithful. *(Metro A: Malostranská. Follow Letecká through Malostranské nám. and continue onto Karmelitská. Open daily 8:30am-7pm. Museum open M-Sa 9:30am-5:30pm, Su 1-6pm. Free.)*

PRAGUE CASTLE (PRAŽSKÝ HRAD)

Prague Castle has been the seat of the Bohemian government for over 1000 years. The main castle entrance is at the end of the lush **Royal Garden** (Královská zahrada), where the Singing Fountain spouts its watery, harp-like tune before the newly renovated **Royal Summer Palace.** Before exploring, pass the main gate to see the **Šternberg Palace,** which houses art from the National Gallery. *(Metro A: Malostranská. Take trams #22 or 23 to Pražský Hrad and go down U Prašného Mostu. Open daily Apr.-Oct. 9am-5pm; Nov.-Mar. 9am-4pm. Buy tickets opposite St. Vitus's Cathedral, inside the castle walls. 1-day ticket valid at Royal Crypt, Cathedral and Powder Tower, Old Royal Palace, and the Basilica. 350Kč, students 175Kč. Royal Gardens open Apr.-Oct.)*

ST. VITUS'S CATHEDRAL. Inside the castle walls stands the colossal St. Vitus's Cathedral (Katedrála sv. Víta), which looks Gothic but was in fact completed in 1929, 600 years after construction began. To the right of the high altar stands the silver **Tomb of St. Jan Nepomucký.** In the main church, the walls of **St. Wenceslas's Chapel** (Svatováclavská kaple) are lined with a painting cycle depicting the legend of Wenceslas. Climb the 287 steps of the **Great South Tower** for a great view, or descend underground to the **Royal Crypt,** which holds the tomb of Charles IV.

OLD ROYAL PALACE. The Old Royal Palace (Starý Královský Palác) is to the right of the cathedral, behind the Old Provost's House and the statue of St. George. The lengthy **Vladislav Hall** once hosted jousting competitions. Upstairs is the **Chancellery of Bohemia,** where the Second Defenestration of Prague took place.

ST. GEORGE'S BASILICA AND ENVIRONS. Across the courtyard from the Old Royal Palace stands St. George's Basilica (Bazilika sv. Jiří), which holds the tomb of St. Ludmila, complete with skeleton on display. The convent next door houses the **National Gallery of Bohemian Art,** which displays art ranging from

Gothic to Baroque. *(Open Tu-Su 10am-6pm. 100Kč, students 50Kč.)* **Jiřská** street begins to the right of the basilica. Halfway down, tiny **Golden Lane** (Zlatá ulička) heads off to the right; alchemists once worked here, attempting to create gold. Kafka later lived at #22.

OUTER PRAGUE

The city's outskirts are packed with green fields, churches, and panoramic vistas, all peacefully tucked away from hordes of tourists. **Vyšehrad** is the former haunt of Prague's 19th-century Romantics; quiet walkways wind between stone walls to the **Vyšehrad Cemetery**, home to the remains of composer Antonín Dvořák. The oldest monastery in Bohemia, **Břevnov Monastery**, was founded in AD 993 by King Boleslav II and St. Adalbert, each of whom was guided by a divine dream to build a monastery atop a bubbling stream. The stream leads to a pond to the right of **St. Margaret's Church** (Bazilika sv. Markéty). *(From Metro A: Malostranská, take tram #22 uphill to Břevnovský klášter. Church open only for mass, M-Sa 7am and 6pm, Su 7:30, 9am, and 6pm.)* The traditional **Prague Market** (Pražskátrznice) has acres of stalls selling all kinds of wares. *(Take tram #3 or 14 from Nám. Republiky to Vozovna Kobylisy and get off at Pražskátrznice.Open M-F 8am-6pm, Sa 8am-1pm.)*

▥ MUSEUMS

The city's museums often have striking facades but mediocre collections. Still, a few quirky museums are worth a visit.

▨MUCHA MUSEUM. The museum is devoted to the work of Alfons Mucha, the Czech Republic's most celebrated artist, who painted some of the pioneering brushstrokes of the Art Nouveau movement. *(Panská 7. Metro A or B: Můstek. Walk up Václavské nám. toward the St. Wenceslas statue. Go left onto Jindřišská and left again onto Panská. ☎224 215 409; www.mucha.cz. Open daily 10am-6pm. 120Kč, students 60Kč.)*

MUSEUM OF COMMUNISM. This gallery is committed to exposing the flaws of the Communist system that suppressed the Czech people from 1948-1989. A model factory and an interrogation office send you behind the Iron Curtain. *(Na Příkopě 10. Metro A: Můstek. ☎224 212 966. Open daily 9am-9pm. 180Kč, students 140Kč.)*

MUSEUM OF MEDIEVAL TORTURE INSTRUMENTS. The collection and highly detailed explanations are sure to nauseate. *(Mostécka 21. Metro A: Malostranská. Follow Letenská from the metro and turn left on Mostécka. Open daily 10am-8pm. 120Kč.)* In the same building, the **Exhibition of Spiders and Scorpions** shows live venomous creatures in their natural habitats. *(Open daily 10am-10pm. 100Kč, children 80Kč.)*

NATIONAL GALLERY. The massive collection of the National Gallery (Národní Galerie) is spread among nine locations throughout Prague; the notable Šternberský palác and Klášter sv. Jiří are in the **Prague Castle** (p. 270). The **Trade Fair Palace and the Gallery of Modern Art** (Veletržní palác a Galerie moderního umwní) exhibit an impressive collection of 20th-century Czech and European art. *(Dukelských hrinů 47. Metro C: Holešovice. All open Tu-Su 10am-6pm. 150Kč, students 70Kč.)*

♫ ENTERTAINMENT

For concerts and performances, consult *Threshold*, *Do města-Downtown*, *The Pill* (all three are free at many cafes and restaurants), or *The Prague Post*. Most performances start at 7pm and offer standby tickets 30min. before curtain. Between mid-May and early June, the **Prague Spring Festival** draws musicians from around the world. For tickets, try **Bohemia Ticket International**, Malé nám. 13, next to Čedok. (☎224 227 832; www.ticketsbti.cz. Open M-F

9am-5pm, Sa 9am-2pm.) The **National Theater** (Národní divadlo), Národní 2/4, stages drama, opera, and ballet. (☎224 901 448; www.narodni-divadlo.cz. Metro B: Národní třída. Box office open daily 10am-6pm and 30min. before performances. 30-1000Kč.) **Estates Theater** (Stavovské divadlo), Ovocný trg 1, is on the pedestrian Na Příkopě. (☎224 921 528. Metro A or B: Můstek.) Mozart's *Don Giovanni* premiered here; shows today are mostly classic theater, opera, and ballet. Use the National Theater box office or show up 30min. before the performance. The **Marionette Theater** (Říše loutek), Žatecká 1, stages a hilarious marionette version of *Don Giovanni*. (☎224 819 322. Metro A: Staroměstská. Performances June-July M-Tu and Th-Su 8pm. Box office open daily 10am-8pm. 490Kč, students 390Kč.)

HIGH CULTURE, LOW BUDGET. Prague's state-run theaters will often hold a group of seats in the higher balconies until the day of the performance before selling them off at reduced prices. By visiting your venue of choice the morning of a performance, you can score tickets for as little as 50Kč.

🎵 NIGHTLIFE

With some of the world's best beers on tap, it's no surprise that pubs and beer halls are Prague's most popular nighttime hangouts. Tourists have overrun the city center, so authentic pub experiences are now largely restricted to the suburbs and outlying metro stops. Although dance clubs abound, Prague is not a clubbing city—locals prefer the many jazz and rock hangouts scattered about the city.

BARS

▧ Vinárna U Sudu, Vodičkova 10. Metro A or B: Můstek. Cross Václavské nám. to Vodičkova and follow the curve left. Infinite labyrinth of cavernous cellars. Red wine 125Kč per 1L. Open M-Th 1pm-2am, F-Sa 1pm-3am, Su 3pm-1am.

▧ Kozička (The Little Goat), Kozí 1. Metro A: Staroměstská. This giant cellar bar is always packed; you'll know why after your first 0.5L of *Krušovice* (30Kč). Czech 20-somethings stay all night. Open M-F noon-4am, Sa 6pm-4am, Su 6pm-3am. MC/V.

U Fleků, Křemencova 11. Metro B: Národní třída. Turn right on Spálená away from Národní, right on Myslíkova, and then right again on Křemencova. The oldest beer hall in Prague. Home-brewed beer 49Kč. Open daily 9am-11pm.

Pivnice u Sv. Tomáše, Letenská 12 (☎257 531 835). Metro A: Malostranská. Walk downhill on Letenská. While meat roasts on a spit, the mighty dungeons echo with boisterous revelry and gushing toasts. Order meats (350-400Kč) a day in advance. Beer 40Kč. Live brass band daily 7-11pm. Open daily 11:30am-midnight. MC/V.

Cafe Marquis de Sade, Melnicka 5. Metro B: Nám. Republiky. Spacious bar decorated in red velvet. Happy Hour M-F 4-6pm (beer 22Kč, wine 25Kč). Open daily 2pm-2am.

Zanzibar, Saská 6. Metro A: Malostranská. Head down Mostecká toward the Charles Bridge, turn right on Lázeňská, and turn left on Saská. The tastiest, priciest, and most exotic cocktails this side of the Vltava (80-190Kč). Open daily 5pm-3am.

Bugsy's Bar, Parížská 10. Sophisticated, American-style speakeasy serving the tastiest mixed drinks in town. Cocktail menu so thick it's hardcover (95-1490Kč). Sushi satisfies your upscale cravings. Live jazz M at 9pm. Open daily 7pm-2am. AmEx/MC/V.

U 3 Cernych Ruzi, Zámecká 5. Metro A: Malostranska. At the foot of the New Castle steps. A small, quirky bar that pours endless pints at low prices (Budvar 18Kč) for an eternally thirsty local crowd. Open 11am-midnight.

CLUBS AND DISCOS

■ **Radost FX,** Bělehradská 120 (☎224 254 776; www.radostfx.cz). Metro C: I. P. Pavlova. Plays the hippest techno, jungle, and house music. Creative drinks such as Frozen Sex with an Alien (140Kč). Cover 100-200Kč. Open M-Sa 10pm-5am.

Roxy, Dlouhá 33. Metro B: Nám. Republiky. In the same building as the Dlouhá 33 Traveler's Hostel (p. 265). Experimental DJs and theme nights. Crowds hang out on the huge staircases. Cover 100-200Kč. M no cover. Open M-Tu and Th-Sa 9pm-late.

Karlovy Lázně, Novotného lávka 1. 4 levels of themed dance floors under the Charles Bridge. Cover 120Kč, 50Kč before 10pm and after 4am. Open daily 9pm-5am.

Palác Akropolis, Kubelíkova 27 (☎296 330 911). Metro A: Jiřího z Poděbrad. Head down Slavíkova and turn right onto Kubelíkova. Live bands several times a week. Top Czech act *Psí vojáci* is an occasional visitor. Open daily 10pm-5am.

U staré paní (The Old Lady's Place), Michalská 9. Metro A or B: Můstek. Some of Prague's finest jazz vocalists in a tiny yet classy venue. Shows daily 9pm-midnight. Cover 150Kč, includes 1 drink. Open for shows 7pm-2am. AmEx/MC/V.

Ungelt, Tyn 2. Metro A or B: Staroměstská. Subterranean vault with live jazz daily from 9pm-midnight. Cover 200Kč, students 150Kč. Open daily 8pm-midnight.

GAY AND LESBIAN NIGHTLIFE

At either of the places below, you can pick up a copy of *Amigo* (69Kč), the most thorough English guide to gay life in the Czech Republic, or *Gayčko* (60Kč), a glossier magazine written mostly in Czech. Check out www.praguegayguide.net for a comprehensive list of attractions.

Tingl Tangl, Karolíny Světlé 12. Metro B: Národní třída. Under the archway on the left, this gay club draws a diverse crowd for its cabarets. Women welcome. Cover 120Kč. Open W and F-Sa 10pm-5am. Shows after midnight.

Cafe Maler, Blanická 28 (☎222 013 116). Metro A: Náměstí Míru. Exit the metro and take a right on Korunní and then the first left on Blanická. The club is on your right, just after the intersection with Vinohradská. This classy café turns into Prague's only lesbian club at night. Men welcome. Club open M-Th 6:30pm-late, F-Sa 7pm-late.

Pinocchio, Seifertova 3 (☎222 710 772). Take tram #5, 9, 26, or 55 uphill. Exit tram at Husinecka and walk back downhill. Complex includes poker machines, strip shows, video arcades, and hotel rooms. Beer 25Kč. Open daily 3pm-6am.

⚡ DAYTRIPS FROM PRAGUE

TEREZÍN (THERESIENSTADT). In 1941, when Terezín became a concentration camp, Nazi propaganda films touted the area as a resort where Jews would live a normal life. In reality, over 30,000 died here while another 85,000 were transported to death camps farther east. Fine sleeping quarters, bathrooms, and even a park were built in order to receive delegations from the Red Cross, though Jews were not allowed to use these facilities. The **Ghetto Museum,** around the corner, to the left of the bus stop, sets Terezín in the wider context of WWII. (Open daily Apr.-Sept. 9am-6pm, Oct.-Mar. 9am-5:30pm. Museum, barracks, and fortress 180Kč, students 140Kč.) Across the river is the **Small Fortress,** which was used as a Gestapo prison. (Open daily Apr.-Sept. 8am-6pm, Oct.-Mar. 8am-4:30pm.) Outside the walls lie the **cemetery** and **crematorium** where Nazis disposed of the remains of the executed. Men should cover their heads. (Open Apr.-Sept. M-F and Su 10am-5pm, Nov.-Mar. 10am-4pm. Free.) Terezín has been repopulated to about half its former size. Families now live in barracks, and supermarkets occupy former Nazi offices. Take the **bus** from

CZECH REPUBLIC

THE LOCAL STORY

BONE-CHILLING CHAPEL

In and around Prague, you will find churches of stone, brick, iron, glass...and bones. **Kutná Hora,** a picturesque village one hour from Prague, is both famous and infamous for its ossuary, a chapel filled with artistic and religious creations made entirely from parts of the human skeleton.

Originally founded around silver mines, the town boomed until the Black Death halted fortune seekers dead in their tracks. The Cistercian Order built a chapel to house the extra corpses from the overflowing cemetery, and in a fit of whimsy (or possibly insanity), one monk began designing flowers from pelvises and crania. He never completed the ossuary, but in 1870, artist František Rint did, adorning the chapel with the remains of over 40,000 people.

Today, tourists admire the chandelier, comprised of every bone imaginable, and suspended from the ceiling by jawplates. While some marvel at the skeletal crest of arms, others find the chapel macabre and disrespectful of the dead. Though the town's residents are similarly divided in their opinion of their claim to fame, make the decision for yourself. If you are in the area, Kutná Hora is a must-see. *Hourly trains run from Hlavni Nadrazi (1hr., round-trip 112Kč). Open daily Apr.-Sept. 8am-6pm; Oct. 9am-noon and 1-5pm; Nov.-Mar. 9am-noon and 1-4pm. 35Kč, students 20Kč).*

Prague's Florenc station to the Terezín stop (1hr., 19 per day, 68Kč), where the **tourist office** is located. (Open Tu-Su 9am-12:30pm and 1-4pm.)

KUTNÁ HORA. East of Prague, the former mining town of Kutná Hora (Mining Mountain) has a history as morbid as the **bone church** that has made the city famous. The interior of the church is decorated with the bones of over 40,000 plague victims. (Open daily Apr.-Sept. 8am-6pm; Oct. 9am-noon and 1-5pm; Nov.-Mar. 9am-noon and 1-4pm. 35Kč, students 20Kč.) Take a **bus** (1½hr., 6 per day, 54-64Kč) from Prague Florenc station or a train from Hlavni Nadrazi (1hr., 1 per hr., 112Kč round-trip). Exit left onto Benešova, continue through the rotary until it becomes Vítězná, then go left on Zámecká.

KARLŠTEJN. A gem of the Bohemian countryside, Karlštejn is a turreted **fortress** built by Charles IV in the 14th century to store his crown jewels and holy relics. (Open July-Aug. Tu-Su 9am-6pm; May-June and Sept. 9am-5pm; Apr. and Oct. 9am-4pm; Nov.-Mar. 9am-3pm. 7-8 English tours per day; 200Kč, students 100Kč.) The **Chapel of the Holy Cross** is inlaid with precious stones and 129 apocalyptic paintings by medieval artist Master Theodorik. (☎02 74 00 81 54; reservace@stc.npu.cz. Open July-Nov. Tu-Su 9am-5pm. Tours by reservation only; 300Kč, students 100Kč.) The area also has beautiful **hiking** trails. A **train** runs to Praha-Hlavní (55min., 1 per hr., 46Kč). To reach the castle, turn right out of the station and go left over the bridge; turn right and walk through the village (25min., mostly uphill).

ČESKÝ RÁJ NATIONAL PRESERVE. The narrow sandstone pillars and deep gorges of **Prachovské skály** (Prachovské rocks) make for climbs and hikes with stunning views. Prachovské skály also boasts the **Pelíšek** rock pond and the ruins of the 14th-century **Pařez** castle. (Open daily 8am-5pm. 45Kč, students 20Kč.) The 588 acres of the park are interwoven by a network of **trails;** green, blue, and yellow signs guide hikers to additional sights, while triangles indicate vistas off the main trails. Red signs mark the "Golden Trail," which connects Prachovské skály to **Hrubá Skála** (Rough Rock), a rock town surrounding a hilltop castle. From the Hrubá Skála castle, the red trail leads up to what remains of **Wallenstein Castle** (Valdštejnský Hrad). The red and blue trails are open to cyclists, but only the blue trail is ideal for biking. **Buses** run from Prague-Florenc station to Jičín (1½hr., 8 per day, 77Kč), while other buses go to Prachovské Skály and Český Ráj (15min., 10Kč). Buses to Český Ráj sometimes run less frequently than scheduled. From Jičín, you can walk along a 6km trail beginning at Motel Rumcajs, Koněva 331.

WEST AND SOUTH BOHEMIA

West Bohemia overflows with curative springs; over the centuries, emperors and intellectuals alike have soaked in the waters of Karlovy Vary (also known as Carlsbad). Those seeking good beer visit the *Pilsner Urquell* brewery in Plzeň or the *Budvar* brewery in České Budějovice. More rustic than West Bohemia, South Bohemia is filled with brooks, virgin forests, and castle ruins.

KARLOVY VARY (CARLSBAD)

A stroll through the spa district or into the hills of Karlovy Vary (pop. 55,000) reveals why this lovely town developed into one of the great "salons" of Europe, frequented by Johann Sebastian Bach, Peter the Great, Sigmund Freud, and Karl Marx. Although older Germans and Russians seeking the therapeutic powers of the springs are the main visitors, film stars from around the world and fans from around the country fill the town for the International Film Festival each July.

TRANSPORTATION AND PRACTICAL INFORMATION. Buses, much more convenient than trains, run from Dolní nádraží, on Západní (☎353 504 516), to Plzeň (1¾hr., 10 per day, 80Kč) and Prague (2¼hr., 10 per day, 120Kč); buy tickets

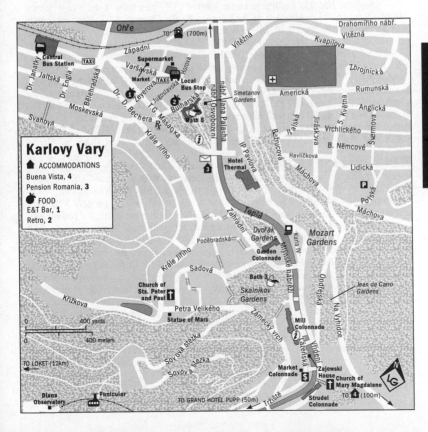

Karlovy Vary

⬆ ACCOMMODATIONS
Buena Vista, 4
Pension Romania, 3

🍎 FOOD
E&T Bar, 1
Retro, 2

on board. To reach the town center from the bus station, turn left and take the left fork of the pedestrian underpass towards Lázně. Turn right at the next fork, following the sign for the supermarket, and go straight up the stairs to reach T. G. Masaryka, which runs parallel to the other main thoroughfare, Dr. Davida Bechera. **Centrum Taxi,** Zeyerova 9, offers 24hr. service (☎353 223 000). **Infocentrum,** Lazenska 1, next to Mill Colonnade, sells maps (39-69Kč) and theater tickets (100-500Kč), and books rooms (from 400Kč) in town. (☎353 224 097. Open Jan.-Oct. M-F 8am-6pm, Sa-Su 10am-4pm; Nov.-Dec. M-F 7am-5pm.) *Promenáda,* a monthly booklet with event schedules and other info, is available here and at kiosks in town (15Kč). The **post office** at T. G. Masaryka 1, offers **Western Union** services. (Open M-F 7:30am-7pm, Sa 8am-1pm, Su 8am-noon.) **Postal Code:** 36001.

⌐⌐ ACCOMMODATIONS AND FOOD. City Info ❸, T. G. Masaryka 9, offers pension singles from 630Kč and hotel doubles from 950Kč. (☎353 223 351. Open daily 10am-6pm.) One of the best deals in the Czech Republic, **◪Buena Vista Backpackers' Hostel ❶,** Moravská 42, offers self-contained apartments with spacious bathrooms, dining and livings areas, and fully equipped kitchens for unusually low prices. To get there from the bus stand, take bus #2, 8, 11, or 13 four stops to Na Vyhlídce. Continue walking, veer right at the fork to the market, and go downhill then uphill. The hostel is at the end of the street on the right. (☎353 239 002; www.premium-hotels.com/buenavista. Internet 1Kč per min. 4- to 6-bed dorms 248Kč.) Next to the post office at the corner of Zahradní and T. G. Masaryka, **Pension Romania ❸,** Zahradní 49, offers luxurious, modern rooms right on the Teplá. (☎353 222 822. Breakfast included. Singles 900Kč, student singles 715Kč; doubles 1480Kč, river view 1630Kč; triples 1900Kč. Oct.-Mar. 15-30% discount.)

Karlovy Vary is known for its sweet *oplatky* (spa wafers); try them at a street vendor (6Kč). Trendy **Retro ❷,** T.G. Masaryka 18, has a diverse menu that includes vegetarian options. (Entrees 49-189Kč. Open M-Th 10am-1am, F 10am-3am, Sa 11am-3am, Su 11am-1am.) Faithful regulars dine on hearty Czech fare at **E&T Bar ❸,** Zeyerova 3. (☎353 226 022. Entrees 75-155Kč. Open M-Sa 9am-2am, Su 10am-2am.) The **supermarket,** Horova 1, is in the building marked "Městská tržnice," behind the bus station. (Open M-F 6am-7pm, Sa 7am-5pm, Su 9am-5pm. MC/V.)

◙⌐ SIGHTS AND ENTERTAINMENT. The **spa district,** which overflows with springs, baths, and colonnades, starts at the Victorian **Bath 5** (Lázně 5), Smetanovy Sady 1, across from the post office, offering thermal baths (355Kč) and underwater massages (495Kč). Reserve a few days in advance. (☎353 222 536; www.spa5.cz. Pool and sauna open M-F 8am-9pm, Sa 8am-6pm, Su 10am-6pm. 90Kč. MC/V.) Follow the Teplá River to **Bath 3,** Mlýnské nábř 5, which offers full-body massages for 735Kč. (Treatments daily 7-11:30am and noon-3pm.) Next door, the imposing **Mill Colonnade** (Mlýnská kolonáda) shelters five springs. Farther down is the **Zawojski House,** Trižiště 9, an Art Nouveau building that houses Živnostenská Banka. Two doors down, **Strudel Spring** (Vřídlo pramen), inside the **Strudel Colonnade** (Vřídelní kolonáda), is Karlovy Vary's hottest and highest-shooting spring, spouting 30L of 72°C (162°F) water each second. (Open daily 6am-7pm.)

Follow Stará Louka to find signs pointing you to the funicular (every 15min. 9am-7pm; 30Kč, round-trip 50Kč), which leads to the **Diana Observatory** and a magnificent panorama of the city. (Observatory tower open daily 9:15am-6:45pm. 10Kč.) *Promenáda* (see above) lists each month's concerts and performances, including info about the **International Film Festival,** which screens independent films in early July. Tickets sell out quickly; get to the box office early. **Routes Berlin,** Jaltská 7, off D. Bechera, attracts a hip young crowd with live music and a seductive red interior. (Beer from 15Kč. Open daily noon-midnight.)

🔁 DAYTRIP FROM KARLOVY VARY: PLZEŇ.
Recent attempts to clean up Plzeň (pop. 175,000) have left its beautiful architecture and gardens looking fresh and new. But it's the world-famous beer, not the architecture that lures so many to Plzeň. A beer lover's perfect day begins at Plzeň's legendary ⊠**Pilsner Urquell Brewery** (Měšťanský Pivovar Plzeňský Prazdroj), where knowledgeable guides lead visitors to the fermentation cellars for samples. After the tour, take a lunch break at the on-site beerhouse **Na spilce**, which pours Pilsner for 20Kč per pint. The entrance to the complex is across the Radbuza River from Staré Město, where Pražská becomes U Prazdroje. Cross the street and take the pedestrian overpass. (Brewery ☎377 062 888. 70 min. tours daily June-Aug. 12:30, 2pm; Sept.-May 12:30pm. 120Kč, students 60Kč. Na spilce open M-Th and Sa 11am-10pm, F 11am-11pm, Su 11am-9pm.) Take Pražská out of the square and turn left on Perlová to visit the **Brewery Museum**, Veleslavínova 6, which traces the history of brewing from ancient times. (Open daily Apr.-Sept. 10am-6pm; Jan.-Mar. 10am-4pm. 100Kč, students 50Kč.) Take a stroll through the **Kopecký gardens** (Kopeckého sady) at the end of Františkánská.

Buses leave from Husova 58 for Karlovy Vary (45min., 16 per day, 70-80Kč) and Prague (2hr., 16 per day, 65-80Kč). The **tourist office**, Nám. Republiky 41, books rooms (from 179Kč), sells phone cards (150-350Kč), and offers free maps. (☎378 035 330; www.icpilsen.cz. Open Apr.-Sept. daily 9am-6pm; Oct.-Mar. M-F 10am-5pm, Sa-Su 10am-3:30pm.) To reach the main square, turn left on Husova, which becomes Smetanovy Sady, then turn left on Bedřicha Smetany. The **Hotel Slovan ❸**, Smetanovy Sady 1, is at the corner with Jungamannova, offering lovely rooms and soft beds. (☎377 227 256; http://hotelslovan.pilsen.cz. Breakfast included. Singles 620Kč; doubles 990Kč. MC/V.) **Euro Café (Kavárna Europa) ❶**, Nám. Republiky 12, provides an alternative to heavy Czech fare. (Sandwiches 55Kč; salads 50Kč. Open M-F 9am-8pm, Sa 10am-6pm.) For groceries, try **Tesco**, Sirkova 47. (Open M-W 7am-7pm, Th-F 7am-8pm, Sa-Su 8am-6pm.) **Postal Code:** 30101.

ČESKÉ BUDĚJOVICE

České Budějovice (pop. 100,000) is a great base for exploring the surrounding region's attractions. The town was known as Budweis in the 19th century, inspiring the name of the popular but pale North American Budweiser, which bears little relation to the malty local Budvar. Today, rivalry lingers between Anheuser-Busch and the **Budvar**

THE ART OF DRINKING *PIVO*

South and West Bohemia are a beer drinker's heaven. Between České Budějovice and Plzeň, the respective homes of Budvar and Pilsner Urquell, this area boasts a high ratio of hops to humans. In fact, many tourists venture outside of Prague solely to visit these breweries. But before setting off for your local pub to down a Budvar, it's important to learn the etiquette of drinking Czech beer.

While you may be tempted to merely order *pivo* (beer), such a request is far too simple. Do you want *pivo svělé* (light beer), *pivo tmavé* (dark beer), or *pivo řezané* (a mixture of light and dark)? Once that's settled, would you prefer your beer to have 10% or 12% of alcoholic strength? Or are you feeling bold enough to try the potent Budvar 16%? If the normal-sized stein is too much to handle, there's no shame in trying the *pivo male*, a half-size glass.

Once you've ordered a beer to your liking, it's time for a toast. Czechs always wish each other well before drinking their beer—it is considered the height of rudeness to take a sip without wishing your neighbors "*na zdraví*." Beer connoisseurs claim that the only appropriate toast is to clink glasses three times and firmly set your stein down on the table, thereby maintaining an appropriate amount of foam head. Whatever your toast, the first sip is sure to go down smoothly.

Brewery, Karoliny Světlé 4, which can be reached from the town center by bus #2, going towards Borek, Točna. (Tours 9am-4pm except Friday. Tours 92Kč, students 70Kč.) **Staré Město** (Old Town) centers around the **Náměstí Přemysla Otakara II,** which is surrounded by colorful Renaissance and Baroque buildings. Nearby is the **Church of the Sacrifice of the Virgin Mary,** in Piaristické Nám. The cobbled square and courtyard garden offer a respite from the more touristed main square. (Open M-Th and Sa 10am-noon and 2-4pm, Su 2-4pm.)

Buses run to: Brno (4½hr., 6 per day, 200Kč); Český Krumlov (50min., 25 per day, 25Kč); and Prague (2½hr., 10 per day, 120-144Kč). **Trains** leave from opposite the bus station (Nádražní 12). The TIC **tourist office,** Nám. Otakara II 2, books private rooms. (☎386 801 413; www.c-budejovice.cz. Open M-F 8:30am-6pm, Sa 8:30am-5pm, Su 10am-noon and 12:30-4pm.) To reach the center of town from the train station, turn right on Nádražní, take a left at the first crosswalk, and follow Lannova třída, which becomes Kanovnická. To reach **AT Penzion ❸,** Dukelská 15, from Nám. Otakara II, hang a right down Dr. Stejskala. The well-furnished rooms feature private bath, TV, and fridge. At the first intersection, turn left and follow Široká, veering right on Dukelská. Penzion is on the left. (☎387 312 529. Breakfast 50Kč. Singles 500Kč; doubles 800Kč.) Under the Maly Pivovar Hotel, the official Budvar brewhouse **Maly Pivovar,** Vilke Karla IV 8-10, offers excellent regional specialties. (Entrees 86-175Kč. Open M-Th 10:30am-8:30pm, F-Sa 10:30am-11pm, Su 10:30am-9pm. MC/V.) **Večerka grocery** is at Palachého 10; enter on Hroznova. (Open M-F 7am-8pm, Sa 7am-1pm, Su 8am-8pm.) **Postal Code:** 37001.

ČESKÝ KRUMLOV

This once-hidden gem of the Czech Republic has finally been discovered—some might say besieged—by tourists seeking refuge from Prague's hectic pace and overcrowded streets. Český Krumlov still won't disappoint those who wander its medieval streets, raft down the meandering Vltava, and explore the enormous 13th-century castle that looms over it all. This UNESCO-protected town, with its countryside charm and beautiful surrounding hills, can be explored for days. Apart from hiking, horseback riding, and kayaking, the town lures visitors with affordable accommodations and burgeoning nightlife.

🖃🖪 TRANSPORTATION AND PRACTICAL INFORMATION. Frequent **buses** arrive from České Budějovice (30min.; M-F 33 per day, Sa-Su 14 per day; 26Kč) and Prague (3hr.; M-F 9 per day, Sa-Su 6 per day; 130-145Kč). To get to the main square, **Náměstí Svornosti,** head up the path from the back of the terminal, to the right of stops #20-25. Go downhill at its intersection with Kaplická, then cross the highway and head onto Horní, which leads into the square. The **tourist office,** Nám. Svornosti 2, books rooms in pensions (from 300Kč) as well as cheaper private rooms. (☎380 704 622; www.ckrumlov.cz/infocentrum. Open Apr.-Oct. M-F 9am-7pm, Sa-Su 9am-1pm and 2-7pm.) **Postal Code:** 38101.

🖪🖸 ACCOMMODATIONS AND FOOD. To reach the Backpacker's Shangri-La, 🟥**Krumlov House ❶,** Rooseveltova 68, run by an American expat couple, follow the directions to the square from the station. Turn left from Horní onto Rooseveltova after the lights and follow the signs. (☎380 711 935; www.krumlovhostel.com. Dorms 250Kč; doubles 600Kč; suites 750Kč.) The comfy beds at **Hostel 99 ❶,** Věžní 99, were acquired from a four-star hotel. From Nám. Svornosti, head down Radniční, which becomes Latrán; at the red and yellow gate, turn right onto Věžní. (☎380 712 812; www.hostel99.com. Dorms 300-390Kč; doubles 700Kč.) Take Panská off of Nám. Svornosti and turn right on Soukenická to reach the conveniently located **Traveller's Hostel ❶**, Soukenická 43, has a kitchen, lounge, satellite TV, pool table, and foosball for guest use. (☎380 711 345; www.travellers.cz. Laundry 150Kč. Internet access 1.50Kč per min. 4-8 bed dorms 300Kč, students 270Kč, 7th night free; doubles 380Kč.) Just off Radniční, on Parkán, the river-front **U dwau Maryi (Two Marys) ❶**, Parkán 104, specializes in medieval Bohemian fare. (Entrees 54-120Kč. Open daily Apr.-Oct. 11am-11pm.) From the right-hand corner of Nám. Svornosti, across from the tourist office, turn left onto Kájovská. Just down the street is **Na louži ❷**, Kájovská 66, which serves generous portions of Czech dishes. (Entrees 59-160Kč. Veggie options 62-81Kč. Open daily 10am-10pm.) Get groceries at **NOVA Potraviny,** Linecká 49. (Open M-Sa 7am-6pm, Su 8am-6pm.)

🄶🄵 **SIGHTS AND NIGHTLIFE.** Towering above Krumlov since the 1200s, the **castle** has been home to a succession of Bohemian and Bavarian noble families. Follow Radniční across the river to the castle's main entrance on Latrán. Two tours cover different parts of the lavish interior, including a frescoed ballroom and a splendid Baroque theater. The eerie galleries of the **crypts** showcase distorted sculptures. Climb the 162 steps of the tower for a fabulous view. (Castle open Tu-Su June-Aug. 9am-noon and 1-6pm; Apr.-May and Sept.-Oct. 9am-noon and 1-5pm. 1hr. English tours 140-50Kč, students 70-80Kč. Crypts open daily June-Aug. 10am-5pm. 20Kč, students 10Kč. Tower open daily June-Aug. 9am-5:30pm; May-Apr. and Sept.-Oct. 9:30am-4:30pm. 30Kč, students 20Kč.) The castle gardens also host the outdoor **Revolving South Bohemia Theater,** where operas and plays are performed in Czech during the summer. (Open June-early Sept. Tu-Su. Shows begin 8:30-9:30pm. Tickets 224-390Kč; purchase at the tourist office.) The Austrian painter Egon Schiele (1890-1918) lived in Český Krumlov until residents ran him out for painting burghers' daughters in the nude. The ▓**Egon Schiele International Cultural Center,** Široká 70-72, displays his work, along with paintings by other 20th-century Central European artists. Parts of the museum will be closed for renovations in 2005. Call ahead for current hours. (☎420 380 704 011; www.schieleartcentrum.cz. Open daily 10am-6pm. 180Kc, students 105Kč.)

Rybárška is lined with lively bars and cafes, including **U Hada (Snake Bar),** Rybárška 37, a cellar bar where locals and backpackers dance the night away. (Open M-Th 7pm-3am, F-Sa 7pm-4am, Su 7pm-2am.) **Cikánská Jizba (Gypsy Bar),** Dlouhá 31, offers Roma cuisine (entrees 45-150Kč), cheap beer (18Kč), and excellent live music. (☎380 717 585. Open M-Th 11am-10pm, F-Sa 11am-midnight.)

🄺 **OUTDOORS.** Whether you'd like to float down the Vltava in a kayak or a canoe, or bike through the Bohemian countryside to the 13th-century **Zlatá Koruna** monastery, stop by **Vltava,** Kájovská 62, for equipment rental and info. Go horseback riding at **Jezdecký klub Slupenec,** Slupenec 1; from the center, follow Horní to the highway, take the second left on Křížová, and take the red trail to Slupenec. (☎380 711 052; www.jk-slupenec.cz. 250Kč per hr. Open Tu-Su 9am-6pm.)

MORAVIA

Wine-making Moravia makes up the easternmost third of the Czech Republic. Home to the country's finest folk-singing and two leading universities, it's also the birthplace of a number of Eastern European notables, including Tomáš G. Masaryk, first president of Czechoslovakia, psychoanalyst Sigmund Freud, and chemist Johann Gregor Mendel, who founded modern genetics in a Brno monastery.

BRNO

Brno (pop. 388,900) has been an international marketplace since the 13th century. Today, global corporations compete with family-owned produce stands, while historic churches soften the glare of casinos and clubs that line the streets.

⌨️🔢 TRANSPORTATION AND PRACTICAL INFORMATION. Trains (☎541 171 111) go to: Bratislava (2hr., 8 per day, 250Kč); Budapest (4hr., 2 per day, 945Kč); Prague (3hr., 16 per day, 294Kč); and Vienna (1½hr., 1 per day, 536Kč). **Buses** (☎543 217 733) leave from the corner of Zvonařka and Plotní for Prague (2½hr., 36 per day, 112-167Kč) and Vienna (2½hr., 2 per day, 250Kč). From the main exit, cross the tram lines on Nádražní, walk left, and then go right on Masarykova to reach **Náměstí Svobody,** the main square. The **tourist office** (Kulturní a informační centrum města Brna), Radnická 8, inside the town hall, books rooms (from 500Kč). From Nám. Svobody, head down Masarykova and turn right onto Průchodní. (☎542 211 090; fax 542 210 758. Open M-F 8am-6pm, Sa-Su 9am-5pm.) **Internet Center Cafe,** Masarykova 2/24, has speedy computers in the center of town. (40Kč per hr. Open M-F 8am-midnight, Sa-Su 9am-11pm.) **Postal Code:** 60100.

🔢📳 ACCOMMODATIONS AND FOOD. From the train station, cross the tram tracks, turn right, then take an immediate left up the stairs. At the top, turn right onto Novobranská to reach the sparkling new, centrally located ▧**Hotel Astorka ❶,** at #3. (☎542 510 370. Open July 1-Sept. 30. Singles, doubles, and triples 520Kč per person, students 260Kč per person. AmEx/MC/V.) The beautifully furnished rooms in **Pension U Leopolda ❸,** Jeneweinova 49, have private baths. Take tram #12 or bus #A12 to Komarov, go left on Studnici, and right on Jeneweinova. (☎545 233 036. Singles 775Kč; doubles 1250Kč; triples 1450Kč.) **Fischer Cafe ❸,** Masarykova 8/10, serves up creative pasta, fish, and steak entrees (113-216Kč), and massive salads (90-147Kč) in this sleek hot spot. (20Kč cover charge. Open M-Th 8am-10pm, F 8am-11pm, Sa 9am-11pm, Su 10am-8pm.) Enjoy a Czech feast amid the medieval atmosphere at **Dávné Časy ❸,** Starobrněnská 20, up Starobrněnská from Zelný trh. (Entrees 79-189Kč. Open daily 11am-11pm. AmEx/V.) Behind the train station is a **Tesco** supermarket. (Open M-F 8am-9pm, Sa 8am-7pm, Su 9am-7pm.)

◩📳 SIGHTS AND NIGHTLIFE. From Nám. Svobody, take Zámečnická and go right on Panenská; after Husova, head uphill to reach the ▧**Špilberk Castle** (Hrad Špilberk), which earned a reputation as the cruelest prison in Habsburg Europe. (Open May-Sept. Tu-Su 9am-6pm; Apr. and Oct. Tu-Su 9am-5pm; Nov.-Mar. W-Su 10am-5pm. 80Kč, students 40Kč.) In the 18th century, monks at the **Capuchin Monastery Crypt** (Hrobka Kapucínského kláštera), just left of Masarykova from the train station, developed a burial technique using a series of air ducts that they used to preserve more than 100 bodies. (Open May-Sept. M-Sa 9am-noon and 2-4:30pm, Su 11-11:45am and 2-4:30pm. 40Kč, students 20Kč.) The newly expanded **Mendelianum,** Mendlovo nám. 1a, documents the life and work of Johann Gregor Mendel, who founded modern genetics in a Brno monastery. (Open May-Oct. Tu-Su 10am-6pm; Nov.-Apr. W-Su 10am-6pm. 80Kč, students 40Kč.) In summer, **techno raves** are announced by posters. After performances in the attached Merry Goose Theater, artsy crowds gather at **Divadelní hospoda Veselá husa,** Zelný trh. 9. (Open M-F 11am-1am, Sa-Su 3pm-1am.) Students frequent dance club **Mersey,** Minská 15. Take tram #3 or 11 from Česká to Tábor. (Beer 25Kč. Open M-Sa 8pm-late.)

TELČ

The Italian aura of Telč (pop. 6000) results from the crew of artists and crafts-men that the town's ruler imported from Genoa in 1546. As you cross the cobble-stone footbridge to the main square—flanked by long arcades of peach gables and time-worn terra-cotta roofs—it's easy to see why UNESCO designated the gingerbread town a World Heritage Monument. Two tours of Telč's glorious cas-tle are available. The more interesting *trasa A* leads you through Renaissance hallways, past the old chapel, and under extravagant ceilings; *trasa B* goes through rooms decorated in later styles. (Open May-Sept. Tu-Su 9am-noon and 1-5pm; Apr. and Oct. closes 1hr. earlier. Tours 70Kč, students 35Kč.) The park at the base of the castle, where the stone walls meet the river, has paths that make for a pleasant stroll overlooking the town. (Open daily dawn-dusk. Free.)

Buses run from the station on Slavíčkova, a 5min. walk from the main square, to Brno (2hr., 8 per day, 88Kč) and Prague (3hr., 7 per day, 100Kč). To reach the main square, **Nám. Zachariáše Hradce,** from the bus station, follow the walkway and turn right on Tyršova, then left on Masarykovo, and pass under the archway on the right. Pick up a map (30-79Kč) and access the Internet (1Kč per min.) at the **tourist office,** Nám. Zachariáše Hradce 10, in the town hall. (☎567 112 407; www.telc-etc.cz. Open M-F 8am-6pm, Sa-Su 10am-6pm.) The best bet for accommodations is **Privát U Šeniglů ❶,** Nám. Zachariáše Hradce 11, which offers doubles with private bath. (☎567 243 406. 300Kč per person.) Unfortunately, Telč's restaurant selection is slim, with a few touristy pizza parlors and cafes where you can eat for 100Kč. Otherwise, the only food you'll find is at the grocery store, **Horacke Potraviny,** Nám. Zachariáše Hradce 65. (Open M-F 7am-6pm, Sa 7am-noon.) **Postal Code:** 58856.

OLOMOUC

Today, Olomouc (pop. 103,372) is the echo of what Prague once was before it was engulfed by hordes of tourists. By day, locals enjoy the rebuilt town center where Baroque architecture lines cobblestone paths. By night, the students keep the clubs thumping well into the morning light.

🖃🎦 TRANSPORTATION AND PRACTICAL INFORMATION. Trains (☎585 785 490) leave from Jeremenkova 23 for Brno (1½hr., 7-8 per day, 120Kč) and Prague (3½hr., 19 per day, 294Kč). **Buses,** Rolsberská 66 (☎585 313 848), go to Brno (1½hr., 10 per day, 75-85Kč) and Prague (4½hr., 3 per day, 310Kč). The **tourist office,** Horní nám., in the town hall, provides maps and books hotel and hostel rooms. (☎685 513 385; www.olomoucko.cz. Open daily Mar.-Nov. 9am-7pm; Dec.-Feb. 9am-5pm.) **Internet u Dominika,** Slovenská 12, has the best connections and the most terminals. (☎777 181 857. 1Kč per min. Open M-F 9am-9pm, Sa-Su 10am-9pm.) **Postal Code:** 77127.

🛏🍴 ACCOMMODATIONS AND FOOD. The small **🏠Poet's Corner Hostel ❶,** with a communal kitchen and laundry, feels more like a friend's home than a hos-tel. To reach it from the train station, take trams #4-7 to Nám. Hridinů and walk two blocks in the direction from which you came. Turn onto Sokolská to reach the hostel, which is on the 4th floor. (☎777 570 730; www.hostelolomouc.com. 7-person dorm July-Aug. 300Kč; Sept.-June 250Kč; doubles 800Kč; triples 1000Kč. To reach the **Penzion Best ❷,** take tram #1 or 4-7 to Nám. Hridinů, then hop on bus #17, 18, or 22 to Na Strelnici. Continue in the same direction until the hotel appears on your right. All rooms have bath and TV. (☎/fax 585 231 450. Break-fast 40Kč. Singles 500Kč; doubles 750Kč. AmEx/MC/V.) Local favorite, **Hanácká**

Hospoda ❶, is always packed with locals devouring the very best in Czech fare. (☎ 777 721 171. Entrees 56-170Kč. Open daily 10am-midnight. AmEx/MC/V.) The **Supermarket Delvita** is in the basement of Prior department store. (8. května 24, at the corner of 28. října. ☎ 685 535 135. Open M-F 7am-8pm, Sa 7am-2pm.)

🎫 💈 SIGHTS AND NIGHTLIFE. The massive 1378 **town hall** and its spired clock tower dominate the town center. The tourist office arranges trips up the tower. (Daily at 11am and 3pm. 15Kč.) A wonderful **astronomical clock** is set in the town hall's northern side. In 1955, Communist clockmakers replaced the mechanical saints with archetypes of "the people"; since then the masses strike the hour with their hammers and sickles. The 35m black-and-gold **Trinity Column** (Sloup Nejsvětější Trojice) soars higher than any other Baroque sculpture in the country. To reach **St. Wenceslas Cathedral** (Metropolitní Kostel sv. Václava) follow its spires. The church interior is in impeccable condition, having been reworked virtually every century since it was damaged by fire in 1265. (Open Tu and Th-Sa 9am-5pm, W 9am-4pm, Su 11am-5pm. Free, but donation requested.) Next door to the cathedral, the walls of the **Přemyslid Palace** (Přemyslovský palác) are covered in pristine, if fading, frescoes. (Open Apr.-Sept. Tu-Su 10am-6pm. 15Kč, students 5Kč. W free.)

The popular **Depo No. 9,** Nám. Republiky 1, pours *Staropramen* (20Kč) in three underground rooms with metallic decor and comfy seats. In the wee hours, the basement becomes Olomouc's most happening dance club, with frequent live performances. (☎ 585 221 273; www.depo9.cz. Occasional cover for more popular acts 50-100Kč. Open M-Th 10am-2am, F 10am-6am, Sa 7pm-6am, Su 7pm-midnight.) For a more low-key spot to relax over a drink or two, head next door to **The Crack,** an upscale Irish pub in the renovated cellar of the old town brewery. (☎ 520 842 829. Open M-Th 11am-midnight, F 11am-2am, Sa 4pm-2am, Su 4pm-1am.)

DENMARK (DANMARK)

Like Thumbelina, the heroine of native son Hans Christian Andersen's fairy tale, Denmark has a vibrant, puckish personality squeezed into a tiny body. Located between Sweden and Germany, the country is the geographic and cultural bridge between Scandinavia and continental Europe. It comprises the Jutland peninsula and the islands of Zealand, Funen, Lolland, Falster, and Bornholm, as well as some 400 smaller islands, some of which are not inhabited. With its Viking past behind it, Denmark now has one of the most comprehensive social welfare structures in the world, and liberal immigration policies have diversified the once-homogeneous population. Today, Denmark has a progressive youth culture that lures travelers to the hip club scene in Copenhagen. Contrary to the suggestion of one waggish Briton, very little seems to be rotten in the state of Denmark.

 DISCOVER DENMARK: SUGGESTED ITINERARIES

Start off in the cosmopolitan capital of **Copenhagen** (p. 288), soaking up some sunshine on a **bike tour** (p. 294) of the central city or waiting out showers in the medieval ruins beneath **Christianborg Slot**. Spend a day on the nude beaches of **Klampenborg** (p. 298), but remember to pull your jeans back on before visiting the castle of Frederiksborg Slot in nearby **Hillerød** (p. 297). Head west to sprightly **Odense** (p. 301) for celebrations of Hans Christian Andersen's birth, and then catch a ferry to the sleepy island hamlet of **Ærøskøbing** (p. 303). Discover the museums and nightlife of little-known **Århus** (p. 303) before indulging your inner child at Legoland in **Billund** (p. 305). End up at the northern tip of Jutland, where the quaint yellow houses of **Skagen** (p. 308) look out on the tumultuous Baltic Sea.

ESSENTIALS

WHEN TO GO

Denmark is best visited May to September, when days tilt sunny and temperatures average 10-16°C (50-61°F). Winter temperatures average 0°C (32°F). Although temperate for its northern location, Denmark can capriciously turn rainy and cool at a moment's notice; pack a sweater and an umbrella, even in summertime.

DOCUMENTS AND FORMALITIES

VISAS. EU citizens do not need a visa. Citizens of Australia, Canada, New Zealand, and the US do not need a visa for stays of up to 90 days, although this three-month period begins upon entry into any of the countries that belong to the EU's freedom of movement zone. For more information, see p. 17.

EMBASSIES. All foreign embassies are in Copenhagen. For Danish embassies at home: **Australia**, Level 14 Gold Fields House, 1 Alfred St., Circular Quay, Sydney NSW 2000 (☎02 92 47 22 24; dtcsydney@dtcsyd.org.au); **Canada**, 47 Clarence St., Ste. 450, Ottawa, ON K1N 9K1 (☎613-562-1811; www.danish-embassy-can-

ada.com); **Ireland,** 121-122 St. Stephen's Green, Dublin 2 (☎01 475 64 04; www.denmark.ie); **New Zealand,** 273 Bleakhouse Rd., Howick P.O. Box 619, 1015 Auckland (☎09 537 30 99; danish.nz@xtra.co.nz); **UK,** 55 Sloane St., London SW1X 9SR (☎020 7333 0200; www.denmark.org.uk); **US,** 3200 Whitehaven St. NW, Washington, D.C. 20008-3683 (☎202-234-4300; www.denmarkemb.org).

TRANSPORTATION

BY PLANE. Kastrup Airport in Copenhagen (CPH; ☎32 31 32 31; www.cph.dk) handles international flights from cities around the world, mostly by Air France, British Airways, Delta, Icelandair, KLM, Lufthansa, SAS, and Swiss Air. **Billund Airport** (BLL; ☎76 50 50 50; www.billund-airport.dk) handles flights to other European cities. **SAS** (Scandinavian Airlines; US ☎800-221-2350; www.scandinavian.net), the national airline company, offers youth discounts to some destinations.

BY TRAIN AND BY BUS. The state-run rail line in Denmark is **DSB;** visit www.dsb.dk/journey_planner to use their extremely helpful **journey planner. Eurail** is valid on all state-run routes. The **Scanrail pass,** purchased outside Scandinavia, is good for rail travel through Denmark, Finland, Norway, and Sweden, as well as many discounted ferry and bus rides. The pass is also available for purchase within Scandinavia, but only three of those days can be used in the country of purchase, so a Scanrail pass purchased at home (p. 63) is more economical for those traveling mostly within Denmark. Visit www.scanrail.com for more info. Remote towns are typically served by buses from the nearest train station. The national **bus** network is reliable and fairly cheap. You can take buses or trains over the **Øresund bridge** from Copenhagen to Malmö, Sweden.

BY FERRY. Railpasses include discounts or free rides on many Scandinavian ferries. The free *Vi Rejser* newspaper, at tourist offices, can help you sort out the dozens of smaller ferries that serve Denmark's outlying islands, although the best bet for overcoming language barriers is just to ask at the station. For more info on connections from Bornholm to Germany and Sweden, see p. 300; for connections from Jutland to Norway and Sweden, see p. 307.

BY CAR. Roads are toll-free, except for the **Storebæltsbro** (Great Belt Bridge; 250kr) and the **Øresund bridge** (around 240kr). Speed limits are 50kph (30mph) in urban areas, 80kph (50mph) on highways, and 110kph (68mph) on motorways. **Service centers** for motorists, called *Info-terias*, are spaced along Danish highways. **Gas** averages 7.96kr per liter. Watch out for bikes, which have the right-of-way. Driving in cities is discouraged by high parking prices and numerous one-way streets. For more info on driving in Denmark, contact the **Forenede Danske Motore-jere (FDM)**, Firskovvej 32, Box 500, 2800 Kgs. Lyngby (☎ 70 13 30 40; www.fdm.dk).

BY BIKE AND BY THUMB. Flat terrain, well-marked bike routes, bike paths in the countryside, and raised bike lanes on most streets in towns and cities make Denmark a cyclist's dream. You can rent **bikes** (50-65kr per day) from some tourist offices, rental shops, and a few train stations. The **Dansk Cyklist Forbund (Danish Cycle Federation)**, Rømersg. 7, 1362 Copenhagen K (☎ 33 32 31 21; www.dcf.dk), provides info about cycling in Denmark and investing in longer-term rentals. For info on bringing your bike on a train (which costs 50kr or less), pick up *Bikes and Trains* at any train station. **Hitchhiking** on motorways is illegal and uncommon. *Let's Go* does not recommend hitchhiking as a safe means of transport.

TOURIST SERVICES AND MONEY

EMERGENCY Police: ☎ 112. Ambulance: ☎ 112. Fire: ☎ 112.

TOURIST OFFICES. Contact the tourist board in Denmark at Islands Brygge 43, 2300 Copenhagen S (☎ 32 88 99 00; www.visitdenmark.dt.dk). **Tourist Boards** at home include: **Australia**, Finnesse Communications Marketing & PR, P.O. Box 1427, North Sydney, NSW 2059 (☎ 02 9929 6044; satu@finnesse.com.au); **UK**, 55 Sloane St., London SW1X 9SY (☎ 7259 5959; www.dtb.dt.dk); **US**, 18th fl., 655 3rd Ave., New York, NY 10017 (☎ 212-885-9700; www.goscandinavia.com). Additional tourist info and helpful maps can be found at www.krak.dk.

MONEY. The Danish unit of currency is the **krona** (plural: kronor), divided into 100 *øre*. The easiest way to get cash is from **ATMs**; cash cards are widely accepted, and many machines give advances on credit cards. Denmark has a high cost of living; expect to pay 90-120kr for a hostel bed, 400-800kr for a hotel room, 75-125kr for a day's groceries, and 50-90kr for a cheap restaurant meal. A bare-bones day in Denmark might cost 250-350kr; a slightly more comfortable day might cost 400-600kr. The European Union imposes a **Value Added Tax (VAT)** on goods and services purchased within the EU, which is included in the price (p. 22). Denmark's VAT is one of the highest in Europe (25%). Non-EU citizens can get a VAT refund upon leaving the country for purchases in any one store that total over 300kr. There are no hard and fast rules for **tipping,** but it's always polite to round up to the nearest 10kr in restaurants and for taxis. In general, service at restaurants is included in the bill, although tipping up to 15% is becoming common in Copenhagen.

DANISH KRONER (KR)		
AUS$1 = 4.35KR	10KR = AUS$2.30	
CDN$1 = 4.72KR	10KR = CDN$2.12	
EUR€1 = 7.45KR	10KR = EUR€1.34	
NZ$1 = 4.04KR	10KR = NZ$2.47	
UK£1 = 11.09KR	10KR = UK£0.91	
US$1 = 6.19KR	10KR = US$1.61	

BUSINESS HOURS. Shops are normally open Monday to Thursday from about 9 or 10am to 5:30 or 6pm and Friday until 7 or 8pm; they are usually open Saturday mornings. Shops in Copenhagen stay open all day Saturday. **Banks** are usually open Monday to Friday 9:30am-4pm, Thursday until 6pm.

COMMUNICATION

PHONE CODES	**Country code: 45. International dialing prefix: 00.** From outside Denmark, dial the int'l dialing prefix (see inside back cover) + 45 + local number. Within the country, always dial city code + local number.

TELEPHONES. Pay phones accept both coins and phone cards, available at post offices or kiosks in 30-100kr denominations. **Mobile phones** are an increasingly popular and economical alternative (p. 35). For domestic directory info, dial ☎118; for international info, dial ☎113. International direct dial numbers include: **AT&T** (☎8001 0010); **Canada Direct** (☎8001 0011); **MCI** (☎8001 0022); **Sprint** (☎8001 0877); **Telecom New Zealand** (☎8001 5469); **Telstra Australia** (☎8088 0543).

MAIL. Mailing a postcard or letter to Australia, Canada, New Zealand, or the US costs 6.75kr; to elsewhere in Europe 5.75kr. Domestic mail costs 6.75kr.

LANGUAGES. Danish is the official language of Denmark, although natives of Greenland and the Faroe Islands still hew to their native dialects. The Danish add æ (pronounced like the "e" in "egg"), ø (pronounced "euh"), and å (sometimes written *aa;* pronounced "oh" with tightly pursed lips) to the end of the alphabet; thus Århus would follow Viborg in an alphabetical listing of cities. *Let's Go* indexes these under "ae," "o," and "a." Nearly all Danes speak flawless English, but for a handful of basic Danish phrases, see p. 1059.

ACCOMMODATIONS AND CAMPING

DENMARK	**❶**	**❷**	**❸**	**❹**	**❺**
ACCOMMODATIONS	under 90kr	90-130kr	130-200kr	200-400kr	over 400kr

Since Denmark's hotels are uniformly expensive, **youth hostels** (*vandrehjem*) tend to be mobbed by budget travelers of all ages. **Danhostels,** which are affiliated with HI, dominate the industry and are often the only option in smaller towns. Facilities are clean, spacious, and very comfortable, but because they have no age limit, they attract vacationing families as well as droves of middle-aged businessmen. The country's **inde-**

pendent hostels, found mostly in cities and larger towns, draw a younger backpacking crowd and tend to be more sociable, although their facilities rarely sparkle in the way that Danhostels do. Pay close attention to Danhostel check-in times, usually a 3-4hr. window that is in no way negotiable. Sheets cost 30-60kr, while breakfast usually runs 45kr. Dorms run about 120kr per night; nonmembers add 30kr. Reserve ahead, especially during summer and near beaches. For more info, contact the Danish Youth Hostel Association, Vesterbrog. 39, 1620 Copenhagen V. (☎33 31 36 12; www.danhostel.dk. Open M-Th 9am-4pm, F 9am-3pm.) Tourist offices book rooms in private homes (125-175kr).Denmark's 510 **campgrounds** (about 60kr per person) rank from one-star (toilets and drinking water) to three-star (showers and laundry) to five-star (swimming, restaurants, and stoves). You'll need either a **Camping Card Scandinavia,** sold at campgrounds (1-year 80kr), or a **Camping Card International.** Both cards, as well as a plethora of camping info, are available at www.dk-camp.dk. Campsites affiliated with hostels generally do not require this card. If you only plan to camp for a night, you can buy a 24hr. pass (20kr). The **Danish Camping Council** (*Campingradet;* ☎39 27 88 44; www.campingraadet.dk) sells passes and the *Camping Denmark* handbook (95kr). Sleeping in train stations, in parks, or on public property is illegal.

FOOD AND DRINK

DENMARK	❶	❷	❸	❹	❺
FOOD	under 40kr	40-70kr	70-100kr	100-150kr	over 150kr

A "Danish" in Denmark is a *wienerbrød* ("Viennese bread"), found in bakeries alongside other flaky treats. In days of yore, the Danes favored open-faced sandwiches called *smørrebrød* for a more substantial meal, although today they have become more of a rarefied delicacy. Herring is served in various forms, usually pickled or raw with onions or a curry mayonnaise. For cheap eats, look for lunch specials (*dagens ret*) and all-you-can-eat buffets. National beers include Carlsberg and Tuborg; bottled brew tends to be cheaper. A popular alcohol alternative is *snaps* (or *aquavit*), a clear distilled liquor flavored with fiery spices, usually served chilled and unmixed. Many vegetarian (*vegetarret*) options are the result of Indian and Mediterranean influences, and both salads and veggies (*grønsager*) can be found on most menus.

HOLIDAYS AND FESTIVALS

Holidays: New Year's Day (Jan. 1); Easter Holidays (Mar. 24-28); Queen's Birthday (Apr. 16); Worker's Day (May 1); Whit Sunday and Monday (May 30-31); Constitution Day (June 5); Valdemar's Day (June 15); Midsummer's Eve (June 23); Christmas (Dec. 25).

Festivals: In February, Danish children assail sweet-filled barrels with birch branches on Fastelavn (Shrovetide), while adults take to the streets for carnivals. Flags will fly high on May 5, the 60th anniversary of Denmark's liberation from Nazi Germany. Yowling guitar solos ring out over Roskilde at the open-air Roskilde Festival in early July, just as Copenhagen and Århus kick off their annual jazz festivals.

FACTS AND FIGURES: DENMARK

Official Name: Kingdom of Denmark.

Capital: Copenhagen.

Major Cities: Aalborg, Århus, Odense.

Population: 5,410,000.

Land Area: 42,000 sq. km.

Time Zone: GMT +1.

Languages: Danish. Pockets of Faroese and Greenlandic, though English is widely spoken as a second language.

Religions: Evangelical Lutheran (95%).

DENMARK

COPENHAGEN (KØBENHAVN)   ☎ 33, 35

Copenhagen (pop. 1,800,000) embodies the laid-back, progressive attitudes that have come to pervade Europe's oldest monarchy. The Strøget, the city's famed pedestrian thoroughfare, now bustles with Middle Eastern restaurants and Internet cafes, while blazing neon signs conceal angels in the architecture. And while Christian VIII may have built the Tivoli amusement park in 1843 to distract his subjects from politics, today rowdy Danes gather in the shadow of the town hall to watch soccer on an outdoor screen. Bread and circuses never go out of style.

▐ TRANSPORTATION

Flights: Kastrup Airport (CPH; ☎ 32 47 47 47; www.cph.dk). **Trains** connect the airport to København H (13min., 6 per hr., 25kr). RyanAir flies cheaply into nearby **Sturup Airport** in Malmö, Sweden (MMX; ☎ 40 613 1000) from London and Frankfurt.

Trains: Trains stop at **København H** (Hovedbanegården or Central Station; domestic travel ☎ 70 13 14 15, international reservations 70 13 14 16; S-train info 33 14 17 01). For travel within the country, www.dsb.dk is indispensable. Fares depend on seat availability, and can drop as low as 25% of the quotes listed below; it is well worth it to ▨ **book at least 14 days in advance.** Travelers under 26 can also purchase a Wildcard (175kr), which guarantees 25-50% discounts on many domestic and international routes. Approximate fares to: **Berlin** (8hr., 9 per day, 724kr); **Hamburg** (4½hr., 5 per day, 508kr); Malmö (35min., every 20min., 65kr), **Oslo** (7¼hr., 2 per day, 928kr); **Stockholm** (5hr., every 1-2hr., 961kr). Seat reservations (23-150kr) are mandatory on all international routes except for Malmö.

Public Transportation: Copenhagen has an extensive and efficient public transport system. **Buses** (info ☎ 36 13 14 15; www.hur.dk) run daily 7am-12:30am. **Trains** (info ☎ 33 14 17 01) run 6:30am-11pm. Buses and **S-trains** (subways and suburban trains; M-Sa 5am-12:30am, Su 6am-12:30am) operate on a zone system. To travel any distance, you must buy a minimum of a 2-zone **ticket** (17kr, additional zones 8.50kr). Most of Copenhagen is within 2 zones. For extended stays or travel in Zealand, the best deal is the **rabatkort** (rebate card; 105kr), available from kiosks and bus drivers, which offers 10 2-zone tickets at a discount; just "clip" the ticket each time you embark the bus or train. For longer travel, you can clip the ticket more than once or purchase a *rabatkort* with more zones. Tickets and clips allow 1hr. of transfers. The **24hr. pass** (100kr), available at any train station, grants unlimited bus and train transport in Northern Zealand, as does the Copenhagen Card (see below). **Night buses,** marked with an "N," run 12:30-5:30am on limited routes and charge double fare; they also accept the 24hr. pass. Copenhagen's newly renovated **metro** system is small but convenient.

Taxis: Københavns Taxa (☎ 35 35 35 35) and **Hovedstadens Taxi** (☎ 38 77 77 77) charge a base fare of 23kr, then add 10-13kr per km. The ride from København H to Kastrup Airport costs around 200kr.

Bike Rental: City Bike (www.bycyklen.dk/engelsk) lends bikes from 110 racks all over the city for a 20kr deposit. Anyone can return your bike and claim your deposit, so lock up your bike or return it to the rack when not in use. **Københavns Cykler,** Reventlowsg. 11 (☎ 33 33 86 13; www.rentabike.dk), in København H. 75kr per day, 340kr per week; 500kr deposit. Open July-Aug. M-F 8am-5:30pm, Sa 9am-1pm, Su 10am-1pm; Sept.-June M-F 8am-5:30pm, Sa 9am-1pm.

◤▞ ORIENTATION AND PRACTICAL INFORMATION

Copenhagen lies on the east coast of the island of **Zealand** (Sjælland), across the Øresund Sound from Malmö, Sweden. The 28km **Øresund bridge and tunnel,** which opened July 1, 2000, established the first "fixed link" between the two countries.

Copenhagen

⬆ ACCOMMODATIONS
Cab Inn City, 28
Cab Inn Copenhagen
  Express, 11
Cab Inn Scandinavia, 10
Hotel Jørgensen, 9
Hotel Rye, 4
Jørgensen's Hostel, 9
København Vandrerhjem
  Amager (HI), 29
København Vandrerhjem
  Bellahøj (HI), 1
Luftmadrassen, 25
Sleep-In, 3
Sleep-In Green, 6
Sleep-In Heaven, 7

🍴 FOOD
Café Europa, 20
Café Norden, 21
Cafe Paludan, 15
Hvilds Vinstue, 18
Kate's Joint, 8
Nyhavns Færgekro, 14
RizRaz, 16, 24

★ NIGHTLIFE
IN, 19
JazzHouse, 17
The Moose Bar, 13
PAN Club and Café, 22
Park, 5

DENMARK

Copenhagen's main train station, København H, lies near the city's heart. North of the station, **Vesterbrogade** passes **Tivoli** and **Rådhuspladsen**, the central square, then cuts through the city center as **Strøget** (STROY-yet), the world's longest pedestrian thoroughfare. As it heads east, Strøget goes through a series of names: **Frederiksberggade, Nygade, Vimmelskaftet, Amagertorv,** and **Østergade.**

Tourist Offices: Wonderful Copenhagen, Vesterbrog. 4a (☎70 22 24 42; www.woco.dk). Head out the main exit of København H, turn left, and cross Vesterbrog. toward the Axelrod building. Open May-June M-Sa 9am-6pm; July-Aug. M-Sa 9am-8pm, Su 10am-6pm; Sept.-Apr. M-F 9am-4pm, Sa 9am-2pm. ◙**Use It,** Rådhusstr. 13 (☎33 73 06 20; www.useit.dk). From the station, follow Vesterbrog., cross Rådhuspl. onto Strøget, and turn right on Rådhusstr. Indispensable info and free services geared toward budget travelers. Be sure to pick up a copy of *Playtime,* a comprehensive budget guide to the city. Provides daytime luggage storage, has free **Internet** access (20min. max.), holds mail, and finds lodgings for free. Open mid-June to mid-Sept. daily 9am-7pm; mid-Sept. to mid-June M-W 11am-4pm, Th 11am-6pm, F 11am-2pm. The **Copenhagen Card** (24hr. card 199kr; 72hr. card 399kr), sold in hotels, tourist offices, and train stations, grants free or discounted admission to most major sights, as well as unlimited travel throughout Northern Zealand; however, cardbearers will need to keep up an almost manic pace to justify the cost.

Budget Travel: Kilroy Travels, Skinderg. 28 (☎70 15 40 15). Open M-F 10am-5:30pm, Sa 10am-2pm. **Wasteels Rejser,** Skoubog. 6 (☎33 14 46 33). Open M-F 9am-5pm, Sa 10am-2pm.

Embassies and Consulates: Australia, Dampfaergev. 26, 2nd fl. (☎70 26 36 76). **Canada,** Kristen Bernikowsg. 1 (☎33 48 32 00). **Ireland,** Østbaneg. 21 (☎35 42 32 33). **New Zealand,** Taarbæk Strandv. 24, Klampenborg (☎39 64 10 00). **UK,** Kastelsv. 36-40 (☎35 44 52 00). **US,** Dag Hammarskjölds Allé 24 (☎35 55 31 44).

Currency Exchange: Numerous locations, especially on Strøget. 25kr commission. **Forex,** in København H. 20kr commission on cash, 10kr per traveler's check. Open daily 8am-9pm. **The Change Group,** Østerg. 61. 35kr commission. Open May-Sept. M-Sa 8:45am-8pm, Su 10am-6pm; daily Oct.-Apr. 10am-6pm.

Luggage Storage: Free at **Use It** (above) and most hostels. At **København H,** 30kr per bag per day; 10-day max. Lockers 25-35kr per 24hr.; 3 day max. Open M-Sa 5:30am-1am, Su 6am-1am.

Laundromats: Look for **Vascomat** and **Møntvask** chains. At Borgerg. 2, Nansensg. 39, Vendersg. 13, and Istedg. 45. Wash and dry 40-50kr. Most open daily 7am-9pm.

GLBT Services: Landsforeningen for Bøsser and Lesbiske (National Association for Gay Men and Women), Teglgårdsstr. 13 (☎33 13 19 48; www.lbl.dk). Open M-F 11am-4pm. The monthly *Out & About,* which lists nightlife options, is available at gay clubs and the tourist office. Also check out www.copenhagen-gay-life.dk.

Emergencies: ☎112. **Police:** ☎33 14 14 48. Headquarters at Polititorvet.

24-Hour Pharmacy: Steno Apotek, Vesterbrog. 6c (☎33 14 82 66). Open 24hr.; ring the bell. Across from the Banegårdspl. exit of København H.

Medical Assistance: Doctors on Call (☎70 27 57 57). **Emergency rooms** at **Amager Hospital,** Kastrup 63 (☎32 34 32 34), and **Bispebjerg Hospital,** Bispebjerg Bakke 23 (☎35 31 35 31).

Internet Access: Free at **Use It** (above). **Copenhagen Hovedbibliotek** (Central Library), Krystalg. 15 (☎33 73 60 60). Free. Open M-F 10am-7pm, Sa 10am-2pm. **Boomtown,** Axeltorv 1 (☎33 32 10 32). 20kr per 30min., 30kr per hr. Open 24hr.

Post Office: In København H. Address mail to be held in the following format: SURNAME First name, Post Denmark, Hovedbanegårdens Posthus, Hovedbanegården, 1570 Copenhagen V, DENMARK. Open M-F 8am-9pm, Sa 9am-4pm, Su 10am-4pm. **Use It** (above) also holds mail. Address mail to: First name SURNAME, *Poste Restante,* Use It, Rådhusstr. 13, 1466 Copenhagen K, DENMARK.

ACCOMMODATIONS

Comfortable and inexpensive accommodations can be hard to find near the city center, but pedestrian-friendly streets and the great public transportation system ensure that you're never far from the action. Many hostels are also vibrant social worlds unto themselves. The price jump between hostels and hotels is significant. In summer, it is wise to reserve well in advance.

HOSTELS

Luftmadrassen, Strandg. 100B (☎70 23 32 74, www.luftkastellet.dk), on the water in Christianshavn. M: Christianshavn. Inside the warehouse-cum-club Luftkastellet ("castle in the air"), clusters of beds come equipped with astroturf "yards" and picket fences. Attached to a laid-back bar and restaurant with a plentiful buffet (20kr per 100g of food). Breakfast, sheets, and Internet access included. Open July-Aug. Be sure to call ahead, as organizers tend to fly by the seat of their pants. Dorms 200kr. ❸

Sleep-In Heaven, Struenseg. 7 (☎35 35 46 48; www.sleepinheaven.com), in Nørrebro. M: Forum. From København H, take bus #250S 2 stops (dir.: Buddinge; every 10min.) to H.C. Ørsteds Vej. Dorms are pleasant, if crowded, with a clamorous social atmosphere. Close to nightlife. Breakfast 40kr. Free lockers. Sheets 30kr. Internet 20kr per 30min. Reception 24hr. Under 35 only. Dorms 125kr; doubles 450kr. MC/V. ❷

Sleep-In Green, Ravnsborgg. 18, Baghuset (☎35 37 77 77). M: Nørreport. From there, take bus #5A. An unassuming exterior gives way to clean, colorful rooms inside this eco-friendly hostel. 30 beds per room. Internet 20kr per 30min. Organic breakfast 30kr. Sheets included; pillow and blanket 30kr. Reception 24hr. Lockout noon-4pm. Open early May to Sept. Dorms 100kr. Cash only. ❷

Jørgensen's Hostel, Rømersg. 11 (☎33 13 81 86), 20min. from København H, close to Strøget, next to Israels Pl. M: Nørreport. Go right along Vendersg.; it's on the left. Clean and cozy rooms in a deliciously central location. 6-14 beds per room. Breakfast included. Sheets 45kr. Max. stay 5 nights. Lockout 11am-3pm. Under 35 only. No reservations. Dorms 130kr. ❸

Sleep-In, Blegdamsvej 132 (☎35 26 50 59). From København H, take bus #1A (dir.: Hellerup; 15min., every 5-7min.) to Trianglen and then walk down Blegdamsvej. Popular hostel in a huge warehouse near Østerbro and Nørrebro nightlife. Kitchen available. Sheets 30kr. Key deposit 20kr. Reception 24hr. Lockout noon-4pm. Open July-Aug. No reservations. Dorms 110kr. ❷

København Vandrerhjem Bellahøj (HI), Herbergvejen 8 (☎38 28 97 15; www.danhostel.dk/bellahoej), in Bellahøj. Take bus #2A (dir.: Tingbjcrg; 15min., every 5-10min.) to Fuglsang Allé. Turn right onto Fuglsang Allé; it's on the right after 50m. Quiet, clean hostel 5km from the city center. Breakfast 45kr. Sheets 35kr. Laundry 35kr. Internet 1kr per min. Reception 24hr. Lockout 10am-2pm. Open Feb.-Dec. Dorms 95kr; doubles 300kr; triples 390kr; quads 460kr; quints 475kr. Nonmembers add 30kr. MC/V. ❷

København Vandrerhjem Amager (HI), Vejlands Allé 200 (☎32 52 29 08). M: Bella Center. Walk all the way through the Bella Center parking lot and turn right. Feels like the wilderness, but the city is just minutes away by metro. 6 beds per room. Breakfast 45kr. Kitchen available. Mandatory sheet rental 35kr. Laundry 25kr. Lockers 25kr. Reception 7am-1am. Check-in 1-5pm. Open mid-Jan. to Nov. Dorms 95kr; singles and doubles 300kr. Nonmembers add 30kr. MC/V. ❷

HOTELS

Cab Inns are very comfortable budget hotels with small, modern rooms. **Cab Inn City,** Mitchellsg. 14 (☎33 46 16 16), is ideally located near København H and Tivoli; turn right out of the station and left onto Polititorvet. To reach **Cab Inn Scandinavia,** Vodroffsvej 55 (☎35 36

11 11), take bus #2A from the station (dir.: Tingbjerg; 5min., every 5min.) to Vodroffsvej.
Cab Inn Copenhagen Express is 5min. away at Danasvej 32-34 (☎33 21 04 00). Breakfast 50kr. Reception 24hr. Singles 510kr; doubles 630kr; triples 750kr; quads 870kr. ❺

Hotel Jørgensen, Rømersg. 11 (☎33 13 81 86). Same ownership and great location as Jørgensen's Hostel (see above). Small, comfortable rooms in a great location. Breakfast included. Reception 24hr. Singles 475-575kr; doubles 575-700kr; triples 900kr. ❺

Hotel Rye, Ryesg. 115 (☎35 26 52 10; www.hotelrye.dk). Take bus #1A (dir.: Hellerup; 15min., every 5-7min.) or 14 to Trianglen, then turn right off Østerbrog. onto Ryesg. Cozy hotel provides a kimono and slippers for each room, and homemade buns at breakfast. Shared showers. Breakfast included. Reception 9am-9pm. Singles 500kr; doubles 700kr; triples 900kr; quads 1000kr. ❺

CAMPING

Bellahøj Camping, Hvidkildevej 66 (☎38 10 11 50), 5km from the city center. Take bus #2A from København H (dir.: Tingbjerg; 15min., every 5-10min.) to Primulavej. Kitchen, cafe, and market. Showers included. Reception 24hr. Open June-Aug. 59kr per person; rental tents 100kr per person. ❶

🍴 FOOD

Good, inexpensive food is plentiful in central Copenhagen. Strøget is lined with all-you-can-eat buffets (pizza, pasta, and Indian being the most popular), while **Fakta** and **Netto** supermarkets are plentiful in the Nørreport area (S-train: Nørreport). **Open-air markets** provide fresh fruits and veggies; try the one at **Israels Plads** near Nørreport Station. (Open M-Th 9am-5:30pm, F 9am-6:30pm, Sa 9am-3pm.) Fruit stalls line Strøget and the side streets to the north. Around **Kongens Nytorv,** elegant cafes serve filling *smørrebrød* (open-faced sandwiches) for about 40kr, along with all the herring you could ever want.

▨ **Nyhavns Færgekro,** Nyhavn 5 (☎33 15 15 88). Upscale fisherman's cottage atmosphere along the canal. Lunch on 10 styles of all-you-can-eat herring (89kr) or pick just one (45kr). Sumptuous dinners from 165kr. Open daily 9:30am-11:30pm. MC/V. ❸

Kate's Joint, Blågårdsg. 12 (☎35 37 44 96). Diverse, extensive selection of pan-Asian cuisine with African and Middle-Eastern accents. Located in trendy Nørrebro. Entrees 88-98kr. Stir-fry, tofu, and other munchies 50-69kr. Open daily 6-10pm. MC/V. ❸

RizRaz, Kompagnistr. 20 (☎33 15 05 75) and Store Kannikestr. 19 (☎33 32 33 45). Extensive, heavily vegetarian Mediterranean buffet in a friendly, upbeat environment. Lunch buffet 59kr. Dinner 69kr. Open daily 11:30am-midnight. AmEx/D/MC/V. ❷

Café Norden, Østerg. 61 (☎33 11 77 91), on Strøget and Nicolaj Pl. A warm, boisterous cafe in the middle of everything. Try the tomato soup (70kr) while you people-watch. Sandwiches 75-95kr. Salads 99-110kr. Kitchen open M-Th and Su until 9pm, F-Sa until 10pm. Open M-Sa 9am-midnight, Su 10am-midnight. V. ❸

Hviids Vinstue, Kongens Nytorv 19 (☎33 15 10 64), in the basement. Copenhagen's oldest pub is a delightful rabbit warren of an establishment. Lunch special includes three varieties of *smørrebrød* and a beer (55kr). Open 10am-midnight. MC/V. ❷

Cafe Paludan, Fiolstr. 10 (☎33 15 07 71). A homey, inviting eatery that doubles as a bookstore. Around the corner from the Hovedbibliotek. Sandwiches 64-79kr. Open M-F 10am-6pm, Sa 10am-3pm. ❷

Café Europa, Amagertorv 1 (☎33 14 28 89), on Nicolaj Pl. Purposefully hip spot across the plaza from the more laid-back Café Norden (see above). Sandwiches 79-99kr. Large selection of gourmet salads 99-129kr. Beer 50kr. Open M-F 9am-midnight, Sa 9am-12:30am, Su 10am-8pm. ❸

☉ SIGHTS

Compact Copenhagen lends itself to exploration by **bike** (p. 294). Various **walking tours** are also detailed in *Playtime* (at **Use It**), covering all sections of the city. Opposite Kongens Nytorv is the multi-colored and picturesque Nyhavn, the "new port" where Hans Christian Andersen penned his first fairy tale. On a clear day, take the 6.4km walk along the five lakes that border the western end of the city center. The lakes, as well as the Rosenborg Have, are great places for a **picnic.** Wednesday is the best day to visit museums, as most are free.

CITY CENTER. The first sight you'll see as you exit the train station is ◪**Tivoli,** the famous 19th-century **amusement park.** It features rides old-fashioned and new, shimmering fountains and colorful gardens, a world-class *Commedia dell'arte* theater, and venues for jazz and rock concerts. Don't miss the **Tivoli Illuminations,** an evocative light show staged each night 30min. before closing. *(www.tivoligardens.com. Open mid-June to mid-Aug. M-Th and Su 11am-midnight, F-Sa 11am-1am; low season reduced hours. Admission 65kr, children 30kr. Rides 15-60kr. Admission with unlimited rides 180kr, children 120kr.)* Across the street from the back entrance of Tivoli, the beautiful **Ny Carlsberg Glyptotek** boasts a fine collection of ancient and Impressionist art and sculpture, complete with an enclosed Mediterranean garden. The museum will be undergoing extensive renovations in 2005; however, the Egyptian collection and most of the Impressionist works will be on temporary exhibit *(Dantes Pl, 7. Open Tu-Su 10am-4pm. 20kr. Free W and Su.)* Across the street, the avant-bare **Danish Design Center** displays trends in Danish fashion and lifestyles. *(H.C. Andersens Blvd. 27. ☎ 33 69 33 69. Open M-F 10am-5pm, Sa-Su 11am-4pm. 40kr, students 20kr.)* To see the vivid modernist tapestries designed by Bjørn Nørgård and given to the Queen for her 50th birthday, tour ◪**Christiansborg Castle,** home of the *Folketing* (Parliament), the royal reception rooms, and some spooky subterranean ruins. *(Prins Jørgens Gård. ☎ 33 92 64 92. Ruins open daily 9:30am-3:30pm. 25kr. Castle tours in English daily May-Sept. 11am, 1pm, and 3pm; Oct.-Apr. Tu, Th, and Sa-Su 3pm. 45kr, students 35kr.)* For a sweeping view of the city, climb the spiral ramp of the **Round Tower,** where astronomer Tycho Brahe once observed the stars. *(Kobmagerg. 52a. Open June-Aug. M-Sa 10am-8pm, Su noon-8pm; Sept.-May M-Sa 10am-5pm, Su noon-5pm. 20kr.)* The tower is attached to the opulent, gold-drenched **Trinitatis Church.** *(Open M-Sa 9:30am-4:30pm. Free.)* Dabble in things carnal at gaudy **Museum Erotica,** where exhibits feature kinky art and dig into the sex lives of historical figures. *(☎ 33 12 03 11; www.museumerotica.dk. Open May-Sept. daily 10am-11pm; Oct.-Apr. M-Th and Su 11am-8pm, F-Sa 10am-10pm.)*

NO BROWNIES HERE, OFFICER

The crop of hippies who founded Christiania in 1971 shared a commitment to communal life and consensus decision-making. Many of them also shared an affection for nudism and hashish, and before long the enclave's drug culture came to outshine any mention of its New Age politics. Armed conflicts in the 1970s resulted in bans on hard drugs and weapons, but even the soft drugs that stayed attracted more stoners from abroad than the authorities liked. So once a new center-right Danish government took power in 2001, people knew that Christiania would soon have to answer for its anarchist ways.

Sure enough, police raided the area in March 2004, arresting 53 on drug charges even after many dealers had pre-emptively torched their own booths back in January. Finance Minister Thor Pedersen ominously pronounced that Christiania would be "normalized," though reporters soon discovered that the government stood to gain as much as 200 million kronor by selling the land to developers. The resulting public outcry led to a compromise solution: Residents will be allowed to stay if they pay for their utilities, and an independent commission will oversee the building of 300 new houses in compliance with building codes. It's clear that 2004 marked the end of an era for Christiania, but it remains to be seen what the new era will have in store.

A BIKING TOUR OF COPENHAGEN

The *Copenhagen Post* estimates that there may be more bikes than Danes in Denmark, and the city of Copenhagen leads the way as one of the most bike-friendly capitals this side of Amsterdam. Rentals from **City Bike** (p. 288) are the most convenient way to go, although you can only ride them in the center city—the eastern banks of the five western lakes are fair game, but crossing over to the

TIME: 4hr., 6hr. with visits to Rosenborg Slot and Christiansborg Slot.

DISTANCE: about 6km.

SEASON: Year-round, although Rosenborg Slot has reduced hours Nov.-Apr.

A tour of the parks, monuments, and canals just outside the central city.

western banks is punishable with a 1000kr fine. You should also avoid pedestrian thoroughfares like Strøget, unless you fancy slaloming around pram-pushing newlyweds and elderly gents out taking their constitutional. If you want to ride out into the countryside, ask your hostel about rental bikes or head over to **Københavns Cykler,** Reventlowsg. 11. You can take your bike onto an S-Train for 10kr. You are legally required to use lights when riding at night, and police are not shy about handing out 400kr fines. Helmets are recommended, but not mandatory.

This tour starts and ends at the **Rådhus.** Begin by carefully picking your way down busy Hans Christian Andersens Boulevard.

1 BOTANISK HAVE. Take a right onto Nørre Voldgade and follow it until you see the gates leading into the University of Copenhagen's lush botanical gardens (p. 296). Wander along paths lined with more than 13,000 species of plant, or else hone in on the **Palm House** for its extravagant orchids and other tropical rarities.

2 STATENS MUSEUM FOR KUNST AND ROSENBORG SLOT. Turn left out of the gardens onto Øster Voldgade. Up at the intersection with Sølvgade, you'll see the gates of the State Museum of Fine Arts (p. 296) to the north and the spires of Rosenborg Slot (p. 296) to the south. The latter served as the 16th-century summer house of King Christian IV, although the royal family took refuge here in 1801 when the British navy was shelling Copenhagen. Lock up your bike and pop inside for a look at Denmark's crown jewels.

3 THE ROUND TOWER. Backtrack down Øster Voldgade and turn left onto Gothersgade. Make a right onto Landemærket and then hop off again to scale the heights of the Round Tower (p. 293), a onetime royal observatory that still affords a sweeping view of the city.

4 AMALIENBORG PALACE. Head back up to Gothersgade and turn right. Pass by **Kongens Nytorv,** the 1670 "new square" that turns into a skating rink each winter, and hang a left onto Bredgade. Keep your eyes peeled for the gilded dome of the **Marmorkirken** (Marble Church; p. 296) on your left, and then turn right to enter the octagonal plaza of Amalienborg Palace (p. 296), a set of four Rococo mansions that the queen and her family call home.

5 NYHAVN. You've rubbed elbows with enough royalty for one day. Continue on through the plaza, turn right on Toldbodgade, and then right before the bridge onto Nyhavn. Part of the city's old waterfront, Nyhavn was known for centuries as a seedy strip for sailors to find grog, women, and a tattoo artist sober enough to wield a firm needle. Within the past 30 years, Copenhagen has embarked on a clean-up campaign, and today you're more likely to find an upscale deli serving open-faced *smørrebrod* than a tumbledown soup kitchen. Whenever a scrap of sunshine can be found, the good people of Copenhagen are soaking it up along the wharf, joined by Swedes from Malmö in search of cheap Danish beer.

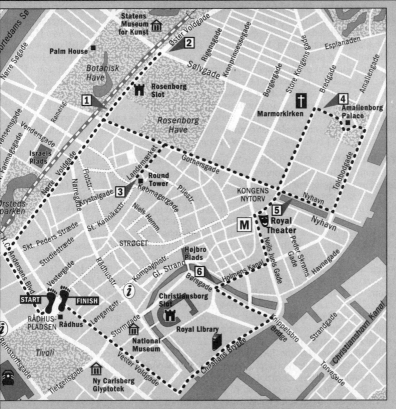

CHRISTIANBORG SLOT. Walk your bike through Kongens Nytorv, and then thread your way between the Royal Theater (p. 296) and the metro station down Neils Juels Gade. Turn right onto Holmens Kanal and cross the bridge to reach Christiansborg Slot (p. 293), seat of the Danish Parliament. Look for the 103m tower; it's difficult to miss. If you arrive before 3:30pm, head down into the ruins of the 12th-century castle underneath the present-day building. The Hanseatic League dismantled the original castle stone by stone after they captured the city of Copenhagen in 1369.

You're in the home stretch. Head east toward the Knippelsbro Bridge and **Christiania** (p. 296), taking in the industrial skyline before lugging your bike down the steps to Christians Brygge below. Mount your trusty steed, turn right, and bike along the canal. Keep watch on the right for the Black Diamond annex of the **Royal Library,** built in 1996 from black marble imported from Zimbabwe. Make a right onto Vester Voldgade and coast back up to the Rådhus. You've earned the right to call it a day.

CHRISTIANSHAVN. Brave the harrowing climb up the airy spire of **Vor Frelsers Kirke** (Our Savior's Church) for a great view of both the city and the water. *(Sankt Annæg. 29. M: Christianshavn or bus #48. Turn left onto Prinsesseg. Tower open Mar.-Nov. M-Sa 11am-4:30pm, Su noon-4:30pm. 20kr.)* Back in 1971, the "free city" of **Christiania** was established in an abandoned Christianshavn fort by a few dozen flower children. Today the thousand or so residents are trying their best to continue a tradition of artistic expression and unconventionality; vendors sell clothing and jewelry out of stalls, while spots like **Woodstock Cafe** and popular **Cafe Nemoland** offer cheap beer and the most mixed crowds in town. Recent government crackdowns have driven **Pusher Street's** once-open drug trade underground; exercise caution, as arrests for possession have become almost commonplace. Never take pictures on Pusher St. *(Main entrance on Prinsesseg. Take bus #48 from København H.)*

FREDERIKSTADEN. Edvard Eriksen's **Lille Havfrue** (Little Mermaid), the tiny statue at the opening of the harbor, honors Hans Christian Andersen's tale and is usually surrounded by tour groups and souvenir hounds. *(S-train: Østerport; turn left out of the station, left on Folke Bernadottes Allé, right on the path bordering the canal, left up the stairs, and then right along the street. Open daily 6am-dusk.)* Head back along the canal and turn left across the moat to reach **Kastellet**, a rampart-enclosed 17th-century fortress that's now a park. Cross through Kastellet to the fascinating **Frihedsmuseet** (Museum of Danish Resistance), which documents the German occupation from 1940-1945, during which the Danes helped over 7000 Jews escape to Sweden and committed thousands of acts of sabotage. *(At Churchillparken. ☎ 33 13 77 14. Open May to mid-Sept. Tu-Sa 10am-4pm; Su 10am-5pm; mid-Sept. to Apr. Tu-Sa 10am-3pm, Su 10am-4pm. 25kr. W free.)* From the museum, walk south down Amalieng. to reach the lovely **Amalienborg Palace,** four enormous mansions that serve as the residences of Queen Margrethe II and the royal family. Most of the interior is closed to the public, but several apartments are open, including the original studies of 19th-century Danish kings. The changing of the guard takes place at noon on the vast plaza. *(☎ 33 12 08 08; www.rosenborg-slot.dk. Open May-Oct. daily 10am-4pm; Nov.-Apr. Tu-Su 11am-4pm. 45kr, students 25kr; combined ticket with Rosenborg Slot 80kr.)* The imposing 19th-century **Marmorkirken** (Marble Church), opposite the palace, features an ornate interior under Europe's third-largest dome. *(Fredriksg. 4. Open M-Tu and Th 10am-5pm, W 10am-6pm, F-Su noon-5pm. Free.)* A few blocks north, the **Statens Museum for Kunst** (State Museum of Fine Arts) displays an eclectic collection of Danish and international art in two buildings linked by a long, glass-roofed gallery nicknamed Sculpture Street. *(Sølvg. 48-50. S-train: Nørreport. Walk up Øster Voldg. ☎ 33 74 84 94; www.smk.dk. Open Tu and Th-Su 10am-5pm, W 10am-8pm. 50kr, under 25 35kr. W free.)* Opposite the museum, the wildly baroque **Rosenborg Slot,** built by King Christian IV as a summer residence, shows off the **crown jewels.** *(Øster Voldg. 4A. S-train: Nørreport. Walk up Øster Voldg. ☎ 33 15 32 86. Open June-Aug. daily 10am-5pm; May and Sept. daily 10am-4pm; Oct. daily 11am-3pm; Nov.-Apr. Tu-Su 11am-2pm. 60kr, students 30kr.)* Nearby, stroll through the 13,000 plant species in the **Botanisk Have** (Botanical Gardens); be sure to visit its iron-and-glass arboretum, the **Palm House.** *(Gardens open June-Aug. daily 8:30am-6pm; Sept.-May Tu-Su 8:30am-4pm. Palm House open June-Aug. daily 10am-3pm; Sept.-May Tu-Su 10am-3pm. Free.)*

🎵 🎎 ENTERTAINMENT AND FESTIVALS

For events, consult *Copenhagen This Week*. The **Royal Theater** is home to the world-famous Royal Danish Ballet; the box office is located at Tordenskjoldsg. 7. (Open M-Sa 10am-6pm.) For same-day half-price tickets, head to the **Tivoli ticket office,** Vesterbrog. 3. (☎33 15 10 12. Open daily mid-Apr. to mid-Sept. 10am-8pm; mid-Sept. to mid-Apr. 9am-7pm.) Tickets for a variety of events are sold online at www.billetnet.dk. The relaxed **Kul-Kaféen,** Teglgårdsstr. 5, is a great place to see live performers, listen to stand-up comedy, and grab a bite. (Sandwiches 51kr. Open M 6pm-midnight, Tu-Sa 6pm-2am.) During early July's world-class ▧Copenhagen Jazz Festival (☎33 93 20 13; http://festival.jazz.dk), the city teems with free outdoor concerts. Programs are available at the tourist office. October brings the well-respected Copenhagen Gay and Lesbian Film Festival (☎22 33 44 24; www.cglff.dk), followed by November's edgy new festival of documentary cinema, cph:dox (☎33 12 00 05; www.cphdox.dk).

◐ NIGHTLIFE

In Copenhagen, weekends often begin on Wednesday, and clubs pulse with activity late enough to serve breakfast with their martinis. On Thursday, many bars and clubs have reduced covers and cheaper drinks. The city center, Nørrebro, and Østerbro reverberate with hip, crowded bars. Fancier options abound along Nyhavn, but loads of Danes just bring beer and sit on the pier. Copenhagen has a thriving gay and lesbian scene; check out *Playtime* or *Out & About* for listings.

▧ Park, Østerbrog. 79, in the Østerbro. A luxurious, enormously popular club with a packed dance floor, live music hall, lavish lounges, and a rooftop patio. Beer 40kr. Th 20+, F 21+, Sa 22+. Cover Th 50kr, F-Sa 60kr. Restaurant open Tu-Sa 11am-10pm. Club open M-Tu and Su 11am-midnight, W 11am-2am, Th-Sa 11am-5am.

JazzHouse, Niels Hemmingsens G. 10. Copenhagen's premier jazz venue becomes one of its hottest clubs after hours. Cover (from 60kr) depends on the evening's performer. Concerts M-Th 8:30pm, F-Sa 9:30pm. Dance club open Th-Sa midnight-5am.

PAN Club and Café, Knabrostr. 3. Gay cafe, bar, and multiple dance floors sprawl out around a seemingly endless staircase. Karaoke Th, with cheap drinks and no cover. Cover F-Sa 50kr. Cafe opens W-Th 9pm, F-Sa 10pm. Disco opens 11pm.

IN, Nørreg. 1. Choose between La Hacienda, a crowded, laid-back lounge, and The Dance Floor, a huge, trance-driven club. Steep cover comes with free champagne once inside. 18+. Cover for men 150kr, women 130kr. Open F 11pm-8am, Sa 11pm-11am.

The Moose Bar, on Sværtevej. Low on chic ambiance, but rowdy local spirit is plentiful. Happy Hour Tu, Th, and Sa 9pm-6am. 2 pints 30kr. 2 mixed drinks 25kr. Open M, W, and Su 11am-2am, Tu and Th-Sa 11am-6am.

◪ DAYTRIPS FROM COPENHAGEN

When it's time for a break from the urban din of Copenhagen, the city's S-trains and other regional lines can whisk you all over northern Zealand. Museums, castles, and well-trodden beaches await less than an hour outside of the city.

HILLERØD. Hillerød is home to ▧Frederiksborg Slot, one of Denmark's largest and most impressive castles. From attic to cellar, close to 90 rooms are open to the public; highlights include the Chapel, the Great Hall, and the Baroque gardens. From the train station, cross the street onto Vibekeg. and follow the signs; at the main plaza, walk to the pond and follow it to reach the castle. (☎48 26 04 39. Castle open daily Apr.-Oct. 10am-5pm; Nov.-Mar. 11am-3pm. 60kr, students 50kr. Gardens open daily May-Aug. 10am-9pm; low season reduced hours. Free. Hillerød is at the end of S-train lines A and E. 40min., every 15min., 68kr or 4 clips.)

HUMLEBÆK AND RUNGSTED. Humlebæk boasts the spectacular ▧Louisiana Museum of Modern Art, 13 Gl. Strandvej, named for the three wives (all named Louisa) of the estate's original owner. The museum rounds out its permanent collection, including works by Warhol, Lichtenstein, and Picasso, with six to eight major exhibitions each year. Landscape architects have lavished attention on the sculpture garden and the sloping lake garden, which would themselves be worth the

DENMARK

trip. Follow signs 5-8min. north from the Humlebæk station. (☎ 49 19 07 19. Open M-Tu and Th-Su 10am-5pm, W 10am-10pm. 74kr, students 67kr.) Near the water in **Rungsted** stands the house where Karen Blixen wrote the autobiographical novel *Out of Africa* under the pseudonym Isak Dinesen. The **Karen Blixen Museum,** Rungsted Strandvej 111, chronicles the author's life in a poignant, but respectful way, while the grounds yield fresh flowers for the museum and are home to 40 species of birds. Follow the street leading out of the train station and turn right on Rungstedsvej, then right again on Rungsted Strandvej; or, take bus #388 and tell the driver your destination. (☎ 45 57 10 57. Open May-Sept. Tu-Su 10am-5pm; Oct.-Apr. W-F 1-4pm, Sa-Su 11am-4pm. 35kr. Audioguide 25kr. Both Humlebæk (45min., every 20min., 68kr or 4 clips) and Rungsted (30min., every 20min., 68kr or 4 clips) are on the Copenhagen-Helsingør rail line. The Rungsted tourist office kiosk is on the corner by the museum.)

KLAMPENBORG. When the Copenhagen scene gets stultifying during the dog days of summer, young Danes head north to the crowded beaches of Klampenborg in order to bronze their fair complexions and flirt. **Bellevue Beach,** to the right out of the station, evolved from a 19th-century sanatorium into a hash-and-hippie haven during the 1970s; clothes remain optional today (as with most Danish beaches), and gays and lesbians cluster on the north end. Klampenborg is also home to the **Jægersborg Dyrehavn,** the royal family's former hunting grounds. Over two thousand deer still meander the overgrown paths around the **Eremitage** summer chateau. Turn left out of the train station. Bordering the preserve is the **Bakken,** the delightfully weatherbeaten great-aunt of the Tivoli; the kid-friendly atmosphere currently prevailing at the world's oldest amusement park is a far cry from the burlesque excesses of yesteryear. After entering the Dyrehavn, take the first path on the left. (☎ 39 63 73 00; www.bakken.dk. Open daily Mar. 17-Aug. 29, 2005. Open July noon-midnight; hours vary otherwise; consult the Danish-language website. Free admission. Rides 10-35kr each; unlimited rides 199kr. Klampenborg is on S-train lines C and F+. 22min., every 20min., 34kr or 2 clips.)

HELSINGØR. Helsingør, just 5km from the coast of Sweden, sits at a strategic entrance to the Baltic Sea, and the majestic 16th-century **Kronborg Slot** peers down at the waters below with unstinting vigilance. Better known as **Elsinore,** the castle is the setting for Shakespeare's *Hamlet* (although neither the historical "Amled" nor the Bard ever came to visit), and today exhibits recall notable productions of the play that have taken place on the castle's grounds. Skip the underwhelming **Danish Maritime Museum** on the first floor, and head down into the dank, forbidding casemates; a statue of Viking chief Holger Danske sleeps there, and legend holds that he will awake to face any threat to Denmark's safety. From the train station, turn right and follow the signs along the waterfront. (☎ 49 21 30 78; www.kronborg.dk. Open May-Sept. daily 10:30am-5pm; Apr. and Oct. Tu-Su 11am-4pm; Nov.-Mar. Tu-Su 11am-3pm. Castle and casemates 50kr. Free guided 45min. tour of castle daily 2pm.) The **tourist office,** Havnepl. 3, is in the Kulturhuset, the large brick building across from the 19th-century train station. (☎ 49 21 13 33. Open mid-June to Aug. M-Th 9am-5pm, F 9am-6pm, Sa 10am-3pm; Sept. to mid-June M-F 9am-4pm, Sa 10am-1pm.) To reach the lovely beachfront **Helsingør Vandrerhjem Hostel (HI)** ❷, Ndr. Strandvej 24, take bus #340 (8min., 1 per hr.). Or take the local train toward Hornbæk, get off at Hojstrup Trinbræt, and follow the path across the park; it's on the other side of the street. (☎ 49 21 16 40; www.helsingorhostel.dk. Breakfast 45kr. Sheets 40kr. Reception 8am-noon and 3-9pm. Curfew 11pm. Open Feb.-Nov. Dorms 110kr; private rooms 350-450kr. Nonmembers add 30kr. Helsingør is at the end of the northern train line. 55min., every 20min., 68kr or 4 clips.)

MØN. To see what Hans Christian Andersen once called the most beautiful spot in Denmark, plan to spend at least one full day on the isle of Møn, south of Copenhagen. The towering **Møns Klint** (chalk cliffs) guard the northeastern section of the island. A scenic 3km hike from the cliffs, **Liselund Slot** sits in a fairytale park populated by peacocks and pastel farm houses. To reach this area in July or early August, take bus #632 from Stege (30min., 3 per day, 14kr), or hike from the hostel (3km). During the rest of the year, bus #52 will take you to Busene, a 10min. walk from the cliffs. (20min., every 1-2hr., 14kr.) To get to Møn, take the **train** from Copenhagen to Vordingborg (1½hr., 102kr), then bus #62 to the town of Stege (45min., 39kr). The **Møns Turistbureau**, Storeg. 2, is next to the Stege bus stop and has a helpful **map** of the cliffs area. (☎ 55 86 04 00; www.visitmoen.com. Open mid-June to Aug. M-F 9:30am-5pm, Sa 9am-6pm; Sept. to mid-June M-F 9:30am-4:30pm, Sa 9am-noon.) Stay at the lakeside **Youth Hostel (HI) ❷**, Langebjergvej 6. From July to early August, take the infrequent bus #632 to the campsite stop, backtrack, then take the first road on the right. During low season, take bus #52 to Magleby and walk 2.5km left down the road. (☎ 55 81 20 30. Breakfast 46kr. Sheets 45kr. Reception 8am-noon and 4-8pm. Dorms 105kr; singles and doubles 300kr.)

ROSKILDE ☎ 46

Roskilde (pop. 53,000), in central Zealand, teems with medieval monasteries and healing springs as the location of Denmark's first Christian church. These days, pilgrims come not to take the waters, but to see everything from Malian desert blues to David Bowie at the ■**Roskilde Music Festival,** northern Europe's largest and best-run outdoor concert. (www.roskilde-festival.dk. June 30-July 3, 2005.) In the town itself, most of the action is on Alg., which becomes Skomagerg. when you pass the Stændertorvet, the main square. The stunning sarcophagi of the red-brick ■**Roskilde Domkirke** house the remains of generations of Danish royalty, just off of the Stændertorvet. (☎ 35 16 24. Open Apr.-Sept. M-F 9am-4:45pm, Sa 9am-noon, Su 1-2pm; Oct.-Mar. Tu-Sa 10am-3:45pm, Su 12:30-3:45pm. 15kr, students 10kr. English tours mid-June to mid-Aug. M-F 11am and 2pm, Sa 11am, Su 2pm.) The **Viking Ship Museum,** Vindeboder 12, houses remnants of authentic Viking ships and builds museum-quality reconstructions, some of which can be sailed out into the harbor. From the Domkirke, walk downhill through the park or take bus #607 from the train station. (☎ 30 02 00; www.vikingeskibsmuseet.dk. Open daily 9am-5pm. 75kr, low season 45kr. Boat trip 50kr with museum ticket.)

Trains depart for Copenhagen (25-30min., every 15min., 60kr). The **tourist office,** Gullandsstr. 15, sells festival tickets and books rooms for a 25kr fee and a 10-15% deposit. Walk through the Stændertorvet

ROSKILDE ROCKS

In AD 800, Vikings put the small town of Roskilde on the map by sailing to continental Europe and annihilating the feudal order. Over a millennium later, the tiny town continues to take Europe by storm with its annual Roskilde Music Festival, once again challenging any semblance of law and order.

The 2004 festival was plagued by unusually heavy rains, so that poncho-clad concert-goers were forced to slog through fields of mud to hear sets by headliners Fatboy Slim, Korn, and Morrissey. Yet 70,000 fans from around the world don't trek to Roskilde just for the big names. Northern Europe's largest outdoor music festival is more than a concert; it's a week-long musical experience, recalling Woodstock and consoling the hemp-bedecked hippies still in mourning over the dissolution of Phish. Although the festival technically begins on a Thursday, the campground opens four days beforehand, offering early-birds a chance to strike up a common vibe before more than 150 bands descend. *Agoras,* open squares scattered around the grounds, become focal points for late-night jam sessions, and with a portion of the festival's profits donated to international charities, fellow-feeling and good karma are flowing in abundance.

Roskilde reconvenes June 30-July 3, 2005. 4-day pass 1050kr, 7-day pass 1150kr. Check details at www.roskilde-festival.dk.

with the Domkirke on your right, and turn left immediately onto Gullandsstr. The office is a block down on the left. (☎31 65 60. Open late June to late Aug. M-F 9am-6pm, Sa 10am-2pm; low season reduced hours.) The bright, clean **Youth Hostel (HI) ❷**, Vindeboder 7, is on the harbor next to the Viking Museum's shipyard. Book far, far in advance during the festival. (☎35 21 84; www.danhostel.dk/roskilde. Kitchen available. Breakfast 45kr. Sheets 40kr. Reception 8am-noon and 4-10pm. Dorms 115kr. Nonmembers add 30kr. AmEx/MC/V.) **Roskilde Camping ❶**, Baunehøjvej 7, is on the beach and has a great view; take bus #603 (15kr) toward Veddelev to Veddelev Byg. (☎75 79 96. Reception 8am-9pm. Open Apr. to mid-Sept. 65kr per person.) **Algade** and **Skomagergade** are lined with restaurants, and boast no fewer than four grocery stores.

BORNHOLM

Bornholm natives like to say that when God was creating Scandinavia, he saved the choice bits for last and then dropped them into the Baltic Sea. After a night or two on Bornholm, you might be inclined to agree. The undulating farmlands of the south are ideal for bikers, while nature-lovers will favor the dramatic, rocky landscape of the north. The sandiest and longest beaches are at Dueodde, on the island's southern tip. Don't miss Bornholm's four round churches, built in the 12th century and recently tied to the rituals of the Knights Templar, predecessors to today's Freemasons. For more info, check out www.bornholm.info.

TRANSPORTATION. Trains from Copenhagen to Ystad, Sweden are timed to meet the **ferry** from Ystad to Rønne, Bornholm's capital. (Train ☎70 13 14 15; 1¾hr., 5-6 per day. Ferry ☎46 411 55 87 00; 70min., 150kr.) Overnight ferries from Copenhagen to Rønne leave at 11:30pm and arrive in Rønne at 6:30am (240kr, add 75kr for a dorm-style bed). **Scandlines** operates ferries from Fährhafen Sassnitz on the northern coast of Germany. (☎49 383 926 44 20. 3½hr., 1-2 per day, 90-135kr.) Bornholm has an efficient local BAT **bus** service, although buses run infrequently on weekends. (☎56 95 21 21. 36-45kr, 24hr. pass 130kr.) Bus #7 makes a circuit of the entire island; it starts at Rønne and ends at Hammershus, stopping at most of the island's towns and attractions along the way. To go directly between Rønne and Hammershus, take bus #1 or 2. There are well-marked **bike** paths between all the major towns; pick up a guide at the tourist office in Rønne (40kr). The rides from Rønne to Sandvig and Rønne to Dueodde are about 28km.

RØNNE. Busy Rønne (pop. 14,000) is Bornholm's principal port of entry. Perched on the island's southwestern coast, the town is a prime outpost for biking trips through the surrounding fields, forests, and beaches. Rent a **bike** from **Bornholms Cykeludlejning,** next door to the tourist office at Ndr. Kystvej 5. (☎56 95 13 59. Reserve ahead in July. 60kr per day. Open daily May-Sept. 7am-4pm and 8:30-9pm.) The **tourist office,** Ndr. Kystv. 3, books private rooms (150-215kr) for free. (☎56 95 95 00. Open mid-June to mid-Aug. M-Sa 10am-5:30pm, Su 10am-3pm; low season reduced hours.) To reach it, head straight out of the ferry terminal and cross toward the gas station; look for the green flag. The charming but noisy **Youth Hostel (HI) ❷**, Arsenalv. 12, is in a wooded area near the coastline. From the ferry, turn right and walk 3min. down Snellemark past the red BAT terminal. Turn right onto Lille Torvet, and walk for 10min.; Arsenalv. is on the right past the rotary. (☎56 95 13 40. Breakfast 45kr. Kitchen available. Sheets 55kr. Reception 8am-noon and 4-5pm. Open mid-June to mid-Aug. Dorms 115kr. Nonmembers add 30kr. Cash only.) **Galløkken Camping ❶**, Strandvejen 4, is near the city center and the beach. (☎56 95 23 20. Bikes 55kr per day. Reception 7:30am-noon and 2-9pm. Open mid-May to Aug. 58kr per person.) **Sam's Corner ❷**, St. Torv 2, is a laid-back burger and pizza joint with low prices (45-60kr) and large portions. Get groceries at **Kvickly,** opposite the tourist office. (Open mid-June to late Aug. daily 9am-8pm; Sept. to mid-June M-F 9am-8pm, Sa 8am-5pm, Su 10am-4pm.)

◪ **SANDVIG AND ALLINGE.** These tony seaside villages, 1km apart, are excellent points of entry for hikes and bike rides through the jagged heights along the northern coast. Less than 2km from Sandvig is ▨**Hammershus,** northern Europe's largest castle ruin, situated on a breathtaking cliff overlooking the sea. Make the pleasant 20min. walk uphill from Sandvig, or catch bus #1, 2, or 7 to Hammershus. Many trails originate in Sandvig; the rocky area around **Hammeren,** northwest of the town, is a beautiful 2hr. walk that can only be covered on foot. Several kilometers east in a field of waving grass, the whitewashed **Østerlars Rundkirke** is the largest of the island's enigmatic round churches. Take bus #3 or 9 to Østerlars Kirke. The **Nordbornholms Turistbureau,** Kirkeg. 4, in Allinge, offers free maps of the Hammeren area and also finds rooms for free. (☎56 48 00 01. Open mid-June to mid-Aug. M-F 10am-5pm, Sa 10am-3pm; mid-Aug. to mid-June M-F 10am-5pm, Sa 10am-noon.) Rent **bikes** at the **Sandvig Cykeludlejning,** Strandvejen 121. (☎56 48 00 60. Open June-Aug. M-F 9am-4pm, Sa 9am-2pm, Su 10am-1pm. 60kr per day.) Just outside Sandvig is the lakeside **Sandvig Vandrerhjem (HI) ❷,** Hammershusv. 94. (☎56 48 03 62. Breakfast 45kr. Sheets 60kr. Reception 9-10am and 4-6pm. Open Apr.-Oct. Dorms 100kr; singles 250kr; doubles 350kr. Cash only.) **Sandvig Familie Camping ❶,** Strandlinien 5, has sites on the sea. (☎56 48 04 47. Bikes 50kr per day, 200kr per week. Reception 8am-11pm. Open Apr.-Oct. 50kr per person, 15kr per tent.) **Riccos ❷,** Strandg. 8, a pleasant cafe near the sea, offers a vast array of coffees and teas as well as free **Internet** access. (Open daily 7am-10pm. MC/V.)

FUNEN (FYN)

Situated between Zealand to the east and the Jutland Peninsula to the west, the island of Funen is Denmark's garden. This once-remote breadbasket is no longer isolated from the rest of Denmark—the magnificent Storebæltsbro bridge and tunnel now connect it to Zealand. Pick up maps (75kr) of the bike paths covering the island at Funen tourist offices.

ODENSE   ☎65, 66

Most tourists are drawn to Odense (OH-n-sa; pop. 185,000) by the legacy of Hans Christian Andersen and his fairytales, but a thriving nightlife and music scene are quickly making this city a destination for the young and trendy.

◪▨ **TRANSPORTATION AND PRACTICAL INFORMATION. Trains** arrive from Copenhagen (1½hr., 270kr) and from Svendborg via Kværndrup (40min., 58kr). Intracity **buses** depart from behind the train station. The **tourist office,** on Rådhuspl., books rooms for a 35kr fee and sells the **Odense Adventure Pass,** good for admission to museums, discounts on plays, and unlimited public transport. (24hr. pass 110kr, 48hr. pass 150kr.) Turn left out of the train station and make a right at the light onto Thomas B. Thriges Gate. Turn right onto Vesterg. after the bank. The office is on the left. (☎66 12 75 20; www.visitodense.com. Open mid-June to Aug. M-F 9:30am-7pm, Sa 10am-5pm, Su 10am-4pm; Sept. to mid-June M-F 9:30am-4:30pm, Sa 10am-1pm.) The library in the station has free **Internet,** but you must reserve time at the info desk. (Open Apr.-Sept. M-Th 10am-7pm, F 10am-4pm, Sa 10am-2pm; Oct.-Mar. M-Th 10am-7pm, Sa-Su 10am-4pm.) **Galaxy Netcafe,** also in the station, offers unlimited Internet and other computer services for a one-time fee of 17kr. Rent **bikes** next door to the station at **Rolsted Cykler.** (85kr per day, 300kr deposit. Open M-Th 10am-5:30pm, F 10am-7pm, Sa 10am-2pm.) A free map with local bike routes is available at the tourist office. **Postal Code:** 5000.

▮▯ ACCOMMODATIONS AND FOOD. The fabulous **Danhostel Odense City (HI) ❸** is attached to the station. (☎63 11 04 25; www.cityhostel.dk. Kitchen available. Breakfast 45kr. Sheets 50kr. Laundry 40kr. Internet 10kr per 15min. Reception 8am-noon and 4-8pm. Dorms 164kr; singles 406kr; doubles 552kr; triples 597kr; quads 644kr. Nonmembers add 30kr. MC/V; 4% credit card surcharge.) To reach **DCU-Camping Odense ❶**, Odensevej 102, take bus #21, 22, or 23 (dir.: Højby) and ask the driver to drop you off. (☎66 11 47 02. Pool. Reception 7:30am-noon and 4-10pm. Open late Mar. to Sept. 64kr per person; 20kr per tent. MC/V.) **Vestergade,** a long pedestrian street, is the center of the city's activity, especially around the intersection with Kongensg.; it swarms with ethnic restaurants and cafes in all price ranges. Don't overlook the small alleys that occasionally wend their way off of Vesterg.; Brandts Passage is the liveliest, while Vintapperstr. is slightly more low-key. Both are on the right as you walk away from the tourist office on Vesterg., just before and after Kongensg. Get groceries at **Aktiv Super,** at the corner of Nørreg. and Skulkenborgg. (Open M-F 9am-7pm, Sa 9am-4pm.)

◨◧ SIGHTS AND ENTERTAINMENT. At **Hans Christian Andersen's Hus,** Hans Jensens Str. 37-45, you can learn about the great author's eccentricities, listen to his timeless children's tales, and follow his rags-to-riches rise to fame; 2005 marks the bicentennial of his birth. From the tourist office, walk right on Vesterg., then turn left on Thomas Thringes Gate and right on Hans Jensens Str. (☎65 51 46 20. Museum open daily mid-June to Aug. 9am-7pm; Sept. to mid-June Tu-Su 10am-4pm. English-language performances W-Th 3pm. 40kr.) At the **Carl Nielsen Museum,** Claus Bergs G. 11, listen to the works of the most famous Danish musician. (☎66 14 88 14. Open Th-F 4-8pm, Su noon-4pm. 15kr.) **Brandts Passage** is home to a number of small, eccentric museums featuring photography and contemporary art. A night out on the town in Odense has two discrete phases. On many weekends, from dinnertime until around 11pm, Vesterg. and other nearby streets are packed with people of all ages shopping, drinking, and listening to live bands on nearly every corner. Once this crowd disperses, the city's growing club and bar scene takes over. **Crazy Daisy,** Skt. Knuds Kirkestr. just past Radhuspl., has four rooms and six bars on three floors. (www.daisy-odense.dk. Open Th-Sa 11pm-late; 30-45kr cover.) **Froggy's Cafe** is a crowded, smoky pub at the corner of Vesterg. and Kongensg. that features live music every weekend. (Open Th-Sa 9am-5am. MC/V.) Farther away from the center, **Boogie Dance Cafe,** on Nørreg. near Thomas B. Thriges Gate, features a young crowd grooving out to Odense's best DJs. (Open Tu-Sa 10:30pm-5:30am. Cover 40kr after midnight. MC/V.)

▶ DAYTRIP FROM ODENSE: KVÆRNDRUP. Just 25min. south of Odense lies Kværndrup, home to ▮**Egeskov Slot,** a magnificent castle that appears to float on the surrounding lake. Spend at least two hours exploring the grounds, which include a series of lovely, imaginative gardens and a grab bag of small museums. (Castle open July M-Tu and Th-Su 10am-7pm, W 10am-11pm; May-June and Aug.-Sept. daily 10am-5pm. Grounds open daily July 10am-8pm; June and Aug. 10am-6pm; Apr.-May and Sept. 10am-5pm. Grounds, maze, and museums 85kr, with castle 140kr.) Take the Svendborg-bound train from Odense to Kværndrup; make sure to ask at Odense which trains stop there. Turn right out of the station and walk up to Bøjdenvej, the main road. Wait for bus #920 (1 per hr.; 18kr, free with connecting train ticket), or turn right and walk 20min. to the castle. The **tourist office,** Egeskovg. 1, is just before the castle. (☎62 27 10 46. Open daily July noon-8pm; June and Aug. noon-6pm; Sept. and Apr.-May noon-5pm.)

TIP In Funen and other rural areas in Denmark, trains do not always stop at every station on the line. Be sure to ask ahead at the ticket counter about exactly which train to take, and whether you need to sit in a particular car. This will prevent you from pressing your nose against the window, forlorn, as your station stop whizzes by.

ÆRØSKØBING ☎62

The wheat fields, harbors, and hamlets of Ærø (EH-ruh), a small island off the southern coast of Funen, quietly preserve an earlier era of Danish history. Cows, rather than real estate developers, lay claim to the land around the quaint southern town of Ærøskøbing (pop. 3900). Rosebushes and half-timbered houses line the town's cobblestone streets, while sleepy one-lane roads and a serene phalanx of windmills lure vacationing Danes into exploring the rest of the island by bicycle. Several **trains** from Odense to Svendborg are timed to meet the **ferry** (☎62 52 40 00) to Ærøskøbing (1¼hr.; 6 per day, 3hr. apart; one-way 79kr, round-trip 132kr). Ferries depart down Frederiksg., which is behind and to the left of the Svendborg train station; tickets are available on board. On the island, **bus** #990 travels between the towns of Ærøskøbing, Marstal, and Søby (20kr, day pass 60kr). Ærøskøbing's **tourist office,** Vesterg. 1, books rooms for a 25kr fee. (☎62 52 13 00; www.arre.dk. Open mid-June to Aug. M-F 9am-5pm, Sa 9am-2pm, Su 9:30am-12:30pm; Sept. to mid-June M-F 9am-4pm, Sa 9:30am-12:30pm.) To get to the **Youth Hostel (HI) ❷,** Smedev. 15, turn left on Smedeg.; at the end, bear right onto Nørreg., which becomes Østerg. and eventually Smedev. (☎62 52 10 44. Kitchen available. Breakfast 40kr. Sheets 40kr. Bikes 45kr per day. Reception 8am-noon and 4-8pm. Check-in 6pm. Open Apr.-Sept. Dorms 100kr; singles 265kr; doubles 270kr. Non-members add 30kr. Cash only.) **Ærøskøbing Camping ❶,** is 10min. to the right along Sygehusvejen, off of Vestre Allé as you leave the ferry. (☎62 52 18 54. Reception 8am-noon and 3-10pm. Open May-Sept. 54kr per person.) Stock up at **Netto,** across from the ferry landing. (Open M-F 9am-7pm, Sa 8am-5pm.) **Postal Code:** 5970.

JUTLAND (JYLLAND)

Homeland of the same Jutes who joined the Angles and Saxons in the conquest of England, the Jutland peninsula is Denmark's only land link to continental Europe. Fertile soil along the eastern coast has nourished Jutland's dairy farms for centuries and spawned cultural centers like Århus and Aalborg. The western half of the peninsula is overall less compelling, although some seaside enthusiasts swear by the sandy beaches north of Esbjerg.

ÅRHUS ☎86, 89

Rather than pouting in the shadow of Copenhagen, Århus (ORE-hoos; pop. 280,000) takes some of the capital's urban sophistication and then tempers it with a refreshingly pull-no-punches provincialism. Pedestrian walkways thread their way through museums, swollen night clubs, and a well-developed art scene in this second-largest city in Denmark.

█▒ TRANSPORTATION AND PRACTICAL INFORMATION. Trains run from Århus to: Aalborg (1½hr., 2 per hr., 145kr); Copenhagen (3hr., 2 per hr., 273kr); Fredericia (1hr., 2 per hr., 110kr); Frederikshavn (2¾hr., 1 per hr., 189kr). All major **buses** leave from the train station or from outside the tourist office. To get to the **tourist office,** exit the train station and go left across Banegardspl., then take the first right on Park Allé.; it's under the clock tower of the ultramodern Radhus. They book private rooms (200-300kr) for a 25kr fee and sell the **Århus pass,** which includes unlimited public transit and admission to most museums and sights (1-day 97kr, 2-day 121kr). If you're not going to many museums, the **24hr. Tourist Ticket** (50kr), also available at the tourist office, is a better bet; it offers unlimited use of the city's extensive bus system. (☎89 40 67 00; www.visitaarhus.com. Open mid-June to early Sept. M-F 9:30am-6pm, Sa 9:30am-5pm, Su 9:30am-1pm; May to mid-June M-F 9:30am-5pm, Sa 10am-1pm; early Sept.-Apr. M-F 9am-4pm, Sa 10am-1pm.) The main **library,** on Vesterg. 55 in Mølleparken, is out-and-out ugly, but it does offer free **Internet** access. (Open May-Sept. M-Th 10am-7pm, F 10am-5pm, Sa 10am-2pm; Oct.-Apr. M-Th 10am-8pm, F 10am-6pm, Sa 10am-3pm, Su noon-4pm.) After hours, try **Boomtown NetCafe,** Åboulevarden 21. (☎89 41 39 30. Open M-Th and Su 10am-2am, F-Sa 10am-8am. 20kr per 30min., 30kr per hr.) The **post office,** Banegardspl. 1A, is next to the train station. **Postal Code:** 8000.

┌┐┌┐ ACCOMMODATIONS AND FOOD. The very popular **Århus City Sleep-In ❸,** Havneg. 20, is 15min. from the train station and in the middle of the city's nightlife. From the train station, follow Ryesg., which becomes Sønderg., all the way to the canal. Take the steps or elevator down to Åboulevarden, cross the canal, and turn right; at the end of the canal, turn left on Mindebrog., then left again on Havneg. (☎86 19 20 55; www.citysleep-in.dk. Bikes 50kr per day; deposit 200kr. Kitchen available. Breakfast 40kr. Sheets 40kr; deposit 30kr. Laundry 25kr. Internet 20kr per hr. Reception 24hr. Dorms 105kr; doubles 320-360kr. MC/V; 4.75% credit card surcharge.) **Blommehaven Camping ❶,** Ørneredevej 35, is a camper's resort located in the Marselisborg forest south of the city, near the beach. In the summer, take bus #19 from the station to the grounds; low season, take bus #6 to Hørhavevej. (☎86 27 02 07; info@blommehaven.dk. Reception 8am-noon and 2-10pm. Open Apr.-Aug. 64kr per person, 20kr per site.) **Frederiksgade** and **Åboulevarden** are lined with restaurants, but the mother-lode of inexpensive food is Skoleg., which becomes Mejlg., just behind City Sleep-in. The New Age vibe at **Under Engle ❷,** Mejlg. 28, means that you can see an astrologer or acupuncturist after sampling their vegetarian fare. (☎86 18 23 30. Open Tu-Sa noon-10pm.) Travelers in a rush can grab good sandwiches at **DeeDee's ❷,** across from the train station. (Open M-F 8am-7pm, Sa 9:30am-4pm, Su 11am-6pm.) Pick up groceries at **Netto,** in St. Knuds Torv. (Open M-F 9am-8pm, Sa 8am-5pm.)

◎┌┐ SIGHTS AND ENTERTAINMENT. A city the size of Århus has no right to harbor a museum as exceptional as the **☒Århus Kunstmuseum (ARoS),** Aros Allé 2, off of Vester Allé. ARoS features eight sinuous levels of gallery space, which play host to installations, multimedia exhibits, and a huge permanent collection of modern art. The view from the roof terrace is excellent. (☎87 30 66 00; www.aros.dk. Open Tu and Th 10am-5pm, W 10am-10pm. 60kr.) Just outside town, the **Moesgård Museum of Prehistory,** Moesgård Allé 20, would be unremarkable except for the eerie, mummified **☒Grauballe Man.** Take bus #6 from the train station to the end. (☎89 42 11 00; www.moesmus.dk. Open Apr.-Sept. daily 10am-5pm; Oct.-Mar. Tu-Su 10am-4pm. 45kr, students 35kr.) The **Prehistoric Trail** is a beautiful walk that leads from behind the museum through dense forest to a sandy **beach** (3km). In summer, bus #19 returns from the beach to the Århus station. The lush gardens of **Marselisborg Slot,** Kongevejen 100, are open to the public, although the palace and storied rose garden are closed in July and whenever the Queen is in residence. From the train station, take bus #1, 18, or 19. Across the street, **Mindepark** is a great spot for a stroll or a picnic. Each summer, Århus hosts its acclaimed **jazz festival** (July 9-16, 2005; www.jazzfest.dk), followed by the **Århus Festuge** (☎89 31 82 70; www.aarhusfestuge.dk), a rollicking celebration of theater, dance, and music held from the last weekend in August through early September. The neighboring **Fever** (☎87 30 33 09; www.fever.dk; open Th-Sa 11pm-6am) and **The Social Club** (☎86 19 42 50; www.socialclub.dk; open Th-Sa 11pm-6am), both at Klosterg. 34, are large clubs that poll well with students. **Train,** Tolbodg. 6, has reinvented an enormous dockside warehouse as a nightclub and concert venue. (☎86 13 47 22; www.train.dk. Concerts all ages, disco 23+. Disco open F-Sa 11pm-late.) The many pubs down Skoleg. offer a laid-back alternative to the club scene.

▶ DAYTRIP FROM ÅRHUS: BILLUND. Billund is best known as the home of **▩Legoland,** an amusement park filled with intricate, sprawling Lego-sculptures made from over 50 million of the tiny candy-colored blocks. Although many of the attractions target young children, the ferocious **Power Builder** ride will flail any skeptic into submission. (☎75 33 13 33; www.legoland.com. Park open daily July to mid-Aug. 10am-9pm; June and late Aug. 10am-8pm; Apr.-May and Sept.-Oct. reduced hours. Day pass 180kr. Free entrance 30min. before rides close.) To get there, take the **train** from Århus to Vejle (45min., 1 per hr.), then take **bus** #244 (dir.: Grinsted; 52kr) to the park.

SILKEBORG AND RY   ☎86

Right in the heart of Jutland, Silkeborg and Ry offer a prime base for canoeing, biking, and hiking. Silkeborg (pop. 38,000) is a charming town between two lakes, and it offers a smattering of culture along with conveniences for those about to strike out into the wilderness. The **Silkeborg Museum,** right next to the tourist office, boasts the **Tollund Man,** a 2500-year-old body found preserved in a local bog. The body is in much better condition than the Grauballe Man in Århus (p. 304), although its presentation is underwhelming. (Museum open May to late Oct. daily 10am-5pm; late Oct. to Apr. M-Tu and Th-F 10am-5pm, W and Sa-Su noon-4pm. 40kr.) **Trains** run from Silkeborg to Århus (1hr., 2 per hr., 40kr) and Ry (15min., 2 per hr., 26kr). To reach the **tourist office,** Åhavev. 2a, and its wealth of info on outdoor activities, turn right out of the train station onto Drewsonsv., left on Chr. 8 V., and right onto Østerg. (☎82 19 11; www.silkeborg.com. Open mid-June to Aug M-F 9am-5pm, Sa-Su 9am-2pm; Sept. to mid-June M-Sa 10am-3pm.) The **Silkeborg Vandrerhjem (HI) ❶** is near both downtown and the water. (☎82 36 42. Breakfast 45kr. Sheets 40kr. Reception 8am-noon and 4-8pm. Open June-Aug. Dorms 85kr; quads 340-532kr; 6-person rooms 708kr. V.)

Ry (pop. 4800) is a promising, if less developed, base for exploration. Rent bikes from **Ry Cykel & Knallertservice,** Parallelv. 9b, up Skanderborgv. 500m from the train station. (☎89 14 91. 60kr per day, 300kr per week. Open M-Th 8am-5:30pm, F 8am-6pm, Sa 8am-noon.) Rent canoes from **Ry Kanofart,** Kyhnsvej 20. (☎89 11 67. 60kr per hr., full-day 300kr. Open daily May-Aug. 9am-6pm.) The **tourist office,** in the train station, has free hiking maps of the area, including one that shows the route to **Himmelbjerget Tower,** one of Denmark's highest points. (☎89 34 22; www.visitry.com. Open July M-F 7am-5pm, Sa 10am-noon; June and Aug. M-F 7am-4pm, Sa 9am-2pm; Sept.-May M-F 7am-4pm, Sa 10am-noon.) Get supplies at **Kvickly,** on Siimtoften near the rotary. (Open M-Th 9am-7pm, F 9am-8pm, Sa 8am-5pm.)

FREDERICIA   ☎75

Fredericia (pop. 49,000) was founded in 1650 by King Frederik III after his defeat in the Thirty Years' War. Convinced that the area needed better protection, Frederik outfitted the town with a ring of moated and cannon-strewn **ramparts.** Two centuries later, these ramparts would help the Danes ward off invaders from the south during the 1849 Battle of Fredericia; the city celebrates this victory each year with parades and concerts on July 5-6. These days, however, no one is in any hurry to invade Fredericia's smokestacks and concrete high-rises; the town is the major railway junction connecting Jutland to the rest of Denmark, and little else recommends it. While waiting for a connection, climb the **White Water Tower,** across the street from the tourist office, for a view of the ramparts and the downtown area. (Open late June to mid-Aug. daily 10am-4pm; May-late June and mid-Aug. to Sept. Sa-Su 10am-4pm. 10kr.)

Trains go to Århus (1hr., 3 per hr., 110kr) and Copenhagen (2¼hr., 2 per hr., 253kr) via Odense (30-50min., 75kr). To get to the **tourist office,** Danmarksg. 2A, go left across the plaza, and then turn right on Vesterbrog and right again on Danmarksport. (☎92 13 77; www.visitfredericia.dk. Open mid-June to Aug. M-F 9am-6pm, Sa 9am-2pm; Sept. to mid-June M-F 10am-5pm, Sa 10am-1pm.) The library, on the corner of Danmarksg. and Prinsesseg., has free **Internet** access. (Open M-Th 10am-7pm, F 10am-5pm, Sa 10am-2pm.) **Fredericia Vandrerhjem and Kursuscenter (HI) ❷,** Vestre Ringvej 98, has many rooms with balconies overlooking an adjoining lake. From the station, go across the plaza, turn left on Vejlevej, go under the bridge, turn right on the first road past the lake, walk for 10min., then take the path on the right. (☎92 12 87; www.fredericia-danhostel.dk. Breakfast 45kr. Sheets 47kr. Reception 8am-noon and 4-8pm. Dorms 118kr; doubles 422-472kr. MC/V; 4.75% credit card surcharge.) **Gothersgade,** a few blocks past the tourist office on the right, has a number of inexpensive cafes.

RIBE   ☎75

Aware of the town's historical importance as Denmark's oldest settlement, Ribe (pop. 18,000) passed preservation laws in 1899 forcing residents to maintain the character of their houses and to live in them year-round. The result is a town that's lovely, if self-consciously medieval, situated on the salt plains near Jutland's west coast. For a breathtaking view of Ribe's red shingle roofs, climb the 248 steps through the clockwork and huge bells of the 12th-century **Domkirke tower.** (☎75 42 06 19. Open July to mid-Aug. M-Sa 10am-5:30pm, Su noon-5:30pm; May-June and mid-Aug. to Sept. M-Sa 10am-5pm, Su noon-5pm; Apr. and Oct. M-Sa 11am-6pm, Su noon-4pm; Nov.-Mar. daily 11am-3pm. 12kr.) Next to the Rådhus, **Von Støckens Plads,** a former debtor's prison, houses a small museum on medieval torture. (☎76 88 11 22. Open daily June-Aug. 1-3pm; May and Sept. M-F 1-3pm. 15kr.) Follow the singing **night watchman** on his rounds for a tour of town, beginning in the Torvet. (35min.; June-Aug. 8 and 10pm; May and Sept. 10pm. Free.) The open-air **Ribe Vikingcenter,** Lustrupvej 4, painstakingly recreates a Viking town that was unearthed near Ribe, complete with a farm and a marketplace. Take bus #51 to Lustrup, or enjoy the 25min. walk south down Hundeg. Pass through two rotaries, and then be on the lookout for signs. (☎41 16 11; www.ribevikingecenter.dk. Open July-Aug. daily 11am-4:30pm; May-June and Sept. M-F 11am-4pm. 60kr.)

Trains run to Esbjerg (40min., 1 per hr., 60kr) and to Fredericia via Bramming (1½hr., every 20-40min., 102kr). The **tourist office,** Torvet 3, books rooms for a 20kr fee. From the train station, walk down Dagmarsg.; it's on the right in the main square. (☎75 42 15 00; www.ribetourist.dk. Open July-Aug. M-F 9:30am-5:30pm, Sa 10am-5pm, Su 10am-2pm; low season reduced hours.) **Ribe Vandrerhjem (HI) ❷,** Sct. Pedersg. 16, offers **bike** rentals (60kr per day). From the station, cross the Viking Museum parking lot, bear right, walk down Sct. Nicolajg. to the end, then turn right on Saltg. and immediately left on Sct. Petersg. (☎42 06 20. Breakfast 45kr. Sheets 42kr. Laundry 45kr. Reception 8am-noon and 4-6pm. Open Feb.-Nov. Dorms 110kr; singles 250-440kr; doubles 325-440kr. AmEx/MC/V; 4% credit card surcharge.) **Ribe Camping ❶,** Farupvej 2, is 1.5km from the town center. Take bus #715 (every 1½hr.) from the station to Gredstedbro. (☎41 07 77. 65kr per person; cabins from 220kr.) **Overdammen,**

which begins at the Torvet and eventually becomes Saltsg., has plenty of inexpensive cafes and pizzerias; **Seminarievej**, at the far end of Saltsg., is home to a number of supermarkets.

AALBORG   ☎99

Modern Aalborg (OLE-borg; pop. 160,000), is a laid-back haven for university students partaking of high and low culture in equal measure. On C. W. Obels Pl., behind the student center, you can tour the beautiful **Monastery of the Holy Ghost**. (Open late June to early Aug.; tours in Danish, German, and English every M, W, and F at 1:30pm. 40kr.) At the corner of Alg. and Molleg., an elevator descends beneath the shopping plaza to the half-excavated ruins of a **Franciscan Friary**. (Open in summer daily 10am-5pm; low season Tu-Su 10am-5pm. 20kr.) North of town, the starkly solemn grounds of **Lindholm Høje**, Vendilavej 11, include 700 ancient Viking graves and a less-than-essential museum detailing life in Viking times. Take bus #2 from the plaza near the tourist office. (☎96 31 04 10. Grounds free and open 24hr. Museum open mid-Apr. to Oct. daily 10am-5pm; Nov. to mid-Apr. Tu 10am-4pm, Su 11am-4pm. 30kr, students 15kr.) After a full day of dusty antiquarianism, turn your attention to the bacchanalia down on **Jomfru Ane Gade**, a teeming pedestrian strip of bars and clubs that's packed with students and partygoers nearly every night.

Trains arrive from Århus (1½hr., 1 per hr., 145kr) and Copenhagen (5hr., 1 per hr., 320kr). Aalborg's recently redesigned bus system is daunting; buses are usually 15kr with an hour's worth of transfers, and most pass through J. F. K. Pl. To find the **tourist office**, Østeråg. 8., head out of the train station, cross J. F. K. Pl. and turn left on Boulevarden, which becomes Østeråg. The office distributes copies of *Musik i Aalborg*, with info on **free concerts** in Mølleparken. (☎30 60 90; www.visitaalborg.com. Open July M-F 9am-5:30pm, Sa 10am-4pm; late June and Aug. M-F 9am-5:30pm, Sa 10am-1pm; Sept. to mid-June M-F 9am-4:30pm, Sa 10am-1pm.) The public library, near the end of Alg., has free **Internet** access. (☎31 44 00. Open mid-June to Aug. M-F 10am-8pm, Sa 10am-2pm; Sept. to mid-June M-F 10am-8pm, Sa 10am-3pm.) After hours, try **NetCafeen**, Nytorv 13a (open M-Th and Su 11am-3am, F-Sa 11am-8am; 20kr per hr.) or head across the street to **Boomtown**, Nytorv 18 (open M-Th 10am-2am, F-Sa 10am-8am, Su 11am-midnight; 30kr per hour). **Aalborg Vandrerhjem and Camping (HI) ❷**, Skydebanevej 50, has cozy private cabins, some of which double as dorms, alongside a windswept fjord. Take bus #13 (dir: Egholm Faergeleje), call for a stop when you pass a triangular church on your right, and then walk 100m further down the road to the hostel. (☎98 11 60 44. Reception mid-June to mid-Aug. 7:30am-11pm; mid-Jan. to mid-June and mid-Aug. to mid-Dec. 8am-noon and 4-9pm. Dorms 118kr; singles 270-480kr; doubles 330-480kr. Camping 49kr.) **Ved Stranden**, which runs parallel to the water, is lined with cheap eateries between Vesterbro and Jomfru Ane G.; farther down toward Østeråg., the restaurants get more expensive.

FREDERIKSHAVN   ☎98

From its days as a fishing village and naval base, Frederikshavn (fred-riks-HOW-n; pop. 35,000) has evolved into a transportation hub for Scandinavian ferry lines. Little else recommends the town. **Stena Line** ferries (☎96 20 02 00; www.stenaline.com) leave for Gothenburg, Sweden (2-3¼hr.; 100-150kr, 30% Scanrail discount) and Oslo, Norway (8½hr.; 140-280kr, 50% Scanrail discount). **Color Line** (☎99 56 20 00; www.colorline.com) sails to Larvik, Norway (6¼hr.; 180-410kr). To reach the Frederikshavn **tourist office**, Skandia Torv 1, turn left out of the train station and follow the path in the old railroad tracks; the office is 5min. down on the right. (☎42 32 66; www.frederikshavn-tourist.dk. Open July to mid-Aug. M-Sa 8:30am-7pm, Su 8:30am-5pm; June and late Aug. daily 8:30am-5pm; Sept.-May M-F

DENMARK

9am-4pm, Sa 11am-2pm.) To get from the station to the **Youth Hostel (HI)** ❷, Buhlsvej 6, walk right on Skipperg. for 10min.; turn left onto Norreg., and right on Buhlsv. (☎42 14 75; www.danhostel.dk/frederikshavn. Reception 8am-noon and 4-8pm. Closed Jan. Dorms 85-100kr; singles 200-250kr; doubles 240-300kr.)

SKAGEN
☎98

Perched on Denmark's northernmost tip, Skagen (SKAY-en; pop. 10,000) is a bucolic, if crowded, summer retreat tucked between long stretches of sea and white sand dunes. With houses painted in vibrant "Skagen yellow" and roofs covered in red tile to welcome local fishermen home from sea, Skagen is a colorful and idyllic vacation spot. The elegant ▧**Skagens Museum,** Brøndumsv. 4, features 19th- and 20th-century work by Skagen-based artists, most notably Anna Archer and P.S. Krøyer. (☎44 18 10; www.skagensmuseum.dk. Open daily June-Aug. 10am-6pm. 40kr.) In nearby **Grenen,** the powerful currents of the North and Baltic Seas violently collide. You can swim along 60km of beaches around Skagen, but Grenen is strictly off-limits to bathers; however, this doesn't stop hordes of vacationing Danes from making the trek out to the sandy point. To get to Grenen, take the bus from the Skagen station (15kr) or walk 2km down Fyrvej; turn left out of the train station and bear left at the fork. About 13km south of Skagen is the spectacular and enormous **Råberg Mile** (ROH-bayrg MEE-lay), a sand dune formed by a 16th-century storm. The vast moonscape migrates 15m east each year. Take bus #79 or the train from Skagen to Hulsig, then walk about 2km down Kandestedvej.

Buses and **trains** run to Frederikshavn (1hr.; 45kr). Biking is by far the best way to experience Skagen's charm, including Grenen and the Råberg Mile; rent **bikes** at **Skagen CykelUdlejning,** Banegardspl., next to the station. (☎44 10 70. 75kr per day. 200kr deposit. Open daily 9am-7pm.) The **tourist office** is in the station. (☎44 13 77; www.skagen.dk. Open July-Aug. M-Sa 9am-6pm, Su 10am-4pm; Sept.-May M 9am-5pm, Tu-Th 9am-4pm, F 9am-3pm, Sa 10am-1pm; June M-Sa 9am-5pm, Su 10am-6pm.) The library, Sct. Laurentii Vej 23., has free **Internet** access. (Open M and Th 10am-6pm, Tu-W and F 1-6pm, Sa 10am-1pm.) The **Skagen Ny Vandrerhjem** ❷, Rolighedsvej 2, is very popular; book in advance. From the station, turn right on Chr. X's Vej, which becomes Frederikshavnvej, then left on Rolighedsvej. (☎44 22 00; www.danhostelnord.dk/skagen. Breakfast 45kr. Kitchen available. Sheets 50kr. Reception 9am-noon and 4-6pm. Open Mar.-Nov. Dorms 118kr; singles 250-470kr; doubles 300-585kr. Cash only.) Bus #79 passes several **campgrounds.** Turn right out of the station onto **Sct. Laurentii Vej** for groceries and sandwich shops.

ESTONIA (EESTI)

Happy to sever its Soviet bonds, Estonia has quickly revived ties with its Nordic neighbors. As a result, Finnish tourism and investment have proven a revitalizing force. The material wealth that has accumulated in Tallinn, however, masks the declining living standards that lurk outside of big cities, as well as the chagrin of the ethnically Russian minority over Estonia's Finnish leanings. Still, having overcome successive centuries of domination by the Danes, Swedes, and Russians, Estonians are now proud to take their place as members of modern Europe.

ESSENTIALS

WHEN TO GO

The best time to visit is from May to September. During summer, Estonia's climate is mild due to its proximity to the Baltic Sea. Winters, however, can be severe.

DOCUMENTS AND FORMALITIES

VISAS. As of May 1, 2004, member states of the EU and the EEA do not require a visa to visit Estonia. Citizens of Australia, Canada, New Zealand, and the US do not need a visa for up to 90 days in a six-month period. Visa extensions are not granted, and visas cannot be purchased at the border. For visa info, consult the **Estonian Ministry of Foreign Affairs** (www.vm.ee/eng).

EMBASSIES. Foreign embassies are all in Tallinn (p. 312). Estonian embassies at home include: **Australia**, 86 Louisa Rd., Birchgrove NSW, 2041 (☎02 9810 7468; eestikon@ozemail.com.au); **Canada**, 260 Dalhousie St., Ste. 216, Ottawa, ON K1N 7E4 (613 789 4222; embassy.ottawa@mfa.ee); **Ireland**, Riversdale House, St. Ann's, Ailesbury Rd., Dublin 4 (01 269 1552; asjur@gofree.indigo.ie); **UK**, 16 Hyde Park Gate, London SW7 5DG (020 7589 3428; www.estonia.gov.uk); **US**, 2131 Massachusetts Ave. NW, Washington, D.C. 20008 (202 588 0101; www.estemb.org).

TRANSPORTATION

BY PLANE, TRAIN, AND FERRY. Several international airlines offer flights to Tallinn; try **Estonian Air, Finnair,** or **SAS.** If you're coming from another Baltic state or Russia, trains may be even cheaper than ferries—which connect to Finland, Sweden, and Germany—but expect more red tape when crossing the border.

BY BUS. Domestically, buses are the best means of transport, as they are cheaper and more efficient than trains. It's even possible to ride buses from the mainland to island towns (via ferry) for less than the price of the ferry ride. During the school year (Sept.-June 25), students receive half-price bus tickets. Internationally, buses can be a painfully slow choice, as clearing the border may take hours.

BY BIKE AND BY TAXI. On the islands, bike rentals (around 100EEK per day) are an excellent means of exploration. Taxis are safe; the average rate is 7EEK per km.

BY THUMB. *Let's Go* does not recommend hitchhiking. Those who choose to do so should stretch out an open hand.

TOURIST SERVICES AND MONEY

EMERGENCY	Police: ☎110. Ambulance and Fire: ☎112.

TOURIST OFFICES. Most towns have tourist offices with English-speaking staff. Small info booths, marked with a green "i," sell maps and give away brochures.

MONEY. The unit of currency is the **kroon (EEK),** divided into 100 *senti.* Though Estonia joined the EU in 2004, it will not officially adopt the euro (€) until at least 2006. Prices and exchange rates are relatively stable. **Hansapank** and **Eesti Ühispank** cash traveler's checks. Credit cards are widely accepted, and **ATMs** are common. When making a purchase, cash is not passed between hands, but placed in a tray on the counter. **Tipping** is uncommon, but a service charge may be included in the bill.

ESTONIAN KROON (EEK)	AUS$1 = 9.14EEK	1EEK = AUS$0.11
	CDN$1 = 9.90EEK	1EEK = CDN$0.10
	EUR€1 = 15.65EEK	1EEK = EUR€0.06
	NZ$1 = 8.44EEK	1EEK = NZ$0.12
	UK£1 = 23.21EEK	1EEK = UK£0.04
	US$1 = 12.92EEK	1EEK = US$0.08

COMMUNICATION

PHONE CODES	**Country code:** 372. **International dialing prefix:** 800. From outside Estonia, dial int'l dialing prefix (see inside back cover) + 372 + city code + local number.

TELEPHONES AND INTERNET ACCESS. Tallinn, unlike other Estonian cities, has no city code. The 0 listed in parentheses before each city code should only be dialed when placing calls within Estonia. Payphones require **digital cards,** available at banks and newsstands. Cards come in denominations of 30, 50, and 100EEK. International calls can also be made from post offices. Phoning the US costs US$1-4 per minute. International access codes include: **AT&T** (☎0 800 12 001); **British Telecom** (800 10442); **Canada Direct** (0800 12011); **MCI** (0800 1122). **Internet** access is common, and usually costs 30-60EEK per hour.

MAIL. Within the EU, an airmail letter or postcard costs 6.50EEK; to the rest of the world, 8EEK. For *Poste Restante*, address envelope as follows: First name SURNAME, *Poste Restante*, Narva mnt. 1, Tallinn 10101, ESTONIA.

LANGUAGES. Estonians speak the best English in the Baltic states; most young people also know Finnish or Swedish, but German is more common among the older set. Russian used to be mandatory, but many Estonians resist its use, except along the eastern border.

ACCOMMODATIONS AND CAMPING

ESTONIA	❶	❷	❸	❹	❺
ACCOMMODATIONS	under 200EEK	200-400EEK	400-550EEK	550-600EEK	over 600EEK

Tourist offices have accommodations listings and can often arrange beds. There is little distinction between hotels, hostels, and guesthouses. For info on HI hostels, contact the **Estonian Youth Hostel Association,** Narva Mantee 16-25, 10120, Tallinn (☎6461 457; www.baltichostels.net). Some **hostels** are part of larger hotels, so ask for the cheaper rooms. Note that even some upscale **hotels** have hall baths. **Homestays** are inexpensive, but the cheapest hostels can be a better deal. The word *võõrastemaja* (guesthouse) often implies that a place is less expensive. **Camping** is a great option on the islands, but camping outside designated areas is illegal.

FOOD AND DRINK

ESTONIA	❶	❷	❸	❹	❺
FOOD	under 50EEK	50-80EEK	80-100EEK	100-140EEK	over 140EEK

Much to the dismay of vegetarians and those trying to keep kosher, *schnitzel* (a breaded and fried pork fillet) appears on nearly every menu, and most cheap Estonian cuisine is fried and doused with sour cream. Estonian specialties include the typical Baltic *seljanka* (meat stew) and *pelmenid* (dumplings), as well as smoked salmon and trout. Bread is usually dark and dense. A delicious, common dessert is pancakes with cheese curd and berries. The national brew *Saku* and the darker *Saku Tume* are excellent, but local beers, like Kuressaare's *Saaremaa*, are less consistent. Carbonated *Värska* mineral water is particularly salty.

HOLIDAYS AND FESTIVALS

Holidays: New Year's Day (Jan. 1); Independence Day (Feb. 24); Good Friday (Mar. 25); Easter (Mar. 27); May Day (May 1); Pentecost (May 15); Victory Day (June 23); Midsummer (June 24); Restoration of Independence (Aug. 20); Christmas (Dec. 25-26).

Festivals: The International New Music Festival, Nyyd, (Oct. 14-21) celebrates contemporary music of Estonian composers as well as the freedoms gained with independence. Conductors and musical groups from around the world are drawn to Pärnu for its summer film and music festivals.

FACTS AND FIGURES: ESTONIA

Official Name: Republic of Estonia.

Capital: Tallinn.

Major Cities: Pärnu, Tartu.

Population: 1,400,000.

Land Area: 45,226 sq. km.

Time Zone: GMT +2.

Languages: Estonian (official); Russian.

Religions: Evangelical Lutheran, Russian Orthodox, Estonian Orthodox.

ESTONIA

TALLINN ☎ 0

In the heart of Tallinn (pop. 371,000), cosmopolitan shops contrast with the serene Vanalinn (old town), where German spires, Danish towers, and Russian domes rise above the sea. Tourists from all over Europe are quickly falling in love with the city's ethnic restaurants, vibrant nightlife, and low prices.

⊏ TRANSPORTATION

Trains: Toompuiestee 35 (☎615 68 51; www.evrekspress.ee). Trams #1 and 5 run between the station and the town center. To **Moscow** (14½hr., 1 per day, 515-723EEK) and **St. Petersburg** (10hr., 1 per day on even-numbered days, 207-390EEK). There are no rail links to Latvia.

Buses: Lastekodu 46 (☎680 09 00), 1.5km southeast of Vanalinn. Trams #2 and 4 run between Hotel Viru and the station. Buy tickets at the station or from the driver. **Eurolines** (www.eurolines.ee) runs to: **Rīga** (5½-6½hr., 5 per day, 200EEK); **St. Petersburg** (8-10hr., 5 per day, 200EEK); **Vilnius** (10½hr., 2 per day, 370EEK).

Ferries: ☎631 85 50. At the end of Sadama, 15min. from the city center. 4 different terminals. Ferries cross to **Helsinki: Eckerö Line,** Terminal B (☎631 86 06; www.eckeroline.ee). 3½hr., 1 per day, 220-620EEK); **Nordic Jet Line,** Terminal C (☎613 70 00; www.njl.info. 1½hr., 6 per day, 295-595EEK); **Silja Line,** Terminal D (☎611 66 61; www.silja.ee. 1½hr.; 5 per day; 250-530EEK, students 200-480EEK); **Tallink,** Terminals A and D (☎640 98 08; www.tallink.ee. 3¼hr.; 3 per day; 315-345EEK, students 284-310EEK. Express ferries 1½hr.; 7 per day; 235-425EEK, students 212-384EEK).

Public Transportation: Buses, trams, and trolleybuses cover the entire metropolitan area 6am-midnight. Buy tickets (*talong;* 10EEK) from kiosks around town and validate them in the metal boxes onboard or risk a 600EEK fine.

Taxis: Klubi Takso (☎648 142 00) or **Tulika Takso** (☎12 00). 5.50-7EEK per km, min. 35EEK. Call ahead to avoid the 8-50EEK "waiting fee."

▓▓ ▓ ORIENTATION AND PRACTICAL INFORMATION

Even locals lose their way along the winding medieval streets of Tallinn's **Vanalinn** (old town), which is surrounded by the major streets **Rannamäe tee, Mere pst., Pärnu mnt., Kaarli pst.,** and **Toompuiestee.** Vanalinn is divided into the larger, busier **All-linn** (lower town) and **Toompea,** a fortified rocky hill. Enter Vanalinn through the 15th-century **Viru ärarad,** the main gates in the city wall, located across from **Hotel Viru,** Tallinn's central landmark. To reach Vanalinn from the ferry terminal, walk 15min. along Sadama, which becomes Põhja pst., and turn left on Pikk through **Paks Margareeta** (Fat Margaret) gate. To get to **Raekoja plats** (Town Hall Square), the center of All-linn, from the train station, cross under Toompuiestee and continue straight on Nunne; turn left on Pikk and then take a right on Kinga.

Tourist Office: Kullassepa 4/Niguliste 2 (☎645 77 77; www.tourism.tallinn.ee). Sells city maps and *Tallinn In Your Pocket* (35EEK). Open July-Aug. M-F 9am-8pm, Sa-Su 10am-6pm; Sept. M-F 9am-6pm, Sa-Su 10am-5pm; Oct.-Apr. M-F 9am-5pm, Sa 10am-3pm; May-June M-F 9am-7pm, Sa-Su 10am-5pm.

Embassies: For more info, contact the Estonian Foreign Ministry (www.vm.ee). **Canada,** Toom-Kooli 13 (☎627 33 11; tallinn@canada.ee). Open M, W, F 9am-noon. **UK,** Wismari 6 (☎667 47 00; www.britishembassy.ee). Open M-F 10am-noon and 2-4:30pm. **US,** Kentmanni 20 (☎668 81 00, emergency 50 921 29; www.usemb.ee). Open M-F 9am-noon and 2-5pm.

Currency Exchange: Throughout the city. **ATMs** are on nearly every street in Vanalinn.

American Express: Suur-Karja 15 (☎626 62 11; www.estravel.ee). Books hotels and tours. Sells airline, ferry, and Scandinavian rail tickets. Offers visa services. Open June-Aug. M-F 9am-6pm, Sa 10am-5pm; Sept.-May M-F 9am-6pm, Sa 10am-3pm.

Tallinn

▲ ACCOMMODATIONS
Meriton Old Town
  Hotel, 1
Oldhouse Guesthouse, 2
Tallinn Old Town
  Backpackers (HI), 4

🌙 NIGHTLIFE
Café VS, 10
Club Hollywood, 9
Hell Hunt, 3
X-Baar, 8

🍴 FOOD
Café Elsebet, 6
Kompressor, 5
Peppersack, 7

Emergency: ☎ 112.

Pharmacy: Raeapteek, Raekoja pl. 11 (☎ 631 48 30). In business since 1422. Open M-F 9am-7pm, Sa 9am-5pm.

Internet Access: Central Library, Estonia pst. 8, 2nd fl. Open M-F 11am-7pm, Sa 10am-5pm. You can often use the computers free for 15min., but at busier times you may have to become a member (5EEK per day). **Kohvik@Grill,** Aia 3 (☎ 627 12 29). 10EEK per 15min. Also serves quick meals and drinks. Open daily 10am-11pm. MC/V. Free wireless access is available at over 80 points throughout the city.

Post Office: Narva mnt. 1. (☎ 661 66 16), opposite Hotel Viru. Open M-F 7:30am-8pm, Sa 8am-6pm, Su 9am-3pm. Address mail to be held as follows: First name SURNAME, *Poste Restante,* Narva mnt. 1, Tallinn 10101, ESTONIA. **Postal Code:** 10101.

🏠🍴 ACCOMMODATIONS AND FOOD

Hostels fill fast, so book ahead. **Rasastra ❷,** Mere pst. 4, 2nd fl., finds private rooms in the city center. (☎ 661 62 91; www.bedbreakfast.ee. Singles 275EEK; doubles 500EEK; triples 650EEK. Open daily 9:30am-6pm.) **◼Tallinn Old Town Backpackers ❷,** Uus 14, features clean dorms, a common kitchen, and a fun-loving staff. (☎ 051 711 337; www.balticbackpackers.com. Sheets 25EEK. Dorms 200EEK. Nonmembers add 25EEK.) **Hotell G9 ❸,** Gonsiori 9, is a short walk from Vanallin. Rooms have private bath, TV, and phone. (☎62 67 100; www.hotelg9.ee. Singles 550EEK; doubles 650EEK; triples 850EEK. Renovated rooms add 100EEK.) **Oldhouse Guest-house ❷**, Uus 22/1, has small but immaculate rooms. From Raekoja pl., follow Viru and turn left on Uus. (☎641 14 64; www.oldhouse.ee. Dorms 290EEK; singles 450-550EEK; doubles 650EEK; quads 1300EEK; apartments 950-2000EEK. 10% ISIC discount.) Brand-new **Meriton Old Town Hotel ❺**, Lai 49, steps from St. Olaf's Church, offers rooms with bath, phone, and satellite TV for prices lower than comparable hotels. (☎614 13 00; www.meritonhotels.com. Breakfast included. Internet in lobby. Singles 750EEK; doubles 900EEK; triples 1200EEK. MC/V.)

■Kompressor ❶, Rataskaevu 3, is the best place in town for real Estonian pancakes, offering giant portions with meat, fish, and veggie fillings. (Pancakes 35-45EEK. Kitchen open F-Sa noon-10pm, Su 11am-10pm; bar stays open to last customer). **Eesti Maja ❷**, Lauteri 1, just 600m southeast of the old town, offers food for thought: It serves folksy favorites and publishes its own history magazine. (www.eestimaja.ee. All-you-can-eat buffet M-F 11am-3pm, 75EEK. Entrees 45-165EEK. Open daily 11am-11pm.) **Peppersack ❹**, Viru 2/Vanaturu 6, serves hearty fare with a medieval flair. (Entrees 110-250EEK. Sword-fighting F-Sa nights. Live music M-Tu at 8 or 9pm. Open daily 11am-midnight. MC/V.) Come early to eat the same food for a fraction of the price upstairs at the affiliated **Café Elsebet ❷**, (Entrees 55-120EEK. Open M-F 8am-8pm, Sa-Su 8am-6pm.) Buy groceries at **Rimi** supermarket, Aia 7, between Uus and Aia (Open daily 8am-10pm.) **Kolmjalg**, Pikk 3, is a 24hr. convenience store.

◖ SIGHTS

ALL-LINN. Enter Vanalinn through the Viru gate and head up Viru to reach **Raekoja plats** (Town Hall Square), where beer flows in cafes and local troupes perform throughout the summer. In July, classical music concerts are held each weekend in the town hall, Europe's oldest; buy tickets at the tourist office. *(Town Hall open July-Aug. M-Sa 10am-4pm. 30EEK, students 20EEK.)* Take Mündi from the square, turn right on Pühavaimu, and then left on Vene to reach the **Tallinn City Museum** (Tallinna Linnamuuseum), which features well-organized exhibits about Tallinn's most colorful characters, from Old Thomas, the town watchman, to Johann von Uexkyll, the infamous serf-beating nobleman. *(Vene 17. Open M and W-Su Mar.-Oct. 10:30am-5:30pm; Nov.-Feb. 11am-4:30pm. 25EEK, students 10EEK.)* Continue up Vene, turn left on Olevimägi, and turn right on Pikk for a view of the medieval **north towers**. Head to the other end of Pikk and turn left on Rataskaevu to see **St. Nicholas Church** (Niguliste kirik) and its mighty spire. The church also houses an exquisite silver treasury. *(Open W-Su 10am-5pm. Organ concerts Sa-Su 4pm. Museum 35EEK, students 20EEK.)*

TOOMPEA. Toompea's **Lossi plats** (Castle Square) is dominated by the onion domes of golden **Aleksander Nevsky Cathedral**. *(From Raekoja pl., head down Kullassepa, right on Niguliste, and uphill on Lühike jalg. Open daily 8am-8pm. Services 9am and 6pm.)* Directly behind **Toompea Castle**, the current seat of the Estonian Parliament (closed to the public), an Estonian flag tops **Tall Hermann** (Pikk Hermann), Tallinn's tallest tower and most impressive medieval fortification. To reach the spires of 13th-century **Toomkirik** that tower over Toompea, follow Toom-Kooli to Kiriku plats. *(Open Tu-Su 9am-5pm. Services Su 10am.)* Next door is the **Art Museum of Estonia** (Eesti Kunstimuuseum), which features 19th- and 20th-century Estonian art. *(Kiriku plats 1. W-Su 11am-6pm. Museum 20EEK, students 5EEK.)*

KADRIORG. Among the quiet paths, shady trees, and fountains of Kadriorg Park is Peter the Great's **■Kadriorg Palace**, whose sumptuous grand hall is a fine example of Baroque architecture. *(www.ekm.ee/kadriorg. Open May-Sept. Tu-Su 10am-5pm; Oct.-*

Apr. W-Su 10am-5pm. 45EEK, students 35EEK.) The grounds also have two superb art museums, as well as the **Peter I (the Great) House Museum** in his former temporary residence. The museum holds many of the tsar's original furnishings, as well as an imprint of his extremely large hand. *(Mäekalda 2. From Vanalinn, follow Narva mnt. and at the fork veer right on Weizenbergi; or, take tram #1 or 3 to Kadriorg. The museum was closed for enlargement in 2004, but is slated to be up and running by 2005.)*

ROCCA-AL-MARE. On the peninsula of Rocca-al-Mare, 10km west of the city center, is the **Estonian Open-Air Museum** (Eesti Vabaõhumuuseum). The park is filled with 17th- to 20th-century wooden mills and homesteads transplanted from all over the country. Estonian folk troupes perform here regularly. *(Vabaõhumuuseumi 12. Take bus #21 or tram #7 to the zoo stop. Open daily May-Oct. 10am-6pm; Nov.-Apr. 10am-5pm; Oct. 10am-4pm. 28EEK, students 12EEK. Last Tu of each month free.)*

🎵 🎭 ENTERTAINMENT AND NIGHTLIFE

Pick up a free copy of *Tallinn This Week* at the tourist office. The **Estonia Concert Hall** and the **Estonian National Opera** are both at Estonia pst. 4. (Concert Hall ☎ 614 77 60. Box office open M-F noon-7pm, Su 1hr. before curtain. Tickets 30-150EEK. Opera ☎ 626 02 60; www.opera.ee. Box office open daily noon-7pm. Tickets 30-270EEK.) Celebrate the power of barley at **Beersummer,** Tallinn's answer to the Oktoberfest. (www.ollesummer.ee. July 6-10, 2005.) ▓**Hell Hunt** ("Gentle Wolf"), Pikk 39, sells its own brand of Saaremaa-brewed light and dark beers for 25EEK per 0.5L. (☎ 681 83 33. Open daily noon-2am.) Wild and crazy **Club Hollywood,** Vana-Posti 8, is known for inspiring occasional bouts of toplessness. (Cover up to130EEK. W women free. Open W-Th 10pm-4am, F-Sa 10pm-5am.) **Café VS,** Pärnu 28, is an excellent Indian restaurant that moonlights as an industrial-style disco and hosts an Internet radio station in the basement. (Entrees 70-110EEK. Live DJs every night. Bands play F-Sa 10pm-1am. No cover. Open M-Th 10am-1am, F 10am-3am, Sa Noon-3am, Su 1pm-1am.) **X-Baar,** Sauna 1, offers a relaxed atmosphere for its largely gay clientele. (Beer 30EEK. Live DJ F-Sa 10pm. Open daily 2pm-1am.)

🔁 DAYTRIP FROM TALLINN: PÄRNU

Famous for its mud baths, beaches, and festivals, Pärnu (pop. 45,000) is known as the summer capital of Estonia. The **Mudaravila** health resort, Ranna pst. 1, features the crème-de-la-crème of mud. (☎ 44 25 525; www.mudaravila.ee. Treatments 100-200EEK.) When you're not soaking in mud, soak up some culture at Pärnu's **Museum of New Art,** Esplanaadi 10, which exhibits unorthodox contemporary art. (Open daily 9am-9pm. 15EEK, students 10EEK.) The clean water of the white-sand **beach** warms up in July and August. At night, crowds dance on the beach at the **Sunset Club,** Ranna pst. 3. (Open M-Th and Su 10pm-4am, F-Sa 10pm-6am.)

Buses (☎ 044 720 02; Eurolines 278 41) go from Ringi 3 to: Rīga (3½hr., 6-8 per day, 110-150EEK); Tallinn (2hr., 42 per day, 55-80EEK); and Tartu (2½hr., 21 per day, 90-100EEK). **Rattapood,** Ringi 14a, rents **bikes** for 150EEK per day. (Open M-F 10am-6pm, Sa 10am-3pm.) The **tourist office,** Rüütli 16, sells *Pärnu In Your Pocket* for 25EEK. (☎ 044 730 00; www.parnu.ee. Open May 15-Sept. 15 M-F 9am-6pm, Sa 9am-4pm, Su 10am-3pm; Sept. 16-May 14 M-F 9am-5pm.) **Tanni-Vakoma Majutus-büroo,** Hommiku ❺, behind the bus station, arranges **private rooms.** (☎ 044 310 70. Open May-Aug. M-F 10am-8pm, Sa 10am-3pm. From 200EEK.) **Trahter Postipoiss ❸,** Vee 12, serves small, but delicious portions of Russian delicacies. (☎ 044 648 64. Entrees 45-175EEK. F-Sa live music 9pm. Open M-Th and Su noon-midnight, F-Sa noon-2am.) Cafeteria-style **Georg ❶,** Rüütli 43, is packed with locals. (Entrees under 35EEK. Open M-F 7:30am-10pm, Sa-Su 9am-10pm.)

TARTU

☎ 027

Tartu (pop. 110,000), Estonia's second largest city, is home to prestigious **Tartu University** (Tartu Ülikool). In **Raekoja plats** (Town Hall Square), the building that houses the **Tartu Art Museum** (Tartu Kunstimuuseum) leans a little to the left (similar to the city's student population). From there, follow Ülikooli behind the town hall to the university's main building at Ülikooli 18. In the attic is the **student lock-up** (*kartser*), which until 1892 was used to detain rule-breaking students; their drawings and inscriptions are still visible. (Open M-F 11am-5pm. 5EEK, students 4EEK.) According to a warning sign, the ruins of the **Cathedral of St. Peter and St. Paul** are "liable to fall down." Next door is the **Tartu University History Museum**, which features a replica of the interior of a 1980s university dorm room, strewn with beer cans and Russian rock posters. (Open W-Su 11am-5pm. 20EEK, students 5EEK.) The **Tartu Toy Museum** (Tartu Manguasjamuuseum) includes a massive **playroom** where visitors can entertain themselves with childhood memorabilia. (Open W-Su 11am-6pm; playroom closes at 4pm. 15EEK, students 10EEK, playroom 5EEK).

Buses (☎ 477 227) leave from Turu 2, on the corner with Riia, 300m southeast of Raekoja pl., for: Pärnu (4hr., 20 per day, 50-95EEK); Rīga (5hr., 1 per day, 190EEK); St. Petersburg (9hr., 1 per day, 160EEK); and Tallinn (2-3hr., 46 per day, 50-80EEK). Some routes offer 30-50% ISIC discounts. **Trains** (☎ 615 68 51), generally less reliable than buses, go from the intersection of Kuperjanovi and Vaksali, 1.5km from the center, to Tallinn (2½-3½hr., 3 per day, 70EEK). Public buses #5 and 6 run from the train stop to the city center and then to the bus station. From the bus station, follow Riia mnt. and turn right on Ülikooli to reach Raekoja pl. Pick up the helpful *Tartu Today* (15EEK) at the **tourist office**, Raekoja pl. 14. (☎ 442 111; www.visitestonia.com. Open June-Aug. M-F 9am-5pm, Sa 10am-3pm; Sept.-May M-F 9am-6pm, Sa-Su 10am-3pm.) The university dorms at **⬛Hostel Pepleri ❷**, Pepleri 14, are more luxurious than many hotels. From the bus station, take Vadabuse toward town, turn left on Vanemuise, and then take a left on Pepleri. (☎ 42 76 08; janikah@ut.ee. Singles 250EEK; doubles 400EEK. Cash only.) The tavern **Püssirohukelder ❷** ("Gunpowder Cellar"), Lossi 28, features hearty fare on its "student menu" and brews its own "Gunpowder Red" beer. (Live music Tu-Sa usually 10pm. Open M-Th noon-2am, F-Sa noon-3am, Su noon-midnight. MC/V.) **⬛Wilde Irish Pub ❸**, Vallikraavi 4, records every order of Saku, the national brew, on a digital billboard; the tally reset when it reached 100,000 in 2003. (Entrees 49-170EEK. Open M-Tu and Su noon-midnight, W-Th noon-1am, F-Sa noon-3am. MC/V.) **Postal Code:** 51001.

ESTONIAN ISLANDS

Afraid that Estonia's 1500 islands would serve as an escape route to the West, the Soviets cordoned them off from foreign and mainland influence; the islands now remain a preserve for all that is distinctly Estonian.

⬛ SAAREMAA. Kuressaare (pop. 16,000), the largest town on the island of Saaremaa, is making a comeback with tourists but remains quiet and tranquil. Head south from Raekoja pl. (Town Hall Square) along Lossi, through the park, and across the moat to reach the 1260 **⬛Bishopric Castle** (Piiskopilinnus). Inside, the **Saaremaa Museum** chronicles the island's history. (Open May-Aug. daily 10am-7pm; Sept.-Apr. W-Su 11am-6pm. 30EEK, students 15EEK.) Rent a **bike** (135EEK per day) at **Bivarix,** Tallinna 26, near the bus station, to pedal to the beaches of southwestern Saaremaa (8-12km) or to Karujärve Lake in western Saaremaa (23km).

Direct **buses** (☎ 045 316 61) leave from Pihtla tee 2, at the corner with Tallinna, for Pärnu (2½hr., 5 per day, 90EEK) and Tallinn (4-6hr., 9-11 per day, 100-160EEK). The **tourist office**, Tallinna 2, in the town hall, offers free **maps** and arranges private rooms. (☎ 045 331 20; www.visitestonia.com. Open May-Sept. 15 M Г 0uil-7pm, Sa

9am-5pm, Su 10am-3pm; Sept. 16-Apr. M-F 9am-5pm.) **Sug Hostel ❶**, Kingu 6, is your best bet for budget accommodations. (☎45 543 88. Open June-Aug. Singles 210-250 EEK; doubles 300-350EEK; quads 480-580EEK.)

⛴ HIIUMAA. By restricting access to Hiiumaa (pop. 11,500) for 50 years, the Soviets unwittingly preserved the island's rare plant and animal species. Creek-laced **Kärdla** (pop. 4100) is the island's biggest town. To explore the interesting sights along the coast, rent a **bike** (150EEK per day) from **Kerttu Sport**, Sadama 15, across the bridge from the bus station. (☎046 321 30. Open M-F 10am-6pm, Sa 10am-3pm.) Bike west from Kärdla toward Kõrgessaare to the chilling **Hill of Crosses** (Ristimägi; 4km). About 2km past the Hill of Crosses, a right turn leads to the **Tahkuna Lighthouse** (11km), brought from Paris in 1874. Return to the main road and turn right again toward Kõrgessaare; continue 20km past the town to reach the impressive 16th-century **Kõpu Lighthouse**, which offers a panoramic view of the Baltic Sea. (20EEK, students 10EEK.) The tiny island of **Kassari** is attached to Hiiumaa by a land bridge from Käina, which can be reached from Kärdla by local buses or a 22km bike ride. The island's most beautiful sight is the 1.3m-wide **⛰Sääretirp** peninsula, covered in wild strawberry and juniper bushes and jutting 3km into the sea.

Direct **buses** run from Sadama 13 (☎046 320 77), north of Kärdla's main square, Keskväljak, to Tallinn (4½hr., 2-3 per day, 140EEK). Once you're on **Hiumaa**, you can get to **Saaremaa** via public transportation, but it's difficult to find transportation in the opposite direction. The **tourist office**, Hiiu 1, in Keskväljak, sells maps (5-40EEK) and *The Lighthouse Tour* (20EEK), a handy guide. (☎046 222 32; www.hiiumaa.ee. Open May-Sept. M-F 9am-6pm, Sa-Su 10am-3pm; Oct.-Apr. M-F 10am-4pm.) **Eesti Posti Hostel ❷**, Posti 13, has modern rooms and clean shared baths. From Keskväljak, turn onto Uus to reach Posti; look for the pink building on the left. (☎046 918 71. May-Sept. 200EEK per person; Oct.-Apr. 150EEK.) Käina boasts Hiiumaa's best restaurant, **Arteesia Kohvik ❶**, Keskväljak 5, which serves generous portions of home-cooked meat and seafood. (Entrees 30-65EEK. Open daily 9am-9pm. MC/V.)

FINLAND (SUOMI)

It's fair to call Finland the forgotten Nordic country. Sweden has its starlets and Norway its slashing fjords, but their neighbor to the east has yet to develop an iconic vocabulary to market itself to the world. This comes as happy news to budget travelers, who will find Finland (outside its stylish capital) more affordable than many other Northern European countries. After lying about for centuries as a loose confederation of Swedish provinces, Finland started thinking as a nation under 19th-century Russian rule. It won its independence in 1917, but fought two fierce, courageous wars against Soviet occupation between 1939 and 1945. Once the dust settled, Finland emerged on the international stage with the 1952 Summer Olympics and never looked back. With thousands of lakes and 68% of its land area carpeted in boreal forest, the country's geography reels in serious hikers even as its southern cities draw students of architecture and art gurus.

 DISCOVER FINLAND: SUGGESTED ITINERARIES

Start things off in the lakeside capital of **Helsinki** (p. 322), ambling along the tree-lined Esplanadi and veering into some of the city's grade-A museums. Leave time to sun yourself on the beaches near **Hanko** (p. 329) or bike down the Pellinge archipelago south of **Porvoo** (p. 329). Out west, the venerable city of **Turku** (p. 329) is worth a look, but today **Tampere** (p. 331) is the rising star of Finnish urbanity, with a lively music scene and museums taking over renovated factories. Picnic on the island of Sulosaari in the heart of **Savonlinna** (p. 333), and daytrip out to the transcendent **Retretti Art Center.** From here, decide between heading back to Helsinki or embarking on the long trek north to **Rovaniemi** (p. 335), the best outpost from which to launch a foray into the wilds of the Arctic Circle.

ESSENTIALS

WHEN TO GO

The long days of Finnish summers make for a tourist's dream, although the two-month *kaamos* (polar night) in the northernmost regions of Finland could give the chirpiest traveler a case of Seasonal Affective Disorder. By early February, though, winter-sport fanatics start hitting the slopes, and the skiing continues well into March and April. Temperatures average about 20-25°C (68-77°F) in the summer, and dip as low as -20°C (-5°F) in the winter.

DOCUMENTS AND FORMALITIES

VISAS. EU citizens do not need a visa. Citizens of Australia, Canada, New Zealand, and the US do not need a visa for stays of up to 90 days, although this three-month period begins upon entry into any of the countries that belong to the EU's freedom of movement zone. For more information, see p. 17.

EMBASSIES AND CONSULATES. All foreign embassies are in Helsinki. Finnish embassies at home include: **Australia,** 12 Darwin Ave., Yarralumla, ACT 2600 (☎26 273 38 00; www.finland.org.au); **Canada,** 55 Metcalfe St., Ste. 850, Ottawa, ON K1P 6L5 (☎613-288-2233; www.finland.ca/en); **Ireland,** Russell House, Stokes Pl., St. Stephen's Green, Dublin 2 (☎01 478 1344); **UK,** 38 Chesham Pl., London SW1X 8HW (☎020 7838 6200; www.finemb.org.uk); **US,** 3301 Massachusetts Ave. NW, Washington, D.C. 20008 (☎202-298-5800; www.finland.org). **New Zealanders** should either contact their consul in Wellington (☎472 65 81; colin.beyer@simpsongrierson.com) or call the Australian embassy directly.

TRANSPORTATION

BY PLANE. Several major airlines fly into **Helsinki** from Europe, North America, and Australia. **Finnair** (Finland ☎0600 140 140, €1.64 per call; US 800-950-5000; UK 087 0241 4411; www.finnair.com) flies from 50 international cities and also covers the domestic market. Finnair gives a domestic discount of up to 50% for ages 17-24, and has summer and snow rates that reduce fares by up to 60%.

BY TRAIN. The national rail company is **VR Ltd., Finnish Railways** (☎0600 41 902; www.vr.fi). Travelers pay high prices for efficient trains; seat reservations (€2.40-11.20) are not required except on *InterCity* and *Pendolino* trains. **Eurail** is valid in Finland. A **Finnrail pass** gives three (€119), five (€159), or ten travel days (€215) in a one-month period. The **Scanrail pass**, purchased outside Scandinavia, is good for rail travel through Denmark, Finland, Norway, and Sweden, as well as many discounted ferry and bus rides. Passes can also be purchased within Scandinavia, but passholders can only use three travel days in the country of purchase, so a Scanrail pass purchased at home is more economical for those traveling mostly within Finland. See p. 61 for more info or visit www.scanrail.com.

BY BUS. Buses are the only way to reach some smaller towns or to travel past the Arctic Circle. **Oy Matkahuolto Ab** (☎02 00 40 00; www.matkahuolto.fi) coordinates bus service across most of Finland. ISIC holders can buy a **student card** (€5.40) at bus stations, which provides a 50% discount on one-way tickets for routes longer than 80km. Some drivers will give the discount to ISIC cardholders without the special student card. **Railpasses** are valid on buses when trains are not in service.

BY FERRY. Viking Line (Helsinki ☎09 123 51, Stockholm 08 452 4000) runs from Stockholm to Helsinki, Mariehamn, and Turku. **Silja Line** (Helsinki ☎09 180 41, Stockholm 08 666 33 30; www.silja.fi) sails from Stockholm to Helsinki, Mariehamn, and Turku. Scanrail holders get 50% off on Viking; Eurailers ride free on Silja. **Birka Lines** (Mariehamn ☎018 270 27, Stockholm 08 702 72 00; www.birkacruises.com) sails daily from Mariehamn to Stockholm (from €46).

BY CAR. Finland honors foreign driver's licenses for visits up to one year in length. **Speed limits** are 120kph on expressways, 50kph in thickly settled areas, and 80-100kph

FINLAND

elsewhere. Headlights must be used at all times. Driving conditions are good, but take extra care in winter weather and be wary of reindeer crossings. For more info on car rental and driving in Europe, see p. 66.

BY BIKE AND BY THUMB. Finland boasts a well-developed network of **cycling** paths, and **Fillari GT** route maps are available at bookstores (€10-16). **Hitchhiking** is fairly uncommon in Finland, although www.cs.helsinki.fi/u/kjokisal/liftaus does recommend a number of routes out of major cities. *Let's Go* does not recommend hitchhiking as a safe means of transport.

TOURIST SERVICES AND MONEY

EMERGENCY	Police: ☎ 10022. Ambulance and Fire: ☎ 112.

TOURIST OFFICES. The **Finnish Tourist Board** (☎ 09 4176 911; www.visitfinland.com) maintains an official online travel guide, with dedicated home pages for travelers from Canada, Ireland, the UK, and the US.

MONEY. On January 1, 2002, the **euro (€)** replaced the **Finnish markka** as the unit of currency in Finland. For exchange rates and more info on the euro, see p. 20. Banks exchange currency for a €2-5 commission, though **Forex** offices and **ATMs** offer the best exchange rates. Food from grocery stores runs €10-17 per day; meals cost somewhere around €6 for lunch and €10 for dinner. Restaurant bills include a service charge, although an extra 5-10% tip can be a classy gesture. Elsewhere in Finland, tips are not expected. All countries who are members of the European Union impose a **Value Added Tax (VAT)** on goods and services purchased within the EU. Prices in Finland already include the country's stiff 22% VAT rate, although partial refunds are available for visitors who are not EU citizens (p. 22).

BUSINESS HOURS. Banks are generally open Monday to Friday 9:30am-4:30pm. **Stores** are open Monday to Friday from 9am to either 5 or 9pm, and Saturday from 9am to 2 or 6pm. During the summer, some shops open on Sundays from noon to 9pm. Most **sights** are open Sundays, but closed Mondays.

COMMUNICATION

PHONE CODES	**Country code: 358. International dialing prefix:** 00. From outside Finland, dial the int'l dialing prefix (see inside back cover) + 358 + city code + local number.

TELEPHONES. To make a long-distance call within Finland, dial 0 and then the number. Prepaid phone cards (€1-10) are available from bus stations, post offices, and R-kiosk convenience stores. **Mobile phones** are extremely popular in the nation that gave the world Nokia, and prepaid cell phone cards can be used to make international calls (never cheap, but cheapest 5pm-8am). For more info on cell phones in Europe, see p. 35. For operator assistance, dial ☎118; for help with international calls, dial ☎020 208. International direct dial numbers include: **AT&T** (☎0800 1100 15); **Canada Direct** (☎0800 1100 11); **MCI** (☎0800 1102 80); **Sprint** (☎0800 1102 84); **Telecom New Zealand** (☎080 110 640); **Telstra Australia** (☎0800 110 610).

MAIL. Mail service is fast and efficient. Postcards and letters under 50g cost €0.65 within Finland, €0.90 within the EU, and €1.20 outside Europe. Both domestic and international letters weighing under 20g cost just €0.65.

LANGUAGES. Finnish is spoken by most of the population, although children learn both Swedish and Finnish from the first grade. Three dialects of Sami are also spoken by an ethnic minority in northern Finland, adding up to roughly 2000 speakers. English is also widely spoken, with 66% of Finns reporting that they can speak at least some English; city-dwellers and those under 35 are generally the most proficient. Travelers should note that some town names take a modified form on train and bus schedules. "To Helsinki" is written *"Helsinkiin,"* while "from Helsinki" is *"Helsingistä."* For basic Finnish words and phrases, see p. 1060.

ACCOMMODATIONS AND CAMPING

FINLAND	❶	❷	❸	❹	❺
ACCOMMODATIONS	under €10	€10-20	€20-45	€45-70	over €70

Finland has more than 100 **youth hostels** (*retkeilymaja*; RET-kay-loo-MAH-yah), although just half of them are open year-round. The **Finnish Youth Hostel Association** (Suomen Retkeilymajajärjestö; ☎09 565 71 50; www.srmnet.org) is Finland's HI affiliate. Prices average €15-50 per person; nonmembers add €2.50. Most have laundry facilities and a kitchen; some have saunas and rent bicycles or skis. **Hotels** are often exorbitantly priced (over €50); *kesähotelli* (summer hotels) are usually student lodgings that are vacant from June to August, and cost about €25 per night. More than 350 **campgrounds** pepper the countryside, 70 of which are open year-round (tent sites €10-25 per night; small cottages from €30). The **Camping Card Scandinavia** (€6) qualifies cardholders for discounts, and includes accident insurance. For a campground guide, contact the **Finnish Camping Site Association** (☎09 477 407 40; www.camping.fi). Finland's *jokamiehenoikeudet* (right to public access) means that even noncitizens can temporarily camp for free in the countryside, as long as they stay a reasonable distance from private homes.

FOOD AND DRINK

FINLAND	❶	❷	❸	❹	❺
FOOD	under €8	€8-15	€15-20	€20-30	over €30

Kebab and pizza joints (from €4) are always an option for budget dining, but the local **Kauppatori** market and **Kauppahali** food court are more likely to serve fresh, recognizably Finnish fare. Finland's traditional diet slants toward hearty grain breads and sausages that last through a winter too long to keep perishable meats around. In season, however, menus feature freshly caught trout, perch, pike, and herring, and a new wave of five-star chefs in Helsinki are starting to pair French and Mediterranean ingredients with the fruits of Finland's fisheries. Bowls of reindeer stew are a staple of Lapland, while Kuopio and the region of North Karelia are known for their pillowy rye pastries. A surprising number of adults drink milk with their meals, followed by interminable pots of coffee; the Finnish market accounts for almost 2% of global coffee consumption. You must be 18 to purchase beer and wine, 20 for liquor; the minimum age in bars is usually 18, but can be as high as 25. All alcohol stronger than light beer must be purchased at state-run **Alko** liquor stores, open weekdays until at least 6pm and Saturdays until at least 4pm.

F
I
N
L
A
N
D

HOLIDAYS AND FESTIVALS

Holidays: New Year's Day (Jan. 1); Epiphany (Jan. 6); Good Friday (Mar. 25); Easter Sunday and Monday (Mar. 27-28); May Day (May 1); Ascension Day (May 5); Whit Sunday (May 15); Midsummer (June 24-25); All Saints' Day (Nov. 1); Independence Day (Dec. 6); Christmas Day (Dec. 25); Boxing Day (Dec. 26).

Festivals: Flags fly high and *kokko* (bonfires) blaze on Midsummer's Eve (June 24), when the Finnish desert their cities for seaside cabins. Those marooned in town still get a touch of the countryside with the birch branches that festoon buses and trams. July is high season for festivals in Finland, with gays and lesbians celebrating Helsinki Pride, Turku's youth taking to the mosh pits of Ruisrock, and Pori launching the 40th edition of its eclectic Jazz Festival. Savonlinna's Opera Festival continues into early Aug., while Oulu's Music Video Festival and Lahti's Sibelius Festival close out the summer. Check out www.festivals.fi for more info.

FACTS AND FIGURES: FINLAND

Official Name: Republic of Finland.

Capital: Helsinki.

Major Cities: Oulu, Tampere, Turku.

Population: 5,210,000.

Land Area: 305,000 sq. km.

Time Zone: GMT +2.

Languages: Finnish, Swedish.

Religions: Evangelical Lutheran (89%).

HELSINKI (HELSINGFORS)   ☎09

With all the appeal of a big city but none of the grime, Helsinki's (pop. 560,000) broad avenues, grand architecture, and green parks make it a model of successful urban planning. The city distinguishes itself with a decidedly multicultural flair: Lutheran and Russian Orthodox cathedrals stand almost face-to-face, and youthful energy mingles with Old World charm. Baltic Sea produce fills the marketplaces and restaurants, while St. Petersburg and Tallinn are only a short cruise away.

▐ TRANSPORTATION

Flights: Helsinki-Vantaa Airport (HEL; ☎020 01 46 36). **Buses** #615 and 617 run between the airport and the train station (35min., every 20min. 5:20am-12:20am, €3). A **Finnair bus** runs between the airport and the Finnair building next to the train station (☎0600 14 01 40; www.finnair.com; 35min., every 15min. 5am-midnight, €5).

Trains: ☎030 072 09 00. Reserve ahead for all long-distance routes. To: **Moscow** (14hr., daily 5:40pm, €85); **Rovaniemi** (10-13hr., 5-8 per day, €66-71); **St. Petersburg** (5½hr., 2 per day, €50); **Tampere** (2hr., 8-12 per day, €19-28); **Turku** (2hr., 12 per day, €19-28). See p. 871 for info on documents you'll need before entering Russia.

Buses: ☎020 040 00. The station is between Salomonk. and Simonk.; from the train station, take Postik. past the statue of Mannerheim. Cross Mannerheimintie onto Salomonk. and the station will be to your left. To: **Lahti** (1½hr.; 2 per hr.; €18, students €9); **Tampere** (2½hr., 1 per hr., €20/€10); **Turku** (2½hr., 2 per hr., €22/€11).

Ferries: Viking Line, Mannerheimintie 14 (☎12 35 77), sails to **Stockholm** (16hr., daily 5:30pm, from €40). Take tram #2 or bus #13 to Katajanokka terminal. **Tallink,** Erottajank. 19 (☎22 83 11), sails to **Tallinn** (3¼hr., 2-3 per day, from €20). Take bus #15 to West terminal.

Local Transportation: ☎010 01 11; www.ytv.fi. **Buses, trams,** and the **metro** run 5:30am-11pm; major bus and tram lines, including tram #3T, run until 1:30am. There is 1 metro line (running approximately east to west), 10 tram lines, and many more bus lines. **Night buses,** marked with an "N," run after 1:30am. A single-fare ticket on the tram without transfers is €1.80. Single-fare tickets with 1hr. of transfers to buses, trams, and the metro are €2. The **City Transport Office** is in the Rautatientori metro station, below the train station. Open in summer M-Th 7:30am-6pm, F 7:30am-4pm, Sa

Helsinki

🏠 **ACCOMMODATIONS**
Eurohostel, **19**
Hostel Erottanjanpuisto, **14**
Hostel Lönnrot, **12**
Hostel Suomenlinna, **18**
Hotel Finn, **6**
Hotel Satakuntatalo, **2**
Stadion Hostel, **1**

🍴 **FOOD**
Amarillo, **10**
Café Ursula, **17**
Kapelli, **16**
Lappi, **4**
Zetor, **8**
Zucchini, **15**

⭐ **NIGHTLIFE**
Copacabana, **11**
DTM, **13**
Fever, **3**
Mother Bar, **5**
On the Rocks/Barfly, **9**
Vanha, **7**

10am-3pm; low season M-Th 7:30am-7pm, F 7:30am-5pm, Sa 10am-3pm. The office sells the **tourist ticket,** a good investment for unlimited bus, tram, metro, and local trains during the period of validity. 1-day ticket €5.40, 3-day €10.80, 5-day €16.20.

Taxis: Taxi Centre Helsinki (☎0100 06 00). **Yellow Line** (☎0600 55 55 55) runs from the airport (20min., about €25).

Bike Rental: Green Bikes, Mannerheimintie 13 (☎85 02 28 50). Bikes from €10 per day. The city also provides over 300 free **city bikes** at major destinations throughout the city; it can be tricky to track one down, but when you do, deposit a €2 coin in the lock and then retrieve it upon returning the bike to any location. Free cycling maps of the city are available from the tourist office.

✳🌀 ORIENTATION AND PRACTICAL INFORMATION

Sea surrounds Helsinki on the south, east, and west, and the city center is bordered on the north by two lakes. Water shapes everything in the Finnish capital, from relaxing city beaches to gorgeous lakeside parks. Helsinki's main street, **Mannerheimintie,** passes between the bus and train stations on its way south to the city center, eventually crossing **Esplanadi.** This tree-lined promenade leads east to **Kauppatori** (Market Square) and the beautiful South Harbor. Both Finnish and Swedish are used on all street signs and maps; *Let's Go* uses the Finnish names.

FINLAND

Tourist Offices: City Tourist Office, Pohjoisesplanadi 19 (☎169 37 57; www.hel.fi/tourism). From the train station, walk 2 blocks down Keskusk. and turn left on Pohjoisesplanadi; from the ferry terminals, head left on Pohjoisesplanadi. Open May-Sept. M-F 9am-8pm, Sa-Su 9am-6pm; Oct.-Apr. M-F 9am-6pm, Sa-Su 10am-4pm. The **Finnish Tourist Board,** across the street at Eteläesplanadi 4 (☎41 76 93 00; www.mek.fi), has info for all of Finland. Open May-Sept. M-F 9am-5pm, Sa-Su 11am-3pm; Oct.-Apr. M-F 9am-5pm. The **Helsinki Card,** sold at the tourist office, provides unlimited local transportation and free or discounted admission to most museums, although cardholders have to keep up a blistering pace to make their purchase worthwhile. 1-day card €25, 2-day €35, 3-day €45. **Finnsov Tours,** Eerikink. 3, arranges trips to Russia and expedites the visa process. Open M-F 8:30am-5pm.

Embassies: Canada, Pohjoisesplanadi 25B (☎22 80 30; www.canada.fi). Open M-F 8:30am-noon and 1-4:30pm. **Ireland,** Erottajank. 7A (☎64 60 06). Open M-F 9am-5pm. **UK,** Itäinen Puistotie 17 (☎22 86 51 00; www.ukembassy.fi). Also handles diplomatic matters for **Australians** and **New Zealanders.** Open M-F 8:30am-5pm. **US,** Itäinen Puistotie 14A (☎61 62 50; www.usembassy.fi). Open M-F 8:30am-5pm.

Currency Exchange: Forex has 5 locations and the best rates in the city. Hours vary; the branch in the train station is open daily 8am-9pm.

Luggage Storage: Train station lockers €2-4 per day.

Laundromat: ▧ **Café Tin Tin Tango,** Töölöntorink. 7 (☎27 09 09 72), a combination bar, cafe, laundromat, and sauna. Laundry €3.50. Sandwiches €4.50-5.50. Sauna €20. Open M-F 7am-2am, Sa-Su 10am-2am. MC/V. More typical is **Easywash,** Runebergink. 47 (☎40 69 82). Open M-Th 10am-9pm, F 10am-6pm, Sa 10am-4pm.

Emergency: ☎112. **Police:** ☎100 22.

Pharmacy: Yliopiston Apteekki, Mannerheimintie 96 (☎41 78 03 00). Open 24hr.

Medical Assistance: 24hr. hotline (☎100 23). 24hr. medical clinic **Mehilainen,** Runebergink. 47A (☎010 414 44 44).

Internet Access: Cable Book Library, Mannerheimintie 22-24, in the mall across from the bus station. Free 30min. slots. Open M-Th 10am-8pm, Sa-Su noon-6pm. **Academic Bookstore,** Keskusk. 2. Free 15min. slots. Open M-F 9am-9pm, Sa 9am-6pm.

Post Office: Mannerheiminaukio 1A (☎98 00 71 00). Open M-F 9am-6pm. Address mail to be held in the following format: First name SURNAME, *Poste Restante,* Mannerheiminaukio 1A, 00100 Helsinki, FINLAND.

▐ ACCOMMODATIONS

Helsinki's hotels tend to be expensive, but budget hostels are often quite nice. In June and July, it's wise to make reservations a few weeks in advance.

▧ **Hostel Erottanjanpuisto (HI),** Uudenmaank. 9 (☎64 21 69). Head right from the train station, turn left on Mannerheimintie, bear right onto Erottajank., and turn right on Uudenmaank. Friendly staff tends well-kept rooms in a beautiful 19th-century building in the heart of the city. Breakfast €5. Kitchen available. Lockers €1. Internet €1 per 10min. Reception 24hr. In summer dorms €20; singles €44; doubles €58. Low season singles €42; doubles €56. Nonmembers add €2.50. AmEx/MC/V. ❷

Eurohostel (HI), Linnank. 9, Katajanokka (☎622 04 70; www.eurohostel.fi), 200m from the ferry terminal. From the train station, head right to Mannerheimintie and take tram #2 or 4 to Katajanokka. From Uspensky Cathedral, head down Kanavank., turn left on Pikku Satamank. (not the same as Satamank.), and then bear right on Linnank. Bright rooms, a cafe, and a sauna with great views of the harbor. Kitchen and sauna available. Breakfast €5. Sheets included. Internet €1 per 10min. Reception 24hr. Dorms €20; singles €34. Nonmembers add €2.50. MC/V. ❷

Stadion Hostel (HI), Pohj. Stadiontie 3B (☎49 60 71). Take tram #7A or 3 to Auroran Sairaala. Walk down Pohj. Stadiontie toward the white tower for 250m, following the signs. The hostel, on the far side of the Olympic stadium, looks like a minimalist high-school locker room and brims with social life. Breakfast and sheets €5.50. Kitchen available. Lockers €1. Laundry €2.50. Internet €1 per 15min. Lockout noon-4pm. Reception June to early Sept. 7am-3am; mid-Sept. to May 8-10am and 4pm-2am. Dorms €13; singles €25; doubles €36. Nonmembers add €2.50. AmEx/MC/V. ❷

Hostel Satakuntatalo (HI), Lapinrinne 1A (☎69 58 52 33). Take the metro to Kampi and walk downhill. Spacious, well-equipped dorms and private rooms close to the city center. Breakfast and sauna included. Sheets €5. Laundry €5. Reception 24hr. Check-in 2pm. Check-out noon. Open June-Aug. Dorms €17; singles €36; doubles €55; triples €68; quads €78. Nonmembers add €2.50. AmEx/MC/V. ❷

Hostel Suomenlinna (HI), Iso Mustasaari (☎684 74 71), by the main quay on Suomen-linna. Comfortable rooms in a squat brick building on Suomenlinna's western island. Breakfast €3. Sheets included. Reception 9am-11pm; call ahead to be let inside for check-in. Dorms €18; doubles and triples €25. Nonmembers add €2.50. MC/V. ❷

Hostel Lönnrot (HI), Lönnrotink. 16 (☎693 25 90). Go right out of the train station, left onto Mannerheimintie, and right onto Lönnrotink. just before the Swedish Theatre. Reception upstairs. Clean, cozy rooms in a very central location. Breakfast and sheets included. Reception 24hr. Check-in 2pm. Dorms €15; singles €49; doubles €59; tri-ples €74. Nonmembers add €2.50. MC/V. ❷

Hotel Finn, Kalevank. 3B (☎68 44 360; fax 68 44 36 10). From the train station, go right, then turn left on Mannerheimintie and right onto Kalevank. Hotel is on the 6th fl. The basic rooms are pricey, but a great location and proximity to nightlife explain why. Breakfast included. Singles €55, with shower €65; doubles €65/€80. MC/V. ❹

Rastila Camping (☎321 65 51), 12km east of the city center. Take the metro east to Rastila (15min.); the campsite is 100m to the right. Beach access, showers, and kitchen. Reception mid-May to mid-Sept. 24hr; mid-Sept. to mid-May daily 8am-10pm. 1 person with tent €11, 2-6 people with tent €17; cabins €43-62. MC/V. ❶

🍴 FOOD

Restaurants and cafes are easy to find on **Esplanadi** and the streets branching off from **Mannerheimintie** and **Uudenmaankatu.** Cheaper options surround the **Hietalahti** flea market at the southern end of Bulevardi. A large **supermarket** is under the train station. (Open M-F 7:30am-10pm, Sa 9am-10pm, Su 10am-10pm.) Get lunch at the open-air market of **🏪Kauppatori,** by the harbor, where stalls sell a variety of fresh fish and farm-fresh produce; it's not hard to assemble a satisfying meal for €6-8. (Open June-Aug. M-Sa 6:30am-5pm; Sept.-May M-F 7am-2pm.) The nearby **Vanha Kauppahalli** is an old-fashioned indoor market. (Open M-F 8am-7pm, Sa 8am-4pm.)

Zetor, Kaivok. 10 (☎66 69 66), in Kaivopiha, the mall opposite the train station. The dishes' names are cheeky and the farm-inspired decor is cheekier, but the authentic Finnish fare is absolutely delicious. Homemade beer €4. Entrees €9-16. 22+ after 9pm. Open M and Su 3pm-1am, Tu-Th 3pm-3am, F 3pm-4am, Sa 1pm-4am. ❷

Kapelli, Eteläesplanadi 1 (☎681 24 40), at the Unionk. end of Esplanadi park. Fre-quented by well-heeled bohemians since 1837, this lovely outdoor cafe serves salads and sandwiches (€6-9); head inside to the left. The restaurant to the right is pricier. Open daily 9am-2am. Kitchen closes at 1am. AmEx/MC/V. ❶

Café Ursula (☎65 28 17), near Kaivopuisto park on Ehrenströmintie. Delicious meals in an idyllic setting on the edge of the Baltic Sea. Sandwiches €5-7. Salads €8-9. Open daily 9am-midnight. AmEx/MC/V. ❶

Lappi, Annank. 22. (☎64 55 50). The wood-and-fur decor may put you in the mood to splurge on Lappish specialties like reindeer, elk, lingonberries, and arctic char. Entrees from €17. Open M-F noon-10:30pm, Sa-Su 1-10:30pm. MC/V. ❸

Amarillo, Mikonk. 9 (☎686 00 00). A Finnish twist on a Texas truck stop, this chain gorges its customers on quesadillas (from €6) and burgers (from €9). Three bars draw revelers by night. Open M-Tu 11am-1am, W-Th 11am-3am, F-Sa 11am-4am, Su 11am-11pm. Kitchen closes at 10pm. AmEx/MC/V. ❶

Zucchini, Fabianink. 4 (☎622 29 07), just south of the tourist office. A casual vegetarian restaurant featuring organic produce as well as vegan and gluten-free options. Daily lunch specials €7.90, with soup €9. Open Aug.-June M-F 11am-4pm. MC/V. ❶

◉ SIGHTS

Helsinki's polished Neoclassical buildings and bold new forms reflect Finnish architect Alvar Aalto's joke: "Architecture is our form of expression because our language is so impossible." Much of the layout and architecture of the old center, however, is the brainchild of a German. After Helsinki became the capital of Finland in 1812, Carl Engel designed a grand city modeled after St. Petersburg. Today, Art Nouveau (*Jugendstil*) and Modernist structures give Helsinki a uniquely cosmopolitan feel. Most of the major sights are packed into the compact center of the city, making it ideal for walking tours; pick up *See Helsinki on Foot* from the tourist office for suggested routes. Trams #3T and 3B loop around the major sights in roughly 1hr., providing a cheap alternative to sightseeing buses. Helsinki is dotted with parks, including **Kaivopuisto** in the south, **Töölönlahti** to the north, and **Esplanadi** and **Tähtitorninvuori** in the center of town.

◪ SUOMENLINNA. Five interconnected islands are home to this 18th-century Swedish military fortification, erected for fear of a Russian invasion of Helsinki. The old fortress's dark passageways are great to explore, as are the **Suomenlinna Museum** and the **Coastal Artillery Museum,** located within one of the ramparts. The islands also feature the world's only combination church and lighthouse, containing Finland's largest bell. The smooth rocks on the southern island are popular with sunbathers and swimmers. *(www.suomenlinna.fi. Museums open May-Aug. daily 10am-6pm; Apr. and Sept. daily 11am-4pm; Mar. Sa-Su 11am-4pm. €5.50, students €2.50. Ferries depart from Market Sq. every 20min. 8am-11pm; round-trip €3.60.)*

SENAATIN TORI (SENATE SQUARE). The square and its gleaming white **Tuomiokirkko** (Dome Church) showcase Engel's work and exemplify the splendor of Finland's 19th-century Russian period. The church's interior is so elegantly simple that every decorative detail becomes magnified tenfold. *(At Aleksanterink. and Unionink. in the city center. Church open June-Aug. M-Sa 9am-midnight, Su noon-midnight; Sept.-May M-Sa 9am-6pm, Su noon-6pm.)* On a dramatic hill to the east, the red-brick **Uspenskinkatedraadi** (Uspensky Orthodox Cathedral) evokes images of Russia with its ornate interior and golden onion domes; it's the largest Orthodox church in Western Europe. *(Open M and W-Sa 9:30am-4pm, Tu 9:30am-6pm, Su 9:30am-3pm.)*

ESPLANADI AND MANNERHEIMINTIE. A lush boulevard spangled with statues and fountains, Esplanadi is an ideal place to people-watch on a sunny day. Turn south onto Korkeavuorenk. to reach the **Museum of Art and Design,** which presents the work of established designers like Aalto and Eliel Saarinen alongside creations by exciting young artists. *(Korkeavuorenk. 3. Open June-Aug. daily 11am-6pm; Sept.-May Tu and Th-Su 11am-6pm, W 11am-8pm. €7.)* At the end of Esplanadi, turn right onto Mannerheimintie and right again onto Kaivok. past the train station to reach the **Ateneum Taidemuseo,** Finland's largest art museum, with comprehensive exhibitions on Finnish art since the 1700s. Don't miss Aksel Gallen-Kallela's work illustrating episodes from the Kalevala. *(Kaivok. 2, opposite the train station. ☎17 33 64 01; www.ateneum.fi. Open Tu and F 9am-6pm, W-Th 9am-8pm, Sa-Su 11am-5pm. €5.50, €7.50 during temporary exhibitions.)* Continue on Mannerheimintie past the post office to **▓Kiasma,** a stark, silvery warehouse that houses top-flight modern art and calibrates the width of its doors to Fibonacci's golden ratio. *(Mannerheiminaukio 2. ☎17 33 65 01; www.kiasma.fi. Open Tu 9am-5pm, W-Su 10am-8:30pm. €5.50, students €4.)* After passing the Parliament on the left, you'll find yourself between two of Helsinki's most beautiful buildings. On the left is Saarinen's **Suomen Kansallismuseo** (National Museum of Finland), featuring a romp through Finnish cultural history and a magnificent lobby-to-ceiling fresco by Gallen-Kallela. *(Mannerheimintie 34. ☎40 50 95 44; www.nba.fi/en/nmf. Open Tu-W 11am-8pm, Th-Su 11am-6pm. €5.50, students €3.50.)* On the right is Aalto's majestic **Finlandia Talo,** the white marble home of Helsinki's Philharmonic and Radio Symphony Orchestra. *(Mannerheimintie 13E. ☎402 41; www.finlandia.hel.fi. Tours in summer daily 1:30pm. €4.)* Head back down Mannerheimintie toward the post office, turn right onto Arkadiank. and right again onto Fredrikink. to reach the stunning **Temppeliaukio Church.** Hewn out of a hill of rock with only the roof visible from the outside, the huge domed ceiling inside appears to be supported only by rays of sunshine. *(Lutherink. 3. Usually open M-F 10am-8pm, Sa 10am-6pm, Su noon-1:45pm and 3:15-5:45pm. Services in English Su 2pm.)*

OTHER SIGHTS. In an industrial area west of the city center, the mammoth, vaguely anarchic **Kaapeli (Cable Factory)** houses three museums, dozens of studios and galleries, and various performance areas. Especially worthwhile are the **Finnish Museum of Photography,** with dramatic photographs from the past century, and the **Theatre Museum,** with dazzling set models and costume designs from the national theater. The complex also hosts major cultural events. *(Tallbergink. 1. ☎47 63 83 00. Take the metro to Ruoholahti and walk 5 blocks down Itämerenk., or take tram #8 to the end of the line. Photography and theater museum open Tu-Su noon-7pm; combined ticket €5.)* Near the western harbor, the well-touristed **Jean Sibelius Monument** pays homage to one of the 20th century's greatest composers with what looks like a stormcloud of organ pipes ascending to heaven. *(On Mechelinink. in Sibelius park. Take bus #24 (dir.: Seurasaari) from Mannerheimintie; get off at Rasjasaarentie and the monument will be behind you on the left.)* Northwest of the monument, across a lovely white bridge, the island of **Seurasaari** is home to farmsteads and churches transplanted from around Finland. An **open-air museum** allows entrance into many of the his-

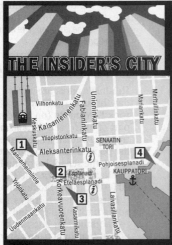

AALTO'S HELSINKI

The curvilinear marble surfaces of Finlandia Hall may be architect Alvar Aalto's most recognizable gift to Helsinki, but a number of his other Modernist creations give a sense of his aesthetic breadth.

1 **Rautaulo** (Iron House), Keskusk. 3. The stark facade conceals an airy atrium meant to recall an Italian *piazza*, one of Aalto's favorite motifs.

2 **Academic Bookstore,** Pohjoisesplanadi 39. The capital's largest bookstore named its upstairs cafe after the architect who designed the building in 1969.

3 **Savoy Restaurant,** Eteläesplanadi 14. The €35 entrees are too pricey for the budget traveler, but the decor is all Aalto's work—right down to the sinuous amber vases.

4 **Stora Enso Headquarters,** Kanavak. 1. This ultramodern "sugar cube" overlooks the South Harbor and provocatively comments on the two churches that flank it.

torical buildings. On Midsummer's Eve, drunken revelers light tall *kokko* (bonfires) to celebrate the mild season. *(Take bus #24 from Erottaja, outside the Swedish Theater, to the last stop. The island is always open for hiking. Museum open M-F 9am-3pm, Sa-Su 11am-5pm. €3.40.)*

🎵 📷 ENTERTAINMENT AND NIGHTLIFE

Helsinki's parks are always animated; jazz fills the **Esplanadi** park all summer Monday through Thursday at 4:30pm (www.kulttuuri.hel.fi/espanlava), while concerts rock **Kaivopuisto** (on the corner of Puistok. and Ehrenstromintie, in the southern part of town) and **Hietaniemi Beach** (down Hesperiank. on the western shore). The free English-language papers *Helsinki This Week*, *Helsinki Happens*, and *City* list popular cafes, nightspots, and events; pick up copies at the tourist office. Also check the schedules of the Helsinki Philharmonic and Radio Symphony Orchestra, the National Opera, and the National Theater; **Lippupiste**, Aleksanterink. 52 (☎ 0600 90 09 00), in the Stockmann department store, sells tickets for most big venues.

Bars and beer terraces start filling up in the late afternoon; most clubs don't get going until midnight and stay hopping until 4am. With the exception of licensed restaurants and bars, only the state-run liquor store **Alko** can sell alcohol more potent than light beer. (Branch at Mannerheimintie 1, in Kaivopiha across from the train station. Open M-F 9am-8pm, Sa 9am-6pm.) Bars and clubs, ranging from laidback neighborhood pubs to sleek discos, line **Mannerheimintie, Uudenmaankatu,** and **Iso Roobertinkatu.** East of the train station, nightlife flourishes around **Yliopistonkatu** and **Kaisaniemenkatu.** One of the hottest spots in town is **DTM (Don't Tell Mama),** Iso Roobertink. 28, a huge, popular gay club that draws a mixed crowd to foam parties and drag bingo. (☎ 67 63 14; www.dtm.fi. 22+ after 11pm. F-Sa cover €6-8. Open M-Sa 9am-4am, Su noon-4am.) On Mikonk. across from the station, the edgy bar **On the Rocks** (23+; cover €6-7; open 8pm-4am) and chic club **Barfly** (F-Sa cover €7; open daily 8pm-4am) share a broad terrace. Nearby **Copacabana,** Yliopistonk. 5, has salsa dancing each Sunday. (☎ 278 18 55. F-Sa cover €8-10. Open daily 8pm-4am.) A student crowd gathers at **Vanha,** Mannerheimintie 3, in the historic Old Students' House, which features club nights every other weekend. (☎ 13 11 43 46. Beer €4-5. F-Sa cover €2-4. Open M-Th 11am-1am, F 11am-2am, Sa 11am-4am.) **Fever,** Annank. 32, is more generic, although it draws a dependably robust crowd with pop and hip-hop tunes. (☎ 68 55 03 00. 23+. F-Sa cover €6-8. Open daily 9pm-4am.) **Mother Bar,** Eerikink. 2, is a relaxed, retro-chic lounge with nightly techno. (☎ 612 39 90; www.mother.to. Open M-Th 11:30am-midnight, F-Sa 2pm-3am.) DJ Orkidea and Unity Tourist Collective play 6hr. sets of trance and progressive house at sporadic, roving **Club Unity** parties. Check www.clubunity.org for details.

📷 DAYTRIPS FROM HELSINKI

LAHTI. World-class winter sports facilities make Lahti (pop. 96,000) a popular destination for the snow-bunny set. All year round, the **Ski Museum** has ski-jump and biathalon simulators, as well as exhibits on the history of skiing in Finland. (☎ 38 14 45 23; www.lahti.fi/museot/ski.html. Open M-F 10am-5pm, Sa-Su 11am-5pm. €4.30.) Towering more than 200m above the museum, the tallest of three **ski jumps** is accessible by a chairlift/elevator combination. (Open in summer M-F 10am-5pm. €5, with ski museum €6.) The extensive network of cross-country **ski trails** (100km) emanating from the sports complex is hikable in summer; the tourist office provides free hiking **maps,** including information about the thickly forested **Ilvesvaellus Trail,** a 30min. bus ride to the northwest. *(Trains arrive from: Helsinki (1½-2hr., 1 per hr., €12-17); Savonlinna (3-3½hr., 5 per day, €31-35); and Tampere (2hr., every*

1-2hr., €18-23). The tourist office, Aleksanterink. 16, provides free Internet access; walk up Rau-tutienk. 7 blocks and turn left on Aleksanterink. ☎03 814 45 66; www.lahtitravel.fi. Open in sum-mer M-F 9am-6pm, Sa 10am-2pm; low season M-F 9am-6pm.)

PORVOO. Picturesque Porvoo (pop. 46,000) hugs the Porvoo River and lies along **Old King Road,** a network of paths that stretched from St. Petersburg west through Turku all the way to the Norwegian port of Bergen. In 1809, Tsar Alexander I granted Finland autonomy at the simple, whitewashed **cathedral** in Porvoo's old town. (Open May-Sept. M-F 10am-6pm, Sa 10am-2pm, Su 2pm-5pm; Oct.-Apr. Tu-Sa 10am-2pm, Su 2-4pm. Free.) The house of Finland's national poet **Johan Ludvig Runeberg,** Aleksanterink. 3, looks much as it did when he called it home in the mid-1800s; the work of his son, sculptor Walter Runeberg, is on display across the street. (Both houses open May-Aug. M-Sa 10am-4pm, Su 11am-5pm; Sept.-Apr. W-Sa 10am-4pm, Su 11am-5pm. €5 for both.) Impressionist painter Albert Edelfelt also called Porvoo home, and some of his graceful canvases are on display at the **Edelfelt-Vallgren Museum,** Välikatu 11, next to the **Historical Museum.** (Both open May-Aug. M-Sa 10am-4pm, Su 11am-4pm; Sept.-Apr. W-Su noon-4pm. €5 for both.) **Porvoo Pyörätalo,** Mannerheimink. 12 (☎019 58 51 04), rents **bikes** to visitors heading south as far as **Pellinki** (30km) on the Pellinge archipelago. *(Buses run from Helsinki (1hr., every 15min., €8.50). The tourist office, Rihkamak. 4, books rooms for free. Follow signs from the bus station. ☎019 520 23 16; www.porvoo.fi. Open mid-June to Aug. M-F 9am-6pm, Sa-Su 10am-4pm; low season reduced hours.)*

HANKO. Occupying a peninsula at the southern tip of Finland, seaside Hanko (pop. 10,000) makes for a refreshing change of pace from the hubbub of Helsinki. The villas and bungalows along the coastline reflect the tastes of the long-gone Russian nobility, while the red **water tower,** uphill from the tourist office, offers a great view of the rocky archipelago. (Open daily noon-6pm. €1.) Choose from over 30km of **beaches;** Bellevue, on Appelgrenintie to the northeast, is the most popular. *(Trains arrive from Helsinki (2hr., 6-8 per day, €19) and Turku (2hr., 6-8 per day, €22). The tourist office, Raatihuoneentori 5, books rooms for free. ☎019 220 34 11; www.hanko.fi. Open June-July M-F 9am-5pm, Sa 10am-4pm; Aug. M-F 9am-5pm; Sept.-May M-F 8am-4pm.)*

TURKU (ÅBO) ☎02

Finland's oldest city, Turku (pop. 163,000) has grown weatherbeaten with the passing of 775 years. It was the focal point of Swedish and Russian power strug-gles, the seat of Finnish governance until Helsinki usurped that honor in 1812, and then the victim of the worst fire in Scandinavian history, which almost wiped the city off the map in 1827. Undaunted, Turku shook off its woes and rebuilt itself into a vibrant cultural and academic center that's proud of what it has endured.

⌂⚡ TRANSPORTATION AND PRACTICAL INFORMATION. Trains run to Hels-inki (2hr., 1 per hr., €19-28) and Tampere (1¾hr., every 1-2hr., €17-26). Viking Line **ferries** sail to Stockholm (10hr., 2 per day, from €24), as do Silja Line ferries (12hr., daily 6:30pm, from €20). To get to the ferry terminal, catch bus #1 from Kauppa-tori (€2) or walk to the end of Linnank. The **tourist office,** Aurak. 2, offers 15min. of free **Internet** access. (☎262 74 44; www.turkutouring.fi. Open Apr.-Sept. M-F 8:30am-6pm, Sa-Su 9am-4pm; Oct.-Mar. M-F 8:30am-6pm, Sa-Su 10am-3pm.)

⌂⬚ ACCOMMODATIONS AND FOOD. The spacious, well-run ▓**Hostel Turku (HI) ❷,** Linnank. 39, is on the Aura River between the train station and the ferry terminal. From the station, walk west four blocks on Ratapihank., turn left on Puistok., and make a right on Linnank. at the river. (☎262 76 80. Breakfast

€4.50. Kitchen available. Sheets €4.70. Laundry €2. Reception 7am-midnight. Check-in 3pm-midnight. Curfew 2am. Dorms €11; doubles €33; quads €47. Nonmembers add €2.50. MC/V.) For well-kept rooms in a peaceful setting, try the nun-run **Bridgettine Convent Guesthouse ❸**, Ursinink. 15A, near the corner of Puutarhak. (☎250 19 10. Breakfast included. Reception 8am-9pm. Singles €42; doubles €61; triples €80. Cash only.) Take bus #8 from Eerikinkatu to **Ruissalo Camping ❶**, on leafy Ruissalo Island. (☎262 51 00. Reception 7am-11pm. Open June-Aug. €10 per person with tent, €8 per extra person. MC/V.) Produce fills the outdoor market at **Kauppatori** (open M-Sa 7am-2pm) and indoor **Kauppahalli** (open M-Th 8am-5pm, F 8am-2pm, Sa 8am-2pm) on Eerikink., while cheap eateries line Humalistonkatu.

◨ ◫ SIGHTS AND ENTERTAINMENT. Blocky **Turku Cathedral** is the spiritual center of Finland's Lutheran Church, and its 101m tower dominates Turku's skyline. Finnish public radio has broadcast the noontime chiming of the bells since 1944. (Open daily 9am-7pm.) Around the corner, the **Sibelius Museum**, Piispank. 17, houses manuscripts and fetish objects like the composer's cigar box, but also an impressive collection of European folk instruments. (☎215 44 94; www.sibeliusmuseum.abo.fi. Open Tu-Su 11am-4pm. €3, students €1. Concerts W 8pm. €7, students €3.) The 700-year-old **Turun Linna** (Turku Castle), 3km from the town center, contains a labyrinthine **historical museum** with dark passageways and medieval artifacts. Catch bus #1 (€2) from Market Square or walk to the end of Linnank. (Open mid-Apr. to mid-Sept. daily 10am-6pm; mid-Sept. to mid-Apr. Tu-Su 10am-3pm. €6.50, students €5.50.) The nearby **Forum Marinum**, Linnank. 72, is a top-notch maritime museum. (☎282 25 11; www.forum-marinum.fi. Open May-Sept. daily 11am-7pm; Oct.-Apr. Tu-Su 10am-6pm. Exhibitions €4-6.) Just over a decade ago, when a tobacco magnate's riverside mansion was being renovated into a museum, workers discovered a medieval city block directly beneath the house. Rather than abandoning the project, the ⧉**Aboa Vetus & Ars Nova Museums**, Itäinen Rantak. 4-6, now house a modern art collection suspended over the archaeological dig. (☎250 05 52; www.aboavetusarsnova.fi. Open Apr. to mid-Sept. daily 11am-7pm; late Sept. to Mar. Tu-Su 11am-7pm. €9.50, students €8.50.)

Turku is known throughout Finland for its pubs and breweries, many of which are housed in unusual spaces: an old apothecary (**Pub Uusi Apteeki**, Kaskenk. 1), a 19th-century girls' school (**Brewery Restaurant Koulu**, Eerikink. 18), and a public restroom (**Restaurant Puutorin Vessa**, Puutori). In summer, Turku's nightlife centers around the river, where Finns and tourists alike crowd the boats docked by the banks to dance and drink. Posh **Prima**, Aurak. 14, is the best place for clubbing until late; it features two dance floors, a bar, and an Indian restaurant in the basement. (☎232 37 11. Cover F-Sa €3-5. Club open W-Th and Su 11pm-4am, F-Sa 10pm-4am. Bar open M-Tu 10am-1am, W-Sa 10am-4am, Su noon-4am. Restaurant open daily 5-10pm.) Power chords have been rattling windowpanes on Ruissalo Island at July's **Ruisrock** festival since 1970. Check www.ruisrock.fi for details.

NEAR TURKU

NAANTALI. Just 15km west of Turku, pleasant Naantali (pop. 13,000) comes alive each summer with vacationing Finns. Mannerheiminkatu leads to the old town, whose wooden buildings date to the late 18th century. On a lush hill overlooking the water, the medieval **Convent Church** is a warm, intimate retreat. *(Open daily June-Aug. 10am-8pm; low season reduced hours.)* Across the harbor is **Kultaranta**, Finnish president Tarja Halonen's granite summer home; keep an eye out for her. During the summer, flocks of Finnish tots, parents in tow, descend upon Naantali's main attraction, the

fantasy theme park **Moomin World,** where kids can interact with Snufkin, Sniff, and other characters from author Tove Janssen's beloved book series. *(☎02 511 11 11; www.muumimaailma.fi. Open daily mid-June to mid-Aug. 10am-6pm. €13-17.)* The junior-high set tends to prefer **Väski,** an adventure island with rock climbing, pirate ships, and a nettlesome obstacle course. *(☎02 511 11 88; www.vaski.com. Open daily mid-June to mid-Aug. 11am-7pm. €7-13.)* These young mischief-makers will inherit the tradition of **Sleepyhead Day** (July 27), when the residents of Naantali get up at 6am and proceed to crown the year's Sleepyhead before throwing him or her into the harbor. *(Buses #11, 110, and 111 run to Naantali from Turku (30-45min., €3.60). The tourist office, Kaivotori 2, books rooms for free. From the bus station, walk southwest on Tullik. to Kaivok. ☎02 435 98 00. Open June to mid-Aug. M-F 9am-6pm, Sa-Su 10am-3pm; mid-Aug. to May M-F 9am-4:30pm.)*

RAUMA. Farther up the Baltic Coast, Rauma (pop. 37,000) is known for the well-preserved wooden buildings that make up the **old town.** Pick up walking tour maps at the tourist office. Nearby, the lavish, subtly asymmetrical **Church of the Holy Cross** is a posterchild for the Reformation, having shed its past as a Franciscan monastery to become a Lutheran chapel. Many islands in Rauma's **archipelago** are excellent for hiking; try the trails on **Kuuskajaskari,** a former military fortress. (Ferries depart twice daily in summer from the harbor. 30min., €7.) Midsummer brings the hugely popular **Finnish Rock Festival** (www.rmj.fi), while festivals dedicated to lace (early July) and the blues (late July) pack Rauma's calendar later in the summer. *(Buses arrive from Turku every hour (1½-2hr.; €16, students €8). To reach the tourist office, Valtak. 2, walk down Nortamonk. and turn right. ☎834 45 51; www.rauma.fi. Open June-Aug. M-F 8am-6pm, Sa 10am-3pm, Su 11am-2pm; Sept.-May M-F 8am-4pm.)*

PORI. Come July, the elegant coastal town of Pori (pop. 76,000) will be mobbed with the 40th anniversary of the **Pori Jazz Festival,** an event that has confounded jazz traditionalists by showcasing Macy Gray and Ladysmith Black Mambazo alongside the usual suspects. *(July 16-24, 2005. ☎626 22 00; www.porijazz.fi. Tickets from €7; some concerts free.)* For modern art installations with ambitious titles like "What Is Important?," head to the **Pori Art Museum,** on the corner of Etelärantak. and Raatihuonek. *(☎621 10 80. Open Tu-Su 11am-6pm, W until 8pm. €5, students €2.50.)* In a graveyard 1.5km west of the center, on Maantiek., the gorgeous **Juselius Mausoleum** is adorned with frescoes painted by Jorma Gallen-Kallela using sketches drawn by his father Akseli. *(☎623 87 46. Open May-Aug. noon-3pm.)* If you have extra time, take bus #2 (20min., €2) northwest to **Yyteri beach,** popular with wind-surfers in summer and cross-country skiers in winter. While lolling about the dunes, pound a bear-labeled bottle of **Karhu** beer, brewed in Pori and popular across Finland. *(Trains arrive from Helsinki (3½-4hr., 5-8 per day, €25-32), while buses pull in from Tampere (2hr., 4 per day, €16) and Turku (2hr., 6-7 per day, €21). The tourist office, Yrjönk. 17, helps find rooms. ☎621 12 73; www.pori.fi. Open June-Aug. M-F 8am-6pm; Sept.-May M-F 8am-4pm.)*

TAMPERE ☎03

A striking example of successful urban renewal, Tampere (pop. 200,000) has filled its old brick factories with art and planted trees along waterways where paddle-wheels and turbines once whirred. As telecommunications and information technology edged out textile and metal plants, a clean and vibrant city emerged to give Turku a run for its money as Finland's second capital.

🖪🖩 TRANSPORTATION AND PRACTICAL INFORMATION. Trains head to: Helsinki (2hr., 2 per hr., €19-29); Oulu (4-5hr., 8 per day, €45-56); and Turku (2hr., every 1-2hr., €17-26). Riding on a **city bus** costs €1.40, and most buses pass

FINLAND

through the main square on Hämeenkatu. The **tourist office**, Verkatehtaank. 2, offers free **Internet**, while its standard-bearers zip around town on green scooters and render assistance. To reach the office from the train station, walk up Hämeenk. four blocks and turn left before the bridge. (☎31 46 68 00; www.tampere.fi. Open June-Aug. M-F 8:30am-8pm, Sa-Su 10am-5pm; Sept. daily 9am-4pm; Oct.-May M-F 9am-4pm.) **Postal Code:** 33100.

⌐⌐ ACCOMMODATIONS AND FOOD. Tampeeren NNKY (HI) ❷, Tuomiokirkonk. 12, offers rickety, bare-bones rooms near the cathedral overlooking the city. From the train station, walk down Hämeenk. and make a right on Tuomiokirkonk. (☎254 40 20. Breakfast €5. Sheets €4.50. Reception 8-10am and 4-11pm. Open June-Aug. Dorms €11-13; singles €29; doubles €42. Nonmembers add €2.50. Cash only.) For cheerier lodgings, make the trek out to **Hostel Uimahallin Maja (HI) ❷**, Pirkank. 10, on the other side of the city center. Walk 1.5km down Hämeenk. and bear right after the library. (☎222 94 60. Breakfast €4.50. Sheets included. Reception 8am-11pm. Dorms €17; singles €35-38; doubles €50; triples €62, quads €84. Nonmembers add €2.50. MC/V.) Bus #1 (€2) goes to **Camping Härmälä ❷**, which overlooks Lake Pyhäjärvi. (☎265 13 55. Open early May to late Aug. Tents €14.50-16.50; cabins €29-64.) Restaurants line **Hämeenkatu** and **Aleksanterinkatu**. The first building to be electrified in Northern Europe now houses **Plevna Panimoravintola ❷**, Itäinenk. 8, a traditional restaurant serving microbrews and heavy local specialties in a converted weaving mill. (☎260 12 00. Entrees €8-16. Beer €4-6. Open M-Th 11am-1am, F-Sa 11am-2am, Su noon-11pm. MC/V.) The city's oldest pizzeria, **Napoli ❶**, Aleksanterink. 31, serves 100 different varieties. (☎223 88 87. Pizza €7-12. Open M-Tu 11am-10pm, W-Th 11am-11pm, F-Sa noon-midnight, Su 1-11pm. MC/V.) The gastronomically bold can also try *mustamakkara*, a black blood sausage, available at Tampere's vast **Kauppahalli**, Hämeenk. 19, the largest market hall in Scandinavia. (Open M-F 8am-6pm, Sa 8am-4pm.)

◎◢ SIGHTS AND ENTERTAINMENT. Most of Tampere's museums are housed in renovated factories, including the **Vapriikki Museum Center**, Veturiaukio 4. Seven collections run the gamut from local history to ice hockey, while temporary exhibitions add heft to the center's offerings. (☎31 46 69 66. Open Tu and Th-Su 10am-6pm, W 11am-8pm. €5, students €1.) Scottish cotton magnate James Finlayson gave his name to the **Finlayson Complex**, which includes the **Media Museum Rupriikki** (open Tu-Su 11am-7pm; €4), the **Central Museum of Labor** (open Tu-Su 11am-6pm; €4), and the interactive **Spy Museum** (open M-F noon-6pm, Sa-Su 10am-4pm; €4). In December 1905, a conference in the Tampere Workers' Hall was the occasion of Lenin and Stalin's first meeting; a century later, the **Lenin Museum**, Hämeenpuisto 28, occupies the same building. (☎276 81 00. Open M-F 9am-6pm, Sa-Su 11am-4pm. €4.) The daring frescoes of the **Tuomiokirkko**, Tuomiokirkonk. 3 (open daily 9am-6pm), are matched only by the vaulted wooden ceiling of **Aleksanterin kirkko**, on Pyynikin kirkkopuisto (open daily May-Aug. 10am-5pm). Finland's most-visited library, **Metso**, Pirkank. 2, bears the name of the wood grouse that it is said to resemble if seen from above. In the basement, the intricate dioramas of **Moomin Valley** pay tribute to the same cast of characters who inhabit Moomin World (p. 330) in Naantali. (☎31 46 14. Library open M-F 9:30am-8pm, Sa 9:30am-3pm. Free Internet. Moomin Valley open M-F 9am-5pm, Sa-Su 10am-6pm. €4.) The city's northern lakefront is home to **Särkänniemi**, a cultural and recreation center that includes the 168m **Näsinneula** observation tower. (Open 11am-11:30pm. €4.) A planetarium, a dolphinarium, and two swooping roller coasters round out the park. (☎248 82 12; www.sarkanniemi.fi. €3.50 each. Check website for hours.)

In March, Tampere will mark the 35th anniversary of its well-regarded **Short Film Festival,** which draws entries from as many as 40 countries each year. (www.tampere.filmfestival.fi; March 9-13, 2005.) August's **International Theater Festival** takes over city parks and squares for performances of Finnish and Baltic works. (www.teatterikesa.fi; August 9-14, 2005.) **Hämeenkatu, Aleksanterinkatu,** and the surrounding streets are energetic at night, and many hotels host discos. ▧**Cafe Europa,** Aleksanterink. 29, serves drinks in a Bohemian lounge with low, rakishly mismatched chandeliers. (☎ 223 55 38. Beer €4. 20+ after 6pm. Dancing W-Sa 9pm-close. F cover €2 for dance floor. Open M-Th and Su noon-2am, F-Sa noon-3am.) **Telakka,** Tullikamarinaukio 3, houses a bar, restaurant, club, and theater in an old warehouse near the train station. (☎ 225 07 00. Live music F-Sa. Open M-Th 11am-2am, F 11am-3am, Sa noon-3am, Su noon-midnight.) **Doris,** Aleksanterink. 20, is a popular rock club featuring live acts most nights. (☎ 272 02 12. Cover from €2. Open Tu-Th and Su 9pm-3am, F-Sa 10pm-3am.)

SAVONLINNA   ☎ 015

Savonlinna (pop. 28,000) sits amid a chain of islands in the heart of Finland's lake region. The Russian aristocracy was the first to discover Savonlinna as a vacation spot, turning it into a fashionable spa town. **Olavinlinna Castle,** built to reinforce the border against the tsars in 1475, has towering spires that rise up out of the lakes. Face away from the train tracks at the Kauppatori, and follow the docks to the left. (Open daily June to mid-Aug. 10am-5pm; mid-Aug. to May 10am-3pm. €5, students €3.50.) Secluded **Sulosaari** island is a peaceful retreat with walking trails. From Kauppatori, go under the train tracks, cross the footbridge, go through the parking lot, and cross the next footbridge; look for the "no cars" sign to the right of the building. Try to make time for a daytrip out to the surreal ▧**Retretti Art Center,** where massive caves display beautiful glasswork and dream-like installations alongside major temporary exhibitions. (☎ 775 22 00; www.retretti.fi. Open daily July 10am-6pm; June and Aug. 10am-5pm. €15, students €9.) Buses (7 per day, €4.50) make the 30min. trip from Savonlinna. From Retretti, walk 20min. along the breathtaking **Punkaharju Ridge** to reach the **Lusto** forestry museum, which details the environmental history of the area and puts on rustic exhibitions like 2004's look at Finnish chainsaw art. (☎ 345 10 30; www.lusto.fi. Open daily June-Aug. 10am-7pm; low season reduced hours. €7, students €6.)

THE BIG SPLURGE

THE HIGH NOTES

Above the sea of well-dressed people filing reverently into Olavinlinna Castle, one whistled melody floats in the air: the haunting tune of *Nessun Dorma.* Puccini left the opera *Turandot* unfinished when he died in 1924, but the crowd of 60,000 that attends the Savonlinna Opera Festival each year has no trouble filling in the blanks. And when the Finnish tenor opens act three with a rousing rendition of *Nessun Dorma,* the stellar cast, skilled orchestra, and lavish sets conspire to produce a moment of inexpressible beauty.

Tracing its history back to 1912 but most recently revived in 1967, the opera festival seized on the idea of using the medieval castle as a commanding backdrop for its productions. Each summer the castle's courtyard turns into a covered auditorium with all the bells and whistles of an indoor opera house, while in town restaurants with names like "Tosca" charge an arm and a leg for their pre-show menus. Budget travelers may feel like part of a conspicuous minority during the festival, but with the 2005 lineup including *Aida, Turandot,* and the 1975 Finnish opera *Ratsumies* (The Horseman), one melodious night might be worth the splurge.

July 8-Aug. 6, 2005. Visit www.operafestival.fi or call ☎ 15 47 67 50 for more info. Tickets start at €31, but the choice seats run a whopping €93-115.

Trains run from Savonlinna to Helsinki (5-6hr., 3 per day, €40-45). When arriving, hop off at Savonlinna-Kauppatori, in the center of town, rather than at the distant Savonlinna station. The **tourist office**, Puistok. 1, across the bridge from the market, is not known for being terribly helpful. (☎51 75 10. Open June-Aug. daily 8am-8pm; Sept.-May M-F 9am-5pm.) **Summer Hotel Vuorilinna ❸**, on Kylpylaitoksentie near the casino, has well-equipped student apartments. From the Kauppatori, walk under the tracks and cross the bridge. (☎739 54 30. Sheets included. Kitchen available. Reception 7am-11pm. Open June-Aug. Dorms €25; singles €55-65; doubles €65-75. AmEx/MC/V.) Bars and cafes line **Olavinkatu** and the marketplace area, while terraces on **Linnankatu** look out over the castle. **Postal Code:** 57100.

KUOPIO   ☎017

Eastern Finland's largest city, Kuopio (pop. 88,000) sits in the midst of the beautiful Saimaa lake system. The archbishop of the Finnish Orthodox Church resides here, and the **Orthodox Church Museum**, Karjalank. 1, shows a collection of textiles and icons. (☎287 22 44. Open May-Aug. Tu-Su 10am-4pm; Sept.-Apr. M-F noon-3pm, Sa-Su noon-5pm. €5, students €3.) The 2km hike uphill to the **🔳Puijo Tower** is rewarded with a ranging view of Lake Kallavesi and the coniferous forests beyond it. From Kauppatori, walk toward the train station on Puijonk., cross the tracks and the highway, and continue up the hill. (Open daily May-Sept. 9am-9pm. €3.) Take bus #16 (€2.50) from the Kauppatori to **Rauhalahti Holiday Center**, with trails for mountain-biking and snowshoeing as well as a large woodsmoke sauna. (☎47 30 00; www.rauhalahti.com. Sauna open in summer Tu and Th 5-10pm; winter Tu 5-10pm. €10.) The **Kuopio Dance Festival** (www.kuopiodancefestival.fi) draws crowds in mid-June, while oenophiles toast early July's **Wine Festival.**

Trains travel to Helsinki (5½hr., 9 per day, €46-53) and Oulu (4½hr., 6 per day, €34-45). The **tourist office**, Haapaniemenk. 17, has a stand at the train station and roving staff members throughout the city. To get to the main office from the station, go right on Asemak., and turn left on Haapaniemenk. (☎18 25 84; www.kuopioinfo.fi. Open July M-F 9:30am-5pm, Sa 9:30am-3pm; June and early Aug. M-F 9:30am-5pm; mid-Aug. to May M-F 9:30am-4pm.) **Rautatie Guest House ❸**, Asemak. 1, offers basic rooms in the train station and in an annex across the street; reception is in the Asemagrilli restaurant in the station. (☎580 05 69. Breakfast and sheets included. Reception 7am-10pm. Singles €36-46; doubles €56-75; triples €93; quads €119. MC/V.) To the right out of the station, **Virkkula Youth Hostel ❷**, Asemak. 3, offers bare-bones accommodations in an old-fashioned schoolhouse. (☎263 18 39. Breakfast €5. Sheets €5. Reception 6pm-9am. Open mid-June to July. Dorms €14.) **Muikkuravintola Sampo ❷**, Kauppak. 13, draws praise for imaginative renderings of *muikku*, a local whitefish. (☎261 46 77. Entrees €9-12. Open M-Sa 11am-midnight, Su noon-midnight. MC/V.) Get fresh produce at the gargantuan **Kauppatori** market in the center of town (open M-Sa 7am-3pm) or inside the lovely **Kauppahalli** market hall (open M-F 8am-5pm, Sa 9am-3pm). **Postal Code:** 70100.

OULU   ☎08

Warm winds off the Gulf of Bothnia tousle the hair of students ambling along Oulu's (pop. 124,000) flower-lined avenues. Despite its young population, Oulu toes the line between relaxed and soporific, so there's no need to tarry for more than a day or two unless you plan on **birdwatching** in the wetlands around the Bay of Liminka, to the south. Just west of the city center, the island of **Pikisaari** draws picnickers with brightly colored wooden cottages and cutesy boutiques; take the footbridge at the end of Kaarlenväylä. **Science Center Tietomaa**, Nahkatehtaank. 6, has interactive science exhibits, an IMAX theater, and a 35m observation tower. (☎55 84 13 40; www.tietomaa.fi. Open July daily 10am-8pm; Mar.-June and Aug. daily 10am-6pm; Sept.-Feb. M-F 10am-4pm, Sa-Su 10am-6pm. €10, students €8.50.) Across the street, the **Oulun Taidemuseo** shows 20th-century Finnish art in a building that has seen duty as a leather factory and as the university library. (☎558 474 50. Open Tu-Su 10am-5pm. €3, students €1.) Nightlife spills out of the pavilion on **Kirkkokatu** and the terraces lining **Otto Karhin Park** and **Kappurienkatu**. Late August kicks off the **Oulu Music Video Festival**, with master classes, screenings, and a competition that draws dozens of Finnish directors. The festival also plays host to the **Air Guitar World Championships**, a gimmicky draw that occasionally achieves moments of Claptonesque transcendence. Visit www.omvf.net for more info.

All **trains** between northern and southern Finland pass through Oulu, heading south to Helsinki (6-7hr., 5-6 per day, €55-66) and north to Rovaniemi (2½hr., 4 per day, €22-26). To reach the **tourist office,** Torik. 10, take Hallitusk. and then the second left after passing through the park. (☎55 84 13 30; www.oulutourism.fi. Open mid-June to mid-Aug. M-F 9am-6pm, Sa 10am-3pm; mid-Aug. to mid-June M-F 9am-4pm.) The **Oppimestari Summer Hotel ❸,** Nahkatehtaank. 3, offers generously furnished rooms with kitchenettes during the summer. From the train station, cross Rautatienk. straight onto Asemak. After four blocks, turn right on Isok., which becomes Kasarmintie, and turn right again onto Nahkatehtaank. (☎884 85 27; oppimestari@merikoski.fi. Breakfast and sheets included. Laundry €3. Open June-July. Singles €37; doubles €55. AmEx/MC/V.) For summer visitors staying longer than one night, the University of Oulu rents out **flats** for €60-70 per week between semesters. (☎553 40 48; housing@oulu.fi. Reserve in advance.) Bus #5 (€2) goes to **Nallikari Camping ❷,** Hietasaari, which has colorful cottages by the water. (☎55 86 13 50; www.nallikaricamping.fi. €11-16 per person; 4-person cabins €32. MC/V.) Cheap food is easy to find; as in many university towns, it's hard to walk 10m without passing a pizza or kebab joint. The **Kauppatori,** at the end of Kauppurienk. by the harbor, sells produce and is flanked by old wooden warehouses that have been pressed into service as yuppie cafes. **Postal Code:** 90100.

ROVANIEMI
☎016

Just south of the Arctic Circle, Rovaniemi (pop. 62,000) is the capital of Finnish Lapland and a gateway to the northern wilderness. After retreating German troops burned the city to the ground in October 1944, architect Alvar Aalto stepped in with the Reindeer Antler Plan, a reconstruction scheme that would use rivers and existing highways to rebuild the settlement in the shape of a reindeer's head. Not all of Aalto's plan was executed, but you can look at a modern map of Rovaniemi with east facing up and see the resemblance. The **Arktikum,** housed in a beautiful glass corridor at Pohjoisranta 4, has a treasure trove of info on Arctic peoples and landscapes. (☎31 78 40; www.arktikum.fi. Open mid-June to mid-Aug. daily 9am-7pm; low season reduced hours. €11, students €8.50.) Think back to the time when you still thought snow globes were magical and then head out to **Santa Claus Village,** 8km north of the center, where rolypoly, multilingual Father Christmas holds court while his minions hawk souvenirs. Take bus #8 (20min., €2.70) from the train station to Arctic Circle. (☎356 20 96; www.santaclausvillage.info. Open daily June-Aug. and Dec. to mid-Jan. 9am-7pm; Sept. 9am-5pm; Oct.-Nov. and mid-Jan. to May 10am-5pm.) **Koskikatu** is lined with cafes and bars.

Trains go south to Helsinki (10hr.; 4 per day; €71, students €36) via Oulu (2½hr., €22/€11) and Kuopio (8hr., 3-4 per day, €54/€27). **Buses** run to destinations throughout northern Finland, and to Nordkapp, Norway (11hr., 1 per day,

€101). The staff of the **tourist office**, Rovak. 21, combs the town on yellow mopeds and speaks flawless English, even though rank-and-file Laplanders may not. (☎34 62 70; www.rovaniemi.fi. Internet €2 per 15min. Open June-Aug. M-F 8am-6pm, Sa-Su 10am-6pm; Dec. M-F 8am-6pm, Sa-Su 10am-2pm; Sept.-Nov. and Jan.-May M-F 8am-6pm.) The **public library,** one of Aalto's signature designs, offers free **Internet** access. (Open in summer M-Th 11am-7pm, F 11am-5pm, Sa 11am-3pm; winter M-Th 11am-8pm, F 11am-5pm, Sa 11am-4pm.) Cheap rooms are hard to come by in Rovaniemi. To reach **Outa Guesthouse ❸,** Ukkoherrantie 16, turn right out of the station, left onto Lapinkävijäntie, and cross the highway at the first overpass on the right; take the first left on Kansank. and go right on Ukkoherrantie. (☎31 24 74. Breakfast and sheets included. Singles €35; doubles €45. MC/V.) **Café Bar Zoomlt ❶,** at the corner of Koskik. and Korkalonk., serves a summer stir-fry menu (€6.50) as well as *panini* and wraps. (☎32 13 21. Open M-Tu and Th 11am-midnight, W 11am-1am, F-Sa 11am-2am, Su noon-11pm. MC/V.) **Postal Code:** 96100.

FRANCE

Every year, France welcomes over 70 million visitors to its cities, chateaux, mountains, and beaches, making it the most popular tourist destination in the world. Yet to the French, it is only natural that outsiders should flock to their beloved homeland so steeped in history and rich in art and architecture. Influential authors like Camus, Hugo, and Proust; visionary artists like Matisse, Monet, and Rodin; and luminary thinkers like Voltaire, Sartre, and Derrida have ensured France's long-standing role as a pioneer of Western culture, while ambitious imperialists and barefoot revolutionaries have placed their country in the driver's seat of history. Even though France may no longer control the course of world events, the vineyards of Bordeaux, the cutting-edge museums of Paris, the sun-soaked beaches of the Riviera, and the crisp air of the Alps will be certain to tickle your senses and capture your imagination.

DISCOVER FRANCE: SUGGESTED ITINERARIES

THREE DAYS Don't even think of leaving **Paris**, the City of Light (p. 342). Explore the shops and cafes of the **Latin Quarter**, then cross the Seine to reach **Ile de la Cité** to admire **Sainte Chapelle.** Visit the wacky **Centre National d'Art et de Culture Georges Pompidou** before seeing a hot spot of 1789, the **Bastille.** Swing through **Marais** for food and fun. The next day, stroll down the **Champs-Elysées**, starting at the **Arc de Triomphe**, meander through the **Jardin des Tuileries,** and over to the **Musée d'Orsay.** See part of the **Louvre** the next morning, then spend the afternoon at **Versailles.**

ONE WEEK After three days in **Paris**, go to **Tours** (1 day; p. 378) a great base for exploring the chateaux of the **Loire Valley** (1 day; p. 376). Head to **Rennes** for medieval sights and modern nightlife (1 day; p. 373), then to the dazzling island of **Mont-St-Michel** (1 day; p. 373).

BEST OF FRANCE, THREE WEEKS
Begin with three days in **Paris,** with a day-trip to the royal residences at **Versailles.** Whirl through the **Loire Valley** (2 days) before traveling to the wine country of **Bordeaux** (1 day; p. 381). Check out the rose-colored architecture of **Toulouse** (1 day; p. 385) and the medieval walls of **Carcassonne** (1 day; p. 386) before sailing through **Avignon** (p. 388), **Aix-en-Provence** (p. 390), and **Nimes** (p. 388) in sunny Provence (3 days). Let loose in **Marseille** (2 days; p. 391), and back in the glitter of the Riviera in **Nice** (2 days; p. 400). Then show off your tan in the Alps as you travel to **Lyon** (2 days; p. 414) and **Chamonix** (1 day; p. 413). Eat your fill in **Dijon** (1 day; p. 420), and finish your trip with a little German flavor in cosmopolitan **Strasbourg** (1 day; p. 421), where trains will whisk you away to your next European adventure.

ESSENTIALS

WHEN TO GO

In July, Paris starts to shrink; by August it is devoid of Parisians, animated only by tourists and the pickpockets who love them. The French Riviera fills with Anglophones from June to September. French natives flee to other parts of the country during these months, especially the Atlantic coast. Early summer and autumn are the best times to visit Paris—the city has warmed up but not completely emptied out. The north and west have cool winters and mild summers, while the less-

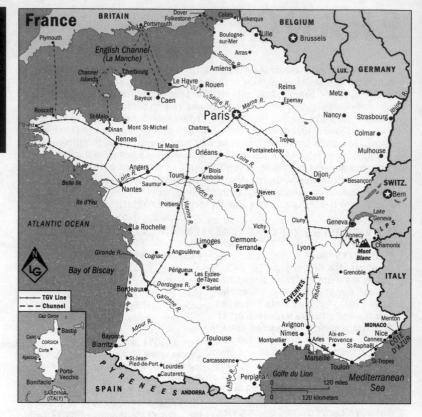

France

BRITAIN · Dover · Folkestone · Portsmouth · Plymouth
Calais · Dunkerque · BELGIUM · Brussels · LUX. · GERMANY
Boulogne-sur-Mer · Lille · Arras · Amiens · Reims · Metz · Nancy · Strasbourg · Colmar · Mulhouse
English Channel (La Manche) · Somme R. · Epernay · Marne R.
Channel Islands · Cherbourg · Le Havre · Rouen · Seine R.
Roscoff · St-Malo · Dinan · Mont St-Michel · Rennes · Chartres · Paris · Troyes · Dijon · Besançon · SWITZ. · Bern
Brest · Quimper · Le Mans · Orléans · Fontainebleau · Loire R.
Angers · Tours · Blois · Amboise · Bourges · Nevers · Beaune · Lake Geneva · ALPS
Belle Ile · Nantes · Saumur · Indre R. · Geneva · Annecy · Mont Blanc · Chamonix
Ile d'Yeu · Poitiers · Vienne R. · Vichy · Cluny · Lyon · ITALY
ATLANTIC OCEAN · La Rochelle · Limoges · Clermont-Ferrand · Grenoble
Gironde R. · Angoulême · Cognac · Lyon
Bay of Biscay · Périgueux · Les Eyzies-de-Tayac · Sarlat · CEVENNES MTS. · Rhône R.
Bordeaux · Dordogne R. · Garonne R.
Cap Corse · Calvi · CORSICA · Corte · Bastia · Ajaccio · Porto-Vecchio · Bonifacio · SARDINIA (ITALY)
Bayonne · Biarritz · St-Jean-Pied-de-Port · Lourdes · Cauterets · Toulouse · Carcassonne · Aude R. · Avignon · Nîmes · Arles · Montpellier · Aix-en-Provence · St-Raphaël · Marseille · Toulon · St-Tropez · Menton · MONACO · Nice · Cannes · CÔTE D'AZUR
SPAIN · ANDORRA · PYRENEES · Perpignan · Golfe du Lion · Mediterranean Sea

— TGV Line
--- Chunnel

N · LG

0 — 120 miles
0 — 120 kilometers

crowded center and east have a more continental climate. From December to February, the Alps provide some of the best skiing in the world, while the Pyrenees offer a calmer, if less climatically dependable, alternative.

DOCUMENTS AND FORMALITIES

VISAS. EU citizens do not need a visa. Citizens of Australia, Canada, New Zealand, and the US do not need a visa for stays of up to 90 days, although this three-month period begins upon entry into any of the countries that belong to the EU's freedom of movement zone. For more information, see p. 17. For stays longer than 90 days, all non-EU citizens need long-stay visas (€101).

EMBASSIES. Foreign embassies in France are in Paris (p. 344). French embassies at home include: **Australia,** Embassy of France, 6 Perth Avenue, Yarralumla, Canberra, ACT 2600 (☎02 62 16 01 27; www.ambafrance-au.org.); **Canada,** French Embassy and Consulate, 42 Sussex Dr., Ottawa, ON K1M 2C9 (613-789-1795; www.ambafrance-ca.org); **Ireland,** French Embassy, Consulate Section, 36 Ailesbury Rd., Ballsbridge, Dublin 4 (01 227 5000; www.ambafrance.ie); **New Zealand,** French Embassy and Consulate, 34-42 Manners St., P.O. Box 11-343, Wellington (04 384 25 55; www.ambafrance-nz.org); **UK,** French Embassy, 58 Knightsbridge, London SW1X 7JT (020 7201 1000; www.ambafrance-uk.org.); **US,** Embassy of France in the United States, 4101 Reservoir Rd. NW, Washington, D.C. 20007 (202-944-6000; www.ambafrance-us.org).

FEATURED ITINERARY: WINETASTING IN FRANCE

Start your tour in **Paris** (p. 342), and preview some of France's most distinctive vintages at **La Belle Hortense**, an egghead wine bar in the Marais. Then set out for **Reims** (p. 425), where the folks at **Champagne Pommery** offer tours of cellars that hold magnums of the bubbly stuff. Spend a night in **Epernay** (p. 425), and saunter down the avenue de Champagne for wine-tastings at blue-blood **Moët & Chandon** and the more populist **Mercier**. Then head for **Strasbourg** (p. 421), the northernmost point on Alsace's legendary **Route du Vin** (p. 422).

Frequent trains will whisk you south to touristy **Colmar** (p. 423), while buses are a better bet as you head to **Riquewihr** and quaint **Kaysersberg.** Catch a train to Dijon—just to the south lies **Beaune** (p. 420), surrounded by the storied Côte de Beaune vineyards. Don't pass up a visit to **Patriarche Père et Fils,** where a tour of the Byzantine cellars includes a mouthful of 13 regional wines. Then dart back to Paris, or extend your itinerary to explore the Médoc region around **Bordeaux** (p. 381) and the ancient vineyards at **St-Emilion** (p. 382).

TRANSPORTATION

BY PLANE. Most transatlantic flights to Paris land at **Roissy-Charles de Gaulle** (CDG; ☎01 48 62 22 80). Many continental and charter flights use **Orly** (ORY; ☎01 49 75 15 15). **Aéroports de Paris** (www.adp.com) has information about both airports. For more info on flying to France, see p. 51. Once in France, you shouldn't need to take a plane unless you're headed for **Corsica** (p. 408).

BY TRAIN. The French national railway company, **SNCF** (☎08 92 35 35 35; www.sncf.fr), manages one of Europe's most efficient rail networks. **TGV** (*train à grande vitesse*, or high-speed) trains now link many major cities in France, as well as some other European destinations, including Brussels, Geneva, Lausanne, and Zurich. **Rapide** trains are slower; local **Express** trains are, oddly, the slowest option. SNCF offers a wide range of discounted round-trip tickets called *tarifs Découvertes*. Get a calendar from a train station detailing *période bleue* (blue period) and *periode blanche* (white period) times and days; blue gets the most discounts. Those under 25 have two great options: The **Découverte 12-25** gives a 25% discount for any blue-period travel, and the **Carte 12-25** (€48), valid for a year, is good for 25-50% off TGV trains, 50% off non-TGV trips that started during a blue period, and 25% off non-TGV trips that started during a white period. Tickets must be validated in the orange machine at the entrance to the platforms at the *gare* (train station) and revalidated at any connections on your trip. Seat reservations are mandatory on EuroCity (EC), InterCity (IC), and TGV trains. All three require a supplement (usually €8-40) and reservation fee (€4-10).

Eurail is valid in France. SNCF's **France Railpass** grants 4-10 days in one month of unlimited rail travel in France (2nd-class US$218-386); the parallel **Youthpass** offers similar perks for those under 26 (US$164-290). The **France Rail 'n' Drive pass** combines two days of rail travel with two days of car rental for two adults traveling together. Prices vary depending on the type of car you choose. (US$205-280 per person; extra traveler US$179; extra rail days US$29; extra car days US$39-99.)

BY BUS. Within France, long-distance buses are a secondary transportation choice, as service is relatively infrequent. However, in some regions buses are indispensable for reaching out-of-the-way towns. Bus services operated by SNCF accept railpasses. *Gare routière* is French for "bus station."

BY FERRY. Ferries across the English Channel (*La Manche*) link France to England and Ireland. The shortest and most popular route is between **Dover** and **Calais** (1-1½hr.), and is run by P&O Stena Line, SeaFrance, and Hoverspeed. Hoverspeed also travels from Newhaven, England to **Dieppe** (2¼-4¼hr.). Brittany Ferries travels from Portsmouth to **Caen** (6hr.) and **St-Malo** (8¾hr.). For more info on English Channel ferries, see p. 55. For info on ferries to **Corsica**, see p. 408.

BY CAR. Drivers in France should have either an **International Driving Permit (IDP;** see p. 69) or a valid EU-issued driving license. Remember that seat belts are mandatory by law. Unless you're traveling in a group of three or more, you won't save money going by car instead of by train, thanks to highway tolls, high gasoline costs, and rental charges. French roads are usually in great condition, but in Corsica and the Alps, rugged landscapes can make for difficult driving.

BY BIKE AND BY THUMB. Of all Europeans, the French may be alone in loving cycling more than soccer. Drivers usually accommodate bikers on wide country roads, and many cities banish cars from select streets each Sunday. Renting a bike (€8-19 per day) beats bringing your own if you're only touring one or two regions. Hitchhiking is illegal on French highways, and many people consider France the hardest country in Europe to get a lift. *Let's Go* does not recommend hitchhiking.

TOURIST SERVICES AND MONEY

EMERGENCY	Police: ☎122. Ambulance: ☎123. Fire: ☎124.

TOURIST OFFICES. The **French Government Tourist Office** (FGTO; www.franceguide.com), also known as **Maison de la France,** runs tourist offices in French cities and offers tourist services to travelers abroad. Tourist offices are called *syndicats d'initiative* or *offices de tourisme*; in the smallest towns, the *mairie* (town hall) may also distribute maps and pamphlets, help travelers find accommodations, and suggest sights and excursions.

MONEY. On January 1, 2002, the **euro (€)** replaced the **franc** (abbreviated FF) as the unit of currency in France. For more information, see p. 20. As a general rule, it's cheaper to exchange money in France than at home. Be prepared to spend at least €20-40 per day, and considerably more in Paris. **Tips** are always included in meal prices in restaurants and cafes and in drink prices at bars and clubs; look for the phrase *service compris* on the menu or just ask. If service is not included, tip 15-20%. Even when service is included, it is polite to leave a *pourboire* of up to 5% at a cafe, bistro, restaurant, or bar. Workers such as concierges may also expect at least a €1.50 tip for services beyond the call of duty; taxi drivers won't expect more than €1. A **Value Added Tax (VAT; TVA** in French) of up to 19.6% is included in the price for a wide range of goods and services (see p. 22).

COMMUNICATION

TELEPHONES. Publicly owned **France Télécom** payphones charge less than their privately owned counterparts. They accept stylish *Télécartes* (phonecards), available in 50-unit (€7.50) and 120-unit (€15) denominations at *tabacs*, post offices, and train stations. Most payphones now also accept credit cards such as Master-Card/EuroCard and Visa. An expensive alternative is to call collect *(faire un appel en PCV)*; an English-speaking operator can be reached by dialing the appropriate service provider listed below. *Décrochez* means pick up; you'll then be asked to *patientez* (wait) to insert your card; at *numérotez* or *composez* you can dial. The information number is ☎12; for an international operator, call ☎00 33 11.

For information on purchasing **cell phones**, see p. 35. International direct dial numbers include: **AT&T**, ☎ 0 800 99 00 11; **British Telecom**, 0 800 14 41 44; **Canada Direct**, 0 800 99 00 16 or 99 02 16; **Ireland Direct**, 0 800 58 05 00; **MCI**, 0 800 99 00 19; **Sprint**, 0 800 99 00 87; **New Zealand Direct**, 0 800 99 00 64; **Telstra Australia**, 0 800 99 00 61.

MAIL. Air mail between France and North America takes 5-10 days; writing "*prioritaire*" on the envelope should ensure delivery in 4-5 days at no extra charge. To send a 20g airmail letter or postcard from France to another EU destination costs €0.50, to a non-EU European country costs €0.75, and to Australia, Canada, New Zealand, or the US costs €0.90. Mail can be held for pickup through *Poste Restante* at almost any city or town with a post office. Address letters to be held according to the following example: SURNAME First name, *Poste Restante*, 52 r. du Louvre, 75001 Paris, France. Mark the envelope HOLD.

INTERNET ACCESS. Most major **post offices** and some branches now offer Internet access at special "cyberposte" terminals, where rechargeable cards provide 1hr. of access for €7. Every hour after that is €4. A large town in France will usually have at least one **cybercafe,** and occasionally there are free terminals in technologically-oriented museums or exhibition spaces. **Cybercafes.com** (www.cybercafes.com) can find a cybercafe near you.

ACCOMMODATIONS AND CAMPING

FRANCE	❶	❷	❸	❹	❺
ACCOMMODATIONS	under €16	€16-25	€25-35	€35-55	over €55

The **French Hostelling International (HI)** affiliate, **Fédération Unie des Auberges de Jeunesse (FUAJ;** ☎ 01 44 89 87 27; www.fuaj.org), operates 160 hostels within France. A bed in a hostel averages around €8-15. Some hostels accept reservations through the International Booking Network (p. 37). Two or more people traveling together will often save money by staying in cheap hotels rather than hostels. The French government employs a four-star hotel ratings system. *Gîtes d'étapes* are rural accommodations for cyclists, hikers, and other ramblers in less-populated areas; they provide beds, a kitchen facility, and a resident caretaker. After 3000 years of settled history, true wilderness in France is hard to find. It's illegal to camp in most public spaces, including national parks. Most campsites have toilets, showers, and electrical outlets, though you may have to pay €2-6 extra for such luxuries; you'll often pay a fee for your car, too (€3-8). In total, expect to pay €8-15 per site.

FOOD AND DRINK

FRANCE	❶	❷	❸	❹	❺
FOOD	under €7	€7-10	€10-15	€15-25	over €25

French chefs cook for one of the most finicky clienteles in the world. The largest meal of the day is *le déjeuner* (lunch). A complete French meal includes an *apéritif* (drink), an *entrée* (appetizer), a *plat* (main course), salad, cheese, dessert, fruit, coffee, and a *digestif* (after-dinner drink). The French drink wine with virtually every meal; *boisson comprise* entitles you to a free drink (usually wine) with your food. Most restaurants offer a *menu à prix fixe* (fixed-price meal) that costs less than ordering *à la carte*. The *formule* is a cheaper, two-course version. Odd-hour cravings between lunch and dinner can be satisfied at *brasseries*, the middle ground between casual cafes and structured restaurants. *Service compris* means the tip is included in *l'addition* (the check). For a picnic, get fresh produce at a *marché* (outdoor market) and then hop between specialty shops. Start with a *boulangerie* (bakery) for bread, proceed to a *charcuterie* (butcher) for meats, and then *pâtisseries* (pastry shops) and *confiseries* (candy shops) to satisfy a sweet tooth. Cafes on a major boulevard are more expensive than smaller places a few steps down a side street. Prices are also cheaper at the *comptoir* (counter) than in the *salle* (seating area). For supermarket shopping, look for the chains Carrefour, Casino, Monoprix, and Prisunic.

HOLIDAYS AND FESTIVALS

Holidays: New Year's Day (Jan. 1); Easter Monday (Mar. 28); Labor Day (May 1); Ascension Day (May 5); Fête de la Victoire (May 8); Whit Monday (May 15); Bastille Day (July 14); Feast of the Assumption (Aug. 15); All Saints' Day (Nov. 1); Armistice Day (Nov. 11); Christmas (Dec. 25).

Festivals: Many cities celebrate a pre-Lenten Carnaval—for the most over-the-top festivities, head to Nice (Feb. 11-27). The Cannes Film Festival (May 11-22; www.festival-cannes.com) caters to directors and stars. Although you may not be competing in the Tour de France (starting July 2; www.letour.fr), you'll enjoy all the hype. The Festival d'Avignon (July-Aug.; www.festival-avignon.com) is famous for theater. The biggest national holiday, Bastille Day (July 14), is marked by parades and fireworks nationwide.

FACTS AND FIGURES: FRANCE	
Official Name: French Republic.	**Land Area:** 547,030 sq. km.
Capital: Paris.	**Time Zone:** GMT+1
Major Cities: Lyon, Marseilles, Nice.	**Language:** French.
Population: 60,000,000.	**Religion:** Roman Catholic (90%).

PARIS

From tortuous medieval alleyways to broad 19th-century boulevards, from the gargoyles of Notre Dame to the futuristic motions of the Parc de la Villette, from the masterpieces of the Louvre to the installations of avant-garde galleries, Paris (pop. 2,100,000) presents itself as both a harbor of tradition and a hotbed of innovation. The city and its inhabitants foster a spirit of revolution alongside a reverence for history, devoting as much energy to preserving conventions as to shattering them. Paris is everything you expected—and a constant surprise.

◪ INTERCITY TRANSPORTATION

Flights: Aéroport Roissy-Charles de Gaulle (CDG; ☎01 48 62 22 80; www.adp.fr), 23km northeast of Paris, services most transatlantic flights. For flight info, call the 24hr. English-speaking information center. **Aéroport d'Orly** (ORY; English recording ☎01 49 75 15 15), 18km south of Paris, is used by charters and many continental flights. The cheapest and fastest ways to get into the city are by **RER** or **bus.**

Trains: Paris has 6 major train stations: **Gare d'Austerlitz** (to the Loire Valley, southwestern France, Spain, and Portugal); **Gare de l'Est** (to Austria, eastern France, southern Germany, Hungary, Luxembourg, Prague, and Switzerland); **Gare de Lyon** (to southern France, Greece, Italy, and Switzerland); **Gare du Nord** (to Belgium, Britain, the Netherlands, northern France, northern Germany, and Scandinavia); **Gare Montparnasse** (to Brittany and southwestern France by TGV); and **Gare St-Lazare** (to Normandy).

Buses: Gare Routière Internationale du Paris-Gallieni, 28 av. du Général de Gaulle, just outside Paris in Bagnolet. Ⓜ Gallieni. Eurolines (☎01 49 72 57 80; www.eurolines.fr) sells tickets to most destinations in France and neighboring countries.

FRANCE

▓ ORIENTATION

The **Ile de la Cité** and **Ile St-Louis** sit at the center of the city, while the **Seine**, flowing east to west, splits Paris into two sections: the **Left Bank (Rive Gauche)** to the south and the **Right Bank (Rive Droite)** to the north. The Left Bank, with its older architecture and narrow streets, has traditionally been considered bohemian and intellectual, while the Right Bank, with grand avenues and designer shops, is more ritzy. Administratively, Paris is divided into 20 **arrondissements** (districts; e.g. 1er, 6ème) that spiral clockwise around the Louvre. Well-known sights are packed into the central *arrondissements* (1er through 8ème), though the peripheral ones should not be overlooked. Refer also to this book's **color maps** of the city.

On the Left Bank, the **Latin Quarter**, encompassing the 5ème and parts of the 6ème, has been home to students for centuries. The northwestern corner of the 6ème is known as **St-Germain-des-Prés**. Further west, the gold-domed **Invalides** and the **Ecole Militaire** recall the military past of the 7ème, now an upscale neighborhood. The 15ème is predominantly residential. **Montparnasse,** mostly contained by the boundaries of the 14ème, is a relatively quiet neighborhood with a bohemian history. Much of the eastern Left Bank, in the 13ème, is working-class or industrial, but the area around **place d'Italie** is an up-and-coming hot-spot.

On the Right Bank, the **Louvre** is located in the sight- and tourist-packed 1er. The 2ème is more business-oriented and contains the old-fashioned **Montorgeuil** neighborhood. The crooked streets of the **Marais**, in the 3ème and 4ème, escaped Baron Haussmann's redesign of Paris and now support many diverse communities. From **place de la Concorde**, at the western end of the 1er, **avenue des Champs-Elysées** bisects the 8ème as it sweeps up toward the **Arc de Triomphe** at **Place Charles de Gaulle-Etoile.** South of the Etoile, old and new money fill the exclusive 16ème, bordered to the west by the **Bois de Boulogne** park and to the east by the Seine and the **Trocadéro**, facing the Eiffel Tower across the river. Back toward central Paris, the 9ème is defined by broad boulevards to the south and a red-light district, **Pigalle**, to the north. The 10ème, not generally frequented by tourists, is known primarily as home to the **Gare du Nord** and **Gare de l'Est.** The **Bastille** area in the 11ème and 12ème claims the newest hip nightlife scene in Paris. East of Bastille, the party atmosphere gives way to the quieter, more residential 20ème and 19ème, while the 18ème is home to the quaint and heavily touristed **Montmartre.** To the east, the 17ème is a mix of wealthy and working-class neighborhoods.

▐ LOCAL TRANSPORTATION

Public Transportation: The efficient **Metro (Ⓜ)** runs 5:30am-12:30am. Lines are numbered and are generally referred to by their number and final destinations; connections are called *correspondances.* **Single-fare tickets** within the city €1.30; **carnet** of 10 €9.60. Buy extras for when ticket booths are closed (after 10pm) and hold onto your ticket until you exit. The **RER (Réseau Express Régional),** the commuter train to the suburbs, serves as an express subway within central Paris; changing to and getting off the RER requires sticking your validated ticket into a turnstile. Watch the signboards next to the RER tracks and check that your stop is lit up before riding. **Buses** use the same €1.30 tickets (bought on the bus; validate in the machine by the driver), but transfer requires a new ticket. Buses run 6:30am-8:30pm, *Autobus de Nuit* until 1am, and *Noctambus* (3-4 tickets) every hr. 1:30-5:30am at stops marked with the bug-eyed moon between the Châtelet stop and the *portes* (city exits). The **Mobilis** pass covers the metro, RER, and buses only (€5 for a 1-day pass in Zones 1 and 2). A weekly pass (*carte orange hebdomadaire*) costs €13.75 and expires every Su; photo ID required. Refer to this book's **color maps** of Paris's transit network.

FRANCE

Taxis: Alpha Taxis (☎01 45 85 85 85). **Taxis Bleus** (☎01 49 36 10 10). Taxis are expensive and take 3 passengers (extra passenger €2.60 surcharge). Meter starts running when you phone. Taxi stands are indicated by a blue light.

Car Rental: Rent-a-Car, 79 r. de Bercy (☎01 43 45 98 99). Open M-Sa 8:30am-noon and 2-6:30pm. AmEx/MC/V.

Bike Rental: Paris Vélo, 2 r. de Fer-à-Moulin, 5ème (☎01 43 37 59 22). ⓜ Censier-Daubenton. €14 per day. Open M-Sa 10am-7pm, Su 10am-2pm and 5-7pm.

🔳 PRACTICAL INFORMATION

TOURIST, FINANCIAL, AND LOCAL SERVICES

Tourist Office: Bureau Gare d'Austerlitz, 13ème (☎01 45 84 91 70). ⓜ Gare d'Austerlitz. Open M-Sa 8am-6pm. **Bureau Gare de Lyon,** 12ème (☎01 43 43 33 24). ⓜ Gare de Lyon. Open M-Sa 8am-6pm. **Bureau Tour Eiffel,** Champs de Mars, 7ème (☎08 92 68 31 12). ⓜ Champs de Mars. Open daily May-Sept. 11am-6:40pm.

Embassies: Australia, 4 r. Jean-Rey, 15ème (☎01 40 59 33 00; www.austgov.fr). ⓜ Bir-Hakeim. Open M-F 9:15am-noon and 2-4:30pm. **Canada,** 35 av. Montaigne, 8ème (☎01 44 43 29 02; www.amb-canada.fr). ⓜ Franklin-Roosevelt. Open M-F 9am-noon and 2-5pm. **Ireland,** 12 av. Foch, 16ème (☎01 44 17 67 00; www.embassyofireland-paris.com). ⓜ Trocadéro. Open M-F 9:30am-noon. **New Zealand,** 7ter r. Léonard de Vinci, 16ème (☎01 45 01 43 43; www.nzembassy.com/france). ⓜ Victor-Hugo. Open July-Aug. M-Th 9am-1pm and 2-4:30pm, F 9am-2pm; Sept.-June M-Th 9am-1pm and 2-5:30pm, F 9am-1pm and 2-4pm. **UK,** 18bis r. D'Anjou, 8ème (☎01 44 51 31 00; www.amb-grandebretagne.fr). ⓜ St-Augustin. Open M and W-F 9:30am-12:30pm and 2:30-5pm, Tu 9:30am-4:30pm. **US,** 2 r. St-Forentin, 1er (☎01 43 12 22 22; www.amb-usa.fr). ⓜ Concorde. Open M-F 9am-12:30pm and 1-3pm; notarial services Tu-F 9am-noon. Skip the long line; go to the right and tell them you're there for American services.

Currency Exchange: Hotels, train stations, and airports offer poor rates but have extended hours; Gare de Lyon, Gare du Nord, and both airports have booths open 6:30am-10:30pm. Most **ATMs** accept **Visa** ("CB/VISA") and **MasterCard** ("EC"). Crédit Lyonnais ATMs take **AmEx;** Crédit Mutuel and Crédit Agricole ATMs are on the **Cirrus** network; and most Visa ATMs accept **PLUS**-network cards.

American Express: 11 r. Scribe, 9ème (☎01 47 77 79 28), opposite the back of the Opéra. ⓜ Opéra or Auber. Mail held for cardholders and AmEx Traveler's Check holders. Open M-Sa 9am-6:30pm; exchange counters open Su 10am-5pm.

Gay and Lesbian Services: Centre Gai et Lesbien, 3 r. Keller, 11ème (☎01 43 57 21 47). ⓜ Ledru Rollin or Bastille. Info hub for all gay services and associations in Paris. English spoken. Open M-Sa 2-8pm, Su 2-7pm.

EMERGENCY AND COMMUNICATIONS

Emergency: Police: ☎17. **Ambulance:** ☎15. **Fire:** ☎18.

Hospitals: Hôpital Américain de Paris, 63 bd. Hugo, Neuilly (☎01 46 41 25 25). ⓜ Port Maillot, then bus #82 to the end of the line. **Hôpital Franco-Britannique de Paris,** 3 r. Barbès, in the suburb of Levallois-Perret (☎01 46 39 22 22). ⓜ Anatole France. Has some English speakers, but don't count on it. **Hôpital Bichat,** 46 r. Henri Buchard, 18ème (☎01 40 25 80 80). ⓜ Port St-Ouen. Emergency services.

Pharmacies: Every *arrondissement* has a **pharmacie de garde** which opens in emergencies. The locations change, but their names are posted on every pharmacy's door. **Pharmacie des Champs,** in the Galerie des Champs 84, av. des Champs-Elysées, 8ème (☎01 45 62 02 41). ⓜ George V. Open 24hr. **British & American Pharmacy,** 1 r. Auber, 9ème (☎01 42 65 88 29). ⓜ Auber or Opéra. Open daily 8am-8:30pm.

Internet Access: easyInternetCafé, 31 bd. de Sébastopol, 1er (☎ 01 40 41 09 10). Ⓜ Les Halles. €3 per hr. Open daily 7:30am-midnight. **Akyrion Net Center,** 19 r. Charlemagne, 4ème (☎01 40 27 92 07). €2.80 per hr. Open M-Th 11am-10:30pm, F-Sa 11am-11pm, Su 2-9:30pm. **Cyber Cube,** 5 r. Mignon, 6ème (☎01 53 10 30 50). Ⓜ St-Michel or Odéon. €0.15 per min., €30 for 5hr. Open M-Sa 10am-10pm.

Post Office: Poste du Louvre, 52 r. du Louvre, 1er (☎01 40 28 20 40). Ⓜ Louvre. Open 24hr. Address mail to be held: SURNAME First name, *Poste Restante,* 52 r. du Louvre, 75001 Paris, FRANCE. **Postal Codes:** 750xx, where "xx" is the *arrondissement* (e.g., 75003 for any address in the 3ème).

⌐ ACCOMMODATIONS

Paris's **hostels** skip many standard restrictions (sheets, curfews, etc.) and tend to have flexible maximum stays. **Hotels** may be the most practical accommodations for most travelers. Expect to pay at least €25 for a single or €35 for a double in the luckiest of circumstances. Rooms fill quickly after morning check-out, so arrive early or reserve ahead. Most hostels and *foyers* include the **taxe de séjour** (€1-1.50 per person per day) in listed prices, but some do not. If you haven't reserved ahead, tourist offices (p. 344) and the organizations below can book rooms.

ACCOMMODATIONS SERVICES

La Centrale de Réservations (FUAJ-HI), 9 r. Brantome, 3ème (☎01 48 04 70 40; www.fuaj.org). Ⓜ Rambuteau. Open M-F 10am-6:30pm, Sa 10am-5:30pm.

OTU-Voyage (Office du Tourisme Universitaire), 119, r. St-Martin 4ème (☎08 20 81 78 17, 01 49 72 57 19 for groups). €1.53 service charge. Open M-F 9:30am-7pm, Sa 10am-noon and 1:30-5pm. Also at 2 r. Malus, 5ème (☎01 44 41 74 74). Ⓜ Place Monge. Open M-Sa 9-6pm.

BY NEIGHBORHOOD

ILE DE LA CITÉ, 1ER, AND 2ÈME ARRONDISSEMENTS

▧ **Hôtel Henri IV,** 25 pl. Dauphine (☎01 43 54 44 53). Ⓜ Pont Neuf. One of Paris's best located and least expensive hotels. Showers €2.50. Reserve 1 month in advance, earlier in summer. Singles €23; doubles €32, with bath €55; triples €43, with shower €69; quads €49. Cash and checks only. ❷

▧ **Hôtel Tiquetonne,** 6 r. Tiquetonne, 2ème (☎01 42 36 94 58; fax 01 42 36 02 94). Ⓜ Etienne-Marcel. This 7-story hotel is affordable. Breakfast €5. Shower €5. Reserve 2 weeks in advance. Singles €28, with toilet €38; doubles with bath €46. AmEx/MC/V. ❸

▧ **Centre International de Paris (BVJ): Paris Louvre,** 20 r. Jean-Jacques Rousseau, 1er (☎01 53 00 90 90). Ⓜ Louvre or Palais-Royal. Bright, dorm-style rooms with 2-10 beds each. Lockers €2. Internet €1 for 10min. Weekend reservations up to 1 week in advance by phone only. Rooms held for 5-10min. after your expected check-in time; call if you'll be late. Doubles €28 per person; other rooms €25 per person. Cash only. ❷

Hôtel Montpensier, 12 r. de Richelieu, 1er (☎01 42 96 28 50; fax 01 42 86 02 70). Ⓜ Palais-Royal. Clean rooms, lofty ceilings, bright decor. Small elevator. TVs in rooms with shower or bath. Breakfast €7. Shower €4. Internet €1 for 4min. Reserve 2 months in advance in high season. Singles and doubles €57-92. AmEx/MC/V. ❺

3ÈME AND 4ÈME ARRONDISSEMENTS

Some of the Marais's 17th-century mansions now house budget hotels close to the **Centre Pompidou** and the **Ile St-Louis;** the area is also convenient for sampling nightlife, as Paris's night buses converge in the 4ème at Ⓜ Châtelet.

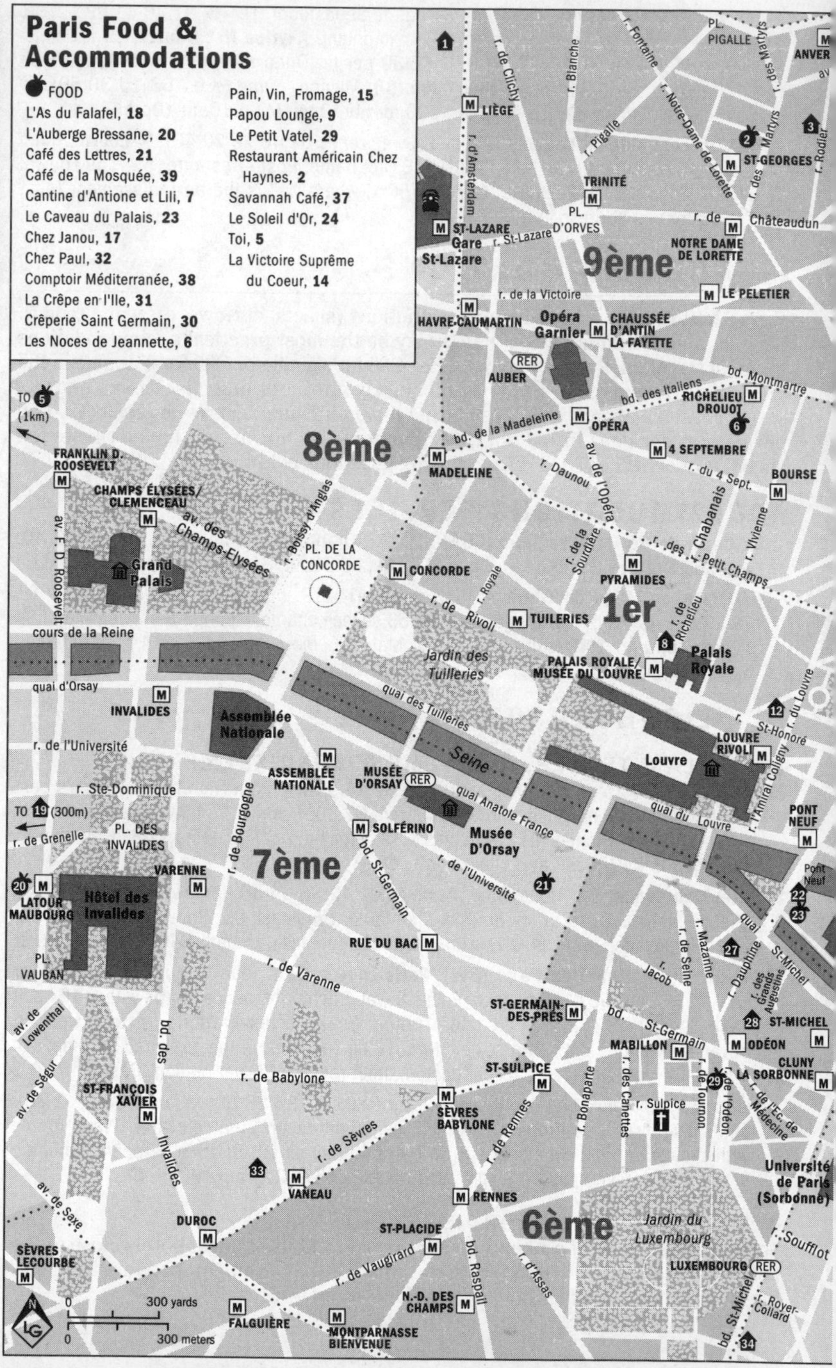

Paris Food & Accommodations
FOOD
L'As du Falafel, 18
L'Auberge Bressane, 20
Café des Lettres, 21
Café de la Mosquée, 39
Cantine d'Antione et Lili, 7
Le Caveau du Palais, 23
Chez Janou, 17
Chez Paul, 32
Comptoir Méditerranée, 38
La Crêpe en l'Ile, 31
Crêperie Saint Germain, 30
Les Noces de Jeannette, 6
Pain, Vin, Fromage, 15
Papou Lounge, 9
Le Petit Vatel, 29
Restaurant Américain Chez Haynes, 2
Savannah Café, 37
Le Soleil d'Or, 24
Toi, 5
La Victoire Suprême du Coeur, 14
9ème
8ème
1er
7ème
6ème
TO 5 (1km)
TO 19 (300m)
LIÈGE
TRINITÉ
ST-GEORGES
PL. PIGALLE
ANVERS
ST-LAZARE
Gare St-Lazare
PL. D'ORVES
NOTRE DAME DE LORETTE
LE PELETIER
HAVRE-CAUMARTIN
Opéra Garnier
CHAUSSÉE D'ANTIN LA FAYETTE
AUBER
RER
OPÉRA
RICHELIEU DROUOT
MADELEINE
4 SEPTEMBRE
BOURSE
FRANKLIN D. ROOSEVELT
CHAMPS ÉLYSÉES/ CLEMENCEAU
Grand Palais
PL. DE LA CONCORDE
CONCORDE
PYRAMIDES
TUILERIES
Jardin des Tuilleries
PALAIS ROYALE/ MUSÉE DU LOUVRE
Palais Royale
LOUVRE RIVOLI
Louvre
Seine
INVALIDES
Assemblée Nationale
ASSEMBLÉE NATIONALE
MUSÉE D'ORSAY
Musée D'Orsay
SOLFÉRINO
PONT NEUF
Pont Neuf
PL. DES INVALIDES
VARENNE
LATOUR MAUBOURG
Hôtel des Invalides
PL. VAUBAN
RUE DU BAC
ST-GERMAIN-DES-PRÉS
MABILLON
ST-MICHEL
ODÉON
CLUNY LA SORBONNE
ST-SULPICE
ST-FRANÇOIS XAVIER
SÈVRES BABYLONE
Université de Paris (Sorbonne)
VANEAU
RENNES
DUROC
ST-PLACIDE
Jardin du Luxembourg
LUXEMBOURG
SÈVRES LECOURBE
N.-D. DES CHAMPS
FALGUIÈRE
MONTPARNASSE BIENVENUE
r. de Clichy
r. Blanche
r. Fontaine
r. Notre-Dame de Lorette
r. des Martyrs
r. Rodier
r. Pigalle
r. d'Amsterdam
r. St-Lazare
r. de Châteaudun
r. de la Victoire
bd. Montmartre
bd. des Italiens
bd. de la Madeleine
r. Daunou
av. de l'Opéra
r. du 4 Sept.
r. Chabanais
r. Vivienne
r. des Petit Champs
r. de la Sourdière
r. Boissy d'Anglas
av. des Champs-Elysées
av. F. D. Roosevelt
r. Royale
r. de Rivoli
r. de Richelieu
cours de la Reine
quai d'Orsay
quai des Tuilleries
r. St-Honoré
r. du Louvre
r. de l'Amiral Coligny
quai Anatole France
quai du Louvre
r. de l'Université
r. Ste-Dominique
r. de Grenelle
r. de Bourgogne
bd. St-Germain
r. de l'Université
quai St-Michel
r. Mazarine
r. de Seine
r. Jacob
r. Dauphine
r. des Grands Augustins
r. de Varenne
av. de Lowenthal
bd. des Invalides
av. de Ségur
r. de Babylone
bd. St-Germain
r. des Canettes
r. de Tournon
r. de l'Odéon
r. de l'Ec. de Médecine
r. Sulpice
r. Bonaparte
r. de Rennes
r. de Sèvres
av. de Saxe
r. de Vaugirard
bd. Raspail
r. d'Assas
r. Soufflot
bd. St-Michel
r. Royer-Collard
0 300 yards
0 300 meters
LG

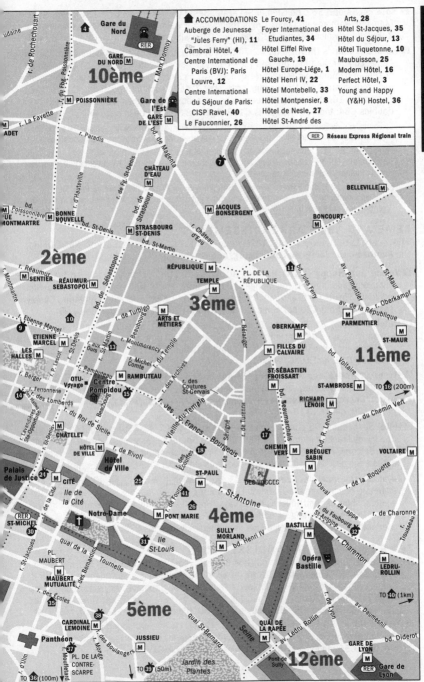

ACCOMMODATIONS
Auberge de Jeunesse "Jules Ferry" (HI), **11**
Cambrai Hôtel, **4**
Centre International de Paris (BVJ): Paris Louvre, **12**
Centre International du Séjour de Paris: CISP Ravel, **40**
Le Fauconnier, **26**

Le Fourcy, **41**
Foyer International des Etudiantes, **34**
Hôtel Eiffel Rive Gauche, **19**
Hôtel Europe-Liège, **1**
Hôtel Henri IV, **22**
Hôtel Montebello, **33**
Hôtel Montpensier, **8**
Hôtel de Nesle, **27**
Hôtel St-André des

Arts, **28**
Hôtel St-Jacques, **35**
Hôtel du Séjour, **13**
Hôtel Tiquetonne, **10**
Maubuisson, **25**
Modern Hôtel, **16**
Perfect Hôtel, **3**
Young and Happy (Y&H) Hostel, **36**

RER Réseau Express Régional train

■ **Hôtel du Séjour,** 36 r. du Grenier St-Lazare, 3ème (☎/fax 01 48 87 40 36). ⓜ Etienne-Marcel or Rambuteau. Clean, bright rooms and a warm welcome. Showers €4. Reserve 1 week in advance. Singles €33; doubles €45, with bath €55, 3rd person add €23. ❸

■ **Hôtel des Jeunes (MIJE;** ☎01 42 74 23 45; www.mije.com). Books beds in Le Fourcy, Le Fauconnier, and Maubuisson (see below), 3 small hostels located on cobblestone streets in beautiful old Marais residences. No smoking. Breakfast, shower, and sheets included. Internet €0.15 per min. Max. stay 7 days. Lockout noon-3pm. Curfew 1am. Quiet after 10pm. Reserve at least 1 week in advance. Dorms €27-28; singles €42; doubles €64; triples €84; quads €108. Ages 18-30 only. Cash only. ❸

Le Fourcy, 6 r. de Fourcy, 4ème. ⓜ St-Paul or Pont Marie. From ⓜ St-Paul, walk opposite the traffic down r. François-Miron and turn left on r. de Fourcy. Light sleepers should avoid rooms on the social courtyard.

Le Fauconnier, 11 r. du Fauconnier, 4ème. ⓜ St-Paul or Pont Marie. From ⓜ St-Paul, take r. du Prevôt, turn left on r. Charlemagne, and turn right on r. du Fauconnier. Ivy-covered building steps away from the Seine and Ile St-Louis.

Maubuisson, 12 r. des Barres, 4ème. ⓜ Hôtel-de-Ville or Pont Marie. From ⓜ Pont Marie, walk opposite traffic on r. de l'Hôtel-de-Ville and turn right on r. des Barres. A half-timbered former convent on a silent street by the St-Gervais monastery.

5ÈME AND 6ÈME ARRONDISSEMENTS

The lively Latin Quarter and St-Germain-des-Prés offer proximity to **Notre-Dame,** the **Panthéon,** the **Jardin du Luxembourg,** and the bustling student cafe culture.

■ **Young and Happy (Y&H) Hostel,** 80 r. Mouffetard, 5ème (☎01 47 07 47 07; www.youngandhappy.fr). ⓜ Monge. A funky, lively hostel with clean rooms. Breakfast included. Sheets €2.50, towels €1. Internet €1 for 10min. Lockout 11am-4pm. Curfew 2am. Dorms from €20 per person; doubles from €23 per person. Cash only. ❷

■ **Hôtel de Nesle,** 7 r. du Nesle, 6ème (☎01 43 54 62 41; www.hoteldenesle.com). ⓜ Odéon. Walk up r. de l'Ancienne Comédie, take a right onto r. Dauphine, and then take a left on r. du Nesle. Friendly staff and unique decor. Singles €50-69; doubles €69-99. Extra bed €12. AmEx/MC/V. ❹

■ **Hôtel St-André des Arts,** 66 r. St-André-des-Arts, 6ème (☎01 43 26 96 16; hsaintand@minitel.net). ⓜ Odéon. Country inn feel. New bathrooms and very friendly owner. Breakfast included. Reservations recommended. Singles €64; doubles €82; triples €100; quads €110. MC/V. ❺

■ **Hôtel St-Jacques,** 35 r. des Ecoles, 5ème (☎01 44 07 45 45; hotelstjacques@wanadoo.fr). ⓜ Maubert-Mutualité or RER: Cluny-La Sorbonne. Spacious, faux-elegant rooms with balcony, renovated bathroom, and TV. English spoken. Breakfast €7. Internet access. Singles €49, with bath €75; doubles with bath €85-€112. AmEx/MC/V. ❹

Foyer International des Etudiantes, 93, bd. St-Michel (☎01 43 54 49 63). RER: Luxembourg. Across from the Jardin du Luxembourg. Library, laundry, and TV lounge. Kitchenettes, showers, and toilets on hallways. Breakfast included in summer. Min. stay 3 nights. Reserve in writing as early as Jan. for summer; €35 deposit. July-Sept. foyer is coed and open 24hr. Oct.-June foyer is women-only. Singles €28; 2-bed dorms €40. ❷

7ÈME TO 10ÈME ARRONDISSEMENTS

■ **Hôtel Eiffel Rive Gauche,** 6 r. du Gros Caillou, 7ème (☎01 45 51 24 56; www.hotel-eiffel.com). ⓜ Ecole Militaire. Walk up av. de la Bourdonnais, turn right onto r. de la Grenelle, then left onto Gros-Caillou. A favorite of Anglophone travelers. Rooms have cable TV, phone, Internet jack, and full bath; some have Eiffel Tower views. Breakfast €9. Safe €3. Singles €69-89; doubles €76-80; triples €96. Extra bed €14. MC/V. ❺

■ **Perfect Hôtel,** 39 r. Rodier, 9ème (☎01 42 81 18 86; perfecthotel@hotmail.com). Hotel-quality rooms at hostel prices. Breakfast free for Let's Go readers. Singles €30, with bath €50; doubles €36/€50; triples €53/€65. MC/V. ❸

Cambrai Hôtel, 129bis bd. de Magenta, 10ème (☎01 48 78 32 13; www.hotel-cambrai.com). ⓜ Gare du Nord. Clean rooms with high ceilings. Breakfast €5. Showers €3. Singles €30-35, with shower €41, with full bath €48; doubles with shower €46, with full bath €54; twins €60; triples €80; quads €90; quints €110. AmEx/MC/V. ❷

Hôtel Montebello, 18 r. Pierre Leroux, 7ème (☎01 47 34 41 18; hmontebello@aol.com). ⓜ Vaneau. Unbeatable rates for this upscale neighborhood. Clean rooms with full bath. Reserve at least 2 weeks in advance. Breakfast served 7:30-9:30am; €4. 1 person €30; 2 people €37-47. Cash only. ❸

Hôtel Europe-Liège, 8 r. de Moscou, 8ème (☎01 42 94 01 51; fax 01 43 87 42 18). ⓜ Liège. Clean and fresh rooms and a lovely interior courtyard. Reserve 15 days in advance. All have TV, hair dryer, phone, and shower or bath. 2 wheelchair-accessible rooms on the ground floor. Breakfast €7. Singles €68; doubles €84. AmEx/MC/V. ❺

Hôtel Palace, 9, r. Bouchardon (☎01 42 06 59 32; hotel.palace@club-internet.fr). ⓜ Strasbourg-St-Denis. Walk against traffic on bd. St-Denis until the small arch; follow r. René Boulanger on the left, then turn left on r. Bouchardon. Clean hotel with the rates of a hostel. Breakfast €3.50. Shower €3.50. Reserve 2 weeks ahead. Singles €19-21, with shower €31; doubles €26/€36; triples €48; quads €58. AmEx/MC/V. ❷

11ÈME AND 12ÈME ARRONDISSEMENTS

These hotels are close to hopping bars and clubs, but be careful at night.

▨ **Auberge de Jeunesse "Jules Ferry" (HI),** 8 bd. Jules Ferry, 11ème (☎01 43 57 55 60; auberge@easynet.fr). ⓜ République. Walk east on r. du Faubourg du Temple and turn right on the far side of bd. Jules Ferry. Wonderful location, party atmosphere. Breakfast and showers included. Lockers €1.55. Internet access in lobby. Max. stay 1 week. Lockout 10am-2pm. No reservations; arrive by 8am. Dorms €20; doubles €20. MC/V. ❷

▨ **Modern Hôtel,** 121, r. de Chemin-Vert (☎01 47 00 54 05; www.modern-hotel.fr). ⓜ Père Lachaise. A few blocks from the metro on r. de Chemin-Vert, on the right. Newly renovated, with modern furnishings, pastel color scheme, and spotless marble bathrooms. All rooms have a hair dryer, modem connection, and safe-deposit box. Breakfast included. Singles €65; doubles €75-78; triples €91. Extra bed €15. AmEx/MC/V. ❺

Centre International du Séjour de Paris: CISP "Ravel," 6 av. Maurice Ravel, 12ème (☎01 44 75 60 00; www.cicp.ccoo.fr). ⓜ Porte de Vincennes. Large, clean rooms (most with fewer than 4 beds) with art exhibited all around. Breakfast, sheets, and towels included. Reception 6:30am-1:30am. Reserve at least 1 month ahead. Dorms €16-20; singles with bath €30; doubles with bath €48. AmEx/MC/V. ❷

13ÈME TO 20ÈME ARRONDISSEMENTS

▨ **Three Ducks Hostel,** 6 pl. Etienne Pernet, 15ème (☎01 48 42 04 05; www.3ducks.fr). ⓜ Félix Faure. Aimed at young Anglo travelers. Breakfast and shower included. Sheets €2.30, towels €0.75. Internet access in lobby. Max. stay 1 week. Reception daily 8am-2am. Lockout 11am-5pm. Reserve with credit card 1 week ahead. Mar.-Oct. dorms €22; doubles €50. Nov.-Feb. reduced prices. MC/V. ❷

▨ **FIAP Jean-Monnet,** 30 r. Cabanis, 14ème (☎01 43 13 17 00, reservations 01 43 13 17 17; www.fiap.asso.fr). ⓜ Glacière. 500-bed student center offers spotless rooms with phone, toilet, and shower. Breakfast included. Max. stay 3 months. Check-in after 2:30pm. Check-out 9am. Curfew 2am. Reserve 2-4 weeks in advance; specify if you want a dorm bed or you'll be booked for a single. €15 deposit per person per night by check or credit card. Dorms €23; singles €52; doubles €66; quads €120. MC/V. ❷

Hôtel de Blois, 5 r. des Plantes, 14ème (☎01 45 40 99 48; fax 01 45 40 45 62). ⓜ Mouton-Duvernet. Elegant rooms. TV, hair dryer, and big, clean bath. Breakfast €6. Reserve 10 days in advance. Singles €41, with shower €44, with bath €47-53; doubles €44/€46/€55-58; triples €64. AmEx/MC/V. ❹

■ **Hôtel Caulaincourt,** 2 sq. Caulaincourt, 18ème (☎01 46 06 46 06; bienvenue@caulaincourt.com). Ⓜ Lamarck-Caulaincourt. Friendly establishment in a pleasant, quiet area of Montmartre. TV and phone in every room. Breakfast €5.50. Reserve up to 1 month in advance. Singles €35, with shower €45, with bath €55; doubles €48-74; twins €52-79; triples with shower €66-82. MC/V. ❸

Eden Hôtel, 7 r. Jean-Baptiste Dumay, 20ème (☎01 46 36 64 22; fax 01 46 36 01 11). Ⓜ Pyrénées. Clean rooms with TVs and toilets. Elevator. Breakfast €4.50. Bath or shower €4. Reserve rooms by fax 1 week in advance. Singles €38, with shower €51; doubles with shower €54-56, 1 double with bath €54. Extra bed €10. MC/V. ❹

◘ FOOD

Don't approach dining in Paris with the assumption that chic equals *cher*. A world-class meal in the capital of cuisine is worth a splurge, but there are also a wealth of ways to eat well on a budget, from rowdy *brasseries* to Chinatown eateries. **CROUS (Centre Regional des Oeuvres Universitaires et Scolaires),** 39 av. Georges Bernanos, 5ème, has info on university restaurants, often a cheap way to get great meals. (☎01 40 51 55 55; www.crous-paris.fr. Ⓜ Port-Royal. Open M-F 9am-5pm.)

BY NEIGHBORHOOD

ILE DE LA CITÉ AND ILE ST-LOUIS

▩ **Le Caveau du Palais,** 19 pl. Dauphine, Ile de la Cité (☎01 43 26 04 28). Ⓜ Cité. A chic, intimate restaurant serving traditional French and Basque food from an old-style brick oven. Open daily noon-3pm and 7-10:30pm. Reservations recommended. MC/V. ❹

Le Soleil d'Or, 15 bd. du Palais, Ile de la Cité (☎01 43 54 22 22). Ⓜ Cité. This classy-looking *brasserie* is a real bargain. Eclectic menu offers delicious crepes (€4.50-5.50) and sandwiches (from €4.50). Sunday brunch €10. Open daily 9am-10pm. MC/V. ❶

La Crêpe en l'Ile, 13 r. des Deux Ponts, Ile St-Louis (☎01 43 26 28 68). Ⓜ Pont Marie. Just off the main drag and less crowded than its island siblings. Choose from among 20 crepe options (€2.50-7.20). Incredible selection of teas. 3-course *menu* €8.80. Open daily in summer 11:30am-midnight; low season 11:30am-11pm. Cash only. ❷

1ER AND 2ÈME ARRONDISSEMENTS

The area around the Louvre is expensive. The **Montorgueil** neighborhood has charming bistros and food shops; **Les Halles** is loud, crowded, and generally cheap.

▩ **Les Noces de Jeannette,** 14 r. Favart and 9 r. d'Amboise, 2ème (☎01 42 96 36 89). Ⓜ Richelieu-Drouot. Elegant bistro. 3-course *menu* €28. Open daily noon-1:30pm and 7-9:30pm. Reservations recommended. AmEx/MC/V. ❺

▩ **Papou Lounge,** 74 r. Jean-Jacques Rousseau, 1er (☎01 44 76 00 03). Ⓜ Les Halles. Papou's cuisine is both flavorful (rumpsteak €13) and inventive (tuna tartar with strawberries €14). Lunch special €10. Beer €3.30. Open daily 10am-2am; kitchen open noon-4:30pm and 7pm-midnight. MC/V. ❸

La Victoire Suprême du Coeur, 41 r. des Bourdonnais 1er (☎01 40 41 93 95). Ⓜ Châtelet. All vegetarian, and very tasty. Meals marked with a "V" can be made vegan. 2-course lunch *menu* €11. Open M-F 11:45am-3pm and 6:40-10pm, Sa noon-3pm and 6:40-10pm. MC/V. ❷

3ÈME AND 4ÈME ARRONDISSEMENTS

The Marais offers chic bistros, kosher delis, and couple-friendly cafes.

▩ **Pain, Vin, Fromage,** 3 r. Geoffrey L'Angevin, 4ème (☎01 42 74 07 52). On a side street near the Centre Pompidou. Seating in the rustic basement wine cellar. Winning wine list. Fondue €14. Salad €7.50-9. Open M-Sa 7-11pm. AmEx/MC/V. ❸

■ **L'As du Falafel,** 34 r. des Rosiers, 4*ème* (☎01 48 87 63 60). Ⓜ St-Paul. Lenny Kravitz reportedly credited this kosher falafel stand and restaurant with "the best falafel in the world." Falafel special €6. Open M-F and Su 11:30am-midnight. MC/V. ❶

Chez Janou, 2 r. Roger Verlomme, 3*ème* (☎01 42 72 28 41). Ⓜ Chemin-Vert. Take r. St-Gilles and turn left almost immediately on r. des Tournelles. The restaurant is on the corner of r. Roger Verlomme. Dishes are listed on blackboards scattered throughout the restaurant, with a new *plat du jour* (€12) every day. Delicious *ratatouille* €8.50. Open daily noon-3pm and 8pm-midnight. Reservations recommended. MC/V. ❸

5ÈME AND 6ÈME ARRONDISSEMENTS

Tiny, low-priced restaurants and cafes pack the quadrangle bounded by bd. St-Germain, bd. St-Michel, r. de Seine, and the Seine river. **Rue de Buci** harbors Greek restaurants and a street market; **rue Gregoire de Tours** has cheap, greasy spoons.

■ **Café de la Mosquée,** 39 r. Geoffrey St-Hilaire, 5*ème* (☎01 43 31 38 20). Ⓜ Censier-Daubenton. Savor Persian mint tea (€2.50) and *maghrebain* pastries (€2) on the exquisite terrace. Couscous €9-25. Tea room open daily 9am-11:30pm. Kitchen open daily noon-3pm and 7:30-10:30pm. MC/V. ❸

Le Petit Vatel, 5 r. Lobineau, 6*ème* (☎01 43 54 28 49). Ⓜ Mabillon. Follow traffic on bd. St-Germain, turn right on r. de Seine, and take the 2nd right onto r. Lobineau. This bistro serves up French-Mediterranean specialties, all for €10. Vegetarian options. No smoking. Lunch *menu* €11. Open Tu-Sa noon-2:30pm and 7-10:30pm. Cash only. ❷

Savannah Café, 27 r. Descartes, 5*ème* (☎01 43 29 45 77). Ⓜ Cardinal Lemoine. Follow r. du Cardinal Lemoine uphill, turn right on r. Clovis, and walk 1 block. Lebanese food and other "selections from around the world." Pasta dishes €13. *Menu* €23. Open M-Sa 7-11pm. MC/V. ❸

Comptoir Méditerranée, 42 r. du Cardinal Lemoine, 5*ème* (☎01 43 25 29 08). Run by the same owner as Savannah Café. Select from 20 dishes to make your own plate (€6). Sandwich or thyme pizza €3.50. Open M-Sa 11am-10pm. MC/V (€16 min.). ❶

Crêperie Saint Germain, 33 r. St-André-des-Arts, 6*ème* (☎01 43 54 24 41). Ⓜ St-Michel. Cross pl. St-Michel and walk down r. St-André-des-Arts. €8.50 *menu* (M-F noon-3pm) includes 2 crepes and cider. Open daily noon midnight. AmEx/MC/V. ❷

7ÈME AND 8ÈME ARRONDISSEMENTS

■ **Toi,** 27 r. de Colisée, 8*ème* (☎ 01 42 56 56 58). Ⓜ Franklin D Roosevelt. Walk toward the Arc on the Champs-Elysées; take 1st street on the right. Deep red sofas, dim lighting, and artfully black-clad waitstaff. *Mikado* of grilled prawns with shrimp *tempura* €17. Crème brulée €10. Open M-Sa noon-2am; Sa closed for lunch. AmEx/MC/V. ❹

■ **Café des Lettres,** 53 r. de Verneuil, 7*ème* (☎01 42 22 52 17). Ⓜ Solférino. Exit the metro onto pl. J. Blainville and take r. de Villersexel; turn right onto r. de l'Université, make a left onto r. de Poitiers, and another right onto r. de Verneuil. Scandinavian cafe located in the same sunny courtyard as the Maison des Ecrivains. Danish seafood dishes €12-20. Su brunch buffet (€26); reservations recommended. Coffee €2.30. Beer €4-6.50. Open M noon-3pm, Tu-F noon-11pm, Sa noon-7pm. MC/V. ❹

L'Auberge Bressane, 16 av. de la Motte Picquet, 7*ème* (☎01 47 05 98 37). Ⓜ Ecole Militaire or Tour Maubourg. A small, luxuriously decorated restaurant full of regular patrons. Weekday lunch *menu* €15-24. Dinner *menu* with wine €25. Open daily noon-2:30pm and 8-10:30pm; Sa closed for lunch. Reservations essential. AmEx/MC/V. ❺

9ÈME TO 11ÈME ARRONDISSEMENTS

Meals close to the Opéra cater to the after-theater and movie crowd and can be quite expensive. **Rue Faubourg-Montmartre** is packed with cheap eateries.

▧ **Restaurant Américain Chez Haynes,** 3 r. Clauzel, 9ème (☎01 48 78 40 63). ⓜ St-Georges. Head uphill on r. Notre Dame de Lorette and turn right on r. H. Monnier, then right on r. Clauzel to the end of the block. Famous for its "original American Soul Food." Generous portions are under €16. Open Tu-Sa 7pm-12:30am. AmEx/MC/V. ❸

▧ **Chez Paul,** 13 r. de Charonne, 11ème (☎01 47 00 34 57). ⓜ Bastille. Go east on r. du Faubourg St-Antoine and turn left on r. de Charonne. Regulars go for the house speciality *steak tartare* (€14), while the very brave give in to St. Antoine's Temptation (€16), a dish of pig ear, foot, tail, and groin. Open daily noon-2:30pm and 7pm-2am; kitchen open until 12:30am. Reservations recommended. AmEx/MC/V. ❸

Cantine d'Antoine et Lili, 95 quai de Valmy, 10ème (☎01 40 37 34 86). ⓜ Gare de l'Est. Go down r. Faubourg St-Martin and make a left on r. Récollets; Cantine is on the corner of quai de Valmy. Canal-side cafe-bistro serves light fare. Salads €6.50. Quiche €7.50. Open M-Tu and Su 11am-8pm, W-Sa 11am-1am. AmEx/MC/V. ❶

12ÈME TO 14ÈME ARRONDISSEMENTS

The 13*ème* is a budget gourmand's dream, with scores of Asian restaurants packing Paris's **Chinatown,** south of pl. d'Italie on av. de Choisy, and numerous affordable French restaurants in the **Butte-aux-Cailles** area. The 14*ème* is bordered at the top by the busy **boulevard du Montparnasse,** lined with diverse restaurants.

▧ **Chez Papa,** 6 r. Gassendi, 14ème (☎01 43 22 41 19). ⓜ Denfert-Rochereau. Walk down Froidevaux along the cemetery; the restaurant is on the left at the intersection with Gassendi. Huge servings, often straight from the pot. *Menu* (M-F until 4pm) €9.15. Open daily 11am-1am. AmEx/MC/V. ❷

▧ **Tricotin,** 15 av. de Choisy, 13ème (☎01 45 84 74 44). ⓜ Porte de Choisy. 6 chefs prepare delicious food from Cambodia, Thailand, and Vietnam. Try the famed Cambodian fried rice with beef (€6.80). Open daily 9:30am-11:30pm. MC/V. ❶

L'Amuse Bouche, 188 r. du Château, 14ème (☎01 43 35 31 61). ⓜ Alésia. Take av. du Maine to r. du Château. French cuisine prepared to perfection. Dinner *menu* €29. Open Tu-Sa noon-2pm and 7:30-10:15pm. Reservations recommended. MC/V. ❺

15ÈME AND 16ÈME ARRONDISSEMENTS

▧ **Thai Phetburi,** 31 bd. de Grenelle, 15ème (☎01 40 58 14 88). ⓜ Bir-Hakeim. Head away from the river on bd. de Grenelle; the restaurant is on your left. Award-winning food, friendly service, and low prices, just minutes from the Eiffel Tower. The *tom yam koung* (shrimp soup with lemongrass; €7) is a favorite. Vegetarian options. Open M-Sa noon-2:30pm and 7-10:30pm. AmEx/MC/V. ❷

▧ **Aux Artistes,** 63 r. Falguière, 15ème (☎01 43 22 05 39). ⓜ Pasteur. Follow Pasteur away from the rails and make a left onto r. Falguière. This lively cafe draws a mix of professionals, students, and artists. Lunch *menu* €9.20. Dinner *menu* €13. Open M-F noon-2:30pm and 7:30pm-midnight, Sa 7:30pm-midnight. ❷

Byblos Café, 6 r. Guichard, 16ème (☎01 42 30 99 99). ⓜ La Muette. Walk down r. Passy 1 block and turn left on r. Guichard. This airy, modern Lebanese restaurant serves cold *mezzes* (think Middle Eastern tapas) for €5.80-8. Vegetarian options. Takeout 15-20% less. Open daily 11am-3pm and 5-11pm. AmEx/MC/V. ❸

17ÈME TO 20ÈME ARRONDISSEMENTS

The 17*ème*'s **Village des Batignolles** is a great place to dine on a budget, far from the tourist traffic of the city. In the 18*ème*, bistros and cafes line **rue des Abbesses** and **rue Lepic.** Ethnic enclaves in the 19*ème* and 20*ème* offer cheap, funky eats.

▧ **Le Soleil Gourmand,** 10 r. Ravignan, 18ème (☎01 42 51 00 50). ⓜ Abbesses. Facing the church in pl. des Abbesses, head right down r. des Abbesses and go right on r. Ravignan. Local favorite with artistic flare. Try the *bricks* (grilled stuffed filo dough; €11). Open daily 12:30-2:30pm and 7:30-11pm. Evening reservations a must. Cash only. ❸

■ **The James Joyce Pub,** 71 bd. Gouvion St-Cyr, 17ème (☎01 44 09 70 32). ⓜ Porte Maillot (exit at Palais de Congrès). Take bd. Gouvion St-Cyr past Palais de Congrès. Upstairs is a friendly restaurant with stained-glass windows depicting scenes from Joyce's novels. Irish meals from €10. Open M-Th 9pm-1:30am, F-Su 10am-2am; kitchen open M-Sa noon-3pm and 7:30-10:30pm, Su noon-5pm. AmEx/MC/V. ❸

Le Bistrot de Théo, 90 r. des Dames, 17ème (☎01 43 87 08 08). ⓜ Villiers. From r. de Lévis, turn right on r. des Dames. A classy, quirky bistro. Lunch *menu* €13. Dinner *menu* €23 or €27. Open M-Sa noon-2:30pm and 7:30-11:30pm. AmEx/MC/V. ❸

Lao Siam, 49 r. de Belleville, 19ème (☎01 40 40 09 68). ⓜ Belleville. A wall full of articles touts the Thai and Chinese cuisine served up at this local favorite. Open daily noon-3pm and 6:30-11:30pm. MC/V. ❷

SALONS DE THÉ

Parisian *salons de thé* (tea rooms) fall into three categories: stately salons straight out of the last century piled high with macaroons, Seattle-inspired joints for brooding intellectuals, and cafes that simply want to signal they also serve tea.

■ **Ladurée,** 16 r. Royale, 8ème (☎01 42 60 21 79). ⓜ Concorde. The rococo decor of this classic tea salon attracts well-groomed shoppers. Famous for the mini macaroons stacked in the window (€3, in 9 different varieties). Specialty tea *Ladurée mélange* €6.50. Su brunch €29. Open daily 8:30am-7pm; lunch served until 3pm. AmEx/MC/V.

Mariage Frères, 30 r. du Bourg-Tibourg, 4ème (☎01 42 72 28 11). ⓜ Hôtel-de-Ville. Also at 13 r. des Grands Augustins, 6ème (☎01 40 51 82 50); and at 260 r. du Faubourg St-Honoré, 8ème (☎01 46 22 18 54). Started by 2 brothers who found British tea shoddy, this salon offers 500 varieties of tea (€7-15). Afternoon tea *menu* includes sandwich, pastry, and tea (€25). Brunch *menu* €25; reservations recommended. Open daily 10:30am-7:30pm. AmEx/MC/V.

SPECIALTY SHOPS

Food shops, particularly *boulangeries* (bakeries) and *pâtisseries* (pastry shops), are on virtually every street in Paris, or at least it seems like it. Not surprisingly, most of them are excellent; the following listings are some of the best.

■ **Ice Cream: Berthillon,** 31 r. St-Louis-en-l'Ile (☎43 54 31 61). ⓜ Cité or Pont Marie. Commonly regarded as the best ice cream and sorbet in Paris (€2-4). Choose from dozens of *parfums,* ranging from passion fruit to gingerbread to the house speciality *nougat miel* (honey nougat). Open Sept.-July 14. Takeout W-Su 10am-8pm; eat-in W-F 1-8pm, Sa-Su 2pm-midnight. Closed 2 weeks in Feb. and Apr.

Cheese: Barthélemy, 51 r. Grenelle, 7ème (☎01 45 48 56 75). ⓜ r. du Bac. A cluttered, old-fashioned store-front; inside, the finest *fromagerie* in Paris. President Chirac has been known to stop in. Open Tu-F 7:30am-7:30pm.

Bread: Julien, 75 r. St-Honoré, 1er (☎01 42 36 24 83). The best of everything: breads, sandwiches, pastries, cakes. For an indulgent breakfast, try the *pain au chocolat* (chocolate croissant) or the very different but equally delicious *pain chocolat* (small loaf of bread with chocolate chips). Long lines at lunch.

MARKETS

Marché Monge, pl. Monge, 5ème. ⓜ Monge. A bustling, friendly, and easy-to-navigate market. You'll find everything from cheese to shoes to jewelry and flowers in these stalls. Look for the very popular prepared foods (perfect for a lunch picnic at the Arènes de Lutèce). Open W, F, and Su 8am-1:30pm.

Marché Montorgueil, 2ème. ⓜ Etienne-Marcel. Walk along r. Etienne Marcel away from the river. r. Montorgueil is the 2nd street on your right. A center of food commerce and gastronomy since the 13th century, this marble market is comprised of wine, cheese, meat, and produce shops. Open Tu-Su 8am-7:30pm.

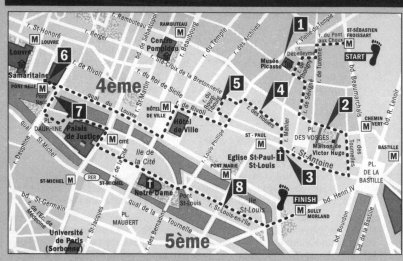

1 MUSÉE PICASSO. This museum traces Picasso's life and work chronologically: from his blue period to his pink period, from his days in Paris to his days in the Riviera, from his first mistress to his last (p. 362).

2 PLACE DES VOSGES. The manicured grass of Paris's oldest public square has been trod by Molière and Victor Hugo (no. 6 is a museum of his life and work), not to mention a good number of royals. An arcade runs around all four of its sides and houses restaurants, art galleries, and shops (p. 357).

START: Ⓜ St-Sébastien Froissart
FINISH: Ⓜ Sully Morland
DISTANCE: 5.2km
DURATION: 3-4hr.
WHEN TO GO: Start in the late morning.

3 EGLISE ST-PAUL-ST-LOUIS. Dominating r. St-Antoine, this Jesuit cathedral offers the weary traveler a break from roadside heat and car exhaust. The church's Baroque interior houses Eugène Delacroix's 1826 *Christ in the Garden of Olives.*

4 RUE DES ROSIERS. This quintessential Marais street is filled with bakeries, off-beat boutiques, and kosher restaurants. For lunch, enjoy a delicious falafel sandwich at the perpetually crowded **L'As du Falafel,** no. 34 (p. 351).

5 MARIAGE FRÈRES. This classic and classy *salon de thé*, 30 r. du Bourg-Tibourg, has 500 varieties of tea for patrons to choose from (p. 353).

6 SAMARITAINE. At 67 r. de Rivoli are 11 floors of shopping for him, her, and home, with an unbeatable panoramic view of the city. Markers name every dot on the horizon, making this Art Deco department store worth a visit even if shopping isn't on the agenda (p. 365).

7 PONT NEUF. By way of the very long, very straight r. de Rivoli and the scenic quai du Louvre, meander over to the Pont Neuf, Paris's oldest bridge (c. 1607). Its gargoyles have seen peddlers, pickpockets, and a whole lot of bubble wrap.

8 RUE ST-LOUIS-EN-ILE. Wander down the charming 17th-century main street of the Ile St-Louis. Pop into **Berthillon,** no. 34, for ice cream (p. 353).

WALKING TOUR

Marché Mouffetard, 5ème. Ⓜ Monge. Walk through pl. Monge and follow r. Ortolan to r. Mouffetard. Cheese, meat, fish, produce, and housewares. The bakeries here are some of the best of all Paris's markets, and don't miss the ice cream at **Octave** near the far end. Open Tu-Su 8am-1:30pm.

⊙ SIGHTS

While it would take weeks to see all of Paris's monuments, museums, and gardens, the city's small size makes sightseeing easy and enjoyable. In a few hours, you can walk from the heart of the Marais in the east to the Eiffel Tower in the west, passing most major monuments along the way. A solid day of wandering will show you how close the medieval Notre Dame is to the modern Centre Pompidou and the funky Latin Quarter to the royal Louvre—Paris's diversity is all the more amazing for the proximity in which it unfolds.

ILE DE LA CITÉ AND ILE ST-LOUIS

ILE DE LA CITÉ

If any one place is the heart of Paris, it is this small island in the Seine. In the 3rd century BC, when it was inhabited by the *Parisii*, a Gallic tribe of merchants and fishermen, the Ile was all there was to Paris. Today, all distance-points in France are measured from *kilomètre zéro*, a sundial in front of Notre-Dame.

CATHÉDRALE DE NOTRE DAME DE PARIS. This 12th- to 14th-century cathedral, begun under Bishop Maurice Sully, is one of the world's most famous and beautiful examples of medieval architecture. After the Revolution, the building fell into disrepair and was even used to shelter livestock until Victor Hugo's 1831 novel *Notre Dame de Paris* (a.k.a. *The Hunchback of Notre Dame*) inspired citizens to lobby for restoration. The apocalyptic facade and soaring, apparently weightless walls, effects produced by brilliant Gothic engineering and optical illusions, are inspiring even for the most church-weary. The cathedral's biggest draws are its enormous stained-glass **rose windows** that dominate the northern and southern ends of the transept. A staircase inside the towers leads to a perch from which gargoyles survey the city. *(Ⓜ Cité. ☎ 01 53 10 07 02, crypt 01 55 42 50 10. Cathedral open M-F 8am-6:45pm and Sa-Su 8am-7:45pm. Towers open July-Aug. 9am-7:30pm; Apr.-June and Sept. 9:30am-7:30pm; Oct.-Mar. 10am-5:30pm. €6, ages 18-25 €4.10. Treasury open M-Sa 9:30am-12:30pm and 1:30-5:30pm, Su 1:30-5:30pm. €2.50, students and ages 12-17 €2. Crypt open daily 10am-5:30pm. €3.90, under 27 €2.20. Free tours begin at the booth to the right as you enter. In English W-Th noon, Sa 2:30pm; in French M-F noon, Sa 2:30pm.)*

PALAIS DE JUSTICE, STE-CHAPELLE, AND CONCIERGERIE. The **Palais de la Cité** contains three vastly different buildings. The opulent, Gothic **Ste-Chapelle** was built by St. Louis (Louis IX) to house Christ's crown of thorns, now in Notre Dame. The phenomenal **Upper Chapel** has glowing stained glass and frescoes of saints and martyrs. *(4 bd. du Palais. Ⓜ Cité. ☎01 53 73 78 50. Open daily Apr.-Sept. 9:30am-6pm. €6.10, seniors and ages 18-25 €4.10. Under 18 free.)* Around the corner is the **Conciergerie,** a prison where Marie-Antoinette and Robespierre were incarcerated during the Revolution. *(Entrance on bd. du Palais, to the right of Palais de Justice. ☎01 53 73 78 50. Open daily Apr.-Sept. 9:30am-6pm; Oct.-Mar. 10am-5pm. €6.10, students €4.10.)* The Palais de Justice has been home to Paris's district courts since the 13th century. *(☎01 44 32 51 51. Courtrooms open M-F 9am-noon and 1:30-6pm. Free.)*

ILE ST-LOUIS

The Ile St-Louis has been home to some of Paris's most privileged elite, from Pompidou to Voltaire, Baudelaire to Marie Curie. Paris's best ice cream is at ▧**Berthillon,** 31 r. St-Louis-en-Ile (see p. 353).

ÉGLISE ST-LOUIS-EN-L'ILE. Louis Le Vau's 17th-century Rococo interior is lit by a surprising number of windows. The third chapel has a splendid gilded wood relief, *The Death of the Virgin*. *(19bis r. St-Louis-en-l'Ile. ☎01 46 34 11 60. Open Tu-Su 9am-noon and 3-7pm. Check with FNAC (www.fnac.com) or call the church for concert details; ticket prices vary, usually around €20 general admission and €15 for students.)*

LOUVRE AND OPÉRA: 1ER, 2ÈME, AND 9ÈME ARRONDISSEMENTS

LOUVRE AND TUILERIES. World-famous art museum and former residence of kings, the **Louvre** (p. 361) occupies about one-seventh of the 1*er arrondissement.* The **Jardin des Tuileries,** at the western foot of the Louvre, was commissioned by Catherine de Médici in 1564 and improved by André Le Nôtre (designer of the gardens at Versailles) in 1649. *(Ⓜ Tuileries. ☎01 40 20 90 43. Open daily Apr.-Sept. 7am-9pm; Oct.-Mar. 7:30am-7:30pm. Tours in English from the Arc de Triomphe du Carrousel.)* Three blocks north along r. de Castiglione, **place Vendôme** hides 20th-century offices and luxury shops behind 17th-century facades. Look out for Napoleon on top of the column in the center of the *place*—he's the one in the toga. *(Ⓜ Tuileries or Concorde.)*

PALAIS-ROYAL. One block north of the Louvre along r. St-Honoré lies the once regal and racy Palais-Royal, constructed in the 17th century as Richelieu's Palais Cardinal. Anne d'Autriche moved in with her son, young Louis XIV. In 1781, the Duc d'Orléans, strapped for cash, rented out the buildings around the palace's garden to boutiques, restaurants, theaters, and gambling joints. *(Fountain open daily June-Aug. 7am-11pm; Sept. 7am-9:30pm; Oct.-Mar. 7am-8:30pm; Apr.-May 7am-10:15pm. Free.)*

LES HALLES. A sprawling market since 1135, Les Halles received a much-needed face-lift in the 1850s with the construction of large iron-and-glass pavilions to shelter the vendors' stalls. In 1970, when authorities moved the old market to a suburb, planners destroyed the pavilions to build a subterranean transfer-point between the metro and the new commuter rail and a subterranean shopping mall, the **Forum des Halles,** with over 200 boutiques and three movie theaters. *(Ⓜ Les Halles.)*

OPÉRA. Located north of the Louvre in the 9*ème* arrondissement, Charles Garnier's grandiose **Opéra Garnier** was built under Napoleon III in the eclectic style of the Second Empire. Gobelin tapestries, gilded mosaics, a 1964 Marc Chagall ceiling, and a six-ton chandelier adorn the magnificent interior. *(Ⓜ Opéra. General info ☎08 36 69 78 68, tours 01 40 01 22 63; www.opera-de-paris.fr. Concert hall and museum open daily Sept. to mid-July 10am-5pm; mid-July to Aug. 10am-6pm. Concert hall closed during rehearsals; call ahead. €6; ages 10-16, students, and over 60 €3. English tours daily at noon and 2pm. €10, students €8.)*

PIGALLE. Farther north, at the border of the 18*ème*, is the infamous Pigalle district. Stretching along bd. de Clichy from pl. Pigalle to pl. Blanche is a salacious, voracious, and generally naughty neighborhood, the home of famous cabarets-*cum*-nightclubs like Folies Bergère and Folies Pigalle. Visitors should exercise caution in the area. *(Ⓜ Pigalle.)*

MARAIS: 3ÈME AND 4ÈME ARRONDISSEMENTS

RUE DES ROSIERS. Until the 13th century, Paris's Jewish community was concentrated in front of Notre Dame. Then the Jewish population was expelled from the city limits, and many families moved to the Marais, just outside the walls. Since then, this quarter has been Paris's Jewish center, with two synagogues at 25 r. des Rosiers and 10 r. Pavée, designed by Art Nouveau architect Hector Guimard. Mediterranean and Eastern European Jewish cultures give the area a unique flavor, with kugel and falafel served side by side. Nearby, the corner of **rue Vieille-de-Temple** and **rue Ste-Croix de la Bretonnerie** is the epicenter of the Marais's gay community. (Ⓜ St-Paul. 4 blocks east of Beaubourg, parallel to r. des Francs-Bourgeois.)

HÔTEL DE VILLE. Paris's grandiose city hall dominates a large square scattered with fountains and *Belle Epoque* lampposts. The present edifice is a 19th-century creation built to replace the original medieval structure, a meeting hall for the cartel that controlled traffic on the Seine. (29 r. de Rivoli. Ⓜ Hôtel-de-Ville. ☎01 42 76 43 43. Open M-F 9am-6:30pm when there is an exhibit, until 6pm otherwise.)

PLACE DES VOSGES. At the end of r. des Francs-Bourgeois sits the magnificent pl. des Vosges, Paris's oldest public square. The manicured central park is surrounded by 17th-century Rennaissance townhouses. The *place* is one of Paris's most charming spots for a picnic or an afternoon siesta. Victor Hugo lived at no. 6, which is now a museum of his life and work. (Ⓜ Chemin Vert or St-Paul.)

THE LATIN QUARTER AND ST-GERMAIN-DES-PRÉS: 5ÈME AND 6ÈME ARRONDISSEMENTS

The student population is the soul of the Latin Quarter, so named for prestigious universities that taught in Latin until 1798. Since the student riots in May 1968, many artists and intellectuals have migrated to the cheaper outer *arrondissements*, and the *haute bourgeoisie* have moved in. The 5*ème* still presents the most diverse array of bookstores, cinemas, and jazz clubs in the city. Designer shops and cutting edge art galleries are situated around St-Germain-des-Prés.

LA SORBONNE. The Sorbonne is one of Europe's oldest universities, founded in 1253 by Robert de Sorbon as a dormitory for 16 theology students. Visitors can stroll through the **Chapelle de la Sorbonne** (entrance off of the pl. de la Sorbonne), which houses temporary exhibits on the arts and letters. Nearby **place de la Sorbonne,** off bd. St-Michel, boasts cafes, bookstores, and—during term-time—students. (45-47 r. des Ecoles. Ⓜ Cluny-La Sorbonne or RER: Luxembourg. Walk away from the Seine on bd. St-Michel and turn left on r. des Ecoles to see the main building.)

JARDIN DU LUXEMBOURG. Parisians flock to these formal gardens to sunbathe or read. A residential area in Roman Paris, the site of a medieval monastery, and later the home of 17th-century French royalty, the gardens were liberated during the Revolution and are now free to all. (Ⓜ Odéon or RER: Luxembourg. The main entrance is on bd. St-Michel. Open daily dawn-dusk.)

PANTHÉON. The **crypt** of the Panthéon, which occupies the highest point on the Left Bank, houses the tombs of Louis Braille, Victor Hugo, Jean Jaurès, Jean-Jacques Rousseau, Voltaire, and Emile Zola. The building's other attraction is **Foucault's Pendulum,** which proves the rotation of the earth. (Pl. du Panthéon. Ⓜ Cardinal Lemoine. ☎01 44 32 18 00. Walk down r. Cardinal Lemoine, turn right on r. Clovis, and walk around to the front of the building. Open daily 10am-6:30pm. Last admission 5:45pm. €7, students €4.50, under 18 free. Tours in French leave from the main door daily at 2:30 and 4pm.)

MOSQUÉE DE PARIS. The *Institut Musulman* houses the beautiful Persian gardens, elaborate minaret, and shady porticoes of the Mosquée de Paris, a mosque constructed in 1920 by French architects to honor the role played by the countries of North Africa in WWI. Exhausted travelers can relax in the steam baths at the exquisite *hammam* (Turkish bath) or sip mint tea at the equally soothing cafe. (Ⓜ Jussieu. Behind the Jardin des Plantes at pl. du Puits de l'Ermite. Walk down r. Daubenton; the mosque is at the end of the street, on the left. ☎01 48 35 78 17. Open daily June-Aug. 10am-noon and 2-6:30pm; Sept.-May until 5:30pm. Guided tour €3, students €2. Hammam open for men Tu 2-9pm; Su 10am-9pm; women M, W-Th, and Sa 10am-9pm, F 2-9pm. €15.)

EGLISE ST-GERMAIN-DES-PRÉS. Having miraculously survived invading Normans, the Revolution, and Baron Haussmann, Eglise St-Germain-des-Prés, begun in 1163, is Paris's oldest standing church. *(3 pl. St-Germain-des-Prés. ☎01 55 42 81 33. Open daily 8am-8pm. Info office open M 2:30-6:45pm, Tu-Sa 10:30am-noon and 2:30-6:45pm.)*

JARDIN DES PLANTES. Opened in 1640 to grow medicinal plants for King Louis XIII, the garden now features science museums, rosaries, and a zoo, which Parisians raided for food during the Prussian siege of 1871. *(Ⓜ Gare d'Austerlitz or Jussieu. ☎01 40 79 37 94. Open daily 7:30am-8pm; in winter 7:30am-5:30pm.)*

7ÈME ARRONDISSEMENT

EIFFEL TOWER. Gustave Eiffel, its designer, wrote: "France is the only country in the world with a 300m flagpole." Designed in 1889 as the tallest structure in the world, the Eiffel Tower was conceived as a monument to engineering that would surpass the Egyptian pyramids in size and notoriety. Before construction had begun, shockwaves of dismay reverberated through the city. Critics dubbed it a "metal asparagus" and a Parisian tower of Babel. Writer Guy de Maupassant ate lunch every day at its ground-floor restaurant—the only place in Paris, he claimed, from which he couldn't see the offensive thing. Nevertheless, when it was inaugurated in March 1889 as the center-piece of the World's Fair, the tower earned the love of Paris; nearly two million people ascended the event. Today, as an icon represented on everything from post-cards to neckties and umbrellas, Eiffel's wonder still takes the heat from some who see it as Maupassant did: an "excruciating nightmare" overrun with tourists and their trinkets. Don't believe the anti-hype, though. The tower may not be beautiful, but it is a wonder of design and engineering. *(Ⓜ Bir-Hakeim or Trocadéro. ☎01 44 11 23 23. Open daily mid-June to Aug. 9am-midnight; Sept.-Dec. 9:30am-11pm (stairs 9:30am-6pm); Jan. to mid-June 9:30am-11pm (stairs 9:30am-6pm). Elevator to 1st fl. €4, to 2nd fl. €7.30, to 3rd fl. €10.40. Stairs to 1st and 2nd fl. €3.50. Last access to top 30min. before close.)*

INVALIDES. The gold-leaf dome of the Hôtel des Invalides shines at the center of the *7ème*. The tree-lined **Esplanade des Invalides** runs from the *hôtel* to the **Pont Alexandre III,** a bridge with gilded lampposts from which you can catch a great view of the Invalides and the Seine. The **Musée de l'Armée, Musée des Plans-Reliefs,** and **Musée de l'Ordre de la Libération** are housed in the Invalides complex, as is **Napoleon's tomb,** in the **Eglise St-Louis.** Enter from either pl. des Invalides or pl. Vauban and av. de Tourville. To the left of the Tourville entrance, the **Jardin de l'Intendant** is a shady break from guns and emperors. *(Ⓜ Invalides, Latour Maubourg, or Varenne.)*

CHAMPS-ELYSÉES AND NEARBY: 8ÈME AND 16ÈME ARRONDISSEMENTS

PLACE DE LA CONCORDE. Paris's most famous public square lies at the eastern end of the Champs-Elysées. Built between 1757 and 1777 as a monument to Louis X, the area soon became the **place de la Révolution,** site of the guillotine that severed 1343 aristocratic heads. After the Reign of Terror, the square was renamed *concorde* (peace). The huge 13th-century BC **Obélisque de Luxor** depicts the deeds of Egyptian pharaoh Ramses II. Given to Charles X by the Viceroy of Egypt, it is Paris's oldest monument. *(Ⓜ Concorde.)*

CHAMPS-ELYSÉES. Anchored by the Arc de Triomphe on one end and the pl. de Concorde on the other, the legendary **avenue des Champs-Elysées** stretches west, lined with luxury shops, chain stores, cafes, and cinemas. The avenue is the work of Baron Haussmann, who was commissioned by Napoleon III to convert Paris into a grand capital with broad avenues, wide sidewalks, new parks, elegant housing, and sanitary sewers. The city's most elegant shopping is on nearby **avenue Montagne** and **rue Faubourg St-Honoré.**

ARC DE TRIOMPHE. Napoleon commissioned the Arc de Triomphe, at the western terminus of the Champs-Elysées, in 1806 to honor his Grande Armée. In 1940, Parisians were brought to tears as Nazis goose-stepped through the Arc; on August 26, 1944, British, American, and French troops liberating the city from Nazi occupation marched through to the cheers of thousands. The **Tomb of the Unknown Soldier** has been under the Arc since November 11, 1920. It bears the inscription, "Here lies a French soldier who died for his country, 1914-1918," representing the 1,500,000 men who died during WWI. *(On pl. Charles de Gaulle. ⓜ Charles-de-Gaulle-Etoile. Open daily Apr.-Sept. 10am-11pm; Oct.-Mar. 10am-10:30pm. €7, ages 18-25 €4.50.)*

THE MADELEINE. Mirrored by the Assemblée Nationale across the Seine, the Madeleine—formally called **Eglise Ste-Marie-Madeleine**—was begun in 1764 by Louis XV and modeled after a Greek temple. Construction was halted during the Revolution and finally completed in 1842. The structure is distinguished by four ceiling domes that light the interior, 52 exterior Corinthian columns, and a curious altarpiece. *(Pl. de la Madeleine. ⓜ Madeleine. ☎01 44 51 69 00. Open daily 7:30am-7pm.)*

PLACE DU TROCADÉRO. In the 1820s, the Duc d'Angoulême built a memorial to his victory in Spain at Trocadéro. Jacques Carlu's designed the **Palais de Chaillot** for the 1937 World's Fair. The Palais features two white stone wings and an Art Deco courtyard that extends over cannon-shaped fountains. The terrace offers brilliant views of the Eiffel Tower and Champs de Mars. *(ⓜ Trocadéro.)*

BASTILLE: 10ÈME, 11ÈME, AND 12ÈME ARRONDISSEMENTS

CANAL ST-MARTIN. The most pleasant area of the 10*ème* is the tree-lined Canal St-Martin. In recent years, the city has made efforts to improve water quality in the canal and clean up its banks, and the result has been a local renaissance. Children line up along the quays to watch the several working locks lift barges and boats. *(ⓜ République or Goncourt will take you to the more beautiful end of the canal.)*

THE BASTILLE PRISON. The Bastille Prison is often visited, but doesn't actually exist. A Parisian mob stormed this symbol of the monarchy's tyranny on July 14, 1789, sparking the French Revolution. Two days later, the National Assembly ordered the prison demolished. Today, pl. de la Bastille is a busy intersection, but the ground plan of the fortress is still visible as a line of paving-stones in the *place*, beneath which some of the cellars are said to survive. *(ⓜ Bastille.)*

OPÉRA DE LA BASTILLE. One of Mitterrand's *Grands Projets*, the Opéra opened in 1989 to loud protests over its unattractive design. It has been described as a huge toilet because of its resemblance to the coin-operated *pissoirs* on the streets of Paris. The opera has not struck a completely sour note, though, as it has helped renew local interest in the arts. The interesting guided tour offers a behind-the-scenes view of the largest theater in the world. *(130 r. de Lyon. ⓜ Bastille. Look for the words "Billeterie" on the building. ☎01 40 01 19 70; www.opera-de-paris.fr. €10, over 60 €8, students and under 26 €5. 1hr. tour almost every day, usually at 1 or 5pm; call ahead. Tours in French, but groups of 10 or more can arrange for English.)*

EASTERN LEFT BANK: 13ÈME ARRONDISSEMENT

QUARTIER DE LA BUTTE-AUX-CAILLES. Historically a working-class neighborhood, the old-fashioned Butte-aux-Cailles quarter has a long-standing tradition of defiance. The area was one of the first to fight during the Revolution of 1848. Later, it was the unofficial headquarters of the *soixante-huitards*, the student and intellectual activists behind the 1968 riots in Paris. Funky new restaurants and galleries have cropped up in recent years. *(ⓜ Corvisart. Exit onto bd. Blanqui, and turn onto r. Barrault, which will meet r. de la Butte-aux-Cailles.)*

CHINATOWN. Paris's Chinatown is bounded by r. de Tolbiac, bd. Masséna, av. de Choisy, and av. d'Ivry. It is home to large Chinese, Vietnamese, and Cambodian communities and a host of Asian restaurants and shops. (Ⓜ *Tolbiac.*)

MONTPARNASSE: 14ÈME AND 15ÈME ARRONDISSEMENTS

BOULEVARD DU MONTPARNASSE. In the early 20th century, Montparnasse became a center for avant-garde artists like Chagall and Modigliani. Political exiles Lenin and Trotsky talked strategy over cognac in cafes along the boulevard, including **Le Dôme, Le Sélect,** and **La Coupole.** After WWI, Montparnasse attracted American expats and artistic rebels like Calder, Hemingway, and Henry Miller. (Ⓜ *Montparnasse-Bienvenue.*)

THE CATACOMBS. A series of tunnels 20m below ground and 1.7km in length, the Catacombs were originally excavated to provide stone for building the city. By the 1770s, much of the Left Bank was in danger of caving in and digging promptly stopped. The former quarry was then used as a mass grave, relieving Paris's foul and overcrowded cemeteries. During WWII, the Resistance set up headquarters among the departed. *(1 pl. Denfert-Rochereau.* Ⓜ *Denfert-Rochereau.* ☎ *01 43 22 47 63. Exit to pl. Denfert-Rochereau and cross av. du Général Leclerc; the entrance is the dark green structure straight ahead. Open Tu-Su 10am-4pm. €5, ages 14-26 €2.50. Tour lasts 45min.)*

PARC ANDRÉ CITROËN. The futuristic Parc André Citroën was created by landscapers Alain Provost and Gilles Clément in the 1970s. Rides in the hot-air balloon that launches from the central garden offer spectacular aerial views of Paris. *(2 r. de la Montagne de la Fage.* ☎ *01 44 26 20 00; www.volenballon.com.* Ⓜ *Javel-André Citroën or Balard. Open M-F 7:30am-9:30pm, Sa-Su 9am-9:30pm. Balloon ride €12, ages 12-17 €10.)*

MONTMARTRE AND PÈRE-LACHAISE: 18ÈME, 19ÈME, AND 20ÈME ARRONDISSEMENTS

MOUNTING MONTMARTRE. Montmartre, comprised mostly of one very large hill, is one of the few Parisian neighborhoods Baron Haussmann left intact when he redesigned the city and its environs. During its Belle Epoque heyday from 1875 to 1905, it attracted bohemians like Erik Satie and Toulouse-Lautrec, as well as performers and impresarios like Aristide Bruant. Later, Apollinaire, Modigliani, Picasso, and Utrillo came into its artistic circle. Nowadays, Montmartre is a mix of upscale bohemia (above r. des Abbesses) and sleaze (along bd. de Clichy). The northwestern part of the area retains some village charm, its breezy streets speckled with interesting shops and cafes. (Ⓜ *Anvers or Abbesses. Funicular runs cars up and down the hill every 2min. Open 6am-12:30am. €1.30 or metro ticket.)*

BASILIQUE DU SACRÉ-COEUR. The Basilique du Sacré-Coeur crowns the butte Montmartre like an enormous white meringue. Its onion dome is visible from almost anywhere in the city, and its 112m bell tower is the highest point in Paris, offering a view that stretches up to 50km. Nearby, pl. du Tertre is full of touristy cafes and amateur artists. *(35 r. du Chevalier de la Barre.* Ⓜ *Anvers, Abbesses, or Château-Rouge.* ☎ *01 53 41 89 00. Open daily 7am-10:30pm. Wheelchair accessible through back. Free. Dome and crypt open daily 9am-6:45pm. €5.)*

BAL DU MOULIN ROUGE. Along the bd. de Clichy and bd. de Rochechouart, you'll find many of the cabarets and nightclubs that were the definitive hangouts of the Belle Epoque, including the infamous cabaret Bal du Moulin Rouge, immortalized by the paintings of Toulouse-Lautrec, the music of Offenbach, and, most recently, Baz Luhrmann's Hollywood blockbuster. (Ⓜ *Blanche. 82 bd. de Clichy. Directly across from the metro.* ☎ *01 53 09 82 82; www.moulin-rouge.com. Shows 7, 9, 11pm.)*

PARC DE LA VILLETTE. La Villette is the product of a successful urban renewal project. Inaugurated by President Mitterrand in 1985 as "the place of intelligent leisure," it contains museums, libraries, and concert halls in the Cité des Sciences and the Cité de la Musique. The **Promenade des Jardins** links several thematic gardens. Every July and August, La Villette hosts a free open-air **film festival.** The **Zénith** concert hall hosts major rock bands, and the **Trabendo** jazz and modern music club holds an extraordinarily popular yearly jazz festival. (Ⓜ *Porte de Pantin. General info including Grande Halle ☎ 01 40 03 75 03. Promenade des Jardins open 24hr. Free.)*

CIMETIÈRE PÈRE LACHAISE. The Cimetière Père Lachaise, located in the 20ème, holds the remains of Balzac, Sarah Bernhardt, Colette, Danton, David, Delacroix, La Fontaine, Haussmann, Molière, Proust, and Seurat within its peaceful, winding paths and elaborate sarcophagi. Foreigners buried here include Modigliani, Gertrude Stein, and Oscar Wilde, but the most visited grave is that of Jim Morrison. French Leftists make ceremonious pilgrimage to the **Mur des Fédérés** (Wall of the Federals), where 147 *communards* were executed and buried. *(16 r. du Repos.* Ⓜ *Père-Lachaise. Open Mar.-Oct. M-F 8am-6pm, Sa 8:30am-6pm, Su and holidays 9am-6pm; Nov.-Feb. M-F 8am-5:30pm, Sa 8:30am-5:30pm, Su and holidays 9am-5:30pm. Free.)*

PERIMETER SIGHTS

LA DÉFENSE. Outside the city limits, west of the 16ème, the skyscrapers and modern architecture of La Défense make up Paris's newest (unofficial) *arrondissement,* home to the headquarters of 14 of France's top 20 corporations. The **Grande Arche,** inaugurated in 1989, completes the *axe historique* running through the Louvre, pl. de la Concorde, and the Arc de Triomphe. There's yet another stunning view from the top. Trees, shops, and sculptures by Calder and Miró line the esplanade. *(M/RER: La Défense, or bus #73. Arch open daily 10am-8pm. €7.50; under 18, students, and seniors €5.50.)*

BOIS DE BOULOGNE. By day, this 846-hectare park, with numerous gardens, several stadiums, and two lakes, is a popular spot for picnics, jogging, and bike-riding. The *bois* is notorious for drugs and prostitution by night. (Ⓜ *Porte Maillot, Sablons, Pont de Neuilly, or Porte Dauphine. On the western edge of the 16ème.)*

🏛 MUSEUMS

The **Carte Musées et Monuments** grants immediate entry to 70 Paris museums (no waiting in line) and will save you money if you plan to visit three or more museums and major sights per day. It's available at major museums and metro stations. (1-day €15; 3-days €30; 5-days €45.)

MUSÉE DU LOUVRE. A short list of its masterpieces includes the *Code of Hammurabi,* Jacques-Louis David's *The Oath of the Horatii,* Delacroix's *Liberty Leading the People,* Vermeer's *Lacemaker,* and da Vinci's *Mona Lisa.* Enter through I.M. Pei's stunning glass **Pyramid** in the Cour Napoléon, or skip lines by entering directly from the metro. The Louvre is organized into three different wings: Sully, Richelieu, and Denon. Each is divided according to the artwork's date, national origin, and medium. *(1er.* Ⓜ *Palais-Royal-Musée du Louvre. ☎01 40 20 51 51; www.louvre.fr. Open M and W 9am-9:45pm, Th-Su 9am-6pm. Last entry 45min. before close, but visitors are asked to leave 15-30min. before close. Admission M and W-Sa 9am-3pm €8.50, M and W-Sa 3pm-close and Su €6, 1st Su of month free.)*

MUSÉE D'ORSAY. While considered the premier Impressionist collection, the museum is dedicated to presenting all major artistic movements between 1848 and WWI. On the ground floor, works from Classicism and Proto-Impressionism are on display, including Manet's *Olympia*, a painting that caused a scandal when it was unveiled in 1865. Other highlights include: Monet's *La Gare St-Lazare* and *Cathédrale de Rouen* series, Renoir's *Le bal du Moulin de la Galette*, Edgar Dégas's *La classe de danse*, and paintings by Sisley, Pissaro, and Morisot. Over a dozen diverse works by van Gogh follow. Cézanne's works experiment with the soft colors and geometric planes that would open the door to Cubism. (*62 r. de Lille. 7ème.* Ⓜ *Solférino; RER: Musée d'Orsay.* ☎ *01 40 49 48 14; www.musee-orsay.fr. Open July-Sept. Tu-Su 9am-6pm; Oct.-May Tu-W and F-Sa 10am-6pm, Th 10am-9:45pm. Last entry 45min. before close. €7, ages 18-25 and Su €5, under 18 and 1st Su of month free.*)

CENTRE POMPIDOU. This inside-out building has inspired debate since its opening in 1977. The exterior's chaotic colored piping and ventilation ducts provide an appropriate shell for the Fauvist, Cubist, and Pop and Conceptual works inside. (*Pl. Georges-Pompidou, 4ème.* Ⓜ *Rambuteau or Hôtel-de-Ville.* ☎ *01 44 78 12 33; www.centrepompidou.fr. Centre open M and W-Su 11am-10pm; museum open M and W-Su 11am-9pm. Last entry 8pm. €7, students and over 60 €5, under 18 and 1st Su of month free.*)

MUSÉE RODIN. Parisians know that this is the best museum in Paris. The 18th-century Hôtel Biron holds hundreds of sculptures by Auguste Rodin (and by his student and lover, Camille Claudel), including the *Gates of Hell*, *The Thinker*, *The Burghers of Calais*, and *The Kiss*. (*77 r. de Varenne, 7ème.* Ⓜ *Varenne.* ☎ *01 44 18 61 10; www.musee-rodin.fr. Open Apr.-Sept. Tu-Su 9:30am-5:45pm; Oct.-Mar. 9:30am-4:45pm. Last entry 30min. before close. €5; seniors, ages 18-25, and Su €3.*)

MUSÉE DE CLUNY. One of the world's finest collections of medieval art, the Musée de Cluny is housed in a medieval monastery built on top of Roman baths. Works include the *La Dame et La Licorne* (The Lady and the Unicorn), a striking medieval tapestry series. (*6 pl. Paul Painlevé, 5ème.* Ⓜ *Cluny-La Sorbonne.* ☎ *01 53 73 78 00. Open M and W-Sa 9:15am-5:45pm. Last entry 5:15pm. €7; students, under 25, over 60, and Su €5.50; under 18 free.*)

EXPLORA SCIENCE MUSEUM. Dedicated to bringing science to young people, the Explora Science Museum is the star attraction of La Villette, in the complex's Cité des Sciences et de l'Industrie. The futuristic architecture of the buildings is impressive on its own, but the displays inside are especially fantastic. (*19ème.* Ⓜ *Porte de la Villette.* ☎ *01 40 05 70 00; www.cite-sciences.fr. Museum open Tu-Sa 10am-6pm, Su 10am-7pm. €7.50, under 25 €5.50, under 7 free. Planetarium €3, under 7 free. Médiathèque open Tu noon-7:45pm, W-Su noon-6:45 pm. Free. 1½hr. Cité des Enfants programs every 2hr. Tu-Su; 1½hr. long. €5. Last admission M-Sa 5:30pm, Su 6pm.*)

MUSÉE PICASSO. When Picasso died in 1973, his family paid the French inheritance tax in artwork. The French government put this collection, which includes work from his Cubist, Surrealist, and Neoclassical years, on display in 1985 in the 17th-century Hôtel Salé. (*5 r. de Thorigny, 3ème.* Ⓜ *Chemin Vert.* ☎ *01 42 71 63 15 or 01 42 71 70 84. Open Apr.-Sept. M and W-Su 9:30am-6pm; Oct.-Mar. 9:30am-5:30pm. Last entry 45min. before close. €5.50, Su and ages 18-25 €4.*)

INSTITUT DU MONDE ARABE. Featuring art from the Maghreb and the Near and Middle East, the IMA is housed in a cool, modern building. The riverside facade is shaped like a boat, representing the migration of Arabs to France. (*1 r. des Fossés St-Bernard, 5ème.* Ⓜ *Jussieu.* ☎ *01 40 51 38 38. Open Tu-Su 10am-7pm. Library open Tu-Sa 1-8pm. €4.*)

FONDATION CARTIER POUR L'ART CONTEMPORAINE. The Fondation Cartier, a gallery of contemporary art, looks like an avant-garde indoor forest, with a stunning glass facade surrounding the grounds' natural greenery. Thursday *Soirées*

Nomades present an eclectic set of performance art. *(261 bd. Raspail, 14ème.* Ⓜ *Raspail or Denfert-Rochereau.* ☎ *01 42 18 56 51; www.fondation.cartier.fr. Open Tu-Su noon-8pm. €6, students and seniors €4.50, under 10 free. Soirées Nomades Th 8:30pm; check website for performance details. Reserve ahead* ☎ *01 42 18 56 72.)*

MUSÉE CARNAVALET. Housed in Mme. de Sévigné's 16th-century *hôtel particulier*, this museum traces Paris's history with exhibits from prehistory to 18th-century extravagance, 19th-century Haussmannization, and Mitterrand's *Grands Projets. (23 r. de Sévigné, 3ème.* ☎ *01 44 59 58 58; www.paris.fr/musees/musee_carnavalet.* Ⓜ *Chemin Vert. Take r. St-Gilles, and turn left on r. de Sévigné. Open Tu-Su 10am-5:40pm. Last entry 5:15pm. Free. Special exhibits €5.50, students and elderly €4, ages 13-18 €2.50.)*

MAISON DE BALZAC. In this three-story hillside *maison*, home of Honoré de Balzac from 1840-47, visitors can see the desk and chair where the author wrote. The picturesque garden is filled with flowers in the summertime. *(47 r. Raynouard, 16ème.* Ⓜ *Passy. Walk up the hill and turn left onto r. Rayonard.* ☎ *01 55 74 41 80. Open Tu-Su 10am-6pm. Last entry 5:40pm. Free.)*

PALAIS DE TOKYO. Part of the magnificent Palais houses the **Musée d'Art Moderne de la Ville de Paris,** one of the world's foremost collections of 20th-century art. Two works stand out: Matisse's *La Danse Inachevée* and Dufy's epic of electricity, *La Fée Electricité.* The Museum is closed for renovations until early 2005. *(13 av. du Président Wilson, 16ème.* Ⓜ *Iéna. Follow av. du Président Wilson with the Seine on your right.* ☎ *01 47 23 54 01; www.palaisdetokyo.com. Open Tu-F 10am-5:30pm, Sa-Su 10am-6:45pm. Free. Special exhibits approximately €5, students €2.20-3.)*

On the other side of the Palais, the **site création contemporaine** displays several exciting, controversial exhibits a year. The large, warehouse-like space accommodates massive abstract sculpture, video displays, and multimedia installations. *(Open Tu-Su noon-midnight. Admission approximately €5. Discounts for students, youth, and seniors; art students free.)*

MUSÉE JACQUEMART-ANDRÉ. The 19th-century home of Nélie Jacquemart and her husband contains a world-class collection of Renaissance art, including *Madonna and Child* by Botticelli and *St-George and the Dragon* by Uccello. *(158 bd. Haussmann, 8ème.* Ⓜ *Miromesnil.* ☎ *01 45 62 11 59. Open daily 10am-6pm. Last entry 5:30pm. €8.50, students and ages 7-17 €6.50. Audio tours in English free with admission.)*

MUSÉE MARMOTTAN MONET. Owing to donations by Monet's family, this Empire-style house has been transformed into a shrine to Impressionism, with some of Monet's famed water lilies in the basement. *(2 r. Louis Boilly, 16ème.* Ⓜ *La Muette.* ☎ *01 44 96 50 33. Follow Chaussée de la Muette, which becomes av. Ranelagh, through the Jardin du Ranelagh park. Open Tu-Su 10am-6pm. €6.50, students €4.)*

GALLERIES. Evidence of its thriving artistic scene, Paris has dozens of galleries displaying the work of international artists both established and up-and-coming. The highest concentrations of hip contemporary art galleries are in the **Marais** and **St-Germain-des-Prés.** The **Champs-Elysées** area in the 8*ème* is loaded with Old Masters. Galleries near Ⓜ Franklin D. Roosevelt on the Champs-Elysées, av. Matignon, r. du Faubourg St-Honoré, and r. de Miromesnil focus on Impressionism and post-Impressionism. The 13*ème* also has new galleries along **rue Louise-Weisse** (Ⓜ Chevaleret) and the perpendicular **rue Duchefdelaville.** The *Portes Ouvertes* festival (May-June; check *Pariscope* for info) allows visitors to witness artists in action in their studios. Almost all galleries close at lunchtime, on Mondays, and in August.

♫ ENTERTAINMENT

Paris's cabarets, cinemas, theaters, and concert halls can satisfy all tastes and desires. The bibles of Parisian entertainment, the weekly *Pariscope* and the *Officiel des Spectacles* (both €0.40), on sale at any newsstand or *tabac*, have every conceivable listing. *Pariscope* includes an English-language section.

FREE CONCERTS

For concert listings, check the free magazine *Paris Selection*, available at tourist offices throughout the city. Free concerts are often held in churches and parks, especially during summer festivals. They are extremely popular, so plan to arrive at the host venue early. The **American Church in Paris**, in the 7*ème*, **Eglise St-Germain-des-Prés**, in the 6*ème*, and **Eglise St-Merri**, in the 4*ème*, host frequent free concerts. Concerts also take place W-Su in the **Jardin du Luxembourg's** band shell, 6*ème* (☎01 42 34 20 23); show up early if you don't want to stand. Occasional free concerts are held in the **Musée d'Orsay**, 1 r. Bellechasse, 7*ème* (p. 361).

CONCERT VENUES

Le Bataclan, 50 bd. Voltaire, 11*ème* (☎01 43 14 35 35). ⓜ Oberkampf. An 800-person concert space and cafe-bar that hosts the likes of Blur, Metallica, Oasis, and Prince, as well as indie rock bands. Tickets start at €15 and vary with show. Call for schedules and reservations. Open Sept.-July. MC/V.

La Cigale, 120 bd. Rochechouart, 18*ème* (☎01 49 25 89 99; www.lacigale.fr). ⓜ Pigalle. One of the 2 large rock clubs in Pigalle, seating 2000 for international indie, punk, and hard-core bands. Also stages modern dance shows. Box office open M-Sa noon-showtime; music starts 8:30pm. Concerts €20-35. MC/V.

L'Olympia, 28 bd. des Capucines, 9*ème* (☎01 55 27 10 00; www.olympiahall.com). ⓜ Opéra. The oldest music hall in Paris. The Beatles and Sinatra played here, and it's still drawing big-name acts. Box office open M-Sa 9am-7pm. Tickets €25-60. MC/V.

OPERA AND THEATER

Opéra de la Bastille, pl. de la Bastille, 12*ème* (☎08 92 69 78 68; www.opera-de-paris.fr). ⓜ Bastille. Opera and ballet with a modern spin. Tickets can be purchased by Internet, mail, fax, phone (M-Sa 9am-7pm), or in person (M-Sa 11am-6:30pm). Tickets €60-105. Rush tickets for students under 25 and seniors 15min. before show. MC/V.

Opéra Garnier, pl. de l'Opéra, 9*ème* (☎ 08 92 89 90 90; www.opera-de-paris.fr). ⓜ Opéra. Hosts symphonies, chamber music, and the Ballet de l'Opéra de Paris. Box office open M-Sa 11am-6pm. Tickets €19-64. Tickets available 2 weeks before shows; last-minute discount tickets available 1hr. ahead. AmEx/MC/V.

La Comédie Française, 2 r. de Richelieu, 1*er* (☎01 44 58 15 15; www.comedie-francaise.fr). ⓜ Palais-Royal. Founded by Molière, now the granddaddy of all French theaters. Expect wildly gesticulated slapstick farce; you don't need to speak French to understand the jokes. Tickets €10-35. Rush tickets for students (€5-6) available 1hr. before show. AmEx/MC/V.

Bouffes du Nord, 37bis bd. de la Chapelle, 10*ème* (☎01 46 07 34 50; www.bouffes-dunord.com). ⓜ La Chapelle. This experimental theater headed by British director Peter Brook and Stephen Lissner produces cutting-edge performances and concerts and offers occasional productions in English. Closed Aug. Box office open M-Sa 11am-6pm. Concerts €19, under 26 and over 60 €12; plays €14-25.

JAZZ AND CABARET

Au Duc des Lombards, 42 r. des Lombards, 1*er* (☎01 42 33 22 88; www.jazzvalley.com/duc). ⓜ Châtelet. Still the best in French jazz, with occasional American soloists, and hot items in world music. 3 sets each night. Beer €5-8. Mixed drinks €9. Cover €12-25. Open M-Sa 8pm-2am. Music 9:30pm-1:30am.

Au Lapin Agile, 22 r. des Saules, 18ème (☎01 46 06 85 87). Ⓜ Lamarck-Coulaincourt. Turn right on r. Lamarck, then right again up r. des Saules. Picasso, Verlaine, Renoir, and Apollinaire hung out here during Montmartre's heyday. Drinks €6-7. Cover €25, M-F and Su students €18; includes 1 drink. Shows Tu-Su at 9pm-2am.

◘ SHOPPING

From the wild clubwear near r. Etienne-Marcel to the unique boutiques of the Marais to the upscale designer shops of St-Germain-des-Prés, shopping in Paris is an intense experience. Each month, the equivalent of Paris's entire population visits the chaotic **Galeries Lafayette** department store, 40 bd. Haussmann, 9ème. (☎01 42 82 34 56. Ⓜ Chaussée d'Antin. Open M-W and F-Sa 9:30am-7:30pm, Th 9:30am-9pm. AmEx/MC/V.) Not quite as chic, **Samaritaine,** 67 r. de Rivoli, on the quai du Louvre, 1er, stocks 4 historic Art Deco buildings with merchandise at down-to-earth prices. (☎01 40 41 20 20. Ⓜ Pont Neuf, Châtelet-Les Halles, or Louvre-Rivoli. Open M-W and F-Sa 9:30am-7pm, Th 9:30am-10pm. AmEx/MC/V.)

Etienne-Marcel and **Les Halles,** in the 1er and 2ème, sport a younger style, especially around **rue Tiquetonne. ▧Le Shop,** 3 r. d'Argout, 2ème, has 1200 sq. m of sleek clubwear plus a live DJ. Shirts and pants start at around €50. (Ⓜ Etienne-Marcel. ☎01 40 28 95 94. Open M 1-7pm, Tu-Sa 11am-7pm. AmEx/MC/V.) From Ⓜ Etienne-Marcel, walk against traffic on r. de Turbigo and go left on r. Tiquetonne to reach ▧**Espace Kiliwatch,** 64 r. Tiquetonne, 2ème. This is one of Paris's most popular shops, with funky new and pre-owned clothes, books, and furnishings. (Ⓜ Etienne-Marcel. ☎01 42 21 17 37. MC/V.) Shopping in the **Marais** is a complete aesthetic experience: boutiques of all colors and flavors brighten up medieval streets. What the area does best is independent designer shops. Vintage stores line **rue Vieille-du-Temple, rue de Sévigné, rue Roi de Sicile,** and **rue des Rosiers.** The deconstructed is *de rigeur* at ▧**Culotte,** 7 r. Malher, 4ème, a cutting-edge, Japanese-inspired boutique. Designs range from ripped rendered tees to 40s-style dresses, all handmade and mostly under €100. (Ⓜ St-Paul. Open Tu-Sa 12:30-7pm, Su 2-7pm. AmEx/MC/V.) **Boy'z Bazaar,** 5 r. Ste-Croix-de-la-Bretonnerie, 4ème, features all that's trendy in casual menswear. (Ⓜ Hôtel-de Ville. ☎01 42 71 94 00. Open M-Th noon-9pm, F-Sa noon-midnight, and Su 2-8pm. AmEx/MC/V.) The **Champs-Elysées** area in the 8ème (Ⓜ Charles de Gaulle-Etoile or Franklin D. Roosevelt) is perfect for a day of window shopping. On the Champs, you can purchase everything from CDs (check out the **Virgin Megastore,** open until midnight) to perfumes to chocolates, usually until a much later hour than in the rest of Paris. Then take a break and walk along **avenue Montaigne** to admire the great *couture* houses; their collections are always innovative, gorgeous, and jaw-droppingly expensive.

Across the river in the **Latin Quarter,** you'll find both chains and boutiques selling chic scarves and jewelry around **boulevard St-Michel.** Bookstores of all kinds are where the 5éme really stands out. ▧**Shakespeare & Co.,** 37 r. de la Bûcherie, 5ème, across the Seine from Notre Dame, is run by *bon vivant* George Whitman. Walt's grandson sells a wide, quirky selection of new and used books. (Ⓜ St-Michel. Open daily noon-midnight.) ▧**Om Kashi,** 7 r. de la Montagne Ste-Geneviève, 5ème, has boxes of henna, 300 kinds of incense, and shelves of unusual clothing, scarves, and jewelry. (Ⓜ Maubert-Mutualité. ☎01 46 33 46 07. Open M 2-7pm, Tu-Sa 10am-7pm. Simple, Asian-inspired women's clothing awaits at **Moloko,** 53 r. du Cherche-Midi, 6ème. (Ⓜ Sèvres-Babylone, St-Sulpice, or Rennes. ☎01 45 48 46 79. Dresses from €120. Open Tu-Sa 11am-1pm and 2-7pm. Closed Aug. MC/V.)

FRANCE

⚑ NIGHTLIFE

CAFES AND BARS

LES HALLES AND MARAIS (1ER, 2ÈME, 3ÈME, 4ÈME)

▨ **Le Champmeslé,** 4 r. Chabanais, 1er. ⓜ Pyramides or Quatre Septembre. This welcoming lesbian bar is Paris's oldest and most famous. Mixed crowd in the front, but women-only in back. Beer €4. Mixed drinks €8. Popular cabaret show Th 10pm. Monthly art exhibits. Open M-Th 2pm-2am, F-Sa 2pm-2am.

▨ **L'Apparemment Café,** 18 r. des Coutures St-Gervais, 3ème. ⓜ St-Paul. Beautiful wood and red lounge with games and a chill, young crowd. Late-night meals €10-13. MC/V.

▨ **Amnésia Café,** 42 r. Vieille-du-Temple, 4ème. ⓜ Hôtel-de-Ville. Amnésia's plush sofas draw a largely gay crowd. 1st floor cafe, 2nd floor bar/club. One of the top see-and-be-seen spots in the Marais. Espresso €2. Open daily 10:30am-2am.

Les Etages, 35 r. Vieille-du-Temple, 4ème. ⓜ St-Paul. Set in an 18th-century hotel-turned-bar. 3 floors of dressed-down, nonthreatening 20-somethings. Limited selection of €4 cocktails during Happy Hour (3:30-9pm). Open daily 3:30pm-2am.

La Belle Hortense, 31 r. Vieille-du-Temple, 4ème. ⓜ St-Paul. Walk with traffic along r. de Rivoli and turn right onto r. Vieille-du-Temple. Intellectual scene offers walls of books and mellow music to go with your merlot. Varied wine selection from €3 per glass, €20-36 per bottle. Coffee €1.30-2. Open daily 5pm-2am.

LATIN QUARTER AND ST-GERMAIN (5ÈME, 6ÈME, 7ÈME)

▨ **Le 10 Bar,** 10 r. de l'Odéon, 6ème. ⓜ Odéon. Walk against traffic on bd. St-Germain and make a left on r. de l'Odéon. A classic student hangout, where Parisian youth indulges in philosophical and political discussion. Jukebox plays everything from Edith Piaf to Aretha Franklin. Their sangria (€3) is famous. Open daily 5:30pm-2am.

▨ **Le Caveau des Oubliettes,** 52 r. Galande, 5ème. ⓜ St-Michel. Head away from pl. St-Michel on quai de Montebello and turn right on r. Petit Pont, then left onto r. Galande. The upstairs bar has sod carpeting, ferns, and a real guillotine; the downstairs cellar is an outstanding jazz club; beneath the club, you can romp through the narrow *"caveau des oubliettes"* (cave of the forgotten ones). Beer €4. Rum Cocktail €4. Free jam session M-Th and Su 10:30pm-1:30am. F-Sa concerts €7.50. Open daily 5pm-2am.

Bob Cool, 15 r. des Grands Augustins, 6ème (☎01 46 33 33 77). ⓜ Odéon. Walk up r. de l'Ancienne Comédie, turn right on r. St-André-des-Arts and left onto r. des Grands Augustins. Friendly bar with a reputation as one of the city's best. Music is at the bartender's discretion; it veers all over the spectrum. Wine €4. Open daily 5pm-2am.

Le Crocodile, 6 r. Royer-Collard, 6ème (☎01 43 54 32 37). ⓜ Cluny-La Sorbonne. Walk 7 blocks up bd. St-Michel and turn left onto r. Royer Collard. A lively crowd of local 20-somethings packs into this unassuming bar in the heart of the 6ème. 238 tasty, potent cocktails (€8, before midnight M-Th €6) to choose from. Open M-Sa 10:30pm-4am.

Le Club des Poètes, 30 r. de Bourgogne, 7ème. ⓜ Varenne. A restaurant by day, Le Club is transformed at 10pm each night when a troupe of readers bewitches the audience with poetry from Baudelaire to Ronsard. Lunch *menu* €15. Drinks €9, students €5-7. Open M-Sa noon-2:30pm and 8pm-1am; kitchen open until 10pm.

CHAMPS-ELYSÉES (8ÈME)

▨ **buddha-bar,** 8 r. Boissy d'Anglas, 8ème. ⓜ Madeleine or Concorde. Gorgeous bar and restaurant frequented by the glitterati. Mixed drinks and martinis €12. Weekday lunch *menu* €32. Open M-F noon-3pm and daily 6pm-2am.

House of Live, 124 r. La Boétie, 8ème. Ⓜ Franklin D. Roosevelt. This friendly American bar has free, first-class live music most nights. Snack bar has good ol' Yankee fare. Beer €6. Mixed drinks €6.80. Coffee €2-4. Open daily 9am-5am.

BASTILLE (11ÈME)

▨ **Boteco,** 131 r. Oberkampf, 11ème. Ⓜ Parmentier. A popular Brazilian bar-restaurant with trendy waitstaff, jungle decor, and avant-garde art. Happy Hour 6-9pm (cocktails €4). Open daily 9am-2am.

Le Bar Sans Nom, 49 r. de Lappe, 11ème. Ⓜ Bastille. Seductive lounge famous for its creative cocktails (€8.50). Beer €5-6.20. Shots €6.20. Open M-Sa 7pm-2am.

MONTPARNASSE (13ÈME, 14ÈME)

▨ **L'Entrepôt,** 7-9 r. Francis de Pressensé, 14ème. Ⓜ Pernety. Proving that intellectualism and good times go together: Cinema, restaurant, art gallery, and bar. Concerts F-Sa; usually around €5. Beer €2.50. Su brunch 11:30am-4:30pm (€15). Open M-Sa 9am-midnight or later, Su 11:30am-midnight; kitchen open noon-3pm and 7:30-11:30pm.

La Folie en Tête, 33 r. de la Butte-aux-Cailles, 13ème. Ⓜ Corvisart. The artsy axis mundi of the 13ème. Crowded concerts Sept.-June on Sa nights, usually Afro-Caribbean music (€8). Beer €2.50. Happy Hour 6-8pm. Open M-Sa 6pm-2am.

MONTMARTRE AND PERIPHERAL ARRONDISSEMENTS (17ÈME, 18ÈME, 20ÈME)

Chez Camille, 8 r. Ravignan, 18ème. Ⓜ Abbesses. From the metro, walk down r. de la Vieuville and make a left on r. Drevet and another left on r. Gabrielle, which becomes r. Ravignan. Small, bright yellow bar on the slopes of Montmartre with a terrace overlooking the Invalides dome. Coffee €1.20. Beer €2.50-3.30. Wine from €2.80. Cocktails €6.50. Open M 11am-2pm, Tu-Sa 9am-2am, Su 9am-8pm.

L'Endroit, 67 pl. du Dr. Félix Lobligeois, 17ème. Ⓜ Rome. Follow r. Boursault to r. Legendre, and turn right. Hip, young 17ème-ers come for the snazzy bar and idyllic location in the tree-lined *place.* Beer €5-6. Wine €3.50-4. Cocktails €6. Open daily noon-2am.

Café Flèche d'Or, 102bis r. de Bagnolet, 20ème (☎ 01 43 72 04 23; www.flechedor.com). Cool, intense, and a little rough around the edges. Live music nightly, from reggae to hip-hop to Celtic rock. Art videos, dance classes, and crazy theater on the tracks below the terrace. North African, French, Caribbean, and South American food. Beer €4-5. Cocktails €4-7. Cover €5-6, no cover with dinner. Open daily 10am-2am.

DANCE CLUBS

Les Bains, 7 r. du Bourg l'Abbé, 3ème. Ⓜ Etienne-Marcel or Réaumur-Sébastopol. Look for the long line of people. Ultra-selective, super-crowded, and expensive. Madonna and Mick Jagger have stopped in. Drinks €5-13. Cover Su-Th €13, includes 1 drink; F-Sa €16. Open daily 11pm-5am.

Barrio Latino, 46/48 r. du Faubourg St-Antoine, 12ème. Ⓜ Bastille. Hot Latin dance floor. Sneakers and jeans will get you in, but the clientele prefers to salsa in style. Margarita €11. Open daily noon-2am; DJ arrives 10pm.

Batofar, facing 11 quai François-Mauriac, 13ème. Ⓜ Quai-de-la-Gare. Facing the river, walk right along the quai—Batofar has the red lights. This barge/bar/club has made it big with the electronic music crowd but maintains a friendly vibe. Cover €7-10, usually includes 1 drink. Open Tu-Th 9pm-3am, F-Sa until 4am; hours vary for special events.

Latina Café, 114 av. des Champs-Elysées, 8ème. Ⓜ George-V. Draws one of the largest nightclub crowds on the Champs with an energetic world music mix. Drinks €10-12. Women free M-Th and Su, men's €7 cover includes 1 drink. F-Sa cover €16, includes first 2 drinks. Cafe open daily 7:30pm-2am; club open daily 10am-5am.

FRANCE

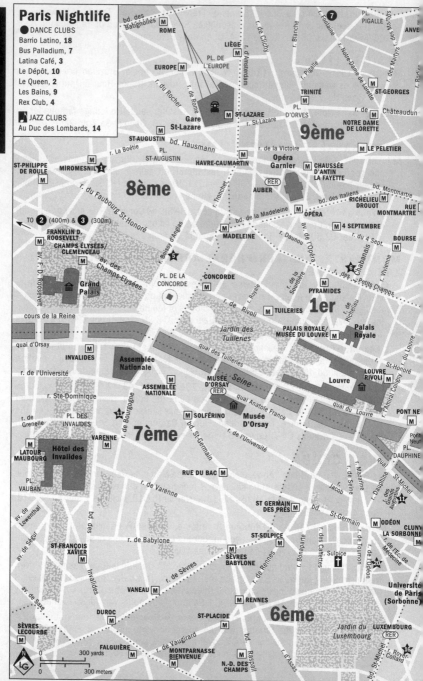

Paris Nightlife

● DANCE CLUBS
Barrio Latino, **18**
Bus Palladium, **7**
Latina Café, **3**
Le Dépôt, **10**
Le Queen, **2**
Les Bains, **9**
Rex Club, **4**

🎵 JAZZ CLUBS
Au Duc des Lombards, **14**

FRANCE

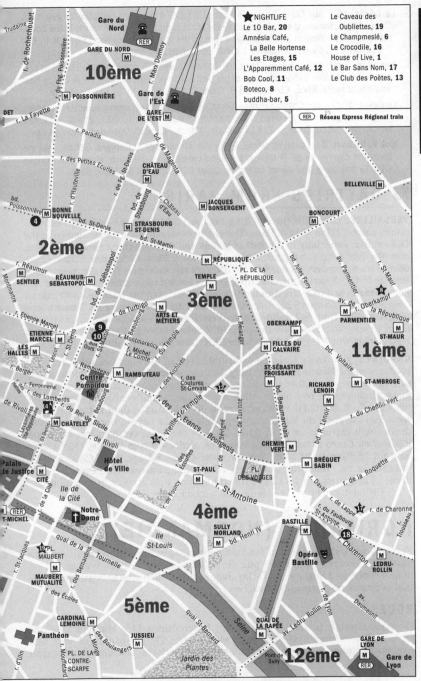

NIGHTLIFE
Le 10 Bar, **20**
Amnésia Café,
 La Belle Hortense
 Les Etages, **15**
L'Apparrement Café, **12**
Bob Cool, **11**
Boteco, **8**
buddha-bar, **5**

Le Caveau des
 Oubliettes, **19**
Le Champmeslé, **6**
Le Crocodile, **16**
House of Live, **1**
Le Bar Sans Nom, **17**
Le Club des Poètes, **13**

RER Réseau Express Régional train

Le Dépôt, 10 r. aux Ours, 3ème. ⓜ Etienne-Marcel. A pleasure complex for gay men. Dance for inspiration, then take your boy toy of the night to one of the rooms in the downstairs labyrinth. Women welcome after 11pm on the upstairs dance floor. Cover M-Th €8, F €12, Sa €14, Su €12; includes 1 drink. Open daily 2pm-8am.

Rex Club, 5 bd. Poissonnière, 2ème. ⓜ Bonne-Nouvelle. A non-selective club that presents very selective DJ line-ups. One of the best sound systems in Paris. Large dance floor and lots of seats. Shots €5. Beer €6-8. Cover €11-13. Open Th-Sa 11:30pm-6am.

Le Queen, 102 av. des Champs-Elysées, 8ème. ⓜ George V. Drag queens, superstars, models, moguls, and go-go boys get down to the mainstream rhythms of a 10,000 gigawatt sound system. All drinks €10. Cover Su-Th €14, includes 1 drink. F-Sa €20. Open daily midnight-dawn.

Bus Palladium, 6 r. Fontaine, 9ème. ⓜ Pigalle, Blanche, or St-Georges. Getting past the bouncers can be tough. A trendy, beautiful crowd rocks this rock 'n' roll club. Drinks €13. Tu free cover and drinks for ladies. Cover €16. Open Tu-Sa 11pm-6am.

▨ DAYTRIPS FROM PARIS

VERSAILLES. Louis XIV, the Sun King, built and held court at Versailles's extraordinary palace, 12km west of Paris. The chateau embodies the extravagance of the Old Regime, especially in the **Hall of Mirrors** and fountain-filled **gardens.** *(Chateau open May-Sept. Tu-Su 9am-6:30pm; Oct.-Apr. Tu-Su 9am-5:30pm. €7.50, after 3:30pm €5.30. Gardens open dawn-dusk; €3, under 18 and after 6pm free. Audio tours €4. 1-2hr. tours meet at entrance D. €4.)* A **shuttle** (round-trip €5) runs behind the palace to the **Grand** and **Petit Trianons,** and to Marie Antoinette's peasant fantasy, the **Hameau.** *(Both Trianons Open Nov.-Mar. Tu-Sa noon-5:30pm; Apr.-Oct. noon-6pm. €5.)* Take any RER C5 **train** beginning with a "V" from ⓜ Invalides to the Versailles Rive Gauche station (30-40min., every 15min., round-trip €5). Buy your RER ticket before getting to the platform; a metro ticket won't get you through the RER turnstiles at Versailles.

CHARTRES. Chartres's stunning cathedral is one of the most beautiful surviving creations of the Middle Ages. Arguably the finest example of early Gothic architecture in Europe, the cathedral retains several of its original 12th-century stained-glass windows; the rest of the windows and the magnificent sculptures on the main portals date from the 13th century, as does the carved floor in the rear of the nave. You can enter the 9th-century **crypt** only from La Crypte, opposite the cathedral's south entrance. *(☎ 02 37 21 75 02. Open daily Easter-Oct. 8am-8pm; Nov.-Easter 8:30am-7pm. Closed to tourists during mass. Free. North Tower open May-Aug. M-Sa 9:30am-noon and 2-5:30pm, Su 2-5:30pm; Sept.-Apr. closes 4:30pm. €4, ages 18-25 €2.50, under 18 and some Su free.)* **Trains** run from Paris's Gare Montparnasse (1hr., every hr., €24, under 26 and groups of 2-4 €18). From the station, walk straight, turn left into the pl. de Châtelet, right on r. Ste-Même, and left on r. Jean Moulin.

NORMANDY (NORMANDIE)

Fertile Normandy is a land of fields, fishing villages, and cathedrals. Invasions have twice secured the region's place in military history: in 1066, William of Normandy conquered England; on D-Day, June 6, 1944, Allied armies began the liberation of France on Normandy's beaches.

ROUEN

However strongly Gustave Flaubert may have criticized his home in *Madame Bovary*, Rouen (pop. 108,000) is no provincial town. The site of Joan of Arc's 1431 execution, Rouen has always entranced artists, writers, and, today, a younger crowd with its splendid Gothic cathedrals and *vieille ville*. The most famous of Rouen's "hundred spires" belong to the ◪**Cathédrale de Notre-Dame**, in pl. de la Cathédrale; one of them, standing at 151m, is the tallest in France. Art lovers may also recognize the cathedral's facade from Monet's celebrated studies of light. (Open M 2-7pm, Tu-Sa 7:45am-7pm, Su 8am-6pm.) Combining the disparate themes of Flaubert, who was raised on the premises, and the history of medicine, the **Musée Flaubert et d'Histoire de la Médicine**, 51 r. de Lecat, down r. de Crosne from pl. de Vieux Marché, houses a large collection of bizarre paraphernalia on both subjects. (☎ 02 35 15 59 95. Open Tu 10am-6pm, W-Sa 10am-noon and 2-6pm. €2.20, ages 18-25 €1.50, under 18 free.) The **Musée des Beaux-Arts**, 26bis r. Jean Lecanuet, down r. Jeanne d'Arc from the train station, houses a worthwhile collection of 16th- to 20th-century art, including works by Monet and Renoir. (☎ 02 35 71 28 40. Open M and W-Su 10am-6pm. €3, ages 18-25 and groups €2, under 18 free.)

Trains leave r. Jeanne d'Arc, on pl. Bernard Tissot, for Lille (3hr., 3 per day, €27) and Paris (1½hr., every hr., €18). Ask for a 25% student discount on train fares. From the station, walk down r. Jeanne d'Arc and turn left on r. du Gros Horloge to reach the **tourist office**, 25 pl. de la Cathédrale. (☎ 02 32 08 32 40; www.rouentourisme.com. Open May-Sept. M-Sa 9am-7pm, Su 9:30am-12:30pm and 2-6pm; Oct.-Apr. M-Sa 9am-6pm, Su 10am-1pm.) **Hôtel Solférino ②**, 51 r. Jean Lecanuet, is between the train station and the center of town. (☎/fax 02 35 71 10 07. Breakfast €5. Singles €25, with shower €28; doubles €28/€32. MC/V.) Cheap eateries crowd **place du Vieux-Marché** and the **Gros Horloge** area. A **Monoprix** supermarket is at 73 r. du Gros Horloge. (Open M-Sa 8:30am-9pm.) **Postal Code:** 76000.

CAEN

Although Allied bombing leveled three-quarters of its buildings during World War II, Caen (pop. 120,000) has skillfully rebuilt itself into a vibrant university town. Its biggest draw is the ◪**Mémorial de Caen**, a powerful, tasteful, and creative exploration of the "failure of peace" and the modern prospects for global harmony. The engaging exhibit unfolds through an artful blend of vintage footage, high-tech audio-visuals, old letters, and paintings. Take bus #2 to Mémorial. (☎ 02 31 06 06 44. Open daily mid-July to late Aug. 9am-8pm; low season reduced hours. Closed first 2 weeks in Jan. Last entry 1¼hr. before closing. €10.50-17; students, seniors, and ages 10-18 €14-16.) Flanking the ruined chateau, **Abbaye-aux-Hommes**, off r. Guillaume le Conquérant, has functioned as a boys' school and a shelter for the town's inhabitants during World War II, and is now the Hôtel de Ville. (☎ 02 31 30 42 81. Open to tourists only during 1½-2hr. tours; daily at 9:30am, 11am, and 2:30pm. €2, students €1, under 18 free.) The adjacent **Eglise St-Etienne** contains William the Conqueror's tomb—now home only to the monarch's right femur following pillaging during the Wars of Religion. (Open M-Sa 8am-5:30pm, Su 9:30am-12:30pm.)

Trains run to: Paris (2¼hr., 12 per day, €26.20); Rennes (3hr., 2 per day, €27.30); Rouen (2hr., 5 per day, €19.40); and Tours (3½hr., 2 per day, €28.40). **Bus Verts** (☎ 08 10 21 42 14) covers the beaches and the rest of Normandy. The **tourist office**, pl. St-Pierre, offers free maps. (Open July-Aug. M-Sa 9am-7pm, Su 10am-1pm and 2-5pm; June and Sept. M-Sa 9:30am-6:30pm, Su 10am-1pm.) The **Auberge de Jeunesse (HI), Foyer Robert Reme ①**, 68bis rue Eustache-Restout, has four-person, single-sex rooms with shower and stove, but is far from town. Take bus #5 (dir.: Fleury Cimitière) to Lycée Fresnel. (☎ 02 31 52 19 96; fax 02 31 84 29 49. Sheets €2.50. Beds €10. Open June-Sept. HI members only. Cash only.) Ethnic restaurants, *crêperies*, and *brasseries* are near the chateau and between **Eglise St-Pierre** and **Eglise St-Jean**. Get groceries at **Monoprix**, 45 bd. du Maréchal Leclerc. (Open M-Th and Sa 9am-8:30pm, F 9am-9pm.) At night Caen's old streets come to life; **rue de Bras, rue des Croisiers**, and **rue St-Pierre** are especially popular. **Postal Code:** 14016.

FRANCE

BAYEUX

Relatively unharmed by WWII, beautiful Bayeux (pop. 15,000) is an ideal base for exploring the nearby D-Day beaches (see below). However, visitors should not miss its 900-year-old ▓**Tapisserie de Bayeux,** 70m of embroidery that relates the tale of William the Conqueror's invasion of England. The tapestry is displayed in the **Centre Guillaume le Conquérant,** on r. de Nesmond. (Open daily May-Aug. 9am-7pm; low season reduced hours. €7.40, students €3.) Nearby is the original home of the tapestry, the extraordinary **Cathédrale Notre-Dame.** (Open daily July-Sept. 8:30am-7pm; Oct.-June 8:30am-6pm. Free.) The **Musée de la Bataille de Normandie,** bd. Fabian Ware, recounts the D-Day landing and subsequent 76-day battle. (Open daily May to mid-Sept. 9:30am-6:30pm; mid-Sept. to Apr. 10am-12:30pm and 2-6pm. Closed last 2 weeks of Jan. €5.50, students €2.60.)

Trains (☎02 31 92 80 50) leave pl. de la Gare for Caen (20min., 15 per day, €5.70) and Paris (2½hr., 12 per day, €28.80). To reach the **tourist office,** pont St-Jean, turn left on bd. Sadi-Carnot, bear right, follow signs to the *centre ville,* and take r. Larcher to r. St-Martin. (☎02 31 51 28 28; www.bayeux-tourism.com. Open June-Aug. M-Sa 9am-7pm, Su 9am-1pm and 2-6pm; Apr.-May and Sept.-Oct. daily 9:30am-12:30pm and 2-6pm; Nov.-Mar. reduced hours.) From the tourist office, turn right onto r. St-Martin, follow through several name changes, and turn left onto r. Général de Dais for the ▓**Family Home/Auberge de Jeunesse (HI) ❷,** 39 r. Général de Dais. (☎02 31 92 15 22; www.fuaj.org. Dorms €18. Nonmembers add €2. Cash only.) Get groceries at **Champion,** on bd. d'Eindhoven. **Postal Code:** 14400.

D-DAY BEACHES

On June 6, 1944, over one million Allied soldiers invaded the beaches of Normandy in the first of a chain of events that liberated France and led to the downfall of Nazi Europe. Today, reminders of that first devastating battle can be seen in somber gravestones, remnants of German bunkers, and the pockmarked landscape.

The Americans first landed at **Utah Beach,** near Ste-Marie du Mont, where they spearheaded the western flank of the invasion. The **Musée du Débarquement** shows how 836,000 troops, 220,000 vehicles, and 725,000 tons of equipment came ashore. (☎02 33 71 53 35. Open daily June-Sept. 9:30am-7pm; Oct.-May reduced hours. €6.) The most difficult landing was at **Pointe du Hoc,** the most heavily fortified of all the coastline strongholds. Here, 225 US Rangers scaled 30m cliffs with ropes and hooks under a rain of gunfire and grenades. The 150 men who made it to the top neutralized a key German position and defended it for two days; only 90 survived. The Pointe is considered a military cemetery because so many casualties remain crushed beneath collapsed sections of the 5m-thick concrete bunkers. Often referred to as "bloody Omaha," **Omaha Beach,** next to Colleville-sur-Mer and east of the Pointe du Hoc, is perhaps the most famous of the beaches. Nothing went right here on D-Day: scouts failed to detect a German presence, and aerial and naval bombardment of the fortifications were ineffective due to foggy conditions. Nearby, 9387 graves stretch across the American Cemetery. (Open daily 9am-5pm.) Just east of Omaha and 10km north of Bayeux is **Arromanches,** a small town at the center of **Gold Beach,** where the British built the artificial Port Winston in one day to provide shelter while the Allies unloaded supplies. The **Arromanches 360° Cinéma** combines images of modern Normandy with those of D-Day. Turn left on r. de la Batterie from the museum and climb the steps. (Open daily June-Aug. 9:40am-6:40pm; Sept.-May reduced hours. Closed Jan. €4, students €3.50.)

Bayeux makes a beautiful base for D-Day beach exploration, but reaching the beaches can be difficult without a car. Some sites are accessible from Caen and Bayeux with **Bus Verts.** (☎08 10 21 42 14; www.busverts14.fr. All buses leave between 9:20 and 9:40am. Caen line runs daily June to mid-Sept. From Bayeux, buses go to Omaha Beach Tu, Th, and Sa; to Utah Beach M, W, and F. €14.; ask about the special "D-Day" line.) A day pass (€17) takes you to four major sites.

MONT-ST-MICHEL

Regarded as a paradise in the Middle Ages, the fortified island of Mont-St-Michel (pop. 42) is a dazzling labyrinth of stone arches, spires, and stairways that climb up to the **abbey**. Adjacent to the abbey church, **La Merveille** (the Marvel), a 13th-century Gothic monastery, encloses a seemingly endless web of corridors and chambers. (Open daily May-Aug. 9am-7pm; Sept.-Apr. 9:30am-6pm. €8, ages 18-25 €5.) The Mont is most stunning at night, but plan ahead; since there's no late-night public transport off the island, consider viewing Mont-St-Michel as a daytrip via a Courriers Bretons **bus,** 104 r. Couesnon in Pontorson (☎02 99 19 70 70), from Rennes (1½hr., 1-6 per day, €11) or St-Malo (1½hr., 2-4 per day, €9). Hotels on Mont-St-Michel are expensive (from €50 a night). The **Pontorson tourist office,** pl. de l'Eglise, helps visitors find affordable accommodations (☎02 33 60 20 65; mont.st.michel.pontorson@wanadoo.fr. Open July-Aug. M-F 9am-noon and 2-6pm, Sa 10am-noon and 3-6pm, Su 10am-noon; Sept.-June reduced hours.) The cheapest beds are at the **Centre Dugusclin (HI)** ❶, r. du Général Patton, Pontorson. (☎/fax 02 33 60 18 65. Dorms €8.50, nonmembers €9.50. Cash only.) **Postal Code:** 50170.

BRITTANY (BRETAGNE)

Lined with spectacular beaches, wild headlands, and cliffs gnawed by the sea into long crags and inlets, Brittany fiercely maintains its Celtic heritage despite Paris's age-old efforts at assimilation. Britons fled Anglo-Saxon invaders for this beautiful peninsula between the 5th and 7th centuries; over the following 800 years, they defended their independence from the Franks, Normans, French, and English. Even today, traditional headdresses appear at folk festivals, and lilting *Brezhoneg* (Breton) is spoken at pubs and ports in the western part of the province.

RENNES

The cultural capital of Brittany, Rennes (pop 212,000), also has a well-deserved reputation as the party capital of northwestern France. Ethnic eateries, colorful nightspots, and crowds of university students lend interest to the picturesque cobblestones and half-timbered houses of the *vieille ville*. At the end of r. St-Guillaume, turn left onto r. de la Monnaie to visit the **Cathédrale St-Pierre,** founded in 1787 on the former site of a pagan temple, a Roman church, and a Gothic cathedral. The center of attention is its intricate altarpiece depicting the life of the Virgin. (Open daily 9:30am-noon and 3-6pm.) Across the street, the **Portes Mordelaises** are the former entrances to the city and the last vestiges of its medieval walls. The **Musée des Beaux-Arts,** 20 quai Emile Zola, houses a small, varied collection, including a few works by Picasso and Gauguin. (Open M and W-Su 10am-noon and 2-6pm. €4, students €2, under 18 free.) Across the river and up r. Gambetta is the lush **Jardin du Thabor,** ranked among the most beautiful gardens in France. Concerts are often held here; a gallery on the northern side exhibits local artwork. (Open June-Sept. 7:30am-8:30pm.) With bars and clubs that draw students from Paris and beyond, Rennes is a partygoer's mecca. Look for action in **place Ste-Anne, place St-Michel,** and the radiating streets. ▩**Le Zing,** 5 pl. des Lices, packs two floors and four bars with the young and beautiful. (Open daily from 3pm, busy midnight-2am.) ▩**Delicatessen,** 7 allée Rallier du Baty, around the corner from pl. St-Michel in a former prison, has swapped jailhouse bars for dance cages to become one of Rennes's hottest clubs. (Cover €8-14. Open Tu-Sa midnight-5am.)

    Trains leave pl. de la Gare for: Caen (3hr., 8 per day, €28); Paris (2hr., 1 per hr., €48); St-Malo (1hr., 15 per day, €12); and Tours (2½-3hr., every 2-3hr., €31) via Le Mans. **Buses** go from the train station to Angers (2½-3hr., 3-4 per day, €16) and Mont-St-Michel (1½hr., 3-5 per day, €12). To get from the train station to the **tourist**

office, 11 r. St-Yves, take av. Jean Janvier to quai Chateaubriand. Turn left, walk through pl. de la République, turn right on r. George Dottin, and right again on r. St-Yves. (☎02 99 67 11 11; www.tourisme-rennes.com. Open Apr.-Sept. M-Sa 9am-7pm; Su 11am-6pm; Oct.-Mar. reduced hours.) Access the **Internet** at **Neurogame, ❶** 2 r. de Dinan. (☎02 99 65 53 85. €3 per hr. Open M 2pm-1am, Tu-Th noon-1am, F noon-3am, Sa noon-5am, Su 2-10pm.) The **Auberge de Jeunesse (HI) ❶,** 10-12 Canal St-Martin, has simple rooms, a kitchen, a TV room, and a cafeteria. Take the metro (dir.: Kennedy) to Ste-Anne. Follow r. de St-Malo downhill; the hostel will be on your right after the bridge. (☎02 99 33 22 33; rennes@fuaj.org. Breakfast included. Dorms €14. AmEx/MC/V.) In general, the best food is on the outskirts of the city center, around **rue St-Georges.** A **Champion** supermarket is in a mall on r. d'Isly, near the train station. (Open M-Sa 9am-8pm.) ■**Café Breton ❷,** 14 r. Nantaise, serves fresh Breton cuisine at reasonable prices. (☎02 99 30 74 95. *Plats* €7.30. Open M and Sa noon-3:30pm, Tu-F noon-3pm and 7-11pm.) **Postal Code:** 35032.

ST-MALO

St-Malo (pop. 52,000) combines sandy beaches with a walled *vieille ville* that holds numerous *crêperies,* boutiques, and cafes. Though 80% of the town was destroyed in 1944, careful reconstruction makes it nearly impossible to distinguish the old from the new. East of the walled city is **Grande Plage,** the most popular beach. The more secluded **Plage de Bon Secours** lies to the west and features the curious **Piscine de Bon-Secours,** three cement walls that hold in a pool's worth of warm salt water even when the tide recedes. The best view of St-Malo is from its **ramparts;** the view from the north side reveals a sea speckled with tiny islands.

 Trains run from sq. Sean Coquelin to: Dinan (1hr., 4 per day, €8); Paris (5hr., 10 per day, €64); and Rennes (1hr., 7-15 per day, €11). From the station, cross bd. de la République and follow av. Louis Martin to esplanade St-Vincent for the **tourist office,** near the *vieille ville's* entrance. (☎02 99 56 64 48; www.saint-malo-tourisme.com. Open July-Aug. M-Sa 9am-7:30pm, Su 10am-6pm; Sept.-June reduced hours.) The 248-bed ■**Auberge de Jeunesse (HI) ❷,** 37 av. du Révérend Père Umbricht, is near the beach. From the train station, take bus #5 (dir.: Paramé or Davier) or bus #1 (dir.: Rothéneuf) to Auberge de Jeunesse. (☎02 99 40 29 80; www.centrevarangot.com. Reception M-F 8:30am-10pm, Sa-Su 8:45am-10pm. Dorms €16.) The best eateries lie close to the center of the *vieille ville.* Try **La Brigantine ❷,** 13 r. de Dinan. (☎02 99 56 82 82. *Galettes* €2-7. Crepes €1.50-6. Open M and Th-F 11am-3pm and 6:30-8pm, Sa-Su noon-11pm. MC/V.) **Marché Plus,** 9 r. St-Vincent, is near the Porte St-Vincent entrance to the city walls. (Open M-Sa 7am-9pm, Su 9am-1pm.) **Postal Code:** 35400.

DINAN

Perhaps the best-preserved medieval town in Brittany, Dinan's (pop. 10,000) cobblestone streets are lined with 15th-century houses inhabited by traditional artisans. On the ramparts, the 13th-century **Porte du Guichet** is the entrance to the **Château de Dinan,** also known as the **Tour de la Duchesse Anne,** which has served as a military stronghold, a residence, and a prison. Included in the ticket is the 15th-century **Tour de Coëtquen,** which houses a collection of funerary ornaments and medieval sculptures. (Open daily June-Sept. 10am-6:30pm; Oct.-May reduced hours. €4, ages 12-18 €1.55.) On the ramparts behind the chateau are the **Jardins "des Petits Diables" du Val Cocherel,** which hold huge bird cages and a chessboard scaled for life-sized pieces. (Open daily 8am-7:30pm.) A long, picturesque walk down the steep r. du Petit Fort will lead you to the ■**Maison d'Artiste de la Grande Vigne,** 103 r. du Quai. This former home of painter Yvonne Jean-Haffen (1895-1993) is a work of art, with exhibitions of her work, murals adorning the walls, and a beautiful hillside garden. (☎02 96 87 90 80. Open daily July-Aug. 10:30am-6pm; Sept.-June reduced hours. €2.60, students and ages 12-18 €1.65.)

Trains run from pl. du 11 Novembre 1918 to Paris (3hr., 8 per day, €54) and Rennes (1hr., 8 per day, €12). To get from the station to the **tourist office,** 9 r. du Château, bear left across pl. 11 Novembre onto r. Carnot, turn right on r. Thiers, turn left into the *vieille ville,* and bear right onto r. du Marchix, which becomes r. de la Ferronnerie; it will be on your right. (☎02 96 87 69 76; www.dinan-tourisme.com. Open mid-June to mid-Sept. M-Sa 9am-7pm, Su 10am-12:30pm and 2:30-6pm; low season reduced hours.) Access the **Internet** at **Aerospace Cybercafe,** 9 r. de la Chaux, off r. de l'Horloge. (☎02 96 87 14 85. Open Tu-Sa 10am-12:30pm and 2-7pm. €1.50 per 15min.) To reach the ▨**Auberge de Jeunesse (HI) ❶,** in an old water mill in Vallée de la Fontaine-des-Eaux, turn left from the station and cross the tracks, then turn right, and follow the tracks downhill for 1km before turning right again; it will be on your right. (☎02 96 39 10 83; fax 02 96 39 10 62. Reception July-Aug. 8am-noon and 5-9pm, Sept.-June reduced hours. Dorms €9.30. MC/V.) **Monoprix** supermarket is at 7 pl. du Marchix. (Open M-Sa 9am-7:30pm.) **Rue de la Cordonnerie** and **place des Merciers** have inexpensive *brasseries.* **Postal Code:** 22100.

BREST

Brest (pop. 156,000) was transformed into a somber wasteland in 1944 by Allied bombers driving out the occupying German flotilla. However, the city has begun to show signs of life with a number of pleasant cafes, a busy shopping district, a summer concert series, and a massive aquarium. Brest's **chateau,** the world's oldest active military institution, was the only building in town to survive WWII. It houses the **Musée de la Marine,** which highlights local maritime history. (Open Apr. to mid-Sept. daily 10am-6:30pm; mid-Sept. to mid-Dec. and Jan.-Mar. M and W-Su 10am-noon and 2-6pm. €4.60, students €3.) **Océanopolis,** at port de Plaisance, has tropical, temperate, and polar pavilions and a coral reef accessible by a glass elevator. From the Liberty terminal, take bus #7 (dir.: Port de Plaisance; M-Sa every 30min. until 7:30pm; €1) to Océanopolis. (☎02 98 34 40 40. Open Apr.-Aug. daily 9am-6pm; Sept.-Mar. Tu-Sa 10am-5pm, Su 10am-6pm. €15.)

Trains (☎02 98 31 51 72) leave pl. du 19*ème* Régiment d'Infanterie for: Paris (€64); Quimper (30min., 5 per day, €14); and Rennes (1½hr., 15 per day, €30). From the station, av. Georges Clémenceau leads to the **tourist office,** at pl. de la Liberté. (☎02 98 44 24 96. Open mid-June to mid-Sept. M-Sa 9:30am-7pm, Su 10am-noon; low season M-Sa 9:30am-12:30pm and 2-6pm.) Access the **Internet** at **@cces.cibles,** 31 av. Georges Clémenceau. (☎02 98 46 76 10. €2.50 per hr. Open M-Sa 11am-1am, Su 2-11pm.) For the luxurious ▨**Auberge de Jeunesse (HI) ❶,** 5 r. de Kerbriant, 4km away near Océanopolis, take bus #7 (dir.: Port de Plaisance) from opposite the station to its final stop; with your back to the bus stop, go left toward the beach, take an immediate left, and follow signs to the hostel. (☎02 98 41 90 41. Breakfast included. Reception July-Aug. M-F 5pm-midnight, Sa-Su 6pm-midnight; low season reduced hours. Dorms €13. MC/V.) One end of **rue de Siam,** near the port, has a variety of restaurants. At the other end is **Le Mont Liban ❸,** 8 pl. de la Liberté, where patrons sample exotic Middle Eastern delicacies. (☎02 98 80 12 76. *Menus* €7.50-13.70. Open M-F noon-2pm and 7:30-10pm, Sa noon-2pm. MC/V.) A **Marché Plus** supermarket is just off r. de Siam at 59 r. Louis Pasteur. (Open M-Sa 7am-9pm, Su 9am-1pm.) **Postal Code:** 29285.

QUIMPER

With a central waterway crisscrossed by flower-adorned pedestrian footbridges, Quimper (kam-PAIR; pop. 63,000) has irrepressible charm to fuel its fierce Breton pride. At ▨**Faïenceries de Quimper HB-Henriot,** r. Haute, guides lead visitors through the studios where potters and painters design each piece of the town's world-renowned earthenware. (☎02 98 90 09 36; www.hb-henriot.com. Open July-Aug. M-Sa 9-11:15am and 1:30-4:45pm; Sept.-June closed Sa. Tours every hr. €3.) The magnificent dual spires of the **Cathédrale St-Corentin,** built between the 13th and

15th centuries, mark the entrance to the old quarter from quai St-Corentin. Inside, the choir is curved to mimic the angle of Jesus's drooping head during his crucifixion. (Open May-Oct. M-Sa 9:30am-noon and 1:30-6:30pm, Su 1:30-6:30pm; Nov.-Apr. M-Sa 9am-noon and 1:30-6pm, Su 1:30-6pm.) At night, head to the cafes near the cathedral, or to ◼**Molly Malone's,** an offbeat Irish pub at pl. St-Mathieu, on r. Falkirk. (Beamish stout €3.10, pint €5.40. Open daily 11am-1am.)

Trains go to Brest (1½hr., 4 per day, €14) and Rennes (2¼hr., 10 per day, €30). From the train station, go right onto av. de la Gare and follow it, with the river on your right, until it becomes bd. Dupleix and leads to pl. de la Résistance. The **tourist office,** 7 r. de la Déesse, will be on your left. (☎02 98 53 04 05; www.quimper-tourisme.com. Open July-Aug. M-Sa 9am-7pm; Sept.-June reduced hours.) To reach the comfortable **Centre Hébergement de Quimper (HI)** ❶, 6 av. des Oiseaux, take bus #1 (dir.: Kermoysan; last bus 7:30pm) from pl. de la Résistance to Chaptal; the hostel will be up the street on your left. (☎02 98 64 97 97; quimper@fuaj.org. Breakfast €3.30. Sheets €3.10. Dorms €9. HI members only. Cash only.) The Les Halles **markets,** off r. Kéréon on r. St-François, have produce, seafood, meat, and cheese. (Open Apr.-Oct. M 7am-8pm, Tu-Th 5:30am-8pm, F-Sa 5am-8pm, Su 7:30am-1pm; Nov.-Mar. opens 30min. later.) **Postal Code:** 29000.

LOIRE VALLEY (VAL DE LOIRE)

The Loire, France's longest and most celebrated river, meanders toward the Atlantic through a valley overflowing with fertile soil and gentle vineyards that produce some of France's best wines. It's hardly surprising that a string of French (and English) kings chose to station themselves in opulent chateaux by these waters rather than in the commotion of their capital cities.

▐ TRANSPORTATION

Faced with such widespread grandeur, many travelers plan overly ambitious itineraries—two chateaux a day is a reasonable goal. The city of Tours is the region's best **rail** hub. However, train schedules are often inconvenient and many chateaux aren't accessible by train. **Biking** is the best way to explore the region. Many stations distribute the invaluable *Châteaux pour Train et Vélo* booklet with train schedules and **bike** and **car** rental information.

ORLÉANS

A pleasant gateway from Paris into the Loire, Orléans (pop. 117,000) clings tightly to its historical connection to Joan of Arc, who marched triumphantly down **Rue de Bourgogne** in 1429 after liberating the city from a seven-month British siege. Most of Orléans's highlights are near **Place Ste-Croix.** With towering Gothic buttresses and stained-glass windows that depict Joan's story, the ◼**Cathédrale Sainte-Croix,** pl. Ste-Croix, is Orléans's crown jewel. (Open daily July-Aug. 9:15am-7pm, Sept.-June reduced hours.) The **Musée des Beaux-Arts,** 1 r. Ferdinand Rabier, has a fine collection of French, Italian, and Flemish works. (☎02 38 79 21 83; museeba@ville-orleans.fr. Open Tu and Th-Sa 9.30am-noon and 1:30-6pm, W 9:30am-noon and 1:30-8pm, Su 2-6:30pm. €3, students €1.50, under 16 free.)

Trains arrive at the Gare d'Orléans on pl. Albert I from: Blois (30min., 15 per day, €8.60); Paris (1¼hr., 4 per hr., €15); and Tours (1hr., 2 per hr., €15). To get from the station to the **tourist office,** 2 pl. de l'Etape, walk straight onto r. de la République until you reach pl. du Martroi, then take r. d'Escures to pl. de l'Etape. (☎02 38 24 05 05; www.ville-orleans.fr. Open May-Sept. Tu-Sa 9:30am-1pm and 2-6pm; Oct.-Apr. reduced hours.) To reach the ◼**Auberge de Jeunesse (HI)** ❶, 1 bd. de la Motte Sanguin, take bus RS (dir.: Rosette) or SY (dir.: Concyr/La Bolière) from pl. Jeanne d'Arc to Pont Bourgogne, then follow bd. de la Motte; the hostel is on the right. (☎02 38 53 60 06. Breakfast €3.50. Reception M-F 8am-7pm, Sa-Su 9-11am and 5-7pm. Dorms €9. Cash only.) You'll find groceries at **Carrefour,** in the back of the mall at pl. Jeanne d'Arc. (Open M-Sa 8:30am-9pm.) **Rue de Bourgogne** and **rue Ste-Catherine** have cheap eateries and a vibrant bar scene at night. **Postal Code:** 45000.

BLOIS

Blois (pop. 50,000) is one of the Loire's most popular and historical cities. Once home to monarchs Louis XII and François I, Blois's gold-trimmed **chateau** was the Versailles of the late 15th and early 16th centuries. Housed within are excellent museums: the **Musée des Beaux-Arts,** featuring a 16th- to 19th-century portrait gallery; the **Musée d'Archéologie,** showcasing locally-excavated glass and ceramics; and the **Musée Lapidaire,** exhibiting sculpted pieces from nearby chateaux. (☎02 54 90 33 33. Open daily Apr.-Sept. 9am-6pm; Jan.-Mar. and Oct.-Dec. 9am-12:30pm and 2-5:30pm. €6.50, students under 25 €4.50.) The **▧Musée de la Résistance, de la Déportation et de la Libération,** 1 pl. de la Grève, is a powerful memorial to the French Holocaust, packed with photos, newspaper clippings, and narratives of Resistance fighters. (☎02 54 56 07 02. Open M-F 9am-noon and 2-6pm, Sa 2-6pm. €3, students €1.) At night, Blois lights up. Move from the cafes of **Place de la Résistance** to the hip combination *discothèque,* lounge bar, and karaoke joint **▧Z 64,** 6 r. Mal. de Tassigny. (☎02 54 74 27 76. Cocktails €5-8. Open Tu-Su 8:30pm-4am.)

Trains leave pl. de la Gare for: Orléans (30min., 14 per day, €8.40); Paris (1¾hr., 8 per day, €20) via Orléans; and Tours (1hr., 13 per day, €8.20). Transports Loir-et-Cher (TLC; ☎02 54 58 55 44) sends **buses** from the station to nearby chateaux (45min., 2 per day; €10, children €8). Or, rent a **bike** from **Amster Cycles,** 7 r. de Desfray, one block from the train station, for the hour-long ride to the valley. (☎02 54 56 07 73. €13 per day. Open M-Sa 9:15am-1pm and 2-6:30pm, Su 10am-1:30pm and 3-6:15pm. MC/V.) The **tourist office** is in pl. du Château. (☎02 54 90 41 41; www.loiredeschateaux.com. Open May-Sept. M and Su 10am-7pm, Tu-Sa 9am-7pm; Oct.-Apr. reduced hours.) **▧Hôtel du Bellay ❷,** 12 r. des Minimes, is at the top of porte Chartraine, 2min. above the city center. This family-run establishment offers spotless, comfortable rooms with rustic decor. (☎02 54 78 23 62; http://hoteldubellay.free.fr. Breakfast €4.50. Closed Jan. 5-25. Singles and doubles €24-30; triples €58; quads €60. MC/V.) To reach rooms with views of the Loire at

AROUND THE LOIRE IN 80 MINUTES

It may take a lot of patience and time to see all the chateaux in the Loire Valley, but it's certainly possible for those up to the challenge. Some determined chateau-crawlers spend hours traveling by bike or car, but more intrepid souls can save themselves the long haul and visit the chateaux via hot air balloon. From the air, all parts of the estates can be fully appreciated, from the gardens' exquisite patterns to the buildings' turrets and facades.

Total excursion time is 3½hr., and actual flight time approximates 1hr. Balloons take off in the early morning, a few minutes after sunrise, and in the evening before sunset. As they prepare for departure, patrons savor the anticipation (and a complimentary champagne toast) before embarking on their once-in-a-lifetime adventure.

For the most fearless travelers, the romance of a hot air balloon may seem too tame. Luckily, some companies also offer helicopter tours of the valley or opportunities to skydive onto the lawns of Chambord or Cheverny.

For hot air balloons, contact France Montgolfières, 24 r. Nationale, 41400 Montrichard. ☎02 54 32 20 48; www.franceballoons.com. €250. For helicopters, contact Jet Systems, Aérodrome d'Amboise, 37150 Dierre. ☎02 47 30 20 21; www.jet-systems.fr. €57-229.

Le Pavillon ❷, 2 av. Wilson, take bus line 3A from the station or walk 20min. on foot. (☎02 54 74 23 27; fax 02 54 74 03 36. Breakfast €6.50. Singles and doubles €20-40; quads €50. MC/V.) Fragrant *pâtisseries* line **rue Denis Papin**, while **rue St-Lubin, place Poids du Roi**, and **place de la Résistance** have more options. An **Intermarché** supermarket is at 16 av. Gambetta. (Open M-Sa 9am-7pm.) **Postal Code:** 41000.

CHAMBORD AND CHEVERNY

Built between 1519 and 1545 to satisfy François I's egomania, **Chambord** is the largest and most imposing of the Loire chateaux. With 440 rooms, 365 fireplaces, and 83 staircases, the castle could accommodate the entire royal court—up to 10,000 people. To cement his claim, François stamped 200 of his trademark stone salamanders throughout this "hunting lodge," which also boasts a spectacular double-helix staircase designed by Leonardo da Vinci. (☎02 54 50 40 00. Open daily Apr.-Sept. 9am-6:15pm; Oct.-Mar. reduced hours. €7, ages 18-25 €4.50, under 18 free.) Take TLC **bus** #2 from Blois (45min., 2 per day, €10) or **bike** south from Blois on D956 for 2-3km, and then turn left on D33 (1hr.).

Cheverny has been privately owned since 1634 by the Hurault family, whose members have served as financiers and officers to the kings of France. The chateau's magnificent furnishings include elegant tapestries and delicate Delft vases. Fans of Hergé's *Tintin* books may recognize Cheverny's Renaissance facade as the inspiration for Marlinspike, Captain Haddock's mansion. The **kennels** hold nearly 90 mixed English-Poitevin hounds who stalk stags in hunting expeditions. (☎02 54 79 96 29. Open daily July-Aug. 9:15am-6:45pm; Apr.-June and early Sept. 9:15am-6:15pm; low season reduced hours. €6.10, students €4.10.) Cheverny is 45min. south of Blois by **bike** and on the route of TLC **bus** #2 (see above). Travelers to Chambord or Cheverny should plan to stay in **Blois** (see above).

AMBOISE

Amboise (pop. 12,000) is guarded by the parapets of the 15th-century **chateau** that six security-minded French kings called home. In the **Logis du Roi**, intricate 16th-century Gothic chairs stand over 2m tall to prevent attacks from behind. The jewel of the grounds is the **Chapelle St-Hubert,** the final resting place of **Leonardo da Vinci.** (☎02 47 57 00 98. Open daily July-Aug. 9am-7pm; Sept.-June reduced hours. €7.50, students €6.50.) Four hundred meters away is ■**Clos Lucé** manor, where da Vinci spent the last three years of his life. Its main attraction is a collection of 40 machines created from da Vinci's visionary designs and built with materials contemporaneous to his lifetime. (☎02 47 57 62 88. Open daily July-Aug. 9am-8pm; Apr.-June and Sept.-Oct. 9am-7pm; Nov.-Mar. reduced hours. €11, students €9.)

Trains leave bd. Gambetta for: Blois (20min., 20 per day, €6); Orléans (1hr., 18 per day, €13); Paris (2½hr., 7 per day, €24); and Tours (20min., 11 per day, €5). To reach the **tourist office** on quai du Général de Gaulle, take a left outside the train station, following r. Jules-Ferry, and cross both bridges past the residential Ile d'Or. (☎02 47 57 09 28; www.amboise-valdeloire.com. Open July-Aug. M-Sa 9am-8pm, Su 10am-6pm; Sept.-June reduced hours.) The **Centre International de Séjour Charles Péguy (HI) ❶**, on Ile d'Or, sits on an island in the Loire. Some rooms have views of the chateau. (☎02 47 30 60 90; www.ucrif.asso.fr. Breakfast €3. Sheets €3.30. Reception M-F 3-7pm. Dorms €8.80.) Buy groceries at **Marché Plus,** 5 quai du Général de Gaulle. (Open M-Sa 7am-9pm, Su 9am-1pm.) **Postal Code:** 35400.

TOURS

Balzac's birthplace and home to 30,000 students, Tours (pop. 253,000) is also a convenient base for nearby Loire chateaux. The **Cathédrale St-Gatien,** on r. Jules Simon, was first erected in the 4th century; it now combines solid Romanesque columns with delicate Gothic carvings, two Renaissance spires, and an intricate facade.

(Cathedral open daily 9am-7pm. Free. Cloister open Easter-Sept. daily 9:30am-12:30pm and 2-6pm; Oct.-Mar. W-Su 9:30am-12:30pm and 2-5pm. €2.50.) The ▨**Musée du Gemmail**, 7 r. du Murier, showcases the brilliantly-colored glass mosaics that are unique to Tours. (Open Apr.-Nov. Tu-Su 10am-noon and 2-6:30pm. €5, students €3.10.) At night, **place Plumereau** (or just pl. Plum) is the place to be, with cheerful students sipping drinks and chatting at cafes and bars.

Trains leave pl. du Général Leclerc for Bordeaux (2½hr., 9 per day, €37) and Paris (2¼hr., 14 per day, €27). To reach the **tourist office**, 78-82 r. Bernard Palissy, from the station, walk through pl. du Général Leclerc, cross bd. Heurteloup, and take a right. (☎02 47 70 37 37; www.ligeris.com. Open mid-Apr. to mid-Oct. M-Sa 8:30am-7pm, Su 10am-12:30pm and 2:30-5pm; mid-Oct. to mid-Apr. reduced hours.) Access the **Internet** at **Cyber Gate**, 11 r. de Président Merville. (☎02 47 05 95 94. €1 for 20min. Open M 1-10pm, Tu-Sa 11am-midnight, Su 2-10pm.) ▨**Hôtel Regina ❷**, 2 r. Pimbert, has owners who make travelers feel like family. (☎02 47 05 25 36; fax 02 47 66 08 72. Breakfast €4.30. Singles and doubles €20-24; triples €23-36. MC/V.) The **Foyer des Jeunes Travailleurs ❷**, 16 r. Bernard Palissy, houses workers, students, and backpackers in the summer. (☎02 47 60 51 51. Singles €17; doubles €31.) Try **place Plumereau** and **rue Colbert** for great restaurants, cafes, and bars. ▨**La Souris Gourmande ❷**, 100 r. Colbert, serves regional cheese dishes and fondues. (Open Tu-Sa noon-2pm and 7-10:30pm.) **Postal Code:** 37000.

CHENONCEAU AND LOCHES

▨**Chenonceau**, sometimes called the *chateau des dames* (castle of the ladies), owes its beauty to the series of women who designed it: first a 16th-century tax collector's wife; then Henri II's lover, Diane de Poitiers; and finally Henri's widowed wife, Catherine de Médici. The part of the chateau bridging the Cher River marked the border between occupied and Vichy France during WWII. (☎02 47 23 90 07. Open daily mid-Mar. to mid-Sept. 9am-7pm; low season reduced hours. €8, students €6.50.) **Trains** from Tours roll into the station in front of the castle. (30min., 8 per day, €5.10). Fil Vert **buses** also run from Amboise (20min., 2 per day, €1.05) and Tours (1¼hr., 2 per day, €2.10).

The chateau of **Loches** is surrounded by a walled medieval town that merits a visit in itself. The chateau's oldest structures are the 11th century keep and watch towers to the north, which were converted into a state prison under Louis XI. The three-story **tower**, whose floors have fallen out, offers fantastic panoramic views of the village below. The extravagant **Logis Royal** (Royal Lodge) honors the famous ladies who held court here, including Charles VII's lover Agnès Sorel, the first officially-declared Mistress of the King of France. (☎02 47 59 01 32. Open daily Apr.-Sept. 9am-7pm; Oct.-Mar. 9:30am-5pm. Dungeon or *Logis Royal* €5, students €3.) **Trains** and **buses** run from Tours to Loches (50 min., 13 per day, €7). Nearby accommodations are in **Tours** (above).

ANGERS

From illustrious aristocratic origins, Angers (pop. 160,000) has grown into a sophisticated modern city. Behind the massive stone walls of the **Château d'Angers**, on pl. Kennedy, the medieval Dukes of Anjou ruled the surrounding area, as well as a certain island across the Channel. The 13th-century chateau remains a well-preserved haven of medieval charm in a city otherwise teeming with shops and sights. Inside the chateau is the 14th-century ▨ **Tapisserie de l'Apocalypse**, the world's largest tapestry. (Open daily May to mid-Sept. 9:30am-7pm; mid-Sept. to Apr. 10am-5:30pm. €6.10, students €4.10.) Angers's other woven masterpiece is the 1930 **Chant du Monde** (Song of the World), in the **Musée Jean Lurçat**, 4 bd. Arago. (☎02 41 24 18 45. Open mid-June to mid-Sept. daily 10am-7pm; mid-Sept. to mid-June Tu-Su 10am-noon and 2-6pm. €4, students €3.) Creator of the famous liqueur since 1849, the **Musée Cointreau** offers tours of the factory, followed by free tastings. Take bus #7 from the train station to Cointreau. (Open daily July-Aug. 10:30am-6:30pm; Sept.-June reduced hours. €5.50.)

From r. de la Gare, **trains** leave for Paris (2-4hr., 15 per day, €42.20-53.80) and Tours (1hr., 10 per day, €14). **Buses** run from pl. de la République to Rennes (3hr., 2 per day, €16). To get from the station to the **tourist office**, at pl. Kennedy, exit straight onto r. de la Gare, turn right at pl. de la Visitation on r. Targot, and turn left on bd. du Roi-René; it's on the right, across from the chateau. (☎ 02 41 23 50 00; www.angers-tourisme.com. Open May-Sept. M-Sa 9am-7pm; Su 10am-6pm; Oct.-Apr. reduced hours.) Access the **Internet** on one of the 45 computers at **LAN Station**, 41 r. Nationale. (☎ 02 43 27 94 56. €2 per hour. Open M-Sa noon-midnight, Su 2-11pm.) **Hôtel de l'Univers ❸**, 2, pl. de la Gare, near the train station, has comfortable rooms. (☎ 02 41 88 43 58; fax 41 86 97 28. Breakfast €5.60. Singles and doubles €26-52. AmEx/MC/V.) Cheap food is abundant along **rue St-Laud** and **rue St-Aubin**. Grab groceries in **Galeries Lafayette**, at r. d'Alsace and pl. du Ralliement. (Open M-Sa 9:30am-7:30pm.) **Postal Code:** 49052.

PÉRIGORD AND AQUITAINE

Périgord's green countryside is splashed with yellow sunflowers, white chalk cliffs, and plates of black truffles. First settled 150,000 years ago, the area around Les Eyzies-de-Tayac has produced more Stone-Age artifacts than anywhere else on Earth, while the Prehistoric painted caves of Lascaux are the most extensive in the world. Farther south, Aquitaine grows its grapes in the world-famous vineyards of the Médoc that surround Bordeaux.

PÉRIGUEUX

Rich with tradition and gourmet cuisine, the lovely old quarters of Périgueux (pop. 65,000) preserve architecture from Gallo-Roman times. The towering steeple and five massive Byzantine cupolas of the **Cathédrale St-Front** dominate the city from above the Isle River. Fifteen-hundred years of rebuilding, restoration, rethinking, and revision have produced the largest cathedral in southwestern France. (Open daily 8am-noon and 2:30-7pm.) Just down r. St-Front, the **Musée du Périgord**, 22 cours Tourny, houses one of France's most important collections of prehistoric artifacts, including a set of 2m mammoth tusks. (☎ 05 53 06 40 70. Open Apr.-Sept. M and W-F 10:30am-5:30pm, Sa-Su 1-6pm; Oct.-Mar. reduced hours. €4, students €2, under 18 free.) The **Musée Gallo-Romain**, 20 r. du 26ème Régiment d'Infanterie, has built an intricate walkway over the excavated ruins of the *Domus de Vésone*, once the home of a wealthy Roman merchant. (☎ 05 53 53 00 92. Open daily July-Aug. 10am-7pm; low season reduced hours; closed Jan. €5.50, under 12 €3.50. Tours in French daily July-Aug. €2. Audio tours in English €2.)

Trains leave r. Denis Papin for: Bordeaux (1½hr., 12 per day, €16.30); Lyon (6-8hr., 2 per day, €46.80); Paris (4-6hr., 12 per day, €45.90); and Toulouse (4hr., 8 per day, €37). The **tourist office**, 26 pl. Francheville, has free maps. From the station, turn right on r. Denis Papin, bear left on r. des Mobiles-de-Coulmiers, which becomes r. du Président Wilson, and take the next right after the Monoprix; it will be on the left. (☎ 05 53 53 10 63; www.ville-perigueux.fr. Open mid-June to mid-Sept. M-Sa 9am-6pm, Su 10am-1pm and 2-6pm; mid-Sept. to mid-June M-Sa 9am-1pm and 2-6pm, Su 10am-1pm and 2-6pm.) Across from the train station, **Hôtel des Voyageurs ❶**, 26 r. Denis Papin, has clean, basic rooms. (☎/fax 05 53 53 17 44. Breakfast €3.50. Singles €14; doubles €16, with shower €19.) ◪**Au Bien Bon ❸**, 15 r. Aubergerie, serves stellar regional eats. (☎ 05 53 09 69 91. Lunch *menus* €10-14, *plats* €9-14. Open Tu-F noon-2pm and 7:30-10pm, Sa noon-2pm.) **Monoprix** supermarket is on pl. de la République. (Open M-Sa 8:30am-8pm.) **Postal Code:** 24070.

FRANCE

SARLAT

The medieval *vieille ville* of Sarlat (pop. 10,800) is the best base for exploring the **Caves of Lascaux** (see below), but it has also been the focus of tourist and movie cameras; Gérard Depardieu's *Cyrano de Bergerac* and *Manon des Sources* were both filmed here. **Trains** go to Bordeaux (2½hr., 4 per day, €21) and Périgueux (3hr., 2 per day, €13). Trans-Périgord **buses** run from pl. Pasteur to Périgueux (1½hr., 1 per day, €11). To reach the **tourist office**, on r. Tourny in the Ancien Evêché, follow av. de la Gare downhill and turn right onto av. Thiers, which becomes r. de la République. Bear right on r. Lakanal and left onto r. de la Liberté; the office is next to the cathedral. (☎05 53 31 45 45; www.ot-sarlat-perigord.fr. Open Apr.-Oct. M-Sa 9am-7pm, Su 10am-noon and 2-6pm; Nov.-Mar. M-Sa 9am-noon and 2-7pm.) Sarlat's tiny, rustic **Auberge de Jeunesse ❶**, 77 av. de Selves, is 40min. from the train station, but only 10min. from the *vieille ville*. From the *vieille ville*, go straight on r. de la République, which becomes av. Gambetta, and bear left onto av. de Selves. (☎05 53 59 47 59. Reception 6-9pm. Open mid-Mar. to Nov. Reserve ahead. Dorms €10, after first night €9; camping €6/€5. Cash only.) **Champion** supermarket is near the hostel on rte. de Montignac; follow av. de Selves away from the town center. (Open M-Sa 9am-7:45pm. MC/V.) **Postal Code:** 24200.

CAVES OF THE VÉZÈRES VALLEY

The most spectacular cave paintings ever found line the **Caves of Lascaux,** near the town of **Montignac**, 25km north of Sarlat. Discovered in 1940 by a couple of teenagers, they were closed to the public in 1963—the breath of millions of visitors had fostered algae and micro-stalactites that ravaged the paintings. **Lascaux II** replicates the original cave in the same pigments used 17,000 years ago. Although they may lack ancient awe and mystery, the new caves—filled with paintings of 5m-tall bulls, horses, and bison—manage to inspire a wonder all their own. The ticket office (☎05 53 05 65 65) shares a building with Montignac's tourist office (☎05 53 51 95 03), on pl. Bertram-de-Born. (Ticket office open 9am until sold-out. Reserve tickets 1-2 weeks ahead. €8.) The **train** station nearest Montignac is at Le Lardin, 10km away. From there, you can call a **taxi** (☎05 53 50 86 61). During the academic year (Sept.-June), CFTA (☎05 55 86 07 07) runs **buses** from Périgueux and Sarlat; call or check at the stations for times and prices. July and August see fewer buses. The best place to sleep is in **Sarlat** (above).

At the **Grotte de Font-de-Gaume**, 1km east of **Les Eyzies-de-Tayac** on D47, amazing 15,000-year-old friezes are still open for viewing. (☎05 53 06 86 00; www.leseyzies.com/grottes-ornees. Open mid-May to mid-Sept. M-F and Su 9am-5:30pm; mid-Sept. to mid-May reduced hours. Tours available in English. Reserve 2-4 weeks in advance. €6.10, ages 18-25 €4.10, under 18 free.) The **tourist office** is on pl. de la Mairie. (☎05 53 06 97 05; www.leseyzies.com. Open July-Aug. M-Sa 9am-8pm, Su 10am-noon and 2-6pm; Sept.-June reduced hours.) From Les Eyzies-de-Tayac, **trains** go to Périgueux (30min., 5 per day, €6.30) and Sarlat (1hr., 3 per day, €7.50) via Le Buisson. Rooms tend to be expensive—consider staying in **Périgueux** (p. 380). The Demaison family runs an exceptional ☀**Chambre d'Hôte ❸**, rte. de Sarlat, 3min. outside town. From the train station, follow signs to Sarlat; the house is past the laundromat on the right. (☎05 53 06 91 43. Breakfast €5. Reservations required. Singles and doubles €25-36; triples and quads €48.)

BORDEAUX

Enveloped by emerald vineyards, Bordeaux (pop. 280,000) toasts the ruby wine that made it famous. A mecca for wine connoisseurs, this university town also has vibrant nightlife, a world-class opera house, and some of the best food in France.

FRANCE

▐▐▌ TRANSPORTATION AND PRACTICAL INFORMATION. Trains leave Gare St-Jean, r. Charles Domercq, for: Lyon (8-10hr., 4 per day, €56.70); Nice (9-10hr., 2 per day, €75); Paris (3hr., 15-25 TGV per day, €61); and Toulouse (2-3hr., 11 per day, €29). From the train station, take tramway line B to pl. Gambetta (€1.30) and walk toward the Monument des Girondins to reach the **tourist office**, 12 cours du 30 juillet, which arranges winery tours and books rooms. (☎05 56 00 66 00; www.bordeaux-tourisme.com. Open July-Aug. M-Sa 9am-7:30pm, Su 9:30am-6:30pm; Sept.-June reduced hours.) **Postal Code:** 33065.

▐▐▌ ACCOMMODATIONS AND FOOD. A favorite among backpackers, ▧**Hôtel Studio ❷**, 26 r. Huguerie, has clean, newly remodeled rooms with phone, bathroom, and cable TV. (☎05 56 48 00 14; www.hotel-bordeaux.com. Breakfast €4. Internet access €2.25 per hr. Singles €16-24; doubles €20-29. MC/V.) **Hôtel de la Boétie ❷**, 4 r. de la Boétie, is run by the same family and offers similar amenities Check-in around the corner at Hôtel Bristol, 4 r. Bouffard. (☎ 05 56 81 76 68; fax 05 56 81 24 72. Breakfast €4. Singles and doubles €24; triples €31. AmEx/MC/V.) The *Bordelais* take their food as seriously as their wine. Hunt around **rue St-Remi** and **place St-Pierre** for regional specialties: oysters, *foie gras*, and beef braised in wine sauce. **La Casuccia ❷**, 49 r. St-Rémi, serves classic Italian food. (☎05 56 51 17 70. Open Tu-Su noon-3pm and 7-11:30pm. MC/V.) **Le Valentino ❸**, 6 r. des Lauriers, is a reasonably priced oasis in an expensive quarter of Bordeaux. (☎05 56 48 11 56. Entrees €8-15. Open daily noon-2pm and 7-11pm. AmEx/MC/V.) **Auchan** supermarket is at the Centre Meriadeck on r. Claude Bonnier. (Open M-Sa 8:30am-10pm.)

◨ ▐▌ SIGHTS AND ENTERTAINMENT. Nearly nine centuries after its consecration, the **Cathédrale St-André**, in pl. Pey-Berland, which hosted the weddings of Louis VII and Louis XIII, is still the centerpiece of Gothic Bordeaux. Its bell tower, the **Tour Pey-Berland,** juts 50m into the sky. (Cathedral open July-Aug. M 10-11:30am and 2-6:30pm, Tu-F 7:30-11:30am and 2-6:30pm, Sa 9-11:30am and 2-7pm, Su 9am-12:30pm and 2:30-8:30pm; Sept.-June closed Su afternoon. €4, under 25 €2.50. Tower open June-Sept. daily 10am-1:15pm and 2-6pm; Oct.-May Tu-Su 10am-12:30pm and 2-5:30pm. €4.60, under 25 €3.10.) Nearby, the **Musée des Beaux Arts,** 20 cours d'Albret, contains works by masters such as Carvaggio, Matisse, and Picasso. The permanent collection is held in the two buildings that frame the Hôtel de Ville; the temporary exhibits are across the street. (Open M and W-Su 11am-6pm. Permanent collection €4, joint pass for permanent and temporary collections €5.50. Students, under 18, and 1st Su of every month free.) Bordeaux's opera house, the **Grand Théâtre**, conceals a breathtakingly intricate interior behind an austere Neoclassical facade, and houses operas, concerts, and plays. (☎05 56 00 66 00; www.opera-bordeaux.com. Tickets €5-100, 50% discount for students and under 25. Open for tours Tu-Sa 11am-6pm. Tours €5, students €4.)

Bordeaux boasts a seemingly endless list of lively bars and clubs, and a gay scene rivaled only by Paris's. For an overview, check out *Clubs and Concerts* at the tourist office (free). **Place de la Victoire** and **place Gambetta** are year-round hot spots. **St-Michel**, where locals gather at cafe tables from around 6pm until midnight, has a more mellow atmosphere. **El Bodegon**, on pl. de la Victoire, has theme nights and giveaways on weekends. (Beer €2.50. Open M-Sa 7am-2am, Su 2pm-2am.) Covered in flashy lights and mirrors, the gay bar **BHV**, 4 r. de l'Hôtel de Ville, is almost always full. (Beer €3.50. Theme nights W. Open daily 6pm-2am.)

▐▌ DAYTRIP FROM BORDEAUX: ST-EMILION. Just 35km northeast of Bordeaux, St-Emilion (pop. 2850) is home to viticulturists who have been refining their technique since Roman times. Today, they gently crush hectares of grapes to produce 23 million liters of wine every year. Vineyards aside, the medieval village is a pleasure to visit, and its **Eglise Monolithe** is the largest subterranean church in Europe. The **tourist office,** pl. des Créneaux, near the church tower, rents **bikes** (€14 per day) and offers guided tours (€9) of the local chateaux. (☎05 57 55 28 28; www.saint-emilion-tourisme.com. Open daily July-Aug. 9:30am-8pm; Sept.-June reduced hours.) **Trains** run from Bordeaux to St-Emilion (35min., 4 per day, €7.20). The only afternoon train back to Bordeaux leaves at 6:26pm—plan accordingly.

THE PAYS BASQUE AND GASCONY

South of Aquitaine, the forests recede and the mountains of Gascony begin, shielded from the Atlantic by the Basque Country. While the Gascons have long considered themselves French, the Basques still struggle to maintain their identity; some separatists see themselves as an independent people rather than a part of France or Spain. Today, people come to Gascony to be healed: Millions of believers descend on Lourdes in search of miracles, while thousands of others undergo natural treatments in the hot springs of the Pyrenees.

BAYONNE

The pace of life in Bayonne (pop. 42,000) has not changed for centuries. Locals rise early to set up lively markets on the banks of the Nive and shop in the *vieille ville.* In the afternoon, they retreat indoors behind exposed wooden beams and colorful shutters. The ■**Musée Bonnat,** 5 r. Jacques Laffitte, showcases works by Bayonnais painter Léon Bonnat alongside others by Degas, Goya, Rembrandt, and Reubens. (Open May-Oct. M and W-Su 10am-6:30pm; Nov.-Apr. reduced hours. €5.50, students €3, under 18 free.) The 13th-century **Cathédrale Ste-Marie** endured fires and destruction during the Revolution, but renovations have erased all traces of decay. (Open M-Sa 7:30am-noon and 3-7pm, Su 3:30-8pm. Free.)

Trains depart from pl. de la Gare for: Bordeaux (2hr., 9 per day, €24); San Sebastián, Spain (1½hr., 5-6 per day, €8); and Toulouse (4hr., 5 per day, €35). Local STAB **buses** (☎05 59 59 04 61) depart from the Hôtel de Ville for Biarritz (#1, 2, and 6; last bus M-Sa 8pm, Su 7pm; €1.20). From the train station, take the middle fork onto pl. de la République, veer right over pont St Esprit, pass through pl. Réduit, cross pont Mayou, and turn right on r. Bernède which becomes av. Bonnat. The **tourist office,** pl. des Basques, is on the left. (☎05 59 46 01 46; www.bayonne-tourisme.com. Open July-Aug. M-Sa 9am-7pm, Su 10am-1pm; Sept.-June M-F 9am-6:30pm, Sa 10am-6pm.) The ■**Hôtel Paris-Madrid ❷,** pl. de la Gare, has large rooms and knowledgeable, English-speaking proprietors. (☎05 59 55 13 98. Breakfast €4. Reception 6am-12:30am. Singles and doubles €17-22, with shower €26, with bath €29-45; triples and quads with bath €41-45. MC/V.) A **Monoprix** supermarket is at 8 r. Orbe. (Open M-Sa 8:30am-7:30pm.) **Postal Code:** 64100.

BIARRITZ ☎05

Once a playground for 19th-century aristocrats, Biarritz (pop. 29,000) can still make a dent in the wallet. Luckily, its sparkling **beaches** are accessible to budget travelers as well as the rich and famous. In summer, thousands of perfect bodies soak up the sun at **Grande Plage,** while thrill-seeking surfers ride its waves. **Plage Miramar,** just to the north, is less crowded. Walk left along av. de l'Impératrice to reach the **Pointe St-Martin** for a fantastic view of the water. **Trains** (☎05 59 50 83 07) leave from Biarritz-la-Négresse, 3km from town, for Bordeaux (2hr., 7 per day, €26) and Paris (5hr., 5 TGV per day, €67). The **tourist office,** 1 sq. d'Ixelles, finds accommodations. (☎05 59 22 37 10; www.biarritz.fr. Open daily July-Aug. 8am-8pm; Sept.-June reduced hours.) Take bus #2 (dir.: Gare SNCF) to Francis Jammes to reach the ◪**Auberge de Jeunesse (HI) ②**, 8 r. de Chiquito de Cambo, which has a friendly staff and a lakefront location. (☎05 59 41 76 00; aubergejeune.biarritz@wanadoo.fr. Internet access €0.50 for 10min. Dorms €17-18, €14-15 each additional night. AmEx/MC/V.) **Rue Mazagran** and **Place Clemenceau** have cheap crepes and sandwiches. **Shopi** supermarket, 2 r. du Centre, is off r. Gambetta. (Open M-Sa 9am-8pm, Su 9am-12:30pm.) **Postal Code:** 64200.

LOURDES

In 1858, 14-year-old Bernadette Soubirous saw the first of 18 visions of the Virgin Mary in the Massabielle grotto in Lourdes (pop. 16,300). Today, five million people from across the globe make the pilgrimage each year. Follow av. de la Gare, turn left on bd. de la Grotte, and follow it to the right and across the River Gave to reach the **Grotte de Massabielle,** where visitors whisper prayers, receive blessings, and carry home water from the spring where Bernadette washed her face. (No shorts or tank tops. Open daily 5am-midnight.) The **Basilique du Rosaire** and the **Upper Basilica** were built double-decker style above the grotto. The **Basilique St-Pius X,** a huge concrete echo chamber designed to resemble an upturned ship, is hidden underground. (Basilicas open daily Easter-Oct. 6am-7pm; Nov.-Easter 8am-6pm.) **Processions** depart daily from the grotto at 5 and 9pm.

Trains leave 33 av. de la Gare for: Bayonne (2hr., 5 per day, €18.40); Bordeaux (3hr., 7 per day, €30-31); Paris (7-9hr., 5 TGV per day, €89); and Toulouse (2½hr., 8 per day, €22). To reach the **tourist office,** on pl. Peyramale, turn right onto av. de la Gare, bear left onto av. Maransin, cross the bridge above bd. du Lapacca, and climb uphill. (☎05 62 42 77 40; www.lourdes-infotourisme.com. Open May-Oct. M-Sa 9am-7pm; Nov.-Apr. reduced hours.) To get to the centrally located **Hôtel Arbizon ①,** 37 r. des Petits Fossés, follow av. Helios away from the station, bear right under the bridge on bd. du Lapacca, take the next left uphill onto r. Basse, and turn right onto r. des Petits Fossés. (☎/fax 05 62 94 29 36. Breakfast €4. Singles €14, with shower €15; doubles €19/€20; triples €24. Cash only.) The cheapest eateries are near the tourist office. Stock up at the **market** at Les Halles, pl. du Champ Commun. (Open daily 8am-1pm, every other Th until 5pm.) **Postal Code:** 65100.

CAUTERETS

Nestled in a narrow, breathtaking valley on the edge of the **Parc National des Pyrénées Occidentales** is tiny, sleepy Cauterets (pop. 1300). Cauterets's sulfuric hot springs (*thermes*) have long been instruments of healing; for more information, contact **Thermes de César,** av. Docteur Domer. (☎05 62 92 51 60. Open M-Sa 7-11:30am and 2:30-8pm.) Today, most visitors come to ski and hike. Multiple half-day **hikes** depart from a trailhead behind the Thermes de César; for more hiking info and advice, head to Parc National des Pyrenees (see below).

SNCF **buses** run from pl. de la Gare to Lourdes (1hr., 8 per day, €6.20). Rent **bikes** at Le Grenier, 4 av. du Mamelon Vert. (☎05 62 92 55 71. Full day €22-53, half-day €16-39. Open daily 8am-1pm and 3-8pm.) The **tourist office,** on pl. Foch, has free maps of ski and hiking trails. (☎05 62 92 50 50; www.cauterets.com. Open July-Aug. M-Sa 9am-12:30pm and 2-7pm, Su 9am-12:30pm and 3-6pm; Sept.-June reduced hours.) ◪**Gite d'Etape UCJG ①,** av. du Docteur Domer, has a great location and a friendly staff. From the Parc National office, cross the street and turn left uphill on a footpath underneath the funicular depot. (☎05 62 92 52 95. Open June 15-Sept. 15. Dorms €8; **camping** and tent rental €6.50.) **Postal Code:** 65110.

THE PYRENEES

The **Parc National des Pyrénées Occidentales** shelters thousands of endangered species in its snow-capped mountains and lush valleys. Touch base with the friendly, helpful **Parc National Office,** Maison du Parc, pl. de la Gare, in Cauterets, before braving the wilderness. The staff has maps (€7-9) and info on the park, the 14 **hiking** trails that begin and end in Cauterets, and various **ski** paths. (☎05 62 92 52 56; www.parc-pyrenees.com. Open June to mid-Sept. daily 9:30am-noon and 3-7pm; mid-Sept. to May M-Tu and F-Sa 9:30am-12:30pm and 3-6pm, Th 3-6pm.) The park's trails are designed for a wide range of skill levels. From Cauterets, the **GR10**, which intersects most other hikes in the area, winds through Luz-St-Saveur, over the mountain, and then on to Gavarnie, another day's trek up the valley; this is also known as the **circuit de Gavarnie.** One of the most spectacular trails follows the GR10 to the turquoise **Lac de Gaube** and then to the end of the glacial valley (2hr. past the lake), where you can spend the night at the **Refuge des Oulettes ❶.** (☎05 62 92 62 97. Open June-Sept. Dorms €14.) Other *gîtes* (shelters) in the park, usually located in towns along the GR10, cost about €11 per night. Reserve at least two days ahead, especially in July and August, when the mountains teem with hikers.

LANGUEDOC-ROUSSILLON

An immense region called Occitania once stretched from the Rhône Valley to the foothills of the Pyrenees. It was eventually integrated into France, the local *langue d'oc* dialect faded, and in 1539, the northern *langue d'oïl*, a predecessor of modern French, became official. Latent nationalism lingers, however, in vibrant cities like Toulouse—many locals speak Catalan, a relative of *langue d'oc*, and feel a stronger cultural connection with Barcelona than Paris.

TOULOUSE

Sassy, headstrong Toulouse—*la ville en rose* (city in pink)—provides a change of pace from surrounding villages with stately rose-colored architecture and a vibrant twenty-something scene. A rebellious city since the 12th century, Toulouse (pop. 390,600) remains a center of independent thought, pushing the frontiers of knowledge as a university town and the capital of France's aerospace industry.

🖪🖬 TRANSPORTATION AND PRACTICAL INFORMATION. Trains leave Gare Matabiau, 64 bd. Pierre Sémard, for: Bordeaux (2-3hr., 14 per day, €28); Lyon (6½hr., 3-4 per day, €51); Marseille (4½hr., 8 per day, €41); and Paris (8-9hr., 4 per day, €60). Eurolines, in the bus station, 68-70 bd. Pierre Sémard, runs **buses** to major European cities. (☎05 61 26 40 04; www.eurolines.fr. Open M-F 9:30am-6:30pm, Sa 9:30am-5pm.) To get from the station to the **tourist office**, r. Lafayette, in pl. Charles de Gaulle, turn left along the canal, turn right on allée Jean Jaurès, bear right around pl. Wilson, and turn right on r. Lafayette; it's in a park near r. d'Alsace-Lorraine. You can also take the metro to Capitole. (☎05 61 11 02 22; www.ot-toulouse.fr. Open June-Sept. M-Sa 9am-7pm, Su 10am-1pm and 2-6:15pm; Oct.-May reduced hours.) Surf the **Internet** at **Nethouse**, 1 r. des 3 Renards. (☎05 61 21 98 42. €3 per hr. Open M-Sa 9am-11pm, Su noon-6pm.) **Postal Code:** 31000.

🖪🖸 ACCOMMODATIONS AND FOOD. While it lacks a youth hostel, Toulouse has a number of well-located budget hotels. To reach the spacious **🖪Hôtel des Arts ❷,** 1bis r. Cantegril, off r. des Arts, take the metro (dir.: Basso Cambo) to pl. Esquirol. Walk away from the river down r. de Metz; r. des Arts is on the left. (☎05 61 23 36 21; fax 05 61 12 22 37. Breakfast €5. Singles €23-26, with shower €29-31; doubles €28-34/€32-38. MC/V.) **Hôtel Beauséjour ❷,** 4 r. Caffarelli, near the station, has bright rooms with new beds at the lowest prices in Toulouse. (☎/fax 05 61 62 77 59. Breakfast €4. Shower €1. Singles and doubles €20, with bath €27; twins €28/€33. MC/V.) Take the metro to Arène, then hop on bus #64 (dir.: Colo-

FRANCE

miers) and ask for "St-Martin-du-Touch" to camp at **La Bouriette ❶**, 199 chemin de Tournefeuille, 5km outside Toulouse along N124. (☎ 05 61 49 64 46. €8.50 per person.) On **rue du Taur,** in the student quarter, cheap eateries serve meals for €5.50-10. **Markets** line **place des Carmes, place Victor Hugo,** and **boulevard de Strasbourg.** (Open Tu-Su 6am-1pm.) There's a **Monoprix** supermarket at 39 r. Alsace-Lorraine (Open M-Sa 9am-10pm.) A cross between a restaurant, an art gallery, and a small theater, **Le Grand Rideau ❸**, 75 r. du Taur, serves a three-course lunch (€9.10) and an evening *menu* (€16) with excellent regional dishes. (☎ 05 61 23 90 19. Open M noon-2pm, Tu-F noon-2pm and 7:30-10pm, Sa 7:30-10pm. Cash only.) **Jour de Fête ❶**, 43 r. du Taur, is a relaxed *brasserie* with brick walls and international music. (☎ 05 61 23 36 48. *Plat du jour* €6.70. Open daily 11am-midnight. Cash only.)

◧ ⬆ SIGHTS AND ENTERTAINMENT. The **Capitole,** the brick palace next door to the tourist office, is Toulouse's most prominent monument. The building was once home to the bourgeois *capitouls*, who unofficially ruled the city for many years. (Open daily 9am-7pm. Free.) R. du Taur leads to the **Basilique St-Sernin,** the longest Romanesque structure in the world; its **crypt** houses ecclesiastical relics from the time of Charlemagne. (Church open July-Sept. M-Sa 8:30am-6:30pm, Su 8:30am-7:30pm; Oct.-June reduced hours. Free. Crypt open July-Sept. M-Sa 10am-6pm, Su 11:30-6pm; Oct.-June reduced hours. €2.) From pl. du Capitole, take a right on r. Romiguières, and turn left on r. Lakanal to get to a 13th-century southern Gothic **church,** where the remains of St. Thomas Aquinas are housed in an elevated, underlit tomb. (Open daily 9am-7pm.) Next door, the **Réflectoire des Jacobins** has rotating exhibitions of archaeological artifacts and modern art. (Open daily 10am-7pm. €5.) The huge **Musée des Augustins,** 21 r. de Metz, displays Romanesque and Gothic sculptures, including 15 snickering gargoyles, in a renovated monastery. (☎ 05 61 22 21 82. Open M and Th-Su 10am-6pm, W 10am-9pm. €2.40, students free.) The restored **Hôtel d'Assézat,** at pl. d'Assézat on r. de Metz, houses the **Fondation Bemberg,** a modest collection of Bonnards, Gauguins, and Pissarros. (Open Tu and F-Su 10am-12:30pm and 1:30-6pm, Th 10am-12:30pm and 1:30-9pm. €4.60, students €2.75.) Toulouse's nightlife is liveliest when students are in town. Numerous cafes flank **place St-Georges** and **place du Capitole,** and late-night bars line **rue de la Colombette** and **rue des Filatiers.** For cheap drinks and a lively atmosphere, try **Café Populaire,** 9 r. de la Colombette, where you can polish off 13 bottles of beer for only €19, €13 on Mondays. (☎ 05 61 63 07 00. Open M-F 9pm-2am, Sa 2pm-4am.) The best dancing is at **Bodega-Bodega,** 1 r. Gabriel Péri, just off bd. Lazare Carnot. (Cover from €6 Th-Sa 10pm-2am. Open M-F and Su 7pm-2am, Sa 7pm-6am. MC/V.)

CARCASSONNE

Walking over the drawbridge and through the stone portals into the medieval city of Carcassonne (pop. 46,000) is like stepping into a fairy tale, where the 1st-century ramparts still seem to resound with the clang of armor and steel. It's almost enough to make you forget that the only battles now are between camera-wielding visitors vying for space on the narrow streets. Built as a palace in the 12th century, the **Château Comtal,** 1 r. Viollet-le-Duc, became a citadel after the royal takeover in 1226. (Open daily Apr.-Sept. 9:30am-6pm; Oct.-Mar. 9:30am-5pm. €6.10, under 25 €4.10.) Converted into a fortress after the city was razed during the Hundred Years' War in 1355, the Gothic **Cathédrale St-Michel,** r. Voltaire, in the bastide St-Louis, still has fortifications on its southern side. (Open M-Sa 7am-noon and 2-7pm, Su 9:30am-noon.) The evening is the best time to experience the *cité* without the crowds. Although nightlife is limited, several bars and cafes along **boulevard Omer Sarraut** and **place Verdun** are open until midnight. Locals dance the night away at **La Bulle,** 115 r. Barbacane. (Cover €9, includes 1 drink. Open F-Sa until dawn.)

Trains depart behind Jardin St-Chenier for: Marseille (3hr., every 2hr., €36); Nice (6hr., 5 per day, €52); Nîmes (2hr., 9 per day, €25); and Toulouse (50min., 20 per day, €14). Shops, hotels, the cathedral, and the train station are in the **bastide St-Louis,** once known as the *basse ville* (lower city). Free **shuttles** run from sq. Gambetta to the citadel gates. From the station, walk down av. de Maréchal Joffre, which becomes r. Clemenceau; after pl. Carnot, turn left on r. de Verdun to reach the **tourist office,** 28 r. de Verdun. (☎04 68 10 24 30; www.carcassonne-tourisme.com. Open daily July-Aug. 9am-7pm; Sept.-June 9am-6pm.) The ▧**Auberge de Jeunesse (HI) ❶,** r. de Vicomte Trencavel, has a fabulous location in the *cité,* with great views of the castle late at night. (☎04 68 25 23 16; carcassonne@fuaj.org. Internet €3 per hr. Dorms €15.50. Nonmembers add €3. MC/V.) Restaurants on **rue du Plô** have *menus* under €10. Regional specialties at ▧**Les Fontaines du Soleil ❷,** 32 r. du Plô, include *cassoulet,* a stew of white beans, herbs, and meat. (☎04 68 47 87 06. Open daily 11:30am-3pm and 7-10:30pm. MC/V.) **Postal Code:** 11000.

MONTPELLIER

Amateur theatrical performances and live music bring every street corner to life in Montpellier (pop. 230,000), the most lighthearted city in southern France. The gigantic **Musée Fabre,** 39 bd. Bonne Nouvelle, is undergoing renovations until 2006; it has one of the largest collections of 14th- to 17th-century painting outside of Paris, with works by Delacroix, Ingres, Poussin, and others. Temporary exhibits are on display at the **pavilion** on the opposite side of Esplanade Charles de Gaulle from the museum. (Hours and ticket prices vary; call in advance.) Bd. Henri IV leads to the **Jardin des Plantes,** France's first botanical garden. (Open June-Sept. M-Sa noon-8pm; Oct.-May noon-6pm. Free.) The liveliest bars are in **place Jean-Jaurès.** The popular ▧**Barberousse "Bar A Shooters,"** 6 r. Boussairolles, just off pl. de la Comédie, sells 73 flavors of rum. (Rum €2. Beer from €3. Open M-Sa 7pm-2am.) **Fizz,** 4 r. Cauzit, is a hot live-music dance club packed with students. (Cover F-Sa €8. Open July-Aug. Tu-Su midnight-4am; Sept.-June midnight-5am.) Gay nightlife is prominent in Montpellier, especially around **place du Marché aux Fleurs.**

Trains leave pl. Auguste Gibert for Avignon (1hr., 12 per day, €14); Marseille (1¾hr., 12 per day, €22); Nice (4hr., 3 per day, €41); Paris (3½hr., 12 per day, €84); and Toulouse (2½hr., 13 per day, €28). From the train station, r. Maguelone leads to **place de la Comédie.** The **tourist office,** 30 allée Jean de Lattre de Tassigny, is to the right. (☎04 67 60 60 60; www.ot-montpellier.fr. Open July-Aug. M-F 9am-7:30pm, Sa 10am-6pm, Su 9:30am-1pm and 2:30-6pm; Sept.-June reduced hours.) Behind a nondescript facade, **Nova Hôtel ❸,** 8 r. Richelieu, hides large, comfortable rooms. (☎04 67 60 79 85; hotelnova@free.fr. Breakfast €4.60. Reception M-Sa 7am-1am, Su 7-11am and 7pm-1am. Singles €21; doubles €24, with shower €28-35, with shower, toilet, and TV €36-41. 5% discount with *Let's Go.* AmEx/MC/V.) A number of ethnic restaurants are on **rue des Ecoles Laïques. Crêperie le Kreisker ❶,** 3 passage Bruyas, serves 80 kinds of crepes (€2-7) topped with everything from buttered snails to bananas. (☎04 67 60 82 50. Open M-Sa 11:45am-2pm and 7-11pm. MC/V.) Get groceries at **INNO,** in the basement of the Polygone commercial center, near the tourist office. (Open M-Sa 9am-8:30pm.) **Postal Code:** 34000.

PROVENCE

Olive groves and vineyards carpet hills dusted with sunflowers and mimosas, while the fierce winds of the *mistral* carry the scents of lavender, rosemary, and sage. From the Roman arena and cobblestoned elegance of Arles to Cézanne's lingering footsteps in Aix-en-Provence, life along Provence's shaded paths tastes as good as a bottomless glass of *pastis.*

NÎMES

Southern France flocks to Nîmes (pop. 132,000) for the *férias*, celebrations featuring bullfights, flamenco dancing, and other hot-blooded fanfare (mid-Sept., mid-Feb., and Pentecost). The city's other attractions are limited, despite some impressive Roman structures. Magnificent **Les Arènes** is a 1st-century Roman amphitheater that still holds bullfights and concerts. (Open in summer M-F 9am-7pm; low season 10am-6pm. €4.65, students €3.40.) North of the arena stands the **Maison Carrée**, a rectangular temple built in the first century BC. (Open daily June-Sept. 9am-7pm; Oct.-May 10am-6pm. Free.) Across the square, the **Carrée d'Art** displays contemporary art. (Open Tu-Su 10am-6pm. €4.65, students €3.40.)

Trains go from bd. Talabot to: Arles (20min., 8 per day, €7); Marseille (1¼hr., 9 per day, €17); and Toulouse (3hr., 8 per day, €32). **Buses** (☎04 66 29 52 00) depart from behind the train station for Avignon (1½hr., 4 per day, €7.30). The **tourist office**, 6 r. Auguste, is near the Maison Carrée. (☎04 66 58 38 00; www.ot-nimes.fr. Open July-Aug. M-F 8:30am-8pm, Sa 9am-7pm, Su 10am-6pm; Sept.-June reduced hours.) The newly renovated ◪**Auberge de Jeunesse (HI)** ❶, 257 chemin de l'Auberge de la Jeunesse, off chemin de la Cigale, is 1.5km from quai de la Fontaine. Take bus I (dir.: Alès) to Stade, Route d'Alès and follow the signs uphill; call for pickup after 8pm. This comfortable, well-kept hostel is worth the trek. (☎04 66 68 03 20; fax 04 66 68 03 21. Breakfast €3.30. Sheets €2.80 per week. Internet €3.80 per hr. Reception 24hr. Mar.-Sept. Dorms €9.50; camping €5.50. Members only. MC/V.) Stock up at **Marché U** supermarket, 19 r. d'Alès, downhill from the hostel. (Open M-Sa 8am-12:45pm and 3:30-8pm.) **Postal Codes:** 30000 and 30900.

PONT DU GARD

In 19 BC, Augustus's close friend and advisor Agrippa built an aqueduct to channel water 50km to Nîmes from the Eure springs near Uzès. The architectural fruit of this 15-year project remains in the Pont du Gard, spanning the gorge of the Gardon River and towering over sunbathers and swimmers. A great way to see the Pont du Gard is to start from **Collias**, 6km toward Uzès. Here **Kayak Vert** rents canoes, kayaks, and bikes. (☎04 66 22 80 76. Canoes and kayaks €18 per day, bikes €15 per day. 10% student discount. €4 discount with stay at the hostel in Nîmes.) STDG **buses** (☎04 66 29 27 29) run to the Pont du Gard from Avignon (45min., 6 per day, €6) and Nîmes (40min., 7 per day, €5.60). **Camping le Barralet** ❶, in Collias, offers a pool and hot showers. (☎04 66 22 84 52; fax 04 66 22 89 17. Closed Oct.-Feb. €8-12 per person. MC/V.) More accommodations are in **Nîmes** (see above).

AVIGNON

Known to most as the home of the bridge immortalized in the children's song, *Sur le pont d'Avignon*, Avignon (pop. 100,000) also hosts Europe's most prestigious theater festival. A reminder of the city's brief stint as the center of the Catholic Church, the golden ◪**Palais des Papes,** the largest Gothic palace in Europe, keeps watch over the city. Although Revolutionary looting stripped the interior of its lavish furnishings, the giant rooms and their frescoed walls are still remarkable. (Open daily July 9am-9pm; Aug.-Sept. 9am-8pm; Oct.-June 9am-7pm. €9.50.) In July and early August, the ◪**Festival d'Avignon** holds theatrical performances in at least 30 different venues, from factories to cloisters to palaces. (☎04 90 14 14 14; www.festival-avignon.com. Tickets under €30. Standby tickets available 45min. before shows; 50% student discount. €8 Carte IN, sold at the tourist office, grants a 30% discount on all tickets.) The almost-as-well-established, more experimental **Festival OFF** also takes place in July. (Office on pl. du Palais. ☎01 48 05 01 19; www.avignon-off.org. Tickets under €16. €13 Carte OFF grants a 30% discount on all tickets.) During the festivals, theatrical performances spill into the streets at night, and many eateries stay open until 2 or 3am. **Place des Corps Saints** has lively bars. **The Cubanito Café,** 52 r. Carnot, hosts dancing to Cuban music in a boisterous atmosphere. (☎ 04 90 27 90 59. Beers from €2.20. Free salsa lessons Tu-Sa 9-10pm. Open daily 8am-1am.)

Trains (☎ 04 90 27 81 89) run from bd. St-Roch, porte de la République to: Arles (30min., 19 per day, €6); Lyon (1hr., 5-7 TGV per day, €36); Marseille (1¼hr., 18 per day, €16); Nîmes (30min., 16 per day, €8); and Paris (3½hr., 17 TGV per day, €80). **Buses** leave to the right of the train station for Arles (45min., 5 per day, €8.50) and Marseille (2hr., 1 per day, €16.40). The **tourist office** is at 41 cours Jean Jaurès. (☎ 04 32 74 32 74; www.avignon-tourisme.com. Open July M-Sa 9am-7pm, Su 10am-5pm; Apr.-June and Aug.-Oct. M-Sa 9am-6pm, Su 10am-5pm; Nov.-Mar. reduced hours.) Avignon's accommodations fill up well before festival season; book ahead or stay in Arles or Nîmes. Pitch your tent at ▨ **Camping du Pont d'Avignon ❶,** 300 Ile de la Barthelasse, which has hot showers, laundry facilities, a restaurant, a supermarket, a pool, a jacuzzi, and tennis and volleyball courts. (☎ 04 90 80 63 50; www.camping-avignon.com. Open Mar.-Oct. High season 1 person and tent €15, 2 people and tent €21, extra person €4.10; low-season prices 60% lower. MC/V.) **Hôtel du Parc ❸,** 18 r. Perdiguier, offers modern, comfortable rooms with handmade bedspreads and views of a nearby park. (☎ 04 90 82 71 55. Singles €28, with shower €35; doubles €35-42; triples with bath €65. MC/V.) Chatty owners and a cheerful crowd of regulars enjoy delicious *tartines* (€4.50) and occasional guitar serenades at ▨**La Cuisine des Méchantes ❶,** 68 r. de la Bonneterie. (☎ 04 90 86 14 81. Open daily noon-2pm and 7:30pm-1:30am.) A variety of restaurants cluster on **Rue des Teinturiers.** R. St-Agricol has a **Petit Casino** supermarket. (Open M-F 8am-8pm, Sa-Su 9am-8pm.) **Postal Code:** 84000.

ARLES

Every street in Arles (pop. 35,000), once the capital of Roman Gaul, seems to run either into or out of the great Roman arena. Built to seat 20,000 spectators in the first century AD, **Les Arènes** is still used for bullfights. (Open daily May-Sept. 9am-6pm; Oct.-Apr. reduced hours. €4, students €3.) The excellent **Musée de l'Arles Antique,** on av. de la 1*er* D. F. L., revives the city's Roman past. (Open daily Mar.-Oct. 9am-7pm; Nov.-Feb. 10am-5pm. €5.50, students €4.) Provençal daily life and folklore are showcased at the **Muséon Arlatan,** 29 r. de la République. (Open June-Aug. daily 9:30am-1pm and 2-6:30pm; Apr.-May and Sept. Tu-Su 9:30am-12:30pm and 2-6pm; Oct.-Mar. Tu-Su 9:30am-12:30pm and 2-5pm. €4, students €3.) The contemporary **Musée Réattu,** r. du Grand Prieuré, houses 57 of Picasso's drawings. (Open daily May-Sept. 10am-12:30pm and 2-7pm; Mar.-Apr. and Oct. 10am-12:30pm and 2-5.30pm; Nov.-Feb. 1-5:30pm. €4, students €3.) The annual **Fête d'Arles** brings traditional costumes, Provençal dancing, bullfights, and horseback riding to town during the last weekend in June and the first in July.

Trains leave av. P. Talabot for: Avignon (20min., 17 per day, €6); Marseille (1hr., 20 per day, €12); Montpellier (1hr., 5 per day, €12.50); and Nîmes (20min., 7 per day, €7). **Buses** (☎ 04 90 49 38 01) depart from next to the station for Avignon (45min., M-Sa 7 per day, €8.10) and Nîmes (1hr., M-Sa 6 per day, €5.20). To get to the **tourist office,** esplanade Charles de Gaulle on bd. des Lices, turn left outside the station, walk to pl. Lamartine, turn left on bd. Emile Courbes, and then take a right on bd. des Lices. (☎ 04 90 18 41 20; www.tourisme.ville-arles.fr. Open daily Apr.-Sept. 9am-6:45pm, Oct.-Mar. reduced hours.) To get from the station to the **Auberge de Jeunesse (HI) ❶,** 20 av. Maréchal Foch, follow directions to the tourist office, but cross bd. des Lices instead of turning onto it and follow the signs down av. des Alyscamps. (☎ 04 90 96 18 25; fax 04 90 96 31 26. Breakfast included. Lockout 10am-5pm. Curfew midnight, in winter 11pm. Dorms €14 first night, each additional night €12. Cash only.) ▨**Saint Trophime ❹,** 16 r. de la Calade, is a 15th-century mansion that feels like a palace. (☎04 90 96 88 38. Singles €35-40; doubles €50-55. AmEx/MC/V.) **Les Sandwiches ❶,** a tiny counter at 46 r. des Arènes, serves sandwiches (€2-4) that are sure to satisfy both vegetarians and meat-lovers. (Open Tu-F 11am-12:30pm and 4-6pm.) **Monoprix** supermarket is on pl. Lamartine. (Open M-Th 8:30am-7:30pm, F-Sa 8:30am-8pm.) **Postal Code:** 13200.

THE CAMARGUE

Pink flamingos, black bulls, and famous white Camargue horses roam freely across this flat expanse of protected wild marshland that stretches between Arles and the Mediterranean coast. The **Parc Ornithologique de Pont de Gau,** along D570, provides paths through the marshes with views of wildlife. (Open daily Apr.-Sept. 9am-sunset; Oct.-Mar. 10am-sunset. €6.) The best way to see the Camargue is on horseback; call the **Association Camarguaise de Tourisme Equestre** for more info. (☎04 90 97 10 40. 1hr. €13-16, 2hr. €26-30, half-day €35-40, full day €55-80.) Other options include jeep safaris (☎04 90 97 89 33; 2hr. €31, 4hr. €37) and boat trips (☎04 90 97 84 72; 1½hr., 2-4 per day, €10). Biking is another way to see the area; trail maps are available from the **tourist office** in Stes-Maries-de-la-Mer, 5 av. van Gogh. (☎04 90 97 82 55. Open daily July-Aug. 9am-8pm; Apr.-June and Sept. 9am-7pm; Oct.-Feb. 9am-5pm.) Arles runs **buses** to **Stes-Maries-de-la-Mer** (1hr., 4-5 per day, €5), the region's largest town. The best places to stay are in **Arles** (above).

AIX-EN-PROVENCE

Famous for festivals, fountains, and former residents Paul Cézanne, Victor Vasarely, and Emile Zola, Aix-en-Provence (pop. 137,000) caters to tourists without being ruined by them. The **Chemin de Cézanne,** 9 av. Paul Cézanne, features a two-hour self-guided walking tour that leads visitors to the artist's birthplace, his favorite cafes, and his studio. (☎04 42 21 06 53. Open daily June-Sept. 10am-6:30pm; Oct.-May reduced hours. €5.50, students €2.) The **Fondation Vasarely,** av. Marcel-Pagnol, in Jas-de-Bouffan, was designed by Victor Vasarely, the father of optical illusion art, and is a must-see for modern art fans. (☎04 42 20 01 09. Open June-Sept. M-Sa 11am-7pm; Oct.-May 11am-6pm. €7, students and under 18 €4.) An eclectic mix of Romanesque, Gothic, and Baroque, the **Cathédrale St-Saveur,** r. Gaston de Saporta, witnessed some misplaced violence during the Revolution, when angry *Aixois* mistook the statues of the apostles for statues of royalty and defiantly chopped off their heads. The statues were recapitated in the 19th century, but are still without necks. (☎04 42 23 45 65. Open daily 8am-noon and 2-6pm.) In June and July, famous performers and rising stars descend on Aix for the **Festival d'Aix-en-Provence,** a series of operas and orchestral concerts. (☎04 42 16 11 70; www.festival-aix.com. Tickets from €6.) Aix also hosts **Danse à Aix,** a two-week dance festival starting in late July. (☎04 42 23 41 24; www.danse-a-aix.com. Tickets €11-38.) **Rue Verrerie,** off r. des Cordiliers, is lined with bars and clubs. **Bistro Aixois,** 37 cours Sextius, packs in international students. (Open daily 6:30pm-4am.) At **Le Scat,** 11 r. Verrerie, a sophisticated crowd enjoys live jazz and rock at free nightly concerts in a funky stone basement. (Open M-Sa 11:30pm-5:30am.)

   Trains, at the end of av. Victor Hugo, run to: Cannes (3½hr., 8 per day, €26); Marseille (40min., 27 per day, €6); and Nice (3-4hr., 8 per day, €30). **TGV** trains also leave for Paris CDG (3½hr., 4 per day, €89) from the TGV station, accessible via a shuttle (20min., every 15min., €4) from the bus station. **Buses** (☎04 42 91 26 80), av. de l'Europe, also run frequently to Marseille (30min., every 10min., €4.20). From the train station, follow av. Victor Hugo, bearing left at the fork, until it feeds into La Rotonde. On the left is the **tourist office,** 2 pl. du Général de Gaulle, which books rooms for free. (☎04 42 16 11 61; www.aixenprovencetourism.com. Open July-Aug. M-Sa 8:30am-8pm, Su 10am-1pm and 2-6pm; Sept.-June reduced hours.)

You can surf the Internet at **Virtu@us**, 40 r. des Cordeliers. (☎04 42 26 02 30. €3.80 per hr. Open M-F 9am-1am, Sa-Su noon-1am.) Aix has few inexpensive hotels, and during festival season they may be fully booked—travelers hoping to find accommodations during July should reserve as early as March or April. The excellent ▓**Hôtel du Globe ❹**, 74 cours Sextius, is five minutes from the *centre ville*. (☎04 42 26 03 58; fax 04 42 26 13 68. Singles €35, with bath €39; doubles €54/€59; triples €63-69; quads €85. AmEx/MC/V.) To **camp** at **Arc-en-Ciel ❶**, on rte. de Nice, take bus #3 from La Rotonde to Trois Sautets. (☎04 42 26 14 28. €5.90 per person, €5.40 per tent.) The roads north of **cours Mirabeau** are packed with reasonably-priced restaurants, as is **rue Verrerie**. You'll find tasty Provençal *tartines* (grilled bread with cheese and toppings; €9.20-11.20) at **Le P'tit Bistrot**, 38 rue Lieutaud. (☎04 42 27 52 20. Open Tu-Sa 9am-3pm and 6pm-1am. MC/V.) Choose from three **Petit Casino** supermarkets at: 3 cours d'Orbitelle (open M-Sa 8am-1pm and 4-7:30pm); 16 r. Italie (open Tu-Sa 8am-8pm, Su 8am-1pm); and 5 r. Sapora (open M and W-Sa 8:30am-7:30pm, Su 8:30am-12:30pm). **Postal Code:** 13100.

MARSEILLE

Dubbed "the meeting place of the entire world" by Alexandre Dumas, Marseille (pop. 800,000), the third-largest city in France, is a jumble of color and commotion. A walk through its sidestreets is punctuated by the vibrant colors of West African fabrics for sale in markets, the sounds of Arabic music from car stereos, and the smells of North African cuisine wafting out of hole-in-the-wall restaurants. A true immigrant city, Marseille offers a taste of both the ancient and modern cultures of the entire Mediterranean.

▐ TRANSPORTATION

Flights: Aéroport Marseille-Provence (MRS; ☎04 42 14 14 14; www.marseille.aeroport.fr). Flights to **Corsica, Lyon** and **Paris.** Buses connect airport to Gare St-Charles (3 per hr. 5:30am-9:50pm, €8.50).

Trains: Gare St-Charles, pl. Victor Hugo (☎08 92 35 35 35). To: **Lyon** (1½hr., 21 per day, €48); **Nice** (2½hr., 21 per day, €25); **Paris** (3hr., 18 per day, €08).

Buses: Gare Routière, pl. Victor Hugo (☎04 91 08 16 40), near the train station. Open M-Sa 6:30am-6:30pm, Su 7:30am-6:30pm. To: **Avignon** (2hr., 5 per day, €15); **Cannes** (2¼-3hr., 4 per day, €21); **Nice** (2¾hr., 1 per day, €23).

Ferries: SNCM, 61 bd. des Dames (☎04 91 56 32 00; www.sncm.fr). Ferries to **Corsica** (12hr., €35-53, reduced price €20-40) and **Sardinia** (20hr., €59-69/€50-65). Open M-F 8am-6pm, Sa 8am-noon and 2-5:30pm.

Local Transportation: RTM, 6 r. des Fabres (☎04 91 91 92 10). Tickets sold at bus and metro stations (€1.50 per ride; day pass €4; 5- to 11-ride **Carte Liberté** €6.50-13). **Metro** runs M-Th 5am-9pm and F-Su 5am-12:30am.

Taxis: (☎04 91 02 20 20) 24hr. €20-30 from the train station to hostels.

▟ ❼ ORIENTATION AND PRACTICAL INFORMATION

Although the city is divided into 16 *arrondissements*, Marseille is understood by *quartier* (neighborhood) names and major streets. **La Canebière** is the main artery, funneling into the **vieux port,** with its upscale restaurants and nightlife, to the west. North of the *vieux port*, working-class residents pile into the hilltop neighborhood of **Le Panier,** east of which lies the **Quartier Belsunce,** the hub of the city's Arab and African communities. A few blocks to the southeast, **Cours Julien** has a

FRANCE

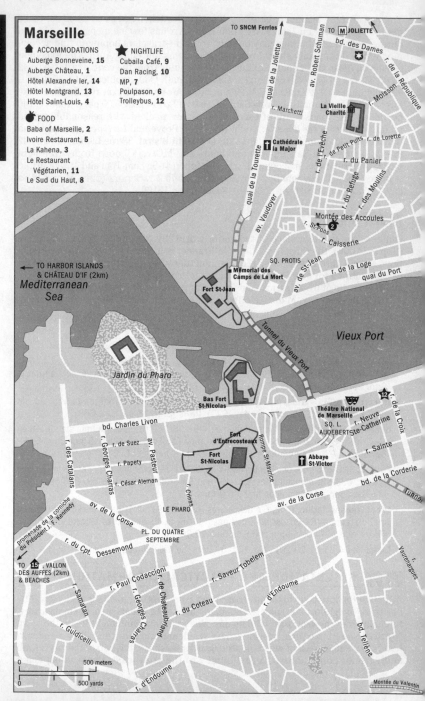

Marseille

🏠 ACCOMMODATIONS
Auberge Bonneveine, **15**
Auberge Château, **1**
Hôtel Alexandre Ier, **14**
Hôtel Montgrand, **13**
Hôtel Saint-Louis, **4**

⭐ NIGHTLIFE
Cubaila Café, **9**
Dan Racing, **10**
MP, **7**
Poulpason, **6**
Trolleybus, **12**

🍅 FOOD
Baba of Marseille, **2**
Ivoire Restaurant, **5**
La Kahena, **3**
Le Restaurant
  Végétarien, **11**
Le Sud du Haut, **8**

TO SNCM Ferries

TO Ⓜ JOLIETTE

bd. des Dames

av. Robert Schuman

r. de la République

r. Moisson

quai de la Joliette

r. Marchetti

r. de Petit Puits

r. de Lorette

La Vieille
Charité

Cathédrale
la Major

r. de l'Evêché

r. du Panier

r. du Refuge

r. des Moulins

quai de la Tourette

av. Vaudoyer

Montée des Accoules

r. St-Pons

r. Caisserie

SQ. PROTIS

av. de St-Jean

r. de la Loge

Mémorial des
Camps de La Mort

Fort St-Jean

quai du Port

TO HARBOR ISLANDS
& CHÂTEAU D'IF (2km)

*Mediterranean
Sea*

Tunnel du Vieux Port

Vieux Port

Jardin du Pharo

Bas Fort
St-Nicolas

Théâtre National
de Marseille

r. de la Croix

SQ. L.
AUDEBERT

r. Neuve

Ste-Catherine

r. Sainte

Fort
d'Entrecosteaux

Rompe St-Maurice

Abbaye
St-Victor

bd. Charles Livon

r. de Suez

av. Pasteur

Fort
St-Nicolas

bd. de la Corderie

r. des Catalans

r. Georges Charras

r. Papety

r. César Aleman

r. Cinnas

av. de la Corse

LE PHARO

av. de la Corse

Tunnel

promenade de la corniche
du Président J. F. Kennedy

r. du Cpt. Dessemond

PL. DU QUATRE
SEPTEMBRE

r. Saveur Tobelem

r. Vaurenargues

TO 15 , VALLON
DES AUFFES (2km)
& BEACHES

r. Paul Codaccioni

r. de Chateaubriand

r. du Coteau

r. d'Endoume

r. Samatan

r. Georges Charras

bd. Tellene

r. Guidicelli

r. d'Endoume

Montée du Valentin

0   500 meters

0   500 yards

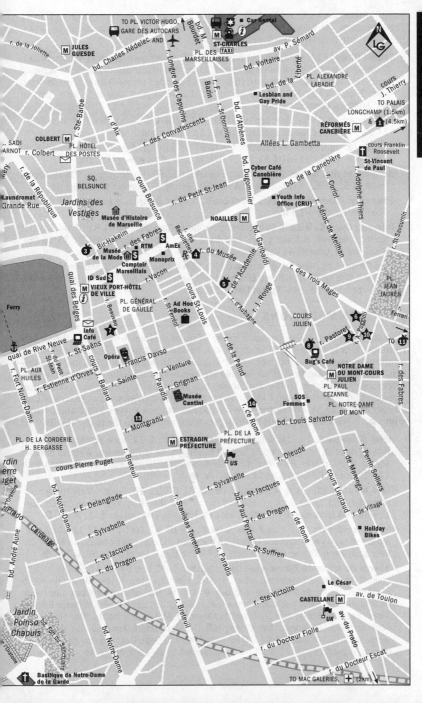

FRANCE

younger, counter-cultural feel. Both **metro** lines go to the train station; line #1 (blue) goes to the *vieux port.* The **bus** system is much more thorough but complex—a route map from the tourist office helps enormously.

Tourist Office: 4 bd. de la Canebière (☎04 91 13 89 00; www.marseille-tourisme.com). Multilingual staff has brochures of walking tours, free maps, accommodations services, and RTM day passes. City tours (€16 by bus, €5 by open-car train) daily at regular intervals. Open July-Aug. M-Sa 9am-7:30pm, Su 10am-6pm; Oct.-June M-Sa 9am-7pm, Su and holidays 10am-5pm.

Consulates: UK, 24 av. du Prado (☎04 91 15 72 10). **US,** 12 bd. Paul Peytral (☎04 91 54 92 00). Both open by appointment M-F 9am-noon and 2-5pm.

Police: 2 r. du Commissaire Becker (☎04 91 39 80 00). Also in the train station on esplanade St-Charles (☎04 91 14 29 97). In case of an **emergency,** Dial ☎17.

Hospital: Hôpital Timone, 246 r. St-Pierre (☎04 91 38 60 00). M: Timone. **SOS Médecins** (☎04 91 52 91 52) and **SOS Dentist** (☎04 91 85 39 39) connect to on-call doctors.

Pharmacy: Pharmacie le Cours Saint-Louis, 5 cours Saint-Louis (☎04 91 54 04 58). Open daily 8:30am-7:30pm.

Internet: Cyber Café de la Canebière, 87 r. de la Canebière (☎04 91 05 94 24). €2 per hr. Open daily 8:30am-11pm. **Info Café,** 1 quai Rive Neuve (☎04 91 33 53 05). €3.80 per hr. Open M-Sa 9am-10pm.

Post Office: 1 pl. Hôtel des Postes (☎04 91 15 47 00). Follow La Canebière toward the sea and turn right onto r. Reine Elisabeth as it becomes pl. Hôtel des Postes. Open M-F 8am-7pm, Sa 8am-noon. **Postal Code:** 13001.

ACCOMMODATIONS

Like any large city, Marseille has a range of hotel options, from pricey three- and four-star hotels scattered throughout the *vieux port* to the less reputable but temptingly cheap accommodations in the quartier Belsunce. Hotels listed here prioritize safety and location. Both hostels are located far from the city center, which offers an escape from traffic and noise, but also makes them considerably less accessible due to infrequent bus service and early curfews. Most places fill up quickly on weekends and in the summer, so call at least a week in advance. Large white signs posted throughout the city provide directions to the major hotels.

Hôtel Saint-Louis, 2 r. des Recollettes (☎04 91 54 02 74; www.hotel-st-louis.com). Brightly-painted, spacious rooms just off bustling r. de la Canebière. Wireless Internet access €10 for 24hr. Breakfast €5. Reception 24hr. Singles €32; doubles with bath €40-49; triples €57. Extra bed €7. AmEx/V. ❸

Hôtel Montgrand, 50 r. Montgrand (☎04 91 00 35 20; www.hotel-montgrand-marseille.com). Quiet, newly renovated rooms near the *vieux port.* Breakfast €5. Singles €36-€43; doubles €43, with 2 beds €47; triples €49; quads €61. MC/V. ❹

Hôtel Alexandre Ier, 111 r. de Rome (☎04 91 48 67 13; fax 04 91 42 11 14). Large, red-toned rooms with showers. Rooms on the cours St-Louis can be noisy. Breakfast €5. Reception 24hr. Singles €37; doubles €38-40; triples €49; quads €65. MC/V. ❹

Auberge de Jeunesse Bonneveine (HI), impasse Bonfils (☎04 91 17 63 30; http://fuaj.net/homepage/marseille), off av. J Vidal. From the station, take Metro line #2 to Rond-Point du Prado and transfer to bus #44 to pl. Bonnefon. At the bus stop, walk back toward the traffic circle and turn left at J. Vidal, then turn left onto impasse Bonfils. A well-organized hostel with an international crowd. Max. stay 6 nights. Reception 9am-noon and 2-6pm. Curfew 1am. Closed late Dec.-Jan. Dorms Apr.-Aug. 1st night €14, thereafter €12.10; doubles €17/€15. Feb.-Mar. and Sept.-Dec. reduced prices. Members only; guests under 18 must be accompanied by an adult. MC/V. ❶

Auberge de Jeunesse Château de Bois-Luzy (HI), allée des Primevères (☎04 91 49 06 18). Take metro #1 to Réformés-Canebière, then transfer to bus #6 from cours J. Thierry at the top of La Canebière to Marius Richard. 10m up the hill from the bus stop, take a right onto bd. de l'Amandière and walk to the soccer fields. Follow the road down to the right and around the fields. A beautiful 19th-century chateau on a hilltop east of Marseille. Breakfast €3.20. Lunch and dinner €9 each. Sheets €2.50. Max. stay 4 nights. Lockout noon-5pm. Curfew 10:30pm. Dorms for first night €11.40, thereafter €9; singles €15.50/€13; doubles €12.50/€10. Members only. Cash only. ●

▐ FOOD

Marseille's restaurants reflect the cultural diversity of its inhabitants. African eateries and kebab stands line **cours St-Louis**, the streets surrounding the **vieux port** are packed with outdoor cafes and restaurants serving the city's famed seafood and trademark *bouillabaisse*, and **Cours Julien** offers an artsy, eclectic collection of food options. Stock up on groceries at the **Monoprix** supermarket across from the AmEx office on bd. de la Canebière. (Open M-Sa 8:30am-8:30pm.)

▨ **Baba of Marseille**, 14 r. St-Pons (☎04 91 90 66 36). Delicious southern French dishes have won a loyal clientele. Photos of past diners as well as an eclectic collection of paper lanterns and glass chandeliers give this welcoming restaurant a homey, familiar feel. Open W-Sa 8pm-midnight. ●

Ivoire Restaurant, 57 r. d'Aubagne (☎04 91 33 75 33). Head to this no-frills restaurant for authentic West African cuisine and helpful advice from owner "Mama Africa." Côte d'Ivoire specialties include *Yassa* (braised fish with plantains and couscous; €7) and *Maffé* (meat or fish in peanut sauce; €7). Open daily noon-midnight. ●

Le Sud du Haut, 80 cours Julien (☎04 91 92 66 64). M: Cours Julien. Beautifully presented, traditional Provençal cuisine. Funky bathrooms supply markers and paper so patrons can add their words of praise to the glowing reviews scrawled on the walls. Open M-Sa noon-1:30pm and 8pm-12:30am. AmEx/MC/V. ●

La Kahena, 2 r. de la République (☎04 91 90 61 93). M: Vieux Port. Tasty couscous dishes (€8-14) are served on hand-painted clay dishes at this sunny Tunisian restaurant on the corner of the vieux port. Blue tile mosaics and smells of warm spicoo complete its North African aura. Open daily noon-2.30pm and 7-11:30pm. MC/V. ●

Le Restaurant Végétarien, 63 rue St-Pierre (04 91 42 61 15 06). M: Cours Julien. Tables in a quiet outdoor courtyard provide a respite from the city. Appetizing *plats du jour* (€10-13) and delicious, homemade desserts (€4.30-5) from the full vegetarian menu make for a pleasant meal. Open M-Sa noon-2pm and 6:30-10:30pm. MC/V. ●

⊙ SIGHTS

A walk through the city's streets tops any other sights-oriented itinerary, providing glimpses of lively African and Arabic communities amid ancient Roman ruins and 17th-century forts. Check www.museum-paca.org for the latest info on the region's museums. Unless otherwise noted, all the museums listed below have the same hours (June-Sept. Tu-Sa 11am-6pm; Oct.-May Tu-Sa 10am-5pm).

▨**BASILIQUE DE NOTRE DAME DE LA GARDE.** A hilltop location has made this church strategically important for centuries, and today offers visitors a stunning view of the city, surrounding mountains, and stone-studded bay. During the WWII liberation of Marseille, a battle raged for days before FFI forces regained the basilica, which remains pocked with bullet holes and shrapnel scars. Towering 230m above the city, the golden statue of Madonna cradling the infant Christ is often considered the symbol of Marseille. *(Open daily in summer 7am-8pm; low season 7am-7pm.)*

COURS JULIEN

An eclectic collection of murals, vintage shops, bookstores, theaters, cafes, and restaurants make cours Julien one of Marseille's most interesting neighborhoods and the perfect place to find a bargain.

1 Peruse dusty paperbacks at **Librairie du Cours Julien**, 51 cours Julien.

2 Street artists have turned **rue Pastoret** and **rue Crudère** into impromptu outdoor galleries that display bright, cartoonish spray-paint murals.

3 Tiny **Baluchon Boutique**, 11 r. des Trois Rois, has the best vintage threads.

4 **La Passerelle**, 26 r. des Trois Mages, features a large selection of comic books and a snappy cafe-bar.

5 **Kaleidoscope**, 3 r. des Trois Mages, offers offbeat used records and CDs.

6 **Black Music**, 2 r. de la Bibliothèque, has a wide collection of soul, funk, and hip-hop.

HARBOR ISLANDS. Resembling a child's sand castle, the **Château d'If** guards the city from its rocky perch outside the harbor. Its dungeon, immortalized in Dumas's *Count of Monte Cristo*, once held a number of hapless Huguenots. Nearby, the **Ile Frioul** quarantined plague infectees for two centuries, beginning in the 1600s. It was only marginally successful, as an outbreak in 1720 killed half of the city's 80,000 citizens. A handful of small shops and restaurants, combined with inlets popular for swimming, make the islands a convenient escape from the city. *(Boats depart from quai des Belges for both islands. Call the Groupement des Armateurs Côtiers at ☎ 04 91 55 50 09. Château ☎ 04 91 59 02 30. Round-trip 20min.; €10 for each island, €15 for both.)*

LA VIEILLE CHARITÉ. A fine example of the 17th-century work of local architect Pierre Puget, La Charité was originally constructed to house the hundreds of beggars congesting the entrances to Marseille's churches. Now a national historical monument and home to many of Marseille's cultural organizations, it contains several of the city's museums, including the anthropological collections held in the **Musée des Arts Africains, Océaniens et Amérindiens.** *(2 r. de la Charité. ☎ 04 91 14 58 80. Temporary exhibits €3, permanent collections €2; students half-price.)*

MUSÉE CANTINI. This memorable museum chronicles the region's artistic successes of the last century, with major Fauvist and Surrealist collections, including limited works by Henri Matisse and Paul Signac. *(19 r. Grignan. ☎ 04 91 54 77 75. €3, students €1.50. Over 65 and under 10 free.)*

MEMORIAL DES CAMPS DE LA MORT. This building for this small but moving museum is located in a blockhouse built by the Germans during their occupation of Marseille. A collection of photos and news articles recalls the death camps of World War II and the deportation of 20,000 Jews from the *vieux port* in 1943. Sobering quotes by Primo Levi, Louis Serre, and Elie Wiesel, and an unsettling collection of ashes are on display. *(Quai de la Tourette. ☎ 04 91 90 73 15. Open Sept.-May Tu-Su 10am-5pm; June-Aug. 11am-6pm. Free.)*

ABBAYE ST-VICTOR. St-Victor, an abbey fortified against pirates and Saracen invaders, is one of the oldest Christian sites in Europe. The eerie 5th-century catacombs and basilica contain both pagan and Christian relics, including the remains of two 3rd-century martyrs. Sarcophagi pile up along the walls; some remain half-embedded in the building's foundations. *(On r. Sainte at the end of quai de Rive Neuve. Follow signs from the quai. ☎ 04 96 11 22 60. Open daily 9am-7pm. Crypt €2.)*

OTHER SIGHTS. The fluctuating exhibits at **Musée de la Mode** pay homage to the fashion world, featuring designers from around the world. *(Espace Mode Méditerranée, 11 La Canebière. ☎04 91 56 59 57. Free tours in French Sa-Su 4pm. €1.50, students €1, over 65 free.)* The remains of Marseille's original port rest peacefully in the quiet **Jardin des Vestiges.** Millennia-old artifacts, including pottery pieces and the skeleton of a 6th-century fishing boat, are displayed in the adjacent **Musée d'Histoire de Marseille.** *(Enter through the lowest level of the Centre Bourse mall. ☎04 91 90 42 22. €2, students €1, over 65 and under 10 free.)* Bus #83 (dir.: Rond-Point du Prado) takes you from the *vieux port* to Marseille's **public beaches.** Get off just after it rounds the statue of David (20-30min.). Both the north and south **plages du Prado** offer wide beaches, clear water, and plenty of grass.

◙ NIGHTLIFE

Late-night restaurants and a few nightclubs center around **place Thiers,** near the *vieux port.* Tables from the bars along the **quai de Rive Neuve** spill out into the sidewalk, and locals rush to grab a drink. A more counter-cultural crowd unwinds along the **cours Julien.** Be cautious at night, particularly on the dimly-lit streets of quartiers Panier and Belsunce, and on the *vieux port.* Night buses are scarce, taxis are expensive, and the metro closes early (M-Th and Su 9pm, F-Sa midnight).

Trolleybus, 24 quai de Rive Neuve. M: Vieux Port. A mega-club in an 18th-century warehouse with three separate rooms for pop-rock, techno, and soul-funk-salsa. Prizewinning French and international DJs have been spinning here for 14 years. Beer from €5, drinks €6-7. F nights no cover; Sa cover €10, includes 1 drink. Open July-Aug. M-Sa 11pm-7am; low season Tu and Th-Sa.

Dan Racing, 17 r. André Poggioli. M: Cours Julien. Let your inner rock star run wild at this fun, casual bar, where drunken revelers can hop onstage to jam on 15 guitars, two drum sets, and countless other instruments. Auto- and bike-racing decor adds to the atmosphere. Drinks €2.50-3.50. Open M-Sa 9pm-2am.

Cubaila Café, 40 r. des Trois Rois (☎04 91 48 97 48). M: Cours Julien. Take your mojito down to the basement, where you'll find a perfect replica of the Malecon boardwalk in Havana, with miniature house facades on one side and a view of the "ocean" on the other. Drinks €3-8. Open M-Sa 9pm-4am.

Poulpason, 2 r. André Poggioli. M: Cours Julien. DJs spin rock, techno, and electro-house. A giant octopus reaching out from the wall, wave mosaics, and a black-lit aquarium make for a trippy underwater theme. Drinks €2.50-5. Open M-Sa 10pm-2am.

MP, 10 r. Beauvau (☎04 91 33 64 79). Both men and women relax on plush velour couches at this quiet gay bar. Tall wire stools, red runner lights, and elaborate metal sconces add a classy touch. Patrons can snack on paella or couscous and use the free Internet kiosk. Drinks €2.50-6.50. Open daily from 5:30pm.

FRENCH RIVIERA (CÔTE D'AZUR)

Between Marseille and the Italian border, the sun-drenched beaches and warm waters of the Mediterranean form the backdrop for this fabled playground of the rich and famous. Chagall, F. Scott Fitzgerald, Matisse, Picasso, and Renoir are among those who flocked to the coast in its heyday. Now, the Riviera is a curious combination of high-handed millionaires and low-budget tourists. High society steps out every May for the Cannes Film Festival and the Monte-Carlo Grand Prix. Less exclusive are Nice's uproarious *Carnaval* and various summer jazz festivals.

ST-TROPEZ

Hollywood stars, corporate giants, and curious backpackers congregate on the spotless streets of St-Tropez (pop. 5400), where the glitz and glamour of the Riviera shine like nowhere else. The young, beautiful, and restless flock to this "Jewel of the Riviera" to flaunt their tans on its infamous **beaches.** The best beaches can be difficult to reach without a car, but a **shuttle** (*navette municipale*) leaves pl. des Lices for **Les Salins,** a secluded sunspot, and **plage Tahiti** (Capon-Pinet stop), the first of the famous **plages des Pampelonne.** (M-Sa, 5 per day, €1.) Take a break from the sun at the **Musée de l'Annonciade,** pl. Grammont, which showcases Fauvist and neo-Impressionist paintings. (Open June-Sept. M and W-Su 10am-1pm and 4-9pm; Oct.-May 10am-1pm and 4-7pm. €4.60, students €2.30.)

Les Bateaux de St-Raphaël **ferries** (☎ 04 94 95 17 46; www.tmr-saintraphael.com), at the *vieux port,* serve St-Tropez from St-Raphaël (1hr.; 2-5 per day; €11 one-way, €20 round-trip). Sodetrav **buses** (☎ 04 94 97 88 51) leave av. Général Leclerc for St-Raphaël (2hr., 10-14 per day, €8.70). The **tourist office,** on quai Jean Jaurès, has schedules of the shuttle transport and copies of *Manifestations,* a guide that lists local events. (☎ 04 94 97 45 21; www.saint-tropez.st. Open daily late June-Aug. 9:30am-12:30pm and 2-7pm; Sept.-late June reduced hours.) Budget hotels do not exist in St-Tropez, and the closest youth hostel is in Fréjus (see below). **Camping** is the cheapest option—**Kon Tiki ❷** has a choice location near the northern stretch of the Pampelonne beaches. In July and August, Sodetrav sends daily buses (4 per day; €1.60) from the station to the campsite; otherwise, take the municipal shuttle from pl. des Lices to Capon-Pinet, then head downhill, follow the signs to the Plage Tahiti, and walk for 30-40min. down the beach to reach the site. Campers can soak up sun by day and the beach's wild nightlife, including Kon Tiki's own bar, after dark. (☎ 04 94 55 96 96; www.campazur.com. Open Apr. to mid-Oct. July-Aug. two people, tent, and car €40; low season €20-27.) For those who prefer not to camp, one of the most budget-friendly and central hotels is **Lou Cagnard ❹,** 18 av. Paul Roussel, offering spacious, cheery rooms. (☎ 04 94 97 04 24; www.hotel-lou-cagnard.com. Breakfast €8. Open Jan.-Oct. 1-week min. stay. Free parking for guests. Singles and doubles €44-53, with toilet €53-100. MC/V.) The *vieux port* and the streets behind the waterfront are lined with incredibly pricey restaurants, so create your own meal at **Monoprix** supermarket, 9 av. du Général Leclerc (open daily July-Aug. 8am-10pm; Sept.-June 8am-7:50pm) or stop by the snack stands and cafes near **place des Lices. Postal Code:** 83990.

ST-RAPHAËL AND FRÉJUS

With affordable accommodations, convenient transport, and proximity to the sea, the twin cities of St-Raphaël (pop. 32,000) and Fréjus (pop. 48,000) provide a good base for exploring the Riviera. In St-Raphaël, golden beaches stretch along the coast, while Fréjus trades sandy shores for Roman ruins. The first weekend in July brings the **Compétition Internationale de Jazz New Orleans** (☎ 04 98 11 89 00) to St-Raphaël. In Fréjus, the **Roman amphitheater,** on r. Henri Vadon, holds concerts and occasional bullfights. (Open Apr.-Oct. M-Tu and Th-Sa 10am-1pm and 2:30-6:30pm; Nov.-Mar. reduced hours.)

St-Raphaël sends **trains** every 30min. from pl. de la Gare to Cannes (25min., €5.30) and Nice (1hr., €8.90). **Buses** leave from behind the train station in St-Raphaël for Fréjus (25min., every hr., €1.10) and St-Tropez (1½hr., 11 per day, €8.70). The **St-Raphaël tourist office,** on r. Waldeck Rousseau, is opposite the train station. (☎ 04 94 19 52 52; www.saint-raphael.com. Open daily July-Aug. 9am-7pm; Sept.-June M-Sa 9am-12:30pm and 2-6:30pm.) Take bus #6 from St-Raphaël to pl. Paul Vernet to get to the **Fréjus tourist office,** 325 r. Jean Jaurès. (☎ 04 94 51 83 83; www.ville-frejus.fr. Open July-Aug. M-Sa 10am-noon and 2:30-6:30pm, Su 10am-noon and 3-6pm; Sept.-June M-Sa 10am-noon and 2-6pm.) Take av. du 15*ème* Corps d'Armée from the Fréjus tourist office and turn left on chemin de Counillier to reach the ■Auberge de Jeunesse de St-Raphaël-Fréjus (HI) ❶, a peaceful, friendly hostel in a superb, secluded location. (☎04 94 53 18 75; frejus-st-raphael@fuaj.org. Sheets €2.80. Lockout 11am-5:30pm. Curfew July-Aug. 11:30pm, Sept.-June 10pm. Closed Dec.-Jan. Dorms €13. Camping €10 per person with tent. Cash only.) In St-Raphaël, the **Hôtel les Pyramides** ❸, 77 av. Paul Doumer., offers well-kept rooms just minutes from the waterfront. To get there, leave the station to the left, make a right onto av. Henri Vadon, and take the first left onto av. Paul Doumer. (☎04 98 11 10 10; www.saint-raphael.com/pyramides. Breakfast €7. Open Mar. 15-Nov. 15. Singles €26; doubles €37-55; triples €57; quads €67. Extra bed €13. MC/V.) St-Raphaël's **Monoprix** supermarket is on 14 bd. de Félix Martin, near the station. (Open M-Sa 8am-8pm.) **Postal Codes:** St-Raphaël 83700; Fréjus 83600.

CANNES

Cannes's name conjures images of its renowned annual film festival, where countless starlets compete for camera time. But at other times of the year, Cannes (pop. 70,000) rolls up the red carpet and becomes the most accessible of all the Riviera's glam-towns. A palm-lined boardwalk, gorgeous sandy beaches, and innumerable boutiques ensure that anyone can sport the famous Cannes style. The **Eglise de la Castre** and its courtyard stand on the hill on which *Vieux Cannes* was built. Of Cannes's three **casinos,** the most accessible is **Le Casino Croisette,** 1 espace Lucien Barrière, next to the Palais des Festivals. (No shorts, jeans, or t-shirts. Jackets required for men. 18+. Cover €10. Gambling daily 8pm-4am; slots open at 10am.) Just as much fun and half the price, cafes and bars near the waterfront stay open all night. Nightlife thrives around **rue Dr. G. Monod.** Try ■Morrison's, 10 rue Teisseire (☎04 92 98 16 17), for casual company in a literary-themed pub. (Beer from €5. Happy Hour 5-8pm. Open daily 5pm-2am.) **Le 7,** 7 rue Rougières (☎04 93 39 10 36), is famous for outrageous nightly drag shows. (F-Sa cover €16, includes one drink. Drag shows start at 1:30am. Open daily 11:30pm-dawn.)

Coastal **trains** depart from 1 r. Jean-Jaurès for: Antibes (15min., €2.30); Marseille (2hr., €23); Monaco (1hr., €7.40); Nice (40min., €5.20); and St-Raphaël (25min., €5.50). The **tourist office,** 1 bd. de la Croisette, helps find accommodations. (☎04 93 39 24 53; www.cannes.fr. Open July-Aug. daily 9am-8pm; Sept.-June M-F 9am-7pm.) There is a branch office at the train station. (☎04 93 99 19 77. Open M-Sa 9am-7pm.) Access the **Internet** at **CyberCafé Institut Riviera Langue,** 26 r. de Mimont. (€4 per hr. Open M-F 10am-9:30pm.) Hostels are 10-20min. farther from the beach than other lodgings, but are the cheapest options in town. Run by a young, English-speaking couple, the **Hostel Les Iris** ❷, 77 bd. Carnot, was converted from an old hotel into a clean, bright hostel with brand-new bunks, a Mexican-themed terrace restaurant, and small cafe. (☎/fax 04 93 68 30 20; www.iris-solola.com. Dorms €20. AmEx/MC/V.) **Hotel Mimont** ❸, 39 r. de Mimont, is the best budget hotel in Cannes. English-speaking owners maintain pleasing rooms two streets behind the train station, off bd. de la République. (☎04 93 39 51 64; canneshotelmimont@minitel.net. Singles €29; doubles €38; triples €51. AmEx/MC/V.) Stock up at **Champion** supermarket, 6 r. Meynadier. (Open M-Sa 8:30am-7:45pm.) The pedestrian zone around **rue Meynadier** has inexpensive restaurants. **Postal Code:** 06400.

ANTIBES

Blessed with beautiful beaches and a charming *vieille ville*, Antibes (pop. 78,000) is less touristy than Nice and more relaxed than St-Tropez; with access to top-notch nightlife in neighboring **Juan-les-Pins,** it has become an undisputed jewel of the Riviera. The excellent ■Musée Picasso, in the Château Grimaldi on pl. Mariejol, displays works by the former Antibes resident and his contemporaries. (Open mid-June to mid-Sept. Tu-Su 10am-6pm; low season 10am-noon and 2-6pm. €3, students €1.50, under 18 free.) The two main public beaches in Antibes, **plage du Pon-**

teil and neighboring **plage de la Salis,** are crowded all summer. Cleaner and more secluded, the rocky beach on **Cap d'Antibes** has a breathtaking landscape of white cliffs and blue water perfect for snorkeling. Come summer, the young and hip Juan-Les-Pins is synonymous with wild nightlife. Frequent **buses** and **trains** run from Antibes, although walking between the two along bd. Wilson is also an option. Boutiques generally remain open until midnight, cafes until 2am, discothèques until 5am, and bars past dawn. ☒**Pam Pam Rhumerie,** 137 bd. Wilson, is a hot Brazilian bar that turns smokin' when bikinied showgirls take the stage to down flaming drinks. (☎04 93 61 11 05. Open daily mid-Mar. to early Nov. 2pm-5am.) In psychedelic **Whisky à Gogo,** 5 r. Jacques Leonetti, bubbling, water-filled columns lit by neon lights frame a young crowd on the intimate dance floor. (Cover €16. Open July-Aug. daily midnight-5am; Apr.-June and Sept.-Oct. Th-Sa.)

Trains leave pl. Pierre Semard, off av. Robert Soleau for: Cannes (20min., 23 per day, €2.30); Marseille (2¼hr., 12 per day, €24); and Nice (15min., 25 per day, €3.50). RCA **buses** leave 200 pl. de Gaulle for Cannes (20min., every 20min., €2.50) and Nice (45min., every 20min., €4.10). From the train station, turn right on av. Robert Soleau, and follow the signs to the **tourist office** at 11 pl. de Gaulle. (☎04 92 90 53 00; www.antibes-juanlespins.com. Open July-Aug. daily 9am-7pm; Sept.-June M-F 9am-12:30pm and 1:30-6pm, Sa 9am-noon and 2-6pm.) Grab a bunk in bright, bare rooms with a rowdy Anglo crowd at **The Crew House ❸.** From the train station, walk down av. de la Libération until it turns into av. de Verdun, then make a right onto av. St-Roch. (☎04 92 90 49 39; workstation_fr@yahoo.com. Internet €0.12 per min. Dorms Apr.-Oct. €20, Nov.-Mar. €15. MC/V.) Instead of trekking back to Antibes, crash in Juan-Les-Pins at **Hôtel Trianon ❹,** 14 av. de l'Estérel, which offers renovated, clean rooms with large windows and free Internet. (☎ 04 93 61 18 11; www.trianon-hotel.com. Breakfast €4. Singles €39; doubles €48; triples €54. Low season reduced prices. AmEx/MC/V.) A variety of tempting restaurants sets up outdoor tables along **boulevard d'Aguillon,** behind the *vieux port.* For cheaper eats and great people-watching, you're better off heading to lively **place Nationale,** a few blocks away. The **Marché Provençal,** on cours Masséna, is considered one of the best markets on the Côte d'Azur. (Open Tu-Su 6am-1pm.) **Postal Code:** 06600.

NICE

Sophisticated and spicy, Nice (pop. 380,000) is the unofficial capital of the Riviera. Its non-stop nightlife, top-notch museums, and bustling beaches are unerring tourist magnets. During the three-week *Carnaval* in February, visitors and *Niçois* alike ring in the spring with wild revelry, grotesque costumes, and raucous song and dance. Prepare to have more fun than you'll remember.

▐ TRANSPORTATION

Flights: Aéroport Nice-Côte d'Azur (NCE; ☎08 20 42 33 33). **Air France,** 10 av. Félix Faure (☎08 02 80 28 02), serves **Bastia, Corsica** (€116; under 25, over 60, and couples €59) and **Paris** (€93; under 25, over 60, and couples €46).

Trains: Gare SNCF Nice-Ville (☎04 93 14 82 12), av. Thiers. Open 5am-12:30am. To: **Cannes** (35min., every 20min., €5.30); **Marseille** (2½hr., 16 per day, €26); **Monaco** (15min., every 10-30min., €3.10); **Paris** (5½hr., 9 per day, €83.50).

Buses: 5 bd. Jean Jaurès (☎04 93 85 61 81). Info booth open M-F 8:30am-5:30pm, Sa 9am-4pm. To **Cannes** (1½hr., every 20min., €6) and **Monaco** (45min., every 15min., €4).

Ferries: Corsica Ferries, Port du Commerce (☎04 92 00 42 93; www.corsicaferries.com). Take bus #1 or 2 (dir.: Port) from pl. Masséna. To **Corsica** (€40).

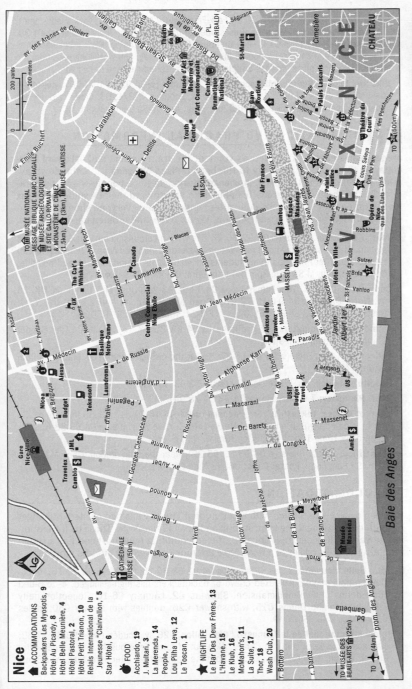

Nice

▲ ACCOMMODATIONS
Backparkers Les Myosotis, **9**
Hôtel Au Picardy, **8**
Hôtel Belle Meunière, **4**
Hôtel Pastoral, **2**
Hôtel Petit Trianon, **10**
Relais International de la
Jeunesse "Clairvallon," **5**
Star Hôtel, **6**

◆ FOOD
Acchiardo, **19**
J. Multari, **3**
La Merenda, **14**
People, **7**
Lou Pilha Leva, **12**
Le Toscan, **1**

★ NIGHTLIFE
Le Bar Des Deux Frères, **13**
L'Havane, **15**
Le Klub, **16**
McMahon's, **11**
La Suite, **17**
Thor, **18**
Wash Club, **20**

Public Transportation: Sunbus, 10 av. Félix Faure (☎04 93 13 53 13; www.sunbus.com), near pl. Leclerc and pl. Masséna. Buses operate daily 7am-8pm. Individual ticket €1.30, day pass €4, 5-day pass €13, week-long pass €17, 8-ticket *carnet* €8.30. Purchase individual tickets and day pass on board the bus; *carnet,* 5-day, and week-long pass from the office. The tourist office provides **Sunplan** bus maps, schedules, and route info.

Bike and Scooter Rental: JML Location, 34 av. Auber (☎04 93 16 07 00), opposite the train station. Bikes €11 per day, €56 per week; scooters €33/€203. Credit card deposit required. Open July-Aug. daily 9am-6:30pm; Sept.-June M-Sa 9am-6:30pm. MC/V.

■*❷ ORIENTATION AND PRACTICAL INFORMATION

Avenue Jean-Médecin, on the left as you exit the train station, and **boulevard Gambetta,** on the right, run directly to the beach. **Place Masséna** is 10min. down av. Jean-Médecin. Along the coast, **promenade des Anglais** is a people-watcher's paradise. To the southeast, past av. Jean-Médecin and toward the bus station, is **Vieux Nice.** Women should not walk alone after sundown, and everyone should exercise caution at night around the train station, *Vieux Nice,* and promenade des Anglais.

Tourist Office: av. Thiers (☎08 92 70 74 07; www.nicetourism.com), next to the train station. Makes same-day hotel reservations. Ask for a map and *Nice: A Practical Guide. Le Pitchoun* (free) has tips from students on restaurants, entertainment, and nightlife. Open June-Sept. M-Sa 8am-8pm, Su 9am-6pm; Oct.-May M-Sa 8am-7pm.

Consulates: Canada, 10 r. Lamartine (☎04 93 92 93 22). Open M-F 9am-noon. **UK,** 26 av. Notre Dame (☎04 91 15 72 10). Open M-F 9am-noon and 2-5pm. **US,** 7 av. Gustave V (☎04 93 88 89 55). Open M-F 9-11:30am and 1:30-4:30pm.

Laundromat: Lavomatique, 7 r. d'Italie (☎04 93 85 88 14). Wash €4, dry €1 per 18min. Open daily 7am-9pm.

Police: 1 av. Mal. Foch (☎04 93 17 22 22), at the opposite end of av. Mal. Foch from av. Jean-Médecin.

Hospital: St-Roch, 5 r. Pierre Devoluy (☎04 92 03 33 75).

24hr. Pharmacy: 7 r. Masséna (☎04 93 87 78 94).

Internet Access: Teknosoft, 16 r. Paganini (☎04 93 16 89 81). €1.50 for 30min., €3 per hr. Open daily 8:30am-11pm. **Alexso Info,** 2 r. de Belgique (☎04 93 88 65 00). Open daily 10am-10pm. €2.35 for 30min., €4 per hr.

Post Office: 23 av. Thiers (☎04 93 82 65 22), near the train station. Open M-F 8am-7pm, Sa 8am-noon. **Postal Code:** 06033 Nice Cédex 1.

⌐ ACCOMMODATIONS

To sleep easy, come to Nice with reservations. The city has two clusters of budget accommodations: near the train station and near *Vieux Nice.* Those by the station are newer but less centrally located; the surrounding neighborhood has a rough reputation. Hotels closer to *Vieux Nice* are more convenient but less modern.

▨ **Hôtel Belle Meunière,** 21 av. Durante (☎04 93 88 66 15; fax 04 93 82 51 76), opposite the train station. A relaxed crowd of backpackers fills high-ceilinged, 4- to 5-bed coed dorms in a former mansion. Showers €2. Laundry €6-10. Reception daily 7:30am-midnight. Dorms €15, with shower €20; doubles with shower €50; triples €60; quads €80. MC/V. ❷

Relais International de la Jeunesse "Clairvallon," 26 av. Scudéri (☎04 93 81 27 63; clajpaca@cote-dazur.com), in Cimiez, 4km out of town. Take bus #15 to Scudéri (dir.: Rimiez; 20min., every 20min., €1.30) from the train station; after 9pm, take the N2 bus

FRANCE

from pl. Masséna. Clean, 160-bed hostel in the luxurious villa of a deceased marquis, with sports field, TV room, and swimming pool. Laundry €6. Lockout 9:30am-5pm. Curfew 11pm. Dorms €15. Cash only. ❶

Hôtel Au Picardy, 10 bd. Jean Jaurès (☎/fax 04 93 85 75 51), across from the bus station. Recently renovated, good-sized rooms, some with soundproof windows, located ideally near *Vieux Nice*. Breakfast €3. Reception 8am-8pm. Singles €25, with bath €33-35; doubles €40; triples €43; quads €49. Extra bed €5. Cash only. ❸

Hôtel Petit Trianon, 11 r. Paradis (☎04 93 87 50 46; hotel.nice.lepetittrianon@wanadoo.fr), off r. Masséna. 8 simple, elegant rooms just off lively pl. Masséna. Reservations essential. Singles €30, with bath €35; doubles €40-43/€50-53; triples €66-75; quads €80-100. 10% discount on stays longer than a week. Extra bed €8. MC/V. ❸

Star Hôtel, 14 r. Biscarra (☎04 93 85 19 03; www.hotel-star.com), in a quiet neighborhood halfway between the train station and *Vieux Nice*. Offers spacious pastel rooms with modern amenities. Closed Nov.-Dec. Singles €38; doubles with shower €48, with bath €53; triples with bath €63. Prices €10-15 higher May-Sept. AmEx/MC/V. ❹

Backpackers Les Myosotis, 19 r. Meyerbeer (☎04 93 88 30 88 or 06 24 72 49 36), on the corner of r. Meyerbeer and r. de la Buffa. A youthful crowd enjoys the communal feel of this converted hotel just minutes from the beach. Clean 2- and 4-bed dorms have bright blue walls, showers, and mini-fridges. Sheets €1.20. Max. stay 4 days. Reception 24hr. Dorms €18. Cash only. ❷

Hôtel Pastoral, 27 r. Assalit (☎04 93 85 17 22), on the far side of av. Jean Médecin near the train station. A modest, comfortable hotel popular with French and international students. Breakfast €3. Reception daily 8am-8pm; access code after hours. Free luggage storage. Singles with shower €20; doubles €25, with bath €30; triples €37.50/€47.50; quads €50. Extra bed €10. Cash only. ❷

▐ FOOD

Niçois cuisine is a collection of unique dishes flavored with Mediterranean spices. Try crusty *pan bagnat*, a round loaf of bread topped with tuna, sardines, vegetables, and olive oil; *pissaladière* pizza loaded with onions, anchovies, and olives; or *socca*, thin, olive-oil-flavored chickpea bread. The famous *salade niçoise* combines tuna, olives, eggs, potatoes, tomatoes, and a spicy mustard dressing. The eateries along the promenade des Anglais and av. Masséna are expensive and unremarkable. Save your euros for olives, cheese, and produce from the **markets** at cours Saleya and av. Maché de la Libération (both open Tu-Su 7am-1pm). **Avenue Jean Médecin** features reasonable *brasseries*, *panini* vendors, and kebab stands. Load up on groceries at **Monoprix**, av. Jean Médecin, next to the Nice Etoile shopping center. (☎04 92 47 72 62. Open M-Sa 8:30am-8:50pm. MC/V.)

▨ **La Merenda,** 4 r. de la Terrasse. The simple brown awning and plain decor are deceptive. Those lucky enough to get a table can savor the work of a culinary master who turned his back on one of the most renowned restaurants in Nice to open this affordable gem. Reserve in the morning, in person, for dinner. 2 seatings at 7 and 9pm. *Plats* €10-15. Open M-F noon-1:30pm and 7-9pm. Cash only. ❸

▨ **Lou Pilha Leva,** 10-13 r. du Collet (☎04 93 13 99 08), in *Vieux Nice*. At lunch and dinner time, a line of locals and tourists hungry for inexpensive, tasty *Niçois* fare extends around the corner and down the street. The lively staff keeps things moving quickly, dishing out plate after plate of *socca* (€2), *pissaladière* (€2), and *salade niçoise* (€7). Open daily 8am-midnight. Cash only. ❶

Acchiardo, 38 r. Droite (☎04 93 85 51 16), in *Vieux Nice*. Family-style tables for simple but appetizing Italian and French dishes served up quickly by a dedicated family team. Open July M-F 7-10pm; Sept.-June M-F noon-1:30pm and 7-10pm. ❶

Le Toscan, 1 r. de Belgique (☎04 93 88 40 54), near the train station. Delicious, generous 4-course *menus* (€12, €14, or €20) use fresh produce purchased daily on the cours Saleya. Open Tu-Sa 11:45am-2pm and 6:45-10pm. MC/V. ❸

People, 12 r. Pastorelli (☎04 93 85 08 43). A trendy setting for traditional cuisine, well worth the short walk from *Vieux Nice*. Tasty regional dishes like *risotto aux truffes* (€13) and *magret de canard* with *foie gras* (€17) fill enormous chalkboard *menus* on deep purple walls. Open M-Sa noon-2:30pm and 5:30-11pm. AmEx/MC/V. ❸

J. Multari, 58bis av. Jean Médecin (☎04 93 92 01 99). No French city is complete without a *salon de thé,* bakery, *crêperie,* and sandwich shop; J. Multari provides Nice with all four in a graceful, elegant setting. Open M-Sa 6am-8:30pm. ❶

◉ SIGHTS

Many visitors to Nice head straight for the beaches and don't retreat from the sun and water until the day is done. Whatever dreams you've had about Nice's beach, though, the hard reality is an endless stretch of pebbles; bring a beach mat if you plan to soak up the sun in comfort. Perfecting your tan has its merits, but don't forget that blue waves and topless sunbathers aren't Nice's only attractions.

▨ MUSÉE NATIONAL MESSAGE BIBLIQUE MARC CHAGALL.
Chagall founded this extraordinary concrete and glass museum in 1966 to showcase his 17 *Message Biblique* paintings. Twelve of these strikingly colorful canvases illustrate the first two books of the Old Testament, and the remaining five, done entirely in shades of red, illustrate the Song of Songs. The museum also includes a small auditorium with stained glass panels illustrating the creation of the world, which occasionally stages concerts and lectures; ask at the entrance for program information. (*Av. du Dr. Ménard. Walk 15min. north of the station, or take bus #15 (dir.: Rimiez) to Musée Chagall.* ☎04 93 53 87 20; www.musee-chagall.fr. Open July-Sept. M and W-Su 10am-6pm; Oct.-June 10am-5pm. Last tickets sold 30min. before closing. €6.70, students ages 18-25 €5.20, under 18 and 1st Su of the month free.)

▨ MUSÉE MATISSE.
Henri Matisse visited Nice in 1916 and never left its shores. Originally a 17th-century Genoese villa, this museum contains a small collection of paintings and a dazzling exhibit of Matisse's three-dimensional work, including lost-wax bronze reliefs and dozens of paper-cutting tableaux. (*164 av. des Arènes de Cimiez. Take bus #15, 17, 20, 22, or 25 to Arènes. Free bus tickets between Musée Chagall and Musée Matisse; ask at either ticket counter.* ☎04 93 81 08 08. Open Apr.-Sept. M and W-Su 10am-6pm; Oct.-Mar. 10am-5pm. €4, students €2.50.)

▨ VIEUX NICE.
Though the tourist industry has brought an inevitable slew of souvenir shops, ice cream stands, and *brasseries*, *Vieux Nice*, southeast of bd. Jean Jaurès, remains the spiritual and historical heart of the city. Its tall buildings, painted in bright Mediterranean blues, yellows, and reds overlook a labyrinth of streets crowded with tiny, pansy-filled balconies, hand-painted awnings, pristine churches, and lively public squares. Artisans and artists of all kinds have shops throughout the neighborhood, particularly on **rue Droight.** In the morning, the area hosts bustling **markets,** including a fish frenzy at **place St-François** and a flower market on **cours Saleya.** In the evening, cafe tables replace the market stalls, and the quarter becomes the center of Nice's lively nightlife.

MUSÉE D'ART MODERNE ET D'ART CONTEMPORAIN.
Wavy steel beams and a glass facade welcome visitors to this museum, which houses the work of French New Realists and American Pop Artists like Lichtenstein, Klein, and Warhol. Minimalist galleries pay homage to avant-garde pieces, including the fantastic statues of Niki de St. Phalle. An exhibit on the "School of Nice" traces the history of local movements that developed in opposition to the Parisian art scene. (*Prom. des Arts, at*

the intersection of av. St-Jean Baptiste and Traverse Garibaldi. Take bus #5, dir.: St-Charles, to Musée Promenade des Arts. ☎*04 93 62 61 62; www.mamac-nice.org. Open Tu-Su 10am-6pm. €4, students €2.50, under 18 and 1st and 3rd Su of every month free.)*

CATHÉDRALE ORTHODOXE RUSSE ST-NICOLAS. Also known as the **Eglise Russe,** the cathedral was commissioned by Empress Marie Feodorovna in memory of her husband, Tsar Nicholas I, who died in Nice in 1865. Built to imitate Moscow's 16th-century churches, the onion-domed structure quickly became a spiritual home for exiled Russian nobles. Its color scheme, however, is straight from the Riviera, dominated by Mediterranean light blue and yellow rather than dark blue and gray. *(17 bd. du Tsarevitch, off bd. Gambetta.* ☎*04 93 96 88 02. Open daily June-Sept. 9am-noon and 2:30-6pm; Oct.-May 9:30am-noon and 2:30-5pm. €2.50.)*

LE CHÂTEAU. At the eastern end of the promenade, Le Château—the formal name for the remains of an 11th-century cathedral—marks the site of the city's birthplace. Don't be fooled: there hasn't been a chateau here since it was destroyed by Louis XIV. The hilltop does, however, provide a spectacular view of the rooftops of Nice and the sparkling Baie des Anges. In the summer, an outdoor theater hosts orchestral and vocal concerts. The vista can be reached by climbing 400 steps or catching the elevator at the Tour Bellanda. *(Park open daily June-Aug. 8am-8pm; Sept. and Apr.-May 8am-7pm; Oct.-Mar. 8am-6pm. Elevator runs daily June-Aug. 9am-8pm; Sept.-Mar 10am-6pm; Apr.-May 9am-7pm. €1.)*

OTHER SIGHTS. Named by the rich English community that commissioned it, the **promenade des Anglais,** a posh, palm-lined seaside boulevard, is Nice's answer to the great pedestrian thoroughfares of Paris, London, and New York. Today the promenade is lined by luxury hotels like the stately **Négresco** (toward the western end), where the staff still don top hats and 19th-century uniforms. Just east of the Négresco, the **Espace Masséna** provides a lovely, shady area where romantic picnickers can flirt beside the fountains. The seashore between bd. Gambetta and the Opéra alternates private **beaches** with crowded public strands, but a large section west of bd. Gambetta is reserved entirely for public use.

🎵🎭 ENTERTAINMENT AND NIGHTLIFE

Nice's **Jazz Festival,** in mid-July at the Parc et Arènes de Cimiez near the Musée Matisse, attracts world-famous performers. (☎08 20 80 04 00; www.nicejazzfest.com. Tickets €33.) The **◼Carnaval,** in late February, gives Rio a run for its money with three weeks of parades, floral processions, confetti, fireworks, and parties.

Lazy days in the sun give visitors a chance to gear up for some of the best nightlife on the entire Riviera. Bars and nightclubs around r. Masséna and *Vieux Nice* pulsate with dance and jazz. Most will turn you away if they catch you wearing shorts, sandals, or a baseball cap. To experience Nice's nightlife without spending a euro, head down to the **promenade des Anglais,** where street performers, musicians, and pedestrians fill the beach and boardwalk. The free brochure *La Côte d'Azur en Fêtes,* available at the tourist office, provides info on nightlife and festivals. Exercise caution after dark. At night, men have a reputation for harassing lone women on the promenade, near the train station, and in the Jardin Albert 1er; the beach also becomes a gathering place for prostitutes and thugs.

BARS

◼ **McMahon's,** 50 bd. Jean Jaurès. Locals and expats stay entertained with nonstop contests, theme parties, and dancing barmaids. Happy Hour daily 6-9pm (pints €3, wine €2). Cheap Tuesday (whisky, vodka, or gin cocktails €2). Theme parties F. Request DJ and free shots on Sa. Open daily 6:30pm-2am.

Thor, 32 cours Saleya. Svelte blonde bartenders pour pints for a youthful crowd amid war shields, long wooden oars, and glasses shaped like Viking horns in this raucous Scandinavian pub. Daily live music starting at 10pm. Happy Hour 6-9pm (pints €4.50). Open daily 6pm-2:30am.

L'Havane, 32 r. de France. A mid-20s crowd enjoys free tapas with mojitos (€7.60) and live salsa bands. Open daily 5pm-2:30am.

Le Bar Des Deux Frères, 1 r. du Moulin. Vinyl records cover the walls of this hip local favorite, where nightly DJs keep a young crowd hopping with reggae, rock, and techno. Open Tu-Sa 9pm-2:30am.

CLUBS

Wash Club, 26 quai Lunel. A crowd of young fashionistas show off their trendy threads against a backdrop of white vinyl stools and blank tile walls, while planning their next purchases from designer outfits in display cases at this brand-new, already popular club. Cover €15. Open Th-Su midnight-5am.

La Suite, 2 r. Brea. With velvet theater curtains and tall white candles, this swanky *boîte* attracts a well-dressed, well-moneyed crowd. Wild go-go girls help to pick up the pace on weekends. Cover €13. Open Tu-Su 11pm-2:30am.

Le Klub, 6 r. Halévy. Nice's most popular gay club features a sleek lounge and video projections on the dance floor. Cocktails €5-10. Cover €11. Open T-Su midnight-5am.

▶ DAYTRIPS FROM NICE: THE CORNICHES

Rocky shores, pebble beaches, and luxurious villas line the coast between hectic Nice and high-rolling Monaco. More relaxing than their glamorous neighbors, these tiny towns have interesting museums, ancient finds, and breathtaking countryside. The train offers a glimpse of the coast up close, while bus rides on the high roads allow bird's-eye views of the steep cliffs and crashing sea below.

VILLEFRANCHE-SUR-MER. This town's narrow streets and red-roofed houses have enchanted artists and writers from Aldous Huxley to Katherine Mansfield. As you stroll from the train station along quai Courbet, a sign for the *vieille ville* points to the spooky 13th-century **rue Obscure,** the oldest street in Villefranche. At the end is the **Chapelle St-Pierre,** decorated by Jean Cocteau, former resident, filmmaker, and jack-of-all-arts. (☎04 93 76 90 70. Open summer Tu-Sa 10am-noon and 4-8:30pm; low season reduced hours. €2.) **Trains** run from Nice. (8min., 2 per hr., €1.40.) To get to the **tourist office** from the train station, exit on quai 1, head inland on av. G. Clémenceau, and take the right-hand branch of av. Sadi Carnot; the office is at the end of the street. (☎04 93 01 73 68; www.villefranche-sur-mer.com. Open June-Sept. daily 9am-7pm; Oct.-May M-Sa 9am-noon and 2-6pm.)

ST-JEAN-CAP-FERRAT. A lovely town with an even lovelier beach, St-Jean-Cap-Ferrat is the trump card of the Riviera. The **Fondation Ephrussi di Rothschild,** just off av. D. Semeria, is a stunning Italian villa that houses the furniture and art collections of the Baroness de Rothschild, including German porcelain, Gobelins tapestries, and Chinese vases. The seven lush gardens range from Japanese to Florentine. (Open July-Aug. daily 10am-7pm; Sept.-Oct. and mid-Feb. to June daily 10am-6pm; Nov. to mid-Feb. M-F 2-6pm, Sa-Su 10am-6pm. €8.50, students €6.50.) The town's beautiful **beaches** have earned the area the nickname *"presqu'île des rêves"* (peninsula of dreams). The tiny **tourist office,** 59 av. Denis Séméria, is in the middle of the peninsula, along the winding street that runs from Nice and Monaco to the port. (☎04 93 76 08 90. Open July-Aug. M-Sa 9am-6pm; Sept.-June 10am-4pm.) RCA **bus #111** runs from Nice (25min., M-Sa 9:10am and 12:15pm, €2.10).

EZE. Three-tiered Eze owes its fame to the Roman-village-turned-medieval-citadel in the middle tier. The **Porte des Maures** was the Moors' golden ticket into Eze during a 10th-century surprise attack; they ended up controlling the village for the following 70 years. Nearby, the **Chapelle de la Saint-Croix** is the oldest building in town. The best views are 40min. up the **Sentier Friedrich Nietzsche,** where its namesake found inspiration; the path begins in Eze Bord-du-Mer, 100m east of the train station and tourist office, and ends at the base of the medieval city, near the Fragonard parfumerie. Frequent **trains** run from Nice (12min., 2 per hr., €3).

MONACO AND MONTE-CARLO

Monaco (pop. 7200) has money—lots of it—invested in ubiquitous surveillance cameras, high-speed luxury cars, and sleek yachts. At Monaco's spiritual heart is its famous casino in Monte-Carlo, a magnet for the wealthy and dissolute since 1885. The sheer spectacle of it all is worth a daytrip from Nice.

CALLING TO AND FROM MONACO	Monaco's country code is 377. To call Monaco from France, dial 00377, then the 8-digit Monaco number. To call France from Monaco, dial 0033 and drop the first zero of the French number.

⬛🚻 TRANSPORTATION AND PRACTICAL INFORMATION. Trains run to: Antibes (1hr., every 30min., €7); Cannes (65min., every 30min., €7.50); and Nice (25min., every 30min., €3.10). **Buses** (☎04 93 85 64 44) leave bd. des Moulins and av. Princesse Alice, near the tourist office, for Nice (45min., every 15min., €4). The enormous **Rocher de Monaco** looms over the harbor, with **Monaco-Ville** clustered at the top. The historical and legislative heart of the city can be found in this district, home to the Palais Princier, the Cathédrale de Monaco, and narrow cafe-lined pedestrian avenues. **La Condamine** quarter, Monaco's port, sits just below Monaco-Ville, with a colorful morning market, lively bars, and lots of traffic. The ritz and glitz for which Monaco is famous is mostly concentrated in **Monte-Carlo,** home to the casino. **Bus #4** links the Ste-Dévote train station entrance to the casino; buy tickets on board (€1.40, *carnet* of 4 €3.30). At the **tourist office,** 2a bd. des Moulins, a friendly, English-speaking staff provides city maps and books hotels free of charge. (☎92 16 61 16; www.monaco-tourisme.com. Open M-Sa 9am-7pm, Su 10am-noon.) **Postal Code:** MC 98000 Monaco.

🍴🏠 ACCOMMODATIONS AND FOOD. There's no need to stay in Monaco itself; the nearby town of **Beausoleil,** in France, has several reasonable options and is only a 10min. walk from the Casino. **Hôtel Cosmopolite ❹,** 19 bd. du Général Leclerc, has comfortable rooms managed by English-speaking Italian owners. (☎04 93 78 36 00; www.hotelcosmopolite.com. Singles €42; doubles €68; triples €84. AmEx/MC/V.) The rooms at **Hôtel Diana ❸,** 17 bd. du Général Leclerc, show some signs of wear and tear, but come with A/C, TV, and firm beds. (☎04 93 78 47 58; www.monte-carlo.mc/hotel-diana-beausoleil. Singles €35; doubles €52; triples €63. AmEx/MC/V.) Not surprisingly, most of Monaco has little budget fare. Try the narrow streets behind the **place du Palais** for reasonably-priced sit-down meals, or fill a picnic basket at the fruit and flower **market** on pl. d'Armes at the end of av. Prince Pierre. (Open daily 6am-1pm.) The bright, bustling **Café Costa Rica ❷,** 40 bd. des Moulins, serves up *bruschetta,* salads, and other flavorful Italian staples at lunchtime, and tea and crepes after 3pm. (☎93 25 44 45. *Plats du jour* €10-11. Open July-Aug. M-F 8am-8pm, Sa-Su 8am-3pm; Sept.-June daily 8am-7pm. Closed Aug. 1-15. V.) Fontvieille's shopping plaza has a huge **Carrefour** supermarket. (☎92 05 57 00. Open M-Sa 8:30am-10pm.)

FRANCE

⊡ ⊡ SIGHTS AND ENTERTAINMENT. The notorious **⊠Monte-Carlo Casino,** at pl. du Casino, is where Richard Burton wooed Elizabeth Taylor and Mata Hari shot a Russian spy. The slot machines open at 2pm, while blackjack, craps, and roulette open at noon (cover €10). The exclusive *salons privés,* where French games such as *chemin de fer* and *trente et quarante* begin at noon, will cost you an extra €10 cover. Next door, the more relaxed **Café de Paris** opens at noon and has no cover. All casinos have **dress codes** (no shorts, sneakers, sandals, or jeans), and the *salons privés* require coat and tie. Guards are strict about the **18 age minimum;** bring a passport as proof. Perched above the casino is the **Palais Princier,** the occasional home of Prince Rainier and his tabloid-darling family. Visitors curious for a glimpse of royal life can tour the small but lavishly decorated palace whose stunning apartments boast silk walls, coffered ceilings, gilt furniture, and Venetian crystal chandeliers. (☎93 25 18 31. Open daily June-Sept. 9:30am-6pm; Oct. 10am-5pm. €6, students €3.) Next door, the **Cathédrale de Monaco,** at pl. St-Martin, is the burial site of 35 generations of the Grimaldi family and was the venue for Prince Rainier and Princess Grace's 1956 wedding. The victim of a car accident, Princess Grace lies behind the altar in a tomb marked with her Latinized name, "Patritia Gracia." (Open daily Mar.-Oct. 8am-7pm; Nov.-Feb. 8am-6pm. Free.) The **Private Collection of Antique Cars of H.S.H. Prince Rainier III,** on les Terraces de Fontvieille, puts the casino's parking lot to shame, showcasing 105 of the sexiest cars ever made. (Open daily 10am-6pm. €6, students €3.) Though Monaco hardly seems like a desert locale, innumerable species of cacti imported from America in the 16th century thrive in the **Jardin Exotique,** 62 bd. du Jardin Exotique. (Open daily mid-May to mid-Sept. 9am-7pm; mid-Sept. to mid-May 9am-6pm or until sundown. €6.60, students €3.20.) The **Musée Océanographique,** on av. St-Martin, founded by Jacques Cousteau and Prince Albert I, holds a 90-tank aquarium full of exotic sea life, including the largest green moray eel in the world. (☎93 15 36 00; www.oceano.mc. Open daily Apr.-Aug. 9:30am-7:30pm; Sept. 9:30am-7pm; Oct.-Mar. 10am-6pm. €11, students €6.) Monaco's nightlife offers the catwalk-ready a great chance to see and be seen. **La Condamine,** near the port, is cheaper and caters to a younger clientele. Pricier bars and clubs near the casino are frequented by a glitzy crowd. **Stars N' Bars,** 6 quai Antoine 1*er,* draws a young, international crowd with vintage decor, video games, and the latest pop and techno beats. (Open daily 11am-midnight. Disco open July-Aug. daily 12:30-5am; Sept.-June F-Sa 12:30-5am.) **Café Grand Prix,** at 1 quai Antoine 1*er,* honors Monaco's famous race with sleek stools, racing-print etched glass, and red walls. (Open daily 10am-5am. AmEx/MC/V.)

CORSICA (LA CORSE)

Napoleon claimed that the smell of the herbs on Corsica's hillsides was so distinctive that he could identify his home island with his eyes shut. Even if your senses aren't that acute, there's no confusing Corsica with the French mainland—despite centuries of invasions by Phoenicia, Carthage, Rome, Pisa, and Genoa, it has managed to preserve a unique, fiercely guarded culture. Natives remain divided over the issue of allegiance to France, and often reject the French language in favor of Corse, the local dialect. Most of Corsica's visitors come for the endless possibilities offered by its unspoiled landscapes, which are easily accessible even from major towns. Nearly one-third of the island is a protected nature reserve, with over 100 summits, far-reaching networks of hiking and ski trails, and unbroken coastlines that beckon to kayakers, windsurfers, sailors, and sunbathers alike.

FRANCE

ⓧ⊏ GETTING THERE AND TRANSPORTATION

Air France and its subsidiary **Compagnie Corse Méditerranée (CCM)** fly to Ajaccio and
Bastia from Paris (round-trip from €173, students €140); Nice (€121, students
€98); and Marseille (€117, students €104). In Ajaccio, the Air France/CCM office
is at 3 bd. du Roi Jérôme (☎ 08 20 82 08 20). **Ferries** between the mainland and Corsica can make for a rough trip, and aren't always much cheaper than a plane. High-
speed ferries (3½hr.) run from Nice. Overnight ferries from Marseille take
upwards of 10 hours. The **Société National Maritime Corse Méditerranée** (☎ 08 91 70
18 01; www.sncm.fr) sends ferries from Marseille (€35-53, under 25 €20-40) and
Nice (€30-41, under 25 €15-26) to Ajaccio and Bastia. Get SNCM schedules and
prices at travel agencies and ports. **Corsica Ferries** (☎ 08 25 09 50 95; www.corsicaf-
erries.com) has similar destinations and prices; it crosses from Livorno and
Genoa, Italy to Bastia (€16-26). **SAREMAR** (☎ 04 95 73 00 96) and **Moby Lines** (☎ 04 95
73 00 29) go from Santa Teresa, Sardinia to Bonifacio. (€6.80-15 per person.)

Train service in Corsica is slow and limited to destinations north of Ajaccio.
Travelers can't use rail passes. **Buses** provide more comprehensive service; call
Eurocorse Voyages (☎ 04 95 21 06 30) for more info. **Hiking** is the best way to
explore the island's mountainous interior. The **GR20** is an extremely difficult 14- to
15-day, 180km trail that takes hikers across the island from Calenzana to Conca.
The popular **Mare e Monti** (7-10 days), **Mare a Mare Sud** (4-6 days), **Mare a Mare Nord**
(12 days), and **Mare a Mare Centre** (7 days) trails are shorter and easier. The **Parc
Naturel Régional de la Corse**, 2 Sargent Casalonga, in Ajaccio (☎ 04 95 51 79 00;
www.parc-naturel-corse.com), has maps and a guide to *gîtes d'étape* (hostels).

AJACCIO (AIACCIU)

Brimming with more urban energy than most Corsican towns, Ajaccio (pop. 60,000)
has excellent museums and nightlife to complement its palm-lined boulevards and yellow sunlit buildings. Inside the ▨**Musée Fesch**, 50-52 r. Cardinal Fesch, you'll find an
impressive collection of 14th- to 19th-century Italian paintings gathered by Napoleon's
art-collecting Uncle Fesch. Also within the complex is the **Chapelle Impériale**, the final
resting place of most of the Bonaparte family—though Napoleon himself is buried in
Paris. (Open July-Aug. M 1:30-6pm, Tu-Th 9am-6:30pm, F 9am-6:30pm and 0pm-mid-
night, Sa-Su 10:30am-6pm; Sept.-June reduced hours. Museum €5.40, students €3.80;
chapel €1.50/€0.75.) Napoleon's first home, the **Musée National de la Maison Bonaparte**,
r. St-Charles, between r. Bonaparte and r. Roi-de-Rome, is now a warehouse of memorabilia. (Open May.-Sept. M 2-6pm, Tu-Su 9am-noon and 2-6pm; Oct.-Apr. M 2-5pm, Tu-
Su 10am-noon and 2-5pm. €4, students and ages 18-25 €2.60, under 18 free.) **Boulevard
Pascal Rossini** is home to several lively bars. At ▨**La Boca Loca**, 2 r. de la Porta, live flamenco and salsa music spices up a red-curtained interior and tree-lined terrace.
(Cocktails €5. Mojitos €5.50. Tapas €2.80. Open Tu-Sa 7pm-2am.)

At **Aéroport Campo dell'Oro** (AJA; ☎ 04 95 23 56 56), flights serve Lyon, Marseille,
Nice, and Paris. **Trains** leave pl. de la Gare for Bastia (3-4hr., 4 per day, €24) and
Corte (2½hr., 4 per day, €13). Eurocorse Voyages **buses** go to: Bastia (3hr., 2 per
day, €18); Bonifacio (3hr., 2 per day, €21); and Corte (1¾hr., 2 per day, €11). The
tourist office is at 3 bd. du Roi Jérôme. (☎ 04 95 51 53 03; www.tourisme.fr/ajaccio.
Open July-Aug. M-Sa 8am-8:30pm, Su 9am-1pm and 4-7pm; Sept.-June reduced
hours.) In June-Aug., hotel rates soar and vacancies plummet. The unbelievably
welcoming ▨**Pension de Famille Tina Morelli ❹**, 1 r. Major Lambroschini, is nearly
always full; book as far in advance as possible. (☎/fax 04 95 21 16 97. Singles with
breakfast €50, with full meals €63; doubles €90/€115. Cash only.) To **camp** at **Barbicaja ❶**, take bus #5 from av. Dr. Ramaroni to Barbicaja. (☎/fax 04 95 52 01 17.
Open May to mid-Sept. €5.85 per person, €2.30 per tent and per car. Electricity

€2.40.) Check out the fabulous ▨**morning market** on pl. du Marché. (Tu-Su 8am-1pm.) Get groceries at **Monoprix,** 31 cours Napoléon. (Open July-Sept. M-Sa 8:30am-8pm; Oct.-June M-Sa 8:30am-7:15pm.) **Postal Code:** 20000.

BONIFACIO (BONIFAZIU)

On the southern tip of Corsica, the stone ramparts of Bonifacio (pop. 3000), perched on 70m-tall limestone cliffs, present an imposing visage to miles of empty turquoise sea. Bonifacio's fantastic **boat tours** reveal multicolored coves, cliffs, and stalactite-filled grottoes. Ferries also run to the pristine sands of **Iles Lavezzi,** a nature reserve with beautiful reefs perfect for **scuba diving.** Companies that offer tours include **Marina Croisières.** (☎04 95 73 12 41. Grottes-Falaises-Calanques tour every 30min. 9:30am-6pm. €14. Iles Lavezzi 7-8 departures per day, return boats every hr. until 6pm. €25.) To explore the *haute ville,* head up the steep, broad steps of the **montée Rastello,** located halfway down the port, where excellent views of the hazy cliffs to the east await. Continue up montée St-Roch to the lookout at **Porte des Gênes,** a drawbridge built by invaders. Then walk to the **place du Marché** to see Bonifacio's famous cliffs and the **Grain de Sable,** an enormous limestone formation that serves as a perch for daring cliff-divers.

Eurocorse Voyages (☎04 95 21 06 30) runs **buses** to Ajaccio (3½hr., 1-3 per day, €21). To reach the **tourist office,** at the corner of av. de Gaulle and r. F. Scamaroni, walk along the port; before the *gare maritime,* climb the stairs. (☎04 95 73 11 88; www.bonifacio.fr. Open May to mid-Oct. daily 9am-8pm; mid-Oct. to Apr. M-F 9am-noon and 2-6pm.) Finding affordable rooms is virtually impossible in summer; avoid visiting in August, when prices soar. Try **Hôtel des Etrangers ❹,** av. Sylvère Bohn. (☎04 95 73 01 09; fax 04 95 73 16 97. Singles and doubles €47-74; triples €70; quads €72-84. MC/V.) **Camping** is by far the cheapest option. **L'Araguina ❶,** av. Sylvère Bohn, is at the entrance to town between Hôtel des Etrangers and the port. (☎04 95 73 02 96; fax 04 95 73 57 04. Open April to mid-Oct. €5.60 per person, €2.10 per car and per tent. Electricity €2.80. Laundry €6.) A few supermarkets dot the port, including **SPAR,** at the start of rte. de Santa Manza. (Open daily July-Aug. 8am-8:30pm; low season reduced hours.) **Postal Code:** 20169.

BASTIA

Bastia (pop. 40,000), Corsica's second-largest city, is a well-trampled gateway with connections to the French mainland and to the island's more removed vacation spots. But despite travelers' constant comings and goings, Bastia deserves more than a passing glance. Its enormous 14th-century **Citadel,** also called Terra Nova, has remained almost intact, with ramparts that reach down the hill toward the *vieux port,* dwarfing adjacent shops and bakeries. The tiny **Eco-Musée,** in the citadel's old powder magazine, contains a detailed replica of a traditional Corsican village. (Open Apr.-Oct. M-Sa 9am-noon and 2-6pm. €3.50, students €3.) The 17th-century **Eglise St-Jean Baptiste,** pl. de l'Hôtel de Ville, is the largest church in Corsica. Shuttle buses (30min., €8) leave from the prefecture, across from the train station, for the **Bastia-Poretta Airport** (BIA; ☎04 95 54 54 54), where flights go to Marseille, Nice, and Paris. **Trains** (☎04 95 32 80 61) run from pl. de la Gare to Ajaccio (4hr., 5 per day, €24) and Calvi (3hr., 4 per day, €19). Eurocorse **buses** (☎04 95 21 06 31) leave rte. du Nouveau Port for Ajaccio (3hr., 2 per day, €18). The **tourist office,** pl. St-Nicolas, has copies of the bus schedule. (☎04 95 54 20 40; www.bastia-tourisme.com. Open daily July-Aug. 8am-9:30pm; Sept.- June 8:30am-noon and 2-6pm.) ▨**Hôtel Central ❺,** 3 r. Miot, has antique furniture in large, well-kept rooms. (☎04 95 31 71 12; www.centralhotel.fr. Breakfast €5.50. May-Oct singles €55-65; doubles €60-78. Low-season prices €10 less. AmEx/MC/V.) To reach **Les Orangiers camping ❶,** take bus #4 (€1.15) from the tourist office to Licciola-Miomo. (☎04 95 33 24 09. Open May to mid-Oct. €4.60 per person, €2.70 per tent, €2.50 per car. Electricity €3.50.) Cheap cafes crowd **place St-Nicolas. SPAR** supermarket is at 14 r. César Campinchi. (Open M-Sa 8am-12:30pm and 4-8:30pm, Su 8am-noon.)

FRANCE

CAP CORSE

North of Bastia stretches the gorgeous Cap Corse peninsula, a necklace of tiny former fishing villages strung together by a narrow road of perilous curves, windswept valleys and sheer oceanside cliffs. The Cap is a dream come true for **hikers;** every forest and cliff lays claim to some decaying Genoese tower or hilltop chapel. If you don't have access to a car, you can take **bus #4** (☎ 04 95 31 06 65) from pl. St-Nicolas in Bastia to Erbalunga (20min., 1-2 per hr., €2), Macinaggio (50min., 3 per day, €6.40), or Sisco (30min., every hr., €2.30). Ask politely and the driver will drop you off wherever you like. Most buses serve coastal towns; you'll have to hike to inland villages. The nearest accommodations are in **Bastia** (see above).

CORTE (CORTI)

Corte (pop. 6000) is an unforgettable eyeful of plunging cliffs, jagged summits, and endless skies. The town's *vieille ville*, with steep streets and a stone **citadel**, has always been a bastion of Corsican patriotism. At the top of r. Scolisca is the engaging **Musée de la Corse**, which provides entrance to the higher fortifications of the citadel. (Open daily June-Sept. 10am-8pm; Nov.-May reduced hours. €5.30, students €3.) Corte's mountains offer spectacular **hiking, biking,** and **horseback riding.** Rent **horses** at **Ferme Equestre Albadu**, 1.5km from town on N193. (☎ 04 95 46 24 55. €14 per hr., €75 per day with picnic.) **Trains** (☎ 04 95 00 80 17) leave from the rotary, at av. Jean Nicoli and N193, for Ajaccio (2½hr., 4 per day, €13) and Bastia (2hr., 5 per day, €12). Eurocorse Voyages (☎ 04 95 31 73 76) runs **buses** to Ajaccio (1¾hr., M-Sa 2 per day, €10) and Bastia (1¼hr., M-Sa 2 per day, €10). To reach the town center from the train station, turn right on N193, then left onto av. Jean Nicoli. Follow the road to cours Paoli, then turn left onto pl. Paoli; at the far right corner, climb the stairs of r. Scolisca to reach the **tourist office.** (☎ 04 95 46 26 70; www.corte-tourisme.com. Open July-Aug. M-Sa 9am-8pm, Su 10am-6pm; low season reduced hours.) Next door, experts at the **Parc Naturel Régional** provide additional info for hikers. (☎ 04 95 46 27 44; www.parc-naturel-corse.com. Open May-Sept. M-F 9am-noon and 2-6pm.) The no-frills **Hôtel-Residence Porette ❷**, 6 allée du 9 Septembre, hides functional, clean rooms and a pleasant garden behind an unattractive facade. Head left from the train station; the hotel is across from the stadium. (☎ 04 95 45 11 11; fax 04 95 61 02 85. Breakfast €5. Singles €21-27, with bath €39; doubles €25-29/€39; triples €55; quads €59. AmEx.) **Place Paoli** has sandwiches and pizza, while **rue Scolisca** and the surrounding streets abound with cheap local fare. A huge **Casino** supermarket is near the station on N193. (Open July-Aug. M-Sa 8:30am-8pm; Sept.-June reduced hours.) **Postal Code:** 20250.

THE ALPS (LES ALPES)

Nature's architecture is the real attraction of the Alps. The curves of the Chartreuse Valley rise to rugged crags in the Vercors range and ultimately crescendo at Europe's highest peak, Mont Blanc. Lyon acts as a major gateway to the region, but TGV trains also whisk travelers directly from Paris to Grenoble or Annecy; scenic trains and slower buses service Alpine towns from there. Service is more frequent from December to April, during ski season.

GRENOBLE

Hordes of university students, expats from all corners of the globe, and sizeable North and West African populations collide in Grenoble (pop. 156,000), a dynamic city whose snow-capped peaks are cherished by athletes and aesthetes alike.

FRANCE

▣⟩ TRANSPORTATION AND PRACTICAL INFORMATION. Trains leave pl. de la Gare for: Annecy (2hr., 18 per day, €15); Lyon (1½hr., 27 per day, €17); Marseille (2½-4½hr., 15 per day, €35); Nice (5-6½hr., 5 per day, €56); and Paris (3hr., 10 per day, €60-80). **Buses** leave from the left of the train station for Geneva, Switzerland (3hr., daily, €26). From the station, turn right into pl. de la Gare, take the third left on av. Alsace-Lorraine, and follow the tram tracks on r. Félix Poulat and r. Blanchard to reach the **tourist office**, 14 r. de la République. (☎ 04 76 42 41 41; www.grenoble-isere.info. Open M-Sa 9am-6:30pm, Su 10am-1pm and 2-5pm.) **Celciuscafe.com**, on r. Gutéal, has **Internet** access. (☎ 04 76 46 43 36. €2.50 per hr. Open daily 9am-11pm.) **Postal Code:** 38000.

▣▢ ACCOMMODATIONS AND FOOD. From the tourist office, follow pl. Ste-Claire to pl. Notre-Dame and take r. du Vieux Temple on the far right to reach ▧**Le Foyer de l'Etudiante ❶**, 4 r. Ste-Ursule. This stately building serves as a dorm during most of the year, but opens its large rooms to travelers from June to August. (☎ 04 76 42 00 84; www.multimania.com/foyeretudiante. Sheets €10. Laundry €2.20. Free Internet access. June-Aug. 3-night min. for room; 5-night max. for dorm. Dorms €8; singles €15; doubles €24. MC/V.) **Hôtel de la Poste ❷**, 25 r. de la Poste, in the pedestrian zone, has amazing rooms. (☎/fax 04 76 46 67 25. Singles €22, with shower €28; doubles €28/€35; triples €32; quads €37. MC/V.) To reach **Camping Les 3 Pucelles ❶**, 58 r. des Allobroges in Seyssins, take tram A (dir.: Fontaine-La Poya) to Louis Maisonnat, then take bus #51 (dir.: Les Nalettes) to Mas des Iles; it's on the left. (☎ 04 76 96 45 73; www.camping-trois-pucelles.com. One person, tent, and car €7.50; extra person €3.) Regional restaurants cater to locals around **place de Gordes,** while Asian eateries abound between **place Notre-Dame** and the river. *Pâtisseries* and North African joints congregate around **rue Chenoise** and **rue Lionne,** between the pedestrian area and the river. **La Belle Etoile ❷**, 2 rue Lionne, has excellent Tunisian dishes. (Open T-Su noon-2pm and 7-11pm. Entrees €7.40-13. AmEx/MC/V.) A **Monoprix** supermarket is opposite the tourist office. (Open M-Sa 8:30am-7:30pm. AmEx/MC/V.)

◩▤ SIGHTS AND ENTERTAINMENT. Téléphériques (cable cars) depart from quai Stéphane-Jay every 10min. for the 16th-century **Bastille,** a fort perched 475m above the city. (Open July-Aug. M 11am-12:15am, Tu-Su 9:15am-12:15am; Sept.-June reduced hours. One-way €3.80, round-trip €5.50; students €3/4.40.) You can walk down via the **Parc Guy Pape,** through the other end of the fortress, to the Jardin des Dauphins (1hr.). Cross the Pont St-Laurent and go up Montée Chalemont for the **Musée Dauphinois,** 30 r. Maurice Gignoux, which offers exhibits on the people of the Alps and the history of skiing. (Open June-Sept. M and W-Su 10am-7pm; Oct.-May 10am-6pm. €3.20, under 25 free.) The **Musée de Grenoble,** 5 pl. de Lavelette, has one of France's most prestigious collections of art. (☎ 04 76 63 44 44; www.museedegrenoble.fr. Open M and W-Su 10am-6:30pm. €5, students €2.) The biggest and most developed **ski areas** are to the east in **Oisans;** the **Alpe d'Huez** boasts 220km of trails. (Tourist office ☎ 04 76 11 44 44; ski area 04 76 80 30 30. Lift tickets €33.50 per day, €202 per week.) The **Belledonne** region, northeast of Grenoble, has both lower elevation and lower prices; its most popular ski area is **Chamrousse.** (Tourist office ☎ 04 76 89 92 65. Lift tickets €24 per day, €108-139 per week.) Whether you've spent your day in the museums or on the slopes, Grenoble's funky cafes, bars, and clubs are a great way to top it off. Most are in the area between **place St-André** and **place Notre-Dame.** Drunken scholars mix it up at **Le Couche-Tard,** 1 r. du Palais, a small, graffiti-covered bar. (Happy Hour 7-10pm; cocktails €2. Open M-Sa 7pm-2am. AmEx/MC/V.)

CHAMONIX

The site of the first winter Olympics in 1924, Chamonix (pop. 10,000) combines the dignity of Mont Blanc, Europe's highest peak (4807m), with the spirit of energetic travelers. Whether you've come to climb up the mountains or ski down them, be cautious—the slopes are as challenging as they are beautiful. The **Aiguille du Midi** *téléphérique* (cable car) offers a pricey, knuckle-whitening ascent over forests and snowy cliffs to a needlepoint peak at the top, revealing a fantastic panorama from 3842m (€34). Bring your passport to continue by gondola to **Helbronner, Italy** for views of three countries and of the **Matterhorn** and **Mont Blanc** peaks. (May-Sept., round-trip €18.) Chamonix has 350km of **hiking**; the tourist office distributes a map with departure points (€4). The mountains that surround Chamonix are also ideal for **skiing.** To the south, **Le Tour-Col de Balme,** above the village of **Le Tour** (☎ 04 50 54 00 58; day pass €27), draws beginner and intermediate skiers, while **Les Grands Montets** (☎ 04 50 54 00 71; day pass €36), to the north, is the *grande dame* of Chamonix skiing, with advanced terrain and **snowboarding** facilities.

Trains leave av. de la Gare (☎ 04 50 53 12 98) for: Annecy (2½hr., 7 per day, €17); Geneva, Switzerland (2½hr., 7 per day, €45); Lyon (4hr., 6 per day, €32); and Paris (6½hr., 7 per day, €50-70). Société Alpes Transports **buses** (☎ 04 50 53 01 15) leave the train station for Annecy (2¼hr., daily M-F, €15) and Geneva, Switzerland (1hr.; May-Nov. 1-3 per day; Dec.-Apr. 4- 5 per day; €33). From the station, follow av. Michel Croz, turn left on r. du Dr. Paccard, and take the first right to reach the **tourist office,** 85 pl. du Triangle de l'Amitié. (☎ 04 50 53 00 24; www.chamonix.com. Open daily July-Aug. 8:30am-12:30pm and 2-7pm; Sept.-June reduced hours.) **Compagnie des Guides,** in Maison de la Montagne facing the tourist office, leads ski trips and hikes. (☎ 04 50 53 00 88. Open daily Jan.-Mar. and July-Aug. 8:30am-noon and 3:30-7:30pm; low season reduced hours.) Chamonix's *gîtes* (mountain hostels) and dorms are cheap, but they fill up fast; call ahead. From the train station, go down av. Michel Croz and turn right on r. Joseph Vallot for the ■**Red Mountain Lodge** ❷, 435 r. Joseph Vallot. The fun-loving, English-speaking staff keeps guests happy with plush furnishings, views of Mont Blanc, and frequent barbeques for €10. (☎ 04 50 53 94 97. Breakfast included. Dorms €16; doubles €40, with bath €50; triples €60/€75. Cash only.) Turn left from the base of the Aiguille du Midi, continue past the main round-about, and look right to camp at **L'Ile des Barrats** ❶, 185 chemin de l'Ile des Barrats, off of rte. des Pélerins. (☎/fax 04 50 53 51 44. Open Feb. to mid-Oct. €5.40 per person, €4.90 per tent, €2.20 per car. MC/V.) Restaurants in Chamonix cluster around the town center on **Rue du Docteur Paccard** and **Rue des Moulins,** which also boast popular nightclubs and bars. Get groceries at **Super U,** 117 r. Joseph Vallot. (Open M-Sa 8:15am-7:30pm, Su 8:30am-noon.) **Postal Code:** 74400.

ANNECY

With narrow cobblestone streets, winding canals, and a turreted castle, Annecy (pop. 50,000) appears more like a fairy-tale fabrication than a modern city. The **Palais de l'Isle,** in the beautiful *vieille ville*, is a 13th-century chateau that served as a prison for Resistance fighters during WWII. (☎ 04 50 33 87 30. Open June-Sept. daily 10:30am-6pm; Oct.-May M and W-Su 10am-noon and 2-5pm. €3.20, students €0.90.) The shaded **Jardins de l'Europe** are the town's pride and joy. In summer, the crystalline **lake** is a popular spot for windsurfing and kayaking, particularly along the ■**plage d'Albigny.** Annecy's Alpine forests boast excellent hiking and biking trails. One of the best hikes begins at the **Basilique de la Visitation,** near the hostel, and a scenic 16km *piste cyclable* (bike route) hugs the eastern shore of the lake.

Trains arrive at pl. de la Gare from: Chamonix (2½hr., 6 per day, €18); Grenoble (2hr., 7 per day, €15); Lyon (2hr., 9 per day, €20); Nice (7-9hr., 7 per day, €67); and Paris (4hr., 6 per day, €71). Autocars Frossard **buses** (☎04 50 45 73 90) leave from next to the station for Geneva, Switzerland (1¼hr., 6 per day, €10). From the train station, take the underground passage to r. Somellier, go left onto r. Vaugelas for four blocks, and enter the Bonlieu shopping mall to reach the **tourist office**, 1 r. Jean Jaurès, in pl. de la Libération. (☎04 50 45 00 33; www.lac-annecy.com. Open daily 9am-6:30pm.) In summer, you can reach the clean, beautifully located ⬛**Auberge de Jeunesse "La Grande Jeanne" (HI) ❶**, on rte. de Semnoz, via the *ligne d'été* (dir.: Semnoz) from the station (€1); otherwise, take bus #1 (dir.: Marquisats) from the station to Hôtel de Police, turn right on av. du Tresum, and follow signs to Semnoz. (☎04 50 45 33 19; annecy@fuaj.org. Breakfast included. Sheets €2.90. Reception Apr.-Nov. 8am-noon and 3-10pm; low season reduced hours. 4- to 5-bed dorms €14. MC/V.) A €10.50 menu at ⬛**Quoi de n'Oeuf ❸**, 19 fbg. Ste-Claire, includes generous portions of *tartiflette*, salad, and dessert. (☎04 50 45 75 42. Open M-Sa noon-2pm and 7-9:45pm. MC/V.) A **Monoprix** supermarket is at pl. de Notre-Dame. (Open M-Sa 8:30am-7:30pm.) **Postal Code:** 74000.

LYON

Laid-back Lyon (pop. 1,200,000), usually a stopping point between the north and south, elicits cries of "forget Paris" from weary backpackers. Friendlier than that other French metropolis, Lyon also boasts a few more centuries of history—it has been a provincial capital of Gaul, a hub of the silk trade, a center of the French Resistance, and now an ultramodern city. France's culinary capital is also a stomping ground for world-renowned chefs. If the way to your heart is through your stomach, Lyon will have you at *bon appétit*.

▐ TRANSPORTATION

Flights: Aéroport Lyon-Saint-Exupéry (LYS; ☎04 72 22 72 21), 25km east of Lyon. The TGV, which stops at the airport, is cheaper and more convenient than the 50 daily flights to Paris. Satobus/Navette Aéroport (☎04 72 68 72 17) shuttles passengers to Gare de Perrache, Gare de la Part-Dieu, and Metro stops Jean Mace, Grange-Blanche, and Mermoz Pinel (every 20min., €8.50). **Air France**, 17 r. Victor Hugo, 2ème (☎08 20 82 08 20), has flights to Paris's Orly and Roissy airports (6 per day, €101-207).

Trains: Trains passing through Lyon stop at **Gare de la Part-Dieu,** bd. Marius Vivier-Merle (M: Part-Dieu), on the east bank of the Rhône. Trains terminating at Lyon also stop at **Gare de Perrache,** pl. Carnot (M: Perrache). TGV trains to Paris stop at both. SNCF trains go from both stations to: **Dijon** (2hr., 16 per day, €22.50); **Geneva,** Switzerland (2hr., 13 per day, €20); **Grenoble** (1¼hr., 19 per day, €16.30); **Marseille** (3hr., 17 per day, €35.20); **Nice** (6hr., 12 per day, €51); **Paris** (2hr., 26 TGVs per day, €55-70); **Strasbourg** (5½hr., 5 per day, €42.30).

Buses: On the lowest level of the Gare de Perrache and at Gorge de Loup in the 9ème (☎04 72 61 72 61 for both). Domestic companies include **Philibert** (☎04 78 98 56 00) and **Transport Verney** (☎04 78 70 21 01), but it's almost always cheaper, faster, and simpler to take the train. **Eurolines,** on the main floor of Perrache train station (☎04 72 56 95 30), travels out of France. Open 9am-9pm M-Sa.

Local Transportation: TCL (☎08 20 42 70 00; www.tcl.fr), has info offices at both train stations and major Metro stops. Pocket maps are available from the tourist office or any TCL branch. The efficient **Metro** runs 5am-midnight, as do **buses** and **trams.** 1hr. single-fare ticket €1.40; *carnet* of 10 €11.50, students €10. The *Ticket Liberté* day pass (€4.20) allows unlimited use of all mass transit for the day.

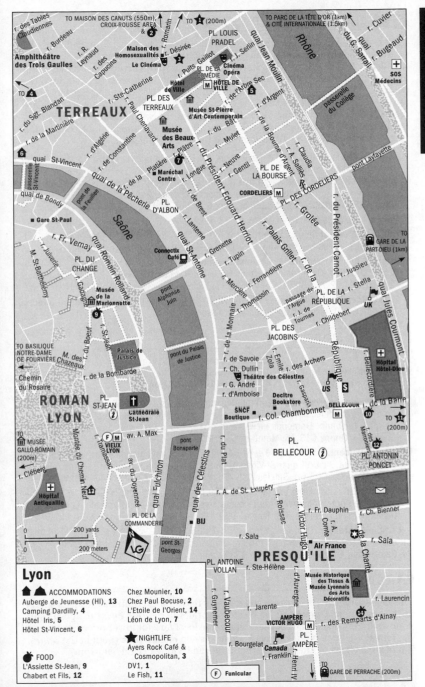

Lyon

ACCOMMODATIONS
Auberge de Jeunesse (HI), **13**
Camping Dardilly, **4**
Hôtel Iris, **5**
Hôtel St-Vincent, **6**

Chez Mounier, **10**
Chez Paul Bocuse, **2**
L'Etoile de l'Orient, **14**
Léon de Lyon, **7**

FOOD
L'Assiette St-Jean, **9**
Chabert et Fils, **12**

NIGHTLIFE
Ayers Rock Café &
Cosmopolitan, **3**
DV1, **1**
Le Fish, **11**

Ⓕ Funicular

FRANCE

⚡📋 ORIENTATION AND PRACTICAL INFORMATION

Lyon is divided into nine **arrondissements** (districts). The 1*er*, 2*ème*, and 4*ème* lie on the **presqu'île** (peninsula), which juts south toward the **Saône** (to the west) and the **Rhône** (to the east) rivers. Starting in the south, the 2*ème* (the *centre ville*) includes the **Gare de Perrache** and **place Bellecour**. The 1*er* houses the nocturnal **Terreaux** neighborhood, with popular cafes and student-packed bars. Farther north are the 4*ème* and the **Croix-Rousse**. The main pedestrian roads on the *presqu'île* are **rue de la République** and **rue Victor Hugo**. West of the Saône, **Fourvière Hill** and its basilica overlook **Vieux Lyon** (5*ème*). East of the Rhône (3*ème* and 6-8*ème*) lie the **Part-Dieu** train station (3*ème*) and most of the city's population.

Tourist Office: In the Tourist Pavilion at pl. Bellecour, 2*ème* (☎04 72 77 69 69; www.lyon-france.com). M: Bellecour. Indispensable *Map and Guide* and free hotel reservation office. The **Lyon City Card** authorizes unlimited public transport along with admission to 14 museums and various tours. Valid for: 1 day €18, 2 days €28, or 3 days €38. Open May-Oct. M-Sa 9am-7pm, Su 10am-6pm; Nov.-Apr. daily 10am-6pm.

Police: 47 r. de la Charité (☎04 78 42 26 56).

Hospital/Medical Service: Hôpital Hôtel-Dieu, 1 pl. de l'Hôpital, 2*ème*, near quai du Rhône, is the most central. The city hospital line (☎08 20 08 20 09) will direct you.

Internet Access: Taxiphone Communications, 15-17 r. Montebello (☎04 78 14 54 25). €2 per hr. Open daily 8:30am-10:30pm. **Connectix Café,** 19 quai St-Antoine, 2*ème* (☎04 72 77 98 85). €6 divisible card allows 1hr. of use. Open M-Sa 10am-7pm.

Post Office: 2 pl. Antonin Poncet (☎04 72 40 65 22), near pl. Bellecour. **Postal Codes:** 69001-69009; last digit indicates *arrondissement*.

🏠 ACCOMMODATIONS

As a major financial center, Lyon has more empty beds on the weekends than during the work week. Fall is the busiest season; it's easier and cheaper to find a place in the summer. Budget hotels cluster east of **place Carnot**.

🏨 **Auberge de Jeunesse (HI),** 41-45 montée du Chemin Neuf (☎04 78 15 05 50). M: Vieux Lyon. Take the funicular from Vieux Lyon to Minimes, walk down the stairs, and go left downhill for 5min. Gorgeous views, a *terrasse*, and a lively bar. Breakfast included. Sheets €3. Dorms €13.25. Members only. MC/V. ❶

🏨 **Hôtel St-Vincent,** 9 r. Pareille, 1*er* (☎04 78 27 22 56; www.hotel-saintvincent.com). M: Hôtel de Ville. Just off quai St-Vincent, north of passerelle St-Vincent. Simple, elegant rooms. Breakfast €5.50. Singles €35-40; doubles €38-47; triples €47. MC/V. ❹

Hôtel Iris, 36 r. de l'Arbre Sec (☎04 78 39 93 80; www.hoteliris.freesurf.fr). A cozy convent-turned-hotel filled with return customers thanks to a sunny breakfast room and friendly owner. Breakfast €5. Singles €29-41; doubles €32-50, triples €51. MC/V. ❸

Camping Dardilly, 10km from Lyon (☎04 78 35 64 55). From the Hôtel de Ville, take bus #19 (dir.: Ecully-Dardilly) to Parc d'Affaires. Pool, TV, and restaurant. Reception 8am-10pm. €3.20 per person, €6.30 per tent. Electricity €3. MC/V. ❶

🍴 FOOD

The galaxy of Michelin stars adorning Lyon's restaurants confirms the city's status as the gastronomic capital of the Western world. But if *haute cuisine* doesn't suit your wallet, try one of the **bouchons** that serve local fare for lower prices; they're in the **Terreaux** district, along **rue des Marronniers** and **rue Mercière** (both in the 2*ème*). There are **markets** on the quais of the Rhône and Saône (Tu-Su 8am-1pm).

FRANCE

▨ **Chez Paul Bocuse,** 50 r. de la Plage, 9km out of town (☎04 72 42 90 90). Take bus #40 to Neuville and tell the driver you are going to Bocuse. The pinnacle of the *lyonnais* food scene charges accordingly, with *menus* in excess of €100. Open daily noon-2pm and 8-9:30pm. ❺

▨ **Léon de Lyon,** 1 r. Pléney, 1er (☎04 72 10 11 12). M: Hotel de Ville. Features the cuisine of master Jean-Paul Lacombe. *Menus* €57, €105, and €136. Open Tu-Sa noon-2pm and 7:30-10pm. MC/V. ❺

▨ **Chez Mounier,** 3 r. des Marronniers, 2ème (☎04 78 37 79 26). M: Bellecour. Tiny gem satisfies a discriminating local clientele with generous traditional specialties. 4-course *menus* €10-16. Open Tu-Sa noon-2pm and 7-10pm, Su noon-1:30pm. MC/V. ❸

Chabert et Fils, 11 r. des Marronniers, 2ème (☎04 78 37 01 94). M: Bellecour. One of the better-known *bouchons* in Lyon. For dessert, try the delicious *guignol* (€5.40). *Menus* €17-33. Open daily noon-2pm and 7-11pm, F-Sa until 11:30pm. MC/V. ❹

L'Assiette St-Jean, 10 r. St-Jean, 5ème (☎04 72 41 96 20). M: Vieux Lyon. An excellent *bouchon,* with unusual, archaic decor. House specialty *gâteau de foies de volaille* (chicken liver custard; €8). *Menus* €13-21. Open summer Tu-Su noon-2pm and 7-10:30pm. Closed Tu in winter. AmEx/MC/V. ❸

L'Etoile de l'Orient, 31 r. des Remparts d'Ainay, 2ème (☎04 72 41 07 87). M: Ampère-Victor Hugo. Intimate Tunisian restaurant serves excellent couscous dishes (€8.50-15). *Menus* €15-19. Open M noon-2pm, Tu-Su noon-2pm and 7-11pm. ❹

🅖 SIGHTS

VIEUX LYON

Stacked against the Saône at the bottom of Fourvière Hill, the narrow streets of *Vieux Lyon* wind between lively cafes, tree-lined squares, and magnificent medieval and Renaissance houses. The colorful *hôtels particuliers,* with their delicate carvings, shaded courtyards, and ornate turrets, sprang up between the 15th and 18th centuries when Lyon controlled Europe's silk and publishing industries.

TRABOULES. The distinguishing features of *Vieux Lyon* townhouses are the *traboules,* indoor pasageways connecting parallel streets through a maze of courtyards, often with vaulted ceilings and statuary niches. Although their original purpose is still debated, many of the later *traboules* were constructed to transport silk safely from looms to storage rooms. During WWII, the passageways proved invaluable as information-gathering and escape routes for the Resistance (though some *résistants* found their way blocked by Germans at the exits). Many are open to the public, especially in the morning. A tour beginning near the cathedral is the ideal way to see them; the tourist office also has a list of addresses. *(Consult tourist office. Tours in summer every few days at 2:30pm; low-season hours vary. €9, students €5.)*

CATHÉDRALE ST-JEAN. The Cathedral's soaring columns dominate the southern end of *Vieux Lyon.* Paris might have been worth a mass, but Lyon got the wedding cake; it was here that Henri IV met and married Maria de Médici in 1600. Some of the stained-glass windows are relatively new replacements, since the originals were destroyed when Lyon's bridges exploded during the hasty Nazi retreat in 1944. Inside, every hour between noon and 4pm, automatons pop out of the 14th-century ▨**astronomical clock** in a charming reenactment of the Annunciation. The clock can calculate Church feast days until 2019. *(Open M-F 8am-noon and 2-7:30pm, Sa-Su 8am-noon and 2-5pm. Free.)*

FOURVIÈRE AND ROMAN LYON

From the corner of r. du Bœuf and r. de la Bombarde in *Vieux Lyon,* climb the stairs heading straight up to reach **Fourvière Hill,** the nucleus of **Roman Lyon.** From the top of the stairs, continue up via the rose-lined **Chemin de la Rosaire,** a series of switchbacks that leads through a garden to the **esplanade Fourvière,** where a model of the city indicates local landmarks. Most prefer to take the less strenuous **funicular** (known as *la ficelle*) to the top of the hill. It leaves from the *Vieux Lyon* Metro station, at the head of av. A. Max. The **Tour de l'Observatoire,** on the eastern edge of the hilltop basilica, offers a more acute angle on the city. On a clear day, scan for Mont Blanc, about 200km to the east. (Jardin de la Rosaire open daily 6:30am-9:30pm. Tour de l'Observatoire open M and W-Su 10am-noon and 2-6:30pm. €2.)

■ **BASILIQUE NOTRE-DAME DE FOURVIÈRE.** During the Franco-Prussian War, Lyon's archbishop vowed to build a church if the city was spared from attack. Now, the basilica's white, meringue-like exterior looms over the entire city—gorgeous or bizarre, depending on taste. Inside are shimmering, gigantic mosaics that depict religious scenes, Joan of Arc at Orléans, and the naval battle of Lepanto. The low, heavy crypt was conceived by architect Pierre Bossan. *(Behind the esplanade at the top of the hill. Open 8am-7pm.)*

MUSÉE GALLO-ROMAIN. With rooms and corridors that cut deep into the historic hillside of Fourvière, this brilliant museum houses a collection of arms, pottery, statues, and jewelry. Highlights include six large, luminous mosaics, a bronze tablet inscribed with a speech by Lyon's favorite son, Emperor Claudius, and a huge, half-cracked eggshell pot. Artifacts are labeled in English and French. *(Open Mar.-Oct. Tu-Su 10am-6pm; Nov.-Feb. 10am-5pm. €3.80, students €2.30, Th free.)*

LA PRESQU'ÎLE AND LES TERREAUX

Monumental squares, statues, and fountains are the trademarks of the *presqu'île,* the lively area between the Rhône and the Saône. At its heart is **place Bellecour,** which is home to the tourist office and links Lyon's two main pedestrian arteries. **Rue Victor Hugo** heads quietly south, lined with boutiques. To the north, crowded **rue de la République,** or "la Ré," is the urban aorta of Lyon. It runs through **place de la République** and ends at **place Louis Pradel** in the 1*er,* at the tip of the Terreaux district. Once a marshy wasteland, this area was filled with soil, creating dry terraces (*terreaux*) and establishing the neighborhood as the place to be for chic locals.

■ **MUSÉE DES BEAUX-ARTS.** This unassuming but excellent museum includes a comprehensive archaeological wing, a distinguished collection of French, Dutch, and Spanish paintings, works by Picasso, a section devoted to the Italian Renaissance, a lovely sculpture garden, and all-star pre-, post-, and just-plain-Impressionist collections. A few nice surprises await explorers of the museum, including a Rodin bust of Victor Hugo at the end of his life (1883) and a huge French coin collection. *(20 pl. des Terreaux. Open M, W-Th, and Sa-Su 10am-6pm, F 10:30am-8pm. Sculptures closed noon-1pm, paintings closed 1-2pm. €6, under 26 €4, students free.)*

LA CROIX-ROUSSE AND THE SILK INDUSTRY

Lyon is proud of its historical dominance of the silk industry in Europe. A few remaining silk workers still perform delicate handiwork, reconstructing and replicating rare patterns for museum and chateau displays.

■ **MUSÉE HISTORIQUE DES TISSUS.** Exhibits about the history of the silk trade are interesting, but everyone comes here for the clothes. In dark rooms, rows of costumes recall skirt-flouting and bosom-baring characters of the past. The collection includes examples of 18th-century elite garb (such as Marie-Antoinette's Versailles winter wardrobe), luxurious Byzantine textiles, and silk wall-hangings that resemble stained-glass windows. *(34 r. de la Charité, 2ème. Open Tu-Su 10am-5:30pm.)*

EAST OF THE RHÔNE AND MODERN LYON

INSTITUT LUMIÈRE. A must for film buffs, the museum's exhibits chronicle the exploits of the brothers Lumière, who invented the motion picture in 1895. It's intriguing factoids: the brothers also invented postsynchronization, and Louis created a forerunner to holograms in 1920. (*25 r. du Premier-Film, 8ème. M: Monplaisir Lumière. Open Su and Tu-Sa 11am-7pm. €5.50, students €4.50.*)

CENTRE D'HISTOIRE DE LA RÉSISTANCE ET DE LA DÉPORTATION. Housed in a building where Nazis tortured detainees during the WWII occupation, this museum presents an impressive but sobering collection of documents, photos, and films of the Resistance, which was based in Lyon. There's also a space set up for children. (*14 av. Bertholet, 7ème. M: Jean Macé. Open W-Su 9am-5:30pm. €4, students €2, under 18 free. Admission includes an audio tour in French, English, or German.*)

MUSÉE D'ART CONTEMPORAIN. This extensive, entertaining mecca of modern art resides in the futuristic **Cité Internationale de Lyon,** a super-modern complex with offices, shops, theaters, and Interpol's world headquarters. (*Quai Charles de Gaulle, 6ème. Take bus #4 from M: Foch. Open W-Su noon-7pm. €5, students €2, under 18 free.*)

🎵 NIGHTLIFE

Nightlife in Lyon is fast and furious; the city is crawling with nightclubs. The best late-night spots are a strip of **riverboat dance clubs** by the east bank of the Rhône. The tourist office lists venues that cater to gay and lesbian communities; the most popular are in the 1er. For tips about gay nightlife, pick up *Le Petit Paumé.*

■ **Le Fish,** across from 21 quai Augagneur. Plays salsa, jungle, hip-hop, disco, and house in a swank boat with a deck and dance floor. F-Sa cover €11 includes 1st drink, free before 11pm. Open W-Sa 10pm-5am. Students only.

Ayers Rock Café, 2 r. Désirée. Aussie bar caters to a melange of international 20-somethings. Right next door, the **Cosmopolitan** serves New-York-themed drinks. Both are usually packed with students, but Cosmo is a little darker, a little less international, and a little more restrained. Shooters from €3. Cocktails from €6. Tu student nights. Ayers open daily 9pm-3am; Cosmo open M-Sa 8pm 3am.

DV1, 6 r. Violi, off r. Royale, north of pl. Louis Pradel. Drag queens nightly, with a huge dance floor and a mostly male crowd. Drinks €3.50-4. Open Tu-Su 11:30pm-5am.

BERRY-LIMOUSIN AND BURGUNDY

Too often passed over for beaches and big cities, Berry-Limousin offers undisturbed countryside and fascinating towns. While Bourges served as a temporary capital of France in the 15th century, Jacques Coeur, King Charles VII's financier, built a string of chateaux through the area. To the east, Burgundy is dotted with abbeys and cathedrals. Today, it draws Epicureans worldwide for its fine wines and delectable dishes like *coq au vin* and *bœuf bourguignon.*

BOURGES

A one-time capital of France, Bourges (pop. 80,000) rose to fame in 1443 when Charles VII's financier, Jacques Coeur, chose it as the site for one of his many chateaux. You'll see more of the **Palais Jacques-Coeur,** 10bis r. Jacques-Coeur, than he ever did, since he was imprisoned for embezzlement before its completion. (Open daily July-Aug. 9:30am-5:45pm; Sept.-June reduced hours. €6.10.) Ask at the tourist office about excursions to 17 other chateaux along the **Route Jacques Coeur.**

Blue and red stained glass lights up the marble interior of the Gothic ■**Cathédrale St-Etienne.** (Open daily Apr.-Sept. 8:30am-7:15pm; Oct.-Mar. 9am-5:45pm. Closed to tourists Su morning. Crypt and tower €6.10, students €4.10.)

Trains leave from pl. du Général Leclerc (☎08 92 35 35 35) for Paris (2½hr., 5-8 per day, €26) and Tours (1½hr., 12 per day, €18). From the station, follow av. H. Laudier at it turns into av. Jean Jaurès; bear left onto r. du Commerce, which becomes r. Moyenne and leads to the **tourist office,** 21 r. Victor Hugo. (☎02 48 23 02 60; www.bourges-tourisme.com. Open July-Aug. M-Sa 9am-7:30pm, Su 10am-7pm; low season reduced hours.) To get from the station to the **Auberge de Jeunesse (HI) ❶,** 22 r. Henri Sellier, bear right from r. du Commerce onto r. des Arènes, which becomes r. Fernault; turn right onto r. René Ménard, then left onto r. Henri Sellier. (☎02 48 24 58 09. Breakfast €3.30. Sheets €2.80. Reception daily 8am-noon and 5-10pm. Dorms €9. Members only. MC/V.) **Place Gordaine, rue des Beaux-Arts, rue Moyenne,** and **rue Mirabeau** are lined with eateries. A **Leclerc** supermarket is on r. Prado off bd. Juraville. (Open M-F 9:15am-8pm, Sa 8:30am-7:20pm.) **Postal Code:** 18000.

DIJON

Dijon (pop. 160,000) isn't just about the mustard. The capital of Burgundy, once home to dukes who wielded a power unmatched by the puny French monarchy, counters its historic grandeur with an irreverent, fun-loving lifestyle. The diverse **Musée des Beaux-Arts** occupies the east wing of the colossal **Palais des Ducs de Bourgogne,** on pl. de la Libération at the center of the *vieille ville.* (Open May-Oct. M and W-Su 9:30am-6pm; Nov.-Apr. 10am-5pm. €3.40, students and Su free.) Built in only twenty years, the **Eglise Notre-Dame,** pl. Notre Dame, is one of France's most famous cathedrals. Its 11th-century cult statue of the Black Virgin is credited with having liberated the city on two desperate occasions: in 1513 from a Swiss siege and in 1944 from the German occupation. The brightly tiled **Cathédrale St-Bénigne,** in pl. St-Bénigne, has a spooky circular crypt. (Open daily 9am-7pm. Crypt €1.)

From the station at cours de la Gare, **trains** run to: Lyon (2hr., 7 per day, €22.50); Nice (6-8hr., 6 per day, €64); and Paris (1¾-3hr., 20 per day, €33). The **tourist office,** in pl. Guillaume Darcy, is straight down av. Maréchal Foch from the station. (☎03 80 44 11 44; www.dijon-tourism.com. Open May to mid-Oct. daily 9am-8pm; mid-Oct. to Apr. M-Sa 10am-6pm, Su 10am-noon and 2-6pm.) ■**Hotel Victor Hugo ❸,** 23 r. des Fleurs, has antique clocks and high-ceilinged comfort. (☎03 80 43 63 45. Breakfast €5. Reception 24hr. Singles €29-38, with shower €38-44; doubles €33-46. MC/V.) Reasonably priced restaurants line **rue Berbisey, rue Monge, rue Musette,** and **place Emile Zola.** Stock up at the **supermarket** in the Galeries Lafayette department store, 41 r. de la Liberté. (Open M-Sa 8:15am-7:45pm.) **Postal Code:** 21000.

BEAUNE

Wine has poured out of the well-touristed town of **Beaune** (pop. 24,000), just south of Dijon, for centuries. Surrounded by the famous Côte de Beaune vineyards, the town itself is packed with wineries offering free *dégustations* (tastings). The largest cellar belongs to ■**Patriarche Père et Fils,** 5-7 r. du Collège, a 5km labyrinth of corridors with over four million bottles. (☎03 80 24 53 78. Open daily 9:30-11:30am and 2-5:30pm. €9.) Those also thirsting for knowledge can learn more about winemaking on the Côte at the **Musée du Vin,** r. d'Enfer, off pl. Général Leclerc. (☎03 80 22 08 19. Open Apr.-Nov. daily 9:30am-6pm; Dec.-Mar. W-Su 9:30am-5pm. €5.10, students €3.10.) **Trains** run from Dijon (25min., 37 per day, €6). The **tourist office,** 1 r. de l'Hôtel-Dieu, lists *caves* that offer tours. (☎03 80 26 21 30; www.ot-beaune.fr. Open mid-June to mid-Nov. M-Sa 9:30am-8pm, Su 10am-12:30pm and 2-5pm; low season reduced hours.) Beaune works best as a daytrip from **Dijon** (above).

ALSACE-LORRAINE AND FRANCHE-COMTÉ

As first prize in the endless Franco-German border wars, France's northeastern frontier has a long and bloody history. Heavily influenced by its tumultuous past, the entire region now maintains a fascinating blend of French and German in the local dialects, cuisine, and architecture. Alsatian towns display half-timbered Bavarian houses, tiny crooked streets, and canals, while Lorraine's wheat fields are interspersed with elegant, well-planned cities. The Jura mountains in Franche-Comté offer some of France's finest cross-country skiing.

STRASBOURG

Just a few kilometers from the Franco-German border, Strasbourg (pop. 451,000) has been annexed so many times by both sides that even its residents seem unsure of their current nationality. The tower of the ornate Gothic ▨**Cathédrale de Strasbourg** stretches skyward at 142m; young Goethe scaled its 332 steps regularly to cure his fear of heights. Inside the cathedral, the **Horloge Astronomique** demonstrates the wizardry of 16th-century Swiss clockmakers. While you wait for the clock to strut its stuff—apostles troop out of the clock-face and a cock crows to greet Saint Peter daily at 12:30pm—check out the **Pilier des Anges** (Angels's Pillar), a Gothic depiction of the Last Judgment. (Cathedral open M-Sa 7-11:40am and 12:40-7pm, Su 12:45-6pm. Tower open Apr.-Oct. M-F 9am-5:30pm; Nov.-Mar. reduced hours. Clock tickets for sale inside cathedral or at southern entrance; €0.80. Tower €3, students €1.50.) **Palais Rohan**, 2 pl. du Château, houses three small but excellent museums: the **Musée des Beaux-Arts**, the **Musée des Arts Décoratifs**, and the **Musée Archéologique.** (All open M and W-Su 10am-6pm. €4 each, students €2.50. Day-pass for all museums in Strasbourg €6, students €3.) Strasbourg, home to an international university, has **bars** everywhere. Students often play jazz piano at ▨**Le Gayot,** 18 r. des Frères, whose terraces spill onto lively pl. Marché Gayot. (Beer €3.10. Live music Th Sept.-June. Open daily June-Aug. 11am-1am; Sept.-May 11am-midnight.) The best gay bar in town, **Le Zoo,** 6 r. des Bouchers, has kitschy decor, bouncing tunes, and an eye catching, mostly male clientele. (Beer €2.20. Mixed drinks €6. Open daily 6pm-2am.)

Strasbourg is a major rail hub. **Trains** (☎08 92 35 35 35) go to: Frankfurt (3hr., 18 per day, €48); Luxembourg (2½hr., 14 per day, €28); Paris (4hr., 16 per day, €43); and Zurich (3hr., 18 per day, €36). The **tourist office,** 17 pl. de la Cathédrale, makes hotel reservations for a €2 fee plus deposit. (☎03 88 52 28 28; www.ot-strasbourg.fr. Open daily 9am-7pm.) There is also a **branch** at pl. de la Gare, near the train station (☎03 88 32 51 49). Get on the **Internet** at **Ultim@,** 31 r. du Fossé (€3 per hr. Open M-Sa 10am-8pm.) There are high-quality, inexpensive hotels all over the city, especially around the train station. Make reservations early, particularly in the summer. The ▨**Centre International d'Accueil de Strasbourg (CIARUS) ❷,** 7 r. Finkmatt, has brightly painted hallways and newly-renovated rooms complete with shower and toilet. From the train station, take r. du Maire-Kuss to the canal, turn left, and follow quai St-Jean through various name-changes; turn left on r. Finkmatt and it's on the left. (☎03 88 15 27 88; www.ciarus.com. Breakfast included. Curfew 1am. 3- to 8-bed dorms €16-20; singles €39. MC/V.) The ▨**La Petite France** neighborhood, especially along r. des Dentelles, is full of informal *winstubs* with Alsatian specialties. Try **place de la Cathédrale, rue Mercière,** or **rue du Vieil Hôpital** for restaurants, and **place Marché Gayot,** off r. des Frères, for cafes. ▨**Crêp' Mili ❶,** 3 r. du Ciel, off r. des

Frères, serves fabulous crepes (€3-6) in an atmospheric cellar. (☎03 88 36 56 88. Open daily 11:30am-2pm and 6:30-11:30pm. MC/V.) Buy groceries at **ATAC**, 47 r. des Grandes Arcades. (Open M and Sa 8:30am-8:30pm, Tu-F 8:30am-8pm.) **Postal Code:** 67000.

LA ROUTE DU VIN

Since the Middle Ages, the wines of Alsace have been highly prized—and priced. Vineyards flourish along a 170km corridor known as La Route du Vin (Wine Route) that begins at **Strasbourg** (p. 421) and stretches south along the foothills of the Vosges, passing through nearly 60 wine-producing towns on its way to Mulhouse. **Colmar** (p. 423) and **Sélestat** (p. 422) are excellent bases, but don't miss smaller, less-touristed villages. The most accessible towns from Strasbourg are **Molsheim**, a medieval university center, and **Barr**, with a vineyard trail that leads through the hills. The more famous towns lie to the south. The most visited sight in Alsace, the **Château de Haut Koenigsbourg,** towers over **Kintzheim.** The 16th-century walled hamlet **Riquewihr** is the Route's most popular village, with many of its best-known wine houses, while beautiful ◼**Kaysersberg** is relatively untouristed. To help plan your tour, pick up the *Alsace Wine Route* brochure from any tourist office in the area.

▐ TRANSPORTATION

Trains from Strasbourg hit many of the towns along the northern half of the Route, including: Barr (40min., every hr., €6); Colmar (30-50min., every hr., €10); and Sélestat (20min.-1hr., every hr., €7). Trains also run to Colmar from Sélestat (15min., 35 per day, €4). From Mulhouse, trains head to: Basel, Switzerland (20min., 7 per day, €6); Paris (4½hr., 8 per day, €48); or Strasbourg (1hr., every hr., €14.40). **Bus** lines pepper the southern half of the Route, running from Colmar to Kaysersberg (20min., 9 per day, €5-10) and Riquewihr (30min., 10 per day, €6-11), as well as many other small towns on the Route.

SÉLESTAT

Sélestat (pop. 17,200), between Colmar and Strasbourg, is a friendly haven of good vines and good vibes often overlooked by tourists on their way to more "authentic" Route cities. The **Bibliothèque Humaniste**, 1 r. de la Bibliothèque, founded in 1452, contains a fascinating collection of illuminated manuscripts and handwritten books produced during Sélestat's 15th-century Humanistic boom. (Open July-Aug. M and W-F 9am-noon and 2-6pm, Sa 9am-noon and 2-5pm, Su 2-5pm; Sept.-June closed Su. €3.60, students €2.) Nearby, on r. du Sel, the **Maison du Pain** reveals the history of breadmaking from 12,500 BC to the present. Master baker François will happily tell you more about his art. (Open July-Aug. Tu-F 10am-12:30pm and 1:30-6pm, Sa-Su 10am-12:30pm and 1:30-5pm; low season reduced hours. €4.60, students €2.30.) The **tourist office**, 10 bd. Général Leclerc, in the Commanderie St-Jean, rents **bikes** (€12.50 per day). From the train station, go straight on av. de la Gare, through pl. Général de Gaulle, to av. de la Liberté. Turn left onto bd. du Maréchal Foch, which becomes bd. Général Leclerc; the office is on your right. (☎03 88 58 87 20; www.selestat-tourisme.com. Open July-Aug. M-F 9:30am-12:30pm and 1:30-6:45pm, Sa 9am-12:30pm and 2-5pm, Su 11am-3pm; low season reduced hours.) **Hôtel de l'Ill ❸**, 13 r. des Bateliers, has 15 cozy rooms with shower, toilet, and TV. (☎03 88 92 91 09. Breakfast €5. Reception daily 7am-3pm and 6:30-11pm. Singles €30; doubles €40; triples €50. MC/V.) **Postal Code:** 67600.

COLMAR

Best used as a base for exploring smaller Route towns, Colmar (pop. 68,000) has bubbling fountains, crooked lanes, waterways, pastel houses—and crowds of tourists. The **Musée Unterlinden**, 1 r. d'Unterlinden, houses Grünewald's *Issenheim Altarpiece*. (Open May.-Oct. daily 9am-6pm; Nov.-Apr. M and W-Su 9am-noon and 2-5pm. €7, students €5.) The **Eglise des Dominicains**, on pl. des Dominicains, is a bare-bones container for Colmar's other masterpiece, Schongauer's *Virgin in the Rose Bower*. (Open daily Apr.-Dec. 10am-1pm and 3-6pm. €1.30, students €1.) To get to the **tourist office**, 4 r. d'Unterlinden, from the train station, turn left on av. de la République (which becomes r. Kléber) and follow it to the right to pl. Unterlinden. (☎03 89 20 68 92; www.ot-colmar.fr. Open July-Aug. M-Sa 9am-7pm, Su 9:30am-2pm; Sept.-June reduced hours.) To reach the **Auberge de Jeunesse (HI) ❶**, 2 r. Pasteur, take bus #4 (dir.: Europe) to Pont Rouge. (☎03 89 80 57 39. Breakfast included. Sheets €3.50. Lockout 10am-5pm. Curfew 11pm. Closed mid-Dec. to mid-Jan. Dorms €12; singles €17; doubles €28. Members only. MC/V.) **La Cassolette ❷**, 70 Grande Rue, has breakfasts, sandwiches, and salads. (Open M-Th 8am-7pm and F-Sa 8am-9:30pm. Closed W afternoon. MC/V.) **Postal Code:** 68000.

BESANÇON

Bounded by the river Doubs on three sides and a steep bluff on the fourth, Besançon (pop. 120,000) baffled Julius Caesar's military strategies and was later made impenetrable by an enormous **citadel**, at the end of r. des Fusilles de la Résistance. Though its mountaintop fortifications are more daunting than pretty, the city hosts a slew of world-class museums and an active student population. Within the citadel, the ▨**Musée de la Résistance et de la Déportation** chronicles the Nazi rise to power and the events of WWII from a distinctly French perspective. (Citadel ☎03 81 87 83 33. Open daily July-Aug. 9am-7pm; Apr.-June and Sept.-Oct. 9am-6pm; Nov.-Mar. 10am-5pm. Closed Tu Nov.-Easter. Admission to all museums €6, students €5.) The **Cathédrale St-Jean**, beneath the citadel, holds two treasures: the white marble **Rose de St-Jean** and the 30,000-part 19th-century **Horloge Astronomique**. (Open M and W-Su 9am-6pm. Cathedral free. Tour of clock €2.50, students and under 18 free.) The **Musée des Beaux-Arts et d'Archéologie**, on pl. de la Révolution, houses an exceptional collection ranging from ancient Egyptian mummies to works by Matisse, Picasso, and Renoir. (☎03 81 87 80 49. Open M and W-Su 9:30am-12pm and 2-6pm. €3, students and under 18 free, Su and holidays free.) The area between **rue Claude Pouillet** and **rue Pont Battant** buzzes with nightlife. Shoot pool and sip beer (€2) at the tacky but hip ▨**Pop**

Hall, 26 r. Proudhon. (Open M-Th and Su 2pm-1am, F-Sa 2pm-2am.) **Le KGB,** 8 av. de Chardonnet, is Besançon's best dance club with a London Underground theme and all kinds of music. (Cover €5, with drink €10. Open Th-Sa 10:30pm-5am.)

Trains (☎08 36 35 35 35) leave av. de la Paix for: Dijon (1hr., 22 per day, €12.40); Paris (2hr., 8 per day, €55.10); and Strasbourg (3hr., 10 per day, €28). Monts Jura **buses,** 4 r. Berthelot (☎08 25 00 22 44), go to Pontarlier (1hr., 3 per day, €8). From the station, walk downhill; turn onto av. Maréchal Foch and continue to the left as it becomes av. de l'Helvétie. Once you reach pl. de la Première Armée Française, the *vieille ville* is across pont de la République; the **tourist office,** 2 pl. de la Première Armée Française, is in the park to the right. (☎08 20 32 07 82; www.besancon-tourisme.com. Open M 10am-7pm, Tu-Sa 9:30am-7pm, Su 10am-5pm.) To reach the **Foyer Mixte de Jeunes Travailleurs (HI) ❷,** 48 r. des Cras, take av. de la Paix, which veers to the left of the train station, and keep left as it turns into r. de Belfort; go right onto av. Carnot, then left onto r. des Chaprais. When you get to pl. de Flore, take bus #7 or night line A (both dir.: Orchamps; 3-5 per hr., €0.90) to the hostel, which has concerts, movies, and other special events, as well as free Internet access in the lobby. (☎03 81 40 32 00; fax 03 81 40 32 01. Singles €20, second night €18; doubles €30/€27. AmEx/MC/V.) A variety of restaurants line **rue Claude-Pouillet.** Buy groceries at **Monoprix** supermarket, 12 Grande Rue. (Open M-Sa 8:30am-8pm.) ▧**La Boite au Sandwich,** 21 r. du Lycée, offers enormous salads and sandwiches (€2.30-6.50), including many vegetarian options. (☎03 81 81 63 23. Open M-F 11:30am-2:30pm and 7-10:30pm, Sa 11:30am-2:30pm. MC/V.) **Postal Code:** 25000.

PONTARLIER AND THE JURA

The sedate town of Pontarlier (pop. 18,400) is a good base from which to explore the oft-overlooked Haut-Jura Mountains. The Jura are best known for **cross-country skiing;** nine trails cover every skill level. (Day pass available at the Le Larmont and Le Malmaison trails €6, under 17 €3.50.) Le Larmont is the closest **Alpine ski** area (☎03 81 46 55 20). **Fishing, hiking,** and **mountain biking** are also popular. Monts Jura **buses** (☎08 25 00 22 44) run to Besançon (1hr., 3 per day, €8). The **tourist office,** 14bis r. de la Gare, has guides and maps. (☎03 81 46 48 33; www.pontarlier.org. Open July-Aug. M-Sa 9am-7pm, Su 10am-noon; Sept.-June reduced hours.) Pontarlier makes a good daytrip from **Besançon** (above). **Postal Code:** 25300.

NANCY

Nancy (pop. 300,000) combines classical beauty and fresh innovation. The city that spawned the Art Nouveau "Nancy School" is today the artistic and intellectual heart of modern Lorraine. The stunning works on display at the ▧**Musée de L'Ecole de Nancy** reject the straight lines of previous art and architecture, instead using organic forms to recreate aspects of the natural landscape. Take bus #122 or 123 (dir.: Vandoeuvre Cheminots) to Sédillot or Paul-Painlevé. The elaborate **Place Stanislas,** unfortunately under construction until April 2005, houses three Neoclassical pavilions, with nightly *son-et-lumière* (sound and light) shows at 10pm in July and August. The collection in the **Musée des Beaux-Arts,** 3 pl. Stanislas, houses works that date from the 14th century to the present, including gems by Monet, Rodin, and Picasso. (☎03 83 85 30 72. Open M and W-Su 10am-6pm. €5, students €2.30, W students free.) **Rue Stanislas** and **Grand Rue** are great places to grab a drink. ▧**Blitz,** 76 r. St-Julien, is smoky coolness at its best. (Shots €2. Absinthe €4. Cocktails €2.50. Open June-Aug. Tu-Sa 2pm-2am; Sept.-May 11am-2am. MC/V.)

Trains (☎03 83 22 10 00) depart from the station at pl. Thiers for Paris (3hr., 14 per day, €40) and Strasbourg (1hr., 17 per day, €20). Head left, follow r. Raymond Poincaré through a stone archway, and then go straight on to pl. Stanislas and the **tourist office.** (☎03 83 35 22 41; www.ot-nancy.fr. Open Apr.-Oct. M-Sa 9am-7pm, Su

10am-5pm; Nov.-Mar. M-Sa 9am-6pm, Su 10am-1pm.) Access the **Internet** at **Copy.com,** 3-5 r. Guerrier de Dumast. (☎03 83 22 90 41. €2 per hr. Open M-Th 9am-8pm, F 9am-1pm and 3-9pm, Sa 10am-9pm, Su 3-8pm.) **Hôtel Carnot ❸,** 2-4 cours Léopold, has a convenient location, rooms with great views, and a friendly bar. (☎03 83 36 59 58; fax 03 83 37 00 19. Breakfast €5. Singles €28-31; doubles €28-50; triples €50. Extra bed €10. MC/V.) A **Shopi** supermarket is at 26 r. St-Georges. (Open M-F 9am-8pm, Sa 9am-7pm.) **Postal Code:** 54000.

CHAMPAGNE AND THE NORTH

Legend has it that when he first tasted champagne, Dom Perignon exclaimed, "Come quickly! I am drinking the stars!" Few modern-day visitors need further convincing as they flock to the wine cellars in Reims and Epernay, where champagne is produced from regional grapes according to a rigorous, time-honored method. As you head north to the ferry ports, don't overlook the intriguing Flemish culture in Arras or the world-class art collections in Lille.

REIMS

From the 26 monarchs crowned in its cathedral to the bubbling champagne of its famed caves, everything Reims (pop. 185,000) touches turns to gold. The **Cathédrale de Notre-Dame,** built with golden limestone taken from the medieval city walls, features sea-blue stained-glass windows by Marc Chagall. (Open daily 7:30am-7:30pm. €6, ages 12-25 €3.50.) The adjacent **Palais du Tau,** pl. du Cardinal Luçon, has original statues from the cathedral's facade alongside 16th-century tapestries. (Open May-Aug. Tu-Su 9:30am-6:30pm; Sept.-Apr. reduced hours. €6.10, ages 18-25 €4.10, under 18 free.) **Champagne Pommery,** 5 pl. du Général Gouraud, gives the best tours of Reims's champagne caves. Its 75,000L *tonneau* (vat) is the largest in the world. (☎03 26 61 62 56. Tours by reservation. €7, students €3.50.) The schoolroom where Germany surrendered to the Allies during WWII is now the **Museé de la Reddition,** 12 r. Franklin Roosevelt. (☎03 26 47 84 19. Open M and W-Su 10am-noon and 2-6pm, Tu 2-6pm. €1.60, students free.) In July, the fantastic 🎵**Flâneries Musicales d'Eté** (☎03 26 77 45 00), feature over 100 free concerts.

   Trains (☎03 26 88 11 65) leave bd. Joffre for Epernay (20min., 11 per day, €5) and Paris (1½hr., 11 per day, €21). To get from the train station to the **tourist office,** 2 r. Guillaume de Machault, follow the right-hand curve of the rotary to pl. Drouet d'Erlon, turn left onto r. de Vesle and right on r. du Trésor; it's on the left before the cathedral. (☎03 26 77 45 00; www.reims-tourisme.com. Open mid-Apr. to mid-Oct. M-Sa 9am-7pm, Su 11am-6pm; mid-Oct. to mid-Apr. reduced hours.) The 🏠**Centre International de Séjour/ Auberge de Jeunesse (HI) ❶,** on chaussée Bocquaine, has comfortable, sunlit rooms. (☎03 26 40 52 60; fax 03 26 47 35 70. Reception 24hr. Dorms €11; singles €18, with shower €28; doubles €24/€32; triples with shower €39. Nonmembers add €3. AmEx/ MC/V.) **Place Drouet d'Erlon** is crowded with cafes, restaurants, and bars. A **Monoprix** supermarket is at 21 r. Chativesle. (Open M-Sa 9am-8pm.) **Postal Code:** 51100.

EPERNAY

Epernay (pop. 30,000), at the juncture of three wealthy grape-growing regions, is appropriately ritzy. The aptly named 🏛**avenue de Champagne** is distinguished by its palatial mansions, lush gardens, and swanky champagne companies. **Moët & Chandon,** 20 av. de Champagne, produces the king of all champagnes: **Dom Perignon.** (☎03 26 51 20 20. Open Mar.-early Nov. daily 9:30-11:30am and 2-4:30pm; early Nov.-Apr. M-F only. 1hr. tour with one glass €7.50.) Five minutes away is **Mercier,** 70 av. de Champagne, the self-proclaimed "most popular champagne in France," which gives tours in laser-guided cars. (☎03 26 51 22 22. Open daily late Mar. to mid-Nov. 9:30-11:30am and 2-4:30pm; low season reduced hours. Tour €6.50.)

Trains leave Cours de la Gare for Paris (1¼hr., 18 per day, €19) and Reims (25min., 16 per day, €5). From the station, walk straight ahead through pl. Mendès France, go one block up r. Gambetta to pl. de la République, and turn left on av. de Champagne to reach the **tourist office,** 7 av. de Champagne. (☎03 26 53 33 00; www.epernay.fr. Open Easter to mid-Oct. M-Sa 9:30am-12:30pm and 1:30-7pm, Su 11am-4pm; low season reduced hours.) Epernay caters to the champagne set—budget hotels are rare. ■**Hôtel St-Pierre ❷,** 14 av. Paul-Chandon, is your best bet with spacious, antique-furnished rooms. (☎03 26 54 40 80; fax 03 26 57 88 68. Breakfast €5. Reception 7am-10pm. Singles and doubles €23, with shower €26-40. MC/V.) **Rue Gambetta** has ethnic eateries. The area around **place des Arcades** and **place Hugues Plomb** is dotted with delis and bakeries. A **Marché Plus** supermarket is at 13 pl. Hugues Plomb. (Open M-Sa 7am-9pm, Su 9am-1pm.) **Postal Code:** 51200.

TROYES

Although the city plan resembles a champagne cork, Troyes (pop. 56,000) shares little with its grape-crazy northern neighbors, combining small-town charm with an energy and social scene equal to cities many times its size. The enormous **Cathédrale St-Pierre et St-Paul,** pl. St-Pierre, down r. Clemenceau past the town hall, is a flamboyant Gothic church, with ornate detail and flying buttresses. Its stained glass, done in the unique Troyes style, has survived fires, bombings, and other disasters. (Open daily 10am-noon and 2-5pm. Closed M morning. Free.) The **Musée d'Art Moderne,** just next door on **pl. St-Pierre,** houses over 2000 works by French artists, including Degas, Rodin, and Seurat, in the former Episcopal palace. (☎03 25 76 95 02. Open Tu-Su 11am-6pm. €6, students and under 25 €0.80. W free.)

Trains run from av. Maréchal Joffre to Paris (1½hr., 14 per day, €19.80). The **tourist office,** 16 bd. Carnot, to the right of the station, helps reserve rooms. (☎03 25 82 62 70; www.tourisme-troyes.com. Open M-Sa 9am-12:30pm and 2-6:30pm. MC/V.) ■**Les Comtes de Champagne ❸,** 56 r. de la Monnaie, is in a 16th-century mansion with lace-curtained windows, sparkling floors, and large, airy rooms. (☎03 25 73 11 70; www.comtesdechampagne.com. Reception 7am-10pm. Singles from €28; doubles from €32; triples from €50; quads from €55. MC/V.) To reach **Camping Municipal ❶,** 2km from Troyes on N60, take bus #1 (dir.: Pont St-Marie) and ask to be let off at the campground. (☎03 25 81 02 64. Open Apr. to mid-Oct. €4 per person, €5.50 per tent or car.) *Crêperies* and inexpensive eateries lie near **rue Champeaux,** in *quartier* St-Jean, and on **rue Général Saussier,** in *quartier* Vauluisant. **Aux Crieurs de Vin ❸,** 4-6 pl. Jean Jaurès, is part restaurant, part wine cellar. This simple eatery offers 10 times as many wine selections as meal choices. A meal and glass of wine run €13. (☎03 25 40 01 01. Open Tu-Sa noon-2pm and 8-10:30pm. MC/V.) Stock up at **Monoprix** supermarket, 78 r. Emile Zola, which also features a cheap but tasty cafeteria. (Open M-Sa 8:30am-8pm. MC/V.) **Postal Code:** 10000.

LILLE

A long-time international hub with a rich Flemish ancestry and the best nightlife in the north, Lille (pop. 214,000) has abandoned its industrial days to become a delightfully untouristed metropolis. The impressive ■**Palais des Beaux-Arts,** on pl. de la République, is the second-largest art collection in France, with a comprehensive display of 15th- to 20th-century French and Flemish masters. (M: République. Open M 2-6pm; Tu, Th, and Sa-Su 10am-6pm; F 10am-7pm. €4.60, students €3.) Housed in a renovated interior pool, the aptly named ■**La Piscine,** 23 r. de L'Espérance (M: Gare Jean Lebas), has a collection that includes paintings and sculptures from the 19th and early 20th centuries. (Open Tu-Th 11am-6pm, F 11am-8pm, Sa-Su 1-6pm. €3, students €2.) The **Musée d'Art Moderne,** 1 allée du musée, displays Cubist and postmodernist works. Take the metro to Pont de Bois, then bus #41 (dir.: Villeneuve d'Ascq) to Parc Urbain-Musée. (Open M and W-Su

10am-6pm. €3.70, under 25 €1.50.) At night, students flock to the pubs along **rue Solférino** and **rue Masséna**. Sip cocktails and shoot billiards at **Gino Pub**, 21 r. Masséna. (Beer €1.50. Open M-Sa noon-2am, Su 5pm-2am.)

Trains leave from Gare Lille Flandres, on pl. de la Gare (M: Gare Lille Flandres), for Brussels, Belgium (1½hr., 20 per day, €21) and Paris (1hr., 21 per day, €35). Gare Lille Europe (☎08 36 35 35 35), on r. Le Corbusier (M: Gare Lille Europe), sends Eurostar trains to Brussels and London (10 per day, €35-188), and TGVs to the south of France. Eurolines **buses** (☎03 20 78 18 88) run to: Amsterdam (round-trip €45); Brussels (round-trip €18); and London (round-trip €52). From Gare Lille Flandres, walk straight down r. Faidherbe and turn left through pl. du Théâtre and pl. de Gaulle; the **tourist office**, pl. Rihour (M: Rihour), is behind the huge war monument. (☎03 20 21 94 21; www.lilletourism.com. Open M-Sa 9:30am-6:30pm, Su 10am-noon and 2-5pm.) To reach the friendly **Auberge de Jeunesse (HI) ❶**, 12 r. Malpart, from Gare Lille Flandres, go around the station, then turn right onto r. du Molinel, left onto r. de Paris, and right onto r. Malpart. (☎03 20 57 08 94; lille@fuaj.org. M: Mairie de Lille. Sheets €2.80. Lockout 10am-3pm. Curfew 1am. Open Feb. to mid-Dec. Dorms €14-17. MC/V.) Restaurants line **rue de Béthune, rue Léon Gambetta** and **place du Théâtre**. A huge **Carrefour** supermarket is in the shopping center next to Gare Lille Europe. (Open M-Sa 9am-10pm.) **Postal Code:** 59000.

CALAIS

Calais (pop. 80,000) is a lively, brash Channel port where English is spoken as often as French. Rodin's famous sculpture **The Burghers of Calais** stands in front of the Hôtel de Ville, at bd. Jacquard and r. Royale. Follow r. Royale to the end of r. de Mer for wide, sandy **beaches**. See p. 55 for the schedules and prices of **ferries** to Dover, England. During the day, free **buses** connect the ferry terminal and Gare Calais-Ville, on bd. Jacquard, where **trains** leave for: Boulogne (45min., 8 per day, €6.70); Lille (1¼hr., 8 per day, €15); and Paris-Nord (3¼hr., 6 per day, €37). To reach the **tourist office**, 12 bd. Clemenceau, turn left from the station and cross the bridge; it's on your right. (☎03 21 96 62 40; www.ot-calais.fr. Open Easter-Aug. M-Sa 9am-7pm, Su 10am-1pm; Sept.-Easter M-Sa 9am-1pm and 2-6:30pm.) The ▉Centre Européen de Séjour/Auberge de Jeunesse (HI) ❶, av. Maréchal Delattre de Tassigny, is near the beach and has a bar, a library, and Internet access. (☎03 21 34 70 20; www.auberge-jeunecooc calais.com. Dorms €14-16; singles €18-20. Nonmembers add €1.60. MC/V.) **Match** supermarket is at 50 pl. d'Armes. (Open July-Aug. M-Sa 9am-7:30pm, Su 9-11:30am; low season closed Su.) **Postal Code:** 62100.

BOULOGNE-SUR-MER

Boulogne-sur-Mer (pop. 46,000) is by far the most attractive of the Channel ports. Its huge aquarium, ▉Le Grand Nausicaä, bd. Ste-Beuve, capitalizes on the town's main source of commerce and nutrition. (Open daily July-Aug. 9:30am-8pm; Sept.-June 9:30am-6:30pm. €13, students €9.50.) Next door is the **beach**. The **Château-Musée**, r. de Bernet, houses an eclectic collection that ranges from an Egyptian mummy to Napoleon's second-oldest hat. (Closed for construction until Jan. 2005; call ahead for hours. €3.50, students €2.50.) **Trains** leave Gare Boulogne-Ville, bd. Voltaire, for: Calais (30min., 13 per day, €7); Lille (2½hr., 11 per day, €19); and Paris-Nord (2-3hr., 11 per day, €29). From the station, turn right on bd. Voltaire, turn left on bd. Danou and follow it to pl. de France, and continue past the roundabout for the **tourist office**, 24 quai Gambetta. (☎03 21 10 88 10; www.tourisme-boulognesurmer.com. Open July-Aug. M-Sa 9am-7pm, Su 10am-1pm and 3-6pm; Sept.-June reduced hours.) ▉Hôtel Au Sleeping ❸, 18 bd. Daunou, has spotless, well-decorated rooms. (☎03 21 80 62 79; fax 03 21 80 63 97. Breakfast €5. Reserve ahead June-Aug. Singles €30; doubles €34-43. MC/V.) **Champion** supermarket is in the shopping center on r. Daunou. (Open M-Sa 8:30am-8pm.) **Postal Code:** 62200.

GERMANY
(DEUTSCHLAND)

History has bequeathed present-day Germany a dual legacy of Goethe and Goebbels: A world power with long-standing humanist traditions has had much of its moral standing undermined by Hitler and the Holocaust. Now, more than

a decade after the fall of the Berlin Wall created a hybrid nation from two disparate halves, Germans must fashion a new identity for themselves. Anyone seeking to avoid the cranes dotting the Berlin horizon, however, will find less changeable attractions in the country's many snowy mountains, half-timbered houses, and medieval castles.

 DISCOVER GERMANY: SUGGESTED ITINERARIES

THREE DAYS Enjoy two days in **Berlin** (p. 433): Stroll along **Unter den Linden** and the **Ku'damm**, gape at the **Brandenburger Tor** and the **Reichstag**, and explore the **Tiergarten**. Walk along the **East Side Gallery** and visit **Checkpoint Charlie** for a history of the Berlin Wall, then pass an afternoon at **Schloß Sanssouci** (p. 456). Overnight it to **Munich** (p. 490) for a stein-themed last day.

ONE WEEK After scrambling through **Berlin** (3 days), head north to racy **Hamburg** (1 day, p. 466). Take in the cathedral of **Cologne** (1 day, p. 475) before slowing down in the bucolic **Lorelei Cliffs** (1 day, p. 484). End your trip Bavarian-style with the castles, cathedrals, and beer gardens of **Munich** (1 day, p. 490).

THREE WEEKS Start in **Berlin** (3 days). Party in **Hamburg** (2 days), then zip to **Cologne** (1 day) and the former West German capital, **Bonn** (1 day, p. 478). Contrast the Roman ruins at **Trier** (1 day, p. 483) with glitzy **Frankfurt** (p. 480), then visit Germany's oldest university in **Heidelberg** (2 days, p. 485). Lose your way in the fairy-tale **Schwarzwald** forest (2 days, p. 489), before finding it again in **Munich** (2 days). Marvel at **Neuschwanstein** (1 day, p. 504) and tour the wineries of the **Romantic Road** (2 days, p. 503). Get cultured in Goethe's **Weimar** (1 day, p. 463)—then dramatize your learnings in Faust's cellar in **Leipzig** (1 day, p. 462). End your trip in the reconstructed splendor of **Dresden** (1 day, p. 456).

ESSENTIALS

WHEN TO GO

Germany's climate is temperate, with rain year-round (especially in summer). The cloudy, moderate months of May, June, and September are the best time to go, as there are fewer tourists and the weather is pleasant. Germans head to summer spots en masse with the advent of school vacations in early July. Winter sports gear up from November to April; high season for skiing is mid-December to March.

DOCUMENTS AND FORMALITIES

VISAS. Citizens of Australia, Canada, the EU, New Zealand, and the US do not need visas for stays of up to 90 days. Residence and work permits are obtainable after entering the country.

EMBASSIES. All foreign embassies are in Berlin (p. 433). German embassies at home include: **Australia,** 119 Empire Circuit, Yarralumla, Canberra, ACT 2600 (☎02 62 70 19 11; www.germanembassy.org.au); **Canada,** 1 Waverly St., Ottawa, ON K2P OT8 (☎613-232-1101; www.ottawa.diplo.de); **Ireland,** 31 Trimleston Ave., Booterstown, Blackrock/Co Dublin (☎01 269 3011; www.germanembassy.ie); **New Zealand,** 90-92 Hobson St., Thorndon, Wellington (☎04 473 6063; www.deutsche-botschaftwellington.co.nz); **UK,** 23 Belgrave Sq., London SW1X 8PZ (☎020 7824 1300; www.germanembassy.org.uk); **US,** 4645 Reservoir Rd., Washington, D.C. NW 20007 (☎202-298-8140; www.germany-info.org).

FEATURED ITINERARY: THE CASTLES OF GERMANY

Depart from Berlin to Potsdam's **Schloß Sanssouci** (p. 456), built by Frederick the Great. From there, head north to Schleswig for **Schloß Gottorf** (p. 472), now a museum complex. Alternatively, skip that former Viking territory in order to head straight for the castle heartland. In Kassel, the intact, hillside **Schloß Wilhelmshöhe** (p. 479) counterpoints a second, nearby castle in ruins. Budget travelers to Bacharach can stay in **Jugendherberge Stahleck** (p. 484) overlooking the Rhine. If you tire of the view, duck into the underground passages of St. Goar's **Burg Rheinfels** (p. 484).

Martin Luther translated the Bible into the vernacular in Eisenach's **Wartburg Fortress** (p. 464). Farther south, the cellar of beautiful **Heidelberger Schloß** (p. 487) contains the largest wine tun ever used. In the foothills of the Alps, Füssen neighbors the famed **Neuschwanstein** (p. 504), which Ludwig II built, as well as the lesser-known **Hohenschwangau** (p. 504), where he summered as a child. To the east, **Schloß Herrenchiemsee** (p. 500) was Ludwig's ambitious attempt to outdo Versailles. End the journey with Ludwig I's scandalous portrait gallery of beauties in Munich's **Schloß Nymphenburg** (p. 496).

TRANSPORTATION

BY PLANE. Most flights land in Frankfurt; Berlin, Munich, and Hamburg also have international airports. **Lufthansa**, the national airline, is not always the best-priced option. Often it is cheaper to travel domestically by plane than by train; check out **Air Berlin** (www.airberlin.com) among other options.

BY TRAIN. The **Deutsche Bahn (DB)** network (www.bahn.de) is Europe's best and one of its most expensive. **RegionalExpress (RE)** and the slightly slower **RegionalBahn (RB)** trains include rail networks between neighboring cities. **InterRegio (IR)** trains, covering larger networks between cities, are speedy and comfortable. **D** trains are foreign trains that serve international routes. **EuroCity (EC)** and **InterCity (IC)** trains zoom between major cities every hour from 6am-10pm. You must purchase a *Zuschlag* (supplement) for IC or EC trains (€3.60). **InterCityExpress (ICE)** trains approach the luxury and kinetics of airplanes, running at speeds up to 280km per hour. All trains have clean and comfy second-class compartments.

Eurail is valid in Germany. Designed for tourists, the **German Railpass** allows unlimited travel for four to 10 days within a four-week period. Non-Europeans can purchase German Railpasses in their home countries and—with a passport—in major German train stations (2nd-class 4-day pass €180, 10-day €316). The **German Rail Youth Pass** is for those under 26 (4-day pass €142, 10-day €216). A **Schönes-Wochenende-Ticket** (€28) gives up to five people unlimited travel on any of the slower trains (RE or RB) from 12:01am Saturday or Sunday until 3am the next day; single travelers often find larger groups who will share their ticket.

BY BUS. Bus service runs from the local **ZOB** (*Zentralomnibusbahnhof*), usually close to the main train station. Buses are usually slightly more expensive than trains. Railpasses are not valid on buses except for a few run by Deutsche Bahn.

BY CAR AND BY BIKE. German road conditions are generally excellent. Rumors are true that there is no speed limit on the *Autobahn*, only a recommendation of 130kph (80mph). Germans drive fast. Watch for signs indicating the right-of-way (usually designated by a yellow triangle). The *Autobahn* is marked by an "A" on signs; secondary highways, where the speed limit is usually 100kph (60mph), are accompanied by signs bearing a "B." In cities and towns, speed limits hover around 30-60kph (20-35mph). **Mitfahrzentralen** are agencies that pair up drivers and riders for a small fee; riders then negotiate payment for the trip with the driver. Seat belts are mandatory. Police strictly enforce driving laws. Germany has designated lanes for **bikers**. *Germany by Bike*, by Nadine Slavinski (Mountaineers Books, 1994; US$15), details 20 tours throughout Germany.

TOURIST SERVICES AND MONEY

EMERGENCY	Police: ☎ 110. **Ambulance** and **Fire:** ☎ 112.

TOURIST OFFICES. Every city in Germany has a tourist office, usually near the *Hauptbahnhof* (main train station) or *Marktplatz* (central square). All are marked by a thick lowercase "*i*" sign. Many offices book rooms for a small fee. Consult also the website of the **National Tourist Board** (www.germany-tourism.de).

MONEY. On January 1, 2002, the **euro (€)** replaced the **Deutschmark (DM)** as the unit of currency in Germany. As a general rule, it's cheaper to exchange money in Germany than at home. Costs for those who stay in hostels and prepare their own food may range anywhere from €20-40 per person per day. **Tipping** is not practiced as liberally in Germany as elsewhere—most natives just round up €1. Tips are handed directly to the server with payment of the bill—if you don't want any change, say "*Das stimmt so*" (das SHTIMMT zo). Germans rarely bargain except at flea markets. As in other EU nations, most goods and services bought in Germany automatically include a **Value Added Tax (VAT);** see p. 22.

COMMUNICATION

TELEPHONES. Most public phones will accept only a *Telefonkarte* (phone card), available at post offices, kiosks, and selected Deutsche Bahn counters in major train stations. **Mobile phones** are a popular and economical alternative (p. 35). Phone numbers have no standard length. International access numbers include **AT&T** (☎ 0800 225 5288), **British Telecom** (☎ 0800 010 0144), **Canada Direct** (☎ 0800 888 0014), **MCI Worldphone** (☎ 0800 888 8000), **Sprint** (☎ 0800 888 0013), **Telecom New Zealand** (☎ 0800 080 0064), and **Telstra Australia** (☎ 0800 080 0061).

MAIL. *Let's Go* lists addresses for mail to be held (*Postlagernde Briefe*) in the practical information sections of big cities. Mail will go to the main post office unless you specify a subsidiary by street address. Airmail (*Luftpost* or *par avion*) usually takes 3-6 days for Ireland and the UK, 4-10 days to Australia and North America. Address mail to be held according to the following example: Firstname Surname, Ludwigstr. 60, 10963 Berlin, GERMANY.

PHONE CODES	**Country code:** 49. **International dialing prefix:** 00. From outside Germany, dial int'l dialing prefix (see inside back cover) + 49 + city code + local number.

INTERNET ACCESS. Almost all German cities, as well as a surprising number of smaller towns, have at least one Internet cafe with web access for about €1-5 per 30min. Some German universities have banks of available computers hooked up to the Internet in their libraries, intended for student use.

LANGUAGE. English speakers are often found among younger generations and residents of Western Germany. Recent spelling reforms did not eliminate the letter ß (the *ess-tset*); it is equivalent to a double "s." German basics are listed on p. 1061.

ACCOMMODATIONS AND CAMPING

GERMANY	❶	❷	❸	❹	❺
ACCOMMODATIONS	under €12	€12-20	€20-30	€30-50	over €50

Germany currently has about 600 **hostels**—more than any other nation on the planet. Official hostels in Germany are overseen by **DJH** (*Deutsches Jugendherbergswerk*), Bismarckstr. 8, 32756 Detmold, Germany (☎05231 740 10; www.jugendherberge.de). A growing number of **Jugendgästehäuser** (youth guesthouses) have more facilities than hostels and attract slightly older guests. DJH publishes *Jugendherbergen in Deutschland*, a guide to all federated German hostels. The cheapest **hotel-style** accommodations are places with *Pension, Gasthof, Gästehaus,* or *Hotel-Garni* in the name. Hotel rooms start at €20 for singles and €25 for doubles; in large cities, expect to pay nearly twice as much. *Frühstück* (breakfast) is almost always available, if not included. The best bet for a cheap bed is often a **Privatzimmer** (a room in a family home), which works best with a rudimentary knowledge of German. Prices can be as low as €15 per person. Reservations are made through the local tourist office or through a private *Zimmervermittlung* (room-booking office), sometimes for a small fee. Germans love **camping**; over 2600 campsites dot the outskirts of even the most major cities. Facilities are well maintained and usually provide showers, bathrooms, and a restaurant or store. Camping costs €3-6 per person, with additional charges for tents and vehicles. Blue signs with a black tent on a white background indicate official sites.

FOOD AND DRINK

GERMANY	❶	❷	❸	❹	❺
FOOD	under €4	€4-8	€8-12	€12-20	over €20

A typical *Frühstück* (breakfast) consists of coffee or tea with *Brötchen* (rolls), *Wurst* (cold sausage), and *Käse* (cheese). Germans' main meal, *Mittagessen* (lunch), includes soup, broiled sausage or roasted meat, potatoes or dumplings, and a salad or vegetable side dish. *Abendessen* or *Abendbrot* (dinner) is a reprise of breakfast, with beer in place of coffee and a wider selection of meats and cheeses. Many older Germans indulge in a daily *Kaffee und Kuchen* (coffee and cake) at 3 or 4pm. To eat cheap, stick to the daily *Tagesmenü* (menu of the day), buy food in supermarkets, or, if you have a student ID, head to a university *Mensa* (cafeteria). Fast-food *Imbiß* stands also have cheap fare; the ubiquitous Turkish *Döner* resembles a gyro. German beer tends to be maltier and more "bread-like" than American beer; a nickname for brew is *Flüßige Brot* (liquid bread).

HOLIDAYS AND FESTIVALS

Holidays: New Year's Day (Jan. 1); Epiphany (Jan. 6); Easter (Mar. 27-28); Good Friday (Mar. 25); Labor Day (May 1); Ascension (May 6); Pentecost (May 15-16); Corpus Christi (May 26); Assumption (Aug. 15); Day of German Unity (Oct. 3); Reformation Day (Oct. 31); All Saints' Day (Nov. 1); Repentance Day (Nov. 17); Christmas (Dec. 25-26).

Festivals: Check out the pre-Lenten bacchanalia during Fasching in Munich (Feb. 7-9; p. 490) and Karneval in Cologne (Feb. 3-9; p. 478); international film in the Berlinale Film Festival (Feb. 10-20; p. 452); parades on Christopher Street Day in major cities (late June); general mayhem in the Love Parade in Berlin (mid-July; see **Who Loves the Love Parade?,** p. 452); vanishing kegs during Oktoberfest in Munich (Sept. 17-Oct. 2; p. 490); and the Christmas Market in Nuremberg (late Dec.).

FACTS AND FIGURES: GERMANY

Official Name: Federal Republic of Germany.
Capital: Berlin.
Major Cities: Cologne, Frankfurt, Hamburg, Munich.
Population: 82,425,000.

Land Area: 357,021 sq. km.
Time Zone: GMT + 1.
Language: German.
Religions: Protestant (38%), Roman Catholic (34%), Muslim (2%), unaffiliated or other (27%).

BERLIN ☎ 030

Dizzying, electric, and dynamic, Berlin is nearing the end of a period of profound transition. At first reeling in the aftermath of the Cold War, it has rapidly moved toward the epicenter of the EU. Today, everything in this city of 3.5 million is still changing, whether it be the demographics of its increasingly diverse population or which *Bezirk* (neighborhood) is currently deemed the trendiest. Its cosmopolitan atmosphere will only increase once the **Lehrter Stadtbahnhof,** slated to open in 2006, makes Berlin home to the largest train station in Europe. Yet while Berlin surges ahead as one of the continent's most vibrant cities, memories of the past century—in particular, the Nazi regime and the DDR— remain etched into residents' daily life. Psychological divisions between East and West Germany—the problem dubbed *"Mauer im Kopf"* (wall in the head)—is still felt more acutely here than anywhere else in the country. Berliners have always been on the nation's most progressive edge, and the atmosphere is Germany's most diverse and most tolerant, with a leading gay and lesbian scene and few racially motivated crimes. If you seek a city in the midst of finding itself, now is the time to visit, as the Berlin of even two years hence will be radically different from the Berlin of today.

⊠ INTERCITY TRANSPORTATION

Flights: Berlin has 3 airports; for info on any of them, call ☎0180 500 01 86. Currently, the city is consolidating its airports into just one, Flughafen Schönefeld, but until at least 2008, **Flughafen Tegel** will remain Western Berlin's main international airport. Take express bus X9 from Bahnhof Zoo, bus #109 from U7: Jakob-Kaiser-Pl., bus #128 from U6: Kurt-Schumacher-Pl., or bus TXL from U2: Potsdamer Pl. **Flughafen Schönefeld** services intercontinental flights and travel to developing countries. Take S9 or 45 to Flughafen Berlin Schönefeld. Or, take the Schönefeld Express, which runs every 30min. through most major Bahn stations, including Bahnhof Zoo, Ostbahnhof, Alexanderpl., and Friedrichstr. **Flughafen Tempelhof,** Berlin's smallest airport, has flights to European destinations. Take U6 to Pl. der Luftbrücke.

Train Stations: While construction continues on **Lehrter Stadtbahnhof,** trains to and from Berlin stop at **Zoologischer Garten** (a.k.a. **Bahnhof Zoo**) in the West and at **Ostbahnhof** in the East. Most trains run to both stations, but some connections to cities in former East Germany only stop at Ostbahnhof. Call ☎0180 599 66 33 or visit www.bahn.de for more info. Trains run every hr. to: **Cologne** (4¼hr., €95); **Frankfurt** (4hr., €92); **Hamburg** (2½hr., €49); **Leipzig** (2hr., €33); **Munich** (6½-7hr., €111). Trains run every 2hr. to **Dresden** (2¼hr., €30). Times and prices for international connections change frequently; check at the computers located in stations. Destinations include: **Amsterdam** (6½hr.); **Brussels** (7½hr.); **Budapest** (12hr.); **Copenhagen** (7½hr.); **Kraków** (8½-11hr.); **Moscow** (27-33hr.); **Paris** (9hr.); **Prague** (5hr.); **Rome** (17½-21hr.); **Stock-**

GERMANY

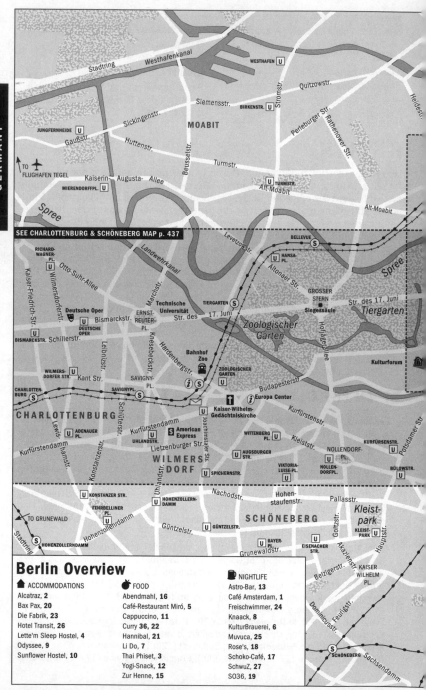

Berlin Overview

🏠 **ACCOMMODATIONS**

Alcatraz, **2**
Bax Pax, **20**
Die Fabrik, **23**
Hotel Transit, **26**
Lette'm Sleep Hostel, **4**
Odyssee, **9**
Sunflower Hostel, **10**

🍖 **FOOD**

Abendmahl, **16**
Café-Restaurant Miró, **5**
Cappuccino, **11**
Curry 36, **22**
Hannibal, **21**
Li Do, **7**
Thai Phiset, **3**
Yogi-Snack, **12**
Zur Henne, **15**

🍺 **NIGHTLIFE**

Astro-Bar, **13**
Café Amsterdam, **1**
Freischwimmer, **24**
Knaack, **8**
KulturBrauerei, **6**
Muvuca, **25**
Rose's, **18**
Schoko-Café, **17**
SchwuZ, **27**
SO36, **19**

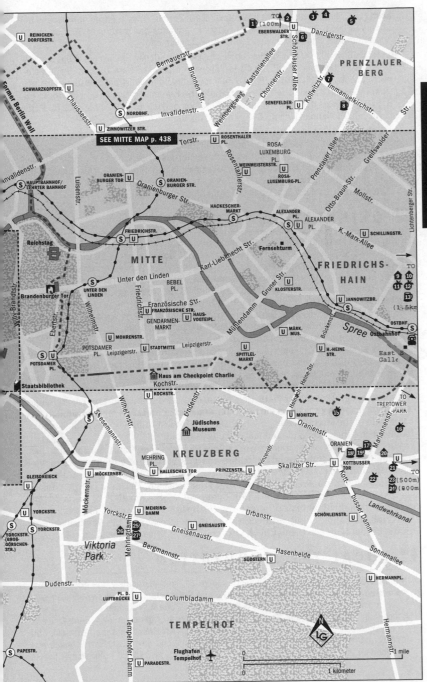

GERMANY

REINICKEN-DORFERSTR.

SCHWARZKOPFSTR.

Former Berlin Wall

Chausseestr.

NORDBHF.

Invalidenstr.

ZINNOWITZER STR.

SEE MITTE MAP p. 438

Torstr.

Bernauerstr.

Brunnen Str.

Weinbergsweg

Kastanienallee

Chornerstr.

Schönhauser Allee

EBERSWALDER STR.

TO (100m)

Danzigerstr.

PRENZLAUER BERG

SENEFELDER-PL.

Kollwitzstr.

Immanuelkirchstr.

ROSENTHALER PL.

ROSA-LUXEMBURG PL.

WEINMEISTERSTR.

Rosenthalerstr.

ROSA-LUXEMBURG-PL.

Prenzlauer Allee

Greifswalder

Lichtenberger Str.

Invalidenstr.

HAUPTBAHNHOF/ LEHRTER BAHNHOF

Luisenstr.

ORANIEN-BURGER TOR

ORANIEN-BURGER STR.

Oranienburger Str.

FRIEDRICHSTR.

HACKESCHER-MARKT

ALEXANDER PL.

ALEXANDER PL.

Otto-Braun-Str.

Mollstr.

K.-Marx-Allee

SCHILLINGSTR.

Reichstag

MITTE

Unter den Linden

BEBEL PL.

Karl-Liebknecht Str.

Fernsehturm

Gruner Str.

KLOSTERSTR.

FRIEDRICHS-HAIN

TO (1.5km)

Brandenburger Tor

UNTER DEN LINDEN

Friedrichstr.

Wilhelmstr.

Franzősische Str.

FRANZÖSISCHE STR.

GENDARMEN-MARKT

HAUS-VOGTEIPL.

Mühlendamm

Spree

JANNOWITZBR.

OSTBHF.

Ostbahnhof

MOHRENSTR.

POTSDAMER PL.

Leipzigerstr.

STADTMITTE

Leipzigerstr.

MÄRK. MUS.

Brückenstr.

East Gall€

POTSDAMER PL.

Ebertstr.

Willy-Brandt-Str.

Staatsbibliothek

SPITTEL-MARKT

H.-HEINE STR.

Haus am Checkpoint Charlie

Kochstr.

KOCHSTR.

Lindenstr.

Heinrich-Heine Str.

MORITZPL.

Oranienstr.

TO TREPTOWER PARK

Jüdisches Museum

Stresemannstr.

Wilhelmstr.

MEHRING PL.

KREUZBERG

Prinzenstr.

Skalitzer Str.

ORANIEN PL.

KOTTBUSSER TOR

Kott.

Marianenstr.

GLEISDREIECK

MÖCKERNBR.

HALLESCHES TOR

PRINZENSTR.

Möckernstr.

Dresel Damm

Landwehrkanal

YORCKSTR.

YORCKSTR.

Yorckstr.

MEHRING-DAMM

GNEISAUSTR.

Urbanstr.

SCHÖNLEINSTR.

Sonnenallee

YORCKSTR. (GROß-GÖRSCHEN-STR.)

Mehringdamm

Gneisenaustr.

Bergmannstr.

Hasenheide

Viktoria Park

Dudenstr.

SÜDSTERN

HERMANNPL.

PL. D. LUFTBRÜCKE

Columbiadamm

Hermannstr.

PAPESTR.

TEMPELHOF

Tempelhofer Damm

Flughafen Tempelhof

PARADESTR.

N

0 _____ 1 mile

0 _____ 1 kilometer

holm (13-16hr.); **Vienna** (9½hr.); **Warsaw** (6hr.); **Zurich** (8½hr.). Prices now depend on when you book tickets. Reserving 3 weeks in advance can save over 30% on listed prices. **Euraide** counters sell tickets and have English info.

Buses: ZOB (☎301 03 80), by the *Funkturm* near Kaiserdamm, is the central bus station. U2 to Kaiserdamm or S4, 45, or 46 to Witzleben. Open M-F 6am-7:30pm, Sa-Su 6am-noon. Check *Zitty* (€2.30) or *Tip* (€2.50) for deals on long-distance buses, which are slower than trains, but usually cheaper. **Gullivers**, Hardenbergpl. 14 (☎0800 48 55 48 37; www.gullivers.de), is at the far end of the bus parking lot in Bahnhof Zoo. To: **Paris** (14hr., €59); **Vienna** (10½hr., €49). Open daily 9am-2:30pm and 3-7pm.

Ride-sharing: Berlin has many ride-sharing centers (*Mitfahrzentralen*). Magazines *Zitty*, *Tip*, and *030* list addresses and phone numbers. Larger centers include: **Citynetz**, Joachimstaler Str. 17 (☎194 44; www.mtz-citynetz.de). U9 or 15 to Kurfürstendamm. To: **Frankfurt** (€29); **Hamburg** (€19); **Hanover** (€19). Open M-F 9am-8pm, Sa-Su 9am-7pm. **Mitfahrzentrale Zoo** (☎194 40; www.mfzoo.de), on the Pankow side of the U2 platform in Bahnhof Zoo. Open M-F 9am-8pm, Sa-Su 10am-6pm.

◢ ORIENTATION

Berlin's main landmarks include the **Spree River,** which flows through the city from west to east, and the narrower **Landwehrkanal** that flows into it from the south. The vast central park, the **Tiergarten,** stretches wide between the waterways. If you see a radio tower it's either the pointed **Funkturm,** in the west, or the globed **Fernseh-turm,** rising above **Alexanderplatz** in the east. Major thoroughfares include **Kur-fürstendamm** (a.k.a. Ku'damm), which is lined with department stores and runs into the **Bahnhof Zoologischer Garten,** the transportation hub of West Berlin. Nearby are the elegant wreck of the **Kaiser-Wilhelm Gedächtniskirche,** and one of Berlin's few real skyscrapers, the **EuropaCenter.**

Grand **Strasse des 17. Juni** runs east-west through the Tiergarten, ending trium-phantly at the **Brandenburger Tor,** on the park's eastern border. Next the street becomes **Unter den Linden,** which runs a beeline through most of Berlin's imperial architecture. Neighboring the gate is the **Reichstag;** several blocks south bustles the über-modern **Potsdamer Platz.** Berlin's streets tend to be short and can change names often; addresses often climb higher and higher and then wrap around to the other side of the street, placing the highest- and lowest-numbered buildings across from one another. Well-indexed maps are invaluable.

What once was West Berlin, including **Charlottenburg** and **Schöneberg,** has become the city's commercial heart. **Kreuzberg,** a bastion of counter-culture, was also part of the West despite lying geographically in the East. In the former East are happening **Mitte, Prenzlauer Berg,** and **Friedrichshain.** Berlin is rightly consid-ered a collection of towns, not a homogeneous city; each *Bezirk* has a strong sense of its individual history. Annually, for instance, citizens of Kreuzberg and Friedrichshain duke it out with vegetables for possession of the **Oberbaumbrücke** on the border between them. Check www.oberbaumbrueckenfest.de for details.

▯ LOCAL TRANSPORTATION

Public Transportation: Berlin is 8 times as large as Paris—fortunately, the extensive **bus, Straßenbahn** (streetcar), **U-Bahn** (subway), and **S-Bahn** (surface rail) systems can take you anywhere. Berlin is divided into 3 transit zones. **Zone A** encompasses central Berlin, including Tempelhof airport. **Zone B** comprises the rest of the downtown. **Zone C** ties in outlying areas, including Potsdam and Oranienburg. **AB tickets** are the best deal, and allow for the purchase of extension tickets for Zone C. A one-way ticket (*Einzelfahrausweis*) is good for 2hr. after validation. (Zones AB €2, BC €2.25, ABC €2.60.) Since single tickets

GERMANY

Charlottenburg and Schöneberg

ACCOMMODATIONS
A&O Hostel, 10
ART-Hotel Charlottenburger Hof, 4
CVJM-Haus, 16
Hotel-Pension Charlottenburg, 13
Hotel-Pension München, 20
Jugendgästehaus am Zoo, 6
Meininger City Hostel, 21
Pension Knesebeck, 9

FOOD & DRINK
Cafe Berio, 18
Café Bilderbuch, 22
Art-Café Miró, 5
Damas Falafel, 7
Die Feinbeckerei, 23
Mario Pasta Bar, 12
Zab Thai Cuisine, 11

BARS & ★ NIGHTLIFE
A-Trane, 8
Metropol, 17
Slumberland, 19

MUSEUMS
Ägyptisches Museum, 2
Gemäldegalerie, 14
Neue Nationalgalerie, 15
Museum Berggruen, 3
Schloß Charlottenburg, 1

GERMANY

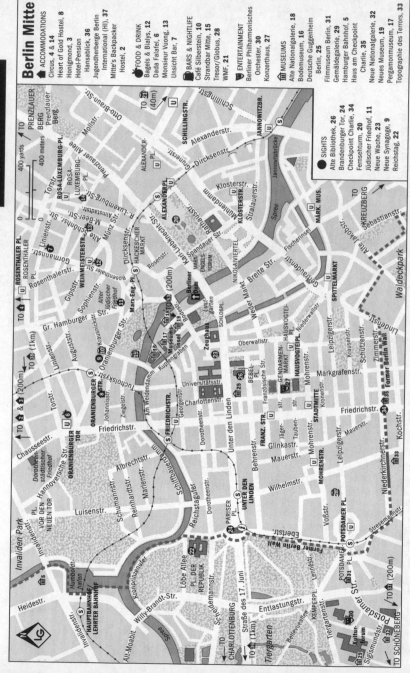

Berlin Mitte

■ ACCOMMODATIONS
Circus, **4 & 14**
Heart of Gold Hostel, **8**
Honigmond, **3**
Hotel-Pension
Hansablick, **36**
Jugendherberge Berlin
International (HI), **37**
Mitte's Backpacker
Hostel, **2**

❖ FOOD & DRINK
Bagels & Bialys, **12**
Dada Falafel, **6**
Monsieur Vuong, **13**
Unsicht Bar, **7**

🍸 BARS & NIGHTLIFE
Café Silberstein, **10**
Strandbar Mitte, **15**
Tresor/Globus, **28**
WMF, **21**

♪ ENTERTAINMENT
Berliner Philharmonisches
Orchester, **30**
Konzerthaus, **27**

🏛 MUSEUMS
Alte Nationalgalerie, **18**
Bodemuseum, **16**
Deutsche Guggenheim
Berlin, **25**
Filmmuseum Berlin, **31**
Gemäldegalerie, **29**
Hamburger Bahnhof, **5**
Haus am Checkpoint
Charlie, **35**
Neue Nationalgalerie, **32**
Neues Museum, **19**
Pergamonmuseum, **17**
Topographie des Terrors, **33**

● SIGHTS
Alte Bibliothek, **26**
Brandenburger Tor, **24**
Checkpoint Charlie, **34**
Fernsehturm, **20**
Jüdischer Friedhof, **11**
Neue Wache, **23**
Neue Synagoge, **9**
Reichstag, **22**

can become pricey, it often makes sense to buy a pass. A **Tageskarte** (AB €5.60, ABC €6) is good until 3am the next day; the **WelcomeCard** (€21, sold at tourist offices) remains valid for 72hr. and additionally discounts sights; the **7-Tage-Karte** (AB €24.30, ABC €30) remains valid for 7 days; and the **Umweltkarte Standard** (AB €64, ABC €79.50) is valid for 1 calendar month. Tickets work on any S-Bahn, U-Bahn, bus, or streetcar. **Bikes** require a supplemental ticket and are permitted on the U- and S-Bahn, but not on buses and streetcars. Buy tickets from *Automaten* (machines), bus drivers, or ticket windows in the U- and S-Bahn stations. When using an *Automat*, make your selection before inserting money. Machines will not give more than €10 change. Validate your ticket in the box marked *"hier entwerfen"* or face a possible €40 fine.

Night Transport: U- and S-Bahn lines shut down from 1-4am on weeknights (with final runs around 12:15am), but **night buses** (with numbers preceded by the letter N) run every 20-30min.; pick up the *Nachtliniennetz* map at a *Fahrscheine und Mehr* office.

Taxis: ☎26 10 26, 21 02 02, or 690 22. Call at least 15min. in advance.

Car Rental: Most companies have counters at all 3 airports and, among train stations, at Bahnhof Zoo, Ostbahnhof, and Friedrichstr. In the EuropaCenter, Budapester Str. 39, are a **Hertz** (☎261 10 53; open M-F 7am-8pm, Sa 8am-4pm, Su 9am-1pm) and an **Avis** (☎230 93 70; open M-F 7am-7pm, Sa 9am-2pm).

Bike Rental: Fahrradstation, in the Friedrichstr. S-Bahn station. €15 per day. Open M-F 8am-8pm, Sa-Su 10am-4pm. **Prenzlberger Orangebikes**, 37 Kollwitz Pl. U2 to Senefelderplatz. €10 per day. Open M-F 2:30-7pm, Sa 10am-7pm, Su 7-8pm. **Deutsche Bahn Call-A-Bike** (☎0800 522 55 22) has locations all over the city, and rents bikes for €0.06 per min. Call for pick-up and drop-off; it's handiest to have a cell phone.

🔢 PRACTICAL INFORMATION

TOURIST AND FINANCIAL SERVICES

The monthly magazine *Berlin Programm* (€1.50) lists opera, theater, and classical music schedules. If you speak German, spring for *Tip* (€2.50) or *Zitty* (€2.30). *Siegessäule*, *Sergej*, and *Gay-yellowpages* have entertainment listings for gays and lesbians. Check www.berlin.de for more info in English.

Tourist Offices: EurAide, in Bahnhof Zoo's *Reisezentrum*, sells rail tickets, maps, phone cards, and walking tour tickets, gives general help in English, and recommends hostels. Open June-Oct. daily 8am-noon and 1-6pm; Nov.-May M-F 8am-noon and 1-4:45pm.

City Tours: ⬛Terry Brewer's Best of Berlin (www.brewersberlin.com). Terry and his guides are legendary for their vast knowledge and engaging personalities. 5hr. tours leave daily at 10:30am from the Neue Synagoge on Oranienburger Str., near the intersection with Tucholskystr. (S1, 2, or 25 to Oranienburger Str.). The tour picks up participants at hostels Odyssee (p. 442) at 9:15am, Circus (p. 440) at 9:40am and 2pm, and Clubhouse at 10:15am. €10. Abridged 4hr. version Apr.-Oct. 12:30pm.

Embassies and Consulates: Australia, Wallstr. 76-79 (☎880 08 80; www.australian-embassy.de). U2 to Märkisches Museum. Open M-F 8:30am-1pm and 2-5pm, F closes 4:15pm. **Canada**, Friedrichstr. 95, 12th fl. (☎20 31 20; www.canada.de). S1 or 3, or U6 to Friedrichstr. Open M-F 8:30am-12:30pm and 1:30-5pm. **Ireland**, Friedrichstr. 200 (☎22 07 20; www.botschaft-irland.de). U2 or 6 to Stadtmitte. Open M-F 9:30am-12:30pm and 2:30-4:45pm. **New Zealand**, Friedrichstr. 60 (☎20 62 10; www.nzembassy.com). U2 or 6 to Stadtmitte. Open M-F 9am-1pm and 2-5:30pm, F closes 4:30pm. **UK**, Wilhelmstr. 70-71 (☎20 18 40; www.britischebotschaft.de). S1-3, 5, 7, 9, 25, or 75, or U6 to Friedrichstr. Open M-F 9am-4pm. **US**, Clayallee 170 (☎832 92 33; fax 83 05 12 15). U1 to Oskar-Helene-Heim. Open M-F 8:30am-noon. Phone advice M-F 2-4pm; after hours emergency advice ☎830 50.

Currency Exchange: The best rates are usually found at exchange offices with "*Wechsel-stube*" signs outside, at most major train stations and large squares.

American Express: Main Office, Bayreuther Str. 37-38 (☎21 47 62 92). U1, 2, or 15 to Wittenbergpl. Long lines F-Sa. Open M-F 9am-7pm, Sa 10am-1pm.

LOCAL SERVICES

Luggage Storage: In Bahnhof Zoo. €0.50-2 per day. 72hr. maximum. If lockers are full, try *Gepäckaufbewahrung* (€2 per piece per day). Open daily 6:15am-10:30pm. Lockers are also available 24hr. at Ostbahnhof and Alexanderplatz stations.

Bookstores: Marga Schöler Bücherstube, Knesebeckstr. 33, between Savignypl. and the Ku'damm. S3 to Savignypl. Off-beat and contemporary reading material in English. Open M-W 9:30am-7pm, Th-F 9:30am-8pm, Sa 9:30am-4pm. **Dussman,** Friedrichstr. 90. U6 to Friedrichstr. English books are on the 2nd fl. Open M-Sa 10am-10pm.

GLBT Services: Lesbenberatung, Kulmer Str. 20 (☎217 22 53), offers lesbian counseling. Open M-Tu and Th 4-7pm, F 2-5pm. **Schwulenberatung,** Mommsenstraße 45 (☎194 46), in Charlottenburg, has similar services for gay men.

EMERGENCY AND COMMUNICATIONS

Emergency: Police: ☎110. **Ambulance** and **Fire:** ☎112.

Crisis Lines: American Hotline (☎0177 814 15 10), is a crisis and referral service. **Berliner Behindertenverband,** Jägerstraße 63d (☎204 38 47), has advice for the handicapped. Open M-F 8am-4pm. **Frauenkrisentelefon** (☎614 22 42), is a women's crisis line. Open M and W noon-2pm, Th 2-4pm.

Pharmacies: Pharmacies are ubiquitous. **Europa-Apotheke,** Tauentzienstr. 9-12 (☎261 41 42), is conveniently located near Bahnhof Zoo. Open M-F 6am-8pm, Sa 9am-4pm.

Medical Assistance: The American and British embassies list English-speaking doctors. **Emergency doctor:** ☎31 00 31. **Emergency dentist:** ☎89 00 43 33. Both 24hr.

Internet Access: Netlounge, Auguststr. 89 (☎24 34 25 97). U-Bahn to Oranienburger Str. €1.50 per hr. Open noon-midnight. **Easy Everything** has locations at: Karl-Marx-Str. 78, Kurfürstendamm 224, Schloßstr. 102, Sony Center, and Rathausstr. 5. **Wireless** access can be found throughout Berlin, sometimes for free.

Post Offices: City-wide general service hotline ☎01802 33 33. **Postamt Charlottenburg,** Joachimstaler Str. 7, near Bahnhof Zoo. Open M-Sa 8am-midnight, Su 10am-6pm. **Postal Code:** 10623. **Postamt Mitte,** Georgenstr. 17. Open M-F 6am-10pm, Sa-Su 8am-10pm. **Postal Code:** 10117.

◪ ACCOMMODATIONS

Longer stays are most conveniently arranged through one of Berlin's many **Mitwohnzentrale,** which can arrange housesits or sublets (from €250 per month); **Home Company Mitwohnzentrale,** Joachimstaler Str. 17, is one of these. (U9 or 15 to Kurfürstendamm. ☎194 45. Open M-F 9am-6pm, Sa 11am-2pm.)

MITTE

▧ **Mitte's Backpacker Hostel,** Chausseestr. 102 (☎28 39 09 65). U6 to Zinnowitzer Str. Look for the giant orange sign. At the zenith of hostel hipness, with gregarious English-speaking staff and themed rooms (ever sleep beneath a huge metal spider?). Bikes €10 per day. Internet €6 per hr. Kitchen available. Sheets €2.50. Laundry €5. Reception 24hr. Dorms €15-18; singles €20-30; doubles €40-60. Winter reduced rates. ❷

▧ **Circus,** Rosa-Luxemburg-Str. 39-41 (☎28 39 14 33). U2 to Rosa-Luxemburg-Pl. Circus was designed with the English-speaking traveler in mind. Laundry, Internet (€0.60 per 10min.), nightlife info, and help booking your next hostel. **Another location** at Weinbergersweg 1a, Rosenthaler Pl., has similar facilities and prices, and rents bikes for €12 per day. Sheets €2. Reception and bar 24hr. 4 to 8-bed dorms €15-18; singles €32, with shower €45; doubles €48/€60; triples €60. Winter reduced rates. ❷

Heart of Gold Hostel, Johannisstr. 11 (☎29 00 33 00; www.heartofgold-hostel.de). S1, 2, or 25 to Oranienburger Str. or U6 to Oranienburger Tor. Designed in tribute to *The Hitchhiker's Guide to the Galaxy*. Internet €0.50 per 10min. Breakfast €3. Laundry €3. Reception and bar 24hr. 3- to 6-bed dorms €17-21; singles €24-28; doubles €48-56. ❷

Honigmond, Tieckstr. 12 (☎284 45 50; www.honigmond-berlin.de). U6 to Zinnowitzer Str. Old-fashioned rooms with canopy beds. Reception 9am-6pm. Check-in 3pm-1am; call if arriving after 8pm. Singles €49-89; doubles €69-89, with bath €89-119. ❺

TIERGARTEN

Jugendherberge Berlin International (HI), Kluckstr. 3 (☎257 99 808; www.hostel.de). U1 to Kurfürstenstr. Walk up Potsdamer Str., go left on Pohlstr., and right on Kluckstr. Big, clean, and modern. Bikes €10 per day. Breakfast and sheets included. Internet €1 per 30min. Reception and cafe 24hr. Dorms €16, under 27 €12; doubles €24/€28. ❷

Hotel-Pension Hansablick, Flotowstr. 6 (☎390 48 00; www.hotel-hansablick.de). S3, 5, 7, 9, or 75 to Tiergarten. Some rooms have balconies over the Spree; all have bath, phone, and cable TV. Riverboat tours stop 200m away. Breakfast included. Reception 24hr. Singles €82; doubles €101-121. *Let's Go* discount 5%. ❹

SCHÖNEBERG AND WILMERSDORF

Meininger City Hostel, Meininger Str. 10 (☎78 71 74 14; www.meininger-hostels.de). U4 or bus #146 to Rathaus Schöneberg. Walk toward the Rathaus tower on Freiherr-vom-Stein-Str., turn left onto Martin-Luther-Str., then right on Meininger Str. Run by students, for students. Breakfast included. Reception 24hr. Dorms €12.50; 4- to 5-bed dorms €21; singles €33; doubles €46. *Let's Go* first-night discount 5%. ❶

CVJM-Haus, Einemstr. 10 (☎264 10 88; www.cvjm-berlin.de). U1 to Nollendorfpl. Book ahead, as this YMCA hostel is popular with student groups. Breakfast included. Sheets €4. Reception M-F 8am-5pm. Quiet hours 10pm-7am and 1-3pm. €25 per person. ❸

Hotel-Pension München, Güntzelstr. 62 (☎857 91 20; www.hotel-pension-muenchen-in-berlin.de). U9 to Güntzelstr. 8 rooms with cable TV and phones; contemporary Berlin art in the foyer. Breakfast included. Garage space €5. Singles €40, with bath €55; doubles with bath €70-80; triples €95; quads €105. ❹

CHARLOTTENBURG

Jugendgästehaus am Zoo, Hardenbergstr. 9a (☎312 94 10; www.jgh-zoo.de), opposite the Technical University Mensa. Bus #145 to Steinpl., or a short walk from Bahnhof Zoo down Hardenbergstr. Reception 9am-midnight. Check-in 10am. Check-out 9am. Lock-out 10am-2pm. Dorms €20, under 27 €17; singles €28/€25; doubles €47/€44. ❷

A&O Hostel, Joachimstaler Str. 1 (☎0800 2 22 57 22; www.aohostel.com), 40m from Bahnhof Zoo. A&O owes its success to a prime location and dirt-cheap dorms. Sheets €3. Reception 24hr. Check-out noon. 16-bed dorm €10; smaller dorms €15-17, with shower €20-24; singles €70; doubles €72. Winter reduced rates. ❷

Pension Knesebeck, Knesebeckstr. 86 (☎312 72 55). S3, 5, 7, or 9 to Savignypl. Follow Kantstr. to Savignypl. and go clockwise around the green until Knesebeckstr. appears on your left. Friendly owners and 9 rooms with personality. Hearty breakfast included. Laundry €4. Reception 24hr. Dorms of 4 or more beds €25-30; singles €35-39, with shower €40-45; doubles €55-61/€65-72. ❸

Hotel-Pension Charlottenburg, Grolmanstr. 32/33 (☎88 03 29 60; www.pension-charlottenburg.de). S3 to Savignypl. Clean and simple rooms with phone and TV. Check-out 11am. Dorms of 3 or more €25 per person; singles €30-48; doubles €54-78. ❸

ART-Hotel Charlottenburger Hof, Stuttgarter Pl. 14 (☎32 90 70; www.charlottenburger-hof.de). S3, 5, 7, or 9 to Charlottenburg or U7 to Wilmersdorfer Str. All rooms have unique decor, phone, TV, and free Internet; some have whirlpool and balcony. Laundry €3. Reception 24hr. Singles €70-90; doubles €85-120; quads €125-160. ❺

KREUZBERG

Die Fabrik, Schlesische Str. 18 (☎611 71 16; www.diefabrik.com). U1 to Schlesisches Tor. A classy former factory with spacious rooms and easy access to nightlife. Reception 24hr. Dorms €18; singles €38; doubles €52-64; triples €69; quads €84. ❷

Hotel Transit, Hagelberger Str. 53-54 (☎789 04 70; fax 78 90 47 77). U6 or 7 or night bus N19 to Mehringdamm. Modern rooms with bath overlook a courtyard in this friendly hotel. Internet €6 per hr. Breakfast included. Reception 24hr. 3- to 6- bed dorms €15; singles €52; doubles €60; triples €78; quads €104. ❷

Bax Pax, Skalitzer Str. 104 (☎69 51 83 22; www.baxpax.de). U1 or 15 to Görlitzer Bahnhof. At the start of Oranienstr., with a pool table and fuzzy blue carpets. One bed is inside a VW Bug. Kitchen facilities. Internet €3 per hr. Sheets €2.50. Reception 24hr. Dorms €12-18; singles €30; doubles €46; triples €60. Winter reduced rates. ❷

FRIEDRICHSHAIN AND PRENZLAUER BERG

▨ Lette'm Sleep Hostel, Lettestr. 7 (☎44 73 36 23; www.backpackers.de). U2 to Eberswalder Str. A common room at street level, laid-back staff, and a big kitchen all make this hostel cozy and social. Free Internet. Wheelchair-accessible. Sheets €3. Dorms €15-16; doubles €48; triples €57. 10% off for stays over 3 nights. ❷

Odyssee, Grünberger Str. 23 (☎29 00 00 81). U1 or 15 to Warschauer Str. or U5 to Frankfurter Tor. Vibrant and spotless. Bar open until dawn. Internet €3 per hr. Reception 24hr. Dorms €13; doubles €45-52; triples €57; quads €68. Winter reduced rates. ❷

Sunflower Hostel, Helsingforser Str. 17 (☎44 04 42 50). U1 or 15 to Warschauer Str., turn right and then left onto Helsingforserstr., closest to the river. With a lounge and a staff well-informed about nightlife. Internet €1.50 per 15min. Laundry €4.50. Reception 24hr. Dorms €13-15; singles €35; doubles €45; triples €57; quads €68. ❷

Alcatraz, Schönhauser Allee 133a (☎48 49 68 15; www.alcatraz-backpacker.de). U2 to Eberswalder Str. In a courtyard close to clubs, with small, spray-painted dorms. Bike rental €5. Internet €3 per hr. Kitchen facilities. Sheets €3. Reception 24hr. Dorms €13; singles from €40; doubles €44; triples €60; quads €76. Winter reduced rates. ❷

◘ FOOD

Berlin's predominant cuisine is more cosmopolitan than archetypally German. Thanks to the city's Indian, Italian, Thai, and Turkish sub-populations, it has excellent ethnic specialties. Streetside cafes extend breakfast well into the afternoon; wake up late over a *Milchkaffee* (a bowl of coffee with foamed milk). Quick bites are supplied by *Currywurst* vendors, but more often by the ubiquitous 24hr. Turkish *Imbiß* stands. Somewhere, every traveler will run into the *Döner*, a toasted flatbread stuffed with veggies and shavings of roast lamb or chicken.

Aldi, Plus, Edeka, and **Penny Markt** are the cheapest supermarket chains, followed by the pricier **Bolle, Kaiser's,** and **Reichelt** (typically open M-F 9am-6pm and Sa 9am-4pm). Almost every neighborhood has an **open-air market;** Bahnhof Zoo's, on Winterfeldtpl., is particularly lively on Saturday mornings. In Kreuzberg along Maybachufer, on the Landwehrkanal, the **Turkish market** sells cheap veggies and huge wheels of *Fladenbrot* every Friday. Take U8 to Schönleinstr.

MITTE

Monsieur Vuong, Alte Schönhauser Allee 46 (☎30 87 26 43). U2 to Rosa Luxembourg Pl. Serves delicious Vietnamese food (glass noodle salad €6.50) to patrons in authentic, all-wood furniture. Entrees €6-9. Open M-Sa noon-midnight, Su 2pm-midnight. ❷

Dada Falafel, Linienstr. 132 (☎27 59 69 27). S1 or 2 to Oranienburgertor. Just off Oranienburgerstr. Caters to executives during the day and clubgoers at night. Falafel and *schawarma* sandwiches €3. Open daily 10am-2am, F-Sa until 4am. ❶

Bagels & Bialys, Rosenthalerstr. 46 (☎283 65 46). U8 to Rosenthaler Pl. Takeout sandwiches (€2.50-4) from all over the world: baguettes, falafel, and bagels. Open 24hr. ❶

Unsicht Bar, Gormannstr. 14 (☎24 34 25 00; www.unsicht-bar-berlin.de). U8 to Weinmeisterstr. Meals here are *unsichtbar*—served in complete darkness. €44 for 4 meat courses, €30 for 3 vegetarian ones. Reservations required. Open daily from 6pm. ❺

SCHÖNEBERG

☒ Cafe Berio, Maaßenstr. 7 (☎216 19 46). U1, 2, 4, or 15 to Nollendorfpl. A Viennese-style cafe with a great breakfast menu (€3.50-8.50) and special business lunch (€4.50; M-F noon-2pm). Open daily 8am-1am. ❷

☒ Die Feinbeckerei, Vorbergstr. 2 (☎784 51 58). U7 to Kleistpark. Swabian cuisine as unassuming as the restaurant's tasteful interior. Unbeatable *Spätzle* (noodles; €6.50) and weekday lunch special (€4.90; M-F noon-5pm). Open daily noon-midnight. ❷

Café Bilderbuch, Akazienstr. 28 (☎78 70 60 57). U7 to Eisenacher Str. Serves tasty brunch baskets in a Venetian library. Sunday buffet €8. Dance to swing and jazz Su afternoons from Oct.-Apr. Open M-Th 9am-1am, F-Sa 9am-2am, Su 10am-1am. ❸

KREUZBERG

☒ Zur Henne, Leuschnerdamm 25 (☎614 77 30). U1 or 15 to Kottbusser Tor. Nearly everyone orders the *Brathänchen* (fried chicken), arguably Berlin's best. Reserve ahead, as this place is always packed. Entrees €2.50-6. Open Tu-Su 7pm-late. ❷

Abendmahl, Muskauer Str. 9 (☎612 51 70; www.abendmahl-berlin.de). U1 or 15 to Görlitzer Bahnhof. Fabulously macabre desserts: A "Last Date" consists of coffin-shaped ice cream petit-fours (€8.50). Vegetarian options. Open daily from 6pm. ❹

Hannibal, on the corner of Wienerstr. and Skalitzerstr. (☎611 23 88). U1, 12, or 15, or night bus N29 to Görlitzer Bahnhof. Excels in leisurely breakfasts, massive burgers (€6), and fruit smoothies (€2.90). Open M-Th 8am-3am, F-Sa 8am-4am, Su 9am-3am. ❷

ON THE MENU

THE BEST *WURST*

So you're finally in Germany and itching to sink your teeth into your first authentic German *Wurst*. With over 1500 varieties, choices abound, but all types have one thing in common: German law mandates that sausages can only be made with meat and spices—if it contains cereal filling, it's not *Wurst*.

Bockwurst: This tasty sausage is commonly roasted or grilled at street stands, and usually served dripping with ketchup and mustard in a soft *Brötchen*. Although "*Bock*" means billy-goat, this *Wurst* is made of finely ground veal with parsley and chives. Complement your *Bockwurst* with some Bock beer.

Thüringer Bratwurst: Similar to the *Bockwurst* both in content and presentation, the *Bratwurst* also contains a little pork, ginger and nutmeg.

Frankfurter: Unlike the American variety (whose origin is believed to be Viennese), the German Frankfurter can only bear this name if made in Frankfurt. It's made of lean pork ground into a paste and then cold-smoked, which gives it an orange-yellow coloring.

Knockwurst: Shorter and plumper, this sausage is served with sauerkraut. It's made of lean pork and beef, and a healthy dose of garlic.

Weißwurst: Cream and eggs give this "white sausage" its paleness. *Weißwurst* goes best with rye bread and mustard.

Curry 36, Mehringdamm 36. U6 or 7 to Mehringdamm. Berlin's best curry sausages and burgers (€2-4). Open M-F 9am-4am, Sa 10am-4am, Su 11am-3am. ❶

FRIEDRICHSHAIN AND PRENZLAUER BERG

▨ **Café-Restaurant Miró,** Raumerstr. 29 (☎44 73 30 17). U2 to Eberswalder Str. Generous portions of Mediterranean cuisine (€8-11). Breakfast €4-7. Soups €3, large appetizers and salads €4-9. Open 10am-late. Kitchen open until midnight. ❸

Cappuccino, Simon-Dach-Str. 7 (☎292 64 57). U5 to Frankfurter Tor. A local favorite that serves pastas and pizzas (€3-5) and gyros (€7). A flaming sambucca shot comes free with most main dishes. Open M-F 10am-1am, Sa-Su noon-1am. ❷

Yogi-Snack, Simon-Dach-Str. 11 (☎29 00 48 38). U5 to Frankfurter Tor. A dark Indian restaurant with entrees for €4-9, and €1 spiced yogi tea. Open daily noon-midnight. ❷

Thai Phiset, Pappelallee 19 (☎41 72 52 75). Noodle dishes from €2.50. Chicken €3.20-4.50. Brunch Su 11am-5pm. Open daily 11am-11pm. ❶

Li Do, Knaackstr. 30-32 (☎440 84 72). U2 to Senefelderpl. The elegant food here is less expensive than surrounding sidewalk sprawlers. A *blini* burger (€8) consists of lox between thin buckwheat pancakes. Pasta specials €5. Open daily 9am-late. ❷

CHARLOTTENBURG

▨ **Damas Falafel,** Goethestr. 4 (☎37 59 14 50). A vegetarian haven in a city of carnivores; most popular are the falafel (€2.50) and *makali* (mixed grilled vegetables; €3). Don't take off without trying the free *Zimttee* (cinnamon tea). Open daily 11am-10pm. ❶

▨ **Zab Thai Cuisine,** Leibnizstr. 43 (☎324 35 16). Bus #149 or 349 to Kantstr/Leibnizstr. or #145 to Otto-Suhr-Allee/Leibnizstr. Try the fruit cocktails (€4.50). Entrees €12-20. Open M-F noon-3pm and 6pm-midnight, Sa 5pm-midnight. ❹

▨ **Mario Pasta Bar,** Leibnizstr. 43 (☎324 35 16). In the same building as Zab (above). A menu would be boring—the cook helps patrons decide what to eat. Meat dishes and handmade pasta. Entrees €6.50-11.50. Open M-Sa noon-3pm and 6:30-11pm. ❸

Art-Café Miró, Stuttgarter Pl. 14 (☎32 90 74 04). S3, 5, 7, 9, or 75 to Charlottenburg, or U7 to Wilmersdorfer Str. Its tapas have been declared *Kunstwerke* (works of art; €2-6). Breakfast buffet €8. Entrees €4.50-14. Open 24hr. ❸

◎ SIGHTS

Most of central Berlin's major sights lie along the route of **bus #100,** which runs every 5min. from Bahnhof Zoo to Prenzlauer Berg. It passes by the **Siegessäule** (p. 445), **Brandenburg Gate** (below), other sights along **Unter den Linden** (below), the **Berliner Dom** (p. 446), and **Alexanderplatz** (p. 446). Remnants of the **Berlin Wall** still survive in only a few places: in **Potsdamer Platz** (p. 446); near the **Haus Am Checkpoint Charlie** (p. 448); in Prenzlauer Berg, next to the sobering **Documentation Center** (p. 449); and memorably at the **East Side Gallery** (p. 448) in Friedrichshain.

MITTE

Mitte, once split by the Wall, was the first district to benefit from post-wall construction projects. It also contains most of Berlin's imperial architecture.

UNTER DEN LINDEN

Unter den Linden, one of Europe's best-known boulevards, was the spine of imperial Berlin. During the Cold War it was known as the "idiot's mile" because it was often all that visitors to the East saw, and gave them little idea of what the city was like. Beginning in Pariser Platz in front of Brandenburger Tor, the street extends east through Bebelplatz and the Lustgarten, punctuated by dramatic squares. *(S1, 2 or 25 to Unter den Linden. Bus #100 runs the length of the boulevard every 4-6 min.)*

▓ BRANDENBURGER TOR. Berlin's only remaining gate, Brandenburger Tor was built as a tribute to peace by Friedrich Wilhelm II in the 18th century. It later became symbolic of the city's division: situated along the wall, in the very center of Berlin, it had become a barricaded gateway to nowhere. Today, it is the most powerful emblem of reunited Germany. In the northern end of the gate, the **Room of Silence** provides a place for meditation and reflection.

NEUE WACHE. The New Guardhouse was designed by Prussian architect Karl Friedrich Schinkel in a Neoclassical style. Under the DDR, it was called the "Memorial to the Victims of Fascism and Militarism," even as East German soldiers kept watch outside. Today, the remains of an unknown soldier and of an unknown concentration camp victim are buried inside. A replica of Käthe Kollwitz's sculpture *Mutter mit totem Sohn* (Mother With Dead Son) memorializes all victims of war. *(Unter den Linden 4. Open daily 10am-6pm.)*

BEBELPLATZ. On May 10, 1933 Nazi students burned nearly 20,000 books here by "subversive" authors such as Heinrich Heine and Sigmund Freud, both of Jewish descent. A plaque in the center of the square bears an engraving of Heine's eerily prescient epigram from 1820: *"Dort wo man Bücher verbrennt, verbrennt man am Ende auch Menschen"* (Where men burn books, there they will finally also burn humans). Currently the memorial is under wraps while a massive parking lot is built underground. On the western side of Bebelpl., the building with a curved facade is the **Alte Bibliothek;** once the royal library, it is now home to Humboldt's law faculty. On the eastern side is the **Deutsche Staatsoper,** one of Berlin's three opera houses, fully rebuilt after the war from the original sketches by the architect Knobelsdorff, who also designed Schloß Sanssouci in Potsdam (p. 456). The distinctive blue dome at the end of the square belongs to **St.-Hedwigs-Kathedrale,** the first Catholic church to be built in Berlin after the Reformation. Completed in 1773, it was destroyed by Allied bombers in 1943. Originally modeled on the Roman Pantheon, the church was rebuilt in the 1950s in a more modern style. *(Cathedral open M-Sa 10am-5pm, Su 1-5pm. Free. Organ concerts W at 3pm.)*

TIERGARTEN

Once a hunting ground for Prussian monarchs, the lush Tiergarten (Animal Park) is the eye of the metropolitan storm. Today extending from Bahnhof Zoo to the Brandenburg Gate, it is frequented by picnickers, joggers, and families out for a walk. **Straße des 17. Juni,** bisecting the park from east to west, is the site of demonstrations like the Love Parade in mid-July (see **Who Loves the Love Parade?,** p. 452).

▓ THE REICHSTAG. Today home to Germany's governing body, the *Bundestag,* the Reichstag has been at the center of critical moments in history. It was here that Philipp Scheidemann proclaimed, in 1918, *"Es lebe die Deutsche Republik"* (Long live the German Republic), and here that in 1933 Adolf Hitler used a fire as a pretext to declare a state of emergency and seize power. Recently a glass dome was added to the roof, surrounding the inverted solar cone that powers the building. A walkway spirals up the inside, leading visitors through several worthwhile vistas of Berlin. *(☎ 22 73 21 52. Open daily 8am-midnight. Last entrance 10pm. Free.)*

SIEGESSÄULE. In the heart of the Tiergarten, this slender 70m victory column commemorates Prussia's crushing victory over France in 1870. The statue at the top—of Victoria, the goddess of victory—is made of melted French cannons. In an affront to the French in 1938, the Nazis moved the monument here from the Reichstag in order to increase its visibility. Climb the 285 steps for a panorama of the city. *(Großer Stern. Take bus #100 or 187 to Großer Stern or S5, 7, or 9 to Tiergarten and walk 5min. on Straße des 17. Juni. ☎ 391 29 61. Open Apr.-Nov. M-F 9:30am-6:30pm, Sa-Su 9:30am-7pm; Nov.-Mar. M-F 10am-5pm, Sa-Su 10am-5:30pm. €2.20, students €1.50.)*

■ POTSDAMER PLATZ

Potsdamer Platz was designed primarily to allow the rapid mobilization of troops. under Friedrich Wilhelm I, but also was an attempt to approximate the effect of wide Parisian boulevards. It lost cachet during the Cold War, caught in the no-man's-land between East and West. After reunification, Potsdamer Platz became the city's commercial center, achieved fame in the 1990s as the city's largest construction site. Overlooking Potsdamer Str., the new central complex includes the towering headquarters of the Deutsche Bahn, the glitzy ■Sony Center, and an off-kilter glass recreation of Mt. Fuji that covers the vast courtyard. Watch a movie, window-shop, or just sit and marvel at it all. *(U2, or S1, 2, or 25 to Potsdamer Pl.)*

MUSEUMSINSEL AND ALEXANDERPLATZ

After crossing the Spree, Unter den Linden becomes Karl-Liebknecht-Str. and cuts through the Museumsinsel (Museum Island), home to five major museums and the **Berliner Dom.** Karl-Liebknecht-Str. then continues onward to Alexanderplatz. Take S3, 5, 7, 9, or 75 to Hackescher Markt, or bus #100 to Lustgarten.

BERLINER DOM. One of Berlin's most recognizable landmarks, this bulky, multi-domed cathedral proves that Protestants can be as dramatic as Catholics. It was built in a faux-Renaissance style during the reign of Kaiser Wilhelm II, but suffered damage in a 1944 air raid. Recently it has emerged from two decades of restoration. Inside, keep an eye out for the likenesses of Protestant luminaries Calvin, Zwingli, and Luther, or search out the glorious view of Berlin from the tower. *(Open M-Sa 9am-8pm, Su noon-8pm. Closed for services 6:30-7:30pm. Organ recitals W-F at 3pm. Admission to Dom, crypt, tower, and galleries €5, students €3. Buy tickets to frequent summer concerts in the church or call ☎ 20 26 91 36. Ticket office open M-Sa 10am-8pm, Su noon-8pm.)*

ALEXANDERPLATZ. At the heart of Berlin life in the Weimar era, this plaza was transformed into a wasteland of pre-fab concrete office blocks under the DDR. In the 1970s, the grey drear was interrupted by enormous neon signs with declarations like "Medical Instruments of the DDR—Distributed In All the World!" to satisfy a need for bright lights. Today chains like **Kaufhof** have replaced the signs and form the backdrop to the legion of bourgeois German shoppers, punks, and tourists.

FERNSEHTURM. Berlin's tallest structure at 368m, this bizarre TV tower was built to prove East Germany's technological capabilities, even though Swedish engineers helped build it. Look at the windows when the sun is out to see a cruciform pattern of glinting light; it is known as the *"Papsts Rache"* (Pope's revenge) because it defied the DDR's attempt to rid the city of religious symbols. An elevator whisks tourists up to a magnificent view from the spherical node 203m above the city. A cafe one floor up serves international meals for €9-13. *(☎ 242 33 33. Open daily Mar.-Oct. 9am-1am; Nov.-Feb. 10am-midnight. €6.80, under 16 €3.50.)*

SCHEUNENVIERTEL AND ORANIENBURGER STRAßE

Northwest of Alexanderpl., near Oranienburger Str. and Große Hamburger Str., is the Scheunenviertel, once the center of Berlin's Orthodox Jewish community. Prior to WWII, Berlin did not have ghettos; the city's more assimilated Jews tended to live in Western Berlin, while Orthodox Jews from Eastern Europe settled here. The district shows traces of Jewish life back to the 13th century, though the Jews were expelled from the city several times before WWII (once for allegedly causing the Black Death). Today, the area is known mainly for its outdoor cafes, but the past few years have seen the opening of several Jewish bookstores and kosher restaurants. *(S1, 2, or 25 to Oranienburger Str., or U6 to Oranienburger Tor.)*

NEUE SYNAGOGE. Berlin architect Eduard Knoblauch modeled this huge, "oriental-style" building after the Alhambra (p. 956). Seating 3200, the synagogue was used for worship until 1940, when the Nazis occupied it and used it for storage.

Amazingly, the building survived *Kristallnacht*—although the SS torched it, a local police chief managed to bluff his way past SS officers and order the fire to be extinguished. Too big for Berlin's current Jewish community, the striking building no longer holds services. Today, it houses exhibits on the history of Berlin's Jews. *(Oranienburger Str. 30. ☎ 88 02 83 00. Open May-Aug. M and Su 10am-8pm, Tu-Th 10am-6pm, F 10am-5pm; Sept.-Apr. M-Th and Sa-Su 10am-6pm, F 10am-2pm. Security checks required. Museum €5, students €3. Permanent exhibit only €3/€2. Dome €1.50/€1.)*

CHARLOTTENBURG

Charlottenburg was originally a separate town huddled around Friedrich I's imperial palace. Now the neighborhood is home to Berlin's main shopping drag, the **Ku'damm** (p. 453), which is full of uppity department stores. Charlottenburg can be expensive; budget travelers come mostly to see the sights near Bahnhof Zoo.

AROUND BAHNHOF ZOO. West Berlin once centered around Bahnhof Zoo, the station that inspired U2's "Zoo TV" tour. (How cute: U-Bahn line U2 runs through the station.) In the surrounding area, a welter of peepshows and department stores mingle with souvenir shops and other G-rated attractions. Many animals at the renowned **Zoologischer Garten** live in open-air habitats; its flamingos have no confines. Gates to the zoo post feeding times. At the second entrance across from EuropaCenter is the famous **Elefantentor,** Budapester Str. 34, a pagoda of pachyderms. *(Open daily May-Sept. 9am-6:30pm; Oct.-Feb. 9am-5pm; Mar.-Apr. 9am-5:30pm. €10, students €7.50, children €5.)* Within the walls of the zoo but independently accessible, an **aquarium** contains insects, reptiles, and miles of fish tanks. A wall of translucent sea nettles has a psychedelic effect. *(Budapester Str. 32. Open daily 9am-6pm. €7.50, students €7, children €4.50. Combination ticket to zoo and aquarium €15/€12/€7.50.)*

KAISER-WILHELM-GEDÄCHTNISKIRCHE. Nicknamed "the hollow tooth" (*Hohler Zahn*), this shattered church has been left in its jagged state as a reminder of WWII. Completed in 1895 in a partly neo-Romanesque, partly Byzantine style, the church has colorful mosaics covering its ceiling, floor, and walls. Inside, an exhibit shows how the church once looked, as well as how Berlin appeared after Allied bombings in WWII. In summer, Berlin's youth, salesmen, and street performers gather in front to hawk their wares, hang out, and play bagpipes and sitars. *(☎ 218 50 23. Exhibit open M-Sa 10am-4pm. Church open daily 9am-7pm.)*

SCHLOß CHARLOTTENBURG. Commissioned by Friedrich I, this broad Baroque palace occupies a park in northern Charlottenburg. Its grounds include the furnished **Altes Schloß,** the marbled receiving rooms of the **Neuer Flugel,** the **Neuer Pavillon,** a museum dedicated to Prussian architect Karl Friedrich Schinkel, the **Belvedere,** which houses the royal family's porcelain collection, and the palace **Mausoleum.** Leave time to stroll the **Schloßgarten** behind the main buildings, a paradise of small lakes, footbridges, and fountains. *(Take bus #145 from Bahnhof Zoo to Luisenpl./Schloß Charlottenburg or U2 to Sophie-Charlotte Pl. and walk about 10-15 min. up Schloßstr. ☎ 320 92 75. Altes Schloß open Tu-F 9am-5pm, Sa-Su 10am-5pm. Mandatory tour €8, students €5. Neuer Flugel open Tu-F 10am-6pm, Sa-Su 11am-6pm. €5, students €4. Neuer Pavillon open Tu-Su 10am-5pm. €2, €1.50. Belvedere open Apr.-Oct. Tu-Su 10am-5pm; Nov.-Mar. Tu-F noon-4pm and Sa-Su noon-5pm. €2, students €1.50. Mausoleum open Apr.-Oct. Tu-Su 10am-noon and 1-5pm. €1. Entire complex €7, students €5. Family card €20.)*

OLYMPIA-STADION. At the western edge of Charlottenburg, the Olympic Stadium is one of the most prominent legacies of the Nazi architectural aesthetic. It was erected for the 1936 Olympic Games, in which African-American Jesse Owens triumphed over Nazi racism by winning four gold medals. Hitler refused to congratulate him, but there's now a Jesse-Owens-Allee nearby. In order to host the

2006 World Cup, the stadium will be under renovations until at least late 2004. A neighboring bell tower (*Glockenturm*) has a view. *(S5 or 7 to Pichelsburg. Turn left onto Schirwindter Allee and left again onto Passenheimerstr. Glockenturm open Apr.-Oct. 9am-6pm.)*

SCHÖNEBERG

South of the Ku'damm, Schöneberg is a pleasant residential district notable for its shopping streets and good restaurants. Locals lounge here for hours in laid-back cafes. Nollendorfpl., where even the military store is draped with rainbow flags, is the nexus of Berlin's gay and lesbian community.

GRUNEWALD. This 745-acre birch forest is home to the **Jagdschloß**, once a royal hunting lodge. Now a one-room museum, it houses paintings by German masters Graff and Cranach, as well as knives, guns, spears, goblets, antlers, and mounted wild boars. *(Am Grunewaldsee 29. U1 or 7 to Fehrbelliner Pl., or S45 or 46 to Hohenzollerndamm, then bus #115 (dir.: Neuruppiner Str.) to Pücklerstr. Walk west 15min. on Pücklerstr. to the lodge. ☎813 35 97. Open Tu-Su 10am-1pm and 1:30-5pm. €2, students €1.50.)*

KREUZBERG

In what was once West Germany, Kreuzberg is counter-culture central. Much of the area was occupied by *Hausbesetzer* (squatters) in the 1960s and 70s, but the city government evicted most of them in the early 80s. Protests are still frequent and intense; the most prominent is an annual demonstration on Labor Day. Still home to a large portion of the city's immigrant population, the district has recently seen an influx of hipsters amid a wider wave of gentrification.

▓HAUS AM CHECKPOINT CHARLIE. A strange mix of earnest eastern sincerity and glossy western salesmanship, Checkpoint Charlie, one of Berlin's most popular attractions, is a wonderfully cluttered museum of artwork, newspaper clippings, and photographs about the Berlin Wall, not to mention a collection of contraptions used to get over, under, or through it. Outside on the street, the checkpoint is overshadowed by photos of one American and one Russian soldier each keeping watch over the other's territory. *(Friedrichstr. 43-45. U6 to Kochstr. ☎253 72 50; www.mauer-museum.com. Museum open daily 9am-10pm. German films every 2hr. from 9:30am. €9.50, students €5.50.)*

FRIEDRICHSHAIN AND LICHTENBERG

As the alternative scene follows the low rents eastward, Friedrichshain is becoming the new hallowed ground of the unpretentiously hip. Relatively unrenovated since reunification, the district retains its pre-fab apartments and large stretches of the wall. **Simon-Dach-Str.** is cluttered with outdoor cafes and a crowd of twenty-somethings. The grungier area surrounding Rigärstr. is one of the strongholds of Berlin's legendary alternative scene, home to squatter bars, makeshift clubs, and lounging grounds for punks.

▓EAST SIDE GALLERY. The longest remaining portion of the Wall, this 1.3km stretch of cement slabs and asbestos also serves as the world's largest open-air art gallery, unsupervised and open at all hours. The murals are not remnants of Cold War graffiti, but efforts of an international group of artists who gathered here in 1989 to celebrate the end of the city's division. It was expected that the wall would be destroyed soon after and the paintings lost, but in 2000, with this portion still standing, many of the artists reconvened to repaint their work, covering others' scrawlings. Unfortunately, the new paintings are being rapidly eclipsed again. *(Along Mühlenstr. Take U1 or 15, or S3, 5, 6, 7, 9, or 75 to Warschauer Str.)*

FORSCHUNGS- UND GEDENKSTÄTTE NORMANNENSTRAßE. The Lichtenberg suburb harbors perhaps the most feared building of the DDR regime: the headquarters of the **secret police** (Staatssicherheit, or Stasi). During the Cold War, the Stasi kept dossiers on six million East Germans. On January 15, 1990, a crowd of 100,000 Berliners stormed the building to protest the police state. After a 1991 law returned the records to the people, the "Horror Files" exposed millions of informants and wrecking careers, marriages, and friendships at all levels of society. Today, the building preserves its Orwellian gloom and worn 70s decor. An exhibit displays a collection of the Stasi's bugging devices and a shrine filled with busts of Lenin. *(Ruschestr. 103, Haus #1. U5 to Magdalenenstr. Walk up Ruschestr. from the exit and take a right on Normannenstr.; it's in the office complex. ☎553 68 54; www.stasimuseum.de. Exhibits in German. Open Tu-F 11am-6pm, Sa-Su 2-6pm. €3.50, students €2.50.)*

PRENZLAUER BERG

Everything in Prenzlauer Berg used to be something else. Brunches unfold every Sunday morning in what were butcher shops, a former power plant stages exhibitions about furniture, and kids cavort in breweries-turned-nightclubs. Prenzlberg was neglected by the city's reconstruction efforts, leaving many buildings covered in graffiti. Relics of the *Bezirk*'s past life are disappearing, but cafe owners know shabby chic when they see it: Plenty of cabbage ads and mismatched sofas remain.

■ **DOKUMENTATIONSZENTRUM DER BERLINER MAUER.** A museum, chapel, and an entire city block of the Berlin Wall—two concrete barriers separated by the open *Todesstreife* (death strip)—make up a controversial memorial to "victims of the communist tyranny." The Documentation Center assembles historic photos, film clips, and sound bites from Wall history. Ascend the spiral staircases for the full desolate effect. *(Bernauer Str. 111. U8 to Bernauer Str. Open W-Su 10am-5pm. Free.)*

JÜDISCHER FRIEDHOF. Prenzlauer Berg was one of the centers of Jewish Berlin, especially during the 19th and early 20th centuries. In the ivied **Jewish cemetery** on Schönhauser Allee are the graves of composer Giacomo Meyerbeer and painter Max Liebermann. *(Open M-Th 8am-4pm, F 8am-3pm. Men must cover their heads before entering.)* Nearby stands the **Synagoge Rykestraße,** Rykestr. 53, a lovely synagogue spared on *Kristallnacht* thanks to its inconspicuous courtyard location.

🏛 MUSEUMS

Berlin is one of the world's great museum cities, with collections from every world-historical epoch. *Berlin Programm* (€1.60) lists museums and galleries.

SMB MUSEUMS

Staatliche Museen zu Berlin (SMB) runs over 20 museums in four major regions—the **Museumsinsel, Kulturforum, Charlottenburg,** and **Dahlem**—and elsewhere in Mitte and around the Tiergarten. All museums sell single admission tickets (€6, students €3) and the *Drei-Tage-Karte* (3-day card; €12, students €6). Admission is free the first Sunday of every month. Unless otherwise noted, all SMB museums are open Tu-Su 10am-6pm, Th until 10pm. All offer free English audiotours.

MUSEUMSINSEL (MUSEUM ISLAND)

Germany's greatest cultural treasures reside in five separate museums, all built in the 19th and 20th centuries and separated from the rest of Mitte by two arms of the Spree. Many of the museums are now undergoing extensive renovations: the **Bodemuseum** should reopen in 2006, the **Neues Museum** in 2008. *(S3, 5, 7, 9 or 75 to Hackescher Markt or bus #100 to Lustgarten. ☎20 90 55 55.)*

■ **PERGAMONMUSEUM.** One of the world's great ancient history museums, the museum is named for Pergamon, the Turkish city from which the enormous **Altar of Zeus** (180 BC) was taken. Collections include artifacts from the ancient Near East, including the colossal blue **Ishtar Gate of Babylon** (575 BC) and the Roman **Market Gate of Miletus.** *(Bodestr. 1-3. ☎ 20 90 55 77. Last entry 30min. before closing.)*

ALTE NATIONALGALERIE. After renovations, this renowned museum is again open to hordes of 19th-century art lovers. Collections showcase everything from German Realism to French Impressionism, and include works by Caspar David Friedrich and Karl Friedrich Schinkel. *(Am Lustgarten. ☎ 20 90 58 01.)*

TIERGARTEN-KULTURFORUM

A complex of museums at the eastern end of the Tiergarten, near the Staatsbibliothek and Potsdamer Pl., the Tiergarten-Kulturforum is a good place to find fine arts students and local aficionados. *(Take S1, 2, or 25, or U2 to Potsdamer Pl. and walk down Potsdamer Str.; look for Matthäikirchpl. on the right. ☎ 20 90 55 55.)*

■ **GEMÄLDEGALERIE.** One of Germany's best-known museums, the Gemälde-galerie houses nearly 3000 masterpieces by Italian, German, Dutch, and Flemish masters from the 13th to 18th centuries, including works by Botticelli, Dürer, Raphael, Rembrandt, Titian, and Vermeer. *(Stauffenbergstr. 40. ☎ 266 29 51.)*

■ **HAMBURGER BAHNHOF/MUSEUM FÜR GEGENWART.** Berlin's foremost modern art collection occupies a full 10,000 sq. m. of this former train station. Its artist roster includes Beuys, Kiefer, and Warhol. With few space constraints, the museum also hosts outrageous sculptures and temporary exhibits. *(Invalidenstr. 50-51. S3, 5, 7, 9, or 75 to Lehrter Stadtbahnhof or U6 to Zinnowitzer Str. ☎ 39 78 34 12. Open Tu-F 10am-6pm, Sa-Su 11am-6pm. Tours Su at 4pm.)*

NEUE NATIONALGALERIE. Designed by Mies van der Rohe, this sleek building contains both interesting temporary exhibits and a formidable permanent collection of 20th century art, including works by Beckmann, Kirchner, Munch, and War-hol, as well as a variety of often grotesque modern selections. Never has roadkill looked so classy. *(Potsdamer Str. 50. Just past the Kulturforum. ☎ 266 26 62.)*

CHARLOTTENBURG

Many excellent museums surround **Schloß Charlottenburg.** Take bus #145 from Bahnhof Zoo to Luisenpl./Schloß Charlottenburg. Or, take U2 to Sophie-Charlotte-Pl. and walk 10-15min. up the tree-lined Schloßstr.

■ **ÄGYPTISCHES MUSEUM.** This stern Neoclassical building holds a huge array of ancient Egyptian art, such as sarcophagi and mummified cats. Best-known in the collection is the limestone bust of **Queen Nefertiti** (1340 BC), from the work-shop of Tuthmosis. *(Schloßstr. 70. ☎ 34 35 73 11. Open M-Su 10am-6pm. Th 2-6pm free.)*

MUSEUM BERGGRUEN. Subtitled "Picasso and His Time," this museum contains three floors of the groundbreaking 20th-century artist's work. Picasso's influences occupy the bottom floor, including African masks and late paintings by Matisse. On the top floor are paintings by Klee and the elongated sculptures of Giacometti. *(Schloßstr. 1. Across from the Ägyptisches Museum. ☎ 32 69 58 11. Open Tu-Su 10am-6pm.)*

INDEPENDENT (NON-SMB) MUSEUMS

DEUTSCHE GUGGENHEIM BERLIN. Located in a newly renovated building oppo-site the Deutsche Staatsbibliothek, this museum features new exhibits of contem-porary art every few months. *(Unter den Linden 13-15. ☎ 202 09 30; www.deutsche-guggenheim-berlin.de. Open daily 11am-8pm. €3, students €2.50. M free.)*

FILMMUSEUM BERLIN. This new museum chronicles the development of German film, with a special focus on older films like *Metropolis* and whole rooms devoted to such superstars as Leni Riefenstahl and Marlene Dietrich. Don't miss the ultra-futuristic entrance. *(Potsdamer Str. 2. On the 3rd and 4th fl. of the Sony Center. S1, 2, 25 or U2 to Potsdamer Pl. ☎300 90 30; www.filmmuseum-berlin.de. Tickets sold on the ground floor. Open Tu-Su 10am-6pm, Th until 8pm. €6, students €4.)*

JÜDISCHES MUSEUM BERLIN. Daniel Libeskind designed this zinc-plated museum in such a way that no facing walls run parallel. Jagged hallways end in windows overlooking "the void." Wander through the labyrinthine "Garden of Exile" or shut yourself in the "Holocaust Tower," a concrete room virtually devoid of light and sound. Exhibits feature modern art, Holocaust memorials, and a history of German Jews. *(Lindenstr. 9-14. U6 to Kochstr. or U1, 6, or 15 to Hallesches Tor. ☎308 78 56 81; www.jmberlin.de. Open daily 10am-8pm, M until 10pm. €5, students €2.50.)*

TOPOGRAPHIE DES TERRORS. In these torture bunkers located beneath the former Gestapo headquarters, photographs and documents detail the Nazis' rise to power and their wartime atrocities. Along the perimeter of the exhibit stand a remaining 200m of the Berlin Wall, a graffitied memorial to the city's division. *(At the corner of Niederkirchnerstr. and Wilhelmstr., behind the Martin-Gropius-Bau. S1 or 2, or U2 to Potsdamer Pl. ☎25 48 67 03. Open daily 10am-6pm. Free. English audioguides available.)*

▣ ENTERTAINMENT

Berlin hosts myriad exhibitions, concerts, plays, and dance performances. Despite recent cutbacks, the city still generously subsidizes its arts. Numerous festivals celebrate everything from Chinese film to West African music; posters for special events plaster city walls and lampposts well in advance. Tickets are usually reasonably priced everywhere, especially for students. Box offices at theaters and concert halls offer student discounts of up to 50% on tickets bought at the *Abendkasse* (evening counter; generally open 1hr. before shows). Other ticket outlets charge 15-18% commissions and offer no discounts. **KaDeWe** (p. 453) has a city-wide ticket counter. (☎217 77 54. Open M-F 10am-8pm, Sa 10am-4pm.) Many venues close from mid-July to late August (*Theaterferien* or *Sommerpause*),

CONCERTS, OPERA, AND DANCE

Berlin's musical calendar peaks in September during the **Berliner Festwochen**, a festival that draws the world's best orchestras. In November, the **Berliner Jazztage** brings in huge crowds. Contact **Berliner Festspiele** (☎25 48 90; www.berlin-erfestspiele.de) for tickets or more info. In mid-July, the **Bachtage** feature classical music, while every Saturday night in August the **Sommer Festspiele** turns the Ku'damm into a multi-faceted concert hall with punk, steel-drum, and folk groups.

The monthlies *Konzerte und Theater in Berlin und Brandenburg* (free) and *Berlin Programm* (€1.50) both have concert listings, as do the biweeklies *Tip* (€2.50) and *Zitty* (€2.30). Tickets for the *Philharmonie* and the *Oper* are nearly impossible to get without writing months in advance, except by standing outside before performances with a small sign marked "*Suche Karte*" (seeking ticket). Of course, unless the seller is desperate, these will be unloaded at scalpers' prices.

▨ **Berliner Philharmonisches Orchester,** Herbert Von Karajanstr. 1 (☎25 48 81 32; www.berlin-philharmonic.com). Take S1, 2, or 25, or U2 to Potsdamer Pl., and walk up Potsdamer Str. Although visually bizarre, this building is acoustically perfect: every seat hears the music as it is meant to sound. The *Berliner Philharmoniker* is one of the world's finest orchestras. Tickets are hard to come by; either check 1hr. before concert time or write at least 8 weeks in advance. No performances late June to early Sept. Box office open M-F 3-6pm, Sa-Su 11am-2pm. Standing room tickets from €7, seats from €15.

WHO LOVES THE LOVE PARADE?

In the aftermath of the Love Parade, beer cans and condoms littered the ground of the Tiergarten every June for 15 consecutive years—until last summer. Inaugurated in 1989 as a gathering of 150 peace-love-and-unity protesters—and costing nothing to attend—the Love Parade rapidly became one of the biggest parties on the planet. It soon attracted over a million people and gave rise to sibling events in San Francisco and Mexico City.

Unfortunately, love now comes at a price. Ever since the Parade lost demonstration status in 2001, raising money to organize the festival of *Friede und Freude* (peace and joy) has been a formidable hurdle. After considering ticketing to help cover costs, the organizers cancelled the event in 2004 rather than destroy its reputation of being "open to anyone."

Luckily, the story doesn't end there, as the organizers put together a much smaller parade called "Fight the Power." Although it consisted of only five wagons and a much shorter route, over 30,000 Berliners attended, and local clubs and bars joined in the effort, creating a "Love Week" of festivities.

"Fight the Power" is a less inviting slogan than free, universal love, however, and it remains to be seen whether a fierce nostalgia for its exponentially larger precursor will prompt a return of the Love Parade in 2005.

Konzerthaus (Schauspielhaus am Gendarmenmarkt), Gendarmenmarkt 2 (☎20 30 90; www.konzerthaus.de). U2 or 6 to Stadtmitte. Berlin's symphony orchestra has its home here. No performances mid-July to Aug. Box office open M-Sa 11am-7pm, Su noon-4pm.

Deutsche Oper Berlin, Bismarckstr. 35 (tickets ☎343 84 01; www.deutscheoperberlin.de). U2 to Deutsche Oper. Berlin's youngest but best opera features newly commissioned works as well as German and Italian classics. Box office open M-Sa 11am until 1hr. before performances, Su 10am-2pm. *Abendkasse* opens 1hr. before performances. No performances July-Aug. Tickets €10-112. Student discounts 25%.

THEATER

Pamphlets *Kultur!news, 030* (free), *Berlin Programm* (€1.50), *Zitty* (€2.30), and *Tip* (€2.50) all list shows city-wide. In addition to the world's best German theater, Berlin has a lively English-language scene. A number of private companies called "off-theaters" also occasionally feature plays in English.

Deutsches Theater, Schumannstr. 13a (☎28 44 12 25; www.deutsches-theater.berlin.net). Take U6 to Friedrichstr., then follow Friedrichstr. north; turn left on Reinhardtstr., then right on Albrechtstr., which curves into Schumannstr. Widely recognized as the best theater in Germany, interpreting playwrights from Büchner to Mamet. The **Kammerspiel** (☎28 44 12 26) stages smaller, provocative productions. Tickets €4-42, students €8. Box office for both open M-Sa 11am-6:30pm, Su 3-6:30pm.

Hebbel-Theater, Stresemannstr. 29 (☎25 90 04 27; www.hebbel-theater.de). U1, 6 or 15 to Hallesches Tor. Producing plays in their original language, the most *avant* of Berlin's avant-garde theaters brings in playwrights to collaborate with the actors. Tickets €11-23, students €11. Box office open daily 4-7pm.

Berliner Ensemble, Bertolt-Brecht-Pl. 1 (☎28 40 81 55; www.berliner-ensemble.de). U6 or S1-3, 5, 7, 9, 25, or 75 to Friedrichstr. Berthold Brecht established this theater; recently its repertoire has included work by Brecht, Heiner Müller, and Americans. Box office open M-F 8am-6pm, Sa-Su 11am-6pm, and 1hr. before shows. Tickets €2-24.

FILM

Berlin is a town for cinéastes—on any given night, moviegoers can choose from over 150 films. Movies listed as "*O.F.*" play undubbed; those listed as "*O.m.U.*" have German subtitles. Check *Tip* (€2.50) or *Zitty* (€2.30) for schedules. Most theaters offer student discounts and reduced rates Monday to Wednesday. Truly avid cinephiles should arrive in mid-winter for the international **Berlinale film festival** (Feb. 12-17 in 2005); check www.berlinale.de for the latest info. Watch blockbusters in English at **CineStar**, Potsdamer Pl. 4, in the Sony Center. (S1 or 2, or U2 to Potsdamer Pl. ☎20 66 62 60. Open 11am-11:30pm. €7.90, Tu and Th €6.)

◪ SHOPPING

With seven stories, the department store **KaDeWe,** Tauentzienstr. 21-24, on Wittenbergpl., is the largest in Europe. Its name abbreviates *Kaufhaus des Westens* (Department Store of the West); for the product-starved East Germans who flooded Berlin in the days after the crumbling of the Wall, KaDeWe *was* the West. *(☎212 10. Open M-F 10am-8pm, Sa 9:30am-8pm.)* Near Bahnhof Zoo, the **Kurfürstendamm** contains almost every shop imaginable. Check the classified *Zweite Hand* (second-hand; €2; distributed Tu, Th, and Sa) to find ads for sundry objects: plane tickets, silk dresses, stray cats, and deals on bikes. **Bergmannstraße,** in Kreuzberg, is a good strip for used clothing and cheap antiques. *(U7 to Gneisenaustr.)*

◪ NIGHTLIFE

Berlin's nightlife is absolute madness. Bars typically open around 6pm and get going around midnight, just as clubs begin to open their doors. Bar scenes wind down anywhere between 1 and 6am. Meanwhile, club dance floors fill up and don't empty out until dawn, when they pass the baton to after-parties and 24hr. cafes. Between 1 and 4am, take advantage of the **night buses** and **U-Bahn** 9 and 12, which run all night on Friday and Saturday. Info about bands and dance venues can be found in the pamphlets *Tip* (€2.50) and *Zitty* (€2.30), available at newsstands, or in *030* (free), distributed in hostels, cafes, and bars.

Kreuzberg's reputation as the national dance capital is now challenged by clubs sprouting up in **Mitte, Prenzlauer Berg,** southern **Friedrichshain,** and **Potsdamer Platz** in the East. Berlin's largest bar scene sprawls down pricey **Oranienburger Straße.** Originally an alternative to trendy Mitte, Prenzlauer Berg has recently become more expensive, especially around **Kollwitzplatz** and **Kastanianallee.** Areas around Schönhauser Allee and Danziger Str. still keep the dream alive, in particular in the **"LSD" zone** of Lychener Str., Schliemannstr., and Dunckerstr. Friedrichshain has a lively bar scene along **Simon-Dach-Str.** and **Gabriel-Max-Str.** Dance venues for younger crowds are scattered between the car dealerships and empty lots of **Mühlenstr.** Businessmen and middle-aged tourists drink at bars along the **Ku'damm.** Gay and lesbian nightlife centers on **Nollendorfplatz,** in the West.

BARS AND CLUBS

MITTE

▧ **WMF,** Karl-Marx-Allee 34. U5 to Schillingstr. In a former East German cabaret, its 2 dance floors fill with electroloungers Th and Sa. Gay night Su. Cover €7-13. Open Th and Sa from 11pm, Su from 10pm.

▧ **Tresor/Globus,** Leipziger Str. 126a. U2 or S1, 2, or 25 or night bus N5, N29, or N52 to Potsdamer Pl. One of the best techno venues in Berlin. Downstairs former bank vaults flicker in strobe light as ravers sweat to hardcore techno; upstairs the music is slower. Cover W €3, F €7, Sa €4. Open W and F-Sa 11pm-6am.

Strandbar Mitte, Monbijoustr. 3. S3, 5, 7, 9, or 75 to Hackescher Markt. In Monbijoupark, across from the Bodemuseum. With deep beach chairs and a huge pit of sand, this bar radiates sunshine. An outdoor sound system blasts hits as locals enjoy beer (€2.50-3) and cocktails (€4-7). Open daily in summer from 10pm.

Café Silberstein, Oranienburger Str. 27. S1, 2, or 25 to Oranienburger Str. Sushi served until midnight. Japanese industrial-chic motifs, chairs with 8ft. backs, and a sophisticated thirty-something crowd. Open daily from 10am.

SCHÖNEBERG

▨ Slumberland, Goltzstr. 24. U1, 2, 4, 12, or 15 to Nollendorfpl. Palm trees, African art, and a sand floor must be seen to be believed. Instant coffee crystals are the secret to the bittersweet frappes. Open M-Th 6pm-2am, F 6pm-4am, Sa 11am-4am, Su 4pm-2am.

Metropol, Nollendorfpl. 5 (www.metropol-berlin.de). U1, 2, 4, or 15, or night buses N5, 19, 26, 48, 52, or 75 to Nollendorfpl. Don't meet a friend here without specifying on which floor. **Tanz Tempel,** the main venue of Metropol, is vast, and has the power to match: 650,000 watts of light and 35,800 of sound. Also check out the **West-Side Club** and **Love Lounge.** Drinks €2.50-4. Music and hours vary.

KREUZBERG

▨ Freischwimmer, vor dem Schlesischen Tor 2. U1 or 15 to Schlesisches Tor or night bus N65 to Heckmannufer. Waterside tables with roses, with sofas, or in boats. Kitchen open daily until midnight, F-Sa until 1am. F a roll of the die determines cover (€1-6). M poetry readings. Su brunch €8.20, 11am-4pm. Open M-F from noon, Sa-Su from 11am.

▨ SO36, Oranienstr. 190 (www.SO36.de). U1, 12, or 15 to Görlitzer Bahnhof or night bus N29 to Heinrichpl. Berlin's best mixed club. A massive dance floor packs in a friendly crowd for techno, hip-hop, and ska; music is often played live. Gay night last Sa of each month. Cover for parties €4-8, concerts €7-18. Open from 11pm.

Muvuca, Gneisenaustr. 2a (www.muvuca.de), in Mehringhof. U6, or night bus N4, N19, or N76 to Mehringdamm. A bar, performance space, Afro-Brazilian eatery, and club, all run by a socialist collective in a steel and concrete courtyard. Also the site of political meetings, lesbian events, and an anarchist bookstore. Open Tu-Su 3pm-late.

FRIEDRICHSHAIN AND PRENZLAUER BERG

Astro-Bar, Simon-Dach-Str. 40 (www.astro-bar.de). At this retro-space locale, DJs spin anything from reggae to electronica. Cocktails €4.50-5.50. Open daily from 6pm.

KulturBrauerei, Knaackstr. 97 (www.kulturbrauerei.de). U2 to Eberswalder Str. An enormous party space in an old East German brewery, housing the popular clubs **Soda** and **Kesselhaus,** a Russian theater, upscale cafes, and an art school. Dance floors and stages abound. Music includes disco, hardcore, reggae, techno, Ostrock, and Schlager. Cover and hours vary between venues.

Knaack, Greifswalderstr. 224 (www.knaack-berlin.de). Tram #2, 3, or 4 to Am Friedrichshain. With 4 floors, Knaack plays disco, rock, and punk—anything but techno. Live music on the ground fl. Billiards upstairs. Internet €1 per hr. Bands often stop here on tour. Cover varies. Dance floors open F-Su and sometimes W from 11pm.

CHARLOTTENBURG (SAVIGNYPLATZ)

A-Trane, Bleibtreustr. 1 (www.a-trane.de). S3, 5, 7, 9, or 75 to Savignypl. Red curtains and dim lights create a mellow glow. Jazz fans are here for the music, not to chat. Cover €8-15. Open 9pm-late. Music daily 10pm-2am, later Sa-Su. Usually closed M and Su.

TREPTOW

▨ Insel der Jugend (Island of Youth), Alt-Treptow 6 (www.insel-berlin.com). S4, 6, 8, or 9 to Treptower Park, then bus #265 or N65 to Rathaus Treptow. Located on an island in the Spree River, the club is a tower of 3 winding stories crammed with gyrating bodies, multiple bars, riverside couches, an open-air movie theater, and a small cafe. Depending on the night, the top 2 floors spin reggae, hip-hop, ska, and house—sometimes all at once—while a techno scene in the basement heats to a fast pace. Cover Th-Sa €4-6. Open W from 7pm, F-Sa from 10pm, sometimes Th from 9pm. Cafe open Sa-Su from 2pm. Movies play M-Tu, Th, and Su. €5-8.

GAY AND LESBIAN NIGHTLIFE

Berlin is one of the most gay-friendly cities in Europe. Thousands of homosexuals flocked to Berlin during the Cold War to take part in the city's left-wing activism, as well as to avoid West Germany's *Wehrpflicht* (mandatory military service). Christopher Isherwood lived at Nollendorfstr. 17, in the famously gay-friendly **Nollendorfplatz,** while he wrote his short-story collection *Goodbye to Berlin;* later this was adapted into the musical *Cabaret.* Goltzstr., Akazienstr., and Winterfeldtstr., have mixed bars and cafes, while the "Bermuda Triangle" of Motzstr., Fuggerstr., and Eisenacherstr. is more exclusively gay.

Mann-o-Meter, Bülowstr. 106, at the corner of Else-Lasker-Schüler-Str., provides counseling, information on gay nightlife, and long-term accommodations, in addition to drinks and Internet access. (☎216 80 08; www.mann-o-meter.de. Open M-F 5-10pm, Sa-Su 4-10pm.) **Spinnboden-Lesbenarchiv,** Anklamer Str. 38, has hip lesbian offerings, with exhibits, films, and other cultural info. (U8 to Bernauer Str. ☎448 58 48. Open W and F 2-7pm.) June culminates in the ecstatic, champagne-soaked floats of the **Christopher Street Day (CSD)** parade, a 6hr.-long street party that draws over 250,000 participants annually (June 27 in 2005). Nollendorferpl. hosts the **Lesbisch-schwules Stadtfest** (lesbian-gay city fair) on the previous weekend.

▨ **Hafen,** Motzstr. 19 (www.hafen-berlin.de), in Schöneberg. U1, 2, 4, or 15 to Nollendorfpl. Artist owners created the decor. Mostly male but not restrictively so. A pub quiz is held in English the first M of each month at 10pm. Open daily 8pm-late.

▨ **Rose's,** Oranienstr. 187 (☎615 65 70), in Kreuzberg. U1, 12, or 15 to Görlitzer Bahnhof. Look for a sign marked "Bar" over the door. A friendly, mixed clientele packs this party spot at all hours. The voluptuous dark-red interior is adorned by hearts, glowing lips, furry ceilings, feathers, and glitter. Margaritas €4. Open daily 10pm-6am.

SchwuZ, Mehringdamm 61 (☎62 90 880; www.schwuz.de), in Kreuzberg. U6 or 7 to Mehringdamm. Hidden behind **Sundström,** a popular gay and lesbian cafe, SchwuZ features 2 small dance floors and a lounge area with its own DJ. A young, chill crowd. Music varies. 2nd F of each month is for lesbians. Cover €4-8. Open F-Sa from 11pm.

Schoko-Café, Mariannenstr. 6 (☎615 15 61; www.schoko-fabrik.de), in Kreuzberg. Lesbian central, the friendly, laid-back Schoko-Café has billiards, Turkish baths, a cultural center, and innumerable other women-only services. Dancing from 10pm every 2nd Sa of each month. Cultural events every weekend. Open daily from 5pm.

Café Amsterdam, Gleimstr. 24 (☎448 07 92), in Prenzlauer Berg. S4, 8, or 85 or U2 to Schönhauser Allee. Gay-friendly with a mixed crowd. Relaxed, with gilt-framed paintings and sweet, creamy cocoa. Pasta dishes (€6-7) until 11:30pm. Brunch Sa-Su from 10am. Open M-F from 4pm.

◪ DAYTRIPS FROM BERLIN

KZ SACHSENHAUSEN. Just north of Berlin, the small town of Oranienburg was the setting for the Nazi concentration camp Sachsenhausen, where more than 100,000 Jews, communists, intellectuals, Roma (Gypsies), and homosexuals were killed between 1936 and 1945. **Gedenkstätte Sachsenhausen,** a memorial preserving the remains of the camp, was opened in 1961 under the DDR. It includes some of the original cramped barracks, the cell block where "dangerous" prisoners were kept in solitary confinement and tortured daily, and a pathology wing where Nazis experimented on inmates. A stone monolith commemorating the camp's victims stands sentinel over the windswept grounds and several small museums. *(Str. der Nationen 22. S1 to Oranienburg (40min.). Follow the signs from Stralsunderstr., turn right on Bernauer Str., left on Str. der Einheit, and right on Str. der Nationen (20min.). ☎03301 20 00; www.gedenkstaette-sachsenhausen.de. Free. Audioguide €3.50. Open mid-Mar. to mid-Oct. 8:30am-6pm; mid-Oct to mid-Mar. 8:30am-4pm.)*

POTSDAM. Anyone disappointed by Berlin's distinctly unroyal demeanor can satisfy cravings for imperial splendor in nearby Potsdam, the glittering city of Friedrich II (the Great). Spread over 600 acres, ■**Park Sanssouci** is palpable testimony to the size of Friedrich's treasury and the diversity of his aesthetic. For info on the park, stop by the **Visitor's Center** at the windmill. *(Open daily May-Oct. 8:30am-5pm; Nov.-Feb. 9am-4pm.)* **Schloß Sanssouci**, the park's main attraction, was Friedrich's answer to Versailles. German tours leave every 20min.; the final tour at 5pm usually sells out hours earlier. The tourist office leads English-language tours of the main Schloß only. *(Take bus #695 to Schloß Sanssouci. ☎969 41 90. Open Apr.-Oct. Tu-Su 9am-5pm; Nov.-Mar. 9am-4pm. Mandatory tours €8, students €5.)* The exotic gold-plated **Chinesisches Teehaus,** complete with a rooftop Buddha carrying a parasol, contains 18th-century *chinoiserie* porcelain. Next door, the **Bildergalerie** gathers Caravaggio, van Dyck, and Rubens into one long hall. *(Open mid-May to mid-Oct. Tu-Su 10am-5pm. €2, students €1.50. Tours €1.)* Perhaps the park's most intricate garden, the stunning **Sizilianischer Garten** is at the opposite end of the park from the largest of the four castles, the 200-chambered **Neues Palais.** *(Open M-Th and Sa-Su Apr.-Oct. 9am-5pm; Nov.-Mar. 9am-4pm. €6, students €5. Summer tours €1.)*

Potsdam's second park, the **Neuer Garten,** contains several royal residences. **Schloß Cecilienhof,** built in the style of an English Tudor manor, documents the **Potsdam Treaty,** which was signed here in 1945. It would have been the "Berlin Treaty" had not the capital been too bombed-out for the Big Three. *(Take bus #692 to Schloß Cecilienhof. Open Apr.-Oct. Tu-Su 9am-5pm; Nov.-Mar. 9am-4pm. €4, students €3. Summer tours €1.)* The garden also contains the huge, marbled **Marmorpalais** and small, eccentric buildings like a replica of an Egyptian pyramid. *(Marmorpalais open Apr.-Oct. Tu-Su 10am-5pm; Nov.-Mar. Sa-Su 10am-4pm. €2, students €1.50. Summer tours €1.)*

EASTERN GERMANY

Saxony *(Sachsen)* envelops Dresden and Leipzig, the largest cities in the East after Berlin. Dresden's surrounding castles attest to the decadence of Saxony's electors, while boxy GDR-era buildings recall the socialist aesthetic. Germany's only national minority, the Sorbs, lend a Slavic influence to many of Saxony's eastern towns. Thuringia *(Thüringen)* includes Weimar, the crucible of German culture from Goethe to the Bauhaus that gave its name to the post-WWI government.

DRESDEN   ☎0351

The stunning buildings of Dresden's Altstadt look ancient, but most are newly reconstructed—the Allied firebombings in February 1945 that claimed over 40,000 lives also destroyed 75% of the center. Its Baroque architecture, world-class museums, and Neustadt nightlife make Dresden (pop. 479,000) one of the most celebrated cities its size, and a frequent stopover on journeys from Berlin to Prague.

▐ TRANSPORTATION

Flights: Dresden's **airport** (☎881 33 60; www.dresden-airport.de) is 9km from the city. S2 runs there from both train stations. (20min., 2 per hr. 4am-11:30pm, €1.50.)

Trains: Nearly all trains stop at both the **Hauptbahnhof** in the Altstadt and **Bahnhof Dresden Neustadt** across the Elbe. Trains to: **Berlin** (3hr., 2 per hr., €30); **Budapest** (11hr., every 2hr., €64); **Frankfurt** (5hr., 2 per hr., €70); **Leipzig** (1½hr., 1-2 per hr., €17); **Munich** (7hr., 1 per hr., €79); **Prague** (2½hr., 12 per day, €20); **Warsaw** (8hr., 8 per day, €27). Buy tickets from the machines in the main halls of stations or pay less at the Reisezentrum desk.

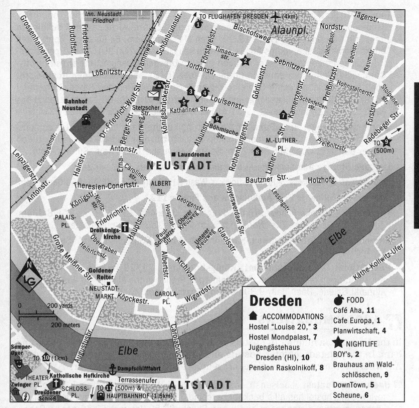

Dresden

🏠 ACCOMMODATIONS
Hostel "Louise 20," 3
Hostel Mondpalast, 7
Jugengästehaus
  Dresden (HI), 10
Pension Raskolnikoff, 8

🍎 FOOD
Café Aha, 11
Cafe Europa, 1
Planwirtschaft, 4

⭐ NIGHTLIFE
BOY's, 2
Brauhaus am Wald-
  schlösschen, 9
DownTown, 5
Scheune, 6

Public Transportation: Most of Dresden is manageable on foot, but **streetcars** cover the whole city. Single ride €1.50; 4 or fewer stops €1. Day pass €4; weekly pass €14. Tickets are available from *Fahrkarte* dispensers at major stops, and on the streetcars. For info and maps, go to one of the **Verkehrs-Info** stands in front of the Hauptbahnhof or at Postpl. Open M-F 8am-7pm, Sa 8am-6pm, Su 9am-6pm. Most major lines run hourly after midnight—look for the moon sign marked "Gute-Nacht-Linie."

Taxis: ☎ 211 211 or 888 88 88.

Bike Rental: In the Hauptbahnhof (☎461 32 62). €6 per day. Open daily 6am-10pm.

Ride-Sharing: Mitfahrzentrale, Dr.-Friedrich-Wolf-Str. 2 (☎194 40). On Slesischen Pl., across from Bahnhof Neustadt. Open M-F 9am-8pm, Sa-Su 10am-2pm.

Hitchhiking: *Let's Go* does not recommend hitchhiking. Those who do hitchhike stand in front of the *Autobahn* signs at on-ramps. To **Berlin:** streetcar #3 or 13 to Liststr., then bus #81 to Am Olter. To **Prague** or **Frankfurt:** bus #72 or 88 to Luga, or bus #76, 85, or 96 to Lockwitz.

✚🚻 ORIENTATION AND PRACTICAL INFORMATION

Dresden is bisected by the **Elbe** river 60km northwest of the Czech border. The **Hauptbahnhof** is on the same side as the **Altstadt,** south of the river. Many of Dresden's main attractions are between **Altmarkt** and the Elbe. Nightlife centers in the **Neustadt** to the north, around **Albertplatz.**

Tourist Office: 2 main branches: Prager Str. 2a, near the Hauptbahnhof (open M-F 10am-6pm, Sa 10am-4pm); and Theaterpl. in the Schinkelwache, a small building in front of the Semper Oper (☎49 19 20; open M-F 10am-6pm, Sa-Su 10am-4pm). Staff books rooms (€3 fee, rooms from €18) and sell city maps (€0.30). Also, 2 cards provide transportation and free or reduced entry to Dresden museums: the **Dresden City-Card**, valid for 48hr. of transport in the city-zone (€18), and the **Dresden Regio-Card**, good for 72hr. in the entire Oberelbe region, including Meißen and Saxon Switzerland (€29). Call the city hotlines for general information (☎49 19 21 00), room reservations (☎49 19 22 22), tours (☎49 19 21 40), and advance tickets (☎49 19 22 33).

Currency Exchange: ReiseBank, in the main hall of the Hauptbahnhof. €1-3 commission for exchanges; 1-1.5% commission to cash **traveler's checks.** Western Union money transfers. Open M-F 8am-7pm, Sa 9am-noon and 12:30-4pm, Su 9am-1pm.

Luggage Storage and Lockers: At all train stations. Lockers €1-2 per 24hr.

Laundromat: Eco-Express, 2 Königsbrückestr. Wash €1.90, dry €0.50. Open M-Sa 6am-11pm.

Emergency: Police: ☎110. **Ambulance** and **Fire:** ☎112.

Pharmacy: Apotheke Prager Straße, Prager Str. 3 (☎490 30 14). Open M-F 8:30am-7pm, Sa 8:30am-4pm. The "*Notdienst*" sign outside lists 24hr. pharmacies.

Internet Access: Groove Station, Katharinenstr. 11-13. €3 per hr. Open M-Sa 7pm-late, Su 4pm-late.

Post Office: The **Hauptpostamt,** Königsbrückerstr. 21/29 (☎819 13 73). In the Neustadt. Open M-F 9am-7pm, Sa 10am-1pm. Branch in the Altstadt on Weberg. at the Altmarkt Galerie. Open daily 9:30am-8pm. **Postal Code:** 01099.

ACCOMMODATIONS

In the Neustadt, a number of hostels with late check-out times neighbor clubs and bars. In the Altstadt, quieter hostels and pricier hotels are nearer to the sights. Anywhere in the city, reservations are a must from April to November.

Hostel Mondpalast, Louisenstr. 77 (☎563 40 50). With a guestbook full of rave reviews, this hostel has all a backpacker could desire: good prices, comfy beds, a large kitchen, a social dining room, and a bar. Sheets €1.50. Internet €3.50 per hr. Reception 24hr. Dorms €13.50-16; singles €29, with bath €39; doubles €37/€50. ❷

Hostel "Louise 20," Louisenstr. 20 (☎889 48 94). Climb the ladder to the beds in the dorm attic (€10) of Dresden's newest hostel. Reception 7am-11pm. Check-out noon. Sheets €2.50. 5-bed room €15; 3-4 bed room €16; singles €26; doubles €37. ❷

Pension Raskolnikoff, Böhmische Str. 34 (☎804 57 06). This 6-room pension is squeezed into the same building as the restaurant and gallery of the same name. The distinctly relaxed bohemian atmosphere is a perfect escape from the hostel scene. Singles €30-35; doubles €40-50. Each additional person €8. ❹

Jugendgästehaus Dresden (HI), Maternistr. 22 (☎49 26 20). From the Hauptbahnhof turn left on Ammonstr. to Rosenstr. Turn right, then take a left onto Maternistr. Come here when everything else is booked—they have 480 beds. Breakfast included. 24hr. reception. Check-in after 4pm. Check-out 9:30am. Dorms €19-23; singles €27-31. ❷

FOOD

It's difficult to find anything in the Altstadt not targeting tourists; the cheapest eats are at the Imbiß stands along **Prager Straße** and around **Postplatz.** The Neustadt area between **Albertplatz** and **Alaunplatz** spawns a new bar every few weeks and is home to most of Dresden's quirky, ethnic, and student-friendly restaurants.

⊠ **Café Aha,** Kreuzstr. 7. Across the street from Kreuzkirche. Introduces food from a different developing country each month—often exotic, always delicious. Vegetarian options. Entrees €3.50-8.40. Open daily 10am-midnight. Kitchen closes 10:30pm. ❶

⊠ **Planwirtschaft,** Louisenstr. 20. German dishes new and traditional with ingredients fresh from local farms. Inventive soups, fresh salads (€3.50-6.90), and entrees (€7-13) from stuffed eggplant to fresh lake fish. Breakfast buffet (€8.60) until 3pm. Open M-Th and Su 9am-midnight, F-Sa 9am-1am. ❸

Cafe Europa, Königsbrücker str. 68 (☎804 48 10). Open 24/7, this self-consciously hip cafe draws a student crowd with 120 different drinks. Free Internet access for customers complements great soups (€2.90-3.20) and traditional entrees (€6-10). ❷

ⓒ SIGHTS

Saxony's electors once ruled nearly all of central Europe from the banks of the Elbe. Despite its demolition in WWII and only partial reconstruction during Communist times, the Altstadt remains one of the continent's major cultural centers.

ZWINGER. The extravagant collection of Saxon elector August the Strong occupies the magnificent Zwinger palace. A glorious example of Baroque design, the palace narrowly escaped destruction in the 1945 bombings. Gottfried Semper, revolutionary activist and master architect, designed the north wing. Now the palace hosts Dresden's finest museums (see **Museums,** below).

SEMPER-OPER. Dresden's opera house, a major attraction, replicates the splendor of the Zwinger's north wing. Painstaking restoration has returned the building to its original state. Tour the interior, or just go to an opera. *(Theaterpl. 2. ☎491 14 96. Tour times usually M-F every 30min. 11am-3pm; check at the entrance. €5, students €3.)*

DRESDENER SCHLOß. Once the proud home of August the Strong, this palace regained its notoriety in 2004, with the return of the ⊠**Grünes Gewölbe** (Green Vault). From a collection of rare medieval chalices to the most lavish Baroque jewels, the vault dazzles the eyes with some of the finest metal and gem work in Europe. *(☎491 47 14. Open Mar.-Oct. M-Th 9am-5pm; F 1-5pm, Sa 10:30am-4pm; Nov.-Apr. M-Sa until 5pm; Su noon-4pm. Free.)* The 100m tall ⊠**Hausmannsturm** hosts a collection of sobering photographs of the city after the firebombings that, combined with the 360° view from the tower, convey the enormity of the reconstruction project. *(Open M and W-Su 10am-6pm. €2.50, students and seniors €1.50.)* To meet the rulers of Saxony from 1123 to 1904, stop by the **Fürstenzug** (Procession of Electors) along Augustsstr., a 102m mural made of 24,000 tiles of Meißen china.

KREUZKIRCHE. After being leveled three times—by fire in 1669, by the Thirty Years' War in 1760, and by fire again in 1897—the Kreuzkirche survived WWII despite the flames that ruined its interior. The tower offers a bird's-eye view of downtown. *(An der Kreuzkirche 6. ☎439 39 20. Church open in summer M-Tu and Th-F 10am-5:30pm, W and Sa 10am-4:30pm, Su noon-5:30pm; winter M-Sa 10am-3:30pm, Su noon-4:30pm. Free. Tower €1.)* The world-class **Kreuzchor** boys' choir has sung here since the 13th century. *(Concerts Sa 6pm. €4-31, students €3-23.)*

🏛 MUSEUMS

After several years of renovations, Dresden's museums are once again ready to compete with the best in Europe. If you plan on visiting more than one in a day, consider a **Tageskarte** (€10, students and seniors €6), which grants one-day admission to the Albertinum museums, the Schloß, most of the Zwinger, and more.

RESURRECTING THE FRAUENKIRCHE

For two centuries, the bell-shaped cupola of Dresden's Frauenkirche (Church of Our Lady) crowned a stunning skyline. Completed in 1743, the Baroque church was built by master architect George Bähr as a symbol of strength, community, and durability. But the Allied firebombing in February 1945 reduced the church to rubble, along with over three quarters of the surrounding city.

The church lay in ruins for 45 years, until German reunification brought about the restoration of many of Dresden's historic buildings. Renovations began in 1994.

In June 2004, the famous dome once more topped the church, and the cross that rose above it 250 years ago was salvaged from the rubble and refurbished by a British craftsman whose father was an RAF pilot in the 1945 air raid. Great Britain then presented it to Dresden as a gesture of reconciliation.

One-sixth of the new exterior is composed of stones from the original church that have been meticulously replaced in their original positions. Although work on the church will continue through 2005, the restored, completed silhouette of the Frauenkirche is a symbol of healing for many Dresdeners, and a sign that the postwar renaissance of their city—and their nation—is almost complete. *(On Neumarkt. ☎ 498 11 31. English tours available every hr. M-F 10am-4pm.)*

ZWINGER. Through the archway from the Semper-Oper, ▧**Gemäldegalerie Alte Meister** has a first-rate collection of Italian and Dutch paintings from 1400 to 1800, including Cranach the Elder's luminous *Adam and Eve*, Rubens's *Leda and the Swan*, and Raphael's *Sistine Madonna*. *(☎ 491 46 19. Open daily 10am-6pm. €6, students €3.50. Tours F and Su 11am and 4pm. €0.50.)* The **Rüstkammer** shows shiny but deadly toys from the court of the Wettin princes: ivory-inlaid guns, chain mail, and the wee armor of the Wettin toddlers. *(Open Tu-Su 10am-6pm. €3, students €2, covered by admission to the Gemäldegalerie Alte Meister.)* With over 20,000 pieces, the ▧**Porzellan-sammlung** boasts the largest collection of European porcelain in the world. *(Open Tu-Su 10am-6pm. €5, students and seniors €3.)* Europe's oldest "science museum," the **Mathematisch-Physikalischer Salon** contains 16th- to 19th-century scientific instruments far more stylish than those in use today. *(Open Tu-Su 10am-6pm. €3, students €2.)*

ALBERTINUM. The **Gemäldegalerie Neue Meister** picks up in the 19th century where the Alte Meister gallery leaves off, with exhibits by hometown Romantic painter Caspar David Friedrich and by the Impressionists Degas, Monet, and Renoir. Check out Otto Dix's renowned *War* triptych, as well as Expressionist and *Neue Sachlichkeit* works. *(Open M and W-Su 10am-6pm. €6, students and seniors €3.50.)* In 2005, the immense **Skulpturensammlung**, comprising works of classical sculpture, will likely have filled the void left by the departure of the Grünes Gewölbe.

▣ ENTERTAINMENT

For centuries, Dresden has been a focal point of theater, opera, and music. Although most theaters break from mid-July to early September, open-air festivals bridge the gap; movies screen during **Filmnächte am Elbufer** in July and August at 9-9:30pm for around €6. (Office at Alaunstr. 62. ☎ 89 93 20.) Like other area palaces, the **Zwinger** has classical concerts on summer evenings. (Shows start at 6:30pm.)

> **Sächsische Staatsoper (Semper-Oper),** Theaterpl. 2 (☎ 491 17 05). Some of the finest opera in the world. It takes work to get a ticket; call ahead. Tickets €3-80. Box office at Schinkelwache open M-F 10am-6pm, Sa 10am-1pm, and 1hr. before performances.

> **Kulturpalast,** Schlossstrasse 2, am Altmarkt (☎ 486 66 66; www.kulturpalast-dresden.de). Home to the **Dresdner Philharmonie** (☎ 486 63 06; www.dresdner-philharmonie.de) and a variety of performances. Open M-F 10am-7pm, Sa 10am-2pm.

Staatsoperette Dresden, Pirnär Landstr. 131 (☎20 79 90; www.staatsoperette-dresden.de). Musicals and operettas from Lerner and Löwe to Sondheim. €4-19. Box office open M 11am-4pm, Tu-Th 10am-7pm, F 11am-7pm, Sa 4-7pm, Su 1hr. before curtain.

projekttheater dresden, Louisenstr. 47 (☎810 76 10; www.projekttheater.de). Cutting-edge, international experimental theater in the heart of the Neustadt. Tickets €11, students €7. Shows at 9pm, box office open 8pm.

💲 NIGHTLIFE

It is as if the entire Neustadt spends the day anticipating 10pm. Little over 10 years ago, the area north of Albertpl. was a maze of gray streets lined with crumbling buildings. Since then a spontaneous alternative community has sprung up in the 50 bars crammed onto Königsbrückerstr., Bischofsweg, Kamenzerstr., and Albertpl. *Kneipen Surfer,* free at Neustadt hostels, describes every bar.

■ **Brauhaus am Waldschlösschen,** am Brauhaus 8b. Tram 11 to Waldschlösschen or walk 25min. up Baunitzerstr. With spectacular views from a hill overlooking the Elbe and the Dresden skyline, this brewery proves Bavaria doesn't have a monopoly on great beer gardens. Beer by the liter (€4.60) and classic German entrees (€6-12).

DownTown, Katharinenstr. 11. Constantly packed. Music is loud, seating hard to come by, and the crowd enthusiastic. Evenings here begin upstairs at the bar, billiard hall, and tattoo parlor. Expect pop, Latin, and electronica. Cover €3.50, students €2.50. Open M-Sa from 7pm, Su from 4pm. Club open Th-Sa 10pm-5am.

Scheune, Alaunstr. 36. From Albertpl., walk up Königsbrücker Str. and turn right onto Katharinenstr.; take a left onto Alaunstr. The granddaddy of the Neustadt bar scene, this huge bar is a starting point for many youth on a night out. Cover varies. Club opens at 8pm. Indian cafe open M-F 5pm-2am, Sa-Su 10am-2am.

BOY's, Alaunstr. 80, just beyond the Kunsthof Passage. A half-clad devil mannequin guards one of Dresden's popular gay bars. Drinks €2.70-6. Open daily 8pm-3am.

▶ DAYTRIP FROM DRESDEN: MEIßEN

In 1710, the Saxon elector contracted severe *Porzellankrankheit* (the porcelain "bug," which still afflicts tourists today) and turned the city's defunct castle into Europe's first porcelain factory. To prevent competitors from learning its techniques, the building was once more tightly guarded than KGB headquarters; today, anyone can tour the **Staatliche Porzellan-Manufaktur,** Talstr. 9. Peruse finished products in the **Schauhalle** (€4.50, students €4), but the real fun is the **Schauwerkstatt** (show workshop) in which porcelain artists paint petal-perfect flowers before your incredulous eyes. (Open daily May-Oct. 9am-6pm; Nov.-Apr. 9am-5pm. €3. English headsets available.) Narrow, romantic alleyways lead up to the ■**Albrechtsburg** castle and cathedral. (Open daily Mar.-Oct. 10am-6pm; Nov.-Feb. 10am-5pm. €3.50, students €2.50.) From the train station, walk straight onto Bahnhofstr. and follow it over the Elbbrücke. Cross the bridge, continue straight to the Markt, and turn right onto Burgstr. Next door looms the **Meißener Dom,** a Gothic cathedral featuring four 13th-century statues by the Naumburg Master, a triptych by Cranach the Elder, and the metal grave coverings of the Wettins. (Open daily Apr.-Oct. 9am-6pm; Nov.-Mar. 10am-4pm. €2, students €1.50.)

Trains run to Dresden (30min., €4.50). The **tourist office,** Markt 3, finds **private rooms** for free. (☎03521 419 40. Open Apr.-Oct. M-F 10am-6pm, Sa-Su 10am-4pm; Nov.-Mar. M-F 10am-5pm, Sa 10am-3pm.) **Postal Code:** 01662.

LEIPZIG ☎0341

Leipzig (pop. 493,000) is one of the few German university cities large enough to have a life outside the academy, but small enough to feel the influence of its students. Every corner is packed with cafes, cabarets, street musicians, and second-hand stores. Once home to Bach and Mendelssohn, Wagner and Nietzsche, Goethe and Leibniz, Leipzig also boasts world-class museums, churches, and restaurants.

▐ ▐ TRANSPORTATION AND PRACTICAL INFORMATION. Leipzig lies on the Berlin-Munich line. **Trains** run to: Berlin (2-3hr., 3 per hr., €33); Dresden (1½hr., 3 per hr., €25); Frankfurt (5hr., 2 per hr., €57); and Munich (7hr., 3 per hr., €90). To find the **tourist office,** Richard-Wagner-Str. 1, cross Willy-Brandt-Pl. in front of the station and hang a left on Richard-Wagner-Str. (☎710 42 30. Open M-F 10am-7pm, Sa 10am-4pm, Su 10am-2pm.) **Postal Code:** 04109.

▐▐ ACCOMMODATIONS AND FOOD. To reach ▉**Hostel Sleepy Lion ❷,** Käthe-Kollwitz-Str. 3, take streetcar #1 (dir.: Lausen) to Gottschedstr. Run by young locals, it draws an international crowd. All rooms with showers and bath. (☎993 94 80. Sheets €2. Internet €2 per hr. Reception 24hr. Dorms €14; singles €24; doubles €36; quads €60.) **Kosmos Hotel ❹,** Gottschedstr. 1, is 12min. from the train station. Cross the street and turn right onto Richard-Wagner-Str.; when it ends, cut left through the parking lot and park. Keep left on Dittrichring and it will be ahead on the right. This funky hotel is part of a larger complex that includes a restaurant and an occasionally loud nightclub. (☎233 44 20. Reception daily 8am-11pm. Singles from €30; doubles from €50.)

Grimmaischestraße in the Innenstadt is full of *Imbiß* stands, bistros, and bakeries. Outside the city center, **Karl-Liebknecht-Straße** (streetcar #10 or 11 to Südpl.) is packed with cafes, bars, and cheap *Döner* stands. ▉**Bellini's ❷,** Markt 3-5, sells baguettes, salads, and pasta in the marketplace. (Open daily 10am-late. AmEx/MC/V.) **Zur Pleißenburg ❷,** Schulstr. 2, down Burgstr. from the Thomaskirche, serves hearty fare with veggie options. (Open daily 9am-5am.) There is a **market** on Richard-Wagner-Pl. at the end of the Brühl. (Open Tu and F 9am-5pm.)

◼◼ SIGHTS AND NIGHTLIFE. The heart of Leipzig is the **Marktplatz,** a cobblestone square guarded by the slanted 16th-century **Altes Rathaus.** Head down Grimmaischestr. to the **Nikolaikirche,** where massive weekly demonstrations accelerated the fall of the GDR. (Open M-Sa 10am-6pm, Su 9am-6pm. Free.) Backtrack to the Rathaus and follow Thomasg. to the **Thomaskirche.** Bach spent his last 27 years here as cantor; his grave is by the altar. (Open daily 9am-6pm. Free.) Just in back is the **Johann-Sebastian-Bach-Museum,** Thomaskirchof 16. (Open daily 10am-5pm. €3, students €2. Free English audiotours.) Head back to Thomasg., turn left, then right on Dittrichring to reach the ▉**Museum in der "Runden Ecke,"** Dittrichring 24, which has stunningly blunt exhibits on the GDR-era secret police. (Open daily 10am-6pm. Free.) Outside the city ring, the **Völkerschlachtdenkmal** memorializes the 1813 Battle of Nations against Napoleon. Climb the 364 steps for a view of Leipzig. (Tram #15 from the station to Völkerschlachtdenkmal. Open daily Apr.-Oct. 10am-6pm; Nov.-Mar. 10am-4pm. €3, students €2.)

Leipzig's **Gewandhaus-Orchester,** Augustuspl. 8, has been a major international orchestra since 1843. (☎127 02 80. Open M-F 10am-6pm, Sa 10am-2pm, and 1hr. before performances. €12-40, 20% student discount.) Free magazines *Fritz* and *Blitz* have nightlife info, as does *Kreuzer* (€1.50 at newsstands). **Barfußgäßchen,** a street just off the Markt, is the place to see and be seen for the student and yuppie crowd. A slightly younger crowd and slightly louder music lie just across Dittrichring on **Gottschedstraße** and **Bosestraße.** Leipzig university students spent eight years excavating a series of medieval tunnels so they could get their groove on in the ▧Moritzbastei, Universitätsstr. 9, with bars and multi-level dance floors under vaulted brick ceilings. (Cover €3, students €2; higher for concerts. Cafe open daily 2pm-midnight. Disco open W and F until late.)

WITTENBERG ☎ 03491

Martin Luther inaugurated the Protestant Reformation here in 1517 when he nailed his *95 Theses* to the door of the Schloßkirche; Wittenberg (pop. 48,000) has been fanatical about its native heretic ever since. All major sights surround **Collegien-straße**. The ▧**Lutherhalle**, Collegienstr. 54, chronicles the Reformation through letters, texts, art, and artifacts. (☎420 30. Open Apr.-Oct. daily 9am-6pm; Nov.-Mar. Tu-Su 10am-5pm. €5, students €3.) Down Schloßstr., the **Schloßkirche** allegedly holds Luther's body and a copy of the *Theses*; its tower has a sumptuous view of the Altstadt, the countryside, and the Elbe. (Open M-Sa 10am-5pm, Su 11:30am-5pm. Free. Tower open M-F noon-4pm, Sa-Su 10am-4pm. €1, students €0.50.)

Trains leave for Berlin (1½hr., every 2hr., €17) and Leipzig (1hr., every 2hr., €9). From the station, follow the street curving right and continue until Collegienstr., the start of the **pedestrian zone**. The **tourist office**, Schloßpl. 2, provides maps, leads tours (€6), and books rooms. (☎49 86 10. Open Mar.-Oct. M-F 9am-6pm, Sa 10am-3pm, Su 11am-4pm; Nov.-Feb. M-F 10am-4pm, Sa 10am-2pm, Su 11am-3pm.) The ▧**Jugendherberge (HI) ❷** is in the castle across from the tourist office. (☎40 32 55. Breakfast included. Sheets €3.50. Reception 3-10pm. Dorms €15, under 27 €12.) Look for cheap meals along the Collegienstr.-Schloßstr. strip. **Postal Code:** 06886.

WEIMAR ☎ 03643

While countless German towns leap at any excuse to build a memorial *Goethe-haus* (claiming that Goethe slept here, Goethe ate here, Goethe asked for directions here, etc.), Weimar (pop. 62,000) has the authentic article. The **Goethehaus** and **Goethe-Nationalmuseum**, Frauenplan 1, preserve the chambers where the poet wrote, entertained guests, and, after a half-century in Weimar, died. (Open Apr.-Oct. Tu-Su 9am-6pm; Nov.-Mar. 9am-4pm. Expect a wait on summer weekends. €6, students €4.50. Museum €2.50/€2.) Always the polymath, Goethe himself landscaped the **Park an der Ilm**, which contains his first Weimar residence, the **Gartenhaus**. (On Corona-Schöfer-Str. Open Apr. to mid-Oct. M and W-Su 9am-6pm; mid-Oct. to Mar. 9am-4pm. €3, students €2.) South of the center is the **Historischer Fried-hof**, where Goethe and Schiller rest together in the basement of the **Fürstengruft** (Ducal Vault). Schiller, who died in an epidemic, was originally buried in a mass grave; later Goethe combed through the remains and had him interred in a tomb. (Cemetery open daily Mar.-Sept. 8am-9pm; Oct.-Feb. 8am-6pm. Free. Tomb open Apr. to mid-Oct. M and W-Su 9am-1pm and 2-6pm; mid-Oct. to Mar. 10am-1pm and 2-4pm. €2, students €1.50.) Weimar's **Bauhaus Museum** showcases weavings, sculptures, furniture, toys, and books that illuminate the Bauhaus philosophy. (On Theaterpl. Open Apr.-Oct. Tu-Su 10am-6pm; Nov.-Mar. 10am-4pm. €3, students and seniors €2.) Directly opposite the museum, the ▧**Deutsches Nationaltheater,** which debuted Goethe and Schiller, still presents *Faust* regularly, along with Mozart and Verdi operas; the Weimar Constitution was signed there in 1919. (☎75 53 34. Box office open M 2-6pm, Tu-Sa 10am-6pm, Su 10am-1pm, and 1hr. before shows.)

Trains run to: Dresden (2hr., 1per hr., €30); Frankfurt (3hr., 1 per hr., €40); and Leipzig (1½hr., 1 per hr., €21). To reach the central **Goetheplatz** from the station, follow Carl-August-Allee downhill to Karl-Liebknecht-Str., which leads into Goethepl. (15min.). The **tourist office**, Marktstr. 10, across from the Rathaus, has free maps, books rooms for a €2.55 fee, and offers German **walking tours**. Its Weimarer Wald desk has info on nearby **outdoor activities**. (☎240

GERMANY

00. Open Apr.-Oct. M-F 9:30am-6pm, Sa-Su 9:30am-3pm; Nov.-Mar. M-F 10am-6pm, Sa-Su 10am-2pm.) **Jugendherberge Germania (HI) ❸**, Carl-August-Allee 13, is in a lovely Jugendstil mansion. (☎85 04 90. Dorms €20, under 27 €17. Cash only.) To reach the relaxed, student-run **Hababusch Hostel ❶**, Geleitstr. 4, in the heart of Weimar, follow Geleitstr. from Goethepl. After a sharp right, you'll come to a statue on your left; the entrance is behind it. (☎85 07 37. Reception 24hr. Dorms €10; singles €15; doubles €24. Cash only.) A combination cafe and gallery, **ACC ❷**, Burgpl. 1-2, is popular with students and vegetarians. (Open M-F 11am-1am, Sa-Su 10am-1am. Cash only.) A daily **produce market** on Marktpl. has groceries. (Open M-Sa 7am-5pm.)

⚡ DAYTRIP FROM WEIMAR: BUCHENWALD. During WWII, Buchenwald labor camp interned 250,000 prisoners, including Jews, Gypsies, homosexuals, Communists, and other political dissidents. Although Buchenwald was not built as an extermination camp, over 50,000 died here from malnutrition, medical experiments, or harsh treatment by the SS. The **Nationale Mahnmal und Gedenkstätte Buchenwald** (National Monument and Memorial) has two principal sites. The **KZ-Lager** is what remains of the camp; a large storehouse documents the history of Buchenwald (1937-1945) and of Nazism. The East German **Mahnmal** (monument) is on the other side of the hill; go up the main road that bisects the two large parking lots or take the footpath uphill from the old Buchenwald train station and then continue on the main road. Camp **archives** are open to anyone searching for records of family and friends between 1937 and 1945; schedule an appointment with the curator. (Archives ☎03643 43 01 54, library 43 01 60. Outdoor camp area open daily until sundown.) Sadly, the suffering at Buchenwald did not end with liberation. Soviet authorities used the site as an internment camp, **Special Camp. No. 2,** where more than 28,000 Germans—mostly Nazi war criminals and opponents of Communism—were held until 1950; an exhibit on this period opened in 1997.

The best way to reach the camp is by **bus #6** from Weimar's train station or from Goethepl. Check the schedule carefully; some #6 buses go to Ettersburg rather than Gedenkstätte Buchenwald. (20min.; M-Sa 1 per hr., Su every 2hr.) Buses back to Weimar stop at the KZ-Lager parking lot and at the road by the *Glockenturm* (bell tower). An **info center** near the Buchenwald bus stop has audioguides (€3, students €2), runs a free walking tour, and shows a 30min. video every hour. (☎43 00. Open May-Sept. Tu-Su 9am-6pm; Oct.-Apr. 8:30am-4:30pm.)

EISENACH   ☎03691

Eisenach (pop. 44,000) is best-known as home to ▓**Wartburg Fortress,** which protected Martin Luther in 1521 after his excommunication. It was here, disguised as a bearded noble named Junker Jörg, that Luther famously fought an apparition of the devil with an inkwell. After renovations, much of the castle's interior is not authentically medieval, but Wartburg is still enchanting and the view from its south tower is spectacular. (Open daily Mar.-Oct. 8:30am-5pm; Nov.-Feb. 9am-3:30pm. Mandatory German tour €6.50, students and children €3.50.) Eisenach is also known as the birthplace of composer **Johann Sebastian Bach.** According to local tradition, Bach was born in 1685 in the **Bachhaus,** Frauenplan 21. Roughly every hour, a guide plays one of the museum's period keyboard instruments and provides historical context in German. (Open daily 10am-6pm. €4, students €3. English translations available on request.) Bach was baptized at the 800-year-old **Georgenkirche,** just off the Markt, where members of his family were organists for 132 years. (Open M-Sa 10am-12:30pm and 2-5pm, Su 11am-12:30pm and 2-5pm.) Up the street is the latticed **Lutherhaus,** Lutherpl. 8, where Luther lived in his school days. (Open daily Apr.-Oct. 9am-5pm; Nov.-Mar. 10am-5pm. €2.50, students €2.)

Trains run to Weimar (1hr., 2 per hr., €11). The **tourist office**, Markt 2, hands out free maps, books rooms for no charge, and runs daily city tours (2pm, €4). From the train station, follow Bahnhofstr. through the tunnel and veer left until taking a right onto Karlstr. (☎194 33. Open M 10am-6pm, Tu-F 9am-6pm, Sa-Su 10am-2pm.) To reach the renovated **Jugendherberge Arthur Becker (HI) ❷**, Mariental 24, take Bahnhofstr. from the station to Wartburger Allee, which runs into Mariental (35min.), or take bus #3 or 10 (dir.: Mariental) to Liliengrund Parkplatz. (☎74 32 59. Reception daily 8am-11pm. Dorms €18, under 27 €15.) There is an **Edeka** supermarket on Johannispl. (Open M-F 7am-7pm, Sa 7am-2pm.) **La Fontana ❶**, Georgenstr. 22, serves €3 pizza and pasta dishes. (☎74 35 39. Open M-Th and Su 11:30am-2:30pm and 5-11pm, F-Sa 11:30am-2:30pm and 5-11:30pm.) **Postal Code:** 99817.

NORTHERN GERMANY

Despite recent hard times, it is clear why Mecklenburg-Vorpommern, the northeasternmost part of Germany, was once a vacation spot for East Germans. Schleswig-Holstein, on the border with Denmark, is Germany's gateway to Scandinavia, while the less idyllic Hamburg is notoriously huge, rich, and radical.

HANOVER (HANNOVER)   ☎0511

Despite its small size, Hanover (pop. 516,000) has the culture and landscape to rival any European city. Wide boulevards and endless gardens make the city an example of all that is good in urban planning. Hanover's highlights are the three bountiful ◼Herrenhausen gardens. Largest among these, the **Großer Garten** contains geometrically pruned shrubbery and the **Große Fontäne**, one of Europe's highest-shooting fountains. (Spurts M-F 11am-noon and 3-5pm, Sa-Su 11am-noon and 2-5pm. Garden open Apr. to mid-Oct. 9am-8pm; mid-Oct. to Mar. 8am-dusk. €2.50.) On the outskirts of the Altstadt stands the **Neues Rathaus;** take the elevator up the tower for a thrilling view. (Open May-Sept. M-F 9am-11pm, Sa-Su 10am-11pm. Elevator €2.) Nearby, the ◼Sprengel Museum, Kurt-Schwitters-Pl., hosts some of the best in 20th-century art, including Dalí, Picasso, and Schwitters. (Open Tu 10am-8pm, W-Su 10am-6pm. Permanent collection €3.50, students €2; with special exhibits €6/€3.50.) **Kestner-Museum**, Trammpl. 3, showcases decorative arts, with a focus on chairs. (Open Tu and Th-Su 11am-6pm, W 11am-8pm. €2.60, students €1.50. F free.) **The Loft**, Georgstr. 50a, fills a chic garden with students on weekends. (Happy Hour M-Th and Su 8-9pm, F-Sa 1-2am. Open W-Sa from 8pm.)

Trains leave at least every hr. for: Amsterdam (4½-5hr., €56); Berlin (2½hr., €49); Frankfurt (3hr., €65); Hamburg (1½hr., €29); and Munich (9hr., €95). To reach the **tourist office**, Ernst-August-Pl. 2, head out the main entrance of the train station; turn right facing the rear of the king's steed. (☎16 84 97 00. Open M-F 9am-6pm, Sa 9am-2pm.) ◼Jugendherberge Hannover (HI) ❷, Ferdinand-Wilhelm-Fricke-Weg. 1, is outside the city center, but worth the trek. Take U3 or 7 to Fischerhof. From the stop, backtrack 10m, turn right, and cross the tracks; follow the path as it curves and cross Stammestr. Go over the red footbridge and turn right. (☎131 7674. Reception daily 7:30am-1am. Dorms €19-30, under 27 €17-28.) To reach **CityHotel am Thielenplatz ❹**, Thielenpl. 2, take a left onto Joachimstr. from the station and go one block to Thielenpl. (☎32 76 91. Check-out 11:30am. Singles €40, with shower €57; doubles with shower €75. MC/V.) **Uwe's Hannenfaß Hannover ❷**, Knochenhauerstr. 36, in the center of the Altstadt, serves German fare for €5-7 and great house brews at €3.65 for 0.5L. (Open M-Th and Su 4pm-2am, F 4pm-4am, Sa noon-4am.) **Jalda ❷**, Limmerstr. 97, serves Greek and Mideastern dishes for €4-8. Take U10 to Ungerstr. (Open M-Th and Su 11:30am-midnight, F-Sa 11:30am-1am.) A **Euro-Spar** supermarket is by the Kröpke U-Bahn stop. (Open M-Sa 7am-8pm.) **Postal Code:** 30159.

HAMBURG ☎040

The largest port city in Germany, Hamburg (pop. 1,700,000) radiates an inimitable recklessness. Hamburg gained the status of Free Imperial City in 1618 and now retains its autonomy as one of Germany's 16 *Länder*, making it one of only three German city-states. Riots and restorations defined the post-WWII landscape; today, Hamburg is a haven for contemporary artists, intellectuals, and party-goers who live it up in Germany's self-declared "capital of lust."

◾ TRANSPORTATION

Flights: Fuhlsbüttel Airport (☎507 50) is a hub for **Lufthansa** (☎0180 380 3803) and **Air France** (☎0180 583 0830). Jasper Airport Express **buses** (☎22 71 06 61) run to the airport from the Kirchenallee exit of the Hauptbahnhof (25min.; every 15min. 5am-7pm, then every 20min. 7-9:20pm; €4.60, under 13 €2). Or, take U1 or S1/S11 to Ohlsdorf, and then an express bus to the airport (every 10min. 4:30am-11pm, then every 30min. 11pm-1am; €2.20, under 13 €0.80).

Trains: The Hauptbahnhof has hourly connections to: **Berlin** (2½hr., €42); **Copenhagen** (5hr., €66); **Frankfurt** (3½hr., €86); **Hanover** (1½hr., €34); **Munich** (6hr., €96); and runs frequently to **Amsterdam** (5hr., 3 per day, €68). **DB Reisezentrum** ticket office open M-F 5:30am-10pm, Sa-Su 7am-10pm. **Dammtor** station is near the university; **Harburg** station is south of the Elbe; **Altona** station is to the west of the city; and **Bergedorf** is to the southeast. **Lockers** are available 24hr. for €1-4 per day at stations.

Buses: The **ZOB** is on Steintorpl. across from the Hauptbahnhof. **Autokraft** (☎280 86 60) runs to **Berlin** (3¼hr., 8 per day, €23). **Gulliver's** (☎24 71 06) to **Amsterdam** (5½hr., 1 per day, €36) and **Paris** (12hr., 1 per day, €55). Student and children discounts. Open M-Th 5am-10pm, F-Sa 5am-midnight, Su 5am-10pm.

Public Transportation: HVV operates an efficient U-Bahn, S-Bahn, and bus network. One-way tickets within the downtown cost €1.50; prices vary with distance and network. Hour pass €4.65, 1-day pass €5.50, 3-day pass €13.30. Tickets can be bought at Automaten, but consider buying a **Hamburg Card** instead (see below).

Bike Rental: Fahrradladen St. Georg, Schmilinskystr. 6 (☎24 39 08), off Lange Reihe towards the Außenalster. €8 per day. Open M-F 10am-7pm, Sa 10am-1pm.

◼✳◪ ORIENTATION AND PRACTICAL INFORMATION

Hamburg's center sits between the Elbe River and the two city lakes, **Außenalster** and **Binnenalster.** Most major sights lie between the **St. Pauli Landungsbrücken** port area in the west and the **Hauptbahnhof** in the east. **Mönckebergstraße,** Hamburg's most famous shopping street, runs all the way to Rathausmarkt. North of downtown, the **university** dominates the **Dammtor** area and sustains a vibrant community of students and intellectuals. To the west of the university, the **Schanzenviertel** is a politically active community home to artists, squatters, and a sizeable Turkish population. At the south end of town, an entirely different atmosphere reigns in **St. Pauli,** where the raucous **Fischmarkt** (fish market) is surpassed only by the wilder **Reeperbahn,** at once home to Hamburg's infamous sex trade and best discos.

Tourist Offices: The **Hauptbahnhof office,** in the Wandelhalle near the Kirchenallee exit (☎300 512 01; www.hamburg-tourism.de), books rooms for a €4 fee. Open daily 7am-10pm. The **St. Pauli Landungsbrücken office,** between piers 4 and 5 (☎300 512 03; fax 31 35 78), is less crowded. Both supply free English maps and sell the **Hamburg Card,** which provides unlimited access to public transportation, reduced admission to museums, and discounts on bus and boat tours. 1-day card €7.

GERMANY

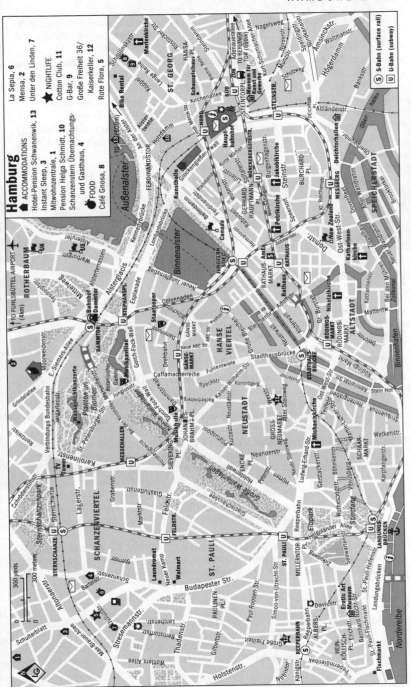

Hamburg

ACCOMMODATIONS
Hotel-Pension Schwanenwik, **13**
Instant Sleep, **3**
Mitwohnzentrale, **1**
Pension Helga Schmidt, **10**
Schanzenstern Übernachtungs-
und Gasthaus, **4**

FOOD
Café Gnosa, **8**
La Sepia, **6**
Mensa, **2**
Unter den Linden, **7**

NIGHTLIFE
Cotton Club, **11**
G-Bar, **9**
Große Freiheit 36/
Kaiserkeller, **12**
Rote Flora, **5**

Ⓢ S-Bahn (surface rail)
Ⓤ U-Bahn (subway)

Currency Exchange: ReiseBank, on the 2nd fl. of the Hauptbahnhof near the Kirchenallee exit (☎32 34 83), has Western Union services, cashes traveler's checks, and exchanges currency for a steep 4-5% fee. Open daily 7:30am-10pm.

American Express: Rathausmarkt 10 (☎30 39 38 11). U3 to Rathaus. Across from the bus stop, on the corner of Hermanstr. All banking services. Mail (letters only) held for members up to 5 weeks. Open M-F 9:30am-6pm, Sa 10am-2pm.

GLBT Services: St. Georg is the center of the gay community. Find the free **hinnerk** magazine and *Friends: The Gay Map* at **Café Gnosa,** Lange Reihe 93 (p. 469).

Laundromat: Schnell und Sauber, Grindelallee 158, in the university district. Take S21 or 31 to Dammtor. Wash €3.50 per 6kg. Dry €1 per 15min. Open daily 7am-10:30pm.

Emergency: Police: ☎110. **Ambulance** and **Fire:** ☎112.

Pharmacy: Senator-Apotheke, Hachmannpl. 14 (☎32 75 27 or 33 92 92). Turn right from the station's Kirchenallee exit. English spoken. Open M-F 7am-8pm, Sa 8am-4pm.

Internet Access: Internet Cafe, Adenauerallee 10 (☎28 00 38 98). €0.70 per 30min. Open M-Sa 10am-midnight, Su 1pm-midnight. **Teletime,** Schulterblatt 39 (☎41 30 47 30). €0.50 per 10min. Open M-Sa 10am-midnight.

Post Office: At the Kirchenallee exit of the Hauptbahnhof. Open M-F 8am-8pm, Sa 9am-6pm. **Postal Code:** 20099.

ACCOMMODATIONS

The dynamic **Sternschanze** area has the city's two best backpacker hostels. Small, relatively cheap pensions line **Steindamm** and the area around the Hauptbahnhof, although the area's prostitutes and wannabe Mafiosi detract from its charm. **Lange Reihe** has equivalent options in a cleaner neighborhood. More expensive hotels line the **Binnenalster** and eastern **Außenalster.** For longer stays, try **Mitwohnzentrale Homecompany,** Schulterblatt 112. (☎194 45; www.homecompany.de.)

Schanzenstern Übernachtungs- und Gasthaus, Bartelsstr. 12 (☎439 84 41; www.schanzenstern.de). S21, S31, or U3 to Sternschanze. Left onto Schanzenstr., right on Susannenstr., and left to Bartelsstr. In the middle of an electrifying neighborhood, the hostel maintains bright, clean rooms on the upper floors of a renovated pen factory. Dorms €18; singles €36; doubles €51; triples €61; quads €74; quints €92. ❷

Instant Sleep, Max-Brauer-Allee 277 (☎43 18 23 10). S21 or U3 to Sternschanze. Everyone is part of a big happy family in this backpacker hostel; rooms are often left open while guests lounge together, read, or cook dinner in the communal kitchen. Bike rental €4 per 6hr. Sheets €2. Internet €1 for 15min. Reception daily 9am-2pm. Dorms €15-18; singles €28; doubles €44; triples €60. ❷

Pension Helga Schmidt, Holzdamm 14 (☎280 83 90). Welcoming pension only 2 blocks from the Hauptbahnhof. All rooms with TV and phone. Cheaper rooms share a hall shower. Singles €35-37; doubles €55-65; triples €82. ❹

Hotel-Pension Schwanenwik, Schwanenwik 29 (☎220 09 18). Bus #6 to Mundsburger Brücke, cross the street, walk down Hartwicusstr., and turn right onto Schwanenwik. Beautiful rooms near the lake. Breakfast included. Singles €44-68; doubles €62-90. ❹

FOOD

Seafood abounds in Hamburg, as would be expected in a port city. **Sternschanze** is the most interesting part of town from a culinary standpoint; here the food and atmosphere of avant-garde cafes and Turkish falafel stands entice hungry passersby. **Schulterblatt, Susannenstraße,** and **Schanzenstraße** have funky cafes and restaurants, while cheaper establishments abound in the **university** area, especially along **Rentzelstraße, Grindelhof,** and **Grindelallee.** In **Altona,** the pedestrian zone approaching the train station packs in ethnic food stands and produce shops.

🗹 **La Sepia,** Schulterblatt 36, is a Portuguese restaurant with some of the city's finest, most reasonably priced seafood. Lunch €4-6. Dinner €8-15. Open daily 11am-3am. ❷

Unter den Linden, Juliusstr 16. Read complimentary papers over Milchkaffee (€3.20), breakfast (€4-7), or enormous salads (€4-6) in a relaxed atmosphere beneath the lindens. Open M-F 11am-11pm, Sa-Su 10am-11pm. ❷

Mensa, Von-Melle-Park 5. S21 or S31 to Dammtor, then bus #4 or 5 to Staatsbibliothek (1 stop). Heaps of cafeteria food and a bulletin board of university events. Meals €2.20-3.70. Student discount €0.70. Open M-Th 10am-5:30pm, F 10am-4:30pm. ❶

Café Gnosa, Lange Reihe 93. A social focal point for the gay community of St. Georg, Gnosa serves up drinks and desserts to 20-somethings of mixed orientation. Drinks €2-5. Open M-Th and Su 10am-1am, F-Sa 10am-2am. ❶

🔘 SIGHTS

ALTSTADT

GROßE MICHAELSKIRCHE. This giant 18th-century Michaelskirche is the symbol of Hamburg, and with good reason. Destroyed successively by lightning, accidents, and Allied bombs, its fate has kept in tandem with the city's. Restored in 1996, the scalloped walls of the interior recall the space of a concert hall. A panoramic view of Hamburg awaits those who climb the 462 stairs of the spire—or those who opt for the elevator. In the crypt, a multimedia presentation on the history of the church screens on weekends. (☎37 67 81 00. Open May-Oct. M-Sa 9am-6pm, Su 11:30am-5:30pm; Nov.-Apr. M-Sa 10am-4:30pm, Su 11:30am-4:30pm. Screenings Th, Sa, and Su every hr. 12:30-3:30pm. €2.50. Tower open until 9pm in summer. €2.50. Crypt open June-Oct. daily 11am-4:30pm; Nov.-May Sa-Su 11am-4:30pm. €1.)

RATHAUS. Both city and state government are sheltered amid the intricate mahogany carvings and two-ton chandeliers of unquestionably the most richly ornamented building in Hamburg. In front, the Rathausmarkt is host to both political demonstrations and medieval fairs. (☎428 31 24 70. English tours every hr. M-Th 10:15am-3:15pm, F-Su 10:15am-1:15pm. €1.50, under 14 €0.50.)

NIKOLAIKIRCHE. Devastated by a July 1943 Allied bomb, the spire of this neo-Gothic ruin has been preserved as a memorial for victims of war and persecution. (Exhibition in the basement open M-F 11am-5pm, Sa-Su 11am-6pm. €2.) Along nearby **Trostbrücke,** buildings sport huge copper models of clipper ships on their spires in testimony to Hamburg's sea-trade wealth. (Just south of the Rathaus, off Ost-West-Str.)

MÖNKEBERGSTRAßE. Two spires punctuate Hamburg's shopping zone, which stretches from the Rathaus to the Hauptbahnhof. The one closest to the Rathaus is St. Petrikirche, the oldest church in Hamburg. (Open M-Tu and Th-F 10am-6:30pm, W 10am-7pm, Sa 10am-5pm, Su 9am-9pm. Frequent free concerts.) The other, St. Jakobikirche, is known for its 14th-century Arp-Schnittger organ. (Open M-Sa 10am-5pm.)

BEYOND THE ALTSTADT

🗹 **PLANTEN UN BLOMEN.** West of the Alster, this huge expanse of manicured flower beds and trees includes the largest Japanese garden in Europe. (S21 or S31 to Dammtor. Open 7am-11pm. Free.) At night, opt for the **Wasserlichtkonzerte,** with a choreographed play of fountains and underwater lights. *(Daily May-Aug. 10pm; Sept. 9pm.)* North of the center, the two **Alster lakes,** bordered by tree-lined paths, provide further refuge from the crowds.

ST. PAULI LANDUNGSBRÜCKEN. Hamburg's harbor lights up at night with ships from all over the world. At the **Fischmarkt,** charismatic vendors haul in and hawk huge amounts of fish, produce, and other goods. Don't shy away if you dislike fish—about 90% of the merchandise is something else. *(U- or S-Bahn to Landungsbrücken or S-Bahn to Königstr. or Reeperbahn. Open Apr.-Oct. Su 5-10am; Nov.-Mar. 7-10am.)*

BEYOND THE CENTER

Outside the city center, public transportation allows access to two very different testaments to the atrocities of the Nazi regime.

KZ NEUENGAMME. An idyllic agricultural village east of Hamburg provided the backdrop for the Neuengamme concentration camp, where Nazis killed 55,000 prisoners through slave labor. In 1989, the Hamburg senate built a memorial on the site. Banners inscribed with the names and death dates of the victims hang in the **Haus des Gedenkens,** and **Walther-Werke** has the recorded testimony of survivors in German, English, French, and Russian. *(Jean-Doldier-Weg 39. S21 to Bergedorf, then bus #227. Bus runs from Bergedorf M-Sa every hr., Su every 2hr. ☎ 428 96 03. Museum and memorial open May-Oct. Tu-F 10am-5pm, Sa-Su 10am-6pm; Oct.-Mar. Tu-Su 10am-5pm. Path always open. Tours Su noon and 2:30pm.)*

GEDENKSTÄTTE BULLENHUSER DAMM UND ROSENGARTEN. Surrounded by warehouses, this schoolhouse is a memorial to 20 Jewish children brought here from Auschwitz for "testing" and murdered by the S.S. only hours before Allied troops arrived. Visitors are invited to plant a rose for the children in the flower garden behind the school. *(Bullenhuser Damm 92. S21 to Rothenburgsort. Follow the signs to Bullenhuser Damm along Ausschläger Bildeich to the intersection with Grossmannstr.; the garden is on the far left side, the school 200m farther. ☎ 428 13 10. Rose garden always open. Exhibition open Th 2-8pm and Su 10am-5pm. Free.)*

🏛 MUSEUMS

The **Hamburg Card** provides access to all museums except the Deichtorhallen, the Hafen Basar, and the Erotic Art Museum. *Museumswelt Hamburg,* a free newspaper, lists exhibitions and events and can be picked up at tourist offices. Most museums close on Mondays.

▓ HAMBURGER KUNSTHALLE. This sprawling, first-rate fine arts museum would require many days to appreciate in full. The lower level presents the Old Masters and extensive special exhibitions. In the connected four-level **Galerie der Gegenwart,** contemporary art takes a stand, and a loud one at that—check out the pneumatic dancing legs on the top floor. *(Glockengießerwall 1. Turn right from the Spitalerstr./City exit of the Hauptbahnhof and cross the street. ☎ 428 13 12 00; www.hamburger.kunsthalle.de. Open Tu-Su 10am-6pm, Th until 9pm. €8.50, students €5, families €11.)*

MUSEUM FÜR KUNST UND GEWERBE. Handicrafts, china, and furnishings from all corners of the earth fill the applied arts museum. A huge exhibit chronicles the evolution of the modern keyboard with dozens of the world's oldest harpsichords, clavichords, and hammerklaviers. Also check out the extensive photography display. *(Steintorpl. 1. 1 block south of the Hauptbahnhof. ☎ 428 54 27 32; www.mkg-hamburg.de. Open Tu-Su 10am-6pm, Th until 9pm. €8.20, students and seniors €4.10, under 16 €2.)*

EROTIC ART MUSEUM. Recently moved off the Reeperbahn and spread over 4 floors, the museum hosts everything from the *Kama Sutra* to Victorian pornography, from loose sketches to gigantic Russian dolls in degrees of undress. Drawings by Picasso add fame and propriety to an otherwise shocking display. *(Bernhard-Nocht-Str. 69. S1 or 3 to Reeperbahn. ☎ 317 47 57; www.erotic-art-museum.de. Open M-Th and Su 10am-midnight, F-Sa 10am-2am. €8, students €5. Under 16 not admitted.)*

🎵 🎭 ENTERTAINMENT AND NIGHTLIFE

The **Staatsoper**, Große Theaterstr. 36, houses one of the best **opera** companies in Germany; the associated **ballet** is the nation's acknowledged star. (☎ 35 68 68. U2 to Gänsemarkt. Open M-Sa 10am-6:30pm.) **Orchestras** abound—the Philharmonie, the Norddeutscher Rundfunk Symphony, and Hamburg Symphonia all perform at the **Musikhalle** on Johannes-Brahms-Pl. (☎ 34 69 20; www.musikhalle-hamburg.de. U2 to Gänsemarkt.) Live music also prospers in Hamburg. Superb traditional jazz swings at the **Cotton Club**. Early on Sundays, musicians talented and otherwise play at the **Fischmarkt**. The **West Port Jazz Festival**, Germany's largest, runs in mid-July; for info, call the Konzertkasse (☎ 32 87 38 54). The huge **G-Move** (May 28, 2005) has been dubbed the "Love Parade of the North." See www.gmove.de for details.

Hamburg's unrepressed nightlife heats up in the Sternschanze and St. Pauli areas. Through the heart of **St. Pauli** runs the infamous **Reeperbahn;** lined with sex shops, strip joints, and peep shows, it is also home to the best bars and clubs. Although the Reeperbahn is generally safe, women especially may want to avoid adjacent streets. Parallel to the Reeperbahn but open only to men over 18 is Hamburg's "official" prostitution strip, **Herbertstraße,** where licensed prostitutes flaunt their flesh; streetwalkers elsewhere are venereal roulette wheels. Students who dislike the hypersexed Reeperbahn head north to the streets of the **Schanzenviertel** for cafes rather than clubs, and an atmosphere more leftist than lustful. **St. Georg,** near Berliner Tor and along Lange Reihe, is the center of Hamburg's **gay scene.** Clubs generally open and close late, with some techno and trance clubs remaining open all night. *Szene* (€2.50), available at newsstands, lists events and parties.

■ **Große Freiheit 36/Kaiserkeller,** Große Freiheit 36 (☎ 31 77 780). Everyone from Ziggy Marley to Matchbox Twenty has performed on the big stage and dance floor upstairs. Live music or DJs usually 10:30pm-5am. Cover €5-6, concerts €10-30. Entry often free until 11pm; if you get your hand stamped, you can return later.

■ **Rote Flora,** Schulterblatt 71. In the heart of the Sternschanze scene, spray paint and posters hold together this looming mansion of graffiti. Beer €1.50. Weekend cover from €3-5. Cafe open M-F 6-10pm. Music starts at around 10pm. Crowds come at midnight.

Cotton Club, Alter Steinweg 10. U3 to Rödingsmarkt. New Orleans, dixie, swing, and big band jazz in a warmly lit setting. Cover €5 for Hamburg bands, around €10 for guest bands. Shows start at 8:30pm. Open M-Th 8pm-midnight, F-Sa 8pm-1am.

G-Bar, Lange Reihe 81. Men in skin-tight shirts serve beer (€2-3) and mixed drinks (€7) with a smile in this comfortable, neon-lit gay bar. Open daily noon-2am.

LÜBECK ☎ 0451

Lübeck (pop. 213,000) is easily Schleswig-Holstein's most beautiful city—you'd never guess that it was mostly razed in WWII. In its heyday it was the capital of the Hanseatic League, controlling trade across all Northern Europe. No longer a center of commercial influence, Lübeck is today a merchant in delicious marzipan and red-blond Dückstein beer. Between the station and the Altstadt stands the massive **Holstentor,** one of Lübeck's four 15th-century gates; the museum inside deals equally in trade and torture. (Open Apr.-Sept. daily 10am-5pm; Oct.-Mar. closed M. €4, students €2.) The skyline is dominated by the twin brick towers of the **Marienkirche,** which houses the world's largest mechanical organ. (Open daily in summer 10am-6pm; low season 10am-4pm. €3.50, students €2.50.) On Domkirchhof, the **Dom** shelters a majestic crucifix. (Open daily Apr.-Sept. 10am-6pm; Mar. and Oct. 10am-5pm; Nov. 10am-4pm; Dec.-Feb. 10am-3pm. Free. €6, students €3.) For a view of the spire-studded Altstadt, take the elevator to the top of **Petrikirche.** (Church open daily 11am-5pm. Tower open daily Apr.-Oct. 9am-7pm. €2.50, students €1.50.) The **Museum für Puppentheater,** Kolk 14, has a huge puppet collection. (Open daily 10am-6pm. €3, students €2.50.) Dance afloat the **"body and soul"** boat at the corner of Kanalstr. and Hohe Glockenstr. (Cover €4. Open Tu and Sa 10pm-late, F 10:30pm-late.)

Trains run to Berlin (3½hr., 1 per hr., €35) and Hamburg (45min., 1 per hr., €9). Lübeck's **tourist office,** by the Holstentor in the Altstadt, books rooms for no commission. (☎122 54 20. Open M-F 9:30am-6pm, Sa-Su 10am-3pm.) Lübeck's **Happy Day Card** (1-day card €5; 3-day card €10) includes free local transport and discounts museums. (☎122 54 20. Open M-F 9:30am-6pm, Sa-Su 10am-3pm.) To reach ▓**Rucksack Hotel ❷**, Kanalstr. 70, take bus #1, 11, 21, or 31 to Pfaffenstr. and turn right at the church onto Glockengießerstr. (☎70 68 92. Sheets €3. Reception daily 10am-1pm and 5-9pm. Dorms €13; doubles with bath €40; quads €60, with bath €68.) The **Baltic Hotel ❹**, Hansestr. 11, is across the street from the station. (☎855 75. Breakfast included. Reception daily 7am-10pm. Singles €35-45; doubles €58-65; triples from €80.) Stop by the famous confectionery ▓**I.G. Niederegger Marzipan Café ❶**, Breitestr. 89, for marzipan, Lübeck's specialty, in the shape of pigs, jellyfish, and even the town gate. (Open M-F 9am-7pm, Sa 9am-6pm, Su 10am-4pm.) **Tipasa ❷**, Schlumacherstr. 12, serves pizza, pasta, and vegetarian dishes, and has a beer garden. (Open M-Th and Su noon-1am, F-Sa noon-2am.) **Postal Code: 23552.**

SCHLESWIG   ☎04621

With its sailboat-filled harbor and cafe-specked shoreline, Schleswig has held the Schlei river in its horseshoe embrace since AD 800. By the harbor, the 18th-century ▓**Schloß Gottorf** and surrounding buildings comprise the **Landesmuseen,** six museums with enough Danish, Dutch, and German art to fill twenty. The surrounding park is an **outdoor sculpture museum.** (Open Apr.-Oct. daily 10am-6pm; Nov.-Mar. Tu-F 10am-4pm, Sa-Su 10am-5pm. Admission to all €6, students €3.) Scale the 240 steps of the **St. Petri Dom** for a bird's-eye view of town. (Open May-Sept. M-Sa 9am-5pm, Su 1:30-5pm; Oct.-Apr. M-Sa 10am-4pm, Su 1:30-5pm. €1.)

Schleswig centers around its **bus terminal** rather than its train station. Single rides cost €1.15, day passes €3.60. Buses #1-3, 6, and 7 run 5min. south of the Altstadt to the **train station.** Trains arrive from Hamburg (2hr., 1 per hr., €18). The **tourist office,** Plessenstr. 7, is up the street from the harbor. (☎98 16 16; room reservations 98 16 17. Open May-Sept. M-F 9:30am-5:30pm, Sa 9:30am-12:30pm; Oct.-Apr. M-Th 10am-4pm, F 10am-1pm.) The **Jugendherberge (HI) ❷**, Spielkoppel 1, is close to the center. Take bus #2 to Schwimmhalle; it's across the street. (☎238 93. Breakfast included. Reception daily 7am-1pm and 5-11pm. Curfew 11pm. Dorms €17, under 27 €14; singles €20/€18.) Nurse cloudy beers at **Asgaard-Brauerei ❸**, Königstr. 27, a popular brewery and restaurant. (Meals €9-10. Open M-Th 5pm-midnight, F 5pm-2am, Sa 11am-2am, Su 11am-midnight.) **Postal Code: 24837.**

CENTRAL AND WEST GERMANY

Lower Saxony (*Niedersachsen*), which stretches from the North Sea to the hills of central Germany, comprises agricultural plains and foggy marshland. Just south, North Rhine-Westphalia is the most heavily populated and economically powerful area in Germany. While the region's squalor kindled the outraged philosophy of Karl Marx and Friedrich Engels, its natural beauty and intellectual energy also inspired the muses of Goethe, Heine, and Böll.

DÜSSELDORF ☎ 0211

As Germany's fashion hub and multinational corporation base, the rich city of Düsseldorf (pop. 571,000) crawls with German patricians and would-be aristocrats. The nation's "Hautstadt"—a pun on "Hauptstadt" (capital) and the French "haute," as in "haute couture"—is a stately metropolis with an Altstadt that features the best nightlife along the Rhine.

🖪🔀 TRANSPORTATION AND PRACTICAL INFORMATION. Trains run to: Amsterdam (3hr., 1-2 per hr., €39); Berlin (4½hr., 1 per hr., €82); Frankfurt (2½hr., 3 per hr., €56); Hamburg (4hr., 2 per hr., €57); and Munich (5hr., 1-2 per hr., €109). Düsseldorf's S-Bahn is integrated into the regional **VRR** (*Verkehrsverbund Rhein-Ruhr*) system, which links most nearby cities and is the cheapest way to get to Aachen and Cologne. Call ☎ 582 28 for schedule info. On the **public transportation system,** single tickets cost €1-7, depending on km traveled. *Tagestickets* (€6.70-17.50) let up to five people travel for 24hr. on any line. To reach the **tourist office,** Immermannstr. 65, head straight out of the train station and to the right; look for the Immermanhof building. It books rooms for a €4 fee. (☎ 172 02 22. Open M-F 8:30am-6pm, Sa 9am-12:30pm.) The **post office,** on Konrad-Adenauer-Pl., is to the right of the tourist office. (Open M-F 8am-6pm, Sa 9am-2pm.) **Postal Code:** 40210.

🖪🖸 ACCOMMODATIONS AND FOOD. Düsseldorf hotels often double their prices during trade fairs, which take place from August to April. **Jugendgästehaus Düsseldorf (HI) ❸,** Düsseldorfer Str. 1, is just over the Rheinkniebrücke from the Altstadt. Take U70, 74, 75, 76, or 77 to Luegpl., then walk 500m down Kaiser-Wilhelm-Ring. (☎ 55 73 10. Reception daily 7am-1am. Dorms €20; singles €32; doubles €50. Cash only.) **Hotel Lindenhof ❹,** Oststr. 124, is close to the train station; follow Friedrich-Ebert-Str. and turn left on Oststr. Spacious rooms with TV, telephone, and private bath. (☎ 36 00 63. Singles €45; doubles €65. AmEx/MC/V.) To reach **Hotel Schaum ❹,** 63 Gustav-Poengsen-Str., exit left from the train station on Graf-Adolf-Str., take your first left, and follow the tracks to Gustav-Poengsen-Str. (☎ 311 65 10. Singles from €30; doubles from €50. MC/V; cash only for bills under €200.) To camp at **Kleiner Torfbruch ❶,** take any S-Bahn to Düsseldorf Gereisheim, then bus #735 (dir.: Stamesberg) to Seeweg. (☎ 899 20 38. Open Apr.-Oct. €4 per person, €5 per tent. Cash only.) For a cheap meal, the endless eateries in the Altstadt can't be beat; rows of pizzerias, *Döner* stands, and Chinese diners reach from Heinrich-Heine-Allee to the banks of the Rhine. **A Tavola ❸,** Wallstr. 11, has meticulously prepared pastas (€7.50-14) and bottomless bread baskets. (Open daily noon-3pm and 6-11pm.) The local outlet of the Czech brewery, **Pilsner Urquell ❷,** Grabenstr. 6, specializes in meaty Eastern European fare. (Open M-Sa 10am-1am, Su 4pm-midnight.) **Otto Mess** is a grocery chain; the most convenient location is at the eastern corner of Carlspl. in the Altstadt. (Open M-F 8am-8pm, Sa 8am-4pm.)

🖸🔳 SIGHTS AND NIGHTLIFE. Glitzy **Königsallee** (the "Kö"), just outside the Altstadt, embodies the vitality and glamor of wealthy Düsseldorf. Midway up is the marble-and-copper **Kö-Galerie,** a mall showcasing one haughty store after another. (Walk 10min. down Graf-Adolf-Str. from the train station.) Baroque **Schloß Benrath,** in the suburbs of Düsseldorf, was originally built as a pleasure palace and hunting grounds for Elector Karl Theodor. Strategically placed mirrors and false exterior windows make the castle appear larger than it is, but the enormous French gardens unremittingly dwarf it. (S6, dir.: Köln, to Schloß Benrath. Open mid-Apr. to Oct. Tu-Su 10am-6pm; Nov. to mid-Apr. 11am-5pm. Tours every hr. €4, students €2.) The **Heinrich-Heine-Institut** is the official shrine of Düsseldorf's melancholic son. (Bilker Str. 12-14. Open Tu-F and Su 11am-5pm, Sa 1-5pm. €2, students €1.) At the upper end of the Kö is the **Hofgarten,** the oldest public park in Germany. At its eastern end, the 18th-century **Schloß Jägerhof** houses a **Goethe Museum.** (Jakobistr. 2. Streetcar #707 or bus #752 to Schloß Jägerhof. Open Tu-F and Su 11am-5pm, Sa 1-5pm. €2, students €1.) The **Kunstsammlung Nordrhein-Westfalen,** within the black glass edifice west of the Hofgarten, houses works by Expressionists, Surrealists, Picasso, and former Düsseldorf resident Paul Klee. (Grabbepl. 5. U70, 75, 76, 78, or 79 to Heinrich-Heine-Allee, and walk 2 blocks north. Open Tu-F 10am-6pm, Sa-Su 11am-6pm. €3, students €1.50. Tours W 3:30pm, Su 11:30am.)

Folklore has it that Düsseldorf's 500 pubs make up *die längste Theke der Welt* (the longest bar in the world). Pubs in the Altstadt are standing-room-only by 6pm; by nightfall it's nearly impossible to see where one pub ends and the next begins. **Bolkerstraße** is jam-packed with street performers. *Prinz* (€3) gives tips on the scene; it's often free at the youth hostel. *Facolte* (€2), a gay and lesbian nightlife magazine, is available at newsstands. **Unique,** Bolkerstr. 30, lives up to its name, drawing a younger, trendier crowd to its red-walled interior. (Cover €5. Open W-Sa 10pm-late.) **Peter-Pam,** Bolkerstr 32, plays house, rock, pop, and plenty of American music. (Open daily 9pm-5am.) **Zum Uel,** Ratinger Str. 16, is the quintessential German pub. (Open M-F 10am-1am, Sa-Su 10am-3am.)

AACHEN
☎**0241**

The capital of Charlemagne's Frankish empire in the 8th century, Aachen (pop. 246,000) is a trove of historical treasures and a polyglot forum for up-and-coming European artists. The three-tiered dome and blue-gold mosaics of Aachen's **Dom** are in the center of the city; Charlemagne's remains lie in the reliquary behind the altar. (Open M-Sa 7am-7pm, Su 12:30-7pm. Closed during services.) Around the corner is the **Schatzkammer,** Klosterpl. 2, a treasury that purportedly contains John the Baptist's hair and ribs, splinters and nails from the True Cross, and the rope that scourged Jesus. A silver bust of Charlemagne built in 1349 holds the emperor's skull. (Open M 10am-1pm, Tu-W and F-Su 10am-6pm, Th 10am-9pm. €4, students €3.) The **Ludwigforum für Internationale Kunst,** Jülicherstr. 97-109, houses international exhibits and a rotating collection of cutting-edge art. (Open Tu-Su 12am-6pm. Last entry 5:30pm. €3, students €1.50. Free German tours Su noon.)

Trains run to Brussels (2hr., every 2hr., €20) and Cologne (1hr., 2-3 per hr., €11). The **tourist office,** on Friedrich-Wilhelm-Pl. in the Atrium Elisenbrunnen, runs tours and finds rooms for no charge. From the station, head up Bahnhofstr.; turn left onto Theaterstr., which becomes Theaterpl., then turn right onto Kapuzinergraben, which becomes Friedrich-Wilhelm-Pl. (☎180 29 60. Open M-F 9am-6pm, Sa 9am-2pm.) **Hotel Cortis ❸,** Krefelderstr. 52, is a comfortable B&B near the Stadtgarten. Take bus #51 to Rolandstr., walk to the intersection, and turn left on Krefelderstr. (☎977 41 10. Singles €28; doubles €50-55, with shower and bath €61. AmEx/MC/V.) **Euroregionales Jugendgästehaus (HI) ❸,** Maria-Theresia-Allee 260, has clean, bright rooms quite a ways from the city center. From the station, walk left on Lagerhausstr. to Finanzamt bus stop and take bus #2 (dir.: Preusswald) to Ronheide. (☎71 10 10. Curfew 1am. Dorms €21; singles €35; doubles €52. Cash only.) **Sausalitos ❸,** Markt 47, is a popular Mexican restaurant with a huge cocktail bar. (Entrees €7-13. Open daily noon-1am.) **Pontstraße,** off Marktpl., and the pedestrian zone also have great restaurants. **Postal Code:** 52062.

COLOGNE (KÖLN) ☎ 0221

Although 90% of inner Cologne (pop. 968,000) crumbled in WWII, the magnificent Gothic *Dom* survived 14 bombings and remains Cologne's main attraction. Today, the city is the largest in North Rhine-Westphalia and is its most important cultural center, with a full range of first-rate museums and theaters.

▣ TRANSPORTATION

Flights: Flights depart from **Köln-Bonn Flughafen** (info ☎ 01803 80 38 03; www.koeln-bonn-airport.de). Shuttles fly to Berlin 24 times per day 6:30am-8:30pm. S13 leaves the train station every 20min. during the week, every 30min. on weekends.

Trains: To: **Amsterdam** (3½hr., €46); **Berlin** (4½hr., 1 per hr., €85); **Düsseldorf** (30-50min., 5-7 per hr., €7); **Frankfurt** (2hr., 2 per hr., €51); **Hamburg** (4hr., 2-3 per hr., €63); **Munich** (4½-5hr., 1-2 per hr., €105); **Paris** (4hr., every 2hr., €78).

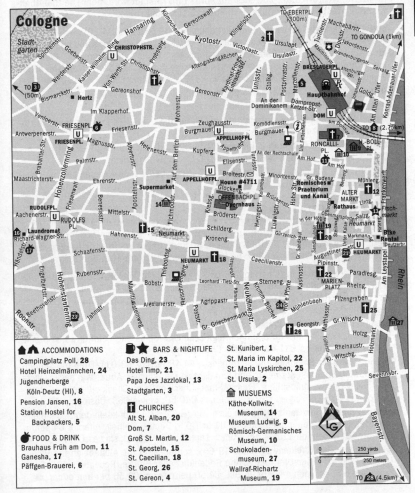

Cologne

▲ ACCOMMODATIONS	🍺 ★ BARS & NIGHTLIFE	St. Kunibert, 1
Campingplatz Poll, **28**	Das Ding, **23**	St. Maria im Kapitol, **22**
Hotel Heinzelmännchen, **24**	Hotel Timp, **21**	St. Maria Lyskirchen, **25**
Jugendherberge	Papa Joes Jazzlokal, **13**	St. Ursula, **2**
Köln-Deutz (HI), **8**	Stadtgarten, **3**	
Pension Jansen, **16**		🏛 MUSUEMS
Station Hostel for	🍴 CHURCHES	Käthe-Kollwitz-Museum, **14**
Backpackers, **5**	Alt St. Alban, **20**	Museum Ludwig, **9**
	Dom, **7**	Römisch-Germanisches
🍎 FOOD & DRINK	Groß St. Martin, **12**	Museum, **10**
Brauhaus Früh am Dom, **11**	St. Aposteln, **15**	Schokoladen-museum, **27**
Ganesha, **17**	St. Caecilian, **18**	Wallraf-Richartz
Päffgen-Brauerei, **6**	St. Georg, **26**	Museum, **19**
	St. Gereon, **4**	

GERMANY

Ride-Sharing: Citynetz Mitfahrzentrale, Maximilianstr. 2 (☎194 40). Turn left from the back of the train station. Open daily 9am-7pm.

Ferries: Köln-Düsseldorfer (☎208 83 18; www.k-d.com) begins popular Rhine cruises here to **Koblenz** (€34) or **Mainz** (€46). Ships to **Bonn** (€11). Eurail valid on most trips.

Public Transportation: VRS (Verkehrsverbund Rhein-Sieg), downstairs in the train station, has free maps of the S- and U-Bahn, bus, and streetcar lines. Day passes €5.50. *Minigruppen-Ticket* (from €7.50) allows up to 5 people to ride M-F from 9am to midnight and all day Sa-Su. Week-long passes €12-20.

Bike Rental: Kölner Fahrradverleih, Markmannsg. (☎0171 629 87 96), in the Altstadt on the Rhine. €2 per hr., €10 per day, €40 per week. Open daily 10am-6pm.

✴🛈 ORIENTATION AND PRACTICAL INFORMATION

Cologne extends across the Rhine, but nearly all sights and the city center can be found on the western side. The Altstadt splits into **Altstadt-Nord,** near the **Hauptbahnhof,** and **Altstadt-Süd,** just south of the **Severinsbrücke** bridge.

Tourist Office: KölnTourismus, Unter Fettenhennen 19 (☎22 13 04 10; www.koelntourismus.de), opposite the main entrance to the *Dom,* has free city maps and books rooms for a €3 fee. Open M-Sa 9am-9pm (July-Sept. until 10pm), Su 10am-6pm. **Köln WelcomeCard** discounts city museum admission, Rhine cruises, and bike rentals and allows free use of the public transportation system (1/2/3-day cards €9/€14/€19).

Currency Exchange: Reisebank, in the train station. Open daily 7am-10pm.

Emergency: Police: ☎110. **Ambulance** and **Fire:** ☎112.

Pharmacy: Apotheke im Hauptbahnhof, near Platform 11 (☎139 11 12), in the train station. Open M-F 6am-8pm, Sa 9am-8pm.

Internet: Telepoint Callshop & Internet C@fe, Komödenstr. 19 (☎250 99 30), by the *Dom.* €1.50 per hr. Open M-F 8am-midnight, Sa-Su 9am-midnight.

Post Office: At the corner of Breite Str. and Tunisstr. in the WDR-Arkaden shopping gallery. **Postal Code:** 50667.

🏠 ACCOMMODATIONS

Conventions fill hotels in spring and fall, and Cologne's hostels often sell out in summer. **Mitwohnzentrale,** Im Ferkulum 4, arranges apartments for longer stays; take the U-Bahn to Chlodwigplatz. (☎194 45. Open M-F 9am-1pm and 2-4pm.)

▩ **Hotel Heinzelmännchen,** Hohe Pforte 5 (☎21 12 17; hotel.koeln@netcologne.de). Bus #132 to Waidmarkt. Fairy-tale pictures decorate this spacious family-run hotel. Breakfast included. Reception 6am-10pm. Singles €35-40; doubles €60-65; triples €75-85. Discounts for stays over 2 nights. MC/V. ❹

▩ **Pension Jansen,** Richard-Wagner-Str. 18 (☎25 18 75). U1, 6, 7, 15, 17, or 19 to Rudolfplatz. Family-run with beautiful, high-ceilinged rooms and colorful walls. Breakfast included. Singles €31-42; doubles €62. Cash only. ❹

Station Hostel for Backpackers, Marzellenstr. 44-48 (☎912 53 01). From the station, walk down Dompropst-Ketzer-Str. and turn right on Marzellenstr. Abuzz with backpackers in a college dorm atmosphere. Free Internet. Check-in 2pm. Check-out noon. 4- to 6-bed dorms €16-18; singles €27-35; doubles €40-50; triples €63. Cash only. ❷

Jugendherberge Köln-Deutz (HI), Siegesstr. 5a (☎81 47 11; jh-koeln-deutz@djh-rheinland.de), over the Hohenzollernbrücke. U1 or 7-9 to Deutzer Freiheit. Internet €4 per hr. Laundry €1. Reception 11am-1am. Curfew 1am. Dorms €22.50; singles €39. MC/V. ❸

Campingplatz Poll, Weidenweg (☎83 19 66), southeast of the Altstadt on the Rhine. U16 to Heinrich-Lübke-Ufer, across the Rodenkirchener Brücke. Reception daily 8am-noon and 5-8pm. Open mid-Apr. to Oct. €4.50 per person; €2.50 per tent or car. ❶

⬤ FOOD

The *Kölner* diet includes *Rievekoochen*, or fried potato dunked in applesauce, and the city's trademark smooth Kölsch beer. Cheap restaurants gather in **Zülpicherstraße** and **Weidengasse** in the Turkish district. Mid-range ethnic restaurants line the perimeter of the Altstadt, particularly from **Hohenzollernring** to **Hohenstaufenring**. German eateries surround **Domplatz**. An **open-air market** on Wilhelmsplatz takes over the Nippes neighborhood in the morning. (Open M-Sa 8am-1pm.)

▧ **Brauhaus Früh am Dom**, Am Hof 14 (☎258 03 97). A required stop on visits to Köln. Regional specialties (€4-18) and cheap Kölsch (€1.35). Open daily 8am-midnight. ❷

Päffgen-Brauerei, Friesenstr. 64. Take U3-6, 12, or 15 to Friesenplatz. Kölsch (€1.25) is brewed on the premises and consumed in cavernous halls and the 600-seat beer garden. Meals €2-16. Open daily 10am-midnight. Kitchen open 11:30am-11pm. ❸

Ganesha, Händelstr. 26, at the corner of Richard-Wagner-Str. Take U1, 6, 7, 12, or 15 to Rudolfplatz. A broad range of Indian specialties, from samosas (€3) to chicken vindaloo (€9). Most entrees €7-12. Open daily 6pm-midnight, Tu-Su also 12:30-3pm. ❷

⬤ SIGHTS

▧ **DOM.** Whether its facade bathes in eerie blue floodlights or its colossal spires eclipse the sun, Germany's greatest cathedral is manifestly the perfect realization of the High Gothic style. Cologne's *Dom*, finished in 1880, took six centuries to complete. A chapel on the inside right houses a 15th-century **triptych** depicting the city's five patron saints. Behind the altar in the center of the choir is the **Shrine of the Magi**, the cathedral's most sacred compartment, which allegedly holds the remains of the Three Kings. Before exiting the choir, stop in the **Chapel of the Cross** to admire the 10th-century **Gero crucifix**, which is the oldest intact sculpture of a crucified Christ with his eyes shut. *(Cathedral open daily 6am-7:30pm. Free. English tours M-Sa 10:30am and 2:30pm, Su 2:30pm. €4, children €2.)* It takes 15min. to scale the 509 steps of the **Südturm** tower. Catch your breath at the **Glockenstube**, a chamber with the tower's nine bells, about three-quarters of the way up. *(Tower open daily May-Sept. 9am-8pm, Nov.-Feb. 9am-4pm, Mar.-Apr. and Oct. 9am-5pm. €2, students €1.)*

MUSEUMS. Heinrich-Böll-Platz houses the **Museum Ludwig**, which spans everything from Impressionism to Picasso to pop art. *(Bischofsgartenstr. 1. Open Tu 10am-8pm, W-F 10am-6pm, Sa-Su 11am-6pm. €6.40, students €3.20.)* Gathered in the **Wallraf-Richartz Museum** are masterpieces from the Middle Ages to Post-Impressionism. *(Martinstr. 39. From the Heumarkt, take Gürzenichtstr. 1 block to Martinstr. Open Tu 10am-8pm, W-F 10am-6pm, Sa-Su 11am-6pm. €5.80, students €3.30.)* The **Römisch-Germanisches Museum** displays a large array of artifacts documenting the daily lives of Romans rich and poor. *(Roncallipl. 4. Open Tu-Su 10am-5pm. €4.50, students €2.70.)* Four words about the ▧**Schokoladenmuseum**: Willy Wonka made real. It presents every step of chocolate production from the rainforests to the gold fountain that spurts streams of silky free samples. *(Rheinauhafen 1a, near the Severinsbrücke. From the train station, head for the river, walk along the Rhine heading right, go under the Deutzer Brücke, and take the 1st footbridge. Open Tu-F 10am-6pm, Sa-Su 11am-7pm. €6, students €3.50.)* The **Käthe-Kollwitz-Museum** houses the world's largest collection of sketches, sculptures, and prints by the brilliant 20th-century artist-activist. *(Neumarkt 18-24. On the top floor in the Neumarkt-Passage. U1, 3, 7-9, 16, or 18 to Neumarkt. Open Tu-F 10am-6pm, Sa-Su 11am-6pm. €5, students €1.50.)*

HOUSE #4711. The fabled **Eau de Cologne**, once prescribed as a drinkable curative, gave the town worldwide recognition. Today the house of its origin, labeled #4711 by a Napoleonic system that abolished street names, is a boutique where a fountain flows with the scented water. Visit the gallery upstairs for a history of the fragrance. *(On Glockeng. at the intersection with Tunisstr. From Hohe Str., turn right on Brücken-str., which becomes Glockeng. Open M-F 9am-7pm, Sa 9am-6pm.)*

RÖMISCHES PRAETORIUM UND KANAL. The excavated ruins of the former Roman military headquarters display remains of Roman idols and an array of rocks left by early inhabitants. *(From the Rathaus, turn right toward the cluster of hotels and then left onto Kleine Budeng. Open Tu-F 10am-4pm, Sa-Su 11am-4pm. €1.50, students €0.75.)*

🎵🎭 ENTERTAINMENT AND NIGHTLIFE

Cologne explodes in celebration during ⬛**Karneval,** a week-long pre-Lenten festival made up of 50 neighborhood processions. **Weiberfastnacht** (Feb. 3, 2005) is the first major to-do; the mayor mounts the platform at Alter Markt and abdicates leadership to the city's women, who then find their husbands at work and chop off their ties. The weekend builds up to the out-of-control parade on **Rosenmontag** (Feb. 8, 2005), where everyone trades a couple dozen *Bützchen* (*Kölnisch* dialect for kisses on the cheek). While most revelers nurse their hangovers on Shrove Tuesday, pubs and restaurants set fire to the straw scarecrows hanging out of their windows. For more info, pick up the Karneval booklet at the tourist office.

Roman mosaics dating back to the third century record the wild excesses of the city's early residents; they've toned it down only a bit since. The best way to know what you'll get is to pick up the monthly magazine *Kölner* (€1). The closer to the Rhine or *Dom* you venture, the more quickly your wallet will empty. After dark in **Hohenzollernring,** crowds of people move from theaters to clubs and finally to cafes in the early morning. Students congregate in the **Bermuda-Dreieck** (Bermuda Triangle), bounded by Zülpicherstr., Zülpicherpl., Roonstr., and Luxemburgstr. Radiating westward from Friesenpl., the **Belgisches Viertel** has slightly more expensive bars and cafes. **Gay nightlife** centers on the area running up Matthiasstr. to Mühlenbach, Hohe Pforte, Marienpl., and the Heumarkt neighborhood by **Deutzer Brücke.**

⬛ **Papa Joes Jazzlokal,** Buttermarkt 37. Papa Joe has a legendary reputation for jazz and good times. Grab some peanuts when the sack comes around. Kölsch (€3.60) in 0.4L glasses, not the usual 0.2L. Live jazz from 9pm. Open daily 7pm-1am, F-Sa until 3am.

Stadtgarten, Venloerstr. 40. Take U3, 5, 6, or 12 to Friesenplatz. Two clubs for the price of one. Downstairs spins techno and house; upstairs, the concert hall is renowned for its live jazz recordings. Cover €7. Open M-Th 9pm-1am, F-Sa 9pm-3am.

Das Ding, Hohenstaufenring 30. Smoky and very *noir*. A popular bar and disco for students with varied music and dirt-cheap drink specials (under €1). Cover €4. Open Tu, Th, Su 9pm-3am; W 9pm-2am; F-Sa 9pm-4am.

Hotel Timp, Heumarkt 25 (www.timp.de), right across from the U-Bahn stop. This gay-friendly club and hotel has become a virtual institution in Cologne for gaudy, glittery travesty theater. Shows daily from 1-4am. No cover, but first drinks €8 on weeknights or €13 on weekends. Open daily 11am-late.

BONN   ☎ 0228

Once derided as *"Hauptdorf,"* or capital village, Bonn (pop. 306,000) became the West German capital because Konrad Adenauer, the first chancellor, resided in its suburbs. In 1999, however, the *Bundestag* returned to Berlin and Bonn to its low profile. Today, the city is home to a respected university and hip cyber-culture.

🚆🚲 TRANSPORTATION AND PRACTICAL INFORMATION. Trains run to:

Cologne (20min., 5 per hr., €5); Frankfurt (2hr., 3 per hr., €25); and Koblenz (45min., 3 per hr., €8). The **tourist office** is at Windeckstr. 1, just off Münsterpl.

(☎ 194 33. Open M-F 9am-6:30pm, Sa 9am-4pm, Su 10am-2pm.) The **Bonn Regio Welcome Card** (1-day €9, 2-day €14, 3-day €19) covers public transportation after 9am and admission to over 20 museums in the Bonn area. The **post office** is at Münsterpl. 17. (Open M-F 9am-8pm, Sa 9am-4pm.) **Postal Code:** 53111.

▐▐ ▐▖ ACCOMMODATIONS AND FOOD. Take bus #621 (dir.: Ippendorf Altenheim) to Jugendgästehaus for the super-modern **Jugendgästehaus Bonn-Venusberg (HI) ❸**, Haager Weg 42. (☎ 28 99 70. Laundry €3.90. Curfew 1am. Dorms €21.50; singles €35.70; doubles €51.20. MC/V.) More central **Hotel Bergmann ❹**, Kasernenstr. 13, is family-run; from the station, follow Poststr., turn left at Münsterpl. on Vivatsgasse, then right on Kasernenstr. (☎ 63 38 91. 1 bath per floor. Singles €35; doubles €50. Cash only.) The **Münsterplatz market** teems with vendors selling meat, fruit, and vegetables. (Open M-Sa 8am-6pm.) Descend to the basement of the Kaufhof on Münsterpl. to find a **supermarket**. (Open M-F 9:30am-8pm, Sa 9am-4pm.) Cheap eats can be had at **Mensa ❶**, Nassestr. 11, a 15min. walk down Kaiserstr. from the station. (Open M-F noon-2pm and 5:30-7:30pm, Sa noon-2pm.)

◖◗ ▐▖ SIGHTS AND NIGHTLIFE. Bonn's lively pedestrian zone has many historic nooks. ▐**Beethovenhaus**, Beethoven's birthplace, houses a collection of the composer's effects, from his first violin to his primitive hearing aids. (Bonng. 20. Open Apr.-Oct. M-Sa 10am-6pm, Su 11am-4pm; Nov.-Mar. M-Sa 10am-5pm, Su 11am-4pm. Last entry 30min. before closing. €4, students €3.) In its heyday as Parliament, the **Bundestag's** see-through walls symbolized transparency in government. (Take U16, 63, or 66 to Heussallee or bus #610 to Bundeshaus.) Students study within the **Kurfürstliches Schloß**, the 18th-century palace that now centers Bonn's **Friedrich-Wilhelms-Universität**. To reach Bonn's other palace, follow Poppelsdorfer Allee to the 18th-century **Poppelsdorfer Schloß**, around which lie **botanical gardens**. (Gardens open Apr.-Sept. M-F 9am-6pm, Su 9am-1pm; Oct.-Mar. M-F 9am-4pm. Free.) WelcomeCards (above) cover admission to most of Bonn's **Museum Mile**. Take U16, 63, or 66 to Heussallee or Museum König. Interactive exhibits at the ▐**Haus der Geschichte** (House of History), Willy-Brandt-Allee 4, examine postwar Germany. (Open Tu-Su 9am-7pm. Free.) A block away, the immense **Kunstmuseum Bonn**, Friedrich-Ebert-Allee 2, houses Expressionist and modern German art. (Open Tu and Th-Su 10am-6pm, W 10am-9pm. €5, students €2.50.)

Schnüss (€1) lists clubs. ▐**Jazz Galerie**, Oxfordstr. 24, is a jumping bar and disco. (Cover €5-7.50. Open Tu and Th 9pm-3am, F-Sa 10pm-5am.) **Boba's Bar,** Josephstr. 17, is a gay and lesbian nightspot. (Open Tu-Su 8pm-3am.)

KASSEL   ☎ 0561

Kassel (pop. 195,000) is unique for its curious monuments and sweeping vistas. Both are in evidence at ▐**Wilhelmshöhe**, an antiquated hillside park. Inside, **Schloß Wilhelmshöhe** is a dressed-down but more authentically furnished version of the Residenz in Würzburg (p. 503). Just uphill, **Schloß Löwenburg** was built by Wilhelm in the 18th century with stones deliberately missing so it would resemble a crumbling medieval castle—he was obsessed with the year 1495 and quixotically imagined himself a knight. Take streetcar #1 from Bahnhof Wilhelmshöhe. (Both castles open Mar.-Oct. Tu-Su 10am-5pm; Nov.-Feb. 10am-4pm. Required tours every hr. Castles each €3.50, students €2.50.) Park paths lead up to the statue **Herkules**, Kassel's emblem; visitors can climb onto the pedestal and, if they're brave enough, into his club. (Access to the base of the statue free. Pedestal and club open daily mid-Mar. to mid-Nov. 10am-5pm. €2, students €1.25.) The **Brüder-Grimm-Museum**, Schöne Aussicht 2, exhibits Jacob and Wilhelm's handwritten copy of *Kinder- und Hausmärchen*. (Open daily 10am-5pm. €1.50, students €1.)

GERMANY

Kassel has two train stations, Bahnhof Wilhelmshöhe and the Hauptbahnhof; most trains stop only at Wilhelmshöhe. **Trains** run to: Düsseldorf (3½hr., 1 per hr., €38); Frankfurt (2hr., 3 per hr., €41); Hamburg (2½hr., 2 per hr., €57); and Munich (4hr., 1 per hr., €78). The **tourist office,** in Bahnhof Wilhelmshöhe, has free maps and books rooms for a €2.50 fee. (☎70 77 07. Open M-F 9am-6pm, Sa 9am-2pm.) To reach **Jugendherberge am Tannenwäldchen (HI) ❸**, Schenkendorfstr. 18, take streetcar #4 from the Wilhelmshöhe station to Annastr., backtrack on Friedrich-Ebert-Str., and turn right on Querallee, which becomes Schenkendorfstr. (☎77 64 55. Sheets €4. Curfew 12:30am. €20.70, under 26 €18.) **Hotel Kö78 ❹**, Kölnische Str. 78, has a garden in back. Follow the directions to the Jugendherberge, but walk up Annastr. from the stop and turn right onto Kölnische Str. (☎716 14; www.koe78.de. Singles €32-51; doubles €51-75. MC/V.) **Postal Code:** 34117.

FRANKFURT AM MAIN ☎069

Frankfurt's role as home to the central bank of the European Union lends it a glitzy vitality—international offices, shiny skyscrapers, and expensive cars define every intersection. Just as important is its role as a major transportation hub for all of Europe. Indeed, the city came into being as a crossing point for the Main River—its name literally means "ford of the Franks." Today, Frankfurt (pop. 641,000) spends more on attractions and tourism than any other city in Germany.

TRANSPORTATION

Flights: The ultra-modern airport, **Flughafen Rhein-Main** (☎01805 372 46 36), is connected to the Hauptbahnhof by S8 and 9 (every 15min.; buy tickets for €3 from the green machines marked "*Fahrkarten*" before boarding).

Trains: Trains run frequently from the Hauptbahnhof to: **Amsterdam** (4hr., 2 per hr., €67-91); **Berlin** (5-6hr., 2 per hr., €74-92); **Cologne** (2½hr., 3 per hr., €34-52); **Hamburg** (3½-5hr., 2 per hr., €67-86); **Munich** (3½-4½hr., 3 per hr., €56-69); **Paris** (6-8hr., 2 per hr., €74-90). Call ☎01805 99 66 33 for schedules, reservations, and info.

Public Transportation: Runs daily until about 1am. Single-ride tickets (€1.70, rush hour €2) are valid for 1hr. in one direction, transfers permitted. **Eurail** is valid only on the S-Bahn. The **Tageskarte** (day pass; valid until midnight of the purchase date) provides unlimited transportation on the S-Bahn, U-Bahn, streetcars, and buses; they can be purchased from machines in any station (€4.70). Ticketless passengers face €40 fines.

Ride-sharing: Mitfahrzentrale, Baseler Str. 7 (☎23 64 44). Turn right onto Baseler Str. from the side exit of the Hauptbahnhof (track 1). Arranges rides to **Berlin** (€29) and elsewhere. Open M-F 8am-6:30pm, Sa 8am-4pm, Su 10am-4pm.

ORIENTATION AND PRACTICAL INFORMATION

Frankfurt's Hauptbahnhof opens into its red light district; from the station, the Altstadt is a 20min. walk down Kaiserstr. or Münchener Str. To the north, the commercial heart of Frankfurt lies along **Zeil**. Students, cafes, and services cluster in **Bockenheim** (U6 or 7 to Bockenheimer Warte). Across the Main River, **Sachsenhausen** draws pub-crawlers and museum-goers (U1, 2, or 3 to Schweizer Pl.).

Tourist Office: ☎21 23 88 00. In the Hauptbahnhof. Sells maps (€0.50-1) and the **Frankfurt Card** (1-day €7.80, 2-day €11.50), which allows unlimited use of public transportation and provides discounts on many sights. It will also book rooms for a €3 fee, or for free if you call ahead. Open M-F 8am-9pm, Sa-Su and holidays 9am-6pm.

Currency Exchange: At banks. Locations in the airport and station have poor rates.

Laundromat: Waschsalon, Wallstr. 8, near the hostel in Sachsenhausen. Wash €3. Dry €0.50 per 15min. Soap included. Open daily 6am-11pm.

Emergency: Police: ☎110. **Ambulance** and **Fire:** ☎112.

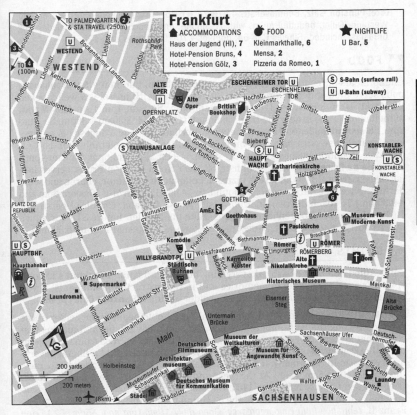

Frankfurt

▲ ACCOMMODATIONS	🍴 FOOD	⭐ NIGHTLIFE
Haus der Jugend (HI), 7	Kleinmarkthalle, 6	U Bar, 5
Hotel-Pension Bruns, 4	Mensa, 2	
Hotel-Pension Gölz, 3	Pizzeria da Romeo, 1	

Ⓢ S-Bahn (surface rail)
Ⓤ U-Bahn (subway)

GERMANY

Pharmacy: ☎ 23 30 47. In the train station's Einkaufspassage. Open M-F 6:30am-9pm, Sa 8am-9pm, Su 9am-4pm. **Emergencies:** ☎ 192 92.

Internet Access: Alpha, in the Hauptbahnhof's gambling salon, past track #24. €3.50 per hr. Open M-Th and Su 9am-11pm, F-Sa 9am-midnight. **Telewave,** Elisabethenstr. 45-47, charges in 1hr. units (each €1.50). Open M-F 10am-8pm, Sa 10am-4pm.

Post Office: Fillale Frankfurt 2, Zeil 90/Schäfer. (☎ 13 81 26 21), inside the Karstadt department store. U- or S-Bahn to Hauptwache. Turn right onto Zeil with your back to the church and follow it to the Karstadt. Open M-Sa 9:30am-8pm. **Postal Code:** 60313.

📷 ACCOMMODATIONS

🏨 **Hotel-Pension Bruns,** Mendelssohnstr. 42 (☎ 74 88 96; www.brunsgallus-hotel.de). U4 to Festhalle. Turn left from the exit onto Beethoven Str.; at the traffic circle, continue on Mendelssohnstr. and look right. Bruns has 9 Victorian rooms with high ceilings, hardwood floors, cable TV, and free breakfast in bed. Ring the bell; it's on the 2nd fl. Showers €1.50. Single €40-45; doubles €50-55; triples €65-70; quads €75-80. ❹

Haus der Jugend (HI), Deutschherrnufer 12 (☎ 610 01 50; www.jugendherberge-frankfurt.de). From the station, take bus #46 to Frankensteiner Pl. Turn left along the river; the hostel is at the end of the block. Popular with students. Breakfast included. Check-in after 1pm. Check-out 9:30am. Curfew 2am. Rooms from €20, under 27 from €15. ❸

Hotel-Pension Gölz, Beethovenstr. 44 (☎74 67 35; www.hotel-goelz.de). U6 or 7 to Westend. Quiet, beautiful rooms with TV, phone, and couch; some have balcony. Big breakfast included. Singles €36-64; doubles €70-105; triples €85-120. ❹

🍴 FOOD

Cheap meals surround the university in **Bockenheim,** and many **Sachsenhausen** pubs serve food at decent prices. Just blocks from the HI hostel is a well-stocked **HL Markt,** Dreieichstr. 56. (Open M-F 8am-8pm, Sa 8am-4pm.) An **Alim Markt,** Münchener Str. 37, is near the Hauptbahnhof. (Open M-F 8:30am-7:30pm, Su 8am-2pm.) **Kleinmarkthalle,** on Haseng. between Berliner Str. and Töngesg., is a three-story warehouse with bakeries, butchers, and fruit and vegetable stands. Cut-throat competition pushes prices way down. (Open M-F 8am-6pm, Sa 8am-4pm.) 🍴**Pizzeria da Romeo ❷,** Mendelssohnstr. 83, near Hotel-Pension Bruns, serves Italian dishes (from €3.50) and fresh pizzas accompanied by humor, charm, and wonderful service. Vegetarian options abound. (☎74 95 01. Open M-F 10:30am-3pm and 4-9:30pm.) To reach the two-floor university **Mensa ❶,** catch U6 (dir.: Heerstr.) or 7 (dir.: Hausen) to Bockenheimer Warte. Take the first left before STA travel; it's in the courtyard to the right. (Guest meals €2.80-4.30. Open M-F 11am-6:30pm.)

👁 SIGHTS

Since Allied bombing destroyed everything but the cathedral, Frankfurt's historic splendor survives mostly in memories and in reconstructed monuments. If you plan on touring Frankfurt's museums, consider buying a **Frankfurt Card** (p. 480).

🏛**RÖMERBERG.** Any voyage through Frankfurt should begin in the center of the Altstadt, among the half-timbered homes and seemingly medieval fountains that somewhat misleadingly cover most postcards of the city. Across from the Römerberg, the **Paulskirche** was the site of the 19th-century attempt at a liberal government over a united Germany; it now memorializes the trials of German democracy. *(Open daily 10am-5pm. Free.)* At the west end of Römerberg, the gables of **Römer** have marked the city hall since 1405. Upstairs, the Kaisersaal is an imperial banquet hall adorned with portraits of the 52 German emperors from Charlemagne to Franz II. *(Entrance from Limpurgergasse. Open daily 10am-1pm and 2-5pm. €2.)* Lone survivor of the WWII bombings, the red sandstone Gothic **Dom** contains several elaborate altarpieces. It was here that the electors of the Holy Roman Empire crowned its emperors. *(Open Tu-F 10am-5pm, Sa-Su 11am-5pm. €2, students €1.)*

🏛**STÄDEL.** With equally important paintings from nearly every period, the Städel exhibits Old Masters, Impressionists, and Moderns. If paintings by Beckmann and Kandinsky aren't your thing, head for the works by Monet and Renoir. *(Schaumainkai 63, between Dürerstr. and Holbeinstr. Open Tu and F-Su 10am-5pm, W-Th 10am-8pm. €6, students €5. Last Sa of each month free. English audioguides €2.)*

MUSEUM FÜR MODERNE KUNST. This triangular museum (dubbed the "slice of cake") displays modern art by Roy Lichtenstein, Jasper Johns, and emerging talents. *(Domstr. 10. Open Tu and Th-Su 10am-5pm, W 10am-8pm. €6, students €3.)*

🎵🎭 ENTERTAINMENT AND NIGHTLIFE

Frankfurt has first-rate theater and opera. The **Alte Oper,** Opernpl. (☎134 04 00; U6 or 7 to Alte Oper), runs the gamut of classical music. The **Städtische Bühne,** Untermainanlage 11 (U1-4 to Willy-Brandt-Pl.; ☎21 23 71 33), hosts ballets and operas. The **English Theatre,** Kaiserstr. 52 (☎24 23 16 20; www.english-theatre.org), plays comedies and musicals in English. *Fritz* and *Strandgut,* free at the tourist office, list schedules. **Frankfurt Ticket** (☎134 04 00) has ticket info at most venues.

A number of prominent techno DJs and discos are situated in the commercial district between **Zeil** and **Bleichstraße**. Wait until midnight for things to really heat up, and wear something dressier than jeans if you plan to slip by the selective bouncers. If you prefer drinks to dancing, head to the **Alt-Sachsenhausen** district between Brückenstr. and Dreieichstr., home to numerous rowdy pubs and taverns. Or yet another alternative, the complex of cobblestoned streets centering on **Grosse** and **Kleine Rittergaße** teems with cafes, restaurants, bars, and Irish pubs. More info on Frankfurt's club scene can be found at www.nachtleben.de. In an old subway station, ■**U Bar** (www.u60311.net), in Roßmarkt on the corner of Goethepl., hosts international stars and Frankfurt's best DJs. (Cover €6-15. Open from 10pm. Techno/house club opens F-Su 11pm. Lines start at 9pm F nights.)

SOUTHWESTERN GERMANY

Much is to be seen in the Rhine and Mosel River valleys, and much to be drunk. The Mosel curls downstream to the Rhine Gorge, a shore of castle-studded hills. Nearby, vineyards upon vineyards grow the best German wines. Just a bit farther south, modern cities fade slowly into the beautiful hinterlands of the Black Forest.

TRIER ☎0651

In the western end of the Mosel Valley, Trier (pop. 100,000) is the oldest town in Germany. Founded by Augustan-Age Romans, it became by the early 4th century both the capital of the Western Empire and a redoubt for Christianity. A one-day **combination ticket** (€6.20, students €3.10) provides access to all the city's Roman monuments. The most impressive is the massive and well-preserved 2nd-century ■**Porta Nigra** (Black Gate); climb it for a view of Trier. (Open daily Apr.-Sept. 9am-6pm; Oct.-Mar. 9am-5pm. €2.10, students €1.60.) The nearby **Dom** shelters the *Tunica Christi* (Holy Robe of Christ) and the tombs of many archbishops. (Open daily Apr.-Oct. 6:30am-6pm; Nov.-Mar. 6:30am-5:30pm. Free.) The enormous **Basilika** was originally the location of Emperor Constantine's throne room. (Open Apr.-Oct. M-Sa 10am-6pm, Su noon-6pm; Nov.-Mar. Tu-Sa 11am-noon and 3-4pm, Su noon-1pm. Free.) Near the southeast corner of the city walls are the 4th-century **Kaiserthermen** (Emperor's baths), with underground passages that once served as Roman sewers. (Open daily Apr.-Sept. 9am-5:30pm; Oct.-Mar. 9am-4:30pm. €2.10, students €1.60.) From there, a 10min. walk uphill along Olewiger Str. leads to the **amphitheater.** Once a gladiatorial arena, it's now a stage for city productions. (Open daily Apr.-Sept. 9am-6pm; Oct.-Mar. 9am-5pm. €2.10, students €1.60.)

Trains run to **Koblenz** (1½hr., 2 per hr., €16) and **Luxembourg City** (45min., 1 per hr., €11). Walk down Theodor-Haus-Allee from the station to reach the **tourist office,** by the Porta Nigra. (☎97 80 80; www.trier.de. Open Apr.-Oct. M-Sa 9am-6pm, Su 10am-3pm; Nov.-Dec. and Mar. M-Sa 9am-6pm, Su 10am-1pm; Jan.-Feb. M-F 10am-5pm, Sa 10am-1pm. English city tours Sa 1:30pm. €6, students €5.) ■**Jugendgästehaus Trier (HI) ❸,** An der Jugendherberge 4, by the river, is a 10min. walk downstream from the Zur Laubener Ufer stop of buses #2, 8, 12, and 87. Its lobby has billiards. (☎292 92. Singles €32; doubles €46; quads €70. MC/V.) Two blocks from Viehmarkt-Pl., ■**Astarix ❷,** Karl-Marx-Str. 11, serves €4 pizza. (Open daily 11am-11:30pm.) **Plus** supermarket, Brotstr. 54, is near the Hauptmarkt. (Open M-F 8:30am-8pm, Sa 8:30am-6pm.) **Postal Code:** 54292.

RHINE VALLEY (RHEINTAL)

Although the Rhine River runs from Switzerland to the North Sea, in the popular imagination it exists only in the 80km of the Rhine Valley. Historical legends, sailors' nightmares, and poets' dreams layer its hills as it flows north from Mainz (an easy journey from Frankfurt) through Bacharach and Koblenz to Bonn.

GERMANY

GERMANY

⌐ TRANSPORTATION

Two different **train** lines traverse the Rheintal, one on each bank; the line on the western side stays closer to the water and has superior views. Although full of tourists, **boats** are probably the best way to see the sights; the **Köln-Düsseldorfer (KD) Line** covers the Mainz-Koblenz stretch four times a day in summer.

MAINZ ☎ 06131

Once the greatest Catholic diocese north of the Alps, Mainz's colossal sandstone **Martinsdom** stands as a memorial to its former ecclesiastical power. (Open Mar.-Oct. Tu-F 9am-6pm, Sa 9am-2pm, Su 1-2:45pm and 4-6:30pm; Nov.-Feb. M-F 9am-5pm, Sa 9am-4pm, Su 12:45-3pm and 4-5pm. Free.) South of the *Dom*, the Gothic **Stephanskirche** is inlaid with stunning stained-glass windows set by Russian exile Marc Chagall. (Stephansberg. Open daily 10am-noon and 2-5pm. Free.) Johannes Gutenberg, the father of movable type, is immortalized at the **Gutenberg-Museum,** which contains a replica of his original press. (Liebfrauenpl. 5, across from the *Dom*. Open Tu-Sa 9am-5pm, Su 11am-3pm. €3, students €2.) **Trains** run to: Frankfurt (30min., €6); Heidelberg (1hr., €17); and Koblenz (1hr., €17). KD **ferries** (☎23 28 00) depart from the wharves on the other side of the Rathaus. The **tourist office,** in Brückenturm, arranges English tours (2hr.; Sa 2 pm, May-Oct. also W and F 2pm; €5), has free maps, and reserves rooms for a €2.50 fee. (☎28 62 10. Open M-F 9am-6pm, Sa 10am-3pm.) To reach **Jugendgästehaus (HI) ❷**, Otto-Brunfels-Schneise 4, take bus #62 (dir.: Weisenau), 63 (dir.: Laubenheim), or 92 (dir.: Ginsheim) to Viktorstift/ Jugendherberge and follow the signs. (☎853 32. Reception daily 6:30am-10pm. Dorms €17; doubles €88.) **Der Eisgrub-Bräu ❷**, Weißliliengaße 1a, on the edge of the Altstadt, serves breakfast and lunch buffets (€2.90 and €5.10) and its own house beer. (Open M-Th and Su 9am-1pm, F-Sa 9am-2pm.) **Postal Code:** 55001.

BACHARACH ☎ 06473

Bacharach (Altar of Bacchus) lives up to its name, with *Weinkeller* (wine cellars) tucked between every other half-timbered house. Try some of the Rhine's best wines and cheeses at **Die Weinstube,** Oberstr. 63. (Open M-F from 11pm, Sa-Su from noon.) Nearby is the 14th-century **Wernerkapelle,** the remains of a red sandstone chapel that took 140 years to build but only hours to destroy during the Palatinate War of Succession in 1689. The **tourist office,** Oberstr. 45, shares a building with the Rathaus. (☎91 93 03. Open Apr.-Oct. M-F 9am-5pm, Sa-Su 10am-2pm; Nov.-Mar. M-F 9am-noon.) Hostels get no better than ▓**Jugendherberge Stahleck (HI) ❷**, a gorgeous 12th-century castle with a panoramic view of the Rhine Valley. The steep 15min. hike to the hostel is worth every step. Turn right from the station, left at the Peterskirche, and take any of the marked paths leading up the hill. (☎12 66. Curfew 10pm. Dorms €15; doubles €74.) At ▓**Café Restaurant Rusticana ❸**, Oberstr. 40, a lovely German couple serves up three-course meals (€6-11) and lively conversation. (Open May-Oct. M-W and F-Su 11:30am-9:30pm.) **Postal Code:** 55422.

LORELEI CLIFFS AND CASTLES

Sailors were once lured to these cliffs by the infamous Lorelei maiden, but her hypnotic song is now superfluous; today, hordes of travelers are seduced by the scenery alone. **St. Goarshausen** and **St. Goar,** two charming towns on either side of the Rhine, host the spectacular **Rhein in Flammen** (Rhine Ablaze) fireworks celebration (May 7, 2005). St. Goarshausen, on the east bank, provides access by foot to the Lorelei statue and the cliffs. Directly above the town, the fierce **Burg Katz** (Cat Castle) eternally stalks its prey, the smaller **Burg Maus** (Mouse Castle). Burg Maus offers daily falconry demonstrations at 11am and 2:30pm; for more info, call ☎76 69 or visit St. Goarshausen's **tourist office,** Bahnhofstr. 8. (☎06771 91 00. Open M

9:30am-noon and 2-4:30pm, Th 2-4:30pm, F 2-5:30pm, Sa-Su 9:30am-noon.) **Trains** run to St. Goarshausen from Cologne (1hr., €18) and Mainz (1hr., €8.40). The "Lorelei V" **ferry** (M-F 6am-11pm, Sa-Su from 7am; round-trip €2) crosses the river to St. Goar, which has a view of the Rhine and surrounding area. St. Goar's **tourist office,** Heerstr. 86, is in the pedestrian zone. (☎ 06741 383. Open M-F 8am-12:30pm and 2-5pm, Sa 10am-noon.) **Burg Rheinfels** is a half-ruined castle with underground passages—it doesn't get more *romantisch* than this. Beware of slippery slopes. (☎ 06741 77 53. Open daily Mar.-Sept. 9am-6pm; Oct. 9am-5pm. €4, students €3.) To reach **Jugendheim Loreley ❶,** on the St. Goarshausen side of the Rhine, walk from the cliffs past the parking gate down the road a few hundred meters and turn left. (☎ 06771 26 19. Sheets €3.50. Curfew 10pm. Dorms €8.50.) **Postal Code:** 56329.

KOBLENZ   ☎ 0261

Koblenz (pop. 108,000) has long been a strategic hot spot; in the two millennia since its birth, the city has hosted every empire seeking to conquer Europe. The city centers around the **Deutsches Eck** (German Corner) at the confluence of the Rhine and Mosel rivers, which purportedly witnessed the birth of the German nation in 1216. To the right, the **Mahnmal der Deutschen Einheit** (Monument to German Unity) is a tribute to Kaiser Wilhelm I. The **Museum Ludwig im Deutschherrenhaus,** Danziger Freiheit 1, behind the Mahnmal, features contemporary French art. (Open Tu-Sa 10:30am-5pm, Su 11am-6pm. €2.50, students €1.50.) Head across the river to the **Festung Ehrenbreitstein,** a fortress at the highest point in the city. Today it's a youth hostel. (Non-hostel guests €1, students €0.60. Tours €1.10. See below.)

    Trains run to: Bonn (30min., 3 per hr., €4.20-8.40); Cologne (1½hr., 4 per hr., €10.50); Frankfurt (2hr., 2-3 per hr., €12.50); Mainz (1hr., 3 per hr., €9); and Trier (2hr., 2-3 per hr., €16). Directly opposite the station is the **tourist office,** Bahnhofpl. 7. (☎ 30 38 80. Open May-Oct. M-F 9am-7pm, Sa-Su 10am-7pm; Nov.-Apr. M-F 9am-6pm, Sa-Su 10am-6pm.) **Jugendherberge Koblenz (HI) ❷,** in the fortress, has views of the Rhine and Mosel. Ride bus #9 or 10 from the bus station by the train station to Charlottenstr., then take the chairlift (daily Mar.-May and Oct. 10am-4:50pm; June-Sept. 9am-5:50pm; round-trip €5.80, students €3.50), or the footpath after following the DJH signs along the main road. (☎ 97 28 70. Reception daily 7:15am-10pm. Curfew 11:30pm. Dorms €16.50; doubles €44. MC/V.) **Ferries** (€0.80) cross the Mosel to **Campingplatz Rhein-Mosel ❶,** Am Neuendorfer Eck. (☎ 827 19. Reception daily 8am-1pm and 3-10pm. Open Apr.-Oct. 15. €4.50 per person, €2.50 per site.) ⛄**Kaffeewirtschaft ❸,** Münzpl. 14, serves meals and desserts amid fresh roses. (Open M-Th 9am-midnight, F-Sa 9am-2am, Su 10am-midnight.) **Postal Code:** 65068.

HEIDELBERG   ☎ 06221

Sun-drenched Heidelberg (pop. 141,000) and its crumbling castle has lured many writers and artists, including Goethe, Hölderlin, Hugo, Schumann, and Twain. Today, legions of camera-toting fannypackers fill the length of Hauptstr., where postcards and T-shirts sell like hotcakes and every sign is posted in four languages. But even mass tourism can't spoil the experience of Heidelberg's beautiful hillside setting, of Germany's oldest university, or of the city's enviable nightlife.

🖵🛈 TRANSPORTATION AND PRACTICAL INFORMATION

Trains run to Frankfurt (50min., 2 per hr., €13) and Stuttgart (40min., 1 per hr., €20). Within Heidelberg, single-ride **bus** tickets cost €2; day passes (€5) are available from the tourist office. Rhein-Neckar-Fahrgastschifffahrt (☎ 201 81), in front of the *Kongresshaus*, runs **cruises** to Neckarsteinach (3hr., Easter to late Oct. every 1½hr. 9:30am-4:50pm, €9.50). Heidelberg's attractions are mostly to the east, along the southern bank of the Neckar. From the station, take any bus or streetcar

GERMANY

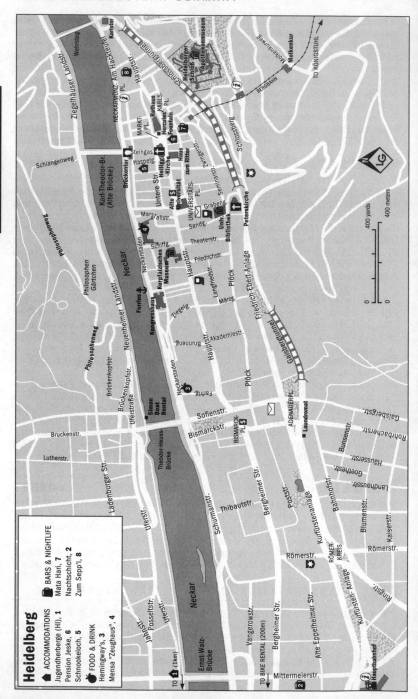

Heidelberg

▲ ACCOMMODATIONS
Jugendherberge (HI), **1**
Pension Jeske, **6**
Schnookeloch, **5**

★ FOOD & DRINK
Hemingway's, **3**
Mensa "Zeughaus", **4**

🛍 BARS & NIGHTLIFE
Mata Hari, **7**
Nachtschicht, **2**
Zum Sepp'l, **8**

to Bismarckpl., then walk east down **Hauptstraße** to the Altstadt. The **tourist office**, in front of the station, books rooms for a €3 fee and a small deposit. (☎ 13 881 21. Open Apr.-Oct. M-Sa 9am-7pm, Su 10am-6pm; Nov.-Mar. M-Sa 9am-6pm.) It also sells the **Heidelberg Card**, which includes unlimited public transit and admission to most sights. (2-day card €12; 4-day card €20.) The **post office** is at Sofienstr. 8-10. (Open M-F 9am-6:30pm, Sa 9:30am-1pm.) **Postal Code:** 69115.

ACCOMMODATIONS AND FOOD

In summer, reserve ahead or arrive early in the day to spare yourself a headache. **Pension Jeske ❸**, Mittelbadgasse 2, has a perfect Altstadt location. Take bus #33 (dir.: Ziegelhausen) to Rathaus/Kornmarkt. (☎ 237 33. Doubles €50, with bath €60; triples €60/€75; quints with bath €100. Cash only.) To reach the large rooms of the **Jugendherberge (HI) ❷**, Tiergartenstr. 5, take bus #33 (dir.: Zoo-Sportzentrum) to Jugendherberge. Located by the zoo—one of Europe's largest—this hostel also teems with wild species, such as *schoolchildus germanius*. (☎ 65 11 90. Reception daily until 11:30pm. Lockout 9am-1pm. Curfew 11:30pm; stragglers admitted until 2am. Reserve ahead. Dorms €23, under 27 €20; singles and doubles add €5.) Luxury at **Schnookeloch ❺**, Haspelgasse 8, carries a corresponding price tag. (☎ 13 80 80. *Let's Go* discounted rates: singles €60-97; doubles €85-120.)

Most restaurants on and around Hauptstr. are expensive. Just outside the central area, good value can be found in historic student pubs. To reach the university **Mensa "Zeughaus" ❶**, in the stone fortress on Marstallstr., take bus #35 to Marstallstr. (Cafeteria meals €0.80 per 100g. CampusCard required; available for €5 deposit at Info Café International, Grabeng. 18. Open M-Sa 11:30am-10pm.) **Hemingway's Bar-Café-Meeting Point ❷**, Fahrtg. 1, has a crowded, shaded patio along the Neckar. (Lunch menu €4.10. Open M-Th and Su 9am-1am, F-Sa 9am-3am.)

SIGHTS

HEIDELBERGER SCHLOß. Tourists lay siege to Heidelberg castle every summer, and for good reason. After 1329 it housed the Prince Electors, whose statues now stand before the entrance. Thrice destroyed, twice by war (1622 and 1693) and once by nature (lightning in 1764), the castle inspired Romantic artists who saw a tension between its ruins and the surrounding forest growth. A cool, musty wine cellar houses the **Großes Faß**, the largest wine tun ever used, holding 221,726L; the **Kleines Faß** holds a mere 125,000L. *(Grounds open daily 8am-5:30pm. €2.50, students €1.20. English tours daily every 15min. 10am-4pm; €3.50.)* Reach the castle by the uphill path or by the **Bergbahn**, one of Germany's oldest cable cars. *(Take bus #11, dir.: Karlstor, to Bergbahn/Rathaus. Trams leave the parking lot next to the bus stop daily Mar.-Oct. every 10min. 9am-8pm; Nov.-Feb. every 20min. 9am-6pm. Round-trip €3.50.)*

UNIVERSITÄT. Heidelberg is home to Germany's oldest university, established in 1386. Its faculty has included over 20 Nobel laureates, and the institution all but gave birth to sociology as an academic subject. The **Museum der Universität Heidelberg** traces the school's history in a building that contains its oldest auditorium, **Alte Aula**. Intriguingly, students were exempt from prosecution by civil authorities until 1914 due to the principle of academic freedom. Instead, their crimes were tried by the faculty and punished in the **Studentenkarzer** jail. *(Grabeng. 1. Open Apr.-Oct. M-Sa 10am-4pm; Nov.-Mar. Tu-F 10am-2pm. Museum and jail €2.50, students €2.)*

MARKTPLATZ. At the center of the Altstadt is the cobblestoned Marktplatz, where accused witches and heretics were burned at the stake in the 15th century. Some of Heidelberg's oldest structures border the square: the 14th-century **Heiliggeistkirche** (Church of the Holy Spirit) and the 16th-century inn **Haus Zum Ritter**, opposite the church. *(Church open M-Sa 11am-5pm, Su 1-5pm. Free. Tower €0.50.)*

GERMANY

PHILOSOPHENWEG. A high path on the opposite side of the Neckar from the Alt-stadt, the Philosophenweg (Philosopher's Way) has unbeatable views of the city. On the top of Heiligenberg (Holy Mountain) lie the ruins of the 9th-century **St. Michael Basilika,** the 13th-century **Stefanskloster,** and an **amphitheater** built under Hitler in 1934 on the site of an ancient Celtic gathering place. *(To get to the path, take streetcar #1 or 3 to Tiefburg, or use the steep spur trail 10m west of the Karl-Theodor-Brücke.)*

⬛ NIGHTLIFE

Most popular nightspots fan out from the **Marktplatz.** On the Neckar side of the Heiliggeistkirche, **Unter Straße** has the highest concentration of bars in the city. A few worthwhile venues also lie along **Hauptstraße.** At **Nachtschicht,** in the Land-fried-Komplex, students dance to a variety of music in a basement resembling an old factory. (☎43 85 50. Cover €3.50; M and F students €1.50. Open M and Th-Sa 10pm-4am, W 10pm-3am.) **Zum Sepp'l,** Hauptstr. 213, is a student lair with stained-glass windows and live piano. (☎230 85. Open daily noon-10:30pm.) **Mata Hari,** on Zwingerstr., near Oberbadg, is a small nightclub for gays and lesbians. Straights are welcome. (☎18 18 08. Beer €2.80. Tu men only. Open daily 10pm-3am.)

⬛ DAYTRIP FROM HEIDELBERG: NECKARSTEINACH

Just 14km upstream from Heidelberg, Neckarsteinach is a fishing village made famous by its four nearly untouristed castles; the two to the west abide in Roman-tic dilapidation, while the two to the east are privately occupied and not open to visitors. All lie within 3km of one another on the Neckar's north bank and can be reached by foot via the **Burgenweg** (castle path). Turn right from the train station onto Bahnhofstr., then take a left on Hauptstr. and follow it until coming to the brick Schloßsteige (castle stairs) on the right, which leads upward to the Burgen-weg. Fireworks set the sky ablaze on the second Saturday after Pentecost in June and on the last Saturday in July for the **Vierburgenbeleuchtung** (four-castle lighting). **Trains** connect Heidelberg to Heilbronn through the Neckar valley, a forested stretch that runs north through Bad Wimpfen, Burg Guttenberg, Hirschhorn am Neckar, and Neckarsteinach. Castles dot the hilltops and form part of the **Burgen-straße** (castle road) stretching from Mannheim to Prague. **Buses** also traverse the valley, and are often faster than trains. Schedules are posted at bus stops. The **tour-ist office,** Hauptstr. 15, lists **private rooms.** (☎920 00. Open M-Tu and Th-F 8:30am-12:30pm and 2:30-6pm, W 8:30am-12:30pm, Sa 8:30am-1pm.) **Postal Code:** 69239.

STUTTGART   ☎0711

Forget about *Lederhosen*—Porsche, Daimler-Benz, and a host of other corporate thoroughbreds keep Stuttgart (pop. 587,000) speeding along in the fast lane. After its almost complete destruction in WWII, Stuttgart was rebuilt in a thoroughly uninspiring style. More to its credit are its amazing **mineral baths** (*Mineralbäder*), fueled by Western Europe's most active mineral springs. **Mineralbad Leuze,** Am Leuzebad 2-6, has indoor and outdoor thermal pools. Take U1 or streetcar #2 to Mineralbäder. (☎216 42 10. Open daily 6am-9pm. Day card €13, students €8.30; 2hr. soak €6.40/€4.80.) ⬛**Staatsgallerie Stuttgart,** Konrad-Adenauer-Str. 30-32, collects Dalí, Kandinsky, and Picasso in its new wing and paintings from the Middle Ages to the 19th century in its old wing. (Open Tu-W and F-Su 10am-6pm, Th 10am-9pm. €4.50, students €3. W free.) The **Mercedes-Benz Museum,** Mercedesstr. 137, is a must for car-lovers. Take S1 (dir.: Ploschingen) to Daimlerstadion. (Open Tu-Su 9am-5pm. Free.) Nightlife clusters around Eberhardstr., Rotebühlpl., and Calwer Str. **Suite 212,** Theodor-Heuss-Str. 15, has DJs and video-mixing on weekends. (Beer €2.50. Open M-W 11am-2am, Th 11am-3am, F-Sa 11am-5am, Su 2pm-2am.)

Trains run to: Basel (3½hr., 2-4 per hr., €37); Berlin (6hr., 2 per hr., €109); Frankfurt (1-2hr., 2 per hr., €39); Munich (2½-3½hr., 2 per hr., €32); and Paris (6½hr., 4 per day, €80). **Tips 'n' trips,** Lautenschlagerstr. 22, is a tourist office. (☎222 27 30. Open M-F noon-7pm, Sa 10am-2pm.) The **post office,** Arnulf-Klett-Pl. 2, is in the station. (Open M-F 8:30am-6pm, Sa 8:30am-12:30pm.) To reach 🏠**Jugendgästehaus Stuttgart (HI) ❷,** Richard-Wagner-Str. 2, take streetcar #15 to Bubenbad. After the next right, the hostel is on the right. (☎24 11 32. Reception 24hr. Dorms €16; singles €21, with bath €26; doubles €37/€42.) Look for mid-range restaurants between Pfarrstr. and Charlottenstr. **Postal Code:** 70173.

THE BLACK FOREST (SCHWARZWALD)

The Black Forest owes its name to the eerie gloom that prevails under its evergreen canopy. Today, the region that once inspired the Grimms' *Hansel and Gretel* lures hikers and skiers with more than just gingerbread. The gateway to the Black Forest is **Freiburg im Breisgau,** most easily accessible by train from Basel and Stuttgart. Visitors tend to favor exploring the area by bike or by car, as public transportation is sparse. Many rail lines encircle it, but only two cut through it. **Bus** service is more thorough, although slow and infrequent.

FREIBURG IM BREISGAU. Green hills can be seen from downtown Freiburg (pop. 208,000), a city without a city's pace. Freiburg's centerpiece is its **Münster,** a 13th- to 16th-century stone cathedral with a 116m spire that shelters Germany's oldest bell. (Open M-Sa 9:30am-5pm, Su 1-5pm. Tower €1.50, students €1.) Surrounding hills have well-marked **hiking** and **mountain biking** trails. **Trains** run to Basel (1hr., 3 per hr., €9-16) and Stuttgart (2hr., every hr., €38). The **tourist office,** Rotteckring 14, down Eisenbahnstr. from the station, has trail maps and free city maps. It also books private rooms, the city's best budget option. (☎0761 388 18 80. Open June-Sept. M-F 9:30am-8pm, Sa 9:30am-5pm, Su 10am-noon; Oct.-May M-F 9:30am-6pm, Sa 9:30am-2pm, Su 10am-noon.) To reach the **Jugendherberge (HI) ❷,** Kartäuserstr. 151, take bus #1 to Lassbergstr. Turn left, then right onto Fritz-Geiges-Str., and follow the signs. (☎0761 676 56. Dorms €22, under 27 €19; doubles €49.) Near the Martinstor, **Freiburger Markthalle ❶** serves ethnic specialties for €3-7. (Open M-F 7am-7pm, Sa 7am-4pm.) **Brennessel ❷,** Eschholzstr. 17, behind the train station, stuffs patrons with everything from ostrich steak to pancakes. (Entrees €1.80-9.20. Open M-Sa 6pm-1am, Su 5pm-1am.) **Postal Code:** 79098.

TRIBERG. Tourists flock in summer to Triberg (pop. 5000), some to see the world's two largest cuckoo clocks, others to hike to the **Gutacher Wasserfall,** cascades that tumble 163m down mossy rocks. Although it is Germany's highest waterfall, it's more of a mountain stream; however, the hike there is indisputably idyllic. (Park always open; admission only 9am-7pm. €1.50, students €1.20.) Signs for **Wallfahrtskirche** lead to the small pilgrimage church, **Maria in der Tanne.** Legend has it that the pious have been miraculously cured here since the 17th century. (☎07722 45 66. Open until 6 or 7pm.) **Trains** run to Freiburg (1½-2hr., 1-2 per hr., €24). The **tourist office,** Luisenstr. 10, is in the *Kurhaus;* from the station, turn right onto Bahnhofstr. and follow the signs, or take any bus to Marktpl. (☎07722 95 32 30. Open M-F 9am-12:30pm and 2-5:30pm, Sa 10am-noon.) **Postal Code:** 79098.

CONSTANCE (KONSTANZ)　　　　　　　　☎07531

Located on the **Bodensee** (Lake Constance) and ranking among Germany's most popular vacation spots, Constance (pop. 79,000) has river promenades and narrow streets that wind around beautiful Baroque and Renaissance facades. Constance emerged unscathed from WWII since part of the city extends into Switzerland and the Allies were leery of striking neutral territory. Under renovation through 2006, the **Münster** displays ancient religious objects beneath its 76m Gothic spire. (Open M-F 10am-6pm, Sa-Su noon-5pm.) Wander down **Seestraße**, near the yacht harbor on the lake, or **Rheinsteig**, along the Rhine, for picturesque promenades. Constance boasts a number of **public beaches**; all are free and open from May to September. **Freidbad Horn** (bus #5) has a section enclosed by hedges for nude sunbathing.

Trains run from Constance to most cities in southern Germany. BSB **ferries** leave hourly from Constance for all ports around the lake. Buy tickets onboard or in the building, Hafenstr. 6, behind the train station. (☎28 13 89. Open daily Apr.-Oct. 7:45am-6:35pm.) The friendly but tiny **tourist office**, Bahnhofspl. 13, to the right of the train station, provides free walking maps and finds private rooms for a €2.50 fee. (☎13 30 30. Open Apr.-Oct. M-F 9am-6:30pm, Sa 9am-4pm, Su 10am-1pm; Nov.-Mar. M-F 9:30am-12:30pm and 2-6pm.) Reserve a few weeks ahead in summer at any lodgings. In the center, **Pension Gretel ❸**, Zollernstr. 6-8, has bright rooms. (☎45 58 25. Singles €36; doubles €64, with bath €75; triples with bath €95; quads with bath €129; low season reduced rates. AmEx/MC/V.) To reach **Jugendherberge Otto-Möricke-Turm (HI) ❸**, Zur Allmannshöhe 18, take bus #4 from the train station to Jugendherberge and backtrack uphill. (☎322 60. Curfew 10pm. Lockout 9:30am-noon. €22.20, under 27 €19.50; additional nights €19.10/€16.40.) **DKV-Campingplatz Brudehofer ❶**, Fohrenbühlweg 50, is by the lake. Take bus #1 to Staad and walk 10min. with the lake to your left. (☎313 88. €3.50 per person. €3.10-4.50 per tent, €2.60 per car.) **Groceries** are in the basement of the Karstadt department store on Augustinerpl. (Open M-F 9:30am-8pm, Sa 9:30am-7pm.) **Postal Code:** 78462.

BAVARIA (BAYERN)

Bavaria is the Germany of Teutonic myth, Wagnerian opera, and Brothers Grimm fairy tales. From the Baroque cities along the Danube to mad King Ludwig's castles high in the Alps, the region attracts more tourists than any other part of the country.

MUNICH (MÜNCHEN)   ☎089

The capital and cultural center of Bavaria, Munich (pop. 1,322,000) is a sprawling, relatively liberal metropolis in the midst of conservative southern Germany. World-class museums, handsome parks and architecture, a vibrant arts scene, and a cosmopolitan population create a city of astonishing vitality. *Müncheners* party zealously during *Fasching*, or Mardi Gras (Feb. 7-9, 2005), shop with abandon during the Christ Child Market (Nov. 26-Dec. 24, 2005), and consume unfathomable quantities of beer during the legendary Oktoberfest (Sept. 17-Oct. 2, 2005).

▶ TRANSPORTATION

Flights: Flughafen München (☎97 52 13 13). S8 runs between the airport and the Hauptbahnhof (40min., every 10min., €8 or 8 stripes on the *Streifenkarte*).

Trains: Munich's **Hauptbahnhof** (☎22 33 12 56) is the transportation hub of southern Germany, with connections to: **Amsterdam** (7-9hr., 1 per hr.); **Berlin** (6½hr., 2 per hr.); **Cologne** (6hr., 2 per hr.); **Frankfurt** (4hr., 2 per hr.); **Füssen** (2hr., every 2hr.); **Hamburg** (6hr., 1 per hr.); **Paris** (8-10hr., 6 per day); **Prague** (6-7hr., 4 per day); **Salzburg** (1¾hr., 2 per hr.); **Vienna** (5hr., 1 per hr.); **Zürich** (4½-5½hr., 4-5 per day). Purchase **Bayern-Ticket** (single €15, 2-5 people €22) for unlimited train transit in Bavaria and parts of Austria on weekdays from 9am-3am, and on weekends from midnight to 3am the following day. **EurAide**, in the station, provides free train info in English and sells train tickets. **Reisezentrum** info counters open daily 7am-9:30pm.

GERMANY

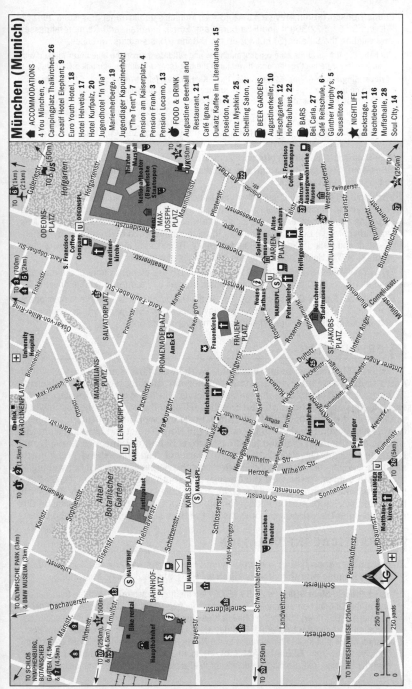

München (Munich)

▲ ACCOMMODATIONS
4 You München, **8**
Campingplatz Thalkirchen, **26**
Creatif Hotel Elephant, **9**
Euro Youth Hotel, **18**
Hotel Helvetia, **17**
Hotel Kurpfalz, **20**
Jugendhotel "In Via"
Marienherberge, **19**
Jugendlager Kapuzinerhölzl
("The Tent"), **7**
Pension am Kaiserplatz, **4**
Pension Frank, **3**
Pension Locarno, **13**

♦ FOOD & DRINK
Augustiner Beerhall and
Restaurant, **21**
Café Ignaz, **1**
Dukatz Kaffee im Literaturhaus, **15**
Poseidon, **24**
Prinz Myshkin, **25**
Schelling Salon, **2**

🍺 BEER GARDENS
Augustinerkeller, **10**
Hirschgarten, **12**
Hofbräuhaus, **22**

BARS
Bei Carla, **27**
Café Reitschule, **6**
Günther Murphy's, **5**
Sausalitos, **23**

★ NIGHTLIFE
Backstage, **11**
Nachtleben, **16**
Muffathalle, **28**
Soul City, **14**

GERMANY

Public Transportation: MVV (☎41 42 43 44), Munich's public transport system, runs M-Th and Su 5am-12:30am and F-Sa 5am-2am. Eurail, InterRail, and German railpasses are valid on the S-Bahn (S) but *not* on the U-Bahn (U), streetcars, or buses.

Tickets: Buy tickets at the blue vending machines and **validate them** in the blue boxes marked with an E before entering the platform. If you jump the fare (*schwarzfahren*), you risk a €40 fine.

Prices: Single ride tickets €2.10 (valid 3hr.). **Kurzstrecke** (short trip) tickets €1.10 (1hr. or 2 stops on the U- or S-Bahn, 4 stops on a streetcar or bus). A **Streifenkarte** (10-strip ticket) costs €9.50 and can be used by more than 1 person. Cancel 2 stripes per person for a normal ride, or 1 strip for a *Kurzstrecke;* beyond the city center, cancel 2 stripes per zone. A **Single-Tageskarte** (single-day ticket) is valid until 6am the next day (€4.50). At €11, the **3-Day Pass** is a great deal. The **Munich Welcome Card** also has transportation discounts. The **XXL Ticket** gives day-long transit on all transport in Munich and surroundings (€6 single; €10.50 for up to 5 individuals).

Ride-Sharing: McShare Treffpunkt Zentrale, Lämmerstr. 6 (☎194 40). Open daily 8am-8pm. **Frauenmitfahrzentrale,** Klenzestr. 57b, arranges ride-shares for women only. Open M-F 8am-8pm.

Hitchhiking: *Let's Go* does not recommend hitchhiking. Munich hitchhikers scan bulletin boards in the **Mensa,** Leopoldstr. 13, or else try *Autobahn* on-ramps; however, anyone standing *Autobahn*-side of a blue sign with a white auto symbol faces **fines.** Hitchhikers to Salzburg take U1 or 2 to Karl-Preis-pl. Those to Nürnberg and Berlin take U6 to Studenstadt and walk 500m to the Frankfurter Ring. Those to the Bodensee and Switzerland take U4 or 5 to Heimeranpl., then bus #33 to Siegenburger Str.

Taxis: Taxi-München-Zentrale (☎216 10 or 194 10) has stands in front of the train station and every 5-10 blocks in the city center. Women can request a female driver.

Bike Rental: Radius Bikes (☎59 61 13), in the Hauptbahnhof behind the lockers opposite tracks 30-36. €3 per hr., €14 per day. Deposit of €50, passport, or credit card. 10% student discount. Open daily May to mid-Oct. 10am-6pm.

▓ ORIENTATION

Downtown Munich is split into quadrants by thoroughfares running east-west and north-south. These intersect at Munich's epicenter, Marienplatz, and link the traffic rings at Karlsplatz (also known as "Stachus") in the west, Isartorplatz in the east, Odeonsplatz in the north, and Sendlinger Tor in the south. In the east beyond the Isartor, the Isar River flows north-south. The Hauptbahnhof (main train station) is just beyond Karlspl. to the west of the Ring. To get to Marienpl. from the station, use the main exit and head east across Bahnhofpl. through Karlspl. and continue straight. Or, take the S-Bahn to Marienpl. The **University** is to the north amid the budget restaurants of the **Schwabing** district; to the east of Schwabing is the **English Garden,** to the west the **Olympiapark.** South of downtown is the **Glockenbachviertel,** filled with night hotspots, including many gay bars. A seedy area with hotels and sex shops surrounds the Hauptbahnhof. Oktoberfest takes place on the large and open **Theresienwiese** southeast of the train station on the U4 and 5 lines.

▐ PRACTICAL INFORMATION

Among publications listing services, events, and museums, the most comprehensive is the English monthly *Munich Found* (€3), available at newsstands.

Tourist Offices: Main Office (☎23 39 65 00), on the front (eastern) side of the train station, next to the SB-Markt on Bahnhofpl. Books rooms for free with a 10-15% deposit, sells English city maps (€0.30), and offers the **Munich Welcome Card** for discounts and passes to transportation and sights (1-day €6.50, 3-day €16). Open M-Sa 9am-8pm, Su 10am-6pm. **Branch office** just inside the entrance to the Neues Rathaus on Marienpl. Open M-F 10am-8pm, Sa 10am-4pm. ▨ **EurAide** (☎59 38 89), room 3 along track 11 of the Hauptbahnhof, near the Bayerstr. exit. Books train tickets for free, explains public transportation, sells maps

(€1), and books English-language city tours. Pick up the free brochure *Inside Track.* Open daily June-Sept. 7:45am-12:45pm and 2-6pm, except Su afternoon; Oct. 7:45am-12:45pm and 2-4pm; Nov.-Apr. 8am-noon and 1-4pm; May 7:45am-12:45pm and 2-4:30pm.

Tours: ⛵ **Mike's Bike Tours** (☎25 54 39 88; www.mikesbiketours.com). If you only have one day in Munich, take this tour. Setting out from the Altes Rathaus on Marienpl., the 4hr., 6.5km city tour (€22) includes a *Biergarten* break; the 7hr., 16km tour (€33) stops at Nymphenburg Palace and Olympic Park. Tours leave daily June-July 10:30am.

Consulates: Canada, Tal 29 (☎219 95 70). Open M-Th 9am-noon and 2-5pm, F 9am-noon. **Ireland,** Dennigerstr. 15 (☎20 80 59 90). Open M-F 9-11am. **UK,** Bürkleinstr. 10, 4th floor. (☎21 10 90). Open M-F 8:45-11:30am and 1-3:15pm. **US,** Königinstr. 5 (☎288 80). Open M-F 8-11am.

Currency Exchange: ReiseBank (☎551 08 37; www.reisebank.de), at the front of the train station on Bahnhofpl. Slightly cheaper than other banks. Open daily 7am-10pm. Branch office at Track 11. Open M-Sa 9:15am-12:30pm and 1-4:15pm.

GLBT Services: Gay services information (☎260 30 56), hotline hours 7-10pm. **Lesbian information** (☎725 42 72). Phone staffed M and W 2:30-5pm, Tu 10:30am-1pm. Also see **Gay and Lesbian Munich** (p. 498).

Laundromat: Waschsalon, Untersbergstrasse 8. U2, 7 or 8 to Untersbergstrasse. Wash €3.50. Detergent €0.30. Dry €0.60 per 10min. Open daily 7am-11pm.

Emergency: Police: ☎110. **Ambulance** and **Fire:** ☎112. **Medical service:** ☎192 22.

Pharmacy: Bahnhofpl. 2 (☎59 41 19 or 59 81 19), on the corner outside the train station. Open M-F 8am-6:30pm, Sa 8am-2pm.

Internet Access: Easy Everything, on Bahnhofspl. across from the station. Open 24hr. Prices depend on demand (around €2.40 per hr.). **Internet Cafe,** Marienpl. 20 (☎20 70 27 37), serves cocktails and food all night. €1 per 30min. Open 24hr.

Post Office: Bahnhofpl. In the yellow building opposite the main train station exit. Open M-F 7:30am-8pm, Sa 9am-4pm. **Postal Code:** 80335.

⌐ ACCOMMODATIONS AND CAMPING

Munich's accommodations tend to fall into one of three categories: seedy, expensive, or booked solid. Only the latter exists during the high seasons, like mid-summer and Oktoberfest, when prices jump 10-15%. In summer, it's usually necessary to book a few weeks in advance or start calling before noon. Don't rely on catching any shuteye in public areas, as police patrol all night long.

HOSTELS AND CAMPING

> **REMINDER.** HI-affiliated hostels in Bavaria generally do not admit guests over age 26, except in families or groups of adults with young children.

⛵ **Euro Youth Hotel,** Senefelderstr. 5 (☎59 90 88 11). From the Hauptbahnhof, make a left on Bayerstr. and a right on Senefelderstr. Friendly and informed English-speaking staff. Breakfast €4.90. Wash €2.80. Dry €1.30. Reception 24hr. Dorms €19.50; 3- to 5-bed rooms €23.50. Breakfast included for: singles €45; doubles €54, with private shower €72; triples with bath and private shower €84; quads €84. Cash only. ❷

⛵ **Jugendlager Kapuzinerhölzl** (The Tent), In den Kirschen 30 (☎141 43 00). Streetcar #17 from the Hauptbahnhof (dir.: Amalienburgstr.) to Botanischer Garten (15min.). Follow the signs straight on Franz-Schrank-Str. and turn left at In den Kirschen. Sleep with 250 others under a big tent on a wooden floor. Evening campfires. Free English city tours. Kitchen available. Lockers free. Wash €2. Dry €1.50. Internet €0.50 per 15min. Reception 24hr. Open June-Aug. €8.50 gets you a foam pad, blankets, a shower, and breakfast. Actual beds €11. Camping €5.50 per person, plus €5.50 per campsite. ❶

GERMANY

4 You München, Hirtenstr. 18 (☎ 552 16 60; www.the4you.de), 200m from the Haupt-bahnhof. Ecological hostel with restaurant and bar. Wheelchair accessible. Breakfast €5. 12-bed dorms €18; 4-, 6-, or 8-bed dorms €20-23; singles €35; doubles €50. ❷

Jugendhotel "In Via" Marienherberge, Goethestr. 9 (☎ 55 58 05), an unmarked yellow building less than a block from the train station. Women only. Breakfast included. Wash €1.50. Dry €1.50. Reception daily 8am-midnight. Curfew midnight-6am. 6-bed dorms €22, over 25 €27; singles €30/€35; doubles €40/€50; triples €60/€75. ❸

Campingplatz Thalkirchen, Zentralländstr. 49 (☎ 723 17 07). U1 or 2 to Sendlinger Tor, then U3 to Thalkirchen, and change to bus #57 (20min.). From the bus stop, cross the street on the left and turn right onto the dirt footpath; the entrance is on the left. 550 sites on the lush banks of the Isar. TV lounge and restaurant. Showers €1. Wash €4. Dry €0.50. Reception 7am-11pm. €4.50 per person, under 14 €1.30. Tent rental €3-4, plus €8 per night. Cars €4.30. Caravans available at €11 per person. ❶

HOTELS AND PENSIONS

▩ **Hotel Helvetia,** Schillerstr. 6 (☎ 590 68 50), at the corner of Bahnhofspl. Just beyond the Vereinsbank, to the right as you exit the station. A friendly hotel with newly reno-vated rooms. Breakfast included. Laundry €6. Free Internet. Reception 24hr. Singles €30-35; doubles €40-55, with shower €50-65; triples €55-69; quads €75-88. ❹

▩ **Creatif Hotel Elephant,** Lammerstr. 6 (☎ 55 57 85; www.munich-hotel.net). Take the Arnulfstr. exit out of the station, hang a quick right, turn left on Hirtenstr., then right on Lammerstr. Uniquely modern rooms, all with bath, telephone, and TV. Free Internet. Reception 24hr. Singles €30-40; doubles €40-65. Extra bed €10. ❹

Pension Frank, Schellingstr. 24 (☎ 28 14 51; www.pension-frank.de). U3 or 6 to Univer-sität. Turn right onto Schellingstr. Rooms with balcony. Internet €2 per hr. Reception 7:30am-10pm. Check-out 11am. 3- to 6-bed dorms €25-28 per person; singles €45-49; doubles €57-60; triples €75-81; quads €100-108; quints €125-135. ❸

Pension am Kaiserplatz, Kaiserpl. 12 (☎ 34 91 90). U3 to Münchener Freiheit. Take the escalator to Herzogstr., then turn left and continue to Viktoriastr.; turn left, and it's at the end of the street on the right. A few blocks from nightlife central. Breakfast included and served in-room. Reception 7am-8pm. Singles €31, with shower €47; doubles €48-53/€55-57; triples €63/€66; quads €84; quints €105; 6-bed rooms €126. ❹

Pension Locarno, Bahnhofspl. 5 (☎ 55 51 64). Cozy rooms, all with cable TV and phone. Reception daily 7:30am-5pm. Singles €43; doubles €56; triples €72. ❹

Hotel Kurfplaz, Schwanthaler Str. 121 (☎ 540 98 60). Turn right on Bayerstr. out of the station, veer left onto Holzapfelstr., and then right onto Schwanthaler Str. Or take street-car #18 or 19 to Holzapfelstr. All rooms with TV, phone, and bath. Breakfast included. Internet €3 per 30min. Reception 24hr. Singles from €30; doubles from €45. ❹

⟨⟩ FOOD

For an authentic Bavarian lunch, spread a *Brez'n* (pretzel) with *Leberwurst* (liv-erwurst) or cheese. **Weißwürste** (white veal sausages) are a regional specialty; don't eat the skin, just slice them open for their tender meat. **Leberkäse** is a pinkish loaf of ground beef and bacon, while **Leberknödel** are liver dumplings.

Just south of Marienpl. the vibrant **Viktualienmarkt** is Munich's gastronomic cen-ter, but don't plan to find any budget groceries here. (Open M-F 10am-8pm, Sa 8am-4pm.) Off **Ludwigstraße,** the university district supplies students with inexpen-sive, filling meals. Many reasonably priced restaurants and cafes cluster on **Schell-ingstraße, Amalienstraße,** and **Türkenstraße** (U3 or 6 to Universität.) Munich is also the place where someone first joined the "beer" concept to the "garden" concept to create the **beer garden.** Now they're all over the city (see **Nightlife,** below).

Dukatz Kaffee im Literaturhaus, Salvatorpl. 1 (☎291 96 00). Munich's unofficial literary hub, this is the place to see and be seen. Gourmet food (€6-8) complements creative drink options (€2-4). Open M-Sa 10am-1pm (Sa 3pm) and 6:30-10:30pm. ❷

Schelling Salon, Schellingstr. 54 (☎272 07 88). Bavarian *Knödel* and billiard balls since 1872. Rack up at the tables where Lenin, Rilke, and Hitler once played (€7 per hr.). A free billiard museum exhibits a Polish noble's table and the game's history since Pharaonic days. Breakfast €3-5.10. Traditional German entrees €4-11. Museum open Su night or on request. Restaurant open M and Th-Su 6:30am-1am. ❷

Café Ignaz, Georgenstr. 67 (☎271 60 93). U2 to Josephspl. Bakery and cafe serves dinners from crepes to stir-fry dishes (€5-9). Buffets during breakfast (€5-7), lunch (€5.50), or on weekends, brunch (€8). Open M-F 8am-10pm, Sa-Su 9am-10pm. ❷

Augustiner Beerhall and Restaurant, Neuhauser Str. 27 (☎23 18 32 57), between Marienpl. and the Hauptbahnhof. Bavarian specialties and the celebrated Augustiner brew (*Maß* €6). English menu. Entrees €4-13.50. Open daily 10am-midnight. ❷

Poseidon, Westenriederstr. 13 (☎29 92 96), off the Viktualienmarkt. Soup bowls of *bouillabaisse* with bread (€10) in a bustling fish-market atmosphere. Th special sushi menu (€20). Open M-W 8am-6:30pm, Th-F 8am-7pm, Sa 8am-4pm. ❹

Prinz Myshkin, Hackenstr. 2 (☎26 55 96). An internationally acclaimed restaurant with Asian-influenced cuisine. Entrees €9.50-15. Open daily 11am-12:30am. ❹

🔥 SIGHTS

RESIDENZ. Down the pedestrian zone from Odeonspl., the ornate rooms of the Residenz (Palace), built from the 14th to 19th centuries, make up the material vestiges of the Wittelsbach dynasty. Behind the Residenz, the manicured **Hofgarten** shelters the lovely temple of Diana. The **Schatzkammer** (treasury) contains jeweled baubles, crowns, swords, china, and ivorywork. *(Open Apr. to mid-Oct. daily 9am-6pm, Th until 8pm; low season daily 10am-4pm. €6, students €5.)* The **Residenzmuseum** comprises the Wittelsbach apartments and State Rooms, a collection of European porcelain, and a 17th-century chapel. In the Ahnengalerie, 120 portraits somehow trace the royal lineage back to Charlemagne. *(Max-Joseph-pl. 3. U3-6 to Odeonspl. ☎29 06 71. Hours same as Schatzkammer. €6, students €5. Combination ticket €9, students €8.)*

MARIENPLATZ. The **Mariensäule,** an ornate 1683 monument to the Virgin Mary, commemorates the city's survival of the Thirty Years' War. At the neo-Gothic

SHEER *BIER*

Although droves of tourists visit Germany to sample its renowned beer, few understand the intricacies of German *Bierkultur*. German beer is typically served by the liter (*Maß*), sometimes by the half-liter (*halb-Maß*). Ask for "*Ein Maß, bitte,*" and if you feel short-changed (most glasses have measurement lines on them), say "*Bitte nachschenken*" for a top-up.

German beer comes in endless varieties. A **Helles** is a typical light, usually Bavarian, beer. The foam-crowned **Pils** is a more bitter and more alcoholic, but less malty brew.

Similar to an English shandy, a **Radlermaß** (bikers brew) is a 50-50 blend of *Helles* and sparkling lemonade, so named because Germans seem to think that it's safe to cycle as long as you are only half drunk. **Weißbier** is a strong, cloudy beer made with wheat (*Weizen*); many like to add a squeeze of lemon.

A maltier lager, the **Dunkeles** is not the strongest beer. If you're aiming for severe inebriation, try a strong **Bock** or an even stronger **Doppelbock.** Both of these beers are often brewed by monks, presumably because they alone have the self-restraint not to drink it all themselves.

Germany's excellence in beer is a double-edged sword, however. Visitors should be warned that for a palate weaned on German brews, watery domestics will never taste as good again.

Neues Rathaus, the **Glockenspiel** chimes with a display of jousting knights and dancing coopers. *(Daily at 11am, noon, and 3pm; in summer also 5pm.)* At 9pm, a mechanical watchman marches out and the Guardian Angel escorts the *Münchner Kindl* (Munich Child) to bed. The Neues Rathaus tower offers a sweeping view. *(Tower open M-F 9am-7pm, Sa-Su 10am-7pm. €1.50, under 19 €0.75.)* Adorning the **Altes Rathaus** tower, to the right of the Neues Rathaus, are all of Munich's coats of arms but one— the swastika emblem of the Nazi era. Be wary passing through Marienplatz; with all the tourists looking upward, pickpockets have a field day.

PETERSKIRCHE AND FRAUENKIRCHE. Across from the Neues Rathaus is the 12th-century Peterskirche, the city's oldest parish church. Scale the over 300 steps to a spectacular view of Munich. *(Open M-Sa 9am-7pm, Su 10am-7pm. Tower €1.50, students €1.)* From the Marienpl., take Kaufingerstr. one block toward the Hauptbahnhof to the onion-domed towers of the 15th-century Frauenkirche—one of Munich's most notable landmarks and now the emblem of the city.

ENGLISCHER GARTEN. Extending from the city center is the vast Englischer Garten (English Garden), Europe's largest public metropolitan park. On sunny days, all of Munich turns out to bike, play badminton, ride horseback, or swim in the Eisbach. The garden includes a Japanese tea house, a Chinese pagoda, a Greek temple, and good old German beer gardens. Nude sunbathing areas are designated FKK *(Frei-Körper-Kultur)* on signs and park maps. More daring *Müncheners* surf the rapids of the Eisbach, which flows artificially through the park.

SCHLOß NYMPHENBURG. After a decade spent trying for an heir, Ludwig I celebrated the birth of his son in 1662 by erecting an elaborate summer playground. Schloß Nymphenburg, to the northwest of town, hides a number of treasures, like Ludwig's "Gallery of Beauties." Whenever a woman caught his fancy, he would have her portrait painted—a scandalous hobby, considering that many of the women were commoners. Four manors and a few lakes also spread over the grounds. In the **Marstallmuseum** (carriage museum), learn about the means of 17th-century royal travel. *(Streetcar #17, dir.: Amalienburgstr., to Schloß Nymphenburg. ☎17 90 80. All attractions open Apr. to mid-Oct. daily 9am-6pm, Th until 8pm; late Oct. to Mar. daily 10am-4pm. Museum and Schloß open Tu-Su 9am-noon and 1-5pm. Schloß €5, students €4. Marstallmuseum €4/€3. Entire complex €10/€8.)*

OLYMPIAPARK. Built for the 1972 Olympic Games in Munich, the Olympiapark contains the architecturally daring, tent-like **Olympia-Zentrum** and the **Olympia Turm** (tower), which is the highest building in Munich at 290m. Two **tours** in English are available: the Adventure Tour of the entire park (daily Apr.-Oct. 2pm; €7, students €5) or a tour of just the soccer stadium (daily Mar.-Oct. 11am; €5, students €3.50). In summer, the stadium also hosts events ranging from concerts to flea markets to bungee jumping. *(U3 to Olympiazentrum. ☎30 67 24 14. Open M-F 10am-6pm, Sa 10am-3pm. Tower open daily 9am-midnight. €3, students €2.)*

🏛 MUSEUMS

Many of Munich's museums require days for exhaustive perusal. The *Münchner Volkshochschule* (☎48 00 62 29) sells tours of many exhibits for €6. A **day pass** to all of Munich's state-owned museums is sold at the tourist office and many larger museums (€15). All state-owned museums are **free on Sunday.**

■ **DEUTSCHES MUSEUM.** Over 50 departments covering 17km spread through the Deutsches Museum. Exhibits include one of the first telephones and a recreated subterranean labyrinth of mining tunnels. *(Museuminsel 1. S1-8 to Isartor or streetcar #18 to Deutsches Museum. ☎217 91; www.deutsches-museum.de. Open daily 9am-5pm. €7.50, students €3, under 6 free. English guidebook €4.)*

PINAKOTHEKE. Newly constructed by *Münchener* Stephan Braunfels, the **Pinakothek der Moderne** is four museums in one. Subgalleries exhibit architecture, design, drawings, and paintings by artists from Picasso to Johns. *(Barerstr. 40. U2 to Königspl. Turn right at Königspl., and then left after 1 block onto Meiserstr. ☎23 80 53 60. Open Tu-Su 10am-5pm, Tu and Th until 8pm.)* Commissioned in 1826 by King Ludwig I, the **Alte Pinakothek** houses Munich's most precious art, such as works by da Vinci, Rembrandt, and Rubens. *(Barerstr. 27. ☎23 80 52 16. Hours same as Pinakothek der Moderne.)* Next door, the **Neue Pinakothek** exhibits artists of the 19th and 20th centuries, including Cézanne, Manet, and van Gogh. *(Barerstr. 29. ☎23 80 51 95. Open M and W-Su 10am-5pm, Th until 10pm. Pinakotheke each €9, students €5. Combination ticket for the Alte and Neue Pinakotheke €8/€5. Day pass to all 3 €12/€7.)*

BMW MUSEUM. This sleek driving museum displays past, present, and future BMW products. *Horizons in Time*, an English brochure, guides you through the path spiraling upward. *(Petuelring 130. U3 to Olympiazentrum. Take the Olympiaturm exit and walk a block up Lerchenauer Str. Open daily 9am-5pm. €3, students €2.)*

ZAM: ZENTRUM FÜR AUSSERGEWÖHNLICHE MUSEEN. Munich's Center for Unusual Museums corrals such treasures as the Peddle-Car Museum, the Museum of Easter Rabbits, and the Chamberpot Museum. *(Westenriederstr. 41. S1-8 or streetcar #17-18 to Isartor. ☎290 41 21. Open daily 10am-6pm. €4, students €3.)*

🎵 🎭 ENTERTAINMENT AND NIGHTLIFE

Munich has world-class cultural cachet. Sixty theaters of various sizes are scattered throughout the city. Styles range from dramatic classics at the **Residenztheater** and **Volkstheater** to comic opera at the **Staatstheater am Gärtnerplatz** to experimental works at the **Theater im Marstall** in Nymphenburg. Munich also reveals a bohemian face in scores of small fringe theaters, cabaret stages, and art cinemas in **Schwabing**. *Monatsprogramm* (€1.50) and *Munich Found* (€3) both list schedules for Munich's stages, museums, and festivals. July sees a magnificent **opera festival** arrive at the **⬛Bayerische Staatsoper** (Bavarian National Theater), Max-Joseph-pl. 2. (Tickets ☎21 85 01, recorded info 21 85 19 19; www.bayerische.staatsoper.de. U3-6 to Odeonspl. or streetcar #19 to Nationaltheater. Standing-room and student tickets €4-10, sold 1hr. before performances. Box office open M-F 10am-6pm, Sa 10am-1pm. No performances Aug. to mid-Sept.)

Munich's nightlife is a curious conglomerate of Bavarian *Gemütlichkeit* (comfort, ease) and trendy cliquishness. A typical odyssey begins at a beer garden or beer hall, which will usually close before midnight. Cafes and bars keep the alcohol flowing, shutting off their taps at 1am (except Friday and Saturday nights). Discos and dance clubs, sedate before midnight, throb relentlessly until 4am. Trendy spots line **Leopoldstraße** in **Schwabing**. Many venues require comers to attempt the jaded hipster look, which doesn't mean shorts, sandals, and a t-shirt.

BEER GARDENS (BIERGÄRTEN)

Munich has six great labels: *Augustiner, Hacker-Pschorr, Hofbräu, Löwenbräu, Paulaner,* and *Spaten-Franziskaner.* Saying *"Ein Bier, bitte"* will order a *Maß* (liter; €4-6). Specify for only a *halb-Maß* (half-liter; €3-4).

⬛Augustinerkeller, Arnulfstr. 52. S1-8 to Hackerbrücke. Many view Augustinerkeller as Munich's finest *Biergarten* for its century-old chestnut trees and sharp Augustiner beer (*Maß* €6). Kitchen open daily 10am-1am. *Biergarten* open daily 10:30am-midnight.

Hirschgarten, Hirschgarten 1 (☎17 25 91). Streetcar #17 (dir.: Amalienburgstr.) to Romanpl. Seating 9000, Europe's largest *Biergarten* is boisterous but remote, near Schloß Nymphenburg. Entrees €5-15. *Maß* €5.50. Open daily 9am-midnight.

Hofbräuhaus, Platzl 9. Many tables are reserved for locals—some keep their personal steins in the hall's safe. *Maß* €6.40. *Weißwürste* €3.50. Open daily 9am-midnight.

BARS

🎵 **Café Reitschule,** Königinstr. 34. U3 or 6 to Giselastr. Overlooking a horseback-riding school. In summer a backyard *Biergarten* teems with students crowding under straw huts and around rose-filled fountains. *Weißbier* €3.20. Open daily 9am-1am.

Günther Murphy's, Nikolaistr. 9a. U3 or 6 to Giselastr. Irish cheer accompanies each plateful of Irish and American food (€6-15). A mostly English-speaking crowd. Guinness €4.40. Karaoke Su. Open M-Th 6pm-1am, F 6pm-3am, Sa noon-3am, Su noon-1am.

Sausalitos, Im Tal 16. U3 or S1-8 to Marienpl. A Mexican bar and restaurant jumping with crowds of 20-somethings. Drinks €6-9. Happy Hour 5-8pm. Open daily 11am-late.

CLUBS

Muffathalle, Zellstr. 4 (☎45 87 59 90), in Haidhausen. S1-8 to Rosenheimerpl. and walk down Rosenheimer Str. toward the river, or take streetcar #18 to Deutsches Museum. In a former power plant, Muffathalle now generates techno, hip-hop, and jazz. It also has a beer garden. Cover from €5. Open M-Sa 7pm-4am, Su 4pm-1am.

Backstage, Wilhelm-Hale Str. 16 (☎126 61 00; www.backstage-online.com). Streetcar #16 or 17 to Steubenpl. or #18 or 19 to Elsenheimerstr. An underground scene playing hardcore, indie rock and electronica. *Maß* €2 from 7-11pm. Check online or call for live concert listings. Open M-Th and Su 7pm-3am, F-Sa 7pm-5am.

Nachtleben, Maximilanstr. 34 (☎22 80 17 00). Once known as *Reich und Schön* (rich and beautiful), this is the place to be for the 18-25 crowd. Music veers between house and Top 40. Entry €5-8. Drinks €3-7. Open W 10pm-4am, F-Sa 10pm-6am.

GAY AND LESBIAN MUNICH

Gay nightlife thrives in Munich, despite Bavaria's reputation as unwelcoming to homosexuality. The gay scene centers in the **Glockenbachviertel,** stretching from south of Sendlinger Tor through the Viktualienmarkt/Gärtnerpl. area to the Isartor. *Our Munich,* a gay and lesbian leaflet, is available at the tourist office. *Sergej,* a magazine, is available at **Max&Milian Bookstore,** Ickstattstr. 2 (☎260 33 20; open M-F 10:30am-2pm and 3:30-8pm, Sa 11am-4pm) and other gay venues.

🎵 **Bei Carla,** Buttermelcherstr. 9. S1-8 to Isartor. Walk south on Zweibrückenstr., then turn right on Rumfordstr., left on Klenzestr., and left again onto Buttermelcherstr. A friendly lesbian cafe and bar. Open M-Sa 4pm-1am, Su 6pm-1am.

Soul City, Maximilianspl. 5, at the intersection with Max-Joseph-Str. Music ranges from 70s to Latin to techno at the biggest gay disco in Bavaria. Straights always welcome. Cover €5-13. Open W 9pm-late, Th and Sa 10pm-late, F 11pm-late, Su 7pm-midnight.

📍 DAYTRIP FROM MUNICH: DACHAU

"Arbeit Macht Frei" (Work Will Set You Free) was the first thing prisoners saw as they passed through the gate of the **Jourhaus** on the way into Dachau, where over 206,000 undesirables were interned between 1933 and 1945. Dachau was primarily a work camp, rather than a death camp like Auschwitz; knowing the Allies would not bomb prisoners, the SS reserved it for the construction of armaments. Once packed beyond capacity, the **barracks** now remain only as foundations, with the exception of two that were rebuilt as a reminder to future generations. Although Dachau has a gas chamber, it was never actually used, because the prisoners who built it worked slowly and purposely made mistakes in order to delay its completion. Surrounding walls, gates, and the crematorium were restored in 1962 and now form a sparse memorial to the victims. Located in the former administrative buildings, the **museum** examines pre-1930s anti-Semitism, the rise of Nazism, the establishment of the concentration camp

system, and the lives of prisoners through a gathering of photographs, documents, and other artifacts. Most exhibits have English captions; a lengthy guide (€26) translates the propaganda posters, SS files, documents, and letters. A **short film** (22min.) screens in English at 11:30am, 2, and 3:30pm. Displays in the **Bunker**, the former prison and torture chamber, chronicle prisoners' lives and the barbarism of SS guards. English **tours** leave from the museum. (2½hr. tours daily June-Aug. 1:30pm; Sept.-May Sa-Su 1:30pm. Free. Camp open Tu-Su 9am-5pm.) *(Take the S2, dir.: Petershausen, to Dachau. 20min., €4 or 4 stripes on the Streifenkarte. Then take bus #724, dir.: Krautgarten, or 726, dir.: Koperni- kusstr., to KZ-Gedenkstätte. 10min., €1 or 1 stripe on the Streifenkarte.)*

GARMISCH-PARTENKIRCHEN   ☎ 08821

Garmisch-Partenkirchen (pop. 28,000) is situated at the foot of the **Zugspitze** (2964m), Germany's highest peak. It should be attempted in fair weather; one way is to take the **cog railway** from the **Zugspitzbahnhof**, behind the main Garmisch station, to Eibsee (1¼hr., 1 per hr. 8:15am-3:15pm), then continue on the **Gletscherbahn** or even steeper **Eibsee Seilbahn** cable car to the top (1½hr., 1 per hr. 8am-3:15pm, round-trip with train and either cable car €43). Climbers can make the ascent in 10-12hr., but first should be sure they have the proper experience.

Trains run to Innsbruck (1½hr., 1 per hr., €10.40) and Munich (1½hr., 1 per hr., €14.20). **Buses** #1084 and 9606 run to Füssen (2hr., 6-7 per day, €7). To reach the **tourist office**, Richard-Strauss-Pl. 2, turn left on Bahnhofstr. from the train station and left again onto Von-Brug-Str.; it's the pink building on the square. The staff distributes maps and will help find rooms at no charge. (☎ 18 07 00. Open M-Sa 8am-6pm, Su 10am-noon.) To reach **◼Naturfreundehaus ❶**, Schalmeiweg 21, from the station, walk straight on Bahnhofstr. as it becomes Ludwigstr., follow the bend to the right and turn left on Sonnenbergstr., and continue as it becomes Prof.-Michael-Sachs-Str. and then Schalmeiweg (25min.). At this hostel, you can sleep in attic lofts with up to 16 other backpackers. (☎ 43 22. Kitchen use €0.50. Reception daily 6-8pm. 10- to 17-bed dorms €8; 3- to 5-bed rooms €10.) **Postal Code:** 82467.

THE CHIEMSEE   ☎ 08051

The region's storybook islands, forests, marshland, and crescent of mountains have drawn visitors for 2000 years. Today, prices have risen and the area has been overrun by resorts for the German *nouveaux riches*. Prien, the largest lake town, offers easy access to the neighboring resort paradises Aschau and Sachrang, the ski areas of the Kampenwand, and the surrounding curtain of mountains.

PRIEN AM CHIEMSEE. Located on the southwestern corner of the Chiemsee, Prien is a good base for exploring the islands. **Trains** depart from the station, a few blocks from the city center, for Munich (1hr., 1 per hr., €12.90) and Salzburg (50min., 1 per hr., €9). **Ferries** run to Herreninsel and Fraueninsel (every 40min. 7:15am-7:30pm, €6-7). To get to the ferry port, turn right from the main entrance of the Prien train station and follow Seestr. for 15min., or at the station hop on the green 19th-century Chiemseebahn steam train (1 per hr. 10am-6pm, round-trip €3). The **tourist office**, Alte Rathausstr. 11, distributes free maps and books private rooms for free. (☎ 690 50; www.prien.chiemsee.de. Open M-F 8:30am-6pm, Sa 8:30am-noon.) Convenient **Jugendherberge (HI) ❷**, Carl-Braun-Str. 66, has cheap beds 10min. from the lake. Turn right from the station, right again onto Seestr., and continue under the overpass; then turn left on Staudenstr., which becomes Carl-Braun-Str. (☎ 687 70. Reception 8-9am, 5-7pm, and 9:30-10pm. Open early Feb.-Nov. 4- to 6-bed dorms €15.90.) To reach **Campingplatz Hofbauer ❶**, Bernauerstr. 110, turn left on Seestr., left again at the next intersection, and then walk 25min. along Bernauerstr. (☎ 41 36. Showers included. Reception 7:30-11am and 2-8pm. Open Apr.-Oct. €5.30 per person, under 15 €2.70. Surcharge of €5.10 per site.)

GERMANY

HERRENINSEL AND FRAUENINSEL. Ludwig's palace on ▨**Herreninsel** (Gentlemen's Island), **Königsschloß Herrenchiemsee,** is a depressed and deluded king's attempt to build a residence larger and more extravagant than Louis XIV's Versailles. Ludwig bankrupted Bavaria building this place—a few unfinished rooms, abandoned after funds ran out, contrast greatly with the completed portion of the castle. (Open daily Apr.-Sept. 9am-6pm; Oct. 9:40am-5pm; Nov.-Mar. 9:40am-4pm. Mandatory tour €5.50, students €4.50.) **Fraueninsel** (Ladies' Island) is home to the **Klosterkirche** (cloister church), the nunnery that complemented the monastery on Herreninsel. The nuns make their own marzipan, beeswax candles, and five kinds of liqueur, all sold in the convent shop. The 8th-century Cross of Bischofhofen and other artifacts are displayed in the Michaelskapelle above the **Torhalle** (gate), the oldest surviving part of the cloister. (Open daily May-Oct. 11am-5pm. €1.50.)

BERCHTESGADEN   ☎08652

Travelers are drawn to Berchtesgaden's natural beauty and to Hitler's well-known mountaintop retreat, the **Kehlsteinhaus.** Now a restaurant, the stone resort house has a spectacular view from the 1834m peak. From the train station, take bus #38 to Kehlstein Busabfahrt (every 30min. 6:45am-6:25pm); then buy a ticket to the summit from the cashier's desk. (Open daily May-Oct.) **Trains** run every hr. to Munich (3hr., €15) and Salzburg (1hr., €6.90). The **tourist office,** Königsseerstr. 2, opposite the station, has tips on **hiking** trails in the Berchtesgaden National Park. (☎96 71 50. Open mid-June to Oct. M-F 8:30am-6pm, Sa 9am-5pm, Su 9am-3pm; Nov. to mid-June M-F 8:30am-5pm, Sa 9am-noon.) To reach the **Jugendherberge (HI) ❷,** Gebirgsjägerstr. 52, turn right from the station, left on Ramsauer Str., right on Gmundbrücke, and left up the steep gravel path. Bus #39 (dir.: Strub Kaserne) works as well. (☎943 70. Check-in until 10pm. Curfew midnight. Closed Nov.-Dec. 26. Dorms €16.) Dirt-cheap **Express-Grill Hendl ❶,** Maximilianstr. 8, serves traditional Bavarian food. (Open daily 11am-9:30pm.) There is an **Edeka** supermarket at Königsseerstr. 22. (Open M-F 7:30am-6pm, Sa 7:30am-noon.) **Postal Code:** 83471.

▨ **HIKING NEAR BERCHTESGADEN.** From Berchtesgaden, the 5½km path to the **Königssee**—which winds through fields of flowers, across bubbling brooks, and past several beer gardens—affords a heart-stopping view of the Alps. From the train station, cross the street, turn right, and take a quick left over the bridge. Pass the green-roofed building to the right, do not ascend the hill, and take a left onto the gravel path near the stone wall; then follow the signs marked "Königssee." Or, take bus #41 from the bus station to Königssee (1 per hr., round-trip €3.70). After arriving in Königssee, walk down Seestr. and look for the **National-park Informationstelle** to your left, which has hiking info. To explore the **Berchtesgaden National Park,** take bus #46 from Berchtesgaden (30min., 2 per hr., €2.50). Get off at Neuhausenbrücke in Ramsau, and head to the **tourist office,** Im Tal 2, for hiking maps. (☎08657 98 89 20; www.ramsau.de. Open July-Sept. M-Sa 8am-noon and 1:15-5pm, Su 9am-noon and 2-5pm; Oct.-June M-F 8am-noon and 1:15-5pm.)

PASSAU   ☎0851

Baroque arches cast long shadows across the cobblestone alleys of Passau (pop. 51,000), a two-millennium-old city situated at the confluence of the Danube, the Inn, and the Ilz rivers. Passau's capstone is the Baroque **Stephansdom,** Dompl., where the world's largest church organ, with 17,774 pipes, looms above the choir. (Open daily in summer 6:30am-7pm; low season 6:30am-6pm. Free. Organ concerts May-Oct. M-F noon, Th also 7:30pm. €3-5, students €1-3.) Behind the cathedral is the **Residenz,** home to the **Domschatz,** an extravagant collection of tapestries and gold. (Enter through the back of the Stephansdom, to the right of the altar. Open Easter-Oct. M-Sa 10am-4pm. €1.50, students €0.50.) Various floods have left their high-water marks on the outer wall of the 13th-century Gothic **Rathaus**. (Open daily Apr.-Oct. 10am-4pm. Free.) Over the Luitpoldbrücke is the former palace of the bishopric, now home to the **Cultural History Museum**. (Open early Apr.-Oct. M-F 9am-5pm, Sa-Su 10am-6pm; Nov.-Mar. Tu-Su 9am-5pm. €5, students €3.)

Trains run to: Frankfurt (4½hr., every 2hr., €50); Munich (2hr., every 2hr., €15); Nuremberg (2hr., every 2hr., €15); Regensburg (1-2hr., 1 per hr., €15); and Vienna (3½hr., 1 per hr., €32). To reach the **tourist office**, Rathauspl. 3, take Bahnhofstr. to Ludwigspl., then bear left downhill to Ludwigstr., which changes its name before becoming Große Messerg.; turn onto Schusterg., then left on Schrottg. (☎95 59 80. Open Easter to mid-Oct. M-F 8:30am-6pm, Sa-Su 9am-4pm; low season M-Th 8:30am-5pm, F 8:30am-4pm.) In a castle high above the Danube, the **Jugendherberge (HI) ❷**, Veste Oberhaus 125, is 30min. from the station. Cross the bridge downstream from the Rathaus and follow the signs. (☎49 37 80. Dorms €17.30.) **Pension Rößner ❸**, Bräug. 19, is more central. (☎93 13 50; www.pension-roessner.de. Singles €35; doubles €50-60.) Cheap eateries can be found near **Innstraße**, parallel to the Inn River. Get baked goods, sandwiches, and salads at **Schmankerl Passage**, Ludwigstr. 6. (Open M-F 7:30am-6pm, Sa 7:30am-4pm.) **Norma** supermarket is at Bahnhofstr. 16b. (Open M-F 8:30am-7pm, Sa 8am-2pm.) **Postal Code:** 94032.

REGENSBURG   ☎0941

Regensburg (pop. 127,000) teems with students and places that feed, souse, and engage them in their idle hours. Per square meter, the city may have more cafes and bars than any other in Europe. Richly colored stained glass dazzles at the **Dom St. Peter**. Inside, the **Domschatz** reliquary displays jewelry purchased by bishops, as well as the preserved hand of Bishop Chrysostomus, who died in AD 407. (Open daily Apr.-Oct. 6:30am-6pm; Nov.-Mar. 6:30am-5pm. Free.) A few blocks away, the **Rathaus** served as the parliament of the Holy Roman Empire until 1803. Downriver from Regensburg, **Walhalla** is an imitation Parthenon honoring Ludwig I's favorite Germans. Take the ferry or bus #5 from Albertspl. to Donaustauf Walhallastr. ◪**Historische Wurstküche**, Thundorfer Str., an 850-year-old beer garden, is ideal for sipping brew (0.5L €2.60) while watching ships on the Danube. Check campus bulletins for student parties. **Cafe Felix**, Fröhliche-Türken-Str. 6, tosses salads (€7-9) with pineapple and prawns. (Open M-Sa 9am-1am, Su 10am-1pm.)

Trains to: Munich (1½hr., 1 per hr., €15); Nuremberg (1½hr., 1-2 per hr., €14.20); and Passau (1½hr., 1 per hr., €15). The **tourist office** is in the Altes Rathaus. From the station, walk down Maximilianstr., turn left on Grasg., then right Obere Bachg.; follow it five blocks. (☎507 44 10. Open M-F 9:15am-6pm, Sa 9:15am-4pm; Apr.-Oct. also Su until 4pm.) From the station, to reach the **Jugendherberge (HI) ❷**, Wöhrdstr. 60, walk to the end of Maximilianstr., turn right on Pflugg., then left at the "*Optik*" sign onto tiny Erhardig.; follow it to the end, descend the steps, turn left over the bridge, then right onto Wöhrdstr. Or, take bus #3, 8, or 9. (☎574 02. Dorms €18.50.) The **Galeria Kaufhof** on Neupfarrpl. has a basement supermarket. (Open M-Sa 9am-8pm.) **Postal Code:** 93047.

NUREMBERG (NÜRNBERG)   ☎0911

Knowing it hosted Imperial Diets in the first *Reich*, Hitler chose Nuremberg (pop. 491,000) for his massive Nazi rallies. After the war, it became the site of the postwar tribunals. New generations have rechristened Nuremberg *Stadt der Menschenrechte* (City of Human Rights). Locally the city is known more for its Christmas market, toy fairs, sausages, and gingerbread than for its politics.

GERMANY

⌐⊒ **TRANSPORTATION AND PRACTICAL INFORMATION.** **Trains** go to: Berlin (5hr., every 2hr., €71); Frankfurt (2½hr., 2 per hr., €40); Munich (1½hr., 2 per hr., €38); and Stuttgart (2hr., every 2hr., €31). DB Reisezentrum, located in the central hall of the station, sells tickets. (Open M-F 6am-9pm, Sa-Su 8am-9pm.) The **tourist office**, Königstr. 93, books rooms for free. Walk through the tunnel from the station to the Altstadt and take a right. (☎ 233 61 31. Open M-Sa 9am-7pm.) **Internet** is available at **Tele Point** on the underground level of the train station. (€2 per hr. Open M-Sa 9am-11pm, Su 10am-11pm.) **Postal Code:** 90402.

⌐□ **ACCOMMODATIONS AND FOOD.** **⊠Jugendgästehaus (HI) ❷**, Burg 2, is in a castle above the city. From the tourist office, follow Königstr. through Lorenzerpl. and over the bridge to the Hauptmarkt, head left, and turn right onto Burgstr. (☎230 93 60. Internet €2.40 per 30min. Dorms €20.) Inside the city walls, **Hotel Garni Probst ❸**, Luitpoldstr. 9, includes a generous breakfast with rooms. (☎249 40. Singles €21, with shower €35-40, with bath €41-51; doubles €43/€57-67.) In the southwestern corner of the Altstadt, **Zum Gulden Stern ❸**, Zirkelschmiedgasse 26, is the world's oldest bratwurst kitchen. (6 for €6. Open daily 11am-10pm.) **Sushi Glas ❹**, Kornmarkt 7, by the National Museum, attracts a yuppie crowd. (Open M-W noon-11pm, Th-Sa noon-midnight, Su 6-11pm.) **Edeka** supermarket, Hauptmarkt 12, is near the Frauenkirche. (Open M-F 8:30am-7pm, Sa 8am-3pm.)

◙⊞ **SIGHTS AND ENTERTAINMENT.** Allied bombing left little of old Nuremberg for posterity, but its churches, castle, and other buildings have been reconstructed. The walled-in **Handwerkerhof** near the station is more mall than medieval; head up Königstr. for the real sights. Take a detour to the left for the pillared **Straße der Menschenrechte** (Avenue of Human Rights) as well as the gleaming glass **Germanisches Nationalmuseum,** Kartäuserg. 1, which chronicles German art since prehistoric times. (Open Tu-Su 10am-6pm, W 10am-9pm. €5, students €4. W 6-9pm free.) Across the river is the **Hauptmarktplatz,** site of the annual **Christmas market.** Walk uphill to the **Rathaus;** the **Lochgefängnisse** (dungeons) beneath contain medieval torture instruments. (Open Tu-Su 10am-4:30pm. Required tours every 30min. €2, students €1.) Atop the hill, the **Kaiserburg** (Fortress of the Holy Roman Emperor), has the best vantage point for a view of the city. (Open daily Apr.-Sept. 9am-6pm; Oct.-Mar. 10am-4pm. Required tours every 30min. €6, students €5.) The Nazi Party Congress held rallies on the **Reichsparteitagsgelände,** now in ruins. Throngs gathered to hear Hitler on the far side of the lake at the **Tribüne,** a marble platform. An exhibit in the ⊠**Kongresshalle,** at the northern end of the park, details the era. (Open M-F 9am-6pm, Sa-Su 10am-6pm. €5, students €2.50.) To reach the park, take S2 (dir.: Feucht/Altdorf) to Dutzendteich, then take the middle exit, descend the stairs, and turn left. Walk past the lake on your left, turn left, then turn right to reach the Kongresshalle. Nazi leaders faced Allied judges during the Nuremberg war crimes trials in room 600 of the **Justizgebäude,** Fürtherstr. 110. (U1 to Bärenschanze. English tours Sa-Su 1, 2, 3, and 4pm. €2, students €1.)

Nuremberg's nightspots cluster in the Altstadt, especially by the river in the west. **Cine Città,** Gewerbemuseumspl. 3, packs in 16 bars and cafes, 17 cinemas, an IMAX, and a disco. (U-Bahn to Wöhrder Wiese. Open M-Th and Su until 3am, F-Sa until 4am.) **Wies'n Biergarten,** on Johann Sörgel Weg in the Wöhrder Wiese, is next to a gigantic grass field where students pretend to study. (Open daily May-Sept. 10am-10pm.) **Frizz,** Weißgerberg. 37, swings to oldies and 80s rock. (Cover €3. Open M and Th 8pm-2am, F-Sa 8pm-4am.) **Cartoon,** An der Sparkasse 6, is a popular gay bar near Lorenzpl. (0.4L beer €3. Open M-Sa 11am-1am, Su 2pm-1am.)

ROMANTIC ROAD

Groomed fields of sunflowers and wheat, vineyards, rolling hills, and dense forests checker the landscape between Würzburg and Füssen. Its beauty was not lost on the German tourist industry, which christened the area the Romantic Road (*Romantische Straße*) in 1950; it's now the most traveled route in Germany.

⌐⌐ TRANSPORTATION

Train travel is the most flexible and economical way to see the Romantic Road. Europabus also has a variety of routes; up-to-date reservations and schedule info can be found at www.touring.de or www.romantischestrasse.de. (10% student and under-26 discount, 60% Eurail and German Railpass discount.)

ROTHENBURG OB DER TAUBER　　　☎ 09861

Possibly the only walled medieval city without a single modern building, Rothenburg (pop. 12,000) is *the* Romantic Roadstop. After the Thirty Years' War, it had no money to modernize and remained unchanged for 250 years. During the war, the conquering general promised not to raze the town if a local could chug a wine keg (3.25L). The mayor himself met the challenge, then passed out for days. In 2005 the **Meistertrunk** will be reenacted May 13-16, Sept. 4, and Oct. 1 and 8; an alternate version takes place every hour by the clock over the Marktpl. For other tidbits of Rothenburg history, take the English tour led by the ▓**night watchman,** which starts from the Rathaus on Marktpl. (Easter-Christmas daily 8pm. €4.) Climb the 60m **Rathaus tower** for a panoramic view of the town. (Open Apr.-Oct. daily 9:30am-12:30pm and 1:30-5pm; Nov. and Jan.-Mar. Sa-Su noon-3pm; Dec. daily noon-3pm. €1.) Anyone who can stomach iron-maiden justice should inspect the torture instruments at the ▓**Medieval Crime Museum,** Burgg. 3-5. (Open daily Apr.-Oct. 9:30am-6pm; Nov. and Jan.-Feb. 2-4pm; Dec. and Mar. 10am-4pm. Last entry 45min. before closing. €3.50, students €2.40.) Alternatively, head to the more anodyne **Weihnachtsdorf** (Christmas Village), Herrng. 1, for a Christmas museum documenting the history of gift-giving. (Open Apr.-Dec. daily 10am-6pm; Jan.-Mar. Sa-Su 10am-5pm. €4, students €2.50.)

　　Trains run to Steinach (15min., 1 per hr., €1.80), which has transfers to Munich and Würzburg. The **Europabus** leaves from the Busbahnhof by the train station. The **tourist office,** Marktpl. 2, books rooms and offers free **Internet** access. (☎ 404 92. Open May-Oct. M-F 9am-noon and 1-6pm, Sa-Su 10am-3pm; Nov.-Apr. M-F 9am-noon and 1-5pm, Sa 10am-1pm.) **Gasthof Goldene Rose ❸,** Spitalgasse 28, has cheery, spacious rooms on the main street. (☎ 09861 46 38. Singles €21-23; doubles €36, with bath €41-62.) **Postal Code:** 91541.

WÜRZBURG　　　☎ 0931

The university town of Würzburg is surrounded by vineyard slopes and bisected by the Main River. In 1895, Wilhelm Conrad Röntgen discovered X-rays here and was awarded the first Nobel Prize. Inside the striking **Fortress Marienburg** are the 11th-century **Marienkirche,** the 40m **Bergfried watchtower,** above the Hole of Fear dungeon, and the **Fürstengarten,** built to resemble a ship. Outside the fortress, the old castle arsenal now houses the **Mainfränkisches Museum,** a collection of wooden sculptures by late Gothic master Tillman Riemenschneider. (Bus #9 from the station to Festung, or a 20min. walk up the hill. Tours Apr.-Oct. Tu-F 11am, 2, and 3pm, Sa-Su every hr. 10am-4pm except noon. €3, students €2.50. Museum open Apr.-Oct. Tu-Su 10am-6pm; Nov.-Mar. 10am-4pm. €3.) The **Residenz** houses the largest ceiling fresco in the world, which is under

GERMANY

restoration until 2006. Inside, see the Baroque gilded moldings and pink marble of the **Residenzhofkirche**. (Open daily Apr. to mid-Oct. 9am-6pm; mid-Oct. to Mar. 10am-4pm. €4, students €3. English tours Sa-Su.)

Trains run to: Frankfurt (1hr., 1 per hr., €14); Munich (3hr., 1 per hr., €15); Nuremberg (1hr., 1 per hr., €15); and Rothenburg ob der Tauber (1hr., 1 per hr., €10). The **tourist office**, in a yellow building on Marktpl., has maps and room info. (☎0931 37 23 98. Open Apr.-Dec. M-F 10am-6pm, Sa 10am-2pm; May-Oct. M-F and Su 10am-2pm; Jan.-Mar. M-F 10am-4pm, Sa 10am-1pm.) **Postal Code:** 97070.

FÜSSEN   ☎08362

Given the little town's position at the foot of the Romantic Road and in the foothills of the Bavarian Alps, its name, Füssen (feet), is apt. Füssen's main attraction is its proximity to Ludwig's famed **Königsschlösser** (below), best seen as daytrips. Inside the town, the inner walls of the **Hohes Schloß** (High Castle) courtyard feature arresting *trompe-l'oeil* windows and towers, and the **Staatsgalerie** in the castle collects regional art. (Open Apr.-Oct. Tu-Su 11am-4pm; Nov.-Mar. Tu-Su 2-4pm. €2.50, students €2.) Inside the **Annakapelle**, macabre paintings depict everyone from the Pope to the smallest child caught up in the *Totentanz* (dance of death), a frenzy of despair that overtook Europe during the plague. (Open Apr.-Oct. Tu-Su 10am-5pm; Nov.-Mar. Tu-Su 1-4pm. €2.50, students €2.)

Trains run to Munich (2hr., every 2hr., €18.20). Füssen can also be reached by bus #1084 or 9606 from Garmisch-Partenkirchen (2¼hr.; M-F 5 per day; €7.20 with a *Tagesticket*, bought on the bus). To reach the **tourist office** from the train station, Kaiser-Maximilian-Pl. 1, walk the length of Bahnhofstr. and head across the rotary to the big yellow building on your left; the staff sells hiking maps (€3-7) and finds rooms for no commission. (☎08362 93 85 32. Open in summer M-F 8:30am-6pm, Sa 10am-1pm; low season M-F 9am-5pm, Sa 10am-noon.) **Postal Code:** 87629.

KÖNIGSSCHLÖßER (ROYAL CASTLES)

King Ludwig II, a lunatic visionary and fervent Wagner fan, used his cash to build fantastic castles. In 1886, a band of nobles and bureaucrats deposed Ludwig, declared him insane, and imprisoned him; three days later, the king and a loyal advisor were mysteriously discovered dead in a nearby lake. The fairy-tale castles that framed Ludwig's life and the enigma of his death still captivate tourists today. Glitzy ◪**Schloß Neuschwanstein** inspired Disney's Cinderella Castle. Its completed chambers—63 remain unfinished—include a Byzantine throne room, an artificial grotto, and an immense *Sängersaal* (singer's hall) built expressly for Wagnerian operas. Hike 10min. up to **Marienbrücke,** a bridge that spans the gorge and waterfall behind the castle, for the fairy godmother of all views. Ludwig aestivated in the bright yellow, neo-Gothic **Schloß Hohenschwangau** across the valley. (Both open daily Apr.-Sept. 9am-6pm; Oct.-Mar. 10am-4pm. Mandatory tours each €9, students €8. Combination ticket €17/€15.) Tickets can be purchased at the **Ticket-Service Center**, Alpseestr. 12, about 100m uphill from the Hohenschwangau bus stop. Arrive early to avoid lines.

Depart from the Füssen train station on **bus** #73 or 78, marked "Königsschlösser" (10min., 2 per hr., €1.40). It will drop you in front of the **info booth.** (Open daily 9am-6pm.) Separate paths lead up to Hohenschwangau and Neuschwanstein. A *Tagesticket* (€5.60, bought on the bus) provides a day's worth of regional bus use.

GREECE (Έλλας)

A land where sacred monasteries are mountainside fixtures, 3hr. seaside siestas are standard issue, and circle dancing and drinking until daybreak is a summer rite: Greece's treasures are impossibly varied. Renaissance men long before their time, the ancient Greeks sprung to prominence with their philosophical, literary, artistic, and athletic mastery. Millennia later, children still dream of Hercules and Medusa; when those youngsters grow up, they hanker for Greece's island beaches, free-flowing booze, and gorgeous natural landscapes that were once the playground for a pantheon of gods. The all-encompassing Greek lifestyle is a frustratingly delicious mix of high speed and sun-inspired lounging, as old men hold lively debates in town *plateias*, young kids zoom on mopeds around the clock, and unpredictable schedules force a go-with-the-flow take on life.

 DISCOVER GREECE: SUGGESTED ITINERARIES

THREE DAYS Spend it all in **Athens** (p. 509). Roam the **Acropolis**, gaze at the treasures of the **National Archaeological Museum**, and pay homage to the gods at the fabulous **Parthenon**. Visit the ancient Athenian **Agora** and the **Roman Agora**, then take a quick trip down to **Poseidon's Temple** at Cape Sounion.

ONE WEEK Begin your week with a sojourn in **Athens** (3 days). Move on to **Corinth** to wander through the 6th-century **Temple of Apollo** (1 day; p. 523). Sprint to **Olympia** to see where the games began—check out the immense **Temple of Zeus** (1 day; p. 520). Take the ferry to **Corfu** (1 day; p. 529) and then soak up Byzantine history in **Thessaloniki** (1 day; p. 524). Ask the **Oracle of Delphi** how to top off your week (1 day; p. 519).

BEST OF GREECE, THREE WEEKS Explore **Athens** (4 days) before strolling among the mansions of **Nafplion** (1 day; p. 522). Race west to **Olympia** (1 day), and then take a ferry from **Patras** to the immortalized beaches of **Corfu** (2 days). Back on the mainland, wander the streets of **Thessaloniki** (2 days), and then climb to the cliffside monasteries of **Meteora** (1 day; p. 528). Be sure to consult the gods at **Mount Olympus** (1 day; p. 527) and the **Oracle of Delphi** (1 day). A ferry from Athens to **Crete** (3 days; p. 536) will let you discover Europe's largest gorge. Seek respite on **Santorini** (1 day; p. 535), debauchery on **Ios** (1 day; p. 535), and suntanning on **Mykonos** (1 day; p. 532). Finally, repent at the famous temples on **Delos** (1 day; p. 533).

ESSENTIALS

WHEN TO GO

June through August is high season in Greece; consider visiting during May, early June, or September, when gorgeous weather smiles on thinner crowds. In ski areas, winter brings another high season: You can hit the slopes at Mt. Parnassos, Kalavrita, or Karpenisi. The low season brings cheaper lodgings and food prices, but many sights and accommodations have shorter hours or close altogether. Ferries, buses, and trains run considerably less frequently, and life is quieter.

Greece

DOCUMENTS AND FORMALITIES

VISAS. Citizens of Australia, Canada, Ireland, New Zealand, the UK, and the US do not need a visa for entrance into Greece. A work permit is needed for employment. Study in Greece requires a special visa.

EMBASSIES. Foreign embassies in Greece are in Athens (p. 509). For Greek embassies at home, contact: **Australia,** 9 Turrana St., Yarralumla, Canberra, ACT 2600 (☎2 6273 3011); **Canada,** 80 MacLaren St., Ottawa, ON K2P 0K6 (☎613-238-6271; www.greekembassy.ca); **Ireland,** 1 Upper Pembroke St., Dublin 2 (☎1 676 7254); **New Zealand,** 5-7 Willeston St., 10th fl., Box 24066, Wellington (☎4 473 7775); **UK,** 1a Holland Park, London W11 3TP (☎020 7229 3850; www.greekembassy.org.uk); and **US,** 2221 Massachusetts Ave. N.W., Washington, D.C. 20008 (☎202-939-1300; www.greekembassy.org).

TRANSPORTATION

BY PLANE. The domestic service offered by **Olympic Airways,** Syngrou 96-100, Athens 11741 (☎210 926 9111; www.olympicairlines.com), has increased greatly. Their website lists info for every office around the globe. A 1hr. flight from Athens

(€60-90) can get you to almost any island in Greece. Even in the low season, remote destinations are serviced several times per week, while developed areas may have several flights per day.

BY TRAIN. Greece is served by a number of international train routes that connect Athens, Larisa, and Thessaloniki to most European cities. Train service within Greece, however, is limited and sometimes uncomfortable, and no lines go to the western coast. The new express, air-conditioned intercity trains, while slightly more expensive and infrequent, are worth the price. **Eurail** passes are valid on all Greek trains. **Hellenic Railways Organization** (OSE; www.osenet.gr) connects Athens to major Greek cities; from Greece, call ☎ 210 529 7777 for schedules and prices.

BY BUS. There are almost no buses running directly from any European city to Greece. **Busabout,** 258 Vauxhall Bridge Rd., London SW1V 1BS (☎ 0207 950 1661; www.busabout.com), is one of the few European bus companies that runs to Greece. Domestic bus service is extensive and fares are cheap. **KTEL** (www.ktel.org) runs most domestic buses; always check with an official source about scheduled departures, as posted schedules are often outdated.

BY FERRY. The most popular way of getting to Greece is by ferry from Italy. Boats travel from Brindisi, Italy, to Corfu (p. 530), Kephalonia (p. 530), and Patras (p. 520) and from Ancona, Italy, to Corfu and Patras. Ferries also run from Greece to various points on the Turkish coast. There is frequent ferry service to the Greek islands, but schedules are irregular and faulty information is common. Check schedules posted at the tourist office or the port police, or at www.ferries.gr. Make reservations and arrive at least 1-2hr. before your departure time. **Flying Dolphins** (www.dolphins.gr) provides extensive hydrofoil service between the islands at twice the cost and speed as ferries.

BY CAR AND MOPED. Ferries charge a transport fee for cars. Rental agencies may quote low daily rates that exclude the 18% tax and **Collision Damage Waiver (CDW)** insurance; expect to pay €30-60 per day for a rental. Foreign drivers are required to have an **International Driving Permit** and an **International Insurance Certificate** to drive in Greece. The **Automobile and Touring Club of Greece (ELPA),** Messogion 395, Athens 11527, provides assistance and offers reciprocal membership to foreign auto club members. (☎ 210 606 8800. 24hr. emergency roadside assistance ☎ 104. Info line for Athens ☎ 174, elsewhere 210 606 8838. Open M-F 7am-3pm.) **Mopeds** can be great for exploring, but they also make you extremely vulnerable to the carelessness of other drivers; wear a helmet.

TOP TEN PLACES TO MEET A GREEK GOD

There once was a time when dinosaurs, centaurs, and gods roamed the earth. Now, finding the divine is hard, but if Hermes, the god of travel, doesn't befriend you, some other deity just might.

1. Visit the active volcanoes of **Nisyros** (p. 540) and **Santorini** (p. 535) to view the forge of Hephaestus, god of fire.

2. Run through the **Vikos Gorge** (p. 529) in search of Artemis, protectress of the woods.

3. Mykonos (p. 532) will put you in the alcoholic stupor needed for bonding with the wine god Dionysus, though **Ios** (p. 535) will do just as well.

4. Seek Athena's wisdom at none other than her patron city, **Athens** (p. 509), or try **Ithaka** (p. 531), home of one of her favorites, Odysseus.

5. Corfu's **Canal d'Amour** (p. 530) might help you find Aphrodite, or a mortal replacement.

6. Longing for Death? A hike through Crete's **Valley of Death** (p. 539) might lead you to Hades.

7. His oracle at **Delphi** (p. 519) or sanctuary at **Delos** (p. 533) will surely allow you to encounter Apollo.

8. Lesvos (p. 541), home of the tenth Muse, Sappho, is a good place to seek the other nine.

9. If you don't meet him on a ferry, find Poseidon at his temple on **Cape Sounion** (p. 518).

10. Mt. Olympus (p. 527). Duh.

TOURIST SERVICES AND MONEY

EMERGENCY	Police: ☎ 100. Hospital: ☎ 106. Ambulance: ☎ 166.

TOURIST OFFICES. Tourism in Greece is overseen by two national organizations: **Greek National Tourist Organization (GNTO)** and the **tourist police** (*touristiki astinomia*). The GNTO, Tsochas 7, Athens (☎ 210 870 7000. www.gnto.gr), known as the **EOT** in Greece, can supply general information about sights and accommodations throughout the country. The tourist police deal with local and immediate problems: bus schedules, accommodations, lost passports, etc. They are open long hours and are willing to help, but their English may be limited.

MONEY. The official currency of Greece is the **euro (€)**. For exchange rates and more information on the euro, see p. 20. If you're carrying more than €1000 in cash when you enter Greece, you must declare it upon entry. A bare-bones day in Greece costs €30-40. A day with more comforts runs €40-50. There is no **tipping** anywhere except restaurants and taxis. Generally, **bargaining** is expected for street wares and in other informal venues, but shop owners whose goods are tagged will consider bargaining rude and disrespectful. The European Union imposes a **Value Added Tax (VAT)** on goods and services purchased within the EU, which is included in the price. For more info, see p. 22.

COMMUNICATION

PHONE CODES	**Country code: 30. International dialing prefix: 00.** The city code must always be dialed, even when calling from within the city. From outside Greece, dial int'l dialing prefix (see inside back cover) + 30 + local number.

TELEPHONES. Payphones in Greece use prepaid phone cards. You can buy the cards at *peripteros* (streetside kiosks) in denominations of €3, €12, and €25. Time is measured in minutes or talk units (100 units equals 30min. of domestic calling). A calling card is the cheapest way to make international phone calls. To place a call with a calling card, contact your service provider's Greek operator. Cell phones are an increasingly popular option; for more info, see p. 35.

MAIL. To send a letter anywhere from Greece weighing up to 20g costs €0.65. Mail sent to Greece from the continent generally takes at least three days to arrive; from Australia, New Zealand, and the US airmail will take up to two weeks. Address mail to be held according to the following example: Firstname SURNAME, Corfu Town Post Office, Corfu, Greece 8900, POSTE RESTANTE.

INTERNET ACCESS. The availability of the Internet in Greece is rapidly expanding. In all big cities, most small cities and large towns, and on most islands, you'll be able to find Internet access. Expect to pay €3-6 per hour. For lists of cybercafes in Greece, check out http://dmoz.org/Computers/Internet/Cybercafes/Greece/.

ACCOMMODATIONS AND CAMPING

GREECE	❶	❷	❸	❹	❺
ACCOMMODATIONS	under €15	€15-25	€25-35	€35-70	above €70

Lodgings in Greece are a bargain. Tourist offices usually maintain lists of inexpensive accommodations. A bed in a **hostel** averages around €9. Those not currently endorsed by HI are in most cases still safe and reputable. In many areas,

domatia (rooms to let) are an attractive and dependable option. Often you'll be approached by locals as you enter town or disembark from your boat, a practice that is common but illegal. Prices vary; expect to pay €16-32 for a single and €35-45 for a double. Always negotiate with *domatia* owners before settling on a price, and never pay more than you would for a hotel in town. If in doubt, ask the tourist police; they may set you up with a room and conduct the negotiations themselves. **Hotel** prices are regulated, but proprietors may try to push you to take the most expensive room. Budget hotels start at €15 for singles and €25 for doubles. Check your bill carefully, and threaten to contact the tourist police if you think you are being cheated. Greece hosts plenty of official **campgrounds**, which run €4-6 per person, plus €3 per tent.

FOOD AND DRINK

GREECE	❶	❷	❸	❹	❺
FOOD	under €3	€3-8	€8-15	€15-25	above €25

Penny-pinching carnivores will thank Zeus for lamb, chicken, or pork *souvlaki*, stuffed into a pita to make *gyros* (yee-RO). Vegetarians can also eat their fill on the cheap, with *horiatiki* (Greek salad) and savory pastries like *tiropita* (cheese pie) and *spanakopita* (spinach and feta pie). Frothy, iced coffee *frappés* take the edge off the summer heat. *Ouzo* (a powerful, licorice-flavored spirit) is served with *mezedes* (snacks of octopus, cheese, and sausage). Breakfast, served only in the early morning, is generally very simple: a piece of toast with *marmelada* or a pastry. Lunch, a hearty and leisurely meal, can begin as early as noon but is more likely eaten sometime between 2 and 5pm. Dinner is a drawn-out, relaxed affair served late. A Greek restaurant is known as a *taverna* or *estiatorio;* a grill is a *psistaria*. Many restaurants don't offer printed menus.

HOLIDAYS AND FESTIVALS

Holidays: Feast of St. Basil/New Year's Day (Jan. 1); Epiphany (Jan. 6); Clean Monday, 1st day of Lent (Mar. 14); Greek Independence Day (Mar. 25); St. George's Day (Apr. 23); Easter (May 1); Labor Day (May 1); Ascension (June 9); Pentecost (June 19); Feast of the Assumption of the Virgin Mary (Aug. 15); The Virgin Mary's Birthday (Sept. 8); Feast of St. Demetrius (Oct. 26); Ohi Day (Oct. 28); Christmas Day (Dec. 25).

Festivals: 3 weeks of Carnival feasting and dancing (starting Feb. 21) precede Lenten fasting. April 23 is St. George's Day, when Greece honors the dragon-slaying knight with horse races, wrestling matches, and dances. The Feast of St. Demetrius (Oct. 26) is celebrated with particular enthusiasm in Thessaloniki.

FACTS AND FIGURES: GREECE

Official Name: Hellenic Republic.
Capital: Athens.
Major Cities: Thessaloniki.
Population: 10,600,000.

Land Area: 131,940 sq. km.
Time: GMT+2.
Language: Greek.
Religion: Eastern Orthodox (98%).

ATHENS Αθήνα ☎210

Athens is a newly transformed city. For the 2004 Summer Olympic Games, Greece's capital underwent an extensive metamorphosis. Tremendous pride and support for the modernization effort coexisted with anti-Olympic parades and anti-Western marches that snaked through the capital, leaving trails of black graffiti in their wake. Still, amid this swift transformation, many of the elements that

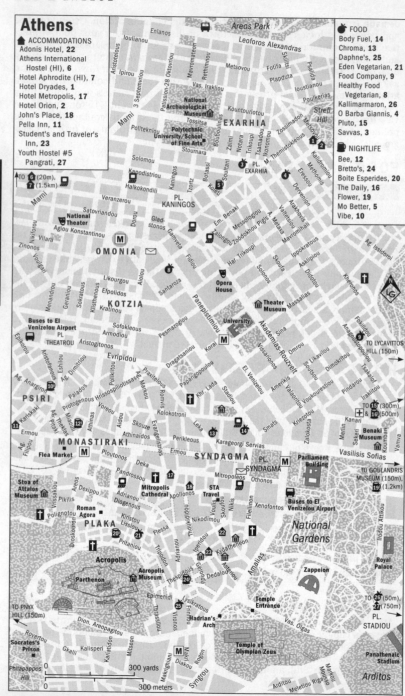

Athens

ACCOMMODATIONS
Adonis Hotel, **22**
Athens International
  Hostel (HI), **6**
Hotel Aphrodite (HI), **7**
Hotel Dryades, **1**
Hotel Metropolis, **17**
Hotel Orion, **2**
John's Place, **18**
Pella Inn, **11**
Student's and Traveler's
  Inn, **23**
Youth Hostel #5
  Pangrati, **27**

FOOD
Body Fuel, **14**
Chroma, **13**
Daphne's, **25**
Eden Vegetarian, **21**
Food Company, **9**
Healthy Food
  Vegetarian, **8**
Kallimarmaron, **26**
O Barba Giannis, **4**
Pluto, **15**
Savvas, **3**

NIGHTLIFE
Bee, **12**
Bretto's, **24**
Boite Esperides, **20**
The Daily, **16**
Flower, **19**
Mo Better, **5**
Vibe, **10**

defined Athens for centuries remain ageless pillars of the proud city's heritage. The Acropolis and the Parthenon, representing the zenith of Classical Greece and the seeds of democracy, still stand guard over the urban landscape, and visitors can still tread the paths of the great philosophers and orators of antiquity.

TRANSPORTATION

Flights: Eleftherios Venizelou (ATH; ☎210 353 0000; www.aia.gr). Greece's new international airport operates as 1 massive yet easily navigable terminal. Arrivals are on the ground floor, departures are on the 2nd. The new **suburban rail** services the airport from the city center in 30min. 4 bus lines run to Athens, Piraeus, and Rafina.

Trains: Hellenic Railways (OSE), Sina 6 (☎210 362 4402; www.ose.gr). **Larisis Train Station** (☎210 529 8837) serves northern Greece. Ticket office open daily 5am-midnight. Take trolley #1 from El. Venizelou in Pl. Syndagma (every 10min. 5am-midnight, €0.45) or the metro to Sepolia. Trains depart for **Thessaloniki** (7hr., 5 per day, €15). **Peloponnese Train Station** (☎210 529 8735) serves **Kalamata** (6½hr., 3 per day, €7); **Nafplion** (3½hr., 2 per day, $4.80); **Patras** (4¼hr., 3 per day, €5.30). From Larisis, exit to your right, and cross the footbridge.

Buses: Terminal A: Kifissou 100 (☎210 512 4910). Take blue bus #051 from the corner of Zinonos and Menandrou near Pl. Omonia (every 15min. 5am-11:30pm, €0.45). Buses to: **Corfu** (10hr., 4 per day, €30); **Corinth** (1½hr., every 30min., €5); **Patras** (3hr., every 30min., €13); **Thessaloniki** (6hr., 11 per day, €30); and other destinations. **Terminal B:** Liossion 260 (☎210 831 7153, M-F only). Take blue bus #024 from Amalias outside the National Gardens (45min., every 20min., €0.45). Buses to **Delphi** (3hr., 6 per day, €11) and other destinations.

Public Transportation: Yellow KTEL (ΚΤΕΛ) **buses** travel all around Attica. Other buses around Athens and its suburbs are blue and designated by 3-digit numbers. Buy bus/trolley tickets at any street kiosk. Hold on to your ticket—you can be fined €18-30 by police if caught without one. **Trolleys** are yellow and crowded, sporting 1- or 2-digit numbers; they are distinguished from buses by their electrical antennae. The Athens **metro** consists of 3 lines. **M1** runs from northern Kifisia to Piraeus. **M2** runs from Sepolia to Ag. Dimitrios. **M3** runs from Ethniki Amyna to Monastiraki in central Athens. Trains run 5am-midnight. Buy tickets (€0.30-0.60) in any station. There are 2 **tram** lines. **Line 1** runs from Pl. Syndagma to the coast and Helliniko. **Line 2** runs from Neo Faliro along the Apollo Coast until Glyfada.

Car Rental: Try the places on **Syngrou.** €35-50 for a small car with 100km mileage (including tax and insurance); prices rise in summer. Up to 50% student discount.

Taxis: Meters start at €0.75, with an additional €0.28 per km; midnight-5am €0.53 per km. There's a €3 surcharge from the airport and a €0.80 surcharge for trips from bus and railway terminals, plus €0.29 for each piece of luggage over 10kg.

PIRAEUS PORT: FERRIES FROM ATHENS The majority of ferries from Athens leave from the Piraeus port. Ferries sail to nearly all Greek islands (except the Ionians and the Sporades). Ferries to Crete: Hania (11hr., 1-2 per day, €20); Iraklion (11hr., 1-3 per day, €24); Rethymno (11hr., 3 per week, €24). Additional ferries to: Chios (9hr., 1-2 per day, €20); Ios (7½hr., 3 per day, €22); Kos (13½hr., 1-2 per day, €28); Lesvos (12hr., 1 per day, €26); Milos (7hr., 1-2 per day, €18); Mykonos (6hr., 2-4 per day, €20); Naxos (6hr., 5-7 per day, €21); Paros (5hr., 4-7 per day, €22); Rhodes (14hr., 2-5 per day, €31); Santorini (9hr., 3-5 per day, €25).

ORIENTATION AND PRACTICAL INFORMATION

Athenian geography mystifies newcomers. If you lose your bearings, ask for directions back to well-lit **Syndagma**. The **Acropolis** serves as a reference point, as does **Mt. Lycavittos**. Syndagma, the central *plateia* containing the Parliament building, is encircled by the other major neighborhoods. Clockwise, they are **Plaka, Monastiraki, Psiri, Omonia, Exarhia, Kolonaki,** and **Pangrati**. Plaka, the center of the old city and home to many accommodations, is bound by the **Temple of Olympian Zeus** and the *plateia* of the Cathedral Mitropolis. Monastiraki is between the outer walls of the ancient Agora and the boulevard **Ermou**; it is the site of a large metro station. Two parallel avenues, **Panepistimiou** and **Stadiou,** connect Syndagma to Omonia. Omonia's neighbor to the east, progressive Exarhia, sports some of Athens's most exciting nightlife, while nearby Kolonaki, on the foothills of Mt. Lycavittos, has plenty of glitz and swanky shops. Pangrati, southeast of Kolonaki, is marked by the **Olympic Stadium** and the **National Cemetery**.

Tourist Office: Information Office, Amalias 26 (☎210 331 0392; www.gnto.gr). Offers brochures on travel throughout Greece; an indispensable Athens map; the most up-to-date bus, train, and ferry schedules; and prices and lists of museums, embassies, and banks. Open M-F 9am-10pm, Sa-Su 10am-3pm. **STA Travel,** Voulis 43 (☎210 321 1188; statravel@robissa.gr). Open M-F 9am-5pm, Sa 10am-2pm. **Consolas Travel,** Aiolou 100 (☎210 321 9228; consolas@hol.gr), on the 9th fl. above the post office. Open M and Sa 9am-2pm, Tu-F 9am-5pm.

Banks: National Bank of Greece, Karageorgi Servias 2 (☎210 334 0500), in Pl. Syndagma. Open M-Th 8am-2:30pm, F 8am-2pm; open for **currency exchange** only M-F 3:30-5pm, Sa 9am-2pm, Su 9am-1pm. Currency exchange available 24hr. at the **airport,** but exchange rates and commissions may be unfavorable.

Laundromats: Most *plintirias* have signs reading "Laundry." **National,** Apollonos 17, in Syndagma. €4.50 per kg. Open M and W 8am-4pm, Tu and Th-F 8am-8pm.

Emergency: Police: ☎100 or 103. **Ambulance:** ☎166. **Medical:** ☎105 from Athens, or 210 646 7811; line available 2pm-7am. *Athens News* lists emergency hospitals. Free emergency health care for tourists. **AIDS Help Line:** ☎210 722 2222.

Tourist Police: Dimitrakopoulou 77 (☎171). English spoken. Open 24hr.

Pharmacies: Marked by a green cross hanging over the street. Many are open 24hr.; check *Athens News* for the day's emergency pharmacy.

Hospitals: Emergency hospitals on duty ☎106. **Geniko Kratiko Nosokomio (Y. Gennimatas; Public State Hospital),** Mesogion 154 (☎210 777 8901). A state hospital, **Aeginitio,** Vas. Sofias 72 (☎210 722 0811) and Vas. Sofias 80 (☎210 777 0501), is closer to Athens's center. Near Kolonaki is the public hospital **Evangelismos,** Ypsilantou 45-47 (☎210 720 1000).

Internet Access: Internet cafes are sprouting in Athens. Expect to pay €2-5 per hr.

Arcade Internet Cafe, Stadiou 5 (☎210 324 8105; sofos1@ath.forthnet.gr), just up Stadiou from the *plateia* in Syndagma, set in a shopping center about 15m from the main thoroughfare. Owner is friendly and PC-proficient. Computer equipped with CD burners. Complimentary coffee. €3 per hr., €0.50 each additional 10min. €2 min. Open M-Sa 9am-10pm, Su noon-8pm.

easyInternetCafé, Filellinon 2 (☎210 331 3034), in Syndagma, on the 2nd fl. above Everest, directly across from the *plateia*. 40 high-speed, flat-screen computers. Purchase "credit" from the automatic machine by the entrance. Since rates depend on the number of customers present at a given time, they range €0.80-3 per hr.

Bits'n Bytes Internet, Kapnikareas 19 (☎210 382 2545 or 330 6590; www.bnb.gr), in Plaka. This mother of new-age Internet cafes has fast connections in a spacious, air-conditioned joint. Midnight-9am €3 per hr., 9am-midnight €5 per hr. Vending machines sell coffee, hot chocolate, juice (€1), and sandwiches (€1-2). Open 24hr.

Cafe 4U, 3 Septemvriou 24 (☎210 520 1564; cafe4u@mail.gr), in Omonia. A refuge off busy Septemvriou, this cafe offers fast access for €2.50 per hr. €1.50 min.

Moc@fe Internet Cafe, Marni 49 (☎210 522 7717), near Pl. Karaiskaki in Omonia. Serves coffee and beer. €4.50 per hr., €1.50 min. Open M-Sa 9am-2am, Su 10am-2am.

Post Office: Syndagma (☎210 622 6253), on the corner of Mitropoleos. Open M-F 7:30am-8pm, Sa 7:30am-2pm. Branch offices in Omonia, at Aiolou 100, Exarhia, at the corner of Zaimi and K. Deligiani, and the Acropolis/Plaka. **Postal Code:** 10300.

ACCOMMODATIONS

The **Greek Youth Hostel Association,** Damareos 75 in Pangrati, lists hostels in Greece. (☎210 751 9530; y-hostels@ote.net.gr. Open M-F 9am-3pm.) The **Hellenic Chamber of Hotels,** Stadiou 24 in Syndagma, provides info and makes reservations for all types of hotels throughout Greece. Reservations require a cash deposit; you must contact them at least one month in advance and inform them of the length of your stay and the number of people. (☎210 323 7193; www.grhotels.gr Open May-Nov. M-F 8:30am-1:30pm.)

GREECE

▓ **Student's and Traveler's Inn,** Kydatheneon 16 (☎210 324 4808; www.studenttravelersinn.com), in Plaka. Unrivaled location and lively atmosphere with around-the-clock Internet access. Reserve ahead. Coed dorms €15; doubles €50, with private bath €60; triples €72/€84; quads €88/€100. ❷

▓ **Pella Inn,** Karaiskaki 1 (☎210 325 0598), in Monastiraki. Walk 10min. down Ermou from Pl. Syndagma; it's 2 blocks from the Monastiraki metro. Features a large terrace with views of the Acropolis. Breakfast included in room prices, €3 extra with dorms. Dorms €15; doubles €40-50; triples €60; quads €80. Credit cards accepted. ❷

Hotel Orion, Em. Benaki 105 (☎210 382 7362; fax 380 5193), in Exarhia. From Pl. Omonia, walk up Em. Benaki or take bus #230 from Pl. Syndagma. Orion rents small rooms with shared baths and A/C. Internet €2 per hr. Laundry €3. Singles €30; doubles €40; triples €48. Bargain for better prices. Credit cards accepted. ❸

Youth Hostel #5 Pangrati, Damareos 75 (☎210 751 9530; y-hostels@ote.net). From Omonia or Pl. Syndagma, take trolley #2 or 11 to Filolaou. There's no sign for this cheery hostel, just a green door. Hot showers €0.50 for 7min. Sheets €2 the 1st night, free thereafter. Laundry (wash only) €4. Quiet hours 2-5pm and 11pm-7am. Dorms €10-12. Bring a sleeping bag to stay on the roof (€6). ❶

Adonis Hotel, Kodrou 3 (☎210 324 9737; fax 323 1602), in Plaka. From Syndagma, follow Filellinon; turn right on Nikodimou and left onto Kodrou. A family hotel with a delightful rooftop lounge. Reserve far in advance. All rooms with bath. Breakfast included. In summer, singles €50; doubles €70; triples €90. Low season €30/€45/€60. A/C €10 extra per person. ❸

John's Place, Patroöu 5 (☎210 322 9719), near Mitropoleos. Off the major streets, John's has basic amenities. Quiet rooms are large and cool. All have A/C. Dim hallways and high ceilings enhance its Old World feel. Singles €35; doubles €50; triples €75. ❸

Hostel Aphrodite (HI), Einardou 12 (☎210 881 0589; www.hostelaphrodite.com), in Omonia. Small, clean rooms with A/C. Free luggage storage. Internet access €5 per hr. Laundry. Reception 24hr. Dorms €17; doubles €45; triples €60; quads €72. Discounts in low season. ❷

Hotel Dryades, Dryadon 4 (☎210 382 7116), in Exarhia. Dryades offers some of Athens's nicest budget accommodations, with large rooms and private baths. Internet €2 per hr. Singles €40-45; doubles €50-€60. Credit cards accepted. ❹

Athens International Hostel (HI), Victor Hugo 16 (☎210 523 2540; www.hostelbooking.com), in Omonia. Walk down 30 Septemvriou from Pl. Omonia and take a left on Veranzerou, which becomes Victor Hugo after crossing Mami. Hot water 6am-midnight. Laundry €6. Common kitchen available. Reservations required. Dorms €8; doubles €16. Members only. ❶

Hotel Metropolis, Mitropoleos 46 (☎210 321 7469; www.hotelmetropolis.gr), in Syndagma. Enjoy full amenities and wonderful views of Cathedral Mitropolis and the Acropolis. Elevator and A/C. Free luggage storage. Laundry €6 per load. Singles €40, with bath €50; doubles €45/€60. Traveler's checks and credit cards accepted. ❹

🍴 FOOD

Athens offers a mix of fast-food stands, open-air cafes, side-street *tavernas*, and intriguing restaurants. Cheap food abounds in **Syndagma** and **Omonia**. Pick up groceries at the markets on **Nikis** in **Plaka**.

🍽 **Eden Vegetarian Restaurant,** Lissiou 12, in Plaka. Fantastic dishes like *boureki* (zucchini with feta; €5), as well as flavorful mushroom *stifado* with onions and peppers (€8.80). Open M and W-Su noon-midnight. ❷

🍽 **Savvas,** Mitropoleos 86, right off of Plateia Monastiraki, across from the flea market. A budget eater's dream with cheap, heavenly *gyros* (€1.70); just don't sit down—prices skyrocket to the €6-9 range if you do. Open daily 10am-3am. Credit cards accepted. ❶

O Barba Giannis, Em. Benaki 94, in Exarhia. From Syndagma, walk up Stadiou and make a right on Em. Benaki. Athenian students, CEOs, and artists all agree that "Uncle John's" is the place for cheap food and great service. Check out what's available at the counter; it's all scrumptious and mostly under €8. Open M-Sa noon-1:30am. ❷

Kallimarmaron, Eforionos 13, in Pangrati. With your back to the old Olympic Stadium, take the closest street on the left and walk 1½ blocks. Some of the best traditional Greek food in the city. Spiced chicken with raisins (€12) is prepared from an ancient recipe. Open Tu-Sa noon-3pm and 8pm-1am, Su noon-3pm. DC/MC/V. ❸

Food Company, Anagnostopoulou 47, in Kolonaki. Translates the casual, gourmet lunch into an art. Try the lentil salad with goat cheese (€4). Open daily noon-11:30pm. ❸

Chroma, Lekka 8 (☎210 331 7793), in Syndagma. Dine on fresh grilled salmon with vegetables and rice (€13) while reclining on leather couches listening to lounge music. Stay late for drinks and dancing. Prices range €6-14. Open daily as a cafe and later as a bar 8am-2am or later; kitchen open 1pm-midnight. Major credit cards accepted. ❸

Pluto, Plutarchou 38, in Kolonaki. Chic, warm ambience with an international menu. Try the grilled eggplant with feta and tomatoes (€9). Open M-Sa noon-3am. ❸

Healthy Food Vegetarian Restaurant, Panepistimiou 57, in Omonia. Serves huge portions of wholesome, fresh Greek food. Open M-Sa 9am-10pm, Su 10am-4pm. ❷

Daphne's, Lysikratous 4 (☎210 322 7971), in Plaka. The most revered kitchen in Plaka serves rabbit in Mavrodaphne wine sauce (€20), a Peloponnesian delicacy, in either a shaded garden or a dining room inside a gorgeous restored 1830s mansion. Chocolate *mousse gateau* €10. Open daily 7:30pm-12:30am. AmEx/DC/MC/V. ❹

Body Fuel, Stadiou 3, in Syndagma. A new-age food bar in a sleek setting with fresh and gourmet delights like salmon and vegetable salad (€4.95) and fresh fruit and vegetable smoothies (€3-5). Open daily 10:30am-8pm. ❷

👁 SIGHTS

ACROPOLIS

Looming majestically over the city, the Acropolis complex has been the heart of Athens since the 5th century BC. Although each Greek *polis* had an *acropolis* (high point of the city), the buildings atop Athens's central peak outshone their imitators and continue to awe visitors today. Visit as early in the day as possible to avoid crowds and the broiling midday sun. (☎ *210 321 0219. Open daily in summer 8am-7pm; low season 8am-2:30pm. Admission includes access to all of the sights below the Acropolis, including Hadrian's Arch, the Temple of Olympian Zeus, and the Agora, within a 48hr. period; tickets can be purchased at any of the sights. €12, students €6.)*

PARTHENON. The **Temple of Athena Parthenos** (Athena the virgin), more commonly known as the Parthenon, keeps vigil over Athens and the modern world. Ancient Athenians saw their city as the capital of civilization, and the **metopes** (scenes in the open spaces above the columns) on the sides of the Parthenon celebrate Athens's rise. On the far right of the southern side—the only side that has not been defaced—the Lapiths battle the Centaurs; on the eastern side, the Olympian gods defeat the giants; the north side depicts the victory of the Greeks over the Trojans; and the western side depicts their triumph against the Amazons.

TEMPLE OF ATHENA NIKE. This tiny temple was raised during the Peace of Nikias (421-415 BC), a respite from the Peloponnesian War. The temple, known as the "jewel of Greek architecture," is ringed by eight miniature Ionic columns and housed a statue of the winged goddess of victory, Nike.

ERECHTHEION. The Erechtheion, to the left of the Parthenon, was completed in 406 BC, just before Sparta defeated Athens in the Peloponnesian War. The building takes its name from the snake-bodied Erechtheus; the eastern half is devoted to the goddess of wisdom, Athena, the western half to the god of the sea, Poseidon.

ACROPOLIS MUSEUM. The museum, which neighbors the Parthenon, houses a superb collection of sculptures, including five of the original Caryatids that supported the southern side of the Erechtheion. The statues seem to be replicas, but a close look at the folds of their drapery reveals delicately individualized detail. Compare the stylized faces and frozen poses of the Archaic period **Moschophoros** (calf-bearer) sculpture to the idealized, more human Classical period **Kritios Boy** to follow the development of Greek sculpture. *(Open in summer M 11am-7pm, Tu-Su 8am-7pm; low season M 11am-2pm, Tu-Su 8am-2pm.)*

ELSEWHERE ON THE ACROPOLIS. The southwestern corner of the Acropolis looks down over the reconstructed **Odeon of Herodes Atticus**, a functional theater dating from the Roman period (AD 160). See the *Athens News* for a schedule of concerts and plays. You'll also see nearby ruins of the Classical Theater of Dionysus, the Asclepion, and the Stoa of Eumenes II. *(Entrance on Dionissiou Areopagitou. ☎ 210 323 2771. Purchase tickets at the door or by phone.)*

OTHER SIGHTS

AGORA. The Agora served as the city's marketplace, administrative center, and hub of daily life from the 6th century BC to AD 500. Here, the debates of Athenian democracy raged; Socrates, Aristotle, Demosthenes, Xenophon, and St. Paul all instructed here. The 415 BC ⬛**Hephaesteion**, on a hill in the northwestern corner of the Agora, is the best-preserved Classical temple in Greece, flaunting **friezes** depicting Hercules's labors and Theseus's adventures. The **Stoa of Attalos** was a multi-purpose building filled with shops and gatherings of philosophers. Reconstructed in the 1950s, it now houses the **Agora Museum,** which contains relics from the site. According to Plato, Socrates's trial was at the **Royal Stoa,** left of the Adrianou exit. *(Enter the Agora off Pl. Thission, from Adrianou, or as you descend from the Acropolis. Open daily 8am-7:30pm. €4, students and EU seniors €2, children and EU students free.)*

ROMAN AGORA. The Roman Agora was a large rectangular structure built between 19 and 11 BC. The ruined columns of the two surviving **prophylae,** a nearly intact entrance gate, and the **gate of Athena Archgetis** stand as testaments to what

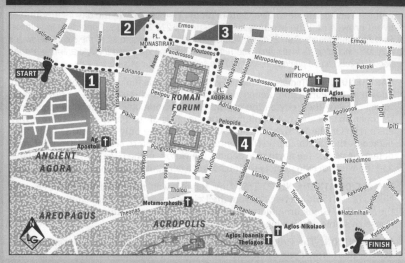

1 ANCIENT AGORA. As you emerge from the bustling streets of Plaka into this wide expanse of marble, crickets, and pines, don't let the quietude fool you—this is not another Byzantine church. Life no less colorful or commonplace than what lies just beyond these gates in the Monastiraki flea market stomped on the very dust you stand on for 1000 continuous years. The

START: Adrianou, entrance to Agora

FINISH: Kydathenenon 41

DISTANCE: 1.5km

DURATION: 2-3hr.

WHEN TO GO: Late morning

Hephaesteion, on the hill to your right, and the reconstructed Stoa of Attalos on your left, are still real enough for you to imagine the generations of Greeks and foreigners who came here to haggle over mandarins. Picture Socrates lounging in the shop of his cobbler-friend Simon on the southwestern part of the square (p. 515).

2 THE POET'S SANDAL SHOP. In the shadow of the Acropolis, Stavros Melissinos works the two crafts that have drawn both Jacqueline Kennedy Onassis and John Lennon, ex-Prime Minister Kanellopoulos and Gary Cooper—sandalmaking, that is, and poetry. His wonderful raw leather sandals line the shop's narrow walls, and samples of his poetry lie around for patrons of his shop to read. "A writer who does nothing but write," the poet once said, "is like the moon which gives off some light, but it's borrowed, taken from the sun. A writer needs first-hand experience which only working in another field can give him. Otherwise, he is rewriting what he's read in other books." *(Melissinos Art, 2 Agias Theklas. ☎ 210 321 9247. Open M-F 10am-6pm, Su 10am-2:30pm. Sandals €13-27, based on size.)*

3 SAVVAS. Perhaps the most widely renowned among Athenians themselves, this is the best place to order souvlaki and run. Why? Well first, it's the best souvlaki out there. Second, it's a sixth of the price (literally) when you take it away (p. 514).

4 BRETTO'S. Barrels of wine on the right side of this one-room, high-ceilinged, 112-year-old wooden distillery are filled with sweet red wine. In midday, you might prefer a chilled glass of *topio* ("local") or a small ice-cubed ouzo cocktail, but whatever you do, you must have a taste, a sip, a drink, a whatever while you're here (p. 518).

was once a lively meeting place. Also nearby are the **vespasianae,** or public toilets, constructed in the 1st century AD, as well as a mosque dating from 1456. By far the most intriguing structure in the site is the well-preserved (and restored) **Tower of the Winds.** (☎ 210 324 5220. Open daily 8am-7:30pm. €2, students €1, EU students free.)

KERAMIKOS. The Keramikos's geometric design is noticeable upon entering the grounds; the site includes a large-scale cemetery built around the **Sacred Way,** the road to Eleusis, and a 40m-wide boulevard that ran to the sanctuary of **Akademes,** where Plato founded his academy. The **Oberlaender Museum** displays finds from the burial sites; it also houses a collection of highly detailed pottery and sculpture. (Northwest of the Agora. From Syndagma, walk toward Monastiraki on Ermou for 1km. Open Tu-Su 8:30am-7pm. €2, students and EU seniors €1. Children and EU students free.)

TEMPLE OF OLYMPIAN ZEUS AND HADRIAN'S ARCH. Right in the center of downtown Athens, you'll spot the traces of the largest temple ever built in Greece. The 15 Corinthian columns of the Temple of Olympian Zeus mark where it once stood. Started in the 6th century BC, it was completed 600 years later by Roman emperor Hadrian, who attached his name to the effort by adding an arch to mark the boundary between the ancient city of Theseus and Hadrian's new city. (Vas. Olgas at Amalias, across from the National Gardens. Open daily 8am-5pm. Temple €2, students and EU seniors €1, children and EU students free. Arch free.)

PANATHENAIC STADIUM. The Panathenaic Olympic Stadium, also known as the Kallimarmaro, is wedged between the National Gardens and Pangrati, carved into a hill. The site of the first modern Olympic Games in 1896, the stadium seats 70,000 and served as both the finish line of the Marathon events as well as the venue for the archery events during the 2004 Summer Olympic Games. (Take the M1. On Vas. Konstantinou. From Syndagma, walk up Amalias 15min. to Vas Olgas, then follow it left. Or take trolley #2, 4, or 11 from Syndagma. Open daily 8am-8:30pm. Free.)

AROUND SYNDAGMA. Be sure to catch the changing of the guard in front of the **Parliament** building. Every hour on the hour, two *evzones* wind up like toy soldiers, kick their tasseled heels in unison, and fall backward into symmetrical guardhouses on either side of the **Tomb of the Unknown Soldier.** Athens's endangered species—greenery and shade—are preserved in the **National Gardens.** Women should avoid strolling here alone.

MT. LYCAVITTOS. Of Athens's seven hills, Lycavittos is the largest. Ascend at sunset to catch a glimpse of the city lighting up for the night. At the top is the **Chapel of St. George,** a popular spot for weddings. A leisurely stroll around the church provides a view of Athens's panoramic expanse.

MUSEUMS

▨ **NATIONAL ARCHAEOLOGICAL MUSEUM.** This astounding collection deserves a spot on even the most packed itinerary. The museum's highlights include the archaeologist Heinrich Schliemann's treasure, the **Mask of Agamemnon,** the death mask of a king who lived at least three centuries earlier than Agamemnon himself. (Patission 44. Take trolley #2, 4, 5, 9, 11, 15, or 18 from the uphill side of Syndagma, or trolley #3 or 13 from the northern side of Vas. Sofias. Open Apr.-Oct. Tu-Su 8:30am-3pm; Nov.-Mar. M 10:30am-5pm, Tu-Su 8:30am-3pm. €6, students and EU seniors €3, EU students and under 19 free. No flash photography.)

BENAKI MUSEUM. This museum represents Antoine Benaki's collection, amassed during his European and Asian travels, boasting an impressive assortment of art and archaeological artifacts. Looking through the exhibits, a visitor gets a sense of the scope of Greek history from prehistoric formation to the modern state, but with an interesting individual bent, as the artifacts were all gathered by one collector. *(Vas. Sofias and 1 Koumbari in Kolonaki. Open M, W, and F-Sa 9am-5pm, Th 9am-midnight, Su 9am-3pm. €6, seniors and adults with children €3, students, teachers free.)*

GOULANDRIS MUSEUM OF CYCLADIC AND ANCIENT GREEK ART. This museum displays a stunning collection of Cycladic figurines: sleek, abstract marble works, some almost 5000 years old. Bronze jewelry from Skyros, a collection of vases, and Corinthian helmets share the space. *(Neophytou Douka 4. Walk toward Kolonaki from Syndagma on Vas. Sofias; turn left on Neophytou Douka. It's half a block up. Accessible by trolleys #3 and 13. Open M and W-F 10am-4pm, Su 10am-3pm. €3.50, seniors and students €1.80, archaeologists and archaeology students free with university pass.)*

🎵 🍷 ENTERTAINMENT AND NIGHTLIFE

The weekly *Athens News* (€1) lists events, as well as news and ferry information. Summertime performances are staged in **Lycavittos Theater** as part of the **Athens Festival**. The **Festival Office**, Stadiou 4, sells tickets. (☎210 322 1459. Open M-Sa 8am-4pm, Su 9am-2pm and 6-9pm. Tickets €10-110. Student discounts available.) Chic Athenians head to the seaside clubs of **Glyfada. Balux** and **Prime** are perfect places to enjoy the night air. (Drinks €4-10. Cover €10-15.) Take the A2, A3, or B3 bus from Vas. Amalias to Glyfada (€0.75), and then catch a cab from there to your club. Taxis to Glyfada run about €8, but the return trip typically costs €10-15.

- 🍸 **Boite Esperides,** Tholou 6, in Plaka at the end of Mniskleous. Aspiring *bouzouki* players and honey-voiced girls "sing about love and the moon." Ouzo €7.50. Cover €7.50. Open Sept.-July Tu-Su 10pm-4am.

- 🍸 **Bretto's,** Kydatheneon 41, between Farmaki and Afroditis in Plaka. This wooden room with stools offers a local-alcohol-only menu. €5 per bottle of sweet red wine; €2 per sizeable glass. Open daily 10am-midnight.

- **Bee,** Miaouli 6, off Ermou at the corner of Themidos, a few blocks from the heart of Psiri. DJs spin while the friendly staff keeps the booze flowing. Drinks €4-7. Open Tu-Th and Su noon-3am, F-Sa noon-6am.

- **Flower,** Dorylaou 2, in Pl. Mavili, in Kolonaki. A popular dive bar with European partiers. Shots €3. Mixed drinks €5. Open daily 6pm-late.

- **Vibe,** Aristofanous 1, just beyond Pl. Iroön in Monastiraki. Unusual lighting makes for a great atmosphere. Open Tu-Su 10:30pm-last customer.

- **Mo Better,** Koleti 32, off Themistokleous, in Exharia. In fall, winter, or spring, find the tall blue wooden door—it's the entrance to the most popular rock bar in Athens. A staple in the nocturnal schedule of alternative university students. Whiskey or vodka tonic €6. Open Oct.-June M-Th and Su 10pm-4am, F-Sa 10pm-dawn.

- **The Daily,** Xenokratous 47. Kolonaki's chic student population converges here to imbibe, listen to Latin and reggae, and watch sports on TV. Fabulous outdoor seating. Mixed drinks €3-6. Open daily 9am-2am.

🔲 DAYTRIPS FROM ATHENS

TEMPLE OF POSEIDON. The Temple of Poseidon has been a dazzling white landmark for sailors at sea for centuries. The temple was constructed around 600 BC, destroyed by the Persians in 480 BC, and rebuilt by Pericles in 440 BC. The temple sits on a promontory at ■**Cape Sounion,** 65km from Athens. (Open daily 10am-sunset. €4, students and seniors €2, EU students and children free.) Two **bus** routes run to Cape Sounion from Athens; the shorter and more scenic route begins at the Mavromateon 14 stop near Areos Park (2hr., 1 per hr., €4.30).

MARATHON. Immediately after running 42km to spread word of the Athenian victory in the 490 BC battle of Marathon, **Phidippides** collapsed and died. Today, runners trace the route between Athens and Marathon twice per year. With a car, you can explore nearby sights and beaches. At **Ramnous,** 15km northeast, lie the ruins of the **Temple of Nemesis,** goddess of divine retribution, and **Thetis,** goddess of law and justice. **Schinias** to the north and **Timvos Marathonas** to the south are popular beaches. **Buses** leave Athens for Marathon from the Mavromateon 29 station (1½hr., 1 per hr. 5:30am-10:30pm, €2.50).

DELPHI. Troubled denizens of the ancient world journeyed to the Oracle of Delphi, where the priestess of Apollo related the cryptic advice of the gods. The treasures of the **Temple of Apollo,** theater, and stadium, the site of the ancient **Pythian Games,** are housed inside the site's fantastic **museum.** Head east out of town to reach the site. (Open daily 7:30am-7:45pm. €6, both the site and the museum €9.) Buses leave Athens for Delphi from Terminal B, Liossion 260 (3hr., 6 per day, €11). Delphi's tourist office, Pavlou 12, is in the town hall. (☎22650 82 900. Open M-F 8am-2:30pm.) If you spend the night, stay at **Hotel Sibylla ❷,** Pavlou 9, which has wonderful views and private baths at the best prices in town. (☎22650 82 335. Singles €16; doubles €22; triples €30. Discount for *Let's Go* readers.)

PELOPONNESE Πελοπόννεσος

Stretching its fingers into the Mediterranean, the Peloponnese transports its visitors to another time and place through its rich history and folklore. Remnants of ancient civilizations and their achievements dot the landscape of the peninsula, and its timeless natural beauty remains unchanged. Here rest the majority of Greece's most significant archaeological sites, including Corinth, Epidavros, Messini, Mycenae, Mystras, and Olympia.

◖ FERRIES TO ITALY

Boats sail from Patras to destinations in Italy, including Ancona, Bari, Brindisi, Trieste, and Venice. Several ferry lines make the trip, each offering different prices, so check the travel offices along Othonas Amalias and make sure to check prices for more than one line. Railpasses won't work for domestic ferries, but for international ferries, **Superfast Ferries,** Oth. Amalias 12 (☎2610 622 500; open 10am-9pm), accepts Eurail passes. Questions about departures from Patras should be directed to the Port Authority (☎2610 341 002).

PATRAS Πάτρας ☎2610

Greece's third-largest city spreads from its harbor in a mixture of urban and classical, Greek and international styles. Location, location, location—on the northwestern tip of the Peloponnese—makes Patras a busy transportation hub. During **Carnival** (mid-Jan. to Ash Wednesday), this port city becomes one gigantic dance floor consumed by pre-Lenten madness. Follow the water to the west end of town to reach **Agios Andreas,** the largest Orthodox cathedral in Greece, which houses magnificent frescoes and St. Andrew's holy head. (Dress modestly. Open daily 7am-dusk.) Sweet black grapes are transformed into Mavrodaphne wine at the ▧**Achaïa Clauss Winery,** the country's most famous vineyard. Take bus #7 (30min., €1) from the intersection of Kanakari and Gerokostopoulou. (Free English tours every hr. Open daily Nov.-Feb. 9am-5pm; Mar. 10am-6pm; Apr. 11am-7pm; May-Aug. 11am-8pm; Sept.-Oct. 10am-6pm. Free.) Built atop ruins of an ancient acropolis and continuously in use from the 6th century to World War II, Patras's **castle** remains relatively intact, considering its turbulent history. Its location also makes it perfect for a bird's-eye view of the entire city. (Open Tu-Sa 8am-7pm. Free.)

Trains (☎2610 639 108) leave from Oth. Amalias 47 for: Athens (3½-5hr., 6 per day, €5.30-10); Kalamata (5½hr., 6:20am, €5); and Pirgos (1½hr., 6 per day, €3-6), where you can catch a bus to Olympia. KTEL **buses** (☎2610 623 886) leave from Othonos Amalias for: Athens (3hr., 33 per day, €13); Ioannina (4hr., 4 per day, €15); Kalamata (4hr., 2 per day, €15); Thessaloniki (8hr., 3 per day, €30); and Tripoli (4hr., 2 per day, €11). **Ferries** go to: Corfu (6-8hr., €21-25); Vathy, Ithaka (3½hr., €12); and Italy. Get free maps at the **tourist office** on Othonos Amalias, between 28 Octovriou and Astingos. (☎2610 461 740. Open daily 8am-10pm.) ⛭**Rooms to Let Spyros Vazouras ❸**, Tofalou 2, across from the new port entrance, has large rooms with A/C and clean baths. (☎2610 452 152. Singles €30; doubles €40. 10% discount for *Let's Go* readers.) The best bet in Patras for price and location is **Pension Nicos ❷**, Patreos 3, two blocks off the waterfront. (☎2610 623 757. Singles €20; doubles €35; triples €50.) The friendly, cafeteria-style **Europa Center ❶**, on Othonos Amalias, serves large portions. (Entrees €3-7.) **Postal Code:** 26001.

OLYMPIA Ολυμπία   ☎26240

In ancient times, every four years city-states would call truces and travel to Olympia for a pan-Hellenic assembly, which was as much about peace and diplomacy as about athletic ability. Modern Olympia, set among meadows and shaded by cypress and olive trees, is also recognized for its pristine natural beauty. The ancient **Olympic arena,** whose central sanctuary was called the **Altis,** draws hordes of tourists. In **Ancient Olympia,** to the north of the **Bouleuterion,** are the ruins of the **Temple of Zeus.** Home to master-sculptor Phidias's awe-inspiring **statue of Zeus** (one of the Seven Wonders of the Ancient World), the 27m long sanctuary was the largest temple completed on the Greek mainland before the Parthenon. The ruins of the ⛭**Temple of Hera,** dating from the 7th century BC, are better preserved than those of Zeus's Temple. The ⛭**Archaeological Museum** has an impressive sculpture collection that includes the **Nike of Paionios** and the **Hermes of Praxiteles.** Maps, available at the site (€2-4), are essential for navigation. (Site open daily in summer 8am-7pm. Museum open M noon-7pm, Tu-Su 8am-7pm. Site or museum €6, both €9; students and seniors €5; under 18 and EU students free.) The **Museum of the Olympic Games,** or the **Sports Museum,** on Angerinou, two blocks uphill from Kondili, houses a collection of Olympic paraphernalia that includes a silver medal from the 1996 games in Atlanta. (☎26240 22 544. Open daily 8am-3:30pm. €2, children and students free.)

Buses run to Tripoli (3½hr., 2-3 per day, €8). The **tourist office,** on Kondili, is on the eastern side of town toward the ruins. (☎26240 23 173. Open daily in high season 9am-8pm.) The friendly **Youth Hostel ❶**, Kondili 18, is a cheap place to get to know international backpackers. (☎26240 22 580. Sheets €2. Dorms €8; doubles €20.) **New Olympia ❸**, on the road that leads diagonally to the train station, is perfect for travelers who like extra amenities at cheap prices. (☎26240 22 506. Breakfast included. Singles €25-40; doubles €45-70.) **Postal Code:** 27065.

TRIPOLI Τρίπολη   ☎2710

The transportation hub of Arcadia, Tripoli is crowded and fast-paced; the *plateias* and huge city park are a break in the city's otherwise urban landscape. Tripoli is best used as a jumping-off point for exploring the lovely villages of **Dimitsana** and **Stemnitsa,** west of Tripoli in Arcadia. The **Archaeological Museum** on Evangelistrias,

Pl. Ag. Vasiliou, has a large collection, including pottery, jewelry, and weaponry from the Neolithic to the Mycenaean periods. (Open Tu-Su 8:30am-2:45pm. €2, students and seniors €1, children free.) **Trains** go to Athens (4½hr., 3 per day, €5) and Corinth (2½hr., €2.90). **Buses** leave at Pl. Kolokotronis, east of the center of town, to Athens (3hr., 14 per day, €11) and Nafplion (1hr., 4 per day, €3.70). Buses at the KTEL Messenia and Laconia depot, across from the train station, go to: Kalamata (1½hr., 1 per hr., €5.50); Patras (3hr., 2 per day, €14); and Sparta (1hr., 9am, €3.70). **Arcadia Hotel ❷**, in Pl. Kolokotronis, offers old-fashioned rooms with unique color schemes, A/C, and private bath. (☎2710 225 551. Singles €25-40; doubles €40-60; triples €50-65.) **Postal Code:** 22100.

KALAMATA Καλαμάτα ☎**27210**

Fast-growing Kalamata has all the characteristics of any other large city, with large beaches, a growing nightlife, and a famous dance festival that will delight visitors who pass through the city. Take a bus from Kalamata to **Ancient Messini** in nearby **Mavromati** (1hr.; leaves M-Sa 5:40am and 2pm, returns 3:30pm; €2), one of Greece's most impressive archaeological sites. (Open daily 8am-8pm. Free.) Near the castle in the old town is one of Kalamata's most famous gems, the **Convent of Ag. Konstantinos and Ag. Elena** (known as *Moni Kalograion*). Founded in 1796, the convent houses nuns who spend their days hand-weaving silks. To reach the train station, walk toward the waterfront in Pl. Georgiou, turn right on Frantzi at the far end of the *plateia*, and walk a few blocks to Sideromikou Stathmou. **Trains** run to: Athens (6½hr., 3 per day, €7) via Tripoli (2½hr., €2.80); Corinth (5¼hr., 3 per day, €5.60); and Patras (5½hr., 4 per day, €5.60). **Buses** leave from the station on Artemidos to: Athens (4hr., 13 per day, €15); Patras (4hr., 2 per day, €15); Sparta (2hr., 2 per day, €2.80); and Tripoli (2hr., €5.50). **Tourist information** is available at **D.E.T.A.K.**, Poliviou 6, just off Aristomenous near the old town. (☎27210 21 700. Open M-F 7am-2:30pm.) **Hotel Haikos ❸**, Navarinou 115, offers bright, carpeted rooms. (☎27210 88 902. Doubles €45-55; triples €55-65.) Good meals can be found along the waterfront. Before leaving town, sample the famous Kalamata olives and figs. The immense **new market,** across the bridge from the bus station, has an assortment of meat, cheese, and fruit shops. **Postal Code:** 24100.

SPARTA Σπάρτη AND MYSTRAS Μυστράς ☎**27310**

Citizens of today's Sparta make olive oil, not war. Pleasant public gardens and broad, palm-lined boulevards make Sparta hospitable, and it is by far the best base for exploring the Byzantine ruins of Mystras. **Ancient Sparta** is only a 1km walk north down Paleolougou. **Buses** from Sparta go to: Areopolis (1½hr., 2 per day, €4.60); Athens (3½hr., 8 per day, €14) via both Corinth (2½hr., €8.30) and Tripoli (1hr., €3.70); and Monemvasia (2hr., 3 per day, €6.80). To reach the town center from the bus station, walk about 10 blocks west on Lykourgou; the **tourist office** is in the *plateia*. (☎27310 24 852. Open M-F 8am-2pm.) **Hotel Cecil ❸**, Paleologou 125, five blocks north of Lykourgou toward Ancient Sparta, on the corner of Paleologou and Thermopilion, has pleasant rooms with A/C, phone, and private bath. (☎27310 24 980. Singles €28-33; doubles €35-45; triples €50-60.) **Parthenon ❶**, on Vrasithou, two blocks east of the intersection with Paleologou, serves unrivaled *gyros* (€1.30-1.50) and *souvlaki*. (☎23767 20 444.) **Postal Code:** 23100.

Mystras, 4km from Sparta, was once the religious center of all Byzantium and the locus of Constantinople's rule over the Peloponnese. Its extraordinary hillside ruins comprise a city of Byzantine churches, chapels, and monasteries. Although churches are the highlight, a visit to the **Palace** is a must, where pointed arches and dressed stone walls tell a history of the region. At some point during your visit to Mystras, make sure to stop at the elegant though small **museum,** in the courtyard of the Metropolis. Modest dress is required at the functioning convent. (Open in summer daily 8am-7pm; low season 8:30am-3pm. €5, children and students €3; EU students free.) **Buses** leave from the station and from the corner of Lykourgou and Leonidou in Sparta for the top of the ruins (20min., 11 per day, €0.90).

MONEMVASIA Μονεμβασία   ☎ 27320

Despite the tourists, an otherworldly quality shrouds the island of Monemvasia. No cars or bikes are allowed on the island, and pack horses bear residents' groceries into the city. Narrow streets hide tiny doorways and flowered courtyards. At the edge of the cliffs perches the **Agia Sofia,** a 12th-century church; to get there, navigate the maze of streets to the inland edge of town, where a path climbs the side of the cliff to the tip of the rock. Stay in more modern and less expensive **New Town Monemvasia,** a 15min. walk down the main road and across the causeway from old Monemvasia. Three **buses** per day leave for: Athens (6hr., €20); Corinth (5hr., €15); Sparta (2½hr., €6.80); and Tripoli (4hr., €10). **Hotel Akrogiali ❷,** directly across from Malvasia Travel on 23 Iouliou, is good for penny-pinching travelers. (☎ 27320 61 260. Singles €20-25; doubles €28-35.) Dining in old Monemvasia is a necessary experience. One of the first *tavernas* on the main road on the right is **Restaurant Matoula ❷,** which serves *dolmas* (€6) and other Greek favorites. (Decadent veal and seafood entrees €6-8. Open daily until midnight. V.)

NAFPLION Ναύφπλιο   ☎ 27520

With its pebbly beaches, Venetian architecture, ancient fortresses, and majestic harbor, Nafplion enchants. The town's crown jewel is the 18th-century **Palamidi fortress,** which provides spectacular views of the town and harbor. To get there, walk or take a taxi up the 3km road; or climb the grueling 999 steps up from Plizoidhou, across the park from the bus station. (Open 8:30am-6:30pm. €4, students €2.) To reach **Bouboulinas,** the waterfront promenade, from the station, go left and follow Syngrou to the harbor and the **old town.** Opened in 2004, the ▨**National Gallery-Nafplion Annex,** Sidiras Merarchias 23, on the left heading toward the new town, houses a wide array of 19th-century oil paintings that depict the 1821 Greek Revolution. (Open M, Th, and Sa 10am-3pm; W and F 10am-3pm and 5-8pm; Su 10am-2pm. €3, seniors €1.50, children 12 and under free. Free on M.) Nafplion's small, pebbly beach, **Arvanitia,** is along the road that curves around the left-hand side of Palamidi; if it gets too crowded, follow the footpath for lovely private coves.

    Buses leave from Syngrou, across from the park, for: Athens (3hr., 1 per hr., €9) via Corinth (2hr., €4); Epidavros (45min., 4 per day, €2); and Mycenae (45min., 3 per day, €2). The **tourist office** is on 25 Martiou across from the telephone office. (☎ 27520 24 444. Open daily 9am-1pm and 4-8pm.) To get to ▨**Pension Marianna ❹,** Potamianou 9, turn onto Potamianou and climb about 100 steps, then follow the signs; expect fabulous views of the city and rooms with excellent amenities. (☎ 27520 24 256. Singles €50; doubles €65.) For the old town rooftop views from **Dimitris Bekas' Domatia ❷,** turn up the stairs on Kokkinou, following the sign for rooms off Staikopoulou; climb to the top and go up 50 steps. (☎ 27520 24 594. Singles €17; doubles from €22; triples €30.) **Ellas ❷,** in Pl. Syndagma, is refreshingly inexpensive and has a cheerful staff. (☎ 27520 27 278. Veal with potatoes €6.50. Pasta dishes €4.) **Postal Code:** 21100.

MYCENAE Μυκήνες AND EPIDAVROS Επίδαυρος ☎27330

The head of the Greek world from 1600 to 1100 BC, **Mycenae** was ruled by the legendary Agamemnon, leader of the attacking forces in the Trojan War. Today, backpackers and senior citizens stampede to the famed ruins. The imposing **Lion's Gate,** the portal into the ancient city, has two lions carved in relief above the lintel and is estimated to weigh 20 tons. The **Tomb of Agamemnon** (a.k.a the Treasury of Atreus) is the large and impressive *tholos.* To the left of the citadel sit the remaining stones of a Hellenistic **Temple of Athena.** At the far end of the city, between the palace and the **postern gate,** is the **underground cistern,** a vital component of the ancient city which guaranteed water during sieges. (Sites open daily Apr.-Sept. 8am-7pm; Oct.-Mar. 8am-5pm. €8, students €4, EU students and children free. Keep your ticket or pay twice.) On the main road to the site, **Hotel Belle Helene ❷** is just uphill from the strip of restaurants. Opened in 1862, it's the oldest hotel in the village. (☎27510 76 225. Singles €20-30; doubles €33-48; triples €40-50. AmEx/MC/ V.) **Postal Code:** 21200.

The grandest structure at the ancient site of **Epidavros** is the **Theater of Epidavros,** built in the 2nd century BC. The amazing acoustics allow you to stand at the top row—14,000 seats back—and hear a match lit on stage. Near the theater and on the road to the sanctuary's ruins is Epidavros's **museum.** (☎27530 22 009. Open M noon-7pm, Tu-Su 8am-7pm. Ticket office open daily 7:30am-7pm, F-Sa until 9pm during festival season. €6, students €3, EU students free.) From late June to mid-Aug., the **Epidavros Theater Festival** hosts performances of classical Greek plays. Shows are Friday and Saturday at 9pm; purchase tickets at the site or by calling the Athens Festival Box Office. (☎210 322 1459. Tickets €17-40, students €9.)

CORINTH Κόρινθος ☎27410

Located on the isthmus between the Corinthian and Saronic Gulfs, Ancient Corinth was once a powerful commercial center and one of the most influential cities in ancient Greece. The ancient city lies at the base of **Acrocorinth,** a large hill, at the top of which stands a magnificent fortress built in the 10th century. Take a taxi to the summit (☎27410 31 464; €6), which will wait an hour before the drive back down (€10). Most conspicuous and breathtaking, seven of the original 38 columns from the **Temple of Apollo** have defiantly endured the trials of time since the 6th century BC. The temple sits down the stairs to the left of the excellent **Archaeological Museum,** which houses statues, mosaics, and figurines. To the left, near the exit at the edge of the site farthest from the museum, a stairway descends into the **Peirene Fountain,** once over 6m tall. Although smoothed by the water that still flows today, the columns and fresco-covered tunnels inside the fountain have survived the centuries unharmed. (☎27410 31 207. Open daily 8am-7pm; low season 8am-5pm. Museum and site €6, students €3, EU students and under 18 free.)

In grimy **New Corinth,** a transportation hub and the logical base for viewing the ruins, **buses** leave from Terminal A, past the train station, for Athens (1½hr., every 30min., €6). Buses run from Terminal B, on Koliatsou, halfway through the park, to Ancient Corinth (20min., 14 per day, €0.90). Buses leave Terminal C, **Argolis Station** (☎27410 24 403), at the intersection of Eth. Antistasis and Aratou, for: Argos (1hr., €3.20); Mycenae (45min., €2.50); and Nafplion (1½hr., €4). **Trains** go from the station on Dimokratias to Athens (2hr., 7 per day, €2.60; express: 1½hr., 6 per day, €5.20). The **tourist police,** Ermou 51, are located in the city's park and provide tourists with maps, brochures, and other assistance. (☎27410 23 282. Open daily 8am-2pm.) **Hotel Akti ❷,** Eth. Antistasis 3, is the best choice for the financially conscious traveler hoping to stay downtown. (☎27410 23 337. Singles €15-20; doubles €30-35.) **Postal Code:** 20100.

GREECE

NORTHERN AND CENTRAL GREECE

For travelers seeking to distance themselves from Athens and the islands, northern and central Greece offer an idyllic escape, ripe with fantastic hiking trails and Byzantine heritage. Countless traditional villages are scattered across the landscape, which is as diverse as the depths of the Vikos Gorge, the heights of Mount Olympus, and the serenity at Meteora. Yet this heartland of Greece also boasts some of the country's great cities, including Thessaloniki, the capital of the region, and Ioannina. A region largely connected, both ethnically and historically, to its Balkan neighbors, the north is where the multicultural Greek state surfaces.

THESSALONIKI Θεσσαλονίκη ☎ 2310

Thessaloniki is one of the most historically diverse, cosmopolitan cities in Greece, second in size only to Athens. With its leafy avenues, charming squares, and interspersed ruins, Thessaloniki dazzles travelers while providing visitors a material timeline for northern Greece's more modern historical periods.

▣ TRANSPORTATION

Flights: The **airport** (☎ 2310 408 400), 16km east of town, can be reached by **bus #78** from the train station or Pl. Aristotelous, or by **taxi** (€10). There's an EOT **tourist office** branch (☎ 2310 985 215) at the airport. The **Olympic Airways** office Koundouriotou 3 (☎ 2310 368 311), is open M-F 8am-3:45pm. Call ☎ 2310 368 666 for reservations. To: **Athens** (55min., 11 per day, €95); **Chios** (3hr., 4 per week, €60); **Corfu** (55min., 4 per week, €64); **Iraklion** (1½hr., 3 per week, €109); **Lesvos** (2hr., 1 per week, €63); **Rhodes** (3hr., 3 per week, €116); and **Samos** (3hr., 4 per week, €70).

Ferries: Buy tickets at **Karacharisis Travel and Shipping Agency,** Koundouriotou 8 (☎ 2310 524 544; fax 532 289), across from the Olympic Airways Office. Open M-F 8:30am-8:30pm, Sa 8:30am-2:30pm. During high season (mid-June to early Sept.), ferries travel to: **Chios** (20hr., Su 1am, €32; 9hr., W 9:30am, €62) via **Lesvos** (14hr., Sa 1pm, €31; 6½hr., €62); **Iraklion** (24hr.; Tu 2:30pm, Th 7pm, Sa 11:30pm; €31) via **Mykonos** (15hr., 3 per week, €31); **Kos** (20hr., Sa, €39); **Naxos** (16hr., Th, €29); **Paros** (17½hr., Tu, Sa, €31); **Rhodes** (24hr., Sa, €46); **Samos** (16hr., 2 per week, €32); **Santorini** (19½hr., 3 per week, €33).

Trains: To reach the **main terminal** (☎ 2310 517 517), on Monastiriou in the western part of the city, take any bus down Egnatia (€0.45). **International trains** go to: **İstanbul, Turkey** (12hr., 7am, €40); **Skopje, FYROM** (4hr., 8am and 6pm, €13); and **Sofia, Bulgaria** (8hr., 11:30pm, €18). Domestic trains to: **Athens** (regular: 7hr., 5 per day 8:25am-midnight, €20; high speed: 5hr., 6 per day 6:40am-2am, €40); **Larisa** (2½hr., 9 per day 7:30am-2am, €4.70); and **Volos** (4hr., 7:40pm, €6.80). The **travel office** (☎ 2310 598 112) can provide updated schedules.

Buses: Most **KTEL** buses leave from one central, dome-shaped bus station west of the city center. **Bus #1** is a shuttle service between the train station and bus station throughout the day (every 15min., €0.45). To: **Athens** (6hr., 11 per day, €30); **Corinth** (7½hr., 11:30pm, €34); **Ioannina** (7hr., 5 per day, €22); **Patras** (8hr., 2-3 per day, €30).

Public Transportation: Local buses cost €0.45 and run throughout the city. Buy tickets at *periptera* or at depot ticket booths. **Taxis** (☎ 2310 551 525) have specific lines at Ag. Sophia and Mitropoleos.

◀✷ ▮ ORIENTATION AND PRACTICAL INFORMATION

Egnatia, an old Roman highway, runs down the middle of town and is home to the cheapest hotels. Running parallel to the water, the main streets are **Ermou, Tsimiski, Mitropoleos,** and **Nikis,** which runs along the waterfront. Inland from Egnatia is

GREECE

Thessaloniki

ACCOMMODATIONS
Hotel Atlantis, 7
Hotel Augustos, 5
Hotel Ilios, 6
Hotel Tourist, 8
Youth Hostel, 1

FOOD
Chatzi, 3
Dore Zythos, 2
Ouzeri Melathron, 4

0   300 yards
0   300 meters

Thermaic Gulf

Agios Dimitriou and the **old city** beyond. Intersecting all these streets are, in order from harbor to the White Tower (*Levkos Pyrgos*), **I. Dragoumi, El. Venizelou, Aristotelous, Ag. Sophias,** and **Eth. Aminis.** Aristotelous, a wide boulevard where breezes sweep unobstructed from the ocean to the acropolis, is the city's center.

Tourist Office: UTS, Mitropoleos 28 (☎2310 286 256; fax 283 156), is near Pl. Aristotelous; ring the bell by the door labeled "28" and go to the 7th fl. Open M-F 9am-5pm.

Banks: Banks with currency exchange and 24hr. **ATMs** line Tsimiski, including **National Bank,** Tsimiski 11 (☎2310 230 783). Open M-Th 8am-2pm, F 8am-1:30pm.

Tourist Police: Dodekanissou 15, 5th fl. (☎2310 554 870). Free maps and brochures. Open 24hr. For the **local police,** call ☎2310 553 800 or 100.

Internet Access: There is no shortage of Internet cafes in Thessaloniki. Behind the shopping complex that houses the American Consulate, **E-Global,** Vasileos Irakliou 40, is 1 block to the right. Midnight-noon €1.80 per hr., noon-6pm €2.30, 6pm-midnight €2.80. **CyberNet,** Pl. Navarinou 14 (☎2310 223 060), overlooks a charming fountain of a young boy perpetually relieving himself. €2 per hr. Open 24hr.

Post Office: Aristotelous 27, just below Egnatia. Open M-F 7:30am-8pm, Sa 7:30am-2pm, Su 9am-1:30pm. It offers *Poste Restante.* **Postal Code:** 54101.

▛ ACCOMMODATIONS

Welcome to the big city—don't expect to find comfort and cleanliness all at one low price. Thessaloniki's less expensive hotels are along the western end of **Egnatia,** between **Pl. Dimokratias** (500m east of the train station) and **Aristotelous.**

▧ **Hotel Atlantis,** Egnatia 14 (☎2310 540 131). Friendly management offers standard budget furnishings and well-maintained hallway bathrooms. Singles €20, with bath €40; doubles €25/€45; triples €35. ❷

Hotel Ilios, Egnatia 27 (☎2310 512 620), on the western Egnatia budget strip, has modern rooms with big windows and A/C. Singles €35; doubles €49; triples €58. ❸

Hotel Augustos, El. Svoronou 4 (☎2310 522 955). From the western end of Egnatia, turn north at the Argo Hotel; Augustos is 20m straight ahead. Cozy rooms with wooden floors. Singles with bath €25; doubles €30/€40; triples with bath €50. ❷

Hotel Tourist, Mitropoleos 21 (☎2310 270 501), west of Aristotelous, has an excellent location. Rooms with phone, A/C, and bath. Singles €55; doubles €70; triples €90. ❹

Youth Hostel, Alex. Svolou 44 (☎2310 225 946). Take bus #8, 10, 11, or 31 west down Egnatia and get off at the Arch of Galerius (Kamara stop). This cheap option finds backpackers talking long into the hot nights on its balconies. €12 per person, July 15-Sept. 15 €15 per person. 10% ISIC discount. ❶

◖ FOOD

The **old city** brims with *tavernas* and restaurants near the **fortress** which have sweeping views of the gulf. Thessaloniki restaurants have a delightful custom of giving patrons watermelon or sweets gratis after a meal.

▧ **Dore Zythos,** Tsiroyianni 7 (☎2310 279 010), behind the grassy triangular plot across from the White Tower. Sea breezes combine with the avant-garde menu to make this a local favorite. Try the *Its Pilaf* (€6.50) for an Anatolian treat. Entrees €4.50-12. ❷

Chatzi, El. Venizelou 50 (☎2310 279 058; www.chatzis.gr), has been satiating Thessaloniki's sweet tooth since 1908. The superb bakery serves interesting adaptations of traditional desserts, like chocolate *kataifi* (€3). Open daily 7am-2am. ❶

Ouzeri Melathron, Karypi 21-34 (☎2310 275 016). From Egnatia, walk past the Ottoman Bedesten on El. Venizelou and make a right into the passageway between storefronts. Witty subtitled menus feature chicken, snails, lamb, octopus, and a variety of cheese dishes. Entrees €4.30-13. ❷

👁 🎵 SIGHTS AND ENTERTAINMENT

The streets of modern Thessaloniki are littered with the reminders of its significance during the Byzantine and Ottoman empires. Originally part of a palatial complex designed to honor the Roman Caesar Galerium, the **Rotunda** became the church **Agios Georgiou** in late Roman times. Its walls were once plastered with some of the city's most brilliant mosaics; unfortunately, very few remain. (Open Tu-Su 8am-7pm. Free.) At the intersection of D. Gounari and Egnatia stands the striking **Arch of Galerius.** The **Heptapyrgion,** a 5th-century Byzantine fortress, is the main attraction of the city's modest acropolis. (Open Tu-Su 8am-7pm. Free.) Farther west down Egnatia, don't miss **Bey Hamami,** a perfectly preserved 15th-century bath house that served the Ottoman governor and his retinue. (Open daily 8am-9pm. Free.) All that remains of a 15th-century Venetian seawall, the **White Tower,** once used for gruesome executions, presides over the eastern edge of the waterfront like an overgrown chess piece. (Open Tu-Su 8:30am-3pm. Free.)

In keeping with its exalted position as second city of the Byzantine Empire, Thessaloniki uses its ▧**Museum of Byzantine Culture** to tell a cosmopolitan and secular tale through the displays of everyday life, economics, engineering, and imperial dynasties. (Stratou 2. Behind the Archaeological Museum, across Septemvriou 3. Open M 10:30am-5pm, Tu-Su 8:30am-3pm. €4, students and seniors €2, EU students and children free.) Thessaloniki's **Archaeological Museum,** at the end of Tsimiski, across from the International Helexpo Fairgrounds, is full of discoveries gleaned from Neolithic tombs, mosaics from Roman houses, and a dazzling display of Macedonian gold. (Open M 12:30-7pm, Tu-Su 8am-7pm; low season reduced hours. €4, students and seniors €2, EU students and under 18 free.)

There are three main hubs for late-night fun in Thessaloniki: the bars and cafes of the **Ladadika** district, once the red-light strip; the bustling **waterfront;** and the dance-till-you-drop open-air discos around the **airport.** Rub elbows with the city's hipsters in **Rodon,** 11km east of the city along the main highway. (Cover €10, includes 1 drink.) **Shark,** Themistokli Sofouli and Argonavton 2, has waterfront views of the skyline that thrill the clientele.

🔁 DAYTRIP FROM THESSALONIKI: ANCIENT VERGINA

The tombs of Vergina (Βέργινα), final home to ancient Macedonian royalty, lie only 30km from Thessaloniki. The principal sight is the **Great Tumulus,** a huge, manmade mount, 12m tall and 110m wide. Check out the bones of **Alexander IV,** son of Alexander the Great, as well as the magnificent **Tomb of Philip II,** Alexander's father. Visitors can stroll into the mound and check out its magnificent burial treasures, intricate gold work, and brilliant frescoes. (Open in summer M noon-7pm, Tu-Su 8am-7pm; winter Tu-Su 8am-7pm. Admission to all of Vergina's sights €8, students €4, EU students free.) **Buses** run from Thessaloniki (55min., 1 per hr. 5:45am-6:55pm, €4.60) to Veria. From Veria, take the bus to Vergina's *plateia* (20min., 8 per day 6:50am-8pm, €1); follow the signs to the sights.

MOUNT OLYMPUS Ολύμπος Όρος   ☎23520

Erupting out of the Thermaic Gulf, the formidable slopes of Mt. Olympus (nearly 3000m) mesmerized the ancients so much that they believed it to be the divine dwelling place of their immortal pantheon. A network of well-maintained **hiking** trails now makes the summit accessible to anyone with sturdy legs and a taste for the divine. Mt. Olympus has eight peaks: Ag. Andonios (2817m), Kalogeros (2701m), Mytikas (the Needle; 2918m), Profitis Ilias (2803m), Skala (2866m), Skolio (2911m), Stefani (the Throne of Zeus; 2907m), and Toumba (2801m). The entire region became Greece's first national park in 1938.

You'll find the most reliable resources for all aspects of hiking—updates on weather and trail conditions, advice on itineraries and routes, and reservations for any of the **Greek Alpine Club (EOS)** refuges—from EOS refuge ■**Zolotas,** known as "Spilios Agapitos," about 800m below Skala and Mytikas peaks. The staff has years of experience and is happy to distribute info over the phone in English. The refuge has 110 beds, making it the largest and cushiest around, with a telephone and very cold showers. (☎23520 81 800. Curfew 10pm. Open mid-May to Oct. 6am-10pm. €10, with any mountain club membership €8. €4.20 to camp nearby and use facilities.) There are three ways to take on Olympus; all originate in **Litochoro** (elev. 340m). The first and most popular trailhead begins at **Prionia** (elev. 1100m), 18km from the village. This trail ascends 4km through a sheltered, forested ravine to Zolotas. The second trailhead is at **Diastavrosi** (also called **Gortsia;** elev. 1300m), 14km away, which leads 11km up to Kakalos and the SEO refuges. There are no buses to Prionia or Diastavrosi so you must walk, drive, or take a taxi (Prionia €20; Diastavrosi €8) along the road that winds upward from the police station in Litochoro. The third route is more challenging and involves hiking to Prionia via a trail along the **Enipeas Gorge;** you begin in Litochoro and eventually arrive at the Prionia trailhead. After spending the night at the Zolotas refuge, you'll ascend to the summit the next day and head around to the SEO and Kakalos refuges.

Trains (☎23520 22 522) run from Litochoro to Athens (6hr., 4 per day, €12) and Thessaloniki (1hr., 4 per day, €3); a **taxi** from the train station to the town costs about €6. KTEL **buses** (☎23520 81 271) go to Athens (5½hr., 3 per day, €25) and Thessaloniki (1½hr., 17 per day, €6). The **tourist office,** which has free maps of the town and a map of the mountain (€4), is on Ag. Nikolaou by the park. (☎23520 83 100. Open daily July-Nov. 8am-2pm and 3-9pm.) The night before your hike, head to **Hotel Park ❷,** Ag. Nikolaou 23, for comfortable rooms with a bath and large balcony. (☎23520 81 252. Singles €20; doubles €30; triples €40.) **Postal Code:** 60200.

METEORA Μετέωρα ☎24230

Atop a series of awe-inspiring pinnacles, which seem to ascend upward from the Thessalian plain to the sky, is the monastic community of Meteora. Believed to be inhabited by hermits as early as the 11th century, these summits were picked as the location of a series of 24 gravity-defying, frescoed Byzantine monasteries in the 14th century. Six of these monasteries are still in use and open to the public. The ■**Grand Meteoro Monastery** is the oldest, largest, and most touristed of the monasteries. It houses a **folk museum** and the 16th-century **Church of the Transfiguration,** whose dome features a *Pantokrator* (a central image of Christ). To escape the hordes of tourists, venture to **Roussanou,** to the right after the fork in the road. Visible from most of the valley, it is one of the most spectacularly situated monasteries in the area. (Dress modestly. Open Apr.-Sept. Sa-Su and W 10am-12:30pm and 3:30-5pm; hours vary during the rest of the week. €2 per monastery.)

Buses leave for Meteora from the fountain in **Kalambaka,** the most popular base for exploring the sight (2 per day, €0.90). **Trains** leave Kalambaka for Athens (4hr., 4 per day, €19) and Thessaloniki (5hr., 4 per day, €8.50). **Buses** depart for: Athens (5hr., 8 per day, €19); Ioannina (3½hr., 2 per day, €7.90);

Patras (6hr., Tu and Th 10am, F-Sa 3pm, €20); and Thessaloniki (6 per day, €13). In the old town at the base of Meteora ⊠**Alsos House ❷**, Kanari 5, has reasonably priced, comfortable suites with breathtaking views of Meteora's pinnacles. It's an 8min. walk from the central *plateia;* follow Vlahava until it ends, then follow the signs. (☎24320 24 097. Internet and laundry available. Singles €25; doubles €35-40; triples €50; apartment with kitchen €60. Discounts for students.) **Postal Code:** 42200.

IOANNINA Ιωάννινα ☎26510

The capital of Epirus and the eighth-largest city in Greece, Ioannina is mostly a modern city that serves as the natural transportation hub for the Epirus region of northern Greece. The city reached its peak after it was captured in 1788 by **Ali Pasha,** an Albanian-born leader and visionary. A historical district occupies the peninsula that extends into Lake Pamvotis and is the site of the **Frourio,** a monumental fortress built in the 14th century, which today is still home to many of Ioannina's residents. To reach the **Itş Kale** (the inner citadel) from the main entrance of the Frourio, veer left, following the signs. To the immediate right along the wall are the remnants of Ali Pasha's **hamam** (baths). Aside from local finds, the highlights of the city's **Archaeological Museum,** off G. Averof, near the city center, are the lead tablets used by ancients to inscribe their questions to the oracle at Dodoni. (Under renovation. Scheduled to re-open in late 2005 or early 2006. Open Tu-Su 8:30am-3pm. €2, students free.) Catch a ferry from the waterfront (10min., €1) for **Nisi** ("the Island") to explore Byzantine monasteries and the **Ali Pasha Museum** (open daily 8am-10pm; €2). A hike through the ⊠**Vikos Gorge,** the world's steepest canyon just north of Ioannina, will rejuvenate anyone tired of city life.

Buses run from the terminal at Zosimadon 4 to Athens (6½hr., 9 per day, €27) and Thessaloniki (7hr., 6 per day, €22). To reach the **tourist office,** walk 500m down Dodonis; the office is on the left, immediately after the playground. Ask for friendly, English-speaking Milton and a free map. (☎26510 46 662. Open M-F 7:30am-2:30pm.) **Hotel Tourist ❸,** Kolleti 18, on the right a few blocks up G. Averof from the *kastro,* offers baths, phones, and A/C. (☎26510 25 070. Singles €30; doubles €40; triples €55.) **Limni ❷,** meaning "lake," has a charming lakeside patio with views of the mountains and mosque. Portions are huge and prices reasonable. (☎26510 78 988. Entrees €5-7.) **Postal Code:** 45110.

DODONI Δωδώνη ☎26510

Ancient Dodoni, the site of mainland Greece's oldest **oracle,** second in importance only to Delphi, is at the base of a mountain 22km southeast of Ioannina. According to myth, Zeus answered queries here from a giant oak tree. There is also a breathtaking 3rd-century **amphitheater** at the site (currently undergoing restoration), which once seated 17,000 people. (Open 8am-7pm. €2, students and seniors €1, EU students free.) Dodoni is best visited as a **daytrip** from Ioannina. **Buses** to Dodoni run from Ioannina's smaller station at Bizaniou 21 (30min., M and F 6:30am and 3:30pm, €1.70). Ask to be let off at the theater. The return bus passes by around 4:45pm.

IONIAN ISLANDS Νησιά Του Ιόνιου

Just to the west of mainland Greece, the Ionian Islands entice weary travelers with their lush, green vegetation that rolls gently to the edge of the shimmering turquoise waters. The islands are a favorite among Western Europeans and ferry-hopping backpackers heading to Italy. Multicultural for millennia, each of the Ionian Islands maintains a unique identity while sharing unparalleled beauty.

🌙 FERRIES TO ITALY

To catch a ferry from Corfu to Italy, buy your ticket at least a day ahead and ask about the port tax. **International Tours** (☎26610 39 007) and **Ionian Cruises** (☎26610 31 649), both located across the street from the old port on El. Venizelou, can help you with your scheduling woes. Ferries go to: Ancona (20hr., 1 per day, €58); Bari (9hr., 1 per day, €46); Brindisi (7hr., 3 per day, €30); Trieste (24hr., 4 per week, €52); and Venice (24hr., 1 per day, €57). Schedules vary; call ahead.

🏛 CORFU Κέρκυρα   ☎26610

Ever since Homer's Odysseus washed ashore and raved about Corfu's lush beauty, the surrounding seas have brought a constant stream of conquerors, colonists, and tourists to the verdant island. **Corfu Town** enchants with the best of Ionian life—a combination, among other things, of Greek and Venetian traditions. Laundry lines stretching from ornate iron balconies, yellow roses, and green-shuttered alleyways complement its two fortresses, varied museums, churches, and winding streets of old town. Make sure to spend time at the **Mon Repos Estate,** the **Palace of St. Michael and St. George,** and the exquisite **Achillion Palace,** south of Corfu Town; to get there, take a bus #10 to Gastouri (30min.; M-Sa 6 per day, Su 4 per day; €0.90). The lovely **Paleokastritsa** beach, where Odysseus supposedly washed ashore, lies west of town; take a KTEL **bus** to Paleokastritsa (45min.; M-Sa 7 per day, Su 5 per day; €1.60). A short walk from there will bring you to the hilltop monastery **Panagia Theotokos.** KTEL buses also run from Corfu Town to **Agios Gordios** (45min.; M-Sa 5 per day, Su 3 per day; €1.50), home to impressive rock formations and the **Pink Palace Hotel ❷,** which is immensely popular with backpackers in search of instant gratification. The Palace has an impressive list of amenities, including a nightclub, clothing-optional cliff-diving (€15), and water sports. (☎26610 53 103; www.thepinkpalace.com. Breakfast, dinner, and ferry pick-up included. Rooms €20, with A/C and bath €25-40.) **Sidari,** north of Corfu Town, is home to Corfu's famous **Canal d'Amour,** a tourist-packed stretch of sand.

Ferries run from Corfu Town to Italy (see above) and Patras (6-7hr., 1-2 per day, €25), and high-speed **flying dolphins** run to Kephalonia (3hr., W and Sa 9am, €38). KTEL inter-city green **buses** depart from between I. Theotaki and the New Fortress; blue municipal buses leave from Pl. San Rocco. **The Association of Owners of Private Rooms and Apartments,** Iak. Polila 24 (☎26610 26 133), has a complete list of rooms in Corfu Town. **Hotel Konstantinoupolis ❹,** K. Savitsianou 1, at the old port, has traditional long Venetian shutters and rooms with A/C. (☎26610 48 716. Doubles €50-70; triples €70-98.) One of the cheaper options in town is **Hotel Europa ❷,** Gitsiali 10. (☎26610 39 304. Singles €25, with bath €35; doubles €35-45; triples €50-60.) **To Paradosiakon ❸,** Odos Solomou 20, serves excellent traditional Greek food. (Open daily 10am-midnight. Entrees €4-8.50.) At **Restaurant Antranik/Pizza Pete ❷,** Arseniou 21, order a large entree (€5-8) or choose between 20 flavors of homemade ice cream. (☎26610 38 858. Open daily 9am-midnight.) The undisputed epicenter of Corfu Town's nightlife is the **Disco Strip,** on Eth. Antistaseos, 2km west of new port. **Postal Code:** 49100.

🏛 KEPHALONIA Κεφαλόνια   ☎26710

Massive mountains, subterranean lakes and rivers, caves, and forests make Kephalonia a nature lover's paradise. Armed with your own transportation, you will uncover picturesque villages perched on lush, green hillsides and never-ending beaches that blend into brilliant sunsets. **Argostoli,** the capital of Kephalonia, is a lively city packed with pastel buildings that offers good shopping and easy access to other points on the island. **Ferries** depart for **Kyllini** on the Peloponnese (1-2 per day, €10). **Buses** leave from the southern end of the waterfront for Fiskardo (2hr., 10am and 2pm, €4) and Sami (4 per day, €3). Internet is available at **Cafeland**, on Andrea Choida in Argostoli. (☎26710 24 064. €4 per hr. €2 min. Open daily 8am-2pm and 5-9pm.) **Hotel Tourist ❸**, on the waterfront near the bus station, has spacious rooms with balcony. (☎26710 22 510. Singles €30-36; doubles €55.) **Captain's Grille ❷** has two large spaces: one on the waterfront (I. Metaxa and 21 Maiou) and one to the right of the *plateia*. (Entrees €6-15.)

Sami is 24km from Argostoli on the east coast. Stunning views stretch in every direction, from waves crashing on the beach to green hills cradling the town. Sami is close to the underground **Melissani Lake** and **Drogarati Cave**, a large cavern filled with stalactites and stalagmites. (Cave open daily 9am-7pm; low season 10am-4pm. Free.) **Fiskardo**, at the northern tip of the island, is the most beautiful of Kephalonia's towns; take a bus from either Sami (10:15am, 2pm, €3) or Argostoli. Buses from Fiskardo stop at the turn-off for ◪**Myrtos Beach,** with its snowy white pebbles and clear, blue water pressed against sheer cliffs. (Beach 4km from turn-off.) **Ferries** run from Sami to: Brindisi, Italy (July-Sept. 1 per day, €35); Patras (2½hr.; 8:30am and 5pm; €12); and Vathy (1hr., 4 per day, €2.50). **Postal Code:** 28100.

◪ ITHAKA Ιθάκη ☎ 26740

Discovering Ithaka means uncovering 6000 years of history, traversing the homeland of legendary Odysseus, and delighting in the island's pebbled beaches, rocky hillsides, and terraced olive groves. **Vathy,** Ithaka's lovely capital, wraps around a circular bay, where garish fishing and pleasure boats bob in the bay and precipitous green hills nudge against the water. The town makes an excellent base for exploring the island's sights; first head 2km outside of Vathy to the archaeological site at the **Cave of the Nymphs,** where, according to legend, Odysseus hid the treasure the Phoenicians gave him. *Sholi Omirou* (Homer's School), the site most widely acknowledged as the place where **Odysseus's Palace** once stood, has a plethora of Mycenaean ruins and intact architectural structures. (Follow signs from the village of Ag. Athanassios. Free.) If you're looking for serene relaxation, bask in the glow of the jaw-dropping beaches of ◪**Filiatro** and **Sarakiniko,** 3.5km and 2.5km out respectively, which have trees that reach the sea.

Ferries depart from Frikes, on the northern tip of Ithaka, to Vasiliki, Lefkada (1½hr., 10:10am, €4.50). Departures from Piso Aetos go to Sami, Kephalonia (45min., 3 per day, €2) and to Patras in the Peloponnese (4½hr., 7am and 4:30pm, €12). **Aktaion Domatia ❸**, across from the ferry dock on the far right side (when facing inland) of the waterfront, has immaculate rooms and waterfront views. (☎26740 32 387. Singles €25-35; doubles €40-50.) Local favorite **Taverna To Trexantiri ❷**, one block off the *plateia*, serves big portions of traditional Greek dishes. (☎26740 33 066. Salads €2.50-3. Entrees under €6. Open 6pm-late.) **Postal Code:** 28300.

◪ ZAKYNTHOS Ζάκυνθος ☎ 26950

Known as the greenest of the Ionian Islands, Zakynthos is home to thousands of plant and flower species and a large population of loggerhead sea turtles. Bustling **Zakynthos Town** maintains a romantic, nostalgic air that makes walking through its streets or along the waterfront a pleasure. Cruises from Zakynthos Town go to many of the island's most spectacular sights, including the glowing, stalactite-filled ◪**Blue Caves** on the northeastern shore past Skinari. Southwest of the Blue Caves is the **Smuggler's Wreck,** a large boat skeleton whose marvel has made the area one of the most photographed beaches in the world, and **Marathonissi,** also called Turtle Island because of its resemblance to a turtle. Travelers should be aware that they share Zakynthos's beaches with a resident population of **endangered sea turtles,** and so should treat the turtle nesting grounds with respect.

GREECE

Ferries for Kyllini in the Peloponnese (1½hr., 7 per day 5:30am-8pm, €6) depart from the southern dock. Tickets for Kyllini ferries can be bought at **Praktoreio Ploion,** next to Hertz on Lomvardou past the police station. (☎26278 22 083. Open daily 8:30am-9pm.) Skinari, north of Zakynthos Town, has ferries to Pesada, Kephalonia (1½hr., 1-2 per day, €5). **Athina Marouda Rooms for Rent ❶,** on Tzoulati and Koutouzi, has simple rooms with fans and small furnishings. (☎26950 45 194. Singles €10-20; doubles €25-40.) Dining in Zakynthos Town is a treat. **Village Inn ❸,** Lomvardou 20, has tables facing the water and a beautiful garden area with live Greek music every evening. (☎26950 26 991. Open noon-late.) **Postal Code:** 29100.

CYCLADES Κυκλάδες

With towns of white-stucco, blue-doored buildings, and cobblestone streets, the Cyclades meet every traveler's dream of the quintessential Greek island vacation. Overly-self-conscious about the potential for tourism, the islands whirl out to provide something for everybody. Whatever your whim, you'll find it next to a cerulean sea under the ever-smiling Greek sun.

▐ TRANSPORTATION

Ferries run from: Athens to Ios, Milos, Mykonos, Naxos, Paros, and Santorini; Crete to Milos, Mykonos, Naxos, Paros and Santorini; and Thessaloniki to Mykonos, Naxos, Paros, and Santorini. Frequent ferries also run between each of the islands in the Cyclades. See below for all ferry information. High-speed ferries and **hydrofoils** typically cover the same routes at twice the cost and speed.

▓ MYKONOS Μύκονος   ☎22890

Coveted by pirates in the 18th century, Mykonos is still lusted after by those seeking revelry and excess. Nightlife, both gay and straight, abounds on this island, the expensive playground of chic sophisticates. Ambling in colorful alleyways at dawn or dusk, among the ▓**disturbingly large pink pelicans,** is the cheapest and most exhilarating way to experience the island, especially **Mykonos Town.** All of Mykonos's beaches are nude, but the degree of bareness varies. **Platis Yialos, Paradise** beach, and **Super Paradise** beach are the most daring; **Elia** is a bit tamer. Buses run south from South Station to Platis Yialos and Paradise (every 30min., €0.90) and to Elia from North Station (30min., 8 per day, €1.10). After 11pm, wild dancing, drag shows, and irresistible hedonism are the norm at **Pierro's** on Matogianni (beer €5). The **Skandinavian Bar** on the waterfront has something for everyone in its two-building party complex. (Beer and shots €3-3.50. Open M-F and Su 8:30pm-3am, Sa 8:30pm-4am.) **Caprice Bar,** on the water in Little Venice, is a popular post-beach hangout with breathtaking sunsets, funky music, and lively company. (Drinks €4-7. Open M-Th and Su 6:30pm-3:30am, F-Sa until 4:30am.) **Cavo Paradiso,** on Paradise beach, is considered one of the world's top dance clubs, hosting internationally renowned DJs. (Open daily 3am-11am. Cover €15.) New clubs open every summer. Follow the crowds to find the most popular places.

Ferries run to: Naxos (3hr., 1-2 per day, €7.90); Piraeus (6hr., 2-3 per day, €25); Samos (2 per week, €19); and Santorini (6hr., 3 per week, €16). The helpful **tourist police** are located at the ferry landing. (☎22890 22 482. Open daily 8am-11pm.) Most budget travelers bed down at Mykonos's several festive campsites, which offer myriad sleeping options beyond the standard plot of grass. **Hotel Philippi ❹,** Kalogera 25, across from Zorzis, provides cheerful rooms with bath, fridge, and A/C around a garden. (☎22890 22 294; chriko@otenet.gr. Open Apr.-Oct. Singles €35-60; doubles €80.) The lively **Paradise Beach Camping ❶,** 6km from the village,

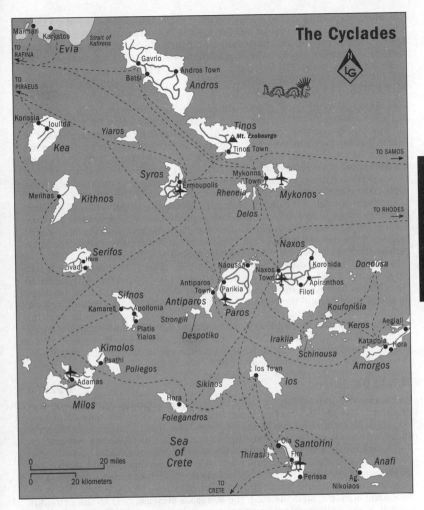

The Cyclades

TO SAMOS

TO RHODES

Marmari Karystos Strait of Kafireos Evia

TO RAFINA

Gavrio Batsi Andros Town Andros

TO PIRAEUS

Korissia Ioulida Yiaros Tinos Mt. Exobourgo Tinos Town

Kea

Merihas Kithnos Syros Ermoupolis Mykonos Town Mykonos Rheneia

Delos

Serifos Hora Livadi Naoussa Naxos Koronida Donousa

Antiparos Town Parikia Naxos Town Apiranthos Filoti

Sifnos Antiparos Paros Koufonisia

Kamares Apollonia Strongili Keros Aegiali

Platis Yialos Despotiko Iraklia Katapola Hora

Kimolos Schinousa Amorgos

Psathi Poliegos

Adamas Sikinos Ios Town Ios

Milos Hora

Folegandros

Sea of Crete Oia Santorini

Thirasia Fira Anafi

Perissa Ag. Nikolaos

TO CRETE

0   20 miles
0   20 kilometers

is directly on the beach. (☎ 22890 25 915. €5-7.50 per person, €3-5 per tent; 2-person beach cabin €20-45.) **Appaloosa ❸**, one block from Taxi Square on Mavrogeneous, serves mostly Mexican selections. (Entrees €8-11. Open daily 8pm-1:30am.) **Ithaki ❹** (☎ 22890 26 850), just past Paradise beach, serves delectable seafood entrees (pasta with shrimp €18) in a beautiful setting. **Postal Code:** 84600.

⚑ DELOS Δήλος ☎ 22890

Delos is the sacred center of the Cyclades. The island-wide **archaeological site's** highlights can be seen in about 3hr. From the dock, head straight to the **Agora of the Competaliasts;** continue in the same direction and turn left onto the wide **Sacred Road** to reach the **Sanctuary of Apollo,** a collection of temples built from Mycenaean times onward. On the right is the biggest and most famous, the **Temple of Apollo.**

Continue 50m past the end of the Sacred Road to the beautiful **Terrace of the Lions.** A path leads to the summit of **Mt. Kythnos** (112m), from which Zeus watched Apollo's birth. A few islands have daily boat trips to Delos, but the island is best visited as a **daytrip** from Mykonos. Excursion **boats** leave the dock near Mykonos Town for Delos (35min., Tu-Su 4 per day, round-trip €6.50-10).

◪ PAROS Πάρος   ☎22840

Paros is famed for its slabs of pure white marble, used for many of the great statues and buildings of the ancient world. Today's visitors know the island for its tall mountains and long, golden beaches. Behind the commercial surface of **Parikia,** Paros's port and largest city, flower-filled streets wind through archways and past one of the most treasured basilicas of the Orthodox faith, the **Panagia Ekatontapiliani** (Church of Our Lady of 100 Gates). Tradition holds that only 99 of the church's 100 doors are visible—when the 100th appears, Constantinople will again belong to the Greeks. (Dress modestly. Open daily 7am-10pm. Free.) Just 10km south of town is the shady, spring-fed ◪**Valley of the Butterflies** (a.k.a. *Petaloudes*), where rare *Panaxiaquadripunctaria* moths congregate during the mating season from June to late September. Take the bus from Parikia to Aliki (12min., 7 per day, €0.90) and ask to be let off at Petaloudes. Follow the signs 2km up the road. (Open daily June-Sept. 9am-8pm. €1.50.)

    Ferries sail to: Crete (3½hr., 2 per week, €43); Ios (2hr., 2-3 per day, €10); Kos (1 per week, €17); Mykonos (5 per week, €8); Naxos (1hr. 4-5 per day, €6); Santorini (3hr., 3-4 per day, €12); and Thessaloniki (1 per week, €35). The **tourist police** are on the *plateia* behind the telephone office. (☎22840 21 673. Open daily 7am-2:30pm.) Turn left at the dock and take a right after the cemetery ruins to reach the pleasant **Rena Rooms ❷**. (☎22840 22 220. Doubles €20-40; triples €30-55. 20% discount for *Let's Go* readers.) The psychedelic **Happy Green Cow ❸**, a block off the *plateia* behind the National Bank, serves tasty vegetarian fare. (Entrees €8-12. Open daily Apr.-Nov. 7pm-midnight.) **Postal Code:** 84400.

◪ NAXOS Νάξος   ☎22850

The ancients believed Naxos, the largest of the Cyclades, was the home of Dionysus. Olive groves, wineries, small villages, and chalky white ruins fill its interior, while sandy beaches line its shores. **Naxos Town,** the capital, is crowned by the **Kastro,** a Venetian castle now home to two museums. The ◪**Venetian Museum** features evening concerts with traditional Greek music, dancing, and shadow theater. (Open daily 10am-3pm and 7-10pm. €3, students and seniors €2.) The **Archaeological Museum** occupies the former Collège Français, which educated Nikos Kazantzakis, author of *The Last Temptation of Christ* and *Zorba the Greek.* (Open Tu-Su 8:30am-3pm. €3, students €2.) The **Mitropolis Museum,** next to the Orthodox Church, is an architectural achievement in itself, built around the excavated site of a 13th-century BC settlement. (Open Tu-Su 8:30am-3pm. Free.) The 6th-century BC **Portara** archway, visible from the waterfront, is one of the few archaeological sites in Greece where you can climb all over the ruins. To experience the island fully, it's essential to escape Naxos Town. A bus goes from the port to the beaches of **Agios Giorgios, Agios Prokopios, Agia Anna,** and **Plaka** (1 per hr., €1.20). Buses also run from Naxos Town to **Apiranthos,** a beautiful village with narrow, marble paths (1hr., €2.10). To get to the **Tragea** highland valley, an enormous olive grove, take a bus from Naxos Town to Halki (30min., 5 per day, €1.20).

    Ferries go from Naxos Town to: Crete (7hr., 1 per week, €20); Ios (1hr., 1 per day, €8.20); Kos (7hr., 1 per week, €16); Mykonos (3hr., 1 per day, €9); Paros (1hr., 4 per day, €5.50); Piraeus (6hr., 4 per day, €20); Rhodes (13hr., 1 per week, €20); Santorini (3hr., 3 per day, €13); and Thessaloniki (14hr., 1 per day, €30). The **tourist office** is

300m up from the dock, by the bus station. (☎22850 24 358. Open daily 8am-11pm.) **Pension Irene ❷**, about 100m from Ag. Giorgios, is near the center of the town. (☎22850 23 169. All rooms with A/C. Singles €15; doubles €20-30; triples €25-35.) Naxos has three **camping ❶** options along the beach; look for representatives along the dock. (€4-8 per person, tents €2.) **Postal Code:** 84300.

🏝 IOS Ιος   ☎22860

On Ios, you'll see everything your mother warned you about—wine swilled from the bottle at 3pm, all-day beachside drinking games, partiers dancing madly in the streets, people swimming less than 30min. after they've eaten, and so much more. The **port** (Yialos) is at one end of the island's sole paved road. The town (Hora) sits above it on a hill; but the beaches are the place to be. Most spend their days at **Mylopotas beach,** a 20min. walk downhill from Ios town or a bus ride from the port or town (every 10-20min. 7:20am-midnight, €0.90). Sunning is typically followed by drinking; head up from the *plateia* to reach the **Slammer Bar** for tequila slammers (€3), then stop by **Disco 69** for some dirty dancing (drinks €5, cover €5 after midnight). Join in the table dancing at **Sweet Irish Dream** (cover after 2:30am) or grind to techno at **Scorpion Disco,** the island's largest club (cover after 1am). A few hours later, crowds begin to gather at the beach, where **Mylopotas** offers windsurfing, water-skiing, and snorkeling (€14-40).

    Ferries go to: Naxos (1¾hr., 3 per day, €9); Paros (3hr., 3 per day, €9); Piraeus (8hr., 3 per day, €20); and Santorini (1¼hr., 3 per day, €6.20). **Acteon Travel,** adjacent to the bus stop in the port, takes the place of the tourist office. (☎22860 91 343. Open daily 8am-midnight.) In the village, take the uphill steps to the left in the *plateia* and take the first left to reach **Francesco's ❶,** where you'll find spectacular harbor views and a terrace bar. (☎22860 91 706; www.francescos.net. Dorms €8-14; doubles €20.) On the end of Mylopotas beach, **Far Out Camping ❶** has a pool, plenty of tents, parties, and activities, including bungee jumping. (☎22860 92 302. Open Apr.-Oct. €4-8 per tent; tent rental €1; small cabins from €5; bungalows €7-18.) **Ali Baba's ❷,** next to Ios Gym, offers delicious *pad thai* (€8.50) and burgers (€5.50). Off the main church's *plateia*, **Lord Byron's ❸** serves creative variations on Greek staples. (Entrees €9-15.) **Postal Code:** 84001.

🏝 SANTORINI Σαντορίνη   ☎22860

Whitewashed towns balanced on cliffs, black-sand beaches, and deeply scarred hills make Santorini's landscape nearly as dramatic as the volcanic explosion that created it. Despite all the kitsch in touristy **Fira,** the island's capital, nothing can ruin the pleasure of wandering the town's cobblestoned streets, browsing its craft shops, and taking in the sunset from its western edge. The town of **Oia** is *the* place in Greece to watch the sunset. Catch a bus from Fira (25min., 23 per day, €0.90). Although the prices are sky-high, it is a spectacular setting not to be missed. On the southwestern side of the island, the Minoan city **Akrotiri** was entirely preserved by lava. (Open Tu-Su 8:30am-3pm. Free) Buses run to Akrotiri from Fira (30min., 14 per day, €1.30). Buses also leave Fira for the black-sand **beaches** of Kamari (20min., 32 per day, €0.90) and Perissa (30min., 21 per day, €1.50). The bus stops before Perissa in Pyrgos; from there, you can hike (40min.) to the **Profitis Ilias Monastery,** whose lofty location provides an island panorama, and continue for 1½hr. to the ruins of **Ancient Thira.** (Open Tu-Su 8:30am-2:30pm. Free.) At night, head to **Murphy's,** which claims to be the first Irish pub in Greece. (Mixed drinks €4.50-6. Cover €5. Open daily Mar.-Oct. noon-4am.) For a mellower evening, check out **Kira Thira Jazz Club.** (Mixed drinks €4-8. Open daily 8:30pm-3:30am.)

GREECE

Ferries from Fira run to: Ios (1hr., 1-3 per day, €6.30); Iraklion, Crete (4hr., 3 per week, €14); Mykonos (6hr., 2 per week, €13); Naxos (3hr., 3-4 per day, €11); Paros (4hr., 2-5 per day, €12); Piraeus (10hr., 2-5 per day, €23); and Thessaloniki (15hr., 5 per week, €35). Most ferries depart from Athinios harbor; frequent buses (25min., €1.50) connect to Fira. Head 300m north from the *plateia* in Fira to reach the friendly **Thira Youth Hostel ❶**, in an old monastery. (☎22860 22 387. Open Apr.-Oct. Dorms €8-12; doubles €20-35.) In Oia, the impeccable rooms at **Youth Hostel Oia ❷** are a good choice. (☎22860 71 465. Breakfast included. Open May-Oct. Dorms €13-15.) The cheery **Mama's Cyclades Cafe ❷**, north of Fira on the road to Oia, serves up a big breakfast special. (☎22860 23 032. Entrees €5-8. Open daily 8am-midnight.) Oia's **1800 ❹**, in a 19th-century mansion, is a special treat. (☎22860 71 485. Entrees €15-30. Open daily 7pm-midnight.) **Postal Code:** 84700.

CRETE Κρήτη

According to a Greek saying, a Cretan's first loyalty is to his island, his second to his country. Since 3000 BC, Crete has maintained an identity distinct from the rest of Greece. Despite this insular mind-set, residents are friendly to visitors who come to enjoy their island's inexhaustible trove of mosques, monasteries, mountain villages, gorges, grottoes, and beaches. Crete is divided into four main prefectures: Iraklion, Hania, Rethymno, and Lasithi.

✈ GETTING TO CRETE

Olympic Airways (☎2810 288 073) and **Aegean Airlines** connect Athens to: Sitia (2-3 per week, €83) in the east; Iraklion (45min., 13-15 per day, €84) in the center; and Hania (4 per day, €53) in the west.

IRAKLION Ηράκλειο   ☎2810

Iraklion is Crete's capital and primary port. The chic locals live life in the fast lane, which translates into an urban brusqueness unique among the cities of Crete and the most diverse nightlife on the island. Iraklion's main attraction after Knossos is

GREECE

the superb ◧**Archaeological Museum,** off Pl. Eleftherias. By appropriating major finds from all over the island, the museum has amassed a comprehensive record of the Neolithic and Minoan stages of Cretan history. (Open M 12:30-7pm, Tu-Su 8am-7pm. €6; students and EU seniors €3; classicists, fine arts students, under 18, and EU students free.) The **Tomb of Nikos Kazantzakis,** on top of the city walls, is a necessary stop for Zorba fans. A maze of streets between **Plateia Venizelou** and **Plateia Eleftherias** houses Iraklion's night spots: At **Cafe Korais,** Korai 8, patrons absorb the hipness and watch the parade of well-dressed bar-hoppers on an expansive deck. (☎2810 346 336. Mixed drinks €6.50. Open daily 9pm-4am.) A walk down D. Boufor takes you to **Privilege** (☎2810 244 850) and **Koo** (☎2810 334 353; opens at midnight). Both have multiple bars serving pricey drinks and their balconies that overlook the port provide a good view for those sober enough to appreciate it.

From Terminal A, between the old city walls and the harbor, **buses** leave for Agios Nikolaos (1½hr., 20 per day, €5) and Hania (3hr., 17 per day, €11) via Rethymno (1½hr., €5.90). Buses leave across from Terminal B for Phaistos (1½hr., 8 per day, €4.50). The **tourist police** are on Dikeosinis 10. (☎2810 283 190. Open daily 8am-11pm.) **Netc@fé,** 1878 4, has Internet access. (€1.50 per hr. Open M-Sa 10am-2am, Su noon-2am.) **Rent Rooms Verginia ❷,** Horatson 32, has sinks in each room and a well-maintained common bath lies just down the hall. (☎2810 242 739. Doubles €25.) The **open-air market** near Pl. Venizelou has stalls piled high with fruit, vegetables, cheeses, and meats. (Open M-Sa 8am-2pm, Tu and Th-F 8am-2pm and 5-9pm.) **Tou Terzaki ❷,** Loch. Marineli 17, has petite portions cooked with delectable freshness. (☎2810 221 444. Open daily 12:30pm-midnight.) **Prassein Aloga ❷,** Handakos 21, serves fresh Mediterranean dishes in its tree-lined courtyard. (Entrees €6-10. Open M-Sa 10am-midnight.) **Postal Code:** 71001.

◧ **DAYTRIP FROM IRAKLION: KNOSSOS.** At Knossos, the most famous archaeological site in Crete, excavations have revealed the remains of the largest and most complicated of Crete's **Minoan palaces.** The original palace dates back to around 1700 BC, but it was partially destroyed by and subsequently forgotten because of a fire around 1450 BC. Sir Arthur Evans, who financed and supervised the excavations, eventually restored large parts of the palace in Knossos; his work

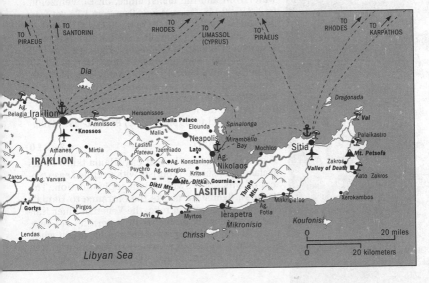

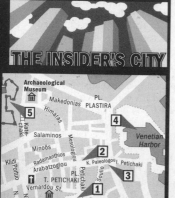

THE INSIDER'S CITY

VENETIAN RETHYMNO

Though the Venetians built all over Crete during their 400-year occupation of the island, their architecture in Rethymno is especially impressive.

1 The **Neratzes Minaret** was first built by the Venetians as a Catholic church. It was converted to a mosque when the Turks invaded in 1646.

2 The **Rimondi Fountain** is still the center of the Old City. Three columns rise out of the three lions' heads that spit water into sinks. The lion symbolizes St. Mark, the patron saint of Venice.

3 The **Loggia** was the central public building of the city.

4 The Venetians worked almost continuously to dredge and improve the **harbor.**

5 The huge **Fortezza** overlooking the Old City stands as the most recognizable reminder of the Venetian period in Rethymno. The city did not fall until the Venetians surrendered the fortress to the Turks in 1646.

often crossed the line from preservation to artistic interpretation, but the site is nonetheless impressive. (Open daily 8am-6pm. €6, students €3; low season free Su.) To reach Knossos from Iraklion, take **bus** #2 from Augustou 25 (€0.90).

RETHYMNO Ρέθυμνο   ☎28310

Crete's many conquerors—Venetians, Ottomans, and even Nazis—have had a profound effect in Rethymno. Arabic inscriptions adorn the walls of the narrow streets, minarets highlight the skyline, and the 16th-century **Venetian Fortezza** stands watch over the harbor. Bring a picnic and explore the fortress ruins. (Open Tu-Su 9am-7pm. €3.) Cloistered beaches, steep gorges, and stunning hikes await in the nearby town of **Plakias.** (4 buses from Rethymno per day, €3.30.) To reach stunning **One Rock beach,** follow the left fork of the main road 1km outside of town, take a right at the signs pointing to Damnoni beach, walk the length of the sand, and take a right on the track at the end; One Rock is the second cove on the right. Look for the underwater tunnel through the cliff on the right side, which leads to **Pig's beach.** To complete the fantastic 2hr. hike to **Preveli Monastery,** ask either in town or at the hostel for directions.

The **Rethymno-Hania bus station** (☎28310 22 212) is south of the fortress on the water, with service to Hania (1hr., 20 per day, €5.60) and Iraklion (1½hr., 21 per day, €6). Climb the stairs behind the bus station, turn left on I. Gavriil, which becomes Kountouriotou, and turn left on Varda Kallergi to reach the waterfront and the **tourist office,** on El. Venizelou. (☎28310 29 148. Open M-F 8:30am-2pm.) To get from the station to the friendly **Youth Hostel ❶,** Tombazi 41-45, walk down I. Gavriil, take the first left at Pl. Martiron; Tombazi is the second right. (☎28310 22 848. Reception 8am-noon and 5-9pm. Dorms €7.50) From the initial entrance into **Taverna Kyria Maria ❷,** Moskovitou 20, to the complimentary *raki* and honey-drizzled cheese pie, Kyria Maria is one of the best bets in town. (☎28310 29 078. Open daily mid-Mar. to Oct. 11am-11pm. MC/V.) **Postal Code:** 74100.

HANIA Χάνια   ☎28210

The island's second largest city, Hania takes on its avalanche of summer tourists with a refined ease typical of this port town's urban sophistication. The **Venetian lighthouse** marks the entrance to Hania's stunning architectural relic, the Venetian Inner Harbor. Nestled away on the northwestern tip of Crete, the heavenly ▧**blue lagoon** of **Balos** offers bright white sand and warm, shallow waters to visitors who trek out to this distant beach. Daily **boat cruises** leave from Kissamos port, 3km outside of town along the main road heading away from Hania (May-Oct. departs daily 10:15am, returns 5:30pm; round-trip €20). Buy tickets at Kissamos port from companies like **Gramvousa-Balos Daily Cruises** (☎28220 24 344; gramvous@in.gr). Before arriving at Balos, the boat stops at nearby **Gramvousa**, a tall island with a large Venetian fortress perched on its summit.

The most popular excursion from Hania and Iraklion is the 5-6hr. hike down ■**Samaria Gorge** (Φράγγι της Σαμαριάς), a spectacular 16km ravine extending through the White Mountains. Sculpted by rainwater over 14 million years, the gorge—the longest in Europe—retains its allure despite having been trampled by thousands of visitors. (Open daily May to mid-Oct. 6am-6pm. €5, children under 15 and organized student groups free. Hang on to your ticket.) For more info, call **Hania Forest Service** (☎28210 92 287). The trail starts at **Xyloskalo;** take the 6:15 or 8:30am **bus** from Hania to Xyloskalo (1½hr., €5.20). The 1:45pm bus from Hania will put you in **Omalos**, ready for the next morning. The trail ends in **Agia Roumeli**, where you can hop on a **boat** to Hora Sfakion (1¼hr., 3-4 per day, €4.60) or take a return bus to Hania (6:30 and 7pm, €5.30).

Ferries arrive in the nearby port of Souda; buses connect from the port to Hania's supermarket on Zymvrakakidon (25min., €1). **Buses** (☎28210 93 306) leave from the station on the corner of Kidonias and Kelaidi for Iraklion (2½hr., 20 per day, €11) and Rethymno (1hr., 20 per day, €6). The **tourist office** is in the city hall. (☎28210 36 155. Open M-F 9am-8pm, Sa 9am-2pm.) To get to ■**Hotel Fidias ❷**, Sarpaki 6, walk toward the harbor on Halidon and turn right onto Athinagora, which becomes Sarpaki. (☎28210 52 494. Singles €9; doubles €15-25.) ■**Anaplous ❷**, near the harbor on Sifaka, claims they serve the only *pilino* (€25, serves 3), a pork and lamb creation, in Greece. (Open daily 7:30pm-12:30am.) **Postal Code:** 73100.

AGIOS NIKOLAOS Άγιος Νικόλαος ☎28210

Catering to beach-obsessed patrons, one-stop holiday-makers, and hikers on their way to more obscure destinations, the town nevertheless provides a relaxing rest stop with its meandering harbor promenades, pedestrian streets, and open-air cafes. For an exciting daytrip, head to the ominous and intriguing island of **Spinalonga**, a former Venetian fortress and leper colony, a few kilometers away by ferry. Catch a bus to Elounda (€1) and take a ferry from Elounda to Spinalonga (Apr.-Oct., every 30min. 9:30am-4:30pm, €8). Once you arrive at Spinalonga, it's €2 (EU students and children under 12 free). A great hike is through the **Valley of Death**. To get there, take the bus to Sitia (1½hr., 7 per day, €5.50) and then to the small village of Zakros (1hr., 3 per day, €2.90). In the city, museums will keep you busy.

Ferries sail to **Piraeus** (12hr., 3 per week, €28) via **Milos** (7hr., 3 per week, €19) and **Rhodes** (12hr., 2 per week, €23). For the **tourist office**, S. Koundourou 21A, cross the bridge at the harbor onto S. Koundourou. (☎28410 22 357. Open daily Apr.-Nov. 8am-9:30pm.) From the tourist office, turn away from the water and turn right onto the street behind the taxi stand. Walk up the hill and turn left onto Stratigou Koraka to reach **Christodoulakis Pension ❷**, Stratigou Koraka 7. The pension, the second building after you turn the corner, is unmarked; look for the profusion of plants. (☎28410 22 525. Singles €15; doubles €20-25; triples €30-36.) **Migomis ❸**, Plastira 24, serves up tasty food with a tremendous panoramic view of the city. (☎28410 24 353. Open daily noon-midnight.) **Postal Code:** 72100.

EASTERN AEGEAN ISLANDS

Scattered along Turkey's coast, the islands of the **Dodecanese** are marked by a history of persistent life in the face of myriad invasions. Eclectic architecture is the most visible legacy of these repeated conquests: Greek and Roman ruins, castles built by crusaders, Ottoman mosques, and stark Italian fascist facades all coexist, undisturbed by the bright blue-and-white modern homes of the locals. The more northern and isolated islands of the **Northeast Aegean** remain sheltered from the cultural creep of globalization. Deck chairs and mass hotels are rarities in this part of Greece, where vast, pristine wilderness and local hospitality are commonplace.

FERRIES TO TURKEY

Ferries for Turkey depart from Chios, Kos, Lesvos, and Samos. From Kos Town, ferries run to Bodrum every morning (round-trip €15-40, port tax included). Daily excursion boats leave to Kuşadası from Samos Town at 8:30am (1¼hr.; €40 round-trip, €8.80 Greek port tax); a guided tour of nearby **Ephesus** is included for an additional €20. Turkish entrance **visas** (US$65) must be purchased at the border. From Chios Town, ferries go to Çesme (45min., 1-2 per day, round-trip €40).

🏛 RHODES Ρόδος   ☎22410

The undisputed tourism capital of the Dodecanese, the island of Rhodes has retained a sense of serenity in the sandy beaches along its eastern coast, the jagged cliffs skirting its western coast, and the green mountains dotted with villages in its interior. Few islands are known for a sight that no longer exists, but Rhodes, with its now-defunct 33m **Colossus** (one of the Seven Wonders of the Ancient World) is one of them. The pebbled inclines of the old town, constructed by the Knights of St. John, lends **Rhodes Town** a medieval flair. At the top of the hill, a tall, square tower marks the entrance to the pride of the city, the **Palace of the Grand Master,** which features moats, drawbridges, battlements, and 300 rooms. (☎22410 25 500. €6, students €3, EU students free.) The beautiful halls and courtyards of the **Archaeological Museum,** dominating the **Plateia Argiokastrou,** shelter small treasures, including the exquisite *Aphrodite Bathing* from the 1st century BC. (☎22410 27 657. Open Tu-Su 8:30am-2:30pm. €3, students €2.) Nightlife in the old town focuses around the street of **Militadou,** off Apelou. **Orfanidou,** in the new town, is popularly known as **Bar Street.** With whitewashed houses clustered at the foot of a castle-capped acropolis, **Lindos,** south of Rhodes Town, is perhaps the most picturesque town on the island. Buses run to Lindos from Rhodes Town (17 per day, €3.40).

Ferries leave Rhodes Town for: Kos (1-2 per day, €15); Patmos (1-2 per day, €29); Piraeus (1 per day, €32); Samos (1 per week, €22); and Sitia, Crete (1 per day, €22). There is a **tourist office** at the intersection of Makariou and Amerikis, a few blocks from Pl. Rimini. **Mama's Pension ❶,** Menekleous 28, has comfortable rooms, and live music performances by the owner. (☎22410 25 359. Dorms €10; doubles €25.) The vine-enclosed garden-bar of **Hotel Anastasia ❷,** 28 Oktovriou 46, complements the bright rooms. (☎22410 28 007. Singles €24-27; doubles €29-36. V.) Flavorful fish at **Sea Star ❷,** in Pl. Sophokleous, arrive fin-flapping fresh and straight off the charcoal. (☎22410 22 117. Entrees €5-7.) **Postal Code:** 85100.

🏛 KOS Κως   ☎22420

Antiquity best knew Kos as the birthplace of Hippocrates, the father of modern medicine. Today **Kos Town** attracts a young, loud, and inebriated crowd more interested in sexual healing than anything else. The more sedate traveler can escape to the sanctuary of ■**Asclepeion,** 4km southwest of Kos Town. Hippocrates's medical school opened in the 5th century BC. In the summer, minitrains run there from Kos Town. (Open Tu-Su 8am-2:30pm. €4, students €2.) For a fiery daytrip, hop a ferry to the island of **Nisyros** (1½hr., 4 per week) to take a peek into the craters of active **Mandraki Volcano,** with its yellow sulfur crystals and hissing steam. The island's best beaches stretch along southern Kos to Kardamene and are all accessible by bus. Most bars are located around **Nafklirou**, in the old city, and along **Porfirou**, in the new city between Averof and Zouroudi. The cavernous, red- and chrome-colored **Fashion Club**, Kanari 2, by the Dolphin Roundabout, hosts Kos's wildest nights. (Cover €10 on weekends, includes 1 drink. Open daily 11pm-4am.)

Ferries run to: Patmos (4hr., 1-2 per day, €10); Piraeus (11-15hr., 1-3 per day, €23); and Rhodes (4hr., 2-3 per day, €15). The **tourist office** is at Vas. Georgiou B' 1 and has free maps. (☎22420 24 460. Open M-F 8am-8:30pm.) Take the first right off Megalou Alexandrou to get to ⊠**Pension Alexis ❷**, Irodotou 9, a beloved travel institution with cheery doubles and a kind owner. (☎22420 28 798. Doubles €20-22; triples €28-38.) A mix of locals and tourists make up the stream of patrons at ⊠**Mummy's Cooking ❷**, where the food really does taste homemade. From the Dolphin Roundabout, walk two blocks down Bouboulinas. (☎22420 28 525. Entrees €6-8. Open M-Sa 7am-11pm.) **Postal Code:** 85300.

⊠ SAMOS Σάμος   ☎22730

Visitors frequently stop in Samos en route to Kuşadası and the ruins of Ephesus on the Turkish coast. Yet the island is an excellent destination itself; hiking paths through mountain forests lead to hidden caves and waterfalls, and luminous beaches lie just minutes from the **Samos Town's** metropolis. The ⊠**Archaeological Museum**, which sits behind the municipal gardens, houses a collection from the Temple of Hera. (☎22730 27 469. Open Tu-Su 8:30am-3pm. €3, seniors and students €2, EU students free. The ancient city of **Pythagorio**, once the island's capital, is 14km south of Vathy. Near the town are the magnificent remains of Polykrates's 6th-century BC engineering project, the **Tunnel of Eupalinos**, which supplied water to the city from a spring 1.3km away. (Open Tu-Su 8:45am-2:45pm. €4, seniors and students €2, EU students free.) Buses run from Samos Town to Pythagorio (9 per day). Polykrates's greatest feat was the **Temple of Hera**, in Heraion, a 30min. bus ride (€1.50) from Pythagorion. Though only one of the original 134 columns is still standing, the temple still merits a visit. (Open Tu-Su 8:30am-3pm. €3, students €2.)

Ferries from Samos Town go to: Chios (3½hr., 3 per week, €11); Kos (1 per week, €15); Mykonos (6hr., 2 per week, €18); Piraeus (5hr., 1-2 per day, €25); and Rhodes (1 per week, €23). The **tourist office** is on a side street a block before Pl. Pythagoras. (☎22730 28 530. Open July-Aug. M-Sa 7am-2:30pm.) **Pension Trova ❷**, Kalomiris 26, has clean, open rooms with shared baths. (☎22730 27 759. Singles €17-20; doubles €20-25; triples €30-40.) **Postal Code:** 83100.

⊠ LESVOS Λέσβος   ☎22510

Ouzo, olive groves, horse-racing, remote monasteries, parched hillsides, lush green expanses, sandy beaches, art colonies, and a petrified forest harmonize on Lesvos in an irresistible siren song. Most travelers pass through modern **Mytilini**, the capital and central port city. At the new ⊠**Archaeological Museum**, on 8 Noemvriou, visitors can walk on preserved mosaic floors dating from Lesvos's Neolithic past. (Open Tu-Su 8am-3pm. €3, students €2, EU students and under 18 free.) Only 4km south of Mytilini along El. Venizelou, the village of **Varia** is home to two excellent museums. **Theophilos Museum** features the work of the Neo-Primitivist Greek painter Theophilos Hadzimichali. (Open Tu-Su 9am-2:30pm and 6-8pm. €2, students and under 18 free.) **Musée Tériade** displays lithographs by Chagall, Matisse, Miró, and Picasso. (Open daily 9am-2pm and 5-8pm. €2, students and children free.) Local **buses** to Varia leave Mytilini every hr. (20min., €0.65). Tell the driver you're going to the museums.

Molyvos breathes the sensibility of an artists' colony; though frequented by tourists, its atmosphere remains serene and its prices reasonable. Take a bus from Mytilini (2hr., 4 per day, €4.70). **Eftalou** has beautiful pebble- and black-sand beaches, accessible by frequent buses from Molyvos. A 20-million-year old ⬛**petrified forest,** 4km from Sigri, one of only two such forests in the world, has fossilized trunks preserved in amazingly precise detail. For more info, call the main parks office in Mytilini. (☎22510 40 132. Open daily July-Aug. 8am-7pm; Sept.-June 8am-4pm. €2, under 15 free.) **Ferries** go from Mytilini to: Chios (3hr., 11 per week, €13); Limnos (5hr., Sa 10am, €17); and Thessaloniki (13hr., Sa 10am, €32). Book tickets at **NEL Lines,** Pavlou Koudourioti 67 (☎22510 46 595), on the far right side of the waterfront facing inland. Mytilini *domatia* are plentiful and well advertised. Be sure to negotiate; doubles should run €20-23. For quality *domatia*, seek out **Arion Rooms to Let ❸,** at Alkaiou and Arionos 4. Hardwood floors grace rooms with A/C and private bath. (☎22510 42 650. Singles €30; doubles €40.) Down Olympou, just off Ermou, **New Life Rooms ❸** keep a handful of somewhat minimalist rooms in an Art Nouveau building. (☎22510 46 100. Singles €30; doubles €35; triples €45.) Fresh octopi hang to dry in front of tables right by the water at **O Stratos ❷.** (☎22510 21 739. Entrees €4.50-6.50. Open daily 11am-late.) **Postal Code:** 81100.

HUNGARY (MAGYARORSZÁG)

Communism was merely a blip in Hungary's 1100 years of repression and renewal. Now one year after its accession to the European Union, Hungary appears at ease with its newfound capitalist identity. Vibrant and teeming Budapest may still be the country's socio-economic keystone, but those who pass over the countryside for the capital risk mistaking Hungary's heart for its soul. Travelers will be rewarded by visits to the rough-and-tumble cowboy plains to the south, the beach resorts to the east, and the rolling hills with wine valleys to the north.

 DISCOVER HUNGARY: SUGGESTED ITINERARIES

THREE DAYS Start in **Budapest** (2 days; p. 548). Lose your way in the labyrinthine streets of downtown Pest until coming upon the palatial **Parliament** (p. 556) or the **Great Synagogue** (p. 556). Crossing the Danube to Buda, descend underground to the **castle labyrinths** (p. 555) or ascend to the citadel on **Gellért Hill** (p. 555) for a city panorama. Wind down from the urban bustle on the lakeside beaches of **Siófok** (1 day, p. 564).

ONE WEEK Arrive in **Budapest** (3 days). Take a break on the beaches of **Siófok** (2 days), before taking in the religious architecture and the vistas from the hiking trails of **Pécs** (2 days; p. 561), in Southern Transdanubia.

THREE WEEKS Spend a week in cosmopolitan **Budapest.** Sail down the river to reach the relaxed villages of the nearby **Danube Bend** (3 days; p. 559). **Eger** (3 days; p. 562) is home to the castle where Dobó István repelled the Ottomans in 1553 and neighbor to the wine cellars of the **Valley of the Beautiful Women** (1 day; p. 562). Curl back westward to **Győr** (2 days; p. 563), which overflows with cultural artifacts; from there, take a daytrip to the **Archabbey of Pannonhalma** (p. 564), founded by Benedictines in AD 996. End with **Lake Balaton** (p. 564) to the south, which hosts the nightlife of **Siófok** (2 days), the hiking of **Tihany** (1 day; p. 565), and the thermal springs of **Keszthely** (1 day; p. 565).

ESSENTIALS

WHEN TO GO

Hungary's most pleasant temperatures fall between May and September, averaging 12-16°C (54-61°F). Budapest never feels crowded, even in the high season, so there is no reason not to visit during summer festivals. Spring and fall see tolerable if chillier weather; winters are frosty, with January, the coldest month, registering an average temperature of –4°C (25°F).

DOCUMENTS AND FORMALITIES

VISAS. Citizens of Canada, Ireland, the UK, and the US do not need visas for stays of up to 90 days, provided their passports do not expire within six months of their trip's end and they do not intend to work. Australians and New Zealanders must obtain 90-day tourist visas from a Hungarian embassy or consulate. Short-term visa prices for US/non-US residents are: single-entry US$40/$65, double-entry

US$75/$100, multiple-entry US$180/$200. Certain visas may require 30 days for processing. Visas may be available at the border, but only at higher prices. Border crossings tend to be efficient, and there is no border fee. Visa extensions are rare; apply at a Hungarian police station.

EMBASSIES. All foreign embassies in Hungary are in Budapest (p. 548). Hungarian embassies at home include: **Australia,** 17 Beale Crescent, Deakin, ACT 2600 (☎02 6282 3226; hungcbr@ozemail.com.au); **Canada,** 299 Waverley St., Ottawa, ON K2P 0V9 (☎613-230-2717; www.docuweb.ca/hungary); **Ireland,** 2 Fitzwilliam Pl., Dublin 2 (☎01 661 2902; www.kum.hu/dublin); **New Zealand** (consulate), 37 Abbott St., Wellington, 6004 (☎04 973 7507; www.hungariancon-sulate.co.nz); **UK,** 35 Eaton Pl., London SW1X 8BY (☎020 7201 3440; www.huemblon.org.uk); and **US,** 3910 Shoemaker St. NW, Washington, D.C. 20008 (☎202-364-8218; www.hungaryemb.org).

TRANSPORTATION

BY PLANE. Several international airlines fly into Budapest. **Malév,** the national airline, offers daily direct flights to the capital from New York and London. It also flies to neighboring countries.

BY TRAIN. Most trains (*vonat*) pass through Budapest and are generally reliable and cheap. Book international tickets in advance. Consult www.elvira.hu for schedules and fares. **Eurail** is valid in Hungary. Students and those under 26 may be eligible for a discount of up to 30% on certain fares; ask ahead and be persistent. **ISIC** holders receive discounts at IBUSZ, Express, and station ticket counters. Flash your card and say *"diák"* (DEE-ahk; student). *Személyvonat* trains are slow; *gyorsvonat* (listed in red on schedules) move twice as fast for the same price. Large towns are accessible by the blue *expressz* lines. Air-conditioned *InterCity* trains are fastest. Trains labeled "R" require seat reservations (*pótjegy*); those without one face fines of 1000Ft. At twice the price of a ticket, it is often possible to purchase a reservation onboard. The *peron* (platform) is rarely indicated until the train approaches the station, and will be announced in Hungarian. Many stations are not marked; ask the conductor what time the train is expected to arrive.

BY BUS AND BY FERRY. Cheap, clean, but crowded, the bus system links many towns with rail connections only to Budapest. The **Erzsébet tér** station in Budapest posts schedules and fares. *InterCity* tickets are purchased on board; arrive early for seat. In larger cities, tickets for local transport must be bought from kiosks; punch the ticket on board or face fines. In smaller cities, pay on board. A **ferry** runs on the Danube between Budapest and Vienna; contact Utinform (☎01 322 3600).

BY TAXI AND BY CAR. Typical **taxi** fares should not exceed a 6am-10pm base fee of 300Ft, 280Ft per km, 70Ft per min. waiting. Make sure that the ride will be metered or fix a lump sum beforehand. Taxis ordered by phone charge less than those hailed on the street. **Driving** is illegal if you have consumed any alcohol. Emergency telephones punctuate Hungarian motorways every 2km. English assistance is available 24hr. from the Magyar Autóklub (MAK; Budapest ☎252 80 00, elsewhere 088). A phone service provides info about road conditions (Budapest ☎117 11 73, elsewhere 322 22 38).

TOURIST SERVICES AND MONEY

EMERGENCY	Police: ☎107. Ambulance: ☎104. Fire: ☎105.

TOURIST OFFICES. Tourinform has branches in most cities, and should be your first stop for local information. In towns, they stock maps and can provide abundant local info; employees generally speak both English and German. Tourinform can't make reservations, but they'll check on vacancies, especially in university dorms and private *panzió*. Most **IBUSZ** offices throughout the country book private rooms, exchange money, and sell train tickets, and charter tours. Pick up the pamphlet *Tourist Information: Hungary* and the monthly entertainment guides *Programme in Hungary* and *Budapest Panorama* (all free and in English).

MONEY. The **forint (Ft)** subdivides into 100 *fillér*, which have almost disappeared from circulation. Given current inflation rates, prices may increase over the next year. Maximum legal **commission** for cash-to-cash exchange is 1%. Never change money on the street. Currency exchange machines have excellent rates, but tend to be slow. OTP Bank and Postabank cash **traveler's checks** at the best rates. **Credit cards** are accepted at expensive hotels and name-brand supermarkets. Rounding up the bill as a **tip** is standard etiquette. In restaurants, hand the tip to the server; it's rude to leave it on the table. Foreigners are expected to tip 15%, although locals never give more than 10%. Bathroom attendants generally get 30Ft. Standard **business hours** in Budapest are Monday to Thursday 9am-4pm, Friday 9am-1pm.

FORINTS (FT) AS OF AUGUST 2004		
AUS$1 = 143.66FT	1000FT = AUS$6.95
CDN$1 = 152.80FT	1000FT = CDN$6.54
EUR€1 = 246.86FT	1000FT = EUR€4.05
NZ$1 = 131.54FT	1000FT = NZ$7.60
UK£1 = 368.49FT	1000FT = UK£2.71
US$1 = 201.84FT	1000FT = US$4.94

COMMUNICATION

PHONE CODES	**Country code: 36. International dialing prefix: 00.** From outside Hungary, dial int'l dialing prefix (see inside back cover) + 36 + city code + local number.

TELEPHONES. For city-to-city calls, wait for the tone and dial slowly; enter ☎06 before the phone code. International calls require red phones or new, digital-display blue phones, which tend to cut calls off after three to nine minutes. Phones often require cards (*telefonkártya*), available at kiosks, train stations, post offices, and certain stores. **Neophone** and **Micronet** are best for international calls. Direct calls can also be placed from Budapest's phone office. International carriers include **AT&T Direct** (☎06 800 01111), **Australia Direct** (☎06 800 06111), **British Telecom** (☎0800 89 0036), **Canada Direct** (☎06 800 01211), **MCI Worldphone** (☎06 800 01411), and **Sprint** (☎06 800 01877).

MAIL. The postal system is somewhat reliable; airmail (*légiposta*) takes seven to 10 days to the US and Europe, two weeks to Australia and New Zealand. Postage costs around 36Ft for domestic, 140-150Ft for international mail. If you're mailing to a Hungarian citizen, the family name precedes the given name. For *Poste Restante*, address mail to be held according to the following example: SURNAME First name, *Poste Restante*, Városház u. 18, 1052 Budapest, HUNGARY.

INTERNET ACCESS. Internet access is available throughout Hungary (usually 150-300Ft per hr.). The Hungarian keyboard differs significantly from English-language keyboards. After first logging on, click the "*Hu*" icon at the lower right corner of the screen to switch the key configuration to "*Angol.*"

LANGUAGES. Hungarian, a Finno-Ugric language, is related distantly to Estonian, Finnish, and Turkish. After Hungarian and German, English is the most commonly spoken language. Hungarian basics are listed on p. 1062.

ACCOMMODATIONS AND CAMPING

HUNGARY	❶	❷	❸	❹	❺
ACCOMMODATIONS	under 2000Ft	2000-3000Ft	3000-6000Ft	6000-10,000Ft	over 10,000Ft

Many travelers stay in **private homes** booked through tourist agencies, which may try to foist their most expensive rooms on you. Singles are scarce—it's worth finding a roommate, since solo travelers often pay for a double room. After staying a few nights you can make arrangements directly with the owner, saving yourself a 20-30% commission. Outside Budapest the best offices are region-specific; see town listings for options. **Hostelling** is becoming more attractive, although it is rare outside Budapest; HI cards are increasingly useful. Many hostels can be booked through the student travel agency **Express** (☎266 32 77) or through a regional tourist office. From June to August, many **university dorms** become hostels; inquire at Tourinform. **Panzió** (pensions), run out of private homes, are common if not always cheap. **Hotels** exist in some towns, but most have disappeared. More than 300 **campgrounds** throughout Hungary are open from May to September. Tourist offices offer the annually updated booklet *Camping Hungary* for free. For more info and maps, contact Tourinform in Budapest (p. 549).

FOOD AND DRINK

HUNGARY	❶	❷	❸	❹	❺
FOOD	under 400Ft	400-800Ft	800-1300Ft	1300-2800Ft	over 2800Ft

Hungarian food is more flavorful and varied than most Eastern European fare. Paprika, Hungary's chief agricultural export, colors most dishes red. In Hungarian restaurants (*vendéglő* or *étterem*), begin your meal with *halászlé*, a deliciously spicy fish stew. As an alternative, try *gyümölcsleves*, a cold fruit soup topped with whipped cream. The Hungarian national dish is *bográcsgulyás* (goulash), a beef stew with dumplings and paprika. *Borjúpaprikás* is veal with paprika and potato-dumpling pasta. Vegetarians can find recourse in the tasty *rántott sajt* (fried cheese) and *gombapörkölt* (mushroom stew) on most menus. In a *cukrászda* (confectionery), you can satisfy your sweet tooth cheaply. *Túrós rétes* is a chewy pastry pocket filled with sweetened cottage cheese. *Somlói galuska* is a rich, rum-soaked sponge cake of chocolate, nuts, and cream. *Unicum*, advertised as the national drink, is a fine herbal liqueur that Habsburg kings used to cure digestive ailments. Hungary also produces a diverse array of fine wines.

SAFETY AND SECURITY

Medical assistance is easily obtained in Budapest, where most hospitals have English-speaking staff; embassies can list Anglophone doctors. Outside Budapest, try to bring a Hungarian speaker with you. **Tourist insurance** is valid and often necessary for many medical services. UK nationals receive certain medical services for free with a valid passport. **Tap water** is usually clean and drinkable. Public toilets vary in cleanliness. Pack toilet paper, soap, and a towel, and be prepared to pay attendants 30Ft. Men's rooms are *férfi*, women's rooms *női*. **Pharmacies** (*gyógyszertar*) stock Western brands and carry tampons and condoms. Violent crime in Hungary is low, but in larger cities foreign tourists are favored targets of petty thieves and pickpockets. Although homosexuality has been legal in Hungary since 1961, **GLBT** travelers may face discrimination, especially outside Budapest.

HOLIDAYS AND FESTIVALS

Holidays: New Year's Day (Jan. 1); National Day (Mar. 15); Easter (Mar. 27); Easter Monday (Apr. 12); Labor Day (May 1); Pentecost (May 15-16); Constitution Day (Aug. 20); Republic Day (Oct. 23); All Saints' Day (Nov. 1); Christmas (Dec. 25-26); New Year's Eve (Dec. 31).

Festivals: In June and July, Budapest's Ferencváros Festival is a diverse celebration of music. At the end of June, the Budapest Farewell Festival holds parades and concerts in celebration of the day the last Russian soldier left the country in 1991. Hotels and tourist offices have English-language guides to Budapest's many summer festivals. Listings and info can also be found at www.fesztivalvaros.hu.

FACTS AND FIGURES: HUNGARY

Official Name: Republic of Hungary.

Capital: Budapest.

Major Cities: Debrecen, Eger, Pécs, Szombathely.

Population: 10,032,000 (90% Magyar, 4% Roma, 3% German, 2% Serb).

Land Area: 92,340 sq. km.

Time Zone: GMT +1.

Language: Hungarian (Magyar).

Religions: Roman Catholic (68%), Calvinist (21%), Lutheran (5%), other (6%).

HUNGARY

BUDAPEST
☎01

Ten times larger than any other Hungarian city, Budapest (pop. 1,900,000) has been busily reassuming its place as a major European capital. After the union in 1872 of two separate cities, Buda and Pest, the Habsburg metropolis soon ranked as the second largest city in the Austro-Hungarian empire after Vienna. Budapest was ravaged in WWII, but Hungarians rebuilt it from the rubble. Over a decade after the end of the Soviet occupation, neon lights now illuminate Ottoman-influenced architecture, making Budapest a vibrant mix of East and West, old and new.

▐ TRANSPORTATION

Flights: Ferihegy Airport (BUD; ☎296 9696). **Malév** (Hungarian Airlines; reservations ☎235 3888) flies to major cities. From the airport, the cheapest way to the city center is by bus #93 (20min., every 15min. 4:55am-11:20pm, 150Ft), and then by the M3 to Köbanya-Kispest (15min. to Deák tér in downtown Pest).

Trains: Major stations are **Keleti pu., Nyugati pu.,** and **Déli pu.** (International info ☎461 5500, domestic 461 5400; www.mav.hu.) Most international trains arrive at Keleti Pályaudvar, but some from Prague go to Nyugati pu. Each station has schedules for the others; for a complete listing of Hungarian rail schedules, see ▨ www.bahn.de. To: **Berlin** (12-15hr.; 2 per day; 26367Ft, 1500Ft reservation fee); **Bucharest** (14hr., 5 per day, 16,000Ft); **Prague** (8hr., 4 per day, 11,700Ft); **Vienna** (3hr.; 17 per day; 6000Ft, 700Ft reservation fee); **Warsaw** (11hr.; 2 per day; 13,899Ft, 2000Ft fee). The daily **Orient Express** stops on its way from Paris to Istanbul. Purchase tickets at an **International Ticket Office.** (Keleti pu. open daily 8am-6pm; Nyugati pu. open daily 5am-9pm.) Or try **MÁV Hungarian Railways,** VI, Andrássy út 35 and at all stations. (☎461 5500. Open M-F 9am-5pm. Say "diák" for student or under 26 discounts on tickets.)

Buses: Most buses to Western Europe leave from **Volánbusz main station,** V, Erzsébet tér (☎117 2966, international tickets 485 2100; www.volanbusz.hu). M1, 2, or 3: Deák tér. Open M-F 6am-6pm, Sa-Su 6am-4pm. Buses to many destinations in Eastern Europe depart from **Népstadion,** Hungária körút 48/52 (☎252 1896). M2: Népstadion. To: **Berlin** (14½hr., 5 per week, 19,900Ft); **Prague** (8hr., 4 per week, 6990Ft); **Vienna** (3-3½hr., 5 per day, 5790Ft).

Commuter Trains: The HÉV commuter railway station is at Batthyány tér, across the river from the Parliament, 1 metro stop past the Danube in Buda. Trains head to **Szentendre** (45min., every 15min. 5am-9pm, 268Ft). Those who do not purchase tickets at the station for transport beyond the city limits will face fines.

Public Transportation: Subways, buses, and **trams** are cheap, convenient, and easy to navigate. The **metro** has three lines: yellow (M1), red (M2), and blue (M3). Night transit (É) buses run midnight-5am along major routes: #7É and 78É follow the M2 route, #6É follows the 4/6 tram line, and #14É and 50É follow the M3 route. **Single-fare tickets** for all public transport (one-way on 1 line 140Ft) are sold in metro stations, in *Trafik* shops, and by sidewalk vendors. Punch them in the orange boxes at the gate of the metro or on buses and trams; punch a new ticket when you change lines, or face fines. Passes: 1-day 1150Ft, 3-day 2200Ft, 1-week 2700Ft.

Taxis: Beware scams; check that the meter is on and inquire about rates. **Budataxi** (☎233 3333) charges 135Ft per km for rides requested by phone. Also reliable are **Főtaxi** (☎222 2222), **6x6 Taxi** (☎266 6666), and **Tele 5 Taxi** (☎355 5555).

▓ ORIENTATION

Originally Buda and Pest, two cities separated by the **Danube River** (Duna), modern Budapest preserves the distinctive character of each. On the west bank, **Buda** has winding streets, breathtaking vistas, a hilltop citadel, and the Castle District. On the east bank, **Pest,** the city's commercial center, is home to shopping boulevards, theaters, Parliament (Országház), and the Opera House. Three main bridges suture together the halves: **Széchenyi Lánchíd,** slender **Erzsébet híd,** and green **Szabadság híd.** Down the north slope of Várhegy (Castle Hill) is **Moszkva tér,** the tram and local bus hub. **Batthyány tér,** opposite Parliament in Buda, is the starting point of the HÉV commuter railway. Metro lines converge at **Deák tér,** next to the main international bus terminal at **Erzsébet tér.** Two blocks west toward the river lies **Vörösmarty tér** and the pedestrian shopping zone, **Váci utca.**

Budapest addresses begin with a Roman numeral representing one of the city's 23 **districts.** Central Buda is I; central Pest is V. To navigate Budapest's often confusing streets, a **map** is essential; pick one up at any tourist office or hostel.

🛈 PRACTICAL INFORMATION

Tourist Offices: All sell the **Budapest Card** (Budapest Kártya), which provides discounts, unlimited public transport, and admission to most museums. (2-day card 4350Ft, 3-day 5400Ft.) Your first stop should be **Tourinform,** V, Sütő u. 2 (☎317 9800; www.hungary.com). M1, 2, or 3: Deák tér. Off Deák tér behind McDonald's. Open daily 8am-8pm. **Vista Travel Center,** Paulay Ede 7 (☎429 9950; www.vista.hu), arranges tours and accommodations. Open M-F 9am-6:30pm, Sa 9am-2:30pm. ▧ **Budapest in Your Pocket** (www.inyourpocket.com; 750Ft) is an up-to-date guide of the city.

Embassies: Australia, XII, Királyhágo tér 8/9 (☎457 9777; www.australia.hu). M2: Déli pu., then bus #21 or tram #59 to Királyhágo tér. Open M-F 9am-noon. **Canada,** XII, Budakeszi út 32 (☎392 3360; www.canadaeuropa.gc.ca/hungary). Take bus #158 from Moszkva tér to the last stop. Entrance at Zugligeti út. 51-53. Open M-F 8:30-10:30am and 2-3:30pm. **Ireland,** V, Szabadság tér 7 (☎302 9600), in Bank Center. M3: Arany J. u. Walk down Bank u. toward the river. Open M-F 9:30am-12:30pm and 2:30-4:30pm. **New Zealand,** VI, Teréz krt. 38, 4th fl. (☎428-2208). M3: Nyugati pu. Open M-F 11am-4pm by appointment only. **UK,** V, Harmincad u. 6 (☎266 2888; www.britishembassy.hu), near the intersection with Vörösmarty tér. M1: Vörösmarty tér. Open M-F 9:30am-12:30pm and 2:30-4:30pm. **US,** V, Szabadság tér 12 (☎475 4400, after hours 475 4703; http://budapest.usembassy.gov). M2: Kossuth tér. Walk 2 blocks down Akadémia and turn on Zoltán. Open M-Th 1-4pm, F 9am-noon and 1-4pm.

Currency Exchange: Banks have the best rates. **Citibank,** V, Vörösmarty tér 4 (☎374 5000). M1: Vörösmarty tér. Cashes traveler's checks for no commission and provides MC/V cash advances (passport required).

American Express: V, Deák Ferenc u. 10 (☎235 4330; amex.retail.buda@exp.com). M2 or 3: Deák tér. Open M-F 9am-5:30pm, Sa 9am-2pm. Cardholders can have mail delivered here. Other services include tourist info and free maps.

Luggage Storage: Lockers at all 3 train stations. 150-480Ft.

English-Language Bookstore: Libri Könyvpalota, VII, Rákóczi u. 12 (☎/fax 267 4843). A floor of English titles. Open M-F 10am-7:30pm, Sa 10am-3pm. M2: Astoria. MC/V.

GLBT Services: GayGuide.net Budapest (☎0630 932 3334; www.budapest.gayguide.net). Volunteers post an online guide and run a hotline (daily 4-8pm) with info about gay- and lesbian-friendly lodgings.

Emergency: ☎112 connects to all. **Police:** ☎107. **Ambulance:** ☎104. **Fire:** ☎105.

Tourist Police: V, Vigadó u. 6 (☎463 9165). M1: Vörösmarty tér. Walk toward the river from the metro to reach the station. Open 24hr.

24hr. Pharmacies: II, Frankel Leó út 22 (☎212 4406); **III,** Szentendrei út 2/a (☎388 6528); **IV,** Pozsonyi u. 19 (☎389 4079); **VI,** Teréz krt. 41 (☎311 4439); **VII,** Rákóczi út 39 (☎314 3695). After-hours service 100-200Ft.

TO
MATYAS
PÁL VÖLGYI CAVES

TO
& OMSZKI LAKE

Árpád Fejedelem

Margit Island
(Margit-sziget)

Bolyai u.
Apostol u.
Rómer Flóris u.
Ady Endre u.
Bimbó u.
Keleti Károly u.
Kis Rókus
Lövőház u.
Margit Körút

Balzac u.
Csanády u.
Radnóti Miklós u.
Raoul Wallenberg u.
Újpesti rakpart
Katona József u.
Visegrádi u.

Szt. István körút

NYUGA
Pt
M
NYÚGAT
TÉR

Mammut
Plaza
Millenáris Park

Bem József u.

Király
Baths

Medve u.
Karsa u.

Bem rakpart

Balaton ul.

Markó u.

Nagy Ignác u.

Bajcsy Zsilinszky út

Weine
7
8
Hajós

MOSZKVA
MOSZKVA TÉR
TÉR
M2

Varsányi Irén u.
Csalogány u.
Hattyú u.

TO VÁROSMAJOR
OPEN AIR THEATER

Batthány u.
Várfok u.
Szabó Ilonka u.

BATTHYÁNY
TÉR
American
Clinic
M2
St. Anne's

Fő u.

Szalay u.
i
Ethnographic
Museum
Parliament
(Országház)

Alkotmány u.
Báthory u.

KOSSUTH
L. TÉR
M2
KOSSUTH
LAJOS TÉR

Garibaldi u.
Zoltán u.
US
9
SZABADSÁG
TÉR

Hold u.

Military History
Museum
Musical History Museum

Fortuna
Országház u.
Úri u.

Fisherman's Bastion

Akadémia u.
Széchenyi rakpart
Széchenyi u.

ARANY
J. U.
M3

State
Opera
House

TO
13
(5km)

i

Matthias Church

Labyrinth
Entrance
CASTLE HILL
(VÁRHEGY)

14

Arany
János u.
Nádor u.
Vigyázó F. u.

15
St. Stephen's
Basilica

i
BAJCSY
ZSILINSZKY U'
M1

DÉLI PU.
M2
Vérmező

Déli Pu.
i

Attila út.

Zrinyi u.
Mérleg u.

ROOSEVELT
TÉR

Széchenyi Lánchíd
(Chain Bridge)

József Attila u.

ERSZÉBET
TÉR
M123

DEÁK
FERENC
TÉR

B U D A

Alagút

Krisztina Körút
Gellérthegy u.
Naphegy u.

National Dance
Theater
Museum of
Contemporary Art
and Ludwig Museum

Lánchíd u.

Danube (Duna)

20
UK
Volánbusz

VÖRÖSMARTY
TÉR
M1
DEÁK
TÉR

Károly
krt.

21
Belgrád rakpart
Deák Ferenc u.

Petőfi S. u.
i
City Hall

Hungarian
National Gallery

NAPHEGY
TÉR

Dezső u.
Tigris u.

Budapest
History
Museum
Royal Castle

Postá
Vigadó

Váci u.
Apácai u.

FERENCIEK
TÉR

Mészáros u.
Avar u.
Győri út.
Csörsz u.

Aladár u.

Hegyalja u.

Inner City
Parish Church
IBUSZ
i
M3

Kossuth L. u.

Károl

Hegyalja u.

Orom u.

Vigadó tér
Boat Station

Irányi u.

24
Ve
Váci u.
Szerb

Schweidel u.
Aitóhegy u.

Szirtes u.

GELLÉRT-
HEGY

Szirtes u.

Erzsébet
híd

Molnár u.

Somlói u.
Kelenhegyi u.
Szirtes u.

Rudas Baths
Szt. Gellért rakpart

Citadel and
Liberation
Monument
(Citadella)

Cave
Church

Szabadság
híd

Budaörsi út.
Ménesi u.
Köbölkút u.
Villányi u.

Somlói ú.
Süret u.

Gellért Hotel
and Baths

Kelenhegyi u.

Bartók Béla u.

Műegyetem
rakpart

TO 26 27
& STATUE PARK

TO 25

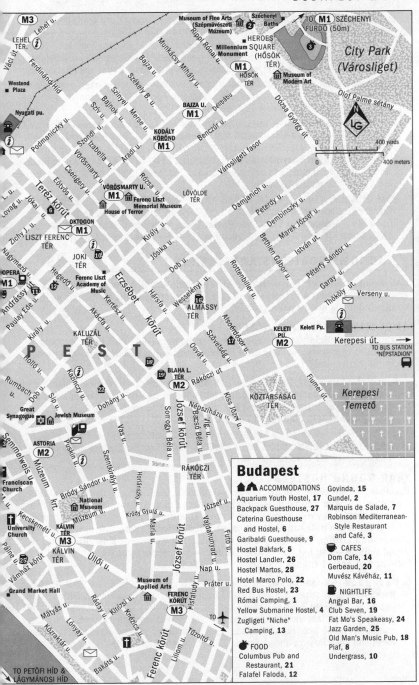

HUNGARY

Budapest

🏠🏠 ACCOMMODATIONS
Aquarium Youth Hostel, **17**
Backpack Guesthouse, **27**
Caterina Guesthouse
  and Hostel, **6**
Garibaldi Guesthouse, **9**
Hostel Bakfark, **5**
Hostel Landler, **26**
Hostel Martos, **28**
Hotel Marco Polo, **22**
Red Bus Hostel, **23**
Római Camping, **1**
Yellow Submarine Hostel, **4**
Zugligeti "Niche"
  Camping, **13**

🍴 FOOD
Columbus Pub and
  Restaurant, **21**
Falafel Faloda, **12**
Govinda, **15**
Gundel, **2**
Marquis de Salade, **7**
Robinson Mediterranean-
  Style Restaurant
  and Café, **3**

☕ CAFES
Dom Cafe, **14**
Gerbeaud, **20**
Muvész Kávéház, **11**

🍺 NIGHTLIFE
Angyal Bar, **16**
Club Seven, **19**
Fat Mo's Speakeasy, **24**
Jazz Garden, **25**
Old Man's Music Pub, **18**
Piaf, **8**
Undergrass, **10**

Medical Assistance: Falck (SOS) KFT, II, Kapy út 49/b (☎200 0100). Ambulance service US$120. **American Clinic,** I, Hattyú u. 14 (☎224 9090; www.americanclinics.com), accepts walk-ins, but calling a day ahead is helpful. Open M 8:30am-7pm, Tu-W 10am-6pm, Th 11:30am-6pm, F 10am-6pm. Direct insurance billing available. 24hr. emergency ☎224 9090. The US embassy (see **Embassies,** above) also lists English-speaking doctors.

Telephones: Most phones require **phone cards,** available at newsstands, post offices, and metro stations. 50-unit card 800Ft, 120-unit card 1800Ft. Domestic operator ☎198. International operator ☎190. Info ☎199.

Internet Access: Cybercafes are everywhere, but access can get expensive and long waits are common. Try a wired hostel. **Ami Internet Coffee,** V, Váci u. 40 (☎267 1644; www.amicoffee.hu). M3: Ferenciek tér. 200Ft per 15min., 700Ft per hr. Open daily 9am-midnight. **Libri Könyvpalota,** VII, Rákóczi út 12 (☎267 4843; www.libri.hu). M2: Astoria. Reserve ahead. Sells coffee and drinks. 250Ft per 30min., 400Ft per hr. Open M-F 10am-7:30pm, Sa 10am-3pm.

Post Office: V, Városház u. 18 (☎318 4811). Open M-F 8am-9pm, Sa 8am-2pm. Branches include: Keleti pu.; Nyugati pu.; VI, Teréz krt. 105/107; VIII, Baross tér 11/c. Open M-F 7am-9pm, Sa 8am-2pm. **Postal Code:** Varies by district, taking the form 1XX2, where XX is the 2-digit district number. (District V translates to 1052.)

⚑ ACCOMMODATIONS AND CAMPING

Call ahead in summer. Travelers arriving at Keleti pu. will be swarmed with hawkers; be cautious and don't believe all promises of special discounts, but keep an open mind if you need a place to stay.

ACCOMMODATION AGENCIES

Private rooms, slightly more expensive than hostels (3000Ft-5000Ft per person; less with longer stays), usually offer what hostels can't: peace, quiet, and private showers. Arrive early, bring cash, and haggle.

Best Hotel Service, V, Sütő u. 2 (☎318 4848; www.besthotelservice.axelero.net). Arranges hotel, apartment, and hostels reservations, as well as car rentals and city tours. M1, 2, or 3: Deák tér. Bus #7 from Keleti pu. Next to McDonald's in the courtyard. Rooms in Pest. 6000Ft and up. Open 8am-8pm. ❹

IBUSZ, V, Ferenciek tér 10 (☎485-2700; accommodation@ibusz.hu). M3: Ferenciek tér. Doubles 5000-10000Ft; triples 6500-12000Ft. 1800Ft surcharge if staying fewer than 4 nights. Open M-F 8:15am-5pm. ❸

YEAR-ROUND HOSTELS

Budapest's hostels are backpacker social centers, each with its own quirks. Hostel common rooms can be as exciting as expat bars and clubs, and especially for solo travelers, they're a great place to pull together a posse of instant friends. Many hostels are now run by the **Hungarian Youth Hostels Association,** which operates from an office in Keleti pu. Representatives who wear Hostelling International t-shirts—and legions of competitors—will accost you as you get off the train and offer free transportation.

▨ Backpack Guesthouse, XI, Takács Menyhért u. 33 (☎209 8406; backpackguest@hotmail.com), in Buda, 12min. from central Pest. From Keleti pu., take bus #7 or 7a toward Buda; get off at Tétenyi u. and walk back under the railway bridge to a sharp left turn. Take the 3rd right at Hamzsabégi út. With a common room full of movies, music, and cheap beer, hostel life doesn't get much better. Internet access 15Ft per min. Reception 24hr. Reserve ahead. Dorms 2200Ft; doubles 6600Ft. ❷

▧ **Red Bus Hostel,** V, Semmelweis u. 14 (☎266 0136; www.redbusbudapest.hu), in Pest. Spacious dorms in downtown Pest. Free luggage storage. Internet access 12Ft per min. Breakfast included. Laundry 1200Ft. Reception 24hr. Check-out 10am. 10-bed dorms 2900Ft; singles 6500-7500Ft; doubles 7500Ft; triples 10,500Ft. AmEx/MC/V. ❷

Hostel Martos, XI, Stoczek u. 5/7 (☎209 4883; reception@hotel.martos.bme.hu), in Buda. From Keleti pu., take bus #7 to Móricz Zsigmond Körtér and walk 300m toward the river on Bartók Béla út. Turn right on Bertalan Lajos and take the 3rd right on Stoczek u.; the hostel is on the corner. A short walk to the outdoor clubs along the river. Free Internet access and satellite TV. Reserve ahead. Singles 4000Ft; doubles 5000Ft, with shower 8000Ft; triples 7500Ft; 2- to 4-bed apartments with bath 15,000Ft. ❸

Aquarium Youth Hostel, VII, Alsoérdósor u. 12 (☎322 0502; aquarium@budapesthostels.com), in Pest. A hidden gem—there are no signs outside. Ring buzzer. Close to Keleti pu. and the metro. Free Internet access and kitchen. Laundry 1200Ft. Reception 24hr. 4- to 5-bed dorms 2600Ft; doubles 8500Ft. ❷

Hotel Marco Polo, VII, Nyár u. 6 (☎413 2555; www.marcopolohostel.com), in Pest. M2: Astoria or M2: Blaha Lujza tér. Luxurious and spotless, dorm bunk beds are in separate compartments blocked off by curtains. Internet access 300Ft per hr. Reception 24hr. Book 1-2 days ahead in summer. Dorms 5000Ft; singles 13,750Ft; doubles 18,900Ft. 10% HI and ISIC discount. MC/V. ❸

Yellow Submarine Hostel, VI, Teréz Körút 56, 3rd fl. (☎331 9896; www.yellowsubmarinehostel.com). Across from Nyugati pu. A great place to crash for a hard day's night. Known as a party hostel. Large dorms with bunk beds and lockers. Doubles and triples in nearby apartments. Internet access 10Ft per min. Breakfast included for dorms. Laundry 1500Ft. Check-out 9am. Dorms 2800Ft; singles 7500Ft; doubles 8000-9000Ft; triples 9900-10,500Ft; quads 13,200Ft. 10% HI discount. MC/V. ❷

SUMMER HOSTELS

Many university dorms moonlight as hostels during July and August. The majority are clustered around Móricz Zsigmond Körtér in district XI.

Hostel Bakfark, II, Bakfark u. 1/3 (☎413 2062), in Buda. M2: Moszkva tér. Comfortable dorms with lofts instead of bunks. Check-out 10am. Call ahead. Open mid-June to late Aug. Dorms 3300Ft. 10% HI discount. ❸

Hostel Landler, XI, Bartók Béla út 17 (☎463 3621), in Buda. Take bus #7 or 7A across the river and get off at Géllert; take Bartók Béla út away from the river. Comfy dorms. Check-out 9am. Open July 1-Sept. 5. Singles 5850Ft; triples 11,700Ft; quads 15,600Ft. 10% HI discount. ❸

GUESTHOUSES

Guesthouses and private rooms add a personal touch for about the same price as hostels. Owners will usually pick travelers up from the train station or airport.

▧ **Garibaldi Guesthouse,** V, Garibaldi u. 5 (☎302 3456; garibaldiguest@hotmail.com). M2: Kossuth tér. Offers a variety of spacious, furnished rooms ranging from singles to quads. Some have kitchenette, TV, and shower. English spoken. Rooms from 6500Ft; apartments 6000-10,000Ft. Reduced prices for longer stays and bigger groups. ❹

▧ **Caterina Guesthouse and Hostel,** III, Teréz krt. 30, apt. #28, ring code: 48 (☎269-5990, www.caterinahostel.hu), in Pest. M1: Oktogon, or trams #4 and 6. Newly renovated, spotless rooms with fresh linens. Reception 24hr. Check-out 10am. Lockout 10am-1pm. Reserve by fax or email. Dorms 2300Ft; doubles 6000Ft; triples 9000Ft. ❷

HUNGARY

CAMPING

Római Camping, III, Szentendrei út 189 (☎388-7167). M2: Batthyány tér. Take HÉV to Római fürdő; walk 100m toward river. Huge complex with a swimming pool and shady park indulges its guests with nearby grocery store and restaurants. Breakfast 880Ft. Laundry 800Ft. Electricity 600Ft. Tents 1950Ft per person; bungalows 1690-15,000Ft. Additional per-person fee (990Ft, children 590Ft). Tourist tax 3%. 10% HI discount. ●

Zugligeti "Niche" Camping, XII, Zugligeti út 101 (☎/fax 200 8346; www.camping-niche.hu). Take bus #158 from Moszkva tér to Laszállóhely, the last stop. Restaurant. Communal showers. Electricity 750Ft. 990Ft per person. Tents 600Ft, large tents 1000Ft. Cars 800Ft, caravans 1990Ft. ●

🄵 FOOD

Cafeterias beneath *"Önkiszolgáló Étterem"* signs serve cheap food (meat dishes 300-500Ft), and any neighborhood *kifőzés* (kiosk) or *vendéglő* (vendor) will give you a real taste of Hungary. Corner markets, many with 24hr. windows, stock basics. The ▨**Grand Market Hall,** IX, Fövam tér 1/3, next to Szabadság híd (M3: Kálvin tér), was built in 1897; it now boasts 10,000 square meters of stalls, making it a tourist attraction in itself. An array of ethnic restaurants inhabits the upper floors of **Mammut Plaza,** just outside of the Moszkva tér metro stop in Buda, and the **West End Plaza,** accessible from the Nyugati metro stop in Pest.

RESTAURANTS

▨ **Columbus Pub and Restaurant** (☎266 9013), V, below the chain bridge on the Danube promenade. If you feel you've neglected the beautiful Danube, enjoy a meal on this moored ship. Open daily noon-midnight. AmEx/MC/V. ❸

▨ **Govinda,** V, Vigyázó Ferenc u. 4 (☎269 1625). An Indian vegetarian restaurant, complete with yoga classes. The best deals are the meal plates (big plate 1600Ft, small plate 1250Ft, student plate 620Ft). Yoga classes Sept.-June M 5-6:30pm (500Ft). Open M-Sa noon-9pm. Cash only. ❷

▨ **Gundel,** XIV, Allatkerti út 2 (☎468 4040). The most famous restaurant in Hungary. Many think the 7-course meal is worth the splurge (13,000-17,500Ft) but there are also delicious sandwiches outside for 400-600Ft. Su brunch buffet 11:30am-3pm (4900Ft). Open daily noon-3:15pm and 6:30-11:15pm. AmEx/MC/V. ❺

Falafel Faloda, VI, Paulay Ede u. 53 (☎351 1243; www.falafel.hu). M1: Opera. From the metro, cross Andrássy, head straight on Nagymező u., and turn left on Paulay Ede. Make-your-own falafel with tons of ingredients. Falafel 540Ft. Salad 530-640Ft. Open M-F 10am-8pm, Sa 10am-6pm. ❷

Robinson Mediterranean-Style Restaurant and Cafe, Városligeti tó (☎422 0222). This scenic restaurant overlooking the lake in City Park is infused with charm. Serves favorites like pan-roasted goose liver (2150Ft) and paprika veal (2600Ft). Vegetarian options available. Entrees 1800-5800Ft. Open daily noon-midnight. AmEx/MC/V. ❹

Marquis de Salade, VI, Hajós u. 43 (☎302 4086). M3: Arany János. At the corner of Bajcsy-Zsilinszky út, 2 blocks from the metro. Huge menu with dishes from Azerbaijan and Russia. Entrees 1800-3500Ft. Open daily noon-midnight. Cash only. ❹

CAFES

Once the haunts of the literary, intellectual, and cultural elite—as well as political dissidents—the city's cafes boast histories as rich as the pastries they serve.

▨ **Dom Cafe,** I, Szentháromság tér. Astonishing views of the Danube and Pest from atop Castle Hill. Beer and coffee start at 360Ft. Pastries and sandwiches also served. Open daily 10am-10pm.

Gerbeaud, V, Vörösmarty tér 7 (☎429 9020). M1: Vörösmarty tér. Perhaps Budapest's largest and most famous cafe, this institution has been serving its layer cakes (620Ft) and homemade ice cream (250Ft) since 1858. Open daily 9am-9pm.

Muvész Kávéház, VI, Andrássy út 29 (☎352 1337). M1: Opera. Diagonally across from the Opera. Before or after a show, stop in for a slice of rich cake (320Ft) and a cup of cappuccino (300Ft) at the polished stone tables. Open daily 9am-11:45pm.

🄖 SIGHTS

In 1896, Hungary's 1000th birthday bash prompted the construction of what are today Budapest's most prominent sights. Among the works commissioned by the Habsburgs were **Heroes' Square** (Hősök tér), **Liberty Bridge** (Szbadság híd), **Vajdahu-nyad Castle** (Vajdahunyad vár), and continental Europe's first **metro** system. Slightly grayer for wear, war, and occupation, these monuments attest to the optimism of a capital on the verge of its Golden Age. See the sights, find your way around the city, and meet other travelers with **Absolute Walking & Biking Tours.** Their basic tour (3½hr.; 4000Ft, under 27 3500Ft) meets daily June-Aug. at 9:30am and 1:30pm on the steps of the yellow church in Deák tér and at 10am and 2pm in Heroes' Sq. Low-season tours (Sept.-May) leave at 10:30am from Deák tér and at 11am from Heroes' Sq. Specialized tours have focuses from Communist Hungary to pub-crawling Budapest. (☎211 8861; www.absolutetours.com. Tours 3½-5½hr. 4000-5000Ft.) **Boat tours** of Budapest can also be taken from Vigadó tér piers 6-7. The evening boat, the *Danube Legend,* costs 4200Ft; its daytime counterpart, the *Duna Bella,* costs 3600Ft. Budapest Card holders receive 20% discounts.

BUDA
On the east bank of the Danube, Buda sprawls between the base of **Castle Hill** and southern **Gellért Hill,** rambling into Budapest's main residential areas. Older than Pest, Buda is filled with parks, lush hills, and islands.

CASTLE DISTRICT. Towering above the Danube on Castle Hill, the Castle District has been razed three times in its 800-year history, most recently in 1945. With its winding, statue-filled streets, breathtaking views, and hodgepodge of architectural styles, the UNESCO-protected district now appears much as it did in Habsburg times. Although the reconstructed **Buda Castle** (*Vár*) now houses a number of fine museums (p. 557), bullet holes in the palace facade recall the 1956 Uprising. *(M1, 2, or 3: Deák tér. From the metro, take bus #16 across the Danube. Alternatively, take the metro to M2: Moszkva tér and walk up to the hill on Várfok u. Becsi kapu marks the castle entrance.)* Beneath Buda castle are the **Castle Labyrinths** (Budvári Labirinths), caverns that provide a spooky glimpse of the subterranean world of the city. *(Úri u. 9. ☎212 0207. Open daily 9:30am-7:30pm. 1200Ft, students 1000Ft.)*

MATTHIAS CHURCH. The multi-colored roof of Matthias Church (Mátyás tem-plom) is one of Budapest's most photographed sights. The church was converted into a mosque in 1541, then reconverted 145 years later when the Habsburgs defeated the Turks. Ascend the spiral steps to the exhibits of the **Museum of Ecclesi-astical Art.** *(On Castle Hill. Open M-Sa 9am-5pm, Su 1-5pm. High Mass 7, 8:30am, and 6pm; Su and holidays 10am and noon. Church and museum 550Ft, students 270Ft.)*

GELLÉRT HILL. After the coronation of King Stephen, the first Christian Hungarian monarch, the Pope sent Bishop Gellért to convert the Magyars. Budapest's principal hill was named Gellérthegy after those unconvinced by the bishop's message hurled him to his death from the summit. The **Liberation Monument** (Szabadság Szobor), which honors Soviet soldiers who died ridding Hungary of Nazis, over-looks Budapest from the hilltop. The view from the adjoining **Citadel,** built as a symbol of Habsburg power after the foiled 1848 revolution, is especially breathtaking at night. At the base of the hill is Budapest's most famous Turkish bath, the **Gellért Hotel and Baths.** *(XI. Tram #18 or 19, or bus #7, to Hotel Gellért; follow Szabó Verjték u. to Jubileumi Park, continuing on marked paths to the summit. Or take bus #27 to the top; get off at Búsuló Juhász and walk 5min. to the peak.)*

PEST

Constructed in the 19th century, the winding streets of Pest now host cafes, corporations, and monuments. The crowded **Belváros** (Inner City) is based around the swarming pedestrian boulevards **Váci utca** and **Vörösmarty tér.**

▓ PARLIAMENT. Standing 96m tall, a number that symbolizes the date of Hungary's millennial anniversary, the palatial Gothic Parliament (Országház) was modeled after the UK's, right down to the riverside location and hieratic facade. The **Hungarian crown jewels,** housed here since 1999, were moved from the National Museum to the center of the Cupola Room amidst national controversy because of the cost of the security required to move them. *(M2: Kossuth Lajos tér. ☎317 9800. English tours M-F 10am, noon, 2, 2:30, 5, and 6pm; Sa-Su 10am only—arrive early. Min. 5 people. Ticket office at Gate X opens at 8am. Entrance with mandatory tour 2000Ft, students 1035Ft. EU citizens free with passport.)*

GREAT SYNAGOGUE. The largest synagogue in Europe and the second-largest in the world after Temple Emmanuel in New York City, Pest's Great Synagogue (Zsinagóga) was designed to hold 3000 worshippers. Renovations begun in 1988 are 95% complete. In the garden the enormous metal **Tree of Life,** a Holocaust memorial, sits above a mass grave for thousands of Jews killed near the end of the war. The Hebrew inscription reads: "Whose pain can be greater than mine?" and the Hungarian beneath: "Let us remember." Each leaf bears the name of a family that perished, but the memorial represents only a fraction of the sufferers. Next door, the **Jewish Museum** (Zsidó Múzeum) documents Hungary's rich Jewish past. *(VII. M2: Astoria. At the corner of Dohány u. and Wesselényi u. Open May-Oct. M-Th 10am-5pm, F 10am-1pm, Su 10am-2pm; Nov.-Apr. M-Th 10am-3pm, F 10am-1pm, Su 10am-1pm. Museum and synagogue 600Ft, with ISIC 200Ft. Services F 6pm. Synagogue tours M-Th 10:30am-3:30pm on the half-hour, F and Su 10:30, 11:30am, 12:30pm. 1900Ft, students 1600Ft.)*

ST. STEPHEN'S BASILICA (SZ. ISTVÁN BAZILIKA). More than the neo-Renaissance facade of the city's largest church was severely damaged by Allied bombs in WWII, but much has been restored. The **Panorama Tower** offers an amazing 360° view. A curious attraction is St. Stephen's mummified right hand, one of Hungary's most revered religious relics; a 100Ft donation dropped in the box will illuminate it for those seeking a closer look. *(V. M1, 2, or 3: Deák tér. Open May-Oct. M-Sa 9am-5pm; Nov.-Apr. M-Sa 10am-4pm. Mass M-Sa 7, 8am, 6pm; Su 8:30, 10am, noon, 6pm. Church free. Mummified hand M-Sa 9am-5pm, Su 1-4pm. 200Ft, students 150Ft. Tower open daily June-Aug. 9:30am-6pm; Sept.-Oct. 10am-5:30pm; Apr.-May 10am-4:30pm. Tower 500Ft, students 400Ft.)*

ANDRÁSSY ÚT AND HEROES' SQUARE. Hungary's grandest boulevard, Andrássy út, extends from Erzsébet tér in downtown Pest to Heroes' Sq. (Hősök tér) to the northeast. The Hungarian State Opera House (Magyar Állami Operaház), the gilded interior of which glows on performance nights, is a vivid reminder of Budapest's Golden Age. Take a tour if you can't see an opera. *(Andrássy út 22. M1: Opera. ☎332 8197. 1hr. English tours daily 3 and 4pm. 2000Ft, students 1000Ft. 20% discount with Budapest Card.)* At the Heroes' Sq. end of Andrássy út, the Millennium Monument (Millenniumi emlékmű) commemorates the nation's most prominent leaders. Also off Heroes' Sq. is the Museum of Fine Arts (see below).

CITY PARK (VÁROSLIGET). Budapest's park is home to a zoo, a circus, an aging amusement park, and the lakeside **Vajdahunyad Castle;** the castle's architectural collage of Baroque, Gothic, Romanesque, and Renaissance styles is intended to chronicle the history of Hungarian design. Outside the castle broods the hooded statue of King Béla IV's **anonymous scribe,** to whom we owe much of our knowledge of medieval Hungary. Rent a **rowboat** or **ice skates** on the lake next to the castle, or a **bike-trolley** to navigate the shaded paths. The park's main road is closed to automobiles on weekends, making the park especially peaceful. *(XIV. M1: Széchenyi Fürdő. Zoo ☎ 343 6075. Open May-Aug. M-Th 9am-6pm, F-Su 9am-7pm; Sept-Oct. daily 9am-5pm; Nov.-Feb. daily 9am-4pm. 1300Ft, students 1000Ft. Amusement Park ☎ 363 8310. Open May-June M-F 11am-7pm, Sa-Su 10am-8pm; July-Aug. daily 10am-8pm. 300Ft.)*

🏛 MUSEUMS

▓ MUSEUM OF FINE ARTS (SZÉPMŰVÉSZETI MÚZEUM). A spectacular collection of European art is housed here, with paintings perhaps not found in the books but memorable nonetheless. Don't miss the El Greco room. *(XIV. Hősök tér. M1: Hősök tér. English ☎ 069 036 9300. Open Tu-Su 10am-5:30pm. Free English tours Tu-F 11am. Museum 900Ft, students 500Ft. Cameras 300Ft, video 1500Ft.)*

▓ NATIONAL MUSEUM (NEMZETI MÚZEUM). An extensive exhibition on the second floor here chronicles the history of Hungary from the founding of the state through the 20th century; the first floor is reserved for temporary exhibits. *(VIII. Múzeum krt. 14/16. M3: Kálvin tér. ☎ 338 2122; www.mng.hu. Open Mar. 1-Oct. 15 Tu-Su 10am-6pm; Oct. 16-Feb. 28 Tu-Su 10am-5pm. 800Ft, students 400Ft.)*

▓ STATUE PARK. After the collapse of Soviet rule, the open-air Statue Park museum (Szoborpark Múzeum) was created from statues removed from Budapest's parks and squares. The indispensable English guidebook (1000Ft) explains the statues' histories. *(XXII. On the corner of Balatoni út and Szabadkai út. Take express bus #7 from Keleti pu. to Étele tér, then take the Volán bus from terminal #2 to Diósd (15min., every 15min.). ☎ 424 7500; www.szoborpark.hu. Open in good weather Mar.-Nov. daily 10am-dusk; Dec.-Feb. weekends and holidays only. 600Ft, students 400Ft.)*

MUSEUM OF APPLIED ARTS (IPARMŰVÉSZETI MÚZEUM). Hungary's 1896 millennium celebration prompted the construction of this Art Nouveau building. Inside is an eclectic collection of impressive hand-crafted objects, including Tiffany glass and furniture, as well as excellent temporary exhibits. *(IX. Üllői út 33-37. M3: Ferenc krt. ☎ 456 5100. Open daily 10am-6pm. 1-2hr. guided tours, under 6 people 2500Ft total, 6-25 people 200Ft each. English pamphlet 100Ft. Museum 600Ft, students 300Ft.)*

BUDA CASTLE. Leveled by the Nazis and later by the Soviets, the reconstructed Buda Castle (see **Castle District,** p. 555) now houses several museums. *(I. Szent György tér 2. M1, 2, or 3: Deák tér, then take bus #16 across the Danube to the top of Castle Hill. ☎ 375 7533.)* Wing A contains the **Museum of Contemporary Art** (Kortárs Művészeti Múzeum), as well as the **Ludwig Museum** upstairs, which is devoted to Warhol, Lichtenstein, and other modern masters. *(☎ 375 9175; www.ludwigmuseum.hu. Open Tu-Su 10am-6pm. 600Ft, students 300Ft. Cameras 1200Ft, video 2000Ft.)* Wings B-D hold the **Hungarian National Gallery** (Magyar Nemzeti Galéria), a collection of the best Hungarian painting and sculpture. *(☎ 375 7533. Open Tu-Su 10am-6pm. English tour by appointment. Museum free.)* Wing E holds artifacts from the 1242 castle in the **Budapest History Museum** (Budapesti Történeti Múzeum). *(English ☎ 375 7533. Open Mar. to mid-Oct. M and W-Su 10am-6pm; Nov.-Feb. M and W-Su 10am-4pm. 800Ft, students 400Ft.)*

🎵 ENTERTAINMENT

Budapest Program, Budapest Panorama, Pesti Est, and the essential *Budapest in Your Pocket* (750Ft) are the best English-language entertainment guides, listing everything from festivals to cinemas to art showings. All are available at most tourist offices and hotels. The "Style" section of the *Budapest Sun* (www.budapestsun.com; 300Ft) has a comprehensive 10-day calendar and film reviews. (Tickets 600-1200Ft; cinema schedules change on Th.) Prices to most performances are reasonable; check the **Music Mix 33 Ticket Service**, V, Ferenciek tér 10. (☎317 7736; www.musicmix.hu. Open M-F 9am-5pm.)

The ▦**State Opera House** (Magyar Állami Operaház), VI, Andrássy út 22, is one of Europe's leading performance centers with a glorious hall. (M1: Opera. ☎331 2550, box office 353 0170. Tickets 800-8700Ft. Box office open M-Sa 11am-7pm, Su 4-7pm; closes at 5pm on non-performance days.) The **National Dance Theater** (Nemzetí Táncszínház), Színház u. 1-3, on Castle Hill, hosts a variety of shows—modern, alternative, Latin, ballet—but Hungarian folklore is the most popular. (☎201 4407, box office 375 8649; www.nemzetitancszinhaz.hu. Most shows 7pm.) Performances in the lovely **Városmajor Open-Air Theater**, XII, Városmajor, include musicals, operas, and ballets. Walk up the big stairs, turn right on Várfok u. and left on Csaba u., then right on Maros u. and left on Szamos u. (M1: Moszkva tér. ☎375 5922. Open June 27-Aug. 18. Box office open W-Su 3-6pm.)

To soak away the city grime, sink into a hot, relaxing thermal bath. First built in 1565, their services—from mud baths to massages—are quite cheap. **Széchenyi**, XIV, Állatkerti u. 11/14, is a welcoming bath with beautiful pools. (M1: Hősök tér. ☎321 0310. Open daily May-Sept. 6am-7pm; Oct.-Apr. M-F 6am-7pm, Sa-Su 6am-5pm. Entrance 1900Ft, 900Ft returned if you leave within 2hr., 500Ft within 3hr., 200Ft within 4hr. Keep your original receipt. 15min. massage 2400Ft.) **Gellért**, XI, Kelenhegyi út 4/6, one of the most elegant baths, has a rooftop sundeck and an outdoor wave pool. Take bus #7 or tram #47 or 49 to Hotel Gellért, at the base of Gellérthegy. (Pools open M-F 6am-7pm, Sa-Su 6am-5pm. Thermal bath and pool 2900Ft. 15min. massage 2400Ft., pedicure 1300Ft, foot massage 800Ft. MC/V.)

🎵 NIGHTLIFE

All-night outdoor parties, elegant after-hours clubs, the nightly thump and grind—Budapest has it all. Pubs and bars bustle until 4am, though given the city's energies the streets remain surprisingly empty and poorly lit. Upscale cafes and restaurants in **VI, Ferencz Liszt tér** (M2: Oktogon) attract Budapest's hip youth.

▨ **Undergrass**, VI, Ferencz Liszt tér 10. M1: Oktogon. The hottest spot in Pest's trendiest area. A soundproof glass door divides a hip bar from a packed disco. Cover F 300Ft, Sa 1000Ft. Open F-Sa 10pm-4am.

▨ **Jazz Garden**, V, Veres Pálné u. 44a. Low-hanging vines and tree branches create a laid-back garden atmosphere; a stage in the midst features live local jazz bands (9pm daily). Beer 500-550Ft. Open daily 6pm-midnight.

Piaf, VI, Nagymező u. 25. A much-loved lounge, and a good place to meet fellow travelers. Knock on the inconspicuous door and kiss cheeks with the club's matron before going inside. Cover 800Ft includes 1 beer. Open M-Th and Su 10pm-6am, F-Sa 10pm-7am, but don't come before 1am.

Angyal (Angel) Bar, VII, Szövetség u. 33 (☎351 6490). M2: Blaha L. tér. Oldest gay bar in Budapest. Huge 3-level disco, cafe, and bar packed for its weekend programs. F-Sa drag shows. F men and women, Sa men only. Cover 1000Ft. Open F-Sa 10pm-5am.

Club Seven, Akácfa u. 7. M2: Blaha Lajos tér. This upscale underground music club is a local favorite and features a casino. Cover for men Sa-Su 2000Ft, women free.

Old Man's Music Pub, VII, Akácfa u. 13. M2: Blaha Lujza tér. Daily blues and jazz start at 11pm. Relax in the restaurant (open 3pm-3am) or hit the dance floor (11pm-late). Open M-Sa 3pm-4:30am.

Fat Mo's Speakeasy, V, Nyári Pal u. 11. M3: Kálvin tér. 14 varieties of draft beer (0.5L 450-1000Ft). Live jazz M-Th and Su 9-11pm. Th-Sa DJ after midnight. Open M-W noon-2am, Th-F noon-4am, Sa 6pm-4am, Su 6pm-2am.

NIGHTLIFE SCAM. There have been reports of a mafia-organized scam involving English-speaking Hungarian women who ask foreign men to buy them drinks. When the bill comes, accompanied by imposing men, it can be as high as US$1000 per round. If victims of the scam claim to have no money, the establishment conveniently has an ATM inside the bar. The US Embassy (see **Embassies,** p. 549) has advised against patronizing a number of places near Váci u. More importantly, if a woman asks you to join her at a bar, either politely refuse or take her to a bar of your choice—not the one she suggests. Unless you know and trust the bar, always verify the price of a drink before ordering. These places change their names rapidly; for the most current list of establishments about which complaints have been received, check with the US Embassy in Budapest or view their list on the web at www.usembassy.hu/conseng/announcements.html. If you are taken in, call the police. You'll probably still have to pay, but can get a receipt to issue a complaint at the Consumer Bureau.

DAYTRIPS FROM BUDAPEST: THE DANUBE BEND

North of Budapest, the Danube sweeps in a dramatic arc called the Danube Bend (Dunakanyar), deservedly one of the most beloved tourist attractions in Hungary.

■ **SZENTENDRE.** Narrow cobblestone streets in Szentendre (pop. 23,000) brim with upscale art galleries and pricey restaurants. Head up **Church Hill** (Templomdomb) in Fő tér, above the town center, for an amazing view from the 13th-century Roman Catholic church. The **Czóbel Museum,** to the left of the church at Templom tér 1, exhibits the work of Béla Czóbel, Hungary's foremost post-Impressionist painter, including his bikini-clad "Venus of Szentendre." English info is available. (Open Tu-Su 10am-6pm. 400Ft, students 200Ft.) The popular **Margit Kovács Museum,** Vastagh György u. 1, off Görög u., which branches from Fő tér, displays whimsical ceramic sculptures and tiles by the 20th-century Hungarian artist. (Open Mar.-Oct. daily 10am-6pm; Nov. daily 9am-5pm; Dec.-Feb. Tu-Su 10am-5pm. 600Ft, students 300Ft.) The real thriller at the ■**Szabó Marzipan Museum and Confectionery,** Dumtsa Jenő u. 12, is the 80kg white chocolate statue of Michael Jackson. (Open daily May-Sept. 10am-7pm; Oct.-Apr. 10am-6pm. 350Ft.) The ■**National Wine Museum** (Nemzeti Bormúzeum), Bogdányi u. 10, is a cellar exhibit of wines from all the wine-making regions in Hungary. (Open daily 10am-10pm. Exhibition 100Ft. Wine tasting (10 samples) and admission to the exhibition 1600Ft.)

HÉV trains travel to Szentendre from Budapest's Batthyány tér (45min., every 20min., 374Ft). **Buses** run to: Budapest's Árpád híd metro station (30min., every 20-40min., 240Ft); Esztergom (1½hr., 1 per hr., 476Ft); and Visegrád (45min., 1 per hr., 316Ft). The train and bus stations are 10min. from Fő tér; descend the stairs past the end of the HÉV tracks and head through the underpass up Kossuth u. At the fork, bear right onto Dumtsa Jenő u., which leads to the town center. MAHART **boats** leave from a pier 20min. north of the town center. With the river on the right, walk along the water to the sign. **Tourinform,** Dumtsa Jenő u. 22, between the town center and the station, has maps. (☎026 31 79 65; www.szentendre.hu. Open mid-Mar. to Oct. M-F 9am-4:30pm, Sa-Su 10am-2pm; Nov. to mid-Mar. M-F 9:30am-4:30pm.) It's usually

THE INSIDER'S CITY

MARGIT ISLAND

In the middle of the Danube River, between Buda and Pest, Margit Island is a secluded refuge with a rich history. Today it is crowded with Hungarian lovers holding hands, but is still big enough that you can make it feel like your own. Below are some highlights you won't want to miss.

1 Lounge by the fountain, grab a snack, and spring on the trampolines (200Ft per 5min.)—but maybe not in that order.

2 Rent and ride around on a pedal car (1800Ft per hr.).

3 Splash in the pools and scream down the slides at Palatinus Strandfürdo.

4 Visit the convent ruins and walk through the statue park, where Hungary's cultural icons are immortalized.

5 Pay to see a show at the theater or just listen as the music carries across the island.

6 Walk in the rose gardens and take a stroll through the small zoo.

cheapest to dine in Budapest or Visegrád. At ▨**Nostalgia Cafe ❶**, Bogdányi u. 2, enjoy a pastry (from 350Ft) and cappuccino (from 300Ft) while serenaded by opera singers. (Open Th-Su 10am-10pm. AmEx/MC/V.)

VISEGRÁD. Host to the royal court in medieval times, Visegrád was devastated when the Habsburgs destroyed its 13th-century **citadel** in a struggle against the freedom fighters. A former Roman outpost, the edifice provides a dramatic view of the Danube and surrounding hills. To reach it, head north on Fő út., make a right on Salamontorony u., and follow the path. Sprawling across the foothills above Fő út are the ruins of King Matthias's **Royal Palace** (Királyi Palota), which was considered a myth until archaeologists discovered it; exhibits inside include a computerized reconstruction of the original castle. (Open Tu-Su 9am-5pm; last admission 4:30pm. Free.) The palace grounds relive their glory days of parades, jousting, and music during the mid-July **Viségrad Palace Games.** (☎ 026 39 81 28; muvelodesihaz@visegrad.hu.) At the end of Salamontorony u., the **King Matthias Museum**, inside Solomon's Tower (Alsóvár Salamon Torony), exhibits artifacts from the palace ruins. (Open May-Oct. Tu-Su 9am-5pm; last admission 4:30pm. Free.)

Buses run to Budapest's Árpád híd metro station (1½hr., 30 per day, 421Ft). The tourist office, **Viségrad Tours,** Rév út 15, sells maps for 300Ft. (☎ 026 39 81 60. Open Apr.-Oct. daily 8am-6pm; Nov.-Mar. M-F 10am-4pm.) Pick up the basics across the street at **CBA Élelmiszer** supermarket. (Open M 7am-6pm, Tu-F 7am-7pm, Sa 7am-3pm, Su 7am-noon. AmEx/MC.) **Gulás Csárda ❸**, Nagy Lajos u. 4, prepares five excellent Hungarian dishes daily; let the garlic aromas tempt you from the garden outside. (Entrees 1050-2050Ft. Open daily noon-10pm.)

ESZTERGOM. A millennium of religious history revolves around the solemn hilltop cathedral, the **Basilica of Esztergom,** which is now the seat of the Catholic Church in Hungary. Ascend the interminable staircases to the ▨**cupola** (200Ft), which offers the best view of the Danube Bend. The **Cathedral Treasury** (Kincstáv) to the right of the main altar has Hungary's most extensive collection of ecclesiastical treasures. The red marble **Bakócz Chapel,** to the left of the nave, is a masterwork of Renaissance craftsmanship. (Open Mar.-Oct. daily 9am-4pm; Nov.-Dec. M-F 11am-3:30pm, Sa-Su 10am-3:30pm. Chapel free. English guidebook 100Ft.)

Trains go to Budapest (1½hr., 22 per day, 436Ft). From the station, turn left on the main street, Baross Gábor út, and make a right onto Kiss János Altábornagy út, which becomes Kossuth Lajos u., to reach the square. **Buses** run to Szentendre (1½hr., 1 per hr., 476Ft) and Visegrád (45min., 1 per hr., 316Ft). From the bus station, walk up Simor János u. toward the street market to reach Rákóczi tér. MAHART **boats** depart from the pier at Gőzhajó u. on Primas Sziget Island for: Budapest (4hr.; 3 per day; 1200Ft, students 900Ft); Szentendre (2¾hr.; 2 per day; 980Ft, students 490Ft); and Visegrád (1½hr.; 2 per day; 700Ft, students 525Ft). **Grantours,** Széchenyi tér 25, at the edge of Rákóczi tér, sells maps (300Ft-500Ft) and arranges accommodations. (☎033 41 70 52; grantour@mail.holop.hu. Open July-Aug. M-F 8am-6pm, Sa 9am-noon; Sept.-June M-F 8am-4pm, Sa 9am-noon.) **Csülök Csárda ❷**, Batthány út 9, offers fine Hungarian cuisine with vegetarian options. (Entrees 480-1800Ft. Open daily noon-10pm. MC/V.)

SOUTHERN TRANSDANUBIA

Once the southernmost portion of the Roman province Pannonia, Southern Transdanubia is framed by the Danube to the west, the Dráva River to the south, and Lake Balaton to the north. Known for its rolling hills, mild climate, and sunflower fields, the region is also filled with magnificent Habsburg architecture.

PÉCS ☎072

Pécs (PAYCH; pop. 180,000), at the foot of the Mecsek mountains, is blessed with a pleasant climate, gorgeous vistas, and lovely architecture. Outdoor activities in the surrounding region and an intense nightlife fueled by university students make Pécs an attractive weekend spot. At the ▨**Zsolnay Museum,** Káptalan u. 2, a family workshop has hand-crafted the world-famous Zsolnay porcelain since the mid-19th century. (Walk up Szepessy I. u. behind the Mosque Church and turn left at Káptalan u. Open Tu-Sa 10am-6pm, Su 10am-4pm. 600Ft, students 300Ft. Photographs 400Ft, video 800Ft.) At nearby Széchenyi tér stands the **Mosque of Ghazi Kassim** (Gázi Khasim Pasa dzsámija). The building was once a Turkish mosque built on the site of an earlier church. Now once again a church, its fusion of Christian and Muslim traditions has become an emblem of the city. (Open mid-Apr. to mid-Oct. M-Sa 10am-4pm, Su 12:30-4pm; mid-Oct. to mid-Apr. M-Sa 10am-noon, Su open for Mass only 9:30, 10:30, and 11:30am. Free; donations requested.) Walk downhill from Széchenyi tér on Irgalmasok u. to Kossuth tér to reach the 1869 **synagogue,** which has intricate ceiling frescoes and a stunning Ark of the Covenant. (Open Mar.-Oct. M-F and Su 10-11:30am and noon-1pm. 300Ft, students 200Ft.) Chill with the artsy crowd at **Cafe Dante,** Janus Pannonis u. 11, in the Csontváry Museum building. (Beer 290-390Ft. Open M-F 10am-1am, later Sa-Su.)

To reach the train station, just south of the historic district, take bus #30, 32, or 33 from the town center. **Trains** run to Budapest (2½hr., 16 per day, 1918-2338Ft), as do **buses** (4½hr., 5 per day, 2088Ft). **Tourinform,** Széchenyi tér 9, sells maps and phone cards. (☎511 232. Open M-F 8am-6pm, Sa-Su 9am-3pm.) Private rooms a small ways from the town center are a good budget option. In the center, spotless ▨**Pollack Mihály Students' Hostel ❶**, Jokai u. 8, has kitchen facilities. (☎315 846. Call ahead. Dorms 1800Ft.) **Janus Pannonius University ❶**, Universitas u. 2, offers clean triples with bathrooms. (☎311 966. Kitchen facilities. Check-out 9am. Call ahead. Open June-Sept. 1800Ft.) Pécs's restaurants, cafes, and bars are among the city's biggest attractions. ▨**Cellarium Étterem ❸**, Hunyadi út 2, is a Hungarian restaurant housed in a wine cellar. (Entrees 950-3200Ft. AmEx/MC/V.) ▨**Afiúm ❸**, Irgalmasok u. 2, has a delicious Italian and Hungarian menu with veggie options. (Entrees 990-2800Ft. Open M-Sa 11am-1am, Su 11am-midnight.) **Postal Code:** 7621.

HUNGARY

LAVA GROOVES

Walking around Eger, one doesn't see neon signs advertising posh dance clubs or tacky discos. It would be understandable if this quiet little town, full of history and overflowing with wine, had no use for such modern diversions. However, the town crawls with them—or more accurately, crawls *on* them. What most tourists would never guess is that a labyrinth of passages threads the ground below Eger, which rests on a 120km bed of hardened lava. Several tunnels have now been converted into nightclubs, hidden to the world above save for a few small, nearly unmarked entrances.

In one of the most popular of these dens, **Broadway Palace,** sacreligious youths dance the night away under the Eger Cathedral, leaving the club only hours before the church above opens for morning services. Look for the entrance on Kossuth L. u., on the left side of the Cathedral. (Cover 400-600Ft. Open W and F-Sa 10pm-4am.)

Another popular underground spot is **Liget Dance Café,** Érsekkert, under Excalibur restaurant in the Archbishop's Gardens. (☎42 77 54. Cover 600Ft. Open F-Sa 10pm-6am.) **Hippolit Club and Restaurant,** Katona tér 2, is classier but also more expensive. (☎41 10 31. Dancing starts around 11pm. Open M-Th noon-midnight, F-Sa noon-4am.)

EGER ☎036

Captain István Dobó's miraculous defeat of the Ottomans besieging Eger Castle in 1553 has secured the town a place in Hungarian lore. According to legend, the key to his victory was the strengthening power of the local wine *Egri Bikavér* (Bull's Blood). A legacy of potent wines continues today in the lively cellars of the Valley of the Beautiful Women. Eger (EGG-air; pop. 57,000) is close enough to Budapest to visit as a daytrip, but constantly tempts travelers to extend their stay with its cobblestone streets, culinary delicacies, and infectious friendliness.

☎ TRANSPORTATION AND PRACTICAL INFORMATION. Trains run frequently to Budapest (2hr.; 21 per day, 6 direct; 1036-1242Ft). From the station, to reach the main square, **Dobó tér** (20 min.), turn right on Deák Ferenc út., walk 10min., turn right on Kossuth Lajos u. and then left on Tokaj u. **TourInform,** Bajcsy-Zsilinszky u. 9, has lodging info. (☎51 77 15; www.ektf.hu/eger. Open June-Sept. M-F 9am-7pm, Sa-Su 10am-6pm; Sept.-June M-F 9am-5pm, Sa 9am-1pm.) **OTP Bank,** Széchenyi u. 2, grants credit card cash advances, cashes **AmEx Traveler's Cheques** for no commission, and has an **ATM.** (☎31 08 66; fax 313 554. Open M-Tu and Th 7:45am-5pm, W 7:45am-6pm, F 7:45am-4pm.) A **24hr. currency exchange** machine is opposite the church on Dobó tér. **Postal Code:** 3300.

☎ ACCOMMODATIONS AND FOOD. Private rooms are best (about 3000Ft); look for *"Zimmer frei"* or *"szòba eladò"* on signs outside the main square, particularly on Almagyar u. and Mekcsey István u. near the castle. **Eger Tourist,** Bajcsy-Zsilinszky u. 9, next to TourInform, arranges private rooms that cost about 3000Ft. (☎51 70 00. Open M-F 9am-5pm.) **Lukács Vendéghaz ❷,** Bárány u. 10, located just next to Eger Castle, has its own garden, an outdoor seating area, and large, comfortable rooms. (☎/fax 411 567. Rooms 2500-4000Ft.) **Hotel Minaret ❹,** Knézich K. u. 4, is centrally located and offers a beauty and massage center, swimming pool, and gym. (☎/fax 410 233. All rooms include satellite TV. Singles 8700Ft; doubles 14,600Ft; triples 19,000Ft; quads 22,300Ft. Surcharge of 300Ft per person per night except in singles. Nov.-Mar. 1000Ft less.) Take bus #5, 11, or 12 north to the Shell station (20min.) to reach **Autós Caravan Camping ❶,** Rákóczi u. 79. (Open daily mid-Apr. to mid-Oct. 9am-10pm. 900Ft, students 700Ft.) **Széchenyi u.** is lined with restaurants. **▨Dobos ❶,** Széchenyi u. 6, offers a mouth-watering selection of pastries and desserts. (Confections 200-400Ft. Ice cream 100Ft. Open daily 9:30am-9pm.) **Gyros Étterem Sörözö ❷,** Széchenyi u. 10, serves gyros (450-950Ft) in a mirrored, well-kept setting with patio seating in summer. In the Valley of the Beautiful Women, crowds dine in the courtyard of **Kulacs Csárda Borozó's ❸**. (Entrees 950-2000Ft. Open M and W-Su noon-10pm. AmEx/MC/V.) There is an **ABC** supermarket between Sandor u. and Szt. Janos u. (Open M-F 6am-7pm, Sa 6am-1pm, Su 6-11am.)

◙ ▓ SIGHTS AND FESTIVALS. Medieval **Eger Castle**, from which Dobó István and his men repelled an attacking Ottoman army, features subterranean barracks, catacombs, a crypt, and a wine cellar. (Open daily 8am-8pm. 200Ft, students 100Ft.) One additional ticket covers the **picture gallery**, the **Dobó István Vármúzeum**, with artifacts and weapons, and the **dungeon exhibition**. (Open Mar.-Oct. Tu-Su 9am-5pm, ticket office closes at 4:20pm; Nov.-Feb. 9am-3pm. 500Ft/250Ft.) Beautiful Baroque architecture graces the **Lyceum**, at the corner of Kossuth Lajos u. and Eszterházy tér.; inside are an astronomical museum and a *camera obscura* that projects a live image of the Eger onto a table. (Open Apr.-Sept. Tu-Su 9:30am-3:30pm; Oct.-Mar. M-F 9:30am-1pm, Sa-Su 9:30am-1:30pm. 450Ft, students 300Ft.)

After a morning exploring Eger's historical sights, spend the afternoon or evening in the wine cellars of the ▨**Valley of the Beautiful Women** (Szépass-zonyvölgy). To reach the cellars, start on Széchenyi u. with Eger Cathedral to your right. Turn right on Kossuth Lajos u., left on Kapu tér, and then right again on Tele-kessy u.; continue until you arrive at Szépasszonyvölgy (20min.). Most of the 25 open cellars consist of little more than a tunnel and a few tables and benches, but each has its own personality. Some are hushed while others burst with Hungarian and Gypsy sing-alongs. (Open from 9am, closing times vary; July-Aug. some stay open till midnight. 0.1L taste either free or 50Ft, 1L 350Ft.)

In summer, **open-air baths** offer a break from the sweltering city heat. (Open May-Sept. M-F 6am-7pm, Sa-Su 8:30am-7pm; Oct.-Apr. daily 9am-7pm. 500Ft, students 350Ft.) The city celebrates its heritage with daily performances of opera and early court music during the **Baroque Festival** (late July to mid-Aug.).

▨ DAYTRIP FROM EGER: SZILVÁSVÁRAD. A perfect outing from Eger, Szil-vásvárad (SEAL-vash-vah-rod) attracts horse and nature lovers. **Horse shows** (800Ft) kick into action on most weekends in the arena on Szalajka u. **Lipicai Stables** is the stud farm for the town's famed Lipizzaner breed. From the park entrance on Egri út., turn left on Enyves u., then follow the signs. (☎ 35 51 55. Open daily 8:30am-noon and 2-4pm. 300Ft.) **Hikers** should head to the nearby **Bükk mountains** and **Szalajka Valley**. A 45min. walk along the green trail leads to the main attraction, the **Fátyol waterfall**; the **Istálósk cave**, home to Stone Age bear-worshippers, is 30min. further. **Bike rentals** and cycling maps are available on Szalajka u.

Szilvásvárad can be reached from Eger by **train** (1hr., 7 per day, 324Ft) or **bus** (45min., every 30min.-1hr., 316Ft). To reach the national park from the train station (Szilvásvárad-Szalajkavölgy), follow Egri út. to Szalajka u. and continue along the road. Szilvásvárad has no bus station; get off at the second stop on Egri út. near Szalajka u. where the road bends sharply. Szilvásvárad has no tourist office either; before heading out, stop by Eger's **TourInform** (p. 562).

GYŐR ☎ 096

In the unspoiled, far western region of Őrség, lively Győr (DJUR; pop. 130,000) overflows with religious monuments, museums, and 17th- and 18th-century architectural highlights. Turn right out of the train station, left before the underpass, and cross the street to reach the pedestrian-only **Baross Gábor útca**. Walking uphill on Czuczor Gergely u., one street to the right of Baross Gábor u., will lead you to the striking **Ark of the Covenant statue** (Frigylada szobor) and **Chapter Hill** (Kápta-landomb). At the top of the hill is the **Episcopal Cathedral** (Székesegyház), which

HUNGARY

holds the **Weeping Madonna of Győr;** legend has it that the icon wept blood for persecuted Irish Catholics on St. Patrick's Day in 1697. The **Diocesan Library and Treasury** (Egyházmegyei Kincstár), Káptalandomb 26, hidden in an alley off the cathedral's square, displays 14th-century gold and silver religious artifacts. (Open Tu-Su 10am-4pm. 300Ft, students 150Ft. English captions.) For contemporary art, head to the **Imre Patkó collection,** Széchenyi tér 4, down Czuczor Gergely u. from the statue; enter at Stelczera u. (Open Tu-Su 10am-6pm. 240Ft, students 120Ft.) Across the river from the town center is the huge and popular **water park,** Cziráky tér 1, supplied by thermal springs. From Bécsi Kapu tér, take the bridge over the small island and make the first right on the other side, then go right again onto Cziráky tér. (Open daily 8am-10pm. 950Ft, students 600Ft; after 3pm 700Ft/500Ft.) At night, music and young people spill from cellar bars onto Győr's streets. The patio at **Komédiás Biergarten,** Czuczor Gergely u. 30, invites drinking and laughing crowds. (Beer 290-460Ft. Open M-Sa 11am-midnight.) **Dublin Gate Irish Pub,** underground at Bécsi kapu tér 8, taps into a lively young crowd and a whole lot of beer. (☎528 466. Guinness 900Ft for 0.5L. Open daily 3pm-late.)

Trains run frequently to Budapest (2½hr., 26 per day, 1284-1646Ft) and Vienna (2hr., 13 per day, 4450Ft). **Buses** also transit to Budapest (2½hr., 1 per hr., 1300Ft). The train station is 3min. from the city center; the underpass that links the rail platforms leads to the bus station. The **Tourinform kiosk,** Árpád u. 32, at the corner with Baross Gabor u., provides free maps and arranges lodgings. (☎ 31 17 71. Open June-Aug. M-F 8am-8pm, Sa-Su 9am-6pm.) 🏠**Katalin's Kert ❹**, Sarkantyú köz 3, off Bécsi Kapu tér, has huge modern rooms with private baths. (☎/fax 45 20 88. Singles 7100Ft; doubles 9100Ft; triples 12500Ft. Tax 300Ft per person. MC/V.) **Matróz Restaurant ❷**, Dunakapu tér 3, off Jedlik Ányos u. facing the river, serves up succulent fish, turkey, and pork dishes. (Entrees 550-1390Ft. Open M-Th and Su 9am-10pm, F-Sa 9am-11pm.) **John Bull Pub ❷**, Aradi út 3, offers a break from the Hungarian diet. (Entrees 780-2350Ft. Open daily 10am-midnight.) **Kaiser's** supermarket is at the corner of Arany János u. and Aradi vértanúk. (Open M 7:30am-7pm, Tu-F 6:30am-7pm, Sa 6:30am-3pm. MC/V.) **Postal Code:** 9021.

⚡ DAYTRIP FROM GYŐR: ARCHABBEY OF PANNONHALMA. Visible on a clear day from Győr, the hilltop Archabbey of Pannonhalma (Pannonhalmi Főapátság) has seen a millennium of destruction and rebuilding since its establishment by the Benedictine order in AD 996. Now a UNESCO World Heritage site, it is home to a 360,000-volume library, a 13th-century basilica, and classical concerts. **Pax Tourist,** to the left of the entrance, leads tours and has concert info. (☎57 01 91; pax@osb.hu. Hungarian tour with English text every hr. 1000Ft. English tours Mar. 21-Nov. 11 Tu-Su 11am and 1pm. 1200Ft.) To reach Pannonhalma from Győr, take the **bus** from stand #11 (45min., 7 per day, 347Ft). Ask for Pannonhalma vár and get off at the huge gates, or you may end up in town a 1km uphill walk away.

LAKE BALATON

A retreat since Roman times, warm Lake Balaton drew the European elite in the 19th century and is now a budget paradise for German and Austrian students. Be aware however that storms roll in quickly—when the yellow lights on harbor buildings speed to one revolution per second, swimmers must get out of the water. Don't worry that storms will ruin your vacation, though: Most last less than 30min.

SIÓFOK. Tourist offices are more densely packed in Siófok than in any other Hungarian city, reflecting the influx every summer of lake-bound vacationers. Bars and nightclubs line the lakefront, and **disco boats** push off nightly. (☎310 050.) Most attractions in Siófok pale in comparison with the **Strand,** a series of park-like lawns running to the shoreline; entry is free to some sections, but others cost 200-400Ft. At the center is the ■**Renegade Pub**, Petőfi sétány 3, a crowded bar and dance club. (Open daily June-Aug. 8pm-5am.) **Palace Disco**, Deák Ferenc sétány 2, is a party complex with discos, bars, and restaurants. Free buses depart every hour from behind the water tower. (☎082 045. Beer from 600Ft. Cover 1500-2500Ft. Pizzeria open 11am-5am. Disco open daily May to mid-Sept. 10pm-5am.) **Trains** run to Budapest (2½hr., 20 per day, 1094Ft). **Buses** head to Budapest (1½hr., 9 per day, 1320Ft) and Pécs (3hr., 4 per day, 2456Ft). **Tourinform**, Fő út. at Szabadság tér, in the base of the water tower opposite the train station, helps find rooms and has free maps. (☎084 315 355; www.siofok.com. Open mid-June to mid-Sept. M-Sa 8am-8pm, Sa-Su 9am-6pm; mid-Sept. to mid-June M-F 9am-4pm.) Take a 25min. bus or train ride to Balatonszéplak felsö for ■**Villa Benjamin Youth Hostel ❷**, Siófoki u. 9, which has garden rooms and a beach-bungalow feel. (☎084 350 704. Singles 2500Ft; doubles 5000Ft; triples 7500Ft; 4- to 6-person apartments 14,000-21,000Ft; 8- to 10-person house 28,000-35,000Ft.) **Park Hotel ❺**, Batthány u. 7, has rooms with A/C right by the Strand. (☎084 310 539. Reception 24hr. July-Aug. doubles 10,000-15,000Ft, Sept.-June 8000-10,000Ft. MC/V.)

TIHANY. Scenic hikes, charming cottages, and panoramic views make the Tihany peninsula the pearl of Lake Balaton. The **Benedictine Abbey** (Bencés Apátság) draws over a million visitors annually with its luminous frescoes, gilded Baroque altars, and crypt sheltering one of Hungary's earliest kings. (Open daily Mar.-Oct. 9am-6pm. 400Ft, students 200Ft. Su free.) Well-marked **hiking** trails across the peninsula take an hour or two to traverse. The ■**green line trail** runs past the Hermit's Place (Barátlakások), where the cells and chapel hollowed out by 11th-century Greek Orthodox hermits are still visible. MAHART **ferries** go to Tihany from Siófok (1-1¼hr.; 6-9 per day; 1000Ft, students 500Ft). To reach the town from the ferry pier and neighboring Strand, walk underneath the elevated road and follow the Apátság signs up the steep hill to the abbey.

KESZTHELY. At the lake's western tip, Keszthely (KEST-hay), once the playground of the powerful Austro-Hungarian Festetics family, is now home to an agricultural college and year-round thermal springs. The ■**Helikon Palace Museum** (Helikon Kastélymúzeum) in the **Festetics Palace** (Kastély) is a storybook Baroque palace with a 90,000-volume library, extravagantly furnished chambers, an exotic arms collection, and a porcelain exhibit. From Fő tér, follow Kossuth Lajos u. toward Tourinform until it becomes Kastély u. (Open Tu-Su 9am-4:30pm. 1500Ft, students 700Ft.) The **Strand**, on the coast to the right as you exit the train station, draws crowds with its giant slide, paddle boats, and volleyball nets. From the center, walk down Erzsébet u. as it curves right into Vörösmarty u.; after the train tracks, go through the park on the left to get to the beach. (Open daily mid-May to mid-Sept. 8:30am-7pm. Entry mid-May to June 350Ft; July to mid-Sept. 440Ft.)

InterCity **trains** run to Budapest (3hr.; 13 per day; 1556Ft, reservations 400Ft). **Buses** run from near the train station to Pécs (4hr., 5 per day, 1486Ft). From the station, take Mártirok u., which ends in Kossuth Lajos u., and turn left to reach the main square, Fő tér. **Tourinform**, Kossuth Lajos u. 28, on the palace side of Fő tér, has free maps and checks room availability. (☎083 31 41 44. Open July-Aug. M-F 9am-8pm, Sa-Su 9am-6pm; Oct.-June M-F 9am-5pm, Sa 9am-1pm.) Central **Kiss-Máté Panzió ❹**, Katona J u. 27, has spacious rooms. (]083 319 072. Kitchen available. Free laundry. Doubles 6000Ft; triples 8000Ft.) **Castrum Camping ❶**, Móra Ferenc u. 48, has large sites and tennis courts. (☎083 31 21 20. 900Ft per person. July-Aug. 600Ft per tent, Sept.-June 480Ft per tent.) ■**Corso Restaurant ❸**, Erzsébet Királyné u. 23, in the Abbázia Club Hotel, serves fish from Balaton. (Entrees 800-2800Ft. Open M-Sa 7am-10pm. AmEx/MC/V.) Just outside the palace, **Kolostor Restaurant ❷**, Katona J. u. 2/c, offers game and seafood dishes on a balcony overlooking the gardens. (Entrees 600-1350Ft. Open 11:30am-9pm. MC/V.)

ICELAND (ÍSLAND)

Born from the collision of the European and North American continents, Iceland's landscape is uniquely warped and contorted, forged by the tempers of still-active volcanoes and raked by the slow advance and retreat of impassive glaciers. Nature is the country's greatest attraction—few other places offer visitors the chance to pick their way through sunken ice kettles, dodge scalding water spewing forth from geysers, and bike 200km between fishing villages with no one but seabirds for company. Icelanders are no strangers to civilization: the geothermal wells beneath their feet have been harnessed to provide hot water and electricity, and style-conscious club kids in the capital city are anything but behind the times. Yet even as the country reaches out to tourists and cracks its door open to immigrants, Iceland remains committed to achieving prosperity without sullying its pristine natural surroundings or sabotaging its deeply rooted sense of community.

DISCOVER ICELAND

Spend two days exploring the heart of **Reykjavík** (p. 570), then daytrip to the rugged natural wonders of **Gullfoss** and **Geysir** (p. 576). Plant one foot on each side of the continental divide in **Þingvellir National Park** (p. 576), then sail out to the **Westman Islands** (p. 578) for a firsthand look at the kind of volcanic activity that formed mainland Iceland just 14 million years ago.

ESSENTIALS

WHEN TO GO

You can make a good argument for visiting most European countries during the low season. Iceland, however, is not one of them. June, July, and August are still the months to go for the broadest range of accommodations and transportation

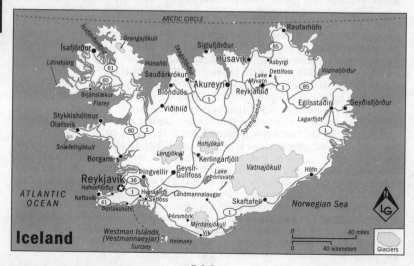

options. The sun dips below the horizon for a few hours each night, but the sky never really gets dark and it's warm enough to camp with a jacket. Conversely, the sun is restricted to brief 4hr. cameo appearances during December and January. With winter temperatures in Reykjavík averaging a far-from-Arctic 0°C (32°F), you won't freeze and you may well see the Northern Lights. Still, you won't be going far, since public transportation in the low season slows to an irregular crawl.

DOCUMENTS AND FORMALITIES

VISAS. EU citizens do not need a visa. Citizens of Australia, Canada, New Zealand, and the US do not need a visa for stays of up to 90 days, although this three-month period begins upon entry into any of the countries that belong to the EU's freedom of movement zone. For more information, see p. 17.

EMBASSIES. Foreign embassies in Iceland are in Reykjavík. Icelandic embassies at home include: **Canada**, 360 Albert St., Ste. 710, Ottawa, ON KIR 7X7 (☎613-482-1944; www.iceland.org/ca); **UK**, 2A Hans St., London SW1X 0JE (☎020 7259 3999; www.iceland.org/uk); **US**, 1156 15th St. NW, Ste. 1200, Washington, D.C. 20005 (☎202-265-6653; www.iceland.org/us).

TRANSPORTATION

BY PLANE. Icelandair (US ☎800-223-5500, UK 207 874 1000; www.icelandair.net) flies to Reykjavík year-round from the US and Europe. Icelandair provides free stopovers of up to seven days on all transatlantic flights, and runs a Lucky Fares e-mail list that makes discounted flights available to members. No-frills **Iceland Express** (UK ☎870 850 0737; www.icelandexpress.com) flies twice daily from London and Copenhagen to Reykjavík from April through late October. Fares vary, but start at €120. Icelandair's domestic counterpart **Air Iceland** (☎570 30 30; www.airiceland.is) flies from Reykjavík to the Faroe Islands, Kulusuk, Greenland, and most major towns in Iceland.

BY BUS. Iceland has no trains; although flying is faster and more comfortable, **Bifreiðastöð Íslands (BSÍ)** buses are usually cheaper and provide a closer look at the terrain. **Destination Iceland** (☎591 10 20; www.dice.is), which has offices in the Reykjavík bus terminal, can help you navigate the schedule, available online at www.bsi.is and at tourist offices. From mid June to August, buses run daily on the **Ring Road**, the highway that circles Iceland, but may only run three times per week in the low season. The going is slow, since some stretches in the east are unpaved.

The **Full Circle Passport** lets travelers circle the island at their own pace on the Ring Road (available mid-May to Sept.; 23,500Ikr). However, it allows travel in only one direction, so travelers must move either clockwise or counter-clockwise around the country. For an extra 11,700Ikr the pass (which has no time limitation) provides access to the Westfjords in the extreme northwest. The **Omnibus Passport** gives a period of unlimited travel on all scheduled bus routes, including non-Ring roads (1-week 26,100Ikr, 2-week 38,000Ikr, 3-week 46,400Ikr, 4-week 51,500Ikr; low-season 1-week pass 15,400Ikr).

BY FERRY. The best way to see Iceland's rugged shores is on the **Norröna** ferry (☎570 86 00; www.smyrlin-line.fo) that crosses the North Atlantic via: Hanstholm, Denmark; Tórshavn in the Faroe Islands; and Seyðisfjörður, Iceland. (Runs mid-May to Aug.; 7 days; 29,900Ikr, students 22,400Ikr). From Tórshavn, you can either continue on to Bergen, Norway or return to Seyðisfjörður. An **Elmskip** cargo ship leaves Reykjavík at 1pm every Thursday from March 1 through October 31, carrying up to three passengers to ports including: Rotterdam, the Netherlands; Hamburg, Germany; and Gothenburg, Sweden. (Reservations ☎585 43 00. Fares from 28,600Ikr. Bicycles 3000Ikr.)

BY CAR. Travelers using cars have the most freedom, and Iceland has plenty of car rental (*bílaleiga*) companies. Prices average 5000-7000Ikr per day for a small car, but are more like 20,000-25,000Ikr for the **4-wheel-drive vehicles** that are imperative outside of settled areas. On these routes, drivers should bring a container of extra fuel, since some roads go 300km without a single refueling station and strong headwinds can significantly affect the rate of fuel consumption. It is not uncommon for drivers to **ford streams** in their vehicles; do not attempt this in a compact car, and cross in a convoy if possible. (24hr. reports on road conditions ☎800 63 16, in English June-Aug.) Drivers are required to wear seatbelts and to keep their headlights on at all times. Iceland recognizes foreign driver's licenses, but you may need to purchase insurance for the rental vehicle (1000-3500Ikr).

BY BIKE AND BY THUMB. Cycling is gaining popularity, but ferocious winds, driving rain, and gravel-strewn roads make it a difficult mode of transport between towns. Hug the Ring Road if you prefer company, branch out to the coastal roads that snake their way through the Eastfjords, or check http://home.wanadoo.nl/erens/icecycle.htm for a wealth of other itineraries. Travels in the country's rugged interior often require mountain bikes; get in touch with the **Icelandic Mountainbike Club** (☎562 00 99; www.mmedia.is/~ifhk) or drop by their clubhouse in Reykjavík, at Brekkustígur 2, Thursday nights after 8pm for some friendly advice. Buses will carry bikes for a 500-900Ikr fee, depending on the route. Hitchhikers sometimes try the roads in summer, but sparse traffic and harsh weather exacerbate the inherent risks. Nevertheless, hitchhikers can find rides with relative ease between Reykjavík and Akureyri; flagging down a ride is harder in the east and the south. *Let's Go* does not recommend hitchhiking as a safe means of transport.

TOURIST SERVICES AND MONEY

EMERGENCY　　Police: ☎112. Ambulance: ☎112. Fire: ☎112.

TOURIST OFFICES. Tourist offices in large towns have maps, brochures, and the must-have BSÍ bus schedule; check at hotel reception desks in smaller towns for local info. The Icelandic Tourist Board maintains a well-designed introduction to the country at www.icetourist.is.

MONEY. Iceland's monetary unit is the **króna** (plural: krónur), which is divided into 100 rarely-used *aurar*. There are 1Ikr, 5Ikr, 10Ikr, 50Ikr, and 100Ikr coins; notes are in denominations of 100Ikr, 500Ikr, 1000Ikr, 2000Ikr, and 5000Ikr. There's no way around it: costs are high. On average, a night in a hostel will cost 1600Ikr, a guesthouse 3000-4000Ikr, and a meal's worth of groceries 700-1200Ikr. Restaurants include a service charge on the bill; **tipping** further is unnecessary and even discouraged. All countries who are members of the European Union impose a **Value Added Tax (VAT)** on goods and services purchased within the EU. Prices in Iceland already include the country's steep 24.5% VAT rate, although partial refunds are available for visitors who are not EU citizens (p. 22).

ICELANDIC KRÓNUR (IKR)		
AUS$1 = 46.98IKR		100IKR = AUS$2.12
CDN$1 = 58.98IKR		100IKR = CDN$1.70
EUR€1 = 89.80IKR		100IKR = EUR€1.11
NZ$1 = 48.09IKR		100IKR = NZ$2.08
UK£1 = 129.77IKR		100IKR = UK£0.77
US$1 = 82.58IKR		100IKR = US$1.21

BUSINESS HOURS. Stores are generally open Monday to Friday 9am-6pm and Saturday mornings. Some supermarkets stay open as late as 11pm every day.

COMMUNICATION

TELEPHONES. **Síminn,** the state-owned telephone monopoly, usually has an office in the same building as the post office; these offices sell **phone cards,** and give the best rates on international calls. Pay phones accept prepaid phone cards, credit cards (cheapest for calls to mobile phones), as well as 10Ikr, 50Ikr, or 100Ikr coins. Iceland uses two different **mobile phone** networks; digital GSM phones service 98% of the country's population, but only a small fraction of its land area, so hikers, fishermen, and others who travel outside of settled areas rely on analog NMT phones. Prepaid GSM phone cards are available at gas stations. For operator assistance within Iceland, dial ☎ 118; for international assistance, dial ☎ 1811. International direct dial numbers include: **AT&T** (☎ 800 222 55 288); **British Telecom** (☎ 800 89 0354); **Canada Direct** (☎ 800 90 10); **MCI** (☎ 800 90 02); **Sprint** (☎ 800 90 03); **Telecom New Zealand** (☎ 800 90 64); **Telstra Australia** (☎ 800 90 61).

PHONE CODES	**Country code: 354. International dialing prefix: 00.** There are no city codes in Iceland. From outside Iceland, dial int'l dialing prefix (see inside back cover) + 354 + local number.

MAIL. Mailing a letter or postcard from Iceland costs 55Ikr to Europe; 60kr outside of Europe. Post offices (*póstur*) are generally open Monday to Friday 9am-4:30pm, although Reykjavík's main office is also open Saturday 10am-2pm.

INTERNET ACCESS. Internet access is widespread in Iceland, although in small towns it may only be available in public libraries.

ACCOMMODATIONS AND CAMPING

ICELAND	❶	❷	❸	❹	❺
ACCOMMODATIONS	under 1500Ikr	1500-3000Ikr	3000-5000Ikr	5000-10,000Ikr	over 10,000Ikr

Iceland's 25 **HI youth hostels** are invariably clean and uniformly priced at 1000Ikr for members and 1950Ikr for nonmembers. Visit www.hostel.is for locations and more info. **Sleeping-bag accommodations** (*svefnpokapláss;* beds with no sheets or blankets included) make guesthouses more affordable and are often the only option when staying in summer hostels or at **farmhouses** (www.farmholidays.is); expect to pay around 2000Ikr. Many remote lodgings will pick up tourists in the nearest town for a small fee. **Campers** can choose between one of Iceland's 125 designated campsites and roughing it on uncultivated land; squatters need to get permission if they set up camp in a nature reserve or near houses. You should also ask permission if more than three people are sleeping in a tent, or if you plan to stay for longer than three nights. Bring a camp stove; open fires are frowned upon. Designated campsites run the gamut from grassy areas with cold water taps to sumptuous facilities around Reykjavík; find the right one at www.camping.is.

FOOD AND DRINK

ICELAND	❶	❷	❸	❹	❺
FOOD	under 800Ikr	800-1200Ikr	1200-2000Ikr	2000-3500Ikr	over 3500Ikr

Fresh fish and gamey free-range lamb continue to be staples of the Icelandic diet, while vitamin-rich vegetables grown in greenhouse towns like Hveragerði (p. 576) are weaning the country off its dependence on starchy roots. A trickle

ICELAND

of Asian immigrants in the past decade have also introduced methods of cooking that retain more flavor than the traditional regimen of boiling and salting everything in sight. On the other hand, *skyr*, a low-fat dessert made from milk curds, is more popular than ever. Food in Iceland is very expensive, and a cheap restaurant meal will cost at least 800Ikr. Grocery stores are the way to go, and virtually every town has a couple. Alcohol presents the same quandary; beer costs 500-600Ikr at pubs and cafes, while hard liquor is even steeper. Perhaps it's no wonder that bootleggers in the countryside cook up batches of *landi*, potent homemade moonshine.

HOLIDAYS AND FESTIVALS

Holidays: New Year's Day (Jan. 1); Good Friday (Mar. 25); Easter Sunday and Monday (Mar. 27-28); Labor Day (May 1); Feast of the Ascension (May 5); Whit Sunday and Monday (May 15-16); Proclamation of the Republic (June 17); Commerce Day (Aug. 1); Christmas Eve and Day (Dec. 24-25); Boxing Day (Dec. 26); New Year's Eve (Dec. 31).

Festivals: Thorri, the fourth winter month in the old Icelandic calendar, begins on Jan. 21, 2005. In past centuries, meager food supplies during mid-winter forced residents to adopt a leaner diet, known as Thorramatur. Today, svið (singed and boiled sheep's head), hrútspungur (ram's testicles), and hákarl (shark meat that has been allowed to rot underground) remain part of the month-long Thorrablót celebration. The Reykjanes peninsula celebrates Sjomannadagur (Seamen's Day) on June 4 with boat races and tug-of-war, while young people head to the countryside on Verslunnarmannahelgi (Labor Day Weekend) for wild parties on the first weekend of Aug.

REYKJAVÍK

Despite its modest size, greater Reykjavík (pop. 180,000) is home to three out of five Icelanders, and it exudes the assured, forward-thinking cosmopolitanism of European capitals several times its size. Bold, modern architecture leans against the searingly blue waters of the Faxaflói bay, and the city's refreshingly clear air circulates through sparkling streets and gardens. Quiet during the week, Reykjavík comes alive on weekends with its legendary nightlife.

▐ TRANSPORTATION

Flights: All international flights arrive at **Keflavík Airport** (KEF), 55km from Reykjavík. From the main exit, catch a **Flybus** (☎562 10 11; 40-50min., 1100Ikr) to the domestic Reykjavík Airport (REK) and then on to the Hótel Loftleiðir; from the hotel, you can take free Flybus minivans to your hostel or hotel or bus #7 downtown to Lækjartorg (M-F every 20min. until 7pm, 1 per hr. after 7pm and Sa-Su; 220Ikr). Flybus minivans en route to the airport stop at Hótel Loftleiðir (2hr. before each departure), and Grand Hótel Reykjavík (2½hr. before each departure). Most hostels and guesthouses can arrange pick-ups.

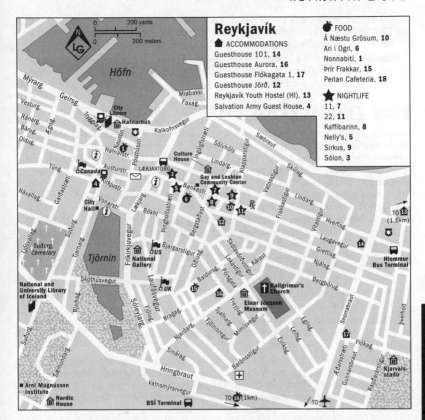

Reykjavík

🏠 ACCOMMODATIONS
Guesthouse 101, **14**
Guesthouse Aurora, **16**
Guesthouse Flókagata 1, **17**
Guesthouse Jörð, **12**
Reykjavík Youth Hostel (HI), **13**
Salvation Army Guest House, **4**

🍴 FOOD
Á Næstu Grösum, **10**
Ari í Ogri, **6**
Nonnabiti, **1**
Þrír Frakkar, **15**
Perlan Cafeteria, **18**

⭐ NIGHTLIFE
11, **7**
22, **11**
Kaffibarinn, **8**
Nelly's, **5**
Sirkus, **9**
Sólon, **3**

Buses: Umferðarmiðstöð (BSÍ Station), Vatnsmýrarvegur 10 (☎552 23 00), off Hringbraut near Reykjavík Airport. Walk 15-20min. south along Tjörnin from the city center, or take bus #7 (every 20min., 220Ikr). Open daily 7am-10pm; tickets sold 7:30am-8pm. The tourist agency **Destination Iceland** (☎591 10 00; www.dice.is) is inside the station. Open June-Aug. M-F 7:30am-6pm, Sa-Su 7:30am-2pm; Sept.-May M-F 9am-5pm.

Public Transportation: Strætisvagnar Reykjavíkur (Strætó; ☎540 27 00) operates yellow city buses (220Ikr). Pick up Strætó's helpful city map and bus schedule at its terminals. Tickets are sold at four locations; the two major terminals are **Lækjargata** in the center of town (open M-F 7am-11:30pm, Sa 8am-11:30pm, Su 10am-11:30pm) and **Hlemmur,** farther east on Hverfisg. (Open M-Sa 8am-11pm, Su noon-11pm.) Buy packages of 9 adult fares (1500Ikr), or else pay fare on the bus with coins; drivers do not give change. Ask the driver for a free transfer ticket (*skiptimiði*), valid for 45min. Buses run M-Sa 7am-midnight, Su and holidays 10am-midnight.

Taxis: BSR, Skogarhilð 18 (☎561 00 00). 24hr. service. BSÍ Station 600-700Ikr; Keflavík Airport 7500Ikr. **Hreyfill,** Fellsmuli 26-28 (☎588 55 22).

Car Rental: Hertz (☎505 06 00), at the Reykjavík Airport. 5800-7100Ikr per day. Pick-up available at Reykjavík Airport for an extra 1300Ikr. **Berg,** Bíldshöfða 10 (☎577 60 50; www.carrental-berg.com). Under 100km 4800-5850Ikr per day, unlimited mileage 8850Ikr per day, reduced rates during low season. Pick-up available at Keflavík and Reykjavík Airports for an extra 1800Ikr.

Bike Rental: At the **youth hostel** (see Accommodations, below). 1000Ikr for under 6hr., 1200Ikr for 6-12hr., 1700Ikr per day, helmet 200 Ikr. **Reykjavík Travel Service** (see below). 700Ikr per 3hr., 1100 per 6hr., 1600Ikr per day.

Hitchhiking: Hitchhiking is uncommon but accepted for young people in Iceland. Those looking for a ride generally head to the east edge of town. *Let's Go* does not recommend hitchhiking as a safe means of transport.

✦✸ 🛈 ORIENTATION AND PRACTICAL INFORMATION

Lækjartorg is Reykjavík's main square and a good base for navigation. **Lækjargata** leads southeast from Lækjartorg to **Tjörnin** (The Pond), which lies halfway between the square and BSÍ Station. Reykjavík's main thoroughfare extends out from Lækjartorg, changing names from **Austurstræti** to **Bankastræti** and then **Laugavegur**, as it is most commonly known. City maps are available at the tourist office, and the monthlies *What's On in Reykjavík* and *Reykjavík This Month* provide info about exploring the city. Both free.

Tourist Office: Upplýsingamiðstöð Ferðamála í Íslandi, Bankastr. 2 (☎562 30 45; www.visitreykjavik.is), at Lækjartorg and Bankastr. Branches at Keflavík Airport and City Hall. Open June-Aug. daily 8:30am-6pm; Sept.-May M-F 9am-5pm, Sa-Su 10am-2pm. All sell the **Reykjavík Card,** which allows unlimited public transportation and free entry to several sights. (1-day card 1000Ikr, 2-day 1500Ikr, 3-day 2000Ikr.) 🔹 **Reykjavík Travel Service,** Lækjarg. 2 (☎511 24 42; www.icelandvisitor.com) rents bikes and has **Internet** access (350Ikr per 30min.). Open June-Aug. daily 9am-10pm; Sept.-May M-Sa 10am-6pm.

Embassies: Canada, Túng. 14 (☎575 65 00). Open M-F 9am-noon. **UK,** Laufásvegur 31 (☎550 51 00). Open M-F 9am-noon. **US,** Laufásvegur 21 (☎562 91 00). Open M-F 8am-12:30pm and 1:30-5pm.

Banks: Most banks are open M-F 9:15am-4pm, and some have extended hours Th until 6pm. On weekends from mid-May to mid-Sept., try the **BSÍ Station.** There are **ATMs** throughout the city, although their currency exchange rates are only slightly lower than those at the bank. The **Exchange Group** located within the tourist office also exchanges money, but charges a steep commission.

Luggage Storage: At BSÍ Station, next to the ticket window. 500Ikr per day. Open M-F 7:30am-7pm, Sa-Su 7:30am-4pm.

GLBT Services: Laugavegur 3, 4th fl. (☎552 78 78; www.gayiceland.com). Includes library and cafe. Offices open M-F 1-5pm; library open M and Th 8-11pm; cafe open M and Th 8-11:30pm, Sa 9-11:30pm.

Laundromat: Þvottahusið Emla, Barónsstíg. 3. 1700Ikr per load. Open M-F 8am-6pm.

Emergency: ☎112.

Police: Hverfisg. 113-115 (☎569 90 00). Station at Tryggvag. 19 (☎569 90 25).

Pharmacies: Lyfja Apótek, Laugavegur 16 (☎552 40 45). Open M-F 9am-7pm, Sa 10am-4pm.

Medical Assistance: National Hospital at Fossvogur (☎525 17 00), on Hringbraut, has a 24hr. emergency ward. From the center of town, take bus #3 southeast.

Internet Access: Reykjavík Public Library, Tryggvegatta 15. Open M-Th 10am-5pm, F 11am-4pm, Sa-Su 10am-3pm. 200Ikr for 30min. **Ground Zero,** Vallarstr. 4. 300Ikr for 30min. Open daily 11am-2am.

Post Office: Íslandspóstur, Pósthússtr. 5 (☎580 11 01), at Austurstr. Address mail to be held in the following format: First name SURNAME, *Poste Restante,* ÍSLANDSPÓSTUR, Pósthússtr. 5, 101 Reykjavík, ICELAND. Open M-F 9am-4:30pm.

☐ ACCOMMODATIONS

Many *gistiheimili* (guesthouses) offer "sleeping-bag accommodations" (bed and pillow in a small room; add 300-500Ikr for a blanket). Hotels cost at least 5500Ikr. Call ahead for reservations, especially from mid-June to August.

▨ **Hjálpræðisherinn Gisti-og Sjómannaheimili (Salvation Army Guest and Seamen's Home),** Kirkjustr. 2 (☎561 32 03; www.guesthouse.is). This pale yellow house, just north of Tjörnin, features a great location and friendly staff. Some rooms include kitchen, and all guests can use a large common kitchen. Breakfast 800Ikr. May-Sept. sleeping-bag accommodations 1900Ikr, blanket 400Ikr; singles 4200Ikr; doubles 5900Ikr; triples 7400Ikr; quads 9000Ikr. Oct.-Apr. reduced prices. ❷

Reykjavík Youth Hostel (HI), Sundlaugavegur 34 (☎553 81 10; www.hostel.is/heimilin/Reykjavik/Eindex.htm). Take bus #5 from Lækjarg. to Sundlaugavegur, or ask to be let off in front of the hostel. A central location, exceptional facilities, and dorm-style camaraderie make this a very desirable location during the summer months. Reserve in advance or you will not get a bed. Kitchen available. Sheets 500Ikr. Laundry 300Ikr. Internet 200Ikr per 15min. Flybus pickup 1000Ikr. Reception 8am-11pm; ring bell after hours. Dorms 1600Ikr; doubles 3200Ikr. Nonmembers add 350Ikr. ❷

Guesthouse Flókagata 1, Flókag. 1 (☎552 11 55; www.eyjar.is/guesthouse). From Hallgrímur's Church, head down Egilsg. and turn left onto Snorrabraut. Breakfast included. Reception 24hr. Sleeping-bag accommodations 2700Ikr; singles 7200Ikr; doubles 10,300Ikr. Extra bed 3300Ikr. Third night free Oct. 1-Apr. 30. ❷

Guesthouse Jörð, Skólavörðustíg 13a (☎562 17 39). Just 2 blocks uphill from Laugavegur. Conveniently located, with spotless, comfortable rooms. TV in each room. Reserve ahead. Breakfast 600Ikr. Extra cot 1000kr. Singles 4000Ikr; doubles 6000Ikr. ❸

Guesthouse Aurora, Freyjug. 24 (☎552 55 15, fax 551 48 94). Head south on Njarðarg. from Hallgrímur's Church and turn right onto Freyjug.; Aurora is the purple house. Homey, rustic digs in a quiet neighborhood 10min. from the city center. Kitchen available. Breakfast included. Laundry 250Ikr. July-Aug. singles 6500Ikr; doubles 8500Ikr; triples 10,500Ikr; Sept.-June reduced prices. ❹

Guesthouse 101, Laugavegur 101 (562 61 01). Located next to the Hlemmer Busterminal, this converted office building is low on atmosphere, but offers small, clean rooms at a reasonable price. Breakfast included. Public phone available. Singles 3900Ikr; doubles 7200Ikr. ❸

Reykjavík Youth Hostel Campsite (☎568 99 44), next to the youth hostel. Take bus #5 from the city center. Campsite in a huge field next to Laugardalslaug. Friendly staff. Bus from the campsite to BSÍ Station at 7:30am (200Ikr). Reception open 8am-1pm and 3-11pm. Ring for assistance 1-3pm. Kitchen available. Breakfast at hostel 250Ikr. Laundry 300Ikr. Electricity 300Ikr. Free showers. Open mid-May to mid-Sept. 750Ikr per person; 3-bed cabins 4000Ikr. ❶

☐ FOOD

An authentic Icelandic meal featuring seafood, lamb, or puffin costs upwards of 1500Ikr, but is worth the splurge at least once. For days on a leaner budget, hit up any one of the stands hawking *pylsur* (hot dogs) west of Lækjartorg, and be sure to ask for "the works"—remoulade and all. Alternately, grab groceries on **Austurstræti, Hverfisgata,** or **Laugavegur.**

▨ **Á Næstu Grösum,** Laugavegur 20B (☎552 84 10). "One woman restaurant" dishes out delicious, heaping portions of vegetarian and vegan fare in a soothing environment. Friendly staff knows many of the customers by name. Daily lunch special 1000Ikr, dinner 1290Ikr. Open M-F 11:30am-10pm, Sa noon-10pm, Su 5-10pm. AmEx/MC/V. ❷

Þrir Frakkar, Baldursg. 14 (☎552 39 39). Serves gourmet traditional Icelandic fare, rounding out a seafarer's menu of whale, monkfish, and puffin with sweet, geyser-cooked brown bread. Worth the splurge. Appetizers 1450-1590Ikr. Entrees 1990-2990Ikr. Open M-F 11:30am-2:30pm and 6-10pm, Sa-Su 11:30am-2:30pm and 6-11pm. AmEx/D/MC/V. ❹

Perlan Cafeteria, Öskjuhlíð (☎562 02 00). Upstairs from the Saga Museum (see below), this sunlit, spacious gallery offers homemade Italian ice cream, unexpectedly cheap greens, and an unrivaled view of the city. Unlimited salad 790Ikr. Ice cream 200Ikr. Open daily 10am-9:30pm. AmEx/D/MC/V. ❷

Nonnabiti, Hafnarstr. 11 (☎551 23 12). An inexpensive sandwich shop favored by locals. Just west of Lækjartorg. Sandwiches 580-660Ikr. Open M-Th and Su 10am-2am, F-Sa 10am-5:30am. MC/V. ❶

Ari í Ögri, Ingólfsstr. 4 (☎551 96 60). The only restaurant in town with a full kitchen open after 10:30pm. Serves traditional Icelandic dishes (1200Ikr) as well as nachos, chicken wings, and an American-style breakfast (950Ikr) all day. Open M-Th 11am-1am, F-Sa 11am-4am, Su 11:30am-1am. MC/V. ❷

🄖 SIGHTS

Well east of the central city, a glaringly white domed gallery houses **Ásmundarsafn,** a collection of sculptures by Iceland's farm-boy-turned-artiste Asmundur Sveinsson, who designed and built the gallery between 1942 and 1950. Ásmundarsafn is one of the three branches of the **Reykjavík Art Museum.** Nearby, **Kjarvalsstaðir** boasts a permanent collection of landscape paintings by 20th-century great Jóhannes Kjarval, and it also features rotating exhibitions of contemporary photography. Take bus #5 to Ásmundarsafn. Downtown **Hafnarhús** may be the most eclectic of the three wings, with performance art and installation pieces staged within the byzantine corridors of a renovated warehouse. (All open daily May-Sept. 10am-4pm; Oct.-Apr. 1-4pm. Combination ticket 500Ikr.) Last year marked the 120th anniversary of the **Listasafn Íslands** (National Gallery of Iceland), Fríkirkjuvegi 7, on the east shore of Tjörnin. The museum supplements its extensive collection of 19th- and 20th-century Icelandic art with rotating exhibitions slanted toward the avant-garde. (Open Tu-Su 11am-5pm. 400Ikr. Free W.)
   Laugardalslaug, on Sundlaugavegur next to the youth hostel campground, is the largest of Reykjavík's geothermally heated pools. Take bus #5 to Laugardalslaug. Facilities include two waterslides and four hot tubs reaching temperatures of 44°C (111°F). (Open Apr.-Sept. M-F 6:30am-10:30pm, Sa-Su 8am-10pm; Oct.-Mar. M-F 6:30am-10:30pm, Sa-Su 8am-8:30pm. 230Ikr. Bathing suit and towel rentals 230Ikr each.) Turn off Laugavegur onto Skólavörðustígur to reach the monolithic **Hallgrímskirkja** church; ride the "elevator to heaven" up to the top of the steeple to survey Reykjavík from the city's highest point. (Open May-Sept. M-W and F-Su 10am-6pm, Th 10am-10pm; Oct.-Apr. daily 10am-5pm. Services Su 11am. Elevator to the top 350Ikr. Stairs free.) Across from the Hallgrímskirkja on Eiriksgata, the **Einar Jónsson Museum** exhibits 300 of the sculptor's allegorical and emotionally charged works. (Open June to mid-Sept. Tu-Su 2-5pm; mid-Sept. to Nov. and Feb.-May Sa-Su 2-5pm. Closed Dec.-Jan. 400Ikr, children 200Ikr.) Back toward the city center, **The Culture House,** 15 Hverfisgata, carefully preserves vellum manuscripts of the Icelandic Eddas and Sagas. (Open daily 11am-5pm. Adults 300Ikr, students 200Ikr.) To see these mytho-historical texts brought to life, take the #7 bus south to the Perlan stop and investigate the **Saga Museum.** Founder Ernst Backman fits

sophisticated silicon mannequins with hand-dyed costumes to recreate Viking tableaux with an eerie, tense realism. (Open daily 10am-6pm; low season reduced hours. 800Ikr, students 600Ikr. Audioguide free.)

 HIKING

South of the city lies the **Heiðmörk Reserve,** a large park and sports complex with picnic spots and easy to intermediate hiking trails. There is, however, no direct public transportation. (Take bus #10 or 11, and ask the driver to let you off at Lake Elliðavatn; from there, you can walk or bike 3-4km south to the reserve.) Quaint and slow-paced **Viðey Island,** home to Reykjavík's oldest house and Iceland's second-oldest church, has been inhabited since the 10th century. (Take bus #4 east from Laekjartorg to Sundahöftn. A **ferry** departs daily at 1, 2, and 3pm. 500Ikr, children 250Ikr.) Across the bay from Reykjavík looms **Mt. Esja,** which you can ascend via a well-maintained trail (2-3hr.). While the trail is not difficult, hikers should be prepared for rain, hail, or even a summertime snow squall. (Take bus #10 or 110 to Artún and transfer to bus #20, exiting at Mógilsá. Bus #20 runs only once every 1-2hr.; consult SVR city bus schedule before departing.)

NIGHTLIFE

Although unnervingly quiet on weeknights, Reykjavík reasserts its reputation as a wild party town each weekend; in few other places on earth can you totter out of a club at 3am to a sky that has barely dimmed to twilight. To avoid vicious drink prices and cover charges, most Icelanders pregame at home and then hit the clubs just before covers kick in; don't even bother showing up before 12:30am, and plan to be out until 4 or 5am. Boisterous crowds tend to bar-hop along vibrant **Austurstræti, Tryggvagata,** and **Laugavegur.**

22, Laugavegur 22. An identity crisis has never been so much fun, with a luminous bar, a spacious dance floor, and a skull-adorned "conversation room" all under one roof. 500Ikr cover after 1am. Open M-Th and Su 11:30am-1am, F-Sa 11am-5:30am.

Kaffibarinn, Bergstaðastr. 1, near Laugavegur. A candlelit mecca for the city's hipster set, this atmospheric lounge is a brainy, chill alternative to the whirling dervish of dancing elsewhere. Coffee 200-260Ikr. Beer 550Ikr. Food served noon-6pm. Live DJ Th-Sa. Open M-Th 11am-1am, F-Sa 11am-5am, Su 1pm-1am.

Pravda, Austurstraeti 22. After reinventing itself with a Soviet-chic moniker in the summer of 2004, Pravda is more than ever the playground for the trendy fashionista. A crowded dance floor reverberates with techno tunes, while strategically placed alcoves lend themselves to canoodling. 300Ikr cover. F-Sa 7pm-4am.

Sólon, Bankastraeti 15. A trendy, Eurotypical cafe during the week, Sólon draws shades over its bay windows on the weekend and morphs into a posh nightclub that bounces with grade-A hip-hop. No cover. Beer 600Ikr. Open M-Th 11am-1am, F-Sa 11am-5:30am, Su noon-1am.

Nelly's, Þingholtsstr. 2. The garish sign outside might fool you into thinking that beer is cheaper here than elsewhere in town, but at 600Ikr you're also paying for the easygoing pub ambiance. No cover or dress code. Open M-Th and Su noon-1am, F-Sa noon-6am.

Sirkus, Klapparstígur 30. An outdoor patio and upstairs bungalow room contribute to a deliciously out-of-place tropical ambiance. Beer 550Ikr. Open M-Th 5pm-1am, F-Sa 5pm-5:30am, Su 7pm-1am.

11, Laugavegur 11. DJs serenade the alternative crowd with rock music at this busy bar. Lounge upstairs. Open M-Th and Su 4pm-1am, F-Sa 4pm-5am.

⚡ DAYTRIPS FROM REYKJAVÍK

Iceland's true attractions are its mesmerizing natural wonders. Iceland Excursions runs the popular Golden Circle tour, which stops at Hveragerði, Kerið, Skálholt, Geysir, Gullfoss, and Þingvellir National Park. (☎562 10 11. 9-10hr. 5900Ikr.) Highlanders offers exciting, if pricey off-road tours in "super jeeps" that can traverse rivers, crags, and even glaciers. (☎568 30 30; www.hl.is. 10,500-17,500Ikr.)

🏔GULLFOSS AND GEYSIR. The glacial river Hvita plunges down 32m to create **Gullfoss**, the "Golden Falls." The thunderous cascades can be viewed from only an arm's length away, although the spray may give you a good drenching. The hill adjacent to the falls also affords a stunning view of the surrounding mountains, plains, cliffs, and glaciers. Only 9km away is the **Geysir** area, a rocky, rugged tundra with steaming pools of hot water scattered across the landscape. The energetic **Strokkur** erupts every 5-10min., spewing sulfurous water at heights up to 20m. Watch your footing; more than one tourist has fallen into the nearby **Blesi pool** and been badly scalded by its steamy waters. *(BSÍ runs a round-trip bus to both sites, departing Reykjavík June-Aug. daily 8:30am and 12:30pm, Sa also 5pm; Sept.-May M-Sa 9:30am, Su 12:30pm. 3800Ikr.)*

BLUE LAGOON. Southwest of Reykjavík lies a primordial paradise: a vast pool of geothermally-heated water hidden in the middle of a lava field. Though the lagoon has become an out-and-out tourist magnet, its cloudy blue waters (rich in silica, minerals, and algae) are probably soothing enough to rejuvenate any crowd-weary traveler. Bathers who have had their fill of the 36-39°C (97-102°F) waters can indulge in a steam bath, skin-soothing mud facial, or an in-water massage (1300Ikr per 10min.). The lagoon rents towels (300Ikr), bathing suits (350Ikr), and bathrobes (700Ikr) if you've forgotten your own. *(Buses arrive from BSÍ station in Reykjavík.; 5 per day; last return 8pm. 850Ikr each way. Open daily mid-May to Aug. 9am-9pm; Sept. to mid-May 10am-8pm. 1200Ikr, locker included. AmEx/MC/V.)*

ÞINGVELLIR NATIONAL PARK. Þingvellir National Park straddles the divide between the European and North American tectonic plates. Stand in the chasm between the continents, but don't linger too long—the plates are moving apart at a rate of 2cm per year. The Öxará River, slicing through lava fields and jagged fissures, leads to the **Drekkingarhylur** (Drowning Pool), where adulterous women were once drowned, and to **Lake Þingvallavatn,** Iceland's largest lake. Not far from the Drekkingarhylur lies the site of the **Alþing** (ancient parliament), where for almost nine centuries Icelanders gathered in the shadow of the **Lögberg** (Law Rock) to discuss matters of blood, money, and justice. *(A bus runs from Reykjavík to Þingvellir's information center. ☎482 26 60. Open daily May-Sept. 8:30am-8pm. Bus runs daily May 20-Sept. 10 at 1:30pm, return 4:50pm. 50min. 900Ikr.)*

HVERAGERÐI. While yuppie homeowners elsewhere in the world save and scrimp to pay for a jacuzzi on the back porch, the citizens of Hveragerði (pop. 2000) already have them built into their yards. The town sits on a geothermal hotbed so volatile that natural geysers have been known to spout up right through the floor of existing houses. However, this source of energy also powers the town's numerous greenhouses, which allow locals to grow peppers, bananas, and other produce that would not survive in Iceland's capricious climate. While most of the greenhouses do not have organized tours, many owners will be happy to show you around upon request. **The Garden of Eden,** Austurmork 25, is one of the few that caters to tourists, boasting a nursery and an ice cream parlor. *(☎483 49 00; www.smart.is/eden. Open daily in summer 9am-11pm; winter 9am-7pm.)* The **information**

center, Breidumork 10, can steer visitors toward guesthouses and campsites or dispatch them on hiking routes in the surrounding area. (☎ 483 46 01. *Open M-F 10am-4pm, Sa-Su 10am-2pm.)*

HAFNARFJÖRÐUR. A small coastal city just 30min. outside of Reykjavík, Hafnarfjörður (pop. 21,000) is said to be a popular gathering place for trolls, dwarves, and other "hidden people." The **Hidden Worlds Tour** leads visitors through **Hellisgerði park** and up to the **Hamarinn cliffs** overlooking the town, pointing out various enchanted warrens along the way. *(Tours in summer M-F 10am, 2:30pm. 60-90min. 1800Ikr. Hidden Worlds map 980kr. Departs from the information center.)* The town also hosts the *Bjartir Dagar* (Bright Days) festival of arts and culture in mid-June, which includes a 4-day **Viking Festival** teeming with burly bowmen, woodcarvers, and stonemasons. Stop by the **information center,** Vesturgata 8, for info on the hiking trails that wend their way through the lava fields and bluffs along the dolphin-dotted bay. (☎ 565 06 61. *Open in summer M-F 8am-5pm, Sa-Su 10am-3pm; low season closed Sa-Su.)*

LANDMANNALAUGAR AND ÞÓRSMÖRK

Wedged between the glaciers, lava fields, and colorful rhyolite mountains of southern Iceland, Landmannalaugar and Þórsmörk (Thor's Woods) are popular jumping-off points for **hikers,** especially the intrepid souls who undertake the demanding 4-day trek between the two areas. The 54km trail poses a number of challenges, including volatile weather conditions, even in the middle of the summer. Other trails take day hikers through gentler terrain, including a 2hr. loop through Landmannalaugar's volcanoes and bubbling hot springs, and a walk from Þórsmörk to the peak of **Valahnjukur,** which overlooks a web of rivers and ash fields. **Ferðafélag Íslands** (Iceland Touring Association) runs guided hikes. (☎ 568 25 33; www.fi.is). The footsore can also soak away their aches and pains in Landmannalaugar's soothing **thermal brook.**

Austurleið SBS (☎ 552 23 00; www.austurleid.is) runs **buses** daily from Reykjavík to Landmannalaugar (4½hr.; June to mid-Sept. 8:30am, return 2:45pm; round-trip 8580Ikr) and Þórsmörk (3½hr.; daily June to mid-Sept. 8:30am, return 3:30pm; round-trip 6940Ikr). Landmannalaugar has a **camp-site ①** and **lodge ②** run by Ferðafélag Íslands. (☎ 854 11 92. Open July-Sept. Camping 600Ikr; mountain huts 1700Ikr.) In Þórsmörk, **Húsadalur Þórsmörk ①** offers hiking tips and simple accommodations. (☎ 852 55 06. Open Apr. to mid-Oct. Breakfast 850Ikr. Camping 500Ikr; sleeping-bag dorms 1600Ikr; 5-person cabin with kitchen 6000Ikr.)

THE LOCAL STORY

I BRAKE FOR ELVES

Hafnarfjörður has certainly seized on the elf industry as a source of tourist revenue. But with 80% of Iceland unwilling to rule out the existence of "hidden people," it's cynical and even disrespectful to dismiss this folk religion out of hand. After all, the staunchly Lutheran nation has worked elves into the book of Genesis; some believe that when God paid Adam and Eve a visit on washing day, Eve had only bathed some of her children. She told the others to stay hidden until God left, but God was irked at the poor turnout and declared that "whomsoever hides from me shall be hidden from me and my people forever."

Excluded from divine favor, some hidden people hope to fall in love with a human and then get baptized. Others just care for their own, as in the tale of a human grandmother who stepped away from milking her cow only to find her bucket half-empty. Puzzled, she left a little milk behind every night for a week, finding it gone the next morning. On the last night, a beautiful elf-woman came to the grandmother in her sleep to say thanks; she had needed the milk for a potion to cure a sick child. In exchange for the grandmother's kindness, the elf gave her a veil with golden embroidery that no human had the skill to make. The old woman's greedy progeny hoped to inherit the veil after she died, but after the funeral they searched her closet and found that the veil was gone.

WESTMAN ISLANDS (VESTMANNAEYJAR)

Jutting from the depths of the North Atlantic, the black cliffs off the Westman Islands are the most recent products of the volcanic fury that created Iceland. In 1973, the fiery **Eldfell** volcano tore through the northern section of **Heimaey**, the only inhabited island, spewing lava and ash in a surprise eruption that forced the population to flee overnight. When the eruption tapered off five months later, a third of the town's houses had been destroyed, but the island itself had grown by the same amount. Visitors can still feel the heat of the cooling lava. The **Volcanic Show** cinema runs a documentary about the eruption. (Shows daily mid-June to Aug. 11am, 3:30, 9pm; Sept. to mid-June 11am and 3:30pm. 55min. 600Ikr.) Head to the **aquarium** on Heiðarvegur, to see some of the island's sea creatures. A combination ticket (450Ikr) also grants admission to the **Folkmuseum,** in the town hall, which re-creates 19th-century Heimaey. (Both open May-Sept. daily 11am-5pm; Sept.-Apr. Sa-Su 3-5pm. 300Ikr each.) Though fewer than 15 sq. km in area, the island offers several spectacular **hikes.** Scenic spots include the cliff's edge at **Há** and the puffin colony at **Stórhöfði,** where the sky fills with birds when southerly winds are blowing. Both volcanic peaks can be scaled by experienced hikers, although strong winds often make for rough going. The three-day **Þjóðhátíð** (People's Feast) draws thousands of young people to the island during the first weekend in August for bonfires, binge drinking, and related revelry. Book transportation well in advance.

During the summer, Flugfélag Islands (Air Iceland) has three daily **flights** from Reykjavík Airport. (20min. One-way from 4500Ikr.) A slower but much cheaper option is the Herjólfur **ferry** (☎481 28 00) departing from Þorlákshöfn. (2¾hr. In summer M-F and Su noon and 7:30pm, Sa noon only; return M-F and Su 8:15am and 4pm, Sa 8:15am only. 1700Ikr, 10% off Internet orders.) **Buses** go from BSÍ Station to the dock in Þorlákshöfn 1hr. before departure (950Ikr). The **tourist office** is in the central harbor. (☎481 35 55; www.eyjar.is/eyjar. Open May-Sept. M-F 8am-4pm, Sa 10am-4pm, Su 11am-4pm; Oct.-Apr. M-F 8am-4pm.) Friendly, centrally located ▓**Guesthouse Hreiðrið ❷,** Faxastigur 33, is just past the cinema on Heiðarvegur. (☎699 89 45. Sleeping-bag accommodations 1700Ikr; singles 3500Ikr; doubles 5600Ikr.) **Guesthouse Sunnuholl ❷,** Vestmannabraut 28b, offers rooms in a house behind Hótel Þorshamar. (☎481 29 00. Sleeping-bag accommodations 2700Ikr; singles 3900Ikr.) The **campground ❶,** 10min. west of town on Dalvegur, has showers and a kitchen. (☎692 69 52. 500Ikr per person.) Pick up groceries at **Krónan** on Strandavegur. (Open daily noon-7pm.)

REPUBLIC OF IRELAND AND NORTHERN IRELAND

Jagged coastal cliffs, thatch-roofed cottages, misty days, and green rolling hills—these are the poetic images of Ireland that dominate the mind. This largely agricultural and sparsely populated island still looks as it did when Celtic bards roamed the land. Windswept scenery lines the coasts and untouched mountain chains stretch across the interior bogland. The landscape is punctuated with pockets of civilization, ranging in size from one-street villages to large cities; Dublin and Belfast are cosmopolitan centers whose international populations greatly influence their immediate surroundings. Some fear this threatens the native culture, but the survival of traditional music, dance, and storytelling proves otherwise. The Irish language lives on in secluded areas known as *gaeltachts*, as well as on road signs, in national publications, and in a growing body of modern literary works. In Northern Ireland, recent negotiations have helped ensure peace for future generations.

 DISCOVER IRELAND: SUGGESTED ITINERARIES

THREE DAYS Spend it all in **Dublin** (p. 584). Wander through **Trinity College,** admire the **Book of Kells,** then have a drink at the **Old Jameson Distillery.** Take a day to visit the **National Museums,** stopping to relax on **St. Stephen's Green.** Get smart at the **James Joyce Centre** and then work your pubbing potential in **Temple Bar** and on **Grafton Street,** stopping by Leopold Bloom's haunt, **Davy Byrne's.**

ONE WEEK From **Dublin** (2 days) head to historic **Belfast** (1 day; p. 609). Don't miss the beautiful **Giant's Causeway** (1 day; p. 614) before heading to artsy **Galway** (1 day; p. 605). Admire the countryside in the **Ring of Kerry** (1 day; p. 601) and return to civilization in **Cork** (1 day; p. 597).

BEST OF IRELAND, THREE WEEKS Land in **Dublin** (4 days) before taking the train up to **Belfast** (3 days). Catch the bus to **Giant's Causeway** (1 day), and stop at Derry (1 day; p. 613). Use **Sligo** (3 days; p. 607) as a base for visiting the surrounding lakes and mountains. From there, head to **Galway** (3 days), the **Ring of Kerry** (2 days), **Killarney National Park** (1 day; p. 600), and **Cork** (2 days). On the way back to Dublin, stop by medieval **Kilkenny** (1 day; p. 596).

IRELAND

REPUBLIC OF IRELAND

ESSENTIALS

WHEN TO GO

Irish weather is subject to frequent changes but relatively constant temperatures. The southeastern coast is the driest and sunniest, while western Ireland is considerably wetter and cloudier. May and June are the sunniest months, July and August the warmest. December and January have the worst weather. Take heart when you wake to clouded, foggy mornings—the weather usually clears by noon. Make sure you bring rain gear, regardless of the season.

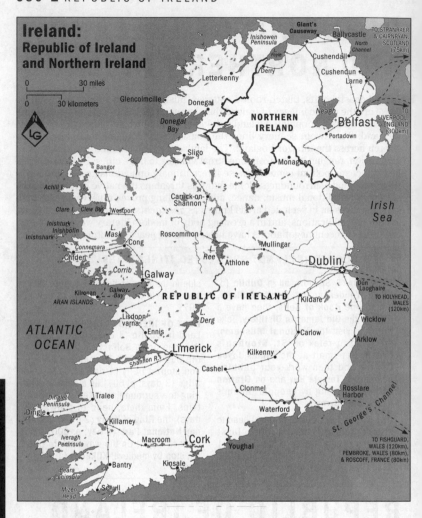

Ireland:
Republic of Ireland
and Northern Ireland

DOCUMENTS AND FORMALITIES

VISAS. Citizens of Australia, Canada, the EU, New Zealand, and the US do not need a visa for stays of up to 90 days.

EMBASSIES. All embassies for the Republic of Ireland are in Dublin (p. 587). For Irish embassies at home, contact: **Australia,** 20 Arkana St., Yarralumla, Canberra ACT 2600 (☎06 273 3022); **Canada,** S. 1105, 130 Albert St., Ottawa, ON K1P 5G4 (☎613-233-6281); **New Zealand,** Honorary Consulate-General, 6th fl., 18 Shortland St. 1001, Auckland (☎0064 9 977 2252; www.ireland.co.nz); **UK,** 17 Grosvenor Pl., London SW1X 7HR (☎020 7235 2171); **US,** 2234 Massachusetts Ave. NW, Washington, D.C. 20008 (☎202-462-3939).

TRANSPORTATION

BY PLANE. Flying to London and connecting to Ireland is often easier and cheaper than flying direct. A popular carrier to Ireland is its national airline, **Aer Lingus** (☎ 081 836 5000, US 800-474-7424; www.aerlingus.com), which has direct flights to London, Paris, and the US. **Ryanair** (☎ 081 830 3030; www.ryanair.ie) is a smaller airline that offers a "lowest-fare guarantee." The web-based phenomenon **easyJet** (UK ☎ 08706 000 000; www.easyjet.com) offers cheap flights into Belfast from all over Europe. **British Airways** (UK ☎ 0845 773 3377, Republic 800 626 747, US 800-247-9297; www.ba.com) flies into most Irish airports daily.

BY TRAIN. Iarnród Éireann (Irish Rail; ☎ 01 836 3333; www.irishrail.ie) is useful only for travel to urban areas. The **Eurail** pass is accepted in the Republic but not in Northern Ireland. The **BritRail** pass does not cover travel in Northern Ireland or the Republic, but the month-long **BritRail+Ireland** pass (€300-500) works in both the North and the Republic, with rail options and round-trip ferry service between Britain and Ireland. **Northern Ireland Railways** (☎ 028 9066 6630; www.nirailways.co.uk) is not extensive but covers the northeastern coastal region well; the major line connects Dublin to Belfast. A valid **Translink Student Discount Card** (UK£6) will get you up to 33% off all trains and 15% discounts on bus fares over UK£1.45 within Northern Ireland. The **Freedom of Northern Ireland** ticket allows unlimited travel by train and Ulsterbus and can be purchased for seven consecutive days (UK£47), three out of eight days (UK£32), or a single day (UK£13).

BY BUS. Bus Éireann (☎ 01 836 6111; www.buseireann.ie), the national bus company, reaches Britain and the Continent by working in conjunction with ferry services and the bus company **Eurolines** (www.eurolines.com). Most buses leave from Victoria Station in London for Belfast (15hr.; €42/UK£28, round-trip €68/UK£46) and Dublin (12hr.; €38/UK£26, round-trip €58/UK£39); other major city stops include Birmingham, Bristol, Cardiff, Glasgow, and Liverpool. Services run to Cork, Derry, Galway, Limerick, Tralee, and Waterford, among others. Discounted fares are available in the low season, as well as for people under 26 or over 60. Bus Éireann operates both long-distance Expressway buses, which link larger cities, and local buses, which serve the countryside and smaller towns.

Ulsterbuc (☎ 028 9066 6630, Belfast office 028 9032 0011; www.ulsterbus.co.uk) runs extensive routes throughout Northern Ireland. The **Irish Rover** pass covers both Bus Éireann and Ulsterbus services (3 of 8 consecutive days €68/UK£46, children €38/UK£26; 8 of 15 €152/UK£102, children €84/UK£56; 15 of 30 €226/UK£152, children €124/UK£83). The **Emerald Card** offers unlimited travel on Ulsterbus, Northern Ireland Railways, Bus Éireann Expressway, and many local services; for more info, see www.buseireann.ie. (8 of 15 consecutive days €198/UK£133, children €99/UK£67; 15 of 30 €341/UK£229, children €170/UK£114).

BY FERRY. Ferries, more economical than air travel, journey between Britain and Ireland several times per day (€28-55/UK£18-35). Weeknight travel promises the cheapest fares. Students, seniors, families, and youth traveling alone typically receive discounts; **ISIC** holders receive a 25% discount from Irish Ferries and a 20-25% discount on Stena Line ferries. Ferries run from Cork to South Wales and Roscoff, France (p. 595), and from Rosslare Harbour to Pembroke, Wales, and Roscoff and Cherbourg, France (p. 595).

BY CAR. Drivers in Ireland use the left side of the road, and their steering wheels are on the right side of the car. Petrol (gasoline) prices are high. Be particularly cautious at roundabouts—give way to traffic from the right. **Dan Dooley** (☎ 0625 3103, UK 0181 995 4551, US 800-331-9301; www.dandooley.com) and **Enterprise**

(☎01 460 5042, UK 0870 350 3000, US 800-261-7331; www.enterprise.com) are the only companies in Ireland that will rent to drivers between 21 and 24, though such drivers incur an added daily surcharge. Prices are €150-370/UK£100-250 (plus VAT) per week, including insurance and unlimited mileage. If you plan to drive a car while in Ireland for longer than 90 days, you must have an **International Driving Permit (IDP)**. If you rent, lease, or borrow a car, you will need a **green card** or **International Insurance Certificate** to certify that you have liability insurance and that it applies abroad. It is always significantly less expensive to reserve a car from the US than from Europe.

BY BIKE, FOOT, AND THUMB. Much of Ireland's countryside is well suited for **biking**, as many roads are not heavily traveled. Single-digit N roads in the Republic and M roads in the North are more busily trafficked; try to avoid these. Ireland's mountains, fields, and heather-covered hills make **walking** and **hiking** arduous joys. The **Wicklow Way** has hostels within a day's walk of each other. Locals do not recommend **hitchhiking** in Northern Ireland, where it is illegal along motorways; some caution against it in Co. Dublin, as well as the Midlands. *Let's Go* does not recommend hitchhiking as a safe means of transport.

TOURIST SERVICES AND MONEY

TOURIST OFFICES. Bord Fáilte (Irish Tourist Board; ☎01 602 4000; www.ireland.ie) operates a nationwide network of offices. Most tourist offices book rooms for a small fee and a 10% deposit, but many fine hostels and B&Bs are not on the board's central list. The **Northern Ireland Tourist Board** (☎028 9023 1221; www.discovernorthernireland.com) offers similar services.

MONEY. On January 1, 2002, the **euro (€)** replaced the Irish pound (£) as the unit of currency in the Republic of Ireland. Legal tender in Northern Ireland is the **British pound;** for more info on conversion rates, see p. 153. Northern Ireland has its own bank notes, identical in value to English and Scottish notes of the same denominations. Although all of these notes are accepted in Northern Ireland, Northern Ireland notes are not accepted in Britain. As a general rule, it is cheaper to exchange money in Ireland than at home.

EMERGENCY	Police: ☎999. Ambulance: ☎999. Fire: ☎999.

If you stay in hostels and prepare your own food, expect to spend about €30/UK£20 per person per day. Menus often indicate whether or not a service charge is included in the price. Most people working in restaurants, however, do not expect a tip, unless the restaurant is targeted exclusively toward tourists. In those incidences, consider leaving 10-15%. Tipping is very uncommon for other services, such as taxis and hairdressers, especially in rural areas. In most cases, people are usually happy if you simply round up the bill to the nearest euro. The European Union imposes a **Value Added Tax (VAT)** on goods and services purchased within the EU, which is included in listed prices; for more info, see p. 22.

COMMUNICATION

TELEPHONES. Both the Irish Republic and Northern Ireland have public phones that accept coins (€0.40/UK£0.27 for about 4min.) and pre-paid phone cards. In the Republic, dial ☎114 for an international operator, 10 for a national operator, or 11850 for a directory. Mobile phones (p. 35) are a popular and economical alternative. International direct dial numbers in the Republic include: **AT&T** (☎800 550 000), **British Telecom** (☎800 550 144), **Canada Direct** (☎800 555 001), **MCI** (☎800 551

PHONE CODES	**Country codes:** 353 (Republic); 44 (Northern Ireland; dial 048 from the Republic). **International dialing prefix:** 00. From outside the Republic of Ireland, dial int'l dialing prefix (see inside back cover) + 353 + city code + local number. From inside the Republic, dial the city code only when calling from outside the city.

001), **New Zealand Direct** (☎800 550 064), and **Telstra Australia** (☎800 550 061). In Northern Ireland, call ☎155 for an international operator, 100 for a national operator, or 192 for a directory. International direct dial numbers in Northern Ireland include: **AT&T** (☎0800 013 0011), **Canada Direct** (☎0800 890 016), **MCI** (☎0800 551 001), **New Zealand Direct** (☎0800 890 064), and **Telstra Australia** (☎0800 856 6161). For more info on making calls to and from Northern Ireland, see p. 609.

MAIL. In the Republic, postcards and letters up to 25g cost €0.60 domestically and to the UK, and €0.65 to the continent and to any other international destination. Airmail letters take about six to nine days between Ireland and North America and cost US$0.80. Dublin is the only place in the Republic with postal codes. Even-numbered codes are for areas south of the Liffey, odd-numbered are for those north. The North has the same postal system as the rest of the UK. Address *Poste Restante* according to the following example: Firstname SURNAME, *Poste Restante*, Enniscorthy, Co. Wexford, Ireland. The mail will go to a special desk in the central post office, unless you specify otherwise.

INTERNET ACCESS. Internet access is available in cafes, hostels, and most libraries. One hour of web time costs about €4-6/UK£2.70-4; an ISIC often earns you a discount. Look into a county library membership in the Republic (€2.50-3), which gives unlimited access to participating libraries and their Internet terminals. Online listings of cybercafes in Ireland and Britain include the **Cybercafe Search Engine** (http://cybercaptive.com) and **Cybercafes.com** (www.cybercafes.com).

ACCOMMODATIONS AND CAMPING

THE REPUBLIC	❶	❷	❸	❹	❺
ACCOMMODATIONS	under €17	€17-26	€26-41	€41-56	over €56

A **hostel** bed will average €10-20 in the Republic and UK£7-13 in the North. **An Óige** (an OYJ), the **HI** affiliate, operates 32 hostels countrywide. (☎01 830 4555; www.irelandyha.org. One-year membership €20, under 18 €10.50.) Many An Óige hostels are in remote areas or small villages and were designed primarily to serve nature-seekers, and do not offer the social environment typical of other European hostels. The North's HI affiliate is **HINI** (Hostelling International Northern Ireland; formerly known as **YHANI**). It operates only eight hostels, all comfortable. (☎028 9031 5435; www.hini.org.uk. One-year membership UK£10, under 18 UK£6.) A number of hostels in Ireland belong to **Independent Holiday Hostels** (**IHH;** ☎01 836 4700; www.hostels-ireland.com). Most IHH hostels have no lockout or curfew, accept all ages, require no membership card, and have a pleasant atmosphere that feels less institutional than that at An Óige hostels. Numerous **B&Bs,** in virtually every Irish town, can provide a break from hosteling; expect to pay €25-30/UK£17-20 for singles and €40-50/UK£27-34 for doubles. "Full Irish breakfasts" are often filling enough to get you through to dinner. **Camping** in Irish State Forests and National Parks is not allowed; camping on public land is permissible only if there is no official campsite nearby. Sites cost €5-13. Northern Ireland treats its campers royally; there are well-equipped campsites throughout (UK£3-9).

FOOD AND DRINK

THE REPUBLIC	❶	❷	❸	❹	❺
FOOD	under €6	€6-10	€10-15	€15-20	over €20

Food in Ireland is expensive, but the basics are simple and filling. Find quick and greasy staples at chippers (fish 'n chip shops) and takeaways (takeout joints). Most pubs serve food like Irish stew, burgers, soup, and sandwiches. Soda bread is delicious and keeps well, and Irish cheeses are addictive. Guinness, a rich, dark stout, is revered in Ireland with a zeal usually reserved for the Holy Trinity. Known as "the dark stuff" or "the blonde in the black skirt," its head is so thick it's rumored that you can stand a match in it. Irish whiskey, which Queen Elizabeth once claimed was her only true Irish friend, is sweeter than its Scotch counterpart. Irish monks invented whiskey, calling it *uisce beatha*, or "water of life."

Ordering at an Irish **pub** is a traditional process. When in a small group, one individual will usually approach the bar and buy a round of drinks for everyone. Once those drinks are downed, another individual will buy the next round. It's considered poor form to refuse someone's offer to buy you a drink.

HOLIDAYS AND FESTIVALS

Holidays: Holidays for the Republic of Ireland include: New Year's Day (Jan. 1); St. Patrick's Day (Mar. 17); Good Friday (Mar. 25); Easter Monday (Mar. 28); and Christmas (Dec. 25 and 27). There are Bank Holidays in the Republic and Northern Ireland during the summer months; check at tourist offices for dates. Northern Ireland has the same national holidays as the Republic; it also observes Orangeman's Day (July 12).

Festivals: All of Ireland goes green for St. Patrick's Day (Mar. 17). On Bloomsday (June 16), Dublin celebrates James Joyce's *Ulysses*. In mid-July, the Galway Arts Festival hosts theater, *trad,* rock, and film. Many return home happy from the Lisdoonvarna Matchmaking Festival in early September.

FACTS AND FIGURES: REPUBLIC OF IRELAND

Official Name: Éire.
Capital: Dublin.
Major Cities: Cork, Galway, Limerick.
Population: 3,900,000.

Land Area: 70,280 sq. km.
Time Zone: GMT.
Languages: English, Gaelic.
Religion: Roman Catholic (92%).

DUBLIN ☎01

In a country known for its rural sanctity, the international flavor and frenetic pace of Dublin stand out. Those who live outside the city worry that it has acquired the crime, rapid social change, and unfriendly demeanor characteristic of metropolises elsewhere. Dublin is gritty, but it's quite accessible for a major city. While it may not resemble the rustic "Emerald Isle" promoted on tourist brochures, its people and pubs do embody the charm that has made their country famous.

▐ TRANSPORTATION

Flights: Dublin Airport (DUB; ☎814 1111; www.aer-rianta.ie). **Dublin buses** #41, 41B, and 41C run from the airport to Eden Quay in the city center (40-45min., every 20min., €1.65). **Airlink shuttle** (☎844 4265) runs non-stop to Busáras Central Bus Station and O'Connell St. (20-25min., every 10min. 5:15am-11:30pm, €5), and to Heuston Station (50min., €4.50). A **taxi** to the city center costs roughly €20-25.

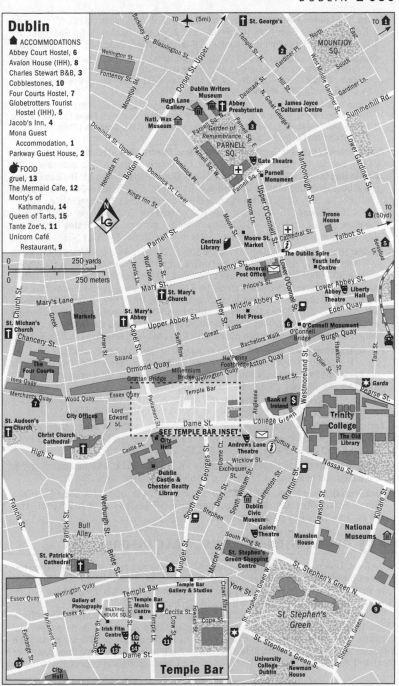

Dublin

ACCOMMODATIONS
Abbey Court Hostel, 6
Avalon House (IHH), 8
Charles Stewart B&B, 3
Cobblestones, 10
Four Courts Hostel, 7
Globetrotters Tourist
  Hostel (IHH), 5
Jacob's Inn, 4
Mona Guest
  Accommodation, 1
Parkway Guest House, 2

FOOD
gruel, 13
The Mermaid Cafe, 12
Monty's of
  Kathmandu, 14
Queen of Tarts, 15
Tante Zoe's, 11
Unicorn Café
  Restaurant, 9

IRELAND

Temple Bar

Trains: The **Iarnród Éireann** travel center, 35 Lower Abbey St., sells tickets. (Center open M-F 9am-5pm, Sa 9am-1pm. Info ☎836 6222; www.irishrail.ie. M-Sa 9am-6pm, Su 10am-6pm.) Dublin's other train station is **Pearse Station**, Pearse St. (☎888 0226).

Connolly Station, Amiens St. (☎703 2358), is north of the Liffey and close to Busáras. **Buses** #20, 20A, and 90 head south of the river, and the DART runs to Tara Station on the south quay. **Trains to: Belfast** (2hr.; M-Sa 8 per day, Su 5 per day; €31); **Sligo** (3hr.; 3-4 per day; M-Th and Sa €22, F and Su €30); **Wexford** (3hr., 2 per day, €20).

Heuston Station (☎703 2132) is south of Victoria Quay, west of the city center (a 25min. walk from Trinity College). **Buses** #26, 51, 90, and 79 run to the city center. **Trains to: Cork** (3hr., 6 per day, €50); **Galway** (2¾hr.; 7 per day; €25, F and Su €35); **Limerick** (2½hr., 9 per day, €38); **Waterford** (2½hr., 4-5 per day, €24.50).

Buses: Intercity buses to Dublin arrive at **Busáras Central Bus Station,** Store St. (☎836 6111), behind the customs house and next to Connolly Station. Info available at the **Dublin Bus Office,** 59 O'Connell St. (☎872 0000; www.dublinbus.ie). The Bus Éireann (www.buseireann.ie) window is open M-F 9am-5pm, Sa 10:30am-2pm. To: **Belfast** (3hr., 6-7 per day, €18); **Derry** (4¼hr., 4-5 per day, €17.50); **Donegal** (4¼hr., 4-5 per day, €15); **Galway** (3½hr., 15 per day, €13); **Limerick** (3½hr., 13 per day, €14.50); **Rosslare** (3hr., 13 per day, €14); **Sligo** (4hr., 4-6 per day, €15); **Tralee** (6hr., 6 per day, €20.50); **Wexford** (2¾hr.; M-Sa 13 per day, Su 10 per day; €11.50).

Ferries: Irish Ferries, 2-4 Merrion Row (☎1890 313 131; www.irishferries.com). Open M-F 9am-5pm, Sa 9:15am-12:45pm. **Ferries** arrive from Holyhead, UK at the **Dublin Port** (☎607 5665), from which **buses** #53 and 53A run every hr. to Busáras station (tickets €1). **Norse Merchant Ferries** (☎819 2999; www.norsemerchant.com) also dock at the Dublin Port and run a route to **Liverpool, UK** (7½hr.; 2 per day; €25-40, with car €105-170). **Stena Line** ferries arrive from **Holyhead** at the Dún Laoghaire ferry terminal (☎204 7777); DART trains run from Dún Laoghaire to the Dublin city center. Dublin Bus also runs connection buses timed to fit the ferry schedules (€2.55-3.20).

Public Transportation: Dublin Bus, 59 O'Connell St. (☎873 4222; www.dublinbus.ie). Open M 8:30am-5:30pm, Tu-F 9am-5:30pm, Sa 9am-1pm. The smaller **City Imp** buses run every 10-15min. Dublin Bus runs the **NiteLink** service to the suburbs (M and W 12:30 and 2am, Th-Sa every 20min. 12:30-4:30am; €4-6; passes not valid). **Travel Wide** passes offer unlimited rides for a day (€7.50) or a week (€18). **DART** trains serve the suburbs and the coast (every 10-15min. 6:30am-11:30pm, €0.80-1.75).

Taxis: Blue Cabs (☎802 2222), **ABC** (☎285 5444), and **City Metro Cabs** (☎872 7272) have wheelchair-accessible cabs (call in advance). €3.25 plus €1.15 every 500m; €1.50 call-in charge. All available 24hr.

Car Rental: Budget, 151 Lower Drumcondra Rd. (☎837 9611; www.budget.ie), and at the airport. Economy from €27 per day, €165-200 per week. Ages 23-75.

Bike Rental: Cycle Ways, 185-6 Parnell St. (☎873 4748). Open M-W and F-Sa 10am-6pm, Th 10am-8pm. €20-40 per day. **Tony Doyle,** 58 Gardiner St. (☎872 5399), rents bikes to people sticking around the area.

◢✦ ⁊ ORIENTATION AND PRACTICAL INFORMATION

In general, Dublin is refreshingly compact. Street names are usually posted on the sides of buildings at most intersections and never on street-level signs. Buying a map with a street index is a smart idea. The tiniest map of all is the *EZ Map Guide* (€1.50), perfect for the traveler who wants to blend in.

The **River Liffey** forms a natural boundary between Dublin's North and South Sides. Heuston Station and the more famous sights, posh stores, and upscale restaurants are on the **South Side.** Connolly Station, the majority of hostels, and the bus station cling to the **North Side.** The North Side is less expensive than the more touristed South, but also has the reputation of being rougher, especially at night.

The streets alongside the Liffey are called **quays** (KEYS); each bridge over the river has its own name, and streets change names as they cross. **O'Connell Street,** three blocks west of the Busáras Central Bus Station, is the primary link between north and south Dublin. **Henry Street** and **Mary Street** comprise a pedestrian shopping zone that intersects with O'Connell St. after the **General Post Office,** two blocks from the Liffey. **Fleet Street** becomes **Temple Bar** one block south of the Liffey. **Dame Street** runs parallel to Temple Bar until **Trinity College,** which defines the southern edge of the district. Trinity College is the nerve center of cultural activity.

Tourist Information: Main Office, Suffolk St. (☎ 1850 230 330 or 605 7700, UK 0171 493 3201, international 669 792 083; www.visitdublin.com), near Trinity College, in a converted church. Open M-Sa 9am-5:30pm; July-Aug. also Su 10:30am-3pm. Reservation desks close 30min. earlier. **Northern Ireland Tourist Board,** 16 Nassau St. (☎ 679 1977 or 1850 230 230). Open M-F 9:15am-5:30pm, Sa 10am-5pm.

Embassies: Australia, Fitzwilton House, 2nd fl. Wilton Terr. (☎ 664 5300; www.australianembassy.ie); **Canada,** 65/68 St. Stephen's Green (☎ 417 4100); **UK,** 29 Merrion Rd. (☎ 205 3700; www.britishembassy.ie); **US,** 42 Elgin Rd. (☎ 668 8777). **New Zealanders** should contact their embassy in London.

Banks: Bank branches with **currency exchange** and 24hr. **ATMs** cluster on Lower O'Connell St., Grafton St., and near Suffolk and Dame St. Most open M-W and F 10am-4pm, Th 10am-5pm.

Luggage Storage: Connolly Station. €4-6 per item per day. Open M-Sa 7:40am-11pm. **Busáras.** €3 per item. Lockers €4-9. Open M-Sa 8am-7:45pm, Su 10am-5:45pm.

Laundromat: Laundry Shop, 191 Parnell St. (☎ 872 3541), near Busáras. Wash and dry around €8. Open M-F 9:30am-7pm, Sa 9:30am-6:30pm.

Emergency: ☎ 999 or 112; no coins required. **Police** (*Garda*): Dublin Metro Headquarters, Harcourt Terr. (☎ 666 9500); Store St. Station (☎ 666 8000); Fitzgibbon St. Station (☎ 666 8400); Pearse St. Station (☎ 666 9000).

Pharmacy: O'Connell's, 56 Lower O'Connell St. (☎ 873 0427). Open M-F 7am-10pm, Sa 8am-10pm, Su 10am-10pm. 2 other branches on Grafton St.

Hospital: St. James's Hospital, James St. (☎ 453 7941). Take bus #123. **Mater Misericordiae Hospital,** Eccles St. (☎ 830 1122), off Lower Dorset St. Buses #10, 11, 13, 16, 121, and 122.

Internet Access: The Internet Exchange, with branches at Cecila St. (☎ 670 3000) and Fownes St. (☎ 635 1680) in Temple Bar. €3 per hr. Cecila location open M-F 8am-2am, Sa-Su 10am-midnight; Fownes location open 24hr.

Post Office: General Post Office, O'Connell St. (☎ 705 7000). Open M-Sa 8am-8pm, Su 10am-6:30pm. Smaller post offices open M-Tu and Th-F 9am-6pm, W 9:30am-6pm. **Postal Code:** Dublin 1. Dublin is the only city in the Republic with postal codes.

ACCOMMODATIONS

Reserve accommodations at least a week in advance, especially during summer and holidays. **Hostel** dorms range €10-24 per night. Quality **B&Bs** are plentiful and most charge €25-40 per person.

HOSTELS

Dublin's hostels lean toward the institutional, especially in comparison to their more personable country cousins. The beds south of the river fill up fastest; they also tend to be more expensive than those to the north.

▨ **Globetrotters Tourist Hostel (IHH),** 46-7 Lower Gardiner St. (☎ 878 8808; www.townhouseofdublin.com). All-you-can-eat Irish breakfast. Free Internet and luggage storage. Towels €6. Dorms €19-22; singles €60-66.50; doubles €102-110. ❷

Four Courts Hostel, 15-17 Merchants Quay (☎672 5839), on the South Side, near O'Donovan Rossa Bridge. Bus #748 from the airport stops next door. Long-term stays available. Free Internet in 6min. increments. Continental breakfast included. Laundry €5. Dorms €15-23; doubles €56-66; family room €23-25. ❶

Jacob's Inn, 21-28 Talbot Pl. (☎855 5660; www.isaacs.ie), 2 blocks north of the customs house. Clean, spacious rooms. Light breakfast included. Lockers €1.50 per night. Towels €2. Lockout 11am-3pm. Dorms €17-25; doubles €65-73. ❷

Abbey Court Hostel, 29 Bachelor's Walk (☎878 0700; www.abbey-court.com), near O'Connell Bridge. Continental breakfast included. Internet €2 per 40min. Free luggage storage; security box €1. Laundry €8. Dorms €18-29; doubles €76-88. ❷

Cobblestones, 29 Eustace St. (☎677 5614). A breath of fresh air in the middle of Temple Bar. Snug rooms and a well-appointed kitchen. Breakfast included. Dorms €16-21; doubles €50-55. Discounts mid-week, for groups, and for longer stays. ❷

Avalon House (IHH), 55 Aungier St. (☎475 0001; www.avalon-house.ie). Turn off Dame St. onto Great Georges St., walk 5min., and look right. Light continental breakfast included. Internet and kitchen. Dorms €13-30; singles €30-37; doubles €56-70. ❶

BED AND BREAKFASTS

B&Bs with a green shamrock sign out front are registered and approved by Bord Fáilte. On the North Side, B&Bs cluster along Upper and Lower **Gardiner Street,** on **Sheriff Street,** and near **Parnell Square.**

▨ **Mona Guest Accommodation,** 148 Clonliffe Rd. (☎837 6723). Charming house run for 38 years by Ireland's most endearing proprietress. Homemade brown bread accompanies the full Irish breakfast. Open May-Oct. Singles €35; doubles €66. ❸

Parkway Guest House, 5 Gardiner Pl. (☎874 0469). High-ceilinged, plush-carpeted, tidy rooms. Ask the owner, a hurling veteran, for advice on the city's restaurants and pubs. Irish breakfast included. Singles €35; doubles €52-62. ❸

Charles Stewart B&B, 5-6 Parnell Sq. E. (☎878 0350; www.charlesstewartinn.com), up O'Connell St. past Parnell St.; close to the Dublin Writers' Museum. Irish breakfast included. Singles €50-63.50; doubles €65-89. Call ahead for specials. ❹

⬕ FOOD

Dublin's **open-air markets** sell fresh and cheap fixings. The cheapest **supermarkets** are in the **Dunnes Stores** chain, with **branches** at St. Stephen's Green (☎478 0188; open M-W and F-Sa 8:30am-7pm, Th 8:30am-9pm, Su noon-6pm), the ILAC Centre, and North Earl St. **Temple Bar** has creative eateries catering to every budget.

▨ **Queen of Tarts,** Dame St. (☎670 7499), across from City Hall. This little red gem offers homemade pastries, scones, cakes, and coffee. Breakfast €4-6. Succulent sandwiches €5. Open M-F 7:30am-6pm, Sa 9am-6pm, Su 10am-6pm. ❷

▨ **Unicorn Café Restaurant,** 12B Merrion Court (☎676 2182). Left off Merrion Row, behind Unicorn Market and Cafe. Legendary Italian restaurant. Entrees €16-25. Open M-Th noon-4pm and 6-11pm, F-Sa noon-4pm and 6-11:30pm. **Unicorn Food Store and Café,** Merrion Row (☎678 8588), offers food from the same kitchen for a fraction of the price. Open daily 8am-7pm. ❷/❹

Tante Zoe's, 1 Crowe St. (☎679 4407), across from the back entrance of the Foggy Dew pub. New Orleans creole food in an elegantly casual setting. Entrees €14-22. Open daily noon-4pm and 6:30pm-midnight. ❹

The Mermaid Cafe, 69-70 Dame St. (☎670 8236), near S. Great Georges St. Outstanding Su brunch. Entrees, like Wexford lamb with minted carrots and mash, €19-30. Open M-Sa 12:30-2:30pm and 6-11pm, Su 12:30-3:30pm and 6-9pm. ❺

gruel, 68 Dame St. (☎670 7119). Their motto: "We gruel, you drool." Popular beef stew (€11) is always on the menu. Entrees €6-12. Heavenly brownies €2.40. Coffee €2. Open M-W 8:30am-9:30pm, Th-F 8:30am-10:30pm, Sa-Su brunch 10:30am-4pm. ❷

Monty's of Kathmandu, 28 Eustace St. (☎670 4911; www.montys.ie), just off Dame St. on the right. Nepalese food with decor to match. Entrees €13-18. Open M-Sa noon-2:30pm and 6-11:30pm, Su 6-11:30pm. ❹

◐ SIGHTS

Most of Dublin's sights lie less than 2km from O'Connell Bridge, and the 2hr. **Historical Walking Tour** stops at many of them. Meet at Trinity College's main gate. (☎878 0227. Tours Apr.-Sept. daily 11am and 3pm; Oct.-Mar. F-Su noon. May-Aug. special themed tours at noon. €10, students €8.)

TRINITY COLLEGE AND GRAFTON STREET. Behind ancient walls sprawls Trinity's expanse of stone buildings, cobblestone walks, and green grounds. The British built Trinity in 1592 as a Protestant seminary that would "civilize the Irish and cure them of Popery;" in the 1960s, the Catholic Church still deemed it a cardinal sin to attend Trinity. *(Between Westmoreland and Grafton St., in the very center of South Dublin. The main entrance fronts the block-long traffic circle now called College Green. Pearse St. runs along the northern edge of the college, Nassau St. to the south. ☎608 1000; www.tcd.ie. Grounds always open. Free.)* Trinity's **Old Library** holds an invaluable collection of ancient manuscripts, including the renowned and beautiful *Book of Kells*. Upstairs, the **Long Room** contains Ireland's oldest harp—the **BrianBorú Harp,** seen on Irish coins—and one of the few remaining **1916 proclamations** of the Republic of Ireland. *(On the southern side of Library Sq. ☎608 2320; www.tcd.ie/library. Open June-Sept. M-Sa 9:30am-5pm, Su 9:30am-4:30pm; Oct.-May M-Sa 9:30am-5pm, Su noon-4:30pm. €7.50, students and seniors €6.50.)* The few blocks south of College Green are off-limits to cars, making them a playground for pedestrians. Street performers on **Grafton Street** range from string octets to jive limbo-ists.

KILDARE STREET AND TEMPLE BAR. The ▨**Natural History Museum** displays fascinating examples of classic taxidermy, including enormous Irish deer skeletons. *(Upper Merrion St. Open Tu-Sa 10am-5pm, Su 2-5pm. Free.)* The **National Museum of Archaeology and History** has extraordinary artifacts spanning the last two millennia, including the **Tara Brooch** and the bloody vest of nationalist **James Connelly.** *(Kildare St., next to Leinster House. Open Tu-Sa 10am-5pm, Su 2-5pm.)* The **National Gallery** has a collection of over 2400 paintings, including canvases by Bruegel, Goya, El Greco, Rembrandt, and Vermeer. *(Merrion Sq. West. Open M-W and F-Sa 9:30am-5:30pm, Th 9:30am-8:30pm, Su noon-5pm. Free.)* West of Trinity, between Dame St. and the Liffey, the Temple Bar neighborhood has rapidly become one of Europe's hottest nightspots. The government-sponsored Temple Bar Properties spent over €40 million to build a fleet of arts-related attractions. Among the most inviting are: **The Irish Film Institute,** which screens specialty and art house film; Ireland's only **Gallery of Photography;** and the **Temple Bar Music Centre.** *(The Irish Film Institute, 6 Eustace St. Gallery of Photography, Meeting House Sq. Temple Bar Music Centre, Curved St.)*

DAME STREET AND THE CATHEDRALS. King John built **Dublin Castle** in 1204 and, for the next 700 years, it would be the seat of British rule in Ireland. Fifty Nationalist insurgents died at the castle's walls on Easter Monday, 1916. Since 1938, each president of Ireland has been inaugurated here. *(On Dame St., at the intersection of Parliament and Castle St. Open M-F 10am-5pm, Sa-Su 2-5pm. €4.50, students and seniors €3.50. Grounds free.)* At the **Chester Beatty Library,** behind Dublin Castle, visitors can see the treasures bequeathed to Ireland by American rags-to-riches mining engineer Alfred Chester Beatty: Asian art, sacred scriptures, illus-

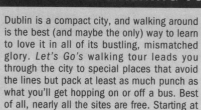

A WALKING TOUR OF DUBLIN

Dublin is a compact city, and walking around is the best (and maybe the only) way to learn to love it in all of its bustling, mismatched glory. *Let's Go's* walking tour leads you through the city to special places that avoid the lines but pack at least as much punch as what you'll get hopping on or off a bus. Best of all, nearly all the sites are free. Starting at 10:30am, and visiting all the sites we list,

START: Mulligan's Pub

FINISH: Arran Quay

TIME: 8hr.

DISTANCE: 3 mi.

SEASON: Year-round

you'll have a full and definitely fulfilling day in the city. Otherwise, tailor the tour to your own desires, stopping to enjoy whatever strikes your fancy.

1 MULLIGAN'S PUB: Begin in Mulligan's Pub, with possibly the best pint of Guinness you'll ever drink. Journalists, writers, and JFK have all crowded into this classic Victorian pub.

2 TRINITY COLLEGE: Wind your way down to Trinity College's front gates, where you can wander through the quads and marvel at the impressive stone buildings and the pristine grass. It stays so green because nobody is allowed to walk on it—stick to the cobblestone pathways.

3 MERRION SQUARE: Exit onto Lincoln Pl. and head down to Merrion Square, a wonderful enclosed garden where a colorful statue of **Oscar Wilde** reclines on a rock. When you've soaked up enough greenery, exit onto Merrion Sq. Rd., where you will pass by the imposing **Government Buildings** and **Natural History Museum.**

4 UNICORN FOOD STORE: At the end of the street, turn right onto Merrion Row, and stop at Unicorn Food Store to grab picnic supplies before heading to **St. Stephen's Green,** Dublin's most bustling and exciting park.

5 DUBLIN CIVIC MUSEUM: Exit at the Northwest corner, where St. Stephen's Shopping Center attracts crowds. Pass the poor fools by, head down William St. South, and stop in the Dublin Civic Museum for a free taste of old Dublin or go to **Powerscourt House** for *chi-chi* shopping.

6 BUTLER'S CHOCOLATE CAFE: By now you might be a bit tired, so hop into Butler's Chocolate Cafe and jolt yourself awake with a cup of their stunning hot chocolate. From there stroll down Exchequer St. and onto South Great George's St. before enjoying Dame St. for a few blocks.

7 DUBLIN CASTLE: Turn left and pass by **City Hall** before entering the gates of Dublin Castle. If the 20th-century wing doesn't impress you (it won't), go to the **circular lawn** behind the State Apartments. This large lawn, with a celtic knot path running through it, covers the spot where the "black pool" from which Dublin derives its name used to stand. This is a good place to lounge, look at your map, and gaze at the colorful turrets of Dublin Castle.

8 CHESTER BEATTY LIBRARY: Next to the lawn is the Chester Beatty Library. With no charge and no lines, this building houses beautiful old manuscripts, including some of the oldest extant pages of the Bible, written on fraying papyrus, and gorgeous illuminated manuscripts.

9 ST. AUDOEN'S GATE: Exit the Castle Grounds the way you came, and turn left to head down Dame St., passing the grand **Christ Church,** and turning right on Winetavern St., to see St. Audoen's Gate, one of the few remaining pieces of the Old City walls. Cross O'Donovan Rossa Bridge, and turn left in front of the **Four Courts,** a masterpiece of Georgian architecture.

10 ST. MICHAN'S CHURCH: From here, if you look across the Liffey, a great view of **Christ Church** and its flying buttresses awaits. Turn right onto Church St. to find St. Michan's Church, and its nightmare-inducing **vaults.**

11 OLD JAMESON DISTILLERY: After all the coffins and cobwebs, you might want a drink, so follow the signs to the Old Jameson Distillery and sample some firewater.

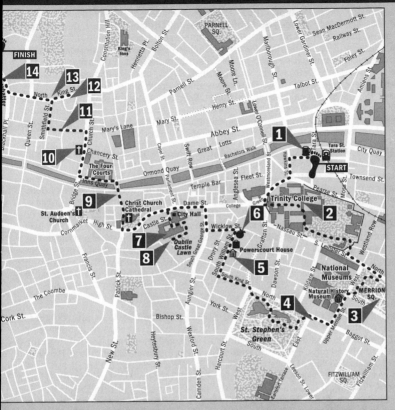

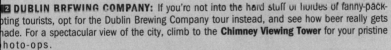
DUBLIN BREWING COMPANY: If you're not into the hard stuff or hordes of fanny-packsporting tourists, opt for the Dublin Brewing Company tour instead, and see how beer really gets made. For a spectacular view of the city, climb to the **Chimney Viewing Tower** for your pristine photo-ops.

CHIEF O'NEILL'S: Dinner is traditional Irish food at Chief O'Neill's, just below the tower, or, for those on a budget, walk down King St. to **Stoneybatter Road,** where takeaway counters abound.

COBBLESTONE: To round out the night in grand fashion, grab a stool and a pint at Cobblestone and settle in for a night of trad (sessions start at 7pm). When you're finally ready for bed or (more likely) when the lights have been dimmed and the musicians sent home, walk the two blocks down to Arran Quay to catch any bus heading back toward O'Connell St.

Tomorrow: Sleep late and make sure to eat a big Irish breakfast—after 8hr. of walking, you certainly deserve it.

trated texts, and much more. *(Open May-Sept. M-F 10am-5pm, Sa 11am-5pm, Su 1-5pm; Oct.-Apr. closed M. Free.)* **St. Patrick's Cathedral,** Ireland's largest, dates to the 12th century, although Sir Benjamin Guinness remodeled much of it in 1864. Jonathan Swift spent his last years as Dean of St. Patrick's, and his crypt is above the south nave. *(On Patrick St. Take a bus from Eden Quay. Open Mar.-Oct. daily 9am-6pm; Nov.-Feb. Sa 9am-5pm, Su 10am-3pm. €4.20, students and seniors €3.20.)* Sitric Silkenbeard, King of the Dublin Norsemen, built a wooden church on the site of the **Christ Church Cathedral** around 1038; Strongbow rebuilt it in stone in 1169. Fragments of the ancient pillars are now scattered about like bleached bones. *(Across from the castle. Take bus #50 from Eden Quay or 78A from Aston Quay. Open daily 9:45am-5:30pm except during services. €5, students and seniors €3.)*

GUINNESS BREWERY AND KILMAINHAM. Guinness brews its black magic at the St. James Gate Brewery, next door to the ▓**Guinness Storehouse.** Take a look at the quirky seven-story-tall atrium containing Arthur Guinness's 9000-year lease on the original brewery. And then drink, pilgrim, drink. *(St. James's Gate. From Christ Church Cathedral, follow High St. west through its name changes: Cornmarket, Thomas, and James. Take bus #51B or 78A from Aston Quay or #123 from O'Connell St. Open daily July-Aug. 9:30am-9pm; low season 9:30am-5pm. €13.50, students over 18 and seniors €9.)* Almost all of the rebels who fought in Ireland's struggle for independence from 1792 to 1921 spent time at **Kilmainham Gaol.** Tours wind through the chilly limestone corridors of the prison and end in the haunting execution yard. *(Inchicore Rd. Take bus #51A from Lower Abbey St., or #68, 69, or 79 from Aston Quay. Open Apr.-Sept. daily 9:30am-4:45pm; Oct.-Mar. M-F 9:30am-4pm, Su 10am-4:45pm. €5, seniors €3.50, students €2. Tours every 35min.)*

O'CONNELL STREET AND PARNELL SQUARE. O'Connell St. is Dublin's biggest shopping thoroughfare and was once Europe's widest street as well. Statues of Irish leaders such as **Daniel O'Connell, Charles Parnell,** and **James Larkin** adorn the street's traffic islands. Follow O'Connell St. to get to Parnell Sq., home of **The Hugh Lane Municipal Gallery of Modern Art.** *(Parnell Sq. N. Buses #3, 10, 11, 13, 16, and 19 all stop near Parnell Sq. Open Tu-Th 9:30am-6pm, F-Sa 9:30am-5pm, Su 11am-5pm. Free.)* The **General Post Office,** O'Connell St., was the nerve center of the 1916 Easter Rising; Patrick Pearse read the Proclamation of Irish Independence from its steps. *(Open M-Sa 8am-8pm, Su 10am-6:30pm.)* The city's rich literary heritage comes to life at **The Dublin Writers' Museum,** which displays rare editions, manuscripts, and memorabilia of Beckett, Wilde, Yeats, and many other famous Irish writers. *(18 Parnell Sq. N. Open June-Aug. M-F 10am-6pm, Sa 10am-5pm, Su 11am-5pm; Sept.-May M-Sa 10am-5pm. €6.25, students and seniors €5.25. Combined ticket with James Joyce Centre €10.50.)* The **James Joyce Cultural Centre** features a wide range of Joyceana, including portraits of the individuals who inspired his characters. *(35 N. Great Georges St. ☎878 8547. Open Sept.-June M-Sa 9:30am-5pm, Su 12:30-5pm; July-Aug. M-Sa 9:30am-5pm, Su 11am-5pm. €10, students and seniors €9.)*

OTHER SIGHTS. Once a private estate, **St. Stephen's Green,** down Grafton St. from Trinity College, was later bequeathed to the city by the Guinness clan. Today, its 22 acres teem with all sorts of life. During the summer, musical and theatrical productions are given near the old bandstand. *(Open M-Sa 8am-dusk, Su 10am-dusk.)* **Four Courts,** Inn's Quay, along the Liffey, has an impressive facade and was once seized by members of the IRA, sparking the Irish Civil War when members of the Free State Government attacked the garrison there. The building now houses Ireland's highest national court. *(Open M-F 9am-4:30pm. Free.)* At the **Old Jameson Distillery,** learn how science, grain, and tradition come together to create **whiskey.** Be quick to volunteer in the beginning and you'll get to sample a whole tray of different whiskeys. Even the unchosen are blessed, however, with a glass of firewater at the end. *(Bow St. From O'Connell St., turn onto Henry St., and continue straight as the street dwindles to Mary St., then Mary Ln., then May Ln.; the warehouse is on a cobblestone street on the left. Tours daily 9am-5:30pm. €8, concessions €6.25.)* **Dublin Zoo,** Europe's largest, is in **Phoenix Park.** It contains 700 animals and the world's biggest egg. *(Take bus #10 from O'Connell St., or #25 or 26 from Wellington Quay. Open M-Sa 9:30am-6pm, Su 10:30am-6pm. Last admission 5pm. Zoo closes at dusk in winter. €12.50, students €10.)*

🎵 🎭 ENTERTAINMENT AND NIGHTLIFE

Whether you fancy poetry or punk, Dublin is equipped to entertain you. The free *Event Guide* is available at the tourist office and Temple Bar restaurants. Dublin has no true Theater District, but smaller theater companies thrive off Dame St. and Temple Bar. **Abbey Theatre,** 26 Lower Abbey St., was founded in 1904 by W. B. Yeats and Lady Gregory to promote Irish culture and modernist theater. Synge's *Playboy of the Western World* was first performed here in 1907. (☎878 7222. Tickets €15-30; Sa 2:30pm matinee €10, students €9.50. Box office open M-Sa 10:30am-7pm.) The **Peacock Theatre,** 26 Lower Abbey St., is the Abbey's experimental downstairs theater, offering evening shows in addition to occasional lunchtime plays, concerts, and poetry. (☎878 7222. Tickets €12.50-17. Doors open M-Sa at 7:30pm.)

PUBS

James Joyce once proposed that a "good puzzle would be to cross Dublin without passing a pub." A radio station later offered €125 to the first person to solve the puzzle. The winner explained that you could take any route—you'd just have to visit them all on the way. Normal **pub hours** in Ireland end at 11:30pm Sunday through Wednesday; 12:30am Thursday through Saturday. Bars post their closing time as "late," meaning at least after midnight. Begin your journey at the gates of Trinity College, moving onto Grafton St., stumble onto Camden St., teeter down S. Great Georges St., and finally, crawl triumphantly into the Temple Bar area. Then again, any port in a storm; drink where ye may.

- 🍺 **The Stag's Head,** 1 Dame Ct. (☎679 3701). Victorian pub with stained glass, mirrors, and deer heads. Excellent pub grub. Entrees €10. Open M-Th 10:30am-11:30pm, F-Su 11am-12:30am. Kitchen open M F noon-3.30pm and 5-7pm, Sa noon-2:30pm.

- 🍺 **Whelan's,** 25 Wexford St. (☎478 0766). Dark wooden pub in front. Stage venue in back hosts big-name acts. Live music nightly from 9:30pm (doors open 8pm); comedy on some W. Cover €7-15. Lunch served 12:30-2pm (€8-12). Open late Th-Sa.

- 🍺 **The Porter House,** 16-18 Parliament St. (☎679 8847). The country's largest selection of beers plus 10 home brews. Live music every night. Open M-Tu and Th 11:30am-11:30pm, W 11:30am-midnight, F-Sa 11:30am-2:30am, Su 11:30am-11pm.

- **Mulligan's,** 8 Poolbeg St. (☎677 5582), behind Burgh Quay off Tara St. A taste of the typical Irish pub: low-key and "strictly drink." Open M-W 10:30am-11:30pm, Th-Sa 10:30am-12:30am, Su noon-11pm.

- **McDaid's,** 3 Harry St. (☎679 4395), off Grafton St. across from Anne St. Center of Ireland's literary scene in the 50s. Incredibly high ceilings, summer patio, and gregarious crowd. Open M-W 10:30am-11:30pm, Th-Sa 10:30am-12:30am, Su 12:30-11pm.

- **Davy Byrne's,** 21 Duke St. (☎677 5217), off Grafton St. Lively, middle-aged crowd fills the pub where Joyce set *Ulysses's* "Cyclops" chapter. Gourmet pub food served all day. Open M-W 11:30am-11:30pm, Th-Sa 11:30am-12:30am, Su 12:30-11pm.

- **The Celt,** 81-82 Talbot St. (☎878 8655). Step out of the city and into Olde Ireland. Small, comfortably worn, and truly welcoming. Nightly *trad*. Open daily 10:30am-late.

THE LOCAL STORY

THE PERFECT PINT

Bartender Glenn, of a local Dublin Pub, helps Let's Go resolve the most elusive question of all...

LG: Tell us, what's the most important thing about pouring a pint?
A: The most important thing is to have the keg as close to the tap as possib▮ ▮loser, the better.
LG: An▮ ▮ that?
A: Well, you don't want the Guinness sitting in a long tube while you wait to pour the next pint. You want to pull it straight out of the keg, without any muck getting in between.
LG: Does stopping to let the Guinness settle make a big difference?
A: Well, you can top it straight off if you want, but you might get too big a head with that. You don't want too small or big a head, so if you stop ¾ of the way, you can adjust the pint until the head is perfect. A true Guinness lover will taste the difference.
LG: Because of the head?
A: No, because of the gas. If you pull the Guinness straight from the tap and get a big head, it means you've gotten too much gas. It kills the taste ▮hat's why you have to tilt the glass. What you don't want is a window-clean glass; you don't want a glass that you can see through when you're done. Good Guinness leaves a healthy film on the glass. If it doesn't, you didn't get a good Guinness.

CLUBS

Because of their later hours, clubs currently have a slight edge over pubs in Dublin's nightlife war. Clubs generally open at 10:30 or 11pm, but the action heats up after the 11:30pm pub closings. Covers run €7-20, and pints are a steep €5. The gay nightclub scene is alive and well, with gay venues (usually rented-out clubs) existing just about every night. Keep up-to-date by checking out the queer pages in *In Dublin* for gay-friendly pubs, restaurants, and clubs, or try **Gay Switchboard Dublin** for event info and updates (☎872 1055; M-F and Su 8-10pm, Sa 3:30-6pm).

🖾 **The PoD,** 35 Harcourt St. (☎478 0225). Spanish-style decor meets hard-core dance music. **The Red Box,** upstairs, is a more intense club with a warehouse atmosphere. Cover €10-20, Th and Sa €5 with ISIC, Th ladies free before midnight. Open until 3am.

🖾 **The George,** 89 S. Great Georges St. (☎478 2983). Dublin's 1st and most prominent gay bar. Attached nightclub open W-Su until 2am. Frequent theme nights. Smart outfit a must. Cover €8-10 after 10pm. Open M-Tu 12:30-11:30pm, W-Su 12:30pm-2:30am.

The Front Lounge, Parliament St. (☎670 4112). The red velvet seats of this gay bar are filled nightly by a mixed, trendy crowd. Open M and W noon-11:30pm, Tu noon-12:30am, F-Sa noon-2am, Su 4-11:30pm.

Traffic, 54 Middle Abbey St. (☎873 4800). Nightly DJ spins hip-hop, house, or techno from his throne at the end of the long, deep bar. Cover €6-10. Open M-W noon-11:30pm, Th and Sa noon-2:30am, F 3pm-2:30am, Su noon-1:30am.

▣ DAYTRIPS FROM DUBLIN

HOWTH. Howth (rhymes with "both") dangles from the mainland about 16km from Dublin. A 3hr. **cliff walk** circles the peninsula, passing heather and thousands of seabird nests. To get to the trailhead, turn left at the DART station and follow Harbour Rd. around the coast for about 20min. Just offshore is **Ireland's Eye,** a former sanctuary for monks that has become an avian refuge. **Ireland's Eye Boat Trips,** on the East Pier, jets passengers across the water. (☎087 267 8211. Round-trip €10, students and children €8.) To reach the private **Howth Castle,** a charming patchwork of architectural styles, go right as you exit the DART station and then left after 400m, at the entrance to the Deer Park Hotel. To get to Howth, take a northbound DART **train** to the end of the line (30min., 6 per hr., €1.80). **Tourist services** are periodically available in a small building next to the DART station; for more info, call the **Old Courthouse** community center (☎844 5976).

BOYNE VALLEY. The thinly populated Boyne Valley hides Ireland's greatest archaeological treasures. Between Slane and Drogheda lie no fewer than 40 Neolithic passage tombs from the 4th millennium BC. **Newgrange** is the most spectacular; a roof box over the entrance allows a solitary beam of sunlight to shine directly into the tomb for 17min. on the winter solstice, a breathtaking experience that is simulated on the tour. You may only enter Newgrange by admission at ▧**Brú na Bóinne Visitors Centre,** near Donore on the south side of the River Boyne, across from the tombs. (☎041 988 0300. Open June to mid-Sept. 9am-7pm; May 9am-6:30pm; late Sept. 9am-6:30pm; Mar.-Apr. and Oct. 9:30am-5:30pm; Nov.-Feb. 9:30am-5pm. Center and Newgrange tour €5.50, students €2.75.) A group of enormous, well-preserved Norman castles—including **Trim Castle,** conquered by Mel Gibson in *Braveheart*—overlooks **Trim** proper on the River Boyne. (☎046 943 8619.Open Easter-Oct. daily 10am-6pm; Nov.-Easter Sa-Su 10am-5pm. Tours every 45min. Grounds €1.50. Tour and grounds €3.50, students €1.25.)

SOUTHEASTERN IRELAND

A base first for the Vikings and then the Normans, the Southeast echoes a fainter Celtic influence than the rest of Ireland. Town and street names in this region reflect Norse, Norman, and Anglo-Saxon influences rather than Gaelic ones. The Southeast's busiest attractions are its beaches, which draw admirers to the coastline stretching from Kilmore Quay to tidy Ardmore.

◀ FERRIES TO FRANCE AND BRITAIN

Irish Ferries (☎053 33158) sails from Rosslare Harbour to Pembroke, Wales (4hr., 1 per day, from €31) and Roscoff and Cherbourg, France (18hr., every other day). **Eurail** passes grant passage on ferries to France. **Stena Line** (☎053 61560) runs from Rosslare Harbour to Fishguard, Wales (3½hr., €30-36).

THE WICKLOW MOUNTAINS   ☎0404

Over 600m tall, carpeted in fragrant heather, and pleated by sparkling rivers, the Wicklow summits are home to grazing sheep, scattered villages, beautiful lakes, and monastic ruins. The blessed valley of **Glendalough** is home to St. Kevin's 6th-century monastery. **St. Kevin's Bus Service** (☎01 281 8119) arrives in Glendalough from St. Stephen's Green in Dublin (2 per day, round-trip €13). The **National Park Information Office,** between the two lakes, is the best source for hiking advice in the area. (☎45425. Open May-Aug. daily 10am-6pm; Sept.-Apr. Sa-Su 10am-dusk.) When the park office is closed, call the **ranger office** (☎45800), located in nearby Trooperstown Wood. Shack up at ▧**The Glendaloch Hostel (An Óige/HI) ❷,** 5min. up the road from the Glendalough Visitor Centre. (☎45342. Internet available. Breakfast €4-6.50. Laundry €5. Dorms €20-22; private rooms €24-25 per person.) Just 1.5km up the road, **Laragh** has groceries, food options, and plenty of B&Bs. Public transportation in the mountains is severely limited.

ROSSLARE HARBOUR   ☎053

Rosslare Harbour is a useful departure point for Wales or France. **Trains** run from the ferry port to Dublin (3hr., 3 per day, €17.50) and Limerick (2½hr., 1-2 per day, €17.50) via Waterford (1¼hr., €9). **Buses** run from the same office to: Dublin (3hr., 10-12 per day, €14.50); Galway via Waterford (4 per day, €23); Limerick (M-Sa 5 per day, Su 3 per day; €19); and Tralee (M-Sa 4 per day, Su 2 per day; €23). Contact Wexford Tourism (☎52900) for **tourist information**. If staying overnight, try the seaside ◪**Mrs. O'Leary's Farmhouse ❷**, off N25 in Kilrane. It's a 15min. drive from town, so call for pickup. (☎33134. Singles €30, low season €27.)

KILKENNY   ☎056

Nine churches share the streets with 80 pubs in Kilkenny (pop. 25,000), Ireland's best-preserved medieval town. **Tynan Walking Tours** explore Kilkenny's folkloric tradition; 1hr. tours depart from the tourist office. (☎087 265 1745. €6, students €5.50.) The 13th-century ◪**Kilkenny Castle** housed the Earls of Ormonde from the 1300s until 1932. The basement shelters the **Butler Gallery's** modern art exhibits. (☎21450. Open daily June-Aug. 9:30am-7pm; Sept. 10am-6:30pm; Oct.-Mar. 10:30am-12:45pm and 2-5pm; Apr.-May 10:30am-5pm. Required tour €5, students €2.) Start your pub crawl at the top of **John Street** or the end of **Parliament Street**.

Trains (☎22024) arrive at Dublin Rd. from Dublin (2hr.) and Waterford (45min.). **Buses** (☎64933) arrive at Dublin Rd. and the city center from: Cork (3hr., 2-3 per day, €16); Dublin (2hr., 5-6 per day, €10); Galway (5hr., 3-6 per day, €19); Limerick (2½hr., 2-4 per day, €13.30); Rosslare Harbour (2hr., 2-3 per day, €7); and Waterford (1½hr., 2 per day, €6.35). The **tourist office** is on Rose Inn St. (☎51500. Open Mar.-Sept. M-F 9am-6pm, Sa 10am-6pm; Oct.-Feb. M-Sa 9am-5pm.) **B&Bs** are concentrated on **Waterford Road**. Stay in former royal quarters at the 15th-century **Foulksrath Castle (An Óige/HI) ❶**, in Jenkinstown, 12.5km north of town on the N77. Buses run to the hostel from the Parade (20min., €2) in Kilkenny. (☎67674. Dorms €11-12.) **Pordylo's ❹**, on Butterslip Ln. between Kieran St. and High St., has excellent world cuisine. (Entrees €17-23. Open daily 5:30-11pm.) A **Dunnes** supermarket is on Kieran St. (☎61655. Open M-Sa 8:30am-10pm, Su 9:30am-7pm.)

WATERFORD   ☎051

Founded by Vikings in AD 914 as a refuge for his longships, Waterford's harbor is now instead filled with massive freighters. The highlight of the town is the ◪**Waterford Crystal Factory**, 3km away on N25. One-hour tours allow you to witness the transformation of molten glass into polished crystal. Catch the City Imp minibus outside Dunnes on Michael St. (10-15min., every 15-20min., €1.20) and request a stop at the factory. (☎332 500. Open daily Mar.-Oct. 8:30am-6pm; Nov.-Feb. 9am-5pm. 1hr. tours every 15min. during high season. Tours €7.50, students €3.50.) Head to **Waterford Treasures** at the granary and see Viking artifacts and the only extant item of Henry VIII's clothing, a velvet hat. (☎304 500. Open May-Sept. M-Sa 9am-6pm, Su 11am-5pm; Oct.-Apr. M-Sa 10am-5pm, Su 11am-5pm. €6, students €4.50.) The Quay is crowded with pubs; try ◪**T&H Doolan's,** on George's St., which has been serving crowds for 300 years. (Pub food €13-19. *Trad* nightly at 9:30pm.)

Trains (☎317 889) leave from The Quay across the bridge for: Dublin (2½hr., M-F 5-6 per day, €17-21); Kilkenny (40min., 3-5 per day, €8); Limerick (2¼hr., M-Sa 2 per day, €15.50); and Rosslare Harbour (1hr., M-Sa 2 per day, €10). **Buses** depart from The Quay for: Cork (2½hr., 10-13 per day, €14.50); Dublin (2¾hr.; M-Sa 10-12 per day, Su 6 per day; €10); Galway (4¾hr., 5-6 per day, €18.50); Kilkenny (1hr., 1 per day, €8); Limerick (2½hr.; M-Th and Su 6 per day, F 7 per day; €14.50); and Rosslare Harbour (1¼hr., 3-5 per day, €12.50). The **tourist office** is on The Quay, across from the bus station. (☎875 823. Open M-F 9am-6pm, Sa 10am-6pm.) Let Mrs. Ryan of **Beechwood ❷**, 7 Cathedral Sq., invite you into her charming house. (☎876 677. Doubles €50.) **Haricot's Wholefood Restaurant ❷**, 11 O'Connell St., serves innovative meals. (Entrees €9.50. Open M-F 10am-8pm, Sa 10am-6pm.)

CASHEL ☎062

Cashel sits at the foot of the 90m ◾**Rock of Cashel** (a.k.a. **St. Patrick's Rock**), a huge limestone outcropping topped by medieval buildings. (Open daily mid-June to mid-Sept. 9am-7pm; mid-Mar. to mid-June 9am-5:30pm; mid-Sept. to mid-Mar. 9am-4:30pm. €5, students €2.) Down the cow path from the Rock lie the ruins of **Hore Abbey**, built by Cistercian monks and presently inhabited by sheep. The **GPA-Bolton Library**, on John St., houses ecclesiastical texts and rare manuscripts. (☎62511. Call for tours.) The internationally acclaimed ◾**Brú Ború Heritage Centre**, at the base of the Rock, stages traditional music and dance performances. (☎61122. Performances mid-June to mid-Sept. Tu-Sa 9pm. €15, with dinner €40.) **Buses** (☎061 33333) leave from the Bake House on Main St. for: Cork (1½hr., 6 per day, €12); Dublin (3hr., 6 per day, €15); and Limerick (1hr., 5 per day, €12). The **tourist office** is in the City Hall on Main St. (☎62511. Open May-Sept. M-F 9:30am-5:30pm, Su 10am-6pm.) Just out of town on Dundrum Rd. is ◾**O'Brien's Farmhouse Hostel ❶**. (☎61003. Laundry €8-10. Dorms €15; doubles €45-50. Camping €7.50 per person.)

SOUTHWESTERN IRELAND

With a dramatic landscape that ranges from lakes and mountains to stark ocean-battered cliffs, Southwest Ireland is a land rich in storytellers and history-makers. Outlaws and rebels once lurked in the hidden coves and glens now overrun by visitors. The Ring of Kerry and Cork's southern coast offer many peaceful stretches.

◼ FERRIES TO FRANCE AND BRITAIN

Swansea-Cork Ferries (☎021 427 1166) goes between Cork and Swansea, South Wales (10hr., 1 per day, from €39). **Brittany Ferries** (☎021 437 8401) sails from Cork to Roscoff, France (14hr., one-way from €79).

CORK ☎021

Cork (pop. 150,000) orchestrates most of the cultural activities in the southwest. River quays and pub-lined streets reveal architecture both grand and grimy, evidence of "Rebel Cork's" history of resistance, ruin, and reconstruction.

◼ TRANSPORTATION

Trains: Kent Station, Lower Glanmire Rd. (☎450 6766; www.irishrail.ie), across the river from the city center. Open M-Sa 6:35am-8pm, Su 7:50am-8pm. To: **Dublin** (3hr.; M-Sa 9 per day, Su 8 per day; €55); **Killarney** (2hr.; M-Sa 7 per day, Su 4 per day; €25.50); **Limerick** (1½hr., 5 per day, €25.50); **Tralee** (2½hr., 3 per day, €30.50).

Buses: Parnell Pl. (☎450 8188), 2 blocks east of Patrick's Bridge on Merchant's Quay. Info desk open daily 9am-6pm. **Bus Éireann** goes to all major cities: **Dublin** (4½hr.; M-Sa 6 per day, Su 5 per day; €23); **Galway** (4hr., 12 per day, €17); **Killarney** (2hr.; M-Sa 13 per day, Su 11 per day; €13); **Limerick** (2hr., 14 per day, €13.20); **Rosslare Harbour** (4hr., 3 per day, €18.50); **Sligo** (7hr., 5 per day, €23); **Tralee** (2½hr., 12 per day, €14); **Waterford** (2¼hr., M-Sa 13 per day, €14.50).

Public Transportation: Downtown **buses** run M-Sa every 10-30min. 7:30am-11:15pm, with reduced service Su 10am-11:15pm. Fares from €1. From downtown, catch buses along St. Patrick St., across from the Father Matthew statue.

IRELAND

◘ 🛈 ORIENTATION AND PRACTICAL INFORMATION

Cork is compact and pedestrian-friendly. **St. Patrick Street** becomes **Grand Parade** to the west; to the north it crosses **Merchant's Quay**, home of the bus station. North across **St. Patrick's Bridge**, **McCurtain Street** runs east to **Lower Glanmire Road** and the train station before becoming the N8 to Dublin. Downtown action concentrates on the vaguely parallel **Paul**, **Oliver Plunkett**, and **St. Patrick Streets.**

Tourist Office: Tourist House, Grand Parade (☎425 5100), near the corner of South Mall, offers accommodations booking (€4), souvenirs, and a free Cork city guide and map. Open June-Aug. M-F 9am-6pm, Sa 9am-5pm; Sept.-May M-Sa 9:15am-5:15pm.

Banks: Ulster Bank Ltd., 88 St. Patrick St. (☎427 0618). Open M 10am-5pm, Tu-F 10am-4pm. **Bank of Ireland**, 70 St. Patrick St. (☎427 7177). Open M 10am-5pm, Tu-F 10am-4pm. Most banks in Cork have 24hr. **ATMs.**

Emergency: ☎999; no coins required. **Police** (*Garda*): Anglesea St. (☎452 2000).

Pharmacies: Regional Late-Night Pharmacy, Wilton Rd. (☎434 4575), opposite the Regional Hospital on bus #8. Open M-F 9am-10pm, Sa-Su 10am-10pm. **Phelan's Late Night**, 9 Patrick St. (☎427 2511). Open M-Sa 9am-10pm, Su 10am-10pm.

Hospitals: Mercy Hospital, Grenville Pl. (☎427 1971). €45 fee for emergency room access. **Cork University Hospital**, Wilton St. (☎454 6400), on the #8 bus route.

Internet Access: 📶 **Web Workhouse** (☎427 3090), near the post office between St. Patrick and Oliver Plunkett St. 8am-noon €3 per hr., noon-5pm €4-5, 5pm-3am €2.50, 3-8am €1.25; Su €2.50 all day. Open daily 24hr.

Post Office: ☎427 2000. On Oliver Plunkett St. Open M-Sa 9am-5:30pm.

🛏 ACCOMMODATIONS

B&Bs cluster along **Patrick's Hill**, on **Glanmire Road** rising upward from St. Patrick's Bridge, and on **Western Road** near University College. Call ahead; Cork is Europe's "Capital of Culture" for 2005 and will undoubtedly draw throngs of visitors.

📶 **Sheila's Budget Accommodation Centre (IHH)**, 4 Belgrave Pl. (☎450 5562; www.sheilashostel.ie), at Wellington Rd. and York Street Hill. Sauna €2. Bike rental €14. Breakfast €3.20. Internet €1 per 20min. Reception 24hr. Check-out 10am. Dorms €14-17; singles €30; doubles €40-50. ❷

Kinlay House (IHH), Bob and Joan Walk (☎450 8966; www.kinlayhouse.ie), to the right of St. Anne's (Shandon) Church. Recently renovated, with a plush lounge area. Continental breakfast included. Internet €1 per 15min. Laundry €7. Free parking. Dorms €14-16; singles €30; doubles €45-50; family rooms €20 per person. ❷

Roman House, 3 St. John's Terr., Upper John St. (☎450 3606), across from Kinlay House. Colorful Roman House is Cork's only B&B catering specifically to gay and lesbian travelers. Walls display proprietor's artwork. Singles €40; doubles €60. ❷

Cork International Hostel (An Óige/HI), 1-2 Redclyffe, Western Rd. (☎454 3289), a 15min. walk from the Grand Parade. Continental breakfast €3.50. Internet €1 per 10min. Check-in 10:30am-midnight. Dorms €17-19; doubles €44. ❷

🍴 FOOD

Restaurants and cafes abound on the lanes connecting **Patrick St., Paul St.,** and **Oliver Plunkett St.** On Paul St., **Tesco** (☎427 0791), is the biggest grocery store in town. (Open M-W 9am-8pm, Th-F 9am-10pm, Sa 8:30am-8pm, Su noon-6pm.)

▨ **Quay Co-op,** 24 Sullivan's Quay (☎431 7660). Delicious vegetarian and vegan meals. Apricot and yogurt flan €2.50. Specials €7.50. Open M-Sa 9am-9pm. ❷

Tribes, Tuckey St. (☎427 6070). Serves full menu into the wee hours. Global spectrum of coffee blends (€1.80). Open M-W noon-12:30am, Th-Sa noon-4am. ❶

Amicus, 14A French Church St. (☎427 6455). Sophisticated decor. Artistic, delicious dishes. Entrees €12-20. Open M-Sa 10am-10:30pm, Su 10am-9:30pm. ❹

📷 SIGHTS

All sights in Cork can be reached by foot; pick up the *Cork Area City Guide* at the tourist office (€1.90). In the western part of town lie the brooding Gothic buildings, manicured lawns, and sculpture-studded grounds of the 1845 ▨**University College Cork.** (☎490 3000; www.ucc.ie.) Across the walkway from UCC's front gate, ▨**Fitzgerald Park** has beautiful rose gardens and art exhibits courtesy of the **Cork Public Museum.** (☎427 0679. Open M-F 11am-1pm and 2:15-5pm, Su 3-5pm; closed for renovation until late 2004. M-F students and seniors free, family €3; Sa-Su €1.50.) At the western end of Fitzgerald Park is a white footbridge; cross it and make a right on Sunday's Well Rd. to reach **Cork City Gaol.** Cork's social history comes alive in multimedia tours of the former prison. (☎430 5022. Open daily Mar.-Oct. 9:30am-6pm; Nov.-Feb. 10am-5pm. €6, students €5.) In the old city, **St. Finbarr's Cathedral,** Bishop St., is a testament to the Victorian obsession with Neo-Gothic bombast and houses contemporary art exhibits in the summer. (☎496 3387. Open M-Sa 10am-5:30pm. €2.50 requested donation.) North across the river in the Shandon neighborhood, the striped steeple of **St. Anne's Church** inspired the red and white "rebel" flag still flying throughout the county. Its four clock faces are notoriously out of sync. (Open June-Sept. M-Sa 10am-5:30pm; closed for renovation until late 2004. €4, students and seniors €3.50.)

📷 NIGHTLIFE

The lively streets of Cork make finding entertainment easy. *List Cork,* free at local shops, helps stay on top of the scene, and **Oliver Plunkett Street, Union Quay,** and **South Main Street** for pubs and live music. ▨**The Lobby,** 1 Union Quay, overlooks the river and hosts live music every night, from *trad* to acid jazz. (☎431 9307. Occasional cover €5-10.) ▨**The Old Oak,** Oliver Plunkett St., across from the General Post Office, is packed and noisy. (☎427 6165. Bar open M-Sa noon-1:45am.) **Half Moon,** Academy Ln., on the left side of the Opera House, attracts a young crowd. (Strictly 18+. Cover €9.) And for those who crave good alternative rock and want to sport an eyebrow ring, **An Brog** (☎427 1392), at the corner of Oliver Plunkett and Grand Parade, is sure to please.

📷 DAYTRIP FROM CORK: BLARNEY

Tourists eager for quintessential Irish scenery and a cold kiss head northwest of Cork to see **Blarney Castle** and its legendary **Blarney Stone.** Despite widespread rumors that locals relieve themselves upon the stone, tourists insist that those who kiss it while leaning over backwards will be granted the gift of persuasion. The top of the castle provides a stunning view of the countryside. (Open June-Aug. M-Sa 9am-7pm, Su 9:30am-5:30pm; Sept. M-Sa 9am-6:30pm, Su 9:30am-sundown; Oct.-Apr. M-Sa 9am-6pm or sundown, Su 9:30am-5pm or sundown; May M-Sa 9am-6:30pm, Su 9:30am-5:30pm. Last admission 30min. before closing. Castle and grounds €7, seniors and students €5.) **Buses** run from Cork to Blarney (10-16 per day, round-trip €4.50).

IRELAND

SCHULL AND THE MIZEN HEAD PENINSULA ☎028

The seaside hamlet of Schull is an ideal base for exploring the craggy southwestern tip of Ireland. A calm harbor and numerous shipwrecks make it a diving paradise; the **Watersports Centre** rents gear. (☎28554. Open Apr.-Oct. M-Sa 9:30am-6pm.) The coastal road winds past the **Barley Coast Beach** and continues on to **Mizen Head.** The Mizen becomes more scenic and less populated the farther west you go from Schull; **Betty Johnson's Bus Hire** offers tours of the area. (☎28410. Call ahead. €12.) In summer, **ferries** (☎28138) depart from Schull for Cape Clear Island (June-Sept. 2-3 per day, round-trip €12). **Buses** arrive in Schull from Cork (2-3 per day, €12) and Goleen (2 per day, €3.50). There is no other public transportation on the peninsula. Confident **cyclists** can daytrip to Mizen Head (29km from Schull). The immaculate ▧**Schull Backpackers' Lodge (IHH) ❶**, on Colla Rd., has a welcoming staff eager to share info on local walks and rides. (☎28681. Bike Rental €11 per day. Dorms €13-15; singles €18-22; doubles €36-40.) **The Courtyard ❷**, on Main St., has delicious food; the fruit scones (€0.60) and the sandwiches on fresh *ciabatta* (€7-9.50) are both perfect for picnics. (☎28390. Open M-Sa 9:30am-6pm.)

CAPE CLEAR ISLAND ☎028

Although the scenery visible from the ferry landing at Cape Clear Island (*Oileán Chléire*) is desolate and foreboding, the main industry of this beautiful island is farming. Cape Clear provides asylum for gulls, petrels, cormorants, and (of course) their attendant flocks of ornithologists at the **Cape Clear Bird Observatory** (☎39189), on North Harbour. The **Cape Clear Heritage Centre** is packed with everything from a family tree of the ubiquitous O'Driscolls to a waterlogged deck chair from the *Lusitania*. (Open June-Aug. M-Sa noon-5pm, Su 2-5pm. €3, students €2.) On the road to the center, **Cléire Goats** (☎39126) claims that its **goat's milk ice cream** (€1.50) is richer and more scrumptious than the generic bovine variety. **Ferries** (☎28138) go to Schull (45min., 1-3 per day, round-trip €11.50). There is an **information office** in the pottery shop to the left of the pier. (☎39100. Open June-Aug. 11am-noon and 3-6pm; Sept. 3-5pm.) **An Óige/HI ❶**, is a 10min. walk from the pier; follow the main road and keep left. (☎41968. Dorms €15.) To reach **Cuas an Uisce Campsite ❶**, on the south pier, walk 5min. uphill from the harbor and bear right before Ciarán Danny Mike's; it's 400m down on the left. (☎39119. Open June-Sept. €6 per person, under 16 €3.) Groceries are available at **An Siopa Beag**, on the pier. (☎39099. Open Sept.-May M-Th 11am-6pm; June-Aug. daily 11am-6pm.)

KILLARNEY AND KILLARNEY NATIONAL PARK ☎064

The town of Killarney is just minutes from some of Ireland's most glorious natural scenery. Outside town, the 95 sq. km national park blends forested mountains with the **Lakes of Killarney.** Five kilometers south of Killarney on Kenmare Rd. is **Muckross House**, a 19th-century manor with a brilliant garden. A path leads to the 20m **Torc Waterfall**, the starting point for several trails along the beautiful **Torc Mountain.** It's a 3.5km stroll in the opposite direction to the **Meeting of the Waters**, a quiet spot where channels from the Upper Lough introduce themselves into the Middle, which then offers its watery handshake to the Lower. The paved path is nice, but the dirt trail through the **Yew Woods** is more secluded and inaccessible to bikes.

To get to the 14th-century **Ross Castle**, the last stronghold in Munster to fall to Cromwell's army, take a right on Ross Rd. off Muckross Rd., 3km from Killarney. The footpaths from Knockreer (out of town on New St.) offer a more scenic route. (☎35851. Open daily June-Aug. 9am-6:30pm; May and Sept. 10am-6pm; mid-Mar. to Apr. and Oct. 10am-5pm. €5, students €2.) Bike around the **Gap of Dunloe**, which borders **Macgillycuddy's Reeks**, Ireland's highest mountain range, or hop on a boat from Ross Castle to the head of the Gap (1½hr., €8-15; book at the tourist office).

From **Lord Brandon's Cottage,** on the Gap, head left over the stone bridge, continue 3km to the church, and then turn right onto a winding road. Climb 2km and enjoy an 11km stroll downhill through the park's most breathtaking scenery.

Trains (☎31067 or 1890 200 493) arrive at Killarney station, off East Avenue Rd., from: Cork (2hr., 4 per day, €20); Dublin (3½hr., 4 per day, €52.50); and Limerick (3hr., 4 per day, €22). **Buses** (☎30011) leave from Park Rd. for: Belfast (2-4 per day, €31); Cork (2hr., 11-14 per day, €13.50); and Dublin (6hr., 5-6 per day, €20.50). **O'Sullivan's,** on Bishop's Ln., rents **bikes.** (☎31282. Free locks and maps. Open daily 8:30am-6:30pm. €12 per day, €70 per week.) The **tourist office** is on Beech St. (☎31633. Open July-Aug. M-Sa 9am-8pm, Su 10am-1pm and 2:15-6pm; June and Sept. M-Sa 9am-6pm, Su 10am-1pm and 2:15-6pm; Oct.-May M-Sa 9:15am-1pm and 2:15-5:30pm.) The immaculate ▦**Neptune's (IHH) ❶,** on Bishop's Ln., up the first walkway off New St. on the right, has an ideal location and professional staff. (☎35255. Breakfast €2.50. Dorms €11-17; doubles €37-40.) ▦**The Fairview Guest House ❷,** College St., near the bus station, pampers guests in luxurious digs. (☎34164. €35-50 per person for *Let's Go* readers.) For delicious food, try ▦**The Stonechat ❸,** Fleming's Ln. The low-key but sophisticated ambience makes this the best eatery in Killarney. (☎34295. Lunch €7-9. Dinner €11-14. Open M-Sa 11am-5:30pm and 6:30-10pm.) *Trad* is a staple in Killarney's pubs. Patrons both foreign and domestic mingle in the upbeat atmosphere of ▦**O'Connor's Traditional Pub,** 7 High St. (☎31115. *Trad* M-F 9-11:30pm, Su 7-9pm; winter F-Su.)

RING OF KERRY
☎066

The Southwest's most celebrated peninsula offers picturesque villages, fabled ancient forts, and rugged mountains. Although tour buses often hog the roads, rewards await those who take the time to explore the landscape on foot or by bike.

▣ TRANSPORTATION

The term "Ring of Kerry" usually describes the entire **Iveragh Peninsula,** though it technically refers to the ring of roads circumnavigating it. Hop on the circuit run by **Bus Éireann,** based in Killarney and stopping at the major towns on the Ring (mid-June to Aug. 2 per day), including Cahersiveen (from Killarney 2½hr., €11.50) and Caherdaniel (from Cahersiveen 1hr., €4.25).

CAHERSIVEEN

Although best known as the birthplace of patriot Daniel O'Connell, Cahersiveen (CAR-sah-veen) serves as an excellent base for jaunts to Valentia Island, the Skelligs, and local archaeological sites. The ruins of **Ballycarbery Castle** are past the barracks on Bridge St., over the bridge, off the main road, and to the left. About 200m past the castle turn-off stands a pair of Ireland's best-preserved stone forts, **Cahergall Fort** and **Leacanabuaile Fort.** The **tourist office** is across from the bus stop, next to the post office. (☎947 2589. Open June to mid-Sept. M, W, F 9:15am-1pm and 2-5:15pm, Tu and Th 9:15am-1pm.) The welcoming **Sive Hostel (IHH) ❶** is at 15 East End, Main St. (☎947 2717. Laundry €5.10. Dorms €13; doubles €31-35. Camping €7 per person.) **O'Shea's B&B ❸,** next to the post office on Main St., boasts comfortable rooms and impressive views. (☎947 2402. Singles €35; doubles €55.) The pubs on **Main Street** serve as both watering holes and the proprietors' main businesses, be it general store, blacksmithy, or leather shop.

Quiet ▦**Valentia Island** makes for a fantastic daytrip. The little roads of this unspoiled gem are perfect for biking or light hiking. Bridges on either end of the island connect it to the mainland; alternatively, a **ferry** runs during the summer (☎947 6141; every 8min. Apr.-Sept. M-Sa 8:15am-10pm, Su 9am-10pm; €1.50, cyclists €2.50) from **Reenard Point,** 5km west of Cahersiveen. Or sail to the **Skellig Rocks,** about 13km off the shore of the Iveragh Peninsula. From the boat, **Little Skellig** may appear snow-capped, but it's actually covered with 24,000 pairs of crooning birds. Climb 630 steps to reach a **monastery** built by 6th-century Christian monks, whose beehive-like dwellings are still intact. The hostel in Cahersiveen can arrange the **ferry** ride (about 1hr.) for €35.

CAHERDANIEL

There's little in the village of **Caherdaniel** to attract the Ring's droves of buses. However, nearby **Derrynane National Park,** 2.5km along the shore from the village, holds 3km of gorgeous beach ringed by picture-perfect dunes. Follow the signs for **Derrynane House,** once the residence of Daniel O'Connell. (☎947 5113. Open May-Sept. M-Sa 9am-6pm, Su 11am-7pm; Apr. and Oct. Tu-Su 1-5pm; Nov.-Mar. Sa-Su 1-5pm. Last admission 45min. before closing. €2.75, students €1.25.) Rest up at **The Travellers Rest Hostel ❶.** (☎947 5175. Dorms €13; private rooms €16.50.)

DINGLE PENINSULA ☎066

For decades, the Ring of Kerry's undertouristed counterpart has remained laden with more ancient sites than tour buses. Only recently has the Ring's tourist blitz begun to encroach upon the spectacular cliffs and sweeping beaches of this Irish-speaking peninsula. Many visitors explore the area by bike.

▐ TRANSPORTATION

Dingle Town is most easily reached by **Bus Éireann** from Tralee (1¼hr.; M-Sa 4-6 per day, Su 2-5 per day; €8.80); other routes run from Dingle to: Ballydavid (Tu and F 3 per day, €4.80); Ballyferriter (M-Sa 2-3 per day, €4.80); Dunquin (M-Sa 3-5 per day, €4.80).

DINGLE TOWN

Lively Dingle Town, adoptive home of **Fungi the Dolphin** (now a focus of the tourist industry), is a good base for exploring the peninsula. **Sciúird Archaeology Tours** leave from the pier for 3hr. whirlwind bus tours of the area's ancient spots. (☎915 1606. 2 per day, €15.) **Moran's Tours** runs great trips to Slea Head, passing through majestic scenery and stopping at historic sites. (☎915 1155. 2 per day, €15.) The **tourist office** is on Strand St. (☎915 1188. Open mid-June to mid-Sept. M-Sa 9am-7pm, Su 10am-5pm; mid-Sept. to mid-June M-Tu and Th-Sa 9:30am-5:30pm.) ▧**Ball-intaggart Hostel (IHH) ❶,** 25min. east of town on Tralee Rd., is supposedly haunted by the murdered wife of the Earl of Cork. (☎915 1454. Dorms €13-20; doubles €48-54. Camping €6-7 per tent, €15 per van.) The menu at busy **Homely House Cafe ❷,** Green St., caters to a range of hunger levels. (☎915 2431. Entrees €4-9.50. Open July-Aug. M-Sa noon-9:30pm; Sept.-June M-Sa noon-5:30pm.)

VENTRY, SLEA HEAD, AND DUNQUIN

By far the most rewarding way to see the cliffs and crashing waves of Dunquin and Slea Head is to **bike** along the predominantly flat **Slea Head Drive.** Past Dingle Town toward Slea Head sits the village of Ventry (Ceann Trá), home to a sandy **beach** and the ▧**Celtic and Prehistoric Museum,** a massive collection that includes a 50,000-year-old woolly mammoth. (☎915 9191. Open daily Mar.-Nov. 10am-5:30pm; other months call ahead. €5, students €3.50.) While in Ventry, stay at the secluded yet convenient ▧**Ballybeag Hostel ❶.** (☎915 9876. Bike rental €7 per day. Laundry €3. Dorms €14; singles €20.)

North of Slea Head and Ventry, the scattered settlement of Dunquin (Dún Chaoin) consists of stone houses, a pub, and little else. Past Dunquin on the road to Ballyferriter, the ⚡Great Blasket Centre has outstanding exhibits about the isolated Blasket Islands. (☎915 6444. Open daily July-Aug. 10am-7pm; Easter-June and Sept.-Oct. 10am-6pm. €3.50, students €1.25.) At An Óige Hostel (HI) ❶, on the Dingle Way across from the turnoff to the Blasket Centre, each bunk has an ocean view. (☎915 6121. Breakfast €3. Reception 9-10am and 5-10pm. Lockout 10am-5pm. Dorms €14-16; doubles €32.) Kruger's ❸ (☎915 6127), the westernmost pub in Europe, features pub grub, music sessions, and great views.

TRALEE

The economic and residential capital of County Kerry, Tralee (pop. 20,000) is a good departure point for the Ring of Kerry or the Dingle Peninsula. ⚡Kerry the Kingdom, in Ashe Memorial Hall on Denny St., features a high-tech history of Ireland from 8000 BC to the present. (☎712 7777. Open June-Aug. daily 9:30am-5:30pm; Apr.-May and Sept.-Dec. Tu-Sa 9:30am-5:30pm; Jan.-Mar. Tu-F 10am-4:30pm. €8, students €6.50.) During the last week of August, the nationally-known Rose of Tralee Festival brings lovely Irish lasses to town to compete for the title "Rose of Tralee." Trains depart from the station on Oakpark Rd. for: Cork (2½hr., 13 per day, €26); Dublin (4hr., 3-4 per day, €52.50); Galway (5-6hr., 3 per day, €52.50); and Killarney (40min., 4 per day, €7.50). Buses leave from the train station for: Cork (2½hr., 13 per day, €14.50); Galway (7-8 per day, €19.50); Killarney (40min., 10-15 per day, €6.70); and Limerick (2¼hr., 8-9 per day, €13.50). To get from the station to the tourist office in Ashe Memorial Hall, head down Edward St., turn right on Castle St., and then left on Denny St. The well-informed staff provides free maps. (☎712 1288. Open July-Aug. M-Sa 9am-7pm, Su 9am-6pm; May-June and Oct. M-Sa 9am-6pm; Nov.-Apr. M-F 9am-5pm.) Westward Court (IHH) ❷, Mary St., has spotless dorms and quality showers. (☎718 0081. Breakfast included. Curfew 3am. Dorms €17; singles €25; doubles €46.) O'Riordans, 9 Russel St., serves a mean full Irish breakfast. (☎710 2759. Open M-Sa 8am-5pm, Su 9am-5pm.)

WESTERN IRELAND

Even Dubliners will say the west is the "most Irish" part of Ireland; in many remote areas you'll hear Gaelic as often as English. The potato famine that plagued the island was most devastating in the west—entire villages emigrated or died. In fact, the current population is still less than half of what it was in 1841. The mountainous landscapes from Connemara north to Ballina are great for hiking and cycling.

LIMERICK   ☎061

Limerick is a city on the rise, even though 20th-century industrial developments lent its 18th-century Georgian streets and parks a featureless, urban feel. The ⚡Hunt Museum, in the Custom House on Rutland St., has a gold crucifix given by Mary Queen of Scots to her executioner and a coin reputed to be one of the infamous 30 pieces of silver paid to Judas by the Romans. (☎312 833. Open M-Sa 10am-5pm, Su 2-5pm. €6, students and seniors €4.75.) Limerick's student population adds spice to the nightlife scene. The area where Denmark Street and Cornmarket Row intersect is a good place to quench your thirst or listen to live music. Dolan's, 4 Dock Rd., hosts nightly *trad* and rambunctious local patrons.

Trains (☎315 555) leave for: Cork (2½hr., 5-6 per day, €20); Dublin (2hr., 7-10 per day, €37); Ennis (2 per day, €8); Killarney (2½hr., 3-5 per day, €22); and Waterford (2hr., 1-2 per day, €15). Buses (☎313 333) leave Colbert Station, off Parnell St., for: Cork (2hr., 14 per day, €13.20); Derry (6½hr., 3 per day, €24); Donegal (6hr., 4

IRELAND

per day, €22); Dublin (3½hr., 13 per day, €14.50); Ennis (45min., 14 per day, €7.50); Galway (2hr., 14 per day, €13.20); Killarney (2½hr.; M-Sa 6 per day, Su 3 per day; €13.50); Rosslare Harbour (4hr., 3-4 per day, €18.50); Tralee (2hr., 8 per day, €13.20); and Waterford (2½hr., 7 per day, €14.50). The **tourist office** is on Arthurs Quay. From the station, walk down Davis St., turn right on O'Connell St. and then go left at Arthurs Quay Mall. (☎361 555. Open July-Aug. M-F 9am-6pm, Sa-Su 9:30am-5:30pm; Sept.-June M-F 9:30am-5:30pm, Sa 9:30am-1pm.) A number of B&Bs can be found on O'Connell St. or the Ennis road. **Cherry Blossom Budget Accommodation ❶**, several blocks south of the Daniel O'Connell statue, has comfortable rooms and serves a delicious breakfast. (☎469 449. Shared rooms €20-25 per person.) Next door, **Alexandra House B&B ❸**, O'Connell St., is a red brick townhouse with a pleasant pastel interior. (☎318 472. Irish breakfast included. Singles €30; shared rooms €25-30 per person.) ◪**Furze Bush Cafe Bistro ❷**, on the corner of Catherine St. and Glentworth St., offers delicious crepes (€12.50) and gourmet sandwiches (€7) in an eccentric atmosphere. (☎411 733. Open June-Aug. M-Sa 10am-5pm; Sept.-May M-W 10:30am-5pm, Th-Sa 10:30am-5pm and 7-10pm.)

ENNIS AND DOOLIN ☎065

Ennis's proximity to Shannon Airport and the Burren makes it a common and exciting stopover for tourists. At ◪**Cruises Pub,** on Abbey St., local musicians appear nightly for cozy *trad* sessions in one of the oldest buildings in Co. Clare (est. 1658). Those with eclectic tastes should stop by **Glor,** a state-of-the-art music center that features nightly performances of music, theater, or dance. (☎684 3103. Box office open M-Sa 9:30am-5:30pm. Tickets €12-22.) **Trains** leave from Station Rd. for Dublin (1-2 per day, €30). **Buses** also leave every hr. from Station Rd. for: Cork (3hr., €14); Dublin (4hr., €14); Galway (1hr., €10); Limerick (40min., €6.70); and Shannon Airport (40min., €7). The **tourist office** is on Arthur's Row, off O'Connell Sq. (☎28366. Open July-Sept. daily 9am-1pm and 2-6pm; Apr.-June and Oct. M-Sa 9:30am-1pm and 2-6pm; Nov.-Mar. M-F 9:30am-1pm and 2-6pm.) **Abbey Tourist Hostel ❶**, Harmony Row, welcomes guests with flowers. (☎682 2620. Dorms €14-16; singles €25; doubles €40.)

Something of a shrine to Irish music, the little village of **Doolin** draws thousands every year to its three pubs. ◪**McDermott's** (in the upper village), **O'Connor's** (in the Lower), and **McGann's** (Upper) all have *trad* sessions nightly at 9:30pm. **Buses** leave from Doolin Hostel for Dublin via Ennis and Limerick (#15; 2 per day) and Galway (#50; 1½hr., 2-4 per day). **Aille River Hostel (IHH) ❶**, halfway between the upper and lower villages, has a friendly atmosphere and a gorgeous location. (☎707 4260. Internet free for guests. Dorms €12; doubles €27. Camping €6.)

THE CLIFFS OF MOHER AND THE BURREN ☎065

Plunging 213m straight down to the open sea, the ◪**Cliffs of Moher** afford views of Loop Head, the Kerry Mountains, the Twelve Bens, and the Aran Islands. **Warning:** *Winds can be extremely strong and blow a few tourists off every year. Let's Go* strongly discourages straying from the established paths. The seasonal **tourist office** houses a tea shop and exchanges currency. (☎708 1171. Open daily May-Sept. 9:30am-5:30pm.) To reach the cliffs, head 5km south of Doolin on R478, or hop on the Galway-Cork **bus** (in summer 2-3 per day).

In the magical 260 sq. km of the nearby **Burren,** limestone stretches end in secluded coves, bright wildflowers peek from cracks in 1.5km long rock planes, and 28 species of butterfly flutter by. **Burren Exposure,** between Kinvara and Ballyvaughn on N67, airs films on the region. (☎707 7277. Open daily 9am-6pm. €6.50, students €5.) The Burren town of **Lisdoonvarna** is synonymous with its **Matchmaking Festival,** a month-long *craic*-and-snogging celebration that attracts over 10,000 singles each September. The **Hydro Hotel** ❹ has nightly music and information on the festival. (☎707 4005. Open Mar.-Oct. €45 per person.) A **bus** (☎682 4177) connects Galway to towns in and near the Burren a few times a day in summer but infrequently in winter. In Ballyvaughan, stay at **O'Brien B&B** ❸, above a pub and restaurant on Main St., and enjoy its fireplaces and hearty Irish breakfasts. (☎707 7292. Doubles €44.)

GALWAY   ☎091

In the past few years, Co. Galway's reputation as Ireland's cultural capital has brought flocks of young Celtophiles to Galway (pop. 70,000). Galway is the fastest-growing city in Europe. Street performers dazzle with homegrown tricks while locals and tourists lounge in outdoor cafes. With its quiet quay-side walks, quality theater, and hot club scene, Galway is also just a skip away from the Clare Coast and beautiful Connemara.

▐▓ TRANSPORTATION AND PRACTICAL INFORMATION. Trains leave the station on Eyre Sq. (☎561 444; open M-Sa 9am-6pm) for Dublin (3hr., 4-5 per day, €25-35) via Athlone (€11-14); transfer at Athlone for all other lines. **Buses**, which also leave from Eyre Sq. (☎562 000), head to: Belfast (7hr., 2-3 per day, €28); Donegal (4hr., 4 per day, €15.20); and Dublin (4hr., 14 per day, €13). The **tourist office** is on Forster St. (☎537 700. Open daily 9am-5:45pm.) Check the **Internet** at **Fun World,** Eyre Sq., above Supermac's. (☎561 415. €5 per hr., 8-11pm €3 per hr. Open M-Sa 10am-11pm, Su 11am-11pm.) The **post office** is on 3 Eglinton St. (☎534 727. Open M and W-Sa 9am-5:30pm, Tu 9:30am-5:30pm.)

▐▐ ACCOMMODATIONS AND FOOD. Salmon Weir Hostel ❶, 3 St. Vincent's Ave., is extremely homey and cozy, with a friendly, laid-back vibe. (☎561 133. Free tea and coffee. Curfew 3am. Dorms €9-15; doubles €35.) **St. Martin's** ❸, 2 Nun's Island Rd., on the western bank of the river at the end of O'Brien's Bridge, is a gorgeous B&B located near Galway's best pubs. (☎568 286. All rooms ensuite. Singles €35; doubles €70; large family room €30 per person.) For a place where the food does all the talking, try **▧Anton's** ❶, just over the bridge near the Spanish Arch. (Open M-F 8am-6pm.) For a lighter meal, try **Java's** ❶, Abbeygate St. (☎567 400. New York-style bagel sandwiches €2.75-6.25. Open M-Sa noon-3am, Su 1pm-3am.)

◉ ▮ SIGHTS AND ENTERTAINMENT. The Nora Barnacle House has hardly changed since James Joyce's life-long companion left. Check out the author's original love letters to Ms. Barnacle. (8 Bowling Green. ☎564 743. Open mid-May to mid-Sept. W-F 10am-1pm and 2-5:30pm, otherwise by appointment; last admission 5pm. €2.50.) Head to **Claddagh,** an area that until the 1930s was an Irish-speaking, thatch-roofed fishing village. The famous **Claddagh rings,** traditionally used as wedding bands, are today's mass-produced reminders of yesteryear. Satiate all aquatic cravings at **Atlantaquaria,** recently opened as the National Aquarium of Ireland. A wax paper-covered jar upstairs holds the gigantic eye of a fin whale. (On Grattan Rd. 200 yd. past Beach Court. ☎585 100. Open M-F 10am-5pm, Sa-Su 10am-6pm.) In mid-July, the **Galway Arts Festival** (☎583 800) attracts droves of *trad* musicians, rock groups, theater troupes, and filmmakers.

Pubs on Quay St. and Eyre Sq. cater to tourists, while locals stick to the more *trad*-oriented **Dominick Street** pubs. Behind the bookshelved front at **▧Roisín Dubh** ("The Black Rose"), Dominick St., hides one of Galway's hottest live music scenes. (☎586 540. Occasional cover €5-23.) **The King's Head** (☎566 630), on High St., has three floors and a huge stage devoted to nightly rock. **Cuba,** past Eyre Sq. on Prospect Hill, is Galway's best club, with live music upstairs. (Cover €5-10.)

ARAN ISLANDS (OILEÁIN ÁRANN) ☎ 099

On the westernmost edge of County Galway, isolated from the mainland by 32km of swelling Atlantic, lie the spectacular Aran Islands (*Oileán Árann*). Dozens of ruins, forts, churches, and holy wells rise from the stony terrain of **Inishmore** (*Inis Mór;* pop. 900). Don't miss the **Dún Aengus** ring fort, where concentric stones circle a sheer 100m drop. The **Inis Mór Way** is a mostly paved route that passes the majority of the island's sights; pick up a map at the tourist office (€2). Windswept **Inishmaan** (*Inis Meáin;* pop. 300) and **Inisheer** (*Inis Oírr;* pop. 300), the smallest island, also feature similar paths.

Island Ferries (☎ 091 561 767) go from **Rossaveal**, west of Galway, to Inishmore (2-4 per day) and Inisheer (2 per day). Queen of Aran II (☎ 566 535), based in the islands, also leaves from Rossaveal for Inishmore (4 per day; round-trip €19, student €14). Both companies run **buses** to Rossaveal (€6, students €5); they depart from Kinlay House, on Merchant St. in Galway, 1½hr. before ferry departure. Ferries to Inishmore arrive at **Kilronan**. The **tourist office** stores luggage (€1) and helps find accommodations. (☎ 61263. Open daily June 10am-6pm; July-Sept. 10am-6:45pm; Oct.-Mar. 11am-5pm; Apr.-May 10am-5pm.) The **Kilronan Hostel ❶**, adjacent to Tí Joe Mac's pub, has great rooms and a helpful staff. (☎ 61255. Bike rental €10. Dorms €16, all ensuite.) The **Spar** in Kilronan functions as an unofficial community center. (☎ 61203. Open in summer M-Sa 9am-8pm, Su 9am-6pm; winter M-Sa 9am-8pm, Su 10am-5pm.)

CONNEMARA

Connemara, a largely Irish-speaking region in northwestern Co. Galway, is comprised of a lacy net of inlets and islands, a gang of inland mountains, and desolate stretches of bog. Offshore islands look out over two major mountain ranges, the **Twelve Bens** and the **Maamturks**.

CLIFDEN (AN CLOCHÁN) ☎ 095

Busy, English-speaking Clifden attracts crowds of tourists, who use it as a base for exploring the region. Visit the **Connemara Walking Centre**, Market St., and take a tour led by Michael Gibbons, the critically acclaimed archaeologist-raconteur. The tours explore the history, folklore, geology, and archaeology of the region. Though closed for renovation, the center should be reopened for the 2005 season. (☎ 21379 or 22278; www.walkingireland.com. Open Mar.-Oct. M-Sa 9am-9pm. Boat tours daily Easter-Oct.) Bus Éireann runs **buses** from the library on Market St. to Galway via Oughterard (2hr., 1-6 per day, €9) and Westport via Leenane (1½hr., late June to Aug. M-Sa 1 per day). Michael Nee buses go from the courthouse to Galway (2hr., 2 per day, €13). Rent a **bike** at **Mannion's**, on Bridge St. (☎ 21160. €15 per day. Open daily 9:30am-6pm.) The **tourist office** is on Galway Rd. (☎ 21163. Open June M-Sa 10am-6pm; July-Aug. M-Sa 9:30am-6pm, Su 10am-6pm; Sept.-Oct. M-Sa 10am-4:50pm; Mar.-May M-Sa 10am-5pm.) **B&Bs** start at €25 per person. **White Heather House ❸**, The Square, boasts panoramic views and an Irish breakfast. (☎ 21655. Singles €25-30; doubles €60.) Tranquil **Shanaheever Campsite ❶** is 1.5km outside Clifden on Westport Rd. (☎ 21018. €13 per person with tent or trailer.) Most restaurants in Clifden are attached to pubs. **Cullen's Bistro & Coffee Shop ❸**, Market St., is a family-run establishment that cooks up hearty meals and delicious desserts. (☎ 21983. Thick Irish stew €14.50. Open daily 11am-10pm.) **O'Connor's SuperValu** is on Market St. (☎ 21182. Open M-Sa 9am-8pm, Su 10am-6pm.)

CONNEMARA NATIONAL PARK   ☎095

Connemara National Park occupies 12½ sq. km of mountainous countryside. Bogs, often thinly covered by a deceptive screen of grass and flowers, constitute much of the park's terrain. The **Snuffaunboy Nature** and **Ellis Wood** trails are easy 20min. hikes. Trails lead from the back of the Ellis Wood trail and along **Bog Road** onto spectacular ◪**Diamond Hill**. The 2hr. Diamond Hill trail has been closed for the past three years for erosion control; call the Visitors' Centre (see below) to check if it's reopened. Experienced hikers often head for the **Twelve Bens** (*Na Benna Beola*; the Twelve Pins), a rugged range that reaches 2200m heights. A tour of all 12 bens takes experienced hikers about 10hr.; the range is not recommended for beginning hikers. **Biking** the 65km circle through Clifden, Letterfrack, and the Inagh Valley is truly captivating, but only appropriate for fit bikers. A guidebook mapping out walks (€6.40) and help in planning hikes is available at the **Visitors' Centre**. (☎41054. Open June-Aug. 9:30am-6:30pm; Mar.-May and Sept. 10am-5:30pm. €2.75, students €1.25.) Hikers often base themselves at the **Ben Lettery Hostel (An Óige/HI) ❶**, in Ballinafad, 13km east of Clifden. (☎51136. Dorms €12.)

WESTPORT   ☎098

Palm trees and steep hills lead down to Westport's busy Georgian streets. Nearby, the conical **Croagh Patrick** rises 650m over Clew Bay. The summit has been revered as a holy site for thousands of years. St. Patrick worked here in AD 441, praying for 40 days and nights to banish snakes from Ireland. Climbers start their excursion from the 15th-century **Murrisk Abbey**, several kilometers west of Westport on R395 toward Louisburgh. **Buses** go to Murrisk (2-3 per day); for groups, cabs (☎27171) are cheaper and more convenient. Sheep calmly rule **Clare Island**, a desolate but beautiful speck in the Atlantic. Take a bus to Roonah Pier, 29km from Westport, and then a ferry to the island. (Bus departs from Westport's tourist office at 10am and returns by 6pm; €25 for bus and ferry combined.) **Matt Molloy's**, on Bridge St., is owned by the flautist of the Chieftains and has nightly *trad.*

    Trains arrive at the Altamont St. Station (☎25253), a 5min. walk up the North Mall, from Dublin (2-4 per day, €22-25) via Athlone. **Buses** leave Mill St. for Galway (2hr., 4-8 per day, €12). The **tourist office** is on James St. (☎25711. Open daily 9am-5:45pm.) **B&Bs** cluster on **Altamont Road** and **The Quay**. Award-winning breakfasts and incredible hospitality at ◪**Altamont House ❶**, Altamont St., have kept travelers coming back for 37 years. (☎25226. Rooms €30, with bath €33.) Restaurants are concentrated on **Bridge Street**. The **SuperValu** supermarket is on Shop St. (☎27000. Open M-W and Sa 8:30am-7:30pm, Th-F 8:30am-9pm, Su 10am-6pm.)

NORTHWESTERN IRELAND

A mere sliver of land connects the mountains, lakes, and ancient monuments of Co. Sligo to Co. Donegal. Among Ireland's counties, Donegal (DUN-ee-gahl) is second to Cork in size and second to none in glorious wilderness. Its *gaeltacht* is the largest sanctuary of the living Irish language in Ireland, and its geographic isolation and natural beauty embrace travelers sick of the tourist hordes.

SLIGO   ☎071

Since the beginning of the 20th century, Sligo has seen a literary pilgrimage of William Butler Yeats devotees; the poet spent summers in town as a child and set many of his poems around Sligo Bay. **Sligo Town,** the commercial center, is an excellent base for exploration. The well-preserved 13th-century **Sligo Abbey** is on Abbey St. (Open daily Apr.-Oct. 10am-6pm; Nov.-Mar. reduced hours. €2, students €1.) ▨**The Model Arts Centre and Niland Gallery,** on the Mall, houses one of the finest collections of modern Irish art. (Open Tu-Sa 10am-5:30pm; June-Oct. also Su noon-5:30pm. Free.) Yeats is buried in **Drumcliffe Churchyard,** on the N15, 6.5km northwest of Sligo. **Buses** from Sligo to Derry stop at Drumcliffe (10min., 5-8 per day, round-trip €5). Over 70 pubs crowd the main streets of Sligo. The trendy ▨**Shoot the Crows,** on Grattan St., has fairies and skulls dangling from the ceiling.

Trains (☎ 69888) go from Lord Edward St. to Dublin (3hr., 4-5 per day, €25.50) via Carrick-on-Shannon and Mullingar. From the same station, **buses** (☎ 60066) head to: Belfast (4hr., 2-3 per day, €24); Derry (3hr., 4-7 per day, €15); Donegal (1hr., 3-7 per day, €11); Dublin (3-4hr., 4-5 per day, €15); and Galway (2½hr., 4-6 per day, €12.50). Turn left on Lord Edward St., then follow the signs right onto Adelaid St. and around the corner to Temple St. to find the **tourist office.** (☎ 61201. Open July-Aug. M-F 9am-6pm, Sa 10am-4pm, Su 10am-2pm; Sept.-May M-F 9am-5pm; June M-F 9am-5pm, Sa 10am-3pm.) **B&Bs** cluster on **Pearse Road,** on the south side. ▨**Eden Hill Holiday Hostel (IHH) ❶,** off Pearse Rd., has Victorian decor and a friendly staff. From the town center, follow Pearse Rd., turn right at the Marymount sign, and take another right after one block. (☎ 43204. Laundry €6. Dorms €14.) A **Tesco** supermarket is on O'Connell St. (☎ 62788. Open M-Tu and Sa 8:30am-7pm, W-F 8:30am-9pm, Su 10am-4pm.)

LETTERKENNY   ☎ 074

Letterkenny, although difficult to navigate, is a lively place to make bus connections to the rest of Donegal, the Republic, and Northern Ireland. **Buses** leave from the junction of Port Rd. and Pearse Rd., in front of the shopping center. Bus Éireann (☎ 21309) runs to: Derry (30min., 3-9 per day, €6.70); Dublin (4½hr., 4-6 per day, €15); Galway (4¾hr., 4 per day, €27.50) via Donegal Town (50min., €7.50); and Sligo (2hr., 4-5 per day, €12). Lough Swilly (☎ 22863) runs to Derry (M-Sa 12 per day, €6) and the Inishowen Peninsula (2-3 per day, €6). The **Chamber of Commerce Visitors' Information Centre** is at 40 Port Rd. (☎ 24866. Open M-F 9am-5pm.) ▨**The Port Hostel (IHO) ❶,** Orchard Crest, is the only hostel in town. (☎ 25315. Laundry €5. Dorms €15.) There is a **Tesco** supermarket behind the bus station. (Open M-Tu and Sa 8:30am-7pm, W 8:30am-8pm, Th-F 8:30am-9pm, Su noon-6pm.)

NORTHERN IRELAND

FACTS AND FIGURES: NORTHERN IRELAND	
Official Name: Northern Ireland.	**Time Zone:** GMT.
Capital: Belfast.	**Language:** English.
Population: 1,700,000.	**Religions:** Protestant (40%), Roman Catholic (40%), other (20%).
Land Area: 14,160 sq. km.	

Media headlines screaming about riots and bombs have long overshadowed the typically calm tenor of life in Northern Ireland. In reality, acts of violence and extremist fringe groups are less visible than the division in civil society that sends Protestants and Catholics to separate neighborhoods, separate stores, separate pubs, and often separate schools, with separate, though similar, traditional songs and slang. The 1998 Good Friday Agreement, an attempt to lead Northern Ireland out of its struggles, has itself been a long journey. The Assembly has been suspended a number of times and the lack of progress on various emotional issues continues to frustrate. London has had to take the reins again, while all sides have renewed their efforts to make their country as peaceful as it is beautiful.

Belfast's bursting nightlife gives way to the thatched-cottage fishing villages dotting the Ards Peninsula, which leads to the rounded peaks of the Mournes and the park retreats of Newcastle. The waterfalls and valleys of the glorious Glens of Antrim lie to the north; nearby, the eighth wonder of the world, the Giant's Causeway, a volcanic staircase, extends out to the Atlantic.

PHONE CODES	The regional code for all of Northern Ireland is 028. From outside Northern Ireland, dial int'l dialing prefix (see inside back cover) + 44 (from the Republic, 048) + 28 + local number. From within Northern Ireland, simply dial the local number.

BELFAST   ☎ 028

Despite the violent associations conjured by the name Belfast, the capital feels more neighborly than most visitors expect. As the second-largest city on the island, Belfast (pop. 330,000) stands in stark contrast to the rest of Ireland. Today, its reputation as a thriving artistic center is maintained by such renowned writers as Nobel Prize-winner Seamus Heaney and an annual arts festival. The Belfast bar scene, a mix of Irish-British pub culture and international trends, entertains locals, foreigners, and a student population as lively as any in the world.

⌐ TRANSPORTATION

Flights: Belfast International Airport (BFS; ☎9442 2448; www.belfastairport.com), in Aldergrove, serves **Aer Lingus** (☎0845 084 4444), **British Airways** (☎0845 850 9850), **British European** (sometimes called **Flybe;** (☎087 0567 6676), and **BMI** (☎0870 607 0555). **Airbus** (☎9066 6630) runs to Laganside and Europa bus stations in the city center (40min.; M-Sa 2 per hr. 5:45am-10:30pm, Su about every hr. 6:15am-9:30pm; £6, round-trip £9). **Belfast City Airport** (☎9093 9093; www.belfastcityairport.com), at the harbor, serves **British European.** Trains run from City Airport to Central Station (M-Sa 25-33 per day, Su 12 per day; £1).

Trains: Infoline ☎9066 6630; www.translink.co.uk. **Trains** arrive at **Central Station,** East Bridge St. Some also stop at **Botanic Station,** Botanic Ave. in the University area, or **Great Victoria Station,** next to Europa Hotel. To **Derry** (2hr.; M-F 9 per day, Sa 6 per day, Su 3 per day; £8.20/£4) and **Dublin** (2hr.; M-Sa 9 per day, Su 5 per day; £20).

Belfast

🏠 ACCOMMODATIONS
The Ark (IHH), **6**
Arnie's Backpackers (IHH) **4**
Belfast Hostel (HINI) **2**
Botanic Lodge, **7**
Camera Guesthouse, **8**

🍴 FOOD
Azzura, **1**
Benedict's, **3**
Bookfinders, **5**

IRELAND

Buses: Buses to the west, the northern coast, and the Republic operate out of **Europa Bus Terminal** (☎9066 6630), off Great Victoria St., behind the Europa Hotel. To: **Derry** (1¾hr.; M-Sa 19 per day, Su 7 per day; £7.50, students £5) and **Dublin** (3hr.; M-Sa 7 per day, Su 6 per day; £12/£10). Buses to Northern Ireland's eastern coast operate out of **Laganside Station** (☎9066 6630), off Donegall Quay.

Ferries: The docks can be unsafe late at night and early in the morning; take a cab.

SeaCat (☎087 0552 3523; www.seacat.co.uk), from the ferry terminal off Donegall Quay, sails to **Isle of Man** (2¾hr.; Apr.-Nov. M, W, F 1 per day) and **Troon, Scotland** (2½hr., 2-3 per day). **Norse Merchant Ferries** (☎087 0600 4321; www.norsemerchant.com) runs to **Liverpool, England** (8hr.).

P&O Irish Ferries (☎0870 242 4777), in Larne, run to **Cairnryan, Scotland. Stena Line** (☎087 0570 7070; www.stenaline.com), up the Lagan River, sails to **Fleetwood, England** and **Stranraer, Scotland.**

Local Transportation: The red **Citybus Network** (☎9066 6630; www.translink.co.uk) is supplemented by **Ulsterbus's** suburban "blue buses." Travel within the city center £1.20, students £0.60. **Centrelink** buses traverse the city (every 12min.; M-F 7:25am-9:15pm, Sa 8:30am-9:15pm; £1.10, free with bus or rail ticket.) **Nightlink** buses shuttle to various small towns outside Belfast (Sa 1 and 2am; £3.50, payable on board).

Taxis: Value Cabs (☎9080 9080); **City Cab** (☎9024 2000); **Fon a Cab** (☎9033 3333).

�># ## ORIENTATION AND PRACTICAL INFORMATION

City Hall is in **Donegall Square.** A busy shopping district extends north for four blocks to the enormous Castlecourt Shopping Centre. In the eastern part of the shopping district, the **Cornmarket** area shows off characteristically Belfastian architecture and pubs in its narrow entries (small alleyways). The stretch of Great Victoria St. between Europa Station and **Shaftesbury Square** is known as the **Golden Mile** for its high-brow establishments and Victorian architecture. **Botanic Avenue** and **Bradbury Place** (which becomes University Rd.) extend south to **Queen's University,** where student pubs and budget accommodations await. In this southern area, the busiest neighborhoods center around **Stranmillis Road, Malone Road,** and **Lisburn Road.** Divided from the rest of Belfast by the **Westlink Motorway,** working-class **West Belfast** is more politically volatile than the city center. There remains a sharp division between sectarian neighborhoods: the Protestant neighborhood stretches along **Shankill Road,** just north of the Catholic neighborhood, which is centered on **Falls Road.** The two are separated by the **peace line.** River Lagan splits industrial **East Belfast** from Belfast proper. During the week, the area north of City Hall is deserted after 6pm. Although muggings are infrequent in Belfast, use taxis after dark, particularly when pubbing in the northeast.

Tourist Office: Belfast Welcome Centre, 47 Donegall Pl. (☎9024 6609; www.gotobelfast.com), books accommodations in Northern Ireland (£2) and the Republic (£3). Open June-Sept. M-Sa 9am-7pm, Su noon-5pm; Oct.-May M-Sa 9am-5:30pm.

Banks: Banks and **ATMs** are plentiful. Most banks are open M-F 9am-4:30pm. **Thomas Cook,** 10 Donegall Sq. West (☎9088 3800). Open M-F 8am-6pm, Sa 10am-5pm.

Laundry: Globe Drycleaners & Launderers, 37-39 Botanic Ave. (☎9024 3956). £4.65 for use of machines. Open M-F 8am-9pm, Sa 8am-6pm, Su 2-6pm.

Emergency: ☎999; no coins required. **Police:** 65 Knock Rd. (☎9065 0222).

Hospital: Belfast City Hospital, 91 Lisburn Rd. (☎9032 9241).

Internet Access: Belfast Central Library. £1 per 15min., £3 per hr., with photo ID. **Revelations Internet Cafe,** 27 Shaftesbury Sq. (☎9032 0337). £4 per hr., students and hostelers £3 per hr. Open M-F 10am-10pm, Sa 10am-6pm, Su 11am-7pm.

Post Office: **Central Post Office,** 25 Castle Pl. (☎0845 722 3344). Open M-Sa 9am-
5:30pm. **Postal Code:** BT1 1BB.

ACCOMMODATIONS

Nearly all of Belfast's budget accommodations are near Queen's University. Walk
10-20min. south from Europa Bus Station or the train stations, or catch a **Centrelink**
bus to Shaftesbury Sq. or, from Donegall Sq. East, **Citybus** #69-71, 83, 84, or 86.

Arnie's Backpackers (IHH), 63 Fitzwilliam St. (☎9024 2867), a short walk from Europa
Station. Impressively clean with a library of travel info. No curfew. Dorms £7-9.50. ●

Camera Guesthouse, 44 Wellington Park (☎9066 0026). Pristine and family-run. Breakfasts offer organic options. Singles £35, ensuite £45; doubles £54/£60. ●

Belfast Hostel (HINI), 22 Donegall Rd. (☎9031 5435; www.hini.org.uk), off Shaftesbury
Sq. Clean and inviting interior. Internet access £1 per 20min. Laundry £3. Reception
24hr. Dorms £8.50-10.50; singles £17-18; triples £33-34. ●

The Ark (IHH), 18 University St. (☎9032 9626), 10min. from Europa Station on Great
Victoria St. Great sense of community: staff of former guest MVPs. Also books tours of
Belfast (£8) and Giant's Causeway (£18). Internet access £1 per 20min. Weekend lug-
gage storage. Laundry £5. Curfew 2am. Dorms £10; doubles £36. ●

Botanic Lodge, 87 Botanic Ave. (☎9032 7682), at the corner of Mt. Charles Ave. Comfortable and close to the city center. Singles £25, ensuite £35; doubles £40/£45. ●

FOOD

Dublin Road, Botanic Road, and the **Golden Mile** have the most options. For produce,
visit **St. George's Market,** East Bridge St., between May St. and Oxford St. (Open F
8am-2pm, Sa 6am-noon.) For gourmet pizzas and pastas fresh from the oven
(under £5), try **Azzura ●,** 8 Church Ln. The owners of this tiny cafe grow their
own peppers. (☎9024 2444. Open M-Sa 9am-5pm.) **Benedict's ●,** 7-21 Bradbury Pl.,
is a swanky hotel restaurant with a "Beat the Clock" meal deal: order fine meals
from 5:30 to 7:30pm, and the time ordered is the price. Curried chicken and vegetarian options delight. (☎9059 1999. Open M-Sa noon-2:30pm and 5:30 10:30pm, Su
noon-3:30pm and 5:30-9pm.) Or, eat at cozy **Bookfinders ●,** 47 University Rd., a
dusty bookstore-cafe with mismatched dishes, counter-culture paraphernalia, and
occasional poetry readings. (☎9032 6677. Open M-Sa 10am-5:30pm.)

SIGHTS

DONEGALL SQUARE. The most impressive piece of architecture in Belfast is,
appropriately, its administrative and geographic center. Removed from the
crowded streets by a grassy square, **City Hall's** green copper dome (52m) is visible
from nearly any point in the city. A foreboding marble statue of **Queen Victoria** gri-
maces formidably at the entrance. *(☎9027 0456. 1hr. tours June-Sept. M-F 11am, 2,
and 3pm, Sa 2:30pm; Oct.-May M-F 11am and 2:30pm, Sa 2:30pm. Tour times subject to
change. Free.)* The **Linen Hall Library** contains a famous collection of Northern Irish
political documents. *(Enter via 52 Fountain St. ☎9087 2214. Free tours available. Open
M-F 9:30am-5:30pm, Sa 9:30am-4pm.)*

CORNMARKET AND ST. ANNE'S CATHEDRAL. North of the city center, this shopping district envelops eight blocks around **Castle Street** and **Royal Avenue.** Relics of
the old city remain in the **entries,** or tiny alleys. **St. Anne's Cathedral,** also known as

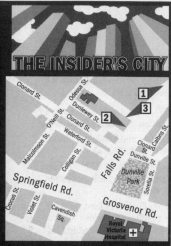

THE INSIDER'S CITY

THE CATHOLIC MURALS

The murals of West Belfast are some of the city's most intriguing attractions. The following are Catholic Belfast's more famous and important; also included is a building closely related to the Troubles.

1 Mural illustrating protestors during **The Hunger Strikes of 1981,** in which 10 IRA members starved themselves to death over the course of six months.

2 Portrayal of **Bobby Sands,** the first hunger striker to die. It is found on Sevastopol St., on the side of the Sinn Féin Office. Sands was elected to British Parliament during this time and is remembered as the North's most famous martyr.

3 Formely known as Northern Ireland's National RUC Headquarters, this bulding is the most bombed police station in England, the Republic, and the North. Its fortified, barbwire facade is on Springfield St.

the **Belfast Cathedral,** was begun in 1899. Each of its interior pillars names one of Belfast's professions: Agriculture, Art, Freemasonry, Healing, Industry, Music, Science, Shipbuilding, Theology, and "Womanhood." *(Donegall St., near the city center. Open M-Sa 10am-4pm, Su before and after services.)*

THE DOCKS AND EAST BELFAST. Belfast's newest mega-attraction, **Odyssey,** 2 Queen's Quay, is a gigantic science center that houses five different science attractions. The best feature is the ■**W5 Discovery Centre,** a science and technology museum that beckons geeks of all ages to play with pulley chairs, laser harps, robots, and the Fire Tornado. *(☎ 9046 7700; www.w5online.co.uk. Open M-Sa 10am-6pm, Su noon-6pm; last admission 5pm. £6, students £4.50, families £17.)*

THE GOLDEN MILE. This strip along Great Victoria St. contains many of Belfast's jewels. Of these, the **Grand Opera House,** is the city's pride and joy, sadly making it a repeated bombing target for the IRA. Tours allow a look behind the ornate facade. *(☎ 9024 1919. Office open 8:30am-9pm. Tours begin across the street at the office Sa 11am. £3, seniors and children £2. Box office open M-Sa 8:30am-6pm. Tours 11am.)* If opera is not your thing, visit the popular **Crown Liquor Saloon,** 46 Great Victoria St., a showcase of carved wood, gilded ceilings, and stained glass recently restored by the National Trust. Finally, check out the **Europa Hotel,** which has the dubious distinction of being "Europe's most bombed hotel," having survived 32 blasts.

WEST BELFAST: THE MURALS OF THE FALLS AND SHANKILL. West Belfast is not a "sight" in the traditional sense. The streets display political **murals,** but be discreet if photographing them. Visitors should definitely take a ■**black cab tour** for fascinating commentary on the murals and sights on both sides of the peace line. **Black Taxi Tours** offers witty, objective presentations *(☎ 0800 052 3914; £8 per person).* The Catholic neighborhood is centered around **Falls Road,** where the **Sinn Féin** office is easily spotted: One side of it is covered with an enormous portrait of Bobby Sands and an advertisement for the Sinn Féin newspaper, *An Phoblacht.* On Divis St., a high-rise apartment building marks the site of **Divis Tower,** formerly an IRA stronghold and now occupied by the British Army. Farther north is **Shankill Road** and the Protestant neighborhood. **Crumlin Road** is the site of the oldest Loyalist murals. Between the Falls and Shankill is the **peace line.**

 Be advised that it is illegal to photograph military installations, and **Marching Season** (July 4-12) is a risky time to visit the area.

🎵 🎭 ENTERTAINMENT AND NIGHTLIFE

Belfast's cultural events and performances are covered in the monthly *Arts Council Artslink* (free at the tourist office). The **Grand Opera House,** on Great Victoria St., stages a mix of opera, ballet, musicals, and drama. Buy tickets at the box office, 2-4 Great Victoria St. (☎9024 1919; www.goh.co.uk. Tickets from £12.50.) The **Queen's University Festival** (☎9066 7687; www.belfastfestival.com) in November draws ballet, comedy, films, and opera.

Pubs close early, so start crawling while the sun's still up; *Let's Go* suggests starting downtown, moving through Cornmarket, and finishing near the university. Begin with a pint at **The Duke of York,** 7-11 Commercial Ctr., which in former days was a boxing venue and a Communist printing press. Today it's home to the city's largest selection of Irish whiskeys. (☎9024 1062. Open M noon-9pm, Tu noon-1am, W noon-midnight, Th-Sa noon-2am.) Move on to **White's Tavern,** 2-4 Winecellar Entry, Belfast's oldest tavern. (☎9024 3080. Open M-Sa 11:30am-11pm.) Farther south, **Apartment** has a cafe-bar downstairs and an upscale lounge upstairs, perfect for pre-clubbing cocktails. (☎9032 5942. Open M-F 8am-1am, Sa 9am-1am, Su noon-midnight.) Explore the club scene at **The Fly,** 5-6 Lower Crescent, and don't let the insect-friendly decor scare you off. The first floor is for pints, the second for mingling, and the third for a 40-flavor vodka test-tube-shot bar. (☎9050 9750. Open M-W 7pm-1am, Th-Sa 5am-1:15am.) **The Kremlin,** 96 Donegall St., is Belfast's hottest gay spot. Doors close at 1am, but the party only heats up inside. (☎9080 9700. Bar open M-Th 4pm-3am, F-Su 1pm-3am.)

CAUSEWAY COAST ☎028

Past Cushendun, the northern coast becomes even more dramatic. Sea-battered cliffs tower 185m over white beaches before giving way to the spectacular geology of **Giant's Causeway,** for which the region is named. Thousands of visitors swarm to the site today, but few venture beyond the Visitors' Centre to the stunning and easily accessible coastline that stretches beyond.

📌 **TRANSPORTATION. Bus** (☎7032 5400) #172 runs between Ballycastle and Portrush along the coast (1hr., 3-7 per day, £3.50). The Antrim Coastor #252 runs from Belfast to Portstewart via most small towns along the coast (2 per day). The open-topped Bushmills Bus traces the coast between Coleraine, 8km south of Portrush, and the Causeway (July-Aug. 5 per day).

BALLYCASTLE AND ENVIRONS. The Causeway Coast leaves the sleepy glens behind when it hits **Ballycastle,** a seaside town that shelters tourists bound for Giant's Causeway. **Bus** #162A goes to Cushendall via Cushendun (50min., M-F 1 per day, £3), and #131 goes to Belfast (3hr., M-Sa 5-6 per day, £6.50). The **tourist office** is in Sheskburn House, 7 Mary St. (☎2076 2024. Open July-Aug. M-F 9:30am-7pm, Sa 10am-6pm, Su 2-6pm; Sept.-June M-F 9:30am-5pm.) Sleep at the friendly and comfortable **Castle Hostel (IHH) ❶,** 62 Quay Rd. (☎2076 2337. Dorms £8.) Just off the coast of Ballycastle, bumpy, boomerang-shaped **Rathlin Island** ("Fort of the Sea") is home to more puffins (pop. 20,000) than people (pop. 100). **Raghery Tours** (☎2076 3949) drives to the **Kebble Bird Sanctuary,** 7km from the harbor (20min., every 45min., £3). Caledonian MacBrayne (☎2076 9299) **ferries** run to the island from the pier at Ballycastle, up the hill from Quay Rd. (45min., 1-3 per day, round-trip £8.60). Eight kilometers west of Ballycastle, the village of **Ballintoy** attracts the crowds on their way to the tiny **Carrick-a-rede Island.** From the mainland, cross the fishermen's rope bridge (about 2m wide) over the dizzying 30m drop to the rocks and sea below; be extremely careful in windy weather. A sign marks the turn-off for the bridge from the coastal road east of Ballintoy. The island's **Larrybane Sea Cliffs** are home to a variety of species of gulls. The **Sheep Island View Hostel (IHH)** ❶ is at 42A Main St. in Ballintoy. (☎2076 9391; www.sheepislandview.com. Laundry £2. Dorms with breakfast £12. Camping £5 per person.)

GIANT'S CAUSEWAY. Advertised as the eighth natural wonder of the world, the ▨**Giant's Causeway** is Northern Ireland's most popular attraction, so don't be surprised to find that 2000 other travelers picked the same day to visit. Geologists believe that the unique rock formations were formed some 60 million years ago. Comprised of over 40,000 perfectly symmetrical hexagonal basalt columns, the site resembles a large descending staircase that leads out from the cliffs to the ocean's floor below. Ulsterbus #172 to Portrush, the #252 Antrim Coaster, and the Bushmills Bus all drop visitors off at the **Giant's Causeway Visitors' Centre. A minibus** (£1.20) runs the 1km from the center to the columns. (Causeway open 24hr. Free. Centre ☎2073 1855. Open May daily 10am-5:30pm; June daily 10am-6pm; July-Aug. daily 10am-7pm; Sept.-Oct. M-F 10am-5pm, Sa-Su 10am-5:30pm.)

ITALY (ITALIA)

One of the few countries whose very geography seems active—it resembles a boot poised to kick Sicily clear across the Mediterranean—Italy has never been inclined to sit back quietly. After bursting onstage as the base for the Roman empire, it became persecutor and popularizer of an upstart religion called Christianity and later served as center to the artistic and philosophical Renaissance. Today it has emerged as a world power that has changed governments more than 50 times since World War II. Countless invasions have left the land rich with examples of nearly every artistic era; Egyptian obelisks, Etruscan huts, Greek temples, Augustan arches, Byzantine mosaics, Renaissance *palazzi*, Baroque fountains, and postmodern structures sprawl across its 20 regions. From perfect pasta to the creation of pizza, Italy knows that the quickest way to a country's heart is through its stomach. Italy is also the champion of romance—passionate lovers shout their *amore* from the rooftops of southern Italy and Venice. Somewhere between the leisurely gondola rides and the frenetic nightlife, you too will fall in love with Italy.

 DISCOVER ITALY: SUGGESTED ITINERARIES

THREE DAYS Spend it all in the Eternal City of **Rome** (p. 620). Go back in time at the **Ancient City**: be a gladiator in the **Colosseum**, explore the **Roman Forum** and stand in the well-preserved **Pantheon**. Spend the next day admiring the fine art in the **Capitoline Museums** and the **Galleria Borghese,** then satiate your other senses in a disco. The next morning, redeem your debauched soul in **Vatican City,** gazing at the ceiling of the **Sistine Chapel,** gaping at **St. Peter's Cathedral,** and enjoying the **Vatican Museums.**

ONE WEEK Spend 3 days taking in the sights in **Rome** before heading north to **Florence** (2 days; p. 681) to immerse yourself in Italy's amazing Renaissance art at the Uffizi Gallery. Move to **Venice** (2 days; p. 665) to float through the canals and explore the lagoon islands.

BEST OF ITALY IN 3 WEEKS Begin among the waterways of **Venice** (2 days). Find your Romeo or Juliet in **Verona** (1 day; p. 678). Take a hike in **Lake Como** (1 day; p. 653) before heading to cosmopolitan **Milan** (2 days; p. 646). Move coastward to **Finale Ligure** (1 day; p. 656), and the beautiful **Cinque Terre** (2 days; p. 658). Next, take in the culture of **Florence** (3 days), then cheer on horses in **Siena** (1 day; p. 692). Immerse yourself in the sights and history of **Rome** (3 days), before heading south to **Naples** (2 days; p. 697); be sure to visit preserved, ancient **Pompeii** (1 day; p. 702). Then hike and swim along the **Amalfi Coast** (1 day; p. 703), and see the Grotto Azzura on the island of **Capri** (1 day; p. 704).

ESSENTIALS

WHEN TO GO

Traveling to Italy in late May or early September, when the temperature drops to a comfortable 77°F (25°C), will assure a calmer and cooler vacation. Also keep weather patterns, festival schedules, and tourist congestion in mind. Tourism enters overdrive in June, July, and August: Hotels are booked solid, with prices limited only by the stratosphere. During *Ferragosto*, a national holiday in August, Italians take

their vacations and flock to the coast; northern cities become ghost towns or tourist-infested infernos. Though many visitors find the larger cities enjoyable even during the holiday, most agree that June and July are better months for a trip to Italy.

DOCUMENTS AND FORMALITIES

VISAS. EU citizens do not need a visa. Citizens of Australia, Canada, New Zealand, and the US do not need a visa for stays of up to 90 days, although this three-month period begins upon entry into any of the countries that belong to the EU's freedom of movement zone. For more information, see p. 17.

EMBASSIES. Foreign embassies are in Rome (p. 620). For Italian embassies at home, contact: **Australia,** 12 Grey St., Deakin, Canberra ACT 2600 (☎ 02 6273 3333; www.ambitalia.org.au); **Canada,** 275 Slater St., 21st fl., Ottawa, ON K1P 5H9 (613-

232-2401; www.italyincanada.com); **Ireland,** 63 Northumberland Rd., Dublin (01 660 1744; www.italianembassy.ie); **New Zealand,** 34-38 Grant Rd., Wellington (0064 4473 5339; www.italy-embassy.org.nz); **UK,** 14 Three Kings Yard, London W1K 4EH (020 73 12 22 00; www.embitaly.org.uk); and **US,** 3000 Whitehaven St. NW, Washington, D.C. 20008 (202 612 4400; www.italyemb.org).

 FEATURED ITINERARY: MASTERWORKS OF ITALY

Though many of the original details have faded in Leonardo da Vinci's depiction of *The Last Supper* in **Milan** (Chiesa di Santa Maria della Gratzie, p. 650), its prestige has never diminished. Among **Venice's** masterworks is Veronese's *Rape of Europa.* (Palazzo Ducale, p. 673). A veritable treasure trove or artistic gems, **Florence** is home to Michelangelo's *David* (Accademia, p. 690), Botticelli's *Birth of Venus* (Uffizi, p. 688), and Donatello's *David* (Bargello, p. 689), the first nude since antiquity. St. Francis may have given up his worldly possessions, but his namesake in **Assisi** retains a wealth of beauty; don't miss Giotto's fresco cycle, *The Life of St. Francis* (Basilica di San Francesco, p. 695). **Rome** played host to Michelangelo, ever the renaissance man, who's paintings grace the ceiling of the Sistine Chapel (Vatican, p. 640), and his sculpture *Pietà* resides in the Basilica of St. Peter (Vatican, p. 639). Along with the ruins scattered throughout the south, **Naples** contains both Titian's *Danae* and Bellini's *Transfiguration of Christ* (Museo and Gallerie di Capodimonte, p. 701). A short trip from Naples and Pompeii, **Herculaneum's** House of the Mosaic of Neptune and Anfitrite displays the breathtaking mosaic that gives the structure its name (p. 702).

TRANSPORTATION

BY PLANE. Rome's international airport, known as both Fiumicino and Leonardo da Vinci, is served by most major airlines. Other hubs are Milan's Malpensa or Linate airports and Florence's Amerigo Vespucci airport. Alitalia (US ☎800-223-5730; UK 870 544 8259; www.alitalia.com) is Italy's national airline and may offer low-season youth fares.

BY TRAIN. The Italian State Railway **Ferrovie dello Stato,** or **FS** (national information line ☎147 88 80 88; www.ts-on-line.com), offers inexpensive and efficient service. There are several types of trains: The *locale* stops at every station on a particular line; the *diretto* makes fewer stops than the *locale;* and the *espresso* stops only at major stations. The air-conditioned *rapido,* an InterCity (IC) train, zips along but costs a bit more. Tickets for the fast, pricey **Eurostar** trains require reservations. If you are under 26 and plan to travel extensively in Italy, the **Carta verde** should be your first purchase. The card (€26) is valid for one year and gives a 15% discount on state train fares. **Eurail** is valid without a supplement on all trains except Eurostar. Other railpasses are seldom cost effective since regular fares are cheap. For more info, contact the **Italian State Railways** in the US (☎212-730-2121).

BY BUS. Intercity buses serve countryside points inaccessible by train and occasionally arrive in more convenient places in large towns. For city buses, buy tickets in *tabacchi* or kiosks and validate them once on board to avoid a hefty fine.

BY FERRY. Portside ferries in Bari, Brindisi, and Ancona (p. 697) connect Italy to Greece. Boats from Trieste (p. 679) serve the Istrian Peninsula down to Croatia's Dalmatian Coast. Ferries also connect Italy's islands to the mainland. For Sardinia, boats go from Genoa (p. 655), La Spezia (p. 659), and Naples (p. 697). Travelers to Sicily (p. 705) take the ferry from Naples (p. 697) or Reggio di Calabria.

BY CAR. There are four kinds of roads: *Autostrada* (superhighways; mostly toll-roads); *strade statali* (state roads); *strade provinciali* (provincial); and *strade communali* (local). Driving in Italy is frightening; congested traffic is common in large cities and in the north. On three-lane roads, be aware that the center lane is for passing. **Mopeds** (€30-40 per day) can be a great way to see the islands and the more scenic areas of Italy, but can be disastrous in the rain and on rough roads. Call the **Automobile Club Italiano** (ACI) at ☎ 116 if you break down.

BY BIKE AND BY THUMB. Bicycling is a popular national sport, but bike trails are rare, drivers are often reckless, and, except in the Po Valley, the terrain is challenging. *Let's Go* does not encourage hitchhiking. It can be particularly unsafe in Italy, especially in areas south of Rome or Naples.

TOURIST SERVICES

EMERGENCY	Police: ☎ 112. Ambulance: ☎ 113. Fire: ☎ 115.

TOURIST OFFICES. In provincial capitals, look for the **Ente Provinciale per il Turismo** (EPT) or **Azienda di Promozione Turistica** (APT) for info on the entire province and the town. Local tourist offices, **Informazione e Assistenza ai Turisti** (IAT) and **Azienda Autonoma di Soggiorno e Turismo** (AAST), are generally the most useful. **Italian Government Tourist Board** (ENIT) has offices in: **Australia,** Level 26, 44 Market St., NSW 2000 Sydney (☎ 02 9262 1666); **Canada,** 175 E. Bloor St., #907 South Tower, Toronto, ON M4W 3R8 (416 925 4882); **UK,** 1 Princes St., London WIB 2AY (020 7399 3562); **US,** 630 Fifth Ave., #1565, New York, NY 10111 (212 245 5618). Visit www.enit.it for a comprehensive list of all ENIT locations.

MONEY. On January 1, 2002, the **euro (€)** replaced the **lira** as the unit of currency in Italy. For more information, see p. 20.

BUSINESS HOURS. Nearly everything closes from around 1 to 3 or 4pm for *siesta*. Most museums are open 9am-1pm and 3-6pm; some are open through lunch, however. Monday is often their *giorno di chiusura* (day of closure).

COMMUNICATION

PHONE CODES	Country code: 39. International dialing prefix: 00. The city code must always be dialed, even when calling from within the city. From outside Italy, dial int'l dialing prefix (see inside back cover) + 39 + city code + local number (drop the leading zero). When calling within a city, dial 0 + city code + local number. When *Let's Go* lists ten-digit numbers it denotes a mobile phone and should not be preceeded by the city code.

TELEPHONES. Pre-paid phone cards, available from *tabacchi*, vending machines, and phone card vendors, carry a certain amount of time depending on the card's denomination (€5, €10, or €20). International calls start at €1.05 and vary depending on where you are calling. A collect call is a *contassa a carico del destinatario* or *chiamata collect*. Using your calling card at a hotel phone instead of a pay phone may give you more minutes and save you the surcharge that payphones may add. For info on purchasing and using a **cell phone** in Italy, see p. 35. International direct dial numbers include: **AT&T,** ☎ 172 10 11; **British Telecom,** 172 00 44; **Canada Direct,** 172 10 01; **MCI,** 172 10 22; **Sprint,** 172 18 77; **Telecom New Zealand,** 172 10 64; 172 10 27; **Telstra Australia,** 172 10 61.

MAIL. Airmail letters sent from Australia, North America, or the UK to Italy take anywhere from three to ten days. Since Italian mail is notoriously unreliable, it is usually safer and quicker to send mail priority (*prioritaria*) or registered (*raccomandata*). To send a letter priority costs €0.62 within Europe, €0.80 to the US and Canada, and €1 to Australia and New Zealand. *Fermo Posta* is Italian for *Poste Restante*.

INTERNET ACCESS. Though Italy had initially lagged behind in constructing the information superhighway, it's now playing the catch-up game like a pro. While Internet cafes are still rare in rural and industrial cities, "Internet points" such as bars and even laundromats are becoming common in well-touristed areas. Rates range from €3-7 per hr. For free Internet access, try the local universities and libraries. For a list of Italian cyberspots, check www.cybercaptive.com.

LANGUAGE. Any knowledge of French, Portuguese, Spanish, or Latin will help you understand Italian. The tourist office staff usually speaks some English. For a list of useful Italian phrases, see p. 1063.

ACCOMMODATIONS AND CAMPING

ITALY	❶	❷	❸	❹	❺
ACCOMMODATIONS	under €15	€15-25	€25-40	€40-60	over €60

Associazione Italiana Alberghi per la Gioventù (AIG), the Italian hostel federation, is a Hostelling International (HI) affiliate, though not all Italian hostels (*ostelli per la gioventù*) are part of AIG. A full list is available from most **EPT** and **CTS** offices and online at www.ostellionline.org. Prices start at about €11 per night for dorms. Hostels are the best option for solo travelers (single rooms are relatively scarce in hotels), but curfews, lockouts, distant locations, and less-than-perfect security detract from their appeal. Italian **hotel** rates are set by the state. Hotel owners will need your passport to register you; don't be afraid to hand it over for a while (usually overnight), but ask for it as soon as you think you will need it. Hotel singles (*camera singola*) usually start at around €26-31 per night, and doubles (*camera doppia*) start at €36-42. A room with a private bath (*con bagno*) usually costs 30-50% more. Smaller **pensioni** are often cheaper than hotels. Be sure to confirm the charges before checking in; Italian hotels are notorious for tacking on additional costs at check-out time. The **Azienda di Promozione Turismo** (APT), provides lists of hotels that have paid to be listed; some of the hotels we recommend may not be on the list. **Affitta-camere** (rooms for rent in private houses) are another inexpensive option. For more info, inquire at local tourist offices. There are over 1700 **campsites** in Italy; the **Touring Club Italiano**, C. Italia 10-20122, Milan (☎02 852 61; www.touringclub.it) publishes numerous books and pamphlets on the outdoors. Rates average €4.20 per person or tent, and €3.70 per car.

FOOD AND DRINK

ITALY	❶	❷	❸	❹	❺
FOOD	under €5	€5-10	€10-15	€15-25	over €25

Breakfast in Italy often goes unnoticed; lunch is the main feast of the day. A *pranzo* (full meal) is a true event, consisting of an *antipasto* (appetizer), a *primo* (first course of pasta or soup), a *secondo* (meat or fish), a *contorno* (vegetable side dish), and then finally a *dolce* (dessert or fruit), a *caffè*, and often an after-dinner liqueur. If you don't have a big appetite, you can buy authentic snacks for a picnic at *salumeria* or *alimentari* (meat and grocery shops). A bar is an excellent place to grab a quick bite. They usually offer *panini* (hot and cold sandwiches), drinks with or without alcohol, and *gelato*. Grab a lighter lunch at an inexpensive *tavola calda* (hot table), *rosticceria* (grill), or *gastronomia* (serving hot prepared dishes). *Osterie, trattorie,* and *ristoranti* are, in ascending order, fancier and more expensive. Many restaurants offer a fixed-price tourist menu *(menù turistico)* that includes *primo, secondo,* bread, water, and wine. Italian dinner is typically a lighter meal. In the north, butter and cream sauces dominate, while Rome and central Italy are notoriously spicy regions. Farther south, tomatoes play a significant role. Coffee is another rich and varied focus of Italian life; for a standard cup of *espresso,* request a *caffè; cappuccino* is the breakfast beverage. *Caffè macchiato* (spotted coffee) has a touch of milk, while *latte macchiato* is heavier on the milk and lighter on the coffee. Wines from the north of Italy, such as the Piedmont's *Asti Spumante* or Verona's *Soave,* tend to be heavy and full-bodied; stronger, fruitier wines come from southern Italy. Almost every shop sells Italy's greatest contribution to civilization: *gelato* (ice cream).

HOLIDAYS AND FESTIVALS

Holidays: New Year's Day (Jan. 1); Epiphany (Jan. 6); Easter Sunday and Monday (Apr. 27 and 28); Liberation Day (Apr. 25); Labor Day (May 1); Assumption of the Virgin (Aug. 15); All Saints' Day (Nov. 1); Immaculate Conception (Dec. 8); Christmas Day (Dec. 25); and Santo Stefano (Dec. 26).

Festivals: The most common excuse for a local festival is the celebration of a religious event. Most include parades, music, wine, obscene amounts of food, and boisterousness. Carnevale, a country-wide celebration, is held during the 10 days leading up to Lent. In Venice, costumed revelers fill the streets and canals. During Scoppio del Carro, held in Florence's P. del Duomo on Easter Sunday, Florentines set off a cart of explosives, remembering Pazziano dei Pazzi who returned from the crusades with a few splinters from the holy sepulchre, which he used to light a simple fireworks display. The Spoleto Festival (known as the Festival dei Due Mondi) is one of the world's most prestigious international arts events. Each June and July it features concerts, operas, ballets, film screenings, and modern art shows (www.spoletofestival.it).

FACTS AND FIGURES: ITALY

Official Name: Italian Republic.

Capital: Rome.

Major Cities: Florence, Milan, Naples, Venice.

Population: 58,060,000.

Land Area: 300,000 sq. km.

Time Zone: GMT+1.

Language: Italian; some German, French, and Slovenian.

Religions: Roman Catholic (98%).

ROME (ROMA)

Centuries of sporadic growth transformed Rome from a fledgling city-state to the capital of the Western world. At its zenith, the glory of Rome transcended human imagination and touched upon the divine; from its legendary founding, to the demi-god emperors who reveled in human form, to the modern papacy's global political influence, earthly ideas have proved insufficient to capture the Eternal City. Looking at Rome today, the phrase "decline and fall" seems preposterous—

though Rome no longer dictates the course of Western history, its claim upon the modes of culture remains firmly intact. Style. Art. Food. Passion. These form Rome's new empire, tying the city to the living moment, rather than relegating it to stagnate in a museum case. Today, while the Colosseum crumbles from industrial pollution, Romans celebrate their city. Concerts animate ancient monuments and children play soccer around the Pantheon. In a city that has stood for nearly three thousand years, Rome's glory is not dimmed, merely altered.

⌦ INTERCITY TRANSPORTATION

Flights: da Vinci International Airport (FCO; ☎ 659 51), known as **Fiumicino**, handles most flights. The **Termini line** runs nonstop to Rome's main station, **Stazione Termini** (30min., at :08 and :38 past the hr., €20). After hours, take the blue COTRAL **bus** to Tiburtina from outside the main doors after customs (€5). From Tiburtina, take bus #492 or Metro B to Termini. Most charter flights arrive at **Ciampino** (CIA; ☎ 79 49 41). To get to Rome, take the COTRAL bus (every 30min., €1) to Anagnina station.

Trains: From Stazione Termini to: **Bologna** (2½-3½hr., €26-33); **Florence** (1½-3¾hr., €14-30); **Milan** (4½-8hr., €30-46); **Naples** (2-2½hr., €10-27); **Venice** (5hr., €35-57). Trains arriving in Rome midnight and 5am arrive at **Stazione Tiburtina** or **Stazione Ostiense**, which are connected to Termini by the #175 bus.

⌦ ORIENTATION

Located two blocks north of the **Termini** train station, **Via Nazionale** is the central artery connecting **Piazza della Repubblica** with **Piazza Venezia**, home to the immense wedding-cake-like Vittorio Emanuele II monument. A few blocks west of P. Venezia, **Largo Argentina** marks the start of **Corso Vittorio Emanuele**, which leads to the *centro storico*, a medieval and Renaissance tangle of sights around the **Pantheon, Piazza Navona, Campo dei Fiori**, and **Piazza Farnese**. From P. Venezia, V. dei Fori Imperiale leads southeast to the **Forum** and **Colosseum**, south of which are the ruins of the **Baths of Caracalla** and the **Appian Way**, and the neighborhoods of southern Rome: The Aventine, Testaccio, Ostiense, and EUR. **Via del Corso** stretches from P. Venezia north to **Piazza del Popolo**. To the east, fashionable streets border the **Piazza di Spagna** and, to the northeast, the **Villa Borghese.** South and east are the **Fontana di Trevi, Piazza Barberini, and the Quirinal Hill.** Across the Tiber to the northwest is **Vatican City**, and, to the southwest, **Trastevere**, the best neighborhood for wandering. It is nearly impossible to navigate Rome without a map. Pick up a free map from a tourist office. The invaluable **Roma Metro-Bus map** (€4.13) is available at newsstands or at the ATAC office, V. Volturno 65 (free).

⌦ LOCAL TRANSPORTATION

Public Transportation: The 2 **Metropolitana** subway lines (A and B) meet at Termini and run 5:30am-11:30pm. **Buses** run 6am-midnight (with limited late-night routes); validate your ticket in the machine when you board. Buy tickets (€0.80) at *tabacchi*, newsstands, and station machines; they're valid for 1 metro ride or unlimited bus travel within 75min. of validation. **BIG daily tickets** (€4) and **CIS weekly tickets** (€16) allow for unlimited public transport, including Ostia but not Fiumicino. For a short stay, buy the €11 3-day tourist pass. Be careful; pickpocketing is rampant on buses and trains.

Taxis: Easily located at stands, or flag them down in the street. Ride only in yellow or white taxis, and make sure your taxi has a meter (if not, settle the price before you get in the car). **Surcharges** apply at night (€2.60), on Su (€1), and when heading to or from Fiumicino (€7.25) or Ciampino (€5.50). Fares run about €7.75 from Termini to Vatican City; between city center and Fiumicino around €35.

Rome Overview

Circ. Trionfale
Via Trionfale
Vie. Angelico
Via Trionfale
Viale delle Milizie
Via Lepanto
Via Cesare
LGO. TRIONFALE
Viale Giulio
PIAZZALE DEGLI EROI
V. Andrea Doria
Via Barletta
Via Ottaviano
Via Leone IV
Via Vespasiano
Via Carlo Marto
Via F. Massimo
Via Germanico
Via M. A. Colonna
PIAZZA DI LIBERTÀ
Ponte Regina Margherita
L. Amaldo da Brescia
Ponte Pietro Nenni
Ponte G. Matteotti
Via Flaminia
Viale G. Washingt
Vi
Via Trion
PIAZZA DEL POPOLO
Via del Babuino
Via di Ripetta
Vie. Trit.
Via Margu
Via del Corso
Via di
Via Candia
PIAZZA COLA DI RIENZO
Via Cicerone
Via Cola di Rienzo
Via Crescenzio
PIAZZA CAVOUR
L.d. Mellini
L. in Augusta
Ponte Cavour
PIAZZA AUGUSTO IMPERATORE
Via Condo
Via Frattl
CITTÀ DEL VATICANO
Castel Sant'Angelo
River
L. Prati
L. Marzio
Via d. Scrofa
PIAZZ COLONN.
Saint Peter's Basilica
Via d. Conciliazione
Castello
Ponte S. Angelo
Ponte Umberto I
L. di Tor di Nona
Tiber
Via Vi
PIAZZ
Viale Vaticano
Ponte V. Emanuele II
L. in Sassia
Via dei Coronari
Via d. Zanardelli
V. d. B. di S. Spirito
PIAZZA NAVONA
Corso d. Rinascimento
Via Giustiani
Pantheon
V. d. Seminario
PZA. DELLA ROTONDA
V. Gregorio VII
V. delle Fornaci
Ponte P.A.S. Aosta
PIAZZA DELLA ROVERE
Gianicolense
Corso Vittorio Emanuele II
S. Maria d'Anima
V. Monterone
V. d. Cestari
V. d. Gesù
Torre Argentina
V. d. Plebisc
Via d. Staz. di S. Pietro
Via d. Cava Aurelia
Via Giulia
L. dei Sangallo
Viat Orti d'Alibert
V. d. Monserrato
Palazzo Farnese
V. d. Giubbonari
Via Arenula
Via Botteghe Oscure
Passeggiata di Gianicolo
Via di S. F. di Sales
Ponte Mazzini
L. della Farnesina
L. de Tebaldi
V. d. Pettinari
MONTE DEL GIANICOLO
L. della Lungara
Ponte Sisto
L. dei Vallati
Teatro Marcello
o di Marcello
Via Garibaldi
V. P. Sisto
L. Sanzio
Ponte Garibaldi
Isola Tiberina
L. dei Cenci
L. di Beffecci
N LG
0   500 yards
0   500 meters
Via Garibaldi
PIAZZA S. SONNINO
Ponte Cestio
L. Anguillara
Ponte Palatino
Via Aurelia Antica
Via Luciano Manara
TRASTEVERE
V. d. Genovesi
Aventino
Villa Doria Pamphili
Via di S. Pancrazio
Via Nicola Fabriz
Viale Glorioso
V. G. Induno
V. Anicia
Via di S. Michele
L. Ripa
Via Giacinto Carini
Via Dandolo
Viale di Trastevere
Porto di Pipa Grande
Ponte Sublico
Lungotevere
Via Fonteiana
Via Nicola Fabrizi
v. Ugo Bassi
Via Alessandro Poeria
V. d. Porta Lavernale
Via Vittelia
Via di Villa Pamphili
Viale di Villa Pamphili
Via dei Quattro Venti
L. Portuense
Via Portuense
Lungotevere Testaccio
Via Marmorata
Via di Donna Olimpia
v. Federico Ozanam
Via Giovanni Branca
V. Nicola Zaboaglia
Via Galvani
Parco Testaccio

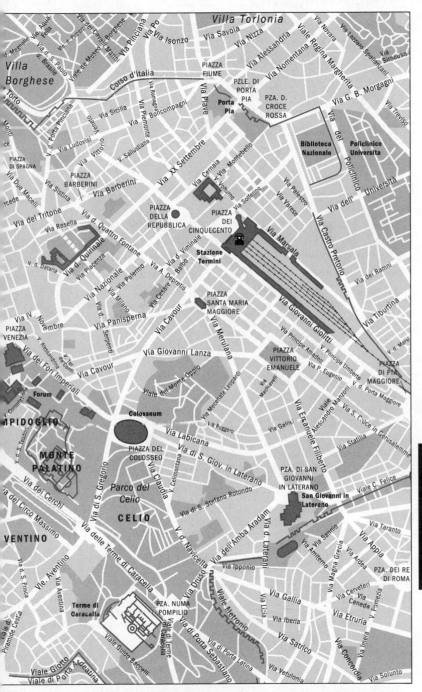

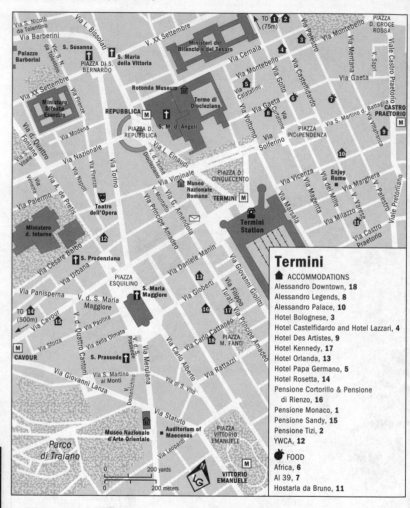

Termini

🏠 ACCOMMODATIONS
Alessandro Downtown, **18**
Alessandro Legends, **8**
Alessandro Palace, **10**
Hotel Bolognese, **3**
Hotel Castelfidardo and Hotel Lazzari, **4**
Hotel Des Artistes, **9**
Hotel Kennedy, **17**
Hotel Orlanda, **13**
Hotel Papa Germano, **5**
Hotel Rosetta, **14**
Pensione Cortorillo & Pensione
 di Rienzo, **16**
Pensione Monaco, **1**
Pensione Sandy, **15**
Pensione Tizi, **2**
YWCA, **12**

🍖 FOOD
Africa, **6**
Al 39, **7**
Hostaria da Bruno, **11**

ITALY

Bike and Moped Rental: Bikes generally cost €3 per hr. or €8 per day, but the length of a "day" varies according to the shop's closing time. In summer, try the stands on V. del Corso at P. di San Lorenzo and V. di Pontifici. Open daily 10am-7pm.

🛈 PRACTICAL INFORMATION

TOURIST, FINANCIAL, AND LOCAL SERVICES

▨ **Tourist Office: Enjoy Rome,** V. Marghera 8/A (☎445 18 43; www.enjoyrome.com). From the middle concourse of Termini, exit right, with the trains behind you; cross V. Marsala and follow V. Marghera 3 blocks. Full-service travel agency books transportation, tours, and lodgings throughout Italy. Open Apr.-Oct. M-F 8:30am-7pm, Sa 8:30am-2pm; Nov.-Mar. M-F 9:30am-6:30pm, Sa 9am-2pm.

Foreign Consulates: Australia, V. Alessandria 215 (☎85 27 21, emergency 800 877 790). Services around the corner at C. Trieste 25. Open M-F 8:30am-noon and 1:30-4:15pm. **Canada,** V. Zara 30 (☎44 59 81; www.canada.it). Open M-F 8:30am-4:30pm. **Ireland,** P. Campitelli 3 (☎697 91 21). Open M-F 10am-12:30pm and 3-4:30pm. **New Zealand,** V. Zara 28 (☎441 71 71; fax 440 29 84). Open M-F 8:30am-12:45pm and 1:45-5pm. **UK,** V. XX Settembre 80/A (☎482 54 41; www.grbr.it). Open M-F 9:15am-1:30pm. **US,** V. Veneto 119/A (☎467 41; www.usembassy.it/mission). Open M-F 8:30am-5:30pm.

American Express: P. di Spagna 38 (☎676 41, lost cards 722 82). Open Aug. M-F 9am-6pm, Sa 9am-12:30pm; Sept.-July M-F 9am-7:30pm, Sa 9am-3pm.

Luggage Storage: In train station Termini, underneath track #24. €3.60.

GLBT Services: Arci-Gay, V. d. Minzoni 18 (☎051 649 30 55; www.arcigay.it). Membership card (€10) gains admission to gay clubs. **Coordinamento Lesbico Italiano,** V. S. Francesco di Sales 1/A (☎686 42 01), off V. d. Lungara in Trastevere. **Circolo Mario Mieli di Cultura Omosessuale,** V. Efeso 2/A (☎541 39 85; www.mariomieli.it). M: B-San Paolo. Walk 1 block to Largo Beato Placido Riccardi, turn left, walk 1½ blocks to V. Corinto, turn right, and walk to V. Efeso. Open Sept.-July M-F 9am-1pm and 2-6pm.

Laundromat: OndaBlu, V. La Mora 7 (☎800 86 13 46). Locations throughout Rome. Wash €3.20 per 6.5kg load; dry €3.20 per 6.5kg load. Open daily 8am-10pm.

EMERGENCY AND COMMUNICATIONS

Emergency: ☎118. **Police:** ☎113. **Carabinieri:** ☎112. **Fire:** ☎115.

24hr. Pharmacies: Farmacia Internazionale, P. Barberini 49 (☎487 11 95). MC/V. **Farmacia Piram,** V. Nazionale 228 (☎488 07 54). MC/V.

Hospitals: International Medical Center, V. Firenze 47 (☎488 23 71, nights and Su 488 40 51). Call first. Paramedic crew on call, referral service to English-speaking doctors. General visit €68. Open M-Sa 8:30am-8pm; on-call 24hr. **Rome-American Hospital,** V. E. Longoni 69 (24hr. service ☎225 51, appointments 22 552 90; www.rah.it). Lab services, HIV tests, and pregnancy tests. No emergency room.

Internet Access: Internet cafes are located throughout the city. **Trevi Internet,** V. d. Lucchesi 31-32 (☎/fax 692 007 99). €2.50 per hr., €4 for 2hr. Open daily 9:30am-10pm. **Splashnet,** V. Varese 33 (☎493 820 73), 3 blocks north of Termini. €1.50 per hr. Open daily in summer 9am-1am; low season 9am-11pm.

Post Office: Main Post Office (Posta Centrale), P. San Silvestro 19 (☎697 663 20). Open M-F 8am-7pm, Sa 8am-1:15pm. **Branch** at V. d. Terme di Diocleziano 30 (☎488 869 20), near Termini.

⌂ ACCOMMODATIONS

Prices vary widely with the time of year, and a proprietor's willingness to negotiate increases with length of stay, number of vacancies, and group size. Termini is swarming with hotel scouts. Many are legitimate and have IDs issued by tourist offices; however, some imposters have fake badges and direct travelers to run-down locations with exorbitant rates, especially at night.

HOTELS BY NEIGHBORHOOD

CENTRO STORICO

If being a bit closer to the sights is worth it to you, then choosing Rome's medieval center over the area near Termini may be worth the higher prices.

ITALY

Via del Corso

TO PIAZZA DEL POPOLO (450m)

TO PZA. DI SPAGNA (300m)

Mausoleum of Augustus

V. Tomacelli
Via dell'Arancio
V. Borghese
PZA. SAN LORENZO IN LUCINA
PZA. DEL PARLAMENTO
V. d. Romano
V. d. Caravia
PIAZZA DI COLLI ROMANO
Via d. Plebiscito
Via d'Asta

V. d. Clementino
V. di Marzio
PIAZZA FIRENZE
V. Rosini
PZA. IN CAMPO MARZIO
Uffici del Vicario
PZA. MONTECITORIO
PIAZZA CAPRANICA
PIAZZA DI PIETRA
Pastini
V. d. Seminario
PIAZZA D. GESÙ

Metastasio
V. d. Maddalena
V. di Pietra
V. d. Pantheon
PIAZZA DELLA ROTONDA
Pantheon
PIAZZA DI MINERVA

Lungotevere Prati
Ponte Cavour
V. Colonna
Via di Monte Brianzo
V. d. Scrofa
Lung. Marzio
V. del Orso
V. d. Scrofa
PZA. S. EUSTACHIO
LGO. TORRE ARGENTINA
V. Torre Argentina
V. d. Rotonda
LGO. ARENULA

Via d. Soldati
Via Zanardelli
PZA. AGOSTINO
Corso de Rinascimento
PIAZZA NAVONA
V. Sediari
Via de Chiavari

PZA. DEI TRIBUNALI
Pte. Umberto
Sant'Agnese in Agone
V. d. Tor Millina
V. Tor Sanguigna
PZA. PASQUINO
LGO. S. PANTALEO
PZA. D. BISCIONE
V. d. Giubbon

Palazzo di Giustizia
PZA. CAVOUR
V. d. Governo Vecchio
DEL FICO
V. di Fossa
della Pace
Corso Vittorio Emanuele II
Via del Pellegrino
CAMPO DE FIORI
PIAZZA FARNESE

PZA. ADRIANA
L. Castello
Fiume Tevere (Tiber River)
Lung. Tor di Nona
Via dei Coronari
Via di Monte Giordano
V. d. Monti
V. PZA. SORA
PZA. CHIESA NUOVA
Via del Cappellari
V. del Monserrato
Palazzo Farnese

Castel Sant'Angelo
Pte. S. Angelo
PZA. CORONARI
V. di Panico
PZA. SFORZA CESARINI
Carini
PZA. S.
Via Giulia
V. Banchi
V. d. Pettinari

L. Vaticano
Pte. V. Emanuele II
L. del Fiorentini
Corso Vittorio Emanuele II
Via d. C. P. Sugorelli
V. d. Giulia
Prigioni
Via Giulia
Villa Farnesina
Lungotevere del Tebaldo

PZA. PAOLI PAOLA
DEL'ORO
LGO. DEI FIORENTINI
Bresciani
V. d. Gonfalone
Scimia
Pte. Mazzini
L. della Farnesina

Borgo Pio
Lung. in Sassia
Pte. Pr. Amadeo Savoia Aosta
L. Sassia
PZA. DE ROVERE
Lungotevere del Sangallo
L. Gianicolense
Via della Lungara
Palazzo Corsini

V. di Conciliazione
Borgo Santo Spirito
Penitenzieri
Borgo
V. d. Orti di Albert
V. d. Mantellate
V. di S. Fr. Di Sales
V. dei Riari

Santo Spirito
PIAZZA PIO
PIAZZA SAN PIETRO
LARGO PORTA CAVALLEGGERI
Parco Gianicolense

ITALY

Monte Gianicolo
V. del Gianicolo
Via

VATICAN CITY
San Pietro
V. Porta Cavalleggeri
Chiesa S. Maria alle Fornaci

V. d. Stazione di San Pietro
PZA. D. STAZIONE DE S. PIETRO
Stazione S. Pietro

Rome: Centro Storico and Trastevere

▲ ACCOMMODATIONS
Albergo della Lunetta, 16
Albergo Pomezia, 17
La Fraterna Domus d Roma, 2
Hotel Carmel, 27
Hotel Trastevere, 26
Santa Maria Alle Forraci, 3

✦ FOOD
Augusto, 20
Bar Da Benito, 18
Bar Giulia, 4
Cul de Sac, 12
Dar Poeta, 19
Giolitti, 6
Pasticceria Ebraica, 23
Pizzeria Baffetto, 8
Pizzeria Corallo, 7
Pizzeria San Callisto, 25
La Taverna del Ghetto, 21
Trattoria Da Giggetto, 22
Trattoria Da Luigi, 10
Trattoria da Settimio all'Arancio, 1
Trattoria dal Cav. Ginc., 5
Zampanò, 15

♪ NIGHTLIFE
Abbey Theatre, 11
Artú Café, 24
Groove, 13
Jonathan's Angels, 9

Orto Botanico
(Botanical Gardens)

Passeggiata
del Gianicolo

TO TRASTEVERE
STATION (1km)

Fiume Tevere (Tiber River)

Circo
Massimo

ITALY

Albergo Pomezia, V. d. Chiavari 13 (☎/fax 686 13 71; www.hotelpomezia.it), off C. V. Emanuele II, behind Sant'Andrea della Valle. 3 floors of recently renovated, clean, and quiet rooms with fans. Breakfast included. Wheelchair-accessible room on the 1st fl. Singles €60-105; doubles €75-125; triples €100-160. AmEx/MC/V. ❹

Albergo della Lunetta, P. d. Paradiso 68 (☎686 10 80; www.albergolunetta.it). The 1st right off V. Chiavari from C. V. Emanuele II. Well-lit rooms; some face a fern-filled courtyard. Great location between Campo dei Fiori and P. Navona. Singles €60, with bath €70; doubles €90/€120; triples €120/€150; quads €150/€180. MC/V. ❺

Hotel "Rosetta," V. Cavour 295 (☎/fax 47 82 30 69). Located just 2 blocks from the Roman Forum, this family-owned hotel offers spacious rooms, each with TV, phone, fan, and bath. Singles €60; doubles €80; triples €90; quads €100. AmEx/MC/V. ❹

NEAR PIAZZA DI SPAGNA

These accommodations might run you a few more euros, but can you really put a price tag on living but a few steps from Prada?

▦**Pensione Panda,** V. della Croce 35 (☎678 01 79; www.hotelpandparadise.com), between P. di Spagna and V. del Corso. Immaculate rooms and arched ceilings. English spoken. Check-out 11am. Mar.-Dec. singles €48, with bath €68; doubles €68/€98; triples with bath €130; quads with bath €170. Jan.-Feb. €6 less. AmEx/MC/V. ❹

Hotel Pensione Suisse S.A.S., V. Gregoriana 54 (☎678 36 49). Turn right at the top of the Spanish Steps. Near the action but not the hubbub. Antique furniture, phone, bath, and fan in every room. Internet available. Breakfast included. Singles €95; doubles €148; triples €198; quads €230. 10-20% discount on long stays Nov.-Feb. MC/V. ❺

Daphne B&B, V. di San Basilio 55 (☎478 235 29; www.daphne-rome.com), off P. Barberini and V. degli Avignonesi. Cell phone rental available. Singles €60-95, with bath €80-120; doubles €70-110/€96-160; triples €90-135/€135-210. AmEx/MC/V. ❹

Hotel Boccaccio, V. d. Boccaccio 25 (☎488 59 62; www.hotelboccaccio.com). M: A-Barberini. Off V. d. Tritone. This quiet, well-situated hotel offers 8 elegantly furnished rooms near many sights. Reception 9am-11pm, late-night access via key. Singles €43; doubles €70, with bath €93; triples €94/€133. AmEx/DC/MC/V. ❹

BORGO AND PRATI (NEAR VATICAN CITY)

While not the cheapest, the *pensioni* near the Vatican have all of the sobriety and quiet that one would expect from an area with this kind of nun-to-tourist ratio.

▦**Colors,** V. Boezio 31 (☎687 40 30; www.colorshotel.com). M: A-Ottaviano, or take a bus to P. Risorgimento. V. Cola di Rienzo to V. Terenzio. 18 beds in rooms painted with a bravado that would put Raphael to shame. Internet €2 per hr. Reservations only for private rooms. Dorms €18-22; doubles €75-90; triples €85-110. Cash only. ❷

Hotel Il San Pietrino, V. G. Bettolo 43, 3rd fl. (☎370 01 32; www.sanpietrino.it) M: Ottaviano. Exit on V. Barletta, walk 3 blocks, and turn left onto V. Bettolo. Friendly staff; spacious rooms have A/C, TV, and Internet. Singles €28-45, with bath €38-48; doubles €48-98; triples €72-125; quads €92-155. AmEx/DC/MC/V. ❸

Pensione Ottaviano, V. Ottaviano 6, 2nd fl. (☎397 381 38; www.ottavianohostel.com). M: Ottaviano. Follow V. Ottaviano toward S. Pietro; hostel is on the left. Simple but roomy dorms in an optimal location. A/C, TV, and Internet. Dorms €12-20; doubles €45-60; triples €50-80. Credit card required for reservations; payment cash only. ❶

Ostello Per La Gioventù Foro Italico (HI), V. delle Olimpiadi 61 (☎323 62 67). M: Ottaviano, then bus #32 to Cadorna. Building holds spacious dorm rooms and large common areas. Dinner €8.50. Flexible 1am curfew. Reception 7am-midnight. Breakfast, sheets, and warm showers included. Dorms €17. Nonmembers add €3. Cash only. ❷

Hotel Lady, V. Germanico 198, 4th fl. (☎324 21 12), between V. F. Massimo and V. Paolo Emilio. 8 rooms, some with ornate ceilings, lack A/C but are cool in summer. Singles without bath €75; doubles €90, with bath €100; triples €120. AmEx/MC/V. ❺

TRASTEVERE

Trastevere is a beautiful old Roman neighborhood famous for its separatism, medieval streets, and pretty-far-from-the-tourist-crowd charm. Hotels here are scattered, most of them too pricey for budget travelers, but the area does offer great nightlife and a location near the Vatican.

Hotel Carmel, V. G. Mameli 11 (☎580 99 21; www.hotelcarmel.it). Take a right onto V. E. Morosini (V. G. Mameli), off V. d. Trastevere. 11 small rooms with bath are a close to central Trastavere. A comfortable sitting room leads to a garden terrace. Breakfast included. Singles €85; doubles €100; triples €140; quads €160. AmEx/MC/V. ●

Hotel Trastevere, V. Luciano Manara 25 (☎581 47 13; fax 588 10 16). From V. d. Trastevere, turn right onto V. d. Fratte di Trastevere, which becomes V. Luciano Manara. Community murals give way to airy rooms with bath, TV, and phone. Breakfast included. Singles €77; doubles €103; triples €130; quads €155. AmEx/DC/MC/V. ●

TERMINI AND SAN LORENZO

Welcome to budget traveler and backpacker central. While Termini is chock-full of traveler's services, use caution in the area south of Termini at night.

▨ **Hotel Papa Germano,** V. Calatafimi 14/A (☎48 69 19; www.hotelpapagermano.com). From the middle concourse of Termini, exit right; turn left onto V. Marsala, which becomes V. Volturno. Clean rooms with TV. English spoken. A/C in dorms €3 per day. Internet €2 per hr. Breakfast €4. Check-out 11am. Dorms €18-22; singles €30-40; doubles €60-72, with bath €70-90; triples €62-78/€78-100. AmEx/MC/V. ●

Hostels Alessandro (www.hostelsalessandro.com). 3 hostels around the Termini station, all offering incredible prices and a fun, knowledgeable staff. Sheets and breakfast included. English, French, Spanish, and German spoken. Reservations are made online or at one of the hostels on the day of arrival. ●

Alessandro Palace, V. Vicenza 42 (☎446 19 58). Exit Termini from track #1. Take a left on V. Marsala, then a right onto V. Vicenza. The Palace houses Alessandro's headquarters, as well as the popular bar and computer lab. 4-person dorms are spacious, each with its own bathroom and A/C. Dorms €18-22; doubles €50-80; triples €60-99; quads €80-120.

Alessandro Downtown, V. C. Cattaneo 23 (☎443 40 147). Exit Termini by track 22, make a left on V. Giolitti, then a right onto V. Cattaneo. Rooms have fan and shared bath. Dorms €15-20; doubles €40-60; quads €68-100.

Alessandro Legends, V. Curatone 12 (☎447 03 217). Farther away from the main streets, provides quieter rooms suitable for families. Private baths and fans. Dorms €19-22; doubles €45-75; quads €80-108. AmEx/MC/V.

Hotel Des Artistes, V. Villafranca 20 (☎445 43 65). From the middle concourse of Termini, exit right, turn left onto V. Marsala, right onto V. Vicenza, and then left onto the 5th cross-street. 3-star hotel with elegant rooms. Free Internet. Breakfast included for rooms with bath, otherwise €12. Singles and doubles €35-155; triples €50-150; quads €90-199. Winter 20-30% less. €10 discount when paying cash. AmEx/MC/V. ●

Hotel Bolognese, V. Palestro 15 (☎/fax 49 00 45). From the middle concourse of Termini, exit right. Walk down V. Marghera and take the 4th left on V. Palestro. This hotel is set apart by the artist-owner's impressive paintings. Some rooms have balcony. Singles €30, with bath €40; doubles €50/€60; triples €60/€75. AmEx/MC/V. ●

VIA XX SETTEMBRE AND ENVIRONS

Dominated by government ministries and private apartments, this area is less noisy and touristy than the nearby Termini.

Pensione Piave, V. Piave 14 (☎474 34 47; www.albergopiave.it). Going north up V. XX Settembre, turn left onto V. Piave. Features key cards, sparkling floors, and modern decor. All rooms with bath, A/C, TV, and phone. Check-in 11:30am. Reservations recommended. Singles €50-75; doubles €70-105. AmEx/MC/V. ●

ITALY

Pensione Tizi, V. Collina 48 (☎482 01 28; fax 474 32 66). A 10min. walk from the station. Go north up V. XX Settembre, and turn left onto V. Servio Tullio, right onto V. Flavia, and left on V. Collina. Or take bus #38 from the train station until the 3rd stop. Marble floors and inlaid ceilings adorn spacious and renovated rooms. Check-out 11am. Singles €45; doubles €60, with bath €70; triples €90; quads €120. Cash only. ❹

Hotel Castelfidardo and **Hotel Lazzari,** V. Castelfidardo 31 (☎446 46 38; www.castelfidardo.com), 2 blocks off V. XX Settembre. From Termini, exit right, cross V. Marsala, and follow V. Marghera. Turn left onto V. Castelfidardo. 3 floors of modern, comfortable rooms. English spoken. Check-out 10:30am. Singles €44, with bath €55; doubles €64/€74; triples €83/€96; quads with bath €110. AmEx/MC/V. ❹

Pensione Monaco, V. Flavia 84 (☎/fax 474 43 35). Go north up V. XX Settembre, turn left onto V. Quintino Sella, and then right onto V. Flavia. Remarkably clean rooms all have bath, A/C, and satellite TV. Lovely courtyard. Check-out 10:30am. Singles €45-65; doubles €75-120; triples €95-105; quads €115-160. 10% discount in winter. ❹

SOUTH AND WEST OF TERMINI

Esquilino (south of Termini) is home to many cheap hotels close to the major sights. The neighborhood west of Termini is slightly more inviting, with busy streets and lots of shopping.

▨ **Pensione Cortorillo,** V. Principe Amedeo 79/A, 5th fl. (☎446 69 34; www.hotelcortorillo.it). Rooms have bath, TV, and A/C; dorms have TV and fan. Breakfast included. Dorms €25; singles €30-70; doubles €40-120. Extra bed €10. AmEx/MC/V. ❸

▨ **Pensione di Rienzo,** V. Principe Amedeo 79/A (☎446 71 31). A family-run retreat with spacious rooms overlooking a courtyard, all with TV and bath, some with balcony. Breakfast €7. Singles €20-50; doubles €30-60, with bath €30-70. AmEx/D/MC/V. ❷

Hotel Kennedy, V. Filippo Turati 62-64 (☎446 53 73; www.hotelkennedy.net). Lounge with leather couches and a large color TV. Private bath, satellite TV, phone, and A/C. Hearty breakfast included. Check-out 11am. Reservations by fax or e-mail only. Singles €60-85; doubles €75-130; triples €90-149. 10% *Let's Go* discount. AmEx/D/MC/V. ❺

Pensione Sandy, V. Cavour 136, 4th fl. (☎488 45 85; www.sandyhostel.com), just past the intersection of V. S. Maria Maggiore. Next door to the Hotel Valle. Free Internet, sheets, and individual lockers (bring a lock) in each room. Simple, hostel-style rooms, usually for 4-8 people. Dorms with bath €12-20. Cash only. ❶

Hotel Orlanda, V. Principe Amedeo 76, 3rd fl. (☎488 01 24; www.hotelorlanda.com). Frequented by Italian businesspeople. Rooms have TV, phone, A/C, and bath. Breakfast included. Check-in noon. Check-out 10am. Singles €30-65, with bath €45-75; doubles €65-105; triples €85-140; quads €100-160. AmEx/MC/V. ❷

OTHER TYPES OF ACCOMMODATIONS

RELIGIOUS HOUSING

Don't automatically think cheap; some religious accommodations run up to €155 for a single. Most are single-sex with curfews, church services, and light chores.

Santa Maria Alle Fornaci, P. S. Maria alle Fornaci 27 (☎393 676 32; ciffornaci@tin.it). Facing St. Peter's Basilica, take a left (through a gate in the basilica walls) onto V. della Fornace. Take the 3rd right onto V. de Gasperi, which leads to P. S. Maria alle Fornaci. This *casa per ferie* has 54 rooms, each with bath and phone. Simple and clean. Breakfast included. No curfew. Singles €50; doubles €80; triples €110. AmEx/MC/V. ❹

La Fraterna Domus di Roma, V. Monte Brianzo 62 (☎688 027 27; domusrm@tin.it). From Ponte Umberto, bear left onto V. Monte Brianzo. Take a right on V. Cancello; the entrance is at V. Cancello 6. Simple rooms, all with bath. A/C €10. Breakfast included. Lunch and dinner €12. Curfew 11pm. Singles €48; doubles €78; triples €98. MC/V. ❹

WOMEN'S HOUSING

YWCA Foyer di Roma, V. C. Balbo 4 (☎ 488 04 60). From Termini, take V. Cavour, turning right onto V. Torino, then left onto V. C. Balbo. The YWCA (known as the *Casa per Studentesse*) is a clean women's hostel. Breakfast included. Curfew midnight. Dorms €26; singles €37, with bath €47; doubles €62/€74. Extra bed €26. Cash only. ❸

🄵 FOOD

Traditional Roman cuisine is not generally ranked among the best in Italy, but the city has excellent restaurants specializing in both regional Italian and international cuisine. Lunch is typically the main meal, although some Romans now eat lunch on the go during the week. Restaurants tend to close between 3 and 7:30pm.

BY NEIGHBORHOOD

ANCIENT CITY

Despite its past glory, this area has yet to discover the noble concept of "affordable food." But along **Via dei Fori Imperiali,** several restaurants offer decent prices.

▨ **I Buoni Amici,** V. Aleardo Aleardi 4 (☎ 70 49 19 93). From the Colosseum, take V. Labicana to V. Merulana. Turn right, then left onto V. A. Aleardi. The food is worth the walk. Choices include the *linguine all'astice* (linguini with lobster sauce; €7). Cover €1. Open M-Sa noon-3pm and 7:30-11:30pm. AmEx/D/MC/V. ❷

Taverna dei Quaranta, V. Claudia 24 (☎ 700 05 50), off P. del Colosseo. Shaded by the trees of Celian Park, outdoor dining at this corner *taverna* is a must. The menu changes weekly and often features the sinfully good *oliva ascolane* (fried olives stuffed with meat; €4). Open daily 12:30-3:30pm and 7:45pm-midnight. AmEx/D/MC/V. ❷

Hostaria da Nerone, V. delle Terme di Tito 96 (☎ 481 79 52). M: B-Colosseo. Take the stairs to the right (with your back to the Colosseum) and walk up to V. N. Salvi. Turn right, and then left onto V. delle Terme di Tito. Outdoor dining near the Colosseum with views of the Baths of Titus. Serves traditional specialties like oven-cooked spring lamb (€13). Pasta €6. Open M-Sa noon-3pm and 7-11pm. Closed Aug. AmEx/D/MC/V. ❷

CENTRO STORICO

The twisting streets of Rome's historic center offer many hidden gems, especially just off the main *piazze*.

▨ **Pizzeria Baffetto,** V. del Governo Vecchio 114 (☎ 686 16 17), at the intersection of V. del Governo Vecchio and V. Sora. Once a meeting place for 60s radicals, Baffetto now overflows with hungry Romans—be prepared to wait a long time for an outdoor table. Pizza €4.50-7.50. Open daily 6:30pm-1am. Cash only. ❷

Trattoria dal Cav. Gino, V. Rosini 4 (☎ 678 34 34), off V. del Campo Marzio across from P. del Parlamente. The very affable Gino will greet you at the door. *Tonnarelli alla ciociala* (€7) is the house specialty. *Primi* €5-7.50. *Secondi* €8-11. Open M-Sa 1-2:45pm and 8-10:30pm. Cash only. ❸

Pizzeria Corallo, V. d. Corallo 10-11 (☎ 683 077 03), off V. del Governo Vecchio near P. del Fico. This *pizzeria* is a great place to grab a cheap, late dinner. Pizzas €4-9. Excellent *primi* pastas €5-7. Open daily 6:30pm-1am. AmEx/DC/MC/V. ❷

CAMPO DEI FIORI AND THE JEWISH GHETTO

▨ **La Taverna del Ghetto,** V. del Portico d'Ottavia 8 (☎ 688 09 771). This lively kosher option offers excellent homemade pasta and sit-down meals. Try the artichoke, a house specialty (€4.50). Cover €1.50. Open M-Th and Sa-Su noon-3pm and 6:30-11pm, F noon-3pm. AmEx/MC/V. ❸

ITALY

▩ **Trattoria Da Luigi,** P. S. Cesarini 24 (☎686 59 46), near Chiesa Nuova. 4 blocks down C. V. Emanuele II from Campo dei Fiori. Enjoy the delicate *carpaccio di salmone fresco con rughetta* (€8). Bread €1. Open Tu-Su noon-3pm and 7pm-midnight. AmEx/MC/V. ❸

Zampanò, P. della Cancelleria 80/83 (☎689 70 80), between C. V. Emanuele II and the Campo. Offers creative pizzas (€7-9) and over 200 wines. *Primi* €7-8. *Secondi* €11-13. Top it all off with a savory dessert (€3.50-7). Open daily noon-2:30pm and 7:30-11pm, closed Tu for lunch. AmEx/MC/V. ❷

Trattoria da Giggetto, V. del Portico d'Ottavia, 21-22 (☎686 11 05). Rightfully famous but increasingly pricey, Giggetto may serve the finest Roman food around. Dare to try the *fritto di cervello d'abbacchino* (brains with vegetables; €12). *Primi* €7.50-10. *Secondi* €11.50-16. Cover €1.50. Open Tu-Su 12:15-3pm and 7:30-11pm; closed the last 2 weeks of July. Dinner reservation required. AmEx/MC/V. ❸

PIAZZA DI SPAGNA

The Spanish Steps may seem very different from the environs of Termini, but there is one big similarity—lousy food. But here, it costs twice as much. Exceptions:

▩ **Trattoria da Settimio all'Arancio,** V. del Arancio 50-52 (☎687 61 19). Take V. dei Condotti from P. di Spagna, the 1st right after V. del Corso, then the 1st left. The less inhibited might try the squid's ink *risotto* (€7.50). Bread €1. *Primi* €7.50-14.50. *Secondi* €8.50-30. Open M-Sa 12:30-3pm and 7:30-11:30pm. AmEx/MC/V. ❸

▩ **PizzaRè,** V. di Ripetta 14 (☎321 14 68). Take V. di Ripetta 1 block away from P. del Popolo. For those looking for a cheap vacation to the south, PizzaRè serves up Neapolitan-style pizza (€6-9.50) as well as regional wines and desserts. The "PizzaRè," with buffalo mozzarella and cherry tomatoes, is a favorite (€9.50). AmEx/MC/V. ❷

Il Brillo Parlante, V. Fontanella 12 (☎324 33 34), near P. del Popolo. The wood-burning oven, fresh ingredients, and excellent wine attract many lunching Italians. Pizza €7-10. Open Tu-Su 12:30pm-1am. MC/V. ❷

Naturist Club Ristorante Bio Vegetariano, V. delle Vite 14, 4th fl. (☎679 25 09). Heading toward P. del Popolo on V. del Corso, turn right on V. delle Vite. A veggie haven with large portions and decent prices. *Primi* €8-9. *Secondi* €7.50-11, salads €5.50. Lunch *menù* €14. Open M-Sa 12:30-3pm and 7:30-11pm. Cash only. ❷

BORGO AND PRATI (NEAR VATICAN CITY)

Establishments near the Vatican serve mediocre sandwiches at hiked-up prices, but just a few blocks northeast, food is much better and reasonably priced.

Cacio e Pepe, V. Giuseppe Avezzana 11 (☎321 72 68). From P. Mazzini, take V. Settembrini to P. dei Martiri di Belfiore, then left on V. Avezzana. Great homemade pasta at low prices; no wonder it's been a neighborhood favorite since 1964. Lunch under €10. Full dinner around €15. M-F 8-11:30pm. Reservations accepted. Cash only. ❷

Franchi, V. Cola di Rienzo 204 (☎687 46 51; www.franchi.it). Delicacies include various croquettes (€1.20), marinated munchies (anchovies, peppers, olives, and salmon, all sold by the kg), and pastas—try the vegetarian lasagna or *cannellini* stuffed with ricotta, spinach, and beef (each €5.90). Open M-Sa 8:15am-9pm. AmEx/MC/V. ❷

"Lo Spuntino" da Guido e Patrizia, V. Borgo Pio 13 (☎687 54 91). There's no sign, but you can recognize it by the men playing cards in the sun. Guido holds court behind a counter filled with all the makings of a beautiful *tavola calda*. A full meal (*primi, secondi,* and unlimited wine) will run less than €8. Open M-Sa 9am-8pm. ❷

San Marco, V. Tacito 27-29 (☎323 55 96), off P. Cavour. San Marco has been dousing hungry Romans with mozzarella for the past 50 years. Perfect Roman crust and fresh toppings €6-12. The conventional pizzas are delicious, or try toppings like smoked swordfish (€9.50). Homemade tiramisu (€4.20) is heavenly. Open daily noon-2am. ❸

TRASTEVERE

The waits are long and the streetside tables are always cramped, but you can't get more Roman than Trastevere.

🍴 **Pizzeria San Calisto,** P. S. Calisto 9/A (☎ 581 82 56), right off P. S. Maria in Trastevere. Simply the best pizza in Rome. Gorgeous thin-crust pizzas so large they hang off the plates (€4.20-7.80). Open Tu-Su 7pm-midnight. MC/V. ❶

Dar Poeta, Vicolo del Bologna 45-46 (☎ 588 05 16; www.darpoeta.it). From P. S. Egidio, head down V. della Scala and turn right. Hardly a tourist in sight. 18 types of *bruschetta* (€2) and unusual pizzas amid old favorites (€4-8.50). Save room for desserts, homemade by the owner's mother (€3.50). Open 7:30pm-1am. AmEx/MC/V. ❶

Augusto, P. de' Renzi 15 (☎ 580 37 98), north of P. S. Maria in Trastevere. Enjoy the daily pasta specials at lunch (around €5), and the *pollo arrosto con patate* (€5.50). The homemade desserts are wonderful. Open M-F 12:30-3pm and 8-11pm, Sa 12:30-3pm. Closed Aug. No reservations. ❶

TERMINI

Tourist traps abound; avoid the torturous €8 "quick lunch" advertised in windows.

🍴 **Africa,** V. Gaeta 26-28 (☎ 494 10 77), near P. Independenza. Excellent Eritrean/Ethiopian food. The meat-filled *sambusas* (€3) are a flavorful starter; both the *zighini beghi* (roasted lamb in a spicy sauce; €7) and the *misto vegetariano* (mixed veggies; €7) make fantastic entrees. Cover €1. Open Tu-Su 8am-1:30am. MC/V. ❷

🍴 **Al 39,** V. Palestro 39/A-41/A (☎ 444 12 13), between the intersection of V. S Martino della Battaglia and V. Gaeta. The locals' lunch joint. Ingredients are fresh, the waiters friendly, and the food a good value. Carnivores should try the specialty, *bistecca Al 39* (€10). Open M-Sa noon-3:30pm and 7pm-midnight. AmEx/MC/V. ❷

Hostaria da Bruno, V. Varese 29 (☎ 49 04 03). From V. Marsala, next to the train station, walk 3 blocks down V. Milazzo and turn right onto V. Varese. Start with the *tortellini con panna e funghi* (with cream and mushrooms; €7). For dessert: the best crepes in town (€3.50). Open M-Sa noon-3:15pm and 7-10:15pm. AmEx/MC/V. ❷

SAN LORENZO

Poor students with discriminating palates in this university district means cheap food and lots of local character. From Termini, walk south on V. Pretoriano to P. Tiburtino, or take bus #492. Avoid walking alone at night.

🍴 **Il Pulcino Ballerino,** V. d. Equi 66-68 (☎ 494 12 55). Take a right off V. Tiburtina. Dishes include *conchiglione al "Moby Dick"* (shells with tuna, cream, and greens; €6.50). Open M-Sa 1-3:30pm and 8pm-midnight. Closed mid-Aug. AmEx/MC/V. ❷

🍴 **Il Tunnel,** V. Arezzo 11 (☎ 442 368 08). From M: B-Bologna, walk down V. delle Province, take the 4th right onto V. Padova, and the 2nd left onto V. Arezzo. A bit of a trek, but all pasta dishes (€4-10) are fresh and the *bistecca alla Fiorentina* is unrivaled in Rome (around €15). Open Tu-Su noon-3pm and 7pm-midnight. Closed Aug. MC/V. ❸

Arancia Blu, V. dei Latini 65 (☎ 445 41 05), off V. Tiburtina. *Tonnarelli con pecorino romano e tartufo* (pasta with sheep cheese and truffles; €6.20) or fried ravioli stuffed with eggplant and smoked *caciocavallo* with pesto sauce (€8.50) make excellent meals. Extensive wine list. Open daily 8:30pm-midnight. MC/V. ❷

TESTACCIO

This working-class southern neighborhood is the center of Roman nightlife, and eateries here offer food made of just about every animal part imaginable.

🍴 **La Cestia,** V. di Piramide Cestia 69 (☎ 574 37 54). M: B-Piramide. Walk across P. di Porta San Paolo to V. di Piramide Cestia; the restaurant is on the right. *Primi* €4.20-8. *Secondi* €6.20-13. Open Tu-Su 12:30-3pm and 7:30-11pm. MC/V. ❸

ITALY

Volpetti Più, V. Alessandro Volta 8 (☎574 43 06). Take a left onto V. A. Volta off V. Marmorata. Join the locals at this authentic *gastronomica* for a quick lunch at one of their self-service tables. Fresh salads (€2.48), pizza (€5.16), and daily specials (from €5). Open M-Sa 10:30am-9:30pm. ❶

DESSERT AND COFFEE

■ **San Crispino,** V. della Panetteria 42 (☎679 39 24), near the Trevi Fountain. Facing the fountain, turn right onto V. Lavatore, and take your 2nd left; it is inset on the right. Crispino is acknowledged as one of the best *gelaterie* in Rome. Every flavor is made from scratch. Cups €1.70-6.30. Open M, W-Th, Su noon-12:30am, F-Sa noon-1:30am.

Giolitti, V. degli Uffici del Vicario 40 (☎699 12 43). 2 blocks north of the Pantheon, find V. della Maddalena and walk to its end; turn right on V. degli Uffici del Vicario. Makes wonderful *gelato* in dozens of flavors (€1.80-3), as well as ices laden with fresh fruit. Festive and crowded at night. Open daily 7am-1am. AmEx/D/MC/V.

Pasticceria Ebraica Boccione, Portico d'Ottavia 1 (☎687 86 37). Little fanfare, just long lines of locals who line up for what they all acknowledge to be the finest pastries in Rome. *Torta Ricotta Vicciole* and *Torta Ricotta Cioccolate* are the most famous of their creations (€10.30 per kg). Open M-Th and Su 8am-8pm, F 8am-5:30pm.

Bar Giulia (a.k.a. Caffè Peru), V. Giulia 84 (☎686 13 10), near P. V. Emanuele II. Giulia serves some of the cheapest (and most delicious) coffee in Rome (€0.70), and they'll add your favorite liqueur at no extra charge. Open M-Sa 4am-9:30pm.

ENOTECHE (WINE BARS)

Roman wine bars range from laid-back and local to chic and international. They often serve excellent food to accompany your bottle.

■ **Bar Da Benito,** V. dei Falegnami 14 (☎686 15 08), off P. Cairoli in the Jewish Ghetto. A *tavola calda* lined with bottles and hungry patrons. Wine from €1; bottles from €5.50. One hot pasta prepared daily (€4.50), along with fresh *secondi* like *prosciutto* with vegetables (€5). Open M-Sa 6:30am-7pm. Closed Aug.

Trimani Wine Bar, V. Cernaia 37/B (☎446 96 30), near Termini, perpendicular to V. Volturno. Rome's oldest wine bar, and probably its most influential. Excellent food includes salads (veggies and smoked cod; €8.50). Wines €2-15 per glass. Happy Hour 11:30am-12:30pm and 4-6:30pm. Open M-Sa 11:30am-12:30am. AmEx/MC/V.

Cul de Sac, P. Pasquino 73 (☎688 010 94), off P. Navona. Specialty pâtés (such as boar and chocolate; €5.60) are exquisite, as is the scrumptious *escargot alla bourguignonne* (€5.10). Open daily noon-4pm and 6pm-12:30am. MC/V.

Enoteca Cavour 313, V. Cavour 313 (☎678 54 96), ashort walk from M: B-Cavour. Wonderful meats and cheeses (€7-9) listed by region or type, fresh salads (€3-7), and rich desserts (€4). Massive wine list (€12.50-300). Open M-Sa 12:30-2:30pm and 7:30pm-1am; kitchen closes 12:30am. Closed Aug. AmEx/DC/MC/V.

◉ SIGHTS

From ancient temples, medieval churches, and Renaissance basilicas to Baroque fountains and contemporary museums, La Città Eterna is a city bursting with masterpieces from every era of Western Civilization. Remember to dress modestly when visiting churches or the Vatican.

ANCIENT CITY

THE COLOSSEUM. This enduring symbol of the Eternal City—a hollowed-out ghost of marble that dwarfs every other ruin in Rome—once held as many as 50,000 spectators. Within 100 days of its opening in AD 80, some 5000 wild beasts

TIME: 3 hr.

DISTANCE: About 3km.

SEASON: Year-round, but spring is best.

A complete tour of the medieval Centro Storico neighborhood.

1 PIAZZA NAVONA. The site of Domitian's stadium, the *piazza* was a special pet project of a number of 17th-century popes. The result was a Baroque masterpiece that today houses Bernini's *Fontana dei Quatto Fiumi* (p. 638) and pushy vendors alike. The Church of Sant'Agnese in Agone (p. 638) is also worth a look, if for nothing else than the saint's head, which is on prominent display.

2 PANTHEON. A 2000-year-old temple currently masquerading under the name "Church of Santa Maria ad Martyres." When the ancient Romans dedicated it to all of the pagan gods, they topped the round temple with the largest masonry dome ever constructed. Enter and marvel at the magnificent structure (p. 638).

3 CHURCH OF SANTA MARIA SOPRA MINERVA. The current structure was built upon (*sopra*) the old Roman temple to Minerva, and is one of the few examples of Gothic architecture in Rome. Under the main altar is the tomb of Catherine de Siena, who convinced the Pope to remove the papacy from wicked, wild France and back to sober, discreet Italy. Other highlights include the final resting place of the artist Fra Angelico and Michelangelo's *Risen Christ*.

4 GALLERIA DORIA PAMPHILJ. Taking V.d. Seminario to the east and a right onto V. Sant'Ignazio will lead you directly to the place where the term "nepotism" was first coined. The Doria Pamphilj's family's relations with Innocent X are largely responsible for the contents of their palace, which can only be described as opulent. Velasquez's painting of Innocent X is one of the finest papal portraits in Rome (p. 642).

5 TREVI FOUNTAIN. All roads lead to this tourist monstrosity. Just face the facts: You'll end up here at some point, bathed in the flashbulbs of thousands of disposable cameras, tossing a coin over your shoulder. If you can, take a moment to enjoy the Neptune Fountain, built into the side of a *palazzo*. A trip to nearby **San Crispino** (p. 634) is reward enough for being a normal tourist for a night.

6 PIAZZA BARBERINI. Bernini's *Fontana del Tritone* is the centerpiece of this square, built for Urban VIII. The fountain is adorned with the same Barberini bees that decorate the bronze canopy in the Vatican. Walking up V. Veneto to the Capuchin Crypt in the Chiesa Santa Maria della Concezione is a spooky (and cool) way to spend a hot afternoon.

7 SPANISH STEPS. Home of all that is Italian chic, the Spanish Steps are host to a number of famous, overpriced cafes, a couple of decent churches (for the materialistic Armani-clad sinners that congregate in the nearby *piazze*), and everything that you need to know about international fashion (p. 639).

WALKING TOUR

perished in the arena (from the Latin word for sand, *harena*, which was put on the floor to absorb blood). The partially-restored floor covers a labyrinth of cells, ramps, and elevators used to transport wild animals from cages up to arena level. Beware the men dressed as gladiators: They want to take a picture with you for €5. *(M: B-Colosseo. Open Mar.-Aug. daily 9am-7:30pm; Oct. 9am-6:30pm; Nov.-Feb. 9am-4pm.)*

THE PALATINE HILL. The best way to attack the Palatine is from the stairs near the Forum's **Arch of Titus.** Throughout the garden complex, terraces provide breathtaking views. Farther down, excavations continue on the 9th-century BC village, the **Casa di Romulo.** To the right of the village is the podium of the 191 BC **Temple of Cybele.** The stairs to the left lead to the **House of Livia,** which is connected to the **House of Augustus** next door. Around the corner, the long **Cryptoporticus** connected Tiberius's palace with the buildings nearby. The path around the House of Augustus leads to the vast ruins of a giant palace which is divided into two wings. The solemn **Domus Augustana** was the private space for the emperors; the adjacent wing, the **Domus Flavia,** once held a gigantic octagonal fountain. Between the Domus Augustana and the Domus Flavia stands the **Palatine Antiquarium,** the museum that houses the artifacts found during the excavations of the Palatine Hill. *(30 people admitted every 20min. starting at 9:10am. Free.)* Outside on the right, the palace's east wing contains the curious **Stadium of Domitian,** or *Hippodrome,* a sunken oval space once surrounded by a colonnade but now decorated with remains of porticoes, statues, and fountains. The **Arch of Constantine** lies between the Colosseum and the Palatine Hill, marking the end of the V. Sacra. One of the best-preserved monuments in the area, it commemorates Constantine's victory over Maxentius at the Milvian Bridge in AD 315. *(The Palatine rises to the south of the Forum. Palatine Hill and the Colosseum €8.)*

ROMAN FORUM. Here, the pre-Romans founded a thatched-hut shantytown in 753 BC. The entrance ramp leads to V. Sacra, Rome's oldest street, near the **Basilica Aemilia,** built in 179 BC, and the area once known as the Civic Forum. Next to the Basilica stands the **Curia** (Senate House); it was converted to a church in AD 630 and restored by Mussolini. The broad space in front of the *Curia* was the **Comitium,** where male citizens came to vote and representatives of the people gathered for public discussion. Bordering the *Comitium* is the large **Rostrum** (speaker's platform) erected by Julius Caesar in 44 BC, just before his death. The **Arch of Septimius Severus,** to the right of the *Rostrum,* was dedicated in AD 203 to celebrate Caesar's victories in the Middle East. The **market square** holds a number of shrines and sacred precincts, including the **Lapis Niger** (Black Stone), where Romulus was supposedly murdered by Republican senators. Below the *Lapis Niger* are the underground ruins of a 6th-century BC altar and the oldest known Latin inscription in Rome. The newest part of the Forum is the **Column of Phocas,** erected in AD 608. The three great temples of the **Lower Forum** have been closed off for excavations; however, the eight columns of the 5th-century BC **Temple of Saturn,** next to the *Rostrum,* have been restored. Around the corner, rows of column bases are all that remain of the **Basilica Julia,** a courthouse built by Julius Caesar in 54 BC. At the far end, three marble columns mark the podium of the recently restored **Temple of Castor and Pollux,** built to celebrate the Roman defeat of the Etruscans. The circular building is the **Temple of Vesta,** where Vestal Virgins tended the city's sacred fire, keeping it lit for more than 1000 years.

In the Upper Forum lies the **House of the Vestal Virgins.** For 30 years, the six virgins who officiated over Vesta's rites lived in seclusion here from the ripe old age of seven. Nearby, V. Sacra runs over the **Cloaca Maxima,** the ancient sewer that still drains water from the otherwise marsh-like valley. V. Sacra continues out of the Forum proper to the Velia and the gargantuan **Basilica of Maxentius.** V. Sacra leads to an exit on the other side of the hill to the Colosseum; the path that crosses before the Arch of Titus heads to the Palatine Hill. *(M: B-Colosseo, or bus to P. Venezia. Main entrance is on V. dei Fori Imperiali, at Largo C. Ricci, between P. Venezia and the Colosseum. Open daily in summer 9am-6:30pm; low season 9am-3:30pm. Guided tour €3.50; audioguide in English, French, German, Italian, Japanese, or Spanish €4.)*

FORI IMPERIALI. Across the street from the Ancient Forum are the **Fori Imperiali,** a conglomeration of temples, basilicas, and public squares constructed in the first and second centuries. Much of the surrounding area is being excavated and is closed to the public, but passersby can still peer over the railing from V. dei Fori Imperiali. Built between AD 107 and 113, the **Forum of Trajan** included a colossal equestrian statue of Trajan and an immense triumphal arch. At one end of the forum, 2500 carved legionnaires march their way up the immaculately preserved ◼**Trajan's Column,** one of the greatest extant specimens of Roman relief-sculpture. The crowning statue is St. Peter, who replaced Trajan in 1588. The gray wall of the **Forum of Augustus** commemorates Augustus's victory over Caesar's murderers in 42 BC. The aptly named **Forum Transitorium** (also called the **Forum of Nerva**) was a narrow space connecting the Forum of Augustus with the Republican Roman Forum. The only remnant of **Vespatian's Forum** is the mosaic-filled **Church of Santi Cosma e Damiano** across V. Cavour, near the Roman Forum. *(Open daily 9am-6:30pm.)*

DOMUS AUREA. This park houses just a portion of Nero's "Golden House," which once covered a huge chunk of Rome. After deciding that he was a god, Nero had architects build a house worthy of his divinity. The forum was reduced to a vestibule of the palace; Nero crowned it with the 35m Colossus, a huge statue of himself as the sun. *(On the Oppian Hill. From the Colosseum, walk up V. della Domus Aurea and make the 1st left. Reservations ☎399 677 00. Open M and W-Su 9am-7:45pm. Groups of 30 admitted every 20min. €5.)*

VELABRUM. The Velabrum is a flood plain south of the Jewish Ghetto. At the bend of V. del Portico d'Ottavia, a shattered pediment and a few ivy-covered columns are all that remain of the once magnificent **Portico d'Ottavia.** The **Teatro di Marcello** next door is named for Augustus's nephew, whose sudden death remains a mystery. Farther down V. di Teatro di Marcello, **Chiesa di San Nicola in Carcere** incorporates Roman temples originally dedicated to Juno, Janus, and Spes. *(☎686 99 72. Open Sept.-July M-Sa 7:30am-noon and 4-7pm.)* Across the street, the **Chiesa di Santa Maria in Cosmedin** harbors beautiful medieval decorations. The Audrey Hepburn film *Roman Holi-*

ROME FOR FREE

So you've got one day left to kill in Rome and have completely maxed out your credit cards and blown your savings. You can either sit in your hostel room sulking or take advantage of the many things Rome offers *da gratis.*

1. A stroll up to the **Colle Oppio** park provides fine views of the Colosseum and contains ruins from the **Domus Aurea.**

2. The **Colosseum,** the grandaddy of Roman sights: Walking around and peering in are free, and also enough to get a sense of its grandeur. Admire the nearby **Arch of Constantine.**

3. The **Roman Forum** displays 2000-year-old ruins, as well as the **Mamertine Prison** where the apostles Peter and Paul were imprisoned. Notice the nearby **Arch of Settimio.**

4. Witness the changing of the guard at the **Tomb of the Unknown Soldier** at the **Monument to Vittorio Emanuele II.** Inside, visit the **Museum of the Italian Renaissance,** housing Italian historical art dating from renaissance times through WWI.

5. Gawk at Michelangelo's **Capitoline Piazza** and **steps.** Enjoy the piazza's copy of the bronze statue, **Marcus Aurelius on Horseback.** View the Roman Forum from the terrace.

6. Finally, on the last Sunday of each month, the **Vatican Museum** and **Sistine Chapel** are free. Visit other **Roman churches** for mosaics, sculptures, paintings, and relics.

day made the portico's relief, the ▨**Bocca della Verità,** famous; according to legend, the hoary face will chomp on the hand of a liar. *(Open daily 9:30am-1pm and 4-7pm. Portico open daily Apr.-Sept. 9am-6:30pm; Oct.-Mar. 9am-5pm.)*

CAPITOLINE HILL. Home to the original capitol, the **Monte Capitolino** still serves as the seat of the city government. Michelangelo designed its **Piazza di Campidoglio,** now home to the **Capitoline Museums** (p. 642). Stairs lead up to the rear of the 7th-century **Chiesa di Santa Maria in Aracoeli.** The gloomy **Mamertine Prison,** consecrated as the **Church of San Pietro in Carcere,** lies down the hill from the back stairs of the Aracoeli. St. Peter, imprisoned here, baptized his captors with the waters that flooded his cell. *(Open daily 9am-12:30pm and 2:30-5:30pm. Donation requested.)* At the far end of the *piazza,* opposite the stairs, lies the turreted **Palazzo dei Senatori,** the home of Rome's mayor. *(To get to the Campidoglio, take any bus that goes to P. Venezia. From P. Venezia, walk around to the right to P. d'Aracoeli, and take the stairs up the hill.)*

CENTRO STORICO

PIAZZA VENEZIA AND VIA DEL CORSO. The **Via del Corso** takes its name from its days as Rome's premier race course, running between P. del Popolo and P. Venezia. **Palazzo Venezia** was one of the first Renaissance *palazzi* built in Rome; Mussolini used it as an office and delivered his orations from its balcony, but today it is little more than a glorified traffic circle dominated by the **Vittorio Emanuele II monument.** Off the northwestern corner of the *piazza* is the **Piazza di Montecitorio,** dominated by Bernini's **Palazzo Montecitorio,** now the seat of the Chamber of Deputies.

THE PANTHEON. Architects still wonder how this 2000-year-old temple was erected; its dome—a perfect half-sphere made of poured concrete without the support of vaults, arches, or ribs—is the largest of its kind. The light that enters the roof was used as a sundial to indicate the passing of the hours and the dates of equinoxes and solstices. In AD 606, it was consecrated as the **Church of Santa Maria ad Martyres.** *(In P. della Rotonda. Open M-Sa 8:30am-7:30pm, Su 9am-6pm. Free.)*

PIAZZA NAVONA. Originally a stadium, the *piazza* once hosted wrestling matches, track and field events, and mock naval battles (in which the stadium was flooded and filled with fleets of convicts). Each of the river god statues in Bernini's **Fountain of the Four Rivers** represents one of the four continents (as known then): the Ganges for Asia, the Danube for Europe, the Nile for Africa (veiled, since the source of the river was unknown), and the Río de la Plata for the Americas. The **Church of Sant'Agnese in Agone** dominates the *piazza*'s western side. *(Open daily 9am-noon and 4-7pm.)*

CAMPO DEI FIORI

Campo dei Fiori lies across C. V. Emanuele II from P. Navona. During papal rule, the area was the site of countless executions; now the only carcasses that litter the *piazza* are the fish in the colorful produce **market** (M-Sa 6am-2pm). South of the Campo lie P. Farnese and the huge, stately **Palazzo Farnese,** the greatest of Rome's Renaissance *palazzi.* To the east of the *palazzo* is the Baroque facade of the **Palazzo Spada** and the collection of the **Galleria Spada** (p. 591).

THE JEWISH GHETTO. The Jewish community in Rome is the oldest in Europe—Israelites came in 161 BC as ambassadors from Judas Maccabei, asking for help against invaders. The Ghetto, the tiny area to which Pope Paul IV confined the Jews in 1555, was closed in 1870 but is still the center of Rome's vibrant Jewish population of 16,000. In the center of the ghetto are **Piazza Mattei** and the 16th-century **Fontana delle Tartarughe.** Nearby is the **Church of Sant'Angelo in Pescheria;** Jews were forced to attend mass here every Sunday and quietly resisted by stuffing their ears with wax. *(Toward the eastern end of V. d. Portico d'Ottavia. Prayer meetings W 5:30pm, Sa 5pm.)*

PIAZZA DI SPAGNA AND ENVIRONS

■ **THE SPANISH STEPS.** Designed by an Italian, funded by the French, named for the Spaniards, occupied by the British, and currently under the sway of American ambassador-at-large Ronald McDonald, the **Scalinata di Spagna** exude an international air. The pink house to the right of the Steps was the site of John Keats's 1821 death; it's now the **Keats-Shelley Memorial Museum.**

■ **FONTANA DI TREVI.** The extravagant **Fontana di Trevi** emerges from the back wall of **Palazzo Poli.** Legend says that a traveler who throws a coin into the fountain is ensured a speedy return to Rome; a traveler who tosses two will fall in love there. Forget about funding your trip with an early morning treasure hunt: Several homeless men were arrested in 2002 and fined €500. Opposite is the Baroque **Chiesa dei Santi Vincenzo e Anastasio,** rebuilt in 1630. The crypt preserves the hearts and lungs of popes from 1590 to 1903. *(Open daily 7:30am-12:30pm and 4-7pm.)*

PIAZZA DEL POPOLO. P. del Popolo, once a favorite venue for public executions, is now the lively "people's square." In the center is the 3200-year-old **Obelisk of Pharaoh Ramses II,** which Augustus brought back as a souvenir from Egypt in the first century BC. Behind an early-Renaissance shell, the **Church of Santa Maria del Popolo** contains Renaissance and Baroque masterpieces. The **Cappella Cerasi** contains two exquisite Caravaggios, *The Conversion of St. Paul* and *Crucifixion of St. Peter.* Raphael designed the **Cappella Chigi** for the Renaissance financier Augustino Chigi.

VILLA BORGHESE. To celebrate his purchase of a cardinalship, Scipione Borghese built the **Villa Borghese** north of P. d. Spagna and V. V. Veneto. Its huge park houses three art museums: world-renowned **Galleria Borghese,** stark **Galleria Nazionale d'Arte Moderna,** and intriguing **Museo Nazionale Etrusco di Villa Giulia.** North of the Borghese are the **Santa Priscilla catacombs.** *(M: A-Spagna and follow the signs. Open M-F 9:30am-6pm, Sa-Su 9:30am-7pm. €8.50.)*

VATICAN CITY

Vatican City is the seat of the Catholic Church and was once the mightiest power in Europe. The nation preserves its independence by running a separate postal system and maintaining an army of Swiss Guards. (M: A-Ottaviano. Alternatively, catch bus #64, 271, or 492 from Termini or Largo Argentina, 62 from P. Barberini, or 23 from Testaccio. ☎69 82.)

BASILICA DI SAN PIETRO (ST. PETER'S). A colonnade by Bernini leads from **Piazza San Pietro** to the church. The **obelisk** in the center is framed by two fountains; stand on the round discs set in the pavement and the quadruple rows of the colonnade will visually resolve into one perfectly aligned row, courtesy of the Reformation popes' battery of architects. Above the colonnade are 140 statues; those on the basilica represent Christ, John the Baptist, and the Apostles (except for Peter, naturally). The pope opens the **Porta Sancta** (Holy Door) every 25 years by knocking in the bricks with a silver hammer; the last opening was in 2000, so don't hold your breath. The basilica itself rests on the reputed site of St. Peter's tomb. To the right, Michelangelo's *Pietà* has been behind bullet-proof glass since 1972, when an axe-wielding fiend smashed Christ's nose and broke Mary's hand. Arnolfo di Cambio's *Peter*, in the central nave of the basilica, was not originally malformed, but centuries' worth of pilgrims rubbing his foot have crippled him. The climb to the top of the **dome** is worth the trip; an elevator will take you up about 300 of the 330 stairs. *(Dress modestly—no shorts, skirts above the knee, sleeveless shirts, or sundresses allowed. Multilingual confession available. Open daily 7am-7pm. Mass M-Sa 9, 10, 11am, noon, 5pm; Su 9, 10:30, 11:30am, 12:10, 1, 4, 5:30pm. Dome: Exit the basilica, and re-enter the door to the far left, with your back to the basilica. Open daily Apr.-Sept. 7am-5:45pm; Oct.-Mar. 7am-4:45pm. €4; elevator €5.)*

▨ SISTINE CHAPEL. Ever since its completion in the 16th century, the **Sistine Chapel** (named for its founder, Pope Sixtus IV) has served as the chamber in which the College of Cardinals elects new popes. Michelangelo's ceiling, at the pinnacle of artistic creation, gleams from its restoration. The simple compositions and vibrant colors hover above, each section depicting a story from Genesis. The scenes are framed by the famous *ignudi* (young nude males). Contrary to legend, Michelangelo did not paint flat on his back, but standing up and craning backward, and he never recovered from the strain to his neck and eyes. *The Last Judgement* fills the altar wall. The figure of Christ as judge hovers in the upper center, surrounded by his saintly entourage and the supplicant Mary. Michelangelo painted himself as a flayed human skin that hangs symbolically between the realms of heaven and hell. The cycle was completed between 1481 and 1483 by a team of artists under Perugino including Botticelli, Ghirlandaio, Roselli, Pinturicchio, Signorelli, and della Gatta. The frescoes on the side walls predate Michelangelo's ceiling; on the right, scenes from the life of Moses complement parallel scenes of Christ's life on the left. *(Admission included with Vatican Museums, p. 642.)*

CASTEL SANT'ANGELO. Built by Hadrian (AD 117-138) as a mausoleum for himself and his family, this mass of brick and stone has served as a fortress, prison, and palace. When the city was wracked with the plague in 590, Pope Gregory the Great saw an angel sheathing his sword at the top of the complex; the plague abated soon after, and the edifice was rededicated to the angel. The fortress offers an incomparable view of Rome and the Vatican. Outside, the marble **Ponte Sant'Angelo,** lined with statues of angels designed by Bernini, is the starting point for the traditional pilgrimage route from St. Peter's to the **Church of San Giovanni in Laterano.** *(Walk along the river with St. Peter's behind you and the towering castle to your left; follow the signs to the entrance. Open Tu-Su 9am-7pm. €5.)*

TRASTEVERE

Right off the **Ponte Garibaldi** stands the statue of the famous dialect poet G. G. Bellie. On V. di Santa Cecilia, behind the cars, through the gate, and beyond the courtyard is the **Basilica di Santa Cecilia in Trastevere;** Carlo Maderno's famous statue of Santa Cecilia lies under the altar. *(Open daily 7am-1pm and 3:30-7pm. Cloister open Tu and Th 10-11:30am, Su 11:30am-noon. Donation requested. Crypt €2.)* From P. Sonnino, V. della Lungaretta leads west to P. S. Maria in Trastevere, home to the **Chiesa di Santa Maria in Trastevere,** built in the 4th century. *(Open M-Sa 9am-5:30pm, Su 8:30-10:30am and noon-5:30pm.)* North of the *piazza* are the Rococo **Galleria Corsini,** V. della Lungara 10, and, across the street, the **Villa Farnesina,** the jewel of Trastevere. Atop the Gianicolo hill is the **Chiesa di San Pietro in Montorio,** built on the spot once believed to be the site of St. Peter's upside-down crucifixion. The church contains del Piombo's *Flagellation*, from designs by Michelangelo. Next door in a small courtyard is Bramante's **▨Tempietto.** Rome's **botanical gardens** contain a **garden for the blind** as well as a rose garden that holds the bush from which all the world's roses are supposedly descended. *(Church and Tempietto open daily 9:30am-12:30pm and 4-6pm.)*

NEAR TERMINI

The sights in this urban part of town are concentrated northwest of the station and to the south, near P. V. Emanuele II.

PIAZZA DEL QUIRINALE. Several blocks south of P. Barberini and northeast of P. Venezia, the statues of Castor and Pollux, Rome's protectors, flank yet another obelisk that served as part of Sixtus V's redecoration plan. The **Chiesa di Sant'Andrea al Quirinale,** full of Bernini's characteristic jolly cherubs, highlights the artist's ability to combine architecture and painting for a single, coherent effect— even if that effect is overdone, as most Baroque work is. *(Open Sept.-July M and W-Su 8am-noon and 4-7pm; Aug. daily 10am-1pm and 3-7pm.)*

BASILICA OF SANTA MARIA MAGGIORE. As one of the five churches in Rome granted extraterritoriality, this basilica, crowning the Esquiline Hill, is officially part of Vatican City. To the right of the altar, a marble slab marks the **tomb of Bernini.** The 14th-century mosaics in the **loggia** recount the story of the August snowfall that showed the pope where to build the church. *(Dress code strictly enforced. Open daily 7am-7pm. Loggia open daily 9:30am-12:30pm. Tickets in souvenir shop €3.)*

SOUTHERN ROME

The area south of the center is a great mix of wealthy and working-class neighborhoods and is home to the city's best nightlife and some of its grandest churches.

CAELIAN HILL. Southeast of the Colosseum, the Caelian, along with the Esquiline, is the biggest of Rome's seven original hills and home to some of the city's greatest chaos. Split into three levels, each from a different era, the **Chiesa di San Clemente** is one of Rome's most intriguing churches. A fresco cycle by Masolino dating from the 1420s graces the **Chapel of Santa Caterina.** *(M: B-Colosseo. Turn left out of the station and walk east on V. Fori Imperiali. Open M-Sa 9am-12:30pm and 3-6pm, Su and holidays 10am-12:30pm and 3-6pm. €3.)* The immense **Chiesa di San Giovanni in Laterano** was the seat of the pope until the 14th century; founded by Constantine in AD 314, it's Rome's oldest Christian basilica. The two golden reliquaries over the altar contain the heads of St. Peter and St. Paul. Across the street is the **Scala Santa,** which houses what are believed to be the 28 steps used by Jesus outside Pontius Pilate's house. *(Dress code enforced. M: A-San Giovanni or bus #16 from Termini. Open daily 7am-7:30pm. €2; museum €1.)*

APPIAN WAY. Since burial inside the city walls was forbidden during ancient times, fashionable Romans made their final resting places along the Appian Way. At the same time, early Christians secretly dug maze-like catacombs under the ashes of their persecutors. *(M: A-San Giovanni. Take bus #218 from P. di S. Giovanni to the intersection of V. Ardeatina and V. delle Sette Chiese.)* **San Callisto,** V. Appia Antica 110, is the largest catacomb in Rome, with nearly 22km of subterranean paths. Its four levels once held 16 popes, St. Cecilia, and 500,000 other Christians. *(Take the private road that runs northeast to the entrance to the catacombs. Open Mar.-Jan. M-Tu and Th-Su 8:30am noon and 2:30 5pm.)* **Santa Domitilla** houses an intact 3rd-century portrait of Christ and the Apostles. *(Facing V. Ardeatina from the exit of S. Callisto, cross the street, and walk up V. d. Sette Chiese. Open Feb.-Dec. M and W-Su 8:30am-noon and 2:30-5pm.)* **San Sebastiano,** V. Appia Antica 136, once held the bodies of Peter and Paul. *(Open Dec.-Oct. M-Sa 9am-noon and 2:30-5pm. Adjacent church open daily 8am-6pm.)*

AVENTINE HILL. The ▓**Roseto Comunale,** Rome's official rose garden, is host to the annual Premio Roma, the worldwide competition for the best blossom. Entries are sent in May. *(V. d. Valle Murcia, across the Circus Maximus from the Palatine Hill. Open daily 8am-7:30pm.)* The nearby **Giardini degli Aranci** is a pleasant place for a stroll. *(Open daily dawn to dusk.)* The 5th-century **Church of Santa Sabina** and its accompanying monastery were home to St. Dominic, Pius V, and St. Thomas Aquinas. *(At the southern end of Parco Savello.)* V. S. Sabina continues along the crest of the hill to **Piazza dei Cavalieri di Malta,** home of the crusading order of the Knights of Malta. Through the ▓**keyhole** in the yellow gate, the dome of St. Peter's is perfectly framed by hedges.

EUR. EUR (AY-oor) is an Italian acronym for the 1942 Universal Exposition of Rome, which Mussolini planned as a showcase of Fascist achievement. The center of the area is **Piazza Guglielmo Marconi.** According to legend, when St. Paul was beheaded at the **Abbazia delle Tre Fontane** (Abbey of the Three Fountains), his head bounced three times, creating a fountain at each bounce. *(M: B-Laurentina. Walk north on V. Laurentina and turn right on V. di Acque Salve; the abbey is at the bottom of the hill. Open daily 8am-1pm and 3-7pm.)*

🏛 MUSEUMS

Etruscans, emperors, popes, and *condottiere* have been busily stuffing Rome full of artwork for several millennia, leaving behind a city teeming with galleries. Museums are generally closed Mondays, Sunday afternoons, and holidays.

VATICAN MUSEUMS. The Vatican Museums contain virtually the entire contents of every art book you've ever seen. The four color-coded routes displayed at the entrance are the only way to see the museums; route C is the most comprehensive. The **Egyptian Museum** contains a small, high-quality sample of Egyptian and pseudo-Egyptian statuary and paintings. The walk through the entire gallery comes out in the **Belvedere Courtyard,** with its gigantic bronze pinecone, and a view of the **Tower of the Winds,** where Queen Christina of Sweden lived briefly before insisting on more comfortable accommodations. The **Pio-Clementine Museum** is the western world's finest collection of antique sculpture and features the Apollo Belvedere. Minor galleries (Candelabra, Tapestries, Maps) abound, and a trip to the Vatican without a sojourn in the 🖂**Raphael Rooms** is no trip at all. The **Stanza della Segnatura** and its companions hold the *School of Athens* and many famous frescoes. The **Pinacoteca,** the Vatican's painting collection, spans eight centuries. *(Walk north from the right-hand side of P. S. Pietro along the wall of Vatican City for about 10 blocks. ☎ 69 88 49 47. Open M-F 8:45am-3:45pm, Sa 8:45am-1:45pm. €10. Free last Su of the month 8:45am-1:45pm. Plan to spend at least 4-5hr.)*

GALLERIA BORGHESE. The exquisite Galleria's **Room I,** on the right, houses Canova's sexy statue of **Paolina Borghese** portrayed as Venus triumphant. The next rooms display the most famous sculptures by Bernini: a magnificent **David,** crouching with his slingshot; **Apollo and Daphne;** the weightless body in **Rape of Proserpina;** and weary-looking Aeneas in **Eneo e Anchise.** Don't miss six **Caravaggio** paintings, including his *Self Portrait as Bacchus* and *St. Jerome,* which grace the side walls. The collection continues in the *pinacoteca* upstairs, accessible from the gardens around the back by a winding staircase. **Room IX** holds Raphael's *Deposition* while Sodoma's *Pietà* graces **Room XII.** Look for self portraits by Bernini, del Conte's *Cleopatra and Lucrezia,* Rubens's *Pianto sul Cristo Morto,* and Titian's *Amor Sacro e Amor Profano. (M: A-Spagna; take the exit labeled "Villa Borghese," walk to the right past the metro stop to V. Muro Torto and then to P. Porta Pinciana; V. del Museo Borghese, ahead, leads to the museum. Open Tu-Su 9am-6pm. Entrance every hr., visits limited to 2hr. €8.50. Audio guide €5.)*

CAPITOLINE MUSEUM. This collection of ancient sculpture is one of the largest in the world. The Palazzo Nuovo contains the original statue of **Marcus Aurelius** that once stood in the center of the *piazza.* The collections continue across the *piazza* in the Palazzo dei Conservatori. See fragments of the **Colossus of Constantine** and the famous **Capitoline Wolf,** an Etruscan statue that has symbolized the city of Rome since antiquity. At the top of the stairs, the **pinacoteca's** masterpieces include Bellini's *Portrait of a Young Man,* Caravaggio's *St. John the Baptist* and *Gypsy Fortune-Teller,* Rubens's *Romulus and Remus Fed by the Wolf,* and Titian's *Baptism of Christ. (On Capitoline Hill behind the Vittorio Emanuele II monument. ☎ 399 678 00. Open Tu-Su 9am-8pm. €7.80. Audioguide €4.)*

OTHER RECOMMENDED COLLECTIONS. Montemartini, Rome's first power plant, was converted to hold displaced sculpture from the Capitoline Museums in the 1990s. *(V. Ostiense 106. M: B-Piramide. Open Tu-Su 9:30am-7pm. €4.20.)* The **Doria Pamphilj** family, whose relations with Pope Innocent X coined the term "nepotism," still owns its stunning private collection. Titian's *Salome* and Velazquez's portrait of Innocent X alone are worth the visit. *(P. del Collegio Romana 2. Open M-W and F-Su 10am-5pm. €8, stu-*

dents and seniors €5.70. Audioguide included.) After overdosing on "artwork" and "culture," get your aesthetic stomach pumped at the one museum dedicated to crime and punishment, the **Museo Criminologico**. Etchings like *A Smith Has His Brains Beaten Out With a Hammer* hang on the walls along with terrorist, spy, and druggie paraphernalia. *(V. del Gonfalone 27. Open Tu-W 9am-1pm, Tu and Th 2:30-6:30pm, F-Sa 9am-1pm. €2; under 18 and over 65 €1.)*

⚡ ENTERTAINMENT

The weekly *Roma C'è* (with a section in English) and *Time Out*, both available at newsstands, have comprehensive and up-to-date club, movie, and event listings.

THEATER AND CINEMA

The **Festival Roma-Europa** in late summer brings a number of world-class acts to Rome (consult www.romace.it for more information), but for year-round performances of classic Italian theater, **Teatro Argentina,** Largo di Torre Argentina 52, is the grand matriarch of all Italian venues. (☎ 688 046 01. Box office open M-F 10am-2pm and 3-7pm, Sa 10am-2pm. Tickets €14-26, depending on performance; students €10-13. AmEx/D/MC/V.) **Teatro Colosseo,** V. Capo d'Africa 5/A, usually features work by foreign playwrights translated into Italian, but also hosts an English theater night. (☎ 700 49 32. M: B-Colosseo. Box office open Sept.-Apr. Tu-Sa 6-9:30pm. Tickets €10-20, students €8.)

Most English-language films are dubbed into Italian; check newspapers or *Roma C'è* for listings with a **v.o.** or **l.o.** These indicate that the film is in the original language. For a sure bet, pay a visit to **Il Pasquino,** P. Sant-Egidio 10, off P. S. Maria in Trastevere. Three screens show a program of English films that changes daily. (☎ 580 36 22. €6.20, students €4.20.)

MUSIC

Founded by Palestrina in the 16th century, the **Accademia Nazionale di Santa Cecilia** remains the best in classical music performances. Concerts are held at the Parco della Musica, V. Pietro di Coubertin 30, near P. del Popolo. (http://www.musicaperroma.it/. Box office open 9am-6pm. Regular season runs Sept.-June. €15, students €8.) **Alexanderplatz Jazz Club,** V. Ostia 9, is the current residence of that *je ne sais quoi* that was expatriate life in Italy during the 50s. Read messages on the wall from old jazz greats. It moves outside to the Villa Celimontana during the summer. (☎ 397 42 171. M: A-Ottaviano, near Vatican City. Required *tessera* €7. Open daily Sept.-May 9pm-2am. Shows start at 10pm.) The **Cornetto Free Music Festival Roma Live** (www.cornettoalgida.it.) has attracted the likes of Pink Floyd and the Backstreet Boys at various venues throughout the city during the summer.

SPECTATOR SPORTS

While other spectator sports may exist in Rome, it's *calcio* (soccer) that brings the scantily-clad fans and the large-scale riots that the world knows and loves. Rome has two teams in Italy's Serie A: **A. S. Roma** and **S. S. Lazio.** Games are played at the Stadio Olimpico in the Foro Italico (M: A-Ottaviano to bus #32). *Tifosi*, as hardcore fans are called, arrive hours or sometimes days ahead of time for big games, to drink, sing, and taunt rivals. Tickets are available at the stadium box office, but they are easier to obtain at the **A. S. Roma Store,** P. Colonna 360. (☎ 678 65 14; www.asroma.it. Open daily 10am-6:30pm. AmEx/MC/V.) Italy is also one of the hosts to the **6 Nations Cup,** Europe's premier Rugby Union tournament. Visitors will find that despite rising interest, good seats are readily available from mid-February through March at the Flaminio Stadium. (Metro A: Flaminio. Then take the #2 tram to the V. Tiziano stop. For more info, visit www.6-nations-rugby.com.)

◻ SHOPPING

Milan might be Italy's fashion hub, but Rome has a sense of style all its own. Check out the sales *(saldi)* in mid-January and mid-July for major deals. A number of boutiques, while not as fashionable as their counterparts on V. dei Condotti, don't require selling a major organ to afford their wares.

BOUTIQUES

Rome's designer shops cluster around the Spanish Steps and V. dei Condotti. Purchases of over €155 at a single store are eligible for a tax refund.

Dolce & Gabbana, V. dei Condotti 52 (☎ 699 249 99). Open M-Sa 10am-7:30pm.

Emporio Armani, V. del Babuino 140 (☎ 360 021 97). Houses the less expensive end of the Armani line. Open M-Sa 10am-7pm.

Gianni Versace, men: V. Borgognona 24-25 (☎ 679 50 37); women: V. Bocca di Leone 25-27 (☎ 678 05 21). Open M-Sa 10am-7pm.

Giorgio Armani, V. dei Condotti 75 (☎ 699 14 60). Same hours as Emporio Armani.

Gucci, V. dei Condotti 8 (☎ 678 93 40). Open Sept.-July M-F 10am-7pm, Sa 10am-2pm; Aug. M 3-7pm.

Prada, V. dei Condotti 92/95 (☎ 679 08 97). Open daily 10am-7pm.

CHEAP AND CHIC

Designer emporiums such as **David Cenci,** V. Campo Marzio 1-7 (☎ 699 06 81; open M 4-8pm, Tu-F 9:30am-1:30pm and 4-8pm, Sa 10am-8pm); **Antonelo & Fabrizio,** C. V. Emanuele 242-243 (☎ 68 80 27 49; open daily in summer 9:30am-1:30pm and 4-8pm; low season 3:30-7:30pm); and **Discount dell'alta Moda,** V. Agostino Depretis 87 (☎ 47 82 56 72; open M 2:30-7:30pm, Tu-Sa 9:30am-7:30pm) stock many lines of designer clothes and shoes—sometimes at half their normal prices.

▨ **Diesel,** V. d. Corso 186 (☎ 678 10 45), off V. d. Condotti. Also at V. d. Babuino 95. *The label in urban European fashion.* Prices are cheaper than elsewhere in the world, so it's worth the visit. Open M-Sa 10:30am-8pm, Su 3:30-8pm.

Mariotti Boutique, V. d. Frezza 20 (☎ 322 71 26). This elegant boutique sells modern, sophisticated clothes in gorgeous fabrics. Prices are steep; watch for significant sales. Open M-F 10am-7pm, Sa 10am-2pm.

Ethic, V. del Corso 85 (☎ 360 021 91), V. d. Pantheon 46, and V. d. Carozze 20. the hip yet less adventurous can find a balance between the avant-garde and the tasteful.

◪ NIGHTLIFE

PUBS

Exactly why the Irish pub became the *de facto* form of Roman nightlife is unclear, but that's the way it is. Rome has more pubs than Dublin, and more are on the way. Not all of Rome's pubs are Irish; some claim to be English, Scottish, American, or Brazilian, and some are distinctly Roman. Nationality is in the eye of the drinker.

▨ **Jonathan's Angels,** V. della Fossa 14-16 (☎ 689 34 26), west of P. Navona. Not since Pope Julius II has there been a case of Roman vanity as severe as that of Jonathan, whose face serves as the theme for the decor in this bar. Medium beer on tap €5. Cocktails/long drinks €8. Open M-F 8pm-3:30am, Sa-Su 6:30pm-3:30am. Cash only.

▨ **Trinity College,** V. del Collegio Romano 6. Off V. del Corso near P. Venezia. Offers degrees in such diverse curricula as Guinness, Harp, and Heineken. Tuition (beer) €5. Happy Hour noon-8pm. Open daily noon-2:30am. AmEx/MC/V.

Shanti, V. dei Conciatori 11. From M: Piramide, go down V. Ostiense and take 2nd street on the right. Great cocktails (€6-7) and hookahs (€2.60 per person). Belly dancing Sept.-Mar. W-F 11pm-1am. Open daily Sept.-June 9pm-1am; July-Aug. M-Sa 9pm-1am.

ITALY

Artù Cafè, Largo Fumasoni Biondi 5. Good selection of drinks. Enjoy specialty cocktails made with fresh juices (€6.20-7.20). Beer €4.50. Wine €3-5.50. Free *apertivi* buffet 6:45-9pm. Open Tu-Su 6pm-2am. MC/V.

Abbey Theatre, V. del Governo Vecchio 51-53 (☎686 13 41). One of the only establishments in Rome where you can drop in for a morning Guinness (€5). Stay for lunch (a lot of vaguely Irish dishes, such as beef in Guinness; €6.50). Happy Hour M-F 3:30-8pm. 40min. Internet access and 1 drink €5. Open daily 11am-3am. AmEx/MC/V.

CLUBS

Although Italian discos can be a flashy, sweaty good time, the scene changes as often as Roman phone numbers. Check *Roma C'è* or *Time Out*. Rome has fewer gay establishments than most cities its size, but those it has are solid and keep late hours. Many gay establishments require an **ARCI-GAY pass** (€10 yearly), available from **Circolo di Cultura Omosessuale Mario Mieli** (☎541 39 85).

Neutra, V. S. Saba 11/A. Uniting the elegant with the eclectic, music (often house or a variant) is selected by resident DJ Giuliano Marchili. Cover men €13, women €10; includes 1 drink. Open Sept.-July Th-Sa 11:30pm-4am.

Classico Village, V. Libetta 3. M: B-Garbatella. Exit onto V. Argonauti and take a left on V. Libetta. Women shouldn't travel alone in this area at night. One of the best-known *centri sociali* in Rome—your one-stop shop for all things counter-cultural. Hosts live music, films, art exhibits, poetry readings, and more. Hours and cover vary (€8-10).

Groove, V. Savelli 10, near Campo dei Fiori. Look for the black door. Lose it to acid jazz, funk, soul, and disco. F-Sa 1-drink min. (€5.16). Open W-Su 10pm-2am. Closed Aug.

Alien, V. Velletri 13-19. This disco attracts a well-dressed crowd. Cover varies (about €15, includes 1 drink; Sa €20). Mostly house, with occasional theme nights. Open Tu-Su 11pm-4:30am. In summer, moves to Gilda on the Beach in Fregene.

Gilda on the Beach, Lungomare di Ponente 11 (☎665 60 649). Operating May 1-Sept. 30, Gilda on the Beach is a favorite among the VIPs and those who normally frequent Alien. 4 dance floors, a private beach, pool, and restaurant are all reasons why Gilda is the place be during the summer. Cover €20. Open 11pm-4am. AmEx/MC/V.

▶ DAYTRIP FROM ROME

PONZA

From Rome, take the train from Termini to Anzio (1hr., 1 per hr., €2.90) and then the Linee Vetor hydrofoil from Anzio to Ponza (1¼hr., €20-23). The ticket office in Anzio is on the quay. (☎984 50 83; www.vetor.it).

As the largest of the Pontine Islands, Ponza was also the one most susceptible to pirate attacks, which were frequent until the arrival of the fierce and wealthy Bourbon monarchs in 1734. The laid-back island lifestyle has resulted in a happy disregard for signs, street names, and maps. *Isole Pontine*, a comprehensive guide to the islands, is available at newsstands for €6.20. Beaches are the reason for the season in Ponza. **Cala dello Schiavone** and **Cala Cecata** (on the bus line) are the best and most accessible spots. The most spectacular views on the island are at **Chiaia di Luna,** a rocky beach set at the bottom of a 200m cliff. Another prime sunbathing spot is the **Piscine Naturale,** just a quick ride through the hillside. Take the bus to Le Foma and ask to be let off at the Piscine. Cross the street and make your way down the steep path. Sea urchins line the rocks, so be careful. A Pro Loco **tourist office** is on V. Molo Musco, at the right of the port in the long red building. (☎07 718 00 31; prolocoponza@libero.it. Open in summer M-Sa 9am-1pm and 4-8:30pm, Su 9am-1pm.)

LOMBARDY (LOMBARDIA)

Ever since the Celts snatched this region from the Etruscans, the fertile land of Lombardy has been under attack. The land has been coveted in turn by the Romans, Goths, French, Spaniards, Austrians, and Corsicans. The disputing powers failed to rob Lombardy of her prosperity, as the region remains the wealthiest in Italy. While Milan may bask in the cosmopolitan spotlight, equally important are the rich culture and beauty of Bergamo, Mantua, and the foothills of the Alps.

MILAN (MILANO)   ☎02

Since its days as capital of the western Roman Empire from AD 286 to 402, Milan (pop. 1,300,000) has embraced modern life more forcefully than any other major Italian city. The pace of life is quick, and *il dolce di far niente* (the sweetness of doing nothing) is an unfamiliar taste. Although Milan's growth has brought petty crime and drugs, the city remains on the cutting edge of finance, fashion, and fun.

▐ TRANSPORTATION

Flights: Malpensa Airport, 45km from town. Handles intercontinental flights. **Malpensa Express** leaves Cadorna metro station for the airport (45min., €9). **Linate Airport,** 7km away, covers domestic and European flights. Take bus #73 from MM1: P. S. Babila (€1). General info for both airports ☎ 748 52 200.

Trains: Stazione Centrale (☎01 478 88 088), in P. Duca d'Aosta on MM2. Trains leave every hr. for: **Bergamo** (1hr., €4); **Florence** (3½hr., €22); **Rome** (7hr., €39); **Turin** (2hr., €8); **Venice** (3hr., €20).

Buses: Stazione Centrale. Intercity buses tend to be less convenient and more expensive than trains. **SAL, SIA, Autostradale,** and other carriers leave from P. Castello and nearby (MM1: Cairoli) for **Bergamo,** the **Lake Country, Trieste,** and **Turin.**

Public Transportation: The **metro** (Metropolitana Milanese, or **MM**) runs 6am-midnight. Use the **bus** system for trips outside the city proper. Metro tickets can also be purchased at station machines. Always keep a few extra tickets, as *tabacchi* close at 8pm and ticket machines can be unreliable. Single-fare tickets €1, 1-day passes €3, 2-day €5.50.

▐ ▐ ORIENTATION AND PRACTICAL INFORMATION

The layout of the city resembles a giant bull's-eye, encircled by a series of ancient concentric city walls. In the outer rings lie suburbs built during the 1950s and 60s to house southern immigrants. Within the inner circle are four central squares: **Piazza Duomo,** at the end of V. Mercanti; **Piazza Cairoli,** near the Castello Sforzesco; **Piazza Cordusio,** connected to Largo Cairoli by V. Dante; and **Piazza San Babila,** the business and fashion district along C. Vittorio Emanuele. The **duomo** and **Galleria Vittorio Emanuele** are roughly at the center of the downtown circle. Radiating from the center are two large parks, the Giardini Pubblici and the Parco Sempione. From the colossal **Stazione Centrale** train station, farther northeast, you can take a scenic ride on bus #60 or the more efficient commute on subway line #3 to the downtown hub, **Via Vito Pisani,** which leads to the mammoth **Piazza della Repubblica,** connects the station to the downtown area.

Tourist Office: APT, V. Marconi 1 (☎ 725 24 300; www.milanoinfotourist.com), in the Palazzo di Turismo in P. Duomo. Pick up the extensive *Milano e Milano* and *Milano Mese* for event info. Open M-Sa 9am-1pm and 2-6pm, Su 9am-1pm and 2-5pm.

Milan

ACCOMMODATIONS
La Cordata, 9
Hotel Aurora, 15
Hotel Cà Grande, 12
Hotel San Tomaso, 16
Hotel Sara, 13
Ostello Piero Rotta (HI), 1
Postello, 2

FOOD
Caffé Vecchia Brera, 5
Il Panino Giusto, 17
Osteria del Binari, 8

★ **NIGHTLIFE**
Alcatraz, 3
Le Biciclette, 7
Hollywood, 4
Maya, 10
Scimmie, 11

Around Stazione Centrale

Milan

ITALY

American Express: V. Larga 4 (☎721 04 010), on the corner of V. Larga and S. Clemente. Handles wire transfers and holds mail (up to 1mo.) for AmEx cardholders. Also **exchanges currency.** Open M-F 9am-5:30pm.

Emergency: ☎118. **Police:** ☎113. **Carabinieri:** ☎112. **Ambulance:** ☎38 83.

Hospital: Ospedale Maggiore di Milano, V. Francesco Sforza 35 (☎550 31).

24hr. Pharmacy: (☎669 07 35). In Stazione Centrale's *galleria.*

Internet Access: Enjoy Internet, V. le Tunisia 11 (☎365 55 805). €2 per hr. Open M-Sa 9am-1am, Su 2pm-midnight.

Post Office: V. Cordusio 4 (☎724 82 223). Address mail to be held as follows: First Name SURNAME, *In Fermo Posta,* Ufficio Postale Centrale di Piazza Cordusio 4, Milano 20100, ITALY. Open M-F 8am-7pm, Sa 8:30am-7pm. **Postal Code:** 20100.

▞ ACCOMMODATIONS

Every season in Milan is high season—except August when many hotels close. A single room in a decent establishment for under €35 is a real find. For the best deals, try the city's southern periphery or the areas south and east of the train station. Women should use caution when traveling alone near the train station at night. When possible, make reservations well ahead of time.

▧ **Hotel Sara,** V. Sacchini 17 (☎20 17 73; www.hotelsara.it). MM1/2: Loreto. Take V. Porpora; V. Sacchini is the 2nd street on the right. Sleek rooms with sparkling windows, bath, and TV. Singles €25-80, depending on A/C; doubles €45-113. AmEx/MC/V. ❹

Hotel Aurora, C. Buenos Aires 18 (☎204 79 60). MM1: Porta Venezia. Exit the station onto C. Buenos Aires. Spotless, modern rooms with phone and TV. Singles €41-46, with shower €46-54; doubles with bath €69-82. AmEx/MC/V. ❹

Ostello Piero Rotta (HI), V. Salmoiraghi 1 (☎392 67 095), northwest of city. MM1: QT8. Turn right facing the white church outside the metro. The hostel will be on the right. Laundry €5.50. 3-night max. stay. Lockout 9:30am-3:30pm. Reserve at www.hostelbooking.com. Closed Dec. 23-Jan. 13. Dorms €18.50. Nonmembers add €3. MC/V. ❷

Hotel Cà Grande, V. Porpora 87 (☎26 14 40 01; www.hotelcagrande.it). MM1/2: Loreto. 6 blocks from P. Loreto in a yellow house. Spotless rooms with TV and phone. Internet €2 per hr. Singles €45, with bath €55; doubles €65/€75. AmEx/MC/V. ❹

La Cordata, V. Burigozzo 11 (☎583 14 675; www.lacordata.it). MM3: Missori. From P. Missori, take the tram 2 stops to Italia S. Lucia, walk same direction for 1 block, and turn right. Whimsical murals cover this hostel which houses mostly college-aged backpackers. 16-bed rooms each have communal bath. Curfew 12:30pm. Dorms €18. ❷

Postello, V. Pergola 5 (☎33 317 522 72). MM2: P. Garibaldi. Go through the train station to the V. Pepe exit, then turn left on V. Pepe and right on V Carmagnola. V. Pergola is 3 blocks ahead. Clean, no-frills dorms. Frequent movies, book talks, and DJ performances in the courtyard, and communal dinners in the coffee shop next door. Free Internet connection (wireless accessibility). Breakfast €2. Dorms and singles €10. ❶

Hotel San Tomaso, V. Tunisia 6, 3rd fl. (☎295 147 47; www.hotelsantomaso.com). MM1: Porta Venezia. From the C. Buenos Aires metro exit, turn left on V. Tunisia. Most rooms have shower or bath. Singles €40; doubles €65; triples €85. AmEx/MC/V. ❸

Camping Città di Milano, V. G. Airaghi 61 (☎482 02 999; www.parcoaquatica.com). MM1 to De Angeli, then bus #72 to S. Romanello Togni. Backtrack 10m and turn right onto V. Tongi. Enter at Aquatica waterpark. Large campground with modern facilities. Laundry €5. Closed Dec.-Jan. €7.50 per person, €6.50-8.50 per tent, €6.50 per car. 2- to 6-person cabins €37-88; deluxe bungalows with bath and A/C €80-120. MC/V. ❶

🔾 FOOD

Like its fine *couture*, Milanese cuisine is often overpriced. Specialties include *risotto alla Milanese* (rice with saffron), *cotoletta alla Milanese* (breaded veal cutlet with lemon), and *osso buco* (shank of lamb, beef, or veal). **Peck**, V. Cantu 3, off V. Orefici near P. Duomo, sells delectables like *foie gras* and Black Forest ham. (Open M 3-7:30pm, Tu-Sa 8:45am-7:30pm.) **PAM** supermarket, V. Piccinni 2, is off C. Buenos Aires. (Open M-Sa 8am-9pm.)

🥙 **Osteria del Binari,** V. Tortona 1 (☎894 09 428). MM2: Porta Genova. Head to the C. Colombo side of P. Stazione Porta Genova. Cross the train tracks to V. Tortona. Binari is the perfect setting for an intimate meal. Unless explicitly refused, a platter of *antipasti* (€7) welcomes guests. *Primi* €10. *Secondi* €12-17. Open M-Sa 8-11pm. MC/V. ❺

🥙 **Trattoria Milanese,** V. S. Marta 11 (☎864 51 991). MM1/3: Duomo. From P. Duomo, take V. Torino; turn right on V. Maurilio and left on V. S. Marta. The *costoletta alla milanese* (breaded rib; €14) is a culinary work of art. *Primi* €5-8. *Secondi* €6-18. Cover €2. Service 11%. Open M and W-Su 12:30-3pm and 7pm-midnight. Closed last 2 weeks of July. AmEx/MC/V. ❸

Caffè Vecchia Brera, V. Dell'Orso 20 (☎864 61 695). MM1: Cordusio. From P. Cordusio take V. Broletto until it becomes V. M. Vetero. This classic spot serves up Parisian chic with an Italian kick. A favorite of the cast of *La Scala,* where crepes range from dreamy desserts to full meals. Service 10%. Crepes €4.50-7. Open daily 8am-2am. ❷

Il Centro Ittico, V. F. Aporti 35 (☎261 43 774). MM2/3: Centrale F. S. A 20min. walk down V. F. Aporti, which runs up the left-hand side of P. Duca d'Aosta. Once a fish market, today it serves the finest of the daily catch. Market prices. *Primi* from €8. *Secondi* from €12. Open M-Sa 12:30-2:30pm and 8pm-midnight. Cover €2.60. MC/V. ❸

Il Panino Giusto, V. Malpighi 3 (☎294 09 297). From MM1: Pta. Venezia, turn onto V. Piave, and then take a left on V. Malpighi. Gourmet sandwiches (€4.50-8) are some of the best in Milan. Open daily noon-12:30am. AmEx/MC/V. ❶

🔾 SIGHTS

🥙 **DUOMO.** The geographical and spiritual center of Milan, the duomo is one of the largest churches in the world. **Gian Galeazzo Visconti** began construction of the duomo in 1386, and it was finally completed at Napoleon's command in 1809. Meanwhile, the cathedral accumulated more than 3400 statues, 135 spires, and 96 gargoyles. Climb (or ride) to the 🥙**roof walkway,** where you'll find turrets and statues with views of the Alps. *(MM1: Duomo. Cathedral open daily Mar.-Oct. 7am-7pm; Nov.-Feb. 9am-4:15pm. Modest dress required. Free. Roof open daily 9am-5pm. €3.50, elevator €5.)*

🥙 **TEATRO ALLA SCALA.** Founded in 1778, La Scala has established Milan as the opera capital of the world. Its understated Neoclassical facade and lavish interior set the stage for premieres of works by Mascagni, Rossini, Puccini, and Verdi, performed by virtuosos like Maria Callas and Enrico Caruso. The theater's renovation was halted amid controversy in 2002, but it is scheduled to reopen in December 2004. *(Through the Galleria Vittorio Emanuele from P. Duomo.)* Visitors can soak up La Scala's historical glow at the **Museo Teatrale alla Scala.** From poster art to a plaster cast of Toscanini's hand, the museum offers a glimpse into the past of opera's premier house. *(C. Magenta 71. MM1: Conciliazione. Open daily 9am-6pm. €5, students €4.)*

■ **PINACOTECA AMBROSIANA.** The 23 palatial rooms of the Ambrosiana display exquisite works from the 14th through 19th centuries, including works by Botticelli, Brueghel, Caravaggio, Raphael, and Titian, and da Vinci. The statue-filled courtyard is also enchanting. *(P. Pio XI 2. Follow V. Spadari off V. Torino and make a left onto V. Cantù. Open Tu-Su 10am-5:30pm. €7.50, under 18 and over 65 €4.50.)*

CASTELLO SFORZESCO. Restored after heavy bomb damage in 1943, the Castello Sforzesco is one of Milan's best-known monuments. Constructed in 1368 as a defense against Venice, it was used as an army barrack, a horse stall, and a storage house before da Vinci converted it into a studio. Inside are the 12 **Musei Civici** (Civic Museums), which include the **Museo Degli Instrumenti Musicali** (Musical Instruments Museum) and the **Museo d'Arte Applicata** (Applied Arts Museum). The ground floor contains a sculpture collection most renowned for Michelangelo's unfinished, angular *Pietà Rondanini* (1564), his last work. *(MM1: Cairoli. Open Tu-Su 9:30am-7:30pm. Combined admission €3.)*

GALLERIA VITTORIO EMANUELE II. Light pours through an immense glass cupola (48m), into an arcade of cafes, shops, and offices. Mosaics adorn floors, walls, and the central octagon's upper portion. Once considered the drawing room of Milan, the statue-filled Galleria is now a mall. Spin on the mosaic bull clockwise three times for good luck, but gyrate in the opposite direction and the luck will go bad. *(On the left, facing the duomo. Open M-Sa 10am-11pm, Su 10am-8pm. Free.)*

CHIESA DI SANTA MARIA DELLA GRAZIE. The church's Gothic nave is dark and elaborately patterned with frescoes, contrasting the splendid, airy Renaissance tribune Bramante added in 1492. Next to the church entrance, in what was once the dining hall, is the **Cenacolo Vinciano** (Vinciano Refectory), home to Leonardo da Vinci's **Last Supper.** Following a 20-year restoration effort, it was re-opened to the public in 1999. Make reservations well in advance or risk missing it. *(P. di S. Maria delle Grazie 2, on C. Magenta, off V. Carducci. MM1: Cadorna Cairoli. Reservations ☎89 42 11 46. Open Tu-Su 8:15am-7pm. €6.50.)*

PINACOTECA DI BRERA. The Brera Art Gallery presents a superb collection of 14th- to 20th-century paintings, with an emphasis on the Lombard School. The collection includes works by Bellini, Caravaggio, Hayez, Mantegna, and Raphael. *(V. Brera 280. MM2: Lanza. Wheelchair accessible. Open daily 8:30am-7:15pm. €5.)*

MUSEO NAZIONALE DELLA SCIENZA E DELLA TECNICA "DA VINCI". This hands-on museum traces the development of technology from the age of Leonardo to the present. The hall of computer technology features an interesting hybrid: a piano converted to a typewriter by Edoardo Hughes of Turin in 1885. The da Vinci room features wooden models of his most innovative inventions. *(V. San Vittore 21, off V. Carducci. MM2: San Ambrogio. Open Tu-F 9:30am-4:50pm, Sa-Su 9:30am-6:20pm. €7.)*

BASILICA DI SANT'AMBROGIO. A prototype for Lombard-Romanesque churches throughout Italy, Sant'Ambrogio is the most influential medieval building in Milan. St. Ambrose once presided over this building from AD 379 to 386. The 4th-century **Cappella di San Vittore in Ciel D'oro,** with exquisite mosaics adorning its cupola, lies through the seventh chapel on the right. The two asymmetrical **bell towers** flanking the facade are not miscalculations but remains of an 8th-century dispute between some Benedictine monks and the church priests. *(MM1: San Ambrogio. Walk up V. G. Carducci, and the church is on the right. Open M-Sa 7:30am-noon and 2:30-7pm, Su 3-7pm. Free. Chapel open Tu-Su 9:30-11:45am and 2:30-6pm. €2.)*

BASILICA DI SANT'EUSTORGIO. Founded in the 4th century to house the bones of the Magi, the church lost its original function when the dead sages were spirited off to Cologne in 1164. The present building, erected in 1278, sports a Lombard-

Gothic interior of brick ribs, low vaults, and substantial columns. The aesthetic pinnacle of the church is the **Portinari Chapel** (1468), attributed to Michelozzo. *(P. S. Eustorigio 3, down C. Ticinese from S. Lorenzo Maggiore. Tram #3. Open M and W-Su 9:30am-noon and 3:30-6pm. Cappella open Tu-Su 10am-6:30pm. €5.)*

GALLERIA D'ARTE MODERNA. Napoleon lived here with Josephine when Milan was the capital of the Napoleonic Kingdom of Italy (1805-1814). The gallery, reminiscent of Versailles, displays modern Lombardian art as well as works by Impressionists. Notable artists include Klee, Modigliani, Morandi, and Picasso. *(V. Palestro 16, in the Villa Reale. MM1/2: Palestro. Currently undergoing restoration. Doors open to the public Tu-Su 9 and 11am only. Free.)* The adjacent **Padiglione D'Arte Contemporanea (PAC),** is an extravaganza of video, photographs, multimedia, and painting. *(Open Tu-Th and Sa-Su 9:30am-5:30pm, F 9:30am-9pm. Free.)*

⬛🔲 SHOPPING AND ENTERTAINMENT

If Milan's status as an international fashion capital has lured you here for shopping, don't despair about the prices. If you can tolerate the stigma of being an entire season behind, purchase your famous designer duds from *blochisti* (wholesale clothing outlets), such as the well-known **Il Salvagente,** V. Bronzetti 16, off C. XXII Marzo. (Bus #60 from MM1: Lima or MM2/3: Stazione Centrale. Open M-Tu 3-7pm, W-Sa 10am-7pm.) Savvy shoppers unearth gems in the shops along **Corso Buenos Aires,** which becomes **Corso Venezia** after MM1: Porta Venezia. The whole city goes on sale during the first week of January and of July. Hard-core window shoppers should head to the world-famous ⬛**fashion district** between **Corso Vittorio Emanuele** near the duomo and **Via Monte Napoleone** off P. San Babila. The dresses come straight from the designers and the selection is more up-to-date than anywhere else in the world, including New York and Tokyo.

Milan Oltre is a festival of drama, dance, and music, held annually in June; call the Ufficio Informazione del Comune (☎86 46 40 94; www.comune.milano.it) for more details. Milan's increasingly popular **Carnevale,** which fills the days preceding Ash Wednesday, is the longest lasting in Italy. The revelry centers around the duomo. Milan's famed tradition and audience enthusiasm makes it one of the best places in the world to see an **opera.** The city's beloved opera house will re-open beginning December 7, 2004. (☎72 023 339; www.teatroallascala.org. Tickets €12-114. Prices reduced at noon the day of a performance. Open daily noon-6pm.)

⬛ NIGHTLIFE

The ⬛**Navigali district** is a particularly popular area for nightlife. Corso di Porta Ticinese is the land of the all-night Happy Hour buffet, where the price of an enormous cocktail (€6-8) also buys dinner.

- ⬛ **Scimmie,** V. Sforza 49 (☎894 02 874; www.scimmie.it). A legendary, energetic bar. Different theme every night and frequent concerts; fusion, jazz, soul, and reggae dominate. Concerts 10:30pm; schedule online. Open daily 8pm-3am.

- ⬛ **Le Biciclette,** V. Conca dei Naviglio 10. A *bici* dangling above the entrance harkens back to the bar's predecessor, a bike shop. Beer and wine €4.50. Mixed Drinks €5.50. Happy Hour buffet 6:30-9:30pm. Open daily 6pm-2am. MC/V.

- **Hollywood,** C. Como 15. Get primped to pout for the bouncer: This disco selects its revellers from the crowd at the door. The mirror in the women's restroom is said to have a view of the men's restroom. Hip-hop, house, and disco. Cover Tu-W €13, Th-Su €16. Women free with student ID before 12:30am. Open Tu-Su 11pm-4am. MC/V.

Alcatraz, V. Valtellina 25. MM2: Porta Garibaldi. Take V. Ferrari and go right on C. Farni. After the train tracks, turn left on V. Valtellina. Biggest club and indoor concert venue in Milan. Cover €14. Open F-Sa 11pm-4am.

Maya, V. A. Sforza 41. Totem poles, funky geometric figures, and entertaining drinks like the *cuccaracha de toro* (€5) fuel the groove. Happy Hour 6-9pm. Open daily 6pm-2am.

MANTUA (MANTOVA)   ☎0376

Mantua (pop. 100,000) owes its literary fame to its celebrated son, the poet Vergil. Its grand *palazzi* and graceful churches come thanks to the Gonzaga family who, after ascending to power in 1328, imported well-known artists to change Mantua's small-town image. Once the largest palace in Europe, the opulent ◪**Palazzo Ducale** towers over **Piazza Sordello,** sheltering the Gothic **Magna Domus** and **Palazzo del Capitano.** Inside, check out a breathtaking array of frescoes, gardens, and facades. Outside the *palazzo,* signs point to the **Castello di San Giorgio** (1390-1406), a formidable fortress before its absorption into the *palazzo* complex. (*Palazzo* open Tu-Su 8:45am-7:15pm. €6.50, students €3.25.) Music lovers first filled the balconies of the **Teatro (Bibiena),** V. Accademia 4, when Mozart inaugurated the building in 1769. (Open Tu-Su 9:30am-12:30pm and 3-5pm. €2.10; students, under 18, or over 60 €1.10.) In the south of the city, down V. P. Amedeo, through P. Veneto, and down Largo Parri, lies the **Palazzo del Te,** built by Giulio Romano in 1534 as a suburban retreat for Federico Gonzaga II. It is widely considered the finest building in the Mannerist style. (Open M 1-6pm, Tu-Su 9am-6pm. €8, students €2.50.) Just south of P. Sordello is the 11th-century Romanesque **Piazza delle Erbe;** opposite the *piazza* is the **Chiesa di Sant'Andrea.** (*Piazza* open daily 10am-12:30pm and 2:30-4:30pm. *Chiesa* open daily 8am-noon and 3-7pm. Both free.)

Trains go from P. Don E. Leoni to Milan (2hr., 10 per day, €8.05) and Verona (40min., 17 per day, €2.30). From the train station, head left on V. Solferino, through P. S. Francesco d'Assisi to V. Fratelli Bandiera, and right on V. Verdi to reach the **tourist office,** P. Mantegna 6, next to Chiesa Sant'Andrea. (☎32 82 53; www.aptmantova.it. Open M-Sa 8:30am-12:30pm and 3-6pm, Su 9:30am-12:30pm.) Charming **Hotel ABC ❸,** P. Don Leoni 25, opposite the station, offers clean rooms and the personal attention of its gregarious owners. (☎32 33 47; www.hotelabcmantova.it. Breakfast included. Singles and doubles €22-77; triples €77-110. MC/V.) **Antica Osteria ai Ranari ❷,** V. Trieste 11, down V. Pomponazzo near Porta Catena, specializes in regional dishes. (☎32 84 31. *Primi* €5-7. *Secondi* €5-11. Cover €1.50. Closed for 3 weeks from late July into Aug. Open Tu-Su noon-2:30pm and 7:30-11:30pm. AmEx/MC/V.) **Postal Code:** 46100.

BERGAMO   ☎035

Bergamo's (pop. 110,000) two sections reflect its colorful history: The *città bassa* (lower city) is a modern metropolis packed with Neoclassical buildings, while the *città alta* (upper city) reveals its origins as a Venetian outpost. Turning left onto V. S. Tomaso and then right on the next street brings you to the **Galleria dell'Accademia Carrara,** which holds works by local greats Botticelli and Lotto, plus Brueghel, van Dyck, Rubens, and Titian. (Open Tu-Su Apr.-Sept. 10am-1pm and 3-6:45pm; Oct.-Mar. 9:30am-1pm and 2:30-5:45pm. €2.60.) From the Galleria, the cobbled **Via Noca** ascends to the medieval *città alta* through the 16th-century **Porta S. Agostino.** Head through the archway near P. Vecchia to P. del Duomo, and see the thickly frescoed **Cappella Colleoni.** (Open Apr.-Oct. daily 9am-12:30pm and 2-6:30pm; Nov.-Mar. Tu-Su 9am-12:30pm and 2:30-4:30pm. Free.) Just left of the Cappella is the ◪**Basilica di Santa Maria Maggiore,** a 12th-century church with an ornate Baroque interior and tapestries depicting Biblical scenes. (Open Apr.-Oct. daily 9am-12:30pm and 2:30-6pm; Nov.-Mar. M-Sa 9am-12:30pm and 2:30-5pm, Su 9am-noon and 3-6pm. Free.)

The train station, bus station, and many budget hotels are in the *città bassa*. **Trains** (1hr., 1 per hr., €3.30) and **buses** (every 30min., €4.20) pull into P. Marconi from Milan. The **airport bus** runs to and from Bergamo's airport, a hub for RyanAir (15min., 5:30am-10:05pm, €1.05). To get to the **tourist office**, Vco. Aquila Nera 2, in the *città alta*, take bus #1a to the top of the *città alta* and walk back down. (☎24 22 26; www.apt.bergamo.it. Open daily 9am-12:30pm and 2-5:30pm.) To get from the train station to **Ostello della Gioventù di Bergamo (HI)** ❶, V. G. Ferraris 1, head to Porta Nuova and take bus #14 to Leonardo da Vinci, then walk up the hill. (☎36 17 24. Internet €5.20 per hr. Dorms €15; singles €21; doubles €20. Nonmembers add €3. MC/V.) **Locanda Caironi** ❷, V. Toretta 6/B, off V. Gorgo Palazzo, is in a quiet neighborhood. Take bus #5 or 7 to V. Angelo Maj. (☎24 30 83. Singles €20; doubles €38. MC/V.) The student-run **Cooperativa Città Alta** ❶, Vco. S. Agata 19, in the *città alta*, serves local favorites like *polenta taragna* (corn pudding with cheese). (☎21 85 68. *Primi* €4. *Secondi* €4-7. Open daily noon-3am.) **Postal Code:** 24122.

THE LAKE COUNTRY

When Italy's monuments and museums start blurring together, escape to the natural beauty of the northern Lake Country, where clear waters lap the encircling mountains. Artistic visionaries like Liszt, Longfellow, and Wordsworth sought rest among the serene shores of the northern lakes. Today, a young crowd descends upon Lake Garda for its watersports by day and thriving club scene at night.

LAKE COMO (LAGO DI COMO)

A heavenly magnificence lingers over the reaches of Europe's deepest lake (410m), peaceful Lake Como. *Bougainvillea* and lavish villas adorn the lake's craggy backdrop, warmed by sunshine and cooled by lakeside breezes. Como, the largest city on the lake, makes an ideal transportation hub. Three lakes form the forked Lake Como, joined at the towns of Centro Lago: Bellagio, Menaggio, and Varenna. These towns are more relaxing than their industrial neighbor, Como.

Trains roll into Stazione San Giovanni (☎0147 88 80 88) from Milan (1hr., every 30min. €4.85) and Venice (4hr., 1 per hr., €22). To get from the train station to the **tourist office**, P. Cavour 16, walk down the steps, turn loft on V. Fratelli Ricchi, and turn right on V. Fratelli Rosselli, which leads to P. Cavour via Lungo Lario Trento. (☎031 26 97 12; www.lakecomo.org. Open M-Sa 9am-1pm and 2:30-6pm, Su 9:30-12;30pm; in winter closed Su.) **Ostello Villa Olmo (HI)** ❶, V. Bellinzona 2, offers cramped but clean rooms at a lakeside location. From the train station, walk 20min. down V. Borgo Vico, which becomes V. Bellinzona. (☎031 57 38 00; hostellocomo@tin.it. Breakfast included. Reception 7-10am and 4-11:30pm. Lockout 10am. Strict curfew 11:30pm. Open Mar-Nov. Dorms €3.50.)

LAKE MAGGIORE (LAGO MAGGIORE)

Lacking the frenzy of its eastern neighbors, Lake Maggiore combines temperate mountain waters with idyllic shores. The romantic town **Stresa** is only 1hr. from Milan by **train** (1 per hr., €4.20). To reach the **tourist office**, P. Martini, exit the station, turn right on V. P. Piemonte, and then left onto V. Genova. Head to the waterfront and turn right. (☎/fax 0323 301 50. Open Mar.-Oct. daily 10am-12:30pm and 3-6:30pm; Nov.-Feb. M-F 10am-12:30pm and 3-6:30pm, Sa 10am-12:30pm.) To reach **Orsola Meublé** ❷, V. Duchessa di Genova 45, turn right from the station, walk downhill to the intersection, and turn left. Rooms have balconies. (☎0323 310 87. Breakfast included. Singles €15, with bath €20; doubles €30/€40. AmEx/MC/V.)

⛴ BORROMEAN ISLANDS. Stresa is a perfect stepping-stone to the gorgeous Borromean Islands. Daily excursion tickets (€9) allow you to hop back and forth between Stresa and the three islands—**Isola Bella, Isola Superiore dei Pescatori,** and **Isola Madre.** The islands boast lush, manicured botanical gardens and elegant villas. The opulent, Baroque **⛴Palazzo e Giardini Borromeo,** on Isola Bella, features six meticulously designed rooms with priceless masterpieces, tapestries, and sculptures. The 10 terraced gardens are punctuated with statues of the gods and topped by one of a unicorn. (Open daily Mar.-Sept. 9am-6pm; Oct. 9am-5pm. €9.)

LAKE GARDA (LAGO DI GARDA)

Garda has staggering mountains and breezy summers. **Desenzano,** the lake's southern transport hub, is only 30min. from Verona, 1hr. from Milan, and 2hr. from Venice. Sirmione and Gardone Riviera, easily accessible by bus and boat, are best explored as daytrips; accommodations are scant and pricey.

SIRMIONE. Exploring Sirmione's 13th-century castle and Roman ruins can fill a leisurely day or a busy afternoon. **Buses** run every hour from Verona (1hr., €2.90). **Ferries** run until 8pm to: Desenzano (20min., €2.60); Gardone (1¼-2hr., €5.50-8); and Riva (2-4hr., €8-11.30). The **tourist office,** V. Guglielmo Marconi 2, is in the disc-shaped building. (☎030 91 61 14; www.comune.sirmione.bs.it. Open Apr.-Oct. daily 9am-9pm; Nov.-Mar. M-F 9am-12:30pm and 3-6pm.) The **Albergo Grifone ❸,** V. Bocchio 4, has country-style rooms with bath and lake views. (☎030 91 60 14; fax 91 65 48. Reserve ahead. Singles €36; doubles €55.) **Postal Code:** 25019.

RIVA DEL GARDA. Riva's calm pebble beaches are Lake Garda's compromise for the budget traveler put off by steep local prices. Visitors **swim, windsurf, hike,** and **climb** near the most stunning portion of the lake, where cliffs crash into the sea. Riva is accessible by **bus** (☎0464 55 23 23) from Trent (1½hr., 20 per day, €3.20) and Verona (2hr., 14 per day, €5). **Ferries** (☎030 914 95 11) leave from P. Matteoti for Gardone (1½-3hr., €6.60). The **tourist office** is at Giardini di Porta Orientale 8. (☎0464 55 44 44; www.gardatrentino.it. Open M-Sa 9am-noon and 3-6pm, Su 10am-noon and 4-6:30pm.) Sleep at **Locanda La Montanara ❷,** V. Montanara 20, off V. Florida. (☎0464 55 48 57. Singles €17; doubles €32-36; triples €49.) **Postal Code:** 38066.

ITALIAN RIVIERA (LIGURIA)

The Italian Riviera stretches 350km along the Mediterranean between France and Tuscany, forming the most famous and most touristed area of the Italian coastline. Genoa divides the crescent-shaped strip into the Riviera di Levante ("Rising Sun") to the east and the Riviera di Ponente ("Setting Sun") to the west. The elegant coast beckons with lemon trees, almond blossoms, and turquoise seas. Especially lovely is the Cinque Terre area (p. 658), just to the west of La Spezia (p. 659).

The coastal towns are linked by the main rail line, which runs west to Ventimiglia (near the French border) and east to La Spezia (near Tuscany), but slow local trains can make short trips take hours. Frequent intercity buses pass through all major towns, and local buses run to inland hill-towns. Boats connect most resort towns. **Ferries** go from Genoa to Olbia, Sardinia and Palermo, Sicily.

GENOA (GENOVA)

☎010

Genoa (pop. 640,000), city of grit and grandeur, has little in common with its resort neighbors. A Ligurian will tell you, *"Si deve conoscerla per amarla"* (you have to know her to love her). While lacking the intimacy of a small-town resort, Genoa more than makes up for it with its rich cultural history and extravagant sights. Since falling into decline in the 18th century, modern Genoa has turned its attention from industry and trade to the restoration of its bygone splendor, and it is once again claiming its position among Italy's most important cultural centers.

⊟⚐ TRANSPORTATION AND PRACTICAL INFORMATION. C. Columbo Internazionale airport (GOA), in Sesti Ponente, services European destinations. Take **Volabus #100** from Stazione Brignole to the airport (every 30min., €2) and get off at Aeroporto. Most visitors arrive at one of Genoa's two **train stations: Stazione Principe**, in P. Acquaverde, or **Stazione Brignole**, in P. Verdi. **Trains** go to Rome (5-6hr., 12 per day, €33) and Turin (2hr., 19 per day, €8-12). AMT **buses** (☎558 24 14) run throughout the city. One-way tickets (€1) are valid for 1½hr.; all-day passes cost €3. **Ferries** depart from the Ponte Assereto section of the port; buy tickets in the port at the **Stazione Marittima**. The **tourist office** is on Porto Antico, in Palazzina S. Maria. From the aquarium, walk toward the complex of buildings to the left. (☎57 67 91; www.genovatouristboard.net. Open M-Sa 9am-1pm and 2-6pm.) Log on to the **Internet** at **Point Nondove**, C. Buenos Ayres 2. (☎58 99 90. €2 per 15min. Open M-Sa 9:30am-7:30pm.) **Postal Code:** 16121.

⚑ ORIENTATION. To get to the center of town, **Piazza de Ferrari**, from Stazione Principe, take **Via Balbi** to **Via Cairoli**, which becomes **Via Garibaldi**, and turn right on **Via XXV Aprile** at P. delle Fontane Marose. From Stazione Brignole, turn right onto **Via Fiume**, and right onto **Via XX Settembre**. Or, take bus #18, 19, or 20 from Stazione Principe, or bus #19 or 40 from Stazione Brignole, to P. de Ferrari in the center of town. The **centro storico** (historic center) contains many of Genoa's monuments.

⚏⛭ ACCOMMODATIONS AND FOOD. ▨Ostello per la Gioventù (HI) ❶, V. Costanzi 120, has a cafeteria, TV, and a view of the city far below. From Stazione Principe, take bus #35 to V. Napoli and transfer to #40, which runs to the hostel. From Stazione Brignole, pick up bus #40 (every 15min.) and ask to be let off at the *ostello*. (☎242 24 57; www.geocities.com/hostelge. Breakfast included. No curfew. HI members only. Dorms €14.50.) **Albergo Carola ❸**, V. Gropallo 4/12, offers meticulously decorated, comfortable rooms, some of which overlook a private garden. (☎839 13 40; albergocarola@libero.it. Singles €28; doubles €52, with bath €55; triples €60/€70; quads €70/€80. Cash only.) **Camping** is popular; check the tourist office for availability, or try **Genova Est ❶**, on V. Marcon Loc Cassa. Take the train from Stazione Brignole to the suburb of Bogliasco (10min., 6 per day, €1); a free van (5min., every 2hr. 8:10am-6pm) will take you from Bogliasco to the campsite. (☎347 20 53; www.camping-genova-est.it. Laundry €3.50 per load. Electricity €1.80 per day. €5.45 per person, €9.60 per tent.) **▨Trattoria da Maria ❷**, V. Testa d'Oro 14r, off V. XXV Aprile, has new selections daily. (☎58 10 80. *Menù* €10. Open M-F and Su noon-2:30pm and 7-9:30pm.)

⛭⛴ SIGHTS AND ENTERTAINMENT. Genoa boasts a multitude of *palazzi* built by its famous merchant families. These are best seen along **Via Garibaldi**, on the edge of *centro storico*, and **Via Balbi**, in the heart of the university quarter. The 17th-century **Palazzo Reale**, V. Balbi 10, 10min. west of V. Garibaldi, is filled with Rococo rooms bathed in gold and upholstered in red velvet. (Open Th-Su 9am-7pm, Tu-W 9am-1:30pm. €4, ages 18-25 €2, under 18 and seniors free.) Follow V. Balbi through P.

LIGHT MY FIRE

It is the clichéd plot of so many movies: Things begin to go wrong, machines turn against humans, and all assume that evil is involved, although no one knows how or why.

Last year, this classic horror film story line became a reality for the small Sicilian village of Canneto di Caronia, whose 150 residents became plagued with a series of unexplainable fires. Fuse boxes, refrigerators, televisions, and even a pile of wedding presents spontaneously combusted, with fires breaking out in over a dozen homes within a span of two months. Strangely, the outbreaks continued even after the town's power supply was cut off. To add to the terror, other machines started to act up: cell phones would ring when no one was calling, computers began to jam, and cars would lock out their owners.

Faced with no other options, the town evacuated, as a team of scientists came in to investigate. After testing every hypothesis, there was still no definitive explanation for the outbreak, although a buildup of static charges was the leading theory.

After a four-month evacuation, villagers finally returned, hopeful that the fires had ended. Many residents reluctantly accepted the theories offered by the scientists, who weren't totally confident themselves, while others, insisting that evil was at play in the town, have threatened to bring in an exorcist at the next spark.

della Nunziata and continue to L. Zecca, where V. Cairoli leads to **Via Garibaldi,** the most impressive street in Genoa, bedecked with elegant *palazzi* that once earned it the names "Golden Street" and "Street of Kings." The **Galleria di Palazzo Bianco,** V. Garibaldi 11, exhibits Ligurian, Dutch, and Flemish paintings. Across the street, the 17th-century **Galleria Palazzo Rosso,** V. Garibaldi 18, has a lavishly frescoed interior. (Both open Tu-Sa 9am-7pm, Su 10am-6pm. One gallery €3.10, €5.20 for both. Su free.) From P. de Ferrari, take V. Boetto to P. Matteotti for the ornate **Chiesa di Gesù.** (Open daily 7:15am-12:30pm and 4-7:30pm. Closed during Su mass. Free.) Head past the Chiesa di Gesù down V. di Porta Soprana to V. Ravecca to reach the medieval twin-towered **Porta Soprana,** the supposed boyhood home of **Christopher Columbus.** Off V. S. Lorenzo lies the **San Lorenzo Duomo,** a church in existence since the 9th century, which boasts a striped Gothic facade with a copiously decorated main entrance. (Modest dress required. Open M-Sa 8am-7pm, Su 7am-7pm. Free.) The **centro storico,** the eerie and beautiful historical center bordered by the port, V. Garibaldi, and P. Ferrari, is a mass of winding and confusing streets containing some of Genoa's most memorable monuments, including the **duomo** and the medieval **Torre Embraici.** However, a dangerous night scene makes visits to the *centro storico* best confined to weekdays when stores are open. From P. Matteotti, go down V. S. Lorenzo toward the water, turn left on V. Chiabrera and left on V. di Mascherona to reach the **Chiesa S. Maria di Castello,** a labyrinth of chapels, courtyards, cloisters, and crucifixes. (Open daily 9am-noon and 3-6pm. Closed Su during mass. Free.) Kids and ocean-lovers will adore the **aquarium** on Porto Antico, just right of the APT tourist office. (Open July-Aug. daily 9:30am-11pm; Sept.-June M-W and F 9:30am-7:30pm. €13.)

RIVIERA DI PONENTE

FINALE LIGURE   ☎019

A beachside plaque proclaims the town of Finale Ligure (pop. 15,000) the place for *"Il riposo del popolo"* (the people's rest). From bodysurfing in choppy waves to browsing through chic boutiques to scaling the 15th-century ruins of **Castello di San Giovanni,** *riposo* takes many forms in Finale Ligure. The city is divided into three sections: **Finalpia** to the east, **Finalmarina** in the center, and inland **Finalborgo.** The station and most sights are in Finalmarina. Climb the trail that starts from Finalborgo's post office to the ruins of **Castel Govone** for a spectacular view. The hamlets near Finale Ligure are also worth exploring. SAR **buses** run from the train station to **Borgo Verezzi**

(10min., every 15min., €1.50). Skip the packed beaches in town and walk east along V. Aurelia through the first tunnel, turning right for a less populated free **beach**. Within the ancient walls, **Finalborgo**, Finale Ligure's historic quarter is a 1km walk or short ACTS bus ride up V. Bruneghi from the station.

Trains leave from P. V. Veneto for Genoa (1hr., 1 per hr., €4). The IAT **tourist office**, V. S. Pietro 14, gives out free maps. (☎68 10 19; www.inforiviera.it. Open M-Sa 9am-12:30pm and 3:30-6:30pm, Su 9am-noon.) Check email at **Net Village Internet Cafe,** near the train station. (☎681 62 83. Open daily 8:15am-10pm. €2 per 20min.) ▓**Castello Wuillerman (HI) ❶**, on V. Generale Caviglia, is well worth the hike. From the train station, cross the street and turn left onto V. Raimondo Pertica, then left onto V. Rossi. After passing a church, take a left onto V. Alonzo and trudge up the steps to a brick castle. (☎69 05 15; www.hostelfinaleligure.com. Breakfast and linens included. Internet €4.50 per hr. Reception daily 7-10am and 5-10pm. Curfew 11:30pm. Dorms €12. MC/V. HI members only.) **Pensione Enzo ❷**, Gradinata d. Rose 3, has jovial owners and a fantastic view. (☎69 13 83. Breakfast included. Open mid-Mar. to Sept. Doubles €40-60.) **Camping Del Mulino ❶**, on V. Castelli, has a restaurant and mini-market on the premises. Take the Calvisio bus from the station to the Boncardo Hotel and follow the signs to the campsite entrance. (☎60 16 69. Open Apr.-Sept. €4.50-6 per person, €5-7 per tent. MC/V.) Cheap restaurants lie along **Via Rossi, Via Roma,** and **Via Garibaldi.** Fill up on huge portions of pasta at **Spaghetteria Il Posto ❷**, V. Porro 21. Bring a friend, as each dish is made for two. (Cover €1. Entrees €7. Open Tu-Su 7-10:30pm. Closed 1st two weeks of Mar.) Di per **Di Express** supermarket, is at V. Alonzo 10. (Open M-Sa 8:30am-1pm and 3:45-7:45pm, Su 9am-1pm. MC/V.) **Postal Code:** 17024.

RIVIERA DI LEVANTE

CAMOGLI. Postcard-perfect Camogli shimmers with color. Sun-faded peach houses crowd the hilltop, red and turquoise boats bob in the water, piles of fishing nets cover the docks, and bright umbrellas dot the dark stone beaches. **Trains** run on the Genoa-La Spezia line to Genoa (40min., 38 per day, €1.60) and La Spezia (1½hr., 24 per day, €4). Golfo Paradiso **ferries**, V. Scalo 3 (☎0185 77 20 91; www.golfoparadiso.it), near P. Colombo, go to Cinque Terre (round-trip €20) and Portofino (round-trip €12). Buy tickets on the dock; call ahead for the schedule. Turn right from the station to find the **tourist office,** V. XX Settembre 33, which helps find rooms. (☎0185 77 10 66. Open M-Sa 9am-12:30pm and 3:30-7pm, Su 9am-1pm; low season reduced hours.) Exit the train station, walk down the stairway to the right, and look for the blue sign for the ▓**Albergo La Camogliese ❹**, V. Garibaldi 55, near the beach. (☎0185 77 14 02; www.lacamogliese.it. Internet access €2 per hr. Singles €50-85; doubles €67-97; triples €90-120. 10% *Let's Go* discount with cash payment. AmEx/MC/V.) **Postal Code:** 16032.

SANTA MARGHERITA LIGURE. Santa Margherita Ligure was a calm fishing village until the early 20th century, when it fell into favor with Hollywood stars. Today, glitz and glamour paint the shore, but the serenity of the town's early days still lingers. If ocean waves don't invigorate your spirit, try the holy water in seashell basins at the **Basilica di Santa Margherita,** at P. Caprera. **Trains** along the Pisa-Genoa line go from P. Federico Raoul Nobili, at the top of V. Roma, to Genoa (50min., 2-4 per hr., €2.10) and La Spezia (1½hr., 1-2 per hr., €4). Tigullio **buses** (☎0185 28 88 34) go from P. V. Veneto to Camogli (30min., 1-2 per hr., €1.20) and Portofino (20min., 3 per hr., €1.50). Tigullio **ferries,** V. Palestro 8/1b (☎0185 28 46 70), have tours to Cinque Terre (July-Sept. W-Th and Sa, €21) and Portofino (1 per hr., €4). Turn right from the train station on V. Roma, left on C. Rainusso, and take a hard right onto V. XXV Aprile from Largo Giusti to find the **tourist office**, V. XXV Aprile 2b, which arranges lodging. (☎0185 28 74 85; www.apttigullio.liguria.it. Open M-Sa 9am-12:30pm and 3-7:30pm, Su 9:30am-12:30pm and 4:30-7:30pm.) ▓**Hotel Terminus ❹**, P. Nobili 4, is to the left as you exit the station. French windows give way to views of the sea. (Singles €80, with bath €85; doubles with bath €95; triples €110; quads €160. AmEx/MC/V.) **Trattoria Da Pezzi ❸**, V. Cavour 21, is a local haunt for home-style *Genovese* cuisine. (☎0185 28 53 03. *Primi* €3-6.50. *Secondi* €3-8. Open M-F and Su 10am-2:15pm and 5-9:15pm. MC/V.) **Postal Code:** 16032.

PORTOFINO. As long as they don't buy anything, princes and paupers alike can enjoy the curved shores and tiny bay of Portofino. A 1hr. walk along the ocean road offers a chance to scout out small rocky **beaches.** The area's only sandy beach, **Paraggi** (where the bus stops), is just a small strip. In town, follow the signs uphill from the bay to escape to the simple **Chiesa di San Giorgio.** A few minutes up the road toward the **castle** is a serene garden with sea views. (Open daily 10am-7pm; in winter Sa-Su 10am-5pm. €3.50.) To get to town, take the bus to Portofino Mare (*not* Portofino Vetta). From P. Martiri della Libertà, Tigullio **buses** go to Santa Margherita (3 per hr., €1.50); buy tickets at the kiosk. **Ferries** go to Camogli (2 per day, €7) and Santa Margherita (1 per hr., €3.50). The **tourist office,** V. Roma 35, is between the waterfront and the bus stop. (☎0185 26 90 24; www.apttigullio.liguria.it. Open daily 10:30am-1:30pm and 2:30-7:30pm.) **Postal Code:** 16034.

CINQUE TERRE   ☎0187

In the five fishing villages of Cinque Terre, man and nature have worked in harmony to produce a place that sweetens and soothes the spirit. Though farmers toiled to produce the terraced hillsides of olive groves and vineyards, and fishermen built the rainbow-colored houses along the harbors, nature created Cinque Terre's greatest sights. Savage cliffs and lush tropical vegetation surround the stone villages, while a vast expanse of dazzling turquoise sea laps against the *cittadine* that cling to the terraced hillsides and steep, crumbling cliffs. Each of these five villages—Monterosso, Vernazza, Corniglia, Manarola, and Riomaggiore—invites the traveler to explore its own unique character. Despite increasing tourism, the towns of the Cinque Terre still feel untouched by time.

▣▨ TRANSPORTATION AND PRACTICAL INFORMATION. Trains run along the Genoa-La Spezia line. A **Cinque Terre Card** (€4.20) allows unlimited trips among the five towns and to La Spezia and Levanto. Monterosso is the most accessible. From the station on V. Fegina, in the northern end of town, trains run to: Florence (3½hr., 1 per hr., €8-17) via Pisa (2½hr., 1 per hr., €4.65); Genoa (1½hr., 1 per hr., €4.45); La Spezia (20min., 2 per hr., €1.20); and Rome (7hr., every 2hr., €27). Frequent local trains connect the five towns (5-20min., 1 per hr., €1-1.50). **Ferries** run from La Spezia to Monterosso (1hr., 2 per day, €18). The five villages stretch along the shore between Levanto and La Spezia, connected by trains, roads (although cars are not allowed inside the towns), and footpaths that traverse the rocky shoreline. **Monterosso** is the northernmost town and the largest, containing most of the services for the area, followed by picturesque **Vernazza,** cliffside **Corniglia,** and the quiet towns of **Manarola** and **Riomaggiore.** The Pro Loco **tourist office,** V. Fegina 38, Monterosso, below the train station, provides information and accommodations service. (☎81 75 06; fax 81 78 25. Open Apr.-Oct. M-Sa 9:15am-noon and 2:30-6:30pm, Su 9am-noon.) Each town also has a **National Park Office** that provides info on hiking and accommodations and sells **Cinque Terre Cards.** The Monterosso office is at P. Garibaldi 20. (☎81 78 38. Open daily 9am-10pm.) **Postal Codes:** Monterosso: 19016; Manarola and Riomaggiore: 19017; Corniglia and Vernazza: 19018.

◾◖ ACCOMMODATIONS AND FOOD. Most hotels are in Monterosso, and they fill quickly during the summer. Try the tourist office for help finding the more plentiful *affitacamere* (private rooms). The ◾**Albergo Della Gioventù-Ostello Cinque Terre ❷**, V. B. Riccobaldi 21 is in Manarola. Turn right from train station and continue up the hill 300m. The new hostel is both beautiful and modern with incredible views. (☎92 02 15; www.hostel5terre.com. Breakfast €3.50. Curfew 1am; in winter midnight. Dorms €17-23. AmEx/DC/MC/V.) **Hotel Gianni Franzi ❸**, P. Marconi 1, in Vernazza, is run by the town's oldest *trattoria* and has lovely rooms. (☎82 10 03; www.giannifranzi.it. Single €42-64; double €60, with bath €76; triple €99. AmEx/DC/MC/V.) **Hotel Souvenir ❸**, V. Gioberti 30, in Monterosso, is friendly and family-run. (☎/fax 81 75 95. Breakfast €5. Rooms €40 per person, students €25.) Cinque Terre has excellent food—Vernazza supposedly has the best. **Trattoria Gianni Franzi ❷**, P. Marconi 1, is famous for its pesto. (☎82 10 03. *Primi* €4-11. *Secondi* €5-16. Open M-Tu and Th-Su noon-3pm, 7:30-9:30pm. AmEx/MC/V.)

◙ ◖ SIGHTS AND ENTERTAINMENT. The best sightseeing in Cinque Terre consists of exploring the five villages and the gorgeous paths that connect them. Monterosso has the Cinque Terre's largest free **beach,** in front of the historic center, sheltered by a cliff cove. The 17th-century **Chiesa Del Convento dei Cappuccini** perched on a hill in the center of town, has expansive vistas. A chapel on the left contains an crucifix by van Dyck, who traveled here during some of his most productive years. (Open daily 9am-noon and 4-7pm. Free.) The hike between Monterosso and Vernazza is considered the hardest of the four because of its steep climbs. The trail winds its way through terraced vineyards and past hillside cottages before steeply descending into town. From there, the trip to Corniglia offers breathtaking views and scents of rosemary, lemon, and lavender. Near Corniglia, the secluded **Guvano Beach,** accessed through a tunnel, is popular for nude sunbathing. The subsequent hike to vibrant Manarola lacks the picturesque vegetation of the previous two, but retains the sweeping views of the turquoise sea. The most famous Cinque Terre hike, the **Via dell'Amore,** from Manarola to Riomaggiore, the smallest of the five towns, is a slate-paved walk that features a stone tunnel painted with love scenes. All together, the hikes take about five hours, not including time spent exploring the towns themselves. At night, the most popular towns are Monterosso, Manarola, and Riomaggiore. In Monterosso, **Il Casello,** V. Lungo Fessario 70, brings in the backpackers with thumping music and a location near the beach, making it far enough from the town to be the only bar open past 1am. (Beer and mixed drinks from €2.50. Internet €1 per hr. Open daily 10am-3am.)

LA SPEZIA
☎0187

A departure point for Corsica and an important transport hub for Cinque Terre, La Spezia (pop. 96,000) is among Italy's most beautiful ports, with regal palms lining the promenade and citrus trees growing in the parks. The unique collection of the **Museo Navale,** in P. Chiodo, features diving suits from WWII. (Open M-Sa 8:30am-1pm and 4:15-9:45pm, Su 8:30am-1:15pm. €1.55.) La Spezia lies on the Genoa-Pisa **train** line. **Navigazione Golfo dei Poeti,** V. d. Minzoni 13, (☎73 29 87; www.navigazionegolfodeipoeti.it) runs ferries that stop in each village of **Cinque Terre** (one-way €11; round-trip M-Sa €19, Su €22). The **tourist office,** V. Mazzini 45, is at the port. (☎77 09 00. Open M-Sa 9:30am-1:30pm and 3:30-7pm, Su 9:30am-12:30pm.) **Albergo Il sole ❸**, V. Cavalloti 3, off V. Prione, offers tidy rooms. (☎73 51 64. Singles €25-36; doubles €39-45, with bath €47-55. AmEx/MC/V.) Reasonably priced *trattorie* line V. del Prione. For groceries and produce, try **Supermercato Spesafacile,** V. Colombo 101-107. (Open daily 8:30am-1pm and 4:15-8pm. MC/V.) **Postal Code:** 19100

EMILIA-ROMAGNA

Go to Florence, Venice, and Rome to sightsee; come to Emilia-Romagna to eat. Italy's wealthy wheat- and dairy-producing region covers the fertile plains of the Po River Valley, and celebrates the finest culinary traditions on the peninsula. The Romans originally settled here, but the towns later fell under the rule of great Renaissance families whose names adorn every *palazzo* and *piazza* in the region.

BOLOGNA   ☎051

Home to Europe's oldest university along with rich, flavorful cuisine, Bologna (pop. 500,000) has been known since ancient times as the *dotta* (learned) and *grassa* (fat) city. Today, academic liberalism drives political activism—minority groups, student alliances, and the national gay organization all find a voice (and attentive ears) in Bologna. All eyes, however, are on Bologna's art. Priceless works inhabit numerous museums and churches, whose porticoes line the wide streets.

⌂⚑ TRANSPORTATION AND PRACTICAL INFORMATION. Bologna is a rail hub for all major Italian cities and the Adriatic coast. **Trains** leave the northern tip of the walled city for: Florence (1½hr., 53 per day, €7.75); Milan (3hr., 53 per day, €10); Rome (4hr., 39 per day, €29); and Venice (2hr., 25 per day, €78). **Buses** #25 and 30 run between the station and the **Piazza Maggiore** (€1). The **tourist office**, P. Maggiore 1, is next to the Palazzo Comunale. (☎648 76 07; www.comune.bologna.it/bolognaturismo. Open daily 9am-8pm.) **Postal Code:** 40100.

⌂⚑ ACCOMMODATIONS AND FOOD. The sparklingly clean **Albergo Panorama ❹**, V. Livraghi 1, 4th fl., has a prime location. Follow V. Ugo Bassi from P. del Nettuno and take the third left. (☎22 18 02; www.hotelpanoramabologna.it. Singles €55; doubles €70; triples €85; quads €95. AmEx/DC/MC/V.) **Ostello due Torre San Sisto (HI) ❶**, V. Viadagola 5, is off V. San Donato, 6km from the town center. Take bus #93 from V. Marconi 69 (M-Sa every 30min.); ask for the San sisto stop. (☎/fax 50 18 10. Lockout 10am-3:30pm. Curfew 11:30pm. Dorms €14.50; doubles €33.) Don't leave without sampling Bologna's signature *spaghetti alla bolognese*. Scout **Via Augusto Righi, Via Piella,** and **Via Saragozza** for traditional *trattorie*. Locals chat over plates of pasta at ▨**Trattoria Da Maro ❷**, V. Broccaindosso 71/B, between Strada Maggiore and V. S. Vitale. (☎22 73 04. *Primi* €5-6. *Secondi* €5-8. Open Tu-Sa noon-2:30pm and 8-11pm. AmEx/DC/MC/V.) **Ristorante Clorofilla ❷**, Strada Maggiore 64/C, is a trendy vegetarian spot. (☎23 53 43. Entrees from €4.50. Open M-Sa 12:15-2:45pm and 7:30-11pm.) A **PAM** supermarket, V. Marconi 26, is by the intersection with V. Riva di Reno. (Open M-Sa 7:45am-8pm.)

◉⚑ SIGHTS AND ENTERTAINMENT. Forty kilometers of porticoed buildings line the streets of Bologna in a mix of Gothic, Renaissance, and Baroque styles. The tranquil ▨**Piazza Maggiore** flaunts both Bologna's historical and modern wealth. The cavernous Gothic interior of the city's duomo, **Basilica di San Petronio,** was meant to be larger than Rome's St. Peter's, but the jealous Church leadership ordered that the funds be used instead to build the nearby Palazzo Archiginnasio. The pomp and pageantry of the exercises at the church allegedly inspired a disgusted Martin Luther to reform religion in Germany. (Open daily 7:30am-1pm and 2:30-6pm. Free.) The **Palazzo Archiginnasio,** behind S. Petronio, was the first home of Bologna's university; the upstairs theater was built in 1637 to teach anatomy to students. (Open daily 9am-1pm. Closed 2 weeks in Aug. Free.) On the northern side of P. Maggiore is the **Palazzo de Podestà.** Next to P. Maggiore, **Piazza del Nettuno** contains Giambologna's famous 16th-century fountain, **Neptune and Attendants.**

From P. Nettuno, go down V. Rizzoli to **Piazza Porta Ravegana**, where seven streets converge to form Bologna's medieval quarter. Two towers that constitute the city's emblem rise magnificently from the *piazza;* you can climb the 498 steps of the **Torre degli Asinelli** for a breathtaking view of the city. (Open daily 9am-6pm. €3.) From V. Rizzoli, follow V. S. Stefano to P. S. Stefano, where four of the original seven churches of the **Chiesa Santo Stefano** remain. Bologna's patron saint, San Petronio, lies buried under the pulpit of the **Chiesa di San Sepolcro.** (Open M-Sa 9am-noon and 3:30-6pm, Su 9am-12:45pm and 3:30-6:30pm. Free.) Take Strada Maggiore to P. Aldrovandi to reach the remarkably intact **Chiesa di Santa Mari dei Servi,** whose columns support a web of arches and vaulting. (Open daily 7am-1pm and 3:30-8pm.) The **Pinacoteca Nazionale,** V. delle Belle Arti 56, off V. Zamboni, traces the history of Bolognese art. (Open Tu-Su 9am-7pm. €4, EU students €2.)

Bologna's hip student population ensures raucous nighttime fun. **Cluricaune,** V. Zamboni 18/B, is an Irish bar packed with students who gather around its pool tables and dart boards. (Pints €3-4.20. Happy Hour W 7-10:30pm. Open M-F and Su 11pm-3am, Sa 4pm-3am.) **Cassero,** in the Porta Saragozza, is a lively gay bar packed with both men and women. (Drinks €3-6. Open M-F 10pm-2am, Sa-Su 10pm-3am.)

PARMA   ☎0521

Famous for its *parmigiano* cheese and *prosciutto* ham, Parma's (pop. 200,000) artistic excellence is not confined to the kitchen. Mannerist painting came into full bloom here, and native Giuseppe Verdi composed some of his greatest works while residing in Parma. The town centers around the 11th-century Romanesque **duomo,** in P. del Duomo, which is filled with masterpieces; from P. Garibaldi, follow Strada Cavour toward the train station and take the third right on Strada al Duomo to reach it. Most spectacular is the dome, where Correggio's *Virgin* ascends to a golden heaven in a spiral of white robes and blue sky. The pink-and-white marble **baptistry** was built between the Romanesque and Gothic periods. (Duomo open daily 9am-12:30pm and 3-7pm. Baptistry open daily 9am-12:30pm and 3-6pm. €3, students €1.50.) Behind the duomo is the frescoed dome of the **Chiesa di San Giovanni Evangelista,** P. S. Giovanni, designed by Correggio. (Open M-F 9-11:45am and 3-6:45pm, Su 8am-12:45pm and 3-7:45pm.) From P. del Duomo, follow Strada al Duomo across Strada Cavour, walk one block down Strada Piscane, and cross P. della Pace to reach the 17th-century **Palazzo della Pilotta,** an artistic treasure chest that houses the **Galleria Nazionale.** (Palace open Tu-Su 8:30am-2pm. €6, students €3.) Downstairs, the **Museo Archeologico Nazionale** displays coins, bronzes, and sculptures of Greek, Etruscan, Roman, and Egyptian origin. (Open Tu-Su 8:30am-7:30pm. €2, students €1.)

Parma is on the Bologna-Milan rail line. **Trains** go from P. Carlo Alberto della Chiesa to Bologna (1hr., 2 per hr., €4.30); Florence (3hr., 4 per day, €14.85); and Milan (1½hr., 1 per hr., €7.20). Walk left from the station, turn right on V. Garibaldi, then turn left on V. Melloni to reach the **tourist office,** V. Melloni 1/a. (☎21 88 89; http://turismo.comune.parma.it. Open M-Tu and Th-Sa 9am-7pm, W 1-3pm, Su and holidays 9am-1pm.) From the station, take bus #9 (€0.85) and get off when the bus turns left on V. Martiri della Libertà for the **Ostello Cittadella (HI) ❶,** on V. Passo Buole. The hostel is situated in a corner of a 15th-century fortress with a campground beside it. (☎96 14 34; ostellocittadella@libero.it. 3-night max. stay. Lockout 9:30am-5pm. Curfew 11pm. Open Apr.-Oct. HI members only. Dorms €10; camping €6.50 per person, €12 per car. Cash only.) **Albergo Leon d'Oro ❸,** V. Fratti 4, off V. Garibaldi, has clean, basic rooms and is only two blocks from the train station. (Closed in Aug., call ahead for exact dates. Singles €33; doubles €50. AmEx/MC/V.) Look near **Via Garibaldi** for fragrant Parmesan cuisine. **Pizzeria La Duchessa ❷,** P. Garibaldi 1/b, has a large variety of pastas and thick-crust pizzas. (☎23 59 62. Pizzas €5-10. *Primi* €5.50-8. *Secondi* €6.50-15. Cover €1.50. Open Tu-Su 10am-2pm and 7:30pm-12:30am. MC/V.) **K2**

❶, Borgo Cairoli 23, next to the Chiesa di San Giovanni Evangelista, tops each cone with the creamiest of gelato, sculpted into a flower. (Cups and cones from €1.50. Open M-Tu and Th-Su 11am-midnight.) **Dimeglio** supermarket is at V. XXII Luglio 27/c. (Open M-W and F-Sa 8:30am-1pm and 4:30-8pm, Th 8:30am-1pm.) **Postal Code:** 43100.

RAVENNA   ☎0544

Ravenna's (pop. 130,000) 15 minutes of historical fame came and went 14 centuries ago, when Justinian and Theodora, rulers of the Byzantine Empire, made it the headquarters of their campaign to restore order in the anarchic west. Take V. Argentario from V. Cavour to reach the 6th-century ▓**Basilica di San Vitale,** V. S. Vitale 17. A courtyard overgrown with greenery leads to the glowing mosaics that coat the interior. Behind S. Vitale, the city's oldest and most intriguing mosaics cover the shimmering interior of the **Mausoleo di Galla Placidia,** which holds the sarcophagi of Costanzo III, Empress Galla Placida, and Valentiniano III. (☎21 62 92. Open daily Apr.-Sept. 9am-7pm; Mar. and Oct. 9am-5:30pm; Nov.-Feb. 9am-4:30pm.) Take bus #4 or 44 across from the train station (€0.75) to Classe, south of the city, to see the pastoral mosaics in the ▓**Basilica di Sant'Apollinare.** (Open M-Sa 8:30am-7:30pm, Su 9am-1pm. Tickets close 30min. before basilica. €2, EU students €1. Su free.) Much to Florence's dismay, Ravenna is also home to the **Tomb of Dante Alighieri,** the final resting place of its exiled native son. In the adjoining **Dante Museum,** Dantephiles pore over illustrations of the poet's works, the chest that held his bones, and 18,000 volumes on his works. From P. del Popolo, cut through P. Garibaldi to V. Alighieri. (☎33 667. Tomb open daily 9am-7pm. Free. Museum open Apr.-Sept. Tu-Su 9am-noon and 3:30-6pm; Oct.-Mar. 9am-noon. €2)

   Trains (☎89 20 21) leave P. Farini for Ferrara (1hr., 22 per day, €4) and Bologna (1hr., 19 per day, €4.60). Follow V. Farini from the station to V. Diaz, which runs to the central P. del Popolo and the **tourist office,** V. Salara 8. (☎354 04; www.turismo.ravenna.it. Open Apr.-Sept. M-Sa 8:30am-7pm, Su 10am-4pm; Oct.-Mar. 8:30am-6pm, Su 10am-4pm.) Take bus #1 or 70 from V. Pallavicini at the train station (1-4 per hr., €0.75) to reach **Ostello Dante (HI) ❶,** V. Nicolodi 12. (☎42 11 64; hostelravenna@hotmail.com. Breakfast included. Lockout 10am-5pm. Curfew 11:30pm. Dorms €13. Nonmembers add €3. MC/V.) Walk down V. Farini, and go right at P. Mameli for the **Albergo Al Giaciglio ❸,** V. Rocca Brancaleone 42. (☎394 03. Breakfast €5. Singles €25-38, with bath €30-43; doubles €42-525/€60-65. MC/V.) Nearby, **Piazza del Popolo** has a number of good restaurants. **Postal Code:** 48100.

RIMINI   ☎0541

The Ibiza of the Adriatic, Rimini is the party town of choice for young European *fashionistas.* Beaches, nightclubs, and boardwalks plastered with boutiques, fortune tellers, and artists all contribute to a society where it is perfectly acceptable—and admirable—to collapse into bed and bid the rising sun goodnight. Rimini's most treasured attraction is its remarkable **beach** of fine sand and mild Adriatic waves. Hotels reserve strips of beach with chairs and umbrellas for their guests; everyone else must use the public beach, located at the top of the shore. After dark, Rimini's nightlife heats up around the *lungomare* in southern Rimini and surrounding areas. **Bus #11** is an institution in and of itself: Early in the evening, families and older locals steel themselves in the seats as the bus fills with scantily-clad teenagers. Some buses play loud disco music to get the raucous passengers going (as if they need assistance) or flood the front of the buses with blue lights. ▓**Embassy,** V. Vespucci 22, 5min. from P. Kennedy, stays dependably active as the only club within walking distance of Rimini *centro.* (☎23 934. Drinks €6. Cover €10-16. Open daily midnight-4am.) Get some love from the friendly staff at **Spazio,** P. Cavour 5, a strikingly trendy bar designed to look like an ultra-mod living room. (☎054 12 34 39. Wine from €4 a glass. Open M-Sa 5pm-2am. MC/V.)

Trains (☎89 20 21) run from P. C. Battisti and V. Dante to Bologna (1½hr., 58 per day, €6.35); Milan (3hr., 25 per day, €15.44); and Ravenna (1hr., 34 per day, €2.80). **Hotel Cirene ❸,** V. Cirene 50, has pleasant owners offering rooms with bath, phone, and TV; some rooms have a balcony. (☎39 09 04; www.hotelcirene.com. Breakfast included. Open May-Sept. Singles €25-52; doubles €30-57; triples €50-62; quads €62-67. AmEx/MC/V.) After spending your budget on drinks and club cover, pick up groceries at the **STANDA** supermarket, V. Vespucci 13. (Open daily 8am-1:30pm. AmEx/DC/MC/V.) **Postal Code:** 47900.

FERRARA   ☎0532

Rome has its mopeds, Venice its gondolas, and Ferrara (pop. 135,000) its bicycles. Wrinkled old men, gum-popping girls in stilettos, and harried businesspeople zip through the city, dodging the cars that race bravely through the winding medieval streets. In the midst of it all, an imposing castle and *palazzi* fill the *centro* with more than enough beauty, romance, and adventure.

▐▞ TRANSPORTATION AND PRACTICAL INFORMATION. Trains go to: Bologna (30min., 52 per day, €3); Padua (1hr., 39 per day, €4.25); Ravenna (1hr., 22 per day, €4.15); Rome (3-4hr., 11 per day, €31); and Venice (2hr., 26 per day, €6). ACFT (☎59 94 92) and GGFP **buses** leave V. Rampari S. Paolo or the train station for Bologna (1½hr., 15 per day, €3.31) and nearby beaches (1½hr., 12 per day, €4.23). Rent **bikes** at **Pirani e Bagni,** P. Stazione 2. (☎77 21 90. €2 per hr., €7 per day. Open M-F 5:30am-8pm, Sa 6:30am-1pm.) To get to the town center, from the train station, turn left onto **Viale Costituzione,** which becomes **Viale Cavour** and runs to the **Castello Estense** (1km). Or, take bus #2 to Castello or bus #1 or 9 to the **post office** (every 20min., €0.83). The **tourist office** is in Castello Estense. (☎20 93 70. Open M-Sa 9am-1pm and 2-6pm, Su 9:30am-1pm and 2-5:30pm.) **Postal Code:** 44100.

▐▗ ACCOMMODATIONS AND FOOD. Ferrara has plenty of inexpensive and comfortable accommodations. **▨Pensione Artisti ❷,** V. Vittoria 66, near P. Lampronti, is in the historic center of Ferrara and has a garden, shared fridge, and gas burners available for guest use. (☎76 10 38. Singles €22; doubles €40, with bath €57. Cash only.) Walk down C. Ercole I d'Este from the *castello* to reach the central **Ostello della Gioventù Estense (HI) ❹,** C. B. Rossetti 24, with spacious rooms. (☎/fax 20 42 27. Breakfast included. Internet €5.16 per hr. Lockout 10am-3:30pm. Curfew 11:30pm. Dorms €15; private rooms for 2-5 people €16 per person. Nonmembers add €3. AmEx/DC/MC/V.) **Hotel de Prati ❹,** V. Padiglioni 5, has a staff as sunny as its warm yellow decor. (☎24 19 05; www.hoteldeprati.com. Singles €47-70; doubles €70-105; suites €110-140. AmEx/DC/MC/V.) Try delicious *panini* with one of 600 varieties of wine at **Osteria Al Brindisi ❸,** V. G. degli Adelardi 11, which has wined and dined the likes of Copernicus and Pope John Paul II since opening in 1435. (☎20 91 42. Cover €2. Open Tu-Su 9am-1am. MC/V.) For picnic supplies, stop by the **Supermercato Conrad,** V. Garibaldi 53. (Open daily 8:30am-8pm. MC/V.)

◙♫ SIGHTS. Bike the tranquil, wooded path atop the city's well-preserved 9km **medieval wall,** which begins at the far end of C. Giovecca. The imposing, 14th-century **▨Castello Estense** towers over the center of town. Inside, duck through damp dungeon tunnels or admire palatial frescoed apartments for the full medieval experience. (☎29 92 33. Open Tu-Su 9:30am-5pm. €6, students €5. Audioguides €3.) From the *castello*, take C. Martiri della Libertà to P. Cattedrale and the ornate **Duomo San Romano,** across V. S. Romano from the **Museo della Cattedrale.** (Duomo open M-Sa 7:30am-noon and 3-6:30pm, Su 7:30am-12:30pm and 3:30-7:30pm. Museum open Tu-Su 9am-1pm and 3-6pm. €4.50, students €2.) From the *castello*, cross Largo Castello to C. Ercole I d'Este and walk to the intersection with C. Rossetti to reach the **Palazzo Diamanti,** built in 1493 and covered with 8500 white spikes. Inside, the **Pinacoteca Nazionale** holds many of the finest works of the Ferrarese school of painting. (Open Tu-W and F-Sa 9am-2pm, Th 9am-7pm, Su 9am-1pm. €4, EU students €2, under 18 free.) Follow C. Ercole I d'Este behind the *castello* and go right on C. Porta Mare to find the **Palazzo Massari,** C. Porta Mare 9, which houses both the **Museo d'Arte Moderna e Contemporanea Filippo de Pisis,** and upstairs, the spectacular **Museo Ferrarese dell'Ottocentro/Museo Giovanni Boldini.** (Both open Tu-Su 9am-1pm and 3-6pm. Joint ticket €6.50, students €4.50.)

THE DOLOMITES (DOLOMITI)

The Dolomites offer a naturally beautiful setting for nearly any outdoor enthusiast, from mountain trails to trendy lodges. The near-impenetrable dolomitic rock has slowed major industrialization, preserving the jagged cliffs and thick forests that Le Corbusier once called "the most beautiful natural architecture in the world."

TRENT (TRENTO)   ☎ 0461

Between the Dolomites and the Veneto, Trent (pop. 105,000) offers an affordable sampling of northern Italian culture. The **Piazza del Duomo,** Trent's bustling epicenter, is stoically regarded by the massive trident-wielding **Fontana del Nettuno** in the center of the *piazza*. The steps at the base offer full views of the rows of cafes and aging frescoed homes. Nearby is the **Cattedrale di San Vigilio,** where the Council of Trent waged the Counter-Reformation. (Open daily 6:40am-12:15pm and 2:30-8pm. Free.) Walk down V. Belenzani and head right on V. Roma to reach the **Castello del Buonconsiglio,** which houses the **Ciclo dei Mesi,** a series of frescoes depicting 11 months of a year in the bishop-prince's ideal feudal system. (Open Tu-Su 9am-noon and 2-5pm. €5, students and seniors €2.50.) **Trains** (☎ 98 36 27) leave V. Dogana for: Bologna (3hr., 9 per day, €11); Bolzano (45min., 35 per hr., €3); Venice (3hr., 12 per day, €11); and Verona (1hr., 2 per hr., €4.70). Atesina **buses** (☎ 82 10 00) go from V. Pozzo, next to the train station, to Roverto (1hr., 1 per hr., €3.20) and Riva del Garda (1¾hr., 1 per hr., €3.20). Turn right as you exit the train station and turn left on V. Roma, which becomes V. Manci, to reach the **tourist office,** V. Manci 2, which offers advice on local trails, festivals, and guided tours. (☎ 98 38 80; www.apt.trento.it. Open daily 9am-7pm.) From the station, turn right on V. Pozzo then right on V. Torre Vanga to get to **Ostello Giovane Europa (HI) ❶,** V. Torre Vanga 11, which has tidy rooms and a friendly staff. (☎ 26 34 84. Breakfast included. Curfew 11:30pm, ask for door code for later entry. Dorms €13; singles €25; doubles €40. AmEx/MC/V.) **Hotel Venezia ❸,** at P. Duomo 45, offers rooms right across from the duomo. (☎/fax 23 41 14. Singles €43; doubles €63. MC/V.) P. Duomo is lined with cafes and hosts a Thursday morning market. **Postal Code:** 38100.

BOLZANO (BOZEN)   ☎ 0471

As German street names begin to appear alongside their Italian equivalents, Bolzano's (pop. 100,000) cultural fusion with Austria becomes increasingly obvious. A spiny Gothic bell tower tops the squat Romanesque **duomo,** off P. Walther. (Open M-F 9:45am-noon and 2-5pm, Sa 9:45am-noon. Free.) The fascinating **South Tyrol Museum of Archaeology,** V. Museo 43, near Ponte Talvera, provides the viewable freezer home of **Ötzi,** the 5000-year-old **Ice Man.** (Open Tu-Su 10am-5pm, Th until 7pm. €8, students €5.50.) **Trains** leave P. Stazione for Trent (45min., 32 per day, €3) and Verona (2hr., 25 per day, €6.80). Walk up V. Stazione from the train station to reach the **tourist office** at P. Walther 8. (☎30 70 00. Open M-F 9am-6:30pm, Sa 9am-12:30pm.) **Croce Bianca ❸,** P. del Grano 3, and its homey rooms, are around the corner from P. Walther. (☎97 75 52. Singles €28; doubles €47.) Sample Bolzano's Austrian-influenced fare around V. Argentieri and the markets of the P. della Erbe. **Postal Code:** 39100.

THE VENETO

From the rocky foothills of the Dolomites to the fertile valleys of the Po River, the Veneto region has a geography as diverse as its historical influences. Once loosely linked to the Venetian Empire, these towns have retained their cultural independence; in fact, visitors are more likely to hear regional dialects than standard Italian when neighbors gossip across their geranium-bedecked windows. The tenacity of local culture and custom may be a pleasant surprise for those who come expecting only mandolins and gondolas.

VENICE (VENEZIA)   ☎041

There is a mystical quality to Venice's (pop. 265,000) decadence. Her lavish palaces stand proudly on a steadily sinking network of wood, treading in the clouded waters of age-old canals lapping at the wet, mossy steps of her abandoned front doors. The maze of knotted streets leads to a treasury of Renaissance art, housed in scores of palaces, churches, and museums that are themselves architectural delights. But the same dim, narrow streets that once earned the name *La Serenissima* (most serene) are now saturated with visitors, as Venice struggles to retain its unique flavor in a climate where 70% of economic growth comes from tourism. All but 70,000 have fled to homes on the mainland, leaving an island where one third of dwellings are owned (and largely uninhabited) by foreigners. Still, those who do stay behind find endless beauty in romantic canals, bridges, and tiny cafes which are nearly impossible to find on any tourist's map. But romanticism dies hard, and the sinking city persists beyond the summer crowds and polluted waters, united by winding canals and the memory of a glorious past.

▐ TRANSPORTATION

The **train station** is on the northwest edge of the city; be sure to get off at **Santa Lucia**, not Mestre on the mainland. Buses and boats arrive at **Piazzale Roma,** just across the Canal Grande from the train station. To get from either station to **Piazza San Marco** or the **Ponte di Rialto** (Rialto Bridge), take *vaporetto* #82 or follow the signs for a 40min. walk—from the train station, exit left on Lista di Spagna.

Flights: Aeroporto Marco Polo (VCE; ☎260 92 60; www.veniceairport.it), 10km north of the city. Take the **ATVO shuttlebus** (☎520 55 30) from the airport to P. Roma (30min., 1 per hr., €3).

Trains: Stazione Santa Lucia, northwest corner of the city. Open daily 3:45am-12:30am. **Info office** (☎78 55 70) at the left as you exit the platforms. Open daily 7am-9pm. To: **Bologna** (2hr., 27 per day, €8); **Florence** (3hr., 9 per day, €19); **Milan** (3hr., 24 per day, €20-30); **Rome** (4½hr., 7 per day, €35-45).

Buses: ACTV (info via the HelloVenezia hotline, ☎24 24), in P. Roma. Local buses and boats. **ACTV long-distance carrier** runs buses to **Padua** (1½hr., 2 per hr., €2.90).

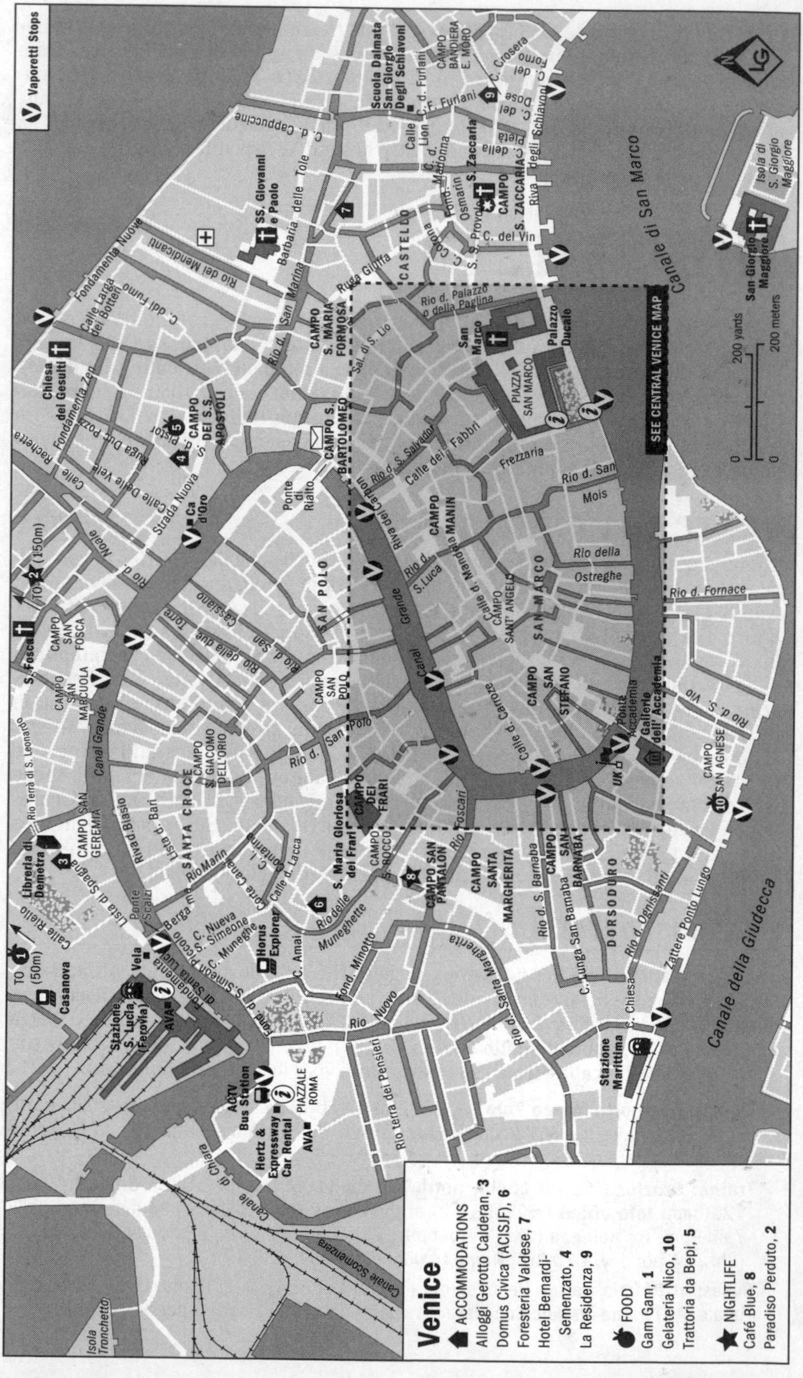

Venice
ACCOMMODATIONS
Alloggi Gerotto Calderan, 3
Domus Civica (ACISJF), 6
Foresteria Valdese, 7
Hotel Bernardi-Semenzato, 4
La Residenza, 9
FOOD
Gam Gam, 1
Gelateria Nico, 10
Trattoria da Bepi, 5
NIGHTLIFE
Café Blue, 8
Paradiso Perduto, 2
Vaporetti Stops
SEE CENTRAL VENICE MAP
200 yards
200 meters
Canal Grande
Canale della Giudecca
Canale di San Marco
SANTA CROCE
SAN POLO
SAN MARCO
CASTELLO
DORSODURO
CAMPO SAN POLO
CAMPO S. MARIA FORMOSA
CAMPO SANTA MARGHERITA
CAMPO SAN STEFANO
CAMPO MANIN
PIAZZA SAN MARCO
Palazzo Ducale
San Marco
Ponte di Rialto
Ponte Accademia
Gallerie dell' Accademia
Stazione S. Lucia (Ferrovia)
Stazione Marittima
PIAZZALE ROMA
ACTV Bus Station
Hertz & Expressway Car Rental
Chiesa dei Gesuiti
SS. Giovanni e Paolo
S. Maria Gloriosa dei Frari
Isola di S. Giorgio Maggiore
San Giorgio Maggiore
Isola Tronchetto
Canale Scomenzera

Public Transportation: The **Canal Grande** can be crossed on foot only at the Scalzi, Rialto, and Accademia *ponti* (bridges). **Vaporetti** (water buses) provide 24hr. service around the city, with reduced service midnight-5am. Single-ride €3.50, €5 for the Grand Canal. 24hr. *biglietto turistico* pass €10.50, 3-day €22 (€13 with Rolling Venice Card), 7-day €31. Buy tickets from booths in front of *vaporetti* stops, self-serve dispensers at the ACTV office in P. Roma and the Rialto stop, or from the conductor. Pick up extra *non timbrati* (non-validated) tickets to use when the booths aren't open. Validate them before boarding to avoid a fine. **Lines #1** (slow) and **82** (fast) run from the station down Canale Grande and Canale della Giudecca; **line #52** goes from the station through Canale della Giudecca to Lido and along the city's northern edge, then back to the station; **line #LN** runs from Fondamente Nuove to Burano, Murano, and Torcello.

✴ ORIENTATION

Venice spans 118 bodies of land in a lagoon and is connected to the mainland by a thin causeway. The city is a veritable labyrinth and can confuse even its natives, most of whom simply set off in a general direction and then patiently weave their way. A few tips will help you to orient yourself. Locate the following landmarks on a map: **Ponte di Rialto** (the bridge in the center), **Piazza San Marco** (central south), **Ponte Accademia** (the bridge in the southwest), **Ferrovia** (the train station, in the northwest), and **Piazzale Roma** (directly south of the station). The Canal Grande winds through the city, creating six *sestieri* (sections): Cannaregio, Castello, Dorsoduro, Santa Croce, San Marco, and San Polo. Within each *sestiere*, there are no street numbers—door numbers in a section form one long, haphazard set consisting of around 6000 numbers. While these boundaries are nebulous, they can give you a general sense of location. **Cannaregio** is in the north and includes the train station, Jewish ghetto, and Cà d'Oro; **Castello** extends east toward the Arsenale; **Dorsoduro,** across the bridge from S. Marco, stretches the length of Canale della Giudecca and up to Campo S. Pantalon; **San Croce** lies west of S. Polo, across the Canal Grande from the train station; **San Marco** fills in the area between the Ponte di Rialto and Ponte Accademia; and **San Polo** runs north from Chiesa S. Maria dei Frari to the Ponte di Rialto. If *sestiere* boundaries prove too vague, Venice's **parrochie** (parishes) provide a more defined idea of where you are; *parrochia* signs, like *sestiere* signs, are painted on the sides of buildings.

🛈 PRACTICAL INFORMATION

Tourist Office: APT, Calle della Ascensione, S. Marco 71/F (☎529 87 40; www.doge.it), directly opposite the Basilica. Open daily 9am-3:30pm. The APT desk at the nearby **Venice Pavilion,** Giardini E Reali, S. Marco 2 (☎522 51 50) sells ACTV tickets. Open daily 10am-6pm. The **Rolling Venice Card** offers discounts on transportation and at over 200 restaurants, cafes, hotels, museums, and shops for ages 14-29. The tourist office provides a list of participating vendors. Cards cost €3 and are valid for 1 yr. from date of purchase. The card can be purchased at the **ACTV VeLa** office (☎274 76 50) in P. Roma. Open daily 7am-8pm. The card is also available at any APT tourist office, and ACTV VeLa kiosks next to the Ferrovia, Rialto, S. Marco, and Vallaresso *vaporetto* stops. **AVA** (☎171 52 88), in the train station. Makes room reservations for a €1 fee. Open daily 8am-10pm. **Branch** in P. Roma (☎523 86 40) and the airport (☎541 51 33).

Budget Travel: CTS, Fondamenta Tagliapietra Dorsoduro, 3252 (☎520 56 60; www.cts.it). From Campo S. Barnaba, cross the bridge and follow the road through the *piazza.* Turn left at the foot of the bridge. Sells discounted student plane tickets and issues ISIC. English spoken. Open M-F 9:30am-1:30pm and 2:30-6pm. MC only.

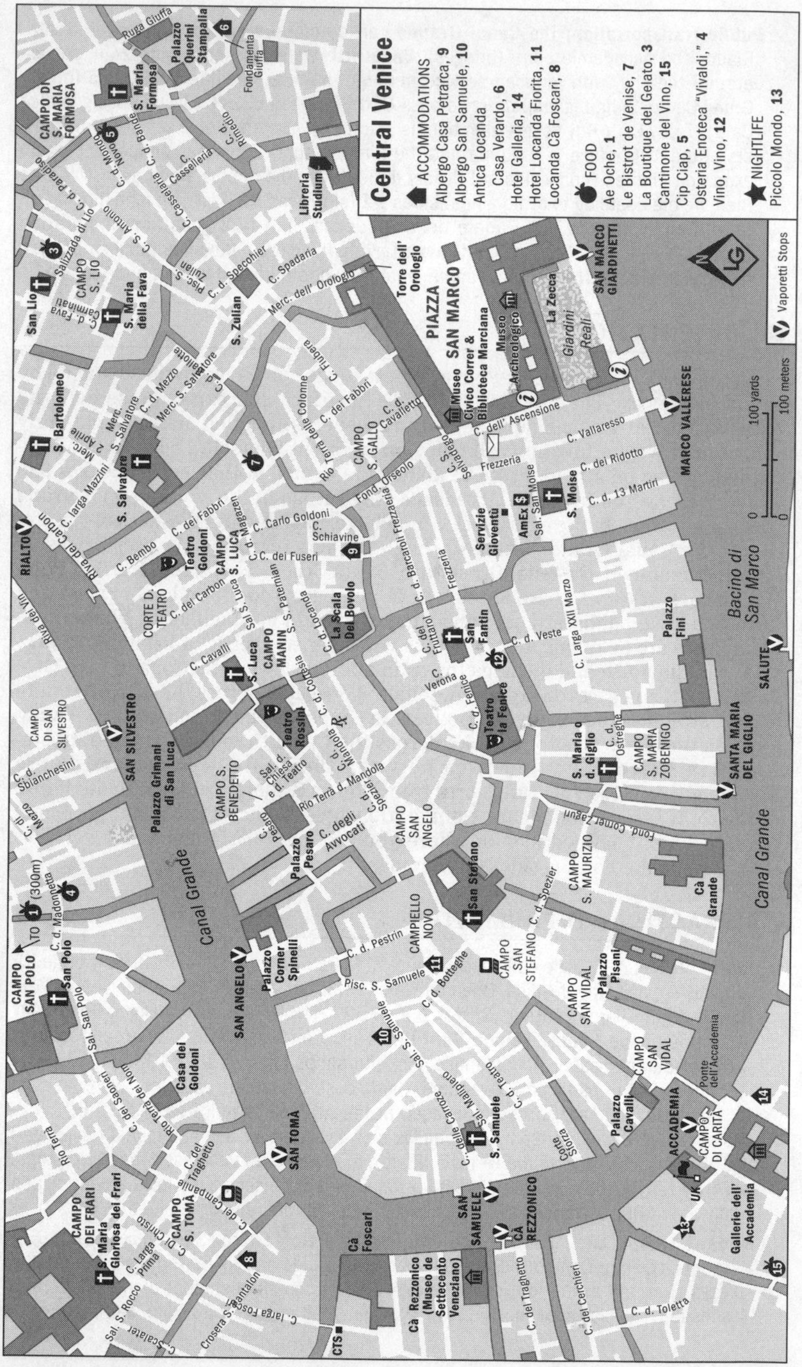

Central Venice
ACCOMMODATIONS
Albergo Casa Petrarca, 9
Albergo San Samuele, 10
Antica Locanda
Casa Verardo, 6
Hotel Galleria, 14
Hotel Locanda Fiorita, 11
Locanda Cà Foscari, 8
FOOD
Ae Oche, 1
Le Bistrot de Venise, 7
La Boutique del Gelato, 3
Cantinone del Vino, 15
Cip Ciap, 5
Osteria Enoteca "Vivaldi," 4
Vino, Vino, 12
NIGHTLIFE
Piccolo Mondo, 13
Vaporetti Stops
100 yards
100 meters
Canal Grande
Bacino di San Marco
PIAZZA SAN MARCO
Torre dell' Orologio
Museo Civico Correr & Biblioteca Marciana
Museo Archeologico
La Zecca
Giardini Reali
SAN MARCO GIARDINETTI
MARCO VALLERESE
SALUTE
SANTA MARIA DEL GIGLIO
RIALTO
SAN SILVESTRO
SAN ANGELO
SAN TOMÀ
SAN SAMUELE
CÀ REZZONICO
ACCADEMIA
Palazzo Querini Stampalia
CAMPO DI S. MARIA FORMOSA
S. Maria Formosa
Libreria Studium
S. Zulian
San Lio
CAMPO S. LIO
S. Maria della Fava
S. Bartolomeo
S. Salvatore
Teatro Goldoni
CAMPO S. LUCA
S. Luca
CAMPO MANIN
La Scala Del Bovolo
Teatro Rossini
San Fantin
Teatro la Fenice
S. Moisè
AmEx
Servizie Gioventù
CAMPO S. GALLO
Palazzo Fini
S. Maria d. Giglio
CAMPO S. MARIA ZOBENIGO
Palazzo Grimani di San Luca
CAMPO DI SAN SILVESTRO
CAMPO S. BENEDETTO
Palazzo Pesaro
CAMPO SAN ANGELO
San Stefano
CAMPIELLO NOVO
CAMPO SAN STEFANO
CAMPO S. MAURIZIO
Cà Grande
Palazzo Corner Spinelli
CAMPO SAN POLO
San Polo
Casa del Goldoni
CAMPO SAN VIDAL
Palazzo Pisani
Palazzo Cavalli
CAMPO DI CARITÀ
Gallerie dell' Accademia
UK
S. Samuele
CAMPO DEI FRARI
S. Maria Gloriosa dei Frari
CAMPO S. TOMÀ
Cà Foscari
Cà Rezzonico (Museo de Settecento Veneziano)
CTS
Ponte dell'Accademia

Currency Exchange: Money exchangers charge high prices for service. Use banks whenever possible and inquire about fees beforehand. The streets around S. Marco and S. Polo are full of **banks** and **ATMs.** Many 24hr. automatic change machines, outside banks and next to ATMs, offer decent rates and low commissions.

Emergency: ☎113. **Ambulance:** ☎118. **Fire:** ☎115.

Police: ☎113 or 112. **Carabinieri,** Campo S. Zaccaria, Castello 4693/A (☎27 41 11). **Questura,** V. Nicoladi 21 (☎271 57 67). Contact the Questura if you have a serious complaint about your hotel.

Pharmacy: Farmacia Italo Inglese, Calle della Mandola, S. Marco 3717 (☎522 48 37). Follow C. Cortesia out of Campo Manin. Open M-F 9am-12:30pm and 3:45-7:30pm, Sa 9am-12:45pm. There are no 24hr. pharmacies in Venice; late-night and weekend pharmacies rotate—check the list posted in the window of any pharmacy.

Hospital: Ospedale Civile, Campo S. S. Giovanni e Paolo, Castello (☎529 41 11).

Internet Access: Casanova, Lista di Spagna, Cannaregio 158/A. This hip bar has Internet access on 5 high-speed computers. €7 per hr., students €4. Internet daily 9am-11:30pm. **Net House,** in Campo S. Stefano, S. Marco 2967 and 2958. Open daily 8am-3am. €7 per hr., with ISIC or Rolling Venice €5. AmEx/MC/V.

Post Office: Poste Venezia Centrale, Salizzada Fontego dei Tedeschi, S. Marco 5554 (☎271 71 11). Open M-Sa 8:30am-6:30pm. **Postal Codes:** Castello: 30122; Cannaregio: 30121; Dorsoduro: 30123; S. Croce: 30135; S. Marco: 30124; S. Polo: 30125.

ACCOMMODATIONS

The heavily touristed Venetian hotels are generally more expensive than other areas of Italy, but savvy travelers can find cheap, quality alternatives if they sniff out options in advance. Dorm-style rooms are sometimes available without reservations even in summer. The **AVA** (see **Tourist Offices,** above) finds rooms with same-day availability, but they will not be cheap. Religious institutions offer dorms and private rooms in the summer for €25-70. Options include: **Casa Murialdo,** Fondamenta Madonna dell'Orto, Cannaregio, 3512 (☎71 99 33); **Domus Cavanis,** Dorsoduro, 896 (☎528 73 74), near the Accademia Bridge; and **Patronato Salesiano Leone XIII,** Cal. S. Domenico, Castello, 1281 (☎240 36 11).

CANNAREGIO AND SANTA CROCE

The station area, around the Lista di Spagna, has some of Venice's best budget accommodations. Although a 20min. *vaporetto* ride and a 15-25min. walk from most major sights, the neighborhood bustles at night with students and travelers.

■ **Alloggi Gerotto Calderan,** Campo S. Geremia 283 (☎71 55 62; www.casagerottocalderan.com). 34 big, bright rooms. Check-out 10am. Curfew 12:30am for dorms. Reserve at least 15 days ahead. Dorms €21; singles €36, with bath €41; doubles €60/€75-93; triples €84/€93. 10% Rolling Venice discount. Cash only. ❷

■ **Hotel Bernardi-Semenzato,** Calle dell'Oca, Cannaregio 4366 (☎522 72 57). From V: Cà d'Oro, turn right on Strada Nuova, left on tiny Calle del Duca, then right on Calle dell'Oca. Antiques decorate this small hotel. Curfew 1am; ask for key if returning later. Singles €30; doubles €50-65, with bath €75-100; triples from €90; quads €85/€110. 10% Rolling Venice discount on larger rooms. AmEx/DC/MC/V. ❸

Ostello di Venezia (HI), Fondamenta Zitelle, Giudecca 86 (☎523 82 11; www.hostelbooking.com). Take V: #82 or 41 to Zitelle. Turn right alongside canal. Large and efficient, with a sweeping view of the water. Must book through website; do not call to reserve. Reception 7-9:30am and 1pm-midnight. Lockout 9:30am-1:30pm. Curfew 11:30pm. HI members only; cards for sale. Dorms €18. MC/V. ❷

Istituto Canosiano, Ponte Piccolo, Giudecca 428 (☎522 21 57). Take V: #82 or 41 to Palanca, and cross the bridge on the left. Women only. 35 beds. Sheets included. Reception 3pm-curfew. Lockout noon-3pm. Strict curfew 10:30pm, in winter 10pm. Large dorms €15. Cash only. ❶

SAN MARCO AND SAN POLO

Surrounded by designer boutiques, souvenir stands, scores of *trattorie* and *pizzerie*, near-domesticated pigeons, and many of Venice's most popular sights, these accommodations are pricey options for those in search of Venice's showy side.

🏨 **Albergo Casa Petrarca,** Calle Schiavine, S. Marco 4386 (☎520 04 30; arcapetra@libero.it). From Campo S. Luca, follow C. Fuseri, take 2nd left and then a right. Tiny hotel has 7 cozy rooms, most with bath and A/C. Sunny sitting room with English books and a quaint breakfast room. Singles €45-48; doubles €90-110. Cash only. ❹

Albergo San Samuele, Salizzada S. Samuele, S. Marco 3358 (☎/fax 522 80 45; www.albergosansamuele.it). Follow Calle delle Botteghe from Campo S. Stefano and turn left on Salizzada S. Samuele. Great location 2min. from V: #82 (S. Samuele) and 10min. from P. S. Marco. Clean rooms, some with balcony views of S. Marco's red rooftops. Singles €26-45; doubles €36-75, with bath €46-105; triples €135. Cash only. ❸

Hotel Locanda Fiorita, Campiello Novo, S. Marco 3457a (☎523 47 54; www.locandafiorita.com). From Campo S. Stefano, take Calle del Pestrin and then climb onto the raised *piazza*. Sunny terrace leads to rooms with lush bedspreads and tapestry wallpaper. All rooms have A/C and TV. Singles €80; doubles €110-180. AmEx/MC/V. ❺

Domus Civica (ACISJF), Campiello Chiovere Frari, S. Polo 3082 (☎72 11 03). From the station, cross Ponte Scalzi and turn right. Turn left on Fondamenta dei Tolentini and left onto Corte Amai. The hostel is to the right, after the bridge. Spartan beds with shared coed bath, TV, and piano. Strict curfew 11:30pm. Open June-Sept. Singles €29; doubles and triples €52. 20% ISIC discount; 15% Rolling Venice discount. Cash only. ❸

CASTELLO

Castello, where most Venetians make their homes, is arguably the most authentic part of Venice. A room with a view of the sculpted skyline is worth the inevitability of getting lost among the city's most narrowest and most tightly clustered streets.

🏨 **Foresteria Valdese,** Castello 5170 (☎528 67 97). From Campo S. Maria Formosa, take Calle Lunga S. Marial; it's immediately over the 1st bridge. Frescoed ceilings ornament the 18th-century Palazzo Cavagnis, a guest house run by Venice's largest Protestant church. No curfew. Closed Nov. Dorms €21-22; doubles €57, with bath €75; quads with bath €104. €1 Rolling Venice discount, 2% discount with cash payment. MC/V. ❷

🏨 **La Residenza,** Campo Bandiera e Moro Castello 3608 (☎528 53 15; www.venicelaresidenza.com). From V: Arsenal, turn left on Riva degli Schiavoni and right on C. del Dose into the *campo.* Luxurious hotel with palatial lobby. All rooms with bath, safe, A/C, TV, and minibar. Singles €60-95; doubles €100-155. MC/V. ❺

Antica Locanda Casa Verardo, Castello 4765 (☎528 61 27; www.casaverardo.it). From the Basilica, take C. Canonica, turn right before the bridge and left over the bridge on Ruga Giuffa into S. Filippo e Giacomo. Follow C. della Chiesa left out of the *campo;* hotel is just across the 1st bridge. Richly colored rooms in a 16th-century *palazzo.* Singles €60-100; doubles €80-240. AmEx/MC/V. ❺

DORSODURO

Spartan facades line the still canals that trace the quiet streets of Dorsoduro. Here, museums draw visitors to canal-front real estate, while the area around C. S. Margherita remains a residential quarter and a vibrant student social hub. Situated near the Grand Canal and the Ponte Accademia, most hotels tend to be pricey.

▓ **Locanda Cà Foscari,** Calle della Frescada, Dorsoduro 3887b (☎71 04 01), in a quiet neighborhood. From V: San Tomà, turn left at the dead end, cross the bridge, turn right, then turn left on the alley. Murano glass chandeliers and *Carnevale* masks embellish this family-run hotel. Breakfast included. Closed Nov. 20-Jan. 20 and 1st wk. in Aug. Singles €62; doubles €72, with bath €93; triples €90/€114; quads €112. MC/V. ❺

Hotel Galleria, Rio Terra Antonio Foscarini, Dorsoduro 878/A (☎523 24 89), on the left facing the Accademia Museum. Oriental rugs and art prints lend an elegance appropriate to its location on the Grand Canal. Breakfast in bed included. Singles €75; doubles €100, with bath €115, with canal view €180; triples €130-190. AmEx/MC/V. ❺

CAMPING

Plan on at least a 20min. boat ride from Venice. In addition to these listings, the Litorale del Cavallino, on the Lido's Adriatic side, has multiple beach campsites.

Camping Miramare, Lungomare Dante Alighieri 29 (☎96 61 50; www.camping-miramare.it). A 40min. ride on *vaporetto* #14 from P. S. Marco to Punta Sabbioni. Campground is along the beach on the right. 3-night min. stay in summer. Reserve bungalows ahead. Open Apr.-Oct. €4.30-6.40 per person, €9-14 per tent; bungalows €27-62 plus per-person charge. 15% Rolling Venice discount only on per-person cost. MC/V. ❶

Camping Fusina, V. Moranzani 93 (☎547 00 55; www.camping-fusina.com), in Malcontenta. From Mestre, take bus #1. Restaurant, garden, laundromat, ATM, Internet, and satellite TV on premises. Call ahead to reserve cabins. Showers included. €7 per person; €4 per tent; €14 per car. Cabin singles €13; doubles €26. AmEx/MC/V. ❶

◖ FOOD

In Venice, dining well on a budget requires exploration. The best and most affordable restaurants are hidden in the less-traveled alleyways—for authenticity, look for restaurants without a *menù turistico*. For an inexpensive option, visit any *osteria* or *bacario* and create a meal from the vast array of *cicchetti* (tidbits of seafood, rice, meat, and sardines; €1-3). The key ingredients of Venetian cuisine come fresh from the sea. *Spaghetti al vongole* (pasta with clams and vegetables) is served on nearly every menu. Good local wines include the sparkling white *prosecco della Marca* or the red *valpolicella*. **DILLA** supermarket, Strada Nuova, Cannaregio 3660, is near Campo Apostoli. (Open daily 9am-8pm. AmEx/MC/V.)

RESTAURANTS

▓ **Cantinone del Vino,** Fondamente Meraviglie, Dorsoduro 992 (☎523 00 34). Individually priced bottles of wine ranging from €3-200 a bottle. Enjoy a glass (from €0.70) at the bar with some *cicchetti* (from €1). Open M-Sa 8:30am-8:30pm. Cash only. ❷

▓ **Le Bistrot de Venise,** Calle dei Fabbri, S. Marco 4685 (☎523 66 51; www.bistrotdevenise.com). Scrumptious, beautifully presented pasta dishes prepared from 14th-century recipes are overshadowed only by the service. *Primi* from €10. *Secondi* from €22. Service 15%. 10% Rolling Venice discount. Open daily noon-1am. MC/V. ❺

Trattoria da Bepi, Cannaregio 4550 (☎528 50 31). Copper pots dangle above patrons enjoying Venetian cuisine and years of expertise at this family-run *trattoria*. *Primi* €7-11. *Secondi* €10-17. Open M-W and F-Su noon-2:30pm and 7-10pm. MC/V. ❹

Vino, Vino, Ponte d. Veste, S. Marco 2007A. Dark bar with over 350 varieties of wine. Seafood menu changes daily. *Primi* €5.50. *Secondi* €9-10.50. Open M and W F and Su 10:30am-midnight, Sa 10:30am-1am. 15% Rolling Venice discount. Cash only. ❸

Osteria al Bomba, Cannaregio 4297/98 (☎520 51 75). From Hotel Bernardi-Semenzato, exit right onto Strada Nuova, then turn right into the next alleyway. Sidle up to the bar and order a glass of *prosecco* (€1) or nab a plate of *cicchetti* (€1 for a skewer, €14 for a large mixture). Open W-Sa 6-10pm, Su 11am-2:30pm and 6-10pm. MC/V. ❶

Pizzeria/Trattoria Al Vecio Canton, Castello 4738/A (☎ 528 51 76). Famed for *pizza Vecio Canton* (with tomatoes, cheese, anchovies, olive oil, garlic, and a spritz of lemon; €6), this *pizzerie* is a bustling neighborhood favorite. Cover €2. Service 12%. *Primi* €6-10. *Secondi* €8-20. Open M and W-Su noon-3pm and 7pm-midnight. MC/V. ❸

Cip Ciap, Calle Mondo Novo, Castello 5799/A (☎ 523 66 21). Generously portioned pizzas and calzones are deliciously greasy and surprisingly filling. Try the *disco volante* (literally, flying saucer), made like a calzone and stuffed with mushrooms, eggplant, ham, egg, and salami (€6.50). Open M and W-Su 9am-9pm. Cash only. ❷

Gam Gam, Canale di Cannaregio, Cannaregio 1122 (☎ 71 52 84). Religious artwork dots the small interior of the only kosher Jewish restaurant in Venice. Join Shabbat service on Friday night and enjoy a free Shabbat dinner after; all are welcome. Pasta €7.50-9. 10% *Let's Go* discount. Open M-Th noon-10pm, Su noon-5pm. Cash only. ❸

Osteria Enoteca "Vivaldi," S. Polo 1457 (☎ 523 81 85). Friendly tavern-style restaurant lined with violins, framed sheets of music, and portraits of its namesake. *Primi* €8-10. *Secondi* from €10. Cover €1.50. Service 10%. Open daily 10:30am-2:30pm and 5:30-10:30pm. Kitchen opens at noon. AmEx/MC/V. ❸

Ae Oche, S. Croce 1552a/b (☎ 524 11 61). From Campo S. Giacomo da l'Orio, take Calle del Trentor. Not for the indecisive, this *trattoria* offers over 100 types of pizza (€3.50-7.80) and a bustling crowd that spills out onto canal-side tables. Open daily noon-3pm and 7pm-midnight. Cover €1.40. Service 12%. MC/V. ❶

GELATERIE

■ **La Boutique del Gelato,** Salizzada S. Lio, Castello 5727 (☎ 522 32 83). Popular stand doles out rich, heavy gelato to scores of passers-by. 1 scoop €0.80, 2 scoops €1.50. Open daily July-Aug. 10am-midnight; Sept.-June 10am-8:30pm. Cash only. ❶

Gelateria Nico, Fondamenta Zattere, Dorsoduro 922. Great view of the Giudecca Canal. For a guilty pleasure that's heavy on the pleasure, try the Venetian ■ **gianduiotto al passagetto** (a chunk of dense chocolate-hazelnut ice cream dropped into a cup of whipped cream; €2.30). 1 scoop €1, 2 scoops €1.50, 3 scoops €2. Open M-W and F-Su 6:45am-11pm. Cash only. ❶

🅖 SIGHTS

AROUND PIAZZA SAN MARCO

■ **BASILICA DI SAN MARCO.** Venice's crown jewel, San Marco, is a spectacular fusion of gold mosaics on marble walls, gracing **Piazza San Marco** with bulbous, symmetrical arches and incomparable mosaic portals. As the city's largest tourist attraction, the **Basilica di San Marco** also has the longest lines. Visit in the early morning for the shortest wait or in late afternoon for the best natural illumination. Begun in the 9th century to house the remains of St. Mark, the interior now sparkles with mosaics from both the 13th-century Byzantine and 16th-century Renaissance periods. Behind the altar, the **Pala D'Oro** relief frames a parade of saints in thick, gem-encrusted gold. Behind this masterpiece, the tomb of St. Mark himself rests within the altar, adorned with a single gold-stemmed rose. To the right rests the **Tesoro** (treasury), containing gold and relics from the Fourth Crusade. Steep stairs in the atrium lead to the **Galleria della Basilica,** which provides an eye-level view of the tiny golden tiles that compose the Basilica's vast ceiling mosaics, an intimate view of the original bronze **Cavalli di San Marco** (Horses of St. Mark), and a balcony overlooking the *piazza* below. (*Basilica open M-Sa 9:30am-5pm, Su 2-4pm. Modest dress required. Free. Pala D'Oro open M-Sa 9:45am-5pm. €2. Treasury open M-Sa 9:45am-5pm. €2. Galleria open M-F 9:45am-4:15pm, Sa-Su 9:45am-4:45pm. €3.*)

■ **PALAZZO DUCALE (DOGE'S PALACE).** Once the home of Venice's *doge* (mayor), the Palazzo Ducale museum contains spectacular artwork including Veronese's *Rape of Europa*. In the courtyard, Sansovino's enormous sculptures, *Mars* and *Neptune*, flank the **Scala dei Giganti** (Stairs of the Giants), upon which new *doges* were crowned. On the balcony stands the **Bocca di Leone** (Lion's Mouth), into which the Council of Ten, the *doge's* assistants, who acted as judges and administrators, would drop the names of those they suspected to be guilty of crimes. The *doge's* private apartments and the massive state rooms of the Republic contain ornate carving, thick gold leaf, and enormous oil canvases. Climb the elaborate **Scala d'Oro** (Golden Staircase) to the **Sala delle Quatro Porte** (Room of the Four Doors), and the **Sala dell'Anticollegio** (Antechamber of the Senate). More doors lead through the courtrooms of the much-feared Council of Ten, the even-more-feared Council of Three, and the **Sala del Maggior Consiglio** (Great Council Room), dominated by Tintoretto's *Paradise*, the largest oil painting in the world. Near the end, thick stone lattices line the **Ponte dei Sospiri** (Bridge of Sighs) and continue into the prisons. Casanova was condemned by the Ten to walk across this bridge, which gets its name from 19th-century Romantic writers' references to the groans of prisoners descending into the cells. (☎ 520 90 70. *Wheelchair accessible. Open daily Apr.-Oct. 9am-7pm; Nov.-Apr. 9am-5pm. €11, students €5.50.*)

■ **PIAZZA SAN MARCO.** Unlike the labyrinthine streets that tangle themselves through most of Venice, P. S. Marco, Venice's only official *piazza*, is a magnificent expanse of light, space, and architectural harmony. Enclosing the *piazza* are rows of cafes and expensive shops along the ground floor of the Renaissance **Procuratie Vecchie** (old treasury offices), the Baroque **Procuratie Nuove** (new treasury offices), and the Neoclassical **Ala Napoleonica** (also treasury offices). The 96m brick **campanile** (bell tower), which stands on Roman foundations, provides one of the best views of the city. In a 1902 restoration project, it collapsed into a pile of bricks only to be reconstructed in 1912 with the enlightened addition of an elevator. On a clear day, Croatia and Slovenia are visible from the top, but a panorama of the entire island is almost guaranteed. (*Campanile open daily 9am-9pm. €6.*)

LA SCALA DEL BOVOLO. This brick and white marble "staircase of the snails," as it translates into English, takes guests up five stories of tightly spiraling marble *loggia* to a circular portico at the top. Legend has it that the staircase was designed by Leonardo da Vinci himself and constructed by his assistants. It once led to the top floors of a now-destroyed palace. Today the top only affords views of the courtyard below, red-tiled rooftops, and the not-especially-sordid lives of various neighbors. (*From the Campo Manin, facing the bridge, take a left down the alley and look for the signs. Open daily Apr.-Oct. 10am-6pm; Nov.-Mar. 10am-4pm. €3. Cash only.*)

AROUND THE PONTE RIALTO

THE GRAND CANAL. The Grand Canal is Venice's "main street." Over 3km long and nearly 50m wide, it loops through the city and passes under three bridges: the **Ponte Scalzi, Rialto,** and **Accademia.** The candy-cane posts used for mooring boats on the canal are called *"bricole";* they are painted with the family colors of the adjoining *palazzo. (For great facade views, ride vaporetto #82 or the slower #1 from the train station to P. S. Marco. The facades are flood-lit at night, producing dazzling reflections.)*

PONTE RIALTO. This impressive architectural construct was named after Rivo Alto, the first colony built in Venice. It was originally built of wood, but after its collapse in the 1500s, Antonio da Ponte designed the current structure (1588-91).

RIVOALTUS LEGATORIA. Step into the book-lined Rivoaltus and hear Wanda Scarpa shouting greetings from the attic, where she has been sewing leather-bound ▓journals for an international cadre of customers for more than 30 years. The shop's floor-to-ceiling shelves overflow with the fruits of Wanda's efforts. *(Ponte di Rialto 11. Basic notebooks €18-31, photo albums €31-78. Open daily 10am-7:30pm.)*

SAN POLO

▓ **SCUOLA GRANDE DI SAN ROCCO.** The most illustrious of Venice's *scuola*, or guild halls, stands as a monument to Jacopo Tintoretto, who left Venice only once in 76 years, and who sought to combine "the color of Titian with the drawing of Michelangelo." The school commissioned Tintoretto to complete all the paintings in the building, which took 23 years. *(Behind Basilica dei Frari in Campo S. Rocco. Open daily Apr.-Oct. 9am-5:30pm; Nov.-Mar. 10am-4pm. €5.50, students €4.)*

DORSODURO

▓ **GALLERIE DELL'ACCADEMIA.** The Accademia houses the most extensive collection of Venetian art in the world. At the top of the double staircase, **Room I,** topped by a ceiling full of cherubim, houses Venetian Gothic art. Among the enormous altarpieces in **Room II,** Giovanni Bellini's *Madonna Enthroned with Child, Saints, and Angels* stands out for its lush serenity. **Rooms IV** and **V** display more Bellinis and **Giorgione's** enigmatic *La Tempesta.* In **Room VI,** three paintings by Tintoretto, *The Creation of the Animals, The Temptation of Adam and Eve,* and *Cain and Abel* get progressively darker as one moves from the glowing God commanding flocks of animals to the graphic murder of Abel by Cain, who stands naked in the darkness. In **Room XX,** works by Gentile Bellini and Carpaccio display Venetian processions and cityscapes so accurately that scholars use them as "photos" of Venice's past. *(V: Accademia. Open M 8:15am-2pm, Tu-Su 9:15am-7:15pm. €6.50.)*

▓ **COLLEZIONE PEGGY GUGGENHEIM.** Guggenheim's Palazzo Venier dei Leoni displays works by Dalí, Kandinsky, Klee, Picasso, and Pollock. The Marini sculpture *Angel in the City,* in front of the *palazzo,* was designed with a detachable penis so that Ms. Guggenheim could make emergency alterations to avoid offending her more prudish guests. *(Fondamenta Venier dei Leoni, Dorsoduro 710. V: Accademia. Turn left and follow the signs. Open M and Th-Su 10am-6pm. €8, ISIC or Rolling Venice €5.)*

CASTELLO

SCUOLA DALMATA SAN GIORGIO DEGLI SCHIAVONI. Some of Carpaccio's finest paintings, including episodes from the lives of St. George, Jerome, and Tryfon, decorate this early 16th-century building. *(Castello, 3259/A. V: S. Zaccaria. Modest dress required. Open Apr.-Oct. Tu-Sa 9:30am-12:30pm and 3:30-6:30pm, Su 9:30am-12:30pm; Nov.-Mar. Tu-Sa 10am-12:30pm and 3-6pm, Su 10am-12:30pm. €3.)*

CANNAREGIO

JEWISH GHETTO. In 1516 the *doge* forced Venice's Jewish population into the old cannon-foundry area, creating the first Jewish ghetto in Europe. The word "ghetto" is the Venetian word for "foundry." The **Schola Grande Tedesca** (German Synagogue), the oldest synagogue in the area, now shares a building with the **Museo Ebraica di Venezia** (Hebrew Museum of Venice) in the Campo del Ghetto Nuovo. *(Cannaregio 2899/B. V: S. Marcuola. Hebrew Museum open M-F and Su June-Sept. 10am-7pm; Oct.-May 10am-4:30pm. €3, students €2. Entrance to synagogues by guided tour only, 40min. Museum and tour €8, students €6.50. MC/V.)*

CÀ D'ORO AND GALLERIA GIORGIO FRANCHETTI. The most spectacular facade on the Canal Grande and the premier example of Venetian Gothic, the Cà d'Oro, built between 1425 and 1440, now houses the Giorgio Franchetti collection. For the best view of the palace, take the *traghetto* across the canal to the Rialto Markets. *(V: Cà d'Oro. Open M 8:15am-2pm, T-Su 8:15am-7:15pm. €5, students €2.50.)*

CHURCHES

The Foundation for the Churches of Venice sells the **Chorus Pass** that provides admission to all of Venice's churches. A yearly pass (€8, students €5) which includes S. Maria dei Miracoli, S. Maria Gloriosa dei Frari, S. Polo, Madonna dell'Orto, Il Redentore, and S. Sebastiano, is available at all participating churches except S. Maria Gloriosa dei Frari. *(☎ 275 0462; www.chorusvenezia.org.)*

■ CHIESA DI SAN ZACCARIA (SAN MARCO). Designed in the late 1400s by Coducci, among others, and dedicated to the father of John the Baptist, this Gothic-Renaissance church holds S. Zaccaria's incorruptible corpse in a glass-windowed sarcophagus along the right wall of the nave. Nearby, watch for Bellini's *Virgin and Child Enthroned with Four Saints*, one of the masterpieces of Venetian Renaissance painting. Its rich tones and shading are a testament to the Venetian attention to detail. *(V: S. Zaccaria. Open daily 10am-noon and 4-6pm. Free.)*

BASILICA DI SANTA MARIA GLORIOSA DEI FRARI (SAN POLO). Franciscans began construction on this enormous Gothic church, also known simply as *I Frari*, in 1340. Today it is a mausoleum of art, boasting two paintings by Titian as well as the master himself, who is entombed within the cathedral's terra-cotta walls. His ■**Assumption** (1516-1518) on the high altar marks the height of the Venetian Renaissance. Titian's elaborate tomb stands across from the enormous pyramid in which the sculptor Canova rests. *(V: S. Tomà. Follow signs back to Campo dei Frari. Open M-Sa 9am-6pm, Su 1-6pm. €2.50.)*

CHIESA DI SANTA MARIA DELLA SALUTE (DORSODURO). The theatrical *Salute* (Italian for "health") is a hallmark of the scattered Venetian skyline: From the church's perch on Dorsoduro's long peninsula just southwest of San Marco, its domes are visible from everywhere in the city. The fat domes, accented with gesturing marble statuary and spiral flourishes, are prime examples of the Baroque style. In 1631, the city commissioned Longhena to build the church for the Virgin, whom they believed would return the favor by ending the plague. *(V: Salute. ☎ 522 55 58. Open daily 9am-noon and 3-5:30pm. Free. Entrance to sacristy with donation.)*

CHIESA DI SAN SEBASTIANO (DORSODURO). The Renaissance painter Veronese took refuge in this small 16th-century church when he fled Verona in 1555 after allegedly killing a man. By 1565, he had filled the church with an amazing cycle of paintings and frescoes. His *Stories of Queen Esther* covers the ceiling, while the artist himself rests under the gravestone by the organ. *(V: S. Basilio. Open M-Sa 10am-5pm, Su 1-5pm. Tickets close at 4:45pm. €2.50. Cash only.)*

CHIESA DI SANTISSIMI GIOVANNI E PAOLO (CASTELLO). This terra-cotta structure is built primarily in the Gothic style, but it has a Renaissance-era portal and an arch supported by columns of Greek marble. Inside, monumental salmon-hued walls and cream-colored stone ceilings enclose the tombs and monuments of the doges. After a fire destroyed the chapel in 1867, Veronese replaced the chapel's lost paintings with ceiling pieces depicting the Adoration, Assumption, and Annunciation. *(V: Fondamenta Nuove. Turn left, then right on Fondamenta dei Mendicanti. ☎ 523 59 13. Open M-Sa 9:30am-7pm, Su 1-7pm. €2.50, students €1.25.)*

CHIESA DI SANTA MARIA DEI MIRACOLI (CASTELLO). This small Renaissance jewel remains one of Venice's prettiest churches, elegantly faced with polychrome marble and brimming inside with gold reliefs, sculpted figures, and lavish colors. *(From S. S. Giovanni e Paolo, cross Ponte Rosse and continue straight. At the dead end, follow the alley to your right. Open M-Sa 10am-5pm, Su 1-5pm. €2.50. Cash only.)*

SAN GIORGIO MAGGIORE AND GIUDECCA

BASILICA DI SAN GIORGIO MAGGIORE. Standing on its own monastic island, S. Giorgio Maggiore contrasts sharply with most other Venetian churches. Palladio ignored the Venetian fondness for color and instead opted for an austere design. Light fills the enormous open space inside, although unfortunately it does not hit Tintoretto's *Last Supper* by the high altar. The beautiful courtyard, to the right of the church, is closed to the public. Take the elevator to the top of the **campanile** for a marvelous view of the city. *(V: S. Giorgio Maggiore. Open M-Sa in summer 9am-12:30pm and 2:30-6:30pm; low season 2:30-5pm. Basilica free. Campanile €3.)*

ISLANDS OF THE LAGOON

⚑ BURANO. Curtains billow from the doorways of bright yellow and electric blue houses in this traditional fishing village, where carefully hand-tatted lace has become a community art. The **Scuola di Merletti di Burano** (Lace Museum), once home of the island's professional lace-making school, displays local handiwork. The basilica, **Chiesa di San Martino,** sits across from the museum. *(40min. boat ride from Venice. V: #12: Burano from either S. Zaccaria or Fond. Nuove. Museum in P. Galuppi. Open M and W-Su 10am-5pm. €4. Church open daily 8am-noon and 3-7pm. Free.)*

⚑ MURANO. Famous for its glass since 1292 (when Venice's artisans were forced off Venice proper because their kilns started fires), the island of Murano affords visitors the opportunity to witness resident artisans blowing and spinning crystalline creations. The **Museo Vetrario** (Glass Museum) houses a collection featuring pieces from the last two millennia. *(V: #12 or 52: Faro from S. Zaccaria. Museo Vetrario: Fond. Giustian 8. ☎ 73 95 86. Open M-Tu and Th-Su Apr.-Oct. 10am-5pm; Nov.-Mar. 10am-4pm. €4, students €2.50. Basilica open daily 8am-noon and 4-7pm. Free.)*

⚑ LIDO. The sunny, breezy resort island of Lido provided the tragic setting for Thomas Mann's haunting novella of love and lust, *Death in Venice.* Today, people flock to Lido to enjoy the surf at the popular **public beach.** An impressive shipwreck looms at one end. *(V #1 and 82: Lido. Beach open 9am-8pm. Free.)*

🎵 ENTERTAINMENT

Admire Venetian houses and *palazzi* via their original canal pathways. Rides are most romantic about 50min. before sunset and most affordable if shared by six people. The rate that a gondolier quotes is negotiable, and the most bargain-able gondoliers are those standing by themselves rather than those in groups at the "taxi-stands" throughout the city. The "official" price starts at €62 per 50min., with a maximum of six people; prices rise at night.

Teatro Goldoni, Calle del Teatro, S. Marco 4650/B (☎240 20 11), near the Ponte di Rialto, showcases varying types of live productions, often with a seasonal theme. Check with the theater for upcoming listings. The **Mostra Internazionale di Cinema** (International Film Festival), held annually from late August to early September, draws established names and rising phenoms. Movies screened in the original language. (☎521 88 78. Tickets €20. Some late-night outdoor showings are free.) The weekly *A Guest in Venice*, free at hotels and tourist offices or online at www.unospitedivenezia.it, lists current festivals, concerts, and gallery exhibits.

Banned by the church for several centuries, Venice's famous **Carnevale** was successfully reinstated in the early 1970s. During the 10 days preceding Ash Wednesday, masked figures jam the streets and outdoor concerts and street performances spring up throughout the city. Venice's second-most colorful festival is the **Festa del Redentore** (3rd Su in July), originally held to celebrate the end of a plague. It kicks off with a magnificent fireworks display at 11:30pm the Saturday before.

🎵 NIGHTLIFE

Though pubs and bars are not uncommon, most residents agree that a truly vibrant nightlife in Venice is virtually non-existent. It seems that locals would rather spend an evening sipping wine or beer and listening to string quartets in P. S. Marco than bumping and/or grinding in a disco, but the island's fluctuating population means that new establishments spring up (and wither and die) with some regularity. Student nightlife is concentrated around **Campo Santa Margherita**, in Dorsoduro, and the areas around the **Lista di Spagna**, in Cannaregio.

■ **Paradiso Perduto**, Fondamenta della Misericordia 2540. Students and locals flood this unassuming bar with conversation and laughter, while the young waitstaff doles out large portions of *cicchetti* (€11). Live jazz Su 9pm. Open Th-Su 7pm-2am. Closed July.

■ **Piccolo Mondo**, Accademia, Dorsoduro 1056/A. (☎520 03 71). Disco, hip-hop, and vodka with Red Bull (€10) keep a full house at this small but popular *discoteca*, while Framed collages of the clientele include notables like Michael Jordan and Mick Jagger. Drinks from €7. Cover varies, free with *Let's Go*. Open nightly 10pm-4am. AmEx/MC/V.

■ **Café Blue**, S. Pantalon, Dorsoduro 3778. Grab some absinthe (€6) and a stool in the brick-walled back room and watch the daytime coffee crowd turn young and trendy as night falls. Free Internet available. Live jazz F and Su evening during the winter. Open daily in summer noon-2am; low season 8am-2am. Cash only.

Orange, Dorsoduro 3054a (☎523 47 40; www.orangebar.it). Across from Duchamp in Campo S. Margherita. Modern art canvases dot the bright walls of this hip new bar, where everything except the aquamarine garden is uniformly orange. Try the tequila sunrise (€5). Beer from €1.20. Wine from €1. Open M-Sa 7am-2pm. AmEx/DC/MC/V.

Cafe Noir, Dorsoduro 3805 (☎71 09 25). Faded images of Marilyn Monroe cover the walls of Cafe Noir, where brown lampo, a blue glass mosaic bar, and tightly packed tables give an artistic vibe. The black leather booth and street-side windows in front are great for coffee and people-watching. Open M-Sa 7am-2am, Su 9am-2am. Cash only.

PADUA (PADOVA)   ☎049

Ancient Padua (pop. 205,000) was once a wealthy center of commerce, but centuries of barbarian attacks and natural disasters left few of her architectural treasures intact. Padua's university, founded in 1222 and second in seniority only to Bologna's, keeps a young and vibrant population buzzing in the streets well past dusk. The starry blue-ceiling of the ■**Cappella degli Scrovegni**, P. Eremitani 8, overlooks Giotto's breathtaking 38-panel fresco cycle, illustrating the lives of Mary, Jesus, St. Anne, and St. Joachim. Buy tickets at the attached **Musei Civici Eremitani**, which displays an overwhelming art collection, including Giotto's beautiful crucifix that once adorned the Scrovegni Chapel. (☎820 45 51; www.padovanet.it/museicivici. Open daily Feb.-Oct. 9am-7pm; Nov.-Jan. 9am-6pm. Museum €10; combined with chapel €12, students €5. AmEx/DC/MC/V.) Thousands of pilgrims are drawn to Saint Anthony's displayed jawbone, tongue, and tomb at the **Basilica di Sant'Antonio**, in P. del Santo, a medieval conglomeration of eight domes filled with beautiful frescoes. (☎878 97 22; www.basilicadelsanto.org. Modest dress required. Open daily Apr.-Sept. 6:30am-7:45pm; Nov.-Mar. 6:30am-6:45pm. Free.)

From the basilica, follow signs to **Orto Botanico,** V. Orto Botanico 15, a circular oasis of colorful water lilies, medicinal herbs, and a 420-year-old palm tree that continues to offer shade. (Open Apr.-Sept. daily 9am-1pm and 3-6pm; Oct.-Mar. M-F 9am-1pm. €4, students €1.) Next to the **duomo,** in P. Duomo, sits the tiny 12th-century **Battistero,** with a domed interior coated with colorful New Testament frescoes. (Duomo open M-Sa 7:30am-noon and 3:45-7:45pm, Su 7:45am-1pm and 3:45-8:30pm. Free. Battistero open daily 10am-6pm. €2.50, students €1.50.) Ancient buildings from the university are scattered throughout the city, especially near the student-heavy **Palazzo Bó,** which also serves as the nexus for nightlife. The cavernous **Highlander Pub,** V. S. Martino e Solferino 69, is a consistently lively Scottish hot spot with pints from €4.50. (Open daily 11am-3pm and 6pm-2am.)

   Trains depart from P. Stazione for Bologna (1½hr., 34 per day, €5.73); Milan (2½hr., 25 per day, €11.21); Venice (30min., 82 per day, €2.45); and Verona (1hr., 44 per day, €4.23). **Buses** (☎820 68 11; fax 820 68 28) leave from P. Boschetti for Venice (45min., 2 per hr., €2.90). The **tourist office** is in the train station. (☎875 20 77. Open M-Sa 9am-7pm, Su 8:30am-12:30pm.) From the train station, follow the main street through town and turn right on V. Rogati. Go to V. Aleardi and turn left; walk to the end of the block and **Ostello Città di Padova (HI) ❶,** V. Aleardi 30, will be on the left. (☎875 22 19; pdyhtl@tin.it. Internet €5.16 per hr. Wheelchair accessible. Lockout 9:30am-4pm. Curfew 11pm. Reserve at least 1 week in advance. Dorms €14.50. Nonmembers add €3. MC/V.) **Locanda la Perla ❸,** V. Cesarotti 67, has large, airy rooms minutes from the Basilica di Sant'Antonio. (☎87 55 89 39. Closed Aug. 15-30. Singles €30-32; doubles €40-42. Cash only.) Enjoy thick, flavorful pizza on the wooden deck of **Pizzeria Al Borgo ❷,** V. L. Belludi, 56, near the Basilica di S. Antonio. (Pizzas from €3.70. Cover €2. Open M and W-Su noon-2:30pm and 7pm-midnight. MC/V.) **Postal Code:** 35100.

VERONA   ☎045

A glorious combination of majestic Roman ruins, colorful Venetian facades, and orange rooftops, Verona (pop. 245,000) is one of the most beautiful cities in Northern Italy. In this city, star-crossed lovers, jaded travelers, and hopeless romantics alike can find verdant gardens and breathtakingly realistic sculptures in the setting of Shakespeare's *Romeo and Juliet.*

🖃🛈 TRANSPORTATION AND PRACTICAL INFORMATION. Trains (☎89 20 21) go from P. XXV Aprile to Bologna (2hr., 27 per day, €6); Milan (2hr., 37 per day, €7); Trent (1hr., 25 per day, €6); and Venice (1½hr., 41 per day, €6). From the train station, walk 20min. up **Corso Porta Nuova** or take bus #11, 12, 13, 72, or 73 (weekends take #91, 92, or 93) to Verona's epicenter, the **Arena** in **Piazza Brà.** The **tourist office** is right of the *piazza* at V. D. Alpini, 9. (☎806 86 80; iatverona@provincia.vr.it. Open M-Sa 9am-7pm, Su 9am-3pm.) **Internet Train,** V. Roma 17/a, has high-speed computers. (☎801 33 94. €2.50 per 30min., €5 per hr. for first-time users, plus 1 bonus hr. Open M-F 11am-10pm, Sa-Su 2-8pm. MC/V.) **Postal Code:** 37100.

🖪🍴 ACCOMMODATIONS AND FOOD. Reserve hotel rooms ahead, especially in opera season (June-Sept.). The ▨**Ostello della Gioventù (HI) ❶,** Villa Francescatti, Salita Fontana del Ferro 15, is in a renovated 16th-century villa with gorgeous gardens; from the station, take bus #73 or night bus #90 to P. Isolo, turn right, and follow the signs uphill. (☎59 03 60. Lockout 9am-5pm. Curfew 11:30pm; flexible for opera-goers. Dorms €13.50.) To get to the **Locanda Catullo ❹,** Vco. Catullo 1, walk from V. Mazzini, turn onto V. Catullo, and turn left on Vco. Catullo. (☎800 27 86. Singles €40; doubles €55-65; triples €81-96. Cash only.) Verona is famous for its wines, including the dry white *soave* and red *valpolicella.* Prices in **Piazza Isolo** are cheaper than those in P. delle Erbe. **Enoteca dal Zuvo ❶,** Vco. S. Marco in Foro 7/5, near P. Brà, was once the private chapel of Verona's arch-bishop. (☎803 43 69. Open M-Th 8am-1pm and 2-8:30pm, F-Su 8am-1pm and 2-9pm. Cash only.) **Pam** supermarket is at V. dei Mutilati 3. (Open M-Sa 8am-8pm, Su 9am-7pm.)

◪ **SIGHTS.** The physical and social heart of Verona is the tiered first-century **Arena** in P. Brà. (☎800 32 04. Open M 1:45-6:30pm, Tu-Su 8:30am-6:30pm. Closes 4:30pm on opera nights. Tickets close 45min. before Arena. €3.10, students €2.10. Cash only.) From late June to early Sept., tourists and singers from around the world descend on the Arena for the city's annual ▨**Opera Festival.** *La Boheme*, *Aida*, and *Turandot* are among the 2005 highlights. (☎800 51 51; www.arena.it. Box office open M-F 9am-noon and 3:15-5:45pm, Su 9am-noon. During 2005 opera season, June 17-Aug. 31, open on performance days from 10am-9pm, non-performance days 10am-5:45pm. General admission M-Th and Su €16.50-24.50, F-Sa €18.50-26.50. AmEx/MC/V.) From P. Brà, V. Mazzini leads to the markets and medieval architecture of **Piazza delle Erbe,** the former Roman forum. The 83m ▨**Torre dei Lambertini,** in P. dei Signori, offers a breathtaking view of Verona. (Open M 1:30-7:30pm, Tu-Su 8:30am-7:30pm. €2.60, students €2.10. Cash only.) The **Giardino Giusti,** V. Giardino Giusti 2, is a magnificent 16th-century garden filled with limbless Roman sculptures, meticulously trimmed hedges, and a thigh-high floral labyrinth. (Open daily 9am-8pm. €5, under 18 free. Cash only.) The della Scala fortress, **Castelvecchio,** down V. Roma from P. Brà, is filled with an impressive art collection. (Open M 1:30-7:30pm, Tu-Su 8:30am-7:30pm. €2.10, students €1.50. Cash only.) Thousands of tourists have immortalized **Casa di Giulietta** (Juliet's House), V. Cappello 23, although the del Cappello (Capulet) family never actually lived there. The famed balcony overlooks a courtyard full of tourists waiting to rub the bronze statue of Juliet while starry-eyed lovers add their love notes to walls covered in scraps of paper and graffiti. (Open M 1:30-7:30pm, Tu-Su 8:30am-7:30pm. Ticket office closes at 6:45pm. €3.10, students €2.10. Courtyard free. Cash only.)

FRIULI-VENEZIA GIULIA

Friuli-Venezia Giulia traditionally receives less than its share of recognition, but this region has served as inspiration to a number of prominent literary figures. James Joyce lived in Trieste for 12 years, during which he wrote most of *Ulysses;* Ernest Hemingway drew part of the plot for *A Farewell to Arms* from the region's role in WWI; and Freud and Rilke both worked and wrote here. The city of Trieste attracts tourists to the most affordable beach resorts on the Adriatic.

TRIESTE (TRIEST)   ☎040

After volleying between Italian, Austrian, and Slavic allegiances for hundreds of years, Trieste (pop. 241,000) celebrated its 50th anniversary as an Italian city in 2004. Still, subtle reminders of Trieste's Eastern European past are manifest in the arches of her architecture, the subtle spices of her cuisine, and the Habsburgian rulers smirking from the portraits that line her museums' walls. While Trieste's fast-paced center is undeniably urban, the surrounding Carsoian hillside and the tranquil Adriatic Sea temper the metropolis with stunning natural beauty. The **Città Nuova,** a grid-like pattern of streets lined with majestic Neoclassical palaces, centers around the **Canale Grande.** Facing the canal is the bright blue-domed Serbian Orthodox **Chiesa di San Spiridione.** (Open Tu-Sa 9am-noon and 5-8pm. Modest dress required.) The ornate **Municipio** faces the Adriatic across the **Piazza dell'Unità d'Italia,** the largest waterfront *piazza* in Italy. Take bus #24 to the last stop (€0.90) to reach the 15th-century Venetian **Castello di San Giusto,** which presides over **Capitoline Hill.** From P. Goldoni, you can ascend the hill by the **Scala dei Giganti** (Steps of

TURIN OLYMPICS 2006

GOING FOR THE GOLD

If you've always dreamt of Olympic glory, but can't land a lutz or drive a bobsled, there's still hope. The organizers of the XX Winter Olympics are recruiting 20,000 volunteers to work in Turin leading up to and during the Olympic Games and subsequent Paralympic competitions.

Organizers began accepting applications in the summer of 2004 and will continue to do so indefinitely, but those hoping to win a spot should apply by mid-2005. Applicants need only be at least 18 years of age and able to work 10 consecutive days February 10-26 or March 10-19, 2006, with training sessions a few days befor ■ ne committee says "passion ■ is the only other requirement, but admits that proficiency in multiple languages is a plus.

Volunteers are assigned to one of more than 350 jobs based on preferences and experience. Duties range from babysitting athletes' children to assisting with security. The perks are excellent: free meals and local transportation, insurance, and a uniform. Notably missing from the benefits, though, are the price of your plane ticket to Turin and lodgings. The latter is not a trivial omission, as every hotel between Turin and Milan will be booked. And no free tickets to the women's figureskating finals or the the men's giant slalom, either—unless you're lucky enough to be working at them. *For info ■ nd applications, visit www.noi2006.org.*

the Giants), a 265-step climb. (☎30 93 62. Castle open daily Apr.-Sept. 9am-7pm; Oct.-Mar. 9am-5pm. Museum open daily 9am-1pm. Free. Some areas closed for renovation until 2007.) **Piazza della Cattedrale** overlooks the town center and the sea from the remains of a Roman basilica. The archaeological **Museo di Storia e d'Arte,** V. Cattedrale 15, is down the hill past the duomo. (☎31 05 00. Open Tu and Th-Su 9am-1pm, W 9am-7pm. €2, students €1.) At the bottom of the hill is the **Teatro Romano,** a crumbling Roman amphitheater, which is illuminated at night.

Trains leave P. della Libertà 8, down C. Cavour from the quays, for Budapest, Hungary (12hr., 2 per day, €85-95) and Venice (2hr., 20 per day, €8). The APT **tourist office** is at P. dell'Unità d'Italia 4/E, near the harbor. (☎347 83 12; fax 347 83 20. Open M-Sa 9:30am-7pm.) **Hotel Alabarda ❸,** V. Valdirivo 22, is near the city center. All rooms have modern furnishings, telephone, and satellite TV. From the train station, head south on Corso Cavour and turn left onto V. Valdirivo. (☎63 02 69; www.hotelalabarda.it. Internet access €5 per hr. Singles €33, with bath €38; doubles €45/€68; triples €60/€91. AmEx/MC/V.) Catch bus #36 (€0.90) from the V. Miramare side of the train station to reach the **Ostello Tergeste (HI) ❶,** V. Miramare 331. Ask for the Ostello stop. From there, walk along the **Barcola** until you see a yellow villa with a terrace on your right. Guests are expected to help with minimal chores. (☎/fax 22 41 02. Breakfast included. Internet €2 per hr. Reception daily 8am-11:30pm. Dorms €13. HI members only. Cash only.) Eat at **Bar Tartini ❶,** V. San Martiri Liberta 2, a local hot spot for families and teen *Triestini* alike, featuring a near-nightly rotation of jazz musicians. (☎63 61 03. Open daily 8am-midnight. V.) For groceries, stop by **Euro Spesa** supermarket, V. Valdirivo 13/F, off C. Cavour. (☎76 39 38. Open M-Sa 8am-8pm.) **Postal Code:** 34100.

PIEDMONT (PIEMONTE)

Piedmont has been a politically influential region for centuries. When Vittorio Emanuele II and Camillo Cavour united Italy, Turin served as the capital from 1861 to 1865. In addition to its political activity, Piedmont has proven itself a producer of fine food and wine, which *Piemontese* insist is the best in Italy.

TURIN (TORINO) ☎011

Turin's (pop. 860,000) elegance is the direct result of centuries of urban planning—graceful, church-lined avenues lead to spacious *piazze*. At the same time, Turin vibrates with modern economic energy as the headquarters of the **Fiat Auto Company** and the host of the 🖳2006 **Winter Olympic Games.** To experience the Turin of the future and relive past Olympic glories in a multi-media extravaganza, hit the ultra-modern **Olympic Atrium,** in P. Solfieri. (Open daily 9:30am-7pm. Free.) The city also possesses one of the more famous relics of Christianity: the **Holy Shroud of Turin,** which is housed in the **Cattedrale di San Giovanni,** behind the **Palazzo Reale.** With rare exceptions, a life-sized photo is as close as anyone gets to the real thing. (Open daily 7am-noon and 3-7pm. Free.) The **Museo Egizio,** in the **Palazzo dell'Accademia delle Scienze,** V. dell'Accademia delle Scienze 6, boasts a world-class collection of Egyptian artifacts. (Open Tu and F-Su 8:30am-2pm, W 2-7:30pm, Th 10am-7:30pm. €6.50, under 18 and over 65 free.) The same building houses the **Galleria Sabauda,** which features a large collection of Renaissance paintings, including van Dyck and Rembrandt. (Same hours as the Egyptian Museum. €4.) Begun as a synagogue in 1863, the **Mole Antonelliana,** V. Montebello 20, dominates Turin's skyline. It's also home to the eccentric **Museo Nazionale del Cinema,** which plays hundreds of movie clips in oddly-designed settings. (Open Tu-F and Su 9am-8pm, Sa 10am-11pm. €5.40. Elevator to the observation deck €3.60. Combined ticket €6.80.) One of Guarini's great Baroque palaces, the **Palazzo Carignano,** V. dell'Accademia delle Scienze 5, houses the **Museo Nazionale del Risorgimento Italiano,** commemorating the 1706-1846 unification of Italy. (Open Tu-Su 9am-7pm. €5, students €3.50.)

Trains (☎53 13 27) leave Porta Nuova on C. Vittorio Emanuele for: Genoa (2hr., 1 per hr., €8); Milan (2hr., 1 per hr., €8); Rome (4½hr., 5 per day, €38); and Venice (4½hr., 3 per day, €31). The Porta Susa station, on C. Inghilterra, will handle the bulk of the city's rail traffic by 2007. The **tourist office,** in the Atrium, has free maps. (☎53 51 81. Open M-Sa 9:30am-7pm, Su 9:30am-3:30pm.) To get to the clean and comfortable **Ostello Torino (HI) ❶,** V. Alby 1, take bus #52 (#64 on Su) from Stazione Porto Nuova to the "Lanza" stop on V. Crimea. Continue along the road 300m, following the signs. (☎660 29 39. Curfew 11:30pm; ask for a key if coming in late. Closed Dec. 20-Feb. 1. Dorms €12.50; doubles €31-35.) The **Pensione Azalea ❸,** V. Mercanti 16, 4th fl., offers immaculate rooms in a prime location. Exit Porta Nuova on the right and take #58 or 72 to Garibaldi. Turn left on V. Caribaldi, then left on V. Mercanti. (☎53 81 15. Singles €30, with bath €35; doubles €35/€55. MC/V.) The huge **open-air market** in Porta Palazzo has fruit, bread, and cheese; for reasonably priced fare, hit the arcade-lined V. Po, which leads to the River and I Murazzi—the riverside strip of all-night, all-year university student hangouts. **Postal Code:** 10100.

TUSCANY (TOSCANA)

The vision of Tuscany has inspired countless artists, poets, and hordes of tourists. Its rolling hills, prodigious olive groves, and cobblestone streets beg visitors to slow their frenetic pace, sip some wine, and relax in fields of brilliant sunflowers. Tuscany fostered some of Italy's, and the world's, greatest cultural achievements under the tender care—and devious machinations—of the powerful Medici family, gaining eternal eminence in the arts for its staggering accomplishments during a scant half-century. Today, tourists flock to Tuscany to witness the glory that was, and the wonder that still is, *Toscana*.

FLORENCE (FIRENZE)   ☎055

The rays of the setting sun shimmer over a sea of burnt-orange roofs and towering domes to reveal the breathtaking concentration of beauty in Florence (pop. 376,000). Once a busy 13th-century wool- and silk-trading town, Florence took a different path under Medici rule. By the mid-15th century, the city was the undisputed European capital of art, architecture, commerce, and political thought. Today, Florence is a mix of young and old: street graffiti quotes Marx and Malcolm X, businessmen whiz by on Vespas, and children play soccer in front of the duomo.

TRANSPORTATION

Flights: Amerigo Vespucci Airport (FLR; ☎30 615), in Peretola. The **ATAF** bus #62 connects the train station to the airport (€1).

Trains: Santa Maria Novella Station, across from S. Maria Novella. Trains depart every hr. for **Bologna** (1hr., €7.75); **Milan** (3½hr., €22); and **Rome** (3½hr., €15-22); less frequently to **Siena** (1½hr., 10 per day, €5.30) and **Venice** (3hr., 4 per day, €16). Check out www.trenitalia.it for the most up-to-date schedules.

Buses: SITA, V. S. Caterina da Siena 15r (☎28 46 61; www.sita-on-line.it), buses run to **San Gimignano** (1½hr., 14 per day, €7.60) and **Siena** (1½hr., 2 per day, €5.90). **LAZZI,** P. Adua, 1-4r (☎35 10 61; www.lazzi.it) sends buses to **Pisa** (1 per hr., €6.10) via Lucca.

Public Transportation: ATAF (☎800 42 45 00; www.ataf.net), outside the train station, runs orange city buses (6am-1am). 1hr. tickets €1, 3hr. €1.80, 24hr. €4, 3-day €7.20. Buy tickets at any newsstand, *tabacchi,* or automated ticket dispenser before boarding. Validate your ticket using the orange machine on board or risk a €50 fine.

Bike/Moped Rental: Alinari Noleggi, V. Guelfa 85r (☎28 05 00). Bikes €15-20 per day, mopeds €30-60 per day.

ORIENTATION AND PRACTICAL INFORMATION

From the train station, a short walk on V. dei Panzani, and a left on V. dei Cerretani leads to the **duomo,** the center of Florence. Major arteries radiate from the duomo and its two *piazze.* A bustling walkway, **Via dei Calzaiuoli** runs south from the duomo to **Piazza Signoria.** V. Roma leads from P. S. Giovanni through **Piazza della Repubblica** to the **Ponte Vecchio** (old bridge), which crosses from central Florence to **Oltrarno,** the district south of the **Arno River.** Note that most streets change names unpredictably. For guidance through Florence's tangled center, grab a free map from the tourist office.

Tourist Office: Informazione Turistica, P. della Stazione 4 (☎21 22 45), across the *piazza* from the main exit. Info on entertainment and cultural events. Ask for a free map with a street index. Open M-Sa 8:30am-7pm, Su and holidays 8:30am-2pm.

Consulates: UK, Lungarno Corsini 2 (☎28 41 33). Open M-F 9:30am-12:30pm and 2:30-4:30pm. **US,** Lungarno Amerigo Vespucci 38 (☎239 82 76), at V. Palestro, near the station. Open M-F 9am-12:30pm. For consulates not listed, see www.corpoconsolarefrienze.it.

Currency Exchange: Local banks offer the best rates. Most are open M-F 8:20am-1:20pm and 2:45-3:45pm. 24hr. **ATMs** common throughout the city.

American Express: V. Dante Alighieri 22r (☎50 98 220). From the duomo, walk down V. dei Calzaiuoli and turn left on V. dei Tavolini. Mail held free for AmEx customers, otherwise €1.55. Open M-F 9am-5:30pm, Sa 9am-12:30pm.

Emergency: ☎113. **Fire:** ☎115. **Police:** ☎49 771. **Medical Emergency:** ☎118.

24hr. Pharmacies: Farmacia Comunale (☎28 94 35), at the train station by track #16. **Molteni,** V. dei Calzaiuoli 7r (☎28 94 90).

Internet Access: Walk down almost any busy street and you'll find an Internet cafe. **Internet Train** has 15 locations in the city listed on www.internettrain.it/citta.isp. Offers telnet, email, and web-cruising. €4 per hr., students €3. Most branches open M-F 9am-midnight, Sa 10am-8pm, Su noon-9pm. AmEx/MC/V. **Libreria Edison,** P. Repubblica 27r, filled with shelves of books and a cafe. €3 per hr. Open daily 10am-8pm.

Florence

▲▲ ACCOMMODATIONS
Albergo Por S. Maria, 28
Albergo Sampaoli, 5
Campeggio Michelangelo, 37
Hotel Abaco/
  Hotel Giappone, 16
Hotel Elite, 10
Hotel Giglio, 1
Hotel Il Perseo, 17
Hotel La Scaletta, 36
Hotel Nazionale, 4
Hotel Visconti, 15
Istituto Gould, 34
Katti House, 9
Locanda Orchidea, 22
Ostello Archi Rossi, 2
Ostello Santa Monaca, 32
Pensionato Pio X, 33
Relais Cavalcanti, 26
Soggiorno Luna Rosse, 8
Via Faenza 56, 3

● FOOD
Acqua al Due, 23
Al Lume di Candela, 27
Enoteca Alessi, 18
Gelateria Triangolo delle
  Bermuda, 6
La Loggia degli Albizi, 21
Oltrarno Trattoria
  Casalinga, 35
Trattoria Anita, 30
Trattoria Contadino, 12
Trattoria da Giorgio, 11
Tre Merli, 19
Vivoli, 24

★ NIGHTLIFE
Central Park, 14
Kikuya, 31
May Day Lounge, 20
Slowly, 25
Tabasco, 29

ITALY

Post Office: V. Pellicceria (☎273 648), off P. della Repubblica. Address mail to be held: First name SURNAME, In Fermo Posta, L'Ufficio Postale, V. Pellicceria, Firenze, 50100 ITALY. Open M-F 8:15am-7pm, Sa 8:15am-12:30pm. **Postal Code:** 50100.

🏠 ACCOMMODATIONS

Lodging in Florence generally doesn't come cheap. **Consorzio ITA,** in the train station, can find rooms for a fee. (☎28 28 93. Open daily 8:45am-8pm.) Because Florence is constantly full of tourists, it is best to make reservations (*prenotazioni*) in advance, especially if you plan to visit during Easter or summer.

HOSTELS

🏠 **Ostello Archi Rossi,** V. Faenza 94r (☎29 08 04; ostelloarchirossi@hotmail.com). Exit left from the station on V. Nazionale and take the 2nd left on V. Faenza. Patio packed with young travelers. Breakfast included. Laundry €5.20. Free Internet. Lockout 11am-2:30pm. No reservations. In summer, arrive before 8am. Dorms €18-26. ❷

🏠 **Istituto Gould,** V. dei Serragli 49 (☎21 25 76; gould.reception@dada.it), in the Oltrarno. Take bus #36 or 37 from the train station to the 2nd stop across the river. Spotless rooms. Reception M-F 9am-1pm and 3-7pm, Sa 9am-1pm. Singles €30, with bath €35; doubles €44/€50; triples €56/€63; quads €72/€80. MC/V. ❸

Pensionato Pio X, V. dei Serragli 106 (☎/fax 22 50 44). Follow directions to Istituto Gould, and walk a few blocks farther; it's on the right—don't be fazed by the construction in the courtyard. Rooms are nothing fancy but they are clean and larger than average. Check-out 9am. Curfew 12:30am. Dorms €16, with bath €18. Cash only. ❷

Ostello Santa Monaca, V. S. Monaca 6 (☎26 83 38; www.ostello.it). Follow the directions to the Istituto Gould, but turn right off V. dei Serragli onto V. S. Monaca. Laundry €6.50 per 5kg. Internet €4 per hr. June-Sept. arrive before 9am. 7-night max. stay. Curfew 1am. Reserve at least 3 days in advance. 10-bed dorms €16. AmEx/MC/V. ❷

OLD CITY (NEAR THE DUOMO)

🏠 **Hotel Il Perseo,** V. de Cerretani 1 (☎21 25 04; www.hotelperseo.com), en route to the duomo from the station, opposite the Feltrinelli bookstore. Immaculate rooms with fans. Bar and TV lounge. Breakfast included. Internet €1.50 per 15min. Singles €55; doubles €75, with bath €95; triples €100/€125; quads €120/€145. MC/V. ❹

Relais Cavalcanti, V. Pellicceria 2 (☎21 09 62; www.relaiscavalcanti.com). Supreme location just steps from P. della Repubblica, near the central post office. Beautiful gold-trimmed rooms with antique wardrobes and immaculate baths. Ask for the *Let's Go* discount. Singles €70-100; doubles €95-125; triples €120-155. MC/V. ❺

Albergo Por S. Maria, V. Calimaruzza 3 (☎21 63 70). Between the Uffizi and P. della Repubblica. Pleasant, airy rooms. Bubbly, matronly proprietor strikes up conversations in Italian. Singles €55; doubles €85, with bath €95. Cash only. ❹

Locanda Orchidea, Borgo degli Albizi 11 (☎248 03 46; hotelorchidea@yahoo.it). Turn left off V. Proconsolo from the duomo. Dante's wife was born in this 12th-century *palazzo,* built around a still-intact tower. Friendly, helpful English-speaking staff. Graceful rooms with marble floors, some of which open onto a garden. Singles €55; doubles €75; triples with shower €100; quads with shower €120. Cash only. ❹

PIAZZA SANTA MARIA NOVELLA AND ENVIRONS

🏠 **Hotel Abaco,** V. dei Banchi 1 (☎ 238 19 19; www.abaco-hotel.it). From train station, cross to the back of S. Maria Novella church. Walk past church into P. S. Maria Novella and go left onto V. dei Banchi. 7 beautiful rooms, each devoted to a Renaissance master, prominently displaying his work. A/C €5. Laundry €7. Free Internet. Ask for the *Let's Go* discount. Singles €70; doubles €75, with bath €90. MC/V. ❺

■ **Hotel Elite,** V. della Scala 12 (☎21 53 95; fax 21 38 32). Exit right from the train station onto V. degli orti Oricellari; turn left on V. della Scala. Brass glows in the lovely rooms. Breakfast €6. Singles €70-80; doubles €90; triples €110; quads €120. ❺

Soggiorno Luna Rossa, V. Nazionale, 7 (☎230 21 85; www.touristhouse.com). Exit train station left on V. Nazionale. Large, airy rooms with TV, fan, and stained-glass windows. Shared baths. Breakfast included. Singles €40; doubles €60; triples €75, with shower €90; quads with shower €100. ❸

Hotel Giappone, V. dei Banchi, 1 (☎21 00 90; www.hotelgiappone.com). Follow directions to Hotel Abaco. 10 clean rooms, centrally located. All rooms have phone, TV, A/C, and Internet jacks. Singles €50, with bath €55-60; doubles €72/€85. MC/V. ❹

Hotel Visconti, P. Ottaviani 1 (☎/fax 21 38 77). Exit the train station from the left, cross behind the church into P. S. Maria Novella, and walk to the left until you reach tiny P. Ottaviani. Look for huge Grecian nudes. Breakfast included. Singles €40; doubles €60, with bath €90; triples €80/€100; quads €90. Cash or traveler's checks. ❸

AROUND PIAZZA SAN MARCO

■ **Albergo Sampaoli,** V. S. Gallo 14 (☎28 48 34; www.hotelsampaoli.it). Helpful reception and a large common area with patterned tile floors and ornate wooden furniture. All with fans, some with balcony. 30min. free Internet. Singles €48, with bath €60; doubles €65/€84; triples €110; quads €140. AmEx/MC/V. ❹

■ **Hotel Giglio,** V. Cavour 85 (☎48 66 21; www.hotelgiglio.it). With a fantastic staff and veritable overflow of luxuries—hardwood floors, embroidered drapes, ornate furnishings, fluffy towels. All rooms have bath, A/C, TV, and phone. Internet €3 per hr. Buffet breakfast included. Singles €65-90; doubles €85-130; triples €105-150; quads €120-170. Ask for the *Let's Go* discount. AmEx/MC/V. ❺

AROUND VIA NAZIONALE

■ **Katti House,** V. Faenza 21 (☎21 34 10). Exit station onto V. Nazionale; walk 1 block and turn right onto V. Faenza. This jewel among Florence's lodgings was recently renovated and now features 400-year-old antiques. Rooms with A/C, TV, and bath. Singles €60; doubles €80; triples and quads €105. Nov.-Mar. prices drop. MC/V. ❺

Hotel Nazionale, V. Nazionale 22 (☎238 22 03; www.nazionalehotel.it). Exit train station and turn left onto V. Nazionale. 9 sunny, spacious rooms with comfy beds and A/C. Renovated in winter of 2004. Breakfast brought to your room from 8 to 9:30am, €6. Singles €47, with bath €57; doubles €72/€88; triples €97/€110. MC/V. ❹

Via Faenza 56 houses 5 *pensioni*, that are among the best deals in the city. From the train station, exit left onto V. Nazionale, walk 1 block, and turn left on V. Faenza.

Pensione Azzi (☎21 38 06; www.hotelazzi.com) has large rooms and a terrace. Styles itself as a *locanda degli artisti* (an artists' inn). Breakfast included. Singles €60, with bath €80; doubles €80/€90. AmEx/MC/V. ❺

Locanda Paola (☎21 36 82) has doubles with views of the surrounding hills. Flexible 2am curfew. Doubles €65. Extra bed €25. Breakfast included. Cash only. ❹

Hotel Merlini (☎21 28 48; www.hotelmerlini.it) has some rooms with views of the duomo. Curfew 1am. Breakfast €5. Doubles €75, with bath €90; triples €105; quads €115. MC/V. ❺

Albergo Marini (☎28 48 24) boasts spotless rooms. Breakfast €5. Singles €48, with bath €75; doubles €65/€96; triples €86/€117. Extra bed €21. Advance payment needed. MC/V. ❹

Albergo Armonia (☎21 11 46). All rooms have high ceilings and wood-framed beds. No curfew. Singles €42; doubles €66; triples €90; quads €100. 25% discount in winter. ❹

OLTRARNO

Hotel La Scaletta, V. Guicciardini 13b (☎28 30 28; www.lascaletta.com). Turn right onto V. Roma from the duomo, cross Ponte Vecchio and take V. Guicciardini. Views of Boboli gardens. Breakfast included. Reception open until midnight. Singles €51, with bath €100; doubles €120/€140. 10% *Let's Go* discount with cash payment. MC/V. ❺

ITALY

CAMPING

Campeggio Michelangelo, V. Michelangelo 80 (☎681 19 77), beneath Piazzale Michelangelo. Take bus #13 from the bus station (15min.; last bus 11:25pm). Crowded, but has a great view of Florence. Apr.-Nov. €9.50 per person, €6 per tent, €5 per car. ❶

☐ FOOD

Florence's hearty cuisine originated in the peasant fare of the countryside. Specialties include *bruschetta* (grilled bread soaked with olive oil and garlic and topped with tomatoes and basil, anchovy, or liver paste) and *bistecca alla Fiorentina* (sirloin steak). No Tuscan meal is complete without wine, and genuine *chianti classico* commands a premium price. Florence's Buontalenti family supposedly invented *gelato;* true or not, Florence serves some of the world's best. For lunch, visit a *rosticceria gastronomia*, peruse the city's pushcarts, or pick up fresh produce or meat at the **Mercato Centrale,** between V. Nazionale and S. Lorenzo. (Open June-Sept. M-Sa 7:30am-2pm; Oct.-May M-F 7am-2pm, Sa 7am-2pm and 4-8pm.) To get to **STANDA** supermarket, V. Pietrapiana 1r, turn right on V. del Proconsolo, take the first left on Borgo degli Albizi, and continue through P. G. Salvemini. (Open M-Sa 8am-9pm, Su 9:30am-1:30pm and 3:30-6:30pm.)

OLD CITY (THE CENTER)

▨ **Trattoria Anita,** V. del Parlascio 2r (☎21 86 98), just behind the Bargello. Dine by candlelight, surrounded by expensive bottles of wine. Traditional Tuscan fare—including filling pastas, chicken, and beefsteak Florentine. *Primi* €5. *Secondi* from €5. Fantastic lunch *menù* €5.50. Cover €1. Open M-Sa noon-2:30pm and 7-10pm. AmEx/MC/V. ❷

▨ **Acqua al Due,** V. Vigna Vecchia 40r (☎28 41 70), behind the Bargello. Popular with young Italians. Serves Florentine specialties, including *assaggio* (selection of 5 pastas; €7.50). *Primi* €7. *Secondi* €7-19. Cover €1. Open daily 7pm-1am. AmEx/MC/V. ❸

Al Lume di Candela, V. delle Terme 23r (☎265 65 61), between P. S. Trinità and P. della Signoria. Candlelit tables illuminate the bright yellow walls of this restaurant that serves Tuscan, Venetian, and southern Italian favorites. *Primi* €6.90-9.20. *Secondi* with *contorni* €7.60-13.20. Open M-Sa noon-2:30pm and 6:30-11pm. AmEx/MC/V. ❸

La Loggia degli Albizi, Borgo degli Albizi 39r (☎247 95 74). From behind the duomo, go right on V. del Proconsolo, take the 1st left onto Borgo degli Albizi, and head 2 blocks down. Coffee and astries from €0.80 each. Open M-Sa 7am-8pm. ❶

PIAZZE SANTA MARIA NOVELLA AND DEL MERCATO CENTRALE

▨ **Trattoria Contadino,** V. Palazzuolo, 71r (☎238 2673). Filling, homestyle meals. Offers fixed price *menù* that includes *primi, secondi*, bread, water, and 0.25L of wine (€9.50). Open 11am-2:30pm and 7-9:30pm. June-July closed Sa-Su. AmEx/MC/V. ❷

Tre Merli, entrances on V. del Moro 11r and V. dei Fossi 12r (☎28 70 62). Beautiful red mushroom lights shine on booths for a candlelit meal. *Primi* €7.50-14. *Secondi* €12-19. Cover €2. Lunch *menù* €12. Open daily 11am-11pm. AmEx/MC/V. ❸

Trattoria da Giorgio, V. Palazzuolo 100r. Generous portions of home-cooked Tuscan food. *Primo, secondo,* bread, water, and house wine included in fixed *menù* for lunch and dinner, €10. Expect a wait. Open M-Sa noon-3:30pm and 7pm-12:30am. ❷

THE STATION AND UNIVERSITY QUARTER

▨ **Trattoria da Zà-Zà,** P. del Mercato Centrale 26r (☎21 54 11). Wooden-beam ceilings, brick archways, and wine racks cover the walls. Try the *tris* (mixed bean and vegetable soup; €6). Cover €1.55. Open M-Sa noon-3pm and 7-11pm. AmEx/MC/V. ❸

Trattoria Mario, V. Rosina 2r (☎21 85 50), around the corner from P. del Mercato Centrale. Informal lunch establishment with a loyal following. *Primi* €3.10-3.40. *Secondi* €3.10-10.50. Cover €0.50. Open M-Sa noon-3:30pm. Closed August. Cash only. ❷

OLTRARNO

Oltrarno Trattoria Casalinga, V. Michelozzi 9r (☎21 86 24), near P. S. Spirito. Basic Tuscan dishes and specialties. Good quality for the price. *Primi* €4-6. *Secondi* €5-9. Cover €1.50. Open M-Sa noon-2:30pm and 7-10pm. MC/V. ❷

La Mangiatoia, P. S. Felice 8r (☎22 40 60). Continue straight on V. Guicciardini from Ponte Vecchio. Quality Tuscan fare. *Primi* €3.50-5.50. *Secondi* €4-5. Pizza €4-6.50. Cover €1.50. Open Tu-Su 11am-3pm and 6:30-10pm. AmEx/MC/V. ❷

GELATERIE

Vivoli, V. Isole della Stinche 7 (☎29 23 34), behind the Bargello. A renowned Florentine *gelateria* and long-time contender for the distinction of the best ice cream in Florence. Cups from €1.50. Open Tu-Sa 7:30am-1am, Su 9:30am-1am.

Gelateria Triangolo delle Bermuda, V. Nazionale 61r (☎28 74 90). *Crema venusiana* has hazelnut, caramel, and meringue. Cones €1.60. Open daily 11am-midnight.

ENOTECHE (WINE BARS)

Enoteca Alessi, V. della Oche 27/29r (☎21 49 66), 1 block from the duomo. Among Florence's finest, stocking over 1000 wines. Doubles as a candy store offering bites between sips. Sizable and cool. Open M-F 9am-1pm and 4-8pm. AmEx/MC/V. ❷

👁 SIGHTS

With the views from Brunelleschi's dome, the perfection of San Spirito's nave and the overwhelming array of art in the Uffizi Galleries, it's hard to take a wrong turn in Florence. For a full list of museum openings, check out www.firenzeturismo.it. For museum reservations call **Firenze Musei** (☎294 883; www.firenzemusei.it).

 VENI, VIDI, MEDICI. Florentine museums charge up to €8.50, so breezing in and out of attractions starts to add up fast. Sadly, most museums no longer offer student discounts. The price of a ticket should not, however, keep any visitor from seeing the best collections of Renaissance art in the world. Choose carefully and plan to spend a few hours at each sight. In the summer, inquire about **Sere al Museo,** evenings when certain museums are free 8:30-11pm. Reserve tickets for Florence's highlights online at **www.florenceart.it.**

PIAZZA DEL DUOMO

THE DUOMO (CATTEDRALE DI SANTA MARIA DEL FIORE). In 1296 the city fathers commissioned Arnolfo di Cambio to erect a cathedral so magnificent that it would be "impossible to make it either better or more beautiful with the industry and power of man." Arnolfo succeeded, completing the massive but domeless nave by 1418. After studying long-neglected classical methods, Filippo Brunelleschi came up with his revolutionary double-shelled construction that utilized self-supporting interlocking bricks in order to construct the enormous dome. *(Open M-Sa 10am-4:45pm, Su 1:30-4:45pm. Mass daily 7am-12:30pm and 5-7pm.)* Climb the 463 steps inside the dome to **Michelangelo's lantern,** which offers an unparalleled view of the city from the 100m high external gallery. *(Open M-F 8:30am-7pm, Sa 8:30am-5:40pm. €6.)* The 82m high **campanile,** next to the duomo, also has spectacular views. *(Open daily 8:30am-7:30pm. €6.)*

THE LOCAL STORY

MEDIEVAL MEDICINE

Sick and tired of that pesky cough? Try some treacle, a potion made with roasted viper skin. Want to get rid of that tooth ache? Hold a candle to the tooth, and heat will cause the worms rotting it to fall from your mouth.

Though perhaps less effective than modern medicine, these far more colorful prescriptions were found at the Antica Spezieria di San Giovanni Evangelista, Parma's 700-year-old pharmacy. Historical sources indicate that the pharmacy dates back as early as the 10th century, when it was developed by Benedictine monks to serve their brothers and the Parman community. It became fully operational in the 13th century, and by the 16th century boasted over 100 syrups, salves, greases, and gums.

While they don't fill prescriptions anymore, the four chambers can still be explored. Massive granite mortar and pestles dominate the Room of Mortars, delicate glass distillers span the height of the Room of Alembics, and porcelain urns used to store volitile ingredients adorn the Room of Sirens. Along the ceiling, 16th-century frescoes offered words of wisdom. One compelling inscription reads, "This is the place to preserve poison so that what is skillfully produced as curative does not become dangerous through an inexperienced hand."
Directly behind the duomo. Open M-F 8:30am-1:45pm. Tickets €2, under 18 and over 60 €1.

BATTISTERO. Built between the 5th and 9th centuries, the *battistero* (baptistry) was the site of Dante's christening; its Byzantine-style mosaics inspired the details of his *Inferno.* The **bronze doors** were products of an intense competition among Florentine artists; Ghiberti was commissioned to forge the last set of doors that depict Biblical scenes. In the resulting products, which Michelangelo dubbed the ■**Gates of Paradise,** Ghiberti exchanged his earlier 28-panel design for 10 large, gilded squares, each of which employs mathematical perspective to create the illusion of deep space. *(Opposite the duomo. Open M-Sa noon-7pm, Su 8:30am-2pm. €3.)*

MUSEO DELL'OPERA DEL DUOMO. Most of the duomo's art resides behind the cathedral in the Museo dell'Opera del Duomo. Up the first flight of stairs is a late *Pietà* by Michelangelo who, according to legend, destroyed Christ's left arm with a hammer in a fit of frustration; soon after, an over-eager pupil touched up the work, leaving visible scars on parts of Mary Magdalene's head. The museum also houses four frames from the baptistry's *Gates of Paradise.* *(P. del Duomo 9, behind the duomo. ☎ 23 02 885. Open M-Sa 9am-7:30pm, Su 9am-1:40pm. €6.)*

PIAZZA DELLA SIGNORIA AND ENVIRONS
From P. del Duomo, the bustling **Via dei Calzaiuoli,** one of the city's oldest streets, runs south through crowds and chic shops to P. della Signoria.

■**PALAZZO VECCHIO.** Arnolfo del Cambio designed this fortress-like *palazzo* in the late-13th century as the governmental seat. Michelangelo decorated the **courtyard** after it became the Medici family home in 1470. The **Monumental Apartments,** which house the *palazzo's* extensive art collections, now function as a museum. The **Activities Tour,** well worth the extra €2 (students €1) on top of the cumulative ticket, includes the **Secret Routes,** which reveal hidden stairwells and chambers tucked behind exquisite oil paintings, and **Invitation to Court,** a reenactment of court life. *(☎276 84 65, tours 276 82 24. Call ahead for tours. Palazzo €6/€4.50. Monumental Apartments €6, ages 18-25 €4.50. Open June-Sept. M and F 9am-11pm, Tu-W and Sa 9am-7pm, Th and Su 9am-2pm; Oct.-May M-W and F-Sa 9am-7pm, Th and Su 9am-2pm.)*

■**THE UFFIZI.** Giorgio Vasari designed this palace in 1554 for the offices (*uffizi*) of Duke Cosimo's administration; today the gallery holds one of the world's finest art collections. Botticelli, da Vinci, Michelangelo, Raphael, Titian, Giotto, Fra Angelico, Caravaggio, Bronzino, Cimabue, della Francesca, Bellini, even Dürer, Rubens, and Rembrandt—you name it, it's here. To avoid disappointment, note that a few rooms are usually closed each day, and famous works often go on loan, so not all works will be available for viewing. A sign outside the ticket office lists the *sale* that will be closed that day; ask if they will reopen the next day. *(Extends from P. della Signoria to the Arno River.* ☎ *23 88 65. Open Tu-Su 8am-6:50pm. €8.50.)*

PIAZZA DELLA SIGNORIA. The destruction of powerful Florentine families' homes in the 13th century created an empty space that cried out *"piazza!"* With the construction of the Palazzo Vecchio in 1299, the square became Florence's civic and political center. In 1497, religious zealot Girolamo Savonarola convinced Florentines to light the Bonfire of the Vanities, a grand roast in the square that consumed some of Florence's best art. A year later, disillusioned citizens sent Savonarola up in smoke on the same spot, marked today by a granite disc. Monumental sculptures cluster in front of the *palazzo*, including a copy of Michelangelo's *David*. From the Uffizi, follow V. Georgofili left and turn right along the river to reach the nearby **Ponte Vecchio** (old bridge), the oldest bridge in Florence. From the neighboring **Ponte alle Grazie,** the view of the Ponte Vecchio melting in the setting sun is nothing less than heart-stopping, and the bridge itself buzzes with pedestrians and street performers, especially at night.

THE BARGELLO AND ENVIRONS

BARGELLO. The heart of medieval Florence lies in this 13th-century fortress which was once the residence of the chief magistrate and later a brutal prison with public executions in the courtyard. It was restored in the 19th century and now houses the sculpture-filled **Museo Nazionale.** Donatello's bronze *David*, the first freestanding nude since antiquity, stands opposite the two bronze panels of the *Sacrifice of Isaac*, submitted by Ghiberti and Brunelleschi in the baptistry door competition (p. 688). Michelangelo's early works, including *Bacchus*, *Brutus*, and *Apollo*, are on the ground floor. *(V. del Proconsolo 4, between the duomo and P. della Signoria.* ☎ *238 86 06. Open daily 8:15am-1:50pm. Closed 2nd and 4th M of each month, though hours and closing days vary by month. €4.)*

CASA DI DANTE. The Casa di Dante is reputedly identical to the house Dante inhabited. Anyone with an interest in Dante and who can read Italian will enjoy the displays, which trace the poet's life from youth to exile to the artistic creation that immortalized him. Check out Giotto's early but representative portrait of Dante on the third floor. Nearby is a facsimile of the abandoned little church where Beatrice, Dante's unrequited love and spiritual guide in *Paradiso*, attended mass. *(Corner of V. Dante Alighieri and V. S. Margherita within 1 block of the Bargello.* ☎ *21 94 16. Open M and W-Sa 10am-5pm, Su 10am-2pm. €3, groups over 15 €2 per person.)*

PIAZZA DELLA REPUBBLICA AND FARTHER WEST

PIAZZA DELLA REPUBBLICA. The largest open space in Florence, this *piazza* teems with crowds and street performers in the evenings. An enormous arch filling in the gap over V. Strozzi marks the western edge of the square. The rest of the *piazza* is lined with overpriced *caffès*, restaurants, and *gelaterie*. The inscription *"Antico centro della città, da secolare squalore, a vita nuova restituito"* ("Ancient center of the city, squalid for centuries, restored to new life") makes a derogatory reference to the fact that the *piazza* is the site of the old Jewish ghetto, which slowly disappeared as a result of the "liberation of the Jews" in Italy in the 1860s that allowed members of the Jewish community to live elsewhere.

CHIESA DI SANTA MARIA NOVELLA. This church, near the train station, houses the chapels of the wealthiest merchants. Santa Maria Novella was home to the order of Dominicans, or *Domini canes* (Hounds of the Lord), who took a bite out of sin and corruption. The 14th-century *chiesa* boasts a green and white Romanesque-Gothic facade, considered one of the greatest masterpieces of early

Renaissance architecture. Thirteenth-century frescoes covered the interior until the Medici commissioned Vasari to paint new ones. Fortunately, Vasari spared Masaccio's powerful ■**Trinity**, the first painting to use geometric perspective. This fresco, on the left side of the nave, creates the illusion of a tabernacle. *(Open M-Th and Sa 9:30am-5pm, F and Su 1-5pm. €2.50, ages 13-18 €1.50.)*

CHIESA DI SANTA TRINITÀ. Hoping to spend eternity as they had lived—in elite company—the most fashionable *palazzo* owners commissioned family chapels in this church. The facade, designed by Bernardo Buontalenti in the 16th century, is an exquisite example of late-Renaissance architecture that verges on Baroque in its ornamentation. Scenes from Ghirlandaio's *Life of St. Francis* decorate the **Sassetti chapel** in the right arm of the transept. The famous altarpiece, Ghirlandaio's *Adoration of the Shepherds*, resides in the Uffizi—this one is a convincing copy. *(In P. S. Trinità. Open M-Sa 8am-noon and 4-6pm, Su 4-6pm.)*

SAN LORENZO AND FARTHER NORTH

BASILICA DI SAN LORENZO. Designed in 1419 by Brunelleschi, the Basilica di San Lorenzo was funded by the Medici family. Because they were footing the bill, the Medicis insisted that they retain artistic control of the project. They cunningly used this authority to place Cosimo Medici's grave in front of the high altar, making the entire church his personal mausoleum. Michelangelo designed the exterior but, disgusted by Florentine politics, he abandoned the project to study architecture in Rome. *(☎21 66 34. Open daily M-Sa 10am-5pm. €2.50.)* To reach the ■**Cappelle dei Medici** (Medici Chapels), walk around to the back entrance on P. Madonna degli Aldobrandini. A glimpse of the Baroque in Florence, the **Cappella dei Principi** (Princes' Chapel) emulates the bapistry in P. del Duomo. Michelangelo sculpted the **Sacrestia Nuova** (New Sacristy) to hold two Medici tombs. *(Open daily 8:15am-5pm. Closed the 2nd and 4th Su and the 1st, 3rd, and 5th M of every month. €6.)*

■ **MUSEO DELLA CHIESA DI SAN MARCO.** Remarkable works by Fra Angelico adorn the Museo della Chiesa di San Marco, one of the most peaceful and spiritual places in Florence. A large room to the right of the lovely courtyard contains some of the painter's major works, including the church's altarpiece. The second floor houses Angelico's famous *Annunciation*, across from the top of the stairwell, as well as the monks' quarters. To the right of the stairwell, Michelozzo's library, modeled on Michelangelo's work, is a fine example of purity and vigor. After visiting, you may want to follow in the footsteps of the convent's patron, Cosimo I, who retired here. In cells 17 and 22, you can see underground artwork through the glass floor, excavated from the medieval period. Towards the exit are two rooms housing the **Museo di Firenze Antica,** which has numerous archaeological fragments on display, most of them from Etruscan and Roman buildings in the area. *(Enter at P. di San Marco 3. ☎238 86 08 or 238 87 04. Open daily 8:15am-6:50pm. Closed 1st, 3rd, and 5th Su and 2nd and 4th M of every month. €4, under 18 and over 65 free.)*

■ **ACCADEMIA.** Michelangelo's triumphant **David** stands in self-assured perfection under the rotunda designed just for him. The photographs peddled by street vendors cannot capture Michelangelo's painstaking attention to detail or the sheer size of this masterwork. In the hallway leading up to the *David* are Michelangelo's four *Slaves* and a *Pietà*. The master left these intriguing statues intentionally unfinished. Remaining true to his theories of living stone, he chipped away only enough to show their figures emerging from the marble. *(V. Ricasoli 60, between the churches of San Marco and S. S. Annunziata. ☎29 48 83. Most areas wheelchair accessible. Open Tu-Su 8:15am-6:50pm. €6.50.)*

PALAZZO MEDICI RICCARDI. The palace's facade is the work of Michelozzo—it stands as the archetype for all Renaissance *palazzi*. The private chapel inside features Benozzo Gozzoli's beautiful, wrap-around fresco of the ■**Three Magi** and several Medici family portraits. The *palazzo* hosts rotating exhibits ranging from Renaissance architectural sketches to Fellini memorabilia. *(V. Cavour 3. ☎ 276 03 40. Open daily 10am-7pm. €4, children €2.50.)*

PIAZZA SANTA CROCE AND ENVIRONS

CHIESA DI SANTA CROCE. The Franciscans built this church as far as possible from their Dominican rivals at S. Maria Novella. Started in 1210 as a small oratory, the ascetic Franciscans ironically produced what is arguably the most splendid church in the city. Among the luminaries buried here are Machiavelli, Galileo, Michelangelo (who rests in the right aisle in a tomb designed by Vasari), and humanist Leonardo Bruni, shown holding his precious *History of Florence*. Note also Donatello's gilded *Annunciation*. *(Open M-Sa 9:30am-5:30pm, Su and holidays 3-5:30pm. €4, under 18 €2.)* Intricate *pietra serena* pilasters and statues of the evangelists by Donatello grace Brunelleschi's small **Cappella Pazzi,** at the end of the cloister next to the church. A humble marvel of perfect proportions, among them are Luca della Robbia's *tondi* of the apostles and Brunelleschi's moldings of the evangelists. The **Museo dell'Opera di Santa Croce** forms three sides of the church's peaceful courtyard. *(Enter through the loggia in front of Cappella Pazzi. Open M-Tu and Th-Su 10am-7pm. Free with entrance to church.)*

THE OLTRARNO

Historically disdained by downtown Florentines, the far side of the Arno remains a lively and unpretentious quarter, even in high season.

PALAZZO PITTI. Luca Pitti, a 15th-century banker, built his *palazzo* east of P. S. Spirito against the Boboli hill. The Medici acquired the *palazzo* and the hill in 1550 and expanded in every way possible. Today, it houses six museums, including the **Galleria Palatina,** one of only a few public galleries when it opened in 1833. Today the gallery houses Florence's most important art collection after the Uffizi. Works by Raphael, Titian, Andrea del Sarto, Caravaggio, and Rubens line the walls. Other museums display Medici family treasures, costumes, porcelain, carriages, and Royal Apartments—lavish reminders of the time when the *palazzo* was the royal House of Savoy's living quarters. *(Open Tu-Su 8:15am-6:50pm. €8.50.)*

BOBOLI GARDENS. With geometrically sculpted hedges, contrasting groves of holly and cypress trees, and bubbling fountains, the elaborate gardens are an exquisite example of stylized Renaissance landscaping. A large oval lawn is just up the hill from the back of the palace, with an Egyptian obelisk in the middle and marble statues in portals dotting the hedge-lined perimeter. *(Open daily June-Aug. 8:15am-7:30pm; Sept.-May 8:15am-4:30pm. €6 includes admission to the Porcellane Museum.)*

SAN MINIATO AL MONTE AND ENVIRONS

SAN MINIATO AL MONTE. One of Florence's oldest churches gloriously surveys the skyline. The inlaid marble facade and 13th-century mosaics provide a prelude to the incredible pavement inside, patterned with lions, doves, and astrological signs. The **Chapel of the Cardinal of Portugal** holds a collection of superlative della Robbia terra-cottas. Be sure to circle the church and spend a moment in the cemetery, which contains an overwhelming profusion of tombs and mausoleums in many architectural styles. *(Take bus #13 from the station or climb the stairs from Piazzale Michelangelo. ☎ 234 27 31. Open daily 8am-7:30pm. Free.)*

PIAZZALE MICHELANGELO. Laid out in 1860, Piazzale Michelangelo offers a fine panorama of the entire city, which is breathtaking at sunset. Unfortunately, the *piazza* doubles as a large parking lot, and is home to hordes of tour buses during summer days. It occasionally hosts concerts as well. *(Cross the Ponte Vecchio and turn left, walk through the piazza, and turn right up V. de Bardi. Follow it uphill as it becomes V. del Monte alle Croci, where a staircase to the left heads to the piazza.)*

🎵 ENTERTAINMENT

In June, the *quartieri* of Florence turn out in costume to play their own medieval version of soccer known as **calcio storico,** in which two teams of 27 players face off over a wooden ball in one of the city's *piazze.* Tickets (€10-40) are sold at the box office across from P. S. Croce. Check with the tourist office for times and locations of matches. The **Festival of San Giovanni Battista,** on June 24, features a fireworks display in P. Michelangelo. May begins the summer music festivals with the classical **Maggio Musicale.** The **Estate Fiesolana** (June-Aug.) fills the Roman theater in Fiesole with concerts, opera, theater, and ballet. September brings the **Festa dell'Unità,** a concert series at Campi Bisenzia (take bus #30). The **Festa del Grillo** (Festival of the Cricket), is held on the Sunday after Ascension Day, when crickets in tiny wooden cages are sold in the Cascine park to be released into the grass.

🎭 NIGHTLIFE

For info on hot nightlife, consult the monthly *Firenze Spettacolo* (€2). Begin your nighttime *passeggiata* along V. dei Calzaiuoli and end it with coffee or *gelato* on **Piazza della Repubblica,** where singers prance about the stage at the **Bar Concerto.** In the Oltrarno, **Piazza San Spirito** has plenty of bars with live music in summer.

May Day Lounge, V. Dante Alighieri 16r (www.maydayclub.it). Aspiring artists display their work on the walls of this eclectic lounge. Play Pong on the early 1980s gaming system or sip mixed drinks (€4.50-6.50) to the beat of the background funk. Beer €4.50. Happy Hour 8-10pm. Open daily 8pm-2am. AmEx/MC/V.

Kikuya, V. Benci 43r (☎ 234 4879). A Japanese name for an Irish pub cherished by local Florentines and foreigners of all ages who engage in lively conversations over a pint (€4.50) and a burger (€5). Open daily 7:30pm-2am. MC/V.

Slowly, V. Porta Rossa 63r (☎264 5354). Leather booths, sleek barstools, blaring pop-jazz and mood candles make this lively bar *the* place for trendy twenty-somethings to see and be seen. Mixed drinks €7. Coffee €3-5. Open daily 7pm-2:30am. MC/V.

Central Park, in Parco della Cascinè. Open-air dance floor pulses with hip-hop, reggae, and rock. Favored by Florentine and foreign teens and college students. No cover for foreign students before 12:30am, after that, the regular €11 cover applies. Mixed drinks €8. Open M-Tu and Th-Sa 11pm-late, W 9pm-late. AmEx/MC/V.

Tabasco Gay Club, P. S. Cecilia 3r, from Palazzo Vecchio. Smoke machines and strobe lights on dance floor. Florence's popular gay disco caters primarily to men. 18 and over. Cover €13, includes 1 drink. Open Tu-Su 10pm-4am. AmEx/MC/V.

SIENA   ☎ 0577

Many travelers rush from Rome to Florence, ignoring gorgeous, medieval Siena (pop. 60,000). The Sienese have a history rich in arts, politics, and trade. One of their proudest celebrations is **Il Palio** (p. 693), an intoxicating display of pageantry in which jockeys from the city's 17 *contrade* (districts) race horses bareback around **Il Campo,** the central square.

🖪🛈 TRANSPORTATION AND PRACTICAL INFORMATION. Trains leave P. Rosselli for Florence (1¾hr., 19 per day, €5.50) and Rome (3hr., 12 per day, €17) via Chiusi. TRA-IN/SITA **buses** (☎20 42 46) depart from P. Gramsci and the train station for Florence (1 per hr., €6.50) and San Gimignano (21 per day, €5). From the train station, cross the street and take TRA-IN/SITA buses #3, 4, 7-10, 14, 17, or 77 (all €0.90) into the center of town at **Piazza del Sale** or **Piazza Gramsci.** The APT **tourist office** is at Il Campo 56. (☎28 05 51. Open daily Mar. 16-Nov. 14 9:30am-1pm and

2:30-6pm; Nov. 15-Mar. 15 8:30am-1pm and 3-7pm.) **Prenotazioni Alberghiere,** in P. S. Domenico, finds rooms for a €2 fee. (☎28 80 84. M-Sa 9am-7pm.) Check email at **Cafe Internet,** Galleria Cecco Angiolieri 16. (€0.99 for 20min., €0.03 per min. thereafter. Open M and Su 11am-10:30pm, Tu-Sa 9:30am-10:30pm.) **Postal Code:** 53100.

☎ ☐ ACCOMMODATIONS AND FOOD. Book rooms months ahead if coming during *Il Palio.* The tastefully furnished **Albergo Tre Donzelle ❸** is at V. Donzelle 5. (☎28 03 58. Curfew 1am. Singles €33; doubles €46-60. AmEx/MC/V.) Bus #15 from P. Gramsci, stops at the **Ostello della Gioventù "Guidoriccio" (HI) ❶,** V. Fiorentina 89, in Località Lo Stellino. (☎522 12. Curfew midnight. Dorms €15. MC/V.) **Piccolo Hotel Etruria ❹,** V. Donzelle 3, is a stone's throw from Il Campo. (☎28 80 88; www.hoteletruria.com. Breakfast €5. Curfew 12:30am. Singles €45-50; doubles €80; triples €105. AmEx/MC/V.) To camp at **Colleverde ❶,** Strada di Scacciapensieri 47, take bus #3 or 8 from P. del Sale; confirm destination with driver. (☎28 00 44; www.terresiena.it. Open Mar. to mid-Nov. €8 per person, €8 per tent. MC/V.)

Siena specializes in rich pastries, of which the most famous is *panforte,* a confection of honey, almonds, and citron. Indulge in this treat at **Bar/Pasticceria Nannini ❶,** V. Banchi di Sopra 22-24, the oldest *pasticceria* in Siena. Next to Santuario di S. Caterina is the divine **Osteria La Chiacchera ❷,** Costa di S. Antonio 4, which serves hearty pasta dishes. (☎28 06 31. *Primi* €4-5. *Secondi* €5-7. Open M and W-Su noon-3:30pm and 7pm-midnight. AmEx/MC/V.) **Consortio Agrario** supermarket, V. Pianigiani 5, is off P. Salimberi. (Open M-F 8am-7:30pm.)

☐ ♫ SIGHTS AND ENTERTAINMENT. Siena offers two **biglietto cumulativi** (cumulative tickets). The first is good for five days (€10) and allows entry into the Museo dell'Opera Metropolitana, baptistry, crypt and oratorio; the second is valid for seven days (€16) and covers four additional sights, including the Museo Civico. Both may be purchased at any of the sights included. Siena radiates from **▧Piazza del Campo (Il Campo),** a shell-shaped brick square designed for civic events. At the top of Il Campo is the **Fonte Gaia,** still fed by the same aqueduct used in the 1300s. At the bottom, the **Torre del Mangia** bell tower looms over the graceful Gothic **Palazzo Pubblico.** Inside the *palazzo,* the **Museo Civico** contains excellent Gothic and early Renaissance paintings; also check out the **Sala del Mappamondo** and the **Sala della Pace.** (*Palazzo,* museum, and tower open daily Mar.-Oct. 10am 7pm; Nov.-Feb. 10am-5:30pm. €6.50, students €4.) From the *palazzo,* take the right-side stairs and cross V. di Città for Siena's Gothic **▧duomo.** the lavish **baptistry** was constructed below the apse to keep it stable. (Open mid-Mar. to Oct. M-Sa 7:30am-7:30pm, Su 2-5pm; Nov. to mid-Mar. M-Sa 7:30am-5:30pm, Su 2-5pm. €3, except when floor is uncovered in Sept. €4-5.50.) The **Museo dell'Opera della Metropolitana,** to the right of the duomo, houses the overflow art from the church. (Open daily mid-Mar. to Sept. 9am-7:30pm; Oct. to mid-Mar. reduced hours. €6.)

Siena's **▧Il Palio** (July 2 and Aug. 16) is a traditional bareback horse race around the packed P. del Campo. Arrive three days early to watch the five trial runs and to pick a *contrada* to root for. At *Il Palio,* the jockeys take about 90 seconds to tear around Il Campo three times. To stay in Siena during the *Palio,* book rooms at least four months in advance, especially for budget accommodations.

▨ DAYTRIP FROM SIENA: SAN GIMIGNANO. The village of San Gimignano looks like an illustration from a medieval manuscript. The city's famous 14 towers, which are all that survive of its original 72, earned San Gimignano its nickname as the *Città delle Belle Torri* (City of Beautiful Towers). The **Museo Civico,** on the second floor of **Palazzo del Popolo,** has an amazing collection of Sienese and Florentine artwork. Within the museum is the entrance to the **Torre Grossa,** the tallest remaining tower; climb its 218 steps for a panoramic view of Tuscany. (Open daily

ITALY

Mar.-Oct. 9:30am-7pm; Nov.-Feb. 10am-7pm. €5, students €4.) Not for the faint of heart, ▇**Museo Della Tortura**, V. del Castello 1, off P. Cisterna, offers a morbidly fascinating history of torture through current times. (Open daily Apr.-Oct. 10am-8pm; Nov.-Mar. 10am-6pm. €8, students €5.50.) TRA-IN **buses** leave P. Montemaggio for Siena (1hr., 1 per hr., €5.20) and Florence (1½hr., 1 per hr., €6) via Poggibonsi. From the bus station, pass through the *porta*, climb the hill, following V. S. Giovanni to the **Piazza della Cisterna**, which runs into P. del Duomo. The **tourist office** is at P. del Duomo 1. (☎94 00 08; prolocsg@tin.it. Open daily Mar.-Oct. 9am-1pm and 3-7pm; Nov.-Feb. 9am-1pm and 2-6pm.) Accommodations are pricey in San Gimignano. *Affitte camere* (private rooms) are a good alternative. The tourist office and the **Associazione Strutture Extralberghiere**, P. della Cisterna 6, both find **private rooms.** (☎94 31 90. Open daily Mar.-Nov. 9:30am-7:30pm.) **Postal Code:** 53037.

PISA ☎050

Tourism hasn't always been Pisa's (pop. 96,000) prime industry. During the Middle Ages, the city was a major port with its own Mediterranean empire, but when the Arno River filled with silt and the tower started to lean, the city's power and wealth declined accordingly. Today the city seems resigned to welcoming tourists to the **Piazza del Duomo**, also known as the **Campo dei Miracoli** (Field of Miracles), a grassy expanse enclosing the tower, duomo, baptistry, Camposanto, Museo delle Sinopie, and Museo del Duomo. An **all-inclusive ticket** to the Campo's sights—excluding the tower—costs €10.50. Begun in 1173, the famous **Leaning Tower** began to tilt when the soil beneath it suddenly shifted. In June 2001, a multi-year stabilization effort was completed; the tower is presently considered stable. Tours of 30 visitors are permitted to ascend the 294 steps once every 30min. (Make reservations at adjacent tourist office. Tours depart daily June-Aug. 8:30am-10:30pm; Sept.-May 8:30am-7:30pm. Make reservations at the ticket office. €15.) Also on the Campo, the dazzling ▇**duomo,** a cache of splendid art, is considered one of the finest Romanesque cathedrals in the world. (Open M-Sa 10am-8pm. €2.) Next door is the **baptistry,** whose precise acoustics allow an unamplified choir to be heard 2km away. (Open daily Apr.-Sept. 8am-8pm; Oct.-Mar. 9am-6pm. €5.) The adjoining ▇**Camposanto,** a cloistered cemetery, has sarcophagi and a series of haunting frescoes about the Black Death by an unidentified 14th-century artist known only as the "Master of the Triumph of Death." (Open daily late Apr. to late Sept. 8am-8pm; Mar. and Oct. 9am-5:40pm; Nov.-Feb. 9am-4:40pm. €5.) The **Museo delle Sinopie**, across the *piazza*, displays preliminary sketches discovered during post-WWII restoration. Behind the tower is the **Museo dell'Opera del Duomo.** (Both open daily Apr.-Sept. 8am-7:20pm; Mar. and Oct. 9am-5:20pm; Nov.-Feb. 9am-4:20pm. €5.)

Trains (☎147 808 88) leave Piazza della Stazione, in the southern end of town, for: Florence (1hr., 1 per hr., €5.05); Genoa (2½hr., €7.90); and Rome (3hr., 12 per day, €16-24). To reach the **tourist office,** walk straight out of the train station and take a left onto P. V. Emanuele. (☎422 91. Open Apr.-Oct. M-Sa 9am-7pm, Su 9:30am-3:30pm; Nov.-Mar. M-Sa 9am-6pm, Su 9:30am-3:30pm.) To reach the *campo* from the train station, take **bus** #3 (€0.75). The **Albergo Helvetia ❸**, V. Don G. Boschi 31, off P. Archivescovado, has large rooms 2min. from the duomo. (☎55 30 84. Singles €35, with bath €52; doubles €45/€62.) **Centro Turistico Madonna dell'Acqua ❶**, V. Pietrasantina 15, is behind an old Catholic sanctuary, 2km from the Tower. Take bus #3 from the station (4 per hr., last bus 9:45pm); ask the driver to stop at *ostello*. (☎89 06 22. Sheets €1. Dorms €15; doubles €42; triples €54; quads €64. MC/V.) Cheap dining options line **Corso Italia,** south of the river, and **Via Santa Maria;** prices skyrocket near the duomo. Try the heavenly *risotto* at the lively ▇**Il Paiolo ❶**, V. Curtatone e Montanara 9. (*Menù* €4-6. Open M-F 12:30-3pm and 7:30pm-1am, Sa-Su 7:30pm-2am. Cash only.) Get groceries at **Pam,** V. Pascoli 8, just off C. Italia. (Open M-Sa 8am-8pm.) **Postal Code:** 56100.

UMBRIA

Umbria is known as the "Green Heart of Italy," a land rich in natural beauty, from wild woods and fertile plains to craggy gorges and tiny villages. Christianity transformed Umbria's architecture along with its regional identity, turning it into a breeding ground for saints and religious movements. It was here that St. Francis of Assisi shamed the extravagant church with his humility.

PERUGIA ☎075

Perugia (pop. 150,000) may boast the most polite people in Italy. With their gorgeous countryside, big-city vitality, and world-renowned chocolate, this city's residents have much to smile about. Perugia's most popular sights frame **Piazza IV Novembre.** In its center, the **Fontana Maggiore** is adorned with sculptures and bas-reliefs by Nicolà and Giovanni Pisano. At the end of the *piazza*, the imposing Gothic **Catedral di San Lorenzo** houses the purported wedding ring of the Virgin Mary. (Open M-Sa 9am-12:45pm and 4-5:15pm, Su 4-5:45pm.) The 13th-century **Palazzo dei Priori** presides over the *piazza* and contains the impressive ◪**Galleria Nazionale dell'Umbria,** C. Vannucci 19, which displays magnificent 13th- and 14th-century religious works. (Open daily 8:30am-7:30pm. Closed 1st M each month. €6.50.) At the end of town past the Porta S. Pietro, the ◪**Basilica di San Pietro,** on Borao XX Guigo, has a beautiful garden. Every centimeter of the interior is covered with brilliant paintings and frescoes. (Open daily 8am-noon and 3-6:30pm.)

Trains leave **Perugia FS** in P. V. Veneto, Fontiveggio, for: Assisi (25min., 1 per hr., €1.65); Florence (2½hr., 18 per day, €8); and Rome (2½hr., 6 per day, €10) via Terontola or Foligno. From the station, take bus #6, 7, 9, 13d, or 15 to the central P. Italia (€0.80), then walk down C. Vannucci to P. IV Novembre and the **tourist office,** P. IV Novembre 3. (☎572 33 2; fax 573 93 86. Open M-Sa 8:30am-1:30pm and 3:30-6:30pm, Su 9am-1pm.) ◪**Ostello della Gioventù/Centro Internazionale di Accoglienza per la Gioventù ❶,** V. Bontempi 13, offers clean rooms, a social setting, and panoramic views. From the tourist office, walk down C. Vannucci past the duomo and P. Danti, take the farthest street directly through P. Piccinino, and turn right on V. Bontempi. (☎572 28 80; www.ostello.perugia.it. Sheets €1.50. Lockout 9:30am-4pm. Curfew midnight. Closed Dec. 15-Jan. 15. Dorms €12. AmEx/MC/V.) Off P. della Repubblica, **Hotel Umbria ❸,** V. Boncambi 37, has narrow rooms with TVs and large baths. (☎572 12 03. Singles €38-48; doubles €55-70. AmEx/MC/V.) Local favorite **Trattoria Dal Mi Cocco ❸,** C. Garibaldi, 12, serve pasta, meats, and desserts at reasonable prices. (*Menù* €13. Open Tu-Su 1-3pm and 8:30pm-midnight. MC/V.) Perugia is full of bakeries peddling local confections and chocolates. The **COOP,** P. Matteotti 15, has groceries. (Open M-Sa 9am-8pm.) **Postal Code:** 06100.

ASSISI ☎079

The undeniable jewel of Assisi (pop. 25,000) is the 13th-century ◪**Basilica di San Francesco.** The subdued art of the lower church celebrates St. Francis's modest lifestyle, while Giotto's renowned fresco cycle, the *Life of St. Francis*, decorates the walls of the upper church, paying tribute to his sainthood and consecration. (Lower basilica open daily 6am-6:45pm. Upper basilica open daily 8:30am-6:45pm. Modest dress code is strictly enforced.) The fortress **Rocca Maggiore** looms above the town, offering a panoramic view of the countryside. (Open daily 10am-dusk. €1.70, students €1.) The pink and white **Basilica of Santa Chiara** houses St. Francis's tunic, sandals, and crucifix. (Open daily 9am-noon and 2-7pm. Free.)

From the station near the Basilica Santa Maria degli Angeli, **trains** go to: Ancona (2hr., 8 per day, €7); Florence (2½hr., 13 per day, €9); and Rome (2½hr., 14 per day, €9). **Buses** run from P. Unita D'Italia to Florence (2½hr., 7am, €6.40) and Perugia

ITALY

(1½hr., 12 per day, €2.70). From P. Matteotti, follow V. del Torrione, bear left in P. S. Rufino, and take V. S. Rufino to **Piazza del Comune,** the town center and location of the **tourist office.** (☎81 25 34; www.assisi.umbria2000.it. Open M-Sa 8am-2pm and 3-6pm, Su 9am-1pm.) ■**Camere Martini ❷,** V. S. Gregorio 6, has a comfy lounge and friendly atmosphere. (☎ 81 35 36. Singles €25; doubles €34-38; triples €55; quads €62. Cash only.) **Ostello Fontemaggio ❶,** V. per L'Eremo delle Carceri 8, has a hostel, hotel, campground, and market. Take V. L'Eremo from P. Matteotti about 1.5km. (☎81 36 36. Curfew 11pm. Camping €5.50; dorms €20; singles €36; doubles €52; triples €72; quads €80. Cash only.) Grab a pizza (€5-7) at **Pizzeria Otello ❷,** V. San Antonio 1. (Open daily noon-3pm and 7-10:30pm. AmEx/MC/V.) **Postal Code:** 06081.

ORVIETO   ☎0763

Perched on a plateau of volcanic rock, **Orvieto** (pop. 25,000) has a view of the rolling farmlands of Umbria. Below the surface, however, caves and tunnels attest to the town's long history; Etruscans began burrowing into the hillside in the 7th century BC. **Underground City Excursions** offers the most complete tour of the ancient Etruscan city buried beneath modern Orvieto. (☎34 48 91. Tours leave the tourist office daily 11am, 12:15, 4, and 5:15pm. €5.50, students €3.50.) 600 years of labor went into the construction of the ■ **Duomo,** whose spires, sculptures, and mosaics are the pride and joy of Orvieto. The **Capella della Madonna di San Brizio,** off the right transept, houses the dramatic Apocalypse frescoes of Luca Signorelli, whose compositions inspired Michelangelo. (Duomo open M-Sa 7:30am-12:45pm and 2:30-7pm, Su 2:30-6:45pm. Modest dress required. *Capella* open Apr.-Sept. M-Sa 10am-12:45pm and 2:30-7:15pm, Su 2:30-6pm; Oct.-Mar. reduced hours. €3.)

Trains run hourly to Florence (2½hr., €9.90) and Rome (1½hr., €7). From the train station, take a shuttle to the **tourist office** at P. del Duomo 24. (☎34 17 72; fax 34 44 33. Open M-F 8:15am-1:50pm and 4-7pm, Sa 10am-1pm and 4-7pm, Su 10am-noon and 4-7pm.) Walk up V. Duomo to reach **Hotel Posta ❸,** V. Luca Signorelli 18, in a grand building with antique decorations. (☎34 19 09. Singles €31; doubles €43/€56. Cash only.) ■**Hostaria Vini e Cucina ❷,** V. del Duomo 25, caters to a devoted clientele. (Pizza €6-7.50. *Primi* €5-7. *Secondi* €7-13. Open daily 7-11pm. Cash only.) For a free tasting of *Orvieto Classico*, try **Cantina Freddano,** C. Cavour 5. (☎30 82 48. Bottles from €4. Open daily 9:30am-7:30pm.) **Postal Code:** 05018.

THE MARCHES (LE MARCHE)

In the Marches, green foothills separate the gray shores of the Adriatic from the Apennine peaks and traditional hill towns from umbrella-laden beaches. Inland towns, easily accessible by train, rely on agriculture and preserve the region's historical legacy in the architectural remains of Gauls and Romans.

URBINO   ☎0722

With picturesque stone dwellings scattered along steep city streets and a turreted palace ornamenting its skyline, Urbino (pop. 15,000) encompasses all that is classic Italy. The city's most remarkable monument is the imposing Renaissance **Palazzo Ducale.** From C. Garibaldi, you can see its delicate balconies flanked by turrets; around the back in P. Rinascimento, stairs in the central courtyard lead to the former private apartments of the duke, which are now home to the **Galleria Nazionale delle Marche.** Watch for Raphael's *Portrait of a Lady* in **Room 25.** (☎32 26 25. Open M 8:30am-2pm, Tu-Su 8:30am-7:15pm. €8, EU students ages 18-25 €4.) Walk back across P. della Repubblica and continue onto V. Raffaello to Raphael's birthplace, the **Casa Natale di Raffaello,** V. Raffaello 57, now a museum full of period furniture, works by local masters, and the *Madonna col Bambino*, by Raphael himself. (☎32 01 05. Open Mar.-Oct. M-Sa 9am-1pm and 3-7pm, Su 10am-1pm; Nov.-Feb. M-Sa 9am-2pm, Su 10am-1pm. €3.)

Bucci **buses** (☎0721 32 401) go from Borgo Mercatale to Rome (5hr., 1 per day, €22). Blue SOGET **buses** (☎223 33) run from P. Matteotti and the train station to Pesaro (55min.; M-Sa 11 per day, Su 6 per day; €2.05), which sends trains on to Ancona (1hr., 55 per day, €2.94). From there, a short walk uphill on V. G. Mazzini leads to **Piazza della Repubblica**, the city center. The **tourist office**, V. Puccinotti 35, is opposite the palace. (☎26 13; iat.urbino@regione.marche.it. Open M-F 9am-1pm and 3-6pm, Sa-Su 9am-1pm.) **Pensione Fosca ❷**, V. Raffaello 67, has large rooms five doors down from Rafael's birthplace. (☎32 96 22. Singles €21; doubles €35; triples €45. Cash only.) **Hotel San Giovanni ❷**, V. Barocci 13, has simple rooms. (☎32 90 55. Closed July. Singles €23, with bath €33; doubles €34/€50.) **Margherita** supermarket, V. Raffaello 37, stocks meats, cheeses, and packaged food. (☎32 97 71. Open M-Sa 7:30am- 2pm and 4:30-8pm. Cash only.) **Postal Code:** 61029.

ANCONA   ☎071

Ancona (pop. 100,000) is Italy's major transportation hub for those heading east. Industry and transportation are the main functions of this busy town. Though the P. del Duomo, atop Monte Guasco, offers a view of the rooftops and sapphire port below, those searching for more than a day of exploration may welcome the view from an outbound train. **Ferries** leave Stazione Marittima for Croatia, Greece, and northern Italy. Adriatica (☎502 11 621; www.adriatica.it.), Jadrolinija (☎20 43 05; www.jadrolinija.tel.hr/jadrolinija), and SEM Maritime Co. (☎20 40 41; www.marittimamauro.it) run to Croatia (from €37). ANEK (☎207 22 75; www.anekitalia.com) ferries go to Patras, Greece (from €50). Consult a schedule in advance, as departure times vary. Schedules and tickets are available at the Stazione. **Trains** leave P. Rosselli for: Bologna (2½hr., 43 per day, €10); Milan (5hr., 24 per day, €19.37); Rome (3-4hr., 10 per day, €13.22); and Venice (5hr., 4 per day, €25.20). Take bus #1/4 (€0.80) along the port to reach P. Cavour, the city center. The **tourist office** in Stazione Marittima provides ferry info. (☎20 11 83. Open daily July-Aug. 9am-7pm.) From the train station, cross the *piazza*, turn left, take the first right, and make a sharp right behind the newsstand to reach the **Ostello della Gioventù ❶**, V. Lamaticci 7. (☎/fax 42 257. Dorms €14. HI members only. AmEx/MC/V.) **CONAD** supermarket is at V. Matteotti 115. (Open M-W and F-Sa 8:15am-1:30pm and 5-7:30pm, Th 8:15am-1:30pm. Cash only.) **Postal Code:** 60100.

SOUTHERN ITALY

South of Rome, the sun gets brighter, the meals longer, and the passion more intense. The introduction to the *mezzogiorno* (Southern Italy) begins in Campania, the fertile cradle of the Bay of Naples and the Gulf of Salerno. The shadow of Mt. Vesuvius hides the famous ruins of Pompeii, lost to time and a river of molten lava, while the Amalfi Coast cuts a dramatic course down the lush Tyrrhenian shore. The region remains justly proud of its open-hearted populace, strong traditions, classical ruins, and relatively untouristed beaches.

NAPLES (NAPOLI)   ☎081

Italy's third-largest city, Naples (pop. 1,000,000) is also its most chaotic—Neapolitans run red lights, drive the wrong way on one-way streets, order things not on the menu, and stand in the middle of the street, blocking traffic, to finish a conversation. At the same time, they believe that they live in the best city in the world, and many travelers agree. As the birthplace of pizza and the modern-day home of tan-

ITALY

talizing seafood and pasta, Naples will please even the pickiest of gourmands. The city moves a mile a minute, but once you give in to the heartbeat of Naples, everywhere else seems a bit slow in comparison.

⊏ TRANSPORTATION

Flights: Aeroporto Capodichino, V. Umberto Maddalena (NAP; ☎789 6111), northeast of the city. Connects to all major Italian and European cities. An **Alibus** (☎531 1706) departs P. Municipio and P. Garibaldi (20min., 6am-10:30pm, €3).

Trains: Ferrovie dello Stato (☎892 021) goes from Stazione Centrale to: **Brindisi** (5hr., 5 per day, €9.25); **Milan** (8hr., 13 per day, €50); **Rome** (2hr., 34 per day, €10). **Circumvesuviana** (772 2444) runs to **Herculaneum** (2 per hr., €1.70) and **Pompeii** (2 per hr., €2.30).

Ferries: Depart from **Molo Angioino** and **Molo Beverello,** at the base of P. Municipio. From P. Garibaldi, take tram #1; from P. Municipio, take the R2 bus. **Caremar,** Molo Beverello (☎551 3882), runs often to **Capri** and **Ischia** (both 1½hr., €5). **Tirrenia Lines,** Molo Angioino (☎199 123 199), goes to **Palermo, Cagliari,** and **Sardinia.** Schedules and prices are inconsistent, check *Qui Napoli* (free at the tourist office).

Public Transportation: Giranapoli tickets (€1 per 1½hr., full-day €3) are valid on **buses, metro, trains,** and **funiculars.**

Taxis: Free (☎551 5151) or **Napoli** (☎556 4444). Only take metered taxis, and inquire about prices up front; even well-known companies may charge dubiously high rates.

⚹ ⁊ ORIENTATION AND PRACTICAL INFORMATION

The main train and bus terminals are in the immense **Piazza Garibaldi** on the east side of Naples. From P. Garibaldi, broad **Corso Umberto I** leads southwest to P. Bovi, from which V. de Pretis leads left to **Piazza Municipio,** the city center, and **Piazza Trieste e Trento** and **Piazza Plebiscito.** Below P. Municipio lie the **Stazione Marittima** ferry ports. From P. Trieste e Trento, **Via Toledo** (also known as **Via Roma**) leads through the Spanish quarter to **Piazza Dante.** Make a right into the historic **Spaccanapoli** neighborhood, which follows **Via dei Tribunali** through the middle of town. While violence is rare in Naples, theft is fairly common, so exercise caution.

Tourist Offices: EPT (☎26 87 79), at Stazione Centrale. Helps with hotels and ferries. Grab ◼ **Qui Napoli,** a monthly tourist publication full of schedules and listings. Open M-Sa 8:30am-8pm, Su 8am-2pm. **Branch** at Stazione Mergellina (☎761 21 02).

Consulates: Canada, V. Carducci 29 (☎40 13 38). **UK,** V. dei Mille 40 (☎423 89 11). **US,** P. della Repubblica (☎583 81 11, emergency 033 794 50 83).

Emergency: ☎113. **Police:** ☎113 or 794 11 11. English spoken.

Hospital: Cardarelli (☎747 28 59), on the R4 line. **Ambulance:** ☎752 82 82.

Internet Access: Internet Point, V. Toledo 59A, across from the Bank of Naples (☎497 60 90). €2 per hr. Open daily 9:30am-8:30pm. **Internet Cafe Multimedia,** V. Pignatelli 34 (☎551 47 08). €1.50 per hr. Open daily 9:30am-9:30pm.

Post Office: P. Matteotti (☎552 42 33), at V. Diaz on the R2 line. Unreliable *Fermo Posta.* Address mail to be held: First name, SURNAME, *In Fermo Posta,* P. Matteotti, Naples 80100, ITALY. Open M-F 8:15am-6pm, Sa 8:15am-noon. **Postal Code:** 80100.

⌂ ACCOMMODATIONS

Although Naples has some fantastic bargain lodgings, especially near **Piazza Garibaldi,** be cautious when choosing a room. Avoid hotels that solicit customers at the station, never give your passport until you've seen the room, agree on

Naples

▲ ACCOMMODATIONS
6 Small Rooms, 8
Casanova Hotel, 1
Hostel Pensione Mancini, 3
Hotel des Artistes, 2

🍴 FOOD
Gino Sorbillo, 5
Pizzeria Brandi, 9
Pizzeria Di Matteo, 4

★ NIGHTLIFE
Itaca, 6
Las Tapas, 7

ITALY

ON THE MENU

PIZZA FIT FOR A QUEEN

Though Neopolitans don't agree on which pizzeria is the best in town, most agree that Brandi is one of the most prestigious. Founded by Enrico Brandi, this pizzeria has been churning out pizzas in the same location (supposedly with the same oven) since 1780. The restaurant eventually passed to Raffaele Esposito, who made the pizzeria famous when Umberto and Margherita, the king and queen of the House of Savoy, passed through Naples in 1889.

To mark the occasion of their visit, Esposito made a special pizza that celebrated the Italian flag, with the red of the tomato sauce, the white of the mozzarella, and the green of basil. Queen Margherita loved it so much that she sent a letter to Esposito thanking him, a letter that is still in the restaurant today. Esposito named the pizza after her, and the rest is history.

The margherita pizza is not the only thing on the menu at Brandi. Special pizzas have been named after the celebrities who have enjoyed them. The Pavarotti pizza, only for the brave, has 20 toppings and is meant for four people, but Pavarotti is rumored to have eaten it all by himself.

Pizzeria Brandi, Salita S. Anna di Palazzo 1 (☎081 41 69 28). Open Tu-Su 12:30-3pm and 7pm-midnight. AmEx/MC/V.

the price *before* unpacking, be alert for unexpected costs, and gauge how secure the lodging seems. The **ACISJF/Centro D'Ascolto,** at Stazione Centrale, helps women find safe rooms. (☎28 19 93. Open M-Tu and Th 3:30-6:30pm.)

◪ **Hostel Pensione Mancini,** V. Mancini 33 (☎553 67 31; www.hostelpensionemancini.com), off the far end of P. Garibaldi from the train station. Renovated rooms. Dorms €18; singles €35; doubles €45, with bath €55; triples €80; quads €90. Cash only. ❷

◪ **6 Small Rooms,** V. Diodato Lioy 18 (☎790 13 78; www.at6smallrooms.com), up from P. Monteolovieto. Friendly atmosphere and larger rooms than its name suggests. No sign; look for the name on the call button. Dorms €18; doubles €54. Cash only. ❷

Ostello Mergellina (HI), V. Salita della Grotta 23 (☎761 23 46; fax 761 23 91). M: Mergellina. From the metro, make 2 sharp rights onto V. Piedigrotta, then a right onto V. Salita della Grotta. Turn right onto driveway after overpass. Laundry €5.20. Lockout 9am-3pm. Strict curfew 12:30am. Dorms €14; doubles from €50. Cash only. ❷

Casanova Hotel, C. Garibaldi 333 (☎26 82 87; www.hotelcasanova.com). From P. Garibaldi, take C. Garibaldi and turn right before V. Casanova. Airy rooms and a rooftop terrace. Breakfast €4. Singles €23-28, with bath €30-35; doubles €39-46/€45-56; triples €60/€65-78; quads €70-84. Ask about *Let's Go* discount. AmEx/MC/V. ❸

Hotel des Artistes, V. Duomo 61 (☎44 61 55; www.hoteldesartistesnaples.it). Conveniently located for exploring the district's sites. Intimate and inviting, all rooms have balconies, luxurious linens, bath, phone, A/C, and TV. Singles €70-80; doubles €80-115; triples €95-120; quads €115-130. 10% *Let's Go* discount. AmEx/MC/V. ❺

🍴 FOOD

If you ever doubted that Neapolitans invented pizza, Naples's *pizzerie* will take that doubt, beat it into a ball, throw it in the air, spin it on their collective finger, punch it down, cover it with sauce and mozzarella, and serve it *alla margherita.* For pizza try the historic district; for cafes and *gelaterie* head to **Via Toledo.** As former customer Bill Clinton can attest, ◪**Pizzeria Di Matteo ❶,** V. Tribunali 94, serves up pies bursting with flavor. (☎45 52 62. Open M-Sa 9am-midnight. Cash only.) ◪**Gino Sorbillo ❶,** V. Tribunali 32, is a family affair that boasts a grandfather who invented the *ripieno al forno* (calzone) and 21 pizza-making children in this generation alone. (Open daily noon-3:30pm and 7-

11:30pm. MC/V.) Raffaele Esposito invented the *margherita* in the oven of **Pizzeria Brandi ❷**, Salita S. Anna di Palazzo 1. The famous *pizzeria* counts Luciano Pavarotti and Isabella Rossellini among its customers. (Open daily 12:30-3pm and 7:30pm-late. AmEx/MC/V.)

👁 SIGHTS

🏛 **MUSEO ARCHEOLOGICO NAZIONALE.** Situated in a 16th-century *palazzo* and former barracks, one of the world's most important archaeological museums houses exquisite treasures from Pompeii and Herculaneum, from the collection of Charles Bourbon. The mezzanine contains the Alexander Mosaic, while a sporadically-open Egyptian Collection inhabits the museum's basement. *(M: P. Cavour. Turn right and walk 2 blocks. Open M and W-Su 9am-7:30pm. €6.50, under 18 and over 65 free.)*

🏛 **MUSEO AND GALLERIE DI CAPODIMONTE.** Housed in a royal *palazzo*, the museum resides inside a pastoral park filled with playful youngsters. In addition to its plush royal apartments, the palace houses the Italian National Picture Gallery. Among these incomparable works are Bellini's *Transfiguration*, Masaccio's *Crucifixion*, and Titian's *Danae. (Open Tu-Su 8:30am-7:30pm. €7.50, after 2pm €6.50.)*

DUOMO. The main attraction of the 14th-century duomo is the **Capella del Tesoro di San Gennaro**, decorated with Baroque paintings. A beautiful 17th-century bronze grille protects the high altar, which possesses a reliquary containing the saint's head and two vials of his coagulated blood. According to legend, disaster will strike the city if the blood does not liquify on the celebration of his **festa**; miraculously, it always does. *(Walk 3 blocks up V. Duomo from C. Umberto I or take bus #42 from P. Garibaldi. Open M-F 9am-noon and 4:30-7pm, Su 9am-noon. Free. Excavation site €3.)*

PALAZZO REALE AND MASCHIO ANGIONO. The 17th-century **Palazzo Reale** contains opulent royal apartments, the **Museo di Palazzo Reale,** and a fantastic view from the terrace of the **Royal Chapel.** The **Biblioteca Nazionale** stores 1.5 million volumes, including the scrolls from the **Villa dei Papiri** in Herculaneum. The **Teatro San Carlo** is reputed to top the acoustics in Milan's La Scala. *(Take the R2 bus from P. Garibaldi to P. Trieste e Trento and go around to the P. Plebiscito entrance. Open M Tu and W Su 9am-8pm. €4.20.)* From P. Trieste e Trento, walk up V. Vittorio Emanuele III to P. Municipio for the five-turreted **Castel Nuovo,** built in 1286 by Charles II of Anjou. Inside, admire the **Museo Civico.** *(Open M-Sa 9am-7pm. €5.)*

CATACOMBS. The catacombs of San Gennaro, San Gaudioso, and San Severo all date back to the early centuries AD. Tours of the subterranean alleys beneath the city are fascinating, but not for the claustrophobic. *(Napoli e La Città office at V. S. Anna di Palazzo. ☎40 02 56. Tours Th 9pm; Sa 10am and 6pm; Su 10, 11am, and 6pm. €5. Napoli Sotterranea, P. S. Gaetano 68. Go down V. Tribunali and turn left before San Paolo Maggiore. ☎29 69 44. Tours every 2hr. M-F noon-4pm, Sa-Su and holidays 10am-6pm. €5.)*

🎵 🎭 ENTERTAINMENT AND NIGHTLIFE

Piazza Vanvitelli in Vomero draws young people to relax and socialize. **Piazza San Domenico Maggiore** is another hot spot. Take the funicular from V. Toledo or bus C28 from P. Vittoria. Outdoor bars and cafes are a popular choice in **Piazza Bellini. Itaca,** P. Bellini 71, mixes trance music with dark decor. (Mixed drinks €6-7. Beer €3-4. Open daily 10am-3am.) **Las Tapas,** V. Paladino 56, is a favorite of university students, near trendy P. S. Domenico Maggiore. (Sangria €2. Open daily 7pm-2:30am.) **ARCI-GAY/Lesbica** (☎552 88 15) has info on gay and lesbian club nights.

DAYTRIPS FROM NAPLES

POMPEII. On the morning of August 24, AD 79, a deadly cloud of volcanic ash from the eruption of nearby Mt. Vesuvius overtook the Roman city of Pompeii, engulfing the city in suffocating black clouds and catching the prosperous residents by surprise. Mere hours after the eruption, stately buildings, works of art, and—ghastliest of all—human bodies were sealed in hardened casts of ash, natural tombs that would remain undisturbed until 1748 when excavations began. The site hasn't changed much since then, and neither have the victims. Walk down V. d. Marina to reach the colonnaded ■Forum, which was once the civic and religious center of the city. Exit the Forum through the upper end by the cafeteria, and head right on V. d. Fortuna to reach the ■House of the Faun, where excavators found a bronze dancing faun and the spectacular Alexander Mosaic (today in the Museo Archeologico Nazionale). Continue on V. d. Fortuna and turn left on V. d. Vettii to reach the **House of the Vettii**, on the left, and the most vivid frescoes in Pompeii. Backtrack on V. d. Vettii, cross V. d. Fortuna to V. Storto, turn left on V. d. Augustali, and take a quick right to reach a small **brothel** (the Lupenar), still popular after 2000 years. V. d. Teatri, across the street, leads to the oldest standing **amphitheater** in the world (80 BC), which once held up to 12,000 spectators. To get to the ■Villa of the Mysteries, head west on V. d. Fortuna, right on V. Consolare, and all the way up Porta Ercolano. (Archaeological site open daily 8:30am-7:30pm. €10.) Take the Circumvesuviana **train** (☎081 772 24 44) from Naples to Pompeii (dir.: Sorrento, 40 min., 2 per hr., €2.30). To reach the site, head downhill and take your first left to the Porta Marina entrance. To reach the **tourist office,** V. Sacra 1, walk right from the station and continue down the hill. (Open M-F 8am-3:30pm, Sa 8am-2pm.)

HERCULANEUM. Herculaneum city is less excavated than Pompeii because it was buried much deeper and a modern city sits on top; one highlight is the **House of Deer.** (Open daily 8:30am-7:30pm. €10.) The **House of the Mosaic of Neptune and Anfitrite** is famous for the breathtaking **mosaic.** The city is 500m downhill from the *Ercolano* stop on the Circumvesuviana **train** from Naples (dir.: Sorrento; 20min., €2). Stop at the **tourist office,** V. IV Novembre 84 (☎081 88 12 43), for a free map.

MOUNT VESUVIUS. You can peer into the only active volcano on mainland Europe at Mt. Vesuvius. Although Vesuvius hasn't erupted since March 31, 1944 (and scientists say volcanoes should erupt every 30 years), experts deem the trip safe. Trasporti Vesuviani **buses** (buy ticket onboard; round-trip €3.80) run from the Ercolano Circumvesuviana station to the crater.

CASERTA. Few palaces, no matter how opulent, can hold a candle to Caserta's glorious ■Reggia, often referred to as "The Versailles of Naples." A world apart from the brutality of Pompeii, the palace and grounds resonate with a passion for art and beauty. When Bourbon King Charles III commissioned the palace in 1751, he intended it to rival Louis XIV's famously spectacular abode. Completed in 1775, the vast expanse of lush lawns filled with fountains and sculptures, culminates in a 75m man-made waterfall—the setting for the final scene of *Star Wars.* To the right are the **English Gardens,** complete with fake ruins inspired by Pompeii and Paestum. The **palazzo** boasts 1200 rooms, 1742 windows, and 34 staircases, and furnishings that are equally grandiose. The Reggia is opposite the train station. (Open Tu-Su 9am-7:30pm. €6.50.) **Trains** run from Naples (40min., 35 per day, €2.80).

AMALFI COAST

Tucked between the jagged rocks of the Sorrentine Peninsula and the waters of the Adriatic, the Amalfi Coast has many alluring aspects. Its lemon groves bask in the sun, its local population is spirited, and its monuments reflect the area's history as a maritime power. Still, the region's natural beauty remains its main asset.

⌨ TRANSPORTATION. The coast is accessible from Naples, Sorrento, Salerno, and the islands by ferry and blue SITA buses. **Trains** run directly to Salerno from Naples (45min., 40 per day, €5-10) and Rome (2½-3hr., 22 per day, €22-33). Trains also run to Sorrento from Naples (1hr., 2 per hr., €3.10). **Buses** link Paestum and Salerno (1hr., 12 per day, €3.20). From Salerno, Travelmar (☎089 87 29 50) runs **ferries** to Amalfi (35min., 6 per day, €4) and Positano (1¼hr., 6 per day, €6). From Sorrento, Linee Marittime Partenopee (☎081 807 18 12) ferries (40min., 5 per day, €7) and **hydrofoils** (20min., 10 per day, €11.10) run to Capri.

AMALFI AND ATRANI. Breathtaking natural beauty surrounds the narrow streets and historic monuments of Amalfi. Visitors crowd P. del Duomo to admire the elegant 9th-century **Duomo di Sant'Andrea** and the nearby **Fontana di Sant'Andrea,** a marble female nude with water spouting from her breasts. **A'Scalinatella ❶,** P. Umberto 12, has hostel beds, regular rooms, and camping all over Amalfi and Atrani. (☎089 87 19 30; www.hostelscalinatella.com. Dorms €10-21; doubles €30-60, with bath €50-83; camping €5 per person. Cash only.) Amalfi's many *paninoteche* are perfect for a tight budget. The tiny beachside village of Atrani is a 15min. walk from Amalfi. The **Path of the Gods,** a spectacular 4hr. hike, follows the coast from Bomerano to Positano and offers spectacular views. The 2hr. hike to **Ravello** via Scalla also makes for a pleasant trip. **Postal Code:** 84011.

RAVELLO. Perched atop 330m cliffs, Ravello has provided a haven for many celebrity artists over the years. The Moorish cloister and gardens of **Villa Rufolo,** off P. Duomo, inspired Boccaccio's *Decameron* and Wagner's *Parsifal.* (Open daily 9am-8pm. €4.) In summer, the villa puts on a concert series in the gardens of the Villa; tickets are sold at the Ravello Festival Box office, V. Roma 10-12 (☎089 85 84 22; www.ravellofestival.com). The small road to the right leads to the impressive **Villa Cimbrone,** whose floral gardens hide temples and statue-filled grottoes, along with spectacular views. (Open daily 9am-7:30pm. €4.50.) **Hotel Villa Amore ❹,** V. dei Fusco 4, has a garden overlooking the sea. (☎089 85 71 35. Follow V. San Francesco out of P. Duomo toward Villa Cimbrone, and turn left onto V. dei Fusco. Breakfast included. Singles €48-60; doubles €74-85. MC/V.) **Postal Code:** 84010.

SORRENTO. The most heavily touristed town on the peninsula, lively Sorrento makes a convenient base for daytrips around the Bay of Naples. The **tourist office,** L. de Maio 35, is off P. Tasso, in the C. dei Forestieri compound. (☎081 807 40 33. Open Apr.-Sept. M-Sa 8:45am-7:45pm; Oct.-Mar. 8:30am-2pm and 4-6:15pm.) Halfway to the **beach** at **Punta del Capo** (bus A), **Hotel Elios ❸,** V. Capo 33, has clean rooms. (☎081 878 18 12. Open Apr.-Oct. Singles €30-40; doubles €50-60.) Savory menus abound. After dark a crowd gathers for drinks in the rooftop lemon grove above **The English Inn,** C. Italia 56. (Open daily 9am-1am.) **Postal Code:** 80067.

SALERNO AND PAESTUM. Industrial **Salerno** is best used as a base for daytrips to nearby **Paestum,** the site of spectacularly preserved **▥Doric temples,** including the **Temple of Ceres** and the **Temple of Poseidon,** as well as a **museum** with artifacts taken from the sites. (Temples open daily 9am-7:30pm. Museum open daily 9am-6:30pm. Both hold reduced hours low season and are closed the 1st and 3rd M of each month. Both sights €6.50, EU students €3.25.) To reach the clean and com-

ITALY

fortable **Ostello Ave Gratia Plena ❷**, V. Canali, take C. V. Emanuele into the old district where it becomes V. dei Mercanti, and head right onto V. Canali. (☎ 089 23 47 76. Curfew 12:30am. Dorms €14; doubles €33. Cash only.) **Postal Code:** 84100.

BAY OF NAPLES ISLANDS

◪ **CAPRI.** There are two towns on the island of Capri—**Capri** proper, near the ports, and **Anacapri,** higher up the mountain. Visitors flock to the **Blue Grotto,** a sea cave whose waters shimmer with neon-blue light. (Open daily 9am-5pm. Boat ride €8.) **Buses** leaving from V. Roma make the trip up the mountain to Anacapri every 15min. until 1:40am. Upstairs from P. Vittoria in Anacapri, **Villa San Michele** sports lush gardens and ancient sculptures. (Open daily 9am-6pm. €5.) Take the chairlift up **Monte Solaro** from P. Vittoria to see the looming Apennines. (Open daily Mar.-Oct. 9:30am-4:45pm. €5.50.) For those who prefer cliff to coastline, Capri's **hiking** trails lead to stunning vistas; try the short but steep hike to the ruins of Emperor Tiberius's **Villa Jovis,** the largest of his 12 Capri villas. The view from the **Cappella di Santa Maria del Soccorso,** built onto the villa, is unrivaled. (Open daily 9am-6pm.) In the evenings, Italians come out for Capri's nightlife; bars around **Piazza Umberto** in Capri keep the music pumping, while cheaper Anacapri draws a younger crowd.
   Caremar (☎ 081 837 07 00) **ferries** run from Marina Grande to Naples (1¼hr., 3 per day, €10) and Sorrento (25min., 4 per day, €8). LineaJet (☎ 081 837 08 19) runs **hydrofoils** to Naples (40-50min., 11 per day, €12) and Sorrento (25min., €9). Ferries and hydrofoils to Ischia and Amalfi run less frequently; check with the lines at Marina Grande for information. The Capri **tourist office** (☎ 081 837 06 34) is at the end of Marina Grande; in Anacapri, it's at V. Orlandi 59 (☎ 081 837 15 24), to the right of the P. Vittoria bus stop. (Both open June-Sept. M-Sa 9am-7pm; Oct.-May reduced hours.) ◪**Bussola di Hermes ❷**, V. Traversa La Vigna 14, in Anacapri, has a friendly proprietor. Call from P. Vittoria in Anacapri for pick-up. (☎ 081 838 20 10. Dorms €20-24 per person; doubles €50-65. AmEx/MC/V.) The **Bed and Breakfast Tirrenia Roberts ❺**, V. Mulo 27, is closer to Capri's center and the beach. From the center of Capri, walk 500m to the gas station; Tirrenia is below the station. (☎ 081 837 61 19. Reserve well in advance. Doubles €90-110.) The **supermarket,** V. G. Orlandi 299, in Anacapri, is well stocked. (Open M-Sa 8:30am-1:30pm and 5-8:30pm, Su 8:30am-noon.) **Postal Codes:** Capri: 80073; Anacapri: 80021.

◪ **ISCHIA.** Augustus fell in love with Capri's fantastic beauty in 29 BC, but later swapped it for its more fertile neighbor. Ischia, just across the bay, offers sandy beaches, natural hot springs, ruins, forests, vineyards, and lemon groves. SEPSA **buses** #1, CD, and CS (every 15-30min.; €1.20, 1-day pass €4) depart from the ferry landing and follow the coast in a circular route, stopping at: **Ischia Porto,** a port formed by the crater of an extinct volcano; **Casamicciola Terme,** with a crowded beach and legendary thermal waters; **Lacco Ameno,** the oldest Greek settlement in the western Mediterranean; and popular **Forio,** home to lively bars. The **Motella Gardens,** V. Calese 39, feature over 800 tropical plants, man-made streams and gorgeous views of Ischia. (Open Tu, Th, and Sa-Su 9am-7pm. €10.) Caremar **ferries** (☎ 081 98 48 18) arrive from Naples (1½hr., 8 per day, €5.70). Alilauro (☎ 081 99 18 88; www.alilauro.it) runs **hydrofoils** to Sorrento (1 per day, €13). The **tourist office** is on V. Iasolino. (☎ 081 98 20 61. Open daily 9am-8pm.) The ◪**Ostello "Il Gabbiano" (HI) ❷**, Strada Statale Forio-Panza 162, is accessible by buses #1, CS, and CD. The hostel has a bar, pool, and beach access. (☎ 081 90 94 22. Curfew 2am. Open Apr.-Sept. Dorms €16.) **Pensione Di Lustro ❸**, V. Filippo di Lustro 9, is near the beach. (☎ 081 99 71 63. €45-55 per person. AmEx/MC/V.) Savor locally-caught fish at **Emiddio ❷**, V. Porto 30. (*Primi* €5-7. *Secondi* €10-16. Cover €1. Open daily noon-3pm and 7pm-midnight. AmEx/MC/V.) **Postal Code:** 80077.

SICILY (SICILIA)

Sicily is a land of sensuous sunshine and sinister shadows. Ancient Greek influences lauded the golden island as the second home of the gods; now eager tourists seek it as the home of *The Godfather*. While the *Cosa Nostra* remains a presence in Sicily, it makes up only the smallest part of the vivacious and varied culture.

⚏ TRANSPORTATION. Tirrenia **Ferries** (☎ 091 602 11 11; www.tirrenia.it) offers extensive service. From southern Italy, take a **train** to Reggio di Calabria, then a Meridiano **ferry** (40min., M-Sa 12 per day, €1.50) or Ferrovie Statale **hydrofoil** (☎ 096 586 35 40. 25min., 12 per day, €2.60) to Messina, Sicily's transport hub. Ferries also go to Palermo from Sardinia (14hr., €39) and Naples (10hr., 2 per day, €38). **SAIS Trasporti** (☎ 091 617 11 41) and SAIS **buses** (☎ 091 616 60 28) serve destinations throughout the island. **Trains** head to Messina directly from Naples (7hr., 11 per day, €22) and Rome (9hr., 17 per day, €42). Trains continue west to Palermo (3½hr., 12 per day, €11).

PALERMO. From ruin-lined streets to the shrinking shadow of organized crime, gritty Palermo's (pop. 700,000) recent history provides shade and texture to a rich cultural heritage. To reach the **Teatro Massimo,** where the opera scene of *The Godfather: Part III* was filmed, walk up V. Maqueda past the intersection of Quattro Canti and C. Vittorio Emanuele. (Open for tours Tu-Su 10am-3:30pm. €3. Closed during rehearsals.) Up C. Vittorio Emanuele, the **Palazzo dei Normanni** contains the ⛪**Cappella Palatina,** full of golden mosaics. (Open M-F 9-11:45am and 3-4:45pm, Sa 9-11:45am, Su 9-9:45am and 11:15am-12:45pm.) The morbid **Cappuchin Catacombs,** in P. Cappuccini, are lined with thousands of corpses and twisted skeletons. To get there, take buses #109 or 318 from Stazione Centrale to P. Indipendenza and transfer to bus #327. (Open daily 9am-noon and 3-5:30pm. €1.50.) **Trains** leave Stazione Centrale, in P. Giulio Cesare, for Florence (15hr., 11 per day, €58) and Rome (11hr., 9 per day, €53). All four **bus** lines leave from V. Balsamo, next to the train station. Pick up a combined metro and bus map from an **AMAT** or **metro** info booth. Buses #101 and 102 (€1 for 2hr.) both circle the downtown area. To reach the **tourist office,** P. Castelnuovo 34, in the Banco di Sicilia building, take a bus from the train station to P. Politeama, at the end of V. Maqueda. (☎ 091 605 81 11. Open June-Sept. M-Sa 8:30am-2pm and 3-7pm; Oct.-May M-F 8:30am-2pm and 2:30-6pm.) **Hotel Regina ❷,** C. Vittorio Emanuele 316, is off V. Maqueda. Be sure to check your reservation before arriving. (☎ 091 611 42 16. Singles €21, with bath €35; doubles €40/€50. AmEx/MC/V.) The area around **Teatro Massimo** has lots of cheap restaurants. **Postal Code:** 90100.

SYRACUSE (SIRACUSA). Never having regained the glory of its Grecian golden days, the modern city of Syracuse (pop. 130,000) takes pride in its extraordinary ruins. Syracuse's one-time role as a Mediterranean superpower is still evident in the **Archaeological Park,** on the northern side of town, which includes several sites. 15,000 spectators saw Aeschylus premiere his *Persians* in the enormous **Greek theater.** To reach the 2nd-century **Roman amphitheater,** follow C. Gelone until it meets V. Teocrito, then walk left down V. Augusto. (Open daily 9am-2hr. before sunset; low season reduced hours. €4.50.) Across from the tourist office on V. S. Giovanni are the **Catacomba di San Giovanni,** displaying 20,000 now-empty tombs carved into the remains of a Greek aqueduct. (Tu-Su 9:10am-12:30pm and 2:30-5:30pm. €3.50, under 15 or over 65 €2.50. MC/V.) More ruins lie over the Ponte Umbertino on **Ortigia,** the serene island on which the Greeks first landed. The ruined **Temple of Apollo** has a few columns still standing, but those at the **Temple of Diana** are much more impressive. **Trains** leave V. Francesco Crispi for Messina (3hr., 9 per day, €8.26) and Rome (12hr., 11 per day, €37.70). Interbus **buses,** V. Trieste 40 (☎ 667 10), leave for Palermo (3hr., 3 per day, €13.40). To get from the train station to the **tourist office,** V. S. Sebastiano 43, take V. F. Crispi to C. Gelone, turn right on V. Teocrite, then left on V. S. Sebastiano. (☎ 48 12

UNREAL RELICS?

Dr. Luigi Garlaschelli is an organic chemist at the University of Pavia. As an extracurricular, he investigates the authenticity of religious blood relics.

LG: Why are relics everywhere in Italy?

A: In the Middle Ages, it was believed that they would protect the city from its enemies. [Such relics include] the milk of the Virgin Mary and Christ's fingernails.

LG: What was your first project?

A: My first work was on the blood of St. Januarius, which is contained in a small vial kept in the *duomo* in Naples. St. Januarius was beheaded in AD 305. The relic appeared in the Middle Ages, 1000 years later, contemporary to the appearance of the shroud of Turin. Normally blood taken from a living body will clot only once; the "miracle" of this blood is that it turns from solid to liquid and back again twice a year during religious ceremonies.

LG: How does that work?

A: Well, using only ferric chloride (an iron salt), which exists naturally near active volcanoes (like Vesuvius, active at the time of the discovery of the blood), calcium carbonate, kitchen salt, and techniques available in the Middle Ages, we created a substance of the same color and properties as the reputed blood of the saint. The matter would be closed were we to open the vial and take samples.

00. Open daily 8:30am-1:30pm and 3-6:30pm.) **Hotel Centrale ②**, C. Umberto I 141, has rooms with gorgeous views. (☎ 0931 605 28. Singles €17; doubles €26-35; triples €37.) For cheap food, try stops along **Via Savoia** and **Via Cavour**, or the **market** in Ortigia, on V. Trento. (Open M-Sa 8am-1pm.) **Postal Code:** 96100.

TAORMINA. Legend has it that Neptune wrecked a Greek boat off the eastern coast of Sicily in the 8th century BC, and the sole survivor, inspired by the spectacular scenery onshore, founded Taormina. As historians tell it, the Carthaginians founded Tauromenium at the turn of the 4th century BC only to have it wrested away by the Greek tyrant Dionysius. Taormina's Greek roots are apparent in its best-preserved treasure, the **Greek theater.** (Open daily 9am-1hr. before sunset. €4.15, EU residents €2.) The 5000-seat theater hosts the annual **Taormina Arte** summer festival. (Box office at C. Umberto, 19. www.taormina-arte.com.) The 13th-century **Duomo** was rebuilt during the Renaissance. (Hours vary.) **Trains** run from Syracuse (2hr., 11 per day, €6.70) and Messina (40min., 22 per day, €3). The **tourist office** is in P. Corvaja, off C. Umberto. (☎ 0942 23 243. Open M-Sa 8:30am-2pm and 4-7pm.) To reach the **🖥Taormina's Odyssey Youth Hostel ②**, go from the intersection of C. Umberto and V. L. Pirandello and take V. C. Patrizio to V. Cappuccini. When it forks, veer right on to V. Fontana Vecchia and follow the signs.The hostel offers clean rooms and a social atmosphere that makes it well worth the hike. (☎ 0942 24 533. Dorms €15-18.) **SMA** supermarket is at V. Apollo Arcageta, near the post office. (Open M-Sa 8:30am-1pm and 4:30-8:30pm.) **Postal Code:** 98039.

AEOLIAN ISLANDS (ISOLE EOLIE)

Homer thought the Aeolian Islands to be the second home of the gods, and indeed, these last few stretches of unspoiled seashore border on the divine. Sparkling seas, smooth beaches, and fiery volcanoes testify to the area's stunning beauty.

🚆 TRANSPORTATION. The *archipelago* lies off the Sicilian coast, north of Milazzo, the principal and least expensive departure point. Hop off a **train** from Palermo (2½hr., €9.20) and onto a free, orange AST **bus** for the port (10min., 1 per hr.). Siremar (☎ 090 928 32 42) and Navigazione Generale Italiana (NGI; ☎ 090 928 40 91) **ferries** depart for Lipari (2hr., €6.20); Stromboli (6hr., €9.90); and Vulcano (1½hr., €5.70). **Hydrofoils** make the trip in half the time but twice the price. Both have ticket offices on V. Dei Mille in Milazzo. Ferries run less frequently from the Molo Beverello port in Naples.

▓ LIPARI. Lipari, the largest of the islands, is renowned for its amazing beaches and stunning hillside views. To reach the popular beaches of **Spiaggia Bianca** and **Porticello,** take the Lipari-Cavedi **bus** north to Canneto; Spiaggia Bianca is *the* spot for topless (and often bottomless) sunbathing. Lipari also offers a splendidly rebuilt medieval **castello,** the site of an ancient Greek acropolis. The fortress shares its hill with the **San Bartolo church,** an **archaeological park,** and the ▓**Museo Archeologico Eoliano.** (Museum open daily May-Oct. 9am-1:30pm and 4-7pm; Nov.-Apr. 9am-1:30pm and 3-6pm. €4.50.) The **tourist office,** C. Vittorio Emanuele 202, is near the ferry dock. (☎090 988 00 95. Open July-Aug. M-F 8am-2pm and 4:30-9:30pm, Sa 8am-2pm; Sept.-June M-F 8am-2pm and 4:30-7:30pm.) **Casa Vittorio ❷,** Vico Sparviero 15, is on a quiet street in the center of town. Rooms range from singles to a five-person penthouse. (☎090 981 15 23. €15-40 per person. Cash only.) ▓**Da Gilberto e Vera ❶,** V. Garibaldi 22-24, has superb sandwiches. (*Panini* from €3.50. Open daily Mar.-Oct. 7am-4am; Nov.-Feb. 7am-2am. AmEx/MC/V.) Stock up at **UPIM** supermarket, C. Vittorio Emanuele 212. (Open M-Sa 8am-10pm.) **Postal Code:** 98050.

▓ VULCANO. Black beaches, bubbling seas, and natural mud spas attract visitors from around the world to Vulcano. A steep 1hr. **hike** to the inactive **Gran Cratere** (Grand Crater) snakes between the volcano's noxious yellow fumaroles. On a clear day, you can see all the other islands from the top. The allegedly therapeutic **Laghetto di Fanghi** (mud pool) is just up V. Provinciale to the right from the port; this natural spa's odor is impossible to miss. If you would prefer not to bathe in sulfuric radioactive mud, you can step gingerly into the scalding waters of the **acquacalda,** with underwater volcanic outlets, or visit the nearby black sands of **Sabbie Nere** (follow the signs off V. Ponente). To get to Vulcano, take the **hydrofoil** from the port at nearby Lipari (10min., 8 per day, €2.60). For more info, see the tourist office, V. Provinciale 41. (☎090 985 20 28. Open daily July-Aug. 8am-1:30pm and 3-5pm.) For **private rooms** (*affittacamere*), call ☎090 985 21 42. The Lipari tourist office also has information on Vulcano. **Postal Code:** 98050.

▓ STROMBOLI. If you find luscious beaches and hot springs a bit tame, a visit to Stromboli's active ▓**volcano,** which spews orange cascades of lava and molten rock about every 10min., will quench your thirst for adventure. **Hiking** the volcano on your own is **illegal** and **dangerous,** but **Magmatrek** offers tours, which also should be taken at your own risk. The group once ran excursions to the craters themselves, but new laws prohibit tours from going any higher than 450m, which still provides a close-up view of the eruptions. Bring sturdy shoes, a flashlight, snacks, water, and warm clothes; don't wear contact lenses, as the wind sweeps dust everywhere. (☎/fax 090 986 57 68. Tours depart from V. Vittorio Emanuele. €13.50.) Siremar (☎090 98 60 16) runs **ferries** and **hydrofoils** from Milazzo to Stromboli. From the main road, follow the side street across from St. Bartholomew's church at the end of town to reach ▓**Casa del Sole ❷,** on V. D. Cincotta, the best value in town. Large rooms face a shared terrace. (☎/fax 090 98 60 17. Open Mar.-Oct. €22; doubles €46. Prices vary by season.) **Postal Code:** 98050.

SARDINIA (SARDEGNA)

An old Sardinian legend says that when God finished making the world, He had a handful of dirt left over. He took the dirt, threw it into the Mediterranean, and stepped on it, creating the island of Sardinia. The contours of His divine foot formed some of the world's most spectacular landscapes.

▗ TRANSPORTATION

Tirrenia **ferries** (☎081 317 29 99; www.tirrenia.it) run to Olbia from Civitavecchia, just north of Rome (4-8hr., 3 per day, from €16-40), and Genoa (9-13hr., 1-2 per day, from €34). They also chug to Cagliari from Civitavecchia (15hr., 1 per day,

ITALY

from €23); Naples (16hr., Jan.-Sept. 1-2 per week, €20-41); and Palermo (13½hr., 1 per week, from €21). **Trains** run from Cagliari to Olbia (4hr., 1 per day, €13) via Oristano (1½hr., 16 per day, €4.55) and to Sassari (4hr., 2 per day, from €12.10). From Sassari, trains run to Alghero (40min., 11 per day, €1.80). PANI **buses** connect Cagliari to Oristano (1½hr., 4 per day, €5.84).

CAGLIARI
☎070

Cagliari combines the bustle and energy of a modern Italian city with the endearing rural atmosphere of the rest of the island. Its Roman ruins, medieval towers, and cobblestone streets contrast with the regal tree-lined streets and sweeping beaches downtown. Climb Largo Carlo Felice to reach the city's impressive **duomo**, P. Palazzo 3, with dazzling gold mosaics topping each of its entryways. (Open daily 8am-12:30pm and 4-8pm.) The 2nd-century **Roman amphitheater** comes alive with concerts, operas, and classic plays during the summer **arts festival** in July and August. If you prefer to sun-worship, take city bus P, PQ, or PF to **Il Poetto** beach (20min., €0.77), which was famous for its pure white sand until the government dumped course brown sand on top to prevent erosion. The **tourist office** is in P. Matteotti. (☎66 92 55. Open M-Sa 8:30am-1:30pm and 2:30-7:30pm; low season reduced hours.) **Albergo Palmas ❷**, V. Sardegna 14, is the town's best budget option, with clean rooms and shared bath. Cross V. Roma and turn right; take the first left on Largo Carlo Felice, and turn right onto V. Sardegna. (☎65 16 79. Singles €23; doubles €31-38. AmEx/MC/V.) **Postal Code:** 09100.

ALGHERO
☎079

Vineyards, ruins, and horseback rides are all a short trip from Alghero's palm-lined parks and twisting medieval streets. The █**Grotte di Nettuno,** a 70-million-year-old, stalactite-filled cavern complex in Capo Caccia, is accessible by bus (1hr., 3 per day, round-trip €1.80) or boat (1hr., 8 per day, round-trip €10). Visitors can descend the 632 steps between massive cliffs. (Open daily Apr.-Sept. 9am-7pm; Oct. 10am-4pm; Nov.-Mar. 8am-2pm. €10.) The **tourist office**, P. Porta Terra 9, is to the right when exiting the bus stop. (☎97 90 54; www.infoalghero.it. Open Apr.-Oct. M-Sa 8am-8pm, Su 10am-1pm; Nov.-Mar. M-Sa 8am-2pm.) Take bus AF from the port to Fertilia for the █**Hostal del'Alguer (HI) ❶**, V. Parenzo 79, which offers bike rental, bar, pool table, and Internet. (☎/fax 93 20 39. Breakfast included. Dorms €13; 2-bed family rooms €16-18. HI members only. **Postal Code:** 07041.

ORISTANO AND THE SINIS PENINSULA
☎0783

The town of Oristano is an excellent base for excursions to the nearby Sinis Peninsula. From the train station, follow V. Vittorio Veneto straight to P. Mariano, then take V. Mazzini to P. Roma to reach the town center. Rent a moped or car to explore the tranquil beaches, stark white cliffs, and ancient ruins on the mystical Sinis Peninsula. At the tip, 17km west of Oristano, lie the ruins of the ancient Phoenician port of **Tharros.** Take the ARST bus to San Giovanni di Sinis (dir.: Is Arutas; 40min., 5 per day, €1.45). Slightly to the north off the road to Cuglieri is **S'Archittu,** where people leap from a 15m limestone arch into the waters of a rocky inlet. ARST **buses** go to S'Archittu (30min., 8 per day, €1.45). The secluded white quartz sands of **Is Arutas** are well worth the trip. The ARST bus to Is Arutas runs only during July and August (50min., 5 per day, €1.50). The **tourist office,** V. Ciutadella de Minorca 8, has maps and information on local festivals. (☎/fax 70 621. Open daily 9am-noon and 4:30-7:30pm.) The spacious **Piccolo Hotel ❸**, V. Martignano 19, is on a quiet side street in the historic center. All rooms have bath; some have TV and balcony. (☎71 500. Singles €32; doubles €53. Cash only.) **SISA** supermarket is on V. Amiscora, 26. (Open M-Sa 8am-8pm. MC/V.) **Postal Code:** 09170.

LATVIA (LATVIJA)

At the Baltic crossroads, Latvia has been caught for hundreds of years in international political struggles. The country has been conquered and reconquered so many times that the year 2005 will only be Latvia's 36th year of independence—ever. National pride, however, abounds, from patriotically renamed streets to a rediscovery of native holidays predating even the Christian invasions. Rīga, Latvia's only large city, is a Westernized capital luring more and more international companies, while the rest of the country is mostly a provincial expanse of green hills dominated by tall birches and pines, dairy pastures, and quiet towns.

ESSENTIALS

DOCUMENTS AND FORMALITIES

VISAS. Citizens of Australia, Canada, Ireland, New Zealand, the UK, and the US can visit Latvia for up to 90 days in six months without a visa. Apply for extensions at the Department of Immigration and Citizenship, 6 Raiņa bul., Rīga (☎ 721 91 81).

EMBASSIES. All foreign embassies are in Rīga (p. 711). For Latvian embassies at home, contact: **Australia,** 38 Longstaff St., Ivanhoe East, 3079 Victoria (☎ 03 9499 6920; fax 9499 7008); **Canada,** 280 Albert St., Ste. 300, Ottawa, ON K1P 5G8 (☎ 613-238-6014; www.ottawa.am.gov.lv/en); **Ireland,** 14 Lower Leeson St., Dublin 2 (☎ 01 662 1610; embassy.ireland@mfa.gov.lv); **UK,** 45 Nottingham Pl., London W1M 3FE (☎ 020 7312 0040; fax 7312 0040); and **US,** 4325 17th St. NW, Washington, D.C. 20011 (☎ 202-726-8213; www.latvia-usa.org).

TRANSPORTATION

Air Baltic, Finnair, KLM, Lufthansa, and **SAS,** among others, fly into Rīga (RIX). **Trains** link Latvia to Berlin, Lviv, Moscow, Odessa, St. Petersburg, Tallinn, and Vilnius. **Eurail** is not valid. Trains are cheap and efficient, but stations aren't well marked—

always carry a map. The **suburban rail** system renders the entire country a suburb of Rīga, and is a better choice than buses for daytrips from the capital. Latvia's quicker **bus** network reaches Prague, Tallinn, Vilnius, and Warsaw. **Ferries** run to Rīga from Kiel, Germany and Stockholm, Sweden. **Hitchhiking** is common, but hitchhikers may be expected to pay. *Let's Go* does not recommend hitchhiking.

TOURIST SERVICES AND MONEY

EMERGENCY	Police: ☎02. Ambulance: ☎03. Fire: ☎01.

Tourist offices are scarce; look for a green "i." Private offices such as **Patricia** (p. 712) are more helpful. The Latvian **Lat** is divided into 100 *santims*. Inflation is around 3%. It's often hard to exchange currencies other than US dollars and euros. As Latvia joined the EU in 2004, it will begin to integrate the euro (€) in 2005. Latvia will not officially adopt the euro until at least 2007. There are many **ATMs** in Rīga and in large towns, most linked to Cirrus, MasterCard, and Visa. Larger businesses, restaurants, and hotels accept MasterCard and Visa. Traveler's checks are harder to use; both AmEx and Thomas Cook can be converted in Rīga, but Thomas Cook is a safer bet elsewhere.

LATVIAN LATS (LS)		
AUS$1 = 0.39 LVL		1LVL = AUS$2.60
CDN$1 = 0.41 LVL		1LVL = CDN$2.44
EUR€1 = 0.66 LVL		1LVL = EUR€1.52
NZ$1 = 0.36 LVL		1LVL = NZ$2.80
UK£1 = 0.97 LVL		1LVL = UK£1.03
US$1 = 0.53 LVL		1LVL = US$1.88

COMMUNICATION

PHONE CODES	**Country code: 371. International dialing prefix:** 00. From outside Latvia, dial int'l dialing prefix (see inside back cover) + 371 + city code + local number.

TELEPHONES AND INTERNET ACCESS. If a number is six digits long, dial a 2 before the number; if it's seven digits, you needn't dial anything before the number. To call abroad from an analog phone, dial 1, then 00, then the country code. From a digital phone, simply dial 00, then the country code. Most telephones take cards (available in 2, 3, 5, or 10Ls denominations) from post offices, telephone offices, kiosks, and state stores. The phone system has been undergoing changes; phone offices and *Rīga in Your Pocket* have the latest info. **International** calls can be made from telephone offices or booths. International access codes include **AT&T Direct** (☎800 2 288) and **MCI WorldPhone** (800 8888). **Internet** access is readily available in major cities and towns and averages 0.5Ls per hr.

MAIL. Ask for *gaisa pastu* to send something by airmail. Letters to the EU cost 0.30Ls, postcards 0.20Ls, elsewhere 0.40Ls/0.30Ls. For *Poste Restante*, address mail to be held as in the following example: First name SURNAME, *Poste Restante*, Stacijas laukums 1, Rīga, LV-1050 LATVIA.

LANGUAGES. Heavily influenced by Estonian, German, Russian, and Swedish, Lettish is one of two languages (the other is Lithuanian) in the Baltic language group. Russian is in disfavor in the countryside but is more widespread in Rīga. Many young Latvians study English. Older Latvians tend to know some German.

ACCOMMODATIONS AND FOOD

LATVIA	❶	❷	❸	❹	❺
ACCOMMODATIONS	under 8Ls	8-15Ls	15-20Ls	20-24Ls	over 24Ls
FOOD	under 2Ls	2-3Ls	3-5Ls	5-7Ls	over 7Ls

College **dormitories,** which open to travelers in the summer, are often the cheapest places to sleep. In Rīga, Patricia (p. 712) arranges **homestays** and **apartment** rentals for around 10Ls per night. There are very few budget-range (3-15Ls) hotels. Latvian food is heavy and starchy, but tasty. Rīga is one of the easiest places to find vegetarian options in all the Baltics. Tasty national specialties include the holiday dish *zirņi* (gray peas with onions and smoked fat), *maizes zupa* (bread soup usually made from corn bread and full of currants, cream, and other goodies), and the warming *Rīgas* (or *Melnais*) *balzams* (a black liquor great with ice cream, Coke, or coffee). Dark rye bread is a staple. Try *speķa rauši*, a warm pastry, or *biezpienmaize*, bread with sweet curds. Latvian beer is stellar, especially *Porteris* and other offerings from the Aldaris brewery.

HOLIDAYS

New Year's Day (Jan. 1); Good Friday (Mar. 25); Catholic Easter (Mar. 27); Labor Day (May 1); Ligo (Midsummer Festival; June 23-24); Independence Day (Nov. 18); Ziemsvetki (Christmas; Dec. 25-26); New Year's Eve (Dec. 31).

FACTS AND FIGURES: LATVIA

Official Name: Republic of Latvia.
Capital: Rīga.
Population: 2,400,000.
Land Area: 64,589 sq. km.

Time Zone: GMT +2.
Languages: Lettish, Lithuanian, Russian.
Religions: Lutheran, Roman Catholic, Russian Orthodox

RĪGA ☎82

Rīga's claim to be the "New Paris" may have more merit than travelers might think: St. Peter's Church is a veritable answer to Notre Dame; the right bank of the Daugava emulates the cafe-lined, cobblestone streets of the Left Bank; and outside the city rests the Baltic Versailles: Rundales Palace. Still, despite the opulent facelift it received in preparation for its 800th anniversary in 2001, Rīga has not shed all evidence of its Communist past.

Rīga's phone code is ☎2 for all 6-digit numbers; there is no phone code for 7-digit numbers. **Info:** ☎800 80 08. **Latvian operator:** ☎116. **International operator:** ☎115. **Directory services:** ☎118, 722 22 22, or 777 07 77.

TRANSPORTATION

Flights: Lidosta Rīga (RIX; ☎720 70 09), 8km southwest of Vecrīga. Take bus #22 from 13 Janvara iela (30min., 0.20Ls).

Trains: Centrālā Stacija (Central Station), Stacijas laukums (☎583 30 95), next to the bus station south of the old town. Long-distance trains depart from the larger building to the left; destinations include: **Moscow** (18hr., 1 per day, 25Ls); **St. Petersburg** (14hr., 1 per day, 22-33Ls); **Vilnius** (8hr.; 2 per day on odd numbered days, no service on even numbered days; 9-11Ls).

Buses: Autoosta, Prāgas 1 (☎900 00 09), 100m from the train station, across the canal from the Central Market. To: **Kaunas** (5-6hr., 2 per day, 5.20Ls); **Minsk** (12hr., 1 per day, 7Ls); **Tallinn** (4-6hr., 8 per day, 7-8.50Ls); **Vilnius** (5hr., 4-6 per day, 4.50-6Ls). **Ecolines** (☎721 45 12; www.ecolines.lv), in the bus station, sends buses to **Prague** (25½hr.; 1 per week; 36Ls, students 24Ls).

⚡❔ ORIENTATION AND PRACTICAL INFORMATION

The city is divided in half by **Brīvības bulvāris,** which leads from the outskirts to the **Freedom Monument** in the center, becomes **Kaļķu iela,** and passes through **Vecrīga** (Old Rīga). To reach Vecrīga from the train station, turn left on Marijas iela and then right on any of the small streets beyond the canal. For reliable info, pick up a free copy of *Rīga This Week* at major hotels or the Tourist Information Center.

Tourist Office: Tourist Information Center, Rātslaukums 6 (☎703 79 00; www.rigatourism.com), in the town square, next to the House of the Blackheads. Sells maps and provides advice and brochures. Open daily 9am-7pm; low season 10am-7pm.

Embassies and Consulates: Canada, Baznicas 20/22 (☎781 39 45; riga@dfait-maeci.qc.ca). Open Tu and Th 10am-1pm. **Ireland,** Brīvības iela 54 (☎702 52 59; fax 702 52 60). Open M-Tu and Th-F 10am-noon. **UK,** Alunāna iela 5 (☎777 47 00; www.britain.lv). Open M-F 9:30am-noon. **US,** Raiņa bul. 7 (☎703 62 00; www.usembassy.lv). Open M-Tu and Th 9-11:30am. US citizen services Tu-Th 2-4pm.

Currency Exchange: At any of the **Valutos Maiņa** kiosks. **Unibanka,** Pils iela 23, gives MC/V cash advances and cashes both AmEx and Thomas Cook traveler's checks without commission. Open M-F 9am-5pm.

24hr. Pharmacy: Vecpilsetas Aptieka, Audeju 20 (☎721 33 40).

Internet Access: Elik, Kaļķu iela 11 (☎722 7079; www.elikkafe.lv), in the center of Vecrīga; **branch** at Čaka iela 26 (☎728 4506). 0.50Ls per hr., 4Ls per day. Open 24hr.

Telephone Office: Brīvības bul. 19 (☎701 87 38). Open M-F 7am-11pm, Sa-Su 8am-10pm. **Branch** at the post office by the train station. Open 24hr.

Post Office: Stacijas laukumā 1 (☎701 88 04; www.riga.post.lv), near the train station. *Poste Restante* at window #9. Open M-F 8am-8pm, Sa 8am-6pm, Su 8am-4pm. **Branch** at Brīvības bul. 19. Address mail to be held: First name SURNAME, *POSTE RESTANTE,* Stacijas laukumā 1, Rīga, LV-1050 LATVIA. **Postal Code:** LV-1050.

⌂ ACCOMMODATIONS

Make reservations well in advance during the high season. **Patricia,** Elizabetes iela 22 (☎728 48 68; tourism@parks.lv), arranges homestays from 20Ls; apartments 35-50Ls. (Open M-F 9am-6pm, Sa-Su 11am-4pm.)

Radi un Draugi, Marstalu 1/3 (☎782 02 00; www.draugi.lv). Head along Audeju toward the heart of the old town. Cozy, tastefully-decorated rooms and top-notch service. Breakfast included. Singles 35Ls; doubles 44Ls; triples 53Ls. MC/V. ❹

Krisjanis & Gertrude, Barona 39/1 (☎750 66 03; kg@mail.teliamtc.lv). Buzz in on Gertudes iela; reception is on the 3rd fl. Charming B&B with English-speaking staff within walking distance of the old town. Singles 20-30Ls; doubles 35-40Ls; triples 45Ls. ❸

Posh Backpackers Hostel, Populu iela 5 (☎602 08 08; www.poshbackpackers.lv). From the bus station, walk through the Central Market, past the ASA on your left; enter through the building marked "Viola." Reliable staff and clean rooms—although some guests may feel uncomfortable walking back at night. 4-6 bed dorms 9Ls. Cash only. ❷

Old Town Hostel, Kaleju iela 50 (☎614 72 14; www.oldtownhostel.lv). Entering Vecrīga on K. Barona/Audeju, turn left on Kaleju. With 4-12 to a room, you'll probably feel closer to your fellow travelers than ever before. Dorms 9-12Ls. MC/V. ❷

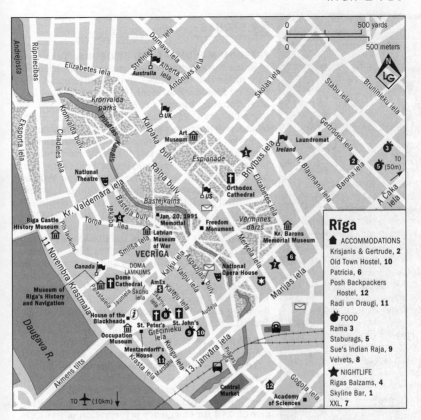

Rīga

🏠 ACCOMMODATIONS
Krisjanis & Gertrude, **2**
Old Town Hostel, **10**
Patricia, **6**
Posh Backpackers
Hostel, **12**
Radi un Draugi, **11**

🍎 FOOD
Rama **3**
Staburags, **5**
Sue's Indian Raja, **9**
Velvets, **8**

⭐ NIGHTLIFE
Rigas Balzams, **4**
Skyline Bar, **1**
XXL, **7**

🗂 FOOD

Any city that claims to be the "New Paris" must prove itself gastronomically, and Rīga does just that with top-notch international cuisine. For midnight snackers, 24hr. food and liquor stores are at Marijas 5 and Brivibas 68. **Centrālais Tirgus** (Central Market), behind the bus station, is the largest market in Europe.

🍽 **Rama,** Barona 56 (☎ 727 24 90). Between Gertrudes and Stabu. Eat well for 1Ls at this Hare-Krishna-run cafeteria, which dishes out hearty Indian-style vegetarian fare. Patrons are always invited to join the owners in meditation. Open M-Sa 11am-7pm. ❶

🍽 **Staburags,** A. Čaka iela 55 (☎ 729 97 87). Follow A. Čaka iela away from Vecrīga until it intersects with Stabu iela. Authentic Latvian cuisine served amidst rustic decor. Try the unprocessed house beer (0.70Ls per 0.5L). Entrees 1.80-7.30Ls. ❷

Sue's Indian Raja, Vecpilsetas iela 3 (☎ 721 26 14). Voted one of the best 100 restaurants in the world by *Conde Nast Traveler*. Serves authentic Indian and Thai food, though vegetarian dishes are not as meatless as one might intuit. Belly dancing most nights. Entrees 3-11Ls. Open daily noon-11pm. MC/V. ❹

Velvets, Skārņu iela 9 (☎ 721 50 75), just off Kaļķu iela in Vecrīga. Stylish old town restaurant with large, but not quite authentic, French entrees (2-7Ls). Open M-Th 10am-2am, F-Sa 10am-4am, Su 11am-2am. MC/V. ❸

LATVIA

THE LOCAL STORY

BEARING IT ALL

Until the late 19th century, two versions of the Lacplesis the Bear-slayer legend circulated through the Latvian countryside. According to one, the hero was the off-spring of a suspiciously amorous relationship between a man and a she-bear. Another version claimed that after Lacplesis's human parents abandoned him, he was reared by a genial bear. Whatever the truth, Lacplesis acquired extraordinary physical strength—and two furry ears.

When Lacplesis confronted the monstrous, three-headed Black Knight in fierce combat, the knight cut off one of Lacplesis's ears. Neither fighter, however, got the last laugh—both combatants drowned in the Daugava River.

In 1888, Latvian writer Andrejs Pumpurs published an enormously popular epic recounting Lacplesis's valor, thereby changing the legend forever. The bard portrayed Lacplesis as a historically accurate figure who fought valiantly against the Teutonic Knights. Decades later, as Latvia struggled for independence from Russia, Lacplesis served as a compelling inspiration. Today, numerous monuments document the bear-warrior's importance in Latvian history and lore. But the tributes, which can be found both at the Freedom Monument and in Majori's central square, depict the hero with a covered head in an effort to keep the legend historically accurate.

🔾 SIGHTS

FREEDOM MONUMENT AND ENVIRONS. Take time to savor the winding streets and unusual architecture of Vecrīga (Old Rīga). In the center stands the beloved **Freedom Monument** (Brīvības Pieminēklis), affectionately known as "Milda." *(At the corner of Raiņa bul. and Brīvības bul.)* Continuing along Kaļķu iela toward the river, you'll see one of the few Soviet monuments not torn down: the **Latvian Riflemen Monument** (Latviešu Strēlnieku Laukums), which honors Lenin's famous bodyguards. Rising behind the statues are the black walls of the ▧**Occupation Museum** (Okupācijas muzejs), Strēlnieku laukums 1, where the initial Soviet occupation is vividly depicted. *(Open May-Sept. daily 11am-6pm; Oct.-Apr. Tu-Su 11am-5pm. Free; donations accepted.)* Just beyond the museum stands the **House of the Blackheads** (Melngalvju nams) Rātslaukums 7. Built in 1344 and completely destroyed by the Nazis and the Soviets, the unusual but magnificent building was reconstructed in honor of Rīga's 800th birthday. The structure, which hosts occasional concerts, now houses a museum and an assembly hall. *(Open Tu-Su 10am-5pm. 1Ls, students 0.50Ls.)*

ELSEWHERE IN VECRĪGA. Follow Kaļķu iela from the Freedom Monument and turn right on Šķūņu iela to reach the cobblestone **Dome Square** (Doma laukums), home of the **Dome Cathedral** (Doma baznīca). Unfortunately, the cathedral, the largest house of worship in the Baltics, closed to visitors in the summer of 2004 for emergency preservation of the 13th-century structure. Adjacent to the cathedral is the **Museum of Rīga's History and Navigation** (Rīgas Vēstures un Kugniecības Muzejs), Palasta iela 4. Established in 1773, this museum is itself a part of history: in the early 1990s, its collection helped rekindle Latvia's cultural heritage after the Soviets' efforts to suppress national identity. *(Open May-Sept. W-Su 10am-5pm; Oct.-Apr. 11am-5pm. 1.20Ls, students 0.40Ls. Tours 3Ls/2Ls.)* From the top of the 123m spire of **St. Peter's Church** (Sv. Pētera baznīca), you can see the entire city and the Baltic Sea. *(On Skāmu iela, off Kaļķu iela. Open Tu-Su 10am-6pm; low season 10am-5pm. Staff sometimes closes ticket office from 1-2:30pm. Church free. Tower 2Ls, students 1Ls.)* The magnificent Neoclassical **State Museum of Art** (Valsts mākslas muzejs), Kr. Valdemāra iela 10a, displays 18th- to 20th-century Latvian art and hosts occasional concerts. *(Near the intersection of Elizabetes iela and Kr. Valdemāra iela. Open Apr.-Oct. M, W, and F-Su 11am-5pm, Th 11am-7pm; Oct.-Apr. M and W-Su 11am-5pm. 0.50Ls, students*

Europe is the source of civilization.

But Eurail Passes give you the freedom.

Let yourself go in Europe with a flexible and fun Eurail Pass! Feel the excitement as the train whisks you from country to country and the ever-changing landscape passes your window. Trains criss-cross the entire continent allowing you to see Europe your way. Meet new friends, take in the nightlife, explore a famous city, and soon you'll be on your way to another adventure.

There's a Eurail Pass for every budget and taste, from the classic 17-country Eurailpass, to the Eurail Selectpass that focuses on fewer countries and saves you money, to the new and highly targeted 2-country pass.

Welcome to Eurail Pass. It truly is *Europe without borders.*

0.40Ls.) The newer areas of Rīga feature fantastic **Art Nouveau** *(Jugendstil)* architecture. Elaborately adorned buildings are scattered throughout the city; most are on Alberta iela, Elizabetes iela, and Strēlnieku laukums.

BASTEJKALNS. Rīga's central park, surrounded by the old city moat (Pilsētas kanāls), houses ruins of the old city walls. Across and around the canal, five red slabs of stone stand as **memorials** to the events of January 20, 1991, when Soviet special forces stormed the Interior Ministry on Raiņa bul. At the northern end of Bastejkalns, on K. Valdemāra iela, sits the **National Theatre,** where Latvia first declared its independence on November 18, 1918. *(Open daily 10am-7pm.)*

🎵🎭 ENTERTAINMENT AND NIGHTLIFE

Rīga offers the best and widest array of music and performance art in the Baltics. Theaters close from mid-June to August, but the Opera House and Dome Cathedral host special events. The **Latvian National Opera** performs in the **Opera House,** Aspazijas bul. 3 (☎707 705; www.opera.lv), where Richard Wagner once presided as director. The **Latvian Symphony Orchestra** (☎722 48 50) holds frequent concerts in the Great and Small Guilds off Filharmonija laukums. Smaller ensembles perform throughout the summer in **Wagner Hall** (Vāgnera zāle), Vāgnera iela 4 (☎721 08 17). The **Rīga Ballet** carries on the proud tradition of native star Mikhail Baryshnikov. The **ticket offices** at Teātra 10/12 (☎722 57 47; open daily 10am-7pm) and Amatu iela 6 (☎721 37 98), on the first floor of the Great Guild, serve most local concerts.

The night scene is centered in Vecrīga. 🎵**Skyline Bar,** Elizabetes iela 55, on the 26th floor of the Reval Hotel Latvija, has the best view in the city. (Open M-Th and Su 3pm-2am, F-Sa 3pm-3am. MC/V.) Try Latvia's national liquor—a mysterious herb and berry brew, at **Rigas Balzams,** Torņa iela 4, in Vecrīga, 100m east of the Powder Tower. (Open M-Th and Su 11am-midnight, F-Sa 11am-1am). The gay bar and club **XXL,** A Kalniņa iela 4, is off K. Barona iela; buzz to be let in. (www.xxl.lv. Cover Tu-Sa 1-5Ls. Open daily 6pm-6am.)

🏞 DAYTRIPS FROM RĪGA

JŪRMALA. Boardwalks and sun-bleached sand cover the narrow spit of Jūrmala Visitors, including the Soviet elite, have been drawn to its warm waters since the 19th century. The coastal towns between **Bulduri** and **Dubulti** are popular for sunning and swimming, but Jūrmala's social center is **Majori,** where masses file to the crowded beach or wander along **Jomas iela,** a pedestrian street lined with cafes and shops. The **commuter rail** runs from Rīga to Jūrmala (30min., every 30min., 0.50Ls). **Public buses** (0.18Ls) and **microbuses** (0.20-0.30Ls) string together Jūrmala's towns. **Bicycles** are a popular mode of transportation; rent one along the beach (1.50Ls per hr.). The **tourist office,** Jomas iela 42, arranges accommodations (from 6Ls) with no booking fee. (☎877 642 76; www.jurmala.lv. Open daily in summer 10am-7pm; low season 10am-5pm.) **Sue's Asia ❹,** Jomas 74, offers Chinese, Indian, and Thai cuisine, serving the same fine fare that scored Rīga's branch a spot on *Conde Naste*'s list of the 100 best restaurants in the world. (☎775 59 00. Entrees 3-10Ls. Open M-Th noon-11pm, F-Su noon-midnight.) **Postal Code:** LV-2105.

SIGULDA. The Knights of the Sword, the Germanic crusaders who Christianized much of Latvia in the 13th century, staked their base at Segewald—now Sigulda. The knights are gone, but the Gauja National Park Administration has planted its headquarters in this picturesque town 50km from Rīga. The area offers great biking, bobsledding, bungee jumping, horseback riding, and hot-air ballooning, as well as skiing in winter; **Makars Tourism Agency,** Peldu 1, arranges all kinds of outdoor excursions. (☎924 49 48; www.makars.lv.) The restored brick fortifications of **Turaida Castle** (Turaidas Pils), Turaidas iela 10, across the river from Sigulda and 2km down the road, are visible throughout the Gauja Valley and from surrounding hilltops. Climb the staircase in the main tower for a scenic view of the region. (Tower open daily 8am-9pm.) Take Turaidas iela 10-15min. back down the hill to reach the famous **caves** of Sigulda. Inscriptions and coats of arms from as early as the 16th century cover the chiseled mouth of **Gutman's Cave** (Gūtmaņa ala). On a ridge to the right of Gaujas iela, on the near side of the gorge, is the **Sigulda Dome** palace, behind which lie the remains of the 13th-century **Sigulda Castle** (Siguldas pilsdrupas). The immense ruins form the backdrop for the renowned **Sigulda Opera Festival** in late July.

Trains run from Rīga on the Rīga-Lugaži commuter rail line (1hr., 9 per day, 0.71Ls). From the station, walk up Raiņa iela to the town center. Continue as it turns into Gaujas iela, which, after the Gaujas Bridge, becomes the steep Turaidas iela and passes Turaida Castle. **Bus** #12 runs directly to Turaida Castle (at least 1 per hr., 0.20Ls). From the station, Raiņa iela runs 1km north to the **Gauja National Park Visitor Centre,** Baznicas 3, which offers the absolutely essential full map of the GNP for 1.20Ls. (☎797 13 45; www.gnp.gov.lv. Open M 9am-5:30pm, Tu-Su 9am-7pm.) **Viesu Nams Livonija ❷,** P. Brieža iela 55, has a kitchen, common room, and sauna available for guest use. (☎797 3066; hotel.livonija@lis.lv. Buffet breakfast 1Ls. Dorms 7Ls; singles with bath 14Ls; doubles 16-20Ls.) **◪Pilsmuižas Restorāns ❸,** Pils iela 16, in Pilseta Dome, serves generous portions of Latvian fare. (Entrees 3-12Ls. Open daily noon-2am. MC/V.) For a cheap bite, try **Trīs Draugi ❶,** Pils iela 9, a Soviet-style cafeteria. (Open daily 8am-10pm. MC/V.) **Postal Code:** LV-2150.

CĒSIS. Sprawling medieval ruins and Cēsu, the local brew, make Cēsis the quintessential Latvian town. Crusading Germans came to town in 1209 and built the famous **Cēsis Castle.** The new castle's **tower** offers stunning views of the Gauja Valley. The old castle's **ruins** were also reopened recently. (☎412 26 15. Open May 15-Sept. Tu-Su 10am-5pm; Nov.-May 14 W-Su 10am-5pm. 1Ls admission includes castle, tower, and ruins.) Cēsis is reached via infrequent suburban **trains** from Rīga via Sigulda (1½-2hr., 2 per day, about 1Ls). **Buses** are more convenient (2hr., 1-2 per hr., 1.30Ls). The **tourist office,** Pils laukums 1, across from the castle, offers free maps and arranges **private rooms** in the Cēsis region for a 0.50Ls booking fee or elsewhere in Latvia for 1Ls. (☎412 18 15; www.cesis.lv. Open May 15-Sept. 15 M-F 9am-6pm, Sa-Su 10am-5pm.) **Madara '89,** Raunas 15, is a well-stocked supermarket. (Open daily 8am-10pm.) **Postal Code:** LV-4101.

LIECHTENSTEIN

A tourist brochure once amusingly mislabeled the already tiny 160-square-kilometer country an even tinier 160 square meters. That's just about how much most tourists see of the world's only German-speaking monarchy, even though its cliff-hugging roads are gateways to unspoiled mountains with great biking and hiking.

ESSENTIALS

DOCUMENTS AND FORMALITIES. Citizens of Australia, Canada, New Zealand, the UK, and the US do not need visas for stays of up to 90 days.

TRANSPORTATION. To enter Liechtenstein, catch a **bus** from Buchs or Sargans in Switzerland, or from Feldkirch just across the Austrian border (20-30min., 3.60SFr). Liechtenstein has no rail system. Instead, its cheap, efficient **Post Bus** system links all 11 villages (short trips 2.40SFr, long trips 3.60SFr; students half-price; SwissPass valid). A **one-week bus ticket** (10SFr, students 5SFr) covers all of Liechtenstein and buses to Swiss and Austrian border towns.

EMERGENCY. Police: ☎117. **Ambulance:** ☎144. **Fire:** ☎118.

MONEY. Liechtenstein uses the **Swiss Franc (SFr).** Go to Switzerland to exchange currency at reasonable rates. Conversion rates for the franc are listed on p. 1021.

FACTS AND FIGURES: LIECHTENSTEIN	
Capital: Vaduz.	**Land Area:** 160 sq. km.
Major Villages: Malbun, Schaan.	**Major Exports:** Dental products.
Population: 33,000.	**Language:** German (see p. 1061).
Form of Government: Hereditary constitutional monarchy.	**Religions:** Roman Catholic (80%), Protestant (7.4%), other (12.6%).

VADUZ AND LOWER LIECHTENSTEIN

As the national capital, Vaduz (pop. 5000) attracts the most visitors of any village in Liechtenstein. Above town, the 12th-century **Schloß Vaduz** (Vaduz Castle) is home to Hans Adam II, Prince of Liechtenstein. After transferring day-to-day running of the country to his son Alois in 2004, he invited the entire country to a garden party to celebrate. Its interior is off-limits, but visitors can hike up to the castle for a closer look and for a view of the entire country; the 15min. trail begins down the street from the tourist office, heading away from the post office. Facing the tourist office is the **Kunstmuseum Liechtenstein**, Städtle 32, with works by Dalí, Kandinsky, and Klee. (Open Tu-W and F-Su 10am-5pm, Th 10am-8pm. 8SFr, students 5SFr.) Stamp your passport (2SFr), or pick up a **hiking map** (8-16SFr) at Liechtenstein's **tourist office**, Städtle 37, just up the hill from the Vaduz Post Bus stop. (☎232 14 43. Open July-Sept. M-F 8am-5:30pm, Sa-Su 9am-5pm; Oct.-June M-F 8am-noon and 1:30-5:30pm.) Nearby **Schaan** has better budget lodgings than Vaduz, such as Liechtenstein's sole **Jugendherberge ❷**, Untere Rüttig. 6. From Vaduz, take bus #1 to Mühleholz, walk toward the intersection with traffic lights, and turn left on Marianumstr. Walk 5min. and follow the signs to this spotless pink hostel on the edge of a farm. (☎232 50 22. Breakfast included. Reception daily 5-10pm. Check-out 10am. Open Feb.-Oct. Dorms

29SFr; doubles 37SFr.) There is a **Migros** supermarket at Aulestr. 20 in Vaduz. (Open M-F 8am-1pm and 1:30-7pm, Sa 8am-6pm.)

UPPER LIECHTENSTEIN

Just when it seems that the roads could not possibly become any narrower or steeper, they do—welcome to Upper Liechtenstein, where the country's real beauty lies. It's a short bus trip to Triesenberg or Malbun (30min. from Vaduz) for spectacular views of the Rhine Valley. **Triesenberg** (take bus #10), the principal town, is spanned by a series of switchbacks and foothills 800m above the river. The **tourist office** shares a building with the **Walser Heimatmuseum**, which chronicles the region. (Both ☎262 19 26. Open Sept.-May Tu-F 1:30-5:30pm, Sa 1:30-5pm; June-Aug. also Su 2-5pm. Museum 2SFr.) Take bus #34 to Gaflei (20min., every hr.) for great hiking. **Malbun** sits in an alpine valley in the southeastern corner of Liechtenstein. It is undoubtedly the hippest place in the principality, home to approachable people, plenty of hiking, and affordable ski slopes (day-pass 33SFr). Contact the **tourist office** for more info. (☎263 65 77; www.malbun.li. Open June-Oct. and mid-Dec. to mid-Apr. M-Sa 9am-noon and 1:30-5pm.) **Hotel Alpen ❸** is close to the bus stop and tourist office. (☎263 11 81. Reception daily 8am-10pm. Open mid-May to Oct. and mid-Dec. to Apr. In summer 45-75SFr per person; in winter add 10SFr.)

LITHUANIA (LIETUVA)

Once part of the largest country in Europe, stretching into modern-day Ukraine, Belarus, and Poland, Lithuania shrank significantly in the face of oppression from Tsarist Russia, Nazi Germany, and the Soviet Union. The first Baltic nation to declare its independence from the USSR in 1990, Lithuania has become more Western with every passing year, culminating in its recent admission to the European Union. The spectacular capital city of Vilnius welcomes hordes of tourists into the largest old town in Europe, recently covered in a bright new coat of paint. In the other corner of the country, the mighty Baltic Sea washes up against Palanga and the towering dunes of the Curonian Spit.

ESSENTIALS

DOCUMENTS AND FORMALITIES

VISAS. Citizens of Australia, Canada, Ireland, New Zealand, the UK, and the US can visit Lithuania **visa-free** for up to 90 days. "Special Visas" (€60), for temporary residence and valid for up to one year, can be purchased from the Migration

Department of the Ministry of the Interior. Avoid crossing through Belarus to enter or exit Lithuania: not only do you need to obtain visa (US$100) for Belarus in advance, but guards may hassle you at the border.

EMBASSIES. Foreign embassies are in Vilnius (p. 722). Embassies at home include: **Australia,** 40B Fiddens Wharf Rd., Killara 2071, NSW (☎02 9498 2571); **Canada,** 130 Albert St., Ste. 204, Ottawa, ON K1P 5G4 (☎613-567-5458; www.lithuanianembassy.ca); **New Zealand,** 28 Heather St., Parnell, Auckland (☎09 336 7711; saul@f1rst.co.nz); **UK,** 84 Gloucester Pl., London W1U 6AU (☎020 7486 6401; http://amb.urm.lt/jk); **US,** 2622 16th St. NW, Washington, D.C. 20009 (☎202-234-5860; www.ltembassyus.org).

TRANSPORTATION

Finnair, LOT, Lufthansa, SAS, and other, smaller airlines fly into Vilnius. **Trains** are more popular for long-distance travel. Two major lines cross Lithuania: One runs north-south from Latvia through Šiauliai and Kaunas to Poland; the other runs east-west from Belarus through Vilnius and Kaunas to Kaliningrad. Domestic **buses** are faster, more common, and only a little more expensive than the often-crowded trains. Whenever possible, try to catch an express bus to your destination. They are typically direct and can be up to twice as fast. Vilnius, Kaunas, and Klaipėda are easily reached by train or bus from Belarus, Estonia, Latvia, Poland, and Russia. **Ferries** connect Klaipėda with Århus, Denmark and Kiel, Germany.

TOURIST SERVICES AND MONEY

EMERGENCY	Police: ☎02. Ambulance: ☎03. Fire: ☎01.

Liniterp is generally the most helpful organization for travel info; they reserve accommodations, usually without a surcharge. Kaunas, Klaipėda, Nida, Palanga, and Vilnius each have an edition of the *In Your Pocket* series, available at newsstands and some hotels. The unit of currency is the **Lita** (1Lt=100 *centas*), plural *Litai*. In February 2002 the **Lita (Lt)** was fixed to the euro at €1 to 3.4528Lt. Prices are stable, with inflation hovering at just under 1%. Except in Vilnius, exchange bureaus near the train station usually have worse rates than banks; it's often difficult to exchange currencies other than US dollars and euros. Most banks cash **traveler's checks** for a 2-3% commission. **Vilniaus Bankas,** with outlets in major cities, accepts major credit cards and traveler's checks for a small commission. **ATMs** are readily available in most cities.

LITHUANIAN LITAI (LT)			
AUS$1 = 2.02LT		1LT = AUS$0.49	
CDN$1 = 2.15LT		1LT = CDN$0.46	
EUR€1 = 3.45LT		1LT = EUR€0.29	
NZ$1 = 1.88LT		1LT = NZ$0.53	
UK£1 = 5.11LT		1LT = UK£0.20	
US$1 = 2.79LT		1LT = US$0.36	

COMMUNICATION

PHONE CODES	**Country code:** 370. **International dialing prefix:** 810. From outside Lithuania, dial int'l dialing prefix (see inside back cover) + 370 + city code + local number.

MAIL AND TELEPHONES. Airmail (*oro pastu*) letters abroad cost 1.70Lt (postcards 1.20Lt) and usually take about one week to reach the US. For *Poste Restante,* address mail to be held as in the following example: First name SURNAME,

Centrinis Paštas, Gedimino pr. 7, Vilnius LT-2000, LITHUANIA. There are two kinds of **public phones:** Rectangular ones accept magnetic strip cards and rounded ones accept chip cards. Both are sold at phone offices and kiosks in denominations of 8.74Lt, 12.96Lt, 16.05Lt, and 30.66Lt. Most countries can be dialed directly. Dial 8, wait for the second tone, dial 10, then enter the country code and number. International direct dialing numbers include: **AT&T** (☎ 8 80 09 28 00); **British Telecom** (☎ 8 80 09 00 44); and **Canada Direct** (☎ 8 80 09 00 04).

ACCOMMODATIONS AND FOOD

LITHUANIA	❶	❷	❸	❹	❺
ACCOMMODATIONS	under 30Lt	30-80Lt	80-130Lt	130-180Lt	over 180Lt
FOOD	under 11Lt	11-20Lt	20-30Lt	30-40Lt	over 40Lt

Lithuania has several **youth hostels.** HI membership is nominally required, but an LJNN guest card (10.50Lt at any of the hostels) will suffice. The head office is in Filaretu St. 17, 2007 Vilnius. (☎ 5 215 46 27; www.lithuanianhostels.org.) Their *Hostel Guide* is a handy booklet with info on bike and car rentals, hotel reservations, and maps. **Litinterp,** with offices in Vilnius, Kaunas, and Klaipėda, assists in finding homestays or apartments for rent. **Camping** is gaining popularity, but is vigorously restricted by law to marked campgrounds. Lithuanian cuisine is heavy and sometimes greasy. Keeping a vegetarian or kosher diet will prove difficult, if not impossible. Restaurants serve various types of *blynai* (pancakes) with *mėsa* (meat) or *varske* (cheese). Good Lithuanian beer flows freely; *Kalnapis* is common. Lithuanian vodka (*degtinė*) is also very popular.

HOLIDAYS

New Year's Day (Jan. 1); Independence Day (Feb. 16); Restoration of Independence (Mar. 11); Easter (Apr. 25-27); May Day (May 1); Day of Statehood (July 6); Feast of the Assumption (Aug. 15); All Saints' Day (Nov. 1); Christmas (Dec. 25-26).

FACTS AND FIGURES: LITHUANIA

Official Name: Republic of Lithuania.

Capital: Vilnius.

Major Cities: Klaipėda, Šiauliai.

Population: 3,600,000.

Land Area: 65,200 sq. km.

Time Zone: GMT +2.

Language: Lithuanian, Polish, Russian.

Religions: Roman Catholic (80%).

VILNIUS   ☎ 5

Encouraging new businesses and foreign investment, Vilnius (pop. 579,000) was the leading force in Lithuania's recent ascension to the EU. Founded in 1321 after a prophetic dream by Grand Duke Gediminas, Vilnius grew and flourished throughout the centuries despite numerous foreign occupations. Scarred but not destroyed by WWII, the Holocaust, and the iron grip of the Soviet Union, Vilnius today remains a rich cultural and commercial center.

▢ TRANSPORTATION

Flights: Vilnius Airport (Vilniaus oro uostas), Rodūnės Kelias 2 (Info ☎ 230 66 66), is 5km south of town. Take bus #1 or 2 to the old town.

Trains: Geležinkelio Stotis, Geležinkelio 16 (☎ 233 00 86; www.litrail.lt). Domestic tickets are sold to the left of the entrance, and international to the right (reservations for Western Europe ☎ 269 37 22). Open daily 6-11am and noon-6pm. All international trains (except those heading north) pass through Belarus, requiring a Belarussian visa (p. 117). To: **Berlin** (22hr., 1 per day, 317Lt); **Minsk** (5½hr., 2 per day, 57Lt); **Moscow** (17hr., 3 per day, 128Lt); **Rīga** (7½hr., 1 per day, 72Lt); **St. Petersburg** (18hr., 3 per day, 110Lt); **Warsaw** (8hr., 2 per day, 115Lt). No direct trains to Tallinn.

Buses: Autobusų Stotis, Sodų 22 (☎290 16 61; reservations 216 29 77), opposite the train station. **Eurolines Baltic International** (☎215 13 77; www.eurolines.lt) serves destinations across Europe. Open daily 6am-10pm. **Minsk** (5hr., 3 per day, 22Lt); **Rīga** (5hr., 4 per day, 40Lt); **St. Petersburg** (18hr., 4 per day, 44Lt); **Tallinn** (10hr., 2 per day, 90Lt); **Warsaw** (9-10hr., 3 per day, 97Lt).

Public Transportation: Buses and **trolleys** run daily 6am-midnight. Buy tickets at any kiosk (0.80Lt) or from the driver (1Lt). Tickets are checked frequently; punch them on board to avoid the 20Lt fine. Monthly passes available for students (5Lt).

Taxis: Vilnius's cheapest company is **Ekipažas** (☎1446). About 1.65Lt per km; negotiate price with driver in advance.

■❼ ORIENTATION AND PRACTICAL INFORMATION

The **train** and **bus stations** are side-by-side. **Geležinkelio** runs right from the train station to **Aušros Vartų,** which leads downhill through the **Aušros Vartai** (Gates of Dawn) and into the **Senamiestis** (old town). Aušros Vartų becomes **Didžioji** and then **Pilies** before reaching the base of Gediminas Hill. Here, the **Gediminas Tower** of the Higer Castle presides over **Arkikatedros Aikštė** (Cathedral Square) and the banks of the river Neris. **Gedimino,** the commercial artery, leads west from the square in front of the cathedral.

Tourist Offices: Tourist Information Center, Didžioji 31 (☎262 64 70; www.vilnius.lt), in the Town Hall, offers info about travel and events and provides free maps, as well as train and bus schedules. Open in summer M-F 9am-6pm, Sa-Su 10am-4pm. **Branch,** Vilniaus 22 (☎262 96 60). Open M-F 9am-6pm, Sa 10am-4pm, Su 9am-4pm.

Embassies: Australia, Vilniaus 23 (☎ 212 33 69; aust.con.vilnius@post.omnitel.net). Open M, W, F 11am-2pm. **Canada,** Gedimino pr. 64 (☎249 09 50; vilnius@canada.lt). Open M, W, F 9am-noon. **Russia,** Latvių 53/54 (☎272 17 63; rusemb@rusemb.lt). Open M-F 8am-noon. **UK,** Antakalnio 2 (☎12 20 70; www.britain.lt). Visas M-F 8:30-11:30am. Open M-Th 8:30am-5pm, F 8:30am-4pm. **US,** Akmenų 6 (☎266 55 00; www.usembassy.lt). Visas M-Th 8:30-11:30am. Open M-T and Th 2-4:30pm, F 9-11:30am and 2-4pm.

Currency Exchange: Pabex Bankas, Geležinkelio 6, left of the train station. Open 24hr. **Vilniaus Bankas,** Vokiečių 9, cashes traveler's checks. Open M-F 8am-6pm.

24hr. Pharmacy: Gedimino Vaistinė, Gedimino pr. 27 (☎261 01 35).

Medical Assistance: Baltic-American Medical & Surgical Clinic, Antakalnio 124 (☎234 20 20). Accepts major insurance plans. Open 7am-11pm. Doctors on call 24hr.

Internet Access: Klubas Lux, Svitrigailos 5 (☎233 37 88). 2Lt per hr., 8Lt. for all-night access from 9pm-8am. Open 24hr. **Pixel,** Sopeno 10-12 (☎ 233 6223). 2Lt per hour. Open M-W and Su 9am-11pm, Th-Sa 24hr.

Post Office: Centrinis Paštas, Gedimino 7 (☎262 54 68; www.post.lt), west of Arkikatedros aikštė. **Poste Restante** at the window marked "iki pareikalavimo." Address mail to be held as in the following example: Firstname SURNAME, Centrinis Paštas, Gedimino pr. 7, Vilnius LT-2000, LITHUANIA. 0.50Lt to pick up mail. Open M-F 7am-7pm, Sa 9am-4pm. **Postal Code:** LT-2000.

▐❒ ACCOMMODATIONS AND FOOD

⬛Litinterp ❸, Bernardinv 7/2, has spacious rooms with clean shared baths. (☎212 38 50; www.litinterp.lt. Breakfast included. Reception M-F 8:30am-5:30pm, Sa 9am-3pm. Singles 80-120Lt; doubles 140-160Lt.; triples 180-210Lt. 5% ISIC discount.

LITHUANIA

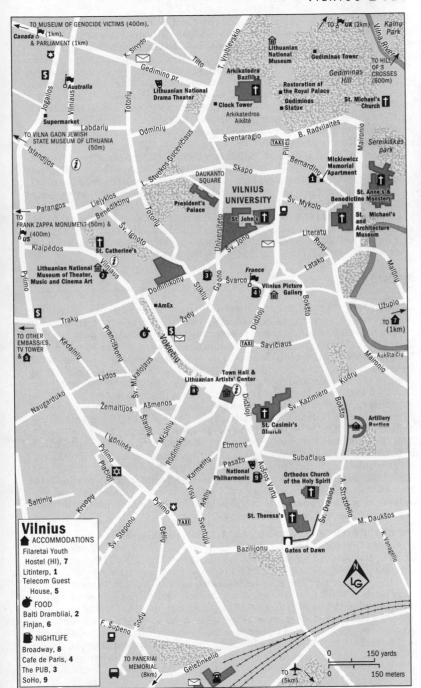

TO MUSEUM OF GENOCIDE VICTIMS (400m),
Canada (1km),
& PARLIAMENT (1km)

K. Sirvydo

Gedimino pr.

TO UK (2km)

Kalnų Park

Vilna River

Lithuanian National Museum

Gediminas Tower

TO HILL OF 3 CROSSES (600m)

Tilto

T. Vrublevskio

Arkikatedra Bazilika

Gediminas Hill

Jogailos

Vilniaus

Australia

Lithuanian National Drama Theater

Clock Tower

Restoration of the Royal Palace

Gediminas Statue

St. Michael's Church

Totorių

Arkikatedros Aikštė

Supermarket

Labdarių

Odminių

Šventaragio

B. Radvilaitės

Sereikiškės park

TO VILNA GAON JEWISH STATE MUSEUM OF LITHUANIA (50m)

Islandijos

TAXI

Maironio

Palangos

Lielyklos

Benediktinų

L. Stuokos-Gucevičiaus

Totorių

DAUKANTO SQUARE

President's Palace

Skapo

VILNIUS UNIVERSITY

Bernardinų

Pilies

Mickiewicz Memorial Apartment

St. Anne's & Benedictine Monastery

Šv. Mykolo

St. John's

St. Michael's and Architecture Museum

TO FRANK ZAPPA MONUMENT (50m) & US (400m)

Klaipėdos

St. Catherine's

Vilniaus

Šv. Ignoto

Universiteto

Šv. Jono

Literatų

Rusų

Lithuanian National Museum of Theater, Music and Cinema Art

Dominikonų

Stiklių

Ga ono

Švarco

France

Vilnius Picture Gallery

Latako

Bokšto

Malūnų

Užupio

TO (1km)

AmEx

Žydų

Didžioji

Traku

Volklečių

Savičiaus

TAXI

Maironio

TO OTHER EMBASSIES, TV TOWER &

Kėdainių

Pranciškonų

Aukštaičių

Naugarduko

Lydos

Šv. Mikalojaus

Žemaitijos

Ašmenos

Šiaulių

Mėsinių

Town Hall & Lithuanian Artists' Center

Didžioji

Artillery Bastion

(Igūninės)

Rūdininkų

Etmonų

St. Casimir's Church

Šv. Kazimiero

Bokšto

Pylimo

Plačioji

Karmelitų

Pasažo

National Philharmonic

Aušros Vartų

Orthodox Church of the Holy Spirit

Subačiaus

Šaltinių

Krūopų

Šv. Stepono

Gėlių

Pylimo

Višų

Arklių

St. Theresa's

Šv. Dvasios

A. Strazdelio

M. Daukšos

TAXI

Sventų

Bazilijonų

Gates of Dawn

K. Vanagėlio

N

LG

F. Šopeno

Sodų

TO PANERIAI MEMORIAL (8km)

Geležinkelio

TO (5km)

0 ——— 150 yards

0 ——— 150 meters

Vilnius

◆ ACCOMMODATIONS
Filaretai Youth
Hostel (HI), **7**
Litinterp, **1**
Telecom Guest
House, **5**

🍴 FOOD
Balti Drambliai, **2**
Finjan, **6**

🍸 NIGHTLIFE
Broadway, **8**
Cafe de Paris, **4**
The PUB, **3**
SoHo, **9**

DC/MC/V.) Hideously hard to find, **Telecom Guest House ❷**, A. Vivulskio 13a, is well worth the search, with newer rooms and private baths. From the city center, follow Traku, which becomes J. Basanaviciaus. Just before you reach an Orthodox church, turn left onto Algirido. After one block, turn right onto A. Vivulskio; the guest house is in a courtyard on your right, 50m from the corner. (☎264 48 61; www.telecomguesthouse.lt. Singles 220Lt; doubles 260Lt. MC/V.) Young travelers converge on **Filaretai Youth Hostel (HI) ❶**, Filaretv 17, 1km east of the old town. (☎215 46 27; www.filaretaihostel.lt. Kitchen, common room, free Internet access and bike rental. Luggage storage 3Lt. Linen 5Lt. Laundry 10Lt. Open 5am-1am. Reservations recommended June-Sept. and weekends. 5-6 bed dorms 24Lt; triples and quads 28Lt. Non-members 3Lt fee. MC/V.)

For a wide selection of local and Western brands, stop by one of the **Iki** supermarkets. (Branch at Sodu 22. Open daily 8am-10pm.) For an authentic Lithuanian shopping experience, visit **Turgus Dirbu**, an indoor market at the intersection of Pylmio and Bazilijonu just 500m from the train station, offering homegrown produce and freshly-baked breads. (Open Tu-Sa 7am-7pm, Su 7am-5pm.) Locals and students linger at **Finjan ❸**, Vokiečių 18, sampling a mix of Middle Eastern and Argentine cuisine. (Entrees 10-45Lt. Open daily 11am-midnight. MC/V.) In a city of carnivores, **Balti Drambliai ❷**, Vilniaus 41, manages to maintain an entirely meatless menu. (Open M-F 11am-midnight, Sa-Su noon-midnight. MC/V.)

◉ SIGHTS

SENAMIESTIS. The 16th-century **Aušros Vartai** (Gates of Dawn) guard the Senamiestis (old town). After the gates, enter the first door on the right to ascend to the 17th-century **chapel** (Koplyčia), packed with locals praying to the gilded Virgin Mary icon, said to have miraculous powers. Around the corner **St. Theresa's Church** (Šv. Teresės bažnyčia), known for its multicolored arches and frescoed ceiling, was built to honor a Carmelite mystic. A few steps farther down, a gateway leads to the bright 17th-century **Church of the Holy Spirit** (Šv. Dvasios bažnyčia), the seat of Lithuania's Russian Orthodox Archbishop. The street merges with the pedestrian Pilies and leads to the main entrance of **Vilnius University** (Vilniaus Universitetas), at Pilies and Šv. Jono. Founded in 1579, the university is the oldest in Eastern Europe. Further north on Pilies is **Arkikatedros aikštė** (Cathedral Square); its **cathedral** contains the ornate **Chapel of St. Casimir** (Šv. Kazimiero koplyčia), the royal mausoleum, and Vilnius's oldest Baroque church. *(Didžioji 34. ☎222 17 15. Open M-Sa 4-6:30pm, Su 9am-1pm. Free.)* From behind the cathedral, walk up the Castle Hill path to **Gedimino Tower** for a great view of Vilnius's spires. Off Pylimo, between Kalinausko 1 and 3, is the continent's most unexpected monument: a 4m steel shaft topped with a bust of the late freak-rock legend **Frank Zappa.**

THE OLD JEWISH QUARTER AND PANERIAL MEMORIAL. Vilnius was once a center of Jewish life comparable to Warsaw and New York, with a Jewish population of 100,000 (in a city of 230,000) at the start of WWII. Nazi persecution left only 6000 survivors. The **synagogue** at Pylimo 39 is the only remaining of 105 that stood before the war. The **Paneriai Memorial**, Agrastų 15, is in **Paneriai**, 10min. away by train (0.90Lt). Head right from the train station and follow Agrastų to the memorial. Between 1941 and 1944, Nazis executed 100,000 Lithuanians, including 70,000 Jews, in this eerie forest. The memorials, at pits that served as mass graves, are connected by paved paths. Return by bus #8, on the other side of the tracks. *(Open M and W-F 11am-5pm. Free.)* The **Holocaust Museum**, locally called "The Green House," provides an honest account of Lithuanian partisan fighters' persecution of their Jewish neighbors on the eve of the German invasion. *(Pamfnkalnio 12. Open M-Th 9am-5pm, F 9am-4pm. Donations requested.)* For info on the Jewish Quarter or on locating ancestors, visit the **Chabad Lubavitch Center**. *(Šaltiniv 12. ☎215 03 87; www.jewish.lt. Open daily 9am-6pm.)*

MUSEUM OF GENOCIDE VICTIMS. The horrors of the Soviet regime are on full display at the former KGB headquarters, which also served as a Gestapo outpost when Germany occupied the city during WWII. The remains of some 706 former prisoners are still stored inside. The only aspect of this museum eerier than the meticulously-preserved execution chamber is the near-total disregard for the building's Nazi past. *(Aukv 2a, at the intersection with Gedimino. Open Tu-Sa 10am-5pm, Su 10am-3pm. 2Lt. 1Lt. with ISIC from Sept. to May.)*

🎭🎵 ENTERTAINMENT AND NIGHTLIFE

Summer is full of festivals, including the National Philharmonic's **Vilniaus Festivalis** that starts in late May (www.filharmonija.lt/vilniausfestivalis); check *Vilnius in Your Pocket, Exploring Vilnius,* distributed at hotels, or the Lithuanian-language paper *Lietuvos Rytas* for more info on performances. For info on gay nightlife, check the **Lithuanian Gay and Lesbian Homepage** (www.gay-line.lt). **SoHo**, Aušros Vartv 7, a cafe and bar, is a charming new feature in the old town night scene. (Live music F-Sa at 8pm. Open M-W and Su 11am-midnight, Th-Sa 11am-2am.) **Broadway** (Broadvejus), Mėsiniu 4, is Vilnius's most crowded dance floor: it's enormously popular with the teenie-bopper crowd, though older folks hang there too. (10Lt cover includes 2 drinks. Open M noon-3am, Tu noon-4am, W-Sa noon-5am. MC/V.) The dungeon-like basement at **The PUB** (Prie Universiteto Baras), Dominikonų 9, hosts Vilnius's wildest dance parties. College students pack this joint. (Open M-Th and Su 11am-2am, F-Sa 11am-5am. MC/V.) On Wednesday nights, live DJs rock the house at **Cafe de Paris**, Didzioji 1, adjacent to the French Embassy. Lithuanian pop stars and French tourists groove on the ad hoc dance floor.

🔁 DAYTRIP FROM VILNIUS: TRAKAI CASTLE

Trakai was crowned capital of Lithuanian in 1410, and the red-brick **Insular Castle** was home to the dukes who ruled the country. Russians destroyed the castle in the 17th century; the Soviet regime began reconstructing it in 1955. The original stone foundations are still visible, but unfortunately the castle now looks like a 20th-century creation and—along with the adjacent **museum**—has morphed into a modern tourist trap. *(Open daily 10am-7pm. 8Lt, 4Lt with ISIC.)* Trakai became home to a community of Karaites, a breakaway sect of Judaism, in the late 14th century. The **Karaite Ethnographic Museum**, Karaimų 22, displays relics from the sect's past, including a *megillah*, the text used by Jews to celebrate the holiday of Purim. *(Open W-Sa 10am-6pm. 2Lt, students 1Lt.)* The best way to see Lake Gavle is by paddleboat. Rental stands are located just beyond the castle's footbridge. *(12-15Lt per hr.)* Buses run to Trakai, 28km west of Vilnius *(30min., 1 per hr., 2.90Lt).* The last bus back departs at 11:30pm. If you plan to catch the last bus, confirm the schedule ahead of time to avoid being stranded.

KAUNAS

Kaunas (pop. 420,000) served as capital of independent Lithuania between world wars and remains a vibrant cultural center today. At the eastern end of **Laisvės**, the city's main pedestrian boulevard, the sparkling blue domes of the late-19th century **Church of St. Michael the Archangel** cast a shadow upon the city. (Open M-F 9am-

3pm, Sa-Su 8:30am-2pm. Free). Nearby, the **Devil Museum** exhibits more than 2000 depictions of the devil, who was revered as a guardian in Lithuanian folklore until the introduction of Christianity. (V. Putvinskio 64. Open Tu-Su 10am-5pm. 5Lt, students 2.50Lt.) On the western end of Laisves is Kaunas's well-preserved **old town;** at its heart stands Lithuania's largest Gothic structure, the 15th-century **Cathedral.** (Open daily 7am-7pm. Free.) Take the bus to reach the **Ninth Fort** (20min, 2 per hr., 1Lt), where 50,000 prisoners—including 30,000 Jews, were executed during WWII. Today, the site also includes a display of the Lithuanians sent to Siberia during Stalin's post-WWII purge. (Open M and W-Su 10am-6pm. 4Lt, students 2Lt.) The **Sugihara House and Foundation** details the courageous effort of Diplomat Sugihara, the "Japanese Schindler," who helped 6000 Jews escape near-certain execution by issuing them visas to travel through Russia. (Valzganto 30. Open M-F 10am-5pm, Sa-Su 11am-6pm. Free.)

To reach Kaunas from Vilnius, take a **train** (2hr., 12 per day, 9.80Lt) or **bus** (1½hr., 2 per hr., 12Lt). The **Tourist Information Center** is at Laisvės 36. (☎40 84 10; www.turinfo.lt. Open M-F 9am-6pm, Sa-Su 9am-12:15pm and 1-6pm.) ◙**Litinterp** ❸, Gedimino 28, arranges private rooms. (☎ 22 87 18; www.litinterp.lt. Open M-F 8:30am-5:30pm, Sa 9:30am-3pm. Singles 80-120Lt; doubles 140-160Lt. MC/V.) **Žalias Ratas ❷,** Laisvės 36b, is an excellent traditional tavern. (Entrees 5-28Lt. Open daily 11am-midnight. MC/V.) Follow the Dalai Lama's footsteps to **Avilys,** Vilniaus 34, an old town microbrewery with a wide selection of Tibetan teas. (Open M-Th 11am-midnight, F-Sa noon-2am, Su noon-midnight.) **Postal Code:** LT-3000.

KLAIPĖDA
☎846

Strategically located on the tip of the Neringa peninsula, Klaipėda (pop. 194,000) was briefly the Prussian capital in the 19th century, and was later handed to France by the 1919 Treaty of Versailles. In WWII, the city served as a German U-boat base before being industrialized by the Soviets after the war. On mainland Klaipėda, the **Clock Museum** (Laikrodžių Muziejus), Liepų 12, displays every conceivable kind of timekeeping device, from Egyptian sundials to Chinese candle clocks. From S. Daukanto, turn right on H. Manto and left on Liepų. (Open Tu-Su noon-6pm. 4Lt, students 2Lt.) **Klaipėda Drama Theater** (Klaipėdos Dramos Teatras), Teatro aikštė, on the other side of H. Manto, was one of Wagner's favorite haunts, as well as the site where Hitler personally proclaimed the town's incorporation into the *Reich.* (Tickets ☎31 44 53. Tu-Su 11am-2pm and 4-7pm.) The main attraction in **Smiltynė,** across the lagoon, is the **Sea Museum** (Lietuvos Jūrų Muziejus), Smiltynė 3, in an 1860s fortress. The Sea Museum's ◙**sea lion show** is spectacular. (www.juru.muziejus.lt. Open June-Aug. Tu-Su 10:30am-6:30pm; Sept. W-Su 10:30am-6:30pm; Oct.-May Sa-Su 10:30am-5pm. 8Lt, students 4Lt.) Forest paths lead west 500m to the **beaches.** The best bars line H. Manto. **Kurpiai,** Kurpių 1a, an excellent jazz club, is a mix between a traditional tavern and a jazz museum. (Live jazz 9:30pm. Cover F-Sa 5-10Lt. Open M-Th and Su noon-1am, F-Sa noon-3am. MC/V.) **Memelis,** Žvejv 4, on the river across the street from the ferry port, is part brewery, part dance club, part bar. (Open M 11am-midnight, Tu-W 11am-2am, Th 11am-3am, F-Sa 11am-4am, Su noon-midnight. MC/V.)

Buses (☎41 15 47, reservations 41 15 40) go from Butkų Juzės 9 to: Kaunas (3hr., 14 per day, 28Lt); Palanga (30-40min., 23 per day, 2.50-3Lt); and Vilnius (4-5hr., 10-14 per day, 41Lt). **Ferries** (☎31 42 17, info 31 11 17) run from Old Port Ferry Terminal, Žveju 8, to Smiltynė (10min., every 30min., 0.75Lt) and connect with microbuses to Nida (1hr., 7Lt). The staff at the **tourist office,** Turgaus 7, arranges tours and offers free maps and guidebooks. (☎41 21 86; www.klaipeda.lt. Open M-F 9am-7pm, Sa-Su 9am-4pm.) **Litinterp ❸,** S. Šimkaus 2¼, arranges rooms. (☎31 14 90. Open M-F 8:30am-5:30pm, Sa 9:30am-3:30pm. Singles 90-120Lt; doubles 140-

180Lt. Low season 20-40Lt discount.) **Klaipėda Traveller's Guesthouse (HI) ❷**, Butkų Juzės 7-4, 50m from the bus station, has spacious dorms, hot showers, and a friendly staff. (☎21 18 79; oldtown@takas.lt. Dorms 32Lt.) Heading away from the Danė River on Tiltų, make a left on Kulių Vartų, then turn left onto Bangų to reach **Aribė Hotel ❹**, Bangų 17a, a modern hotel with private bathrooms. (☎49 09 40; vitetur@klaipeda.omnitel.net. Singles 140Lt; doubles 180Lt; luxury suite 260Lt. Low season 20Lt less. MC/V.) **Trys Mylimos ❸**, Taikos 23, 500m southeast of the old town, is a traditional Lithuanian beer hall, dishing out generous portions of deep-fried regional cuisine. (☎41 14 79. Entrees 6-16Lt. Live music F-Sa 8-11pm. Open daily 11am-midnight. MC/V.) **Postal Code:** LT-5800.

NIDA AND PALANGA

Windswept white sand dunes have long drawn summer vacationers to **Nida**, only 3km north of the Kaliningrad region on the Curonian Spit. From the remains of the town's immense sundial on the highest of the ▧**Drifting Dunes of Parnidis,** you can look down on the Curonian Lagoon and the Baltic. Take a walk along the beach or through the forest paths to see surreal mountains and sheets of white sand from the dunes blowing gracefully into the sea. From the center of town, follow the promenade by the water and bear right on Skruzdynės to reach the **Thomas Mann House** (Thomo Manno Namelis) at #17. Mann built the cottage in 1930 and wrote *Joseph and His Brothers* here, but had to abandon it when Hitler invaded. (Open June-Aug. daily 10am-6pm, Sept.-May Tu-Sa 11am-5pm. 2Lt, students 0.50Lt.) The **Thomas Mann Cultural Center** puts on classical concerts for the **Thomas Mann Festival** in mid-July. From Naglių 18e, **microbuses** (☎ 524 72) run to Klaipeda/Smiltynė (1hr., 1 per hr., 7Lt). The **Tourist Info Center,** Taikos 4, opposite the bus station, arranges private rooms for a 5Lt fee and offers free Internet access. (☎523 45; www.neringainfo.lt. Open June 1-Sept. 1 M-F 10am-7pm, Sa 10am-6pm, Su 10am-3pm; low season M-F 9am-1pm and 2-6pm, Sa-Su 10am-3pm.) The **TIC ❶** arranges rooms (from 40-50Lt) and is the best option for inexpensive accommodations.

The largest park in the country, over 20km of shoreline, and an exuberant nightlife make **Palanga** (pop. 20,000) the hottest summer spot in Lithuania. While the beach is the main attraction, Palanga's pride and joy is the **Amber Museum** (Gintaro Muziejus) in a mansion at the Botanical Gardens. The collection consists of 15,000 pieces of fossilized resin known as "Baltic Gold" that have primeval flora and fauna trapped inside. (Open June-Aug. Tu-Sa 10am-8pm, Su 10am-7pm; Sept.-May daily 11am-4:30pm. 5Lt, students 2.50Lt.) Palanga's main streets are **Vytauto,** which runs parallel to the beach and passes the bus station, and **J. Basanavičiaus,** which runs perpendicular to Vytauto, ending at the boardwalk. Pedestrian-only **Meilės alėja** runs south of the pier along the beach, becoming **Birutės alėja** in the Palanga Park and Botanical Garden. Vytauto and J. Basanavičiaus g. are lined with cafes and restaurants that have outdoor seating. **Buses** (☎533 33) from Klaipėda (30min., every 30min., 2.50Lt) arrive at Kretinjos 1. Info is available at the **tourist office** to the right of the station; they also book private rooms by email. (☎488 11; palanga-turinfo@is.lt. Open daily 9am-1pm and 2-6pm.) **Palanga Welcome Host ❶,** Vytauto 21, maintains a catalogue with listings and pictures of most available rooms. Catalogue prices are generally lower than those printed in the agency's pamphlet. (☎487 23; svetingas@service.lt. Singles from 15Lt.)

LITHUANIA

LUXEMBOURG

The forgotten "lux" of the Benelux countries, tiny Luxembourg is often overlooked by travelers smitten by Dutch windmills or impatient to press east into Germany. Yet Luxembourg's castles can go toe to toe with those of the Rhineland, and the charming villages of the Ardennes are less touristed than their Belgian cousins to the northwest. White-collar financiers keep prices in Luxembourg City high, but the eminently walkable capital remains a promising destination for those who have drunk their fill of Bruges or Ghent.

DISCOVER LUXEMBOURG

Budget two days for **Luxembourg City** (p. 731), exploring the capital's maze of well-fortified tunnels by day and its lively nightlife after hours. The towns of **Echternach** (p. 736) and **Clervaux** (p. 735) should be your next stops, the former for its historic basilica and the latter for its hilltop chateau, restored to medieval splendor from a honest-to-goodness pile of rubble. From here, the route coils south to the flyspeck village of **Esch-sur-Sûre** (p. 736) for hiking through wooded river valleys.

ESSENTIALS

WHEN TO GO

The sea winds that routinely douse Belgium with rain have usually shed their moisture by the time they reach Luxembourg; good weather prevails from May through October, although travelers leery of crowds may want to avoid July and August. Temperatures average 17°C (64°F) in summer, and 1°C (34°F) in winter.

DOCUMENTS AND FORMALITIES

VISAS. EU citizens do not need a visa. Citizens of Australia, Canada, New Zealand, and the US do not need a visa for stays of up to 90 days, although this three-month period begins upon entry into any of the countries that belong to the EU's freedom of movement zone. For more information, see p. 17.

EMBASSIES AND CONSULATES. All foreign embassies and consulates are in Luxembourg City. For Luxembourg's embassies and consulates at home: **Australia,** Level 4, Quay West, 111 Harrington St.,

Sydney NSW 2000 (☎02 92 53 47 08); **Ireland,** Pension Systems Limited, Estate House, 51 Dawson St., Dublin 2 (☎353 1 671 98 11); **UK,** 27 Wilton Crescent, London SW1X 8SD (☎20 7235 6961); **US,** 2200 Massachusetts Ave. NW, Washington, D.C. 20008 (☎202-265-4171). **Canadians** can reach their ambassador at the American embassy in Washington, while **New Zealanders** should contact the Dutch embassy with questions.

TRANSPORTATION

BY PLANE. The Luxembourg City airport (LUX) is serviced by **Luxair** (☎2456 42 42; www.luxair.lu) and a slew of other European airlines. Cheap last-minute flights on Luxair (from €129) are available online.

BY TRAIN AND BUS. A **Benelux Tourrail Pass** allows five days of unlimited train travel in a one-month period in Belgium, the Netherlands, and Luxembourg (p. 63), and is discounted 33% for travelers under 26. Within Luxembourg itself, the **Billet Réseau** (€4.60, book of 5 €18.50) is good for one day of unlimited bus and train travel. The **Luxembourg Card** (€9-22) includes 1-3 days of unlimited transportation along with free or discounted admission to 50+ sights around the country.

BY BIKE AND THUMB. An 460km network of **cycling paths** already snakes its way through Luxembourg, and plans are in place to add another 440km in the near future. Domestic tains will transport bikes for €1.20. While *Let's Go* does not recommend hitchhiking as a safe means of transport, service areas in Luxembourg are popular places to hitch rides into Belgium, France, and the Netherlands, since many motorists stop to take advantage of relatively low fuel prices.

TOURIST SERVICES AND MONEY

EMERGENCY	Police: ☎113. Ambulance: ☎112. Fire: ☎112.

TOURIST OFFICES. For general info, contact the **Luxembourg National Tourist Office,** P.O. Box 1001, L-1010 Luxembourg (☎42 82 82 10; www.ont.lu).

MONEY. On January 1, 2002, the **euro (€)** replaced the **Luxembourg Franc** as the unit of currency in Luxembourg. For exchange rates and more info on the euro, see p. 20. The cost of living in Luxembourg City is high, although the surrounding countryside is more reasonable. All countries who are members of the European Union impose a **Value Added Tax (VAT)** on goods and services purchased within the EU. Prices in Luxembourg already include the country's 15% VAT rate, one of the lowest in Europe. Partial refunds are also available for visitors who are not EU citizens (p. 22). Restaurant bills usually include a service charge, although an extra 5-10% tip can be a classy gesture. Tip taxi drivers 10%.

BUSINESS HOURS. Most **banks** are open M-F 8:30am-4:30pm, while most **shops** are open Monday through Saturday 10am-6pm, with shorter hours on Sunday. Some banks and shops close at noon for two hours, especially in the countryside.

COMMUNICATION

TELEPHONES. Public phones require phone cards, available at post offices and train stations. **Mobile phones** are an increasingly popular and economical alternative (p. 35). International direct dial numbers include: **AT&T** (☎8002 0111); **British Telecom** (☎0800 89 0352); **Canada Direct** (☎8002 0119); **MCI** (☎8002 0112); **Sprint** (☎0800 0115); **Telecom New Zealand** (☎800 20064); **Telstra Australia** (☎0800 0061).

LUXEMBOURG

PHONE CODES	Country code: 352. International dialing prefix: 00. Luxembourg has no city codes.

MAIL. Mailing a letter (weighing up to 50g) within Luxembourg costs €0.70, within the EU €0.80, and to the rest of the world €1.20.

LANGUAGES. French and German are the administrative languages, but most citizens use a dialect called *Lëtzebuergesch* in everyday conversation. The dialect is almost never written, however, so signs and official documents appear in French. German is favored in smaller towns.

ACCOMMODATIONS AND CAMPING

LUXEMBOURG	❶	❷	❸	❹	❺
ACCOMMODATIONS	under €12	€12-16	€16-30	€30-40	over €40

Luxembourg's 12 **HI youth hostels** (*Auberges de Jeunesse*) are often booked solid with large school groups during the summertime, so it is wise to reserve ahead. Half of the hostels close from mid-November to mid-December, and the other half close from mid-January to mid-February. Prices range from €14-16; nonmembers pay €3 extra. Contact **Centrale des Auberges de Jeunesse Luxembourgeoises** (☎26 29 35 00; www.youthhostels.lu) for more info. **Hotels** are typically expensive, costing upwards of €40 per night. Happily, Luxembourg is a **camper's** paradise, and most towns have campsites close by. Two people with a tent will typically pay €8-12 per night. Contact **Camprilux** (www.camping.lu/gb/gbstart.htm) for more info.

FOOD AND DRINK

LUXEMBOURG	❶	❷	❸	❹	❺
FOOD	under €5	€5-9	€9-14	€14-20	over €20

Traditional Luxembourgish cuisine combines elements of French and German cooking. Some specialties include **Judd mat Gaardenbou'nen** (smoked neck of pork with beans), **Friture de la Moselle** (fried fish), **Gromperekichelcher** (potato fritters), and **Quetscheflued** (plum tart). Fruity **Riesling wines** are produced in the Moselle Valley, and show up most Chardonnays in terms of subtlety.

HOLIDAYS AND FESTIVALS

Holidays: New Year's Day (Jan. 1); Easter Sunday and Monday (Mar. 27-28); Labor Day (May 1); Ascension Day (May 5); Whit Sunday and Monday (May 15-16); National Day (June 23); Assumption Day (Aug. 15); All Saints' Day (Nov. 1); Christmas (Dec. 25).

Festivals: The weeks leading up to Lent bring parades and masked balls under the guise of Carnival. Echternach hosts the International Music Festival in May and June, while Riesling Open wine festivals kick off in Wormeldange on the third weekend of Sept.

FACTS AND FIGURES: LUXEMBOURG	
Official Name: Grand Duchy of Luxembourg.	**Time Zone:** GMT +1.
Capital: Luxembourg City.	**Languages:** Lëtzebuergesch; French and German are widely spoken.
Population: 463,000.	**Religions:** Roman Catholic (87%).
Land Area: 2,600 sq. km.	

LUXEMBOURG CITY

With a medieval fortress perched on a cliff that overlooks high bridges and a lush river valley, Luxembourg City (pop. 84,000) is one of the most beautiful capitals in Europe. As an international banking capital, it is home to thousands of frenzied business executives; even so, most visitors find it surprisingly relaxed and idyllic.

▄ TRANSPORTATION

Flights: Findel International Airport (LUX), 6km from the city. Bus #9 (€1.20) is the cheapest option to get from the airport to the train station, and runs the same route every 10-20min. Taxis are around €20 from the airport to the city center.

Trains: Gare CFL, av. de la Gare (toll-free info ☎49 90 49 90; www.cfl.lu), 15min. walk south of the city center. To: **Amsterdam** (6hr.; 1 per hr.; €46.40, under 26 €35); **Brussels** (2¾hr., 1 per hr., €26/€14.50); **Ettelbrück** (25min., 2 per hr., €3.60); **Frankfurt** (4½hr., 1 per hr., €46); **Paris** (4hr., every 2hr., €43/€32.30).

Buses: For travel exclusively within the city, buy a *billet courte distance* (short-distance ticket; €1.20, package of 10 €9.20), which is valid for 1hr. A *billet réseau* (network pass; €4.60, package of 5 €18.50) allows for unlimited travel within Luxembourg City and throughout the rest of the country for one day. Accepted on both buses and domestic trains, a *billet réseau* is the most economical option for intercity travel. Buses run until midnight; night buses run on weekends from midnight-4am.

Taxis: Colux Taxis, ☎48 22 33. €2.04 per km. 10% premium 10pm-6am. 25% premium on Sundays. **InterTaxis,** ☎40 52 52. Same prices.

Bikes: Rent from **Vélo en Ville,** 8 r. Bisserwé (☎47 96 23 83), in the Grund. Open daily Apr.-Nov. 10am-noon and 1-8pm. €5 per hr., €12.50 per half-day, €20 per day, €37.50 per weekend, €75 per week. Under 26 20% discount for full day and longer.

▄▟ ORIENTATION AND PRACTICAL INFORMATION

Five minutes by bus and 15min. by foot from the train station, Luxembourg City's historic center revolves around the **Place d'Armes.** From the train station, follow av. de la Gare or av. de la Liberté, then watch for signs giving directions to the city's main sights. Facing the City Tourist Office in the **Place d'Armes,** the Pétrusse Valley is to your right; take r. Chimay to reach **Place de la Constitution** and the historic **Pétrusse Casemates.** The city's lower areas, the **Grund** and the **Clausen,** are located diagonally to your right and left, 10min. and 15min. on foot, respectively. Halfway between these areas are the **Bock Casemates;** walk straight down r. du Curé, which becomes r. Boucherie and then r. Sigefroid.

Tourist Offices: Grand Duchy National Tourist Office (☎42 82 82 20; www.ont.lu), in the train station. Open daily June-Sept. 8:30am-6:30pm; Oct.-May 9:15am-12:30pm and 1:45-6pm. **Luxembourg City Tourist Office,** pl. d'Armes (☎22 28 09; www.lcto.lu). Open Apr.-Sept. M-Sa 9am-7pm, Su 10am-6pm; Oct.-Mar. M-Sa 9am-6pm, Su 10am-6pm. **Centre Information Jeunes,** 26 pl. de la Gare (☎26 29 32 00), inside Galerie Kons across from the train station, is a great service for young people, providing free **Internet** access for students (30min. max.) and info on finding jobs in the area. Open M-F 10am-6pm.

Embassies: Ireland, 28 rte. d'Arlon (☎45 06 10). Open M-F 10am-12:30pm and 2:30-5pm. **UK,** 14 bd. Roosevelt (☎22 98 64). Open M-F 9am-12:30pm. **US,** 22 bd. Emmanuel Servais (☎46 01 23). Open M-F 8:30am-5:30pm. **Australians, Canadians,** and **New Zealanders** should contact their embassies in France or Belgium.

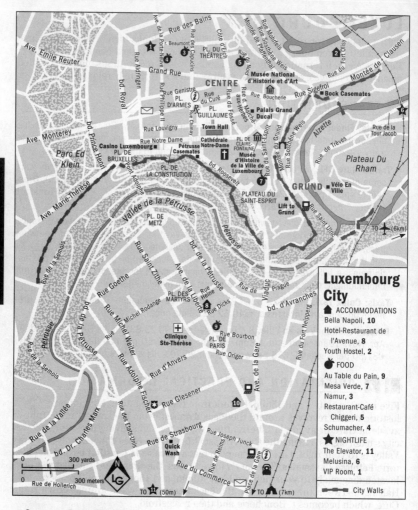

Luxembourg City

⌂ ACCOMMODATIONS
Bella Napoli, **10**
Hotel-Restaurant de
l'Avenue, **8**
Youth Hostel, **2**

🍎 FOOD
Au Table du Pain, **9**
Mesa Verde, **7**
Namur, **3**
Restaurant-Café
Chiggeri, **5**
Schumacher, **4**

★ NIGHTLIFE
The Elevator, **11**
Melusina, **6**
VIP Room, **1**

▬▬ City Walls

Currency Exchange: Banks are the only option for changing money or cashing traveler's checks. Most are open M-F 8:30am until 4 or 4:30pm. All are closed on weekends. Expect to pay commissions of €5 for cash and €8 for traveler's checks.

Luggage Storage: In train station. €2-4 per day, depending on the size of the locker. Storage for up to 48hr. Open daily 6:30am-9:30pm.

Laundromat: Quick Wash, 31 r. de Strasbourg, near the station. Wash and dry €10. Open M-F 8:30am-6:30pm, Sa 8am-6pm.

Pharmacy: Pharmacie Goedert, 5 pl. d'Armes (☎22 23 99). Open M-F 8am-6:15pm, Sa 8am-12:30pm. After hours, check the window for a schedule of 24hr. pharmacies.

Medical Services: Doctors and pharmacies on call ☎112. **Clinique Ste-Therese,** r. Ste-Zithe 36 (☎49 77 61 or 49 77 65). Open M-F 2-8pm for office visits. Doctors are available for emergencies M-W and F 7am-7pm, Th 24hr.

Internet Access: Centre Information Jeunes has free Internet for students. **Cyber-Grund,** 2 r. Saint Ulric (☎26 20 39 98), in the Grund. €2 for 30min., €3 per hr. Rates discounted to €2 per hr. Tu-F noon-3pm. Open Tu-F noon-6:30pm, Sa 1-5pm.

Post Office: 38 pl. de la Gare, across the street and to the left of the train station. Open M-F 6am-7pm, Sa 6am-noon. Address mail to be held in the following format: Firstname SURNAME, *Poste Restante,* L-1009 Luxembourg G-I Gare, LUXEMBOURG. **Branch office,** 25 r. Aldringen, near the pl. d'Armes.

ACCOMMODATIONS

The city hostel is the only budget option in Luxembourg City. Hotels are cheaper near the train station than in the city center but are often a splurge nonetheless.

Youth Hostel (HI), 2 r. du Fort Olisy (☎22 19 20). Take bus #9 and ask to get off at the hostel; head under the bridge and turn right down the steep path. Open, but under renovation until spring 2005. Breakfast and sheets included. 5-night max. stay in summer. Reception 24hr. Dorms €17. Nonmembers add €3. AmEx/MC/V. ❸

Bella Napoli, 4 r. de Strasbourg (☎48 46 29). From the train station, go straight down r. de la Liberté and turn left onto r. de Strasbourg. Simple rooms with hardwood floors and full bath. Breakfast included. Reception 8am-midnight. Singles €38; doubles €45; triples €60. AmEx/MC/V. ❹

Hotel-Restaurant de l'Avenue, 43 ave. de la Liberté (☎40 68 12; hotelav@pt.lu). Straight down r. de la Liberté from the train station. Rooms are small but comfortable, and some have spacious bathrooms. For less noise, avoid the rooms overlooking the main street. Singles €50; doubles €75; triples €90. MC/V. ❺

Camping Kockelscheuer (☎47 18 15), 7km outside Luxembourg City. Take bus #5 from the station to Kockelscheuer-Camping. Showers included. Snack bar on location. Open Easter-Oct. €3.50 per person, €4 per site. Cash only. ❶

FOOD

Although the area around the pl. d'Armes teems with a strange mix of fast-food joints and upscale restaurants, there are a few affordable and appealing alternatives. Stock up on groceries at **Supermarché Boon,** in Galerie Kons across from the train station. (Open M-F 8am-8pm, Sa 8am-6pm, Su 8am-noon.)

Restaurant-Café Chiggeri, 15 r. du Nord (☎22 82 36). From Place du Théâtre, walk down r. du Nord; Chiggeri is on the right after the bend. Serves traditional French food in a shimmery, night-sky decor. Wine list offers an amazing 2200 vintages. Entrees €11-14. Open M-Th 8am-1am, F-Sa 8am-3am, Su 10am-1am. AmEx/MC/V. ❸

Mesa Verde, 11 r. du St-Esprit (☎46 41 26), down the street from the Place de Clairefontaine. A local favorite, this bright vegetarian restaurant features an ever-changing array of hand-painted murals and fabrics. Entrees €18-25. Open Tu-Sa 6:30pm-midnight. Open for lunch W-F noon-2pm. MC/V. ❹

Namur, 27 r. des Capuchins (☎22 34 08), down the street from Place d'Armes. Marble floors and an elegant ambience make Namur's selection of pastries, chocolates, and sundaes (€1-5) even sweeter. Open M 11:30am-6pm, Tu-Sa 8:30am-6pm. MC/V. ❶

Au Table du Pain, 37 av. de la Liberté (☎29 56 63), on the way to the train station. Serves up soups, salads (€8-10), sandwiches (€4-8), and baked goods on wooden tables in a country-home atmosphere. Open M-F 7am-6pm. Cash only. ❷

Schumacher, 18 av. de la Porte-Neuve (☎22 90 09). Popular spot to grab a sandwich (€2-4) and go. Perfect for last-minute picnics in the Pétrusse Valley. Open M-F 7am-7pm, Sa 7am-6pm. MC/V. ❶

MAKE A WISH, YOUR HIGHNESS

Luxembourg's diminutive size doesn't stop it from throwing one enormous royal birthday party. The circumstances around the June 23 bash are a little puzzling, since Grand Duke Henri was born on April 16, 1955. But Henri inherited the tradition from his grandmother, Grand Duchess Charlotte, born on January 23, 1896. When her court realized that mid-winter doesn't lend itself to open-air wingdings, they nudged official celebrations up by five months. Reluctant to further befuddle their subjects, both Grand Duke Henri and his father Jean took June 23 as their own.

A long procession through the old city starts things off early in the evening on June 22. At 11pm, fireworks rip through the air, and waterfalls of fire make silhouettes out of the city's tall bridges. Then, in a twinkle, the narrow streets are transformed into impromptu bars and dance floors; alcohol flows like water, spirits are high, and it takes the rising sun to finally break up the party. The disheveled revelers pour into the Place d'Armes for breakfast before staggering home to sleep. June 23 is a public holiday, so once the city wakes around noon, everyone heads downtown to see Henri strolling through the streets. With his aged parents in tow and royal security out of sight, the duke restores calm and a sense of routine to a city unaccustomed to such glorious commotion.

◉ SIGHTS

Luxembourg City is compact enough to be explored on foot; just by wandering around, you'll bump into most of the major sights. The most spectacular views of the city can be seen from the bridge closest to the Bock Casemates and from **Place de la Constitution.** For guidance, follow the signs pointing out the **Wenzel Walk.** It leads visitors through 1000 years of history as it winds around the old city, from the **chemin de la Corniche** down into the casemates.

FORTRESSES AND THE OLD CITY. The city's first fortress may have been built in 963, but the Burgundians, the French, the Spaniards, and the Austrians all expanded the network of fortifications, earning the city the nickname "Gibraltar of the North." The casemates, a 23km network of underground tunnels, were among the most distinctive features of the city's defenses, and when Luxembourg was declared a neutral state in 1867, the casemates were almost dismantled. This plan proved to be impractical, and during World War II the remaining tunnels sheltered 35,000 people during bombing raids. Start with the **Bock Casemates** fortress, part of Luxembourg's original castle, which looms over the Alzette river valley and offers a view of the **Grund** and the **Clausen.** (Entrance on r. Sigefroi, just past the bridge leading to the hostel. Open daily Mar.-Oct. 10am-5pm. €1.75, students €1.50.) The **Pétrusse Casemates** were built by the Spanish in the 1600s, and improved by the Austrian Habsburgs. By the 19th century, a second ring of fortifications had been extended and a third was springing up around the expanding city. (On pl. de la Constitution. Tours every hr. July-Sept. 11am-4pm. €1.75, students €1.50.) The peaceful paths of the green **Pétrusse** valley beckon for a jog or an afternoon picnic in the shadow of the towering fortress walls. More sedentary visitors can also catch one of the green **tourist trains** that depart from pl. de la Constitution and meander through the city and into the valley. (☎26 65 11. Runs mid-Mar. to Oct. every 30min. 10am-6pm except 1pm. €7.50.)

MUSEUMS. The **Luxembourg Card** covers entrance to 51 museums and tourist attractions throughout the country. (Available at tourist offices and most train stations. www.luxembourgcard.lu. 1-day card €9, 2-day €16, 3-day €22.) The more modest **Museum Card** includes five museums over three days. (Available at the City Tourist Office. €7, students €5.) The eclectic collection at the **Musée National d'Histoire et d'Art** chronicles the influences of the various empires that controlled Luxembourg through history. (Marché-aux-Poissons, at r. Boucherie and Sigefroi. ☎479 33 01; www.mnha.lu.

Open Tu-Su 10am-5pm. €5, students €3.) The only gamble at **Casino Luxembourg** is on the changing exhibitions of contemporary art. *(41 r. de Notre Dame, near pl. de la Constitution. ☎22 50 45; www.casino-luxembourg.lu. Open M and W-Su 11am-6pm, Th until 8pm. €4, under 26 €3.)*

ENTERTAINMENT AND NIGHTLIFE

At night, the **place d'Armes** comes to life with free concerts and stand-up comedy. Pick up a copy of *Nico* at the tourist office for a list of nightlife action and events. There is no central location for nightlife in Luxembourg City, so an evening of bar-hopping also involves hopping on and off of the city's night bus. On weekends, dance the night away at **Melusina**, 145 r. de la Tour Jacob, a cafe that becomes a popular nightspot when the sun sets. (☎43 59 22. Entrees €8-17. Open M-Th 11:30am-2pm and 7-11pm, F-Sa 11:30am-2pm and 7pm-3am.) To get there, cross the bridge from the Grund lift, follow r. de Trèves, and veer left as it becomes r. de la Tour Jacob. The clubbing scene's new kid on the block is the glitzy **VIP Room**, 19 r. des Bains (☎18 78 67), modeled after playboy-promoter Jean-Roch's other VIP clubs in Paris and Saint-Tropez. (Located near the Place du Théatre. No cover. Open M-F 6pm-late, Sa-Su 7pm-late.) **The Elevator**, 48 r. de Hollerich (☎29 14 64), is a local favorite for its lively crowds and outside-the-mainstream electronic music. Open M-F 5pm-1am, Sa-Su 7pm-1am. Drinks are 50% off during Happy Hour W 5-8 pm. Take bus #1 or 22, or walk down r. de la Gare away from the city center.

THE ARDENNES

Six decades ago, the Battle of the Bulge (1944) mashed Luxembourg into the mud. Today, quiet towns, looming castles, and pleasant hiking trails are powerful draws.

ETTELBRÜCK. The main railway line linking Luxembourg City to Liège, Belgium runs through Ettelbrück (pop. 7000), making the town the transportation hub for the Ardennes. Little else recommends the place, although history buffs waiting out a layover might investigate the **General Patton Memorial Museum**, 5 r. Dr. Klein, which commemorates Luxembourg's liberation during WWII. (☎81 03 22. Open daily June to mid-Sept. 10am-5pm; mid-Sept. to June Su 2-5pm. €2.50.) **Trains** go to: Clervaux (30min., 1 per hr.); Liège (2 hr., every 2hr.); Luxembourg City (25min., 3 per hr.). The **tourist office** is in the train station. (☎81 20 68. Open M-F 9am-noon and 1:30-5pm, Sa 10am-noon and 2-4pm; Sept.-May closed Sa.) **Auberge de la Gare ❺**, 45 r. Prince Henri, offers the most affordable rooms in town, across the road from the station. (☎81 21 80. Singles €41; doubles €45. MC/V.) However, **Camping Kalkesdelt ❶**, 22 r. du Camping, is far more affordable for travelers with tents. (☎81 21 85. Open Apr.-Oct. Reception 7:30am-noon and 2-10pm. €5 per person, €5.50 per site.) Pick up groceries at **Match**, near the train station. (Open M-Th 7:30am-7:30pm, F 7:30am-8pm, Sa 7:30am-6 pm, Su 9am-12:30pm.)

CLERVAUX. You'll see more faces in Clervaux's **chateau** than in the tiny town (pop. 1000); the castle houses Edward Steichen's moving ▨**Family of Man,** an exhibition of 500 photos from 68 countries, depicting milestones of everyday life and emphasizing the common bonds of human experience. (☎92 96 57. Open Apr.-Sept. daily 10am-6pm; Mar. and Oct.-Dec. Tu-Su 10am-6pm. €4.50, students €2.50.) To get to the chateau, turn left out of the train station onto r. de la Gare, which becomes Grand Rue, and walk 10min. to the place du Marché. The red roof of the **Benedictine Abbey** noses its way above the treeline on a hill overlooking Clervaux; reach it by walking 15min. up Montée de l'Abbaye, the narrow road behind the parish church. (Abbey open daily 9am-7pm. Free.) **Trains** run to: Ettelbrück

(25min., 1 per hr.); Liège, Belgium (1¾hr., every 2hr.), Luxembourg City (50min., 1 per hr.). Hotels are pricey in Clervaux; think about heading back to Ettelbrück for accommodations. The **tourist office,** in the castle, finds rooms. (☎92 00 72; www.tourisme-clervaux.lu. Open daily July-Aug. 9:45-11:45am and 2-6pm; low season reduced hours.) **Camping Officiel ❶,** 33 Klatzewe, is near the river. (☎92 00 42. Open Apr.-Nov. €4.30 per person, €4.30 per tent.)

ESCH-SUR-SURE. Cradled by the green Ardennes and almost encircled by the Sûre River, this tiny village (pop. 320) is an ideal base of operations for those looking to explore the **Haute-Sûre nature reserve** (☎89 93 311; www.naturpark-sure.lu). The ruins of a 10th-century **castle** overlook the village, and are floodlit well into the evening in summer. Otherwise, visitors can rent **bikes** and **canoes** from **Hotel de la Sûre ❸,** 1 r. du Pont, the village's unofficial tourist office and best bet for lodgings. (☎83 91 10; www.hotel-de-la-sure.lu. Breakfast included. Singles from €28. Bikes €12 per half-day, €21 per day; canoes free to borrow for guests. AmEx/MC/V.) **Camping im Aal ❶** is a 5min. walk from the bus drop-off point; just cross the bridge and turn right. (Open Mar.-Dec. Reception 8am-5pm. €5 per person, €5 per site.) The bus from Ettelbrück runs only on weekdays (25min., every 2-4hr., €2), although Hotel de la Sûre runs overpriced shuttles from Ettelbrück for its guests seven days a week (€15 per person, call ahead to arrange pickup).

ECHTERNACH. In the heart of the Little Switzerland region, Echternach (pop. 5200) is a paradise for **hikers** and **bikers** who venture out into the surrounding woodlands. In town, the turrets of the 15th-century **town hall** share the skyline with the towering **Basilica of St. Willibrord.** (Basilica open daily 8:30am-7:30pm.) Widely considered the most important church in Luxembourg, St. Willibrord draws more than 10,000 pilgrims every Whit Tuesday (the 7th Tuesday after Easter) for a **Dancing Procession** of penance and healing. The basilica also plays host to Echternach's renowned **International Music Festival,** held in May and June. The festival highlights a different classical instrument each year, and Echternach's own Georges Lentz has composed a special piece for 2005's 30th anniversary festival. (☎72 83 47; www.echternachfestival.lu. Student tickets from €7.)

Buses run to Ettelbrück (50min., 1 per hr.) and Luxembourg City (1hr., 2 per hr.). To get from the bus station to the town center, walk past the cafes and hotels that line r. de la Gare. Rent **bikes** at **Trisport,** 31 rte. de Luxembourg. (☎72 00 86. €2.50 per hr., €15 per day.) The **tourist office** provides information on hiking and biking routes nearby. (☎72 02 30; www.echternach-tourist.lu. Open daily July-Aug. 9:30am-12:30pm and 1:30-5:30pm; low season M-F 9:30am-12:30pm and 1:30-5:30pm.) The **Youth Hostel (HI) ❷,** is conveniently located near the center of town. From the bus station, head down r. de la Gare, turn right onto r. André Duchscher, and look on the right for number 9. (☎72 01 58. Breakfast and sheets included. Reception 8-10am and 5-9pm. Lockout 10am-5pm. Curfew 11pm. Open May-Dec. Dorms €15; singles €23; doubles €34. Nonmembers add €3. AmEx/MC/V.) A new hostel is being built near the lake for the summer of 2005; check with the tourist office for details. **Camping Officiel ❶,** 5 rte. de Diekirch, is near the bus station. (☎72 02 72. €4.80 per person, €5 per tent.) Pick up groceries at **Match,** near the place du Marché. (Open M-F 8am-7pm, Sa 8am-6pm, Su 8am-noon.)

MOROCCO (المغرب)

At the crossroads of Africa, Europe, and the Middle East, Morocco has carved its identity from a host of influences. Drawing from its neighbors' cultures, religions, and languages, the North African country oscillates between the past and present as both an ancient civilization descended from nomadic tribes and a modern nation that has only recently won its struggle for sovereignty. Travelers to the region find Morocco to be a mesmerizing gateway between two continents, and for those weary of another visit to a Spanish cathedral, traversing the Moroccan border can unexpectedly become the highlight of the trip. While Morocco is only a few hours from Europe, it's an entirely different world.

ESSENTIALS

WHEN TO GO

Weather in the coastal regions is generally mild, although it can be rainy in the winter. From October to April, the weather is nice all around, making this a popular time to visit. During the high season (June-Sept.) be sure to book ahead.

DOCUMENTS AND FORMALITIES

VISAS. Citizens of Australia, Canada, Ireland, New Zealand, the UK, and the US do not need a visa for stays of up to 90 days.

EMBASSIES. Foreign embassies in Morocco are in Rabat. Moroccan embassies at home include: **Canada,** 38 Range Rd., Ottawa, ON K1N 8J4 (☎613-236-7391; www.ambassade-maroc.ottawa.on.ca); **Ireland,** 53 Raglan Rd., Ballsbridge, Dublin 4 (☎353 1 660 9449); **UK,** 49 Queens Gate Gardens, London SW7 5NE (☎171 581 5001); **US,** 1601 21st St. NW, Washington, D.C. 20009 (☎202-462-7979).

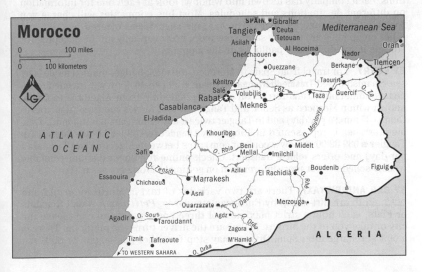

TRANSPORTATION

BY PLANE. Royal Air Maroc (RAM; ☎ 022 32 11 22; www.royalairmaroc.com), Morocco's national airline, flies to and from most major cities in Europe, including Madrid. Domestically, a network of flights radiates from the Mohammed V Airport outside Casablanca. Planes fly daily to Agadir, Fez, Marrakesh, Tangier, and occasionally to Ouarzazate. If you hope to see a lot of Morocco in a short time, flying can be a convenient option. **Air France** (in Casablanca ☎ 022 43 18 18; www.airfrance.com) also flies to all major domestic cities, as well as some international destinations. For more information on flying to Morocco, see p. 51.

BY TRAIN. Trains in Morocco are faster and more comfortable than buses, fairly reliable, and prompt. Second-class train tickets are slightly more expensive than corresponding CTM bus fares. First-class tickets cost around 50% more than second-class tickets; however, there is no great difference between the two compartments besides extra space. Check the Moroccan Railway website (www.oncf.ma) for schedules and prices. The main route runs from Tangier to Marrakesh via Rabat and Casablanca. A spur connects Fez, Meknes, and points east. There is one couchette train between Tangier and Marrakesh. No student fares are available. Rail lines are presently non-existent south of Marrakesh. **Eurail** is not valid in Morocco. **InterRail** is valid, but train fares are so low that it's not worth it. For more information on getting to Morocco by train, see p. 57.

BY BUS. In Morocco, bus travel is less frequent and less reliable than in Spain or Portugal. Plan well ahead if you wish to use buses as your method of transport. They're not extremely fast or comfortable, but they are very cheap and travel to nearly every corner of the country. The state-owned line, **Compagnie de Transports du Maroc (CTM;** www.ctm.co.ma), has the fastest and most reliable buses, but is slightly more expensive than other lines. In many cities, CTM has a station separate from other lines; reservations are usually unnecessary. Several dozen private companies operate as well; they have more departures and are cheaper, but are also slower and less comfortable than CTM. In bus stations, each company has its own info window; look at each one for information on different destinations and schedules. Most bus companies will charge you for bringing luggage on board. The **baggage checkrooms** offered by CTM and other companies are usually safe. Your bags, however, may not be accepted for storage if you don't have padlocks on the zippers.

BY FERRY. For travel from Spain to Morocco, the most budget-minded mode is by sea. Spanish-based **Trasmediterránea** (in Spain ☎ 902 45 46 45; www.trasmediterranea.es/homei.htm) runs ferries on a shuttle schedule from Algeciras to **Ceuta,** known within Morocco as Sebta, and Tangier. "Fast" ferries run from Algeciras to Ceuta (35 min.; 4 per day) and to Tangier twice a day (1 hr.; 9am and 1:45pm). Trasmediterránea is represented in Tangier by **Limadet** (☎ 039 93 11 42). **Comarit** (in Tangier ☎ 039 32 00 32; www.comarit.com) runs between Algeciras and Tangier (4 per day) and offers **vehicle transport.** Check online for Comarit's unpredictable weekly schedule. For more information on getting to Morocco, see p. 69.

BY CAR AND BY TAXI. There are two varieties of taxi in Morocco: *grand* and *petit*. Both are dirt-cheap by European standards. *Petit taxis*, small Renaults or Fiats, each hold a strict maximum of three passengers and can't leave the city or take you to the airport. Make sure the driver turns the meter on. There is a 50% surcharge after 8pm. Drivers may stop for other passengers or pick you up with other passengers in the car; if you are picked up after the meter has been started, note the initial price. *Grand taxis*, typically beige or dark-blue Mercedes sedans, are more expensive, but go just about anywhere. They usually congregate at a central area in town and won't go until filled with passengers going in the same direction. Rent a car in Morocco only for large group travel or travel to areas inaccessible by Moroccan bus lines.

BY THUMB. Almost no one in Morocco **hitchhikes,** though flagging down buses can feel like hitchhiking. Transportation is dirt cheap by European and North American standards. If Moroccans do pick up a foreigner, they are likely to expect payment. Hitchhiking is more frequent in the south and in the mountains, where transportation is irregular. *Let's Go* does not recommend hitchhiking.

TOURIST SERVICES AND MONEY

EMERGENCY	Police: ☎ 19. Ambulance: ☎ 15. Fire: ☎ 15.

TOURIST OFFICES. Tourist offices in Morocco tend to be few and far between. However, existing offices have lists of available accommodations and an official tour-guide service. *Let's Go* does not recommend hiring unofficial guides. The official website for tourism in Morocco is www.tourism-in-morocco.com.

MONEY. The **dirham (DH),** Morocco's unit of currency, is divided into 100 centimes. Coins are issued in denominations of 10, 20, and 50 centimes, and 1, 5, and 10 DH. Notes come in denominations of 10, 20, 50, 100, and 200 DH. Do not try the **black market** for currency exchange—you'll be swindled. As in Europe, **ATMs** are the best way to change money. Also know that it is very difficult to change back upon departure. Morocco has a 10% **Value Added Tax (VAT)** on accommodations which is usually included in the listed price. VAT on consumer goods varies 0-20% and is usually included in the listed price. It is customary to **tip** 10% in nicer restaurants; in cafes it is fine to round up and leave the change. **Bargaining** is a legitimate part of the Moroccan shopping experience—it is most commonly accepted in outdoor markets. Decide what the item is actually worth to you and use that as a benchmark. Do not try to bargain in supermarkets or established stores.

DIRHAM (DH)		
	AUS$1 =DH6.39	DH1 = AUS$0.16
	CDN$1 = DH6.83	DH1 = CDN$0.15
	EUR€1 = DH11	DH1 = EUR€0.09
	NZ$1 = DH5.93	DH1 = NZ$0.17
	US$1 = DH8.93	DH1 = US$0.11

COMMUNICATION

PHONE CODES	**Country code:** 212. **International dialing prefix:** 00. From outside Morocco, dial int'l dialing prefix (see inside back cover) + 212+ city code (leaving out the first 0) + local number. When dialing within Morocco from one city to another, dial city code + local number. When calling within a city, omit the city code.

MOROCCO

TELEPHONES. Morocco has invested hundreds of millions of dollars into modernizing its telephone system, markedly improving services. Pay phones accept only phone cards, which are sold at phone offices and *tabacs*. To use the card, insert and dial 00. Once the dial tone turns into a tune, dial the number. The best way to call home is with an international calling card issued by your phone company. For more information on calling out of Europe, see p. 32.

MAIL. Sending something **air mail** (*par avion*) can take a week to a month to reach the US or Canada. Less reliable **surface mail** (*par terre*) takes up to two months. **Express mail** (*recommandé* or *exprès postaux*) is faster than regular air mail and more reliable. Post offices and *tabacs* sell **stamps.** For fast service (2 days to the US), your best bet is DHL (www.dhl.com) or FedEx (www.fedex.com). Moroccan post offices often misplace or automatically return held mail (*Poste Restante*). If you want to try, mail should be addressed as follows: SURNAME, First Name; Poste Restante; Post Office Address; City; MOROCCO; PAR AVION.

INTERNET ACCESS. Cybercafes can be found in major cities and touristed towns.

LANGUAGE. Although Classical Arabic is the official language of Morocco, it is rarely spoken and has become an almost exclusively written language. Most Moroccans speak *Darija*, a French-influenced dialect of Arabic specific to Morocco, as well as French proper. In addition to these, there are three main dialects of Berber used throughout the country. Spanish is also spoken in the more northern regions of Morocco. As Moroccan Arabic is quite difficult to pronounce and differs greatly from both Classical and Modern Standard Arabic, *Let's Go* recommends communicating in French.

ACCOMMODATIONS AND CAMPING

Hotels in Morocco are rated by an official star system; the number of stars, however, reflects little more than price. Hotels not part of the system are not necessarily worse and are usually cheaper. The quality of rooms can vary widely—even within a particular hotel. Cheap hotels in Morocco are really cheap—as little as DH50 per night. Hot showers, when available, may cost extra (usually less than DH10). The **Federation Royale des Auberges de Jeunesse (FRMAJ)** is the Moroccan Hostelling International (HI; www.hihostels.com) affiliate. Beds cost DH30-60 per night, and there is a surcharge for non-members. Some hostels sell HI memberships on the spot. Call ahead for reservations. You'll probably need to bring your own sleepsack and towel, and there are usually curfew and lock-out times. **Camping** is popular and cheap (about DH15 per person), especially in the desert, mountains, and beaches. Like hotels, conditions vary widely. You can usually expect to find restrooms, but electricity is not as readily available. Use caution if camping unofficially, especially on the beaches, as theft is a problem.

FOOD AND DRINK

Moroccan chefs lavish aromatic and colorful spices on their dishes—pepper, ginger, cumin, saffron, honey, and sugar are culinary staples. The distinctive flavor comes from a blend of spices known as *ras al-hanut*. No matter how delicious everything taste, be prepared to get sick at least once, as Morocco is full of parasites and bacteria to which tourists are not immune. Taking extra precautions may help. Bottled mineral water is the way to go, as is peeling all fruits and vegetables. The truly cautious may avoid salads as well, or ensure that their vegetables are washed in purified water. Most food sold on the street can be quite risky.

HOLIDAYS AND FESTIVALS

Holidays: New Year's Day (Jan. 1); Independence Manifesto (Jan. 11); Aïd al-Adha (Jan. 21); Fatih Mouharram (Feb. 10); Aïd al-Mawid (Apr. 21); Labor Day (May 1); Feast of the Throne (June 30); Reunification Day (Aug. 14); the King and the People's Revolution Day (Aug. 20); Youth Day (Aug. 21); Aïd al-Fitr (Nov. 3-5); Anniversary of the Green March (Nov. 6); Independence Day (Nov. 18).

Festivals: Morocco's most important religious festival is Ramadan (Oct. 4-Nov. 2). During this period, Muslims refrain from food and drink for the entire day; between sunset and sunrise, restrictions are lifted. In the secular realm, Morocco hosts several interesting festivals. June brings the World Sacred Music Festival to Fez and the National Festival of Popular Arts to Marrakesh. In September, the matchmaking festival in Imilchil arranges marriages for the eligible youths of the town.

FACTS AND FIGURES: MOROCCO

Official Name: Kingdom of Morocco.

Capital: Rabat.

Major Cities: Agadir, Casablanca, Fez, Marrakesh, Tangier.

Population: 30,000,000.

Land Area: 446,500 sq. km.

Time Zone: GMT.

Languages: Arabic (official), French, Berber dialects.

Religion: Islam (98.7%).

MOROCCO

THE NETHERLANDS
(NEDERLAND)

The Dutch are given to saying that although God created the rest of the world, *they* created the Netherlands. With most of their country's land area below sea level, the task of keeping their iconic tulips and windmills on dry ground has become something of a national pastime. Early planners built dikes higher and higher in order to hold the sea back, but a new "flexible coast" policy depends on spillways and reservoirs to contain potentially calamitous floods. For a nation treading water beneath the sword of Damocles, the Dutch have deep cultural roots and a down-to-earth friendliness that keep them better grounded than most land-locked nations. Time-tested art, ambitious architecture, and dynamic nightlife make the Netherlands one of the most popular destinations in Western Europe.

 DISCOVER THE NETHERLANDS: SUGGESTED ITINERARIES

The canal houses and coffeeshops of **Amsterdam** (p. 746) are a logical place to begin, especially if you can wake early enough to see flower trading in **Aalsmeer** (p. 757). Zip west to the beach parties at **Bloemendaal aan Zee** (p. 765), then recover for a day in historic **Haarlem** (p. 764). Spend a low-key day ambling through **The Hague** (p. 766), and brace yourself for the onslaught of futuristic architecture in **Rotterdam** (p. 767).

It'll be no surprise to find a slew of worthwhile museums in the college town of **Utrecht** (p. 768), but you might not expect to run across a major modernist sculpture garden in the middle of **Hoge Veluwe National Park** (p. 769). Swing north through trendy, underappreciated **Groningen** (p. 771), and then take your sweet time pedaling through the grassy dunes and cranberry bogs of the **Wadden Islands** (p. 771).

ESSENTIALS

WHEN TO GO

July and August are lovely months to travel to the Netherlands, as the crowded hostels and lengthy queues during those months will confirm. If you fancy a bit more elbow room, April, May, and early June may be more to your liking, as tulips and fruit trees roar into bloom amid temperatures hovering between 12-20°C (53-68°F). The Netherlands are famously drizzly year-round, so travelers would be well-advised to bring an umbrella.

DOCUMENTS AND FORMALITIES

VISAS. EU citizens do not need a visa. Citizens of Australia, Canada, New Zealand, and the US do not need a visa for stays of up to 90 days, although this three-month period begins upon entry into any of the countries that belong to the EU's freedom of movement zone. For more information, see p. 17.

EMBASSIES. All foreign embassies and most consulates are in The Hague. Both the US and the UK have consulates in Amsterdam. For Dutch embassies at home: **Australia,** 120 Empire Circuit, Yarralumla Canberra, ACT 2600 (☎ 02 62 20 94 00;

The Netherlands

North Sea

TO NEWCASTLE, ENGLAND

TO HARWICH, ENGLAND
AND HULL, ENGLAND

Schiermonnikoog
Ameland
Terschelling
Wadden Islands
Vlieland
Waddenzee
Texel
Leeuwarden
Groningen
Harlingen
Heerenveen
Den Helder
IJsselmeer
Assen
Hoorn
Hoogeveen
Alkmaar
Zaansee Schans
IJmuiden
Edam
Meppel
Vecht R.
Haarlem
Zwolle
Zandvort
Amsterdam
IJssel R.
Noordwijk-aan-Zee
Lisse
Aalsmeer
Scheveningen
Leiden
Utrecht
Apeldoorn
The Hague
Amersfoort
Hoge Veluwe
National Park
Hoek van Holland
Delft
Gouda
Rijn R.
Arnhem
Rotterdam
Waal R.
Nijmegen
Maas R.
Maas R.
Rhine R.
Breda
GERMANY
Eindhoven
Antwerp
Roermond
Cologne
BELGIUM
Maastricht
Brussels

0   25 miles
0   25 kilometers

www.netherlands.org.au); **Canada,** 350 Albert St., Ste. 2020, Ottawa ON K1R 1A4 (☎613-237-5030; www.netherlandsembassy.ca); **Ireland,** 160 Merrion Rd., Dublin 4 (☎012 69 34 44; www.netherlandsembassy.ie); **New Zealand,** P.O. Box 840, at Ballance and Featherston St., Wellington (☎04 471 63 90; www.netherlandsembassy.co.nz); **UK,** 38 Hyde Park Gate, London SW7 5DP (☎020 75 90 32 00; www.netherlands-embassy.org.uk); **US,** 4200 Linnean Ave., NW, Washington, D.C. 20008 (☎202-244-5300; www.netherlands-embassy.org).

TRANSPORTATION

BY PLANE. Many major airlines fly into Amsterdam's sleek, glassy **Schiphol Airport** (AMS) from Europe, North America, and Australia, including the Dutch carrier **KLM. RyanAir** flies from London-Stansted into secondary airports in Aachen (AAH), Eindhoven (EIN), and Groningen (GRQ), all accessible by rail.

BY TRAIN. The national rail company is **Nederlandse Spoorwegen** (NS; Netherlands Railways; www.ns.nl). *Sneltreinen* are the fastest, while *stoptreinen* make many local stops. One-way tickets are called *enkele reis;* same-day round-trip tickets (*dagretour*) are valid only on the day of purchase, but are roughly 15% cheaper than normal round-trip tickets. *Weekendretour* tickets are not quite as cheap, but are valid from Friday at 7pm through Monday at 4am. **Eurail** is valid in the Netherlands. The **Holland Railpass** (US$80-122, under 26 US$60-96) is good for three or five travel days in any one-month period. Although available in the US, the Holland Railpass is cheaper in the Netherlands at RailEurope offices. **One-day train passes** cost €38.70, about as much as the most expensive one-way domestic fare.

BY BUS. A nationalized fare system covers city buses, trams, and long-distance buses. The country is divided into zones; a trip between destinations in the same zone costs two strips on a *strippenkaart* (strip card), while a trip that traverses two zones will set you back three strips. On buses, tell the driver your destination and he or she will cancel the correct number of strips; on trams and subways, stamp your own *strippenkaart* in a yellow box at the back of the tram or in the subway station. Tram and bus drivers sell cards with two, three, and eight strips, but it's cheaper to buy 15-strip (€6.40) or 45-strip (€18.90) cards at tourist offices, post offices, and some newsstands. *Dagkarten* (day passes) are valid for travel throughout the country (€12.80) and are discounted as *zomerzwerfkaarten* (special summer tickets) during the months of June, July, and August (€8.50).

BY CAR. As a general rule, tourists with a driver's license valid in their home country may use that license to drive in the Netherlands for less than 185 days. The country has well-maintained roadways, although drivers may cringe at high fuel prices and at congestion around Amsterdam, Rotterdam, and The Hague. **Speed limits** are 120kph on motorways, except where posted as 100kph around urban areas. Other main roads call for 80kph, although the limits can drop as low as 30-50kph. The yellow cars of the **Royal Dutch Touring Association** (ANWB) patrol many major roads, and will offer prompt roadside assistance. In the case of a breakdown, call the ANWB (☎ 080 08 88) toll-free from any yellow phone booth.

BY BIKE AND BY THUMB. Cycling is the way to go in the Netherlands—distances between cities are short, the countryside is absolutely flat, and most streets have separate bike lanes. Bikes run €6-7 per day or €25-40 per week. For a database of bike rental shops across the country, visit www.holland.com/global/discover/active/cycling/geninfo/huur.html. **Hitchhiking** is illegal on motorways, but common elsewhere; droves of hitchhikers are common along roads leading out of Amsterdam. Those choosing this mode of transport often take public transportation to a nearby town and then try their luck there. *Let's Go* does not recommend hitchhiking as a safe means of transport.

TOURIST SERVICES AND MONEY

EMERGENCY	Police: ☎ 112. Ambulance: ☎ 112. Fire: ☎ 112.

TOURIST OFFICES. VVV (vay-vay-vay) tourist offices are marked by triangular blue signs. The website www.visitholland.com is also a useful resource.

MONEY. On January 1, 2002, the **euro (€)** replaced the guilder as the unit of currency in the Netherlands. For exchange rates and more info on the euro, see p. 20. A bare-bones day traveling in the Netherlands will cost €35-40; a slightly more comfortable day will run €50-60. All countries who are members of the European Union impose a **Value Added Tax (VAT)** on goods and services purchased within the EU. Prices in the Netherlands already include the country's 19% VAT rate, although partial refunds are available for visitors who are not EU citizens (p. 22). Hotels and restaurants always include a service charge in the bill, so extra tips are appreciated but not necessary. Tip taxi drivers 10%.

BUSINESS HOURS. Banks and **stores** are generally open 9am-5pm on weekdays, although banks in smaller towns may close at 4pm and many stores close for part of Monday. **Supermarkets** stay open until 8pm, and some stores remain open until 9pm on Thursday and Friday. **Museums** generally close on Monday.

COMMUNICATION

PHONE CODES	**Country code: 31. International dialing prefix:** 00. From outside the Netherlands, dial int'l dialing prefix (see inside back cover) + 31 + city code + local number.

TELEPHONES. Some pay phones still accept coins, but phone cards are the rule. KPT and Telfort are the most widely accepted varieties, the former available at post offices and the latter at train stations (from €5). **Mobile phones** are an increasingly popular and economical alternative (p. 35). For directory assistance, dial ☎09 00 80 08; for collect calls, dial ☎08 00 01 01. International direct dial numbers include: **AT&T** (☎0800 022 91 11); **British Telecom** (☎0800 089 00 31); **Canada Direct** (☎0800 022 91 16); **MCI** (☎0800 023 5103); **Sprint** (☎0800 022 91 19); **Telecom New Zealand** (☎0800 022 44 64); **Telstra Australia** (☎0800 022 00 61).

MAIL. Post offices are generally open Monday to Friday 9am-5:30pm, while in larger towns some remain open Thursday night, Friday night, or Saturday 10am-1pm. Mailing a postcard or letter (up to 20g) in the EU or a postcard outside of Europe costs €0.61; letters outside of Europe cost €0.77.

INTERNET ACCESS. Email is easily accessible within the Netherlands. In small towns where Internet access is not listed, try the public library.

ACCOMMODATIONS AND CAMPING

NETHERLANDS	❶	❷	❸	❹	❺
ACCOMMODATIONS	under €30	€30-50	€50-70	€70-100	over €100

VVV offices supply accommodation listings, and can almost always reserve rooms (for a €2-5 fee). **Private rooms** cost about two-thirds as much as hotels, but they are harder to find; check with the VVV. During July and August, many cities add a tourist tax (€1-2) to the price of all rooms. The country's 30 **HI youth hostels,** run by **Stayokay,** are dependably clean and modern. Visit www.stayokay.com for profiles of individual hostels and booking information. **Camping** is available across the country, although campsites tend to be crowded during the summer months; **City-Camps Holland** has a network of 17 well-maintained sites. Visit www.stadscamping.nl/algemeen/en for more information.

FOOD AND DRINK

NETHERLANDS	❶	❷	❸	❹	❺
FOOD	under €7	€7-10	€10-14	€14-20	over €20

Traditional Dutch cuisine is usually hearty, heavy, meaty, and wholesome. Expect bread and cheese for breakfast and lunch, and generous portions of meats and fishes for dinner, traditionally the only hot meal of the day. Popular seafood choices include all sorts of grilled fish and shellfish, fish stews, and raw herring. To round out a truly authentic Dutch meal (especially in May and June), ask for white asparagus, served with potatoes, ham, and eggs. Light snacks include *tostjes* (hot grilled cheese sandwiches, sometimes with ham) and *broodjes* (light, cold sandwiches), while colonial history has added Surinamese and Indonesian cuisine into the mix. Wash it all down with a small, foamy glass of Heineken or Amstel.

HOLIDAYS AND FESTIVALS

Holidays: New Year's Day (Jan. 1); Good Friday (Mar. 25); Easter Sunday and Monday (Mar. 27-28); Liberation Day (May 5); Ascension Day (May 5); Whitsunday and Whitmonday (May 15-16); Christmas Day (Dec. 25); Boxing Day (Dec. 26).

Festivals: Koninginnedag (Queen's Day; Apr. 30) turns the country into a huge carnival. The Holland Festival (in June) features more than 30 productions in a massive celebration of the arts. Bloemen Corso (Flower Parade; first Sa in Sept.) runs from Aalsmeer to Amsterdam. Many historical canal houses and windmills are open to the public for National Monument Day (2nd Sa in Sept.). The Cannabis Cup (November) celebrates the magical mystery weed that brings millions of visitors to Amsterdam every year.

FACTS AND FIGURES: THE NETHERLANDS

Official Name: Kingdom of the Netherlands.

Capital: Amsterdam.

Major Cities: The Hague, Rotterdam, Utrecht.

Population: 16,320,000.

Land Area: 34,000 sq. km.

Time Zone: GMT+1.

Language: Dutch; English is spoken almost universally.

Religions: Catholic (31%), Protestant (21%), Muslim (4%).

AMSTERDAM
☎ 020

Amsterdam (pop. 730,000) is not merely the city of garish sin. While the aroma of marijuana smoke does waft out of coffeeshops and prostitutes do pose provocatively behind windows bathed in red light, these vices have to be understood in a broader context. The same culture of acceptance that tolerates cannabis use and a commercial sex trade has also turned the city into a multicultural capital; countless immigrants from Spain to Suriname have called this city home, and today less than 45% of its population identify themselves as ethnically Dutch. A Golden Age of art flourished in Amsterdam, and art remains in many forms—Rembrandt's shadowy portraits, Vermeer's luminous women, and the post-Impressionist swirls of van Gogh's brush. Tall, narrow canal houses sit primly along long waterways, while subtle remnants of WWII Nazi occupation give pause to the observant. In short, this supremely relaxed capital of northern Europe is alluring for all sorts of travelers: eagerly experimenting youth, pot pilgrims, businesspeople, art aficionados, and history buffs. Each group, in turn, would do well to remember that although Amsterdam *is* a place for indulging desires, the best trip to Amsterdam isn't necessarily the one you won't remember.

▣ TRANSPORTATION

Flights: Schiphol Airport (AMS; ☎ 0800 72 44 74 65). Light rail **sneltrains** connect the airport to Centraal Station (20min., every 10min., €3.20).

Trains: Centraal Station, Stationspl. 1 (☎ 09 00 92 92, €0.30 per min.; www.ns.nl), at the northern end of the Damrak. To: **Brussels** (2½-3hr., 1-2 per hr., €32); **Groningen** (2½hr., 2 per hr., €26); **Haarlem** (20min., 6-7 per hr., €3); **The Hague** (50min., 2-3 per hr., €9); **Leiden** (35min., 2-4 per hr., €7); **Paris** (4hr., 10 per day, €90); **Rotterdam** (1hr., 1 per hr., €12); **Utrecht** (40min., 3-8 per hr., €6).

Buses: Trains are quicker, but the **GVB** (see below) will direct you to a bus stop for domestic destinations not on a rail line. **Muiderpoort** (2 blocks east of Oosterpark) sends buses east; **Marnixstation** (at the corner of Marnixstr. and Kinkerstr.) west; and the **Stationsplein depot** north and south.

Public Transportation: GVB (☎09 00 92 92, €0.30 per min.), on Stationspl. in front of Centraal Station. Open M-F 7am-9pm, Sa-Su 8am-9pm. **Tram, metro,** and **bus** lines radiate from Centraal Station. Trams are most convenient for inner-city travel; the metro leads to farther-out neighborhoods. Normal public transportation runs daily 6am-12:30am; **night buses** traverse the city 12:30am-6am—pick up a schedule and map at the GVB. *Strippenkaarten* are used on all public transportation in Amsterdam; 2 strips (€1.40) will get you to almost all sights within the city center and include unlimited transfers for 1hr. *Strippenkaarten* are cheapest when bought in bulk (up to bundles of 45) and are available everywhere, especially at newsstands and VVV offices.

Bike Rental: Frederic Rent a Bike, Brouwersgr. 78 (☎624 55 09; www.frederic.nl), in the Shipping Quarter. Bikes €10 per day, €40 per week. Lock, theft insurance, and personalized map of the city included. Open daily 9am-6pm. Cash only. **MacBike Rentals,** Stationspl. 12 (☎620 09 85; www.macbike.nl), has 2 locations in the south of the city at Weteringschans 2, near Museumpl., and Mr. Visserpl. 2. Bikes €6.50-9.75 per day, plus €3-5 for theft insurance. €50 deposit. Open daily 9am-5:45pm. AmEx/MC/V.

◢ ORIENTATION

Welcome to Amsterdam, the "Venice of the North," whose confusing neighborhoods can be easily explored by following the horseshoe shape of its canals. Water runs in concentric circles, radiating from Centraal Station. The **Singel** canal runs around the **Centrum,** which includes the **Oude Zijde,** the infamous **Red Light District,** and the **Nieuwe Zijde.** In a space not even a kilometer in diameter, brothels, bars, clubs, and tourists compete for oxygen with clouds of pungent marijuana smoke. The next three canals are the **Herengracht,** the **Keizersgracht,** and the **Prinsengracht,** lined by streets of the same name. The land around them is known as the **Canal Ring,** home to Renaissance canal houses and classy nightlife, including bars and traditional *bruin cafés* (brown cafes). On the eastern end of the Canal Ring, **Rembrandtplein** is the city's gay district and home to some raucous nightlife, while on the western end, at the corner of Leidsegracht and Singelgracht, **Leidseplein** boasts some of the city's best restaurants. Just over the Singel, **Museumplein** is home to the city's famous art museums as well as the sprawling **Vondelpark.** Farther out lie residential neighborhoods: to the west the **Jordaan, Oud-West,** and **Westerpark;** to the east **Plantage** and the **Jodenbuurt;** and to the south **De Pijp.** These densely populated districts have their own museums and neighborhood eateries, many of which possess a rough charm that souvenir stands have drained from the city center.

◢ PRACTICAL INFORMATION

TOURIST, FINANCIAL, AND LOCAL SERVICES

Tourist Office: VVV, Stationspl. 10 (☎0900 400 40 40, €0.55 per min.), to the left when exiting Centraal Station. Books rooms for a €3.50 fee and sells maps for €2. Open daily 9am-5pm. **Branches** inside Centraal Station (open M-Sa 8am-7:45pm, Su 9am-5pm) and Leidsepl. 1 (open M-Th 9am-6pm, F-Sa 9am-7pm, Su 9am-5pm).

Budget Travel: Eurolines, Rokin 10 (☎560 87 88; www.eurolines.nl), books coach travel throughout Europe. Office open M-F 9:30am-5:30pm, Sa 10am-4pm. Phone bookings M-F 9am-7pm, Sa 9am-5pm.

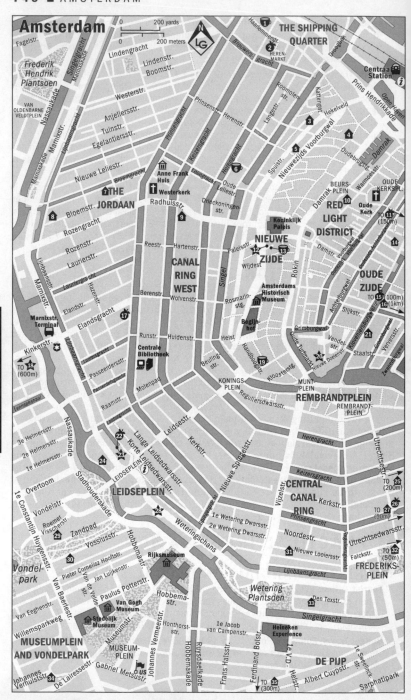

Amsterdam

Consulates: All foreign embassies are in **The Hague** (p. 766). **UK Consulate,** Koningslaan 44 (☎676 43 43). Open M-F 9am-noon and 2-5:30pm. **US Consulate,** Museumpl. 19 (☎575 53 09). Open M-F 8:30am-11:30am.

Currency Exchange: American Express, Damrak 66, offers the best rates, with no commission on AmEx traveler's checks and a €4 flat fee for all non-euro cash and non-AmEx traveler's checks. Open M-F 9am-5pm, Sa 9am-noon.

GLBT Resources: Pink Point (☎428 10 70; www.pinkpoint.org), a kiosk in front of the Westerkerk, provides info on nightlife and events. Open daily noon-6pm. The **Gay and Lesbian Switchboard** (☎623 65 65) takes calls daily 10am-10pm.

English-Language Bookstores: The Book Exchange, Kloveniersburgwal 58, has a good, if pricey, selection of used books, particularly fiction and poetry. Bring in old books to trade. Open M-Sa 10am-6pm, Su 11:30am-4pm. **Waterstone's,** Kalverstr. 152, sells new titles and is the biggest English-language bookstore in the country. Open M 10am-6pm, Tu-W and F 9am-7pm, Th 9am-9pm, Sa 10am-7pm, Su 11am-6pm.

Laundromats: Happy Inn, Warmoesstr. 30 (☎624 84 64). 5kg load €3, dry €1. Also offers drop-off service (€8-10 per load). Open M-W and F 8am-7pm, Th 8am-9pm, Sa 8am-10pm, Su 9am-10pm. Drop-off hours M-F 9am-6pm. In the south of the city, head for **Be-Jo,** Kerkstr. 276 (☎023 12 26). 5kg load €3.50, dry €0.50 for 15min. Open M-F 8am-7pm, Sa 10am-7pm, Su 11am-7pm.

EMERGENCY AND COMMUNICATIONS

Emergency: ☎112.

Police: Headquarters, Elandsgr. 117 (☎08 00 88 44), at the intersection with Marnixstr. Call here for the **Rape Crisis Department.**

Crisis Lines: General counseling at **Telephone Helpline** (☎675 75 75). Open 24hr. For drug counseling, call **Jellinek Clinic** (☎408 77 77). Open M-F 9am-5pm. For phone counseling about sexually transmitted diseases, call the **STD Line,** Groenburgwal 44 (☎555 58 22). Free testing clinic. Open for calls M-F 8am-noon and 1-4pm.

Medical Assistance: For hospital care, **Academisch Medisch Centrum,** Meibergdreef 9 (☎566 91 11), is easily accessible by bus #59, 60, 120, or 158 from Centraal Station (ask the driver to announce the medical center). **Kruispost Medisch Helpcentrum,** Oudezijds Voorburgwal 129 (☎624 90 31), is a walk-in clinic offering first aid to non-insured travelers daily 10am-12:30pm and 7-9pm. €25 per visit. For 24hr. medical help, call **Centrale Doktorsdienst** (☎592 34 34).

24hr. Pharmacy: A hotline (☎694 87 09) will direct you to the nearest pharmacy, including 24hr. pharmacies after hours.

Internet Access: Many coffeeshops and hostels offer Internet access for customers and guests, charging €1-2 for 30min. **easyInternetCafe,** Reguliersbreestr. 22 and Damrak 34, generally offers 26min. of access for €1, although rates vary according to demand. Open 24hr. Free 30min. slots are also available at the **Centrale Bibliotheek** (☎523 09 00; www.oba.nl), Prinsengracht 587, although lines sometimes form on rainy days. Open M 1-9pm, Tu-Th 10am-9pm, F-Sa 10am-5pm, Su 1-5pm.

Post Office: Singel 250, at Radhuisstr. Address mail to be held in the following format: First name, SURNAME, *Poste Restante,* Singel 250, 1016 AB, Amsterdam, THE NETH-ERLANDS. Open M-W and F 9am-6pm, Th 9am-8pm, Sa 10am-1:30pm.

⌂ ACCOMMODATIONS

The chaos of the Red Light District prompts accommodations near **Centraal Station** to enforce strong security measures, while hostels and hotels near **Museumplein** and out in the **Jordaan** can afford to be more laissez-faire. These locations are close to bars and coffeeshops and are a mere 2min. by tram from the heart of the city. Accommodations in the heart of the **Red Light District** (surrounded by the Oude Zijde) are often bars with beds over them. Before signing up for a bunk, consider just how much noise and drug use you can tolerate from your neighbors.

NIEUWE ZIJDE, OUDE ZIJDE, AND THE RED LIGHT DISTRICT

▓ **Anna Youth Hostel,** Spuistr. 6 (☎620 11 55). Simply the most beautiful hostel in the city, with high ceilings and shimmering drapery. Quiet, drug-free ambience is surprising given its location. Sheets, towel, and small safe-deposit box included. Free Internet. 2-night min. stay on weekends. Lockout 1-5pm. No reservations; arrive before 11am for a room. Closed during part of Dec. Dorms €20; doubles €70-80. Cash only. ❶

▓ **Flying Pig Downtown,** Nieuwendijk 100 (☎420 68 22; www.flyingpig.nl). Helpful staff, a great location, and the happening, funky lounge overlooking the street keep backpack-ers coming year after year. Kitchen available. Breakfast and sheets included. Free Inter-net. Key deposit €10. Online reservations strongly recommended. Dorms €23-29; queen-sized beds for two €34-43; singles €38; doubles €76. AmEx/MC/V. ❶

▓ **Hotel Winston,** Warmoesstr. 129 (☎623 13 80; www.winston.nl). Rooms painted by local artists and designers make every room feel like an installation art piece. Breakfast included. Singles €60-72; doubles €74-96; triples €113-128. AmEx/MC/V. ❸

StayOkay Amsterdam Stadsdoelen (HI), Kloveniersburgwal 97 (☎624 68 32; www.stayokay.com/stadsdoelen). Clean, drug-free canalside lodgings in a quiet cor-ner of Oude Zijde. Kitchen available. Breakfast and sheets included. Laundry €4.50. Internet €1 per 12min. Reception 7am-midnight. Dorms €20. Nonmembers add €2.50. AmEx/MC/V. ❶

Tourist Inn, Spuistr. 52 (☎421 58 41; www.tourist-inn.nl). Sparkling-clean bathrooms adjoin comfortable rooms with hardwood floors and rose-tinted walls. Breakfast and sheets included. Call ahead for a firm price quote. Dorms €20-35; singles and doubles €60-100; triples and quads €105-150. AmEx/MC/V. ❶

The Shelter City, Barndesteeg 21 (☎625 32 30; www.shelter.nl). A bastion of virtue amid the city's temptations, this Christian hostel welcomes guests of all faiths. You can't miss the brightly lit sign when exiting Centraal Station. No drugs. Under 35 only. Breakfast and sheets included. Locker deposit €5. Internet €0.50 per 20min. Curfew M-Th and Su midnight, F-Sa 1am. Dorms €18.50. MC/V; 5% credit card surcharge. ❶

SHIPPING QUARTER, CANAL RING WEST, AND THE JORDAAN

Hotel van Onna, Bloemgr. 104 (☎626 58 01; www.vanonna.nl). Get a peaceful night's rest in a restored historic building, situated on the prettiest canal in the Jordaan. Small but very comfortable rooms with shiny white bathrooms. Breakfast included. Reception 8am-11pm. Singles €40; doubles €80; triples €120; quads €160. Cash only. ❷

Hotel Clemens, Raadhuisstr. 39 (☎624 60 89; www.clemenshotel.nl). Each renovated, elegant suite has a safe for valuables. Breakfast €7. Key deposit €20. Book well in advance. Min. stay 3 nights on weekends. Singles €55; doubles €70, €110 with bath; triples €125/€150. Cash only for singles and rooms without bath. AmEx/MC/V. ❸

The Shelter Jordan, Bloemstr. 179 (☎624 47 17; www.shelter.nl). Religious but not proselytizing, this Christian hostel provides a quiet retreat. No smoking or alcohol. Under 35 only. Breakfast included. Lockers €5 deposit. Internet €0.50 per 20min. Curfew 2am. July-Aug. dorms €18.50; low season €16.50-17. MC/V. ❶

LEIDSEPLEIN AND MUSEUMPLEIN

StayOkay Amsterdam Vondelpark (HI), Zandpad 5 (☎589 89 96; www.stayokay.com/vondelpark). One of the most palatial hostels in the StayOkay empire, in a lovely parkside location. Breakfast and sheets included. Lockers €2. Laundry €4.50. Internet €5 per hr. Reception 7:30am-midnight. Reserve well in advance. Dorms €23-28; doubles €77. Low season reduced rates. €2.50 HI discount. AmEx/MC/V. ❶

Flying Pig Palace, Vossiusstr. 46-47 (☎400 41 87; www.flyingpig.nl). Laid-back, friendly attitude with views of Vondelpark. Online bookings don't guarantee you the room you reserved, so be prepared to switch rooms or pay extra for an upgrade. Popular bar downstairs. Under 35 only. Breakfast and sheets included. Free Internet. Reception 8am-9pm. Max. stay 7 nights. Dorms €22-27; queen-sized beds for two €33-41; doubles €62; triples €87. Low season reduced rates. AmEx/MC/V. ❶

Quentin Hotel, Leidsekade 89 (☎626 21 87). A chic lobby leads to white, almost minimalist rooms with canal views. Reception 24hr. Singles €40, with bath €70; doubles €80-100; triples €125. AmEx/MC/V; 4% credit card surcharge. ❷

Bema Hotel, Concertgebouwplein 19b (☎679 13 96; www.bemahotel.com). Charming 7-room hotel with skylights and neo-hippie style. Breakfast included. Reception 8am-midnight. Singles €50-65; doubles €70-85; triples €85-120; quads €105-160. AmEx/MC/V; 5% credit card surcharge. ❸

CENTRAL CANAL RING AND REMBRANDTPLEIN

Hemp Hotel, Frederikspl. 15 (☎625 44 25; www.hemp-hotel.com). Only 5 rooms, but each is lovingly done up to celebrate one of the world's major hemp-producing regions: Afghanistan, the Caribbean, India, Morocco, and Tibet. Everything is made of hemp—bedclothes, curtains, and even soap. Breakfast included. Reception 11am-3am. Singles €50; doubles €65-70. MC/V; 5% credit card surcharge. ❸

Radio Inn Youth Hostel, Utrechtsedwarsstr. 79 (☎625 03 45; www.radioinn.nl). Lots of character at this cheerfully idiosyncratic hostel—somewhere between a 70s garage sale and a budget hotel. Housed in an old radio store, the homey lobby contains mounds of defunct gadgets, as well as 2 resident cats. Kitchen available. Laundry free. Dorms €21; singles €35; doubles €52; triples €69; quads €80. Cash only. ❶

Euphemia Budget Hotel, Fokke Simonszstr. 1-9 (☎622 90 45; www.euphemiahotel.com). Quiet, bright budget digs draw an older crowd to this former monastery. Internet €1 per 15min. Reception 8am-11pm. Dorms €30; doubles €80; triples €105. Low season reduced rates. AmEx/MC/V; 5% credit card surcharge. ❷

Hotel Asterisk, Den Texstr. 16 (☎626 23 96; www.asteriskhotel.nl). Quiet, friendly hotel with clean rooms that verge on quaint. All rooms with phone and safe. Breakfast included. Min. stay 3 nights on weekends. Singles €44-48; doubles €65-115; triples €130-136; quads €150. MC/V; credit card surcharge 4%. ❷

DE PIJP, JODENBUURT, AND THE PLANTAGE

Hotel Fantasia, Nieuwe Keizersgr. 16 (☎623 82 59; www.fantasia-hotel.com). Clean, friendly, family-owned establishment in an 18th-century house on a quiet canal. Ask for a room on the top floor. Breakfast included. Reception 8am-10pm. Closed Dec. 14-27 and Jan. 6-Mar. 1. Singles €55-65; doubles €84-100; triples €120; quads €140. AmEx/MC/V; 3% credit card surcharge. ❸

Bicycle Hotel, Van Ostadestr. 123 (☎679 34 52; www.bicyclehotel.com). Clean digs, spotless bathrooms, and a leafy garden. Bicycle-friendly hotel furnishes guests with a bike garage and trip recommendations. Breakfast included. Free Internet. Singles €65; doubles €70-75, with bath €105; triples €95/€130; quads €150. AmEx/MC/V; 4% credit card surcharge. ❸

Hotel Pension Kitty, Plantage Middenlaan 40 (☎622 68 19). Look out for the small sign. Gentle, aged proprietress provides for those seeking a peaceful stay in this historic house. Grandmotherly warmth and tranquility abound. No children. Singles €50; doubles €60-70; triples €75. Cash only. ❸

◘ FOOD

Cheap restaurants cluster around **Leidseplein, Rembrandtplein,** and the **Spui.** Cafes, especially in the **Jordaan,** serve inexpensive sandwiches (€2-5) and good meat-and-potatoes fare (€5.50-9). Bakeries line **Utrechtsestraat,** south of Prinsengracht, and De Pijp is home to a collection of ethnic restaurants with budget-friendly prices. **Albert Heijn** supermarkets are scattered throughout Amsterdam; there is a large one near Dam Square, at Nieuwezijds Voorburgwal 226, and another off of Museumplein, at Van Baerlestr. 33a. (Both open M-Sa 8am-10pm, Su 11am-7pm.)

NIEUWE ZIJDE AND OUDE ZIJDE

◪ In de Waag, Nieuwmarkt 4 (☎452 77 72; www.indewaag.nl). In the late 1400s, this castle served as the eastern entrance to the city. Today, sandwiches and salads (€4-8.50) are served on the patio for lunch. For heavier fare, come back at night for richly flavored Italian, French, and Norwegian specialties served by the light of hundreds of candles. Entrees €17-22. Open M-Th and Su 10am-midnight, F-Sa 10am-1am; often open until 3am on busy evenings. Kitchen closes at 10:30pm. AmEx/MC/V. ❷

Broodje Bert, Singel 321 (☎623 03 82). The cast of Sesame Street decorates the walls of this canalside eatery, popular with locals for omelettes (€4.50-5) and open-faced sandwiches (€3-4) worthy of a knife and fork. Open daily 8am-7pm. Cash only. ❶

Pannenkoekenhuis Upstairs, Grimburgwal 2 (☎626 56 03). Scale the steep staircase to this tiny nook, serving sweet, filling pancakes (€5-9) that are the talk of the town. Open M-F noon-7pm, Sa noon-6pm, Su noon-5pm. Cash only. ❶

De Keuken van 1870, Spuistr. 4 (☎620 40 18). Doling out hearty soup to the city's working class since the late 19th century, this kitchen recently reopened after renovations with its mission unchanged: serving heavy, traditional Dutch fare at unexpectedly cheap prices. Menu of the day €7.50. Open M-Sa noon-midnight. AmEx/MC/V. ❷

Taste of Culture, Zeedijk 109 (☎638 14 66). Many an eating contest has been inspired by the gauntlet that Taste of Culture throws down: all the Chinese food you can eat in 1hr., €7.50. Open M-W noon-11pm, Th-Su until midnight. Another location at Rokin 152 (☎638 12 49). Cash only. ❷

SHIPPING QUARTER, CANAL RING WEST, AND THE JORDAAN

▨ **Der Bolhoed,** Prinsengr. 60-62 (☎626 18 03). An Edenic decor, complete with murals of squash and pumpkin vines, sets the tone for fresh, flavorful vegetarian and vegan fare. Lunch menu €4-9. Pastas, casseroles, and daily special €12.50-15. Fresh-squeezed juices €2-4. Dinner reservations a must. Open daily noon-10pm, last reservation 9pm. Cash only. ❸

Harlem: Drinks and Soulfood, Haarlemmerstr. 77 (☎330 14 98). When American-style soul food collides with Cajun and Caribbean flavors, the crowds arrive. Enormous plates of nachos (from €6) will sate the most grievous case of post-coffeeshop munchies. Soups and sandwiches €5-8. Open M-Th 10am-1am, F-Sa 10am-3am, Su 11am-1am. Kitchen closes at 10pm. Cash only. ❷

Lunchcafe Nielson, Berenstr. 19 (☎330 60 06). Prop yourself up on one of the stools by the window and dig into the breakfast menu (€7.50), served all day. Sandwiches €4.50. Omelettes €5-7. Open Tu-F 8am-4pm, Sa 8am-6pm, Su 9am-5pm. Kitchen closes 30min. before restaurant. MC/V. ❶

The Pancake Bakery, Prinsengr. 191 (☎625 13 33). Pricier than Pannenkoekenhuis Upstairs (see above), but offers more elbow room and can seat larger parties with ease. Vintage photographs adorn the dark brick walls. Omelettes €5-8. Pancakes €8-11. Open daily noon-9:30pm. AmEx/MC/V. ❷

LEIDSEPLEIN AND MUSEUMPLEIN

▨ **Eat at Jo's,** Marnixstr. 409 (☎624 17 77; www.melkweg.nl), inside Melkweg (see **Night-life,** below). Jo may hail from the American Midwest, but her restaurant's multi-ethnic menu and arty, modular decor suggest that she's seen the world outside Milwaukee. Large bowls of soup (€3.40) make for a satisfying lunch, while vegetarian and meat entrees (€11-14) leave the dinner crowd content. Open W-Su noon-9pm. Cash only. ❸

Cafe Vertigo, Vondelpark 3 (☎612 30 21; www.vertigo.nl). Pop over to Vertigo's tree-lined terrace for some sunshine before you get too pasty watching movies at the Filmmu-seum next door. The dinner menu's pricier than it needs to be, but light sandwiches (€4) and pastries (€2) hit the spot around mid-afternoon. Open Apr.-Sept. daily 10am-1am; Oct.-Mar. M-F 11am-1am, Sa-Su 10am-1am. MC/V. ❶

Het Blauwe Theehuis, Vondelpark 5 (☎662 02 54; www.blauwetheehuis.nl). Peering through the trees in Vondelpark, you may glimpse a blue structure shaped like a flying saucer, brimming with a convivial crowd. Reach for your ray gun, or else pull up a chair on this teahouse's outdoor terrace. Tea €1.70. Sandwiches €4. DJs spin July-Aug. F night. Open M-Th and Su 9am-midnight, F-Sa 9am-2am. Kitchen closes at 10pm. Cash only. ❶

Go Sushi, Johannes Verhulststr. 35 (☎471 00 35). Tiny sushi joint in a city that tends to prefer spicy South Asian fare to the more restrained flavors of Japan. Sit on stools by a bay window overlooking a quiet residential street. 3 pieces of *maki* €1.90-2.60. *Nigiri* €1.20-2.95. 10-piece sushi "lunchbox" €9. Open M-F noon-7pm. Cash only. ❷

CENTRAL CANAL RING AND REMBRANDTPLEIN

Coffee & Jazz, Utrechtsestr. 113 (☎624 58 51). Dutch-Indonesian fusion turns colonialism on its ear, as fruity *pannenkoeken* (€10) share the menu with tender lamb and chicken satay (€9-15). Nurse a cup of strong, dark coffee by the window on a rainy day, or talk a waiter into taking out the glass once some sunshine arrives. Open Tu-F 9:30am-11pm. Cash only. ❸

Maoz Falafel, Regulierbreestr. 45 (☎624 92 90). Crisp, flavorful falafel and all-you-can-stack toppings bar make this string of kiosks a reliable bet for budget meals on the go. Falafel €3.50. Other locations: outside Centraal Station; Ferdinand Bolstr. 67; Leidsestr. 85; Muntpl. 1. Open daily at least 11am-11pm; hours vary by location. ❶

THE NETHERLANDS

Lanskroon, Singel 385 (☎623 77 43). Traditional Dutch pastries, including a cinnamon croissant (€0.90) that disappears from the menu at noon. If you're a late riser, try the *vijgenwafel* (2 thin, crispy waffles with a sweet syrup in the middle; €1.35). Open Tu-W 8am-5:30pm, Th-Sa 8am-8pm, Su 10am-8pm. Cash only. ❶

DE PIJP, JODENBUURT, AND THE PLANTAGE

Soup En Zo, Jodenbreestr. 94a (☎422 22 43). Once this tiny soupery lures you in with their free sample cups, there's no escaping. Choose between several soups and sizes (€2.20-5.50), and then dress up your broth with free bread and fresh toppings from coriander and dill to cheese and nuts. Another location at Nieuwe Spiegelstr. 54. Open M-F 11am-8pm, Sa 11am-7pm, Su 1-7pm. Cash only. ❶

Zagros, Albert Cuypstr. 50 (☎670 04 61). Armenia, Iran, Iraq, Syria, and Turkey have all left their imprint on earthy Kurdish cuisine. Spartan Zagros serves up tender lamb dishes (€10-14) and veggie options (€10.50) in a quiet, candlelit dining room. Open daily 3pm-midnight. AmEx/MC/V. ❸

Peppino Gelateria, 1e Sweelinckstr. 16 (☎676 49 10). Lines out the door testify to the popularity of this gelato shack. Gelato from €0.75 per scoop. Cappuccino €1.80. Open M-F 11am-11pm, Sa 10am-11pm, Su noon-11pm. Cash only. ❶

⑥ SIGHTS

Amsterdam is fairly compact, so tourists can easily explore the area from the Rijksmuseum to the Red Light District on foot. For those not inclined to pedestrian navigation, the tram system will get you to any of the city's major sights within minutes. For a peaceful, if pricey, view of the city from the water, **Museumboot Canal Cruise** allows you to hop on and off along its loop from the VVV to the Anne Frank Huis, the Bloemenmarkt, the Rijksmuseum, Waterlooplein, and the old shipyard. (☎530 10 90. Boats pass every 15-40min. Day pass €16.)

NIEUWE ZIJDE, OUDE ZIJDE, AND THE RED LIGHT DISTRICT

THE RED LIGHT DISTRICT. No trip to Amsterdam would be complete without witnessing the notorious spectacle that is the Red Light District. After dark, the area actually takes on a red radiance—sex theaters throw open their doors, and the main streets are thick with people gawking at lingerie-clad prostitutes pressing themselves against the windows where they work; **Warmoesstraat** and **Oudezijds Achterburgwal** boast wall-to-wall brothels. There are also **sex shows,** in which actors perform strictly choreographed fantasies on stage; the most famous live sex show takes place at **Casa Rosso,** Oudezijds Achterburgwal 106-108, where €25 will buy you admission to eight or nine consecutive acts and €40 includes complimentary drinks. The show is quite tame, and probably not worth the money. Still, the Casa's **marble penis fountain** across from the theater remains the Red Light District's most recognizable landmark. (☎627 89 54; www.janot.com. *Afternoon shows daily 1:30-7:30pm. €20. Evening shows M-Th and Su 7:30pm-2am, F-Sa 7:30pm-3am.*)

OUDE KERK. Amsterdam's Old Church may come as a welcome, wholesome shock, smack in the middle of the otherwise lurid Red Light District. The stunning structure began as a narrow, rude basilica around 1300 and took on new features well into the 16th century. Today, Oude Kerk's enormous interior and magnificent stained-glass windows host photography and modern art exhibitions. At the head of the church is the massive Vater-Müller organ, built in 1724 and still played for public concerts every Saturday or Sunday, depending on the week. Check the schedule posted in the church. (*Oudekerkspl. 23.* ☎625 82 84; www.oudekerk.nl. *Open M-Sa 11am-5pm, Su 1-5pm. €4, students €3. Exhibitions usually €5. Concerts €6, students €5.*)

NIEUWMARKT. On the border between the Oude Zijde and the Jodenbuurt, Nieuwmarkt is worth a visit simply to take a look at the **Waag,** Amsterdam's largest surviving medieval building. Dating from the 15th century, the Waag was one of Amsterdam's fortified city gates and later housed the Surgeons Guild's amphitheater. Public dissections and private anatomy lessons were once held there, as Rembrandt's *The Anatomy Lesson of Dr. Tulp* famously depicts.

DAM SQUARE AND KONINKLIJK PALEIS. The **Koninklijk Paleis** (Royal Palace) was completed in 1655 and functioned as the town hall until Louis Napoleon had it renovated to better look the part of a royal residence. Today Queen Beatrix still uses the building for official receptions. The palace's indisputable highlight is the **Citizen's Hall,** designed to replicate the universe in a single room. Across the large Dam Square is the Dutch **Nationaal Monument,** unveiled on May 4, 1956, to honor Dutch victims of WWII. Inside the 21m white stone obelisk is soil from all 12 of Holland's provinces as well as the Dutch East Indies. *(Koninklijk Paleis ☎ 620 40 60; www.koninklijkhuis.nl. Open daily July-Aug. 11am-5pm; low season hours vary. €4.50.)*

BEGIJNHOF AND SPUI. You don't have to take vows to enter this secluded courtyard—the 14th-century home of the Beguines, a sect of religiously devoted laywomen—but you will have to get up early. Begijnhof's rose-lined gardens and beautifully manicured lawns afford a welcome respite from the excesses of the Nieuwe Zijde. *(Open daily July-Aug. 8am-1pm; Sept.-June 9am-5pm. Free.)* Just to the south, Spui (pronounced "spow") is a tree-lined square perfect for lounging on a summer afternoon. Walled in by bookstores, Spui is home to a Friday book market as well as a Sunday art market.

CANAL RING WEST AND THE JORDAAN

WESTERKERK. This stunning Protestant church was designed by Roman Catholic architect Hendrick de Keyser and completed in 1631. It is one of the last structures to be built in the Dutch Renaissance style, although the bare, white interior raises the question of whether Classicism was such a bad idea after all. Rembrandt is believed to be buried here, though his exact resting place has not yet been located. Climb the **Westerkerkstoren** tower in a 30min. tour for a great view of the city. *(Prinsengr. 281. ☎ 624 77 66. Church open July-Aug. M-Sa 11am-3pm; Apr.-June and Sept. M-F 11am-3pm. Free. Tower open M-Sa 10am-5:30pm. €5. Tours every 30min.)*

HOMOMONUMENT. **Homomonument,** in front of Westerkerk, serves as a memorial to people of all genders persecuted for being anything other than happily heterosexual. Since 1987, the monument has stood in the center of Amsterdam as a testament to the strength and resilience of the city's queer community. Karin Daan's design, three pink granite triangles, allude to the emblem that homosexuals were forced to wear in Nazi concentration camps. During Amsterdam Pride, held in the first week of August, the monument takes on a happier cast, drawing DJs and performers for a four-night "Summer Camp" party.

LEIDSEPLEIN AND MUSEUMPLEIN

LEIDSEPLEIN. Leidseplein proper is a crush of street musicians, blaring neon lights, and open-air urinals. Daytime finds the square packed with shoppers, smokers, and drinkers lining the sidewalks around the square. When night falls, tourists and locals emerge in packs of skin-tight jeans and greased-down hair. **Max Euweplein,** a square along Weteringschans named for the famous Dutch chess master, sports an enormous chess board with people-sized pieces.

VONDELPARK. With meandering walkways skirting meadows and rose gardens, this English-style park is a lovely meeting place for children, seniors, soccer players, and stoners alike. Bikers and skaters traverse the 1.5km paved path. Named after 17th-century poet and playwright Joost van den Vondel, Vondelpark is home to the open-air **Openluchttheater** (☎ 673 14 99; www.openluchttheater.nl), where visitors can enjoy free summer concerts from Wednesday through Sunday. Check the schedule posted beside the theater. *(In the southwestern corner of the city, outside the Singelgr. A short walk across the canal and to the left from the Leidsepl.)*

CENTRAL CANAL RING AND REMBRANDTPLEIN

CENTRAL CANAL RING. You haven't seen Amsterdam until you've spent some time wandering the Central Canal Ring, the city's highest rent district and arguably its most beautiful. Collectively, **Prinsengracht** (Prince's canal), **Keizersgracht** (Emperor's canal), and **Herengracht** (Gentlemen's canal) are known as the *gracht-engordel* (literally "canal girdle"). The Ring is home to some of Amsterdam's most important and breathtaking architecture, particularly on a stretch of the Herengrt. between Leidsegrt. and Vijzelstr. known as the **Golden Bend** for its wide, lavish homes. *(Over the Singel and just south of Centrum.)*

REMBRANDTPLEIN. Rembrandtplein proper consists of a grass rectangle surrounded by scattered flowerbeds. A bronze likeness of the famed master, Rembrandt van Rijn, peers at the hordes of out-of-towners who elbow their way into the bars and cafes in the surrounding area. South and west of the square you'll find **Reguliersdwarsstraat,** ground zero for Amsterdam's gay nightlife. *(In the northeastern corner of the Central Canal Ring, just south of the Amstel.)*

DE PIJP, JODENBUURT, AND THE PLANTAGE

▧ HEINEKEN EXPERIENCE. Heineken stopped producing beer at their original Amsterdam brewery in 1988, opting to turn the place into a sort of multimedia amusement park devoted to their green-bottled lager. A visit includes three beers and a free gift. *(Heinekenpl. ☎ 523 96 66; www.heinekenexperience.com. Open Tu-Su 10am-6pm; last entry at 5pm. Guests under 18 must be accompanied by a parent. €10.)*

PORTUGEES-ISRAELIETISCHE SYNAGOGUE. This beautifully maintained Portuguese synagogue dates to 1675, when it was founded by Jews fleeing the Spanish Inquisition. It has remained largely unchanged since then and still holds services every Saturday at 9am. *(Mr. Visserpl. 1-3. ☎ 624 53 51; www.esnoga.com. Open Apr.-Oct. M-F and Su 10am-4pm; Nov.-Mar. M-Th and Su 10am-4pm, F 10am-3pm. €6.50.)*

HOLLANDSCHE SCHOUWBURG. In 1941, Nazi occupiers converted this historic theater into the Joodsche Schouwburg, the sole establishment to which the city's Jewish performers and patrons were granted access. Before long, the building took on a more sinister purpose as an assembly point for Jews about to be deported to transit camps. Today a memorial to victims of the Holocaust brings the theater's history full circle. *(Plantage Middenlaan 24. ☎ 626 99 45; www.hollandscheschouwburg.nl. Open daily 11am-4pm. Free.)*

HORTUS BOTANICUS. Founded in 1638, these gardens were originally established as "Hortus Medicus," medicinal gardens for the city's physicians. Among 6000 flourishing species, one of the highlights is the *Victoria amazonica*, the world's largest water lily, strong enough to hold a baby on its blossoms. When it blooms on summer evenings, it emits a strong pineapple scent. *(Plantage Middenlaan 2A. ☎ 638 16 70; www.dehortus.nl. Open July-Aug. M-F 9am-9pm, Sa-Su 10am-9pm; Feb.-June and Sept.-Nov. daily 9am-5pm; Dec.-Jan. daily 9am-4pm. €6. Guided tours Su 2pm. €1.)*

DE PIJP. De Pijp (pronounced "pipe") is a work in progress, a gritty immigrant neighborhood gentrifying into bohemian-bourgeois respectability. New high-design bars and cafes are opening up next to Moroccan souks and Indonesian bodegas, creating a lively, syncretic atmosphere best experienced by wandering through the neighborhood's skinny streets. The best place to start is amid the crowded din of the **Albert Cuypmarkt**, a vibrant market and home to some of the best no-name eateries in the city. The market is along Albert Cuypstr., between **Ferdinand Bolstraat** (the district's largest thoroughfare) and Van Woustr.

AALSMEER

Easily accessible by bus, the quiet, quaint town of Aalsmeer is home to the planet's largest flower auction. With a huge trading floor the size of 150 American football fields, **Bloemenveiling Aalsmeer**, Legmeerdijk 313, is the central market where Dutch growers sell over 19 million flowers every single day. The price of flowers as a global commodity is determined here. (☎ 0297 39 21 85; www.vba-aalsmeer.nl. Open M-F 7:30-11am. €4.50.) From Amsterdam's Centraal Station, take **bus** #172 (45min., every 15min., 7 strips). Arrive by 8am to witness the busiest trading; buses begin leaving Amsterdam at 6:10am.

🏛 MUSEUMS

There's no shortage of Serious Museums in Amsterdam, the kind that the upper middle class visits on Sunday afternoon to consider a still life of three kumquats and then feel pompous and cultured. However, the city has just as many museums which creatively sabotage the whole idea of collecting art, whether that means devoting an entire gallery to paintings of cats or opening up a vandalized church to ask why people wage religious wars on sacred artwork. Amsterdam is versatile enough to make room for all of these and more.

NIEUWE ZIJDE, OUDE ZIJDE, AND THE RED LIGHT DISTRICT

AMSTERDAM HISTORISCH MUSEUM. The Amsterdam Historical Museum offers an introduction to Amsterdam's historical development through medieval manuscripts, Baroque paintings, and multimedia displays. In the covered passageway between this converted orphanage and Begijnhof, be sure to catch the extensive collection of 17th-century paintings depicting Amsterdam's civic guards. *(Nieuwezijds Voorburgwal 357 and Kalverstr. 92. ☎ 523 18 22; www.ahm.nl. Open M-F 10am-5pm, Sa-Su 11am-5pm; closed Apr. 30. €6.)*

THE VICES. If it's weed that interests you, far and away your best bet is the staggeringly informative ▨**Cannabis College**, Oudezijds Achterburgwal 124. The center for "higher" education offers info on

THE HIDDEN DEAL

MORE PAINTINGS, LESS POVERTY

Somewhere between hours three and four, visiting a museum can start to be a drag. Your kneecaps hurt, you resent paying a fortune for wilted greens in the gallery cafe, and you've just stared at too much art to emotionally engage with any more. But with museums in the Netherlands charging €6-9, it's hard for the budget traveler to justify taking an hour-long jaunt through two exhibition halls before flitting back out into the sunshine. Unless, that is, the traveler in question is brandishing the Holy Grail of Dutch art buffs.

The decidedly underpublicized *Museumkaart* gives cardholders one year of free entrance to more than 400 museums throughout the Netherlands, including big-marquee names like Amsterdam's Rijksmuseum and Van Gogh Museum. Yet this potent piece of plastic will set you back just €25, and travelers under 25 can nab one for an astonishing €12.50. The longer you're in the country, the more you'll save, but you'll likely come out ahead on any visit longer than a few days. Starving artists may be chic, but museumgoers who can afford to buy themselves dinner are even better.

Call ☎ 0900 40 40 910 from inside the country to sign up, or struggle through the Dutch-only website www.museumkaart.nl for a list of participating museums.

everything from the uses of medicinal marijuana to facts about the war on drugs to creative applications of industrial hemp. Downstairs, artificial lighting in the Cannabis Garden simulates the summer and autumn growing season so that visitors can always see a plant in full bloom. For a curated taste of the seaminess that runs down Amsterdam's underbelly, head to the **Amsterdam Sex Museum,** Damrak 18, less than a 5min. walk from Centraal Station. If walls plastered with pictures of bestiality and S&M are not your cup of tea, you may wish to look elsewhere for a cup of tea. *(Cannabis College open daily 11am-7pm. Free. Sex Museum open daily 10am-11:30pm. 16+. €2.50.)*

MUSEUM AMSTELKRING "ONS' LIEVE HEER OP SOLDER" ("OUR LORD IN THE ATTIC"). This 17th-century secret church was built after the Reformation swept into the Netherlands. Catholics forbidden to practice their faith gathered in a small chapel spanning the attics of three adjacent buildings, which were camouflaged as shop fronts down at street level. *(Oudezijds Voorburgwal 40. ☎ 624 66 04; www.museum-mamstelkring.nl. Open M-Sa 10am-5pm, Su and holidays 1-5pm. €7, students €5.)*

NIEUWE KERK. Closed for six months to allow emergency repairs, this extravagant 15th-century "New Church" reopened in November 2004 to resume its role as religious edifice, historical monument, and art museum. When Queen Beatrix steps down from the Dutch throne and Prince Willem-Alexander is crowned king, his coronation will take place in the Nieuwe Kerk, as did his mother's. *(Adjacent to Dam Sq., beside Koninklijk Palace. ☎ 638 69 09; www.nieuwekerk.nl. Open M-W, F, and Su 10am-6pm, Th 10am-10pm. Organ recitals June-Sept. Th 12:30pm, Su 8pm. €8.)*

CANAL RING WEST AND THE JORDAAN

■ **ANNE FRANK HUIS.** A visit to the Anne Frank House is a must, whether or not you've read the famous diary. The museum chronicles the two years the Frank family and four other Jews spent hiding in the annex of this warehouse on the Prinsengracht. The rooms are no longer furnished, but personal objects in display cases and text panels with excerpts from the diary bring the story of the eight inhabitants to life. Arrive around 5 or 6pm for the shortest lines. *(Prinsengr. 267. ☎ 556 71 00; www.annefrank.nl. Open daily Apr.-Aug. 9am-9pm; Sept.-Mar. 9am-7pm. Closed on Yom Kippur. Last admission 30min. before closing. €7.50.)*

ELECTRIC LADYLAND: THE FIRST MUSEUM OF FLUORESCENT ART. Endearingly eccentric owner Nick Padalino has collected a singularly impressive assortment of fluorescent objects. These include gorgeous rocks that glow green in black light and an array of everyday objects that reveal hidden shades. During personal guided tours, visitors are encouraged to dive into the interactive space and play with the many switches and buttons that turn various lights on and off. *(2e Leliedwarsstr. 5. ☎ 420 37 76; www.electric-lady-land.com. Open Tu-Sa 1-6pm. €5.)*

MUSEUMPLEIN

■ **VAN GOGH MUSEUM.** This architecturally breathtaking museum houses the largest collection of van Goghs in the world and a diverse group of 19th-century paintings by contemporaries like Gaugin and friend Emile Bernard. While the Rijksmuseum and the Stedelijk are juggling their collections during renovations, this museum's substantial collection of Impressionist, post-Impressionist, Realist, and Symbolist art acquires a new luster. *(Paulus Potterstr. 7. ☎ 570 52 00; www.vangoghmuseum.nl. Open daily 10am-6pm; ticket office closes 5:30pm. €9. Audioguides €4. Tickets become more expensive during major temporary exhibitions.)*

▨ **RIJKSMUSEUM AMSTERDAM.** Amsterdam's "state museum" has long been known as the Continent's preeminent destination for art from the Dutch Golden Age. Even though the museum's main building closed for renovations in December 2003, the Rijksmuseum is still a mandatory outing. During the restoration, the smaller Philips Wing will remain open to show 400 masterpieces of 17th-century painting, including works by Rembrandt, Vermeer, Frans Hals, and Jan Steen. Unfortunately, the bulk of the museum's collection will not be on display until renovations are completed in 2008, though you may be able to catch a glimpse of certain works on loan to venues around the city and elsewhere in the Netherlands. Check the website for details on the location of these venues. *(Jan Luijkenstr. 1.* ☎ *674 70 00; www.rijksmuseum.nl. Open daily 10am-5pm. €9. Audioguides €4.)*

▨ **STEDELIJK MUSEUM OF MODERN ART.** The Stedelijk has amassed a world-class collection on par with MoMA or the Tate Modern. But new art deserves a new home just as surely as old art does, and a distinguished jury spent the summer of 2004 choosing a Dutch architect to design a new museum building, to open on Museumplein in 2008. Meanwhile, selected pieces are being shown on the second and third floors of the Post-CS Building, to the left when exiting Centraal Station. Dinner at **Restaurant Club 11,** up on the 11th floor, will set you back at least €30, although the spectacular view of the city is free. *(Oosterdokskade 5.* ☎ *573 27 45; www.stedelijk.nl. Open M-W and F-Su 10am-6pm, Th 10am-9pm. €8.)*

CENTRAL CANAL RING

FOAM PHOTOGRAPHY MUSEUM. Inside a traditional canal house, Foam stages a fearless exploration of modern photography. Every genre of the photographed image is fair game—from the purely aesthetic to the explicitly political, from fashion photography to historical exhibits. *(Keizersgr. 609.* ☎ *551 65 00; www.foam.nl. Open M-W and Sa-Su 10am-5pm, Th-F 10am-9pm. €5, students €4. Cafe open W-Su 10am-5pm.)*

DE APPEL. This contemporary art museum houses a small permanent collection and draws compelling, cutting-edge temporary exhibits that make even the Stedelijk look old-fashioned. *(Nieuwe Spiegelstr. 10.* ☎ *625 56 51; www.deappel.nl. Open Tu-Su 11am-6pm, F 11am-10pm. €2.50.)*

CAT'S CABINET. Housed in the only public building on the Golden Bend, the Cat's Cabinet is a temple to all things feline—including statuary, portraiture, pop art, and assorted knick-knacks. The collection was started by a businessman with an unusually strong 18-year attachment to his cat named J. P. Morgan; check out his feline face gracing the dollar bill in the museum. *(Herengrt. 497.* ☎ *626 53 78; www.kattenkabinet.nl. Open M-F 10am-2pm, Sa-Su 1-5pm. €4.50.)*

JODENBUURT AND PLANTAGE

▨ **NEMO (NEW METROPOLIS).** The half-submerged green structure shaped like a ship's hull by the Oosterdok is NEMO, the coolest science museum you have ever seen. Renzo Piano's whimsical architecture pays tribute to the Netherlands' seafaring past, and inside four stories littered with science exhibits just beg to be poked at, jumped on, and experimented with. NEMO targets children ages 4-16, but adult visitors soon find themselves shooting each other conspiratorial grins as they blow meter-wide bubbles. Afterwards, don't miss the spectacular view of the shipyard and the historic city; a staircase traverses the structure's slanted roof on the eastern side. *(Oosterdok 2, east of Centraal Station on the Oosterdok.* ☎ *0900 919 11 00, €0.35 per min.; www.e-nemo.nl. Open Tu-Su 10am-5pm. €11, students €6.)*

JOODS HISTORISCH MUSEUM. In the heart of Amsterdam's oldest Jewish neighborhood, the Jewish Historical Museum aims to document the religious heritage and cultural legacy of Dutch Jews. The museum presents a comprehensive picture of Jewish life through a permanent collection of photographs, religious artifacts, artwork, and traditional clothing. *(Jonas Daniel Meijerpl. 2-4. ☎626 99 45; www.jhm.nl. Open daily 11am-5pm. Closed Yom Kippur. €6.50, students €4. Audioguides €1.)*

VERZETSMUSEUM (DUTCH RESISTANCE MUSEUM). Though the Nazis quickly overran Dutch armed forces in May 1940, the Netherlands maintained an active resistance throughout WWII. The Resistance Museum focuses on the members of this secret army, providing visitors with the details of their lives and struggles. Model streets, buildings, and tape-recorded radio reports recreate the rebels' experiences—from smuggling food to issuing counterpropaganda on an illicit printing press. *(Plantage Kerklaan 61. ☎620 25 35; www.verzetsmuseum.org. Open M and Sa-Su noon-5pm, Tu-F 10am-5pm, public holidays noon-5pm. €5.)*

🎵 ENTERTAINMENT

The **Amsterdams Uit Buro (AUB),** Leidsepl. 26, is stuffed with flyers, pamphlets, and guides to help you sift through upcoming events; pick up the free monthly *Uitkrant* to see what's on. The AUB also sells tickets and makes reservations for just about any cultural event, although they charge a small commission. (☎09 00 01 91, €0.55 per min.; www.uitlijn.nl. Office open M-W and F-Sa 10am-6pm, Th 10am-9pm, Su noon-6pm. Phones open daily 9am-8pm.) If you're hungry for more info on bars, coffeeshops, gay life, and other events, sink your teeth into a copy of *Shark* (www.underwateramsterdam.com; print versions available throughout the city).

CONCERTS

In summer, the **Vondelpark Openluchttheater** (☎673 14 99; www.openluchttheater.nl) hosts free rock and jazz concerts, as well as performances aimed at children, daily Wednesday through Sunday. The **Royal Concertgebouw Orchestra,** regarded as one of the world's finest, plays in the **Concertgebouw,** Concertgebouwpl. 2-6. (Take tram #316 to Museumplein. ☎671 83 45; www.concertegebouw.nl. Tickets from €11. Music buffs under 27 can try to get last-minute tickets for just €7. Free lunchtime concert Sept.-June W 12:30pm. No tickets necessary. Ticket office open daily 10am-7pm. Guided tours Su at 9:30am. €7.)

FILM

Check out www.movieguide.nl for movie listings. In the Vondelpark, head left from the main entrance on Stadhouderskade to see what's on at the **Filmmuseum** independent movie theater, or show up on Friday night for an outdoor screening. (☎589 14 00; www.filmmuseum.nl. Open M-F 10am-10pm; Sa-Su box office opens 1hr. prior to first showing. €7.20-7.80.) Young indie filmmakers show their work each week at ▣**Diatoom Cinema,** Overtoom 301. Check the website for info and schedule. (☎779 49 13; www.squat.net/overtoom301. Screenings €4.)

🍁 COFFEESHOPS AND SMART SHOPS

COFFEESHOPS

The coffee at Amsterdam's coffeeshops is rarely the focal point. Establishments calling themselves coffeeshops often sell pot or hash or will let customers buy a drink and smoke their own. Look for the **green-and-white sticker** signifying the shop's affiliation with the Bond voor Cannabisdetaillisten (BCD), an organized union of coffeeshops. Reputable independent shops do exist, and between fairly steep union dues and a decade-long freeze on new licenses, it's easy to understand why not all shops get union-certified. Still, establishments with the BCD sticker remain the safest bet for visitors new to the city. While Amsterdam was once known as the **hashish** capital of the world, **marijuana** has increasingly become the soft drug of choice. Technically, pot is illegal in the Netherlands, but the country's tolerance policy means that you are unlikely to face legal action if you carry no more than 30g (1.05 oz) on your person, and buy no more than 5g (0.17 oz) at a time. Possession of harder drugs like cocaine and heroin can and will be severely punished. For more info on the legal ins and outs, call the **Jellinek clinic** (☎408 77 77). If you're more interested in how cannabis gets from seed to spliff, the staff at **Cannabis College** (p. 757) can tell you anything you want to know.

Let's Go does not recommend illegal drug use in any form. Those who decide to partake should use common sense and remember that any experimentation with drugs can be dangerous. **Never buy drugs from street dealers,** because there is no way of knowing whether they are laced with more harmful drugs or are simply expensive oregano. Coffeeshops are licensed to sell cannabis and hashish, and the good ones carefully regulate the quality of their smokeables. When customers walk into a coffeeshop, they should ask for a menu, because the shops are not allowed to leave menus out or otherwise advertise their wares. The legal age to enter a coffeeshop is 18, and it's not unusual for staff to ask for ID when you enter.

Marijuana is the dried, cured flower of the cannabis plant, and costs €5-12 per gram. Different strains fall in and out of favor, but are divided into two main subspecies: Sativa strains (like "Kali Mist" or anything marked "Thai") gets users high, giggly, and energized, while Indica strains (like "Northern Lights") gets users really stoned and relaxed. Increasingly popular hybrid strains (like "White Widow" or "AK-47") combine both effects. Pot in the Netherlands is very potent; visitors report that they smoke noticeably less than they would at home and still achieve the same high. Pre-rolled joints are sometimes available, but smoking one clearly identifies its user as a tourist, as does smoking out of a pipe. Staff at coffeeshops are unlikely to explain how to roll a joint, but they will be happy to explain different options on the menu.

Hashish is made from resin crystals extracted from the flowers of the cannabis plant, and it comes in three varieties: black (Indian), blonde (Moroccan), and Dutch (also called ice-o-lator). The first two grades run €4-20 per gram, averaging somewhere around €7, while increasingly popular **ice-o-lator hash** tops out at €20-40 per gram. Typically, the cost of the hash is proportional to its quality and strength; black hash hits harder than blonde, and ice-o-lator can send even a seasoned smoker off his head. Hash can be smoked directly out of a glass hash pipe, or sprinkled into a joint containing either tobacco or marijuana. Both hash and weed can be used to make **space cakes** and other fortified food items, available at Chocolata (see below) and elsewhere in the city. Because these treats need to be digested, they take longer to affect the body (up to 2hr.) and longer to rinse out. Experts warn against eating another brownie just because you don't feel effects immediately.

SMART SHOPS

Smart shops peddle a variety of "herbal enhancers" that walk the line between soft and hard drugs. Always remember that experimentation with drugs is dangerous and can cause either short or long-term damage. If you're interested in experimenting with magic mushrooms ('shrooms), it is crucial, as with all soft drugs, that you do your research beforehand. Here's a brief rundown of the types of mushrooms and a few guidelines. **Magic mushrooms** start to work 30-60min. after consumption and act on your system for 4-8hr., depending on how much you weigh. Different types give different highs: **Mexican** and **Thai** mushrooms are the least potent and give a laughing, colorful high with some visual hallucination. **Philosophers' stones** (colors and lights swirl together as you think deep thoughts) and **Hawaiians** (a visual trip similar to LSD) are more intense, and should be taken only by experienced users. Wandering the city tripping on mushrooms can be a majestic, mind-expanding experience, but it can also leave you unable to think straight enough to find your way home. It's often more pleasant to stay in familiar surroundings, like a favorite coffeeshop or a corner of the Vondelpark. Never look for mushrooms in the wild and never buy from a street dealer; it's very difficult to tell the difference between hallucinogenic mushrooms and flat-out poisonous ones. **Don't mix mushrooms with alcohol,** and if you have a bad trip, call ☎ 122 to go to the hospital or ask someone for help—you won't be arrested, and they've seen it all before.

WHERE TO GO

▨ **Barney's Coffeeshop,** Haarlemmerstr. 102. Wine and cheese, coffee and cigarettes—some pairings are just meant to be. Pot and all-day breakfast (€5.50-12.50) fall into the same category, especially when the coffeeshop in question is a three-time "best marijuana strain" winner at the Cannabis Cup. Open daily 7am-8pm.

▨ **Dampkring,** Handboogstr. 29. Several scenes from the 2004 film *Ocean's Twelve* were filmed in this chill, subterranean space. But don't take Brad Pitt's word for it; locals are unanimously enthusiastic. Open M-Th 10am-1am, F-Sa 10am-2am, Su 11am-1am.

▨ **Abraxas,** J. Roelensteeg 12-14. Hotspots come and go, but Abraxas has remained one of Amsterdam's largest, most beautiful coffeeshops. Plush couches fill 3 floors decorated by abstract designs and a stylized tree-branch motif. Open daily 10am-1am.

▨ **Amnesia,** Herengr. 133. Fuschia walls, pink tabletops, and cushioned benches make for a comfortable, newbie-friendly atmosphere that has found a niche in a city with many standoffish, veterans-only shops. Vaporizer available for guests looking for alternatives to smoking. Open daily 9am-1am.

Yo Yo, 2e van der Heijdenstr. 79. Sunflowers and long wooden tables contribute to a country-kitchen atmosphere, where twee, corduroy-clad locals partake of famous apple pie (€1.75) and organic smokeables. Open M-Sa noon-7pm.

Conscious Dreams Kokopelli, Warmoesstr. 12. Perhaps the best place to begin with psychedelic experimentation, this smart shop features a staff with background in neurobiology and botany—they give great information to the uninitiated, then steer the tripping toward beanbag chairs underneath a ceiling mural. Open daily 11am-10pm.

Chocolata, Spuistr. 51. The one-stop shop for Amsterdam's best eatables: vanilla and chocolate spacecakes (€4), space bonbons (€2), and hash hot chocolate (€3.80). Open M-Th and Su 11am-midnight, F-Sa 11am-1am.

▨ NIGHTLIFE

Leidseplein and **Rembrandtplein** remain the liveliest areas for nightlife, with coffeeshops, loud bars, and tacky clubs galore. Near Leidseplein, pricey discos abound on **Prinsengracht,** near **Leidsestraat,** and on **Lange Leidsedwarsstraat.** Some clubs charge a membership fee in addition to normal cover. Amsterdam's finest cafes are the old, dark, wood-paneled *bruin cafe* (brown cafes) mainly on the **Jordaan;** those lining **Prinsengracht** often have outdoor seating. In Amsterdam, the concept of a completely "straight" nightlife versus a "gay" nightlife does not really apply; most establishments are gay-friendly and have a mixed-orientation crowd. Around Rembrandtpl., gay bars almost exclusively for men line **Amstelstraat** and **Reguliersdwarsstraat. Kerkstraat,** five blocks north of Leidseplein, is another gay hot spot. Pick up a wallet-sized *Clu* guide, free at cafes and coffeeshops, for a club map of the city, or the monthly *Gay and Night.*

BARS AND CAFES

▨ **NL Lounge,** Nieuwezijds Voorburgwal 169. This is the unmarked destination where some of Amsterdam's slickest, best-dressed, and most savvy insiders hang out. Music varies, but at 1am, the beat invariably switches over to what the staff likes to call "power lounge." Cocktails €8. Open M-Th and Su 10pm-3am, F-Sa 10pm-4am.

Café de Jaren, Nieuwe Doelenstr. 20-22. Spacious, glamorous cafe on par with the best of Paris or Vienna. Two sprawling floors offer various seating options, from long, blonde-wood tables to outdoor patio tables an arm's length away from the Klovenierburgswal canal. Cocktails and beer €1.90-3.10. Open M-Th and Su 10am-1am, F-Sa 10am-2am.

Lux, Marnixstr. 403. Kitschy red velour walls and leopard-print curtains draw a crowd night after night. There's not much dancing, but DJs will get you pumped to go hit the clubs Th-Su. Beer €2. Cocktails €6. Open M-Th and Su 8pm-3am, F-Sa 8pm-4am.

Café 't Smalle, Egelantiersgrt. 12. Founded in 1780 as the tasting room of a neighboring distillery, and one of the most popular *bruin cafes* in the city's western end. A steep, narrow staircase leads to the upstairs seating area, although canalside seating is available in summer. Draft beer €1.95. Open M-Th and Su 10am-1am, F-Sa 10am-2am.

Montmartre, Halvemaarsteg 17. Rococo interior bedecked with flowers and rich draperies houses some of the wildest gay parties in the city. Voted best gay bar in Amsterdam by *Gay Krant* 7 years running. Happy Hour daily 6-8pm. *Heugemeug* (the house shooter) €3. Open M-Th and Su 5pm-1am, F-Sa 5pm-3am.

Arc Bar, Reguliersdwarsstr. 44. A hip, cutting-edge lounge where black tabletops get lowered to form go-go blocks as the evening progresses. Cocktails €6.50-7.50. Happy Hour daily 5-7pm and W all night. Open M-Th and Su 4pm-1am, F-Sa 4pm-3am.

CLUBS AND DISCOS

De Trut, Bilderdijkstr. 165. A low-ceilinged basement in an apartment building west of the city center hosts Su night parties for gay and lesbian locals skipping the cruisy downtown scene. Don't be chased off by 2m pictures of genitalia on the doors; the emphasis inside is on dancing and mingling. Beer €1. Cover €1.50. Doors open at 11pm and close once the club fills, so join the queue on the sidewalk by 10:30pm.

Meander, Voetboogstr. 3b. Smoky atmosphere, constant clamor, and dense crowds make for a raucous, high-energy good time. Beer €2. M student night, F-Sa disco with live music. Cover €2.50-5. Open M-Th and Su 9pm-3am, F-Sa 9pm-4am.

Escape, Rembrandtpl. 11. Party animals pour into this massive venue, one of the city's nightlife institutions with 6 bars on 2 floors. Well-dressed club kids groove to house, trance, and disco tunes. Beer €2.30. Cocktails €7.50. Cover €10-15. Open Th and Su 11pm-4am, F-Sa 11pm-5am.

Dansen Bij Jansen, Handboogstr. 11-13. *The* student dance club in Amsterdam, popular with locals from the University of Amsterdam and backpackers too. You must show a student ID or be accompanied by a student. Beer €1.70-3.30. Cocktails from €3.30. Cover M-W and Su €2, Th-Sa €4. Open M-Th and Su 11pm-4am, F-Sa 11pm-5am.

Bitterzoet, Spuistr. 2. Dreadlocks and skateboard style prevail at this popular club, which reels in alternafolks fleeing from the Kylie Minogue remixes on Rembrandtpl. and Leidsepl. Dance floor downstairs; lounge in the upstairs balcony. Beer €1.90. Live music M-Th and Su. 21+. Cover €5. Open M-Th and Su 8pm-3am, F-Sa 8pm-4am.

LIVE MUSIC

Melkweg, Lijnbaansgrt. 234a (☎531 81 81; www.melkweg.nl). Legendary nightspot in an old milk factory, it's one-stop shopping for live music, food (see **Eat At Jo's,** p. 753), films, and dance parties. Concert tickets €5-22 plus €2.50 monthly membership fee. Box office open M-F 1-5pm, Sa-Su 4-6pm; show days from 7:30pm to end of show.

Paradiso, Weteringschans 6-8 (☎626 45 21; www.paradiso.nl). When big-name rock, punk, and reggae bands come to Amsterdam, they almost invariably play in this former church. Tickets €5-35 plus €2.50 monthly membership fee. Usually open daily 8pm-4am; check website for details.

Cafe Alto, Korte Leidsedwarsstr. 115 (☎623 34 40; www.jazz-cafe-alto.nl). Crowded, dark, and smoky-noir, this jazz cafe features intimate live performances nightly. Beer €5. No cover. Open M-Th and Su 9pm-3am, F-Sa 9pm-4am.

THE NETHERLANDS

HAARLEM
☎ 023

Haarlem's narrow cobblestone streets, rippling canals, and fields of tulips make for a great escape from the urban frenzy of Amsterdam. Most visitors come to Haarlem (pop. 150,000) for its Renaissance facades, medieval architecture, and varied museums, but the city possesses more than yesteryear charm. Haarlem also bustles with a relaxed energy that befits its urban size, as coffeeshops and a slew of restaurants ensure that there's fun to be had even after the sun goes down.

🖃🖬 TRANSPORTATION AND PRACTICAL INFORMATION. Reach Haarlem from Amsterdam by **train** from Centraal Station (20min.; every 30min.; €3.20, same-day round-trip €5.70). The VVV **tourist office,** Stationspl. 1, just to your right as you walk out of the train station, sells maps of the city (€2) and finds private rooms (from €20) for a €5 fee. (☎ 090 06 16 16 00; www.vvvzk.nl. Open Apr.-Sept. M-F 9am-5:30pm, Sa 10am-4pm; Oct.-Mar. M-F 9am-5pm, Sa 10am-2pm.)

🖪🖸 ACCOMMODATIONS AND FOOD. Hotel Carillon ❷, Grote Markt 27, is ideally located on the town square, to the left of the Grote Kerk. Despite their small size, most rooms include a shower, phone, and TV, and all are extremely clean. (☎ 531 05 91; www.hotelcarillon.com. Breakfast included. Reception 7:30am-1am. Singles €33, with bath €55; doubles €57/€76; triples €97. AmEx/MC/V.) To stay at the more remote **Stayokay Haarlem (HI) ❶,** Jan Gijzenpad 3, take bus #2 (dir.: Haarlem-Noord; every 10min. until 6pm, every 15min. 6pm-12:30am) or rent a bike at the hostel and then pedal 15min. into town. (☎ 537 3793; www.stayokay.com/haarlem. Breakfast and sheets included. Bikes €8 per day. Laundry €4.50. Dorms €24-26.50, low season €21-23.50. AmEx/MC/V.) For cheap meals, try cafes in the **Grote Markt** or **Botermarkt;** many offer outdoor patios. Stylish **Lakoniek ❸,** Oude Groenmarkt 24, serves tapas-sized portions from several European countries, allowing you to customize your meal into an early-evening snack or a table-bending feast. (☎ 532 83 22. Entrees €4.35-7. Open daily 5:30-10pm. MC/V.)

🄶🄳 SIGHTS AND ENTERTAINMENT. The action centers on the **Grote Markt,** Haarlem's vibrant main square, which gets taken over by a flea market on Saturday and Monday mornings. To get there from the train station, head south along Kruisweg, which becomes Kruisstr. and then Barteljorisstr. A 2min. walk from the Grote Markt is the moving **Corrie Ten Boomhuis,** Barteljorisstr. 19, a museum in the former headquarters of Corrie Ten Boom's movement to protect Jews during WWII. The savior of an estimated 800 lives, Corrie was caught and sent to a concentration camp but survived to write *The Hiding Place,* later made into an evangelical Christian film. (Open Apr.-Oct. Tu-Sa 10am-4pm; Nov.-Mar. Tu-Sa 10am-3pm. Free.) The **Grote Kerk,** on the Grote Markt, houses portraitist Frans Hals's tomb, a mammoth Müller organ once played by Handel and Mozart, and even a small cafe. (Open M-Sa 10am-4pm. €1.50.) From the front of the church, take a right onto Warmoestr. and walk three blocks to the **Frans Hals Museum,** Groot Heiligland 62, which houses 11 of Hals's canvases and work by other Golden Age Dutchmen in a 17th-century almshouse and orphanage. (☎ 511 57 75; www.franshalsmuseum.nl. Open Tu-Sa 11am-5pm, Su noon-5pm. €5.40, under 19 free.) The museum also organizes modern art exhibitions at **De Hallen,** Grote Markt 16. (Open Tu-Sa 11am-5pm, Su noon-5pm. €4, under 19 free.) Nightlife clusters on the streets surrounding the Grote Markt. **Cafe Stiel's,** Smedestr. 21, features live music from soul and jazz to alternative rock. (Open M-Th and Su 8pm-2am, F-Sa 8pm-4am.)

DAYTRIPS FROM HAARLEM: ZANDVOORT AND BLOEMENDAAL AAN ZEE. Just 11 kilometers from Haarlem, the seaside town of **Zandvoort** (pop. 16,000) draws the sun-starved hoi polloi to its sandy beaches. From the train station, walk straight through the Koper Passarel; the surf awaits just beyond the high-rise hotel. More than 20 **beach clubs** boast patios where revelers carouse on lounge chairs. **Mango's Beachbar,** Boulevard Barnaart 15, serves high-octane Caribbean cocktails and turns into a salsa lounge during **Zandvoort (A)live,** a four-club party staged once a month each summer. Check www.zandvoortalive.nl for more info. (☎571 27 88; www.mangosbeachbar.com. Open daily 10am-midnight, kitchen closes at 10pm.) Nearby **Bloemendaal aan Zee** isn't even a town; it's simply a collection of five or six beach clubs, which operate from April to September and then close up shop for the winter. To get there from Zandvoort, walk 30min. to your right when facing the water. Back in 1998, the irresistible hippie-style club ▨**Woodstock 69,** Zeedijk 8, launched **Beach Bop,** the party that takes over the beach the last Sunday of every month. (Tickets €15; check www.beachbop.info for details.) ▨**Republiek,** Zeeweg 1, is equal parts Bali and postmodern chic, with flat black couches equipped with tiki-hut sunshades. (☎573 07 30; www.republiek.tv.) **Trains** arrive in Zandvoort from Haarlem (10min., 2-4 per hr., round-trip €2.80), although **bikes** can cover the same distance in 30min. The VVV **tourist office,** Schoolpl. 1, is just east of the town square, off Louis Davidstr. (☎571 79 47. Open June-Aug. M-F 9:30am-4:30pm, Sa 10am-4pm; Sept.-May M-F 9:30am-4:30pm, Sa 10am-2pm.) Most visitors stay the night in Haarlem, although **B&Bs** line Burg. Engelbertstr. and rent cheap rooms (€17-20); look for window signs reading "*zimmer.*"

LEIDEN   ☎071

Home to one of the oldest universities in Europe, Leiden (pop. 117,000) brims with bookstores, windmills, gated gardens, and hidden walkways. The city that gave the world Rembrandt has more than its fair share of outstanding museums, while the botanical gardens where Carolus Clusius first cultivated **tulips** still draw admirers of the Netherlands' beloved bulbs. Make your own pilgrimage to the **Hortus Botanicus,** Rapenburg 73, and picnic on the grassy knolls alongside the **Witte Singel** canal. (☎527 72 49. Open Apr.-Nov. daily 10am-6pm; Dec.-Mar. M-F and Su 10am-4pm, €4.) Once your green thumb has been appeased, head indoors to the spacious ▨**Museum Naturalis,** a natural history museum that traces the formation of the earth and its inhabitants through splashy, interactive displays. (☎568 76 00; www.naturalis.nl. Open July-Aug. daily 10am-6pm; Sept.-June Tu-Su 10am-6pm. Treasure room open 1:30-4:30pm. €9.) The **Rijksmuseum van Oudheden** (National Antiquities Museum), Rapenburg 28, traces the history of the Netherlands up through the Middle Ages, and holds the restored Egyptian Temple of Taffeh, transplanted from the reservoir basin of the Aswan Dam. (☎516 31 63; www.rmo.nl. Open Tu-F 10am-5pm, Sa noon-5pm, Su noon-5pm. €6.)

Trains run to: Amsterdam (30min., every 30min., €7); Haarlem (20min., 4-6 per hr., €4.50); and The Hague (20min., every 30min., €3.70). To get to the VVV **tourist office,** Stationsweg 2d, take the city center exit from the train station and walk straight ahead. (☎090 02 22 23 33; www.leidenpromotie.nl. Open M 11am-5:20pm, Tu-F 10am-5:20pm, Sa 10am-4:30pm.) The **Hotel Pension Witte Singel ❷,** Witte Singel 80, overlooks serene canals and gardens. (☎512 45 92; www.pensionws.demon.nl. Singles €37-44; doubles €55-67.50. V.) Students pack the popular **de Oude Harmonie ❷,** Breestr. 16, just off Rapenburg, where candlelight and stained glass set the mood. (Entrees €6.50-13.50. Open M-Th 3pm-1am, F-Sa 3pm-2am, Su 3pm-1am. Cash only.) **Super de Boer** supermarket, Stationsweg 40, is opposite the train station. (Open M-F 7am-9pm, Sa 9am-8pm, Su noon-7pm.) **Postal Code:** 2300.

THE NETHERLANDS

THE HAGUE (DEN HAAG)   ☎ 070

Think of the seat of the Dutch government as the capital city's fussy older brother; The Hague (pop. 470,000) is too mature and pulled-together for Amsterdam's juvenile antics. There are precious few coffeeshops amid the city's historic buildings, though institutions like the Peace Palace and the International Criminal Court are perhaps best appreciated with a clear head. Besides, The Hague's museums and its extensive network of parks can go toe to toe with any city in the Low Countries.

▄▓ TRANSPORTATION AND PRACTICAL INFORMATION. Trains run from Amsterdam (50min., €8) and Rotterdam (25min., €3.60) to both of The Hague's major stations, **Centraal Station** and **Holland Spoor.** Trams #1, 9, and 12 connect the two stations. The VVV **tourist office,** Kon. Julianapl. 30, just outside the north entrance to Centraal Station and right next to the Hotel Sofitel, sells detailed city maps (€2) and books rooms (€5 fee). You can book hotels on the computer outside the tourist office 24hr. (☎090 03 40 35 05; www.denhaag.com. Open June-Sept. M and Sa 10am-5pm, Tu-F 9am-6pm, Su 10am-2pm; Oct.-May M 10am-6pm, Tu-F 9am-5:30pm, Sa 10am-5pm.) Another branch is located at Wagenstr. 193, closer to the hostel. (☎402 33 36. Open Tu-Sa 11am-5pm.)

▐▐ ACCOMMODATIONS AND FOOD. The StayOkay City Hostel Den Haag (HI) ❶, Scheepmakerstr. 27, is near Holland Spoor; turn right from the station, follow the tram tracks, go straight through the big intersection, and Scheepmakerstr. is the second street on your right after the big pink building. From Centraal Station, take tram #1 (dir.: Delft), 9 (dir.: Vrederust), or 12 (dir.: Duindrop) to Holland Spoor (2 strips) and then follow the above directions. (☎315 78 88; www.stayokay.com/denhaag. Breakfast and sheets included. Laundry €6. Reception 7:30am-10pm. Dorms €24; singles €49; doubles €70. Nonmembers add €2.50. AmEx/MC/V.) Budget fare is plentiful on **Lange Poten** and **Korte Poten** near the Binnenhof. The cavernous **De Boterwaag ❷,** Grote Markt 8a, serves pasta (€6), salads (€7.50-9.50), and meat dishes (€13.50) under a high ceiling held up by thick stone pillars. (☎365 96 86. Open M-W and Su 10am-1am, Th-Sa 10am-1:30am. AmEx/MC/V.) Tasty *tapas* await at the antiqued **Cafe de Oude Mol ❸,** Oude Molstr. 61, a few blocks from Grote Halstr., although the bill can get steep at €2-7.50 per dish. (☎345 16 23. Open M-W 5pm-1am, Th-Sa 5pm-2am, Su 5pm-1am. Cash only.)

◙ ▐ SIGHTS AND ENTERTAINMENT. The Hague's **Peace Palace** (Het Vredespaleis), at Carnegiepl., was donated in 1903 by American industrialist Andrew Carnegie and is today the opulent home of the International Court of Justice. (☎302 41 37; www.vredespaleis.nl. Take tram #1 to Vredespaleis. Tours usually M-F 10, 11am, 2, and 3pm, but call ahead to reserve a spot. €5.) Bask in the sunshine in the courtyard of the **Binnenhof,** The Hague's Parliament complex. Tours of the complex leave from Binnenhof 8a and visit the 13th-century **Ridderzaal** (Hall of Knights) as well as the chambers of the States General. (☎364 61 44. Open M-Sa 10am-4pm, last tour leaves at 3:45pm. Call ahead. Tour €5.) Near the Binnenhof's entrance, the 17th-century **Mauritshuis,** Korte Vijverberg 8, features an impressive collection of Dutch paintings, including works by Rembrandt and bawdy Jan Steen, as well as Vermeer's famous *Girl With a Pearl Earring.* (☎302 34 56; www.mauritshuis.nl. Open Tu-Sa 10am-5pm, Su 11am-5pm. €7.50, under 19 free. Audioguide €1.) Piet Mondrian's 1944 canvas *Victory Boogie Woogie* stands out from his earlier sketches at the **Gemeentemuseum,** Stadhouderslaan 41, which also features early musical instruments and historical costume. Take tram #17 to Gemeentemuseum/Museon. (☎338 11 11; www.gemeentemuseum.com. Open Tu-Su 11am-5pm. €9.50, students €7.) Windsurfers and kite-flying tots pack the beach in nearby **Scheveningen,** which doubles as a popular nightlife destination.

Back in The Hague, young clubgoers pile into cinema-turned-discotheque **Asta,** Spui 27, where multiple rooms play pop, hip-hop, and R&B. Beer sells for €1 on Thursdays in honor of student night. (☎364 42 22; www.asta.nl. Cover Tu-Th €3-4, F-Sa €7.50-20. Open Tu and Th 11pm-4am, F-Sa 11pm-late.) Close to the Grote Markt, the hipster-cool **Paard van Troje,** Prinsegracht 10-12, features local alternative bands in the **cafe** every Wednesday and bigger names in the **poppodium** next door. (☎360 18 38; www.paard.nl. Open W 4pm-2am, Th 4pm-3am, F-Sa 4pm-late. Cafe concerts free. Poppodium concerts €5-20.) In early July, Paard van Troje and other venues throughout the city host the **State-X New Forms Festival,** which showcases experimental pop music from around the world. In 2004, the festival saw a stirring performance of "Happy Metal" on dozens of vacuum cleaners and other household appliances. (www.state-x.nl. Tickets €25, or €40 for two days.)

▓ DAYTRIP FROM THE HAGUE: DELFT. The lilied canals and stone footbridges that line the streets of Delft (pop. 97,000) offer the same views that native Johannes Vermeer immortalized in paint over 300 years ago. It's best to visit on Thursdays and Saturdays, when townspeople flood the marketplace. The town is renowned for **Delftware,** blue-on-white earthenware developed in the 16th century. Watch Delftware being made from scratch at homey **De Candelaer,** Kerkstr. 13a-14, located in the center of town. (☎213 18 48; www.candelaer.nl. Open M-F 9am-5:30pm, Sa 9am-5pm, Su 10am-5:30pm. Free.) To see a larger factory, take tram #1 to Vrijenbanselaan and take in the free demonstration at **De Delftse Pauw,** Delftweg 133. (☎212 49 20; www.delftsepauw.com. Open Apr.-Oct. daily 9am-4:30pm; Nov.-Mar. M-F 9am-4:30pm, Sa-Su 11am-1pm.) The easiest way into Delft is the 15min. ride on **tram** #1 from The Hague (4 strips) to Delft station. **Trains** also arrive from Amsterdam (1hr., €10) and Rotterdam (15min., €2.50). The **Tourist Information Point,** Hippolytusbuurt 4, near the Stadhuis, distributes a free map of the city. (☎215 40 51; www.delft.nl. Open M 10am-4pm, Tu-F 9am-6pm, Sa 9am-5pm, Su 10am-4pm.) Even the campgrounds in Delft have sky-high rates; take the tram back to The Hague before you crash for the night, and you'll save a bundle.

ROTTERDAM   ☎010

The second-largest city in the Netherlands and the busiest port city in the world, Rotterdam (pop. 660,000) lacks the quaint, gingerbread-house feel that characterizes neighboring areas. Unapologetically hypermodern and daring the rest of the world to catch up, Rotterdam is poised to become one of the new cultural centers of 21st-century Europe; get to know it now, so you can say that you loved it back when. Brush up on Dali, Magritte, and Rothko at the ▓**Museum Boijmans van Beuningen,** Museumpark 18-20. (☎441 91 75; www.boijmans.rotterdam.nl. Take the metro to Eendractspl. Open Tu-Sa 10am-5pm, Su 11am-5pm. €7. Audioguide €3.) Walk through the Museumpark to reach the linear **Kunsthal,** Westzeekijk 341, which Rem Koolhaas designed to feature temporary exhibitions on architecture, photography, and painting. (☎440 03 00; www.kunsthal.nl. Open Tu-Sa 10am-5pm, Su 11am-5pm. €7.50, students €4.50.) Step aboard a 19th-century turret ship at the **Maritiem Museum,** Leeuvehaven 1, or peruse hundreds of finely detailed models. (☎413 26 80; www.maritiemmuseum.nl. Take the metro to Beurs. Open July-Aug. M-Sa 10am-5pm, Su 11am-5pm; Sept.-June Tu-Sa 10am-5pm, Su 11am-5pm. €3.50.) Just to the left of the museum, the powerful **Zadkine Monument** was erected only 11 years after the bombing of 1944; it depicts a man with a hole in his heart. Down by the wharf, floodlights illuminate the cables of the **Erasmus Bridge** each night in a ghostly white haze. Speaking of haze, coffeeshops line **Oude Binnenweg** and **Nieuwe Binnenweg.** For something more uptempo, dance the night away at the onetime

SHAPES AND SPACE

After Germany's *Luftwaffe* leveled the city in May 1940, Rotterdam became the blank slate for a new school of architects to make their mark upon. They wasted no time.

1 Start off at Jo Coenen's subtle **Netherlands Architecture Institute,** Museumpark 25.

2 Turn right on Museumpark, left after the canal, and walk 15min. to **Schouwburgplein,** which human geographers at Rotterdam's West 8 firm divided into "sunlight zones."

3 Head up Mauritsweg, but turn left on Weena. On your right is **Groothandelsgebouw,** a 1951 concrete megabuilding that rang in the era of post-war experimentation.

4 Take the metro to Blaak, and crane your neck to see Piet Blom's yellow **Kijk-Kubus** (Cube Houses).

5 Follow signs to **Witte Huis,** Wijnhaven 3. Built in the days before steel support beams, some of the walls in Europe's first skyscraper are 1.4m thick.

moviehouse **off_corso,** Kruiskade 22, today Rotterdam's hottest club phenomenon. (Beer €2. Mixed drinks €6. Cover €6, students €4. Open Th-Sa 11pm-5am.)

Trains run to: Amsterdam (1¼hr., €11.60); The Hague (25min., €3.70); and Utrecht (45min., €7.90). The VVV **tourist office,** Coolsingel 67, opposite the Stadhuis, books rooms for a €5 fee per person. (☎414 00 00; www.rotterdam.info. Open M-Th 9:30am-6pm, F 9:30am-9pm, Sa 9:30am-5pm.) **Use-It,** Schaatsbaan 41-45, is also a great service for young, budget-conscious backpackers, providing free **lockers,** publishing the *Simply the Best* guide to the city, and booking last-minute hotel rooms at discounts of up to 70%. Veer to the right behind the grey building immediately upon exiting the station, and walk 150m. (☎3110 240 91 58; www.use-it.nl. Open May-Sept. Tu-Su 9am-6pm; Oct.-Apr. Tu-Sa 9am-5pm.) If the Continent's getting you down, escape to the Middle East, Africa, or South America in one of the intricately themed rooms of ◪**Hotel Bazar ❸,** Witte de Withstr. 16. (☎206 51 51. Free bikes. Reception M-F 8am-11pm, Sa-Su 9am-11pm. Singles €60-120; doubles €68-120. AmEx/MC/V.) More modest digs are available at the centrally-located **Sleep-In De Mafkees ❶,** Schaatsbaan 41-45, with 119 beds lined up in one arena-sized room. Starry-eyed couples should ask about the honeymoon suite. (☎240 91 58; www.sleep-in.nl. Breakfast included. Sheets €2. Women-only dorm upstairs. Use-It office in basement. Reception 24hr. Open July-Aug. Dorms €10. Cash only.) Schwarma and Chinese food await along **Witte de Withstraat,** where you can grab a meal for around €5. Try **Lijbaan** for its array of pubs, bars, and culinary charm. ◪**Bazar ❷,** on the first floor of the hotel (see above), shines with glittering colored lights, bright blue tables, and amazing Middle Eastern fusion cuisine. (☎206 51 51. Sandwiches €4. Entrees €8-15. Open M-Th 8am-1am, F 8am-2am, Sa 10am-2am, Su 10am-midnight. AmEx/MC/V.) Shop for groceries at **Spar,** Witte de Withstr. 36. (Open M-F 8:30am-7pm, Sa 8:30am-5pm.) **Postal Code:** 3000.

UTRECHT ☎030

Sitting roughly in the center of the Netherlands, Utrecht (pop. 250,000) is the country's oldest city, with a well-preserved commercial district hemmed in by the north-south Oudegracht and Nieuwegracht. Get info on Utrecht's churches and museums at **RonDom,** Dompl. 9, the visitors center for cultural history. (Open M-Sa 10am-5pm, Su noon-5pm.) Then make your first stop the awe-inspiring **Domkerk,** started in 1254 and finished a good 250 years later. (Open May-Sept. M-F 10am-5pm, Sa 10am-3:30pm, Su 2-4pm; Oct.-Apr. M-F 11am-4pm, Sa

11am-3:30pm, Su 2-4pm. Free.) The 112m **Domtoren,** the tallest tower in the Netherlands, was attached to the cathedral until a medieval tornado blew away the nave in 1674. (Tickets for tours sold at RonDom. Tours Apr.-Sept. every hr. M-Sa 10am-4pm, Su noon-4pm; Oct.-Mar. daily 1 and 3pm. €6.80.) The **Museum Quarter** includes the labyrinthine **Centraal Museum,** Nicolaaskerkhof 10, with collections ranging from oil paintings in the style of Caravaggio to Gerrit Thomas Rietveld's 1918 *Red and Blue Chair.* (☎236 23 62; www.centraalmuseum.nl. Open Tu-Su 11am-5pm. €9, students €4.50.) The nearby **Aboriginal Art Museum,** Oudegracht 176, is the only museum in Europe devoted to native art from Australia. Most info is in Dutch, but ask for the walkthrough pamphlet in English. (☎238 01 00. Open Tu-F 10am-5pm, Sa-Su 11am-5pm. €8.) Utrecht is the Netherlands's largest college town, and it has the social scene to prove it. Thursday's the big night for stepping out among students, although Saturday draws an spirited crowd from the provinces after students head elsewhere for the weekend. **De Winkel van Sinkel,** Oudegracht 158, is the city's most popular grand-cafe, with martini glasses lining the walls of this huge, mandarin-colored complex. (Beer €2-3. Open M-W and Su 11am-midnight, Th-F 11am-1am, Sa 11am-6am. DJs spin house music Sa. Cover €12.50.) In **'t Oude Pothuys,** Oudegracht 279, musical instruments hang from the ceiling in a converted cellar that hosts live music nightly. (Beer €1.80. Open daily 10pm-1:30am.)

Trains depart from Hoog Catharijne station to Amsterdam (30min., 3-6 per hr., €6.30); Arnhem (40min., 2-4per hr., €8.60); and Rotterdam (30min., 2-4 per hr., €6.80). To get to the VVV **tourist office,** Vinkenbrugstr. 19, follow the signs to Vredenberg, which leads to the town center. It's located near the Neude festival square. Pick up a map of the city and a complete listing of museums and sights for €2. (☎0900 128 87 32; www.utrechtstad.com. Open M noon-6pm, Tu-W and F 10am-6pm, Th 9am-9pm, Sa 9:30am-5pm; May-Sept. Su 10am-2pm.) **█B&B Utrecht City Centre ❶,** Lucasbolwerk 4, offers guests musical instruments, an inflatable pool, and a 24hr. breakfast buffet. From the station, walk toward the city center down Smakkelaarsveld, which eventually turns into Nobelstr. (☎0650 43 48 84; www.hostelutrecht.nl. Free Internet. Coed showers. Dorms €16; singles €55; doubles €65; triples €90; quads €110. AmEx/MC/V.) Farther from downtown, the same owners run quieter **B&B Utrecht ❶,** Egelantierstr. 25. Take bus #3 to Watertoren (€1), cross the street and head to Anemoonstr., then go two blocks to the end and turn left. The street turns into Egelantierstr. and the hostel is on your left. (☎0650 43 48 84; www.hotelinfo.nl. Breakfast 24hr. Free Internet. Dorms €12; singles €45; doubles €50; triples €70; quads €80; quints €90. AmEx/MC/V.) **Mr. Jacks ❶,** Voorstr. 61, polls well with students for a candlelit, vine-draped decor. Pizzas are all €4.50, while the pasta is just €5. (Open daily 4pm-midnight. Cash only.) Sit out by the canal or inside the cozy lounge at **Het Nachtrestaurant ❷,** Oudegrt. 158, which boasts great tapas (€2.40-6.80) and sangria (€3.20) by the glass. (☎230 30 36. Open M-W 6-11pm, Th-F 6pm-midnight, Sa 6-10:30pm. MC/V.) **Postal Code:** 3512.

HOGE VELUWE NATIONAL PARK ☎0318

The impressive **Hoge Veluwe National Park** (HO-geh VEY-loo-wuh) is a 13,565-acre preserve of woods, heath, dunes, red deer, and wild boars. (☎0900 464 38 35; www.hogeveluwe.nl. Park open daily June-July 8am-10pm; May and Aug. 8am-9pm; low season reduced hours. €6.) Deep in the park, the **Rijksmuseum Kröller-Müller** has troves of van Goghs from the founding family's collection, while the striking **sculpture garden** has exceptional works by Dubuffet, Rodin, and Serra. (☎03 18 59 12 41; www.kmm.nl. Open Tu-Su 10am-5pm, sculpture garden closes at 4:30pm. €6, children €3.) Explore over 40km of paths with one of the 1700 free **bikes** in the park and a map (€2.50) from the **visitors center.** Find your way to the center by following signs reading "*Bezoekerscentrum.*" (Open daily 10am-5pm.)

Arnhem (pop. 141,000) is a good base for exploring the park; **bus** #107 (6 strips) traverses the 15km from Arnhem and drops visitors at the park's northwestern Otterlo entrance. From the Otterlo stop, you can walk to the park entrance and grab a bike, or else transfer to bus #110 (free), which heads through the middle of the park and stops at both the museum and the visitors center. Contact Arnhem's **tourist office,** Willemspl. 8, for more information. (☎ 0900 202 40 75; www.vvvarnhem.nl. Open M 11am-5:30pm, Tu-F 9am-5:30pm, Sa 10am-5pm.) To get to the **Stayokay Hostel (HI) ❶,** Diepenbrocklaan 27, take bus #3 (2 strips) from the Arnhem train station to Rijnstate Hospital; as you face the hospital, turn right and then left on Cattepoelseweg. About 150m ahead, turn right up the brick steps, and right again at the top. (☎ 026 442 01 14; www.stayokay.com/arnhem. Breakfast and sheets included. Reception 8am-11pm. Dorms €22; singles €37; doubles €59; triples €80; quads €101. Nonmembers add €2.50. AmEx/MC/V.) **Postal Code:** 6800.

MAASTRICHT
☎ 043

Situated on a narrow strip of land between Belgium and Germany, Maastricht (pop. 122,000) has a strategic location that has been a target for military conquest throughout history. More recently, however, the city has been a symbol of international cooperation, as it was the Treaty of Maastricht that created the European Union in 1991. The futuristic design of the **Bonnefantenmuseum,** ave. Ceramique 250, strikes an intriguing contrast with the building's traditional Dutch brickwork. (☎ 329 01 99; www.bonnefanten.nl. Open Tu-Su 11am-5pm. €7.) Centuries of conflict prompted Maastricht to invest in an innovative subterranean defense system; the underground passages of the ▧**Mount Saint Pieter Caves** were used as a siege shelter as late as WWII, and they contain inscriptions and artwork by generations of inhabitants. Access to the caves is possible at two locations, and only with a tour guide. The **Northern System,** Luikerweg 71, will have to suffice during the low season (English-language tours mid-Apr. to June and Sept. to late Oct. at 2pm; €3.50), but opt for the **Zonneberg Caves,** Slavante 1, during high season (English-language tours July-Aug. at 2:45pm; €3.50). When night falls, throw back a pint at **In de Moriaan,** Stokstr. 12, reputedly the smallest bar in the Netherlands. (Beer €1.60-3. Open daily 11am-2am.) Then get pious at **Nightlive,** Kesselskade 43, a former church where clubgoers dance beneath an illuminated cross. (☎ 362 82 78; www.nightlive.nl. Open Th 10pm-4am, F-Sa 11pm-5am. Cover €10.)

The train station is located on the east side of town. **Trains** go to Amsterdam (2½hr., 3 per hr., €26) and Brussels (2 hr., 1 per hr., €19) via Liège (30min., 5 per hr., €7.20). To get from the station to the VVV **tourist office,** Kleine Str. 1, walk straight on Stationstr., cross the bridge, go one more block, take a right, and walk down a block; the office will be on the right, and it books rooms for a €1.75 fee. (☎ 325 21 21; www.vvvmaastricht.nl. Open May-Oct. M-Sa 9am-6pm, Su 11am-3pm; Nov.-Apr. M-F 9am-6pm, Sa 9am-5pm.) Maastricht's popularity with gourmands and monocled art dealers means that budget accommodations can be hard to find. The tiny cabins of the floating **Botel ❶,** Maasboulevard 95, are the best bet in town, although some of them are reminiscent of a roomy telephone booth. Try to land a room above deck. (☎ 321 90 23. Reception 24hr. Breakfast €4. Singles €27-30; doubles €43-45; triples €63; quads €84. Cash only.) After a trip to the caves, stop by **Chalet Bergrust ❶,** Luikerweg 71, a homespun eatery with beautiful views of the city. Sandwiches and omelettes run about €5. (☎ 325 54 12. Open daily in summer 10am-10pm; winter M, W, F-Su 11am-8pm. Cash only.) **Postal Code:** 6200.

GRONINGEN
☎ 050

Groningen, easily the most happening city in the northern Netherlands, pulses with new life. More than half of the city's 175,000 inhabitants are under 35, adding to Groningen's reputation as a great party town. Heavily bombed during WWII,

Groningen rebuilt itself completely and yet managed to keep the Old World appeal that Rotterdam consciously kicked to the curb. The city's spectacular ▓Groninger Museum, housed in three whimsical pavilions, cultivates a futuristic laboratory atmosphere for daring exhibitions of contemporary art. (☎366 65 55; www.groninger-museum.nl. Open July-Aug. M 1-5pm, Tu-Su 10am-5pm; Sept.-June Tu-Su 10am-5pm. €7, students €6. Audioguides €2.50.) Admire the city from atop the Grote Markt's Martinitoren, a 97m tower that weathered the German attacks of WWII. Book tickets at the tourist office. (Open daily Apr.-Oct. 11am-5pm; Nov.-Mar. noon-4pm. €2.50.) Soak up the sun in the serene Prinsenhoftuin (Princes' Court Gardens); the entrance is on the canal by the Maagden bridge. (Open daily Apr. to mid-Oct. 10am-dusk.) Inside the gardens, the Theeschenkerij Tea Hut offers 130 kinds of tea (€0.80) under canopied underpasses. (Open M-F 10-6pm, Sa-Su noon-6pm. Closed during inclement weather.) Groningen parties harder than its modest size would let on. For bars packed shoulder-to-shoulder, head to the southeastern corner of the Grote Markt on Poelestr. and Peperstr., where students boast that the bars close when people stop drinking. The staff at Vera, Oosterstr. 44, proclaim the club to be "the rock temple of the entire world," although the shows that Nirvana and U2 have played on the premises lend the pronouncement some credibility. (☎313 46 81; www.vera-groningen.nl. Open Tu, Th and Sa; sometimes other days. Concerts 11pm. Cover usually €6-8.) You'll want to see and be seen beneath the wire chandeliers at trendy News Cafe, Waagpl. 5. (Open M-W 10am-1am, Th 10am-3am, F 10am-4am, Sa 10am-5am, Su 11am-1am.)

Trains arrive from Amsterdam (2½hr., 2 per hr., €26), though passengers sometimes need to switch trains at Amersfoot; ask the conductor to be sure. To get to the VVV tourist office, Grote Markt 25, turn right as you exit the station, walk along the canal, turn left at the first bridge, and keep heading straight on Herestr. until it hits Grote Markt. The office is in the far corner of the Markt next to the Martinitoren, and it books accommodations for free. (☎313 97 41; www.vvvgroningen.nl. Open M-W 9am-6pm, Th 9am-8pm, F 9am-6pm, Sa 10am-5pm.) A staff of heavy-metal enthusiasts tends imaginatively decorated rooms at Simplon Youthhotel ❶, Boterdiep 73-2. Take bus #1 from the station (dir.: Korrewegwijk) to Boterdiep; the hostel is through the yellow- and black-striped entranceway. (☎313 52 21; www.simplonjongerenhotel.nl. Breakfast €4; included with private room. Free lockers. Sheets €2.50. Reception 3pm-2am. Lockout noon-3pm. All-female dorm available. Dorms €13.75; singles €29; doubles €43; triples €61; quads €77. Cash only.) At ▓Ben'z ❷, Peperstr. 17, dinner is served by lantern-light in a Bedouin tent. Recline on Turkish cushions after your meal and take a puff on the *nargila*, a traditional water pipe. (☎313 79 17; www.restaurantbenz.nl. Student menu €7.60-9.10. Open daily 4:30-10pm. Cash only.) While your palate is attuned to the spices of the East, try ▓De Kleine Moghul ❷, Nieuwe Boteringstr. 62, which serves inventive Indian fare to guests surrounded by lengths of drapery and shimmery walls. (☎318 89 05. Entrees €8-11. Open daily 5-10pm. MC/V.) Postal Code: 9700.

WADDEN ISLANDS (WADDENEILANDEN)

Wadden means "mudflat" in Dutch, but sand is the defining characteristic of these islands; gorgeous beaches hide behind dunes covered in golden grass. Deserted, tulip-lined bike trails carve through vast, flat stretches of grazing land to the sea. Sleepy and isolated, these islands are truly the Netherlands' best-kept secret.

▐ TRANSPORTATION The islands arch clockwise around the northwestern coast of the Netherlands: Texel (closest to Amsterdam), Vlieland, Terschelling, Ameland, and Schiermonnikoog. To reach Texel, take the train from Amsterdam to Den Helder (1½hr., 2 per hr., €11.20), then grab bus #33 (2 strips) and a ferry to 't Hoorntje, the island's southernmost town (15min., 1 per hr. 6:30am-9:30pm, round-trip €3). **Buses** depart from the ferry dock to various locales around the island, though the best way to travel is to rent a **bike** from **Verhuurbedrijf Heijne,** opposite the ferry dock. (☎02 22 31 95 88. Bikes from €4.50 per day. Open daily Apr.-Oct. 9am-8pm; Nov.-Mar. 9am-5pm.) To reach the other islands from Amsterdam, catch a **train** from Centraal station to Harlingen Haven (3hr., €27). From Harlingen, **ferries** (☎05 17 49 15 00; www.doeksen.nl) depart for Terschelling (1-2 hr., 3-5 per day, round-trip €22.50). Daily **ferries** also run between Texel, Vlieland, and Terschelling. From Texel, ferries depart for Vlieland at 5:15pm (€11.50). From Vlieland, ferries depart for Terschelling at 7pm (€5.70).

▓ **TEXEL** The largest and most populous of the Wadden Islands, Texel (pop. 14,000) is still home to more sheep than people. Birdwatchers bundle up to see the thousands of Brent geese that winter in the island's Zeeburg reserve. Stunning **beaches** lie near De Koog, on the western side of the island, and *naakstranden* (nude beaches) beckon the uninhibited; you can bare it all near paal 9 (2km southwest of Den Hoorn) or paal 27 (5km west of De Cocksdorp). Watch the frolicsome seals being fed at the **EcoMare Museum and Aquarium,** Ruijslaan 92, in De Koog. (☎02 22 31 77 41; www.ecomare.nl. Take bus #230. Open daily 9am-5pm. Seal feeding 11am and 3pm. €7.50.) A **Texel Ticket** (€4.50), for sale on any bus, allows one day of unlimited travel on the island's bus system. The VVV **tourist office,** Emmaln 66, is located 300m south of the main bus stop in Den Burg; look for the blue signs. (☎02 22 31 47 41; www.texel.net. Open M-Th 9am-6pm, F 9am-9pm, Sa 9am-5:30pm, Su 10am-1:30pm; Sept.-June closed Su.) At press time, traveling from the ferry landing to **StayOkay Texel (HI) ❶**, Schansweg 7, meant a long ride on bus #29. However, StayOkay is preparing to move the hostel into a new building with bathrooms in each room; check the website for details. (☎02 22 31 54 41; www.stayokay.com/texel. Breakfast and sheets included. Bikes €5. Reception daily 8:30am-10:15pm. Dorms €20; low season reduced rates. Nonmembers add €2.50. AmEx/MC/V.) **Campgrounds** cluster south of De Koog and near De Cocksdorp.

▓ **TERSCHELLING** With 80% of the island covered by protected nature reserves, Terschelling (pop. 5000) offers secluded **beaches,** stretches of mudflat, and cranberry bogs dotted by migratory gulls. To explore the island's scenery, rent a **bike** from **Haantjes Fietsverhuur,** W. Barentzskade 23 and other locations around the island. (☎05 62 44 29 29. Bikes €4.50 per day, €20 per week. M-Sa 9am-5:30pm, Su 9:30am-5:30pm.) The VVV **tourist office,** W. Barentzkade 19, opposite the ferry landing, books rooms for a €2 fee and arranges 3hr. tours of the island in horse-drawn carriages. (☎05 62 44 30 00; www.vvv-terschelling.nl. Carriage tours €15. Open M-Sa 9:30am-5:30pm.) The **Terschelling Hostel (HI) ❶**, van Heusdenweg 39, is located just out of town on the waterfront. From the boat dock, turn right and walk for 15min. (☎05 62 44 23 38; www.stayokay.com/terschelling. Breakfast and sheets included. Laundry €7. Reception 9am-10pm. Dorms €24; low season €18-22. Add €1.50 F-Sa. AmEx/MC/V.) The most convenient place to grab a bite is in the main village, West Terschelling. However, it's worth the 13km trek out to ▓**The Heartbreak Hotel ❷**, in Oosterend, which doubles as a shrine to Elvis. Rent a bike or take the hourly night bus (€4.50 round-trip). The restaurant serves great diner-style food (Burning Love Burger €4.50) in red pleather booths, and hosts live music each night in summer. (☎05 62 44 86 34. Open daily 10am-2am. AmEx/MC/V.) From mid-July to mid-August, every wild child in the Netherlands flocks to Terschelling; head to **Braskoer,** Torenstr. 32, to join a young crowd on the sweaty, packed dance floor. (☎05 62 44 21 97. Beer €1.50-3. Cover €4. Open daily 10am-2am.) If the high-energy pop music leaves you feeling a bit long in the tooth, take your brooding thoughts on mortality over to dimly-lit **Cafe De Zeevaart,** Torenstr. 22, a traditional Dutch *bruin café* (brown cafe) where classic rock prevails. The kitchen serves snack fare until close. (☎05 62 44 26 77. Beer €1.50. Open daily 10am-2am.)

NORWAY (NORGE)

The rugged fjords and remote mountain farms of Norway gave birth to one of the most fabled and feared seafaring civilizations of pre-medieval Europe. The Vikings of modern-day Denmark sailed south into France and the Swedes pointed their longboats east toward Russia, but Norway's Vikings headed west centuries before Columbus to settle Greenland, Iceland, and Canada's Newfoundland. Modern-day Norwegians have inherited their Norse ancestors' independent streak, voting against joining the EU in 1994 and drawing the ire of environmental groups for being the only nation to authorize commercial whaling. And although much of the country's oil revenues get socked away to pay for social programs, Norway is a place that values self-reliance. After all, scaling the unforgiving face of a heaving blue glacier is not an exercise in consensus decision-making.

 DISCOVER NORWAY: SUGGESTED ITINERARIES

Oslo (p. 778) is the classic jumping-off point for travels in Norway, although the capital city's many museums and ethnic restaurants may leave you spoiling to stay. Tear yourself away long enough to visit seaside **Stavanger** (p. 786), and then catch a westbound train for the long, scenic ride to **Bergen** (p. 787). Let yourself get sidetracked by a trip up the **Flåm Railway** (p. 792), or try hiking on the unspoiled Hardangervidda plateau near **Eidfjord** (p. 793). Plan a few days to explore Bergen's museums and relaxed cafes, but then head north to picture-postcard **Geirangerfjord** (p. 797) and less-trafficked **Sognefjord** (p. 794). Soak up some civilization in **Ålesund** (p. 798) or **Trondheim** (p. 799) before shooting north to the tumbledown fishing villages of the **Lofoten Islands** (p. 801). Vibrant **Tromsø** (p. 802) ties it all together with echoes of the cosmopolitan south.

ESSENTIALS

WHEN TO GO

Oslo averages 18°C (63°F) in July and 4°C (24°F) in January. In the north, average temperatures drop and it is wetter than the south and east; Bergen and the surrounding mountains, in particular, see more than their share of rain. For a few weeks around the summer solstice (June 21), the area north of Bodø basks in the midnight sun. You stand the best chance of seeing the **Northern Lights** from above the Arctic Circle (Nov.-Feb.). Skiing is best just before Easter.

DOCUMENTS AND FORMALITIES

VISAS. EU citizens do not need a visa. Citizens of Australia, Canada, New Zealand, and the US do not need a visa for stays of up to 90 days, although this three-month period begins upon entry into any of the countries that belong to the EU's freedom of movement zone. For more information, see p. 17.

EMBASSIES. Foreign embassies for Norway are in Oslo. For Norwegian embassies at home: **Australia** and **New Zealand,** Royal Norwegian Embassy, 17 Hunter St., Yarralumla, Canberra, ACT 2600 (☎ 02 6273 3444; www.canberra.mfa.no); **Canada,** 90 Sparks St., Suite 532, Ottawa, ON K1P 5B4 (☎ 613-238-6571; www.emb-noway.ca); **Ireland,** 34 Molesworth St., Dublin 2 (☎ 01 662 18 00; www.norway.ie/

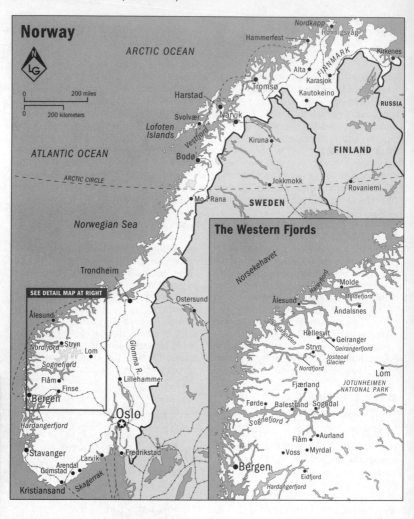

info/embassy.htm); **UK,** 25 Belgrave Sq., London SW1X 8QD (☎020 7591 5500; www.norway.org.uk/info/embassy.htm); **US,** 2720 34th St. NW, Washington, D.C. 20008 (☎202-333-6000; www.norway.org/embassy).

TRANSPORTATION

BY PLANE. The main international airport is in Oslo, though a few international flights land at Trondheim and Bergen. **Scandinavian Airlines** (Norway ☎815 20 400; UK 870 6072 7727; US 800-221-2350; www.scandinavian.net) flies to Norway, as do **Finnair** and **Icelandair.** Flying between cities in Norway is becoming increasingly popular, especially since students and travelers under 25 qualify for special fares from 100kr. SAS offers domestic standby tickets (*sjanse billetter*).

BY TRAIN. Norway's train system includes an extensive commuter train network around Oslo and long-distance lines running from Oslo to Bergen and to Stavanger via Kristiansand. Overnight trains may be your best option for travel as far north as Bodø and Trondheim; from there, you'll need buses or ferries to get farther north. Trains do run southeast from Narvik, going through Kiruna, Sweden (p. 1017). Seat reservations (30kr) are compulsory on many trains, including high-speed **Signatur** trains, which cover some of the long-distance lines. **Eurail** is valid in Norway. The **Norway Railpass** allows three days of unlimited travel in a one-month period (US\$209, under 26 US\$151), while the **Scanrail pass** purchased in Norway allows five travel days in a 15-day period (1956kr, under 26 1360kr) or 21 consecutive travel days (3044kr, under 26 2117kr) of unlimited rail travel, as well as heavily discounted fares on many ferries and buses. However, only three of those days can be used in the country of purchase, so a Scanrail pass purchased at home (p. 63) is more economical for those traveling mostly within Norway.

BY BUS. Buses can be quite expensive but are the only land option north of Bodø and in the fjords. **Norway Bussekspress** (☎81 54 44 44; www.nor-way.no) operates 75% of the domestic bus routes and publishes a free timetable (*Rutehefte*) with schedules and prices, available at bus stations and on buses. Scanrail holders are entitled to a 50% discount on most bus routes, and students with a valid student card are eligible for a 25-50% discount—be insistent, and follow the rules listed in the *Norway Bussekspress* booklet. Bus passes, valid for 21 consecutive travel days (2300kr), are good deals for those exploring the fjords or the north.

BY FERRY. Car ferries (*ferjer*) are usually much cheaper (and slower) than the many passenger express boats (*hurtigbat* or *ekspressbat*) cruising the coasts and fjords; both often have student, Scanrail, and InterRail discounts. The **Hurtigruten** (☎76 96 76 00; www.hurtigruten.com) takes six days for the incredible voyage from Bergen to Kirkenes on the Russian border; there is one northbound and one southbound departure daily from each of its 34 stops (round-trip from 3600kr in high season, 1800kr in low season). There are no railpass discounts, but some ferry lines offer a 50% discount for students. The most common ports for international ferries are Oslo, Bergen, Kristiansand, and Stavanger; destinations include: Copenhagen and Hanstholm, Denmark; Newcastle, England; Iceland; and Sweden.

BY CAR. Citizens of Canada, the EU, and the US need only a valid driver's license in their home country to drive in Norway for less than one year. Insurance is required and is usually included in the price of rental. Roads in Norway are in good condition, although blind curves are common and roads are frighteningly narrow in some places. Drivers should remember to be cautious, especially on mountain roads and in tunnels. Driving around the fjords can be frustrating, as only Nordfjord has a road completely circumnavigating it; there are numerous car ferries, but check timetables in advance to connect with the boats. Rental cars are expensive, but can be more affordable than trains and buses for groups. Vehicles are required to keep headlights on at all times. For more info on driving in Europe, see p. 66.

BY BIKE AND BY THUMB. Biking is becoming increasingly common. The beautiful scenery is rewarding for cyclists, although the hilly terrain can be rough on bikes. Contact **Syklistenes Landsforening** (☎22 47 30 30) for maps, suggested routes, and other info. **Hitchhiking** is notoriously difficult in Norway. Some successfully hitchhike beyond the rail lines in northern Norway and the fjord areas of the west, but many others try for hours and end up exactly where they started. Hitchhikers should bring several layers of clothing, rain gear, and a warm sleeping bag. *Let's Go* does not recommend hitchhiking as a safe means of transport.

NORWAY

TOURIST SERVICES AND MONEY

EMERGENCY	Police: ☎112. Ambulance: ☎113. Fire: ☎110.

TOURIST OFFICES. Virtually every town and village has a **Turistinformasjon** office; look for a white lower-case "i" on a square green sign. In July and the first half of August, most tourist offices are open daily; expect reduced hours in low season. Check out www.visitnorway.com for a directory of local offices, and the very good www.norwaythepoorway.com for tips on traveling cheaply.

MONEY. The Norwegian **krone** (plural: kroner) is divided into 100 *øre*. Coins come in 50 *øre*, as well as 1kr, 5kr, 10kr, and 20kr denominations; bills are in 50kr, 100kr, 200kr, 500kr, and 1000kr denominations. Banks and large post offices change money, usually for a commission (but at fair rates). As a general rule, it's cheaper to exchange money in Norway than at home. **Tipping** is not essential, but an extra 5-15% is always welcome for good restaurant service. Hotel bills often include a 15% service charge. Refunds for the 24% **Value Added Tax (VAT)** are available for single-item purchases of more than 250kr in a single store.

NORWEGIAN KRONER (KR)	AUS$1 = 4.83KR	10KR = AUS$2.07
	CDN$1 = 5.26KR	10KR = CDN$1.90
	EUR€1 = 8.30KR	10KR = EUR€1.21
	NZ$1 = 4.45KR	10KR = NZ$2.25
	UK£1 = 12.30KR	10KR = UK£0.81
	US$1 = 6.87KR	10KR = US$1.46

BUSINESS HOURS. Business hours are short in summer, especially on Fridays and in August, when Norwegians vacation. Shop hours are Monday to Friday 10am-5pm, Saturday 10am-2pm; hours may be extended on Thursday. Banks are generally open Monday to Wednesday and Friday 8am-3pm, Thursday 8am-5pm.

COMMUNICATION

PHONE CODES	**Country code: 47. International dialing prefix:** 095. There are no city codes in Norway. From outside Norway, dial int'l dialing prefix (see inside back cover) + 47 + local number.

TELEPHONES. There are three types of **public phones;** the black and gray phones accept 1kr, 5kr, 10kr, and 20kr coins; green phones accept only phone cards; and red phones accept coins, phone cards, and major credit cards. **Phone cards** (*telekort;* 40kr, 90kr, or 140kr at post offices and Narvesen kiosks) are the most economical option, especially when prices drop 5pm-8am. **Mobile phones** are an increasingly popular and economic option; for more info, see p. 35. For help with domestic calls, dial ☎117; for help with international calls, dial ☎115. International direct access numbers include: **AT&T** (☎800 190 11); **British Telecom** (☎800 199 44); **Canada Direct** (☎800 191 11); **MCI** (☎800 199 12); **Sprint** (☎800 198 77); **Telecom New Zealand** (☎800 140 58); **Telstra Australia** (☎800 199 61).

MAIL. Mailing a postcard or letter within Norway costs 5.50kr; to Sweden or Finland 7.50kr; within Europe 9.50kr; to regions outside Europe 10.50kr. Most post offices offer Poste Restante. Address mail to be held in the following format: First name SURNAME, *Poste Restante*, 5811 Bergen, NORWAY.

INTERNET ACCESS. There are a good number of Internet cafes in Oslo and Bergen. Smaller cities might have one or two Internet cafes, but most have a public library open on weekdays that offers free Internet access in 15-30min. time slots.

LANGUAGE. Norwegian is universally spoken, although most Norwegians also speak flawless English. The Sami languages are spoken by the indigenous people of northern Norway. For basic Norwegian words and phrases, see p. 1063.

ACCOMMODATIONS AND CAMPING

NORWAY	❶	❷	❸	❹	❺
ACCOMMODATIONS	under 200kr	200-350kr	350-500kr	500-650kr	over 650kr

HI youth hostels (*vandrerhjem*) are run by **Norske Vandrerhjem**, Torggata 1, in Oslo (☎23 13 93 00; www.vandrerhjem.no). Beds run 150-210kr, though hostels out on the Lofoten Islands are closer to 100kr. Sheets typically cost 45-60kr per stay. Only rural or smaller hostels have curfews (though quiet hours are usually 11pm-7am), and only a few are open year-round. Most open in mid- to late June and close after the third week in August. Most tourist offices book **private rooms** and last-minute hotel rooms for a fee (usually 30kr).

Norwegian law allows free **camping** anywhere on public land for less than three nights, provided that you keep 150m from buildings and leave no trace behind. **Den Norske Turistforening** (DNT; Norwegian Mountain Touring Association) sells excellent maps (60-70kr), offers various guided hiking trips for novice and experienced hikers alike, and maintains more than 350 **mountain huts** (*hytter*) throughout the country. (☎22 82 28 00; www.dntoslo.no. One-year membership 365kr, under 25 175kr.) The 43 staffed huts are open in summer; most have showers and serve dinner around 7pm. Unstaffed huts are open from mid-February until mid-October, and a sizable minority have basic provisions for sale on the honor system. Leave a 200kr deposit at any tourist office to borrow a key. Official campgrounds ask 60-130kr for small tents, and 400-700kr for cabins.

FOOD AND DRINK

NORWAY	❶	❷	❸	❹	❺
FOOD	under 60kr	60-135kr	135-200kr	200-300kr	over 300kr

Eating in Norway is pricey; markets and bakeries are the way to go. **Rema 1000** and **Rimi** supermarkets have the best prices (usually open M-F 9am-8pm, Sa 9am-6pm), while outdoor markets provide cheap seafood and fruit. Many restaurants have inexpensive *dagens ret* (dish of the day; 70-80kr); otherwise, you'll rarely spend less than 150kr on a full Norwegian meal. Fish in Norway—cod, salmon, and herring—is fresh and relatively inexpensive. National specialties include *ost* (cheese); *kjøttkaker* (pork and veal meatballs) with boiled potatoes; and, for more adventurous carnivores, reindeer, ptarmigan, and *hval* (whale meat). Around Christmas, steel yourself for a special meal of *lutefisk* (dried fish soaked in water and lye). Beer is very expensive in bars (45-60kr for 0.5L), though 0.33L bottles hover around 10-13kr in supermarkets. Try the local favorite Frydenlund, or go rock-bottom with Danish Tuborg. You must be 18 to buy beer, 20 to buy wine and alcohol at aptly-named **Vinmonopolet** ("wine monopoly") stores.

HOLIDAYS AND FESTIVALS

Holidays: New Year's Day (Jan. 1); Maundy Thursday (Mar. 24); Good Friday (Mar. 25); Easter Sunday and Monday (Mar. 27-28); Labor Day (May 1); Ascension Day (May 5); Whit Sunday and Monday (May 15-16); Constitution Day (May 17); Christmas Eve and Day (Dec. 24-25); Boxing Day (Dec. 26).

Festivals: Norway throws festivals virtually year-round, from the Tromsø International Film Festival (Jan. 18-23) to Lillehammer's DølaJazz Festival in mid-October. David Bowie was struck by an airborne lollipop during 2004's Norwegian Wood festival, but dauntless Oslo will roll out the 2005 festival in mid-June. Heavy metal enthusiasts might prefer Inferno, held in the capital over Easter weekend. A searchable database of other festivals can be found online at www.norwayfestivals.com.

FACTS AND FIGURES: NORWAY	
Official Name: Kingdom of Norway.	**Land Area:** 310,000 sq. km.
Capital: Oslo.	**Time Zone:** GMT +1.
Major Cities: Bergen, Stavanger, Tromsø, Trondheim.	**Language:** Norwegian; Swedish and English widely spoken.
Population: 4,570,000.	**Religions:** Evangelical Lutheran (86%).

OSLO
☎ 22

Scandinavian capitals consent to being urban without renouncing the landscape around them, and Oslo (pop. 550,000) is no exception. The pine-covered hills to the north and the limpid Oslofjord to the south bracket the cultural institutions, classy cafes, and Eurochic boutiques that give the city its metropolitan edge. A wave of immigrant workers from Pakistan and Turkey arrived in Oslo in the early 1970s, followed later by refugees from Somalia, Vietnam, and Iran. Most of these new arrivals still live in or around the capital, and while numerically they remain a small minority, their presence has both challenged and enriched the largest city in a nation that remains ethnically homogeneous and wedded to its Nordic past.

▐ TRANSPORTATION

Flights: The high-speed **FlyToget** train runs between **Gardermoen Airport** (GEN; ☎ 815 50 250) and downtown Oslo (20min.; M-F every 10min., Sa-Su every 20min. 4:45am-midnight from train station to airport, 5:36am-12:36am from airport to downtown; 110-180kr). White SAS **Flybussen** drive a similar route (40min.; every 20-30min. 4:05am-9:50pm from bus terminal to airport, 5:20am-1am from airport to downtown; 110kr, round-trip 160kr).

Trains: Oslo Sentralstasjon (Oslo S; ☎ 81 50 08 88). Trains run to: **Bergen** (6-7hr., 3-4 per day, 670kr); **Copenhagen** (7-8hr.; 2 per day; 1158kr, under 26 809kr); **Stockholm** (4¾hr.; 3 per day; 1014kr, under 26 709kr); **Trondheim** (6-7hr., 3-5 per day, 748kr). Mandatory seat reservations for all long-distance domestic trains cost 41-71kr.

Buses: Norway Bussekspress, Schweigårdsgt. 8 (☎ 81 54 44 44). Follow the signs from the train station through the Oslo Galleri Mall to the Bussterminalen Galleriet. Schedules available at the info office. 25-50% student discount on tickets to major cities.

Ferries: Color Line (☎ 22 94 44 00). To **Hirtshals, Denmark** (12½hr., 7:30pm, from 580kr) and **Kiel, Germany** (20hr., 1:30pm, from 1430kr). 50% student discount daily except F. **DFDS Seaways** (☎ 21 62 10 00) goes to **Copenhagen, Denmark** (16hr.) and **Helsingborg, Sweden** (14hr.) daily at 5pm (both from 995kr). Color Line departs from 20min. west of the train station, DFDS from 10min. south.

Public Transportation: Bus, tram, subway, and **ferries** all cost 30kr per ride, or 20kr in advance. Tickets include 1hr. of unlimited transfers. If you are caught traveling without a valid ticket, you can be fined 750kr. **Trafikanten** (☎ 177), in front of Oslo S, also sells the **Dagskort** (day pass) for 55kr, **Flexicard** (8 trips) for 150kr, and **7-day Card** for 190kr. Open M-F 7am-8pm, Sa-Su 8am-6pm. Tickets also available at Narvesen kiosks and Automat machines. The **Oslo Pass** is available at the Main Tourist Office (see below) and includes unlimited public transportation as well as admission to most of the city's museums. (1-day pass 195kr, 2-day 285kr, 3-day 375kr.)

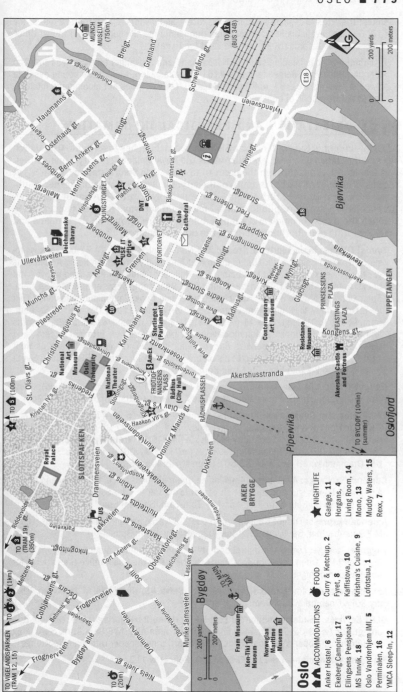

NORWAY

Oslo

🏠 ACCOMMODATIONS
Anker Hostel, **6**
Ekeberg Camping, **17**
Ellingsens Pensjonat, **3**
MS Innvik, **18**
Oslo Vandrerhjem IMI, **5**
Perminalen, **16**
YMCA Sleep-In, **12**

🍴 FOOD
Curry & Ketchup, **2**
Fyret, **8**
Kaffistova, **10**
Krishna's Cuisine, **9**
Lofotstua, **1**

★ NIGHTLIFE
Garage, **11**
Horgans, **4**
Living Room, **14**
Mono, **13**
Muddy Waters, **15**
Rexx, **7**

Bikes: The city's bike-share system allows locals and visitors alike to borrow one of the 1000+ bikes available at racks scattered throughout the city center. Main Tourist Office sells enrollment cards (50kr) that are valid for 1 year.

Hitchhiking: Those heading south to Kristiansand and Stavanger take bus #31 or 32 to Maritim. Hitchers to Bergen take bus #161 to the last stop, while those bound east into Sweden ride bus #81, 83, or 85 to Bekkelaget. *Let's Go* does not recommend hitchhiking as a safe means of transport.

ORIENTATION AND PRACTICAL INFORMATION

At Oslo's center is the garden plaza **Slottsparken,** which lies just beside **Oslo University** and the **National Theater,** and surrounds the **Royal Palace.** The city's main street, **Karl Johans gate,** runs through the heart of town to **Oslo Sentralstasjon** ("Oslo S") at the eastern end. The harbor is south of the city, the **Bygdøy** peninsula farther southwest. Parks are scattered throughout Oslo, especially north of the Nationaltheatret. An excellent network of public trams, buses, and subways makes transportation through the outskirts quick and simple; don't get mired down on Karl Johans and miss exploring neighborhoods outside the downtown area.

Tourist Offices: Main Tourist Office, Fridtjof Nansenspl. 5 (☎23 14 77 00; www.visitoslo.com). From Oslo S, walk 15min. down Karl Johans gt., turn left on Roald Amundsens gt.; the office is on the right just before City Hall. Sells the Oslo Pass (see above) and books hotels (45kr fee). Open daily June-Aug. 9am-7pm; Sept. and May M-Sa 9am-5pm; Oct.-Apr. M-F 9am-4pm. Branch at Oslo S also books last-minute pensions (45kr fee). Open daily May-Aug. 8am-11pm; Sept. M-Sa 8am-11pm; Oct.-Apr. M-Sa 8am-5pm. **✉ Use It,** Møllergt. 3 (☎41 51 32; http://unginfo.oslo.no/useit) targets students and backpackers. Books accommodations for free, offers free **Internet** access, and puts out the invaluable *Streetwise Budget Guide to Oslo.* Go up Karl Johans gt. from Oslo S and turn right onto Møllergt.; it's on the left. Open July-Aug. M-F 9am-6pm; Sept.-June M-W and F 11am-5pm, Th 11am-6pm.

Budget Travel: STA Travel, Karl Johans gt. 8 (☎81 55 99 05; www.statravel.no), a few blocks up from Oslo S. Books student airfares. Open M-F 10am-5pm, Sa 11am-3pm.

Embassies and Consulates: Australia, Jermbanetorg. 2 (☎22 47 91 70). Open M-F 9am-noon and 2-4pm. **Canada,** Wergelandsv. 7, 4th fl. (☎22 99 53 00). Open June-Aug. M-F 8am-3:30pm, Sept.-May M-F 8:30am-4:45pm. **Ireland,** Haakon VII's gt. 1 (☎22 01 72 00). **UK,** Thomas Heftyes gt. 8 (☎23 13 27 00). Open M-F 8:30am-4pm. **US,** Drammensv. 18 (☎22 44 85 50). Open M-F 8:30am-5pm.

Currency Exchange: Available at AmEx office, the main post office, the banks and hotels along Karl Johans gt., and the branch of **Nordea Bank** in Oslo S. Open May-Sept. M-F 7am-7pm, Sa-Su 8am-5pm; Oct.-Apr. M-F 7am-7pm, Sa 8am-5pm.

American Express: Fridtjof Nansens pl. 6 (☎98 37 35), across from the Rådhus. Open M-F 9am-4:30pm, Sa 10am-3pm; July-Aug. also Su 11am-3pm.

Luggage Storage: Lockers at Oslo S and at the Nationalteateret station. 7-day max. 20-45kr per 24hr. Open M-F 9am-3pm. Bags can be left in the Use It office (see above) for an afternoon or night.

Laundromat: Look for the word *"myntvaskeri."* **Selva AS,** Ullevålsveien 15. Wash 40kr, dry 30kr. Open daily 8am-9pm.

GLBT Services: Landsforeningen for Lesbisk og Homofil fri gjøring (LLH), Nordahl Breuns gt. 22 (☎23 32 73 73; www.llh.no). Open June-Aug. M-F 8am-3pm, Sept.-May 8am-4pm. Cafe open W 6-9pm. Sells *Blikk* (50kr), a newspaper with nightlife listings.

Emergency: Ambulance: ☎ 113. **Fire:** ☎ 110. **Police:** ☎ 112.

Pharmacy: Jernbanetorvets Apotek (☎ 23 35 81 00), opposite the train station. Open 24hr. **Apoteket Sfinxen**, Bogstadveien 51 (☎ 46 34 44). Open M-F 8:30am-11pm, Sa 9am-8pm, Su 5-8pm.

Medical Assistance: Oslo Kommunale Legevakt, Storgt. 40 (☎ 11 80 80). Open 24hr.

Internet Access and Library: Free terminals at **Use It** (see above) and at the stately **Deichmanske Library**, Henrik Ibsensgt. 1; sign up in advance for 15min. slots. Open June-Aug. M-F 10am-6pm, Sa 9am-2pm; Sept.-May M-F 10am-8pm, Sa 9am-3pm. **Studenten**, Karl Johans gt., is conveniently located. 20kr per 15min., 30kr per 30min., 55kr per hr. Open M-Tu 11am-11pm, W-Sa 11am-9pm, Su noon-11pm.

Post Office: Main post office at Kirkegt. 20 (☎ 23 35 86 90). From Oslo S, head down Karl Johans gt. and turn left on Kirkegt. Address mail to be held in the following format: First name SURNAME, *Poste Restante*, Oslo Central Post Office, N-0101 Oslo, NORWAY. Open M-F 9am-5pm, Sa 10am-2pm.

ACCOMMODATIONS

Hostels in Oslo fill up quickly in the summer—make reservations, especially if traveling in a group. The **private rooms** available through **Use It** (see above) are a good deal at upwards of 125kr. **Pensions** *(pensjonater)* are centrally located, but can be more expensive since they do not offer dorm options. Check with the tourist office for last-minute deals on accommodations. You can **camp** for free in the forest north of town; try the end of the Sognsvann line.

Anker Hostel, Storgt. 55 (☎ 99 72 00, bookings 99 72 10; www.ankerhostel.no). Walk 15min. from the city center or take tram #10, 11, 12, 13, or 17 to Hausmanns gt.; it's 100m up Storgt., behind the Anker Hotel. Comfortable rooms with well-equipped kitchenettes. Convivial atmosphere around the TV area, foosball table, and cafe. Sheets 45kr. Internet 10kr per 10min., 25kr per hr. Reception 24hr. in summer. Dorms 145-170kr; doubles 430kr. AmEx/D/V. ❶

MS Innvik, Langkaia 49 (☎ 41 95 00; www.msinnvik.no). Cross the large white overpass and head right along the harbor. Let the waters of Bjørvika Bay rock you to sleep in this boatborne B&B. Well-kept cabins with a resolutely 80s color scheme. Live music Sa in summer. Breakfast included. Reception 24hr. Singles 350kr; doubles 600kr. MC/V. ❷

Perminalen, Øvre Slottsgt. 2 (☎ 23 09 30 81). Clean rooms only 5min. from the heart of Oslo. No alcohol. Breakfast included. Internet 15kr per 15min. Reception 24hr. Dorms 280kr; singles 495kr; doubles 650kr. AmEx/D/MC/V. ❷

Oslo Vandrerhjem IMI, Staffeldgt. 4 (☎ 98 62 00). Walk 20min. down Karl Johans gt., staying to the right of Slottsparken, and turn right on Linstows gt. Or take tram #17 or 18 to Holberg. Though a fair walk away from the city center, a warm community atmosphere makes the trek worthwhile. Open June to mid-Aug. Breakfast included. Sheets 50kr. Internet 20kr per 30min. Reception 24hr. Dorms 190kr; singles 295kr; doubles 470kr; triples 670kr; quads 790kr. AmEx/MC/V. ❶

YMCA Sleep-in, Grubbegata 4 (☎ 42 10 66). Well-worn dormitories greet high-season travelers with rock-bottom prices (130kr). Open mid-July to mid-Aug. Bring your own sleeping bag. Kitchen available. Cash only. ❶

Ellingsens Pensjonat, Holtegt. 25 (☎ 60 03 59). Take tram #19 to Briskeby. From the intersection of Holtegt. and Uranienborgveien, walk away from the church; it's an unmarked off-white house on the right. Helpful, cheery staff. Reception M-F 7:30am-10:30pm, Sa-Su 8am-10:30pm. Singles 300kr; doubles 490kr, with bath 590kr. Cash only. ❷

Ekeberg Camping, Ekebergveien 65 (☎ 19 85 68; www.ekebergcamping.no). 3km from town. Take bus #34A or 40 (10min.). Grocery store open daily 8am-9pm. Laundry 40kr. Free showers. Reception 7:30am-11pm. Open late May to Aug. Two-person tent 130kr, four-person tent 190kr. ❶

FOOD

Visitors to Oslo can choose between authentic Norwegian fare and a wide array of ethnic dishes, but either way will usually feel as if they have been robbed blind once the check arrives. The smart backpacker will raid the city's **grocery stores** for essentials; look for the chains **Rema 1000** or **Kiwi** throughout the city, or invest in fresh produce at the **open-air market** on Youngstorget (M-Sa 7am-2pm). Vendors in the **Grønland** district east of the train station hawk **kebabs** (40kr) and **falafel** (35kr), while the district's halal butchers can provide Muslim travelers with cooking meat.

Kaffistova (☎20 51 82), at the intersection of Rosenkrantz gt. and Kristian IV gt. Quiet, convenient cafeteria-style eatery with traditional Norwegian meat, fish, porridges, and desserts. Popular with rural Norwegians in town for the day. Vegetarian options. Sandwiches 50-60kr. Entrees 120kr. Open M-F 9:30am-8pm, Sa-Su 10:30am-5pm. ❷

Lofotstua, Kirkeveien 40 (☎46 93 96). One of Oslo's best fish restaurants, drawing on the cuisine and the spare aesthetic of the Lofoten Islands (p. 801). The only place in town serving whale and seal. Entrees 150-210kr. Open M-F 3-10pm. AmEx/D/MC/V. ❸

Fyret, Youngstorg. 6 (☎20 51 82). Down the stairs at the intersection of Møllergt. and Pløens gt. Cozy restaurant and bar serves fresh meat, shellfish, and Oslo's largest selection of potent aquavit. Try the house special Skipper Burger (70kr). Live jazz M 8pm. Open M-W 11am-1am, Th-Sa 11am-2am. AmEx/MC/V. ❷

Curry & Ketchup, Kirkeveien 51 (☎69 05 22). Traditional Indian food, including *naan* and *tikka masala*. Generous portions 70-100kr. Open daily 1-11pm. Cash only. ❷

Krishna's Cuisine, Kirkeveien 59b (☎60 62 50). Huge portions of spicy, mercifully inexpensive Indian fare. Exclusively vegetarian, although their reliance on *ghee* (clarified butter) rules out vegans. Entrees from 80kr. Open M-F noon-8pm. Cash only. ❷

SIGHTS

Although visitors can wander Oslo's tree-lined streets and extensive network of parks for free, access to museums and other sights often comes at a hefty price. Select one or two that particularly pique your interest, or take advantage of discounts afforded by the Oslo Pass (see **Transportation,** above).

VIGELANDSPARKEN. This 80-acre expanse is home to over 200 of Gustav Vigeland's sculptures, which depict each stage of the human life cycle. Each year the park draws more than a million visitors, who read and rollerblade amid works like the *Monolith,* a towering granite column of intertwining bodies. *(Entrance on Kirkeveien. Take bus #20 or tram #12 or 15 to Vigelandsparken. Open 24hr. Free.)*

ART MUSEUMS. Armed robbers stole two valuable paintings from the **Munch Museum** in August 2004, including one version of Edvard Munch's meditation on existential dread, **The Scream** *(Shrik)*. Security's tighter these days, but the paintings, prints, and watercolors that Munch bequeathed to the city of Oslo before his death in 1944 still add up to an impressive collection. *(Tøyengt. 53. Take the subway to Tøyen. Open June-Aug daily 10am-6pm; Sept.-May Tu-F 10am-4pm, Sa-Su 11am-5pm. 65kr, students 35kr. Free with Oslo Pass.)* The definitive version of The Scream can still be found at the **National Art Museum** *(Nasjonalgalleriet),* which boasts an impressive collection of Norwegian and foreign works. *(Universitetsgt. 13. Open M, W, F 10am-6pm, Th 10am-8pm, Sa-Su 11am-4pm. Free.)* Next door at Oslo University's **Assembly Hall,** several of Munch's late, dreamy murals show his interest in bringing art to the masses; in 1929, he wrote that "the small picture with its broad frame belongs to the living room: it is bourgeois art." *(Enter through the door by the columns off Karl Johans gt. Open mid-June to mid-Aug. M-F 10am-2:45pm. Free.)* Living-room art is nowhere in sight at the **Contemporary Art Museum** *(Museet for Samtidskunst)*, in Kvadraturen, Oslo's old town. Spacious halls display works from the museum's heavily Norwegian, many-genred permanent collection, as well as avant-garde temporary exhibits from abroad. *(Take bus #60 or tram #10, 12, 13, 15, or 19 to Koongens Gt. Open Tu-W and F 10am-5pm, Th 10am-8pm, Sa 11am-4pm, Su 11am-5pm. Free.)*

AKERSHUS CASTLE AND FORTRESS. Originally built in 1299, this waterfront complex was rebuilt as a Renaissance palace after most of Oslo burned to the ground in 1624. Norway's most famous traitor, Vidkun Quisling, was imprisoned here prior to his execution for collaborating with the Nazi invasion of 1940. *(Take bus #60 to Bankplassen or tram #10 or 15 to Christiania torv. Fortress complex open daily 6am-9pm. Free. Castle open May to mid-Sept. M-Sa 10am-4pm, Su 12:30-4pm. 30kr, students 10kr. Free with Oslo Pass. Guided tours M-Sa 11am, 1 and 3pm; Su 1 and 3pm.)* The castle grounds include the powerful **Hjemmefrontmuseet** (Resistance Museum), which documents the country's efforts to subvert Nazi occupation. *(Open mid-June to Aug. M, W, F 10am-5pm, Tu and Th 10am-6pm, Sa 10am-4pm, Su 11am-5pm; Sept. to mid-June closes 1-2hr. earlier. 25kr, students 10kr.)*

BYGDØY. The Bygdøy peninsula is directly across the inlet from downtown Oslo; although mainly residential, it counts a few beaches and some intriguing museums to its credit. In the summer, a public ferry leaves from Pier 3 in front of City Hall for the peninsula. *(10min.; runs late May to mid-Aug. every 15-30min. M-F 7:45am-8:45pm, Sa-Su 8:45am-8:45pm; 20kr. Ferry info ☎ 177; www.boatsightseeing.com. Or take bus #30 from Oslo S to Folkemuseet or Bygdøynes.)* Uphill from the ferry port is the **Norsk Folkemuseum**, one of Europe's largest open-air museums, which traces Norwegian everyday life since 1200 through its architecture. Nearby, the **Viking Ship Museum** showcases three wooden burial vessels promoted as the best-preserved of their kind. *(Walk away from the dock up the hill and follow signs to the right (10min.), or take bus #30 to Folkemuseet. Folkmuseum open mid-May to mid-Sept. daily 10am-6pm; mid-Sept. to mid-May M-F 11am-3pm, Sa-Su 11am-4pm. Summer 75kr, students 45kr. Winter 55kr/35kr. Ship Museum open daily May-Sept. 9am-6pm; Oct.-Apr. 11am-4pm. 40kr, students 20kr.)* Other maritime exploits are celebrated at the **Fram Museum,** home to the sturdy schooner that carried Roald Amundsen to the South Pole. Venture below deck to explore the cabins and engine room. The **Kon-Tiki Museum** details Oscar-winning documentarian Thor Heyerdahl's daring 1947 ocean crossing from South America to Polynesia on a papyrus raft, a voyage that strengthened anthropologists' hypotheses about migration between the continents. *(Walk 10min. toward Bygdøynes, or take bus #30b. Fram Museum open daily mid-June to Aug. 9am-6:45pm; Sept. to early June 11am-3:45pm. 35kr, students 25kr. Kon-Tiki Museum open daily June-Aug. 9:30am-5:45pm; Apr.-May and Sept. 10:30am-5pm; Oct.-Mar. 10:30am-4pm. 40kr, students 20kr. Both museums free with Oslo Pass.)* The southwestern side of Bygdøy is home to two popular beaches: **Huk** appeals to a younger crowd, while **Paradisbukta** is more family-oriented. The stretch of shore between them is a nude beach. *(Take bus #30 or walk south for 25min. from the Bygdøynes ferry stop.)*

OTHER SIGHTS. The **Royal Palace**, on a hill at the western end of Karl Johans gt., is open to the public via guided tours, although tickets sell out well in advance. *(Open late June to mid-Aug. Tours in English daily at 2 and 2:20pm. Purchase tickets at any post office. Reservations ☎ 81 33 31 33. 80kr, students 70kr.)* You can watch the changing of the guard daily at 1:30pm in front of the palace. *(Tram #12, 15, or 19, or bus #30-32 or 45 to Slottsparken. Free.)* For a panoramic view of Oslofjord and the city, bound up the stairs of the Holmenkollen ski jump and explore 4000 years of skiing history at the world's oldest **Ski Museum,** Kongeveien 5. A simulator recreates the rush of a leap off a ski jump and a blisteringly swift downhill run. *(Take subway #1 on the Frognerseteren line to Holmenkollen, and walk 10min. uphill. Open daily June-Aug. 9am-8pm; Sept. and May 10am-5pm; Oct.-Apr. 10am-4pm. Museum 50kr. Free with Oslo Pass. Simulator 45kr.)*

🎵 📷 ENTERTAINMENT AND NIGHTLIFE

The monthly *What's On in Oslo* (free at tourist offices), follows the latest in opera, symphony, and theater. **Filmens Hus,** Dronningens gt. 16 (☎47 45 00), is the center of Oslo's indie film scene. In addition to the countless bars along **Karl Johans gate** and in the **Aker Brygge** harbor complex, Oslo boasts a number of nightclubs and cafes featuring DJs and live music. Since alcohol tends to be egregiously expensive out on the town, young Norwegians have taken to the custom of the *Vorspiel* (pregame)—gathering at private homes to sip comparatively cheap, store-bought liquor before wobbling outside to paint the town red.

Mono, Pløens gt. 4, livens up a relaxed, funky bar atmosphere with frequent concerts. (Beer 48kr. M-Th and Su 20+, F-Sa 22+. Cover for concerts 50kr. Open M-Sa 3pm-3am, Su 6pm-3am.) **Garage,** Grensen 9, caters to the Norwegian metal scene but has also drawn international acts, including American smirk-rockers Death Cab for Cutie. (Beer 48kr. Courtyard open in summer. F-Sa 22+. Cover for concerts 50-150kr. M-Sa 2pm-3:30am, Su 4pm-3:30am.) A few blocks away, the dance floor and bar at **Rexx,** Grensen 7, have become a dressy haunt for the young and stylish. (Beer 57kr. 24+. Cover Sa 100kr. Open F-Su 10pm-3am.) A more mixed crowd gathers at **Muddy Waters,** Grensen 13, for basement rock concerts and blues upstairs. (Cover for concerts 90kr. Open daily noon-3am.) If it's a boisterous, sports-bar vibe that you're after, **Horgans,** Hegdehaugsv. 24, is a good bet. (23+. Open M-Tu and Su 5pm-2am, W-Th 5pm-1:30am, F-Sa 5pm-2:30am.) On week-nights, **Living Room,** Olav V's gt. 1, is a fixture on the city's lounge scene and an appealing spot for a post-cinema nightcap. (Beer 50kr. 24+. Cover F-Sa 50-80kr. Open M-Sa 10pm-3:30am.) Mellowness also prevails at the cafe-by-day, bar-by-night lounges along **Thorvald Meyers gate** in Grüner Løkka.

📷 DAYTRIPS FROM OSLO

Short, scenic harbor cruises show off the nearby islands of inner **Oslofjord,** which are themselves cheap, delightful daytrip destinations. The ruins of a **Cistercian Abbey,** as well as a picnic-friendly southern shore, lie on the landscaped island of **Hovedøya,** while **Langøyene** has Oslo's best **beach.** Take bus #60 (22kr) from City Hall to Vippetangen to catch a ferry to either island. **The Wilderness House** *(Villmarkshuset),* Christian Krohgs gt. 16, rents canoes and kayaks for trips on the Akerselva river. (☎22 05 05 22; www.schlytter.no. Open M-F 10am-6pm, Sa 10am-3pm. 200kr for 2hr., 650kr for full weekend.) The well-preserved fortress town of **Fredrikstad** is less than 2hr. south of Oslo. Explore the 28km **Glommastien** bike path that wends its way through abandoned brickyards and timber mills along the Glomma River, or else hop a ferry bound for seaside resorts on the lovely **Hvaler Islands**. Take the **train** to Fredrikstad (1hr., every 2hr., 155kr). The **tourist information office,** Voldgaten 98, rents bikes and has ferry schedules. (☎69 30 46 00. Open M-F 9am-5pm, Sa-Su 11am-5pm.)

LILLEHAMMER. A small city set in the Lagen River valley at the edge of Lake Mjøsa, Lillehammer (pop. 25,000) still cherishes the laurels it earned as host of the 1994 Winter Olympics. The **Norwegian Olympic Museum** in Olympic Park traces the history of the Games from their genesis in ancient Greece and their rebirth in 1896 through their return to Athens in the summer of 2004. From the train station, it's a 15-20min. walk; head two blocks uphill, turn left on Storgt., right on Tomtegt., go up the stairs and follow the road uphill to the left. Or take bus #5 to Sigrid Undsetsveg (5min., 17kr). The museum is in the farther dome. (Open late May to mid-Aug. daily 10am-6pm; late Aug. to mid-May Tu-Su 11am-4pm. 60kr, students 50kr.) Climb up the endless steps of the Olympic **ski jump,** or give your spine a jolt on the **bobsled simulator** at the bottom of the hill. (Open daily mid-June to mid-Aug. 9am-8pm; early June and late Aug. 9am-5pm; Sept. and Mar-May 11am-4pm. Ski jump 15kr. Simulator 40kr, students 30kr. Combination ticket including chairlift ride 65kr, students 45kr.) **Gjeste Bu ❶,** Gamleveien 110, offers the cheapest accommodations in town with a dose of mountainside charm. (☎61 25 43 21. Dorms 100kr. Singles 225kr; doubles 350kr. Cash only.) Most restaurants are on the pedestrian section of **Storgata,** two blocks uphill from the station. *(Trains run to Oslo (2¼hr., 1 per hr., 282kr) and Trondheim (4½hr., 4 per day, 556kr). The tourist office, in the station, has info on hiking and attractions. ☎61 28 98 00; www.lillehammerturist.no. Open mid-June to mid-Aug. M-Sa 9am-7pm, Su 11am-6pm; mid-Aug. to mid-June M-F 9am-4pm, Sa 10am-2pm.)*

SOUTHERN NORWAY

Norway's southern coastline has become a summer holiday destination, and town after tidy town whispers "moneyed leisure" with red-tiled bungalows and jetties full of small powerboats. Sandy beaches are scarce outside of Kristiansand, but boaters weave their way through the *skjærgarden,* archipelagos of water-worn rock that hug the shore and are fine spots to fish or picnic.

KRISTIANSAND ☎38

One of the jewels of the Norwegian Riviera, Kristiansand (pop. 75,000) convinces many Scandinavian vacationers to tarry for a few days each year, even if many tourists from abroad just disembark from the Jutland ferry (see below) and make a beeline for Oslo. Families flock to the **Dyreparken,** 11km east of the city, which includes carnival games, an amusement park, and a zoo with elevated boardwalks affording glimpses of prowling lynxes and Nordic wolves. Catch bus #1 (dir.: Sørlandsparken) just around the corner from the tourist office. (☎04 97 00; www.dyreparken.com. Open June to late Aug. daily 10am-7pm; late Aug.-May M-F 10am-3pm, Sa-Su 10am-5pm; 240kr, children 195kr; low season reduced rates.) Back in Kristiansand, meander through the old town of **Posebyen,** where the single-story wooden houses quartered soldiers over the centuries and also hid Jewish refugees during WWII. Walking tour pamphlets and free guided tours are both available at the tourist office. The **skerries,** a string of tiny islands and coves just off the coast, break the waves of the Skagerrak before they wash up on Kristiansand's harbor; take in the view on a ferry cruise (2½hr.), or else befriend a local and sail out on your own for a secluded swim or **camping** spot. (Ferry departs at noon from Nupen Park in East Harbor; round-trip 100kr.)

FIG LEAVES AND POWER CHORDS

Decorum reigns for most of the year in sedate Kristiansand. During the first week of July, however, up to 80,000 music fans descend for the Quart Festival, a six-day extravaganza that focuses on two main stages but also spills over into the city's clubs and cinemas. In 2004, British hipsters Franz Ferdinand and Morrissey joined Alicia Keys and Jamaican reggae-thug Sean Paul, though the headliners were almost overshadowed by an X-rated publicity stunt.

A Norwegian band invited two environmental activists up on stage to have sex during their set. Tommy Holm Ellingsen and Leona Johansson advocate using sex to raise awareness about saving the rain forest—the philosophy behind their nonprofit Internet porn site. After 10 orgiastic minutes, the pair was finally removed from the stage, and courts later slapped them with a 10,000kr fine. Shortly afterwards, the World Wildlife Fund rejected a sizable donation from the duo, citing a reluctance to associate itself with "certain sectors of industry." This intrigue aside, Kristiansand is once again gearing up for the 2005 festival, sure to focus more on music and the famously chill atmosphere than on any risqué acts of civil disobedience.

Check www.quart.no for schedule and info on festival-sponsored campsites. 1-day pass 380-450kr, 5-day 1500kr.

Trains run to Oslo (4½-5½hr.; 7 per day; 531kr, students from 266kr) and Stavanger (3hr.; 8 per day; 379kr, students from 190kr). Color Line **ferries** (☎81 00 08 11) sail to Hirsthals, Denmark. (2½-4hr.; 2-5 per day; in summer M-F 400kr, Sa-Su 440kr; low season 190-280kr; students 50% off.) The **tourist office,** opposite the train station and upstairs at Henrik Wegerlandsgt. and Vestre Strandgt., books rooms and can arrange elk safaris. (☎38 12 13 14. Internet 15kr per 15min. Safari 250kr; min. 4 persons; call ahead. Open mid-June to mid-Aug. M-Sa 8:30am-6pm, Su noon-6pm; mid-Aug. to mid-June M-F 8:30am-3:30pm.) The public library on Rådhusgaten offers free **Internet** access. The **Kristiansand Youth Hostel (HI) ❶,** Skansen 8, is a solid 25min. from the harbor and train station. Walk away from the water until you reach Elvegt., turn right, then turn left onto Skansen. Quiet and clean, this hostel draws travelers of all ages and is next to a popular beach. (☎02 83 10. Breakfast included. Kitchen available. Sheets 50kr. Internet 10kr per 15min. Reception June-Aug. 24hr.; Sept.-May 5-11pm. Dorms 185kr; singles 395kr; doubles 430kr. Nonmembers add 25kr.) Restaurants are expensive in this resort town, even by Norwegian standards; head down to the **harbor** between 11am and 4pm, when the families of fishermen cook up part of the morning's catch and sell it out of stalls. Find the other four food groups at **Joker,** Skippergata 21. (Open M-W and F 8:30am-6pm, Th 8:30am-7pm, Sa 8:30am-4pm.) **Postal Code:** 4601.

STAVANGER

☎51

A delightful port town with cobblestone streets and a lively fish market, Stavanger (pop. 110,000) is known for its cultural history and its proximity to great hikes. On the western side of the harbor is **Gamle Stavanger,** the old town where narrow lanes nose their way between well-preserved cottages by old world lamplight. The 12th-century **Stavanger Domkirke** is Norway's oldest cathedral, although time and over-zealous renovations have not been kind to its Anglo-Norman towers. Even so, they solemnly dominate the modern town center from the northern banks of the Breia-vatnet pond. (Cathedral open June-Aug. daily 11am-7pm; Sept.-May Tu-Th and Sa 11am-4pm.) A short walk down Kirkegt. from the church, the architecturally inno-vative, kid-friendly **Norsk Oljemuseum** (Norwegian Petroleum Museum) explains drilling and refining with interactive, if vaguely propangandist displays. Find your way out of the pitch-black "Catastrophe Room" in under 2min., or else your future as a firefighter may be in doubt. (☎93 93 00; www.norskolje.museum.no. Open June-Aug. daily 10am-7pm; Sept.-May M-F 10am-4pm, Sa-Su 10am-5pm. 75kr, stu-dents 35kr.) A perennial postcard pick, ▨**Preikestolen** (Pulpit Rock), in nearby **Lysefjord,** boasts a magnificent view from an altitude of 600m. If the crowds and your sense of vertigo permit, lie flat on this mountain plateau and look down into the abyss below. Take the **ferry** to Tau from the Fiskepiren dock (M-Su 8 and 9am, Su 8:25 and 9:25am; 33kr), catch the waiting bus (50kr) and then make the easy hike up the well-marked trail (1½-2hr.). Ferries return at 2:50 and 4:25pm.

Trains run to Kristiansand (3hr., every 3hr., 379kr) and Oslo (8hr., 4 per day, 783kr), but the 16hr. train ride to Bergen makes alternate arrangements a must. **Buses** to Ber-gen (5½hr., 400kr, students 300kr) leave from Stavanger Byterminal every 30min., although the Flaggruten **express boat** (4hr., 560kr) sails past many a fjord and still makes the trip in record time. (☎86 87 87; www.hsd.no. M-F 4 per day, Sa-Su 1-2 per day. Eurail and Scanrail holders 50% off.) Fjordline **ferries** (☎86 87 87; www.fjord-line.co.uk) also go to Newcastle, England (19½/hr.; 2-3 per week; one-way from 760kr, students 50% off). Fjordline ferries depart and arrive from Strandkaien, on the west-ern side of the harbor. The **tourist office,** Rosenkildetorg. 1, books rooms (30kr fee) and provides info about bike rental. (☎85 92 00; www.visitstavanger.com. Open June-Aug. daily 9am-8pm; Sept.-May M-F 9am-4pm, Sa 9am-2pm.) Accommodations fill up quickly, so your best bet may be the distant, bare-bones **Jæren Vandrerhjem (HI) ❶,** Nordsjøvegen. Take bus #4 from the train station to Vigrestad, then walk across the road and through the small tunnel to your right. Head through the camping grounds and then turn left. (☎43 57 55. Breakfast 60kr. Sheets 50kr. Dorms 155kr; doubles 320kr. Nonmembers add 25kr. MC/V.) Back in town, head for the **market** opposite the cathedral for native strawberries (open M-F 8am-5pm), or consider taking a **Stavanger Cruise** around the harbor for fresh mussels and a glittering view of the shoreline. (☎71 48 00. Departure Th-Sa 7pm. 100kr, including mussels.) **Postal Code:** 4001.

THE FJORDS AND WEST COUNTRY

Spectacular views and charming towns await at the end of the scenic train ride from Oslo to Bergen. From the rugged peaks of Jotunheim National Park to the humbling depths of Sognefjord, western Norway possesses a dramatic natural grandeur that makes the region's settlements almost beside the point.

GETTING AROUND

Although transportation around the fjords can be complicated, the scenery out the window is half the fun. Plan your route ahead of time, as times vary from day to day. Call ☎177 for transportation info; tourist offices, boat terminals, and bus stations can also help plan itineraries. **Bergen** is the major port serving the region; HSD **express boats** (☎55 23 87 80; www.hsd.no; ticket office at Strandkaiterminalen) run to Stavanger and points south of the city, while **Fylkesbaatane** (☎55 90 70 71; www.fylkesbaatane.no; ticket office at Strandkaiterminalen) sails north into Sognefjord. Almost all destinations around the fjords connect via **bus** to Bergen.

BERGEN   ☎55

Situated in a narrow valley between steep mountains and the waters of the Puddefjorden, Bergen (pop. 235,000) bills itself as the "Gateway to the Fjords." Norway's second-largest metropolis, the city has a compact, pedestrian-friendly downtown and a slew of international students who contribute to its relaxed, shirt-sleeves dynamic—a pleasant departure from the rush of Oslo and the east.

TRANSPORTATION

Trains: The **station** (☎96 69 00) is a 7-10min. walk south of the harbor. Trains run to: **Myrdal** (2¼hr.; 6-8 per day; 209kr, students 153kr); **Oslo** (6½hr.; 4-5 per day; 670kr, students 503kr); **Voss** (1¼hr.; every 1-2hr.; 142kr, students 107kr).

Buses: Busstasjon, Strømgtn. 8. Inside the Bergen Storsenter mall at the corner of Strømgt. and Fjøsangermeien (☎177, outside Bergen ☎55 55 90 70). Buses run to: **Ålesund** (10hr., 3 per day, 545kr); **Oslo** (11hr., Th-Su at 2:05pm, 585kr); **Trondheim** (14½hr., 2 per day, 695kr). 25% student discount.

Ferries: The **Hurtigruten** coastal steamer (☎81 03 00 00; www.hurtigruten.com) begins its journey up the coast from **Bergen** and stops in **Ålesund**, the **Lofoten Islands, Tromsø,** and **Trondheim,** as well as other northern towns. (Leaves daily Apr.-Sept. 8pm, 495-5212kr; Oct.-Apr. 10:30pm, 400-2616kr. 50% student discount.) **Flaggruten** express boats (☎51 86 87 80; www.flaggruten.no) head south to Stavanger (4hr.; 4 per day M-F, 1-2 per day Sa-Su; 590kr, students 350kr; 50% Scanrail discount). **Fjord Line** (☎55 54 88 00; www.fjordline.co.uk) sends ships to **Hanstholm, Denmark** (16hr.; 3-4 per week; mid-June to mid-Aug. M-Th 800kr, F-Su 920kr; low season from 340kr) and **Newcastle, England** (22-24hr.; 2-3 per week; mid-June to early Aug. M-W 1100kr, Th-Su 1300kr; low season from 500kr). **Smyril Line** (☎59 65 20; www.smyril-line.no) departs Tu 3pm for: the **Faroe Islands** (27hr.; mid-June to early July from

Bergen

🏠 ACCOMMODATIONS
Intermission, 13
Marken Gjestehus, 9
Skandia
  Sommerpensjonat, 5
YMCA InterRail Center, 2

🍎 FOOD
Godt Brød, 3, 8
KroaThai, 12
Stjernesalen Kafé, 10
Vågen Fetevare, 4

⭐ NIGHTLIFE
Café Opera, 7
Det Akademiske
  Kvarteret, 10
Garage Bar, 11
Metro, 1

224kr, low season from 168kr); **Iceland** (45hr., from 336kr/240kr); and the **Shetland Islands** (10hr., from 517kr/392kr). All international ferries depart from **Skoltegrunns-kaien,** a 10-15min. walk past Bryggen along the right side of the harbor.

Public Transportation: Buses are 23kr within the city center, 31-38kr outside. The **Bergen Card,** available at the train station, includes unlimited rides on city buses as well as free admission to most of the city's museums. (1-day 165kr, 2-day 245kr.)

✱ 🔢 ORIENTATION AND PRACTICAL INFORMATION

Central Bergen is small enough for visitors to explore on foot. Using the **Torget** (fish market) by the harbor as a basis for navigation, the city can be broken down into a few basic areas. North of the Torget where the main street **Bryggen** curves around the harbor, the well-tended old city features artisans from an earlier era; southwest of the Torget is **Torgalmenningen,** the city's main shopping street. Locals tend to stay farther down Torgalmenningen, past **Håkons gaten** and **Nygårdsgaten.** The train and bus stations are about 10min. south of the Torget.

Tourist Office: Vågsalmenningen 1 (☎55 20 00; www.visitbergen.com), just past the Torget in the Fresco Hall. Crowded in summer, but friendly, dedicated staff make it worth the wait. Books private rooms for a 30kr fee, distributes the free *Bergen Guide*, and helps visitors plan travel through the fjords. Open June-Aug. daily 8:30am-10pm; May and Sept. daily 9am-8pm; Oct.-Apr. M-Sa 9am-4pm. **DNT,** Tverrgt. 4-6 (☎33 58 10), off Marken, sells maps (77-99kr) and provides comprehensive hiking info. Open M-W and F 10am-4pm, Th 10am-6pm.

Currency Exchange: At banks near the harbor (usually open M-W and F 9am-3pm, Th 9am-5:30pm; low season reduced hours) and the post office. The tourist office changes currency at a rate less favorable than the bank's, but without commission.

Luggage Storage: At train and bus stations. 20-40kr per day depending on locker size.

Budget Travel: STA Travel, Vaskerelven 32 (☎55 99 05; bergen@statravel.no). Take Torgalmenningen southwest from the Torget; turn left on Vaskerelven. Sells discounted tickets for international flights and books accommodations. Open M-F 10am-5pm.

Laundry: Jarlens Vaskoteque, Lille Øvregt. 17. Wash 45kr; dry 5kr per 15min. Open M-Tu and F 10am-6pm, W-Th 10am-8pm, Sa 10am-3pm.

Emergency: Ambulance: ☎113. **Fire:** ☎110. **Police:** ☎112.

Pharmacy: Apoteket Nordstjernen (☎21 83 84), on 2nd fl. of the bus station. Open M-Sa 8am-midnight, Su 9:30am-midnight.

Medical Assistance: 24-Hour Clinic, Vestre Strømkai 19 (☎56 87 00).

Internet Access: Bibliotek (public library), Strømgt. 6, at the intersection of Strømgt. and Vestre Strømkai. Free 15min. slots. Open May-Aug. M-Th 10am-6pm, F 10am-4:30pm, Sa 10am-4pm; Sept.-Apr. M-Th 10am-8pm, F 10am-4:30pm, Sa 10am-4pm. **CyberHouse,** Vetrlidsalm. 13, between the Torget and the funicular. 20kr per 30min. Open daily 9am-midnight.

Post Office: Småstrandgt. (☎54 15 00). Open M-F 8am-6pm, Sa 9am-3pm. Address mail to be held in the following format: First name SURNAME, *Poste Restante,* 5014 Bergen, NORWAY. *Poste Restante* office closes at 3pm M-Sa.

⌐ ACCOMMODATIONS

In the summer, it's wise to reserve ahead. The tourist office books **private rooms** in local homes for a 30kr fee, a good deal for duos who can sometimes nab doubles for as little as 300kr. You can also **camp** for free on the far side of the hills above town; walk 30min. up the slopes of Mount Fløyen or take the funicular. Interested in spending the entire summer in Bergen? Email the YMCA InterRail Center in the winter and ask about volunteering in exchange for a free room.

▓ **Intermission,** Kalfarveien 8 (☎30 04 00; www.intermissionhostel.com). The summer staff, mostly students from a Christian college in the American Midwest, cultivates a chatty, open-hearted vibe. Breakfast 30kr. Free waffle night M and Th. Kitchen available. Sheets 30kr deposit. Laundry free. Reception M-Th and Su 7-11am and 5pm-midnight, F-Sa until 1am. Lockout 11am-5pm. Curfew M-Th and Su midnight, F-Sa 1am. Open mid-June to mid-Aug. Dorms 110kr. **Camping** in backyard 70kr. Cash only. ❶

YMCA InterRail Center, Nedre Korskirkealm. 4 (☎31 72 52; ymca@online.no). Young backpackers clamber up to the rooftop balcony for a great view. 40+ bed dormitory can be noisy. Kitchen available. Internet 20kr per 30min. Reception 7am-midnight. Lockout 11am-3:30pm. Dorms 125kr; 4- to 6-person room 160-175kr per person. MC/V. ❶

Marken Gjestehus, Kong Oscars gt. 45 (☎31 44 04; www.marken-gjestehus.com). Don't be put off by the creaky elevator; immaculate, sunny rooms await on the upper floors, drawing travelers of all ages. Breakfast 55kr. Kitchen available. Sheets 55kr. Reception May-Sept. 9am-11pm; Oct.-Apr. 9am-7pm. All dorms single-sex. 6-person dorms 165kr; 4-person dorms 195kr; singles 355kr; doubles 470kr. AmEx/D/MC/V. ❶

Vandrerhjem Montana (HI), Johan Blyttsvei 30 (☎20 80 70; www.montana.no). Take bus #31 from the tourist office to Laudas. Backpackers and traveling families trek 5km out of the city for clean, basic digs. Breakfast included. Kitchen available. Sheets 60kr. Dorms 150kr; doubles 570kr; quads 780kr. Nonmembers add 25kr. MC/V. ❶

Skandia Sommerpensjonat, Kong Oscars gt. 22 (☎21 00 35). Bright student flats get converted into private rooms in summer; ask to see the available rooms, since some are more spacious than others. Laundry 30kr. Reception 8am-midnight. Open mid-June to mid-Aug. Singles 375kr; doubles 500kr, with kitchen 600kr. MC/V. ❸

🍴 FOOD

Bergen's irresistible **fish market** panders to tourists on the Torget with colorful tents, raucous fishmongers, and free samples of salmon, caviar, and wild shrimp. (Open June-Aug. M-W and F 7am-5pm, Th 7am-7pm, Sa 7am-4pm; low season M-Sa 7am-4pm.) **Godt Brød ❶,** Vestre Torggt. 6 and Nedre Korskirkealm. 12, prepares thick sandwiches (28-59kr) on fresh organic bread. The N. Korskirkealm. location has outdoor seating. (V. Torggt. branch open M-F 8am-6pm, Sa 8am-4:30pm. N. Korskirkealm. branch open M-F 7am-6pm, Sa-Su 7am-4:30pm. Cash only.) Cozy **Vågen Fetevare ❶,** Kong Oscars gt. 10, is the favorite for leisurely morning coffee (15-33kr) while browsing through secondhand books. (☎31 65 13. Open M-Th 8am-11pm, F 8am-8pm, Sa 9am-6pm, Su 11am-8pm.) **Stjernesalen Kafé ❶,** inside 🏛Det Akademiske Kvarteret (see **Nightlife,** below), Olav Kyrresgt. 49-53, serves a rotating menu of soups and snack fare (30-55kr) until late. (☎58 99 10. Open M-F noon-1am, Sa-Su noon-2am. MC/V.) Students also recommend the counter service at **KroaThai ❷,** Nygardsgt. 29, for cheap Asian fare (from 60kr) on the go. (☎32 58 50. Open M-Sa 2-10pm. Cash only.)

👁 SIGHTS

BRYGGEN AND BERGENHUS. Gazing down the right side of the harbor from the Torget brings **Bryggen's** signature pointed gables into view. This row of medieval buildings, with its narrow alleys and balconies all askew, has survived numerous fires and the explosion of a Nazi munitions ship to remain a shining example of the architecture of the Middle Ages. The town's preservation and restoration efforts have hinged on traditional methods and tools to safeguard (and market) the area's authenticity. The **Bryggens Museum** displays archaeological artifacts, including fragments from the foundations of the oldest buildings in Bergen, and gives the visitor a strong impression of the city's attachment to its Viking roots. *(Dreggsalm. 3, behind a small park at the end of the Bryggen houses. Open May-Aug. daily 10am-5pm; Sept.-Apr. M-F 11am-3pm, Sa noon-3pm, Su noon-4pm. 40kr, students 20kr.)* Tickets for walking tours of Bryggen are available at the museum. *(1½hr.; daily June-Aug. 10am; 80kr.)* The tours bypass **Bergenhus,** the city's fortress, but visitors will not want to miss the late medieval splendor of the 16th-century **Rosenkrantz Tower,** nor the cavernous **Håkonshallen,** where King Magnus the Lawmender was married and crowned in 1261. *(Walk along the harbor away from the Torget. Hall and tower open daily mid-May to Aug. 10am-4pm; Sept. to mid-May tower open Su noon-3pm, hall open M-W and F-Su noon-3pm, Th 3-6pm. Guided tours every hr. in summer. 20kr, students 10kr.)*

MUSEUMS. Three branches of the **Bergen Art Museum** line the western side of the Lille Lungegårdsvann. The 13th-century Russian icons and 15th-century Dutch Masters in **Lysverket** anticipate the canvases of Munch, Dahl, and Norway's Neo-Impressionists in the **Rasmus Meyers Collection,** while the **Stenersen Collection** chimes in with temporary exhibitions as well as Northern Europe's most extensive collection of Paul Klee's work. *(Rasmus Meyers allé 3, 7, and 9. ☎56 80 00; www.berge-nartmuseum.no. Open Tu-Su 11am-5pm. 50kr for all 3 museums, students 35kr; temporary exhi-bitions 15kr.)* Bergen's **Leprosy Museum,** Kong Oscars gt. 59, is on the site of one of the first hospitals dedicated to the study of the disease. Visit the homespun chapel, then cross the courtyard and poke your nose into the tiny cells where as many as three patients were kept and observed into the 1940s. *(☎96 11 55. Open mid-June to Aug. 11am-3pm; Sept. to mid-June by appointment. 30kr, students 15kr.)*

🔼 THE OUTDOORS

A vast archipelago spreads westward from the only side of Bergen not bordered by towering mountains. **Hiking** trails surrounding the city are well kept and easily accessible; free maps are available at the tourist office and DNT office. The **Fløibanen funicular** runs up **Mt. Fløyen** to a spectacular lookout point, although the steep 45min. hike to the peak is manageable on a paved road. (Funicular runs June-Aug. M-F 7:30am-midnight, Sa 8am-midnight, Su 9am-midnight; Sept.-May closes at 11pm. Round-trip 50kr.) At the summit, you'll find terrific views and the requisite ice-cream stand, as well as several well-marked **trailheads** that lead away from the crowds into a forest dotted by mammoth kerns, springy moss, and quiet ponds—the foliage occasionally parts to reveal stunning vistas. A demanding 4hr. trek from Fløyen leads to the top of **Mt. Ulriken,** the highest peak above Bergen, which affords a panoramic view over the city, fjords, mountains, and nearby islands. A **bus/cable car combination** also runs to the top of Mt. Ulriken from the city center. (Cable car runs daily every 7min. May-Sept. 9am-10pm; Oct.-Apr. 10am-5pm. 70kr.)

🎵 📷 ENTERTAINMENT AND NIGHTLIFE

As spring sets up shop in western Norway, Bergen gears up for two simultaneous festivals: late May's **Festspillene,** a 12-day program of music and dance that has attracted notables like choreographer Merce Cunningham (www.festspillene.no), and **Nattjazz,** a series of more than 60 jazz concerts held in a converted sardines factory and around the city (late May to early June; www.nattjazz.no). October rings in the up-and-coming **Bergen International Film Festival** (www.biff.no). Bergen rarely picks up until around 11:30pm on weekend nights; many locals throw back a round or two at home to avoid high beer prices at bars and clubs. Steer clear of the harborside tourist traps and take Torgallm. to **Nygårdsgaten,** home to an array of pubs and cafes. **图Det Akademiske Kvarteret,** Olav Kyrresgt. 49-53, is half salon, half cultural center and is run by student volunteers from the University of Bergen. The happening **Grøhndals** bar sells the cheapest beer in Bergen (29kr before 10pm, 42kr after 10pm), while the **Teglverket** stage hosts jazz and rock concerts (80-100kr) on F and Sa nights. (☎58 99 10; www.kvarteret.no. Bar open M-W and Su 7pm-1am, Th-Sa 7pm-3am. Concerts usually at 10pm; brave the Norwegian-language website for details.) **Metro,** Ole Bulls pl. 4, draws the young and trendy with hip-hop beats and spicy "mixology" fruit drinks in summer. (20+ M-Th and Su, 24+ F-Sa. 90kr cover. Open daily 10pm-3am.) The city that gave the world the winsome indie-pop duo The Kings of Convenience was also bound to produce the pricklier **Garage Bar,** at the corner of Nygårdsgt. and Christies gt., where a friendly, pierced crowd queues up for Bergen's most popular alt-rock pub. (20+. Cover 30kr after 1am.

Open M-Th 1pm-3am, F-Sa 1pm-3:30am, Su 3pm-1am.) **Café Opera,** Engen 18, draws a mixed clientele with light meals, drinks, and DJs spinning after 11pm. (No cover. Open M and Su noon-12:30am, Tu-Th noon-3am, F-Sa noon-3:30am.)

ALONG THE OSLO-BERGEN RAIL LINE

The 7hr. rail journey from Oslo to Bergen is one of the most famous scenic rides in the world. From Oslo, trains climb 1222m to remote Finse, stop in Myrdal for transfers to the Flåm railway, and then pass through Voss en route to Bergen. A hush invariably falls over passengers during the 100km stretch along the desolate Hardangervidda plateau.

FINSE. Outdoor enthusiasts hop off at Finse and hike several days north through the Aurlandsdalen valley into **Aurland,** 53km from Flåm. Before you set out, be sure to ask about trail conditions at Finse's train station or at the DNT offices in Oslo and Bergen; the trails are usually snow-free and accessible between early July and late September. You can sleep in DNT mountain huts (p. 777), spaced one day's walk apart along the Aurland trail. **Bikers** can pick up the rutted **Rallarvegen** trail, which parallels the Oslo-Bergen train and extends 81km west to Voss. Most of the ride is downhill, and bikers should exercise extreme caution on the steep curves in the **Flåmdalen valley.** Break up the ride by staying in a DNT *hytte* in Hallingskeid (21km from Finse) or forge on to Flåm (53km). Rent bikes (495kr per day, min. 2 days) at **Finsehytta** (☎56 52 67 32).

FLÅM AND THE FLÅM RAILWAY. The historic railway connecting Myrdal, a stop on the Oslo-Bergen line, to the tiny fjord town of Flåm (pop. 450) is one of Norway's most celebrated attractions. The railway is an incredible feat of engineering, boasting the steepest descent of any railway in the world and ducking through hand-excavated tunnels. The highlight of the ride is a view of the thunderous **Kjosfossen** waterfall, whose grandeur could easily stand on its own without faux ruins and a dancing-nymph routine to amuse tourists. A 20km **hike** (4-5hr.), on the well-tended paths between Myrdal to Flåm, more or less mirrors the train route and allows hikers to tarry by smaller cascades before camping along the valley's goat-dotted knolls. Taking the train uphill to Myrdal opens up the possibility of cycling back down; check your brakes beforehand, or be ready to dismount on the steepest sections. **Trains** run regularly in both directions (55min.; 8-10 per day; 150kr, round-trip 250kr, 30% discount with ScanRail or Eurail). Flåm's **tourist office** is beside the train station. (☎57 63 21 06. Open daily July-Aug. 8:30am-8pm; May-June and Sept. 8:30am-3:30pm and 5-8pm.) During the rest of the year, direct Flåm questions to the tourist office in nearby Aurland, 9km to the north. (☎57 63 33 13; www.alr.no. Bikes 30kr per hr., 175kr per day. Open M-F 8am-4pm.) Fylkesbaatane **express boats** run daily to Aurland (15min.), Balestrand (1½hr.), and Bergen (5hr.); check www.fylkesbaatane.no for an updated schedule. **Postal Code:** 5742.

VOSS. Stretched along a glassy lake that serves as a reflecting pool for snow-capped peaks, Voss (pop. 14,000) is an adventurer's dream. In late June, **Extreme Sport Week** (www.ekstremsportveko.com) descends on the town, goading more than 1000 participants from 30 countries into death-defying feats in the air and on the water. Festival tickets run 300-350kr for a day pass, although splurging on a "Try It" ticket (4500kr) buys you a 5-day festival pass, paragliding lessons, and a helicopter ride up to a basejumping ledge. Deep powder and 40km of marked trails attract British skiers during the winter, while in summer the safety-conscious staff at **Nordic Ventures,** behind the Park Hotel in a mini-mall, runs white-water rafting trips from 750kr. (☎56 51 00 17; www.nordicventures.com. Open daily May to mid-Oct. 9am-7pm; mid-Oct. to Apr. 10am-5pm. AmEx/MC/V.) If you'd rather stick to *terra firma*, take the easy 30min. walk to **Bordal Gorge,** where water rushes through a narrow path lined by overhanging cliffs. Turn left from the train station, walk along the shore, and turn right onto the gravel path; after crossing the bridge, turn right and follow the signs to Bordalgjelet. **Trains** leave for Oslo (5½-6hr., 4-5 per day, 582kr) and Bergen (1¼hr., every 1-2hr., 142kr). The central train station is just west of downtown, up a small hill. To get to the **tourist office,** Hestavangen 10, turn left as you exit the station and bear right at the fork by the church. Ask for maps on local hikes. (☎56 52 08 00; www.visitvoss.no. Open June-Aug. M-Sa 9am-7pm, Su 2-7pm; Sept.-May M-F 9am-3:30pm.) Turn right as you exit the station and walk along the lakeside road to reach Voss's modern **Youth Hostel (HI) ●**, home to a sauna and a terrific view. If money is short, economize by sleeping on one of the foam mattresses up in the attic for just 145kr. (☎56 51 20 17. Bike, canoe, and kayak rental. Breakfast included. Internet 1kr per min. Reception 24hr. Dorms 195kr; singles 420kr; doubles 540kr. Nonmembers add 25kr. AmEx/MC/V.) Those bent on **camping** can head left from the station, stick to the lake shore, and turn right onto the gravel path at the church. Follow the path to **Voss Camping ●**. (☎56 51 15 97; www.vosscamping.no. Reception May-Sept. 8am-10pm. Small tent 95kr. 5-person cabin 400kr. Cash only.) Pick up groceries at **Kiwi,** on the main street past the post office. (Open M-F 9am-9pm, Sa 9am-6pm.) **Postal Code:** 5702.

⬛ NORWAY IN A NUTSHELL. Hoping to spend a few days sampling Norway's charms, but paralyzed about where to start? The immensely popular "Norway in a Nutshell" tour (☎81 56 82 22; www.fjordtours.no) combines a ride along the **Flåm railway** (see above), a cruise through narrow Aurlandsfjord and Nærøyfjord to the port of Gudvangen (2hr.; 1-4 per day; 180kr, 50% student discount), and a twisting **bus** ride over the mountains to Voss (1¼hr., 8-10 per day, 70kr). The tour is unguided and extremely flexible, allowing "nutshellers" to customize the trip, completing it in one day or taking stopovers at transfer points. From Voss, dart west to Bergen (1¼hr., every 1-2hr., 142kr) or drink in the scenery on the ride east to Oslo (5½-6hr., 4-5 per day, 582kr). Either final destination caps off a whirlwind tour that partakes of both rustic splendor and cosmopolitan flair—hardly the last word on Norway, but a worthwhile introduction just the same. **Tickets** can be bought separately for each leg of the journey while traveling, or purchased in advance as a package from tourist offices or train stations in Oslo and Bergen.

EIDFJORD. Tucked into an eastern arm of the orchard-lined Hardangerfjord, tiny Eidfjord (pop. 950) draws hikers to the nearby **Hardangervidda** mountain plateau. Greenhorns stick to the plateau's eastern half,

NO VEGANS HERE

Dine at the farm of Ivar Løne, and nights spent counting sheep will never be the same. You'll eat in a converted meat storeroom where the forks and candlesticks are stamped with sheep heads. "In Voss," Løne's daughter-in-law explains, "there have always been sheep." Then Løne himself turns up, carrying half a cooked sheep's head on a long platter. "And as long as there have been sheep, there has been *smalahove!*"

Smalahove is a specialty of western Norway, eaten by farmers who used every scrap of meat on their sheep in the lean winter months. Løne's farm, 8km north of Voss, uses both old and new techniques to prepare the gory masterpiece. Instead of scraping the heads clean by hand, a large spinning rack allows them to be shaved en masse. Each head gets sawed in half, cleaned, soaked in salt for three days, and cured in a traditional smokehouse.

Løne gives his guests a tour of the facilities before sitting them down for the feast, flashing a sweet smile as they devour the sheep's eye in a single bite. Falafel may have taken Oslo by storm, but in Voss carnivores still rule the roost. Løne's farm sells 55,000 heads a year, satisfying local demand but also shipping *smalahove* overseas to soldiers and oil executives jonesing for a taste of home.

Call ☎56 51 69 65 to arrange a farm visit. Dinner from 275kr.

while more seasoned adventurers might head for the Hardangerjøkulen glacier up north or to the virtually untouched southern tip. In Eidfjord itself, the austere 14th-century **old church** hugs the harbor. (Open July-Aug. M-F 9am-3:30pm.) A 2hr. walk along a trail from the harbor leads to a **Viking burial place** on top of a plateau in **Hereid;** the gravestones are nondescript enough, but the walk up to the field is scenic and not too demanding. Pick up a map of the trail from the tourist office (see below) and then head out along Simadalvegen. After passing the bridge, turn right and walk along the river; follow the path as it goes by the lake and winds uphill. A **mini-tour** whisks families to the kid-friendly **Hardangervidda Nature Center,** although parents would do well to keep a close eye on their progeny when the tour continues on to the roaring **Vøringfossen** waterfall, which plummets 182m into a serrated glacial valley. The stones are slippery, and safety rails are few and far between. (Mini-tour daily mid-June to mid-Aug. Departs after ferry arrival. 195kr, children 105kr.)

To get to Eidfjord from Bergen take a **bus/ferry** combo, transferring at Norheimsund (4¼hr., M-F and Su 7:30am, 300kr). **HSD** also offers a bus tour of Eidfjord and Vøringfossen, ending with a cruise through the Hardangerfjord. (☎55 96 69 00; www.hsd.no. Mid-May to mid-Sept.; leave Bergen 8:40am, return 7pm. 590kr.) Ask at the **tourist office,** in the town center, for info about hiking on the plateau. (☎53 67 34 00. Open mid-June to mid-Aug. M-F 9am-6pm, Sa-Su noon-6pm; May to mid-June and mid-Aug. to Sept. M-F 8:30am-4pm; low season M, W, and every other F 10am-4pm.) The office also rents **bikes** (half-day 100kr, full-day 150kr) and finds accommodations for a 30kr fee. For a spectacular lakeside location, try ◨**Sæbø Camping ❶,** 7km from town. Buses leave from the HSD station across the street from the tourist office; ask the driver to let you off at the campground. (☎53 66 59 27. Open mid-May to mid-Sept. Showers 5kr per 2min. 65kr per person and tent, 90kr per car. Cabins from 350kr. MC/V.)

SOGNEFJORD

The slender fingers of Sognefjord, the longest and deepest fjord in Europe, reach all the way to the foot of the Jotunheimen Mountains in central Norway. **Fylkesbaatane** (☎55 90 70 70; www.fylkesbaatane.no) sends boats on daytrips to towns on Sognefjord and back to Bergen, and offers day tours of Sognefjord and the Flåm valley. The boats depart from Bergen's Strandkaiterminalen; buy tickets there or at the city's tourist office. Overland transportation is likely to be more confusing than it's worth, due to uncertain road conditions and the limited number of bus routes. If you've rented a car, the mountainous **Sognefjellvegen** (Highway 55) is a good way to explore the northern shores of the fjord; pick up the road in Lom.

BALESTRAND. Balestrand (pop. 1400) is an ideal base for exploration of Sognefjord. **Jostedalen Breførarlag** (☎57 68 31 11; www.bfl.no) runs glacier walks (from 140kr), mountain hikes (from 650kr), and courses (from 2000kr) lasting 3-6 days. **Icetroll** (☎57 68 32 50; www.icetroll.com) also runs kayaking trips on two glacial lakes within Jostedalsbreen National Park (from 650kr); during the summer, kayakers often see huge ice-boulders splintering off of glaciers and tumbling down into the water. In front of the ferry docks, **Sognefjord Akvarium** showcases the rarely-seen marine life of the fjords. Admission includes a short slideshow and a full hour of canoeing on the fjord. (☎57 69 13 03. Open daily late June to mid-Aug. 9am-10pm; May to late June and mid-Aug. to early Sept. 10am-6pm. 60kr.) It's a bit macabre, but the aquarium also serves affordable seafood plates (95-140kr) with seating on the pier overlooking the fjord. **Hiking** in the area around Balestrand is excellent, with clear, color-coded trails guaranteeing exquisite views. From the harbor, head uphill to the right, take your second left, and walk along the main road for 7-10min.; turn right on Sygna and follow the signs. The trails, described at the trailhead, range from gentle strolls to arduous treks for experienced hikers. The 5hr. hike to **Raudmelen** culminates in a far-ranging 360° view on a clear day.

Fylkesbaatane **express boats** connect Bergen and Balestrand (4hr.; 2 per day M-Sa; 387kr, students 193kr). By car, follow Highway 55 to Hella and then take a **car ferry** (10min.; 40kr, plus 17kr for each additional passenger) to Dragsvik, just north of Balestrand. For free hiking maps and other info, stop by the **tourist office** near the quay. (☎57 69 12 55. Internet 20kr per 15min. Open mid-June to mid-Aug. M-F 7:30am-7pm, Sa-Su 10am-5:30pm; low season daily 10am-5:30pm.) Walk 100m up the hill past the office and take your second left to reach the **Kringsjå Hotel and Youth Hostel (HI) ❶**, where large windows and balconies look out on the mountains. (☎57 69 13 03; www.kringsja.no, Breakfast included. Kitchen available. Sheets 50kr. Laundry 15kr. Open July to mid-Aug. Dorms 190kr; doubles 560kr; triples 690kr. Nonmembers add 20kr. V.) **Sjøtun Camping ❶**, past the brown church on the coastal road, has tent sites and huts near the center of town. (☎57 69 12 23. Open June to early Sept. Reception 9-9:30am, 6-6:30pm and 9-9:30pm; call for other arrival times. 20kr per person, 30kr per tent. Cabins 150-325kr. Cash only.)

FJÆRLAND AND FJÆRLANDSFJORD. Fjærlandsfjord branches off Sognefjord in a thin northward line past Balestrand to the tiny town of **Fjærland** (pop. 300), perched at the base of the looming **Jostedalsbreen glacier.** Don't get too comfortable; Jostedalsbreen is the fastest-moving glacier in western Norway, migrating 2m per day. The **Glacier Museum** *(Norsk Bremuseum)*, 3km outside town, screens a beautiful panoramic film about the glacier and national park. (Open daily June-Aug. 9am-7pm; Apr.-May and Sept.-Oct. 10am 4pm. 80kr, students 40kr.) Back in town, **The Norwegian Booktown** supplements the region's farm economy with a network of 12 secondhand bookstores; **Bok and Bilde,** in the same building as the tourist office, stocks novels in many languages, while down the road on the left **Seriesalget** focuses on Norwegian comic books and children's stories. (☎57 69 22 10. Stores open daily May-Sept. 10am-6pm.) Accommodations are cheaper back in Balestrand, and **ferries** connect the two towns (1¼hr.; 2 per day; 152kr, students 76kr). Buses shuttle passengers to the Glacier Museum, whisk them to view two Jostedalsbreen outcroppings, then return them to the harbor. (9:25am bus 120kr, 1:25pm bus 90kr.) From the Glacier Museum, **buses** run to Ålesund (6hr.; 4 per day; 320kr, students 233kr) and Sogndal (30min.; 2-5 per day M-Sa; 56kr, students 41kr). The **tourist office,** near the harbor, solves transportation woes, rents bikes (125kr per day), and provides hiking maps. (☎57 69 32 33. Open daily 10am-6pm.)

FROM THE ROAD

SCALING BRIKSDAL

So you know the basic facts about glaciers, huge mountains of compressed ice that flow and slide across the landscape. There's something about them that commands our respect, as they crush boulders and split mountains without breaking a sweat. Still, it's a different story to see one up close. Conquering even part of the Briksdalbreen glacier felt like taking my place in history: woman versus nature, a conflict for the ages.

After some brief instruction, I buckled crampons to my shoes, hefted my ice axe, and walked across the base with a safety line linking me to my guide. I knew that I was by no means the first to try this climb, but my adrenaline still surged as I prepared to scale the first slippery face.

"You are mine," I thought, and kicked as hard as I could, driving the spiked tip of my boot into the frozen wall. I used this leverage to swing the axe deep into the ice above my head, and then pulled myself up, all my weight hanging from one sharp point. With an axe in each hand and grips on my boots, I felt like I was winning a battle of wills against a worthy adversary. My limbs grew tired, but I would not let the glacier see me falter. In the life of the Briksdalbreen I was just a gadfly, but I reached the summit reeling from my own immensity.

— Regina Schwartz

LOM AND JOTUNHEIMEN NATIONAL PARK

Between the last tributaries of the western fjords and the remote towns of the interior lies the pristine landscape of Jotunheimen National Park. Hunters chased wild reindeer across its heights for thousands of years, but Norwegian writers and painters discovered it anew in the 19th century, channeling its rugged beauty into a National Romantic artistic movement. In 1862, the poet Aasmund Olavsson Vinje christened the region "Jotunheimen," the home of the giants in Norse mythology.

LOM. The town of Lom (pop. 2500) has grown into a valued hub for excursions farther into the park. Residents continue to worship at the 13th-century **stave church,** whose tumbledown, wood-carved interior includes graffiti carved in runes by some medieval wag. (Open daily mid-June to mid-Aug. 9am-8pm; mid-May to mid-June and mid-Aug. to mid-Sept. 10am-6pm. 40kr.) The **Norwegian Mountain Museum** (*Fjellmuseum*) takes a stab at documenting the history and ecology of Jotunheimen, although its collection of ephemera isn't anything to write home about. (☎61 21 16 00; www.fjell.museum.no. Open mid-June to mid-Aug. M-F 9am-8pm, Sa-Su 10am-8pm; early June and late Aug. M-F 9am-5pm, Sa-Su 10am-5pm; Sept. and May M-F 9am-4pm, Sa-Su 10am-5pm; Oct.-Apr. M-F 9am-4pm. 50kr, students 30kr.) The park itself is the main attraction here, including the popular trek to the summit of **Galhøpiggen,** northern Europe's tallest mountain at 2469m, and the **Memurubu-Gjendsheim** trail mentioned in Henrik Ibsen's *Peer Gynt.* Ask at the tourist office for the best location from which to base your excursions; options include **Juvashytta, Krossbu, Leirvassbu,** and **Spiterstulen.**

Buses run to: Bergen (8½hr., 2 per day, 508kr); Oslo (6-6½hr., 5 per day, 475kr); Sogndal (3½hr., 2 per day, 200kr); and Trondheim (5½hr., 2 per day, 380kr). From the bus station, turn left and cross the bridge to reach the church and museum. The **tourist office,** in the same building as the museum, provides crucial transportation info, suggests outdoor activities for all levels of experience, and directs travelers to the hostels and campgrounds dotting the park. (☎61 21 29 90; www.visitlom.com. Open on the same schedule as the museum.) Across the street, sign up for a free 30min. slot on the **Internet** at the public library. With the nearest HI hostel more than 20km away, opt for a room at **Furulund Camping ❶,** just 600m away from the center of town. Walk left as you exit the tourist office and follow the right branch of the main road. (☎61 21 10 57. Outdoor trampoline. Showers 5kr per 5min. Laundry available. Doubles 200kr; quads without running water 300kr, with running water 450kr. AmEx/MC/V.)

NORDFJORD AND JOSTEDALSBREEN

Although Nordfjord places third compared to Geirangerfjord and Sognefjord, the icy 800km expanse of Jostedalsbreen is becoming an increasingly popular destination for guided excursions. The glacier is difficult to miss as it winds through mountain passes in frozen cascades of luminous blue. Adventurous travelers should note that it is dangerous to venture onto the glacier without a guide, as all glaciers have hidden soft spots and crevices.

STRYN. Stryn (pop. 6600) is wedged between mountains near the eastern end of Nordfjord. Despite a small, unexceptional town center, Stryn provides a good base for glacier walks and other outdoor excursions. The young, energetic staff of **Olden Aktiv** (☎57 87 38 88; www.briksdalsbreen.com) runs a variety of glacier tours and ice climbs for different fitness and skill levels (230-400kr; reserve ahead). The **Glacier Bus** (60kr) from Stryn out to the base of the glacier leaves daily from the main terminal at 9:30am, returning at 1:40pm. This timetable makes it difficult to squeeze in any of Olden Aktiv's longer tours and still make it back to Stryn for the night; consider staying at Melkevoll Bretun (below) if you plan to spend most of the day on the glacier. Hitchhiking back to Stryn is also possible, although *Let's Go* does not recommend hitchhiking as a safe means of transport.

Bus #440 leaves Stryn daily at 3pm for Lom (2hr., 175kr) and Trondheim (7½hr., 490kr). Buses also run to Ålesund (3½hr., 4-5 per day, 220kr) and Bergen (6hr., 6 per day, 398kr). All fares are discounted 25% for students. Check www.nor-way.no for a schedule. The knowledgeable staff at Stryn's **tourist office,** Perhusveien 19, past the Esso station, sells mountain maps (30kr) and recommends hikes. (☎57 87 40 40; www.nordfjord.no. **Internet** 15kr per 15min. Open July daily 8:30am-8pm; June and Aug. daily 8:30am-6pm; Sept.-May M-F 8:30am-3:30pm.) **Melkevoll Bretun ❶** sits almost in the shadow of the Briksdalbreen glacier, 45min. from Stryn. In addition to camping huts (from 270kr) and palatial holiday cabins (from 570kr), the campsite also features an open-air ❚cave dorm, where guests sleep on wooden slabs swaddled in reindeer skins with 800 tons of rock overhead. Bring an insulated sleeping bag. (☎57 87 38 64. Showers 10kr for 5min. Firewood 50kr. Kitchen available. Cave dorm 90kr. AmEx/MC/V.) To reach Stryn's **Youth Hostel (HI) ❶** from the town's bus station, turn left onto Setrevegen, head up the long, winding hill and then look for signs. (☎57 87 11 06. Breakfast included. Kitchen available. Laundry 20kr. Reception 8-11am and 4-11pm. Lockout 11am-4pm. Open June-Aug. Dorms 170kr; singles 250kr; doubles 400kr, with bath 500kr. Nonmembers add 25kr. V.)

GEIRANGERFJORD

Only 16km long, Geirangerfjord is lined with narrow cliffs and waterfalls that make it one of the prettiest places in Norway. While cruising through the iridescent water, watch for the Seven Sisters waterfalls and the Suitor geyser opposite them. Geirangerfjord can be reached from the north via the famous Trollstigen road from Åndalsnes or by the bus from Ålesund that stops in sleepy Hellesylt.

GEIRANGER. A tiny jewel of a Norwegian town, Geiranger (pop. 210) is situated at Geirangerfjord's glorious eastern end. An endpoint of the famous Trollstigen road splintered by sheer inclines, the town is one of this nation's most visited destinations. It's impossible not to wish that you'd happened upon the place before the rest of the world did, but even hordes of high-season tourists can't spoil the picture-perfect views just outside of town. **Hikers** can peer down from **Flydalsjuvet Cliff** (1½hr.), sidle behind the **Storseter Waterfall** (2½hr.), or catch a glimpse of the Seven Sisters waterfalls from **Skagoflå Farm** (5hr.), abandoned in 1916. **Buses** (2 per day 9am and 2pm, 140kr) make the 1hr. ride to Lanfvaten, where hikers disembark and climb up into the cloud cover that shrouds the top of the **Dalsnibba Mountain Plateau.** All of these hikes are well-marked, and visitors who make them in July or August will not be alone. To the right of the tourist office, 1km uphill, Geiranger's **Fjord Center** screens the requisite slideshow and maintains an interactive exhibit about life on the fjords hundreds of years ago. (☎70 26 18 00. Open daily mid-June to mid-Aug. 10am-7pm; mid-Aug. to mid-June 10am-5pm. 75kr.) If it's historical authenticity you're after, try **fishing** in the fjord for your supper with equipment from **Holenaustet.** (☎70 26 00 80. Poles 50kr per hr., 150kr per day. Lures 25-80kr. MC/V.) **Buses** run directly to Ålesund (3hr., 2-4 per day, 169kr), but getting to Oslo or Trondheim requires connecting through Åndalsnes (3hr., 2 per day 1 and 6:10pm, 146kr). There's no bus station; buy tickets on the bus with cash. For hiking maps and travel help, head to the **tourist office,** up the path from the ferry landing. The office can also help find private rooms (from 300kr) for a 30kr fee. (☎70 26 30 99; www.geiranger.no. Open daily mid-June to Aug. 9am-7pm, mid-May to mid-June 9am-4pm.) The nearest **hostel** is in Hellesylt, 1hr. away by ferry (8 per day, last ferry 7:35pm, 90kr). In Geiranger itself, one of the only true budget options is **Geiranger Camping ❶,** 100m from the town center down by the water. (☎70 26 31 20. Open mid-May to early Sept. 14kr per person, 60kr per tent. Cash only.)

NORWAY

ROMSDAL AND TRØNDELAG

Between the western fjords and the long, sparsely inhabited stretch of Norway extending up past the Arctic Circle, a string of small coastal cities forms the third point of a triangle with Oslo and Bergen. Hemmed in by the spiny Trollstigen range and the fertile valleys along the Trondheimsfjord, this region is something of a Norwegian heartland that travelers are only beginning to discover.

ÅLESUND   ☎ 70

Often compared to a scaled-down version of Bergen, Ålesund (OH-less-oont; pop. 40,000) welcomes travelers emerging from fjord country with splashy Art Nouveau architecture and a breezy seaside location. The best view of the city and the distant mountains calls for scampering up 418 steps to the **Aksla** viewpoint. Head through the small park across from the youth hostel and then start climbing; the 25min. walk to the top is well worth the exertion, especially late at night when the city's lights sear the inky, expansive sky. Step into the time machine exhibit at the centrally located ▨**Art Nouveau Center,** Apotekergrt. 16, and be transported back to the city's devastating fire of 1904. This informative and engaging introduction to the city traces its century-long renaissance, manifested on a smaller scale in the stylish living quarters of the pharmacist who once lived upstairs. (☎ 10 49 70. Open June-Aug. M-F 10am-7pm, Sa-Su noon-5pm; Aug.-May Tu-F 11am-5pm, Sa 11am-4pm, Su noon-4pm. 50kr, students 40kr.) To telescope back even further, the open-air **Sunnmøre Museum** features reconstructed farmhouses and the excavated remains of the 11th-century Borgundkaupangen trading post. On Wednesdays, locals demonstrate traditional handicrafts and a replica Viking ship takes visitors out on the water at 1:30pm for a short cruise. Take bus #13 or 18 to Sunnmøre. (☎ 17 40 00; www.museumsnett.no/sunnmore. Open in summer M-Sa 11am-7pm, Su noon-5pm; low season M-Sa 11am-5pm, Su noon-6pm.) Children flock to the **Atlantic Sea Park,** where tanks are submerged in the ocean and illuminated by natural daylight. Scuba divers feed the fish by hand daily at 1pm. To reach the park, take bus #13 or 18 (10min., 6-7 per day, 22kr) from St. Olavs pl. to Atlanterhavsparken. (Open mid-June to mid-Aug. M-F and Su 10am-7pm, Sa 10am-4pm; mid-Aug. to mid-June M-Sa 11am-4pm, Su noon-5pm. 90kr, students 75kr.)

Buses go to Stryn (3½hr., 1-2 per day, 220kr) and Trondheim (8hr., 2 per day, 490kr). A slightly shorter, but more expensive route to Trondheim involves a bus to Åndalsnes (2½hr., 3 per day, 175kr) and then a seat on the waiting train to Trondheim (4hr., 480kr). Hurtigruten **express boats** are costly, but since trips include one night of accommodations, they can be an affordable alternative to overland routes. The dock is a 5min. walk to the right of the tourist office. (Departs daily 6:45pm, arrives in Trondheim 8:15am. 822kr, students 411kr.) The **tourist office** on Keiser Wilhelms gt. has **Internet** access (10kr per 10min.) and arranges walking tours of the city (departs daily 2pm; 60kr, students 35kr). (☎ 70 15 76 00. Open June-Aug. M-F 8:30am-7pm, Sa 9am-5pm, Su 11am-5pm; Sept.-May M-F 9am-4pm.) It's a 5-7min. walk from the bus station to the plain, but convenient **Ålesund Vandrerhjem (HI)** ❶, Parkgt. 14, where triple-decker bunk beds and too-wide common spaces conspire to nip community in the bud. Head down Keiser Wilhelms gt., keeping the water on your right, turn left onto Rådstugt. and head uphill to Parkgt; the hostel is around the corner to the right. (☎ 70 11 58 30. Breakfast included. Sheets 50kr. Laundry free. Reception 8:30-11am and 3:30pm-midnight. Open May-Sept. Dorms 150kr; singles 390kr; doubles 510kr. Nonmembers add 25kr. V.) Grab a sandwich at trendy **Tango** ❷, Keyser Wilhelmsg. 23, or return at night for a chatty bar scene clustered around outdoor tables. (☎ 12 10 12. Open M-Th 11am-1am, F 11am-2am, Sa noon-2am, Su 4pm-1am.)

ÅNDALSNES ☎71

Romsdalsfjord slashes east as far as the town of Åndalsnes (pop. 2700), a brawny, lightly industrialized port on the northeastern perimeter of fjord country. **Hikes** along the **Trollstigen** (Troll's Road) climb to altitudes more than 850m above sea level, sometimes describing zigzag turns to negotiate the incline more gradually. The trail becomes enwreathed in mist as it passes the 180m **Stigfossen** waterfall and approaches the sheer **Trollveggen** (Troll's Wall), with an alluring lip that drew base jumpers for years until the town went into debt making helicopter rescues and outlawed the activity. Thrill-seeking scofflaws continue to make jumps on the sly. Trace your way back down to Åndalsnes (5hr.) on the **Kløvstien path,** recently smoothed over for walkers but still steep enough to require a hand-rail on certain segments. During the first week of August, Åndalsnes holds the **Rauma Rock Festival** (www.raumarock.com; 2-day pass 510kr), while the outdoor theater in nearby Klungnes hosts the **Sinclairfestival,** an open-air reenactment of a 1612 battle between Scottish mercenaries and Norwegian farmers. Sean Connery film screenings occupy the evenings, while participants nosh on haggis prepared at the local high school. (www.sinclairfestivalen.com. Tickets from 100kr.) **Trains** run to Oslo (5½hr., 2-4 per day, 644kr). **Buses** depart outside the train station on the square for Ålesund (2hr.; 1-2 per day; 135kr, students 89kr), where the Hurtigruten stops en route to Bergen. For hiking maps and help booking private rooms, duck into the **tourist office,** in the same building as the train station. (☎22 16 22; www.visitandalsnes.com. Open M-F 9am-6pm, Sa 10am-6pm, Su noon-6pm.) The wooden cabins and friendly proprietor of **Andalsnes Vandrerhjem (HI) ❶,** Setnes, make for a homey place to stay just 2km outside of town. (☎22 13 82. Sheets 50kr. Internet 15kr per 15min. Reception 4pm-10am. Dorms 190kr; singles 350kr; doubles 500kr. V.)

TRONDHEIM ☎73

A thousand years have come and gone since Viking kings turned Trondheim (pop. 150,000) into Norway's seat of power. Norway's *axis mundi* runs farther south today, between Oslo and Bergen, but the elegant boulevards laid out by Caspar von Cicignon after the fire of 1681 still bespeak this harbor city's order and grace. More than 25,000 university students lend Trondheim vivacity during termtime, although by no means does summer leave this technology center and gateway to the north country a ghost town.

NORWAY

TRANSPORTATION AND PRACTICAL INFORMATION. **Trains** go to Bodø (11hr., 2 per day, 861kr) and Oslo (6½hr., 3-5 per day, 748kr). **Buses** leave the train station for Ålesund (7¼hr., 4 per day, 488kr) and Bergen (14hr.; 2 per day; 695kr, students 347kr). The **Hurtigruten** sails to Stamsund, in the Lofoten Islands (31hr.; departs daily at noon, arrives in Stamsund 7pm the next day; 1682kr, students 841kr). Trondheim is bike-friendly; the city keeps 300 serviceable **bikes** parked at stations in town (20kr deposit). Maps showing the station locations are available at the **tourist office,** Munkegt. 19. To get there from the train station, cross the bridge, walk six blocks down Søndregt., turn right on Kongensgt., and look to your left as you approach the rotary. (☎80 76 60; www.visit-trondheim.com. Open July to early Aug. M-F 8:30am-8pm, Sa-Su 10am-6pm; mid-May to June and early Aug. to late Aug. M-F 8:30am-4pm, Sa-Su 10am-2pm; late Aug. to mid-May M-F 9am-4pm.) **DNT,** Sandgt. 30, has maps and hiking info. (☎92 42 00. Open Mar.-Oct. M-F 8am-4pm, Th 8am-6pm.) **Postal Code:** 7411.

ACCOMMODATIONS AND FOOD. **Trondheim InterRail Centre ❶,** Elgesetergt. 1, in the Studentersamfundet, is a lively, student-run hostel 10-12min. from the tourist office. Cross the roundabout to Kongensgt., turn left onto Prinsens gt., and the hostel will be on your left after the bridge. (☎89 95 38; tirc@samfundet.no. Free Internet. Breakfast included. Dinner 45kr. Sheets 60kr deposit. Does not rent pillow or quilts. Open late June to early Aug. Sleeping-bag dorms 115kr. Cash only.) For equally basic, if quieter lodging, take Lillegårdsbakken, off Øvre Bakklandet, uphill to **Singsaker Sommerhotell ❶**, Rogertsgt. 1. (☎89 31 00; http://sommerhotell.singsaker.no. Breakfast included. Sheets 35kr. Open June to mid-Aug. Sleeping-bag dorms 150kr; singles 375-480kr; doubles 570-680kr; triples 780kr. V.) During the low season, your best bet is **Trondheim Vandrerhjem (HI) ❷**, Weidemmamsv. 41, a 10min. walk from the train station. Turn left and cross the bridge, then continue to the top of the hill and turn left. (☎87 44 50; www.trondheim-vandrerhjem.no. Internet 1.50kr per min. Breakfast included. Kitchen available. Sheets 40kr. Dorms 210kr; singles 395kr; doubles 500kr. V.) Gluttony may be one of the seven deadly sins, but the all-you-can-eat ▨**cake buffet** (54kr) at cottage-style **Mormors Stue ❷**, Nedre Enkeltskillingsveita 2, is more fun than wrath and sloth combined. Throw in all-you-can-eat pasta for an extra 55kr, and then nestle down into the restaurant's plush couches as your starch headache sets in. (☎52 20 22. Buffet Su 1-7pm. Open M-Sa 10am-11:30pm, Su 1-11:30pm. MC/V.) The early-bird dinner crowd can snap up fresh fish platters for a paltry 99kr at the riverside pub **Den Gode Nabo ❷**, Øvre Bakklandet 66, just over the old bridge. (☎87 42 40. Dinner special daily 4-6pm. Open daily 1pm-1am. MC/V.) Alternakids nibble on eco-friendly lamb burgers (55kr) at eclectic **Ramp ❶**, Strandv. 25a. Nab groceries at **Rema 1000**, on the main square. (Open M-F 8am-9pm, Sa 9am-8pm.)

🄶 🄳 **SIGHTS AND ENTERTAINMENT.** Most sights huddle in the southern end of town around **Nidaros Cathedral**, finished around 1300 and unquestionably one of the most magnificent churches in Norway. Savaged by fire and left to vandals who ran off with countless liturgical treasures, the cathedral took on new importance during the 19th-century National Romantic period, when King Carl III Johan ordered crown jewels made and then donned them at an 1818 coronation ceremony in the church. The jewels remain here, as does one of only five large organs built by Joachim Wagner, one of Bach's contemporaries. Free organ concerts take place Monday through Saturday at 1pm. Guided tours also ascend the cathedral's soaring spire throughout the day; arrive at 15 or 45min. past the hour. (Open mid-June to mid Aug. M-F 9am-6pm, Sa 9am-2pm, Su 1-4pm; low season reduced hours. 40kr, includes admission to the nearby Archbishop's Palace.) To the north, the **Nordenfjeldske Kunstindustrimuseum** (National Museum of Decorative Arts), Munkeg. 3-7, features textiles, furniture, and a robust collection of 20th-century tapestries. (☎80 89 50; www.nkim.museum.no. Open June to late Aug. M-Sa 10am-5pm, Su noon-5pm; late Aug. to May Tu-Sa 10am-3pm, Th 10am-5pm, Su noon-4pm. 50kr, students 25kr.) Across the scenic **Gamle Bybro** (Old Town Bridge) to the east is the **old district's** former fishing houses, which have subtly morphed into chic galleries and cafes even as they outwardly maintain their weather-worn maritime charm. On the hill above the old district, Trondheim's proto-Haussmann figure Caspar von Cicignon built **Kristiansen Fortress**, offering a splendid view of the city. Take the precarious bike lift up from the base of the Gamle Bybro; you'll need a bike (20kr deposit) from a nearby bike rack and a key card (100kr deposit; available at the tourist office and adjacent cafes). Mastery of this conveyance requires patience. The **Solsiden** ("sunny side") district is home to popular **Club Blæst**, TMV kaia 17, which holds concerts most weekends and hosts DJs other nights of the week. (☎60 01 06; www.blaest.no. Open daily noon-3am.) When school is in session, the clubs and bars along **Brattorgata** offer everything from tapas to fine malt whiskey.

FARTHER NORTH

LOFOTEN ISLANDS

A jumble of emerald mountains, glassy waters, and colorful villages, the Lofotens prove that there is more to Norwegian beauty than the western fjords. As late as the 1950s, isolated fishermen lived in *rorbuer*, raised red wooden shacks along the coast; today, the same shacks are rented out to tourists venturing above the Arctic Circle to visit fishing villages aglow with the sallow rays of the midnight sun.

■ ▐ GETTING THERE AND TRANSPORTATION. To get to the Lofotens from Trondheim, take the **Hurtigruten** to Stamsund (31hr.; departs daily at noon, arrives at 7pm the next day; 1682kr, students 841kr) or take a **train** to Bodø (11hr., 2 per day, 861kr) and then a **car ferry** to Moskenes (3-4hr.; 4-7 per day; 127kr, students 63kr), an **express boat** to Svolvær (3½hr.; daily except Sa; 257kr, students 130kr), or the **Hurtigruten** to Svolvær (6hr., daily 3pm, 358kr) via Stamsund (4hr., 334kr). Bodø's **tourist office** is down Sjogt. from the train station. (Open June-Aug. M-F 9am-8pm, Sa 10am-8pm, Su noon-8pm; Sept.-May M-W and F 9am-4pm, Th 9am-6pm, Sa 10am-3pm.) Within the islands, **local buses** are the main form of transport; pick up the *Lofoten Trafikklag* timetable at the tourist office. Hitchhiking is not uncommon, either by boat or by car. However, *Let's Go* does not recommend hitchhiking as a safe means of transport.

◢ MOSKENES AND FLAKSTAD. The southernmost inhabited islands, Moskenes (pop. 1300) and Flakstad (pop. 1600) are linked by the north-south E10 highway. The Lofotens are not overzealous about marking trails through the western wilderness, but challenging mountainous **hikes** are one of the principal reasons to visit; pick up a hiking map (95kr) at the tourist office. Make the 3hr. trek up to the DNT's **Munkebu cabin** and stay the night if you prefer running water and beds to sleeping bags in the rough. (170kr, plus 200kr deposit. Key available at the tourist office.) South of Moskenes, the lovely, well-preserved fishing village of **Å** (OH) is the posterchild for the Lofotens' tourist industry. **Buses** depart from behind the tourist office 5-15min. after boat landings. The **Norsk Fiskeværsmuseum** uses reenactments to explain the island's maritime economy, and offers visitors with strong stomachs a spoonful of homemade cod-liver oil. For a less noxious snack, sample cinnamon rolls from the birch-fired oven at the museum's historic bakery. (☎76 09 14 88. Open mid-June to mid-Aug. daily 11am-6pm; mid-Aug. to mid-June M-F 11am-3pm. 65kr, students 45kr.) Experienced hikers can tackle the 8hr. **Stokkvikka hike** by heading down the southern bank of Lake Ågvatnet and up 400m to cross the Stokkvikskaret Pass. Bring a map. The **tourist office,** 100m from the Moskenes ferry landing, offers rafting tours (3-6hr., 600-900kr) that go through the **Maelstrom,** one of the most dangerous ocean currents in the world, past the abandoned fishing hamlet of **Hell,** and into the ancient **Refsvikhula caves** to view their 3000-year-old drawings. The office also arranges 3hr. fishing trips with locals for 300kr. (☎76 09 15 99; www.lofoten-info.no. Internet 15kr per 15min. Open late June to early Aug. daily 10am-7pm; early June to late June and early Aug. to late Aug. M-F 10am-5pm.) The dorms at **Å Lofoten Vandrerhjem (HI) ❶** are in a converted attic above the bakery, while private residences around town let out double rooms. (☎76 09 11 21; aa.hostel@vandrerhjem.no. Dorms 140kr; doubles 250kr. V.) Groups of four or more should consider renting out one of the comfortable *rorbu* cabins offered by **Å Hamna Rorbuer As.** (☎76 09 11 21. June-Sept. reception 24hr. Cabins 600-950kr. V.)

◪ VESTVÅGØY. Farther north is Vestvågøy (pop. 11,000), an island worth visiting if only to stay at the seaside ◪**Stamsund Vandrerhjem (HI) ❶**. A 15min. walk from the Stamsund ferry dock, this hostel's two common rooms have kindled enough friendships between travelers to have cultivated a reputation throughout Norway. The endearingly gruff, knowledgeable proprietor Roar Justad is at least half the reason why. (☎76 08 93 34. Fishing gear and rowboats 100kr deposit. Bikes 100kr per day. Showers 5kr per 5min. Laundry 30kr. Closed mid-Oct. to mid-Dec. Dorms 90kr; doubles 300kr; *rorbuer* 400-650kr. Cash only.) The gas station uphill from the hostel offers **Internet** access (20kr per 15min.) and rents cars (300kr per day); given the island's sporadic bus schedules, a car may the best way to go, as long as you drive carefully on the one-lane roads. **Hikers** are serenaded by ptarmigans on the way up to the peaks of **Stein Tinden** (500m) or **Justad Tinden** (732m); both treks take roughly 6hr. round-trip and provide panoramic views of the Lofotens. Visiting during June and the first two weeks of July means tanning into the wee hours under the midnight sun. Clear nights in late autumn or early spring could mean seeing the **Northern Lights,** spectacular night-time displays formed when solar flares produce plasma clouds that collide with gases in the Earth's atmosphere.

TROMSØ
☎77

The undisputed capital of northern Norway, Tromsø (pop. 60,000) exudes a worldly savoir-faire unexpected from a craggy island 720km north of the Arctic Circle. With Hurtigruten express boats connecting the town to southern Norway and a major university drawing students from across Scandinavia, perhaps the lively atmosphere of the town's pedestrian-friendly downtown shouldn't come as a surprise. The **Arctic Cathedral** resembles a glacier with light, metallic plates that reflect natural light in long, diaphanous streaks; 11 tons of glass were used to fashion the huge, triangular stained-glass window behind the altar. (Open June to mid-Aug. M-Sa 10am-8pm, Su 1-8pm; mid-Aug. to May daily 4-6pm. 22kr. Services Su 11am.) Across the bridge, **Polaria,** Hjarlmar Johansens gt. 12, is a sleek, interactive museum and aquarium focused on Arctic ecosystems; watch the bearded seals strut their stuff at the daily feeding. (☎75 01 00; www.polaria.no. Open daily mid-May to mid-Aug. 10am-7pm; Sept.-Apr. noon-5pm. Seal meals 12:30 and 3:30pm. 80kr, students 40kr.) The **Tromsø University Museum** delves into geology, zoology, and the indigenous Sami culture, then dazzles visitors with a mesmerizing video about the Northern Lights. (Take bus #28 from the city center. ☎64 50 00. Open mid-June to mid-Aug. daily 9am-8pm; mid-May to mid-June and mid-Aug. to mid-Sept. daily 9am-6pm; mid-Sept. to mid-May M-F 9am-3:30pm, Sa-Su 11am-5pm. 30kr.) To see the midnight sun hovering above Tromsø in June and early July, take the **Fjellheisen** (cable car) up 420m to the top of Mt. Storsteinen. Students are fond of taking the lift late at night for a serene, introspective evening, sipping tea and talking in low tones at the **Fjellstua** cafe. (Cafe open daily mid-May to mid-Aug. 10am-1am; Apr. to mid-May and mid-Aug. to Sept. 10am-5pm. Cable car daily every 30min. 10am-1am. 70kr.) Nightlife crackles on the **Storgoret** and along **Sjøgata.**

The **Hurtigruten** arrives in Tromsø from Stamsund, in the Lofoten Islands (departs 7:30pm, arrives 2:30pm the next day; 980kr, students 490kr). **Buses** go to Narvik (4½hr.; 2-4 per day; 320kr, students and Scanrail holders 160kr), a transportation hub for travelers continuing on to Finland and Sweden. The very helpful **tourist office,** Storgt. 63, books private rooms as well as excursions by dogsled, snowmobile, or white-water raft. (☎61 00 00; www.destinasjon-tromso.no. Open June-Aug. M-F 10am-6pm, Sa-Su noon-5pm; low season reduced hours.) To reach **Tromsø Vandrerhjem (HI) ❶**, Åsgårdv. 9, from the tourist office, turn right and walk two blocks down Storgt., take another right on Fr. Langes gt., and then catch bus #26 up until 11:40pm; after that, it's a 25min. walk. (☎65 76 28. Sheets 60kr. Reception 8-11am and 5-11pm. Open mid-June to mid-Aug. Dorms 150kr; doubles 380kr. V.) Mountainside **Tromsø Camping ❶**, across the river, has comfortable cabins and convenient access to outdoor activities. Take bus #20 or 24 to Kraftforsyninga, walk back across the red bridge, turn left and follow the road 400m. (☎63 80 37; www.tromsocamping.no. Reception 7am-11pm. Tents 150kr; 2- to 5-person cabins 400-950kr, low season 400-700kr. Cash only.) Cappuccino and Norwegian board games await at **Amt-mandens Datter ❷**, Grønne gt. 81, a student hangout with leather chairs straight out of a professor's study. (☎68 49 06. Internet 20kr per 20min. DJ spins Sept.-May F-Sa. Open June-Aug. M-Th and Su 3pm-1:30am, F 3pm-3am, Sa noon-3am; Sept.-May M-Sa noon-3am, Su 3pm-3am. Kitchen closed Su. V.) The **Tromsø Inter-national Film Festival** is Norway's largest, and will showcase "Films from the North" shot in arctic Scandinavia and Russia. (January 18-23, 2005. ☎75 30 90; www.tiff.no.) **Postal Code:** 9253.

NORWAY

POLAND (POLSKA)

Caught at the threshold of East and West, Poland's moments of independence have always been brief. Between 1795 and 1918, the country did not exist on any map of Europe. After being ravaged in WWII, it was subsumed into the USSR. Today, finally given a bit of breathing room, Poland has used the opportunity to raise its economic output and to enter both NATO and the EU. Although capitalism has brought with it rising crime and unemployment—the shocks of transition—Poles have also disbursed their new wealth on projects to reinvent their cultural roots and restore their war-smitten architecture to glory.

 DISCOVER POLAND: SUGGESTED ITINERARIES

THREE DAYS Start in **Warsaw** (1 day, p. 808). Stroll along the bustling **Royal Way** (p. 813), stop by a cafe, and then explore the city's **former ghetto** and **synagogues** (p. 814). Depart soon for Poland's cultural capital, **Kraków** (2 days, p. 816), the only Polish city to make it unscathed through the 20th century. Wander through the intact **Stare Miasto** (old town), visit **Jagellonian University**, and gape at the magnificent **Wawel Castle.** In the south of the city is the Jewish quarter, **Kazimierz,** rich in history after 600 years.

ONE WEEK Arrive in cosmopolitan **Warsaw** (2 days). Rest amid the lush parks and 19th-century architecture of **Wrocław** (2 days, p. 824), before ending your trip in **Kraków** (3 days).

THREE WEEKS After exhausting **Warsaw** proper (3 days), take a daytrip to the extravagant palace at **Wilanów** (p. 816). Head southeast to **Lublin** (2 days, p. 822) for the intact Stare Miasto and 14th-century castle. Dip south to **Zakopane** (2 days, p. 823) for hiking in the Tatras, then board the express line to **Kraków** (4 days). From there, take a sobering daytrip to **Auschwitz** (p. 821), or experience a different kind of wonderment in the salt mines of **Wieliczka** (1 day, p. 822). **Wrocław** (2 days) and Copernicus's birthplace, **Toruń** (1 day, p. 825), are on the way to the lively port city of **Gdańsk** (3 days, p. 828). End your trip on the nearby beaches of **Sopot** (1 day, p. 832), on the coast of the Baltic Sea.

ESSENTIALS

WHEN TO GO

Winter temperatures average –3 to –6°C (20-26°F), while summer temperatures tend to fall in the range 16-19°C (61-66°F). Visit the Tatras between November and February to ski, or in August to hike. Elsewhere, summer and autumn are the best times to visit, as winter can be dreary.

DOCUMENTS AND FORMALITIES

VISAS. Citizens of Australia, Canada, Ireland, New Zealand, and the US do not need a visa for stays of up to 90 days, citizens of the UK for stays of up to 180 days. To extend your stay, apply to the regional government branch (*voi vodine*) of the city you are staying in, or to the **Ministry of Internal Affairs** at ul. Stefana Batorego 5, Warsaw 02-591 (☎ 022 621 02 51; fax 849 74 94).

EMBASSIES. All foreign embassies are in Warsaw (p. 808) and Kraków (p. 816). Polish embassies at home include: **Australia,** 7 Turrana St., Yarralumla ACT 2600 Canberra (☎02 6273 1208; www.poland.org.au); **Canada,** 443 Daly Ave., Ottawa, ON

KIN 6H3 (☎613-789-0468; www.polishembassy.ca); **Ireland,** 5 Ailesbury Rd., Ballsbridge, Dublin 4 (☎01 283 0855; www.polishembassy.ie); **New Zealand,** 17 Upland Rd., Kelburn, Wellington (☎04 475 9453; polishembassy@xtra.co.nz); **UK,** 47 Portland Pl., London W1B 1JH (☎087 0774 2700; www.polishembassy.org.uk); **US,** 2640 16th St. NW, Washington, D.C. 20009 (☎202-234-3800; www.polandembassy.org).

TRANSPORTATION

BY PLANE. LOT (www.lot.com) flies into Warsaw's modern Okęcie Airport (WAW) from London, New York, and Toronto, among other cities.

BY TRAIN. Trains are generally faster and more convenient than buses. Be alert—stations are not announced and can be poorly marked. Stations have boards that list towns alphabetically and posters that list trains chronologically. For a complete **timetable,** see www.pkp.pl/english. *Odjazdy* (departures) are in yellow, *przyjazdy* (arrivals) in white. **InterCity** and **ekspresowy** (express) trains are listed in red with an "IC" or "Ex" before the train number. *Pośpieszny* (direct; also in red) are almost as fast. *Osobowy* (in black) are the slowest and have no restrooms but are cheaper than *pośpieszny*. *InterCity, ekspresowy,* and some *pośpieszny* trains require seat reservations, indicated by a boxed R on the schedule; ask the clerk for a *miejscówka* (myay-TSOOF-kah; reserva-tion). Allocate time for long, slow lines or buy your ticket in advance at the station or an Orbis office. On board, the *konduktor* sells surcharged tickets. **Eurail** passes are not valid in Poland. While Polish students and seniors can buy *ulgowy* (half-price) tickets, foreign travelers are not eligible for discounts; there is a hefty fine for traveling with an *ulgowy* ticket without Polish ID. **BIJ-Wasteels** tickets and **Eurotrain** passes, sold at Almatur and Orbis, give under-26 travelers 40% off international tickets.

BY BUS AND BY FERRY. **PKS buses** are cheapest and fastest for short trips. Like trains, buses may be *pośpieszny* (direct; marked in red) or *osobowy* (slow; in black). Purchase advance tickets at the station and expect long lines. Tickets for many routes can be bought only from the driver. In the countryside, PKS markers (steering wheels that look like upside-down, yellow Mercedes-Benz symbols) indi-cate bus stops; drivers will also often stop if you flag them down. Traveling with a backpack can be a problem if the bus is full, since there are no storage compart-ments. The private **Polski Express** has more luxurious buses, but the area of service is limited. **Ferries** (p. 70) run from Denmark and Sweden to Gdańsk.

BY TAXI AND BY THUMB. Arrange cabs by phone rather than hailing one on the street. Taxi drivers generally try to rip off foreigners; arrange the price before get-ting in or ensure that the meter has been turned on. The going rate is 1.50-3zł per km. Hand-waving is the accepted sign for hitchhiking. Although it is common in Poland, *Let's Go* does not recommend hitchhiking.

TOURIST SERVICES AND MONEY

EMERGENCY Police: ☎997. **Ambulance:** ☎999. **Fire:** ☎998.

TOURIST OFFICES. City-specific offices are generally more helpful than the larger chains. All offices provide free info in English and should be of some help with accommodations. **Orbis** (www.orbis-use.com), the state-sponsored travel bureau staffed by English speakers, operates luxury hotels and sells transportation tick-ets. **Almatur** (www.almatur.com.pl), the Polish student travel organization, sells ISIC (p. 18), arranges summer dorms, and sells discounted transportation tickets. Both provide maps, as do **PTTK** and **IT** (*Informacji Turystycznej*) bureaus.

MONEY. The Polish **złoty** (plural *złotych*) is composed of 100 *groszy*. For cash, private **kantors** offices offer better exchange rates than banks, except at transpor-tation hubs. **Bank PKO SA** also has decent rates; they cash **traveler's checks** and give MasterCard and Visa **cash advances** for a small commission. **ATMs** (*bankomat*) are almost everywhere. **Credit cards** are rarely accepted.

BUSINESS HOURS. Business hours tend to be Monday to Friday 8am-4pm and Saturday 9am-1pm; shops distinguish "working" (*pracująca*) Saturdays from "free" (*wolna*) ones, when hours are shorter. Very few stores are open on Sunday.

POLAND

ZŁOTYCH (ZŁ)		
AUS$1 = 2.58ZŁ		1ZŁ = AUS$0.39
CDN$1 = 2.70ZŁ		1ZŁ = CDN$0.37
EUR€1 = 4.42ZŁ		1ZŁ = EUR€0.23
NZ$1 = 2.37ZŁ		1ZŁ = NZ$0.42
UK£1 = 6.58ZŁ		1ZŁ = UK£0.15
US$1 = 3.60ZŁ		1ZŁ = US$0.28

COMMUNICATION

PHONE CODES	Country code: 48. International dialing prefix: 00. From outside Poland, dial int'l dialing prefix (see inside back cover) + 48 + city code + local number.

TELEPHONES AND INTERNET ACCESS. Most public phones use cards, which come in several denominations and are sold at post offices, Telekomunikacja Polska offices, and most kiosks. To make a collect call, write the name of the city or country, the number, and *"Rozmowa 'R'"* on a slip of paper and hand it to a post office clerk. International access codes include **AT&T Direct** (☎ 00 800 111 11 11), **Australia Direct** (☎ 00 800 611 11 61), **BT Direct** (☎ 00 800 89 0036), **Canada Direct** (☎ 00 800 111 41 18), **MCI WorldPhone** (☎ 00 800 111 21 22), **Sprint** (☎ 00 800 111 31 15), and **Telkom SA WorldCall** (☎ 00 800 271 11 27). Most mid-sized towns have an Internet cafe, and larger cities have several. Costs run about 3-8zł per hr.

MAIL. Mail service is efficient; airmail (*lotnicza*) reaches most overseas locations in seven to 10 days. Letters abroad cost about 2.20zł, depending on weight. When picking up mail received via *Poste Restante*, you may have to pay a fee (1.10zł) or show your passport. Address mail to be held as follows: First name SURNAME, *Poste Restante*, ul. Swiętokrzyska 31/33, Warsaw 1, 00-001 POLAND.

LANGUAGES. Polish varies little across the country; the exceptions are Kaszuby, which has a Germanic dialect, and Karpaty, where the highlanders have thick accents. In western Poland, German is the best-known foreign language, although many Poles in big cities speak English. Polish basics are listed on p. 1064.

ACCOMMODATIONS AND FOOD

POLAND	❶	❷	❸	❹	❺
ACCOMMODATIONS	under 45zł	45-65zł	65-80zł	80-120zł	over 120zł
FOOD	under 8zł	8-18zł	18-30zł	30-45zł	over 45zł

Private rooms (*wolne pokoje;* around 20-60zł per night) are available in most towns but are not regulated; tourist offices can usually find reputable renters. **PTSM** is the national organization of **youth hostels** (*schroniska młodzieżowe*), which average 15-40zł per night. Call at least a week in advance. **University dorms** transform into spartan budget housing in July and August; these are an especially good option in Kraków. **PTTK** runs a number of hotels called **Dom Turysty,** which have multi-bed rooms as well as budget singles and doubles. **Hotels** generally cost 80-150zł per night. **Campsites** average 10-15zł per person; **bungalows** are also often available (20-30zł). *Polska Mapa Campingów,* available at tourist offices, lists all campsites.

Polish staples include meat, potatoes, cabbage, and butter. **Meals** always begin with soup, often *barszcz* (clear broth), *chłodnik* (a cold beet soup with buttermilk and hard-boiled eggs), *kapuśniak* (cabbage soup), or *żurek* (barley-flour soup loaded with eggs and sausage). Hearty main courses include *gołąbki* (cabbage rolls stuffed with meat and rice), *kotlet schabowy* (pork cutlets), *naleśniki* (cream-topped crepes filled with cottage cheese or jam), and *pierogi* (stuffed dumplings). Poland bathes in beer, vodka, and spiced liquor. Żywiec is the most popular strong beer; EB is its excellent, gentler peer. The Wyborowa, Żytnia, and Poloncz brands of Wódka usually decorate private bars, while Belweder (Belvedere) is Poland's most prized alcoholic export.

POLAND

SAFETY AND SECURITY

Public restrooms, which can cost up to 0.70zł, are marked with an upward-pointing triangle for men and a circle for women. Pharmacies are well-stocked, and at least one in each large city stays open 24hr. Avoid state hospitals. There are usually **clinics** in major cities with private English-speaking doctors; expect to pay around 50zł per visit. **Tap water** is theoretically drinkable, but bottled mineral water, available carbonated (*gazowana*) or flat (*nie gazowana*), will spare you from some unpleasant metals and chemicals. Always be on your guard against **pickpockets,** especially at big train stations and on crowded public buses and trams.

HOLIDAYS AND FESTIVALS

Holidays: New Year's Day (Jan. 1); Easter (Mar. 28); Labor Day (May 1); Constitution Day (May 3); Corpus Christi (May 26); Assumption Day (Aug. 15); All Saint's Day (Nov. 1); Independence Day (Nov. 11); Christmas (Dec. 25-26).

Festivals: Kraków is Poland's festival capital, especially in summer. The most notable include the International Short Film Festival (late May), the Festival of Jewish Culture (late June and early July), and jazz festivals (notably July-Aug. and Oct.-Nov.).

FACTS AND FIGURES: POLAND

Official Name: Republic of Poland.	**Land Area:** 312,685 sq. km.
Capital: Warsaw.	**Time Zone:** GMT +1.
Major Cities: Gdańsk, Kraków, Łódź.	**Language:** Polish.
Population: 38,626,000.	**Religion:** Roman Catholic (95%).

WARSAW (WARSZAWA)   ☎ 022

Proud and resilient Warsaw (pop. 1,676,600) rebuilt itself from rubble at the end of WWII after two-thirds of the population had been killed and 83% of the city destroyed. Now having weathered the further blow of a half-century of Communist rule, the city has sprung to life as a dynamic center of business, politics, and culture. UNESCO's inclusion of the Polish capital on its World Heritage list in 1980 marked the authenticity of its city-wide restorations. Things have only improved since then, and Warsaw's current revival, though less obvious to the eye, is in many ways just as impressive as its postwar reconstruction.

▐ TRANSPORTATION

Flights: Port Lotniczy Warszawa-Okęcie (Terminal 1), ul. Żwirki i Wigury (☎650 41 00). Take bus #175 (bus #611 after 10:40pm) for a 20min. ride to the city center. Buy tickets at the *Ruch* kiosk in the departure hall. Open M-F 6am-10pm.

Trains: Warszawa Centralna, al. Jerozolimskie 54 (☎94 36), is the most convenient of Warsaw's 4 train stations. Services include a **cafe, 24hr. pharmacy, ATM, telephones, baggage check,** and a **post office** (urząd poctowy). The **IT office** helps with schedules and translations. Yellow signs list departures (*odjazdy*), white signs arrivals (*przyjazdy*). English is rare; write down when and where you want to go, then ask "*Który peron?*" (Which platform?). Domestic trains to: **Gdańsk** (4hr., 12 per day, 43-117zł); **Kraków** (2½-5hr., 10 per day, 55-101zł); **Łódź** (2hr., 10 per day, 27-40zł); **Lublin** (2½hr., 11 per day, 19-92zł); **Poznań** (2½-3hr., 15 per day, 42-114zł); **Toruń** (2½-4½hr., 7 per day, 35-105zł); **Wrocław** (4½hr., 9 per day, 45-125zł). International trains to: **Berlin** (6hr., 4 per day, 160zł); **Budapest** (11hr., 2 per day, 280zł); **Prague** (9-11hr., 2 per day, 270-310zł); **St. Petersburg** (27-30hr., 2 per day, 300zł).

Buses: Both PKS and Polski Express buses serve Warsaw.

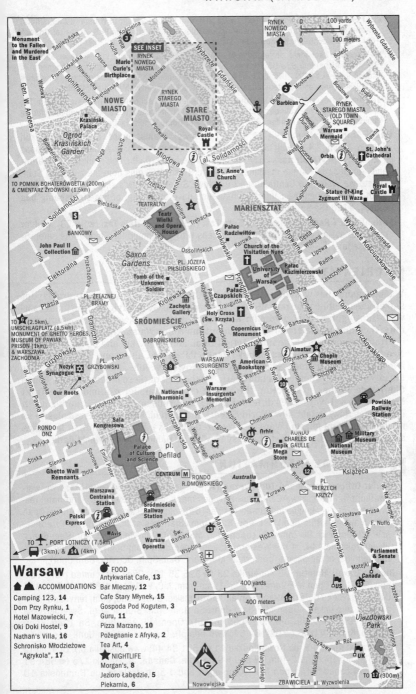

RYNEK NOWEGO MIASTA
0   100 yards
0   100 meters

Monument to the Fallen and Murdered in the East

Marie Curie's Birthplace

NOWE MIASTO

RYNEK NOWEGO MIASTA

RYNEK STAREGO MIASTA

STARE MIASTO

Royal Castle

Krasiński Palace

Ogród Krasińskich Garden

TO POMNIK BOHATERÓW GETTA (200m) & CMENTARZ ŻYDOWSKI (1.5km)

Barbican

RYNEK STAREGO MIASTA (OLD TOWN SQUARE)

Warsaw Mermaid

Orbis

St. John's Cathedral

Statue of King Zygmunt III Waza

Royal Castle

al. Solidarności

St. Anne's Church

PL. TEATRALNY

Teatr Wielki and Opera House

MARIENSZTAT

Pałac Radziwiłłów

Church of the Visitation Nuns

University of Warsaw

Pałac Kazimierzowski

PL. BANKOWY

John Paul II Collection

Saxon Gardens

PL. JÓZEFA PIŁSUDSKIEGO

Tomb of the Unknown Soldier

Pałac Czapskich

Zachęta Gallery

Holy Cross (Św. Krzyża)

ŚRÓDMIEŚCIE

Copernicus Monument

TO (2.5km), UMSCHLAGPLATZ (1.5km), MONUMENT OF GHETTO HEROES, MUSEUM OF PAWIAK PRISON (1km), & WARSZAWA ZACHODNIA

PL. ŻELAZNEJ BRAMY

PL. DĄBROWSKIEGO

Świętokrzyska

American Bookstore

Almatur

Chopin Museum

Nożyk Synagogue

Our Roots

PL. GRZYBOWSKI

PL. PRÓŻNA

WARSAW INSURGENTS' SQ.

Warsaw Insurgents' Memorial

National Philharmonic

Sala Kongresowa

Powiśle Railway Station

RONDO ONZ

Palace of Culture and Science

pl. Defilad

Orbis

RONDO CHARLES DE GAULLE

Empik Mega Store

Military Museum

National Museum

Ghetto Wall Remnants

CENTRUM M RONDO R.DMOWSKIEGO

Australia

STA

PL. TRZECH KRZYŻY

Książęca

Warszawa Centralna Station

Polski Express

Avis

Śródmieście Railway Station

Warsaw Operetta

Parliament & Senate

US

Canada

TO ✈, PORT LOTNICZY (7.5km), (3km), & (4km)

Al. Jerozolimskie

Hoża

PL. KONSTYTUCJI

Ujazdowski Park

UK

TO (300m)

Warsaw

ACCOMMODATIONS
Camping 123, **14**
Dom Przy Rynku, **1**
Hotel Mazowiecki, **7**
Oki Doki Hostel, **9**
Nathan's Villa, **16**
Schronisko Młodzieżowe "Agrykola", **17**

FOOD
Antykwariat Cafe, **13**
Bar Mleczny, **12**
Cafe Stary Młynek, **15**
Gospoda Pod Kogutem, **3**
Guru, **11**
Pizza Marzano, **10**
Pożegnanie z Afryką, **2**
Tea Art, **4**

NIGHTLIFE
Morgan's, **8**
Jezioro Łabędzie, **5**
Piekarnia, **6**

POLAND

Polski Express, al. Jana Pawła II (☎620 03 20), in a kiosk adjacent to Warszawa Centralna. A private, domestic-only company faster and cushier than the state-run PKS. Buses to: **Gdańsk** (6hr., 2 per day, 68zł); **Kraków** (8hr., 2 per day, 60zł); **Wrocław** (6hr., 3 per day, 65zł).

PKS Warszawa Zachodnia, al. Jerozolimskie 144 (☎822 48 11, domestic info and reservations 94 33, international info 823 55 70; www.pks.pl), in same building as Warszawa Zachodnia train station. Take bus #127, 130, 508, 517, or E5 to the center. PKS runs to many of the same cities as Polski Express and to international destinations, including **Kyiv, Minsk,** and **Vilnius.**

Centrum Podróży AURA, al. Jerozolimskie 144, at the Zachodnia station (☎823 55 70; www.aura.pl), may be your best bet internationally with service to cities all over Europe, including **Amsterdam, Geneva, London, Paris, Prague,** and **Rome.** Open M-F 9am-6pm, Sa 9am-2pm.

Public Transportation: ☎94 84; www.ztm.waw.pl. **Trams, buses,** and the **metro** run 4:30am-11pm. 2.40zł, with ISIC 1.20zł; extra ticket required for large baggage. **Day pass** 7.20zł/3.70zł. **Weekly pass** 26zł/12zł. Punch the ticket (on the end marked by the arrow and "*tu kasować*") in the machines on board. Bus #175 runs from the airport to Stare Miasto via Warszawa Centralna and ul. Nowy Świat. Warsaw's single **metro** line runs north-south through the center. Tourists also have the option of two **sightseeing bus routes,** #100 (Sa-Su) and 180 (M-F).

Taxis: Try **MPT Radio Taxi** (☎919), **Euro Taxi** (☎96 62), or **Halo Taxi** (☎96 23). Call for pickup to avoid overcharging. State-run cabs with a mermaid logo tend to be safer. 5-6zł base fare, 1.80-3zł per km. MC/V.

✴ ORIENTATION

Warsaw mainly lies west of the **Wisła River.** Although the city is large, its grid layout and efficient public transportation system make it easy to navigate. The main east-west thoroughfare is **al. Jerozolimskie,** which intersects several north-south avenues, including **ul. Marszałkowska,** a major tram route. **Warszawa Centralna,** the busiest train station, sits at the intersection of al. Jerozolimskie and **al. Jana Pawła II.** Nearby the gargantuan **Pałac Kultury i Nauki** (Palace of Culture and Science) looms above **pl. Defilad** (Parade Square); its clock tower, visible almost anywhere near the city center, can serve as a landmark. To the east of these landmarks lies **Rondo Charles de Gaulle.** Intersecting the traffic circle at al. Jerozolimskie, the **Trakt Królewski** (Royal Way) takes different names as it runs north-south. Running north it becomes **Nowy Świat** (New World Street) and then **ul. Krakówskie Przedmieście** as it leads into **Stare Miasto** (Warsaw's restored old city). Running south, it becomes **al. Ujazdowskie** as it runs past embassy row, more palaces, and **Łazienki Park.**

☷ PRACTICAL INFORMATION

Tourist Offices: Informacji Turystyczna (IT), al. Jerozolimskie 54 (☎94 31; www.warsawtour.pl), in Warszawa Centralna. Provides maps, currency exchange, and hotel reservations. English-language *Warsaw Insider* (6zł) sold in kiosks outside the office. Open daily May-Sept. 8am-8pm; Oct.-Apr. 8am-6pm. Branches at ul. Krakowskie Przedmieście 89, opposite Pl. Zamkowy (open daily May-Sept. 9am-8pm; Oct.-Apr. 9am-6pm); al. Jerozolimkie 144, at the Western Station (open daily 9am-5pm); and in the departure terminal of the airport (open daily May-Sept. 8am-8pm; Oct.-Apr. 8am-6pm).

Budget Travel: Almatur, ul. Kopernika 23 (☎826 35 12). Offers discounted plane tickets. ISIC 44zł. Open M-F 9am-7pm, Sa 10am-3pm. MC/V. **Orbis,** ul. Bracka 16 (☎827 07 30; fax 827 76 05), entrance on al. Jerozolimskie. Sells plane, train, ferry, and international bus tickets. Open M-F 8am-6pm, Sa 9am-3pm. Branch at ul. Świętokrzyska 23/25 (☎831 82 99; orbis.bis@pbp.com.pl). Open M-F 9am-6pm, Sa 10am-3pm. **STA,** ul. Krucza 41/43 (☎622 62 64; www.eria.pl). Open daily 10am-6pm.

Embassies: Australia, ul. Nowogrodzka 11 (☎521 34 44; www.australia.pl). Open M-Tu and Th 9am-1pm and 2-4pm, W and F 9am-1pm. **Canada,** al. Matejki 1/5 (☎584 31 00; www.canada.pl). Open M-F 10am-noon and 1-3pm. **Ireland,** ul. Humanska 10

(☎849 66 33). Open M-F 9am-1pm. **UK**, ul. Emilii Plater 28, 2nd fl. (☎625 30 30; www.britishembassy.pl). Open M-F 10:30am-4:30pm. **US**, al. Ujazdowskie 29/31 (☎628 30 41; www.usinfo.pl). Open M and W-F 9am-noon, Tu 9am-3pm.

Currency Exchange: 24hr. ATMs (*bankomat*) accepting Cirrus, Maestro, Plus, and other cards are abundant. **Kantori** have the best rates for exchanging both currency and **traveler's checks** except at tourist sights. **24hr. currency exchange** at Warszawa Centralna station or Al. Jerozolimskie 61. **Bank PKO S.A.**, pl. Bankowy 2 (☎635 05 00), in the blue glass skyscraper, and ul. Grójecka 1/3 (☎658 82 17), in Hotel Sobieski, cashes AmEx/V **traveler's checks** for 1-2% commission and gives MC/V **cash advances.** Open M-F 8am-6pm, Sa 10am-2pm. All branches open M-F 8am-6pm, Sa 10am-2pm.

American Express: al. Jerozolimskie 65/79 (☎630 69 52/53). Will send and receive **Western Union** money transfers. Open M-F 9am-7pm, Sa 10am-6pm. Branch at ul. Sienna 39 (☎581 51 53). Open M-F 9am-6pm.

Luggage Storage (Kasa Bagażowa): At Warszawa Centralna train station. 6zł per item per day; insurance 2.25zł per 50zł of declared value. Open 24hr. Storage also available in Zachodnia Station. 5zł for a large pack. Open daily 7am-7pm.

English-Language Bookstores: American Bookstore (Księgarnia Ameryańska), ul. Nowy Świat 61 (☎827 48 52; www.americanbookstore.pl). A good but pricey selection. Open M-Sa 10am-7pm, Su 10am-6pm. **Empik Megastore,** ul. Nowy Świat 15-17 (☎627 06 50). Outstanding selection of maps. Open M-Sa 9am-10pm, Su 11am-5pm.

Laundromat: Ul. Karmelicka 17 (☎831 73 17). Take bus #180 or 516 north from ul. Marszałkowska and get off at ul. Anielewicza; backtrack 1 block to ul. Karmelicka. Detergent 3zł. Wash and dry 26.60zł. Open M-F 9am-5pm, Sa 9am-1pm.

24hr. Pharmacy: Apteka Grabowskiego "21" (☎825 69 86), at Warszawa Centralna.

Medical Services: Centrum Medyczyne LIM, al. Jerozolimskie 65/79, 9th fl. (24hr. emergency line ☎458 70 00, 24hr. ambulance 430 30 30; www.cm-lim.com.pl), at the Marriott. English-speaking doctors. 85zł. Open M-F 7am-9pm, Sa 8am-8pm, Su 9am-1pm. Branch at ul. Domaniewski 41 (☎458 70 00). Open M-F 7am-9pm, Sa 8am-8pm.
Central Emergency Station, ul. Hoża 56 (☎999) has a 24hr. ambulance.

Telephones: Phones can be found at the post office and scattered throughout the city. Most only accept cards, available at the post office and kiosks. Ask for a *karta telefoniczna.* Directory assistance ☎913.

Internet Access: ▨Simple Internet Cafe, at the corner of al. Jerozolimskie and ul. Marszałkowska, has English-speaking staff and the best hourly rates. Open daily 24hr. Rates vary from 1zł per hr. late at night to 4zł per hr. in the day. Several 24hr. Internet cafes can be found in the bowels of the main train station.

Post Office: Main branch, ul. Świętokrzyska 31/33 (☎827 00 52). Take a number at the entrance. Push "D" for stamps and letters, "F" for packages. Inquire at window #42 for *Poste Restante.* Open 24hr. *Kantori* are open daily 7am-10pm. Most other branches open daily 8am-8pm. **Postal Code:** 00-001.

◤ ACCOMMODATIONS AND CAMPING

Although accommodations options are rapidly improving, demand still outpaces supply; reserve ahead, especially in summer. The **IT** (p. 810) maintains a list of accommodations in the city, including private rooms, and can also arrange stays in **university dorms.** (25-30zł. Available July-Sept.)

▨ **Oki Doki,** pl. Dąbrowskiego 3 (☎826 51 12; www.okidoki.pl). From the center, take any tram north on Marszałkowska to Świętokrzyska. Walk 1 block north on Marszałkowska and turn right on Rysia. In the heart of town but facing a quiet park, this is half hostel, half dazzling Varsovian art gallery. Multilingual staff. Laundry 10zł. Kitchen available. Internet free. Reception 24hr. Check-out 11am. Check-in 3pm. Dorm beds 45-60zł; singles 110zł; doubles 135zł, with bath 185zł. Prices lower Sept.-Apr. MC/V. ❷

■ **Nathan's,** ul. Piękna 24/26 (☎622 29 46; www.nathansvilla.com). From the center, take any train south on ul. Marszałkowska to Płac Konstytucji. Go left on ul. Piękna; the hostel will be on your left. Near the downtown, Nathan's has cheery dorms and restrooms that could pass for Ikea showcases. Amenities include free breakfast, laundry, lockers, and Internet access (30min. per day). English-speaking, fun-loving staff eager to advise. Reception 24hr. No fixed check-out. Dorm beds 45-60zł; private rooms 120-140zł. Reserve ahead. Cots will be rented to the truly desperate. MC/V. ❷

Dom Przy Rynku, Rynek Nowego Miasta 4 (☎/fax 831 50 33; www.cityhostel.net). Take bus #175 from the center to Franciszkańska; turn right on Franciszkańska, then right into the *Rynek;* the hostel is downhill on your left. In summer, this school for disadvantaged children helps finance itself by becoming one of Warsaw's most spotless budget accommodations. TV room and kitchenette. Reception 24hr. Flexible lockout for cleaning 10am-4pm. Open late-June to late-Aug. only. Dorms 45zł per person. Cash only. ❷

Schronisko Młodzieżowe "Agrykola," ul. Myśliwiecka 9 (☎622 91 10; www.hotel-agrykola.pl). Near Łazienki Park. Take bus #151 from the train station, or bus #107, 420, or 520 from Marszałkowska to Rozbrat. From the bus stop, walk downstairs to the corner of ul. Myśliwiecka and al. Armii Ludowej; enter from the al. Armii Ludowej side of the corner. Serene parkside Agrykola includes both a hostel and a mid-range hotel. Hostel beds 47zł; hotel singles 270zł; hotel doubles 320zł. Cash only. ❷

Hotel Mazowiecki, ul. Mazowiecka 10 (☎/fax 827 23 65; www.mazowiecki.com.pl), off ul. Świętokrzyska, next to Stare Miasto. Rooms with bath have been recently renovated; other rooms are more basic. Singles 150zł, with bath 198zł; doubles 200zł/248zł. Weekend discount 20%. Cash only. ❺

Camping 123, ul. Bitwy Warszawskiej 15/17 (☎/fax 823 37 48). By Warszawa Zachodnia bus station. Take bus #508, 127, 130, or 517 to Zachodnia, cross Al. Jerozolismie, turn right, walk to the traffic circle and turn left on Bitwy Warszawskiej. Near the city center. Swimming pool and tennis courts. Open May-Sept. 10zł per person, per tent, and per vehicle. Singles 40zł; doubles 70zł; triples 100zł; quads 120zł. Cash only. ❶

◖ FOOD

At the countless roadside stands dotting the city the food of choice is the **kebab turecki,** a pita stuffed with spicy meat, cabbage and pickles (5-10zł). Kebab Bar, ul. Nowy Świat 31, serves up an excellent version, as do many others; look for long lines. **Domowy Okruszek,** ul. Bracka 3, just south of Aleje Jerozolimskie, sells baked goods and ready-to-cook dishes like *naleśniki* (pancakes) and *pierogi* (dumplings) for 15-20zł per kg. (☎628 70 77. Open M-Sa 10am-6pm, Su 10am-3pm.) Grocery stores open 24hr. include **MarcPol** by the central train station and **Albert** on ul. Marszałkowska in the Galleria Centrum.

■ **Gospoda Pod Kogutem,** ul. Freta 48 (☎635 82 82). A rare treat in touristy Stare Miasto: delectable local food. Beer 6zł. Entrees 15-40zł. Open daily 11am-midnight. MC/V. ❷

■ **Guru,** ul. Bracka 18 (☎827 27 88). Warsaw's best vegetarian fare is a stone's throw from Nowy Świat. Guru serves Indian food with a dash of Polish influence. Live music Sa-Su. Entrees 15-25zł. Open M-Sa 10am-10pm, Su noon-10pm. AmEx/MC/V. ❷

■ **Pożegnanie z Afryką,** ul. Freta 4/6, ul. Ostrobranmska 75c, and ul. Dobra 56/66. Local chain brews incredible coffee (8-15zł) and unparalleled iced coffee (8zł). Indoor tables are worth the wait. Open M-Th 10am-9pm, F-Su 10am-10pm. ❶

Pizza Marzano, ul. Nowy Świat 42 (☎826 21 33). This trustworthy local chain cooks up a score of richly flavored pizzas (15-25zł), with Polish spiced meats adding a local touch, and the salads and appetizers are also worth trying. Serves beer, wine, and coffee. Open M-Th and Su 11am-11pm, F-Sa 11am-midnight. AmEx/MC/V. ❷

Bar Vega, ul. Jana Pawła II 36c (☎654 41 11). A full vegetarian meal here (8-10zł) costs as much as coffee on Nowy Świat. Cafeteria-style offerings include both Indian dishes and vegetarian versions of Polish favorites. Open daily noon-8pm. Cash only. ❷

Cafe Stary Młynek, al. Ujazdowskie 6 (☎622 92 64). Traditional Polish food in the cellar of a renovated old mill. Sample a range of small dishes, each 10-25zł. Open M-F 10am-10pm, Sa noon-11pm, Su noon-9pm. Cash only. ❸

Bar Mleczny, ul. Nowy Świat 5. Locals praise this subsidized, Communist-era milk bar as one of the best of its dying breed. Ridiculously cheap "rations" and long lines make it an authentic Soviet experience, if not an advertisement for socialism. Meat-heavy *danie* (main courses) go for 3-5zł. Open M-F 8am-8pm, Sa-Su 9am-5pm. Cash only. ❶

Antykwariat Cafe, ul. Żurawia 45 (☎629 99 29), 2 blocks south of Rondo Charles de Gaulle. Staff welcomes lingerers to lounge amid book-lined walls. Coffees 5-17zł; also serves cocktails, and desserts. Open M-F 11am-11pm, Sa-Su 1-11pm. Cash only. ❷

Tea Art, ul. Bednarska 28/30 (☎826 24 16). Just outside Stare Miasto, this mellow cellar cafe serves teas (small pot 8zł, large pot 14zł) and scrumptious desserts (6-12zł) like *szarlotka* (apple tart) and ginger cake. Open daily 11am-10pm. Cash only. ❷

🜨 SIGHTS

At a glance, the cityscape comprises two strains of architecture: impeccably restored historical facades and unattractive Soviet-era concrete blocks. But first impressions don't do justice to Warsaw. From the Neoclassical splendor of the Palace on the Isle to the sobering stillness of the Jewish Cemetery, the Polish capital holds out compelling sights to those who get to know it well. Tour buses will help to orient newcomers. **Routes #100** and **180** begin at pl. Zamkowy and run along pl. Teatralny, ul. Marszałkowska, al. Ujazdowskie, Łazienki Park, then back up the Royal Way before looping through Praga and returning to pl. Zamkowy.

STARE MIASTO. Warsaw's postwar reconstruction shows its finest face in the narrow cobblestone streets and colorful facades of Stare Miasto (old town). *(Take bus #175 or E3 from the city center to Miodowa.)* The landmark **Statue of King Zygmunt III Waza**, constructed in 1644 to honor the king who transferred the capital from Kraków to Warsaw, towers over the entrance to Stare Miasto. To the right stands the impressive **Royal Castle** (Zamek Królewski), the royal residence since the late 16th century. When it was plundered and burned by the Nazis in September 1939, many Varsovians risked their lives hiding priceless works in the hope they might one day be returned. Today the palace houses the ◪**Royal Castle Museum,** which has paintings, artifacts, and the stunning Royal Apartments. *(Pl. Zamkowy 4. ☎657 21 70; www.zamek-krolewski.art.pl. Route 1 open M 11am-4pm, Tu-Sa 10am-4pm. 10zł, students 5zł. Route 2 (Royal Apartments) open M 11am-6pm, Tu-Sa 10am-6pm. 15zł, students 8zł. Highlights tour Su 11am-6pm. Free.)* Across ul. Świętojańska sits Warsaw's oldest church, **St. John's Cathedral** (Katedra św. Jana), decimated in the 1944 uprising but rebuilt after the war. *(Open daily 10am-1pm and 3-5:30pm. Entrance to crypt 1zł.)* Ul. Świętojańska leads to the restored Renaissance and Baroque **Rynek Starego Miasta** (old town square); the statue of the **Warsaw Mermaid** (Warszawa Syrenka) still marks the center. According to legend, a greedy merchant kidnapped the mermaid from the Wisła River, but local fishermen rescued her from her captivity. In return, she swore to defend the city, and now protects it with a shield and raised sword. Ul. Krzywe Koło starts in the northeast corner of the *Rynek* and leads to the restored **Barbican** (*barbakan*), a rare example of 16th-century Polish fortification and a popular spot to relax. The *barbakan* opens onto ul. Freta, the edge of **Nowe Miasto** (new town). Nobel prize-winning physicist and chemist **Marie Curie** was born at ul. Freta 16.

TRAKT KRÓLEWSKI. The Trakt Królewski (Royal Way) begins at the entrance to the Stare Miasto on pl. Zamkowy and stretches 4km south toward Kraków, Poland's former capital. On the left as you leave pl. Zamkowy looms the 15th-century **St. Anne's Church** (Kościół św. Anny). Rebuilt in Baroque style, its most striking feature is a gilded altar. *(Open daily dawn-dusk.)* Frederick Chopin spent his childhood in the neighborhood near ul. Krakówskie Przedmieście. He gave his first public concert in **Pałac Radziwiłłów**, ul. Krakówskie Przedmieście 46/48, the building guarded by four stone lions; it is now known as **Pałac Namiestnikowski**, the Polish presidential mansion. **Pałac Czapskich**, where Chopin wrote some of his best-known works, was his last home before he left for France in 1830; today, the palace houses his preserved drawing room (Salonik Chopinów) and the Academy of Fine Arts. *(ul. Krakówskie Przedmieście 5; entrance on the left. ☎826 62 51, ext. 267. Open M-F 10am-2pm. 3zł, students 2zł.)* Chopin died abroad at the age of 39 and was buried in Paris, but his heart belongs to Poland; it now rests in an urn in **Holy Cross Church** (Kościół św. Krzyża), next to the Academy. *(Ul. Krakówskie Przedmiescie 3. Open daily dawn-dusk.)* For Chopin relics, visit the **Frederick Chopin Museum** (Muzeum Fryderyka Chopina), which has a collection of original letters, scores, paintings, and keepsakes, including the composer's last piano and a section of his first polonaise, penned when he was seven years old. *(Ul. Okólnik 1; entrance on ul. Tamka. ☎827 54 71. Open May-Sept. M, W, F 10am-5pm, Th noon-6pm, Sa-Su 10am-2pm; Oct.-Apr. M-W and F-Sa 10am-2pm, Th noon-6pm. 8zł, students 4zł. Audioguide 4zł. Concerts 30zł, students 15zł.)*

The Royal Way continues down fashionable **ul. Nowy Świat**. Turn left just after Rondo Charles de Gaulle to reach Poland's largest museum, the **National Museum** (Muzeum Narodowe), which collects 16th- to 20th-century Polish paintings and ancient statuary. *(Al. Jerozolimskie 3. Open T-W and F 10am-5pm; Th and Sa-Su 10am-6pm. Permanent exhibits 11zł, students 6zł. Special exhibits 15zł, students 8zł.)* Further down, the Royal Way turns into al. Ujazdowskie and runs alongside **Łazienki Park**. In the park is the striking Neoclassical **Palace on Water** (Pałac na Wodzie or Pałac na Wyspie), while outbuildings house rotating art exhibits. *(Take bus #116, 180, or 195 from ul. Nowy Świat or #119 from the city center to Bagatela. Park open daily dawn-dusk. Palace open Tu-Su 9am-4pm. 12zł, students 9zł.)* Just north of the park, off ul. Agrykola, the **Center of Contemporary Art** (Centrum Sztuki Współczesnej), al. Ujazdowskie 6, hosts installations of contemporary Polish art in the reconstructed 17th-century Ujazdowskie Castle. *(Open Tu-Th and Sa-Su 11am-5pm, F 11am-9pm. 3.5zł, students 2.5zł.)*

THE FORMER WARSAW GHETTO AND SYNAGOGUE. Still referred to as the Ghetto, the modern **Muranów** (walled) neighborhood north of the city center holds few traces of the nearly 400,000 Jews who made up one-third of the city's population prior to WWII. The **Umschlagplatz**, at the corner of ul. Dzika and ul. Stawki, was the railway platform where the Nazis gathered 300,000 Jews for transport to death camps. *(Take tram #35 from ul. Marszałkowska to Dzika.)* With the Umschlag pl. monument to your left, continue down Stawki and turn right on ul. DuBois, which becomes ul. Zamenhofa; along the road, a stone monument marks the location of the command bunker of the 1943 Ghetto Uprising. Farther on, in a large park to your right, the large **Monument of the Ghetto Heroes** (Pomnik Bohaterów) pays homage to the leaders of the uprising. Continue along ul. Zamenhofa for two blocks and then take a right on Dzielna. On the corner of Dzielna and al. Jana Pawall, the **Museum of Pawiak Prison** (Muzeum Więzienia Pawiaka) exhibits photographs and artifacts, including the artwork and poetry of many former prisoners. Over 100,000 Polish Jews were imprisoned here from 1939 to 1944; 37,000 were executed and 60,000 were transferred to concentration camps. *(ul. Dzielna 24/26. ☎/fax 831 13 17. Open W 9am-5pm, Th and Sa 9am-4pm, F 10am-5pm, Su 10am-4pm. Donation requested.)* Follow al. Jana Pawall, take a left on ul. Anielewicza, and continue for five blocks to reach the **Jewish Cemetery** (Cmentarz Żydowski), in the western corner of Muranów. The thickly-wooded cemetery is the final resting place of 250,000 Polish Jews. *(Tram #22 from the center to Cm. Żydowski. ☎838 26 22; www.jewishcem.waw.pl. Open Apr.-Oct. M-Th 10am-5pm, F 9am-1pm, Su 11am-4pm; Nov.-Mar. cemetery closes at dusk. Closed Jewish holidays. 4zł.)* The beautifully reconstructed **Nożyk Synagogue** (Synagoga Nożyka) is a living remnant of Warsaw's Jewish heritage. Today, the only synagogue to survive the war is the spiritual home for the few hundred observant Jews remaining in Warsaw. *(ul. Twarda 6. From the center, take any tram along ul. Jana Pawła II to Rondo Onz. Turn right on Twarda and left at the Jewish Theater (Teatr Żydowski).* ☎ *620 43 24. Open M-F and Su 10am–7pm. Closed on Jewish holidays. 5zł. Morning and evening prayer daily.)* **ELSEWHERE IN CENTRAL WARSAW.** The center of Warsaw's commercial district, southwest of Stare Miasto near the Warszawa Centralna train station, is dominated by the 70-story Stalinist **Palace of Culture and Science** (Pałac Kultury i Nauki) on ul. Marszałkowska. Locals claim the view from the top is the best in Warsaw— partly because it's the only place from which you can't see the building itself. *(*☎ *656 60 00. Open daily 9am-midnight. Observation deck on 33rd floor. 18zł, students 12zł. After 9pm, 20zł.)* Below is **pl. Defilad** (Parade Sq.), Europe's largest square. Adjacent to **Saxon Garden** (Ogród Saski) is the **John Paul II Collection**, with works by Dalí, van Gogh, Goya, Rembrandt, Renoir, and others. *(Pl. Bankowy 1. Open May-Oct. Tu-Su 10am-5pm; Nov.-Apr. 10am-4pm. 8zł, students 4zł.)*

🎵 🎭 ENTERTAINMENT AND NIGHTLIFE

For the latest schedule of performances, call the tourist info line (☎ 94 31). Inquire about concerts at the **Warsaw Music Society** (Warszawskie Towarzystwo Muzyczne), ul. Morskie Oko 2. (☎ 849 56 51. Take tram #4, 18, 19, 35, or 36 to Morskie Oko from ul. Marszałkowska.) The **Warsaw Chamber Opera** (Warszawska Opera Kameralna), al. Solidarności 76B (☎ 831 22 40), hosts a Mozart festival each year in early summer. Łazienki Park hosts free performances at the **Chopin Monument** (Pomnik Chopina) on Sundays. (May-Oct. noon and 4pm.) **Teatr Wielki,** pl. Teatralny 1 (☎ 826 32 88; www.teatrwielki.pl), Warsaw's main opera and ballet hall, offers performances almost every day. (Tickets 10-100zł. AmEx/MC/V.) **Sala Kongresowa** (☎ 620 49 80), on the train station side of the Pałac Kultury, hosts jazz and rock concerts with famous international bands; enter from ul. Emilii Plater. **Warsaw Summer Jazz Days** (☎ 620 12 19; www.adamiakjazz.pl) take place annually in June. **Teatr Dramatyczny** (☎ 620 21 02), in the Pałac Kultury, has a stage for large productions and a studio theater playing more avant-garde works. **Kinoteka** (☎ 826 1961), in the Pałac Kultury, shows Hollywood blockbusters in a surreal Stalin-era setting. Head to **Kino Lab,** ul. Ujazdowskie 6 (☎ 628 12 71), for independent films.

In the evening, Warsaw is full of energy. Cafes (*kawiarnie*) around Stare Miasto and ul. Nowy Świat continue serving until late into the night, and a variety of pubs attract crowds with live music. In summer, large outdoor beer gardens complement the pub scene. Kiosks sell *Gazeta Wyborcza,* a magazine that lists gay nightlife info. ◪**Morgan's,** ul. Okólnik 1, is a friendly Irish joint with live music on weekends and a mean shepherd's pie. (Pie 20zł. Guinness 15zł. Open daily 10am-late.) **Piekarnia,** ul. Młocinska 11, has a packed dance floor and expert DJs. (☎ 636 49 79. Cover F 20zł, Sa 25zł. Open F-Sa 10pm-late.) At Swan Lake-themed **Jezioro Łabędzie,** ul. Moliera 4/6, beautiful Warsaw gathers to sip sophisticated cocktails (10-30zł) made from local mead and berry vodka. (☎ 826 65 99. Open M-Th 11am-2am, F 11am-4am, Sa 1pm-4am, Su 3pm-4am.)

🏛 DAYTRIPS FROM WARSAW

ŻELAZOWA WOLA. Twisting paths wind through the expansive, well-maintained gardens of **Frederick Chopin's birthplace.** (☎ 46 863 33 00. Open May-Sept. Tu-Su 9:30am-5:30pm; Oct.-Apr. Tu-Su 9:30am-4pm. English audio tour 20zł. 12zł, students 6zł. Park only 4zł/2zł.) In warmer months Polish musicians perform free **concerts** of Chopin's works. (May-Sept. Su at 11am and 3pm.) Schedules are posted throughout Warsaw and at the Chopin Museum (p. 813). The **Wyszogród bus** runs from Warszawa Zachodnia (9.1zł). Arrive early; no direct buses return after 4:30pm.

WILANÓW. In 1677, King Jan III Sobieski bought the sleepy village of Milanowo, had its existing mansion rebuilt into a Baroque palace, and named the new residence Villa Nova (Wilanów). Since 1805, **Pałac Wilanowski** has functioned both as a public museum and as a residence for the highest-ranking guests of the Polish state. Surrounded by elegant formal gardens, the palace is filled with lovely frescoed rooms, portraits, and extravagant royal apartments. English captions along the way allow you to break off from the slow-moving Polish-language tour to explore on your own. *(Take bus #180 from ul. Krakówskie Przedmiesce, #516 or 519 from ul. Marszalkowska south to Wilanów, or #116 south along the Royal Way; then cross the highway and follow the signs for the Pałac. ☎842 07 95. Open mid-May to mid-Sept. M and W-Su 9:30am-4:30pm; mid-Sept. to mid-May M and W-Su 9:30am-4pm. 20zł, students 10zł. Th free. English tour 135zł for fewer than 6 people, 25zł per person for 6-35 people. Gardens open M and W-F 9:30am-dusk. 4.5zł, students 2.5zł. Orangery open M, W-F, and Su 9:30am-3:30pm.)*

KRAKÓW ☎012

Home to 100,000 students and scores of museums, galleries, and underground pubs, Kraków (KRAH-koof; pop. 745,000) draws throngs of foreign visitors to its rich cafe culture, regal architecture, and spirited nightlife. Although it emerged only recently as a trendy international hot spot, the city has always figured prominently in Polish history. Wedged between Stalinist-era Nowa Huta steelworks to the east and the Auschwitz-Birkenau death camp to the west, Kraków endured much darkness in the 20th century. In a brighter period the city protected centuries of Central European kings and feats of architecture, many of which still stand in Stare Miasto (old town) and the rejuvenated Jewish quarter of Kazimierz.

▐▀ TRANSPORTATION

Flights: Balice Airport (☎411 19 55; www.lotnisko-balice.pl), 15km west of the center. Take northbound bus #192 (40min.) or 208 (1hr.) to the main train station. Taxis to downtown Kraków cost 30-50zł.

Trains: Kraków Główny, pl. Kolejowy 1 (☎624 54 39, info 624 15 35). Trains to: **Bratislava** (8hr., 1 per day, 167zł); **Budapest** (11hr., 1 per day, 227zł); **Gdańsk** (7-10hr., 4 per day, 52-100zł); **Kyiv** (22hr., 21 per day, 149zł); **Poznań** (6-8hr., 4 per day, 46-70zł); **Prague** (9hr., 2 per day, 226zł); **Vienna** (8½hr., 2 per day, 183zł); **Warsaw** (4½-5hr., 10 per day, 45-70zł); **Zakopane** (3-5hr., 4 per day, 30zł).

Buses: ul. Worcella (☎93 16), across from Kraków Główny. Open 5am-11pm. Buses to: **Łódź** (6½hr., 1 per day, 31zł); **Warsaw** (6hr., 3 per day, 40zł); **Wrocław** (6½hr., 2 per day, 35zł); **Zakopane** (2hr., 33 per day, 10zł). **Sindbad,** in the main hall, sells international tickets. (☎421 02 40. Open M-F 8am-5:30pm, Sa 9am-2pm.) Buses to **Prague** (9hr., 2 per week, 98zł) and **Vienna** (9hr., 7 per week, 115zł).

Public Transportation: Buy **bus** and **tram** tickets at *Ruch* kiosks (2.40zł) or from drivers (2.90zł) and punch them onboard. Large backpacks need their own tickets. Night buses (from 11pm) 4zł. Day pass 9zł; week 22zł.

Taxis: Barbakan Taxi (☎96 61, toll-free 0800 400 400); **Euro Taxi** (☎96 64); **Express Taxi** (☎96 29, toll-free 0800 111 111); **Radio Taxi** (☎919, toll-free 0800 500 919).

▐▞ ORIENTATION

The true heart of the city is the huge **Rynek Główny** (main marketplace) in the center of **Stare Miasto** (old town). The **Planty gardens** and a ring of roads including **Basztowa, Dunajewskiego, Podwale,** and **Westerplatte** encircle Stare Miasto. The gigantic **Wawel Castle** looms south of the *Rynek*. The **Wisła** (VEE-swa; Vistula)

Kraków: Stare Miasto

🏠 ACCOMMODATIONS
Bling Bling Hostel, 3
Hotel Eden, 16
Hostel Express, 4
Hotel Polonia, 5
Mama's Hostel, 14
Nathan's Villa Hostel, 17
Strawberry Youth
  Hostel, 1

🍴 FOOD
Dym, 9
Fabryka Pizzy, 19
Gruzińskie
  Chaczapuri, 8
Pierogarnia, 2
Restauracja
  Samoobsługowa
  "Polakowski," 18
Vega Bar Restaurant, 7

🛏 NIGHTLIFE
Alchemia, 21
Faust, 12
Kredens, 11
Propaganda, 20
Prozak, 15
Stalowe Magnolie, 6
Klub pod
  Jaszczurami, 13

River snakes past the castle and borders the old Jewish village of **Kazimierz**, accessible from the market by ul. Starowiślna and ul. Stradomska. The **bus** and **train** stations are located just to the northeast of the Planty ring. To reach the *Rynek* from either, follow the "*do centrum*" signs through the underpass to the Planty gardens. A number of streets lead from there to the square.

🛈 PRACTICAL INFORMATION

Tourist Offices: MCI, Rynek Główny 1/3 (☎421 77 06; www.mcit.pl). Multilingual staff sells maps and the incredibly handy guide *Kraków in Your Pocket* (5zł, English 10zł). Open May-Sept. M-F 9am-7pm, Sa 9am-1pm; Oct.-Apr. M-F 9am-5pm, Sa 9am-1pm.

Budget Travel: Orbis, Rynek Główny 41 (☎422 40 35; www.orbis.krakow.pl). Sells train tickets, arranges trips to Wieliczka and Auschwitz (115zł, both 220zł), cashes traveler's checks, and exchanges currency. Open M-F 9am-7pm, Sa 9am-3pm.

Consulates: UK, Św. Anny 9, 4th fl. (☎421 70 30; ukconsul@bci.krakow.pl). Open M-F 9am-2pm. **US,** ul. Stolarska 9 (☎424 51 00; www.usinfo.pl/krakow). Open M-F 8:30am-5pm.

Currency Exchange: *Kantory,* except those around the train station, have the best rates. **Bank PKO SA,** Rynek Główny 31 (☎422 60 22), cashes **traveler's checks** for a 1-2% commission and gives MC/V **cash advances.** Open M-F 8am-6pm, Sa 9am-2pm.

POLAND

American Express: ul. św. Marka 25 (☎423 12 02; www.americanexpress.pl). Directs those seeking help with traveler's checks to the Warsaw office. Open M-F 9am-5pm.

Luggage Storage: At the train station. 1% of value per day plus 3.90zł for the 1st day and 2zł for each additional day. Lockers near the exit. Small 4zł. Large 8zł. Open 24hr.

English Bookstore: Szawal, ul. Krupnicza 3. Open M-F 10am-7pm, Sa 10am-2pm.

Laundromat: ul. Piastowska 47, in Hotel Piast basement. Tram #4, 13, or 14 to "WKS Wawel" and turn left. Wash 15zł, dry 15zł. Open Tu and Th 11am-4pm, Sa 11am-2pm.

Pharmacy: Apteka Pod Złotym Tygrysem, Szczepańska 1 (☎422 92 93), just off Rynek Główny. Posts a list of 24hr. pharmacies. Open M-F 8am-8pm, Sa 8am-3pm.

Medical Assistance: Medicover, ul. Krótka 1 (☎430 00 34). English-speaking staff. Ambulance services available. Open M-F 8am-8pm, Sa 9am-2pm.

Telephones: At the post office and throughout the city. **Telekomunikacja Polska,** ul. Wielpole 2 (☎421 64 57; www.telekomunikacja.pl), sells phone cards and offers free Internet access. Open M-F 9am-7pm, Sa 10am-2pm.

Internet Access: Enter Internet Cafe, ul. Basztowa 23 (☎429 42 25). 8am-11am 2zł per hr.; 11am-11pm, 3zł per hr. Full nights 10pm-6am 10zł. **Internet Point,** ul. Sławkowska 12, 3rd floor. (☎422 22 64). 2zł per hr. Open M-F 8am-8pm.

Post Office: ul. Westerplatte 20 (☎422 24 97). *Poste Restante* at counter #1. Open M-F 7:30am-8:30pm, Sa 8am-2pm, Su 9am-11am. **Postal Code:** 31-075.

▛ ACCOMMODATIONS

Call ahead in summer. **Travel Agency Jordan,** ul. Długa 9 (☎421 21 25; www.jordan.krakow.pl), arranges private rooms. (Open M-F 8am-6pm, Sa 9am-2pm. Singles 65-100zł; doubles 130-160zł; triples 180-240zł. AmEx/MC/V.) **University dorms** open up in July and August; the booklet *Kraków in Your Pocket* has a list.

■ **Mama's Hostel,** ul. Bracka 4 (☎429 59 40; www.mamashostel.com.pl). Centrally located with excellent facilities. Beautiful kitchen. Breakfast, storage, linen, and laundry included. Reception 24hr. Check-in and check-out flexible. Dorms 50zł. MC/V. ❷

■ **Bling Bling Hostel,** ul. Pędzichow 7 (☎634 05 32; www.blingbling.pl). Small, familial hostel with warm staff. Full kitchen. Breakfast, storage, linen, and laundry included. Free Internet. Reception 24hr. Check-in and check-out flexible. Dorms 45zł. MC/V. ❷

■ **Nathan's Villa Hostel,** ul. św. Agnieszki 1 (☎422 35 45; www.nathansvilla.com). Kraków's most social hostel. Full kitchen. Breakfast, storage, sheets, and laundry included. Reception 24hr. Check-in before midnight. Dorms 50-60zł. MC/V. ❷

Hostel Express, ul. Wrocławska 91 (☎633 88 62). Spacious bungalows, spotless baths, kitchens, and washing machines (7zł per load). Breakfast 9zł. Reception 24hr. Check-in 3pm. Check-out 10am. Quiet hours 10pm-6am. 6-bed dorms 29-35zł. MC/V. ❶

Strawberry Youth Hostel, ul. Racławicka 9 (☎294 53 63 or 294 63 64). Well-kept student dorm open during July and Aug. only. TV room and kitchen. Dorms 40zł. ❶

Hotel Polonia, ul. Basztowa 25 (☎422 12 33). Opposite the train station and a 5min. walk from Rynek Główny. Elegant exterior and modern rooms. Breakfast 17zł, included for rooms with bath. Reception 24hr. Check-in 2pm. Check-out noon. Singles 99zł, with bath 268zł; doubles 119zł/319zł; triples 139zł/380zł; suites 484zł. MC/V. ❹

Hotel Eden, ul. Ciemna 15 (☎430 65 65). In the heart of Kazimierz. Eden offers the only *mikveh* in Poland, kosher meals, and tours of Kazimierz. All rooms include bathroom, telephone, and satellite television. Free Internet. Kosher breakfast included. Wheelchair accessible. Singles 200zł; doubles 280zł; triples 370zł; suites 450zł. AmEx/MC/V. ❺

▜ FOOD

Many restaurants, cafes, and grocery stores are located on and around the *Rynek*. More grocery stores surround the bus and train stations.

Pierogarnia, ul. Szpitalnia 30/32 (☎422 74 95). Window offers a view of the cook making both classic and innovative varieties of *pierogi*. Also serves excellent *gołabki* (6zł) and Polish fruit juices (4zł). All *pierogi* 5.90-6.90zł. Open daily 10am-9pm. ❶

Navara, ul. Podbrzezie 2 (☎431 19 42). The bagel returns to its birthplace in triumph: these are the best anywhere east of New York City, with a full range of fresh spreads (4-5zł). Also serves *chili con carne* and burritos (10-15zł). Open Tu-Su 10am-7pm. ❶

Dym (Smoke), ul. św. Jana 5 (☎429 66 61). Sophisticated locals gather for the best coffee in town (4.50zł) or to chat over a beer (5.50zł). Open daily 10am-midnight. ❶

Camelot, ul. św. Tomasza 17 (☎421 01 23). A legend in Stare Miasto. Cafe serves sandwiches (3-6zł) and salads (19-21zł). Cabaret F 9pm. Open daily 9am-midnight. ❶

Gruzińskie Chaczapuri, ul. Sławkowska 19. Richly spiced Georgian dishes. Specialties include grilled meats (5zł); paprika eggplant stuffed with meat, mushrooms, or spinach (6.90zł); and meat- or veggie-filled *lavash* (5.90-7.90zł). Open daily 9am-midnight. ❶

Restauracja Samoobsługowa "Polakowski," ul. Miodowa 39 (☎421 21 17). Polish cooking in a homey setting. Meals 10-15zł. Soup 4zł. Open daily 10am-10pm. ❷

Vega Bar Restaurant, ul. Krupnicza 22 (☎430 08 46). Soups, salads, and delightful vegetarian cuisine (2-5zł). 36 varieties of tea (2.50zł each). Branch at ul. św. Gertrudy 7 (☎422 34 94). Both open daily 9am-9pm. MC/V. ❶

Fabryka Pizzy, ul. Józefa 34 (☎433 80 80). Popular in Kazimierz. Pizzas (12-20zł) have surreal English translations. Open M-Th and Su 11am-11pm, F-Sa noon-midnight. ❷

⊙ SIGHTS

STARE MIASTO. In center of Stare Miasto is Rynek Główny, a sea of cafes and bars surrounded by particolored row houses. Nearby, **Collegium Maius** of Kraków's **Jagiellonian University** (Uniwersytet Jagielloński) dates from 1364, making it the second oldest institution of higher learning in Eastern Europe (after Prague's Charles University). Alumni include astronomer Mikołaj Kopernik, or Copernicus, and painter Jan Matejko. Once a lecture hall and professors' quarters, the Collegium became a museum in 1964. *(At ul. Jagiellońska 15. Walk down św. Anny in the corner of the Rynek near the Town Hall and turn left onto Jagiellońska. ☎422 05 49. Open M-F 10am-3pm, Sa 11am-2pm. University Museum tours every 20min. 16zł, students 12zł. Sa free. English tours daily at 1pm.)* A trumpet call blares from the towers of **St. Mary's Church** (Kościół Mariacki) once in each direction every hour; the call's abrupt ending reflects the near-destruction of Kraków in

THE BIRTH OF THE BAGEL

According to legend, a Jewish baker in Vienna molded the first bagel in 1683 as a gift to Polish king Jan Sobieski to thank him for routing Turkish invaders. The bread (or so the story goes) was shaped like a stirrup "beugal" in honor of Sobieski's heroic horsemanship. The historical record, however, first spots the bagel in Kraków in 1610: community regulations decreed that bagels be given to teething babies and to pregnant women for easy childbirth. Whatever the bagel's origins, it thrived in Poland, especially in the Kraków region. A 1915 chronicle of the Kazimierz neighborhood recalls that the smell of freshly baked bagels often wafted through the streets, especially near the Tempel Synagogue, where a tiny shop called Pan Bejgul (Mr. Bagel) stood at the end of Podbrzezie Street.

In Kraków today, street vendors hawk the Polish descendent of the original bagel, a crisp ring of bread known as "*obwarzanki*," for less than a złoty. The aroma of the bagel bakery, meanwhile, has returned to ul. Podbrzezie. **Navara,** Podbrzezie 2, facing the Tempel Synagogue, is run by an American expat chef and is currently the only shop in all of Poland that sells fresh bagels as they now appear among Polish Jewish immigrants to North America: soft and chewy, with cream cheese spreads. See left.

1241, when (following legend) the invading Tartars shot down the herald as he tried to warn the city. A stunning blue and gold interior encases the world's oldest Gothic altarpiece, a 500-year-old treasure once dismantled by the Nazis. *(At the corner of the Rynek closest to the train station. Cover shoulders and knees. Open daily 11:30am-6pm. Altar 4zł, students 2zł.)* In the middle of the *Rynek*, the yellow Italianate **Cloth Hall** (Sukiennice) houses hawkers of souvenirs and a gallery of Polish painting and sculpture. *(Open Tu, F, Sa 10am-7pm, W-Th 10am-4pm, Su 10am-3pm. 7zł, students 4zł. Th free.)* Letters by Copernicus and paintings by Matejko, da Vinci, and Rembrandt can be found in the **Czartoryskich Museum.** *(Św. Jana 19, parallel to ul. Florianska. Open Tu and Th 10am-4pm, W and F 11am-7pm, Sa-Su 10am-3pm. Closed 3rd Su of each month. 8zł, students 5zł. Su usually free.)* **Ulica Floriańska** runs to the *Rynek* from the **Barbakan** and **Floriańska Gate,** which once formed the old entrance to the city and are now the only remnants of the city's medieval fortifications. From the *Rynek*, walk down Grodzka and turn right to reach the vibrantly colored **Franciscan Church,** which displays Stanisław Wyspiański's stained-glass window *God the Father*. *(Open daily until 7:30pm. English tours.)*

WAWEL CASTLE AND SURROUNDINGS. ⬛**Wawel Castle** (Zamek Wawelski) is an architectural masterpiece and arguably *the* sight to see in Poland. Begun in the 10th century and remodeled in the 16th, the castle contains 71 chambers, including a magnificent sequence of 16th-century tapestries commissioned by the royal family. Royal treasures can be seen in the **Komnaty** (state rooms), the royal lifestyle in the **Apartamenty** (royal chambers). Also see the treasury's cache of armor, swords, spears, and ancient guns. *(☎ 422 64 64; www.wawel.krakow.pl. Open Apr.-Oct. M 9:30am-noon, Tu and F 9:30am-4pm, W-Th and Sa 9:30am-3pm, Su 10am-3pm; Nov.-Mar. Tu-Sa 9:30am-3pm, Su 10am-3pm. State rooms and treasury 12zł, students 7zł; royal chambers same prices.)* Next door is **Wawel Cathedral** (Katedra Wawelska), which once hosted the coronations and funerals of Polish monarchs. Kraków native Karol Wojtyła, now John Paul II, was archbishop here before his papacy. Steep wooden stairs from the church lead to **Sigismund's Bell** (Dwon Zygmunta); the view of the city rewards the climb. *(Open May-Sept. M-Sa 9am-5pm, Oct.-Apr. 9am-3pm, Su and holy days 12:15-5:15pm. 8zł, students 4zł.)* In the complex's southwest corner is the entrance to the **Dragon's Den** (Smocza Jama). Legend has it that a shepherd left a poisoned sheep outside the cave as bait; the dragon ate it and became so thirsty that it drank itself to death at the Wisła River. *(Open daily Apr.-Oct. 10am-5pm. 3zł.)*

KAZIMIERZ. South of Stare Miasto lies Kazimierz, Kraków's 600-year-old **Jewish quarter.** On the eve of WWII, 68,000 Jews lived in the Kraków area, many of them in Kazimierz. The Nazis deported all by March 1943, many to the nearby Płaszów (where parts of *Schindler's List* were filmed) and Auschwitz-Birkenau concentration camps. Today, Kazimierz is a focal point for the 5000 Jews remaining in Poland, and a starting place for those seeking their roots. *(The walk from the Rynek leads down ul. Sienna past St. Mary's Church; ul. Sienna turns into Starowiślna. After 1km, turn right onto Miodowa, then left onto Szeroka.)* The tiny **Remuh Synagogue** is surrounded by **Remuh's Cemetery,** which has graves dating to the plague of 1551-1552 and a wall constructed from tombstones recovered after WWII. *(At ul. Szeroka 40. Open Su-F 9am-6pm. Services F at sundown and Sa morning. 5zł, students 2zł.)* Back on Szeroka is Poland's earliest example of Jewish religious architecture, the **Old Synagogue,** which houses a museum of traditions and art. *(At ul. Szeroka 24. ☎ 422 09 62. Open Apr.-Oct. M 10am-2pm, W-Th and Sa-Su 9am-3:30pm, F 10am-5pm; Nov.-Mar. M 10am-2pm, W-Th and Sa-Su 9am-3:30pm, F 10am-5pm. 6zł, students 4zł. M free.)* The **Center for Jewish Culture** organizes cultural events and arranges heritage tours. *(Rabina Meiselsa 17, off pl. Nowy. ☎ 430 64 49; www.judaica.pl. Open M-F 10am-6pm, Sa-Su 10am-2pm.)*

ENTERTAINMENT

The **Cultural Information Center,** ul. św. Jana 2, sells the comprehensive monthly guide *Karnet* (3zł; www.karnet.krakow2000.pl) and tickets for upcoming events. (☎421 77 87. Open M-F 10am-6pm, Sa 10am-4pm.) Summer festivals are especially abundant, including the **International Short Film Festival** (late May), **Children's Day Celebrations** (early June), the **Floating of Wreaths on the Wisła** (June), **Festival of Jewish Culture** (early July), the **Street Theater Festival** (early July), and the **Jazz Festival** (late July). The opera performs at **J. Słowacki Theater,** pl. św. Ducha 1. (☎422 40 22; www.slowacki.krakow.pl. Box office open M-Sa 11am-2pm and 3-7pm, Su 2hr. before performances.) **Stary Teatr** stages host movies, plays, and other exhibits. (Tickets at pl. Szczepański 1. ☎422 40 40. Open Tu-Sa 10am-1pm and 5-7pm.) European films roll at **Kino Mikro,** ul. Lea 5. (☎634 28 97; www.apollofilm.pl. Open daily 30min. before first showing. M-F 10zł, Sa-Su 12zł.)

NIGHTLIFE

With thousands of students milling through its streets, Kraków offers more than just sightseeing. At night, clubs come alive in the brick basements of 14th-century buildings near the *Rynek*, while laid-back bars are scattered through Kazimierz.

- **Alchemia,** ul. Estery 5, is the quintessential Kazimierz bar. Patrons arrive for a beer and leave after dawn. Beer 6-10zł. Open M-Sa 11am-4am, Su 10am-4am.

- **Stalowe Magnolie,** ul. św Jana 15. Locals relax and listen to live jazz Tu-Th and contemporary rock on the weekends. Beer 6-10zł. Open Tu-W 7pm-1am, Th-Su 7pm-3am.

- **Prozak,** ul. Dominikańska 6, the hottest club in town, attracts international DJs and a young, beautiful crowd. Beer 6-10zł. Cover F-Sa averages 10zł. Open daily 4pm-2am.

- **Propaganda,** ul. Miodowa 20, mixes posters of Stalin with the guitars of Polish rockers, some of whom have been known to tend bar here. Brave the rabid "Mad Dog" (10zł) of vodka, Tabasco, and sweet syrup. Open daily 2pm-last customer.

- **Faust,** Rynek Główny 6, has closed-circuit cameras and TV sets that let you witness the crowd go wild as you chat with friends at a candle-lit table. Beer 4zł. Disco W-Sa. F-Sa cover 5zł. Open M-Th and Su noon-1am, F-Sa noon-4am.

- **Klub pod Jaszczurami (Club under the Lizards),** Rynek Główny 8 (☎292 22 02). Cafe by day, club by night. Over the dance floor waits smoke from tables of animated twentysomethings. Beer 5.50zł. Open Su-Th 10am-1am, F-Sa 10am-last customer.

- **Kredens,** Rynek Główny 12, is a casual club packed with multinational party-goers. 21+. Cover F-Sa 5zł. Open daily 5pm-3am.

DAYTRIPS FROM KRAKÓW

AUSCHWITZ-BIRKENAU. An estimated 1.5 million people, mostly Jews, were murdered—and thousands more suffered unthinkable horrors—in the Nazi concentration camps at **Auschwitz** (in Oświęcim) and **Birkenau** (in Brzezinka). The gates over the smaller **Konzentrationslager Auschwitz I** are inscribed with the ironic dictum "*Arbeit Macht Frei*" (Work Will Set You Free). Tours begin at the **museum** at Auschwitz. As you walk past the leavings of thousands of lives—suitcases, shoes, glasses, kilos upon kilos of women's hair—the sheer enormity of the atrocity begins to come into focus. A 15min. English-language **film** (2zł), with footage shot by the Soviet Army that liberated the camp on January 27, 1945, is shown at 11am and 1pm. (☎843 20 22; www.um.oswiecim.pl. Open daily June-Aug. 8am-7pm; May and Sept. 8am-6pm; Apr. and Oct. 8am-5pm; Mar. and Nov. to mid-Dec. 8am-4pm; mid-Dec. to Feb. 8am-3pm. Free. 3½hr. English tour daily 11:30am. 25zł, film and bus included. English guidebook 3zł.)

POLAND

The larger, starker Konzentrationslager Auschwitz II-Birkenau is located in the countryside 3km from the original camp. A 30min. walk along a well-marked route or a quick **shuttle** ride from the parking lot of the Auschwitz museum (hourly 11:30am-5:30pm, 2zł) will get you there. Birkenau was built later in the war, when the Nazis developed a more brutally efficient means of exterminating the massive numbers of people brought to the area. Little is left of the camp today; most was destroyed by retreating Nazis to conceal the genocide. The train tracks, reconstructed after the liberation, lead to the ruins of the crematoria and gas chambers, where a memorial pays tribute to all who died in the Auschwitz system. Near the monument lies a pond still gray from the ashes deposited there half a century ago.

Auschwitz Jewish Center and Synagogue features exhibits on pre-war Jewish life in the town of Oświęcim, films based on survivors' testimonies, genealogy resources, and a reading room. Guides offer tours of the compound. Take a taxi for about 17zł, or take bus #1, 3-6, or 8 from the train station in the town center, get off at the first stop after the bridge, and backtrack. (Pl. Ks. Jana Skarbka 5. ☎ 844 70 02; www.ajcf.pl. Open daily Apr.-Sept. 8:30am-8pm; Oct.-Mar. M-F and Su 8:30am-6pm.)

Buses from Kraków's central bus station go to **Oświęcim** (1½-2hr., 5 per day, 10zł). Return buses leave from the stop on the other side of the parking lot; turn right out of the museum. Less convenient **trains** leave from Kraków Płaszów, south of the town center. Buses #2-5, 8-9, and 24-29 connect the Oświęcim train station to the Muzeum Oświęcim stop; alternatively, walk a block to the right out of the station, turn left onto ul. Więźniów Oświęcimia, and continue 1.6km to Auschwitz.

WIELICZKA. A 700-year-old ▥**salt mine** sits at ul. Daniłowicza 10 in the tiny town of Wieliczka, 13km southeast of Kraków. Pious Poles carved the immense underground complex of chambers out of salt; in 1978, UNESCO declared the mine one of the 12 most priceless monuments in the world. The most spectacular cavern is **St. Kinga's Chapel,** complete with salt chandeliers, an altar, and relief works. (☎ 278 73 02; www.kopalnia.pl. Open daily Apr.-Oct. 7:30am-7:30pm; Nov.-Mar. 8am-4pm. English tours available July-Aug. 5 per day; June and Sept.-Oct. 3 per day; Nov.-May 2 per day. 2hr. 47zł, students under 25 36zł.) Most travel companies, including **Orbis** (p. 817), organize trips to the mines, but it's cheapest to take a private **minibus,** like "Lux-Bus," that departs from between the train and bus stations (30min., every 15min., 2zł). Look for "Wieliczka" marked on the door. In Wieliczka, follow the path of the former tracks, then signs marked "*do kopalni.*"

LUBLIN ☎ 081

Unlike most cities in Poland, Lublin (LOO-bleen; pop. 400,000) survived WWII with cobblestones and medieval buildings intact. The 14th-century **Lublin Castle** (Zamek Lubelski), in the **Rynek** (main square) of the **Stare Miasto** (old town), was used as a Gestapo jail during the Nazi occupation. The adjacent **Holy Trinity Chapel** contains stunning Russo-Byzantine frescoes from 1418. (Castle museum open W-F 9am-4pm, Sa 10am-5pm, Su 9am-5pm. Chapel open M-Sa 9am-3:30pm, Su 9am-4:30pm. Entry to each 6.50zł, students 4.50zł.) Take eastbound bus #28 from the train station, trolley #153 or 156 from al. Racławickie, or walk along Droga Męczenników Majdanka (Road of the Martyrs of Majdanek; 30min.) to Zamość in order to reach **Majdanek,** the second-largest concentration camp during WWII. Nazis did not have time to destroy it, so the original structures still stand. (☎ 744 26 48; www.majdanek.pl. Open May-Sept. Tu-Su 8am-6pm; Mar.-Apr. and Oct.-Nov. Tu-Su 8am-3pm. Free. Children under 14 not permitted. English tours 100zł per group; call ahead. English guidebooks 7zł. Maps free.)

Trains (☎ 94 36) run from pl. Dworcowy 1 to: Berlin (13hr., 1 per day, 158-234zł); Kraków (4hr., 4 per day, 43zł); Warsaw (3hr., 14 per day, 32zł); and Wrocław (9½hr., 3 per day, 48zł). The **tourist office,** ul. Jezuica 1/3, is near the Kraków Gate. (☎ 532 44 12; itlublin@onet.pl. Open May-Aug. M-Sa 9am-6pm, Su 10am-3pm; Sept.-Apr. M-F 9am-5pm, Sa-Su 10am-3pm.) From the bus station, walk through

Zamkowy Square, past the castle, and through the gate to reach ⊠**Domu Rekole-kcyjnym ❶**, ul. Podwale 15, a rectory with tranquil gardens. (☎532 41 38; j.halasa@kuria.lublin.pl. No curfew. Dorms 20-40zł.) Lublin's eateries cluster near **ul. Kraków skie Przedmieście;** a dozen beer gardens can be found in Stare Miasto. **Café Szeroka 28 ❹**, ul. Grodzka 21, looks out onto the castle and hosts live Klezmer on Saturday. (Entrees 30zł. Open M-Th and Su 11am-11pm, F-Sa 11am-late. AmEx/MC/V.) **Cafe Vanilla ❷**, ul. Krakowskie Przedmieście 12, serves *naleśniki* (Polish crepes) for 8-20zł. (Open daily 10am-11pm. AmEx/MC/V.) **Postal Code:** 20-950.

ZAKOPANE   ☎018

Zakopane (zah-ko-PAH-neh; pop. 28,000), Poland's premier year-round resort, lies in a valley framed by jagged Tatran peaks and alpine meadows. During peak seasons (Jan.-Feb. and June-Sept.), the town swells with skiers and hikers who come for the magnificent **Tatra National Park.** (Tatrzański Park Narodowy; 3zł, students 1.50zł.) The bus station sits on the corner of ul. Kościuszki and ul. Jagiellońska, facing the train station. **Buses** (☎201 46 03) run to Kraków (2-2½hr., 22 per day, 8zł) and Warsaw (8½hr., 2 per day, 53zł). A private **express line** runs between Zakopane and Kraków (2hr., 15 per day, 10zł); buses leave from a stop on ul. Kościuszki, 50m toward the center from the station. **Trains** (☎201 45 04) go to Kraków (3-4hr., 19 per day, 20zł) and Warsaw (8hr., 8 per day, 46-80zł). Walk down ul. Kościuszki, which intersects the central ul. Krupówki (15min.). **Tourist Agency Redykołka**, ul. Kościeliska 1, can help with private rooms (30-50zł), English-language tours (4hr., 320zł per group), and rafting trips. (☎201 32 53; www.tatratours.pl. Open M-Sa 9am-5pm, Su 9am-1pm.) Signs marked "*pokój,*" "*noclegi,*" and "*Zimmer*" indicate private rooms; owners may greet you at the station. **Schronisko Morskie Oko ❶**, by the Morskie Oko lake, is a gorgeous hostel in an ideal hiking location. Take a bus (45min., 11 per day, 4zł) from the station to Palenice Bialczanska or a direct minibus (20min., 5zł) from opposite the bus station. (☎207 76 09. Reserve well in advance. June-Oct. 3- to 6-bed dorms 41zł; 8- to 12-bed dorms 32zł; Nov.-June 32zł/22zł.) **PTTK Dom Turysty ❶**, ul. M. Zaruskiego 5, is a large and popular chalet in the center of town. From the bus station, walk down ul. Kosciuszki, which turns into ul. M. Zaruskiego. (☎206 32 07. Curfew midnight. Dorms 18-30zł.) Waiters at ⊠**Czarny Staw ❸**, ul. Krupówki 2, serve a smorgasbord of Western and Polish fare in traditional costume. (☎201 38 52. Open 10am-midnight. MC/V.) At ul. Krupówki 41 is a **Delikatooy** grocery store. (Open M-Sa 7am-8pm.) *Oscypek* cheese, a local delicacy, can be found at the stalls that line the street. **Postal Code:** 34-500.

🅽 **HIKING NEAR ZAKOPANE. Kuźnice,** south of central Zakopane, is the best and most popular place to begin hikes. Walk from the train station up ul. Jagiellońska, which becomes ul. Chałubińskiego, then continue down ul. Przewodników Tatrzańskich to the trailheads. Alternatively, catch the 1987m Kasprowy Wierch **cable car,** which runs between Zakopane and Kuźnice. (Round-trip 28zł, students 18zł; up 18zł/13zł; down 10zł/5zł. Open July-Aug. 7am-7pm; June and Sept. 7:30am-4pm; Oct. 7:30am-3pm.) Trails are well-marked, but pick up the map *Tatrzański Park Narodowy* (7zł) at a kiosk or bookstore before hiking. The ⊠**Valley of the Five Polish Tarns** (Dolina Pięciu Stawów Polskich; full-day) is an intense, beautiful hike. It starts at Kuźnice and follows the blue trail to Hala Gąsienicowa. After several steep ups and downs, the blue trail ends at Morskie Oko. From here, it's 2km further to a parking lot in Palenica Białczańska, where buses return to Zakopane (10zł). **Mount Glewont** (1894m; 6½hr.) has a silhouette that looks like a man lying down. It's crowded and the final ascent is steep, so be careful. From Kuźnice, take the moderately difficult blue trail (7km) to the peak for a view of Zakopane, the Tatras, and Slovakia. **Morskie Oko** (Sea Eye; 1406m; 5-6hr.) is a dazzling glacial lake. Take a bus from the Zakopane station (45min., 11

POLAND

per day, 4zł) or a private minibus from opposite the station (30-40min., 5zł) to Palenica Białczańska. Hike the popular 18km round-trip on a paved road or take the green trail to the blue trail (4hr.) for a majestic view of the lake.

WROCŁAW ☎ 071

Wrocław (pop. 657,000), the capital of Lower Silesia, is a city of spires, stone bridges, islands, and gardens. Passed among competing powers for centuries, in WWII the city became *Festung Breslau* (Fortress Wrocław), one of the last Nazi holdouts en route to Berlin. Today, the rejuvenated city captivates visitors with the antique grace of its 19th-century buildings and lush parks. The Gothic **Ratusz** (Town Hall) towers over the **Rynek** (main square) in the heart of the city. Past the *Rynek* runs the beautiful central street **Ulica Świdnicka.** The rotunda containing the 120-by-5m ⬛**Racławice Panorama,** ul. Purkyniego 11, wraps viewers in the action of a legendary 18th-century peasant insurrection led by Tadeusz Kościuszko against the Russian occupation. To reach it, face away from the *Ratusz*, bear left onto Kuźnicza and then turn right onto Kotlarska, which becomes ul. Purkyniego. (Viewings every 30min. M-Tu and Su 9:30am-3:30pm. 19zł, students 15zł.) Across the street is the **National Museum** (Muzeum Narodowe), pl. Powstańców Warszawy 5, which has permanent modern art exhibits, medieval statuary, and other paintings. (Open W and F 10am-4pm, Th 9am-4pm, Sa-Su 10am-6pm. 15zł, students 10zł.) Wrocław's cultural center, the **Uniwersytet Wrocławski** (Wrocław University) has lovely architecture; the **mathematical tower,** pl. Uniwersytecka 1, provides a sweeping view of the city. (Open M-Tu and Th-Su 10am-3pm. 4zł, students 2zł.) Across the Oder River lies the serene **Cathedral Square** (Plac Katedralny). With your back to the *Ratusz*, walk until you hit ul. Piaskowy; turn left over Piakowsky Bridge to **Cathedral Island,** then right onto Tumski bridge to pl. Katedralny to reach the spires of the 13th-century **Cathedral of St. John the Baptist** (Katedra Św. Jana Chrzciciela; open daily 10am-6pm.) Students crowd into ⬛**REJS Pub,** ul. Kotlarska 32a. (Beer 3.50zł. Open M-Sa 9:30am-late, Su 11am-late.) Artsy **Kawiarnia "Pod Kalamburem,"** ul. Kuźnicza 29a, includes a bar, cafe, and cinema. (Beer 3-10zł Open M-Th 1pm-midnight, F-Sa 1pm-late, Su 4pm-midnight.)

Trains, ul. Piłsudskiego 105 (☎367 58 82), run from Wrocław Główny to: Berlin (6¼hr., 2 per day, 185zł); Bratislava (7½hr., 10:30pm, 167zł); Kraków (4½hr., 14 per day, 40-61zł); Poznań (3¼hr., 25 per day, 32zł); Prague (5¼hr., 2 per day, 140zł); and Warsaw (4¼hr., 12 per day, 44-89zł). **Buses** leave from behind the train station. From the train station, turn left on ul. Piłsudskiego, take a right on ul. Świdnicka, and go past Kościuszki pl. over the Fosa River to reach the *Rynek*. **IT,** Rynek 14, can help find rooms in student dorms. (☎344 11 09; fax 344 29 62. Open M-F 10am-6pm, Sa 9am-2pm.) Surf the web at **Internet Klub Navig@tor Podziemia,** ul. Kuźnicza 11/13. (3zł per hr. Open daily 9am-10pm.) The cheerful **Youth Hostel Mlodziezowy Dom Kultury im. Kopernika (HI) ❶,** ul. Kołłątaja 20, is opposite the train station on the road perpendicular to ul. Piłsudskiego. (☎343 88 56. Lockout 10am-5pm. Curfew 10pm. Call ahead. Dorms 22zł; doubles 58zł. Discount after 2 nights.) Art Nouveau **Hotel Monopol ❹,** ul. Modrzejewskiej 2, has satellite TV, telephones, and a princely breakfast buffet. (☎343 70 40. Check-in and check-out 2pm. Singles 115zł, with bath 180zł; doubles 260zł/290zł; triples with bath 310zł. AmEx/MC/V.) **Bazylia ❶,** ul. Kuźniczna 42, is a traditional Polish milk bar serving cheap, nourishing meals. (Open M-F 7am-7pm, Sa 8am-5pm.) **Postal Code:** 50-900.

KARPACZ ☎ 075

Karpacz (pop. 8000) is a beautiful gateway to **Karkonosze National Park** (Karkonoski Park Narodowy; 4zł, students 2zł; 3-day pass 8/4zł), where several 2¼-3hr. trails lead to the stop **Pod Śnieżka** (1394m) on **Śnieżka** (Mt. Snow; 1602m), the highest peak in the Czech Republic (the Polish-Czech border runs across the summit). As a substitute for the trails, take the 2-3hr. Kopa chairlift. (Follow the black trail from Hotel Biały Jar. Daily June-Aug. 8:30am-5:30pm; Sept.-May 8am-4pm. Before 1pm 17zł, students 14zł; round-trip 22zł/18zł. After 1pm 15zł/10zł; round-trip 18zł/13zł.) **Trains** run to Jelenia Góra from Kraków (8hr., 1 per day, 40zł); Póznan (6-7hr., 1 per day, 35zł); Warsaw (9hr., 2-3 per day, 42zł); and Wrocław (4-5hr., 7 per day, 16zł). **PKS buses** from Jelenia Góra (45min., every 30min.-1hr., 5-6zł) stop at eight points in Karpacz (2.20zł). Get off at the Karpacz Bacchus stop and head downhill to the **tourist office**, ul. 3-go Maja 25a, for maps, currency exchange, and info about various outdoor activities. (☎761 86 05. Open M-F 9am-5pm, Sa 9am-4pm; July-Aug. also Su 10am-4pm.) The office also reserves rooms at **D.W. Szczyt ❶**, ul. Na Śnieżkę 6, at the Karpacz Wang stop. (Singles 25zł; doubles 50zł.) There is a **Delikatesy** supermarket at ul. 3-go Maja 29. (Open M-Sa 8:30am-9pm, Su 10am-6pm.) **Postal Code:** 58-540.

POZNAŃ   ☎061

International trade fairs throughout the year fill Poznań (pop. 600,000), the capital of Wielkopolska (Greater Poland), with businessmen and tourists. Opulent 15th-century merchant homes surround the Renaissance **Town Hall** (*Ratusz*), a multi-colored building with an ornately painted ceiling and history museum. (Open M-Sa 10am-4pm, Su 10am-3pm. Museum 5.50zł, students 3.50zł. Sa free.) The **National Museum** (Muzeum Narodowe), ul. Marcinkowskiego 9, contains a marvelous collection of 13th- to 19th-century paintings. (Open Tu 10am-6pm, W 9am-5pm, Th and Su 10am-4pm, F-Sa 10am-5pm. 10zł, students 6zł. Sa free.) The **❏Museum of Musical Instruments** (Muzeum Instrumentów Muzycznych), Stary Rynek 45, exhibits antique and foreign instruments, including one of Chopin's pianos. (Open Tu-Sa 11am-5pm, Su 11am-4pm. 5.50zł, students 3.50zł. Sa free.) Sculpted ceilings and columns spiral heavenward in the **Parish Church of the City of Poznań of St. Mary Magdalene**, at the end of ul. Świętosławska off Stary Rynek. (Free concerts Sa 12:15pm.) On the outskirts of town stands the first Polish cathedral, the **Cathedral of St. Peter and St. Paul** (Katedra Piotra i Pawła). In the **Golden Chapel** (Kaplica Złota) are the tombs of Prince Mieszko I and his son Bolesław Chrobry, the first king of Poland. (Cathedral open M-Sa 9am-6pm, Su 1:15pm-6:30pm. Crypt 2zł.)

Trains run from Poznań Główny, Ul. Dworcowa 1 (☎866 12 12), to: Berlin (3½hr., 7 per day, 138zł); Kraków (5hr., 10 per day, 45-79zł); and Warsaw (3hr., 23 per day, 57-87zł). To reach **Stary Rynek** (Old Market), take any tram heading down św. Marcin (to the right) from the end of ul. Dworcowa, and get off at ul. Marcinkowskiego. **Centrum Informacji Turystycznej (CIT),** Stary Rynek 59/60, provides free maps and lodging info. (☎852 61 56. Open June-Aug. M-F 9am-6pm, Sa 10am-4pm; Sept.-May M-F 9am-5pm, Sa 10am-2pm.) **❏Przemysław ❶**, ul. Głogowska 16, arranges private rooms near the center. (☎866 35 60; przemyslaw@przemyslaw.com.pl. Singles 42zł; doubles 64zł. Open M-F 8am-6pm, irregularly Sa 10am-2pm.) **Hotel Dom Turysty ❷**, Stary Rynek 91, occupies the attic of a former nobleman's home. (☎852 88 93; www.domturysty-hotel.com.pl. Check-in noon. Check-out 10am. Dorms 50zł; singles with bath 150zł; doubles 150zł, with bath 250zł; triples with bath 300zł. Sa-Su discounts. MC/V.) **❏W Starem Kinie,** ul. Nowowieskiego 8, draws students and artists with its film screenings and live rock and jazz shows. (Beer 6.50zł. Open M-Sa 10am-1am, Su 6pm-midnight. 18+.) Contact **Centrum Informacji Miejskiej,** ul. Ratajczka 44, for info on cultural events. (☎94 31. Open M-F 10am-7pm, Sa-Su 10am-5pm.) **Postal Code:** 61-890.

TORUŃ   ☎056

Toruń (pop. 210,000) can bill itself as the birthplace and childhood home of Mikołaj Kopernik, or Copernicus. Before the astronomer eclipsed its other attractions, his hometown was known far and wide as "beautiful red Toruń" for its brick and stone structures. **Stare Miasto** (old town), on the right bank of the Wisła River, was constructed by the Teutonic Knights in the 13th century. The 14th-century **Town Hall** (*Ratusz*) dominating **Rynek Stromiejski** (old town square) is one of the finest examples of monumental burgher architecture in Europe. (Museum open May-Aug. Th and Su 10am-4pm, Tu-W and Sa noon-6pm; Sept.-Apr. Tu-Su 10am-4pm. 6zł, students 4zł. Su free. Medieval tower open May-Sept. Tu-Su. 6zł/4zł.) Copernicus was born at ul. Kopernika 15/17; the meticulously restored **Dom Kopernika** features historical artifacts and a sound-and-light show. (Open Su, W, F 10am-4pm; Tu, Th, Sa noon-6pm. 7zł, students 5zł. Sound-and-light show 8zł/5zł. Both 12zł/8zł.) A city-wide revolt in 1454 led to the destruction of the **Teutonic Knights' Castle**, but its ruins, on ul. Przedzamcze, still impress. (Open daily 9am-8pm. 1zł, students 0.5zł.) The 15m **Leaning Tower** (Krzywa Wieża), ul. Krzywa Wieża 17, was built in 1271 by a Teutonic Knight as punishment for infringing his order's rule of celibacy. The **Cathedral of St. John the Baptist and St. John the Evangelist** (Bazylika Katedralna pw. św. Janów), at the corner of ul. Żeglarska and św. Jana, is the most impressive of the many Gothic churches in the area. (Open Apr.-Oct. M-Sa 8:30am-5:30pm, Su 2-5:30pm. 2zł, students 1zł.) Just across the *Rynek* are the slender stained-glass windows of the **Church of the Virgin Mary** (Kościół św. Marii) on ul. Panny Marii. (Open M-Sa 8am-5pm. Free.) ◪**Niebo,** Rynek Staromiejski 1, a Gothic cellar in the Old Town Hall, has *szarlotka*, live jazz and cabaret shows, and outdoor seating in summer. (Beer 4-5zł. Open M-Th and Su noon-midnight, F-Sa noon-2am.)

Across the Wisła River from the city center, the **train station**, ul. Kujawska 1, serves: Gdańsk (3¼hr., 7 per day, 36zł); Łódź (2¾hr., 4 per day, 32zł); Poznań (2¼hr.; 5 per day; 31zł); and Warsaw (2¾hr., 6 per day, 37zł). **Dworzec PKS buses,** ul. Dąbrowskiego 26, leave for Berlin (9½hr., 1 per day, 120zł) and Kołobrzeg (7hr., 2 per day, 40zł). **Polski Express buses** leave from Ruch Kiosk just north of pl. Teatralny for many of the same destinations, with student discounts. The IT **tourist office,** Rynek Staromiejski 25, offers helpful advice in English and helps find lodgings. From the train station, take city bus #22 or 27 across the river to Pl. Rapackiego and head through the park. (☎621 09 31; www.it.torun.pl. Open May-Dec. M and Sa 9am-4pm, Tu-F 9am-6pm, Su 9am-1pm; Sept.-Apr. closed Su.)

◪**Hotel Kopernik ❸,** ul. Wola Zamkowa 16, decks out its rooms with satellite TVs and fluffy towels. (☎652 25 73. Reception 24hr. Check-in and check-out 2pm. Breakfast 10zł. Singles 76zł, with bath 115zł; doubles 136zł/180zł. MC/V.) **Hotel "Gotyk" ❺,** ul. Piekary 20, has beautiful rooms with Internet access. (☎658 40 00; gotyk@ic.torun.pl. Reception 24hr. Singles 170zł; doubles 250-300zł; apartments 300-350zł.) To reach the student-filled **PTTK Dom Turystyczny ❶,** ul. Legionów 24, from the *Rynek*, follow ul. Chełmińska past pl. Teatralny; take the second right after the park and turn left onto ul Legionów. (☎/fax 622 38 55. Dorms 30zł; singles 70zł; doubles 80zł; triples 99zł.) ◪**U Sołtysa ❷,** ul. Mostowa 17, serves traditional food from the Pomorze region. (*Pierogi* 9.50-12zł. Open daily noon-midnight.) **Kopernik Factory Store ❷,** Rynek Staromiejski 6, sells gingerbread effigies of Polish kings, saints, and astronomers. (0.70-26zł. Open M-F 9am-7pm, Sa-Su 10am-2pm. MC/V.) Look for a 24hr. **grocery store** at ul. Chełmińska 22. **Postal Code:** 87-100.

ŁÓDŹ ☎042

Poland's second-largest city, Łódź (WOODGE; pop. 1,055,000) has few postcard-worthy attractions but nonetheless exudes a charisma of its own. It has always been a working-class town, at one time holding the largest Jewish ghetto in Europe (see **The Łódź Ghetto**, p. 827). The **Jewish cemetery** (Cmentarz Żydowski), on ul. Zmienna, encloses over 200,000 graves. Near the entrance is a memorial to the Jews killed in the Łódź ghetto; signs lead the way to the **Ghetto Fields** (Pole Ghettowe), which are lined with the faintly marked graves of those who died there. (Take tram #1 from ul. Kilinskiego or #6 from ul. Kosciuszki or Zachnodnia north to the end of the line (20min.). Continue up the street, take a left on ul. Zmienna, and enter through the small gate in the wall on your right. ☎656 70 19. Open May-Sept. M-F and Su 9am-5pm, Oct.-Apr. M-F and Su 9am-3pm. Closed on Jewish holidays. 4zł; free for those visiting the graves of relatives.) The **Jewish Community Center** (Gmina Wyznaniowa Żydowska), ul. Pomorska

18, in the center of town, has info about those buried in the cemetery. (☎ 633 51 56. Open M-F 10am-2pm. Services daily. English spoken.) Łódź's main thoroughfare, **ul. Piotrkowska,** is a bustling pedestrian shopping drag by day and a lively pub land by night.
Trains run from the **Łódź Fabryczna** (☎ 664 54 67), pl. B. Sałacinskiego 1, to Kraków (3¼hr., 3 per day, 41zł) and Warsaw (2hr., 17 per day, 28zł), and from **Łódź Kaliska,** al. Unii 1 (☎ 41 02), to Gdańsk (7½hr., 4 per day, 45zł) and Wrocław (3¾hr., 5 per day, 39zl). Polski Express **buses** also depart from Łódź Fabryczna to Kraków (5hr., 3 per day, 31zł) and Warsaw (2½hr., 5 per day, 24zł). **IT,** al. Kosciuszkiul 88, has tourist info and can help book lodgings, including university dorms, in summer. (☎/fax 638 59 56; cit@uml.lodz.pl. Open M-F 8:30am-4:30pm, Sa 9am-1pm.). Quiet, convenient **PTSM Youth Hostel (HI) ❶,** ul. Legionów 27, has spacious rooms and baths. (☎ 630 66 80; www.youthhostel-lodz.w.pl. Flexible curfew 11pm. Dorms 30zł; singles 45-65zł; doubles with TV 80zł; triples with TV 120zł.) **Anatewka ❸,** ul. 6 Sierpnia 2/4, elegantly evokes the rich Jewish culture of prewar Łódz. (Meals 20-50zł. Open daily 11am-11pm). Designed by an arts collective, legendary bar and club **Łódz Kaliska,** ul. Piotrowska 102, has a dance floor as offbeat as its decor. (Beer 7zł. Open daily noon-3am). **Postal Code:** 90-001.

KOŁOBRZEG   ☎ 094

Long known as the "Pearl of the Baltic," Kołobrzeg (koh-WOH-bzheg) was recently voted Poland's most popular holiday resort for its excellent beaches and healing salt springs. Ready to celebrate its 750th birthday in 2005, the city is full of history. In March 1945, the Poles battled fiercely with the Nazis over the port, and although most of the city was destroyed, the Poles ultimately triumphed. They threw a wedding ring into the Baltic to symbolize Poland's claims on Kołobrzeg; a monument near the beach commemorates the event, known as Poland's **Marriage to the Sea** (Zaślubiny z Morzem). An expansive view of the Baltic can be seen from the nearby 1745 **lighthouse,** *Latarnia Morska.* (Open daily July-Aug. 10am-sunset; Sept.-June 10am-5pm. 3zł.) The **Museum Oręza Polskiego,** ul. Emilii Gierczak 5, features an impressive array of military paraphernalia from Poland and elsewhere. (Open M-Tu and Th-Su 9:30am-5pm, W 9:30am-6pm. 6zł, students 3zł. W noon-6pm free.) The **Gallery of Modern Art** (Galeria Sztuki Współczesnej), in the town hall, ul. Armii Krajowej 12, has rotating exhibits of international modern paintings; don't miss the gift shop's selection of paintings and crafts by Polish artists and artisans. (Open Tu-Su 10am-6pm. 8zł, students 6zł.) **Beaches** are obscured by train tracks and tricky to reach; visit the **IT** office (see below) for free English maps.

THE LOCAL STORY

THE ŁÓDŹ GHETTO

In February 1940, the Nazis established Europe's largest Jewish ghetto in Łódź. In order to confine the city's 230,000 Jews to the 4.3 sq. km area, the Nazis drove out non-Jewish residents with warnings of infectious diseases, then ordered all of the city's Jews into the cramped district, and after surrounding the area with a wall, announced that the ghetto was "closed."

After the Nazis proclaimed that residents of the ghetto must work in exchange for their meager rations of food, the overcrowded ghetto became a massive textile factory: young girls even hand-stitched the emblems on Nazi officers' uniforms. Conditions worsened when 20,000 more Jews and 5000 Gypsies joined the original internees. In 1942, deportations of the infirm and children began. Until 1944, though, Łódź managed to escape the total liquidation that had been the fate of other ghettos.

With the approach of the Red Army in August 1944, Heinrich Himmler deported the ghetto's 70,000 remaining residents to Auschwitz and Majdanek, sparing only 800 Jews who stayed back as a cleaning crew. As the Russians were about to capture Łódź, the Nazis resolved to execute them also. Fortunately, the Russians' swift advance interrupted their plans, saving all 800 Jews. Of those deported, 20,000 survived—the highest number of survivors of any European ghetto.

Dworzec PKP **trains** (☎352 35 76) run from ul. Kolejowa to: Gdynia (3½hr., 8 per day, 39zł); Kraków (11½hr., 5 per day, 51zł); Poznań (6hr., 5 per day, 40zł); and Warsaw (8hr., 9 per day, 49-83zł). Dworzec PKS **buses** (☎352 39 28) depart from next door for: Gdańsk (6hr., 1 per day, 40zł); Gdynia (5hr., 2 per day, 35zł); Poznań (5hr., 4 per day, 45zł); and Warsaw (11hr., 5 per day, 65zł). To reach the city center from the stations, take ul. Dworcowa, turn left onto ul. Armii Krajowej, the main thoroughfare, and continue to the town hall (15min.). **Private rooms** are the best lodging options, but avoid aggressive locals holding *"wolne pokoje"* signs at the train station; decent rooms can be arranged through the **IT tourist office**, ul. Dworcowa 1, just outside. (☎352 79 39; www.kolobrzeg.turystyka.pl. Open June-Aug. daily 7am-7pm; Sept.-May M-F 7am-3pm.) **Jadłodajnia Całoroczna ❷**, ul. Budowlana 28, is a delightful milk bar hidden off the main square. Try the daily *zestawy*. From the town hall, turn left on ul. Armii Krajowej, right on Budowlana, and pass under the arch; enter through the back. (Entrees 12-15zł. Open M-F 10am-7pm, Sa-Su 10am-5pm.) **Postal Code:** 78-100.

GDAŃSK ☎058

Gdańsk (pop. 481,000) has a strategic location at the mouth of the Wisła River, on the Baltic Coast, that has put it at the forefront of Polish history. As the free city of Danzig, it was the Polish gateway to the sea during years of occupation in the 18th and 19th centuries. In WWII, it was the site of the first casualties and of the Germans' last stand. In the early 1980s, it saw the birth of Lech Wałęsa's Solidarity trade union. Recently, reconstruction has restored the Hanseatic charm of the quayside old town, and efficient transport makes it a starting point to explore Sopot and Gdynia, which with Gdańsk form the Trójmiasto (Tri-City Area).

▐ TRANSPORTATION

Trains: Gdańsk Główny, ul. Podwale Grodzkie 1 (☎94 36). To: **Kołobrzeg** (2¾hr., 8 per day, 41zł); **Kraków** (7hr., 9 per day, 42zł); **Łódź** (8hr., 2 per day, 42zł); **Lublin** (8hr., 2 per day, 42zł); **Malbork** (50min., 36 per day, 15-30zł); **Poznań** (4½hr., 7 per day, 42-73zł); **Toruń** (3¼hr., 7 per day, 36zł); **Warsaw** (4hr., 18 per day, 46-79zł); **Wrocław** (6-7hr., 6 per day, 47-80zł). **SKM** (Fast City Trains; ☎628 57 78) run to **Gdynia** (35min.; 4zł, students 2zł) and **Sopot** (20min.; 2.80zł/1.40zł) every 10min. during the day and less frequently at night. Punch your ticket in a *kasownik* machine before boarding.

Buses: Ul. 3-go Maja 12 (☎302 15 32), behind the train station, connected by an underground passageway. To: **Kołobrzeg** (6hr., 1 per day, 47zł); **Kraków** (10¾hr., 1 per day, 65zł); **Łódź** (8hr., 4 per day, 44zł); **Malbork** (1hr., 8 per day, 9.40-13zł); **Toruń** (2½hr., 4 per day, 31zł); **Warsaw** (5¾hr., 7 per day, 55zł). Comfortable **Polski Express** buses run to **Warsaw** (4½hr., 2 per day, 45zł).

Ferries: Żegluga Gdańska (☎301 49 26; www.zegluga.gda.pl) runs summer ferries that depart from the Green Gate (Zielona Brama) for **Gdynia** (2hr.; 2 per day; 39zł, students 28zł) and **Sopot** (1hr.; 5 per day; 33zł, students 22zł). **DFDS Seaways,** ul. Sucharskiego 70 (☎340 50 00), sails to **Copenhagen** (17¼hr., 4 per week, 190-495zł).

Local Transportation: Gdańsk has an extensive **bus** and **tram** system. Transport 10min. 1.10zł; 30min. 2.20zł; 45min. 2.70zł; 1hr. 3.30zł; day pass 6.20zł. **Night buses** 30min. 3.30zł; night pass 5.50zł. Bags over 60cm need their own tickets.

Taxis: MPT (☎96 33; www.artusmpt.gda.pl) is a state-run taxi service.

✴ ▐ ORIENTATION AND PRACTICAL INFORMATION

While Gdańsk technically sits on the Baltic Coast, its center is 5km inland. Just blocks southeast of the **Gdańsk Główny** train and bus stations, the center borders **Wały Jagiellońskie** on the west, and the **Motława River** on the east. Take the under-

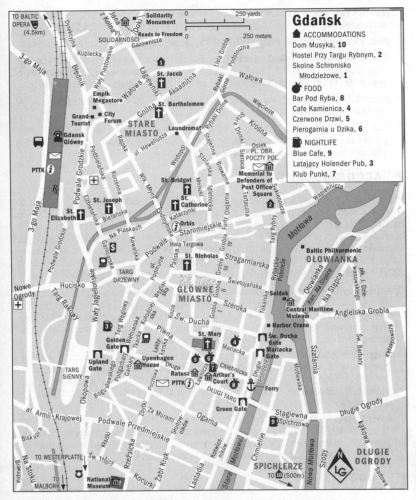

Gdańsk

🏠 ACCOMMODATIONS
Dom Musyka, **10**
Hostel Przy Targu Rybnym, **2**
Skolne Schronisko
  Młodzieżowe, **1**

🍴 FOOD
Bar Pod Ryba, **8**
Cafe Kamienica, **4**
Czerwone Drzwi, **5**
Pierogarnia u Dzika, **6**

🌙 NIGHTLIFE
Blue Cafe, **9**
Latajacy Holender Pub, **3**
Klub Punkt, **7**

pass in front of the station, go right, and turn left on **ul. Heweliusza.** Turn right on **ul. Rajska** and follow the signs to **Główne Miasto** (main town), turning left on **ul. Długa.** Długa becomes **Długi Targ** as it widens near the Motława. Gdańsk's suburbs all lie north of Główne Miasto.

Tourist Offices: PTTK Gdańsk, ul. Długa 45 (☎301 91 51; www.pttk-gdansk.com.pl), in Główne Miasto, has free maps. Tour guides (☎301 60 96) available daily May-Sept. 12:30pm. Open May-Sept. M-F 9am-6pm, Sa-Su 9am-3pm; Oct.-Apr. M-F 9am-6pm.

Budget Travel: Almatur, ul. Długi Targ 11, 2nd fl. (☎301 29 31; www.almatur.gda.pl), in Główne Miasto. Sells **ISIC** (52zł), offers hostel info, and books international air and ferry tickets. Open M-F 10am-5pm, Sa 10am-2pm.

Currency Exchange: Bank Pekao SA, ul. Garncarska 31 (☎801 365 365), cashes **traveler's checks** for 1% commission and provides MC/V **cash advances** for no commission. Open M-F 9am-5pm and the 1st and last Sa of each month 10am-2pm.

English-Language Bookstore: Empik, ul. Podwale Grodzkie 8 (☎301 62 88, ext. 115), sells maps and *Gdańsk in Your Pocket* (5zł). Open M-Sa 9am-9pm, Su 11am-8pm.

24hr. Pharmacy: Apteka Plus (☎763 10 74), at the train station. Ring bell at night.

Medical Assistance: Private doctors, ul. Podbielańska 16 (☎301 51 68). The sign reads "Lekarze Specjaliści." 50zł per visit. Open daily 7am-7pm. **Szpital Specjalistyczny im. M. Kopernika,** ul. Nowe Ogrody 5 (☎302 30 31), offers emergency care.

Internet Access: Jazz 'n' Java, ul. Tkacka 17/18 (☎305 36 16; www.cafe.jnj.pl), in the old town. 3zł per 30min., 5zł per hr. Open daily 10am-10pm.

Post Office: Ul. Długa 23/28 (☎301 88 53). Exchanges currency and has fax and telephone services. Open M-F 8am-8pm, Sa 9am-3pm. For *Poste Restante,* use the entrance on ul. Pocztowa. **Postal Code:** 80-801.

▐ ACCOMMODATIONS

With Gdańsk's limited tourist infrastructure and increasing popularity, it's best to reserve ahead, especially in summer. **University dorms** open to travelers in July and August; for further info consult **PTTK** (see above). Private rooms (20-80zł) can be arranged through either PTTK or **Grand-Tourist** (Biuro Podróży i Zakwaterowania), ul. Podwale Grodzkie 8, connected to the train station. (☎301 26 34; www.grand-tourist.pl. Singles 43-60zł; doubles 75-100zł; 2-person apartments 160-170zł; 3-person 220zł; 4-person 250zł. Open July-Aug. daily 8am-8pm; Sept.-June M-Sa 10am-6pm.)

▒ **Hostel Przy Targu Rybnym,** ul. Grodzka 21 (☎301 56 27; www.gdanskhostel.com). Off Targ Rybny, along the waterfront just south of Podwale Staromieskie and across from the *baszta* (tower). Guests arrive for a night and then stay for weeks to enjoy the common room and the free Internet, laundry, and bicycle and kayak use. Kitchen available. Reception 24hr. Dorms 40zł; doubles 120-140zł; quads 250zł. ❶

Skolne Schronisko Młodzieżowe (HI), ul. Wałowa 21 (☎301 23 13). From the train station, follow ul. Karmelicka, turn left on ul. Rajska, and then right on ul. Wałowa. Near the train station, with unusually spacious rooms, a full kitchen, common room, and lockers. No smoking or drinking. Reception 8am-10pm. Curfew midnight. Dorms 12-25zł; singles 25-30zł; doubles 50-60zł. ❶

Dom Musyka, ul. Łąkowa 1/2 (☎300 92 60; www.amuz.gda.pl). From the train station, take tram #8, 13, or 63 to Łąkowa; the hotel is on the corner with Podwale Przedmiejskie, behind the gate of the yellow building. Just a block across the Motława from the old town. Singles 120zł; doubles 180-200zł; suites 300zł. ❹

▐ FOOD

Gdańsk has a welter of options for excellent traditional food. For fresh produce, try **Hala Targowa** on ul. Panska, just off Podwale Staromiejskie. (Open M-F 9am-6pm, first and last Sa of each month 9am-3pm.)

▒ **Cafe Kamienica,** ul. Mariacka 37/39, in the shadow of St. Mary's Church. Try the superb *szarlotka* (apple pie) for 5zł. Tea 4zł. Coffee 5zł. Entrees 12-19zł. Open June-Sept. 9am-midnight; Oct.-May 10am-10pm. ❷

Pierogarnia u Dzika, ul. Piwna 59/60. Locals swear by these *pierogi* (10-20zł) stuffed with everything from soy to caviar. Open daily 10am-10pm. ❷

Bar Pod Ryba, Długi Targ 35/38/1. Stuffed baked potatoes and fish and chips. Entrees 6-15zł. Open daily July-Aug. 11am-10pm; Sept.-June 11am-7pm. AmEx/MC/V. ❶

Czerwone Drzwi, ul. Piwna 52. Elegant decor and a rotating menu with staples of herring and Baltic salmon. Entrees 17-32zł. Open daily noon-11pm. MC/V. ❸

⊙ SIGHTS

DŁUGI TARG. Długi Targ (Long Market) is the handsome square at the heart of **Główne Miasto** (main town). Gdańsk's row houses line the cobblestone ul. Mariacka, ul. Chlebnicka, and ul. Św. Ducha. The stone Upland Gate and the elegant blue-gray Golden Gate, emblazoned with gold leaf moldings and the shields of Poland, Prussia, and Germany, mark the entrance to ul. Długa. In the square proper, the **Fontanna Neptuna** (Neptune Fountain) faces the 16th-century facade of **Dwór Artusa** (Arthur's Court), a palace with a Renaissance interior and woodcarved spiral staircase that were restored in 1997. By the fountain, at the intersection of ul. Długa and Długi Targ, is the 14th-century **Ratusz** (Town Hall), which houses a branch of the **Gdańsk History Museum** (Muzeum Historii Gdań ska) containing exhibits on the city's past from its first historical mention to the rubble that overspread it after WWII. *(Court and museum open June-Sept. M 10am-3pm, Tu-Sa 10am-6pm, Su 11am-6pm; Oct.-May Tu-Sa 10am-4pm, Su 11am-4pm. Each branch 6zł, students 3zł; combined ticket 12zł/6zł. W free.)* A block toward the train station is Poland's largest brick church, the **Church of the Blessed Virgin Mary** (Kościół Najświętszej Marii Panny), which has an intricate 15th-century astronomical clock. Climb the steeple's 405 steps for a blessed vista. *(Open June-Aug. M-Sa 9am-5:30pm, Su 1-5:30pm; low-season hours vary. 3zł, students 1.50zł.)*

ELSEWHERE IN GŁÓWNE MIASTO. In the vaulted chambers of a former Franciscan monastery, the ☒**National Museum** (Muzeum Narodowe Gdańsku) has a large collection of 16th- to 20th-century art and furniture, including Hans Memling's *Last Judgment.* *(Signs lead from opposite the Town Hall down Lawnicza and Żabi Kruk, under Podwale Przedmiejskie, and to the right onto Toruńska. Open June to mid-Sept. Tu-F 9am-4pm, Sa-Su 10am-5pm; mid-Sept. to May Tu-Su 9am-4pm. 8zł, students 4zł.)* The **Memorial to the Defenders of the Post Office Square** (Obrońców Poczty) honors the postal workers who bravely defended themselves on September 1, 1939, at the start of WWII. *(From Podwale Staromiejskie, go north on Olejarna and turn right at the sign for Urząd Poctowy Gdańsk 1. Open M and W-F 10am-4pm, Sa-Su 10:30am-2pm. 3zł, students 2zł.)* Cobblestone ul. Mariacka, with Gdańsk's famous stone porch steps and gaping dragon'shead gutter-spouts, leads to riverside ul. Długie Pobrzeże. To the left is the huge **Gothic Harbor Crane** (Żuraw), part of **Central Maritime Museum** (Centralne Muzeum Morskie), which spans both banks of the Motława. The other two branches lie across the river: one on land, the other onboard the ship *Sołdek.* *(☎301 86 11. Open June-Aug. daily 10am-6pm; Sept.-May Tu-Su 9:30am-4pm. Crane 5zł, students 3zł. Museum 5zł/3zł. Sołdek 4zł/2.50zł. Shuttle boat round-trip 3zł/1.50zł. All museums and shuttle boat 12zł/7zł.)* The flags of Lech Wałęsa's trade union *Solidarność* (Solidarity), the Soviet bloc's first, fly high once again at the **Solidarity Monument,** on pl. Solidarności, north of the city center at the end of ul. Wały Piastowskie, and at the **Gdańsk Shipyard** (Stocznia Gdańska), where a permanent exhibit documents the movement's rise. *(Ul. Doki 1. ☎308 42 80. Open Tu-Su 10am-4pm. 5zł, students 3zł. W free.)*

WESTERPLATTE. When Germany attacked Poland on September 1, 1939, the little island fort guarding Gdańsk's harbor gained the unfortunate distinction of being the first target of WWII. Its defenders held out bravely for a week until lack of food and munitions forced them out—they were outnumbered 20 to one. **Guardhouse #1** has been converted into a museum. *(Take bus #106 or 606 south from the train station to the last stop. 20-25min., every 25-40min. Open daily May-Sept. 9am-6pm. 2zł, students 1.50zł.)* The path beyond the museum passes the bunker ruins and, farther up, the massive **Memorial to the Defenders of the Coast** (Pomnik Obrońców Wybrzeża). Giant letters below spell out "Nigdy Więcej Wojny" (No More War). On March 31, 1945, Westerplatte also became the site of the Germans' last resistance.

⚡ NIGHTLIFE

Długi Targ hums at night as crowds of all ages pack its pubs, clubs, and beer gardens. *City* magazine lists events and venues in the Tri-City area, and *Gdańsk in Your Pocket* has the latest club listings. Debaucherous, bohemian **Klub Punkt,** ul. Chlebnicka 2, stands apart from Gdańsk's other, tamer bars. (Beer 7zł. Open M-Th and Su 4pm-1am, F-Sa 4pm-3am.) Eclectically decorated ▓**Latający Holender Pub,** ul. Wały Jagiełłońskie 2/4, is toward the end of ul. Długa in the basement of the LOT building. (Beer 6zł. Coffee 4zł. Open daily noon-midnight.) **Blue Cafe,** ul. Chmielna 103/104, just across the first bridge at the end of Długi Targ, packs its dance floor nightly for hip-hop and R&B. (Beer 5-12zł. Open daily 11am-late.)

🔁 DAYTRIPS FROM GDAŃSK

MALBORK. Malbork (pop. 40,000) is home to the largest brick **castle** in the world, built by the Teutonic Knights in the 14th century. Spectacular collections of amber and weaponry lie inside. Turn right out of the station onto ul. Dworcowa, then left at the fork. Go around the corner to the roundabout and cross to ul. Kościuszki, then veer right on ul. Piasłowska and follow the signs for the castle. (☎055 647 08 00. Open May-Sept. Tu-Su 9am-7pm; Oct.-Apr. 9am-3pm. 23zł, students 14zł. Polish tour included. Courtyards, terraces, and moats open May-Sept. Tu-Su 9am-8pm; Oct.-Apr. 9am-4pm. 6zł, students 4zł. Kiosks sell English guide booklets (7zł). Call ahead for an English tour (150zł). Both **trains** (40min.-1hr., 36 per day; 9.80zł, express 15zł) and **buses** (1hr., 8 per day, 9.40-13zł) run from Gdańsk to Malbork.)

SOPOT. Sopot (pop. 50,000) is Poland's premier seaside spa town. The most popular golden sands lie at the end of **ulica Bohaterów Monte Cassino,** lined with cafes, pubs, and discos. (Beach M-F 2.50zł, Sa-Su 3.30zł.) The **SKM commuter rail** connects Sopot to Gdańsk (20min.; every 10-60min.; 2.80zł, students 1.40zł). Ul. Dworcowa begins at the station and leads to ul. Bohaterów Monte Cassino, which runs along the sea to the 512m pier (*molo*). **Ferries** (☎058 551 12 93) run from the end of the pier to Gdańsk (1hr.; 1 per day; round-trip 46zł, students 32zł) and Gdynia (35min., 4 per day, 45zł/34zł). **IT tourist office,** ul. Dworcowa 4, by the train station, sells maps (4-5zł) and arranges **rooms.** (☎058 550 37 83. Lodgings bureau open June to mid-Sept. daily 10am-5pm; mid-Sept. to May M-F 10am-3pm.)

GDYNIA. Prosperous Gdynia is Poland's major port. The highlight of the massive pier off Skwer Kościuzki is the destroyer **Błyskawica** (Lightning), where sailors lead tours on Polish naval history. (Open Tu-Su 10am-12:30pm and 2-4:30pm. 4zł, students 2zł.) The 1909 sailboat **Dar Pomorza** (Gift of Pomerania), once "the fastest and most beautiful ship of the seas," at one time took first honors at the Cutty Sark Tall Ships Race. (Open daily 9:30am-4pm. 5zł, students 3zł. June-Aug. Sa free.) At the end of the pier, the **Museum of Oceanography and Aquarium** (Muzeum Oceanograficzne i Akwarium Morskie) reels in children with reef sharks, anemones, and a model of the Baltic sea floor. (Open daily May-Aug. 9am-7pm; Sept.-Apr. 10am-5pm. 10zł, students 6zł.) The beach extends to the right of the pier. Gdynia's most intimate pub is ▓**Cafe Strych,** pl. Kaszubski 7B, at the end of ul. Jana z Kolna. (Live piano music Th-F and Su 7-10pm. Live rock M 7-10pm, Sa 7-11pm. Open June-Aug. daily 4pm-1am; Sept.-May Tu-Su noon-midnight.) SKM Commuter **trains** run every 10min. from platform #1 at Gdynia Główna (☎94 36) to Gdańsk (35min.; 4zł, students 2zł) and Sopot (15min., 2.80zł/1.40zł). **IT tourist office,** pl. Konstytucji 1, in the train station, has free maps. (☎058 628 54 66. Open May-Sept. M-F 8am-6pm, Sa 9am-4pm, Su 9am-3pm; Oct.-Apr. M-F 10am-5pm, Sa 10am-4pm.) All of the roads running away from the train station on your right lead toward the waterfront.

PORTUGAL

In the era of Christopher Columbus, Vasco da Gama, and Magellan, Portugal was one of the world's most powerful nations, ruling a wealthy empire that stretched from Africa to America to Asia. Today, it is often overshadowed by its larger neighbor Spain. But while it shares the beaches, nightlife, and strong architectural heritage of the Iberian Peninsula, Portugal is culturally and geographically unique. It contains some of the most pristine wilderness areas in all of Europe, and some villages in the northeast have not changed in over 800 years. Despite ongoing modernization, Portugal's rich, age-old traditions seem destined to stay—rows of olive trees surround ancient castles, and Porto's wines are as fine as ever.

 DISCOVER PORTUGAL: SUGGESTED ITINERARIES

THREE DAYS Make your way through **Lisbon's** (1 day; p. 837) famous Moorish district, the Alfama, up to the Castelo de São Jorge, and then to the Parque das Nações. Daytrip to **Sintra's** fairy-tale castles (1 day; p. 846) before sipping sweet wine in **Porto** (1 day; p. 852).

ONE WEEK After wandering the streets of **Lisbon** (2 days) and **Sintra** (1 day), lounge on the beaches of **Lagos** (1 day; p. 849) and admire the windswept cliffs of **Sagres** (1 day; p. 851). From there, move on to the university town of **Coimbra** (1 day; p. 847) before ending your week in **Porto** (1 day).

BEST OF PORTUGAL, TWO WEEKS After the sights, sounds, and cafes of **Lisbon** (2 days), daytrip to enchanting **Sintra** (1 day). Head down to the infamous beach-and-bar town **Lagos** (2 days), where hordes of visitors dance the night away, and take an afternoon in **Sagres,** once considered the edge of the world. Check out the macabre bone chapel in **Évora** (1 day; p. 849) and the impressive monastery in **Batalha** (1 day; p. 848). Head north to vibrant **Coimbra** (2 days) and **Porto** (2 days), then finish your tour in the impressive squares of **Viana do Castelo** (1 day; p. 854).

ESSENTIALS

WHEN TO GO
Summer is high season, but the southern coast draws tourists March through November. In the low season, many hostels cut their prices by 50% or more, and reservations are seldom necessary. But while Lisbon and some of the larger towns (especially Coimbra with its university) burst with vitality year-round, many smaller towns virtually shut down, and sights cut their hours nearly everywhere.

DOCUMENTS AND FORMALITIES

VISAS. EU citizens do not need a visa. Citizens of Australia, Canada, New Zealand, and the US do not need a visa for stays of up to 90 days, although this three-month period begins upon entry into any of the countries that belong to the EU's freedom of movement zone. For more information, see p. 17.

EMBASSIES. Most foreign embassies in Portugal are in Lisbon. For Portuguese embassies at home, contact: **Australia** and **New Zealand,** 23 Culgoa Circuit, O'Malley, ACT 2606; P.O. Box 9092, Deakin, ACT 2600 (☎612 6290 1733); **Canada,** 645 Island Park Dr., Ottawa, ON K1Y 0B8 (☎613-729-0883); **Ireland,** Knocksinna Mews,

7 Willow Park, Foxrock, Dublin 18
(☎289 4416); **UK,** 11 Belgrave Sq.,
London SWIX 8PP (☎0207 235 5331;
www.portembassy.gla.ac.uk/info/
embassy.html); **US,** 2125 Kalorama
Rd. NW, Washington, D.C. 20008
(☎202-328-8610).

TRANSPORTATION

BY PLANE. Most major international airlines serve Lisbon; some
serve Faro, the Madeiras, and Porto.
TAP Air Portugal (in US and Canada
☎800-221-7370, in UK 845 601 09 32,
in Lisbon 707 205 700; www.tap.pt)
is Portugal's national airline, serving
all domestic locations and many
major international cities. **Portugália**
(☎218 425 559, 60, 61, or 62;
www.pga.pt) is a smaller Portuguese
airline that flies between Faro, Lisbon, Porto, all major Spanish cities,
and other Western European destinations. For more information on
flying to Portugal, see p. 51.

**BY TRAIN. Caminhos de Ferro Portu-
gueses** (☎808 20 82 08; www.cp.pt) is
Portugal's national railway, and
serves Paris and Madrid as well as domestic destinations. For long-distance travel outside of the Braga-Porto-Coimbra-Lisbon line, however, the bus is better. The exception
is around Lisbon, where local trains are fast and efficient. Trains often leave at irregular hours, and posted schedules (*horarios*) aren't always accurate; check station
ticket booths upon arrival. Don't ride without a ticket; if caught, you'll be fined exorbitantly. Children under 12 and adults over 65 receive a 50% discount. **Youth discounts** are
only available to Portuguese citizens. Though there is a Portugal Flexipass, it is not
worth buying. For more information on getting to Portugal, see p. 57.

BY BUS. Buses are cheap, frequent, and connect just about every town in Portugal. **Rodoviária,** the national bus company, has been privatized. Each company
name corresponds to a particular region of the country, such as Rodoviária
Alentejo or Minho e Douro, with notable exceptions such as EVA in the Algarve.
Private regional companies also operate. Be wary of non-express buses in small
regions like Estremadura and Alentejo, which stop every few minutes. Express
coach service (*expressos*) between major cities is especially good; inexpensive
city buses often run to nearby villages. Portugal's main **Euroline** affiliates are Internorte, Intercentro, and Intersul. **Busabout** stops in Portugal at Lisbon and Lagos.

BY CAR. Portugal has the highest rate of automobile accidents per capita in Western Europe. The new highway system (IP) is quite good, but off the main arteries,
the narrow roads are difficult to negotiate. Speed limits are ignored, recklessness
is common, and lighting and road surfaces are often inadequate. Buses are safer
options. Portugal's national automobile association, the **Automóvel Clube de Portugal (ACP),** Shopping Center Amoreiras, Loja 1122 Lisbon (☎213 714 720), provides
breakdown and **towing service** and **first aid.**

BY THUMB. In Portugal, **hitchhikers** are rare. Rides are easiest to come by between smaller towns and at gas stations near highways and rest stops. *Let's Go* does not recommend hitchhiking.

TOURIST SERVICES AND MONEY

EMERGENCY	Police: ☎112. Ambulance: ☎112. Fire: ☎112.

TOURIST OFFICES. The official tourism website is www.portugalinsite.pt. When in Portugal, stop by municipal and provincial tourist offices for maps and advice.

MONEY. On January 1, 2002, the **euro (€)** replaced the **escudo** as the unit of currency in Portugal. For more information, see p. 20. As a general rule it's cheaper to exchange money in Portugal than at home. Expect to spend €40-60 per day. Modest **tipping** is customary in Portugal. Most restaurants include a 10% service charge. In nicer restaurants, waiters expect an additional 5-10%; in cheaper restaurants it is fine to round up and leave the change. It is customary to tip taxi drivers 10%. Retail goods in Portugal bear a 19% **Value Added Tax (VAT),** usually included within the listed price. Upon departure, non-EU citizens who have stayed in the EU fewer than 180 days can claim back the tax paid on purchases made at participating stores, provided the total amount spent at each store is over €59.36. Ask the shop where you have made the purchase to supply you with a tax return form. **Bargaining** is not customary in shops, but you can try it when looking for a room (*quarto*).

COMMUNICATION

PHONE CODES	Country code: 351. International dialing prefix: 00. From outside Portugal, dial int'l dialing prefix (see inside back cover) + 351 + city code + local number. Within Portugal, always dial city code + local number.

TELEPHONES. Portugal's national telephone company is **Portugal Telecom.** Pay phones are either coin-operated or require a phone card. The country uses the **Credifone** and Portugal Telecom systems. For both systems, the basic unit for all calls (and the price for local ones) is €0.10. Telecom phone cards, using "patch" chips, are most common in Lisbon and Porto and increasingly elsewhere. Credifone cards, with magnetic strips, are most useful outside these two big cities. City codes all begin with a 2. **Calling cards** probably remain the best method of making international calls. For information on using a **cell phone** in Portugal, see p. 35.

MAIL. From Portugal, **air mail** (*via aerea*) can take from one to two weeks (or longer) to reach the US or Canada. It is slightly quicker for Europe and longer for Australia and New Zealand. **Surface mail** (*superficie*), for packages only, takes up to two months. **Registered** or **blue mail** takes five to eight business days (for roughly 3 times the price of air mail). **EMS** or **Express Mail** will probably get there in three to four days for more than double the blue mail price. Mail to be held should be addressed as follows: SURNAME, First Name; Posta Restante; Post Office Street Address; City; Postal Code; PORTUGAL; PAR AVION.

INTERNET ACCESS. Cybercafes, listed in all cities and most towns, generally charge €1.20-4 per hour for Internet access. When in doubt, try the library, where there is often at least one computer equipped for Internet access.

LANGUAGE. Portuguese is the official language of Portugal. Although many residents speak English or French, the Portuguese appreciate it when travelers try to speak at least a few phrases of their language.

PORTUGAL

ACCOMMODATIONS AND CAMPING

PORTUGAL	❶	❷	❸	❹	❺
ACCOMMODATIONS	under €15	€15-25	€26-35	€36-45	over €45

Movijovem, Av. Duque de Ávila, 137, 1069-017 Lisbon (☎ 707 20 30 30; www.pousadasjuventude.pt), the Portuguese Hostelling International affiliate, oversees the country's HI hostels. All bookings can be made through them. A bed in a *pousada da juventude* (not to be confused with plush *pousadas*) costs €9-15 per night and slightly less in the low season (breakfast and sheets included). To reserve a bed in the high season, obtain an **International Booking Voucher** from Movijovem (or your country's HI affiliate) and send it from home to the desired hostel four to eight weeks in advance. In the low season (Oct.-Apr.), double-check to see if the hostel is open. **Hotels** in Portugal tend to be pricey. Room prices typically include breakfast and showers, and most rooms without bath or shower have a sink. When business is weak, try bargaining in advance. **Pensões**, also called **residencias**, are a budget traveler's mainstay. They're far cheaper than hotels and only slightly more expensive than youth hostels. During high season, many *pensões* do not take reservations, but for those that do, booking a week ahead is advisable. **Quartos** are rooms in private residences, similar to Spain's *casas particulares*. These rooms may be the only option in smaller towns or the cheapest one in bigger cities; tourist offices can help you. Portugal has over 150 **official campgrounds** (*parques de campismo*). Urban and coastal parks may require reservations. Police are strict about illegal camping. Tourist offices stock *Portugal: Camping and Caravan Sites*, a free guide to official campgrounds. Otherwise, write the **Federação de Campismo e Montanhismo de Portugal**, Av. Coronel Eduardo Galhardo, 24D, 1199-007 Lisbon (☎ 218 12 68 90; www.fpcampismo.pt).

FOOD AND DRINK

PORTUGAL	❶	❷	❸	❹	❺
FOOD	under €6	€6-10	€11-15	€16-25	over €25

Portuguese dishes are seasoned with olive oil, garlic, herbs, and sea salt, but few spices. The fish selection includes *choco grelhado* (grilled cuttlefish), *linguado grelhado* (grilled sole), and *peixe espada* (swordfish). Portugal's renowned *queijos* (cheeses) are made from the milk of cows, goats, and ewes. For dessert, try *pudim*, or *flan* (caramel custard). The hearty *almoço* (lunch) is eaten between noon and 2pm and *jantar* (dinner) is served between 9pm and midnight. *Meia dose* (half-portions) are often adequate; full portions may satisfy two. The *prato do dia* (special of the day) and the *ementa* (*menú*) of appetizer, bread, entree, and dessert are also filling choices. *Vinho do porto* (port) is a dessert in itself. Coffees include *bica* (black espresso), *galão* (with milk, served in a glass), and *café com leite* (with milk, in a cup).

HOLIDAYS AND FESTIVALS

Holidays: New Year's Day (Jan. 1); Good Friday (Mar. 25); Easter (Mar. 27); Easter Monday (Mar. 28); Liberation Day (Apr. 25); Labor Day (May 1); Corpus Christi (May 26); Portugal Day (June 10); Feast of the Assumption (Aug. 15); Republic Day (Oct. 5); All Saints' Day (Nov. 1); Restoration of Independence Day (Dec. 1); Feast of the Immaculate Conception (Dec. 8); Christmas (Dec. 25).

Festivals: All of Portugal celebrates *Carnaval* (Feb. 8) and Holy Week (Mar. 20-27). Coimbra holds the *Queima das Fitas* (Burning of the Ribbons) festival in early May, celebrating the end of the school year. In June, Batalha holds a *Feira International* celebrating the food, wine, and traditional handicrafts of the region, and Lisbon hosts the *Festas da Cidade,* honoring the birth of St. Anthony with music, games, and parades. For more information on Portuguese festivals, see www.portugal.org.

FACTS AND FIGURES: PORTUGAL

Official Name: Portuguese Republic.	**Land Area:** 92,000 sq. km.
Capital: Lisbon.	**Time Zone:** GMT.
Major Cities: Coimbra, Porto.	**Language:** Portuguese.
Population: 10,100,000.	**Religion:** Roman Catholic (94%).

LISBON (LISBOA) ☎21

Once the center of the world's richest and farthest-reaching empire, Lisbon (pop. 2,500,000) hit its peak at the end of the 15th century when Portuguese navigators pioneered explorations of Asia, Africa, and South America. Aching with *saudade* (nostalgia) for its past, the city works to preserve its rich history, continually renovating its monuments and meticulously maintaining its black-and-white mosaic sidewalks, pastel facades, and cobbled medieval alleys.

✈ INTERCITY TRANSPORTATION

Flights: Aeroporto de Lisboa (LIS; ☎841 3500). From the terminal, turn right and follow the path to the bus stop. Take bus #44 or 45 (20min., every 12-15min. 7am-9pm, €1) to Pr. dos Restauradores and Rossio. Or, take the express AeroBus #91 to the same locations (15min., every 20min. 7am-9pm, €1). A taxi from downtown costs €7.50 at low traffic hours. Trips are billed by time. Ask at the tourist office (☎845 0660) inside the airport about buying pre-paid vouchers for taxi rides from the airport. Major airlines have offices at Pr. Marquês de Pombal and along Av. da Liberdade.

Trains: Caminhos de Ferro Portugueses (☎800 20 09 04 for Lisbon connections, 808 20 82 08 elsewhere; www.cp.pt). 5 main stations, each serving different destinations.

Estação do Barreiro, across the Rio Tejo. Services southern destinations. Station accessible by ferry from the Terreiro do Paço dock off Pr. do Comércio. (Ferry ride 30min., every 30min., €1.30.) To **Évora** (2½hr., 6 por day, €12) and **Lagos** (5½hr., 5 per day, €12).

Estação Cais do Sodré (☎347 0181), just beyond the end of R. do Alecrim, 5min. from Baixa. M: Cais do Sodré. Take the metro or bus #1, 44, or 45 from Pr. dos Restauradores or bus #28 from Estação Santa Apolónia. To: the monastery in **Belém** (10min., every 15min., €1); **Cascais** and **Estoril** (30min., every 15min., €2); the youth hostel in **Oeiras** (20min., every 15min., €2).

Estação Oriente, in the Parque des Nações. M: Oriente. Services international destinations. To **Madrid** (14½hr., daily 6:10pm, €53-180) and **Porto** (14hr., 16 per day, €16-24).

Estação Rossio (☎346 5022). M: Rossio or Restauradores. Services western destinations. Information on ground level open daily 10am-1pm and 2-8pm. English spoken. To **Sintra** (45min., every 15-30min. 6am-2am, €1.30).

Estação Santa Apolónia (☎888 4025), Av. Infante Dom Henrique, runs the international, northern, and eastern lines. All trains to Santa Apolónia also stop at Estação Oriente (M: Oriente) by the Parque das Nações. To reach downtown, take bus #9, 39, 46, or 90 to Pr. dos Restauradores and Rossio. To: **Braga** (5hr., 19 per day, €25); **Coimbra** (2½hr., 23 per day, €15); **Madrid** (10hr., daily 10:05pm, €54); **Porto** (4½hr., 20 per day, €13.50).

Buses: Arco do Cego, Av. João Crisóstomo. M: Saldanha. Exit the metro onto Av. da República, walk 1 block up from Pr. Duque de Saldanha, and take a right onto Av. João Crisóstomo. The bus station is on the corner of Av. João Crisóstomo and Av. Defensores de Chaves. **Saldanha** buses (#36, 44, 45) stop in Pr. Duque de Saldanha (€0.60). **Rede Expressos** buses (☎707 22 33 44 or 213 58 14 70; www.rede-expressos.pt) go

PORTUGAL

Lisbon

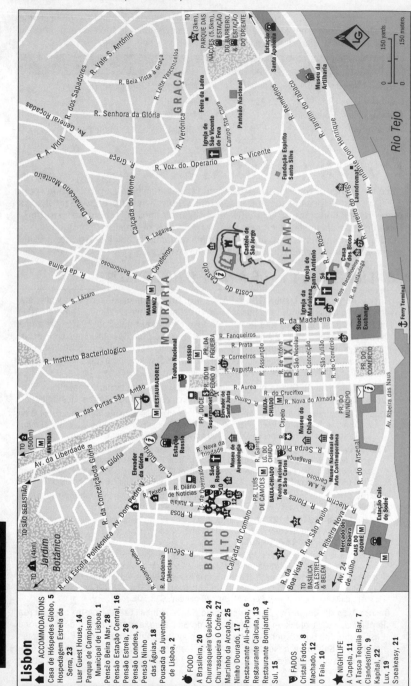

to: **Braga** (5hr., 13 per day, €15); **Coimbra** (2½hr., every 15min., €10); **Évora** (2hr., 26 per day, €10); **Faro** (5hr., 16 per day, €15); **Lagos** (5hr., 16 per day, €15); **Porto** (4hr., 19 per day, €14) via **Leiria** (2hr., €8).

ORIENTATION

The city center is made up of three neighborhoods: **Baixa** (low district), **Bairro Alto** (high district), and hilly **Alfama.** Other areas of interest, several kilometers from downtown, include **Belém** (p. 843), **Alcântara,** whose docks are home to much of Lisbon's party scene, and the **Parque das Nações,** the site of the 1998 World Expo. Baixa's grid of mostly pedestrian streets is bordered to the north by Rossio (a.k.a. Praça Dom Pedro IV). **Avenida da Liberdade** runs north, uphill from Pr. dos Restauradores. At Baixa's southern end is the **Praça do Comércio,** on the Rio Tejo (River Tagus). On the other side of Baixa is **Alfama,** Lisbon's labyrinthine oldest district. Across Baixa from Alfama is **Barrio Alto** and its upscale shopping district the **Chiado,** which is traversed by R. do Carmo and R. Garrett.

LOCAL TRANSPORTATION

Public Transportation: CARRIS (☎361 3000; www.carris.pt) runs **buses, trams,** and **funiculars** (each €1). If you plan to stay in Lisbon for any length of time, consider a *passe turístico,* good for unlimited travel on all CARRIS transports. 1-, 3-, 4-, and 7-day passes are sold in CARRIS booths located in most network train stations and the busier metro stations. (€2.35/€5.65/€9.95/€14.10.) The 4 lines of the **metro** (☎355 8457; www.metrolisboa.pt) cover downtown and the modern business district. Single ride €0.65; unlimited daily use ticket €1.40; book of 10 tickets €5.10; 1-week pass €4.80. Trains run daily 6:30am-1am, though some stations close earlier.

Taxis: Rádio Táxis de Lisboa (☎811 9000), **Autocoope** (☎793 2756), and **Teletáxis** (☎811 1100). Along Av. da Liberdade and Rossio. Luggage €1.50.

PRACTICAL INFORMATION

TOURIST, FINANCIAL, AND LOCAL SERVICES

Tourist Office: Palácio da Foz, Pr. dos Restauradores (☎346 3314). M: Restauradores. The largest tourist office. Open daily 9am-8pm. The **Welcome Center,** Pr. do Comércio (☎031 2810) is the city's main office. It sells the "Lisboa Card," which includes transportation and entrance to most sights (€13.25 for 24hr., €23 for 48hr., €28 for 72hr.; children €6/€9.10/€12). English spoken. Open daily 9am-8pm.

Embassies: Australia, Av. da Liberdade 200, 2nd fl., 1250-147 (☎310 1500; fax 310 1555; www.portugal.embassy.gov.au); **Canada,** Av. da Liberdade 196-200, 3rd fl., 1269-121 (☎316 4600; fax 316 4692); **Ireland,** R. da Imprensa à Estrela, 4th fl., Ste. 1, 1200 (☎392 9440; fax 397 7363); **New Zealand** (consulate), Av. Antonio Augusta de Aguia 122, 9th fl., 1097 (☎350 9690; fax 357 2004); **UK,** R. de São Bernardo 33, 1249-082 (☎392 4000; fax 392 4183); **US,** Av. das Forças Armadas, 1600-081 (☎727 3300; www.american-embassy.pt).

Currency Exchange: Banks are open M-F 8:30am-3pm. **Cota Câmbio,** Pr. Dom Pedro IV 41 (☎322 0480). Open M-Sa 9am-8pm. The main post office, most banks, and travel agencies also change money. Exchanges line the streets of Baixa. Fees can be high.

Laundromat: Lavandaria Clin, R. de São João da Praça 5-7 (☎886 6444), in Alfama. Wash, dry, and fold €4 per kg. Open M-F 8:30am-7:30pm, Sa 8am-3pm.

EMERGENCY AND COMMUNICATIONS

Police: R. Capelo 13 (☎346 6141 or 342 1634). English spoken.

Late-Night Pharmacy: Farmácia Azevedos, Pr. Dom Pedro IV 31 (☎343 0402).
Medical Services: Hospital Inglês, R. Saraiva de Carvalho 49 (☎395 5067). **Cruz Vermelha Portuguesa,** R. Duarte Galvão 54 (**ambulance** ☎942 1111 or 771 4000).
Internet Access: Web C@fé, R. Diário de Notícias 126 (☎342 1181). €2 per 15min., €2.50 per 30min., €3.50 per 45min., €4 per hr. Open daily 4pm-2am.
Post Office: Pr. dos Restauradores (☎328 8700; fax 323 8976). Open daily 8am-7pm. Often crowded. Central Lisbon has **Postal Code:** 1100.

⋒ ACCOMMODATIONS

Several hotels are in the center of town on **Avenida da Liberdade,** while many hostels are in **Baixa** along the **Rossio** and on **Rua da Prata, Rua dos Correeiros,** and **Rua Aurea.** Lodgings near the **Castelo de São Jorge** are quieter and closer to the sights. At night, be careful in Baixa, Bairro Alto, and Alfama; many streets are poorly lit.

BARRIO ALTO
▨ **Luar Guest House,** R. das Gáveas 101 (☎/fax 346 0909). Offers simple, clean rooms far enough from the nightlife to ensure a good night's sleep. Check-out 11:30am. Check-in from noon. Singles €15; doubles €20-30; triples €35; quads €40. ❷
▨ **Casa de Hóspedes Globo,** R. Teixeira 37 (☎/fax 346 2279), near Parque São Pedro de Alcântara. Popular with young travelers. Singles €15, with bath €22.50; doubles €25/€30; triples with bath €40; quads with bath €50; quints with bath €55. Cash only. ❷
Pensão Londres, R. Dom Pedro V 53, 2nd-5th fl. (☎346 2203; www.pensaolondres.com.pt), on the corner of R. da Rosa. High ceilings and marble bathrooms. Breakfast included. Singles €31, with bath €50; doubles €42/€70; triples with bath €84; quads with bath €94. Low season reduced prices. MC/V. ❸

BAIXA
Pensão Estação Central, Calçada da Carmo 17, 2nd-3rd fl. (☎342 3308). M: Rossio. Small, plain rooms are inexpensive and centrally located. Singles have shared bath. June-Sept. singles €20; doubles €35; triples €45. Low season €10 less. Cash only. ❷
Hospedagem Estrela da Serra, R. dos Fanqueiros 122, 4th fl. (☎887 4251), at the end of R. São Nicolau. Worth the 5-floor hike; half the rooms have terraces with a view of Baixa. June-Aug. singles €15-20; doubles €25-30. Sept.-May €5 less. Cash only. ❷

ALFAMA
Pensão Ninho das Águias, Costa do Castelo 74 (☎885 4070), behind the Castelo. Canary-filled garden looks out over the old city. Call ahead in the summer. Singles €25; doubles €42, with bath €45; triples €60. Low season reduced prices. Cash only. ❷
Pensão Beira Mar, R. Terreiro do Trigo 16 (☎887 1528). Some rooms with a view of the river. June-Aug. singles €15-20; doubles €30-40; quads €60. Oct.-May singles €10-15; doubles €20-30; quads €40. Bargain for lower prices in low season. Cash only. ❶
Pensão Estrela, R. dos Bacalhoeiros 8 (☎886 9506), in the lower part of Alfama. Breezy rooms look out on the square below. Check-out 11am. June-Sept. singles €20-25; doubles €40; 1 triple €60. Oct.-May singles €15; doubles €30-35; triple €45. ❷

ELSEWHERE AND CAMPING
Pousada da Juventude de Lisboa (HI), R. Andrade Corvo 46 (☎353 2696). M: Picoas. Call ahead for reservations. June-Sept. dorms €15; doubles with bath €42. Oct.-May dorms €12.50; doubles €35. HI members only. MC/V. ❷
Parque de Campismo Municipal de Lisboa (☎760 9620; fax 762 3106), on the road to Benfica. Take bus #14 to Parque Florestal Monsanto; campsite is at entrance to park. Pool and supermarket. Reception 9am-9pm. July-Aug. €4.80 per person, €5 per tent, €3.20 per car. Sept.-June prices vary, but generally run €3.20-3.70. ❶

◘ FOOD

Lisbon has some of the best wine and least expensive restaurants of any European capital. Dinner costs about €10 per person; the *prato do dia* (daily special) is often only €5. Head to the **Calçada de Sant'Ana** and **Rua dos Correeiros** to find restaurants that cater to locals. The city's culinary specialties include *amêjoas à bulhão pato* (steamed clams), *creme de mariscos* (seafood chowder), and *bacalhau cozido com grão e batatas* (cod with chickpeas and potatoes). For groceries, look for any **Pingo Doce** supermarket. (Most open M-Sa 8:30am-9pm. AmEx/MC/V.)

BARRIO ALTO

▩ **A Brasileira,** R. Garrett 120-122 (☎346 9541). A former stomping ground of early 20th-century poets and intellectuals (and their contemporary successors). Specialty is *bife à brasileira* (€11). Mixed drinks €5. Open daily 8am-2am. AmEx/MC/V. ❸

▩ **Sul,** R. do Norte 13 (☎/fax 346 2449). Dark wood paneling and candlelight give this restaurant and wine bar a romantic feel. Turns into a swank bar at 10pm. Entrees €12-16. Open Tu-Su noon-midnight. Kitchen open noon-7pm. Cash only. ❸

Restaurante Calcuta, R. do Norte 17 (☎342 8295), near Lg. Camões. Indian restaurant with a wide selection of vegetarian entrees (€5.50-6). Meat entrees €6.50-9. Open M-F noon-3pm and 7-11pm, Sa-Su 7-11pm. AmEx/MC/V. ❷

Restaurante Ali-a-Papa, R. da Atalaia 95 (☎347 4143). Serves generous helpings of traditional Moroccan food in a quiet atmosphere; dishes include couscous and tagine. Vegetarian-friendly. Entrees €9-11.50. Open M-Sa 7-11pm. AmEx/MC/V. ❸

BAIXA AND ALFAMA

▩ **Martinho da Arcada,** Pr. do Comércio 3 (☎887 9259). Lisbon's oldest restaurant (est. 1782), and a famed haunt of poet Fernando Pessoa. Adjacent cafe has lunch special (€4-5). Entrees €11-17. *Pratos do dia* €4. Open M-Sa 7am-10pm. AmEx/MC/V. ❸

▩ **Churrasqueira Gaúcha,** R. Bacalhoeiros 26C-D (☎887 0609), 1 block from the river toward Alfama, near Pr. do Comércio. Argentine-style *churrasco* (grilled meat) dishes. Entrees €7-10. Open M-Sa 9am-midnight. AmEx/MC/V. ❷

Churrasqueira O Cofre, R. dos Bacalhoeiros 2C-D (☎886 8935), near Pensão Estrela. A display case at the entrance shows everything available for grilling. Entrees €7-13. Open daily noon-11pm. Kitchen open noon-4pm and 7-11:30pm. AmEx/MC/V. ❸

Restaurante Bomjardim, Tv. Santo Antão 12, off Pr. dos Restauradores. Living up to its self-proclaimed title of *Rei da Brasa* (king of the grill), this eatery satiates customers with savory grilled meats (€8-11). Open daily noon-11:30pm. AmEx/MC/V. ❷

Ninho Dourado, R. Augusta 278. Pleasant outdoor seating, a huge menu, and decent prices (sandwiches €3-4, pizzas €7.50, entrees €8) make Ninho Dourado perfect for a dinner at sunset. Huge pitchers of beer €6. Open daily 10am-midnight. AmEx/MC/V. ❷

◎ SIGHTS

BAIXA

Though Baixa has few historic sights, the lively atmosphere and dramatic history surrounding its three main *praças* make Baixa a monument in its own right.

AROUND THE ROSSIO. Once a cattle market, the site of public executions, a bullring, and carnival ground, the Rossio (also known as the Praça Dom Pedro IV) is now the domain of tourists and ruthless local motorists who circle a statue of Dom Pedro IV. A statue of Gil Vicente, Portugal's first great dramatist, peers from the top of the **Teatro Nacional de Dona Maria II** at one end of the *praça*. Adjoining the Rossio is the elegant **Praça da Figueira,** which lies on the border of Alfama.

PORTUGAL

AROUND PRAÇA DOS RESTAURADORES. Just past the Rossio train station, an obelisk and a bronze sculpture of the "Spirit of Independence" commemorate Portugal's independence from Spain in 1640. Numerous shops line the *praça* and C. da Glória—the hill that leads to Barrio Alto. Pr. dos Restauradores also begins **Avenida da Liberdade,** Lisbon's most elegant promenade. This shady avenue ends at **Praça do Marquês de Pombal,** where a statue of the Marquês overlooks the city.

BAIRRO ALTO

In the Bairro Alto, the only place in Lisbon that never sleeps, pretentious intellectuals mix with idealistic university students. At the center of the neighborhood is **Praça Luís de Camões,** which adjoins **Largo do Chiado** at the top of R. Garrett. (To reach R. Garrett from the Rossio, take R. do Carmo uphill; it's the 1st street on the right.)

■ BASÍLICA DA ESTRELA. Directly across from the Jardim da Estrela, the Basílica da Estrela dates back to 1796. Its dome, behind a pair of tall belfries, towers over surrounding buildings and trees to take its place in the Lisbon skyline. Half-mad Dona Maria I, desiring a male heir, promised God anything and everything if she were granted a son. When a baby boy was finally born, she built this church, and admirers of beautiful architecture and ornate decor have been grateful ever since. (*Pr. da Estrela. Accessible by metro or tram #28 from Pr. do Comércio. ☎ 396 0915. Open daily 7:30am-1pm and 3-8pm. Free.*)

MUSEU DO CHIADO. The Museu do Chiado's collection features works from Portugal's most famous post-1850 artists, juxtaposing art from the Fascist era with pre- and post-Salazar works. The museum also showcases 19th- and 20th-century French art as well as famous contemporary artists. (*R. Serpa Pinto 4. ☎ 343 2148. Open Tu 2-6pm, W-Su 10am-6pm. €3, students and seniors €1.50, Su before 2pm free.*)

ALFAMA

Alfama, Lisbon's medieval quarter, was the lone neighborhood to survive the infamous 1755 earthquake. This charming labyrinth of *escandinhas* (narrow stairways), alleys, and unmarked streets is a challenge to navigate; be especially wary after nightfall and leave handbags in hostel lockers. Tram #28 leaves from Pr. do Comércio (€1) and winds through the neighborhood past most of its sights.

■ CASTELO DE SÃO JORGE. At the end of an uphill walk lies the Castelo de São Jorge, which offers superb views of Lisbon and the ocean. Built in the 5th century by the Visigoths and enlarged in the 9th century by the Moors, this castle was again improved and converted into a playground for the royal family between the 14th and 16th centuries; today, a lively village bustles within its walls. Wander around the ruins, soak in the views, explore the ponds, or gawk at the exotic birds in the gardens. (*☎ 882 3670. Castle open daily Apr.-Sept. 9am-9pm; Oct.-Mar. 9am-6pm. Free.*)

THE LOWER ALFAMA. Rua da Alfândeo, which begins two blocks away from Pr. do Comércio, connects Baixa and lower Alfama. Veer right when you see **Igreja da Madalena** in Lg. da Madalena. Take R. de Santo António da Sé and follow the tram tracks to the **Igreja de Santo António,** built in 1812 over the beloved saint's alleged birthplace. The construction was funded with money collected by the city's children. (*☎ 886 9145. Open daily 8am-7pm.*) In the square beyond the church is the 12th-century **Sé de Lisboa,** whose relic-filled treasury makes it worth a visit. (*☎ 886 6752. Open M 10am-5pm, Tu-Su 10am-6pm. Treasury open 10am-1pm and 2-5pm. €2.50.*)

GRAÇA

■ PANTEÃO NACIONAL. The building that is now the Panteão Nacional (National Pantheon) was originally meant to be the Igreja da Santa Engrácia; the citizens of Graça started building the church in 1680 to honor their patron saint. Their ambitions soon outstripped their finances and the building project was abandoned. The military regime led by General Salazar eventually took over construction, completing the project and dedicating it in 1966 as the Panteão Nacional, the burial ground for important statesmen. Ironically, when democracy was restored in 1975, the new government relocated the remains of prominent anti-Fascist opponents to this building and prohibited those that had worked with Salazar from entering. Today, the building houses the honorary tombs of explorers like Vasco da Gama, as well as the remains of Portuguese artists, including Amália Rodrigues, the queen of *fado*. *(To reach Graça and the Panteão, take the #12 bus or the #28 tram from the bottom of R. dos Correeiros. ☎885 4820. Open Tu-Su 10am-5pm. €2, children and seniors €1.)*

IGREJA DE SÃO VICENTE DE FORA. Built between 1582 and 1629, the Igreja is dedicated to Lisbon's patron saint. Ask the church attendant to see the sacristy with inlaid walls of Sintra marble. At the base of the center dome are geometrically confused walls. *(From the bottom of R. dos Correeiros in Baixa, take bus #12 or tram #28; €1. Open Tu-Sa 9am-6pm, Su 9am-12:30pm and 3-5pm. Free. Chapel next door €3.)*

SÃO SEBASTIÃO

Located north of Baixa, this area features a setting of busy avenues, department stores, and scores of stripmalls. São Sebastião, however, also houses two of the finest art museums in Portugal (both legacies of oil tycoon Calouste Gulbenkian).

■ MUSEU CALOUSTE GULBENKIAN. When oil tycoon Calouste Gulbenkian died in 1955, he left his extensive art collection to his beloved Portugal. Though the philanthropist was a British citizen of Armenian descent, it was Portugal he chose to call home. The collection is divided into sections of ancient art—Egyptian, Greek, Roman, Mesopotamian, Islamic, and Oriental—and European pieces from the 15th to 20th centuries. *(Av. Berna 45. M: São Sebastião. Exit the metro onto R. Testa and take a right when you reach El Corte Inglés. Follow the road until it ends and then take another right. Bus #18, 46, or 56. ☎782 3000; www.museum.gulbenkian.pt. Open Tu-Su 10am-6pm. €3, Sa free.)*

CENTRO DE ARTE MODERNA. Though not as famous as its neighbor the Museu Calouste Gulbenkian, this museum, also funded by Mr. Gulbenkian's foundation, houses an extensive modern collection dedicated to promoting Portuguese talent. Don't miss the sculpture gardens. *(R. Dr. Nicolau Bettencourt. M: São Sebastião. From the station, head downhill. Bus #16, 31, or 46. ☎795 0241. Open Tu-Su 10am-5pm. €3, Sa free.)*

BELÉM

Belém is more of a suburb than a neighborhood of Lisbon, but its concentration of monuments and museums makes it a crucial stop on any tour of the capital. To reach Belém, take tram #15 from Pr. do Comércio (15min.) or bus #28 or 43 from Pr. da Figueira (15min.) to the Mosteiro dos Jerónimos stop. Or, take the train from Estação Cais do Sodré (10min., every 15min., €1). From the train station, cross the tracks, then cross the street and go left. The Padrão dos Descobrimentos is to your left, while the Mosteiro dos Jerónimos is to your right.

■ MOSTEIRO DOS JERÓNIMOS. The Mosteiro dos Jerónimos was established in 1502 to give thanks for the success of Vasco da Gama's expedition to India. The monastery showcases Portugal's Manueline style, combining Gothic forms with Renaissance detail. On the main door of the church, to the right of the monastery entrance, Prince Henry the Navigator mingles with the Twelve Apostles. The symbolic tombs of Luís de Camões and Vasco da Gama lie in two opposing transepts. Inside the monastery, the octagonal cloisters of the courtyard surround rose gardens. *(☎362 0034. Open daily in summer 10am-6:30pm; in winter 10am-5pm. €4.50, students €2, Su 10am-2pm free. Cloisters open daily 10am-5pm. Free.)*

■**TORRE DE BELÉM.** The best known tower in all of Portugal, the Torre de Belém rises from the north bank of the Rio Tejo and is surrounded by the ocean on three sides. Built under Manuel I from 1515-1520 as a harbor fortress, it originally sat directly on the shoreline; today, due to the receding beach, it is only accessible by a small bridge. *(A 10min. walk along the water from the monastery away from Lisbon. Take the underpass by the gardens to cross the highway. ☎362 0034. Open daily in summer 10am-6:30pm; in winter 10am-5pm. €3, students and seniors €1.50.)*

■**PARQUE DAS NAÇÕES**

The Parque das Nações (Park of Nations) inhabits the former Expo '98 grounds. Until the mid-1990s, the area was a muddy wasteland with a few run-down factories and warehouses along the banks of the Tejo. However, the city transformed it to prepare for the 1998 World Exposition. After Expo '98, the government spent millions converting the grounds into the Parque das Nações. (To reach the park from Lisbon, take the metro to Oriente at the end of the red line. City buses #5, 10, 19, 21, 25, 28, 44, 50, 68, and 114, €1, all stop at the Oriente station. Parque ☎893 0601; www.parquedasnacoes.pt. Open daily 10am-midnight.)

■**OCEANÁRIO.** The enormous new aquarium is one of the largest oceanariums in Europe. Interactive sections showcase the four major oceans; every section connects to the main tank, which houses fish, sharks, and other sea creatures. Visitors can get within a meter of sea otters and penguins. The multilevel design allows for views of sea life from underneath the tank. *(☎891 7002; www.oceanario.pt. Open daily Apr.-Sept. 10am-7pm; Oct.-Mar. 10am-6pm. €9, under 12 €4.50, over 65 €5.)*

PAVILIONS. The numerous pavilions scattered around the park appeal to a variety of interests. The **Pavilhão do Conhecimento** (Pavilion of Knowledge) hosts an interactive science museum *(☎891 7100; www.paconhecimento.pt; open Tu-F 10am-6pm, Sa-Su 11am-7pm; €5, under 18 and over 65 €2.50)* while the **Virtual Reality Pavilion** holds a ride which challenges the senses. The **Atlantic Pavilion** hosts many of Lisbon's concerts and the **International Fairgrounds** accommodate rotating exhibits.

🎵 ENTERTAINMENT

Portuguese bullfighting differs from the Spanish variety in that the bull is not killed in the ring, a tradition that dates back to the 18th century. These spectacles take place most Thursdays from late June to late September at ■**Praça de Touros de Lisboa**, Campo Pequeno. (☎793 2143. Open daily 10pm-2am.) If you're interested in bullfighting, check out our **featured itinerary** for Spain and Portugal (p. 918).

Lisbon's trademark is **fado**, an art combining singing and narrative poetry that expresses sorrowful *saudade* (nostalgia). The Bairro Alto has many *fado* joints off R. da Misericórdia and on streets by the Igreja de São Roque, but the prices alone may turn a knife in your heart. All of the popular houses have high minimum consumption requirements (normally €15-20). To avoid these, explore nearby streets; various bars and small venues often offer free shows.

■ **O Faia,** R. Barroca 56 (☎342 6742; www.ofaia.com), between R. Atalaia and R. Diário de Notícias. O Faia offers performances by famous *fadistas* like Anita Guerreiro as well as excellent Portuguese cuisine. Minimum consumption €17.50, includes 2 drinks. Entrees €20-25. *Fado* at 9:30pm. Open M-Sa 8pm-2am. AmEx/MC/V. ❹

Machado, R. do Norte 91 (☎322 4640). Machado (est. 1937) is one of the larger *fado* restaurants and features some of the most well-known artists. Minimum consumption €16. Entrees €25-35. *Fado* at 9:15pm. Open Tu-Su 8pm-3am. AmEx/MC/V. ❺

Cristal Fados, Tv. da Queimada 9 (☎342 6787). Less famous singers and less luxurious meals mean you can have dinner without blowing your budget. Minimum consumption €8. Entrees €12. *Fado* Th-Su. Open daily 8:30pm-1am. AmEx/MC/V. ❸

▓ FESTIVALS

In June, the people of Lisbon spill into the city for a summer's worth of revelry. Open-air *feiras* (fairs)—smorgasbords of eating, drinking, live music, and dancing—fill the streets. On the night of June 12, the streets explode in song and dance in honor of St. Anthony during the **Festa de Santo António.** Banners are strung between streetlights, confetti falls like snow, and crowds pack the streets of Alfama. Lisbon also has a number of commercial *feiras*. From late May to early June, bookworms enjoy three weeks of the **Feira do Livro** in the Parque Eduardo VII. The **Feira Internacional de Lisboa** occurs every few months in the Parque das Nações. Year-round *feiras* include the **Feira de Oeiras** (antiques) on the fourth Sunday of every month and the **Feira de Carcanelos** (clothes; Th 8am-2pm). Packrats will enjoy the **Feira da Ladra** (flea market), held behind the Igreja de São Vicente de Fora in Graça (Tu and Sa 7am-3pm). To get there, take bus #104 or 105 or tram #28.

▓ NIGHTLIFE

Bairro Alto, where a plethora of small bars and clubs fills the side streets, is the first place to go for nightlife. **Rua do Norte, Rua do Diário Notícias,** and **Rua Atalaia** have many small clubs packed into three short blocks, making club-hopping as easy as crossing the street. Several gay and lesbian clubs are found between Pr. de Camões and Tv. da Queimada, as well as in the **Rato** area near the edge of Bairro Alto. **Avenida 24 de Julho** and **Rua das Janelas Verdes** have some of the most popular bars and clubs. Newer hot spots include the area along the river across from the **Santa Apolónia** train station. Crowds flow in around 2am and stay until dawn.

▓ **A Tasca Tequila Bar,** Tv. da Queimada 13-15 (☎343 3431). This classy Mexican bar is the perfect stopover between dinner and the louder bars and clubs. Specialty shots €3. Mixed drinks €5. Open daily 6pm-2am.

▓ **Speakeasy,** Docas de St. Amaro (☎395 77308). M: Santos or Alcântara. Lisbon's premier jazz and blues center. Beer €3. Open M-Sa 9pm-4am. AmEx/MC/V.

Lux, Av. Infante D. Henrique A (☎882 0890). Take a taxi to the area across from the St. Apolónia train station. In a class of its own, Lux is one of the hottest spots in Lisbon. Beer €1.50-2.50. Minimum consumption €10. Open Tu-Sa 6pm-6am. AmEx/MC/V.

Clandestino, R. da Barroca 99 (☎397 2341). Catering to a younger crowd, this cavernous bar stands out with messages scrawled by former patrons on its rock walls. Beer €2. Mixed drinks €4-5. Open Tu-Su 10pm-3am. AmEx/MC/V.

A Capela, R. Atalaia 45. A spacious bar with gold walls and red velvet cushions. Popular in the late hours. Beer €3. Mixed drinks €5. Open daily 9pm-2am. MC/V.

Kapital, Av. 24 de Julho 68. The most refined club in Lisbon. Admission is a competitive sport. 3 floors. Cover €15. Mixed drinks €5-8. Open M-Sa 11pm-6am. AmEx/MC/V.

▓ DAYTRIPS FROM LISBON

ESTORIL AND CASCAIS

Trains from Lisbon's Estação Cais do Sodré (☎213 42 48 93; M: Cais do Sodré) run to Estoril (30min., every 20min. 5:30am-2:30am, €1.30) continuing to Cascais. Cascais is also a pleasant 20min. walk from Estoril; take a right onto the walkway at Praia Estoril Tamariz and walk along the coast. Stagecoach bus #418 to Sintra leaves Estoril from Av. Marginal, in front of the train station (35min., 1 per hr. 6:10am-11:40pm, €2.50). From Cascais, take Stagecoach bus #417 to Sintra; it leaves from outside the train station (40min., 1 per hr. 6:35am-7:08pm, €2.80).

Glorious beaches draw sun-loving tourists and locals alike to Estoril (pop. 24,000) and neighboring Cascais (pop. 33,000). In balmy weather, Cascais's beaches, especially **Praia da Ribeira, Praia da Rainha,** and **Praia da Duquesa,** are filled with tanners. To reach Praia da Ribeira from the tourist office, take a right and walk down Av. dos Combatentes de Grande Guerra until you see the water. Praia da Rainha and the large Praia da Duquesa are a short walk out of town towards Estoril. For the beach-weary, the marvelous (and air-conditioned) ▧**Casino Estoril,** one of Europe's largest casinos, is a welcome relief. The casino, in Pr. José Teodoro dos Santos directly across from Estoril's train station, is well worth a visit even for non-gamblers. Every Wednesday at 11:30pm in the Wonder-Bar, a *fado* concert features some of Portugal's most acclaimed singers. Reserve at least a day in advance. (☎214 66 77 00; www.casino-estoril.pt. Dress code: no sneakers, jeans, shorts, swimwear, or hats anywhere in the casino; jackets required for the game room, with tie during the winter. Can be borrowed at the entrance if you leave an ID. 18+ to gamble; passport required for game room. Open daily 3pm-3am.)

Estoril's **tourist office,** on Arcadas do Parque, is across the street from its train station and to the left of the park. (☎214 66 38 13; www.estorilcoast.com. Multilingual staff. Wheelchair accessible. Luggage storage. Open in summer M-Sa 9am-8pm, Su 10am-6pm; in winter M-Sa 9am-7pm, Su 10am-6pm.) To get to Cascais's **tourist office,** Av. dos Combatentes de Grande Guerra 25, exit the train station through the ticket office, cross Lg. da Estaçaõ, and take a right at McDonald's onto Av. Valbom; the office is at the end of the street. (☎214 86 82 04. Multilingual staff. Luggage storage. Open in summer M-Sa 9am-8pm, Su 10am-6pm; in winter M-Sa 9am-7pm, Su 10am-6pm.) A block away from the tourist office, you'll find free **bicycle rentals;** exit the office, turn right, and at the beach you'll see a big stand of bicycles. (Rentals with ID for 1 day only. Open daily 8am-10pm.)

SINTRA

Trains (☎ 219 23 26 05) arrive at Av. Dr. Miguel Bombarda from Lisbon's Estação Rossio and Estação Sete Rios (45min., every 15min. 5am-1am, €1.30). Stagecoach buses (☎ 214 83 20 55) leave from Av. Dr. Miguel Bombarda for Cascais (#417; 40min., 1 per hr. 7:13am-8:23pm; €3) and Estoril (#418; 40min., 1 per hr. 6:50am-midnight; €3).

With fairy-tale castles, enchanting gardens, and spectacular mountain vistas, Sintra (pop. 20,000) is a favorite among backpackers. Overlooking the old town, the ▧**Castelo dos Mouros** provides stunning views of the mountains and coast. Follow the blue signs 3km up the mountain (1-1½hr.) or take bus #434 (15min., every 30min., day pass €3.50), which runs to the top from the tourist office. (Open June-Sept. 9am-7pm; Oct.-May 9:30am-5pm. €3.50, seniors and children €1.50.) A mix of architectural styles, the **Palácio Nacional de Sintra,** in Pr. da República, was once the summer residence of Moorish sultans. (☎219 10 68 40. Open M-Tu and Th-Su 10am-5:30pm. €3, seniors and students €1.50, Su before 2pm free.) Farther uphill is the ▧**Palácio da Pena,** a Bavarian castle decorated with Arabic minarets, Gothic turrets, Manueline windows, and a Renaissance dome. (Open June-Sept. Tu-Su 9am-7pm; Oct.-June Tu-Su 9:30am-6pm. €6, seniors and students €4.)

Tourist offices are located in Pr. da República 23 (☎219 23 11 57) and in the train station (☎219 24 16 23). Both are staffed with English, French, and Spanish speakers. (Both open daily June-Sept. 9am-8pm; Oct.-May 9am-7pm.) ▧**Casa Adelaide ❷,** R. Guilherme G. Fernandes 11, offers well-kept rooms. (☎219 23 08 73. English spoken. Singles and doubles €25; triples and quads €35. €5-10 less in the winter. Cash only.) Restaurants crowd **Rua João de Deus** and **Avenida Heliodoro Salgado.**

CENTRAL PORTUGAL

Jagged cliffs and whitewashed fishing villages line the Costa de Prata of Estremadura, with beaches that rival even those in the Algarve. In the fertile region of the Ribatejo (banks of the Rio Tejo), lush greenery surrounds historic sights.

COIMBRA   ☎239

Despite its small size, Coimbra (pop. 200,000) has cosmopolitan charm. Home to the country's only university from the mid-16th to the early 20th century, vibrant Coimbra continues to attract backpackers and youth from around the world.

TRANSPORTATION AND PRACTICAL INFORMATION. Trains (☎808 20 82 08) from other regions stop only at Estação Coimbra-B (Velha), 3km northwest of town, while regional trains stop at both Coimbra-B and Estação Coimbra-A (Nova), two blocks from the lower town center. A train connects the two stations, departing after trains arrive (4min., €0.70). Trains run to Lisbon (3hr., 22 per day, €8.50-9.50) and Porto (2hr., 30 per day, €5.60-6.40). **Buses** (☎82 70 81) go from the end of Av. Fernão de Magalhães, 15min. past Coimbra-A, to Lisbon (2½hr., 25 per day, €9.40) and Porto (1½hr., 17 per day, €9). From the bus station, turn right, follow the avenue to Coimbra-A, then walk to Largo Portagem to reach the **tourist office.** The multilingual staff distributes maps and provides short-term **luggage storage.** (☎85 59 30. Open June-Sept. M-F 9am-7pm, Sa-Su 10am-1pm and 2:30-5:30pm; Oct.-May M-F 9am-6pm, Sa-Su 10am-1pm and 2:30-5:30pm.) **Espaço Internet,** Pr. 8 de Maio, offers free **Internet** access but requires a same-day sign up in advance. (Open M-F 10am-8pm, Sa-Su 10am-10pm.) **Postal Code:** 3000.

ACCOMMODATIONS AND FOOD. The friendly owners and excellent view of the square make **Pensão Santa Cruz ❷,** Pr. 8 de Maio 21, 3rd fl., the best deal in town. (☎/fax 82 61 97. Singles and doubles €20, with bath €30; triples €25/€40. Reduced prices in low season. Cash only.) The **Pousada da Juventude de Coimbra ❶,** R. Henrique Seco 14, has a kitchen and a TV room. (☎82 59 55. Dorms €11; doubles with bath €30.) **Residência Solar Navarro ❶,** Av. Emídio Navarro 60-A, 2nd fl., offers simple rooms with bath and TV; some have balconies and views of the park. (☎82 79 99. Reception 24hr. Singles €12.50; doubles €25; triples €38; 2 enormous rooms with 5 beds each €60. Cash only.) The best cuisine in Coimbra lies off Pr. 8 de Maio around **Rua Direita,** on the side streets between the river and Largo Portagem, and around **Praça República** in the university district. **Restaurante Barca Serrana ❷,** R. Direita 46, is a popular lunch spot. (☎82 06 16. Open M-F 9:30am-10:30pm, Sa 9:30am-3:30pm. Cash only.) **Supermercado Minipreço** is located at R. António Granjo 6C. (Open M-Sa 8:30am-8pm, Su 9am-1pm and 3-7pm.)

SIGHTS AND ENTERTAINMENT. Take in the sights in the **old town** by taking the narrow stone steps from the river to the university. Begin your ascent at the **Arco de Almedina,** a remnant of the Moorish town wall, one block uphill from Lg. da Portagem. The 12th-century Romanesque **Sé Velha** (Old Cathedral) is at the top. (Open M-Th 10am-noon and 2-7:30pm, F-Su 10am-1pm. Cloister €0.75.) Follow signs to the late 16th-century **Sé Nova** (New Cathedral), built by the Jesuits (open Tu-Sa 9am-noon and 2-6:30pm; free), just a few blocks from the 16th-century **University of Coimbra.** The **Porta Férrea** (Iron Gate), off R. São Pedro, opens onto the old university, whose buildings once constituted Portugal's royal palace. (Open daily May-Sept. 9am-7:30pm; Oct.-Apr. 9:30am-12:30pm and 2-5:30pm.) The stairs to the right lead to the **Sala dos Capelos,** which houses portraits of Portugal's

FADO, WITHOUT THE HEARTBREAK

Those in search of good *fado* in Portugal have often found that the pain they feel in their hearts comes not from the songs' melancholy lyrics, but from the steep minimum consumption requirements at typical *casas de fado*. Fortunately for those on a budget, Coimbra hosts *Noites de Fado de Coimbra*, a yearly *fado* festival with free weekly concerts from mid-July to August. Every Saturday at 9:30pm, either the Pátio do Castilho or the Galeria Almedina holds *fado* concerts which showcase Coimbra's unique version of the Portuguese art.

In contrast to Lisboan *fadistas*, Coimbra's *fado* artists are exclusively male—a tradition dating back to the days when the Universidade de Coimbra was open only to men. Unlike the tales of heartbreak and woe sung in Lisbon, the songs of the male groups of Coimbra lament the hard lives led by university students. Though Coimbra's version of *fado* is not as well-known as that of the capital, it is the hope of the city that through festivals such as *Noites de Fado*, Coimbra's artists will receive the international reknown they deserve.

For more information, inquire at the tourist office, Lg. da Portagem. (☎239 85 59 30. Open June-Sept. M-F 9am-7pm, Sa-Su 10am-1pm and 2:30-5:30pm; Oct.-May M-F 9am-6pm, Sa-Su 10am-1pm and 2:30-5:30pm.)

kings. (Open daily 9:30am-12:30pm and 2-5:30pm. €2.50.) The **Capela de São Miguel** (university chapel), adorned with *talha dourada* (gilded wood) carvings, and the 18th-century **Biblioteca Joanina** (university library) lie past the clock tower. (Open daily May-Sept. 9am-7:30pm; Oct.-Apr. 9:30am-noon and 2-5:30pm. €2.50, students free. Ticket to all university sights €4; buy tickets in the main quad.)

Nightlife in Coimbra gets highest honors. ▨**Bar Quebra Costas**, R. Quebra Costas, blasts jazz and funk. (☎821 661. Beer €1-3. Mixed drinks €4-5. Open daily noon-4am. AmEx/MC/V.) The recently renovated **Pitchclub**, Lg. da Sé Velha 4-8, is one of Coimbra's newest dance spots. (☎83 81 64. Beer €1. Mixed drinks €2.50. Open June-Sept. 15 M-Sa 11am-4am; Sept. 16-May M-Sa 9pm-4am. AmEx/MC/V.) In early May, university graduates burn the narrow ribbons they got as first-years and get wide ones in return during Coimbra's **Queima das Fitas.**

LEIRIA ☎244

Capital of the surrounding district and an important transport hub, Leiria (pop. 120,000) fans out from a fertile valley, 22km from the coast. The city's most notable sight is its **Castelo de Leiria**, a granite fort that Dom Afonso Henriques built atop the crest of a hill after he snatched the town from the Moors. (Castle open Tu-Su 10am-6pm, Torre closes at 5pm. €2.14; students, children, and seniors €1.07.)

Leiria makes a practical base for exploring the nearby region. **Trains** (☎88 20 27) run from the station 3km outside town to Coimbra (2hr., 7 per day, €3.60) and Lisbon (1¾hr., 10 per day, €7.60-8.50). **Buses** (☎81 15 07), just off Pr. Paulo VI, next to the main park, run to: Batalha (20min., 9 per day, €1.30); Coimbra (1hr., 11 per day, €6.50); Lisbon (2hr., 13 per day, €7.80); and Porto (3½hr., 10 per day, €10.20). Buses also run between the train station and the **tourist office** (15min., daily 1 per hr. 7am-7:20pm, €0.80), in the Jardim Luís de Camões. (☎84 87 70. Open daily May-Sept. 10am-1pm and 3-7pm; Oct.-Apr. 10am-1pm and 2-6pm.) **Residencial Dom Dinis ❷**, Tr. Tomar 2, has rooms with large bathtubs, phones, and cable TV. (☎81 53 42. Singles €21; doubles €33; triples €42. AmEx/MC/V.) **Postal Code:** 2400.

BATALHA ☎244

The centerpiece of Batalha (pop. 75,000) is the ▨**Mosteiro de Santa Maria da Vitória.** Built in 1386, the Gothic and Manueline complex remains one of Portugal's greatest monuments. (Open daily Apr.-Sept. 9am-6pm; Oct.-Mar. 9am-5pm. €4.50, under 25 and seniors €2.25, under 14 and Su before 2pm free.) **Buses** run from across from the monastery to: Leiria (20min., 16 per day, €1.50) and Lisbon (2hr., 5 per day, €7). The **tourist office**, in Pr. Mouzinho de Albuquerque, is opposite the monastery. (☎76 51 80. Open daily May-Sept. 10am-1pm and 3-7pm; Oct.-Apr. 10am-1pm and 2-6pm.) Travelers to Batalha should stay in Leiria. **Postal Code:** 2440.

ÉVORA   ☎266

Évora (pop. 55,000) is the capital and largest city of the Alentejo region. Attached to the pleasant **Igreja Real de São Francisco**, the bizarre ▓**Capela dos Ossos** (Chapel of Bones) was built by three Franciscan monks out of the bones of 5000 people. From Pr. Giraldo, follow R. República; the church is around back to the right. (Open Apr.-Oct. M-Sa 9am-1pm and 2:30-6pm, Su 10am-1pm; Oct.-Apr. M-Sa 9am-1pm and 2:30-5:30pm, Su 10am-1pm. €1.) According to legend, the second-century **Templo Romano**, on Largo Conde do Vila Flor, was built for the goddess Diana. Facing the temple is the **Igreja de São João Evangelista**, whose interior is covered with tiles. (Open Su and Tu-Sa 10am-12:30pm and 2-6pm. €2.50.) From Pr. Giraldo, head up R. 5 de Outubro to the colossal 12th-century **cathedral**. The **Museu de Arte Sacra**, above the nave, houses religious artifacts. (Cathedral open daily 9am-noon and 2-5pm. Cloisters open daily 9am-noon and 2-4:30pm. Museum open Su and Tu-Sa 9am-12:30pm and 2-4:30pm. Cathedral free. Cloisters and museum €3.)

Trains (☎74 23 36) run from Av.' dos Combatentes de Grande Guerra to Lisbon (2½hr., 5 per day, €8.15). **Buses** (☎76 94 10; www.rede-expressos.pt) go from Av. São Sebastião to Faro (5hr., 4 per day, €12) and Lisbon (3hr., every 1-1½hr., €8.80). The **tourist office** is at Pr. Giraldo 73. (☎73 00 33. Open Apr.-Oct. M-F 9am-7pm, Sa-Su 9am-5:30pm; Nov.-Mar. M-F 9am-6pm.) Free **Internet** access is available at **Instituto Português da Juventude**, R. da República 105. (Open M-F 9am-10pm.) *Pensões* cluster around **Praça do Giraldo**. Take a right out of the tourist office and then the first right onto R. Bernardo Mato to get to cozy **Casa Palma ❷**, R. Bernardo Matos 29A. (☎70 35 60. Singles €20-25; doubles €30-35.) Budget restaurants cluster near Pr. Giraldo, particularly along **Rua Mercadores**. ▓**Restaurante Burgo Velho ❷**, R. de Burgos 10, serves large portions of local dishes. (☎22 58 58. Entrees €5-9. Open M-Sa noon-3pm and 7-10pm. AmEx/MC/V.) **Postal Code:** 7999.

ALGARVE

Nearly 3000 hours of sunshine per year have transformed the Algarve, a desert on the sea, into a popular vacation spot. In July and August, sun-seeking tourists mob the resorts, packing the bars and discos from sunset until way past dawn. In the low season, the resorts become pleasantly de-populated.

LAGOS   ☎282

As the town's countless international expats will attest, Lagos (pop. 17,500) is a black hole: come for two days and you'll stay for two months. Lagos keeps you soaking in the view from the cliffs, the sun on the beach, and the drinks at the bars.

▓▓ **TRANSPORTATION AND PRACTICAL INFORMATION. Trains** (☎79 23 61) run from across the river to Évora (5-5½hr., 3 per day, €16) and Lisbon (3½-4½hr., 5-6 per day, €16). The EVA bus station (☎76 29 44), off Av. dos Descobrimentos, is across the channel from the train station. **Buses** run to Faro (2½hr., 6 per day, €4); Lisbon (5hr., 6 per day, €15); and Sagres (1hr., 16 per day, €3). Running along the channel, **Avenida dos Descobrimentos** is the main road that carries traffic to and from Lagos. From the train station, walk through the marina and cross the suspension bridge; turn left onto Av. Descobrimentos. From the bus station, walk straight until Av. Descobrimentos, then turn right; after 15m, take another right onto R. Porta de Portugal to reach **Praça Gil Eanes,** the center of the old town. The local **tourist office** is on Largo Marquês de Pombal, up from R. Lima Leitão, which extends from Pr. Gil Eanes. (☎76 41 11. Open July-Aug. M-Sa 10am-8pm; June and Sept. M-Sa 10am-8pm; Oct.-May M-F 10am-6pm.) Use the **Internet** at **The Em@il Box (Caixa de Correio),** R. Cândido dos Reis 112. (☎76 89 50. €1.25 per 15min., €3.50 per hr. Open M-F 9:30am-8pm, Sa-Su 10am-3pm.) **Postal Code:** 8600.

⌧ ACCOMMODATIONS AND FOOD. In the summertime, *pensões* and the youth hostel fill up quickly; reserve more than a week in advance. If full, the youth hostel will happily refer you to a *quarto* near the hostel for about the same price. Locals renting rooms in their homes will probably greet you at the station. Though these rooms are often inconveniently located, at €10-15 per person in summer, they are often the best deals. ▨**Pousada da Juventude de Lagos (HI) ❷,** R. Lançarote de Freitas 50, features a kitchen, common room, and Internet access. (☎76 19 70; www.hostalbooking.com. In summer, book through the central Movijovem office ☎213 59 60 00. June 16-Sept. 15 dorms €15; doubles with bath €45. Sept. 16-June 15 dorms €10; doubles with bath €28. MC/V.) **Olinda Teresa Maria Quartos ❸,** R. Lançarote de Freitas 37, lets dorms and doubles with shared bath. Guests have access to a kitchen, common room, and terrace. (☎08 23 29. June 16-Sept. 15 dorms €15; doubles €24. Sept. 16-June 15 dorms €10; doubles €30.) Peruse multi-lingual menus around **Praça Gil Eanes** and **Rua 25 de Abril.** Hordes of backpackers enjoy €4.50-7.50 meals at ▨**Casa Rosa ❷,** Tv. Ferrador 22. (☎968 37 71 15. Many vegetarian options. Open daily 6pm-midnight.) **Mediterraneo ❸,** R. Senhora da Graça 2, serves delicious Mediterranean and Thai cuisine. (☎76 84 76. Entrees €7.50-9. Open Tu-Sa 6:30-10:30pm.) The **market** is on Av. Descobrimentos, 5min. from the town center. (Open Sa.) **Supermercado São Toque,** R. Portas de Portugal 61, is near the post office. (☎76 28 55. Open M-F 9am-7:30pm, Sa 9am-7pm.)

◧ SIGHTS AND BEACHES. Though sunbathing and non-stop debauchery have long erased memories of Lagos's rugged, seafaring past, it's worth taking some time away from the beach or bars to visit the city's sights. The **Forte da Ponta da Bandeira,** a 17th-century fortress which holds maritime exhibitions, overlooks the marina. (☎76 14 10. Open Tu-Sa 10am-1pm and 2-6pm, Su 10am-1pm. €2, students €1, under 13 free.) Also on the waterfront is the old **Mercado dos Escravos** (slave market), where the first sale of African slaves in Portugal took place in 1441. Opposite the Mercado dos Escravos is the gilded **Igreja de Santo António,** which houses a museum filled with artifacts from several ruling powers in Lagos. (Church and museum open Tu-Su 9:30am-12:30pm and 2-5pm. Church free. Museum €2.) For a lazier day, head to one of Lagos's many beaches. Smooth sands can be found at the 4km-long **Meia Praia,** across the river from town. Hop on the 30-second ferry near Pr. Infante Dom Henrique (€0.50 each way). To find less-crowded beaches, caves, and beautiful cliffs, follow Av. Descobrimentos toward Sagres to **Praia de Pinhão** (20min.). A bit farther, **Praia Dona Ana** features the sculpted cliffs and grottoes that grace the majority of Algarve postcards.

If you're up for more than lounging on the beach, Lagos offers a wide variety of outdoor sports—from scuba diving, to surfing, to (booze) cruising. Companies offering tours of the coastal cliffs and grottoes (caves) line Av. dos Descobrimentos. Most tours last 45min. and begin at €25 for two people. **Surf Experience,** R. dos Ferreiros 21, offers one- or two-week surfing trips including lessons, transportation, and accommodations in Lagos. All levels are welcome. (☎76 19 43; www.surf-experience.com. Apr.-Nov. 1 week €424; 2 weeks €727. Dec.-Mar. 1 week €378; 2 weeks €682. Board and wet suit rental 1 week €75; 2 weeks €114.) The extremely popular **Booze Cruise** offers swimming, snorkeling, tours of the nearby grottoes, a live DJ, and, of course, cheap drinks. (☎963 01 26 92. Cruises on M, W, and Sa. €15. For tickets, call or purchase at the youth hostel.)

☑ NIGHTLIFE. As the sun sets on Lagos, there is a mass exodus of beachgoers to the streets. The cafes in the area between **Praça Gil Eanes** and **Praça Luis de Camões** fill quickly. For late-night bars and clubs, try **Rua Cândido dos Reis** and **Rua do Ferrador,** as well as the intersection of **Rua 25 de Abril, Rua Silva Lopes,** and **Rua Soeiro da Costa.** Backpackers, expats, and rugby enthusiasts mingle with the amicable staff at **Taverna Velha,** R. Lançarote de Freitas 34. (☎76 92 31. Beer €1.25-2.50. Mixed drinks €3.50-4. Open M-Sa 4pm-2am, Su 8pm-2am.) Around midnight, Brits and Aussies flood **The Red Eye,** R. Cândido dos Reis 63, in search of classic rock, cheap liquor, and casual games of pool. (Happy Hour 8-10pm. Free shot with first drink. Beer €3. Mixed drinks €3-4. Shots €2.50-3. Open daily 8pm-2am.) **Metro Bar,** R. Lançarote de Freitas 30, boasts a stylish cosmopolitan atmosphere enhanced by acid jazz mixes. (Beer €1.75. Mixed drinks €2.25-3. Open daily 7pm-2am.)

SAGRES ☎282

Marooned atop a desert plateau at the most southwestern point in Europe, desolate Sagres (pop. 2500) and its cape were once considered the edge of the world. Near the town stands the ☑**Fortaleza de Sagres,** the fortress where Prince Henry stroked his beard, decided to map the world, and founded his famous school of navigation. (Open May-Sept. 10am-8:30pm; Oct.-Apr. 10am-6:30pm. Closed May 1 and Dec. 25. €3, under 25 €1.50.) Six kilometers west lies the dramatic **Cabo de São Vicente,** where the second-most powerful lighthouse in Europe shines over 100km out to sea. To get there on weekdays, take the bus from the bus station on R. Comandante Matos near the tourist office (10min.; 11:15am, 12:30, 4:15pm; €1). Alternatively, hike 1hr. past the fortresses perched atop the cliffs. The most notable **beach** in the area is **Mareta,** at the bottom of the road leading from the town center. The nearby coves of **Salema** and **Luz** are intimate and picturesque. At night, a young crowd fills **Água Salgada,** on R. Comandante Matoso, 75m beyond the tourist office, away from the fortress. (☎62 42 97. Beer €1-2. Mixed drinks €4.50. Open June-Aug. daily 10am-4am; Sept.-May closed Tu.) Next door is **O Dromedário,** where a request-taking DJ keeps the party bumping. By day, O Dromedário serves tasty crepes. (☎62 42 97. Crepes €2.20-4. Beer €1-2. Mixed drinks €3.50-5. Open M-Th and Su 10am-2am, F-Sa 10am-4am.)

EVA **buses** (☎76 29 44) run from Lagos (1hr., 17 per day, €3). From July to September, buses also run to Lisbon (daily 4pm, €15). The **tourist office,** on R. Comandante Matoso, is up the street from the bus stop. (☎62 48 73. Open Tu-Sa 9:30am-1pm and 2-5:30pm.) Finding a bed in Sagres is not hard; windows everywhere display multilingual signs for rooms, many in boarding houses with guest kitchens. Follow R. Comandante Matoso toward the tourist office and take a left on R. Patrão António Faustino to reach ☑**Atalaia Apartamentos ❷,** which features beautiful, fully furnished rooms with bath, TV, and refrigerator. Apartments for rent have bath, kitchen, living room, and terrace. (☎62 46 81. Rooms: July-Sept. doubles €40, Oct.-June doubles €25. Apartments: July-Sept. €50 for 2 people, €70-80 for 4 people; Apr.-June €30/€50-60; Oct.-Mar. €25/€40-50.) For groceries, try **Alisuper,** on R. Comandante Matoso. (☎62 44 87. Open daily 9am-8pm). **Postal Code:** 8650.

FARO ☎289

The Algarve's capital, largest city, and transportation hub, Faro (pop. 55,000) is untouristed despite its charm. Its **Cidade Velha** (old town) is a medley of museums, shops, and churches. On Largo do Carmo is the **Igreja de Nossa Senhora do Carmo** and its **Capela dos Ossos** (Chapel of Bones), built from the remains of monks originally buried in the church's former cemetery. (☎82 44 90. Open May-Sept. daily 10am-1pm and 3-6pm; Oct.-Apr. M-F 10am-1pm and 3-5pm, Sa 10am-1pm. Chapel €0.75. Church free.) To get to Faro's **beach,** take bus #16 from the bus station or the stop in front of the tourist office. (5-10min.; 5 per day, return 9 per day; €1.)

Trains (☎82 64 72) run from Largo Estação to Évora (4½-6hr., 2-4 per day, €11) and Lagos (2hr., 9 per day, €14). EVA **buses** (☎89 97 00) go from Av. República to Lagos (1½hr., 8 per day, €4.30). Renex (☎81 29 80), across the street, sends buses to Porto (7½hr., 6-13 per day, €22) via Lisbon (4hr., 12-15 per day, €17). From the stations, turn right down Av. República and left past the garden to reach the **tourist office,** R. da Misericórdia 8. (☎80 36 04. Open daily May-Sept. 9:30am-7pm; Oct.-Apr. 9:30am-5:30pm.) **Pousada da Juventude (HI) ❶** is on R. Polícia de Segurança Pública. (☎82 65 21. Breakfast included. Dorms €10; doubles €24, with bath €30. Low season reduced prices. AmEx/MC/V.) Stock up at **Minipreço,** Lg. Terreiro do Bispo 8-10. (☎80 77 34. Open M-Sa 9am-8pm.) **Postal Code:** 8000.

NORTHERN PORTUGAL

The unspoiled Costa da Prata (Silver Coast), plush greenery of the interior, and rugged peaks of the Serra Estrela comprise the Three Beiras region. Beyond trellised vineyards, *azulejo*-lined houses grace charming streets.

PORTO (OPORTO)   ☎22

Porto (pop. 264,200) is famous for its namesake product—a strong, sugary wine. Developed by English merchants in the early 18th century, the port industry is at the root of the city's successful economy. The city retains traditional charm with granite church towers, orange-tiled houses, and graceful bridges.

◧⑦ TRANSPORTATION AND PRACTICAL INFORMATION. Most **trains** pass through Porto's main station, **Estação Campanhã** (☎536 4141), on R. da Estação. Trains run to: Coimbra (2hr., 14 per day, €7.50-12); Lisbon (3½-4½hr., 14 per day, €15-23); and Madrid, Spain (13-14hr., daily 6:10pm, €60). **Estação São Bento** (☎200 2722), Pr. Almeida Garrett, located one block off Pr. Liberdade, is the terminus for trains with local and regional routes. Internorte (☎605 2420), Pr. Galiza 96, sends **buses** to Madrid, Spain (10½hr.; Tu, Th, Sa 9am; €34) and other international cities. Rede Expresso buses (☎205 2459), R. Alexandre Herculano 366, travel to Coimbra (1½hr., 11 per day, €7.50) and Lisbon (4hr., 12 per day, €14). REDM (☎200 3152), R. Dr. Alfredo Magalhães 94, two blocks from Pr. República, sends buses to Braga (1hr., 9-26 per day, €3.30). Renex (☎200 3395), Campo Mártires da Pátria, has express service to Lagos (8½hr., 6 per day, €18) via Lisbon. Buy tickets for the **intracity buses** and **trams** from small kiosks around the city or at the **STCP** office, Pr. de Almeida Garrett 27, across the street from Estação São Bento (pre-purchased single ticket €0.55, day-pass purchased onboard €2.10). The **tourist office,** R. Clube dos Fenianos 25, is off Pr. da Liberdade. (☎339 3472. Open July-Sept. M-F 9am-7pm, Sa-Su 9:30am-6:30pm; Oct.-June M-F 9am-5:30pm, Sa-Su 9:30am-4:30pm.) **Portweb,** Pr. Gen. Humberto Delgado 291, offers **Internet** access. (€1.20 per hr. Open M-Sa 10am-2am, Su 3pm-2am.) **Postal Code:** 4000.

☊⏏ ACCOMMODATIONS AND FOOD. For good accommodation deals, look west of **Avenida dos Aliados** or on **Rua Fernandes Tomás** and **Rua Formosa.** ▧**Pensão Duas Nações ❶,** Pr. Guilherme Gomes Fernandes 59, offers a variety of rooms at low rates. (☎208 9621. Reserve ahead. Singles €13.50, with bath €22.50; doubles

€22.50/€30; triples €33/€40; quads €44/€48.) From the tourist office, climb the hill past the Igreja de Trinidade and turn left on the second street to reach **Hospedaria Luar ❷**, R. Alferes Malheiro 133, which offers spacious rooms with private bath and cable TV. (☎208 7845. Singles €20-25; doubles €25-30. Discounts available for extended stays. Cash only.) Look near the river in the **Ribeira** district for restaurants. The **⬛Majestic Café ❷**, R. de Santa Catarina 112, is the oldest, most famous cafe in Porto. (Open M-Sa 9:30am-midnight. AmEx/MC/V.) The **Mercado de Bolhão** has a huge selection of fresh food, including bread, cheese, produce, and meat. (Open M-F 8:30am-5pm, Sa 8:30am-1pm.)

⬛ 🎵 SIGHTS AND ENTERTAINMENT. Your first brush with Porto's rich stock of fine artwork may be the celebrated collection of *azulejos* in the **São Bento train station.** Walk past the station and uphill on Av. Afonso Henriques to reach Porto's Romanesque **cathedral.** (☎205 9028. Open M-Sa 9am-12:30pm and 2:30-6pm, Su 2:30-6pm. Cloister €1.25.) From the station, follow signs on R. Mouzinho da Silveira to R. Ferreira Borges and the **⬛Palácio da Bolsa** (Stock Exchange), the epitome of 19th-century elegance. The most striking room of the *Palácio* is the opulent **Sala Árabe** (Arabian Hall). Its gold and silver walls are covered with the oddly juxtaposed inscriptions "Glory to Allah" and "Glory to Dona Maria II." (☎339 9000. Open daily Apr.-Oct. 9am-7pm; Nov.-Mar. 9am-1pm and 2-6pm. €5, students €3.) Next door, the Gothic **Igreja de São Francisco** has an elaborately gilded wooden interior. The neighboring museum houses religious art and artifacts. (☎206 2100. Open daily 9am-6pm. €3, students €1.50.) Up R. dos Clérigos from Pr. Liberdade rises the **Torre dos Clérigos** (Tower of Clerics), adjacent to the 18th-century **Igreja dos Clérigos**, which is adorned with Baroque carvings. (☎200 1729. Tower open daily Sept.-July 10am-noon and 2-5pm; Aug. 9:30am-1pm and 2:30-7pm. €1.50. Church open M-Th 10am-noon and 2-5pm, Sa 10am-noon and 2-8pm, Su 10am-1pm. Free.) From there, head up R. da Restauração, turn right on R. Alberto Gouveia, and go left on R. Dom Manuel II to reach the **Museu Nacional de Soares dos Reis**, R. Dom Manuel II 44. This former royal residence now houses an exhaustive collection of 19th-century Portuguese art. (☎339 3770. Open Tu 2-6pm, W-Su 10am-6pm. €3, seniors and students €1.50, Su before 2pm free.)

BRAGA
☎ 253

Braga (pop. 166,000) originally served as the capital of a region founded by Celtic tribes in 300 BC; it later became the seat of Portugal's archbishops. The city's

PORT TASTING: A CRASH COURSE

We know what drew you to Porto, and you won't be fully satisfied until you've crossed the river into the Vila Nova da Gaia district and visited at least one of the city's celebrated port lodges. Fortunately for your wallet, most offer tours (and tastings) for only a few euros. If you want to look like a pro, keep in mind the characteristics that are used to judge port: smell, taste, and appearance.

Begin by taking a quick whiff of the wine. Don't linger too long over the glass; your nose quickly becomes used to smells, which hinders your ability to distinguish subtle aromas. Once you've gathered your impressions, take a generous sip of the port. Because different parts of your tongue are wired to detect different flavors (sweet, salty, bitter, sour), be sure that there is enough wine to stimulate each area. Lastly, hold your glass, 1/3 full, at a 45° angle against a white background; the color shows up truest near the rim. Vintage ports, which are the finest, vary from dark purple to brown, eventually fading to orange. Tawny ports, which gain their reddish-brown color from the wooden casks in which they are aged, fade to a tawny orange. For more info, go to www.taylor.pt.

Taylor's, R. do Choupelo 250, offers free tours (every 20-30min.) and tastings. (☎223 74 28 00. Open Aug. M-Sa 10am-6pm; Sept.-July M-F 10am-6pm. Last tour at 5pm. AmEx/MC/V.)

beautiful gardens, plazas, and museums have earned it the nickname "Portuguese Rome." In Portugal's oldest **cathedral**, the treasury showcases precious paintings and relics. (☎26 33 17. Open daily June-Aug. 8:30am-6:30pm; Sept.-May 8:30am-5pm. Cathedral free. Treasury and chapels €2.) Braga's most famous landmark, **Igreja do Bom Jesús**, is 5km outside of town. To visit Bom Jesús, take the bus labeled "#02 Bom Jesús" (€1.10) from in front of Farmácia Cristal, Av. da Liberdade 571. At the site, either take the 285m ride on the funicular (8am-8pm, €1) or walk 20-25min. up the path that leads to a 365-step staircase.

To reach the train station, **Estação da Braga** (☎808 20 82 08), take R. do Souto and pass through the town gate; the station is 400m on the left. **Trains** run to Lisbon via Porto and Coimbra (4hr., 3 per day, €25) and Vigo, Spain (4hr., 2 per day, €12.25). **Buses** (☎61 60 80) leave Central de Camionagem for: Coimbra (3hr., 6-9 per day, €10); Faro (12-15hr., 3-6 per day, €20); Guimarães (1hr., every 30min., €2.15); Lisbon (5¼hr., 10-11 per day, €15); and Porto (1¼hr.; M-F every 30min., Sa-Su 5-7 per day; €4). The **tourist office** is on Av. da Liberdade 1. (☎26 25 50. Open June-Sept. M-F 9am-7pm, Sa-Su 9am-12:30pm and 2-5:30pm; Oct.-May M-Sa 9am-12:30pm and 2-5:30pm.) ◪**Pensão Grande Residência Avenida ❷**, Av. da Liberdade 738, 2nd fl., has handsome rooms. (☎60 90 20. July-Aug. singles €25, with bath €40; doubles €35/€45; triples €45/€52. Low season reduced prices. MC/V.) Numerous cafes can be found on **Praça da República**. The **market** sets up in Pr. do Comércio. (Open M-Sa 7am-3pm.) **Postal Code:** 4700.

GUIMARÃES
☎253

Guimarães (pop. 60,000) is home to one of Portugal's most gorgeous palatial estates, the ◪**Paço dos Duques de Bragança** (Ducal Palace), which is modeled after the manor houses of northern Europe. (☎41 22 73. Open daily 9:30am-12:30pm and 2-5:30pm. €3, ages 15-25 and seniors €1.50, Su mornings free.) Guimarães is best reached by **bus** from Braga. REDM buses (☎51 62 29) run frequently between the cities (40min., 13-19 per day, €2.15). The **tourist office**, Alameda de São Dâmaso 83, distributes maps. (☎41 24 50. English spoken. Open M-F 9:30am-12:30pm and 2-6:30pm.) Travelers to Guimarães should stay in Braga. **Postal Code:** 4800.

VIANA DO CASTELO
☎258

Viana do Castelo (pop. 37,000) is one of the loveliest coastal cities in all of Portugal. Though visited mainly as a beach resort, Viana also has a lively historic district centered around the **Praça da República**. Here, granite columns support the facade of the **Igreja da Misericórdia**, known for its *azulejo* interior. (Open daily 9:30am-12:30pm and 2-5:30pm. Free.) The ◪**Monte de Santa Luzia**, overlooking the city, is crowned by Celtic ruins and the **Templo de Santa Luzia**, an early 20th-century neo-Byzantine church. (Templo open daily in summer 8am-7pm; in winter 8am-5pm. Free.) The view from the hill is fantastic; either brave the hundreds of stairs (20-30min.) or take a taxi (€5) to the top. Viana do Castelo features excellent beaches.

Trains (☎82 13 15) run from the station, at the top of Av. dos Combatentes da Grande Guerra, to Porto (2hr., 13-14 per day, €5.50) and Vigo, Spain (2½hr., 2 per day, €8.15). **Buses** (☎82 50 47) run from the **Central de Camionagem** on the eastern edge of town to: Braga (1½hr., 4-9 per day, €3.15); Lisbon (5½hr., 2-3 per day, €14); and Porto (2hr., 9-11 per day, €5). The **tourist office**, Trav. do Hospital Velho 9, has maps and accommodation listings. (☎82 26 20. Open M-F 9am-12:30pm and 2:30-6pm, Sa 9:30am-1pm and 2:30-6pm, Su 9:30am-1pm.) For accommodation and restaurants, try the streets off Av. dos Combatentes da Grande Guerra. A 15min. walk from the town center, you'll find ◪**Pousada de Juventude de Viana do Castelo (HI) ❶**, R. de Límia, off R. da Argaçosa and Pr. da Galiza; its balconies have great views. (☎80 02 60. Breakfast included. Check-out 10:30am. Mid-June to mid-Sept.

dorms €13; doubles with bath €35. Mid-Sept. to mid-June dorms €10; doubles with bath €28.) Buy groceries at **Estacão Supermercado** in the basement of the mall next to the train station. (Open daily 9am-11pm.) **Postal Code:** 4900.

PARQUE NATURAL DE DOURO INTERNACIONAL

While the name may be a mouthful, the phenomenal views that Parque Natural de Douro Internacional offers will leave you speechless. Designated in May 1998, the park covers 85,150 hectares on the border of Portugal and Spain and is home to several endangered species. Flowering almond trees soften the rough terrain, and favorite pastimes among locals include trout fishing and hunting partridge and hare. Several hikes leave from the town of Miranda do Douro to neighboring *pueblos*. Before heading out, consult the park's **information office** in Miranda do Douro, on Rua do Convento, which offers advice about hiking in the park and sells topographic maps (€0.50) outlining the trails. From the tourist office in Miranda do Douro, take Av. Aranda del Duero, which becomes Rua da Alfandega and Rua da Trinidade. Turn left when you reach the *Biblioteca Municipal;* the office will be immediately on your left. (☎273 43 14 57; www.pndi.pt. Open M-F 9am-12:30pm and 2-5:30pm.) Trails are well maintained and well marked with two horizontal yellow and red lines. To begin a day hike from the tourist office, take Rua 25 de Abril and follow the trail when you reach the end of the road after 5-10min.

MIRANDA DO DOURO   ☎273

Perched precariously atop a cliff overlooking the Rio Douro, Miranda do Douro (pop. 4500) attracts visitors primarily for its convenient access to the natural park. In the northern corner of the park, the town provides an excellent base for exploring the undisturbed beauty of eastern Portugal. Miranda do Douro provides a refreshing respite from surrounding urban centers, as well as an opportunity to explore the villages and trails of the natural park. The town's main attraction is its 16th-century **cathedral.** (Open Tu-Su 10am-12:30pm and 2-6pm. Free).

Rodonorte runs **buses** to Miranda do Douro from Bragança (1½hr.; M-F 11am and 5pm, return to Bragança M-F 6:40am and 1:30pm; €5.20). The Miranda do Douro bus stop is located just off of the central rotary, Lg. de Moagem. (Ticket office open daily 8am-7:30pm.) The **tourist office** is across the street from the bus stop. (☎43 11 32. Open Sept.-June M-Sa 10am-12:30pm and 2-5:30pm; July-Aug. M-Sa 9am-12:30pm and 2-7pm.) For luxury at a bargain, head to **Hospedaria Flor do Douro ❷**, Rua do Mercado 7. From the tourist office, approach the rotary from the left and turn left onto Rua do Mercado. The big rooms have TV and bath. (☎43 11 86. Breakfast included. Singles €15; doubles €30.) The quiet **campsite ❶** has trails leading to several neighboring villages. From the rotary, head downhill on Rua D. Dinia, keeping the castle ruins on your left. Take a sharp right just before the next rotary, cross the stone bridge, veer left at the fork in the road, and turn right as the road becomes a dirt path. (☎43 12 73. Open June-Sept. €1.50 per person, under 10 €0.75; €2-3 per tent; €2 per car. Electricity €2.) **Postal Code:** 5210.

ROMANIA (ROMÂNIA)

Devastated by the lengthy reign of Nicolae Ceauşescu, Romania today suffers from a sluggish economy. Some are eager to Westernize while others try to reclaim an ancestral way of life in the countryside. The resulting state of flux, combined with a partly undeserved reputation for poverty and crime, has discouraged many foreigners from visiting. But travelers who dismiss Romania do themselves an injustice. An upbeat candidate for accession to the EU, it is a country rich in history, rustic beauty, and hospitality, not to mention host to the colorful frescoes of the Bucovina monasteries and to Dracula's castle.

DISCOVER ROMANIA: SUGGESTED ITINERARIES

THREE DAYS Start in **Bucharest** (2 days; p. 860). Try to wrap your eyes around the world's second-largest edifice, the **Parliamentary Palace,** or relive the Revolution at **Piaţă Revoluţiei,** where Ceauşescu delivered his final speech. Nineteenth-century Bucharest comes to life near Str. Lipscani and Str. Gabroveni. Spend your last day touring Dracula's castle in **Bran** (p. 866).

ONE WEEK After visiting **Bucharest** (4 days), head north to **Braşov** (2 days; p. 865), a picturesque town with paths and cable cars leading into the Transylvanian mountains. End the week with the famed castle in **Bran** (1 day).

THREE WEEKS Pass the first week in **Bucharest** before stopping in **Sinaia** (2 days; p. 864), once an alpine getaway for Romanian royalty and home to Peleş Castle. Compare that with the castle in **Bran** (1 day), a daytrip from **Braşov** (2 days). **Sibiu** (3 days; p. 866), Transylvania's ancient capital, is midway from there to **Timişoara** (3 days; p. 867), where the most recent revolution began in 1989. In **Cluj-Napoca** (3 days; p. 865) the student culture enlivens a city otherwise pacified by cathedrals, churches, and gardens. Make a pilgrimage to the **Bucovina monasteries** as daytrips from **Gura Humorului** (3 days; p. 868). End near the former capital of Moldavia, **Suceava** (1 day; p. 869), in the white monastery founded by Ştefan cel Mare in **Putna** (p. 869).

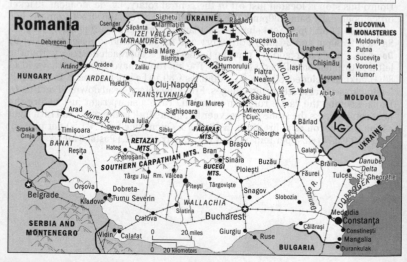

ESSENTIALS

WHEN TO GO

Romania has one of the harsher European climates. Summer heat and humidity can cause discomfort; winters can be very snowy, rainy and cold. Spring and fall are milder, and may prove a better time climate-wise. Bucharest temperatures have reached as low as –32°C (–26°F) in January, and as high as 41°C (106°F) in August. Along the Black Sea Coast the climate is less severe year-round.

DOCUMENTS AND FORMALITIES

VISAS. Citizens of Canada, Ireland, the UK, and the US do not need visas for stays of up to 90 days. Citizens of Australia and New Zealand need visas. **Visa extensions** are available at police headquarters in large cities or at Bucharest's passport office, Str. Luigi Cazzavillan 11. Apply early to allow the bureaucratic process to run its slow, frustrating course.

EMBASSIES. Foreign embassies in Romania are in Bucharest (p. 860). Romanian embassies at home include: **Australia,** 4 Dalman Crescent, O'Malley ACT 2606, Canberra (☎061 2 6286 2343; www.roembau.org); **Canada,** 655 Rideau St., Ottawa, ON K1N 6A3 (☎613-789-5345; www.cyberus.ca/~romania); **Ireland,** 47 Ailesbury Rd., Ballsbridge, Dublin 4 (☎01 269 2852; romemb@iol.ie); **UK,** 4 Palace Green, Kensington Gardens, London W8 4QD (☎020 7937 9666; www.roemb.co.uk); **US,** 1607 23rd St. NW, Washington, D.C. 20008 (☎202-332-4848; www.roembus.org).

TRANSPORTATION

BY PLANE. Numerous airlines fly into Bucharest; **TAROM** (Romanian Airlines), which is in the process of renovating its fleet, flies direct from Bucharest to New York, Chicago, and major European cities (☎21 201 4000; www.tarom.ro). Bucharest's **Otopeni International Airport** (www.otp-airport.ro), despite improvements to ground services, is still far from ideal. Several airlines also offer domestic flights.

BY TRAIN. Trains, a better option for international travel than buses, head daily to Western Europe via Budapest. **Interrail** and **Eurail** have pass options for travel in Romania. English timetables are available online from Romania's national railway, **CFR,** at www.cfr.ro; paper copies are distributed as *Mersul Trenurilor* (L12,000). CFR offices in larger towns sell international and domestic tickets up to 24hr. before departure, after which only train stations sell tickets. International trains (often blue) are usually indicated by an *"i"* on timetables. *Inter-City* trains ("IC" on timetables) stop only at major cities. *Rapid* trains (green) are the next-fastest option. *Accelerat* trains (red), which have four digits starting with "1," come in third. All three types require reservations. Only on the slow but cheap *Personal* trains (black), used locally, is there a marked difference between first class (*clasa întâi;* cars marked with a "1" on the side; 6 people per compartment) and second class (*clasa dova;* 8 people). **Overnight trains** have sleepers (*vagon de dormit*).

BY BUS. Buses connect major cities in Romania to Athens, Prague, and certain Western European locations. Price- and speed-wise, those using buses internationally should consider taking a domestic train to the border and catching an international bus from there. Local bus systems should be a last resort; they depart from the *autogară* (bus station) in each town. Buying tickets straight from the carrier allows savings on commissions. **Minibuses** are worthwhile for short distances.

BY TAXI, BY CAR, AND BY THUMB. It is always cheaper to call a **taxi** instead of hailing one from a stand. If the ride is not metered, fix prices beforehand and haggle; rates vary by city. Tips are not expected. **Roadside assistance** for those driving cars is available 24hr. from the Romanian Automobile Association (ACR) at ☎01 222 22 22 or 01 222 15 52. Holding out the palm as if waving is the accepted sign for **hitchhiking.** Drivers expect payment comparable to the price of a train ticket for the distance traveled. *Let's Go* does not recommend hitchhiking.

TOURIST SERVICES AND MONEY

EMERGENCY	Police: ☎955. Ambulance: ☎961. Fire: ☎981.

TOURIST OFFICES. Most tourist offices are intended for Romanians traveling abroad, and much of the country has poor resources for foreigners. For info, the best idea is to walk into the most expensive hotel in town and pretend to be important. Cluj-Napoca, however, has numerous tourist offices. Online, www.romania-tourism.com has country info and sets of links both to regional offices of the Ministry of Transportation and Tourism and to national tourist offices abroad.

LEI (L)		
AUS$1 = L23,720		L100,000 = AUS$4.22
CDN$1 = L24,974		L100,000 = CDN$4.00
EUR€1 = L40,750		L100,000 = EUR€2.45
NZ$1 = L21,895		L100,000 = NZ$4.57
UK£1 = L60,644		L100,000 = UK£1.64
US$1 = L33,247		L100,000 = US$3.01

MONEY. The Romanian unit of currency is the **leu (L)**, plural *lei*. It is issued in standard banknote denominations of L10,000, L50,000, L100,000, and L500,000. Pay for everything in *lei* to avoid rip-offs and to save your reliable currency for emergencies and bribes. Private **exchange bureaus** litter the country, but few take credit cards or traveler's checks. Shop around for good rates. US dollars are preferred, although euros can usually be exchanged as well. **ATMs** have reasonable exchange rates; they generally accept MasterCard, and Visa less frequently. It is customary to give inexact change for purchases, generally rounding to the nearest L500; this usually suffices as a **tip** in restaurants.

COMMUNICATION

PHONE CODES	**Country code: 40. International dialing prefix: 00.** From outside Romania, dial international dialing prefix (see inside back cover) + 40 + city code + local number.

TELEPHONES AND INTERNET ACCESS. Nearly all public phones are orange and accept phone cards, although a few archaic blue phones take L500 coins. Phone cards are available at telephone offices, major Bucharest subway stops, and some post offices and kiosks. Orange phones in major cities will operate in English when you press "i." Local calls cost L595 per minute and can be made from any phone; a busy signal may just indicate a connection problem. To make a phone call *prin commandă* (with the help of the operator) at the telephone office, write down the destination, duration, and phone number for your call. Pay up front, and ask for the rate per minute. Numbers for the operator and general information are respectively ☎ 930 and 931. Internet cafes are easy to find in major cities; rates average around L10,000-20,000 per hour.

MAIL. Airmail (*par avion*) takes 2-3 weeks to reach international destinations. Mail can be received general delivery through *Poste Restante*. Address mail to be held according to the following example: First name SURNAME, *Poste Restante*, Str. Nicolae Iorga 1, Braşov 2200, ROMANIA.

LANGUAGES. Romanian is a Romance language; speakers of French, Italian, Spanish, or Portuguese should be able to decipher signs. German and Hungarian are widespread in Transylvania. German and French are second languages for the older generation, English for the younger. Romanian basics are listed on p. 1065.

ACCOMMODATIONS AND CAMPING

ROMANIA	❶	❷	❸	❹	❺
ACCOMMODATIONS	under L400,000	L400,000-700,000	L700,000-1,000,000	L1,000,000-2,000,000	over L2,000,000

While some **hotels** charge foreigners up to twice as much as natives, lodging is still relatively inexpensive (€6-20). Youth hostels are usually nicer than one-star hotels, two-star establishments are decent, and three-star places are good but expensive. **Private accommodations** are generally the best option; be aware that renting "together" means sharing a bed. Rooms run US$5-12 per person in the countryside and start from US$15 in larger cities. Visit the room and fix a price before accepting. Many towns allow foreign students to stay in **university dorms** at low prices, but these can be hard to find without some knowledge of Romanian. **Campgrounds** are crowded and often have intolerable bathrooms. Relatively cheap **bungalows** are generally full in summer, so reserve in advance.

FOOD AND DRINK

ROMANIA	❶	❷	❸	❹	❺
FOOD	under L70,000	L70,000-110,000	L110,000-150,000	L150,000-200,000	over L200,000

Lunch usually starts with a soup, called *supă* or *ciorbă*, followed by a main dish (typically grilled meat) and dessert. Soups can be very tasty; try *ciorbă de perişoare* (vegetables and ground meatballs) or *supă cu găluşte* (fluffy dumplings). Pork comes in several cuts, of which *muşchi* and *cotlet* are the best quality. For dessert, *clătite* (crepes), *papanaşi* (doughnuts with jam and sour cream), and *tort* (creamy cakes) are all fantastic. Some restaurants charge by weight (usually 100g) rather than by portion. *Garnituri*, the extras that come with a meal, are usually charged separately, even down to that dollop of mustard. As a rule, you will pay for everything the waiter puts in front of you. "Fast food" means precooked and microwaved. Check expiration dates on everything you buy.

SAFETY AND SECURITY

Bucharest has a few American medical clinics with English-speaking doctors that accept payment in cash. UK nationals receive free medical care with a valid passport. **Pharmacies** (*farmacies*) sometimes have what you need; *antinevralgic*, sometimes called *tylenol*, is for headaches, *aspirină* or *piramidon* for colds and the flu, and *saprosan* for diarrhea. Most **public toilets** lack soap, towels, and toilet paper; it may help to bring supplies along.

HOLIDAYS AND FESTIVALS

Holidays: New Year's (Jan. 1-2); Epiphany (Jan. 6); Easter (Mar. 27-28); Labor Day (May 1); National Unity Day (Dec. 1); Christmas (Dec. 25-26).

Festivals: Summer festivals abound in Transylvania. Sibiu's many festivals include the **International Theatre Festival** in late May-early June (see www.sibfest.ro). Sighişoara holds a huge **medieval festival** in July, while Braşov hosts the **International Chamber Music Festival** in late June-early July.

FACTS AND FIGURES: ROMANIA

Official Name: Romania.

Capital: Bucharest.

Major Cities: Braşov, Bucharest, Cluj-Napoca, Constanţa.

Population: 22,356,000.

Land Area: 230,340 sq. km.

Time Zone: GMT +2.

Languages: Romanian (official), Hungarian, German.

Religions: Romanian Orthodox (70%), Catholic (6%), Protestant (6%).

BUCHAREST (BUCUREŞTI) ☎ 021

Bucharest (pop. 2,000,000) was once a fabled beauty on the Orient Express. Then Communist dictator Nicolae Ceauşescu rose to power and for a quarter-century systematically replaced the grand boulevards and Ottoman ruins with wide highways and concrete blocks. Although Bucharest is no longer the beautiful *"Micul Paris"* (Little Paris) it once was, historic neighborhoods, secluded parks, and a thriving club scene keep the capital attractive for travelers worldwide.

⌐ TRANSPORTATION

Flights: Otopeni Airport (☎ 204 10 00), 16km from the city. Bus #783 to Otopeni runs from Piaţa Unirii with stops throughout the center. Buy **tickets** at the **TAROM office,** Spl. Independenţei 7 (☎ 337 04 00). Open M-F 9am-7pm, Sa 9am-1pm.

Trains: Gara de Nord (☎ 223 08 80) is the main station. M1: Gara de Nord. Tickets on sale 1hr. before departure. To: **Braşov** (4hr., 12 per day, L160,000); **Budapest** (14hr., 5 per day, L2,000,000); **Cluj-Napoca** (10hr., 5 per day, L272,000); **Iaşi** (7hr., 4 per day, L272,000); **Kraków** (27hr., 1 per day, L2,500,000); **Prague** (36hr., 1 per day, L3,200,000); **Sighişoara** (6hr., 7 per day, L203,000); **Sofia** (13hr., 2 per day, L1,300,000). **CFR,** Str. Domniţa Anastasia 10-14 (☎ 313 26 43; www.cfr.ro) books domestic tickets. Open M-F 7:30am-7:30pm, Sa 8am-noon. Inside Gara de Nord, **Wasteels** (☎ 222 78 44; www.wasteelstravel.ro), books international tickets. Open M-F 8am-6pm, Sa 8am-2pm.

Buses: Filaret, Cuţitul de Argint 2 (☎ 335 11 40). M2: Tineretului. South of the center. To **Athens,** buy tickets from **Ager Agency** (☎ 336 67 83). To **Istanbul,** try a **Toros** (☎ 223 18 98; 1 per day) or **Murat** (☎ 224 92 93; 2 per day) from outside Gara de Nord (both L1,250,000). **Double T,** Calea Victoriei 2 (☎ 313 36 42), a Eurail affiliate, and **Eurolines Touring,** Str. Ankara 6 (☎ 230 03 70), travel to Western Europe.

Public Transportation: Buses, trolleys, and **trams** run daily 5:30am-11:30pm. Tickets (L8000) sold at kiosks only; validate onboard or face fines. **Express buses** take only magnetic cards (L40,000 for two trips; sold at kiosks). Pickpocketing is a problem during peak hours. The **metro** offers reliable and less-crowded service to major points. (Open daily 5am-11:30pm. Magnetic cards L16,000 for 2 trips, L50,000 for 10 trips.)

Taxis: Taxi drivers will cheerfully rip off foreigners; only use taxis with a company name, phone number, and per-km rate posted in the window. Official rates run L7000-9000 base fee plus an equal amount per km. Drivers rarely speak English. More reliable companies include **Meridien** (☎ 94 44), **ChrisTaxi** (☎ 94 61), and **Taxi2000** (☎ 94 94).

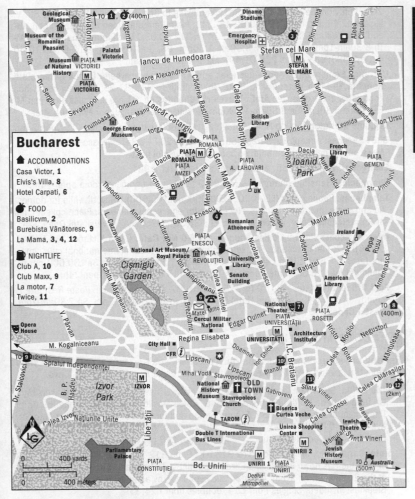

Bucharest

▲ ACCOMMODATIONS
Casa Victor, 1
Elvis's Villa, 8
Hotel Carpaţi, 6

🍴 FOOD
Basilicvm, 2
Burebista Vânătoresc, 9
La Mama, 3, 4, 12

🍸 NIGHTLIFE
Club A, 10
Club Maxx, 9
La motor, 7
Twice, 11

ORIENTATION AND PRACTICAL INFORMATION

One main street changes its name from **Stradă Lascăr** to **Bulevardul General Magheru** to **Bulevardul Nicolae Bălcescu** to **Bulevardul I.C. Brătianu** as it runs north-south through Bucharest's four main squares: **Piaţa Victoriei, Piaţa Romană, Piaţa Universi-tăţii,** and **Piaţa Unirii. Gara de Nord,** the train station, lies along the M1 line. From there, to reach the city center take the M1 (dir.: Dristor) one stop to Piaţa Victoriei, then change to the M2 (dir.: Depoul IMGB). One stop reaches Piaţa Romană, two stops Piaţa Universităţii, and three stops Piaţa Unirii. The helpful *Bucharest In Your Pocket* is available for free at museums, bookstores, and hotels.

Tourist Info: Gara de Nord has a booth but hotels tend to be better sources of info.
Embassies and Consulates: Australia, Bd. Unirii 74, 5th fl. (☎320 98 26). M2: Piaţa Unirii, then bus #104, 123, or 124 to Lucian Blaga. Open M-Th 9:30am-12:30pm.
Canada, Str. Nicolae Iorga 36 (☎307 50 63). M2: Piaţa Romană. Open M-Th 8am-

2pm. Verify before going; the embassy is moving to Sos. Pavel Kisileff. **Ireland,** Str. V. Lascăr 42-44, 6th floor. (☎210 89 48). M2: Piața Romană. Open M-F 10am-noon. **UK** and **New Zealand,** Str. Jules Michelet 24 (☎312 03 03). M2: Piața Romană. Open M-Th 8:30am-1pm and 2-5pm, F 8:30am-1:30pm. **US,** Str. Tudor Arghezi 7-9 (☎210 40 42, ext. 403; after hours 210 01 49). M2: Piața Universității.

Currency Exchange: Exchange agencies and **ATMs** are everywhere. **Banca Comercială Română,** in Piața Victoriei and Piața Universității (☎315 82 99; www.bcr.com), has good rates and exchanges **AmEx Traveler's Cheques** for a 1.5% commission. Open M-F 8:30am-5:30pm, Sa 8:30am-12:30pm. It is illegal to change money on the street.

Luggage Storage: Gara de Nord. Small bags L25,000. Large bags L50,000. Open 24hr.

GLBT Services: Accept Bucharest, Str. Lirei 10 (☎252 16 37; www.accept-romania.ro). News on gay rights in Romania, social info, and useful links.

Emergency: Police: ☎955. **Ambulance:** ☎961. **Fire:** ☎981.

Pharmacies: Sensiblu pharmacies (☎203 90 09) are everywhere, some open 24hr.

Telephones: Phone cards (L80,000, L100,000, or L160,000) are worthwhile for domestic and some international calls. Necessary for emergency numbers. Place collect calls at **Romtelecom,** Calea Victoriei 35 (☎313 36 35). M2: Piața Universității. Open 24hr.

Internet Access: Internet cafes abound. Try **P-C Net Café,** Calea Victoriei 136 (☎315 51 86). M2: Piața Romană. Fax, xerox, printer, and phones for international calls. Internet rates M-F 6am-11pm L40,000 per hr., M-F 11pm-6am and Sa-Su L30,000 per hr. Minimum fee L10,000. International calls from L10,000 per min. Open 24hr.

Post Office: Str. Matei Millo 10 (☎315 90 30). M2: Pță. Universității. *Poste Restante* is nearby on the right, just before Hotel Carpați. Open M-F 7:30am-8pm, Sa 7:30am-2pm. **Postal Code:** 010144.

▐ ACCOMMODATIONS

Renting private rooms is uncommon. Travelers won't go wrong with established hostels, but should avoid "representatives" that greet them at Gara de Nord.

▨ **Elvis's Villa,** Str. Avram Iancu 5 (☎312 16 53; www.elvisvilla.ro). M2: Piața Universității. Or, from Gara de Nord, take trolley #85 to "Calea Moșilor." Continuing along Bd. Carol I, turn right at the park onto Str. Sfântul Ștefan and then left at the playground onto Str. Avram Iancu. Newer hostel in a quiet, older part of town. A/C. Laundry facilities and breakfast included. Reservations recommended. €10 per day, €72 per week. ❷

Hotel Carpati, Str. Matei Millo 16 (☎315 01 40; fax 312 18 57). M2: Universitatii. Walk or take the bus down Bd. Regina Elizabeta until Str. I. Brezoianu. Turn right; the hotel is at the 2nd corner. An aging, one-star relic kept clean by an agreeable, multilingual staff. Breakfast included. Singles from €14; doubles from €24. ❷

Casa Victor, Str. Emanoil Porumbaru 44 (☎222 57 23). M2: Piața Aviatorilor. A touch of luxury in a fashionable northern neighborhood. Free transport to and from the airport or train station (call ahead). Singles €40-55; doubles €70; apartment €80-90. ❹

▐ FOOD

Open-air markets all over Bucharest sell meat, cheese, flowers, and oodles of fresh fruits and vegetables. Try the one at Piața Amzei, next to Piața Romană. Better supermarkets can be found in the basement of the Unirea mall (M1-2: Unirii) or at the **Mega Image** at the corner of Calea Călărășilor and Traian (M2: Universității).

▨ **La Mama,** Str. Barbu Văcărescu 3 (☎212 40 86; www.lamama.ro). M1: Ștefan cel Mare. **Branches** at Str. Del Veche 51 (☎320 52 13); M1: Piața Muncii, off of Calea Călărașilor; and at Str. Episcopiei 9 (☎312 97 97); M2: Piața Universității, off of Piața

Revoluţiei. Motto: "Like at Mom's house." Top-notch traditional Romanian cuisine in a pleasant setting. No jeans or shorts. Reservations recommended. Entrees L70,000-95,000. Open daily 10am-2am. ❷

Burebista Vânătoresc, Str. Batistei 14 (☎211 89 29). M2: Piaţa Universităţii. Turn right off Bd. Nicolae Bălcescu. Taxidermy, live folk music, and bearskin rugs drive home the rustic theme. Menu is game-oriented, but if you hunger for bear meat then look no further. Entrees L100,000-230,000. Open daily noon-midnight. ❸

Basilicvm, Str. Popa Savu 7 (☎222 67 79). M2: Aviatorilor. Refined setting, Italianate menu, praiseworthy food, attentive service, well decorated building, lovely terrace and a weekend lunch special (50% off everything). Entrees L150,000-350,000. Open daily 11am-1am. MC/V. ❹

🄶 SIGHTS

CIVIC CENTER. To create his ideal Socialist capital, Ceauşescu destroyed five sq. km of Bucharest's historical center, demolishing over 9000 19th-century houses and displacing more than 40,000 Romanians. The Civic Center (Centru Civic) lies at the end of the 6km Bd. Unirii, which was purposely built 1m wider than its inspiration, the Champs-Elysées. Its centerpiece, the █**Parliamentary Palace** (Palatul Parlamentului), is the world's second-largest building after the Pentagon in Washington, D.C. Between 1984 and 1989, in the last years of the Ceauşescu regime, over 20,000 workers assembled it from Romanian wood and marble. *(M1 or 3: Izvor. Enter from Calea Izvor, on the right side of the building as seen from Bd. Unirii. Open daily 10am-4pm. Tours L100,000, students L50,000.)*

SIGHTS OF THE REVOLUTION. The first shots of the Revolution were fired at **Piaţa Revoluţiei** on December 21, 1989. The square contains the **University Library,** the **National Art Museum,** and the **Senate Building** (formerly Communist Party Headquarters), on whose balcony Ceauşescu delivered his final speech. A white marble triangle with the inscription "*Glorie martirilor nostri*" (Glory to our martyrs) commemorates the rioters who overthrew the dictator. *(M2: Piaţa Universităţii. With Hotel Intercontinental on your left, turn right on Bd. Regina Elisabeta and then right again on Calea Victoriei.)* **Piaţa Universităţii** houses memorials to victims of both the 1989 revolution and the protests of 1990. Crosses honoring the fallen line the center of Bd. Nicolae Bălcescu—the black one marks the spot where the first victim died. In June of 1990, the *piaţa* was again gripped by student riots. Ceauşescu's replacement, Ion Iliescu, bussed in over 10,000 miners to put down the protest, killing 21 students. Iliescu has since been elected president democratically, but anti-Iliescu graffiti persists on the walls of **Bucharest University** and of the **Architecture Institute.** *(M2: Piaţa Universităţii. Behind the fountain.)*

MUSEUMS. The █**Village Museum** (Muzeul Satului), Şos. Kiseleff 28-30, is an open-air replica of a rural village. *(M2: Aviatorilor. ☎222 91 06. Open Tu-Su 9am-6pm. L40,000, students L15,000.)* The two-wing **National Art Museum** (Muzeul Naţional de Artă al României) has works by Monet, van Eyck, El Greco, and Romania's most famous painter, Nicolae Grigorescu. *(Calea Victoriei 49-53, in Pţă. Revolutiei. M2: Pţă. Universitatii. ☎313 30 30. Open summer W-Su 11am-7pm, winter 10am-6pm. L80,000 for one gallery, L120,000 for both. Students L60,000/L40,000.)* The **Museum of the Romanian Peasant** (Muzeul Ţăranului Român) captures Romanian rural life. *(Şos. Kiseleff 3. M2 or 3: Piaţa Victoriei. Open Tu-Su 10am-6pm. Last entrance 5pm. L50,000, students L15000.)* The **National History Museum** (Muzeul Naţional de Istorie al României) offers a thorough look at Romanian history. *(Calea Victoriei 12. M2: Pţă. Universităţii. ☎311 33 56. Open summer W-Su 10am-6pm, winter 9am-5pm. L31,000, students L15,500.)*

OTHER SIGHTS. Several of modern Bucharest's most fashionable streets, including **Calea Victoriei, Şoseauna Kiseleff, Bulevardul Aviatorilor,** and **Bulevardul Magheru,** are sights in themselves. Sidestreets just off Piaţa Victoriei and Piaţa Dorobanţilor brim with villas and houses typical of beautiful 19th-century Bucharest. The sole vestiges of Bucharest's **old center** lie west of Bd. Brătianu and south of Bd. Regina Elisabetha, in the vicinity of Str. Lipscani and Str. Gabroveni.

🎵 🎭 ENTERTAINMENT AND NIGHTLIFE

Bucharest often hosts huge **rock festivals** (Michael Jackson once greeted screaming fans here with "Hello, Budapest!"). **Theater** and **opera** performances are cheap (L10,000-150,000); tickets go on sale at box offices two Saturdays before shows. No performances play from June to September.

At night, pack a map and cab fare—streets are poorly lit and public transportation stops at 11:30pm. **La motor,** Bd. Bălcescu 2, atop the National Theater, has a lively terrace in summer. (M2: Piaţa Universităţii. Open daily noon-2am.) Nightclub **Twice,** Str. Sfânta Vineri 4, has two dance floors. (M2: Piaţa Universităţii. Cover for men L100,000; women free. Open daily 9pm-5am.) **Club A,** Str. Blănari 14, Bucharest's most famous nightspot, has absurdly cheap drinks. (M2: Piaţa Universităţii. F-Sa Cover for men L50,000; women L20,000. Open daily 8pm-5am.) **Club Maxx,** Str. Independenţei 290, an excellent *discotecă*, attracts a university crowd. (M1: Grozăveşti. Cover L30,000, students free. Open daily 10pm-late.) Staff at **Accept** (p. 862) can provide info on **GLBT nightlife.**

SINAIA
☎0244

Sinaia (sih-NAI-uh; pop. 15,000) first made its mark in the late 1880s as an alpine getaway for Romania's royal family. Carol I, king of the newly independent country, oversaw construction of the opulent **Peleş Castle** (Castelul Peleş), completed in 1883. (Open Tu 11am-5pm, W-Su 9am-5pm. English tours. L100,000, students L50,000.) The equally striking **Pelişor Castle,** built in 1902, was furnished in the Art Nouveau style by the wife of Carol's cousin Ferdinand, Queen Maria. (Open W noon-5pm, Th-Su 9am-5pm. L80,000, students L30,000. English tours available.) The nearby **Bucegi Mountains** are good for hiking in the summer and skiing in the winter. A *telecabină* (cable car) to the mountains leaves from behind Hotel New Montana, Bd. Carol I 24. (Open 8:30am-5pm. Round-trip L120,000.) After a long dayhike, grab a beer at the British-style pub **Old Nick,** Bd. Carol I 22, by the Hotel New Montana. (☎31 54 12. Open daily 9:30am-late.)

Trains (☎31 00 40) run to Braşov (1hr., 22 per day, L92,000); Bucharest (2hr., 19 per day, L175,000); and Cluj-Napoca (5hr., 5 per day, L310,000). To get to the center of town, climb the second set of stone steps across from the station. In summer, the station is mobbed by locals offering private rooms for around €7-12. **Cabana Miorita ❶,** with a bar and restaurant, is the queen of the mountain cabin system. (Bed in 12-person room L150,000; in smaller room L350,000; private doubles L600,000; triples L700,000.) For traditional fare, including a wild game menu, head to **Restaurant Bucegi ❶,** adjacent to Hotel Sinaia, near the top of the stairs by the station. (Entrees L60,000-100,000. Open daily 11am-11pm.) **Postal Code:** 106100.

TRANSYLVANIA (TRANSILVANIA)

In the Western imagination, the name evokes a dark land of black magic and vampires, the nest of Nosferatu. Those seeking the Transylvania of legend will not be disappointed by the region's architecture: Its buildings are tilted, jagged, and more harshly Gothic than any others in Europe. More timid travelers will be relieved to learn that Transylvania is actually a relatively Westernized region with beautiful green hills descending from the Carpathians to the Hungarian Plain.

CLUJ-NAPOCA ☎ 0264

Cluj-Napoca (pop. 400,000) is Transylvania's student center and unofficial capital. Colorful, relaxed, and home to a sizable Hungarian minority, the city is a good starting point for a journey into Transylvania or north to Maramureş. The 80m Gothic steeple of the Catholic **Church of St. Michael** (Biserica Sf. Mihail) rises from **Piaţa Unirii.** Take Str. Regele Ferdinand across the river, turn left on Str. Dragalina, and climb the stairs to your right to reach the city view from **Cetăţuie Hill.** In the **Botanical Garden** (Grădina Botanica), Str. Republicii 42, off Str. Napoca, there grow over 12,000 plant species. (Open daily 9am-7pm. L15,000.) Students shoot pool to rock, jazz, and techno at **Music Pub,** Str. Horea 5. (Live music F-Sa 9 or 10pm. Open in summer daily 6pm-3am; low season M-Sa 9am-4am, Su noon-4am.) Hotels distribute the free *Şapte Seri,* a good source for the latest nightlife info.

Trains run to: Bucharest (8-13hr., 9 per day, L400,000) via Braşov (5-7hr., L222,000); Budapest (6½-7hr., 2 per day, L1,130,000); Sibiu (4hr., 2 per day, L204,000); and Timişoara (6hr., 3 per day, L255,000). Local **buses** and **trams** run 5am-10pm; buy tickets (2 trips L19,000) at **RATUC** kiosks. **ATMs** lie along Bd. Ferdinand. Check email at the **Net Zone Internet Cafe,** Pţă. Muzeului 5. (7am-10pm L12,000 per hr., 10pm-7am L6000 per hr. Open 24hr.) **Retro Youth Hostel ❷,** Str. Potaissa 13, has handsome, dorm-style rooms near the university and arranges excursions into the countryside. (☎45 04 52; www.retro.ro. Breakfast €2. Laundry €2. Dorms €10. MC/V.) Location doesn't get any better than at **Hotel Continental ❸,** Str. Napoca 1, which has both budget and luxury options. (☎59 14 41. Singles €17, with bath €50; doubles €25/€75. MC/V.) **Roata ❷,** Str. Alexandru Ciura 6a, off Str. Emil Isac, is a traditional Romanian restaurant. (Entrees L60,000-200,000. Open M and Su 1pm-midnight, Tu-Sa noon-midnight. MC/V.) **Postal Code:** 400110.

SIGHIŞOARA ☎ 0265

Vlad Ţepeş, the model for Bram Stoker's *Dracula* (see **Bran,** p. 866), was born in enchanting Sighişoara (pop. 39,000). Surrounded by mountains and crowning a green hill, its gilded steeples and old clock tower have survived centuries of attacks, fires, and floods. The **Citadel** (Cetatea), built by the Saxons in 1191, is now a tiny medieval city-within-a-city. Enter through the **Clock Tower** (Turnul cu Ceas), off Str. O. Goga; pass by the museum and ascend for the view. (Open M 10am-4:30pm, Tu-F 9am-6:30pm, Sa-Su 9am-4:30pm. L36,000, students L20,500.) The second weekend in July brings the **Medieval Festival;** a **Folk Art Festival** takes place in late August. **Trains** run to Bucharest (5hr., 8 per day, L305,000) and Cluj-Napoca (3½hr., 8 per day, L260,000). To reach the center, turn right on Str. Libertăţii and left onto Str. Gării; veer left at the Russian cemetery, turn right, take the footbridge over Târana Mare, and walk down Str. Morii. Turn right from the station to reach **Nathan's Villa Hostel ❶,** Str. Libertatii 8. (☎77 25 46. Dorms €8.) **Postal Code:** 545400.

BRAŞOV ☎ 0268

Braşov (pop. 353,000) is an ideal starting point for trips into the mountains. A *tele-cabină* (cable car) goes up **Muntele Tâmpa;** to reach it from **Piaţa Sfatului,** walk down Apollonia Hirscher, make a left on Str. Castelui, a right on Suişul Castelui, and head up the stairs to the off-white building on the right. (Cable car runs M 9:30am-noon and 5-5:45pm, Tu-Su 9:30am-5:45pm. Round-trip L40,000.) Alternatively, follow the red triangle markings to hike to the top (1½hr.). Braşov itself is a picturesque town with peaceful side streets. Beyond the square along Str. Gh.

Bariţiu is Romania's most celebrated Gothic edifice, the Lutheran **Black Church** (Biserica Neagră), which received its name when it was charred by fire in 1689. (Open M-Sa 10am-5pm. L30,000, students L15,000.) Piaţa Sfatului, Str. Republicii, and Piaţa Unirii are nice areas to take a stroll. The box office, Str. Republicii 4, sells tickets for the symphony orchestra and the summer **International Chamber Music Festival,** held in the first week of September. (☎41 59 90. Open late Aug. to mid-June M-F 10am-5pm, Sa 10am-1pm. L50,000-200,000.) In the third week of July, Pţă. Sfatului also hosts the **Golden Stag Festival** (Cerbul de Aur), which attracts musicians from around the world.

Trains run to Bucharest (3-4hr., 13 per day, L195,000); Cluj-Napoca (5-6hr., 5 per day, L300,000); Iaşi (9-10hr., 1 per day, L272,000); and Sibiu (4hr., 7 per day, L145,000). Buy tickets at **CFR,** Bd. 15 Noiembrie 43. (☎47 70 18. Open M-F 8am-7pm, Sa 10am-1pm.) To get to town from the station, take bus #4 (dir.: Piaţă Unirii) to Piaţă Sfatului (10min.); get off in front of the Black Church. Maps (L40,000) are sold at *librarie* (bookstores) around town. For a private room, expect to pay €8-10. **Kismet Dao Villa Hostel ❷,** Str. Democraţiei 2b, is clean with free perks such as breakfast, laundry service, a daily drink, and 1hr. of Internet access at a nearby cafe. From Pţă. Unirii, walk up Str. Bâlea and turn right. (☎51 42 96. Dorms Apr.-Dec. €10, Jan.-Mar. €8; doubles €25. Cash only.) **Bella Musica ❷,** Str. G. Bariţiu 2, has an eclectic Romanian-Mexican menu, with everything from goulash to fajitas to free shots of *palincă*. (Entrees L65,000-200,000. Open daily noon-midnight.) **Taverna ❷,** Str. Politehnicii 6, serves Romanian, Hungarian, and Italian fare. (Entrees L90,000-300,000. Open daily noon-midnight. MC/V.) **Postal Code:** 500057.

BRAN ☎0268

Vlad Ţepeş, the model for the hero-villain of Bram Stoker's novel *Dracula*, once lived in Bran. Dracula's exploits pale in comparison with Ţepeş's: As a local governor of the Wallachia region, he protected the Bran pass from encroaching Turks, and became infamous for impaling his enemies. Turks invading Wallachia in 1462 swiftly retreated in horror after they were welcomed to Ţepeş's territory by the sight of some 20,000 of their kinsmen on stakes. Ţepeş was piously defending Catholicism, however, as had his father before him. (Also named Vlad, his father was a member of the Order of the Dragon, which undertook to defend the faith from infidels—hence the name "Dracula," from Vlad Dracul, or "Dragon.") While Ţepeş may have been a guest at **Bran Castle,** built under Hungarian rule in 1377-1382, he didn't live there—nor, in fact, did Stoker ever visit Romania. (Castle open M 11am-6pm, Tu-Su 9am-6pm. L90,000, students L40,000.) To reach Bran from Braşov, take a taxi or city bus #5 or 9 to Autogară 2 (officially Gară Bartolomeu; 45min., every 30min. 7am-6pm, L20,000). Get off at the souvenir market or at the sign marked "Cabana Bran Castle—500m." Backtrack along the road toward Braşov; the castle is on the right. **Postal Code:** 507025.

SIBIU ☎0269

Sibiu (SEE-bee-oo; pop. 170,000), the ancient capital of Transylvania, is a city of medieval monuments and colorfully ornate houses. Nearby, the **Făgăraş Mountains** offer some of the best hiking in Romania. Take the train from Sibiu to Ucea (1½hr., 4 per day, L25,000), where a bus connects to Victoria (25min., 7 per day, L20,000). From there, many itineraries are possible. **Libraria Friedrich Schiller,** in Pţă. Mare, sells maps and guides to the mountains in English (L70,000-200,000). Hiking season lasts from July to mid-September. The range is cold year-round and in some places very challenging. In case of **emergency,** or for expert help planning your trip, contact **Salvamont,** Nicolae Balcescu 9 (☎21 64 77). Sibiu has many **summer festivals,** including the International Theater Festival in early June and the Medieval Festival in late August. Summer Fest rages near Piaţă Unirii with free open-air concerts Thursday and Friday nights from mid-June to mid-September.

Trains from Sibiu run to: Braşov (3½hr., 7 per day, L145,000); Bucharest (6hr., 4 per day, L222,000); and Cluj-Napoca (4hr., 1 per day, L186,000). Buy tickets at **CFR,** Str. N. Bălcescu 6. (Open M-F 7:30am-7:30pm, Sa 9am-1pm.) **Buses** go to Bucharest (5hr., 5 per day, L200,000) and Cluj-Napoca (3½hr., 9 per day, L110,000). From the stations, take Str. General Magheru and turn right onto Str. Avram Iancu to reach **Piaţă Mare,** the main square. Thick mattresses and private bathrooms make brand-new **Hotel Ela ❶,** on Str. Novâ, worth the walk. From Pţă. Mare, go through the clock tower, cross Pţă. Mica, and descend Str. Ocnei, taking a right onto Str. Novâ. (☎21 51 97. Breakfast L150,000. Dorms L300,000; singles L500,000; doubles L700,000; triples L900,000. Book ahead.) Sibiu has good traditional cuisine. Don't be fooled by the no-frills decor of **Kon-Tiki ❶,** Str. Tudor Vladimescu 10; locals love its Romanian food. (☎22 03 50. Entrees L24,000-60,000. Open M-F 10am-10pm, Su noon-10pm.) To reach the **open-air market,** walk to the end of Str. S. Brukenthall from Pţă. Mare, continue down the staircase on the right, and follow the road. (Open dawn-dusk.) **Postal Code:** 550159.

TIMIŞOARA   ☎0256

Timişoara (pop. 334,000), Romania's westernmost city, is also one of the country's largest and liveliest. In 1989 it ignited the revolution that overthrew the Communist regime; anti-Ceauşescu protestors gathered in **Piaţă Victoriei.** At one end of the square stands the **Metropolitan Cathedral,** designed in Byzantine and Moldavian folk style with a rainbow-tiled roof. (Open daily 6:30am-8pm.) Across the square is the **National Theater** (Teatrul Naţional) and **Opera House** (Opera Timişoara), with a box office down the street on Str. Mărăşeşti. (Open daily Sept.-May 10am-1pm and 5-7pm.) Nearby in **Huniade Castle** is the **Banat Museum** (Muzeul Banatului), which traces Timişoara's history. (Open Tu-Su 10am-4:30pm. L20,000, students L10,000.)

Trains run from Timişoara Nord to: Braşov (9hr., 1 per day, L310,000); Bucharest (8hr., 5 per day, L485,000); Budapest (5hr., 3 per day, L1,000,000); Cluj-Napoca (7hr., 4 per day, L265,000). **Trams** #1, 8, and 11, and **trolleybuses** #11 and 14 go to the city center (2 trips L17,000). **Libraria Mihai Eminescu,** in Piaţă Victoriei, sells English books and maps for L60,000-100,000. (Open M-F 9am-7pm, Sa 9am-1pm.) **Hotel Nord ❷,** in the yellow-and-pink building just across the street from the train station, has comfy rooms with TV and fridge. (☎49 75 04. Breakfast included. Singles €17; doubles €24; suites €42.) Many good restaurants surround Piaţă Victoriei in the center of town. **Postal Code:** 300005.

MOLDAVIA AND BUKOVINA

Eastern Romania, known as Moldavia (Moldova), extends from the Carpathians to the Prut River. Starker than Transylvania but more developed than Maramureş, Moldavia also contains the painted monasteries of Bukovina (Bucovina). Built 500 years ago by Moldavia's ruler Ştefan cel Mare (Stephen the Great) and his successors, the monasteries are hidden among green hills and farming villages. Their exquisite structures mix Moldavian and Byzantine architecture with Romanian Christian images. Often the best way to see the monasteries is to take an organized tour from Gura Humorului or Suceava. Dress modestly.

IAŞI   ☎0232

Iaşi (YAHSH; pop. 340,000) rose to prominence in the 19th century as the home of the Junimea Society, a literary club that built up the city with Neoclassical architecture. Bd. Ştefan cel Mare leads south from the main square, **Piaţă Unirii,** past the gorgeous 1637 **Trei Ierarchi church,** whose walls display Moldavian and Turkish patterns in raised relief. The boulevard then continues to the massive, neo-Gothic

Palace of Culture (Palatul Culturii), which contains historical, ethnographic, polytechnic, and art museums. (Open Tu-Su 10am-5pm. Each museum L15,000, students L10,000. Combination L50,000/L30,000.) North of Pţă. Unirii, Bd. Copou leads from Piaţă Eminescu past some of the most beautiful buildings in Iaşi to **Copou Park.** Inside the park is the **Eminescu Museum,** which exhibits documents of the great poet Mihai Eminescu. (Open Tu-Su 10am-5pm. L10,000.)

Trains go from Str. Silvestru to: Braşov (6hr., 1 per day, L272,000); Bucharest (7½hr., 6 per day, L372,000); Cluj-Napoca (9hr., 4 per day, L272,000); and Timişoara (17hr., 3 per day, L373,000). **CFR,** Pţă. Unirii 9/11, sells train tickets. (☎14 52 69. Open M-F 8am-8pm.) **Buses** leave from Iaşi Vest, Str. Moara de Foc 15, for Braşov (8hr., 1 per day, L230,000). **Libraria Junimea,** Pţă. Unirii 4, sells maps. (Open M-F 8:30am-8pm, Sa 9am-4pm, Su 9am-2pm.) Conveniently located **Casa Bucovineana ❷,** Str. Cuza Voda 30-32, has clean, basic rooms. From the train station, pass Pţă. Unirii and the post office. (☎0740 31 44 93 or 53 90 84. Doubles L400,000, with bath L700,000.) Founded centuries ago, **Bolta Rece ❶,** Str. Rece 10, has some of the best traditional food in Iaşi. From Pţă. Unirii, take Bd. Independentei past Pţă. Academiei, turn left onto Str. M. Eminescu, and again onto Str. Rece. (Entrees L40,000-90,000. Open daily 8am-midnight.) **Postal Code:** 700037.

GURA HUMORULUI   ☎0230

Within walking distance of the Humor and Voroneţ monasteries, small Gura Humorului is an ideal base to see them. Tourist info is available from **Dispecerat de Cazare,** where Str. Câmpului ends at Str. Voroneţ; from the train station, head left off Str. Ştefan cel Mare and left onto Str. Câmpului. The office also arranges villa rooms and car tours for €30-35 per day. (☎23 38 63. Open Mar.-Nov. 11am-9pm.) **Trains** go to: Bucharest (6hr., 1 per day, L300,000); Cluj-Napoca (5hr., 4 per day, L200,000); Iaşi (3hr., 4 per day, L190,000); and Suceava (1hr., 9 per day, L25,000-70,000). To reach the center from the station, turn right onto Str. Ştefan cel Mare and continue over the bridge. **Pensiune Casa Ella ❷,** Str. Cetaţii 7, off Bd. Bucovina, offers soft beds and home-cooked meals. (☎23 29 61. Meals L75,000-150,000. Singles L450,000; doubles L550,000. Cash only.) The more luxurious **Vila Fabian ❷** is across Str. Voroneţ from Dispecerat de Cazare. (☎23 23 87. Singles €15; doubles €25. Cash only.) **Postal Code:** 725300.

█ DAYTRIPS FROM GURA HUMORULUI: THE HUMOR, MOLDOVIŢA, AND VORONEŢ MONASTERIES. Bukovina's oldest frescoes are at **Humor,** known for a depiction of the life of the Virgin Mary on the south wall. The mural, based on a poem by the patriarch of Constantinople, shows Mary saving Constantinople from a Persian attack in 626. From Gura Humorului, walk right on Ştefan cel Mare from the train or bus station to the center of town. At the fork near a park on the right, take Str. Manasteria Humorului to the left and continue 6km to the monastery. (Open daily 8am-8pm. L40,000, students L20,000. Cameras L60,000.)

Moldoviţa is the largest of the monasteries and has the best-preserved frescoes. Painted in 1537, the frescoes portray the Last Judgment, Jesse's Tree, and a monumental Siege of Constantinople. In the first room is a calendar depicting a saint for each day of the year. (Open daily 7am-9pm. L40,000, students L20,000.) Take a **train** from Gura Humorului to Vama (20min., 9 per day, L39,000) and continue to Vatra Moldoviţei (45min., 3 per day, L24,000).

Ştefan cel Mare built **Voroneţ** in 1488, but it was his illegitimate son, Petru Rareş, who in 1524 added the frescoes that led it to be called the "Sistine Chapel of the East." The concoction of the monastery's rich blue pigment still baffles art historians. Take a **bus** from Gura Humorului (15min., mid-Sept. to mid-June M-F 3 per day, L10,000). Or, walk left from the Gura Humorului train station, turn left again onto Cartierul Voroneţ, and follow the signs for a scenic 5km. (Open daily 8am-8pm. L40,000, students L20,000. Cameras L60,000.)

SUCEAVA

☎0230

Moldavia's capital under Ştefan cel Mare, Suceava has many noteworthy museums, as well as the grand 1388 **Citadel of the Throne** (Cetatea de Scaun). Climb the
ramparts for a spectacular view. Taxis (5min., L30,000) from the main square,
Piaţă 22 Decembrie, spare travelers the 10min. walk through the park, which is not
always safe. (Citadel open in summer daily 8am-8pm; low season 9am-5pm.
L30,000, students L15,000.) At night, two of the citadel's terraces serve food and
drinks. (Entrees L50,000-100,000. Open daily 8am-10:30pm.)

Trains run to: Braşov (8hr., 1 per day, L300,000); Bucharest (6hr., 8 per day,
L410,000); Cluj-Napoca (6hr., 4 per day, L250,000); Gura Humorului (1hr., 10 per
day, L25,000); and Iaşi (2hr., 8 per day, L80,000-160,000). Buy tickets at **CFR**, Str. N.
Bălcescu 4. (☎21 43 35. Open M-F 7:30am-7pm.) **Buses** (☎52 43 40) run from the
intersection of Str. N. Bălcescu and Str. V. Alecsandri to: Bucharest (8hr., 4 per
day, L226,000); Cluj-Napoca (7hr., 1 per day, L185,000); Gura Humorului (1hr., 10
per day, L30,000); and Iaşi (3hr., 4 per day, L100,000). **Librăria Alexandria,** Aleea
Ion Grămadă 5, in the main square, sells maps. (L70,000. Open M-F 7am-
7:30pm, Sa 9am-6pm.) New **Class Hostel ❷,** Str. Aurel Vlaicu 195, 1km from the
train station in the Itcani district, arranges monastery car tours and cooks for vegetarians. (☎78 23 28. Breakfast €2. Beds €10. MC/V.) **Postal Code:** 720005.

PUTNA

☎0230

Constructed around 1469, pure-white Putna was the first of 38 monasteries
founded by Ştefan cel Mare, who built one church for each battle he won. He left
the monastery's location up to God: Climbing a nearby hill (now marked with a
cross) to the left of the monastery, he shot an arrow into the air and determined to
build where it fell. A slice of the oak it struck is on display at the museum, along
with various manuscripts, icons, and tapestries. (Museum open daily 9am-8pm.
L40,000, students L5000.) Ştefan cel Mare's tomb is in Putna's church. (Monastery
and church open daily 6am-8pm. Free.) Putna is best seen as a daytrip from
Suceava. **Trains** from Suceava run to Putna (2½hr., 4 per day, L31,000). Turn right
exiting the platform, then left at the first intersection, and keep walking.

RUSSIA (РОССИЯ)

More than a decade after the collapse of the Soviet Union, vast Russia stumbles along with no clear direction; former Communists run the state, while impoverished pensioners long for a rose-tinted Soviet past. Heedless of surrounding provinces, cosmopolitan Moscow gorges on hyper-capitalism, while majestic St. Petersburg struggles to remain one of Europe's major cultural centers. Although traveling here can be a bureaucratic nightmare, Russia is in many ways the ideal destination for a budget traveler—inexpensive and well served by public transportation, with hundreds of monasteries, kremlins, and onion-domed churches.

DISCOVER RUSSIA

Russia's capital, **Moscow** (p. 874) is more than memories of revolution: Marvel at the onion-dome spires of St. Basil's, the Kremlin's collections of Fabergé eggs, or the nearby monastery at **Sergiyev Posad** (p. 885). To the north, **St. Petersburg** (p. 886) remains magnificent despite 20th-century ravages: Art lovers spend fruitful decades exploring the Hermitage, concerts enliven the banks of the Neva during White Nights, and peasants still shudder at the opulence of the Tsars' palaces. A convenient daytrip, nearby **Peterhof** (p. 894) is no less obscenely extravagant.

ESSENTIALS

DOCUMENTS AND FORMALITIES

 BEFORE YOU GO. In March 1998, the US State Department issued a travel advisory regarding the bringing of Global Positioning Systems (GPS), cellular phones, and other radio transmission devices into Russia. Failure to register such devices can and does result in search, seizure, and arrest.

VISAS. Citizens of Australia, Canada, Ireland, New Zealand, the UK, and the US require visas to enter Russia; a visa application requires an **invitation** stating the planned itinerary and dates of travel. Russian law requires that you **register** your visa within three days of arrival. Many hotels will do this for you, as should the organizations listed below; some travel agencies in Moscow and St. Petersburg charge around €30 for the service. Otherwise, to register you'll have to free-fall into the seventh circle of bureaucratic hell known as **OVIR** (ОВИР; in Moscow: UVIR; УВИР). To obtain a visa, apply in person or by mail to an embassy or consulate; travel agencies that advertise discounted tickets to Russia will often also provide visas. Single-, double-, and multiple-entry visas currently cost $100 without rush service. Private organizations also issue invitations and/or visas to tourists:

Host Families Association (HOFA), 5-25 Tavricheskaya ul., 193015 St. Petersburg (☎812 275 19 92; www.hofa.us). Arranges invitations, visas, homestays, language lessons, and more in the former Soviet Union.

Info Travel, 387 Harvard St., Brookline, MA 02446, USA (☎617 566 2197; www.infortravel.com). Invitations and visas to Russia start at US$175. Also provides visas and invitations throughout the CIS.

Red Bear Tours/Russian Passport, 401 St. Kilda Rd., Ste. 11, Melbourne 3004, Australia (☎9867 3888; www.travelcentre.com.au). Provides invitations to Russia and the Central Asian Republics. Also sells rail tickets for the Trans-Siberian, Trans-Manchurian, Trans-Mongolian, and Silk routes and arranges tours.

Russia House, 1800 Connecticut Ave., NW, Washington, D.C. 20009, USA (☎202-986-6010; www.russiahouse.org). **Branch,** 44 Bolshaya Nikitskaya, Moscow 121854, RUS (☎+095 290 34 50). Invitations and visas to Russia start at US$250.

VISAtoRUSSIA.com, 309A Peters St. Atlanta, GA 30313, USA (☎404-837-0099; www.visatorussia.com). Russian visa invitations start at US$30. Also provides visas and invitations throughout the CIS.

EMBASSIES. All foreign embassies are in Moscow (p. 877); many consulates are also in St. Petersburg (p. 887). Russian embassies at home include: **Australia,** 78 Canberra Ave., Griffith ACT 2603 (☎026 295 90 33; www.australia.mid.ru); **Canada,** 285 Charlotte St., Ottawa, ON K1N 8L5 (☎613-235-4341; www.canada.mid.ru); **Ireland,** 184-186 Orwell Rd., Rathgar, Dublin 14 (☎01 492 2048; www.ireland.mid.ru); **New Zealand,** 57 Messines Rd., Karori, Wellington (☎04 476 61 13; www.rus.co.nz); **UK,** 13 Kensington Palace Gardens, London W8 4QX (☎020 7229 2666; www.greatbritain.mid.ru); **US,** 2650 Wisconsin Ave. NW, Washington, D.C. 20007 (☎202-298-5700; www.russianembassy.org).

TRANSPORTATION

BY PLANE. Most major international carriers fly into **Sheremetyevo-2 (SVO)** in Moscow or **Pulkovo-2 (LED)** in St. Petersburg. **Aeroflot** (☎095 245 3851; www.aeroflot.ru) is the most commonly used domestic airline.

BY TRAIN AND BY BUS. If you take a train that passes through Belarus, you will need a US$100 **transit visa**. Trains are best for **domestic travel;** weekend trains between Moscow and St. Petersburg often sell out a week in advance. Of the four classes of train cars, *lyuks* (люкс) has two beds; second-class *kupeyny* (купейний) has four bunks; and *platskartny* (плацкартный) has 52 shorter, harder bunks. Aim for bunks 1-33; bunks 34-37 are next to the restrooms, and bunks 38-52 get hot in summer. **Women** traveling alone can try to buy out a *lyuks* compartment for security, or can travel *platskartny* and depend on the crowds to shame would-be harassers. Riding *platskartny* is also wise on the thief-ridden St. Petersburg-Moscow line, as foreigners are less conspicuous. *Elektrichka* (commuter rail; marked on signs as пригородные поезда; *prigorodnye poezda*) has its own platforms; buy tickets at the *kassa*. *Obshchy* (общий), the fourth class, is for livestock. **Buses,** cheaper than trains, are better for shorter distances, but can be crowded and overbooked; don't hesitate to eject anyone who's taken your seat.

BY TAXI AND BY THUMB. In Russia, hailing a taxi resembles hitchhiking and should be treated with equal caution. *Let's Go* does not recommend it. To hail a car, stand off the curb, hold out one hand palm-down, and when a car stops—usually a private citizen—tell the driver your destination. Drivers will either refuse the destination altogether or ask *"Skolko?"* (How much?), and then haggle. If you do not speak Russian, be sure to fix a price firmly beforehand. If the driver agrees without asking a price, you must ask *"Skolko?"* yourself and trace out digits with your fingers. Never enter a vehicle with more than one person in it.

TOURIST SERVICES AND MONEY

EMERGENCY Police: ☎02. Ambulance: ☎03. Fire: ☎01.

TOURIST OFFICES. Russia has two types of tourist offices: those that only arrange tours, and those that offer general travel services. Offices of the former type are often unhelpful, but those of the latter are often eager to help, especially with visa registration. Travel agencies usually hide out in larger hotels, and often have English-speaking staff; street kiosks can provide the most accurate maps.

MONEY. Since the revaluation in 1998 of the official currency, the **ruble,** old denominations have been phased out. **Inflation** rates mean that prices and exchange rates listed are volatile. Law requires you to show your passport when changing money. Never transact on the street. An *Obmen Valyuty* (Обмен Валюты; currency exchange) will change euros or US dollars; many take credit cards. **Banks** also offer both security and good rates. Main branches usually accept traveler's checks and give cash advances on credit cards. **ATMs** (банкомат; *bankomat*) link to all major networks and credit cards. Although most places only accept rubles, it's wise to keep €20 on hand. Many establishments will not accept crumpled, torn, or written-on bills. One day of budget travel runs between €30-40. In St. Petersburg and Moscow only, a **tip** of 5-10% is becoming customary.

RUBLES (R)		
AUS$1 = 20.93R	100R = AUS$4.78	
CDN$1 = 21.99R	100R = CDN$4.55	
EUR€1 = 35.89R	100R = EUR€2.79	
NZ$1 = 19.28R	100R = NZ$5.19	
UK£1 = 53.37R	100R = UK£1.87	
US$1 = 29.28R	100R = US$3.42	

BUSINESS HOURS. Most establishments close for a lunch break, even train ticket offices and stores billed as open 24hr. Most also close at least 30min. earlier than posted, if they choose to open at all.

COMMUNICATION

PHONE CODES	**Country code: 7. International dialing prefix: 810.** From outside Russia, dial int'l dialing prefix (see inside back cover) + 7 + city code + local number.

TELEPHONES AND INTERNET ACCESS. Telephone offices in St. Petersburg and Moscow place direct international calls; these run €1-1.50 per min. to Europe and US$1.50-2 per min. to Australia and the US. Card-operated phones, often with instructions in English, continue to replace the older token-operated standard. **Phone cards** are sold at central telephone offices, metro stations, and newspaper kiosks; the attendant might ask "*Na ulitse?*" (On the street?) to distinguish between phones in the station or office and outdoor public phones. Insert a "2" between the dialing code and the phone number for 5-digit numbers. International access codes for Moscow (M) and St. Petersburg (SP) include: **AT&T** (M ☎ 755 5042, SP ☎ 325 5042), **British Telecom** (M/SP ☎ 810 800 110 1044), **Canada Direct** (M ☎ 755 5045, SP ☎ 810 800 110 1012), **MCI WorldPhone** (M ☎ 960 2222, SP ☎ 747 3322), **Sprint** (M ☎ 747 3324, SP ☎ 8095 747 3324), **Telecom NZ** (M ☎ 747 3364; SP ☎ 810 800 110 1064). Since calling is expensive, email is your best bet for keeping in touch. **Internet** cafes are common in both cities (from 20-70R per hr.).

MAIL. Service is much more reliable for outgoing than incoming mail. Airmail (авиа; *avia*) to the US will arrive as soon as a week after mailing; to other destinations, two to three weeks. Sending mail certified (заказное; 16R) reduces the chance that it will be lost. Regular letters to the US cost 16R; postcards cost 11R. *Poste Restante* is Писмо До Востребования (*pismo do vostrebovania*). Address mail to be held according to the following example: SURNAME First name, 103 009 Москва (Moscow), Писмо До Востребования, RUSSIA.

LANGUAGE. Russian is spoken in Moscow and St. Petersburg, though pronunciation varies by region. Some familiarity with the **Cyrillic alphabet** (p. 1057) will make getting around immeasurably easier. Russian basics are listed on p. 1065.

ACCOMMODATIONS

RUSSIA	❶	❷	❸	❹	❺
ACCOMMODATIONS	under 400R	400-700R	700-1200R	1200-2000R	over 2000R

Only Moscow and St. Petersburg have **hostels,** which average around US$18-25 per night. Reserve well in advance, especially in summer. Most **hotels** only accept cash. Singles have budget ranges of 300-450R, and vary by class. *Lux,* usually two-room doubles with TV, phone, fridge, and bath, cost the most. *Polu-lux* rooms are singles or doubles with TV, phone, and bath. At the cheapest end, *bez udobstv* (без удобств) are singles with a sink. Hot water, and sometimes all water, is only on for a few hours a day. **University dorms** offer cheap rooms, but don't expect sparkling bathrooms or a reliable boiler room. Some accept foreign students for €5-10 per night; make arrangements through an institution at home. A reasonably-priced option in larger cities, **private rooms** and **apartments** can cost around 200R per night. **Homestays,** arranged through a tourist office, are often the cheapest (50-100R per night) and best option for stays not in a megalopolis.

FOOD AND DRINK

RUSSIA	❶	❷	❸	❹	❺
FOOD	under 70R	70-150R	150-300R	300-500R	over 500R

Russian dishes can be both delectable and disgusting to describe; tasty *borscht* sometimes comes with *salo* (pig fat). Russians' largest meal, *obed* (обед; lunch), includes: *salat* (салат; salad), usually cucumbers and tomatoes or beets and potatoes with mayonnaise or sour cream; *sup* (суп; soup); and *kuritsa* (курица; chicken) or *myaso* (мясо; meat), often called *kotlyety* (котлеты) or *bifshteks* (бифштекс). Ordering a few *zakuski* (закуски; small appetizers) instead of a main dish can save money. *Blini* (stuffed crepes), s*hashlyki* (шашлыки; skewered meat), and *kvas* (квас), a dark-brown alcoholic drink, are sold on the streets.

HEALTH, SAFETY, AND SECURITY

In **medical emergencies,** either leave the country or go to the **American Medical Centers** in Moscow (p. 878) or St. Petersburg (p. 887), which have American doctors. Traveler's **health insurance** is essential (p. 27). **Pharmacies** (Аптека; *Apteka*) abound and offer a range of Western medicine and hygiene products. **Water** in much of Russia is drinkable in small doses, but not in Moscow and St. Petersburg; boil it for 10min. to be safe. Russian bottled water is often mineral water. Men's **toilets** are marked with an "М," women's with a "Ж;" toilet paper is uncommon in public restrooms. **Crime** against foreigners is reportedly on the rise, particularly in cities. Although it is hard to look Russian (especially with a big pack), try not to flaunt your nationality. Reports of mafia warfare are scaring off tourists, but shops are more likely targets than individuals. Due to the recent eruption of violence in the Northern Caucasus, avoid the Dagestan and Chechnya regions.

HOLIDAYS AND FESTIVALS

Holidays: New Year's (Jan. 1-2); Orthodox Christmas (Jan. 7); Defenders of the Motherland Day (Feb. 23); International Women's Day (Mar. 8); Orthodox Easter (May 1); Labor Day (May 1-2); Victory Day (May 9); Independence Day (June 12); Day of Accord and Reconciliation (Nov. 7); Constitution Day (Dec. 12).

Festivals: Moscow and St. Petersburg celebrate White Nights with concerts and fireworks in the summer days when the sun barely touches the horizon (June 21-July 11).

FACTS AND FIGURES: RUSSIA

Official Name: Russian Federation.

Capital: Moscow.

Major Cities: St. Petersburg, Ulan Ude, Vladivostok.

Population: 143,782,000.

Land Area: 16,995,800 sq. km.

Time Zone: GMT +3.

Language: Russian.

Religions: Unaffiliated (74%), Russian Orthodox (16%), Muslim (10%).

MOSCOW (MOCKBA)   ☎ 8095

Moscow (pop. 9,000,000) has long regulated the pulse of Russia. When Communism swept through Moscow, it leveled most of the capital's golden domes and left behind massive buildings, crumbling outskirts, and countless statues of Lenin. But things change quickly in this audacious city, and in the midst of its debauchery and corruption, Moscow is recreating itself using the same resourcefulness that helped it engineer, and then survive, the most ambitious social experiment in history.

RUSSIA

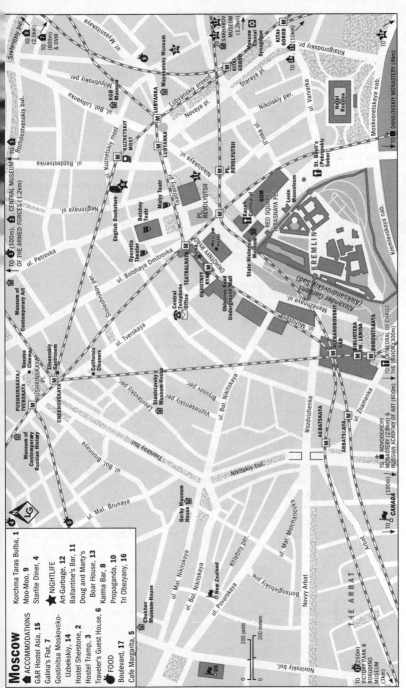

MOSCOW

▲ ACCOMMODATIONS
G&R Hostel Asia, **15**
Galina's Flat, **7**
Gostinitsa Moskovsko-
Uzbekskiy, **14**
Hostel Sherstone, **2**
Hostel Tramp, **3**
Traveler's Guest House, **6**

Korchma Taras Bulba, **1**
Moo-Moo, **9**
Starlite Diner, **4**

★ NIGHTLIFE
Art-Garbage, **12**
Ballantine's Bar, **11**
Doug and Marty's
Boar House, **13**
Karma Bar, **8**
Propaganda, **10**
Tri Obezyany, **16**

● FOOD
Boulevard, **17**
Cafe Margarita, **5**

RUSSIA

▗ TRANSPORTATION

Flights: International flights arrive at **Sheremetyevo-2** (Шереметьево-2; ☎956 46 66). Take the van under the "автолайн" sign in front of the station to M2: Rechnoy Vokzal (Речной Вокзал), or take bus #551 or 851 to M2: Rechnoy Vokzal or bus #517 to M8: Planyornaya (Планёрная; 10R). Buses run 24hr., but the metro closes at 1am. Purchase bus tickets at the *kassa* (касса) at **Tsentralnyy Aerovokzal** (Центральный Аэровокзал; Central Airport Station), Leningradskiy pr. 37, corpus 6 (☎941 99 99), 2 stops on almost any tram or trolley from M2: Aeroport (the sign on the front of the bus should read "Центральный Аэровокзал"). **Taxis** to the center tend to be overpriced; bargain down at least to US$30. **Yellow Taxi** (☎940 88 88) has fixed prices. Cars outside the departures level charge US$15-20. Always agree on a price before getting in.

Trains: Moscow has 8 train stations arranged around the M5 line. Tickets for longer trips within Russia can be bought at the **Tsentralnoye Zheleznodorozhnoye Agenstvo** (Центральное Железнодорожное Агенство; Central Train Agency; ☎266 93 33; www.mza.ru), to the right of Yaroslavskiy Vokzal (see below). Tickets specify passengers' name, seat, and station (*vokzal*) of departure. Cyrillic schedules of trains, destinations, departure times, and station names are posted on both sides of the hall. (*Kassa* open M-F 7am-8pm, Sa-Su 7am-5pm.) If you buy the more expensive tickets through a hotel, the extra cost is what spares you the hassle of the *vokzal* experience.

Belorusskiy Vokzal (Белорусский), pl. Tverskoi Zastavy 7 (☎973 81 91). To: **Berlin** (27hr., 1 per day, 3500R); **Minsk** (10hr., 3-4 per day, 750R); **Prague** (35hr., 1 per day, 2860R); **Vilnius** (16hr., 1-2 per day, 1950R); **Warsaw** (21hr., 2 per day, 2520R).

Kazanskiy Vokzal (Казанский), Komsomolskaya pl. 2 (Комсомольская; ☎264 31 81), opposite Leningradskiy Vokzal. Serves: **Kazan** (12hr., 2 per day, 1950R).

Kievskiy Vokzal (Киевский), pl. Kievskovo Vokzala (Киевского; ☎240 11 15). To: **Kyiv** (14hr., 4 per day, 950R); **Lviv** (26hr., 2 per day, 1100R); **Odessa** (25-28hr., 1-2 per day, 1100R).

Kurskiy Vokzal (Курский), ul. Zemlyanoy Val 29/1 (Земляной Вал; ☎917 31 52), serves **Sevastopol** (26hr., 1-2 per day, 1100R) and the **Caucasus**.

Leningradskiy Vokzal (Ленинградский), Komsomolskaya pl. 3. To: **Helsinki** (13hr., 1 per day, 2720R); **St. Petersburg** (8hr., 10-15 per day, 700R); **Tallinn** (14hr., 1 per day, 1550R).

Paveletskiy Vokzal (Павелецкий), Paveletskaya pl. 1 (Павелецкая; ☎235 05 22), serves the **Crimea** and eastern **Ukraine**.

Rizhskiy Vokzal (Рижский), Pr. Mira 79/3. To **Rīga** (16hr., 2 per day, 2050R) and **Estonia**.

Yaroslavskiy Vokzal (Ярославский), Komsomolskaya pl. 5a, begins the **Trans-Siberian Railroad**.

Public Transportation: The **Moscow Metro** (Метро) is fast, clean, and efficient—a masterpiece of Soviet urban planning. Trains run daily 6am-1am. A station serving multiple lines may have multiple names. Buy token-cards (10R, 10 trips for 75R) from the *kassas* in stations. Buy **bus** and **trolley** tickets from kiosks labeled "проездные билеты" or from the driver (10R). Punch your ticket when you get on, or risk a 100R fine.

Taxis: Most taxis do not use meters and tend to overcharge. **Yellow Taxis** charge 10R per km (15R after midnight) and are easily picked out on the street. It is common and cheaper to hail a private car, done by holding your arm out horizontally. Before getting in, tell the driver your destination and agree on a price (usually 50-100R across town). *Let's Go* does not recommend hitchhiking.

METRO MADNESS. Moscow's subway system can seem bewildering. *Let's Go* has tried to simplify navigation by artificially numbering each line; for correspondences, consult this guide's color map of the Moscow Metro. When speaking with Russians, however, use the color or name, and not the number.

ORIENTATION AND PRACTICAL INFORMATION

A series of concentric rings radiates outward from the **Kremlin** (Кремль; Kreml) and **Red Square** (Красная Площадь; Krasnaya ploshchad). The outermost **Moscow Ring Road** marks the city limits, but most sights lie within the smaller **Garden Ring** (Садовое Кольцо; Sadovoe Koltso). Main streets include **Ulitsa Tverskaya** (Тверская), which extends north along the metro's green line, and **Arbat** (Арбат) and **Novyy Arbat** (Новый Арбат), which run west parallel to the blue lines. Orient yourself using the metro; it helps to have some familiarity with Cyrillic. All over the city, kiosks sell English and Cyrillic maps (35-60R). Be careful when crossing streets, as drivers are notoriously oblivious to pedestrians; for safety's sake, most intersections have an underpass (*perekhod;* переход).

> **PAYING IN RUSSIA.** Due to the fluctuating value of the Russian ruble, some establishments list their prices in US dollars. Likewise, some prices in this book also appear in US dollars, but travelers should expect to pay in rubles.

TOURIST, FINANCIAL, AND LOCAL SERVICES

Tours: People with loudspeakers on the northern end of Red Square offer walking tours of the area (1hr., every 30min. 10am-12:30pm, 80R) and bus tours of the main sights (1½hr., 150R). Russian only; translators may be available at extra cost.

Budget Travel: Student Travel Agency Russia (STAR), Baltiyskaya ul. 9, 3rd fl. (Балтийская; ☎ 797 95 55; www.startravel.ru). M2: Sokol (Сокол). Discount plane tickets, ISICs, and worldwide hostel booking. Open M-F 10am-7pm, Sa 11am-4pm.

Embassies: Australia, Podkoloniy per. 10 (☎ 956 60 70; 956 61 62). M6: Kitai Gorod (Китай Город). M3 or 5: Smolenskaya/Park Kultury (Смоленская/Парк Культуры). Open M-F 9:30am-12:30pm. **Canada,** Starokonyushennyy per. 23 (Староконюшенный; ☎ 105 60 00; fax 232 99 50). M1: Kropotkinskaya or M4: Arbatskaya (Арбатская). Open M-F 8:30am-1pm and 2-5pm. **Ireland,** Grokholskiy per. 5 (Грохольский; ☎ 937 59 11, consular section 937 59 02). M5 or 6: Prospekt Mira. Open M-F 9:30am-1pm and 2:30-5:30pm. **New Zealand,** Povarskaya ul. 44 (Поварская; ☎ 956 35 79). M7: Barikadnaya (Барикадная). Open M-F 9am-5:30pm. Consular section (☎ 956 26 42) open M-F 9:30-10:30am and 4-5pm. **UK,** Smolenskaya nab. 10 (Смоленская; ☎ 956 72 00; www.britemb.msk.ru). M3: Smolenskaya. Open M-F 9am-1pm and 2-5pm. Consular section (☎ 956 72 50) open M-F 8am-noon. **US,** Novinskiy 19/23 (Новинский; ☎ 728 50 00; www.usembassy.ru). M5: Krasnoprenenskaya (Краснопресненская). Flash a US passport and cut the long lines. Open M-F 9am-6pm. Consular section (☎ 728 55 60) open M-F 9am-noon. **American Citizen Services** (☎ 728 55 77, after-hours emergency 728 50 00; fax 728 50 84) connects citizens to a variety of organizations. Open M-F 9-10:30am and 2-4pm.

Currency Exchange: Banks are everywhere; check for ads in English-language newspapers. Typically only main branches change **traveler's checks** and issue **cash advances.** Almost all banks and hotels have **ATMs.** Avoid machines protruding from buildings; they work erratically, and withdrawing cash on busy streets makes you a target for muggers.

American Express: ul. Usacheva 33 (☎ 933 84 00). M1: Sportivnaya. Use the exit at the front of the train, turn right, and then right again after the Global USA shop onto Usacheva. Open M-F 9am-6pm.

English Bookstore: Angliya British Bookshop, Vorotnikovskiy per. 6 (Воротниковский; www.anglophile.ru). Open M-F 10am-7pm, Sa 10am-6pm, Su 11am-5pm. AmEx/MC/V.

EMERGENCY AND COMMUNICATIONS

Emergency: Police: ☎ 02. **Ambulance:** ☎ 03. **Fire:** ☎ 01.

24hr. Pharmacies: Look for signs marked "круглосуточно" (*kruglosutochno;* always open). Locations include: Tverskaya ul. 25 (☎299 24 59), M2: Tverskaya/Mayakovskaya; ul. Zemlyanoi Val 25 (☎917 12 85), M5: Kurskaya; Kutozovskiy Prospekt 24 (Кутозовский; ☎249 19 37), M4: Kutuzovskaya (Кутузовская).

Medical Assistance: American Medical Center (AMC), Prospekt Mira 26 (☎933 77 00; fax 933 77 01). M5 or 6: Prospekt Mira. Turn left out of the metro onto Grokholskiy per. Walk-in medical care US$120 per visit. Open 24hr. AmEx/MC/V. **American Clinic,** Grokholskiy per. 31 (☎937 57 57; www.klinik.ru). M5 or 6: Prospekt Mira. Same directions as for AMC. American board-certified doctors; family and internal medicine services. Consultations US$100. House calls US$150. Open 24hr. MC/V. **European Medical Clinic,** Spiridoniyevskiy Per. 5/1 (☎933 65 55; www.emcmos.ru) offers dental, gynecological, pediatric, and psychiatric care. Consultations US$120. Open 24hr.

Internet Access: Timeonline (☎363 00 60), on the bottom level of the Okhotnyy Ryad underground mall. M1: Okhotnyy Ryad. At night, enter through the metro underpass. Over 100 computers in the center of the city. 30-75R per hr. Open 24hr. **Cafemax** (☎787 68 58; www.cafemax.ru) has 3 locations: ul. Pyatnitskaya 25/1m (M2: Novokuznetskaya), Akademika Khokhlova 3 (M1: Universitet), and ul Novoslobodskaya 3 (M9: Novoslobodskaya). 70R per hr. Open 24hr.

Telephones: Moscow Central Telegraph (see **Post Offices,** below). Go to the 2nd hall with telephones to place international calls. Prepay at the counter or buy a prepaid phonecard. Collect calls and calling card calls not available. Calls to the US 9-20R per min., to Europe 12-35R per min. **Local calls** require phone cards, available at kiosks and some metro stops. Dial ☎09 for directory assistance.

Post Offices: Moscow Central Telegraph, Tverskaya ul. 7, uphill from the Kremlin. M1: Okhotnyy Ryad. International mail at window #23; faxes at #11-12; telegram service available. Open M-F 8am-2pm and 3-8pm, Sa-Su 7am-2pm and 3-7pm. *Poste Restante* at window #24. Bring packages unwrapped. **Postal Code:** 103 009.

▐ ACCOMMODATIONS

As both the Russian capital and the point of departure for the Trans-Siberian Railway, Moscow attracts droves of hostelers. Although the best deals can often be found in Soviet standard-issue hotels, these tend to have receptionists with more limited English. Older women standing outside major rail stations often rent private rooms (сдаю комнату) or apartments (сдаю квартиру)—be sure to haggle.

▨ **Galina's Flat,** ul. Chaplygina 8, #35 (Чаплыгина; ☎921 60 38; galinas.flat@mtu-net.ru). M1: Chistyye Prudy. Head down Chistoprudnyy bul., turn left on Kharitonevskiy per., and then right on Chaplygina. Go into the courtyard at #8, veer right, and enter the building marked "Уникум;" it's on the 5th fl. Superb location and real Russian hospitality. Galina owns cats. Kitchen access. Breakfast 50R. Book in advance. Airport transfer US$30. 5-bed dorms US$10; singles US$18; doubles US$25. ❶

Traveler's Guest House (TGH), Bolshaya Pereslavskaya ul. 50, 10th fl. (Большая Переславская; ☎631 40 59; www.tgh.ru). M5 or 6: Prospekt Mira. Take the 2nd right across from Prospekt Mira 61, walk to the end of the *pereulok,* and go left on B. Pereyaslavskaya. Friendly English-speaking staff. Kitchen access. Airport transport US$40. Internet 1R per min. Laundry 130R per 3kg. Visa invitations for guests US$30. Check-out 11am. Dorms US$23; singles US$45; doubles US$55, with bath US$60. MC/V. ❷

Gostinitsa Moskovsko-Uzbekskiy, Zelenodolskaya ul. 3/2 (Зеленодольская; ☎378 33 92 or 378 21 77; hotel@caravan.ru). M7: Ryazanskiy Prospekt (Рязанский). Take the metro exit near the back car of the outbound train. As you exit, a "Гостиница" sign will be visible on top of the hotel to your left. A wide range of rooms; unrefurbished ones are clean and ultra-cheap. Singles 650-930R; doubles 1000-1500R. 500R key deposit. ❷

G&R Hostel Asia, Zelenodolskaya ul. 3/2 (Зеленодольская; ☎378 00 01; www.hostels.ru). M7: Ryazanskiy Prospekt (Рязанский). On the 5th fl. of the Gostinitsa Moskovsko-Uzbekskiy (see above). Clean rooms. Helpful staff. Transport to/from airport €30/€35. Internet 2R per min. Visa invitations €35. Reception 8am-midnight. Dorms €18; singles €25; doubles €40; triples €54. HI discount €1. 10th day free. MC/V. ❷

Hostel Sherstone, Gostinichny proezd 8 (Гостиничны; ☎797 80 75). M9: Vladykino. Walk along the railway turning left from the metro as far as the overpass, then take a left and go past a post office. On the 3rd fl. of the Hotel Sherstone. Visa invitations €30. Breakfast included. Private showers. Internet 2R per min. Reception (room 324) 8am-midnight. Dorms €17; singles €35; doubles €22. HI discount €1. ❷

Hostel Tramp, Selskohozyaistvennaya ul. 17/2 (☎187 54 33; www.hostelling.ru). M6: Botanicheskiy Sad. Turn left from the metro onto ul. Vilgelma Pika and continue to the Gostinitsa Turist. Hostel Tramp is in building 7; reception is in room 524. Airport transfer US$35. Dorms US$22-25; singles with bath $45; doubles with bath $50. ❷

🄵 FOOD

Restaurants range from the expensive to the outrageous. Those that serve local cuisine tend to be more affordable, and many higher-priced places now offer business lunch specials (бизнес ланч; typically noon-3pm; US$4-8). Russians dine in the late evening; avoid crowds by eating earlier.

RESTAURANTS

🄱 Boulevard, Ul. Petrovka 30/7 (☎209 68 87). M2, 7, or 9: Pushkinskaya. Serving for the most part French-inspired cuisine, Boulevard has survived with the new Russians due to the quality of its food. 10% off before 4pm. Wildfowl entrees US$26. Live harp music Th. French singers F. Open daily noon-midnight. AmEx/DC/MC/V. ❺

Korchma Taras Bulba (Корчма Тарас Бульба), Sadovaya-Samotechnaya ul. 13 (☎200 00 56). M9: Tsvetnoy Bulvar (Цветной Бульвар). Turn left from the metro and walk up Tsvetnoy Bulvar. Any place with a 24hr. feedback hotline must take its service seriously. English menu. Entrees 140-400R. Open 24hr. MC/V. ❸

Cafe Margarita (Кафе Маргарита), Malaya Bronnaya ul. 28 (Малая Вронная; ☎299 65 34), at the intersection with Malyy Kozikhinskiy per. (Малый Козихинский). M2: Mayakovskaya. Turn left on Bolshaya Sadovaya, then again left on Malaya Bronaya. Locals love this Russian cafe and restaurant. Entrees 250-450R. Open daily 1pm-midnight. ❸

Moo-Moo (My-My), with many locations: Koroviy Val 1 (☎237 29 00), M5 Dobryninskaya; ul. Arbat 45/42 (☎241 13 64), M3:Smolenskaya; Komsomolskiy pr. 26 (☎245 78 20), M1: Fruznetskaya; Masnyatskaya ul. 14 (☎923 45 03), M1 or 7: Lubyanka; Pr. Mira 114 (☎287 49 15), M6: Alekseevskaya; Leningradskiy pr. 62a (☎152 13 73), M2: Aeroport. Cheap and fairly healthy European and Russian homecooking served cafeteria-style. *Pelmeni* 46R. Pork cutlets 54R. Open daily 9am-11pm. ❶

Starlite Diner, Bolshaya Sadovaya 16 (☎290 96 38). M2: Mayakovskaya. Walk down Bolshaya Sadovaya toward the Mayakovskiy statue. Often packed with expats, this American-style diner serves a good cheeseburger with fries (250R) and a milkshake (190R). Breakfast is served all day. Entrees 250-599R. Open 24hr. AmEx/MC/V. ❸

MARKETS AND SUPERMARKETS

Vendors bring everything from a handful of cherries to an entire produce section to Moscow's **markets.** A visit is worthwhile just for the sights: Sides of beef, grapes, and pots of flowers crowd together in a visual bouquet. Impromptu markets spring up by metro stations; the best are at Turgenyevskaya and Kuznetskiy most. Vendors arrive around 10am and leave by 8pm. Bring your own bag. **Eliseevskiy Gas-**

tronom (Елисеевский), ul. Tverskaya 14, is Moscow's most famous supermarket. (☎209 07 60. Open M-Sa 8am-9pm, Su 10am-8pm.) Other supermarkets are scattered all over; look for signs marked "продукти" (produkty; groceries).

◉ SIGHTS

Moscow's sights reflect the city's interrupted history: because St. Petersburg was the tsar's seat for 200 years, there are 16th-century churches and Soviet-era museums, but little in between. Although Moscow has no grand palaces and 80% of its pre-revolutionary splendor was demolished by the Soviet regime, the city's museums contain the very best of Russian art, and sights still abound city-wide.

THE KREMLIN

The Kremlin (Кремль; Kreml) is the geographical and historical center of Moscow. It was here that Ivan the Terrible reigned and Stalin ruled from behind the Iron Curtain. Napoleon simmered at this fortress while the rest of Moscow burned, and the USSR dissolved itself here in 1991. In the Kremlin's Armory and in its magnificent churches, the glory and the riches of the Russian Empire are on display. Besides the sights listed below, the only other place in the triangular complex visitors may enter is the **Kremlin Palace of Congresses,** the white square monster built by Khrushchev in 1961 for Communist Party Congresses. Now it's a theater. English-speaking guides offer **tours** of the complex at insane prices; haggle away. (*☎202 37 76. Complex open M-W and F-Su 10am-5pm. Last admission 4:30pm. Buy tickets at the kassa in the Alexander Gardens, on the western side of the Kremlin.*)

▓ARMORY MUSEUM AND DIAMOND FUND. At the southwest corner of the Kremlin complex, the Armory Museum (Оружейная Палата; Oruzheynaya Palata) exemplifies the opulence of the Russian court. Among imperial thrones, coaches, and crowns are the legendary Fabergé Eggs in Room 2, each revealing an intricate jewelled miniature. In an annex, the Diamond Fund (Выставка Алмазного Фонда; Vystavka Almaznogo Fonda) has even more glitter, including a 190-carat diamond given to Catherine the Great by her lover Gregory Orlov. Soviet finds, including the world's largest chunks of platinum, are also on display. (*The Armory lets in groups for 1½hr. visits at 10am, noon, 2:30, and 4:30pm. Diamond Fund open 10am-1pm and 2-6pm. Armory 350R, students 175R. Diamond Fund 350R/250R.*)

CATHEDRAL SQUARE. Russia's most famous golden domes can be seen in Cathedral Square. The church closest to the Armory is the **Annunciation Cathedral** (Благовещуиский Собор; Blagoveshchenskiy Sobor), which guards luminous icons by Andrei Rublev and Theophanes the Greek. The square **Archangel Cathedral** (Азчангельский Собор; Arkhangelskiy Sobor), gleaming with vivid icons and metallic coffins, is the final resting place for many tsars who ruled before Peter the Great, including Ivans III (the Great) and IV (the Terrible), and Mikhail Romanov. The 15th-century **Assumption Cathedral** (Успенский Собор; Uspenskiy Sobor), at the center of the square, was used by Napoleon as a stable in 1812. Nearby are the small **Patriarch's Palace** (Патриарший Дворец; Patriarshiy Dvorets), which now houses a museum, and the even smaller **Church of the Deposition of the Robe.** To the right of Assumption Cathedral, the **Ivan the Great Belltower** (Колокольная Ивана Великого; Kolokolnya Ivana Velikovo) now houses temporary exhibits. Directly behind the tower is the **Tsar Bell** (Царь-колокол; Tsar-kolokol), the world's largest bell. It has never rung and probably never will—a 1737 fire caused an 11½-ton piece to break off. (*All cathedrals 250R, students 125R.*)

AROUND RED SQUARE

The 700m-long Red Square (Красная площадь; Krasnaya Ploshchad) has hosted everything from farmer's markets to public hangings, from Communist parades to renegade Cessna landings. Across from the Kremlin is **GUM**, once the world's largest purveyor of Soviet "consumer goods," now an upscale shopping mall. Also flanking the square are **St. Basil's Cathedral,** the **State Historical Museum,** the **Lenin Mausoleum,** and the pink-and-green **Kazan Cathedral.**

ST. BASIL'S CATHEDRAL. Moscow has no more familiar symbol than the colorful onion domes of St. Basil's Cathedral (Собор Василия Блаженного; Sobor Vasiliya Blazhennovo). Ivan the Terrible commissioned it to celebrate his victory over the Tatars in Kazan in 1552, and it was completed in 1561. "Basil" is the English equivalent of Vasily, the name of a holy fool who correctly predicted that Ivan would murder his own son. St. Basil's labyrinthine interior, unusual for Orthodox churches, is filled with both decorative and religious frescoes. *(M3: Ploshchad Revolutsii (Площадь Революции). Open daily 11am-6pm. Buy tickets from the kassa to the left of the entrance, then proceed upstairs. 100R, students 50R.)*

LENIN'S TOMB. Lenin's likeness can be seen in bronze all over the city, but he appears in the eerily luminescent flesh in Lenin's Mausoleum (Мавзолей В.И. Ленина; Mavzoley V.I. Lenina). In the Soviet era, this squat red structure was guarded fiercely, and the wait to get in took three hours. Today's line is still long, and the guards remain stone-faced, but the atmosphere is characterized by curiosity rather than reverence. Entrance includes access to the **Kremlin wall,** where Stalin, Brezhnev, Andropov, Gagarin, and John Reed, the author of *Ten Days That Shook the World,* are buried. *(Open Tu-Th and Sa-Su 10am-1pm. Free.)*

NORTH OF RED SQUARE

Just outside the main gate to Red Square is an elaborate gold circle marking **Kilometer 0,** the spot from which all distances from Moscow are measured. Don't be fooled by this tourist attraction—the real Kilometer 0 lies underneath the Lenin Mausoleum. Just a few steps away, the **Alexander Gardens** (Александровский Сад; Aleksandrovskiy Sad) are a green respite from the pollution of central Moscow. At the northern end of the gardens is the **Tomb of the Unknown Soldier** (Могила Неизвестного Солдата; Mogila Neizvestnovo Soldata), where an **eternal flame** burns in memory of the catastrophic losses suffered in WWII, known in Russia as the Great Patriotic War. To the west is **Manezh Square** (Манежная Площадь; Manezhnaya Ploshchad), only recently converted into a pedestrian area. The famous **Moscow Hotel**—which may be demolished and rebuilt under Mayor Luzhdoz's city renovation plans—overlooks the square and separates it from the older, smaller **Revolution Square** (Площадь Революции; Ploshchad Revolyutsii). Both squares are connected in the north by **Okhotnyy Ryad** (Охотный Ряд; Hunters' Row), a ritzy underground mall. *(Open daily 11am-10pm. Enter directly from the square or through the underpass.)* Across Okhotnyy Ryad from the Moscow Hotel is the **Duma,** the lower house of Parliament, and across from Revolution Square is **Theater Square** (Театральная Площадь; Teatralnaya Ploshchad), home of the **Bolshoy** and **Malyy Theatres** (see **Entertainment,** p. 884). More posh hotels, chic stores, and government buildings line **Tverskaya Street,** which starts at Manezh Square and runs northwest. Tverskaya is Moscow's main street and home to some of its richest residents.

CHURCHES, MONASTERIES, AND SYNAGOGUES

CATHEDRAL OF CHRIST THE SAVIOR. Moscow's most controversial landmark is the enormous gold-domed Cathedral of Christ the Savior (Храм Христа Спасителя; Khram Khrista Spasitelya). Stalin demolished Nicholas I's original cathedral on this site to make way for a gigantic Palace of the Soviets, but Khrushchev abandoned the project and built a heated outdoor pool instead. In 1995, after the pool's water vapors damaged paintings in the nearby Pushkin Museum, Mayor Yury Luzhkov and the Orthodox Church won the renewed battle for the site and built the US$250 million cathedral in a mere two years. It was completed in 2000. *(Volkhonka 15, between ul. Volkhonka (Волхонка) and the Moscow River. M1: Kropotkinskaya. Open daily 10am-5pm. Service schedule varies. Cathedral free.)*

NOVODEVICHY MONASTERY AND CEMETERY. Moscow's most famous monastery (Новодевичий Монастырь; Novodevichiy Monastyr) is hard to miss thanks to its high brick walls, golden domes, and tourist buses. In the center, the **Smolensk Cathedral** (Смоленский Собор; Smolenskiy Sobor) shows off Russian icons and frescoes. As you exit the gates, turn right and follow the exterior wall back around to the **cemetery** (кладбище; kladbishche), a pilgrimage site that holds the graves of such famous figures as Bulgakov, Chekhov, Gogol, Mayakovsky, Shostakovich, and Stanislavsky. *(M1: Sportivnaya. Take the metro exit that does not lead to the stadium, turn right, and walk several blocks. ☎ 246 85 26. Open M and W-Su 10am-5:30pm; kassa closes at 4:45pm. Closed 1st M of each month. Cathedral closed on humid days; call in advance. English tour 300R. Grounds 40R, students 20R. Smolensk Cathedral and special exhibits 93R/53R each. Cemetery open daily in summer 9am-7pm; low season 9am-6pm. 30R.)*

DANILOV MONASTERY. The seat of the Patriarch, head of the Russian Orthodox Church, is at the Danilov Monastery (Даниловский Монастырь). A mosaic of a stern-looking man marks the Patriarch's office. The white exterior is complemented by stunning grounds and long-robed monks; unfortunately, visitors can only enter the church and the small museum, both to the left of the main entrance. *(M9: Tulskaya (Тульская). From the square, follow the trolley tracks down Danilovskiy val., away from the gray buildings, past a small park. Open daily 6:30am-7pm. Services M-F 6, 7am, and 5pm; Sa-Su 6:30, 9am, and 5pm. Museum open W and Su 11am-1pm and 1:30-4pm.)*

MOSCOW CHORAL SYNAGOGUE. Constructed in the 1870s, the synagogue is a break from the city's ubiquitous onion domes. Though it functioned during Soviet rule, all but the bravest Jews were deterred by KGB agents who photographed anyone who entered. According to official statistics, today more than 200,000 Jews live in Moscow. Services are increasingly well attended, but the occasional graffiti is a sad reminder that anti-Semitism in Russia is not dead. *(M6 or 7: Kitai-Gorod. Go north on Solyanskiy Proyezd (Солянский Проезд) and take the first left. Open daily 8am-10pm. Services M-F 8:30am and 8pm, Sa-Su 9am and 9pm.)*

CHURCH OF ST. NICHOLAS OF THE WEAVERS. The maroon-and-green trim of the Church of St. Nicholas of the Weavers (Церковь Николы в Хамовниках; Tserkov Nikoly v Khamovnikakh) makes it look like a gingerbread house. Enter off ul. Lva Tolstovo (Лва Толстого) for a view of the low ceilings and vivid interior. *(M1 or 5: Park Kultury. Open daily 8am-8pm. Services M-Sa 8am and 5pm; Su 7, 10am, 5pm.)*

OTHER SIGHTS

MOSCOW METRO. All the beautiful Moscow Metro (Московское Метро) stations are unique. Those inside the circle line have sculptures, stained glass, elaborate mosaics, and unusual chandeliers. See the baroque elegance of **Komsomolskaya** (Космомолская), the stained glass of **Novoslobodskaya** (Новослободская), and the bronze statues of revolutionary archetypes, from farmer to factory worker, in the station on **Ploshchad Revolutsii** (Площадь Революции).

THE ARBAT. Now a commercial pedestrian shopping arcade, the Arbat (Арбат) was once a showpiece of *glasnost* and a haven for political radicals, Hare Krishnas, street poets, and *metallisty* (heavy metal rockers). Some of the old flavor remains in the street performers and guitar-playing teenagers. Intersecting but nearly parallel to the Arbat runs the bigger, newer, and uglier **Novyy Arbat**, lined with gray high-rises and massive Russian stores. *(M3: Arbatskaya or Smolenskaya.)*

VICTORY PARK. On the left past the **Triumphal Arch**, which celebrates the victories of 1812, is Victory Park (Парк Победы; Park Pobedy), built as a lasting monument to WWII. It includes the **Museum of the Great Patriotic War** (Музей Отечественной Войны; Muzey Otechestvennoy Voyny) and the gold-domed **Church of St. George the Victorious** (Храм Георгия Победаносного; Khram Georgiya Pobedonosnova). *(M4: Kutuzovskaya.)*

KOLOMENSKOYE SUMMER RESIDENCE (КОЛОМЕНСКОЕ). The tsars' summer residence sits on a wooded slope above the Moskva River. The centerpieces of the grounds are the cone-shaped, 16th-century **Assumption Cathedral** (Успенский Собор; Uspenskiy Sobor) and the seven blue-and-gold cupolas of the nearby **Church of Our Lady of Kazan** (Церковь Казанской Богоматери; Tserkov Kazanskoy Bogomateri). Noteworthy among the park's small museums is Peter the Great's 1702 log cabin. *(M2: Kolomenskaya. Follow the exit signs to "к музею Коломенское," turn right from the metro, and walk down the tree-shaded path, through the small black gate, and 10min. uphill on the left-most path. Museums open Tu-Su 10am-6pm. Each 90R, students 45R. Grounds open daily Apr.-Oct. 7am-10pm; Nov.-Mar. 9am-9pm. Free.)*

▥ MUSEUMS

Moscow's museum scene remains the most patriotic and least Westernized part of the city. Government museums and small galleries alike proudly display Russian art, and dozens of historical and literary museums are devoted to the nation's past.

GALLERIES AND HISTORICAL EXHIBITS

■ **STATE TRETYAKOV GALLERY.** A treasury of 18th- to early 20th-century Russian art, the Tretyakov Gallery (Государственная Третьяковская Галерея; Gosudarstvennaya Tretyakovskaya Galereya) also has a superb collection of icons, including works by Andrei Rublev and Theophanes the Greek. *(M8: Tretyakovskaya (Третьяковская). Turn left out of the metro, then left again, then take an immediate right on Bolshoy Tolmachevskiy per.; turn right after 2 blocks onto Lavrushinskiy per. Open Tu-Su 10am-7:30pm. Kassa closes at 6:30pm. 225R, students 130R. English tours ☎ 953 52 23. 640R.)*

■ **NEW TRETYAKOV GALLERY.** Where the first Tretyakov chronologically leaves off, the new gallery (Новая Третьяковская Галерея; Novaya Tretyakovskaya Galereya) begins. The collection starts on the third floor with early 20th-century art and moves through the Neo-Primitivist, Futurist, Suprematist, Cubist, and Social Realist schools. The second floor holds temporary exhibits that draw huge crowds; it's best to go on weekday mornings. Behind the gallery to the right lies a graveyard for Soviet statues. Once the main dumping ground for decapitated Lenins and Stalins, it now contains captioned sculptures of Gandhi, Einstein, Niels Bohr, and the founder of the Soviet secret police, Dzerzhinsky. *(Ul. Krymskiy Val 10 (Крымский Вал). M5: Oktyabraskaya. Walk toward the big intersection at Kaluzhskaya pl. (Калужская пл.) and turn right onto ul. Krymskiy. Open Tu-Su 10am-7:30pm; kassa closes at 6:30pm. 225R, students 130R. English tours ☎ 238 20 54. 640R.)*

PUSHKIN MUSEUM OF FINE ARTS. Moscow's most important collection of non-Russian art, the Pushkin Museum (Музей Изобразительных Искусств им. А.С. Пушкина; Muzey Izobrazitelnykh Iskusstv im. A.S. Pushkina) houses major Renaissance, Egyptian, and classical works, as well as superb pieces by Van Gogh, Chagall, and Picasso. *(Ul. Volkhonka 12 (Волхонка). M1: Kropotkinskaya. Open Tu-Su 10am-7pm; kassa closes at 6pm. 190R, students 60R. Audioguide 250R, deposit 200R.)*

KGB MUSEUM. Documenting the history and strategies of Russian secret intelligence from Ivan the Terrible to Putin, the KGB Museum (Музей КГБ; Muzey KGB) features guides with intriguing anecdotes and a chance to quiz a current FSB agent. *(Ul. Bul. Lubyanka 12. M1: Lubyanka. It's the building behind the concrete behemoth that towers over the northeast side of the square. Pre-arranged tours only. Patriarshy Dom Tours (from the US ☎ 650 678 70 76) periodically leads 2hr. group tours. US$18.)*

STATE HISTORICAL MUSEUM. A comprehensive exhibit on Russian history, from the Neanderthals through Kyivan Rus to modern Russia, is accessible to anglophone travelers at the State Historical Museum (Государственный Исторический Музей; Gosudarstvennyy Istoricheskiy Muzey) due to its extensive printed info in English. *(Krasnaya pl. 1/2. M1: Okhotnyy Ryad. Entrance by Red Square. Open M and W-Sa 10am-6pm, Su 11am-8pm. Kassa closes 1hr. earlier. Closed first M of each month. Audioguides 50R, deposit 200R. Museum 150R, students 75R.)*

CENTRAL MUSEUM OF THE ARMED FORCES. At the Armed Forces Museum (Центральный Музей Вооруженных Сил; Tsentralnyy Muzey Vooruzhennykh Sil) you can see collections of weapons, uniforms, and artwork since Peter the Great. *(Ul. Sovetskoy Armii 2 (Советской Армии). M5: Novoslobodskaya. Walk along Seleznyovskaya ul. (Селезнёвская) to the rotary. Turn left after the theater and bear right at the fork. Open W-Su 10am-5pm. English tours 300R; call ahead. Museum 30R, students 10R.)*

HOMES OF THE LITERARY AND FAMOUS

■ **PUSHKIN LITERARY MUSEUM.** (Литературный Музей Пушкина; Literaturnyy Muzey Pushkina.) If you've never seen Pushkin-worship first-hand, this large collection of Pushkin memorabilia will either convert or frighten you. *(Ul. Prechistenka 12/2 (Пречистенка). Entrance on Khrushchevskiy per. M1: Kropotkinskaya. Open Tu-Su 11am-7pm; kassa closes at 6pm. 25R.)*

MAYAKOVSKY MUSEUM. (Музей им. В. В. Маяковского; Muzey im. V. V. Mayakovskovo.) A walk-through work of Futurist art, the museum was created as a reminder of Mayakovsky's ideas, life, and death. *(Lubyanskiy pr. 3/6 (Лубянский). M1: Lubyanka. Behind a bust of Mayakovsky on ul. Myasnitskaya (Мясницкая). Open M-Tu and F-Su 10am-6pm, Th 1-9pm. Closed last F of each month. 60R.)*

TOLSTOY MUSEUM. (Музей Толстого; Muzey Tolstovo.) This museum in the neighborhood of Tolstoy's first Moscow residence displays original texts, paintings, and letters related to the author's masterpieces. *(Ul. Prechistenka 11 (Пречистенка). M1: Kropotkinskaya. Open Tu-Su 11am-7pm; kassa closes at 6pm. Closed last F of each month. 100R, students 15R. English captions.)*

GORKY MUSEUM-HOUSE. (Музей-дом Горкого; Muzey-dom Gorkovo.) Built by F. O. Shekhtel in 1900, the museum is a pilgrimage site as much for its Art Nouveau architecture as for its exhibit of Maksim Gorky's possessions. *(Malaya Nikitskaya ul. 6/2 (Малая Никитская). M3: Arbatskaya. Cross Novyy Arbat and turn right on Merelyakovskiy per. (Мереляковский пер.), and cross the small park. Open W-Su 10am-6pm. Closed last Th of each month. Free, but donations requested.)*

🎵 ENTERTAINMENT

From September to June, Moscow boasts some of the world's best theater, ballet, opera, and orchestral performances. Tickets can be purchased from the theater *kassa* or from city kiosks; advance tickets are often very cheap (from US$5).

Bolshoy Theater (Большой Театр), Teatralnaya pl. 1 (☎ 250 73 17; www.bolshoi.ru). M2: Teatralnaya. Home to both the opera and the world-renowned ballet companies. *Kassa* open M-W and F-Su 11am-3pm and 4-7pm, Th 11am-3pm and 4-9pm. Performances daily Sept.-June noon, 2, and 7pm. Tickets 250-3500R. MC/V.

Malyy Teatr (Малый Театр), Teatralnaya pl. 1/6 (☎923 26 21). M2: Teatralnaya. Just to the right of the Bolshoy. Moscow's premier dramatic theater. *Kassa* open daily 10am-8pm, until 7pm in low season. Performances daily Sept.-June 7pm. Tickets 100-400R.

Moscow Operetta Theater (Оперетты Театр), ul. Bolshaya Dmitrovka 6 (Большая Дмитровка; ☎292 12 37; www.operetta.org.ru), to the left of the Bolshoy. M2: Teatralnaya. *Kassa* open M-Th noon-3pm and 4-7pm, F-Su noon-3pm and 4-6pm. Performances M-Th 7pm, F-Su 6pm, and some in daytime. Tickets 100-500R.

⚡ NIGHTLIFE

Moscow's bacchanalian nightlife is the most varied, expensive, and dangerous in Eastern Europe. More interesting clubs enjoy flaunting their exclusivity and their cover charges; more sedate, inexpensive venues attract bohemians and absinthe-seeking students. Check the weekend editions of *The Moscow Times* or *The Moscow Tribune* for club reviews and music festival listings. The Friday pull-out section of *The Moscow Times*, the nightlife section of *The eXile* (www.exile.ru), and *The Beat* have weekly calendars and up-to-date restaurant, bar, and club reviews.

▨ **Propaganda** (Пропаганда), Bolshoy Zlatoustinskiy per. 7 (Большой Златоустинский). M6 or 7: Kitai Gorod. Dance to good house without feeling like you're in a meat market. Beer 70R. Sangria 120R per 0.5L. Cover Sa-Su 100R. Open daily noon-6am.

Karma Bar, ul. Pushechnaya 3. M: Kuznetzky Most. Walk through the archway on your left and turn right onto ul. Pushechnaya. English-speaking waitstaff. Su hip-hop night. Beer 100-140R per 0.33L. Cover F-Sa men 200R, women 100R. Open Th-Su 7pm-6am.

Doug and Marty's Boar House, Zemlyanoi val. 26 (Земляной). M3: Kurskaya, opposite the train station. An American-style bar packed with expats on weekends. Billiards 50R per game. Happy Hour 6-9pm. 50% discount on food noon-8pm. Entrees 190-450R. Beer 90-145R. Cover men 150R, women 100R. Open 24hr. AmEx/MC/V.

Art-Garbage, Starosadskiy per. 5 (☎928 87 45; www.art-garbage.ru). M6 or 7: Kitay Gorod. Art gallery, restaurant, and club, Art-Garbage is refreshingly laid-back in comparison with the more chic and trendy Moscow establishments. Vodka tonic 90R. Cover men 200R, women 150R. Disco daily 10pm-6am. Open 24hr.

Ballantine's Bar, Nikolskaya ul. 17 (Никольская; ☎928 46 92). M3: Ploshchad Revolyutsii. Follow the signs to Nikolskaya ul. away from Red Sq. Great dance music and a lively student crowd. Beer 65-165R. Live DJ Th-Sa at 10pm; occasional live music. Cover F-Sa 100R; concerts up to 500R. Open daily 11am-6am. MC/V.

Tri Obezyany (Three Monkeys), ul. Sadovnicheskaya 71/2 (☎953 09 09). M2 or 5: Paveletskaya. Moscow's premier gay club. Open daily 9pm-9am.

🏛 DAYTRIP FROM MOSCOW: SERGIYEV POSAD

Russia's most famous pilgrimage point, Sergiyev Posad (Сергиев Посад; pop. 200,000) attracts believers to several churches huddled around its main sight: **St. Sergius's Trinity Monastery** (Свято-Троицкая Сергиева Лавра; Svyato-Troitskaya Sergiyeva Lavra). After decades of state-propagated atheism, the stunning monastery, founded circa 1340, is again a thriving religious center. The splendid **Assumption Cathedral** (Успенский Собор; Uspenskiy Sobor) was modeled after its namesake cathedral in Moscow's Kremlin (p. 880). The magnificent frescoes of the **Refectory** (Трапезная; Trapeznaya) and the gilded icons by Andrei Rublev at **Trinity Cathedral** (Троицкий Собор; Troitskiy Sobor) are equally colorful and captivating. (Monastery open daily 9am-6pm.) **Commuter trains** (*elektrichki*) run to Sergiyev Posad from Moscow's Yaroslavskiy Vokzal (1½-2hr., every 20-50min., round-trip 61R). To reach the monastery from the station, turn right and look for the domes, cross the street, and walk down the road until you see the city (10-15min.).

ST. PETERSBURG (САНКТ-ПЕТЕРБУРГ) ☎ 8812

St. Petersburg's splendid, wide boulevards and bright facades are exactly what Peter the Great envisioned when he founded his "window on the West." The curtain drew closed, however, when St. Petersburg (pop. 4,600,000) became the birthplace of the 1917 February Revolution, turning Russia into a Communist state. Not only Lenin and Trotsky have been inspired by St. Petersburg's sophistication and majesty, however. Recently, the city has also rediscovered the artistic genius of its former residents Dostoevsky, Gogol, Tchaikovsky, and Stravinsky.

⌐ TRANSPORTATION

Flights: The main airport, **Pulkovo** (Пулково), has 2 terminals: Pulkovo-1 (☎ 104 38 22) for domestic flights, and Pulkovo-2 (☎ 104 34 44) for international flights. M2: Moskovskaya (Московская), take bus #39 to Pulkovo-1 (25min.) or bus #13 to Pulkovo-2 (20min.). Hostels can arrange taxis (usually US$30-35).

Trains: Central Ticket Offices (Центральные Железнодорожные Кассы; Tsentralnye Zheleznodorozhnye Kassy), Canal Griboyedova 24 (Грибоедого). International tickets at windows #4-6. Tickets are sold at **Intourist** offices in train stations. Check the ticket to see from which station the train leaves. Open M-Sa 8am-8pm, Su 8am-6pm.

Finland Station (Финляндский Вокзал; Finlyandskiy Vokzal; ☎ 168 76 87). M1: Pl. Lenina (Ленина). To: **Helsinki** (6hr., 2 per day, 1375R).

Moskovskiy Vokzal (Московский Вокзал; Moscow Station; ☎ 168 45 97). M1: Pl. Vosstaniya (Восстания). To: **Moscow** (5-8hr., 12-15 per day, 300-1300R); **Novgorod** (3-4hr., 2 per day, 66R); **Sevastopol** (35hr., 1 per day, 754-1186R).

Vitebskiy Vokzal (Витебский Вокзал; Vitebskiy Station; ☎ 168 58 07). M1: Pushkinskaya (Пушкинская). To: **Kaliningrad** (26hr., 550-3300R, 1 per day); **Kyiv** (25hr., 2 every 2 days, 506-637R); **Odessa** (36hr., 1 per day, 654R); **Rīga** (13hr., 1 per day, 887R); **Tallinn** (9hr., 1 per day, 350R); **Vilnius** (14hr., every 2 days, 647R).

Buses: Nab. Obvodnovo Kanala 36 (Обводного Канала; ☎ 166 57 77). M4: Ligovskiy pr. Take tram #19, 25, 44, or 49 or trolley #42 to the stop just across the canal. Facing the canal, turn right and walk 2 long blocks alongside it. The station will be on your right, behind the abandoned building. Surcharge for advance tickets. Open daily 6am-8pm.

Local Transportation: St. Petersburg's **metro** (метро) is the deepest in the world, efficient, cheap, and generally busy, especially 8-9am and 5-6pm. **Tokens** (жетон; zheton) cost 7R. Stock up, as lines are often long and cutting is common. Drivers sell tickets to **buses, trams,** and **trolleys** (6R). Licensed private **minibuses** (маршрутки; marshrutki) follow a set route through the city and cost more (7-20R) but move much more quickly through traffic and will stop on request.

Taxis: Marked cabs are 11R per km; add 35R if you call ahead. Many people hail private cars, which are usually cheaper but less safe, and negotiate the fare before getting in.

✦ ❷ ORIENTATION AND PRACTICAL INFORMATION

St. Petersburg's center lies on the mainland between the south bank of the **Neva River** and the **Fontanka Canal**. It is easiest to get around using the metro. Most major sights, including the Hermitage and the three main cathedrals, are on or near **Nevsky prospekt** (Невский Проспект), the city's main artery; **Moscow Train Station** (Московский Вокзал; Moskovsky Vokzal) is near the midpoint. Trolleys #1, 5, and 22 run along Nevsky pr. On the north side of the Neva is the **Petrograd Side** archipelago, where the **Peter and Paul Fortress** stands.

Museums and sights often charge several times more for "foreigners" than for Russians. Avoid paying the higher price by handing the cashier the exact amount for a Russian ticket, and saying "adeen" (one). Walk as if you know where you are going, and do not keep your map, camera, or *Let's Go* in plain view. Dress like a local and try to speak Russian when you can.

Tourist Office: City Tourist Information Center, ul. Sadovaya 14/52 (☎310 82 62 or 310 22 31; www.ctic.spb.ru). M: Gostinyy Dvor. English-language advice, free brochures, postcards, and souvenir books. Open M-F 10am-7pm. Also helpful are the free English-language *Neva News* and *St. Petersburg Times.*

Budget Travel: Sindbad Travel (FIYTO), ul. 3-ya Sovetskaya 28 (3-я Советская; ☎327 83 84; www.sindbad.ru), in the International Hostel. Books plane, bus, and train tickets. Student discounts on flights. Open M-F 9am-10pm, Sa-Su 10am-6pm.

Consulates: Australia: Italyanskaya ul. 1 (☎325 73 33; oz@consulteast.com). M2: Nevsky Pr. Open M-F 9am-6pm. **Canada:** Malodetskoselskiy pr. 32 (Малодетскосельский; ☎325 84 48; fax 325 83 93). M2: Frunzenskaya. Open M-F 9am-1pm and 2-5pm. **UK:** Pl. Proletarskoy Diktatury 5 (Пролетарской Диктатуры; ☎320 32 00; www.britain.spb.ru). M1: Chernyshevskaya. Open M-F 9:30am-1pm, 2-5:30pm. **US:** Furshtatskaya ul. 15 (Фурштатская; 24hr. ☎331 26 00; www.stpetersburg-usconsulate.ru). M1: Chernyshevskaya. Services for US citizens open M-Tu and Th-F 2-5pm, W 10am-1pm. Citizens of **Ireland** and **New Zealand** can contact the UK consulate in emergencies.

Currency Exchange: Look for "обмен валюты" (obmen valyuty) signs everywhere. Sberbank (☎329 87 87), Dumskaya ul. 1 (right at M2: Nevsky pr.), Nevsky pr. 82/99. American Express: Malaya Morskaya ul. 23 (☎326 45 00). Open M-F 9am-5pm.

Emergency: Police: ☎02. **Ambulance:** ☎03. **Fire:** ☎01.

Tourist Police: ☎ 164 97 87 or 278 30 14.

24hr. Pharmacy: Nevsky pr. 22. Stocks Western medicines and toiletries. MC/V.

Medical Assistance: American Medical Center, nab. Reki Moyki 78, #78 (Реки Мойки; ☎140 20 90). M2/4: Sennaya Pl./Sadovaya. Follow per. Grivtsova across Griboyedov Canal to the Moyka River. English-speaking doctors provide comprehensive services, including house calls. Consultation US$50. Open 24hr. AmEx/MC/V.

Internet and Telephones: Cafemax, Nevsky pr. 90 92 (☎273 66 55; spb@c-max.ru). M3/1; Mayakovskaya. Massive, modern cafe. Access 70R per hr., nights (11pm-7am) 120R. Open 24hr. **Red Fog Internet Cafe,** Kazanskaya ul. 30-32 (☎595 41 38). M2: Nevsky pr. Access 40R per hr., nights (11:30pm-8:30am) 100R. Open 24hr. **Quo Vadis,** Nevsky pr. 24 (☎311 80 11; www.quovadis.ru). Internet 80R per hr., 70R with ISIC. Long-distance calls to the US 12R per min. Open 24hr.

Post Office: Pochtamtskaya ul. 9 (Почтамтская; ☎312 83 02). From Nevsky pr., go west on ul. Malaya Morskaya, which becomes Pochtamtskaya ul.; the office is about 2 blocks past St. Isaac's Cathedral. **Currency exchange** and **telephone** service. International mail at windows #24-30. *Poste Restante* held up to 1 month at windows #1 and 2. Open M-Sa 9am-7:45pm, Su 10am-5:45pm. **Postal Code:** 190 000.

■ ACCOMMODATIONS

▨ **Sleep Cheap,** Mokhovaya ul. 18/32 (☎ 115 13 04; www.sleepcheap.spb.ru). M1: Chernyshevskaya. Enter the courtyard at 18 Mokhovaya; the hostel is 30m inward. St. Petersburg's newest hostel has A/C. English spoken. Airport and train transfer available. Laundry 150R. Internet 50R. Open 24hr. Dorms 700R. ❸

RUSSIA

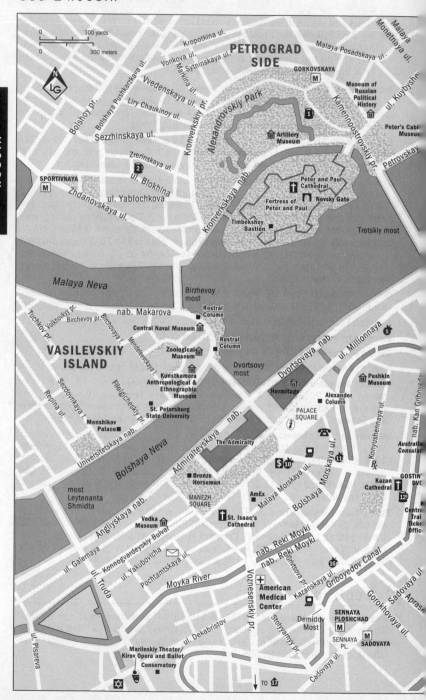

0 300 yards
0 300 meters

N LG

Kropotkina ul.
Vonkova ul.
Sytninskaya ul.
Markina ul.
Vvedenskaya ul.
Bolshoy pr.
Bolshaya Pushkarskaya ul.
Liry Chaukinoy ul.
Sezzhinskaya ul.
Kronverkskiy pr.

PETROGRAD SIDE

Malaya Posadskaya ul.

Malaya Monetnaya ul.

Malaya Monetnaya ul.

GORKOVSKAYA M

Museum of Russian Political History 血

ul. Kuybyshe

Peter's Cabi Museum

Petrovsky

Alexandrovskiy Park

血 **Artillery Museum**

Kamennoostrovskiy pr.

Zrerinskaya ul.

ul. Blokhina

SPORTIVNAYA M

Zhdanovskaya ul.

ul. Yablochkova

Kronverkskaya nab.

Peter and Paul Cathedral †

Nevsky Gate

Fortress of Peter and Paul

Timbekshoy Bastion

Trotskiy most

Malaya Neva

Birzhevoy most

nab. Makarova

Rostral Column

Tuchkov Volkhovkiy pr.

Birchevoy pr.

Birchevaya l.

Central Naval Museum 血

Mendeleevskaya l.

Zoological Museum 血

Rostral Column

VASILEVSKIY ISLAND

Fitologicheskiy pr.

Kunstkamera Anthropological & Ethnographic Museum 血

Dvortsovy most

Dvortsovaya nab.

ul. Millionnaya

5

Pushkin Museum 血

Sezdovnkaya l.

Repina ul.

St. Petersburg State University ■

Menshikov Palace ■

Universitetskaya nab.

Admiralteyskaya nab.

Hermitage 血

Alexander Column

PALACE SQUARE

i

☎

Konyushennaya ul.

nab. Kan Gribc

Australia Consular

Bolshaya Neva

The Admiralty ■

$ 10

11

Rx

most Leytenanta Shmidta

Angliyskaya nab.

Bronze Horseman ■

MANEZH SQUARE

AmEx

Malaya Morskaya ul.

Bolshaya Morskaya ul.

Kazan Cathedral †

GOSTIN' DVO

12

ul. Galernaya

Vodka Museum 血

Konnogvardeyskiy Bulvar

ul. Yakubovicha

Pochtamtskaya ul.

✉

† **St. Isaac's Cathedral**

nab. Reki Moyki

nab. Reki Moyki

Rdgntsova pr

Centra Trai Ticke Offic

ul. Truda

Voznesensky pr.

Moyka River

16

Griboyedov Canal

Sadovaya l.

ul. Pisareva

ul. Dekabristov

✚ **American Medical Center**

Kazanskaya ul.

Stolyarmyy pr.

Demidov Most

SENNAYA PLOSHCHAD M

SENNAYA PL.

M **SADOVAYA**

Gorokhovaya ul.

Gorokhovaya ul.

Sadovaya Apras

Cadovaya ul.

Marlinskiy Theater/ Kirov Opera and Ballet Conservatory ■

✡

☺

↓ TO 血

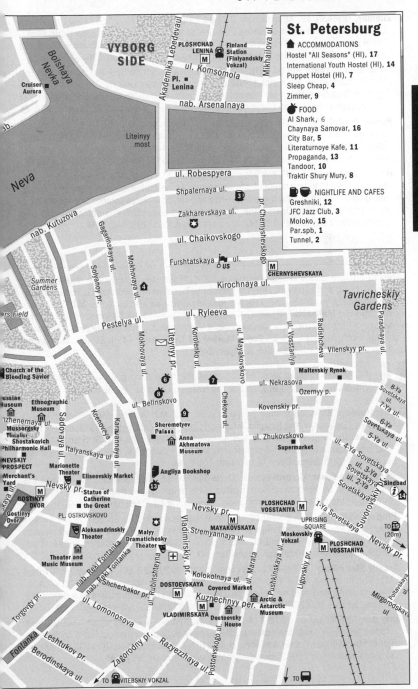

RUSSIA

St. Petersburg

🏠 ACCOMMODATIONS
Hostel "All Seasons" (HI), **17**
International Youth Hostel (HI), **14**
Puppet Hostel (HI), **7**
Sleep Cheap, **4**
Zimmer, **9**

🍴 FOOD
Al Shark, **6**
Chaynaya Samovar, **16**
City Bar, **5**
Literaturnoye Kafe, **11**
Propaganda, **13**
Tandoor, **10**
Traktir Shury Mury, **8**

☕🍷 NIGHTLIFE AND CAFES
Greshniki, **12**
JFC Jazz Club, **3**
Moloko, **15**
Par.spb, **1**
Tunnel, **2**

RUSSIA

Zimmer, Lityenniy 46, Appartement 23 (☎273 08 67 or 973 37 57; www.zimmer.ru). Check in with the English-speaking manager in the front hall. Clean rooms and sensational prices. Showers, bathrooms, TV, refrigerator, kitchen, and free laundry. Check-out noon. Open 24hr. May-Sept. dorms US$15; singles $30; Oct.-Apr. $10/$20. ❷

International Youth Hostel (HI), 3-ya Sovetskaya ul. 28 (☎329 80 18; www.ryh.ru). M1: Pl. Vosstaniya. Walk along Suvorovskiy pr. (Суворовский) for 3 blocks, then turn right on 3-ya Sovetskaya ul. Internet 1R per min. English spoken. Laundry US$4 per 5kg. Reception 8am-1am. Check-out 11am. 3- to 5-bed dorms US$21; doubles $26. ❷

Puppet Hostel (HI), ul. Nekrasova 12, 4th fl. (Некрасова; ☎272 54 01). M3: Mayakovskaya. Walk up ul. Mayakovskaya (Маяковская) and take the 2nd left on Nekrasova. English spoken. Breakfast included. Reception 8am-midnight. Open 24hr. Check-out noon. Mar.-Oct. 3- to 5-bed dorms US$19, doubles $48; low season reduced rates.❷

Hostel "All Seasons" (HI), Yakovlevskiy pr. 11 (☎327 10 70). M2: Park Pobedy. As you exit the metro turn right along ul. Moskovskaya. At the end of the park turn right on Kuznetsovskaya ul. and follow signs when they appear. Low prices compensate for the location. English spoken. Open 24hr. TV and kitchen available. In summer 5- to 8-bed dorms US$10.50; singles $32.50; low season reduced rates. MC/V. ❶

FOOD

Russian cuisine is not known for innovation. Most menus have the staples: pike, sturgeon, beef, and sausage. Don't be afraid to bargain at markets. The **covered market,** Kuznechny pr. 3 (Кузнечьный), just around the corner from M1: Vladimirskaya, and the **Maltsevskiy Rynok** (Мальцевский Рынок), ul. Nekrasova 52 (M1: pl. Vosstaniya), at the top of Ligovskiy pr. (Лиговский), are the largest and most exciting. For groceries, try **24 Super Market,** at the corner of ul. Zhukovskovo and ul. Vosstaniya. (M3: pl. Vosstaniya. Open 24hr.)

> **!** St. Petersburg lacks an effective water purification system, making exposure to **giardia** (p. 29) very likely, so boil tap water, use iodine, or buy bottled water.

Literaturnoye Kafe, 18 Nevsky pr. (☎312 60 57). M2 Gostinyy Dvor. Clientele have included Dostoevsky and Pushkin, who came here the night before his fatal duel. Now sumptuously decorated, the cafe has a reasonable menu with beef Stroganoff (250R) and black caviar (450R). Live classical music plays during the day, Russian romances at night. English menu. Open M-Su 11am-11pm. ❸

Chaynaya Samovar, Gorokovaya ul. 27 (☎314 39 45). M2: Sennaya Pl. Perhaps the best place in St. Petersburg for pancakes (with butter: *blini s myaslom* 16R). Pop hits in the background offset the rustic decor. Russian menu. Open daily 10am-9pm. ❶

Propaganda, nab. Reki Fontanka 40 (Реки Фонтанка; ☎275 35 58). M2: Gostinyy Dvor. Walk toward pl. Vosstaniya on Nevsky pr.; crossing the Fontanka, turn left on nab. Reki Fontanka. American and Russian food in a Soviet-themed interior. Entrees 150-350R. English menu. Open daily 1pm-3am. ❸

Traktir Shury Mury, ul. Belinskovo 8 (Белинского; ☎279 85 50). M2: Gostinyy Dvor or M1: Vladimirskaya. From Vladimirskaya, walk toward the Admiralty, turn right on nab. Reki Fontanka and right on Belinskovo. Russian and European cuisine in a dacha-like setting. Entrees 100-200R. Russian menu. Open 11am-last customer. MC/V. ❷

City Bar, Millionnaya ul. 10 (☎314 10 37; www.citybar.ru). Owned by an American and staffed largely by American students, this expat hangout will dish you up a cheeseburger (150-280R) and other American culinary standbys. Breakfast 90-150R. Amerikanskiy business lunch 150R. Open daily noon-last customer. MC/V. ❸

Tandoor (Тандур), Voznesenskiy pr. 2 (Вознесенский; ☎312 38 86). M2: Nevsky Prospekt. At the end of Nevsky pr., on the corner of Admiralteyskiy pr. (Адмиралтейский). Amid the Indian decor and English conversation, it's easy to forget that Russia is just outside. Veggie options. Entrees US$10-18. Open daily noon-11pm. AmEx/DC/MC. ●

Al Shark, Lityennyy pr. 67 (☎272 90 73). A fixture on the St. Petersburg restaurant scene for kebab sandwiches (*schvarma v pite* 50R). Few places combine low prices, taste, and Mideastern authenticity with the effectiveness of Al Shark. Open 24hr. ●

◙ SIGHTS

▨ THE HERMITAGE. Originally a collection of 255 paintings bought by Catherine the Great in 1764, the State Hermitage Museum (Эрмитаж; Ermitazh) houses the world's largest art collection; it rivals the Louvre and the Prado in architectural, historical, and artistic significance. The **Winter Palace** (Зимний Дворец; Zimny Dvorets) was commissioned in 1762. The complex later expanded to include the Small Hermitage (Малый Эрмитаж; Malyy Ermitazh), the Large Hermitage (Большой Эрмитаж; Bolshoy Ermitazh), the Hermitage Theater (Эрмитажный Театр; Ermitazhny Teatr), and the New Hermitage (Новый Эрмитаж; Novy Ermitazh). Tsars lived in the complex with their collections until 1917, when the museum was nationalized. Only 5% of the three-million-piece collection is on display at a time. English floor plans are available at the info desk near the *kassa*.

Palace Square (Дворцовая Площадь; Dvortsovaya Ploshchad), the huge, windswept expanse in front of the Winter Palace, has witnessed many turning points in Russia's history. Catherine took the crown here after overthrowing Tsar Peter III, her husband; far later, Nicholas II's guards fired into a crowd of peaceful demonstrators on "Bloody Sunday," which precipitated the 1905 revolution. Finally, Lenin's Bolsheviks seized power from the provisional government during the storming of the Winter Palace in October 1917. The 700-ton **Alexander Column**, held in place by its massive weight alone, commemorates Russia's defeat of Napoleon in 1812. Across the bridge from the Hermitage, **Vasilevskiy Island** splits the Neva River in two; most of its sights lie on the eastern edge in the **Strelka** neighborhood. The area closest to the Hermitage was a center for sea trade and now houses many of the city's best museums. *(Nab. Dvortsovaya 34 (Дворцовая). ☎311 34 20; www.hermitagemuseum.org. M2: Nevsky pr. Turn left out of the metro and walk down Nevsky pr. to the Admiralty. The Hermitage is to the right; enter on the river side. Open Tu-Sa 10:30am-6pm, Su 10:30am-5pm; cashier and upper floors close 1hr. earlier. Cameras 100R. Long lines; arrive early. 350R, students free.)*

▨ ST. ISAAC'S CATHEDRAL. Glittering, intricately carved masterpieces of iconography are housed under the awesome dome of St. Isaac's Cathedral (Исаакиевский Собор; Isaakievskiy Sobor), a 101.5m exemplar of 19th-century architecture. On a sunny day, the 100kg of pure gold that coats the dome is visible for miles. The 360° view of the city from atop the **colonnade** is stunning. *(M2: Nevsky pr. Turn left out of the metro and walk almost to the end of Nevsky pr.; turn left onto ul. Malaya Morskaya. ☎315 97 32. Cathedral open M-Tu and Th-Su summer 10am-8pm; winter 11am-7pm. Colonnade open M-Tu and Th-Su summer 10am-7pm; winter 11am-3pm. 100R, students 50R. Last entry 1hr. before closing. Foreigners buy tickets inside.)*

PETER AND PAUL FORTRESS. Across the river from the Hermitage stand the walls and golden spire of the Peter and Paul Fortress (Петропавловская Крепость; Petropavlovskaya Krepost). Construction of the fortress, supervised by Peter the Great himself, began on May 27, 1703, which is considered his city's birthday. Originally built as a defense against the Swedes, the fortress came to be used as a prison for political dissidents. Inside, the **Peter and Paul Cathedral** (Петропавловский Собор; Petropavlovskiy Sobor) glows with rosy marble walls and a breathtaking Baroque partition covered with intricate iconography. The cathedral holds the remains of Peter the Great and his successors. Before the main vault sits the **Chapel of St. Catherine the Martyr.** The bodies of the last Romanovs—Tsar Nicholas II and his family—were entombed here on July 17, 1998, on the 80th anniversary of their murder at the hands of the Bolsheviks. Condemned prisoners awaited their common fate at **Trubetskoy Bastion** (Труецкой Бастон), where Peter the Great held and tortured his first son, Aleksei. Dostoevsky, Gorky, Trotsky, and Lenin's older brother also spent time here. *(M2: Gorkovskaya. Turn right out of the metro onto Kamennoostrovskiy pr. (Каменноостровский), the unmarked street just ahead. Continue to the river and cross the wooden bridge to the island fortress. Open M and W-Su 11am-6pm, Tu 11am-5pm; closed last Tu of each month. Available at the kassa in the "boathouse" in the middle of the complex or in the smaller kassa just inside the main entrance, a single ticket covers most sights. 120R, students 60R. Fortress wall 50R.)*

ALEXANDER NEVSKY MONASTERY. A major pilgrimage site and peaceful strolling ground, Alexander Nevsky Monastery (Александро-невская Лавра; Aleksandro-Nevskaya Lavra) became one of four Orthodox monasteries to receive the highest monastic title of *lavra* in 1797. The **Artists' Necropolis** (Некрапол Мастеров Искусств; Nekropol Masterov Iskusstv) is the resting place of Fyodor Dostoevsky and composers Tchaikovsky, Rimsky-Korsakov, and Mussorgsky. The nearby **Lazarus Cemetery** (Лазаревское Кладбище; Lazarevskoye Kladbishche), also known as the 18th-century Necropolis, is the city's oldest burial ground. The **Church of the Annunciation** (Благовещенская Церков; Blagoveshchenskaya Tserkov), farther along the central stone path on the left, holds the remains of war heroes and is the original burial place of the Romanovs, who were moved to Peter and Paul Cathedral in 1998. At the end of the path is the **Holy Trinity Cathedral** (Свято-Тротский Собор; Svyato-Troitskiy Sobor), teeming with devout *babushki. (M3/4: pl. Aleksandra Nevskovo. The 18th-century Necropolis lies behind and to the left of the entrance, the Artists' Necropolis behind and to the right. ☎ 274 04 09; www.lavra.spb.ru. Grounds open daily 6am-10pm. Cathedral open daily 6am-8pm. 18th-century Necropolis open daily 9:30am-5:45pm. Artists' Necropolis open daily 9:30am-6pm. Admission to both 60R, students 30R. Annunciation Church kassa open Tu-W and F-Su 11am-4:30pm.)*

ALONG NEVSKY PROSPEKT. Many sights cluster around the western end of vibrant Nevsky pr., the city's 4.5km main thoroughfare. Unfortunately, there is no metro station immediately nearby; one was built, but after the station was completed, local residents refused to allow the construction of an entrance or exit connecting it to the surface. The **Admiralty** (Адмиралтейство; Admiralteystvo) towers over the surrounding gardens and most of Nevsky pr. During WWII the golden spire of this former naval headquarters was painted black to disguise it from German artillery bombers. In the park to the left of the Admiralty is the **Bronze Horseman** statue of Peter the Great, one of the most widely recognized symbols of the city. *(M2: Nevsky pr. Walk to the end of Nevsky pr. toward the golden spire.)* Walking back east on Nevsky pr., the enormous, Roman-style **Kazan Cathedral** (Казанский Собор; Kazanskiy Sobor) looms to the right. *(M2: Nevsky pr. Open daily 8:30am-7:30pm. Free.)* Half a block down, looking up Canal Griboyedova to the left, you can see the brilliantly colored ▇**Church of the Bleeding Savior** (Спас На Крови; Spas Na Krovi), which sits on the site of the 1881 assassination of Tsar Aleksandr II. *(Open in summer Tu-Th 10am-8pm; low season 11am-7pm. Kassa closes 1hr. earlier. 250R, students 125R, under 7 free.)* The 220-year-old **Merchants' Yard** (Гостиный Двор; Gostiny Dvor) is to the right. *(M3: Gostinyy Dvor. Open daily 10am-9pm.)* Nearby **Ostrovskovo Square** (Островского) houses the historic Aleksandrinskiy Theater and an impressive statue of Catherine the Great. Much farther down Nevsky pr. is **Uprising Square** (Площадь Восстания; Ploshchad Vosstaniya), where the bloodiest confrontations of the February Revolution of 1917 took place. *(M1: pl. Vosstaniya.)*

SUMMER GARDENS AND PALACE. The long, shady paths of the Summer Gardens and Palace (Летний Сад и Дворец; Letny Sad i Dvorets) are a lovely place to rest and cool off. Peter's small Summer Palace, in the northeast corner, has decor reflecting his diverse tastes, with everything from Spanish and Portuguese chairs to Dutch tile and German clocks. **Mars Field** (Марсово Поле; Marsovo Pole), a memorial to the victims of the Revolution and the Civil War (1917-1919), extends out from the Summer Gardens. *(M2: Nevsky Prospekt. Turn right on nab. Kanala Griboyedova (Канала Грибоедова), pass the Church of the Bleeding Savior, cross the Moyka, and turn right on ul. Pestelya (Пестеля); look for the sights on your left. ☎ 314 03 74. Garden open daily May-Oct. 10am-9:30pm; Nov.-Apr. 10am-8pm. Free. Palace open Tu-Su 11am-6pm; closed last Tu of each month. English signs. 270R, students 135R. 3rd Th of each month free.)*

OTHER MUSEUMS. The ▓**Russian Museum** (Русский Музей; Russkiy Muzey) boasts the world's second-largest collection of Russian art. *(M3: Gostiny Dvor. Down ul. Mikhailovskaya past the Grand Hotel Europe. Open M 10am-5pm, W-Su 10am-6pm; kassa closes 1hr. earlier. 270R, students 135R.)* The **Pushkin Museum** (Музей Пушкина; Muzey Pushkina) displays the personal effects of Russia's adored poet and tells the tragic story of his last days. *(M2: Nevsky pr. Walk toward the Admiralty and turn right onto nab. Reki Moyki. Follow the canal; the museum is the yellow building on the right. Open M and W-Su 10:30am-5pm. Closed last F of the month. 200R, students 50R.)* **Dostoevsky's House** (Дом Достоевского; Dom Dostoyevskovo) is where the author penned *The Brothers Karamazov*. *(M1: Vladimirskaya. On the corner of ul. Dostoevskovo, just past the market. ☎ 311 40 31. Open Tu-Su 11am-6pm; closed last W of each month. Kassa closes 5pm. 90R, students 45R.)* The **Museum of Russian Political History** (Музей Политической Истории России; Muzey Politicheskoi Istorii Rossii) has a vast collection of Soviet propaganda and artifacts from WWII. *(M2: Gorkovskaya. Go down Kamennoostrovskiy toward the mosque and turn left on Kuybysheva. ☎ 233 70 52. Open M-W and F-Su 10am-6pm. 80R, students 40R.)* The **Russian Vodka Museum** (Музей Водки; Muzey Vodki) is the world's first museum devoted to the history of vodka; a cafe offers a chance for hands-on learning. *(Konnogvardeyskiy bul. 5. From the Manezh, walk 1 block toward the river and turn left; the museum is 1 block down on the right. Open daily 11am-10pm. 25R. Vodka shots 20-60R. MC/V.)*

▓ ♫ FESTIVALS AND ENTERTAINMENT

Throughout June, when the evening sun barely touches the horizon, the city holds a series of outdoor concerts as part of the **White Nights Festival.** Bridges over the Neva River go up at 1:30am; most don't touch back down until 4:30 to 5:30am.

The home of Tchaikovsky, Prokofiev, and Stravinsky still lives up to its reputation as a mecca for the performing arts. Scalpers sell cheap Russian tickets to shows, but to enter with them you must pose as a Russian. The **Mariinskiy Teatr** (Мариинский; a.k.a."Kirov"), Teatralnaya pl. 1 (Театральная), can be reached by M4 (dir.: Sadovaya) or bus #3, 22, or 27. Perhaps the world's most famous ballet hall, the Mariinskiy Teatr premiered Tchaikovsky's *Nutcracker* and *Sleeping Beauty.* Baryshnikov and Nizhinsky both started here. Tickets go on sale 20 days in advance. *(☎ 114 43 44. 160-3200R for foreigners. Kassa open Tu-Su 11am-3pm and 4-9pm.)* **Mussorgsky Opera and Ballet Theater** (Театр Имени Муссоргского; Teatr Imeni Mussorgskovo), pl. Iskusstv 1, is open from July to August, when the Mariinskiy is closed. *(☎ 595 42 82. Bring your passport. Tickets 240-1800R for foreigners. Kassa open M and W-Su 11am-7pm, Tu 11am-6pm.)* **Shostakovich Philhar-**

WHITE NIGHTS

During St. Petersburg's beloved White Nights, held from May 25 to June 17, the city barely sleeps, partly because of summer's hardcore partying, but also because of the 22½hr. of sunlight per day that induces a wakeful indifference to the body's natural rhythms.

If you arrive at the beginning of the summer, you can attend one of the shows in repertory for the White Nights Festival in the Mariinskiy Theater. Afterward, leave some time to stroll around the sleepless, dusky metropolis.

The natural festival peaks with the summer solstice on June 22, when there is only 1½hr. of diminished twilight. Municipal festivities consist mostly of expensive ballets, operas, and concerts in the city's most renowned theaters, like the Mariinskiy and Shostakovich Philharmonia. Thankfully, however, simply by delaying bedtime just a few hours, everyone can afford to enjoy the early-morning spectacle of the Neva's bridges rising high to allow cruisers, liners, and other vessels to pass. (Take care to stay on the same side of the Neva as your accommodations, though, as the bridges may not come down as soon as you'd like.) Despite taking place in the wee hours of the morning, it's a great time to drink beer, chat with expats and Russians on the riverbanks, and watch the ships sail on.

monic Hall, ul. Mikhailovskaya 2, opposite the Russian Museum, has classical and modern concerts. (☎110 42 57. M3: Gostinyy Dvor. Tickets from 480-800R. *Kassa* open daily 11am-3pm and 4-7:30pm.) **Aleksandrinskiy Teatr** (Александринский Театр), pl. Ostrovskovo 2, attracts famous Russian actors and companies. (☎311 15 33. M3: Gostiny Dvor. Tickets 70-680R. *Kassa* open daily noon-6pm.)

🎵 NIGHTLIFE

JFC Jazz Club, Shpalernaya ul. 33 (Шпалерная; ☎272 98 50). M1: Chernyshevskaya. Turn right on pr. Chernyshevskovo (Чернышевского) and after 4 blocks left on Shpalernaya; the club is in courtyard 33. A variety of jazz in a relaxed atmosphere. Beer 50R. Live music 8-10pm. Cover 60-100R. Open daily 7-11pm. Arrive early for a table.

Par.spb, 5B Alexandrovskiy Park (☎233 33 74; www.par.spb.ru). M2: Gorkovskaya. Turn right from the metro and cross the park toward the Peter and Paul Fortress; look for the brick building inside the park. Beer from 30R. Cover 100-500R. Open F-Su 11pm-late.

Tunnel, ul. Blokhina 16 (Блохина; ☎233 40 15; www.tunnelclub.ru). M2: Gorkovskaya. Bear left out of the metro, walking along Kronverskiy pr. (Кронверский) in Alexandrinskiy Park toward Vasilevskiy Island. Turn right on ul. Blokhina and right at the fork; it's in the bomb shelter. Beer and vodka 40R. Cover 150-300R. Open Th-Sa midnight-6am.

Moloko (Milk), Perekupnoy per. 12 (Перекупной; ☎274 94 67). Off Nevsky pr., halfway between M1: Pl. Vosstaniya and M3/4: Pl. Aleksandra Nevskovo. Mix with the student crowd. Beer 25R. Cover 60-80R. Open W-Su 7pm-midnight; music starts at 8pm.

Greshniki (Грешники; Sinners), nab. Canala Griboyedova 28 (☎318 42 91), 2 blocks off Nevsky pr., past the Kazan Cathedral. M2: Nevsky Prospekt. Gay club with 4 floors playing techno, and disco. Primarily for men. Drinks 40-250R. Male strip-shows daily midnight-4am. 18+. Cover men 50-150R, women 300-500R. Open daily 10pm-6am.

🔁 DAYTRIPS FROM ST. PETERSBURG

PETERHOF (ПЕТЕРГОФ). Now the largest and the best-restored of the Russian palaces, Peterhof was burned to the ground during the Nazi retreat, but Soviet authorities provided the staggering sums needed to rebuild it. The gates open onto the **Lower Gardens,** a perfect place for a picnic along the shores of the Gulf of Finland. (Open daily 10:30am-6pm. 280R, students 140R.) Wanting to create his own Versailles, Peter started building the first residence in 1714, the **Grand Palace** (Большой Дворец; Bolshoy Dvorets); his daughter Empress Elizabeth and later Catherine the Great expanded and remodeled it. (Open Tu-Su 10am-6pm. Closed last Tu of each month. 420R, students 210R.) The elegant, gravity-powered fountains of the **Grand Cascade** shoot from the palace into the Grand Canal. To enter the impressive stone grotto underneath the fountains, buy tickets just outside the palace. (Grotto open daily 11am-5pm. *Kassa* open 10:30am-noon and 2-4:15pm. 100R, students 50R.) Peter did not actually live in his showroom, the Grand Palace, but in the modest Dutch-style **Monplaisir.** (Open M-Tu and Th-Su 10:30am-6pm. *Kassa* closes at 5pm. Closed 3rd Tu of each month. 190R, students 95R.) Next door is the **Catherine Building** (Екатерининский Корпус; Ekaterininskiy Korpus), where Catherine the Great reposed while her husband was overthrown on her orders. (Open Tu-Su 10:30am-6pm. *Kassa* closes at 5pm. 100R, students 50R.)

Take the **train** from Baltiyskiy station (Балтийский; M1: Baltiyskaya; 35min., every 10-50min., 12R). Tickets are sold at the courtyard office (Пригородная касса; *prigorodnaya kassa*). Get off at Novy Peterhof (Новый Петергоф). From the station, take any minivan (5min.; 10R) or bus (10min.; 7R) to Petrodvorets (Петродворец; Peter's Palace) and get off when you see the palace. Or, in summer, take the **hydrofoil** from the quay on nab. Dvortsovaya (Дворцовая) in front of the Hermitage (30-35min.; every 20min. 9:30am-6pm; 200R, round-trip 360R.)

TSARSKOYE SELO (PUSHKIN). About 25km south of St. Petersburg, Tsarskoye Selo (Царское Село; Tsar's Village) surrounds Catherine the Great's summer residence—an azure, white, and gold Baroque **palace** overlooking English-style parks. (Open M and W-Su 10am-6pm. *Kassa* closes 5pm. Closed last M of each month. 500R, students 250R.) Under the Soviets the surrounding area was renamed Pushkin (Пушкин), although the train station kept its old name, Detskoye Selo (Детское Село; Children's Village). In the sprawling **parks,** Catherine once strolled with her dogs, whom some believed she loved more than her own children. (Open daily May-Sept. 9am-11pm; Oct.-Apr. 10am-11pm. 70R, students 35R, free after 6pm.) In summer, a ferry runs across the Great Pond to the **Island Pavilion.** (Ferry every 40min. noon-6pm; round-trip 200R, students 100R. All island buildings open May-Sept.) The **Cold Bath Pavilion,** which contains the exotic Agate Rooms, stands in front of the palace to the left. (Open W-Su 10am-5pm. Closed last W of each month. 160R, students 80R.) Opposite the palace, the **lycée** schooled a 12-year-old Pushkin. His classrooms and spartan dorm can still be seen through the hordes of awed Russians. (Open M and W-Su 11am-6pm. *Kassa* closes 5pm. Closed last F of each month. 200R, students 100R.) The *elektrichka* runs from Vitebskiy Station (M1: Pushkinskaya). All **trains** from platforms 1-3 go to Pushkin, the first stop that looks like a real station (30min.). From the station, take bus #371 or 382 (10min., 5R), and watch for the palace through the trees to the right.

SLOVAK REPUBLIC
(SLOVENSKA REPUBLIKA)

After centuries of nomadic invasions and Hungarian domination, as well as 40 years of Soviet rule, Slovakia has finally emerged as an independent nation. While still part of Czechoslovakia, Slovaks rejected Communism in the 1989 Velvet Revolution, then split from the Czechs in 1993 only to rejoin them again more broadly in 2004 by acceding to the European Union. Now in flux between industry and agriculture, many rural Slovaks still cling to peasant traditions, while their children trickle away to the cities. Meanwhile, both in and out of Bratislava, budget travelers continue to discover breathtaking castle ruins and spectacular terrain.

DISCOVER THE SLOVAK REPUBLIC

Slovakia is an outdoor-lover's paradise. Begin with the sparsely populated Low Tatras, near **Liptovský Mikuláš** (p. 905) in the west, where day hikes thread the foothills and overnight treks cross the tree line. International tourists fill one of the finest and cheapest mountain playgrounds in Europe, the snow-capped High Tatras near **Starý Smokovec** (p. 904). Farther south, **Slovenský Raj National Park** (p. 905) contains miles of ravines, cliffs, and rock faces; spelunkers will enjoy the 475m path through the Dobšinská ice caves. A well-off and often-overlooked capital, **Bratislava** (p. 899) has man-made treasures such as the ruined Devín Castle towering over the Danube and Morava Rivers. In the east, Slovakia's second-largest city, Košice, is home to the gigantic Cathedral of St. Elizabeth.

ESSENTIALS

WHEN TO GO

Southern Slovakia has mild winters and moderate summers punctuated by thunderstorms; the most pleasant Bratislavan temperatures occur from May to September. In the Carpathians temperatures are more variable and winters harsher.

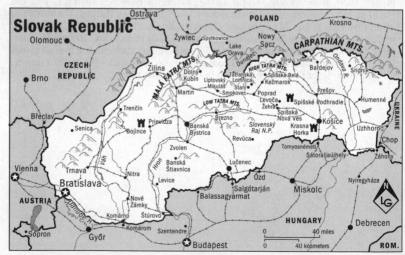

DOCUMENTS AND FORMALITIES

VISAS. Citizens of Australia, Canada, Ireland, New Zealand, the UK, and the US do not need visas for stays of up to 90 days. Temporary residence permits may be necessary for those in Slovakia to work, study, or visit family. Embassies can provide price info and details; processing will take at most three months. Local **Border and Alien Police** deal with foreigner registration and visa extensions.

EMBASSIES. All foreign embassies are in Bratislava (p. 899). Slovakian embassies at home include: **Australia,** 47 Culgoa Ct., O'Malley, ACT 2606 (☎02 6290 1516; www.slovakemb-aust.org); **Canada,** 50 Rideau Terr., Ottawa, ON K1M 2A1 (☎613-749-4442; www.ottawa.mfa.sk); **Ireland,** 20 Clyde Rd., Ballsbridge, Dublin 4 (☎01 660 0012; fax 660 0014); **UK,** 25 Kensington Palace Gardens, London W8 4QY (☎020 7313 6470; www.slovakembassy.co.uk); **US,** 3523 International Ct. NW Washington, D.C. 20008 (☎202-237-1054; www.slovakembassy-us.org).

TRANSPORTATION

BY PLANE. It can be inconvenient and expensive to enter the country through Bratislava's international airport (www.letiskobratislava.sk). One alternative is to travel to Vienna by plane and then on to Slovakian destinations by bus or train.

BY TRAIN. Slovakia's national railway, **ŽSR** (www.zsr.sk), has **timetables** online and in print as *cestovný poriadok* (58Sk), copies of which can be found at info desks and posted on large, round boards in stations. Tickets must be bought before boarding the train except in the tiniest towns. **EastPass** is valid, but **Eurail** has only limited options. **BIJ-Wasteels** offices at larger stations sell discounted tickets to those under 26. *InterCity* and *EuroCity* trains are costlier but faster. A train with a boxed "R" on the timetable requires a reservation (*miestenka;* 7Sk); those without one will face fines. Other trains subdivide into four categories: *expresný* (express), *rychlík* (fast), *spešný* (not quite so fast), and *osobný* (local). Reservations are recommended for express trains and for first-class seats, but are otherwise unnecessary. Second-class arrangements tend also to be comfortable.

BY BUS. In many hilly regions, **ČSAD** or **SAD** buses are the best and sometimes the only option. **Timetables** can be found online at www.eurolines.sk. Buy tickets onboard except for longer trips. Important symbols on schedules include: "X," weekdays only; "a," Sa-Su only; "b," M-Sa; "n," Su only; "r" and "k," excluding holidays. Numbers refer to the days of the week on which the bus runs—"1" is Monday, "2" is Tuesday, etc. *"Premava"* means "including" and *"nepremava"* is "except;" following those words are often lists of dates (day then month).

BY BIKE AND BY THUMB. Slovaks love to ride **bikes,** especially in the Tatras, the western foothills, and Šariš. **VKÚ** publishes color maps of most regions (70-80Sk). **Hitchhiking** is neither convenient nor common; hitchhikers should write their destination on a sign. *Let's Go* does not recommend hitchhiking.

TOURIST SERVICES AND MONEY

EMERGENCY	Police: ☎ 158. Ambulance: ☎ 155. Fire: ☎ 150.

TOURIST OFFICES. The main tourist offices form a conglomeration called **Asociácia Informačných Centier Slovenska (AICES);** look for the green logo. Offices often have English-speaking staff and can be found near the town's main square; dial ☎186 to find the nearest, or consult www.infoslovak.sk. **Slovakotourist** (www.sacr.sk), a travel agency, helps arrange transport and accommodations.

MONEY. One hundred *halér* make up one **Slovak koruna (Sk)**. **Banks** tend to be the best places to exchange currency. **Všeobecná Úverová Banka (VÚB)**, with offices in most towns, cashes American Express Traveler's Cheques for a 1% commission and often gives MasterCard cash advances. **Slovenská Sporiteľňa** bureaus usually handle Visa cash advances. All but the smallest towns have 24hr. **ATMs.** In restaurants most people simply round up to **tip.** Attempts to bargain usually offend.

KORUNY (SK)		
AUS$1 = 23.35SK	10SK = AUS$0.43
CDN$1 = 24.53SK	10SK = CDN$0.41
EUR€1 = 40.02SK	10SK = EUR€0.25
NZ$1 = 21.50SK	10SK = NZ$0.47
UK£1 = 59.54SK	10SK = UK£0.17
US$1 = 32.64SK	10SK = US$0.30

COMMUNICATION

PHONE CODES	**Country code:** 421. **International dialing prefix:** 00. From outside the Slovak Republic, dial int'l dialing prefix (see inside back cover) + 421 + city code + local number.

TELEPHONE AND INTERNET ACCESS. Pay phones are either card- or coin-operated. Cards (100-500Sk) can be found at kiosks and post offices; international callers should opt for GlobalPhone. International direct access numbers include **AT&T** (☎08 00 00 01 01), **British Telecom** (☎08 00 00 44 01), **Canada Direct** (☎08 00 00 01 51), **MCI** (☎08 00 00 01 12), and **Sprint** (☎08 00 08 71 87). Internet is common even in small towns; wired cafes tend to have the best rates and connections.

MAIL. Slovakia has an efficient mail service. International mail spends two to three weeks in transit depending on the destination. Almost every post office (*pošta*) provides **Express Mail Services.** A customs office (*colnice*) will send **packages** abroad. When sending mail *Poste Restante*, put a "1" after the city name to indicate the main post office. Address mail to be held as follows: First name SURNAME, *Poste Restante*, Nám. SNP 35, 81000 Bratislava 1, SLOVAK REPUBLIC.

LANGUAGES. Slovak, closely related to Czech, has complex Slavic origins; natives appreciate attempts to speak it. English is often spoken at tourist offices and by Bratislavan youth; German predominates as a second language elsewhere. Russian is often understood, but is not always welcome.

ACCOMMODATIONS AND CAMPING

SLOVAK REPUBLIC	❶	❷	❸	❹	❺
ACCOMMODATIONS	under 250Sk	251-500Sk	501-800Sk	801-1000Sk	over 1000Sk

Proprietors often charge foreigners up to twice as much as Slovaks for the same room. It is nearly impossible to find cheap accommodations in Bratislava before student dorms open in July, and without reservations, the outlook in Slovenský Raj and the Tatras can be bleak. In other regions, it's not difficult to find a bed as long as you call ahead. A tourist office or Slovakotourist agency can usually help. **Juniorhotels (HI)**, though uncommon, are a step up from the typical hostel. **Hotels** rarely fill, and prices fall dramatically outside Bratislava and the High Tatras. **Pensions** (*penzióny*) are smaller and less expensive than hotels. **Campgrounds** can be found on the outskirts of most towns, and many rent out bungalows. It is illegal to camp in national parks. In the mountains, **chaty** (mountain huts/cottages) range from a friendly bunk and outhouse for 200Sk per night to plush quarters for 600Sk.

FOOD AND DRINK

SLOVAK REPUBLIC	❶	❷	❸	❹	❺
FOOD	under 120Sk	121-190Sk	191-270Sk	271-330Sk	over 330Sk

The national dish, *bryndžové halusky*, is a plate of dumpling-like pasta smothered in a thick sauce of sheep or goat cheese, often flecked with bacon. *Knedliky* (dumplings) frequently accompany entrees, but it is possible to opt for *zemiaky* (potatoes) or *hranolky* (fries) instead. Slovak avoids misnomers: a cheeseburger (*syrový burger*) contains cheese only; hamburgers contain ham. *Kolačky* (pastry) is baked with cheese, jam or poppy seeds, and honey. Enjoy flavorful wines at a *vináreň* (wine hall); the western Slovak Republic produces the celebrated full-bodied *Modra*. *Pivo* (beer) is served at a *pivnica* or *pivareň* (tavern). The preferred Slovak beer is *Zlatý Bažant*, a light, slightly bitter Tatran brew.

SAFETY AND SECURITY

Tap water varies in quality and appearance but is generally safe. **Pharmacies** (*drogerie*) stock Western brands. Bandages are *obväz*, aspirin *aspirena*, tampons *tampony*, and condoms *kondómy*. **Lone women travelers** may encounter stares, but these will likely be the worst of their problems. **Minority** travelers with darker skin may be associated with the stigmatized Roma (Gypsies) and should exercise caution. **GLBT** couples may also face stares or insults.

HOLIDAYS

Independence Day (Jan. 1); Epiphany (Jan. 6); Good Friday (Mar. 25); Easter (Mar. 27-28); Labor Day (May 1); Liberation Day (May 8); Sts. Cyril and Methodius Day (July 5); Anniversary of Slovak Uprising (Aug. 29); Constitution Day (Sept. 1); Our Lady of the Seven Sorrows (Sept. 15); All Saints' Day (Nov. 1); Christmas (Dec. 24-26).

FACTS AND FIGURES: SLOVAK REPUBLIC

Official Name: Slovak Republic.
Capital: Bratislava.
Population: 5,424,000.
Land Area: 48,845 sq. km.
Time Zone: GMT +1.
Languages: Slovak, Hungarian.
Religions: Roman Catholic (60%), Protestant (8%), atheist (10%), other (22%).

BRATISLAVA   ☎02

One of only two regions in Eastern Europe with living standards above the European Union average, Bratislava (pop. 450,000) surprises those who take the time to discover it. While villages, vineyards, and castles lace the city's outskirts, inside, its streets are lined with shops, restaurants, and chic cafes. After the Velvet Revolution of 1989, the fall of Communism, and the dissolution of Czechoslovakia in 1993, Bratislava has been in bloom far more than its neighbors.

Bratislava

🔺 ACCOMMODATIONS
Downtown Backpacker's
  Hostel, **2**
Družba, **10**
Orange Hostel, **12**
Slovenská Zdravotnicka
  Univerzita, **1**

🍎 FOOD
Archa, **6**
Bagetky, **9**
Black Rose Restaurant, **5**
Chez David, **4**

🍴 NIGHTLIFE
Elam Klub, **11**
Jazz Café, **8**
Klub Laverna, **7**
Medusa Cocktail
  Bar, **3**

▐ TRANSPORTATION

Trains: Bratislava Hlavná Stanica. To get downtown, take tram #2 to the 6th stop. International tickets at counters #5-13. **Wasteels** (☎52 49 93 57; www.wasteels.host.sk) sells discounted tickets to those under 26. Open M-F 8:30am-4:30pm. MC/V. To **Prague** (4½-5½hr., 3 per day, 750-840Sk) and **Warsaw** (8hr., 1 per day, 1456Sk).

Buses: Mlynské nivy 31 (☎55 42 16 67). Take trolley #202 to the center, or turn right on Mlynské nivy and continue to Dunajská, which leads to Kamenné nám. and the center of town. To: **Berlin** (12hr., 1 per day, 1200Sk); **Budapest** (4hr., 1 per day, 550Sk); **Prague** (4¾hr., 5 per day, 410Sk); **Vienna** (1½hr., every 1-2 hr., 380Sk); **Warsaw** (13hr., 1 per day, 670Sk). Check ticket for bus number (č. aut.) since several different buses may depart from the same stand.

Public Transportation: Tickets for daytime **trams** and **buses** (4am-11pm) are sold at kiosks and orange ticket machines in bus stations (10min. ticket 14Sk, 30min. 16Sk, 1hr. 22Sk). **Night buses** (midnight-4am), marked with black and orange numbers in the 500s, require 2 tickets. Stamp tickets on board or face a 1200Sk fine. **Tourist passes** are sold at kiosks: 1-day pass 80Sk, 2-day 150Sk, 3-day 185Sk, 1-week 275Sk.)

Taxis: BP (☎16 999); **FunTaxi** (☎16 777); **Profi Taxi** (☎16 222).

Hitchhiking: Those hitching to **Vienna** cross Most SNP (SNP Bridge) and walk down Viedenská cesta. This road also heads to **Hungary** via Győr, though fewer cars head in that direction. Hitchhikers to **Prague** take bus #21 from the center to Patronka. For destinations within the Slovak Republic, take tram #2 or 4 to Zlaté Piesky. Hitchhiking is legal except on major highways. *Let's Go* does not recommend hitchhiking.

■*⃰🛈 ORIENTATION AND PRACTICAL INFORMATION

The **Dunaj** (Danube) flows east-west across Bratislava. **Nový Most** (New Bridge), the largest of the four bridges spanning the Danube, ties together the riven sections of **Staromestská**, the commercial district and entertainment area on the river's southern bank. **Bratislavský Hrad** (Bratislava Castle) towers on a hill to the west. Bratislava's center of gravity lies between the river and **Námestie Slovenského Národného Povstania** (Nám. SNP; Slovak National Uprising Square).

Tourist Office: Bratislavská Informačná Služba (BIS), Klobúčnicka 2 (☎161 86; www.bis.bratislava.sk). Books private rooms and hotels (50Sk commission), sells maps (60Sk), and runs city tours (1000Sk per hr.). A **museum pass** (75Sk) gives admission to 4 major museums and the zoo. Open June to mid-Oct. M-F 8:30am-7pm, Sa-Su 10am-6pm; mid-Oct. to May M-F 8am-6pm, Sa 9am-2pm.

Embassies: Ireland, Mostová 2 (☎59 30 96 11; mail@ireland-embassy.sk). Open M-F 9am-12:30pm. **UK,** Panská 16 (☎59 98 20 00; www.britishembassy.sk). Visa office open M-F 9-11am. **US,** Hviezdoslavovo nám. 4 (☎54 43 08 61, emergency 09 03 70 36 66; www.usembassy.sk). Open M-F 8am-4:30pm. Visa office open M-F 8-11:30am. In an emergency, citizens of **Australia** and **New Zealand** should contact the UK embassy. **Canadians** should consult their embassy in Vienna (p. 94).

Currency Exchange: Ľudová Banka, Jesenkého 2 (☎54 41 89 84; www.luba.sk) cashes AmEx/V **traveler's checks** for 1% commission and offers MC/V **cash advances.** Open M-F 7am-9pm. 24hr. MC/V. **ATMs** are at the train station and throughout the city center.

Emergency: Police: ☎158. **Ambulance:** ☎155. **Fire:** ☎150.

24hr. Pharmacy: Lekáreň Pod Manderlom, Nám. SNP 20 (☎54 43 29 52). Open M-F 7:30am-7pm, Sa 8am-5pm, Su 9am-5pm. Ring bell after hours for emergency service.

Internet Access: Megainet, Šancová 25, is a relaxed cafe with state-of-the-art PCs. 1Sk per min. Open daily 9am-10pm. **Internet Centrum,** Michalská 2, is a 6-computer cafe. M-F 10am-9pm 2Sk per min., off hours 1Sk per min. Open daily 9am-midnight.

Post Office: Nám. SNP 34 (☎59 39 33 30). Has fax service. Open M-F 7am-8pm, Sa 7am-6pm, Su 9am-2pm. *Poste Restante* and phone cards at counters #5-6. *Poste Restante* M-F 7am-8pm, Sa 7am-2pm. **Postal Code:** 81000.

▐ ACCOMMODATIONS

In July and August, several **university dorms** open as hostels; they are sometimes run-down but quite cheap (from 150Sk). Pensions or private rooms are an inexpensive and comfy alternative. **BIS** (see **Practical Information,** above) has more info.

▓ **Downtown Backpacker's Hostel,** Panenska 31 (☎54 64 11 91; www.backpackers.sk). Rooms are spacious, comfy, social, and central. In the common room, recline with a pint (35Sk) on worn-in sofas under a bust of Lenin. Laundry 100Sk. Internet 2Sk per min. Reception 24hr. Check-out noon. Reserve ahead. Dorms 600Sk, with HI card 530Sk; doubles 900Sk. Tourist tax 15Sk. ❸

Orange Hostel, Dobrovicova 14 (☎902 842 900; www.hostelinbratislava.com). Clean and just minutes from the main square. Internet free. Laundry free. Reception 24hr. Check-out 10am. Open July 9-Aug. 25. Dorms 550Sk. AmEx/MC/V. ❸

HOW TO BE A SLOVAK IN ONE QUEASY STEP

One staple of almost every Slovak menu is *bryndza*, a creamy sheep's-milk cheese that the country has made for over two centuries. It is an acquired taste; visitors often wonder whether their serving dates back to the original batch.

Don't be too hasty to judge, however. Slovaks take their *bryndza* seriously, churning out about 3500 tons per year. Indeed, natives assess a Slovak's patriotism by his or her enjoyment of the dish. *Bryndza*-eating contests are common in rural areas. A national soft spot for these curds has even inspired newspaper editorials such as "*Bryndza* is a Part of Our Identity."

Bryndza is never found far from *halusky*, a starchy, potato-like dough smeared in a cheese sauce. *Bryndzove* and *halusky* are respectively the nation's pride and joy, and a necessary rite of passage for foreigners with intrepid stomachs. Many come to appreciate the dish's pungent kick, but vegetarians should approach it with caution, as it frequently comes sprinkled with bacon bits. If you don't want meat, order the dish "*bez slaniny*" (without bacon). To temper the taste of the *bryndza*, you can also order it "*s oprazenymi cibulami*" (with fried onions), or do as the locals do and just wash it down with a strong shot of Becherovka.

Slovenská Zdravotnicka Univerzita, Limbová 12 (☎59 37 01 00; www.szu.sk). From the train station, take bus #32 or electric cable bus #204 5 stops to Nemocnica Kramárel. Breakfast 35Sk. Reception 24hr. Checkout 11am. Singles 600Sk; doubles 700Sk; apartments 1000-1200Sk. ❸

Družba, Botanická 25 (Dorms: ☎60 29 92 61; recepcia@sdjdr.uniba.sk. Hotel: ☎65 42 00 65; www.ubytujsa.sk). Tram #1 (dir.: Pri Kríži) to Botanická Záhrada. One of the more luxurious student dorms, Družba has clean rooms with shared baths. Dorms open July 5-Aug. 25. Reception 24hr. 315Sk, students 130Sk. Hotel open year-round. Reception M-Th 7am-3:30pm, F 7am-1pm. Singles 590Sk; doubles 840Sk. ❸

🍴 FOOD

In a square otherwise full of fast-food stalls, look for groceries at **Tesco Potraviny,** Kamenné nám. 1. (Open M-F 8am-9pm, Sa 8am-7pm, Su 9am-7pm.)

Black Rose Restaurant, Jurigovo nám. 1. Relax outside and people-watch with a dish of anything from Slovak fare to fish and chips. Entrees 89-250Sk. Open M-F 10am-1am, Sa 11am-1am, Su 11am-midnight. ❷

Archa, Urslínska 6 (☎54 43 08 65). Attentive staff offers world cuisine with outstanding salads. Entrees 60-200Sk. Open M-F 9am-midnight, Sa-Su 10am-midnight. ❶

Bagetky, Zelená 8. A relaxed sandwich bar, Bagetsky keeps it simple. Limited seating. Entrees 50-90Sk. Open M-Sa 9:30am-9pm, Su 2-9pm. ❶

Chez David, Zámocká 13 (☎54 41 38 24). The only kosher restaurant in Bratislava. Offers kosher and vegetarian favorites such as falafel (67Sk). Entrees 67-197Sk. Open M-Th and Su 11:30am-10pm, F 11:30am-3pm. ❶

🔅 SIGHTS

NÁMESTIE SNP AND ENVIRONS. With the exception of Devín Castle, most of the city's major attractions are in **Old Bratislava** (Stará Bratislava). From Nám. SNP, which commemorates the bloody 1944 Slovak National Uprising against Fascism, walk down Uršulínska to reach the Baroque █**Primate's Palace** (Primaciálný Palác). In the palace's **Hall of Mirrors** (Zrkadlová Sieň), Napoleon and Austrian Emperor Franz I signed the 1805 Peace of Pressburg. *(Primaciálné nám. 1. Open Tu-Su 10am-5pm. 40Sk, students free.)* Turn left down Kostolná as you exit the palace to reach **Hlavné námestie.** Turn left entering the square to find the **Town History Museum**

(Muzeum Histórie Mesta), which has an impressive 1:500 scale model of Bratislava in the era 1945-1955. *(Open Tu-F 10am-5pm, Sa-Su 11am-6pm. 30Sk, students 10Sk.)* Continue to the opposite end of the square and take a left onto Rybárska Brana to **Hviezdoslavovo námestie,** in which stands the gorgeous 1886 **Slovak National Theater** (Slovenské Národné Divadlo). Go through the square, take Mostová, and turn left at the Danube to reach the **Slovak National Gallery,** which displays artwork from the Gothic and Baroque periods as well as some modern sculptures. *(Rázusovo nábr. 2. www.sng.sk. Open Tu-Su 10am-5:30pm. 80Sk, students 40Sk.)* With the Danube on your left, continue to the gaudy neon-lit **Nový Most** (New Bridge), designed by the Communist government in the 1970s. Backtrack from the bridge and turn left on Rigoleho, continue straight onto Strakova (which becomes Ventúrska, then Michalská), and pass through **St. Michael's Tower** (Michalská Brána), Bratislava's last remaining medieval gateway. Keep going as Michalská becomes Župnénám and take a left onto Kapucínska; cross the pedestrian bridge over the highway to reach the **Museum of Jewish Culture** (Múzeum Zidovskej Kultúry). *(Židovská 17. Open M-F and Su 11am-5pm. Last admission 4:30pm. 200Sk, students 50Sk.)*

CASTLES. Visible from much of the city, the four-towered **Bratislava Castle** (Bratislavský hrad) is the city's defining landmark. The castle burned in 1811 and was bombed during World War II; what's left today is a Communist-era restoration. Its towers provide fantastic views of the Danube. From Nový Most, climb the stairs to Židovská; turn right on Zámocké schody and head uphill. *(www.snm-hm.sk. Castle open daily Apr.-Sept. 9am-8pm; Oct.-Mar. 9am-6pm. Free. Museum open Tu-Su 9am-5pm. Last admission 4:15pm. 60Sk, students 30Sk.)* **Devín Castle's** ruins perch on an imposing cliff above the Danube and Morava Rivers, a stone's throw from Austria. Take bus #29 from below Nový Most to the last stop, 9km west of Bratislava. Originally a Celtic fortification, the castle passed through the hands of Romans, Slavs, and Hungarians before Napoleon destroyed it in 1809. A museum highlights its history. *(Open July-Aug. Tu-F 10am-5pm, Sa-Su 10am-6pm; May-June and Sept.-Oct. Tu-Su 10am-5pm. Last admission 30min. before closing. English info available. Museum 60Sk, students 20Sk.)*

🎵 🎭 ENTERTAINMENT AND NIGHTLIFE

The regular theater season runs from September through June. BIS (p. 901) has the monthly *Kam v Bratislave,* which provides film, concert, and theater schedules. Ballets and operas at the **Slovak National Theatre,** Hviezdoslavovo nám. 1, draw crowds from neighboring Austria. (☎54 43 30 83; www.snd.sk. Box office open Sept.-June M-F 8am-5:30pm, Sa 9am-1pm. Tickets 100-200Sk.) The **Slovak Philharmonic** (Slovenská Filharmónia) plays regularly at the Medená 3; the box office is around the corner at Palackého 2. (☎54 43 33 51; www.filharm.sk. Box office open Sept.-June M-Tu and Th-F 1-7pm, W 8am-2pm. Tickets 100-200Sk.)

By day, **Hlavné námestie** features souvenir stands and free outdoor concerts; by night, it fills with strolling couples and teens preparing for an evening out. Revel in Bratislava's place to see and be seen at **Medusa Cocktail Bar,** Michalská 89, just after St. Michael's Tower. (Open M-Th 11am-1am, F-Sa 11am-3am, Su 11am-midnight.) **Klub Laverna,** Laurinská 19, has a packed dance floor and a slide between its two levels. (Cover 100Sk. Open daily 8pm-6am.) Look for the student crowd at **Elam Klub,** Stare Grunty 53. Take bus #31 or 39 from Nám. Mája to the end of the line. (☎65 42 63 04; www.elam.sk. Cover 39-100Sk depending on DJ. Open daily 9pm-6am.) **Jazz Café,** Ventúrska 5, has cocktails and live jazz. (Beer 40Sk. Jazz Th-Sa 9pm-1am. Cafe open daily 10am-2am. Club open daily 2pm-2am.)

THE TATRA MOUNTAINS (TATRY)

The mesmerizing High Tatras, which span the border between the Slovak Republic and Poland, offer hundreds of hiking and skiing trails along the highest Carpathian peaks (2650m). One of the most compact ranges in the world, the High Tatras feature sky-scraping hikes, glacial lakes, and deep snows. Cheap mountain railways and accommodations add to the allure for the budget hiker.

 The Tatras are a great place to hike, but many of the hikes are extremely demanding and require experience, even in summer. In winter, a guide is almost always necessary. For current conditions, check **www.tanap.sk**.

STARÝ SMOKOVEC. Spectacular trails run from Starý Smokovec, the High Tatras' most central resort. To reach **Hrebienok** (1285m), which leads to hiking country, ride the funicular. (High season 90Sk up, 40Sk down, 100Sk round-trip; low season 70Sk/40Sk/80Sk.) Or, from the funicular station behind the train station, hike 35min. up the green trail. The green trail continues 20min. north from Hrebienok to the foaming **Cold Stream Waterfalls** (Volopáday studeného potoka). From the falls, take the red trail, which connects with the eastward blue trail to **Tatranská Lomnica** (1¾hr.). The hike to **Little Cold Valley** (Malá studená dolina) is also fairly relaxed; take the red trail (40min.) from Hrebienok to **Zamkovského chata (hut)** ❷ (☎052 442 26 36; rooms 290Sk per person) and onto the green trail (2hr.) which climbs above the treeline to a high lake and **Téryho chata** ❷ (☎052 442 52 45; rooms 280Sk per person).

TEŽ trains run to Poprad (30min., every hr., 20Sk). **Buses** run to: Bratislava (6hr., 2 per day, 409Sk); Košice (3hr., 2-3 per day, 132Sk); and Levoča (20-50min., 2-4 per day, 67Sk). The **Tatranská Informačná Kancelária (TIK)**, in Dom Služieb, has weather info and sells the essential *VKÚ sheet #113* (89Sk), among other hiking maps. (☎442 34 40; www.zcrvt.szm.sk. Open July-Aug. daily 8am-6pm; Sept.-Dec. 26 and Jan. 12-June M-F 9am-noon and 12:30-4pm, Sa 9am-1pm; Dec. 27-Jan. 11 daily 8am-5pm. Private rooms 200-250Sk; pensions 400Sk; hotels 600Sk.) Most budget accommodations are down the road in **Horný Smokovec.** From the station, turn right on the main road and walk 5min. to reach **Hotel Šport** ❷, which shares a cafe, sauna, pool, and massage parlor with neighboring Hotel Bellevue. (☎052 442 23 61. Breakfast 80Sk. English-speaking reception 24hr. Check-out 10am. July-Aug. book a month in advance. Jan. 2-Feb. 28, Apr. 8-10, June 19-Sept. 30 singles 430Sk; doubles 750Sk; Dec. 26-Jan. 1. 770Sk/1240Sk; Mar. 1-Apr. 7, Apr. 11-June 18, Oct. 1-Dec. 25 310Sk/550Sk. Tourist tax 15Sk.) To reach the well-furnished, family-run **Penzión Gerlach** ❸, turn left out of the TEŽ station onto the main road and continue past the church, with the tracks on your left; it's near the street on the right. (☎442 32 80; www.penziongerlach.sk. Reception 10am-6pm. Call ahead in high season. Singles 600-800Sk; doubles 800-1000Sk; triples 1200-1500Sk; low season 300-400Sk/400-500Sk/500Sk.) Worthwhile restaurants are clustered above the bus and train stations.

ŠTRBSKÉ PLESO. Many beautiful **hikes** begin from the town. Overlooking the valleys behind placid Štrbské Pleso (Štrbské Lake) is **Chata pod Soliskom** (1840m); a lift hoists climbers to the top in summer. (☎449 22 21. One-way 130Sk, round-trip 190Sk. Open 8:30am-4pm; last lift up 3:30pm.) The challenging **yellow route** (8-9hr.) heads from the eastern side of the lake out along Mlynická dolina to mountain ponds and the Vodopády Skok waterfalls. It then mounts Bystré Sedlo (2314m) and Veľke Solisko (2412m) before returning to the lake. TEŽ **trains** arrive from Starý Smokovec (30min., every 30min., 30Sk).

LIPTOVSKÝ MIKULÁŠ. Liptovský Mikuláš (pop. 33,000) is a good springboard for hiking in the **Low Tatras** (Nízke Tatry). To scale **Mt. Ďumbier,** the region's tallest peak (2043m), catch an early bus from platform #11 at the bus station to Liptovský Ján (25-30min., 1 per hr., 13-16Sk), then follow the blue trail up the Štiavnica River to the **Svidovské Sedlo** (5hr.). Next, bear left on the red trail to the ridge, which leads to panoramic views from the summit (45min.). Descend the ridge and follow the red sign to neighboring peak **Chopok** (2024m), the second-highest in the range. From Chopok, it's a winding walk down the blue trail to the **bus** stop behind the Hotel Grand at Otupné (1¾hr.). **Trains** to Liptovský Mikuláš from Bratislava (4hr., 12 per day, 330Sk) are cheaper and more frequent than buses. Get to the town center by following Štefánikova toward the gas station at the far end of the lot, then turn right onto Hodžu. The **tourist office,** Nám. Mieru 1, in the Dom Služieb complex on the northern side of town, books private rooms, which run from 245-400Sk, and sells dozens of hiking maps. (☎044 552 24 18; www.lmikulas.sk. Open mid-June to mid-Sept. and mid-Dec. to Mar. M-F 8am-7pm, Sa 8am-2pm, Su noon-6pm; low season reduced hours.) **Hotel Kriváň ❷,** Štúrova 5, is across from the tourist office. (☎044 552 24 14. Singles 300Sk, with bath 400Sk; doubles 480Sk/600Sk.) **Liptovská Izba Reštaurácia ❶,** nám. Osloboditeľov 22, serves delicious local dishes. (☎044 551 48 53. Entrees 55-115Sk. Open daily 10am-10pm.)

SLOVENSKÝ RAJ. Southeast of the Nízke Tatry is the less-touristed Slovenský Raj (Slovak Paradise) National Park, filled with forested hills, deep ravines, and fast-flowing streams. The excellent trail guide *VKÚ sheet #4* is available at many hotels. The ▓**Dobšinská Ice Caves** (Dobšinská ľadová jaskyňa) are composed of 110,000 cubic meters of water still frozen from the last Ice Age. Tours cover 475m, passing halls of frozen columns, gigantic ice wells, and hardened waterfalls. From **Dedinky** (pop. 400), the largest town on the park's southern border, take the **train** for two stops (15min., 3 per day, 11Sk). From the station, head 100m out to the main road. Turn left, and the parking lot is 250m ahead. From there, the blue trail (20min.) leads up a steep incline to the caves. (☎788 14 70; www.ssj.sk. Open June-Aug. Tu-Su 9am-4pm; late May and Sept. 9:30am-2pm. 120Sk, students 100Sk.)

The **bus** to Poprad (dir.: Rožňava; 1hr., 4 per day, 65Sk) stops at a junction 2km south of Dedinky. Watch for the huge blue road signs at the intersection just before the bus stop. From the intersection, walk down the road that the bus did *not* take, turn right at the next intersection, cross the dam after the train station, turn left, and walk 10min. to Dedinky. Signs marked *"Privat," "ubytowanie,"* or *"Zimmer frei"* indicate private rooms (200-300Sk), often the best bases for trails. **Penzión Pastierňa ❶,** Dedinky 42, has a restaurant serving Slovakian cuisine, and tasteful rooms with shared baths. (☎058 798 11 75. Breakfast 40-60Sk. Entrees 60-170Sk. Reception daily 8:30am-9:30pm. Check-out 11am. 2- to 4-bed rooms 300Sk.)

KOŠICE
☎055

Košice (KO-shih-tseh; pop. 236,000), Slovakia's second-largest city, has a modern cosmopolitan flair to match the enchantments of its **Staré Mesto** (old town). To get to the center, exit the train station and follow the *"Centrum"* signs across the park. Walk down **Mlynská** to reach the main **Hlavná nám.** High Gothic at its founding in 1378, the ▓**Cathedral of St. Elizabeth** (Dom sv. Alžbety) has since been renovated repeatedly in styles from Baroque to Rococo. Now it is the final resting place of revolutionary hero and Košice native Ferenc Rakóczi II. Climb the north tower for a view of the detailed cathedral roof and the old town. (☎090 866 70 83. Crypt and tower open M-F 9:30am-4:30pm; Apr.-Nov. tower only. Cathedral tours 35Sk, students 20Sk.) The **East Slovak Museum** (Východoslovenské Múzeum), Hrnčiarska 7, partitions into **Rakóczi's House** and **Mikluš's Prison** (Miklušova väznica), an exposé of life behind bars from the 17th to 19th centuries. Walking up Hlavná, take a right at the state theater onto Univerzitná. (Open Tu-Sa 9am-5pm, Su 9am-1pm. Mandatory tours every hr. 30Sk, students 10Sk. English infosheet.) An **archaeological branch,** Hviezdoslavova 2, chronicles the Sariš region. (☎622 05 71. Open Tu-Sa 9am-5pm, Su 9am-1pm. 30Sk, students 10Sk. English guidebook 30Sk.) **■Jazz Club,** Kováčska 39, divides its genres between disco Tuesday, Thursday, and Saturday; jazz and funk Wednesday and Friday; and classical piano Monday and Sunday. (☎622 42 37. Beer 25-35Sk. Cover disco nights 30Sk. Open daily 4pm-2am, disco nights until 3am.) **Aloha Cocktail Club,** Hlavná 69, attracts a younger crowd with its cocktail menu and R&B, rap, and pop playlist. (Open M-Th and Su 2-11pm, F 2pm-3am, Sa 5pm-3am.)

Trains run from the station on Predstaničné nám to: Bratislava (6hr., 13 per day, 550Sk); Budapest (5hr., 3 per day, 827Sk); Kraków (6-7hr., 3 per day, 901Sk); and Poprad (1¼hr., 1 per day, 138Sk). **Buses** priced per km run to many of the same destinations from the terminal to the left of the train station. From the station, to reach the **tourist office,** Hlavná 58, cross the park, walk down Mlynská, and turn right on Hlavná nám. (☎625 88 88; www.kosice.sk/icmk. Internet 40Sk per hr. Open M-F 9am-6pm, Sa 9am-1pm). Košice's **post office,** Poštová 20, has *Poste Restante* at window #16. (☎617 14 01. Open M-F 7am-7pm, Sa 8am-noon.) **University dorms ❶** are the cheapest option in July and August, but farther from the center. (☎643 94 84. 200-400Sk per night). **K2 Tourist Hotel ❷,** Štúrova 32, is the best bargain in walking distance from town. Head down Hlavná from the main square and turn right on Štúrova. (☎625 59 48. Restaurant attached. Reception 24hr. Check-in and check-out noon. Triples 900Sk; quads 1200Sk. Tax 15Sk per day.) At a remove from the city center, **Hotel Kohal ❸,** Trieda SNP 61, contains a hostel with plain-vanilla singles and doubles. Hotel rooms have TV, apartments have private bath. Take tram #6 from the train/bus station to Ferrocentrum. (☎/fax 642 55 72. Breakfast 90Sk. Laundry service. Reception 24hr. Check-out 11am. Hostel singles 330Sk; doubles 610Sk. Hotel singles 580Sk; doubles 1120Sk. Apartments 1300Sk. Tax 15Sk per day. AmEx/MC/V.) **■Restaurant Ethno ❶,** Hlavná 102, dishes up a medley of international foods and Slovakian specialties. (Entrees 89-140Sk. Open daily noon-10pm.) **Tesco** supermarket can be found at Hlavná 109, by Pizza Hut. (☎670 48 10. Open M-F 8am-8pm, Sa-Su 8am-4:30pm. MC/V.) **Postal Code:** 04001.

SLOVENIA (SLOVENIJA)

Slovenia, the most prosperous of Yugoslavia's breakaway republics, has reveled in its new independence and quickly separated itself from its neighbors. With a hungry eye westward, Slovenia has used its liberal politics and high economic output to enter coveted alliances like NATO and the EU. Modernization has not adversely affected the tiny country's natural beauty and diversity, however. It is still possible to eat breakfast on an Alpine peak, lunch under the Mediterranean sun, and dinner in a Pannonian vineyard all in one day.

DISCOVER SLOVENIA

Any visit should start with the Habsburg majesty and lively cafe culture of youthful **Ljubljana** (p. 910). In the Julian Alps, **Bled** (p. 914) and **Lake Bohinj** (p. 914) traverse miles of hikes varying from the casual to the treacherous; in winter, the range offers snowy, steep, and relatively cheap skiing. Descend to seaside **Piran** (p. 915), on the Istrian Peninsula, for scuba diving and the national marine preserve.

ESSENTIALS

WHEN TO GO

Slovenia has a varied climate. Along the Adriatic, as along much of the Mediterranean, winters are not severe and summers (except for the occasional thunderstorm) suited for basking. In Ljubljana, temperatures average –4-5°C (25-41°F) in mid-winter and 14-27°C (57-81°F) in mid-summer. Inland weather is more comparable to nearby landlocked nations.

DOCUMENTS AND FORMALITIES

VISAS. Australian, Canadian, Irish, New Zealand, UK, and US citizens do not need visas for stays of up to 90 days. Apply in your home country.

EMBASSIES. Foreign embassies are in Ljubljana (p. 910). Embassies at home include: **Australia,** Level 6, St. George's Building, 60 Marcus Clarke St., Canberra, ACT 2601 (☎02 6243 4830; www.gov.si/mzz/dkp/vca/eng/); **Canada,** 150 Metcalfe St., Ottawa, ON K2P 1P1 (☎613-565-5781; www.gov.si/mzz/dkp/vot/eng/); **Ireland,** Morrison Chambers, 2nd Floor, 32 Nassau St., Dublin 2 (☎01 670 5240; www.gov.si/mzz/dkp/vdb/); **New Zealand** (consulate; refer to Australia for the embassy), P.O. Box 30247 Eastern Hutt Rd., Pomare, Lower Hutt, Wellington (☎04 567 0027; fax 04 567 0024); **UK,** 10 Little College St., London SW1P 3SH (☎020 7222 5400; www.gov.si/mzz/dkp/vlo/eng/); **US,** 1525 New Hampshire Ave. NW, Washington, D.C. 20036 (☎202-667-5363; www.embassy.org/slovenia).

TRANSPORTATION

BY PLANE. Commercial flights arrive at the Ljubljana Airport (www.lju-airport.si/eng/). **British Airways** flies direct to Slovenia; other major lines offer connections to Slovenia's national carrier, **Adria Airways** (☎01 36 91 010; www.adria.si). Traveling to Vienna by plane and then to Ljubljana by train saves money, but not time.

BY TRAIN. Trains are cheap, clean, and reliable. Relative to the extra money, differences between first and second class are negligible. For most international destinations, travelers under 26 can get a 20% discount; check at the Ljubljana station (look for the BIJ-Wasteels logo). Domestic tickets are 30% off for ISIC holders—ask for a *popust* (discount). **Eurail** has limited options. *"Vlak"* means train, *"prihodi vlakov"* means arrivals, and *"odhodi vlakov"* means departures. Schedules usually list trains by direction; look for those that run *dnevno* (daily).

BY BUS. Slovenia's bus network is extensive. Though usually more expensive than trains, buses are often the only option in mountainous regions. Tickets are sold at the station or on board. Put your luggage in the passenger compartment if it's not too crowded. Large backpacks cost 220Sit extra.

BY BOAT, CAR, BIKE, OR THUMB. In the summer, a regular **hydrofoil** runs between Venice and Portorož. When not traveling by bus or train, most Slovenes transport themselves by **bike;** most towns have a rental office. Drivers can call the emergency number for the **Automobile Association of Slovenia** at ☎987. *Let's Go* does not recommend **hitchhiking,** which is uncommon throughout the country.

TOURIST SERVICES AND MONEY

EMERGENCY	Police: ☎113. **Ambulance** and **Fire:** ☎112.

TOURIST OFFICES. The main tourist organization is **Kompas.** Tourist offices, which can usually help with accommodations, are located in most major cities and tourist spots. Staffs generally speak English, German, and on the coast, Italian.

MONEY. The national currency is the **Slovenian tolar (Sit).** Given inflation, prices may alter by next year. Exchange rates vary, but tend to be better at **exchange offices;** post offices have the worst rates. **ATMs** are common. Major credit cards are not accepted reliably, but American Express Traveler's Cheques and Eurocheques usually work. **Tipping** is not expected, but rounding up is appreciated; 10% is sufficient for good service. Attempts to bargain are often considered offensive.

TOLARS (SIT)		
AUS$1 = 140SIT	100SIT = AUS$0.71
CDN$1 = 147SIT	100SIT = CDN$0.68
EUR€ = 240SIT	100SIT = EUR€0.42
NZ$1 = 129SIT	100SIT = NZ$0.78
UK£1 = 357SIT	100SIT = UK£0.28
US$1 = 196SIT	100SIT = US$0.51

COMMUNICATION

PHONE CODES	**Country code: 386. International dialing prefix: 00.** From outside Slovenia, dial int'l dialing prefix (see inside back cover) + 386 + city code + local number.

TELEPHONES AND INTERNET ACCESS. Slovenia **changed** all of its phone numbers in 2001; check the date of older listings. All phones now take **phone cards,** which are sold at post offices, kiosks, and gas stations (750Sit per 50 impulses, which yields 1½min. to the US). Dial ☎ 115 for collect calls assisted by an English-speaking operator. Try the phones at the post office for international calls. An international access number exists for **MCI WorldPhone** (☎ 080 8808). **Internet** access is very common in Slovenia, even outside the capital.

MAIL. Airmail (*letalsko*) takes 1-2 weeks to reach North America, Australia, and New Zealand. Letters abroad cost 107Sit, postcards 83Sit. Address mail to be held *Poste Restante* according to the following example: Firstname SURNAME, *Poste Restante*, Slovenska 32, 1000 Ljubljana, SLOVENIA.

LANGUAGES. Slovenian is a Slavic language that uses the Roman alphabet. Younger people tend to speak some English, but the older generation is more likely to understand German in the north or Italian along the Adriatic. Serbian and Croatian are also commonly spoken.

ACCOMMODATIONS AND FOOD

SLOVENIA	❶	❷	❸	❹	❺
ACCOMMODATIONS	under 2800Sit	2800-4400Sit	4400-6000Sit	6000-7600Sit	over 7600Sit
FOOD	under 600Sit	600-1000Sit	1000-1400Sit	1400-1800Sit	over 1800Sit

Pensions, the most common form of lodgings, usually have private singles as well as inexpensive triples and dorms. Youth **hostels** and student **dormitories** are cheap (2500-3000Sit), but generally open only in summer (June 25-Aug. 30). While hostels are often the cheapest option inland, **private rooms** are the only budget lodgings on the coast and at Lake Bohinj; inquire at the tourist office or look for signs marked "*Zimmer frei*" or "*sobe.*" Prices vary by location, but rarely exceed €30, and most rooms are very comfortable. **Campgrounds** can be crowded but are in excellent condition. Anyone who pitches a tent outside designated areas faces fines.

For homestyle cooking, try a *gostilna* or *gostišče* (both refer to a restaurant with a country flavor). Meals start with *jota*, a soup with potatoes, beans, and sauerkraut. *Svinjska pečenka* (roast pork) is tasty, but vegetarians should look for *štruklji*—large, slightly sweet dumplings. Pizzerias usually have meatless dishes. A favorite dessert is *potica*, a pastry with a rich filling (usually walnut). The country's wine-making tradition dates from antiquity. *Renski Rizling* and *Šipon* are popular whites, while *Cviček* and *Teran* are well-known reds. Good

SLOVENIA

beers include *Lasko* and *Union*. For something stronger, try the fruit brandy *žganje*. The most enchanting alcoholic concoction is *viljamovka*, distilled by monks who manage to fit a full pear inside the bottle.

SAFETY AND SECURITY

Medical facilities are of high quality, and most have English-speaking doctors. UK nationals receive free medical care with a valid passport; other foreigners must pay cash. **Pharmacies** are also stocked to Western standards. *"Obliž"* means band-aids; *"tamponi,"* tampon; and *"vložki,"* sanitary pads. **Tap water** is safe to drink everywhere. **Crime** is rare. Even in the largest cities, too-friendly drunks and bad drivers are the greatest public menace. There are few **minorities** in Slovenia; while incidents of discrimination are uncommon, minority travelers may be greeted with stares, especially in rural areas. **Homosexuality** is legal but may elicit uncertain or unfriendly reactions from adult generations or from residents of suburban and rural areas.

HOLIDAYS AND FESTIVALS

Holidays: New Year's (Jan. 1-2); Pust (beginning of Lent; Feb. 5-8); Culture Day (Prešeren Day; Feb. 8); Easter (Mar. 27-28); National Resistance Day (Apr. 27); Labor Day (May 1-2); Pentecost (May 15); National Day (June 25); Assumption (Aug. 15); Reformation Day (Oct. 31); Remembrance Day (Nov. 1); Christmas (Dec. 25); Independence Day (Dec. 26).

Festivals: The International Summer Festival (Jul.-Aug.; www.festival-lj.si) in Ljubljana is an extravaganza of opera, theater, and classical music.

FACTS AND FIGURES: SLOVENIA

Official Name: Republic of Slovenia.
Capital: Ljubljana.
Population: 2,011,000.
Land Area: 20,151 sq. km.

Time Zone: GMT +1.
Language: Slovenian.
Religions: Roman Catholic (71%), atheist (5%), other (24%).

LJUBLJANA

☎01

According to legend, Ljubljana (pop. 280,000) was founded when Jason and the Argonauts sailed into the Ljubljana River and slew the horrible Ljubljana dragon. Today, dragons on the bridge guard both sides of the river, surrounded by a mix of Baroque monuments, Art Nouveau facades, and modern high rises—all architectural testimony to the city's richly layered history.

▐ TRANSPORTATION

Trains: Trg O. F. 6 (☎291 33 32). To: **Bled** (1hr., 11 per day, 890Sit); **Budapest** (9hr., 1 per day, 14,836Sit); **Munich** (6-7hr., 3 per day, 15,200Sit); **Sarajevo** (11hr., 1 per day, 8315Sit) via **Zagreb** (2hr., 9 per day, 2700Sit); **Trieste** (3hr., 2-3 per day, 4836Sit); **Venice** (6hr., 3 per day, 7900Sit); **Vienna** (5-6hr., 2 per day, 12,800Sit).

Buses: Trg O. F. 4 (☎090 42 30; www.ap-ljubljana.si). To: **Bled** (1½hr., 14 per day, 1400Sit); **Sarajevo** (9¾hr., 1 per day, 9230Sit); **Zagreb** (3hr., 3 per day, 2920Sit).

Public Transportation: Buses run daily until midnight. Drop 300Sit in the box by the driver or buy 190Sit tokens (*žetoni*) at a post office or kiosk. **Day passes** (900Sit) are sold at **Ljubljanski Potniški Promet,** Trdinova 3. Open M-F 7am-7pm, Sa 7am-1pm.

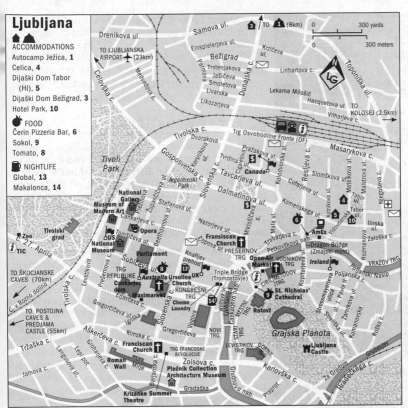

Ljubljana

▲▲ ACCOMMODATIONS
Autocamp Ježica, **1**
Celica, **4**
Dijaški Dom Tabor
(HI), **5**
Dijaški Dom Bežigrad, **3**
Hotel Park, **10**

🍎 FOOD
Čerin Pizzeria Bar, **6**
Sokol, **9**
Tomato, **8**

🍸 NIGHTLIFE
Global, **13**
Makalonca, **14**

S L O V E N I A

✦🛈 ORIENTATION AND PRACTICAL INFORMATION

The train and bus stations are on **Trg Osvobodilne Fronte** (Trg O. F. or O. F. Square). Turn right as you exit the train station, then left on **Miklošičeva cesta** and follow it to **Prešernov Trg**, the main square. Cross the **Tromostovje** (Triple Bridge) over the **Ljubljanica River** to **Stare Miasto** (Old Town) at the base of the castle hill.

Tourist Office: Tourist Info Center (TIC), Stritarjeva 1 (☎306 12 15; www.ljubljana.si). English brochures and free maps. Open daily June-Sept. 8am-9pm; Oct.-May 8am-7pm.

Embassies and Consulates: Australia, Trg Republike 3 (☎425 42 52; fax 426 47 21). Open M-F 9am-1pm. **Canada,** Miklošičeva 19 (☎430 35 70; fax 430 35 77). Open M-F 9am-1pm. **Ireland,** Poljanski nasip 6 (☎300 89 70; fax 282 10 96). Open M-F 9am-noon. **UK,** Trg Republike 3 (☎200 39 10; fax 425 01 74). Open M-F 9am-noon. **US,** Prešernova 31 (☎200 55 00; fax 200 55 55). Open M-F 9am-noon and 2-4pm.

Currency Exchange: 24hr. MC/V **ATMs** can be found throughout the city. **Ljubljanska banka** branches exchange currency for free and cash **traveler's checks** for 1.5% commission. Open M-F 9am-noon and 2-7pm, Sa 9am-noon.

Luggage storage: At the train station; look for *garderoba*. 400Sit per day. Open 24hr.

24hr. Pharmacy: Lekarna Miklošič, Miklošičeva 24 (☎231 45 58).

THAT COUNTRY CAN DANCE

Unlike the typical Ljubljana raves, where Slovenian youth bump and grind deep into the night, this party isn't held in a disco or warehouse, nor is it set to the beat of thumping drum 'n' bass. It happens in broad daylight on the last day of school each May, and takes place on city streets across the nation. It is the largest synchronized dance in the world, and is growing larger every year.

Taking their cue from a dance tune played on the radio (last year's was excerpted from Richard Strauss Jr.'s opera *The Bat*), thousands of upper-classmen begin the *quadrille,* a traditional square dance of French lineage performed in groups of four. Accompanied by live, festive folk music, an equal number of Slovenians turn out into the streets either to spectate or follow suit; the dance's momentum has been impressive, considering that it has only taken place for three consecutive years.

Shortly after high noon on May 21, 2004, there were a projected 1250 *quadrille* groups—for a total of 5000 dancers—spinning through Ljubljana alone. Now the event claims over 15,000 participants in 14 towns across Slovenia, and satellite groups have begun to fall into step in nearby Trieste, Italy. At this rate of expansion, the annual school's-out *quadrille* will become a pan-European event in a matter of years.

Internet: Cyber Cafe Xplorer, Petkovško nab. 23 (☎430 19 91; www.sisky.com), has fast connections. 530Sit per 30min., students 477Sit. 20% discount 10am-noon. Open M-F 10am-10pm, Sa-Su 2-10pm.

Post Office: *Poste Restante,* Slovenska 32 (☎426 46 68), at the counter labeled *"izročitev pošiljk."* Open M-F 7am-8pm, Sa 7am-1pm. **Postal Code:** 1000.

ACCOMMODATIONS

Finding cheap accommodations in Ljubljana is easier in July and August, when university dorms open their doors to travelers. The **Slovene National Hostel Association** (PZS; ☎231 21 56) provides info on youth hostels throughout Slovenia. The **Tourist Info Center** (see above) can help find private rooms (singles 4000-10,000Sit; doubles 5000-15,000Sit.) There is a daily **tourist tax** (240Sit) at all establishments.

▩ Celica, Metelkova 8. (☎430 18 90; www.souhostel.si). With your back to the train station, walk left down Masarykova, then right on Metelkova. Look for the red and yellow building on your left. Local and foreign artists have transformed this former military prison into a creative living space. Bar, cafe, free Internet access, and cultural arts programs. Breakfast included. Reception 24hr. Reserve ahead July-Aug. 3500-5250Sit. ❷

Dijaški Dom Tabor (HI), Vidovdanska 7 (☎234 88 40; ssljddta1s@guest.arnes.si). Turn left out of the train station, right on Resljeva, left on Komenskega, and left on Vidovdanska. Clean and popular with backpackers. Breakfast included. Internet free. Open June 25-Aug. 25. Dorms 2500-3700Sit per person. 200Sit HI discount. ❶

Dijaški Dom Bežigrad, Kardeljeva pl. 28 (☎534 00 61; www2.arnes.si). From the train station, cross the street and turn right; at the intersection with Slovenska, take bus #6 (Črnuče) or #8 (Ježica) and get off at Stadion (5min.), then walk 1 block to the crossroads. Negotiable check-out. Open June 20-Aug. 25. Singles 3600Sit, with shower 4800Sit; doubles 4800Sit/7200Sit; triples 7200Sit/8400Sit. ❷

Autocamp Ježica, Dunajska 270 (☎568 39 13; ac.jezica@gpl.si). Take bus #6 or 8 to Ježica's wooded campgrounds. Bungalows have spacious, impeccably clean rooms with TV and private shower. Reception 24hr. Reserve ahead. Camping 1680-2160Sit per person. Bungalow singles 11,000Sit; doubles 15,000Sit. MC/V. ❶

Hotel Park, Tabor 9 (☎232 13 98; hotel.park@siol.et). The cheapest hotel option for the low-season backpacker. Knowledgeable staff. Singles 11,520-12,480Sit; doubles 14,640-16,320Sit. ISIC discount 10%. ❺

🗋 FOOD

Maximarket, on Trg Republike, has a basement grocery store. (Open M-Th 9am-8pm, F 9am-10pm, Sa 8am-3pm.) Buy fruits and vegetables at the **open-air market** by St. Nicholas's Cathedral. (Open June-Aug. M-Sa 6am-6pm; Sept.-May 6am-4pm).

🔳 **Sokol,** Ciril Metodov trg 18 (☎439 68 55), dishes out Slovenian meals like grilled squid. Entrees 1290-2590Sit. Open M-Sa 9am-11pm, Su 10am-11pm. AmEx/MC/V. ❸

Čerin Pizzeria Bar, Trubarjeva 52 (☎232 09 90), includes 10min. Internet access with a drink purchase in the cafe upstairs. Pizzeria open Sept.-June M-F 10am-11pm, Sa noon-10pm; July-Aug. M-F 10am-9pm, Sa noon-9pm. AmEx/MC/V. ❸

Tomato, Šubičeva ul. 1. (☎252 75 55), serves huge sandwiches (390-820Sit), salads (1050-1150Sit), and entrees (1150-1500Sit). Open M-F 7am-10pm, Sa 9am-4pm. ❷

🔘 🗋 SIGHTS AND ENTERTAINMENT

A good way to see the city is to meet in front of the *rotovž* (city hall), Mestni Trg 1, for the 2hr. **walking tour** in English and Slovenian. (June-Sept. daily 5pm; July-Aug. also Su 11am; Oct.-Apr. F-Su only 11am. 1500Sit, students 700Sit.) A short walk from the *rotovž* down Stritarjeva across **Tromostovje** (Triple Bridge), which majestically guards Stare Miasto, leads to the main square, **Prešernov Trg,** with its pink 17th-century **Franciscan Church** (Frančiškanska cerkev). Cross the bridge back to Stare Miasto and take a left; continue along the river to Vodnikov Trg, where 🔳**Zmajski most** (Dragon Bridge) stretches back across the Ljubljanica. On the far side of Vodnikov Trg, the narrow path Studentovska leads uphill to 🔳**Ljubljana Castle** (Ljubljanski Grad), which has a breathtaking view of Ljubljana. (Open daily May-Oct. 10am-9pm; Nov.-Apr. 10am-7pm. English tours 1100Sit, students 790Sit.) Cross the Dragon Bridge back to Resljeve cesta, turn left on Tubarjea cesta, continue to Prešernov trg, take a left onto Wolfova (which becomes Gosposka), then take a right onto Zoisova cesta and a left onto Emonska ul. Across a bridge is the **Plečnik Collection** (Plečnikova zbrika), Karunova 4, which exhibits the works of Ljubljana's best-known architect. (Open Tu and Th 10am-2pm. 1000Sit, students 800Sit.) Walking back from the museum, take a left onto Zoistova and a right onto Slovenska; after the Ursuline Church, take a left to find **Trg Republike,** home to the National Parliament and **Cankarjev Dom,** the city's cultural center.

Ljubljana International Summer Festival hosts musical, operatic, and theatrical performances from mid-June to mid-September. Hidden on a terrace below the waterfront's main drag, the cavernous bar 🔳**Makalonca,** Hribarjevo nab., just past the Triple Bridge, has gorgeous views of the river with fewer crowds and more attitude than its neighbors. (Mixed drinks 500-900Sit. Sangria 350Sit. Open M-Sa 10am-1am, Su 10am-3pm.) With castle views, rooftop 🔳**Global** is one of the city's trendiest dance clubs. (Mixed drinks 900-1400Sit. Cover 1000Sit Sept.-June after 9pm; no cover July-Aug. Bar open M-Sa 8am-9pm. Disco open Th-Sa 9pm-5am.)

🔁 DAYTRIPS FROM LJUBLJANA: ŠKOCJANSKE CAVES

Škocjanske is an amazing system of UNESCO-protected **caverns** with limestone formations and a 120m gorge created by the Reca River. Be prepared; this physically demanding trip is only for the most adventurous. (☎057 63 28 40; www.gov.si/parkskj. Tours daily June-Sept. 10am-5pm; Oct.-May 10am, 1, and 3:30pm. 2200Sit, students 1200Sit.) **Trains** run from Ljubljana to Divača (1½hr., 10 per day, 1340Sit). Follow signs out of town, over the highway, through the village, and onto a narrow path across the woods to the ticket booth (40min.).

BLED
☎ 04

Alpine hills, snow-covered peaks, a turquoise lake, and a stately castle make Bled (pop. 6000) one of Slovenia's most striking destinations. The **Church of the Assumption** (Cerkev Marijinega Vnebovzetja) rises from the island in the center of the lake. To get there, either rent a boat (2400-2880Sit per hr.), hop on a gondola (round-trip 2400Sit), or just swim. Rising 100m above the water is **Bled Castle** (Blejski grad), built in 1004. Now it houses a museum detailing the history of the Bled region. (Open daily May-Sept. 8am-8pm; Oct.-Apr. 9am-5pm. 1000Sit, students 800Sit.) ▨**Blejski Vintgar,** a 1.6km gorge traced by the waterfalls and rapids of the Radovna River, carves through the rocks of the **Triglav National Park** (Triglavski Narodni Park). To see the 16m-high **Šum Waterfall,** go over the hill on Grajska cesta and turn right at the bottom. After 100m, turn left and follow the signs for Vintgar.

Trains from Ljubljana arrive at the Lesce-Bled station, about 4km from Bled (1hr., 11 per day, 1150Sit). **Buses** run to Ljubljana (1½hr., 1 per hr. 7am-9pm, 1400Sit). The **tourist office,** cesta Svobode 11, sells maps (1100-1600Sit) of Bled and nearby hiking trails. (☎ 578 05 00. Open June-Sept. M-Sa 8am-7pm; Nov.-Feb. 9am-5pm; Mar.-May 9am-7pm.) To find private rooms, look for "*sobe*" signs on Prešernova cesta and Ljubljanska. With comfortable beds and spotless private baths, ▨**Bledec Youth Hostel (HI) ❸,** Grajska cesta 17, has a pension atmosphere. Turn left out of the bus station and follow the street to the top, bearing left at the fork. (☎ 574 52 50; bledec@mlino.si. Reception 24hr. Reserve ahead July-Aug. 4560Sit, HI members 4080Sit.) To reach **Camping Bled ❶,** Kidričeva 10c, walk downhill on cesta Svobode from the bus station, then turn left and walk 25min. along the lake. (☎ 575 20 00; info@camping.bled.si. Reception 24hr. Open Apr.-Oct. 1600-2400Sit.) A **Mercator** supermarket is in the complex at Ljubljanska cesta 13. (Open M-Sa 7am-8pm, Su 8am-noon.) **Postal Code:** 4260.

LAKE BOHINJ (BOHINJSKO JEZERO)
☎ 04

Although it is only 30km southwest of Bled, Bohinjsko Jezero (BOH-heen-sko YEH-zeh-roh) feels worlds away. The three farming villages that border the glacial lake, Ribčev Laz, Stara Fužina, and Ukranc, retain a traditional Slovene atmosphere. Surrounded by **Triglav National Park,** Lake Bohinj is Slovenia's center for alpine tourism. Hikes from its shores range from casual to nearly impossible. Trails are marked with a white circle inside a red circle; look for blazes on trees and rocks. Maps are available at the tourist office (see below). The most popular and accessible destination is **Savica Waterfall** (Slap Savica). Take a bus from Ribčev Laz to Bohinj-Zlatorog (15min., 1 per hr., 290Sit), get off at Hotel Zlatorog, and follow signs 1hr. uphill to the trailhead at Dom Savica, where visitors must pay 400Sit before proceeding another 20min. to the waterfall.

Bohinjska Bistrica, 6km to the east, is the nearest town. **Trains** arrive there from Ljubljana (2½hr., 8 per day, 1250Sit). **Buses** from Ljubljana (2hr., 1 per hr., 1950Sit) pass through Bled (35min., 740Sit) and Bohinjska Bistrica (15min., 1 per hr., 380Sit) on their way to the lake; they stop at Hotel Jezero in Ribčev Laz or at Hotel Zlatorog in Ukanc, on the other side of the lake. The über-helpful **tourist office,** Ribčev Laz 48, sells maps, arranges accommodations, and plans guided excursions. (☎ 574 60 10; www.bohinj.si. Open July-Aug. M-Sa 8am-8pm, Su 8am-7pm; Sept.-June M-Sa 8am-6pm, Su 9am-3pm.) It also books for **AvtoCamp Zlatorog ❶,** Ukanc 2. Take the bus to Hotel Zlatorog and backtrack a bit. (☎ 572 34 82. May-Sept. and July-Aug. 1800-2300Sit; May-June and Sept. 1300-1700Sit. Tourist tax 81Sit.) Look out over the lake from cafe **Gostišče Kramar ❶,** Stara Fužina 3. From Ribčev Laz, walk over the stone bridge and follow the first path on your left 7min.

through the woods. (Entrees 200-900Sit. Open M-Th and Su 11am-midnight, F-Sa 11am-9pm.) A **Mercator** supermarket neighbors the tourist office. (Open M-F 7am-8pm, Sa 7am-8pm.) **Postal Code:** 4265.

PIRAN
☎05

Unlike other more modern towns on the Istrian Peninsula, Piran has retained its Venetian old world charm, with beautiful churches and dilapidated medieval architecture. A short walk uphill from the commercial center, Tartinijev trg, leads to the Gothic **Church of St. George** (Crkva sv. Jurja) and the 17th-century **St. George's Tower,** which commands a spectacular view of Piran and the Adriatic. (Church and tower open daily 10am-10pm. Church free. Tower 100Sit.) From the tower, head uphill away from the church and continue parallel to the shoreline and to the right to the old **city walls.** Piran's real attraction, however, is the sea. **Scuba diving** can be arranged through **Sub-net,** Prešemovo nab. 24, which runs certification classes and guided dives. (☎ 673 22 18; www.sub-net.si. 6000-8400Sit plus equipment. Open M-F 10am-noon and 2-6pm, Sa 10am-noon and 2-7pm.) The **Maritime Museum** (Pomorski Muzej), just off Tartinijev trg on Cankarjevo nab, has three stories of exhibits on marine archaeology and seamanship, and an impressive collection of ship replicas. (Open Tu-Su 9am-noon and 6-9pm. 600Sit, students 500Sit.) July welcomes the **Primoska Summer Festival,** featuring outdoor plays, ballets, and concerts; inquire at the tourist office (see below) for event schedules.

Buses arrive from Ljubljana (2¾hr., 9 per day, 2950Sit). The **tourist office,** Tartinijev trg 2, in the square's far corner, has bus schedules and free maps. (☎ 673 02 20. Open daily 9am-1pm and 3-9pm.) Private rooms can be found through **Maona Travel Agency,** Cankarjevo nabrezje 7, on the waterfront before Tartinijev trg. (☎ 673 45 20; www.maona.si. Open daily 8am-8pm. Singles 4300-5500Sit; doubles 6900-8000Sit.) ⊠**Youth Hostel Val ❸,** Gregorčičeva 38a, has spotless suites (2-4 beds). From the bus station, follow the waterfront past Tartinijev trg as it curves away from the harbor; look for the sign three blocks up. (☎ 673 25 55; www.hostel-val.com. Breakfast included. Reception 8am-10pm. Mid-May to mid-Sept. 5760Sit per person; low season 4800Sit.) Waterfront cafes line Prešemovo nab., but **Tri Vdove ❷** stands out for its generous seafood, meat, and pasta dishes. (☎ 673 02 90. Entrees 1300-3600Sit. Open daily 10am-midnight.) There is a **Mercator** supermarket at Levstikova 5. (Open M-F 7am-8pm, Sa 7am-1pm, Su 8am-11am. AmEx/MC/V.)

S L O V E N I A

SPAIN (ESPAÑA)

Fiery flamenco dancers, noble bullfighters, and a rich history blending Christian and Islamic culture set Spain apart from the rest of Europe and draw almost 50 million tourists each year. The raging nightlife of Madrid, Barcelona, and the Balearic Islands has inspired the popular saying "Spain never sleeps," yet the afternoon siestas of Andalucía attest to the country's laid-back, easy-going approach to life. Spain houses stunning Baroque, Mudéjar, and Mozarabic cathedrals and palaces; hangs the works of Velázquez, Dalí, and Picasso on its hallowed walls; and boasts a beautifully varied landscape of long sunny coastlines, snowy mountain peaks, and the dry, golden plains wandered by Don Quixote. You can do Spain in one week, one month, or one year. But you must do it at least once.

 DISCOVER SPAIN: SUGGESTED ITINERARIES

THREE DAYS Soak in **Madrid's** (p. 921) blend of art and cosmopolitan life as you walk through the **Retiro's** garden and peruse the famed halls of the **Prado, Thyssen-Bornemisza,** and **Nacional Centro de Arte Reina Sofía.** By night, move from the tapas bars of Santa Ana to Malasaña and Chueca. Daytrip to **Segovia** (p. 937) or **Valle de los Caídos** (p.933). Alternatively, spend your time in **Barcelona** (p. 960) admiring the fabulously strange architecture of Antoni Gaudí and soaking up the sun at the beach.

ONE WEEK Begin in southern Spain, exploring the Alhambra's Moorish palaces in **Granada** (1 day; p. 954) and the mosque in **Córdoba** (1 day; p. 942). After two days in **Madrid,** travel northeast to **Barcelona** (2 days) and the beaches of **Costa Brava** (1 day; p. 974).

BEST OF SPAIN, THREE WEEKS Begin in **Madrid** (3 days), with daytrips to **El Escorial** (p. 933) and **Valle de los Caídos.** Take the high-speed train to **Córdoba** (2 days), and on to **Seville** (2 days; p. 945). Catch the bus to the white town of **Arcos de la Frontera** (1 day; p. 951) before heading south to charming **Málaga,** on the **Costa del Sol** (1 day, p.p. 953). Head inland to vibrant **Granada** (2 days), then seaward again to **Valencia** (1 day; p. 958) before traveling up the coast to **Barcelona** (3 days). Daytrip to the **Costa Brava,** taking care not to miss the Teatre-Museu Dalí or the Casa-Museu Salvador Dalí. From Barcelona, head to the beaches and tapas bars of **San Sebastián** (1 day; p. 978) and **Bilbao** (2 days; p. 982), home of the world-famous Guggenheim Museum.

ESSENTIALS

WHEN TO GO

Summer is high season for the coastal and interior regions. In many parts of the country, high season includes *Semana Santa* (Holy Week; March 20-27 in 2005) and festival days. Tourism peaks in August; the coastal regions overflow while inland cities empty out. Traveling in the low season has the advantage of lighter crowds and lower prices, but tourist offices and sights cut their hours.

DOCUMENTS AND FORMALITIES

VISAS. EU citizens do not need a visa. Citizens of Australia, Canada, New Zealand, and the US do not need a visa for stays of up to 90 days, although this three-month period begins upon entry into any of the countries that belong to the EU's freedom of movement zone. For more information, see p. 17.

Spain

EMBASSIES. Foreign embassies in Spain are in Madrid. All countries have consulates in Barcelona. Australia, the UK, and the US also have consulates in Seville. Spanish embassies at home include: **Australia** and **New Zealand,** 15 Arkana St., Yarralumba, ACT 2600; P.O. Box 9076, Deakin, ACT 2600 (☎612 6273 3555; www.embaspain.com); **Canada,** 74 Stanley Ave., Ottawa, ON K1M 1P4 (☎613-747-2252; www.embaspain.ca); **Ireland,** 17a Merlyn Park, Ballsbridge, Dublin 4 (☎353 269 1640; www.mae.es/embajadas/dublin); **UK,** 39 Chesham Pl., London SW1X 8SB (☎0207 235 5555); **US,** 2375 Pennsylvania Ave. NW, Washington, D.C. 20037 (☎202-452-0100; www.spainemb.org).

TRANSPORTATION

BY PLANE. Most flights into Spain that originate outside Europe land at Madrid's Barajas (☎913 05 83 43, 44, 45, or 46) or Barcelona's El Prat (☎932 98 38 38) airports. Details of international airports in Spain can be found at www.aena.es. See p. 51 for more information on flying to Spain.

BY TRAIN. Direct trains are available to Madrid and Barcelona from several European cities, including Geneva, Lisbon, and Paris. Spain's national railway is **RENFE** (☎902 24 02 02; www.renfe.es). Spanish trains are clean, relatively punctual, and reasonably priced. However, most train routes do tend to bypass small towns.

Avoid *transvía, semidirecto*, or *correo* trains—they are very slow. *Alta Velocidad Española* (AVE) trains are the fastest and the most comfortable from Madrid to Córdoba (1¾hr., €48) and Seville (2½hr., €65). *Altaria* trains are also high-speed, cheaper, and from Madrid go to Algeciras (6hr., €53), Cádiz (5hr., €56), and Huelva (5hr., €55), in addition to Córdoba (2¼hr., €43) and Seville (3¼hr., €52). *Talgos* are even cheaper, almost as fast as AVE trains and go from Madrid to Córdoba (2hr., €36-40) as well as to Málaga (4¼hr., €49-54). *Intercity* is cheaper, but substantially slower (from Madrid to Córdoba 4¾hr., €26; to Málaga 7¼hr, €32). *Estrecho* is also slow and cheap (Madrid to Algeciras 10¼hr., €35; to Córdoba 5½hr., €26). *Estrellas* are slow night trains with bunks. *Cercanías* (commuter trains) go from cities to suburbs and nearby towns. There is no reason to buy a **Eurail** if you are planning on traveling only within Spain and Portugal. However, there are several Rail-Europe passes that cover travel within Spain. **Spain Flexipass** offers three days of unlimited travel in a two-month period (first-class US$225, 2nd-class US$175). The **Spain Rail 'n' Drive** pass is good for three days of unlimited first-class train travel and two days of unlimited mileage in a rental car (US$315-578). The **Iberic Railpass** is good for three days of unlimited first-class travel in Spain and Portugal (US$249). The **France 'n' Spain** offers four days of unlimited travel in France or Spain within a two-month period (first-class US$299, 2nd-class US$259). See www.raileurope.com for more information.

 FEATURED ITINERARY: BULLFIGHTING

Begin in **Madrid** (p. 921), where the Plaza de Toros de las Ventas holds *corridas* (professional bullfights) every Sunday night from mid-March to October. If you aren't there on a Sunday, the *novilladas*, bullfights featuring amateur *toreros* (matadors), are held on some Fridays (see www.las-ventas.com for more information). From Madrid, head to **Lisbon** (p. p. 837), where the Praça do Touros do Campo Pequeno holds bullfights every Thursday evening from April to September. Unlike Spanish matadors, Portuguese *cavaleiros* are mounted on horseback and don't personally execute the bull. (The bull is killed only after being led out of the ring.) If you plan your trip for July, be sure to visit **Pamplona** (p. 977) for the most famous bullfighting event in Spain. The festival of *San Fermines*, July 6-14, honors the patron saint of Navarra with daily *encierros* (bull runs) and bullfights (see www.feriadeltoro.com for more information). After you've experienced both types of bullfights, make your way to **Seville** (p. 945) to learn about the history of the bullfight at the Museo Taurino de la Real Maestranza (p. 949). The Real Maestranza, one of Spain's most beautiful bullrings, holds *novilladas* every Sunday in May, June, and September; *corridas* occur less regularly (see www.realmaestranza.com for more information). From Seville, daytrip out to **Ronda** (p. 951) to see Spain's oldest bullring, the Plaza de Toros (est. 1785), which holds *corridas goyescas* (bullfights in traditional costume) during the *Feria de Ronda* in early September. Unless you come during this month, however, you'll have to settle for learning about bullfighting at Ronda's Museo Taurino.

BY BUS. In Spain, buses are cheaper and provide far more comprehensive routes than trains. In addition, bus routes also provide the only public transportation to many isolated areas. Spain has numerous private companies; the lack of a centralized bus company may make itinerary planning an ordeal. **Alsa** (☎902 42 22 42; www.alsa.es) serves Asturias, Castilla y León, Galicia, and Madrid, as well as international destinations in France, Germany, Italy, Morocco, and Portugal, among others. **Auto-Res/Cunisa, S.A.** (☎902 02 09 99; www.auto-res.net) serves Castilla y León, Cataluña, Extremadura, Galicia, Madrid, and Valencia.

BY FERRY. Ferries leave from **Algeciras** for **Tangier** and **Ceuta** in **Morocco** (p. 737) and from Valencia and Barcelona for the **Balearic Islands** (p. 984).

BY CAR. Spain's highway system connects major cities by four-lane *autopistas*. **Speeders beware:** police can "photograph" the speed and license plate of your car and issue a ticket without pulling you over; if you are pulled over, any fines must be paid on the spot (though usually with a 20% discount). Purchase **gas** in super (97-octane), normal (92-octane), diesel, and unleaded. Gas prices range €.80-1.10 per liter. **Renting** a car in Spain is considerably cheaper than in many other European countries. The driver must be 21 and have had a license for at least a year. Spain accepts Canadian, EU, and US driver's licenses; otherwise, an International Driver's License is required. Try **Atesa** (in Spain ☎902 100 101, elsewhere 100 515; www.atesa.es), Spain's largest national rental agency. The Spanish automobile association is **Real Automóvil Club de España (RACE;** in Madrid ☎915 94 74 00). For more info on renting and driving a car in Europe, see p. 67.

BY THUMB. Hitchers report that hitchhiking in Castilla, Andalucía, and Madrid is very difficult. The Mediterranean Coast and the islands are much more promising. *Let's Go* does not recommend hitchhiking.

TOURIST SERVICES AND MONEY

EMERGENCY	General Emergency: ☎112. Local Police: ☎092. National Police: ☎091. Ambulance: ☎061. Fire: ☎080.

TOURIST OFFICES. Spain's official tourism website is www.tourspain.es. **Tourist offices** within Spain usually have free maps and advice for travelers.

MONEY. On January 1, 2002, the **euro (€)** replaced the **peseta** as the unit of currency in Spain. For more information, see p. 20. As a general rule it's cheaper to exchange money in Spain than at home. Expect to spend €40-70 per day. **Tipping** is not very common. In restaurants, all prices include service charge; satisfied customers occasionally toss in some spare change. Many people give train, airport, and hotel porters €1 per bag, while taxi drivers sometimes get 5-10%. **Bargaining** is only common at flea markets and with street vendors. Spain has a 7% **Value Added Tax (VAT),** known as IVA, on all restaurants and accommodations. The prices listed in *Let's Go* include VAT unless otherwise mentioned. Retail goods bear a 16% VAT, although listed prices are usually inclusive. Upon departure, non-EU citizens who have stayed in the EU fewer than 180 days can claim back the tax paid on purchases, provided the total amount spent at each store is over €90.15. Ask the shop where you have made the purchase to supply you with a tax return form.

COMMUNICATION

PHONE CODES	Country code: 34. International dialing prefix: 00. From outside Spain, dial int'l dialing prefix (see inside back cover) + 34 + city code + local number. Within Spain, dial city code + local number, even when calling inside the city.

TELEPHONES. The central Spanish phone company is *Telefónica*. The best way to make local calls is with a phone card, issued in denominations between €5-20 and sold at kiosks, tobacconists (*estancos* or *tabacos*, identifiable by brown signs with yellow lettering and tobacco leaf icons), and most post offices. Calling internationally with a Spanish phone card is quite inexpensive and easy; however, you may prefer to call home with an international calling card issued by your phone company. For information on using a cell phone in Spain, see p. 35.

MAIL. Air mail (*por avión*) takes five to eight business days to reach the US or Canada; service is faster to the UK and Ireland and slower to Australia and New Zealand. Standard postage is €0.77 to North America. Surface mail (*por barco*), while less expensive than air mail, can take over a month, and packages take two to three months. Registered or express mail (*registrado* or *certificado*) is the most reliable way to send a letter or parcel home and takes four to seven business days. Address mail to be held (*Poste Restante*) as follows: SURNAME, First Name; Lista de Correos; City Name; Postal Code; SPAIN; AIR MAIL.

INTERNET ACCESS. Email is easily accessible within Spain and quicker and more reliable than the regular mail system. Cybercafes are listed in most towns and all cities. If Internet access is not listed, check the library or the tourist office. Visit www.cybercafes.com and www.cybercaptive.com for lists of cybercafes in Spain.

LANGUAGES. Castilian Spanish is the official language of Spain, but each region has its own specific language which, in addition to Castilian, is official in that region. This freedom of language, which was prohibited under the dictatorship of Francisco Franco, is now protected under the Spanish Constitution. Most Spaniards are at least bilingual; all speak Castilian in addition to their regional language. The languages with the highest number of speakers are Catalan (spoken in Cataluña), Euskera (spoken in Basque Country), and Galician (spoken in Galicia). However, there are many other region-specific languages.

ACCOMMODATIONS AND CAMPING

SPAIN	❶	❷	❸	❹	❺
ACCOMMODATIONS	under €15	€15-25	€26-35	€36-45	over €45

The cheapest and barest options are *casas de huéspedes* and *hospedajes*, while *pensiones* and *fondas* tend to be a bit nicer. All are essentially just boarding houses. Higher up the ladder, *hostales* generally have sinks in bedrooms and provide sheets and lockers, while *hostal-residencias* are similar to hotels in overall quality. The government rates *hostales* on a two-star system; even establishments receiving one star are typically quite comfortable. The system also fixes *hostal* prices, posted in the lounge or main entrance. **Red Española de Albergues Juveniles (REAJ)** the Spanish **Hostelling International (HI)** affiliate (in Madrid ☎91 347 7700; www.reaj.com), runs over 200 youth hostels year-round. Prices depend on season, location, and services offered, but are generally €10-20 for guests under 26 and higher for those 26 and over. Breakfast is usually included; lunch and dinner are occasionally offered at an additional charge. Hostels usually lock guests out around 11:30am and have curfews between midnight and 3am. As a rule, don't expect much privacy—rooms typically have four to 20 beds in them. To reserve a bed in high season (July-Aug. and during festivals), call in advance. A national **Youth Hostel Card** is usually required. **Campgrounds** are generally the cheapest choice for two or more people. Most charge separate fees per person, per tent, and per car; others charge for a *parcela* (a small plot of land), plus per-person fees. Tourist offices can provide more info, including the *Guía de Campings*.

FOOD AND DRINK

SPAIN	❶	❷	❸	❹	❺
FOOD	under €6	€6-10	€11-15	€16-25	over €25

Spanish food is becoming increasingly sophisticated and cosmopolitan, but fresh local ingredients are still an integral part of the cuisine, varying according to each region's climate, geography, and history. Most experts, in fact, argue that one can speak of Spanish food only in local terms.

Spaniards breakfast lightly and wait for a several-course lunch, served between 2 and 3pm. Supper at home (*la cena*) is light, while eating out begins anywhere between 9pm and midnight. Some restaurants are "open" from 8am until 1 or 2am, but most serve meals only from 1 to 4pm and from 8pm until midnight. A full meal starts at about €5 in the cheapest places. Many restaurants offer a *plato combinado* (main course, side dishes, bread, and sometimes a beverage) or a *menú del día* (two or three set dishes, bread, beverage, and dessert) for roughly €5-9. If you ask for a *menú*, this is what you may receive; *carta* is the word for menu.

Tapas (savory meats and vegetables cooked according to local recipes) are quite tasty and in some regions complimentary with beer or wine. *Raciones* are large tapas served as entrees. *Bocadillos* are sandwiches on hunks of bread. Spanish specialties include *tortilla de patata* (potato omelette), *jamón serrano* (smoked ham), *calamares fritos* (fried squid), *arroz* (rice), *chorizo* (spicy sausage), *gambas* (shrimp), *lomo de cerdo* (pork loin), *paella* (steamed saffron rice with seafood, chicken, and vegetables), and *gazpacho* (cold tomato-based soup). Vegetarians should learn the phrase *"yo soy vegetariano"* (I am a vegetarian) and specify that means no *jamón* (ham) or *atún* (tuna). *Vino blanco* is white wine and *tinto* is red. *Cerveza* is beer; Mahou and Cruzcampo are the most common brands. *Sangría* is a drink of red wine, sugar, brandy, and fruit.

HOLIDAYS AND FESTIVALS

Holidays: New Year's Day (Jan. 1); Epiphany (Jan. 6); Holy Thursday (Mar. 24); Good Friday (Mar. 25); Easter (Mar. 27); Easter Monday (Mar. 28); Labor Day (May 1); Corpus Christi (May 29); Feast of St. James (July 25); Assumption Day (Aug. 15); National Day (Oct. 12); All Saints' Day (Nov. 1); Constitution Day (Dec. 6); Feast of the Immaculate Conception (Dec. 8); Christmas (Dec. 25).

Festivals: Nearly everything closes during festivals. All of Spain celebrates *Carnaval* the week before Ash Wednesday; the biggest parties are in Cataluña and Cádiz. During the *Las Fallas*, in mid-March, Valencia honors St. Joseph with parades, fireworks, and the burning of effigies. March 20-27, the entire country honors the Holy Week, or *Semana Santa*. Seville's *Feria de Abril* (April 12-17) has events showcasing many different Andalusian traditions. *San Fermines* (Running of the Bulls) takes over Pamplona July 6-14. For more information, see www.tourspain.es or www.gospain.org/fiestas.

FACTS AND FIGURES: SPAIN

Official Name: Kingdom of Spain.

Capital: Madrid.

Major Cities: Barcelona, Granada, Seville, Valencia.

Population: 40,220,000.

Land Area: 500,000 sq. km.

Time Zone: GMT+1.

Languages: Spanish (Castilian), Catalan, Galician, Basque, and other regional languages.

Religions: Roman Catholic (94%).

MADRID ☎ 91

After Franco's death in 1975, young *madrileños* celebrated their liberation from totalitarian repression with raging, all-night parties in bars and on streets across the city. This revelry became so widespread that it defined an era, and *la Movida* (the Movement) is recognized as a world-famous nightlife renaissance. While the

SPAIN

TO
MUSEO DE
AMÉRICA

VENTURA
RODRÍGUEZ

Centro Cultural
Conde Duque

Tr. Conde Duque

C. Conde Duque

C. de Limón

C. San Bernardino

C. San Bernardo

TO 1
(500m)

C. de la Palma

C. de la Palma

C. del Norte

C. de San Vicente Ferrer

C. de Acuerdo

NOVICIADO

C. Velarde

PL. DOS
DE MAYO

TO BILBAO (800m)
& C. DE LUCHANA
(200m)

C. de San Andrés

Lucia

TRIBUNAL

C. de San Vicente Ferrer

C. Espíritu Santo

C. Espíritu Santo

Cta. Alta San Pablo

C. Martín

C. la Princesa

C. los Héroes

C. Ventura Rodríguez

ARGÜELLES

San
Marcos

C. S. Leonardo

C. Amigos

C. los Reyes

C. Noviciado

C. Tesoro

C. Marqués de Santa Ana

C. Jesús del Valle

C. Madera

C. Don Felipe

C. DE S.
ILDEFON.

Torre de
Madrid

Edificio de
España

C. los Reyes

C. Poncado

C. Amaniel

C. del Pez

C. Manzana

C. Pozas

C. Andrés Borrego

C. Escorial

C. Molino de Viento

C. Coló

Museo
Cerralbo

C. Ferraz

Pl. de
España

PLAZA DE
ESPAÑA

C. Gen. Mitre

C. A. Grilo

C. San Bernardo

C. Pizarro

C. del Pez

MALASAÑA

Jardines
Ferraz

C. Cadarso

6

C. Flor Baja

C. Rº. León

Gran Vía

7

C. Isabel la Católica

C. Parada

C. la Luna

C. San Roque

C. Corrida Baja San Pablo

C. Puebla

C. Barco

C. Río

C. Relaj

C. de Fomento

C. Leganitos

C. la Estrella

C. de Leganes

C. Flor Alta

C. Libreros

C. de Silva

C. Ballesta

TO CAMPO DEL
MORO (400m)

Cuesta San Vicente

PL. DE LA
MARINA ESPAÑOLA

C. Encarnación

C. Guillermo
Rolland

C. Tudesco

C. del Desengaño

Jardines de
Sabatini

Convento de
la Encarnación

SANTO
DOMINGO

PL. SANTO
DOMINGO

C. Jacometrezo

PL. DEL
CALLAO

CALLAO

C. del Carmen

GRAN VÍA

C. Miguel
Moya

9

11

PL. DE RE
DE SAN LI

Museo de
Carruajes
Reales

C. de la Bola

SANTO
DOMINGO

Cuesta Santo Domingo

C. Preciados

C. Chinchilla

C. de la Salud

GRAN
VÍA

Jardines
Cabo Noval

C. de Arrieta

C. de Campomanes

C. Caños del peral

CALLAO

C. S. Alberto

C. Montera

PL.
DEL
CARMEN

Palacio
Real

Teatro
Real

PL. DE
ORIENTE

PL. DE
ISABEL II

ÓPERA

C. Priora

C. Flora

C. Donados

Convento de las
Descalzas Reales

PL. SAN
MARTÍN

PL.
DESCALZAS

C. Preciados

Museo de la Real
Academia de Bellas Artes
de San Fernand.

Carlos III

14

PL.
ARMERÍA

Jardines
Lepanto

C. Loperto

15

C. Vergara

16

C. Amnistía

C. Clara

C. Fuentes

C. de Arenal

C. Tetuán

SOL

PUERTA
DEL SOL

C. de Alc

C. Espoz

Catedral de
Almudena

C. Bailén

C. Requena

C. San Nicolás

C. Unión

C. Independencia

C. Espejo

C. Escalinata

17

C. las Hileras

C. Bordadores

C. Pasadizo
de Sanoles

15

C. Mayor

CENTRO

C. Postas

20

C. Esparteros

C. Correo

C. Cádiz

C. de la

C. Factor

C. Herrera

19

PL. DE
LA VILLA

C. Santiago

C. Cava San
Miguel

C. Marqués Viudo de Pontejos

PL. SANTA
CRUZ

C. Carretas

C. Espoz y Mina

Ayuntamiento

C. Mayor

C. de la Vega

C. de Sacramento

C. Cordón

C. Conde
Miranda

Zaragoza

PL.
MAYOR

Santa Cruz

PL.
JACINTO
BENAVENTE

C. Bolsa

C. de Atoc

C. Villa

C. Segovia

C. Segovia

C. Segovia

Justo

C. de Toledo

C. Imperial

C. Concepción Jerónima

Salvador de
Rivas

C. Doctor
Cortezo

C. Conde Romanones

C. de Atoc

Jardines de
las Vistillas

26

PL. DE LA
PAJA

Capilla
del Obispo

C. Gratal

C. Grafal

C. Cava Baja

C. Duque
de Rivas

PL.
SEGOVIA
NUEVA

TIRSO DE
MOLINA

27

Corral de la
Morería

Cost. de
San Andrés

San
Andrés

PL. DE
HUMILLADERO

C. Estudios

C. la Colegiata

C. de Magdale.

C. de Cabeza

C. Bailén

C. Don Pedro

PUERTA
DE MOROS

LA
LATINA

Catedral de
San Isidro

C. San Millán

C. Duque de Alba

PL. TIRSO
DE MOLINA

C. S. Pedro Mártir

C. Calvario

C. de Lavapiés

C. Redondilla

PL. DE LA
CEBADA

C. Maldonadas

C. Juanelo

PL. DE
CASCORRO

C. Encomienda

C. Jesús y María

C. S. Francisco

C. Aguas

C. Humilladero

Oriente

C. la
Cebada

C. Santa Ana

C. Dos Hermanas

C. Abades

C. del Amparo

Gran Vía San Francisco

C. de Calatrava

C. Ángel

Tabernillas

C. Luciente

C. Mediodía

C. Irlandese

C. Toledo

C. Mira el Río Alta

C. Oso

Mesón de Paredes

Cabestreros

C. Rosario

C. Águila

C. de Calatrava

C. la Arganzuela

El
Rastro

C. Ribera de Curtidores

Embajadores

C. Caravaca

LA LATINA

C. Sombrer.

TO 32
(12km)

C. Carnero

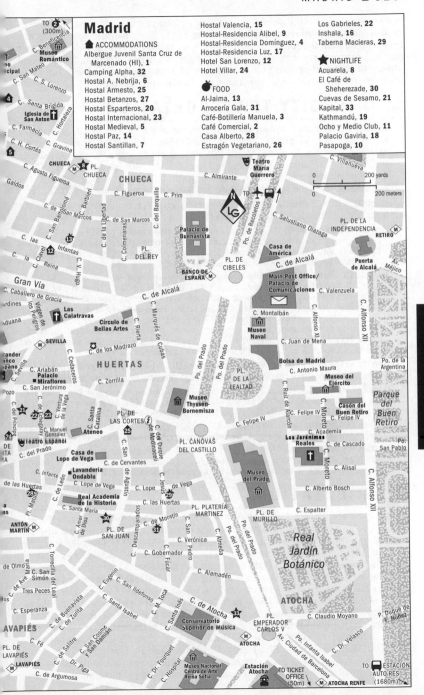

Madrid

🏠 ACCOMMODATIONS

Albergue Juvenil Santa Cruz de
  Marcenado (HI), **1**
Camping Alpha, **32**
Hostal A. Nebrija, **6**
Hostal Armesto, **25**
Hostal Betanzos, **27**
Hostal Esparteros, **20**
Hostal Internacional, **23**
Hostal Medieval, **5**
Hostal Paz, **14**
Hostal Santillan, **7**
Hostal Valencia, **15**
Hostal-Residencia Alibel, **9**
Hostal-Residencia Domínguez, **4**
Hostal-Residencia Luz, **17**
Hotel San Lorenzo, **12**
Hotel Villar, **24**

🍎 FOOD

Al-Jaima, **13**
Arrocería Gala, **31**
Café-Botillería Manuela, **3**
Café Comercial, **2**
Casa Alberto, **28**
Estragón Vegetariano, **26**

Los Gabrieles, **22**
Inshala, **16**
Taberna Macieras, **29**

⭐ NIGHTLIFE

Acuarela, **8**
El Café de
  Sheherezade, **30**
Cuevas de Sesamo, **21**
Kapital, **33**
Kathmandú, **19**
Ocho y Medio Club, **11**
Palacio Gaviria, **18**
Pasapoga, **10**

SPAIN

newest generation is too young to recall the Franco years, it has kept the spirit of *la Movida* alive. Not particularly cognizant of the city's historic landmarks nor preoccupied with the future, young people have taken over the streets, shed their parents' decorous reserve, and captured the present. Bright lights and a perpetual stream of cars and people blur the distinction between 4pm and 4am, and infinitely energized party-goers crowd bars and discos until dawn.

✈ INTERCITY TRANSPORTATION

Flights: All flights land at **Aeropuerto Internacional de Barajas** (MAD; general info ☎305 8343, 44, 45, or 46), 20min. northeast of Madrid. The Barajas metro line connects the airport to all of Madrid (€1.20). Another option is the blue Bus-Aeropuerto #89 (look for EMT signs just outside the airport doors), which leaves from the national and international terminals and runs to the city center (every 10-15min., €2.50). The bus stops beneath the Jardines del Descubrimiento in Plaza de Colón (M: Colón).

Trains: Call **RENFE** (☎902 24 02 02; www.renfe.es) for reservations and info. Try the Main Office, C. de Alcalá 44, at Gran Vía (M: Banco de España), for schedules.

Estación Atocha (☎506 6137). M: Atocha-Renfe. No international service. AVE (☎902 24 02 02) offers high-speed service to the south of Spain, including **Seville** (2½hr., 20 per day, €59-65) via **Córdoba** (1¾hr., €43-48) and **Málaga** (3hr., 6 per day, €49-54). Daytime *Grandes Lineas* for **Barcelona** leave from Atocha (4½-5hr., 5 per day, €35-59).

Estación Chamartín (☎300 69 69). M: Chamartín. For international destinations, call **RENFE** or ☎902 24 34 02. For domestic destinations, call RENFE ☎902 24 02 02, Spanish only. Chamartín services international and domestic destinations in the northeast and south. Major destinations include: **Bilbao** (6hr., 2 per day, €30-38); **Lisbon, Portugal** (9½hr., daily 10:45pm, €53-70); **Paris, France** (13½hr.; daily 7pm; €112-135, seniors and students with ISIC €90-108). Chamartín has many useful services, including **currency exchange, post office, car rental, police, luggage storage** (*consignas;* €2.40-4.50; open daily 7am-11pm) and a **tourist office.** (Vestíbulo, Puerta 14. ☎315 9976. Open M-Sa 8am-8pm, Su 8am-2pm.)

Intercity Buses: Numerous private companies, each with its own station and set of destinations, serve Madrid; many buses pass through the **Estación Sur de Autobuses.**

Estación Auto-Res: C. Fernández Shaw 1 (☎902 02 09 99; www.auto-res.net). M: Conde de Casal. Info open daily 6:30am-1am. To: **Cuenca** (2½hr., 5-10 per day, €9); **Salamanca** (2½-3¼hr., 9-16 per day, €11-15); **Valencia** (5hr., 4 per day, €20; express 4hr., 10-11 per day, €24).

Estación La Sepulvedana: Po. de la Florida 11 (☎530 4800; www.sepulvedana.es). M: Príncipe Pío (via extension from M: Ópera). To **Segovia** (1½hr., every 30min. 6:30am-10:15pm, €6).

Estación Sur de Autobuses: C. Méndez Álvaro (☎468 4200). M: Méndez Álvaro. Info open daily 7am-11pm. **ATMs,** food, and **luggage storage** (€1.25 per bag per day) are available. National destinations include: **Algeciras, Alicante, Santiago de Compostela,** and **Toledo.**

✚ ORIENTATION

Marking the epicenter of both Madrid and Spain, **"Kilometro 0"** in **Puerta del Sol** ("Sol" for short) is within walking distance of most sights. To the west are the **Plaza Mayor,** the **Palacio Real,** and the **Ópera** district. East of Sol lies **Huertas,** the heart of cafe, theater, and museum life. The area north of Sol is bordered by **Gran Vía,** which runs northwest to **Plaza de España.** North of Gran Vía are three club- and bar-hopping districts, linked by Calle de Fuencarral: **Malasaña, Bilbao,** and **Chueca.** Modern Madrid is beyond Gran Vía and east of Malasaña and Chueca. East of Sol, the tree-lined thoroughfares **Paseo de la Castellana, Paseo de Recoletos,** and **Paseo del Prado** split Madrid in two, running from **Atocha** in the south to **Plaza Castilla** in the north, passing the Prado, the fountains of **Plaza Cibeles,** and **Plaza Colón.** Refer to the color map of Madrid's metro. Madrid is safer than its European counterparts, but Sol, Pl. España, Pl. Chueca, and Malasaña's Pl. Dos de Mayo are still intimidating late at night. As a general rule, travel in groups, avoid the parks and quiet streets after dark, and always watch for thieves and pickpockets in crowds.

☰ LOCAL TRANSPORTATION

Public Transportation: Metro (☎902 44 44 03; www.metromadrid.es). Individual metro tickets cost €1.15; a **bonotransporte** (ticket of 10 rides for metro or bus system) is €5.40. Buy both at machines in any metro stop, *estanco* (tobacco shop), or newsstand. Travelers found without tickets are fined exorbitantly. **Bus** info ☎406 8810 (Spanish only). Buses run 6am-11:30pm; single ride €1.15. *Buho* (owl), the **night bus** service, runs every 20min. midnight-3am, 1 per hr. 3-6am. Look for buses N1-20.

Taxis: Call **Radio Taxi** (☎447 5180), **Radio-Taxi Independiente** (☎405 1213), or **Teletaxi** (☎371 3711). A *libre* sign in the window or a green light indicates availability. Base fare €1.60, plus €0.70-0.90 per km 6am-10pm and €1 per km 10pm-6am. Teletaxi charges a flat rate of €1 per km.

◪ PRACTICAL INFORMATION

TOURIST AND FINANCIAL SERVICES

Tourist Offices: Municipal, Plaza Mayor 3 (☎/fax 366 5477), will be expanding and relocating to a location across the Pl. Mayor in 2005. M: Sol. Open M-Sa 10am-8pm, Su 10am-3pm. **Regional/Provincial Office of the Comunidad de Madrid,** C. del Duque de Medinaceli 2 (☎429 4951; www.comadrid.es/turismo). Open M-Sa 9am-7pm, Su 9am-3pm. **Branches** at Estación Chamartín and the airport.

General Info Line: ☎901 30 06 00. Tons of information. Ask for *inglés* to speak with an English-speaking operator. Also try ☎010, run by the Ayuntamiento.

Embassies: Australia, Pl. Descubridor Diego de Ordás 3 (☎441 6025; www.spain.embassy.gov.au). **Canada,** C. Núñez de Balboa 35 (☎423 3250; www.canada-es.org). **Ireland,** Po. Castellana 46, 4th fl. (☎436 4093; fax 435 1677). **New Zealand,** Pl. Lealtad 2, 3rd fl. (☎523 0226; fax 523 0171). **UK,** C. Fernando el Santo 16 (☎700 8200; fax 700 8272). **US,** C. Serrano 75 (☎587 2200; www.embusa.es).

Currency Exchange: In general, credit and ATM cards offer the best exchange rates. Avoid changing money at airport and train station counters; they tend to charge exorbitant commissions on horrible rates. **Santander Central Hispano** charges no commission on cash or **traveler's checks** up to €600. **Main branch,** Pl. Canalejas 1 (☎558 1111). M: Sol. Follow Carrera de San Jerónimo to Pl. Canalejas. Open Apr.-Sept. M-F 8:30am-2pm; Oct.-Mar. M-Th 8:30am-4:30pm, F 8:30am-2pm, Sa 8:30am-1pm.

LOCAL SERVICES

Luggage Storage: Barajas Airport. Follow the signs to *consigna*. One day €3; 2-15 days €3-5 per day; after day 15, €0.60-1.40 per day. **Estación Chamartín** and **Estación Atocha.** Lockers €2.40-4.50 per day. Open daily 6:30am-10:15pm.

GLBT Services: Colectivo de Gais y Lesbianas de Madrid (COGAM), C. Fuencarral 37 (☎/fax 522 4517; www.cogam.com), M: Gran Vía, provides a wide range of services. Reception M-Sa 5-10pm. Also check out *Shanguide,* a free guide to gay nightlife.

Laundromat: Lavandería Ondablu, C. León 3 (☎369 5071). M: Antón Martín, Sol, or Sevilla. Open daily 9am-10:30pm. Wash €2, dry €1. Just up the street is **Lavandería Cervantes,** C. León 6. Wash €2, dry €1. Open daily 9am-9pm.

EMERGENCY AND COMMUNICATIONS

Police: C. de los Madrazo 9 (☎541 7160). M: Sevilla. From C. Alcalá take a right onto C. Cedacneros and a left onto C. de los Madrazo. To report crimes committed in the metro, go to the office in the Sol station (open daily 8am 11pm).

Medical Services: Equipo Quirúrgico Municipal No. 1, C. Montesa 22 (☎588 5100). M: Manuel Becerra. **Hospital de Madrid,** Pl. del Conde del Valle Suchil 16 (☎447 6600; www.hospitaldemadrid.com). For non-emergency concerns, call **Anglo-American Medical Unit,** Conde de Aranda 1, 1st fl. (☎435 1823).

Internet Access: Easy Internet Café, C. Montera 10 (www.easyeverything.com). M: Sol. From the Plaza del Sol, look for C. Montera, which goes toward Gran Vía. Open daily 8am-1am. Hundreds of computers, fast connections, good music, and a cafe. Access from €0.50. **Oficina13,** C. Mayor 1, 4th fl., office 13 (☎523 2089). M: Sol. Take the elevator up and buzz the office. Free coffee. €1 per hr. Open daily 10am-10pm.

Post Office: Palacio de Comunicaciones, C. de Alcalá 51, on Pl. de Cibeles (☎902 19 71 97). M: Banco de España. Windows open M-Sa 8:30am-9:30pm, Su 9am-2pm for stamp purchases, certified mail, telex, and fax service. Poste Restante (*Lista de Correos*) at windows #80-82; passport required. **Postal Code:** 28080.

ℿ ACCOMMODATIONS

Make reservations for summer visits. Expect to pay €17-50 per person, depending on location, amenities, and season. Tourist offices provide information about the 13 or so **campsites** within 50km of Madrid. **El Centro,** the triangle between Puerta del Sol, Ópera, and Plaza Mayor, is full of *hostales,* but you'll pay for the prime location. The cultural hotbed of **Huertas,** framed by C. de San Jerónimo, C. las Huertas, and C. de Atocha, is almost as central and more fun. Festive **Malasaña** and **Chueca,** bisected by C. Fuencarral, host cheap rooms in the heart of the action, but the sleep-deprived should beware; the party doesn't quiet down for rest. *Hostales,* like temptations, are everywhere among **Gran Vía's** sex shops and scam artists.

EL CENTRO: SOL, ÓPERA, AND PLAZA MAYOR

▨ **Hostal-Residencia Luz,** C. Fuentes 10, 3rd fl. (☎542 0759), off C. Arenal. M: Ópera. Bright, modern, and friendly. Singles €15; doubles €34-39; triples €39-45. ❷

▨ **Hostal Paz,** C. Flora 4, 1st and 4th fl. (☎547 3047). M: Ópera. Parallel to C. Arenal. Rooms with large windows are sheltered from street noise and lavished with amenities. Reservations recommended. Singles €20; doubles €32-38; triples €45. MC/V. ❷

Hostal Esparteros, C. Esparteros 12, 4th fl. (☎/fax 521 0903). M: Sol. Sparkling rooms with balcony or large windows; some have private bath. English-speaking owner. Singles €20-25; doubles €35; triples €42. 10% discount after 1 week. ❷

Hostal Valencia, Pl. Oriente 2, 3rd fl. (☎559 8450). M: Ópera. Narrow glass elevator leads to elegant rooms. Singles €42; doubles €72; master suite €92. Cash only. ❹

HUERTAS

▨ **Hostal Villar,** C. del Príncipe 18 (☎531 6600; www.villar.arrakis.es). M: Sol or Sevilla. Villar offers perfect location, low prices, and unintentionally retro rooms. Big lounge for socializing. Singles €23, with bath €26; doubles €31/€42; triples €43/€57. MC/V. ❷

Hostal Armesto, C. de San Agustín 6, 1st fl. (☎/fax 429 9031). M: Banco de España or Antón Martín. This hostel offers a quiet night's sleep for an older crowd. All rooms with bath, TV, and fan. Singles €45; doubles €50; triples €65. AmEx/MC/V. ❹

Hostal Internacional, C. de Echegaray 5, 2nd fl. (☎429 6209). M: Sol. Recently renovated. All rooms with TV, A/C, safe, and shower. Singles €25-30; doubles €40. ❸

Hostal Betanzos, C. Luis de Guevera 8, 3rd fl. (☎369 1440). M: Antón Martín. This pension boasts high ceilings and French windows. Singles €15; doubles €25. Cash only. ❷

GRAN VÍA

Hostal A. Nebrija, Gran Vía 67, 8th fl., elevator A (☎547 7319). M: Pl. España. Pleasant, spacious rooms offering magnificent views of the city landscape. Singles €26; doubles €36; triples €49. AmEx/MC/V. ❸

Hostal-Residencia Alibel, Gran Vía 44, 8th fl. (☎521 0051). M: Callao. Well-lit, spacious rooms with great views, high ceilings, and a cool blue color scheme. All have private bath, TV, fan, and balcony. Free wireless Internet. Doubles €40; triples €50. ❷

Hostal Santillan, Gran Vía 64, 8th fl. (☎/fax 548 2328; www.hostalsantillan.com). M: Pl. España. Friendly management and eclectic decor. Simple rooms all have shower, sink, TV, fan, and safe. Singles €30; doubles €45; triples €60. MC/V. ❸

MALASAÑA AND CHUECA

Hostal-Residencia Domínguez, C. Santa Brígida 1, 1st fl. (☎/fax 532 1547). M: Tribunal. The hospitable young owner is always ready with tips on local nightlife. English spoken. Singles €22, with bath €29.45; doubles with bath and A/C €40. ❷

Hostal Medieval, C. de Fuencarral 46, 2nd fl. (☎522 2549). M: Tribunal. Wonderful, classic-feeling rooms with high ceilings, big windows, showers, and sinks. Central location. Singles €22; doubles €30, with bath €36; triples €44. ❷

Hotel San Lorenzo, C. Clavel 8 (☎521 3057). M: Gran Vía. Renovated rooms have new furniture, modern bath, A/C, TV, phone, and sound-proof windows. Other amenities include a lounge, coffee bar, room service, and laundry. Reservations recommended. Singles €50; doubles €75-85. AmEx/MC/V. ❺

ELSEWHERE AND CAMPING

Albergue Juvenil Santa Cruz de Marcenado (HI), C. de Santa Cruz de Marcenado 28 (☎547 4532). M: Argüelles. From the metro, walk 1 block down C. Alberto Aguilera, turn right on C. de Serrano Jóver, then left on C. de Santa Cruz de Marcenado. Separate floors for men and women. Breakfast included. 3-day max. stay. Curfew 1:30am. Reserve in advance. Dorms €12, under 26 €7.80. Nonmembers add €3.50. ❶

Camping Alpha (☎695 8069; fax 683 1659), 12km down Ctra. de Andalucía in Getafe. M: Legazpi. From the metro station take bus #447 (10min., every 20min. until 10pm, €1.20); cross the bridge and walk 1.5km back toward Madrid; camping signs lead the way. Pool, showers, and laundry. €5 per person, €5.80 per tent, €5.40 per car. ❶

◨ FOOD

In Madrid, it's not hard to fork it down without forking over too much. Most restaurants offer a *menú del día,* which includes bread, one drink, and one choice from each of the day's selection of appetizers, main courses, and desserts (€7-9). Many small eateries line **Calles Echegaray, Bentura de la Vega,** and **Manuel Fernández González** in Huertas; **Calle Agurrosa** at Lavapiés has outdoor cafes; **Calle Fuencarral** in Gran Vía is lined with cheap eats. **Bilbao** boasts ethnically diverse culinary choices. Bars along **Calle Hartzenbusch** and **Calle Cisneros** offer cheap tapas. Keep in mind the following buzz words for quicker, cheaper *madrileño* fare: *bocadillo* (a sandwich on a long, hard roll, €2-3); *ración* (a large tapa, served with bread €2-4); and *empanada* (a puff pastry with meat fillings, €1.30-2). The *Guía del Ocio* has a complete listing of Madrid's vegetarian options under the section *"Otras Cocinas."* The website www.mundovegetariano.com also has valuable information. For groceries, **%Dia** and **Simago** are the cheapest supermarket chains.

▦ **Taberna Macieras,** C. Jesus 7 (☎429 1584), also Huertas 66 (☎429 5818). M: Antón Martín. Tasty Galician seafood served in a lively atmosphere. Open M 8pm-12:45am, Tu-F 1-4:30pm and 8pm-12:45am, Sa-Su 1-4:45pm and 8:30pm-1:30am. ❸

▦ **Al-Jaima, Cocina del Desierto,** C. Barbieri 1 (☎523 1142). M: Gran Vía or Chueca. Lebanese, Moroccan, and Egyptian food in an intimate North African setting. Entrees €8. Open daily 1:30-4pm and 9pm-midnight. Reservations recommended. AmEx/MC/V. ❷

▦ **Casa Alberto,** C. de las Huertas 18 (☎429 9356). M: Antón Martín. Patrons spill out into the night air to wait for a spot at the bar. All tapas are original house recipes. Open Tu-Sa noon-5:30pm and 8pm-1:30am. AmEx/MC/V. ❷

▦ **El Estragón Vegetariano,** Pl. de la Paja 10 (☎365 8982). M: La Latina. Vegetarian food that could convert even the most die-hard carnivores. Delicious *menú* M-F €9.50; Sa-Su and evenings €25. Open daily 1:30-4:30pm and 8pm-1am. AmEx/MC/V. ❹

TAPAS FROM A TO Z

Tapas—these tasty little dishes are Spain's answer to *hors d'oeuvres*, with more taste and less pretension. To experience the *madrileño* lifestyle, you have to give them a try. The only question is: What are you going to order?

To the untrained reader, tapas menus are often undecipherable—and that's if the bar bothered to print them in the first place. To make sure you don't end up eating the stewed parts of the ox you rode in on, keep the following in mind before you *tapear:*

Servings come in three sizes:
— *pincho* (eaten with toothpicks between sips of beer)
— *tapa* (small plate)
— *ración* (meal portion)

Among the standard offerings on any tapas menu, you'll find:
— *aceitunas* (olives)
— *albóndigas* (meatballs)
— *anchoas* (anchovies)
— *callos* (tripe)
— *chorizo* (sausage)
— *croquetas* (croquettes)
— *gambas* (shrimp)
— *jamón* (ham)
— *patatas bravas* (fried potatoes with spicy sauce)
— *pimientos* (peppers)
— *pulpo* (octopus)
— *tortillla española* (onion and potato omelette)

Many tapas are served with thick mayonnaise; ask for them *"sin mayonesa"* if you're not a fan.

Café-Botillería Manuela, C. de San Vicente Ferrer 29 (☎531 7037). M: Tribunal. Upbeat music and occasional impromptu piano playing add to Manuela's atmosphere. Coffees €3.50-4.50. Mixed drinks €3-5. Traditional tapas €2-8. Open July-Aug. Tu-Su 6pm-2:30am; Sept.-June daily 4pm-2am. ❷

Inshala, C. Amnistia 10 (☎548 2632). M: Ópera. Eclectic, ethnically diverse menu. Lunch *menú* €9. Dinner *menú* €8-15. Reservations recommended. Open M-Th noon-2pm, F-Sa noon-3am. MC/V. ❸

Los Gabrieles, C. de Echegaray 17 (☎429 6261). The tiled mural at the back depicts famous artists like Velázquez and Goya as drunks. Serves tapas by afternoon and drinks by night. Flamenco night Tu. Open M-W and Su 1pm-2:30am, Th-Sa 1pm-3:30am. ❶

Arrocería Gala, C. de Moratín 22 (☎429 2562; www.paellas-gala.com). M: Antón Martín. *Menú* (€13) offers choice of paella, along with salad, bread, wine, and dessert. Reservations recommended. Open daily 1:30-3:45pm and 9-11pm. Cash only. ❸

Café Comercial, Glorieta de Bilbao 7 (☎521 5655). M: Bilbao. Founded in 1887, Madrid's oldest cafe boasts high ceilings, cushioned chairs, and huge mirrors. Coffee €1.15-1.85. Open M-Th 8am-1am, F-Sa 8am-2am, Su 10am-1am. ❶

🅖 SIGHTS

Madrid, large as it may seem, is a walker's city. Its fantastic public transportation system should only be used for longer distances or between the day's starting and ending points. Although the word *"paseo"* refers to a major avenue (such as *Paseo del Prado*) it literally means "a stroll." Do just that from Sol to Cibeles and from Plaza Mayor to the Palacio Real. While Madrid is perfect for walking, it also offers some of the world's best places to relax. Whether soothing tired feet after perusing the *triángulo de arte* or seeking shelter from the summer's sweltering heat, there's nothing better than a shaded sidewalk cafe or a romantic park.

EL CENTRO

The area known as El Centro, spreading out from Puerta del Sol (Gate of the Sun), is the gateway to the history and spirit of Madrid. Although several rulers carved the winding streets, the Habsburgs and Bourbons left El Centro's most celebrated monuments. As a result, easily-navigable El Centro is divided into two major sections: Madrid de los Habsburgos and Madrid de los Borbones.

PUERTA DEL SOL

Kilómetro 0, the origin of six national highways, marks the center of the city in the most chaotic of Madrid's plazas. Puerta del Sol blazes with taxis, bars, and street performers. Spaniards and tourists alike converge upon **El oso y el madroño,** a bronze statue of the bear and berry tree that grace the city's coat of arms. *(M: Sol.)*

HABSBURG MADRID

PLAZA MAYOR. Juan de Herrera, architect of El Escorial, also designed this plaza. Its elegant arcades, spindly towers, and open verandas came to define "Madrid-style" architecture. Toward evening, Plaza Mayor awakens as *madrileños* resurface, tourists multiply, and cafes fill with patrons. Live flamenco performances are common. *(M: Sol. From Pta. Sol, walk down C. Mayor. The plaza is on the left.)*

CATEDRAL DE SAN ISIDRO. Designed in the Jesuit Baroque style at the beginning of the 17th century, the cathedral received San Isidro's remains in 1769. During the Civil War, rioting workers burned the exterior and damaged much of the cathedral—all that survived were the main Capilla, a 17th-century banner, and the mummified remains of San Isidro and his wife, Maria de la Cabeza. *(M: Latina. From Pta. del Sol, take C. Mayor to Pl. Mayor, cross the plaza, and exit onto C. de Toledo. The cathedral is located at the intersection of C. de Toledo and C. de Sacramento. Open daily in summer 7:30am-1:30pm and 5:30-9pm; in winter 7:30am-1pm and 5:30-8:30pm. Free.)*

PLAZA DE LA VILLA. Plaza de la Villa marks the heart of what was once old Madrid. Though only a few medieval buildings remain, the plaza still features a stunning courtyard (around the statue of Don Alvara de Bazón), beautiful tile-work, and eclectic architecture. Across the plaza is the 17th-century **Ayuntamiento (Casa de la Villa),** designed in 1640 by Juan Gomez de Mora as both the mayor's home and the city jail. *(M: Sol. From Pta. del Sol, go down C. Mayor and past Pl. Mayor.)*

BOURBON MADRID

PALACIO REAL. The luxurious Palacio Real lies at the western tip of central Madrid, overlooking the Río Manzanares. Felipe V commissioned Giovanni Sachetti to replace the Alcázar, which had burned down in 1734, with a palace that would dwarf all others. The **Salón de Gasparini** houses Goya's portrait of Carlos IV. The **Salón del Trono** (Throne Room) contains a ceiling fresco. The **Biblioteca** shelves first editions of *Don Quixote.* Also open to the public is the **Real Armería** (armory), which displays the armor of Carlos V and Felipe II. *(M: Ópera. From Pl. de Isabel II, head toward the Teatro Real. ☎ 454 8800. Open Apr.-Sept. M-Sa 9am-6pm, Su 9am-3pm; Oct.-Mar. M-Sa 9:30am-5pm, Su 9am-2pm. €8, with tour €9, students €3.50/€8, W EU citizens free. Arrive early to avoid lines.)* Next door to the palace is the **Catedral de Nuestra Señora de la Almudena,** begun in 1879 and finished a century later. *(M: Ópera. Left of the Palacio Real on C. Bailén. Open daily 9am-9pm; closed during mass. Free.)*

PLAZA DE ORIENTE. A minor architectural miscalculation was responsible for this sculpture park. Most of the statues here were designed for the palace roof, but because they were too heavy (and the queen had a nightmare about the roof collapsing), they were placed in this shady plaza instead. Treat yourself to a pricey coffee on one of the elegant *terrazas* that fringe the plaza. The **Jardines de Sabatini,** just to the right as you face the palace, is the romantic's park of choice. *(M: Ópera. From Pl. Isabel II, walk past Teatro Real. Across the street from the Palacio Real.)*

HUERTAS

The area east of Sol is a wedge bounded by C. de Alcalá to the north, C. de Atocha to the south, and Po. del Prado to the east. Huertas's sights, from authors' houses to famous cafes, reflect its artistic focus. Home to Calderón, Cervantes, Góngora, Moratín, and Quevedo in the *Siglo de Oro* (Golden Age; 1500-1700), Huertas enjoyed a fleeting return to literary prominence when Hemingway frequented the neighborhood in the 1920s. **Plaza Santa Ana** and its *terrazas* are the center of this old literary haunt. **Casa de Lope de Vega** is the home where the prolific playwright and poet spent the last 25 years of his life. *(C. de Cervantes 11. With your back to Pl. de Santa Ana, turn left onto C. del Prado, right onto C. de León, and left onto C. de Cervantes.* ☎ *429 9216. Open Th-F 9:30am-2pm, Sa 10am-2pm. Entrance and tour €2, students €1.)*

ARGÜELLES

The area known as Argüelles and the zone surrounding Calle San Bernardo form a cluttered mixture of elegant middle-class houses, student apartments, and bohemian hangouts, all brimming with cultural activity. The **Parque de la Montaña** is home to Spain's only Egyptian temple. Built by Pharaoh Zakheramon in the 4th century BC, the **Temple de Debod** was a gift from the Egyptian government commemorating the Spanish archaeologists who helped rescue monuments in the Aswan Dam floods. *(M: Pl. de España or Ventura Rodríguez. Buses #1 and 74. From the metro, walk down C. Ventura Rodríguez to Parque de la Montaña; the temple is on the left.* ☎ *765 1008. Open Apr.-Sept. Tu-F 10am-2pm and 4-8pm, Sa-Su 10am-2pm; Oct.-Feb. Tu-F 9:45am-1:45pm and 4:15-5:15pm, Sa-Su 10am-2pm. Free. Parque open daily. Free.)*

OTHER SIGHTS

▓**PARQUE DEL BUEN RETIRO.** Join an array of vendors, palm-readers, soccer players, and sunbathers in what Felipe IV converted from a hunting ground into a *buen retiro* (nice retreat). The finely landscaped 300-acre Parque del Buen Retiro is centered around a magnificent monument to King Alfonso XII and a rectangular lake, the **Estanque Grande.** Built by Ricardo Velázquez to exhibit Filipino flowers, the exquisite steel-and-glass **Palacio de Cristal** now hosts a variety of art shows. *(Open Apr.-Sept. M and W-Sa 11am-8pm, Su 11am-6pm; Oct.-Mar. M and W-Sa 10am-6pm, Su 10am-4pm. Free.)* All artists should dream of having their art displayed in the **Palacio de Velázquez,** with its billowing ceilings, marble floors, and ideal lighting. *(Past the Estanque, turn left on Paseo del Venezuela. Open Apr.-Sept. M and W-Sa 11am-8pm, Su 11am-6pm; Oct.-Mar. M and W-Sa 10am-6pm, Su 10am-4pm. Free.)* Avoid the park at night.

EL PARDO. Built as a hunting lodge for Carlos I in 1547, El Pardo was enlarged by generations of Habsburgs and Bourbons. El Pardo gained attention in 1940 when Franco made it his home, in which he resided until his death in 1975. It is renowned for its collection of tapestries—several of which were designed by Goya—but the palace also holds paintings by Velázquez and Ribera. *(Take bus #601 from the stop above M: Moncloa (every 15min., €1.10).* ☎ *376 1500. Palace open Apr.-Sept. M-Sa 10:30am-5:45pm, Su 9:30am-1:30pm; Oct.-Mar. M-Sa 10:30am-4:45pm, Su 9:55am-1:30pm. €5, students and over 65 €2.50, W EU citizens free. Mandatory 45min. tour in Spanish.)*

☶ MUSEUMS

Madrid's great museums need no introduction. If you're not a student and plan on visiting the big three, your best bet is the **Paseo del Arte** ticket (€7.66), which grants admission to the Museo del Prado, Museo Thyssen-Bornemisza, and Museo Nacional Centro de Arte Reina Sofía. The pass is available at all three museums.

▓**MUSEO DEL PRADO.** The Prado is Spain's pride and joy, as well as one of Europe's finest museums of Spanish, Flemish, and Venetian art. On the second floor, keep an eye out for the works of **Diego Velázquez** (1599-1660). The court portraitist **Francisco de Goya y Lucientes** (1746-1828) created the stark *Dos de Mayo* and *Fusilamientas de Tres de Mayo.* The Prado also displays many of **El Greco's** religious paintings. On the second floor are works by other Spanish artists, including **Murillo** and **Ribera.** The Prado also has a collection of Italian works, including pieces by **Botticelli, Raphael, Rubens, Tintoretto,** and **Titian.** The Flemish holdings are top-notch and include works by **van Dyck, Albrecht Durer,** and **Peter Breugel the Elder.**

Hieronymus Bosch's *The Garden of Earthly Delights* depicts hedonism and the destiny that awaits its practitioners. *(Po. del Prado at Pl. Cánovas del Castillo. M: Banco de España or Atocha. ☎ 330 2800; http://museoprado.mcu.es. Open Tu-Su 9am-7pm. €3; students €1.50; under 18, over 65, and Su free.)*

■ **MUSEO THYSSEN-BORNEMISZA.** The Thyssen-Bornemisza covers a wide range of periods and media. Baron Heinrich Thyssen-Bornemisza donated his collection in 1993, and today the museum, with over 775 pieces, is the world's most extensive private showcase. The top floor is dedicated to the **Old Masters** collection, which includes El Greco's *Annunciation*. The **Baroque** collection, including pieces by Caravaggio, outshines that of the Prado. The **Impressionist** and **Post-Impressionist** collections explode with texture and color. The highlight of the museum is the **20th-century** collection on the first floor. *(On the corner of Po. del Prado and C. San Jerónimo. M: Banco de España. Bus #1, 2, 5, 9-10, 14-15, 20, 27, 34, 37, 45, 51-53, 74, 146, or 150. ☎ 369 0151; www.museothyssen.org. Open Tu-Su 10am-7pm. Last entrance 6:30pm. €4.80, students with ISIC and seniors €3, under 12 free.)*

■ **MUSEO NACIONAL CENTRO DE ARTE REINA SOFÍA.** Since Juan Carlos I decreed this renovated hospital a national museum in 1988, the Reina Sofía's collection of **20th-century art** has grown steadily. Rooms dedicated to Salvador Dalí, Juan Gris, and Joan Miró display Spain's vital contributions to the Surrealist movement. Picasso's masterwork **Guernica** is the centerpiece of the Reina Sofía's permanent collection. It depicts the Basque town (p. 984) bombed by the Germans at Franco's request during the Spanish Civil War. Picasso denounced the bloodshed in a huge, colorless work. He gave the canvas to New York's Museum of Modern Art on the condition that they return it to Spain when democracy was restored. The subsequent move to the Reina Sofía sparked an international controversy—Picasso's other stipulation had been that the painting hang only in the Prado. *(C. Santa Isabel 52. M: Atocha. ☎ 467 5062; http://museoreinasofia.mcu.es. Open M and W-Sa 10am-9pm, Su 10am-2:30pm. €3, students €1.50; Sa after 2:30pm, Su, and holidays free.)*

🎵 ENTERTAINMENT

▨ EL RASTRO (FLEA MARKET)

For hundreds of years, *El Rastro* has been a Sunday morning tradition in Madrid. The market begins in La Latina at Pl. Cascorro off C. de Toledo and ends at the bottom of C. Ribera de Curtidores. Get lost in the insanity and the excitement as your senses become overwhelmed with sights, sounds, and smells from every direction. Seek out that zebra hide, antique tool, or pet bird you've been dying for since your first day in Madrid and haggle for it until you're blue in the face. The flea market is a pickpocket's paradise, so leave the camera in your room and bust out the money belt. Fortunately, police are ubiquitous. *(Open Su and holidays 9am-2pm.)*

MUSIC AND FLAMENCO

Anyone interested in live entertainment should stop by the **Círculo de Bellas Artes.** *(C. de Alcalá 42. From Pl. de Santa Ana, go up C. del Príncipe, cross C. San Jerónimo, and continue toward C. de Alcalá. Turn right onto C. de Alcalá. ☎ 360 5400. Open Tu-F 5-9pm, Sa 11am-2pm and 5-9pm, Su 11am-2pm. €1.)* Check the *Guía del Ocio* for information on movies, plays, and concerts. **Flamenco** in Madrid is tourist-oriented and expensive. A few nightlife spots are authentic, but pricey. **Casa Patas,** C. Cañizares 10, is well-priced for the quality. *(C. Cañizares 10. M: Antón Martín. ☎ 369 0496; www.casapatas.com. Call ahead for prices.)* Flamenco enthusiasts should also check out **Corral de la Morería.** *(C. Morería 17. M: Ópera or La Latina. ☎ 365 8446. Cover €32. Shows 9:45pm-2am.)*

BULLFIGHTS

Bullfighters are either loved or loathed. So, too, are the bullfights themselves. Nevertheless, bullfights are a Spanish tradition. Hemingway-toting Americans and true fans of the contorted struggle between man and beast clog Pl. de las Ventas for the heart-pounding, albeit gruesome, events. If you're fascinated by bullfighting, check out our **featured itinerary** for Portugal and Spain (p. 918).

The yearly **Fiestas de San Isidro**, May 15-22, involve daily *corridas* (bullfights) with the top *matadores* and the fiercest bulls. There are also bullfights every Sunday from March to October and less frequently throughout the rest of the year. Look for posters in bars and cafes for upcoming *corridas*. **Plaza de las Ventas,** C. de Alcalá 237, is the biggest ring in Spain. *(M: Ventas. ☎356 2200; www.las-ventas.com. Seats €5-92, more expensive in the shade (sombra) than in the sun (sol). Tickets available F and Sa before and Su of the bullfight.)* **Plaza de Toros Palacio de Vista Alegre** hosts bullfights and cultural events. *(M: Vista Alegre. ☎422 0780. Call for schedule and prices.)* To watch amateurs, head to the **bullfighting school,** which has its own *corridas. (M: Batán. ☎470 1990. Open Sa 7:30pm. Tickets €7, children €3.50.)*

⬛ NIGHTLIFE

Spaniards average one hour less sleep per night than other Europeans, and *madrileños* claim to need even less than that. *Madrileños* start in the tapas bars of **Huertas,** move to the youthful scene in **Malasaña,** and end at the wild parties of **Chueca** or late-night clubs of **Gran Vía.** Students fill the streets of **Bilbao** and **Moncloa.** Madrid's gay scene, centered on **Plaza Chueca,** is fantastic. Most clubs don't heat up until around 2am; don't be surprised by a line waiting outside at 5:30am. The *entrada* (cover) can be as high as €15, but usually includes a drink. Dress well to avoid being overcharged or denied. Women may not be charged at all.

■ **Palacio Gaviria,** C. Arenal 9 (☎526 6069). M: Sol or Ópera. A red carpet leads to 3 ballrooms-turned-club spaces. Cover €9-15; includes 1 drink, additional drinks €9. Open M-W 11pm-4am, Th 10:30pm-6am, F-Sa 11pm-6am, Su 9pm-2:30am.

■ **Kathmandú,** C. de Señores de Luzón 3 (☎635 873 896). M: Ópera. Jammed with locals dancing to funk, soul, hip-hop, reggae, and acid jazz until the wee hours of the morning. Cover €7, includes 1 drink. Open Th midnight-5am, F-Sa 1-6am.

■ **Ocho y Medio Club,** C. Mesonero Romanos 13 (☎541 3500). The cool kids' *discoteca.* Th is **Pink Flamingo,** a gay disco; F local hipsters dance to techno; Sa is **Dark Hole,** a goth-themed party. Mixed drinks €7. Cover €8, includes 1 drink. Open Th-Sa 1am-6am.

■ **El Café de Sheherezade,** C. Santa María 18 (☎369 2474), a block from C. de las Huertas. M: Antón Martín. Surrounded by Middle Eastern decor, groups cluster around *pipas* (€7-10) that filter sweet smoke through whiskey or water. Open in summer M-Th and Su 6pm-2:30am, F-Sa 6pm-3:30am; in winter M-Th and Su 5pm-2am, F-Sa 5pm-3am.

Cuevas de Sesamo, C. Principe 7 (☎429 0542). M: Antón Martín. Cheap pitchers of sangria (€5-8.50) and live jazz piano draw suave crowds of all ages to this smoke-filled gem of the Huertas underground. Open M-Th and Su 6pm-2am, F-Sa 6pm-2:30am.

Acuarela, C. de Gravina 10 (☎522 2143). M: Chueca. Buddhas and candles surround cushy furniture. Liquor €3.20-5. Open daily in summer 3pm-3am; in winter 11pm-3am.

Kapital, C. de Atocha 125 (☎420 2906). M: Atocha. 7 floors of *discoteca* insanity, from hip-hop to house and open *terrazas* to cinemas. Dress to impress. Drinks €10. Cover €12-16, includes 1 drink. Open Th-Su midnight-6am, F-Su also 6-10:30pm. **Kapital Love** draws a mostly gay crowd on Su. Gets going around 2am.

Pasapoga, Gran Vía 37, (☎547 5711), near Pl. de Callao. M: Callao. Gay nightlife explodes here on weekends. Cover €15. Disco F-Sa. Open Tu-Su 6pm-dawn.

⚡ DAYTRIPS FROM MADRID

▨ EL ESCORIAL. Though "El Escorial" roughly translates to "The Slag Heap," the enormous complex was better described by Felipe II as "majesty without ostentation." The **Monasterio de San Lorenzo del Escorial** was a gift from Felipe II to God, the people, and himself, commemorating his victory over the French at the battle of San Quintín in 1557. Near the town of **San Lorenzo,** El Escorial is filled with artistic treasures, two palaces, two pantheons, a church, and a magnificent library. Enter via the gate on C. Floridablanca, on the western side. The adjacent **Museo de Arquitectura and Pintura** has an exhibition comparing El Escorial's construction to that of other related structures. Though masterpieces by Bosch, Durer, El Greco, and Titian still adorn the walls, most of the collection is now housed in Madrid's Museo del Prado (p. 930). The **Palacio Real,** lined with 16th-century *azulejos* (tiles), includes the majestic **Salón del Trono** (Throne Room), Felipe II's spartan 16th-century apartments, and the luxurious 18th-century rooms of Carlos III and Carlos IV. *(Autocares Herranz buses run between El Escorial and Madrid's Moncloa metro station. 50min.; every 15min. M-F 6:00am-10:30pm, Sa 7:30am-9pm, Su 7:45am-10pm; €3. Complex ☎ 918 90 59 03. Open Apr.-Sept. Tu-Su 10am-7pm; Oct.-Mar. 10am-5pm. Last admission 1hr. before closing. Monastery €7, students and seniors €3.50.)*

EL VALLE DE LOS CAÍDOS. In a valley of the Sierra de Guadarrama, fascist dictator Francisco Franco built the overpowering **Santa Cruz del Valle de los Caídos** (Valley of the Fallen) ostensibly as a memorial to those who died during the Civil War. The granite cross, however, honors only those who died "serving *Dios* and *España*" (i.e., the Fascist Nationalists). Many of those forced to build the monument died during its construction. Beneath the high altar, underneath the cross, lies the body of Franco himself. It is accessible only via El Escorial. *(An Autocares Herranz bus runs to the monument from El Escorial, C. Juan de Toledo. 20min.; Tu-Su 3:15pm, return 5:30pm; round-trip plus admission to monument €7.70. Funicular to the cross €2.50. Mass M-Sa 11am; Su 11am, 12:30, 1, 5:30pm. Entrance gate open Tu-Su 10am-6pm. €5, seniors and students €2.50, W EU citizens free.)*

CENTRAL SPAIN

Medieval cities and olive groves fill Castilla La Mancha, the land south and east of Madrid. Castilla y León's dramatic cathedrals are testaments to its glorious history. Farther west, bordering Portugal, stark Extremadura was birthplace to world-famous explorers such as Hernán Cortés and Francisco Pisarro.

CASTILLA LA MANCHA

Castilla La Mancha, a battered, wind-swept plateau, is one of Spain's least-developed regions. Its austere beauty surfaces through its tumultuous history, gloomy medieval fortresses, and awesome crags.

TOLEDO   ☎925

Cossío called Toledo (pop. 66,000) "the most brilliant and evocative summary of Spain's history." Today, the city may be marred by armies of tourists, but this former capital of the Holy Roman, Visigoth, and Muslim empires remains a treasure trove of Spanish culture. Toledo's numerous churches, synagogues, and mosques share twisting alleyways, emblematic of a time when Spain's three religions coexisted peacefully.

⊟ 🔁 TRANSPORTATION AND PRACTICAL INFORMATION

From the station on Po. de la Rosa (RENFE info ☎902 24 02 02), **trains** run to Madrid (½hr., 2-6 per day, €5-6). **Buses** run from Av. Castilla-La Mancha (☎21 58 50), 5min. from Puerta de Bisagra, to Madrid (1½hr., every 30min., €4) and Valencia (5½hr., M-F 3pm, €19). Local buses #5 and 6 service the bus and train stations and the central **Plaza de Zocodóver.** Buses (€0.80) stop to the right of the train station and underneath and across the street from the bus station.

Toledo is an almost unconquerable maze of narrow streets. To get to the central Plaza de Zocodóver from the train station, turn right and follow the left fork uphill to a smaller bridge, **Puente de Alcántara.** Cross the bridge to the stone staircase (through a set of arches); after climbing the stairs, turn left and continue upward, veering right at C. Cervantes, which leads to Pl. de Zocodóver. From the bus station, exit the cafeteria, head straight toward the traffic circle, and take the first right on the steep highway that surrounds the city. Despite well-labeled streets, it's easy to lose your way; get a map at the **tourist office,** located at Pta. de Bisagra. (☎22 08 43. English spoken. Open July-Sept. M-Sa 9am-7pm, Su 9am-3pm; Oct.-June M-F 9am-6pm, Sa 9am-7pm, Su 9am-3pm.) **Banco Santander Central Hispano,** C. del Comercio 47, offers **currency exchange** without commission and has a 24hr. **ATM.** (☎22 98 00. Open Apr.-Sept. M-F 8:30am-2pm; Oct.-Mar. M-F 8:30am-2pm, Sa 8:30am-1pm.) **Internet** access is available at the **Public Library,** located in the Alcázar. (Open M-Sa 9am-2pm and 5-9pm.) **Postal Code:** 45070.

🛋 🍴 ACCOMMODATIONS AND FOOD

Toledo is full of accommodations, but finding a bed during the summer can be a hassle, especially on weekends. Last-minute planners should try the tourist office for help. ▨**Residencia Juvenil San Servando (HI) ❶,** Castillo San Servando, uphill from the train station, is housed inside a 14th-century castle. (☎22 45 54. Dorms €11, under 30 €9. HI members only.) From Pl. de Zocodóver, take C. des Armas downhill, then take the first left to get to **Pensión Castilla ❷,** C. Recoletos 6. (☎25 63 18. Singles €15; doubles with bath €25. Cash only.) Take bus #7 from Pl. de Zocodóver to get to **Camping El Greco ❶,** 1.5km from town on Ctra. CM-4000, km0.7. The shady, wooded site features a restaurant, a bar, and a supermarket. (☎22 00 90. €4.75 per person, €4.55 per tent and per car. VAT not included. MC/V.)

Toledo is famous for its marzipan, which is formed into treats of every shape and size; *pastelería* windows beckon on every corner. The **market** is in Pl. Mayor, behind the cathedral. (Open M-Sa 9am-8pm.) To reach ▨**La Abadía ❷,** Pl. de San Nicolás 5, bear left when C. de la Sillería splits; Pl. de San Nicolás is on the right. Dine on the delicious lunch *menú* (€10) in a maze of cave-like underground rooms. (Open M-Th 8am-12:30am, F 8am-1:30am, Sa noon-1:30am. AmEx/MC/V.) From Pl. de Zocodóver take C. del Comercio and keep right to get to **Pastucci ❷,** C. Sinagoga 10, which serves pasta (€5.70-7.50) and pizza (€6-8.45) in a cheerful atmosphere. (☎25 77 42. Open Tu-Su noon-4pm and 7pm-midnight. MC/V.)

👁 SIGHTS

Toledo's vast collection of museums, churches, synagogues, and mosques make the city impossible to see in one day. Most sights are closed Mondays.

▨**CATHEDRAL.** Built between 1226 and 1498, Toledo's cathedral boasts five naves, delicate stained glass, and unapologetic ostentation. Noteworthy pieces include the 14th-century Gothic *Virgen Blanca,* El Greco's *El Espolio,* and Narciso Tomés's *Transparente.* In the **Capilla Mayor,** the Gothic altarpiece stretches to the ceiling. The tomb of Cardinal Mendoza, founder of the Spanish Inquisition,

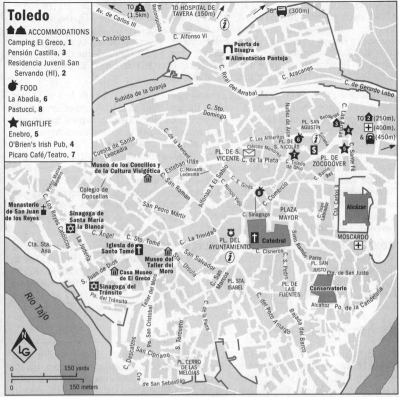

Toledo

🏠🏠 ACCOMMODATIONS
Camping El Greco, **1**
Pensión Castilla, **3**
Residencia Juvenil San
  Servando (HI), **2**

🍴 FOOD
La Abadía, **6**
Pastucci, **8**

⭐ NIGHTLIFE
Enebro, **5**
O'Brien's Irish Pub, **4**
Picaro Café/Teatro, **7**

Map labels: TO ⓘ (1.5km); Av. de Carlos III; Po. Canónigos; TO HOSPITAL DE TAVERA (150m) ⓘ; C. Alfonso VI; TO 🚌 (300m); Av. Reconquista; Puerta de Bisagra; Alimentación Pantoja; C. Real del Arrabal; C. Azacanes; C. de Gerardo Lobo; Subida de la Granja; C. Sto. Domingo; Nuñez de Arce; PL. SAN AGUSTIN; Recoletos; C. LAS AGUILAS; TO 🚌 (250m), ✚ (400m), & (450m); Cuesta de Santa Leocadia; C. de la Merced; C. de la Plata; PL. DE S. VICENTE; C. Los Alfileritos; Clérigos Menores; PL. DE S. NICOLÁS; Iglesia; PL. DE ZOCODÓVER; C. Sante Fé; Museo de los Concilios y de la Cultura Visigótica; C. Esteban Illán; C. San Roman; C. Navarro Ledesma; Alfonso X El Sabio; C. Nuncio Viejo; C. S. Ginés; C. Toledo de Ohio; C. Barrio Rey; Colegio de Doncellas; San Pedro Mártir; C. Comercio; C. Sinagoga; Alcázar; Monasterio de San Juan de los Reyes; Pintor Matías Moreno; C. Los Reyes Católicos; Sinagoga de Santa María la Blanca; C. Ángel; La Judería; C. Sto. Tomé; C. La Trinidad; PLAZA MAYOR; C. Juan Labrador; Cta. Carlos V; MOSCARDÓ; Cta. Sta. Ana; Iglesia de Santo Tomé; Museo del Taller del Moro; Casa Museo de El Greco; Sinagoga del Tránsito; Po. del Tránsito; S. Juan de Dios; C. San Salvador; Sta. Ursula; PL. DEL AYUNTAMIENTO; ⓘ; Catedral; C. Cisneros; Sixto Ramón; Parro PL. SAN JUSTO; Cta. de San Justo; Rio Tajo; Taller del Moro; C. San Cristobal; C. Descalzos; S. Torcuato; C. de la Plata; C. San Marcos; PL. STA. ISABEL; PL. DE LAS FUENTES; C. del Pozo Amargo; Conservatorio; Alcahoz; Po. de la Candelaria; San Cipriano; PL. CERRO DE LAS MELOJAS; C. de la Plata; C. de San Sebastián; Bajada del Barco; 0 150 yards; 0 150 meters

lies to the left. Beneath the dome is the **Capilla Mozárabe,** the only place where the ancient Visigoth Mass (in Mozarabic) is still held. The **treasury** houses a replica of one of Columbus's ships and a 400 lb., 16th-century gold monstrance (Eucharistic receptacle) carried through the streets during the annual Corpus Christi procession (June 10). The **sacristía** is home to 18 El Grecos, two Van Dycks, and a Caravaggio. Portraits of every archbishop of Toledo can be found in the **Sala Capitular.** *(At Arco de Palacio, up C. Comercio from Pl. de Zocodóver. ☎22 22 41. Cathedral open daily 10am-noon and 4-6pm. Sacristía and the capillas open June-Aug. M-Sa 10:30am-6:30pm, Su 2-6pm; Sept.-May M-Sa 10:30am-6pm, Su 2-6pm. Cathedral free. Sacristía and capillas €5.50. Tickets sold at the store opposite the entrance. Modest dress required.)*

📷ALCÁZAR. Toledo's most formidable landmark, the Alcázar, served as a military stronghold for the Romans, Visigoths, Moors, and Spaniards. Much of the building was reduced to rubble during the Civil War, when Fascist troops used it as their refuge. Visit the dark, windowless basement where over 500 civilians hid during the siege. The rooms above ground have been turned into a military museum with armor, swords, guns, knives, and comparatively benign dried plants. *(Cuesta Carlos V 2, a block down from Pl. de Zocodóver. ☎22 16 73. Open Tu-Su 9:30am-2:30pm. €2, W free.)*

EL GRECO. Greek painter Doménikos Theotokópoulos, commonly known as El Greco, spent most of his life in Toledo. His works are displayed throughout town, but the majority of his masterpieces have been carted off to the Prado and other big-name museums. The best place to start is the **Casa Museo de El Greco,** which contains

19 works. *(C. Samuel Leví 2. ☎ 22 40 46. Open Tu-Sa 10am-2pm and 4-6pm, Su 10am-2pm. €2.40; students, under 18, and over 65 €1.20; Sa afternoon and Su free.)* Up the hill and to the right is the **Iglesia de Santo Tomé,** which houses El Greco's famous painting *The Burial of Count Orgaz. (Pl. Conde 1. ☎ 25 60 98; www.santome.org. Open daily Mar. to mid-Oct. 10am-6:45pm; mid-Oct. to Feb. 10am-5:45pm. €1.50.)* Outside handsome **Puerta Nueva de Bisagra,** the **Hospital de Tavera** displays five El Grecos. *(C. Cardenal Tavera 2. ☎ 22 04 51. Open daily 10:30am-1:30pm and 3:30-6pm. €3.)*

LA JUDERÍA. Only two of the many synagogues original to Toledo's *judería* (Jewish quarter) have been preserved. Samuel Ha Leví, diplomat to Pedro el Cruel, built the **Sinagoga del Tránsito** in 1366. Its simple exterior hides an ornate sanctuary. Inside, the **Museo Sefardí** documents early Jewish history in Spain; highlights include a Torah (parts of which are over 400 years old) and a set of Sephardic wedding costumes. *(C. Samuel Leví. ☎ 22 36 65; www.museosefardi.net. Open Tu-Sa 10am-2pm and 4-9pm, Su 10am-2pm. €2.40, students and under 18 €1.20, Sa after 4pm and Su free.)* **Sinagoga de Santa María la Blanca,** down the street, was built in the 12th century as a Mudéjar-style synagogue. After the Jews were expelled in the late 15th century, the synagogue was converted into a church. Now secular, its Moorish arches and tranquil garden make for a pleasant retreat. *(C. Reyes Católicos 2. ☎ 22 72 57. Open daily June-Aug. 10am-7pm; Sept.-May 10am-6pm. €1.50, students and over 65 €1.20.)*

MONASTERIO DE SAN JUAN DE LOS REYES. This monastery was commissioned by Ferdinand and Isabella to commemorate their victory over the Portuguese in the Battle of Toro (1476). The cloister melds Gothic and Mudéjar architecture. The monarchs planned to use the church as their crypt, but later decided instead on Granada, the site of their 1492 victory over the Moorish kingdom. *(☎ 22 38 02. Open daily Apr.-Sept. 10am-1:45pm and 3:30-6:45pm; Oct.-Mar. 10am-2pm and 3:30-6pm. €1.50.)*

⬛ NIGHTLIFE

For nightlife, head through the arch and to the left from Pl. Zocodóver to **Calle Santa Fé,** where beer and local youth can be found in abundance. **Enebro,** on Pl. Santiago Balleros off C. Cervantes, serves free tapas in the evenings. (Open daily 11am-4pm and 7pm-1:30am.) Also try **Calle de la Sillería** and **Calle Alfileritos,** west of Pl. de Zocodóver. Techno-funk remixes play at **Picaro Cafe/Teatro,** C. Núñez. (☎ 22 13 01. *Copas* €5. Pints €3. Open daily 3pm-4am.) **O'Brien's Irish Pub,** C. Armas 12, has live music on Thursdays. (Open M-Th and Su noon-2:30am, F-Sa noon-4am.)

CUENCA   ☎969

Cuenca (pop. 50,000) is a hilltop city flanked by two rivers and the stunning rock formations they created. The enchanting **old city** safeguards most of Cuenca's unique charm, including the famed ⬛**casas colgadas** (hanging houses) that dangle high above the Río Huécar. Cross the San Pablo bridge to **Hoz del Huécar** for a spectacular view of the *casas* and cliffs. Many of the *casas* house museums; on Pl. Ciudad de Ronda is the excellent **Museo de Arte Abstracto Español.** (☎ 21 29 83. Open Tu-F 11am-2pm and 4-6pm, Sa 11am-2pm and 4-8pm, Su 11am-2pm. €3, students and seniors €1.50.) The perfectly square **Cathedral de Cuenca** sits in the Plaza Mayor. (Open daily 9am-2pm and 4-6pm. Free.)

Trains (☎ 902 24 02 02) run to Madrid (2½-3hr., 5-6 per day, €9.15) and Valencia (3-4hr., 3-4 per day, €10.05). **Buses** (☎ 22 70 87) depart from C. Fermín Caballero 20 to: Barcelona (9hr.; 1-2 per day; €31); Madrid (2½hr., 8-9 per day, €8.20-11); and Toledo (2¼hr., 1-2 per day, €10). To get to Plaza Mayor from either station, take a left onto C. Fermín Caballero, continuing as it becomes C. Cervantes and C. José Cobo and then bearing left through Pl. Hispanidad. The **tourist office** is in Pl. Mayor. (☎ 23 21 19. Open July-Sept. M-Sa 9am-9pm, Su 9am-2pm; Oct.-June M-Sa 9am-2pm and 4-6:30pm, Su 9am-2pm.) ⬛**Posada de San José ❷,** C. Julián Romero 4, is near the cathedral. (☎ 21 13

00. Singles €22, with bath €43; doubles €32/€62; triples with sink €43; quads with bath €100. *Semana Santa* increased prices; low season reduced prices. AmEx/MC/V.) Budget eateries line **Calle Cervantes** and **Calle República Argentina.** Stock up at **%Día,** on Av. Castilla La Mancha and Av. República Argentina. (Open M-Th 9:30am-2pm and 5:30-8:30pm, F-Sa 9am-2:30pm and 5:30-9pm.) **Postal Code:** 16002.

CASTILLA Y LEÓN

Castilla y León's cities rise like green oases from a desert of burnt sienna. The aqueduct of Segovia, the Gothic cathedrals of Burgos and León, the sandstone of Salamanca, and the city walls of Ávila stand out as regional and national images.

SEGOVIA   ☎ 921

Legend has it that the devil built Segovia's (pop. 56,000) famed aqueduct in an effort to win the soul of a Segovian water-seller named Juanilla. Devil or not, Segovia's attractions and winding alleyways draw their share of Spanish and international tourists, as well as students seeking language practice.

☞ ▨ TRANSPORTATION AND PRACTICAL INFORMATION. Trains (RENFE ☎ 902 24 02 02), Po. Obispo Quesada, run to Madrid (2hr., 7-9 per day, €5.10). **Buses** (☎ 42 77 07) run from Estación Municipal de Autobuses, Po. Ezequiel González 12. La Sepulvedana (☎ 42 77 07) goes to Madrid (1½hr., every 30min. M-F 6am-9:30pm, Sa 7:30am-9:30pm, Su 8:30am-10:30pm; €6). Linecar (☎ 42 77 06) sends buses to Salamanca (3hr., 1-3 per day, €9). From the train station, take any bus (€0.70) to the **Plaza Mayor,** the city's center and site of the regional **tourist office.** (☎ 46 03 34. Open daily July to mid-Sept. 9am-8pm; mid-Sept. to June 9am-2pm and 5-8pm.) The Po. del Salón **bus** (every 30min. M-F 7:45am-10:15pm) runs to the steps of **Puerta del Sol.** To access the **Internet,** try the **Public Library,** C. Juan Bravo 11. (☎ 46 35 33. Free. Limit 30min. Open M-F 9am-9pm, Sa 9am-2pm.) **Postal Code:** 40001.

▨ ▢ ACCOMMODATIONS AND FOOD. Reservations are a must for any of Segovia's hotels, especially those in or around major plazas. Arrive early to ensure space and expect to pay €21 or more for a single. *Pensiones* are significantly cheaper, but feature fairly basic rooms and shared bathrooms. To reach **Hospedaje El Gato ❷,** Pl. del Salvador 10, which has private baths, TV, and A/C, follow the aqueduct up the hill, turning left on C. Ochoa Ondategui; it meets San Alfonso Rodríguez, which leads into Pl. del Salvador. (☎ 42 32 44. Doubles €35; triples €49. MC/V.) For more luxurious rooms, try **Hotel Las Sirenas ❺,** C. Juan Bravo 30, down C. Cervantes. (☎ 46 26 63. July-Sept. singles €48-53; doubles €70; triples €90. Oct.-June singles €40-45; doubles €50; triples €80. AmEx/MC/V.) **Camping Acueducto ❶,** C. Borbón 49/Ctra. Nacional 601, km 112, is 2km toward La Granja. Take the Autobus Urbano (€0.70) from Pl. Azoguejo to Nueva Segovia. (☎/fax 42 50 00. Open late Mar.-Sept. €4.30 per person, per tent, and per car.)

Sample Segovia's famed lamb, but steer clear of pricey Plaza Mayor and Pl. Azoguejo. Buy groceries at **%Día,** C. Gobernador Fernández Giménez 3, off C. Fernández Ladreda. (Open M-Th 9:30am-8:30pm, F-Sa 9am-9pm). ▨**Bar-Meson Cueva de San Esteban ❸,** C. Vadelaguila 15, off Pl. Esteban and C. Escuderos, is casual but classy. (☎ 46 09 82. Lunch *menús* M-F €8, Sa-Su €10. Entrees €7-14. Open daily 10am-midnight. MC/V.) For tasty vegetarian options (€3.60-9), try **Restaurante La Almuzara ❷,** C. Marqués del Arco 3, past the cathedral. (Open Tu 8pm-midnight, W-Su 12:45-4pm and 8pm-midnight. MC/V.)

◪ ▤ SIGHTS AND ENTERTAINMENT. Segovia rewards the wanderer. Its picturesque museums, palaces, churches, and streets beg closer observation. The serpentine ▨**Roman aqueduct,** built in 50 BC, commands the entrance to the old city. Its two tiers of 163 arches, spanning 813m and reaching a height of 29m near Pl. del

Azoguejo, are supported by 128 pillars. The aqueduct used some 20,000 granite blocks, but no mortar, in its construction. The **cathedral,** commissioned by Carlos V in 1525, towers over the Plaza Mayor. Its 23 chapels and gilt treasury earned it the nickname "The Lady of all Cathedrals." The **Sala Capitular,** hung with 17th-century tapestries, displays an ornate chariot. Off the cloister is the **Capilla de Santa Catalina,** filled with crucifixes, chalices, and candelabras. (☎46 22 05. Open daily Apr.-Oct. 9am-6:30pm; Nov.-Mar. 9:30am-6pm. €2, under 14 and Su until 2:30pm free.) The ⚑**Alcázar,** a late medieval castle and site of Isabella's coronation in 1474, dominates the northern end of the old quarter. In the **Sala de Solio** (throne room), an inscription reads: *Tanto monta, monta tanto* ("she mounts, as does he"). Get your mind out of the gutter—this means Ferdinand and Isabella had equal authority as sovereigns. The **Torre de Juan II,** 140 steps up a spiral staircase, affords a marvelous view of Segovia. (Pl. de la Reina Victoria Eugenia. ☎46 07 59. Open Apr.-Sept. daily 10am-7pm; Oct. M-F 10am-6pm, Sa-Su 10am-7pm; Nov.-Mar. daily 10am-6pm. Tower closed Tu. €3.30, seniors and students €2.50, tower only €1.)

Though the city isn't particularly known for its sleepless nights, native Segovians know how to party. Packed with bars and cafes, the **Plaza Mayor** is the center of nightlife. **Calle Infanta Isabel** earns its nickname "calle de los barres" (street of the bars); a casual crowd frequents **Bar Santana,** C. Infanta Isabel 18. (☎46 35 64. Open daily 9am-midnight.) Clubs abound on **Calle Ruíz de Alda,** off Pl. del Azoguejo. You can count on a party every night at **La Luna,** C. Puerta de la Luna 8, where a young crowd downs cheap shots (€1) and Heineken. (☎46 26 51. Beer €1.50. Open daily 4:30pm-4am.) June 24-29, Segovia celebrates a **fiesta,** with free open-air concerts, dances, and fireworks, in honor of San Juan and San Pedro.

SALAMANCA ☎923

Salamanca la blanca, city of scholars, saints, royals, and rogues, showcases the best examples of Spanish Plateresque by day and a vivacious club scene by night. The prestigious Universidad de Salamanca, grouped in medieval times with Bologna, Paris, and Oxford as one of the "four leading lights of the world," continues to add the energy of its thousands of students to the already well-touristed city.

▐▟ TRANSPORTATION AND PRACTICAL INFORMATION

Trains leave from Po. de la Estación (☎12 02 02) to Lisbon, Portugal (6hr., daily 4:51am, €45.40) and Madrid (2½hr., 5-6 per day, €14.15). **Buses** (☎23 67 17) leave from the station, Av. Filiberto Villalobos 71-85, for: Barcelona (11hr., 2 per day, €43); Madrid (3hr., 16 per day, €10.15-15); and Segovia (3hr., 2 per day, €9).

Plaza Mayor is the social and geographic center of Salamanca. Most budget hostels lie south of the plaza around Rúa Mayor and **Plaza de Anaya,** as do the **Universidad** and most tourist sights. From the train station, catch bus #1 (€0.70) to Gran Vía and ask to be let off at Pl. San Julián, a block from Pl. Mayor. The **tourist office** is at Pl. Mayor 32. (☎21 83 42. Open M-F 9am-2pm and 4:30-8pm, Su 10am-2pm.) Also look for *DGratis,* a free weekly newspaper about events in Salamanca. It's available from newsstands, tourist offices, and pretty girls in Plaza Mayor. **ATMs** are on every major street. For free **Internet** access, try the **Public Library,** located in the Casa de las Conchas, C. Compañía 2. (☎26 93 17. Limit 30min. Open M-F 9am-9pm, Sa 9am-2pm.) The **post office,** Gran Vía 25-29, has *Lista de Correos.* (☎26 30 11. Open M-F 8:30am-8:30pm, Sa 9:30am-2pm.) **Postal Code:** 37080.

▐▌ ACCOMMODATIONS AND FOOD

Reasonably priced *hostales* and *pensiones* cater to the floods of student visitors, especially off Plaza Mayor and C. Meléndez. **Pensión Las Vegas ❷,** C. Meléndez 13, 1st fl., has friendly owners. (☎21 87 49; www.lasvegascentro.com. Singles with bath €18;

doubles €24, with bath €30-36; triples with bath €45. MC/V.) Nearby **Pensión Barez ❶**, C. Meléndez 19, 1st fl., has a common room with a terrace. (☎21 87 49. Singles €12; doubles €22; triples €33. Cash only.) Four kilometers toward Madrid on Ctra. Salamanca is **Regio ❶**, which offers first-class camping sites with hot showers. (☎13 88 88. Albertur buses run from Gran Vía every 30min. €3 per person, per tent, and per car. MC/V.) Cafes and restaurants surround **Plaza Mayor,** where three-course meals run about €9. The closest supermarket is **Champion,** C. Zamora 52. (Open M-F 10am-2pm and 5-8pm, Sa 10am-2pm.) Crowded **El Patio Chico ❷**, C. Meléndez 13, serves large, delicious meals. (☎26 51 03. *Menú* €11. Entrees €4-8. *Bocadillos* €2-3. Open daily 1-4pm and 8pm-midnight.) For traditional Spanish food at low prices, try **Restaurante El Bardo ❷**, C. Compañía 8, between the Casa de las Conchas and the Clerecía. (☎21 90 89. *Menú* €9. Entrees €6-13. Open daily 1:30-4pm and 9-11:30pm. MC/V.)

👁 SIGHTS

▦**CATEDRAL NUEVA.** It's not surprising it took 220 years to build this awesome example of the Spanish Gothic (1513-1733). The church is best viewed from the ground first, but be sure to climb the tower to get a spectacular ▦ **view** from above. From the tower balcony, one can compare the old and new cathedrals. Admission includes an exhibit contrasting the architecture of the two structures. Architects of modern renovations have also left their marks; look for an astronaut and a dragon eating an ice cream cone on the left side of the main door. *(Pl. de Anaya. Open daily Apr.-Sept. 9am-8pm; Oct.-Mar. 10am-2:30pm and 4-5:30pm. Free. Tower ☎ 28 11 23. Open daily 10am-7:30pm. €2.)*

▦**CATEDRAL VIEJA.** The smaller Catedral Vieja (1140) was built in the Romanesque style. The cupola, assembled from intricately carved miniature pieces, is one of the most detailed in Spain. Gargoyles peer down from the columns' capitals. Above the high altar, angels separate the damned from the saved. The oldest original part of the cathedral is the **Capilla de San Martín,** with brilliant frescoes dating from 1242. The **museum** is home to works by Fernando Gallego, who decorated the original ceiling of the University Library. Be sure to check out the famed **Patio Chico** behind the cathedral, where students congregate to chat and play music and tourists head for a spectacular view of both cathedrals. *(Enter through the Catedral Nueva. Museum ☎ 21 74 76. Cathedral open daily Oct.-Mar. 10am-1:30pm and 4-7:30pm; Apr.-Sept. 10am-7:30pm. €3, students €2.25, children €1.50.)*

PLAZA MAYOR. Salamanca's Plaza Mayor is considered one of the most beautiful squares in Spain. Designed and built by Alberto Churriguera between 1729 and 1755, the plaza contains 88 towering arches, the **Ayuntamiento,** and three pavilions dedicated to historical figures. The **Pabellón Real,** to the right of the Ayuntamiento, honors the Spanish monarchy (and, quite controversially, 20th-century dictator Francisco Franco); the **Pabellón del Sur,** in front of the Ayuntamiento, is dedicated to famous Spanish conquistadors; and the **Pabellón del Oeste,** to the left of the Ayuntamiento, pays homage to important *salmantinos* like Santa Teresa and Miguel de Unamuno. The square once served as the town bullring.

THE UNIVERSITY. The university, established in 1218, is the focal point of Salamanca. The university's entryway at C. Libreros is one of the greatest examples of Spanish Plateresque, a style named for the delicate filigree work of *plateros* (silversmiths). The central medallion represents Ferdinand and Isabella, while the higher one is generally thought to represent the Pope. Hidden in the sculptural work lies a tiny frog; according to legend, those who can spot the frog without assistance will be blessed with good luck, or possibly marriage.

The old lecture halls inside are open to the public; entering the cool stone foyer feels like stepping into another era. The **Paraninfo** (auditorium) has Baroque tapestries and a portrait of Carlos IV attributed to Goya. Located on the second floor atop a magnificent Plateresque staircase is the **Antigua Biblioteca,** one of Europe's oldest libraries. The staircase is thought to represent the ascent of the young student through playfulness, *amor*, and adventure to the true love of knowledge.

Don't miss the **University Museum,** which is through the hallway on the left corner of the patio. Preserved here is Fernando Gallego's **Cielo de Salamanca,** a 15th-century fresco of the zodiac which was painted on the library's original ceiling. *(From Plaza Mayor follow R. Mayor, veer right onto R. Antigua, then left onto C. Libreros. University ☎ 29 44 00, museum 29 12 25. Open M-F 9:30am-1:30pm and 4-7:30pm, Sa 9:30am-1:30pm and 4-7pm, Su 10am-1:30pm. University and museum €2.40, students and seniors €1.20.)*

🎵🎸 ENTERTAINMENT AND NIGHTLIFE

According to *salmantinos*, Salamanca is the best place in Spain to party; it is said that there is one bar for every one hundred people living in the city. There are *chupiterias* (shot bars), *barres*, and *discotecas* on nearly every street, and while some close at 4am, others go all night. Nightlife centers on **Plaza Mayor** and spreads out to side streets. **Calle Prior** and **Rúa Mayor** are also full of bars.

Begin your night at ▓ **Bar La Chupitería,** Pl. Monterrey. Make your way through crowds of students to order candy-colored shots from *Los Exóticos*, the ever-changing list of specialty shots (€0.90-1). Later, wander from club to club on C. Prior and C. Compañía, where young Americans mingle with tireless *salmantinos*. Once you get past the picky bouncers, **Niebla, Gatsby, Camelot,** and **Cum Laude** all offer an ambience of tight pants and loose morals. While the dance hits start blasting between 10:30-11pm, the party doesn't peak until 2:30-3:30am and stays strong for another two hours. (Beer €2-3. Mixed drinks €4.50-7. Dress to impress. All clubs are cash only.) If you need a break from all that club-hopping, take five and casually sip drinks while enjoying modern funk and jazz at **Birdland,** C. Azafranal 57, facing Pl. España. (Beer €1.50-2.40. Mixed drinks €3-6. Open M-Th and Su 4pm-3am, F-Sa 4pm-4:30am; opens 6:30pm in summer. Cash only.)

🔆 DAYTRIP FROM SALAMANCA: ZAMORA

Perched atop a rocky cliff, Zamora (pop. 70,000) is an intriguing mix of the modern and the medieval: 15th-century palaces harbor Internet cafes and luxury hotels, while the 12th-century cathedral overlooks modern subdivisions and steel bridges in the distance. While Zamora owes its character to the medieval churches dotting its streets, the ▓ **Museo de Semana Santa,** Pl. Santa María la Nueva 9, is a rare find. (☎ 980 53 22 95. Open M-Sa 10am-2pm and 5-8pm, Su 10am-2pm. €2.70.) Twelve striking **Romanesque churches** remain within the walls of the old city. Almost all were built in the 11th and 12th centuries, though their ornate altars were not added until the 15th and 16th centuries. (All cathedrals open Mar.-Sept. Tu-Sa 10am-1pm and 5-8pm. Free.) Zamora's foremost monument is its Romanesque **cathedral,** built between the 12th and 15th centuries. Inside the cloister, the **Museo de la Catedral** features the 15th-century *Black Tapestries*, which tell the story of Achilles's defeat during the Trojan War. (☎ 980 53 06 44. Cathedral and museum open Tu-Su 10am-2pm and 5-8pm. Cathedral free, museum €2.) **Buses** run from Av. Alfonso Peña to Salamanca and back (1hr.; M-F 15 per day, Sa 10 per day, Su 6 per day; €3.75.) More information on sights can be found at the **tourist office,** Pl. Arias Gonzalo 6. (☎ 987 53 36 94. Open daily Apr.-Sept. 10am-2pm and 5-8pm; Oct.-Mar. 10am-2pm and 4-7pm.)

LEÓN ☎ 987

Formerly the center of Christian Spain, today León (pop. 165,000) is best known for its 13th-century Gothic ▓ **cathedral,** arguably the most beautiful in Spain. Its spectacular stained-glass windows have earned León the nickname

La Ciudad Azul (The Blue City). The cathedral's **museum** displays gruesome wonders, including a sculpture depicting the skinning of a saint. (Cathedral open July-Sept. M-Sa 8:30am-1:30pm and 4-8pm, Su 8:30am-2:30pm and 5-8pm; Oct.-June M-Sa 8:30am-1:30pm and 4-7pm, Su 8:30am-2:30pm and 5-7pm. Free. Museum open June-Sept. M-F 9:30am-2pm and 4-7:30pm, Sa 9:30am-2pm and 4-7pm; Oct.-May M-F 9:30am-1:30pm and 4-7pm, Sa 9:30am-1:30pm. €3.50.) The **Basílica San Isidoro,** dedicated to San Isidoro of Seville, houses the bodies of countless royals in the *Panteón Real*. From Pl. Santo Domingo, walk up C. Ramón y Cajal; the basilica is up the flight of stairs on the right just before C. La Torre. (Open M-Sa 9am-1:30pm and 4-6:30pm, Su 9am-1:30pm. €3.) For bars, discos, and techno music, head to the *barrio húmedo* (drinker's neighborhood) around **Plaza de San Martín** and **Plaza Mayor.**

Trains (☎902 24 02 02) run from Av. de Astorga 2 to Barcelona (9½hr., 2-3 per day, €39-50) and Madrid (4½hr., 7 per day, €22-29). **Buses** (☎21 00 00) leave from Po. del Ingeniero Sáenz de Miera for Madrid (4½hr., 7-12 per day, €18-30) and Salamanca (2½hr., 5-6 per day, €12). The **tourist office**, Pl. Regla 3, has free maps. (☎23 70 82. Open M-F 9am-2pm and 5-7pm, Sa-Su 10am-2pm and 5-8pm.) Many accommodations cluster on **Avenida de Roma, Avenida Ordoño II,** and **Avenida República Argentina,** which lead into the old town from Pl. Glorieta Guzmán el Bueno. ■**Hostal Bayón ❶,** C. Alcazar de Toledo 6, 2nd fl., is just off C. Ancha. The sun-drenched rooms feature hardwood floors. Shared bathrooms are very clean. (☎23 14 46. Singles €12; doubles €20.) Inexpensive eateries can be found near the cathedral and on the small streets off C. Ancha. **Postal Code:** 24004.

EXTREMADURA

Arid plains bake under the intense summer sun, relieved only by scattered patches of golden sunflowers. This land of harsh beauty and cruel extremes hardened New World conquistadors such as Hernán Cortés and Francisco Pizarro.

TRUJILLO   ☎927

The gem of Extremadura, hill-top Trujillo (pop. 10,000) is an enchanting old-world town. Its most impressive monument is a 10th-century **Moorish castle** that offers a panoramic view of the surrounding plains. The **Plaza Mayor** inspired the Plaza de Armas in Cuzco, Perú, which was constructed after Francisco Pizarro defeated the Incas. Festooned with stork nests, the **Iglesia de San Martín** sits on the northeastern corner of the plaza. (Open M-Sa 10am-2pm and 4:30-7:30pm, Su 10am-2pm and 4:30-7pm. €1.30.) To reach the **Iglesia de Santa María la Mayor,** take C. de las Cambroneras from the plaza in front of the Iglesia de San Martín and turn right on C. de Sta. María. The tiny steps leading to the top of the Romanesque church tower are exhausting, but the ■**360° view** from the top is worth the effort. (Open May-Oct. 10am-2pm and 4:30-8pm; Nov.-Apr. 10am-2pm and 4-7pm. €1.25.)

Buses (☎32 18 22) run from the corner of C. de las Cruces and C. del M. de Albayada to Madrid (2½hr., 14-16 per day, €14) and Salamanca (5hr., daily 10:30am, €15). The **tourist office** is in Plaza Mayor; info is posted in the windows. (☎32 26 77. English spoken. Open daily June-Sept. 9:30am-2pm and 4:30-7:30pm; Oct.-May 9:30am-2pm and 4-7pm.) **Camas Boni ❷,** C. Domingo Ramos 117, is off Pl. Mayor on the street across from the church. (☎32 16 04. Singles €15; doubles €28, with bath €30-35.) The **Plaza Mayor** teems with tourist eateries. Head to **La Tahona ❶,** C. Afueras 2 (exit Pl. Mayor by the church and walk four blocks), for homemade pasta (€4-5.20) and other tasty meals (☎32 18 49. Open M 7:30pm-midnight, Tu-Su 1-4pm and 7:30pm-midnight.) **Postal Code:** 10200.

SOUTHERN SPAIN

Southern Spain (Andalucía) is all that you expect Spain to be—flamenco shows, bullfighting, tall pitchers of sangria, white-washed villages, and streets lined with orange trees. The Moors arrived in AD 711 and bequeathed the region with far more than the flamenco music and gypsy ballads proverbially associated with southern Spain, sparking the European Renaissance and reintroducing the wisdom of Classical Greece and the Near East. Despite (or perhaps because of) the poverty and high unemployment of their homeland, Andalusians have always maintained a passionate dedication to living the good life. The *festivales*, *ferias*, and *carnavales* of Andalucía are world-famous for their extravagance.

CÓRDOBA   ☎957

Charming Córdoba (pop. 310,000), perched on the south bank of the Río Guadalquivir, was once the largest city in Western Europe. Córdoba remembers its heyday with amazingly well-preserved Roman, Jewish, Islamic, and Catholic monuments. Today, springtime festivals, flower-filled patios, and a steady nightlife make Córdoba one of Spain's most beloved cities.

🖿📶 TRANSPORTATION AND PRACTICAL INFORMATION. Trains (RENFE info ☎902 24 02 02; www.renfe.es) run from Pl. de las Tres Culturas, off Av. de América, to: Barcelona (10-11hr., 4 per day, €47-65); Madrid (2-4hr., 21-31 per day, €26-48); and Seville (1hr., 20-30 per day, €7-24). **Buses** (☎40 40 40) leave from Estación de Autobuses, Av. de América, across from the train station. Alsina Graells Sur (☎27 81 00) sends buses to: Cádiz (4-5hr., 1-2 per day, €19) via Seville (2hr., 10-13 per day, €9); Granada (3hr., 8 per day, €11); and Málaga (3-3½hr., 5 per day, €11). Bacoma (☎45 65 14) runs to Barcelona (10hr., 3 per day, €69). Secorbus (☎902 22 92 92) sends cheap buses to Madrid (4½hr., 3-6 per day, €12). Autocares Priego (☎40 44 79) and Empresa Rafael Ramírez (☎42 21 77) run buses to nearby towns and camping sites. The easiest way to reach the **old city** from the adjacent train and bus stations is to take bus #3 to **Plaza Campo Santo de los Mártires** (€0.85). To walk (20min.), exit left from the station, cross the parking plaza and take a right onto Av. de los Mozárabes. When you reach the Roman columns, turn left and cross Gta. Sargentos Provisionales. Take a right on Po. de la Victoria and continue until you reach Puerto Almodóvar and the old city.

To get to the **tourist office**, C. Torrijos 10, from the train station, take bus #3 along the river until a stone arch appears on the right. (☎47 12 35. English spoken. Open May-Sept. M-F 9:30am-7pm, Sa 10am-7pm, Su 10am-2pm; Oct.-Apr. M-F 9:30am-6pm, Su 10am-2pm.) **Banks** and **ATMs** can be found on the streets around the Mezquita and Pl. de las Tendillas. In the old city, **NavegaWeb**, Pl. Judá Leví, has **Internet** access at €1.20 per hr. Enter through the HI youth hostel. (☎29 30 89. Open daily 10am-10pm.) The **post office**, C. Cruz Conde 15, has *Lista de Correos*. (☎47 97 96. Open M-F 8:30am-8:30pm, Sa-Su 9:30am-2pm.) **Postal Code:** 14070.

🖿🗔 ACCOMMODATIONS AND FOOD. Most accommodations cluster around the whitewashed walls of the Judería and in old Córdoba between the Mezquita and C. de San Fernando, a quieter and more residential area. Reserve well in advance of *Semana Santa* and summer. Popular **🛏Residencia Juvenil Córdoba (HI) ❷**, Pl. Judá Leví, is a former mental asylum converted into a backpacker's paradise. There's even an Internet cafe. The large rooms all have A/C and bath. (☎29 01 66. Wheelchair accessible. Breakfast included. Mar.-Oct. dorms €19, under 26 €14. Nov.-Feb. dorms €17, under 26 €12. €3.50 extra per day for nonmembers. MC/V.) **🛏Hostal Bagdad ❷**, C. Fernández Ruano 11, has a serene atmosphere and a teahouse. All rooms have bath. (☎20 28 54.

SPAIN

Córdoba

🏠 ACCOMMODATIONS
Hostal Bagdad, **3**
Hostal El Triunfo, **9**
Residencia Juvenil
   Córdoba (HI), **7**
🍎 FOOD
El Churrasco, **6**
El Picantón, **4**
Taberna Casa Salinas, **5**
★ NIGHTLIFE
La Bulería, **10**
Soul, **2**
Tablao Cardenal, **8**
Velvet, **1**

THE HIDDEN DEAL

HISTORICAL
HYDROTHERAPY

Water was key in medieval Muslim culture: It purified worshippers before prayer, gave a serene ambience to royal courtyards, and was, in the form of Arab baths (*hammam*), a means of washing one's burdens away in a pleasant social atmosphere.

Though most Arab baths were unfortunately abandoned, destroyed, or left to ruin after the *Reconquista*, many around the country have been restored and opened for public usage. the *hammam* of Córdoba, with its gorgeous, rich Moorish decor and gracious service, is certain to charm you. The traditional structure of the Arab bath suggests that you proceed from the dressing room to the cold room, and from there to the temperate and hot rooms. You are, of course, free to experiment with temperature as you see fit. If you feel like pampering yourself further, opt for a professional full-body massage, complete with scented oil. For just a few extra euros, you can enjoy the tea room, complete with soothing music, pastries, and bellydancing.

Hammam Baños Árabes, Medina Caliphal. C. Corregidor Luis de la Cerda 51. ☎*957 48 47 46; www.hammamspain.com/cordoba. Open daily 10am-midnight. Bath €15; bath and massage €22, with student ID €18.50. Reservations required.*

Singles €20; doubles €36; triples €45. MC/V.) Across from the southern side of the Mezquita is **Hostal El Triunfo ❸**, C. Corregidor Luís de la Cerda 79, which offers luxury at reasonable prices. All rooms have A/C, bath, phone, safe, and TV. (☎49 84 84; www.htriunfo.com. Wheelchair accessible. Singles €28-34; doubles €48-60; ask about triples. AmEx/DC/MC/V.)

Cheap eateries cluster in **Barrio Cruz Conde**, around **Avenida Menéndez Pidal** and **Plaza de las Tendillas. El Corte Inglés,** Av. Ronda de los Tejeres 30, has a grocery store. (Open M-Sa 10am-10pm.) The tiny ◨**El Picantón ❶**, C. Fernández Ruano 19, serves tapas (€1-3) in a roll with homemade *salsa picante*. (☎629 58 28 64. Open daily 10am-3:30pm and 8pm-midnight.) ◨**El Churrasco ❸**, C. Romero 16, has a variety of themed dining rooms to complement its extensive menu. (☎29 08 19; www.elchurrasco.com. Entrees €9-20. Open 1-4pm and 8pm-midnight. Closed in Aug. AmEx/DC/MC/V.) Ask for a table on the romantic outdoor patio of **Taberna Casa Salinas ❷**, Puerto de Almodóvar. (☎29 08 46. Entrees €4-10. Open M-Sa 11:30am-4:30pm and 8:30pm-12:30am, Su 11:30am-4:30pm. Closed in Aug.)

◨ **SIGHTS.** Built in AD 784, Córdoba's famous ◨**Mezquita** is considered the most important Islamic monument in the Western Hemisphere. Visitors enter through the **Patio de los Naranjos,** an arcaded courtyard featuring carefully spaced orange trees and fountains; inside the mosque, 850 granite and marble columns support hundreds of striped arches. At the far end of the Mezquita lies the **Capilla Villaviciosa,** where Caliphal vaulting appeared for the first time. In the center, intricate pink-and-blue marble Byzantine mosaics—a gift from Emperor Constantine VII—shimmer across the arches of the *Mihrab* (prayer niche), which is covered in Kufic inscriptions of the 99 names of Allah. Although the town rallied violently against the proposed erection of a **cathedral** in the center of the mosque, after the Crusaders conquered Córdoba in 1236 the towering **crucero** (transept) and **coro** (choir dome) were built. (☎47 05 12. Open July-Oct. daily 10am-7pm; Apr.-June M-Sa 10am-7:30pm, Su 2-7:30pm; Nov.-Mar. daily 10am-6pm. €6.50, under 10 free. Wheelchair accessible. Opens M-Sa 8:30am for 9:30am mass. Su mass 11am, noon, 1pm. Admission free during mass M-Sa 8:30am-10am. Strict silence is enforced.)

The **Judería** is the historic area northwest of the Mezquita. Just past the statue of Maimónides, the small **Sinagoga,** C. Judíos 20, is one of Spain's few remaining synagogues, a solemn reminder of the 1492 expulsion of the Jews. (☎20 29 28. Open M-Sa 9:30am-2pm and 3:30-5:30pm, Su 9:30am-1:30pm. €0.30, EU citizens free.) To the south, along the river on the left side of the Mezquita, is the ◨**Alcázar.** Ferdinand and Isabella bade Columbus *adios* here, and the building later served as Inquisition headquarters. The gardens, open June-Sept. 8pm-midnight, feature two big ponds and beautiful greenery. (☎42 01 51. Open Tu-Sa 10am-2pm and 4:30-6:30pm, Su 9:30am-2:30pm. €2, students €1, F free.) The **Museo Taurino y de Arte Cordobés,** on Pl. Maimónides, highlights the history of the bullfight. (☎20 10 56. Open Tu-Sa 10:30am-2pm and 5:30-7:30pm, Su 9:30am-2pm. €3, students €1.50, F free.) There is a **combined ticket** for the Alcázar, Museo Taurino y de Arte Cordobés, and the **Museo Julio Romero,** which displays Romero's sensual portraits of Córdoban women (€7.10, students €3.60, F free.)

🎭🎶 **ENTERTAINMENT AND NIGHTLIFE.** For the latest cultural events, pick up a free copy of the *Guía del Ocio* at the tourist office. Hordes of tourists flock to see the flamenco dancers at the **Tablao El Cardenal,** C. Torrijos 10, facing the Mezquita. The price is high, but a bargain compared to similar shows in Seville and Madrid. (€18 includes 1 drink. Shows M-Sa 10:30pm.) **La Bulería,** C. Pedro López 3, is even more affordable. (€11 includes 1 drink. Shows daily 10:30pm.) 🎵**Soul,** C. Alfonso XIII 3, has cozy tables and friendly bartenders. (☎49 15 80. Beer €1.50-2.10. Mixed drinks €4.50. Open daily Sept.-June 9am-3am.) **Velvet,** C. Alfaros 29, is a popular retro-style pub. (☎48 60 92. Beer €1.50-2.40. Mixed drinks €4-5. Open in summer 10pm-5am; in winter 5pm-4am.) Starting in June, the **Barrio Brillante,** uphill from Av. América, is packed with young *córdobeses* hopping between dance clubs and outdoor bars. Bus #10 goes to Brillante from the train station until about 11pm, but the bars don't wake up until around 1am; a lift from **Radio Taxi** (☎76 44 44) costs €4-6. If you're walking, head up Av. Brillante; be prepared, however, for the 45min. uphill hike. A string of popular discos runs along Av. Brillante.

Of Córdoba's festivals, floats, and parades, **Semana Santa** (Holy Week; Mar. 20-27 in 2005) is the most extravagant. During the **Festival de las Cruces,** in early May, residents make crosses decorated with flowers. During the **Festival de los Patios** in the first two weeks of May, the city erupts with concerts, flamenco, and a patio-decorating contest. Late May brings the **Feria de Nuestra Señora de Salud** (*La Feria de Córdoba*), a week of colorful garb, dancing, music, and wine-drinking.

SEVILLE (SEVILLA) ☎954

Site of a Roman acropolis, capital of the Moorish empire, focal point of the Spanish Renaissance, and guardian of traditional Andalusian culture, Seville (pop. 700,000) never disappoints. Flamenco, tapas, and bullfighting are at their best here, and Seville's cathedral is among the most impressive in Spain.

🚌 TRANSPORTATION

Flights: All flights arrive at **Aeropuerto San Pablo** (SVQ; ☎44 90 00), 12km out of town on Ctra. Madrid. A taxi ride to the town center costs €15-18. Los Amarillos (☎98 91 84) runs a bus to the airport from outside Hotel Alfonso XIII at Pta. Jerez (1-2 per hr., €2.40). **Iberia,** C. Guadaira 8 (☎22 89 01, nationwide 902 40 05 00; open M-F 9am-1:30pm) books 6 flights per day to **Barcelona** (1hr.) and **Madrid** (45min.).

Trains: Estación Santa Justa (☎902 24 02 02), on Av. de Kansas City. Near Pl. Nueva is the **RENFE** office, C. Zaragoza 29. (☎54 02 02. Open M-F 9am-1:15pm and 4-7pm.) Trains run to: **Barcelona** (10½-13hr., 3 per day, €66); **Cádiz** (2hr., 7-12 per day, €8.50); **Córdoba** (45min.-1½, 16-20 per day, €7-20); **Granada** (3hr., 4 per day, €18); **Madrid** (2½-3½hr., 16-20 per day, €62-65); **Valencia** (9hr., 1 per day, €42).

Buses: The old bus station at **Prado de San Sebastián,** C. Manuel Vázquez Sagastizabal, mainly serves Andalucía. (☎41 71 11. Open daily 5:30am-1am.) **Estación Plaza de Armas** (☎90 80 40) primarily serves areas outside of Andalucía.

Alsa, Estación Plaza de Armas (☎90 78 00 or 902 42 22 42). To: **León** (11hr., 3 per day, €36); **Salamanca** (8hr., 5-6 per day, €25.30); **Valencia** (9-11hr., 3 per day, €40). Under 26 and seniors 10% discount, under 12 50% discount.

Autocares Anibal, Estación Plaza de Armas (☎902 36 00 73). To **Lisbon, Portugal** (6½hr., 1-2 per day, €29). 10% student discount.

Los Amarillos, Estación Prado de San Sebastián (☎98 91 84). To **Arcos de la Frontera** (2hr., 2 per day, €6) and **Ronda** (2½hr., 3-5 per day, €9).

Socibus, Estación Prado de San Sebastián (☎ 902 22 92 92 or 954 90 11 60; fax 90 16 92). To **Madrid** (6hr., 14 per day, €17).

Transportes Alsina Graells, Estación Prado de San Sebastián (☎41 88 11). To: **Córdoba** (2hr., 12-15 per day, €9); **Granada** (3hr., 8 per day, €16); **Málaga** (3hr., 10-12 per day, €14).

Public Transportation: TUSSAM (☎900 71 01 71; www.tussam.es) is the city **bus** network. Most lines run every 10min. (6am-11:15pm) and converge on Pl. Nueva, Pl. Encarnación, or in front of the cathedral. Night service departs from Pl. Nueva (M-Th and Su 1 per hr. midnight-2am, F-Sa 1 per hr. all night). €1, *bonobús* (10 rides) €4.50.

Taxis: TeleTaxi (☎62 22 22); **Radio Taxi** (☎58 00 00). Base rate €1, €0.40 per km, Su 25% surcharge. Extra charge for luggage and night taxis.

■✦ ② ORIENTATION AND PRACTICAL INFORMATION

The **Río Guadalquivir** flows roughly north to south through the city. Most of the touristed areas of Seville, including the **Barrio de Santa Cruz** and **El Arenal,** are on the east bank. The **Barrio de Triana,** the **Barrio de Santa Cecilia, Los Remedios,** and the **Expo '92 fairgrounds** occupy the west bank. **Avenida de la Constitución** runs alongside the **cathedral. El Centro,** a busy commercial pedestrian zone, lies north of the cathedral, starting where Av. Constitución hits **Plaza Nueva,** site of the Ayuntamiento.

Tourist Offices: Centro de Información de Sevilla, Po. de las Delicias 9 (☎23 44 65; www.turismo.sevilla.org), has maps. English spoken. Open M-F 8am-7pm. **Turismo Andaluz,** Av. de la Constitución 21B (☎22 14 04), has info on all of Andalucía. English spoken. Open M-F 9am-7pm, Sa 10am-2pm and 3-7pm, Su 10am-2pm.

Currency Exchange: Santander Central Hispano, C. la Campaña 19 (☎902 24 24 24). Open M-F 8:30am-2pm, Sa 8:30am-1pm. **Banks** and **ATMs** can be found along Av. de la Constitución and near Pl. Nueva.

Laundromat: Lavandería Auto-servicio, C. Castelar 2 (☎21 05 35). Wash and dry €6 per 5kg. Open M-Sa 9:30am-1:30pm and 5-8:30pm.

Medical Assistance: Red Cross (☎913 35 45 45). **Ambulatorio Esperanza Macarena** (☎42 01 05). **Hospital Universitario Virgen Macarena** (☎24 81 81), Av. Dr. Fedriani.

Internet Access: Seville Internet Center, C. Almirantazgo 2, 2nd fl. (☎50 02 75). €3 per hr., €1.80 per hr. with prepaid cards. Open M-F 9am-10pm, Sa-Su 10am-10pm.

Post Office: Av. Constitución 32 (☎21 64 76), opposite the cathedral. *Lista de Correos* and fax. Open M-F 10am-8:30pm, Sa 8:30am-2pm. **Postal Code:** 41080.

▐ ACCOMMODATIONS

Rooms vanish and prices soar during *Semana Santa* and the *Feria de Abril;* reserve ahead. The streets east of the cathedral around **Calle Santa María la Blanca** are full of cheap, centrally located hostels. Hostels by the **Plaza de Armas** bus station are convenient for visits to **El Centro** and the lively **Calle Betis** across the river.

▧ **Pensión Vergara,** C. Ximénez de Enciso 11, 2nd fl. (☎21 56 68). Beautiful rooms of varying size. Singles, doubles, triples, and quads available. €20 per person. Cash only. ❷

▧ **Airesevilla,** C. Aire (☎500 905; www.airesevilla-gay.com). This gorgeous gay guest house merges old Andalusian styles with refreshing modern art. Singles €35-45; doubles €55-75. Prices vary with season. MC/V. ❹

Hostal Macarena, C. San Luis 91 (☎37 01 41). Homey hostel in a quieter area. All rooms with A/C. Singles €20; doubles €30, with bath €36; triples €51. MC/V. ❷

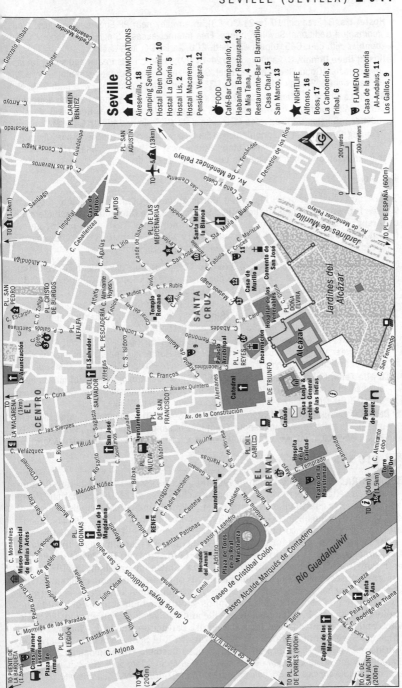

Seville

▲ ACCOMMODATIONS
Airesevilla, 18
Camping Sevilla, 7
Hostal Buen Dormir, 10
Hostal La Gloria, 5
Hostal Lis, 2
Hostal Macarena, 1
Pensión Vergara, 12

◆ FOOD
Café-Bar Campanario, 14
Habanita Bar Restaurant, 3
La Mia Tana, 4
Restaurante-Bar El Barratillo/
Casa Chari, 15
San Marco, 13

★ NIGHTLIFE
Alfonso, 16
Boss, 17
La Carbonería, 8
Tribal, 6

◐ FLAMENCO
Casa de la Memoria
Al-Andalus, 11
Los Gallos, 9

SPAIN

Hostal Lis, C. Escarpín 10 (☎21 30 88), in an alley near Pl. Encarnación. Cozy, tiled rooms in a traditional Sevillian house. Free Internet access. Singles with shower €24; doubles with bath €45; triples with bath €66. AmEx/DC/MC/V. ❷

Hostal Buen Dormir, C. Farnesio 8 (☎21 74 92). Quilted bedspreads and sunny rooms make Hostal "Good Sleep" a great deal. Singles have fans. Doubles and triples have A/C. Laundry €6. Singles €18; doubles €35; triples with shower €50, with bath €55. ❷

Hostal La Gloria, C. San Eloy 58, 2nd fl. (☎22 26 73), at the end of a lively shopping street. Airy rooms. The lively owner will make you feel at home. Reserve 3 days in advance. Singles €20; doubles €30, with bath €36; limited triples €45. ❷

Camping Sevilla, Ctra. Madrid-Cádiz km 534 (☎51 43 79), near the airport. From Pr. San Sebastián, take bus #70 (stops 800m away at Parque Alcosa). Hot showers, supermarket, and pool. One-person tent €6.42, car €7. ❶

🍴 FOOD

Tapas bars cluster around **Plaza San Martín** and along **Calle San Jacinto.** Popular venues for *el tapeo* (tapas barhopping) are **Barrio Santa Cruz** and **El Arenal. Mercado del Arenal,** near the bullring on C. Pastor y Leandro, has fresh meat and produce. (Open M-Sa 9am-2pm.) For a supermarket, try **%Día,** C. San Juan de Ávila, near El Corte Inglés. (Open M-F 9:30am-2pm and 6:30-9pm, Sa 9am-1pm.)

🍴 **Habanita Bar Restaurant,** C. Golfo 3 (☎606 71 64 56), on a tiny street off C. Perez Galdos, next to Pl. Alfalfa. Exquisite Cuban fare. Entrees €4.80-10. Open daily 12:30-4:30pm and 8pm-12:30am. Closed Su evenings. MC/V. ❶

🍴 **San Marco,** C. Mesón del Moro 6 (☎21 43 90), in Santa Cruz's *casco antiguo.* Amazing pizzas, pastas, and desserts in an 18th-century house with 17th-century Arab baths. Entrees €5-10. Open Tu-Su 1:15-4:30pm and 8:15pm-12:30am. AmEx/DC/MC/V. ❷

Restaurante-Bar El Baratillo/Casa Chari, C. Pavía 12 (☎22 96 51), off C. Dos de Mayo. Order 1hr. in advance for the *tour-de-force:* Homemade paella with a jar of wine, beer, or sangria (€18 serves 2). *Menú* €4-9. Open M-F 10am-10pm, Sa 10am-5pm. ❷

La Mia Tana, C. Pérez Galdós 24 (☎22 68 97). This charming restaurant makes even pizza seem romantic, as evidenced by the multitudes of couples. Pizzas €4-12. Pastas €4.10-4.60. Open daily 1-4:30pm and 8pm-1am. DC/MC/V. ❶

Café-Bar Campanario, C. Mateos Gago 8 (☎56 41 89), near the cathedral. Modern cafe-bar is quite vegetarian-friendly. Great jugs of sangria (half-liter €7.30, 1L €9.70). Tapas €1-2.40. *Raciones* €6.40-9.60. Open daily noon-midnight. AmEx/DC/MC/V. ❷

👁 SIGHTS

🏛 **CATEDRAL.** Legend has it that in 1401 the *Reconquistadores* wished to demonstrate their religious fervor by constructing a church so great, they said, that "those who come after us will take us for madmen." With 44 individual chapels, the cathedral of Seville is the biggest Gothic edifice ever constructed. Not surprisingly, it took more than a century to build. In 1401, a 12th-century Almohad mosque was destroyed to clear space for the massive cathedral. All that remains is the **Patio de Los Naranjos,** where the faithful would wash before prayer; the **Puerta del Perdón** entryway from C. Alemanes; and the famed **La Giralda** minaret built in 1198. In the center of the cathedral, the **Capilla Real** stands opposite mahogany **choir stalls.** The **retablo mayor** is a golden wall of intricately wrought saints and disciples. Nearby is the **Sepulcro de Cristóbal Colón** (Columbus's tomb), which supposedly holds the explorer's remains, brought back to Seville after Cuba's independence in 1902 (the tomb had been located in Havana's cathedral). Farther on stands the **Sacristía Mayor** (treasury), which holds gilded panels of Alfonso X el Sabio, works by Ribera and Murillo, and a glittering Corpus Christi icon, **La Custodia Processional.** (☎21 49 71. *Entrance by the Pl. de la Virgen de los Reyes. Open M-Sa 11am-5pm, Su 2:30-6pm. Last entrance 1hr. before closing. €6, seniors and students €1.50, under 12 and Su free.)*

ALCÁZAR. The oldest European palace still used as a private residence for royals, Seville's Alcázar is nothing short of magnificent. Though the Alhambra in Granada gets more press, Seville's Alcázar features equally impressive architecture. Built by the Moors in the 7th century, the palace was embellished greatly during the 15th century and now displays an interesting mix of Moorish and Christian architecture. The *Reyes Católicos* (Catholic Monarchs) Ferdinand and Isabella are the palace's most well-known former residents; their grandson Carlos V also lived here and married his cousin Isabella of Portugal in the **Salón Carlos V.**

Visitors enter through the **Patio de la Montería,** directly across from the Moorish palace. Through the archway lie the Arabic residences, including the **Patio del Yeso** and the **Patio de las Muñecas** (Patio of the Dolls), so named because of miniature faces carved into the bottom of one of the room's pillars. Of the Christian additions, the most notable is the **Patio de las Doncellas** (Patio of the Maids). Court life in the Alcázar revolved around this colonnaded quadrangle, which is adorned with tilework. The golden-domed **Salón de los Embajadores** (Embassadors' Room) is allegedly the site where Ferdinand and Isabella welcomed Columbus back from the New World. Prince Juan, their son, was born in the red-and-blue tiled **Cuarto del Príncipe;** the room was named for him after his untimely death.

The upstairs **private residences,** the official home of the king and queen of Spain and their accommodations when they visit Seville, have been renovated and redecorated throughout the centuries; most of the furniture today dates from the 18th and 19th centuries. These residences are accessible only by 25min. guided tours (see info below). Peaceful **gardens** stretch in all directions from the residential quarters. *(Pl. del Triunfo 7. ☎50 23 23. Open Tu-Sa 9:30am-7pm, Su 9:30am-5pm. €5; handicapped, residents, students, over 65, and under 16 free. Tours of the upper palace living quarters every 30min. June-July 10am-1:30pm; Aug.-May 10am-1:30pm and 3:30-5:30pm; €3. 15 people max. per tour, so buy tickets in advance.)*

CASA DE PILATOS. Inhabited continuously by Spanish aristocrats since the 15th century, this large private residence has only recently been opened to the public. On the ground floor, Roman artifacts and tropical gardens coexist in Mudéjar patios. The second floor features rooms decorated with oil portraits, sculptures, painted ceilings, and tapestries. *(Pl. Pilatos 1. ☎22 52 98. Open daily 9am-7pm. €5 ground level only, €8 ground level and upper chambers. Guided tours every 30min. 10am-6:30pm.)*

MUSEO PROVINCIAL DE BELLAS ARTES. This museum contains Spain's finest collection of works by painters of the *Sevillana* School (most notably Murillo), as well as El Greco and Dutch master Jan Breughel. Although the art (displayed more or less chronologically) is biased toward religious themes, later works include some landscapes and portraits depicting Seville, its environs, and residents. The building itself is a work of art; take time to sit in one of its courtyards. *(Pl. del Museo 9. ☎22 07 90. Open Tu 3-8pm, W-Sa 9am-8pm, Su 9am-2pm. €1.50, EU citizens free.)*

PLAZA DE TOROS DE LA REAL MAESTRANZA. Home to one of the two great bullfighting schools (the other is in Ronda, p. 951), Plaza de Toros de la Real Maestranza fills to capacity (13,800) for weekly fights and the 13 *corridas* of the *Feria de Abril.* Multilingual tours take visitors through the small but informative Museo Taurino de la Real Maestranza, as well as behind the ring to the chapel where *matadores* pray before fights and the medical emergency room used when their prayers go unanswered. *(☎22 45 77. Open non-bullfight days 9:30am-7pm, bullfight days 9:30am-3pm. Mandatory tours in English and Spanish every 20min., €4.)*

♫ ENTERTAINMENT

The tourist office distributes *El Giraldillo,* a free monthly magazine with complete listings on music, art exhibits, theater, dance, fairs, and film. It can also be found online at www.elgiraldillo.es.

FLAMENCO

Flamenco, originally brought to Spain by the Roma (Gypsies), is at its best in Seville. Traditionally consisting of dance, guitar, and song, it expresses the passion and soul of the region. Flamenco can be seen either in *tablaos*, where skilled professional dancers perform, or in *tabernas*, bars where locals dance *sevillanas*. Both have merit, but the *tabernas* tend to be free. The tourist office provides a complete list of both *tablaos* and *tabernas*. Small, intimate **Los Gallos**, Pl. Santa Cruz 11, is probably the best tourist show in Seville. (☎21 69 81. Shows daily 9 and 11:30pm. Cover €27, includes 1 drink.) Less expensive alternatives are the impressive one-hour shows at the cultural center ⬛**Casa de la Memoria Al-Andalus**, C. Ximénez de Enciso 28. Ask at the tourist office or swing by their ticket office for a schedule of different themed performances. (☎/fax 56 06 70. Flamenco shows daily at 9pm. Very limited seating, so buy tickets in advance. €11, students €9.)

BULLFIGHTING

Seville's bullring, one of the most beautiful in Spain, hosts bullfights from *Semana Santa* through October. The cheapest place to buy tickets is at the ring on Po. Alcalde Marqués de Contadero. However, when there's a good *cartel* (line-up), the booths on C. las Sierpes, C. Velázquez, and Pl. de Toros might be the only source of advance tickets. Ticket prices can run from €18 for a *grada de sol* (nosebleed seat in the sun) to €75 for a *barrera de sombra* (front-row seat in the shade). *Corridas de toros* (professional bullfights) and *novilladas* (bullfights featuring apprentice bullfighters and younger bulls) are held around the *Feria de Abril* and into May, every Sunday April-June and September-October, and during the *Feria de San Miguel* near the end of September. During July and August, *corridas* occur on occasional Thursdays at 9pm; check posters around town. (For current info and ticket sales, call ☎50 13 82.) If you're interested in bullfighting, check out our **featured itinerary** for Spain and Portugal (p. 918).

✿ FESTIVALS

If you're in Spain during any of the major festivals, head straight to Seville—you won't regret it (if you can remember it, that is). Reserve a room a few months in advance, and expect to pay up to two or three times the normal rate.

⬛**SEMANA SANTA.** Seville's world-famous *Semana Santa* lasts from Palm Sunday to Easter Sunday (Mar. 20-27 in 2005). In each neighborhood of the city, thousands of penitents in hooded cassocks guide *pasos* (stunning, extravagant floats) through the streets, illuminated by hundreds of candles. The climax is on Good Friday, when the entire city turns out for the procession along the bridges and through the oldest neighborhoods. The tourist office has a helpful booklet on where to eat and sleep during the week's festivities.

⬛**FERIA DE ABRIL.** Two or three weeks after *Semana Santa*, the city rewards itself for its Lenten piety with the *Feria de Abril* (Apr. 12-27 in 2005). Circuses, bullfights, and flamenco performances showcase local customs and camaraderie. A spectacular array of flowers and lanterns decorates over 1000 kiosks, tents, and pavilions, collectively called *casetas*. Locals stroll from one to the next, sharing drinks and food amid the music and dance. The city holds bullfights daily during the festival; buy tickets in advance. *(The fairgrounds are on the southern end of Los Remedios.)*

◗ NIGHTLIFE

Popular bars can be found around **Calle Mateos Gago** near the cathedral, **Calle Adriano** by the bullring, and **Calle Betis** across the river in Triana.

▨ **La Carbonería**, C. Levies 18, off C. Santa María La Blanca. Guitar-strumming Romeos abound on the huge outdoor patio. Tapas €1.50-2. Beer €1.50. Mixed drinks €5. Open July-Aug. M-Sa 8pm-4am, Su 8pm-2:30am; Sept.-May M-Sa 8pm-4am, Su 7pm-3am.

▨ **Boss**, C. Betis. Sensual, irresistible beats and hazy blue lights make this a wildly popular destination. Beer €3.50. Mixed drinks €6. Open daily 9pm-5am. MC/V.

Tribal, Av. de los Descubrimientos, next to Pte. de la Barqueta. Popular *discoteca* plays American hip-hop and Latin favorites. Drinks €5-10. Open W-Sa midnight-6am.

Alfonso, Av. la Palmera (☎23 37 35). Spacious outdoor club. Beer €1.50. Mixed drinks €4.50-6. Open M-Th and Su 10pm-5am, F-Sa 10pm-7am. AmEx/DC/MC/V.

▶ DAYTRIPS FROM SEVILLE

CÁDIZ

RENFE trains (☎956 25 43 01) run to the station at Pl. de Sevilla from Seville. 2hr., 12 per day, €8.50-20. Transportes Generales Comes buses (☎956 22 78 11) arrive at Pl. de la Hispanidad 1 from Seville. (2hr., 14 per day, €9.72.)

Founded by the Phoenicians in 1100 BC, Cádiz (pop. 155,000) is thought to be the oldest inhabited city in Europe. **Carnaval** is perhaps Spain's most dazzling party (Feb. 4-13 in 2005), but year-round Cádiz offers golden sand **beaches. Playa de la Caleta** is the most convenient beach to the old city, but better sand awaits in the new city; take bus #1 from Pl. España to Pl. Glorieta Ingeniero (€0.80), or walk along the *paseo* by the water (20-30min. from behind the Cathedral) to reach ▨**Playa de la Victoria**, whose clean expanse of gorgeous sand has made it a local favorite. Back in town is the gold-domed, 18th-century **cathedral**, on Pl. de la Catedral. (☎956 28 61 64. Open Tu-F 10am-1:30pm and 4:30-7:30pm, Sa 10am-1:30pm. €3, children €2.) To get to the **tourist office**, Pl. San Juan de Dios 11, from the bus station, walk 5min. down Av. Puerto with the port on your left; the plaza is after the park on the right. (☎956 24 10 01. Open M-F 9am-2pm and 5-8pm.)

ARCOS DE LA FRONTERA

Buses (☎956 70 49 77) run from C. Corregidores to: Cádiz (1½hr., 6 per day, €4.75); Ronda (1¾hr., 3 per day, €6); and Seville (2hr., 7am and 5pm, €6.30). From Seville, Los Amarillos (☎954 98 91 84) sends buses to Arcos (2hr., 8am and 4:30pm, €15).

One of Spain's *pueblos blancos*, Arcos (pop. 33,000) is a historic and romantic gem. Wander the winding alleys of ruins and hanging flowers in the **old quartor** and marvel at the view from ▨**Plaza Cabildo**. In the square is the **Basilica de Santa María de la Asunción**, built in a mix of architectural styles. (Open M-F 10am-1pm and 3:30-6:30pm, Sa 10am-2pm. €1.50.) The late Gothic **Iglesia de San Pedro** stands on the site of an Arab fortress in the old quarter. A collection of religious paintings by Murillo, Ribera, and Zurbarán decorates the interior. (Open M-Sa 10am-1:30pm, Su 10am-1:30pm. €1.) To reach the old quarter from the bus station, exit left, follow the road, turn left, and continue uphill on C. Josefa Moreno Seguro. Take a right on C. Muñoz Vásquez, continue until reaching Pl. de España, then veer left onto C. Debajo del Coral, which becomes C. Corredera; the old quarter is 500m ahead. **Minibuses** run every 30min. from the bus station to C. Corredera (€1). The **tourist office** is on Pl. del Cabildo. (☎956 70 22 64. Open mid-Mar. to mid-Oct. M-Sa 10am-2pm and 4-8pm; mid-Oct. to mid-Mar. M-Sa 10am-2pm and 3:30-7:30pm.) Cheap cafes and tapas bars cluster along **Calle Corredera**.

RONDA

Trains (☎902 24 02 02) depart from Av. Alférez Provisional for Granada (3hr., 3 per day, €11) and Madrid (4½hr., 2 per day, €40-49). Buses (☎952 18 70 61) go from Pl. Concepción García Redondo 2, near Av. Andalucía, to: Cádiz (4hr., 3 per day, €11.80) and Seville (2½hr., 3-5 per day, €9.30). From Seville's Estación Prado de San Sebastián, Los Amarillos sends buses to Ronda (2½hr., 3-5 per day, €9).

Picturesque Ronda (pop. 35,000) has all the charm of a small, medieval town with the amenities and cultural opportunities of a thriving city. Ancient bridges, pretty views, old dungeons, and the famed bullring attract many visitors to Ronda. A precipitous 100m gorge, carved by the Río Guadalevín, dips below the **Puente Nuevo,** opposite Pl. España. The views from the Puente Nuevo, and its neighboring **Puente Viejo** and **Puente San Miguel,** are unparalleled. Descend the steep stairs of the ▓**Casa Del Rey Moro** into the 14th-century water mine for an otherworldly view of the river ravine. (Cuesta de Santo Domingo 17. Take the first left after crossing the Puente Nuevo. ☎952 18 72 00. Open daily in summer 10am-8pm; in winter 10am-7pm. €4, children €2.) Bullfighting aficionados charge over to Ronda's ▓**Plaza de Toros,** Spain's oldest bullring (est. 1785) and cradle of the modern *corrida.* In early September, the Plaza de Toros hosts *corridas goyescas* (bullfights in traditional costumes) as part of the **Feria de Ronda.** The town fills to capacity—book rooms months in advance. (☎952 87 15 39; www.rmcr.org. Open daily Apr. 16-Oct. 10am-8pm; Nov.-Feb. 10am-6pm; Mar.-Apr. 15 10am-7pm. €5.) The **tourist office** is at Po. Blas Infante, across from the bullring. (☎952 18 71 19; www.turismoronda.es. Open June-Aug. M-F 9:30am-7:30pm, Sa-Su 10am-2pm and 3:30-6:30pm; Sept.-May M-F 9:30am-6:30pm, Sa-Su 10am-2pm and 3:30-6:30pm. English spoken.)

GIBRALTAR

From the morning mist just off the southern shore of Spain emerges the Rock of Gibraltar. Bastion of empire and Jerusalem of Anglophilia, this rocky peninsula is among history's most contested plots of land. After numerous squabbles between Moors, Spaniards, and Turks, the English successfully stormed Gibraltar in 1704 and have remained in possession ever since.

PHONE CODES	☎350 from the UK or the US. ☎9567 from Spain.

▉▊ TRANSPORTATION AND PRACTICAL INFORMATION. Buses arrive in the Spanish border town of **La Línea** from: Algeciras (40min., every 30min., €1.60); Cádiz (3hr., 4 per day, €10.20); Granada (5hr., 2 per day, €18); Madrid (7hr., 2 per day, €23); and Seville (6hr., 3 per day, €19). Turner & Co., 65/67 Irish Town St. (☎783 05; fax 720 06), runs **ferries** to Tangier, Morocco (1¼hr.; 1 per day; ₤18/€32, under 12 ₤9/€16.20). Gibraltar's **airport** (GIB; ☎730 26) also sends daily 20min. flights to Morocco (p. 737). From the bus station, walk toward the Rock; the border is 5min. away. Catch bus #9 or 10 (₤0.60/€1) or walk across the airport tarmac into town (20min.). Stay left on Av. Winston Churchill when the road forks. The **tourist office** is at Duke of Kent House, Cathedral Sq. (☎450 00; www.gibraltar.gi. Open M-F 9am-5:30pm, Sa 10am-3pm, Su 10am-1pm.) Though **euros** are accepted almost everywhere (except pay phones and public establishments), the **pound sterling (£)** is preferred. Merchants sometimes charge a higher price in euros than in the pound's exchange equivalent. As of press date, **£1 = €1.48.**

▐▌ ACCOMMODATIONS AND FOOD. Gibraltar is best seen as a daytrip. Its few accommodations are pricey and often full. **Emile Youth Hostel Gibraltar ❷,** Montague Bastian, has clean shared bathrooms. (☎511 06. Breakfast included. Lockout 10:30am-4:30pm. Dorms and singles ₤15/€25; doubles ₤30/€50.) La Línea, across the border, may be a cheaper place to stay. Restaurants are easy to find, but you may choke on the prices. Buy groceries at the **Checkout** on Main St., next to Marks & Spencer. (Open M-F 8:30am-8pm, Sa 10am-6pm, Su 1am-3pm. MC/V.)

◧ SIGHTS. No trip to Gibraltar is complete without a visit to the legendary **Rock.** About halfway up the Rock is the infamous **Apes' Den,** where Barbary Macaques cavort on the sides of rocks, the tops of taxis, and the heads of tourists. At the northern tip of the Rock facing Spain are the **Great Siege Tunnels.** Originally used to fend off a combined Franco-Spanish siege at the end of the American Revolution, the underground tunnels were later expanded during WWII to span 33 miles. The eerie chambers of **St. Michael's Cave,** located 500m from the siege tunnels, were cut into the rock by thousands of years of water erosion. At the southern tip of Gibraltar, guarded by three machine guns and a lighthouse, **Europa Point** commands a view of the straits; the lighthouse can be seen from 37km away at sea. (Cable car to above sights daily every 10min. 9:30am-5:15pm. Combined admittance ticket, including one-way cable car ride, £14.50/€21.50.)

ALGECIRAS   ☎956

Algeciras (pop. 101,000) is a city best seen only in transit, as its concrete wharfs and gray high-rises don't make for thrilling sightseeing. RENFE **trains** (☎902 24 02 02) run from C. Juan de la Cierva to Granada (4hr., 3 per day, €16) and Ronda (1½hr., 4 per day, €5.80). Daibus (☎65 34 56) sends **buses** from C. San Bernardo 1 to Madrid (9hr., 4 per day, €24) via La Línea (every 30min.). Empresa Portillo buses (☎65 43 04) leave from Av. Virgen del Carmen 15 for: Córdoba (6hr., 2 per day, €21); and Granada (4hr., 5 per day, €18). Transportes Generales Comes (☎65 34 56) goes from C. San Bernardo 1 to Cádiz (2½hr., 10 per day, €9). To reach the **ferries** from either station, follow C. San Bernardo to C. Juan de la Cierva and turn left at its end. The **tourist office** is on C. Juan de la Cierva. (☎57 26 36. Open M-F 9am-2pm.) Clean rooms, all with bath, can be found at **Hostal Residencia Versailles ❷**, C. Montero Rios 12, off C. Cayetano del Toro. (☎/fax 65 42 11. Singles €15; doubles €24-27. Prices vary with season.) A **supermarket** is on the corner of C. José Santacana and C. Maroto. (Open daily 9am-2pm and 5-8pm.) **Postal Code:** 11203.

COSTA DEL SOL

The Costa del Sol mixes rocky beaches with chic promenades and swank hotels. While some spots have been over-developed and can be hard on the wallet, the coast's stunning natural beauty has elsewhere been left untouched.

MÁLAGA   ☎952

Once celebrated by Hans Christian Andersen, Málaga (pop. 550,000) is the largest Andalusian city on the coast and the birthplace of Pablo Picasso. Today this transportation hub offers a charming *casco antiguo* (old city) and beautiful nearby beaches like the whitewashed Nerja. (Buses run from Málaga, 1hr., approx. every 45min., €3.05.) The ▓Alcazaba exudes a medieval tranquility and offers views of the harbor. (Open June-Aug. Tu-Su 9:30am-8pm; Sept.-May Tu-Sa 8:30am-7pm. €1.80, students €0.60, children under 7 free.) Chronologically arranged exhibitions at the **Museo Picasso,** C. San Agustín 8, allow visitors to observe the evolution of the artist's style. (☎902 44 33 77. Open Tu-Th and Su 10am-8pm, F-Sa 10am-9pm. €6, students and children 10-16 €3, children under 10 free.)

Buses run from Po. de los Tilos (☎31 82 95), one block from the RENFE station along C. Roger de Flor, to: Cádiz (5hr., 5 per day, €18); Córdoba (3hr., 5 per day, €11); Granada (2hr., 17 per day, €8.04); Madrid (7hr., 12 per day, €18); and Seville (3hr., 11-12 per day, €13.03). To get to the city center from the bus station, exit right onto Callejones del Perchel, walk straight through the big intersection, take a right on Av. de Andalucía, and cross Puente de Tetuán. From here, Alameda Principal leads into Pl. de la Marina, where the **tourist office** is located. (☎12 20 20. Open M-F 9am-7pm.) **Pensión Córdoba ❷** is delightfully unpretentious and offers clean and simple rooms; some even have tiny terraces. (☎21 44 69. Singles €19; doubles €36; triples €54.) Vegetarian ▓Restaurante Cañadú ❶, Pl. de la Merced 21, features a heavenly four-course *menú* that changes daily. (☎22 90 56; www.cuidate.com/canadu. Open M-Th and Su 1:30-4pm and 8-11pm, F-Sa 1:30-4pm and 8pm-midnight. Closed Tu evening. AmEx/MC/V.) **Postal Code:** 29080

GRANADA
☎958

Legend says that in 1492, when Moorish ruler Boabdil fled Granada (pop. 240,000), the last Muslim stronghold in Spain, his mother berated him for casting a longing look back at the Alhambra. "You do well to weep as a woman," she told him, "for what you could not defend as a man." A spectacular palace celebrated by poets and artists throughout the ages, the Alhambra continues to inspire melancholy in those who must leave its timeless beauty. The Albaicín, an enchanting maze of Moorish houses and twisting alleys, is Spain's best-preserved Arab quarter and the only part of the Muslim city to survive the *Reconquista*. Since then, Granada has grown into a university city and tourist destination infused with the energy brought by crowds of international students, backpackers, and Andalusian youth.

▐ TRANSPORTATION

Trains: RENFE Station, Av. Andaluces (☎902 24 02 02; www.renfe.es). To: **Algeciras** (5-7hr., 3 per day, €16); **Barcelona** (12-13hr., 1-2 per day, €49); **Madrid** (5-6hr., 2 per day, €28-44); **Seville** (4-5hr., 4 per day, €17).

Buses: The **bus station** is on the outskirts of Granada on Ctra. Madrid, near C. Arzobispo Pedro de Castro. **Alsa** (☎902 42 22 42) goes to: **Alicante** (6hr., 6 per day, €24); **Barcelona** (14hr., 6 per day, €58.12); **Valencia** (10hr., 6 per day, €36). **Alsina Graells** (☎18 54 80) runs to: **Algeciras** (5hr., 4 per day, €18); **Córdoba** (3hr., 7 per day, €11); **Madrid** (5hr., 10 per day, €13); **Seville** (3hr., 7 per day, €17).

Public Transportation: From the bus station take bus #10 to the youth hostel, C. de Ronda, C. Recogidas, or C. Acera de Darro; or take bus #3 to Av. Constitución, Gran Vía, or Pl. de Isabel la Católica. From Pl. Nueva catch #30 to the Alhambra or #31 to the Albaicín. Rides €0.85, *bonobús* (10 tickets) €5.02. Free map at tourist office.

▟ ▐ ORIENTATION AND PRACTICAL INFORMATION

The geographic center of Granada is the small **Plaza de Isabel la Católica,** at the intersection of the city's two main arteries, **Calle de los Reyes Católicos** and **Gran Vía de Colón.** The **cathedral** is on Gran Vía. Two blocks uphill on C. Reyes Católicos sits **Plaza Nueva.** Downhill on C. Reyes Católicos lies Pl. Carmen, site of the **Ayuntamiento** and **Puerta Real.** The **Alhambra** commands the steep hill above Pl. Nueva.

Tourist Office: Oficina Provincial, Pl. Mariana Pineda 10 (☎24 71 28; www.turismode-granada.org). From Pta. Real, turn right onto C. Angel Ganivet, then take a right 2 blocks later to reach the plaza. Open M-F 9am-8pm, Sa 10am-7pm, Su 10am-4pm.

Laundromat: C. Paz 19. Wash €5, dry €1 per 15min. Open M-F 10am-2pm and 5-8pm.

Police: C. Duquesa 21 (☎80 80 00). English spoken.

Medical Assistance: Clínica de San Cecilio, C. Dr. Olóriz 16 (☎28 02 00 or 27 20 00), on the road to Jaén. **Ambulance** (☎28 44 50).

Internet Access: Net (☎22 69 19) has 2 locations: Pl. de los Girones 3, up C. Pavaneras from Pl. de Isabel la Católica; and C. Buensucesco 22, 1 block from Pl. Trinidad. €0.75-1 per hr. Both open M-F 9am-11pm, Sa-Su 10am-11pm.

Post Office: Pta. Real (☎22 48 35). *Lista de Correos* and fax service. Wires money M-F 8:30am-2:30pm. Open M-F 8am-9pm, Sa 9:30am-2pm. **Postal Code:** 18009.

▐ ACCOMMODATIONS

▨ **Hospedaje Almohada,** C. Postigo de Zarate 4 (☎20 74 46; www.hospetajealmo-hada.com). A successful experiment in communal living. Laundry €3. Dorms €14; singles €16; doubles €30; triples €40. ❶

▨ **Hostal Venecia,** Cuesta de Gomérez 2, 3rd fl. (☎22 39 87). Wake up to a soothing cup of tea and a hint of incense. Singles €15; doubles €26; triples €39; quads €52. ❷

Granada

ACCOMMODATIONS
Albergue Juvenil
Granada (HI), **15**
Hospedaje Almohada, **12**
Hostal Antares, **5**
Hostal Austria, **9**
Hostal Residencia Britz, **7**
Hostal Venecia, **8**

FOOD
Botánico Café, **14**
El Ladrillo II, **1**
Naturi Albaicín, **3**
Restaurante Asador
Corrala del Carbón, **13**
Restaurant Sonymar, **10**
Samarcanda, **6**

★ **NIGHTLIFE**
Fondo Reservado, **2**
Granero, **11**
Kasbah, **4**
Planta Baja, **16**

TO SACROMONTE

ALHAMBRA

Puerta de las
Granadas

PL. DEL
REALEJO

Cta. Realejo

C. de Sagrta

C. Solare

C. Serie Lucena

Paseo de la Bomba

Humilladero

paseo de la bomba

San Domingo

PL. MARIANA
PINEDA

C. Ángel Gavinet

C. Varela

PL. STA.
ESCOLÁSTICA

C. Sta.
Escolástica

TO EL CORTE INGLÉS/
SUPERMERCADO T. MARISCAL (20m)

PL.
PADRE
SUÁREZ

PL. ISABEL
LA CATÓLICA

C. del Carmen

C. San Matías

PL.
CARMEN

C. Pavaneras

Corral del Carbón

C. Mariana
Pineda

Museo
Arqueológico

Carrera del Darro

Río Darro

Arab Baths

Santa Ana

H. Santa
Ana

PL.
SANTA
ANA

Cuesta de Gomérez

Real
Cancillería

C. San Juan de los Reyes

PLAZA
NUEVA

C. de los Reyes Católicos

Palacio
de la
Madraza

AmEx

Almirecaros

Cuesta de Sta. Inés

Ctra. Chapiz

Pso. Padre Manjón

Mirador de
San Nicolás

San
Nicolás

ALBAICÍN

PL.
LARGA

Horno San
Agustín

C. Nuevo S. Nicolás

Cuesta de Sta. Inés

C. Ayuntamiento

Ctra. Algibe Trillo

Cárcel Alta

Monasterio Santa
Isabel la Real

Walls of the Albaicín

Mirador de
San Cristóbal

Walls of
the Albaicín

Cta. Ma. de la Miel

PL. SAN
MIGUEL

Gallo BAJO

Tiña

Cta. Gitana

Aljibe de
la Gitana

Pita Minas

Gijón

San Gregorio

San Cecilio

Cta. Marañas

Cárcel Baja

Catedral

PL. DE
Alonso Cano Capilla Real

Palacio de la
Alonso Cano Capilla Real

Puerta
Real

Real

PL.
BIB-RAMBLA

PL.
TRINIDAD

TO C. BUENSUCESO

C. de los Mesones

C. Postigo
de Zarate

C. San Jerónimo

C. Marqués de Falces

C. de Elvira

Cta. Bajeta Caldereta

Cta. Bateta

Álvaro de Bazán

Arteaga

Santa Paula

Arandas

PL.
UNIVERSIDAD

Santos Justo
y Pastor

Universidad

C. Duquesa

PL.
LOBOS

C. Málaga

Cárcel Baja

C. San Jerónimo

TO C. PEDRO ANTONIO
DE ALARCÓN (150m)

TO C. GRAN CAPITÁN

Gran Vía de Colón

PL.
TRIUNFO

C. de Elvira

Cuesta Alhacaba

Cuesta Alhacaba

Carril Zenete

Darro

PL.
BOQUERO

C. la Tinajilla

Basílica San
Juan de Dios

Av. Capitán
Moreno

Av. Hospicio

Hospital
Real

Murcia

Ctra.

C. Real de Cartuja

C. Parra Alta de Cartuja

C. Agua

C. del Cristo de la Yedra

Av. de Madrid

Av. de Ancha de Capuchinos

PL. SAN
ISIDRO

Paseo de la Cartuja

Av. de Murcia

Av. de Pulianas

TO
(750m)

C. San Juan de Dios

San Jerónimo

C. Santa Bárbara

C. Gran Capitán

C. Rector López Argüeta

Av. Fuente
Nueva

C. Doctor Severo Ochoa

CAMPUS
UNIVERSITARIO

Av. de la Constitución

Av. de Madrid

Av. Andaluces

RENFE

Av. Doctor
Oloriz

TO
(1.5km)

200 yards
200 meters

TO LAUNDROMAT
(300m)

TO
JUVENUS (300m)

TO
(150m)

TO
(300m)

SPAIN

Hostal Antares, C. Cetti Meriém 10 (☎22 83 13). Large, bright, and spotless rooms, some with A/C and TV. Singles €18; doubles €28, with bath €36. ❷

Hostal Austria, Cuesta de Gomérez 4 (☎22 70 75). Delightful, spacious rooms. Singles €25; doubles €28, with bath €36. ❷

Hostal Residencia Britz, Cuesta de Gomérez 1 (☎22 36 52). Spacious, clean rooms. Reception 24hr. Singles €19; doubles €29, with bath €42. MC/V. ❷

Albergue Juvenil Granada (HI), C. de Ramón y Cajal 2 (☎00 29 00). From the bus station take #10; from the train station, take #11; ask the driver to stop at "El Estadio de la Juventud." Dorms €14-16, under 26 €10-12. Nonmembers add €3.50. ❶

FOOD

Cheap North African cuisine can be found around the Albaicín, while more typical *menú* fare awaits in Pl. Nueva and Pl. Trinidad. Get groceries at **Supermercado T. Mariscal,** on C. Genil. (Open M-F 9:30am-2pm and 5-9pm, Sa 9:30am-2pm.)

▨ **Naturi Albaicín,** C. Calderería Nueva 10 (☎22 73 83). Excellent vegetarian cuisine in a Moroccan ambience. *Menús* €6.90-8.30. Open daily 1-3:30pm and 8-11pm. MC/V. ❷

▨ **Botánico Café,** C. Málaga 3 (☎27 15 98), near Pl. Trinidad. This hip cafe is a major student hangout. Entrees €6-14. Open M-Th and Su noon-1am, F-Sa noon-2am. MC/V. ❷

Restaurante Asador Corrala del Carbón, C. Mariana Pineda 8 (☎22 38 10). Savor traditional Andalusian grilled meat in a setting decorated as an old neighborhood courtyard. Entrees €11-18. Open daily 1-4pm and 8:30pm-midnight. MC/V. ❸

Samarcanda, C. Calderería Vieja 3 (☎21 00 04). Delicious Lebanese food. Appetizers €3-6. Entrees €10. Open M-Tu and Th-Su 1-4:30pm and 7:30pm-midnight. MC/V. ❸

El Ladrillo II, C. Panaderos 13 (☎29 26 51). Generous portions of tasty seafood. Entrees €6-12. Open daily 12:30pm-1:30am. MC/V. ❷

Restaurant Sonymar, Pl. Boquero 6 (☎27 10 63). Relish in the nouveau Moorish decor and amazing service of this secluded neighborhood eatery. *Menú* €6. Entrees €7.20-12.60. Open daily 1-4pm and 8-11:30pm. AmEx/V. ❷

SIGHTS

▨ **THE ALHAMBRA.** From the streets of Granada, the Alhambra appears simple and faded. Up close, however, you will discover an elaborate and detailed piece of architecture, one that unites water, light, wood, stucco, and ceramics to create a fortress-palace of rich aesthetic and symbolic grandeur. Many would argue that the age-old saying, *"Si mueres sin ver la Alhambra, no has vivido"* ("If you die without seeing the Alhambra, you have not lived"), still holds true. Follow signs to the *Palacio Nazaries* to see the **Alcázar,** a 14th-century palace full of stalactite archways, multicolored tiles, and sculpted fountains. The engraved walls of the *Patio del Cuarto Dorado* (Patio of the Gilded Hall) are topped by the shielded windows of the women's chambers. Off the far side of the patio, horseshoe archways open onto the *Cuarto Dorado* (Gilded Hall). The *Sala de los Abencerrajes* is where Boabdil killed 37 sons of the Abencerrajes family after one of them allegedly had amorous encounters with the sultana.

When the Christians drove the first Nasrid King Alhamar from the Albaicín, he built the series of rust-colored brick towers which form the **Alcazaba** (fortress). A dark, spiraling staircase leads to the *Torre de la Vela* (watchtower), where visitors have a splendid 360° view of Granada and the surrounding mountains.

Over a bridge, across the *Callejón de los Cipreses,* are the vibrant blossoms, towering cypresses, and streaming waterways of **El Generalife,** the sultan's vacation retreat. Over the centuries, the estate passed through private hands until it was finally repatriated in 1931. The two buildings of El Generalife, the *Palacio* and the *Sala Regia,* connect across the *Patio de la Acequia* (Courtyard of the Irrigation Channel), embellished with a narrow pool fed by fountains.

After the Reconquista drove the Moors from Spain, Ferdinand and Isabella restored the Alcázar. Two generations later, Emperor Charles V demolished part of it to make way for his **Palacio.** Although it is incongruous with the surrounding Moorish splendor, scholars concede that the palace is one of the most beautiful Renaissance buildings in Spain. *(Walk up C. Cuesta de Gomérez from Pl. Nueva (20min.), or take the quick Alhambra-Neptuno microbus from Pl. Nueva (every 5min., €1). ☎ 22 15 03, reservations 902 22 44 60; online reservations www.alhambratickets.com. Open Apr.-Sept. daily 8:30am-8pm; Oct.-Mar. M-Sa 9am-5:45pm. Nighttime visits Mar.-Oct. Tu-Sa 10-11:30pm; Nov.-Feb. F-Sa 8-9:30pm; ask for details at the information desk. €10, over 65 €7, the handicapped and under 8 free. Admission is limited, so arrive early or reserve tickets in advance at local banks (reservation fee €0.75) or BBVA branches across the country.)*

■ **THE ALBAICÍN.** A labyrinth of steep streets and narrow alleys, the Albaicín was the only Moorish neighborhood to escape the torches of the *Reconquista.* After the fall of the Alhambra, a small Muslim population remained here until being expelled in the 17th century. Today, with its abundance of North African cuisine, outdoor bazaars blasting Arabic music, teahouses, and the mosque near Pl. San Nicolás, the Albaicín attests to the persistence of Islamic influence in Andalucía.

The best way to explore this maze is to proceed along Carrera del Darro off Pl. Santa Ana, climb the Cuesta del Chapiz on the left, then wander through the Muslim ramparts, cisterns, and gates. On Pl. Santa Ana, the 16th-century **Real Cancillería** (or **Audiencia**), with its beautiful arcaded patio and stalactite ceiling, was the Christians' Ayuntamiento. Farther uphill are the 11th-century **Arab baths.** *(Carrera del Darro 31. ☎ 02 78 00. Open Tu-Sa 10am-2pm. Free.)* The ■mirador (lookout terrace) adjacent to the **Iglesia de San Nicolás** affords the city's best view of the Alhambra. *(From C. Elvira, go up C. Calderería Nueva to C. San Gregorio and continue uphill past Pl. Algibe de Trillo, where the street becomes Cta. Algibe de Trillo. At Pl. Camino, take a left on Cta. Tomasa and another left on Atarazana Cta. Cabras. The mirador will be on your right.)* Although generally safe, the Albaicín is disorienting and should be approached with caution at night. *(Bus #12 runs from beside the cathedral to C. Pagés at the top of the Albaicín.)*

■ **CAPILLA REAL.** Downhill from the Alhambra's Arab splendor, the Capilla Real (Royal Chapel), Ferdinand and Isabella's private chapel, exemplifies Christian Granada. During their prosperous reign, the Catholic Monarchs funneled almost a quarter of the royal income into the chapel's construction to build a proper burial place. Intricate Gothic masonry and meticulously rendered figurines, as well as **La Reja,** the gilded iron grille of Master Bartolomé, grace the couple's resting place. The adjacent **Sacristía** houses Isabella's private **art collection.** *(The Capilla is on C. Oficios through the Pta. Real off Gran Vía de Colón. ☎ 22 92 39. Capilla and Sacristía open M-Sa 10:30am-1pm and 4-7pm, Su 11am-1pm and 4-5pm. €2.50 for both.)*

CATHEDRAL. Behind the Capilla Real and the sacristy is Granada's cathedral. After *la Reconquista,* construction of the cathedral began upon the smoldering embers of Granada's largest mosque and was not completed until 1704. *(☎ 22 29 59. Open Apr.-Sept. M-Sa 10:45am-1:30pm and 4-7pm, Su 4-7pm; Oct.-Mar. M-Sa 10:30am-1:30pm and 3:30-6:30pm, Su 11am-1:30pm. €2.50.)*

◪ NIGHTLIFE

Granada's "free tapas with a drink" tradition lures students and tourists out to its many pubs and bars. The most boisterous nightspots belong to **Calle Pedro Antonio de Alarcón,** from Pl. Albert Einstein to Ancha de Gracia, while hip new bars and clubs line **Calle Elvira** from Cárcel to C. Cedrán. **Gay bars** cluster around Carrera del Darro. The *Guía del Ocio,* sold at newsstands (€0.85), lists clubs, pubs, and cafes.

■ **Granero,** Pl. Luis Rosales (☎ 22 89 79). A new-age bar pulsing with energy and high on style. Beer €2.50. Mixed drinks €6. Open M-Th and Su 8am-3am, F-Sa 8am-4am.

■ **Fondo Reservado,** Cuesta de Sta. Inés, off Carrera del Darro. Gay-friendly bar with a hip crowd. Beer €2.60. Mixed drinks €4-5. Open Tu-Th 11pm-3am, F-Sa 11pm-4am.

Planta Baja, C. Homo de Abad 11 (☎25 35 09). Techno blasts in a futuristic underground garage. Beer €1.80. Open Th 11pm-3:30am, F-Sa 11pm-4:30am.

Kasbah, C. Calderería Nueva 4 (☎22 79 36). Candlelit cafe offers Arab pastries and an exhaustive selection of Moroccan teas (€1.80). Open daily noon-1:30am.

EASTERN SPAIN

Rich soil and famous orange groves, fed by Moorish irrigation systems, have earned Eastern Spain (Valencia) the nickname *Huerta de España* (Spain's Orchard). Dunes, sandbars, jagged promontories, and lagoons mark the grand coastline, while lovely fountains and pools grace carefully landscaped public gardens in Valencian cities. The famed rice dish paella was born in this region.

ALICANTE (ALICANT)   ☎965

Sun-drenched Alicante (pop. 306,000) has it all: relaxing beaches, fascinating historical sites, and an unbelievable collection of bars and port-side discos. The ancient **Castell de Santa Bárbara** features drawbridges, dark passageways, and hidden tunnels. A paved road from Alicante leads to the top, but most people take the **elevator** on Av. Jovellanos, just across the street from Playa Postiguet. (Castle open daily Apr.-Sept. 10am-7:30pm; Oct.-Mar. 9am-6:30pm. Elevator €2.40.) The **Museu de Arte del Siglo XX La Asegurada,** Pl. Santa María 3, at the eastern end of C. Mayor, showcases modern art pieces, including works by Picasso and Dalí. (Open mid-May to mid-Sept. Tu-F 10am-2pm and 5-9pm, Sa-Su 10:30am-2:30pm; mid-Sept. to mid-May Tu-F 10am-2pm and 4-8pm, Sa-Su 10:30am-2:30pm.) Alicante's **Playa del Postiguet** attracts beach lovers, as do nearby **Playa de San Juan** (TAM bus #21, 22, or 31) and **Playa del Mutxavista** (TAM bus #21). Buses (€0.80) depart every 15min. Nightlife in Alicante is fantastic. Try ■**Coscorrón,** C. Tarifa 3, for a famous mojito (€2.50) served in an antique teapot. (Open M-Th and Su 10:30pm-2:30am, F-Sa 11pm-4:30am.) While Alicante nightlife has plenty to offer, for an even crazier time the **Trensnochador** night train runs from Estació Marina to *discotecas* and other stops along the beach. (July-Aug. F-Sa 1 per hr.) During the **Festival de Sant Joan** (June 20-29), *fogueres* (satirical effigies) are erected and then burned in the streets during *la Cremà;* afterwards, firefighters soak everyone during *la Banyà.*

RENFE **trains** (☎902 24 02 02) run from Estación Término on Av. Salamanca to: Barcelona (4½-6hr., 5-6 per day, €43-67); Madrid (4hr., 4-9 per day, €36-56); and Valencia (1½hr., 10 per day, €9-35). **Buses** run from C. Portugal 17 (☎13 07 00) to: Barcelona (7hr., 15 per day, €35-40); Granada (6hr., 10 per day, €24-30); and Madrid (5hr., 15 per day, €23-30). The **tourist office** is at C. Portugal 17 (☎92 98 02; www.alicanteturismo.com. English spoken. Open M-Sa 9am-2pm and 4-8pm.) Use the **Internet** at **Fundación BanCaja,** Rbla. de Méndez Núñez 4, 2nd fl. (Open M-F 10am-2pm and 5-9pm, Sa 9am-2pm.) ■**Habitaciones México** ❶, C. General Primo de Rivera 10, off the end of Av. Alfonso X El Sabio, has a friendly atmosphere and small, cozy rooms. (☎20 93 07. Free Internet access noon-10pm. Singles €12-15; doubles €27; triples €33.) Buy basics at **Mercadona,** C. Alvarez Sereix 5, off Av. Federico Soto. (Open M-Sa 9am-9pm.) **Postal Code:** 03070.

VALENCIA   ☎963

Stylish and cosmopolitan, Valencia (pop. 750,000) presents a striking contrast to the surrounding orchards and mountain range. Yet despite its modern facade, Valencia retains a small-town charm. It seems to possess all the best of its sister cities: the bustling energy of Madrid, the vibrant spirit of Alicante, the offbeat sophistication of Barcelona, and the friendly warmth of Seville.

⌨🔌 TRANSPORTATION AND PRACTICAL INFORMATION. Trains arrive at C. Xàtiva 24 (☎52 02 02). RENFE (24hr. ☎902 24 02 02) runs to: Alicante (2-3hr., 11 per day, €11-23); Barcelona (3hr., every 1-2hr., €29-35); Madrid (3½hr., 12 per day, €19-37); and Seville (8½hr., 1 per day 11:30am, €43). **Buses** (☎49 72 22) go from Av. Menéndez Pidal 13 to: Alicante via the Costa Blanca (4½hr., 9 per day, €15-17.10); Barcelona (4½hr., 9 per day, €21); Madrid (4hr., 13 per day, €20-24.20); and Seville (11hr., 3-4 per day, €43-50). Trasmediterránea **ferries** (☎902 45 46 45) sail to the Balearic Islands (p. 984). Bus #8 (€1) connects to the train station. The main **tourist office**, C. de la Paz 46-48, has branches at the train station and Pl. del Ajuntament. (☎98 64 22; www.valencia.es. Open M-F 9am-7pm, Sa 10am-7pm.) **Internet** access is at **Ono**, C. San Vicente Mártir 22. (☎28 19 02. €1.80 per 45min. 9am-2pm, €1.80 per 30min. 2-10pm, €1.80 per hr. 10pm-1am. Open M-Sa 9am-1am, Su 10am-1am.) The **post office** is at Pl. del Ajuntament 24. (☎51 67 50. Open M-F 8:30am-8:30pm, Sa 9:30am-2pm.) **Postal Code:** 46080.

🏠🍴 ACCOMMODATIONS AND FOOD. The best lodgings are around **Plaza del Ajuntament** and **Plaza del Mercado.** The ▧**Home Youth Hostel ❶**, C. Lonja 4, is behind the Lonja and across from the Mercado Central, off Pl. Dr. Collado. Brightly painted rooms, a common living room, and a kitchen create a homey atmosphere for road-weary guests. (☎91 62 29; www.likeathome.net. Laundry €5.50. Internet €0.50 per 15min. Dorms €14; singles €21; doubles €32; triples €48; quads €64.) To get to **Hostal Antigua Morellana ❸**, C. En Bou 2, walk past Pl. Dr. Collado; it's on one of the small streets behind the Lonja. This quiet and comfortable hostel caters to an older crowd. Rooms have bath and A/C. (☎/fax 91 57 73. Doubles €58.)

Paella is the most famous of Valencia's 200 rice dishes; try as many of them as you can before leaving. ▧**La Lluna ❶**, C. San Ramón 23, in El Carme, serves a huge menu of delicious vegetarian options, all €3-5. (☎92 21 46. Open M-Sa 1:30-3:30pm and 9-11:30pm.) **Sol i Lluna ❷**, C. del Mar 29, just off the Pl. de la Reina, serves creative, gourmet tapas (€5-9) made from scratch. (☎92 22 16. Open M-F 9am-1:30am, Sa 5pm-1:30am.) Fresh fish, meat, and fruit (including Valencia's famous oranges) are sold at the **Mercado Central**, on Pl. Mercado. (Open M-Sa 7am-3pm.) For groceries, try the basement of **El Corte Inglés**, on C. Colón. (Open M-Sa 10am-10pm.)

RICE A LA VALENCIA

Paella is known throughout the world as a quintessentially Spanish dish, but any *valenciano* can tell you where it started—here, in the homes of fishermen around L'Albufera. The technique of preparation have been perfected by rice cultivators, processors, and traditionally male *paelleros*. Don't call it all paella, however; there are hundreds of different rice dishes, unique in ingredients and preparation.

Paella, for example, is the Valenciano word for the typical pan in which the rice dish (originally called *arroz en paella*) is cooked. The most common is *paella de mariscos*, paella with a variety of fish and shellfish. *Paella valenciana*, though, is made with chicken and rabbit. *Arroz a banda*, similar to paella, is a more humble dish traditionally enjoyed by fishermen. The fish is cooked separately from the rice, saffron, garlic, and tomato.

If you prefer your rice baked, try *arroz al horno*, popular in la Ribera and la Huerta for its slightly simpler recipe. Also popular is *arroz negro*, cooked with squid and blackened from the ink. If you don't like rice at all, try *fideuá*, paella's cousin, made with noodles instead of rice. Whichever you choose, you are certain not to be disappointed, as long as you go for the authentic version. Avoid restaurants bearing pictures of pre-made paellas on signs; what you see is what you get, and it's not the real thing.

◙ **SIGHTS.** Most of Valencia's sights line Río Turia or cluster near Pl. Reina, which is linked to Pl. Ayuntamiento by C. San Vicente Mártir. EMT bus #5, dubbed the **Bus Turístic** (€1), makes a loop around the old town sights. Head toward the beach along the riverbed off C. Alcalde Reig., or take bus #35 from Pl. Ayuntamiento to reach the modern, airy, and thoroughly fascinating ▓**Ciudad de las Artes y las Ciencias.** The complex is divided into four large attractions, but the **Palau de les Arts** will not open until at least 2005. The **Museu de Les Ciències Príncipe Felipe** is an interactive playground for technology fiends; **L'Hemisfèric** has an IMAX theater and planetarium; **L'Oceanogràfic** is a huge aquarium. (☎ 902 10 00 31; www.cac.es. Museum open June 15-Sept. 15 daily 10am-9pm; Sept. 16-June 14 M-F and Su 10am-8pm, Sa 10am-9pm. €7, students €5.50. IMAX shows €7/€5.50. Aquarium open June 21-Sept. 7 daily 10am-midnight; Sept. 8-Oct. 21 and Mar. 15-June 20 M-F 10am-8pm, Sa-Su 10am-10pm; Jan. 1-Mar. 14 and Oct. 13-Mar. 14 M-F 10am-6pm, Sa-Su 10am-8pm. €10.) The 13th-century **cathedral,** in Pl. de la Reina, displays a melange of architectural styles. Incredible views of Valencia can be seen from atop the **Miguelete** (the cathedral tower). The **Museu de la Catedral** squeezes a number of treasures into three tiny rooms. (Cathedral ☎91 01 89. Open daily 7:30am-1pm and 4:30-8:30pm. Closes earlier in winter. Free. Tower open daily 10am-1pm and 4:30-7pm. €2. Museum ☎91 81 27. Open Dec.-Feb. daily 10am-1pm; Mar.-Nov. M-Sa 10am-1pm and 4:30-6pm, Su 10am-1pm. €2.) Across the river, the **Museu Provincial de Belles Artes,** C. Sant Pius V, displays superb Valencian art. Its collection includes works by El Greco and Goya. (☎60 57 93. Open Tu-Sa 10am-8pm. Free.) Across the river is the **Institut Valencià d'Art Modern,** C. Guillem de Castro 118. (☎86 30 00. Open Tu-Su 10am-10pm. €2, students €1, Su free.)

♫ ▓ **ENTERTAINMENT AND NIGHTLIFE.** The most popular **beaches** are **Las Arenas** and **Malvarrosa**—buses #20, 21, 22, and 23 all pass through. To get to the **Salér,** 14km from town, take an Autobuses Buñol **bus** (☎49 14 25) from the corner of Gran Vía de Germanias and C. Sueca (25min., every 30min. 7am-10pm, €1). Follow C. Bolsería out of Pl. Mercado, bearing right at the fork, to guzzle *agua de Valencia* (orange juice, champagne, and vodka) in Pl. Tossal. **Cafe Negrito,** Pl. del Negrito 1, off C. Caballeros, is popular with locals. (Open daily 10pm-3am.) Near the university is ▓**Warhol,** Av. Blasco Ibáñez 111. (Open daily 1-7am. M-Th and Su cover €6, F-Sa €9; includes 1 drink.) For more info, consult the weekly *Qué y Dónde* (€1), the weekly *La Cartelera* (€0.75), or the free *24/7 Valencia,* available at hostels and cafes. The most famed festival in Valencia is **Las Fallas** (Mar. 12-19), which culminates with the burning of papier-mâché effigies.

NORTHEASTERN SPAIN

Northeastern Spain encompasses the country's most avidly regionalistic areas. From rocky Costa Brava to chic Barcelona, the prosperous Cataluña is graced with the nation's richest resources. However, Cataluña isn't the only reason to head northeast. The area is also home to the awesome mountains of the Pyrenees, the running bulls of Navarra, the industrious cities of Aragón, the beautiful coasts of Basque Country, and the crazy parties of the Balearic Islands.

BARCELONA ☎ 93

Barcelona loves to indulge in the fantastic. From the urban carnival that is Las Ramblas to buildings with no straight lines, from wild festivals to even wilder nightlife, the city pushes the limits of style and good taste in everything it does—and with amazing results. The center of the whimsical and daring *Modernisme* architectural movement and once home to Pablo Picasso and Joan Miró, Barcelona is grounded in an alternate reality even through its art. Yet the draw of Barcelona extends beyond its paintings and architecture. The energy and attention to the visual is just as alive in its people. In the quarter-century since Spain was freed from Franco's oppressive regime, Barcelona has led the autonomous region of Cataluña in the resurgence of a culture so esoteric and unique it even puzzles the rest of Spain. The result is a vanguard city where rooftops drip toward the sidewalk, serpentine park benches twist past fairy-tale houses, and an unfinished cathedral captures imaginations around the world.

◪ INTERCITY TRANSPORTATION

Flights: El Prat de Llobregat Airport (BCN; ☎298 3838; www.barcelona-airport.com), 13km southwest of Barcelona. To get to the central Pl. de Catalunya, take the Aerobus (☎415 6020, 40min., every 12-13min., €3.50) or a RENFE train (17min. to Estació Sants, 23min. to Pl. de Catalunya; every 30min.; €2.20).

Trains: Barcelona has 2 main train stations. **Estació Barcelona-Sants,** in Pl. Països Catalans (M: Sants-Estació), is the main terminal for domestic and international traffic. **Estació França,** on Av. Marquès de l'Argentera (M: Barceloneta), services regional destinations and some international arrivals. **RENFE** (☎902 24 02 02, international 934 90 11 22; www.renfe.es) has extensive service. To: **Bilbao** (8-9hr., 5 per day, €35-44); **Madrid** (7-9hr., 8 per day, €34-59); **San Sebastián** (8-9hr., 5 per day, €34-43); **Seville** (11-12hr., 6 per day, €50-78); **Valencia** (3-5hr., 15 per day, €29-35). International destinations include **Milan, Italy** (via Figueres and Nice), and **Montpellier, France** with connections to Geneva, Paris, and various stops along the French Riviera.

Buses: Most buses arrive at **Barcelona Estació Nord d'Autobuses,** C. Alí Bei 80 (☎265 6132). M: Arc de Triomf. Buses also depart from Estació Sants and the Airport. **Sarfa** (☎902 30 20 25) goes to **Cadaqués** (2½hr., 6 per day, €16). **Linebus** (☎265 0700; www.movelia.es) travels to **Paris, France** via Tours or Lyon (15hr., M-Sa 2 per day, €84), southern France, and Morocco. **Alsa/Enatcar** (☎902 42 22 42; www.alsa.es) goes to: **Madrid** (8hr., 20 per day, €24); **Naples, Italy** (24hr., daily 4:45pm, €115); **Paris, France** (15hr., 1-3 per day, €84); **Valencia** (4hr., 16 per day, €21).

Ferries: Trasmediterránea (☎902 45 46 45), in Estació Marítima-Moll Barcelona, Moll Sant Bertran. In summer only to: **Ibiza** (5-8hr., 1 per day, €50); **Mahón** (8-9hr., 1 per day, €50); **Palma** (3½hr., 1 per day, €70).

◪ ORIENTATION

Barcelona's layout is simple. Imagine yourself perched on Columbus's head at the **Monument a Colom** (on Passeig de Colom), viewing the city with the sea at your back. From the harbor, the city slopes upward to the mountains. From the Monument a Colom, **Las Ramblas,** the main thoroughfare, runs from the harbor up to **Plaça de Catalunya** (M: Catalunya). The **Ciutat Vella** (old city), the heavily touristed historic neighborhood, centers around Las Ramblas and includes the Barri Gòtic, La Ribera, and El Raval. The **Barri Gòtic** is east of Las Ramblas (to your right), enclosed on the other side by **Vía Laietana.** East of V. Laietana lies the neighborhood of **La Ribera,** which borders Parc de la Ciutadella and the Estació França (train station). To the west of Las Ramblas (to your left) is **El Raval.** Beyond La Ribera—farther east, outside the Ciutat Vella—are **Poble Nou** and **Port Olímpic.** Beyond El Raval (to the west) rises **Montjuïc,** with museums, the 1992 Olympic grounds, and a military fortress. Directly behind the Monument a Colom is the **Port Vell** (old port) development, where a bridge leads across to the shopping and entertainment complexes **Moll d'Espanya** and **Maromàgnum.** Beyond the Ciutat Vella is **l'Eixample,** a neighborhood created during the expansion of the 1860s, which runs toward the mountains. **Gran Via de les Corts Catalanes** defines its lower edge and the **Passeig de Gràcia** bisects the neighborhood. **Avinguda Diagonal** marks the border between l'Eixample and the **Zona Alta** (uptown), which includes **Gràcia.**

Pg. Manuel Girona

Col·legi de les
Teresianes

SARRIÀ

BONANOVA Ⓜ

C. Ravella

Parc
Monterol

C. Vico

C. Copèrnic

C. Modolell

C. Capità

PL.
PAPA PIUS
XII

**PL. PRAT
DE LA RIBA**

C. les Escoles

Vallmajor

C. Plató

C. Desc

Via Augusta

PL. DE LA
REINA MARIA
CRISTINA

MARIA CRISTINA Ⓜ

Av. Sarrià

C. J.S. Bach

MUNTANER

C. Parroco Ubach

C. Maternitat

Av. Diagonal

Gran Via de Carles III

Parc de Poeta
Eduard de
Marquina

C. Madrazo

C. Laforja

Museo del Fútbol
Club Barcelona 🏛

Camp Nou

LES CORTS

C. de Galileu

C. Numància

C. d'Entença

C. Santaló

Tr. de Gràcia

PL. DE
FRANCESC
MACIÀ

C. de l'A

Tr. de les Corts

LES CORTS Ⓜ

C. Dr. Ibáñez

Av. Madrid

C. Joan Güell

C. Marqués de Sentmenat

Filmoteca

C. Roger

C. Brasil

C. Tenor

C. Vallespir

C. Robrenyo

Av. la Infanta Carlota

C. Londres

C. Londres

💻

PL. DEL CENTRE Ⓜ

C. Berlin

C. Paris

C. Paris

PL. DEL SANTS

**MERCAT
NOU** Ⓜ

C. Sants Creu Coberta

Estació
Barcelona-
Sants 🏛

SANTS ESTACIÓ Ⓜ

C. Còrsega

ENTENÇA Ⓜ
C. Rosselló

Hospital
Clínic ✚

**L'EIXAMPLE
ESQUERRA**

**HOSPITAL
CLÍNIC** Ⓜ

PL.
PAÏSOS
CATALANS

Av. Roma

C. Provença

C. Provença

Parc de la
Espanya
Industrial

C. dels Jocs
Florals

Sagunt

C. Olzinelles

C. Guadiana

C. del Rector Triadó

Béjar

C. de

C. Mallorca

C. Mallorca

C. València

TARRAGONA Ⓜ

C. d'Aragó

HOSTAFRANCS

C. Consell de Cent

C. Tarragona

Parc
Joan
Miró

C. de Rocafort

C. de Calàbria

C. Villarroel

C. Comte Borrell

C. Comte d'Urgell

C. Villarroel

C. Casanova

C. Muntaner

C. de Gavà

C. Molines

C. de la Bordeta

ESPANYA

C. de la Diputació

URGELL

ROCAFORT Ⓜ

Gran Via de les Corts Catalanes

TO ✈

Gran Via Corts Catalanes

PL.
D'ESPANYA

C. de Vilamarí

Av. Paral·lel

C. Sepúlveda

C. Floridablanca

Ronda de Sant Antoni

C. Joaquín Costa

Av. Marqués de Comillas

**Poble
Espanyol** 🏛

Av. la Reina
Maria Cristina

C. de Tamarit

Mercat de
Sant Antoni ■

C. Car

PL.
DE SANT
JORDI

PL. DE LES
CASCADES

Palau
Alfonso
XIII

C. de Lleida

C. Manso

POBLE SEC

C. de Sant Pau

C. de l'Hospital

EL RAVAL

Pg. los Cascades

Museo 🏛
Arqueològic

MNAC (Palau
Nacional) 🏛

POBLE SEC Ⓜ

C. Sant Pau

PL.
EUROPA

Palau
Sant Jordi

Jardins de
Joan
Maragall

Museo 🏛
Etnològic

Pg. l'Exposició

C. Magalhaes

🏛 C. Blai

C. Nou de la Rmb

C. Pelai
Güe

Pg. Olímpic

Fundació 🏛
Miró

Av. Miramar

Funicular ••••••••••

PARAL·LEL Ⓜ

Av. l'Estadi

Estadi
Olímpic

Camí dels Tres Pins

MONTJUÏC

Cablecar

Pg. Montjuïc

Museu
Marítim 🏛

Cura. Mondials

0 _____ 450 yards

0 _____ 450 meters

Castell de Montjuïc

Museo
Militar 🏛

Jardins de
Miramar

Ctra.
Montjuïc

Josep Carner

TO TORRE SAN
SEBASTIÀ (800m)

Teleferic

Barcelona

▲▲ ACCOMMODATIONS

Apart. Rembrandt, **20**
BCN Hostal Central, **16**
Filipinas, **1**
Hostal Benidorm, **33**
Hostal Lesseps, **2**
Hostal Levante, **36**
Hostal Malda, **27**
Hostal Qué Tal, **11**
Hostal-Residencia
  Oliva, **13**
Hostal-Residencia
  Rembrandt, **24**
Hostal de Ribagorza, **22**
Hotel Pelayo, **15**
Pensión L'Isard, **14**
Pensión San Medín, **5**

🍴 FOOD

L'Antic Bocoi del
  Gòtic, **38**
Attic, **23**
Bar Ra, **26**
Café de l'Òpera, **32**
HBN BCN, **44**
Orígens 99.9%, **41**
El Pebre Blau, **37**
Pla dels Àngels, **19**
Els Quatre Gats, **21**
Les Quinze Nits, **35**
El Racó d'en Baltá, **8**
El Salón, **40**
Xaloc, **28**

★ NIGHTLIFE

Átame, **10**
Bar Marcel, **3**
El Bosc de les
  Fades, **41**
Buenavista
  Salsoteca, **7**
Casa Almirall, **18**
El Copetín, **42**
Dietrich, **12**
La Fira, **9**
Gasterea, **6**
Jamboree, **34**
Molly Malone, **31**
Nayandei, **43**
Otto Zutz, **4**
L'Ovella Negra, **29**
Razzmatazz, **30**
La Terrazza, **17**
Tinta Roja, **25**

SPAIN

Map of Barcelona showing L'Eixample Dreta, Ciutat Vella, Barri Gòtic, La Ribera, Parc de la Ciutadella, Barceloneta, and Port Olímpic neighborhoods, with streets including Gran Via de les Corts Catalanes, Av. Diagonal, Av. Meridiana, and landmarks such as La Sagrada Família, Casa Milà (La Pedrera), Casa Vicens, Plaça de Toros Monumental, L'Aquàrium de Barcelona, and Monument a Colom.

☲ LOCAL TRANSPORTATION

Public Transportation: ☎010. Barcelona's public transportation is quick and cheap. There are several passes available, all of which work interchangeably for the metro, bus, urban lines of the FGC commuter trains, and the Nitbus. A **T-1 Pass** (€6) is valid for 10 rides; a **T-Día pass** entitles you to unlimited bus and metro travel for 1 (€4.60), 2 (€8.40), 3 (€11.80), 4 (€15.20), or 5 days (€17.30).

Metro: ☎486 0752; www.tmb.net. Trains run M-Th 5am-midnight, F-Sa 5am-2am, Su and holidays 6am-midnight. €1.10 per *sencillo* (single ride).

Ferrocarrils de la Generalitat de Catalunya (FGC): ☎205 1515; www.fgc.es. Commuter trains to local destinations; main stations at Pl. de Catalunya and Pl. d'Espanya. FGC charges the same as the metro (€1.10) until Tibidabo. After that, rates go up by zone. Info office at the Pl. de Catalunya station open M-F 7am-9pm.

Buses: Go just about anywhere, usually from 5am-10pm. €1.10. Most stops have maps posted; buses come every 10-15min. in central locations.

Nitbus: ☎901 511 151. 16 different lines run every 20-30min. 10:30pm-4:30am, depending on the line. All buses depart from Pl. de Catalunya and stop in front of most of the club complexes.

Taxis: RadioTaxi (☎225 0000); **ServiTaxi** (☎330 0300).

⁊ PRACTICAL INFORMATION

TOURIST AND FINANCIAL SERVICES

Tourist Offices: ☎907 30 12 82; www.barcelonaturisme.com. In addition to several tourist offices, Barcelona has numerous mobile information kiosks.

Aeroport El Prat de Llobregat, terminals A and B (☎478 0565). Info and last-minute accommodation booking. Open daily 9am-9pm.

Estació Barcelona-Sants, Pl. Països Catalans. M: Sants-Estació. Info and last-minute accommodation booking. Open in summer daily 8am-8pm; in winter M-F 8am-8pm, Sa-Su 8am-2pm.

Oficina de Turisme de Catalunya, Pg. de Gràcia 107 (☎238 4000; www.gencat.es/probert). M: Diagonal. Open M-Sa 10am-7pm, Su 10am-2:30pm.

Plaça de Catalunya, Pl. de Catalunya 17S. M: Catalunya. The biggest, best, and busiest tourist office. Free map, brochures on sights and public transportation, booking service for last-minute accommodations, gift shop, money exchange, and box office. Open daily 9am-9pm.

Plaça Sant Jaume, Pl. Sant Jaume 1. M: Jaume I. Open M- Sa 10am-8pm, Su 10am-2pm.

Currency Exchange: ATMs give the best rates; the next best rates are available at banks. General banking hours are M-F 8:30am-2pm.

LOCAL SERVICES

Luggage Storage: Estació Barcelona-Sants. M: Sants-Estació. €4.50. Open daily 5:30am-11pm. **Estació de França.** M: Barceloneta. €3. Open daily 7am-10pm.

Libraries: Biblioteca Sant Pau, C. de l'Hospital 56 (☎302 0797). M: Liceu. The library is on the left at the far end of the courtyard. Do not confuse it with the Catalan library you'll see first. Open M and F 3:30-8:30pm, W, Th, Sa 10am-2pm. Closed July-Aug.

Laundromat: Tintorería Ferrán, C. Ferran 11. M: Liceu. Open M-F 9am-8pm.

EMERGENCY AND COMMUNICATIONS

Police: Las Ramblas 43 (☎344 1300). M: Liceu. Multilingual officers. Open 24hr. **Turisme Atenció,** C. Nou de la Rambla 80 (☎344 1300), off La Rambla in El Raval 3 blocks from the port, is a police station specifically for tourists.

Hospital: Hospital Clìnic, C. de Villarroel, 170 (☎227 5400). M: Hospital Clìnic. Main entrance at the intersection of C. Roselló and C. Casanova.

Internet Access:

　▨ **Easy Internet Café,** Las Ramblas 31 (www.easyinternetcafe.com). M: Liceu. With reasonable prices and over 300 terminals in a bright, modern center, this is Internet heaven. Downloading digital camera pictures, CD burning, faxing, copying, and scanning. €1.80 per hr., 24hr. unlimited pass €4, 7-day €10, 30-day €20. Open 8am-2:30am. **Branch** at Ronda Universitat 35. M: Catalunya. €1.60 per hr., 24hr. pass €3, 7-day €7, 30-day €15. Open 8am-2am. Cash only.

Navegaweb, Las Ramblas 88-94 (☎317 9193; navegabarcelona@terra.es). M: Liceu. Good rates on international calls. Internet €0.90 per 30min., €1.80 per hr. Open daily 10am-10pm.

Cybermundo Internet Centre, C. Bergara 3, and C. de Balmes 8. M: Catalunya. Just off Pl. de Catalunya, 2 branches behind the Triangle shopping mall. Disks allowed. €1.20 per hr. (before noon, for students before 5pm). Open M-F 9am-1am, Sa 10am-1am, Su 11am-1am.

Post Office: Pl. d'Antoni López (☎902 19 71 97). M: Jaume I or Barceloneta. Fax and *Lista de Correos.* Open M-F 8:30am-9:30pm, Su 8:30am-2:30pm. **Postal Code:** 08003.

⌐ ACCOMMODATIONS

The **Ciutat Vella**—the **Barri Gòtic, El Raval,** and **La Ribera**—offers budget beds, but reservations are a must. Last-minute travelers can crash in **Gràcia** or **l'Eixample,** outer boroughs with more vacancies.

CIUTAT VELLA
Be careful in the areas near the port and farther from Las Ramblas.

▨ **Hostal Levante,** Baixada de San Miquel 2 (☎317 9565; www.hostallevante.com). M: Liceu. The best deal in the Barri Gòtic. Also has six 4-8 person apartments. Singles €33; doubles €56, with bath €65. Apartments €30 per person per night. MC/V. ❸

▨ **Hostal-Residencia Rembrandt,** C. de la Portaferrissa 23 (☎/fax 318 1011; hostrembrandt@yahoo.es). M: Liceu. Nicest rooms in the area; some with TV, large bath, or patio. Fans €2 per night. Reception 9am-11pm. Reservation requires credit card. Singles €28, with bath €38; doubles €45/€55; triples €65/€70. MC/V. ❸

▨ **Pensión L'Isard,** C. Tallers, 82 (☎/fax 302 5183). M: Universitat. Offers the lowest price in the region. Singles €21; doubles €39, with bath €53; triples €55. AmEx/MC/V. ❷

▨ **Hostal de Ribagorza,** C. Trafalgar, 39 (☎/fax 319 1968; www.hostalribagorza.com). M: Urquinaona. Rooms in a Modernist building have TV, fan, and homey decorations. Doubles €40, with bath €50-55; low season reduced prices. MC/V. ❷

Apart. Rembrandt, C. Canuda 13 (☎301 3157). This hotel offers enormous, brand-new rooms with A/C, TV, luxurious baths, balconies facing the plaza, and even small kitchens. Reception 9am-10pm. Singles €50; doubles €90; suites €120. MC/V. ❺

Hostal Benidorm, Las Ramblas 37 (☎/fax 302 2054). M: Drassanes or Liceu. From lobby, go left and up 3 floors. A great value. Complete bath in each room. Singles €35; doubles €55; triples €75; quads €90; quints €105. Prices rise €5 in Aug. MC/V. ❸

Hostal Malda, C. Pi 5 (☎317 3002), entrance inside a small shopping center. M: Liceu. Quality rooms at a great price. No reservations; show up between 9-11am to claim a room. Singles €13; doubles €28; triples with shower €40. Cash only. ❶

Hotel Pelayo, C. Pelai 9, 1st fl. (☎302 3727). M: Universitat. Amazing location. Each spotless room has bath, TV, A/C, and phone. Singles €55; doubles €75. MC/V. ❺

L'EIXAMPLE
Though L'Eixample may be far from the sights of Las Ramblas and the Barri Gòtic, accommodations in this area tend to be much nicer than those in Ciutat Vella.

▨ **Hostal Residencia Oliva,** Pg. de Gràcia 32, 4th fl. (☎488 0162; www.lasguias.com/hostaloliva). M: Pg. de Gràcia. Wood-worked bureaus and a marble floor give this hostel a classy ambience. Singles €32; doubles €55, with bath €62; triple with bath €90. ❸

▨ **Hostal Qué Tal,** C. Mallorca 290 (☎/fax 459 2366; www.quetalbarcelona.com). M: Pg. de Gràcia or Verdaguer. A high-quality gay- and lesbian-friendly hostel with a great interior. Reception 24hr. Singles €39; doubles €58, with bath €74. Cash only ❹

BCN Hostal Central, Ronda Universitat 11, 1st fl. (☎ 302 2420 or 412 7857; www.bcnhostalcentral.com). M: Universitat. In an old building with marble staircases and ornate ceilings. Great location. Extra bed €12-18. Singles with shared bath €25-33; doubles €50-55, with bath €60-65; triples €54/€78; quads €60/€85-90. ❷

SPAIN

ZONA ALTA: GRÀCIA AND OUTER *BARRIS*

Gràcia is Barcelona's "undiscovered" quarter, so last-minute arrivals may find vacancies here, although options are few.

Pensión San Medín, C. Gran de Gràcia 125 (☎217 3068). M: Fontana. Embroidered curtains and ornate tiling adorn this family-run *pensión*. Reception 8am-midnight. Singles €30, with bath €39; doubles €48/€60. MC/V. ❸

Hostal Lesseps, C. Gran de Gràcia 239 (☎218 4434; fax 217 1180). M: Lesseps. Spacious, classy rooms sport red velvet wallpaper. All 16 rooms have TV and bath; 4 have A/C (€5 extra). Singles €40; doubles €65; triples €80; quads €95-100. MC/V. ❹

CAMPING

A handful of sites lie on the outskirts of the city, accessible by intercity buses (€1.50; 20-45min.). The **Associació de Càmpings de Barcelona,** Gran Via de les Corts Catalanes, 608 (☎93 412 59 55; www.campingsbcn.com) has more info.

Filipinas, Autovía de Castelldefels km12 (☎658 2895; reservas@infonegocio.com). Take bus L95 (€2) from Pl. de Catalunya to the campsite. €5.25 per person, €5.25 per 2-person tent, €5.75 per larger tent, €5.25 per vehicle. Electricity €4. AmEx/MC/V. ❶

◧ FOOD

Available at newsstands, the *Guia del Ocio* (www.guiadelociobcn.es; €1) is an invaluable source of culinary suggestions. **Port Vell** and **Port Olímpic** are known for seafood. The restaurants on **Carrer Aragó** near Pg. de Gràcia have great lunchtime *menús*, and the **Passeig de Gràcia** has beautiful outdoor dining. Gràcia's **Plaça Sol** and La Ribera's **Santa Maria del Mar** are the best places to head for tapas. For fruit, cheese, and wine, head to **La Boqueria** (Mercat de Sant Josep), outside M: Liceu. For groceries, try **Champion,** Las Ramblas 13. (M: Liceu. Open M-Sa 9am-10pm.)

BARRI GÒTIC

▨ **L'Antic Bocoi del Gòtic,** Baixada de Viladecols 3 (☎310 5067). M: Jaume I. This rustic restaurant is tiny and romantic. Open M-Sa 8:30pm-midnight. AmEx/MC/V. ❸

▨ **Les Quinze Nits,** Pl. Reial 6 (☎317 3075). M: Liceu. Delicious Catalan dishes. Entrees €3.30-9. Open daily 1-3:45pm and 8:30-11:30pm. AmEx/MC/V. ❷

Els Quatre Gats, C. Montsió 3 (☎302 4140). M: Catalunya. An old hangout of Picasso with lots of bohemian character. High-quality cuisine. Entrees €12-26. Lunch *menú* €11. Open daily 1pm-1am. Closed Aug. AmEx/MC/V. ❹

Attic, Las Ramblas 120 (☎302 4866). M: Liceu. Chic, modern restaurant with top-rate service. Offers fusion Mediterranean cuisine, including fish (€10-13), meat (€6-14), and rice (€6-9) dishes. Open daily 1-4:30pm and 7:30pm-12:30am. AmEx/MC/V. ❸

Xaloc, C. de la Palla 13-17 (☎301 1990). M: Liceu. This big, classy delicatessen popular with locals is centered around a butcher counter. Sandwiches on tasty baguettes €4-14. Lunch *menú* €9.80. Open daily 9am-midnight. AmEx/MC/V. ❷

El Salón, C. l'Hostal d'en Sol 6-8 (☎315 2159). M: Jaume I. A red-hued mellow bar-bistro serving *gnocchi,* chicken, pork, and fish. Entrees €8-18. Wine €2-8. Cocktails €4-5. *Menú* €20. Open M-Sa 8:30pm-12am; bar open 7pm-2am. AmEx/MC/V. ❸

Café de l'Ópera, Las Ramblas 74 (☎317 7585). M: Liceu. A drink in this antique-mirror-covered cafe used to be a post-opera bourgeois tradition. Delicious, rich hot chocolate €2.70. *Churros* €2.20. Tapas €2-4. Salads €2-8. Open daily 8am-2:30am. ❶

ELSEWHERE IN BARCELONA

▨ **Orígens 99.9%,** C. Enric Granados 9 (☎/fax 453 1120), and at C. Vidrieria 6-8 (☎310 7531). M: Jaume I. This hip restaurant and gourmet store sticks to natural, fresh ingredients. Soups €3-9. Entrees €3-5. Open 12:30pm-1:30am. MC/V. ❷

▓ **Bar Ra,** Pl. de la Garduña (☎301 4163, reservations 615 95 98 72). M: Liceu. Everything about Ra exudes cool, from the clientele to the incense-infused outdoor seating. Many vegetarian options. Entrees €9-15. Open daily 9:30am-1:30am. Kitchen open daily 1:30-4pm and 9:30pm-midnight. Dinner by reservation only. AmEx/MC/V. ❸

▓ **El Racó d'en Baltá,** C. Aribau 125 (☎453 1044). M: Hospital Clínic. Offers innovative Mediterranean dishes. Fish and meat entrees €12-18. Open M 9-11pm, Tu-Th 1-3:30pm and 9-10:45pm, F 1-3:30pm and 9-11pm, Sa 9-11pm. AmEx/D/MC/V. ❸

HBN BCN, C. Escar 1 (☎225 0263), on Platja Sant Sebastià in Barceloneta. Offers Mediterranean and Cuban fare. Live band Th and Su at 6pm. Dinner reservations recommended. Kitchen open daily 1-4pm and 9pm-midnight. AmEx/MC/V. ❸

Pla dels Àngels, C. Ferlandina 23 (☎349 4047). M: Universitat. Colorful, inexpensive eatery has funky decor and a large vegetarian selection. Entrees €5-6. Open M-Th 1:30-4pm and 9-11:30pm, F-Sa 1:30-4pm and 9pm-midnight. MC/V. ❷

El Pebre Blau, C. Banys Vells 21 (☎319 1308). M: Jaume I. Ring the doorbell to get into this hidden gourmet restaurant. Kitchen open daily 8:30pm-midnight. Reservations recommended on weekends. Wheelchair accessible. MC/V. ❹

◉ SIGHTS

Barcelona is defined by its unique *Modernisme* architecture. The tourist areas are **Las Ramblas,** a bustling avenue smack in the city center, and the **Barri Gòtic,** Barcelona's "old city." Don't neglect vibrant **La Ribera** and **El Raval,** the upscale Modernist avenues of **l'Eixample,** the panoramic city views from **Montjuïc** and **Tibidabo,** and the harborside **Port Olímpic.** The **Ruta del Modernisme pass** is the cheapest and most flexible option for those with a few days and an interest in seeing all the biggest sights. Passes (€3.60; students, over 65, and groups of 11 or more €2.60) are good for a month and give holders discounts on entrance to Fundació Antoni Tàpies, the Museu d'Art Modern, tours of l'Hospital de la Santa Creu i Sant Pau, tours of the facades of La Manzana de la Discòrdia, and other attractions. The pass comes with a map and a pamphlet that gives a history of the sights. Buy passes at **Casa Amatller,** Pg. de Gràcia 41. (☎488 0139; www.rutamodernisme.com. M: Pg. de Gràcia.)

LAS RAMBLAS

Las Ramblas, a pedestrian-only median strip roughly 1km long, is a world-famous cornucopia of street performers, fortune-tellers, human statues, pet and flower stands, and artists, all for the benefit of the visiting droves of tourists. The wide, tree-lined thoroughfare dubbed Las Ramblas is actually composed of five (six if you count the small Rambla de Mar) distinct *ramblas* (promenades) that together form one boulevard starting at the Pl. de Catalunya and the **Font de Canaletes** (more a pump than a fountain). Visitors who wish to eventually return to Barcelona are supposed to sample the water.

GRAN TEATRE DEL LICEU. Once one of Europe's leading stages, the Liceu has been ravaged by anarchists, bombs, and fires. This theater, focusing on Catalan opera, is adorned with palatial ornamentation, gold facades, sculptures, and grand rooms—including a fantastic Spanish hall of mirrors. (*Las Ramblas 51-59, by C. de Sant Pau. M: Liceu. ☎485 9913, tours 485 9914; www.liceubarcelona.com. Tickets sold at box office M-F 2-8:30pm and Sa 1hr. before show. Also by ServiCaixa ☎902 33 22 11. Open to public daily 10am-1pm. Guided 30min. tours at 10am by reservation only; call 9am-2pm. €5.*)

CENTRE D'ART DE SANTA MÓNICA. One can only imagine what the nuns of this former convent would have thought of the edgy art installations that rotate through this large gallery, which is worth a visit for modern art fans. (*Las Ramblas 7. M: Drassanes. ☎316 2727. Open Tu-Sa 11am–2pm and 5-8pm. Call for info on exhibitions. Free.*)

MONUMENT A COLOM. Ruis i Taulet's Monument a Colom towers at the port end of Las Ramblas. Nineteenth-century *Renaixença* enthusiasts convinced themselves that Columbus was Catalan, from a town near Girona. The fact that Columbus proudly points toward Libya, not the Americas, doesn't help their claim; historians agree that Columbus was from Italy. Take the elevator to the top to enjoy a stunning view. *(Portal de la Pau. M: Drassanes. Elevator open daily June-Sept. 9am-8:30pm; Oct.-May 10am-6:30pm. €2, children and over 65 €1.30.)*

BARRI GÒTIC

The Barri Gòtic is the oldest part of Barcelona. While its ancient cathedrals and palaces may give the impression that this neighborhood's time has passed, its ever-crowded streets prove that the area is still very much alive.

■ **MUSEU D'HISTÒRIA DE LA CIUTAT.** There are two components to the Museu d'Història de la Ciutat (Museum of the History of Barcelona): the Palau Reial Major and the subterranean excavations of the Roman city Barcino. Built on top of the 4th-century city walls, the **Palau Reial Major** served as the residence of the Catalan-Aragonese monarchs. The second part of the museum lies underground; this 4000 sq. m **archaeological exhibit** displays incredibly intact 1st- to 6th-century remains of the Roman city of Barcino. *(Pl. del Rei. M: Jaume I. ☎315 1111; www.museuhistoria.bcn.es. Pamphlets available in English. Open May 11-Oct. M-Sa 10am-8pm, Su 10am-3pm; Oct.-May 10 Tu-Sa 10am-2pm and 4-8pm, Su 10am-3pm. Museum €4, students €2.50. Exhibition €3.50/€2. Combined museum and exhibition €6/€4.)*

ESGLÉSIA CATEDRAL DE LA SANTA CREU. This cathedral is one of Barcelona's most recognizable monuments. Beyond the choir are the altar with a bronze cross, designed by Frederic Marès in 1976, and the sunken Crypt of Santa Eulalia, one of Barcelona's patron saints. Catch a performance of the *sardana* in front of the cathedral on Sundays after mass. *(M: Jaume I. In Pl. Seu, up C. Bisbe from Pl. St. Jaume. Cathedral open daily 8am-12:45pm and 5:15-7:30pm. Cloister open daily 9am-12:30pm and 5:15-7pm. Elevator to the roof open M-Sa 10:30am-12:30pm and 5:15-6pm. €2. Choir area open M-F 9am-12:30pm and 5:15-7pm, Sa-Su 9am-12:30pm. €2. Guided tours 1-5pm, €4.)*

LA RIBERA

This neighborhood has recently evolved into Barcelona's bohemian nucleus, with art galleries, chic eateries, and exclusive bars.

■ **MUSEU PICASSO.** This museum traces the artistic development of Picasso, with the world's most comprehensive collection of work from his Barcelona period. Picasso donated over 1700 works to the museum; it now boasts 3600. *(C. Montcada 15-19. M: Jaume I. Open Tu-Sa 10am-8pm, Su 10am-3pm. €5, students and seniors €2.50, under 16 and 1st Su of each month free. €8/€4.70 includes temporary exhibition.)*

■ **PALAU DE LA MÚSICA CATALANA.** In 1891, the Orfeo Catalan choir society commissioned Modernist Luis Domènech i Montaner to design this concert venue. The music hall boasts stained-glass windows, an ornate chandelier, marble reliefs, intricate woodwork, and ceramic mosaics. Concerts given at the Palau include symphonic and choral music in addition to pop, rock, and jazz. *(C. Sant Francesc de Paula 2. ☎295 7200; www.palaumusica.org. M: Jaume I. Open daily Aug. 10am-6pm; Sept.-July 10am-3:30pm. €7, students and seniors €6. Mandatory tours in English, 1 per hr. Reserve 1 day in advance. Check the Guía del Ocio for concert listings. Concert tickets €6-330. MC/V.)*

PARC DE LA CIUTADELLA. Host of the 1888 World's Fair, the park harbors several museums, the **Cascada fountains**, a pond, and a zoo. The sprawling lawns are filled with strolling families, smoking students, and affectionate couples. Buildings of note include Domènech i Montaner's **Castell dels Tres Dracs** (now the Museu de Zoologia), the geological museum, and Josep Amergós's **Hivernacle.** The **Parc Zoològic** is home to several threatened and endangered species, including the Iberian wolf and the Sumatran tiger. *(M: Ciutadella. Open daily May-Aug. 9:30am-7:30pm; Apr. and Sept. 10am-7pm; Mar. and Oct. 10am-6pm; Nov.-Feb. 10am-5pm. €13, over 65 €7.20.)*

SANTA MARIA DEL MAR. This 14th-century architectural wonder was built in a quick 55 years. At a distance of 13m apart, the supporting columns span a width greater than any other medieval building in the world. It's a beautiful and fascinating example of the limits of Gothic architecture—were it 1m taller, the roof would collapse from structural instability. *(Pl. Santa Maria 1. M: Jaume 1. Open M-Sa 9am-1:30pm and 4:30-8pm, Su 10am-1:30pm and 4:30-8pm. Free.)*

EL RAVAL

Located next to Las Ramblas and the Barri Gòtic, the northern part of El Raval tends to be a favorite of Barcelona's natives rather than its tourists. Revitalization efforts, especially since the '92 Olympic games, have worked wonders; today El Raval is emerging as one of Barcelona's most dynamic areas.

▨ PALAU GÜELL. Gaudí's recently renovated 1886 Palau Güell—the Modernist residence built for patron Eusebi Güell (of Park Güell fame)—has one of Barcelona's most spectacular interiors. Güell spared no expense on this house, considered to be the first where Gaudí's unique style truly showed. *(C. Nou de La Rambla 3-5. M: Liceu. Mandatory tour every 15min. Open Mar.-Oct. M-Sa 10am-8pm, Su 10am-2pm, M-Sa last tour 6:15pm; Nov.-Dec. M-Sa 10am-6pm. €3, students €1.50.)*

MUSEU D'ART CONTEMPORANI (MACBA). This cleanly-designed building was constructed with the idea that sparse decor would allow the art to speak for itself. The MACBA has received worldwide acclaim for its focus on avant-garde art between the two world wars, as well as for its Surrealist and contemporary art. The main attraction is not the limited permanent exhibition, but the rotating 3-month exhibitions. *(Pl. dels Àngels 1. M: Catalunya. ☎ 412 0810; www.macba.es. Open July-Sept. M-F 11am-8pm, Sa 10am-8pm, Su 10am-3pm; Oct.-June M and W-F 11am-8pm, Sa 10am-8pm, Su 10am-3pm. €7, students €3, under 17 free; temporary exhibitions €2.50.)*

L'EIXAMPLE

The Catalan Renaissance and the growth of Barcelona during the 19th century pushed the city past its medieval walls and into modernity. Ildefons Cerdà drew up a plan for a new neighborhood where people of all social classes could live side by side; however, l'Eixample (luh-SHOMP-luh) did not thrive as a utopian community but rather as a playground for the bourgeois.

▨ LA SAGRADA FAMÍLIA. Although Antoni Gaudí's unfinished masterpiece is barely a shell of the intended finished product, La Sagrada Família is without a doubt the world's most visited construction site. Despite the fact that only eight of the 18 planned towers have been completed and the church still doesn't have an "interior," millions of people make the touristic pilgrimage to witness its work-in-progress majesty. Of the three proposed facades, only the Nativity Facade was finished under Gaudí. *(C. Mallorca 401. M: Sagrada Família. Open daily Apr.-Sept. 9am-8pm, elevator open 9:30am-7:45pm; Oct.-Mar. 9:30am-5:45pm, elevator open 9:30am-5:45pm. €8, students with ISIC €5. Combined ticket with Casa-Museu Dalí €8/€6. Elevator €2. Cash only.)*

▨ CASA MILÀ (LA PEDRERA). Modernism buffs argue that the spectacular Casa Milà apartment building, an undulating mass of granite popularly known as *La Pedrera* (the Stone Quarry), is Gaudí's most refined work. Note the intricate ironwork around the balconies and the irregularity of the front gate's egg-shaped window panes. The roof sprouts chimneys that resemble soldiers. Rooftop tours provide a closer look. The brick attic has been transformed into the **Espai Gaudí,** a multimedia presentation of Gaudí's life and works. *(Pg. de Gràcia 92. ☎ 902 40 09 73. Open daily 10am-8pm. Free guided tours in English M-F 4pm. €7, students and over 65 €3.50.)*

LA MANZANA DE LA DISCÒRDIA. A short walk from Pl. de Catalunya, the odd-numbered side of Pg. de Gràcia between C. Aragó and Consell de Cent is popularly known as *la manzana de la discòrdia* (block of discord), referring to the stylistic clashing of three buildings. Regrettably, the bottom two floors of **Casa**

LA RIBERA

This walking tour is a trip through the Parc de la Ciutadella and La Ribera, one of the oldest sections of the city. Begin your day early with breakfast at a restaurant or cafe near your room, and stop by your local grocery store for picnic fixings. Take the metro to Arc de Triomf and get ready to roll.

START: M: Arc de Triomf, L1

FINISH: M: Jaume I, L4

DISTANCE: 2½km

DURATION: 5hr.

WHEN TO GO: A sunny weekday morning

1 ARC DE TRIOMF. This Modernist work was created by Josep Vilaseca to welcome visitors to the 1888 Exposition.

2 MUSEU DE ZOOLOGIA. Follow Pg. Lluís Companys toward Parc de la Ciutadella (four blocks south), one of Barcelona's most beautiful public spaces. The park is a favorite of families with young children and couples on romantic outings. Domènech i Montaner's Museu de Zoologia (formerly the Castell dels Tres Dracs; p. 968) is one of the first creations that spawned Barcelona's famous architectural movement, Modernisme.

3 CASCADE FOUNTAINS. Across the park from the Museu de Zoologia are the whimsical Cascade Fountains (p. 968). Unpack your lunch and relax by the water as children chase pigeons and orange trees sway in the wind. If all the splashing has gotten you in the mood for water sports, rent a boat at the nearby pond.

4 MUSEU D'ART MODERN. Continuing south in the park, follow signs for the Museu D'Art Modern (p. 971). Gaze at one of the finest collections of Noucentiste sculpture in the world, or study some of Dalí's early paintings (the only works of his still left in Barcelona).

5 PARC ZOOLÒGIC. Barcelona's zoo is home to some 7500 animals, representing over 400 species (p. 968). Bet you've never heard of the lowland anoa.

6 ESGLÉSIA SANTA MARIA DEL MAR. "Mary of the Sea," a church built in the 14th century to serve the sailors of La Ribera, features the widest Medieval nave in the world (p. 969). Another architectural feat of note: If the roof were 1m higher, it would collapse from structural instability.

Visit us at http://www.letsgo.com

LET'S GO
Travel Guides

Be sure to check out our new
website, beyondtourism.com,
for a searchable database of
international volunteer, work
and study opportunities, a
blog from fellow travelers
and feature articles
highlighting a variety of
destination-specific
opportunities.

Purchase one of our 48 guides
online or at your local bookstore

Alaska - Amsterdam - Australia - Austria & Switzerland - Barcelona - Brita
& Ireland - Brazil - California - Central America - China - Chile - Costa Rica
Ecuador - Eastern Europe - Egypt - Europe - France - Germany - Greece -
Hawaii - India & Nepal - Ireland - Israel & the Palestinian Territories - Italy
Japan - London - Mexico - Middle East - New York City - New Zealand &
Fiji - Paris - Peru - Pacific Northwest - Puerto Rico - Roadtrip USA - Rom
San Francisco - South Africa - Southeast Asia - Southwest USA - Spain
Portugal & Morocco - Thailand - Turkey - Vietnam - USA - Washington
D.C. - Western Europe

http://www.letsgo.com

Lleó i Morera, by Domènech i Montaner, were destroyed to make room for a fancy store, but with the Ruta del Modernisme pass you can take a short tour of the upper floors, where sprouting flowers, stained glass, and legendary doorway sculptures adorn the interior. Puig i Cadafalch opted for a geometric, Moorish-influenced pattern on the facade of **Casa Amatller** at #41. Gaudí's balconies ripple like water and purple-blue tiles sparkle on **Casa Batlló,** #43. The ChupaChups lollipop company now owns the Casa Batlló, and it is closed to the public except for tours. *(Open M-Sa 9am-2pm, Su 9am-8pm. €8, students €6.)*

MONTJUÏC

Throughout Barcelona's history, whoever controlled Montjuïc (mon-joo-EEK; Hill of the Jews) controlled the city. Dozens of rulers have modified the **fortress,** built atop an ancient Jewish cemetery; Franco made it one of his "interrogation" headquarters. The fort was not re-dedicated to the city until 1960. Since then, Barcelona has given Montjuïc a new identity, transforming it from a military stronghold into a vast park by day and a playground by night.

■ **FUNDACIÓ MIRÓ.** Designed by Miró's friend Josep Lluis Sert, the Fundació links modern interior and exterior spaces with massive windows and outdoor patios. Skylights illuminate an extensive collection of statues and paintings from Miró's career, ranging from small sketches to wall-sized canvases. Room 13 displays experimental works by young artists. The Fundació also sponsors music and film festivals; check the *Guía del Ocio* for listings. *(Av. Miramar 71-75. Take the funicular from M: Paral·lel. Open Tu-W and F-Sa 10am-7pm, Th 10am-9:30pm, Su and holidays 10am-2:30pm. €7.20, students and seniors €4. Temporary exhibitions €3.60/€1.80. Under 14 free.)*

■ **MUSEU NACIONAL D'ART DE CATALUNYA (PALAU NACIONAL).** Designed by Enric Catá and Pedro Cendoya for the 1929 World's Fair, the beautiful Palau Nacional has housed the Museu Nacional d'Art de Catalunya (MNAC) since 1934. Its main hall is a public event space, while the wings are home to the world's finest collection of Catalan Romanesque art and a wide variety of Gothic pieces. As soon as 2005, the historical art of the museum will be complemented by modern art from the Museu d'Art Modern, which is being moved into the Palau Nacional from its previous home in the Parc de la Ciutadella. In front of the building are the **Fonts Luminoses** (the Illuminated Fountains), dominated by the central **Font Màgica**. *(From M: Espanya, walk up Av. Reina María Cristina, away from the brick towers, and take the escalators to the top. Open Tu–Sa 10am-7pm, Su 10am-2:30pm. €5 for permanent Romanesque exhibit. Temporary exhibits €3 4.20; both temporary exhibits €5; 1 temporary plus permanent €6; all exhibits €7.50. 30% discount for students and seniors.)*

WATERFRONT

■ **TORRE SAN SEBASTIÀ.** One of the easiest and best ways to view the city is on the cable cars which span the entire Port Vell. The full ride, which takes about 10min. each way and makes an intermediate stop at the Jaume I tower near Colom, gives an aerial perspective of the entire city. *(Pg. Joan de Borbó. M: Barceloneta. In Port Vell, as you walk down Joan de Borbó and see the beaches to the left, stay right and look for the high tower. Open daily 11am-8pm. To Jaume I round-trip €7.50; to Montjuïc one-way €7.50, round-trip €9; short trip to the other tower €7.50; elevator to the top €3.50.)*

■ **L'AQUÀRIUM DE BARCELONA.** Barcelona's aquarium—the largest in Europe—is an aquatic wonder, featuring a large number of octopi and penguins. The highlight is a 75m glass tunnel through an ocean tank of sharks, sting rays, and a two-dimensional fish. *(Moll d'Espanya, next to Maremàgnum. Advanced tickets ☎ 221 7474; www.aquariumbcn.com. M: Drassanes or Barceloneta. Open daily July-Aug. 9:30am-11pm; Sept.-June 9:30am-9:30pm. €13.50, students €12.50, under 12 and seniors €9.25.)*

VILA OLÍMPICA. The Vila Olímpica, beyond the eastern side of the zoo, was built to house 15,000 athletes and entertain millions of tourists for the 1992 Summer Olympics. It's home to several public parks, a shopping center, and business offices. This is the newest, most modern part of Barcelona. *(M: Ciutadella/Vila Olímpica. Walk along the waterfront on Ronda Litoral toward the two towers.)*

ZONA ALTA

Zona Alta (uptown) is the section of Barcelona that lies at the top of most maps: past l'Eixample and away from the low-lying waterfront districts. The most visited part of Zona Alta is Gràcia, which was incorporated into Barcelona in 1897, despite the protest of its residents. Gràcia packs a surprising number of Modernist buildings, international cuisine, and chic shops into a relatively small area.

■ **PARK GÜELL.** This fantastic park was designed entirely by Gaudí but—in typical Gaudí fashion—was not completed until after his death. Gaudí intended Park Güell to be a garden city; its dwarfish buildings and sparkling ceramic-mosaic stairways were designed for the elite. Only one house was actually built; it is now the **Casa-Museu Gaudí.** Two mosaic staircases flank the park, leading to a towering Modernist pavilion that Gaudí originally designed as an open-air market. The longest park bench in the world, a multicolored serpentine wonder made of tile shards, decorates the top of the pavilion. *(Bus #24 from Pl. Catalunya stops at the upper entrance. Park free. Open daily May-Sept. 10am-9pm; Mar.-Apr. and Oct. 10am-7pm; Nov.-Feb. 10am-6pm. Museum open daily Apr.-Sept. 10am-8pm; Oct.-Mar. 10am-6pm. €4, students with ISIC €3.)*

MUSEU DEL FÚTBOL CLUB BARCELONA. A close second to the Picasso Museum as Barcelona's most-visited museum, the FCB museum merits all the attention it gets. Sports fans will appreciate the storied history of the team. The high point is the chance to enter the stadium and take in the enormity of Camp Nou. To see the facilities, such as the dressing room and the field, costs extra. *(C. Arístides Maillol, next to the stadium. ☎ 496 3608. M: Collblanc. Enter through access gates 7 or 9. Open M-Sa 10am-6:30pm, Su and holidays 10am-2pm. €5.30, students and seniors €4.50, under 13 €3.70. Facilities and museum €9.50, students and seniors €8.10, under 13 €7.)*

♫ ▓ ENTERTAINMENT AND FESTIVALS

For tips on entertainment, nightlife, and food, pick up the *Guía del Ocio* (www.guiadelociobcn.es) at any newsstand. The best shopping in the city is in the **Barri Gòtic,** but if you feel like dropping some extra cash, check out the posh **Passeig de Gràcia** in l'Eixample. Grab face paint to join Barça at the Camp Nou stadium for **fútbol.** (Box office C. Arístedes Maillol 12-18. ☎ 902 18 99 00. Tickets €30-60.) **Barceloneta** and **Poble Nou** feature tons of sand for topless tanning, as well as plenty of places to rent sailboats and other water-sports equipment. Head up to Montjuïc to take advantage of the **Olympic Facilities,** which are now open for public use, including **Piscines Bernat Picornell,** the gorgeous pool complex. (☎ 423 4041. Open M-F 7am-midnight, Sa 7am-9pm, Su 7am-8pm.)

Festivals in Barcelona, as in the rest of Spain, occur often. Remember to double check sight and museum hours during festival times, as well as during the Christmas season and during *Semana Santa* (Holy Week; the week before Easter). The **Festa de Sant Jordi** (St. George; Apr. 24) celebrates Cataluña's patron saint with a feast. The **Sónar** music festival comes to town in mid-June, attracting renowned DJs and electronic enthusiasts from all over the world for three days of concerts. On September 11, the **Festa Nacional de Catalunya** brings traditional costumes, dancing, and Catalan flags hanging from balconies. **Festa de Sant Joan** takes place the night before June 24; ceaseless fireworks will prevent any attempts to sleep. The largest Barcelona celebration, however, is the **Festa de Mercè,** the week before and after September 24. To honor the Patron Saint of the city, *barceloneses* revel with fireworks, *castellers, sardana* dancing, and concerts.

▓ NIGHTLIFE

Nightlife in Barcelona needs no introduction: whether you're looking for emerald absinthe shots, a great place for grunge rock, a sunrise foam party, or just some-place quiet to sit back and enjoy a drink, the city has it all. Check the *Guía del Ocio*, available at newsstands, for up-to-date listings.

CIUTAT VELLA

In the **Barri Gòtic**, main streets such as C. Ferran hold cookie-cutter *cervecerías* and *bar-restaurantes* every five steps. **La Ribera** has recently evolved into a hip, artsy district, attracting a young crowd of locals and a few expats and tourists in the know. The streets of **El Raval** are packed with every variety of bar-hopper.

▓ **Jamboree,** Pl. Reial 17. (☎301 7564) M: Liceu. What was once a convent now serves as a popular live music venue. Converted into a crowded hip-hop club later at night. Drinks €8-10. Cover M €3, Tu-Sa €8. Open daily 11pm-1am; nightclub open daily 2-5am.

▓ **El Copetín,** Pg. del Born 19. M: Jaume I. Cuban rhythm infuses everything in this small, casual nightspot. Mojitos €5. Open M-Th and Su 7pm-2:30am, F-Sa 7pm-3am.

▓ **Casa Almirall,** C. Joaquim Costa 33. M: Universitat. Cavernous space. The staff will walk you through your first glass of absinthe (€6.50)—and cut you off after your second. Beer €3-4. Mixed drinks €6-8. Open M-Th and Su 7pm-2:30am, F-Sa 7pm-3am.

El Bosc de les Fades, Pg. de la Banca 5 (☎317 2649). M: Drassanes, near the Wax Museum. This bar features gnarled trees and gnomes. A good place to hang out before hitting a club. Open M-Th 2pm-1am, F 2pm-2am, Sa 11am-2am, Su 11am-1am.

Molly Malone, C. Ferran 7. (☎342 4026). M: Liceu. The place to go if you want to meet English-speaking tourists guzzling pricey but strong mixed drinks. Guinness on tap €5. Bottled beer €4. Mixed drinks €7-8. Open M-Th and Su 8pm-2:30am, F-Sa 7pm-3am.

L'EIXAMPLE

L'Eixample has upscale bars and some of the best gay nightlife in Europe, as evidenced by the area's nickname, "Gaixample."

▓ **Buenavista Salsoteca,** C. Rosselló 217 (☎237 6528). M: Diagonal. This over-the-top club manages to attract a chill crowd. Free salsa lessons W 10:30pm. Cover F-Sa €9, includes 1 drink. Open W-Th 11pm-4am, F-Sa 11pm-5am, Su 8:30pm-2am.

Dietrich, C. Consell de Cent 255. M: Pg. de Gràcia. An unflattering painting of Marlene Dietrich in the semi-nude greets a mostly gay crowd. Nightly dance and trapeze show 1:30am. Beer €3.50. Mixed drinks €5-8. Open M-F and Su 6pm-2:30am, Sa 6pm 3am.

La Fira, C. Provença 171. M: Hospital Clínic or FGC: Provença. Bartenders serve a hip crowd Open Tu-Th 10pm-3am, F-Sa 7pm-4:30am, Su 6pm-1am.

Átame, C. Consell de Cent 257. M: Pg de Gràcia. Next to Dietrich, this bar, frequented mainly by gay men, is not as scandalous as its name ("tie me up") might imply. A great spot for relaxed drinks. Beer €3. Mixed drinks €3-8. Open daily 5pm-3am.

MONTJUÏC

Lower Montjuïc is home to **Poble Espanyol,** Av. Marqués de Comillas, a recreation of famous buildings and sights from all regions of Spain. At night the complex becomes a disco theme park. (☎508 6300; www.poble-espanyol.com. M: Espanya.)

▓ **Tinta Roja,** C. Creus dels Molers 17 (☎443 3243), near Poble Espanyol. Live tango show. Open W-Su 8pm-2:30am.

La Terrazza, Poble Espanyol (☎423 1285). Fantastic outdoor dance floor. Cover €15, includes 1 drink. Open May-Oct. F-Sa 1am-7am.

Discothèque, Poble Espanyol. (☎423 1285). Winter counterpart of La Terrazza. Dress to impress. Cover €18, includes 1 drink. Open Oct.-Apr. F-Sa 1-7am, Su 7pm-12am.

SPAIN

WATERFRONT

Poble Nou and **Port Olímpic** are home to docked sailboats, restaurants, and a long strip of nightclubs. The entire waterfront area, which stretches from **Maremàgnum** to **Port Vell**, is perhaps as hedonistic and touristy as Barcelona gets. At night Maremàgnum turns into a tri-level maze of clubs; crowds are guaranteed even on weeknights. There is no cover; clubs make their money by charging exorbitant drink prices (beer €5, mixed drinks €8-10). Catching a cab home can be difficult.

L'Ovella Negra (Megataverna del Poble Nou), C. Zamora 78. (☎309 5938). The place to come for the first few beers of the night. Large beers €2. Mixed drinks from €2. Open F-Sa 5pm-3am, Su 5-10:30pm. Kitchen open F-Sa 5pm-12:30am.

Razzmatazz, C. Pamplona 88 and Almogàvers 122, across the street (☎272 0910). M: Marina. A huge warehouse-turned-entertainment complex now houses 5 clubs. Beer €3. Mixed drinks from €5. Cover €12. Open F-Sa and holidays 1-5am. MC/V.

Nayandei, Maremàgnum. 2 clubs in one: **Disco** has an open-door policy, while **Boîte** has a more exclusive dress code. Spanish and American dance-pop. No cover. Open M-Th and Su 9pm-4:30am, F-Sa 9pm-6am.

ZONA ALTA

The area around C. de Marià Cubí has great nightlife undiscovered by tourists, but you'll have to take a taxi. For more accessible fun in Gràcia, head to Pl. Sol.

Otto Zutz, C. Lincoln 15 (☎238 0722; www.ottozutz.com). FGC: Pl. Molina. Groove to house, hip-hop, and funk. Beer €5. Cover €15, includes 1 drink; email ahead or look for flyers for a discount. Open Tu-W midnight-5am, Th-Sa midnight-6am.

Gasterea, C. Verdi 39. M: Fontana. Yellow walls cast a warm glow in this table-less bar. Tapas €1.05. Mixed drinks €5. M-Tu, Th, and Su 7pm-1am; F-Sa 7pm-2am. Cash only.

Bar Marcel, C. Santaló 42. When midnight strikes, locals pack this place in search of cheap booze. Certainly not the fanciest bar in the neighborhood, but possibly the most loved. Beer €1.60. Mixed drinks €5. Open daily 8pm-3am.

▣ DAYTRIPS FROM BARCELONA

THE COSTA BRAVA: FIGUERES AND CADAQUÉS

From Figueres, trains (☎902 24 02 02) run from Pl. de l'Estació to Barcelona (2hr., 23 per day, €8.40) and Girona (30min., 13-23 per day, €2.50). Buses (☎972 67 33 54) run from Pl. de l'Estació to: Barcelona (2¼hr., 2-4 per day, €13); Cadaqués (1¼hr., 3-5 per day, €3.65); and Girona (1hr., 2-5 per day, €3.60). Buses arrive in Cadaqués from: Barcelona (2½hr., 2 per day, €16.20); Figueres; and Girona (2hr., 1-2 per day, €7.10).

The Costa Brava's jagged cliffs cut into the Mediterranean Sea from Barcelona to the French border. Though rugged by name, the Brave Coast is tamed in July and August by the planeloads of Europeans dumped onto its once-tranquil beaches.

In 1974, Salvador Dalí chose his native, beachless **Figueres** (pop. 35,000) as the site to build a museum to house his works, catapulting the city into international fame. His personal tribute is a Surreal masterpiece—and the second most popular museum in Spain. The ▣**Teatre-Museu Dalí** is in Pl. Gala. From La Rambla, take C. Girona, which becomes C. Jonquera, and climb the steps to your left. The museum contains the artist's nightmarish landscapes and bizarre installations, as well as his tomb. (☎972 67 75 00; www.salvador-dali.org. Open daily July-Sept. 9am-7:45pm; Oct.-June 10:30am-5:45pm. Call ahead about night hours during the summer. €9, students €6.50, nights €10.) The **tourist office** is in Pl. Sol. (☎972 50 31 55. Open July-Aug. M-Sa 9am-8pm, Su 9am-3pm; Sept. M-Sa 9am-8pm; Nov.-Mar. M-F 9am-3pm; Apr.-June and Oct. M-F 9am-3pm and 4:30-7pm, Sa 10am-2pm and 3:30-6:30pm.) **Hostal La Barretina ❷,** C. Lasauca 13, is a lesson in luxury. (☎972 67 64 12. Singles €23; doubles €39. AmEx/MC/V.) **Postal Code:** 17600.

The whitewashed houses and rocky beaches of **Cadaqués** (pop. 2000) have attracted artists, writers, and musicians—not to mention tourists—ever since Dalí built his summer home in nearby Port Lligat. **⬛Casa-Museu Salvador Dalí,** Dalí's home until 1982, houses a lip-shaped sofa and a pop-art miniature Alhambra. Follow the signs to Port Lligat (bear up and to the right with your back to the Sarfa office) and then to the Casa de Dalí (30min.), or take a trolley to Port Lligat (1hr.; 4 per day; €6, children €5) from Pl. Frederic Rahola. (☎972 25 10 15. Open daily June 15-Sept. 15 10am-9pm; Sept. 16-Nov. and Mar. 15-June 14 Tu-Su 10am-6pm. Tours are the only way to see the house; make reservations 1-2 days in advance. Last tour 45-50min. before closing. €8, students €5.) With your back to the Sarfa office at the bus stop, walk right along Av. Caritat Serinyana to find a signboard map at Plaça Frederic Rahola; the **tourist office,** C. Cotxe 2, is to the right of the *plaça,* opposite the beach. (☎972 25 83 15. Open July-Aug. M-Sa 9am-2pm and 3-8pm, Su 10:30am-1pm; Sept.-June M-Sa 9am-2pm and 4-7pm.) **Postal Code:** 17488.

THE COSTA DORADA: SITGES

RENFE trains (☎934 90 02 02) run from Barcelona to Sitges (40min., every 15-30min. 5:30am-11pm, €2.20). Mon Bus (☎938 93 70 60) runs late-night buses from Pg. Villa-granca in Sitges to Rbla. Catalunya in Barcelona (and back) midnight-4am (€2.85).

A mecca of gay nightlife, the town of Sitges is perhaps better seen as a night trip from Barcelona rather than as a day trip. Sitges's gorgeous beaches are often less crowded than those of nearby towns. The places to be at sundown are **Calle Primer de Maig** (which runs directly from the beach and Pg. Ribera) and **Calle Marquès Montroig,** off C. Parellades. Bars and clubs welcoming a mixed crowd line both sides of the small street, blasting pop and house from 10pm until 3am. Bar- and club-hopping is made easy by the universal lack of cover charge. At most places, drinks cost €3-6. A wilder party can be found at the "disco-beach" **Atlàntida,** in Sector Terramar (☎938 94 26 77), or **Pachá,** on Pg. Sant Didac in nearby Vallpineda (☎938 94 22 98). Buses run all night on weekends to the two discos from C. Primer de Maig. **Calle Bonaire** and **Calle Sant Pau** are home to other popular night spots, but most are open only on weekends. For more info on nightlife, pick up a *Guía del Ocio* from the **tourist office,** Sínia Morera 1. (☎938 94 50 04. Open daily July-Sept. 9am-9pm; Oct.-June M-F 9am-2pm and 4-6:30pm.) **Postal Code:** 08870.

GIRONA

RENFE trains (☎902 24 02 02), Pl. de Espanya, run to Barcelona (1½hr., 25 per day, €6) and Figueres (40min., 23 per day, €2.50). Baroolona Buses (☎972 20 24 32) run from next door to Barcelona (1¼hr., 3-6 per day, €12) and Figueres (1hr., 3-6 por day, €5).

A world-class city patiently waiting to be noticed, Girona (pop. 81,000) is really two cities in one: a hushed medieval masterpiece on one riverbank and a thriving, modern metropolis on the other. Nine bridges connect the two banks of the **Riu Onyar,** including **Pont de Pedra,** which heads into the old quarter by way of C. Ciutadans, which eventually becomes C. Força and leads to the cathedral and ⬛**El Call,** the medieval Jewish neighborhood. A thriving community in the Middle Ages, El Call was virtually wiped out by the 1492 Inquisition and expulsion. The entrance to **Centre Bonastruc Ça Porta,** the site of the last synagogue in Girona (today a museum), is off C. Força, about halfway up the hill. (☎972 21 67 61. Open June-Oct. M-Sa 10am-8pm, Su 10am-3pm; Nov.-May M-Sa 10am-6pm, Su 10am-3pm. Museum €2, students and seniors €1.) Uphill on C. Força, the imposing Gothic **cathedral** rises 90 steps from the plaza below. Within, the **Tesoro Capitular** contains some of Girona's most precious art. (Both open July-Sept. Tu-Sa 10am-8pm, Su 10am-2pm; Oct.-Feb. Tu-Sa 10am-2pm and 4-6pm, Su 10am-2pm; Mar.-June Tu-Sa 10am-2pm and 4-7pm, Su 10am-2pm. Cathedral free. Tesoro €3, students €2.) The expansive **Parc de la Devesa** explodes during the summer with *carpas,* temporary outdoor bars. (Open June to mid-Sept. M-Th and Su 10pm-3:30am, F-Sa 10pm-4:30am.)

The **tourist office** is at Rbla. de la Libertat 1. (☎972 22 65 75. Open M-F 8am-8pm, Sa 8am-2pm and 4-8pm, Su 9am-2pm.) Most budget accommodations are in the old quarter. The **Pensió Viladomat ❸**, C. Ciutadans 5, has well-furnished rooms. (☎972 20 31 76. Singles €17; doubles €33-35, with bath €56. Cash only.) **Calle Cort Reial** is the best place to find good, cheap food. Pick up groceries at **Caprabo**, C. Sequia 10, a block from C. Nou off Gran Vía. (Open M-Sa 9am-9pm.) **Postal Code:** 17070.

THE PYRENEES

The jagged green mountains, Romanesque churches, and tranquil towns of the Pyrenees draw hikers and skiers in search of outdoor adventure. Spectacular views make driving through the countryside an incredible experience.

VAL D'ARAN   ☎973

Some of the Catalan Pyrenees' most dazzling peaks cluster around the Val d'Aran, in the northwest corner of Cataluña. The Val d'Aran is best known for its chic ski resorts. The Spanish royal family's favorite slopes are those of **Baquiera-Beret**. The **Auberja Era Garona (HI) ❷**, on Ctra. de Vielha, is 4km downhill in the lovely town of Salardú. (☎64 52 71; www.aranweb.com/garona. Breakfast included. May-June and Sept. 16-Nov. €13, under 26 €12.60. Dec.-Apr. Sa-Su and *Semana Santa* €19.40/€17; Dec.-Apr. M-F and July-Sept. 15 €17.20/€15.) Salardú's 13th-century **church** houses beautifully restored 16th-century murals. For skiing info and reservations, contact the **Oficeria de Baquiera-Beret**. (☎63 90 00; fax 64 44 88.)

The biggest town in the valley, **Vielha** (pop. 7000) welcomes hikers and skiers to its street. It's only 13km from Baquiera-Beret; **shuttle buses** connect the two during July and August (schedules at the tourist office). Alsina Graells (in Lleida ☎27 14 70) runs **buses** to Barcelona (5hr., 2-3 per day, €24) and Lleida (2hr., 5:30am and 1:30pm). The **tourist office**, C. Sarriulèra 10, is one block upstream from the plaza. (☎64 01 10; www.aran.org. Open daily 9am-9pm.) Several inexpensive *pensiones* cluster at the end of C. Reiau, off Pg. Libertat (which intersects Av. Casteiro at Pl. Sant Antoni); try **Casa Vicenta ❷**, at C. Reiau 3. (☎64 08 19. Dec.-*Semana Santa* and July 15-Sept. 15 singles €22; doubles €33, with bath €37. Rest of the year singles €19; doubles €27/€32. Closed Oct.-Nov.)

PARQUE NACIONAL DE ORDESA   ☎974

The beauty of Ordesa's Aragonese Pyrenees will enchant even the most seasoned traveler; its well-maintained trails cut across idyllic forests, jagged rock faces, snow-covered peaks, rushing rivers, and magnificent waterfalls. The main **trail** that runs up the Río Arazas to the foot of Monte Perdido and Refugio Góriz, with three spectacular waterfalls within 1hr. of the trailhead, is the most practical and rewarding hike, especially for inexperienced hikers. For more information, visit www.ordesa.net. The **Visitors' Center** is on the left, 1.8km past the park entrance. (Open daily Apr. to mid-Sept. 9am-2pm and 4-7pm.) The **park info center** in Torla, across the street from the bus stop, takes over in low season. Here you can pick up free maps and the **Senderos Sector** trail guide. (☎48 64 72. Open Oct.-June M-F 8am-3pm; July-Sept. M-F 8am-3pm, Sa-Su 9am-2pm and 4:30-7pm.) La Oscense (☎48 00 45) sends a **bus** from Jaca to Sabiñánigo (20min., 4-6 per day, €1.50). Sabiñánigo is also easily accessible by **train;** all trains on the Zaragoza-Huesca-Jaca line stop here. From there, Compañía Hudebus (☎21 32 77) runs to Torla (55min., 1-2 per day, €2.50). During the high season, a bus shuttles between Torla and Ordesa (15min.; approx. every 15min. 6am-7pm; €2.10, round-trip €3.10). In low season, you'll have to hike 8km to the park entrance or catch a Jorge Soler **taxi** (☎48 62 43; €12). To exit the park area, catch the bus from Torla to Sabiñánigo (daily 3:30pm, July-Aug. also 6pm). In the park, many *refugios* (mountain huts) allow overnight stays. Across from the tourist office is **La Casa de Laly ❶**, C. Fatas. (☎48 61 68. Doubles €26, with bath €32.) Stock up at **Supermercado Torla**, on C. Francia. (☎48 63 88. Open daily May-Oct. 8:30am-2pm and 5-8:30pm; Nov.-Apr. closed Su. MC/V.)

NAVARRA

Bordered by Basque Country to the west and Aragón to the east, Navarra's villages—from the rustic Pyrenean *pueblos* on the French border to bustling Pamplona—are seldom visited apart from the festival of *San Fermines*. These mellow towns welcome non-bullrunning tourists with enthusiasm and open arms.

PAMPLONA (IRUÑA)   ☎948

While the lush parks, impressive museums, and medieval churches of Pamplona (pop. 200,000) await exploration, it's an annual, eight-minute event that draws visitors from around the world. Since the publication of Ernest Hemingway's *The Sun Also Rises*, hordes of travelers have come the week of July 6-14 to witness and experience *San Fermines*, the legendary "Running of the Bulls."

> Although Pamplona is usually very safe, crime skyrockets during *San Fermines*. Beware of assaults and muggings, and do not walk alone at night.

TRANSPORTATION AND PRACTICAL INFORMATION. Trains (☎902 24 02 02) run from the inconveniently located station, on Av. de San Jorge, to Barcelona (6-8hr., 3-9 per day, €30-38) and Madrid (3¾hr., 3 per day, €46). **Buses** go from C. Conde Oliveto, at C. Yanguas y Miranda, to: Barcelona (5½hr., 4 per day, €20); Bilbao (2hr., 4-6 per day, €12); Madrid (5hr., 4-7 per day, €23); and San Sebastián (1hr., 8-9 per day, €5.50). From Pl. del Castillo, take C. San Nicolás, turn right on C. San Miguel, and walk through Pl. San Francisco to get to the **tourist office**, C. Hilarión Eslava 1. (☎20 65 40; www.navarra.es. Open during *San Fermines* daily 8am-8pm; July-Aug. M-Sa 9am-8pm, Su 10am-2pm; Sept.-June M-F 10am-2pm and 4-7pm, Sa 10am-2pm.) During *San Fermines*, **store luggage** at the Escuelas de San Francisco, at the end of Pl. San Francisco. (€2 per day. Open 24hr.) Check email at **Kuria.Net,** C. Curia 15. (☎22 30 77. €3 per hr. Open M-Sa 10am-10pm, Su 1-10pm; during *San Fermines* daily 9am-11pm.) **Postal Code:** 31001.

ACCOMMODATIONS AND FOOD. Smart *San Ferministus* book their rooms up to a year (or at least three months) in advance to avoid paying rates up to four times higher than those listed below; without a reservation, it's difficult to find a room. Check the newspaper *Diario de Navarra* for *casas particulares;* be aware, though, that many owners prefer Spanish guests. Many roomless backpackers are forced to sleep outside. Be careful—if you can't store your backpack, sleep on top of it. During the rest of the year, finding a room in Pamplona is easy. Budget accommodations line **Calle San Nicolás** and **Calle San Gregorio** off Pl. del Castillo. **Pensión Eslava ❶**, C. Eslava 13, 2nd fl., is quieter and less crowded than other *pensiones*. (☎22 15 58. Singles €10-15; doubles €20-30. *San Fermines* doubles €100. Discounts for longer stays. Cash only.) To get to **Camping Ezcaba ❶**, in Eusa, 7km from the city, take city bus line 4-1 (4 per day; 26 per day, 24hr. during *San Fermines;* €1) from Pl. de las Merindades. (☎33 03 15. €3.50 per person, per tent, and per car. *San Fermines* €9 per person, per tent, and per car. AmEx/MC/V.) Aside from C. San Nicolás and **Plaza del Castillo,** look for food around **Plaza San Francisco** and **Paseo Ronda. Calle Navarrería** and **Paseo Sarasate** have good *bocadillo* bars. Stock up at **Vendi,** C. Hilarión Eslava and C. Mayor. (Open M-F 9am-2pm and 5:30-7:30pm, Sa 9am-2pm. MC/V.)

◙ ▣ **SIGHTS AND NIGHTLIFE.** Pamplona's rich architectural legacy is reason enough to visit during the 51 other weeks of the year. The restored 14th-century Gothic **cathedral** is at the end of C. Navarrería. (Open M-F 10am-7pm, Sa 10am-2:30pm. Free. Guided tours €4.) The walls of the pentagonal **Ciudadela** once humbled Napoleon; today the Ciudadela hosts free exhibits and summer concerts. Follow Po. Sarasate to its end and take a right on Navas de Tolosa; take the next left onto C. Chinchilla and follow it to its end. (Open M-Sa 7:30am-9:30pm, Su 9am-9:30pm. Closed for *San Fermines.* Free.) **Plaza del Castillo** is the heart of the social scene. Hemingway's favorite haunt was **Café-Bar Iruña,** immortalized in *The Sun Also Rises.* (Open M-Th 8am-11pm, F 8am-2pm, Sa 9am-2am, Su 9am-11pm. MC/V.) A young crowd boozes up in the *casco antiguo,* around **Calle San Nicolás, Calle de Jarauta,** and **Calle de San Gregorio,** before hitting the **Travesia de Bayona,** a plaza of bars and *discotecas* off Av. Bayona (follow Av. del Ejército past the Ciudadela for 600m).

▨ **LOS SAN FERMINES (JULY 6-14).** Visitors overcrowd the city as Pamplona delivers an eight-day frenzy of bullfights, concerts, dancing, fireworks, parades, parties, and wine. Pamplonese, clad in white with red sashes and bandanas, literally throw themselves into the merry-making, displaying obscene levels of both physical stamina and tolerance for alcohol. The "Running of the Bulls," called the *encierro,* is the highlight of *San Fermines;* the first *encierro* takes place on July 7 at 8am and is repeated at 8am every day for the next seven days. Hundreds of bleary-eyed, hungover, hyper-adrenalized runners flee from large bulls as bystanders cheer from barricades, windows, balconies, and doorways. Both the bulls and the mob are dangerous; terrified runners react without concern for those around them. **Be very careful; follow the tourist office's guidelines for running.** To participate in the bullring excitement without the risk of the *enceierro,* line up by the Pl. de Toros well before 7:30am and run in *before* the bulls are in sight; be prepared, however, for jeers from locals. Hemingway had the right idea: Don't run. Instead, arrive at the bullring around 6:45am to watch the *encierro.* Tickets for the Grada section of the ring are available before 7am (M-F €3.80, Sa-Su €4.40). You can watch for free, but the free section is overcrowded, making it hard to see and breathe. To watch a bullfight, wait in the line that forms at the bullring around 6:30pm. As one fight ends, the next day's tickets go on sale. (Prices vary from €5 to €888; check www.feriadeltoro.com for details). Once the running ends, insanity spills into the streets and gathers steam until nightfall, when it explodes with singing in bars, dancing in alleyways, spontaneous parades, and a no-holds-barred party in Pl. del Castillo, Europe's biggest open-air dance floor.

BASQUE COUNTRY (PAÍS VASCO)

Basque Country's varied landscape resembles a nation complete in itself, combining cosmopolitan cities, verdant hills, industrial wastelands, and quaint fishing villages. Many believe that the strongly nationalistic Basques are the native people of Iberia, as their culture and language cannot be traced to any known source.

SAN SEBASTIÁN (DONOSTIA) ☎943

Glittering on the shores of the Cantabrian Sea, coolly elegant San Sebastián (pop. 180,000) is known for its world-famous beaches, bars, and scenery. Locals and travelers down *pintxos* (tapas) and drinks in the *parte vieja* (old city), which claims the most bars per square meter in the world.

Mar Cantábrico

Isla de Santa Clara

Monte Igueldo

TO (5 km)

Funicular

Parque del Palacio Real de Miramar

Playa de Ondarreta

Playa de la Concha

Bahía de la Concha

Cementerio de los Ingleses

Camino de la Batería Elbira

Po. Nuevo

Monte Urgull

Castillo de Santa Cruz de la Mota

PUERTO

Real Club Náutico

Parte Vieja

Museo de San Telmo

Sant. María del Coro

Aquarium

C. Sta. Cecilia
C. Soraluze
C. 31 de Agosto
San Juan de Bilbao
C. Juan de Bilbao
C. Narrica
San Vicente
C. General Jauregi
Po. de Salamanca
C. San Lorenzo
C. Esterlines
C. San Jerónimo
C. Embeltran
C. Puerto Yeleria
C. F. Calbetón
C. Mayor
C. Igentea
C. Koruko Andra Mari

PL. DE LA CONSTITUCIÓN
PL. DE SARRIEGI
Ayuntamiento

Mercado de la Bretxa
Super Todo Todo
C. Aldamar
C. Euskal Herria
C. R. Regente

TO MONTE ULÍA (1km)

Playa de la Zurriola

Puente de Zurriola

Pukas Surf Club
Bici Rent Donosti
PL. DE LA ZURRIOLA
Po. de la Zurriola
C. Usandizaga
Po. Colón
PL. DE CATALINA
C. Zabaleta
PL. DE SAN FRANCISCO
C. Secundino Esnaola

GROS

TO (20km)

C. Miracruz
C. Virgen del Carmen
Parque Cristina Enea

C. Ramón M. Lili

Puente de Santa Catalina

Río Urumea

Estación del Norte (RENFE)

Po. de Francia

Puente de María Cristina

Po. del Árbol de Guernica
Po. del Urumea

Bus to Museo Chillida-Leku
Po. Rep. Argentina
C. Oquendo
C. Etxaide
C. Legarpi
PL. DE GIPUZKOA
C. Bergara
PL. DE BILBAO
C. Andía
C. Getaria
C. Elkano
C. Txurruka
Ikurraka
C. San Juan
C. San Jerónimo
Parque de Alderdi Eder
C. Peñaflorida
C. Bengoetxea
Garibai
C. Hernani
Av. de la Libertad
C. Fuenterrabia
C. Loiola
Catedral del Buen Pastor
Reyes Católicos
C. Urbieta
C. San Marcial
C. Arrasate
C. Urdaneta
C. Easo
PL. DE CERVANTES
PL. DE ZARAGOZA
C. Manterola
C. San Martín
C. San Bartolomé
C. Triunfo
Po. de la Concha
Po. de los Fueros
Po. del Urumea

Estación de Amara (Euskotren)
TO PALACIO DE AIETE (600m), MUSEO CHILLIDA-LEKU (4km)
TO (200m)

Po. de Concha

SEE PARTE VIEJA INSET

TO ULÍA (1km)

SPAIN

San Sebastián (Donostia)

ACCOMMODATIONS
Camping Igueldo, 11
Pensión Amaiur, 1
Pensión Boulevard, 10
Pensión La Perla, 14
Pensión Larrea, 6
Pensión San Lorenzo, 8
Pensión Urkia, 13

FOOD
Arrai Txiki, 4
Bar Intxa, 5
La Cueva, 2
Juantxo, 9
Kursaal, 15

NIGHTLIFE
Molly Malone, 12
Ostadar, 7

0   200 yards
0   200 meters

0   150 meters
0   150 yards

☞ TRANSPORTATION

Trains: San Sebastián has 2 train stations. **Estación de Amara** runs *cercanías* to local destinations. **RENFE, Estación del Norte,** Po. de Francia (☎902 24 02 02), sends trains to: **Barcelona** (9hr., 1-2 per day, €34); **Madrid** (8hr., 2-3 per day, €33-41); **Paris, France** (9-11hr., 4 per day, €85); **Salamanca** (6½hr., 2-3 per day, €28-37).

Buses: San Sebastián has no actual bus station, only a platform and a series of ticket windows on Av. de Sancho el Sabio 31-33 and Po. de Vizcaya 16.

Alsa, Po. de Vizcaya 16 (☎902 42 22 42), runs to **Paris** (12hr., 8pm, €61).

Continental Auto, Av. de Sancho el Sabio 31 (☎46 90 74). To: **Burgos** (3-3½hr., 7 per day, €13) and **Madrid** (6hr., 7-9 per day, €26.70).

Transportes PESA, Av. de Sancho el Sabio 33 (☎902 10 12 10), to **Bilbao** (1¼hr.; M-F 2 per hr., Sa-Su 1 per hr.; €8).

La Roncalesa, Po. de Vizcaya 16 (☎46 10 64). To **Pamplona** (1hr., 6-10 per day, €6).

Vibasa, Po. de Vizcaya 16 (☎45 75 00). To **Barcelona** (7hr., 3 per day, €25).

Public Transportation: Local **buses** (☎28 71 00). €1. Map/schedule available at tourist office. **Bus #16** runs from Alameda del Boulevard to campground and beaches.

Taxis: Vallina (☎40 40 40) and **Donostia** (☎46 46 46).

⊞ ❷ ORIENTATION AND PRACTICAL INFORMATION

The **Río Urumea** splits San Sebastián. The city center, most monuments, and the two most popular beaches, Playa de la Concha and Playa de Ondaretta, line the peninsula on the western side of the river. At the tip of the peninsula sits **Monte Urgull.** Inland lies the *parte vieja*, San Sebastián's restaurant, nightlife, and budget accommodation nexus. South of the *parte vieja*, at the base of the peninsula, is the commercial district. The **bus station** is south of the city center on Pl. Pío XII, while the RENFE **train station** and Playa de la Zurriola are across the river from the *parte vieja*. To get to the *parte vieja* from the train station, head straight to Puente María Cristina, cross the bridge, and turn right at the fountain. Continue four blocks north to Av. Libertad, then take a left and follow it to the port; the *parte vieja* fans out to the right and Playa de la Concha sits to the left.

Tourist Office: Centro de Atracción y Turismo, C. Reina Regente 3 (☎48 11 66; www.sansebastianturismo.com), in front of Puente de la Zurriola. English, French, and German spoken. Open June-Sept. M-Sa 8am-8pm, Su 10am-2pm and 3-8pm; Oct.-May M-Sa 9am-1:30pm and 3:30-7pm, Su 10am-2pm.

Bike Rental: Bici Rent Donosti, Po. de la Zurriola 22 (☎29 08 54). Has bike trail maps. Bikes €18 per day, €12 for 4hr. Tandem bikes €36 per day, €20 for 4hr., €6 for 1hr.

Laundromat: 5 á Sec, inside Mercado de la Bretxa. Open M-Sa 9am-9pm.

Police: C. Easo (☎45 00 00).

Medical Services: Casa de Socorro, C. Bengoetxea 4 (☎44 06 33). Services only available to EU citizens, but others should come here to be redirected to a private clinic.

Internet Access: Zarr@net, C. San Lorenzo 6 (☎43 33 81). €0.05 per min., €3 per hr. Also sells **phone cards.** Open M-Sa 10am-10pm, Su 4-10pm.

Post Office: C. Urdaneta (☎902 19 71 97), behind the cathedral. Open M-F 8:30am-8:30pm, Sa 9:30am-2pm. **Postal Code:** 20012.

⌂ ACCOMMODATIONS

A bevy of small *pensiones* scatters the streets throughout the noisy *parte vieja*. For a more restful night's sleep, look for hostels and *pensiones* on the outskirts of El Centro. Desperate backpackers will scrounge for rooms in July and August, particularly during *San Fermines* (July 6-14) and *Semana Grande* (Aug. 20-28 in 2005); September's film festival is just as booked. The tourist office has lists of accommodations and most hostel owners know of *casas particulares*.

Pensión Amaiur, C. 31 de Agosto 44, 2nd fl. (☎42 96 54). From Alameda del Boulevard, follow C. San Jerónimo to its end and turn left. Friendly owner and uniquely decorated rooms. Internet €1 per 18min. Singles €18-35; doubles €28-45, with balcony €32-50; triples €39-72; quads €48-85. MC/V. ❷

Pensión San Lorenzo, C. San Lorenzo 2 (☎42 55 16), off C. San Juan. Sunny doubles with TV and minifridge. July-Aug. doubles €48; June and Sept. €36; Oct.-May €24. ❷

Pensión La Perla, C. Loyola 10, 2nd fl. (☎42 81 23), on the street directly ahead of the cathedral. English spoken. Private baths and TVs. July-Sept. singles €30-32; doubles €45. Oct.-June singles €24; doubles €32. ❸

Pensión Urkia, C. Urbieta 12, 3rd fl. (☎42 44 36), between C. Marcial and C. Arrasate. Borders the construction site of a new department store. Big rooms have bath and TV. June-Sept. doubles €45; triple €60. Oct.-May singles €28; doubles €35; triple €42. ❸

Pensión Boulevard, Alameda del Boulevard 24 (☎42 94 05). Spacious rooms all have bath and balcony. Reception 24hr. July-Aug. doubles €60. June and Sept. doubles €42. Oct.-May doubles €36. Cash only. ❸

Pensión Larrea, C. Narrica 21, 2nd fl. (☎42 26 94). This comfortable and welcoming *pensión* has rooms with balconies, and a kitchen for guests. July-Aug. singles €24; doubles €45; triples €50. Sept.-June singles €18; doubles €30; triples €45. ❷

Camping Igueldo (☎21 45 02), 5km west of town. Beautiful views of the ocean. Bus #16 (dir.: Barrio de Igueldo-Camping) runs between the site and Alameda del Boulevard (1 per hr. 7:30am-10pm, €1). June-Aug. and *Semana Santa* plots €12, extra person €3.50. Water and electricity €8.80. Rest of year call for prices. MC/V. ❶

🍴 FOOD

Pintxos (tapas; around €1.50 each), chased down with the fizzy regional white wine *txacoli*, are a religion here. **Mercado de la Bretxa,** Alameda del Boulevard at C. San Juan, sells fresh produce. (Open M-Sa 9am-9pm.) Across the street, **Super Todo Todo** sells groceries. (Open M-Sa 8:30am-9pm, Su 10am-2pm.)

Arrai Txiki, C. del Campanario 3 (☎43 13 02). Delicious, organic vegetarian cuisine in a simple, elegant setting. Entrees €3-6. Open M and W-Su 1-4pm and 8-11pm. ❶

Kurcaal, Po 7urriola 1 (☎00 31 62). Enjoy a gourmet lunch on the breezy patio. *Menú* €14-17. Entrees €12-30. Open daily 10am-3:30pm and 8-11pm, MC/V. ❹

Juantxo, C. Esterlines (☎42 74 05). Best *bocadillos* in San Sebastián. Try the *fillete* with onions, cheese, and peppers (€3). Wide selection of *bocadillos* (€2-3), *pintxos* (€1-2), and *raciones* (€2-5). Open M-Th 9am-11:30pm, F-Su 9am-1:45am. ❶

Bar Intxa, C. Esterlines 12 (☎42 48 33), across from Juantxo. Friendly service and great food make Intxa a must. Open Tu-Su 11am-4:30pm and 7pm-midnight. ❶

La Cueva, Pl. Trinidad (☎42 54 37), off C. 31 de Agosto. A cavernous restaurant serving traditional seafood cuisine. Grilled tuna, cod, and squid entrees €8-15. M-F *menú* €15. Open Tu-Su 1-3:30pm and 7-11pm. MC/V. ❸

👁 SIGHTS

MUSEO CHILLIDA-LEKU. The Museo Chillida-Leku features a beautiful permanent exhibit of Eduardo Chillida's work spread throughout the extensive garden of a 16th-century farmhouse restored by the sculptor himself. The farmhouse, a spectacular construction of huge wood beams and arching stone, is home to some of the artist's earliest works. (*Bo. Jauregui 66.* ☎33 60 06; *www.museochillidaleku.com.*

SPAIN

Autobuses Garayar, line G2, leave from C. Oquendo every 30min., €1.20. Open July-Aug. and Semana Santa M and W-Sa 10:30am-7pm, Su 10:30am-3pm; Sept.-June M and W-Su 10:30am 3pm. Closed Christmas and New Year's Day. €6, under 12 and seniors €3.)

▓ **MONTE IGUELDO.** Though the views from both of San Sebastián's mountains are spectacular, those from Monte Igueldo are superior. The sidewalk toward the mountain ends just before the base of Monte Igueldo with Eduardo Chillida's sculpture *El Peine de los Vientos* (Comb of the Winds). The road leading to the top is bordered by a low stone wall. The funicular provides a quick trip to the summit. *(☎21 02 11. Open June-Sept. daily 10am-10pm; Oct.-Feb. Sa-Su 11am-8pm; Mar.-June Sa 11am-8pm, Su 11am-9pm. Funicular runs every 15min.; €0.90, round-trip €1.60.)*

PALACES. When Queen Isabella II started vacationing here in the mid-19th century, fancy buildings sprang up like wildflowers. The **Palacio de Miramar** has passed through the hands of the Spanish court, Napoleon III, and Bismarck; it now serves as the País Vasco University. The adjacent **Parque de Miramar** has beautiful views of the bay. *(Between Playa de la Concha and Playa de Ondarreta. Open daily June-Aug. 8am-9pm; Sept.-May 8am-7pm. Free.)* The other royal residence, **Palacio de Aiete,** is also closed to the public, but surrounding trails are not. *(Head up Cuesta de Aldapeta or take bus #19 or 31. Grounds open daily June-Aug. 8am-9pm; Sept.-May 8am-7pm. Free.)*

BEACHES AND WATER SPORTS. The gorgeous **Playa de la Concha** curves from the port to the **Pico del Loro,** the promontory home of the Palacio de Miramar. The virtually flat beach disappears during high tide. Sunbathers crowd onto the smaller and steeper **Playa de Ondarreta,** beyond the Palacio de Miramar, and surfers flock to **Playa de la Zurrida,** across the river from Mt. Urgull. Picnickers head for the **Isla de Santa Clara** in the center of the bay. *(Motorboat ferry 5min., June-Sept. every 30min., round-trip €2.)* Check at the portside kiosk for more info. Several sports-related groups offer a variety of activities and lessons. **Surfers** can check out the Pukas Surf Club, Po. de la Zurriola 23, for info on lessons and rentals. *(☎42 12 05. Open M-Sa 9:30am-9pm. AmEx/MC/V.)* For general info on all sports, pick up a copy of the *UDA-Actividades Deportivas* brochure at the tourist office.

🎵 🎭 ENTERTAINMENT AND NIGHTLIFE

The weekly *Kalea* (€1.40), available at tobacco stands and newsstands, has information on **theater** and special events. The *parte vieja* pulls out all the stops in July and August, particularly on **Calle Fermín Calbetón,** three blocks in from Alameda del Boulevard. During the year, when students outnumber backpackers, nightlife tends to move beyond the *parte vieja.* Look out for discount coupons. **Ostadar,** C. Fermín Calbetón 13, attracts locals and tourists alike with its hip dance mix. (Beer €1.80. Mixed drinks €4.50.) **Molly Malone,** C. San Martín 55, is an Irish pub with an impressive brew selection. (Open M-F 11am-4am, Sa-Su 3pm-4am).

BILBAO (BILBO)   ☎944

Bilbao (pop. 370,000) is a city transformed; what was once industry is now new, avant-garde, and futuristic. Twentieth-century success showered the city with a sleek new subway system, a stylish riverwalk, and other additions designed by renowned international architects. Above all else, the shining Guggenheim Museum has most powerfully fueled Bilbao's rise to international prominence.

🚆 🛈 TRANSPORTATION AND PRACTICAL INFORMATION. Flights depart from the **airport** (BIO; ☎86 93 00), 8km from Bilbao. To reach the airport, take the Bizkai bus (☎902 22 22 65) marked *Aeropuerto* from P. Moyúa, in front of the

Hacienda building (25min., daily every 30min. 6am-10pm, €1.10). Buses return from the airport to Pl. Moyúa (daily every 30min. 6:45am-10:45pm). RENFE **trains** (☎902 24 02 02) arrive at the Estación de Abando del Norte, Pl. Circular 2, and travel to: Barcelona, 2 per day, €44); Madrid (5½-8½hr., 2 per day, €30-39); and Salamanca (5½hr., daily 2:05pm, €24). From Pl. Circular, head right around the station and cross Puente del Arenal to reach Pl. Arriaga, the entrance to the *casco viejo* and Pl. Nueva. Most **bus** companies leave from the Termibús terminal, C. Gurtubay 1 (☎39 50 77; M: San Mamés), to: Barcelona (7¼hr., 4 per day, €35); Madrid (4-5hr.; M-F and Su 10-18 per day; €23.20); Pamplona (1¼hr., 4-6 per day, €11.20); and San Sebastián (1¼hr., 1 per hr., €8).

The city's main thoroughfare, **Gran Vía de Don Diego López de Haro**, or just **Gran Vía**, connects three of Bilbao's main plazas. Heading east from Pl. de Sagrado Corazón, Gran Vía continues through the central Pl. Moyúa, and ends at Pl. Circular. Past Pl. Circular, you will cross the Río de Bilbao on **Puente del Arenal**, which deposits you on **Plaza de Arriaga**, the entrance to the **casco viejo** and **Plaza Nueva**. The **tourist office** is on C. Rodriguez Arias 3. (☎79 57 60; www.bilbao.net. Open M-F 9am-2pm and 4-7:30pm.) Near the old city, surf the **Internet** at **Net House**, C. Villarías 6. (☎23 71 53. €1.50 for 1st 30min., €0.05 per additional min. Open M-F 10:30am-10:30pm, Sa 10:30am-11:30pm, Su 11:30am-10:30pm.) **Postal Code:** 48008.

ACCOMMODATIONS AND FOOD. Plaza Arriaga and **Calle Arenal** have many budget accommodations, while upscale hotels are in the new city off **Gran Vía**. Rates climb during *Semana Grande* (Aug. 20-28 in 2005). **Albergue Bilbao Aterpetxea (HI) ❷**, Ctra. Basurto-Kastrexana Errep. 70, is a great place to stay. Take bus #58 from Pl. Circular or Pl. Zabalburu. The hostel offers bike rental (€6 per day), laundry (€3), and Internet. (☎27 00 54; fax 27 54 79. July-Sept. rooms €15-19, under 25 €13.20-17.25; Oct.-June rooms €13-17.25/€12-16. HI members only. MC/V.) **Hotel Arriaga ❺**, C. Ribera 3, has spacious rooms with A/C, private bath, and TV. (☎79 00 01; fax 79 05 16. Singles €48; doubles €60; triples €72. AmEx/MC/V.)

Restaurants and bars in the *casco viejo* offer a wide selection of local dishes, *pintxos*, and *bocadillos*. ◙**New Inn Urrestarazu ❶**, Alameda de Urquijo 9, is perfect when you can't decide between local cuisine and comfort food. (Open M-Th 7am-11pm, F 7am-midnight, Sa 8am-1am, Su 10am-10pm.) **Restaurante Peruano Ají Colorado ❸**, Barrenkale 5, specializes in *ceviche* (€10-12), a marinated raw fish salad. (☎15 22 09. Tu-F lunch *menú* €12. Open Tu-Sa 1:30-3:30pm and 9-11:30pm, Su 1:30-3:30pm. MC/V.) **Mercado de la Ribera,** on the riverbank, is the biggest indoor market in Spain. (Open M-Th and Sa 8am-2:30pm, F 8am-2:30pm and 4:30-7:30pm.)

SIGHTS. Frank Gehry's ◙**Museo Guggenheim Bilbao** can only be described as breathtaking. Lauded in the international press with every superlative imaginable, it has catapulted Bilbao straight into cultural stardom. Sheathed in titanium, limestone, and glass, the US$100 million building is said to resemble an iridescent fish or a blossoming flower. The amazingly light, dramatically spacious interior features a towering atrium and a series of unconventional exhibition spaces. The museum hosts rotating exhibits drawn from the Guggenheim Foundation's collection. (Av. Abandoibarra 2. ☎35 90 80 or 35 90 00; www.guggenheim-bilbao.es. Open July-Aug. daily 10am-8pm; Sept.-June Tu-Su 10am-8pm. Guided tours in English Tu-Su 11am, 12:30, 4:30, and 6:30pm. Sign up 30min. before tour at the info desk. Audiotour €4. €12, students and seniors €7, under 12 free.) The **Museo de Bellas Artes,** though it can't boast the name-recognition of the Guggenheim, is favored by residents. Hoarding aesthetic riches behind an unassuming facade, the museum boasts an impressive collection of 12th- to 20th-century art. (Pl. del Museo 2. Take C. Elcano to Pl. del Museo or bus #10 from Pte. del Arenal. ☎39 60 60, guided tours 39 61 37. Open Tu-Sa 10am-8pm, Su 10am-2pm. €4.50, seniors and

SPAIN

students €3, under 12 and W free.) Located in the *casco viejo*, the **Museo Vasco** celebrates the region's oldest inhabitants, the Basques. (Pl. Miguel de Unamuno 4 Across from the metro stop. ☎ 15 54 23; http://euskal-museoa.org. Open Tu-Sa 11am-5pm, Su 11am-2pm. Temporary exhibition open Tu-Sa 11am-8pm, Su 11am-2pm. €3; students €1.50; seniors, under 12, and Th free.)

🎭 🎟 **ENTERTAINMENT AND NIGHTLIFE.** Bilbao has a thriving bar scene. In the *casco viejo*, revelers spill out into the streets to sip their *txikitos* (chee-KEE-tos; small glasses of wine), especially on **Calle Barrenkale.** Teenagers and twenty-somethings fill **Calle Licenciado Poza,** especially between C. General Concha and Alamede de Recalde, where a covered alleyway connecting C. Licenciado Poza and Alameda de Urquijo teems with bars. For a more mellow scene, munch on *pintxos* (€1-1.20) and people-watch at Bilbao's oldest coffee shop, **Café Boulevard,** C. Arenal 3. (☎ 15 31 28. Open M-Th 7:30am-11pm, F-Sa 8am-2am, Su 11am-11pm. MC/V.) The massive fiesta in honor of *Nuestra Señora de Begoña* takes place during **Semana Grande,** a nine-day party complete with fireworks, concerts, and theater (Aug. 20-28 in 2005). Documentary filmmakers from all over the world gather for a week in fall for the **Festival Internacional de Cine Documental y Cortometraje de Bilbao.** Pick up a *Bilbao Guide* from the tourist office for event listings.

🔢 **DAYTRIP FROM BILBAO: GUERNICA (GERNIKA).** Founded in 1366, Guernica (pop. 15,600) long served as the ceremonial seat of Basque Country. On April 26, 1937, at the behest of General Francisco Franco, the Nazi "Condor Legion" released 29,000kg of explosives on Guernica. The atrocity, which killed nearly 2000 people, is immortalized in Pablo Picasso's masterpiece *Guernica*, now in Madrid's Museo Nacional Centro de Arte Reina Sofía (p. 931). The 🏛**Gernika Peace Museum,** Pl. Foru 1, features a variety of multimedia exhibits. (From the train station, walk 2 blocks up C. Adolfo Urioste and turn right on C. Artekale. ☎ 946 27 02 13. Open July-Aug. Tu-Sa 10am-7pm, Su 10am-2pm; Sept.-June Tu-Sa 10am-2pm and 4-7pm, Su 10am-2pm. Guided tours in Basque, Spanish, English, and French at noon and 5pm, or call for an appointment. €4, students and seniors €2.) To reach the **tourist office,** C. Artekale 8, from the train station, walk three blocks up C. Adolfo Urioste and turn right on C. Barrenkale. Turn left at the alleyway and look for the signs. (☎ 946 25 58 92; www.gernika-lumo.net. M-Sa 10am-2pm and 4-7pm, Su 10am-2pm.) **Trains** (☎ 902 54 32 10; www.euskotren.es) roll in from Bilbao (45min.; M-F every 45min., Sa-Su every 30min.; €2). Bizkai Bus (☎ 902 22 22 65) sends **buses** between Guernica and Bilbao's Estación Abando (45min., lines A-3514 and A3515, buses leave from Hdo. Amezaga in front of RENFE station, every 15-30min., return buses leave from train station, €2.05).

BALEARIC ISLANDS ☎ 971

Each year, beaches, nightlife, and unparalleled natural beauty draw millions of tourists to the *Islas Baleares*. Mallorca absorbs the bulk of high-class, package-tour invaders. Ibiza affords the best nightlife in Europe, while quieter Menorca offers spectacular empty white beaches, hidden coves, and Bronze Age megaliths.

✈ GETTING THERE

Flying is the easiest way to reach the islands. Students with an ISIC can often get discounts from **Iberia** (☎ 902 40 05 00; www.iberia.com), which flies to Palma de Mallorca and Ibiza from Barcelona (1hr., €65-200) and Madrid (1-2hr., €100-200). 🔷**Vueling** (☎ 902 33 39 33; www.vueling.com), **Air Europa** (☎ 902 24 00 42; www.aireuropa.com), and **Spanair** (☎902 13 14 15; www.spanair.com) offer budget flights to and between the islands. Most cheap round-trip **charters** include a week's stay in a hotel. Prices during summer are higher than in low season.

Ferries to the islands are less popular. Trasmediterránea (☎902 45 46 45; www.trasmediterranea.com) departs from Barcelona's Estació Marítima Moll and Valencia's Estació Marítima for Mallorca, Menorca, and Ibiza (€68-100). Fares between the islands run €28-47. Buquebus (☎902 41 42 42) sends **buses** from Barcelona to Palma (4hr., 2 per day, €49). The three major islands have extensive **bus** systems. **Car** rental costs about €36 per day, **mopeds** €18, and **bikes** €6-10.

🏝 MALLORCA

A favorite of Spain's royal family, Mallorca has been popular with the in-crowd since Roman times. Lemon groves and olive trees adorn the jagged cliffs of the northern coast, while lazy beaches sink into calm bays to the east. The capital of the Balearics, **Palma** (pop. 323,000) embraces conspicuous consumption and pleases with its well-preserved old quarter, colonial architecture, and mix of local flavor and international crowds. The tourist office (see below) distributes a list of over 40 nearby **beaches,** many a mere bus ride away; one popular choice is **El Arenal** (Platja de Palma; bus #15), 11km southeast of town toward the airport. For fantastic cookies during the day and a chill scene at night, try ▨**Costa Galana,** C. Argentina 45. (Beer €2. Mixed drinks €3-5. Open daily 8am-3am.) After sunset, **La Bodeguita del Medio,** C. Vallseca 18, keeps its crowd dancing to Cuban rhythms. (Open M-W and Su 8pm-1am, Th-Sa 8pm-3am.) Palma's clubbers start their night in the *bares-musicales* lining the **Paseo Marítimo** strip. When the bar scene fades at 3am, partiers move down the strip to the *discotecas*.

From the airport, take bus #1 to **Plaza Espanya** (15min., every 20min., €2). To reach the **tourist office,** Pg. del Born 27, in the book shop of Casa Solleric, walk up Pg. del Born from Pl. de la Reina about a block and a half. (☎72 40 90. Open M-F 9am-8pm, Sa 9am-1:30pm.) Branches are at the airport and in Pl. Espanya. **Hostal Cuba ❷,** C. San Magí 1, offers spotless rooms with high ceilings and wood furniture. From Pl. Joan Carles I, turn left and walk down Av. Jaume III, cross the river, and turn left on C. Argentina; the hostel is several blocks down. Bus #1 from the airport drops you at the Sa Faixima stop, half a block away. (☎73 81 59. Singles €20; doubles €36.) When hungry, those on a budget tend to try the side streets off **Passeig del Born,** the cafes along **Avenida Joan Miró,** or the carbon-copy pizzerias along **Paseo Marítimo. Servicio y Precios,** on C. Felip Bauzá, sells groceries. (Open M-F 8:30am-8:30pm, Sa 9am-2pm.) **Postal Code:** 07080.

🏝 IBIZA

Perhaps nowhere on Earth does style rule over substance (or substances over style) more than on the island of Ibiza (pop. 84,000). None of Ibiza's beaches are within quick walking distance of **Eivissa** (Ibiza City), but most are at most a 20min. bike ride away; buses leave from Av. Isidor Macabich 20 for **Platja d'en Bossa** (every 30min., €0.75). One of the most beautiful beaches near Eivissa is ▨**Playa de Las Salinas.** The bar scene centers around **Calle Barcelona,** while **Calle de la Virgen** is the nexus of gay nightlife. Refer to *DJ,* free at many hostels, bars, and restaurants, for a list of nightlife options. The **Discobus** runs to and from all the major hot spots (leaves Eivissa from A. Isidor Macabich; schedule available at tourist office; €1.50). Elegant **Pachá,** on Pg. Perimitral, is a 15min. walk or a 2min. cab ride from the port. (Cover €50. Open daily midnight-7:30am.) At **Amnesia,** on the road to San Antonio, you can forget who you are and who you came with. (W drag performances and foam party. Th house. Cover from €40. Open daily midnight-7am.)

SPAIN

The local paper *Diario de Ibiza* (www.diariodeibiza.es; €0.75) features an *Agenda* page with information on the island. The **tourist office,** C. Antoni Riquer 2, is by the water. (☎30 19 00. Open in summer M-F 9am-9pm, Sa 9:30am-7:30pm.) Email friends while washing the beer out of your clothes at **Wash and Dry,** Av. España 53. (☎39 48 22. Laundry €13 for 8kg, €10 for 8kg self service. Internet access €1 per 15min., €1.50 per 30min. Open M-Sa 10am-9pm.) The letters **"CH"** (*casa de huespedes*) mark many doorways; call the owners at the phone number on the door. **Hostal Residencia Sol y Brisa ❷,** Av. B. V. Ramón 15, parallel to Pg. Vara de Rey, has clean rooms, a central location, and a social atmosphere. (☎31 08 18; fax 30 30 32. Singles €25; doubles €44.) The **Mercat Vell** sells fruit, meat, and vegetables. (Open M-Sa 7am-1pm.) **Postal Code:** 07815.

🏖 MENORCA

Menorca's (pop. 72,000) coastline of raw beaches, rustic landscapes, and well-preserved ancient monuments draws ecologists, photographers, and wealthy young families. Atop a steep bluff, **Mahón** (pop. 25,000) is the gateway to the island. The popular **beaches** outside **Mahón** are accessible by bus. Transportes Menorca **buses** leave from the station, up C. Vasallo from the Pl. Esplanada and on the left, for **Platges de Son Bou** (7 per day, €2). Autocares Fornells buses leave for the breathtaking **Arenal d'en Castell** (30min., 3-5 per day, €2), while TMSA buses go to touristy **Cala'n Porter** (7 per day, €1.10). While there, don't miss the 🏖**Covas d'en Xoroi,** a collection of caves in the cliffs above the sea. The caves are inhabited by several bars during the day (cover €5-9, includes 1 drink; open daily Apr.-Oct. 10:30am-10:30pm) and a crowded disco at night (cover €15-25; open daily 11pm-late.)

In **Mahón,** the **tourist office** is at Sa Rovellada de Dalt 24. (☎36 37 90; www.e-menorca.org. Open M-F 9am-1pm and 5-7pm, Sa 9am-1pm. Additional offices open during the summer at the port and the airport.) To get to the beautiful rooms of 🏖**Posada Orsi ❷,** C. de la Infanta 19, from Pl. de s'Esplanada, take C. Moreres, which becomes C. Hannover; turn right at Pl. Constitució; and follow C. Nou through Pl. Reial. (☎36 47 51. Singles €17-33; doubles €28-38, with shower €35-47.) **Grand General (G.G.) Delicatessen ❶,** Moll. De Llevant 319, serves mouthwatering Italian food. To get there, head down to the port, take a right, and continue for 20min. (Open M-Sa noon-midnight.) **Postal Code:** 07700.

NORTHWESTERN SPAIN

Northwestern Spain is the country's best-kept secret; its seclusion is half its charm. Rainy Galicia hides mysterious Celtic ruins, and on the northern coast tiny Asturias allows access to the dramatic Picos de Europa mountain range.

GALICIA (GALIZA)

If, as the Galician saying goes, "rain is art," then there is no gallery more beautiful than the Northwest's misty skies. Often veiled in silvery drizzle, it is a province of fern-laden eucalyptus woods, slate-roofed fishing villages, and endless white beaches. Locals speak *gallego*, a linguistic hybrid of Castilian and Portuguese.

SANTIAGO DE COMPOSTELA   ☎981

Santiago (pop. 94,000) is a city of song. Perhaps these are the celebrations of pilgrims who have just finished the *Camino de Santiago*. More likely, these are just the sounds of joy at waking up to another day in this lovely city. Santiago's **cathedral** has four facades, each a master-piece from a different era, with entrances opening to four different plazas: Inmaculada, Obradoiro, Praterías, and Quintana. The remains of **St. James** (Santiago) lie beneath the high altar in a silver coffer. (☎58 35 48. Open daily 7am-7pm. Free.) Inside the **museum** are manuscripts from the *Codex Calixtinus*, five volumes of the stories of the Apostle James. (☎58 11 55. Open June-Sept. M-Sa 10am-2pm and 4-8pm, Su and holidays 10am-2pm; Oct.-May M-Sa 10am-1:30pm and 4-6:30pm, Su and holidays 10am-1:30pm. €5, students €3; includes entrance to crypt.) Those curious about the *Camino de Santiago* can head to the **Museo das Peregrinacións**, Pl. de San Miguel. (☎58 15 58. Open Tu-F 10am-8pm, Sa 10:30am-1:30pm and 5-8pm, Su 10:30am-1:30pm. €2.40, children and seniors €1.20, special expositions and most of the summer free.) At night, take R. Montero Ríos to the bars and clubs off **Praza Roxa** to party with local students. **Casa oas Crechas,** Vía Sacra 3, just off Pr. da Quintana, is a smoky pub with a witchcraft theme. It's also known for its Galician folk concerts. (☎56 07 51. Beer €1.90-2.10. Open daily in summer noon-4am; in winter 4pm-3am.)

Trains (☎52 02 02) run from R. do Hórreo to Madrid (8hr., 2 per day, €39). To reach the city, take bus #6 to Pr. Galicia or walk up the stairs across the parking lot from the main entrance, bear right onto R. do Hórreo, and continue uphill for 10min. **Buses** (☎58 77 00) run from R. de Rodríguez to Madrid (8-9hr.; 4-6 per day; €36, round-trip €58) and San Sebastián (13½hr.; 3 per day; €50, round-trip €94) via Bilbao (11¼hr., €44/€59). From the station, take bus #10 to Pr. de Galicia. The **tourist office** is at R. do Vilar 63. (☎55 51 29; www.santiagoturismo.com. Multilingual staff. Open daily June-Sept. 9am-9pm; Oct.-May 10am-3pm and 5-8pm). Use the **Internet** at **CyberNova 50,** R. Nova 50. (☎57 51 88. €1-1.20 per hr. Open M-Sa 9am-1am, Su 10am-1am.) Nearly every street in the *ciudad vieja* has at least one *pensión*. **Hospedaje Ramos ❷,** R. da Raíña 18, 2nd fl., above O Papa Una restaurant, is in the center of the *ciudad vieja*. (☎58 18 59. Singles €16; doubles €28.) Most restaurants are on R. do Vilar, R. do Franco, R. Nova, and R. da Raíña. **O Cabaliño do Demo ❷,** R. Ayer Ulloa 7, serves global vegetarian entrees. (☎58 81 46. *Menú* €8. Entrees €4.75-6.50. Open M-W 2-4pm and 9-11:30pm, Th-Sa 2-4pm and 9pm-midnight.) Santiago's **market** is located between Pl. San Felix and Convento de Santo Agostiño. (Open M Sa 7:30am-2pm.) **Postal Code:** 15701.

THE WHITE KING

Like many kings, it is short-lived and inbred. It has thousands of devotees who laud its charm, grace, and taste. Since the 1980s, when wine producers in Galicia shifted their attention to this difficult-to-grow grape, *El Albariño* has become the king of Spanish white wines, transforming Galicia's hillsides forever.

The mild temperatures and high rainfall in Galicia have always hampered attempts to grow red wine grapes. The sturdy, rot-resistant *albariño* grape, however, thrives in the region. Not only is it well-suited to the climate, but its wine—light, with a distinctive perfume and crisp taste—perfectly complements Galicia's celebrated seafood.

The controversy over *albariño's* bloodline only adds to its mystique. Some believe that French monks brought it to Santiago during the 12th- and 13th-century crusades, further asserting that *albariño* is genetically linked to Germany's Riesling grape. Locals, however, hold steadfastly to the claim that *albariño* is indigenous to Galicia. No matter what region gave birth to the grape, though, Galicia's Rías Baixas (Low Estuaries) are now the uncontested parents of the regal wine. The production of *albariño,* considered the best white wine in Spain and one of the best in the world, is now Galicia's fastest growing industry.

ASTURIAS

Spaniards call the tiny land of Asturias a *paraíso natural* (natural paradise). Surrounded by centuries of civilization, its impenetrable peaks and dense alpine forests have remained untouched. Unlike tourists in the rest of the country, travelers don't come here to see the sights; they come here to brave them.

PICOS DE EUROPA

This mountain range is home to **Picos de Europa National Park,** the largest national park in Europe. The most popular trails and peaks lie near the **Cares Gorge** (Garganta del Cares) in the *Macizo Central* (Central Massif). For a list of mountain *refugios* (cabins with bunks but no blankets) and general park info, contact the **Picos de Europa National Park Visitors' Center** in Cangas de Onís. (☎/fax 985 84 86 14. Open M-Sa 9am-2pm and 4-6:30pm, Su 9am-3:30pm.)

CANGAS DE ONÍS ☎985

During the summer months the streets of Cangas (pop. 6370) are packed with mountaineers and vacationing families looking to spelunk and hang glide in the Picos de Europa National Park. Cangas itself is, if not particularly thrilling, a relaxing town rich in history. The town's sights evidence the impact of its former Paleolithic, Celtic, and Roman inhabitants. Alsa (☎84 81 33), Av. de Covadonga 18, across from the tourist office, runs **buses** to Madrid (7hr., daily 2:35pm, €27). Find information on accommodations and adventure tourism at the **tourist office,** Jardines del Ayuntamiento 2, in the Pl. del Ayuntamiento. (☎/fax 84 80 05. Open daily May-Sept. 10am-10pm; Oct.-Apr. 9am-2pm and 4-7pm.) There are few *pensiones* along Av. de Covadonga. **Hospedaje Principádo ❶,** Av. de Covadonga, 16, 3rd fl., has immaculate rooms. (☎84 83 50; fax 84 83 15. Singles €12-19; doubles €20-30, with bath €33-39.) Get groceries at **Alimerka Supermercado,** Av. de Covadonga, 13. (Open Su-M 9am-2pm, Tu-Sa 9am-9:30pm.) **Postal Code:** 33550.

SWEDEN
(SVERIGE)

With the design world cooing over bright, blocky Swedish furniture and college students donning faux-designer wear from H&M, Scandinavia's largest nation has galvanized a reputation for cosmopolitan style that errs on the side of accessible, rather than abstruse. Indeed, Sweden's struggle to balance a market economy with one of the world's most generous social welfare systems stems from its belief that all citizens should have access to education and affordable health care. Cradle-to-grave programs like these come at a price, and top wage-earners can pay out as much as 60% of their annual incomes in taxes. Yet this resolutely neutral nation's zest for spending money on butter instead of guns has also shored up a strong sense of national solidarity, whether you're talking to grain farmers in Skåne or grizzled loggers in Norrland's desolate interior.

DISCOVER SWEDEN: SUGGESTED ITINERARIES

Plan for three days in the capital city of **Stockholm** (p. 993), including one sunny afternoon out on the rocky **Skärgård archipelago** (p. 1004). Daytrip north to the university town of **Uppsala** (p. 1004), or else take an eastbound ferry out to the island of **Gotland** (p. 1005), where serene bike paths and medieval towns overlook the Baltic Sea. Neither **Malmö** (p. 1007) nor **Lund** (p. 1008) are known for their serenity, with clamorous ethnic markets in the former and bombastic student nightlife in the latter. Soak up some high culture in the museums of elegant **Gothenburg** (p. 1010), then get ready to rough it on hikes out of **Åre** (p. 1015) and **Örnsköldsvik** (p. 1015). **Kiruna** (p. 1017) is the end of the line up in mountainous Lappland, where ore miners and the indigenous Sami share vast stretches of Arctic wilderness.

ESSENTIALS

WHEN TO GO

July and August are the most popular months to visit Sweden, when temperatures average 20°C (68°F) in the south and 16°C (61°F) in the north. However, travelers who show up for May and early June can take advantage of low season prices and drink in the late-spring wildflowers, although some attractions will not open until the end of June. If you go during the winter, keep an eye out for the northern lights and bring heavy cold-weather gear; temperatures are frequently below -5°C (23°F). The midnight sun is best seen between early June and mid-July.

DOCUMENTS AND FORMALITIES

VISAS. EU citizens do not need a visa. Citizens of Australia, Canada, New Zealand, and the US do not need a visa for stays of up to 90 days, although this three-month period begins upon entry into any of the countries that belong to the EU's freedom of movement zone. For more information, see p. 17.

EMBASSIES AND CONSULATES. All foreign embassies are in Stockholm. Swedish embassies at home include: **Australia,** 5 Turrana St., Yarralumla, Canberra, ACT 2600 (☎62 70 27 00; www.embassyofsweden.org.au); **Canada,** 377 Dalhousie St.,

Ottawa, ON K1N 9N8 (☎613-241-8553; www.swedishembassy.ca); **Ireland,** 13-17 Dawson St., Dublin 2 (☎474 44 00; www.swedenabroad.com/dublin); **UK,** 11 Montagu Pl., London W1H 2AL (☎020 79 17 64 00; www.swedish-embassy.org.uk); and **US,** 1501 M St. NW, Ste. 900, Washington, D.C. 20005 (☎202-467-2600; www.swedish-embassy.org). **New Zealanders** should contact the Consulate-General at the Vogel Building, Level 13, Wellington (☎04 499 98 95; sweden@extra.co.nz).

TRANSPORTATION

BY PLANE. Most international flights arrive at the airports around Stockholm, although domestic and charter flights connect to other airports throughout the country. **Scandinavian Airlines** (☎08 797 4000; www.scandinavian.net) offers youth fares (ages 12-25) on flights within Scandinavia.

BY TRAIN. Statens Järnväger (SJ), the state railway company, runs reliable trains throughout southern Sweden (☎771 75 75 75; www.sj.se). 30% discount for travelers under 26. Seat reservations (28-55kr) are required on InterCity trains and are recommended on all other routes. Reservations are also mandatory on the sleek, high-speed **X2000** trains; they are included in the ticket price but not in railpasses. In northern Sweden, **Connex** runs trains from Stockholm through Umeå, Lulea, and Kiruna to Narvik, Norway (☎771 26 00 00; www.connex.info/booking/booking_en). The 35min. trip over the **Øresund bridge** connecting Malmö to Copenhagen (70kr) is the fastest way to arrive from continental Europe; the timetable for this train, as well as all SJ and Connex trains, can be found at www.resplus.se. **Eurail** is valid on all of these trains. In the south, purple **pågatågen** trains service local traffic between Helsingborg, Lund, Malmö, and Ystad; **Scanrail** and **Eurail** passes are valid, but otherwise tickets are only available at special vending machines. A **Scanrail pass** purchased in Scandinavia allows five travel days in a 15-day period (2100kr, under-26 1470kr) or unlimited travel for 21 consecutive days (3280/2280kr) throughout Scandinavia, and free or discounted ferry rides. Only three of those days can be used in the country of purchase, however, so a Scanrail pass purchased at home is more economical for those traveling mostly in Sweden.

BY BUS. In the north, buses may be a better option than trains. **Swebus** (☎08 546 30 00; www.swebus.se) is the main carrier nationwide, and its **Swebus Express** arm serves the region around Stockholm and Gothenburg exclusively. **Bus Stop,** inside Stockholm's Cityterminalen, will reserve bus tickets for routes originating in Stockholm (☎08 440 85 70). Students and travelers aged 17-21 get a 30% discount on express buses. Bicycles are not allowed on board.

BY FERRY. Ferries run from Stockholm (p. 993) to the Åland Islands, Gotland, Finland, and the Baltic states. Ystad (p. 1009) sends several ferries a day to Bornholm, Denmark. Ferries from Gothenburg (p. 1010) serve Frederikshavn, Denmark; Kiel, Germany; and Newcastle, England.

BY CAR. Sweden honors foreign driver's licenses for a period up to one year, although drivers under 18 cannot take the wheel, even if they have a valid license in their home country. **Speed limits** are 110kph on expressways, 50kph in thickly settled areas, and 70-90kph elsewhere. Headlights must be used at all times. Swedish roads are remarkably uncrowded and in good condition, but take extra care in winter weather and be wary of reindeer or elk in the road. Many gas stations are open until 10pm, but after hours, look for cash-operated pumps marked *sedel automat.* For more info on car rental and driving in Europe, see p. 66.

BY BIKE AND THUMB. Bicycles and Sweden get along famously; city and regional bike paths are common, while both the **Sverigeleden** (National Route) and the **Cykelspåret** (Bike Path) traverse the entire country. The Stockholm bike group **Cykelfrämjandet,** at Tulegaten 43, publishes a brochure with descriptions of many routes (☎08 545 910 30). **Hitchhiking** is uncommon in Sweden, and *Let's Go* does not recommend hitchhiking as a safe means of transport.

TOURIST SERVICES AND MONEY

TOURIST OFFICES. Nearly every village and town has a tourist office. For more info, consult the **Swedish Tourist Board** (www.visit-sweden.com).

MONEY. In a referendum held in September 2003, Sweden's voters rejected the idea of adopting the euro as the country's currency. Therefore, the unit of Swedish currency for the foreseeable future is the **krona** (plural: kronor), divided into 100 *öre.* Bills come in denominations of 20kr, 50kr, 100kr, 500kr, and 1000kr; coins come in 1kr, 5kr, and 10kr, as well as 50 *öre*. Banks and post offices exchange currency; expect to pay 20-35kr for cash, and 5-15kr for traveler's checks. Although a service charge is usually added to the bill at restaurants, **tipping** is becoming more common and a 7-10% tip is now considered standard. Tip taxi drivers 5-10%. All countries who are members of the European Union impose a **Value Added Tax (VAT)** on goods and services purchased within the EU. Prices in Sweden already include the country's whopping 25% tax rate, although partial refunds are available for visitors who are not EU citizens (p. 22).

SWEDISH KRONOR (KR)		
AUS$1 = 5.38KR	10KR = AUS$1.86
CDN$1 = 5.78KR	10KR = CDN$1.73
EUR€1 = 9.17KR	10KR = EUR€1.09
NZ$1 = 5.00KR	10KR = NZ$2.00
UK£1= 13.66KR	10KR = UK£0.73
US$1 = 7.56KR	10KR = US$1.32

BUSINESS HOURS. Banks are usually open Monday to Friday 9:30am-3pm. Stores generally stay open Monday to Friday 10am-6pm, Saturday and Sunday noon-4pm. Museums open Tuesday to Sunday anywhere from 10am-noon and close between 4 and 6pm. Some are open until 9pm on Wednesday.

COMMUNICATION

PHONE CODES	**Country code:** 46. **International dialing prefix:** 00. From outside Sweden, dial int'l dialing prefix (see inside back cover) + city code without the initial zero + local number. From within the country, always dial city code with the initial zero + local number.

TELEPHONES. Payphones only accept *Telefonkort* (phone cards); buy them at newsstands or other shops (30-250kr). **Mobile phones** are an increasingly popular and economical alternative; for more info, see p. 35. International direct dial numbers include: **AT&T** (☎020 79 91 11); **British Telecom** (☎0800 89 0046); **Canada Direct** (☎020 79 90 15); **MCI** (☎020 79 59 22); **Sprint** (☎020 79 90 11); **Telecom New Zealand** (☎020 79 90 64); **Telstra Australia** (☎020 79 90 61).

MAIL. Postcards and letters under 50g can be sent for 14kr within Europe, and 15kr elsewhere in the world.

LANGUAGE. Sweden has no official language, although Swedish is universally spoken. The region around Kiruna is home to a small minority of Finnish speakers, as well as 7000 speakers of the Sami languages. Almost all Swedes speak English fluently. For basic Swedish words and phrases, see p. 1066.

ACCOMMODATIONS AND CAMPING

SWEDEN	❶	❷	❸	❹	❺
ACCOMMODATIONS	under 150kr	150-220kr	220-350kr	350-500kr	over 500kr

Youth hostels (*vandrarhem*) cost between 120-200kr per night. The 315 hostels run by the **Svenska Turistföreningen (STF)** and affiliated with HI are uniformly top-notch. Nonmembers pay 45kr extra per night. Most hostels have kitchens, laundry facilities, and common areas. To reserve ahead, call the hostel directly or contact STF headquarters in Stockholm (☎08 463 21 00). Tourist offices often book beds in hostels for no fee, and can help find private rooms (200-350kr). STF also manages

mountain huts in the northern wilds (150-350kr). Many **campgrounds** (80-110kr per site; www.camping.se) also offer multi-occupant *stugor* (cottages) for 100-300kr per person (www.stuga.nu). International Camping Cards are not valid in Sweden; **Swedish Camping Cards,** available at all SCR campgrounds, are mandatory (90kr for a one-year sticker of validity). The Swedish tradition of *allemansrätten* (right of public access) means that even noncitizens can camp for free in the countryside, as long as they stay a reasonable distance from private homes. For more info on how to exercise this right responsibly, check out www.allemansratten.se.

FOOD AND DRINK

SWEDEN	❶	❷	❸	❹	❺
FOOD	under 50kr	50-75kr	75-110kr	110-180kr	over 180kr

Restaurant fare is sure to be expensive in Sweden, but **saluhallen** (food halls), open-air markets, and *varmkorv* (hot dog) stands make budget eating easy enough. Many restaurants offer affordable **dagens rätt,** daily lunch specials for 55-70kr. The Swedish palate was long attuned to simple, hearty meat-and-potatoes fare, but enclaves of immigrants in Malmö and Stockholm have spiced things up for budget travelers, while a coterie of five-star chefs in Gothenburg are tossing off increasingly imaginative riffs on herring and salmon. The Swedish love **drip coffee** (as opposed to espresso) and have institutionalized coffee breaks as a near-sacred rite of the workday. Aside from light beer containing less than 3.5% alcohol, booze can be purchased only at **Systembolaget** liquor stores and in licensed bars and restaurants. You can buy light beer at 18, but it's 20+ otherwise and you will be carded. Tonier bars and clubs have age restrictions as high as 25.

HOLIDAYS AND FESTIVALS

Holidays: New Year's Day (Jan. 1); Epiphany (Jan. 6); Good Friday (Mar. 25); Easter Sunday and Monday (Mar. 27-28); May Day (May 1); Ascension Day (May 5); Whit Sunday and Monday (May 15-16); National Day (June 6); All Saints' Day (Nov. 1); Christmas Eve and Day (Dec. 24-25); Boxing Day (Dec. 26).

Festivals: Valborgsmässoafton (Walpurgis Eve; Apr. 30) celebrates the arrival of spring with roaring bonfires in Dalarna and choral singing in Lund and Uppsala. Dalarna also erects flowery maypoles in time for Midsummer (June 24-25), while young people take to the islands of Gotland, Öland, and the Skärgård archipelago for parties well into the night. July brings the Stockholm Jazz Festival to the capital city, while crayfish parties in August and eel parties in September leave the timid swimming for sanctuary.

FACTS AND FIGURES: SWEDEN

Official Name: Kingdom of Sweden.

Capital: Stockholm.

Major Cities: Gothenburg, Malmö.

Population: 8,990,000.

Land Area: 410,000 sq. km.

Time Zone: GMT +1.

Language: Swedish.

Religions: Lutheran (87%).

STOCKHOLM ☎08

Architecture, water, and swaths of greenspace strike a harmonious, elegant balance in Sweden's capital city. Stockholm (pop. 1,250,000) exists by virtue of a delicate latticework of bridges that connects its islands and peninsulas, meaning that individual neighborhoods have developed characters of their own. Even so, sophistication and style are the orders of the day, regardless of which quarters of the city you happen upon during your visit.

▛ TRANSPORTATION

Flights: Arlanda Airport (ARN; ☎ 797 60 00), 45km north of the city. **Flygbussar** shuttles (☎ 686 37 87) run between Arlanda and the bus station (40min., every 15min. 4am-10pm; 89kr, students 59kr), as do **Arlanda Express** trains (☎ 020 22 22 24; 20min.; every 15min. 5am-midnight; 180kr, students 90kr). **Bus** #583 runs to T-bana: Märsta (10min., 35kr or 5 coupons); T-Centralen is 40min. farther by T-bana. Flygbussar also operates shuttles to **Vasteras Airport** (VST; ☎ 021 80 56 10) that are timed to line up with RyanAir departures (100kr).

Trains: Centralstationen (☎ 762 25 80). T-bana: T-Centralen. Trains go to: **Copenhagen** (5-6hr.; 5-6 per day; 1099kr, under 26 948kr); **Gothenburg** (3-5hr.; every 1-2hr.; 512-1110kr, under 26 437-955kr); **Oslo** (5-7hr.; 5-6 per day; 1151kr, under 26 826kr).

Buses: Cityterminalen, upstairs on the north end of Centralstationen. **Terminal Service** (☎ 762 59 97) to airport (80kr) and Gotland ferries (70kr). **Biljettservice** (☎ 762 59 79) makes reservations with Sweden's numerous bus companies for longer routes. **Swebus,** one of the largest, runs to: **Copenhagen** (9hr., 3 per day, 380kr); **Gothenburg** (7hr., 7 per day, 295kr); **Malmö** (8½hr., 3 per day, 370kr).

Ferries: Silja Line, Kungsg. 2 (☎ 22 21 40), sails overnight to Finland: **Helsinki** (16hr., daily, from 395kr); **Mariehamn** (5hr., 2 per day, 99kr); **Turku (Åbo)** (12hr., 2 per day, from 180kr). To get to the terminal, take T-bana to Gärdet and follow signs to Värtahamnen, or take the Silja bus (20kr) from Cityterminalen. 50% Scanrail discount. **Viking Line** (☎ 452 40 00) sails to **Helsinki** (15hr.; daily; mid-June to mid-Aug. 405kr, late Aug. to mid-June 284-495kr) and **Turku (Åbo)** (12hr.; 2 per day; mid-June to mid-Aug. 216-306kr, late Aug. to mid-June 126-261kr). There is a Viking Line office in Cityterminalen; take the T-bana to Slussen to reach the terminal at Stadsgården on Södermalm. **Tallink** (☎ 666 60 01; www.tallink.se) ferries sail to **Tallinn, Estonia** (16hr.; daily; from 410kr, low season 300kr). Shuttle buses (20kr) run from Cityterminalen to the Tallink port. See p. 1005 for info on ferries to **Gotland.**

Public Transportation: T-bana (*Tunnelbana;* subway) runs 5am-12:30am. Nightbuses (which cover many of the same routes as daytime buses) run 12:30am-5:30am. Most destinations cost 2 coupons (30kr, 1hr. unlimited bus/subway transfer). *Rabattkuponger* (books of coupons) are sold at Pressbyrån news agents. 10 coupons 80kr; 20 coupons 145kr. The **SL Turistkort** (Tourist Card) is valid on all public transportation. 1-day 95kr; 3-day 180kr. The **Stockholmskortet** (Stockholm Card), available at Sweden House and Centralstationen, offers use of public transportation, admission to 75 museums and attractions, and discounts on boat tours. 1-day 260kr; 2-day 390kr; 3-day 540kr. The **SL Office,** in the basement of Centralstationen (☎ 600 10 00), offers transportation info. T-bana: T-Centralen. Open M-Sa 6:30am-11:15pm, Su 7am-11:15pm.

Taxis: Many cabs have fixed prices to certain destinations; ask beforehand. It's 450kr from Arlanda to Centralstationen. Major companies include **Taxi 020** (☎ 020 20 20 20), **Taxikurir** (☎ 30 00 00), and **Taxi Stockholm** (☎ 15 00 00).

Bike Rental: Sjöcaféet (☎ 660 57 57), on Djurgårdsbron. Bikes 250kr per day; inline skates 200kr per day; canoes and kayaks 300-500kr per day. Open daily 9am-9pm.

◖▟ ORIENTATION AND PRACTICAL INFORMATION

This compact city spans seven small islands (linked by bridges and the T-bana) at the junction of **Lake Mälaren** to the west and the **Baltic Sea** to the east. The large northern island is divided into two sections: **Norrmalm,** home to Centralstationen and the shopping district around Drottningg., and **Östermalm,** which boasts the elegant **Strandvägen** waterfront and vibrant nightlife fanning out from **Stureplan.** The mainly residential western island, **Kungsholmen,** holds grassy beaches and the majestic Stadhuset (city hall). The southern island of **Södermalm** retains an old neighborhood feel in the midst

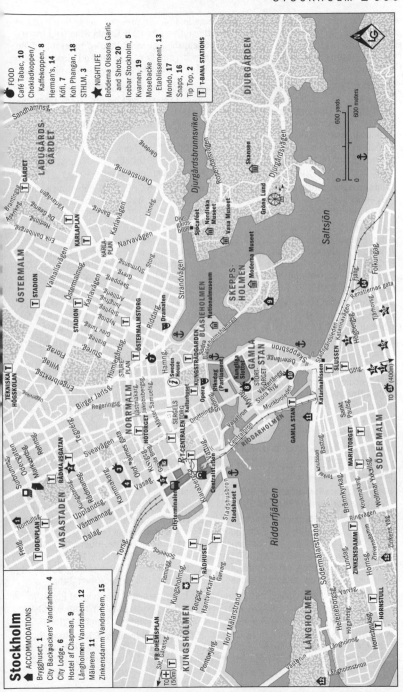

Stockholm

⌂ ACCOMMODATIONS
Brygghuset, 1
City Backpackers' Vandrarhem, 4
City Lodge, 6
Hostel af Chapman, 9
Långholmen Vandrarhem, 12
Mälarens 11
Zinkensdamm Vandrarhem, 15

♥ FOOD
Café Tabac, 10
Chokladkoppen/
Kaffekoppen, 8
Herman's, 14
Köfi, 7
Koh Phangan, 18
STHLM, 3

★ NIGHTLIFE
Bröderna Olssons Garlic
and Shots, 20
Icebar Stockholm, 5
Kvarnen, 19
Mosebacke
Etablissement, 13
Mondo, 17
Snaps, 16
Tip Top, 2

Ⓣ T-BANA STATIONS

SWEDEN

of a budding cafe culture. Nearby **Långholmen** is a nature preserve, as is much of the eastern island **Djurgården**. At the center of these five islands is **Gamla Stan** (old town). Gamla Stan's neighbor (via Norrmalm) is **Skeppsholmen**, an island of museums. The city's streets are easy to navigate: each begins with number "1" at the end closest to the City Palace in Gamla Stan; the lower the numbers, the closer you are to Gamla Stan.

Tourist Offices: Sweden House, Hamng. 27 (☎789 24 90; www.stockholmtown.com), temporarily located in the basement of the Kulturhuset in Sergels Torg until Feb. 2005. From Centralstationen, walk up Klarabergsg. to Sergels Torg (the plaza with the 37m glass obelisk) and bear right on Hamng. Friendly, multilingual agents sell the **SL** and **Stockholm Cards**, and are uniformly helpful. Open June-Aug. M-F 8am-7pm, Sa 9am-5pm, Su 10am-4pm; May and Sept. M-F 9am-6pm, Sa-Su 10am-4pm; Oct.-Apr. M-F 9am-6pm, Sa-Su 10am-3pm. The **HotellCentralen** branch, located in Centralstationen (☎789 24 56), books rooms for a 60kr fee. Open June-Aug. daily 8am-8pm; Sept.-May M-Sa 9am-6pm, Su noon-4pm.

Budget Travel: Kilroy Travels, Kungsg. 4 (☎0771 54 57 69; www.kilroytravels.com). Open M-F 10am-6pm. **STA Travel,** Kungsg. 30 (☎0771 61 10 10; www.statravel.se). Open M-F 10am-6pm.

Embassies: Australia, Sergels Torg 12, 11th fl. (☎613 29 00; www.sweden.embassy.gov.au). Open M-F 8:30am-4:50pm. **Canada,** Tegelbacken 4, 7th fl. (☎453 30 00; www.canadaemb.se). Open 8:30am-noon and 1-5pm. **Ireland,** Ostermalmsg. 97 (☎661 80 05). Open M-F 10am-noon and 2:30-4pm. **UK,** Skarpög. 6-8 (☎671 30 00; www.britishembassy.se). Open M-F 9am-5pm. **US,** Daghammarskjölds Väg 31 (☎783 53 75; www.usemb.se). Open M-F 9-11am.

Currency Exchange: Forex offices in **Centralstationen** (☎411 67 34; open daily 7am-9pm), **Cityterminalen** (☎21 42 80; open M-F 7am-10pm, Sa 8am-5pm), and **Sweden House** (☎20 03 89; open M-F 8am-7pm, Sa-Su 9am-5pm). 15-20kr commission.

Luggage Storage: Lockers are available at Centralstationen (20-60kr per day) and Cityterminalen (25-35kr per day).

GLBT Services: RFSL, Sveav. 57-59 (☎457 13 20; www.rfsl.se). T-bana: Rådmansgatan. Located above Tip Top, a popular club (see **Nightlife,** below). Open M-F 9am-5pm. **Rosa Rummet,** Sveav. 57 (☎736 02 15), is a gay and lesbian bookstore on the same block. Queer Extra (QX) and the **QueerMap,** available at Rosa Rummet and Sweden House, give info about Stockholm's gay hot spots.

Emergencies: ☎112.

Pharmacy: Look for green and white Apoteket signs. **Apoteket C. W. Scheele,** Klarabergsg. 64 (☎454 81 30), at the overpass over Vasag. T-bana: T-Centralen. Open 24hr.

Medical Assistance: ☎32 01 00.

Hospitals: Karolinska (☎517 700 00), north of Norrmalm near Solnavägen. T-Bana: Skt. Eriksplan. **Sankt Göran** (☎587 100 00), on Kungsholmen. T-Bana: Fridhemsplan.

Internet Access: Stadsbiblioteket (library), Odeng. 59, in the annex. T-bana: Odenplan. 10min. free. Open M-F 9am-7pm, Sa noon-4pm. **Sweden House** (see above) provides free access to their own comprehensive website. **Inferno Online,** Odeng. 60, across from the library, has more than 100 terminals. 19kr per hr. Open daily 10am-midnight. **Sidewalk Express** Internet stations are located throughout the city, including one in Cityterminalen, and are spreading across Sweden rapidly. 19kr per hr. Open 24hr.

Telephones: Almost all public phones require Telia phone cards; buy them at Pressbyrån newsstands in increments of 50 (50kr) or 120 (100kr) units. Local calls are 6 units for 1st min., 2 for each additional min.; international calls use up to 12 units per min.

Post Office: In Centralstationen (☎781 24 25). Open in summer M-F 7am-8pm, Sa-Su 10am-4pm; winter M-F 7am-8pm, Sa-Su 9am-6pm. Address mail to be held in the following format: First name SURNAME, Poste Restante, 10110 Stockholm 1, SWEDEN.

⚠ ACCOMMODATIONS

Reservations are absolutely indispensable in summer, and many HI hostels limit stays to five nights. If you haven't booked ahead, arrive around 8am. Many independent (non-HI) hostels are hotel/hostels; specify if you want to stay in a dorm-style hostel, or risk paying hotel rates. Stockholm's several **botels** (boat-hotels) are a novel solution to space issues, but they can be cramped, noisy, and a recipe for seasickness—request a room on the water side of the boat. There are also various **B&B booking services**, including the **Bed & Breakfast Agency** (☎643 80 28; www.bba.nu; open M 10am-5pm, Tu-W 9am-5pm). An SL bus pass (or Stockholm Card) is the cheapest way for **campers** to reach some of the more remote campsites. Note that the right of public access does not apply within the city limits, although camping is allowed on most islands in the archipelago (p. 1004).

🏠 **Hostel af Chapman/Skeppsholmens Vandrarhem (HI)**, Flaggmansväg. 8 (☎463 22 66; www.stfchapman.com), on Skeppsholmen. T-bana: Kungsträdgården. Exit the station toward Kungsträdgården, walk to the water, and cross the bridge to Skeppsholmen. Modern on-shore hostel and a 19th-century schooner pinch-hitting as a roomy botel. Great view of Gamla Stan. Kitchen available. Breakfast 55kr. Sheets 40kr. Laundry 35kr. Internet 1kr per min. Reception 24hr. Lockout 11am-3pm. Dorms 150-210kr; doubles from 420kr. Nonmembers add 45kr. MC/V. ❷

🏠 **City Backpackers' Vandrarhem**, Upplandsg. 2A (☎20 69 20; www.citybackpackers.se). From Centralstationen, go left on Vasag. and bear right on Upplandsg. Dorms are a bit crowded, but a friendly staff and great amenities make up for it. Sauna 20kr. Kitchen available. Sheets 50kr. Laundry 50kr. Internet free. Reception 9am-noon and 2-7pm. Dorms from 180kr; doubles 490kr. MC/V. ❷

Långholmen Vandrarhem (HI), Långholmsmuren 20 (☎668 05 10; www.langholmen.com). T-bana: Hornstull. Walk north on Långholmsg., turn left onto Högalidsg., and then right onto Långholmsbron. Located on the tranquil island of Långholmen, this former prison has renovated its cells into small, cozy rooms. Kitchen, cafe, pub, and laundry. Breakfast 65kr. Sheets 40kr. Reception 24hr. Check-out 10am. Dorms 195kr; doubles 495kr. Nonmembers add 45kr. MC/V. ❷

Mälarens, Södermälarstrand, Kajplats 6 (☎644 43 85; www.theredboat.com). T-bana: Gamla Stan. Take Centralbron across the river and walk 100m to the right along the shore—it's the red boat. Very small rooms with low ceilings, although a lovely view and the maritime decor help. Breakfast 60kr. Reception 8am-11pm. Dorms from 195kr; singles 430kr; doubles 980kr; triples and quads 920kr. MC/V. ❷

Brygghuset, Nortullsg. 12N (☎545 472 30). T-bana: Odenplan. A solicitous staff tends spacious, clean rooms on a quiet street in a former brewery. Take a peek into the 2-level ballroom, and scan the newspaper in one of this hostel's large common rooms. Sheets 50kr. Laundry 50kr. Reception 8am-noon and 3-10pm. Open late June to Aug. Dorms from 150kr. MC/V. ❶

City Lodge, Klara Norra Kyrkog. 15 (☎22 66 30; www.citylodge.se). T-bana: T-Centralen. Head north on Vasag., turn right onto Bryggarg. and then left onto Klara Norra Kyrkog. Clean, modern hostel hidden on a side street very close to Centralstationen. Sheets 50kr. Reception M-F 8am-noon and 2-10pm, Sa-Su 9am-noon and 4-7pm. Dorms 180kr; doubles 700kr; quads 1000kr. MC/V. ❷

Zinkensdamm Vandrarhem (HI), Zinkens Väg 20 (☎616 81 00; www.zinkensdamm.com). T-bana: Zinkensdamm. Head south on Ringv. and turn right onto Zinkens Väg. Immense, colorful, and clean, in a beautiful park setting. Kitchen, restaurant, and laundry. Communal showers only. Breakfast 65kr. Sheets 50kr. Bikes 100kr per day. Reception 24hr. Dorms 175kr. Nonmembers add 45kr. MC/V. ❷

Ängby Camping, Blackebergsv. 24 (☎37 04 20; www.angbycamping.se), on Lake Mälaren. T-bana: Ängbyplan. Go downstairs, turn left on Färjestadsvägen, and bear left at the fork; it's at the bottom of the road. Wooded campsite with swimming area and walking paths. Reception daily in summer 7am-11pm; low season 8am-10pm. 115kr per couple with tent; 80kr per extra person. Cabins 400-725kr. AmEx/MC/V. ●

Bredäng Camping, Stora Sällskapets Väg (☎97 70 71; www.camping.se/plats/A04), near Lake Mälaren. T-bana: Bredäng. Turn left under the tunnel onto Stora Sällskapets Väg and follow the street 700m, past Ålgrytevägen. Reception daily 7am-10pm, on the right. Open mid-Apr. to late Oct. Single tents 90-105kr; group tents 170-205kr; 4-bed cottage 450kr. AmEx/MC/V. ●

◘ FOOD

Fuel up on the all-you-can-eat breakfasts offered by most hostels, and then track down lunch specials (*dagens rätt;* 50-80kr) to save money. Ethnic restaurants line **Götgatan** and **Folkunggatan** in Södermalm, while pizza and kebabs are plentiful on Vasastaden's **Odengatan.** Grocery stores are easy to find around any T-bana station—popular chains include **Coop** and **Vivo.** The huge **Östermalms Saluhall,** Nybrog. 31 (T-bana: Östermalmstorg), contains bustling fish and meat markets, as well as restaurants serving Swedish dishes. (Open M-Th 9:30am-6pm, F 9:30am-6:30pm, Sa 9:30am-2pm.) Get your daily allowance of Vitamin C at the **fruit market** on Hötorg. (Open M-Sa 7am-6pm.)

▩ Herman's, Fjällg. 23A (☎64 39 80), in Södermalm. T-bana: Slussen. Excellent vegetarian fare, served buffet-style, with phenomenal views of Stockholm off the Söder cliffs. Lunch (78-98kr) and dinner (128-168kr) include dessert and a drink. Open in summer daily 11am-11pm; low season M-F 11am-9pm, Sa-Su noon-10pm. MC/V. ❸

▩ Koh Phangan, Skåneg. 57 (☎642 50 40). T-Bana: Skanstull. Head north on Götg. and turn right onto Skåneg. Splurge on Thai food in the city's trendy SoFo ("south of Folkungagata") neighborhood. A stream runs between tables in what looks like a tree-house transplanted from a South Asian jungle, and a simulated monsoon may interrupt your waiter in mid-sentence. Vegetarian entrees 125-140kr. Meat dishes 150-165kr. Seafood 180-195kr. Open M-Th 11am-11pm, F-Su 2-11pm. MC/V. ❹

Chokladkoppen and **Kaffekoppen,** Stortorg. 18-20 (☎20 31 70). T-bana: Gamla Stan. Friendly staff serves light meals (34-65kr), generous desserts (from 34kr), and hot drinks. The best people-watching spots in Gamla Stan. Open in summer M-Th and Su 9am-11pm, F-Sa 9am-midnight; low season M-Th and Su closes 10pm. Cash only. ●

Café Tabac, Stora Nyg. 46 (☎10 15 34). T-bana: Gamla Stan. Chic cafe by the waterfront serves huge grilled sandwiches (46-60kr) and offers an extensive tapas menu (52-65kr). Open M-Th 10am-midnight, F-Sa 10am-1am, Su noon-midnight. MC/V. ❷

STHLM, Drottningg. 73c (☎22 56 66), 7 blocks north of T-Centralen. Urbane, spartan-hip cafe on Normalm's main pedestrian avenue serves large portions of pasta (69-85kr) and salads (79kr), as well as tempting desserts (20-30kr). Open M-F 8am-8pm, Sa 10am-8pm, Su 10am-6pm. AmEx/MC/V. ❷

Kófi, Birger Jarlsg. 11 (☎650 90 85). T-bana: Östermalmstorg. The rent must be sky-high in this tony part of town, but Kófi keeps things affordable with sandwiches (36-49kr) for a light lunch. Open daily in summer 7am-1am; low season 7am-11pm. MC/V. ●

☺ SIGHTS

Break up your walking tour (p. 1000) of Stockholm's inner neighborhoods with T-bana rides to more remote locations in order to get a sense of the capital's sweeping scope. The T-bana has been called the world's longest art exhibition, since over the past 50 years the city has commissioned more than 140 artists to decorate

PEDESTRIAN TACTICS 101. Stockholm lends itself to exploration on foot, but the network of elevated streets and footbridges can be bemusing. To get from Centralstationen to Sergels Torg, turn left out of the station onto Vasag., take the stairs up to Klarag. and head straight. To get to the Stadhuset, turn right out of the station and walk to Vasabron, then walk down the steps to the water just before the bridge and follow the quay under Centralbron. There are different ways to navigate the cloverleaf bridge from Gamla Stan to Söder-malm, depending on your destination; to reach Södermalmstorg or the cliffs, stay on the bridge to the left. To reach Söder Malerstrand, stay as far to the right as possible and then take the ramp down to the water.

its stations. The murals and sculptures of T-Centralen remain the best-recognized example of T-bana artistry, although Madonna cast her vote for the space-age Hötorget station when she featured it in her 1998 "Ray of Light" music video.

GAMLA STAN (OLD TOWN). The Baltic trading port of Stockholm was once confined to the small island of Staden. Today the island is the epicenter of the city and is dominated by the magnificent 1754 **Kungliga Slottet** (Royal Palace), one of the largest palaces in Europe and the winter home of the Swedish royal family. The extravagant **Royal Apartments** and the adjacent **Rikssalen** (State Hall) and **Slottskyr-kan** (Royal Chapel) are dizzyingly lavish. In the former wine cellar, the **Skattkam-maren** (Royal Treasury) houses a small but remarkable collection of jewel-encrusted objects, including the 16th-century sword of King Gustav Vasa. The statues in the **Gustav III Antikmuseum** are forgettable, but the **Museum Tre Konor,** on the lower level, includes the foundation of the 13th-century castle that once stood on the same site. Expect lines in summer. *(The main ticket office and information area are at the rear of the complex, near the Storkyrkan.* ☎ *402 61 30; www.royalcourt.se. Open mid-May to June daily 10am-4pm; July to mid-Aug. daily 10am-5pm; Sept. to early May Tu-Su noon-3pm. Each attraction 70kr, students 35kr; combination ticket 110kr/65kr.)* The **Livrustkammaren** (Armory) presents an extensive collection of swords, suits of armor, and carriages that are straight out of Cinderella. *(Open June–Aug. daily 10am-5pm; Sept.-May Tu-Su 11am-5pm. 40kr.)* A broad plaza separates the palace from the **Storkykan** church, where royals get married and winners of the Nobel Peace Prize speak after accepting their awards. Don't miss the statue of St. George slaying the dragon. *(Open daily 9am-4pm. 20kr. Tower tours in summer 2 and 3pm. 30kr.)* Around the corner on **Stortorget,** the main square, the small **Nobelsmuseum** traces the story of the Nobel Prize and its winners through engrossing multimedia exhibits. *(*☎ *534 818 00; www.nobelprize.org/nobelmuseum. Open mid-May to mid-Sept. M and W-Su 10am-6pm, Tu 10am-8pm; mid-Sept. to mid-May Tu 11am-8pm, W-Su 11am-5pm. 50kr, students 40kr.)* Gamla Stan's main pedestrian street, **Västerlånggatan,** is a lively, good-natured mob scene of tourists during the summer. *(T-bana: Gamla Stan. Tours of Gamla Stan June-Aug. M and W-Th 7:30pm. Meet at the obelisk in front of Storkyrkan. 60kr.)*

KUNGSHOLMEN. Perched on the eastern tip of Kungsholmen, the **Stadshuset** offers more than its muscular red brick exterior lets on. The required tour of the interior takes you through the council room, whose roof suggests an inverted Viking ship, and then into the enormous Blue Hall, where a 10,000-pipe organ overlooks what is in essence a miniature Italian *piazza.* The breathtaking Gold Room uses millions of shimmering tiles to make up an Art Deco mosaic celebrating the history of Stockholm. The 106m **tower** may provide the best panoramic view of the city center. *(Hantverkarg. 1. T-bana: T-Centralen. Walk toward the water and turn right on Stad-shusbron. Tower open daily May-Sept. 10am-4:30pm. 20kr. Tours daily June-Aug. 10, 11am, noon, 2, and 3pm; May 10am, noon, and 2pm; Sept.-Apr. 10am and noon. 50kr.)*

SWEDEN

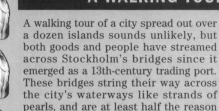

A WALKING TOUR OF STOCKHOLM

A walking tour of a city spread out over a dozen islands sounds unlikely, but both goods and people have streamed across Stockholm's bridges since it emerged as a 13th-century trading port. These bridges string their way across the city's waterways like strands of pearls, and are at least half the reason why Stockholm is such a consummately walkable city. Factor in a network of

TIME: 4hr., 5-6hr. with visits to the Stadhuset, Moderna Museet, or Kungliga Slottet.

DISTANCE: about 6km.

SEASON: Mid-April to late October.

A leisurely traipse through the city center and selected adjoining islands.

parks and thoroughly continental boulevards, and it's not hard to see why residents of Stockholm happily hoof it during the summer months—even though comfortable mass transit options are never very far away.

This tour starts at **Sweden House** (p. 996), Stockholm's main tourist office, and ends in the old town of **Gamla Stan.**

1 SERGELS TORG. Begin by walking west on Hamngatan past the exclusive **NK** department store. Make for the 37m glass obelisk at the center of Sergels Torg, the plaza that was carved out of Lower Norrmalm after WWII in what the Swedes called "the great demolition wave." Modernist city planners were convinced that they could arbitrarily designate a new city center and have civic life revolve around it, but they got more than they bargained for with the covey of drug dealers who flocked to the western side of Sergels Torg. Known as the **Plattan,** this sunken plaza should be avoided at night. The glassy **Kulturhuset** (p. 1002), on the southern side of the square, is a more savory point of interest; check the schedule of events posted inside **Lava,** a popular hangout with Stockholm's university students.

2 STADHUSET. Turn left onto Drottninggatan, Norrmalm's main pedestrian thoroughfare, and then turn right just before the bridge onto Strömgatan. Take the steps down to the quay just before the Centralbron overpass, go under the bridge, and walk toward the majestic Stadshuset (p. 999). Guided tours leave on the hour, lasting around one hour and costing 50kr. If time or money is short, however, make a point of walking around the manicured waterside grounds before continuing on your way.

3 RIDDARHOLMEN. Head back to Centralbron, take the steps up, and then turn right onto the bridge. Make a right into the plaza on Riddarholmen (The Knight's Island). Stockholm's 17th-century elite built private palaces around the **Riddarholmskyrkan** church. Parts of the church date back to the 13th century, when it was used as a Franciscan monastery, although Lutherans threw the Franciscans out on their ears after the Protestant Reformation and then set aside the church as the burial place for Swedish monarchs in 1807. Today the island's elegant palaces are used as courthouses and offices for government agencies.

4 SKEPPSHOLMEN. Head straight out of the plaza, cross Centralbron, and make a right onto charming Stora Nygatan. Turn left down any of the side streets and then left onto Västerlånggatan, lined with shops and confectionaries. Cross two bridges, cutting through the back of the **Riksdag** (Parliament), then turn right onto Strömgatan and right again back across the water, this time past the Riksdag's long east-facing facade. Turn left onto Slottskajen alongside the royal palace of **Kungliga Slottet** (p. 999), and left again onto the bridge toward the Grand Hotel. Bear right onto Södra Blasieholmshamnen and then cross the scenic Skeppsholmbron bridge onto the island of Skeppsholmen. The main attraction here is the **Moderna Museet** (p. 1002), home to one of Marcel Duchamp's infamous fountains and plenty of other work from both ends of the 20th century. Admission is deliciously free.

WALKING TOUR

KUNGLIGA SLOTTET. Retrace your steps and turn left back onto Gamla Stan, flanking palace on Skeppsbron this time. You could spend a full day wandering through the palace's museums and courtyards, but for the sake of time confine your visit to the **Royal Apartments.** Turn into the plaza leading up to Storkyrkan; the ticket office is on the right.

SÖDERMALM. Hug the waterfront as you make your way south to the bridge connecting Gamla Stan to the southern island of Södermalm. Keep to the left as you cross the bridge, to the **Katarinahissen lift** (10kr), and cross the bridge to the north-facing cliffs for one of the best views of the city. Head straight to intimate Mosebacke Torg and continue south down Götgatagatan. Take your first left onto Högbergsgatan, passing by the octagonal tower of the **Katarina kyrka,** devastated by fire in 1990 but rebuilt to its former Baroque splendor. At the end of Högbergsgatan, turn right onto Nytorgsgatan, left onto Tjärhovsgatan, and then right onto Renstiernas gata. As the street begins its languid arch to the west, a beautiful view of Stockholm's spires spreads out before you. Finish by heading down to Slussen and crossing back onto Gamla Stan to rest your weary legs.

BLASIEHOLMEN AND SKEPPSHOLMEN. A short peninsula jutting out from Norrmalm, Blasieholmen is home to the **Nationalmuseum.** Stockholm's major art museum is no slouch, but its collections are hardly in the league of those held by other European capitals; Rembrandt's *Conspiracy of the Batavians* and the folkloric canvases of Anders Zorn are highlights. *(☎51 95 43 00; www.nationalmuseum.se. T-bana: Kungsträdgården. Museum is on the left before Skeppsh. Olmsbron bridge. Open Tu 11am-8pm, W-Su 11am-5pm. 75kr, students 60kr.)* Over on the island of Skeppsholmen (FSHEPS-hole-men), the ▓**Moderna Museet** picks up the slack for its counterpart across the bridge. A huge, well-organized collection spans canvases by Matisse, Picasso, Klee, and Rauschenberg, as well as more recent, lesser-known work. In the same building, the permanent collection of **Arkitekturmuseet** focuses on Swedish design, while temporary exhibitions examine cross-cultural aesthetics. *(Both museums open Tu-W 10am-8pm, Th-Su 10am-6pm. Free.)*

DJURGÅRDEN. Djurgården is a lush national park in the heart of the city, a perfect spot for a summer picnic. The main attraction is the haunting ▓**Vasa Museet,** which contains a massive salvaged warship that sank in the middle of Stockholm's harbor on its maiden voyage in 1628. *(Galärvarvet. Take bus #44, 47, or 69. Open mid-June to mid-Aug. daily 9:30am-7pm; mid-Aug. to mid-June M-Tu and Th-Su 10am-5pm, W 10am-8pm. English-language tours daily every hr. 10:30am-6:30pm. 70kr, students 40kr.)* Across the street, the everything-but-the-kitchen-sink **Nordiska Museet** displays Sami clothing, Viking artifacts, and modern furniture in a kind of multimedia paean to Swedish culture. *(Djurgårdsvägen 6-16. Take bus #44, 47, or 69. Open late June to Aug. daily 10am-5pm; Jan. to late June Tu and Th-Sa 10am-5pm, W 10am-9pm. 75kr, students 40kr.)* The **Gröna Lund** amusement park features a handful of exciting rides, including the 80m Fritt Fall Tilt, which offers a great view of the city before catapulting you downward at high G-forces. *(Open daily mid-May to late Aug., usually 11am-11pm; check www.gronalund.se for detailed schedule. Admission 60kr. Rides 15-60kr each.)* Djurgården is also home to **Skansen,** a huge open-air museum featuring 150 historical buildings, handicrafts, and a small zoo. Costumed actors inhabit the homes, and their attention to period authenticity somehow redeems the project from kitschiness. *(Take bus #44 or 47. Park and zoo open daily June-Aug. 10am-10pm; Sept.-Apr. 10am-4pm; May 10am-8pm. Homes open daily May-Aug. 11am-5pm; Sept.-Apr. 11am-3pm. 70kr, low season 35kr.)*

♫ ▒ ENTERTAINMENT AND FESTIVALS

Stockholm offers a number of venues for theater and music, many of which are small establishments showcased in *What's On,* available at the tourist office. There are also a number of larger, more widely known performance spots. The six stages of the national theater, **Dramaten,** Nybroplan (☎667 06 80), feature Swedish- and English-language performances of works by August Strindberg and other playwrights (50-260kr). Check out **Backstage** for more experimental material. The **Kulturhuset** at Sergels Torg (☎508 15 08), an arts complex built in the 1960s, houses art galleries, performance spaces, and a variety of cultural venues that are often free to the public. It also plays host to **Lava** (☎508 31 44), a popular, just-renovated hangout with a stage, library, and cafe that lend themselves to poetry readings and other student events. Check www.kulturhuset.se for details. The **Operan,** Jakobs Torg 2 (☎24 82 40), stages operas and ballets from late August through mid-June. (Tickets 135-460kr. Student, obstructed-view, and rush tickets available.) The imposing **Konserthuset,** Hötorg. 8 (☎10 21 10), hosts the Stockholm Philharmonic, which just last year agreed to start playing concerts at the venue over the summer (100-270kr). Culture buffs on a budget should also ask at Sweden House about **Parkteatern,** a summer-long program of free theater, dance, and music staged in parks around the city. Call **BiljettDirect** (☎07 7170 7070; www.ticnet.se) for tickets to events and performances. The world-class ▓**Stockholm Jazz Festival** arrives in mid- to late July; the 2004 line-up included international Alisters like Dave Brubeck, Ladysmith Black Mambazo, and Stevie Wonder. (☎556 924 40; www.stockholmjazz.com.) Other festivals include the gay blowout **Stockholm Pride** (late July or early Aug.; ☎33 59 55; www.stockholmpride.org) and late August's **Strindberg Festival** for the turtlenecked, furrowed-brow literati.

 NIGHTLIFE

For a city where "night" barely exists during the summer, Stockholm knows a thing or two about nightlife. In posh, upscale Östermalm (T-bana: Östermalmtorg), celebrities party with beautiful people until 5am. Expect long lines outside nearly every club. High up on the cliffs across the river, Södermalm's nightlife is a little less glitzy and more student-friendly, with a diverse mix of bars and clubs around Medborgspl. A grab bag of nightlife options line **Sveavägen** and the **Vasastaden** area (T-bana: Odenplan or Rådmansgtn.). Stockholm is compact enough to walk between all three areas, although night buses cover most of the city. Pick up *Queer Extra (QX)* and the QueerMap for invaluable tips on gay nightlife.

Mondo, Medborgarpl. 8 (☎641 22 69). T-bana: Medborgarpl. On the left across from the station. This massive complex (5 bars, 4 dance floors, and 3 stages) gets packed with well-dressed young Swedes listening to live rock, hip-hop, or reggae. Drinks from 50kr. 20+. Cover 40-150kr M and F-Sa, no cover Tu-Th. Open M-Sa 10pm-3am.

Tip Top, Sveav. 57 (☎32 98 00). T-bana: Rådmansg. Walk 1 block left of the station. This popular gay club's large dance floor draws a mixed crowd on the weekends. Beer 34-44kr. 18+. Cover F-Sa 50kr after 10pm, 70kr after 11pm. Bar open M-Tu and Th 8pm-1am. Club open W and F-Sa 8pm-3am.

Mosebacke Etablissement, Mosebacke Torg 3 (☎55 60 98 90). T-bana: Slussen. Take the Katarina lift (10kr) to Söder Heights. Next to the Söder Teatern. Eclectic array of live music and a terrace with a spectacular view. Beneath the terrace, the Kagelbana stage features live music in low season. Beer 44-60kr. 20+. Cover 60-100kr. Terrace open daily in summer 11am-1am. Bar and club open Th-Sa 9pm-2am.

Snaps, Medborgarpl. (☎640 28 68). T-bana: Medborgarpl. The free-standing blue-gray house across from the station. Intimate basement dance floor starts to get surreal around midnight, with luminescent walls and skittering jungle beats. Beer 42kr, mixed drinks from 70kr. W-Th 21+, F-Sa 23+. Cover F-Sa 60kr. Open W-Sa 9pm-3am.

Kvarnen, Tjärhovsg. 4 (☎643 03 80). T-bana: Medborgarpl. A 200-year-old beer hall, the slick cocktail lounge **H2O,** and the energetic **Eld** dance club somehow coexist under the same roof. 21+, F-Sa 23+. Beer hall open daily 5pm-3am. Lounge open M-Sa 7pm-3am, Su 9pm-3am. Club open W-Th 11pm-3am, F-Sa 10pm-3am.

Bröderna Olssons Garlic and Shots, Folkungag. 84 (☎640 84 46). T-bana: Medborgarpl. Walk 3 blocks up Folkungag. Quirky bar draws a crowd sporting both leather and sport coats, while tattooed bartenders serve up garlic-flavored beer (35-50kr) and a repertoire of 101 shots (each 35kr). Vampires tend to feel unwelcome. Cafe area 18+, bar 23+. Open daily 5pm-1am.

Icebar Stockholm, Vasaplan 4 (☎505 635 51), inside the Nordic Sea Hotel. T-bana: T-Centralen. The glasses, the tables, and the bar itself are all carved out of ice. As touristy as Stockholm gets, but a fun splurge if you have an extra night in the city. Wear warm clothing. Cover 125kr, includes 1 drink. Open M-Sa 3pm-midnight, Su 3-9pm. Reservations mandatory; call M-F 9am-5pm for a 45min. booking.

 DAYTRIPS FROM STOCKHOLM

Stockholm is situated in the center of an archipelago, where the mainland gradually crumbles into the Baltic. The islands in either direction—east toward the Baltic or west toward Lake Mälaren—are well worth exploration. Visit the **Excursion Shop** in Sweden House (p. 996) for more info. **Ferries** to the archipelago leave from in front of the Grand Hotel on the **Stromkajen** docks between Gamla Stan and Skeppsholmen (T-Bana: Jakobskyrka) or the **Nybrohamnen** docks (T-Bana: Östermalmstorg; walk down Birger Jarlsg. toward the water).

■**THE ARCHIPELAGO (SKÄRGÅRD).** The wooded islands of the Stockholm archipelago get sparser and less developed as the chain coils its way out into the Baltic Sea. **Waxholmsbolaget** (☎08 679 58 30; www.waxholmsbolaget.se) runs boats to 270 ports-of-call, serving even the tiniest islands year-round. Sweden House (p. 996) sells the **Båtluffarkort** (385kr), good for 16 days of unlimited travel on Waxholmsbolaget boats; the pass pays for itself with just a few long rides. Ask at Sweden House about **hostels** on the archipelago; they tend to be booked up months in advance, but the islands are a promising place to exercise the right of public access (p. 992) and set up **camp** under the midnight sun. Ritzy **Vaxholm** is the most popular island to visit, although the beaches and the 16th-century fortress have spawned pricey sidewalk cafes and hordes of tourists. Three hours away from the city center, **Sandhamn** is a little quieter, although the white sands of Trouville Beach have plenty of devotees. Hikers can escape the crowds by exploring the coastal trails on **Finnhamn** and **Tjockö** to the north.

LAKE MÄLAREN. The island of **Björkö** on Lake Mälaren is home to **Birka**, an 8th-century trading port where St. Ansgar established the first Christian congregation in Sweden. The settlement was abandoned by the late 10th century, but excavation continues in the surrounding bay as new artifacts are uncovered and displayed in the **Birka Museum.** A **ferry** departs Stockholm from the Stadshusbron docks next to the Stadshuset. (July-Aug. 10am and 2pm, return 3:30 and 6:30pm; Sept. and May 10am, return 3:30pm. Guided tour, museum admission, and round-trip ferry 200kr.) Closer to the city center, **Drottningholm Palace** was built for the queens of Sweden in the late 17th century and has served as the royal family's residence since 1981, when they quit their apartment in Kungliga Slottet (p. 999). The Rococo interior and sprawling formal gardens are impressive, but the 1766 **Court Theater** takes the cake with artistic director Per-Erik Öhrn using 18th-century sets and stage equipment to mount provocative modern productions. Tickets start at 165kr, but a guided tour (60kr, students 30kr) is a good way to have a look-see. (Palace open May-Aug. daily 10am-4:30pm; Sept. daily noon-3:30pm; Oct-Apr. Sa-Su noon-3:30pm. 60kr, students 30kr. English-language tours mid-June to Aug. daily every hr. 11am-3pm; May to mid-June Sa-Su every hr. 11am-3pm.) Strömma Kanalbolaget **ferries** depart from Stadshusbron from May to early September. (☎08 587 140 00. 1hr.; M-F 1 per hr., Sa-Su more frequently.)

UPPSALA   ☎018

Archbishop Jakob Ulvsson founded Uppsala University in 1477, but the Reformation wrested control away from the Catholic Church and set the stage for secular inquiry in this consummate college town. Today, the footbridges and side streets of Uppsala (pop. 127,000) teem with almost 40,000 undergraduates. Rome may no longer be calling the shots in Uppsala's classrooms, but the city's red-brick **Domkyrka** is still the largest cathedral in Sweden; its 118m towers are as tall as the cathedral is long. Many famous Swedes, ranging from philosopher Emanuel Swedenborg to scientist Carolus Linnaeus, are buried within. (Open daily 8am-6pm. Free. Tours mid-June to Aug. 10am and 2pm.) Just across Akademig. from the church, the **Gustavianum** houses the university's collection of artifacts and scientific curiosities. Make your way to the top floor to see the **Anatomical Theater,** where public dissections were conducted from the late 17th century onwards. (Open late June to late Aug. Tu-Su 11am-5pm; Jan. to late June Tu-Su 11am-4pm. 40kr, students 30kr.) A walk through the center of town along the Fyrisån River is an excellent way to get a taste of the city's flourishing gardens and cafes. Wander down Drottning. to **Carolina Rediviva,** Dag Hammarskjölds v. 1, the university's august humanities library. (☎471 39 00. Free Internet. Open M-F 8:30am-9pm, Sa 9am-6pm.) On the other side of the river, the **Linnéträdgården,** Svartbäcksg.

27, reconstructs the botanical gardens tended by Carolus Linnaeus using his own 1745 sketch. The grounds also include a small **museum** in Linnaeus's former home. (☎471 25 76; www.linnaeus.uu.se. Gardens open daily May-Aug. 9am-9pm; Sept. 9am-7pm. 20kr. Museum open June to mid-Sept. Tu-Su noon-4pm. 25kr.) The *M/S Kung Carl Justaf* sails 2hr. south of Uppsala to **Skoklosters Slott,** a lavish 17th-century castle with an impressive armory. (☎018 38 60 77; www.lsh.se/skokloster. Tours daily mid-June to mid-Aug. every hr. 11am-4pm; May to mid-June and late Aug. 1 per hr. noon-3pm; reduced hours Apr. and Sept.-Oct. 65kr, students 50kr. Boat departs Tu-Su 11:30am from Islandsbron on Östra Åg. and Munkg.; returns 5:15pm. Round-trip 145kr. Purchase tickets at the tourist office.) Bars cluster around **Stortorget,** especially on **Sysslomansgatan, Västra Ågatan,** and the pedestrian areas of **Svartbäcksgatan** and **Kungsgatan.** Many bars require student ID for entry.

Trains run to Stockholm (40min., 1-4 per hr., 64kr). To get from the station to the **tourist office,** Fyristorg 8, walk right on Kungsg., left on St. Persg., and across the bridge. The office books rooms for free. (☎27 48 00; www.uppland.nu. Free Internet. Open in summer M-F 10am-6pm, Sa 10am-3pm, Su noon-4pm; winter closed Su.) **McDonald's,** Dragarbrunnsg. 29, has 24hr. Internet access for 19kr per hr. The dorms at **Hotel Uppsala ❷,** Kungsg. 27, are luxurious, with in-room shower and TV. (☎480 50 00. Breakfast 60kr. Sheets 90kr. Dorms 185kr; singles 370kr; doubles 500kr. AmEx/MC/V.) Pick up groceries at **Rätt Pris,** Kungsg. 95. (Open M-F 7am-9pm, Sa-Su 9am-9pm.) **Postal Code:** 75320.

GOTLAND ☎0498

Swedish families flock to sandy beaches on the eastern shores of their country's largest island, while the town of Visby recalls the Middle Ages with its winding alleyways and impregnable gates. The summer months are busy ones, but even in high season visitors can leave the crowds behind to walk along the northern limestone cliffs or track ospreys and terns by the southern coast. Each May, Gotland's 30+ species of orchids come into bloom.

■ ▌**GETTING THERE AND TRANSPORTATION.** Destination Gotland **ferries** (☎0771 22 33 00; www.destinationgotland.se) sail to Visby from **Nynäshamn,** 3hr. south of Stockholm, and **Oskarshamn,** 2½hr. north of Kalmar. Fares are highest on weekends and in summer, and lowest for early-morning and late-night departures. (June-Aug. 2-5 per day; Oct.-May 1-3 per day. 218-496kr, students 166-372kr; 40% Scanrail discount.) To get to Nynäshamn from **Stockholm,** take the Båtbussen **bus** from Cityterminalen (1hr.; leaves 1¾hr. before ferry departures; 75kr, 100kr on bus) or the **Pendeltåg** from Centralstationen (1hr.; 90kr, SL passes valid). To get to Oskarshamn, hop a KLT bus (1½hr., every 1-2hr., 70kr) from **Kalmar.** If you're planning your trip from Stockholm, **Gotland City,** Kungsg. 57A, books ferries. (☎08 406 15 00. Open June-Aug. M-F 9:30am-6pm, Sa 10am-2pm; Sept.-May M-F 9:30am-5pm.) On Gotland, it's worth picking up a bus timetable at the ferry terminal or at the Visby **bus station** (☎21 41 12), Kung Magnusväg 1, outside the wall east of the city. However, buses are fairly expensive (59kr) and only three or four buses cover the routes each day, making it almost impossible to daytrip. **Cycling** is a far better way to explore Gotland's flat terrain; extensive paths and bike-friendly motorways can be supplemented by strategic bus rides, since buses will carry bikes for an extra 40kr. Bike rental shops are plentiful in Visby and across the island.

◪ **VISBY.** The sleepy town of Visby (pop. 21,500) seems straight out of a fairy tale. Its medieval **Ringmuren** (ring wall) encloses knotted cobblestone streets and nine ruined churches; both **Skt. Karins** and **Skt. Drottens** can be explored by visitors. (Open daily in summer 11am-5pm.) Behind the towering **Domkyrka,** stairs lead to a scenic terrace; follow the path along the cliff for a far-flung view of the town and sea. Visby awakens during the first week of August for **Medieval Week,** complete with jousting tournament, a seminar on runes, and wandering minstrels strumming their lutes. (☎29 19 70; www.medeltidsveckan.com.)

From the ferry terminal, walk 10min. to the left to get to the **tourist office,** Hamng. 4., which arranges guided tours (65kr) and tends to be jam-packed after summer ferry arrivals. (☎20 17 00. Open mid-June to mid-Aug. daily 8am-7pm; low season reduced hours.) Dozens of **bike rental** shops surround the ferry terminal; prices start at 65kr per day for a three-speed bike. **Gotlandsresor,** Färjeleden 3, 75m to the right of the ferry terminal, books ferries, rents bikes, and finds private rooms. (☎20 12 60; www.gotlandsresor.se. Open daily June-Aug. 6am-10pm; Sept.-May 8am-6pm.) Private rooms generally cost 240-290kr for singles and 380-430kr for doubles. **Visby Fängelse Vandrarhem ❷**, Skeppsbron 1, is 300m to the left as you exit the ferry terminal. You'll recognize it by the barbed wire atop its yellow walls, the only remnants of the 19th-century prison that preceded this airy, whimsically decorated hostel. (☎20 60 50. Reception in summer 4-7pm; low season 11am-2pm. Call ahead if arriving at another time. Dorms 170-200kr; doubles 300-500kr; quads 800-1100kr.) Outdoor bars and cafes are everywhere in Visby, but especially on **Stora Torget** and down by the harbor, as well as on Adelsg. as it winds toward the south wall. Take advantage of lunch specials (70-90kr), or else stock up on groceries at the **ICA** on Stora Torg. (Open daily 8am-10pm.) **Postal Code:** 62101.

⬛ ELSEWHERE ON GOTLAND. Use Visby as a launchpad to popular **Tofta** beach, the village of **Klintehamn** (bus #31, 30min.; 1hr. on bike), or the calcified cliffs of **Hoburgen,** at the island's southernmost tip (bus #11, 3hr.). Bus #23 runs from Visby to Fårösund (2hr.), connecting passengers to a free 15min. ferry ride past the monoliths of austere **Fårö,** a small island off Gotland's northern tip. Take the earliest bus to Hoburgen and Fårösund unless you plan to stay overnight. **Gotlandsresor** (see above) can book accommodations at more than 30 hostels and campgrounds outside of Visby, although hardier souls take advantage of the right of public access and **camp** by the brackish waters of the Baltic Sea.

SOUTHERN SWEDEN

Once a fiercely contested no-man's-land during the 17th century's series of wars between Sweden and Denmark, this region still bears witness to its martial past with well-preserved castles and fortifications. Today, however, it is armies of cranes and cormorants that nest alongside marshes and lakes, even as armies of vacationers savor seaside zephyrs at the region's beaches and exult in Malmö and Gothenburg's cosmopolitan flair.

KALMAR ☎0480

An important border city in the days when southern Sweden was part of Denmark, Kalmar (pop. 33,000) is no longer at the center of Scandinavian politics but still retains much of the dignity of its halcyon days. Perched elegantly across from downtown Kalmar is its greatest attraction, the medieval castle of ⬛**Kalmar Slott.** In 1397, the castle witnessed the birth of the Union of Kalmar, a short-lived arrangement that united Denmark, Norway, and Sweden under the rule of Queen Margaret I. King Johann III gave the castle a Renaissance makeover in the 1580s, and today it houses lavish exhibits on its own fascinating history. (Open daily July 10am-6pm; June and Aug. 10am-5pm; Apr.-May and Sept. 10am-4pm; Oct.-Mar. 11am-3:30pm. 75kr, students 50kr.) The castle hosts an annual **Renaissance Festival** in late June and early July. (☎45 06 62 for info and tickets.) Adjoining the castle's seaside grounds are the tree-lined **Kyrkogarden** cemetery and the lush **Stadspark.** In the center of town, Kalmar's luminous **Domkyrkan** is a beautiful example of a 17th-century Baroque church. If you have an extra day, duck across the Kalmar Sound to the long, thin island of **Öland,** whether to laze about on the white sand beaches of Böda in the northeast or to bike through the orchid-dotted steppe of Stora Alvaret in the south. Öland's **tourist office** can furnish a list of shops that rent bikes; follow signs from the 1st bus stop after the bridge to the mainland. (☎ 04 85 56 06 00; www.olandsturist.se. Open M-F 9am-6pm, Sa 9am-4pm, Su 10am-3pm; low season reduced hours.) **Buses** #101 and 106 go from Kalmar's train station to Borgholm, the island's main town (40min., 46kr).

Trains and buses arrive in Kalmar south of the center, across the bay from the castle. Trains go to: Gothenburg (4-5hr.; every 2hr.; 400kr, under 26 297kr); Malmö (3hr.; every 2hr.; 337kr, under 26 235kr); and Stockholm (4½hr.; every 2hr.; 1150kr, under 26 940kr). Buses run directly to Stockholm (3 per day; 325kr, students 260kr). The **tourist office,** Ölandskajen 9, books rooms for a steep 100kr fee and offers **Internet** access (10kr per 15min.). From the train station, turn right onto Stationsg., and then right onto Ölandskajen. (☎ 41 77 00; www.kalmar.se. Open July to mid-Aug. M-F 9am-9pm, Sa-Su 10am-5pm; June and late Aug. M-F 9am-7pm, Sa-Su 10am-4pm; Sept.-May M-F 9am-5pm.) To get from the tourist office to **Vandrarhem Svanen (HI) and Hotel ❷,** Rappeg. 1, on the island of Ängö, turn left onto Larmg., turn right on Södra Kanalg., continue to the end, and turn left across the bridge onto Ängöleden; it will be on the right. (☎ 129 28. Breakfast 55kr. Sheets 45kr. Laundry 25kr. Internet 1kr per min. Reception mid-June to mid-Aug. M-F 7am-10pm, Sa-Su 7:30am-9pm; mid-Aug. to mid-June M-F 7am-9pm, Sa-Su 7:30am-9pm. Dorms 190kr, nonmembers add 45kr; singles 490kr.) For a more central location, **Söderportshotellet ❹,** Slottsväg. 1, near Kalmar Slott, rents out student housing during the summer. (☎ 125 01. Breakfast included. Open mid-June to mid-Aug. Check-in 2-4pm; reception in the cafe. Singles 395kr; doubles 595kr.) Seaside **Stensö Camping ❶** is 2km south of Kalmar; take bus #121 to Lanssjukhuset, turn right onto Stensbergsv., and right onto Stensöv. (☎ 888 03. 105kr per tent; cabins 400kr.) You can hunt up cheap eats along **Larmtorget, Larmgata,** and **Storgata,** or else pick up groceries at **ICP** in the Baronen plaza near the station. (Open M-F 10am-8pm, Sa 10am-5pm, Su 11am-4pm.) **Postal Code:** 39101.

MALMÖ   ☎ 040

Within a (vigorous) stone's throw of Copenhagen, Sweden's third-largest city has a cultural diversity unmatched elsewhere in the country. Malmö (pop. 265,000) melds Arabic and Vietnamese panache with Swedish traditionalism. Intimate and full of outdoor cafes, Lilla Torg, which adjoins the larger Stortorget, is a mecca for people-watching. Möllevångstorget, south of the city center, has a lively open-air market, folksy local bars, and affordable ethnic eateries.

◨◪ TRANSPORTATION AND PRACTICAL INFORMATION. The train station and harbor lie north of the old town. **Trains** go to: Copenhagen (35min., every 20min., 65kr); Gothenburg (3½hr., 1 per hr., 250-335kr); and Stockholm (4½hr., 1 per hr., 300-1000kr). Malmö has an efficient **bus** system; rides within most of the city are 18kr, and many buses pass by the train station. The **tourist office** is located in the station and offers the **Malmö Card,** which provides free public transportation, parking, and admission to various museums. (1-day 130kr, 2-day 160kr, 3-day 190kr.) The office also books rooms for a 50-70kr fee. (☎ 34 12 00. Open June-Aug. M-F 9am-7pm, Sa-Su 10am-5pm; low season reduced hours.) **Internet** access can be found at the atmospheric **Cyberspace Cafe,** on Engelbrektsg. between Lilla Torg and Gustav Adolfs Torg. (☎ 23 81 28. 44kr per hr. until 6pm, 30kr per hr. after 6pm. Open daily 10am-midnight.) **Postal Code:** 20110.

◪◖ ACCOMMODATIONS AND FOOD. Vandrarhem Malmö (HI) ❶, Backav. 18, is the cheapest option in town, although decidedly out of the way. Roadside rooms are noisy, so ask for a room on the yard, and brace yourself for the communal showers.

Take bus #21 from the train station to Vandrarhemmet. (☎822 20; www.malmohostel.com. Breakfast 50kr. Kitchen available. Sheets 40kr. Reception May-Aug. 8-10am and 4-10pm; Sept.-Apr. 8-10am and 4-8pm. Dorms 130kr; singles 285kr; doubles 350kr; triples 450kr. Nonmembers add 45kr.) **Hotel Pallas ❹**, Norra Vallg. 74, across from the train station and to the right, is pricier but has a great location. (☎611 50 77. Breakfast 30kr. Singles 395kr; doubles 455-535kr. Cash only.) **Gök Boet ❶**, Lilla Torg 3, is an intimate spot that serves creative sandwiches and salads at very reasonable prices (35-55kr) and turns into a popular bar at night. (Open M-Th 11am-midnight, F-Sa 11am-2am, Su 11am-11pm.) Next door, the **Saluhallen** is a massive food court with inexpensive restaurants ranging from Greek to Japanese. (Open M-Sa 10am-6pm, Su 10am-3pm.) **Vegegården ❷**, Stora Nyg. 18, features all-vegetarian Chinese dishes (65-75kr) and a buffet (M-F 55kr, Sa-Su 88kr) for the thrifty herbivore. (☎611 38 88. Open M-W 11am-5pm, Th-F 11am-9pm, Sa-Su noon-9pm. Buffet M-F 11am-3pm, Sa-Su 4-8pm.)

◙ ⬒ **SIGHTS AND ENTERTAINMENT.** Malmö's west end is dominated by the **Malmöhus Castle** complex, which encompasses a clutch of five eclectic museums. Within the castle walls, the **Stadsmuseet** documents the city's history and opens onto the fun-house interior of the castle proper. Breeze through the **Konstmuseet's** iffy collection of Swedish and international artwork, and check out the aquariums and terrariums at the **Naturmuseet.** Across the moat, the **Kommendanthuset** has rotating exhibits on popular culture, and down the road the **Tekniska och Sjöfartsmuseum** (Technology and Maritime Museum) is an orgy of shiny ships and airplane mock-ups. Squeeze inside the **U3 Submarine,** part of Sweden's navy from 1943 to 1964; on Sunday and Tuesday afternoons, veterans gather by the vessel to swap old war stories. (All five museums ☎040 34 44 37. Open daily June-Aug. 10am-4pm; Sept.-May noon-4pm. 40kr, students 20kr.) The **Form Design Center,** Lilla Torg 9, shows off the cutting edge of Swedish design for the Ikea generation. (☎664 51 50; www.scandinaviandesign.com. Open Tu-W and F 11am-5pm, Th 11am-6pm, Sa 10am-4pm, Su noon-4pm. Late June to July closed M and Su. Free.) The sprawling **Malmö Konsthall,** St. Johannesg. 7, hosts exhibitions of challenging modern art. (☎34 12 94. Open M-Tu and Th-Su 11am-5pm, W 11am-9pm. Guided tours daily 2pm. Free.) After trawling your way through all these museums, kick back at the **bars** on Lilla Torg and Möllevångstorget, or case the **club** scene around Stortorg.

LUND
☎046

What Oxford and Cambridge are to England, Lund (pop. 72,500) and Uppsala are to Sweden. **Lund University's** antagonism toward its scholarly northern neighbor in Uppsala has inspired countless pranks, drag shows, and drinkfests in Lund's busy streets. With its vibrant student life and proximity to Malmö and Copenhagen, Lund makes an excellent base for exploring Skåne. The Romanesque cathedral, **St. Laurentius,** is a massive 900-year-old reminder of the time when Lund was the religious center of Scandinavia. Its floor-to-ceiling astronomical clock rings on the hour at noon and 3pm, and its 7074-pipe organ is Sweden's largest. To reach the cathedral from the train station, turn right onto Bang. and left onto Klosterg. (Open M-Sa 8am-6pm, Su 9am-6pm.) The **university campus** is just across the park from the cathedral; get briefed on upcoming events at **Student Info,** Sang. 2, in the *Akademiska Föreningen* building. (☎38 49 49; af.lu.se. Open late Aug. to May M-F 10am-4pm.) **Kulturen,** behind the Student Union at the end of Sankt Anneg. on Tegnerplastén, is an engrossing open-air museum with 17th- and 18th-century homes, churches, and historical displays. (Open daily mid-Apr. to Sept. 11am-5pm, Oct. to mid-Apr. Tu-Su noon-4pm. 50kr.) Lund's nightlife revolves around the "nations," student clubs that throw parties and more generally serve as social centers; stop by Student Info for tips on snagging a guest pass. Students should not have much trouble getting into the nations, but others may have more difficulty. One good option that doesn't require a pass is **Mejeriet,** Stora Söderg. 64, an art-house cinema, concert venue, and bar that is popular with students. (☎211 00 23; www.kulturmejeriet.se. Films Th 7pm. Free. Concerts 25-100kr.) **Stortorget,** Stortorg. 1, started off as a bank and morphed into a bar and nightclub with themed nights. (☎13 92 90. 22+, 20+ with student ID. Bar open M-W and Su 11:30am-midnight, Th 11:30am-1am, F-Sa 11:30am-2am. Club open Th-Sa 11pm-3am.)

Lund is accessible from Malmö on SJ **trains** and by local **pågatågen** (10min., 1-5 per hr., 36kr). Trains also run to: Gothenburg (3hr., 1 per hr., 360kr); Kalmar (3hr., every 2hr., 335kr); and Stockholm (4-6hr.; every 1-2hr.; 1065kr, under 26 730kr). The **tourist office,** Kyrkog. 11, across from the cathedral, books rooms for a 50kr fee and sells maps (50-120kr) of the nearby **Skåneleden trail.** (☎35 50 40. Open June-Aug. M-F 10am-6pm, Sa-Su 10am-2pm; May and Sept. M-F 10am-6pm, Sa 10am-2pm; Oct.-Apr. M-F 10am-6pm.) The delightful but cramped **Hostel Tåget (HI)** ❶, Vävareg. 22, is housed in the sleeping compartments of a 1940s train. Take the overpass to the park side of the station. (☎14 28 20. Breakfast 50kr. Sheets 50kr. Reception Apr.-Oct. 8-10am and 5-8pm, Nov.-Mar. 8-10am and 5-7pm. Dorms 130kr. Nonmembers add 45kr. Cash only.) To get to **Källby Camping** ❶, take bus #1 (dir.: Klostergården, 18kr) 2km south of the city center. (☎35 51 88. Open mid-June to Aug. 50kr per tent. MC/V.) The **open-air market** at Mårtenstorg. (open daily 7am-2pm) and the adjoining **Saluhallen** (open M-F 9:30am-6pm, Sa 9am-3pm) are the best bet for budget food; cafes around Stortorg. and the cathedral are pricier. **Conditori Lundagård** ❶, Kyrkog. 17, a charming cafe decorated with caricatures of professors, serves tasty salads (63kr), sandwiches (27-37kr), and pastries. (☎211 13 58. Open M-F 7:30am-8pm, Sa 8:30am-6pm, Su 10am-6pm.) **Postal Code:** 22101.

AUGUST AND EVERYTHING AFTER. Many establishments in Lund, from clubs and restaurants to museums and the otherwise-invaluable Student Info office, are **closed** in the months of June, July, and August. Consult www.lund.se before planning a trip.

YSTAD   ☎0411

Best known as a ferry port for those heading on to Bornholm, Denmark (p. 300), Ystad (pop. 27,000) also has one of Sweden's best-preserved downtowns, a tight network of cobblestone streets just inland of the terminal. A handful of the town's half-timbered houses date back to the 15th century; you'll find the oldest one in Scandinavia at the corner of Pilgr. and Stora Österg. The **Klostret** (monastery), on Klosterg., showcases rotating exhibitions about church and town history, and has a lovely rose garden. From the tourist office, turn left onto Lingsg., left onto Stora Österg., and right out of the Stortorg. onto Klosterg. (Open June-Aug. Tu-F 10am-5pm, Sa-Su noon-4pm; low season reduced hours. 30kr.) Next to the tourist office, the **Konstmuseum** features work by Swedish and Danish artists. (☎57 72 85. Open Tu-F noon-5pm, Sa-Su noon-4pm. 30kr.) 18km southeast of town, near the village of Kåseberga, **Ales Stenar** may have been something of a Nordic Stonehenge; its 59 stones are set in the shape of a ship, with the bow and stern aligned to the position of the sun at the solstices. Take bus #322 (30min., 3 per day, 24kr), but resist the temptation to scale one of the stones for a photo-op; it's considered disrespectful.

Bornholms Trafikken (☎55 87 00) **ferries** sail to Bornholm (70min., up to 6 per day, 185kr). **Trains** run to Malmö (45min., 1 per hr., 74kr). The **tourist office** across from the station offers 15min. of free **Internet** access. (☎57 76 81. Open mid-June to mid-Aug. M-F 9am-8pm, Sa 10am-7pm, Su 11am-6pm; low season reduced hours.) The train station houses the **Vandrarhemmet Stationen** ❷, a sunny hostel conveniently located for travelers passing through. (☎07 08 57 79 95. Sheets 60kr. Reception June-Aug. 9-10am and 5-7pm, Oct.-May 5-6pm. Dorms 185kr; doubles 360kr. Cash only.) Stora Österg., or **Gågatan** (pedestrian street), passes through the main square and teems with cafes and shops. The **Saluhallen** market is just off Stortorg. (Open daily 8am-9pm.) **Postal Code:** 27101.

HELSINGBORG   ☎ 042

Warring armies carrying the standards of the Swedish and Danish crowns passed Helsingborg (pop. 119,000) back and forth fully 12 times during the 17th century. Magnus Stenbock gained the town for the Swedes once and for all in 1710, but it was a Pyrrhic victory, since most of the town's buildings lay in shambles and the population had dwindled to just 700. These hardy souls guided the harbor town into the industrial era, and their descendants have transformed Helsingborg into an elegant cultural center. The city's urban renewal showpiece, **Knutpunkten,** houses train, bus, and ferry terminals, restaurants, and shops under one glass roof. Exit Knutpunkten and make a right to reach **Stortorget,** the long, wide main square that branches out into pedestrian shopping streets like swanky **Kullagatan.** Stortorget ends at the majestic **Terrassen,** a fountain-strewn series of steps that climb the rocky ridge leading up to the **Kärnan** (keep). A remnant of the 12th-century fortress that once loomed over the city, the Kärnan tower offers a ranging view all the way to Copenhagen for those who mount its 154 twisting steps on a clear day. (Open June-Aug. daily 11am-7pm; low season reduced hours. 20kr.) Closer to sea level, the harborside **Dunkers Kulturhus,** Kungsg. 11, has a multimedia installation on the city's history as well as modern art exhibitions. From the tourist office, turn right onto Drottningg. and left into Sundstorg. (☎10 74 00. Open Tu-W and F-Su 10am-5pm, Th 10am-8pm. 70kr, students 35kr.) Just north of Helsingborg, the former royal retreat of ◪**Sofiero Slott** sits on a hillside overlooking the sound. The castle is nothing to write home about, but ponds and grottoes on the densely forested grounds beg for exploration on a sunny afternoon. Take bus #219 (18kr) from Knutpunkten to Sofiero Huvudentréen. (☎13 74 00. Open daily May-Aug. 10am-6pm; Sept.-Apr. 11am-5pm. Grounds 65kr, with castle 75kr.)

Trains depart for: Gothenburg (2½hr.; every 2hr.; 285kr, under 26 240kr); Malmö (50min., 1 per hr., 88kr); and Stockholm (4-6hr.; 2-4 per day; 1085kr, under 26 930kr). **Ferries** leave almost continuously for Helsingør, Denmark (p. 298); the popular Scandlines boats depart every 20min. (☎18 61 00. 20min.; 22kr, 40kr round-trip.) Most **city buses** (16kr) pass Knutpunkten and include 1hr. of free transfers. To reach the **tourist office,** which books rooms for free, exit the station in the direction of the towering Rådhuset; the office is through the doors next to the closest turret. (☎10 43 50; www.helsingborgsguiden.com. Open mid-June to mid-Aug. M-F 9am-8pm, Sa-Su 9am-5pm; low season reduced hours.) **Vandrarhem Miatorp (HI) ②,** Planteringsväg. 69-71, is a comfortable hostel 2.5km south of the city center; take bus #2 (dir.: Ättekulla) to Hästhagsväg., or take bus #1 (dir.: Ättekulla) to Miatorp and backtrack 50m. (☎13 11 30. Breakfast 50kr. Sheets 50kr. Reception 8-10am and 4-9pm. Dorms 160kr; singles and doubles 390kr. Nonmembers add 45kr. MC/V.) Inexpensive cafes line S. Storg., the last right off of Stortorg. before Terrassen. The cream of the crop may be stylish **Cafe Mmmums ①,** just behind the Mariakyrkan, which brings sandwiches (30-37kr) and large salads (48-58kr) out to the outdoor tables. (☎14 33 40. Open M-F 10am-7pm, Sa 10am-5pm. AmEx/MC/V.) The harbor area has a handful of clubs and late-night bars, although the rowdy Helsingør ferries (see above) are probably more fun during the summer. **Postal Code:** 25225.

GOTHENBURG (GÖTEBORG)   ☎ 031

Much more than just Sweden's industrial center, Gothenburg (YO-teh-bor-ee; pop. 460,000) is a sprawling, youthful metropolis threaded with parks, bristling with museums and theaters, and girdled by a famous, urbane thoroughfare that slashes its way through the city center like a glittering, showy sash. Gothenburg is easily overlooked on whirlwind tours of northern Europe, but in truth it measures up to any of the Scandinavian capitals as a thoroughly exciting, continental destination.

SWEDEN

🖃🔢 TRANSPORTATION AND PRACTICAL INFORMATION. Trains run from Central Station to: Malmö (2¾-3¾hr.; every 1-2hr.; 344kr, under 26 293kr); Oslo, Norway (4hr.; 3 per day; 508kr, under 26 356kr); and Stockholm (3-5½hr.; every 1-2hr.; 512kr, under 26 437kr). Stena Line **ferries** (☎704 00 00; www.stenaline.com) sail to Frederikshavn, Denmark (2-3¼hr.; 6-10 per day; 140-200kr, 50% Scanrail or Eurail discount) and Kiel, Germany (13½hr., daily at 7:30pm, 340-780kr). DFDS Seaways (☎65 06 50; www.dfdsseaways.co.uk) sails to Newcastle, England (24hr., Th and Su 10am, 695-1195kr). Gothenburg has an extensive **tram** system; rides are 20kr, and most trains pass by the train station or through Brunnsparken, south of the Nordstan mall. A day pass, available at kiosks throughout the city, is just 50kr.

Central Gothenburg is on the south bank of the Göta River. The busy central districts of Nordstan and Inom Vallgraven are bordered on the south by the Vallgraven canal and bisected by the Hamn Canal. The main street, Kungsportsavenyn (or just "Avenyn") begins just north of the Vallgraven canal at Kungsportsplatsen and continues south 1km to Götaplatsen. Nya Allén, Avenyn's first cross street, leads west to the neighborhood of Masthugget; Vasagatan, a wide boulevard that also crosses Avenyn, leads west to the Haga neighborhood. The crowded **tourist office**, Kungsportspl. 2, books rooms for a 60kr fee and sells the **Göteborg pass**, which includes public transit and admission to numerous attractions, although it may not be worthwhile for those planning to see fewer than three or four sights. From the station, cross Drottningtorg. and follow Östra Larmag. from the right of the Radisson. (☎61 25 00; www.goteborg.com. 1-day pass 175kr, 2-day 295kr. Open daily late June to early Aug. 9:30am-8pm; low season M-F 9am-5pm, Sa 10am-2pm.) The **Stadsbibliotek** (public library), on Götapl., provides free **Internet** access; book time at the desk. (Open M-F 10am-8pm, Sa 11am-5pm.) **Postal Code:** 40401.

🖬🖸 ACCOMMODATIONS AND FOOD. Gothenburg's hostels are mainly in the west end of the city, near Masthugget. It's wise to book ahead, especially in July. **⬛Slottsskogens Vandrarhem (HI) ❶**, Vegag. 21., is a bit of a trek from the city center, but makes up for it with beautiful rooms and large common spaces. Take bus #60 (dir.: Masthugget) to Vegagatan. (☎42 65 20; www.sov.nu. Breakfast 55kr. Sheets 50kr. Internet 1kr per min. Bikes 90kr per day. Reception 8am-noon and 3pm-6pm. Dorms 110kr; singles 240kr; doubles 300kr. MC/V.) A jovial couple tends the well-decorated rooms at **Masthuggsterrassen ❷**, Masthuggsterr. 8. Take tram #3, 9, or 11 to Masthuggstorget, cross the square diagonally, walk up the stairs, and follow the signs. (☎42 48 20; www.mastenvandrarhem.com. Breakfast 55kr. Sheets 55kr. Laundry 40kr. Reception 8-10am and 5-8pm. Dorms 160kr; doubles 400kr; triples 480kr; quads 580kr. MC/V.) **Vandrarhem Stigbergsliden (HI) ❶**, Stigbergsl. 10, features cozy rooms around a lovely courtyard, even if its common areas are somewhat cramped. Take tram #3, 9, or 11 to Masthuggstorget, walk the way the tram is going, and then bear right up the hill. (☎24 16 20. Breakfast 45kr. Sheets 50kr. Bikes 50kr per day. Reception 8am-noon and 4-10pm. Dorms 120kr; singles 250kr. AmEx/MC/V.) The right of public access (p. 992) makes camping outside the city limits a cinch, but the closest organized campsite is **Kärralund Camping ❶**. Take tram #5 to Welanderg. and turn right onto Olbersg. (☎84 02 00. Reception May-Aug. 7am-11pm; low season reduced hours. Tents 60-150kr. AmEx/MC/V.)

The Avenyn is a great place for a stroll, but steer clear of the pricey eats in favor of the affordable restaurants and cafes on **Vasagatan**, **Linnégatan**, and around **Haga**. One of the few exceptions to this rule is **Eva's Paley ❷**, Kungsportsavenyn 39, where large portions and a quality location for people-watching still don't add up to an astronomical tab. (☎16 30 70. Sandwiches 58kr. Salads 75-85kr. Open M-Th 8am-11pm, F 8am-1am, Sa 10am-1am, Su 10am-11pm. MC/V.) **Solrosen ❷**, Kaponjärg. 4, means "sunflower" in Swedish and gets rave reviews for its all-vegetarian menu. (☎711 66 97. Open M-F 11:30am-1am, Sa 2pm-1am. Kitchen closes at 9pm. AmEx/MC/V.) Over in

Masthugget, **Thai Garden ❸**, Andra Långg. 18, was singled out as the best Thai restaurant in town by *GP*, Gothenburg's news daily. Fill up on the 98kr buffet. (☎ 12 76 60. Open daily 11am-11pm. AmEx/MC/V.) While Malmö teems with cheap kebab and falafel stands, Gothenburg's more uniform ethnic makeup means that establishments like these are in short supply. **Rendez Vous Kebab and Grill House ❶**, Vasag. 43, rules the roost with its proximity to Avenyn and its barfly-friendly business hours. (☎ 330 52 30. Open M-Th 10am-4am, F 10am-6am, Sa noon-6am, Su noon-4am. AmEx/MC/V.) For fresh produce, the **Saluhallen,** in Kungstorg., has the iron arches and a glass ceiling of a huge train station. (Open M-F 9am-6pm, Sa 9am-3pm.)

■ **SIGHTS.** Just across from the train station sits **Nordstan,** Scandinavia's largest indoor shopping center and a city unto itself. (Open M-F 10am-7pm, Sa 10am-5pm, Su noon-4pm.) Follow Norra Hamng. along the smaller Hamn canal to reach the **Stadsmuseum,** Norra Hamng. 12, a large and lavish showcase for the city's history from its Viking past to its post-industrial rebirth. (☎ 61 27 70. Open May-Aug. daily 10am-5pm; Sept.-Apr. Tu and Th-Su 10am-5pm, W 10am-8pm. 40kr, students 10kr.) Make a right at the end of Norra Hamng. and go through the casino parking lot to reach the **Göteborg Maritime Centrum,** a floating museum of seafaring that has taken over more than a dozen moored vessels. (☎ 10 59 50. Open daily May-Aug. 10am-6pm, Sept.-Oct. 10am-4pm. 70kr.) A congenial series of parks lines the southern bank of the main canal, including **Trädgårdsföreningens Park,** to the left as you cross the Avenyn bridge. Wend your way down the garden paths to the balmy, fecund **Palm House,** built in 1878 as a reproduction of London's Crystal Palace. (Park open daily Sept.-Apr. 7am-9pm, May-Aug. 10am-6pm. 15kr. Palm House open daily 10am-5pm. 20kr.) Avenyn ends at **Götaplatsen,** the site of Carl Milles's famous **sculpture fountain** of Poseidon. Still, even the bronze sea god is dwarfed by the imposing ▓**Konstmuseum,** which encompasses a spectacular sculpture collection, minor works by Picasso and van Gogh, as well as a 6th-floor bonanza of French Impressionism and Scandinavian landscapes. The photography exhibitions at the adjacent **Hasselblad Center** are icing on the cake. (Both open Tu and Th 11am-6pm, W 11am-9pm, F-Su 11am-5pm. 40kr, under 20 free.)

Westward, the gentrifying **Haga** district boasts art galleries, bookstores, and cafes along its pedestrian streets. A steep flight of steps at the southern end of Kaponjärg. leads to **Skansen Kronen,** the most impressive of the hilltop towers that ring Gothenburg; the military museum inside is unremarkable, but the view of the city from the tower's base is stellar. Take tram #3, 6, 9, or 11 to Hagakyrkan. For a bird's eye view of Gothenburg's harbor, head out to the **Masthuggskyrkan,** a brick church with a timber ceiling that suggests the inside of a Viking ship. Take tram #3, 9, or 11 to Masthuggstorg. South of the church, the vast **Slottsskogsparken** invites you to lose yourself among its ponds, meadows, and aviaries, or to investigate the city's highly-regarded **Botanical Gardens,** Carl Skottsbergs g. 22a. Take tram #1, 7, 8, or 13 to Botaniska Trädgården. Other excursions include a pilgrimage to **Liseberg,** Scandinavia's largest amusement park, less than 1km from Götaplatsen. Strap yourself in good and tight for a ride on **Balder,** the park's bone-rattling wooden roller coaster. Take tram #4, 5, 6, 8, 13, or 14 to Korsvägen. (Open mid-May to late Aug. daily; Sept. Th-Su. Hours vary; consult www.liseberg.se for schedule. Entry 50kr; rides 20-50kr each; 1-day ride pass 255kr.) Beachgoers should venture out onto the **Göteborgs Skärgård,** a string of islands dribbling out into the waters of the Kattegat bay. The islands of Brännö and Styrsö have shops and other resort amenities, while the cliffs and beaches of Vargö are wilder and more secluded. Take tram #9 or 11 to Saltholmen (30min.), and transfer to the ferry (20-50min.) for free.

◨ ◧ **ENTERTAINMENT AND NIGHTLIFE.** The enormous **Opera House,** at Lilla Bommen, hosts opera, musical theater, and concerts from August through May. (☎ 13 13 00; www.opera.se. Tickets from 105-215kr, students 25% off except F-Sa.) Gothenburg's **Stadsteatern** (☎ 61 50 50) and **Konserthus** (☎ 726 53

00) round out its highbrow theater and music scene; swing by the tourist office for the latest issue of *What's on in Göteborg* for details. Gothenburg's annual **film festival,** the largest in Scandinavia, will draw more than 100,000 cinéastes to the city for 10 days, starting January 28, 2005. The summer of 2005 will also be given over to the third **International Biennial for Contemporary Art;** check www.biennal.goteborg.se for details. Gothenburg's club scene is one of the most exclusive and chic in Scandinavia. Many posh restaurants on Avenyn morph into equally posh clubs after nightfall; expect lines, steep covers, and strict dress codes. **Nivå,** Avenyn 9, and **Avenyn 10,** Avenyn 10, are among the standard-bearers of this scene, although on weeknights the latter spot lets down its hair a bit. For a little less attitude, head for ■**Trädgår'n,** on Nye Allén, an ivy-clad concert venue, club, and patio bar that spills out into the Trädgårdsföreningens park. (☎ 10 20 80. 21+. Cover from 100kr. Club open F-Sa 10pm-5am.) A younger crowd packs the two levels of **Kompaniet,** Kungsg. 34, and jives out to an eclectic mix of music. (☎711 99 46. Beer 49kr; 2-for-1 special daily 5-10pm. 18+. Cover 40-100kr. Club open Tu 10pm-3am, F-Sa 10pm-5am.) Gays and lesbians flock to **Gretas,** Drottningg. 35, especially now that the just-renovated second floor gives guests some welcome elbow room. (☎ 13 69 49; www.gretas.nu. 20+. Cover for club 50-60kr. Restaurant and bar open daily 5-11pm. Club open W 10pm-2am, F-Sa 10pm-3am.) On a more downtempo evening, head to ■**Nefertiti,** Hvitfeldtspl. 6, an intimate jazz bar that reinvents itself as a dance club after 1am. (☎711 15 33; www.nefertiti.se. 20+. Cover for club 70kr. Tickets 120-250kr. Concerts in summer Tu-W and F-Sa 9pm, low season 8pm.)

◪ **DAYTRIP FROM GOTHENBURG: VARBERG.** Between Gothenburg and Helsingborg beckons this summer paradise, a sunny town replete with expansive beaches and charming bath houses. Varberg's spectacular 13th-century **fortress** is home to a number of attractions; the **museum** features the **Bocksten Man,** a bog corpse from 1360 found with his clothing intact. To reach the fortress, turn right out of the station and right onto S. Hamnv. (Museum open June-Aug. daily 10am-6pm; Sept.-May M-F 10am-4pm, Sa-Su noon-4pm. 50kr.) Follow the boardwalk 2km south of town to reach the shallow **Apelviken** bay, which offers some of the best surfing and windsurfing in Northern Europe. **Surfers Paradise,** Söderg. 22, rents gear and gives both formal lessons and informal tips. Turn right out of the station, pass the tourist office, and turn right onto Söderg. (☎03 40 67 70 55. Open May-June and Aug. M-F 1-7pm, Sa 10am-2pm, Su noon-4pm; July M-F noon-6pm, Sa 10am-2pm, Su noon-4pm; low season reduced hours.) The boardwalk also passes several **nude beaches:** Karringhalan for women and Skarpa Nord and Goda Hopp for men. **Trains** arrive from Gothenburg (45min., 77kr) and Helsingborg (1½hr., 250kr). To reach the **tourist office,** in Brunnsparken, turn right out of the station and walk four blocks. (☎03 40 887 70. Open mid-June to mid-Aug. M-Sa 9am-7pm, Su 3-7pm; mid-Aug. to mid-June M-F 9am-6pm.) **Postal Code:** 43201.

DALARNA

Well west of Stockholm, the county of Dalarna extends from swampy foothills along the Norwegian border through sleepy lakeside villages down to the copper mines around Falun. With a larger population than the farmland could support, Dalarna turned to handicrafts to bolster its regional economy; by the 19th century, stylized religious paintings and garish wooden horses graced the walls and shelves of the eastern urban bourgeoisie.

MORA. Hollowed out by a meteorite more than 300 million years ago, shimmering **Lake Siljan** extends south and east of Mora (pop. 20,000). The **Siljansleden** network of trails enwreathes the lake, including a well-marked 310km bike trail skirting the shore and a 340km **walking trail** that edges its way farther inland, past grazing pastures and

shady creeks. Back in Mora, **Zorngården,** Vasag. 37, is the 19th-century home of Anders
Zorn, the Swedish painter best remembered for his nude portraits. Tour the estate and
then move on to the **Zornmuseet,** long on Zorn's work but rounded out by canvases by
his contemporaries from the Zorn family's collection. (☎ 0250 59 23 10; www.zorn.se.
English-language tours of Zorngården daily 2:10pm. 50kr, students 45kr. Museum
open mid-May to mid-Sept. M-Sa 9am-5pm, Su 11am-5pm; mid-Sept. to mid-May M-Sa
noon-5pm, Su 1-5pm. 40kr, students 35kr.) On the first Sunday in March, Mora serves
as the terminus of the **Vasaloppet,** a 90km cross-country skiing race that draws 15,000
contestants each year. The **Vasaloppsmuseet** screens a 30min. film about the race, and
chases the hero worship of past winners with warm blueberry soup. (☎ 0250 392 25.
Open mid-June to mid-Aug. daily 7am-5pm; mid-Aug. to mid-June M-F 7am-5pm.
30kr.) **Trains** run to Östersund (6hr., 2 per day mid-June to early Aug., 347kr) and
Stockholm (4hr., 7 per day, 303kr). **Buses** also head to Östersund year-round (5¼hr., 2
per day, 170kr). The **tourist office,** in Mora's train station, books rooms (200-345kr) for
a 25kr fee. (☎ 0250 592 020. Open mid-June to mid-Aug. M-F 9am-7pm, Sa-Su 10am-
5pm; mid-Aug. to mid-June M-F 10am-5pm.) Homey **Vandrarhem Mora (HI) ❷,** Fredsg.
6, is 500m from the train station; turn left on the main road and turn right on Fredsg.
(☎ 0250 381 96. Breakfast 60kr. Kitchen available. Sheets 60kr. Reception 8-10am and
5-7pm. Dorms 185kr; doubles 320kr. Nonmembers add 45kr. V.) Get groceries at **ICA**
on Kyrkog. (Open M-Sa 9am-8pm, Su 11am-8pm.) **Postal Code:** 79200.

◪ ÖSTERSUND. Travelers heading north into Lappland often tarry for a few days
in hilly Östersund (pop. 58,000). Deep, reedy Lake Storsjön laps against the town's
western shores, and many residents sincerely believe the lake to contain the
Storsjöodjuret monster. In 1894, the town called in a Norwegian harpoonist to flush
out the creature, but appeals by local Quakers and then the tourist office resulted
in an 1986 ban on future hunting. The steamer *S/S Thomée* runs cruises and mon-
ster-spotting tours. (2-3 per day. 65-75kr. Tickets at the tourist office.) Rent a **bike**
at **Cykelogen,** Kyrkg. 45 (☎ 063 12 20 80; open M-F 10am-1pm and 2-6pm, Sa 10am-
2pm; 100kr per day), and pedal over the footbridge to **Frösön Island,** named for the
Norse god of crops and fertility. Swedish couples have taken the hint by making
the island's 12th-century **church** one of the country's most popular wedding chapels. (Open Tu-Sa 11am-8pm.) Just north of town, the Disney-style **Jamtli** complex
encompasses a Viking tapestry collection, an open-air museum with 18th-century
farmhouses, and a 1950s gas station. (☎ 063 15 01 00; www.jamtli.com. Open June-
Aug. daily 11am-5pm; Sept.-May Tu-F 10am-4pm, Sa-Su 11am-5pm.)

    Trains run to Stockholm (6hr.; 6 per day; 572kr, under 26 482kr) and Trondheim,
Norway (4hr.; 2 per day; 268kr, under 26 187kr). From mid-June to early August,
the *Inlandsbanan* railway runs to Gällivare (14hr., 1 per day, 697kr) and Mora
(6hr., 2 per day, 347kr). Check www.inlandsbanan.se for schedules or call ☎ 0771
53 53 53. The **tourist office,** Rådhusg. 44, books rooms for free. From the station,
walk up the hill on your left and continue down Prästg.; take a right one block up
Postgränd. (☎ 063 14 40 01; www.turist.ostersund.se. Open July M-Sa 9am-9pm, Su
10am-7pm; June and Aug. usually M-F 9am-5pm, Sa-Su 10am-3pm; Sept-May M-F
9am-5pm.) Wild strawberries grow on the roofs of old log cabins at ◪**Frösötornets
Härbärge ❶,** Utsiktv. 10, Frösön. Bus #5 runs from the city center 8am-10:20pm,
and stops at the bottom of a long, steep hill. It's worth the climb. (☎ 063 51 57 67.
Reception 9am-9pm. Open May-Oct. Dorms 140kr. Cash only.) **Youth Hostel Ral-
laren ❶,** 300m from the station along the tracks, has less character but is centrally
located and open year-round. (☎ 063 13 22 32. Dorms 150kr. Cash only.) Entrees at
dim, stylish **NEWS Bar & Kitchen ❸,** Samuel Permansg. 9, are overpriced, but students dip in for strong coffee (20kr) or cocktails (from 48kr) late into the evening.
(☎ 063 10 11 31. Open M-Tu and Th 11am-11pm, W 11am-midnight, F-Sa 11am-1am,
Su noon-6pm. AmEx/MC/V.) Pick up groceries at **Hemköp,** Kyrkg. 56. (Open M-F
8am-8pm, Sa 9am-6pm, Su noon-4pm.) **Postal Code:** 83100.

ÅRE. The **Åre ski resort** (☎ 0647 177 00; www.skistar.com/english/are) is the largest in Sweden, with a rich variety of beginner and intermediate trails as well as an excellent ski school. However, the town of Åre (pop. 10,000) is a promising base for outdoor activities even after the snows melt. Ambitious **hikers** make their way up the 6km **Åreskutan trail** from the town square to a 1420m peak, while the **Kabinbanan** cable car makes the same trip during high season. (Lift runs June 25-Aug. 22 9:30am-4:30pm. 100kr round-trip. Free descent for hikers.) The 26km **Åreskutan Runt** hike cuts a broad circle around the mountain via cabins by the Bjelke mines, while the gentle 2.5km walk to **Totthummeln** can be completed in 2hr. Serious cyclists can take a gander at **downhill mountain biking,** a sport so extreme that bike rental prices are sky-high (300-800kr per day) on account of the maintenance that must be done after every outing. Rental shops abound around the base of the mountain, and the **World Cup** chairlift brings you halfway up the mountain to a number of trailheads. (Lift runs late June to mid-Aug. daily 11am-3pm; late Aug. to early Sept. Sa-Su 11am-3pm. 60kr.) **Trains** run from Åre to Östersund (1¼hr., 2 per day, 113kr) and Trondheim, Norway (2¾hr., 2 per day, 180kr). The **tourist office,** in the station, sells essential hiking maps (90kr) and organizes outdoor activities. (☎ 0647 177 20; www.areturistbyra.com. Free Internet. Open June-Aug. daily 9am-6pm; Sept.-May M-F 9-11:30am and 12:30-5pm, Sa-Su 10am-3pm.) The **Åre Ski Lodge ❶,** Trondheimsleden 44, accents well-equipped rooms with vintage photographs. (☎ 0647 510 29. Sheets 90kr. Kitchen and laundry available. Dorms 110kr; doubles 290kr. Reserve ahead during ski season. Cash only.) **Postal Code:** 83013.

GULF OF BOTHNIA

The Gulf of Bothnia region is deservedly well-known for its sprawling forests, stark ravines, and stretches of pristine coastline. Yet its quiet, friendly cities are also worthy destinations for visitors who want to see workaday Sweden outside of the glittery metropolitan centers to the south.

GÄVLE. Two hours north of Stockholm, Gävle (pop. 90,000) is the first stop on the way to northern Sweden. Just south of the train station lie the cobblestoned streets and 17th-century houses of **Gamle Gefle,** the only part of Gävle that survived a ravaging 19th-century fire. On the edge of the old town next to the canal, **Länsmuseet Gävleborg,** Södra Strandg. 20, houses 300 years of Swedish paintings daringly grouped by theme rather than era or style. (☎ 026 65 56 00. Open June-Aug. M-F 10am-4pm, Sa-Su noon-4pm; Sept.-May Tu and Th-F 10am-4pm, W 10am-9pm, Sa-Su noon-4pm. 40kr.) Neo-Nazis may have rung in 2004 by tossing Molotov cocktails at the tiny **Joe Hill Museum,** Nedre Bergsg. 28, but the attack only made this shrine to the slain American labor activist and Gävle native all the more poignant. (☎ 026 61 20 22. Open mid-June to July Tu-Sa 11am-3pm; low season by appointment. Free.) **Trains** run from Gävle to Östersund (4-5hr., 2-4 per day, 252kr) and Stockholm (1½hr., 1 per hr., 177kr). The **tourist office,** Drottningg. 37, is across from the train station. (☎ 026 14 74 30. Free Internet. Open M-F 9am-6pm, Sa 9am-2pm, Su 11am-4pm.) Smack in the middle of Gamle Gefle, **⊠Vandrarhem Gävle (HI) ❶,** Södra Rådmansg. 1, has well-lit rooms and a flower-drenched courtyard. From the train station, turn left, cross the canal, turn right onto Södra Strandg., turn left at the library, go through the square and up the stairs; the hostel is on the left. (☎ 026 62 17 45. Breakfast 55kr. Kitchen available. Sheets 55kr. Reception 8-10am and 5-7pm. Dorms 125kr. Nonmembers add 45kr. V.) **Postal Code:** 80250.

ÖRNSKÖLDSVIK. Burly gray high-rises dominate the center of drab Örnsköldsvik (urn-SHULDS-vik; "Ö-vik" to locals; pop. 30,000), although the town is a popular base for **hiking** excursions. The 127km **Höga Kusten Leden** (High Coast Trail) winds south through Skuleskogen National Park as far as Veda, just north of Sundsvall. Flanked by sea cliffs that drop dizzyingly into the Gulf of Bothnia, the trail is divided into 13 segments with free mountain huts at the end of each leg; bring an insulated sleeping bag or arrive early enough to cut firewood. Day hikes are also plentiful, including the **Yellow Trail** loop (6km); the hike itself is easy, but adventurers nervous around heights should be advised of the steep drop-offs along the trail. You'll find the trailhead on Hantverkareg.; from the tourist office, walk uphill on Nyg. and turn right. Back in town, the **Örnsköldsviks Museum,** Läroverksg. 1, shows off regional folk art and opens onto the studio of sculptor Bror Marklund, well-known in Kiruna (p. 1017) for designing the town's intricate clock tower. (☎06 60 886 01. Head down Hamng. away from the harbor and cross through the garden. Open in summer daily noon-4pm; winter Tu-Su noon-4pm. 20kr.)

Buses run to Östersund (4½hr.; 3 per day M-F, 1 per day Sa-Su; 252kr) and Umeå (2hr., 7 per day, 107kr). The **tourist office,** Nyg. 18, books rooms for a 40kr fee. (☎06 60 881 00. Free Internet. Open mid-June to mid-Aug. M-F 9am-6pm, Sa-Su 10am-2pm; mid-Aug. to mid-June M-F 10am-5pm.) To get there, walk up the steps behind the bus station, follow Fabriksg., and turn left on Nyg. **Vandrarhem Örnsköldsvik (HI) ❶,** Högsnäsgården, is outside town in a gracious country house. Take bus #421 out to the hostel, although the last bus leaves town at 9pm on weekdays and 3pm on weekends; plan accordingly. (☎06 60 702 44. Reception 9-10am and 5-7pm. Dorms 130kr. Nonmembers add 45kr. MC/V.) Pick up groceries at **Hemköp** on Stortorg. (Open M-F 10am-7pm, Sa 10am-3pm, Su noon-4pm.) **Postal Code:** 89188.

UMEÅ. In the 1970s, lefty students in Umeå (OOM-eh-oh; pop. 110,000) earned their alma mater the nickname of "the red university." Times change, though, and today northern Sweden's largest city is better known for its birch-lined boulevards and genial youth culture than its Marxist leanings. A 20min. walk east of the city center, the **Västerbottens Museum** complex includes the ▨**Gammlia** open-air museum, which gives visitors a crack at 19th-century crafts like churning butter and working a pre-industrial loom. (Open daily mid-June to mid-Aug 10am-5pm. Free. Guided tours daily 1pm.) In the same complex, the **Fishing and Nautical Museum** sheds light on the history of seal hunting in the region. (Open daily 10am-5pm. Free. Guided tours daily 2:30pm.) Southwest of the city, the 30km **Umeleden** bike and car trail snakes past old hydropower stations, ancient rock carvings, and **Baggböle Herrgård,** a delightful cafe in a 19th-century manor house that opens during the summer. Pick up the trail at the Gamla Bron (Old Bridge) and veer across the Norvarpsbron to cut the route in half. **Cykel och Mopedhandlaren,** Kungsg. 101, rents **bikes.** (☎090 14 01 70. 70kr per day, 195kr per week. Open M-F 9:30am-5:30pm, Sa 10am-1pm.) Hikers can follow the **Tavelsjöleden** trail (30km) along a boulder ridge, or brave the **Isälvsleden** trail (60km), carved out by melting pack ice. Mingle with the city's students at the **bars** along Rådhusgata and Kungsgata.

Trains run to Gothenburg (14½hr.; 1 per day; 490kr, 670kr with couchette) and Luleå (4½hr., 3 per day, 290kr). Ybuss **buses** (☎090 70 65 00) run to Stockholm (10hr.; 3 per day; 330kr, students 240kr). The bus terminal is across from the train station. To get to the **tourist office** from the stations, Renmarkstorg. 15, walk straight down Rådhusesplanaden and turn right on Skolg. (☎090 16 16 16; www.umea.se. Free Internet. Open mid-June to late Aug. M-F 8:30am-7pm, Sa 10am-4pm, Su noon-4pm; low season reduced hours.) The conveniently located **Youth Hostel (HI) ❷,** V. Esplanaden 10, is to the left off Skolg. (☎090 77 16 50. Breakfast 50kr. Sheets 45kr. Reception M-F 8am-noon and 5-8pm, Sa-Su 8-10am and 5-8pm. Dorms 165kr. Nonmembers add 45kr. V.) **Starz Coffee ❸,** Kungsg. 55, brings large salads (69kr) out to the outdoor seating on the plaza. (☎090 14 14 90. Open M-Th 10am-10pm, F-Sa 10am-midnight, Su 11am-10pm. V.) **Postal Code:** 90326.

LULEÅ. After the salmon-laden waters of the Lule River make their way through Boden's hydropower dam, they empty into the Bay of Bothnia at the university town of Luleå (LOOL-eh-oh; pop. 72,000). A low cost of living and unusually sunny climate for a settlement so far north make Luleå a pleasant, if not terribly edgy, place to visit. In 1649, the town migrated 10km south to seize on a more auspicious harbor, but the 15th-century **Nederluleå Church** kept townspeople coming back to the original settlement for Sunday worship. ⌘**Gammelstad** became a "church town" with cottages that housed families who traveled a full day's ride to attend services. Today the cottages and the adjacent **Hägnan** open-air museum provide a vivid look at everyday life on what was once Sweden's northern frontier. (Take bus #6 from the tourist office; 25kr. Church open June-Aug. M-Tu and Sa-Su 9am-8pm, W-F 9am-6pm; Sept.-May M-F 10am-4pm. Museum open June to mid-Aug. daily 9am-6pm; Sept.-May Tu-Th 10am-4pm.) Moose, seabirds, and gray seals have the run of the **Luleå Archipelago,** although the inner islands of **Sandön** and **Junkön** have their fair share of fishermen and beach bums. Take a **tour boat** out to the islands or else go your own way with a rented **kayak** from the **Luleå Kayak Club,** Kanotv. 14 (☎ 0920 22 24 32). During the winter, the bay freezes over deeply enough for snowplows to clear **ice roads** that allow visits to the islands on cross-country skis or snowmobiles. Ask at the tourist office for info on tour boats or rentals. **Storgatan** has cafes that morph from laid-back daytime haunts to energetic nightspots.

Trains run to Kiruna (4hr., 5 per day, 250kr) and Umeå (4½hr., 2 per day, 290kr). The **tourist office,** Storg. 43b, books rooms for free. From the train station, cross Prästg. and follow it to the right, walk diagonally across the park, cross Hermalingsg., and tromp up Storg. (☎ 0920 29 35 00. Internet 10kr per 15min. Open June to mid-Aug. M-F 9am-7pm, Sa-Su 10am-4pm; mid-Aug. to May M-F 10am-6pm, Sa 10am-2pm.) The **Luleå Youth Hostel and Mini-Hotel ❶,** Sandviksg. 26, has cramped dorm rooms with three-bed bunks, but also comfortable singles and doubles for a comparable price. From the tourist office, walk down Storg., turn left onto Rådhusg., and follow it until the highway; the hostel is 50m to the right. (☎ 0920 22 26 60. Laundry 30kr. Sheets 50kr. Reception 9-10am and 5-7pm. Dorms 150kr; singles 175kr; doubles 360kr. Cash only.) **Postal Code:** 97101.

LAPPLAND (SÁPMI)

Known as "Europe's last wilderness," Lappland's mountains and alpine dales sprawl across northern Sweden, largely untouched except for the very hardiest of mosquito-proof hikers. Today, the region's indigenous Sami people use modern technology like helicopters and snowmobiles to tend their herds of reindeer, yet continue to wrangle with Stockholm over hunting and grazing rights that their ancestors enjoyed centuries before Sweden consolidated its nationhood.

▐ TRANSPORTATION

There are two **rail** routes to Lappland. Connex runs trains along the **coastal route** from Stockholm through Boden, Umeå, and Kiruna to Narvik, Norway, along the ore railway. Head to www.connex.info/booking/booking_en for more info. From late June to early August, the privately run **Inlandsbanan** runs north from Mora (p. 1013) through the northern countryside. (☎ 063 19 44 12; www.inlandsbanan.se.) **Buses** are the only way to reach smaller towns; call ☎ 020 47 00 47 for schedules.

KIRUNA   ☎ 098

The only large settlement in Lappland, Kiruna (pop. 23,000) retains the rough edges of a mining town, even as ski teams headed for the 2006 Winter Olympics descend to practice at **Riksgänsen,** the northernmost ski resort in the world. The state-owned mining company LKAB hauls an astonishing 20 million tons of iron ore out of the ground each year and caters to visitors with **InfoMine** tours, which descend 540m to

COLD COMFORT

Rising out of the Torne River in tiny Jukkasjärvi, the remarkable Icehotel melts away each May and then crystallizes anew in November. Take the name at face value—the entire building is made out of ice. Artists spray tall metal frames with snow cannons to form walls, while ice pillars support the cavernous ceiling from which ice chandeliers dangle. The masterminds behind the Icehotel also allow for innovation; each year it's built with a new set of blueprints, so that artists are never simply replicating the same design.

However, innovation has yet to reveal how to pipe hot water into an ice hotel. Washroom facilities are outside, but the hotel gives its guests thermal suits for the wintry dash to the showers. Reindeer skins line the ledges that serve as beds, and thermal sleeping bags keep guests toasty until the staff shows up mid-morning with cups of hot lingonberry juice. More potent drinkables are on tap at the Absolut Icebar, while the nearby Ice Chapel has become a popular wedding spot for the matching-parka set. Meanwhile, the Ice Globe Theater stages the Bard's plays inside a faithful reproduction of the original. Except that Hamlet wears mittens.

☎ *980 668 00; www.icehotel.com. Take bus #501 from Kiruna M-F. Breakfast and sauna included. Open mid-Dec. to Apr. Doubles 2800kr. Tours daily noon-6pm. 120kr, students 80kr.*

an informative museum. (☎07 10 16. 3hr. tours every hr. 9am-4pm leave from outside the tourist office. 195kr.) Scientists at **Esrange**, a space center 40km outside Kiruna, launch short-range sounding rockets to study the Northern Lights and conduct research on the ozone layer using high-altitude weather balloons. (4hr. tours June-Aug. M-F 9am. Reserve at the tourist office at least 24hr. in advance. 290kr.) Hikers take bus #92 from Kiruna out to Nikkaluokta (1¼hr., 1-2 per day, 67kr) and then pick up the well-marked **Kungsleden** trail at Kebnekaise Fjällstation, staying at cabins spaced 10-20km apart on a week's trek north into the mountain passes of Abisko National Park. Closer to Kiruna, the village of Jukkasjärvi is home to a 1608 **wooden church** used to convert the Sami to Christianity. (Open 8am-8pm. Free.) Nearby, an open-air **Sami Museum** affords the opportunity to talk with guides about their struggle to preserve a Sami cultural identity in between lessons on how to lasso a reindeer. (☎02 13 29; www.nutti.se. Open daily 10am-6pm. 75kr. Tours daily 11am, 12:30, and 2pm.)

Buses run to Luleå (5hr., 2 per day, 250kr) via Gällivare (1½hr., 117kr). Connex **trains** run to Luleå (3½hr., 3-4 per day, 250kr) and Narvik, Norway (2¾hr., 3-4 per day, 210kr). **Flights** to Stockholm depart from Kiruna Flygplats. (KRN; ☎028 48 10. 3-4 per day; 500kr, students 350kr.) The Kiruna-Lappland **tourist office**, Lars Janssonsgat. 17, is in the Folkets Hus in the town center. Walk straight from the train station, follow the footpath through the tunnel, and then walk up through the park to the top of the hill and across the plaza. The office arranges dogsled excursions, moose safaris, and other wilderness outings. (☎01 88 80; www.lappland.se. Internet 25kr per 20min. Open June-Aug. M-F 8:30am-8pm, Sa-Su 8:30am-6pm; Sept.-May M-F 9am-5pm, Sa 10am-4pm.) The **Yellow House Hostel ❶**, Hantverkareg. 25, resembles an old farmhouse with bright, spacious rooms. (☎01 37 50. Breakfast 50kr. Sheets 50kr. Dorms 130kr; singles 300kr; doubles 400kr. Cash only.) From the tourist office, walk uphill and turn left onto Vänortsg., which turns into Steinholtzg., which then turns into Hantverkareg. Pull up to one of the outdoor tables at **Kaffekoppen ❷**, Föreningsg. 13B, for sandwich fare (from 55kr) and mugs of hot chocolate (25kr) the size of small mixing bowls. (Open M-Sa 9am-10pm, Su 10am-10pm. Cash only.) **Postal Code:** 98122.

SWITZERLAND
(SCHWEIZ, SUISSE, SVIZZERA)

The natural beauty of Switzerland entices outdoor enthusiasts from around the globe to romp in its Alpine playground. Three-fifths of the country is dominated by mountains: The Jura cover the northwest region bordering France, the Alps stretch gracefully across the lower half of Switzerland, with the eastern Rhaetian Alps bordering Austria. While the stereotypes of Switzerland as a "Big Money" banking and watch-making mecca are to some extent true, its energetic youth culture belies its staid reputation. Although the country is not known for being cheap, the best things—warm hospitality and Europe's highest peaks—remain priceless.

 DISCOVER SWITZERLAND: SUGGESTED ITINERARIES

THREE DAYS Experience the great outdoors at **Interlaken** (1 day; p. 1026), and then head to **Lucerne** (1 day; p. 1032) for the perfect combination of city culture and natural splendor before jetting to international **Geneva** (1 day; p. 1038).

ONE WEEK Begin in **Lucerne** (1 day), where your vision of a typical Swiss city will, strangely, be all too true. Then head to the capital, **Bern** (1 day; p. 1023), before getting your adventure thrills in **Interlaken** (1 day). Get a taste of Italian Switzerland in **Locarno** (1 day; p. 1045), then traverse northern Italy to reach **Zer**-matt (1 day; p. 1037). End your trip in the cosmopolitan city of **Geneva** (2 days).

TWO WEEKS Start in **Geneva** (2 days), then check out **Lausanne** (1 day; p. 1042) and **Montreux** (1 day; p. 1043). Tackle the Matterhorn in **Zermatt** (1 day) and keep hiking above **Interlaken** (1 day). Bask in **Locarno's** Mediterranean climate (1 day) then explore the **Swiss National Park** (1 day; p. 1037). Head to **Zurich** (2 days; p. 1028) and nearby **Lucerne** (1 day). Unwind in tiny, romantic **Stein am Rhein** (2 day; p. 1033) and then return to civilization via the capital, **Bern** (1 day).

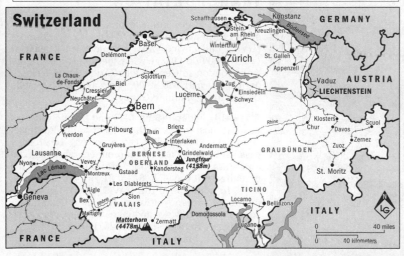

A SAINTLY BREED

In AD 1050, the Archdeacon Bernard de Menthon founded a hospice in a mountain pass in the Jungfrau region and brought with him a breed of large, furry dogs of Gallic origin. In addition to providing shelter for passing merchants, Bernard and the monks working under him would venture into blizzards in search of stranded travelers. Though it is uncertain whether the dogs accompanied the monks on their rescue missions—early accounts relate that dogs were used to run an exercise wheel that turned a cooking spit—by the time of Bernard's canonization, the dogs bearing his name had become famous for regularly patrolling the pass (now also named after Bernard).

Gifted with a fine sense of smell, a thick coat, an amiable attitude, and a neck that just begs to have a barrel of brandy tied to it, the St. Bernards made a name for themselves by saving over 2000 lives over several hundred years. In the 1810s, a single dog named Barry saved 40 travelers who had lost their way. Today, few St. Bernards still work as rescue dogs; smaller, lighter breeds less liable to sink in the snow have taken their place. Today the St. Bernard is a common household pet, and though it has entered the popular imagination through cartoons and children's movies, it will always have dignity as the Alpine fixture it once was.

ESSENTIALS

WHEN TO GO

November to March is ski season; prices in eastern Switzerland double and travelers need reservations well in advance. The reverse occurs in the summer, when the western half of Switzerland fills up. July and August are the prime months for hiking. Sights and accommodations are cheaper and less crowded in late spring and early fall, though many mountain towns shut down completely in May and June. Call ahead to make sure that the attractions you want to visit will be open.

DOCUMENTS AND FORMALITIES

VISAS. EU citizens do not need a visa. Citizens of Australia, Canada, New Zealand, and the US do not need a visa for stays of up to 90 days.

EMBASSIES. Most foreign embassies are in **Bern** (p. 1023). Swiss embassies abroad include: **Australia,** 7 Melbourne Ave., Forrest, Canberra, ACT 2603 (☎06 6273 3977); **Canada,** 5 Marlborough Ave., Ottawa, ON K1N 8E6 (☎613-235-1837); **Ireland,** 6 Ailesbury Rd., Ballsbridge, Dublin 4 (☎353 12 18 63 82); **New Zealand,** 22 Panama St., Wellington 6001 (☎04 472 15 93); **UK,** 16-18 Montague Pl., London W1H 2BQ (☎020 76 16 60 00); and **US,** 2900 Cathedral Ave. NW, Washington, D.C. 20008-3499 (☎202-745-7900).

TRANSPORTATION

BY PLANE. Major international airports for overseas connections are in Bern (BRN), Geneva (GVA), and Zurich (ZRH). From the UK, **easyJet** (☎0870 600 00 00; www.easyjet.com) has flights from London to Geneva and Zurich. From Ireland, **Aer Lingus** (☎01 886 32 00; www.aerlingus.ie) sells tickets from Dublin to Geneva.

BY TRAIN. Federal **(SBB, CFF)** and private railways connect most towns, with frequent trains. For times and prices, check online (www.sbb.ch). **Eurail, Europass,** and **Interrail** are all valid on federal trains. The **SwissPass,** sold worldwide, offers five options for unlimited rail travel: 4, 8, 15, 21, or 30 consecutive days. In addition to rail travel, it entitles you to unlimited transportation within 36 cities and on some private railways and lake steamers. (2nd-class 4-day pass US$160, 8-day US$225, 15-day US$270, 21-day US$315, 1-month US$350.)

BY BUS. **PTT Post Buses,** a barrage of government-run banana-hued coaches, connect rural villages and towns that trains don't service. **SwissPasses** are valid on many buses; **Eurail** passes are not. Even with the SwissPass, you might have to pay extra (5-10SFr) if you're riding one of the direct, faster buses.

BY CAR. With armies of mechanized road crews ready to remove snow at a moment's notice, roads at altitudes of up to 1500m generally remain open throughout winter. The speed limit is 50kph in cities, 80kph on open roads, and 120kph on highways. Many small towns forbid cars to enter; some require special permits or restrict driving hours. Call ☎140 for roadside assistance.

BY BIKE. Cycling, though strenuous, is a splendid way to see the country; most train stations rent bikes and let you return them at another station. The **Touring Club Suisse,** Chemin de Blandonnet 4, Case Postale 820, 1214 Vernier (☎022 417 27 27; www.tcs.ch), is a good source for maps and route descriptions.

TOURIST SERVICES AND MONEY

EMERGENCY	Police: ☎117. Ambulance: ☎144. Fire: ☎118.

TOURIST OFFICES. The **Swiss National Tourist Office,** marked by a standard blue "i" sign, is represented in nearly every town in Switzerland; most agents speak English. The official tourism website for Switzerland is www.myswitzerland.com.

MONEY. The Swiss monetary unit is the **Swiss Franc (SFr/CHF),** which is divided into 100 *centimes* (called *rappen* in German Switzerland). Coins come in 5, 10, 20, and 50 *centimes* and 1, 2, and 5SFr; bills come in 10, 20, 50, 100, 500, and 1000SFr. Switzerland is not cheap; if you stay in hostels and prepare your own food, expect to spend 45-100SFr per day. Generally, it's cheaper to exchange money in Switzerland than at home. There is no **Value Added Tax (VAT),** although there is often a small tourist tax for a hostel stay. **Gratuities** are automatically factored into prices; however, it is polite to round up your bill 1-2SFr as a nod of approval for good service.

SWISS FRANCS		
AUS$1 = 0.88SFR	1SFR = AUS$1.13
CDN$1 = 0.96SFR	1SFR = CDN$1.08
EUR€1 = 1.52SFR	1SFR = EUR€0.66
NZ$1 = 0.843FR	1SFR = NZ$1.19
UK£1 = 2.45SFR	1SFR = UK£0.44
US$1 = 1.22SFR	1SFR = US$0.82

COMMUNICATION

TELEPHONES. Whenever possible, use a calling card for international phone calls, as long-distance rates for national phone services are often exorbitant. For info about using cell phones abroad, see p. 35. Most pay phones in Switzerland accept only prepaid phone cards, available at kiosks, post offices, and train stations. Direct access numbers include: **AT&T** (☎0800 89 00 11), **British Telecom** (☎0800 55 25 44), **Canada Direct** (☎0800 55 83 30), **Ireland Direct** (☎0800 40 00 00), **MCI** (☎0800 89 02 22), **Sprint** (☎0800 89 97 77), **Telecom New Zealand** (☎0800 55 64 11).

MAIL. Airmail from Switzerland averages 4-7 days to North America, although times are unpredictable from smaller towns. Domestic letters take 1-3 days. Address mail to be held according to the following example: Firstname SURNAME, *Postlagernde Briefe*, CH-8021 Zürich, SWITZERLAND.

LANGUAGES. German, French, Italian, and Romansch are the national languages. Most urban Swiss speak English fluently. For basic German words and phrases, see p. 1061; for French, see p. 1060; for Italian, see p. 1063.

PHONE CODES	**Country code: 41. International dialing prefix:** 00. From outside Switzerland, dial int'l dialing prefix (see inside back cover) + 41 + city code + local number.

ACCOMMODATIONS AND CAMPING

SWITZERLAND	❶	❷	❸	❹	❺
ACCOMMODATIONS	under 23SFr	23-54SFr	54-85SFr	85-170SFr	over 170SFr

There are **hostels** (*Jugendherbergen* in German, *Auberges de Jeunesse* in French, *Ostelli* in Italian) in all big cities and in most small towns. **Schweizer Jugendherbergen** (SJH; www.youthhostel.ch) runs HI hostels in Switzerland, where beds are usually 20-34SFr. Non-HI members can stay in any HI hostel but usually pay a surcharge. The more informal **Swiss Backpackers (SB)** organization (www.backpacker.ch) has 31 hostels for the young, foreign traveler interested in socializing. Most Swiss **campgrounds** are not isolated areas but large plots glutted with RVs. Prices average 6-9SFr per person and 4-10SFr per tent site. **Hotels** and **pensions** tend to charge at least 50-75SFr for a single room and 80-150SFr for a double. The cheapest have *Gasthof, Gästehaus,* or *Hotel-Garni* in the name. **Privatzimmer** (rooms in a family home) run about 25-60SFr per person. Breakfast is included at most hotels, pensions, and *Privatzimmer.*

FOOD AND DRINK

SWITZERLAND	❶	❷	❸	❹	❺
FOOD	under 12SFr	12-23SFr	23-37SFr	37-52SFr	over 52SFr

Switzerland is not for the lactose-intolerant. The Swiss are serious about dairy products, from rich and varied **cheeses** to decadent **milk chocolate**—even the major Swiss soft drink, rivella, is dairy. Swiss dishes vary from region to region and what your waiter brings you is most likely related to the language he is speaking. Bernese *rösti,* a plateful of hash-brown potatoes (sometimes flavored with bacon or cheese), is prevalent in the German regions; cheese or meat **fondue** is popular in the French part. Try Valaisian *raclette,* made by melting cheese over a fire, scraping it onto a baked potato, and garnishing it with meat or vegetables. **Supermarkets Migros** and **Co-op** double as cafeterias; stop in for a cheap meal as well as groceries. Each canton has its own local beer—it's often less expensive than Coca-Cola.

 HIKING AND SKIING. Nearly every town has **hiking trails;** consult the local tourist office. Lucerne (p. 1034), Interlaken (p. 1026), Grindelwald (p. 1027), and Zermatt (p. 1037) offer particularly good hiking opportunities. Trails are usually marked with either red-white-red markers (only sturdy boots and hiking poles needed) or blue-white-blue markers (mountaineering equipment needed). **Skiing** in Switzerland is often less expensive than in North America—if you avoid pricey resorts. **Ski passes** run 30-50SFr per day, 100-300SFr per week; a week of lift tickets, equipment rental, lessons, lodging, and *demi-pension* (breakfast plus one other meal) averages 475SFr. **Summer skiing** is less common than it once was but is still available in a few towns such as Zermatt and Saas Fee.

HOLIDAYS AND FESTIVALS

Holidays: New Year's Day (Jan. 1); Good Friday (Mar. 25); Easter Monday (Mar. 28); Labor Day (May 1); Swiss National Day (Aug. 1); Christmas (Dec. 25).

Festivals: Two raucous festivals are the Fasnacht (Carnival; mid-Feb.) in Basel and the Escalade (early Dec.) in Geneva. Music festivals occur throughout the summer, including Open-Air St. Gallen (late June) and the Montreux Jazz Festival (July).

FACTS AND FIGURES: SWITZERLAND

Official Name: Swiss Confederation.

Capital: Bern.

Major Cities: Basel, Geneva, Zurich.

Population: 7,450,000 (65% German, 18% French, 10% Italian).

Land Area: 41,000 sq. km.

Time Zone: GMT + 1.

Languages: German, French, Italian, Romansch.

Religions: Roman Catholic (46%), Protestant (40%), unaffiliated (9%).

GERMAN SWITZERLAND

BERNESE OBERLAND

The Swiss are fiercely proud of the Bernese Oberland. When WWII threatened to engulf the country, the Swiss army resolved to defend the area to the death; they were aided in their endeavor by the natural fortress of mountains. The jutting peaks now shelter a pristine wilderness that lends itself to discovery through scenic hikes up the mountains and around the twin lakes, the Thunersee and Brienzersee. Not surprisingly, the area's opportunities for paragliding, mountaineering, and whitewater rafting are unparalleled. North of the mountains and lakes lies exuberant Bern, Switzerland's capital and the metropolitan heartbeat of the region.

BERN   ☎ 031

Bern (pop. 127,000) has been Switzerland's capital since 1848, but don't expect fast tracks, power politics, or men in suits—the Bernese prefer to focus on the lighter things in life, nibbling the local Toblerone chocolate and lolling along the banks of the serpentine Aare.

▐▟ TRANSPORTATION AND PRACTICAL INFORMATION. Bern's **airport** (BRN; ☎960 21 11) is 20min. from the city. An **airport bus** runs from the train station 50min. before each flight (10min., 14SFr). **Trains** run from the station at Bahnhofpl. to: Geneva (2hr., 3 per hr., 47SFr); Lucerne (1½hr., every 30min., 30SFr); Munich (6hr., 1 per hr., 120SFr); Paris (6hr., approx. 1 per hr., 111SFr); Salzburg (7¼hr., 2 per day, 133SFr); and Zurich (1¼hr., every 30min., 45SFr). Bernmobil **buses** run from 5:45am-midnight. (☎321 86 41. 24 hr. pass 7.50SFr.)

Most of medieval Bern lies in front of the train station and along the Aare River. Bern's main train station is a tangle of essential services and extraneous shops. Take extra caution around the Parliament park, especially at night. The **tourist office** is on the street level of the station. (☎328 12 12. Open June-Sept. daily 9am-8:30pm; Oct.-May M-Sa 9am-6:30pm, Su 10am-5pm.) For information on GLBT establishments, visit **Homosexuelle Arbeitsgruppe die Schweiz (HACH)**, Mühlenpl. 11, the headquarters of Switzerland's largest gay organization. The **post office**, Schanzenpost 1, is one block from the train station. (Open M-F 7:30am-9pm, Sa 8am-4pm, Su 5-9pm.) **Postal Codes:** CH-3000 to CH-3030.

SWITZERLAND

Bern

ACCOMMODATIONS
Backpackers Bern/
Hotel Glocke, 4
Jugendherberge, 7

FOOD
Café du Nord, 2
Manora, 6

NIGHTLIFE
Altes Tramdepot, 5
Pery Bar/Räblus, 3
Reitschule, 1

Laubeggstr.

Rosengarten

Aargauerstalden

Klösterlistutz

Mahogany Hall
Untertorbr.
Bärengraben
(Bear Pits)
Nydeggr.

Schänzlistr.

Aare

Mattenenge

Nr. Deigasalden

Wasserwerg

Gerbeng.

Englische Anlagen
(English Garden)

Jungfraustr.

Dufourstr.

Luisenstr.

Kollerweg

Schifflaube

Altenbergstr.

Langmauerweg

Postgasshalde

Posts.
Oberegggässchen
Gerechtigkeitsg.
Junkerng.

Rathausg.

Münster
(Cathedral)

Herreng.

Nydeggrain
Gübenbergstr.

Badg.

Marienstr.

Helvetiastr.

TO SWISS NATIONAL
LIBRARY (300m)

Rabbentalstr.

Botanical
Gardens

TO ① (75m)

Kornhausbr.

Schüttestr.

Nägelig.

Stadttheater

Brunngasshalde
Brunng.

Albert
Einstein's
House

Münsterg.

Schaalg.

Meat and
Cheese Market

Münstergasse

Hotelg.

Kramg.

KORNHAUSPL.

Zytglogge
(Clock Tower)

THEATERPL.

CASINOPL.

MÜNSTERPL.

Frickw.

Aarstr.

Kirchenfeldbr.

Schwellenmättstr.

Aare

Bernastr.

Bernesisches
Historische
Museum

HELVETIAPL.

Swiss
Alpine
Museum

TO NATURAL
HISTORY
MUSEUM (200m)

Dalmazibr.

Dalmaziquai

TO ZOO
(1.25km)

Kunstmuseum

Lorrainebr.

Hodlerstr.

Speicherg.

Genferg.

STA

Zeughausg.

Waisenhausplatzgässchen

WAISENHAUS-
PLATZ

Migros
Supermarkt

Marktg.

Käfigturm

Bärenpl.

Aarbergerg.

Co-op
Neueng. Pronto

Fruit and
Vegetable Market

Hang Loose

Jäggibücher

Spitalg.

BUNDESPL.

Bundeshaus

Bundesterrasse

Bundesrain

Münzraben

Kocherg.

Inselg.

Amthausg.

Münzgraben

Schauplatzg.

Gurteng.

Marzilibad
(Public Pool)

Marzili

Gassstr.

Weherg.

Aarstr.

TO CO-OP
SHOPPING
CENTER
(1.75km)

Marzilistr.

Marzilibahn
(Funicular Train)

Bundesrain

Bollwerk

Neubrückstr.

Hauptbahnhof

Co-op Pronto

BAHNHOFPL.

Heiliggeistkirche

Bubenbergpl.

Bernmobil
Office

Christoffelg.

Bundesg.

Kleine
Schanze

Taubenstr.

Sulgeneckstr.

Synagogue

Brückenstr.

Schwarztorstr.

Kapellenstr.

Monbijoustr.

Monbijoustr.

Effingerstr.

Hirschengraben

Maulbeer Str.

Laupen Str.

Schanzenstr.

Universität

Hochschulstr.

Sidlerstr.

FALKEN-
PLATZ

Falken-str.

Gesellschaftsstr.

Stud. Bächstr.

Länggass Str.

300 yards

300 meters

N

LG

ⲅⲂ ACCOMMODATIONS AND FOOD. Bern has responded to the influx of backpackers with several new hostels. All offer clean beds with varying services, prices, and personal touches. If the cheaper options are all full, check the tourist office for a list of private rooms. To reach the █**Backpackers Bern/Hotel Glocke ❷**, Rathausg. 75, from the train station, cross the tram lines and turn left on Spitalg., continuing onto Marktg; turn left at Kornhauspl., then right on Rathausg. (☎311 37 71. Internet 2SFr per 15min. Dorms 39SFr; singles 75SFr; doubles 120SFr, with bath 150SFr. AmEx/MC/V.) From the station, go down Christoffelg; take the stairs by the park gates, go down the steep slope, and turn left onto Weiherg. to reach **Jugendherberge (HI) ❷**, Weiherg. 4. (☎311 63 16. Breakfast included. Closed 2nd and 3rd weeks of Jan. Dorms 31-36SFr; singles from 50SFr; doubles from 80SFr. Nonmembers add 6SFr. MC/V.) Try one of Bern's hearty specialties: *gschnätzlets* (fried veal, beef, or pork), *suurchabis* (sauerkraut), or Toblerone chocolate. Produce **markets** sell their wares daily at Bärenpl. and every Tuesday and Saturday on Bundespl. (May-Oct.) A diverse crowd socializes over creative dishes at **Café du Nord ❸**, Lorrainestr. 2. (Meat entrees 22-32SFr. Pasta from 17SFr. Open M-F 8am-12:30am, Sa 9am-12:30am. Kitchen open M-Sa 11:30am-2pm and 6:30-10pm, Su 4:30-10pm. MC/V.) **Manora ❶**, Bubenbergpl. 5a, near the station, is a self-service chain with large portions of nutritious food. (Open daily 6:30am-11pm.)

◪ SIGHTS. The massive █**Bundeshaus**, center of the Swiss government, dominates the Aare. (45min. tour every hr. M-Sa 9-11am and 2-4pm. Free.) From the Bundeshaus, Kocherg. and Herreng. lead to the 15th-century Protestant **münster** (cathedral), which has a fantastic view from its 100m spire. (Open Easter-Oct. Tu-Sa 10am-5pm; Nov.-Easter Tu-F 10am-noon and 2-4pm, Sa 10am-noon and 2-5pm, Su 11am-2pm. Tower 3SFr.) Several walkways lead steeply down from the Bundeshaus to the **Aare River.** On hot days, locals dive from the banks and the bridges to take a ride on the river's swift currents, but only experienced swimmers should join in. Bern's **Kunstmuseum** includes the world's largest Paul Klee collection and a smattering of other 20th-century masters. (Hodlerstr. 8-12, near Lorrainebrücke. Open Tu 10am-9pm, W-Su 10am-5pm. 7SFr, students and seniors 5SFr.) Across the Nydeggbr. lie the **Bärengraben** (bear pits), which were recently renovated. (Open daily June-Sept. 9am-5:30pm; Oct.-May 10am-4pm.) The path snaking up the hill to the left leads to the █**Rosengarten** (rose garden), which provides one of the best views of Bern's Altstadt (Old Town). **Albert Einstein's house,** Kramg. 49, where he conceived the theory of general relativity, is now filled with his photos and letters. (Open Feb.-Nov. Tu-F 10am-5pm, Sa 10am-4pm. 3SFr, students 2SFr.)

◪◪ ENTERTAINMENT AND NIGHTLIFE. Check out *Bewegungsmelder*, available at the tourist office, for events. July's **Gurten Festival** (www.gurtenfestival.ch) has attracted such luminaries as Bob Dylan, Elvis Costello, and Björk, while jazz-lovers arrive in early May for the **International Jazz Festival** (www.jazzfestivalbern.ch). However, Bern's best-known festival is probably the off-the-wall **onion market** on the fourth Monday in November. The orange grove at **Stadgärtnerei Elfnau** (take tram #19 to Elfnau) has free Sunday concerts in summer. From mid-July to mid-August, **OrangeCinema** (www.orangecinema.ch) screens recent films in the open air; tickets are available from the tourist office in the train station.

At night, the fashionable folk linger in the Altstadt's bars and cafes while a leftist crowd gathers under the gargoyles of the Lorrainebrücke, behind the station. **Pery Bar,** Schmiedenpl. 3, is the perfect place to see and be seen. (Open M-W 5pm-1:30am, Th 5pm-2:30am, F-Sa 5pm-3:30am.) The **Altes Tramdepot,** across Nydeggbr. to the right of the bear pits, is great for early evening beers. (Open daily in summer 10am-12:30am; in winter 11am-12:30am.) The **Reitschule** club, Neubrückestr. 8, is a center for Bern's counterculture. (Open daily 8pm-late.)

JUNGFRAU REGION

The Jungfrau area has attracted tourists for hundreds of years with glorious hiking trails and snow-capped peaks. From Interlaken, the valley splits at the foot of the Jungfrau: The eastern valley contains Grindelwald, while the western valley hosts many smaller towns. The two valleys are divided by an easily hikeable ridge.

INTERLAKEN   ☎ 033

Interlaken (pop. 21,000) lies between the Thunersee and the Brienzersee at the foot of the largest mountains in Switzerland. With easy access to these natural playgrounds, Interlaken has earned its rightful place as one of Switzerland's prime tourist attractions and its top outdoor adventure spot.

▐▐ TRANSPORTATION AND PRACTICAL INFORMATION. The *Westbahnhof* (☎ 826 47 50) and *Ostbahnhof* (☎ 828 73 19) have **trains** to: Basel (5:30am-10:30pm, 56SFr); Bern (6:00am-10:30pm, 24SFr); Geneva (5:30am-9:30pm, 63SFr); Lucerne (5:30am-8:35pm, 26SFr); Lugano/Locarno (5:30am-4:35pm, 87SFr); and Zurich (6:45am-10:30pm, 62SFr). The *Ostbahnhof* also sends trains to Grindelwald (June-Sept. every 30min., Sept.-May 1 per hr.; 9.80SFr).
The **tourist office,** Höheweg 37, in Hotel Metropole, has free maps. (☎ 826 53 00. Open July-Aug. M-F 8am-7pm, Sa 8am-5pm, Su 10am-noon and 4-6pm; Sept.-June M-F 8am-6pm, Sa 8am-noon.) Both train stations rent **bikes.** (30SFr per day. Open daily 6am-7pm.) For **snow** and **weather info,** call ☎ 828 79 31. In case of **emergency,** call the **police** ☎ 117 or the **hospital** ☎ 826 26 26. **Postal Code:** CH-3800.

▐▌ ACCOMMODATIONS AND FOOD. ▨**Backpackers Villa Sonnenhof ❷,** Alpenstr. 16, diagonally across the Höhenmatte from the tourist office, is friendly and low-key. (☎ 826 71 71. Mountain bikes 28SFr per day. Breakfast and lockers included. Laundry 10SFr. Internet 1SFr per 5min. Reception 7:30-11am and 4-10pm. Dorms 29-32SFr; doubles 82-88SFr; triples 111-120SFr. 5SFr extra for balcony. AmEx/MC/V.) **Balmer's Herberge ❷,** Hauptstr. 23, is thoroughly American: It is a place to party, not to relax. Services include mountain bike rental (35SFr per day), nightly movies, TV, free sleds, and a bar. (☎ 822 19 61. Breakfast included. Internet 12SFr per hr. Reception in summer 6:30am-noon and 4-10pm; in winter 6:30-10am and 4:30-10pm. Dorms 24-26SFr; doubles 68-72SFr; triples 90-112SFr; quads 120-128SFr.) **Swiss Adventure Hostel ❷,** in the tiny town of Boltigen, has made this quiet valley a sporty alternative to Interlaken's party scene. A free shuttle runs to and from Interlaken each day (40min.). The hostel's adventure company offers the same activities as the Interlaken companies, but with a more personal touch. (☎ 773 73 73. Dorms 20-25SFr; doubles with shower 70SFr; quad with shower 100SFr. Special deals if combined with adventure sports.) Most hostels serve cheap food, and there are **Migros** supermarkets by both train stations. (Open M-Th 8am-6:30pm, F 8am-9pm, Sa 7:30am-5pm.)

▟ OUTDOOR ACTIVITIES. Interlaken offers a wide range of adrenaline-pumping activities. **Alpin Raft** (☎ 823 41 00), the most established company in Interlaken, has qualified, personable guides and offers: paragliding (150SFr), canyoning (215SFr), river rafting (205SFr), skydiving (380SFr), bungee jumping (125-295SFr), and hang gliding (180SFr). All prices include transportation to and from any hostel in Interlaken. A number of horse and hiking tours, as well as rock-climbing lessons, are also available upon request. **Outdoor Interlaken** (☎ 826 77 19) offers rock-climbing lessons (89SFr per half-day) and white-water kayaking tours (155SFr per half-day). **Swissraft** (☎ 823 02 10; www.swissraft.ch.), in Boltingen, offers similar adventures, as well as hydro-speeding (aided body-surfing down the river; 120SFr), and all-day combinations of multiple activities. The owner of **Skydiving Xdream,** Stefan Heuser, has been on the Swiss skydiving team for 17 years. (☎ 079 75 93 48 34. Skydiving 380SFr per tandem jump. Open Apr.-Oct.)

Interlaken's most traversed trail climbs to the Harder Kulm (1310m). From the *Ostbahnhof*, head toward town, take the first road bridge right across the river, and follow the yellow signs that later give way to white-red-white markings on the rocks. From the top, signs lead back down to the *Westbahnhof*. In summer, a funicular runs from the trailhead near the *Ostbahnhof* to the top. (2½hr. up, 1½hr. down. Daily May to mid-Oct. 13.40SFr, round-trip 21SFr; 25% Eurail and SwissPass discount.) For flatter trails, turn left from the train station and left before the bridge, then follow the canal over to the nature reserve on the shore of the Thunersee. The trail winds along the Lombach River, through pastures at the base of the Harder Kulm, and back toward town (3hr.).

 Interlaken's adventure sports industry is thrilling, but accidents do happen. On July 27, 1999, 19 tourists were killed by a sudden flash flood while canyoning. Be aware that you participate in all adventure sports at your own risk.

GRINDELWALD ☎ 033

Grindelwald (pop. 4500), the launching point to the only glaciers accessible by foot in the Bernese Oberland, crouches beneath the north face of the Eiger. The town has all kinds of hikes, from easy valley walks to challenging peaks for top climbers. The **Bergführerbüro** (Mountain Guides Office), in the sports center near the tourist office, sells hiking maps and coordinates glacier walks, ice climbing, and mountaineering. (☎853 12 00. Open June-Oct. M-F 9am-noon and 2-5pm.) The **Untere Grindelwaldgletscher** (lower glacier) hike is moderately steep (5hr.). To reach the trailhead, walk up the main street away from the station and follow the signs downhill to Pfinstegg. Hikers can either walk the first forested section of the trail (1hr.), following signs up to Pfinstegg., or take a funicular to the Pfinstegg. hut (July to mid-Sept. 8am-7pm; mid-Sept. to June 8am-4pm; 9.80SFr). From the hut, signs lead up the glacier-filled valley to Stieregg., a hut that offers food.

The **Jungfraubahn** runs to Grindelwald from Interlaken's *Ostbahnhof* (40min., 6:35am-10:30pm, 9.80SFr). The **tourist office,** located in the Sport-Zentrum to the right of the station, provides chairlift information and a list of free guided excursions. (☎854 12 12. Open July-Aug. M-F 8am-noon and 1:30-6pm, Sa 8am-noon, 1:30-5pm, Su 9-12am and 3:30-5pm; Sept.-June M-F 8am-noon and 2-6pm, Sa 8am-noon and 2-5pm.) **Hotel Hirschen ❹,** to the right of the tourist office, offers comfortable beds and a bowling alley. (☎854 84 84. Breakfast included. Reception daily 8am-10pm. Singles 90-135SFr; doubles 150-220SFr.) To reach the **Jugendherberge (HI) ❷,** head left out of the train station for 400m, then cut uphill to the right and follow the steep trail all the way up the hill. (☎853 10 09. Breakfast included. Reception daily 7:30-10am and 3pm-midnight. Dorms 28-30SFr; doubles 70SFr, with toilet and shower 102SFr. Nonmembers add 6SFr. AmEx/MC.) **Hotel Eiger ❷,** near the tourist office, is a huge complex of eateries and bars. (Open 8:30am-1:30am.) There's a **Co-op** supermarket on Hauptstr., across from the tourist office. (Open M-F 8am-noon and 1:30-6:30pm, Sa 8am-6pm.) **Postal Code:** CH-3818.

CENTRAL SWITZERLAND

A cosmopolitan area, central Switzerland is considerably more populous than the mountainous cantons to the south. The greater population density and diversity brings a greater mass of cultural artifacts, as evidenced by innovative museums, enchanting castles, and medieval *Altstädte* in Zurich, Lucerne, and other towns along the shores of the region's lakes.

ZURICH (ZÜRICH)   ☎01

Battalions of briefcase-toting executives charge daily through the world's largest gold exchange and fourth-largest stock exchange, pumping enough money into the economy to keep Zurich's upper-crust boutiques thriving. Once the focal point of the Reformation in German Switzerland, 20th-century Zurich (pop. 363,000) enjoyed an avant-garde radicalism that attracted progressive thinkers; while James Joyce wrote *Ulysses* in one corner of the city, an exiled Vladimir Lenin read Marx and dreamt of revolution in another. A walk through Zurich's student quarter immerses you in the energetic counter-culture that encouraged such thinkers, only footsteps away from the deep capitalism of the Bahnhofstr. shopping district.

⌐ TRANSPORTATION

Flights: Kloten Airport (ZRH; ☎816 25 00) is a major stop for Swiss International Airlines (☎084 885 20 00). Daily connections to **Frankfurt, Paris, London,** and **New York.** Trains connect the airport to the Hauptbahnhof in the city center (every 10-20min., 5.40SFr. Eurail and SwissPass valid).

Trains: Bahnhofpl. To: **Basel** (1hr., 1-2 per hr., 30SFr); **Bern** (1¼hr., 1-2 per hr., 45SFr); **Geneva** via Bern (3hr., every hr. 6am-10pm, 76SFr); **Lucerne** (1hr., 2 per hr. 6am-midnight, 19.80SFr); **Milan** (4hr., every hr. 6:30am-10pm, 72SFr); **Munich** (5hr., every hr. 6am-10:30pm, 86SFr); **Paris** (5hr., every hr. 6:30am-midnight, 133SFr); **Salzburg** (5hr., every hr. 6am-7pm, 97SFr); **Vienna** (9hr., every hr. 6am-6pm, 124SFr). Under 26 discount on international trains.

Public Transportation: Trams criss-cross the city, originating at the Hauptbahnhof. Tickets for rides of more than 5 stops cost 3.60SFr and are valid for 1hr. (press the blue button on automatic ticket machines); rides of fewer than 5 stops cost 2.10SFr (yellow button). Police will fine you 60SFr if you ride without a ticket. If you plan to ride several times, buy a 24hr. **Tageskarte** (7.20SFr), valid on trams, buses, and ferries. **Night buses** run from the city center to outlying areas (F-Su 1-4am).

Bike Rental: Bike loans are free at **Globus** (☎079 336 36 10); **Enge** (☎079 336 36 12); and **Hauptbahnhof** (☎210 13 88), at the very end of track 18. Passport and 20SFr deposit. Same day return. Open daily May-Oct. 7am-9:30pm.

◼✱🛈 ORIENTATION AND PRACTICAL INFORMATION

Zurich is in north-central Switzerland, close to the German border and on some of the lowest land in the country. The **Limmat River** splits the city down the middle on its way to the **Zürichsee.** On the western side of the river are the **Hauptbahnhof** and **Bahnhofstraße.** Two-thirds of the way down Bahnhofstr. lies **Paradeplatz,** the town center. On the eastern side of the river is the University district, which stretches above the narrow **Niederdorfstraße** and pulses with bars, restaurants, and hostels.

Tourist Offices: Main office (☎215 40 00, free hotel reservation service 215 40 40; www.zuerich.com), in the main station. An electronic hotel reservation board is at the front of the station. Open May-Oct. M-Sa 8am-8:30pm, Su 8:30am-6:30pm; Nov.-Apr. M-Sa 8:30am-7pm, Su 9am-6:30pm. **Touring Club des Schweiz (TCS),** Alfred-Escher-Str. 38 (☎286 86 86), offers maps and travel info to bikers and backpackers.

Currency Exchange: At the main train station. Cash advances for MC/V with photo ID, 200SFr min. Open daily 6:30am-10pm. **Crédit Suisse,** Paradepl. 2.50SFr commission. Open M-W and F 8:15am-4:30pm, Th 8:15am-6pm.

GLBT Services: Homosexuelle Arbeitsgruppe Zürich (HAZ), Sihlquai 67 (☎271 22 50; www.haz.ch), offers a library, meetings, and the free newsletter *InfoSchwül.* Open W 2-6pm. **Frauenzentrum Zürich,** Matteng. 27 (☎272 85 03), provides information for lesbians and a library of magazines and other resources. Open Tu and Th 6-8pm.

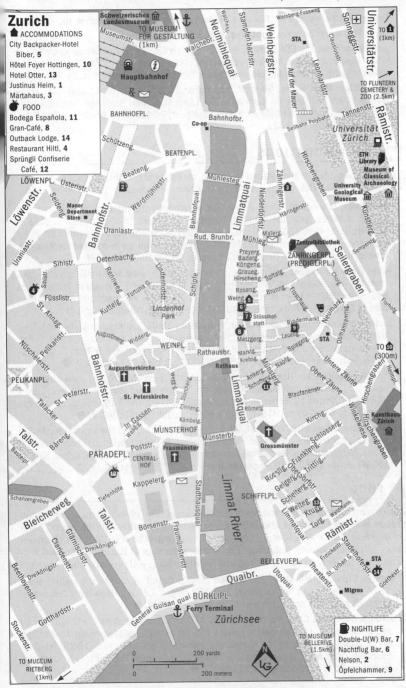

Zurich

ACCOMMODATIONS
City Backpacker-Hotel
  Biber, 5
Hôtel Foyer Hottingen, 10
Hotel Otter, 13
Justinus Heim, 1
Martahaus, 3

FOOD
Bodega Española, 11
Gran-Café, 8
Outback Lodge, 14
Restaurant Hiltl, 4
Sprüngli Confiserie
  Café, 12

NIGHTLIFE
Double-U(W) Bar, 7
Nachtflug Bar, 6
Nelson, 2
Öpfelchammer, 9

Schweizerisches Landesmuseum
TO MUSEUM FÜR GESTALTUNG (1km)
Hauptbahnhof
Universitätstr.
TO (1km)
TO FLUNTERN CEMETERY & ZOO (2.5km)
Rämistr.
Universität Zürich
ETH Library
Museum of Classical Archaeology
University Geological Museum
Seilbahn Polybahn
BAHNHOFPL.
Co-op
Bahnhofbr.
BEATENPL.
Mühlesteg
Zentralbibliothek
ZÄHRINGERPL. (PREDIGERPL.)
LÖWENPL.
Usterstr.
Manor Department Store
Bahnhofstr.
Uraniastr.
Rud. Brunbr.
Lindenhof Park
Stüssihofstatt
Neumarkt
Rindermarkt
Metzgerg.
WEINPL.
Rathausbr.
Rathaus
Augustinerkirche
St. Peterskirche
MÜNSTERHOF
Münsterbr.
Grossmünster
Kunsthaus Zürich
PARADEPL.
CENTRAL-HOF
Fraumünster
Limmatquai
SCHIFFLPL.
BELLEVUEPL.
Rämistr.
Quaibr.
BÜRKLIPL.
Ferry Terminal
Zürichsee
TO MUSEUM BELLERIVE (1.5km)
TO MUSEUM RIETBERG (1km)

0   200 yards
0   200 meters

SWITZERLAND

Emergency: Police: ☎117. **Fire:** ☎118. **Ambulance:** ☎144. **First Aid:** ☎360 44 44.

24hr. Pharmacy: Bellevue Apotheke, ☎266 62 22, on Bellevuepl.

Internet Access: The ETH Library, Ramistr. 101 (☎632 21 35; info@library.ethz.ch), in the *Hauptgebäude,* has free Internet access. Take tram #6, 9, or 10 to "ETH," enter the main building, and take the elevator to floor H. Open M-F 8:30am-9pm, Sa 9am-2pm.

Post Office: Main office, Sihlpost, Kasernestr. 95-97, just behind the station. Open M-F 6:30am-10:30pm, Sa 6am-8pm, Su 11am-10:30pm. Branches throughout the city. Address mail to be held as follows: Sihlpost, Postlagernde Briefe, CH-8021 Zurich. **Postal Code: CH-8021.**

ACCOMMODATIONS

The few budget accommodations in Zurich are easily accessible by foot or via public transportation. Reserve at least a day in advance, especially during the summer.

Martahaus, Zähringerstr. 36 (☎251 45 50; www.martahaus.ch). Popular with American college students. Breakfast included. Dorms 38SFr; singles 75-85, with shower 115SFr; doubles 98-114SFr/150-160SFr; triples 135SFr; quads 200SFr; studio with kitchen for 1-2 people 150SFr, 3 people 185SFr. The owners also run the nearby **Luther Pension,** a **women-only** residence. Dorms 30SFr; singles 50SFr. AmEx/MC/V. ❸

Hôtel Foyer Hottingen, Hottingenstr. 31 (☎256 19 19; www.foyer-hottingen.ch). Take tram #3 (dir.: Kluspl.) to "Hottingerpl." Dorm is women-only. Breakfast, lockers, and kitchen included. 11-bed dorm 35SFr; singles 70-85SFr, with bath 105-120SFr; doubles 110SFr/150-165SFr; triples 140SFr/190SFr; quads 180SFr. MC/V. ❷

Justinus Heim Zürich, Freudenbergstr. 146 (☎361 38 06; justinuszh@bluewin.ch). Take tram #9 or 10 (dir.: Haldenegg) to "Seilbahn Rigiblick," then take the funicular. Quiet, private rooms. Breakfast included. Reception daily 8am-noon and 5-9pm. Singles 35-50SFr, with shower 60SFr; doubles 85SFr/100SFr; triples 120-140SFr. V. ❸

The City Backpacker-Hotel Biber, Niederdorfstr. 5 (☎251 90 15; www.city-backpacker.ch). With the nightlife outside, you may not even need your bunk. Sheets, towels 3SFr each. Internet 12SFr per hr. Reception daily 8-11am and 3-10pm. Strict check-out 10am. 4- to 6-bed dorms 31SFr; singles 66SFr; doubles 92SFr. MC/V. ❷

Hotel Otter, Oberdorfstr. 7 (☎251 22 07; www.wueste.ch), and the swanky Wuste Bar below it attract an eclectic crowd. Floor bathrooms. Breakfast included. Rooms have TV, phone, fridge, and sink. Reception 8am-6pm in hotel, and until midnight in bar. Singles 100SFr; doubles 130-160SFr; private apartment 180SFr. AmEx/MC/V. ❹

FOOD

Zurich's more than 1300 restaurants run the gamut. The cheapest meals are available at *würstli* stands for about 5SFr. For heartier appetites, Zurich prides itself on *geschnetzeltes mit rösti,* thinly-sliced veal (often liver or kidney) in cream sauce with hash-brown potatoes. The **farmer's markets** at Burklipl. (Tu and F 6-11am) and Rosenhof (Th 10am-8pm and Sa 10am-5pm) sell produce and flowers.

▨ **Bodega Española,** Münsterg. 15. Catalan delights served by charismatic waiters since 1874. Egg-and-potato tortilla dishes 15.50SFr. Tapas 4.80SFr. Open daily 10am-midnight. Kitchen open noon-2pm and 6-10pm. AmEx/MC/V. ❷

▨ **Sprüngli Confiserie Café,** Paradepl. (☎224 47 11), a Zurich landmark, was founded by one of the original Lindt chocolate makers. Pick up a handful of the bite-size *Luxemburgerli* (8.20SFr per 100g), try the homemade sundaes, or eat a full meal (19-28SFr). Confectionery open M-F 7:30am-8pm, Sa 8am-4pm. Cafe open M-F 7:30am-6:30pm, Sa 8am-6pm, Su 9:30am-5:30pm. AmEx/MC/V. ❷

Restaurant Hiltl, Sihlstr. 28 (☎227 70 00; www.hitl.ch). Munch carrot sticks with the vegetarian elite. All-day salad buffet and nightly Indian buffet both 4.60SFr per 100g. Open M-Sa 7am-11pm, Su 11am-11pm. AmEx/MC/V. ❷

Outback Lodge, Stadelhoferstr. 18. Foster's beer on tap (4.20SFr), crocodile dishes (35SFr), and a generally Aussie atmosphere. 18+ after 6pm. Open M-F 9am-midnight, Sa-Su 11:30am-2am. AmEx/V/MC. ❹

Gran-Café, Limmatquai 66. Across from the rushing Limmat River. Think *Great Gatsby.* Save room for sundaes (8-10SFr). Open M-Th 6am-11:30pm, F 6am-midnight, Sa 7am-midnight, Su 7:30am-11:30pm. AmEx/MC/V. ❷

🔵 SIGHTS

It's virtually inconceivable to start a tour of Zurich anywhere but the stately **Bahnhofstraße.** The famous causeway of capitalism bustles with shoppers during the day but falls dead quiet at 6pm. At the Zürichsee end of Bahnhofstr., **Bürkliplatz** is a good place to explore the lake shore. The *platz* itself hosts a colorful Saturday **flea market** (May-Oct. 6am-3pm). On the other side of the river, the pedestrian zone continues on Niederdorfstr. and Münsterg., where shops run from the ritzy to the erotic. Off Niederdorfstr. **Spiegelgasse** was once home to Goethe, Buchner, and Lenin. **Fraumünster, Grossmünster,** and **St. Peterskirche** straddle the Limmat river.

▧ KUNSTHAUS ZÜRICH. The largest privately funded museum in Europe houses a collection ranging from 21st-century American pop art to religious pieces. Highlights include works by Chagall, Dalí, Dégas, Gaugin, Munch, Picasso, Rembrandt, Renoir, Rubens, and van Gogh. (*Heimpl. 1. Take tram #3, 5, 8, or 9 to "Kunsthaus." ☎253 84 84; www.kunsthaus.ch. English audiotours and brochures. Bag storage required. Call ahead for wheelchair access. After 2005, fully accessible without prior arrangements. Open Tu-Th 10am-9pm, F-Su 10am-5pm. 12SFr, students and seniors 6SFr, W free. Free tours W 6:30pm, Sa 3pm.*)

▧ MUSEUM RIETBERG. In contrast to the Kunsthaus, Rietberg presents non-European art housed in two mansions in the Rieter-Park. **Park-Villa Rieter** features internationally acclaimed exhibits of Chinese, Japanese, and Indian paintings. **Villa Wesendonck** houses a sculpture collection. (*Gablerstr. 15. Take tram #7 to Museum Rietberg. Villa Wesendonck open Apr.-Sept. Tu and Th-Su 10am-5pm, W 10am-8pm; Oct.-Mar. daily 10am-5pm. Audioguide 5SFr. Park-Villa Rieter open Tu-Su 10am-5pm. 6SFr, students 3SFr, under 16 free.*)

FRAUMÜNSTER. This 13th-century cathedral's Gothic style is juxtaposed with **Marc Chagall's** stained-glass windows, which depict stories from the Old and New Testament. Outside the church, a mural decorating the courtyard's archway pictures Felix and Regula (the decapitated patron saints of Zurich) with their heads in their hands. (*Off Paradepl. Open daily May-Nov. 9am-6pm; Nov.-Apr. 10am-4pm. Free.*)

GROSSMÜNSTER. The twin Neo-Gothic towers of this mainly Romanesque church are best viewed from the bridge near the Fraumünster. Considered the mother church of the Swiss-German Reformation, it has come to be a symbol of Zurich. (*Church open daily mid-Mar. to Oct. 9am-6pm; Nov. to early Mar. 10am-5pm. Tower open Mar.-Oct. daily 9am-5pm; Nov.-Feb. Sa-Su 9:15am-5pm. Entrance to the tower 2SFr.*)

ST. PETERSKIRCHE. St. Peterskirche has the largest clock face in Europe. (*Open M-F 8am-6pm, Sa 8am-4pm, Su 11am-5pm.*) Recently excavated Roman baths from the 1st century are visible beneath the iron stairway. (*Down Thermeng. from St. Peter's.*)

🎵 🎭 ENTERTAINMENT AND NIGHTLIFE

Niederdorfstraße rocks as the epicenter of Zurich's nightlife. Beware the "night club"—it's a euphemism for strip club. As with any nightlife center, women should be cautious about walking alone at night. Other hot spots include **Münsterg.** and

Limmatquai, both lined with overflowing cafés and bars. Beer in Zurich is pricey (from 6SFr), but a number of cheap bars have established themselves on Niederdorfstr. near Muhleg. From mid-July to mid-August, the Orange Cinema, an open-air cinema at Zürichhorn (take tram #4 or 2 to "Fröhlichstr."), attracts huge crowds to its lakefront screenings. Every August, the Street Parade brings together ravers from all over the world for a giant techno party.

🔲 **Nelson,** Beateng. 11. Expats, locals, backpackers, and businessmen alike chug beer (8.50SFr per pint) at this large and vibrant bar/club. Upstairs, **Lady Hamilton's,** where wine and whiskey are preferred to brews, is more sedate. (Both 20+. Nelson's open M-W 11:30am-2am, Th 11:30am-3am, F 11:30am-5am, Sa 3pm-5am, Su 3pm-2am. Lady Hamilton's open M-W 5pm-midnight, Th 5pm-1am, F-Sa 5pm-4am.)

Double-U (W) Bar, Niederdorfstr. 21, on the 1st floor of Hotel Schafli. Popular with locals and students. Beer (from 5SFr) and mixed drinks (from 14SFr) rise 2SFr in price after midnight. Open M-F and Su 4pm-2am, Sa 4pm-4am. AmEx/MC/V.

Nachtflug Bar, Café, and Lounge, Stüssihofstaff 4, boasts a popular outdoor bar. Wine from 7SFr. Beer from 4.90SFr. Open M-Th and Su 11am-midnight, F-Sa 11am-1:30am. Outdoor bar Th-Su 10pm-midnight.

Öpfelchammer, Rindermarkt 12. This popular Swiss wine bar (3-5SFr per glass) has low ceilings and wooden crossbeams covered with initials and messages from 200 years of merry-making. Those who climb the rafters and drink a free glass of wine from the beams get to engrave their names on the furniture. It's harder than it looks. Open mid-Aug. to mid-July Tu-Sa 11am-12:30am. AmEx/MC/V.

LUCERNE (LUZERN)   ☎041

Lucerne (pop. 60,000) is the Swiss traveler's dream come true. The old city is engaging, the lake is placid, and sunrise over the famous Mount Pilatus has hypnotized hikers and artists—including Twain, Wagner, and Goethe—for centuries.

▣🔃 TRANSPORTATION AND PRACTICAL INFORMATION. Trains leave Bahnhofpl. for: Basel (1hr., 1-2 per hr., 29SFr); Geneva (3½hr., every 2-3hr., 64SFr); and Zurich (1hr., 2 per hr., 20SFr). VBL **buses** depart from in front of the station and provide extensive coverage of Lucerne; route maps are available at the tourist office. The **tourist office,** in the station, offers free city guides, sells the **Museum Pass** (30SFr), and makes reservations. (☎220 11 00. Open May-Oct. M-F 8:30am-6:30pm, Sa-Su 9am-6:30pm; Nov.-Apr. M-F 8:30am-5:30pm, Sa-Su 9am-1pm.) **C&A Clothing,** on Hertensteinstr. at the top of the Altstadt, has two free but busy **Internet** terminals. (Open M-W 9am-6:30pm, Th-F 9am-9pm, Sa 8:30am-4pm.) The **post office** is by the train station. Address mail to be held: First name SURNAME, *Postlagernde Briefe*, Hauptpost, CH-6000 Luzern 1, SWITZERLAND. (Open M-F 7:30am-6:30pm, Sa 8am-noon.) **Postal Code:** CH-6000.

🔒🛏 ACCOMMODATIONS AND FOOD. To reach 🔲**Backpackers ❷,** Alpenquai 42, turn right from the station on Inseliquai and follow it until it turns into Alpenquai (20min.); the hostel is on the right. (☎360 04 20. Bikes 16SFr per day. Internet 10SFr per hr. Reception daily 7:30-10am and 4-11pm. Dorms 28-34SFr.) Until 1998, **Hotel Löwengraben ❹,** Löwengraben 18, was a prison; now it's a trendy, clean hotel with a bar, a restaurant, and dance parties every Saturday in summer. (☎417 12 12. Breakfast 15SFr. Singles 110-160SFr; doubles 160-220SFr.) **Markets** along the river sell cheap, fresh goods on Tuesday and Saturday mornings. There's also a **Migros** supermarket at the train station. (Open M-Sa 6:30am-9pm, Su 8am-9pm.)

◙🎵 SIGHTS AND ENTERTAINMENT. The Altstadt, across the river over Spreuerbrücke from the station, is famous for its frescoed houses; the best examples are those on Hirschenpl. and Weinmarkt. The 14th-century **Kapellbrücke,** a wooden-roofed bridge, runs from left of the train station to the Altstadt and is decorated with Swiss historical scenes; farther down the river, the **Spreuerbrücke** is decorated by Kaspar Meglinger's eerie *Totentanz* (Dance of Death) paintings. On the hills above the river, the **Museggmauer** and its towers are all that remain of the medieval city's ramparts. Three of the towers are accessible to visitors and provide panoramas of the city; walk along St. Karliquai, head uphill to the right, and follow the brown castle signs. (Open daily in summer 8am-7pm.) To the east is the magnificent **Löwendenkmal** (Lion Monument), the dying lion of Lucerne, which is carved into a cliff on Denkmalstr. The **⬛Picasso Museum,** Am Rhyn Haus, Furreng. 21, displays 200 intimate photographs of Picasso as well as a large collection of his lesser-known works. From Schwanenpl., take Rathausquai to Furreng. (Open daily Apr.-Oct. 10am-6pm; Nov.-Mar. 11am-5pm. 8SFr, students 5SFr.) The **⬛Verkehrshaus der Schweiz** (Swiss Transport Museum), Lidostr. 5, has interactive displays on all kinds of vehicles, but the real highlight is the warehouse of trains. Take bus #6, 8, or 24 to *Verkehrshaus*. (Open daily Apr.-Oct. 10am-6pm; Nov.-Mar. 10am-5pm. 26SFr, students 22SFr, with Eurail 14SFr.)

Although Lucerne's nightlife is more about chilling than club-hopping, **The Loft,** Haldenstr. 21, hosts special DJs and theme nights. (Beer 8-9SFr. Open W 9pm-2am, Th-Su 10am-4am.) The mellower **Jazz Cantine,** Grabenstr. 8, is a product of the Jazz School of Lucerne. (Sandwiches 6-8SFr. Open M-Sa 7am-12:30am, Su 4pm-12:30am.) Lucerne attracts big names for its two jazz festivals: **Blue Balls Festival** (July 22-30 in 2005) and **Blues Festival** (2nd week of Nov.).

▶ DAYTRIP FROM LUCERNE: MOUNT PILATUS. The view of the Alps from the top of **Mount Pilatus** (2132m) is absolutely phenomenal. For the most memorable trip, catch a boat from Lucerne to Alpnachstad (1½hr.), ascend by the world's steepest **cogwheel train,** then descend by cable car to Krienz and take the bus back to Lucerne (entire trip 79SFr, with Eurail or SwissPass 40-43SFr). For less money, take a train or boat to Hergiswill and hike up to Fräkmüntegg (3hr.), then get on the cable car at the halfway point. (23SFr round-trip, with Eurail 19SFr.) Fräkmüntegg also operates central Switzerland's longest *Rodelbahn* course; for 7SFr, you whizz down the hillside on a plastic slide at surprising speed.

STEIN AM RHEIN ☎ 052

The tiny medieval Altstadt of Stein am Rhein (pop. 3000) is postcard-perfect, with traditional Swiss architecture framed by hills and river. All the houses of the square date back to the 15th century and are marked by facade paintings depicting the animal or scene after which each house is named. However, it was the 12th-century establishment of the **Kloster St. George** that first made Stein am Rhein prominent. You can reach the Benedictine monastery by heading up Chirchhofpl. from the Rathauspl. Less austere is the vibrant **Festsaal,** whose tiled floor is off-limits to feet. As lights are dim, try to go when it is bright outside for the best view of delicate paintings and engravings. (☎741 21 42. Open Mar.-Oct. Tu-Su 10am-5pm. 3SFr, students 1.50SFr.) The **Rathaus,** at the corner of Rhig. and Rathauspl., is more stately.

Trains connect Stein am Rhein to Konstanz (40min., 1 per hr., 10SFr) via Kreuzlingen. **Boats** (☎634 08 88) depart for Schaffhausen (1¼hr., 20SFr) and other Bodensee towns. The **tourist office,** Oberstadt. 3, lies on the other side of the Rathaus. (☎742 20 90. Open July-Aug. M-F 9:30am-noon and 1:30-5pm, Sa 9:30am-noon and 1:30-4pm; Sept.-June M-F 9:30am-noon and 1:30-5pm.) The family-oriented **Jugendherberge (HI) ❷** is at Hemishoferstr. 87. From the train station, take the bus (#7349, dir.: Singen) to Strandbad and walk 5min. farther in the same direction. (☎052 741 12 55. Breakfast, showers, and sheets included. Curfew 10:30pm, keys available. Reception daily 8-10am and 5-10pm. Open Mar.-Nov. Dorms 25SFr; singles 40SFr; doubles 60SFr; family rooms 34SFr per person. Nonmembers add 6SFr. AmEx/MC/V.) The **Rothen Ochsen Wine Bar ❶**, Rathauspl. 9, a wooden hall built in

1466, is the oldest public house in the town. Though full meals are not available, their regional soups, appetizers, and wines are sustenance enough. (☎741 23 28. Open Tu-Sa 11:30am-late, Su 10:30am-6pm.) **Postal Code:** CH-8260.

NORTHWESTERN SWITZERLAND

The cantons of Basel-Stadt, Basel-Land, Solothurn, and Aargau inspire peaceful contentment. Odds are, you'll pass through Basel, as it is a transportation hub for Germany and France, so why not slow down to enjoy excellent museums and delightful Altstadt? Nearby Solothurn offers a stunning Italian cathedral and outdoor activities. Despite their proximity to France and the occasional French town name, the cantons of northwestern Switzerland are German-speaking.

BASEL (BÂLE)   ☎061

Situated on the Rhine near France and Germany, Basel is home to a large medieval quarter as well as one of the oldest universities in Switzerland—graduates include Erasmus and Nietzsche. Visitors can view art from Roman times to the 20th century and be serenaded by musicians on every street corner year-round.

■■ TRANSPORTATION AND PRACTICAL INFORMATION. Basel has three **train stations:** the French (SNCF) and Swiss (SBB) stations on Centralbahnpl., near the Altstadt, and the German (DB) station across the Rhine. **Trains** leave from the SBB to: Bern (1¼hr., every hr. 5:50am-11:07pm, 34SFr); Geneva (3hr., 1 per hr., 71SFr); Lausanne (2½hr., 1 per hr., 60SFr); and Zurich (1hr., every 15-30min., 30SFr). Make international connections at the French (SNCF) or German (DB) stations. The **tourist office** Steinenbergstr., is in the Stadt Casino building on Barfüsserpl. From the SBB station, take any tram headed to "Barfüsserpl." (☎268 68 68; www.baseltourismus.ch. Open M-F 8:30am-6pm, Sa-Su 10am-5pm.) For information on **GLBT** establishments, stop by **Arcados,** Rheing. 69, at Clarapl. (☎681 31 32. Open Tu-F 1-7pm, Sa noon-4pm.) To reach the **post office,** Rüdeng 1., take tram #1 or 8 to Marktpl. and backtrack one block, away from the river. (Open M-W and F 7:30am-6:30pm, Th 7:30am-8pm, Sa 8:30-11:30am.) Address mail to be held as follows: *Postlagernde Briefe für* First name SURNAME, Rüdeng., CH-4001 Basel, Switzerland. **Postal Codes:** CH-4000 to CH-4059.

■■ ACCOMMODATIONS AND FOOD. The **Jugendherberge (HI) ❷,** St. Alban-Kirchrain 10, is a mecca for weary travelers. To get there, take tram #2 to Kunstmuseum; turn right on St. Alban-Vorstadt, then follow the signs. (☎272 05 72. Internet 5SFr per 25min. Breakfast included. Laundry 7SFr. Reception daily Mar.-Oct. 7-10am and 2-11:30pm; Nov.-Feb. 2-11pm. Dorms 32.50SFr; singles 80SFr; doubles 100SFr. Nonmembers add 6SFr. AmEx/MC/V.) Though **Basel Back Pack ❷,** Dornacherstr. 192, Basel's newest hostel, is far from the city center, it is serviced by a convenient tram. (☎333 00 37; www.baselbackpack.ch. Breakfast 7SFr. Sheets, showers, kitchen, and locker included. Reception daily 8am-1pm and 7pm-midnight. Dorms 30SFr; singles 80SFr; doubles 94SFr; triples 120SFr; quads 150SFr.)

   Barfüsserpl., Marktpl., and the streets connecting them are full of satisfying restaurants. **Wirtshaus zum Schnabel ❷,** Trillengässlein 2, serves tasty German fare. (Open M-Sa 10:30am-midnight. AmEx/MC/V.) Vegetarians can dine at **Restaurant Gleich ❸,** Leonhardsberg 1. (Open M-F 10:30am-9:30pm.) Head to **Migros,** in the SBB station, for groceries. (Open M-F 6am-10pm, Sa-Su 7:30am-10pm.)

◐ ◪ SIGHTS AND ENTERTAINMENT. *Groß-Basel* (Greater Basel) and the train station are separated from *Klein-Basel* (Lesser Basel) by the Rheine. The very red **Rathaus** brightens Marktpl. in *Groß-Basel* with its blinding façade and gold-and-green statues. Behind the Marktpl. is the 775-year-old **Mittlere Rheinbrücke** (Middle

Rhine Bridge) which connects the two halves of Basel. At the other end of Marktpl. is the spectacular ◪**Jean Tinguely Fountain,** also known as the **Fasnachtsbrunnen.** Behind Marktpl. stands the red sandstone **Münster,** where you can visit the tomb of Erasmus. (Open Easter to mid-Oct. M-F 10am-5pm, Sa 10am-4pm, Su 1-5pm; mid-Oct. to Easter M-Sa 11am-4pm, Su 2-4pm. Free. Tower closes 30min. before the church. 3SFr.) Basel has over 30 museums; pick up the comprehensive museum guide at the tourist office. The **Basel Card** provides admission to all museums as well as discounts around town. (24hr. card 20SFr, 48hr. card 27SFr, 72hr. card 35SFr.) The **Kunstmuseum** (Museum of Fine Arts), St. Alban-Graben 16, houses an outstanding collection; admission also gives access to the **Museum für Gegenwartskunst** (Museum of Modern Art), St. Alban-Rheinweg 60. (Kunstmuseum open Tu and Th-Su 10am-5pm, W 10am-7pm. Gegenwartskunst open Tu-Su 11am-5pm. Both 10SFr, students 8SFr, 1st Su of every month free.) The **Fondation Beyeler,** Baselstr. 101, is one of Europe's finest private art collections, housing works by many major artists. Take tram #6 to Riehen Dorf then walk toward the tram. (Open M-Tu and Th-Su 9am-6pm, W 9am-8pm. M-F 16SFr, Sa-Su 20SFr; students 5SFr.)

In a year-round party town, Basel's carnival, or **Fasnacht,** still manages to distinguish itself. The festivities commence the Monday before Lent with the *Morgestraich*, a 72hr. parade with a 600-year tradition; the parade begins at 4am. The goal is to scare away winter, though it is rarely accomplished. During the rest of the year, head to **Barfüsserplatz** for an evening of bar-hopping. **Atlantis,** Klosterberg 10, is a multi-level, sophisticated bar with reggae, jazz, and funk. (Open Tu-Th 11am-midnight, F 11:30am-4am, Sa 6pm-4am.) **Brauerei Fischerstube,** Rheing. 45, brews the delectably sharp *hell spezial* (light special) beer. (Open M-Th 10am-midnight, F-Sa 10am-1am, Su 5pm-midnight. Full dinner menu from 6pm.)

GRAUBÜNDEN

The largest, highest, and least populous of the Swiss cantons, Graubünden features rugged gorges, fir forests, and eddying rivers give the region a wildness seldom found in ultra-civilized Switzerland. Visitors should plan their trips carefully, especially in ski season, when reservations are absolutely required. Beware: Almost everything shuts down in May and June.

DAVOS   ☎081

Davos (pop. 12,000) sprawls along the valley floor under seven mountains laced with chair-lifts and cable cars. Originally a health resort, the city catered to such *fin-de-siècle* giants as Robert Louis Stevenson and Thomas Mann, who, while in Davos, wrote *Treasure Island* and *The Magic Mountain,* respectively. The influx of tourists in recent decades has given the city an impersonal feel, but the thrill of carving down the famed, wickedly steep ski slopes may make up for it. Europe's largest natural **ice rink** (22,000 sq. m), between Platz and Dorf, has curling, figure skating, hockey, ice dancing, and speed skating. (☎415 36 04. Open Dec. 15-Feb. 15. M-W and F-Su 10am-4pm, Th 8-10pm. 5SFr. Skate rental 6.50SFr.) For joggers, birdwatchers, and aspiring windsurfers, the **Davosersee** is the place to be. At the **Davosersee Surfcenter,** board rentals are 30SFr per hr., 60SFr per day. (Take bus #1 to Flueelastr. and follow the yellow signs to the lake. Open daily mid-June to mid-Sept. 11am-6:30pm.) Davos provides direct access to two mountains—**Parsenn** and **Jakobshorn**—and four skiing areas. Parsenn, with long runs and fearsome vertical drops, is the mountain around which Davos built its reputation. (www.fun-mountain.ch. Day pass 60SFr.) Jakobshorn has found a niche with the younger crowd since the opening of a snow-boarding park with two half-pipes. (Day pass 52SFr.) In the valley run 75km of cross-country trails, one of which is lit at night. In the summer, ski lifts connect to **hikes,** such as the 2hr. **Panoramweg.** To get a little culture with your sweat, visit the **Kirchner Museum,** on the Promenade. It houses an extensive collection of Ernst Ludwig Kirchner's artwork, whose harsh colors and long figures defined 20th-century German Expressionism. (Take the bus to Kirchner Museum. Open Tu-Su 10am-6pm; Sept.-Dec. 24 and Easter-July 7 Tu-Su 2-6pm. 8SFr, students 5SFr.)

Davos is accessible by **train** from Chur (1½hr., 7 per day, 25SFr) via Landquart or from Klosters (25min., 2 per hr., 8.60SFr) on the Rhätische Bahn lines. The town is divided into two areas, Davos-Dorf and Davos-Platz, each with its own train station; Platz has the tourist office, post office, and most places of interest to budget travelers. Dorf is closer to the Davosersee. **Buses** (2.70SFr) run between the two train stations and stop near major hotels and at the hostel on the Davosersee. The main **tourist office,** Promenade 67, is up the hill from the *Platz* station. (☎415 21 21. Open Dec. to mid-Apr. and mid-June to mid-Oct. M-F 8:30am-6:30pm, Sa 9am-5pm, Su 10am-noon and 3-5:30pm; mid-Oct. to Dec. and mid-Apr. to mid-June M-F 8:30am-5pm, Sa-Su 8:30am-noon.) At Jakobshorn Ski Mountain's **Snowboardhotel Bolgenschanze ❸,** Skistr. 1, dorm rooms are sold as a package with ski passes. (☎414 90 20; www.fun-mountain.ch. 1-night, 2-day ski pass 145-195SFr; 6-night, 7-day pass 570-690SFr. AmEx/MC/V.) **Postal Code:** CH-7270.

KLOSTERS   ☎081

Davos's sister resort, Klosters (pop. 3000), lies across the Gotschna and Parsenn mountains. Though Klosters is only 10min. from Davos by train, it's a world away in atmosphere. Davos makes every effort to be cosmopolitan, while Klosters capitalizes on its natural serenity and cozy chalets. Most ski packages include mountains from both towns, and Klosters's main lift leads to a mountain pass where one can ski down to either. In summer, Klosters has better access to fantastic biking trails. **Ski passes** for the Klosters-Davos region run 121SFr for 2 days and 279SFr for 6 days (including public transportation). The **Madrisabahn** leaves from Klosters-Dorf (1-day pass 33SFr). The **Grotschnabahn** gives access to Parsenn and Strela in Davos and Madrisa in Klosters. (1-day pass 60SFr, 6-day pass 324SFr.) Summer cable car passes (valid on Grotschna and Madrisabahnen) are also available. (4-day pass 80SFr.) **Bananas,** operated out of Duty Boardsport, Bahnhofstr. 16, gives snowboard lessons. (☎422 66 60. Lessons 70SFr per 4hr. Board rental 38SFr per day.) **Ski rental** is also available at **Sport Gotschna,** across from the tourist office. (☎422 11 97. Skis and snowboards 28-50SFr per day plus 10% insurance. Open M-F 8am-noon and 2-6:30pm, Sa 8am-12:30pm and 2-6pm, Su 9am-noon and 3-6pm.) On the luscious green valley floor, **hikers** can make a loop, from the Protestant church on Monbielstr. to Monbiel. The route continues to an elevation of 1488m and turns left, passing through Bödmerwald, Fraschmardintobel, and Monbieler Wald before climbing to its highest elevation of 1634m and returning to Klosters via Pardels. Several adventure companies offer a variety of activities including **river rafting, canoeing, horseback riding, paragliding,** and **glacier trekking.**

Klosters-Platz and Klosters-Dorf are connected to Chur by **train** via Landquart (1¼hr., every hr. 5:20am-9:30pm, 19SFr). The same line connects Klosters and Davos (30min., every hr. 5:30am-11:30pm, 9SFr.) The main **tourist office,** in Platz by the station, sells area hiking (15.50SFr) and biking (7.50SFr) maps. (Open May-Nov. M-F 8:30am-noon and 2-6pm, Sa 8:30am-noon and 2-4pm; July to mid-Aug. also Su 9-11am; Dec.-Apr. M-Sa 8:30am-noon and 2-6pm, Su 9-11:30am and 4-6pm.) **Andrist Sport** on Gotschnastr, rents **bikes.** (☎410 20 80. 38SFr per day, 6 days 130SFr. Open M-F 9am-noon and 2-6:30pm, Sa 8am-noon and 2-4pm.) To get to **Jugendherberge Soldanella (HI) ❷,** Talstr. 73, from the station, go left uphill past Hotel Alpina to the church, then cross the street and head up the alley to the right of the Kirchplatz bus sign. Walk 10min. along the gravel path. This massive chalet has a comfortable reading room and a flagstone terrace. (☎422 13 16. Breakfast included. Reception daily 7-10am and 5-10pm. Open mid-Dec. to mid-Apr. and late June to mid-Oct. Dorms 28SFr; singles 38SFr; doubles 76SFr; family rooms 38SFr per person. Nonmembers add 6SFr. AmEx/MC/V.) **Postal Code:** CH-7250.

THE SWISS NATIONAL PARK   ☎ 081

The Swiss National Park offers hikes that rival the best in Switzerland, but no other area can match the park's isolation from man-made structures, which allows hikers to experience the undiluted wildness of the terrain. A network of hiking trails runs throughout the park, concentrated in the center. Few trails are level; most involve a lot of climbing, often into snow-covered areas. All trails are clearly marked, and it is against park rules to wander off the designated trails. Trails that require no mountaineering gear are marked with white-red-white blazes. Keep in mind, though, that even some of the no-gear routes can be tricky.

Zernez is the main gateway to the park and home to the main headquarters of the park, the **National Parkhouse.** The staff provides helpful trail maps as well as up-to-date information on which trails are navigable—take their advice seriously; when they say a trail is too dangerous, they mean it. (☎856 13 78. Open June-Oct. M and W-Su 8:30am-6pm. Tu 8:30am-10pm) From Zernez, **trains** and **post buses** run to other towns in the area, including Scuol, Samedan, and S-chanf. The park is closed November through May. The Swiss National Park is one of the most strictly regulated nature reserves in the world. Camping and campfires are prohibited in the park, as is collecting flowers and plants. A team of wardens patrols the park at all times, so it's better not to test the rules. Zernez, Scuol, and S-chanf have campsites right outside the park boundaries.

VALAIS

The Valais occupies the deep and wide glacial gorge traced by the Rhône River. The clefts of the valley divide the land linguistically: in the west, French predominates, and in the east, Swiss-German is used. Though its mountain resorts can be over-touristed, the region's spectacular peaks and skiing, hiking, and climbing make fighting the traffic worthwhile.

ZERMATT AND THE MATTERHORN   ☎ 027

The shape of the valley blocks out most of the great Alpine summits that ring Zermatt (pop. 3500), allowing the monolithic **Matterhorn** (4478m) to rise alone above town. The area has attained mecca status with Europe's longest **ski** run, the 13km trail from Klein Matterhorn to Zermatt, and more **summer ski trails** than any other Alpine ski resort. A one-day ski pass for f the area's mountains runs 60-72SFr. The **Zermatt Alpine Center,** which houses both the **Bergführerbüro** (Mountain Guide's Office; ☎966 24 60) and the **Skischulbüro** (Ski School; ☎966 24 66), is located past the post office. The Bergführerbüro provides ski passes, weather forecasts, and info on guided climbing. (Open July-Sept. M-F 8:30am-noon and 4-7pm, Sa 3:30-7pm, Su 10am-noon and 3:30-7pm; late Dec. to mid-May daily 5-7pm.) Rental prices for skis and snowboards are standardized throughout Zermatt (28-50SFr per day). **Freeride Film Factory** (☎213 38 07) offers custom **hiking, biking,** and **climbing** expeditions (160-250SFr) that come with a videotape of your trek. The only company to lead expeditions above Zermatt is the **Bergführerbüro.** Groups scale Breithorn (150SFr), Pollux (260SFr), and Castor (270SFr) daily in summer. Climbing the Matterhorn is expensive and requires a guide, peak physical condition, and lots of experience (at least PD+). ◪**The Pipe Surfer's Cantina,** on Kirchstr., has the area's craziest parties. Don't leave without downing a shot of Moo (6SFr), their specialty caramel vodka. (Happy Hour daily 6-7pm. Open daily 3:30pm-2:30am.)

To preserve the Alpine air, cars and buses are banned in Zermatt; the only way in is the hourly **BVZ** (Brig-Visp-Zermatt) rail line, which connects to Lausanne (73SFr). The **tourist office,** in the station, sells hiking maps for 26SFr.

SWITZERLAND

(☎966 81 00. Open mid-June to mid-Oct. M-Sa 8:30am-6pm, Su 9:30am-noon and 4-6pm; mid-Oct. to mid-Dec. and May to mid-June M-F 8:30am-noon and 2-6pm, Sa 9:30am-noon; mid-Dec. to Apr. 8:30am-noon and 2-6pm, Sa 8:30am-6:30pm, Su 9:30am-noon and 4-6pm.) **Hotel Bahnhof ❷**, on Bahnhofstr. to the left of the station, provides hotel housing at hostel rates. (☎967 24 06. Dorms 30SFr; singles 60SFr, with shower 71SFr; doubles 88SFr/99SFr. MC/V.) Treat yourself to Swiss fare at **Walliserkanne ❸**, on Bahnhofstr. next to the post office. (Open 9am-midnight. MC/V.) Get groceries at the **Co-op Center,** opposite the station. (Open M-F 8:15am-12:15pm and 1:45-6:30pm, Sa 8:15am-12:15pm and 1:45-6pm.) **Postal Code:** CH-3920.

FRENCH SWITZERLAND

All around Lac Léman and Lac Neuchâtel, hills sprinkled with villas and blanketed by patchwork vineyards sewn with garlands of ripening grapes seem tame and settled...until the haze clears. Many travelers suffer financial anxiety when they consider venturing to refined French Switzerland, since high prices are the general rule in tourist-infested Geneva, Lausanne, Neuchâtel, and Montreux. However, adventurers find that tranquility is just a short stroll along a tree-lined quai or into hilltowns along the lakes.

GENEVA (GENÈVE)   ☎022

A stay in Geneva will likely change your definition of diversity. The most international city in Switzerland, Geneva is a mix of 178,000 unlikely neighbors: wealthy businessmen speed past dreadlocked skaters, while families stroll by struggling artists: Only one-third of the city's residents are natives of the canton. Birthplace of the League of Nations and current home to many multinational organizations (including the Red Cross and the United Nations), Geneva emanates worldliness.

▐▀ TRANSPORTATION

Flights: Cointrin Airport (GVA; ☎717 71 11, flight info 799 31 11) is a hub for **Swiss Airlines** (☎0848 85 20 00) and also serves **Air France** (☎827 87 87) and **British Airways** (☎0848 80 10 10). Several direct flights per day to **Amsterdam, London, New York, Paris,** and **Rome.** Bus #10 runs to the Gare Cornavin (15min., every 5-10min., 2.60SFr). The train provides a shorter trip (6min., every 10min., 2.70-7.40SFr).

Trains: Trains run approximately 4:30am-1am. **Gare Cornavin,** pl. Cornavin, is the main station. To: **Basel** (2¾hr., 1 per hr., 71SFr); **Bern** (2hr., 1 per hr., 47SFr); **Interlaken** (3hr., 1 per hr., 63SFr); **Lausanne** (40min., every 15-30min., 19SFr); **Montreux** (1hr., 2 per hr., 29SFr); **Zurich** (3½hr., every 30min., 76SFr). Ticket counter open M-F 8:30am-6:30pm, Sa 9am-5pm. **Gare des Eaux-Vives** (☎736 16 20), on av. de la Gare des Eaux-Vives (tram #12 to *Amandoliers SNCF*), connects to France's regional rail through **Annecy** (1½hr., 6 per day, 14SFr) or **Chamonix** (2½hr., 4 per day, 24SFr).

Public Transportation: Geneva has an efficient bus and tram network. **Day passes** 6SFr-12SFr. Stamp multi-use tickets before boarding. Buses run roughly 5:30am-midnight; **Noctambus** (1:30-4:30am, 3SFr) runs when the others don't.

Bike Rental: Geneva has well-marked bike paths and special traffic lights for spoked traffic. Behind the station, **Genève Roule,** pl. Montbrillant 17 (☎740 13 43), has free bikes available (50SFr deposit; hefty fine if bike is lost or stolen). Slightly nicer bikes from 5SFr per day. Open in summer 7:30am-9:30pm; in winter 7:30am-6pm.

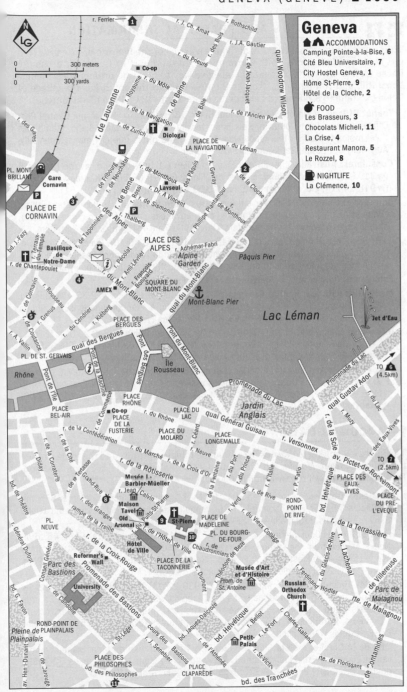

Geneva

🏠🏕 **ACCOMMODATIONS**
Camping Pointe-à-la-Bise, **6**
Cité Bleu Universitaire, **7**
City Hostel Geneva, **1**
Hôme St-Pierre, **9**
Hôtel de la Cloche, **2**

🍴 **FOOD**
Les Brasseurs, **3**
Chocolats Micheli, **11**
La Crise, **4**
Restaurant Manora, **5**
Le Rozzel, **8**

🍸 **NIGHTLIFE**
La Clémence, **10**

SWITZERLAND

✳ 🄻 ORIENTATION AND PRACTICAL INFORMATION

The labyrinthine cobbled streets and quiet squares of the historic *vieille ville* (old city), around **Cathédrale de St-Pierre,** make up the heart of Geneva. Across the **Rhône River** to the north, five-star hotels give way to lakeside promenades, **International Hill,** and rolling parks. Across the **Arve River** to the south lies the village of **Carouge,** home to student bars and clubs (take tram #12 or 13 to pl. du Marché).

Tourist Offices: Main office, r. du Mont-Blanc 18 (☎909 70 00), in the Central Post Office Building. From Cornavin, walk 5min. toward the Pont du Mont-Blanc. Staff books hotel rooms for a 5SFr fee, leads walking tours, and offers free city maps. Open July-Aug. daily 9am-6pm; Sept.-June M-Sa 9am-6pm.

Consulates: Australia, chemin des Fins 2 (☎799 91 00). **Canada,** av. de l'Ariana 5 (☎919 92 00). **New Zealand,** chemin des Fins 2 (☎929 03 50). **UK,** r. de Vermont 37 (☎918 24 26). **US,** r. Versonnex 5 (☎840 51 60, recorded info 840 51 61).

Currency Exchange: ATMs offer the best rates. **Gare Cornavin** has good rates with no commission on traveler's checks, makes cash advances on credit cards (min. 200SFr), and arranges **Western Union** transfers. Open M-Sa 7am-7:40pm, Su 9:15am-6pm.

GLBT Services: Diologai, r. de la Navigation 11-13 (☎906 40 40). From Gare Cornavin, turn left on r. de Lausanne, and turn right onto r. de la Navigation. Resource with programs from support groups to outdoor activities. Mostly male, but women welcome.

Emergency: Police: ☎117. **Ambulance:** ☎144. **Fire:** ☎118.

Medical Assistance: Hôpital Cantonal, r. Micheli-du-Crest 24 (☎372 33 11). Bus #1 or 5 or tram #12. Door #2 is for emergency care, door #3 for consultations. For info on walk-in clinics, contact the **Association des Médecins** (☎320 84 20).

Internet Access: Point 6, r. de Vieux-Billard 7a, off r. des Bains (☎800 26 00). 5SFr per hr. Open daily noon-midnight. **Connections Net World,** r. de Monthoux 58. 3SFr per 30min., 5SFr per hr. Copier available. Open M-Sa 9:30am-2:30am, Su 1pm-2am.

Post Office: Poste Centrale, r. de Mont-Blanc 18, 1 block from Gare Cornavin. Open M-F 7:30am-6pm, Sa 8:30am-noon. Address mail to be held as follows: First name SUR-NAME, *Poste Restante,* Genève 1 Mont-Blanc, CH-1211, Geneva, SWITZERLAND. **Postal Code:** CH-1211.

⌐ ACCOMMODATIONS

The indispensable *Info Jeunes* lists about 50 budget options, and the tourist office publishes *Budget Hotels,* which stretches the definition to 120SFr per person. Even for short stays, reservations are a must.

City Hostel Geneva, r. Ferrier 2 (☎901 15 00). TV room and kitchen. Internet 8SFr per hr. Sheets 3.50SFr. Reception daily 7:30am-noon and 1pm-midnight. Check-out 10am. Single-sex dorms 28SFr; singles 58SFr; doubles 85SFr. MC/V. ❷

Hôme St-Pierre, Cour St-Pierre 4 (☎310 37 07; info@stpierre.ch). Take bus #5 to pl. Neuve or walk from the station. Be aware, though, that a church bell next door rings every 15min. Breakfast M-Sa 7SFr. Reception M-Sa 9am-noon and 4-8pm, Su 9am-noon. Dorms 23SFr; singles 36-45SFr; doubles 50-60SFr. MC/V. ❸

Cité Bleu Universitaire, av. Miremont 46 (☎839 22 11). Take bus #3 (dir.: Crets-de-Champel) from the station to the last stop. TV rooms, restaurant, disco (Th and Sa, free to guests), and a small grocery store. Hall showers. Check-out 10am. Dorm lockout 11am-6pm. Dorm curfew 11pm. Dorms (July-Sept. only) 22SFr; singles 55SFr; doubles 84SFr; studios with kitchenette and bathroom 75SFr. ❷

Hôtel de la Cloche, r. de la Cloche 6 (☎732 94 81), off quai du Mont-Blanc in a converted mansion. Breakfast included. Reception daily 8am-10pm. Singles 50-70SFr; doubles 85-95SFr; triples 110-130SFr; quads 140SFr. AmEx/MC/V. ❹

Camping Pointe-à-la-Bise, chemin de la Bise (☎752 12 96). Take bus #8 to Rive, then bus E north to Bise and walk 10min. to the lake. Open Apr.-Sept. 6.20SFr per person, 9SFr per site. No tents provided. Beds 15SFr. 4-person bungalows 60SFr. ❶

🍴 FOOD

You can find anything from sushi to paella in Geneva, but you may need a banker's salary to foot the bill. Do-it-yourselfers can pick up basics at *boulangeries*, *pâtisseries*, or at the ubiquitous supermarkets. Many supermarkets also have attached cafeterias; try the **Co-op** on the corner of r. du Commerce and r. du Rhône, in the Centre Rhône Fusterie. In the **Les Paquis** area, bordered by the r. de Lausanne and Gare Cornavin on one side and the Quais Mont-Blanc and Wilson on the other, are a variety of relatively cheap ethnic foods. Around **pl. du Cirque** and **plaine de Plain-palais** are cheap, student-oriented tea rooms. To the south, the neighborhood of **Carouge** is known for its cozy pizzerias and funky brasseries.

▧ **Chocolats Micheli,** r. Micheli-du-Crest 1 (☎329 90 06). Take tram #13 to Plainpalais and walk up bd. des Philosophes until it intersects r. Micheli-du-Crest. Confectionery masterpieces abound in this homey cafe. Open Tu-F 8am-7pm, Sa 8am-5pm. MC/V. ❶

Restaurant Manora, r. de Cornavin 4, to the right of the station in the Placette department store. This huge self-serve restaurant has a varied selection and free water (rare in Switzerland). Entrees from 8SFr. Open M-Sa 7:30am-9:30pm, Su 9am-9:30pm. ❶

Le Rozzel, Grand-Rue 18. Take bus #5 to pl. Neuve, then walk up the hill past the cathedral on r. Jean-Calvin to Grand-Rue. Savory crepes 4-18SFr. Sweet crepes 5-9SFr. Open M 7am-4pm, Tu-W 7am-7pm, Th-F 7am-10pm, Sa 9am-10pm. AmEx/MC/V. ❷

La Crise, r. de Chantepoulet 13. Small but popular snack bar dishes and tasty quiches and soups at reasonable prices. Open M-F 6am-3pm and 5-8pm, Sa 6am-3pm. ❷

Les Brasseurs, pl. Cornavin 20. Go left from the station. Serves *flammeküchen,* an Alsatian specialty similar to pizza but topped with cream and onions (11.60-23SFr), and home-brewed towers of beer (31SFr for 2L). Open M-W 11am-1am, Th-Sa 11am-2am, Su 5pm-1am. Kitchen open 11:30am-2pm and 6-10:45pm. AmEx/MC/V. ❸

👁 SIGHTS

The city's most interesting historical sites are in a dense, easily walkable area. The tourist office offers 2hr. walking tours. (Mid-June to Sept. M-Sa 10am; Oct. to mid-June Sa 10am. 12SFr, students and seniors 8SFr.)

SAMICHLAUS IS COMING...FOR YOU!

December 5 means one thing for naughty children across Switzerland: a day of reckoning. On this day, Samichlaus (St. Nicholas) parades through the streets, stopping for a visit at each house along the way. In snowy mountain towns, sleighs bedecked with festive decorations bear the magical man, while a walk on foot must suffice in lower regions. As night falls, children frantically tidy themselves up in order to impress their visitor; after all, they have more than just presents at stake here.

Legend (kept alive by aggravated parents) has it that Samichlaus and his helpers cart disobedient children off to the Black Forest for a year of unspeakable horrors. Children tremble to hear Samichlaus's heavy knock on the door, and stand wide-eyed as he recounts the worst of their capers for the year. It seems that not a thing escapes the watchful eye of this fear-inducing man. (Unbeknownst to the youngsters, the parents hand the visitor a list of their little ones' transgressions for the year when they usher him into the house.) The Black Forest looms closer and closer as the guest recounts mischief after mischief. Luckily, the visit ends in treats all around, and, much to their parents' dismay, the children most likely return to their old dreadful habits...that is, until December 5 rolls around again.

VIEILLE VILLE. From 1536 to 1564, Calvin preached at the **Cathédrale de St-Pierre.** *(Open June-Sept. daily 9am-7pm; Oct.-May M-Sa 10am-noon and 2-5pm, Su 11am-12:30pm and 1:30-5pm. Tower 3SFr.)* Ruins, including a Roman sanctuary and a 4th-century basilica, rest in an **archaeological site** below the cathedral. *(Open June-Sept. Tu-Sa 11am–5pm, Su 10am-5pm; Oct.-May Tu-Sa 2-5pm, Su 10am-noon and 2-5pm. 5SFr, students 3SFr.)* Across the street is the **Hôtel de Ville** (town hall), where world leaders met on August 22, 1864 for the Geneva Convention, the results of which still govern war conduct today. The **Grand-Rue,** which begins at the Hôtel de Ville, is lined with medieval workshops and 18th-century mansions; plaques commemorate famous residents like Jean-Jacques Rousseau, who was born at #40. Below the cathedral, along r. de la Croix-Rouge, the **Parc des Bastions** stretches from pl. Neuve to pl. des Philosophes and includes **Le Mur des Réformateurs** (Reformers' Wall), a sprawling collection of bas-relief figures of the Reformers. The park's center walkway leads to the ▧**Petit-Palais,** Terrasse St-Victor 2, a beautiful mansion containing art by Chagall, Gauguin, Picasso, and Renoir. *(Bus #36 to Petit Palais or #1, 3, or 5 to Claparède. Open M-F 10am-6pm, Sa-Su 10am-5pm. 10SFr, students 5SFr.)*

WATERFRONT. As you descend from the cathedral to the lake, medieval lanes give way to wide quais. Down quai Gustave Ador, the **Jet d'Eau,** Europe's highest fountain, spews a 7-ton plume of water 134m into the air. The **floral clock** in the **Jardin Anglais** pays homage to Geneva's watch industry. On the northern shore, locals head to the beach at **Pâquis Plage,** quai du Mont-Blanc 30. *(Open 9am-8:30pm. 2SFr.)*

INTERNATIONAL HILL. The International Red Cross building contains the moving ▧**International Red Cross and Red Crescent Museum,** Av. de la Paix 17. *(Bus #8 or F to Appia or bus V or Z to Ariana. Open M and W-Su 10am-5pm. 10SFr, students 5SFr.)* The nearby European headquarters of the **United Nations** is in the same building that sheltered the now-defunct League of Nations. The constant traffic of international diplomats (often in handsome non-Western dress) provides more excitement than the dull guided tour. *(Open July-Aug. daily 10am-5pm; Apr.-June and Sept.-Oct. daily 10am-noon and 2-4pm; Nov.-Mar. M-F 10am-noon and 2-4pm. 8.50SFr, seniors and students 6.50SFr.)*

🎵 🍸 ENTERTAINMENT AND NIGHTLIFE

Genève Agenda, available at the tourist office, is your guide to fun, with event listings ranging from major festivals to movies (be warned—a movie runs about 16SFr). In July and August, the **Cinelac** turns Genève Plage into an open-air cinema screening mostly American films. Free **jazz concerts** take place in July and August in Parc de la Grange. Geneva hosts the biggest celebration of **American Independence Day** outside the US (July 4), and the **Fêtes de Genève** in early August fills the city with international music and fireworks. The best party is **L'Escalade** in early December, which commemorates the repulsion of invading Savoyard troops.

   Place Bourg-de-Four, in the *vieille ville* below the cathedral, attracts students and professionals to its charming terraces and old-world atmosphere. **Place du Molard,** on the right bank by the pont du Mont-Blanc, offers terrace cafes and big, loud bars and clubs. **Les Paquis,** near Gare Cornavin and pl. de la Navigation, is the city's red-light district, but it also has a wide array of rowdy, low-lit bars, many with an ethnic flavor. **Carouge,** across the river Arve, is a student-friendly locus of nightlife activity. Generations of students have eaten at the famous ▧**La Clémence,** pl. du Bourg-de-Four 20. (Open M-Th 7am-12:30am, F-Sa 7am-1:30am.)

LAUSANNE   ☏ 021

The unique museums, distinctive neighborhoods, and lazy Lac Léman waterfront of Lausanne (pop. 125,000) make it well worth a stay. In the *vieille ville,* two flights of medieval stairs lead to the Gothic **Cathédrale.** (Open July to mid-Sept. M-F 7am-7pm, Sa-Su 8am-7pm; mid-Sept. to June daily 8am-5:30pm.) Below the cathedral is the **Hôtel de Ville,** on pl. de la Palud, the meeting point for guided tours of the town. (Tours M-Sa 10am and 3pm. 10SFr, students free.) The **⑤Collection de l'Art Brut,** av. Bergières 11, is filled with disturbing sculptures, drawings, and paintings by artists on the fringe—institutionalized schizophrenics, uneducated peasants, and convicted criminals. Take bus #2 or 3 to Jomini. (Open July-Aug. daily 11am-6pm; Sept.-June Tu-F 11am-1pm and 2-6pm, Sa-Su 11am-6pm. 6SFr, students 4SFr.) The **Musée Olympique,** Quai d'Ouchy 1, is a high-tech shrine to modern Olympians with an extensive video collection, allowing visitors to relive almost any moment of the games. Take bus #2 to Ouchy. (Open M-W and F-Su 9am-6pm, Th 9am-8pm; Oct.-Apr. closed M. 14SFr, students 9SFr.) In Ouchy, several booths along quai de Belgique and pl. de la Navigation rent **pedal boats** (10SFr per 30min.) and offer **water skiing** or **wake boarding** (30SFr per 15min.) on Lake Léman.

Trains leave from pl. de la Gare 9 for: Basel (2½hr., every hr. 5:25am-11:25pm, 64SFr); Geneva (50min., every 20min. 4:55am-12:45am, 19SFr); Montreux (20min., every 30min. 5:25am-2:25am, 10SFr); Paris (4hr., 4 per day 7:35am-5:50pm, 71SFr); and Zurich (2½hr., 3 per hr. 5:25am-10:25pm, 65SFr). The **tourist office** in the train station reserves rooms. (☎613 73 73. Open daily 9am-7pm.) Home to the world's oldest hotel school, Lausanne has a well-deserved reputation for service-industry excellence. **⑤Lausanne Guesthouse & Backpacker ❷,** chemin des Epinettes 4, is conveniently located and has comfortable rooms. Head left and downhill out of the station on W. Fraisse; take the first right on chemin des Epinettes. (☎601 80 00. Sheets for dorms 5SFr. 4-bed dorms 34SFr; singles 81SFr, with bathroom 89SFr; doubles 88SFr/100SFr. MC/V.) Restaurants, cafes, and bars cluster around pl. **St-François** and the *vieille ville,* while *boulangeries* sell cheap sandwiches on every street and grocery stores abound. Stop by **Le Barbare ❶,** Escaliers du Marché 27, for a sandwich (5.50SFr), omelette (7.50-10SFr), or pizza (12-16SFr) while staying on budget. (☎312 21 32. Open M-Sa 8:30am-midnight.)

MONTREUX
☎021

Montreux (pop. 22,500) is a resort town past its Jazz Age heyday. Fortunately, the music still swings; world-famous for drawing and discovering exceptional talent, the **⑤Montreux Jazz Festival** erupts for 15 days starting the first Friday of July. (www.montreuxjazz.com. Tickets 49-79SFr.) Icons Neil Young, Bob Dylan, Paul Simon, and Miles Davis have all played here. If you can't get tickets, come anyway for **Montreux Jazz Under the Sky,** 500 hours of free, open-air concerts. The **Château de Chillon,** a medieval island fortress, is one of Switzerland's most visited attractions. Take the CGN **ferry** (13.80SFr) or **bus** #1 (2.80SFr) to Chillon. (Open daily Apr.-Sept. 9am-6pm; Mar. and Oct. 9:30am-5pm; Nov.-Feb. 10am-4pm. 9SFr, students and seniors 7SFr.)

Trains leave the station on av. des Alpes for: Bern (1½hr., 2 per hr. 5:30am-11pm, 37SFr); Geneva (1hr., 2 per hr. 5:30am-11:30pm, 26SFr); and Lausanne (20min., 3-5 per hr. 5:25am-midnight, 9.80SFr). Descend the stairs opposite the station, head left on Grand Rue for 5-10min., and look to the right for the **tourist office,** pl. du Débarcadère. (☎962 84 84. Open mid-June to mid-Sept. M-F 9am-6pm, Sa-Su 10am-5pm; late Sept. to early June M-F 8:30am-5pm, Sa-Su 10am-3pm.) **⑤Riviera Lodge ❷,** pl. du Marché 5, in the neighboring town of Vevey, is worth the commute. Take bus #1 to Vevey (20min., every 10min., 2.80SFr). Head away from the train station on the main road to the square. (☎923 80 40. Sheets 5SFr. Laundry 7SFr. Internet 3SFr per 15min. Reception daily 8am-noon and 5-8pm. Call ahead if arriving late. Dorms 24SFr; doubles 80SFr. MC/V.) To get to **Hôtel Pension Wilhelm ❸,** r. du Marché 13-15, turn left on ave. des Alpes from the Montreux station, walk uphill., and go left on r. du Marché. (☎963 14 31. Breakfast included. Open Mar.-Sept. Singles 60SFr; with shower 70SFr; doubles 100SFr/120SFr.) **Babette's ❷,** Grand Rue 60, downstairs from the station and to the left, serves sweet (7-10SFr) and savory (11-14SFr) crepes. (Open daily 7am-7pm.) There's a **Co-op** supermarket at Grand Rue 80. (Open M-F 8am-12:15pm and 2-6:30pm, Sa 8am-5pm.) **Postal Code:** CH-1820.

NEUCHÂTEL ☎ 032

Alexandre Dumas once said that Neuchâtel (pop. 164,000) appeared to be carved out of butter. He was referring to its yellow stone architecture, but his comment could easily be taken as a reference to the rich treats in its famous *pâtisseries*. The old town centers around **place des Halles,** a block from **place Pury,** the hub of every bus line. From pl. des Halles, turn left onto r. de Château and climb the stairs on the right to reach **Collégiale church** and the **chateau** that gives the town its name. (Church open daily Apr.-Sept. 9am-8pm; Oct.-Mar. 9am-6:30pm.) Entrance to the chateau is available only through a free tour. (1 per hr. Apr.-Sept. M-F 10am-noon and 2-4pm, Sa 10-11am and 2-4pm, Su 2-4pm.) The nearby **Tour des Prisons** (Prison Tower), on r. Jeanne-Hochberg, has a prime view. (Open daily Apr.-Sept. 8am-6pm. 1SFr.) The **Musée d'Histoire Naturelle,** off r. de l'Hôpital, is an innovative version of the standard natural history museum. Turn right from pl. des Halles onto Croix du Marché, which becomes r. de l'Hôpital. (Open Tu-Su 10am-6pm. 6SFr, students 3SFr.) The **Musée des Beaux Arts et d'Histoire,** esplanade Léopold-Robert 1, houses an eclectic collection of paintings, weapons, and textiles. (Open June-Mar. Tu-Su 10am-6pm; Apr.-May daily 10am-6pm. 7SFr, students 4SFr. W free.)

Trains run to: Basel (1¾hr., every hr. 5:30am-midnight, 34SFr); Bern (45min., every hr. 5:15am-11:20pm, 18SFr); and Geneva (1½hr., every hr. 6am-11:00pm, 35-40SFr). An underground **tram** runs from the station to the shore area, where you can catch bus #1 to pl. Pury and the **tourist office,** in the same building as the post office. (☎889 68 90. Open July-Aug. M-F 9am-6:30pm, Sa 9am-4pm, Su 10am-4pm; Sept.-May M-F 9am-noon and 1:30-5:30pm, Sa 9am-noon.) From the underground tram exit, walk a block toward the city center on av. du Premier-Mars and turn left onto r. Pourtalès to reach **Hôtel des Arts ❹,** r. Pourtalès 3. Most rooms have TV; all have phone. (☎727 61 61. Breakfast included. Reception 24hr. Singles 87SFr, with bath 98-126SFr; doubles 112SFr/140-166SFr. AmEx/MC/V.) At **A.R. Knecht Boulangerie et Pâtisserie ❶,** on the corner of pl. des Halles and r. du Coq d'Inde, locals munch croissants stuffed with ham (3SFr), fruit tarts (3.50SFr), and *pain noix* (bread with nuts; 3SFr) while enjoying a vibrant atmosphere. (Open Tu-Sa 6am-6:30pm.) **Migros,** r. de l'Hôpital 12, sells groceries. (Open M-W 8am-6:30pm, Th 8am-10pm, F 7:30am-6:30pm, Sa 7:30am-7pm.) **Postal Code:** CH-2001.

ITALIAN SWITZERLAND

Ever since Switzerland won Ticino, the only Italian-speaking Swiss canton, from Italy in 1512, the region has been renowned for its mix of Swiss efficiency and Italian *dolce vita*. It's no wonder the rest of Switzerland vacations here among jasmine-laced villas painted in the vibrant colors of Italian gelato.

LUGANO ☎ 091

Set in a valley between two mountains, Lugano (pop. 114,000) draws plenty of visitors with its seamless blend of religious beauty, artistic flair, and natural spectacle. The frescoes of the 16th-century **Cattedrale San Lorenzo,** just south of the train station, are still vivid despite their advanced age. The most spectacular fresco in town, however, is the gargantuan *Crucifixion* in the **Chiesa Santa Maria degli Angiuli,** to the right of the tourist office. Armed with topographic maps and trail guides (sold at the tourist office), **hikers** can tackle the rewarding Monte Boglio (5hr.), while tamer soles can reach the peaks of Monte Brè (933m) and Monte San

Salvatore (912m) by **funicular**. Alpine guides at the **ASBEST Adventure Company**, V. Basilea 28 (☎966 11 14), offer everything from snowshoeing and skiing (full-day 90SFr) to paragliding (165SFr) and canyoning (from 90SFr).

Trains leave p. della Stazione for: Locarno (1hr., every 30min., 16.60SFr); Milan (45min., 21SFr); and Zurich (3hr., 60SFr). The **tourist office** is across from the ferry station at the corner of P. Rezzonico. (☎913 32 32. Open Apr.-Oct. M-F 9am-7pm, Sa 9am-5pm, Su 10am-3pm; Nov.-Mar. M-F 9am-noon and 1-5pm.) ▧**Hotel & Backpackers Montarina ❷**, V. Montarina 1, is a palm-tree-surrounded hostel with a pool, kitchen, and terrace. (☎966 72 72. Laundry 4SFr. Reception daily 8am-10:30pm. Open Mar.-Oct. Dorms 25SFr; singles 70SFr, with bath 80SFr; doubles 100SFr/ 120SFr.) The **Migros** supermarket, V. Pretoria 15, also has a food court. (Open M-W and F 8am-6:30pm, Th 8am-9pm, Sa 7:30am-5pm.) **Postal Code:** CH-6900.

LOCARNO   ☎091

A Swiss vacation spot on the shores of Lago Maggiore, Locarno (pop. 30,000) gets over 2200 hours of sunlight per year—more than anywhere else in Switzerland. For centuries, visitors have journeyed here solely to see the church of **Madonna del Sasso** (Madonna of the Rock), founded in 1487. A 20min. walk up the Via al Sasso leads to the top, passing life-sized wooden statues along the way. Hundreds of heart-shaped medallions on the church walls commemorate acts of Mary's intervention in the lives of worshippers who have journeyed here. (Grounds open daily 6:30am-7pm.) Each summer (Aug. 3-13 in 2005), Locarno swells with pilgrims of a different sort; its world-famous **film festival** draws over 150,000 annually.

Trains run from P. Stazione to: Lucerne (2½hr., every 30min., 54SFr); Lugano (1hr., every 30min., 17SFr); and Milan (2hr., every hr., 34SFr) via Bellinzona. The **tourist office**, on P. Grande in the *kursaal* (casino), makes hotel reservations. (☎791 00 91. Open Apr.-Oct. M-F 9am-6pm, Sa 10am-6pm, Su 10am-1:30pm and 2:30-5pm; Nov.-Mar. closed Su.) To reach **Pensione Città Vecchia ❷**, V. Toretta 13, turn right onto V. Toretta from P. Grande. (☎751 45 54. Breakfast included. Check-in 1-6pm. Dorms 29-40SFr; doubles 70-80SFr; triples 120SFr.) The rooms of **Garni Sempione ❸**, V. Rusca 6, are set around an enclosed courtyard. To reach the hotel, walk to the end of P. Grande, turn right onto v. della Motta, and take the left fork onto V. Rusca. (☎751 30 64. Breakfast included. Singles 60SFr, with shower 65SFr; doubles 100SFr/120SFr; triples 150/165SFr. Prices drop in winter. AmEx/MC/V.) Left of the station, **Ristorante Manora ❶**, V. della Stazione 1, offers cheap, self-service dining. (Salad bar 4.50-10SFr. Pasta buffet 8.50-10SFr. Open Nov.-Feb. M-Sa 7:30am-9pm, Su 8am-9pm; Mar.-Oct. M-Sa 7:30am-10pm, Su 8am-9pm.) Get groceries at the **Aperto** in the station. (Open daily 6am-10pm.) **Postal Code:** CH-6600.

UKRAINE (УКРАЇНА)

"Ukraine" literally means "borderland," and the country has occupied this precarious position for most of its history. Vast and fertile, perpetually tempting to invaders, Ukraine is now poised between overbearing Russia to the east and a bloc of *nouveau riche* countries to the west. With no beaten path from which to stray, travelers are rewarded by fascinating, uncrowded museums, age-old castles, and the magnificent, spirited Black Sea coast.

DISCOVER UKRAINE

Start any trip to Ukraine in **Kyiv** (p. 1050). Once the seat of medieval Rus, the modern city's parks and riverside vistas form a backdrop to its mix of urban bustle and provincial charm. Lesser-known **Lviv** (p. 1053), to the west, is a crucible for Ukrainian culture. Unfortunately for the Russians, no one objected when Khrushchev gave **Yalta** (p. 1055) to their neighbor: they lost a seaside resort city. West of Yalta is storied **Odessa** (p. 1054), a lively port once home to Babel and Pushkin.

ESSENTIALS

WHEN TO GO

The best time to visit is between May and September, when it's warmer. Spring and fall can be unpredictable; flurries are always possible. Winter is bitterly cold.

DOCUMENTS AND FORMALITIES

VISAS. Visas are required of all travelers to Ukraine. Citizens of Australia and New Zealand also require an **invitation.** All visas are valid for three months. Without rush service, single-entry visas cost US$100, double-entry US$110, multiple-entry US$165. Transit visas cost US$10, not including the US$100 processing fee. Fees are waived for

children under 16 years of age and for American students with proper documents. Visas cannot be obtained on the border; they must be applied for in advance. **Diane Sadovnikov,** a former missionary living and working in Ukraine, arranges invitations (US\$30). **Janna Belousova,** of Eugenia Travel in Odessa, can help with invitations (☎380 182 21 85 83; www.eugeniatravel.com). Janna can arrange for you to obtain a two-week visa upon arrival at Kyiv's Borispil Airport, Odessa Airport, or Simferopol Airport. When proceeding through **customs** you will be required to declare all jewelry and foreign currency (including traveler's checks). To bring Ukrainian currency into Ukraine, it is necessary to have a customs declaration stating that the amount brought into the country is no more than that originally brought out. Visa extensions can be arranged through the **Offices of Visas and Registration** (OVIR; ОВИР), in Kyiv at blv. Tarasa Shevchenka 34 (Тараса Шевченка; ☎044 224 9051), and in police stations in smaller cities. Do not lose the visa supplement given to you on arrival; it is required to leave the country. Carry your passport and visa at all times.

EMBASSIES AND CONSULATES. All foreign embassies are in Kyiv (p. 1050). Ukrainian embassies at home include: **Australia,** Suite 12:1, St. George Centre, 60 Marcus Clarke St., Canberra ACT 2601 (☎02 6230 5789; www.ukremb.info); **Canada,** 331 Metcalfe St., Ottawa, ON K2P 1S3 (☎613-230-8015; www.infoukes.com/ukremb); **UK,** Ground Floor, 78 Kensington Park Rd., London W11 2PL (☎020 7243 8923; www.ukremb.org.uk); **US,** 3350 M St. NW, Washington, D.C. 20007 (☎202-333-0606; www.ukremb.com).

TRANSPORTATION

BY PLANE. Ukraine International Airlines (US ☎800-876-0114, in Kyiv 044 461 5050; www.ukraine-international.com/eng) flies to Kyiv, Lviv, and Odessa from several European capitals. Other international carriers also have flights to Kyiv.

BY TRAIN. Trains run frequently from Ukraine's neighboring countries, and are the best way to travel. Prepare for a two-hour stop at the border, and have your ticket and ID ready at boarding. Most domestic trains have three classes: *Platzkart, coupé,* and *SV.* Paying the extra \$2 for *coupé* is usually more than worth it.

BY BUS. Buses cost about the same as trains, but are often much shabbier. Modern **AutoLux** (АвтоЛюкс) buses are an exception. Schedules are generally reliable, but low demand can cause cancellations. Buy tickets at the *kasa* (box office); if they are sold out, try the driver himself, who might be able to find an extra seat.

BY TAXI AND BY THUMB. In cities, private minibuses called *marshrutki* run along the same routes as public transportation; they are faster but slightly more expensive. **Taxi** drivers may try to rip off foreigners, so negotiate the price beforehand. **Hitchhiking** is uncommon; those who do hold a sign with their destination. *Let's Go* does not recommend hitchhiking.

TOURIST SERVICES AND MONEY

EMERGENCY	Police: ☎02. Ambulance: ☎03. Fire: ☎01.

TOURIST OFFICES. Although there is no state-run tourist office, local travel agencies often have English-speaking staff. Remnants of the Soviet-era **Intourist** can be found in some hotels, but their employees tend not to speak English.

MONEY. Since 1996, Ukraine's official currency has been the **hryvnia** (гривна; hv; plural *hryvny*). **Obmin Valyut** (Обмін Валют) kiosks in the center of most cities change money at the best rates; fancier hotel lobbies usually exchange US dollars at lousy rates. Western Union offices and **ATMs** are widespread. Most banks will give Visa and MasterCard cash advances for large commissions. Illegitimate private money changers often lurk near legitimate kiosks; it is illegal to transact with them. Locals may not usually leave **tips,** but most expats give 10%. Accommodations in Ukraine average €10-20; cheaper meals run from €5-7.

HRYVNY (HV)		
AUS$1 = 2.93HV	1HV = AUS$0.34
CDN$1 = 3.42HV	1HV = CDN$0.29
EUR€1 = 5.24HV	1HV = EUR€0.19
NZ$1 = 2.49HV	1HV = NZ$0.40
UK£1 = 8.26HV	1HV = UK£0.12
US$1 = 5.33HV	1HV = US$0.19

COMMUNICATION

PHONE CODES	**Country code: 380. International dialing prefix: 810.** From outside Ukraine, dial int'l dialing prefix (see inside back cover) + 380 + city code + local number.

TELEPHONES AND INTERNET. To call internationally, use a **Utel** phone card, available at Utel outlets. Central telephone offices also have phone services; give a clerk an estimate of the call's duration and your money. Ukrainian international calling cards are available (15hv for 30min.). Local calls from gray pay phones generally cost 10-30hv. Dialing ☎8 192 reaches an English-speaking operator. International access codes include **AT&T Direct** (☎8 10 011), **British Telecom** (☎8 10 044 1), **Canada Direct** (☎8 10 017), **MCI WorldPhone** (☎8 10 013), and **Sprint** (☎8 100 15 or 8 100 16). Wait for a second dial tone after entering the first "8." Try post offices for **email,** the best way to communicate internationally.

MAIL. Mail is cheap and reliable, taking 10 to 14 days to reach North America. Sending a letter internationally costs about 2-3hv. Pre-stamped envelopes, available at the post office, expedite the sending of letters. Address mail to be held *Poste Restante* (До Запитание) according to the following example: First name SUR-NAME, До Запитание, Ul. Sadovaya 10, 01 001 Odessa, UKRAINE.

LANGUAGES. It can be hard to get by without knowing Ukrainian or Russian. In Kyiv, Odessa, and the Crimea, Russian is more common than Ukrainian, though all official signs are in Ukrainian. In Transcarpathia Ukrainian is preferred.

ACCOMMODATIONS AND FOOD

UKRAINE	❶	❷	❸	❹	❺
ACCOMMODATIONS	under 55hv	55-105hv	106-265hv	266-480hv	over 480hv
FOOD	under 11hv	11-27hv	28-54hv	55-105hv	over 105hv

No youth hostels exist in Ukraine, and budget accommodations are usually in unrenovated Soviet-era buildings. **Hotels** that accept foreigners often charge them many times more than they charge natives. Room prices in Kyiv are stratospheric; elsewhere singles may run from 5 to 90hv. Prices do not always correspond to luxury; standard amenities include TVs, phones, and refrigerators. Guests receive a *vizitka* (визитка; hotel card) to show to the hall monitor (дежурная; *dezhurnaya*) to get a key; surrender it upon leaving the building. In certain places, women lodging alone may be mistaken for prostitutes. Valuables should never be left unattended; the reception will sometimes provide access to a safe. Hot water is a rarity. **Private rooms** can be arranged through overseas agencies or bargained for at the train station. Most cities have a **campground;** it is illegal to camp outside of designated areas, and enforcement is merciless.

After fancy restaurants, Ukraine offers little other than **stolovayas** (cafeterias), dying bastions of cheap, hot food. Old *stolovaya* food can knock you out of commission for hours, but a good *stolovaya* meal is a triumph of the human spirit. Vegetarians can create their own meals from potatoes, mushrooms, and cabbage sold at markets; bring your own bag. State food stores are classified by content: *hastronom* (гастроном) sell packaged goods; *moloko* (молоко) milk products; *ovochi-frukty* (овочі-фрукты) fruits and vegetables; *myaso* (мясо) meat; *hlib* (хліб) bread; *kolbasy* (колбаси) sausage; and *ryba* (риба) fish. Tea is a popular national drink, as is the beer-like *kvas*.

SAFETY AND SECURITY

HEALTH AND EMERGENCIES. Ukraine's limited hospital facilities do not meet Western standards; patients may be required to supply their own basic supplies, like bandages. Medical insurance is necessary to receive health care, but foreigners should nonetheless be prepared to front the bill themselves. National embassies can find adequate care, though at a cost. Medical evacuations to Western nations can cost anywhere from US$25,000-50,000. **Water** is unreliable and hard to find in bottled form; either boil what flows from the tap or learn to love brushing your teeth with soda water. Fresh produce is generally safe, although storage conditions and pesticides make thorough washing imperative. Meat should be examined carefully and cooked thoroughly. Embassy officials say that **Chernobyl**-related radiation poses minimal risk to short-term travelers, but the region should be given a wide berth. Public **toilets** are disgusting; pay toilets (платній; *platnyi*) are cleaner and sometimes have toilet paper, but bring your own just in case. **Pharmacies** are common and carry basic Western products. At the irregular kiosk, travelers can find sanitary napkins (гігієнічні пакети; *hihienchni paketi*), condoms (презервативи; *prezervativy*), and tampons (прокладки; *prokladki*).

SAFETY AND SPECIAL CONCERNS. While Ukraine is neither violent nor politically volatile, it is poor; it is wise to **register** with your embassy upon arrival. Pickpocketing and wallet scams are the most common crimes, but travelers have been assaulted or robbed at gunpoint. Accepting drinks from strangers can result in your being drugged and robbed. Never exchange money on the street, and beware that credit card and ATM fraud are endemic. Take note that drivers do not stop for pedestrians. **Women** traveling alone should expect to be addressed by men almost anywhere, whether on the street or in restaurants (where Ukrainian women rarely eat alone). They may request to ride in female-only compartments during long train rides. Although non-Caucasians may experience **discrimination,** profiling problems mostly come from the militia, which often stops persons of non-Slavic ethnicity. Discretion is advised for **GLBT** travelers, as homosexuality is rarely accepted.

HOLIDAYS

New Year's (Jan. 1-2); Orthodox Christmas (Jan. 7); Orthodox New Year (Jan. 14); Women's Day (Mar. 8); Good Friday (Apr. 29); Easter (May 1); Labor Day (May 1-2); Victory Day (May 9); Holy Trinity (June 19); Constitution Day (June 28); Independence Day (Aug. 24).

FACTS AND FIGURES: UKRAINE	
Official Name: Ukraine.	**Land Area:** 603,700 sq. km.
Capital: Kyiv.	**Time Zone:** GMT +2.
Major cities: Kyiv, Lviv, Odessa.	**Languages:** Ukrainian, Russian, Tatar.
Population: 47,732,000.	**Religions:** Ukrainian Orthodox (85%).

UKRAINE

KYIV (КИЇВ) ☎ 8044

Straddling the wide Dniper River and layered with hills, Kyiv (pop. 2,600,000) greets visitors with golden-domed churches, winding streets, and a sprawling old town. The cradle of Slavic-Orthodox culture and once the USSR's third-largest city, Kyiv has been struggling to adjust to its new role as the capital of an independent and nationalist Ukraine. Recovery from the Soviet era doesn't happen overnight, but extensive remodeling projects promise great changes to come.

⌐ TRANSPORTATION

Flights: Boryspil International Airport (Бориспіль; ☎296 72 43), 30km southeast of the capital. **Polit** (Політ; ☎296 73 67) sends buses every 30min.-1hr. to Ploscha Peremohi and the train station; buy tickets (10hv) onboard. Taxis downtown cost 70-100hv.

Trains: Kyiv-Pasazhyrskyy (Київ-Пасажирський), Vokzalna pl. (☎005). MR: Vokzalna (Вокзальна). Ticket counters in the main hall require passports. An **Advance-Ticket Office** is next to Hotel Express, blv. Shevchenka 38, up vul. Kominternu from the train station. Some travel agencies book tickets. To: **Bratislava** (18hr., 1 per day, 453hv); **Budapest** (24hr., 1 per day, 586hv); **Lviv** (10hr., 20 per day, 50hv); **Minsk** (13hr., 1 per day, 104hv); **Moscow** (17hr., 20 per day, 195hv); **Prague** (35hr., 1 per day, 832hv); **Odessa** (11hr., 5 per day, 40hv); **Warsaw** (17hr., 2 per day, 305hv).

Buses: Tsentralny Avtovokzal (Центральний Автовокзал), Moskovska pl. 3 (Московська; ☎265 04 30), 10min. from MB: Libidska. Turn right and then left out of the metro; take trolley #4 or walk 100m down the big highway and follow it 500m right.

Public Transportation: The 3 intersecting lines of the **metro**—blue (MB), green (MG), and red (MR)—cover the city center. Purchase blue tokens (0.50hv), good on all public transport, at the каса (*kasa*). "Вхід" (*vkhid*) indicates an entrance, "перехід" (*perekhid*) a walkway to another station, and "вихід у місто" (*vykhid u misto*) an exit onto the street. **Trolleys, buses,** and **marshrutki** (private vans) go where the metro doesn't. Bus tickets are sold at kiosks; punch your ticket onboard or face a 10hv fine. *Marshrutki* tickets (0.60-1hv) are sold onboard. Public transport runs 6am-midnight.

◢✦ 🔢 ORIENTATION AND PRACTICAL INFORMATION

Most attractions and services lie on the west bank of the Dniper River. Three metro stops from the train station is the main avenue **vulitsa Khreshchatyk** (Хрещатик; MR line). Today the center of Kyiv is vul. Khreshchatyk's fountained **Independence Square** (Майдан Незалежності; Maidan Nezalezhnosti; MB line).

Tourist Office: Kyiv still lacks official tourist services. Representatives of various agencies at the airport offer vouchers, excursion packages, hotel arrangements, tours, and other services. Try **Carlson Wagonlit Travel,** vul. Ivana Franka 34/33, 2nd fl. (☎238 61 56). Open M-F 9am-6pm. Or, head to **Yana Travel Group,** vul. Saksahanskoho 42 (Саксаганського; ☎246 62 13; www.yana.kiev.ua). Open M-F 9am-7pm, Sa 10am-5pm, Su 10am-3pm. Students and youth should try **STI Ukraine,** vul. Priorizna 18/1, #11 (☎490 59 60; www.sticom.ua). Open M-F 9am-9pm, Sa 10am-4pm.

Embassies: Australia, vul. Kominternu 18/137 (Комінтерну; ☎/fax 235 75 86). Open M-Th 10am-1pm. **Canada,** vul. Yaroslaviv Val 31 (Ярославів Вал; ☎464 11 44; fax 464 11 33). Open M-Th 8:30am-noon. **UK,** vul. Desyatynna 6 (Десятинна; ☎462 00 11; fax 462 00 13). Consular section at vul. Glybochytska 6 (Глибочицька; ☎494 34 00; fax 494 34 18). Open M-F 9am-noon. **US,** vul. Yu. Kotsyubynskoho 10 (Ю. Коцюбинського; ☎490 40 00; www.usinfo.usemb.kiev.ua). Consular section on vul.

Pymonenka (Пимоненка; ☎490 44 22; fax 216 33 93). From Maidan Nezalezhnosti, take trolley #16 or 18 for 4 stops. Walk down vul. Artema (Артема) until it curves to the right, then take the 1st right onto vul. Pymonenka. Call ahead. Open M-Th 9am-6pm.

Medical Assistance: Ambulance (☎03). The **American Medical Center,** vul. Berdycher-ska 1 (Бердичерска; ☎/fax 490 76 00; www.amcenters.com), has English-speaking doctors. Open 24hr. AmEx/MC/V.

Internet Access: Orbita (Орбіта), vul. Khreshchatyk 46, 2nd fl. (☎234 16 93). 6hv. per hr., unlimited use at night (11pm-8am) for 10hv. Ring bell after 11pm. Open 24hr. The main **post office** (see below) houses 2 Internet cafes. 10hv per hr. Pay in advance. Open M-Sa 8am-9pm, Su 9am-7pm.

Telephones: Myzhmiskyy Perehovornyy Punkt (Мижміський Переговорний Пункт), at the post office, or **Telefon-Telefaks** (Телефон-Телефакс), around the corner (enter on Khreshchatyk). Both open 24hr. **Public telephones** (Таксофон; *taksofon*) require cards, which are available at any post office. **English operator** (☎8192).

Post Office: Vul. Khreshchatyk 22 (☎228 11 67), by Independence Sq. *Poste Restante* at counters #29-30. Open M-Sa 8am-9pm, Su 9am-7pm. **Postal Code:** 01001.

ACCOMMODATIONS AND FOOD

Hotels in Kyiv tend to be expensive; the *Kyiv Post* (www.kyivpost.com) lists short-term apartment rentals and private rooms. People at train stations offer even cheaper rooms (from US$5). Another way to find budget lodging is through the commission-free telephone service **Okean-9.** (☎443 61 67. Open M-F 9am-5pm, Sa 9am-3pm.) **Hotel St. Petersburg** ❷ (Санкт-Петербург), bul. T. Shevchenka 4, has an ideal location just up the street from Bessarabska Square. Rooms without bath have reasonable prices. (☎229 73 64; s-peter@i.kiev.ua. Reserve ahead. Singles 73hv; doubles 182hv; triples 213hv. MC/V.) **Hotel Express** ❸ (Експрес), bul. Shevchenka 38/40, is straight up vul. Kominternu from the train station and has some clean, inexpensive rooms. (☎239 89 95; www.railwayukr.com. Internet 4hv per 30min. Train tickets sold next door. Shower 5hv. Singles 145hv; doubles 230hv.) The conveniently located rooms at **Hotel Druzhba** ❸, bul. Druzhby Narodiv 5 (Дружби Народів), have shower, phone, TV, and fridge. Turn left on bul. Druzhby Narodiv and walk 200m to the hotel. (MB: Lybidska (Либідська). ☎268 34 06; fax 268 33 87. Singles 190hv; doubles 342hv.) ◙**Taras** ❸ (Тарас), Tereshchen-kivska vul. 10, in the Taras Shevchenko Park, serves Ukrainian dishes amid beau-tiful decor. (☎235 21 32. Entrees 30-50hv. Open Sept.-May 10am-1am; June-Aug. 10am-2am. MC/V.) **OsteriaPantagruel** ❹, vul. Lysenko 1, has the best Italian food in Kyiv. (MG: Zoloti Vorota. ☎228 81 42. Pasta 44-95hv. English menu. Open daily 11am-11pm. MC/V.) In summer Pantagruel also manages a popular outdoor **terrace cafe** ❸ down the street, around the large fountain in front of Zoloti Vorota. (Open daily 10am-11pm. Cash only.) Inexpensive, cafeteria-style Ukrainian food is served at **Dva Gusya** ❶ (Два Гуся; Two Geese), vul. Khreshchatyk 42, upstairs in the *Gas-tronom* on the right side. (☎229 76 83. Entrees 3-8hv. Open daily 10am-10pm.)

SIGHTS

◙**KYIV-PECHERSKA MONASTERY.** Allot a full day for Kyiv's oldest and holiest religious site, the mysterious Kyiv-Pecherska Monastery (Киево-Печерська Лавра; Kyivo-Pecherska Lavra). Inside the complex are the **Refectory Church** and the 12th-century **Holy Trinity Gate Church,** as well as several **museums** and **caves** where monks lie mummified. The **Great Lavra Bell Tower** has views of the river and the churches' golden domes. *(MR: Arsenalna. Turn left out of the metro and walk 10min.*

down vul. Sichnevoho Povstaniya. Open daily May-Aug. 9am-7pm; Sept.-Apr. 9:30am-6pm. 10hv, students 5hv. English tours from 160hv, students from 80hv. Caves open daily May-Sept. 9am-5:30pm; Oct.-Apr. 9am-4:30pm. English tours from 60hv. Museums each 5-7hv, students 3hv.)

ST. SOPHIA MONASTERY. Once the religious center of Kyivan Rus, the St. Sophia Monastery complex is now the focal point of Ukrainian nationalism. Small wonder, for its golden onion domes, ornamented facades, and Byzantine mosaics make it one of Kyiv's main attractions. *(Vulitsa Volodymyrska. MG: Zoloti Vorota or trolley #16 from Maidan Nezalezhnasti. Grounds open daily 9am-7pm. 1hv. Museums open Apr.-Oct. daily 10am-6pm; Nov.-Mar. M-W and F-Su 10am-6pm. 11hv, students 4hv. English tour 40hv.)*

VULITSA KHRESHCHATYK AND ENVIRONS. Kyiv's spinal cord, vulitsa Khreshchatyk (Хрещатик), begins at the intersection with bul. Shevchenka and extends to **Independence Sq.** (Майдан Незалежності; Maidan Nezalezhnosti), which is full of fountains and covers an underground mall. **Khreshchaty Park,** past the silver **Friendship of the Peoples Arch,** contains a monument to Prince Volodymyr, the man who converted Kyivan Rus to Christianity. *(MR: Khreshchatyk; Хрещатик.)*

ANDRIYIVSKYY PATH AND THE PODIL DISTRICT. Full of cafes, vendors, and galleries, the cobblestone Andriyivskyy path (Андріївский узвіз; Andriyivskyy uzviz) can be reached by funicular from the subway or by walking from Mikhaylivska Sq. *(MB: Poshtova. Funicular operates daily 6:30am-11pm, every 5min., 0.50hv.)* The **Museum of One Street,** Andriyivskyy 2b, chronicles the history of Kyiv's most famous street. *(Open Tu-Su noon-6pm. 5hv. English tour 50hv.)* Ascend the gray steps at the corner of Desyatinna and vul. Volodymyrska to see the ruins of **Tithe Church** (Десятинна Церква; Desyatinna Tserkva), the oldest stone church of Kyivan Rus. It neighbors the **National Museum of Ukrainian History.** *(Open M-Tu and Th-Su 10am-5pm. 4.20hv.)* Nearby is the 18th-century **St. Andrew's Church.** The path opens onto the Podil district, the center of Kyiv in the 10th and 11th centuries. To the east, the **Chernobyl Museum,** Provulok Khoryva 1, details the aftermath of the nuclear disaster. *(Open M-F 10am-6pm, Sa 10am-5pm. Closed last M of each month. 5hv, students 1hv.)*

🎵 🎭 ENTERTAINMENT AND NIGHTLIFE

In May, a two-week theater festival leads up to the final weekend, the **Kyiv Days,** when stages for drama, folklore, jazz, and rock music performances are set up all over town. The famed **Kyiv International Film Festival** comes to town in July. Any time between late spring and fall, don't miss **Dynamo Kyiv,** one of Europe's top soccer teams. (Tickets 5-30hv at the stadium.) Hot summer days invite a boat ride down the Dniper or a trip to **Hydropark** (Гідропарк), an amusement park (rides 8-16hv) and beach on an island on the river (MR: Hidropark). The **National Philharmonic,** Volodymyrsky uzviz 2, holds regular concerts. (☎228 16 97. *Kasa* open Tu-Su noon-3pm and 4-7pm.) **Shevchenko Opera and Ballet Theater,** vul. Volodymyrska, puts on several shows each week. (MR: Teatralna. ☎224 71 65. Shows at noon and 7pm. Ticket office open M 11am-3pm, Tu-Su 11am-3pm and 4:30-7pm.)

Check out *What's On* (www.whatson-kiev.com) and the *Kyiv Post* (www.kyivpost.com) for the latest listings. ▓**O'Brien's Pub,** vul. Mykhaylivska 17a (Михайлівська), up the street from Maidan Nezalezhosti, is Kyiv's most popular expat bar. (☎229 15 84. Satellite TV, darts, and billiards. Beer 6-22hv. Live music Th-Sa 9:30pm-12:30am. Open daily 8am-2am. AmEx/MC/V.) Jazz plays at **Artclub 44,** vul. Khreshchatyk 44, in the courtyard through an unmarked brown door on the left. (☎229 41 37. Live music daily 10pm-midnight. Cover Th-Sa 10-40hv. Open daily 10am-2am.) At sexy **Mojo,** vul. Khreshchatyk 15, in the Passage alley, guests can try pole dancing on the bar. (☎228 17 17. Cocktails 25-30hv. Cover F-Sa women 20hv, men 40hv. Open daily 9am-8am.) **Androhyn,** vul. Harmatna 26/2, is a gay-friendly club. (MR: Shulyavska. Cover 20-30hv. Open Th-Su 8pm-8am.)

LVIV (ЛЬВІВ)   ☎ 80322

Poland conquered it, Austria rebuilt it, and the USSR neglected it. Now free of the Soviet yoke, more affordable than Kyiv, and teeming with energy, Lviv (pop. 830,000) is Ukraine's patriotic and cultural center. Meander down cobblestone streets, sip coffee in a cafe, and watch Lviv come into its own before your eyes.

🖭📶 **TRANSPORTATION AND PRACTICAL INFORMATION. Trains** (☎748 20 68; info 005) go from pl. Vokzalna (Вокзальна) to: Bratislava (18hr., 1 per day, 355hv); Budapest (13½hr., 1 per day, 405hv); Kraków (7½hr., 1 per day, 136hv); Minsk (14hr., 1 per day, 95hv); Moscow (25hr., 2 per day, 185hv); Prague (24hr., 1 per day, 390hv); and Warsaw (12hr., 1 per day, 220hv). Tickets can be bought at the railway *kasa* at Hnatyuka 20. (Гнатюка; ☎35 25 79. Open M-Sa 8am-2pm and 3-8pm, Su until 6pm.) **Buses** run from the main station, vul. Stryyska 189 (Стрийська; ☎63 24 93), to Kraków (8-9hr., 1 per day, 75hv) and Warsaw (10hr., 4 per day, 90hv). From the bus station, *marshrutka* #18 goes to the train station, from which trams run to town. English-speaking staff at **Lviv Tourist Info Center,** vul. Pidvalna 3, charges for info and maps. (☎97 57 51; www.tourism.lviv.ua. Open M-F 10am-1pm and 2-6pm.) **Internet Klub,** vul. Dudaeva 12, has 24hr. high-speed Internet access. (8am-midnight 4hv per hr., midnight-8am 2hv per hr.) If and only if **dialing locally,** prefix a "2" to numbers that begin with a "9." **Postal Code:** 79 000.

📷🍴 **ACCOMMODATIONS AND FOOD.** Most backpackers stay at the Soviet-style **Hotel Lviv ❸,** vul. Chornovola 7 (Чорновола), located behind the opera house in the city center, just past the end of pr. Svobody. Take tram #6 from the train station. (☎79 22 70; fax 72 86 51. Singles 50hv, with bath 100hv; doubles 80hv/140hv.) Located in the city center where pr. Svobody meets pr. Shevchenko, **Hotel George ❸** (Готель Жорж), pl. Mitskevycha 1, has reasonably priced rooms without bath. (☎74 21 82; info@georgehotel.com.ua. Breakfast included. Singles 149-161hv, with bath 357-455hv; doubles 126-138hv, with bath 333-432hv. MC/V.) A cheap place to find Ukrainian cuisine is **Smachna Plitka ❶** (Смачна Плітка), vul. Kurbasa 3, between vul. Tiktora and vul. Hnatyuka. (☎40 33 37. Entrees 5-12hv. Open daily 11am-11pm.) **Oselya ❷** (Оселя), vul. Hnatyuka 11, serves traditional dishes with veggie options, sometimes accompanied by live folk music. (☎72 16 01. Entrees 7-70hv. Open daily 11am-11pm. MC/V.) Try the kangaroo (120hv) at **Cactus ❸** (Кактус), vul. O. Nyzhankivskoho 18,

WILD DANCES

In late May 2005, Kyiv will host the 50th anniversary of the Eurovision contest. Perhaps not the likeliest place for the event, Ukraine owes the opportunity to its native singer Ruslana Lyzychko, who joined the ranks of ABBA and Celine Dion last year by winning the contest with a performance of her composition "Wild Dances." Because the contest is traditionally held in the homeland of the previous year's victor, Lyzychko's win became a windfall for all Kyiv.

Hugely popular throughout the continent, Eurovision was the only Western program broadcast on Eastern European television during the Cold War. But though Ukrainians could watch the contest, they couldn't sing in it. Although the event was inaugurated in 1956, last year's lineup in Istanbul was only the second with Ukrainian contestants. Lyzychko's victory has brought an unforeseen spotlight to Ukraine's vibrant but long-neglected culture. "Wild Dances" was inspired by the rhythms of the Hutsuls, an ethnic group native to the Carpathian Mountains, where Lyzychko's father was born. Its success has raised the profile of Ukrainian music and taken the singer to the top of European charts.

For concert dates and the latest info on the Eurovision Song Contest, check the unofficial website www.esctoday.com.

near Hotel George. (☎74 50 61. Entrees 22-150hv. Business lunch M-F noon-3pm, 22hv. Open M-Th and Su 7am-11pm, F-Sa 7am-2am. MC/V.) ▓**Veronika** ❶ (Вероніка), pr. Shevchenko 21, serves cakes (4.50-7hv), pastries (2-3hv), and coffee and tea (3-15hv). Downstairs is a pricier European restaurant. (☎97 81 28. Entrees 26-88hv. Open daily 10am-11pm. MC/V.)

◼◰ **SIGHTS AND ENTERTAINMENT.** Climb up to **High Castle Hill** (Високий Замок; Vysokyy Zamok), the former site of the Galician King's Palace, for a panoramic view of Lviv. To get there, follow vul. Krivonoca (Кривоноса) from its intersection with Hotny and Halytskono until you pass #39, then take a left down the long dirt road to circle up and around the hill counterclockwise. After surveying the breadth of the city, return to the heart of the city and begin a walking tour from pr. Svobody, which is dominated by the dazzling exterior of the **Theater of Opera and Ballet.** (Театр Опери та Балету; Teatr Opery Ta Baletu; ☎72 88 60. Tickets from 10hv.) **Ploschad Rynok,** the historic market square, is surrounded by churches and richly decorated merchant homes dating from the 16th to 18th centuries; its central **tower** has a view of Lviv. (Open Tu-F 10am-5pm, Sa-Su 11am-7pm. 10hv, children 2.50hv.) The **History Museum** (Історичний Музей; Istorychnyy Muzey) complex is at pl. Rynok #4, 6, and 24. Exhibits at #4 recount the history of WWII: Ukrainian citizens first fought for the Nazis, then for the Soviets, and later were oppressed by both. King Jan III Sobieski lived at building #6 in the 17th century; museum #24 chronicles Ukraine from Kyivan Rus to the Polish annexation in 1686. (Open Tu and Th-Su 10am-5:30pm. Each museum 3.50hv.) Walk up vul. Staroyevrejska (Old Jewish Road) to reach the ruins of the **Golden Rose Synagogue,** long a center for Jewish culture before its destruction by the Nazis. The 14th-century dome of the **Armenian Cathedral** rises from vul. Virmenska 7-9. (Open M-F 9am-5pm.) Lviv has a humming cafe culture. **Club-Cafe Lyalka** (Клуб-Кафе Лялька), vul. Halytskoho 1, often has live music and is a popular disco at night. (☎98 08 09. Wine 4hv. Cover 7-25hv. Open daily 1pm-7am.) US-inspired **Red Bull Dancing Club,** vul. Ivana Franka 15, is full of red trucks and has a "war room" in back. (☎96 51 51. Beer 3-14hv. Minimum consumption 20-40hv. Open daily 24hr.)

ODESSA (ОДЕСА)   ☎80482

Odessa (pop. 1,100,000) has been blessed by prosperity and cursed with corruption ever since its founding by Catherine the Great in 1794. With a full set of European influences, life in this port town has been kept lively by intellectuals and *mafiosi,* inspiring writers from Alexander Pushkin to Isaac Babel.

◧◲ **TRANSPORTATION AND PRACTICAL INFORMATION. Trains** run from pl. Privokzalnaya 2 (Привокзальная), at the northern end of ul. Pushkinskaya, to: Kyiv (10hr., 6 per day, 59hv); Moscow (25hr., 2-3 per day, 210hv); and Warsaw (24hr., even days of the month, 340hv). From there, to reach the bus station, take tram #5 to the last stop. **Buses** run from ul. Kolontayevskaya 58 (Колонтаевская) to Kyiv (8-10hr., 11 per day, 36hv). **Ferries** run from Morskoy Vokzal (Морской Вокзал; Sea Terminal), ul. Primorskaya 6 (Приморская) to Yalta (10-15hr., 3-5 per week, 171hv) and Varna (20-25hr., 2-4 per week, 267hv). **FGT Travel,** ul. Rishelyevskaya 4, in a wax museum, runs tours and has accommodations info. (☎37 52 01; www.odessapassage.com. Open daily 8:30am-8pm.) **Postal Code:** 65 001.

◤◪ **ACCOMMODATIONS AND FOOD.** Comfort isn't cheap in Odessa, especially in summer, when only the best hotels have hot water. Private rooms (from US$5) are the cheapest, but not the safest option. To reach downtown hotels from the train station, take tram #3 or 12, or a minibus. **Hotel Passage ❸** (Пассаж), ul. Preobrazhenskaya 34, is the best budget option, but shared bathrooms may lack toilet seats. (☎22 48 49. Singles 41hv, with bath 75hv; doubles 60hv/96hv; triples 83hv/122hv.) **Hotel Centralnyy ❹** (Центральний), ul. Preobrazhenskaya 40, is higher-end. (☎26 84 06. Breakfast included. Singles 92hv, with bath 100hv; doubles 92/150-300hv.) **Hotel Frapolli ❹**, ul. Deribasovskaya 13, has rooms with private bath, hot water, Internet, TV, and A/C. (☎35 68 01. Breakfast included. Singles US$60; doubles US$90. MC/V.) **🅼Pulcinella ❷**, ul. Lanzheronovskaya 17, is an Italian brick oven pizzeria. (☎777 30 10. Pizzas 13-28hv. Open daily 11am-last customer. MC/V.) Try **Kumanets ❷** (Куманець), ul. Gavanna 7 (Гаванна), for traditional dishes. (Entrees 15-54hv. Open 11am-midnight.) A **Privoz** (Привоз) supermarket is across from the train station on ul. Privoznaya. (Open daily 6am-6pm.)

◉🍴 SIGHTS AND ENTERTAINMENT. Street performers of all kinds gather on **ulitsa Deribasovskaya.** Turn right on Preobrazhenska, left on Sofiyevskaya (Софиевская), and walk up two blocks to reach the **Odessa Art Museum** (Художний музей; Khudozhniy muzey), ul. Sofiyevskaya 5a, which has a storied grotto below. (☎23 84 62. Museum 2hv. Grotto tour with guide only 2hv plus negotiable guide fee. Open M and W-Su 10:30am-6pm.) To the left off ul. Deribasovskaya on ul. Yekaterinskaya, a statue of the **Duc de Richelieu,** the city's first governor, looks down the **Potemkin Steps** toward the shining port, **Morskoy Vokzal.** Odessa's most beautiful street is **ulitsa Pushkinskaya;** the **Pushkin Museum and Memorial** (Литературно-мемориальный музей Пушкина; Literaturno-memorialny muzey Pushkina) at #13, is the former hotel where Pushkin lived during his 1823-1824 exile from St. Petersburg. (Open Tu-Su 10am-5pm. 3.50hv, students 1.50hv.) Directly underneath the city is the world's longest series of **🅼catacombs.** During the Nazi occupation, the resistance based itself here; Odessa has established a subterranean **museum** in its honor. FGT (see **Practical Information,** above) runs 2hr. English tours. (75hv. Dress warmly.) Most **beaches** are accessible by public transportation and on foot. Tram #5 goes to **Arkadiya** (Аркадия), the most popular on summer nights. Tram #4 runs to **Lanzheron** (Ланжерон), closest to Odessa proper, and **Otrada** (Отрада). Tram #18 goes to **Golden Shore** (Золотой Берег; Zolotoy Bereg) and **Kurortny** (Курортный). Tram #17 runs to the beach **Chaika** (Чайка).

Buy theater tickets for all shows at the **box office** at ul. Preobrazhenskaya 28. (☎22 02 45. Open daily 10am-5pm.) At the end of ul. Rishelyevskaya, the **Opera and Ballet Theater** (Театр Оперы и балета; Teatr Opery i Baleta) performs almost daily. Restaurants, cafes, and bars stay open late on **ulitsa Deribasovskaya,** with music from techno to Slavic folk. **Arkadiya** beach attracts dancers nightly to its open-air discos.

YALTA (ßЁÒÀ)   ☎80654

A former respite for the Russian elite, Yalta's beautiful beaches and palatial sanatoria now bustle with the throngs the rich came here to evade. Its tree-lined avenues, serene mountains, and open sea give visitors a hint of the city that inspired Chekhov, Rachmaninov, and Tolstoy.

▢🏾 TRANSPORTATION AND PRACTICAL INFORMATION. Yalta is not accessible by train. **Buses** run from ul. Moskovskaya to Kyiv (17½hr., 1 per day, 110hv) and Odessa (14½hr., 1 per day, 110hv). **Eugenia Travel,** ul. Rusvelta 12, offers tours and assists with accommodations. (☎32 81 40; www.eugeniatours.com.ua. Open M-F 9am-6pm.) **Postal Code:** 98 600.

ACCOMMODATIONS AND FOOD. Reserve at least two months ahead if you plan to stay in a Yalta hotel between June and August. Don't even bother calling hotels if you arrive without a booking; instead, negotiate with bus station middlemen for private rooms (25-50hv) or contact **Eugenia Travel** (☎/fax 27 18 29) to rent an **apartment** (150hv). In low season, hotels become much cheaper and availability is not a problem. **Gostinitsa Krym ❷**, ul. Moskovskaya 1/6, between pl. Lenina and pl. Sovetskaya, is cheap and central. (☎27 17 10. Singles 20-90hv; doubles 50-350hv.) **Pension T. M. M. ❸**, ul. Lesi Ukrayinki 16, has views of the sea and its own courtyard. Rooms have balcony, TV, and bath. (☎/fax 23 09 50. Rates include 3 meals. Singles 160hv; doubles 300-415hv.) Several Soviet-style **cafeterias ❶** (столовая; stolovaya) in the center serve cheap fare (10-20hv); **Stolovaya Krym**, next to Gostinitsa Krym, is one of the better ones. (Open daily 9am-9pm.) **Cafe Voschod ❷**, ul. Ignatenko 2, near pl. Sovetskaya, serves Turkish and Russian cuisine. (☎32 75 46. Entrees 10-45hv. Open daily June-Sept. 24hr.; Oct.-May 8am-midnight.)

SIGHTS AND ENTERTAINMENT. Many of the area's most worthwhile sights are best seen as daytrips. ◪**Massandra Palace** was once a residence of the tsars, then of Stalin and other Soviet officials. Take trolleybus #2 from Yalta, cross the street, and go uphill until you see the sign marked "Дворец" and an arrow pointing to a forest path on the right; follow the path. (☎32 17 28. Open July-Aug. Tu-Su 9am-6pm; May-June and Sept.-Oct. Tu-Su 9am-5pm; Nov.-Apr. W-Su 9am-4pm. 15hv, students 7hv.) The **Great Livadiya Palace,** which hosted the Yalta conference in WWII, and **Vorontsov Palace,** built for Count Mikhail Vorontsov, are also daytrip-worthy excursions from the city. **Anton Chekhov** spent his last five years in Yalta. At ul. Kirova 112, explore the ◪ **white dacha** he built in 1899, the desk at which he wrote *Three Sisters, The Cherry Orchard,* and *Lady with a Dog,* and a museum. Take *marshrutka* #8 from Kinoteatr Spartak on ul. Pushkinskaya. The **Nikitskiy Botanical Gardens** (Никицкий Сад; Nikitskiy Sad), founded in 1812, boast over 15,000 species of flora. Take bus #34 past Massandra to Nikitskiy Sad. (Open daily June-Aug. 8am-8pm; Sept.-May 9am-4pm. 6hv, students 3.50hv.) Follow the shore either way from the harbor to reach one of Yalta's many **beaches** (entrance 1.50-5hv).

Nightlife centers on beachfront bars. Overlooking the waterfront is the nightclub **Tornado,** nab. Lenina 11, upstairs through the arch and to the left. (☎32 20 36. Beer 8hv. Nightly laser shows. Cover 50-100hv; women free until 11pm. Open June-Sept. daily 10pm-5am; Oct.-Nov. Th-Sa 10am-5pm; Dec.-May F-Sa 10am-5pm.)

APPENDIX

LANGUAGE PHRASEBOOK

CYRILLIC ALPHABET

CYRILLIC	ENGLISH	PRONUNCIATION	CYRILLIC	ENGLISH	PRONUNCIATION
А а	a	*ah* as in **Pra**gue	Р р	r	*r* as in **R**evolution
Б б	b	*b* as in **B**osnia	С с	s	*s* as in **S**erbia
В в	v	*v* as in **V**olga	Т т	t	*t* as in **t**ank
Г г	g	*g* as in **G**lasnost	У у	u	*oo* as in B**u**dapest
Д д	d	*d* as in **d**ictatorship	Ф ф	f	*f* as in **F**ormer USSR
Е е	e	*yeh* as in **ye**llow	Х х	kh	*kh* as in *Ba***ch**
Ё ё	yo	*yo* as in **yo!**	Ц ц	ts	*ts* as in Le**t's** Go
Ж ж	zh	*zh* as in mira**ge**	Ч ч	ch	*ch* as in Khrush**ch**ev
З з	z	*z* as in communi**sm**	Ш ш	sh	*sh* as in Khru**sh**chev
И и	i	*ee* as in Gr**ee**k	Щ щ	shch	*shch* in Khru**shch**ev
Й й	y	*y* as in bo**y** or ke**y**	Ъ ъ	(hard sign)	(not pronounced)
К к	k	*k* as in **K**remlin	Ы ы	y	*y* as in s**i**lver
Л л	l	*l* as in **L**enin	Ь ь	(soft sign)	(not pronounced)
М м	m	*m* as in **M**acedonia	Э э	e	*eh* as in **E**stonia
Н н	n	*n* as in **n**uclear	Ю ю	yu	*yoo* as in **U**kraine
О о	o	*o* as in Cr**o**atia	Я я	ya	*yah* as in **Ya**roslavl
П п	p	*p* as in **P**oland			

Belarus, Bulgaria, and **Ukraine** use variations of the Russian Cyrillic alphabet.

GREEK ALPHABET

SYMBOL	NAME	PRONUNCIATION	SYMBOL	NAME	PRONUNCIATION
α A	alpha	*a* as in **f**ather	ν N	nu	*n* as in **n**et
β B	beta	*v* as in **v**elvet	ξ Ξ	xi	*x* as in mi**x**
γ Γ	gamma	*y* as in **yo** or *g* as in **go**	o O	omicron	*o* as in r**o**w
δ Δ	delta	*th* as in **th**ere	π Π	pi	*p* as in **p**eace
ε E	epsilon	*e* as in **je**t	ρ P	rho	*r* as in **r**oll
ζ Z	zeta	*z* as in **z**ebra	σ (ς) Σ	sigma	*s* as in **s**ense
η H	eta	*ee* as in qu**ee**n	τ T	tau	*t* as in **t**ent
θ Θ	theta	*th* as in **th**ree	υ Y	upsilon	*ee* as in gr**ee**n
ι I	iota	*ee* as in tr**ee**	φ Φ	phi	*f* as in **f**og
κ K	kappa	*k* as in **k**ite	χ X	chi	*h* as in **h**orse
λ Λ	lambda	*l* as in **l**and	ψ Ψ	psi	*ps* as in oo**ps**
μ M	mu	*m* as in **m**oose	ω Ω	omega	*o* as in Let's G**o**

CROATIAN

ENGLISH	CROATIAN	PRONOUNCE
Yes/No	Da/Ne	da/neh
Please	Molim	MO-leem
Thank you	Hvala lijepa	HVAH-la lye-pa
Good day	Dobardan	Do-bar-DAHN
Goodbye	Zbogom	ZBO-gohm
Sorry/Excuse me	Oprostite	o-PRO-sti-teh
Help!	U pomoć!	OO po-moch!
Police	Policija	po-LEE-tsee-ya
Embassy	Ambasada	ahm-bah-sah-da

ENGLISH	CROATIAN	PRONOUNCE
Ticket	Karta	KAR-tah
Train/Bus	Vlak/Autobus	vlahk/aw-TOH-bus
Station	Kolodvor	KOH-loh-dvor
Airport	Zračna Luka	ZRA-chna lu-kah
Taxi	Taksi	TAH-ksi
Grocery	Trgovina	ter-GOH-vee-na
Hotel	Hotel	HOH-tel
Pharmacy	Ljekarna	lye-KHAR-na
Bathroom	WC	VAY-tsay

ENGLISH	CROATIAN	PRONOUNCE
Where is...?	Gdje je?	GDYE yeh?
How do I get to...?	Kako mogu doći do ...?	KA-ko MOH-goo DOH-chee do...?
How much does this cost?	Koliko to košta?	KO-li-koh toh KOH-shta?
Do you have...?	Imate li...?	EEM-a-teh lee...?
Do you speak English?	Govorite li engleski?	GO-vor-i-teh lee eng-LEH-ski?

CZECH

ENGLISH	CZECH	PRONOUNCE
Yes/No	Ano/ne	AH-no/neh
Please	Prosím	PROH-seem
Thank you	Děkuji	DYEH-koo-yih
Hello	Dobrý den	DO-bree den
Goodbye	Nashledanou	NAH sleh-dah-noh-oo
Sorry/Excuse me	Promiňte	PROH-mihn-teh
Help!	Pomoc!	POH-mots!
Police	Policie	PO-lits-iye
Passport	Cestovní pas	TSE-stov-neeh pas
Open/Closed	Otevřeno/Zavřeno	O-te-zheno/ZAV-rzhen-o
Pharmacy	Lékárna	LEE-khaar-nah
Doctor	Lékař	LEK-arzh

ENGLISH	CZECH	PRONOUNCE
Ticket	Lístek	LIS-tek
Train/Bus	Vlak/Autobus	vlahk/OUT-oh-boos
Station	Nádraží	NA-drah-zhee
Airport	Letiště	LEH-tish-tyeh
Taxi	Taxi	TEHK-see
Bank	Banka	BAN-ka
Exchange	Směnárna	smyeh-NAR-na
Grocery	Potraviny	PO-tra-vee-nee
Tourist office	Turistické informace	TOO-rist-it-skeh IN-for-mat-tseh
City center	Centrum měšţá	TSEN-troom MNEHST-skeh
Hotel	Hotel	HOH-tel
Bathroom	WC	VEE-TSEE

ENGLISH	CZECH	PRONOUNCE
Where is...?	Kde je...?	k-DEH...?
How do I get to...?	Jak se dostanu do...?	YAK seh dohs-TAH-noo doh...?
How much does this cost?	Kolik to stojí?	KOH-lihk STOH-yee?
Do you have...?	Máte...?	MAH-teh...?
Do you speak English?	Mluvíte anglicky?	MLOO-vit-eh ahng-GLIT-ski?
I'd like to order...	Prosím...	PROH-seem...

DANISH

ENGLISH	DANISH	PRONOUNCE
Yes/No	Ja/ne	yah/nay
Please	Vær så venlig	vair soh VEN-li
Thank you	Tak	tahk
Hello	Hallo	HAH-lo
Goodbye	Farvel	fah-VEL
Sorry/Excuse me	undskyld	OHN-scoolt
Help!	Hjælp!	yailp!
Police	Politiet	poh-lee-TEE-ehht
Embassy	Ambassade	ahm-bah-SAH-theh

ENGLISH	DANISH	PRONOUNCE
Ticket	Billet	bih-LEHD
Train/Bus	Tog/Bus	too/boos
Airport	Lufthavn	LOFD-haown
Departure	Afgang	OW-gahng
Market	Marked	MAH-gehth
City center	Centrum	SEHN-trum
Hotel/Hostel	Hotel/Van-drerhjem	ho-TEL/VAN-druh-yem
Pharmacy	Apotek	ah-poh-TAYG
Toilet	Toilet	toe-ah-LEHD

ENGLISH	DANISH	PRONOUNCE
Where is...?	Hvor er...?	voa air...?
How do I get to...?	Hvordan kommer jeg til...?	vo-DAN KOM-ah yay tee...?
How much does this cost?	Hvad koster det?	vah KOS-ter day?
I'd like a...	Jeg vil gerne have en...	yay vee GEHR-neh hah en?
Do you speak English?	Taler du engelsk?	TAY-luh doo ENG-elsk?

DUTCH

ENGLISH	DUTCH	PRONOUNCE
Yes/No	Ja/Nee	yah/nay
Please/ You're welcome	Alstublieft	ahl-stoo-BLEEFT
Thank you	Dank u	DAHNK oo
Hello	Hallo	hah-LOW
Goodbye	Tot ziens	TOT seens
Excuse me	Neem me niet kwalijk	naym muh neet KWAH-lek
Help!	Help!	haylp!
Police	Politie	pu-LEET soo
Embassy	Ambassade	ahm-bah-SAH-duh
Pharmacy	Apotheek	ah-po-TAYK

ENGLISH	DUTCH	PRONOUNCE
Ticket	Kaartje	KAHR-chuh
Train/Bus	Trein/Bus	train/boos
Station	Station	stah-SHON
Taxi	Taxi	TAHK-see
Grocery	Kruidenier	kruh-oo-duh-NEER
Tourist office	VVV	vay-vay-VAY
Town Center	Centrum	SEHN-trum
Hotel	Hotel	ho-TEL
Toilet	Toilet	twah-LAYT
Handwriting on a slant	Schuinschrift	SKEUHN-skrift

ENGLISH	DUTCH	PRONOUNCE
Where is...?	Waar is...?	WAHR iss...?
How much does this cost?	Wat kost het?	wat KOST het?
Do you have...?	Heeft u...?	HAYFT oo...?
Do you speak English?	Sprekt u Engels?	SPRAYKT oo EN-gels?

FINNISH

ENGLISH	FINNISH	PRONOUNCE
Yes/No	Kyllä/Ei	KEW-la/ay
Please	Olka hyvä	OHL-ka HEW-va
Thank you	Kiitos	KEE-tohss
Hello	Hei	hay
Goodbye	Näkemiin	NA-keh-meen
Sorry/Excuse me	Anteeksi	ON-take-see
Help!	Apua!	AH-poo-ah!
Police	Poliisi	POH-lee-see
Embassy	Suurlähetystö	SOOHR LA-heh-toos-ter

ENGLISH	FINNISH	PRONOUNCE
Ticket	Lipun	LIP-ooh
Train/Bus	Juna/Bussi	YU-nuh/BUS-si
Boat	Vene	VEH-nay
Departures	Lähtevät	lah-teh-VAHT
Market	Tori	TOH-ree
Hotel/hostel	Hotelli/Retkeilymaja	HO-tehl-lee/reht-kayl-oo-MAH-yuh
Pharmacy	Apteekki	UHP-teehk-kee
Bathroom	Vessa	VEHS-sah
Telephone	Puhelin	POO-heh-lin

ENGLISH	FINNISH	PRONOUNCE
Where is...?	Missä on...?	MEE-sah OHN...?
How do I get to...?	Miten mä pääsen...?	MEE-ten ma PA-sen...?
How much does this cost?	Paljonko se maksaa?	PAHL-yon-ko SEH MOCK-sah?
I'd like to buy...	Haluaisin ostaa...	HUH-loo-ay-sin OS-tuh...
Do you speak English?	Puhutteko englantia?	POO-hoot-teh-kaw ENG-lan-tee-ah?

FRENCH

ENGLISH	FRENCH	PRONOUNCE
Yes/No	Oui/Non	wee/noh
Please	S'il vous plaît	see voo PLAY
Thank you	Merci	mehr-SEE
Hello	Bonjour	bohn-ZHOOR
Goodbye	Au revoir	oh re-VWAHR
Excuse me	Excusez-moi	ex-KU-zay-MWAH
Help!	Au secours!	oh seh-COOR!
Police	La police	la poh-LEES
Embassy	L'ambassade	lahm-bah-SAHD
Passport	Le passeport	le pass-POR
Open/Closed	Ouvert/Fermé	oo-VEHR/fer-MAY
Pharmacy	La pharmacie	la far-ma-SEE
Doctor	Le médecin	le mehd-SEN

ENGLISH	FRENCH	PRONOUNCE
Ticket	Le billet	le bee-AY
Train/Bus	Le train/Le bus	le tran/le boos
Station	La gare	la gahr
Airport	L'aéroport	la-ehr-o-POR
Taxi	Le taxi	le tax-EE
Bank	La banque	la bahnk
Exchange	L'échange	lay-SHANZH
Grocery	L'épicerie	lay-PEES–ree
Tourist office	Le bureau de tourisme	le byur-OH de toor-EESM
Town hall	L'hôtel de ville	lo-TEL de VEEL
Hotel	L'hôtel	lo-TEL
Hostel	L'auberge	lo-BERZH
Toilet	Les toilettes	lay twa-LET

ENGLISH	FRENCH	PRONOUNCE
Where is...?	Où se trouve...?	OO seh TROOV...?
How much does this cost?	Ça fait combien?	sa FAY com-bee-EN?
Do you have...?	Avez vous...?	AH-vay-VOO...?
Do you speak English?	Parlez-vous anglais?	PAR-lay VOO ahn-GLAY?
I would like ...	Je voudrais...	zhe voo-DRAY...

GERMAN

ENGLISH	GERMAN	PRONOUNCE
Yes/No	Ja/Nein	yah/nain
Please/ You're welcome	Bitte	BIH-tuh
Thank you	Danke	DAHNG-kuh
Hello	Hallo	HAH-lo
Goodbye	Auf Wiedersehen	owf VEE-derzayn
Excuse me	Entschuldigung	ent-SHOOL-digung
Help!	Hilfe!	HIL-fuh!
Police	Polizei	poh-lit-ZAI
Embassy	Botschaft	BOT-shaft
Open/Closed	Geöffnet/ Geschlossen	geh-UHF-net/ geh-shlos-sen
Pharmacy	Apotheke	AH-po-TAY-kuh
Doctor	Arzt	ARTZT

ENGLISH	GERMAN	PRONOUNCE
Ticket	Fahrkarte	FAR-kar-tuh
Train/Bus	Zug/Bus	tsug/boos
Station	Bahnhof	BAHN-hohf
Airport	Flughafen	FLOOG-hahf-en
Ferry	Fährschiff	FAYHR-shif
Bank	Bank	bahnk
Exchange	Wechseln	VEHK-zeln
Grocery	Lebensmittelgeschäft	LAY-bens-mittel-guh-SHEFT
Tourist office	Touristbüro	TOR-ist-byur-oh
Hotel/Hostel	Hotel/ Jugendherberge	ho-TEL/YOOgend-her-BERguh
With shower	Mit Dusche	miht DOO-shuh
Bathroom	Badezimmer	BAH-deh-tsimmuh

ENGLISH	GERMAN	PRONOUNCE
Where is...?	Wo ist...?	vo ist...?
How much does that cost?	Wieviel kostet das?	VEE-feel KOS-tet das?
Do you have...?	Haben Sie...?	HAB-en zee...?
Do you speak English?	Sprechen Sie Englisch?	SHPREK-en zee EHNG-lish?
I would like...	Ich möchte...	ish MOOSH-teh...

GREEK

ENGLISH	GREEK	PRONOUNCE
Yes/No	Ναι/Οχι	NEH/OH-hee
Please	Παρακαλω	pah-rah-kah-LO
Thank you	Ευχαριστω	ef-khah-ree-STO
Hello/Goodbye	Γεια σας	YAH-sas
Sorry/Excuse me	Συγνομη	sig-NO-mee
Help!	ΒοηθειαΆ	vo-EE-tee-ah!
Police	Αστυνομεια	as-tee-no-MEE-a
Embassy	Πρεσβεια	prez-VEE-ah
Passport	Διαβατηριο	dhee-ah-vah-TEE-ree-o
Open/closed	Ανοικτο/ κλειστο	ah-nee-KTO/ klee-STO
Pharmacy	Φαρμακειο	fahr-mah-KEE-o
Doctor	Γιατροσ	yah-TROSE

ENGLISH	GREEK	PRONOUNCE
Train/Bus	Τραινο/ Λεωφορειο	TREH-no/leh-o-fo-REE-o
Station	Σταθμοζ	stath-MOS
Airport	Αεροδρομιο	ah-e-ro-DHROmee-o
Taxi	Γαξι	tah-XFF
Ferry	Πλοιο	PLEE-o
Bank	Τραπεζα	TRAH-peh-zah
Exchange	Αντα– λλασσω	an-da-LAS-so
Market	Αγορα	ah-go-RAH
Tourist office	Τουριστικο Γραψειο	tou-ree-stee-KO graf-EE-o
Hotel/Hostel	Ξενοδοχειο	kse-no-dho-HEE-o
Bathroom	Τουαλεττα	tou-ah-LET-ta
Room to let	Δωματια	do-MA-tee-ah

ENGLISH	GREEK	PRONOUNCE
Where is...?	Που ειναι...?	poo-EF-neh...?
How much does this cost?	Ποσο κανει?	PO-so KAH-nee?
Do you have...?	Μηπως εχετε...?	mee-POSE EK-he-teh...?
Do you speak English?	Μιλας αγγλικα?	mee-LAHS ahn-glee-KAH?
I would like ...	Θα ηθελα...	THAH EE-the-lah...

For the Greek alphabet, see p. 1057.

HUNGARIAN

ENGLISH	HUNGARIAN	PRONOUNCE
Yes/No	Igen/Nem	EE-ghen/Nehm
Please	Kérem	KAY-rehm
Thank you	Köszönöm	KUH-suh-nuhm
Hello	Szervusz	SAYHR-voose
Goodbye	Viszontlátásra	Vi-sohnt-lah-tah-shraw
Excuse me	Elnézést	EHL-nay-zaysht
Police	Rendőrség	REN-dur-shayg
Passport	Az útlevelemet	ahz OOT-leh-veh-leh-meht
Open/Closed	Nyitva/Zárva	NYEET-vah/ZAHR-vuh
Pharmacy	Gyógyszertár	DYAW-dyser-tar

ENGLISH	HUNGARIAN	PRONOUNCE
Ticket	Jegyet	YEHD-eht
Train/Bus	Vonat/Autóbusz	VAW-noht/OW-toh-boos
Station	Pályaudvar	pah-yoh-OOT-vahr
Airport	Repülőtér	rehp-ewlu-TAYR
Bank	Bank	bohnk
Exchange	Pénzaváltó	pehn-zah-VAHL-toh
Grocery	Élelmiszerbolt	AY-lel-meser-balt
Travel agency	Utazási iroda	UH-toh-zah-see EE-raw-dah
Hotel	Szálloda	SAH-law-dah
Toilet	WC	VAY-tsay

ENGLISH	HUNGARIAN	PRONOUNCE
Where is...?	Hol van...?	hawl von...?
How much does this cost?	Mennyibe kerül?	MEHN-ye-behe KEH-rewl?
Can I have...?	Kaphatok...?	KAH-foht-tohk...?
Do you speak English?	Beszél angolul?	BESS-ayl ON-goal-ool?

ITALIAN

ENGLISH	ITALIAN	PRONOUNCE	ENGLISH	ITALIAN	PRONOUNCE
Yes/No	Sì/No	see/no	Ticket	Il biglietto	eel beel-YEHT-toh
Please	Per favore/Per piacere	pehr fah-VOH-reh/pehr pyah-CHAY-reh	Train/Bus	Il treno/Auto-bus	eel TRAY-no/aow-toh-BOOS
Thank you	Grazie	GRAHT-see-yeh	Station	La stazione	lah staht-see-YOH-neh
Hello	Ciao	chow	Airport	L'aeroporto	LAYR-o-PORT-o
Goodbye	Arrivederci	ah-ree-veh-DAIR-chee	Taxi	Il tassì	eel tahs-SEE
Sorry/Excuse me	Mi dispiace/Scusi	mee dees-PYAH-cheh/SKOO-zee	Ferry	Il traghetto	eel tra-GHEHT-toh
Help!	Aiuto!	ah-YOO-toh!	Bank	La banca	lah bahn-KAH
Police	La Polizia	lah po-LEET-ZEE-ah	Exchange	Il cambio	eel CAHM-bee-oh
Embassy	L'Ambasciata	lahm-bah-shee-AH-tah	Grocery	Gli alimentari	li ah-li-mehn-TA-ri
Passport	Il passaporto	eel pahs-sah-POHR-toh	Tourist office	L'azienda Promozione Turistica	lah-tzi-EHN-da pro-mo-tzi-O-nay tur-EES-tee-kah
Open/Closed	Aperto/Chiuso	ah-PAIR-toh/KYOO-zoh	Hotel/Hostel	L'lbergo	lal-BEHR-go
Pharmacy	La f armacia	lah far-mah-SEE-ah	With shower	Con doccia	kohn DOH-cha
Doctor	Il Medico	eel MEH-dee-koh	Bathroom	un gabinetto/un bagno	oon gah-bee-NEHT-toh/oon BAHN-yoh

ENGLISH	ITALIAN	PRONOUNCE
Where is...?	Dov'è...?	doh-VEH...?
How much does this cost?	Quanto costa?	KWAN-toh CO-stah?
Do you have...?	Hai...?	HI...?
Do you speak English?	Parla inglese?	PAHR-lah een-GLAY-zeh?
I'd like...	Vorrei...	VOH-ray...

NORWEGIAN

ENGLISH	NORWEGIAN	PRONOUNCE	ENGLISH	NORWEGIAN	PRONOUNCE
Yes/No	Ja/Nei	yah/nay	Ticket	Billett	bee-LEHT
Please	Vær så snill	vay sho SNEEL	Train/Bus	Toget/Buss	TOR-guh/büs
Thank you	Takk	tuhk	Airport	Lufthavn	LUFT-hahn
Hello	Goddag	gud-DAHG	Departures	Avgang	AHV-gahng
Goodbye	Ha det bra	HUH deh brah	Market	Torget	TOHR-geh
Sorry/Excuse me	Unnskyld	ÜN-shül	Hotel/Hostel	Hotell/Vandrerhjem	hoo-TEHL/VAN-drair-yaim
Help!	Hjelp!	yehlp	Pharmacy	Apotek	ah-pu-TAYK
Police	Politit	po-lee-TEE-uh	Toilets	Toalettene	tuah-LEHT-tuh-nuh
Embassy	Ambassade	uhm-bah-SAH-duh	City center	Sentrum	SEHN-trum

ENGLISH	NORWEGIAN	PRONOUNCE
Where is...?	Hvor er...?	VORR ayr...?
How do I get to...?	Hvordan kommer jeg til...?	voor-duhn KOM-morr yay teel...?
How much is...?	Hvor mye koster det...?	vorr moo-yuh KOS-tor deh...?
Do you speak English?	Snakker du engelsk?	sna-koh du EHNG-olsk?

POLISH

ENGLISH	POLISH	PRONOUNCE
Yes/No	Tak/Nie	tahk/nyeh
Please	Proszę	PROH-sheh
Thank you	Dziękuję	jen-KOO-yeh
Hello	Cześć	cheshch
Goodbye	Do widzenia	doh veedz-EN-yah
Sorry/Excuse me	Przepraszam	psheh-PRAH-shahm
Help!	Na pomoc!	nah POH-mots!
Police	Policja	poh-LEETS-yah

ENGLISH	POLISH	PRONOUNCE
Ticket	Bilet	BEE-leht
Train	Pociąg	POH-chawnk
Bus	Autobus	ow-TOH-booss
Bank	Bank	bahnk
Grocery	Sklep spożywczy	sklehp spoh-ZHIV-chih
Hostel	Schronisko młodzieżowe	srah-NIHS-kah mwa-jee-eh-SHAH-veh
Pharmacy	Apteka	ahp-TEH-ka
Bathroom	Toaleta	toh-uh-LEH-tuh

ENGLISH	POLISH	PRONOUNCE
Where is...?	Gdzie jest...?	g-JEH yest...?
How much does this cost?	Ile to kosztuje?	EE-leh toh kohsh-TOO-yeh?
Do you have...?	Czy są...?	chih sawn...?
Do you (male/female) speak English?	Czy pan(i) mówi po angielsku?	chih PAHN(-ee) MOO-vee poh ahn-GYEL-skoo?

PORTUGUESE

ENGLISH	PORTUGUESE	PRONOUNCE
Yes/No	Sim/Não	seeng/now
Please	Por favor	pur fah-VOR
Thank you	Obrigado (m)/ Obrigada (f)	oh-bree-GAH-doo/dah
Hello	Olá	oh-LAH
Goodbye	Adeus	ah-DAY-oosh
Sorry/Excuse me	Desculpe	desh-KOOLP
Help!	Socorro!	so-KO-ro!
Police	Polícia	po-LEE-see-ah

ENGLISH	PORTUGUESE	PRONOUNCE
Ticket	Bilhete	beel-YEHT
Train/Bus	Comboio/Auto-carro	kom-BOY-yoo/ OW-to-KAH-roo
Airport	Aeroporto	aye-ro-POR-too
Exchange	Câmbio	CAHM-bee-yoo
Market	Mercado	mer-KAH-doo
Hotel	Pousada	poh-ZAH-dah
Pharmacy	Farmácia	far-MAH-see-ah
Bathroom	Banheiro	bahn-YAY-roo

ENGLISH	PORTUGUESE	PRONOUNCE
Where is...?	Onde é que é ...?	OHN-deh eh keh eh...?
How much does this cost?	Quanto custa?	KWAHN-too KOOSH-tah?
I want...	Quero...	KAY-roo...
Do you speak English?	Fala inglês?	FAH-lah een-GLAYSH?

ROMANIAN

ENGLISH	ROMANIAN	PRONOUNCE
Yes/No	Da/Nu	dah/noo
Please/ Thank you	Vă rog/ Mulţumesc	vuh rohg/ mool-tsoo-MESK
Hello	Bună ziua	BOO-nuh zee-wah
Goodbye	La revedere	lah reh-veh-DEH-reh
Sorry	Îmi pare rău	im PA-reh rau
Excuse me	Scuzaţi-mă	skoo-ZAH-ts muh
Help!	Ajutor!	AH-zhoot-or!
Police	Poliţie	poh-LEE-tsee-eh

ENGLISH	ROMANIAN	PRONOUNCE
Ticket	Bilet	bee-LEHT
Train/Bus	Trenul Autobuz	TRAY-nool aw-toh-BOOS
Station	Gară	GAH-ruh
Grocery	Alimentar	AH-lee-mehn-tar
Taxi	Taxi	tak-SEE
Hotel	Hotel	ho-TEHL
Bathroom	Toaletă	toh-ahl-EH-tah
Child	Kopil	KO-pill

ENGLISH	ROMANIAN	PRONOUNCE
Where is...?	Unde e...?	OON-deh YEH...?
How much does this cost?	Cât costă?	kyht KOH-stuh?
Do you have...?	Aveţi...?	a-VETS...?
Do you speak English?	Vorbiţi englezeşte?	vor-BEETS ehng-leh-ZESH-te?

RUSSIAN

ENGLISH	RUSSIAN	PRONOUNCE
Yes/No	Да/нет	Dah/Nyet
Please	Пожалуйста	pa-ZHAL-sta
Thank you	Спасибо	spa-SEE-bah
Hello	Добрый день	DOH-bri DYEHN
Goodbye	До свидания	da svee-DAHN-ya
Sorry/ Excuse me	Извините	iz-vi-NEET-yeh
Help!	Помогите!	pah-mah-GIT-yeh!
Embassy	посольство	pah-SOHL'-stva
Police	милиция	mee-LEE-tsi-ya
Passport	паспорт	PAS-pahrt
Open/Closed	открыт/ закрыт	ot-KRIHT/ za-KRIHT
Pharmacy	аптека	ahp-TYE-kah

ENGLISH	RUSSIAN	PRONOUNCE
Ticket	билет	bil-YET
Train/Bus	поезд/ автобус	PAH-yizt/av-TOH-boos
Station	вокзал	VOK-zal
Airport	аэропорт	ay-airoh-PORT
Bank	банк	bahnk
Exchange	обмен валюты	ab-MYEHN val-iy-YU-tee
City center	центр города	TSEHN-tehr GOR-rah-dah
Grocery	гастроном	gah-stroh-NOM
Market	рынок	REE-nohk
Hotel	гостиница	gahs-TEE-nee-tsah
Dorm/Hostel	общежитие	ob-sheh-ZHEE-tee-yeh
Bathroom	туалет	twah-LYET

ENGLISH	RUSSIAN	PRONOUNCE
Where is...?	Где находится...?	gdyeh nah-KHOH-di-tsah...?
How much does this cost?	Сколько это стоит?	SKOHL-ka EH-ta STOY-it?
Do you have...?	У вас есть...?	oo vas YEST...?
Do you speak English?	Вы говорите по-английски?	vy gah-vah-REE-tyeh pa-an-GLEE-ski?
I'd like (male/female)...	Я хотел(а) бы	ya khah-TYEL(a) bwee...

For the Cyrillic alphabet, see p. 1057.

APPENDIX

SPANISH

ENGLISH	SPANISH	PRONOUNCE
Yes/No	Sí/No	see/noh
Please	Por favor	pohr fah-VOHR
Thank you	Gracias	GRAH-see-ahs
Hello	Hola	OH-lah
Goodbye	Adiós	ah-di-OHS
Sorry/Excuse me	Perdón	pehr-DOHN
Help!	¡Ayuda!	¡ay-YOOH-duh!
Police	Policía	poh-lee-SEE-ah
Embassy	Embajada	em-bah-HA-dah
Passport	Pasaporte	pas-ah-POR-teh
Open/Closed	Abierto(a)/Cerrado(a)	ah-bee-AYR-toh/sehr-RAH-doh
Pharmacy	Farmácia	far-MAH-see-ah
Doctor	Médico	MEH-dee-koh

ENGLISH	SPANISH	PRONOUNCE
Ticket	Boleto	boh-LEH-toh
Train/Bus	Tren Autobús	trehn ow-toh-BOOS
Station	Estación	es-tah-see-OHN
Airport	Aeropuerto	ay-roh-PWER-toh
Taxi	Taxi	tahk-SEE
Ferry	Transbordador	trahns-bor-dah-DOHR
Bank	Banco	BAHN-koh
Exchange	Cambio	CAHM-bee-oh
Grocery	Supermercado	soo-pehr-mer-KAH-doh
Tourist Office	Oficina de turismo	oh-fee-SEE-nah day toor-EEZ-moh
Hotel/Hostel	Hotel/Hostal	oh-TEL/OH-stahl
Dorm	Dormitorio	dor-mih-TOR-ee-oh
Bathroom	Baño	BAHN-yoh

ENGLISH	SPANISH	PRONOUNCE
Where is...?	Dónde está...?	DOHN-day eh-STA...?
How much does this cost?	Cuánto cuesta?	KWAN-toh KWEHS-tah?
Do you have...?	Usted tiene....?	ooh-STED tee-EN-ay...?
Do you speak English?	Habla inglés?	AH-blah een-GLEHS?
I'd like...	Me gustaría...	may goos-tah-REE-ah...

SWEDISH

ENGLISH	SWEDISH	PRONOUNCE
Yes/No	Ja/Nej	yah/nay
Please	Tack	tahk
Thank you	Tack	tahk
Hello	Hej	hay
Goodbye	Hejdå	TOHR-yet
Excuse me	Ursäkta mig	oor-SHEHK-tuh MAY
Help!	Hjälp!	yehlp!
Police	Polisen	poo-LEE-sehn
Embassy	Ambassad	uhm-bah-SAHD

ENGLISH	SWEDISH	PRONOUNCE
Ticket	Biljett	bil-YEHT
Train/Bus	Tåget/Buss	TOH-get/boos
Ferry	Färjan	FAR-yuhn
Departure	Avgångar	uhv-GOANG-er
Market	Torget	TOHR-yet
Hotel/Hostel	Hotell/Vandrarhem	hoo-TEHL/vun-DRAR-um
Pharmacy	Apotek	uh-poo-TEEK
Toilets	Toaletten	too-uh-LEHT-en
Post office	Posten	POHS-tehn

ENGLISH	SWEDISH	PRONOUNCE
Where is...?	Var finns det...?	vahr FINS deh...?
How much does this cost?	Hur mycket kostar det?	hurr MÜK-keh KOS-tuhr deh?
I'd like to buy...	Jag skulle vilja köpa...	yuh SKOO-leh vil-yuh CHEU-pah...
Do you speak English?	Talar du engelska?	TAH-luhr du EHNG-ehl-skuh?

WEATHER CHART

Average Temp. and Precipitation	January			April			July			October		
	°C	°F	in	°C	°F	in	°C	°F	in	°C	°F	in
Amsterdam	5/1	41/34	3.1	11/4	53/40	1.5	20/12	69/55	2.9	13/7	57/46	4.1
Athens	12/6	55/44	1.9	18/11	66/52	0.9	31/22	89/73	0.2	22/15	73/60	2.1
Berlin	1/-3	35/26	1.6	12/2	54/37	1.6	22/13	73/56	2.0	13/5	56/42	1.0
Budapest	2/-3	36/25	1.2	15/5	60/41	1.5	26/15	79/59	2.3	15/6	59/43	1.4
Copenhagen	2/-1	37/30	1.7	9/2	49/36	1.6	20/12	69/55	2.6	11/6	53/44	2.1
Dublin	7/2	46/37	2.5	11/5	52/41	1.9	18/12	66/54	2.6	12/7	55/46	2.9
Kraków	0/-5	33/22	1.3	12/3	54/38	1.9	21/12	71/55	3.5	12/4	55/40	1.7
London	7/2	45/36	2.4	12/5	55/41	1.7	22/13	72/56	1.8	14/7	58/46	2.9
Madrid	10/0	51/32	1.8	17/5	63/42	1.8	32/16	90/61	0.4	20/8	68/47	1.8
Moscow	-6/-11	21/11	1.4	9/1	49/34	1.5	21/12	71/55	3.2	7/0	45/33	2.0
Paris	6/1	43/34	0.2	13/5	57/42	0.2	23/14	75/58	0.2	15/7	59/46	0.2
Prague	1/-4	34/24	0.8	12/2	54/36	1.4	22/12	72/54	2.6	12/3	54/39	1.2
Rome	12/3	55/39	3.2	17/8	63/47	2.6	28/18	83/66	0.6	21/13	71/56	4.5
Stockholm	0/-5	31/22	1.2	8/0	47/31	1.1	21/12	70/54	2.5	8/3	48/38	2.0
Vienna	2/-2	36/27	1.5	13/5	57/41	2.0	25/15	77/59	2.9	13/6	57/43	1.9

INDEX

LONG ON WEEKEND. SHORT ON CASH.

The fastest way to the best fare.

MAP INDEX

MAP LEGEND

▪ Point of Interest	✈ Airport	ⵜ Convent/Monastery	℞ Pharmacy
🛏 Accommodation	⌿ Arch/Gate	⚓ Ferry Landing	Police
▲ Camping	$ Bank	(347) Highway Sign	✉ Post Office
🍎 Food	⛱ Beach	⊞ Hospital	⛷ Skiing
☕ Café	🚌 Bus Station/Stop	⌨ Internet Cafe	Synagogue
🏛 Museum	✪ Capital City	📖 Library/Bookstore	☎ Telephone Office
● Sight	♜ Castle	⟨M⟩ M Metro Station	Theater
Bar/Pub	⛪ Church	▲ Mountain	ⓘ Tourist Office
★ Nightlife	⚑ Consulate/Embassy	Mosque	🚉 Train Station

Park	Water	Beach	----- Pedestrian Zone
			Stairs

The Let's Go compass always points NORTH.